The Norton Anthology
of World Masterpieces

SIXTH EDITION

VOLUME 1

VOLUME 1

Masterpieces of the Ancient World • Knox
Masterpieces of the Middle Ages • McGalliard
Masterpieces of the Renaissance • Pasinetti

VOLUME 2

Masterpieces of the Enlightenment • Hugo/Spacks

Masterpieces of the Nineteenth Century:
Varieties of Romanticism • Hugo/Spacks

Masterpieces of the Nineteenth Century:
Realism, Naturalism, and the New Poetry • Wellek

Masterpieces of the Twentieth Century:
Varieties of Modernism • Douglas/Lawall

Masterpieces of the Twentieth Century:
Contemporary Explorations • Lawall

VOLUME 1

Masterpieces of the Ancient World • Knox

Masterpieces of the Middle Ages • McClure

Masterpieces of the Renaissance • Pasinetti

VOLUME 2

Masterpieces of the Enlightenment • Hugo Spacks

Masterpieces of the Nineteenth Century:
Varieties of Romanticism • Hugo Spacks

Masterpieces of the Nineteenth Century:
Realism, Naturalism, and the New Poetry • Wellek

Masterpieces of the Twentieth Century:
Varieties of Modernism • Douglas Lawall

Masterpieces of the Twentieth Century:
Contemporary Explorations • Lawall

The Norton Anthology of World Masterpieces

SIXTH EDITION

Maynard Mack, *General Editor*

Bernard M. W. Knox

John C. McGalliard

P. M. Pasinetti

Howard E. Hugo

Patricia Meyer Spacks

René Wellek

Kenneth Douglas

Sarah Lawall

VOLUME 1
Literature of Western Culture Through the Renaissance

W · W · NORTON & COMPANY · *New York* · *London*

The text of this book is composed in Electra, with display type set in Bernhard
Modern. Composition by Maple-Vail Book Manufacturing Group. Manufacturing
by R. R. Donnelley. Book design by Antonina Krass.

Library of Congress Cataloging-in-Publication Data

The Norton anthology of world masterpieces / Maynard Mack, general
   editor. — 6th ed.
     p. cm.
  Includes index.
  Contents: v. 1. Literature of Western culture through the
Renaissance — v. 2. Literature of Western culture since the
Renaissance.
  0-393-96140-0 Vol. I-cloth
  0-393-96141-9 Vol. I-paper
  1. Literature—Collections. I. Mack, Maynard, 1909–
PN6014.N66 1992
808.8—dc20   91-12777
                                        CIP

W.W. Norton & Company, Inc., 500 Fifth Avenue, New York, N.Y. 10110
W.W. Norton & Company Ltd., 10 Coptic Street, London WC1A 1PU

5 6 7 8 9 0

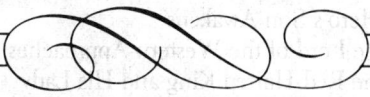

Contents

PREFACE TO THE SIXTH EDITION   xv

ACKNOWLEDGMENTS   xxi

Masterpieces of the Ancient World

INTRODUCTION   1

The Epic of Gilgamesh   11
(Translated by N. K. Sandars)

THE OLD TESTAMENT   45
Genesis 1-3. (The Creation—The Fall)   49
Genesis 4. (The First Murder)   53
Genesis 6-9. (The Flood)   53
Genesis 11. (The Origin of Languages)   57
Genesis 37-46. (The Story of Joseph)   57
From Job   69
Psalm 8   86
Psalm 19   86
Psalm 23   87
Psalm 104   87
Psalm 137   89
Isaiah 52-53. (The Song of the Suffering Servant)   89
Jonah   90
(The King James Version)

HOMER   92
The Iliad   98
  Book I. The Rage of Achilles   98
  From Book VI. Hector Returns to Troy   116
  From Book VIII. The Tide of Battle Turns   124
  Book IX. The Embassy to Achilles   124
  Book XVIII. The Shield of Achilles   145
  Book XIX. The Champion Arms for Battle   161
  Book XXII. The Death of Hector   173
  Book XXIV. Achilles and Priam   187
  (Translated by Robert Fagles)
The Odyssey   208
  Book I. A Goddess Intervenes   208

Book II. A Hero's Son Awakens   220
Book III. The Lord of the Western Approaches   231
Book IV. The Red-Haired King and His Lady   244
Book V. Sweet Nymph and Open Sea   266
Book VI. The Princess at the River   278
Book VII. Gardens and Firelight   286
Book VIII. The Songs of the Harper   295
Book IX. New Coasts and Poseidon's Son   310
Book X. The Grace of the Witch   325
Book XI. A Gathering of Shades   340
Book XII. Sea Perils and Defeat   359
Book XIII. One More Strange Island   372
Book XIV. Hospitality in the Forest   385
Book XV. How They Came to Ithaka   400
Book XVI. Father and Son   417
Book XVII. The Beggar at the Manor   431
Book XVIII. Blows and a Queen's Beauty   450
Book XIX. Recognitions and a Dream   462
Book XX. Signs and a Vision   479
Book XXI. The Test of the Bow   490
Book XXII. Death in the Great Hall   502
Book XXIII. The Trunk of the Olive Tree   515
Book XXIV. Warriors, Farewell   525
       (Translated by Robert Fitzgerald)

SAPPHO OF LESBOS (born ca. 630 B.C.)   540
"Throned in splendor, deathless, O Aphrodite"   541
"Like the very gods in my sight is he . . ."   542
"Some there are who say that the fairest things seen"   542
       (Translated by Richmond Latimore)

AESCHYLUS (524?-456 B.C.)   543
The Oresteia   548
    Agamemnon   548
    The Libation Bearers   594
    The Eumenides   623
       (Translated by Robert Fagles)

SOPHOCLES (496-406 B.C.)   652
Oedipus the King   658
Antigone   701
       (Translated by Robert Fagles)

EURIPIDES (480-406 B.C.)   739
Medea   740
       (Translated by Rex Warner)

ARISTOPHANES (450?-385? B.C.)   772
Lysistrata   774
       (Translated by Charles T. Murphy)

PLATO (429-347 B.C.)   806
    The Apology of Socrates   807
    From Phaedo (The Death of Socrates)   827
    (Translated by Benjamin Jowett)

ARISTOTLE (384-322 B.C.)   831
    From Poetics   831
    (Translated by James Hutton)

CATULLUS   835
    "Come, Lesbia, let us live and love"   836
    "There are many who think of Quintia . . ."   836
    "No woman, if she is honest, can say . . ."   837
    "When at last after long despair . . ."   837
    "My life, my love, you say our love will last forever"   837
    "Lesbia speaks evil of me . . ."   837
    "My woman says that she would rather wear the
        wedding-veil for me"   838
    "There was a time, O Lesbia . . ."   838
    "Were you born of a lioness . . ."   838
    "I hate and love"   838
    "You are the cause of this destruction, Lesbia"   839
    "Poor damned Catullus, here's no time for nonsense"   839
    "Caelius, my Lesbia, that one, that only Lesbia"   839
    "Furius, Aurelius, bound to Catullus"   839
    "If man can find rich consolation . . ."   840
    (Translated by Horace Gregory)

VIRGIL (70-19 B.C.)   841
    The Aeneid   844
        From Book I. (Aeneas Arrives in Carthage)   844
        Book II. How They Took the City   853
        Book IV. The Passion of the Queen   877
        From Book VI. (Aeneas in the Underworld)   900
        From Book VIII. (The Shield of Aeneas)   907
        From Book XII. (The Death of Turnus)   911
    (Translated by Robert Fitzgerald)

OVID (43 B.C.-A.D. 17)   917
    Metamorphoses   918
    Book I   918
        The Creation   918
        The Four Ages   920
        Jove's Intervention   922
        The Story of Lycaon   923
        The Flood   924
        Deucalion and Pyrrha   926
        Apollo and Daphne   929
        Jove and Io   932

Book XV 937
    The Teachings of Pythagoras 937
    (Translated by Rolfe Humphries)

THE NEW TESTAMENT 947
    Luke 2 (The Birth and Youth of Jesus) 948
    Matthew 5-7 (The Teaching of Jesus: The Sermon on the
        Mount) 950
    Luke 15 (The Teaching of Jesus: Parables) 954
    Matthew 26 (The Betrayal of Jesus) 956
    Matthew 27 (The Trial and Crucifixion of Jesus) 958
    Matthew 28 (The Resurrection) 961
    (The King James Version)

PETRONIUS (died A.D. 65) 961
    The Satyricon 963
        Dinner with Trimalchio 963
    (Translated by J. P. Sullivan)

ST. AUGUSTINE (A.D. 354-430) 980
    Confessions 982
        From Book I. (Childhood) 982
        From Book II. (The Pear Tree) 986
        From Book III. (The Student at Carthage) 988
        From Book VI. (Worldly Ambitions) 990
        From Book VIII. (Conversion) 993
        From Book IX. (Death of His Mother) 996
    (Translated by F. J. Sheed)

Masterpieces of the Middle Ages

INTRODUCTION 1009

From The Koran 1014
    Sura 1. The Exordium 1014
    Sura 4. Women 1014
    Sura 5. The Table 1017
    Sura 10. Jonah 1027
    Sura 12. Joseph 1033
    Sura 19. Mary 1039
    Sura 55. The Merciful 1043
    Sura 62. Friday, or the Day of Congregation 1045
    Sura 71. Noah 1045
    Sura 76. Man 1045
    (Translated by N. J. Dawood)

Beowulf 1052
    (Translated by Burton Raffel)

The Wanderer   1124
(Translated by Charles W. Kennedy)

The Story of Deirdre   1129
(Translated by Jeffrey Gantz)

The Song of the Seeress   1137
(Translated by Paul B. Taylor and W. H. Auden)

Thorstein the Staff-Struck   1148
(Translated by Hermann Pálsson)

From The Song of Roland   1159
(Translated by Frederick Goldin)

MARIE DE FRANCE (Twelfth Century)   1216
   Eliduc   1218
   (Translated by John Fowles)

   Aucassin and Nicolette   1231
   (Translated by Glyn S. Burgess)

   Medieval Latin Lyric Poetry   1259
      Boethius • Saint Venantius Fortunatus • Alcuin • Sedulius
      Scottus • Mss. of Salzburg, Canterbury, and Limoges
      Pierre Abélard • The Archpoet • *From* Carmina Burana
      Thomas Aquinas

DANTE ALIGHIERI (1265-1321)   1273
   The Divine Comedy   1284
      Inferno   1284
      From Purgatorio   1423
      From Paradiso   1447
      (Translated by John Ciardi)

GIOVANNI BOCCACCIO (1313-1375)   1467
   The Decameron   1470
      The First Day   1470
      The Second Tale of the Fourth Day   1482
      The Ninth Tale of the Fifth Day   1488
      (Translated by Mark Musa and Peter E. Bondanella)

   Sir Gawain and the Green Knight   1492
   (Translated by Marie Borroff)

GEOFFREY CHAUCER (1340?-1400)   1551
   The Canterbury Tales   1558
      General Prologue   1558
      Prologue to the Miller's Tale   1577
      The Miller's Tale   1578

Prologue to the Pardoner's Tale   1592
The Pardoner's Tale   1595
(The Knight's Interruption of the Monk's Tale)   1606
The Nun's Priest's Tale   1607
(Translated by Theodore Morrison)

FRANÇOIS VILLON (1431-?)   1621
Ballade   1622
From The Testament   1623
(Translated by Galway Kinnell)

Everyman (ca. 1485)   1637
(Text by E. Talbot Donaldson)

Masterpieces of the Renaissance

INTRODUCTION   1661

FRANCIS PETRARCH (1304-1374)   1668
Letter to Dionisio da Borgo San Sepolcro (The Ascent of
    Mount Ventoux)   1670
(Translated by James H. Robinson and Henry W. Rolfe)
Sonnet 3: It Was the Morning   1676
Sonnet 61: Blest Be the Day   1677
(Translated by Joseph Auslander)
Sonnet 62: Father in Heaven   1677
(Translated by Vernard Bergonzi)
Sonnet 90: She Used to Let Her Golden Hair Fly Free   1677
(Translated by Morris Bishop)
Sonnet 292: The Eyes That Drew from Me   1678
Sonnet 300: Great Is My Envy of You   1678
(Translated by Edwin Morgan)
Sonnet 333: Go, Grieving Rimes of Mine   1679
(Translated by Morris Bishop)

DESIDERIUS ERASMUS (1466-1536)   1679
The Praise of Folly   1682
    Part I. Folly Herself   1682
    Part II. The Powers and Pleasures of Folly   1683
    Part IV. The Christian Fool   1698
(Translated by Leonard F. Dean)

NICCOLÒ MACHIAVELLI (1469-1527)   1702
Letter to Francesco Vettori ("That Food Which Alone
    Is Mine")   1705
The Prince   1706
    (Princely Virtues)   1706

("Fortune Is a Woman")   1713
(The Roman Dream)   1715
(Translated by Allan H. Gilbert)

BALDESAR CASTIGLIONE (1478-1529)   1718
The Book of the Courtier   1719
(The Setting)   1719
("Everything He May Do or Say Shall Be Stamped
    with Grace")   1722
(Translated by Leonard E. Opdycke)

MARGUERITE DE NAVARRE (1492-1549)   1730
The Heptameron   1734
Story Three   1734
Story Thirty   1739
Story Forty   1744
(Translated by P. A. Chilton)

FRANÇOIS RABELAIS (1495?-1553)   1750
Gargantua and Pantagruel, Book I   1753
(Education of a Giant Humanist)   1753
(The Abbey of Thélème)   1766
Gargantua and Pantagruel, Book II   1775
(Pantagruel: Birth and Education)   1775
(Father's Letter from Home)   1777
(Adventures of Panurge)   1780
(Translated by Burton Raffel)

MICHEL DE MONTAIGNE (1533-1592)   1789
Essays   1793
Of Cannibals   1793
Of the Inconsistency of Our Actions   1803
From Apology for Raymond Sebond   1808
Of Repentance   1816
(Translated by Donald Frame)

MIGUEL DE CERVANTES (1547-1616)   1819
Don Quixote, Part I   1823
("I Know Who I Am, and Who I May Be, If I Choose")   1823
(Fighting the Windmills and a Choleric Biscayan)   1845
(Of Goatherds, Roaming Shepherdesses, and
    Unrequited Loves)   1860
(Fighting the Sheep)   1884
("To Right Wrongs and Come to the Aid of the
    Wretched")   1888
("Set Free at Once That Lovely Lady . . .")   1896
Don Quixote, Part II   1902
("Put Into a Book")   1902

(A Victorious Duel)   1908
("For I Well Know the Meaning of Valor")   1936
(Last Duel)   1943
(Homecoming and Death)   1947
(Translated by Samuel Putnam)

CHRISTOPHER MARLOWE (1564-1593)   1955
  The Tragical History of the Life and Death of Doctor
    Faustus   1958
  (Text by Hallett Smith)

WILLIAM SHAKESPEARE (1564-1616)   2010
  Hamlet, Prince of Denmark   2014

JOHN DONNE (1572-1631)   2110
  The Good-Morrow   2112
  Song ("Go and catch a falling star")   2112
  The Indifferent   2113
  The Canonization   2114
  The Apparition   2115
  The Funeral   2115
  Holy Sonnets
    Sonnet 7: "At the round earth's imagined corners, blow"   2116
    Sonnet 10: "Death, be not proud, though some have
      callèd thee"   2116

PEDRO CALDERÓN DE LA BARCA (1600–1681)   2117
  Life Is a Dream   2120
  (Translated by Roy Campbell)

JOHN MILTON (1608-1674)   2176
  Paradise Lost   2179
    From Book I. ("This Great Argument")   2179
    Book IX. (Temptation and Fall)   2180
    From Book X. (Acceptance, Reconciliation, Hope)   2208
    From Book XII. ("The World Was All Before Them")   2217

A NOTE ON TRANSLATION   2221

INDEX   2229

Preface
to the Sixth Edition

The book in your hands is the new Sixth Edition of *The Norton Anthology of World Masterpieces*—rethought, redesigned, minutely corrected, and richly enlarged.

The additional works that our new format allows us to bring you in this edition have been chosen individually to propagate lively class discussions and collectively to confer on what many users tell us is already the best teaching instrument in the business an unparalleled variety and scope. This without in any way impairing the carefully considered inner coherencies of theme and genre that for thirty-five years have made this anthology an inimitable classroom success.

New authors in this edition include, from Greece, Sappho; from Rome, Catullus; from France, Villon, Marguerite de Navarre, Chateaubriand, Hugo, and Duras; from Spain, Calderón; from Italy, Leopardi; from Germany, Heine; from Austria, Freud and Bachmann; from Russia, Pushkin and Akhmatova; from Mexico, Sor Juana; from Egypt, the Nobel prize-winner Mahfouz; and from Nigeria, Achebe. Four authors *not* new in this edition appear here in important new selections: Browning in two additional poems that allow for a deeper exploration of the dramatic monologue ("My Last Duchess") and open up an entirely different side to his poetic genius (" 'Childe Rolande to the Dark Tower Came' "); Baudelaire in more and different poems (including several prose poems from *Paris Spleen*) as well as new translations; Mann in one of the seminal short novels of our century, *Death in Venice*; and Lessing in an African story evoking most poignantly the pain and confusion that result when a society, or an age, or a person of settled traditions and cherished values goes down to destruction under the destabilizing forces of time and change.

Add to the above names the most prolific of all authors, "Anonymous," on whom we draw in this edition for the Babylonian *Epic of Gilgamesh* (at least eight centuries older than Homer), the Anglo-Saxon epic *Beowulf*, and the Provençal romance of *Aucassin and Nicolette*; add further a florilegium of medieval Latin poems by authors as various as Boethius, Alcuin, Aquinas, and the poets of the *Carmina Burana*; add as well a liberal selection from the Koran, and we believe you will agree with us that a challenging year of choices lies ahead.

Of the world's great plays, you may choose here among twenty, representing nine literatures and proceeding from the complete *Oresteia* of Aeschylus (458 B.C.) to Samuel Beckett's *Endgame* (1957) and Marguerite Duras's ground-breaking screenplay *Hiroshima Mon Amour* (1959). We like to think, moreover, that our shift to Duras's brilliant and pertinent script will encourage teachers and students who have not already done so to enter into serious study of what is more and more clearly the preponderant art form of our times: film.

Of the world's "heroic" poems—those narratives of large substance that in earlier times reflected the frailties and aspirations of an entire people or culture through the vicissitudes of a single protagonist or group (a task that in later times has fallen to the greater novelists)—we are able to give you either whole or in extended abridgments, eight: *Gilgamesh* (complete), the *Iliad*, the *Odyssey* (complete), the *Aeneid* (Book IV treating the love affair between Aeneas and Dido is now complete), *Beowulf* (complete), the *Song of Roland*, the *Divine Comedy* (here the entire *Inferno* is complete), and *Paradise Lost* (Book IX treating the Fall of Eve and Adam is complete). Other works supplied here that affiliate easily with these, and sometimes have a comparable cultural reach despite their (usually) shorter compass, range from Cervantes' parody of the chivalric romances in his *Don Quixote* (in extensive selections) through such satiric narratives as Swift's *Gulliver's Travels*, Pope's mock-heroic *Rape of the Lock*, and Samuel Johnson's *Rasselas* to Eliot's *The Waste Land*.

In other choices, you may wish to draw on autobiography: the *Confessions* of St. Augustine and Rousseau or the painful and moving *Narrative of the Life of Frederick Douglass, an American Slave* (complete). Or on a range of human wisdom in the essays and quasi-essays of Aristotle, Plato, Castiglione, Machiavelli, Montaigne. Or on expressions of religious experience: the Old Testament or Hebrew Bible, the New Testament or Greek Bible, the Koran. Or on perhaps the most famous psychological case study ever made: Freud's *"Dora"* (first written up in 1901, first published in 1905), which ushers in this century's persistent fascination with the scientific analysis of human motivations and desires.

As for prose fiction and lyric poetry, you have before you, as the poet Dryden once said of Chaucer, "God's plenty." Contained here are stories or what amount to stories, short and long, by Petronius, Rabelais, Cervantes, Swift, Johnson, Chateaubriand, Pushkin, Woolf, Lawrence, Porter, Faulkner, Camus, Borges, Mahfouz, Ellison, Solzhenitsyn, Lessing, Robbe-Grillet, Bachmann, and García Márquez. Contained here also are eight short novels, complete: Madame de La Fayette's *The Princess of Clèves*, Voltaire's *Candide*, Melville's *Billy Budd*, Dostoevski's *Notes from Underground*, Tolstoy's *The Death of Iván Ilyich*, Kafka's *The Metamorphosis*, Mann's *Death in Venice*, and Achebe's *Things Fall Apart*. From the three writers who perhaps more than any others have shaped our twentieth-century understanding of what a "novel" is—Flaubert, Proust, and Joyce—we give you *Madame Bovary* complete in addition to the substantial initial sections, both self-contained, of *Remembrance of Things Past* and of *A Portrait of the Artist as a Young Man*.

With lyric poetry, our own collective classroom experience and that of many others warned us long ago that translations must be approached with care. Simply put, lyric poetry cannot be translated without losing the unique and marvelously condensed expression that such poetry has in its original language. (We examine the problem in detail in the Note on Translation printed at the back of each volume.) We have accordingly been as generous as space allows with lyric poetry in English, especially when in the nineteenth century it becomes a dominant form. But we have been wary of including too many English translations of lyric poetry composed in another tongue. We do include in this edition, by popular demand, the few poems of Sappho that survive in an undamaged or all but undamaged text, being careful to exclude the many printed under her name that have in fact been manufactured by an editor and / or translator from a few splinters or even three or four words. Catullus, also new here, offers a Roman counterpart to Sappho and like her appears by popular demand.

From Petrarch we have always included selections because so much that follows later in the literary expression of male feelings toward beloved women derives from him. (See, for example, the tone with which Hamlet's letter to Ophelia begins, which is also the tone that Donne in *his* love poetry reacts against and Pope wittily plays off of in his *Rape of the Lock*.) Likewise, we have always included selections from Baudelaire, without whose disturbing imagery much in twentieth-century poetry cannot be understood. Now, in this Sixth Edition, widening our representation of Romantic subject-matter and subjectivity, we add examples from France, Germany, and Italy by Hugo, Heine, and Leopardi.

These short poetic forms we give you in the best translations currently to be found, and in future editions we will be constantly on the lookout for improvements. Still, it can never be insisted too often that a poem such as Hugo's "Reverie" or Heine's "The Silesian Weavers"—or, for that matter, Baudelaire's "The Voyage" or Rilke's "Archaic Torso of Apollo"—tends to become in even the most "adequate" translation a pale simulacrum of the original. We have also included, then, selected poems or passages—in the original languages—from Baudelaire, Rilke, and Lorca in order to clarify the total re-visioning a poem must undergo in the act of translation.

With respect to translation generally, one point requires emphasis. An anthology containing masterpieces from several languages is only as useful as its translations are authoritative, alive to the specific energies of the work in hand, and conveyed in an English idiom that brings those energies to its readers with a minimum of loss. Thus you will find Homer's *Iliad* in this Sixth Edition in the fire-new translation of Robert Fagles, published in 1990, cheek by jowl with Robert Fitzgerald's older translation of the *Odyssey*, published in 1961—the reason being that each so far is the absolute best of its kind. On similar grounds, we give you Burton Raffel's racy and raunchy new Rabelais, likewise published in 1990; Richard Wilbur's sparkling *Phaedra* (1986); David Luke's surpassingly acute rendering of *Death in Venice* (1988); and Judith Hemschemeyer's deeply felt version of Anna Akhmatova's *Requiem* (1989); while at the same time turning for *Faust* to Walter Kaufman's translation of thirty years ago and for *Madame Bovary* to Francis Steegmuller's of 1957. Our reason once again is that no translations come close to Kaufman's in catching the kaleidoscopic play of idea, wit, sentiment, and sheer verbal highjinks that makes the original German such a singular delight, or to Steegmuller's in capturing the exquisite balance of Flaubert's French. We are confident you will be as pleased as we are to find them here at last.

The actual dates in the above paragraph are immaterial. What matters is that an anthology of this kind has a moral responsibility to provide you with the best literature in the best of translations regardless of vintage or cost. We of the Norton anthology take this responsibility seriously.

A word now about the future. At thirty-five, this anthology is in the prime of life and burning for a new adventure. Those of you who have noticed that our Fifth Edition had selections from Africa, Japan, and India and that this Sixth Edition opens with an epic from the ancient Middle East and closes with a great novel from modern Africa (or any of you who have used the separate volume entitled *Masterpieces of the Orient* published long ago as a supplement to these volumes) will be aware that for a very long time we have been experimenting with ways to expand this anthology into a collection of "world" masterpieces in the fullest contemporary sense.

In 1993, the fruit of these experiments will appear. An Expanded Sixth Edition of this anthology will be issued containing (with only rare exceptions) everything that this edition contains, plus approximately two thousand pages devoted to outstanding literary landmarks in the cultures of China; India; Japan; Iran, Egypt, and the Arab and Islamic worlds generally; Africa and the Caribbean; and Native America. As is true of all Norton anthologies, the works presented will be chosen, edited, annotated, and discussed by scholar-teachers with internationally recognized credentials. As is also true of Norton books, the Expanded Sixth Edition will avoid cumbrousness of weight and size by the cunning of its design.

We fully understand that even the Expanded Edition can never do entire justice to these great literatures. To accomplish that would call for a five-foot shelf of anthologies of encyclopedic size. Nonetheless, our added pages will afford those of you who wish it a steeper challenge and an exciting further range. We also fully understand that many of you, for reasons both philosophical and personal, will be in no rush to change. Nor need you be. This Sixth Edition and its successors will continue as in the past to evolve and grow, responding to the needs and preferences of those who wish to stress in the limited time at their disposal the Judaic-Greek-Roman-European-American traditions of thought and feeling from which a majority of the institutions of the United States and Canada derive.

Looking out on the controversies now raging between advocates of "canonicity" and "multiculturalism," we find it useful to remember that a sound democracy, like an effective orchestra, needs diversity and consensus equally. Without diversity the music thins. Without consensus, as Achebe registers so movingly in the novel we conclude with, it "falls apart." Heraclitus put the point memorably some twenty-five hundred years ago: "As with the bow and the lyre, so with the world. It is the tension of opposing forces that makes the structure one."

The Editors

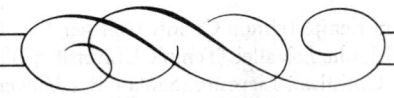

Acknowledgments

We would like, first, to thank Jerome Clinton (Princeton University), for the introductions and notes to *The Epic of Gilgamesh* and the Koran. We need also to thank two eagle-eyed friends, Robert McCoy (Kent State University) and Evan Radcliffe (Villanova University), whose generous help enabled us to correct many of the typographical errors that, to our embarrassment and chagrin, marred the first printings of the last edition.

Among our many critics, advisers, and friends, the following were of special help in providing suggestions and corrections: Richard Adicks (University of Central Florida); Tamara Agha-Jaffar (Kansas City Community College); Kerry Ahearn (Oregon State University); Sarah Bahous Allen (North Georgia College); David Anderson (Texas A & M University); Denise Baker (University of North Carolina—Greensboro); William F. Belcher (University of North Texas); L. Michael Bell (University of Colorado); Ernest Bernhardt (Indiana University); Craig Bernthal (Fresno State University); Gene Blanton (Jacksonville State University); Betsy Bowden (Rutgers University—Camden); Max Braffett (Southwest Texas State University); Edythe Briggs (Santa Rosa Junior College); Gary Brodsky (Northeastern Illinois University); Byron Brown (Valdosta State College); James L. Brown (Kansas City Kansas Community College); Corbin S. Carnell (University of Florida); Michael Carson (University of Evansville); Rose-Ann Cecere (Broward Community College); John Cech (University of Florida); Howard Clarke (University of California—Santa Barbara); Stephen Cooper (Troy State University); T. A. Copeland (Youngstown State University); Walter Coppedge (Virginia Commonwealth University); Bill Crider (Alvin Community College); George Crosland (California State University—Chico); Lennet Daigle (Georgia Southwestern College); Charles Daniel (Valdosta State College); Rosemary DePaolo (Augusta State College); Joseph DeRocco (Bridgewater State College); Ronald DiLorenzo (St. Louis University); Brooks Dodson (University of North Carolina—Wilmington); Patricia Doyle (Lynchburg College); Francis X. Duggan (Santa Clara University); Caroline D. Eckhardt (Pennsylvania State University); Seth Ellis (University of North Carolina—Charlotte); Tom Ferte (Western Oregon State College); Joyce Field; Rowena Flanagan (Kansas City Community College); Marco Fraschella (San Joaquin Delta College); Ruth Fry (Auburn University); Michael Fukuchi (Atlantic Christian College); Robert Gariepy (Eastern Washington University); Robert Garrity (St. Joseph's College); Bruce Golden (California State University—San Bernardino); Gerald Gordon (Kirkwood Community College); Richard Guzman (North Central College); Richard Hannaford (University of Idaho); Stephen Hemenway (Hope College); Beverly Heneghan (Northern Virginia Community College—Annandale); John Hennedy (Providence College); John Hiers (Valdosta State College); Robert Hogan (Rhode Island College); Rebecca Hogan (University of Wisconsin—Whitewater); Phil Holcomb (Angelo State University); Julia Bolton Holloway (University of Colorado); Wallace Hooker (Houston Baptist University); Marjorie Hoskinson (Los Angeles Pierce College); Richard Keithley (Georgia Southern College); Steven G. Kellman (University of Texas at

San Antonio); Barbara Kemps (Union County College); Eric LaGuardia (University of Washington); Marthe LaVallee (Temple University); William Levison (Valdosta State College); Christiaan Lievestro (Santa Clara University); William Lutz (Rutgers University—Camden); Kathleen Lyons (Bellarmine College); Marianne Mayo (Valdosta State College); Barry McAndrew (Mercyhurst College); Glenn McCartney; James McKusick (University of Maryland—Baltimore College); David Middleton (Trinity University); Robert Miller (North Harris Community College, South); James Misenheimer (Indiana State University); David Neff (University of Alabama—Huntsville); Kurt Olsson (University of Idaho); Robert Oxley (Embry-Riddle Aeronautical University); Richard Pacholski (Milliken University); Frank Palmeri (University of Miami); Elysee Peavy (Houston Baptist University); Larry H. Peer (Brigham Young University); John Pennington (Valdosta State College); K. J. Phillips (University of Hawaii); Ira Plybon (Marshall University); Willard Potts (Oregon State University); Victoria Poulakis (Northern Virginia Community College); Joseph Price (Northern Kentucky University); Richard Priebe (Virginia Commonwealth University); Otto Reinert (University of Washington); Janet Robinson (St. Petersburg Community College); James Rolleston (Duke University); Roberta Rosenberg (Christopher Newport College); John Rudy (Indiana University—Kokomo); Pamela Sheridan (Moorpark College); Judith P. Shoaf (University of Florida); Jack Shreve (Allegany Community College); Martha Simonsen (William Rainey Harper College); George Simson (University of Hawaii at Manoa); Melvin Storm (Emporia State University); Frank Stringfellow (University of Miami); Norman Stroh (Angelo State University); Nathaniel Teich (University of Oregon); Eric Thorn (Marshall University); Bruce Thornton (California State University—Fresno); Mason Tung (University of Idaho); Linnea Vacca (St. Mary's College); Robert Vuturo (Kansas City Community College); Sidney Wade (University of Florida); Martha Waller (Butler University); Roger Weaver (Oregon State University); Gibb Weber (Anderson University); Henry Weinfield (New Jersey Institute of Technology); Michael White (Odessa College); Gary Williams (University of Idaho); J. Wooliscroft (Edinboro University of Pennsylvania).

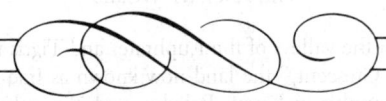

Masterpieces of the
Ancient World

This section represents, not the ancient world as a whole, but its most significant area and period. The area is the Mediterranean basin, and the period the twelve hundred years from, roughly, 800 B.C. to A.D. 400. In this place and time the intellectual and religious foundations of the modern Western outlook were laid.

The literature of that world, which, whether or not we are acquainted with it, is still the background of our institutions, attitudes, and thought, was written in three languages—Hebrew, Greek, and Latin. The peoples who spoke these languages created their civilizations independently in place and time, but the development of the Mediterranean area into one economic and political unit brought them into contact with one another and produced a fusion of their typical attitudes that is the basis of all subsequent Western thought. This process of independent development, interaction, and final fusion is represented in the arrangement of this section: In the last part of it the three separate lines converge, and they finally meet in the figure of St. Augustine, who had the intellectual honesty and curiosity of the Greek at his best, the social seriousness and sense of order of the Roman, and the Hebrew's feeling of man's inadequacy and God's omnipotent justice.

THE ANCIENT WORLD

Though Rome at the height of her power was to extend her rule northward through France as far as Britain and eastward to the Euphrates, the ancient world was centered on the Mediterranean Sea—"We live around the sea," said the Greek philosopher Socrates, "like frogs around a pond." Climate and basic crops were (and still are) similar over most of the area: a dry hot summer and a comparatively mild winter, more favorable to sheep and goats than cattle, to vine and olive rather than cereal crops. Though metal was mined and worked, what we know as heavy industry did not exist; coal and oil were not exploited for energy, and the war galleys were propelled by sail and human oarsmen, the armies moved on foot. All the advanced civilizations of the ancient world depended for their existence on a slave class to do their heavy work, on the land, in the mines, and in the house; this institution, widely varied in its forms—peasants tied to the land as in Egypt, bought slaves as in Greece and Rome, or men enslaved for debt as in Greece and Israel— lasted until the end of the ancient world, to be gradually replaced in Europe by the feudal system with a peasantry technically free but in practice working the land for the benefit of an overlord.

Civilization began, not on the shores of the Mediterranean, but east and south of that sea: in Babylon and Egypt. Ancient civilization was based on agriculture and it flourished first in regions where the soil gave rich rewards: in the valley of the Nile, where annual floods left large tracts of land moist and fertile under the

1

Egyptian sun, and in the valleys of the Euphrates and Tigris rivers, which flowed through the "Fertile Crescent," the land now known as Iraq and Iran. Great cities—Thebes and Memphis in Egypt, Babylon and Nineveh in the Fertile Crescent—came into being as centers for the complicated administration of the irrigated fields. Supported by the surplus the land produced, they became centers also for government, religion, and culture. Civilization begins with cities; the word itself is derived from a Latin word which means "citizen." As far back as 3000 B.C. the pharaohs of Egypt began to build their splendid temples and gigantic pyramids, as well as to record their political acts and religious beliefs in hieroglyphic script. The Sumerians, Babylonians, and Assyrians began to build the palaces and temples of Babylon, as well as to record their laws in cuneiform script on clay tablets.

These civilizations were already immemorially old when Israel, Greece and, later, Rome became conscious of their national character and destiny, yet it was to the younger nations that the future belonged. Babylon, Nineveh, and Egypt as the centuries went by were all but lost to memory, as *Gilgamesh* exemplifies. The pyramids and the Sphinx remained but it was not until the nineteenth century A.D. that the hieroglyphic writing of the Egyptians and the cuneiform records of Babylon and Nineveh were deciphered and their contents read again after a lapse of thousands of years. The cultural history of the ancient world came to medieval Europe in the languages not of Babylon and Egypt but in Hebrew, Greek, and Latin.

THE HEBREWS

There was, of course, contact between the old civilizations and the new. The Hebrews, in fact, early in their history, spent some years as government slaves in Egypt before their Exodus, their migration, under the leadership of Moses, through the Sinai desert to Palestine. This new home of the Hebrews was of no particular strategic importance, and their record is not that of an imperial people. In their period of independence, from their beginnings as a pastoral tribe to their high point as a kingdom with a splendid capital in Jerusalem, they accomplished little of note in the political or military spheres. Their later history was a bitter and unsuccessful struggle for freedom against a series of foreign masters—Babylonian, Greek, and Roman.

After the period of expansion and prosperity under the great kings, David and Solomon (1005–925 B.C.), the kingdom fell apart again into warring factions, which called in outside powers. The melancholy end of a long period of internal and external struggle was the destruction of the cities and the deportation of the population to Babylon (586 B.C.). This period of exile (it ended in 539 when Cyrus, the Persian conqueror of Babylon, released the Hebrews from bondage) was a formative period for Hebrew religious thought, which was enriched and refined by the teachings of the prophet Ezekiel and the unknown prophet known as the Second Isaiah (pp. 48, 89). The return to Palestine was crowned by the rebuilding of the Temple and the creation of the canonical version of the Pentateuch or Torah, the first five books of the Old Testament. The religious legacy of the Hebrew people was now codified for future generations.

But the independent state of Israel was not destined to last long. By 300 B.C. the Macedonian successors of Alexander the Great had encroached on its borders and prerogatives; in spite of a heroic resistance, the territory eventually became part of a Hellenistic Greek-speaking kingdom and, finally, was absorbed by the Roman Empire. A desperate revolt against Rome was crushed in A.D. 70 by the emperor Titus (on the arch of Titus in Rome a relief shows the legionaries carrying the menorah, the seven-branched candlestick, in Titus' triumph). A second revolt, against the emperor Hadrian (A.D. 131–134) resulted in the final extermination or removal from Palestine of the Hebrew people. Henceforward, they were the people of the *diaspora*, the "scattering": religious communities in the great cities of the ancient world maintaining local cohesion and universal religious solidarity but stateless, as they were to be all through the centuries until the creation, in our time, of the state of Israel.

The political history of the ancient Hebrews ended in a series of disasters. In the field of the arts they left behind them no painting or sculpture and little or no secular literature—no drama, for example, no epic poetry. What they did leave us is a religious literature, written down probably between the eighth and second centuries B.C., which is informed by an attitude different from that of any other nation of the ancient world. It is founded on the idea of one God, the creator of all things, all-powerful and just—a conception of the divine essence and the government of the universe so simple that to those of us who have inherited it it seems obvious. But in its time it was so revolutionary that it made the Hebrews a nation apart, sometimes laughed at, sometimes feared, but always alien.

THE GREEKS

The origin of the peoples who eventually produced the great literature of the eighth to the fourth centuries B.C. is still a mystery. The language they spoke clearly belongs to the great Indo-European family (which includes the Germanic, Celtic, Italic, and Sanskrit language groups), but many of the ancient Greek words and place names have terminations that are definitely not Indo-European—the word for sea (*thalassa*), for example. The Greeks of historic times were presumably a blend of the native tribes and the Indo-European invaders, en route from the European landmass.

In the last hundred years archeology has given us a clearer picture than our forefathers had of the level of civilization in early Greece. The second millennium B.C. saw a brilliant culture, called Minoan after the mythical king Minos, flourishing on the large island of Crete, and the citadel of Mycenae and the palace at Pylos show that mainland Greece, in that same period, had centers of wealth and power unsuspected before the excavators discovered the gold masks of the buried kings and the clay tablets covered with strange signs. The decipherment of these signs (published in 1953) revealed that the language of these Myceneans was an early form of Greek. It must have been the memory of these rich kingdoms that inspired Homer's vision of "Mycenae rich in gold" and the splendid armed hosts that assembled for the attack on Troy.

It was a blurred memory (Homer does not remember the writing, for example, or the detailed bureaucratic accounting recorded on the tablets) and this is easy to understand: some time in the last century of the millennium the great palaces were destroyed by fire. With them disappeared not only the arts and skills that had created Mycenean wealth but even the system of writing. For the next few hundred poverty-stricken years the Greeks were illiterate and so no written evidence survives for what, in view of our ignorance about so many aspects of it, we call the Dark Age of Greece.

One thing we do know about it: it produced a body of oral epic poetry which was the raw material Homer shaped into the two great poems, the *Iliad* and *Odyssey*. These Homeric poems seem from internal evidence to date from the eighth century B.C.—which is incidentally, or perhaps not incidentally, the century in which the Greeks learned how to write again. They played in the subsequent development of Greek civilization the same role that the Old Testament writings had played in Palestine: they became the basis of an education and therefore of a whole culture. Not only did the great characters of the epic serve as models of conduct for later generations of Greeks, but the figures of the Olympian gods retained, in the prayers, poems, and sculpture of the succeeding centuries, the shapes and attributes set down by Homer. The difference between the Greek and the Hebrew hero, between Achilles and Joseph, for example, is remarkable, but the difference between "the God of Abraham and of Isaac" and the Olympians who interfere capriciously in the lives of Hector and Achilles is an unbridgeable chasm. The two conceptions of the power that governs the universe are irreconcilable; and in fact the struggle between them ended, not in synthesis, but in the complete victory of the one and the disappearance of the other. The Greek conception of the nature of the gods and of their relation to humanity is so alien to us that it is difficult for the modern reader to take it seriously. The Hebrew basis of European religious thought has made it almost impossible for us to imagine a god who can be feared and laughed at, blamed and admired, and still sincerely worshiped. Yet all these are proper attitudes toward the gods on Olympus; they are all implicit in Homer's poems.

The Hebrew conception of God emphasizes those aspects of the universe that imply a harmonious order. The elements of disorder in the universe are, in the story of Creation, blamed on man, and in all Hebrew literature the evidences of disorder are something the writer tries to reconcile with an *a priori* assumption of an all-powerful, just God; he never tampers with the fundamental datum. Just as clearly, the Greeks conceived their gods as an expression of the disorder of the world in which they lived. The Olympian gods, like the natural forces of sea and sky, follow their own will even to the extreme of conflict with each other, and always with a sublime disregard for the human beings who may be affected by the results of their actions. It is true that they are all subjects of a single more powerful god, Zeus. But his authority over them is based only on superior strength; though he cannot be openly resisted, he can be temporarily deceived by his fellow Olympians. And Zeus, although by virtue of his superior power his will is finally accomplished in the matter of Achilles' wrath, knows limits to his power too. He cannot save the life of his son the Lycian hero Sarpedon. Behind Zeus stands the mysterious power of Fate, to which even he must bow.

Such gods as these, representing as they do the blind forces of the universe which man cannot control, are not thought of as connected with morality. Morality is a human creation, and though the gods may approve of it, they are not bound by it. And violent as they are, they cannot feel the ultimate consequence of violence: death is a human fear, just as the courage to face it is a human quality. There is a double standard, one for gods, one for men, and the inevitable consequence is that our real admiration and sympathy is directed not toward the gods but toward the men. With Hector, and even with Achilles at his worst, we can sympathize; but the gods, though they may excite terror or laughter, can never have our sympathy. We could as easily sympathize with a blizzard or the force of gravity. Homer imposed on Greek literature the anthropocentric emphasis which is its distinguishing mark and its great contribution to the Western mind. Though the gods are ever-present characters in the incidents of his poem, his true concern, first and last, is with men and women.

THE CITY-STATES OF GREECE

The stories told in the Homeric poems are set in the age of the Trojan War, which archeologists (those, that is, who believe that it happened at all) date to the twelfth century B.C. Though the poems do perhaps preserve some faded memories of the Mycenaean age, there is no doubt that the poems as we have them are the creation of later centuries, the tenth to the eighth B.C., the so-called Dark Age which succeeded the collapse (or destruction) of Mycenaean civilization. This was the time of the final settlement of the Greek peoples, an age of invasion and migration, which saw the foundation and growth of many small independent cities. The geography of Greece—a land of mountain barriers and scattered islands—encouraged this fragmentation. The Greek cities never lost sight of their common Hellenic heritage, but it was not enough to unite them except in the face of unmistakable and overwhelming danger, and even then only partially and for a short time. They differed from each other in custom, political constitution, and even dialect: their relations with each other were those of rivals and fierce competitors.

In these cities, constantly at war in the pursuit of more productive land for growing populations, the kings of Homeric society gave way to aristocratic oligarchies, which maintained a stranglehold on the land and the economy of which it was the base. An important safety valve was colonization. In the eighth and seventh centuries B.C. landless men founded new cities (always near the sea and generally owing little or no allegiance to the home base) all over the Mediterranean coast—in Spain, southern France (Marseilles, Nice, and Antibes were all Greek cities), in South Italy (Naples), Sicily (Syracuse), North Africa (Cyrene), all along the coast of Asia Minor (Smyrna, Miletus), and even on the Black Sea as far as Russian Crimea. Many of these new outposts of Greek civilization experienced a faster economic and cultural development than the older cities of the mainland. It was in the cities founded on the Asian coast that the Greeks adapted to their own language the Phoenician system of writing, adding signs for the vowels to create the first efficient alphabet. Its first use was probably for commercial records and transactions, but as literacy became a general condition all over the Greek world in the course of the seventh century B.C., treaties and political decrees were inscribed on stone and literary works written on rolls of paper made from the Egyptian papyrus plant.

ATHENS AND SPARTA

By the beginning of the fifth century B.C. the two most prominent city-states were Athens and Sparta. These two cities led the combined Greek resistance to the Persian invasion of Europe in the years 490 to 479 B.C. The defeat of the solid Persian power by the divided and insignificant Greek cities surprised the world and inspired in Greece, and particularly in Athens, a confidence that knew no bounds.

Athens was at this time a democracy, the first in Western history. It was a direct, not a representative, democracy, for the number of free citizens was small enough to permit the exercise of power by a meeting of the citizens as a body in assembly. Athens' power lay in the fleet with which she had played her decisive part in the struggle against Persia, and with this fleet she rapidly became the leader of a naval alliance which included most of the islands of the Aegean Sea and many Greek cities on the coast of Asia Minor. Sparta, on the other hand, was a totalitarian state, rigidly conservative in government and policy, in which the individual citizen was reared and trained by the state for the state's business, war. The Spartan land army was consequently superior to any other in Greece, and the Spartans controlled, by direct rule or by alliance, a majority of the city-states of the Peloponnese.

These two cities, allies for the war of liberation against Persia, became enemies when the external danger was eliminated. The middle years of the fifth century were disturbed by indecisive hostilities between them and haunted by the probability of full-scale war to come. As the years went by, this war came to be accepted as "inevitable" by both sides, and in 431 B.C. it began. It was to end in 404 B.C. with the total defeat of Athens.

Before the beginning of this disastrous war Athenian democracy provided its citizens with a cultural and political environment that was without precedent in the ancient world. The institutions of Athens encouraged the maximum development of the individual's capacities and at the same time inspired the maximum devotion to the interests of the community. It was a moment in history of delicate and precarious balance between the freedom of the individual and the demands of the state. Its uniqueness was emphasized by the complete lack of balance in Sparta, where the necessities of the state annihilated the individual as a creative and independent being. It was the proud boast of the Athenians that without sacrificing the cultural amenities of civilized life they could yet when called upon surpass in policy and war their adversary, whose citizen body was an army in constant training. The Athenians were, in this respect as in others, a nation of amateurs. "The individual Athenian," said Pericles, Athens' great statesman at this time, "in his own person seems to have the power of adapting himself to the most varied forms of action with the utmost versatility and grace." But the freedom of the individual did not, in Athens' great days, produce anarchy. "While we are . . . unconstrained in our private intercourse," Pericles had observed earlier in his speech, "a spirit of reverence pervades our public acts."

This balance of individual freedom and communal unity was not destined to outlast the century. It went down, with Athens, in the war. Under the mounting pressure of the long conflict, the Athenians lost the "spirit of reverence" that Pericles saw as the stabilizing factor in Athenian democracy. They subordinated all considerations to the immediate interest of the city and surpassed their enemy in the logical ferocity of their actions. They finally fell victim to leaders who carried the process one step further and subordinated all considerations to their own private interest. The war years saw the decay of that freedom in unity which is celebrated in Pericles' speech. By the end of the fifth century Athens was divided internally as well as defeated externally. The individual citizen no longer thought of himself and Athens as one and the same; the balance was gone forever.

One of the solvents of traditional values was an intellectual revolution which was taking place in the advanced Athenian democracy of the last half of the fifth century, a critical re-evaluation of accepted ideas in every sphere of thought and action. It stemmed from innovations in education. Democratic institutions had created a demand for an education that would prepare men for public life, especially by training them in the art of public speaking. The demand was met by the appearance of the professional teacher, the Sophist, as he was called, who taught, for a handsome fee, not only the techniques of public speaking but also the subjects that gave a man something to talk about—government, ethics, literary criticism, even astronomy. The curriculum of the Sophists, in fact, marks the first appearance in European civilization of the liberal education, just as they themselves were the first professors.

The Sophists were great teachers, but like most teachers they had little or no control over the results of their teaching. Their methods placed an inevitable emphasis on effective presentation of a point of view, to the detriment, and if necessary the exclusion, of anything which might make it less convincing. They produced a generation that had been trained to see both sides of any question and to argue the weaker side as effectively as the stronger, the false as effectively as the true. They taught how to argue inferentially from probability in the absence of concrete evidence; to appeal to the audience's sense of its own advantage rather than to accepted moral standards; and to justify individual defiance of general prejudice and even of law by making a distinction between "nature" and "convention." These methods dominated the thinking of the Athenians of the last half of the century. Emphasis on the technique of effective presentation of both sides of any case encouraged a relativistic point of view and finally produced a cynical mood which denied the existence of any absolute standards. The canon of probability (which implies an appeal to human reason as the supreme authority) became a critical weapon for an attack on myth and on traditional conceptions of the gods; though it had its constructive side, too, for it was the base for historical reconstruction of the unrecorded past and of the stages of human progress from savagery to civilization. The rhetorical appeal to the self-interest of the audience, to expediency, became the method of the political leaders of the wartime democracy and the fundamental doctrine of new theories of power-politics. These theories served as cynical justification for the increasing severity of the measures Athens took to terrorize her rebellious subjects. Their distinction between "nature" and "convention" is the source of the doctrine of the superman, who breaks free of the conventional restraints of society and acts according to the law of his own "nature." The new spirit in Athens has magnificent achievements to its credit, but it undermined old solid moral convictions. At its roots was a supreme confidence in the human intelligence and a secular view of man's position in the universe that is best expressed in the statement of Protagoras, the most famous of the Sophists: "Man is the measure of all things."

THE DECLINE OF THE CITY-STATE

In the last half of the fifth century the whole traditional basis of individual conduct, which had been concern for the unity and cohesion of the city-state, was undermined—gradually at first by the critical approach of the Sophists and their pupils, and then rapidly, as the war accelerated the process of moral disintegration. "In peace and prosperity," says Thucydides, "both states and individuals are actuated by higher motives . . . but war, which takes away the comfortable provision of daily life, is a hard master, and tends to assimilate men's characters to their conditions." The war brought to Athens the rule of new politicians who were schooled in the doctrine of the new power-politics and initiated savage reprisals against Athens' rebellious subject-allies, launching the city on an expansionist course which ended in disaster in Sicily (411 B.C.). Seven years later Athens, her last fleet gone, surrendered to the Spartans. A pro-Spartan antidemocratic regime, the Thirty Tyrants, was installed, but soon overthrown. Athens became a democracy again but the confidence and unity of its great age were gone forever. Community and individual were no longer one, and the individual, cast on his own resources for guidance, found only conflicting attitudes which he could not refer to any absolute standards. The mood of postwar Athens oscillated between a fanatic, unthinking reassertion of traditional values and a weary cynicism which wanted only to be left alone. The only thing common to the two extremes was a distrust of intelligence.

In the disillusioned gloom of defeat, Athenians began to feel more and more exasperation with a voice they had been listening to for many years. This was the voice of Socrates, a stonemason who for most of his adult life had made it his business to discuss with his fellow citizens the great issues of which the Athenians were now so weary—the nature of justice, of truth, of piety. Unlike the Sophists, he did not lecture nor did he charge a fee: his method was dialectic, a search for truth through questions and answers, and his dedication to his mission had kept him poor. But the initial results of his discussions were often infuriatingly like the results of sophistic teaching. By questions and answers he exposed the illogicality of his opponent's position, but did not often provide a substitute for the belief he had destroyed. Yet it is clear that he did believe in absolute standards, and what is more, believed they could be discovered by a process of logical inquiry and supported by logical proof. His ethics rested on an intellectual basis. The resentment against him, which came to a head in 399 B.C., is partly explained by the fact that he satisfied neither extreme of the postwar mood. He questioned the old standards in order to establish new, and he refused to let the Athenians live in peace, for he preached that it was every man's duty to think his way through to the truth. In this last respect he was the prophet of the new age. For him, the city and the accepted code were no substitute for the task of self-examination which each individual must set himself and carry through to a conclusion. The characteristic statement of the old Athens was public, in the assembly or the theater; Socrates proclaimed the right and duty of each individual to work out his own salvation and made clear his distrust of public life: "he who will fight for the right . . . must have a private station and not a public one."

The Athenians sentenced him to death on a charge of impiety. They hoped, no doubt, that he would go into exile to escape execution but he remained, as he put it himself, at his post, and they were forced to have the sentence carried out. If they thought they were finished with him, they were sadly mistaken. In the next century Athens became the center for a large group of philosophical schools, all of them claiming to develop and interpret the ideas of Socrates.

The century that followed his death saw the exhaustion of the Greek city-states in constant internecine warfare. Politically and economically bankrupt, they fell under the power of Macedon in the north, whose king, Philip, combined a ferocious energy with a cynicism that enabled him to take full advantage of the corrupt governments of the city-states. Greek liberty ended at the battle of Chaeronea in 338 B.C., and Philip's son Alexander inherited a powerful army and the political control of all Greece. He led his Macedonian and Greek armies against Persia, and in a few brilliant campaigns became master of an empire that extended into Egypt in the south and to the borders of India in the east. He died at Babylon in 323 B.C., and his empire broke up into a number of independent kingdoms ruled by his generals; but the results of his fantastic achievements were more durable than might have been expected. Into the newly conquered territories came thousands of Greeks who wished to escape from the political futility and economic crisis of the homeland. Wherever they went they took with them their language, their culture, and their typical buildings, the gymnasium and the theater. At Alexandria in Egypt, for example, a Greek library was formed to preserve the texts of Greek literature for the scholars who edited them, a school of Greek poetry flourished, Greek mathematicians and geographers made new advances in science. The Middle East became, as far as the cities were concerned, a Greek-speaking area; and when, some two or three centuries later, the first accounts of the life and teaching of Jesus of Nazareth were written down, they were written in Greek, the language on which the cultural homogeneity of the whole area was based.

ROME

When Alexander died at Babylon in 323 B.C., the Italian city of Rome, situated on the Tiber in the western coastal plain, was engaged in a struggle for the control of central Italy. Less than a hundred years later (269 B.C.) Rome, in control of the whole Italian peninsula, was drawn into a hundred-year war against the Phoenician city of Carthage, on the North African coast, from which it emerged master of the western Mediterranean. At the end of the first century B.C., in spite of a series of civil wars fought with savage vindictiveness and on a continental scale, Rome was the capital of an empire that stretched from the Straits of Gibraltar to the frontiers of Palestine. This empire gave peace and orderly government to the Mediterranean area for the next two centuries, and for two centuries after that maintained a desperate but losing battle against the invading savage tribes moving in from the north and east. When it finally went down, it left behind it the ideal of the world-state, an ideal that was to be reconstituted as a reality by the medieval church, which ruled from the same center, Rome, and with a spiritual authority as great as the secular authority it replaced.

The achievements of the Romans, not only their conquests but also their success in consolidating the conquests and organizing the conquered, are best understood in the light of the Roman character. Unlike the Greeks, Romans were above all a practical people. They might have no aptitude for pure mathematics, but they could build an aqueduct to last two thousand years. Though they were not notable as political theorists, they organized a complicated yet stable federation that held Italy loyal to them in the presence of invading armies. Romans were conservative to the core; their strongest authority was *mos maiorum*, the custom of predecessors. A monument of this conservatism, the great body of Roman law, is one of their greatest contributions to Western civilization. The quality Romans most admired was *gravitas*, seriousness of attitude and purpose, and their highest words of commendation were "manliness," "industry," "discipline." Pericles, in his funeral speech, praised the Athenian for his adaptability, versatility, and grace. This would have seemed strange praise to a Roman, whose idea of personal and civic virtue was different. "By her ancient customs and her men the Roman state stands," says Ennius the Roman poet, in a line that by its metrical heaviness emphasizes the stability implied in the key word "stands": *moribus antiquis res stat Romana virisque.*

Greek history begins, not with a king, a battle, or the founding of a city, but with an epic poem; the literary achievement preceded the political by many centuries. The Romans, on the other hand, had conquered half the world before they began to write. The stimulus to the creation of Latin literature was the Greek literature that the Romans discovered when, in the second century B.C., they assumed political responsibility for Greece and the Near East. Latin literature began with a translation of the *Odyssey*, made by a Greek prisoner of war, and with the exception of satire, until Latin literature became Christian, the model was always Greek. The Latin writer (especially the poet) borrowed wholesale from his Greek original, not furtively, but openly and proudly, as a tribute to the master from whom he had learned. But this frank acknowledgment of indebtedness should not blind us to the fact that Latin literature is original, and sometimes profoundly so. This is true above all of Virgil, who chose as his theme the coming of the Trojan prince Aeneas to Italy, where he was to found a city from which, in the fullness of time, would come "the Latin race, ... and the walls of lofty Rome."

When Virgil was born in 70 B.C. the Roman republic, which had conquered and now governed the Mediterranean world, had barely recovered from one civil war and was drifting inexorably toward another. The institutions of the city-state proved inadequate for world government. The civil conflict which had disrupted the republic for more than a hundred years ended finally in the establishment of a powerful executive. Although the Senate, which had been the controlling body of the republic, retained an impressive share of the power, the new arrangement developed inevitably toward autocracy, the rule of the executive, the emperor, as he was called once the system was stabilized. The first of the long line of Roman emperors who gave stable government to the Roman world during the first two centuries A.D. was Octavius, known generally by his title, Augustus. He had made his way cautiously through the intrigues and bloodshed that followed the murder of his uncle Julius Caesar in 44 B.C. until by 31 B.C. he controlled the western half of the empire. In that year he fought a decisive battle with the ruler of the eastern half of the empire, Mark Antony, who was supported by Cleopatra, queen of Egypt. Octavius's victory at Actium united the empire under one authority and ushered in an age of peace and reconstruction.

For the next two hundred years the successors of Augustus, the Roman emperors, ruled the ancient world with only occasional disturbances, most of them confined to Rome, where emperors who flagrantly abused their immense power—Nero, for example—were overthrown by force. The second half of this period was described by Gibbon, the great historian of imperial Rome, as the period "in the history of the world during which the condition of the human race was most happy and prosperous." The years A.D. 96–180, those of the "five good emperors," were in fact remarkable: this was the longest period of peace that has ever been enjoyed by the inhabitants of an area that included Britain, France, all southern Europe, the Middle East, and the whole of North Africa. Trade and agriculture flourished, and the cities with their public baths, theaters, and libraries offered all the amenities of civilized life. Yet there was apparent, especially in the literature of the second century, a spiritual emptiness. Petronius's *Satyricon* paints a sardonic portrait of the vulgar display and intellectual poverty of the newly rich who can think only in terms of money and possessions. The old religion offered no comfort to those who looked beyond mere material ends; it had been too closely knit into the fabric of the independent city-state and was inadequate for a time in which men were citizens of the world. New religions arose or were imported from the East, universal religions that made their appeal to all nations and classes: the worship of the Egyptian goddess Isis, of the Persian god Mithras, who offered bliss in the life to come, and of the Hebrew prophet Jesus, crucified in Jerusalem and believed risen from the dead. This was the religion that, working underground and often suppressed (there was a persecution of the Christians under Nero in the first century, another under the last of the "good emperors" Marcus Aurelius in the second), finally triumphed and became the official and later the exclusive religion of the Roman world. As the empire in the third and fourth centuries disintegrated under the never-ending invasions by barbarian tribes from the north, the Church, with its center and spiritual head in Rome, converted the new inhabitants and so made possible the preservation of much of that Latin and Greek literature that was to serve the European Middle Ages and, later, the Renaissance, as a model and a basis for their own great achievements in the arts and letters.

FURTHER READING

H. M. Orlinsky, *Ancient Israel*, 2nd ed. (1960) is a short but clearly written outline of the history of Israel up to the return from Babylonian exile. John Boardman, Jasper Griffin, and Oswyn Murray, eds., *The Oxford History of the Classical World* (1986) is a superb survey, by many different specialists, of the whole sweep of classical culture—social, political, literary, artistic, and religious. It is also handsomely and lavishly illustrated. For the political history of Greece to the death of Alexander, see J. B. Bury, *A History of Greece*, 4th ed., revised by Russell Merggs (1975). Michael Grant, *History of Rome* (1978), presents a well-illustrated, eminently readable survey.

THE EPIC OF GILGAMESH

The Epic of Gilgamesh is a poem of unparalleled antiquity, the first great heroic narrative of world literature. Its origins stretch back to the margins of prehistory, and its evolution spans millennia. When it was known it was widely known. Tablets containing portions of *Gilgamesh* have been found at sites throughout the Middle East and in all the languages written in cuneiform characters, wedge-shaped characters incised in clay or stone. But then, at a time when the civilizations of the Hebrews, Greeks, and Romans had only just developed beyond their infancy, *Gilgamesh* vanished from memory. For reasons that scholars have not yet fathomed, the literature of the cuneiform languages was not translated into the new alphabets that replaced them. Some portions of this once famous work survived in subsequent traditions, but they did so as scattered and anonymous fragments. They became a kind of invisible substratum that was buried under what was previously believed to be the earliest level of our common tradition. Until Utnapishtim's "Story of the Flood," a portion of *Gilgamesh*, was accidentally rediscovered and published in 1872, no one suspected that the biblical story of Noah and the Great Flood was neither original nor unique.

A great lost work like *The Epic of Gilgamesh* poses particular problems of understanding beyond those posed by the discovery of a lost masterpiece by a known author or of a known time. The meaning of a work of literature is partly contextual—it is established by the culture that produced that work. Yet the whole context of *Gilgamesh* was lost along with the text. The names of the gods and humans who people the epic, the cities and lands in which they lived, and the whole of their history vanished for thousands of years from common memory. The story of Gilgamesh and his companion Enkidu speaks to contemporary readers with astonishing immediacy. Its moving depiction of the bonds of friendship, of the quest for worldly renown, and of the tragic attempt to escape that death which is the common fate of humanity has a timeless resonance and appeal. Yet despite this immediate recognition of something profoundly familiar there is, because of this millennial gap in the history of its transmission, a strangeness and remoteness about the work that strikes us in virtually every line. That strangeness has diminished each year as more tablets have been discovered and translated, and as our understanding of the languages and cultures of the ancient Middle East has increased, but what we know is still relatively slight compared to what we know of the cultures that succeeded them. Today the names of Ulysses and Achilles and the gods and goddesses of Mount Olympus are familiar even to many who have not read Homer. The names of Gilgamesh, Enkidu, Utnapishtim, Enlil, and Eanna are virtually unknown outside the poem itself.

The Epic of Gilgamesh developed over a period of nearly a thousand years. In the version discovered in the city of Ninevah amidst the ruins of the great royal library of Assurbanipal, the last great king of the Assyrian empire—what modern scholars now call the Standard Version—it circulated widely throughout the ancient Middle East for a millennium or more. While the history of the text is a long and complex one, and is still far from fully understood, it is possible to identify three principal stages in its development. The first begins in roughly 2700 B.C. when the historical Gilgamesh ruled in Uruk, a city in ancient Mesopotamia. Tales both mythical and legendary grew up around him and were repeated and copied for centuries. The stories that were later incorporated into the *Gilgamesh* epic existed in this literature, albeit in different form, as well as other material concerning the historical Gilgamesh that was not included in the epic. The earliest written versions of these stories date from roughly 2000 B.C., but oral versions of the stories both preceded them and continued on, parallel with the written tradition. The language of these materials was Sumerian, the earliest written language in Mesopotamia, and one that has little if any connection to any other known language.

The history of the epic itself begins sometime before 1600 B.C., some eight centuries before Homer, when a Babylonian author (Mesopotamian tradition identifies a priest-exorcist named Sîn-leqi-unninni) assembled free translations of the oral versions of some of these tales into a connected narrative. This new work was not simply a sequence of tales linked by the character of Gilgamesh, but a conscious selection and recasting of the Sumerian materials into a new form. Some Gilgamesh tales were ignored while elements from stories not associated with him in the Sumerian accounts were incorporated. This earliest version of the epic, which exists only in fragmentary form, continued to develop for the next few centuries. However, no comparable recasting of the poem was made. By the time of Assurbanipal (668–627 B.C.) the text was essentially stabilized.

Assurbanipal's synthetic version—the Standard Version—was also the first discovered. It was written on twelve hardened clay tablets in Akkadian, a Semitic language like Hebrew and Arabic and one of the principal languages of Babylonia and Assyria. The first eleven of these tablets make up the story as you have it here. The twelfth tells another story of Gilgamesh, "Gilgamesh and the Underworld," and since it is unclear how it is to be incorporated into the preceding tablets, it is usually presented as a kind of appendix to the story.

The tablets of the Standard Version are poorly preserved at a number of points, most notably in the adventure in the Cedar Forest, and the translation relies heavily on the earlier, Old Babylonian version, as well as fragments from a number of other versions.

The epic narrates the legendary deeds of Gilgamesh, King of Uruk, but it begins with a prologue that emphasizes not his adventures but the wisdom he acquired and the monuments he constructed at the end of his epic journey. It also tells us that Gilgamesh was endowed by his divine creators with extraordinary strength, courage, and beauty. He is more god than man. His father, however, is mortal, and that fact is decisive in shaping the narrative that follows. The prologue also suggests that Gilgamesh himself has written this account of his and left the tablet in the foundation of the city wall of Uruk for all to read.

In our first view of him, Gilgamesh is the epitome of a bad ruler: arrogant, oppressive, and brutal. The people of Uruk complain of his oppression to the Sumerian gods, and the gods' response is to create Enkidu as a foil or counterweight to Gilgamesh. Where the latter is a mixture of human and divine, Enkidu, who also appears godlike, is a blend of human and wild animal with the animal predominating at first. He is raised by wild beasts and lives as they do, eating only uncooked food, and embodies the conflict between animal and human natures that is a recurrent theme in Mesopotamian literature and myth. When he becomes a kind of protector for them, breaking the hunter's traps and filling in his pits, Enkidu poses a threat to the human community. This threat is neutralized by civilizing him. First a prostitute seduces him across the line separating animal from human, and educates him in the elements of human society. Then shepherds teach him to eat prepared food and wear clothing and anoint himself as humans do. He is weakened somewhat by this transformation, and estranged from his animal companions; but he is also glorified and made greater than he was. The prostitute leads him to Uruk and the confrontation with Gilgamesh for which the gods have created him. His coming has been announced to Gilgamesh in one of the many dreams that play such an important role in the poem. Although the two are bent on destroying each other at first, their encounter results, as it was meant to, in a deep bond of friendship. Each finds in the other the true companion he has sought. The consequence of their union is that their prodigious energies are directed outward toward heroic achievements.

Gilgamesh proposes the first of their adventures both to gain them universal renown and to refresh the spirit of Enkidu who has been weakened and confused by civilization. He suggests that they go to the great Cedar Forest in the Country of the Living and there slay the terrible giant Humbaba. Enkidu is reluctant at first because he knows the danger in this adventure better than Gilgamesh. But the latter prevails and, with the blessing of the sun god, Shamash, they succeed. Their victory is not a simple, glorious triumph, however, and its meaning is unclear. Humbaba poses no apparent threat to Uruk and its people, and he curses them before he dies. Enlil, the god of wind and storm, is enraged by the slaying of his creature, curses the heroes, and gives to others the seven splendors that had been Humbaba's.

Their second adventure is not of their choosing and also leads to another ambiguous success. Gilgamesh's just but harsh rejection of Ishtar's advances provokes her to send the Bull of Heaven against the people of Uruk. The terrible destruction the Bull causes obliges Gilgamesh and Enkidu to destroy it, but that victory brings about the slow and painful death of Enkidu.

The death of his companion reveals to Gilgamesh the hollowness of mortal fame and leads him to undertake a solitary journey in search of immortality. This journey sets *The Epic of Gilgamesh* apart from more straightforward heroic narratives and gives it a special appeal to modern readers. Gilgamesh's specific goal is to discover the secret of immortality from the one man, Utnapishtim, who has survived the Flood. His journey begins with a conventional challenge, the fierce lions who guard the mountain passes. But the challenges he faces subsequently—the dark tunnel that brings him to a prototypical garden of paradise, the puzzling and perilous voyage to Dilmun—have a different and more magical character. He is discouraged at every step, but Gilgamesh perseveres. Although he at last finds Utnapishtim and hears his story, his goal eludes him. He fails a simple test of his potential for immortality when he cannot remain awake for six days and seven nights. Moreover, he fails a second test as well when he first finds the plant that assures eternal rejuvenation, and then, in a moment of carelessness, loses it to the serpent. Discouraged and defeated, Gilgamesh returns at last to Uruk empty handed. His consolation is the assurance that his worldly accomplishments will endure beyond his own lifetime.

In long belated retrospect we can see that *Gilgamesh* explores many of the mysteries of the human condition for the first time in our literature—the complex and perilous relations between gods and mortals, and between nature and civilization, the depths of friendship, and the immortality of art. It is both humbling and thrilling to hear so familiar a voice from so vast a distance.

The introduction to the present translation by N. K. Sandars in *The Epic of Gilgamesh* (1972) is readily available and contains a wealth of useful information. A. Leo Oppenheim gives a comprehensive interpretation of Mesopotamian civilization in *Ancient Mesopotamia* (1977), and Alexander Heidel addresses the importance of *Gilgamesh* for biblical studies in *The Gilgamesh Epic and Old Testament Parallels* (1963).

The Epic of Gilgamesh

Gilgamesh King in Uruk

I will proclaim to the world the deeds of Gilgamesh. This was the man to whom all things were known; this was the king who knew the countries of the world. He was wise, he saw mysteries and knew secret things, he brought us a tale of the days before the flood. He went on a long journey, was weary, worn-out with labour, returning he rested, he engraved on a stone the whole story.

When the gods created Gilgamesh they gave him a perfect body. Shamash the glorious sun[1] endowed him with beauty, Adad the god of the storm endowed him with courage, the great gods made his beauty perfect, surpassing all others, terrifying like a great wild bull. Two thirds they made him god and one third man.

In Uruk[2] he built walls, a great rampart, and the temple of blessed Eanna[3] for the god of the firmament Anu,[4] and for Ishtar the goddess of love. Look at it still today: the outer wall where the cornice runs, it shines with the brilliance of copper; and the inner wall, it has no equal. Touch the threshold, it is ancient. Approach Eanna the dwelling of Ishtar, our lady of love and war, the like of which no latter-day king, no man alive can equal. Climb upon the wall of Uruk; walk along it, I say; regard the foundation terrace and examine the masonry: is it not burnt brick and good? The seven sages[5] laid the foundations.

1

The Coming of Enkidu

Gilgamesh went abroad in the world, but he met with none who could withstand his arms till he came to Uruk. But the men of Uruk muttered in their houses, "Gilgamesh sounds the tocsin for his amusement, his arrogance has no bounds by day or night. No son is left with his father, for Gilgamesh takes them all, even the children; yet the king should be a shepherd to his people. His lust leaves no virgin to her lover, neither the warrior's daughter nor the wife of the noble; yet this is the shepherd of the city, wise, comely, and resolute."

The gods heard their lament, the gods of heaven cried to the Lord of Uruk, to Anu the god of Uruk: "A goddess made him, strong as a savage bull, none can withstand his arms. No son is left with his father, for Gilgamesh takes them all; and is this the king, the shepherd of his people? His lust leaves no virgin to her lover, neither the warrior's daughter nor the

1. Also judge and lawgiver, with some fertility attributes. Shamash is the husband and brother of Ishtar, goddess of love and fertility, goddess of war, and Queen of Heaven.   2. City in southern Babylonia between Fara and Ur. Shown by excavation to have been an important city from very early times, with great temples to the gods Anu and Ishtar. After the flood it was the seat of a dynasty of kings, among whom Gilgamesh was the fifth and most famous.   3. The temple precinct in Uruk sacred to Anu and Ishtar.   4. Also father of the gods. He had an important temple in Uruk.   5. Wise men who brought civilization to the seven oldest cities of Mesopotamia.

wife of the nobel." When Anu had heard their lamentation the gods cried to Aruru, the goddess of creation, "You made him, O Aruru, now create his equal; let it be as like him as his own reflection, his second self, stormy heart for stormy heart. Let them contend together and leave Uruk in quiet."

So the goddess conceived an image in her mind, and it was of the stuff of Anu of the firmament. She dipped her hands in water and pinched off clay, she let it fall in the wilderness, and noble Enkidu was created. There was virtue in him of the god of war, of Ninurta himself. His body was rough, he had long hair like a woman's; it waved like the hair of Nisaba, the goddess of corn. His body was covered with matted hair like Samuqan's, the god of cattle. He was innocent of mankind; he knew nothing of the cultivated land.

Enkidu ate grass in the hills with the gazelle and lurked with wild beasts at the water-holes; he had joy of the water with the herds of wild game. But there was a trapper who met him one day face to face at the drinking-hole, for the wild game had entered his territory. On three days he met him face to face, and the trapper was frozen with fear. He went back to his house with the game he had caught, and he was dumb, benumbed with terror. HIs face was altered like that of one who has made a long journey. With awe in his heart he spoke to his father: "Father, there is a man, unlike any other, who comes down from the hills. He is the strongest in the world, he is like an immortal from heaven. He ranges over the hills with wild beasts and eats grass; he ranges through your land and comes down to the wells. I am afraid and dare not go near him. He fills in the pits which I dig and tears up my traps set for the game; he helps the beasts to escape and now they slip through my fingers."

His father opened his mouth and said to the trapper, "My son, in Uruk lives Gilgamesh; no one has ever prevailed against him, he is strong as a star from heaven. Go to Uruk, find Gilgamesh, extol the strength of this wild man. Ask him to give you a harlot, a wanton from the temple of love; return with her, and let her woman's power overpower this man. When next he comes down to drink at the wells she will be there, stripped naked; and when he sees her beckoning he will embrace her, and then the wild beasts will reject him."

So the trapper set out on his journey to Uruk and addressed himself to Gilgamesh saying, "A man unlike any other is roaming now in the pastures; he is as strong as a star from heaven and I am afraid to approach him. He helps the wild game to escape; he fills in my pits and pulls up my traps." Gilgamesh said, "Trapper, go back, take with you a harlot, a child of pleasure. At the drinking-hole she will strip, and when he sees her beckoning he will embrace her and the game of the wilderness will surely reject him."

Now the trapper returned, taking the harlot with him. After a three days' journey they came to the drinking-hole, and there they sat down; the harlot and the trapper sat facing one another and waited for the game to come. For the first day and for the second day the two sat waiting, but on the third day the herds came; they came down to drink and Enkidu was with

them. The small wild creatures of the plains were glad of the water, and
Enkidu with them, who ate grass with the gazelle and was born in the hills;
and she saw him, the savage man, come from far-off in the hills. The
trapper spoke to her: "There he is. Now, woman, make your breasts bare,
have no shame, do not delay but welcome his love. Let him see you naked,
let him possess your body. When he comes near uncover yourself and lie
with him; teach him, the savage man, your woman's art, for when he
murmurs love to you the wild beasts that shared his life in the hills will
reject him."

She was not ashamed to take him, she made herself naked and welcomed his eagerness; as he lay on her murmuring love she taught him the
woman's art. For six days and seven nights they lay together, for Enkidu
had forgotten his home in the hills; but when he was satisfied he went back
to the wild beasts. Then, when the gazelle saw him, they bolted away;
when the wild creatures saw him they fled. Enkidu would have followed,
but his body was bound as though with a cord, his knees gave way when
he started to run, his swiftness was gone. And now the wild creatures had
all fled away; Enkidu was grown weak, for wisdom was in him, and the
thoughts of a man were in his heart. So he returned and sat down at
the woman's feet, and listened intently to what she said. "You are wise,
Enkidu, and now you have become like a god. Why do you want to run
wild with the beasts in the hills? Come with me. I will take you to strong-
walled Uruk, to the blessed temple of Ishtar and of Anu, of love and of
heaven: there Gilgamesh lives, who is very strong, and like a wild bull he
lords it over men."

When she had spoken Enkidu was pleased; he longed for a comrade, for
one who would understand his heart. "Come, woman, and take me to that
holy temple, to the house of Anu and of Ishtar, and to the place where
Gilgamesh lords it over the people. I will challenge him boldly, I will cry
out aloud in Uruk, 'I am the strongest here, I have come to change the
old order, I am he who was born in the hills, I am he who is strongest of
all.' "

She said, "Let us go, and let him see your face. I know very well where
Gilgamesh is in great Uruk. O Enkidu, there all the people are dressed in
their gorgeous robes, every day is holiday, the young men and the girls are
wonderful to see. How sweet they smell! All the great ones are roused from
their beds. O Enkidu, you who love life, I will show you Gilgamesh, a
man of many moods; you shall look at him well in his radiant manhood.
His body is perfect in strength and maturity; he never rests by night or day.
He is stronger than you, so leave your boasting. Shamash the glorious sun
has given favours to Gilgamesh, and Anu of the heavens, and Enlil, and
Ea the wise has given him deep understanding. I tell you, even before you
have left the wilderness, Gilgamesh will know in his dreams that you are
coming."

Now Gilgamesh got up to tell his dream to his mother, Ninsun, one of
the wise gods. "Mother, last night I had a dream. I was full of joy, the
young heroes were round me and I walked through the night under the

stars of the firmament, and one, a meteor of the stuff of Anu, fell down from heaven. I tried to lift it but it proved too heavy. All the people of Uruk came round to see it, the common people jostled and the nobles thronged to kiss its feet; and to me its attraction was like the love of woman. They helped me, I braced my forehead and I raised it with thongs and brought it to you, and you yourself pronounced it my brother."

Then Ninsun, who is well-beloved and wise, said to Gilgamesh, "This star of heaven which descended like a meteor from the sky; which you tried to lift, but found too heavy, when you tried to move it it would not budge, and so you brought it to my feet; I made it for you, a goad and spur, and you were drawn as though to a woman. This is the strong comrade, the one who brings help to his friend in his need. He is the strongest of wild creatures, the stuff of Anu; born in the grass-lands and the wild hills reared him; when you see him you will be glad; you will love him as a woman and he will never forsake you. This is the meaning of the dream."

Gilgamesh said, "Mother, I dreamed a second dream. In the streets of strong-walled Uruk there lay an axe; the shape of it was strange and the people thronged round. I saw it and was glad. I bent down, deeply drawn towards it; I loved it like a woman and wore it at my side." Ninsun answered, "That axe, which you saw, which drew you so powerfully like love of a woman, that is the comrade whom I give you, and he will come in his strength like one of the host of heaven. He is the brave companion who rescues his friend in necessity." Gilgamesh said to his mother, "A friend, a counsellor has come to me from Enlil, and now I shall befriend and counsel him." So Gilgamesh told his dreams; and the harlot retold them to Enkidu.

And now she said to Enkidu, "When I look at you you have become like a god. Why do you yearn to run wild again with the beasts in the hills? Get up from the ground, the bed of a shepherd." He listened to her words with care. It was good advice that she gave. She divided her clothing in two and with the one half she clothed him and with the other herself; and holding his hand she led him like a child to the sheepfolds, into the shepherds' tents. There all the shepherds crowded round to see him, they put down bread in front of him, but Enkidu could only suck the milk of wild animals. He fumbled and gaped, at a loss what to do or how he should eat the bread and drink the strong wine. Then the woman said, "Enkidu, eat bread, it is the staff of life; drink the wine, it is the custom of the land." So he ate till he was full and drank strong wine, seven goblets. He became merry, his heart exulted and his face shone. He rubbed down the matted hair of his body and anointed himself with oil. Enkidu had become a man; but when he had put on man's clothing he appeared like a bridegroom. He took arms to hunt the lion so that the shepherds could rest at night. He caught wolves and lions and the herdsmen lay down in peace; for Enkidu was their watchman, that strong man who had no rival.

He was merry living with the shepherds, till one day lifting his eyes he saw a man approaching. He said to the harlot, "Woman, fetch that man here. Why has he come? I wish to know his name." She went and called the man saying, "Sir, where are you going on this weary journey?" The man answered, saying to Enkidu, "Gilgamesh has gone into the marriage-house and shut out the people. He does strange things in Uruk, the city of great streets. At the roll of the drum work begins for the men, and work for the women. Gilgamesh the king is about to celebrate marriage with the Queen of Love, and he still demands to be first with the bride, the king to be first and the husband to follow, for that was ordained by the gods from his birth, from the time the umbilical cord was cut. But now the drums roll for the choice of the bride and the city groans." At these words Enkidu turned white in the face. "I will go to the place where Gilgamesh lords it over the people, I will challenge him boldly, and I will cry aloud in Uruk, 'I have come to change the old order, for I am the strongest here.'"

Now Enkidu strode in front and the woman followed behind. He entered Uruk, that great market, and all the folk thronged round him where he stood in the street in strong-walled Uruk. The people jostled; speaking of him they said, "He is the spit of Gilgamesh." "He is shorter." "He is bigger of bone." "This is the one who was reared on the milk of wild beasts. His is the greatest strength." The men rejoiced: "Now Gilgamesh has met his match. This great one, this hero whose beauty is like a god, he is a match even for Gilgamesh."

In Uruk the bridal bed was made, fit for the goddess of love. The bride waited for the bridegroom, but in the night Gilgamesh got up and came to the house. Then Enkidu stepped out, he stood in the street and blocked the way. Mighty Gilgamesh came on and Enkidu met him at the gate. He put out his foot and prevented Gilgamesh from entering the house, so they grappled, holding each other like bulls. They broke the doorposts and the walls shook, they snorted like bulls locked together. They shattered the doorposts and the walls shook. Gilgamesh bent his knee with his foot planted on the ground and with a turn Enkidu was thrown. Then immediately his fury died. When Enkidu was thrown he said to Gilgamesh, "There is not another like you in the world. Ninsun, who is as strong as a wild ox in the byre, she was the mother who bore you, and now you are raised above all men, and Enlil has given you the kingship, for your strength surpasses the strength of men." So Enkidu and Gilgamesh embraced and their friendship was sealed.

2

The Forest Journey

Enlil of the mountain, the father of the gods,[6] had decreed the destiny of Gilgamesh. So Gilgamesh dreamed and Enkidu said, "The meaning of the dream is this. The father of the gods has given you kingship, such is your destiny, everlasting life is not your destiny. Because of this do not be sad at heart, do not be grieved or oppressed. He has given you power to bind and to loose, to be the darkness and the light of mankind. He has given you unexampled supremacy over the people, victory in battle from

6. Enlil is the breath and "word" of Anu. He is also god of earth, wind, and spirit.

which no fugitive returns, in forays and assaults from which there is no going back. But do not abuse this power, deal justly with your servants in the palace, deal justly before Shamash."

The eyes of Enkidu were full of tears and his heart was sick. He sighed bitterly and Gilgamesh met his eye and said, "My friend, why do you sigh so bitterly?" But Enkidu opened his mouth and said, "I am weak, my arms have lost their strength, the cry of sorrow sticks in my throat, I am oppressed by idleness." It was then that the lord Gilgamesh turned his thoughts to the Country of the Living; on the Land of Cedars the lord Gilgamesh reflected. He said to his servant Enkidu, "I have not established my name stamped on bricks as my destiny decreed; therefore I will go to the country where the cedar is felled. I will set up my name in the place where the names of famous men are written, and where no man's name is written yet I will raise a monument to the gods. Because of the evil that is in the land, we will go to the forest and destroy the evil; for in the forest lives Humbaba whose name is 'Hugeness,' a ferocious giant." But Enkidu sighed bitterly and said, "When I went with the wild beasts ranging through the wilderness I discovered the forest; its length is ten thousand leagues in every direction. Enlil has appointed Humbaba to guard it and armed him in sevenfold terrors, terrible to all flesh is Humbaba. When he roars it is like the torrent of the storm, his breath is like fire, and his jaws are death itself. He guards the cedars so well that when the wild heifer stirs in the forest, though she is sixty leagues distant, he hears her. What man would willingly walk into that country and explore its depths? I tell you, weakness overpowers whoever goes near it: it is not an equal struggle when one fights with Humbaba; he is a great warrior, a battering-ram. Gilgamesh, the watchman of the forest never sleeps."

Gilgamesh replied: "Where is the man who can clamber to heaven? Only the gods live for ever with glorious Shamash, but as for us men, our days are numbered, our occupations are a breath of wind. How is this, already you are afraid! I will go first although I am your lord, and you may safely call out, 'Forward, there is nothing to fear!' Then if I fall I leave behind me a name that endures; men will say of me, 'Gilgamesh has fallen in fight with ferocious Humbaba.' Long after the child has been born in my house, they will say it, and remember." Enkidu spoke again to Gilgamesh, "O my lord, if you will enter that country, go first to the hero Shamash, tell the Sun God, for the land is his. The country where the cedar is cut belongs to Shamash."

Gilgamesh took up a kid, white without spot, and a brown one with it; he held them against his breast, and he carried them into the presence of the sun. He took in his hand his silver sceptre and he said to glorious Shamash, "I am going to that country, O Shamash, I am going; my hands supplicate, so let it be well with my soul and bring me back to the quay of Uruk. Grant, I beseech, your protection, and let the omen be good." Glorious Shamash answered, "Gilgamesh, you are strong, but what is the Country of the Living to you?"

"O Shamash, hear me, hear me, Shamash, let my voice be heard. Here in the city man dies oppressed at heart, man perishes with despair in his heart. I have looked over the wall and I see the bodies floating on the river, and that will be my lot also. Indeed I know it is so, for whoever is tallest among men cannot reach the heavens, and the greatest cannot encompass the earth. Therefore I would enter that country: because I have not established my name stamped on brick as my destiny decreed, I will go to the country where the cedar is cut. I will set up my name where the names of famous men are written; and where no man's name is written I will raise a monument to the gods." The tears ran down his face and he said, "Alas, it is a long journey that I must take to the Land of Humbaba. If this enterprise is not to be accomplished, why did you move me, Shamash, with the restless desire to perform it? How can I succeed if you will not succour me? If I die in that country I will die without rancour, but if I return I will make a glorious offering of gifts and of praise to Shamash."

So Shamash accepted the sacrifice of his tears; like the compassionate man he showed him mercy. He appointed strong allies for Gilgamesh, sons of one mother, and stationed them in the mountain caves. The great winds he appointed: the north wind, the whirlwind, the storm and the icy wind, the tempest and the scorching wind. Like vipers, like dragons, like a scorching fire, like a serpent that freezes the heart, a destroying flood and the lightning's fork, such were they and Gilgamesh rejoiced.

He went to the forge and said, "I will give orders to the armourers; they shall cast us our weapons while we watch them." So they gave orders to the armourers and the craftsmen sat down in conference. They went into the groves of the plain and cut willow and box-wood; they cast for them axes of nine score pounds, and great swords they cast with blades of six score pounds each one, with pommels and hilts of thirty pounds. They cast for Gilgamesh the axe "Might of Heroes" and the bow of Anshan;[7] and Gilgamesh was armed and Enkidu; and the weight of the arms they carried was thirty score pounds.

The people collected and the counsellors in the streets and in the market-place of Uruk; they came through the gate of seven bolts and Gilgamesh spoke to them in the market-place: "I, Gilgamesh, go to see that creature of whom such things are spoken, the rumour of whose name fills the world. I will conquer him in his cedar wood and show the strength of the sons of Uruk, all the world shall know of it. I am committed to this enterprise: to climb the mountain, to cut down the cedar, and leave behind me an enduring name." The counsellors of Uruk, the great market, answered him, "Gilgamesh, you are young, your courage carries you too far, you cannot know what this enterprise means which you plan. We have heard that Humbaba is not like men who die, his weapons are such that none can stand against them; the forest stretches for ten thousand leagues in every direction; who would willingly go down to explore its depths? As for Humbaba, when he roars it is like the torrent of the storm, his breath is like fire and his jaws are death itself. Why do you crave to do this thing,

7. A district of Elam in southwest Persia; probably the source of supplies of wood for making bows. Gilgamesh has a "bow of Anshan."

Gilgamesh? It is no equal struggle when one fights with Humbaba, that battering-ram."

When he heard these words of the counsellors Gilgamesh looked at his friend and laughed, "How shall I answer them; shall I say I am afraid of Humbaba, I will sit at home all the rest of my days?" Then Gilgamesh opened his mouth again and said to Enkidu, "My friend, let us go to the Great Palace, to Egalmah,[8] and stand before Ninsun the queen. Ninsun is wise with deep knowledge, she will give us counsel for the road we must go." They took each other by the hand as they went to Egalmah, and they went to Ninsun the great queen. Gilgamesh approached, he entered the palace and spoke to Ninsun. "Ninsun, will you listen to me; I have a long journey to go, to the Land of Humbaba, I must travel an unknown road and fight a strange battle. From the day I go until I return, till I reach the cedar forest and destroy the evil which Shamash abhors, pray for me to Shamash."

Ninsun went into her room, she put on a dress becoming to her body, she put on jewels to make her breast beautiful, she placed a tiara on her head and her skirts swept the ground. Then she went up to the altar of the Sun, standing upon the roof of the palace; she burnt incense and lifted her arms to Shamash as the smoke ascended: "O Shamash, why did you give this restless heart to Gilgamesh, my son; why did you give it? You have moved him and now he sets out on a long journey to the Land of Humbaba to travel an unknown road and fight a strange battle. Therefore from the day that he goes till the day he returns, until he reaches the cedar forest, until he kills Humbaba and destroys the evil thing which you, Shamash, abhor, do not forget him; but let the dawn, Aya, your dear bride, remind you always, and when day is done give him to the watchman of the night to keep him from harm." Then Ninsun the mother of Gilgamesh extinguished the incense, and she called to Enkidu with this exhortation: "Strong Enkidu, you are not the child of my body, but I will receive you as my adopted son; you are my other child like the foundlings they bring to the temple. Serve Gilgamesh as a foundling serves the temple and the priestess who reared him. In the presence of my women, my votaries and hierophants,[9] I declare it." Then she placed the amulet for a pledge round his neck, and she said to him, "I entrust my son to you; bring him back to me safely."

And now they brought to them the weapons, they put in their hands the great swords in their golden scabbards, and the bow and the quiver. Gilgamesh took the axe, he slung the quiver from his shoulder, and the bow of Anshan, and buckled the sword to his belt; and so they were armed and ready for the journey. Now all the people came and pressed on them and said, "When will you return to the city?" The counsellors blessed Gilgamesh and warned him, "Do not trust too much in your own strength, be watchful, restrain your blows at first. The one who goes in front protects his companion; the good guide who knows the way guards his friend. Let

8. Home of the goddess Ninsun, the mother of Gilgamesh.   9. Priests.

Enkidu lead the way, he knows the road to the forest, he has seen Humbaba and is experienced in battles; let him press first into the passes, let
him be watchful and look to himself. Let Enkidu protect his friend, and
guard his companion, and bring him safe through the pitfalls of the road.
We, the counsellors of Uruk entrust our king to you, O Enkidu; bring him
back safely to us." Again to Gilgamesh they said, "May Shamash give you
your heart's desire, may he let you see with your eyes the thing accomplished which your lips have spoken; may he open a path for you where it
is blocked, and a road for your feet to tread. May he open the mountains
for your crossing, and may the nighttime bring you the blessings of night,
and Lugulbanda, your guardian god, stand beside you for victory. May
you have victory in the battle as though you fought with a child. Wash
your feet in the river of Humbaba to which you are journeying; in the
evening dig a well, and let there always be pure water in your water-skin.
Offer cold water to Shamash and do not forget Lugulbanda."

Then Enkidu opened his mouth and said, "Forward, there is nothing to
fear. Follow me, for I know the place where Humbaba lives and the paths
where he walks. Let the counsellors go back. Here is no cause for fear."
When the counsellors heard this they sped the hero on his way. "Go,
Gilgamesh, may your guardian god protect you on the road and bring you
safely back to the quay of Uruk."

After twenty leagues they broke their fast; after another thirty leagues
they stopped for the night. Fifty leagues they walked in one day; in three
days they had walked as much as a journey of a month and two weeks.
They crossed seven mountains before they came to the gate of the forest.
Then Enkidu called out to Gilgamesh, "Do not go down into the forest;
when I opened the gate my hand lost its strength." Gilgamesh answered
him, "Dear friend, do not speak like a coward. Have we got the better of
so many dangers and travelled so far, to turn back at last? You, who are
tried in wars and battles, hold close to me now and you will feel no fear of
death; keep beside me and your weakness will pass, the trembling will leave
your hand. Would my friend rather stay behind? No, we will go down
together into the heart of the forest. Let your courage be roused by the
battle to come; forget death and follow me, a man resolute in action, but
one who is not foolhardy. When two go together each will protect himself
and shield his companion, and if they fall they leave an enduring name."

Together they went down into the forest and they came to the green
mountain. There they stood still, they were struck dumb; they stood still
and gazed at the forest. They saw the height of the cedar, they saw the way
into the forest and the track where Humbaba was used to walk. The way
was broad and the going was good. They gazed at the mountain of cedars,
the dwelling-place of the gods and the throne of Ishtar. The hugeness of
the cedar rose in front of the mountain, its shade was beautiful, full of
comfort; mountain and glade were green with brushwood.

There Gilgamesh dug a well before the setting sun. He went up the
mountain and poured out fine meal on the ground and said, "O mountain, dwelling of the gods, bring me a favourable dream." Then they took

each other by the hand and lay down to sleep; and sleep that flows from the night lapped over them. Gilgamesh dreamed, and at midnight sleep left him, and he told his dream to his friend. "Enkidu, what was it that woke me if you did not? My friend, I have dreamed a dream. Get up, look at the mountain precipice. The sleep that the gods sent me is broken. Ah, my friend, what a dream I have had! Terror and confusion; I seized hold of a wild bull in the wilderness. It bellowed and beat up the dust till the whole sky was dark, my arm was seized and my tongue bitten. I fell back on my knee; then someone refreshed me with water from his water-skin."

Enkidu said, "Dear friend, the god to whom we are travelling is no wild bull, though his form is mysterious. That wild bull which you saw is Sha-mash the Protector; in our moment of peril he will take our hands. The one who gave water from his water-skin, that is your own god who cares for your good name, your Lugulbanda.[1] United with him, together we will accomplish a work the fame of which will never die."

Gilgamesh said, "I dreamed again. We stood in a deep gorge of the mountain, and beside it we two were like the smallest of swamp flies; and suddenly the mountain fell, it struck me and caught my feet from under me. Then came an intolerable light blazing out, and in it was one whose grace and whose beauty were greater than the beauty of this world. He pulled me out from under the mountain, he gave me water to drink and my heart was comforted, and he set my feet on the ground."

Then Enkidu the child of the plains said, "Let us go down from the mountain and talk this thing over together." He said to Gilgamesh the young god, "Your dream is good, your dream is excellent, the mountain which you saw is Humbaba. Now, surely, we will seize and kill him, and throw his body down as the mountain fell on the plain."

The next day after twenty leagues they broke their fast, and after another thirty they stopped for the night. They dug a well before the sun had set and Gilgamesh ascended the mountain. He poured out fine meal on the ground and said, "O mountain, dwelling of the gods, send a dream for Enkidu, make him a favourable dream." The mountain fashioned a dream for Enkidu; it came, an ominous dream; a cold shower passed over him, it caused him to cower like the mountain barley under a storm of rain. But Gilgamesh sat with his chin on his knees till the sleep which flows over all mankind lapped over him. Then, at midnight, sleep left him; he got up and said to his friend, "Did you call me, or why did I wake? Did you touch me, or why am I terrified? Did not some god pass by, for my limbs are numb with fear? My friend, I saw a third dream and this dream was alto-gether frightful. The heavens roared and the earth roared again, daylight failed and darkness fell, lightning flashed, fire blazed out, the clouds low-ered, they rained down death. Then the brightness departed, the fire went out, and all was turned to ashes fallen about us. Let us go down from the mountain and talk this over, and consider what we should do."

When they had come down from the mountain Gilgamesh seized the

---

1. Hero of a cycle of Sumerian poems; protector of Gilgamesh.

axe in his hand: he felled the cedar. When Humbaba heard the noise far off he was enraged; he cried out, "Who is this that has violated my woods and cut down my cedar?" But glorious Shamash called to them out of heaven, "Go forward, do not be afraid." But now Gilgamesh was overcome by weakness, for sleep had seized him suddenly, a profound sleep held him; he lay on the ground, stretched out speechless, as though in a dream. When Enkidu touched him he did not rise, when he spoke to him he did not reply. "O Gilgamesh, Lord of the plain of Kullab,[2] the world grows dark, the shadows have spread over it, now is the glimmer of dusk. Shamash has departed, his bright head is quenched in the bosom of his mother Ningal. O Gilgamesh, how long will you lie like this, asleep? Never let the mother who gave you birth be forced in mourning into the city square."

At length Gilgamesh heard him; he put on his breastplate, "The Voice of Heroes," of thirty shekels' weight; he put it on as though it had been a light garment that he carried, and it covered him altogether. He straddled the earth like a bull that snuffs the ground and his teeth were clenched. "By the life of my mother Ninsun who gave me birth, and by the life of my father, divine Lugulbanda, let me live to be the wonder of my mother, as when she nursed me on her lap." A second time he said to him, "By the life of Ninsun my mother who gave me birth, and by the life of my father, divine Lugulbanda, until we have fought this man, if man he is, this god, if god he is, the way that I took to the Country of the Living will not turn back to the city."

Then Enkidu, the faithful companion, pleaded, answering him, "O my lord, you do not know this monster and that is the reason you are not afraid. I who know him, I am terrified. His teeth are dragon's fangs, his countenance is like a lion, his charge is the rushing of the flood, with his look he crushes alike the trees of the forest and reeds in the swamp. O my Lord, you may go on if you choose into this land, but I will go back to the city. I will tell the lady your mother all your glorious deeds till she shouts for joy: and then I will tell the death that followed till she weeps for bitterness." But Gilgamesh said, "Immolation and sacrifice are not yet for me, the boat of the dead shall not go down, nor the three-ply cloth be cut for my shrouding. Not yet will my people be desolate, nor the pyre be lit in my house and my dwelling burnt on the fire. Today, give me your aid and you shall have mine: what then can go amiss with us two? All living creatures born of the flesh shall sit at last in the boat of the West, and when it sinks, when the boat of Magilum[3] sinks, they are gone; but we shall go forward and fix our eyes on this monster. If your heart is fearful throw away fear; if there is terror in it throw away terror. Take your axe in your hand and attack. He who leaves the fight unfinished is not at peace."

Humbaba came out from his strong house of cedar. Then Enkidu called out, "O Gilgamesh, remember now your boasts in Uruk. Forward, attack, son of Uruk, there is nothing to fear." When he heard these words his

2. Part of Uruk.   3. Unclear; perhaps "the boat of the dead."

courage rallied; he answered, "Make haste, close in, if the watchman is there do not let him escape to the woods where he will vanish. He has put on the first of his seven splendours[4] but not yet the other six, let us trap him before he is armed." Like a raging wild bull he snuffed the ground; the watchman of the woods turned full of threatenings, he cried out. Humbaba came from his strong house of cedar. He nodded his head and shook it, menacing Gilgamesh; and on him he fastened his eye, the eye of death. Then Gilgamesh called to Shamash and his tears were flowing, "O glorious Shamash, I have followed the road you commanded but now if you send no succour how shall I escape?" Glorious Shamash heard his prayer and he summoned the great wind, the north wind, the whirlwind, the storm and the icy wind, the tempest and the scorching wind; they came like dragons, like a scorching fire, like a serpent that freezes the heart, a destroying flood and the lightning's fork. The eight winds rose up against Humbaba, they beat against his eyes; he was gripped, unable to go forward or back. Gilgamesh shouted, "By the life of Ninsun my mother and divine Lugulbanda my father, in the Country of the Living, in this Land I have discovered your dwelling; my weak arms and my small weapons I have brought to this Land against you, and now I will enter your house."

So he felled the first cedar and they cut the branches and laid them at the foot of the mountain. At the first stroke Humbaba blazed out, but still they advanced. They felled seven cedars and cut and bound the branches and laid them at the foot of the mountain, and seven times Humbaba loosed his glory on them. As the seventh blaze died out they reached his lair. He slapped his thigh in scorn. He approached like a noble wild bull roped on the mountain, a warrior whose elbows are bound together. The tears started to his eyes and he was pale, "Gilgamesh, let me speak. I have never known a mother, no, nor a father who reared me. I was born of the mountain, he reared me, and Enlil made me the keeper of this forest. Let me go free, Gilgamesh, and I will be your servant, you shall be my lord; all the trees of the forest that I tended on the mountain shall be yours. I will cut them down and build you a palace." He took him by the hand and led him to his house, so that the heart of Gilgamesh was moved with compassion. He swore by the heavenly life, by the earthly life, by the underworld itself: "O Enkidu, should not the snared bird return to its nest and the captive man return to his mother's arms?" Enkidu answered, "The strongest of men will fall to fate if he has no judgement. Namtar, the evil fate that knows no distinction between men, will devour him. If the snared bird returns to its nest, if the captive man returns to his mother's arms, then you my friend will never return to the city where the mother is waiting who gave you birth. He will bar the mountain road against you, and make the pathways impassable."

Humbaba said, "Enkidu, what you have spoken is evil: you, a hireling, dependent for your bread! In envy and for fear of a rival you have spoken evil words." Enkidu said, "Do not listen, Gilgamesh: this Humbaba must

4. Unclear; perhaps warlike attributes.

die. Kill Humbaba first and his servants after." But Gilgamesh said, "If we touch him the blaze and the glory of light will be put out in confusion, the glory and glamour will vanish, its rays will be quenched." Enkidu said to Gilgamesh, "Not so, my friend. First entrap the bird, and where shall the chicks run then? Afterwards we can search out the glory and the glamour, when the chicks run distracted through the grass."

Gilgamesh listened to the word of his companion, he took the axe in his hand, he drew the sword from his belt, and he struck Humbaba with a thrust of the sword to the neck, and Enkidu his comrade struck the second blow. At the third blow Humbaba fell. Then there followed confusion for this was the guardian of the forest whom they had felled to the ground. For as far as two leagues the cedars shivered when Enkidu felled the watcher of the forest, he at whose voice Hermon and Lebanon[5] used to tremble. Now the mountains were moved and all the hills, for the guardian of the forest was killed. They attacked the cedars, the seven splendours of Humbaba were extinguished. So they pressed on into the forest bearing the sword of eight talents. They uncovered the sacred dwellings of the Anunnaki[6] and while Gilgamesh felled the first of the trees of the forest Enkidu cleared their roots as far as the banks of Euphrates. They set Humbaba before the gods, before Enlil; they kissed the ground and dropped the shroud and set the head before him. When he saw the head of Humbaba, Enlil raged at them. "Why did you do this thing? From henceforth may the fire be on your faces, may it eat the bread that you eat, may it drink where you drink." Then Enlil took again the blaze and the seven splendours that had been Humbaba's: he gave the first to the river, and he gave to the lion, to the stone of execration, to the mountain and to the dreaded daughter of the Queen of Hell.

O Gilgamesh, king and conqueror of the dreadful blaze; wild bull who plunders the mountain, who crosses the sea, glory to him, and from the brave the greater glory is Enki's![7]

3

Ishtar and Gilgamesh, and the Death of Enkidu

Gilgamesh washed out his long locks and cleaned his weapons; he flung back his hair from his shoulders; he threw off his stained clothes and changed them for new. He put on his royal robes and made them fast. When Gilgamesh had put on the crown, glorious Ishtar lifted her eyes, seeing the beauty of Gilgamesh. She said, "Come to me Gilgamesh, and be my bridegroom; grant me seed of your body, let me be your bride and you shall be my husband. I will harness for you a chariot of lapis lazuli and of gold, with wheels of gold and horns of copper; and you shall have mighty demons of the storm for draft-mules. When you enter our house in the fragrance of cedar-wood, threshold and throne will kiss your feet. Kings,

5. Mountains in Lebanon.   6. Gods of the underworld, judges of the dead and offspring of Anu.
7. Or Ea: god of the sweet waters, also of wisdom, a patron of arts and one of the creators of mankind, towards whom he is usually well disposed.

rulers, and princes will bow down before you; they shall bring you tribute from the mountains and the plain. Your ewes shall drop twins and your goats triplets; your pack-ass shall outrun mules; your oxen shall have no rivals, and your chariot horses shall be famous far-off for their swiftness."

Gilgamesh opened his mouth and answered glorious Ishtar, "If I take you in marriage, what gifts can I give in return? What ointments and clothing for your body? I would gladly give you bread and all sorts of food fit for a god. I would give you wine to drink fit for a queen. I would pour out barley to stuff your granary; but as for making you my wife—that I will not. How would it go with me? Your lovers have found you like a brazier which smoulders in the cold, a backdoor which keeps out neither squall of wind nor storm, a castle which crushes the garrison, pitch that blackens the bearer, a water-skin that chafes the carrier, a stone which falls from the parapet, a battering-ram turned back from the enemy, a sandal that trips the wearer. Which of your lovers did you ever love for ever? What shepherd of yours has pleased you for all time? Listen to me while I tell the tale of your lovers. There was Tammuz,[8] the lover of your youth, for him you decreed wailing, year after year. You loved the many-coloured roller, but still you struck and broke his wing; now in the grove he sits and cries, "kappi, kappi, my wing, my wing." You have loved the lion tremendous in strength: seven pits you dug for him, and seven. You have loved the stallion magnificent in battle, and for him you decreed whip and spur and a thong, to gallop seven leagues by force and to muddy the water before he drinks; and for his mother Silili[9] lamentations. You have loved the shepherd of the flock; he made meal-cake for you day after day, he killed kids for your sake. You struck and turned him into a wolf; now his own herd-boys chase him away, his own hounds worry his flanks. And did you not love Ishullanu, the gardener of your father's palm-grove? He brought you baskets filled with dates without end; every day he loaded your table. Then you turned your eyes on him and said, 'Dearest Ishullanu, come here to me, let us enjoy your manhood, come forward and take me, I am yours.' Ishullanu answered, 'What are you asking from me? My mother has baked and I have eaten; why should I come to such as you for food that is tainted and rotten? For when was a screen of rushes sufficient protection from frosts?' But when you had heard his answer you struck him. He was changed to a blind mole deep in the earth, one whose desire is always beyond his reach. And if you and I should be lovers, should not I be served in the same fashion as all these others whom you loved once?"

When Ishtar heard this she fell into a bitter rage, she went up to high heaven. Her tears poured down in front of her father Anu, and Antum her mother. She said, "My father, Gilgamesh has heaped insults on me, he has told over all my abominable behaviour, my foul and hideous acts." Anu opened his mouth and said, "Are you a father of gods? Did not you quarrel with Gilgamesh the king, so now he has related your abominable behaviour, your foul and hideous acts?"

8. The dying god of vegetation.   9. Perhaps a divine horse.

Ishtar opened her mouth and said again, "My father, give me the Bull of Heaven to destroy Gilgamesh. Fill Gilgamesh, I say, with arrogance to his destruction; but if you refuse to give me the Bull of Heaven I will break in the doors of hell and smash the bolts; there will be confusion of people, those above with those from the lower depths. I shall bring up the dead to eat food like the living; and the hosts of dead will outnumber the living." Anu said to great Ishtar, "If I do what you desire there will be seven years of drought throughout Uruk when corn will be seedless husks. Have you saved grain enough for the people and grass for the cattle?" Ishtar replied, "I have saved grain for the people, grass for the cattle; for seven years of seedless husks there is grain and there is grass enough."

When Anu heard what Ishtar had said he gave her the Bull of Heaven to lead by the halter down to Uruk. When they reached the gates of Uruk the Bull went to the river; with his first snort cracks opened in the earth and a hundred young men fell down to death. With his second snort cracks opened and two hundred fell down to death. With his third snort cracks opened, Enkidu doubled over but instantly recovered, he dodged aside and leapt on the Bull and seized it by the horns. The Bull of Heaven foamed in his face, it brushed him with the thick of its tail. Enkidu cried to Gilgamesh, "My friend, we boasted that we would leave enduring names behind us. Now thrust in your sword between the nape and the horns." So Gilgamesh followed the Bull, he seized the thick of its tail, he thrust the sword between the nape and the horns and slew the Bull. When they had killed the Bull of Heaven they cut out its heart and gave it to Shamash, and the brothers rested.

But Ishtar rose up and mounted the great wall of Uruk; she sprang on to the tower and uttered a curse: "Woe to Gilgamesh, for he has scorned me in killing the Bull of Heaven." When Enkidu heard these words he tore out the Bull's right thigh and tossed it in her face saying, "If I could lay my hands on you, it is this I should do to you, and lash the entrails to your side." Then Ishtar called together her people, the dancing and singing girls, the prostitutes of the temple, the courtesans. Over the thigh of the Bull of Heaven she set up lamentation.

But Gilgamesh called the smiths and the armourers, all of them together. They admired the immensity of the horns. They were plated with lapis lazuli two fingers thick. They were thirty pounds each in weight, and their capacity in oil was six measures, which he gave to his guardian god, Lugulbanda. But he carried the horns into the palace and hung them on the wall. Then they washed their hands in Euphrates, they embraced each other and went away. They drove through the streets of Uruk where the heroes were gathered to see them, and Gilgamesh called to the singing girls, "Who is most glorious of the heroes, who is most eminent among men?" "Gilgamesh is the most glorious of heroes, Gilgamesh is most eminent among men." And now there was feasting, and celebrations and joy in the palace, till the heroes lay down saying, "Now we will rest for the night."

When the daylight came Enkidu got up and cried to Gilgamesh, "O my

brother, such a dream I had last night. Anu, Enlil, Ea and heavenly Shamash took counsel together, and Anu said to Enlil, 'Because they have
killed the Bull of Heaven, and because they have killed Humbaba who
guarded the Cedar Mountain one of the two must die.' Then glorious
Shamash answered the hero Enlil, 'It was by your command they killed
the Bull of Heaven, and killed Humbaba, and must Enkidu die although
innocent?' Enlil flung round in rage at glorious Shamash, 'You dare to say
this, you who went about with them every day like one of themselves!' "

So Enkidu lay stretched out before Gilgamesh; his tears ran down in
streams and he said to Gilgamesh, "O my brother, so dear as you are to
me, brother, yet they will take me from you." Again he said, "I must sit
down on the threshold of the dead and never again will I see my dear
brother with my eyes."

While Enkidu lay alone in his sickness he cursed the gate as though it
was living flesh, "You there, wood of the gate, dull and insensible, witless,
I searched for you over twenty leagues until I saw the towering cedar.
There is no wood like you in our land. Seventy-two cubits high and twenty-
four wide, the pivot and the ferrule and the jambs are perfect. A master
craftsman from Nippur has made you; but O, if I had known the conclusion! If I had known that this was all the good that would come of it, I
would have raised the axe and split you into little pieces and set up here a
gate of wattle instead. Ah, if only some future king had brought you here,
or some god had fashioned you. Let him obliterate my name and write his
own, and the curse fall on him instead of on Enkidu."

With the first brightening of dawn Enkidu raised his head and wept
before the Sun God, in the brilliance of the sunlight his tears streamed
down. "Sun God, I beseech you, about that vile Trapper, that Trapper of
nothing because of whom I was to catch less than my comrade; let him
catch least, make his game scarce, make him feeble, taking the smaller of
every share, let his quarry escape from his nets."

When he had cursed the Trapper to his heart's content he turned on the
harlot. He was roused to curse her also. "As for you, woman, with a great
curse I curse you! I will promise you a destiny to all eternity. My curse
shall come on you soon and sudden. You shall be without a roof for your
commerce, for you shall not keep house with other girls in the tavern, but
do your business in places fouled by the vomit of the drunkard. Your hire
will be potter's earth, your thievings will be flung into the hovel, you will
sit at the cross-roads in the dust of the potter's quarter, you will make your
bed on the dunghill at night, and by day take your stand in the wall's
shadow. Brambles and thorns will tear your feet, the drunk and the dry
will strike your cheek and your mouth will ache. Let you be stripped of
your purple dyes, for I too once in the wilderness with my wife had all the
treasure I wished."

When Shamash heard the words of Enkidu he called to him from heaven:
"Enkidu, why are you cursing the woman, the mistress who taught you to
eat bread fit for gods and drink wine of kings? She who put upon you a
magnificent garment, did she not give you glorious Gilgamesh for your

companion, and has not Gilgamesh, your own brother, made you rest on a royal bed and recline on a couch at his left hand? He has made the princes of the earth kiss your feet, and now all the people of Uruk lament and wail over you. When you are dead he will let his hair grow long for your sake, he will wear a lion's pelt and wander through the desert."

When Enkidu heard glorious Shamash his angry heart grew quiet, he called back the curse and said, "Woman, I promise you another destiny. The mouth which cursed you shall bless you! Kings, princes and nobles shall adore you. On your account a man though twelve miles off will clap his hand to his thigh and his hair will twitch. For you he will undo his belt and open his treasure and you shall have your desire; lapis lazuli, gold and carnelian from the heap in the treasury. A ring for your hand and a robe shall be yours. The priest will lead you into the presence of the gods. On your account a wife, a mother of seven, was forsaken."

As Enkidu slept alone in his sickness, in bitterness of spirit he poured out his heart to his friend. "It was I who cut down the cedar, I who levelled the forest, I who slew Humbaba and now see what has become of me. Listen, my friend, this is the dream I dreamed last night. The heavens roared, and earth rumbled back an answer; between them stood I before an awful being, the sombre-faced man-bird; he had directed on me his purpose. His was a vampire face, his foot was a lion's foot, his hand was an eagle's talon. He fell on me and his claws were in my hair, he held me fast and I smothered; then he transformed me so that my arms became wings covered with feathers. He turned his stare towards me, and he led me away to the palace of Irkalla, the Queen of Darkness,[1] to the house from which none who enters ever returns, down the road from which there is no coming back.

"There is the house whose people sit in darkness; dust is their food and clay their meat. They are clothed like birds with wings for covering, they see no light, they sit in darkness. I entered the house of dust and I saw the kings of the earth, their crowns put away for ever; rulers and princes, all those who once wore kingly crowns and ruled the world in the days of old. They who had stood in the place of the gods like Anu and Enlil, stood now like servants to fetch baked meats in the house of dust, to carry cooked meat and cold water from the water-skin. In the house of dust which I entered were high priests and acolytes, priests of the incantation and of ecstasy; there were servers of the temple, and there was Etana, that king of Kish whom the eagle carried to heaven in the days of old. I saw also Samuqan, god of cattle, and there was Ereshkigal the Queen of the Under-world; and Belit-Sheri squatted in front of her, she who is recorder of the gods and keeps the book of death. She held a tablet from which she read. She raised her head, she saw me and spoke: 'Who has brought this one here?' Then I awoke like a man drained of blood who wanders alone in a waste of rushes; like one whom the bailiff has seized and his heart pounds with terror."

1. Also Ereshkigal, Queen of the Underworld.

Gilgamesh had peeled off his clothes, he listened to his words and wept quick tears, Gilgamesh listened and his tears flowed. He opened his mouth and spoke to Enkidu: "Who is there in strong-walled Uruk who has wisdom like this? Strange things have been spoken, why does your heart speak strangely? The dream was marvellous but the terror was great; we must treasure the dream whatever the terror; for the dream has shown that misery comes at last to the healthy man, the end of life is sorrow." And Gilgamesh lamented, "Now I will pray to the great gods, for my friend had an ominous dream."

This day on which Enkidu dreamed came to an end and he lay stricken with sickness. One whole day he lay on his bed and his suffering increased. He said to Gilgamesh, the friend on whose account he had left the wilderness, "Once I ran for you, for the water of life, and I now have nothing." A second day he lay on his bed and Gilgamesh watched over him but the sickness increased. A third day he lay on his bed, he called out to Gilgamesh, rousing him up. Now he was weak and his eyes were blind with weeping. Ten days he lay and his suffering increased, eleven and twelve days he lay on his bed of pain. Then he called to Gilgamesh, "My friend, the great goddess cursed me and I must die in shame. I shall not die like a man fallen in battle; I feared to fall, but happy is the man who falls in the battle, for I must die in shame." And Gilgamesh wept over Enkidu. With the first light of dawn he raised his voice and said to the counsellors of Uruk:

> Hear me, great ones of Uruk,
> I weep for Enkidu, my friend,
> Bitterly moaning like a woman mourning
> I weep for my brother.
> O Enkidu, my brother,
> You were the axe at my side,
> My hand's strength, the sword in my belt,
> The shield before me,
> A glorious robe, my fairest ornament;
> An evil Fate has robbed me.
> The wild ass and the gazelle
> That were father and mother,
> All long-tailed creatures that nourished you
> Weep for you,
> All the wild things of the plain and pastures;
> The paths that you loved in the forest of cedars
> Night and day murmur.
> Let the great ones of strong-walled Uruk
> Weep for you;
> Let the finger of blessing
> Be stretched out in mourning;
> Enkidu, young brother. Hark,
> There is an echo through all the country

Like a mother mourning.
Weep all the paths where we walked together;
And the beasts we hunted, the bear and hyena,
Tiger and panther, leopard and lion,
The stag and the ibex, the bull and the doe.
The river along whose banks we used to walk,
Weeps for you,
Ula of Elam and dear Euphrates
Where once we drew water for the water-skins.
The mountain we climbed where we slew the Watchman,
Weeps for you.
The warriors of strong-walled Uruk
Where the Bull of Heaven was killed,
Weep for you.
All the people of Eridu
Weep for you Enkidu.
Those who brought grain for your eating
Mourn for you now;
Who rubbed oil on your back
Mourn for you now;
Who poured beer for your drinking
Mourn for you now.
The harlot who anointed you with fragrant ointment
Laments for you now;
The women of the palace, who brought you a wife,
A chosen ring of good advice,
Lament for you now.
And the young men your brothers
As though they were women
Go long-haired in mourning.
What is this sleep which holds you now?
You are lost in the dark and cannot hear me.

He touched his heart but it did not beat, nor did he lift his eyes again. When Gilgamesh touched his heart it did not beat. So Gilgamesh laid a veil, as one veils the bride, over his friend. He began to rage like a lion, like a lioness robbed of her whelps. This way and that he paced round the bed, he tore out his hair and strewed it around. He dragged off his splendid robes and flung them down as though they were abominations.

In the first light of dawn Gilgamesh cried out, "I made you rest on a royal bed, you reclined on a couch at my left hand, the princes of the earth kissed your feet. I will cause all the people of Uruk to weep over you and raise the dirge of the dead. The joyful people will stoop with sorrow; and when you have gone to the earth I will let my hair grow long for your sake, I will wander through the wilderness in the skin of a lion." The next day also, in the first light, Gilgamesh lamented; seven days and seven nights he wept for Enkidu, until the worm fastened on him. Only then he gave him up to the earth, for the Anunnaki, the judges, had seized him.

Then Gilgamesh issued a proclamation through the land, he summoned them all, the coppersmiths, the goldsmiths, the stone-workers, and commanded them, "Make a statue of my friend." The statue was fashioned with a great weight of lapis lazuli for the breast and of gold for the body. A table of hard-wood was set out, and on it a bowl of carnelian filled with honey, and a bowl of lapis lazuli filled with butter. These he exposed and offered to the Sun; and weeping he went away.

4

The Search for Everlasting Life

Bitterly Gilgamesh wept for his friend Enkidu; he wandered over the wilderness as a hunter, he roamed over the plains; in his bitterness he cried, "How can I rest, how can I be at peace? Despair is in my heart. What my brother is now, that shall I be when I am dead. Because I am afraid of death I will go as best I can to find Utnapishtim[2] whom they call the Faraway, for he has entered the assembly of the gods." So Gilgamesh travelled over the wilderness, he wandered over the grasslands, a long journey, in search of Utnapishtim, whom the gods took after the deluge; and they set him to live in the land of Dilmun, in the garden of the sun; and to him alone of men they gave everlasting life.

At night when he came to the mountain passes Gilgamesh prayed: "In these mountain passes long ago I saw lions, I was afraid and I lifted my eyes to the moon; I prayed and my prayers went up to the gods, so now, O moon god Sin, protect me." When he had prayed he lay down to sleep, until he was woken from out of a dream. He saw the lions round him glorying in life; then he took his axe in his hand, he drew his sword from his belt, and he fell upon them like an arrow from the string, and struck and destroyed and scattered them.

So at length Gilgamesh came to Mashu, the great mountains about which he had heard many things, which guard the rising and the setting sun. Its twin peaks are as high as the wall of heaven and its paps reach down to the underworld. At its gate the Scorpions stand guard, half man and half dragon; their glory is terrifying, their stare strikes death into men, their shimmering halo sweeps the mountains that guard the rising sun. When Gilgamesh saw them he shielded his eyes for the length of a moment only; then he took courage and approached. When they saw him so undismayed the Man-Scorpion called to his mate, "This one who comes to us now is flesh of the gods." The mate of the Man-Scorpion answered, "Two thirds is god but one third is man."

Then he called to the man Gilgamesh, he called to the child of the

---

2. A wise king and priest who, like the Biblical Noah, survived the flood along with his family and with "the seed of all living creatures." Afterwards he was taken by the gods to live forever in Dilmun, the Sumerian paradise.

gods: "Why have you come so great a journey; for what have you travelled
so far, crossing the dangerous waters; tell me the reason for your coming?"
Gilgamesh answered, "For Enkidu; I loved him dearly, together we endured
all kinds of hardships; on his account I have come, for the common lot of
man has taken him. I have wept for him day and night, I would not give
up his body for burial, I thought my friend would come back because of
my weeping. Since he went, my life is nothing; that is why I have travelled
here in search of Utnapishtim my father; for men say he has entered the
assembly of the gods, and has found everlasting life. I have a desire to
question him concerning the living and the dead." The Man-Scorpion
opened his mouth and said, speaking to Gilgamesh, "No man born of
woman has done what you have asked, no mortal man has gone into the
mountain; the length of it is twelve leagues of darkness; in it there is no
light, but the heart is oppressed with darkness. From the rising of the sun
to the setting of the sun there is no light." Gilgamesh said, "Although I
should go in sorrow and in pain, with sighing and with weeping, still I
must go. Open the gate of the mountain." And the Man-Scorpion said,
"Go, Gilgamesh, I permit you to pass through the mountain of Mashu
and through the high ranges; may your feet carry you safely home. The
gate of the mountain is open."

When Gilgamesh heard this he did as the Man-Scorpion had said, he
followed the sun's road to his rising, through the mountain. When he had
gone one league the darkness became thick around him, for there was no
light, he could see nothing ahead and nothing behind him. After two
leagues the darkness was thick and there was no light, he could see nothing
ahead and nothing behind him. After three leagues the darkness was thick,
and there was no light, he could see nothing ahead and nothing behind
him. After four leagues the darkness was thick and there was no light, he
could see nothing ahead and nothing behind him. At the end of five leagues
the darkness was thick and there was no light, he could see nothing ahead
and nothing behind him. At the end of six leagues the darkness was thick
and there was no light, he could see nothing ahead and nothing behind
him. When he had gone seven leagues the darkness was thick and there
was no light, he could see nothing ahead and nothing behind him. When
he had gone eight leagues Gilgamesh gave a great cry, for the darkness was
thick and he could see nothing ahead and nothing behind him. After nine
leagues he felt the north wind on his face, but the darkness was thick and
there was no light, he could see nothing ahead and nothing behind him.
After ten leagues the end was near. After eleven leagues the dawn light
appeared. At the end of twelve leagues the sun streamed out.

There was the garden of the gods; all round him stood bushes bearing
gems. Seeing it he went down at once, for there was fruit of carnelian with
the vine hanging from it, beautiful to look at; lapis lazuli leaves hung thick
with fruit, sweet to see. For thorns and thistles there were haematite and
rare stones, agate, and pearls from out of the sea. While Gilgamesh walked
in the garden by the edge of the sea Shamash saw him, and he saw that he
was dressed in the skins of animals and ate their flesh. He was distressed,

and he spoke and said, "No mortal man has gone this way before, nor will, as long as the winds drive over the sea." And to Gilgamesh he said, "You will never find the life for which you are searching." Gilgamesh said to glorious Shamash, "Now that I have toiled and strayed so far over the wilderness, am I to sleep, and let the earth cover my head for ever? Let my eyes see the sun until they are dazzled with looking. Although I am no better than a dead man, still let me see the light of the sun."

Beside the sea she lives, the woman of the vine, the maker of wine; Siduri sits in the garden at the edge of the sea, with the golden bowl and the golden vats that the gods gave her. She is covered with a veil; and where she sits she sees Gilgamesh coming towards her, wearing skins, the flesh of the gods in his body, but despair in his heart, and his face like the face of one who has made a long journey. She looked, and as she scanned the distance she said in her own heart, "Surely this is some felon; where is he going now?" And she barred her gate against him with the cross-bar and shot home the bolt. But Gilgamesh, hearing the sound of the bolt, threw up his head and lodged his foot in the gate; he called to her, "Young woman, maker of wine, why do you bolt your door; what did you see that made you bar your gate? I will break in your door and burst in your gate, for I am Gilgamesh who seized and killed the Bull of Heaven, I killed the watchman of the cedar forest, I overthrew Humbaba who lived in the forest, and I killed the lions in the passes of the mountain."

Then Siduri said to him, "If you are that Gilgamesh who seized and killed the Bull of Heaven, who killed the watchman of the cedar forest, who overthrew Humbaba that lived in the forest, and killed the lions in the passes of the mountain, why are your cheeks so starved and why is your face so drawn? Why is despair in your heart and your face like the face of one who has made a long journey? Yes, why is your face burned from heat and cold, and why do you come here wandering over the pastures in search of the wind?"

Gilgamesh answered her, "And why should not my cheeks be starved and my face drawn? Despair is in my heart and my face is the face of one who has made a long journey, it was burned with heat and with cold. Why should I not wander over the pastures in search of the wind? My friend, my younger brother, he who hunted the wild ass of the wilderness and the panther of the plains, my friend, my younger brother who seized and killed the Bull of Heaven and overthrew Humbaba in the cedar forest, my friend who was very dear to me and who endured dangers beside me, Enkidu my brother, whom I loved, the end of mortality has overtaken him. I wept for him seven days and nights till the worm fastened on him. Because of my brother I am afraid of death, because of my brother I stray through the wilderness and cannot rest. But now, young woman, maker of wine, since I have seen your face do not let me see the face of death which I dread so much."

She answered, "Gilgamesh, where are you hurrying to? You will never find that life for which you are looking. When the gods created man they allotted to him death, but life they retained in their own keeping. As for you, Gilgamesh, fill your belly with good things; day and night, night and day, dance and be merry, feast and rejoice. Let your clothes be fresh, bathe yourself in water, cherish the little child that holds your hand, and make your wife happy in your embrace; for this too is the lot of man."

But Gilgamesh said to Siduri, the young woman, "How can I be silent, how can I rest, when Enkidu whom I love is dust, and I too shall die and be laid in the earth. You live by the sea-shore and look into the heart of it; young woman, tell me now, which is the way to Utnapishtim, the son of Ubara-Tutu? What directions are there for the passage; give me, oh, give me directions. I will cross the Ocean if it is possible; if it is not I will wander still farther in the wilderness." The wine-maker said to him, "Gilgamesh, there is no crossing the Ocean; whoever has come, since the days of old, has not been able to pass that sea. The Sun in his glory crosses the Ocean, but who beside Shamash has ever crossed it? The place and the passage are difficult, and the waters of death are deep which flow between. Gilgamesh, how will you cross the Ocean? When you come to the waters of death what will you do? But Gilgamesh, down in the woods you will find Urshanabi, the ferryman of Utnapishtim; with him are the holy things, the things of stone. He is fashioning the serpent prow of the boat. Look at him well, and if it is possible, perhaps you will cross the waters with him; but if it is not possible, then you must go back."

When Gilgamesh heard this he was seized with anger. He took his axe in his hand, and his dagger from his belt. He crept forward and he fell on them like a javelin. Then he went into the forest and sat down. Urshanabi saw the dagger flash and heard the axe, and he beat his head, for Gilgamesh had shattered the tackle of the boat in his rage. Urshanabi said to him, "Tell me, what is your name? I am Urshanabi, the ferryman of Utnapishtim the Faraway." He replied to him, "Gilgamesh is my name, I am from Uruk, from the house of Anu." Then Urshanabi said to him, "Why are your cheeks so starved and your face drawn? Why is despair in your heart and your face like the face of one who has made a long journey; yes, why is your face burned with heat and with cold, and why do you come here wandering over the pastures in search of the wind?"

Gilgamesh said to him, "Why should not my cheeks be starved and my face drawn? Despair is in my heart, and my face is the face of one who has made a long journey. I was burned with heat and with cold. Why should I not wander over the pastures? My friend, my younger brother who seized and killed the Bull of Heaven, and overthrew Humbaba in the cedar forest, my friend who was very dear to me, and who endured dangers beside me, Enkidu my brother whom I loved, the end of mortality has overtaken him. I wept for him seven days and nights till the worm fastened on him. Because of my brother I am afraid of death, because of my brother I stray through the wilderness. His fate lies heavy upon me. How can I be silent, how can I rest? He is dust and I too shall die and be laid in the earth for ever. I am afraid of death, therefore, Urshanabi, tell me which is the road to Utnapishtim? If it is possible I will cross the waters of death; if not I will wander still farther through the wilderness."

Urshanabi said to him, "Gilgamesh, your own hands have prevented you from crossing the Ocean; when you destroyed the tackle of the boat you destroyed its safety." Then the two of them talked it over and Gilgamesh said, "Why are you so angry with me, Urshanabi, for you yourself cross the sea by day and night, at all seasons you cross it." "Gilgamesh, those things you destroyed, their property is to carry me over the water, to prevent the waters of death from touching me. It was for this reason that I preserved them, but you have destroyed them, and the *urnu* snakes with them. But now, go into the forest, Gilgamesh; with your axe cut poles, one hundred and twenty, cut them sixty cubits long, paint them with bitumen, set on them ferrules and bring them back."

When Gilgamesh heard this he went into the forest, he cut poles one hundred and twenty; he cut them sixty cubits long, he painted them with bitumen, he set on them ferrules, and he brought them to Urshanabi. Then they boarded the boat, Gilgamesh and Urshanabi together, launching it out on the waves of Ocean. For three days they ran on as it were a journey of a month and fifteen days, and at last Urshanabi brought the boat to the waters of death. Then Urshanabi said to Gilgamesh, "Press on, take a pole and thrust it in, but do not let your hands touch the waters. Gilgamesh, take a second pole, take a third, take a fourth pole. Now, Gilgamesh, take a fifth, take a sixth and seventh pole. Gilgamesh, take an eighth, and ninth, a tenth pole. Gilgamesh, take an eleventh, take a twelfth pole." After one hundred and twenty thrusts Gilgamesh had used the last pole. Then he stripped himself, he held up his arms for a mast and his covering for a sail. So Urshanabi the ferryman brought Gilgamesh to Utnapishtim, whom they call the Faraway, who lives in Dilmun at the place of the sun's transit, eastward of the mountain. To him alone of men the gods had given everlasting life.

Now Utnapishtim, where he lay at ease, looked into the distance and he said in his heart, musing to himself, "Why does the boat sail here without tackle and mast; why are the sacred stones destroyed, and why does the master not sail the boat? That man who comes is none of mine; where I look I see a man whose body is covered with skins of beasts. Who is this who walks up the shore behind Urshanabi, for surely he is no man of mine?" So Utnapishtim looked at him and said, "What is your name, you who come here wearing the skins of beasts, with your cheeks starved and your face drawn? Where are you hurrying to now? For what reason have you made this great journey, crossing the seas whose passage is difficult? Tell me the reason for your coming."

He replied, "Gilgamesh is my name. I am from Uruk, from the house of Anu." Then Utnapishtim said to him, "If you are Gilgamesh, why are your cheeks so starved and your face drawn? Why is despair in your heart and your face like the face of one who has made a long journey? Yes, why is your face burned with heat and cold; and why do you come here, wandering over the wilderness in search of the wind?"

Gilgamesh said to him, "Why should not my cheeks be starved and my face drawn? Despair is in my heart and my face is the face of one who has

made a long journey. It was burned with heat and with cold. Why should
I not wander over the pastures? My friend, my younger brother who seized
and killed the Bull of Heaven and overthrew Humbaba in the cedar forest,
my friend who was very dear to me and endured dangers beside me, Enkidu,
my brother whom I loved, the end of mortality has overtaken him. I wept
for him seven days and nights till the worm fastened on him. Because of
my brother I am afraid of death; because of my brother I stray through the
wilderness. His fate lies heavy upon me. How can I be silent, how can I
rest? He is dust and I shall die also and be laid in the earth for ever." Again
Gilgamesh said, speaking to Utnapishtim, "It is to see Utnapishtim whom
we call the Faraway that I have come this journey. For this I have wandered over the world, I have crossed many difficult ranges, I have crossed
the seas, I have wearied myself with travelling; my joints are aching, and I
have lost acquaintance with sleep which is sweet. My clothes were worn
out before I came to the house of Siduri. I have killed the bear and hyena,
the lion and panther, the tiger, the stag and the ibex, all sorts of wild game
and the small creatures of the pastures. I ate their flesh and I wore their
skins; and that was how I came to the gate of the young woman, the maker
of wine, who barred her gate of pitch and bitumen against me. But from
her I had news of the journey; so then I came to Urshanabi the ferryman,
and with him I crossed over the waters of death. O, father Utnapishtim,
you who have entered the assembly of the gods, I wish to question you
concerning the living and the dead, how shall I find the life for which I
am searching?"

Utnapishtim said, "There is no permanence. Do we build a house to
stand for ever, do we seal a contract to hold for all time? Do brothers divide
an inheritance to keep for ever, does the flood-time of rivers endure? It is
only the nymph of the dragon-fly who sheds her larva and sees the sun in
his glory. From the days of old there is no permanence. The sleeping and
the dead, how alike they are, they are like a painted death. What is there
between the master and the servant when both have fulfilled their doom?
When the Anunnaki, the judges, come together, and Mammetun the mother
of destinies, together they decree the fates of men. Life and death they
allot but the day of death they do not disclose."

Then Gilgamesh said to Utnapishtim the Faraway, "I look at you now,
Utnapishtim, and your appearance is no different from mine; there is nothing
strange in your features. I thought I should find you like a hero prepared
for battle, but you lie here taking your ease on your back. Tell me truly,
how was it that you came to enter the company of the gods, and to possess
everlasting life?" Utnapishtim said to Gilgamesh, "I will reveal to you a
mystery, I will tell you a secret of the gods."

5

The Story of the Flood

"You know the city Shurrupak, it stands on the banks of Euphrates?
That city grew old and the gods that were in it were old. There was Anu,

lord of the firmament, their father, and warrior Enlil their counsellor, Ninurta the helper, and Ennugi watcher over canals; and with them also was Ea. In those days the world teemed, the people multiplied, the world bellowed like a wild bull, and the great god was aroused by the clamour. Enlil heard the clamour and he said to the gods in council, 'The uproar of mankind is intolerable and sleep is no longer possible by reason of the babel.' So the gods agreed to exterminate mankind. Enlil did this, but Ea because of his oath warned me in a dream. He whispered their words to my house of reeds, 'Reed-house, reed-house! Wall, O wall, hearken reed-house, wall reflect; O man of Shurrupak, son of Ubara-Tutu; tear down your house and build a boat, abandon possessions and look for life, despise worldly goods and save your soul alive. Tear down your house, I say, and build a boat. These are the measurements of the barque as you shall build her: let her beam equal her length, let her deck be roofed like the vault that covers the abyss; then take up into the boat the seed of all living creatures.'

"When I had understood I said to my lord, 'Behold what you have commanded I will honour and perform, but how shall I answer the people, the city, the elders?' Then Ea opened his mouth and said to me, his servant, 'Tell them this: I have learnt that Enlil is wrathful against me, I dare no longer walk in his land nor live in his city; I will go down to the Gulf to dwell with Ea my lord. But on you he will rain down abundance, rare fish and shy wild-fowl, a rich harvest-tide. In the evening the rider of the storm will bring you wheat in torrents.'

"In the first light of dawn all my household gathered round me, the children brought pitch and the men whatever was necessary. On the fifth day I laid the keel and the ribs, then I made fast the planking. The ground-space was one acre, each side of the deck measured one hundred and twenty cubits, making a square. I built six decks below, seven in all, I divided them into nine sections with bulkheads between. I drove in wedges where needed, I saw to the punt-poles, and laid in supplies. The carriers brought oil in baskets, I poured pitch into the furnace and asphalt and oil; more oil was consumed in caulking, and more again the master of the boat took into his stores. I slaughtered bullocks for the people and every day I killed sheep. I gave the shipwrights wine to drink as though it were river water, raw wine and red wine and oil and white wine. There was feasting then as there is at the time of the New Year's festival; I myself anointed my head. On the eleventh day the boat was complete.

"Then was the launching full of difficulty; there was shifting of ballast above and below till two thirds was submerged. I loaded into her all that I had of gold and of living things, my family, my kin, the beast of the field both wild and tame, and all the craftsmen. I sent them on board, for the time that Shamash had ordained was already fulfilled when he said, 'In the evening, when the rider of the storm sends down the destroying rain, enter the boat and batten her down.' The time was fulfilled, the evening came, the rider of the storm sent down the rain. I looked out at the weather and it was terrible, so I too boarded the boat and battened her down. All was now complete, the battening and the caulking; so I handed the tiller to Puzur-Amurri the steersman, with the navigation and the care of the whole boat.

"With the first light of dawn a black cloud came from the horizon; it thundered within where Adad, lord of the storm was riding. In front over hill and plain Shullat and Hanish, heralds of the storm, led on. Then the gods of the abyss rose up; Nergal pulled out the dams of the nether waters, Ninurta the war-lord threw down the dykes, and the seven judges of hell, the Annunaki, raised their torches, lighting the land with their livid flame. A stupor of despair went up to heaven when the god of the storm turned daylight to darkness, when he smashed the land like a cup. One whole day the tempest raged, gathering fury as it went, it poured over the people like the tides of battle; a man could not see his brother nor the people be seen from heaven. Even the gods were terrified at the flood, they fled to the highest heaven, the firmament of Anu; they crouched against the walls, cowering like curs. Then Ishtar the sweet-voiced Queen of Heaven cried out like a woman in travail: 'Alas the days of old are turned to dust because I commanded evil; why did I command this evil in the council of all the gods? I commanded wars to destroy the people, but are they not my people, for I brought them forth? Now like the spawn of fish they float in the ocean.' The great gods of heaven and of hell wept, they covered their mouths.

"For six days and six nights the winds blew, torrent and tempest and flood overwhelmed the world, tempest and flood raged together like war-ring hosts. When the seventh day dawned the storm from the south subsided, the sea grew calm, the flood was stilled; I looked at the face of the world and there was silence, all mankind was turned to clay. The surface of the sea stretched as flat as a roof-top; I opened a hatch and the light fell on my face. Then I bowed low, I sat down and I wept, the tears streamed down my face, for on every side was the waste of water. I looked for land in vain, for fourteen leagues distant there appeared a mountain, and there the boat grounded; on the mountain of Nisir the boat held fast, she held fast and did not budge. One day she held, and a second day on the mountain of Nisir she held fast and did not budge. A third day, and a fourth day she held fast on the mountain and did not budge; a fifth day and a sixth day she held fast on the mountain. When the seventh day dawned I loosed a dove and let her go. She flew away, but finding no resting-place she returned. Then I loosed a swallow, and she flew away but finding no resting-place she returned. I loosed a raven, she saw that the waters had retreated, she ate, she flew around, she cawed, and she did not come back. Then I threw everything open to the four winds, I made a sacrifice and poured out a libation on the mountain top. Seven and again seven cauldrons I set up on their stands, I heaped up wood and cane and cedar and myrtle. When the gods smelled the sweet savour, they gathered like flies over the sacrifice. Then, at last, Ishtar also came, she lifted her necklace with the jewels of heaven that once Anu had made to please her. 'O you gods here present, by the lapis lazuli round my neck I shall remember these days as I remember the jewels of my throat; these last days I shall not forget. Let all the gods gather round the sacrifice, except Enlil. He shall not approach this offering, for without reflection he brought the flood; he consigned my people to destruction."

"When Enlil had come, when he saw the boat, he was wrath and swelled with anger at the gods, the host of heaven, 'Has any of these mortals escaped? Not one was to have survived the destruction.' Then the god of the wells and canals Ninurta opened his mouth and said to the warrior Enlil, 'Who is there of the gods that can devise without Ea? It is Ea, alone who knows all things.' Then Ea opened his mouth and spoke to warrior Enlil, 'Wisest of gods, hero Enlil, how could you so senselessly bring down the flood?

> Lay upon the sinner his sin,
> Lay upon the transgressor his transgression,
> Punish him a little when he breaks loose,
> Do not drive him too hard or he perishes;
> Would that a lion had ravaged mankind
> Rather than the flood,
> Would that a wolf had ravaged mankind
> Rather than the flood,
> Would that famine had wasted the world
> Rather than the flood,
> Would that pestilence had wasted mankind
> Rather than the flood.

It was not I that revealed the secret of the gods; the wise man learned it in a dream. Now take your counsel what shall be done with him.'

"Then Enlil went up into the boat, he took me by the hand and my wife and made us enter the boat and kneel down on either side, he standing between us. He touched our foreheads to bless us saying, 'In time past Utnapishtim was a mortal man; henceforth he and his wife shall live in the distance at the mouth of the rivers.' Thus it was that the gods took me and placed me here to live in the distance, at the mouth of the rivers."

6

The Return

Utnapishtim said, "As for you, Gilgamesh, who will assemble the gods for your sake, so that you may find that life for which you are searching? But if you wish, come and put it to the test: only prevail against sleep for six days and seven nights." But while Gilgamesh sat there resting on his haunches, a mist of sleep like soft wool teased from the fleece drifted over him, and Utnapishtim said to his wife, "Look at him now, the strong man who would have everlasting life, even now the mists of sleep are drifitng over him." His wife replied, "Touch the man to wake him, so that he may return to his own land in peace, going back through the gate by which he came." Utnapishtim said to his wife, "All men are deceivers, even you he will attempt to deceive; therefore bake loaves of bread, each day one loaf, and put it beside his head; and make a mark on the wall to number the days he has slept."

So she baked loaves of bread, each day one loaf, and put it beside his head, and she marked on the walls the days that he slept; and there came a day when the first loaf was hard, the second loaf was like leather, the third was soggy, the crust of the fourth had mould, the fifth was mildewed, the sixth was fresh, and the seventh was still on the embers. Then Utnapishtim touched him and he woke. Gilgamesh said to Utnapishtim the Faraway, "I hardly slept when you touched and roused me." But Utnapishtim said, "Count these loaves and learn how many days you slept, for your first is hard, your second like leather, your third is soggy, the crust of your fourth has mould, your fifth is mildewed, your sixth is fresh and your seventh was still over the glowing embers when I touched and woke you." Gilgamesh said, "What shall I do, O Utnapishtim, where shall I go? Already the thief in the night has hold of my limbs, death inhabits my room; wherever my foot rests, there I find death."

Then Utnapishtim spoke to Urshanabi the ferryman: "Woe to you Urshanabi, now and for ever more you have become hateful to this harbourage; it is not for you, nor for you are the crossings of this sea. Go now, banished from the shore. But this man before whom you walked, bringing him here, whose body is covered with foulness and the grace of whose limbs has been spoiled by wild skins, take him to the washing-place. There he shall wash his long hair clean as snow in the water, he shall throw off his skins and let the sea carry them away, and the beauty of his body shall be shown, the fillet on his forehead shall be renewed, and he shall be given clothes to cover his nakedness. Till he reaches his own city and his journey is accomplished, these clothes will show no sign of age, they will wear like a new garment." So Urshanabi took Gilgamesh and led him to the washing-place, he washed his long hair as clean as snow in the water, he threw off his skins, which the sea carried away, and showed the beauty of his body. He renewed the fillet on his forehead, and to cover his nakedness gave him clothes which would show no sign of age, but would wear like a new garment til he reached his own city, and his journey was accomplished.

Then Gilgamesh and Urshanabi launched the boat on to the water and boarded it, and they made ready to sail away; but the wife of Utnapishtim the Faraway said to him, "Gilgamesh came here wearied out, he is worn out; what will you give him to carry him back to his own country?" So Utnapishtim spoke, and Gilgamesh took a pole and brought the boat in to the bank. "Gilgamesh, you came here a man wearied out, you have worn yourself out; what shall I give you to carry you back to your own country? Gilgamesh, I shall reveal a secret thing, it is a mystery of the gods that I am telling you. There is a plant that grows under the water, it has a prickle like a thorn, like a rose; it will wound your hands, but if you succeed in taking it, then your hands will hold that which restores his lost youth to a man."

When Gilgamesh heard this he opened the sluices so that a sweet-water current might carry him out to the deepest channel; he tied heavy stones to his feet and they dragged him down to the water-bed. There he saw the plant growing; although it pricked him he took it in his hands; then he cut the heavy stones from his feet, and the sea carried him and threw him on to the shore. Gilgamesh said to Urshanabi the ferryman, "Come here, and see this marvellous plant. By its virtue a man may win back all his former strength. I will take it to Uruk of the strong walls; there I will give it to the old men to eat. Its name shall be 'The Old Men Are Young Again'; and at last I shall eat it myself and have back all my lost youth." So Gilgamesh returned by the gate through which he had come, Gilgamesh and Urshanabi went together. They travelled their twenty leagues and then they broke their fast; after thirty leagues they stopped for the night.

Gilgamesh saw a well of cool water and he went down and bathed; but deep in the pool there was lying a serpent, and the serpent sensed the sweetness of the flower. It rose out of the water and snatched it away, and immediately it sloughed its skin and returned to the well. Then Gilgamesh sat down and wept, the tears ran down his face, and he took the hand of Urshanabi; "O Urshanabi, was it for this that I toiled with my hands, is it for this I have wrung out my heart's blood? For myself I have gained nothing; not I, but the beast of the earth has joy of it now. Already the stream has carried it twenty leagues back to the channels where I found it. I found a sign and now I have lost it. Let us leave the boat on the bank and go."

After twenty leagues they broke their fast, after thirty leagues they stopped for the night; in three days they had walked as much as a journey of a month and fifteen days. When the journey was accomplished they arrived at Uruk, the strong-walled city. Gilgamesh spoke to him, to Urshanabi the ferryman, "Urshanabi, climb up on to the wall of Uruk, inspect its foundation terrace, and examine well the brickwork; see if it is not of burnt bricks; and did not the seven wise men lay these foundations? One third of the whole is city, one third is garden, and one third is field, with the precinct of the goddess Ishtar. These parts and the precinct are all Uruk."

This too was the work of Gilgamesh, the king, who knew the countries of the world. He was wise, he saw mysteries and knew secret things, he brought us a tale of the days before the flood. He went a long journey, was weary, worn out with labour, and returning engraved on a stone the whole story.

7

The Death of Gilgamesh

The destiny was fulfilled which the father of the gods, Enlil of the mountain, had decreed for Gilgamesh: "In nether-earth the darkness will show him a light: of mankind, all that are known, none will leave a monument for generations to come to compare with his. The heroes, the wise men, like the new moon have their waxing and waning. Men will say, 'Who has ever ruled with might and with power like him?' As in the dark month, the month of shadows, so without him there is no light. O Gilgamesh, this was the meaning of your dream. You were given the kingship, such was your destiny, everlasting life was not your destiny. Because of this do not be sad at heart, do not be grieved or oppressed; he has given you power to bind and to loose, to be the darkness and the light of mankind. He has given unexampled supremacy over the people, victory in battle from which no fugitive returns, in forays and assaults from which there is no going back. But do not abuse this power, deal justly with your servants in the palace, deal justly before the face of the Sun."

> The king has laid himself down and will not rise again,
> The Lord of Kullab will not rise again;
> He overcame evil, he will not come again;
> Though he was strong of arm he will not rise again;
>
> He had wisdom and a comely face, he will not come again;
> He is gone into the mountain, he will not come again;
> On the bed of fate he lies, he will not rise again,
> From the couch of many colours he will not come again.

The people of the city, great and small, are not silent; they lift up the lament, all men of flesh and blood lift up the lament. Fate has spoken; like a hooked fish he lies stretched on the bed, like a gazelle that is caught in a noose. Inhuman Namtar is heavy upon him, Namtar that has neither hand nor foot, that drinks no water and eats no meat.

For Gilgamesh, son of Ninsun, they weighed out their offerings; his dear wife, his son, his concubine, his musicians, his jester, and all his household; his servants, his stewards, all who lived in the palace weighed out their offerings for Gilgamesh the son of Ninsun, the heart of Uruk. They weighed out their offerings to Ereshkigal, the Queen of Death, and to all the gods of the dead. To Namtar, who is fate, they weighed out the offering. Bread for Neti the Keeper of the Gate, bread for Ningizzida the god of the serpent, the lord of the Tree of Life; for Dumuzi also, the young shepherd, for Enki and Ninki, for Endukugga and Nindukugga, for Enmul and Ninmul, all the ancestral gods, forbears of Enlil. A feast for Shulpae the god of feasting. For Samuqan, god of the herds, for the mother Ninhursag, and the gods of creation in the place of creation, for the host of heaven, priest and priestess weighed out the offering of the dead.

Gilgamesh, the son of Ninsun, lies in the tomb. At the place of offerings he weighed the bread-offering, at the place of libation he poured out the wine. In those days the lord Gilgamesh departed, the son of Ninsun, the king, peerless, without an equal among men, who did not neglect Enlil his master. O Gilgamesh, lord of Kullab, great is thy praise.

THE OLD TESTAMENT

The religious attitudes of the Hebrews appear in the story that they told of the creation of the world and of man. This creation is the work of one God, who is omnipotent and omniscient, and who creates a perfect and harmonious order. The disorder that we see all around us, physical and moral, is not God's creation but Adam's; it is the consequence of man's disobedience. The story not only reconciles the undeniable existence of evil and disorder in the world with the conception of God's infinite justice; it also attributes to man himself an independence of God, free will, which in this case he had used for evil. The Hebrew God is not limited in His power by other deities, who oppose His will (as in the Greek stories of Zeus and his undisciplined family); His power over inanimate nature is infinite. In all the range of His creation there is only one being able to resist Him—man.

Since God is all-powerful, even this resistance on Adam's part is in some mysterious way a manifestation of God's will. How this can be is not explained by the story, and we are left with the mystery that still eludes us, the coexistence of God's prescient power and man's unrestricted free will.

The story of the Fall of Man ends with a situation in which Adam has earned for himself and his descendants a short life of sorrow relieved only by death. It was the achievement of later Hebrew teachers to carry the story on and develop the concept of a God who is as merciful as He is just, who watches tenderly over the destinies of the creatures who have rebelled against Him, and who brings about the possibility of atonement and full reconciliation.

Adam's son Cain is the first man to shed human blood, but though God drives him out to be a wanderer on the face of the earth, He does not kill him. The brand on Cain's forehead, while it marks him as a murderer, also protects his life—no man is to touch him. Later when the descendants of Adam grow so wicked that God is sorry He has created the human race, He decides to destroy it by sending a universal flood. But He spares one man, Noah, with his family, to beget a new human race, on which God pins His hopes. His rainbow in the sky reminds men of His promise that He will never again let loose the waters. But men do not learn their lesson: they start to build a tower high enough to reach to Heaven, and God is afraid that if they succeed they will then recognize no limit to their ambitions. Yet He does not destroy them; He merely frustrates their purpose by depriving them of their common language.

And yet Man must eventually atone for Adam's act: human guilt must be wiped out by sacrifice. The development of this idea was extended over centuries of thought and suffering. For the Christians, it reached its culmination in the figure of Christ, the Son of God, who as a man pays the full measure due in human suffering and human death. But the idea of the one who suffers for all had long been a major theme in Hebrew religious literature. Not only did there emerge slowly a concept of the Hebrews as a chosen nation that suffers for the rest, but individual figures of Hebrew history and imagination embodied this theme in the form of the story of the suffering servant whose suffering brings relief to his fellow men and ultimate glory to himself. This is the idea behind the story of Joseph.

JOSEPH

Joseph, his father's favorite son, has a sense of his own great destiny, confirmed by his dreams, which represent him as the first of all his race. He is indeed to be the first, but to become so he must also be the last. He is sold into slavery by his brothers; the savior is rejected by those whom he is to save, as the Hebrews were rejected by their neighbors and as they rejected their own prophets.

With the loss of his liberty, Joseph's trials have only begun. In Egypt after making a new and successful life for himself, he is thrown into prison on a false accusation. He interprets the dream of Pharaoh's butler, who promises, if his interpretation is correct, to secure his release; the butler is restored to freedom and royal favor, but, as is the way of the world, forgets his promise and leaves his comforter in jail. Joseph stays in prison two more years but finally obtains his freedom and becomes Pharaoh's most trusted adviser. When his brothers come from starving Palestine and bow down before him asking for help, he saves them; not only does he give them grain but he also provides a home for his people in Egypt. "I am Joseph your brother, whom ye sold into Egypt," he says to them when he reveals his identity. "God sent me before you to preserve you a posterity in the earth, and to save your lives by a great deliverance."

One of the essential points of this story, and the whole conception of the suffering servant, is the distinction that it emphasizes between an external, secular standard of good and a spiritual, religious standard. In the eyes of the average person, prosperity and righteousness are connected, if not identified; and the sufferer is felt to be one whose misfortune must be explained as a punishment for his wickedness. This feeling is strong in ancient (and especially in Greek) literature, but we should not be unduly complacent about our superiority to the ancients in this respect, for the attitude is still with us. It is in fact a basic assumption of the competitive society—the view, seldom expressed but strongly rooted, that the plight of the unfortunate is the result of their own laziness, the wealth of the rich the reward of superior virtue.

The writer of the Joseph story sees in the unfortunate sufferer the savior who is the instrument of God's will. It is because of what he suffers that the sun and the moon and the eleven stars will bow down to Joseph. Yet the story does not emphasize the sufferings of Joseph; he is pictured rather as the man of action who through native ability and divine protection turns the injuries done him into advantages. We are not made to feel the torment in his soul. When he weeps it is because of the memory of what he had suffered and his yearning for his youngest brother, and he is in full control of the situation. And his reward in the things of this world is great. Not only does he reveal himself as the savior of his nation, but he becomes rich and powerful beyond his brothers' dreams, and in a great kingdom. The spiritual and secular standards are at the end of the story combined; Joseph's suffering is neatly balanced by his worldly reward.

JOB

Later Hebrew writers developed a sadder and profounder view. The greatest literary masterpiece of the Old Testament, the Book of Job, is also concerned with the inadequacy of worldly standards of happiness and righteousness; but the suffering of Job is so overwhelming and so magnificently expressed, that even with our knowledge of its purpose and its meaning it seems excessive. Joseph suffered slavery, exile, and imprisonment, but turned them all to account. Job loses his family and wealth in a series of calamities, which strike one on the other like hammer blows, and is then plagued with a loathsome disease. Unlike Joseph, he is old; he cannot adapt himself and rise above adverse circumstances, and he no longer wishes to live. Except for one thing: he wishes to understand the reason for his suffering.

For his friends the explanation is simple. With the blindness of men who know no standards other than those of this world, they are sure that Job's misfortune must be the result of some wickedness on his part. But Job is confident in his righteousness; his torture is as much mental as physical. He cannot reconcile the fact of his innocence with the calamities that have come upon him with all the decisive suddenness of the hand of God.

The full explanation is never given to him, but it is given to the reader in the two opening chapters of the book. This prologue to the dramatic section of the work gives us the knowledge that is hidden from the participants in the ensuing dialogue. The writer uses the method characteristic of Greek tragedy—irony, the deeper understanding of the dramatic spoken word which is based on the superior knowledge of the audience. The prologue explains God's motive in allowing Job to suffer. It is an important one: God intends to use Job as a demonstration to His skeptical subordinate, Satan, of the fact that a human being can retain faith in God's justice in the face of the greatest imaginable suffering. This motive, which Job does not know and which is never revealed to him, gives to the dialogue between Job and his friends its suspense and its importance. God has rested His case—that humanity is capable of keeping faith in divine justice, against all appearances to the contrary—on this one man.

The arguments of Job's friends are based on the worldly equation, success = virtue. They attempt to undermine Job's faith, not in God, but in himself. "[W]ho ever perished, being innocent?" asks Eliphaz, "or where were the righteous cut off?" Job's misfortune is a proof that he must have sinned; all he has to do is to admit his guilt and ask God for pardon, which he will surely receive. He refuses to accept this easy way out, and we know that he is right. In fact, we know from the prologue that he has been selected for misfortune not because he has sinned, but precisely because of his outstanding virtue. "There is none like him in the earth," God says, "a perfect and an upright man, one that feareth God, and escheweth evil." What Job must do is to persevere not only in his faith in God's justice but also in the conviction of his own innocence. He must believe the illogical, accept a paradox. His friends are offering him an easy way out, one that seems to be the way of humility and submission. But it is a false way. And God finally tells them so. "The Lord said to Eliphaz the Temanite, My wrath is kindled against thee, and against thy two friends: for ye have not spoken of me the thing that is right, as my servant Job hath."

Job's confidence in his own righteousness is not pride, but intellectual honesty. He sees that the problem is much harder than his friends imagine. To let them persuade him of his own guilt would lighten his mental burden by answering the question that tortures him, but his intelligence will not let him yield. Like Oedipus, he refuses to stop short of the truth. He even uses the same words: "let me alone, that I may speak, and let come on me what will." He finally expresses his understanding and acceptance of the paradox involved in the combination of his suffering with his innocence, but he does so with a human independence and dignity: "Though he slay me, yet will I trust in him: but I will maintain mine own ways before him." He sums up his case with a detailed account of the righteousness of his ways, and it is clear that this account is addressed not only to his three friends but also to God. "My desire is, that the Almighty would answer me," he says. His friends are silenced by the majesty and firmness of his statement. They "ceased to answer Job, because he was righteous in his own eyes," but God is moved to reply.

The magnificent poetry of that reply, the voice out of the whirlwind, still does not give Job the full explanation, God's motive in putting him to the torture. It is a triumphant proclamation of God's power and also of His justice, and it silences

Job, who accepts it as a sufficient answer. That God does not reveal the key to the riddle even to the man who has victoriously stood the test and vindicated His faith in humanity is perhaps the most significant point in the poem. It suggests that there is not and never will be an explanation of human suffering that man's intelligence can comprehend. The sufferer must, like Job, cling to his faith in himself and in God; he must accept the inexplicable fact that his own undeserved suffering is the working of God's justice.

THE PROPHETS

In the last days of Israel's independence, before conquerors overran the land and transported the population to captivity in the East (an exile mourned in Psalm 137—"By the rivers of Babylon . . ."), a series of prophets reproved the children of Israel for their transgressions and foretold the wrath to come, the end of the kingdom of Israel, and, beyond that, the overthrow of the neighboring kingdoms. The prophet was a man who believed himself to be the spokesman of God, the messenger of a terrifying vision. The horror of the vision of destruction was often too heavy a load for the human mind, and the disbelief and mockery of his hearers tipped the precarious balance so that what might have been merely a strange urgency came often close to madness. The vision of things to come was expressed in magnificent but disconnected images which to the workaday mind of the man in the street seemed only to confirm the suspicion that the prophet was deranged. Amos, Nahum, Jeremiah, and many others poured out their charged and clotted imagery of catastrophe to an unbelieving people.

But the story of Jonah shows us a prophet who was believed. When they heard his message, the people and ruler of Nineveh repented of their sins and made amends to God. They were spared, but Jonah objected and God had to rebuke him; God was more forgiving to sinners than the human prophet to his people.

The prophets were not always messengers of doom; it is in the words of an unnamed prophet (whose writings are included in the Book of Isaiah) that the theme of the one who suffers for others finds its most profound and moving expression. In the earlier versions the sufferer has it all made up to him in the end: Job, like Joseph, has his reward. Job's suffering is greater than Joseph's, and it is clear that the writer of the Book of Job shows, alike in the speeches and in the ironic framework of the whole, a profounder understanding of the nature and meaning of suffering than the narrator of the story of Joseph, but like Joseph, Job lives to see the end of his troubles and has his material reward. "The Lord gave Job twice as much as he had before. . . . After this lived Job an hundred and forty years, and saw his sons, and his sons' sons, even four generations."

But in the Song of the Suffering Servant there is no recompense in this life: the suffering ends in death. In this deeper vision there is no reconciliation between the standards of this world and the standards of the higher authority behind the suffering. The one who is to save Israel and the world is not well favored like Joseph: "he hath no form nor comeliness." Nor is he, like Job, "the greatest of all the men of the east"; he is "despised and rejected of men." He suffers for his fellow men: "the Lord hath laid on him the iniquity of us all." His suffering knows no limit but death; he is oppressed and afflicted, imprisoned and executed. "He was cut off out of the land of the living" and "he made his grave with the wicked."

The circumstances described here are familiar from other cultures than the Hebrew; they are found in the primitive ritual of many peoples, and ceremonial relics of them still existed in civilized fifth-century Athens. In certain primitive societies, to rid the group of guilt a scapegoat was chosen, who was declared responsible for the misdeeds of all, and who was then mocked, beaten, driven out of the community, and killed. The scapegoat was hated and despised as the embodiment of the guilt of the whole community; his death was the most ignominious imaginable. The memory of some such primitive ritual is unmistakable in the Hebrew song; but its meaning has been utterly changed. It is precisely in the figure of the hated and suffering scapegoat that the Hebrew prophet sees the savior of mankind—an innocent sufferer, "he had done no violence, neither was any deceit in his mouth"—and the prophet sees this without visible confirmation. There is no recognition by the brothers, no vindication by a voice out of the whirlwind. It is the highest expression of the Hebrew vision at its saddest and most profound, this portrayal of the savior who comes not in pomp and power but in suffering and meekness, who dies rejected and despised, and who atones for human sin and makes "intercession for the transgressors."

The student will find good background in *The Cambridge History of the Bible*, edited by R. R. Ackroyd and C. F. Evans, vol. I (1970). R. H. Rowley, *The Growth of the Old Testament* (1950), concentrates on the Old Testament as a whole. For Job, see P. Sanders, ed., *Twentieth-Century Interpretations of the Book of Job* (1968). See also Robert Alter and Frank Kermode, eds., *The Literary Guide to the Bible* (1987), especially pp. 283–303 (Job) and 244–261 (Psalms).

The Old Testament[1]

GENESIS 1–3

(The Creation—The Fall)

1. In the beginning God created the heaven and the earth. And the earth was without form, and void; and darkness was upon the face of the deep. And the Spirit of God moved upon the face of the waters.

And God said, Let there be light: and there was light. And God saw the light, that it was good: and God divided the light from the darkness. And God called the light Day, and the darkness he called Night. And the evening and the morning were the first day.

And God said, Let there be a firmament in the midst of the waters,[2] and let it divide the waters from the waters. And God made the firmament, and divided the waters which were under the firmament from the waters which were above the firmament: and it was so. And God called the firmament Heaven. And the evening and the morning were the second day.

And God said, Let the waters under the heaven be gathered together

---

1. The text of these selections is that of the King James, or Authorized, Version of 1611, so called because it was the work of a team of fifty-four scholars named by King James I of England to produce a new translation "appointed to be read in churches." Since that time advances in biblical scholarship have corrected some of the translators' mistakes and substituted clearer versions where their prose is obscure. Yet the superiority of the Authorized Version as literature remains unquestioned; it is one of the greatest literary texts in the history of our language. It was written at a time when English was at a creative peak—the age of William Shakespeare, Ben Jonson, and John Donne. It was written to be read aloud, as it was in churches and homes, to be learned by heart, as it was in schools in the English-speaking world for centuries. The echoes of its magnificent rhythms and cadences can be heard in the verse of English poets from John Milton to T. S. Eliot, in the prose of John Bunyan and the speeches of Abraham Lincoln.
2. The firmament is the sky, which seen from below has the appearance of a ceiling; the waters above it are those which come down in the form of rain.

unto one place, and let the dry land appear: and it was so. And God called
the dry land Earth; and the gathering together of the waters called he Seas:
and God saw that it was good. And God said, Let the earth bring forth
grass, the herb yielding seed, and the fruit tree yielding fruit after his kind,
whose seed is in itself, upon the earth: and it was so. And the earth brought
forth grass, and herb yielding seed after his kind, and the tree yielding fruit,
whose seed was in itself, after his kind: and God saw that it was good. And
the evening and the morning were the third day.

And God said, Let there be lights in the firmament of the heaven to
divide the day from the night; and let them be for signs, and for seasons,
and for days, and years: and let them be for lights in the firmament of the
heaven to give light upon the earth: and it was so. And God made two
great lights; the greater light to rule the day, and the lesser light to rule the
night: he made the stars also. And God set them in the firmament of the
heaven to give light upon the earth, and to rule over the day and over the
night, and to divide the light from the darkness: and God saw that it was
good. And the evening and the morning were the fourth day. And God
said, Let the waters bring forth abundantly the moving creature that hath
life, and fowl that may fly above the earth in the open firmament of heaven.
And God created great whales, and every living creature that moveth, which
the waters brought forth abundantly, after their kind, and every winged
fowl after his kind: and God saw that it was good. And God blessed them,
saying, Be fruitful, and multiply, and fill the waters in the seas, and let
fowl multiply in the earth. And the evening and the morning were the fifth
day.

And God said, Let the earth bring forth the living creature after his kind,
cattle, and creeping thing, and beast of the earth after his kind: and it was
so. And God made the beast of the earth after his kind, and cattle after
their kind, and everything that creepeth upon the earth after his kind: and
God saw that it was good.

And God said, Let us make man in our image, after our likeness: and
let them have dominion over the fish of the sea, and over the fowl of the
air, and over the cattle, and over all the earth, and over every creeping
thing that creepeth upon the earth. So God created man in his own image,
in the image of God created he him; male and female created he them.
And God blessed them, and God said unto them, Be fruitful, and multiply, and replenish the earth, and subdue it: and have dominion over the
fish of the sea, and over the fowl of the air, and over every living thing that
moveth upon the earth.

And God said, Behold, I have given you every herb bearing seed, which
is upon the face of all the earth, and every tree, in which is the fruit of a
tree yielding seed; to you it shall be for meat. And to every beast of the
earth, and to every fowl of the air, and to every thing that creepeth upon
the earth, wherein there is life, I have given every green herb for meat: and
it was so. And God saw every thing that he had made, and, behold, it was
very good. And the evening and the morning were the sixth day.

2. Thus the heavens and the earth were finished, and all the host of them. And on the seventh day God ended his work which he had made; and he rested on the seventh day from all his work which he had made. And God blessed the seventh day, and sanctified it: because that in it he had rested from all his work which God created and made.

These are the generations of the heavens and of the earth when they were created,[3] in the day that the Lord God made the earth and the heavens, and every plant of the field before it was in the earth, and every herb of the field before it grew: for the Lord God had not caused it to rain upon the earth, and there was not a man to till the ground. But there went up a mist from the earth, and watered the whole face of the ground. And the Lord God formed man of the dust of the ground, and breathed into his nostrils the breath of life; and man became a living soul.

And the Lord God planted a garden eastward in Eden; and there he put the man whom he had formed. And out of the ground made the Lord God to grow every tree that is pleasant to the sight, and good for food; the tree of life also in the midst of the garden, and the tree of knowledge of good and evil. And a river went out of Eden to water the garden; and from thence it was parted, and became into four heads. The name of the first is Pison: that is it which compasseth the whole land of Havilah, where there is gold; and the gold of that land is good: there is bdellium and the onyx stone. And the name of the second river is Gihon: the same is it that compasseth the whole land of Ethiopia. And the name of the third river is Hiddekel: that is it which goeth toward the east of Assyria. And the fourth river is Euphrates. And the Lord God took the man, and put him into the garden of Eden to dress it and to keep it. And the Lord God commanded the man, saying, Of every tree of the garden thou mayest freely eat: but of the tree of the knowledge of good and evil, thou shalt not eat of it: for in the day that thou eatest thereof thou shalt surely die.

And the Lord God said, It is not good that the man should be alone; I will make him an help meet for him. And out of the ground the Lord God formed every beast of the field, and every fowl of the air; and brought them unto Adam to see what he would call them: and whatsoever Adam called every living creature, that was the name thereof. And Adam gave names to all cattle, and to the fowl of the air, and to every beast of the field; but for Adam there was not found an help meet for him. And the Lord God caused a deep sleep to fall upon Adam, and he slept: and he took one of his ribs, and closed up the flesh instead thereof; and the rib, which the Lord God had taken from man, made he a woman, and brought her unto the man. And Adam said, This is now bone of my bones, and flesh of my flesh: she shall be called Woman, because she was taken out of Man. Therefore shall a man leave his father and his mother, and shall cleave unto his wife: and they shall be one flesh. And they were both naked, the man and his wife, and were not ashamed.

3. This is the beginning of a different account of the Creation, which does not agree in all respects with the first.

3. Now the serpent was more subtil than any beast of the field which the Lord God had made. And he said unto the woman, Yea, hath God said, Ye shall not eat of every tree of the garden? And the woman said unto the serpent, We may eat of the fruit of the trees of the garden: but of the fruit of the tree which is in the midst of the garden, God hath said, Ye shall not eat of it, neither shall ye touch it, lest ye die. And the serpent said unto the woman, Ye shall not surely die: for God doth know that in the day ye eat thereof, then your eyes shall be opened, and ye shall be as gods, knowing good and evil. And when the woman saw that the tree was good for food, and that it was pleasant to the eyes, and a tree to be desired to make one wise, she took of the fruit thereof, and did eat, and gave also unto her husband with her; and he did eat. And the eyes of them both were opened, and they knew that they were naked; and they sewed fig leaves together, and made themselves aprons. And they heard the voice of the Lord God walking in the garden in the cool of the day: and Adam and his wife hid themselves from the presence of the Lord God amongst the trees of the garden. And the Lord God called unto Adam, and said unto him, Where art thou? And he said, I heard thy voice in the garden, and I was afraid, because I was naked; and I hid myself. And he said, Who told thee that thou wast naked? Hast thou eaten of the tree, whereof I commanded thee that thou shouldest not eat? And the man said, The woman whom thou gavest to be with me, she gave me of the tree, and I did eat. And the Lord God said unto the woman, What is this that thou hast done? And the woman said, The serpent beguiled me, and I did eat. And the Lord God said unto the serpent, Because thou hast done this, thou art cursed above all cattle, and above every beast of the field; upon thy belly shalt thou go, and dust shalt thou eat all the days of thy life: and I will put enmity between thee and the woman, and between thy seed and her seed; it shall bruise thy head, and thou shalt bruise his heel. Unto the woman he said, I will greatly multiply thy sorrow and thy conception; in sorrow thou shalt bring forth children; and thy desire shall be to thy husband, and he shall rule over thee. And unto Adam he said, Because thou hast hearkened unto the voice of thy wife, and hast eaten of the tree, of which I commanded thee, saying, Thou shalt not eat of it: cursed is the ground for thy sake; in sorrow shalt thou eat of it all the days of thy life; thorns also and thistles shall it bring forth to thee; and thou shalt eat the herb of the field; in the sweat of thy face shalt thou eat bread, till thou return unto the ground; for out of it wast thou taken: for dust thou art, and unto dust shalt thou return. And Adam called his wife's name Eve; because she was the mother of all living. Unto Adam also and to his wife did the Lord God make coats of skins, and clothed them.

And the Lord God said, Behold, the man is become as one of us, to know good and evil: and now, lest he put forth his hand, and take also of the tree of life, and eat, and live forever: therefore the Lord God sent him forth from the garden of Eden, to till the ground from whence he was taken. So he drove out the man; and he placed at the east of the garden of

Eden Cherubims, and a flaming sword which turned every way, to keep the way of the tree of life.

GENESIS 4

(The First Murder)

4. And Adam knew Eve his wife; and she conceived, and bare Cain, and said, I have gotten a man from the Lord. And she again bare his brother Abel. And Abel was a keeper of sheep, but Cain was a tiller of the ground. And in process of time it came to pass, that Cain brought of the fruit of the ground an offering unto the Lord. And Abel, he also brought of the firstlings of his flock and of the fat thereof. And the Lord had respect unto Abel and to his offering: but unto Cain and to his offering he had not respect. And Cain was very wroth, and his countenance fell. And the Lord said unto Cain, Why art thou wroth? and why is thy countenance fallen? If thou doest well, shalt thou not be accepted? and if thou doest not well, sin lieth at the door. And unto thee shall be his desire, and thou shall rule over him.[4] And Cain talked with Abel his brother: and it came to pass, when they were in the field, that Cain rose up against Abel his brother, and slew him.

And the Lord said unto Cain, Where is Abel thy brother? And he said, I know not: am I my brother's keeper? And he said, What hast thou done? the voice of thy brother's blood crieth unto me from the ground. And now art thou cursed from the earth, which hath opened her mouth to receive thy brother's blood from thy hand; when thou tillest the ground, it shall not henceforth yield unto thee her strength, a fugitive and a vagabond shalt thou be in the earth. And Cain said unto the Lord, My punishment is greater than I can bear. Behold, thou hast driven me out this day from the face of the earth; and from thy face shall I be hid; and I shall be a fugitive and a vagabond in the earth; and it shall come to pass, that every one that findeth me shall slay me. And the Lord said unto him, Therefore whosoever slayeth Cain, vengeance shall be taken on him sevenfold. And the Lord set a mark upon Cain, lest any finding him should kill him.

GENESIS 6–9

(The Flood)

6. . . . And God saw that the wickedness of man was great in the earth, and that every imagination of the thoughts of his heart was only evil continually. And it repented the Lord that he had made man on the earth, and it grieved him at his heart. And the Lord said, I will destroy man whom I have created from the face of the earth; both man, and beast, and

---

4. An obscure sentence. It seems to mean something like: "It (i.e., sin) shall be eager for you, but you must master it."

the creeping thing, and the fowls of the air; for it repenteth me that I have
made them. But Noah found grace in the eyes of the Lord.

These are the generations of Noah: Noah was a just man and perfect in
his generations, and Noah walked with God. And Noah begat three sons,
Shem, Ham, and Japheth.

The earth also was corrupt before God, and the earth was filled with
violence. And God looked upon the earth, and, behold, it was corrupt; for
all flesh had corrupted his way upon the earth. And God said unto Noah,
The end of all flesh is come before me; for the earth is filled with violence
through them; and, behold, I will destroy them with the earth. Make thee
an ark of gopher wood;[5] rooms shalt thou make in the ark, and shalt pitch
it within and without with pitch. And this is the fashion which thou shalt
make it of: The length of the ark shall be three hundred cubits,[6] the breadth
of it fifty cubits, and the height of it thirty cubits. A window[7] shalt thou
make to the ark, and in a cubit shalt thou finish it above; and the door of
the ark shalt thou set in the side thereof; with lower, second, and third
stories shalt thou make it. And, behold, I, even I, do bring a flood of waters
upon the earth, to destroy all flesh, wherein is the breath of life, from
under heaven; and every thing that is in the earth shall die. But with thee
will I establish my covenant; and thou shalt come into the ark, thou, and
thy sons, and thy wife, and thy sons' wives with thee. And of every living
thing of all flesh, two of every sort shalt thou bring into the ark, to keep
them alive with thee; they shall be male and female. Of fowls after their
kind, and of cattle after their kind, of every creeping thing of the earth after
his kind, two of every sort shall come unto thee, to keep them alive. And
take thou unto thee of all food that is eaten, and thou shalt gather it to
thee; and it shall be for food for thee, and for them. Thus did Noah;
according to all that God commanded him, so did he.

7. . . . And Noah was six hundred years old when the flood of waters
was upon the earth. And Noah went in, and his sons, and his wife, and
his sons' wives with him, into the ark, because of the waters of the flood.
Of clean beasts, and of beasts that are not clean, and of fowls, and of every
thing that creepeth upon the earth, There went in two and two unto Noah
into the ark, the male and the female, as God had commanded Noah.
And it came to pass after seven days, that the waters of the flood were upon
the earth. In the six hundredth year of Noah's life, in the second month,
the seventeenth day of the month, the same day were all the fountains of
the great deep broken up, and the windows of heaven were opened. And
the rain was upon the earth forty days and forty nights. In the selfsame day
entered Noah, and Shem, and Ham, and Japheth, the sons of Noah, and
Noah's wife, and the three wives of his sons with them, into the ark; they,
and every beast after his kind, and all the cattle after their kind, and every
creeping thing that creepeth upon the earth after his kind, and every fowl
after his kind, every bird of every sort. And they went in unto Noah into

5. Cypress.   6. A Hebrew measure of length, about one and a half feet.   7. The text is obscure; it
may refer to a skylight in the roof.

the ark, two and two of all flesh, wherein is the breath of life. And they that went in, went in male and female of all flesh, as God had commanded him: and the Lord shut him in. And the flood was forty days upon the earth; and the waters increased, and bare up the ark, and it was lift up above the earth. And the waters prevailed, and were increased greatly upon the earth; and the ark went upon the face of the waters. And the waters prevailed exceedingly upon the earth; and all the high hills, that were under the whole heaven, were covered. Fifteen cubits upward did the waters prevail; and the mountains were covered. And all flesh died that moved upon the earth, both of fowl, and of cattle, and of beast, and of every creeping thing that creepeth upon the earth, and every man: all in whose nostrils was the breath of life, of all that was in the dry land, died. And every living substance was destroyed which was upon the face of the ground, both man, and cattle, and the creeping things, and the fowl of the heaven; and they were destroyed from the earth: and Noah only remained alive, and they that were with him in the ark. And the waters prevailed upon the earth an hundred and fifty days.

8. And God remembered Noah, and every living thing, and all the cattle that was with him in the ark: and God made a wind to pass over the earth, and the waters assuaged; The fountains also of the deep and the windows of heaven were stopped, and the rain from heaven was restrained; And the waters returned from off the earth continually: and after the end of the hundred and fifty days the waters were abated. And the ark rested in the seventh month, on the seventeenth day of the month, upon the mountains of Ararat. And the waters decreased continually until the tenth month: in the tenth month, on the first day of the month, were the tops of the mountains seen.

And it came to pass at the end of forty days, that Noah opened the window of the ark which he had made: and he sent forth a raven, which went forth to and fro, until the waters were dried up from off the earth. Also he sent forth a dove from him, to see if the waters were abated from off the face of the ground; but the dove found no rest for the sole of her foot, and she returned unto him into the ark, for the waters were on the face of the whole earth: then he put forth his hand, and took her, and pulled her in unto him into the ark. And he stayed yet another seven days; and again he sent forth the dove out of the ark; and the dove came in to him in the evening; and, lo, in her mouth was an olive leaf plucked off: so Noah knew that the waters were abated from off the earth. And he stayed yet other seven days; and sent forth the dove; which returned not again unto him any more.

And it came to pass in the six hundredth and first year, in the first month, the first day of the month, the waters were dried up from off the earth: and Noah removed the covering of the ark, and looked, and, behold, the face of the ground was dry. And in the second month, on the seven and twentieth day of the month, was the earth dried.

And God spake unto Noah, saying, Go forth of the ark, thou, and thy wife, and thy sons, and thy sons' wives with thee. Bring forth with thee every living thing that is with thee, of all flesh, both of fowl, and of cattle, and of every creeping thing that creepeth upon the earth; that they may breed abundantly in the earth, and be fruitful, and multiply upon the earth. And Noah went forth, and his sons, and his wife, and his sons' wives with him: every beast, every creeping thing, and every fowl, and whatsoever creepeth upon the earth, after their kinds, went forth out of the ark. And Noah builded an altar unto the Lord; and took of every clean beast, and of every clean fowl, and offered burnt offerings on the altar. And the Lord smelled a sweet savour; and the Lord said in his heart, I will not again curse the ground any more for man's sake; for the imagination of man's heart is evil from his youth; neither will I again smite any more every thing living, as I have done. While the earth remaineth, seedtime and harvest, and cold and heat, and summer and winter, and day and night shall not cease.

9. And God blessed Noah and his sons, and said unto them, Be fruitful, and multiply, and replenish the earth. And the fear of you and the dread of you shall be upon every beast of the earth, and upon every fowl of the air, upon all that moveth upon the earth, and upon all the fishes of the sea; into your hand are they delivered. Every moving thing that liveth shall be meat for you; even as the green herb have I given you all things. But flesh with the life thereof, which is the blood thereof, shall ye not eat.[8] And surely your blood of your lives will I require; at the hand of every beast will I require it, and at the hand of man; at the hand of every man's brother will I require the life of man. Whoso sheddeth man's blood, by man shall his blood be shed, for in the image of God made he man. And you, be ye fruitful, and multiply; bring forth abundantly in the earth, and multiply therein.

And God spake unto Noah, and to his sons with him, saying, And I, behold, I establish my covenant with you, and with your seed after you; And with every living creature that is with you, of the fowl, of the cattle, and of every beast of the earth with you; from all that go out of the ark, to every beast of the earth. And I will establish my covenant with you; neither shall all flesh be cut off any more by the waters of a flood; neither shall there any more be a flood to destroy the earth. And God said, This is the token of the covenant which I make between me and you and every living creature that is with you, for perpetual generations: I do set my bow in the cloud, and it shall be for a token of a covenant between me and the earth. And it shall come to pass, when I bring a cloud over the earth, that the bow shall be seen in the cloud: and I will remember my covenant, which is between me and you and every living creature of all flesh; and the waters shall no more become a flood to destroy all flesh. And the bow shall be in the cloud; and I will look upon it, that I may remember the everlasting covenant between God and every living creature of all flesh that is upon

8. This sentence refers to the dietary laws: blood was drained from the slaughtered animal.

the earth. And God said unto Noah, This is the token of the covenant, which I have established between me and all flesh that is upon the earth.

Genesis 11

(The Origin of Languages)

11. And the whole earth was of one language, and of one speech. And it came to pass, as they[9] journeyed from the east, that they found a plain in the land of Shinar;[1] and they dwelt there. And they said one to another, Go to, let us make brick, and burn them throughly. And they had brick for stone, and slime[2] had they for mortar. And they said, Go to, let us build us a city and a tower,[3] whose top may reach unto heaven; and let us make us a name, lest we be scattered abroad upon the face of the whole earth. And the Lord came down to see the city and the tower, which the children of men builded. And the Lord said, Behold, the people is one, and they have all one language; and this they begin to do: and now nothing will be restrained from them, which they have imagined to do. Go to, let us go down, and there confound their language, that they may not understand one another's speech. So the Lord scattered them abroad from thence upon the face of all the earth: and they left off to build the city. Therefore is the name of it called Babel;[4] because the Lord did there confound the language of all the earth: and from thence did the Lord scatter them abroad upon the face of all the earth.

Genesis 37–46

(The Story of Joseph)

37. . . . Joseph, being seventeen years old, was feeding the flock with his brethren; and the lad was with the sons of Bilhah, and with the sons of Zilpah, his father's wives: and Joseph brought unto his father their evil report.[5] Now Israel loved Joseph more than all his children, because he was the son of his old age: and he made him a coat of many colours. And when his brethren saw that their father loved him more than all his brethren, they hated him, and could not speak peaceably unto him.

And Joseph dreamed a dream, and he told it his brethren: and they hated him yet the more. And he said unto them, Hear, I pray you, this dream which I have dreamed: for, behold, we were binding sheaves in the field, and, lo, my sheaf arose, and also stood upright; and, behold, your sheaves stood round about, and made obeisance to my sheaf. And his brethren said to him, Shalt thou indeed reign over us? or shalt thou indeed have dominion over us? And they hated him yet the more for his dreams, and for his words.

And he dreamed yet another dream, and told it his brethren, and said,

9. The human race.   1. In Mesopotamia.   2. Bitumen.   3. This story is based on the Babylonian practice of building temples in the form of terraced pyramids (ziggurats).   4. Babylon.   5. Joseph reported their misdeeds. *Father:* Israel.

Behold, I have dreamed a dream more; and, behold, the sun and the moon and the eleven stars made obeisance to me. And he told it to his father, and to his brethren: and his father rebuked him, and said unto him, What is this dream that thou hast dreamed? Shall I and thy mother and thy brethren indeed come to bow down ourselves to thee to the earth? And his brethren envied him; but his father observed the saying.

And his brethren went to feed their father's flock in Shechem. And Israel said unto Joseph, Do not thy brethren feed the flock in Shechem? come, and I will send thee unto them. And he said to him, Here am I. And he said to him, Go, I pray thee, see whether it be well with thy brethren, and well with the flocks; and bring me word again. So he sent him out of the vale of Hebron, and he came to Shechem.

And a certain man found him, and, behold, he was wandering in the field: and the man asked him, saying, What seekest thou? And he said, I seek my brethren: tell me, I pray thee, where they feed their flocks. And the man said, They are departed hence; for I heard them say, Let us go to Dothan. And Joseph went after his brethren, and found them in Dothan. And when they saw him afar off, even before he came near unto them, they conspired against him to slay him. And they said one to another, Behold, this dreamer cometh. Come now therefore, and let us slay him, and cast him into some pit, and we will say, Some evil beast hath devoured him: and we shall see what will become of his dreams. And Reuben heard it, and he delivered him out of their hands; and said, Let us not kill him. And Reuben said unto them, Shed no blood, but cast him into this pit that is in the wilderness, and lay no hand upon him; that he might rid him out of their hands, to deliver him to his father again.

And it came to pass, when Joseph was come unto his brethren, that they stripped Joseph out of his coat, his coat of many colours that was on him; and they took him, and cast him into a pit: and the pit was empty, there was no water in it. And they sat down to eat bread: and they lifted up their eyes and looked, and, behold, a company of Ishmeelites came from Gilead with their camels bearing spicery and balm and myrrh, going to carry it down to Egypt. And Judah said unto his brethren, What profit is it if we slay our brother, and conceal his blood? Come, and let us sell him to the Ishmeelites, and let not our hand be upon him; for he is our brother and our flesh. And his brethren were content. Then there passed by Midianites merchantmen;[6] and they[7] drew and lifted up Joseph out of the pit, and sold Joseph to the Ishmeelites for twenty pieces of silver: and they[8] brought Joseph into Egypt.

And Reuben returned unto the pit; and, behold, Joseph was not in the pit; and he rent his clothes. And he returned unto his brethren, and said, The child is not; and I, whither shall I go? And they took Joseph's coat, and killed a kid of the goats, and dipped the coat in the blood; and they sent the coat of many colours, and they brought it to their father; and said, This have we found: know now whether it be thy son's coat or no. And he

6. The confusion in this passage may be due to the fact that the text we have is a composite of two different versions.   7. The brothers.   8. The Ishmeelites.

knew it, and said, It is my son's coat; an evil beast hath devoured him; Joseph is without doubt rent in pieces. And Jacob rent his clothes, and put sackcloth upon his loins, and mourned for his son many days. And all his sons and all his daughters rose up to comfort him; but he refused to be comforted; and he said, For I will go down into the grave unto my son mourning. Thus his father wept for him.

39. And Joseph was brought down to Egypt; and Potiphar, an officer of Pharaoh, captain of the guard, an Egyptian, bought him of the hands of the Ishmeelites, which had brought him down thither. And the Lord was with Joseph, and he was a prosperous man; and he was in the house of his master the Egyptian. And his master saw that the Lord was with him, and that the Lord made all he did to prosper in his hand. And Joseph found grace in his sight, and he served him: and he made him overseer over his house, and all that he had he put into his hand. And it came to pass from the time that he had made him overseer in his house, and over all that he had, that the Lord blessed the Egyptian's house for Joseph's sake; and the blessing of the Lord was upon all that he had in the house, and in the field. And he left all that he had in Joseph's hand; and he knew not ought he had, save the bread which he did eat. And Joseph was a goodly person, and well favoured.

And it came to pass after these things, that his master's wife cast her eyes upon Joseph; and she said, Lie with me. But he refused, and said unto his master's wife, Behold, my master wotteth not what is with me in the house, and he hath committed all that he hath to my hand; there is none greater in this house than I; neither hath he kept back any thing from me but thee, because thou art his wife: how then can I do this great wickedness, and sin against God? And it came to pass, as she spake to Joseph day by day, that he hearkened not unto her, to lie by her, or to be with her. And it came to pass about this time, that Joseph went into the house to do his business; and there was none of the men of the house there within. And she caught him by his garment, saying, Lie with me: and he left his garment in her hand, and fled, and got him out. And it came to pass, when she saw that he had left his garment in her hand, and was fled forth, that she called unto the men of her house, and spoke unto them, saying, See, he hath brought in an Hebrew unto us to mock us; he came in unto me to lie with me, and I cried with a loud voice: and it came to pass, when he heard that I lifted up my voice and cried, that he left his garment with me, and fled, and got him out. And she laid up his garment by her, until his lord came home. And she spake unto him according to these words, saying, The Hebrew servant, which thou hast brought unto us, came in unto me to mock me: and it came to pass, as I lifted up my voice and cried, that he left his garment with me, and fled out. And it came to pass, when his master heard the words of his wife, which she spake unto him, saying, After this manner did thy servant to me; that his wrath was kindled. And Joseph's master took him, and put him into the prison, a place where the king's prisoners were bound: and he was there in the prison.

But the Lord was with Joseph, and showed him mercy, and gave him favour in the sight of the keeper of the prison. And the keeper of the prison committed to Joseph's hand all the prisoners that were in the prison; and whatsoever they did there, he was the doer of it. The keeper of the prison looked not to any thing that was under his hand; because the Lord was with him, and that which he did, the Lord made it to prosper.

40. And it came to pass after these things that the butler of the king of Egypt and his baker had offended their lord the king of Egypt. And Pharaoh was wroth against two of his officers, against the chief of the butlers, and against the chief of the bakers. And he put them in ward in the house of the captain of the guard, into the prison, the place where Joseph was bound. And the captain of the guard charged Joseph with them, and he served them: and they continued a season in ward.

And they dreamed a dream both of them, each man his dream in one night, each man according to the interpretation of his dream, the butler and the baker of the king of Egypt, which were bound in the prison. And Joseph came in unto them in the morning, and looked upon them, and, behold, they were sad. And he asked Pharaoh's officers that were with him in the ward of his lord's house, saying, Wherefore look ye so sadly to day? And they said unto him, We have dreamed a dream, and there is no interpreter of it. And Joseph said unto them, Do not interpretations belong to God? tell me them, I pray you. And the chief butler told his dream to Joseph, and said to him, In my dream, behold, a vine was before me; and in the vine were three branches: and it was as though it budded, and her blossoms shot forth; and the clusters thereof brought forth ripe grapes: and Pharaoh's cup was in my hand: and I took the grapes, and pressed them into Pharaoh's cup, and I gave the cup into Pharaoh's hand. And Joseph said unto him, This is the interpretation of it: the three branches are three days: yet within three days shall Pharaoh lift up thine head, and restore thee unto thy place: and thou shalt deliver Pharaoh's cup into his hand, after the former manner when thou wast his butler. But think on me when it shall be well with thee, and shew kindness, I pray thee, unto me, and make mention of me unto Pharaoh, and bring me out of this house: for indeed I was stolen away out of the land of the Hebrews: and here also have I done nothing that they should put me into the dungeon. When the chief baker saw that the interpretation was good, he said unto Joseph, I also was in my dream, and, behold, I had three white baskets on my head: and in the uppermost basket there was of all manner of bakemeats for Pharaoh; and the birds did eat them out of the basket upon my head. And Joseph answered and said, This is the interpretation thereof: the three baskets are three days: yet within three days shall Pharaoh lift up thy head from off thee, and shall hang thee on a tree; and the birds shall eat thy flesh from off thee.

And it came to pass the third day, which was Pharaoh's birthday, that he made a feast unto all his servants: and he lifted up the head of the chief butler and of the chief baker among his servants. And he restored the chief butler unto his butlership again; and he gave the cup into Pharaoh's hand. But he hanged the chief baker: as Joseph had interpreted to them. Yet did not the chief butler remember Joseph, but forgat him.

41. And it came to pass at the end of two full years, that Pharaoh dreamed: and, behold, he stood by the river. And, behold, there came up out of the river seven well favoured kine[9] and fatfleshed; and they fed in a meadow. And, behold, seven other kine came up after them out of the river, ill favoured and leanfleshed; and stood by the other kine upon the brink of the river. And the ill favoured and leanfleshed kine did eat up the seven well favoured and fat kine. So Pharaoh awoke. And he slept and dreamed the second time: and, behold, seven ears of corn came up upon one stalk, rank[1] and good. And, behold, seven thin ears and blasted with the east wind sprung up after them. And the seven thin ears devoured the seven rank and full ears. And Pharaoh awoke, and, behold, it was a dream. And it came to pass in the morning that his spirit was troubled; and he sent and called for all the magicians of Egypt, and all the wise men thereof: and Pharaoh told them his dream; but there was none that could interpret them unto Pharaoh.

Then spake the chief butler unto Pharaoh, saying, I do remember my faults this day: Pharaoh was wroth with his servants, and put me in ward in the captain of the guard's house, both me and the chief baker: and we dreamed a dream in one night, I and he; we dreamed each man according to the interpretation of his dream. And there was there with us a young man, an Hebrew, servant to the captain of the guard; and we told him, and he interpreted to us our dreams; to each man according to his dream he did interpret. And it came to pass, as he interpreted to us, so it was; me he restored unto mine office, and him he hanged.

Then Pharaoh sent and called Joseph, and they brought him hastily out of the dungeon: and he shaved himself, and changed his raiment, and came in unto Pharaoh. And Pharaoh said unto Joseph, I have dreamed a dream, and there is none that can interpret it: and I have heard say of thee that thou canst understand a dream to interpret it. And Joseph answered Pharaoh, saying, It is not in me: God shall give Pharaoh an answer of peace. And Pharaoh said unto Joseph, In my dream, behold, I stood upon the bank of the river; and, behold, there came up out of the river seven kine, fatfleshed and well favoured; and they fed in a meadow: and, behold, seven other kine came up after them, poor and very ill favoured and lean-fleshed, such as I never saw in all the land of Egypt for badness: and the lean and the ill favoured kine did eat up the first seven fat kine: and when they had eaten them up, it could not be known that they had eaten them; but they were still ill favoured, as at the beginning. So I awoke. And I saw in my dream, and, behold, seven ears came up in one stalk, full and good: and, behold, seven ears, withered, thin, and blasted with the east wind, sprung up after them: and the thin ears devoured the seven good ears: and

9. Cattle.   1. Fat.

I told this unto the magicians; but there was none that could declare it to me.

And Joseph said unto Pharaoh, The dream of Pharaoh is one: God hath shewed Pharaoh what he is about to do. The seven good kine are seven years; and the seven good ears are seven years: the dream is one. And the seven thin and ill favoured kine that came up after them are seven years; and the seven empty ears blasted with the east wind shall be seven years of famine. This is the thing which I have spoken unto Pharaoh: what God is about to do he sheweth unto Pharaoh. Behold, there come seven years of great plenty throughout all the land of Egypt: and there shall arise after them seven years of famine; and all the plenty shall be forgotten in the land of Egypt; and the famine shall consume the land; and the plenty shall not be known in the land by reason of that famine following; for it shall be very grievous. And for that the dream was doubled unto Pharaoh twice; it is because the thing is established by God, and God will shortly bring it to pass. Now therefore let Pharaoh look out a man discreet and wise, and set him over the land of Egypt. Let Pharaoh do this, and let him appoint officers over the land, and take up the fifth part of the land[2] of Egypt in the seven plenteous years. And let them gather all the food of those good years that come, and lay up corn under the hand of Pharaoh, and let them keep food in the cities. And that food shall be for store to the land against the seven years of famine, which shall be in the land of Egypt; that the land perish not through the famine.

And the thing was good in the eyes of Pharaoh, and in the eyes of all his servants. And Pharaoh said unto his servants, Can we find such a one as this is, a man in whom the Spirit of God is? And Pharaoh said unto Joseph, Forasmuch as God hath shewed thee all this, there is none so discreet and wise as thou art: thou shalt be over my house, and according unto thy word shall all my people be ruled: only in the throne will I be greater than thou. And Pharaoh said unto Joseph, See, I have set thee over all the land of Egypt. And Pharaoh took off his ring from his hand, and put it upon Joseph's hand, and arrayed him in vestures of fine linen, and put a gold chain about his neck; and he made him to ride in the second chariot which he had; and they cried before him, Bow the knee: and he made him ruler over all the land of Egypt. And Pharaoh said unto Joseph, I am Pharaoh, and without thee shall no man lift up his hand or foot in all the land of Egypt. And Pharaoh called Joseph's name Zaphnath-paaneah; and he gave him to wife Asenath, the daughter of Poti-pherah priest of On. And Joseph went out over all the land of Egypt.

And Joseph was thirty years old when he stood before Pharaoh king of Egypt. And Joseph went out from the presence of Pharaoh, and went throughout all the land of Egypt. And in the seven plenteous years the earth brought forth by handfuls. And he gathered up all the food of the seven years, which were in the land of Egypt, and laid up the food in the cities: the food of the field, which was round about every city, laid he up

2. I.e., of the crop.

in the same. And Joseph gathered corn as the sand of the sea, very much, until he left numbering; for it was without number. And unto Joseph were born two sons before the years of famine came, which Asenath, the daughter of Poti-pherah priest of On, bare unto him. And Joseph called the name of the first born Manasseh:[3] For God, said he, hath made me forget all my toil, and all my father's house. And the name of the second called he Ephraim:[4] For God hath caused me to be fruitful in the land of my affliction.

And the seven years of plenteousness, that was in the land of Egypt, were ended. And the seven years of dearth began to come, according as Joseph had said: and the dearth was in all lands; but in all the land of Egypt there was bread. And when all the land of Egypt was famished, the people cried to Pharaoh for bread: and Pharaoh said unto all the Egyptians, Go unto Joseph; what he saith to you, do. And the famine was over all the face of the earth. And Joseph opened all the storehouses, and sold unto the Egyptians; and the famine waxed sore in the land of Egypt. And all countries came into Egypt to Joseph for to buy corn; because that the famine was so sore in all lands.

42. Now when Jacob saw that there was corn in Egypt, Jacob said unto his sons, Why do ye look one upon another? And he said, Behold, I have heard that there is corn in Egypt: get you down thither, and buy for us from thence; that we may live, and not die.

And Joseph's ten brethren went down to buy corn in Egypt. But Benjamin, Joseph's brother, Jacob sent not with his brethren; for he said, Lest peradventure mischief befall him. And the sons of Israel came to buy corn among those that came: for the famine was in the land of Canaan. And Joseph was the governor over the land, and he it was that sold to all the people of the land: and Joseph's brethren came, and bowed down themselves before him with their faces to the earth. And Joseph saw his brethren, and he knew them, but made himself strange unto them, and spake roughly unto them; and he said unto them, Whence come ye? And they said, From the land of Canaan to buy food. And Joseph knew his brethren, but they knew not him. And Joseph remembered the dreams which he dreamed of them, and said unto them, Ye are spies; to see the nakedness of the land ye are come. And they said unto him, Nay, my lord, but to buy food are thy servants come. We are all one man's sons; we are true men, thy servants are no spies. And he said unto them, Nay, but to see the nakedness of the land ye are come. And they said, Thy servants are twelve brethren, the sons of one man in the land of Canaan; and, behold, the youngest is this day with our father, and one is not. And Joseph said unto them, That is it that I spake unto you, saying, Ye are spies: Hereby ye shall be proved: By the life of Pharaoh ye shall not go forth hence, except your youngest brother come hither. Send one of you, and let him fetch your brother, and ye shall be kept in prison, that your words may be

3. Meaning "causing to forget."   4. Meaning "fruitfulness."

proved, whether there be any truth in you: or else by the life of Pharaoh surely ye are spies. And he put them all together into ward three days. And Joseph said unto them the third day, This do, and live; for I fear God: if ye be true men, let one of your brethren be bound in the house of your prison: go ye, carry corn for the famine of your houses: but bring your youngest brother unto me; so shall your words be verified, and ye shall not die. And they did so.

And they said one to another, We are verily guilty concerning our brother, in that we saw the anguish of his soul, when he besought us, and we would not hear; therefore is this distress come upon us. And Reuben answered them, saying, Spake I not unto you, saying, Do not sin against the child; and ye would not hear? therefore, behold, also his blood is required. And they knew not that Joseph understood them; for he spake unto them by an interpreter. And he turned himself about from them, and wept; and returned to them again, and communed with them, and took from them Simeon, and bound him before their eyes.

Then Joseph commanded to fill their sacks with corn, and to restore every man's money into his sack, and to give them provision for the way: and thus did he unto them. And they laded their asses with the corn, and departed thence. And as one of them opened his sack to give his ass provender in the inn, he espied his money; for, behold, it was in his sack's mouth. And he said unto his brethren, My money is restored; and, lo, it is even in my sack: and their heart failed them, and they were afraid, saying one to another, What is this that God hath done unto us?

And they came unto Jacob their father unto the land of Canaan, and told him all that befell unto them; saying, The man, who is lord of the land, spake roughly to us, and took us for spies of the country. And we said unto him, We are true men; we are no spies: we be twelve brethren, sons of our father; one is not, and the youngest is this day with our father in the land of Canaan. And the man, the lord of the country, said unto us, Hereby shall I know that ye are true men; leave one of your brethren here with me, and take food for the famine of your households, and be gone: and bring your youngest brother unto me: then shall I know that ye are no spies, but that ye are true men: so will I deliver you your brother, and ye shall traffick in the land.

And it came to pass as they emptied their sacks, that, behold, every man's bundle of money was in his sack: and when both they and their father saw the bundles of money, they were afraid. And Jacob their father said unto them, Me have ye bereaved of my children: Joseph is not, and Simeon is not, and ye will take Benjamin away: all these things are against me.

And Reuben spake unto his father, saying, Slay my two sons, if I bring him not to thee: deliver him into my hand, and I will bring him to thee again. And he said, My son shall not go down with you; for his brother is dead, and he is left alone: if mischief befall him by the way in the which ye go, then shall ye bring down my gray hairs with sorrow to the grave.

43. And the famine was sore in the land. And it came to pass, when they had eaten up the corn which they had brought out of Egypt, their father said unto them, Go again, buy us a little food. And Judah spake unto him, saying, The man did solemnly protest unto us, saying, Ye shall not see my face, except your brother be with you. If thou wilt send our brother with us, we will go down and buy thee food: but if thou wilt not send him, we will not go down: for the man said unto us, Ye shall not see my face, except your brother be with you. And Israel said, Wherefore dealt ye so ill with me, as to tell the man whether ye had yet a brother? And they said, The man asked us straitly of our state, and of our kindred, saying, Is your father yet alive? have ye another brother? and we told him according to the tenor of these words: could we certainly know that he would say, Bring your brother down? And Judah said unto Israel his father, Send the lad with me, and we will arise and go; that we may live, and not die, both we, and thou, and also our little ones. I will be surety for him; of my hand shalt thou require him: if I bring him not unto thee, and set him before thee, then let me bear the blame for ever: for except we had lingered, surely now we had returned this second time. And their father Israel said unto them, If it must be so now, do this; take of the best fruits in the land in your vessels, and carry down the man a present, a little balm, and a little honey, spices, and myrrh, nuts, and almonds: and take double money in your hand: and the money that was brought again in the mouth of your sacks, carry it again in your hand; peradventure it was an oversight: take also your brother, and arise, go again unto the man: and God Almighty give you mercy before the man, that he may send away your other brother, and Benjamin. If I be bereaved of my children, I am bereaved.

And the men took that present, and they took double money in their hand, and Benjamin; and rose up, and went down to Egypt, and stood before Joseph. And when Joseph saw Benjamin with them, he said to the ruler of his house, Bring these men home, and slay,[5] and make ready; for these men shall dine with me at noon. And the man did as Joseph bade; and the man brought the men into Joseph's house. And the men were afraid, because they were brought into Joseph's house; and they said, Because of the money that was returned in our sacks at the first time are we brought in; that he may seek occasion against us, and fall upon us, and take us for bondmen, and our asses. And they came near to the steward of Joseph's house, and they communed with him at the door of the house, and said, O sir, we came indeed down at the first time to buy food; and it came to pass, when we came to the inn, that we opened our sacks, and behold, every man's money was in the mouth of his sack, our money in full weight: and we have brought it again in our hand. And other money have we brought down in our hands to buy food: we cannot tell who put our money in our sacks. And he said, Peace be to you, fear not: your God, and the

5. Kill an animal for meat.

God of your father, hath given you treasure in your sacks: I had your money. And he brought Simeon out unto them. And the man brought the men into Joseph's house, and gave them water, and they washed their feet; and he gave their asses provender. And they made ready the present against Joseph came at noon: for they heard that they should eat bread there.

And when Joseph came home, they brought him the present which was in their hand into the house, and bowed themselves to him to the earth. And he asked them of their welfare, and said, Is your father well, the old man of whom ye spake? Is he yet alive? And they answered, Thy servant our father is in good health, he is yet alive. And they bowed down their heads, and made obeisance. And he lifted up his eyes, and saw his brother Benjamin, his mother's son, and said, Is this your younger brother, of whom ye spake unto me? And he said, God be gracious unto thee, my son. And Joseph made haste; for his bowels did yearn upon his brother: and he sought where to weep; and he entered into his chamber, and wept there. And he washed his face, and went out, and refrained himself, and said, Set on bread. And they set on for him by himself, and for them by themselves, and for the Egyptians, which did eat with him, by themselves: because the Egyptians might not eat bread with the Hebrews; for that is an abomination unto the Egyptians. And they sat before him, the firstborn according to his birthright, and the youngest according to his youth: and the men marvelled one at another. And he took and sent messes[6] unto them from before him: but Benjamin's mess was five times so much as any of theirs. And they drank, and were merry with him.

44. And he commanded the steward of his house, saying, Fill the men's sacks with food, as much as they can carry, and put every man's money in his sack's mouth. And put my cup, the silver cup, in the sack's mouth of the youngest, and his corn money. And he did according to the word that Joseph had spoken. As soon as the morning was light, the men were sent away, they and their asses. And when they were gone out of the city, and not yet far off, Joseph said unto his steward, Up, follow after the men; and when thou dost overtake them, say unto them, Wherefore have ye rewarded evil for good? Is not this it in which my lord drinketh, and whereby indeed he divineth?[7] ye have done evil in so doing.

And he overtook them, and he spake unto them these same words. And they said unto him, Wherefore saith my lord these words? God forbid that thy servants should do according to this thing: behold, the money, which we found in our sacks' mouths, we brought again unto thee out of the land of Canaan: how then should we steal out of thy lord's house silver or gold? With whomsoever of thy servants it be found, both let him die, and we also will be my lord's bondmen. And he said, Now also let it be according unto your words: he with whom it is found shall be my servant; and ye shall be blameless. Then they speedily took down every man his sack to the ground, and opened every man his sack. And he searched, and began

6. Portions.   7. Joseph's servant is to claim that this is the cup Joseph uses for clairvoyance: the diviner stared into a cup of water and foretold the future.

at the eldest, and left at the youngest: and the cup was found in Benjamin's sack. Then they rent their clothes, and laded every man his ass, and returned to the city.

And Judah and his brethren came to Joseph's house; for he was yet there: and they fell before him on the ground. And Joseph said unto them, What deed is this that ye have done? wot ye not that such a man as I can certainly divine? And Judah said, What shall we say unto my lord? what shall we speak? or how shall we clear ourselves? God hath found out the iniquity of thy servants: behold, we are my lord's servants, both we, and he also with whom the cup is found. And he said, God forbid that I should do so: but the man in whose hand the cup is found, he shall be my servant; and as for you, get you up in peace unto your father.

Then Judah came near unto him, and said, Oh my lord, let thy servant, I pray thee, speak a word in my lord's ears, and let not thine anger burn against thy servant: for thou art even as Pharaoh. My lord asked his servants, saying, Have ye a father, or a brother? And we said unto my lord, We have a father, an old man, and a child of his old age, a little one; and his brother is dead, and he alone is left of his mother, and his father loveth him. And thou saidst unto thy servants, Bring him down unto me, that I may set mine eyes upon him. And we said unto my lord, The lad cannot leave his father: for if he should leave his father, his father would die. And thou saidst unto thy servants, Except your youngest brother come down with you, ye shall see my face no more. And it came to pass when we came up unto thy servant my father, we told him the words of my lord. And our father said, Go again, and buy us a little food. And we said, We cannot go down: if our youngest brother be with us, then will we go down: for we may not see the man's face, except our youngest brother be with us. And thy servant my father said unto us, Ye know that my wife bare me two sons: and the one went out from me, and I said, Surely he is torn in pieces; and I saw him not since: and if ye take this also from me, and mischief befall him, ye shall bring down my gray hairs with sorrow to the grave. Now therefore when I come to thy servant my father, and the lad be not with us; seeing that his life is bound up in the lad's life; it shall come to pass, when he seeth that the lad is not with us, that he will die: and thy servants shall bring down the gray hairs of thy servant our father with sorrow to the grave. For thy servant became surety for the lad unto my father, saying, If I bring him not unto thee, then I shall bear the blame to my father for ever. Now therefore, I pray thee, let thy servant abide instead of the lad a bondman to my lord; and let the lad go up with his brethren. For how shall I go up to my father, and the lad be not with me? lest peradventure I see the evil that shall come on my father.

45. Then Joseph could not refrain himself before all them that stood by him; and he cried, Cause every man to go out from me. And there stood no man with him, while Joseph made himself known unto his brethren. And he wept aloud: and the Egyptians and the house of Pharaoh heard. And Joseph said unto his brethren, I am Joseph; doth my father yet live?

And his brethren could not answer him; for they were troubled at his presence. And Joseph said unto his brethren, Come near to me, I pray you. And they came near. And he said, I am Joseph your brother, whom ye sold into Egypt. Now therefore be not grieved, nor angry with yourselves, that ye sold me hither: for God did send me before you to preserve life. For these two years hath the famine been in the land: and yet there are five years, in the which there shall neither be earing nor harvest. And God sent me before you to preserve you a posterity in the earth, and to save your lives by a great deliverance. So now it was not you that sent me hither, but God: and he hath made me a father to Pharaoh, and lord of all his house, and a ruler throughout all the land of Egypt. Haste ye, and go up to my father, and say unto him, Thus saith thy son Joseph, God hath made me lord of all Egypt: come down unto me, tarry not: and thou shalt dwell in the land of Goshen, and thou shalt be near unto me, thou, and thy children, and thy children's children, and thy flocks, and thy herds, and all that thou hast: and there will I nourish thee; for yet there are five years of famine; lest thou, and thy household, and all that thou hast, come to poverty. And, behold, your eyes see, and the eyes of my brother Benjamin, that it is my mouth that speaketh unto you. And ye shall tell my father of all my glory in Egypt, and of all that ye have seen; and ye shall haste and bring down my father hither. And he fell upon his brother Benjamin's neck, and wept; and Benjamin wept upon his neck. Moreover he kissed all his brethren, and wept upon them: and after that his brethren talked with him.

And the fame thereof was heard in Pharaoh's house, saying, Joseph's brethren are come: and it pleased Pharaoh well, and his servants. And Pharaoh said unto Joseph, Say unto thy brethren, This do ye; lade your beasts, and go, get you unto the land of Canaan; and take your father and your households, and come unto me: and I will give you the good of the land of Egypt, and ye shall eat the fat of the land. Now thou art commanded, this do ye; take you wagons out of the land of Egypt for your little ones, and for your wives, and bring your father, and come. Also regard not your stuff; for the good of all the land of Egypt is yours. And the children of Israel did so: and Joseph gave them wagons, according to the commandment of Pharaoh, and gave them provision for the way. To all of them he gave each man changes of raiment; but to Benjamin he gave three hundred pieces of silver, and five changes of raiment. And to his father he sent after this manner; ten asses laden with the good things of Egypt, and ten she-asses laden with corn and bread and meat for his father by the way. So he sent his brethren away, and they departed: and he said unto them, See that ye fall not out by the way.

And they went up out of Egypt, and came into the land of Canaan unto Jacob their father, and told him, saying, Joseph is yet alive, and he is governor over all the land of Egypt. And Jacob's heart fainted, for he believed them not. And they told him all the words of Joseph, which he had said unto them: and when he saw the wagons which Joseph had sent to carry him, the spirit of Jacob their father revived. And Israel said, It is enough; Joseph my son is yet alive: I will go and see him before I die.

46. And Israel took his journey with all that he had, and came to Beersheba, and offered sacrifices unto the God of his father Isaac. And God spake unto Israel in the visions of the night, and said, Jacob, Jacob. And he said, Here am I. And he said, I am God, the God of thy father: fear not to go down into Egypt; for I will there make of thee a great nation: I will go down with thee into Egypt; and I will also surely bring thee up again: and Joseph shall put his hand upon thine eyes. And Jacob rose up from Beer-sheba: and the sons of Israel carried Jacob their father, and their little ones, and their wives, in the wagons which Pharaoh had sent to carry him. And they took their cattle, and their goods, which they had gotten in the land of Canaan, and came into Egypt, Jacob, and all his seed with him: his sons, and his sons' sons with him, his daughters, and his sons' daughters, and all his seed brought he with him into Egypt.

JOB[8]

1. There was a man in the land of Uz whose name was Job, and that man was perfect and upright, and one that feared God, and eschewed evil. And there were born unto him seven sons and three daughters. His substance also was seven thousand sheep, and three thousand camels, and five hundred yoke of oxen, and five hundred she asses, and a very great household; so that this man was the greatest of all the men of the east. And his sons went and feasted in their houses, every one his day;[9] and sent and called for their three sisters to eat and to drink with them. And it was so, when the days of their feasting were gone about, that Job sent and sanctified them, and rose up early in the morning, and offered burnt offerings according to the number of them all: for Job said, It may be that my sons have sinned, and cursed God in their hearts. Thus did Job continually.

Now there was a day when the sons of God came to present themselves before the Lord, and Satan came also among them. And the Lord said unto Satan, Whence comest thou? Then Satan answered the Lord, and said, From going to and fro in the earth, and from walking up and down in it. And the Lord said unto Satan, Hast thou considered my servant Job, that there is none like him in the earth, a perfect and an upright man, one that feareth God, and escheweth evil? Then Satan answered the Lord, and said, Doth Job fear God for nought? Hast not thou made an hedge about him, and about his house, and about all that he hath on every side? thou hast blessed the work of his hands, and his substance is increased in the land. But put forth thine hand now, and touch all that he hath, and he will curse thee to thy face. And the Lord said unto Satan, Behold, all that

---

8. Chapters 1–14, 29–31, 38–42. 9. In rotation at each son's house.

he hath is in thy power; only upon himself put not forth thine hand. So Satan went forth from the presence of the Lord.

And there was a day when his sons and his daughters were eating and drinking wine in their eldest brother's house: and there came a messenger unto Job, and said, The oxen were plowing, and the asses feeding beside them: and the Sabeans fell upon them, and took them away; yea, they have slain the servants with the edge of the sword; and I only am escaped alone to tell thee. While he was yet speaking, there came also another, and said, The fire of God is fallen from heaven, and hath burned up the sheep, and the servants, and consumed them; and I only am escaped alone to tell thee. While he was yet speaking, there came also another, and said, The Chaldeans made out three bands,[1] and fell upon the camels, and have carried them away, yea, and slain the servants with the edge of the sword; and I only am escaped alone to tell thee. While he was yet speaking, there came also another, and said, Thy sons and thy daughters were eating and drinking wine in their eldest brother's house: and, behold, there came a great wind from the wilderness, and smote the four corners of the house, and it fell upon the young men, and they are dead; and I only am escaped alone to tell thee.

Then Job arose and rent his mantle,[2] and shaved his head, and fell down upon the ground, and worshipped, and said, Naked came I out of my mother's womb, and naked shall I return thither: the Lord gave, and the Lord hath taken away; blessed be the name of the Lord. In all this Job sinned not, nor charged God foolishly.

2. Again there was a day when the sons of God came to present themselves before the Lord, and Satan came also among them to present himself before the Lord. And the Lord said unto Satan, From whence comest thou? And Satan answered the Lord, and said, From going to and fro in the earth, and from walking up and down in it. And the Lord said unto Satan, Hast thou considered my servant Job, that there is none like him in the earth, a perfect and an upright man, one that feareth God, and escheweth evil? and still he holdeth fast his integrity, although thou movedst me against him, to destroy him without cause. And Satan answered the Lord, and said, Skin for skin, yea, all that a man hath will he give for his life. But put forth thine hand now, and touch his bone and his flesh, and he will curse thee to thy face. And the Lord said unto Satan, Behold, he is in thine hand; but save his life.

So went Satan forth from the presence of the Lord, and smote Job with sore boils from the sole of his foot unto his crown. And he took him a potsherd to scrape himself withal; and he sat down among the ashes.

Then said his wife unto him, Dost thou still retain thine integrity? curse God, and die. But he said unto her, Thou speakest as one of the foolish women speaketh. What? shall we receive good at the hand of God, and shall we not receive evil? In all this did not Job sin with his lips.

---

1. Split up into three groups.   2. Tore his cloak.

Now when Job's three friends heard of all this evil that was come upon him, they came every one from his own place; Eliphaz the Temanite, and Bildad the Shuhite, and Zophar the Naamathite: for they had made an appointment together to come to mourn with him and to comfort him. And when they lifted up their eyes afar off, and knew him not, they lifted up their voice, and wept; and they rent every one his mantle, and sprinkled dust upon their heads toward heaven. So they sat down with him upon the ground seven days and seven nights, and none spake a word unto him: for they saw that his grief was very great.

3. After this opened Job his mouth, and cursed his day. And Job spake, and said, Let the day perish wherein I was born, and the night in which it was said, There is a man child conceived. Let that day be darkness; let not God regard it from above, neither let the light shine upon it. Let darkness and the shadow of death stain it; let a cloud dwell upon it; let the blackness of the day terrify it. As for that night, let darkness seize upon it; let it not be joined unto the days of the year, let it not come into the number of the months. Lo, let that night be solitary, let no joyful voice come therein. Let them curse it that curse the day,[3] who are ready to raise up their mourning. Let the stars of the twilight thereof be dark; let it look for light, but have none; neither let it see the dawning of the day: because it shut not up the doors of my mother's womb, nor hid sorrow from mine eyes. Why died I not from the womb? Why did I not give up the ghost when I came out of the belly? Why did the knees prevent[4] me? or why the breasts that I should suck? For now should I have lain still and been quiet, I should have slept: then had I been at rest, with kings and counsellors of the earth, which built desolate places for themselves; or with princes that had gold, who filled their houses with silver: or as an hidden untimely birth I had not been; as infants which never saw light. There the wicked cease from troubling; and there the weary be at rest. There the prisoners rest together; they hear not the voice of the oppressor. The small and great are there; and the servant is free from his master. Wherefore is light given to him that is in misery, and life unto the bitter in soul; which long for death, but it cometh not; and dig for it more than for hid treasures; which rejoice exceedingly, and are glad, when they can find the grave? Why is light given to a man whose way is hid, and whom God hath hedged in? For my sighing cometh before I eat, and my roarings are poured out like the waters. For the thing which I greatly feared is come upon me, and that which I was afraid of is come unto me. I was not in safety, neither had I rest, neither was I quiet; yet trouble came.

4. Then Eliphaz the Temanite answered and said, If we assay to commune with thee, wilt thou be grieved? But who can withhold himself from speaking? Behold, thou hast instructed many, and thou hast strengthened the weak hands. Thy words have upholden him that was falling, and thou

3. Sorcerers, magicians. A more literal translation of the next clause would read, "who are ready to rouse up leviathan," a dragon that was thought to produce darkness. 4. Receive.

hast strengthened the feeble knees. But now it is come upon thee, and
thou faintest; it toucheth thee, and thou art troubled. Is not this thy fear,
thy confidence, thy hope, and the uprightness of thy ways?[5] Remember, I
pray thee, who ever perished, being innocent? or where were the righteous
cut off? Even as I have seen, they that plow iniquity, and sow wickedness,
reap the same. By the blast of God they perish, and by the breath of his
nostrils are they consumed. The roaring of the lion, and the voice of the
fierce lion, and the teeth of the young lions, are broken. The old lion
perisheth for lack of prey, and the stout lion's whelps are scattered abroad.
Now a thing was secretly brought to me, and mine ear received a little
thereof. In thoughts from the visions of the night, when deep sleep falleth
on men, fear came upon me, and trembling, which made all my bones to
shake. Then a spirit passed before my face; the hair of my flesh stood up:
It stood still, but I could not discern the form thereof: an image was before
mine eyes, there was silence, and I heard a voice, saying, Shall mortal
man be more just than God? Shall a man be more pure than his maker?
Behold, he put no trust in his servants; and his angels he charged with
folly: How much less in them that dwell in houses of clay, whose foundation is in the dust, which are crushed before the moth? They are destroyed
from morning to evening: they perish for ever without any regarding it.
Doth not their excellency which is in them go away? They die, even without wisdom.

5. Call now, if there be any that will answer thee; and to which of the
saints wilt thou turn? For wrath killeth the foolish man, and envy slayeth
the silly one. I have seen the foolish taking root: but suddenly I cursed his
habitation. His children are far from safety, and they are crushed in the
gate, neither is there any to deliver them. Whose harvest the hungry eateth
up, and taketh it even out of the thorns, and the robber swalloweth up
their substance. Although affliction cometh not forth of the dust, neither
doth trouble spring out of the ground; yet man is born unto trouble, as the
sparks fly upward. I would seek unto God, and unto God would I commit
my cause: which doeth great things and unsearchable; marvellous things
without number: who giveth rain upon the earth, and sendeth waters upon
the fields: to set up on high those that be low; that those which mourn may
be exalted to safety. He disappointeth the devices of the crafty, so that their
hands cannot perform their enterprise. He taketh the wise in their own
craftiness: and the counsel of the froward is carried headlong. They meet
with darkness in the daytime, and grope in the noonday as in the night.
But he saveth the poor from the sword, from their mouth, and from the
hand of the mighty. So the poor hath hope, and iniquity stoppeth her
mouth. Behold, happy is the man whom God correcteth: therefore despise
not thou the chastening of the Almighty: for he maketh sore, and bindeth
up: he woundeth, and his hands make whole. He shall deliver thee in six
troubles: yea, in seven there shall no evil touch thee. In famine he shall

---

5. A more literal translation of this sentence would read, "Is not thy fear of God thy confidence, and thy
hope the uprightness of thy ways?"

redeem thee from death: and in war from the power of the sword. Thou shalt be hid from the scourge of the tongue: neither shalt thou be afraid of destruction when it cometh. At destruction and famine thou shalt laugh: neither shalt thou be afraid of the beasts of the earth. For thou shalt be in league with the stones of the field: and the beasts of the field shall be at peace with thee. And thou shalt know that thy tabernacle[6] shall be in peace; and thou shalt visit thy habitation, and shalt not sin. Thou shalt know also that thy seed shall be great, and thine offspring as the grass of the earth. Thou shalt come to thy grave in a full age, like as a shock of corn cometh in in his season. Lo this, we have searched it, so it is; hear it, and know thou it for thy good.

6. But Job answered and said, Oh that my grief were thoroughly weighed, and my calamity laid in the balances together! For now it would be heavier than the sand of the sea: therefore my words are swallowed up.[7] For the arrows of the Almighty are within me, the poison whereof drinketh up my spirit: the terrors of God do set themselves in array against me. Doth the wild ass bray when he hath grass? or loweth the ox over his fodder?[8] Can that which is unsavoury be eaten without salt? or is there any taste in the white of an egg? The things that my soul refused to touch are as my sorrowful meat.[9] Oh that I might have my request; and that God would grant me the thing that I long for! Even that it would please God to destroy me; that he would let loose his hand, and cut me off! Then should I yet have comfort; yea, I would harden myself in sorrow: let him not spare; for I have not concealed[1] the words of the Holy One. What is my strength, that I should hope? and what is mine end, that I should prolong my life? Is my strength the strength of stones? or is my flesh of brass? Is not my help in me? and is wisdom driven quite from me?[2] To him that is afflicted pity should be shewed from his friend; but he forsaketh the fear of the Almighty. My brethren have dealt deceitfully as a brook, and as the stream of brooks they pass away; which are blackish by reason of the ice, and wherein the snow is hid: what time they wax warm, they vanish: when it is hot, they are consumed out of their place. The paths of their way are turned aside; they go to nothing, and perish. The troops of Tema looked, the companies of Sheba waited for them. They were confounded because they had hoped;[3] they came thither, and were ashamed. For now ye are nothing; ye see my casting down, and are afraid. Did I say, Bring unto me? or, Give a reward for me of your substance? or, Deliver me from the enemy's hand? or, Redeem me from the hand of the mighty? Teach me, and I will hold my tongue: and cause me to understand wherein I have erred. How forcible are right words! But what doth your arguing reprove? Do ye imagine to

6. Tent.   7. A more literal translation of this clause would read, "therefore have my words been rash." Job recognizes the exaggeration of his first outburst.   8. Animals do not complain without reason; therefore when a rational man complains, he must have some justification for it.   9. More literally, "My soul refuseth to touch them, they are as loathsome meat to me." He is referring to the statements of his friends.   1. More literally, "denied."   2. More literally, "Is not my help within me gone, and is not wisdom driven quite away from me."   3. The caravans reached the springs they had counted on and found them dry.

reprove words, and the speeches of one that is desperate, which are as
wind? Yea, ye overwhelm the fatherless, and ye dig a pit for your friend.
Now therefore be content, look upon me; for it is evident unto you if I lie.
Return, I pray you, let it not be iniquity; yea, return again, my righteousness is in it. Is there iniquity in my tongue? Cannot my taste discern
perverse things?

7. Is there not an appointed time to man upon earth? Are not his days
also like the days of an hireling? As a servant earnestly desireth the shadow,[4]
and as an hireling looketh for the reward of his work: so am I made to
possess months of vanity, and wearisome nights are appointed to me. When
I lie down, I say, When shall I arise, and the night be gone? and I am full
of tossings to and fro unto the dawning of the day. My flesh is clothed with
worms and clods of dust; my skin is broken, and become loathsome. My
days are swifter than a weaver's shuttle, and are spent without hope. O
remember that my life is wind: mine eye shall no more see good. The eye
of him that hath seen me shall see me no more: thine eyes are upon me,
and I am not. As the cloud is consumed and vanisheth away: so he that
goeth down to the grave shall come up no more. He shall return no more
to his house, neither shall his place know him any more. Therefore I will
not refrain my mouth; I will speak in the anguish of my spirit; I will complain in the bitterness of my soul. Am I a sea, or a whale, that thou settest
a watch over me?[5] When I say, My bed shall comfort me, my couch shall
ease my complaint; then thou scarest me with dreams, and terrifiest me
through visions: so that my soul chooseth strangling, and death rather than
my life. I loathe it; I would not live alway: let me alone; for my days are
vanity. What is man, that thou shouldest magnify him? and that thou
shouldest set thine heart upon him? and that thou shouldest visit him every
morning, and try him every moment? How long wilt thou not depart from
me, nor let me alone till I swallow down my spittle?[6] I have sinned; what
shall I do unto thee, O thou preserver[7] of men? Why hast thou set me as
a mark against thee, so that I am a burden to myself? And why dost thou
not pardon my transgression, and take away mine iniquity? For now shall
I sleep in the dust; and thou shalt seek me in the morning, but I shall not
be.

8. Then answered Bildad the Shuhite, and said, How long wilt thou
speak these things? and how long shall the words of thy mouth be like a
strong wind? Doth God pervert judgment? or doth the Almighty pervert
justice? If thy children have sinned against him, and he have cast them
away for their transgression; if thou wouldest seek unto God betimes, and
make thy supplication to the Almighty; if thou wert pure and upright;
surely now he would awake for thee, and make the habitation of thy righteousness prosperous. Though thy beginning was small, yet thy latter end

4. Evening, the end of the working day.   5. Job, now addressing God directly, compares his situation
with that of the sea monster whom a god fought against in the Babylonian myth. He reproves God for
exerting His power against anything as small as himself.   6. Even for a moment.   7. More literally,
"watcher."

should greatly increase. For enquire, I pray thee, of the former age, and prepare thy self to the search of their fathers: (For we are but of yesterday, and know nothing, because our days upon earth are a shadow:) shall not they teach thee, and tell thee, and utter words out of their heart? Can the rush grow up without mire?[8] Can the flag grow without water? Whilst it is yet in his greenness, and not cut down, it withereth before any other herb. So are the paths of all that forget God; and the hypocrite's hope shall perish: whose hope shall be cut off, and whose trust shall be a spider's web. He shall lean upon his house, but it shall not stand: he shall hold it fast, but it shall not endure. He is green before the sun, and his branch shooteth forth in his garden. His roots are wrapped about the heap, and seeth the place of stones. If he destroy him from his place, then it shall deny him, saying, I have not seen thee. Behold, this is the joy of his way, and out of the earth shall others grow. Behold, God will not cast away a perfect man, neither will he help the evil doers: till he fill thy mouth with laughing, and thy lips with rejoicing. They that hate thee shall be clothed with shame; and the dwelling place of the wicked shall come to nought.

9. Then Job answered and said, I know it is so of a truth: but how should man be just with God? If he will contend with him, he cannot answer him one of a thousand.[9] He is wise in heart, and mighty in strength: who hath hardened himself against him, and hath prospered? Which removeth the mountains, and they know not: which overturneth them in his anger. Which shaketh the earth out of her place, and the pillars thereof tremble. Which commandeth the sun, and it riseth not; and sealeth up the stars. Which alone spreadeth out the heavens, and treadeth upon the waves of the sea. Which maketh Arcturus, Orion, and Pleiades, and the chambers of the south. Which doeth great things past finding out; yea, and wonders without number. Lo, he goeth by me, and I see him not: he passeth on also, but I perceive him not. Behold, he taketh away, who can hinder him? Who will say unto him, What doest thou? If God will not withdraw his anger, the proud helpers do stoop under him. How much less shall I answer him, and choose out my words to reason with him? Whom, though I were righteous, yet would I not answer, but I would make supplication to my judge. If I had called, and he had answered me; yet would I not believe that he had hearkened unto my voice. For he breaketh me with a tempest, and multiplieth my wounds without cause. He will not suffer me to take my breath, but filleth me with bitterness. If I speak of strength, lo, he is strong: and if of judgment, who shall set me a time to plead? If I justify myself, mine own mouth shall condemn me: if I say, I am perfect, it shall also prove me perverse. Though I were perfect, yet would I not know my soul: I would despise my life. This is one thing, therefore I said it, He destroyeth the perfect and the wicked. If the scourge slay suddenly, he will laugh at the trial of the innocent. The earth is given into the hand of the wicked: he covereth the faces of the judges thereof; if not, where, and who

8. The papyrus which grows rapidly when the Nile is high, but withers at once when the waters go down.   9. One of a thousand questions.

is he? Now my days are swifter than a post:[1] they flee away, they see no good. They are passed away as the swift ships: as the eagle that hasteth to the prey. If I say, I will forget my complaint, I will leave off my heaviness, and comfort myself: I am afraid of all my sorrows, I know that thou wilt not hold me innocent. If I be wicked, why then labour I in vain? If I wash myself with snow water, and make my hands never so clean; yet shalt thou plunge me in the ditch, and mine own clothes shall abhor me. For he is not a man, as I am, that I should answer him, and we should come together in judgment. Neither is there any daysman[2] betwixt us, that might lay his hand upon us both. Let him take his rod away from me, and let not his fear terrify me: then would I speak, and not fear him; but it is not so with me.

10. My soul is weary of my life; I will leave my complaint upon[3] myself; I will speak in the bitterness of my soul. I will say unto God, Do not condemn me; shew me wherefore thou contendest with me. Is it good unto thee that thou shouldest oppress, that thou shouldest despise the work of thine hands, and shine upon the counsel of the wicked? Hath thou eyes of flesh? or seest thou as man seeth? Are thy days as the days of man? Are thy years as man's days,[4] that thou enquirest after mine iniquity, and searchest after my sin? Thou knowest that I am not wicked; and there is none that can deliver out of thine hand. Thine hands have made me and fashioned me together round about; yet thou dost destroy me. Remember, I beseech thee, that thou hast made me as the clay; and wilt thou bring me into dust again? Hast thou not poured me out as milk and curdled me like cheese? Thou hast clothed me with skin and flesh, and hast fenced me with bones and sinews. Thou hast granted me life and favour, and thy visitation hath preserved my spirit. And these things hast thou hid in thine heart: I know that this is with thee.[5] If I sin, then thou markest me, and thou wilt not acquit me from mine iniquity. If I be wicked, woe unto me; and if I be righteous, yet will I not lift up my head. I am full of confusion; therefore see thou mine affliction; for it increaseth. Thou huntest me as a fierce lion: and again thou shewest thyself marvellous upon me. Thou renewest thy witnesses against me,[6] and increasest thine indignation upon me; changes and war are against me. Wherefore then hast thou brought me forth out of the womb? Oh that I had given up the ghost, and no eye had seen me! I should have been as though I had not been; I should have been carried from the womb to the grave. Are not my days few? Cease then, and let me alone, that I may take comfort a little before I go whence I shall not return, even to the land of darkness and the shadow of death: a land of darkness, as darkness itself; and of the shadow of death, without any order, and where the light is as darkness.

1. Courier.　2. Arbitrator.　3. On behalf of. *Leave:* Give free course to.　4. Is your time, like man's, short, so that you have to judge hastily?　5. The meaning is: "My destruction (*this*) is your purpose." Job accuses God of planning his destruction while showing favor to him.　6. His afflictions, which prove (to his friends) his guilt.

11. Then answered Zophar the Naamathite, and said, Should not the multitude of words be answered? And should a man full of talk be justified? Should thy lies make men hold their peace? And when thou mockest, shall no man make thee ashamed? For thou hast said, My doctrine is pure, and I am clean in thine eyes. But oh that God would speak, and open his lips against thee; and that he would shew thee the secrets of wisdom, that they are double to that which is! Know therefore that God exacteth of thee less than thine iniquity deserveth. Canst thou by searching find out God? Canst thou find out the Almighty unto perfection? It is as high as heaven; what canst thou do? Deeper than hell; what canst thou know? The measure thereof is longer than the earth, and broader than the sea. If he cut off, and shut up, or gather together,[7] then who can hinder him? For he knoweth vain men: he seeth wickedness also; will he not then consider it? For vain man would be wise, though man be born like a wild ass's colt. If thou prepare thine heart, and stretch out thine hands toward him; if iniquity be in thine hand, put it far away, and let not wickedness dwell in thy tabernacles. For then shalt thou lift up thy face without spot; yea, thou shalt be stedfast, and shalt not fear: because thou shalt forget thy misery, and remember it as waters that pass away: and thine age shall be clearer than the noonday; thou shalt shine forth, thou shalt be as the morning. And thou shalt be secure, because there is hope; yea, thou shalt dig about thee,[8] and thou shalt take thy rest in safety. Also thou shalt lie down, and none shall make thee afraid; yea, many shall make suit unto thee. But the eyes of the wicked shall fail, and they shall not escape, and their hope shall be as the giving up of the ghost.

12. And Job answered and said, No doubt but ye are the people, and wisdom shall die with you. But I have understanding as well as you; I am not inferior to you: yea, who knoweth not such things as these? I am as one mocked of his neighbour, who calleth upon God, and he answered him: the just upright man is laughed to scorn. He that is ready to slip with his feet is as a lamp despised in the thought of him that is at ease. The tabernacles of robbers prosper, and they that provoke God are secure; into whose hand God bringeth abundantly. But ask now the beasts, and they shall teach thee; and the fowls of the air, and they shall tell thee: or speak to the earth, and it shall teach thee: and the fishes of the sea shall declare unto thee. Who knoweth not in all these that the hand of the Lord hath wrought this? In whose hand is the soul of every living thing, and the breath of all mankind. Doth not the ear try words? and the mouth taste his meat? With the ancient is wisdom; and in length of days understanding. With him is wisdom and strength, he hath counsel and understanding. Behold, he breaketh down, and it cannot be built again: he shutteth up a man, and there can be no opening. Behold, he withholdeth the waters, and they dry up: also he sendeth them out, and they overturn the earth. With him is strength and wisdom: the deceived and the deceiver are his.

7. For judgment.   8. Search. The master inspects his property before retiring.

He leadeth counsellors away spoiled, and maketh the judges fools. He
looseth the bond of kings, and girdeth their loins with a girdle. He leadeth
princes away spoiled, and overthroweth the mighty. He removeth away the
speech of the trusty, and taketh away the understanding of the aged. He
poureth contempt upon princes, and weakeneth the strength of the mighty.
He discovereth deep things out of darkness, and bringeth out to light the
shadow of death. He increaseth the nations, and destroyeth them: he
enlargeth the nations, and straiteneth them again.[9] He taketh away the
heart of the chief of the people of the earth, and causeth them to wander
in a wilderness where there is no way. They grope in the dark without
light, and he maketh them to stagger like a drunken man.

13. Lo, mine eye hath seen all this, mine ear hath heard and understood it. What ye know, the same do I know also: I am not inferior unto
you. Surely I would speak to the Almighty, and I desire to reason with
God. But ye are forgers of lies, ye are all physicians of no value. O that ye
would altogether hold your peace! and it should be your wisdom. Hear
now my reasoning, and hearken to the pleadings of my lips. Will ye speak
wickedly for God? and talk deceitfully for him? Will ye accept[1] his person?
Will ye contend for God? Is it good that he should search you out? or as
one man mocketh another, do ye so mock him? He will surely reprove
you, if ye do secretly accept persons.[2] Shall not his excellency make you
afraid? and his dread fall upon you? Your remembrances[3] are like unto
ashes, your bodies to bodies of clay. Hold your peace, let me alone, that I
may speak, and let come on me what will. Wherefore do I take my flesh
in my teeth,[4] and put my life in mine hand? Though he slay me, yet will
I trust in him: but I will maintain mine own ways before him. He also
shall be my salvation: for an hypocrite shall not come before him. Hear
diligently my speech, and my declaration with your ears. Behold now, I
have ordered my cause; I know that I shall be justified. Who is he that will
plead with me?[5] for now, if I hold my tongue, I shall give up the ghost.
Only do not two things unto me: then will I not hide myself from thee.[6]
Withdraw thine hand far from me: and let not thy dread make me afraid.
Then call thou, and I will answer: or let me speak, and answer thou me.
How many are mine iniquities and sins? Make me to know my transgression and my sin. Wherefore hidest thou thy face, and holdest me for thine
enemy? Wilt thou break a leaf driven to and fro? and wilt thou pursue the
dry stubble? For thou writest bitter things against me, and makest me to
possess the iniquities of my youth. Thou puttest my feet also in the stocks,
and lookest narrowly unto all my paths; thou settest a print upon the heels
of my feet. And he, as a rotten thing, consumeth, as a garment that is
moth eaten.

9. Contracts their boundaries.   1. Respect.   2. This phrase seems to mean something like, "back the
winning side for personal reasons."   3. Memorable sayings.   4. Like a wild beast at bay, defending
its life with its teeth.   5. Accuse me.   6. He now addresses himself directly to God.

14. Man that is born of a woman is of few days, and full of trouble. He cometh forth like a flower, and is cut down: he fleeth also as a shadow, and continueth not. And dost thou open thine eyes upon such an one, and bringest me into judgment with thee? Who can bring a clean thing out of an unclean? not one. Seeing his days are determined, the number of his months are with thee, thou hast appointed his bounds that he cannot pass; turn from him, that he may rest, till he shall accomplish, as an hireling, his day. For there is hope of a tree, if it be cut down, that it will sprout again, and that the tender branch thereof will not cease. Though the root thereof wax old in the earth, and the stock thereof die in the ground; yet through the scent of water it will bud, and bring forth boughs like a plant. But man dieth, and wasteth away: yea, man giveth up the ghost, and where is he? As the waters fail from the sea, and the flood decayeth and drieth up: so man lieth down, and riseth not: till the heavens be no more, they shall not awake, nor be raised out of their sleep. O that thou wouldest hide me in the grave, that thou wouldest keep me secret, until thy wrath be past, that thou wouldest appoint me a set time, and remember me! If a man die, shall he live again? All the days of my appointed time will I wait, till my change[7] come. Thou shalt call, and I will answer thee: thou wilt have a desire to[8] the work of thine hands. For now thou numberest my steps: dost thou not watch over my sin? My transgression is sealed up in a bag, and thou sewest up mine iniquity. And surely the mountain falling cometh to nought, and the rock is removed out of his place. The waters wear the stones: thou washest away the things which grow out of the dust of the earth; and thou destroyest the hope of man. Thou prevailest for ever against him, and he passeth; thou changest his countenance, and sendest him away. His sons come to honour, and he knoweth it not; and they are brought low, but he perceiveth it not of them. But his flesh upon him shall have pain, and his soul within him shall mourn.

29. Moreover Job continued his parable, and said, Oh that I were as in months past, as in the days when God preserved me; when his candle shined upon my head, and when by his light I walked through darkness; as I was in the days of my youth, when the secret of God was upon my tabernacle; when the Almighty was yet with me, when my children were about me; when I washed my steps with butter and the rock poured me out rivers of oil; when I went out to the gate[9] through the city, when I prepared my seat in the street! The young men saw me, and hid themselves: and the aged arose, and stood up. The princes refrained talking, and laid their hand on their mouth. The nobles held their peace, and their tongue cleaved to the roof of their mouth. When the ear heard me, then it blessed me; and when the eye saw me, it gave witness to me: because I delivered the poor that cried, and the fatherless, and him that had none to help him.

7. Release.   8. For.   9. The town meeting place and law court was just inside the gate.

The blessing of him that was ready to perish came upon me: and I caused the widow's heart to sing for joy. I put on righteousness, and it clothed me: my judgment was as a robe and a diadem. I was eyes to the blind, and feet was I to the lame. I was a father to the poor: and the cause which I knew not I searched out. And I brake the jaws of the wicked, and plucked the spoil out of his teeth. Then I said, I shall die in my nest, and I shall multiply my days as the sand. My root was spread out by the waters, and the dew lay all night upon my branch. My glory was fresh in me, and my bow was renewed in my hand. Unto me men gave ear, and waited, and kept silence at my counsel. After my words they spake not again; and my speech dropped upon them. And they waited for me as for the rain; and they opened their mouth wide as for the latter rain. If I laughed on them, they believed it not; and the light of my countenance they cast not down. I chose out their way, and sat chief, and dwelt as a king in the army, as one that comforteth the mourners.

30. But now they that are younger than I have me in derision, whose fathers I would have disdained to have set with the dogs of my flock. Yea, whereto might the strength of their hands profit me,[1] in whom old age was perished? For want and famine they were solitary; fleeing into the wilderness in former time desolate and waste. Who cut up mallows by the bushes, and juniper roots for their meat. They were driven forth from among men, (they cried after them as after a thief;) to dwell in the cliffs of the valleys, in caves of the earth, and in the rocks. Among the bushes they brayed; under the nettles they were gathered together. They were children of fools, yea, children of base men: they were viler than the earth. And now am I their song, yea, I am their byword. They abhor me, they flee far from me, and spare not to spit in my face. Because he hath loosed my cord, and afflicted me, they have also let loose the bridle before me. Upon my right hand rise the youth; they push away my feet, and they raise up against me the ways of their destruction. They mar my path, they set forward my calamity, they have no helper. They came upon me as a wide breaking in of waters: in the desolation they rolled themselves upon me. Terrors are turned upon me: they pursue my soul as the wind: and my welfare passeth away as a cloud. And now my soul is poured out upon[2] me; the days of affliction have taken hold upon me. My bones are pierced in me in the night season: and my sinews take no rest. By the great force of my disease is my garment changed: it bindeth me about as the collar of my coat. He hath cast me into the mire, and I am become like dust and ashes. I cry unto thee, and thou dost not hear me: I stand up, and thou regardest me not. Thou art become cruel to me: with thy strong hand thou opposest thyself against me. Thou liftest me up to the wind; thou causest me to ride upon it, and dissolvest my substance. For I know that thou wilt bring me to death, and to the house appointed for all living. Howbeit he will not stretch out his hand to the grave, though they cry in his destruction. Did

1. They were too old to work.   2. Within.

not I weep for him that was in trouble? Was not my soul grieved for the poor? When I looked for good, then evil came unto me: and when I waited for light, there came darkness. My bowels boiled, and rested not: the days of affliction prevented me. I went mourning without the sun: I stood up, and I cried in the congregation. I am a brother to dragons, and a companion to owls. My skin is black upon me, and my bones are burned with heat. My harp also is turned to mourning, and my organ[3] into the voice of them that weep.

31. I made a covenant with mine eyes; why then should I think upon a maid? For what portion of God is there from above? and what inheritance of the Almighty from on high? Is not destruction to the wicked? and a strange punishment to the workers of iniquity? Doth not he see my ways, and count all my steps? If I have walked with vanity, or if my foot hath hasted to deceit; let me be weighed in an even balance, that God may know mine integrity. If my step hath turned out of the way, and mine heart walked after mine eyes, and if any blot hath cleaved to mine hands; then let me sow, and let another eat; yea, let my offspring be rooted out. If mine heart have been deceived by a woman, or if I have laid wait at my neighbour's door; then let my wife grind unto another, and let others bow down upon her. For this is an heinous crime; yea, it is an iniquity to be punished by the judges. For it is a fire that consumeth to destruction, and would root out all mine increase.

If I did despise the cause of my manservant or of my maidservant, when they contended with me; what then shall I do when God riseth up? and when he visiteth, what shall I answer him? Did not he that made me in the womb make him? and did not one fashion us in the womb? If I have withheld the poor from their desire, or have caused the eyes of the widow to fail; or have eaten my morsel myself alone, and the fatherless hath not eaten thereof; (For from my youth he was brought up with me, as with a father, and I have guided her from my mother's womb;) if I have seen any perish for want of clothing, or any poor without covering; if his loins have not blessed me, and if he were not warmed with the fleece of my sheep; if I have lifted up my hand against the fatherless, when I saw my help in the gate:[4] then let mine arm fall from my shoulder blade, and mine arm be broken from the bone. For destruction from God was a terror to me, and by reason of his highness I could not endure. If I have made gold my hope, or have said to the fine gold, Thou art my confidence; if I rejoiced because my wealth was great, and because mine hand had gotten much; if I beheld the sun when it shined, or the moon walking in brightness; and my heart hath been secretly enticed, or my mouth hath kissed my hand:[5] this also were an iniquity to be punished by the judge: for I should have denied the God that is above.

If I rejoiced at the destruction of him that hated me, or lifted up myself when evil found him: neither have I suffered my mouth to sin by wishing

3. Pipe.   4. The gate is the court; the clause means, "when I had influence in the court."   5. Idolatrous acts of worship of the sun and moon.

a curse to his soul. If the men of my tabernacle said not, Oh that we had of his flesh! We cannot be satisfied. The stranger did not lodge in the street: but I opened my doors to the traveller. If I covered my transgressions as Adam, by hiding mine iniquity in my bosom: did I fear a great multitude, or did the contempt of families terrify me, that I kept silence, and went not out of the door? Oh that one would hear me! Behold, my desire is, that the Almighty would answer me, and that mine adversary had written a book. Surely I would take it upon my shoulder, and bind it as a crown to me. I would declare unto him the number of my steps; as a prince would I go near unto him. If my land cry against me, or that the furrows likewise thereof complain; if I have eaten the fruits thereof without money, or have caused the owners thereof to lose their life: let thistles grow instead of wheat, and cockle instead of barley. The words of Job are ended.

38. Then the Lord answered Job out of the whirlwind, and said, Who is this that darkeneth counsel by words without knowledge? Gird up now thy loins like a man; for I will demand of thee, and answer thou me. Where wast thou when I laid the foundations of the earth? Declare, if thou hast understanding. Who hath laid the measures thereof, if thou knowest? or who hath stretched the line upon it? Whereupon are the foundations thereof fastened? or who laid the corner stone thereof; when the morning stars sang together, and all the sons of God shouted for joy? Or who shut up the sea with doors, when it brake forth, as if it had issued out of the womb? When I made the cloud the garment thereof, and thick darkness a swaddlingband for it, and brake up for it my decreed place,[6] and set bars and doors, and said, Hitherto shalt thou come, but no further: and here shall thy proud waves be stayed? Hast thou commanded the morning since thy days; and caused the dayspring[7] to know his place; that it might take hold of the ends of the earth, that the wicked might be shaken out of it? It is turned as clay to the seal;[8] and they[9] stand as a garment. And from the wicked their light is withholden, and the high arm shall be broken. Hast thou entered into the springs of the sea? or hast thou walked in the search of the depth? Have the gates of death been opened unto thee? or hast thou seen the doors of the shadow of death? Hast thou perceived the breadth of the earth? Declare if thou knowest it all. Where is the way where light dwelleth? And as for darkness, where is the place thereof, that thou shouldest take it to the bound thereof, and that thou shouldest know the paths to the house thereof? Knowest thou it, because thou wast then born? or because the number of thy days is great? Hast thou entered into the treasures of the snow? or hast thou seen the treasures of the hail, which I have reserved against the time of trouble, against the day of battle and war? By what way is the light parted, which scattereth the east wind upon the earth? Who hath divided a watercourse for the overflowing of waters, or a way for the lightning of thunder; to cause it to rain on the earth, where no man is; on the wilderness, wherein there is no man; to satisfy the desolate and waste

6. The broken coastline.   7. Dawn.   8. More literally, "changed as clay under the seal."   9. All things. God is describing the moment of the creation of the universe.

ground; and to cause the bud of the tender herb to spring forth? Hath the
rain a father? or who hath begotten the drops of dew? Out of whose womb
came the ice? And the hoary frost of heaven, who hath gendered it? The
waters are hid as with a stone, and the face of the deep is frozen. Canst
thou bind the sweet influences of Pleiades, or loose the bands of Orion?
Canst thou bring forth Mazzaroth[1] in his season? or canst thou guide Arcturus with his sons? Knowest thou the ordinances of heaven? Canst thou
set the dominion thereof in the earth? Canst thou lift up thy voice to the
clouds, that abundance of waters may cover thee? Canst thou send light-
nings, that they may go, and say unto thee, Here we are? Who hath put
wisdom in the inward parts? or who hath given understanding to the heart?
Who can number the clouds in wisdom? or who can stay the bottles of
heaven, when the dust groweth into hardness, and the clods cleave fast
together? Wilt thou hunt the prey for the lion? or fill the appetite of the
young lions, when they couch in their dens, and abide in the covert to lie
in wait? Who provideth for the raven his food? when his young ones cry
unto God, they wander for lack of meat.

   39. Knowest thou the time when the wild goats of the rock bring forth?
or canst thou mark when the hinds do calve? Canst thou number the
months that they fulfil? or knowest thou the time when they bring forth?
They bow themselves, they bring forth their young ones, they cast out their
sorrows. Their young ones are in good liking, they grow up with corn; they
go forth, and return not unto them. Who hath sent out the wild ass free?
or who hath loosed the bands of the wild ass? Whose house I have made
the wilderness, and the barren land his dwellings. He scorneth the multitude of the city, neither regardeth he the crying of the driver. The range
of the mountains is his pasture, and he searcheth after every green thing.
Will the unicorn[2] be willing to serve thee, or abide by thy crib? Canst thou
bind the unicorn with his band in the furrow? or will he harrow the valleys
after thee? Wilt thou trust him, because his strength is great? or wilt thou
leave thy labour to him? Wilt thou believe him, that he will bring home
thy seed, and gather it into thy barn? Gavest thou the goodly wings unto
the peacocks? or wings and feathers unto the ostrich? Which leaveth her
eggs in the earth, and warmeth them in dust, and forgetteth that the foot
may crush them, or that the wild beast may break them. She is hardened
against her young ones, as though they were not hers: her labour is in vain
without fear;[3] because God hath deprived her of wisdom, neither hath he
imparted to her understanding. What time she lifteth up herself on high,
she scorneth the horse and his rider. Hast thou given the horse strength?
Hast thou clothed his neck with thunder? Canst thou make him afraid as
a grasshopper? The glory of his nostrils is terrible. He paweth in the valley,
and rejoiceth in his strength: he goeth on to meet the armed men. He
mocketh at fear, and is not affrighted; neither turneth he back from the

1. Meaning disputed; it may be a name for the signs of the zodiac, or for some particular constellation.
2. The Hebrew has "wild ox."   3. Though her labor is in vain, she is without fear.

sword. The quiver rattleth against him, the glittering spear and the shield. He swalloweth the ground with fierceness and rage: neither believeth he that it is the sound of the trumpet. He saith among the trumpets, Ha, ha; and he smelleth the battle afar off, the thunder of the captains, and the shouting. Doth the hawk fly by thy wisdom, and stretch her wings toward the south? Doth the eagle mount up at thy command, and make her nest on high? She dwelleth and abideth on the rock, upon the crag of the rock, and the strong place. From thence she seeketh the prey, and her eyes behold afar off. Her young ones also suck up blood: and where the slain are, there is she.

40. Moreover the Lord answered Job, and said, Shall he that contendeth with the Almighty instruct him? He that reproveth God, let him answer it.

Then Job answered the Lord, and said, Behold, I am vile; what shall I answer thee? I will lay mine hand upon my mouth. Once have I spoken; but I will not answer: yea, twice; but I will proceed no further.

Then answered the Lord unto Job out of the whirlwind, and said, Gird up thy loins now like a man: I will demand of thee, and declare thou unto me. Wilt thou also disannul my judgment? Wilt thou condemn me, that thou mayest be righteous? Hast thou an arm like God: or canst thou thunder with a voice like him? Deck thyself now with majesty and excellency; and array thyself with glory and beauty. Cast abroad the rage of thy wrath: and behold every one that is proud, and abase him. Look on every one that is proud, and bring him low; and tread down the wicked in their place. Hide them in the dust together; and bind their faces in secret. Then will I also confess unto thee that thine own right hand can save thee.

Behold now behemoth,[4] which I made with thee; he eateth grass as an ox. Lo now, his strength is in his loins, and his force is in the navel of his belly. He moveth his tail like a cedar: the sinews of his stones[5] are wrapped together. His bones are as strong pieces of brass; his bones are like bars of iron. He is the chief of the ways of God: he that made him can make his sword to approach unto him. Surely the mountains bring him forth food, where all the beasts of the field play. He lieth under the shady trees, in the covert of the reed, and fens. The shady trees cover him with their shadow; the willows of the brook compass him about. Behold, he drinketh up a river, and hasteth not: he trusteth that he can draw up Jordan into his mouth. He taketh it with his eyes:[6] his nose pierceth through snares.

41. Canst thou draw out leviathan[7] with an hook? or his tongue with a cord which thou lettest down? Canst thou put an hook into his nose? or bore his jaw through with a thorn? Will he make many supplications unto thee? will he speak soft words unto thee? Will he make a covenant with thee? wilt thou take him for a servant for ever? Wilt thou play with him as with a bird? or wilt thou bind him for thy maidens? Shall the companions

---

4. Generally identified with the hippopotamus.   5. More literally, "thighs."   6. Obscure in the original; probably, "None can attack him in the eyes."   7. Here probably the crocodile.

make a banquet of him? Shall they part him among the merchants? Canst thou fill his skin with barbed irons? or his head with fish spears? Lay thine hand upon him, remember the battle, do no more. Behold, the hope of him is in vain: shall not one be cast down even at the sight of him? None is so fierce that dare stir him up: who then is able to stand before me? Who hath prevented[8] me, that I should repay him? Whatsoever is under the whole heaven is mine. I will not conceal his parts, nor his power, nor his comely proportion. Who can discover the face of his garment?[9] or who can come to him with his double bridle? Who can open the doors of his face? His teeth are terrible round about. His scales are his pride, shut up together as with a close seal. One is so near to another, that no air can come between them. They are joined one to another, they stick together, that they cannot be sundered. By his neesings[1] a light doth shine, and his eyes are like the eyelids of the morning. Out of his mouth go burning lamps, and sparks of fire leap out. Out of his nostrils goeth smoke, as out of a seething pot or caldron. His breath kindleth coals, and a flame goeth out of his mouth. In his neck remaineth strength, and sorrow is turned into joy before him. The flakes of his flesh are joined together: they are firm in themselves; they cannot be moved. His heart is as firm as a stone; yea, as hard as a piece of the nether millstone. When he raiseth up himself, the mighty are afraid: by reason of breakings they purify themselves.[2] The sword of him that layeth at him cannot hold: the spear, the dart, nor the habergeon. He esteemeth iron as straw, and brass as rotten wood. The arrow cannot make him flee: slingstones are turned with him into stubble. Darts are counted as stubble: he laugheth at the shaking of a spear. Sharp stones are under him: he spreadeth sharp pointed things upon the mire. He maketh the deep to boil like a pot: he maketh the sea like a pot of ointment. He maketh a path to shine after him; one would think the deep to be hoary.[3] Upon earth there is not his like, who is made without fear. He beholdeth all high things: he is a king over all the children of pride.

42. Then Job answered the Lord, and said, I know that thou canst do every thing, and that no thought can be withholden from thee. Who is he that hideth counsel without knowledge? Therefore have I uttered that I understood not; things too wonderful for me, which I knew not. Hear, I beseech thee, and I will speak: I will demand of thee, and declare thou unto me. I have heard of thee by the hearing of the ear: but now mine eye seeth thee. Wherefore I abhor myself, and repent in dust and ashes.

And it was so, that after the Lord had spoken these words unto Job, the Lord said to Eliphaz the Temanite, My wrath is kindled against thee, and against thy two friends: for ye have not spoken of me the thing that is right, as my servant Job hath. Therefore take unto you now seven bullocks and seven rams, and go to my servant Job, and offer up for yourselves a burnt

---

8. Given anything to me first.   9. His scales. *Discover:* strip off.   1. His breath (compare, "sneeze"). The vapor exhaled by the crocodile appears luminous in the sunlight.   2. A corrupt text. The clause probably should read, "in consternation they are beside themselves."   3. White (with foam).

offering; and my servant Job shall pray for you: for him will I accept: lest I
deal with you after your folly, in that ye have not spoken of me the thing
which is right, like my servant Job. So Eliphaz the Temanite and Bildad
the Shuhite and Zophar the Naamathite went, and did according as the
Lord commanded them: the Lord also accepted Job. And the Lord turned
the captivity[4] of Job, when he prayed for his friends: also the Lord gave Job
twice as much as he had before. Then came there unto him all his brethren, and all his sisters, and all they that had been of his acquaintance
before, and did eat bread with him in his house: and they bemoaned him,
and comforted him over all the evil that the Lord had brought upon him:
every man also gave him a piece of money, and every one an earring of
gold. So the Lord blessed the latter end of Job more than his beginning:
for he had fourteen thousand sheep, and six thousand camels, and a thousand yoke of oxen, and a thousand she asses. He had also seven sons and
three daughters. And he called the name of the first, Jemima; and the
name of the second, Kezia; and the name of the third, Kerenhappuch.
And in all the land were no women found so fair as the daughters of Job:
and their father gave them inheritance among their brethren. After this
lived Job an hundred and forty years, and saw his sons, and his sons' sons,
even four generations. So Job died, being old and full of days.

PSALM 8

1. O Lord our Lord, how excellent is thy name in all the earth! who
hast set thy glory above the heavens.

2. Out of the mouth of babes and sucklings hast thou ordained strength
because of thine enemies, that thou mightest still the enemy and the avenger.

3. When I consider thy heavens, the work of thy fingers, the moon and
the stars, which thou hast ordained;

4. What is man, that thou art mindful of him? and the son of man, that
thou visitest him?

5. For thou hast made him a little lower than the angels, and hast crowned
him with glory and honour.

6. Thou madest him to have dominion over the works of thy hands;
thou hast put all things under his feet:

7. All sheep and oxen, yea, and the beasts of the field;

8. The fowl of the air, and the fish of the sea, and whatsoever passeth
through the paths of the seas.

9. O Lord our Lord, how excellent is thy name in all the earth!

PSALM 19

1. The heavens declare the glory of God; and the firmament sheweth
his handywork.

---

4. Put an end to the suffering.

2. Day unto day uttereth speech, and night unto night sheweth knowledge.

3. There is no speech nor language, where their voice is not heard.

4. Their line is gone out through all the earth, and their words to the end of the world. In them hath he set a tabernacle for the sun,

5. Which is as a bridegroom coming out of his chamber, and rejoiceth as a strong man to run a race.

6. His going forth is from the end of the heaven, and his circuit unto the ends of it: and there is nothing hid from the heat thereof.

7. The law of the Lord is perfect, converting the soul: the testimony of the Lord is sure, making wise the simple.

8. The statutes of the Lord are right, rejoicing the heart: the commandment of the Lord is pure, enlightening the eyes.

9. The fear of the Lord is clean, enduring for ever: the judgments of the Lord are true and righteous altogether.

10. More to be desired are they than gold, yea, than much fine gold: sweeter also than honey and the honeycomb.

11. Moreover by them is thy servant warned: and in keeping of them there is great reward.

12. Who can understand his errors? cleanse thou me from secret faults.

13. Keep back thy servant also from presumptuous sins; let them not have dominion over me: then shall I be upright, and I shall be innocent from the great transgression.

14. Let the words of my mouth, and the meditation of my heart, be acceptable in thy sight, O Lord, my strength, and my redeemer.

PSALM 23

1. The Lord is my shepherd; I shall not want.

2. He maketh me to lie down in green pastures: he leadeth me beside the still waters.

3. He restoreth my soul: he leadeth me in the paths of righteousness for his name's sake.

4. Yea, though I walk through the valley of the shadow of death, I will fear no evil: for thou art with me; thy rod and thy staff they comfort me.

5. Thou preparest a table before me in the presence of mine enemies: thou anointest my head with oil; my cup runneth over.

6. Surely goodness and mercy shall follow me all the days of my life: and I will dwell in the house of the Lord for ever.

PSALM 104

1. Bless the Lord, O my soul. O Lord my God, thou art very great; thou art clothed with honour and majesty.

2. Who coverest thyself with light as with a garment: who stretchest out the heavens like a curtain:

3. Who layeth the beams of his chambers in the waters: who maketh the clouds his chariot: who walketh upon the wings of the wind:

4. Who maketh his angels spirits; his ministers a flaming fire:

5. Who laid the foundations of the earth, that it should not be removed for ever.

6. Thou coveredst it with the deep as with a garment: the waters stood above the mountains.

7. At thy rebuke they fled; at the voice of thy thunder they hasted away.

8. They go up by the mountains; they go down by the valleys unto the place which thou hast founded for them.

9. Thou hast set a bound that they may not pass over; that they turn not again to cover the earth.

10. He sendeth the springs into the valleys, which run among the hills.

11. They give drink to every beast of the field: the wild asses quench their thirst.

12. By them shall the fowls of the heaven have their habitation, which sing among the branches.

13. He watereth the hills from his chambers: the earth is satisfied with the fruit of thy works.

14. He causeth the grass to grow for the cattle, and herb for the service of man: that he may bring forth food out of the earth;

15. And wine that maketh glad the heart of man, and oil to make his face to shine, and bread which strengtheneth man's heart.

16. The trees of the Lord are full of sap; the cedars of Lebanon, which he hath planted;

17. Where the birds make their nests: as for the stork, the fir trees are her house.

18. The high hills are a refuge for the wild goats; and the rocks for the conies.

19. He appointed the moon for seasons: the sun knoweth his going down.

20. Thou makest darkness, and it is night: wherein all the beasts of the forest do creep forth.

21. The young lions roar after their prey, and seek their meat from God.

22. The sun ariseth, they gather themselves together, and lay them down in their dens.

23. Man goeth forth unto his work and to his labour until the evening.

24. O Lord, how manifold are thy works! in wisdom hast thou made them all: the earth is full of thy riches.

25. So is this great and wide sea, wherein are things creeping innumerable, both small and great beasts.

26. There go the ships: there is that leviathan, whom thou hast made to play therein.

27. These wait all upon thee; that thou mayest give them their meat in due season.

28. That thou givest them they gather: thou openest thine hand, they are filled with good.

29. Thou hidest thy face, they are troubled: thou takest away their breath, they die, and return to their dust.

30. Thou sendest forth thy spirit, they are created: and thou renewest the face of the earth.

31. The glory of the Lord shall endure for ever: the Lord shall rejoice in his works.

32. He looketh on the earth, and it trembleth: he toucheth the hills, and they smoke.

33. I will sing unto the Lord as long as I live: I will sing praise to my God while I have my being.

34. My meditation of him shall be sweet: I will be glad in the Lord.

35. Let the sinners be consumed out of the earth, and let the wicked be no more. Bless thou the Lord, O my soul. Praise ye the Lord.

PSALM 137

1. By the rivers of Babylon,[5] there we sat down, yea, we wept, when we remembered Zion.

2. We hanged our harps upon the willows in the midst thereof.

3. For there they that carried us away captive required of us a song; and they that wasted us required of us mirth, saying, Sing us one of the songs of Zion.

4. How shall we sing the Lord's song in a strange land?

5. If I forget thee, O Jerusalem, let my right hand forget her cunning.

6. If I do not remember thee, let my tongue cleave to the roof of my mouth; if I prefer not Jerusalem above my chief joy.

7. Remember, O Lord, the children of Edom[6] in the day of Jerusalem; who said, Rase it, rase it, even to the foundation thereof.

8. O daughter of Babylon, who art to be destroyed; happy shall he be, that rewardeth thee as thou hast served us.

9. Happy shall he be, that taketh and dasheth thy little ones against the stones.

ISAIAH 52–53

(The Song of the Suffering Servant)

52:13–15. Behold, my servant shall deal prudently, he shall be exalted and extolled, and be very high. As many were astonied at thee; his visage was so marred more than any man, and his form more than the sons of men: so shall he sprinkle many nations; the kings shall shut their mouths at him: for that which had not been told them shall they see; and that which they had not heard shall they consider.

5. On the river Euphrates. Jerusalem was captured and sacked by the Babylonians in 586 B.C. The Jews were taken away into captivity in Babylon.   6. The Edomites helped the Babylonians to capture Jerusalem.

53. Who hath believed our report? and to whom is the arm of the Lord revealed? For he shall grow up before him as a tender plant, and as a root out of a dry ground: he hath no form nor comeliness; and when we shall see him, there is no beauty that we should desire him. He is despised and rejected of men; a man of sorrows, and acquainted with grief: and we hid as it were our faces from him; he was despised, and we esteemed him not. Surely he hath borne our griefs, and carried our sorrows: yet we did esteem him stricken, smitten of God, and afflicted. But he was wounded for our transgressions, he was bruised for our iniquities: the chastisement of our peace was upon him; and with his stripes we are healed. All we like sheep have gone astray; we have turned every one to his own way; and the Lord hath laid on him the iniquity of us all. He was oppressed, and he was afflicted, yet he opened not his mouth: he is brought as a lamb to the slaughter, and as a sheep before her shearers is dumb, so he openeth not his mouth. He was taken from prison and from judgment: and who shall declare his generation? for he was cut off out of the land of the living: for the transgression of my people was he stricken. And he made his grave with the wicked, and with the rich[7] in his death; because he had done no violence, neither was any deceit in his mouth. Yet it pleased the Lord to bruise him; he hath put him to grief: when thou shalt make his soul an offering for sin, he shall see his seed, he shall prolong his days, and the pleasure of the Lord shall prosper in his hand. He shall see of the travail of his soul, and shall be satisfied: by his knowledge shall my righteous servant justify many; for he shall bear their iniquities. Therefore will I divide him a portion with the great, and he shall divide the spoil with the strong; because he hath poured out his soul unto death: and he was numbered with the transgressors; and he bare the sin of many, and made intercession for the transgressors.

JONAH

1. Now the word of the Lord came unto Jonah the son of Amittai, saying, Arise, go to Nineveh,[8] that great city, and cry against it; for their wickedness is come up before me. But Jonah rose up to flee unto Tarshish[9] from the presence of the Lord, and went down to Joppa;[1] and he found a ship going to Tarshish: so he paid the fare thereof, and went down into it, to go with them unto Tarshish from the presence of the Lord. But the Lord sent out a great wind into the sea, and there was a mighty tempest in the sea, so that the ship was like to be broken. Then the mariners were afraid, and cried every man unto his god, and cast forth the wares that were in the ship into the sea, to lighten it of them. But Jonah was gone down into the sides of the ship; and he lay, and was fast asleep. So the shipmaster came to him, and said unto him, What meanest thou, O sleeper? arise, call upon thy God, if so be that God will think upon us, that we perish not. And they said every one to his fellow, Come, and let us cast lots, that

7. Some editors emend the Hebrew to give the meaning, "evildoers." 8. On the river Tigris, the capital city of the Assyrians. 9. Probably Tartessus, in Spain. Jonah intends to go west (instead of east to Nineveh) and as far away as he can. 1. Seaport on the coast of Palestine.

we may know for whose cause this evil is upon us. So they cast lots, and the lot fell upon Jonah. Then said they unto him, Tell us, we pray thee, for whose cause this evil is upon us; What is thine occupation? and whence comest thou? what is thy country? and of what people art thou? And he said unto them, I am an Hebrew; and I fear the Lord, the God of heaven, which hath made the sea and the dry land. Then were the men exceedingly afraid, and said unto him, Why hast thou done this? For the men knew that he fled from the presence of the Lord, because he had told them. Then said they unto him, What shall we do unto thee, that the sea may be calm unto us? for the sea wrought, and was tempestuous. And he said unto them, Take me up, and cast me forth into the sea; so shall the sea be calm unto you: for I know that for my sake this great tempest is upon you. Nevertheless the men rowed hard to bring it to the land; but they could not: for the sea wrought, and was tempestuous against them. Wherefore they cried unto the Lord, and said, We beseech thee, O Lord, we beseech thee, let us not perish for this man's life, and lay not upon us innocent blood: for thou, O Lord, hast done as it pleased thee. So they took up Jonah, and cast him forth into the sea: and the sea ceased from her raging. Then the men feared the Lord exceedingly, and offered a sacrifice unto the Lord, and made vows.

Now the Lord had prepared a great fish to swallow up Jonah. And Jonah was in the belly of the fish three days and three nights.

2. Then Jonah prayed unto the Lord his God out of the fish's belly, and said, I cried by reason of mine affliction unto the Lord, and he heard me; out of the belly of hell cried I, and thou heardest my voice. For thou hadst cast me into the deep, in the midst of the seas; and the floods compassed me about; all thy billows and thy waves passed over me. Then I said, I am cast out of thy sight; yet I will look again toward thy holy temple. The waters compassed me about, even to the soul: the depth closed me round about, the weeds were wrapped about my head. I went down to the bottoms of the mountains; the earth with her bars was about me for ever: yet hast thou brought up my life from corruption, O Lord my God. When my soul fainted within me I remembered the Lord: and my prayer came in unto thee, into thine holy temple. They that observe lying vanities forsake their own mercy.[2] But I will sacrifice unto thee with the voice of thanksgiving; I will pay that that I have vowed. Salvation is of the Lord. And the Lord spake unto the fish, and it vomited out Jonah upon the dry land.

3. And the word of the Lord came unto Jonah the second time, saying, Arise, go unto Nineveh, that great city, and preach unto it the preaching that I bid thee. So Jonah arose, and went unto Nineveh, according to the word of the Lord. Now Nineveh was an exceeding great city of three days' journey. And Jonah began to enter into the city a day's journey, and he cried, and said, Yet forty days, and Nineveh shall be overthrown.

2. The general sense: "those that worship false gods forfeit their claim to mercy."

So the people of Nineveh believed God, and proclaimed a fast, and put on sackcloth, from the greatest of them even to the least of them. For word came unto the king of Nineveh, and he arose from his throne, and he laid his robe from him, and covered him with sackcloth, and sat in ashes. And he caused it to be proclaimed and published through Nineveh by the decree of the king and his nobles, saying, Let neither man nor beast, herd nor flock, taste any thing: let them not feed, nor drink water: but let man and beast be covered with sackcloth, and cry mightily unto God: yea, let them turn every one from his evil way, and from the violence that is in their hands. Who can tell if God will turn and repent, and turn away from his fierce anger, that we perish not?

And God saw their works, that they turned from their evil way; and God repented of the evil, that he had said that he would do unto them; and he did it not.

4. But it displeased Jonah exceedingly, and he was very angry. And he prayed unto the Lord, and said, I pray thee, O Lord, was not this my saying, when I was yet in my country? Therefore I fled before unto Tarshish: for I knew that thou art a gracious God, and merciful, slow to anger, and of great kindness, and repentest thee of the evil.[3] Therefore now, O Lord, take, I beseech thee, my life from me; for it is better for me to die than to live. Then said the Lord, Doest thou well to be angry? So Jonah went out of the city, and sat on the east side of the city, and there made him a booth,[4] and sat under it in the shadow, till he might see what would become of the city. And the Lord God prepared a gourd,[5] and made it to come up over Jonah, that it might be a shadow over his head, to deliver him from his grief. So Jonah was exceeding glad of the gourd. But God prepared a worm when the morning rose the next day, and it smote the gourd that it withered. And it came to pass, when the sun did arise, that God prepared a vehement east wind; and the sun beat upon the head of Jonah, that he fainted, and wished in himself to die, and said, It is better for me to die than to live. And God said to Jonah, Doest thou well to be angry for the gourd? And he said, I do well to be angry, even unto death. Then said the Lord, Thou hast had pity on the gourd, for the which thou hast not laboured, neither madest it grow; which came up in a night, and perished in a night: and should not I spare Nineveh, that great city, wherein are more than sixscore thousand persons that cannot discern between their right hand and their left hand;[6] and also much cattle?

3. Jonah is quoting Scripture (Exodus 34:6).   4. A tent shelter.   5. Some kind of climbing plant.
6. I.e. children.

HOMER

Greek literature begins with two masterpieces, the *Iliad* and the *Odyssey*, which cannot be accurately dated (the conjectural dates range over three centuries), and which are attributed to a poet, Homer, about whom nothing is known except his name. The Greeks believed that he was blind, perhaps because the bard Demodokos in the *Odyssey* was blind (see p. 297) and seven different cities put forward claims to be his birthplace. They are all in what the Greeks called Ionia, the Western coast of Asia Minor, which was heavily settled by Greek colonists. It does seem likely that he came from this area: the *Iliad* contains several accurate descriptions of natural features of the Ionian landscape and, on the other hand, his grasp of the geography of mainland, especially western, Greece is unsure. But even this is a guess, and all the other stories the Greeks told about him are obvious inventions.

The two great epics that have made his name supreme among poets may have been fixed in something like their present form before the art of writing was in general use in Greece; it is certain that they were intended not for reading but for oral recitation. The earliest stages of their composition date from long before the beginnings of Greek literacy—the late eighth century B.C. The poems exhibit the unmistakable characteristics of oral composition.

The oral poet had at his disposal not reading and writing, but a vast and intricate system of metrical formulas—phrases that would fit in at different places in the line—and a repertoire of standard scenes (the arming of the warrior, the battle of two champions) as well as the known outline of the story. Of course he could and did invent new phrases and scenes as he recited—but his base was the immense poetic reserve created by many generations of singers before him. When he told again for his hearers the old story of Achilles and his wrath, he was recreating a traditional story that had been recited, with variations, additions, and improvements, by a long line of predecessors. The poem was not, in the modern sense, his creation, still less an expression of his personality. Consequently there is no trace of his identity to be found in it: the poet remains as hidden behind the action and speech of his characters as if he were a dramatist.

The poems as we have them, however, are unlike most of the oral literature we know from other times and places. The poetic organization of each of the two epics, the subtle interrelationship of the parts, which creates their structural and emotional unity, suggests that they owe their present form to the shaping hand of a single poet, the architect who selected from the enormous wealth of the oral tradition and fused what he took with original material to create, perhaps with the aid of the new medium of writing, the two magnificently ordered poems known as the *Iliad* and the *Odyssey*.

THE ILIAD

Of these two the *Iliad* is perhaps the earlier. Its subject is war; its characters are men in battle and women whose fate depends on the outcome. The war is fought by the Achaeans* against the Trojans for the recovery of Helen, the wife of the

*The transcription of Greek names is, unfortunately, a game with no rules. It used to be the convention that Greek names would be spelled according to the form they were given in Latin (and as they appear in our selections from Virgil and Ovid): Achaeans, Achilles. Recently it has become fashionable to stay closer to the Greek—Akhaians, Akhilleus; this is the system followed by Robert Fitzgerald in his translation of the *Odyssey*. Robert Fagles in our selections from the *Iliad* has turned back to the old conventions, the

Achaean chieftain Menelaus; the combatants are heroes who in their chariots engage
in individual duels before the supporting lines of infantry and archers. This romantic war aim and the outmoded military technique suggest to the modern reader a
comparison with chivalrous engagements between medieval knights—a vision of
individual prowess in combat which the nostalgia of our mechanized age contrasts
sentimentally with the mass slaughter of modern war. But there is no sentimentality in Homer's description of battle. "Patroclus rising beside him stabbed his right
jawbone, ramming the spearhead square between his teeth so hard he hooked him
by that spearhead over the chariot-rail, hoisted, dragged the Trojan out as an angler
perched on a jutting rock ledge drags some fish from the sea, some noble catch,
with line and glittering bronze hook. So with the spear Patroclus gaffed him off his
car, his mouth gaping round the glittering point and flipped him down facefirst,
dead as he fell, his life breath blown away." This is meticulously accurate; there is
no attempt to suppress the ugliness of Thestor's death. The bare, careful description
creates the true nightmare quality of battle, in which men perform monstrous
actions with the same matter-of-fact efficiency they display in their normal occupations; and the simile reproduces the grotesque appearance of violent death—the
simple spear thrust takes away Thestor's dignity as a human being even before it
takes his life. He is gaping, like a fish on the hook.

The simile does something else too. The comparison of Patroclus to an angler
emphasizes another aspect of battle, its excitement. Homer's lines here combine
two contrary emotions, the human revulsion from the horror of violent death and
the human attraction to the excitement of violent action. This passage is typical of
the poem as a whole. Everywhere in it we are conscious of these two poles, of war's
ugly brutality and its "terrible beauty." The poet accepts violence as a basic factor
in human life, and accepts it without sentimentality; for it is equally sentimental
to pretend that war is not ugly or to pretend that it does not have its beauty. Three
thousand years have not changed the human condition in this respect. We are still
both lovers and victims of the will to violence, and as long as we are, Homer will
be read as its greatest interpreter.

The *Iliad* describes the events of a few weeks in the ten-year siege of Troy. The
particular subject of the poem, as its first line announces, is the anger of Achilles,
the bravest of the Achaean chieftains encamped outside the city. Achilles is a man
who lives by and for violence, who is creative and alive only in violent action. He
knows that he will be killed if he stays before Troy, but rather than decay, as he
would decay, in peace, he accepts that certainty. His inadequacy for peace is shown
by the fact that even in war the violence of his temper makes him a man apart and
alone. His anger cuts him off from his commander and his fellow princes; to spite
them he withdraws from the fighting, the only context in which his life has any
meaning. He is brought back into it at last by the death of his one real friend,
Patroclus; the consequences of his wrath and withdrawal fall heavily on the Achaeans,
but most heavily on himself.

The great champion of the Trojans, Hector, fights bravely, but reluctantly. War,
for him, is a necessary evil, and he thinks nostalgically of the peaceful past, though
he has little hope of peace to come. His pre-eminence in peace is emphasized by
the tenderness of his relations with his wife and child and also by his kindness to
Helen, the cause of the war which he knows in his heart will bring his city to
destruction. We see Hector always against the background of the patterns of civilized life—the rich city with its temples and palaces, the continuity of the family.
Achilles' background is the discord of the armed camp on the shore, his loneliness,

---

Latin forms that have been standard in English verse and prose for many centuries. These are the forms
used in the introduction.

and his certainty of early death. The duel between these two men is the inevitable crisis of the poem, and just as inevitable is Hector's defeat and death. For against Achilles in his native element of violence nothing can stand.

At the climactic moment of Hector's death, as everywhere in the poem, Homer's firm control of his material preserves the balance in which our contrary emotions are held; pity for Hector does not entirely rob us of sympathy for Achilles. His brutal words to the dying Hector and the insults he inflicts on his corpse are truly savage, but we are never allowed to forget that this inflexible hatred is the expression of his love for Patroclus. And the final book of the poem shows us an Achilles whose iron heart is moved at last; he is touched by the sight of Hector's father clasping in suppliance the terrible hands that have killed so many of his sons. He remembers that he has a father, and that he will never see him again; Achilles and Priam, the slayer and the father of the slain, weep together:

> . . . And overpowered by memory
> both men gave way to grief. Priam wept freely
> for man-killing Hector, throbbing, crouching
> before Achilles' feet as Achilles wept himself,
> now for his father, now for Patroclus once again,
> and their sobbing rose and fell throughout the house.

Achilles gives Hector's body to Priam for honorable burial. His anger has run its full course and been appeased. It has brought death, first to the Achaeans and then to the Trojans, to Patroclus and to Hector, and so to Achilles himself, for his death is fated to come "soon after Hector's." The violence to which he is dedicated will finally destroy him too.

This tragic action is the center of the poem, but it is surrounded by scenes that remind us that the organized destruction of war, though an integral part of human life, is still only a part of it. Except for Achilles, whose worship of violence falters only in the final moment of pity for his enemy's father and his own, the yearning for peace and its creative possibilities is never far below the surface. This is most poignantly expressed by the scenes that take place in Troy, especially the farewell between Hector and Andromache; but it is made clear that the Achaeans too are conscious of what they have sacrificed. Early in the poem, when Agamemnon, the Achaean commander, tests the morale of his troops by suggesting that the war be abandoned, they rush for the ships so eagerly and with such heartfelt relief that their commanders are hard put to it to stop them. These two poles of the human condition, war and peace, with their corresponding aspects of human nature, the destructive and the creative, are implicit in every situation and statement of the poem, and they are put before us, in symbolic form, in the shield that the god Hephaestus makes for Achilles. Its emblem is an image of human life as a whole. Here are two cities, one at peace and one at war. In one a marriage is celebrated and a quarrel settled by process of law; the other is besieged by a hostile army and fights for its existence. Scenes of violence—peaceful shepherds slaughtered in an ambush, Death dragging away a corpse by its foot—are balanced by scenes of plowing, harvesting, work in the vineyard and on the pasture, a green on which young people dance. And around the outermost rim of the shield runs "the might of the Ocean stream," a river that is at once the frontier of the known and the imagined world and the barrier between the quick and the dead. The shield of Achilles is the total background for the tragic violence of the central figures; it provides a frame that gives the wrath of Achilles and the death of Hector their just proportion and true significance.

The other Homeric epic, the *Odyssey,* is concerned with the peace that followed the war, and in particular with the return of the heroes who survived. Its subject is the long drawn out return of one of the heroes, Odysseus of Ithaca, who had come farther than most (all the way from western Greece) and who was destined to spend ten years wandering in unknown seas before he returned to his rocky kingdom. When Odysseus' wanderings began, Achilles had already received, at the hands of Apollo, the death that he had chosen, and that was the only appropriate end for his fatal and magnificent violence. Odysseus chose life, and his outstanding quality is a probing and versatile intelligence, which, combined with long experience, keeps him safe and alive through the trials and dangers of twenty years of war and seafaring. To stay alive he has to do things that Achilles would never have done, and use an ingenuity and experience that Achilles did not possess; but his life is just as much a struggle. Troy has fallen, but "there is no discharge in the war." The way back is as perilous as the ten-year siege.

The opening lines of the poem state the theme:

> Sing in me, Muse, and through me tell the story
> of that man skilled in all ways of contending
> the wanderer, harried for years on end,
> after he plundered the stronghold
> on the proud height of Troy.
>   He saw the townlands
> and learned the minds of many distant men,
> and weathered many bitter nights and days
> in his deep heart at sea, while he fought only
> to save his life. . . .

In this world it is a struggle even to stay alive, and it is a struggle for which Odysseus is naturally endowed. But his objective is not life at any price. Where honor demands, he can be soberly courageous in the face of death (as on Circe's island, where he goes alone and against his mate's advice to save his sailors), and he can even be led into foolhardiness by his insatiable curiosity (as in the expedition to see the island of the Cyclopes). Much as he clings to life, it must be life with honor; what he is trying to preserve is not just existence but a worldwide reputation. His name has become a byword for successful courage and intelligence, and he must not betray it. When he reveals his identity at the palace of the Phaeacians, he speaks of his fame in an objective manner, as if it were something apart from himself:

> I am Laertes' son, Odysseus.
>   Men hold me
> formidable for guile in peace and war:
> this fame has gone abroad to the sky's rim.

This is not boasting, but a calm recognition of the qualities and achievements for which he stands, and to which he must be true.

Ironically enough, to be true to his reputation, he is often forced to conceal his name. In the Cyclopes' cave, he calls himself "Nobody," in order to assure his escape, and it is clear how hard he finds this denial of his reputation when, out of the cave and on board ship, he insists on telling Polyphemus his name. Not only does this reassertion of his identity bring himself, his ship, and his crew back within reach of Polyphemus' arm, but it also enables the blinded giant to call down on his enemy the wrath of his father Poseidon, who, from this point on, musters the full might of the sea against Odysseus' return. Warned by the consequences of this boastful revelation of his name, he conceals his identity even from the hospitable Phaeacians, until his emotional reaction to the singer's tale of Troy gives him away. And when he finally returns home, to a palace full of violent suitors for his wife's hand who think that he is dead and who have presumed so far that they will kill him if they now find out that he is alive, he has to become Nobody again. He disguises himself as an old dirty beggar, to flatter and fawn on his enemies for bread in his own house.

The trials of the voyage home are not just physical obstacles to his return, they are also temptations. Odysseus is tempted, time after time, to forget his identity, to secede from the life of struggle and constant vigilance for which his name stands. The lotus flower which makes a man forget home and family is the most obvious form of temptation; it occurs early in the voyage and is easily resisted. But he is offered more attractive bait. Circe gives him a life of ease and self-indulgence on an enchanted island. His resistance has by this time been lowered, and he stays a full year before his sailors remonstrate with him and remind him of his home. At the Phaeacian palace where he tells the story of his voyages, he is offered the love of a young princess, Nausicaa, and her hand in marriage by her father Alkinoös— a new life in a richer kingdom than his rocky Ithaca. The Sirens tempt him to live in the memory of the glorious past. "Come here, famous Odysseus," they sing, "great glory of the Achaeans, and hear our song. . . . For we know all that at broad Troy the Argives and the Trojans suffered by the will of the gods." If he had not been bound to the mast, he would have gone to hear and join the dead men whose bones rot on the Sirens' island. Calypso, the goddess with whom he spent seven years, longing all the time to escape, offers him the greatest temptation of all, immortality. If he will stay as her husband, he will live forever, a life of ease and tranquility, like that of the gods. Odysseus refuses this too; he prefers the human condition, with all its struggle, its disappointments, and its inevitable end. And the end, death, is an ever-present temptation. It is always near him; at the slightest slackening of effort, the smallest failure of intelligence, the first weakness of will, death will bring him release from his trials. But he hangs on tenaciously, and, toward the end of his ordeals, he is sent living to the world of the dead to see for himself what death means. It is dark and comfortless; Homer's land of the dead is the most frightening picture of the afterlife in European literature. Odysseus talks to the dead and any illusion he had about death as repose is shattered when he comforts the shade of Achilles with talk of his everlasting glory and hears him reply:

> Let me hear no smooth talk
> of death from you, Odysseus, light of councils.
> Better, I say, to break sod as a farm hand
> for some poor country man, on iron rations,
> than lord it over all the exhausted dead.

When he hears these words Odysseus does not yet understand their full significance (that he, the living man, will taste the depths of degradation, not as a serf, but as a despised beggar, mocked and manhandled in his own palace), but he is prepared now to face everything that may be necessary, to push on without another look behind.

In this scene Homer brings his two great prototypes face to face, and poses the tragic fury of Achilles against the mature intelligence of Odysseus. There can be little doubt where his sympathy lies. Against the dark background of Achilles' regret for life lost the figure of Odysseus shines more warmly: a man dedicated to life, accepting its limitations and making full use of its possibilities, a man who is des-

tined to endure to the end and be saved. He finds in the end the home and the
peace he fought for, his wife faithful, a son worthy of his name ready to succeed
him, and the knowledge that the death which must come at last will be gentle:

> Then a seaborne death
> soft as this hand of mist will come upon you
> when you are wearied out with rich old age,
> your country folk in blessed peace around you.

A very short but thoughtful discussion of the basic themes of the two poems is
found in J. Griffin, *Homer* (1980); his *Homer on Life and Death* (1980) is a full
and rewarding exploration of Homer's vision of the human condition and the nature
of the gods. Martin Mueller, *The Iliad* (1984), is a highly readable and thoughtful
discussion of almost every aspect of the *Iliad*, from the problem of its composition
to its influence on later literature. Mark W. Edwards, *Homer: Poet of the Iliad*
(1987), attempts, in his words, "to combine the advantages of a general introduction to Homer and a commentary on the *Iliad*." The first part discusses traditional
oral style and the ways in which Homer "used, adapted or ignored it for his own
purposes," and the second is a detailed literary commentary on "the most important books of the poem" (including I, VI, IX, XVIII, XXII, and XXIV). Jasper
Griffin, *Homer: The Odyssey* (1987), is a short but comprehensive guide to the
background and riches of the poem. George E. Dimock, *Unity of the Odyssey*
(1989), is a brilliant reading, full of original insights and authoritative in its demonstration of the poem's thematic coherence. Sheila Murnaghan, *Disguise and
Recognition in the Odyssey* (1987), is an enlightening guide through the intricacies
of the second half of the poem.

The Iliad[1]

BOOK I

The Rage of Achilles

Rage—Goddess,[2] sing the rage of Peleus' son Achilles,
murderous, doomed, that cost the Achaeans[3] countless losses,
hurling down to the House of Death so many sturdy souls,
great fighters' souls, but made their bodies carrion,
feasts for the dogs and birds,   5
and the will of Zeus was moving toward its end.
Begin, Muse, when the two first broke and clashed,
Agamemnon lord of men and brilliant Achilles.

What god drove them to fight with such a fury?
Apollo the son of Zeus and Leto. Incensed at the king   10
he swept a fatal plague through the army—men were dying
and all because Agamemnon spurned Apollo's priest.
Yes, Chryses[4] approached the Achaeans' fast ships
to win his daughter back, bringing a priceless ransom
and bearing high in hand, wound on a golden staff,   15
the wreaths of the god, the distant deadly Archer.

1. Translated by Robert Fagles.   2. The Muse, inspiration for epic poetry.   3. The Greeks. Homer
also calls them Danaans and Argives.   4. His daughter is called Chryseis, and the place where he lives,
Chryse.

He begged the whole Achaean army but most of all
the two supreme commanders, Atreus' two sons,
"Agamemnon, Menelaus—all Argives geared for war!
May the gods who hold the halls of Olympus give you   20
Priam's city[5] to plunder, then safe passage home.
Just set my daughter free, my dear one . . . here,
accept these gifts, this ransom. Honor the god
who strikes from worlds away—the son of Zeus, Apollo!"

     And all ranks of Achaeans cried out their assent: 25
"Respect the priest, accept the shining ransom!"
But it brought no joy to the heart of Agamemnon.
The king dismissed the priest with a brutal order
ringing in his ears: "Never again, old man,
let me catch sight of you by the hollow ships!   30
Not loitering now, not slinking back tomorrow.
The staff and the wreaths of god will never save you then.
The girl—I won't give up the girl. Long before that,
old age will overtake her in *my* house, in Argos,
far from her fatherland, slaving back and forth   35
at the loom, forced to share my bed!
                                    Now go,
don't tempt my wrath—and you may depart alive."

     The old man was terrified. He obeyed the order,
trailing away in silence down the shore
where the battle lines of breakers crash and drag.   40
And moving off to a safe distance, over and over
the old priest prayed to the son of sleek-haired Leto,
lord Apollo, "Hear me, Apollo! God of the silver bow
who strides the walls of Chryse and Cilla sacrosanct—
lord in power of Tenedos[6]—Smintheus,[7] god of the plague! 45
If I ever roofed a shrine to please your heart,
ever burned the long rich bones of bulls and goats
on your holy altar, now, now bring my prayer to pass.
Pay the Danaans[8] back—your arrows for my tears!"

     His prayer went up and Phoebus Apollo heard him.   50
Down he strode from Olympus' peaks, storming at heart
with his bow and hooded quiver slung across his shoulders.
The arrows clanged at his back as the god quaked with rage,
the god himself on the march and down he came like night.
Over against the ships he dropped to a knee, let fly a shaft 55
and a terrifying clash rang out from the great silver bow.
First he went for the mules and circling dogs but then,

---

5. Priam was king of Troy. *Olympus:* The mountain in northern Greece which was supposed to be the
home of the gods.   6. An island off the Trojan coast. *Chryse and Cilla:* cities near Troy.   7. A cult
name of Apollo, probably a reference to his role as the destroyer of field mice. The Greek *sminthos* means
"mouse."   8. Greeks.

launching a piercing shaft at the men themselves,
he cut them down in droves—
and the corpse-fires burned on, night and day, no end in sight.   60

    Nine days the arrows of god swept through the army.
On the tenth Achilles called all ranks to muster—
the impulse seized him, sent by white-armed Hera[9]
grieving to see Achaean fighters drop and die.
Once they'd gathered, crowding the meeting grounds,   65
the swift runner Achilles rose and spoke among them:
"Son of Atreus, now we are beaten back, I fear,
the long campaign is lost. So home we sail . . .
if we can escape our death—if war and plague
are joining forces now to crush the Argives.   70
But wait: let us question a holy man,
a prophet, even a man skilled with dreams—
dreams as well can come our way from Zeus—
come, someone to tell us why Apollo rages so,
whether he blames us for a vow we failed, or sacrifice.   75
If only the god would share the smoky savor of lambs
and full-grown goats, Apollo might be willing, still,
somehow, to save us from this plague."
                      So he proposed
and down he sat again as Calchas rose among them,
Thestor's son, the clearest by far of all the seers   80
who scan the flight of birds. He knew all things that are,
all things that are past and all that are to come,
the seer who had led the Argive ships to Troy
with the second sight that god Apollo gave him.
For the armies' good the seer began to speak: 85
"Achilles, dear to Zeus . . .
you order me to explain Apollo's anger,
the distant deadly Archer? I will tell it all.
But strike a pact with me, swear you will defend me
with all your heart, with words and strength of hand.   90
For there is a man I will enrage—I see it now—
a powerful man who lords it over all the Argives,
one the Achaeans must obey . . . . A mighty king,
raging against an inferior, is too strong.
Even if he can swallow down his wrath today,   95
still he will nurse the burning in his chest
until, sooner or later, he sends it bursting forth.
Consider it closely, Achilles. Will you save me?"

    And the matchless runner reassured him: "Courage!
Out with it now, Calchas. Reveal the will of god,   100

9. Sister and wife of Zeus, the father of the gods: she was hostile to the Trojans.

whatever you may know. And I swear by Apollo
dear to Zeus, the power you pray to, Calchas,
when you reveal god's will to the Argives—no one,
not while I am alive and see the light on earth, no one
will lay his heavy hands on you by the hollow ships.   105
None among all the armies. Not even if you mean
Agamemnon here who now claims to be, by far,
the best of the Achaeans."
                         The seer took heart
and this time he spoke out, bravely: "Beware—
he casts no blame for a vow we failed, a sacrifice.   110
The god's enraged because Agamemnon spurned his priest,
he refused to free his daughter, he refused the ransom.
That's why the Archer sends us pains and he will send us more
and never drive this shameful destruction from the Argives,
not till we give back the girl with sparkling eyes   115
to her loving father—no price, no ransom paid—
and carry a sacred hundred bulls to Chryse town.
Then we can calm the god, and only then appease him."

    So he declared and sat down. But among them rose
the fighting son of Atreus, lord of the far-flung kingdoms,   120
Agamemnon—furious, his dark heart filled to the brim,
blazing with anger now, his eyes like searing fire.
With a sudden, killing look he wheeled on Calchas first:
"Seer of misery! Never a word that works to my advantage!
Always misery warms your heart, your prophecies—   125
never a word of profit said or brought to pass.
Now, again, you divine god's will for the armies,
bruit it out, as fact, why the deadly Archer
multiplies our pains: because I, I refused
that glittering price for the young girl Chryseis.   130
Indeed, I prefer *her* by far, the girl herself,
I want her mine in my own house! I rank her higher
than Clytemnestra, my wedded wife—she's nothing less
in build or breeding, in mind or works of hand.
But I am willing to give her back, even so,   135
if that is best for all. What I really want
is to keep my people safe, not see them dying.
But fetch me another prize, and straight off too,
else I alone of the Argives go without my honor.
That would be a disgrace. You are all witness,   140
look—*my* prize is snatched away!"
                         But the swift runner
Achilles answered him at once, "Just how, Agamemnon,
great field marshal . . . most grasping man alive,
how can the generous Argives give you prizes now?

I know of no troves of treasure, piled, lying idle,   145
anywhere. Whatever we dragged from towns we plundered,
all's been portioned out. But collect it, call it back
from the rank and file? *That* would be the disgrace.
So return the girl to the god, at least for now.
We Achaeans will pay you back, three, four times over,   150
if Zeus will grant us the gift, somehow, someday,
to raze Troy's massive ramparts to the ground."

      But King Agamemnon countered, "Not so quickly,
brave as you are, godlike Achilles—trying to cheat *me*.
Oh no, you won't get past me, take me in that way!   155
What do you want? To cling to your own prize
while I sit calmly by—empty-handed here?
Is that why you order me to give her back?
No—if our generous Argives *will* give me a prize,
a match for my desires, equal to what I've lost,   160
well and good. But if they give me nothing
I will take a prize myself—your own, or Ajax'
or Odysseus' prize—I'll commandeer her myself
and let that man I go to visit choke with rage!
Enough. We'll deal with all this later, in due time.   165
Now come, we haul a black ship down to the bright sea,
gather a decent number of oarsmen along her locks
and put aboard a sacrifice, and Chryseis herself,
in all her beauty . . . we embark her too.
Let one of the leading captains take command.   170
Ajax, Idomeneus, trusty Odysseus[1] or you, Achilles,
you—the most violent man alive—so you can perform
the rites for us and calm the god yourself."

                                        A dark glance
and the headstrong runner answered him in kind: "Shameless—
armored in shamelessness—always shrewd with greed!   175
How could any Argive soldier obey your orders,
freely and gladly do your sailing for you
or fight your enemies, full force? Not I, no.
It wasn't Trojan spearmen who brought me here to fight.
The Trojans never did *me* damage, not in the least,   180
they never stole my cattle or my horses, never
in Phthia[2] where the rich soil breeds strong men
did they lay waste my crops. How could they?
Look at the endless miles that lie between us . . .
shadowy mountain ranges, seas that surge and thunder.   185
No, you colossal, shameless—we all followed you,

1. The most subtle and crafty of the Greeks. *Ajax:* the bravest of the Greeks after Achilles.   2. Achilles'
home in northern Greece.

to please you, to fight for you, to win your honor
back from the Trojans—Menelaus[3] and you, you dog-face!
What do *you* care? Nothing. You don't look right or left.
And now you threaten to strip me of my prize in person—   190
the one I fought for long and hard, and sons of Achaea
handed her to me.

        My honors never equal yours,
whenever we sack some wealthy Trojan stronghold—
my arms bear the brunt of the raw, savage fighting,
true, but when it comes to dividing up the plunder   195
the lion's share is yours, and back I go to my ships,
clutching some scrap, some pittance that I love,
when I have fought to exhaustion.

                No more now—
back I go to Phthia. Better that way by far,
to journey home in the beaked ships of war.   200
I have no mind to linger here disgraced,
brimming your cup and piling up your plunder."

    But the lord of men Agamemnon shot back,
"*Desert*, by all means—if the spirit drives you home!
I will never beg you to stay, not on *my* account.   205
Never—others will take my side and do me honor,
Zeus above all, whose wisdom rules the world.
You—I hate you most of all the warlords
loved by the gods. Always dear to your heart,
strife, yes, and battles, the bloody grind of war.   210
What if you are a great soldier? That's just a gift of god.
Go home with your ships and comrades, lord it over your Myrmidons![4]
You *are* nothing to me—you and your overweening anger!
But let this be my warning on your way:
since Apollo insists on taking my Chryseis,   215
I'll send her back in my own ships with *my* crew.
But I, I will be there in person at your tents
to take Briseis in all her beauty, your own prize—
so you can learn just how much greater I am than you
and the next man up may shrink from matching words with me,   220
from hoping to rival Agamemnon strength for strength!"

    He broke off and anguish gripped Achilles.
The heart in his rugged chest was pounding, torn . . .
Should he draw the long sharp sword slung at his hip,
thrust through the ranks and kill Agamemnon now?—   225
or check his rage and beat his fury down?
As his racing spirit veered back and forth,

3. The aim of the expedition was to recapture Helen, the wife of Menelaos, who had run off to Troy with Priam's son Paris.   4. The name of Achilles' people.

just as he drew his huge blade from its sheath,
down from the vaulting heavens swept Athena,[5]
the white-armed goddess Hera sped her down: 230
Hera loved both men and cared for both alike.
Rearing behind him Pallas seized his fiery hair—
only Achilles saw her, none of the other fighters—
struck with wonder he spun around, he knew her at once,
Pallas Athena! the terrible blazing of those eyes,   235
and his winged words went flying: "Why, why now?
Child of Zeus with the shield of thunder,[6] why come now?
To witness the outrage Agamemnon just committed?
I tell you this, and so help me it's the truth—
he'll soon pay for his arrogance with his life!"   240

     Her gray eyes clear, the goddess Athena answered,
"Down from the skies I come to check your rage
if only you will yield.
The white-armed goddess Hera sped me down:
she loves you both, she cares for you both alike.   245
Stop this fighting, now. Don't lay hand to sword.
Lash him with threats of the price that he will face.
And I tell you this—and I *know* it is the truth—
one day glittering gifts will lie before you,
three times over to pay for all his outrage.   250
Hold back now. Obey us both."
                              So she urged
and the swift runner complied at once: "I must—
when the two of you hand down commands, Goddess,
a man submits though his heart breaks with fury.
Better for him by far. If a man obeys the gods   255
they're quick to hear his prayers."
                              And with that
Achilles stayed his burly hand on the silver hilt
and slid the huge blade back in its sheath.
He would not fight the orders of Athena.
Soaring home to Olympus, she rejoined the gods   260
aloft in the halls of Zeus whose shield is thunder.

     But Achilles rounded on Agamemnon once again,
lashing out at him, not relaxing his anger for a moment:
"Staggering drunk, with your dog's eyes, your fawn's heart!
Never once did you arm with the troops and go to battle   265
or risk an ambush packed with Achaea's picked men—
you lack the courage, you can see death coming.

---

5. A goddess, daughter of Zeus, a patron of human ingenuity and resourcefulness, whether exemplified
by handicrafts, such as spinning, or by skill in human relations, such as her favorite among the Greeks,
Odysseus, possessed. She supported the Greek side in the war.   6. A terrible shield with which Zeus (or
any other god to whom it was entrusted) stirred up storms or threw panic into human beings.

Safer by far, you find, to foray all through camp,
commandeering the prize of any man who speaks against you.
King who devours his people! Worthless husks, the men you rule—   270
if not, Atrides,[7] this outrage would have been your last.
I tell you this, and I swear a mighty oath upon it . . .
by this, this scepter, look,
that never again will put forth crown and branches,
now it's left its stump on the mountain ridge forever,   275
nor will it sprout new green again, now the brazen ax
has stripped its bark and leaves, and now the sons of Achaea
pass it back and forth as they hand their judgments down,
upholding the honored customs whenever Zeus commands—
This scepter will be the mighty force behind my oath: 280
someday, I swear, a yearning for Achilles will strike
Achaea's sons and all your armies! But then, Atrides,
harrowed as you will be, *nothing* you do can save you—
not when your hordes of fighters drop and die,
cut down by the hands of man-killing Hector![8] Then—   285
then you will tear your heart out, desperate, raging
that you disgraced the best of the Achaeans!"
                                        Down on the ground
he dashed the scepter studded bright with golden nails,
then took his seat again. The son of Atreus smoldered,
glaring across at him, but Nestor rose between them,   290
the man of winning words, the clear speaker of Pylos[9] . . .
Sweeter than honey from his tongue the voice flowed on and on.
Two generations of mortal men he had seen go down by now,
those who were born and bred with him in the old days,
in Pylos' holy realm, and now he ruled the third.   295
He pleaded with both kings, with clear good will,
"No more—or enormous sorrow comes to all Achaea!
How they would exult, Priam and Priam's sons
and all the Trojans. Oh they'd leap for joy
to hear the two of you battling on this way,   300
you who excel us all, first in Achaean councils,
first in the ways of war.
                         Stop. Please.
Listen to Nestor. You are both younger than I,
and in my time I struck up with better men than you,
even you, but never once did they make light of me.   305
I've never seen such men, I never will again . . .
men like Pirithous, Dryas, that fine captain,
Caeneus and Exadius, and Polyphemus, royal prince,
and Theseus,[1] Aegeus' boy, a match for the immortals.
They were the strongest mortals ever bred on earth,   310

7. Son of Atreus, i.e., Agamemnon.   8. Son of Priam; the foremost warrior of the Trojans.   9. On
the western shore of the Peloponnese.   1. Names of heroes of an older generation.

the strongest, and they fought against the strongest too,
shaggy Centaurs, wild brutes of the mountains—
they hacked them down, terrible, deadly work.
And I was in their ranks, fresh out of Pylos,
far away from home—they enlisted me themselves   315
and I fought on my own, a free lance, single-handed.
And none of the men who walk the earth these days
could battle with those fighters, none, but they,
they took to heart my counsels, marked my words.
So now you listen too. Yielding is far better   320
Don't seize the girl, Agamemnon, powerful as you are—
leave her, just as the sons of Achaea gave her,
his prize from the very first.
And you, Achilles, never hope to fight it out
with your king, pitting force against his force: 325
no one can match the honors dealt a king, you know,
a sceptered king to whom great Zeus gives glory.
Strong as you are—a goddess was your mother[2]—
he has more power because he rules more men.
Atrides, end your anger—look, it's Nestor!   330
I beg you, cool your fury against Achilles.
Here the man stands over all Achaea's armies,
our rugged bulwark braced for shocks of war."

   But King Agamemnon answered him in haste,
"True, old man—all you say is fit and proper—   335
but this soldier wants to tower over the armies,
he wants to rule over all, to lord it over all,
give out orders to every man in sight. Well,
there's one, I trust, who will never yield to him!
What if the everlasting gods have made a spearman of him?   340
Have they entitled him to hurl abuse at *me*?"

   "Yes!"—blazing Achilles broke in quickly—
"What a worthless, burnt-out coward I'd be called
if I would submit to you and all your orders,
whatever you blurt out. Fling them at others,   345
don't give me commands!
Never again, I trust, will Achilles yield to *you*.
And I tell you this—take it to heart, I warn you—
my hands will never do battle for that girl,
neither with you, King, nor any man alive.   350
You Achaeans gave her, now you've snatched her back.
But all the rest I possess beside my fast black ship—
not one bit of it can you seize against my will, Atrides.

---

2. Achilles' mother was Thetis, a sea nymph. She was married to a mortal, Peleus (Achilles' father), but later left humankind and went to live with her father, Nereus, in the depths of the Aegean Sea.

Come, try it! So the men can see, that instant,
your black blood gush and spurt around my spear!"

　Once the two had fought it out with words,
battling face-to-face, both sprang to their feet
and broke up the muster beside the Argive squadrons.
Achilles strode off to his trim ships and shelters,
back to his friend Patroclus and their comrades.   360
Agamemnon had a vessel hauled down to the sea,
he picked out twenty oarsmen to man her locks,
put aboard the cattle for sacrifice to the god
and led Chryseis in all her beauty amidships.
Versatile Odysseus took the helm as captain.
　　　　　　　　　　　　　All embarked,   365
the party launched out on the sea's foaming lanes
while the son of Atreus told his troops to wash,
to purify themselves from the filth of plague.
They scoured it off, threw scourings in the surf
and sacrificed to Apollo full-grown bulls and goats   370
along the beaten shore of the fallow barren sea
and savory smoke went swirling up the skies.

　So the men were engaged throughout the camp.
But King Agamemnon would not stop the quarrel,
the first threat he hurled against Achilles.   375
He called Talthybius and Eurybates briskly,
his two hearlds, ready, willing aides:
"Go to Achilles' lodge. Take Briseis at once,
his beauty Briseis by the hand and bring her here.
But if he will not surrender her, I'll go myself,   380
I'll seize her myself, with an army at my back—
and all the worse for him!"
　　　　　　　　　　He sent them off
with the strict order ringing in their ears.
Against their will the two men made their way
along the breaking surf of the barren salt sea   385
and reached the Myrmidon shelters and their ships.
They found him beside his lodge and black hull,
seated grimly—and Achilles took no joy
when he saw the two approaching.
They were afraid, they held the king in awe   390
and stood there, silent. Not a word to Achilles,
not a question. But he sensed it all in his heart,
their fear, their charge, and broke the silence for them:
"Welcome, couriers! Good heralds of Zeus and men,
here, come closer. You have done nothing to me.   395
You are not to blame. No one but Agamemnon—
he is the one who sent you for Briseis.

Go, Patroclus, Prince, bring out the girl
and hand her to them so they can take her back.
But let them both bear witness to my loss . . .   400
in the face of blissful gods and mortal men,
in the face of that unbending, ruthless king—
if the day should come when the armies need *me*
to save their ranks from ignominious, stark defeat.
The man is raving—with all the murderous fury in his heart.   405
He lacks the sense to see a day behind, a day ahead,
and safeguard the Achaeans battling by the ships."

    Patroclus obeyed his great friend's command.
He led Briseis in all her beauty from the lodge
and handed her over to the men to take away.   410
And the two walked back along the Argive ships
while she trailed on behind, reluctant, every step.
But Achilles wept, and slipping away from his companions,
far apart, sat down on the beach of the heaving gray sea
and scanned the endless ocean. Reaching out his arms,   415
again and again he prayed to his dear mother: "Mother!
You gave me life, short as that life will be,
so at least Olympian Zeus, thundering up on high,
should give me honor—but now he gives me nothing.
Atreus' son Agamemnon, for all his far-flung kingdoms—   420
the man disgraces me, seizes and keeps my prize,
he tears her away himself!"

                          So he wept and prayed
and his noble mother heard him, seated near her father,
the Old Man of the Sea in the salt green depths.
Suddenly up she rose from the churning surf   425
like mist and settling down beside him as he wept,
stroked Achilles gently, whispering his name, "My child—
why in tears? What sorrow has touched your heart?
Tell me, please. Don't harbor it deep inside you.
We must share it all."

                          And now from his depths   430
the proud runner groaned: "You know, you know,
why labor through it all? You know it all so well . . .
We raided Thebe once, Eetion's[3] sacred citadel,
we ravaged the place, hauled all the plunder here
and the armies passed it round, share and share alike,   435
and they chose the beauty Chryseis for Agamemnon.
But soon her father, the holy priest of Apollo
the distant deadly Archer, Chryses approached
the fast trim ships of the Argives armed in bronze
to win his daughter back, bringing a priceless ransom   440

---

3. King of the Cilicians, and father of Hector's wife Andromache. *Thebe* was the Cilician capital city.

and bearing high in hand, wound on a golden staff,
the wreaths of the god who strikes from worlds away.
He begged the whole Achaean army but most of all
the two supreme commanders, Atreus' two sons,
and all ranks of Achaeans cried out their assent,   445
'Respect the priest, accept the shining ransom!'
But it brought no joy to the heart of Agamemnon,
our high and mighty king dismissed the priest
with a brutal order ringing in his ears.
And shattered with anger, the old man withdrew   450
but Apollo heard his prayer—he loved him, deeply—
he loosed his shaft at the Argives, withering plague,
and now the troops began to drop and die in droves,
the arrows of god went showering left and right,
whipping through the Achaeans' vast encampment.   455
But the old seer who knew the cause full well
revealed the will of the archer god Apollo.
And I was the first, mother, I urged them all,
'Appease the god at once!' That's when the fury
gripped the son of Atreus. Agamemnon leapt to his feet   460
and hurled his threat—his threat's been driven home.
One girl, Chryseis, the fiery-eyed Achaeans
ferry out in a fast trim ship to Chryse Island,
laden with presents for the god.[4] The other girl,
just now the heralds came and led her away from camp,   465
Briseus' daughter, the prize the armies gave me.
But you, mother, if you have any power at all,
protect your son! Go to Olympus, plead with Zeus,
if you ever warmed his heart with a word or any action . . .

     Time and again I heard your claims in father's halls,   470
boasting how you and you alone of all the immortals
rescued Zeus, the lord of the dark storm cloud,[5]
from ignominious, stark defeat.
That day the Olympians tried to chain him down,
Hera, Poseidon[6] lord of the sea, and Pallas Athena—   475
you rushed to Zeus, dear Goddess, broke those chains,
quickly ordered the hundred-hander to steep Olympus,
that monster whom the immortals call Briareus[7]
but every mortal calls the Sea-god's son, Aegaeon,
though he's stronger than his father. Down he sat,   480
flanking Cronus' son, gargantuan in the glory of it all,
and the blessed gods were struck with terror then,
they stopped shackling Zeus.
                              Remind him of that,

4. Apollo.   5. Zeus, the god of the sky, brings rain and sunshine.   6. Brother of Zeus; god of the
sea.   7. A giant, son of Poseidon.

now, go and sit beside him, grasp his knees . . .
persuade him, somehow, to help the Trojan cause,   485
to pin the Achaeans back against their ships,
trap them round the bay and mow them down.
So all can reap the benefits of their king—
so even mighty Atrides can see how mad he was
to disgrace Achilles, the best of the Achaeans!"   490

     And Thetis answered, bursting into tears,
"O my son, my sorrow, why did I ever bear you?
All I bore was doom . . .
Would to god you could linger by your ships
without a grief in the world, without a torment!   495
Doomed to a short life, you have so little time.
And not only short, now, but filled with heartbreak too,
more than all other men alive—doomed twice over.
Ah to a cruel fate I bore you in our halls!
Still, I shall go to Olympus crowned with snow   500
and repeat your prayer to Zeus who loves the lightning.
Perhaps he will be persuaded.
                              But you, my child,
stay here by the fast ships, rage on at the Achaeans,
just keep clear of every foray in the fighting.
Only yesterday Zeus went off to the Ocean River[8]   505
to feast with the Aethiopians, loyal, lordly men,
and all the gods went with him. But in twelve days
the Father returns to Olympus. Then, for your sake,
up I go to the bronze floor, the royal house of Zeus—
I'll grasp his knees, I think I'll win him over."
                              With that vow   510
his mother went away and left him there, alone,
his heart inflamed for the sashed and lovely girl
they'd wrenched away from him against his will.
Meanwhile Odysseus drew in close to Chryse Island,
bearing the splendid sacrifice in the vessel's hold.   515
And once they had entered the harbor deep in bays
they furled and stowed their sails in the black ship,
they lowered the mast by the forestays, smoothly,
quickly let it down on the forked mast-crutch
and rowed her into a mooring under oars.   520
Out went the bow-stones—cables fast astern—
and the crew themselves climbed out in the breaking surf,
leading out the sacrifice for the archer god Apollo,
and out of the deep-sea ship Chryseis stepped too.
Then tactful Odysseus led her up to the altar,   525

---

8. The river that was believed to encircle the whole world. The Aethiopians were thought to live at the
extreme edges of the world.

placing her in her loving father's arms, and said,
"Chryses, the lord of men Agamemnon sent me here
to bring you daughter back and perform a sacrifice,
a grand sacrifice to Apollo—for all Achaea's sake—
so we can appease the god   530
who's loosed such grief and torment on the Argives."

    With those words he left her in Chryses' arms
and the priest embraced the child he loved, exultant.
At once the men arranged the sacrifice for Apollo,
making the cattle ring his well-built altar,   535
then they rinsed their hands and took up barley.
Rising among them Chryses stretched his arms to the sky
and prayed in a high resounding voice, "Hear me, Apollo!
God of the silver bow who strides the walls of Chryse
and Cilla sacrosanct—lord in power of Tenedos!   540
If you honored me last time and heard my prayer
and rained destruction down on all Achaea's ranks,
now bring my prayer to pass once more. Now, at last,
drive this killing plague from the armies of Achaea!"

    His prayer went up and Phoebus Apollo heard him.   545
And soon as the men had prayed and flung the barley,
first they lifted back the heads of the victims,
slit their throats, skinned them and carved away
the meat from the thighbones and wrapped them in fat,
a double fold sliced clean and topped with strips of flesh.   550
And the old man burned these on a dried cleft stick
and over the quarters poured out glistening wine
while young men at his side held five-pronged forks.
Once they had charred the thighs and tasted the organs
they cut the rest into pieces, pierced them with spits,   555
roasted them to a turn and pulled them off the fire.
The work done, the feast laid out, they ate well
and no man's hunger lacked a share of the banquet.
When they had put aside desire for food and drink,
the young men brimmed the mixing bowls with wine   560
and tipping first drops for the god in every cup
they poured full rounds for all. And all day long
they appeased the god with song, raising a ringing hymn
to the distant archer god who drives away the plague,
those young Achaean warriors singing out his power,   565
and Apollo listened, his great heart warm with joy.

    Then when the sun went down and night came on
they made their beds and slept by the stern-cables . . .
When young Dawn with her rose-red fingers shone once more,
they set sail for the main encampment of Achaea.   570

The Archer sent them a bracing following wind,
they stepped the mast, spread white sails wide,
the wind hit full and the canvas bellied out
and a dark blue wave, foaming up at the bow,
sang out loud and strong as the ship made way,   575
skimming the whitecaps, cutting toward her goal.
And once offshore of Achaea's vast encampment
they eased her in and hauled the black ship high,
far up on the sand, and shored her up with timbers.
Then they scattered, each to his own ship and shelter.   580

But he raged on, grimly camped by his fast fleet,
the royal son of Peleus, the swift runner Achilles.
Now he no longer haunted the meeting grounds
where men win glory, now he no longer went to war
but day after day he ground his heart out, waiting there,   585
yearning, always yearning for battle cries and combat.

But now as the twelfth dawn after this shone clear
the gods who live forever marched home to Olympus,
all in a long cortege, and Zeus led them on.
And Thetis did not forget her son's appeals.   590
She broke from a cresting wave at first light
and soaring up to the broad sky and Mount Olympus,
found the son of Cronus gazing down on the world,
peaks apart from the other gods and seated high
on the topmost crown of rugged ridged Olympus.   595
And crouching down at his feet,
quickly grasping his knees with her left hand,
her right hand holding him underneath the chin,[9]
she prayed to the lord god Zeus, the son of Cronus:
"Zeus, Father Zeus! If I ever served you well   600
among the deathless gods with a word or action,
bring this prayer to pass: honor my son Achilles!—
doomed to the shortest life of any man on earth.
And now the lord of men Agamemnon has disgraced him,
seizes and keeps his prize, tears her away himself. But you—   605
exalt him, Olympian Zeus: your urgings rule the world!
Come, grant the Trojans victory after victory
till the Achaean armies pay my dear son back,
building higher the honor he deserves!"
                                     She paused
but Zeus who commands the storm clouds answered nothing.   610
The Father sat there, silent. It seemed an eternity . . .
But Thetis, clasping his knees, held on, clinging,
pressing her question once again: "Grant my prayer,

9. The posture of the suppliant, who by this physical pressure emphasized his desperation and the urgency
of the request. Zeus was above all other gods the protector of suppliants.

once and for all, Father, bow your head in assent!
Or deny me outright. What have you to fear?   615
So I may know, too well, just how cruelly
I am the most dishonored goddess of them all."
                                            Filled with anger
Zeus who marshals the storm clouds answered her at last:
"Disaster. You will drive me into war with Hera.
She will provoke me, she with her shrill abuse.   620
Even now in the face of all the immortal gods
she harries me perpetually, Hera charges *me*
that I always go to battle for the Trojans.
Away with you now. Hera might catch us here.
I will see to this. I will bring it all to pass.   625
Look, I will bow my head if that will satisfy you.
That, I remind you, that among the immortal gods
is the strongest, truest sign that I can give.
No word or work of mine—nothing can be revoked,
there is no treachery, nothing left unfinished   630
once I bow my head to say it shall be done."

    So he decreed. And Zeus the son of Cronus bowed
his craggy dark brows and the deathless locks came pouring
down from the thunderhead of the great immortal king
and giant shock waves spread through all Olympus.   635

    So the two of them made their pact and parted.
Deep in the sea she dove from radiant Mount Olympus.
Zeus went back to his own halls, and all the gods
in full assembly rose from their seats at once
to meet the Father striding toward them now.   640
None dared remain at rest as Zeus advanced,
they all sprang up to greet him face-to-face
as he took his place before them on his throne.
But Hera knew it all. She had seen how Thetis,
the Old Man of the Sea's[1] daughter, Thetis quick   645
on her glistening feet was hatching plans with Zeus.
And suddenly Hera taunted the Father, son of Cronus:
"So, who of the gods this time, my treacherous one,
was hatching plans with you?
Always your pleasure, whenever my back is turned,   650
to settle things in your grand clandestine way.
You never deign, do you, freely and frankly,
to share your plots with me—never, not a word!"

    The father of men and gods replied sharply,
"Hera—stop hoping to fathom all my thoughts.   655
You will find them a trial, though you are my wife.

1. Nereus.

Whatever is right for you to hear, no one, trust me,
will know of it before you, neither god nor man.
Whatever I choose to plan apart from all the gods—
no more of your everlasting questions, probe and pry no more."   660

    And Hera the Queen, her dark eyes wide, exclaimed,
"Dread majesty, son of Cronus, what are you saying?
Now surely I've never probed or pried in the past.
Why, you can scheme to your heart's content
without a qualm in the world for me. But now   665
I have a terrible fear that she has won you over,
Thetis, the Old Man of the Sea's daughter, Thetis
with her glistening feet. I know it. Just at dawn
she knelt down beside you and grasped your knees
and I suspect you bowed your head in assent to her—   670
you granted once and for all to exalt Achilles now
and slaughter hordes of Achaeans pinned against their ships."

    And Zeus who marshals the thunderheads returned,
"Maddening one . . . you and your eternal suspicions—
I can never escape you. Ah but tell me, Hera,   675
just what can you *do* about all this? Nothing.
Only estrange yourself from me a little more—
and all the worse for you.
If what you say is true, that must be my pleasure.
Now go sit down. Be quiet now. Obey my orders,   680
for fear the gods, however many Olympus holds,
are powerless to protect you when I come
to throttle you with my irresistible hands."

                                        He subsided
but Hera the Queen, her eyes wider, was terrified.
She sat in silence. She wrenched her will to his.   685
And throughout the halls of Zeus the gods of heaven
quaked with fear. Hephaestus[2] the Master Craftsman
rose up first to harangue them all, trying now
to bring his loving mother a little comfort,
the white-armed goddess Hera: "Oh disaster . . .   690
that's what it is, and it will be unbearable
if the two of you must come to blows this way,
flinging the gods in chaos just for mortal men.
No more joy for us in the sumptuous feast
when riot rules the day.   695
I urge you, mother—you know that I am right—
work back into his good graces, so the Father,
our beloved Father will never wheel on us again,
send our banquets crashing! The Olympian lord of lightning—

---

2. God of fire and the patron of craftspeople, especially workers in metal.

what if he would like to blast us from our seats?   700
He is far too strong. Go back to him, mother,
stroke the Father with soft, winning words—
at once the Olympian will turn kind to us again."

Pleading, springing up with a two-handled cup,
he reached it toward his loving mother's hands   705
with his own winning words: "Patience, mother!
Grieved as you are, bear up, or dear as you are,
I have to see you beaten right before my eyes.
I would be shattered—what could I do to save you?
It's hard to fight the Olympian strength for strength.   710
You remember the last time I rushed to your defense?
He grabbed my foot, he hurled me off the tremendous threshold
and all day long I dropped, I was dead weight and then,
when the sun went down, down I plunged on Lemnos,[3]
little breath left in me. But the mortals there   715
soon nursed a fallen immortal back to life."

At that the white-armed goddess Hera smiled
and smiling, took the cup from her child's hands.
Then dipping sweet nectar[4] up from the mixing bowl
he poured it round to all the immortals, left to right.   720
And uncontrollable laughter broke from the happy gods
as they watched the god of fire breathing hard
and bustling through the halls.
                              That hour then
and all day long till the sun went down they feasted
and no god's hunger lacked a share of the handsome banquet   725
or the gorgeous lyre Apollo struck or the Muses[5] singing
voice to voice in choirs, their vibrant music rising.

At last, when the sun's fiery light had set,
each immortal went to rest in his own house,
the splendid high halls Hephaestus built for each   730
with all his craft and cunning, the famous crippled Smith.
And Olympian Zeus the lord of lightning went to his own bed
where he had always lain when welcome sleep came on him.
There he climbed and there he slept and by his side
lay Hera the Queen, the goddess of the golden throne.   735

[The Greeks, in spite of Achilles' withdrawal, continued to fight. They
did not suffer immoderately from Achilles' absence; on the contrary, they
pressed the Trojans so hard that Hector, the Trojan leader, after rallying
his men, returned to the city to urge the Trojans to offer special prayers
and sacrifices to the gods.]

---

3. An island in the Aegean Sea.   4. The drink of the gods.   5. The nine Muses were goddesses of
the arts, and the source of artistic inspiration.

From BOOK VI

(Hector Returns to Troy)

          . . . And now,
when Hector reached the Scaean Gates[6] and the great oak,
the wives and daughters of Troy came rushing up around him,
asking about their sons, brothers, friends and husbands.
But Hector told them only, "Pray to the gods"—   5
all the Trojan women, one after another . . .
Hard sorrows were hanging over many.

                     And soon
he came to Priam's palace, that magnificent structure
built wide with porches and colonnades of polished stone.
And deep within its walls were fifty sleeping chambers   10
masoned in smooth, lustrous ashlar, linked in a line
where the sons of Priam slept beside their wedded wives,
and facing these, opening out across the inner courtyard,
lay the twelve sleeping chambers of Priam's daughters,
masoned and roofed in lustrous ashlar, linked in a line   15
where the sons-in-law of Priam slept beside their wives.
And there at the palace Hector's mother[7] met her son,
that warm, goodhearted woman, going in with Laodice,
the loveliest daughter Hecuba ever bred. His mother
clutched his hand and urged him, called his name: 20
"My child—why have you left the bitter fighting,
why have you come home? Look how they wear you out,
the sons of Achaea—curse them—battling round our walls!
And that's why your spirit brought you back to Troy,
to climb the heights and stretch your arms to Zeus.   25
But wait, I'll bring you some honeyed, mellow wine.
First pour out cups to Father Zeus and the other gods,
then refresh yourself, if you'd like to quench your thirst.
When a man's exhausted, wine will build his strength—
battle-weary as *you* are, fighting for your people."   30

    But Hector shook his head, his helmet flashing:
"Don't offer me mellow wine, mother, not now—
you'd sap my limbs, I'd lose my nerve for war.
And I'd be ashamed to pour a glistening cup to Zeus
with unwashed hands. I'm splattered with blood and filth—   35
how could I pray to the lord of storm and lightning?
No, mother, you are the one to pray.
Go to Athena's shrine, the queen of plunder,
go with offerings, gather the older noble women
and take a robe, the largest, loveliest robe   40
that you can find throughout the royal halls,

---

6. One of the entrances to Troy.   7. Hecuba, Priam's queen.

a gift that far and away you prize most yourself,
and spread it out across the sleek-haired goddess' knees.
Then promise to sacrifice twelve heifers in her shrine,
yearlings never broken, if only she'll pity Troy,   45
the Trojan wives and all our helpless children,
if only she'll hold Diomedes[8] back from the holy city—
that wild spearman, that invincible headlong terror!
Now, mother, go to the queen of plunder's shrine
and I'll go hunt for Paris,[9] summon him to fight   50
if the man will hear what I have to say . . . .
Let the earth gape and swallow him on the spot!
A great curse Olympian Zeus let live and grow in him,
for Troy and high-hearted Priam and all his sons.
That man—if I could see him bound for the House of Death,   55
I could say my heart had forgot its wrenching grief!"

　　But his mother simply turned away to the palace.
She gave her servants orders and out they strode
to gather the older noble women through the city.
Hecuba went down to a storeroom filled with scent   60
and there they were, brocaded, beautiful robes . . .
the work of Sidonian women. Magnificent Paris
brought those women back himself from Sidon,[1]
sailing the open seas on the same long voyage
he swept Helen off, her famous Father's child.   65
Lifting one from the lot, Hecuba brought it out
for great Athena's gift, the largest, loveliest,
richly worked, and like a star it glistened,
deep beneath the others. Then she made her way
with a file of noble women rushing in her train.   70

　　Once they reached Athena's shrine on the city crest
the beauty Theano opened the doors to let them in,
Cisseus' daughter, the horseman Antenor's wife
and Athena's priestess chosen by the Trojans. Then—
with a shrill wail they all stretched their arms to Athena   75
as Theano, her face radiant, lifting the robe on high,
spread it out across the sleek-haired goddess' knees
and prayed to the daughter of mighty Father Zeus:
"Queen Athena—shield of our city—glory of goddesses!
Now shatter the spear of Diomedes! That wild man—   80
hurl him headlong down before the Scaean Gates!
At once we'll sacrifice twelve heifers in your shrine,
yearlings never broken, if only you'll pity Troy,
the Trojan wives and all our helpless children!"

8. One of the Greek champions, who has just distinguished himself in the fighting.   9. Hector's brother.
His seduction and abduction of Helen, the wife of Menelaus, is the cause of the war.   1. Sidon was a
Phoenician city on the coast of what is now Lebanon.

But Athena refused to hear Theano's prayers.   85
And while they prayed to the daughter of mighty Zeus
Hector approached the halls of Paris, sumptuous halls
he built himself with the finest masons of the day,
master builders famed in the fertile land of Troy.
They'd raised his sleeping chamber, house and court   90
adjoining Priam's and Hector's aloft the city heights.
Now Hector, dear to Zeus, strode through the gates,
clutching a thrusting-lance eleven forearms long;
the bronze tip of the weapon shone before him,
ringed with a golden hoop to grip the shaft.   95
And there in the bedroom Hector came on Paris
polishing, fondling his splendid battle-gear,
his shield and breastplate, turning over and over
his long curved bow. And there was Helen of Argos,
sitting with all the women of the house, directing   100
the rich embroidered work they had in hand.
                                    Seeing Paris,
Hector raked his brother with insults, stinging taunts:[2]
"What on earth are you doing? Oh how wrong it is,
this anger you keep smoldering in your heart! Look,
your people dying around the city, the steep walls,   105
dying in arms—and all for you, the battle cries
and the fighting flaring up around the citadel.
You'd be the first to lash out at another—anywhere—
you saw hanging back from this, this hateful war.
                              Up with you—
before all Troy is torched to a cinder here and now!"   110

    And Paris, magnificent as a god, replied,
"Ah Hector, you criticize me fairly, yes,
nothing unfair, beyond what I deserve. And so
I will try to tell you something. Please bear with me,
hear me out. It's not so much from anger or outrage   115
at our people that I keep to my rooms so long.
I only wanted to plunge myself in grief.
But just now my wife was bringing me round,
her winning words urging me back to battle.
And it strikes me, even me, as the better way.   120
Victory shifts, you know, now one man, now another.
So come, wait while I get this war-gear on,
or you go on ahead and I will follow—
I think I can overtake you."
                         Hector, helmet flashing,
answered nothing. And Helen spoke to him now,   125

2. Paris, like Achilles, was sulking at home. He had been worsted in a duel with Menelaus, but the
goddess Aphrodite saved him from the consequences of his defeat and brought him to his house in Troy.
Paris was hated by his countrymen as the cause of the war

her soft voice welling up: "My dear brother,
dear to me, bitch that I am, vicious, scheming—
horror to freeze the heart! Oh how I wish
that first day my mother brought me into the light
some black whirlwind had rushed me out to the mountains   130
or into the surf where the roaring breakers crash and drag
and the waves had swept me off before all this had happened!
But since the gods ordained it all, these desperate years,
I wish I had been the wife of a better man, someone
alive to outrage, the withering scorn of men.   135
This one has no steadiness in his spirit,
not now, he never will . . .
and he's going to reap the fruits of it, I swear.
But come in, rest on this seat with me, dear brother.
You are the one hit hardest by the fighting, Hector,   140
you more than all—and all for me, slut that I am,
and this blind mad Paris. Oh the two of us!
Zeus planted a killing doom within us both,
so even for generations still unborn
we will live in song."
                    Turning to go,   145
his helmet flashing, tall Hector answered,
"Don't ask me to sit beside you here, Helen.
Love me as you do, you can't persuade me now.
No time for rest. My heart races to help our Trojans—
they long for me, sorely, whenever I am gone.   150
But rouse this fellow, won't you?
And let him hurry himself along as well,
so he can overtake me before I leave the city.
For I must go home to see my people first,
to visit my own dear wife and my baby son.   155
Who knows if I will ever come back to them again?—
or the deathless gods will strike me down at last
at the hands of Argive fighters."
                    A flash of his helmet
and off he strode and quickly reached his sturdy,
well-built house. But white-armed Andromache—   160
Hector could not find her in the halls.
She and the boy and a servant finely gowned
were standing watch on the tower, sobbing, grieving.
When Hector saw no sign of his loyal wife inside
he went to the doorway, stopped and asked the servants,   165
"Come, please, tell me the truth now, women.
Where's Andromache gone? To my sisters' house?
To my brothers' wives with their long flowing robes?
Or Athena's shrine where the noble Trojan women
gather to win the great grim goddess over?"   170

A busy, willing servant answered quickly,
"Hector, seeing you want to know the truth,
she hasn't gone to your sisters, brothers' wives
or Athena's shrine where the noble Trojan women
gather to win the great grim goddess over.   175
Up to the huge gate-tower of Troy she's gone
because she heard our men are so hard-pressed,
the Achaean fighters coming on in so much force.
She sped to the wall in panic, like a madwoman—
the nurse went with her, carrying your child."   180

At that, Hector spun and rushed from his house,
back by the same way down the wide, well-paved streets
throughout the city until he reached the Scaean Gates,
the last point he would pass to gain the field of battle.
There his warm, generous wife came running up to meet him,   185
Andromache the daughter of gallant-hearted Eetion
who had lived below Mount Placos rich with timber,
in Thebe below the peaks, and ruled Cilicia's people.
His daughter had married Hector helmed in bronze.
She joined him now, and following in her steps   190
a servant holding the boy against her breast,
in the first flush of life, only a baby,
Hector's son, the darling of his eyes
and radiant as a star . . .
Hector would always call the boy Scamandrius,   195
townsmen called him Astyanax,[3] Lord of the City,
since Hector was the lone defense of Troy.
The great man of war breaking into a broad smile,
his gaze fixed on his son, in silence. Andromache,
pressing close beside him and weeping freely now,   200
clung to his hand, urged him, called him: "Reckless one,
my Hector—your own fiery courage will destroy you!
Have you no pity for him, our helpless son? Or me,
and the destiny that weighs me down, your widow,
now so soon. Yes, soon they will kill you off,   205
all the Achaean forces massed for assault, and then,
bereft of you, better for me to sink beneath the earth.
What other warmth, what comfort's left for me,
once you have met your doom? Nothing but torment!
I have lost my father. Mother's gone as well.   210
Father . . . the brilliant Achilles laid him low
when he stormed Cilicia's city filled with people,
Thebe with her towering gates. He killed Eetion,
not that he stripped his gear—he'd some respect at least—
for he burned his corpse in all his blazoned bronze,   215

3. The name does literally mean "lord of the city." *Scamandrios:* After the Trojan river Scamander.

then heaped a grave-mound high above the ashes
and nymphs of the mountain planted elms around it,
daughters of Zeus whose shield is storm and thunder.
And the seven brothers I had within our halls . . .
all in the same day went down to the House of Death,   220
the great godlike runner Achilles butchered them all,
tending their shambling oxen, shining flocks.
                                        And mother,
who ruled under the timberline of woody Placos once—
he no sooner haled her here with his other plunder
than he took a priceless ransom, set her free   225
and home she went to her father's royal halls
where Artemis,[4] showering arrows, shot her down.
You, Hector—you are my father now, my noble mother,
a brother too, and you are my husband, young and warm and strong!
Pity me, please! Take your stand on the rampart here,   230
before you orphan your son and make your wife a widow.
Draw your armies up where the wild fig tree stands,
there, where the city lies most open to assault,
the walls lower, easily overrun. Three times
they have tried that point, hoping to storm Troy,   235
their best fighters led by the Great and Little Ajax,
famous Idomeneus, Atreus' sons, valiant Diomedes.
Perhaps a skilled prophet revealed the spot—
or their own fury whips them on to attack."

        And tall Hector nodded, his helmet flashing: 240
"All this weighs on my mind too, dear woman.
But I would die of shame to face the men of Troy
and the Trojan women trailing their long robes
if I would shrink from battle now, a coward.
Nor does the spirit urge me on that way.   245
I've learned it all too well. To stand up bravely,
always to fight in the front ranks of Trojan soldiers,
winning my father great glory, glory for myself.
For in my heart and soul I also know this well:
the day will come when sacred Troy must die,   250
Priam must die and all his people with him,
Priam who hurls the strong ash spear . . .
                                Even so,
it is less the pain of the Trojans still to come
that weighs me down, not even of Hecuba herself
or King Priam, or the thought that my own brothers   255
in all their numbers, all their gallant courage,
may tumble in the dust, crushed by enemies—
That is nothing, nothing beside your agony

---

4. A virgin goddess, dispenser of natural and painless death to women.

when some brazen Argive hales you off in tears,
wrenching away your day of light and freedom!   260
Then far off in the land of Argos you must live,
laboring at a loom, at another woman's beck and call,
fetching water at some spring, Messeis or Hyperia,[5]
resisting it all the way—
the rough yoke of necessity at your neck.   265
And a man may say, who sees you streaming tears,
'There is the wife of Hector, the bravest fighter
they could field, those stallion-breaking Trojans,
long ago when the men fought for Troy.' So he will say
and the fresh grief will swell your heart once more,   270
widowed, robbed of the one man strong enough
to fight off your day of slavery.
                    No, no,
let the earth come piling over my dead body
before I hear your cries, I hear you dragged away!"

    In the same breath, shining Hector reached down   275
for his son—but the boy recoiled,
cringing against his nurse's full breast,
screaming out at the sight of his own father,
terrified by the flashing bronze, the horsehair crest,
the great ridge of the helmet nodding, bristling terror—   280
so it struck his eyes. And his loving father laughed,
his mother laughed as well, and glorious Hector,
quickly lifting the helmet from his head,
set it down on the ground, fiery in the sunlight,
and raising his son he kissed him, tossed him in his arms,   285
lifting a prayer to Zeus and the other deathless gods:
"Zeus, all you immortals! Grant this boy, my son,
may be like me, first in glory among the Trojans,
strong and brave like me, and rule all Troy in power
and one day let them say, 'He is a better man than his father!'—   290
when he comes home from battle bearing the bloody gear
of the mortal enemy he has killed in war—
a joy to his mother's heart."
                    So Hector prayed
and placed his son in the arms of his loving wife.
Andromache pressed the child to her scented breast,   295
smiling through her tears. Her husband noticed,
and filled with pity now, Hector stroked her gently,
trying to reassure her, repeating her name: "Andromache,
dear one, why so desperate? Why so much grief for me?
No man will hurl me down to Death, against my fate.   300
And fate? No one alive has ever escaped it,

5. One in central, the other in northern, Greece.

neither brave man nor coward, I tell you—
it's born with us the day that we are born.
So please go home and tend to your own tasks,
the distaff and the loom, and keep the women   305
working hard as well. As for the fighting,
men will see to that, all who were born in Troy
but I most of all."
                    Hector aflash in arms
took up his horsehair-crested helmet once again.
And his loving wife went home, turning, glancing   310
back again and again and weeping live warm tears.
She quickly reached the sturdy house of Hector,
man-killing Hector,
and found her women gathered there inside
and stirred them all to a high pitch of mourning.   315
So in his house they raised the dirges for the dead,
for Hector still alive, his people were so convinced
that never again would he come home from battle,
never escape the Argives' rage and bloody hands.

    Nor did Paris linger long in his vaulted halls.   320
Soon as he buckled on his elegant gleaming bronze
he rushed through Troy, sure in his racing stride.
As a stallion full-fed at the manger, stalled too long,
breaking free of his tether gallops down the plain,
out for his favorite plunge in a river's cool currents,   325
thundering in his pride—his head flung back, his mane
streaming over his shoulders, sure and sleek in his glory,
knees racing him on to the fields and stallion-haunts he loves—
so down from Pergamus'[6] heights came Paris, son of Priam,
glittering in his armor like the sun astride the skies,   330
exultant, laughing aloud, his fast feet sped him on.
Quickly he overtook his brother, noble Hector
still lingering, slow to turn from the spot
where he had just confided in his wife . . .
Magnificent Paris spoke first: "Dear brother,   335
look at me, holding you back in all your speed—
dragging my feet, coming to you so late,
and you told me to be quick!"

    A flash of his helmet as Hector shot back,
"Impossible man! How could anyone fair and just   340
underrate your work in battle? You're a good soldier.
But you hang back of your own accord, refuse to fight.
And that, that's why the heart inside me aches

6. The citadel of Troy.

when I hear our Trojans heap contempt on you,
the men who bear such struggles all for you.
                                          Come,   345
now for attack! We'll set all this to rights,
someday, if Zeus will ever let us raise
the winebowl of freedom high in our halls,
high to the gods of cloud and sky who live forever—
once we drive these Argives geared for battle out of Troy!"   350

[The Trojans rallied successfully and went over to the offensive. They
drove the Greeks back to the light fortifications they had built around their
beached ships. The Trojans lit their watchfires on the plain, ready to deliver
the attack in the morning.]

From BOOK VIII

(The Tide of Battle Turns)

    And so their spirits soared
as they took positions down the passageways of battle
all night long, and the watchfires blazed among them.
Hundreds strong, as stars in the night sky glittering
round the moon's brilliance blaze in all their glory   5
when the air falls to a sudden, windless calm . . .
all the lookout peaks stand out and the jutting cliffs
and the steep ravines and down from the high heavens bursts
the boundless bright air and all the stars shine clear
and the shepherd's heart exults—so many fires burned   10
between the ships and the Xanthus[7] whirling rapids
set by the men of Troy, bright against their walls.
A thousand fires were burning there on the plain
and beside each fire sat fifty fighting men
poised in the leaping blaze, and champing oats   15
and glistening barley, stationed by their chariots,
stallions waited for Dawn to mount her glowing throne.

BOOK IX

The Embassy to Achilles

So the Trojans held their watch that night but not the Achaeans—
godsent Panic seized them, comrade of bloodcurdling Rout:
all their best were struck by grief too much to bear.
As crosswinds chop the sea where the fish swarm,
the North Wind and the West Wind blasting out of Thrace[8]   5
in sudden, lightning attack, wave on blacker wave, cresting,

---

7. One of the rivers of the Trojan plain.   8. The region northwest of Troy.

heaving a tangled mass of seaweed out along the surf—
so the Achaeans' hearts were torn inside their chests.

Distraught with the rising anguish, Atreus' son
went ranging back and forth, commanding heralds   10
to sound out loud and clear and call the men to muster,
each by name, but no loud outcry now. The king himself
pitched in with the lead heralds, summoning troops.
They grouped on the meeting grounds, morale broken.
Lord marshal Agamemnon rose up in their midst,   15
streaming tears like a dark spring running down
some desolate rock face, its shaded currents flowing.
So, with a deep groan, the king addressed his armies:
"Friends . . . lords of the Argives, all my captains!
Cronus' son has entangled me in madness, blinding ruin—   20
Zeus is a harsh, cruel god. He vowed to me long ago,
he bowed his head that I should never embark for home
till I had brought the walls of Ilium crashing down.
But now, I see, he only plotted brutal treachery:
now he commands me back to Argos in disgrace,   25
whole regiments of my men destroyed in battle.
So it must please his overweening heart, who knows?
Father Zeus has lopped the crowns of a thousand cities,
true, and Zeus will lop still more—his power is too great.
So come, follow my orders. Obey me, all you Argives.   30
Cut and run! Sail home to the fatherland we love!
We'll never take the broad streets of Troy."

Silence held them all, struck dumb by his orders.
A long while they said nothing, spirits dashed.
Finally Diomedes lord of the war cry broke forth: 35
"Atrides—I will be first to oppose you in your folly,
here in assembly, King, where it's the custom.
Spare me your anger. My courage—
mine was the first you mocked among the Argives,
branding me a coward, a poor soldier.[9] Yes, well,   40
they know all about that, the Argives young and old.
But you—the son of Cronus with Cronus' twisting ways
gave you gifts by halves: with that royal scepter
the Father gave you honor beyond all other men alive
but he never gave you courage, the greatest power of all.   45
Desperate man! So certain, are you, the sons of Achaea
are cowards, poor soldiers, just because you say so?
Desert—if your spirit drives you to sail home,
then sail away, my King! The sea-lanes are clear,
there are your ships of war, crowded down the surf,   50

9. This happened during Agamemnon's review of his forces before the battle.

those that followed you from Mycenae,[1] your own proud armada.
But the rest of the long-haired Achaeans will hold out,
right here, until we've plundered Troy. And they,
if they go running home to the land they love,
then the two of us, I and Sthenelus[2] here   55
will fight our way to the fixed doom of Troy.
Never forget—we all sailed here with god."

    And all the Achaeans shouted their assent,
stirred by the stallion-breaking Diomedes' challenge.
But Nestor the old driver rose and spoke at once: 60
"Few can match your power in battle, Diomedes,
and in council you excel all men your age.
So no one could make light of your proposals,
not the whole army—who could contradict you?
But you don't press on and reach a useful end.   65
How young you are . . . why, you could be my son,
my youngest-born at that, though you urge our kings
with cool clear sense: what you've said is right.
But it's my turn now, Diomedes.
I think I can claim to have some years on you.   70
So I *must* speak up and drive the matter home.
And no one will heap contempt on what I say,
not even mighty Agamemnon. Lost to the clan,
lost to the hearth, lost to the old ways, that one
who lusts for all the horrors of war with his own people.   75
But now, I say, let us give way to the dark night,
set out the evening meal. Sentries take up posts,
squads fronting the trench we dug outside the rampart.[3]
That's the command I give the younger fighters.
                                 Then,
Atrides, lead the way—you are the greatest king—   80
spread out a feast for all your senior chiefs.
That is your duty, a service that becomes you.
Your shelters overflow with the wine Achaean ships
bring in from Thrace, daily, down the sea's broad back.
Grand hospitality is yours, you rule so many men.   85
Come, gather us all and we will heed that man
who gives the best advice. That's what they need,
I tell you—all the Achaeans—good sound advice,
now our enemies, camping hard against the ships,
kindle their watchfires round us by the thousands.   90
What soldier could warm to that? Tonight's the night
that rips our ranks to shreds or pulls us through."

---

1. A city near Argos.   2. The companion of Diomedes.   3. The Greeks are now besieged beside their
ships; Zeus's promise to Thetis is being fulfilled.

The troops hung on his words and took his orders.
Out they rushed, the sentries in armor, forming
under the son of Nestor, captain Thrasymedes,   95
under Ascalaphus, Ialmenus, sons of Ares,[4]
under Meriones, Aphareus and Deipyrus,
under the son of Creon, trusty Lycomedes.
Seven chiefs of the guard, a hundred under each,
fighters marching, grasping long spears in their hands,   100
took up new positions between the trench and rampart.
There they lit their fires, each man made his meal.

Meanwhile marshal Agamemnon led his commanders,
a file of senior chiefs, toward his own lodge
and set before them a feast to please their hearts.   105
They reached out for the good things that lay at hand
but when they had put aside desire for food and drink
the old man began to weave his counsel among them:
Nestor was first to speak—from the early days
his plans and tactics always seemed the best.   110
With good will to the chiefs he rose and spoke,
"Great marshal Atrides, lord of men Agamemnon . . .
with you I will end, my King, with you I will begin,
since you hold sway over many warriors, vast armies,
and Zeus has placed in your hands the royal scepter   115
and time-honored laws, so you will advise them well.
So you above all must speak your mind, and listen,
and carry out the next man's counsel too,
whenever his spirit leads him on to speak
for the public good. Credit will go to you   120
for whatever he proposes.
Now I will tell you what seems best to me.
No one will offer a better plan than this . . .
the plan I still retain, and I've been forming,
well, for a good long while now, from the very day   125
that you, my illustrious King, infuriated Achilles—
you went and took from his tents the girl Briseis,
and not with any applause from us, far from it:
I for one, I urged you against it, strenuously.
But you, you gave way to your overbearing anger,   130
disgraced a great man the gods themselves esteem—
you seized his gift of honor and keep her still.
But even so, late as it is, let us contrive
to set all this to rights, to bring him round
with gifts of friendship and warm, winning words."   135

4. God of war.

And Agamemnon the lord of men consented quickly:
"That's no lie, old man—a full account you give
of all my acts of madness. Mad, blind I was!
Not even I would deny it.
Why look, that man is worth an entire army,   140
the fighter Zeus holds dear with all his heart—
how he exalts him now and mauls Achaea's forces!
But since I *was* blinded, lost in my own inhuman rage,
now, at last, I am bent on setting things to rights:
I'll give a priceless ransom paid for friendship.
                                                    Here,   145
before you all, I'll name in full the splendid gifts I offer.
Seven tripods[5] never touched by fire, ten bars of gold,
twenty burnished cauldrons, a dozen massive stallions,
racers who earned me trophies with their speed.
He is no poor man who owns what they have won,   150
not strapped for goods with all that lovely gold—
what trophies those high-strung horses carried off for me!
Seven women I'll give him, flawless, skilled in crafts,
women of Lesbos[6]—the ones I chose, my privilege,
that day he captured the Lesbos citadel himself: 155
they outclassed the tribes of women in their beauty.
These I will give, and along with them will go
the one I took away at first, Briseus' daughter,
and I will swear a solemn, binding oath in the bargain:
I never mounted her bed, never once made love with her—   160
the natural thing for mankind, men and women joined.
Now all these gifts will be handed him at once.
But if, later, the gods allow us to plunder
the great city of Priam, let him enter in
when we share the spoils, load the holds of his ship   165
with gold and bronze—as much as his heart desires—
and choose for his pleasure twenty Trojan women
second only to Argive Helen in their glory.
And then, if we can journey home to Achaean Argos,
pride of the breasting earth, he'll be my son-by-marriage!   170
I will even honor him on a par with my Orestes,
full-grown by now, reared in the lap of luxury.
Three daughters are mine in my well-built halls—
Chrysothemis and Laodice and Iphianassa—
and he may lead away whichever one he likes,   175
with no bride-price asked, home to Peleus' house.
And I will add a dowry, yes, a magnificent treasure
the likes of which no man has ever offered with his daughter!
Seven citadels I will give him, filled with people,

---

5. Three-footed kettles; such metal equipment was rare and highly valued.   6. A large island off the coast of what is now Turkey.

Cardamyle, Enope, and the grassy slopes of Hire,   180
Pherae the sacrosanct, Anthea deep in meadows,
rolling Aepea and Pedasus green with vineyards.
All face the sea at the far edge of sandy Pylos
and the men who live within them, rich in sheep-flocks,
rich in shambling cattle, will honor him like a god   185
with hoards of gifts and beneath his scepter's sway
live out his laws in sleek and shining peace.
                                                    All this—
I would extend to him if he will end his anger.
Let him submit to me! Only the god of death[7]
is so relentless, Death submits to no one—   190
so mortals hate him most of all the gods.
Let him bow down to me! I am the greater king,
I am the elder-born, I claim—the greater man."

     Nestor the noble charioteer embraced his offer:
"Generous marshal Atrides, lord of men Agamemnon!   195
No one could underrate these gifts of yours, not now,
the treasure trove you offer Prince Achilles.
Come—we'll send a detail of picked men.
They'll go to Achilles' tent with all good speed.
Quick, whomever my eye will light on in review,   200
the mission's theirs. And old Phoenix[8] first—
Zeus loves the man, so let him lead the way.
Then giant Ajax and tactful royal Odysseus.
Heralds? Odius and Eurybates, you escort them.
Water for their hands! A reverent silence now . . .   205
a prayer to Zeus. Perhaps he'll show us mercy."

     The brisk commands he issued pleased them all.
Heralds brought the water at once and rinsed their hands,
and the young men brimmed the mixing bowls with wine
and tipping first drops for the god in every cup   210
they poured full rounds for all. Libations finished,
each envoy having drunk to his heart's content,
the party moved out from Atrides' shelters.
Nestor the old driver gave them marching orders—
a sharp glance at each, Odysseus most of all: 215
"Try hard now, bring him round—invincible Achilles!"

     So Ajax and Odysseus made their way at once
where the battle lines of breakers crash and drag,
praying hard to the god who moves and shakes the earth[9]
that they might bring the proud heart of Achilles   220
round with speed and ease.

---

7. Hades.   8. He is especially suited for this embassy since he was tutor to the young Achilles.
9. Poseidon, who was believed to be responsible for earthquakes.

Reaching the Myrmidon shelters and their ships,
they found him there, delighting his heart now,
plucking strong and clear on the fine lyre—
beautifully carved, its silver bridge set firm—   225
he won from the spoils when he razed Eetion's city.
Achilles was lifting his spirits with it now,
singing the famous deeds of fighting heroes . . .
Across from him Patroclus sat alone, in silence,
waiting for Aeacus' son to finish with his song.   230
And on they came, with good Odysseus in the lead,
and the envoys stood before him. Achilles, startled,
sprang to his feet, the lyre still in his hands,
leaving the seat where he had sat in peace.
And seeing the men, Patroclus rose up too   235
as the famous runner called and waved them on:
"Welcome! Look, dear friends have come our way—
I must be sorely needed now—my dearest friends
in all the Achaean armies, even in my anger."

So Prince Achilles hailed and led them in,   240
sat them down on settles with purple carpets
and quickly told Patroclus standing by, "Come,
a bigger winebowl, son of Menoetius, set it here.
Mix stronger wine. A cup for the hands of each guest—
here beneath my roof are the men I love the most."   245

He paused. Patroclus obeyed his great friend,
who put down a heavy chopping block in the firelight
and across it laid a sheep's chine, a fat goat's
and the long back cut of a full-grown pig,
marbled with lard. Automedon[1] held the meats   250
while lordly Achilles carved them into quarters,
cut them well into pieces, pierced them with spits
and Patroclus raked the hearth, a man like a god
making the fire blaze. Once it had burned down
and the flames died away, he scattered the coals   255
and stretching the spitted meats across the embers,
raised them onto supports and sprinkled clean pure salt.
As soon as the roasts were done and spread on platters,
Patroclus brought the bread, set it out on the board
in ample wicker baskets. Achilles served the meat.   260
Then face-to-face with his noble guest Odysseus
he took his seat along the farther wall,
he told his friend to sacrifice to the gods
and Patroclus threw the first cuts[2] in the fire.
They reached out for the good things that lay at hand   265

1. Achilles' charioteer.   2. The portion of the meat reserved for the gods.

and when they had put aside desire for food and drink,
Ajax nodded to Phoenix. Odysseus caught the signal,
filled his cup and lifted it toward Achilles,
opening with this toast: "Your health, Achilles!
We have no lack of a handsome feast, I see that,   270
either in Agamemnon's tents, the son of Atreus,
or here and now, in yours. We can all banquet here
to our heart's content.
                              But it's not the flowing feast
that is on our minds now—no, a stark disaster,
too much to bear, Achilles bred by the gods,   275
that is what we are staring in the face
and we are afraid. All hangs in the balance now:
whether we save our benched ships or they're destroyed,
unless, of course, you put your fighting power in harness.
They have pitched camp right at our ships and rampart,   280
those brazen Trojans, they and their far-famed allies,
thousands of fires blaze throughout their armies . . .
Nothing can stop them now—that's their boast—
they'll hurl themselves against our blackened hulls.
And the son of Cronus sends them signs on the right,   285
Zeus's firebolts flashing. And headlong Hector,
delirious with his strength, rages uncontrollably,
trusting to Zeus—no fear of man or god, nothing—
a powerful rabid frenzy has him in its grip!
Hector prays for the sacred Dawn to break at once,   290
he threatens to lop the high horns of our sterns
and gut our ships with fire, and all our comrades
pinned against the hulls, panicked by thick smoke,
he'll rout and kill in blood!
A nightmare—I fear it, with all my heart—   295
I fear the gods will carry out his threats
and then it will be our fate to die in Troy,
far from the stallion-land of Argos . . .
                              Up with you—
now, late as it is, if you *want* to pull our Argives,
our hard-hit armies, clear of the Trojan onslaught.   300
Fail us now? What a grief it will be to you
through all the years to come. No remedy,
no way to cure the damage once it's done.
Come, while there's still time, think hard:
how can you fight off the Argives' fatal day?   305
Oh old friend, surely your father Peleus urged you,
that day he sent you out of Phthia to Agamemnon,
'My son, victory is what Athena and Hera will give,
if they so choose. But you, you hold in check
that proud, fiery spirit of yours inside your chest!   310

Friendship is much better. Vicious quarrels are deadly—
put an end to them, at once. Your Achaean comrades,
young and old, will exalt you all the more.'
That was your aged father's parting advice.
It must have slipped your mind.
                                            But now at last,   315
stop, Achilles—let your heart-devouring anger go!
The king will hand you gifts to match his insults
if only you'll relent and end your anger . . .
So come then, listen, as I count out the gifts,
the troves in his tents that Agamemnon vows to give you.   320
Seven tripods never touched by fire, ten bars of gold,
twenty burnished cauldrons, a dozen massive stallions,
racers who earned him trophies with their speed.
He is no poor man who owns what they have won,
not strapped for goods with all that lovely gold—   325
what trophies those high-strung horses carried off for him!
Seven women he'll give you, flawless, skilled in crafts,
women of Lesbos—the ones he chose, his privilege,
that day you captured the Lesbos citadel yourself:
they outclassed the tribes of women in their beauty.   330
These he will give, and along with them will go
the one he took away at first, Briseus' daughter,
and he will swear a solemn, binding oath in the bargain:
he never mounted her bed, never once made love with her . . .
the natural thing, my lord, men and women joined.   335
Now all these gifts will be handed you at once.
But if, later, the gods allow us to plunder
the great city of Priam, you shall enter in
when we share the spoils, load the holds of your ship
with gold and bronze—as much as your heart desires—   340
and choose for your pleasure twenty Trojan women
second only to Argive Helen in their glory.
And then, if we can journey home to Achaean Argos,
pride of the breasting earth, you'll be his son-by-marriage . . .
He will even honor you on a par with his Orestes,   345
full-grown by now, reared in the lap of luxury.
Three daughters are his in his well-built halls,
Chrysothemis and Laodice and Iphianassa—
and you may lead away whichever one you like,
with no bride-price asked, home to Peleus' house.   350
And he will add a dowry, yes, a magnificent treasure
the likes of which no man has ever offered with his daughter . . .
Seven citadels he will give you, filled with people,
Cardamyle, Enope, and the grassy slopes of Hire,
Pherae the sacrosanct, Anthea deep in meadows,   355
rolling Aepea and Pedasus green with vineyards.

All face the sea at the far edge of sandy Pylos
and the men who live within them, rich in sheep-flocks,
rich in shambling cattle, will honor you like a god
with hoards of gifts and beneath your scepter's sway   360
live out your laws in sleek and shining peace.
                                    All this . . .
he would extend to you if you will end your anger.
But if you hate the son of Atreus all the more,
him and his troves of gifts, at least take pity
on all our united forces mauled in battle here—   365
they will honor you, honor you like a god.
Think of the glory you will gather in their eyes!
Now you can kill Hector—seized with murderous frenzy,
certain there's not a single fighter his equal,
no Achaean brought to Troy in the ships—   370
now, for once, you can meet the man head-on!"

   The famous runner Achilles rose to his challenge:
"Royal son of Laertes, Odysseus, great tactician . . .
I must say what I have to say straight out,
must tell you how I feel and how all this will end—   375
so you won't crowd around me, one after another,
coaxing like a murmuring clutch of doves.
I hate that man like the very Gates of Death
who says one thing but hides another in his heart.
I will say it outright. That seems best to me.   380
Will Agamemnon win me over? Not for all the world,
I swear it—nor will the rest of the Achaeans.
No, what lasting thanks in the long run
for warring with our enemies, on and on, no end?
One and the same lot for the man who hangs back   385
and the man who battles hard. The same honor waits
for the coward and the brave. They both go down to Death,
the fighter who shirks, the one who works to exhaustion.
And what's laid up for me, what pittance? Nothing—
and after suffering hardships, year in, year out,   390
staking my life on the mortal risks of war.

   Like a mother bird hurrying morsels back
to her wingless young ones—whatever she can catch—
but it's all starvation wages for herself.
                                    So for me.
Many a sleepless night I've bivouacked in harness,   395
day after bloody day I've hacked my passage through,
fighting other soldiers to win their wives as prizes.
Twelve cities of men I've stormed and sacked from shipboard,
eleven I claim by land, on the fertile earth of Troy.
And from all I dragged off piles of splendid plunder,   400

hauled it away and always gave the lot to Agamemnon,
that son of Atreus—always skulking behind the lines,
safe in his fast ships—and he would take it all,
he'd parcel out some scraps but keep the lion's share.
Some he'd hand to the lords and kings—prizes of honor—   405
and they, they hold them still. From me alone, Achilles
of all Achaeans, he seizes, he keeps the wife I love . . .
Well *let* him bed her now—
enjoy her to the hilt!
                              Why must we battle Trojans,
men of Argos? Why did he muster an army, lead us here,   410
that son of Atreus? Why, why in the world if not
for Helen with her loose and lustrous hair?
Are *they* the only men alive who love their wives,
those sons of Atreus? Never! Any decent man,
a man with sense, loves his own, cares for his own   415
as deeply as I, I loved that woman with all my heart,
though I won her like a trophy with my spear . . .
But now that he's torn my honor from my hands,
robbed me, lied to me—don't let him try me now.
I know *him* too well—he'll never win me over!
                                        No, Odysseus,   420
let him rack his brains with you and the other captains
how to fight the raging fire off the ships. Look—
what a mighty piece of work he's done without *me*!
Why, he's erected a rampart, driven a trench around it,
broad, enormous, and planted stakes to guard it. No use!   425
He still can't block the power of man-killing Hector!
No, though as long as *I* fought on Achaea's lines
Hector had little lust to charge beyond his walls,
never ventured beyond the Scaean Gates and oak tree.
There he stood up to me alone one day—   430
and barely escaped my onslaught.
                              Ah but now,
since I have no desire to battle glorious Hector,
tomorrow at daybreak, once I have sacrificed
to Zeus and all the gods and loaded up my holds
and launched out on the breakers—watch, my friend,   435
if you'll take the time and care to see me off,
and you will see my squadrons sail at dawn,
fanning out on the Hellespont that swarms with fish,
my crews manning the oarlocks, rowing out with a will,
and if the famed god of the earthquake grants us safe passage,   440
the third day out we raise the dark rich soil of Phthia.
There lies my wealth, hoards of it, all I left behind
when I sailed to Troy on this, this insane voyage—
and still more hoards from here: gold, ruddy bronze,

women sashed and lovely, and gleaming gray iron,   445
and I will haul it home, all I won as plunder.
All but my prize of honor . . .
he who gave that prize has snatched it back again—
what outrage! That high and mighty King Agamemnon,
that son of Atreus!

           Go back and tell him all,   450
all I say—out in the open too—so other Achaeans
can wheel on him in anger if he still hopes—
who knows?—to deceive some other comrade.

                                   Shameless,
inveterate—armored in shamelessness! Dog that he is,
he'd never dare to look me straight in the eyes again.   455
No, I'll never set heads together with that man—
no planning in common, no taking common action.
He cheated me, did me damage, wrong! But never again,
he'll never rob me blind with his twisting words again!
Once is enough for him. Die and be damned for all I care!   460
Zeus who rules the world has ripped his wits away.
His gifts, I loathe his gifts . . .
I wouldn't give you a splinter for that man!
Not if he gave me ten times as much, twenty times over, all
he possesses now, and all that could pour in from the world's end—   465
not all the wealth that's freighted into Orchomenos,[3] even into Thebes,
Egyptian Thebes where the houses overflow with the greatest troves of
    treasure,
Thebes with the hundred gates and through each gate battalions,
two hundred fighters surge to war with teams and chariots—
no, not if his gifts outnumbered all the grains of sand   470
and dust in the earth—no, not even then could Agamemnon
bring my fighting spirit round until he pays me back,
pays full measure for all his heartbreaking outrage!

           His daughter . . . I will marry no daughter of Agamemnon.
Not if she rivaled Aphrodite in all her golden glory,   475
not if she matched the crafts of clear-eyed Athena,
not even then would I make her my wife! No,
let her father pitch on some other Argive—
one who can please him, a greater king than I.
If the gods pull me through and I reach home alive,   480
Peleus needs no help to fetch a bride for me himself.
Plenty of Argive women wait in Hellas and in Phthia
daughters of lords who rule their citadels in power.
Whomever I want I'll make my cherished wife—at home.
Time and again my fiery spirit drove me to win a wife,   485
a fine partner to please my heart, to enjoy with her

---

3. Great city north of Athens.

the treasures my old father Peleus piled high.
I say no wealth is worth my life! Not all they claim
was stored in the depths of Troy, that city built on riches,
in the old days of peace before the sons of Achaea came—   490
not all the gold held fast in the Archer's rocky vaults,
in Phoebus Apollo's house on Pytho's[4] sheer cliffs!
Cattle and fat sheep can all be had for the raiding,
tripods all for the trading, and tawny-headed stallions.
But a man's life breath cannot come back again—   495
no raiders in force, no trading brings it back,
once it slips through a man's clenched teeth.
                                        Mother tells me,
the immortal goddess Thetis with her glistening feet,
that two fates bear me on to the day of death.
If I hold out here and I lay siege to Troy,   500
my journey home is gone, but my glory never dies.
If I voyage back to the fatherland I love,
my pride, my glory dies . . .
true, but the life that's left me will be long,
the stroke of death will not come on me quickly.   505

   One thing more. To the rest I'd pass on this advice:
sail home now! You will never set your eyes
on the day of doom that topples looming Troy.
Thundering Zeus has spread his hands above her—
her armies have taken heart!
                                        So you go back   510
to the great men of Achaea. You report my message—
since this is the privilege of senior chiefs—
let *them* work out a better plan of action,
use their imaginations now to save the ships
and Achaea's armies pressed to their hollow hulls.   515
This maneuver will never work for them, this scheme
they hatched for the moment as I raged on and on.
But Phoenix can stay and rest the night with us,
so he can voyage home, home in the ships with me
to the fatherland we love. Tomorrow at dawn.   520
But only if Phoenix wishes.
I will never force the man to go."
                                        He stopped.
A stunned silence seized them all, struck dumb—
Achilles' ringing denials overwhelmed them so.
At last Phoenix the old charioteer spoke out,   525
he burst into tears, terrified for Achaea's fleet:
"Sail home? Is *that* what you're turning over in your mind,
my glorious one, Achilles? Have you no heart at all

4. Apollo's shrine at Delphi. The treasures consisted of offerings made to the god by grateful worshipers.

to fight the gutting fire from the fast trim ships?
The spirit inside you overpowered by anger!   530
How could I be severed from you, dear boy,
left behind on the beachhead here—alone?
The old horseman Peleus had me escort you,
that day he sent you out of Phthia to Agamemnon,
a youngster still untrained for the great leveler, war,   535
still green at debate where men can make their mark.
So he dispatched me, to teach you all these things,
to make you a man of words and a man of action too.
Cut off from you with a charge like that, dear boy?
I have no heart to be left behind, not even   540
if Zeus himself would swear to scrape away
the scurf of age and make me young again . . .
As fresh as I was that time I first set out
from Hellas where the women are a wonder,
fleeing a blood feud with my father, Amyntor,   545
Ormenus' son. How furious father was with me,
over his mistress with her dark, glistening hair.
How he would dote on her and spurn his wedded wife,
my own mother! And time and again she begged me,
hugging my knees, to bed my father's mistress down   550
and kill the young girl's taste for an old man.
Mother—I did your bidding, did my work . . .
But father, suspecting at once, cursed me roundly,
he screamed out to the cruel Furies[5]—'Never,
never let me bounce on my knees a son of his,   555
sprung of his loins!'—and the gods drove home that curse,
mighty Zeus of the Underworld[6] and grim Persephone.
So I, I took it into my head to lay him low
with sharp bronze! But a god checked my anger,
he warned me of what the whole realm would say,   560
the loose talk of the people, rough slurs of men—
they must not call me a father-killer, our Achaeans!
Then nothing could keep me there, my blood so fired up.
No more strolling about the halls with father raging.
But there was a crowd of kin and cousins round me,   565
holding me in the house, begging me to stay . . .
they butchered plenty of fat sheep, banquet fare,
and shambling crook-horned cattle, droves of pigs,
succulent, rich with fat—they singed the bristles,
splaying the porkers out across Hephaestus' fire,   570
then wine from the old man's jars, all we could drink.
Nine nights they passed the hours, hovering over me,
keeping the watch by rounds. The fires never died,

5. Avenging spirits, particularly concerned with crimes committed by kin against kin.   6. The god
Hades. *Persephone:* Wife of Hades.

one ablaze in the colonnade of the walled court,
one in the porch outside my bedroom doors.
                                      But then,   575
when the tenth night came on me, black as pitch,
I burst the doors of the chamber bolted tight
and out I rushed, I leapt the walls at a bound,
giving the slip to guards and women servants.
And away I fled through the whole expanse of Hellas   580
and gaining the good dark soil of Phthia, mother of flocks,
I reached the king, and Peleus gave me a royal welcome.
Peleus loved me as a father loves a son, I tell you,
his only child, the heir to his boundless wealth,
he made me a rich man, he gave me throngs of subjects,   585
I ruled the Dolopes, settling down on Phthia's west frontier.
And I made you what you are—strong as the gods, Achilles—
I loved you from the heart. You'd never go with another
to banquet on the town or feast in your own halls.
Never, until I'd sat you down on my knees   590
and cut you the first bits of meat, remember?
You'd eat your fill, I'd hold the cup to your lips
and all too often you soaked the shirt on my chest,
spitting up some wine, a baby's way . . . a misery.
Oh I had my share of troubles for you, Achilles,   595
did my share of labor. Brooding, never forgetting
the gods would bring no son of mine to birth,
not from my own loins.
                        So you, Achilles—
great godlike Achilles—I made you my son, I tried,
so someday *you* might fight disaster off my back.   600
But now, Achilles, beat down your mounting fury!
It's wrong to have such an iron, ruthless heart.
Even the gods themselves can bend and change,
and theirs is the greater power, honor, strength.
Even the gods, I say, with incense, soothing vows,   605
with full cups poured and the deep smoky savor
men can bring them round, begging for pardon
when one oversteps the mark, does something wrong.
We do have Prayers, you know, Prayers for forgiveness,
daughters of mighty Zeus . . . and they limp and halt,   610
they're all wrinkled, drawn, they squint to the side,
can't look you in the eyes, and always bent on duty,
trudging after Ruin, maddening, blinding Ruin.
But Ruin is strong and swift—
She outstrips them all by far, stealing a march,   615
leaping over the whole wide earth to bring mankind to grief.
And the Prayers trail after, trying to heal the wounds.
And then, if a man reveres these daughters of Zeus

as they draw near him, they will help him greatly
and listen to his appeals. But if one denies them,   620
turns them away, stiff-necked and harsh—off they go
to the son of Cronus, Zeus, and pray that Ruin
will strike the man down, crazed and blinded
until he's paid the price.
                Relent, Achilles—you too!
See that honor attend these good daughters of Zeus,   625
honor that sways the minds of others, even heroes.
If Agamemnon were not holding out such gifts,
with talk of more to come, that son of Atreus,
if the warlord kept on blustering in his anger, why,
I'd be the last to tell you, 'Cast your rage to the winds!   630
Defend your friends!'—despite their desperate straits.
But now, look, he gives you a trove of treasures
right away, and vows there are more to follow.
He sends the bravest captains to implore you,
leaders picked from the whole Achaean army,   635
comrades-in-arms that you love most yourself.
Don't dismiss their appeal, their expedition here—
though no one could blame your anger, not before.
So it was in the old days too. So we've heard
in the famous deeds of fighting men, of heroes,   640
when seething anger would overcome the great ones.
Still you could bring them round with gifts and winning words.
There's an old tale I remember, an ancient exploit,
nothing recent, but this is how it went . . .
We are all friends here—let me tell it now.   645

    The Curetes were fighting the combat-hard Aetolians,
armies ringing Calydon,[7] slaughtering each other,
Aetolians defending their city's handsome walls
and Curetes primed to lay them waste in battle.
It all began when Artemis throned in gold   650
loosed a disaster on them, incensed that Oeneus[8]
offered her no first fruits, his orchard's crowning glory.
The rest of the gods had feasted full on oxen, true,
but the Huntress alone, almighty Zeus's daughter—
Oeneus gave her nothing. It slipped his mind   655
or he failed to care, but what a fatal error!
How she fumed, Zeus's child who showers arrows,
she loosed a bristling wild boar, his tusks gleaming,
crashing his savage, monstrous way through Oeneus' orchard,
ripping up whole trunks from the earth to pitch them headlong,   660
rows of them, roots and all, appleblossoms and all!

7. A city in northwestern Greece. The Curetes and Aetolians were the local tribes, once allied, now at odds.
8. King of Calydon.

But the son of Oeneus, Meleager, cut him down—
mustering hunters out of a dozen cities,
packs of hounds as well. No slim band of men
could ever finish him off, that rippling killer,   665
he stacked so many men atop the tear-soaked pyre.
But over his body the goddess raised a terrific din,
a war for the prize, the huge beast's head and shaggy hide—
Curetes locked to the death with brave Aetolians.
                                        Now,
so long as the battle-hungry Meleager fought,   670
it was deadly going for the Curetes. No hope
of holding their ground outside their *own* city walls,
despite superior numbers. But then, when the wrath
came sweeping over the man, the same anger that swells
the chests of others, for all their care and self-control—   675
then, heart enraged at his own dear mother Althaea,
Meleager kept to his bed beside his wedded wife,
Cleopatra . . . that great beauty. Remember her?
The daughter of trim-heeled Marpessa,[9] Euenus' child,
and her husband Idas, strongest man of the men   680
who once walked the earth—he even braved Apollo,
he drew his bow at the Archer, all for Marpessa
the girl with lovely ankles. There in the halls
her father and mother always called Cleopatra Halcyon,
after the seabird's name . . . grieving once for her own fate   685
her mother had raised the halcyon's thin, painful cry,
wailing that lord Apollo the distant deadly Archer
had whisked her[1] far from Idas.
                        Meleager's Cleopatra—
she was the one he lay beside those days,
brooding over his heartbreaking anger.   690
He was enraged by the curses of his mother,
volleys of curses she called down from the gods.
So racked with grief for her brother he had killed[2]
she kept pounding fists on the earth that feeds us all,
kept crying out to the god of death and grim Persephone,   695
flung herself on the ground, tears streaking her robes
and she screamed out, 'Kill Meleager, kill my son!'
And out of the world of darkness a Fury[3] heard her cries,
stalking the night with a Fury's brutal heart, and suddenly—
thunder breaking around the gates, the roar of enemies,   700

9. The story to which Homer alludes runs as follows: Idas, the famous archer, carried off and married
Marpessa, daughter of Euenys. Apollo also had been her suitor, and he overtook Idas and carried off
Marpessa. Idas defied Apollo to combat, but Zeus decided that the choice was up to Marpessa, who
preferred Idas. They gave their daughter Cleopatra the nickname Halcyon, the name of a sea-bird that is
supposed to mourn for its mate, to commemorate the time when Marpessa, carried off by Apollo, mourned
for Idas.   1. Marpessa.   2. In the course of the battles Meleager had killed one of his mother's brothers.   3. The personified spirit of vengeance.

towers battered under assault. And Aetolia's elders
begged Meleager, sent high priests of the gods,
pleading, 'Come out now! defend your people now!'—
and they vowed a princely gift.
Wherever the richest land of green Calydon lay,   705
there they urged him to choose a grand estate,
full fifty acres, half of it turned to vineyards,
half to open plowland, and carve it from the plain.
And over and over the old horseman Oeneus begged him,
he took a stand at the vaulted chamber's threshold,   710
shaking the bolted doors, begging his own son!
Over and over his brothers and noble mother
implored him—he refused them all the more—
and troops of comrades, devoted, dearest friends.
Not even they could bring his fighting spirit round   715
until, at last, rocks were raining down on the chamber,
Curetes about to mount the towers and torch the great city!
And then, finally, Meleager's bride, beautiful Cleopatra
begged him, streaming tears, recounting all the griefs
that fall to people whose city's seized and plundered—   720
the men slaughtered, citadel burned to rubble, enemies
dragging the children, raping the sashed and lovely women.
How his spirit leapt when he heard those horrors—
and buckling his gleaming armor round his body,
out he rushed to war. And so he saved them all   725
from the fatal day, he gave way to his own feelings,
but too late. No longer would they make good the gifts,
those troves of gifts to warm his heart, and even so
he beat off that disaster . . . empty-handed.

    But you, you wipe such thoughts from your mind.   730
Don't let your spirit turn you down that path, dear boy.
Harder to save the warships once they're up in flames.
Now—while the gifts still wait—go out and fight!
Go—the Achaeans all will honor you like a god!
But enter this man-killing war without the gifts—   735
your fame will flag, no longer the same honor,
even though you hurl the Trojans home!"

    But the swift runner Achilles answered firmly,
"Phoenix, old father, bred and loved by the gods,
what do I need with honor such as that?   740
I say my honor lies in the great decree of Zeus.
That gift will hold me here by the beaked ships
as long as the life breath remains inside my chest
and my springing knees will lift me. Another thing—
take it to heart, I urge you. Stop confusing   745
my fixed resolve with this, this weeping and wailing

just to serve his pleasure, Atreus' mighty son.
It degrades you to curry favor with that man,
and I will hate you for it, I who love you.
It does you proud to stand by me, my friend,   750
to attack the man who attacks me—
be king on a par with me, take half my honors!
These men will carry their message back, but you,
you stay here and spend the night in a soft bed.
Then, tomorrow at first light, we will decide   755
whether we sail home or hold out here."
                                        With that,
he gave Patroclus a sharp glance, a quiet nod
to pile the bedding deep for Phoenix now,
a sign to the rest to think of leaving quickly.
Giant Ajax rose to his feet, the son of Telamon,   760
tall as a god, turned and broke his silence:
"Ready, Odysseus? Royal son of Laertes,
great tactician—come, home we go now.
There's no achieving our mission here, I see,
not with this approach. Best to return at once,   765
give the Achaeans a full report, defeating as it is.
They must be sitting there, waiting for us now.
                                        Achilles—
he's made his own proud spirit so wild in his chest,
so savage, not a thought for his comrades' love—
we honored him past all others by the ships.   770
Hard, ruthless man . . .
Why, any man will accept the blood-price paid
for a brother murdered, a child done to death.
And the murderer lives on in his own country—
the man has paid enough, and the injured kinsman   775
curbs his pride, his smoldering, vengeful spirit,
once he takes the price.
                          You—the gods have planted
a cruel, relentless fury in your chest! All for a girl,
just one, and here we offer you seven—outstanding beauties—
that, and a treasure trove besides. Achilles,   780
put some human kindness in your heart.
Show respect for your own house. Here we are,
under your roof, sent from the whole Achaean force!
Past all other men, all other Achaean comrades,
we long to be your closest, dearest friends."   785

    And the swift runner Achilles answered warmly,
"Ajax, royal son of Telamon, captain of armies,
all well said, after my own heart, or mostly so.
But my heart still heaves with rage

whenever I call to mind that arrogance of his—   790
how he mortified me, right in front of the Argives—
that son of Atreus treating me like some vagabond,
like some outcast stripped of all my rights!
You go back to him and declare my message:
I will not think of arming for bloody war again,   795
not till the son of wise King Priam, dazzling Hector
batters all the way to the Myrmidon ships and shelters,
slaughtering Argives, gutting the hulls with fire.
But round my own black ship and camp this Hector
will be stopped, I trust, blazing for battle   800
as he goes—stopped dead in his tracks!"
                                        So he finished.
Then each man, lifting his own two-handled cup,
poured it out to the gods, and back they went
along the ships, Odysseus in the lead.
Patroclus told his friends and serving-women   805
to pile a deep warm bed for Phoenix, quickly.
They obeyed and spread the bed as he ordered,
with fleeces, woolen throws and soft linen sheets.
There the old man lay, awaiting shining Dawn.
And deep in his well-built lodge Achilles slept   810
with the woman he brought from Lesbos, Phorbas' daughter,
Diomede in all her beauty sleeping by his side.
And over across from him Patroclus slept
with the sashed and lovely Iphis by his side,
whom Price Achilles gave him the day he took   815
the heights of Scyros, Enyeus' rocky stronghold.

   But once the envoys reached Atrides' shelters,
comrades leapt to their feet, welcomed them back
and clustering round them, lifted golden cups.
One after another pressed them with questions,   820
King Agamemnon most urgent of all: "Come—
tell me, famous Odysseus, Achaea's pride and glory—
will he fight the fire off the ships? Or does he refuse,
does rage still grip his proud, mighty spirit?"

   And the steady, long-enduring Odysseus replied,   825
"Great marshal Atrides, lord of men Agamemnon,
that man has no intention of quenching his rage.
He's still bursting with anger, more than ever—
he spurns you, spurns all your gifts. Work out
your own defense, he says, you and your captains   830
save the Argive armies and the ships. Himself?
Achilles threatens, tomorrow at first light,
to haul his well-benched warships out to sea.
And what's more, he advises all the rest,

'Sail home now. You will never set your eyes   835
on the day of doom that topples looming Troy.
Thundering Zeus has spread his hands above her . . .
her armies have taken heart.'
                                        That's his answer.
And here are men to confirm it, fellow envoys.
Ajax and two heralds, both clear-headed men.   840
But old Phoenix passes the night in camp
as Achilles bids him, so he can voyage home,
home in the ships with him to the fatherland they love.
Tomorrow at dawn. But only if Phoenix wishes.
He will never force the man to go."
                                        So he reported.   845
Silence held them all, struck dumb by his story,
Odysseus' words still ringing in their ears.
A long while they said nothing, spirits dashed.
Finally Diomedes lord of the war cry broke forth:
"Great marshal Atrides, lord of men Agamemnon—   850
if only you'd never begged the dauntless son of Peleus,
holding out to Achilles trove on trove of gifts!
He's a proud man at the best of times, and now
you've only plunged him deeper in his pride.
I say have done with the man—   855
whether he sails for home or stays on here.
He'll fight again—in his own good time—whenever
the courage in him flares and a god fires his blood.
So come, follow my orders. And all of us unite.
Go to sleep now, full to your heart's content   860
with food and wine, a soldier's strength and nerve.
Then when the Dawn's red fingers shine in all their glory,
quickly deploy your chariots and battalions, Agamemnon,
out in front of the ships—you spur them on
and you yourself, you fight in the front ranks!"   865

    And Achaea's kings all shouted their assent,
stirred by the stallion-breaking Diomedes' challenge.
Pouring cups to the gods, each warlord sought his shelter.
There they spent the night and took the gift of sleep.

    [After Achilles' refusal, the situation of the Greeks worsened rapidly.
Agamemnon, Diomedes, and Odysseus were all wounded. The Trojans
breached the stockade and fought beside the ships. Patroclus tried to bring
Achilles to the aid of the Greeks, but the most he could obtain was per-
mission for himself to fight, clad in Achilles' armor, at the head of the
Myrmidons. He turned the tide of battle and drove the Trojans back to
their walls, only to fall himself through the direct intervention of Apollo.
Hector stripped Achilles' armor from the body. A fierce fight for the body

itself ended in partial success for the Greeks; they took Patroclus' body but
had to retreat to their camp, with the Trojans at their heels.]

BOOK XVIII

The Shield of Achilles

So the men fought on like a mass of whirling fire
as swift Antilochus[4] raced the message toward Achilles.
Sheltered under his curving, beaked ships he found him,
foreboding, deep down, all that had come to pass.
Agonizing now he probed his own great heart: 5
"Why, why? Our long-haired Achaeans routed again,
driven in terror off the plain to crowd the ships, but why?
Dear gods, don't bring to pass the grief that haunts my heart—
the prophecy that mother revealed to me one time . . .
she said the best of the Myrmidons—while I lived—   10
would fall at Trojan hands and leave the light of day.
And now he's dead, I know it. Menoetius'[5] gallant son,
my headstrong friend! And I told Patroclus clearly,
'Once you have beaten off the lethal fire, quick,
come back to the ships—you must not battle Hector!' "   15
    As such fears went churning through his mind
the warlord Nestor's son drew near him now,
streaming warm tears, to give the dreaded message:
"Ah son of royal Peleus, what you must hear from me!
What painful news—would to god it had never happened!   20
Patroclus has fallen. They're fighting over his corpse.
He's stripped, naked—Hector with that flashing helmet,
Hector has your arms!"
                        So the captain reported.
A black cloud of grief came shrouding over Achilles.
Both hands clawing the ground for soot and filth,   25
he poured it over his head, fouled his handsome face
and black ashes settled onto his fresh clean war-shirt.
Overpowered in all his power, he sprawled in the dust.
Achilles lay there, fallen . . .
tearing his hair, defiling it with his own hands.   30
And the women he and Patroclus carried off as captives
caught the grief in their hearts and keened and wailed,
out of the tents they ran to ring the great Achilles,
all of them beat their breasts with clenched fists,
sank to the ground, each woman's knees gave way.   35
Antilochus kneeling near, weeping uncontrollably,
clutched Achilles' hands as he wept his proud heart out—
for fear he would slash his throat with an iron blade.

4. A son of Nestor.   5. Patroclus.

Achilles suddenly loosed a terrible, wrenching cry
and his noble mother heard him, seated near her father,   40
the Old Man of the Sea in the salt green depths,
and she cried out it turn. And immortal sea-nymphs
gathered round their sister, all the Nereids swelling
down the sounding depths, they all came rushing now—
Glitter, blossoming Spray and the swells' Embrace,   45
Fair-Isle and shadowy Cavern, Mist and Spindrift,
ocean nymphs of the glances pooling deep and dark,
Race-with-the-Waves and Headlands' Hope and Safe Haven,
Glimmer of Honey, Suave-and-Soothing, Whirlpool, Brilliance,
Bounty and First Light and Speeder of Ships and buoyant Power,   50
Welcome Home and Bather of Meadows and Master's Lovely Consort,
Gift of the Sea, Eyes of the World and the famous milk-white Calm
and Truth and Never-Wrong and the queen who rules the tides in beauty
and in rushed Glory and Healer of Men and the one who rescues kings
and Sparkler, Down-from-the-Cliffs, sleek-haired Strands of Sand   55
and all the rest of the Nereids swelling down the depths.
The silver cave was shimmering full of sea-nymphs,
all in one mounting chorus beating their breasts
as Thetis launched the dirge: "Hear me, sisters,
daughters of Nereus, so you all will know it well—   60
listen to all the sorrows welling in my heart!
I am agony—
                    mother of grief and greatness—O my child!
Yes, I gave birth to a flawless, mighty son . . .
the splendor of heroes, and he shot up like a young branch,
like a fine tree I reared him—the orchard's crowning glory—   65
but only to send him off in the beaked ships to Troy
to battle Trojans! Never again will I embrace him
striding home through the doors of Peleus' house.
And long as I have him with me, still alive,
looking into the sunlight, he is racked with anguish.   70
And I, I go to his side—nothing I do can help him.
Nothing. But go I shall, to see my darling boy,
to hear what grief has come to break his heart
while he holds back from battle."
                              So Thetis cried
as she left the cave and her sisters swam up with her,   75
all in a tide of tears, and billowing round them now
the ground swell heaved open. And once they reached
the fertile land of Troy they all streamed ashore,
row on row in a long cortege, the sea-nymphs
filing up where the Myrmidon ships lay hauled,   80
clustered closely round the great runner Achilles . . .
As he groaned from the depths his mother rose before him
and sobbing a sharp cry, cradled her son's head in her hands

and her words were all compassion, winging pity: "My child—
why in tears? What sorrow has touched your heart?   85
Tell me, please. Don't harbor it deep inside you.
Zeus has accomplished everything you wanted,
just as you raised your hands and prayed that day.
All the sons of Achaea are pinned against the ships
and all for want of you—they suffer shattering losses."   90

     And groaning deeply the matchless runner answered,
"O dear mother, true! All those burning desires
Olympian Zeus has brought to pass for me—
but what joy to me now? My dear comrade's dead—
Patroclus—the man I loved beyond all other comrades,   95
loved as my own life—I've lost him—Hector's killed him,
stripped the gigantic armor off his back, a marvel to behold—
my burnished gear! Radiant gifts the gods presented Peleus
that day they drove you into a mortal's marriage bed . . .
I wish you'd lingered deep with the deathless sea-nymphs,   100
lived at ease, and Peleus carried home a mortal bride.
But now, as it is, sorrows, unending sorrows must surge
within your heart as well—for your own son's death.
Never again will you embrace him striding home.
My spirit rebels—I've lost the will to live,   105
to take my stand in the world of men—unless,
before all else, Hector's battered down by my spear
and gasps away his life, the blood-price for Patroclus,
Menoetius' gallant son he's killed and stripped!"

     But Thetis answered, warning through her tears,   110
"You're doomed to a short life, my son, from all you say!
For hard on the heels of Hector's death your death
must come at once—"
                    "Then let me die at once"—
Achilles burst out, despairing— "since it was not my fate
to save my dearest comrade from his death! Look,   115
a world away from his fatherland he's perished,
lacking me, my fighting strength, to defend him.
But now, since I shall not return to my fatherland . . .
nor did I bring one ray of hope to my Patroclus,
nor to the rest of all my steadfast comrades,   120
countless ranks struck down by mighty Hector—
No, no, here I sit by the ships . . .
a useless, dead weight on the good green earth—
I, no man my equal among the bronze-armed Achaeans,
not in battle, only in wars of words that others win.   125
If only strife could die from the lives of gods and men
and anger that drives the sanest man to flare in outrage—
bitter gall, sweeter than dripping streams of honey,

that swarms in people's chests and blinds like smoke—
just like the anger Agamemnon king of men   130
has roused within me now . . .
                              Enough.
Let bygones be bygones. Done is done.
Despite my anguish I will beat it down,
the fury mounting inside me, down by force.
But now I'll go and meet that murderer head-on,   135
that Hector who destroyed the dearest life I know.
For my own death, I'll meet it freely—whenever Zeus
and the other deathless gods would like to bring it on!
Not even Heracles[6] fled his death, for all his power,
favorite son as he was to Father Zeus the King.   140
Fate crushed him, and Hera's savage anger.
And I too, if the same fate waits for me . . .
I'll lie in peace, once I've gone down to death.
But now, for the moment, let me seize great glory!—
and drive some woman of Troy or deep-breasted Dardan[7]   145
to claw with both hands at her tender cheeks and wipe away
her burning tears as the sobs come choking from her throat—
they'll learn that I refrained from war a good long time!
Don't try to hold me back from the fighting, mother,
love me as you do. You can't persuade me now."   150

    The goddess of the glistening feet replied,
"Yes, my son, you're right. No coward's work,
to save your exhausted friends from headlong death.
But your own handsome war-gear lies in Trojan hands
bronze and burnished—and Hector in that flashing helmet,   155
Hector glories in your armor, strapped across his back.
Not that he will glory in it long, I tell you:
his own destruction hovers near him now. Wait—
don't fling yourself in the grind of battle yet,
not till you see me coming back with your own eyes.   160
Tomorrow I will return to you with the rising sun,
bearing splendid arms from Hephaestus, god of fire!"

    With that vow she turned away from her son
and faced and urged her sisters of the deep,
"Now down you go in the Ocean's folding gulfs   165
to visit father's halls—the Old Man of the Sea—
and tell him all. I am on my way to Olympus heights,
to the famous Smith Hephaestus—I pray he'll give my son
some fabulous armor full of the god's great fire!"

6. The son of Zeus by a mortal woman; pursued by the jealousy of Hera, he was forced to undertake
twelve great labors and finally died in agony from the effects of a poisoned garment.   7. Trojan.

And under a foaming wave her sisters dove   170
as glistening-footed Thetis soared toward Olympus
to win her dear son an immortal set of arms.
                                                    And now,
as her feet swept her toward Olympus, ranks of Achaeans,
fleeing man-killing Hector with grim, unearthly cries,
reached the ships and the Hellespont's long shore.   175
As for Patroclus, there seemed no hope that Achaens
could drag the corpse of Achilles' comrade out of range.
Again the Trojan troops and teams overtook the body
with Hector son of Priam storming fierce as fire.
Three times illustrious Hector shouted for support,   180
seized his feet from behind, wild to drag him off,
three times the Aeantes, armored in battle-fury
fought him off the corpse. But Hector held firm,
staking all on his massive fighting strength—
again and again he'd hurl himself at the melee,   185
again and again stand fast with piercing cries
but he never gave ground backward, not one inch.
The helmed Aeantes could no more frighten Hector,
the proud son of Priam, back from Patroclus' corpse
than shepherds out in the field can scare a tawny lion   190
off his kill when the hunger drives the beast claw-mad.
And now Hector would have hauled the body away
and won undying glory . . .
if wind-swift Iris[8] had not swept from Olympus
bearing her message—Peleus' son must arm—   195
but all unknown to Zeus and the other gods
since Hera spurred her on. Halting near
she gave Achilles a flight of marching orders:
"To arms—son of Peleus! Most terrifying man alive!
Defend Patroclus! It's all for him, this merciless battle   200
pitched before the ships. They're mauling each other now,
Achaeans struggling to save the corpse from harm,
Trojans charging to haul it back to windy Troy.
Flashing Hector far in the lead, wild to drag it off,
furious to lop the head from its soft, tender neck   205
and stake it high on the city's palisade.
                                            Up with you—
no more lying low! Writhe with shame at the thought
Patroclus may be sport for the dogs of Troy!
Yours, the shame will be yours
if your comrade's corpse goes down to the dead defiled!"   210

8. Messenger of the gods, particularly of Hera.

But the swift runner replied, "Immortal Iris—
what god has sped you here to tell me this?"

Quick as the wind the rushing Iris answered,
"Hera winged me on, the illustrious wife of Zeus.
But the son of Cronus throned on high knows nothing,   215
nor does any other immortal housed on Olympus
shrouded deep in snow."
                                    Achilles broke in quickly—
"How can I go to war? The Trojans have my gear.
And my dear mother told me I must not arm for battle,
not till I see her coming back with my own eyes—   220
she vowed to bring me burnished arms from the god of fire.
I know of no other armor. Whose gear could I wear?
None but Telamonian Ajax'[9] giant shield.
But he's at the front, I'm sure, engaging Trojans,
slashing his spear to save Patroclus' body."   225

Quick as the wind the goddess had a plan:
"We know—we too—they hold your famous armor.
Still, just as you are, go out to the broad trench
and show yourself to the Trojans. Struck with fear
at the sight of you, they might hold off from attack   230
and Achaea's fighting sons get second wind,
exhausted as they are . . .
Breathing room in war is all too brief."

And Iris racing the wind went veering off
as Achilles, Zeus's favorite fighter, rose up now   235
and over his powerful shoulder Pallas slung the shield,
the tremendous storm-shield with all its tassels flaring—
and crowning his head the goddess swept a golden cloud
and from it she lit a fire to blaze across the field.
As smoke goes towering up the sky from out a town   240
cut off on a distant island under siege . . .
enemies battling round it, defenders all day long
trading desperate blows from their own city walls
but soon as the sun goes down the signal fires flash,
rows of beacons blazing into the air to alert their neighbors— 245
if only they'll come in ships to save them from disaster—
so now from Achilles' head the blaze shot up the sky.
He strode from the rampart, took his stand at the trench
but he would not mix with the milling Argive ranks.
He stood in awe of his mother's strict command.   250
So there he rose and loosed an enormous cry
and off in the distance Pallas shrieked out too
and drove an unearthly panic through the Trojans.

9. The more famous of the two heroes called Ajax was the son of Telamon.

Piercing loud as the trumpet's battle cry that blasts
from murderous raiding armies ringed around some city—   255
so piercing now the cry that broke from Aeacides.
And Trojans hearing the brazen voice of Aeacides,
all their spirits quaked—even sleek-maned horses,
sensing death in the wind, slewed their chariots round
and charioteers were struck dumb when they saw that fire,   260
relentless, terrible, burst from proud-hearted Achilles' head,
blazing as fiery-eyed Athena fueled the flames. Three times
the brilliant Achilles gave his great war cry over the trench,
three times the Trojans and famous allies whirled in panic—
and twelve of their finest fighters died then and there,   265
crushed by chariots, impaled on their own spears.
And now the exultant Argives seized the chance
to drag Patroclus' body quickly out of range
and laid him on a litter . . .
Standing round him, loving comrades mourned,   270
and the swift runner Achilles joined them, grieving,
weeping warm tears when he saw his steadfast comrade
lying dead on the bier, mauled by tearing bronze,
the man he sent to war with team and chariot
but never welcomed home again alive.   275

Now Hera the ox-eyed queen of heaven drove the sun,
untired and all unwilling, to sink in the Ocean's depths
and the sun went down at last and brave Achaeans ceased
the grueling clash of arms, the leveling rout of war.

And the Trojans in turn, far across the field,   280
pulling forces back from the last rough assault,
freed their racing teams from under chariot yokes
but before they thought of supper, grouped for council.
They met on their feet. Not one of them dared to sit
for terror seized them all—the great Achilles   285
who held back from the brutal fighting so long
had just come blazing forth.
Panthous' son Polydamas led the debate,
a good clear head, and the only man who saw
what lay in the past and what the Trojans faced.[1]   290
He was Hector's close comrade, born on the same night,
but excelled at trading words as he at trading spear-thrusts.
And now, with all good will, Polydamas rose and spoke:
"Weigh both sides of the crisis well, my friends.
What I urge is this: draw back to the city now.   295
Don't wait for the holy Dawn to find us here afield,
ranged by the ships—we're too far from our walls.

1. He was a prophet; he knew the past and foresaw the future.

As long as that man kept raging at royal Agamemnon
the Argive troops were easier game to battle down.
I too was glad to camp the night on the shipways,   300
hopes soaring to seize their heavy rolling hulls.
But now racing Achilles makes my blood run cold.
So wild the man's fury he will never rest content,
holding out on the plain where Trojans and Argives
met halfway, exchanging blows in the savage onset—   305
never: *he* will fight for our wives, for Troy itself!
So retreat to Troy. Trust me—we will face disaster.
Now, for the moment, the bracing godsent night
has stopped the swift Achilles in his tracks.
But let him catch us lingering here tomorrow,   310
just as he rises up in arms—there may be some
who will sense his fighting spirit all too well.
You'll thank your stars to get back to sacred Troy,
whoever escapes him. Dogs and birds will have their fill—
of Trojan flesh, by heaven. Battalions of Trojans!   315
Pray god such grief will never reach my ears.
So follow my advice, hard as it may seem . . .
Tonight conserve our strength in the meeting place,
and the great walls and gates and timbered doors we hung,
well-planed, massive and bolted tight, will shield the city.   320
But tomorrow at daybreak, armed to the hilt for battle,
we man the towering ramparts. All the worse for him—
if Achilles wants to venture forth from the fleet,
fight us round our walls. Back to the ships he'll go,
once he's lashed the power out of his rippling stallions,   325
whipping them back and forth beneath our city walls.
Not even *his* fury will let him crash our gates—
he'll never plunder Troy.
Sooner the racing dogs will eat him raw!"

    Helmet flashing, Hector wheeled with a dark glance: 330
"No more, Polydamas! Your pleading repels me now.
You say go back again—be crammed inside the city.
Aren't you sick of being caged inside those walls?
Time was when the world would talk of Priam's Troy
as the city rich in gold and rich in bronze—but now   335
our houses are stripped of all their sumptuous treasures,
troves sold off and shipped to Phrygia, lovely Maeonia,
once great Zeus grew angry . . .
but now, the moment the son of crooked Cronus
allows me to seize some glory here at the ships   340
and pin these Argives back against the sea—
you fool, enough! No more thoughts of retreat
paraded before our people. Not that one Trojan

will ever take your lead—I'll never permit it.
Come, follow my orders! All obey me now.   345
Take supper now. Take your posts through camp.
And no forgetting the watch, each man wide awake.
And any Trojan so weighed down, so oppressed
by his own possessions, let him collect the lot,
pass them round to the people—a grand public feast.   350
Far better for one of ours to reap the benefits
than all the marauding Argives. Then, as you say,
'tomorrow at daybreak, armed to the hilt for battle'—
we slash to attack against their deep curved hulls!
If it really *was* Achilles who reared beside the ships,   355
all the worse for him—if he wants his fill of war.
I for one, I'll never run from his grim assault,
I'll stand up to the man—see if he bears off glory
or I bear it off myself! The god of war is impartial:
he hands out death to the man who hands out death."   360

   So Hector finished. The Trojans roared assent,
lost in folly. Athena had swept away their senses.
They gave applause to Hector's ruinous tactics,
none to Polydamas, who gave them sound advice.
And now their entire army settled down to supper   365
but all night long the Argives raised Patroclus' dirge.
And Achilles led them now in a throbbing chant of sorrow,
laying his man-killing hands on his great friend's chest,
convulsed with bursts of grief. Like a bearded lion
whose pride of cubs a deer-hunter has snatched away,   370
out of some thick woods, and back he comes, too late,
and his heart breaks but he courses after the hunter,
hot on his tracks down glen on twisting glen—
where can he find him?—gripped by piercing rage . . .
so Achilles groaned, deeply, crying out to his Myrmidons,   375
"O my captains! How empty the promise I let fall
that day I reassured Menoetius in his house—
I promised the king I'd bring him back his son,
home to Opois,[2] covered in glory, Troy sacked,
hauling his rightful share of plunder home at last.   380
But Zeus will never accomplish all our best-laid plans.
Look at us. Both doomed to stain red with our blood
the same plot of earth, a world away in Troy!
For not even *I* will voyage home again. Never.
No embrace in his halls from the old horseman Peleus   385
nor from mother, Thetis—this alien earth I stride
will hold me down at last.

---

2. Ancient city on the eastern coast of the Greek mainland and home of Menoetius, father of Patroclus.

                        But now, Patroclus,
since I will follow you underneath the ground,
I shall not bury you, not till I drag back here
the gear and head of Hector, who slaughtered you,   390
my friend, greathearted friend . . .
Here in front of your flaming pyre I'll cut the throats
of a dozen sons of Troy in all their shining glory,
venting my rage on them for your destruction!
Till then you lie as you are beside my beaked ships   395
and round you the Trojan women and deep-breasted Dardans
will mourn you night and day, weeping burning tears,
women we fought to win—strong hands and heavy lance—
whenever we sacked rich cities held by mortal men."

    With that the brilliant Achilles ordered friends   400
to set a large three-legged cauldron over the fire
and wash the clotted blood from Patroclus' wounds
with all good speed. Hoisting over the blaze
a cauldron filled to the brim with bathing water,
they piled fresh logs beneath and lit them quickly.   405
The fire lapped at the vessel's belly, the water heated
and soon as it reached the boil in the glowing bronze
they bathed and anointed the body sleek with olive oil,
closed each wound with a soothing, seasoned unguent
and then they laid Patroclus on his bier . . .   410
covered him head to foot in a thin light sheet
and over his body spread the white linen shroud.
Then all night long, ringing the great runner Achilles,
Myrmidon fighters mourned and raised Patroclus' dirge.

    But Zeus turned to Hera, his wife and sister, saying,   415
"So, my ox-eyed Queen, you've had your way at last,
setting the famous runner Achilles on his feet.
Mother Hera—look, these long-haired Achaeans
must be sprung of your own immortal loins."

    But her eyes widening, noble Hera answered,   420
"Dread majesty, son of Cronus, what are you saying?
Even a mortal man will act to help a friend,
condemned as a mortal always is to death
and hardly endowed with wisdom deep as ours.
So how could I, claiming to be the highest goddess—   425
both by birth and since I am called your consort
and you in turn rule all the immortal gods—
how could I hold back from these, these Trojans,
men I loathe, and fail to weave their ruin?"

    Now as the King and Queen provoked each other,   430
glistening-footed Thetis reached Hephaestus' house,

indestructible, bright as stars, shining among the gods,
built of bronze by the crippled Smith[3] with his own hands.
There she found him, sweating, wheeling round his bellows,
pressing the work on twenty three-legged cauldrons,   435
an array to ring the walls inside his mansion.
He'd bolted golden wheels to the legs of each
so all on their own speed, at a nod from him,
they could roll to halls where the gods convene
then roll right home again—a marvel to behold.   440
But not quite finished yet . . .
the god had still to attach the inlaid handles.
These he was just fitting, beating in the rivets.
As he bent to the work with all his craft and cunning,
Thetis on her glistening feet drew near the Smith.   445
But Charis[4] saw her first, Charis coming forward,
lithe and lovely in all her glittering headdress,
the Grace the illustrious crippled Smith had married.
Approaching Thetis, she caught her hand and spoke her name:
"Thetis of flowing robes! What brings you to our house?   450
A beloved, honored friend—but it's been so long,
your visits much too rare. Follow me in, please,
let me offer you all a guest could want."
                                        Welcome words,
and the radiant goddess Charis led the way inside.
She seated her on a handsome, well-wrought chair,   455
studded with silver, under it slipped a stool
and called the famous Smith: "Hephaestus, come—
look who's here! Thetis would ask a favor of you!"

   And the famous crippled Smith exclaimed warmly,
"Thetis—here? Ah then a wondrous, honored goddess   460
comes to grace our house! Thetis saved my life
when the mortal pain came on me after my great fall,
thanks to my mother's will, that brazen bitch,
she wanted to hide me—because I was a cripple.
What shattering anguish I'd have suffered then   465
if Thetis had not taken me to her breast, Eurynome too,
the daughter of ocean's stream that runs around the world.
Nine years I lived with both, forging bronze by the trove,
elegant brooches, whorled pins, necklaces, chokers, chains—
there in the vaulted cave—and round us Ocean's currents   470
swirled in a foaming, roaring rush that never died.
And no one knew. Not a single god or mortal,
only Thetis and Eurynome knew—they saved me.
And here is Thetis now, in our own house!
So I *must* do all I can to pay her back,   475

3. Hephaestus was lame.   4. Her name means "grace" or "beauty."

the price for the life she saved . . .
the nymph of the sea with sleek and lustrous locks.
Quickly, set before her stranger's generous fare
while I put away my bellows and all my tools."

                                                With that
he heaved up from the anvil block—his immense hulk   480
hobbling along but his shrunken legs moved nimbly.
He swung the bellows aside and off the fires,
gathered the tools he'd used to weld the cauldrons
and packed them all in a sturdy silver strongbox.
Then he sponged off his brow and both burly arms,   485
his massive neck and shaggy chest, pulled on a shirt
and grasping a heavy staff, Hephaestus left his forge
and hobbled on. Handmaids ran to attend their master,
all cast in gold but a match for living, breathing girls.
Intelligence fills their hearts, voice and strength their frames,   490
from the deathless gods they've learned their works of hand.
They rushed to support their lord as he went bustling on
and lurching nearer to Thetis, took his polished seat,
reached over to clutch her hand and spoke her name:
"Thetis of flowing robes! What brings you to our house?   495
A beloved, honored friend—but it's been so long,
your visits much too rare.
Tell me what's on your mind. I am eager to do it—
whatever I _can_ do . . . whatever can be done."

       But Thetis burst into tears, her voice welling: 500
"Oh Hephaestus—who of all the goddesses on Olympus,
who has borne such withering sorrows in her heart?
Such pain as Zeus has given me, above all others!
_Me_ out of all the daughters of the sea he chose
to yoke to a mortal man, Peleus, son of Aeacus,   505
and I endured his bed, a mortal's bed, resisting
with all my will. And now he lies in the halls,
broken with grisly age, but now my griefs are worse.
Remember? Zeus also gave me a son to bear and breed,
the splendor of heroes, and he shot up like a young branch,   510
like a fine tree I reared him—the orchard's crowning glory—
but only to send him off in the beaked ships to Troy
to battle Trojans! Never again will I embrace him
striding home through the doors of Peleus' house.
And long as I have him with me, still alive,   515
looking into the sunlight, he is racked with anguish.
I go to his side—nothing I do can help him. Nothing.
That girl the sons of Achaea picked out for his prize—
right from his grasp the mighty Agamemnon tore her,
and grief for her has been gnawing at his heart.   520
But then the Trojans pinned the Achaeans tight

against their sterns, they gave them no way out,
and the Argive warlords begged my son to help,
they named in full the troves of glittering gifts
they'd send his way. But at that point he refused   525
to beat disaster off—refused himself, that is—
but he buckled his own armor round Patroclus,
sent him into battle with an army at his back.
And all day long they fought at the Scaean Gates,
that very day they would have stormed the city too,   530
if Apollo had not killed Menoetius' gallant son
as he laid the Trojans low—Apollo cut him down
among the champions there and handed Hector glory.
So now I come, I throw myself at your knees,
please help me! Give my son—he won't live long—   535
a shield and helmet and tooled greaves with ankle-straps
and armor for his chest. All that he had was lost,
lost when the Trojans killed his steadfast friend.
Now he lies on the ground—his heart is breaking."

And the famous crippled Smith replied, "Courage!   540
Anguish for all that armor—sweep it from your mind.
If only I could hide him away from pain and death,
that day his grim destiny comes to take Achilles,
as surely as glorious armor shall be his, armor
that any man in the world of men will marvel at   545
through all the years to come—whoever sees its splendor."

With that he left her there and made for his bellows,
turning them on the fire, commanding, "Work—to work!"
And the bellows, all twenty, blew on the crucibles,
breathing with all degrees of shooting, fiery heat   550
as the god hurried on—a blast for the heavy work,
a quick breath for the light, all precisely gauged
to the god of fire's wish and the pace of the work in hand.
Bronze he flung in the blaze, tough, durable bronze
and tin and priceless gold and silver, and then,   555
planting the huge anvil upon its block, he gripped
his mighty hammer in one hand, the other gripped his tongs.

And first Hephaestus makes a great and massive shield,
blazoning well-wrought emblems all across its surface,
raising a rim around it, glittering, triple-ply   560
with a silver shield-strap run from edge to edge
and five layers of metal to build the shield itself,
and across its vast expanse with all his craft and cunning
the god creates a world of gorgeous immortal work.

There he made the earth and there the sky and the sea   565
and the inexhaustible blazing sun and the moon rounding full

and there the constellations, all that crown the heavens,
the Pleiades and the Hyades, Orion in all his power too
and the Great Bear[5] that mankind also calls the Wagon:
she wheels on her axis always fixed, watching Orion,   570
and she alone is denied a plunge in the Ocean's baths.

And he forged on the shield two noble cities filled
with mortal men. With weddings and wedding feasts in one
and under glowing torches they brought forth the brides
from the women's chambers, marching through the streets   575
while choir on choir the wedding song rose high
and the young men came dancing, whirling round in rings
and among them the flutes and harps kept up their stirring call—
women rushed to the doors and each stood moved with wonder.
And the people massed, streaming into the marketplace   580
where a quarrel had broken out and two men struggled
over the blood-price for a kinsman just murdered.
One declaimed in public, vowing payment in full—
the other spurned him, he would not take a thing—
so both men pressed for a judge to cut the knot.   585
The crowd cheered on both, they took both sides,
but heralds held them back as the city elders sat
on polished stone benches, forming the sacred circle,
grasping in hand the staffs of clear-voiced heralds,
and each leapt to his feet to plead the case in turn.   590
Two bars of solid gold shone on the ground before them,
a prize for the judge who'd speak the straightest verdict.

But circling the other city camped a divided army
gleaming in battle-gear, and two plans split their ranks:
to plunder the city or share the riches with its people,   595
hoards the handsome citadel stored within its depths.
But the people were not surrendering, not at all.
They armed for a raid, hoping to break the siege—
loving wives and innocent children standing guard
on the ramparts, flanked by elders bent with age   600
as men marched out to war. Ares and Pallas led them,
both burnished gold, gold the attire they donned, and great,
magnificent in their armor—gods for all the world,
looming up in their brilliance, towering over troops.
And once they reached the perfect spot for attack,   605
a watering place where all the herds collected,
there they crouched, wrapped in glowing bronze.
Detached from the ranks, two scouts took up their posts,
the eyes of the army waiting to spot a convoy,
the enemy's flocks and crook-horned cattle coming . . .   610

5. The Big Dipper, which never descends below the horizon. It is a female bear (Ursa Major), hence
"she" in l. 570. *Pleiades, Hyades, Orion:* All constellations; Orion was a giant hunter of Greek myth.

Come they did, quickly, two shepherds behind them,
playing their hearts out on their pipes—treachery
never crossed their minds. But the soldiers saw them,
rushed them, cut off at a stroke the herds of oxen
and sleek sheep-flocks glistening silver-gray   615
and killed the herdsmen too. Now the besiegers,
soon as they heard the uproar burst from the cattle
as they debated, huddled in council, mounted at once
behind their racing teams, rode hard to the rescue,
arrived at once, and lining up for assault   620
both armies battled it out along the river banks—
they raked each other with hurtling bronze-tipped spears.
And Strife and Havoc plunged in the fight, and violent Death—
now seizing a man alive with fresh wounds, now one unhurt,
now hauling a deadman through the slaughter by the heels,   625
the cloak on her back stained red with human blood.
So they clashed and fought like living, breathing men
grappling each other's corpses, dragging off the dead.

And he forged a fallow field, broad rich plowland
tilled for the third time, and across it crews of plowmen   630
wheeled their teams, driving them up and back and soon
as they'd reach the end-strip, moving into the turn,
a man would run up quickly
and hand them a cup of honeyed, mellow wine
as the crews would turn back down along the furrows,   635
pressing again to reach the end of the deep fallow field
and the earth churned black behind them, like earth churning,
solid gold as it was—that was the wonder of Hephaestus' work.

And he forged a king's estate where harvesters labored,
reaping the ripe grain, swinging their whetted scythes.   640
Some stalks fell in line with the reapers, row on row,
and others the sheaf-binders girded round with ropes,
three binders standing over the sheaves, behind them
boys gathering up the cut swaths, filling their arms,
supplying grain to the binders, endless bundles.   645
And there in the midst the king,
scepter in hand at the head of the reaping-rows,
stood tall in silence, rejoicing in his heart.
And off to the side, beneath a spreading oak,
the heralds were setting out the harvest feast,   650
they were dressing a great ox they had slaughtered,
while attendant women poured out barley, generous,
glistening handfuls strewn for the reapers' midday meal.

And he forged a thriving vineyard loaded with clusters,
bunches of lustrous grapes in gold, ripening deep purple   655

and climbing vines shot up on silver vine-poles.
And round it he cut a ditch in dark blue enamel
and round the ditch he staked a fence in tin.
And one lone footpath led toward the vineyard
and down it the pickers ran   660
whenever they went to strip the grapes at vintage—
girls and boys, their hearts leaping in innocence,
bearing away the sweet ripe fruit in wicker baskets.
And there among them a young boy plucked his lyre,
so clear it could break the heart with longing,   665
and what he sang was a dirge for the dying year,
lovely . . . his fine voice rising and falling low
as the rest followed, all together, frisking, singing,
shouting, their dancing footsteps beating out the time.

And he forged on the shield a herd of longhorn cattle,   670
working the bulls in beaten gold and tin, lowing loud
and rumbling out of the farmyard dung to pasture
along a rippling stream, along the swaying reeds.
And the golden drovers kept the herd in line,
four in all, with nine dogs at their heels,   675
their paws flickering quickly—a savage roar!—
a crashing attack—and a pair of ramping lions
had seized a bull from the cattle's front ranks—
he bellowed out as they dragged him off in agony.
Packs of dogs and the young herdsmen rushed to help   680
but the lions ripping open the hide of the huge bull
were gulping down the guts and the black pooling blood
while the herdsmen yelled the fast pack on—no use.
The hounds shrank from sinking teeth in the lions,
they balked, hunching close, barking, cringing away.   685

And the famous crippled Smith forged a meadow
deep in a shaded glen for shimmering flocks to graze,
with shepherds' steadings, well-roofed huts and sheepfolds.

And the crippled Smith brought all his art to bear
on a dancing circle, broad as the circle Daedalus   690
once laid out on Cnossos' spacious fields
for Ariadne[6] the girl with lustrous hair.
Here young boys and girls, beauties courted
with costly gifts of oxen, danced and danced,
linking their arms, gripping each other's wrists.   695
And the girls wore robes of linen light and flowing,
the boys wore finespun tunics rubbed with a gloss of oil,
the girls were crowned with a bloom of fresh garlands,

6. Daughter of Minos, king of Crete. *Cnossos*: In Crete, the site of the great "palace of Minos." *Daedalus*:
The "fabulous artificer" who built the labyrinth and, with his son Icarus, escaped from Crete on wings.

the boys swung golden daggers hung on silver belts.
And now they would run in rings on their skilled feet,   700
nimbly, quick as a crouching potter spins his wheel,
palming it smoothly, giving it practice twirls
to see it run, and now they would run in rows,
in rows crisscrossing rows—rapturous dancing.
A breathless crowd stood round them struck with joy   705
and through them a pair of tumblers dashed and sprang,
whirling in leaping handsprings, leading out the dance.

    And he forged the Ocean River's mighty power girdling
round the outmost rim of the welded indestructible shield.

    And once the god had made that great and massive shield   710
he made Achilles a breastplate brighter than gleaming fire,
he made him a sturdy helmet to fit the fighter's temples,
beautiful, burnished work, and raised its golden crest
and made him greaves of flexing, pliant tin.
                                        Now,
when the famous crippled Smith had finished off   715
that grand array of armor, lifting it in his arms
he laid it all at the feet of Achilles' mother Thetis—
and down she flashed like a hawk from snowy Mount Olympus
bearing the brilliant gear, the god of fire's gift.

                    BOOK XIX

            The Champion Arms for Battle

As Dawn rose up in her golden robe from Ocean's tides,
bringing light to immortal gods and mortal men,
Thetis sped Hephaestus' gifts to the ships.
She found her beloved son lying facedown,
embracing Patroclus' body, sobbing, wailing,   5
and round him crowded troops of mourning comrades.
And the glistening goddess moved among them now,
seized Achilles' hand and urged him, spoke his name:
"My child, leave your friend to lie there dead—
we must, though it breaks our hearts . . .   10
The will of the gods has crushed him once for all.
But here, Achilles, accept this glorious armor, look,
a gift from the god of fire—burnished bright, finer
than any mortal has ever borne across his back!"
                                        Urging,
the goddess laid the armor down at Achilles' feet   15
and the gear clashed out in all its blazoned glory.
A tremor ran through all the Myrmidon ranks—none dared
to look straight at the glare, each fighter shrank away.
Not Achilles. The more he gazed, the deeper his anger went,
his eyes flashing under his eyelids, fierce as fire—   20

exulting, holding the god's shining gifts in his hands.
And once he'd thrilled his heart with looking hard
at the armor's well-wrought beauty,
he turned to his mother, winged words flying:
"Mother—armor sent by the god—you're right,   25
only immortal gods could forge such work,
no man on earth could ever bring it off!
Now, by heaven, I'll arm and go to war.
But all the while my blood runs cold with fear—
Menoetius' fighting son . . . the carrion blowflies   30
will settle into his wounds, gouged deep by the bronze,
worms will breed and seethe, defile the man's corpse—
his life's ripped out—his flesh may rot to nothing."

    But glistening-footed Thetis reassured him:
"O my child, wipe these worries from your mind.   35
I'll find a way to protect him from those swarms,
the vicious flies that devour men who fall in battle.
He could lie there dead till a year has run its course
and his flesh still stand firm, even fresher than now . . .
So go and call the Argive warriors to the muster: 40
renounce your rage at the proud commander Agamemnon,
then arm for battle quickly, don your fighting power!"

    With that she breathed in her son tremendous courage
then instilled in Patroclus' nostrils fresh ambrosia,
blood-red nectar too, to make his flesh stand firm.   45

    But brilliant Achilles strode along the surf,
crying his piercing cry and roused Achaean warriors.
Even those who'd kept to the beached ships till now,
the helmsmen who handled the heavy steering-oars
and stewards left on board to deal out rations—   50
even they trooped to the muster: great Achilles
who held back from the brutal fighting so long
had just come blazing forth.
And along came two aides of Ares limping in,
the battle-hard Tydides flanked by good Odysseus   55
leaning on their spears, still bearing painful wounds,
and slowly found their seats in the front ranks.
And the lord of men Agamemnon came in last of all,
weighed down by the wound he took in the rough charge
when Coon, son of Antenor, slashed his arm with bronze.   60
And now, as all the Achaean armies massed together,
the swift runner Achilles rose among them, asking,
"Agamemnon—was it better for both of us, after all,
for you and me to rage at each other, raked by anguish,
consumed by heartsick strife, all for a young girl?   65

If only Artemis had cut her down at the ships—
with one quick shaft—
that day I destroyed Lyrnessus, chose her as my prize.
How many fewer friends had gnawed the dust of the wide world,
brought down by enemy hands while I raged on and on.   70
Better? Yes—for Hector and Hector's Trojans!
Not for the Argives. For years to come, I think,
they will remember the feud that flared between us both.
Enough. Let bygones be bygones. Done is done.
Despite my anguish I will beat it down,   75
the fury mounting inside me, down by force.
Now, by god, I call a halt to all my anger—
it's wrong to keep on raging, heart inflamed forever.
Quickly, drive our long-haired Achaeans to battle now!
So I can go at the Trojans once again and test their strength   80
and see if they still long to camp the night at the ships.
They'll gladly sink to a knee and rest at home, I'd say—
whoever comes through alive from the heat of combat,
out from under my spear!"

                              Welcome, rousing words,
and Achaeans-at-arms roared out with joy to hear   85
the greathearted Achilles swearing off his rage.
Now it was King Agamemnon's turn to address them.
He rose from his seat, not moving toward the center.
The lord of men spoke out from where he stood:
"My friends, fighting Danaans, aides of Ares . . .   90
when a man stands up to speak, it's well to listen.
Not to interrupt him, the only courteous thing.
Even the finest speaker finds intrusions hard.
Yet how can a person hear or say a word?—
this howling din could drown the clearest voice.   95
But I will declare my inmost feelings to Achilles.
And you, the rest of you Argives, listen closely:
every man of you here, mark each word I say.
Often the armies brought this matter up against me—
they would revile me in public. But I am not to blame!   100
Zeus and Fate and the Fury stalking through the night,
they are the ones who drove that savage madness in my heart,
that day in assembly when I seized Achilles' prize—
on my own authority, true, but what could *I* do?
A god impels all things to their fulfillment: 105
Ruin, eldest daughter of Zeus, she blinds us all,
that fatal madness—she with those delicate feet of hers,
never touching the earth, gliding over the heads of men
to trap us all. She entangles one man, now another.
Why, she and her frenzy blinded *Zeus* one time,   110
highest, greatest of men and gods, they say:

even Father Zeus! Hera deceived him blind—
feminine as she is, and only armed with guile—
that day in Thebes, ringed with tower on tower,
Alcmena[7] was poised to bear invincible Heracles.   115
So the proud Father declared to all immortals,
'Hear me, all you gods and all goddesses too,
as I proclaim what's brooding deep inside me.
Today the goddess of birth pangs and labor
will bring to light a human child, a man-child   120
born of the stock of men who spring from *my* blood,
one who will lord it over all who dwell around him.'
But teeming with treachery noble Hera set her trap,
'You will prove a liar . . .
when the time arrives to crown your words with action.   125
Come now, my Olympian, swear your inviolate oath
that he shall lord it over all who dwell around him—
that child who drops between a woman's knees today,
born of the stock of men who spring from Zeus's blood.'
And Zeus suspected nothing, not a word of treachery.   130
He swore his mighty oath—blinded, from that hour on.
Speeding down in a flash from Mount Olympus' summit
Hera reached Achaean Argos in no time, where,
she knew for a fact, the hardy wife of Sthenelus,
Perseus'[8] own son, was about to bear her child,   135
but only seven months gone. So into the light
Queen Hera brought the baby, two months shy,
and the goddess stopped Alcmena's hour of birth,
she held back the Lady of Labor's birthing pangs
and rushed in person to give the word to Zeus: 140
'Zeus, Father, lord of the lightning bolt—
here is a piece of news to warm your heart!
Today an illustrious son is born to rule the Argives . . .
Eurystheus,[9] son of Sthenelus, descended of Perseus—
so he is born of our own stock and immortal blood   145
and it's only right for him to rule the Argives!'
With that, a stab of agony struck his deep heart.
Suddenly seizing Ruin by her glossy oiled braids—
he was furious, raging—now he swore his inviolate oath
that never again would she return to Olympus' starry skies,   150
that maddening goddess, Ruin, Ruin who blinds us all.
With that he whirled her round in his massive hand
and flung her out of the brilliant, starry skies
and she soon found herself in the world of men.
But Zeus could never think of Ruin without a groan   155

---

7. Mortal woman who, though married to Amphitryon, King of Thebes, was pregnant by Zeus.   8. A
son of Zeus.   9. He became king of Argos, and taskmaster of Heracles, who performed twelve great
labors for him.

whenever he saw Heracles, his own dear son endure
some shameful labor Eurystheus forced upon him.

  And so with me, I tell you!
When tall Hector with that flashing helmet of his
kept slaughtering Argives pinned against our ships—   160
how could I once forget that madness, that frenzy,
the Ruin that blinded *me* from that first day?
But since I *was* blinded and Zeus stole my wits,
I am intent on setting things to rights, at once:
I'll give that priceless ransom paid for friendship.   165
Gear up for battle now! And rouse the rest of your armies!
As for the gifts, here I am to produce them all,
all that good Odysseus promised you in full,
the other day, when he approached your tents.
Or if you prefer, hold off a moment now . . .   170
much as your heart would spur you on to war.
Aides will fetch that treasure trove from my ship,
they'll bring it here to you, so you can behold
what hoards I'll give to set your heart at peace."

  But the swift runner Achilles broke in sharply—   175
"Field marshal Atrides, lord of men Agamemnon,
produce the gifts if you like, as you see fit,
or keep them back, it's up to you. But now—
quickly, call up the wild joy of war at once!
It's wrong to malinger here with talk, wasting time—   180
our great work lies all before us, still to do.
Just as you see Achilles charge the front once more,
hurling his bronze spear, smashing Troy's battalions—
so each of you remember to battle down your man!"

  But Odysseus fine at tactics answered firmly,   185
"Not so quickly, brave as you are, godlike Achilles.
Achaea's troops are hungry: don't drive them against Troy
to fight the Trojans. It's no quick skirmish shaping,
once the massed formations of men begin to clash
with a god breathing fury in both sides at once.   190
No, command them now to take their food and wine
by the fast ships—a soldier's strength and nerve.
No fighter can battle all day long, cut-and-thrust
till the sun goes down, if he is starved for food.
Even though his courage may blaze up for combat,   195
his limbs will turn to lead before he knows it,
thirst and hunger will overtake him quickly.
his knees will cave in as the man struggles on.
But the one who takes his fill of food and wine
before he grapples enemies full force, dawn to dusk—   200

the heart in his chest keeps pounding fresh with courage,
nor do his legs give out till all break off from battle.
Come, dismiss your ranks, have them make their meal.
As for the gifts, let the king of men Agamemnon
have the lot of them hauled amidst our muster,   205
so all the troops can see the trove themselves
and you, Achilles, you can warm your heart.
And let the king stand up before the entire army,
let Agamemnon swear to you his solemn, binding oath:
he never mounted her bed, never once made love with her,[1]   210
the natural thing, my lord, men and women joined.
And you, Achilles, show some human kindness too,
in your own heart. Then, as a peace offering,
let him present you a lavish feast in his tents
so you won't lack your just deserts at last.   215
And you, great son of Atreus . . .
you be more just to others, from now on.
It is no disgrace for a king to appease a man
when the king himself was first go give offense."

     The lord of men Agamemnon answered warmly,   220
"Son of Laertes, I delight to hear your counsel!
You have covered it all fairly, point by point.
I'll gladly swear your oath—the spirit moves me now—
nor will I break that oath in the eyes of any god.
But let Achilles remain here, for the moment,   225
much as his heart would race him into war.
The rest remain here too, all in strict formation,
till the treasure trove is hauled forth from my tents
and we can seal our binding oaths in blood.[2]
And you, Odysseus, I tell you, I command you: 230
pick out young men, the best in our joint forces,
bring forth the gifts from my ship, all we promised
Achilles just the other day, and bring the women too.
Here in the presence of our united armed contingents
let Talthybius[3] quickly prepare a wild boar for me—   235
we must sacrifice to the Sun and Father Zeus."

     But the swift runner Achilles interjected,
"Field marshal Atrides, lord of men Agamemnon,
better busy yourself with that some other time,
when a sudden lull in the fighting lets us rest   240
and the fury's not such fire inside my heart.
Now our men are lying mauled on the field—
all that Hector the son of Priam overwhelmed
when Zeus was handing Hector his high glory—

1. Briseis.   2. Animal sacrifice.   3. Agamemnon's herald.

but you, you and Odysseus urge us to a banquet!   245
I, by god, I'd drive our Argives into battle *now*,
starving, famished, and only then, when the sun goes down,
lay on a handsome feast—once we've avenged our shame.
Before then, for me at least, neither food nor drink
will travel down my throat, not with my friend dead,   250
there in my shelter, torn to shreds by the sharp bronze . . .
His feet turned to the door, stretched out for burial,
round him comrades mourning.
                              You talk of food?
I have no taste for food—what I really crave
is slaughter and blood and the choking groans of men!"   255

    But Odysseus, cool tactician, tried to calm him:
"Achilles, son of Peleus, greatest of the Achaeans,
greater than I, stronger with spears by no small edge—
yet I might just surpass you in seasoned judgment
by quite a lot, since I have years on you   260
and I know the world much better . . .
So let your heart be swayed by what I say.
Now fighting men will sicken of battle quickly:
the more dead husks the bronze strews on the ground
the sparser the harvest then, when Zeus almighty   265
tips his scales and the tide of battle turns—
the great steward on high who rules our mortal wars.
You want the men to grieve for the dead by *starving*?
Impossible. Too many falling, day after day—battalions!
When could we find a breathing space from fasting?   270
No. We must steel our hearts. Bury our dead,
with tears for the day they die, not one day more.
And all those left alive, after the hateful carnage,
remember food and drink—so all the more fiercely
we can fight our enemies, nonstop, no mercy,   275
durable as the bronze that wraps our bodies.
Let no one hold back now, waiting further summons—
these *are* your summons: pain and death to the man
who skulks beside the ships! Now, all in a mass,
drive hard against them—rousing battering war   280
against these stallion-breaking Trojans!"
                                        He led an escort
formed of the brave old soldier Nestor's sons,
Meges the son of Phyleus, Meriones and Thoas,
Lycomedes the son of Creon, Melanippus too.
Off they went to the tents of Agamemnon—   285
a few sharp commands and the work was done.
Seven tripods hauled from the tents, as promised,
twenty burnished cauldrons, a dozen massive stallions.

They quickly brought out women, flawless, skilled in crafts,
seven, and Briseis in all her beauty made the eighth.   290
Then Odysseus weighed out ten full bars of gold
and led the princes back, laden with other gifts,
and they set them down amid the meeting grounds.
Agamemnon rose to his feet.
The crier Talthybius, his voice clear as a god's,   295
holding the boar in his arms, flanked the great commander.
And Atreus' son drew forth the dagger always slung
at his battle-sword's big sheath, he cut some hairs
from the boar's head, first tufts to start the rite,
and lifting up his arms to Zeus on high he prayed   300
while the armies held fast to their seats in silence,
all by rank and file, listening to their king.
He scanned the vaulting skies as his voice rang in prayer:
"Zeus be my witness first, the highest, best of gods!
Then Earth, the Sun, and Furies stalking the world below   305
to wreak revenge on the dead who broke their oaths—
I swear I never laid a hand on the girl Briseis,
I never forced her to serve my lust in bed
or perform some other task . . .
Briseis remained untouched within my tents.   310
True. If a word of what I say is falsely sworn,
may the gods deal out such blows to me, such agonies
as they deal out to the men who break sworn oaths
and take their names in vain!"
                          On those terms
he dragged his ruthless dagger across the boar's throat.   315
Talthybius whirled the carcass round about his head
and slung it into the yawning gulf of the gray sea
for swarming fish to eat. Then Prince Achilles stood
and addressed the Argives keen for battle: "Father Zeus—
great are the blinding frenzies you deal out to men!   320
If not, I swear, Atrides could never have roused
the fury in me, the rage that would not die,
or wrenched the girl away against my will—
stubborn, implacable man. But Zeus, somehow,
was bent on his awesome slaughter of Achaeans.   325
Go now, take your meal—the sooner to bring on war."

    This brusque command dispersed the muster quickly.
The contingents scattered, each to its own ship.
Exultant Myrmidons took charge of the gifts
and bore them off to their royal captain's moorings.   330
They stowed them safe in his shelters, settled the women
and proud henchmen drove the teams to his herds.

And so Briseis returned, like golden Aphrodite,
but when she saw Patroclus lying torn by the bronze
she flung herself on his body, gave a piercing cry   335
and with both hands clawing deep at her breasts,
her soft throat and lovely face, she sobbed,
a woman like a goddess in her grief, "Patroclus—
dearest joy of my heart, my harrowed, broken heart!
I left you alive that day I left these shelters,   340
now I come back to find you fallen, captain of armies!
So grief gives way to grief, my life one endless sorrow!
The husband to whom my father and noble mother gave me,
I saw him torn by the sharp bronze before our city,
and my three brothers—a single mother bore us: 345
my brothers, how I loved you!—
you all went down to death on the same day . . .
But you, Patroclus, you would not let me weep,
not when the swift Achilles cut my husband down,
not when he plundered the lordly Mynes' city—   350
not even weep! No, again and again you vowed
you'd make me godlike Achilles' lawful, wedded wife,
you would sail me west in your warships, home to Phthia
and there with the Myrmidons hold my marriage feast.
So now I mourn your death—I will never stop—   355
you were always kind."
                    Her voice rang out in tears
and the women wailed in answer, grief for Patroclus
calling forth each woman's private sorrows.
But Achaea's warlords clustered round Achilles,
begging him to eat. He only spurned them, groaning,   360
"I beg you—if any comrade will hear me out in this—
stop pressing me now to glut myself with food and drink,
now such painful grief has come and struck my heart!
I'll hold out till the sun goes down—enduring—
fasting—despite your appeals."
                    His voice so firm   365
that Achilles caused the other kings to scatter.
But the two Atridae stayed, and good Odysseus,
Nestor, Idomeneus, Phoenix the old charioteer,
all trying to comfort Achilles deep in sorrow.
But no comfort could reach the fighter's heart   370
till he went striding into the jaws of bloody war.
The memories swept over him . . .
sighs heaved from his depths as Achilles burst forth,
"Ah god, time and again, my doomed, my dearest friend,
you would set before us a seasoned meal yourself,   375
here in our tents, in your quick and expert way,

when Argive forces rushed to fight the Trojans,
stampeding those breakers of horses into rout.
But now you lie before me, hacked to pieces here
while the heart within me fasts from food and drink   380
though stores inside are full—
                    I'm sick with longing for you!
There is no more shattering blow that I could suffer.
Now even if I should learn of my own father's death,
who, this moment, is weeping warm tears in Phthia,
I know it, bereft of a son as loved as this . . .   385
and here I am in a distant land, fighting Trojans,
and all for that blood-chilling horror, Helen!—
or the death of my dear son, reared for me in Scyros,
if Prince Neoptolemus is still among the living.
Till now I'd hoped, hoped with all my heart   390
that I alone would die
far from the stallion-land of Argos, here in Troy,
but you, Patroclus, would journey back to Phthia
and then you'd ferry Neoptolemus home from Scyros,[4]
fast in your black ship, and show him all my wealth,   395
my servingmen, my great house with the high vaulting roof.
For father, I fear—if he's not dead and buried yet—
just clings, perhaps, to his last breath of life,
ground down now by the hateful siege of years,
waiting, day after day, for painful news of me—   400
until he learns his only son is dead."

    His voice rang out in tears and the warlords mourned in answer,
each remembering those he had left behind at home.
Seeing their grief the Father, filled with pity,
quickly turned to Athena with winging words: 405
"My child, have you abandoned him forever?
Your favorite man of war. Is it all lost now?—
no more care for Achilles left inside your heart?
There he huddles before his curving, beaked ships,
racked with grief for his dear friend while others scatter,   410
settling down to their meal. He's fasting, never fed.
Go. Run and install some nectar and sweet ambrosia
deep within his chest. Stave off his hunger now."

    So he urged Athena already poised for action.
Down the sky she swooped through the clear bright air   415
like a shrieking, sharp-winged hawk, and while Achaeans
quickly armed throughout the encampment, she instilled
some nectar and sweet ambrosia deep in Achilles' chest
so the stabbing pangs of hunger could not sap his knees.

4. An island in the North Aegean.

Then back to her mighty Father's sturdy halls she went   420
as troops moved out, pouring out of the fast trim ships.
Thick-and-fast as the snow comes swirling down from Zeus,
frozen sharp when the North Wind born in heaven blasts it on—
so massed, so dense the glistening burnished helmets shone,
streaming out of the ships, and shields with jutting bosses,   425
breastplates welded front and back and the long ashen spears.
The glory of armor lit the skies and the whole earth laughed,
rippling under the glitter of bronze, thunder resounding
under trampling feet of armies. And in their midst
the brilliant Achilles began to arm for battle . . .   430
A sound of grinding came from the fighter's teeth,
his eyes blazed forth in searing points of fire,
unbearable grief came surging through his heart
and now, bursting with rage against the men of Troy,
he donned Hephaestus' gifts—magnificent armor   435
the god of fire forged with all his labor.
First he wrapped his legs with well-made greaves,
fastened behind his heels with silver ankle-clasps,
next he strapped the breastplate round his chest
then over his shoulder Achilles slung his sword,   440
the fine bronze blade with its silver-studded hilt,
then hoisted the massive shield flashing far and wide
like a full round moon—and gleaming bright as the light
that reaches sailors out at sea, the flare of a watchfire
burning strong in a lonely sheepfold up some mountain slope   445
when the gale-winds hurl the crew that fights against them
far over the fish-swarming sea, far from loved ones—
so the gleam from Achilles' well-wrought blazoned shield
shot up and hit the skies. Then lifting his rugged helmet
he set it down on his brows, and the horsehair crest   450
shone like a star and the waving golden plumes shook
that Hephaestus drove in bristling thick along its ridge.
And brilliant Achilles tested himself in all his gear,
Achilles spun on his heels to see if it fit tightly,
see if his shining limbs ran free within it, yes,   455
and it felt like buoyant wings lifting the great captain.
And then, last, Achilles drew his father's spear
from its socket-stand—weighted, heavy, tough.
No other Achaean fighter could heft that shaft,
only Achilles had the skill to wield it well: 460
Pelian ash it was, a gift to his father Peleus
presented by Chiron once, hewn on Pelion's[5] crest
to be the death of heroes.
                    Now the war-team—

---

5. A heavily wooded mountain in central Greece. *Chiron:* A centaur famous as a wise teacher.

Alcimus and Automedon worked to yoke them quickly.
They cinched the supple breast-straps round their chests   465
and driving the bridle irons home between their jaws,
pulled the reins back taut to the bolted chariot.
Seizing a glinting whip, his fist on the handgrip,
Automedon leapt aboard behind the team and behind him
Achilles struck his stance, helmed for battle now,   470
glittering in his armor like the sun astride the skies,
his ringing, daunting voice commanding his father's horses:
"Roan Beauty and Charger, illustrious foals of Lightfoot!
Try hard, do better this time—bring your charioteer
back home alive to his waiting Argive comrades   475
once we're through with fighting. Don't leave Achilles
there on the battlefield as you left Patroclus—dead!"

    And Roan Beauty the horse with flashing hoofs
spoke up from under the yoke, bowing his head low
so his full mane came streaming down the yoke-pads,   480
down along the yoke to sweep the ground . . .
The white-armed goddess Hera gave him voice:
"Yes! we will save your life—this time too—
master, mighty Achilles! But the day of death
already hovers near, and we are not to blame   485
but a great god *is* and the strong force of fate.
Not through our want to speed or any lack of care
did the Trojans strip the armor off Patroclus' back.
It was all that matchless god, sleek-haired Leto's son[6]—
he killed him among the champions and handed Hector glory.   490
Our team could race with the rush of the West Wind,
the strongest, swiftest blast on earth, men say—
still *you* are doomed to die by force, Achilles,
cut down by a deathless god and mortal man!"[7]

    He said no more. The Furies struck him dumb.[8]   495
But the fiery runner Achilles burst out in anger,
"Why, Roan Beauty—why prophesy my doom?
Don't waste your breath. I know, well I know—
I am destined to die here, far from my dear father,
far from mother. But all the same I will never stop   500
till I drive the Trojans to their bloody fill of war!"

    A high stabbing cry—
and out in the front ranks he drove his plunging stallions.

---

6. Apollo.   7. Achilles will eventually fall by the hand of Paris as a result of the intervention of Apollo.
8. One of the functions of these goddesses was to ensure that all the creatures of the universe observed
their proper limits.

[Achilles' return to the fighting brought terror to the Trojans and turned the battle into a rout in which Achilles killed every Trojan that crossed his path. As he pursued Agenor, Apollo tricked him by rescuing his intended victim (he spirited him away in a mist) and assumed Agenor's shape to lead Achilles away from the walls of Troy. The Trojans took refuge in the city, all except Hector.]

BOOK XXII

The Death of Hector

So all through Troy the men who had fled like panicked fawns
were wiping off their sweat, drinking away their thirst,
leaning along the city's massive ramparts now
while Achaean troops, sloping shields to shoulders,
closed against the walls. But there stood Hector,   5
shackled fast by his deadly fate, holding his ground,
exposed in front of Troy and the Scaean Gates.
And now Apollo turned to taunt Achilles:
"Why are you chasing *me*? Why waste your speed?—
son of Peleus, you a mortal and I a deathless god.   10
You still don't know that I am immortal, do you?—
straining to catch me in your fury! Have you forgotten?
There's a war to fight with the Trojans you stampeded,
look, they're packed inside their city walls, but you,
you've slipped away out here. You can't kill *me*—   15
I can never die—it's not my fate!"
                                        Enraged at that,
Achilles shouted in mid-stride, "You've blocked my way,
you distant, deadly Archer, deadliest god of all—
you made me swerve away from the rampart there.
Else what a mighty Trojan army had gnawed the dust   20
before they could ever straggle through their gates!
Now you've robbed me of great glory, saved their lives
with all your deathless ease. Nothing for you to fear,
no punishment to come. Oh I'd pay you back
if I only had the power at my command!"   25

    No more words—he dashed toward the city,
heart racing for some great exploit, rushing on
like a champion stallion drawing a chariot full tilt,
sweeping across the plain in easy, tearing strides—
as Achilles hurtled on, driving legs and knees.   30

    And old King Priam was first to see him coming,
surging over the plain, blazing like the star
that rears at harvest, flaming up in its brilliance—
far outshining the countless stars in the night sky,

that star they call Orion's Dog[9]—brightest of all   35
but a fatal sign emblazoned on the heavens,
it brings such killing fever down on wretched men.
So the bronze flared on his chest as on he raced—
and the old man moaned, flinging both hands high,
beating his head and groaning deep he called,   40
begging his dear son who stood before the gates,
unshakable, furious to fight Achilles to the death.
The old man cried, pitifully, hands reaching out to him,
"Oh Hector! Don't just stand there, don't, dear child,
waiting that man's attack—alone, cut off from friends!   45
You'll meet your doom at once, beaten down by Achilles,
so much stronger than you—that hard, headlong man.
Oh if only the gods loved him as much as I do . . .
dogs and vultures would eat his fallen corpse at once!—
with what a load of misery lifted from my spirit.   50
That man who robbed me of my sons, brave boys,
cutting them down or selling them off as slaves,
shipped to islands half the world away . . .
Even now there are two, Lycaon and Polydorus[1]—
I cannot find them among the soldiers crowding Troy,   55
those sons Laothoë[2] bore me, Laothoë queen of women.
But if they are still alive in the enemy's camp,
then we'll ransom them back with bronze and gold.
We have hoards inside the walls, the rich dowry
old and famous Altes[3] presented with his daughter.   60
But if they're dead already, gone to the House of Death,
what grief to their mother's heart and mine—we gave them life.
For the rest of Troy, though, just a moment's grief
unless you too are battered down by Achilles.
Back, come back! Inside the walls, my boy!   65
Rescue the men of Troy and the Trojan women—
don't hand the great glory to Peleus' son,
bereft of your own sweet life yourself.
                              Pity me too!—
still in my senses, true, but a harrowed, broken man
marked out by doom—past the threshold of old age . . .   70
and Father Zeus will waste me with a hideous fate,
and after I've lived to look on so much horror!
My sons laid low, my daughters dragged away
and the treasure-chambers looted, helpless babies
hurled to the earth in the red barbarity of war . . .   75
my sons' wives hauled off by the Argives' bloody hands!
And I, I last of all—the dogs before my doors

9. Sirius, the "dog star," in the constellation *Canis Major*.   1. Both already killed by Achilles in the
fighting outside the city.   2. Priam has more than one wife.   3. Father of Laothoë.

will eat me raw, once some enemy brings me down
with his sharp bronze sword or spits me with a spear,
wrenching the life out of my body, yes, the very dogs   80
I bred in my own halls to share my table, guard my gates—
mad, rabid at heart they'll lap their master's blood
and loll before my doors.
                Ah for a young man
all looks fine and noble if he goes down in war,
hacked to pieces under a slashing bronze blade—   85
he lies there dead . . . but whatever death lays bare,
all wounds are marks of glory. When an old man's killed
and the dogs go at the gray head and the gray beard
and mutilate the genitals—that is the cruelest sight
in all our wretched lives!"
                   So the old man groaned   90
and seizing his gray hair tore it out by the roots
but he could not shake the fixed resolve of Hector.
And his mother wailed now, standing beside Priam,
weeping freely, loosing her robes with one hand
and holding out her bare breast with the other,   95
her words pouring forth in a flight of grief and tears:
"Hector, my child! Look—have some respect for *this!*
Pity your mother too, if I ever gave you the breast
to soothe your troubles, remember it now, dear boy—
beat back that savage man from safe inside the walls!   100
Don't go forth, a champion pitted against him—
merciless, brutal man. If he kills you now,
how can I ever mourn you on your deathbed?—
dear branch in bloom, dear child I brought to birth!—
Neither I nor your wife, that warm, generous woman . . .   105
Now far beyond our reach, now by the Argive ships
the rushing dogs will tear you, bolt your flesh!"

   So they wept, the two of them crying out
to their dear son, both pleading time and again
but they could not shake the fixed resolve of Hector.   110
No, he waited Achilles, coming on, gigantic in power.
As a snake in the hills, guarding his hole, awaits a man—
bloated with poison, deadly hatred seething inside him,
glances flashing fire as he coils round his lair . . .
so Hector, nursing his quenchless fury, gave no ground,   115
leaning his burnished shield against a jutting wall,
but harried still, he probed his own brave heart:
"No way out. If I slip inside the gates and walls,
Polydamas will be first to heap disgrace on me—
he was the one who urged me to lead our Trojans   120
back to Ilium just last night, the disastrous night

Achilles rose in arms like a god. But did I give way?
Not at all. And how much better it would have been!
Now my army's ruined, thanks to my own reckless pride,
I would die of shame to face the men of Troy   125
and the Trojan women trailing their long robes . . .
Someone less of a man than I will say, 'Our Hector—
staking all on his own strength, he destroyed his army!'
So they will mutter. So now, better by far for me
to stand up to Achilles, kill him, come home alive   130
or die at his hands in glory out before the walls.
But wait—what if I put down my studded shield
and heavy helmet, prop my spear on the rampart
and go forth, just as I am, to meet Achilles,
noble Prince Achilles . . .   135
why, I could promise to give back Helen, yes,
and all her treasures with her, all those riches
Paris once hauled home to Troy in the hollow ships—
and they were the cause of all our endless fighting—
Yes, yes, return it all to the sons of Atreus now   140
to haul away, and then, at the same time, divide
the rest with all the Argives, all the city holds,
and then I'd take an oath for the Trojan royal council
that we will hide nothing! Share and share alike the hoards
our handsome citadel stores within its depths and—   145
Why debate, my friend? Why thrash things out?
I must not go and implore him. He'll show no mercy,
no respect for me, my rights—he'll cut me down
straight off—stripped of defenses like a woman
once I have loosed the armor off my body.   150
No way to parley with that man—not now—
not from behind some oak or rock to whisper,
like a boy and a young girl, lovers' secrets
a boy and girl might whisper to each other . . .
Better to clash in battle, now, at once—   155
see which fighter Zeus awards the glory!"
                              So he wavered,
waiting there, but Achilles was closing on him now
like the god of war, the fighter's helmet flashing,
over his right shoulder shaking the Pelian ash spear,
that terror, and the bronze around his body flared   160
like a raging fire or the rising, blazing sun.
Hector looked up, saw him, started to tremble,
nerve gone, he could hold his ground no longer,
he left the gates behind and away he fled in fear—
and Achilles went for him, fast, sure of his speed   165
as the wild mountain hawk, the quickest thing on wings,
launching smoothly, swooping down on a cringing dove

and the dove flits out from under, the hawk screaming
over the quarry, plunging over and over, his fury
driving him down to beak and tear his kill—   170
so Achilles flew at him, breakneck on in fury
with Hector fleeing along the walls of Troy,
fast as his legs would go. On and on they raced,
passing the lookout point, passing the wild fig tree
tossed by the wind, always out from under the ramparts   175
down the wagon trail they careered until they reached
the clear running springs where whirling Scamander
rises up from its double wellsprings bubbling strong—
and one runs hot and the steam goes up around it,
drifting thick as if fire burned at its core   180
but the other even in summer gushes cold
as hail or freezing snow or water chilled to ice . . .
And here, close to the springs, lie washing-pools
scooped out in the hollow rocks and broad and smooth
where the wives of Troy and all their lovely daughters   185
would wash their glistening robes in the old days,
the days of peace before the sons of Achaea came . . .
Past these they raced, one escaping, one in pursuit
and the one who fled was great but the one pursuing
greater, even greater—their pace mounting in speed   190
since both men strove, not for a sacrificial beast
or oxhide trophy, prizes runners fight for, no,
they raced for the life of Hector breaker of horses.
Like powerful stallions sweeping round the post for trophies,
galloping full stretch with some fine prize at stake,   195
a tripod, say, or woman offered up at funeral games
for some brave hero fallen—so the two of them
whirled three times around the city of Priam,
sprinting at top speed while all the gods gazed down,
and the father of men and gods broke forth among them now: 200
"Unbearable—a man I love, hunted round his own city walls
and right before my eyes. My heart grieves for Hector.
Hector who burned so many oxen in my honor, rich cuts,
now on the rugged crests of Ida,[4] now on Ilium's heights.
But now, look, brilliant Achilles courses him round   205
the city of Priam in all his savage, lethal speed.
Come, you immortals, think this through. Decide.
Either we pluck the man from death and save his life
or strike him down at last, here at Achilles' hands—
for all his fighting heart."
                         But immortal Athena,   210
her gray eyes wide, protested strongly: "Father!

4. The great mountain range near Troy.

Lord of the lightning, king of the black cloud,
what are you saying? A man, a mere mortal,
his doom sealed long ago? You'd set him free
from all the pains of death?
     Do as you please—   215
but none of the deathless gods will ever praise you."

 And Zeus who marshals the thunderheads replied,
"Courage, Athena, third-born of the gods, dear child.
Nothing I said was meant in earnest, trust me,
I mean you all the good will in the world. Go.   220
Do as your own impulse bids you. Hold back no more."

 So he launched Athena already poised for action—
down the goddess swept from Olympus' craggy peaks.

 And swift Achilles kept on coursing Hector, nonstop
as a hound in the mountains starts a fawn from its lair, 225
hunting him down the gorges, down the narrow glens
and the fawn goes to ground, hiding deep in brush
but the hound comes racing fast, nosing him out
until he lands his kill. So Hector could never throw
Achilles off his trail, the swift racer Achilles—   230
time and again he'd make a dash for the Dardan Gates,
trying to rush beneath the rock-built ramparts, hoping
men on the heights might save him, somehow, raining spears
but time and again Achilles would intercept him quickly,
heading him off, forcing him out across the plain   235
and always sprinting along the city side himself—
endless as in a dream . . .
when a man can't catch another fleeing on ahead
and he can never escape nor his rival overtake him—
so the one could never run the other down in his speed 240
nor the other spring away. And how could Hector have fled
the fates of death so long? How unless one last time,
one final time Apollo had swept in close beside him,
driving strength in his legs and knees to race the wind?
And brilliant Achilles shook his head at the armies, 245
never letting them hurl their sharp spears at Hector—
someone might snatch the glory, Achilles come in second.
But once they reached the springs for the fourth time,
then Father Zeus held out his sacred golden scales:
in them he placed two fates of death that lays men low— 250
one for Achilles, one for Hector breaker of horses—
and gripping the beam mid-haft the Father raised it high
and down went Hector's day of doom, dragging him down
to the strong House of Death—and god Apollo left him.
Athena rushed to Achilles, her bright eyes gleaming, 255

standing shoulder-to-shoulder, winging orders now:
"At last our hopes run high, my brilliant Achilles—
Father Zeus must love you—
we'll sweep great glory back to Achaea's fleet,
we'll kill this Hector, mad as he is for battle!   260
No way for him to escape us now, no longer—
not even if Phoebus the distant deadly Archer
goes through torments, pleading for Hector's life,
groveling over and over before our storming Father Zeus.
But you, you hold your ground and catch your breath   265
while I run Hector down and persuade the man
to fight you face-to-face."
                          So Athena commanded
and he obeyed, rejoicing at heart—Achilles stopped,
leaning against his ashen spearshaft barbed in bronze.
and Athena left him there, caught up with Hector at once,   270
and taking the build and vibrant voice of Deiphobus
stood shoulder-to-shoulder with him, winging orders:
"Dear brother, how brutally swift Achilles hunts you—
coursing you round the city of Priam in all his lethal speed!
Come, let us stand our ground together—beat him back."   275

    "Deiphobus!"[5]—Hector, his helmet flashing, called out to her—
"dearest of all my brothers, all these warring years,
of all the sons that Priam and Hecuba produced!
Now I'm determined to praise you all the more,
you who dared—seeing me in these straits—   280
to venture out from the walls, all for *my* sake,
while the others stay inside and cling to safety."

    The goddess answered quickly, her eyes blazing,
"True, dear brother—how your father and mother both
implored me, time and again, clutching my knees,   285
and the comrades round me begging me to stay!
Such was the fear that broke them, man for man,
but the heart within me broke with grief for you.
Now headlong on the fight! No letup, no lance spared!
So now, now we'll *see* if Achilles kills us both   290
and hauls our bloody armor back to the beaked ships
or he goes down in pain beneath your spear."

    Athena luring him on with all her immortal cunning—
and now, at last, as the two came closing for the kill
it was tall Hector, helmet flashing, who led off: 295
"No more running from you in fear, Achilles!
Not as before. Three times I fled around

---

5. One of Hector's brothers.

the great city of Priam—I lacked courage then
to stand your onslaught. Now my spirit stirs me
to meet you face-to-face. Now kill or be killed!   300
Come, we'll swear to the gods, the highest witnesses—
the gods will oversee our binding pacts. I swear
I will never mutilate you—merciless as you are—
if Zeus allows me to last it out and tear your life away.
But once I've stripped your glorious armor, Achilles,   305
I will give your body back to your loyal comrades.
Swear you'll do the same."
                          A swift dark glance
and the headstrong runner answered, "Hector, stop!
You unforgivable, you . . . don't talk to me of pacts.
There are no binding oaths between men and lions—   310
wolves and lambs can enjoy no meeting of the minds—
they are all bent on hating each other to the death.
So with you and me. No love between us. No truce
till one or the other falls and gluts with blood
Ares who hacks at men behind his rawhide shield.   315
Come, call up whatever courage you can muster.
Life or death—now prove yourself a spearman,
a daring man of war! No more escape for you—
Athena will kill you with my spear in just a moment.
Now you'll pay at a stroke for all my comrades' grief,   320
all you killed in the fury of your spear!"
                                      With that,
shaft poised, he hurled and his spear's long shadow flew
but seeing it coming glorious Hector ducked away,
crouching down, watching the bronze tip fly past
and stab the earth—but Athena snatched it up   325
and passed it back to Achilles
and Hector the gallant captain never saw her.
He sounded out a challenge to Peleus' princely son:
"You missed, look—the great godlike Achilles!
So you knew nothing at all from Zeus about my death—   330
and yet how sure you were! All bluff, cunning with words,
that's all you are—trying to make me fear you,
lose my nerve, forget my fighting strength.
Well, you'll never plant your lance in my back
as I flee *you* in fear—plunge it through my chest   335
as I come charging in, if a god gives you the chance!
but now it's for you to dodge *my* brazen spear—
I wish you'd bury it in your body to the hilt.
How much lighter the war would be for Trojans then
if you, their greatest scourge, were dead and gone!"   340

    Shaft poised, he hurled and his spear's long shadow flew
and it struck Achilles' shield—a dead-center hit—

but off and away it glanced and Hector seethed,
his hurtling spear, his whole arm's power poured
in a wasted shot. He stood there, cast down . . .   345
he had no spear in reserve. So Hector shouted out
to Deiphobus bearing his white shield—with a ringing shout
he called for a heavy lance—
                              but the man was nowhere near him,
vanished—
              yes and Hector knew the truth in his heart
and the fighter cried aloud, "My time has come!   350
At last the gods have called me down to death.
I thought he was at my side, the hero Deiphobus—
he's safe inside the walls, Athena's tricked me blind.
And now death, grim death is looming up beside me,
no longer far away. No way to escape it now. This,   355
this was their pleasure after all, sealed long ago—
Zeus and the son of Zeus, the distant deadly Archer—
though often before now they rushed to my defense.
So now I meet my doom. Well let me die—
but not without struggle, not without glory, no,   360
in some great clash of arms that even men to come
will hear of down the years!"
                              And on that resolve
he drew the whetted sword that hung at his side,
tempered, massive, and gathering all his force
he swooped like a soaring eagle   365
launching down from the dark clouds to earth
to snatch some helpless lamb or trembling hare.
So Hector swooped now, swinging his whetted sword
and Achilles charged too, bursting with rage, barbaric,
guarding his chest with the well-wrought blazoned shield,   370
head tossing his gleaming helmet, four horns strong
and the golden plumes shook that the god of fire
drove in bristling thick along its ridge.
Bright as that star amid the stars in the night sky,
star of the evening, brightest star that rides the heavens,   375
so fire flared from the sharp point of the spear Achilles
brandished high in his right hand, bent on Hector's death,
scanning his splendid body—where to pierce it best?
The rest of his flesh seemed all encased in armor,
burnished, brazen—*Achilles'* armor that Hector stripped   380
from strong Patroclus when he killed him—true,
but one spot lay exposed,
where collarbones lift the neckbone off the shoulders,
the open throat, where the end of life comes quickest—*there*
as Hector charged in fury brilliant Achilles drove his spear   385
and the point went stabbing clean through the tender neck
but the heavy bronze weapon failed to slash the windpipe—

Hector could still gasp out some words, some last reply . . .
he crashed in the dust—
                              godlike Achilles gloried over him:
"Hector—surely you thought when you stripped Patroclus' armor   390
that you, you would be safe! Never a fear of me—
far from the fighting as I was—you fool!
Left behind there, down by the beaked ships
his great avenger waited, a greater man by far—
that man was I, and I smashed your strength! And you—   395
the dogs and birds will maul you, shame your corpse
while Achaeans bury my dear friend in glory!"

    Struggling for breath, Hector, his helmet flashing,
said, "I beg you, beg you for your life, your parents—
don't let the dogs devour me by the Argive ships!   400
Wait, take the princely ransom of bronze and gold,
the gifts my father and noble mother will give you—
but give my body to friends to carry home again,
so Trojan men and Trojan women can do me honor
with fitting rites of fire once I am dead."   405

    Staring grimly, the proud runner Achilles answered,
"Beg no more, you fawning dog—begging me by my parents!
Would to god my rage, my fury would drive me now
to hack your flesh away and eat you raw—
such agonies you have caused me! Ransom?   410
No man alive could keep the dog-packs off you,
not if they haul in ten, twenty times that ransom
and pile it here before me and promise fortunes more—
no, not even if Dardan Priam should offer to weigh out
your bulk in gold! Not even then will your noble mother   415
lay you on your deathbed, mourn the son she bore . . .
The dogs and birds will rend you—blood and bone!"

    At the point of death, Hector, his helmet flashing,
said, "I know you well—I see my fate before me.
Never a chance that I could win you over . . .   420
Iron inside your chest, that heart of yours.
But now beware, or my curse will draw god's wrath
upon your head, that day when Paris and lord Apollo—
for all your fighting heart—destroy you at the Scaean Gates!"

    Death cut him short. The end closed in around him.   425
Flying free of his limbs
his soul went winging down to the House of Death,
wailing his fate, leaving his manhood far behind,
his young and supple strength. But brilliant Achilles
taunted Hector's body, dead as he was, "Die, die!   430

For my own death, I'll meet it freely—whenever Zeus
and the other deathless gods would like to bring it on!"

    With that he wrenched his bronze spear from the corpse,
laid it aside and ripped the bloody armor off the back.
And the other sons of Achaea, running up around him,   435
crowded closer, all of them gazing wonder-struck
at the build and marvelous, lithe beauty of Hector.
And not a man came forward who did not stab his body,
glancing toward a comrade, laughing: "Ah, look here—
how much softer he is to handle now, this Hector,   440
than when he gutted our ships with roaring fire!"

    Standing over him, so they'd gloat and stab his body.
But once he had stripped the corpse the proud runner Achilles
took his stand in the midst of all the Argive troops
and urged them on with a flight of winging orders: 445
"Friends—lords of the Argives, O my captains!
Now that the gods have let me kill this man
who caused us agonies, loss on crushing loss—
more than the rest of all their men combined—
come, let us ring their walls in armor, test them,   450
see what recourse the Trojans still may have in mind.
Will they abandon the city heights with this man fallen?
Or brace for a last, dying stand though Hector's gone?
But wait—what am I saying? Why this deep debate?
Down by the ships a body lies unwept, unburied—   455
Patroclus . . . I will never forget him,
not as long as I'm still among the living
and my springing knees will lift and drive me on.
Though the dead forget their dead in the House of Death,
I will remember, even there, my dear companion.
                                Now,   460
come, you sons of Achaea, raise a song of triumph!
Down to the ships we march and bear this corpse on high—
we have won ourselves great glory. We have brought
magnificent Hector down, that man the Trojans
glorified in their city like a god!"
                      So he triumphed   465
and now he was bent on outrage, on shaming noble Hector.
Piercing the tendons, ankle to heel behind both feet,
he knotted straps of rawhide through them both,
lashed them to his chariot, left the head to drag
and mounting the car, hoisting the famous arms aboard,   470
he whipped his team to a run and breakneck on they flew,
holding nothing back. And a thick cloud of dust rose up
from the man they dragged, his dark hair swirling round
that head so handsome once, all tumbled low in the dust—

since Zeus had given him over to his enemies now   475
to be defiled in the land of his own fathers.

So his whole head was dragged down in the dust.
And now his mother began to tear her hair . . .
she flung her shining veil to the ground and raised
a high, shattering scream, looking down at her son.   480
Pitifully his loving father groaned and round the king
his people cried with grief and wailing seized the city—
for all the world as if all Troy were torched and smoldering
down from the looming brows of the citadel to her roots.
Priam's people could hardly hold the old man back,   485
frantic, mad to go rushing out the Dardan Gates.
He begged them all, groveling in the filth,
crying out to them, calling each man by name,
"Let go, my friends! Much as you care for me,
let me hurry out of the city, make my way,   490
all on my own, to Achaea's waiting ships!
I must implore that terrible, violent man . . .
Perhaps—who knows?—he may respect my age,
may pity an old man. He has a father too,
as old as I am—Peleus sired him once,   495
Peleus reared him to be the scourge of Troy
but most of all to me—he made my life a hell.
So many sons he slaughtered, just coming into bloom . . .
but grieving for all the rest, one breaks my heart the most
and stabbing grief for him will take me down to Death—   500
my Hector—would to god he had perished in my arms!
Then his mother who bore him—oh so doomed,
she and I could glut ourselves with grief."

So the voice of the king rang out in tears,
the citizens wailed in answer, and noble Hecuba   505
led the wives of Troy in a throbbing chant of sorrow:
"O my child—my desolation! How can I go on living?
What agonies must I suffer now, now *you* are dead and gone?
You were my pride throughout the city night and day—
a blessing to us all, the men and women of Troy: 510
throughout the city they saluted you like a god.
You, you were their greatest glory while you lived—
now death and fate have seized you, dragged you down!"

Her voice rang out in tears, but the wife of Hector
had not heard a thing. No messenger brought the truth   515
of how her husband made his stand outside the gates.
She was weaving at her loom, deep in the high halls,
working flowered braiding into a dark red folding robe.

And she called her well-kempt women through the house
to set a large three-legged cauldron over the fire   520
so Hector could have his steaming hot bath
when he came home from battle—poor woman,
she never dreamed how far he was from bathing,
struck down at Achilles' hands by blazing-eyed Athena.
But she heard the groans and wails of grief from the rampart now   525
and her body shook, her shuttle dropped to the ground,
she called out to her lovely waiting women, "Quickly—
two of you follow me—I must see what's happened.
that cry—that was Hector's honored mother I heard!
My heart's pounding, leaping up in my throat,   530
the knees beneath me paralyzed—Oh I know it . . .
something terrible's coming down on Priam's children.
Pray god the news will never reach my ears!
Yes but I dread it so—what if great Achilles
has cut my Hector off from the city, daring Hector,   535
and driven him out across the plain, and all alone?—
He may have put an end to that fatal headstrong pride
that always seized my Hector—never hanging back
with the main force of men, always charging ahead,
giving ground to no man in his fury!"
                                        So she cried,   540
dashing out of the royal halls like a madwoman,
her heart racing hard, her women close behind her.
But once she reached the tower where soldiers massed
she stopped on the rampart, looked down and saw it all—
saw him dragged before the city, stallions galloping,   545
dragging Hector back to Achaea's beaked warships—
ruthless work. The world went black as night
before her eyes, she fainted, falling backward,
gasping away her life breath . . .
She flung to the winds her glittering headdress,   550
the cap and the coronet, braided band and veil,
all the regalia golden Aphrodite gave her once,
the day that Hector, helmet aflash in sunlight,
led her home to Troy from her father's house
with countless wedding gifts to win her heart.   555
But crowding round her now her husband's sisters
and brothers' wives supported her in their midst,
and she, terrified, stunned to the point of death,
struggling for breath now and coming back to life,
burst out in grief among the Trojan women: "O Hector—   560
I am destroyed! Both born to the same fate after all!
You, you at Troy in the halls of King Priam—
I at Thebes, under the timberline of Placos,

Eetion's house . . . He raised me as a child,
that man of doom, his daughter just as doomed—   565
would to god he'd never fathered *me!*
                              Now you go down
to the House of Death, the dark depths of the earth,
and leave me here to waste away in grief, a widow
lost in the royal halls—and the boy only a baby,
the son we bore together, you and I so doomed.   570
Hector, what help are you to him, now you are dead?—
what help is he to you? Think, even if he escapes
the wrenching horrors of war against the Argives,
pain and labor will plague him all his days to come.
Strangers will mark his lands off, stealing his estates.   575
The day that orphans a youngster cuts him off from friends.
And he hangs his head low, humiliated in every way . . .
his cheeks stained with tears, and pressed by hunger
the boy goes up to his father's old companions,
tugging at one man's cloak, another's tunic,   580
and some will pity him, true,
and one will give him a little cup to drink,
enough to wet his lips, not quench his thirst.
But then some bully with both his parents living
beats him from the banquet, fists and abuses flying: 585
'You, get out—you've got no father feasting with us here!'
And the boy, sobbing, trails home to his widowed mother . . .
Astyanax!
            And years ago, propped on his father's knee,
he would only eat the marrow, the richest cuts of lamb,
and when sleep came on him and he had quit his play,   590
cradled warm in his nurse's arms he'd drowse off,
snug in a soft bed, his heart brimmed with joy.
Now what suffering, now he's lost his father—
                              Astyanax!
The Lord of the City , so the Trojans called him,
because it was you, Hector, you and you alone   595
who shielded the gates and the long walls of Troy.
But now by the beaked ships, far from your parents,
glistening worms will wriggle through your flesh,
once the dogs have had their fill of your naked corpse—
though we have such stores of clothing laid up in the halls, 600
fine things, a joy to the eye, the work of women's hands.
Now, by god, I'll burn them all, blazing to the skies!
No use to you now, they'll never shroud your body—
but they will be your glory
burned by the Trojan men and women in your honor!"   605

    Her voice rang out in tears and the women wailed in answer.

[Achilles buried Patroclus, and the Greeks celebrated the dead hero's fame with athletic games, for which Achilles gave the prizes.]

BOOK XXIV

Achilles and Priam

The games were over now. The gathered armies scattered,
each man to his fast ship, and fighters turned their minds
to thoughts of food and the sweet warm grip of sleep.
But Achilles kept on grieving for his friend,
the memory burning on . . .   5
and all-subduing sleep could not take him,
not now, he turned and twisted, side to side,
he longed for Patroclus' manhood, his gallant heart—
What rough campaigns they'd fought to an end together,
what hardships they had suffered, cleaving their way   10
through wars of men and pounding waves at sea.
The memories flooded over him, live tears flowing,
and now he'd lie on his side, now flat on his back,
now facedown again. At last he'd leap to his feet,
wander in anguish, aimless along the surf, and dawn on dawn   15
flaming over the sea and shore would find him pacing.
Then he'd yoke his racing team to the chariot-harness,
lash the corpse of Hector behind the car for dragging
and haul him three times round the dead Patroclus' tomb,
and then he'd rest again in his tents and leave the body   20
sprawled facedown in the dust. But Apollo pitied Hector—
dead man though he was—and warded all corruption off
from Hector's corpse and round him, head to foot,
the great god wrapped the golden shield of storm
so his skin would never rip as Achilles dragged him on.   25

And so he kept on raging, shaming noble Hector,
but the gods in bliss looked down and pitied Priam's son.
They kept on urging the sharp-eyed giant-killer Hermes
to go and steal the body, a plan that pleased them all,
but not Hera, Poseidon or the girl with blazing eyes.[6]   30
They clung to their deathless hate of sacred Troy,
Priam and Priam's people, just as they had at first
when Paris in all his madness launched the war.[7]
He offended Athena and Hera—both goddesses.
When they came to his shepherd's fold he favored Love   35
who dangled before his eyes the lust that loosed disaster.
But now, at the twelfth dawn since Hector's death,
lord Apollo rose and addressed the immortal powers:

6. Athena.   7. He was appointed judge in a contest of beauty between Aphrodite, Hera, and Athena. All three goddesses offered bribes, but Aphrodite's promise to give him Helen proved the most attractive.

"Hard-hearted you are, you gods, you live for cruelty!
Did Hector never burn in your honor thighs of oxen   40
and flawless, full-grown goats? Now you cannot
bring yourselves to save him—even his corpse—
so his wife can see him, his mother and his child,
his father Priam and Priam's people: how they'd rush
to burn the body on the pyre and give him royal rites!   45
But murderous Achilles—you gods, you *choose* to help Achilles.
That man without a shred of decency in his heart . . .
his temper can never bend and change—like some lion
going his own barbaric way, giving in to his power,
his brute force and wild pride, as down he swoops   50
on the flocks of men to seize his savage feast.
Achilles has lost all pity! No shame in the man,
shame that does great harm or drives men on to good.
No doubt some mortal has suffered a dearer loss than this,
a brother born in the same womb, or even a son . . .   55
he grieves, he weeps, but then his tears are through.
The Fates have given mortals hearts that can endure.
But this Achilles—first he slaughters Hector,
he rips away the noble prince's life
then lashes him to his chariot, drags him round   60
his beloved comrade's tomb. But why, I ask you?
What good will it do him? What honor will he gain?
Let that man beware, or great and glorious as he is,
we mighty gods will wheel on him in anger—look,
he outrages the senseless clay in all his fury!"   65

     But white-armed Hera flared at him in anger:
"Yes, there'd be some merit even in what *you* say,
lord of the silver bow—if all you gods, in fact,
would set Achilles and Hector high in equal honor.
But Hector is mortal. He sucked a woman's breast.   70
Achilles sprang from a goddess—one I reared myself:
I brought her up and gave her in marriage to a man,
to Peleus, dearest to all your hearts, you gods.
All you Gods, you shared in the wedding rites,
and so did you, Apollo—there you sat at the feast   75
and struck your lyre. What company you keep now,
these wretched Trojans. You—forever faithless!"

     But Zeus who marshals the storm clouds warned his queen,
"Now, Hera, don't fly into such a rage at fellow gods.
These two can never attain the same degree of honor.   80
Still, the immortals loved Prince Hector dearly,
best of all the mortals born in Troy . . .
so *I* loved him, at least:
he never stinted with gifts to please my heart.

Never once did my altar lack its share of victims,   85
winecups tipped and the deep smoky savor. These,
these are the gifts we claim—they are our rights.
But as for stealing courageous Hector's body,
we must abandon the idea—not a chance in the world
behind Achilles' back. For Thetis is always there,   90
his mother always hovering near him night and day.
Now would one of you gods call Thetis to my presence?—
so I can declare to her my solemn, sound decree:
Achilles must receive a ransom from King Priam,
Achilles must give Hector's body back."
                    So he decreed   95
and Iris, racing a gale-wind down with Zeus's message,
mid-sea between Samos and Imbros'[8] rugged cliffs
dove in a black swell as groaning breakers roared.
Down she plunged to the bottom fast as a lead weight
sheathed in a glinting lure of wild bull's horn,[9]   100
bearing hooked death to the ravenous fish.
And deep in a hollow cave she came on Thetis.
Gathered round her sat the other immortal sea-nymphs
while Thetis amidst them mourned her brave son's fate,
doomed to die, she knew, on the fertile soil of Troy,   105
far from his native land. Quick as the wind now
Iris rushed to the goddess, urging, "Rise, Thetis—
Zeus with his everlasting counsels calls you now!"
Shifting on her glistening feet, the goddess answered,
"Why . . . what does the great god want with me?   110
I cringe from mingling with the immortals now—
Oh the torment—never-ending heartbreak!
But go I shall. A high decree of the Father
must not come to nothing—whatever he commands."

    The radiant queen of sea-nymphs seized a veil,   115
blue-black, no robe darker in all the Ocean's depths,
and launched up and away with wind-swift Iris leading—
the ground swell round them cleaved and opened wide.
And striding out on shore they soared to the high sky
and found farseeing Zeus, and around him all the gods   120
who live in bliss forever sat in a grand assembly.
And Thetis took a seat beside the Father,
a throne Athena yielded. Hera placed in her hand
a burnished golden cup and said some words of comfort,
and taking a few quick sips, Thetis gave it back . . .   125
The father of men and gods began to address them:
"You have come to Olympus now, immortal Thetis,
for all your grief—what unforgettable sorrow

8. Two islands in the North Aegean.   9. A lure for big fish.

seizes on your heart. I know it well myself.
Even so, I must tell you why I called you here.   130
For nine whole days the immortals have been feuding
over Hector's corpse and Achilles, scourge of cities.
They keep urging the sharp-eyed giant-killer Hermes
to go and steal the body. But that is not my way.
I will grant Achilles glory and so safeguard   135
your awe and love of me for all the years to come.
Go at once to the camp, give your son this order:
tell him the gods are angry with him now
and I am rising over them all in deathless wrath
that he in heartsick fury still holds Hector's body,   140
there by his beaked ships, and will not give him back—
perhaps in fear of me he'll give him back at once.
Then, at the same time, I am winging Iris down
to greathearted Priam, commanding the king
to ransom his dear son, to go to Achaea's ships,   145
bearing gifts to Achilles, gifts to melt his rage."
                                                    So he decreed
and Thetis with her glistening feet did not resist a moment.
Down the goddess flashed from the peaks of Mount Olympus,
made her way to her son's camp, and there he was,
she found him groaning hard, choked with sobs.   150
Around him trusted comrades swung to the work,
preparing breakfast, steadying in their midst
a large fleecy sheep just slaughtered in the shelter.
But his noble mother, settling down at his side,
stroked Achilles gently, whispering his name: "My child—   155
how long will you eat your heart out here in tears and torment?
All wiped from your mind, all thought of food and bed?
It's a welcome thing to make love with a woman . . .
You don't have long to live now, well I know:
already I see them looming up beside you—death   160
and the strong force of fate. Listen to me,
quickly! I bring you a message sent by Zeus:
he says the gods are angry with you now
and he is rising over them all in deathless wrath
that you in heartsick fury still hold Hector's body,   165
here by your beaked ships, and will not give him back.
O give him back at once—take ransom for the dead!"

    The swift runner replied in haste, "So be it.
The man who brings the ransom can take away the body,
if Olympian Zeus himself insists in all earnest."   170

    While mother and son agreed among the clustered ships,
trading between each other many winged words,
Father Zeus sped Iris down to sacred Troy:

"Quick on your way now, Iris, shear the wind!
Leave our Olympian stronghold—   175
take a message to greathearted Priam down in Troy:
he must go to Achaea's ships and ransom his dear son,
bearing gifts to Achilles, gifts to melt his rage.
But let him go alone, no other Trojan attend him,
only a herald with him, a seasoned, older one   180
who can drive the mules and smooth-running wagon
and bring the hero's body back to sacred Troy,
the man that brilliant Achilles killed in battle.
Let him have no fear of death, no dread in his heart,
such a powerful escort we will send him—the giant-killer   185
Hermes will guide him all the way to Achilles' presence.
And once the god has led him within the fighter's shelter,
Achilles will not kill him—he'll hold back all the rest:
Achilles is no madman, no reckless fool, not the one
to defy the gods' commands. Whoever begs his mercy   190
he will spare with all the kindness in his heart."
                                                So he decreed
and Iris ran his message, racing with gale force
to Priam's halls where cries and mourning met her.
Sons huddled round their father deep in the courtyard,
robes drenched with tears, and the old man amidst them,   195
buried, beaten down in the cloak that wrapped his body . . .
Smeared on the old man's head and neck the dung lay thick
that he scraped up in his own hands, groveling in the filth.
Throughout the house his daughters and sons' wives wailed,
remembering all the fine brave men who lay dead now,   200
their lives destroyed at the fighting Argives' hands.
And Iris, Zeus's crier, standing alongside Priam,
spoke in a soft voice, but his limbs shook at once—
"Courage, Dardan Priam, take heart! Nothing to fear.
No herald of doom, I come on a friendly mission—   205
I come with all good will.
I bring you a message sent by Zeus, a world away
but he has you in his heart, he pities you now . . .
Olympian Zeus commands you to ransom royal Hector,
to bear gifts to Achilles, gifts to melt his rage.   210
But you must go alone, no other Trojan attend you,
only a herald with you, a seasoned, older one
who can drive the mules and smooth-running wagon
and bring the hero's body back to sacred Troy,
the man that brilliant Achilles killed in battle.   215
But have no fear of death, no dread in your heart,
such a powerful escort will conduct you—the giant-killer
Hermes will guide you all the way to Achilles' presence.
And once the god has led you within the fighter's shelter,

Achilles will not kill you—he'll hold back all the rest: 220
Achilles is no madman, no reckless fool, not the one
to defy the gods' commands. Whoever begs his mercy
he will spare with all the kindness in his heart!"

And Iris racing the wind went veering off
and Priam ordered his sons to get a wagon ready,   225
a good smooth-running one, to hitch the mules
and strap a big wicker cradle across its frame.
Then down he went himself to his treasure-chamber,
high-ceilinged, paneled, fragrant with cedarwood
and a wealth of precious objects filled its chests.   230
He called out to his wife, Hecuba, "Dear woman!
An Olympian messenger came to me from Zeus—
I must go to Achaea's ships and ransom our dear son,
bearing gifts to Achilles, gifts to melt his rage.
Tell me, what should I do? What do *you* think?   235
Myself—a terrible longing drives me, heart and soul,
down to the ships, into the vast Achaean camp."

But his wife cried out in answer, "No, no—
where have your senses gone?—that made you famous once,
both among outland men and those you rule in Troy!   240
How can you think of going down to the ships, alone,
and face the glance of the man who killed your sons,
so many fine brave boys? You have a heart of iron!
If he gets you in his clutches, sets his eyes on you—
that savage, treacherous man—he'll show no mercy,   245
no respect for your rights!
                              Come, all we can do now
is sit in the halls, far from our son, and wail for Hector . . .
So this, this is the doom that strong Fate spun out,
our son's life line drawn with his first breath—
the moment I gave him birth—   250
to glut the wild dogs, cut off from his parents,
crushed by the stronger man. Oh would to god
that I could sink my teeth in his liver, eat him raw!
That would avenge what he has done to Hector—
no coward the man Achilles killed—my son stood   255
and fought for the men of Troy and their deep-breasted wives
with never a thought of flight or run for cover!"

But the old and noble Priam answered firmly,
"I will go. My mind's made up. Don't hold me back.
And don't go flying off on your own across the halls,   260
a bird of evil omen—you can't dissuade me now.
If someone else had commanded me, some mortal man,
some prophet staring into the smoke, some priest,

I'd call it a lie and turn my back upon it.
Not now. I heard her voice with my own ears,   265
I looked straight at the goddess, face-to-face.
So I am going—her message must not come to nothing.
And if it is my fate to die by the beaked ships
of Achaeans armed in bronze, then die I shall.
Let Achilles cut me down straightway—   270
once I've caught my son in my arms and wept my fill!"

He raised back the carved lids of the chests
and lifted out twelve robes, handsome, rich brocades,
twelve cloaks, unlined and light, as many blankets,
as many big white capes and shirts to go with them.   275
He weighed and carried out ten full bars of gold
and took two burnished tripods, four fine cauldrons
and last a magnificent cup the Thracians gave him once—
he'd gone on an embassy and won that priceless treasure—
but not even *that* did the old man spare in his halls,   280
not now, consumed with desire to ransom back his son.
Crowds of Trojans were mobbing his colonnades—
he gave them a tongue-lashing, sent them packing:
"Get out—you good-for-nothings, public disgraces!
Haven't you got enough to wail about at home   285
without coming here to add to all my griefs?
You think it nothing, the pain that Zeus has sent me?—
he's destroyed my best son! You'll learn too, in tears—
easier game you'll be for Argive troops to slaughter,
now my Hector's dead. But before I have to see   290
my city annihilated, laid waste before my eyes—
oh let me go down to the House of Death!"

He herded them off with his staff—they fled outside
before the old man's fury. So he lashed out at his sons,
cursing the sight of Helenus, Paris, noble Agathon,   295
Pammon, Antiphonus, Polites loud with the war cry,
Deiphobus and Hippothous, even lordly Dius—
the old man shouted at all nine, rough commands:
"Get to your work! My vicious sons—my humiliations!
If only you'd all been killed at the fast ships   300
instead of my dear Hector . . .
But I—dear god, my life so cursed by fate!—
I fathered hero sons in the wide realm of Troy
and now, now not a single one is left, I tell you.
Mestor the indestructible, Troilus, passionate horseman   305
and Hector—a god among men—no son of a mortal man,
he seemed a deathless god's. But Ares killed them all
and all he left me are these, these disgraces—liars,
dancers, heroes only at beating the dancing-rings,

you plunder your own people for lambs and kids!
Why don't you get my wagon ready—now, at once?
Pack all these things aboard! We must be on our way!"

　　Terrified by their father's rough commands
the sons trundled a mule-wagon out at once,
a good smooth-running one,   315
newly finished, balanced and bolted tight,
and strapped a big wicker cradle across its frame.
They lifted off its hook a boxwood yoke for the mules,
its bulging pommel fitted with rings for guide-reins,
brought out with the yoke its yoke-strap nine arms long   320
and wedged the yoke down firm on the sanded, tapered pole,
on the front peg, and slipped the yoke-ring onto its pin,
strapped the pommel with three good twists, both sides,
then lashed the assembly round and down the shaft
and under the clamp they made the lashing fast.   325
Then the priceless ransom for Hector's body:
hauling it up from the vaults they piled it high
on the wagon's well-made cradle, then they yoked the mules—
stamping their sharp hoofs, trained for heavy loads—
that the Mysians[1] once gave Priam, princely gifts.   330
And last they yoked his team to the king's chariot,
stallions he bred himself in his own polished stalls.

　　No sooner were both men harnessed up beneath the roofs,
Priam and herald, minds set on the coming journey,
than Hecuba rushed up to them, gaunt with grief,   335
holding a gold cup of mellow wine in her right hand
so the men might pour libations before they left.
She stood in front of the horses, crying up at Priam,
"Here, quickly—pour a libation out to Father Zeus!
Pray for a safe return from all our mortal enemies,   340
seeing you're dead set on going down to the ships—
though you go against my will. But if go you must,
pray, at least, to the great god of the dark storm cloud,
up there on Ida, gazing down on the whole expanse of Troy!
Pray for a bird of omen, Zeus's wind-swift messenger,   345
the dearest bird in the world to his prophetic heart,
the strongest thing on wings—clear on the right
so you can see that sign with your own eyes
and trust your life to it as you venture down
to Achaea's ships and the fast chariot-teams.   350
But if farseeing Zeus does not send you that sign—
his own messenger—then I urge you, beg you,

1. A people of central Asia Minor.

don't go down to the ships—
not for all the passion in your heart!"

The old majestic Priam gave his answer: 355
"Dear woman, surely I won't resist your urging now.
It's well to lift our hands and ask great Zeus for mercy."

And the old king motioned a steward standing by
to pour some clear pure water over his hands,
and she came forward, bearing a jug and basin.   360
He rinsed his hands, took the cup from his wife
and taking a stand amidst the forecourt, prayed,
pouring the wine to earth and scanning the high skies,
Priam prayed in his rich resounding voice: "Father Zeus!
Ruling over us all from Ida, god of greatness, god of glory!   365
Grant that Achilles will receive me with kindness, mercy.
Send me a bird of omen, your own wind-swift messenger,
the dearest bird in the world to your prophetic heart,
the strongest thing on wings—clear on the right
so I can see that sign with my own eyes   370
and trust my life to *it* as I venture down
to Achaea's ships and the fast chariot-teams!"

And Zeus in all his wisdom heard that prayer
and straightaway the Father launched an eagle—
truest of Zeus's signs that fly the skies—   375
the dark marauder that mankind calls the Black-wing.
Broad as the door of a rich man's vaulted treasure-chamber,
well-fitted with sturdy bars, so broad each wing of the bird
spread out on either side as it swept in through the city
flashing clear on the right before the king and queen.   380
All looked up, overjoyed—the people's spirits lifted.

And the old man, rushing to climb aboard his chariot,
drove out through the gates and echoing colonnades.
The mules in the lead hauled out the four-wheeled wagon,
driven on by seasoned Idaeus. The horses came behind   385
as the old man cracked the lash and urged them fast
throughout the city with all his kinsmen trailing . . .
weeping their hearts out, as if he went to his death.
But once the two passed down through crowded streets
and out into open country, Priam's kin turned back,   390
his sons and in-laws straggling home to Troy.
But Zeus who beholds the world could hardly fail
to see the two men striking out across the plain.
As he watched the old man he filled with pity
and quickly summoned Hermes, his own dear son: 395
"Hermes—escorting men is your greatest joy,
you above all the gods,

and you listen to the wish of those you favor.
So down you go. Down and conduct King Priam there
through Achaea's beaked ships, so none will see him,   400
none of the Argive fighters recognize him now,
not till he reaches Peleus' royal son."
                                        So he decreed
and Hermes the giant-killing guide obeyed at once.
Under his feet he strapped the supple sandals,
never-dying gold, that wing him over the waves   405
and boundless earth with the speed of gusting winds.
He seized the wand that enchants the eyes of men
whenever Hermes wants, or wakes them up from sleep.
That wand in his grip he flew, the mighty giant-killer
touching down on Troy and the Hellespont in no time   410
and from there he went on foot, for all the world
like a young prince, sporting his first beard,
just in the prime and fresh warm pride of youth.
                                        And now,
as soon as the two drove past the great tomb of Ilus[2]
they drew rein at the ford to water mules and team.   415
A sudden darkness had swept across the earth
and Hermes was all but on them when the herald
looked up, saw him, shouted at once to Priam,
"Danger, my king—think fast! I see a man—
I'm afraid we'll both be butchered on the spot—   420
into the chariot, hurry! Run for our lives
or fling ourselves at his knees and beg for mercy!"

    The old man was stunned, in a swirl of terror,
the hairs stood bristling all over his gnarled body—
he stood there, staring dumbly. Not waiting for welcome   425
the running god of luck went straight up to Priam,
clasped the old king's hands and asked him warmly,
"Father—where do you drive these mules and team
through the godsent night while other mortals sleep?
Have you no fear of the Argives breathing hate and fury?   430
Here are your deadly enemies, camping close at hand.
Now what if one of them saw you, rolling blithely
on through the rushing night with so much tempting treasure—
how would you feel then? You're not so young yourself,
and the man who attends you here is far too old   435
to drive off an attacker spoiling for a fight.
But I would never hurt you—and what's more,
I'd beat off any man who'd do you harm:
you remind me of my dear father, to the life."

---

2. The tomb of Priam's grandfather, a landmark on the Trojan plain.

And the old and noble Priam said at once,   440
"Our straits are hard, dear child, as you say.
But a god still holds his hands above me, even me.
Sending such a traveler here to meet me—
what a lucky omen! Look at your build . . .
your handsome face—a wonder. And such good sense—   445
your parents must be blissful as the gods!"
    The guide and giant-killer answered quickly,
"You're right, old man, all straight to the mark.
But come, tell me the truth now, point by point:
this treasure—a king's ransom—do you send it off   450
to distant, outland men, to keep it safe for you?
Or now do you all abandon sacred Troy,
all in panic—such was the man who died,
your finest, bravest man . . . your own son
who never failed in a fight against the Argives."   455

    But the old majestic Priam countered quickly,
"Who are *you*, my fine friend?—who are your parents?
How can you speak so well of my doomed son's fate?"

    And the guide and giant-killer answered staunchly,
"You're testing me, old man—asking of noble Hector.   460
Ah, how often I watched him battling on the lines
where men win glory, saw the man with my own eyes!
And saw him drive Achaeans against the ships that day
he kept on killing, cutting them down with slashing bronze
while we stood by and marveled—Achilles reined us in: 465
no fighting for us while he raged on at Agamemnon.
I am Achilles' aide, you see,
one and the same good warship brought us here.
I am a Myrmidon, and my father is Polyctor,
and a wealthy man he is, about as old as you . . .   470
He has six sons—I'm the seventh—we all shook lots
and it fell to me to join the armies here at Troy.
I've just come up from the ships to scout the plain—
at dawn the fiery-eyed Achaeans fight around the city.
They chafe, sitting in camp, so bent on battle now   475
the kings of Achaea cannot hold them back."

    And the old and noble Priam asked at once,
"If you really are the royal Achilles' aide,
please, tell *me* the whole truth, point by point.
My son—does he still lie by the beached ships,   480
or by now has the great Achilles hacked him
limb from limb and served him to his dogs?"

    The guide and giant-killer reassured him:
"So far, old man, no birds or dogs have eaten him.

No, there he lies—still there at Achilles' ship,   485
still intact in his shelters.
This is the twelfth day he's lain there, too,
but his body has not decayed, not in the least,
nor have the worms begun to gnaw his corpse,
the swarms that devour men who fall in battle.   490
True, dawn on fiery dawn he drags him round
his beloved comrade's tomb, drags him ruthlessly
but he cannot mutilate his body. It's marvelous—
go see for yourself how he lies there fresh as dew,
the blood washed away, and no sign of corruption.   495
All his wounds sealed shut, wherever they struck . . .
and many drove their bronze blades through his body.
Such pains the blissful gods are lavishing on your son,
dead man though he is—the gods love him dearly!"

    And the old man rejoiced at that, bursting out,   500
"O my child, how good it is to give the immortals
fit and proper gifts! Now take my son—
or was he all a dream? Never once in his halls
did he forget the gods who hold Olympus, never,
so now they remember *him* . . . if only after death.   505
Come, this handsome cup: accept it from me, I beg you!
Protect me, escort me now—if the gods will it so—
all the way till I reach Achilles' shelter."

    The guide and giant-killer refused him firmly,
"You test me again, old man, since I am young,   510
but you will not persuade me,
tempting me with a gift behind Achilles' back.
I fear the man, I'd die of shame to rob him—
just think of the trouble I might suffer later.
But I'd escort you with all the kindness in my heart,   515
all the way till I reached the shining hills of Argos
bound in a scudding ship or pacing you on foot—
and no marauder on earth, scorning your escort,
would dare attack you then."
                                        And the god of luck,
leaping onto the chariot right behind the team,   520
quickly grasped the whip and reins in his hands
and breathed fresh spirit into the mules and horses.
As they reached the trench and rampart round the fleet,
the sentries had just begun to set out supper there
but the giant-killer plunged them all in sleep . . .   525
he spread the gates at once, slid back the bars
and ushered Priam in with his wagon-load of treasure.
Now, at last, they approached royal Achilles' shelter,
the tall, imposing lodge the Myrmidons built their king,

hewing planks of pine, and roofed it high with thatch,   530
gathering thick shaggy reeds from the meadow banks,
and round it built their king a spacious courtyard
fenced with close-set stakes. A single pine beam
held the gates, and it took three men to ram it home,
three to shoot the immense bolt back and spread the doors—   535
three average men. Achilles alone could ram it home himself.
But the god of luck now spread the gates for the old man,
drove in the glinting gifts for Peleus' swift son,
climbed down from behind the team and said to Priam,
"Old man, look, I am a god come down to you,   540
I am immortal Hermes—
my Father sent me here to be your escort.
But now I will hasten back. I will not venture
into Achilles' presence: it would offend us all
for a mortal man to host an immortal face-to-face.   545
But you go in yourself and clasp Achilles' knees,
implore him by his father, his mother with lovely hair,
by his own son—so you can stir his heart!"
                                        With that urging
Hermes went his way to the steep heights of Olympus.
But Priam swung down to earth from the battle-car   550
and leaving Idaeus there to rein in mules and team,
the old king went straight up to the lodge
where Achilles dear to Zeus would always sit.
Priam found the warrior there inside . . .
many captains sitting some way off, but two,   555
veteran Automedon and the fine fighter Alcimus
were busy serving him. He had just finished dinner,
eating, drinking, and the table still stood near.
The majestic king of Troy slipped past the rest
and kneeling down beside Achilles, clasped his knees   560
and kissed his hands, those terrible, man-killing hands
that had slaughtered Priam's many sons in battle.
Awesome—as when the grip of madness seizes one
who murders a man in his own fatherland and flees
abroad to foreign shores, to a wealthy, noble host,   565
and a sense of marvel runs through all who see him—
so Achilles marveled, beholding majestic Priam.
His men marveled too, trading startled glances.
But Priam prayed his heart out to Achilles:
"Remember your own father, great godlike Achilles—   570
as old as I am, past the threshold of deadly old age!
No doubt the countrymen round about him plague him now,
with no one there to defend him, beat away disaster.
No one—but at least he hears you're still alive
and his old heart rejoices, hopes rising, day by day,   575

to see his beloved son come sailing home from Troy.
But I—dear god, my life so cursed by fate . . .
I fathered hero sons in the wide realm of Troy
and now not a single one is left, I tell you.
Fifty sons I had when the sons of Achaea came,   580
nineteen born to me from a single mother's womb
and the rest by other women in the palace. Many,
most of them violent Ares cut the knees from under.
But one, one was left me, to guard my walls, my people—
the one you killed the other day, defending his fatherland,   585
my Hector! It's all for him I've come to the ships now,
to win him back from you—I bring a priceless ransom.
Revere the gods, Achilles! Pity me in my own right,
remember your own father! I deserve more pity . . .
I have endured what no one on earth has ever done before—   590
I put to my lips the hands of the man who killed my son."

     Those words stirred within Achilles a deep desire
to grieve for his own father. Taking the old man's hand
he gently moved him back. And overpowered by memory
both men gave way to grief. Priam wept freely   595
for man-killing Hector, throbbing, crouching
before Achilles' feet as Achilles wept himself,
now for his father, now for Patroclus once again,
and their sobbing rose and fell throughout the house.
Then, when brilliant Achilles had had his fill of tears   600
and the longing for it had left his mind and body,
he rose from his seat, raised the old man by the hand
and filled with pity now for his gray head and gray beard,
he spoke out winging words, flying straight to the heart:
"Poor man, how much you've borne—pain to break the spirit!   605
What daring brought you down to the ships, all alone,
to face the glance of the man who killed your sons,
so many fine brave boys? You have a heart of iron.
Come, please, sit down on this chair here . . .
Let us put our griefs to rest in our own hearts,   610
rake them up no more, raw as we are with mourning.
What good's to be won from tears that chill the spirit?
So the immortals spun our lives that we, we wretched men
live on to bear such torments—the gods live free of sorrows.
There are two great jars that stand on the floor of Zeus's halls   615
and hold his gifts, our miseries one, the other blessings.
When Zeus who loves the lightning mixes gifts for a man,
now he meets with misfortune, now good times in turn.
When Zeus dispenses gifts from the jar of sorrows only,
he makes a man an outcast—brutal, ravenous hunger   620
drives him down the face of the shining earth,

stalking far and wide, cursed by gods and men.
So with my father, Peleus. What glittering gifts
the gods rained down from the day that he was born!
He excelled all men in wealth and pride of place,   625
he lorded the Myrmidons, and mortal that he was,
they gave the man an immortal goddess for a wife.
Yes, but even on him the Father piled hardships,
no powerful race of princes born in his royal halls,
only a single son he fathered, doomed at birth,   630
cut off in the spring of life—
and I, I give the man no care as he grows old
since here I sit in Troy, far from my fatherland,
a grief to you, a grief to all your children . . .
And you too, old man, we hear you prospered once: 635
as far as Lesbos, Macar's kingdom,[3] bounds to seaward,
Phrygia east and upland, the Hellespont vast and north—
that entire realm, they say, you lorded over once,
you excelled all men, old king, in sons and wealth.
But then the gods of heaven brought this agony on you—   640
ceaseless battles round your walls, your armies slaughtered.
You must bear up now. Enough of endless tears,
the pain that breaks the spirit.
Grief for your son will do no good at all.
You will never bring him back to life—   645
sooner you must suffer something worse."

    But the old and noble Priam protested strongly:
"Don't make me sit on a chair, Achilles, Prince,
not while Hector lies uncared-for in your camp!
Give him back to me, now, no more delay—   650
I must see my son with my own eyes.
Accept the ransom I bring you, a king's ransom!
Enjoy it, all of it—return to your own native land,
safe and sound . . . since now you've spared my life."

    A dark glance—and the headstrong runner answered,   655
"No more, old man, don't tempt my wrath, not now!
My own mind's made up to give you back your son.
A messenger brought me word from Zeus—my mother,
Thetis who bore me, the Old Man of the Sea's daughter.
And what's more, I can see through you, Priam—   660
no hiding the fact from me: one of the gods
has led you down to Achaea's fast ships.
No man alive, not even a rugged young fighter,
would dare to venture into our camp. Never—
how could he slip past the sentries unchallenged?   665

---

3. Macar was the legendary first king of Lesbos, a large and fertile island off the coast of Asia Minor.

Or shoot back the bolt of my gates with so much ease?
So don't anger me now. Don't stir my raging heart still more.
Or under my own roof I may not spare your life, old man—
supplicant that you are—may break the laws of Zeus!"

   The old man was terrified. He obeyed the order.   670
But Achilles bounded out of doors like a lion—
not alone but flanked by his two aides-in-arms,
veteran Automedon and Alcimus, steady comrades,
Achilles' favorites next to the dead Patroclus.
They loosed from harness the horses and the mules,   675
they led the herald in, the old king's crier,
and sat him down on a bench. From the polished wagon
they lifted the priceless ransom brought for Hector's corpse
but they left behind two capes and a finely-woven shirt
to shroud the body well when Priam bore him home.   680
Then Achilles called the serving-women out:
"Bathe and anoint the body—
bear it aside first. Priam must not see his son."
He feared that, overwhelmed by the sight of Hector,
wild with grief, Priam might let his anger flare   685
and Achilles might fly into fresh rage himself,
cut the old man down and break the laws of Zeus.
So when the maids had bathed and anointed the body
sleek with olive oil and wrapped it round and round
in a braided battle-shirt and handsome battle-cape,   690
then Achilles lifted Hector up in his own arms
and laid him down on a bier, and comrades helped him
raise the bier and body onto the sturdy wagon . . .
Then with a groan he called his dear friend by name:
"Feel no anger at me, Patroclus, if you learn—   695
even there in the House of Death—I let his father
have Prince Hector back. He gave me worthy ransom
and you shall have your share from me, as always,
your fitting, lordly share."
                So he vowed
and brilliant Achilles strode back to his shelter,   700
sat down on the well-carved chair that he had left,
at the far wall of the room, leaned toward Priam
and firmly spoke the words the king had come to hear:
"Your son is now set free, old man, as you requested.
Hector lies in state. With the first light of day   705
you will see for yourself as you convey him home.
Now, at last, let us turn our thoughts to supper.
Even Niobe[4] with her lustrous hair remembered food,
though she saw a dozen children killed in her own halls,

---

4. Wife of Amphion, one of the two founders of the great Greek city of Thebes.

six daughters and six sons in the pride and prime of youth.   710
True, lord Apollo killed the sons with his silver bow
and Artemis showering arrows killed the daughters.
Both gods were enraged at Niobe. Time and again
she placed herself on a par with their own mother,
Leto[5] in her immortal beauty—how she insulted Leto: 715
'All you have borne is two, but I have borne so many!'
So, two as they were, they slaughtered all her children.
Nine days they lay in their blood, no one to bury them—
Cronus' son had turned the people into stone . . .
then on the tenth the gods of heaven interred them.   720
And Niobe, gaunt, worn to the bone with weeping,
turned her thoughts to food. And now, somewhere,
lost on the crags, on the lonely mountain slopes,
on Sipylus[6] where, they say, the nymphs who live forever,
dancing along the Achelous River run to beds of rest—   725
there, struck into stone,[7] Niobe still broods
on the spate of griefs the gods poured out to her.

    So come—we too, old king, must think of food.
Later you can mourn your beloved son once more,
when you bear him home to Troy, and you'll weep many tears."   730

    Never pausing, the swift runner sprang to his feet
and slaughtered a white sheep as comrades moved in
to skin the carcass quickly, dress the quarters well.
Expertly they cut the meat in pieces, pierced them with spits,
roasted them to a turn and pulled them off the fire.   735
Automedon brought the bread, set it out on the board
in ample wicker baskets. Achilles served the meat.
They reached out for the good things that lay at hand
and when they had put aside desire for food and drink,
Priam the son of Dardanus gazed at Achilles, marveling   740
now at the man's beauty, his magnificent build—
face-to-face he seemed a deathless god . . .
and Achilles gazed and marveled at Dardan Priam,
beholding his noble looks, listening to his words.
But once they'd had their fill of gazing at each other,   745
the old majestic Priam broke the silence first:
"Put me to bed quickly, Achilles, Prince.
Time to rest, to enjoy the sweet relief of sleep.
Not once have my eyes closed shut beneath my lids
from the day my son went down beneath your hands . . .   750
day and night I groan, brooding over the countless griefs,

5. Mother of Apollo and Artemis.   6. A mountain in Asia Minor. The legend is thought to have had
its origin in a rock face that resembled a weeping woman, like Niobe, who wept inconsolably for the loss
of her children.   7. She was changed into a rock. *Achelous:* The river near Mount Sipylos in Asia
Minor.

groveling in the dung that fills my walled-in court.
But now, at long last, I have tasted food again
and let some glistening wine go down my throat.
Before this hour I had tasted nothing."
                                    He shook his head   755
as Achilles briskly told his men and serving-women
to make beds in the porch's shelter, to lay down
some heavy purple throws for the beds themselves
and over them spread blankets and thick woolly robes,
a warm covering laid on top. Torches held in hand,   760
they went from the hall and fell to work at once
and in no time two good beds were spread and made.
Then Achilles nodded to Priam, leading the king on
with brusque advice: "Sleep outside, old friend,
in case some Achaean captain comes to visit.   765
They keep on coming now, huddling beside me,
making plans for battle—it's their duty.
But if one saw you here in the rushing dark night
he'd tell Agamemnon straightaway, our good commander.
Then you'd have real delay in ransoming the body.   770
One more point. Tell me, be precise about it—
how many days do you need to bury Prince Hector?
I will hold back myself
and keep the Argive armies back that long."

And the old and noble Priam answered slowly,   775
"If you truly want me to give Prince Hector burial,
full, royal honors, you'd show me a great kindness,
Achilles, if you would do exactly as I say.
You know how crammed we are inside our city,
how far it is to the hills to haul in timber,   780
and our Trojans are afraid to make the journey.
Well, nine days we should mourn him in our halls,
on the tenth we'd bury Hector, hold the public feast,
on the eleventh build the barrow high above his body—
on the twelfth we'd fight again . . . if fight we must."   785

The swift runner Achilles reassured him quickly:
"All will be done, old Priam, as you command.
I will hold our attack as long as you require."

With that he clasped the old king by the wrist,
by the right hand, to free his heart from fear.   790
Then Priam and herald, minds set on the journey home,
bedded down for the night within the porch's shelter.
And deep in his sturdy well-built lodge Achilles slept
with Briseis in all her beauty sleeping by his side.

Now the great array of gods and chariot-driving men   795
slept all night long, overcome by gentle sleep.
But sleep could never hold the running Escort—
Hermes kept on turning it over in his mind . . .
how could he convoy Priam clear of the ships,
unseen by devoted guards who held the gates?   800
Hovering at his head the Escort rose and spoke:
"Not a care in the world, old man? Look at you,
how you sleep in the midst of men who'd kill you—
and just because Achilles spared your life. Now, yes,
you've ransomed your dear son—for a king's ransom.   805
But wouldn't the sons you left behind be forced
to pay three times as much for *you* alive?
What if Atrides Agamemnon learns you're here—
what if the whole Achaean army learns you're here?"

The old king woke in terror, roused the herald.   810
Hermes harnessed the mules and team for both men,
drove them fast through the camp and no one saw them.

Once they reached the ford where the river runs clear,
the strong, whirling Xanthus sprung of immortal Zeus,
Hermes went his way to the steep heights of Olympus   815
as Dawn flung out her golden robe across the earth,
and the two men, weeping, groaning, drove the team
toward Troy and the mules brought on the body.
No one saw them at first, neither man nor woman,
none before Cassandra, golden as goddess Aphrodite.   820
She had climbed to Pergamus heights and from that point
she saw her beloved father swaying tall in the chariot,
flanked by the herald, whose cry could rouse the city.
And Cassandra saw *him* too . . .
drawn by the mules and stretched out on his bier.   825
She screamed and her scream rang out through all Troy:
"Come, look down, you men of Troy, you Trojan women!
Behold Hector now—if you ever once rejoiced
to see him striding home, home alive from battle!
He was the greatest joy of Troy and all our people!"   830

Her cries plunged Troy into uncontrollable grief
and not a man or woman was left inside the walls.
They streamed out at the gates to meet Priam
bringing in the body of the dead. Hector—
his loving wife and noble mother were first   835
to fling themselves on the wagon rolling on,
the first to tear their hair, embrace his head
and a wailing throng of people milled around them.

And now, all day long till the setting sun went down
they would have wept for Hector there before the gates   840
if the old man, steering the car, had not commanded,
"Let me through with the mules! Soon, in a moment,
you can have your fill of tears—once I've brought him home."

So he called and the crowds fell back on either side,
making way for the wagon. Once they had borne him   845
into the famous halls, they laid his body down
on his large carved bed and set beside him singers
to lead off the laments, and their voices rose in grief—
they lifted the dirge high as the women wailed in answer.
And white-armed Andromache led their songs of sorrow,   850
cradling the head of Hector, man-killing Hector
gently in her arms: "O my husband . . .
cut off from life so young! You leave me a widow,
lost in the royal halls—and the boy only a baby,
the son we bore together, you and I so doomed.   855
I cannot think he will ever come to manhood.
Long before *that* the city will be sacked,
plundered top to bottom! Because you are dead,
her great guardian, you who always defended Troy,
who kept her loyal wives and helpless children safe,   860
all who will soon be carried off in the hollow ships
and I with them—
                        And you, my child, will follow me
to labor, somewhere, at harsh, degrading work,
slaving under some heartless master's eye—that,
or some Achaean marauder will seize you by the arm   865
and hurl you headlong down from the ramparts[8]—horrible death—
enraged at you because Hector once cut down his brother,
his father or his son, yes, hundreds of armed Achaeans
gnawed the dust of the world, crushed by Hector's hands!
Your father, remember, was no man of mercy . . .   870
not in the horror of battle, and that is why
the whole city of Troy mourns you now, my Hector—
you've brought your parents accursed tears and grief
but to me most of all you've left the horror, the heartbreak!
For you never died in bed and stretched your arms to me   875
or said some last word from the heart I can remember,
always, weeping for you through all my nights and days!"

Her voice rang out in tears and the women wailed in answer
and Hecuba led them now in a throbbing chant of sorrow:
"Hector, dearest to me by far of all my sons . . .   880
and dear to the gods while we still shared this life—

8. After the fall of Troy Astyanax was, in fact, hurled from the walls.

and they cared about you still, I see, even after death.
Many the sons I had whom the swift runner Achilles
caught and shipped on the barren salt sea as slaves
to Samos, to Imbros, to Lemnos shrouded deep in mist!   885
But you, once he slashed away your life with his brazen spear
he dragged you time and again around his comrade's tomb,
Patroclus whom you killed—not that he brought Patroclus
back to life by that. But I have you with me now . . .
fresh as the morning dew you lie in the royal halls   890
like one whom Apollo, lord of the silver bow,
has approached and shot to death with gentle shafts."

    Her voice rang out in tears and an endless wail rose up
and Helen, the third in turn, led their songs of sorrow:
"Hector! Dearest to me of all my husband's brothers—   895
my husband, Paris, magnificent as a god . . .
he was the one who brought me here to Troy—
Oh how I wish I'd died before that day!
But this, now, is the twentieth year for me
since I sailed here and forsook my own native land,   900
yet never once did I hear from *you* a taunt, an insult.
But if someone else in the royal halls would curse me,
one of your brothers or sisters or brothers' wives
trailing their long robes, even your own mother—
not your father, always kind as my own father—   905
why, you'd restrain them with words, Hector,
you'd win them to my side . . .
you with your gentle temper, all your gentle words.
And so in the same breath I mourn for you and me,
my doom-struck, harrowed heart! Now there is no one left   910
in the wide realm of Troy, no friend to treat me kindly—
all the countrymen cringe from me in loathing!"

    Her voice rang out in tears and vast throngs wailed
and old King Priam rose and gave his people orders:
"Now, you men of Troy, haul timber into the city!   915
Have no fear of an Argive ambush packed with danger—
Achilles vowed, when he sent me home from the black ships,
not to do us harm till the twelfth dawn arrives."

    At this command they harnessed oxen and mules to wagons,
they assembled before the city walls with all good speed   920
and for nine days hauled in a boundless store of timber.
But when the tenth Dawn brought light to the mortal world
they carried gallant Hector forth, streaming tears,
and they placed his corpse aloft the pyre's crest,
flung a torch and set it all aflame.
                    At last,   925

when young Dawn with her rose-red fingers shone once more,
the people massed around illustrious Hector's pyre . . .
And once they'd gathered, crowding the meeting grounds,
they first put out the fires with glistening wine,
wherever the flames still burned in all their fury.   930
Then they collected the white bones of Hector—
all his brothers, his friends-in-arms, mourning,
and warm tears came streaming down their cheeks.
They placed the bones they found in a golden chest,
shrouding them round and round in soft purple cloths.   935
They quickly lowered the chest in a deep, hollow grave
and over it piled a cope of huge stones closely set,
then hastily heaped a barrow, posted lookouts all around
for fear the Achaean combat troops would launch their attack
before the time agreed. And once they'd heaped the mound   940
they turned back home to Troy, and gathering once again
they shared a splendid funeral feast in Hector's honor,
held in the house of Priam, king by will of Zeus.

And so the Trojans buried Hector breaker of horses.

The Odyssey[1]

BOOK I

A Goddess Intervenes

Sing in me, Muse, and through me tell the story
of that man skilled in all ways of contending,
the wanderer, harried for years on end,
after he plundered the stronghold
on the proud height of Troy.
                              He saw the townlands   5
and learned the minds of many distant men,
and weathered many bitter nights and days
in his deep heart at sea, while he fought only
to save his life, to bring his shipmates home.
But not by will nor valor could he save them,   10
for their own recklessness destroyed them all—
children and fools, they killed and feasted on
the cattle of Lord Hêlios,[2] the Sun,
and he who moves all day through heaven
took from their eyes the dawn of their return.   15

Of these adventures, Muse, daughter of Zeus,
tell us in our time, lift the great song again.

1. Translated by Robert Fitzgerald.   2. This is described in Book XII.

Begin when all the rest who left behind them
headlong death in battle or at sea
had long ago returned,[3] while he alone still hungered   20
for home and wife. Her ladyship Kalypso[4]
clung to him in her sea-hollowed caves—
a nymph, immortal and most beautiful,
who craved him for her own.
                              And when long years and seasons
wheeling brought around that point of time   25
ordained for him to make his passage homeward,
trials and dangers, even so, attended him
even in Ithaka,[5] near those he loved.
Yet all the gods had pitied Lord Odysseus,
all but Poseidon, raging cold and rough[6]   30
against the brave king till he came ashore
at last on his own land.
                          But now that god
had gone far off among the sunburnt races,
most remote of men, at earth's two verges,
in sunset lands and lands of the rising sun,   35
to be regaled by smoke of thighbones burning,
haunches of rams and bulls, a hundred fold.
He lingered delighted at the banquet side.

In the bright hall of Zeus upon Olympos
the other gods were all at home, and Zeus,   40
the father of gods and men, made conversation.
For he had meditated on Aigísthos,[7] dead
by the hand of Agamémnon's son, Orestês,
and spoke his thought aloud before them all:

"My word, how mortals take the gods to task!   45
All their afflictions come from us, we hear.
And what of their own failings? Greed and folly
double the suffering in the lot of man.
See how Aigísthos, for his double portion,
stole Agamémnon's wife and killed the soldier   50
on his homecoming day. And yet Aigísthos
knew that his own doom lay in this. We gods
had warned him, sent down Hermês Argeiphontês,[8]
our most observant courier, to say:
'Don't kill the man, don't touch his wife,   55
or face a reckoning with Orestês
the day he comes of age and wants his patrimony.'

---

3. From the siege of Troy.   4. Her name is formed from a Greek verb which means "cover, hide."
5. An island off the northwest coast of Greece, Odysseus' home.   6. The reason for his rage is given by
Zeus below in lines 87–90.   7. The story of Agamémnon's return and death will be told in detail later,
in Book XI.   8. Both the meaning and origin of this epithet are uncertain.

Friendly advice—but would Aigísthos take it?
Now he has paid the reckoning in full."

The grey-eyed goddess Athena replied to Zeus: 60

"O Majesty, O Father of us all,
that man is in the dust indeed, and justly.
So perish all who do what he had done.
But my own heart is broken for Odysseus,
the master mind of war, so long a castaway   65
upon an island in the running sea;
a wooded island, in the sea's middle,
and there's a goddess in the place, the daughter
of one whose baleful mind knows all the deeps
of the blue sea—Atlas,[9] who holds the columns   70
that bear from land the great thrust of the sky.
His daughter will not let Odysseus go,
poor mournful man; she keeps on coaxing him
with her beguiling talk, to turn his mind
from Ithaka. But such desire is in him   75
merely to see the hearthsmoke leaping upward
from his own island, that he longs to die.
Are you not moved by this, Lord of Olympos?
Had you no pleasure from Odysseus' offerings
beside the Argive[1] ships, on Troy's wide seaboard?   80
O Zeus, what do you hold against him now?"

To this the summoner of cloud replied:

"My child, what strange remarks you let escape you.
Could I forget that kingly man, Odysseus?
There is no mortal half so wise; no mortal   85
gave so much to the lords of open sky.
Only the god who laps the land in water,
Poseidon, bears the fighter an old grudge
since he poked out the eye of Polyphêmos,[2]
brawniest of the Kyklopês. Who bore   90
that giant lout? Thoösa, daughter of Phorkys,
an offshore sea lord: for this nymph had lain
with Lord Poseidon in her hollow caves.
Naturally, the god, after the blinding—
mind you, he does not kill the man;   95
he only buffets him away from home.
But come now, we are all at leisure here,
let us take up this matter of his return,

9. A Titan, whose punishment for his part in the war against Zeus was to hold up the sky on his shoulders.
His daughter is Kalypso, who lives on the island of Ogýgia.   1. One of the collective names for the
Greeks fighting at Troy.   2. He had one central eye in his forehead. The encounter with Kyklopês (or
Cyclops) will be told in detail in Book IX.

that he may sail. Poseidon must relent
for being quarrelsome will get him nowhere,   100
one god, flouting the will of all the gods."

The grey-eyed goddess Athena answered him:

"O Majesty, O Father of us all,
if it now please the blissful gods
that wise Odysseus reach his home again,   105
let the Wayfinder, Hermês, cross the sea
to the island of Ogýgia; let him tell
our fixed intent to the nymph with pretty braids,
and let the steadfast man depart for home.
For my part, I shall visit Ithaka   110
to put more courage in the son, and rouse him
to call an assembly of the islanders,
Akhaian[3] gentlemen with flowing hair.
He must warn off that wolf pack of the suitors
who prey upon his flocks and dusky cattle.   115
I'll send him to the mainland then, to Sparta
by the sand beach of Pylos; let him find
news of his dear father where he may
and win his own renown about the world."

She bent to tie her beautiful sandals on,   120
ambrosial, golden, that carry her over water
or over endless land on the wings of the wind,
and took the great haft of her spear in hand—
that bronzeshod spear this child of Power can use
to break in wrath long battle lines of fighters.   125

Flashing down from Olympos' height she went
to stand in Ithaka, before the Manor,
just at the doorsill of the court. She seemed
a family friend, the Taphian[4] captain, Mentês,
waiting, with a light hand on her spear.   130
Before her eyes she found the lusty suitors
casting dice inside the gate, at ease
on hides of oxen—oxen they had killed.

Their own retainers made a busy sight
with houseboys mixing bowls of water and wine,   135
or sopping water up in sponges, wiping
tables to be placed about in hall,
or butchering whole carcasses for roasting.

3. Another of the collective names for the Greeks.   4. The name of a nearby sea-faring people.

Long before anyone else, the prince Telémakhos
now caught sight of Athena—for he, too,   140
was sitting there unhappy among the suitors,
a boy, daydreaming. What if his great father
came from the unknown world and drove these men
like dead leaves through the place, recovering
honor and lordship in his own domains?   145
Then he who dreamed in the crowd gazed out at Athena.

Straight to the door he came, irked with himself
to think a visitor had been kept there waiting,
and took her right hand, grasping with his left
her tall bronze-bladed spear. Then he said warmly: 150

"Greetings, stranger! Welcome to our feast.
There will be time to tell your errand later."

He led the way, and Pallas Athena followed
into the lofty hall. The boy reached up
and thrust her spear high in a polished rack   155
against a pillar where tough spear on spear
of the old soldier, his father, stood in order.
Then, shaking out a splendid coverlet,
he seated her on a throne with footrest—all
finely carved—and drew his painted armchair   160
near her, at a distance from the rest.
To be amid the din, the suitors' riot,
would ruin his guest's appetite, he thought,
and he wished privacy to ask for news
about his father, gone for years.
                       A maid   165
brought them a silver finger bowl and filled it
out of a beautiful spouting golden jug,
then drew a polished table to their side.
The larder mistress with her tray came by
and served them generously. A carver lifted   170
cuts of each roast meat to put on trenchers
before the two. He gave them cups of gold,
and these the steward as he went his rounds
filled and filled again.
                    Now came the suitors,
young bloods trooping in to their own seats   175
on thrones or easy chairs. Attendants poured
water over their fingers, while the maids
piled baskets full of brown loaves near at hand,
and houseboys brimmed the bowls with wine.
Now they laid hands upon the ready feast   180

and thought of nothing more. Not till desire
for food and drink had left them were they mindful
of dance and song, that are the grace of feasting.
A herald gave a shapely cithern harp
to Phêmios, whom they compelled[5] to sing—   185
and what a storm he plucked upon the strings
for prelude! High and clear the song arose.

Telémakhos now spoke to grey-eyed Athena,
his head bent close, so no one else might hear:

"Dear guest, will this offend you, if I speak?   190
It is easy for these men to like these things,
harping and song; they have an easy life,
scot free, eating the livestock of another—
a man whose bones are rotting somewhere now,
white in the rain on dark earth where they lie,   195
or tumbling in the groundswell of the sea.
If he returned, if these men ever saw him,
faster legs they'd pray for, to a man,
and not more wealth in handsome robes or gold.
But he is lost; he came to grief and perished,   200
and there's no help for us in someone's hoping
he still may come; that sun has long gone down.
But tell me now, and put it for me clearly—
who are you? Where do you come from? Where's your home
and family? What kind of ship is yours,   205
and what course brought you here? Who are your sailors?
I don't suppose you walked here on the sea.
Another thing—this too I ought to know—
is Ithaka new to you, or were you ever
a guest here in the old days? Far and near   210
friends knew this house; for he whose home it was
had much acquaintance in the world."

                              To this
the grey-eyed goddess answered:

                                   "As you ask,
I can account most clearly for myself.
Mentês I'm called, son of the veteran   215
Ankhíalos; I rule seafaring Taphos.
I came by ship, with a ship's company,
sailing the winedark sea for ports of call
on alien shores—to Témesê, for copper,

---

5. He belonged to the household of Odysseus.

bringing bright bars of iron in exchange.   220
My ship is moored on a wild strip of coast
in Reithron Bight, under the wooded mountain.
Years back, my family and yours were friends,
as Lord Laërtês[6] knows; ask when you see him.
I hear the old man comes to town no longer,   225
stays up country, ailing, with only one
old woman to prepare his meat and drink
when pain and stiffness take him in the legs
from working on his terraced plot, his vineyard.
As for my sailing here—   230
the tale was that your father had come home,
therefore I came. I see the gods delay him.
But never in this world is Odysseus dead—
only detained somewhere on the wide sea,
upon some island, with wild islanders;   235
savages, they must be, to hold him captive.
Well, I will forecast for you, as the gods
put the strong feeling in me—I see it all,
and I'm no prophet, no adept in bird-signs.
He will not, now, be long away from Ithaka,   240
his father's dear land; though he be in chains
he'll scheme a way to come; he can do anything.

But tell me this now, make it clear to me:
You must be, by your looks, Odysseus' boy?
The way your head is shaped, the fine eyes—yes,   245
how like him! We took meals like this together
many a time, before he sailed for Troy
with all the lords of Argos in the ships.
I have not seen him since, nor has he seen me."

And thoughtfully Telémakhos replied: 250

"Friend, let me put it in the plainest way.
My mother says I am his son: I know not
surely. Who has known his own engendering?
I wish at least I had some happy man
as father, growing old in his own house—   255
but unknown death and silence are the fate
of him that, since you ask, they call my father."

Then grey-eyed Athena said:

                    "The gods decreed
no lack of honor in this generation:

6. Father of Odysseus.

such is the son Penélopê bore in you.   260
But tell me now, and make this clear to me:
what gathering, what feast is this? Why here?
A wedding? Revel? At the expense of all?
Not that, I think. How arrogant they seem,
these gluttons, making free here in your house!   265
A sensible man would blush to be among them."

To this Telémakhos answered:

"Friend, now that you ask about these matters,
our house was always princely, a great house,
as long as he of whom we speak remained here.   270
But evil days the gods have brought upon it,
making him vanish, as they have, so strangely.
Were his death known, I could not feel such pain—
if he had died of wounds in Trojan country
or in the arms of friends, after the war.   275
They would have made a tomb for him, the Akhaians,
and I should have all honor as his son.
Instead, the whirlwinds got him, and no glory.
He's gone, no sign, no word of him; and I inherit
trouble and tears—and not for him alone,   280
the gods have laid such other burdens on me.
For now the lords of the islands,
Doulíkhion and Samê, wooded Zakýnthos,[7]
and rocky Ithaka's young lords as well,
are here courting my mother; and they use   285
our house as if it were a house to plunder.
Spurn them she dare not, though she hates that marriage,
nor can she bring herself to choose among them.
Meanwhile they eat their way through all we have,
and when they will, they can demolish me."   290

Pallas Athena was disturbed, and said:

"Ah, bitterly you need Odysseus, then!
High time he came back to engage these upstarts.
I wish we saw him standing helmeted
there in the doorway, holding shield and spear,   295
looking the way he did when I first knew him.
That was at our house, where he drank and feasted
after he left Ephyra, homeward bound
from a visit to the son of Mérmeris, Ilos.
He took his fast ship down the gulf that time   300
for a fatal drug to dip his arrows in

---

7. Islands close to Ithaka.

and poison the bronze points; but young Ilos
turned him away, fearing the gods' wrath.
My father gave it, for he loved him well.
I wish these men could meet the man of those days!   305
They'd know their fortune quickly: a cold bed.
Aye! but it lies upon the gods' great knees
whether he can return and force a reckoning
in his own house, or not.
                              If I were you,
I should take steps to make these men disperse.   310
Listen, now, and attend to what I say:
at daybreak call the islanders to assembly,
and speak your will, and call the gods to witness:
the suitors must go scattering to their homes.
Then here's a course for you, if you agree: 315
get a sound craft afloat with twenty oars
and go abroad for news of your lost father—
perhaps a traveller's tale, or rumored fame
issued from Zeus abroad in the world of men.
Talk to that noble sage at Pylos, Nestor,   320
then go to Meneláos, the red-haired king
at Sparta, last man home of all the Akhaians.
If you should learn your father is alive
and coming home, you could hold out a year.
Or if you learn that he is dead and gone,   325
then you can come back to your own dear country
and raise a mound for him, and burn his gear,
with all the funeral honors due the man,
and give your mother to another husband.

When you have done all this, or seen it done,   330
it will be time to ponder
concerning these contenders in your house—
how you should kill them, outright or by guile.
You need not bear this insolence of theirs,
you are a child no longer. Have you heard   335
what glory young Orestês won
when he cut down that two-faced man, Aigísthos,
for killing his illustrious father?
Dear friend, you are tall and well set-up, I see;
be brave—you, too—and men in times to come   340
will speak of you respectfully.
                         Now I must join my ships;
my crew will grumble if I keep them waiting.
Look to yourself; remember what I told you."

Telémakhos replied:

"Friend, you have done me
kindness, like a father to his son,   345
and I shall not forget your counsel ever.
You must get back to sea, I know, but come
take a hot bath, and rest; accept a gift
to make your heart lift up when you embark—
some precious thing, and beautiful, from me,   350
a keepsake, such as dear friends give their friends."

But the grey-eyed goddess Athena answered him:

"Do not delay me, for I love the sea ways.
As for the gift your heart is set on giving,
let me accept it on my passage home,   355
and you shall have a choice gift in exchange."

With this Athena left him
as a bird rustles upward, off and gone.
But as she went she put new spirit in him,
a new dream of his father, clearer now,   360
so that he marvelled to himself
divining that a god had been his guest.
Then godlike in his turn he joined the suitors.

The famous minstrel still sang on before them,
and they sat still and listened, while he sang   365
that bitter song, the Homecoming of Akhaians—
how by Athena's will they fared from Troy;
and in her high room careful Penélopê,
Ikários' daughter, heeded the holy song.
She came, then, down the long stairs of her house,   370
this beautiful lady, with two maids in train
attending her as she approached the suitors;
and near a pillar of the roof she paused,
her shining veil drawn over across her cheeks,
the two girls close to her and still,   375
and through her tears spoke to the noble minstrel:

"Phêmios, other spells you know, high deeds
of gods and heroes, as the poets tell them;
let these men hear some other; let them sit
silent and drink their wine. But sing no more   380
this bitter tale that wears my heart away.
It opens in me again the wound of longing
for one incomparable, ever in my mind—
his fame all Hellas[8] knows, and midland Argos."

8. The ancient name for Greece.

But Telémakhos intervened and said to her: 385

"Mother, why do you grudge our own dear minstrel
joy of song, wherever his thought may lead?
Poets are not to blame, but Zeus who gives
what fate he pleases to adventurous men.
Here is no reason for reproof: to sing   390
the news of the Danaans![9] Men like best
a song that rings like morning on the ear.
But you must nerve yourself and try to listen.
Odysseus was not the only one at Troy
never to know the day of his homecoming.   395
Others, how many others, lost their lives!"

The lady gazed in wonder and withdrew,
her son's clear wisdom echoing in her mind.
But when she had mounted to her rooms again
with her two handmaids, then she fell to weeping   400
for Odysseus, her husband. Grey-eyed Athena
presently cast a sweet sleep on her eyes.

Meanwhile the din grew loud in the shadowy hall
as every suitor swore to lie beside her,
but Telémakhos turned now and spoke to them: 405

"You suitors of my mother! Insolent men,
now we have dined, let us have entertainment
and no more shouting. There can be no pleasure
so fair as giving heed to a great minstrel
like ours, whose voice itself is pure delight.   410
At daybreak we shall sit down in assembly
and I shall tell you—take it as you will—
you are to leave this hall. Go feasting elsewhere,
consume your own stores. Turn and turn about,
use one another's houses. If you choose   415
to slaughter one man's livestock and pay nothing,
this is rapine; and by the eternal gods
I beg Zeus you shall get what you deserve:
a slaughter here, and nothing paid for it!"

By now their teeth seemed fixed in their under-lips,   420
Telémakhos' bold speaking stunned them so.
Antínoös, Eupeithês' son, made answer:

"Telémakhos, no doubt the gods themselves
are teaching you this high and mighty manner.

9. Another name for the Greeks as a whole.

Zeus forbid you should be king in Ithaka,   425
though you are eligible as your father's son."

Telémakhos kept his head and answered him:

"Antínoös, you may not like my answer,
but I would happily be king, if Zeus
conferred the prize. Or do you think it wretched?   430
I shouldn't call it bad at all. A king
will be respected, and his house will flourish.
But there are eligible men enough,
heaven knows, on the island, young and old,
and one of them perhaps may come to power   435
after the death of King Odysseus.
All I insist on is that I rule our house
and rule the slaves my father won for me."

Eurýmakhos, Pólybos' son, replied:

"Telémakhos, it is on the gods' great knees   440
who will be king in sea-girt Ithaka.
But keep your property, and rule your house,
and let no man, against your will, make havoc
of your possessions, while there's life on Ithaka.
But now, my brave young friend,   445
a question or two about the stranger.
Where did your guest come from? Of what country?
Where does he say his home is, and his family?
Has he some message of your father's coming,
or business of his own, asking a favor?   450
He left so quickly that one hadn't time
to meet him, but he seemed a gentleman."

Telémakhos made answer, cool enough:

"Eurýmakhos, there's no hope for my father.
I would not trust a message, if one came,   455
nor any forecaster my mother invites
to tell by divination of time to come.
My guest, however, was a family friend,
Mentês, son of Ankhíalos.
He rules the Taphian people of the sea."   460

So said Telémakhos, though in his heart
he knew his visitor had been immortal.
But now the suitors turned to play again
with dance and haunting song. They stayed till nightfall,

indeed black night came on them at their pleasure,   465
and half asleep they left, each for his home.

Telémakhos' bedroom was above the court,
a kind of tower, with a view all round;
here he retired to ponder in the silence,
while carrying brands of pine alight beside him   470
Eurýkleia went padding, sage and old.
Her father had been Ops, Peisênor's son,
and she had been a purchase of Laërtês
when she was still a blossoming girl. He gave
the price of twenty oxen for her, kept her   475
as kindly in his house as his own wife,
though, for the sake of peace, he never touched her.
No servant loved Telémakhos as she did,
she who had nursed him in his infancy.
So now she held the light, as he swung open   480
the door of his neat freshly painted chamber.
There he sat down, pulling his tunic off,
and tossed it into the wise old woman's hands.
She folded it and smoothed it, and then hung it
beside the inlaid bed upon a bar;   485
then, drawing the door shut by its silver handle
she slid the catch in place and went away.
And all night long, wrapped in the finest fleece,
he took in thought the course Athena gave him.

BOOK II

A Hero's Son Awakens

When primal Dawn spread on the eastern sky
her fingers of pink light, Odysseus' true son
stood up, drew on his tunic and his mantle,
slung on a sword-belt and a new-edged sword,
tied his smooth feet into good rawhide sandals,   5
and left his room, a god's brilliance upon him.
He found the criers with clarion voices and told them
to muster the unshorn Akhaians in full assembly.
The call sang out, and the men came streaming in;
and when they filled the assembly ground, he entered,   10
spear in hand, with two quick hounds at heel;
Athena lavished on him a sunlit grace
that held the eye of the multitude. Old men
made way for him as he took his father's chair.

Now Lord Aigýptios, bent down and sage with years,   15
opened the assembly. This man's son

had served under the great Odysseus, gone
in the decked ships with him to the wild horse country
of Troy—a spearman, Ántiphos by name.
The ravenous Kyklops in the cave destroyed him   20
last in his feast of men. Three other sons
the old man had, and one, Eurýnomos,
went with the suitors; two farmed for their father;
but even so the old man pined, remembering
the absent one, and a tear welled up as he spoke: 25

"Hear me, Ithakans! Hear what I have to say.
No meeting has been held here since our king,
Odysseus, left port in the decked ships.
Who finds occasion for assembly, now?
one of the young men? one of the older lot?   30
Has he had word our fighters are returning—
news to report if he got wind of it—
or is it something else, touching the realm?
The man has vigor, I should say; more power to him.
Whatever he desires, may Zeus fulfill it."   35

The old man's words delighted the son of Odysseus,
who kept his chair no longer but stood up,
eager to speak, in the midst of all the men.
The crier, Peisênor, master of debate,
brought him the staff and placed it in his hand;[1]   40
then the boy touched the old man's shoulder, and said:

"No need to wonder any more, Sir,
who called this session. The distress is mine.
As to our troops returning, I have no news—
news to report if I got wind of it—   45
nor have I public business to propose;
only my need, and the trouble of my house—
the troubles.

          My distinguished father is lost,
who ruled among you once, mild as a father,
and there is now this greater evil still: 50
my home and all I have are being ruined.
Mother wanted no suitors, but like a pack
they came—sons of the best men here among them—
lads with no stomach for an introduction
to Ikários, her father across the sea;   55
he would require a wedding gift, and give her
to someone who found favor in her eyes.

1. As in the assembly in Book I of the *Iliad*, the man who is given the floor to speak has a staff, the symbol
of authority, placed in his hand by the herald.

No; these men spend their days around our house
killing our beeves and sheep and fatted goats,
carousing, soaking up our good dark wine,   60
not caring what they do. They squander everything.
We have no strong Odysseus to defend us,
and as to putting up a fight ourselves—
we'd only show our incompetence in arms.
Expel them, yes, if I only had the power;   65
the whole thing's out of hand, insufferable.
My house is being plundered: is this courtesy?
Where is your indignation? Where is your shame?
Think of the talk in the islands all around us,
and fear the wrath of the gods,   70
or they may turn, and send you some devilry.
Friends, by Olympian Zeus and holy Justice
that holds men in assembly and sets them free,
make an end of this! Let me lament in peace
my private loss. Or did my father, Odysseus,   75
ever do injury to the armed Akhaians?
Is this your way of taking it out on me,
giving free rein to these young men?
I might as well—might better—see my treasure
and livestock taken over by you all;   80
then, if you fed on them, I'd have some remedy,
and when we met, in public, in the town,
I'd press my claim; you might make restitution.
This way you hurt me when my hands are tied."

And in hot anger now he threw the staff to the ground,   85
his eyes grown bright with tears. A wave of sympathy
ran through the crowd, all hushed; and no one there
had the audacity to answer harshly
except Antínoös, who said:

                              "What high and mighty
talk, Telémakhos! No holding you!   90
You want to shame us, and humiliate us,
but you should know the suitors are not to blame—
it is your own dear, incomparably cunning mother.
For three years now—and it will soon be four—
she has been breaking the hearts of the Akhaians,   95
holding out hope to all, and sending promises
to each man privately[2]—but thinking otherwise.

Here is an instance of her trickery:
she had her great loom standing in the hall

2. Her tactic is to divide the suitors and so put off the day that they will unanimously demand a decision.

and the fine warp of some vast fabric on it;   100
we were attending her, and she said to us:
'Young men, my suitors, now my lord is dead,
let me finish my weaving before I marry,
or else my thread will have been spun in vain.
It is a shroud I weave for Lord Laërtês,   105
when cold death comes to lay him on his bier.
The country wives would hold me in dishonor
if he, with all his fortune, lay unshrouded.'
We have men's hearts; she touched them; we agreed.
So every day she wove on the great loom—   110
but every night by torchlight she unwove it;
and so for three years she deceived the Akhaians.
But when the seasons brought the fourth around,
one of her maids, who knew the secret, told us;
we found her unraveling the splendid shroud.   115
She had to finish then, although she hated it.

Now here is the suitors' answer—
you and all the Akhaians, mark it well:
dismiss your mother from the house, or make her marry
the man her father names and she prefers.   120
Does she intend to keep us dangling forever?
She may rely too long on Athena's gifts—
talent in handicraft and a clever mind;
so cunning—history cannot show the like
among the ringleted ladies of Akhaia,   125
Mykênê with her coronet, Alkmênê, Tyro.[3]
Wits like Penélopê's never were before,
but this time—well, she made poor use of them.
For here are suitors eating up your property
as long as she holds out—a plan some god   130
put in her mind. She makes a name for herself,
but you can feel the loss it means for you.
Our own affairs can wait; we'll never go anywhere else,
until she takes an Akhaian to her liking."

But clear-headed Telémakhos replied: 135

"Antínoös, can I banish against her will
the mother who bore me and took care of me?
My father is either dead or far away,
but dearly I should pay for this
at Ikários' hands, if ever I sent her back.   140
The powers of darkness would requite it, too,

---

3. Famous ladies of the past (Alkmênê was the mother of Herakles): Odysseus sees the ghosts of Tyro and Alkmênê in the lower world in Book IX.

my mother's parting curse would call hell's furies[4]
to punish me, along with the scorn of men.
No: I can never give the word for this.
But if your hearts are capable of shame,   145
leave my great hall, and take your dinner elsewhere,
consume your own stores. Turn and turn about,
use one another's houses. If you choose
to slaughter one man's livestock and pay nothing,
this is rapine; and by the eternal gods   150
I beg Zeus you shall get what you deserve:
a slaughter here, and nothing paid for it!"

Now Zeus who views the wide world sent a sign to him,
launching a pair of eagles[5] from a mountain crest
in gliding flight down the soft blowing wind,   155
wing-tip to wing-tip quivering taut, companions,
till high above the assembly of many voices
they wheeled, their dense wings beating, and in havoc
dropped on the heads of the crowd—a deathly omen—
wielding their talons, tearing cheeks and throats;   160
then veered away on the right hand through the city.
Astonished, gaping after the birds, the men
felt their hearts flood, foreboding things to come.
And now they heard the old lord Halithersês,
son of Mastor, keenest among the old   165
at reading birdflight into accurate speech;
in his anxiety for them, he rose and said:

"Hear me, Ithakans! Hear what I have to say,
and may I hope to open the suitors' eyes
to the black wave towering over them. Odysseus   170
will not be absent from his family long:
he is already near, carrying in him
a bloody doom for all these men, and sorrow
for many more on our high seamark, Ithaka.
Let us think how to stop it; let the suitors   175
drop their suit; they had better, without delay.
I am old enough to know a sign when I see one,
and I say all has come to pass for Odysseus
as I foretold when the Argives massed on Troy,
and he, the great tactician, joined the rest.   180
My forecast was that after nineteen years,
many blows weathered, all his shipmates lost,
himself unrecognized by anyone,
he would come home. I see this all fulfilled."

4. *Erinyes* is the Greek word for these creatures who avenge injured parents, especially (since they themselves are female) a mother. They appear as the chorus in the final play of the *Oresteia*.   5. The royal
bird, the emblem of Zeus.

But Pólybos' son, Eurýmakhos, retorted: 185

"Old man, go tell the omens for your children
at home, and try to keep them out of trouble.
I am more fit to interpret this than you are.
Bird life aplenty is found in the sunny air,
not all of it significant. As for Odysseus,   190
he perished far from home. You should have perished with him—
then we'd be spared this nonsense in assembly,
as good as telling Telémakhos to rage on;
do you think you can gamble on a gift from him?
Here is what I foretell, and it's quite certain: 195
if you, with what you know of ancient lore,
encourage bitterness in this young man,
it means, for him, only the more frustration—
he can do nothing whatever with two eagles—
and as for you, old man, we'll fix a penalty   200
that you will groan to pay.
Before the whole assembly I advise Telémakhos
to send his mother to her father's house;
let them arrange her wedding there, and fix
a portion[6] suitable for a valued daughter.   205
Until he does this, courtship is our business,
vexing though it may be; we fear no one,
certainly not Telémakhos, with his talk;
and we care nothing for your divining, uncle,
useless talk; you win more hatred by it.   210
We'll share his meat, no thanks or fee to him,
as long as she delays and maddens us.
It is a long, long time we have been waiting
in rivalry for this beauty. We could have gone
elsewhere and found ourselves very decent wives."   215

Clear-headed Telémakhos replied to this:

"Eurýmakhos, and noble suitors all,
I am finished with appeals and argument.
The gods know, and the Akhaians know, these things.
But give me a fast ship and a crew of twenty   220
who will see me through a voyage, out and back.
I'll go to sandy Pylos, then to Sparta,
for news of Father since he sailed from Troy—
some traveller's tale, perhaps, or rumored fame
issued from Zeus himself into the world.   225
If he's alive, and beating his way home,

6. I.e. a dowry. In other passages (e.g., VIII. 327) it is the suitors who offer gifts to the bride's father. Such a cultural amalgam, customs from different periods or places side by side, is characteristic of oral epic traditions.

I might hold out for another weary year;
but if they tell me that he's dead and gone,
then I can come back to my own dear country
and raise a mound for him, and burn his gear,   230
with all the funeral honors that befit him,
and give my mother to another husband."

The boy sat down in silence. Next to stand
was Mentor, comrade in arms of the prince Odysseus,
an old man now. Odysseus left him authority   235
over his house and slaves, to guard them well.
In his concern, he spoke to the assembly:

"Hear me, Ithakans! Hear what I have to say.
Let no man holding scepter as a king
be thoughtful, mild, kindly, or virtuous;   240
let him be cruel, and practice evil ways;
it is so clear that no one here remembers
how like a gentle father Odysseus ruled you.
I find it less revolting that the suitors
carry their malice into violent acts;   245
at least they stake their lives
when they go pillaging the house of Odysseus—
their lives upon it, he will not come again.
What sickens me is to see the whole community
sitting still, and never a voice or a hand raised   250
against them—a mere handful compared with you."

Leókritos, Euênor's son, replied to him:

"Mentor, what mischief are you raking up?
Will this crowd risk the sword's edge over a dinner?
Suppose Odysseus himself indeed   255
came in and found the suitors at his table:
he might be hot to drive them out. What then?
Never would he enjoy his wife again—
the wife who loves him well; he'd only bring down
abject death on himself against those odds.   260
Madness, to talk of fighting in either case.
Now let all present go about their business!
Halithersês and Mentor will speed the traveller;
they can help him: they were his father's friends.
I rather think he will be sitting here   265
a long time yet, waiting for news of Ithaka;
that seafaring he spoke of is beyond him."

On this note they were quick to end their parley.
The assembly broke up; everyone went home—

the suitors home to Odysseus' house again.   270
But Telémakhos walked down along the shore
and washed his hands in the foam of the grey sea,
then said this prayer:

        "O god of yesterday,
guest in our house, who told me to take ship
on the hazy sea for news of my lost father,   275
listen to me, be near me:
the Akhaians only wait, or hope to hinder me,
the damned insolent suitors most of all."

Athena was nearby and came to him,
putting on Mentor's figure and his tone,   280
the warm voice in a lucid flight of words:

"You'll never be fainthearted or a fool,
Telémakhos, if you have your father's spirit;
he finished what he cared to say,
and what he took in hand he brought to pass.   285
The sea routes will yield their distances
to his true son, Penélopê's true son,—
I doubt another's luck would hold so far.
The son is rare who measures with his father,
and one in a thousand is a better man,   290
but you will have the sap and wit
and prudence—for you get that from Odysseus—
to give you a fair chance of winning through.
So never mind the suitors and their ways,
there is no judgment in them, neither do they   295
know anything of death and the black terror
close upon them—doom's day on them all.
You need not linger over going to sea.
I sailed beside your father in the old days,
I'll find a ship for you, and help you sail her.   300
So go on home, as if to join the suitors,
but get provisions ready in containers—
wine in two-handled jugs and barley meal,
the staying power of oarsmen,
in skin bags, watertight. I'll go the rounds   305
and call a crew of volunteers together.
Hundreds of ships are beached on sea-girt Ithaka;
let me but choose the soundest, old or new,
we'll rig her and take her out on the broad sea."

This was the divine speech Telémakhos heard   310
from Athena, Zeus's daughter. He stayed no longer,
but took his heartache home,

and found the robust suitors there at work,
skinning goats and roasting pigs in the courtyard.
Antínoös came straight over, laughing at him,   315
and took him by the hand with a bold greeting:

"High-handed Telémakhos, control your temper!
Come on, get over it, no more grim thoughts,
but feast and drink with me, the way you used to.
The Akhaians will attend to all you ask for—   320
ship, crew, and crossing to the holy land
of Pylos, for the news about your father."

Telémakhos replied with no confusion:

"Antínoös, I cannot see myself again
taking a quiet dinner in this company.   325
Isn't it enough that you could strip my house
under my very nose when I was young?
Now that I know, being grown, what others say,
I understand it all, and my heart is full.
I'll bring black doom upon you if I can—   330
either in Pylos, if I go, or in this country.
And I will go, go all the way, if only
as someone's passenger. I have no ship,
no oarsmen: and it suits you that I have none."

Calmly he drew his hand from Antínoös' hand.   335
At this the suitors, while they dressed their meat,
began to exchange loud mocking talk about him.
One young toplofty gallant set the tone:

                        "Well, think of that!
Telémakhos has a mind to murder us.
He's going to lead avengers out of Pylos,   340
or Sparta, maybe; oh, he's wild to do it.
Or else he'll try the fat land of Ephyra—
he can get poison there, and bring it home,
doctor the wine jar and dispatch us all."

Another took the cue:

                        "Well now, who knows?   345
He might be lost at sea, just like Odysseus,
knocking around in a ship, far from his friends.
And what a lot of trouble that would give us,
making the right division of his things!
We'd keep his house as dowry for his mother—   350
his mother and the man who marries her."

That was the drift of it. Telémakhos
went on through to the storeroom of his father,
a great vault where gold and bronze lay piled
along with chests of clothes, and fragrant oil.   355
And there were jars of earthenware in rows
holding an old wine,
mellow, unmixed, and rare; cool stood the jars
against the wall, kept for whatever day
Odysseus, worn by hardships, might come home.   360
The double folding doors were tightly locked
and guarded, night and day, by the serving woman,
Eurýkleia, grand-daughter of Peisênor,
in all her duty vigilant and shrewd.
Telémakhos called her to the storeroom, saying: 365

"Nurse, get a few two-handled travelling jugs
filled up with wine—the second best, not that
you keep for your unlucky lord and king,
hoping he may have slipped away from death
and may yet come again—royal Odysseus.   370
Twelve amphorai will do; seal them up tight.
And pour out barley into leather bags—
twenty bushels of barley meal ground fine.
Now keep this to yourself! Collect these things,
and after dark, when mother has retired   375
and gone upstairs to bed, I'll come for them.
I sail to sandy Pylos, then to Sparta,
to see what news there is of Father's voyage."

His loving nurse Eurýkleia gave a cry,
and tears sprang to her eyes as she wailed softly: 380

"Dear child, whatever put this in your head?
Why do you want to go so far in the world—
and you our only darling? Lord Odysseus
died in some strange place, far from his homeland.
Think how, when you have turned your back, these men   385
will plot to kill you and share all your things!
Stay with your own, dear, do. Why should you suffer
hardship and homelessness on the wild sea?"

But seeing all clear, Telémakhos replied:

"Take heart, Nurse, there's a god behind this plan.   390
And you must swear to keep it from my mother,
until the eleventh day, or twelfth, or till
she misses me, or hears that I am gone.
She must not tear her lovely skin lamenting."

So the old woman vowed by all the gods,   395
and vowed again, to carry out his wishes;
then she filled up the amphorai with wine
and sifted barley meal into leather bags.
Telémakhos rejoined the suitors.
                                Meanwhile
the goddess with grey eyes had other business: 400
disguised as Telémakhos, she roamed the town
taking each likely man aside and telling him:
"Meet us at nightfall at the ship!" Indeed,
she asked Noêmon, Phronios' wealthy son,
to lend her a fast ship, and he complied.   405
Now when at sundown shadows crossed the lanes
she dragged the cutter to the sea and launched it,
fitted out with tough seagoing gear,
and tied it up, away at the harbor's edge.
The crewmen gathered, sent there by the goddess.   410
Then it occurred to the grey-eyed goddess Athena
to pass inside the house of the hero Odysseus,
showing a sweet drowsiness on the suitors,
whom she had presently wandering in their wine;
and soon, as they could hold their cups no longer,   415
they straggled off to find their beds in town,
eyes heavy-lidded, laden down with sleep.
Then to Telémakhos the grey-eyed goddess
appeared again with Mentor's form and voice,
calling him out of the lofty emptied hall: 420

"Telémakhos, your crew of fighting men
is ready at the oars, and waiting for you;
come on, no point in holding up the sailing."

And Pallas Athena turned like the wind, running
ahead of him. He followed in her footsteps   425
down to the seaside, where they found the ship,
and oarsmen with flowing hair at the water's edge.
Telémakhos, now strong in the magic, cried:

"Come with me, friends, and get our rations down!
They are all packed at home, and my own mother   430
knows nothing!—only one maid was told."

He turned and led the way, and they came after,
carried and stowed all in the well-trimmed ship
as the dear son of Odysseus commanded.
Telémakhos then stepped aboard; Athena   435
took her position aft, and he sat by her.
The two stroke oars cast off the stern hawsers

and vaulted over the gunnels to their benches.
Grey-eyed Athena stirred them a following wind,
soughing from the north-west on the winedark sea,   440
and as he felt the wind, Telémakhos
called to all hands to break out mast and sail.
They pushed the fir mast high and stepped it firm
amidships in the box, made fast the forestays,
then hoisted up the white sail on its halyards   445
until the wind caught, booming in the sail;
and a flushing wave sang backward from the bow
on either side, as the ship got way upon her,
holding her steady course.
Now they made all secure in the fast black ship,   450
and, setting out the winebowls all a-brim,
they made libation to the gods,
                    the undying, the ever-new,
most of all to the grey-eyed daughter of Zeus.
And the prow sheared through the night into the dawn.

BOOK III

The Lord of the Western Approaches

The sun rose on the flawless brimming sea
into a sky all brazen—all one brightening
for gods immortal and for mortal men
on plowlands kind with grain.
                    And facing sunrise
the voyagers now lay off Pylos town,   5
compact stronghold of Neleus.[7] On the shore
black bulls were being offered by the people
to the blue-maned god[8] who makes the islands tremble:
nine congregations, each five hundred strong,
led out nine bulls apiece to sacrifice,   10
taking the tripes to eat, while on their altars
thighbones in fat lay burning for the god.
Here they put in, furled sail, and beached the ship;
but Telémakhos hung back in disembarking,
so that Athena turned and said: 15

"Not the least shyness, now, Telémakhos.
You came across the open sea for this—
to find out where the great earth hides your father
and what the doom was that he came upon.
Go to old Nestor, master charioteer,   20
so we may broach the storehouse of his mind.
Ask him with courtesy, and in his wisdom
he will tell you history and no lies."

---

7. Mortal son of the god Poseidon and father of Nestor.   8. Poseidon.

But clear-headed Telémakhos replied:

"Mentor, how can I do it, how approach him?   25
I have no practice in elaborate speeches, and
for a young man to interrogate an old man
seems disrespectful—"

                              But the grey-eyed goddess said:

"Reason and heart will give you words, Telémakhos;
and a spirit will counsel others. I should say   30
the gods were never indifferent to your life."

She went on quickly, and he followed her
to where the men of Pylos had their altars.
Nestor appeared enthroned among his sons,
while friends around them skewered the red beef   35
or held it scorching. When they saw the strangers
a hail went up, and all that crowd came forward
calling out invitations to the feast.
Peisístratos in the lead, the young prince,
caught up their hands in his and gave them places   40
on curly lambskins flat on the sea sand
near Thrasymêdês, his brother, and his father;
he passed them bits of the food of sacrifice,
and, pouring wine in a golden cup,
he said to Pallas Athena, daughter of Zeus: 45

"Friend, I must ask you to invoke Poseidon:
you find us at this feast, kept in his honor.
Make the appointed offering then, and pray,
and give the honeyed winecup to your friend
so he may do the same. He, too,   50
must pray to the gods on whom all men depend,
but he is just my age, you are the senior,
so here, I give the goblet first to you."

And he put the cup of sweet wine in her hand.
Athena liked his manners, and the equity   55
that gave her precedence with the cup of gold,
so she besought Poseidon at some length:

"Earthshaker, listen and be well disposed.
Grant your petitioners everything they ask:
above all, honor to Nestor and his sons;   60
second, to every man of Pylos town
a fair gift in exchange for this hekatomb;[9]

9. Strictly, the word denotes a sacrifice of a hundred animals, but it is often used to refer to smaller
offerings.

third, may Telémakhos and I perform
the errand on which last night we put to sea."

This was the prayer of Athena— 65
granted in every particular by herself.
She passed the beautiful wine cup to Telémakhos,
who tipped the wine and prayed as she had done.
Meanwhile the spits were taken off the fire,
portions of crisp meat for all. They feasted, 70
and when they had eaten and drunk their fill, at last
they heard from Nestor, prince of charioteers:

"Now is the time," he said, "for a few questions,
now that our young guests have enjoyed their dinner.
Who are you, strangers? Where are you sailing from, 75
and where to, down the highways of sea water?
Have you some business here? or are you, now,
reckless wanderers of the sea, like those corsairs
who risk their lives to prey on other men?"

Clear-headed Telémakhos responded cheerfully, 80
for Athena gave him heart. By her design
his quest for news about his father's wandering
would bring him fame in the world's eyes. So he said:

"Nestor, pride of Akhaians, Neleus' son,
you ask where we are from, and I can tell you: 85
our home port is under Mount Neion, Ithaka.
We are not here on Ithakan business, though,
but on my own. I want news of my father,
Odysseus, known for his great heart, and I
will comb the wide world for it. People say 90
he fought along with you when Troy was taken.
As to the other men who fought that war,
we know where each one died, and how he died;
but Zeus allotted my father death and mystery.
No one can say for sure where he was killed, 95
whether some hostile landsmen or the sea,
the stormwaves on the deep sea, got the best of him.
And this is why I come to you for help.
Tell me of his death, sir, if perhaps
you witnessed it, or have heard some wanderer 100
tell the tale. The man was born for trouble.
Spare me no part of it for kindness' sake,
but put the scene before me as you saw it.
If ever Odysseus my noble father
served you by promise kept or work accomplished 105

in the land of Troy, where you Akhaians suffered,
recall those things for me the way they were."

Then Nestor, prince of charioteers, made answer:

"Dear friend, you take me back to all the trouble
we went through in that country, we Akhaians: 110
rough days aboard ship on the cloudy sea
cruising away for pillage after Akhilleus;
rough days of battle around Priam's town.
Our losses, then—so many good men gone:[1]
Arês' great Aias lies there, Akhilleus lies there,   115
Patróklos, too, the wondrous counselor,
and my own strong and princely son, Antílokhos—
fastest man of them all, and a born fighter.
Other miseries, and many, we endured there.
Could any mortal man tell the whole story?   120
Not if you stayed five years or six to hear
how hard it was for the flower of the Akhaians;
you'd go home weary, and the tale untold.
Think: we were there nine years, and we tried everything,
all stratagems against them,   125
up to the bitter end that Zeus begrudged us.
And as to stratagems, no man would claim
Odysseus' gift for those. He had no rivals,
your father, at the tricks of war.
                              Your father?
Well, I must say I marvel at the sight of you: 130
your manner of speech couldn't be more like his;
one would say No; no boy could speak so well.
And all that time at Ilion,[2] he and I
were never at odds in council or assembly—
saw things the same way, had one mind between us   135
in all the good advice we gave the Argives.
But when we plundered Priam's town and tower
and took to the ships, God scattered the Akhaians.
He had a mind to make homecoming hard for them,
seeing they would not think straight nor behave,   140
or some would not. So evil days came on them,
and she who had been angered,[3]
Zeus's dangerous grey-eyed daughter, did it,

---

1. Nestor, who was the oldest of the warriors at the siege of Troy, lists the great heroes who fell there:
Akhilleus, the bravest of the Akhaians; Patroklos, his closest friend; Aias, who committed suicide because
the armor of the dead Akhilleus, a prize awarded to the bravest after Akhilleus, was given to Odysseus.
Odysseus will meet the ghosts of Akhilleus and Aias in the Underworld (Book XI). Priam, King of Troy,
was killed when the city fell.   2. Troy.   3. Athena. The Trojan princess Cassandra took refuge in
Athena's temple when the Akhaians captured Troy, but she was raped by Aias (not the great Aias but
another chieftain of the same name). Athena was angry not just with him, but with the whole Akhaian
army because they did not punish him.

starting a fight between the sons of Atreus.[4]
First they were fools enough to call assembly   145
at sundown, unheard of hour;
the Akhaian soldiers turned out, soaked with wine,
to hear talk, talk about it from their commanders:
Meneláos harangued them to get organized—
time to ride home on the sea's broad back, he said;   150
but Agamémnon wouldn't hear of it. He wanted
to hold the troops, make sacrifice, a hekatomb,
something to pacify Athena's rage.
Folly again, to think that he could move her.
Will you change the will of the everlasting gods   155
in a night or a day's time?
The two men stood there hammering at each other
until the army got to its feet with a roar,
and no decision, wanting it both ways.
That night no one slept well, everyone cursing   160
someone else. Here was the bane from Zeus.
At dawn we dragged our ships to the lordly water,
stowed aboard all our plunder
and the slave women in their low hip girdles.
But half the army elected to stay behind   165
with Agamémnon as their corps commander;
the other half embarked and pulled away.
We made good time, the huge sea smoothed before us,
and held our rites when we reached Ténedos,[5]
being wild for home. But Zeus, not willing yet,   170
now cruelly set us at odds a second time,
and one lot turned, put back in the rolling ships,
under command of the subtle captain, Odysseus;
their notion was to please Lord Agamémnon.
Not I. I fled, with every ship I had;   175
I knew fate had some devilment brewing there.
Diomêdês[6] roused his company and fled, too,
and later Meneláos, the red-haired captain,
caught up with us at Lesbos,
while we mulled over the long sea route, unsure   180
whether to lay our course northward of Khios,
keeping the Isle of Psyria off to port,
or inside Khios, coasting by windy Mimas.[7]
We asked for a sign from heaven, and the sign came
to cut across the open sea to Euboia,   185

---

4. Meneláos and Agamémnon.   5. An island off the coast, southwest of Troy.   6. One of the Greek
champions: his home was Argos.   7. In their frail ships and without benefit of compass, Greek sailors
preferred to hug the shore: the normal route would have been inside (i.e., to the east) of the island of
Khios, past the headland of Mimas on the coast of Asia Minor, and across the Aegean along the island
chain of the Cyclades. But Nestor is in a hurry; he goes northward of Khios and directly across the northern
Aegean to Geraistos on the long island of Euboia, which hugs the coast of the Greek mainland.

and lose no time putting our ills behind us.
The wind freshened astern, and the ships ran
before the wind on paths of the deep sea fish,
making Geraistos before dawn. We thanked Poseidon
with many a charred thighbone for that crossing.   190
On the fourth day, Diomêdês' company
under full sail put in at Argos port,
and I held on for Pylos. The fair wind,
once heaven set it blowing, never failed.

So this, dear child, was how I came from Troy,   195
and saw no more of the others, lost or saved.
But you are welcome to all I've heard since then
at home; I have no reason to keep it from you.
The Myrmidon[8] spearfighters returned, they say,
under the son of lionhearted Akhilleus;   200
and so did Poias' great son, Philoktêtês.[9]
Idómeneus[1] brought his company back to Krete;
the sea took not a man from him, of all
who lived through the long war.
And even as far away as Ithaka   205
you've heard of Agamémnon—how he came
home, how Aigísthos waited to destroy him
but paid a bitter price for it in the end.
That is a good thing, now, for a man to leave
a son behind him, like the son who punished   210
Aigísthos for the murder of his great father.
You, too, are tall and well set-up, I see;
be brave, you too, so men in times to come
will speak well of you."

Then Telémakhos said:

"Nestor, pride of Akhaians, Neleus' son,   215
that was revenge, and far and wide the Akhaians
will tell the tale in song for generations.
I wish the gods would buckle his arms on me!
I'd be revenged for outrage
on my insidious and brazen enemies.   220
But no such happy lot was given to me
or to my father. Still, I must hold fast."

To this Lord Nestor of Gerênia said:

8. The tribal contingent led by Akhilleus, whose son, Neoptolemos, came to Troy to avenge his father: it
was he who killed Priam on the altar in his palace.   9. He had been abandoned on a desert island by
the Greeks because he fell sick of a loathsome disease; cured, he was brought to Troy for the final assault.
1. Leader of the Greek troops from Crete.

"My dear young friend, now that you speak of it,
I hear a crowd of suitors for your mother   225
lives with you, uninvited, making trouble.
Now tell me how you take this. Do the people
side against you, hearkening to some oracle?
Who knows, your father might come home someday
alone or backed by troops, and have it out with them.   230
If grey-eyed Athena loved you
the way she did Odysseus in the old days,
in Troy country, where we all went through so much—
never have I seen the gods help any man
as openly as Athena did your father—   235
well, as I say, if she cared for you that way,
there would be those to quit this marriage game."

But prudently Telémakhos replied:

"I can't think what you say will ever happen, sir.
It is a dazzling hope. But not for me.   240
It could not be—even if the gods willed it."

At this grey-eyed Athena broke in, saying:

"What strange talk you permit yourself, Telémakhos.
A god could save the man by simply wishing it—
from the farthest shore in the world.   245
If I were he, I should prefer to suffer
years at sea, and then be safe at home;
better that than a knife at my hearthside
where Agamémnon found it—killed by adulterers.
Though as for death, of course all men must suffer it: 250
the gods may love a man, but they can't help him
when cold death comes to lay him on his bier."

Telémakhos replied:

"Mentor, grievously though we miss my father, why
go on as if that homecoming could happen?   255
You know the gods had settled it already,
years ago, when dark death came for him.
But there is something else I imagine Nestor
can tell us, knowing as he does the ways of men.
They say his rule goes back over three generations,   260
so long, so old, it seems death cannot touch him.
Nestor, Neleus' son, true sage, say how
did the Lord of the Great Plains, Agamémnon, die?
What was the trick Aigísthos used
to kill the better man? And Meneláos,   265

where was he? Not at Argos in Akhaia,
but blown off course, held up in some far country,
is that what gave the killer nerve to strike?"

Lord Nestor of Gerênia made answer:

"Well, now, my son, I'll tell you the whole story.   270
You know, yourself, what would have come to pass
if red-haired Meneláos, back from Troy,
had caught Aigísthos in that house alive.
There would have been no burial mound for him,
but dogs and carrion birds to huddle on him   275
in the fields beyond the wall, and not a soul
bewailing him, for the great wrong he committed.
While we were hard-pressed in the war at Troy
he stayed safe inland in the grazing country,
making light talk to win Agamémnon's queen.   280
But the Lady Klytaimnéstra, in the first days,
rebuffed him, being faithful still;
then, too, she had at hand as her companion
a minstrel Agamémnon left attending her,
charged with her care, when he took ship for Troy.   285
Then came the fated hour when she gave in.
Her lover tricked the poet and marooned him
on a bare island for the seabirds' picking,
and took her home, as he and she desired.
Many thighbones he burned on the gods' altars   290
and many a woven and golden ornament
hung to bedeck them, in his satisfaction;
he had not thought life held such glory for him.

Now Meneláos and I sailed home together
on friendly terms, from Troy,   295
but when we came off Sunion Point[2] in Attika,
the ships still running free, Onêtor's son
Phrontis, the steersman of Meneláos' ship,
fell over with a death grip on the tiller:
some unseen arrow from Apollo hit him.[3]   300
No man handled a ship better than he did
in a high wind and sea, so Meneláos
put down his longing to get on, and landed
to give this man full honor in funeral.
His own luck turned then. Out on the winedark sea   305

---

2. The southern cape of Attica: They would round this to go toward the Peloponnese.   3. A formula
for a sudden death which has no obvious explanation. (For women the arrow comes from Artemis.)

in the murmuring hulls again, he made Cape Malea,[4]
but Zeus who views the wide world sent a gloom
over the ocean, and a howling gale
came on with seas increasing, mountainous,
parting the ships and driving half toward Krete[5]   310
where the Kydonians live by Iardanos river.
Off Gortyn's coastline in the misty sea there
a reef, a razorback, cuts through the water,
and every westerly piles up a pounding
surf along the left side, going toward Phaistos—   315
big seas buffeted back by the narrow stone.
They were blown here, and fought in vain for sea room;
the ships kept going in to their destruction,
slammed on the reef. The crews were saved. But now
those five that weathered it got off to southward,   320
taken by wind and current on to Egypt;
and there Meneláos stayed. He made a fortune
in sea traffic among those distant races,
but while he did so, the foul crime was planned
and carried out in Argos by Aigísthos,   325
who ruled over golden Mykênai[6] seven years.
Seven long years, with Agamémnon dead,
he held the people down, before the vengeance.
But in the eighth year, back from exile in Attika,
Orestês killed the snake who killed his father.   330
He gave his hateful mother and her soft man
a tomb together, and proclaimed the funeral day
a festal day for all the Argive people.
That day Lord Meneláos of the great war cry
made port with all the gold his ships could carry.   335
And this should give you pause, my son:
don't stay too long away from home, leaving
your treasure there, and brazen suitors near;
they'll squander all you have or take it from you,
and then how will your journey serve?   340
I urge you, though, to call on Meneláos,
he being but lately home from distant parts
in the wide world. A man could well despair
of getting home at all, if the winds blew him
over the Great South Sea—that weary waste,   345
even the wintering birds delay
one winter more before the northward crossing.

4. The most westerly of the three capes in which the Peloponnese ends. Meneláos would have to round it to get into a harbor for Sparta. It is still a place of storms.   5. Meneláos is blown southeast, toward Egypt where he eventually arrives. Gortyn and Phaistos (site of a Minoan palace) are inland from the south coast of Crete.   6. Argos and Mykênai are close to each other and Homer sometimes does not discriminate between them.

Well, take your ship and crew and go by water,
or if you'd rather go by land, here are
horses, a car, and my own sons for company   350
as far as the ancient land of Lakedaimon[7]
and Meneláos, the red-haired captain there.
Ask him with courtesy, and in his wisdom
he will tell you history and no lies."

While Nestor talked, the sun went down the sky   355
and gloom came on the land,
and now the grey-eyed goddess Athena said:

"Sir, this is all most welcome and to the point,
but why not slice the bulls' tongues[8] now, and mix
libations for Poseidon and the gods?   360
Then we can all retire; high time we did;
the light is going under the dark world's rim,
better not linger at the sacred feast."

When Zeus's daughter spoke, they turned to listen,
and soon the squires brought water for their hands,   365
while stewards filled the winebowls and poured out
a fresh cup full for every man. The company
stood up to fling the tongues and a shower of wine
over the flames, then drank their thirst away.
Now finally Telémakhos and Athena   370
bestirred themselves, turning away to the ship,
but Nestor put a hand on each, and said:

"Now Zeus forbid, and the other gods as well,
that you should spend the night on board, and leave me
as though I were some pauper without a stitch,   375
no blankets in his house, no piles of rugs,
no sleeping soft for host or guest! Far from it!
I have all these, blankets and deep-piled rugs,
and while I live the only son of Odysseus
will never make his bed on a ship's deck—   380
no, not while sons of mine are left at home
to welcome any guest who comes to us."

The grey-eyed goddess Athena answered him:

"You are very kind, sir, and Telémakhos
should do as you ask. That is the best thing.   385
He will go with you, and will spend the night
under your roof. But I must join our ship

---

7. Sparta.   8. The tongue was one of the parts of the meat reserved for the gods; it was thrown on the
fire.

and talk to the crew, to keep their spirits up,
since I'm the only senior in the company.
The rest are boys who shipped for friendship's sake,   390
no older than Telémakhos, any of them.
Let me sleep out, then, by the black hull's side,
this night at least. At daybreak I'll be off
to see the Kaukonians about a debt they owe me,
an old one and no trifle. As for your guest,   395
send him off in a car,[9] with one of your sons,
and give him thoroughbreds, a racing team."

Even as she spoke, Athena left them—seeming
a seahawk, in a clap of wings—and all
the Akhaians of Pylos town looked up astounded.   400
Awed then by what his eyes had seen, the old man
took Telémakhos' hand and said warmly:

"My dear child, I can have no fears for you,
no doubt about your conduct or your heart,
if, at your age, the gods are your companions.   405
Here we had someone from Olympos—clearly
the glorious daughter of Zeus, his third child,
who held your father dear among the Argives.
O, Lady, hear me! Grant an illustrious name
to me and to my children and my dear wife!   410
A noble heifer shall be yours in sacrifice,
one that no man has ever yoked or driven;
my gift to you—her horns all sheathed in gold."

So he ended, praying; and Athena heard him.
Then Nestor of Gerênia led them all,   415
his sons and sons-in-law, to his great house;
and in they went to the famous hall of Nestor,
taking their seats on thrones and easy chairs,
while the old man mixed water in a wine bowl
with sweet red wine, mellowed eleven years   420
before his housekeeper uncapped the jar.
He mixed and poured his offering, repeating
prayers to Athena, daughter of royal Zeus.
The others made libation, and drank deep,
then all the company went to their quarters,   425
and Nestor of Gerênia showed Telémakhos
under the echoing eastern entrance hall
to a fine bed near the bed of Peisístratos,
captain of spearmen, his unmarried son.

9. A horse-drawn chariot.

Then he lay down in his own inner chamber   430
where his dear faithful wife had smoothed his bed.

When Dawn spread out her finger tips of rose,
Lord Nestor of Gerênia, charioteer,
left his room for a throne of polished stone,
white and gleaming as though with oil, that stood   435
before the main gate of the palace; Neleus here
had sat before him—masterful in kingship,
Neleus, long ago a prey to death, gone down
to the night of the underworld.
So Nestor held his throne and scepter now,   440
lord of the western approaches to Akhaia.
And presently his sons came out to join him,
leaving the palace: Ekhéphron and Stratíos,
Perseus and Arêtós and Thrasymêdês,
and after them the prince Peisístratos,   445
bringing Telémakhos along with him.
Seeing all present, the old lord Nestor said:

"Dear sons, here is my wish, and do it briskly
to please the gods, Athena first of all,
my guest in daylight at our holy feast.   450
One of you must go for a young heifer
and have the cowherd lead her from the pasture.
Another call on Lord Telémakhos' ship
to invite his crewmen, leaving two behind;
and someone else again send for the goldsmith,   455
Laerkês, to gild the horns.
The rest stay here together. Tell the servants
a ritual feast will be prepared in hall.
Tell them to bring seats, firewood and fresh water."

Before he finished, they were about these errands.   460
The heifer came from pasture,
the crewmen of Telémakhos from the ship,
the smith arrived, bearing the tools of his trade—
hammer and anvil, and the precision tongs
he handled fiery gold with,—and Athena   465
came as a god comes, numinous, to the rites.

The smith now gloved each horn in a pure foil
beaten out of the gold that Nestor gave him—
a glory and delight for the goddess' eyes—
while Ekhéphron and Stratíos held the horns.   470
Arêtós brought clear lustral water[1]

1. Water for sprinkling.

in a bowl quivering with frest-cut flowers,
a basket of barley in his other hand.
Thrasymêdês, who could stand his ground in war,
stood ready, with a sharp two-bladed axe,   475
for the stroke of sacrifice, and Perseus
held a bowl for the blood. And now Nestor,
strewing the barley grains, and water drops,
pronounced his invocation to Athena
and burned a pinch of bristles from the victim.   480
When prayers were said and all the grain was scattered
great-hearted Thrasymêdês in a flash
swung the sxe, at one blow cutting through
the neck tendons. The heifer's spirit failed.
Then all the women gave a wail of joy[2]—   485
daughters, daughters-in-law, and the Lady Eurydíkê,
Klyménos' eldest daughter. But the men
still held the heifer, shored her up
from the wide earth where the living go their ways,
until Peisístratos cut her throat across,   490
the black blood ran, and life ebbed from her marrow.
The carcass now sank down, and they disjointed
shoulder and thigh bone, wrapping them in fat,
two layers, folded, with raw strips of flesh.
These offerings Nestor burned on the split-wood fire   495
and moistened with red wine. His sons took up
five-tined forks in their hands, while the altar flame
ate through the bones, and bits of tripe went round.
Then came the carving of the quarters, and they spitted
morsels of lean meat on the long sharp tines   500
and broiled them at arm's length upon the fire.

Polykástê, a fair girl, Nestor's youngest,
had meanwhile given a bath to Telémakhos—
bathing him first, then rubbing him with oil.
She held fine clothes and a cloak to put around him   505
when he came godlike from the bathing place;
then out he went to take his place with Nestor.
When the best cuts were broiled and off the spits,
they all sat down to banquet. Gentle squires
kept every golden wine cup brimming full.   510
And so they feasted to their heart's content,
until the prince of charioteers commanded:

"Sons, harness the blood mares for Telémakhos;
hitch up the car, and let him take the road."

---

2. The ritual cry at the moment of sacrifice.

They swung out smartly to do the work, and hooked   515
the handsome horses to a chariot shaft.
The mistress of the stores brought up provisions
of bread and wine, with victuals fit for kings,
and Telémakhos stepped up on the painted car.
Just at his elbow stood Peisístratos,   520
captain of spearmen, reins in hand. He gave
a flick to the horses, and with streaming manes
they ran for the open country. The tall town
of Pylos sank behind them in the distance,
as all day long they kept the harness shaking.   525

The sun was low and shadows crossed the lanes
when they arrived at Phêrai. There Dióklês,
son of Ortílokhos whom Alpheios fathered,
welcomed the young men, and they slept the night.
But up when the young Dawn's finger tips of rose   530
opened in the east, they hitched the team
once more to the painted car,
and steered out eastward through the echoing gate,
whipping their fresh horses into a run.
That day they made the grainlands of Lakedaimon,   535
where, as the horses held to a fast clip,
they kept on to their journey's end. Behind them
the sun went down and all the roads grew dark.

BOOK IV

The Red-Haired King and His Lady

By vales and sharp ravines in Lakedaimon
the travellers drove to Meneláos' mansion,
and found him at a double wedding feast
for son and daughter.
                    Long ago at Troy
he pledged her to the heir[3] of great Akhilleus,   5
breaker of men—a match the gods had ripened;
so he must send her with a chariot train
to the town and glory of the Myrmidons.
And that day, too, he brought Alektor's daughter
to marry his tall scion, Megapénthês,   10
born of a slave girl during the long war—
for the gods had never after granted Helen
a child to bring into the sunlit world
after the first, rose-lipped Hermionê,
a girl like the pale-gold goddess Aphrodítê.   15

3. His son Neoptolemos. Akhilleus asks for news of him from Odysseus in the lower world.

Down the great hall in happiness they feasted,
neighbors of Meneláos, and his kin,
for whom a holy minstrel harped and sang;
and two lithe tumblers moved out on the song
with spins and handsprings through the company.   20
Now when Telémakhos and Nestor's son
pulled up their horses at the main gate,
one of the king's companions in arms, Eteóneus,
going outside, caught sight of them. He turned
and passed through court and hall to tell the master,   25
stepping up close to get his ear. Said he:

"Two men are here—two strangers, Meneláos,
but nobly born Akhaians, they appear.
What do you say, shall we unhitch their team,
or send them on to someone free to receive them?"   30

The red-haired captain answered him in anger:

"You were no idiot before, Eteóneus,
but here you are talking like a child of ten.
Could we have made it home again—and Zeus
gave us no more hard roving!—if other men   35
had never fed us, given us lodging?
                        Bring
these men to be our guests: unhitch their team!"

Eteóneus left the long room like an arrow,
calling equerries after him, on the run.
Outside, they freed the sweating team from harness,   40
stabled the horses, tied them up, and showered
bushels of wheat and barley in the feed box;
then leaned the chariot pole
against the gleaming entry wall of stone
and took the guests in. What a brilliant place   45
that mansion of the great prince seemed to them!
A-glitter everywhere, as though with fiery
points of sunlight, lusters of the moon.
The young men gazed in joy before they entered
into a room of polished tubs to bathe.   50
Maidservants gave them baths, anointed them,
held out fresh tunics, cloaked them warm; and soon
they took tall thrones beside the son of Atreus.
Here a maid tipped out water for their hands
from a golden pitcher into a silver bowl,   55
and set a polished table near at hand;
the larder mistress with her tray of loaves
and savories came, dispensing all her best,

and then a carver heaped their platters high
with various meats, and put down cups of gold.   60
Now said the red-haired captain, Meneláos,
gesturing:

    "Welcome; and fall to; in time,
when you have supped, we hope to hear your names,
forebears and families—in your case, it seems,
no anonymities, but lordly men.   65
Lads like yourselves are not base born."

                    At this,
he lifted in his own hands the king's portion,
a chine of beef, and set it down before them.
Seeing all ready then, they took their dinner;
but when they had feasted well,   70
Telémakhos could not keep still, but whispered,
his head bent close, so the others might not hear:

"My dear friend, can you believe your eyes?—
the murmuring hall, how luminous it is
with bronze, gold, amber, silver, and ivory!   75
This is the way the court of Zeus must be,
inside, upon Olympos. What a wonder!"

But splendid Meneláos had overheard him
and spoke out on the instant to them both:

"Young friends, no mortal man can vie with Zeus.   80
His home and all his treasures are for ever.
But as for men, it may well be that few
have more than I. How painfully I wandered
before I brought it home! Seven years at sea,
Kypros, Phoinikia, Egypt, and still farther   85
among the sun-burnt races.
I saw the men of Sidon and Arabia
and Libya, too, where lambs are horned at birth.
In every year they have three lambing seasons,
so no man, chief or shepherd, ever goes   90
hungry for want of mutton, cheese, or milk—
all year at milking time there are fresh ewes.
But while I made my fortune on those travels
a stranger killed my brother, in cold blood,—
tricked blind, caught in the web of his deadly queen.   95
What pleasure can I take, then, being lord
over these costly things?
You must have heard your fathers tell my story,

whoever your fathers are; you must know of my life,
the anguish I once had, and the great house   100
full of my treasure, left in desolation.
How gladly I should live one third as rich
to have my friends back safe at home!—my friends
who died on Troy's wide seaboard, far
from the grazing lands of Argos.   105
But as things are, nothing but grief is left me
for those companions. While I sit at home
sometimes hot tears come, and I revel in them,
or stop before the surfeit makes me shiver.
And there is one I miss more than the other   110
dead I mourn for; sleep and food alike
grow hateful when I think of him. No soldier
took on so much, went through so much, as Odysseus.
That seems to have been his destiny, and this mine—
to feel each day the emptiness of his absence,   115
ignorant, even, whether he lived or died.
How his old father and his quiet wife,
Penélopê, must miss him still!
And Telémakhos, whom he left as a new-born child."

Now hearing these things said, the boy's heart rose   120
in a long pang for his father, and he wept,
holding his purple mantle with both hands
before his eyes. Meneláos knew him now,
and so fell silent with uncertainty
whether to let him speak and name his father   125
in his own time, or to inquire, and prompt him.
And while he pondered, Helen came
out of her scented chamber, a moving grace
like Artemis,[4] straight as a shaft of gold.
Beside her came Adrastê, to place her armchair,   130
Alkippê, with a rug of downy wool,
and Phylo, bringing a silver basket, once
given by Alkandrê, the wife of Pólybos,
in the treasure city, Thebes of distant Egypt.
He gave two silver bathtubs to Meneláos   135
and a pair of tripods, with ten pure gold bars,
and she, then, made these beautiful gifts to Helen:
a golden distaff, and the silver basket
rimmed in hammered gold, with wheels to run on.
So Phylo rolled it in to stand beside her,   140
heaped with fine spun stuff, and cradled on it

4. A virgin goddess, sister of Apollo. She was associated with wild animals, and women called on her for
help in childbirth.

the distaff swathed in dusky violet wool.
Reclining in her light chair with its footrest,
Helen gazed at her husband and demanded:

"Meneláos, my lord, have we yet heard   145
our new guests introduce themselves? Shall I
dissemble what I feel? No, I must say it.
Never, anywhere, have I seen so great a likeness
in man or woman—but it is truly strange!
This boy must be the son of Odysseus,   150
Telémakhos, the child he left at home
that year the Akhaian host made war on Troy—
daring all for the wanton that I was."

And the red-haired captain, Meneláos, answered:

"My dear, I see the likeness as well as you do.   155
Odysseus' hands and feet were like this boy's;
his head, and hair, and the glinting of his eyes.
Not only that, but when I spoke, just now,
of Odysseus' years of toil on my behalf
and all he had to endure—the boy broke down   160
and wept into his cloak."

                        Now Nestor's son,
Peisístratos, spoke up in answer to him:

"My lord marshal, Meneláos, son of Atreus,
this is that hero's son as you surmise,
but he is gentle, and would be ashamed   165
to clamor for attention before your grace
whose words have been so moving to us both.
Nestor, Lord of Gerênia, sent me with him
as guide and escort; he had wished to see you,
to be advised by you or assisted somehow.   170
A father far from home means difficulty
for an only son, with no one else to help him;
so with Telémakhos:
his father left the house without defenders."

The king with flaming hair now spoke again: 175

"His son, in my house! How I loved the man,
and how he fought through hardship for my sake!
I swore I'd cherish him above all others
if Zeus, who views the wide world, gave us passage
homeward across the sea in the fast ships.   180
I would have settled him in Argos, brought him
over with herds and household out of Ithaka,

his child and all his people. I could have cleaned out
one of my towns to be his new domain.
And so we might have been together often   185
in feasts and entertainments, never parted
till the dark mist of death lapped over one of us.
But God himself must have been envious,
to batter the bruised man so that he alone
should fail in his return."   190

A twinging ache of grief rose up in everyone,
and Helen of Argos wept, the daughter of Zeus,[5]
Telémakhos and Meneláos wept,
and tears came to the eyes of Nestor's son—
remembering, for his part, Antílokhos,   195
whom the son of shining Dawn had killed in battle.
But thinking of that brother, he broke out:

"O son of Atreus, when we spoke of you
at home, and asked about you, my old father
would say you have the clearest mind of all.   200
If it is not too much to ask, then, let us not
weep away these hours after supper;
I feel we should not: Dawn will soon be here!
You understand, I would not grudge a man
right mourning when he comes to death and doom: 205
what else can one bestow on the poor dead?—
a lock of hair sheared, and a tear let fall.
For that matter, I, too,
lost someone in the war at Troy—my brother,
and no mean soldier, whom you must have known,   210
although I never did,—Antílokhos.
He ranked high as a runner and fighting man."

The red-haired captain Meneláos answered:

"My lad, what you have said is only sensible,
and you did well to speak. Yes, that was worthy   215
a wise man and an older man than you are:
you speak for all the world like Nestor's son.
How easily one can tell the man whose father
had true felicity, marrying and begetting!
And that was true of Nestor, all his days,   220
down to his sleek old age in peace at home,
with clever sons, good spearmen into the bargain.
Come, we'll shake off this mourning mood of ours
and think of supper. Let the men at arms

5. Helen was the daughter of Leda, whom Zeus seduced in the shape of a swan.

rinse our hands again! There will be time   225
for a long talk with Telémakhos in the morning."

The hero Menieláos' companion in arms,
Asphalion, poured water for their hands,
and once again they touched the food before them.
But now it entered Helen's mind   230
to drop into the wine that they were drinking
an anodyne, mild magic of forgetfulness.
Whoever drank this mixture in the wine bowl
would be incapable of tears that day—
though he should lose mother and father both,   235
or see, with his own eyes, a son or brother
mauled by weapons of bronze at his own gate.
The opiate of Zeus's daughter bore
this canny power. It had been supplied her
by Polydamna, mistress of Lord Thôn,   240
in Egypt,[6] where the rich plantations grow
herbs of all kinds, maleficent and healthful;
and no one else knows medicine as they do,
Egyptian heirs of Paian, the healing god.
She drugged the wine, then, had it served, and said—   245
taking again her part in the conversation—

"O Menieláos, Atreus' royal son,
and you that are great heroes' sons, you know
how Zeus gives all of us in turn
good luck and bad luck, being all powerful.   250
So take refreshment, take your ease in hall,
and cheer the time with stories. I'll begin.
Not that I think of naming, far less telling,
every feat of that rugged man, Odysseus,
but here is something that he dared to do   255
at Troy, where you Akhaians endured the war.
He had, first, given himself an outrageous beating
and thrown some rags on—like a household slave—
then slipped into that city of wide lanes
among his enemies. So changed, he looked   260
as never before upon the Akhaian beachhead,
but like a beggar, merged in the townspeople;
and no one there remarked him. But I knew him—
even as he was, I knew him,
and questioned him. How shrewdly he put me off!   265
But in the end I bathed him and anointed him,
put a fresh cloak around him, and swore an oath

6. The Greeks had great respect for Egyptian doctors, and Egyptian papyri document their skill as surgeons
and their expertise with drugs.

not to give him away as Odysseus to the Trojans,
till he got back to camp where the long ships lay.
He spoke up then, and told me   270
all about the Akhaians, and their plans—
then sworded many Trojans through the body
on his way out with what he learned of theirs.
The Trojan women raised a cry—but my heart
sang—for I had come round, long before,   275
to dreams of sailing home, and I repented
the mad day Aphroditê
drew me away from my dear fatherland,
forsaking all—child, bridal bed, and husband—
a man without defect in form or mind."   280

Replied the red-haired captain, Meneláos:

"An excellent tale, my dear, and most becoming.
In my life I have met, in many countries,
foresight and wit in many first rate men,
but never have I seen one like Odysseus   285
for steadiness and a stout heart. Here, for instance,
is what he did—had the cold nerve to do—
inside the hollow horse, where we were waiting,
picked men all of us, for the Trojan slaughter,
when all of a sudden, you came by—I dare say   290
drawn by some superhuman
power that planned an exploit for the Trojans;
and Deïphobos,[7] that handsome man, came with you.
Three times you walked around it, patting it everywhere,
and called by name the flower of our fighters,   295
making your voice sound like their wives, calling.
Diomêdês and I crouched in the center
along with Odysseus; we could hear you plainly;
and listening, we two were swept
by waves of longing—to reply, or go.   300
Odysseus fought us down, despite our craving,
and all the Akhaians kept their lips shut tight,
all but Antiklos. Desire moved his throat
to hail you, but Odysseus' great hands clamped
over his jaws, and held. So he saved us all,   305
till Pallas Athena led you away at last."

Then clear-headed Telémakhos addressed him:

"My lord marshal, Meneláos, son of Atreus,
all the more pity, since these valors

7. A Trojan prince whom Helen married after Paris was killed in battle.

could not defend him from annihilation—   310
not if his heart were iron in his breast.
But will you not dismiss us for the night now?
Sweet sleep will be a pleasure, drifting over us."

He said no more, but Helen called the maids
and sent them to make beds, with purple rugs   315
piled up, and sheets outspread, and fleecy
coverlets, in the porch inside the gate.
The girls went out with torches in their hands,
and presently a squire led the guests—
Telémakhos and Nestor's radiant son—   320
under the entrance colonnade, to bed.
Then deep in the great mansion, in his chamber,
Meneláos went to rest, and Helen,
queenly in her long gown, lay beside him.

When the young Dawn with finger tips of rose   325
made heaven bright, the deep-lunged man of battle
stood up, pulled on his tunic and his mantle,
slung on a swordbelt and a new edged sword,
tied his smooth feet into fine rawhide sandals
and left his room, a god's brilliance upon him.   330
He sat down by Telémakhos, asking gently:

"Telémakhos, why did you come, sir, riding
the sea's broad back to reach old Lakedaimon?
A public errand or private? Why, precisely?"

Telémakhos replied: 335

"My lord marshal Meneláos, son of Atreus,
I came to hear what news you had of Father.
My house, my good estates are being ruined.
Each day my mother's bullying suitors come
to slaughter flocks of mine and my black cattle;   340
enemies crowd our home. And this is why
I come to you for news of him who owned it.
Tell me of his death, sir, if perhaps
you witnessed it, or have heard some wanderer
tell the tale. The man was born for trouble.   345
Spare me no part for kindness' sake; be harsh;
but put the scene before me as you saw it.
If ever Odysseus my noble father
served you by promise kept or work accomplished
in the land of Troy, where you Akhaians suffered,   350
recall those things for me the way they were."

Stirred now to anger, Meneláos said:

"Intolerable—that soft men, as those are,
should think to lie in that great captain's bed.
Fawns in a lion's lair! As if a doe   355
put down her litter of sucklings there, while she
quested a glen or cropped some grassy hollow.
Ha! Then the lord returns to his own bed
and deals out wretched doom on both alike.
So will Odysseus deal out doom on these.   360
O Father Zeus, Athena, and Apollo!
I pray he comes as once he was, in Lesbos,
when he stood up to wrestle Philomeleidês—[8]
champion and Island King—
and smashed him down. How the Akhaians cheered!   365
If only that Odysseus met the suitors,
they'd have their consummation, a cold bed!
Now for your questions, let me come to the point.
I would not misreport it for you; let me
tell you what the Ancient of the Sea,   370
who is infallible, said to me—every word.

During my first try at a passage homeward
the gods detained me, tied me down to Egypt—
for I had been too scant in hekatombs,
and gods will have the rules each time remembered.   375
There is an island washed by the open sea
lying off Nile mouth—seamen call it Pharos—
distant a day's sail in a clean hull
with a brisk land breeze behind. It has a harbor,
a sheltered bay, where shipmasters   380
take on dark water for the outward voyage.
Here the gods held me twenty days becalmed.
No winds came up, seaward escorting winds
for ships that ride the sea's broad back, and so
my stores and men were used up; we were failing   385
had not one goddess intervened in pity—
Eidothea, daughter of Proteus,
the Ancient of the Sea. How I distressed her!
I had been walking out alone that day—
my sailors, thin-bellied from the long fast,   390
were off with fish hooks, angling on the shore—
then she appeared to me, and her voice sang:

8. A king of Lesbos who challenged all comers to wrestle with him.

'What fool is here, what drooping dunce of dreams?
Or can it be, friend, that you love to suffer?
How can you linger on this island, aimless   395
and shiftless, while your people waste away?'

To this I quickly answered:

                                    'Let me tell you,
goddess, whatever goddess you may be,
these doldrums are no will of mine. I take it
the gods who own broad heaven are offended.   400
Why don't you tell me—since the gods know everything—
who has me pinned down here?
How am I going to make my voyage home?'

Now she replied in her immortal beauty:

'I'll put it for you clearly as may be, friend.   405
The Ancient of the Salt Sea haunts this place,
immortal Proteus of Egypt; all the deeps
are known to him; he serves under Poseidon,
and is, they say, my father.
If you could take him by surprise and hold him,   410
he'd give you course and distance for your sailing
homeward across the cold fish-breeding sea.
And should you wish it, noble friend, he'd tell you
all that occurred at home, both good and evil,
while you were gone so long and hard a journey.'   415

To this I said:

                                    'But you, now—you must tell me
how I can trap this venerable sea-god.
He will elude me if he takes alarm;
no man—god knows—can quell a god with ease.'

That fairest of unearthly nymphs replied: 420

'I'll tell you this, too, clearly as may be.
When the sun hangs at high noon in heaven,
the Ancient glides ashore under the Westwind,
hidden by shivering glooms on the clear water,
and rests in caverns hollowed by the sea.   425
There flippered seals, brine children, shining come
from silvery foam in crowds to lie around him,
exhaling rankness from the deep sea floor.
Tomorrow dawn I'll take you to those caves
and bed you down there. Choose three officers   430
for company—brave men they had better be—

the old one has strange powers, I must tell you.
He goes amid the seals to check their number,
and when he sees them all, and counts them all,
he lies down like a shepherd with his flock.   435
Here is your opportunity: at this point
gather yourselves, with all your heart and strength,
and tackle him before he bursts away.
He'll make you fight—for he can take the forms
of all the beasts, and water, and blinding fire;   440
but you must hold on, even so, and crush him
until he breaks the silence. When he does,
he will be in that shape you saw asleep.
Relax your grip, then, set the Ancient free,
and put your questions, hero: 445
Who is the god so hostile to you,
and how will you go home on the fish-cold sea.'

At this she dove under a swell and left me.
Back to the ships in the sandy cove I went,
my heart within me like a high surf running;   450
but there I joined my men once more
at supper, as the sacred Night came on,
and slept at last beside the lapping water.
When Dawn spread out her finger tips of rose
I started, by the sea's wide level ways,   455
praying the gods for help, and took along
three lads I counted on in any fight.
Meanwhile the nereid[9] swam from the lap of Ocean
laden with four sealskins, new flayed
for the hoax she thought of playing on her father.   460
In the sand she scooped out hollows for our bodies
and sat down, waiting. We came close to touch her,
and, bedding us, she threw the sealskins over us—
a strong disguise; oh, yes, terribly strong
as I recall the stench of those damned seals.   465
Would any man lie snug with a sea monster?
But here the nymph, again, came to our rescue,
dabbing ambrosia under each man's nose—
a perfume drowning out the bestial odor.
So there we lay with beating hearts all morning   470
while seals came shoreward out of ripples, jostling
to take their places, flopping on the sand.
At noon the Ancient issued from the sea
and held inspection, counting off the sea-beasts.
We were the first he numbered; he went by,   475

9. Sea nymph.

detecting nothing. When at last he slept
we gave a battlecry and plunged for him,
locking our hands behind him. But the old one's
tricks were not knocked out of him; far from it.
First he took on a whiskered lion's shape,   480
a serpent then; a leopard; a great boar;
then sousing water; then a tall green tree.
Still we hung on, by hook or crook, through everything,
until the Ancient saw defeat, and grimly
opened his lips to ask me:

                    'Son of Atreus,   485
who counselled you to this? A god: what god?
Set a trap for me, overpower me—why?'

He bit it off, then, and I answered:

                              'Old one,
you know the reason—why feign not to know?
High and dry so long upon this island   490
I'm at my wits' end, and my heart is sore.
You gods know everything; now you can tell me:
which of the immortals chained me here?
And how will I get home on the fish-cold sea?'

He made reply at once:

                              'You should have paid   495
honor to Zeus and the other gods, performing
a proper sacrifice before embarking:
that was your short way home on the winedark sea.
You may not see your friends, your own fine house,
or enter your own land again,   500
unless you first remount the Nile in flood
and pay your hekatomb to the gods of heaven.
Then, and then only,
the gods will grant the passage you desire.'

Ah, how my heart sank, hearing this—   505
hearing him send me back on the cloudy sea
in my own track, the long hard way of Egypt.
Nevertheless, I answered him and said:

'Ancient, I shall do all as you command.
But tell me, now, the others—   510
had they a safe return, all those Akhaians
who stayed behind when Nestor and I left Troy?
Or were there any lost at sea—what bitterness!—
any who died in camp, after the war?'

To this he said:

                'For you to know these things   515
goes beyond all necessity, Meneláos.
Why must you ask?—you should not know my mind,
and you will grieve to learn it, I can tell you.
Many there were who died, many remain,
but two high officers alone were lost—   520
on the passage home, I mean; you saw the war.
One is alive, a castaway at sea;
the other, Aias,[1] perished with all hands—
though first Poseidon landed him on Gyrai
promontory, and saved him from the ocean.   525
Despite Athena's hate, he had lived on,
but the great sinner in his insolence
yelled that the gods' will and the sea were beaten,
and this loud brag came to Poseidon's ears.
He swung the trident in his massive hands   530
and in one shock from top to bottom split
that promontory, toppling into the sea
the fragment where the great fool sat.
So the vast ocean had its will with Aias,
drunk in the end on salt spume as he drowned.   535
Meanwhile your brother[2] left that doom astern
in his decked ships—the Lady Hera[3] saved him;
but as he came round Malea
a fresh squall caught him, bearing him away
over the cold sea, groaning in disgust,   540
to the Land's End of Argos, where Thyestês
lived in the days of old, and then his son,
Aigísthos. Now, again, return seemed easy:
the high gods wound the wind into the east,
and back he sailed, this time to his own coast.   545
He went ashore and kissed the earth in joy,
hot tears blinding his eyes at sight of home.
But there were eyes that watched him from a height—
a lookout, paid two bars of gold to keep
vigil the year round for Aigísthos' sake,   550
that he should be forewarned, and Agamémnon's
furious valor sleep unroused.
Now this man with his news ran to the tyrant,
who made his crooked arrangements in a flash,
stationed picked men at arms, a score of men   555
in hiding; set a feast in the next room;

---

1. The Lesser Aias, the one who raped Cassandra in Athene's temple. The other Aias, the great warrior of the *Iliad*, committed suicide at Troy when the award of valor, Akhilleus' armor, was given to Odysseus instead of to him. Odysseus meets his ghost in the lower world (Book XI).   2. Agamémnon.   3. The wife and sister of Zeus.

then he went out with chariots and horses
to hail the king and welcome him to evil.
He led him in to banquet, all serene,
and killed him, like an ox felled at the trough;   560
and not a man of either company
survived that ambush in Aigísthos' house.'

Before the end my heart was broken down.
I slumped on the trampled sand and cried aloud,
caring no more for life or the light of day,   565
and rolled there weeping, till my tears were spent.
Then the unerring Ancient said at last:

'No more, no more; how long must you persist?
Nothing is gained by grieving so. How soon
can you return to Argos? You may take him   570
alive there still—or else meanwhile Orestês
will have despatched him. You'll attend the feast.'

At this my heart revived, and I recovered
the self command to question him once more:

'Of two companions now I know. The third?   575
Tell me his name, the one marooned at sea;
living, you say, or dead? Even in pain
I wish to hear.'

                    And this is all he answered:

'Laërtês' son, whose home is Ithaka.
I saw him weeping, weeping on an island.   580
The nymph Kalypso has him, in her hall.
No means of faring home are left him now;
no ship with oars, and no ship's company
to pull him on the broad back of the sea.
As to your own destiny, prince Meneláos,   585
you shall not die in the bluegrass land of Argos;
rather the gods intend you for Elysion[4]
with golden Rhadamanthos at the world's end,
where all existence is a dream of ease.
Snowfall is never known there, neither long   590
frost of winter, nor torrential rain,
but only mild and lulling airs from Ocean
bearing refreshment for the souls of men—
the West Wind always blowing.

---

4. A paradise reserved for a few of the heroes who were related to gods (Menelaos is married to Helen,
daughter of Zeus). *Rhadamanthos* was son of Zeus.

                    For the gods
hold you, as Helen's lord, a son of Zeus.'   595

At this he dove under a swell and left me,
and I went back to the ship with my companions,
feeling my heart's blood in me running high;
but in the long hull's shadow, near the sea,
we supped again as sacred Night came on   600
and slept at last beside the lapping water.

When Dawn spread out her finger tips of rose,
in first light we launched on the courtly breakers,
setting up masts and yards in the well-found ships;
went all on board, and braced on planks athwart   605
oarsmen in line dipped oars in the grey sea.
Soon I drew in to the great stream fed by heaven[5]
and, laying by, slew bulls in the proper number,
until the immortal gods were thus appeased;
then heaped a death mound on that shore against   610
all-quenching time for Agamémnon's honor,
and put to sea once more. The gods sent down
a sternwind for a racing passage homeward.

So ends the story. Now you must stay with me
and be my guest eleven or twelve days more.   615
I'll send you on your way with gifts, and fine ones:
three chariot horses, and a polished car;
a hammered cup, too, so that all your days,
tipping the red wine for the deathless gods,
you will remember me."

                Telémakhos answered: 620

"Lord, son of Atreus, no, you must not keep me.
Not that a year with you would be too long:
I never could be homesick here—I find
your tales and all you say so marvellous.
But time hangs heavy on my shipmates' hands   625
at holy Pylos, if you make me stay.
As for your gift, now, let it be some keepsake.
Horses I cannot take to Ithaka;
let me bestow them back on you, to serve
your glory here. My lord, you rule wide country,   630
rolling and rich with clover, galingale
and all the grains: red wheat and hoary barley.
At home we have no level runs or meadows,

5. The river Nile.

but highland, goat land—prettier than plains, though.
Grasses, and pasture land, are hard to come by   635
upon the islands tilted in the sea,
and Ithaka is the island of them all."

At this the deep-lunged man of battle smiled.
Then he said kindly, patting the boy's hand:
"You come of good stock, lad. That was well spoken.   640
I'll change the gift, then—as indeed I can.
Let me see what is costliest and most beautiful
of all the precious things my house contains:
a wine bowl, mixing bowl, all wrought of silver,
but rimmed with hammered gold. Let this be yours.   645
It is Hephaistos'[6] work, given me by Phaidimos,
captain and king of Sidon. He received me
during my travels. Let it be yours, I say."

This was their discourse on that morning. Meanwhile
guests were arriving at the great lord's house,   650
bringing their sheep, and wine, the ease of men,
with loaves their comely kerchiefed women sent,
to make a feast in hall.
                        At that same hour,
before the distant manor of Odysseus,
the suitors were competing at the discus throw   655
and javelin, on a measured field they used,
arrogant lords at play. The two best men,
Antínoös and Eurýmakhos, presided.
Now Phronios' son, Noêmon, came to see them
with a question for Antínoös. He said: 660

"Do any of us know, or not, Antínoös,
what day Telémakhos will be home from Pylos?
He took my ship, but now I need it back
to make a cruise to Elis, where the plains are.
I have a dozen mares at pasture there   665
with mule colts yet unweaned. My notion is
to bring one home and break him in for labor."

His first words made them stare—for they knew well
Telémakhos could not have gone to Pylos,
but inland with his flocks, or to the swineherd.   670
Eupeithês' son, Antínoös, quickly answered:

"Tell the story straight. He sailed? Who joined him—
a crew he picked up here in Ithaka,

6. The smith-god, who made Akhilleus' armor. He was married to the goddess Aphrodite.

or his own slaves? He might have done it that way.
And will you make it clear   675
whether he took the ship against your will?
Did he ask for it, did you lend it to him?"

Now said the son of Phronios in reply:

"Lent it to him, and freely. Who would not,
when a prince of that house asked for it, in trouble?   680
Hard to refuse the favor, it seems to me.
As for his crew, the best men on the island,
after ourselves, went with him. Mentor I noted
going aboard—or a god who looked like Mentor.
The strange thing is, I saw Lord Mentor here   685
in the first light yesterday—although he sailed
five days ago for Pylos."

                        Turning away,
Noêmon took the path to his father's house,
leaving the two men there, baffled and hostile.
They called the rest in from the playing field   690
and made them all sit down, so that Antínoös
could speak out from the stormcloud of his heart,
swollen with anger; and his eyes blazed:

"A bad business. Telémakhos had the gall
to make that crossing, though we said he could not.   695
So the young cub rounds up a first rate crew
in spite of all our crowd, and puts to sea.
What devilment will he be up to next time?—
Zeus blast the life out of him before he's grown!
Just give me a fast ship and twenty men;   700
I'll intercept him, board him in the strait
between the crags of Samê and this island.
He'll find his sea adventure after his father
swamping work in the end!"

                        They all cried "Aye!"
and "After him!" and trailed back to the manor.   705

Now not much time went by before Penélopê
learned what was afoot among the suitors.
Medôn the crier told her. He had been
outside the wall, and heard them in the court
conspiring. Into the house and up the stairs   710
he ran to her with his news upon his tongue—
but at the door Penélopê met him, crying:

"Why have they sent you up here now? To tell
the maids of King Odysseus—'Leave your spinning:
Time to go down and slave to feed those men'?   715
I wish this were the last time they came feasting,
courting me or consorting here! The last!
Each day you crowd this house like wolves
to eat away my brave son's patrimony.
When you were boys, did your own fathers tell you   720
nothing of what Odysseus was for them?
In word and act impeccable, disinterested
toward all the realm—though it is king's justice
to hold one man abhorred and love another;
no man alive could say Odysseus wronged him.   725
But your own hearts—how different!—and your deeds!
How soon are benefactions all forgotten!"

Now Medôn, the alert and cool man, answered:

"I wish that were the worst of it, my Lady,
but they intend something more terrible—   730
may Zeus forfend and spare us!
They plan to drive the keen bronze through Telémakhos
when he comes home. He sailed away, you know,
to hallowed Pylos and old Lakedaimon
for news about his father."

                        Her knees failed,   735
and her heart failed as she listened to the words,
and all her power of speech went out of her.
Tears came; but the rich voice could not come.
Only after a long while she made answer:

"Why has my child left me? He had no need   740
of those long ships on which men shake out sail
to tug like horses, breasting miles of sea.
Why did he go? Must he, too, be forgotten?"

Then Medôn, the perceptive man, replied:

"A god moved him—who knows?—or his own heart   745
sent him to learn, at Pylos, if his father
roams the wide world still, or what befell him."

He left her then, and went down through the house.
And now the pain around her heart benumbed her;
chairs were a step away, but far beyond her;   750
she sank down on the door sill of the chamber,

wailing, and all her women young and old
made a low murmur of lament around her,
until at last she broke out through her tears:

"Dearest companions, what has Zeus given me?   755
Pain—more pain than any living woman.
My lord, my lion heart, gone, long ago—
the bravest man, and best, of the Danaans,
famous through Hellas and the Argive midlands—
and now the squalls have blown my son, my dear one,   760
an unknown boy, southward. No one told me.
O brute creatures, not one soul would dare
to wake me from my sleep; you knew
the hour he took the black ship out to sea!
If I had seen that sailing in his eyes   765
he should have stayed with me, for all his longing,
stayed—or left me dead in the great hall.
Go, someone, now, and call old Dólios,
the slave my father gave me before I came,
my orchard keeper—tell him to make haste   770
and put these things before Laërtês; he
may plan some kind of action; let him come
to cry shame on these ruffians who would murder
Odysseus' son and heir, and end his line!"

The dear old nurse, Eurýkleia, answered her: 775

"Sweet mistress, have my throat cut without mercy
or what you will; it's true, I won't conceal it,
I knew the whole thing; gave him his provisions;
grain and sweet wine I gave, and a great oath
to tell you nothing till twelve days went by,   780
or till you heard of it yourself, or missed him;
he hoped you would not tear your skin lamenting.
Come, bathe and dress your loveliness afresh,
and go to the upper rooms with all your maids
to ask help from Athena, Zeus's daughter.   785
She it will be who saves this boy from death.
Spare the old man this further suffering;
the blissful gods cannot so hate his line,
heirs of Arkêsios;[7] one will yet again
be lord of the tall house and the far fields."   790

She hushed her weeping in this way, and soothed her.
The Lady Penélopê arose and bathed,

7. Father of Laërtês, Odysseus' father.

dressing her body in her freshest linen,
filled a basket with barley, and led her maids
to the upper rooms, where she besought Athena: 795

"Tireless child of Zeus, graciously hear me!
If ever Odysseus burned at our altar fire
thighbones of beef or mutton in sacrifice,
remember it for my sake! Save my son!
Shield him, and make the killers go astray!"   800

She ended with a cry, and the goddess heard her.
Now voices rose from the shadowy hall below
where the suitors were assuring one another:

"Our so-long-courted Queen is even now
of a mind to marry one of us, and knows   805
nothing of what is destined for her son."

Of what was destined they in fact knew nothing,
but Antínoös addressed them in a whisper:

"No boasting—are you mad?—and no loud talk:
someone might hear it and alarm the house.   810
Come along now, be quiet, this way; come,
we'll carry out the plan our hearts are set on."

Picking out twenty of the strongest seamen,
he led them to a ship at the sea's edge,
and down they dragged her into deeper water,   815
stepping a mast in her, with furled sails,
and oars a-trail from thongs looped over thole pins,
ready all; then tried the white sail, hoisting,
while men at arms carried their gear aboard.
They moored the ship some way off shore, and left her   820
to take their evening meal there, waiting for night to come.

Penélopê at that hour in her high chamber
lay silent, tasting neither food nor drink,
and thought of nothing but her princely son—
could he escape, or would they find and kill him?—   825
her mind turning at bay, like a cornered lion
in whom fear comes as hunters close the ring.
But in her sick thought sweet sleep overtook her,
and she dozed off, her body slack and still.

Now it occurred to the grey-eyed goddess Athena   830
to make a figure of dream in a woman's form—

Iphthimê, great Ikários' other daughter,
whom Eumêlos of Phêrai took as bride.
The goddess sent this dream to Odysseus' house
to quiet Penélopê and end her grieving.   835
So, passing by the strap-slit through the door,[8]
the image came a-gliding down the room
to stand at her bedside and murmur to her:

"Sleepest thou, sorrowing Penélopê?
The gods whose life is ease no longer suffer thee   840
to pine and weep, then; he returns unharmed,
thy little one; no way hath he offended."

Then pensive Penélopê made this reply,
slumbering sweetly in the gates of dream:

"Sister, hast thou come hither? Why? Aforetime   845
never wouldst come, so far away thy dwelling.
And am I bid be done with all my grieving?
But see what anguish hath my heart and soul!
My lord, my lion heart, gone, long ago—
the bravest man, and best, of the Danaans,   850
famous through Hellas and the Argive midlands—
and now my son, my dear one, gone seafaring,
a child, untrained in hardship or in council.
Aye, 'tis for him I weep, more than his father!
Aye, how I tremble for him, lest some blow   855
befall him at men's hands or on the sea!
Cruel are they and many who plot against him,
to take his life before he can return."

Now the dim phantom spoke to her once more:

"Lift up thy heart, and fear not overmuch.   860
For by his side one goes whom all men else
invoke as their defender, one so powerful—
Pallas Athena; in thy tears she pitied thee
and now hath sent me that I so assure thee."

Then said Penélopê the wise:

                              "If thou art   865
numinous and hast ears for divine speech,
O tell me, what of Odysseus, man of woe?
Is he alive still somewhere, seeth he day light still?
Or gone in death to the sunless underworld?"

8. As we would say, "through the keyhole." The inside bolt could by closed from outside by means of a strap which came through a slit in the door.

The dim phantom said only this in answer:　　　　870

"Of him I may not tell thee in this discourse,
alive or dead. And empty words are evil."
The wavering form withdrew along the doorbolt
into a draft of wind, and out of sleep
Penélopê awoke, in better heart　　　　　　　875
for that clear dream in the twilight of the night.

Meanwhile the suitors had got under way,
planning the death plunge for Telémakhos.
Between the Isles of Ithaka and Samê
the sea is broken by an islet, Asteris,　　　　　880
with access to both channels from a cove.
In ambush here that night the Akhaians lay.

BOOK V

Sweet Nymph and Open Sea

Dawn came up from the couch of her reclining,
leaving her lord Tithonos'[9] brilliant side
with fresh light in her arms for gods and men.
And the master of heaven and high thunder, Zeus,
went to his place among the gods assembled　　　5
hearing Athena tell Odysseus' woe.
For she, being vexed that he was still sojourning
in the sea chambers of Kalypso, said:

"O Father Zeus and gods in bliss forever,
let no man holding scepter as a king　　　　　10
think to be mild, or kind, or virtuous;
let him be cruel, and practice evil ways,
for those Odysseus ruled cannot remember
the fatherhood and mercy of his reign.
Meanwhile he lives and grieves upon that island　15
in thralldom to the nymph; he cannot stir,
cannot fare homeward, for no ship is left him,
fitted with oars—no crewmen or companions
to pull him on the broad back of the sea.
And now murder is hatched on the high sea　　20
against his son, who sought news of his father
in the holy lands of Pylos and Lakedaimon."

To this the summoner of cloud replied:

"My child, what odd complaints you let escape you.
Have you not, you yourself, arranged this matter—　25

9. A mortal man whom Eos, the dawn goddess, took for her husband.

as we all know—so that Odysseus
will bring these men to book, on his return?
And are you not the one to give Telémakhos
a safe route for sailing? Let his enemies
encounter no one and row home again." 30

He turned then to his favorite son and said:

"Hermês, you have much practice on our missions,
go make it known to the softly-braided nymph
that we, whose will is not subject to error,
order Odysseus home; let him depart. 35
But let him have no company, gods or men,
only a raft that he must lash together,
and after twenty days, worn out at sea,
he shall make land upon the garden isle,
Skhería,[1] of our kinsmen, the Phaiákians. 40
Let these men take him to their hearts in honor
and berth him in a ship, and send him home,
with gifts of garments, gold, and bronze—
so much he had not counted on from Troy
could he have carried home his share of plunder. 45
His destiny is to see his friends again
under his own roof, in his father's country."

No words were lost on Hermês the Wayfinder,
who bent to tie his beautiful sandals on,
ambrosial, golden, that carry him over water 50
or over endless land in a swish of the wind,
and took the wand with which he charms asleep—
or when he wills, awake—the eyes of men.
So wand in hand he paced into the air,
shot from Pieria[2] down, down to sea level, 55
and veered to skim the swell. A gull patrolling
between the wave crests of the desolate sea
will dip to catch a fish, and douse his wings;
no higher above the whitecaps Hermês flew
until the distant island lay ahead, 60
then rising shoreward from the violet ocean
he stepped up to the cave. Divine Kalypso,
the mistress of the isle, was now at home.
Upon her hearthstone a great fire blazing
scented the farthest shores with cedar smoke 65
and smoke of thyme, and singing high and low
in her sweet voice, before her loom a-weaving,

1. Later Greeks identified it as the island of Corcyra (modern Corfu) off the northwest coast of mainland
Greece.   2. The vicinity of Mount Olympus.

she passed her golden shuttle to and fro.
A deep wood grew outside, with summer leaves
of alder and black poplar, pungent cypress.   70
Ornate birds here rested their stretched wings—
horned owls, falcons, cormorants—long-tongued
beachcombing birds, and followers of the sea.
Around the smoothwalled cave a crooking vine
held purple clusters under ply of green;   75
and four springs, bubbling up near one another
shallow and clear, took channels here and there
through beds of violets and tender parsley.
Even a god who found this place
would gaze, and feel his heart beat with delight: 80
so Hermês did; but when he had gazed his fill
he entered the wide cave. Now face to face
the magical Kalypso recognized him,
as all immortal gods know one another
on sight—though seeming strangers, far from home.   85
But he saw nothing of the great Odysseus,
who sat apart, as a thousand times before,
and racked his own heart groaning, with eyes wet
scanning the bare horizon of the sea.
Kalypso, lovely nymph, seated her guest   90
in a bright chair all shimmering, and asked:

"O Hermês, ever with your golden wand,
what brings you to my island?
Your awesome visits in the past were few.
Now tell me what request you have in mind;   95
for I desire to do it, if I can,
and if it is a proper thing to do.
But wait a while, and let me serve my friend."

She drew a table of ambrosia near him
and stirred a cup of ruby-colored nectar—   100
food and drink for the luminous Wayfinder,
who took both at his leisure, and replied:[3]

"Goddess to god, you greet me, questioning me?
Well, here is truth for you in courtesy.
Zeus made me come, and not my inclination;   105
who cares to cross that tract of desolation,
the bitter sea, all mortal towns behind
where gods have beef and honors from mankind?
But it is not to be thought of—and no use—
for any god to elude the will of Zeus.   110

_____

3. The translator puts Hermes' speech into rhymed couplets; there is no rhyme in the original Greek.

He notes your friend, most ill-starred by renown
of all the peers who fought for Priam's town—
nine years of war they had, before great Troy was down.
Homing, they wronged the goddess with grey eyes,
who made a black wind blow and the seas rise,   115
in which his troops were lost, and all his gear,
while easterlies and current washed him here.
Now the command is: send him back in haste.
His life may not in exile go to waste.
His destiny, his homecoming, is at hand,   120
when he shall see his dearest, and walk on his own land."

That goddess most divinely made
shuddered before him, and her warm voice rose:

"Oh you vile gods, in jealousy supernal!
You hate it when we choose to lie with men—   125
immortal flesh by some dear mortal side.
So radiant Dawn once took to bed Orion
until you easeful gods grew peevish at it,
and holy Artemis, Artemis throned in gold,
hunted him down in Delos with her arrows.   130
Then Dêmêtêr of the tasseled tresses yielded
to Iasion, mingling and making love
in a furrow three times plowed;[4] but Zeus found out
and killed him with a white-hot thunderbolt.
So now you grudge me, too, my mortal friend.   135
But it was I who saved him—saw him straddle
his own keel board, the one man left afloat
when Zeus rent wide his ship with chain lightning
and overturned him in the winedark sea.
Then all his troops were lost, his good companions,   140
but wind and current washed him here to me.
I fed him, loved him, sang that he should not die
nor grow old, ever, in all the days to come.
But now there's no eluding Zeus's will.
If this thing be ordained by him, I say   145
so be it, let the man strike out alone
on the vast water. Surely I cannot 'send' him.
I have no long-oared ships, no company
to pull him on the broad back of the sea.
My counsel he shall have, and nothing hidden,   150
to help him homeward without harm."

To this the Wayfinder made answer briefly:

4. Demeter was the goddess associated with the growth of the crops, especially wheat.

"Thus you shall send him, then. And show more grace
in your obedience, or be chastised by Zeus."

The strong god glittering left her as he spoke,   155
and now her ladyship, having given heed
to Zeus's mandate, went to find Odysseus
in his stone seat to seaward—tear on tear
brimming his eyes. The sweet days of his life time
were running out in anguish over his exile,   160
for long ago the nymph had ceased to please.
Though he fought shy of her and her desire,
he lay with her each night, for she compelled him.
But when day came he sat on the rocky shore
and broke his own heart groaning, with eyes wet   165
scanning the bare horizon of the sea.
Now she stood near him in her beauty, saying:

"O forlorn man, be still.
Here you need grieve no more; you need not feel
your life consumed here; I have pondered it,   170
and I shall help you go.
Come and cut down high timber for a raft
or flatboat; make her broad-beamed, and decked over,
so you can ride her on the misty sea.
Stores I shall put aboard for you—bread, water,   175
and ruby-colored wine, to stay your hunger—
give you a seacloak and a following wind
to help you homeward without harm—provided
the gods who rule wide heaven wish it so.
Stronger than I they are, in mind and power."   180

For all he had endured, Odysseus shuddered.
But when he spoke, his words went to the mark:

"After these years, a helping hand? O goddess,
what guile is hidden here?
A raft, you say, to cross the Western Ocean,   185
rough water, and unknown? Seaworthy ships
that glory in god's wind will never cross it.
I take no raft you grudge me out to sea.
Or yield me first a great oath, if I do,
to work no more enchantment to my harm."   190

At this the beautiful nymph Kalypso smiled
and answered sweetly, laying her hand upon him:

"What a dog you are! And not for nothing learned,
having the wit to ask this thing of me!

My witness then be earth and sky   195
and dripping Styx[5] that I swear by—
the gay gods cannot swear more seriously—
I have no further spells to work against you.
But what I shall devise, and what I tell you,
will be the same as if your need were mine.   200
Fairness is all I think of. There are hearts
made of cold iron—but my heart is kind."

Swiftly she turned and led him to her cave,
and they went in, the mortal and immortal.
He took the chair left empty now by Hermês,   205
where the divine Kalypso placed before him
victuals and drink of men; then she sat down
facing Odysseus, while her serving maids
brought nectar and ambrosia to her side.
Then each one's hands went out on each one's feast   210
until they had had their pleasure; and she said:

"Son of Laërtês, versatile Odysseus,
after these years with me, you still desire
your old home? Even so, I wish you well.
If you could see it all, before you go—   215
all the adversity you face at sea—
you would stay here, and guard this house, and be
immortal—though you wanted her forever,
that bride for whom you pine each day.
Can I be less desirable than she is?   220
Less interesting? Less beautiful? Can mortals
compare with goddesses in grace and form?"

To this the strategist Odysseus answered:

"My lady goddess, here is no cause for anger.
My quiet Penélopê—how well I know—   225
would seem a shade before your majesty,
death and old age being unknown to you,
while she must die. Yet, it is true, each day
I long for home, long for the sight of home.
If any god has marked me out again   230
for shipwreck, my tough heart can undergo it.
What hardship have I not long since endured
at sea, in battle! Let the trial come."

5. One of the rivers of the Underworld.

Now as he spoke the sun set, dusk drew on,
and they retired, this pair, to the inner cave   235
to revel and rest softly, side by side.

When Dawn spread out her finger tips of rose
Odysseus pulled his tunic and his cloak on,
while the sea nymph dressed in a silvery gown
of subtle tissue, drew about her waist   240
a golden belt, and veiled her head, and then
took thought for the great-hearted hero's voyage.
A brazen axehead first she had to give him,
two-bladed, and agreeable to the palm
with a smooth-fitting haft of olive wood;   245
next a well-polished adze; and then she led him
to the island's tip where bigger timber grew—
besides the alder and poplar, tall pine trees,
long dead and seasoned, that would float him high.
Showing him in that place her stand of timber   250
the loveliest of nymphs took her way home.
Now the man fell to chopping; when he paused
twenty tall trees were down. He lopped the branches,
split the trunks, and trimmed his puncheons true.
Meanwhile Kalypso brought him an auger tool   255
with which he drilled through all his planks, then drove
stout pins to bolt them, fitted side by side.
A master shipwright, building a cargo vessel,
lays down a broad and shallow hull; just so
Odysseus shaped the bottom of his craft.   260
He made his decking fast to close-set ribs
before he closed the side with longer planking,
then cut a mast pole, and a proper yard,
and shaped a steering oar to hold her steady.
He drove long strands of willow in all the seams   265
to keep out waves, and ballasted with logs.
As for a sail, the lovely nymph Kalypso
brought him a cloth so he could make that, too.
Then he ran up his rigging—halyards, braces—
and hauled the boat on rollers to the water.   270

This was the fourth day, when he had all ready;
on the fifth day, she sent him out to sea.
But first she bathed him, gave him a scented cloak,
and put on board a skin of dusky wine
with water in a bigger skin, and stores—   275
boiled meats and other victuals—in a bag.
Then she conjured a warm landbreeze to blowing—
joy for Odysseus when he shook out sail!

Now the great seaman, leaning on his oar,
steered all the night unsleeping, and his eyes   280
picked out the Pleiadês, the laggard Ploughman,[6]
and the Great Bear, that some have called the Wain,[7]
pivoting in the sky before Orion;
of all the night's pure figures, she alone
would never bathe or dip in the Ocean stream.[8]   285
These stars the beautiful Kalypso bade him
hold on his left hand as he crossed the main.
Seventeen nights and days in the open water
he sailed, before a dark shoreline appeared;
Skhería then came slowly into view   290
like a rough shield of bull's hide on the sea.

But now the god of earthquake,[9] storming home
over the mountains of Asia from the Sunburned land,
sighted him far away. The god grew sullen
and tossed his great head, muttering to himself: 295

"Here is a pretty cruise! While I was gone,
the gods have changed their minds about Odysseus.
Look at him now, just offshore of that island
that frees him from the bondage of his exile!
Still I can give him a rough ride in, and will."   300

Brewing high thunderheads, he churned the deep
with both hands on his trident—called up wind
from every quarter, and sent a wall of rain
to blot out land and sea in torrential night.
Hurricane winds now struck from the South and East   305
shifting North West in a great spume of seas,
on which Odysseus' knees grew slack, his heart
sickened, and he said within himself:

"Rag of man that I am, is this the end of me?
I fear the goddess told it all too well—   310
predicting great adversity at sea
and far from home. Now all things bear her out:
the whole rondure of heaven hooded so
by Zeus in woeful cloud, and the sea raging
under such winds. I am going down, that's sure.   315
How lucky those Danaans were who perished
on Troy's wide seaboard, serving the Atreidai!
Would God I, too, had died there—met my end
that time the Trojans made so many casts at me
when I stood by Akhilleus after death.   320

6. The constellation Boötes (which means "ploughman"). *Pleiadês*: A cluster of stars in the constellation Taurus.   7. The Big Dipper.   8. It is visible all year long.   9. Poseidon.

I should have had a soldier's burial
and praise from the Akhaians—not this choking
waiting for me at sea, unmarked and lonely."

A great wave drove at him with toppling crest
spinning him round, in one tremendous blow,   325
and he went plunging overboard, the oar-haft
wrenched from his grip. A gust that came on howling
at the same instant broke his mast in two,
hurling his yard and sail far out to leeward.
Now the big wave a long time kept him under,   330
helpless to surface, held by tons of water,
tangled, too, by the seacloak of Kalypso.
Long, long, until he came up spouting brine,
with streamlets gushing from his head and beard;
but still bethought him, half-drowned as he was,   335
to flounder for the boat and get a handhold
into the bilge—to crouch there, foiling death.
Across the foaming water, to and fro,
the boat careered like a ball of tumbleweed
blown on the autumn plains, but intact still.   340
So the winds drove this wreck over the deep,
East Wind and North Wind, then South Wind and West,
coursing each in turn to the brutal harry.

But Ino saw him—Ino, Kadmos' daughter,
slim-legged, lovely, once an earthling girl,   345
now in the seas a nereid, Leukothea.
Touched by Odysseus' painful buffeting
she broke the surface, like a diving bird,
to rest upon the tossing raft and say:

"O forlorn man, I wonder   350
why the Earthshaker, Lord Poseidon, holds
this fearful grudge—father of all your woes.
He will not drown you, though, despite his rage.
You seem clear-headed still; do what I tell you.
Shed that cloak, let the gale take your craft,   355
and swim for it—swim hard to get ashore
upon Skhería, yonder,
where it is fated that you find a shelter.
Here: make my veil your sash; it is not mortal;
you cannot, now, be drowned or suffer harm.   360
Only, the instant you lay hold of earth,
discard it, cast it far, far out from shore
in the winedark sea again, and turn away."

After she had bestowed her veil, the nereid
dove like a gull to windward   365
where a dark waveside closed over her whiteness.
But in perplexity Odysseus
said to himself, his great heart laboring:

"O damned confusion! Can this be a ruse
to trick me from the boat for some god's pleasure?   370
No I'll not swim; with my own eyes I saw
how far the land lies that she called my shelter.
Better to do the wise thing, as I see it.
While this poor planking holds, I stay aboard;
I may ride out the pounding of the storm,   375
or if she cracks up, take to the water then;
I cannot think it through a better way."

But even while he pondered and decided,
the god of earthquake heaved a wave against him
high as a rooftree and of awful gloom.   380
A gust of wind, hitting a pile of chaff,
will scatter all the parched stuff far and wide;
just so, when this gigantic billow struck
the boat's big timbers flew apart. Odysseus
clung to a single beam, like a jockey riding,   385
meanwhile stripping Kalypso's cloak away;
then he slung round his chest the veil of Ino
and plunged headfirst into the sea. His hands
went out to stroke, and he gave a swimmer's kick.
But the strong Earthshaker had him under his eye,   390
and nodded as he said:

                "Go on, go on;
wander the high seas this way, take your blows,
before you join that race the gods have nurtured.[1]
Nor will you grumble, even then, I think,
for want of trouble."

                Whipping his glossy team   395
he rode off to his glorious home at Aigai.[2]
But Zeus's daughter Athena countered him:
she checked the course of all the winds but one,
commanding them, "Be quiet and go to sleep."
Then sent a long swell running under a norther   400
to bear the prince Odysseus, back from danger,
to join the Phaiákians, people of the sea.

1. The Phaiákians, favored by the gods.   2. An island off Euboia, which gave its name to the Aegean
Sea.

Two nights, two days, in the solid deep-sea swell
he drifted, many times awaiting death,
until with shining ringlets in the East   405
the dawn confirmed a third day, breaking clear
over a high and windless sea; and mounting
a rolling wave he caught a glimpse of land.
What a dear welcome thing life seems to children
whose father, in the extremity, recovers   410
after some weakening and malignant illness:
his pangs are gone, the gods have delivered him.
So dear and welcome to Odysseus
the sight of land, of woodland, on that morning.
It made him swim again, to get a foothold   415
on solid ground. But when he came in earshot
he heard the trampling roar of sea on rock,
where combers, rising shoreward, thudded down
on the sucking ebb—all sheeted with salt foam.
Here were no coves or harborage or shelter,   420
only steep headlands, rockfallen reefs and crags.
Odysseus' knees grew slack, his heart faint,
a heaviness came over him, and he said:

"A cruel turn, this. Never had I thought
to see this land, but Zeus has let me see it—   425
and let me, too, traverse the Western Ocean—
only to find no exit from these breakers.
Here are sharp rocks off shore, and the sea a smother
rushing around them; rock face rising sheer
from deep water; nowhere could I stand up   430
on my two feet and fight free of the welter.
No matter how I try it, the surf may throw me
against the cliffside; no good fighting there.
If I swim down the coast, outside the breakers,
I may find shelving shore and quiet water—   435
but what if another gale comes on to blow?
Then I go cursing out to sea once more.
Or then again, some shark of Amphitritê's[3]
may hunt me, sent by the genius of the deep.
I know how he who makes earth tremble hates me."   440

During this meditation a heavy surge
was taking him, in fact, straight on the rocks.
He had been flayed there, and his bones broken,
had not grey-eyed Athena instructed him:
he gripped a rock-ledge with both hands in passing   445
and held on, groaning, as the surge went by,

3. A sea-goddess.

to keep clear of its breaking. Then the backwash
hit him, ripping him under and far out.
An octopus, when you drag one from his chamber,
comes up with suckers full of tiny stones: 450
Odysseus left the skin of his great hands
torn on that rock-ledge as the wave submerged him.
And now at last Odysseus would have perished,
battered inhumanly, but he had the gift
of self-possession from grey-eyed Athena.   455
So, when the backwash spewed him up again,
he swam out and along, and scanned the coast
for some landspit that made a breakwater.
Lo and behold, the mouth of a calm river
at length came into view, with level shores   460
unbroken, free from rock, shielded from wind—
by far the best place he had found.
But as he felt the current flowing seaward
he prayed in his heart:

                    "O hear me, lord of the stream:
how sorely I depend upon your mercy!   465
derelict as I am by the sea's anger.
Is he not sacred, even to the gods,
the wandering man who comes, as I have come,
in weariness before your knees, your waters?
Here is your servant; lord, have mercy on me."   470

Now even as he prayed the tide at ebb
had turned, and the river god made quiet water,
drawing him in to safety in the shallows.
His knees buckled, his arms gave way beneath him,
all vital force now conquered by the sea.   475
Swollen from head to foot he was, and seawater
gushed from his mouth and nostrils. There he lay,
scarce drawing breath, unstirring, deathly spent.
In time, as air came back into his lungs
and warmth around his heart, he loosed the veil,   480
letting it drift away on the estuary
downstream to where a white wave took it under
and Ino's hands received it. Then the man
crawled to the river bank among the reeds
where, face down, he could kiss the soil of earth,   485
in his exhaustion murmuring to himself:

"What more can this hulk suffer? What comes now?
In vigil through the night here by the river
how can I not succumb, being weak and sick,
to the night's damp and hoarfrost of the morning?   490

The air comes cold from rivers before dawn.
But if I climb the slope and fall asleep
in the dark forest's undergrowth—supposing
cold and fatigue will go, and sweet sleep come—
I fear I make the wild beasts easy prey."   495

But this seemed best to him, as he thought it over.
He made his way to a grove above the water
on open ground, and crept under twin bushes
grown from the same spot—olive and wild olive—
a thicket proof against the stinging wind   500
or Sun's blaze, fine soever the needling sunlight;
nor could a downpour wet it through, so dense
those plants were interwoven. Here Odysseus
tunnelled, and raked together with his hands
a wide bed—for a fall of leaves was there,   505
enough to save two men or maybe three
on a winter night, a night of bitter cold.
Odysseus' heart laughed when he saw his leaf-bed,
and down he lay, heaping more leaves above him.

A man in a distant field, no hearthfires near,   510
will hide a fresh brand in his bed of embers
to keep a spark alive for the next day;
so in the leaves Odysseus hid himself,
while over him Athena showered sleep
that his distress should end, and soon, soon.   515
In quiet sleep she sealed his cherished eyes.

BOOK VI

The Princess at the River

Far gone in weariness, in oblivion,
the noble and enduring man slept on;
but Athena in the night went down the land
of the Phaiákians, entering their city.
In days gone by, these men held Hypereia,[4]   5
a country of wide dancing grounds, but near them
were overbearing Kyklopês, whose power
could not be turned from pillage. So the Phaiákians
migrated thence under Nausíthoös
to settle a New World across the sea,   10
Skhería Island. That first captain walled
their promontory, built their homes and shrines,

---

4. An imaginary place, probably, and the one-eyed Kyklopês are certainly mythical but the migration
under pressure and the founding of the new city (fortification, homes, temples, division of the land) suggest
the atmosphere of the great age of Greek colonization (eighth century B.C.).

and parcelled out the black land for the plow.
But he had gone down long ago to Death.
Alkínoös ruled, and Heaven gave him wisdom,   15
so on this night the goddess, grey-eyed Athena,
entered the palace of Alkínoös
to make sure of Odysseus' voyage home.
She took her way to a painted bedchamber
where a young girl lay fast asleep—so fine   20
in mould and feature that she seemed a goddess—
the daughter of Alkínoös, Nausikaa.
On either side, as Graces[5] might have slept,
her maids were sleeping. The bright doors were shut,
but like a sudden stir of wind, Athena   25
moved to the bedside of the girl, and grew
visible as the shipman Dymas' daughter,
a girl the princess' age, and her dear friend.
In this form grey-eyed Athena said to her:

"How so remiss, and yet thy mother's daughter?   30
leaving thy clothes uncared for, Nausikaa,
when soon thou must have store of marriage linen,
and put thy minstrelsy in wedding dress!
Beauty, in these, will make the folk admire,
and bring thy father and gentle mother joy.   35
Let us go washing in the shine of morning!
Beside thee will I drub, so wedding chests
will brim by evening. Maidenhood must end!
Have not the noblest born Phaiákians
paid court to thee, whose birth none can excel?   40
Go beg thy sovereign father, even at dawn,
to have the mule cart and the mules brought round
to take thy body-linen, gowns and mantles.
Thou shouldst ride, for it becomes thee more,
the washing pools are found so far from home."   45

On this word she departed, grey-eyed Athena,
to where the gods have their eternal dwelling—
as men say—in the fastness of Olympos.
Never a tremor of wind, or a splash of rain,
no errant snowflake comes to stain that heaven,   50
so calm, so vaporless, the world of light.
Here, where the gay gods live their days of pleasure,
the grey-eyed one withdrew, leaving the princess.

And now Dawn took her own fair throne, awaking
the girl in the sweet gown, still charmed by dream.   55

5. Goddesses (usually three) personifying charm and beauty.

Down through the rooms she went to tell her parents,
whom she found still at home: her mother seated
near the great hearth among her maids—and twirling
out of her distaff yarn dyed like the sea—;
her father at the door, bound for a council   60
of princes on petition of the gentry.
She went up close to him and softly said:

"My dear Papà, could you not send the mule cart
around for me—the gig with pretty wheels?
I must take all our things and get them washed   65
at the river pools; our linen is all soiled.
And you should wear fresh clothing, going to council
with counselors and first men of the realm.
Remember your five sons at home: though two
are married, we have still three bachelor sprigs;   70
they will have none but laundered clothes each time
they go to the dancing. See what I must think of!"

She had no word to say of her own wedding,
though her keen father saw her blush. Said he:

"No mules would I deny you, child, nor anything.   75
Go along, now; the grooms will bring your gig
with pretty wheels and the cargo box upon it."

He spoke to the stableman, who soon brought round
the cart, low-wheeled and nimble;
harnessed the mules, and backed them in the traces.   80
Meanwhile the girl fetched all her soiled apparel
to bundle in the polished wagon box.
Her mother, for their luncheon, packed a hamper
with picnic fare, and filled a skin of wine,
and, when the princess had been handed up,   85
gave her a golden bottle of olive oil
for softening girls' bodies, after bathing.
Nausikaa took the reins and raised her whip,
lashing the mules. What jingling! What a clatter!
But off they went in a ground-covering trot,   90
with princess, maids, and laundry drawn behind.
By the lower river where the wagon came
were washing pools, with water all year flowing
in limpid spillways that no grime withstood.
The girls unhitched the mules, and sent them down   95
along the eddying stream to crop sweet grass.
Then sliding out the cart's tail board, they took
armloads of clothing to the dusky water,
and trod them in the pits, making a race of it.

All being drubbed, all blemish rinsed away,   100
they spread them, piece by piece, along the beach
whose pebbles had been laundered by the sea;
then took a dip themselves, and, all anointed
with golden oil, ate lunch beside the river
while the bright burning sun dried out their linen.   105
Princess and maids delighted in that feast;
then, putting off their veils,
they ran and passed a ball to a rhythmic beat,
Nausikaa flashing first with her white arms.

So Artemis goes flying after her arrows flown   110
down some tremendous valley-side—
                              Taÿgetos, Erymanthos—[6]
chasing the mountain goats or ghosting deer,
with nymphs of the wild places flanking her;
and Lêto's[7] heart delights to see them running,
for, taller by a head than nymphs can be,   115
the goddess shows more stately, all being beautiful.
So one could tell the princess from the maids.

Soon it was time, she knew, for riding homeward—
mules to be harnessed, linen folded smooth—
but the grey-eyed goddess Athena made her tarry,   120
so that Odysseus might behold her beauty
and win her guidance to the town.
                              It happened
when the king's daughter threw her ball off line
and missed, and put it in the whirling stream,—
at which they all gave such a shout, Odysseus   125
awoke and sat up, saying to himself:

"Now, by my life, mankind again! But who?
Savages, are they, strangers to courtesy?
Or gentle folk, who know and fear the gods?
That was a lusty cry of tall young girls—   130
most like the cry of nymphs, who haunt the peaks,
and springs of brooks, and inland grassy places.
Or am I amid people of human speech?
Up again, man; and let me see for myself."
He pushed aside the bushes, breaking off   135
with his great hand a single branch of olive,
whose leaves might shield him in his nakedness;
so came out rustling, like a mountain lion,
rain-drenched, wind-buffeted, but in his might at ease,

6. Taÿgetos is the mountain range west of Sparta; Erymanthos, a mountain in Arcadia—both places rich
in game.   7. Mother of Artemis and Apollo.

with burning eyes—who prowls among the herds   140
or flocks, or after game, his hungry belly
taking him near stout homesteads for his prey.
Odysseus had this look, in his rough skin
advancing on the girls with pretty braids;
and he was driven on by hunger, too.   145
Streaked with brine, and swollen, he terrified them,
so that they fled, this way and that. Only
Alkínoös' daughter stood her ground, being given
a bold heart by Athena, and steady knees.

She faced him, waiting. And Odysseus came,   150
debating inwardly what he should do:
embrace this beauty's knees in supplication?
or stand apart, and, using honeyed speech,
inquire the way to town, and beg some clothing?
In his swift reckoning, he thought it best   155
to trust in words to please her—and keep away;
he might anger the girl, touching her knees.
So he began, and let the soft words fall:

"Mistress: please: are you divine, or mortal?
If one of those who dwell in the wide heaven,   160
you are most near to Artemis, I should say—
great Zeus's daughter—in your grace and presence.
If you are one of earth's inhabitants,
how blest your father, and your gentle mother,
blest all your kin. I know what happiness   165
must send the warm tears to their eyes, each time
they see their wondrous child go to the dancing!
But one man's destiny is more than blest—
he who prevails, and takes you as his bride.
Never have I laid eyes on equal beauty   170
in man or woman. I am hushed indeed.
So fair, one time, I thought a young palm tree
at Delos⁸ near the altar of Apollo—
I had troops under me when I was there
on the sea route that later brought me grief—   175
but that slim palm tree filled my heart with wonder:
never came shoot from earth so beautiful.
So now, my lady, I stand in awe so great
I cannot take your knees. And yet my case is desperate:
twenty days, yesterday, in the winedark sea,   180
on the ever-lunging swell, under gale winds,
getting away from the Island of Ogýgia.
And now the terror of Storm has left me stranded

8. A small island in the middle of the Aegean sea, the birthplace of Apollo and a center for his worship.

upon this shore—with more blows yet to suffer,
I must believe, before the gods relent.   185
Mistress, do me a kindness!
After much weary toil, I come to you,
and you are the first soul I have seen—I know
no others here. Direct me to the town,
give me a rag that I can throw around me,   190
some cloth or wrapping that you brought along.
And may the gods accomplish your desire:
a home, a husband, and harmonious
converse with him—the best thing in the world
being a strong house held in serenity   195
where man and wife agree. Woe to their enemies,
joy to their friends! But all this they know best."

Then she of the white arms, Nausikaa, replied:

"Stranger, there is no quirk or evil in you
that I can see. You know Zeus metes out fortune   200
to good and bad men as it pleases him.
Hardship he sent to you, and you must bear it.
But now that you have taken refuge here
you shall not lack for clothing, or any other
comfort due to a poor man in distress.   205
The town lies this way, and the men are called
Phaiákians, who own the land and city.
I am daughter to the Prince Alkínoös,
by whom the power of our people stands."

Turning, she called out to her maids-in-waiting: 210

"Stay with me! Does the sight of a man scare you?
Or do you take this one for an enemy?
Why, there's no fool so brash, and never will be,
as to bring war or pillage to this coast,
for we are dear to the immortal gods,   215
living here, in the sea that rolls forever,
distant from other lands and other men.
No: this man is a castaway, poor fellow;
we must take care of him. Strangers and beggars
come from Zeus: a small gift, then, is friendly.   220
Give our new guest some food and drink, and take him
into the river, out of the wind, to bathe."

They stood up now, and called to one another
to go on back. Quite soon they led Odysseus
under the river bank, as they were bidden;   225
and there laid out a tunic, and a cloak,

and gave him olive oil in the golden flask.
"Here," they said, "go bathe in the flowing water."
But heard now from that kingly man, Odysseus:

"Maids," he said, "keep away a little; let me   230
wash the brine from my own back, and rub on
plenty of oil. It is long since my anointing.
I take no bath, however, where you can see me—
naked before young girls with pretty braids."

They left him, then, and went to tell the princess.   235
And now Odysseus, dousing in the river,
scrubbed the coat of brine from back and shoulders
and rinsed the clot of sea-spume from his hair;
got himself all rubbed down, from head to foot,
then he put on the clothes the princess gave him.   240
Athena lent a hand, making him seem
taller, and massive too, with crisping hair
in curls like petals of wild hyacinth,
but all red-golden. Think of gold infused
on silver by a craftsman, whose fine art   245
Hephaistos taught him, or Athena: one
whose work moves to delight: just so she lavished
beauty over Odysseus' head and shoulders.
Then he went down to sit on the sea beach
in his new splendor. There the girl regarded him,   250
and after a time she said to the maids beside her:

"My gentlewomen, I have a thing to tell you.
The Olympian gods cannot be all averse
to this man's coming here among our islanders.
Uncouth he seemed, I thought so, too, before;   255
but now he looks like one of heaven's people.
I wish my husband could be fine as he
and glad to stay forever on Skhería!

But have you given refreshment to our guest?"

At this the maids, all gravely listening, hastened   260
to set out bread and wine before Odysseus,
and ah! how ravenously that patient man
took food and drink, his long fast at an end.

The princess Nausikaa now turned aside
to fold her linens; in the pretty cart   265
she stowed them, put the mule team under harness,
mounted the driver's seat, and then looked down
to say with cheerful prompting to Odysseus:

"Up with you now, friend; back to town we go;
and I shall send you in before my father   270
who is wondrous wise; there in our house with him
you'll meet the noblest of the Phaiákians.
You have good sense, I think; here's how to do it:
while we go through the countryside and farmland
stay with my maids, behind the wagon, walking   275
briskly enough to follow where I lead.
But near the town—well, there's a wall with towers
around the Isle, and beautiful ship basins
right and left of the causeway of approach;
seagoing craft are beached beside the road   280
each on its launching ways. The agora,[9]
with fieldstone benches bedded in the earth,
lies either side Poseidon's shrine—for there
men are at work on pitch-black hulls and rigging,
cables and sails, and tapering of oars.   285
The archer's craft is not for the Phaiákians,
but ship designing, modes of oaring cutters
in which they love to cross the foaming sea.
From these fellows I will have no salty talk,
no gossip later. Plenty are insolent.   290
And some seadog might say, after we passed:
'Who is this handsome stranger trailing Nausikaa?
Where did she find him? Will he be her husband?
Or is she being hospitable to some rover
come off his ship from lands across the sea—   295
there being no lands nearer. A god, maybe?
a god from heaven, the answer to her prayer,
descending now—to make her his forever?
Better, if she's roamed and found a husband
somewhere else: none of our own will suit her,   300
though many come to court her, and those the best.'
This is the way they might make light of me.
And I myself should hold it shame
for any girl to flout her own dear parents,
taking up with a man, before her marriage.   305

Note well, now, what I say, friend, and your chances
are excellent for safe conduct from my father.
You'll find black poplars in a roadside park
around a meadow and fountain—all Athena's—
but Father has a garden in the place—   310
this within earshot of the city wall.
Go in there and sit down, giving us time
to pass through town and reach my father's house.

9. Place of assembly.

And when you can imagine we're at home,
then take the road into the city, asking   315
directions to the palace of Alkínoös.
You'll find it easily: any small boy
can take you there; no family has a mansion
half so grand as he does, being king.
As soon as you are safe inside, cross over   320
and go straight through into the mégaron¹
to find my mother. She'll be there in firelight
before a column, with her maids in shadow,
spinning a wool dyed richly as the sea.
My father's great chair faces the fire, too;   325
there like a god he sits and takes his wine.
Go past him, cast yourself before my mother,
embrace her knees—and you may wake up soon
at home rejoicing, though your home be far.
On Mother's feeling much depends; if she   330
looks on you kindly, you shall see your friends
under your own roof in your father's country."

At this she raised her glistening whip, lashing
the team into a run; they left the river
cantering beautifully, then trotted smartly.   335
But then she reined them in, and spared the whip,
so that her maids could follow with Odysseus.
The sun was going down when they went by
Athena's grove. Here, then, Odysseus rested,
and lifted up his prayer to Zeus's daughter: 340

"Hear me, unwearied child of royal Zeus!
O listen to me now—thou so aloof
while the Earthshaker wrecked and battered me.
May I find love and mercy among these people."

He prayed for that, and Pallas Athena heard him—   345
although in deference to her father's brother
she would not show her true form to Odysseus,
at whom Poseidon smoldered on
until the kingly man came home to his own shore.

BOOK VII

Gardens and Firelight

As Lord Odysseus prayed there in the grove
the girl rode on, behind her strapping team,
and came late to the mansion of her father,

---

1. The great hall of the palace.

where she reined in at the courtyard gate. Her brothers
awaited her like tall gods in the court,   5
circling to lead the mules away and carry
the laundered things inside. But she withdrew
to her own bedroom, where a fire soon shone,
kindled by her old nurse, Eurymedousa.
Years ago, from a raid on the continent,   10
the rolling ships had brought this woman over
to be Alkínoös' share—fit spoil for him
whose realm hung on his word as on a god's.
And she had schooled the princess, Nausikaa,
whose fire she tended now, making her supper.   15

Odysseus, when the time had passed, arose
and turned into the city. But Athena
poured a sea fog around him as he went—
her love's expedient, that no jeering sailor
should halt the man or challenge him for luck.   20
Instead, as he set foot in the pleasant city,
the grey-eyed goddess came to him, in figure
a small girl child, hugging a water jug.

Confronted by her, Lord Odysseus asked:

"Little one, could you take me to the house   25
of that Alkínoös, king among these people?
You see, I am a poor old stranger here;
my home is far away; here there is no one
known to me, in countryside or city."

The grey-eyed goddess Athena replied to him: 30

"Oh yes, good grandfer, sir, I know, I'll show you
the house you mean; it is quite near my father's.
But come now, hush, like this, and follow me.
You must not stare at people, or be inquisitive.
They do not care for strangers in this neighborhood;   35
a foreign man will get no welcome here.
The only things they trust are the racing ships
Poseidon gave, to sail the deep blue sea
like white wings in the sky, or a flashing thought."

Pallas Athena turned like the wind, running   40
ahead of him, and he followed in her footsteps.
And no seafaring men of Phaiákia
perceived Odysseus passing through their town:
the awesome one in pigtails barred their sight
with folds of sacred mist. And yet Odysseus   45
gazed out marvelling at the ships and harbors,

public squares, and ramparts towering up
with pointed palisades along the top.
When they were near the mansion of the king,
grey-eyed Athena in the child cried out: 50

"Here it is, grandfer, sir—that mansion house
you asked to see. You'll find our king and queen
at supper, but you must not be dismayed;
go in to them. A cheerful man does best
in every enterprise—even a stranger.   55
You'll see our lady just inside the hall—
her name is Arêtê; her grandfather
was our good king Alkínoös' father—
Nausíthoös by name, son of Poseidon
and Periboia. That was a great beauty,   60
the daughter of Eurymedon, commander
of the Gigantês[2] in the olden days,
who led those wild things to their doom and his.
Poseidon then made love to Periboia,
and she bore Nausíthoös, Phaiákia's lord,   65
whose sons in turn were Rhêxênor and Alkínoös.
Rhêxênor had no sons; even as a bridegroom
he fell before the silver bow of Apollo,
his only child a daughter, Arêtê.
When she grew up, Alkínoös married her   70
and holds her dear. No lady in the world,
no other mistress of a man's household,
is honored as our mistress is, and loved,
by her own children, by Alkínoös,
and by the people. When she walks the town   75
they murmur and gaze, as though she were a goddess.
No grace or wisdom fails in her; indeed
just men in quarrels come to her for equity.
Supposing, then, she looks upon you kindly,
the chances are that you shall see your friends   80
under your own roof, in your father's country."

At this the grey-eyed goddess Athena left him
and left that comely land, going over sea
to Marathon, to the wide roadways of Athens
and her retreat in the stronghold of Erekhtheus.[3]   85
Odysseus, now alone before the palace,
meditated a long time before crossing
the brazen threshold of the great courtyard.

2. The Giants, an older race of gods who battled, unsuccessfully, against the Olympians. 3. King of
Athens. *Marathon:* A village north of Athens near the coast. It was the site of the famous battle at which
the Athenians repulsed a Persian invasion force (490 B.C.).

High rooms he saw ahead, airy and luminous
as though with lusters of the sun and moon,   90
bronze-paneled walls, at several distances,
making a vista, with an azure molding
of lapis lazuli. The doors were golden
guardians of the great room. Shining bronze
plated the wide door sill; the posts and lintel   95
were silver upon silver; golden handles
curved on the doors, and golden, too, and silver
were sculptured hounds, flanking the entrance way,
cast by the skill and ardor of Hephaistos
to guard the prince Alkínoös' house—   100
undying dogs that never could grow old.
Through all the rooms, as far as he could see,
tall chairs were placed around the walls, and strewn
with fine embroidered stuff made by the women.
Here were enthroned the leaders of Phaiákia   105
drinking and dining, with abundant fare.
Here, too, were boys of gold on pedestals
holding aloft bright torches of pitch pine
to light the great rooms, and the night-time feasting.
And fifty maids-in-waiting of the household   110
sat by the round mill, grinding yellow corn,
or wove upon their looms, or twirled their distaffs,
flickering like the leaves of a poplar tree;
while drops of oil glistened on linen weft.
Skillful as were the men of Phaiákia   115
in ship handling at sea, so were these women
skilled at the loom, having this lovely craft
and artistry as talents from Athena.

To left and right, outside, he saw an orchard
closed by a pale—four spacious acres planted   120
with trees in bloom or weighted down for picking:
pear trees, pomegranates, brilliant apples,
luscious figs, and olives ripe and dark.
Fruit never failed upon these trees: winter
and summer time they bore, for through the year   125
the breathing Westwind ripened all in turn—
so one pear came to prime, and then another,
and so with apples, figs, and the vine's fruit
empurpled in the royal vineyard there.
Currants were dried at one end, on a platform   130
bare to the sun, beyond the vintage arbors
and vats the vintners trod; while near at hand
were new grapes barely formed as the green bloom fell,
or half-ripe clusters, faintly coloring.

After the vines came rows of vegetables   135
of all the kinds that flourish in every season,
and through the garden plots and orchard ran
channels from one clear fountain, while another
gushed through a pipe under the courtyard entrance
to serve the house and all who came for water.   140
These were the gifts of heaven to Alkínoös.

Odysseus, who had borne the barren sea,
stood in the gateway and surveyed this bounty.
He gazed his fill, then swiftly he went in.
The lords and nobles of Phaiákia   145
were tipping wine to the wakeful god, to Hermês—
a last libation before going to bed—
but down the hall Odysseus went unseen,
still in the cloud Athena cloaked him in,
until he reached Arêtê, and the king.   150
He threw his great hands round Arêtê's knees,
whereon the sacred mist curled back;
they saw him; and the diners hushed amazed
to see an unknown man inside the palace.
Under their eyes Odysseus made his plea: 155

"Arêtê, admirable Rhêxênor's daughter,
here is a man bruised by adversity, thrown
upon your mercy and the king your husband's,
begging indulgence of this company—
may the gods' blessing rest on them! May life   160
be kind to all! Let each one leave his children
every good thing this realm confers upon him!
But grant me passage to my father land.
My home and friends lie far. My life is pain."

He moved, then, toward the fire, and sat him down   165
amid the ashes.[4] No one stirred or spoke
until Ekhenêos broke the spell—an old man,
eldest of the Phaiákians, an oracle,
versed in the laws and manners of old time.
He rose among them now and spoke out kindly: 170

"Alkínoös, this will not pass for courtesy:
a guest abased in ashes at our hearth?
Everyone here awaits your word; so come, then,
lift the man up; give him a seat of honor,
a silver-studded chair. Then tell the stewards   175
we'll have another wine bowl for libation

---

4. The fire, the hearth, was the sacred center of the home: the suppliant who sits there is, so to speak, on consecrated ground and cannot be forcibly removed.

to Zeus, lord of the lightning—advocate
of honorable petitioners. And supper
may be supplied our friend by the larder mistress."

Alkínoös, calm in power, heard him out,   180
then took the great adventurer by the hand
and led him from the fire. Nearest his throne
the son whom he loved best, Laódamas,
had long held place; now the king bade him rise
and gave his shining chair to Lord Odysseus.   185
A serving maid poured water for his hands
from a gold pitcher into a silver bowl,
and spread a polished table at his side;
the mistress of provisions came with bread
and other victuals, generous with her store.   190
So Lord Odysseus drank, and tasted supper.
Seeing this done, the king in majesty
said to his squire:

                    "A fresh bowl, Pontónoös;
we make libation to the lord of lightning,
who seconds honorable petitioners."   195

Mixing the honey-hearted wine, Pontónoös
went on his rounds and poured fresh cups for all,
whereof when all had spilt they drank their fill.
Alkínoös then spoke to the company:

"My lords and leaders of Phaiákia: 200
hear now, all that my heart would have me say.
Our banquet's ended, so you may retire;
but let our seniors gather in the morning
to give this guest a festal day, and make
fair offerings to the gods. In due course we   205
shall put our minds upon the means at hand
to take him safely, comfortably, well
and happily, with speed, to his own country,
distant though it may lie. And may no trouble
come to him here or on the way; his fate   210
he shall pay out at home, even as the Spinners[5]
spun for him on the day his mother bore him.
If, as may be, he is some god, come down
from heaven's height, the gods are working strangely:
until now, they have shown themselves in glory   215
only after great hekatombs—those figures
banqueting at our side, throned like ourselves.

5. The Fates, who spin the pattern of each individual; destiny.

Or if some traveller met them when alone
they bore no least disguise; we are their kin; Gigantês,
Kyklopês, rank no nearer gods than we." 220

Odysseus' wits were ready, and he replied:

"Alkínoös, you may set your mind at rest.
Body and birth, a most unlikely god
am I, being all of earth and mortal nature.
I should say, rather, I am like those men 225
who suffer the worst trials that you know,
and miseries greater yet, as I might tell you—
hundreds; indeed the gods could send no more.
You will indulge me if I finish dinner—?
grieved though I am to say it. There's no part 230
of man more like a dog than brazen Belly,
crying to be remembered—and it must be—
when we are mortal weary and sick at heart;
and that is my condition. Yet my hunger
drives me to take this food, and think no more 235
of my afflictions. Belly must be filled.
Be equally impelled, my lords, tomorrow
to berth me in a ship and send me home!
Rough years I've had; now may I see once more
my hall, my lands, my people before I die!" 240

Now all who heard cried out assent to this:
the guest had spoken well; he must have passage.
Then tipping wine they drank their thirst away,
and one by one went homeward for the night.
So Lord Odysseus kept his place alone 245
with Arêtê and the king Alkínoös
beside him, while the maids went to and fro
clearing away the wine cups and the tables.
Presently the ivory-skinned lady
turned to him—for she knew his cloak and tunic 250
to be her own fine work, done with her maids—
and arrowy came her words upon the air:

"Friend, I, for one, have certain questions for you.
Who are you, and who has given you this clothing?
Did you not say you wandered here by sea?" 255

The great tactician carefully replied:

"Ah, majesty, what labor it would be
to go through the whole story! All my years
of misadventures, given by those on high!

But this you ask about is quickly told: 260
in mid-ocean lies Ogýgia, the island
haunt of Kalypso, Atlas' guileful daughter,
a lovely goddess and a dangerous one.
No one, no god or man, consorts with her;
but supernatural power brought me there   265
to be her solitary guest: for Zeus
let fly with his bright bolt and split my ship,
rolling me over in the winedark sea.
There all my shipmates, friends were drowned, while I
hung on the keelboard of the wreck and drifted   270
nine full days. Then in the dead of night
the gods brought me ashore upon Ogýgia
into her hands. The enchantress in her beauty
fed and caressed me, promised me I should be
immortal, youthful, all the days to come;   275
but in my heart I never gave consent
though seven years detained. Immortal clothing
I had from her, and kept it wet with tears.
Then came the eighth year on the wheel of heaven
and word to her from Zeus, or a change of heart,   280
so that she now commanded me to sail,
sending me out to sea on a craft I made
with timber and tools of hers. She gave me stores,
victuals and wine, a cloak divinely woven,
and made a warm land breeze come up astern.   285
Seventeen days I sailed in the open water
before I saw your country's shore, a shadow
upon the sea rim. Then my heart rejoiced—
pitiable as I am! For blows aplenty
awaited me from the god who shakes the earth.   290
Cross gales he blew, making me lose my bearings,
and heaved up seas beyond imagination—
huge and foundering seas. All I could do
was hold hard, groaning under every shock,
until my craft broke up in the hurricane.   295
I kept afloat and swam your sea, or drifted,
taken by wind and current to this coast
where I went in on big swells running landward.
But cliffs and rock shoals made that place forbidding,
so I turned back, swimming off shore, and came   300
in the end to a river, to auspicious water,
with smooth beach and a rise that broke the wind.
I lay there where I fell till strength returned.
Then sacred night came on, and I went inland
to high ground and a leaf bed in a thicket.   305
Heaven sent slumber in an endless tide

submerging my sad heart among the leaves.
That night and next day's dawn and noon I slept;
the sun went west; and then sweet sleep unbound me,
when I became aware of maids—your daughter's—   310
playing along the beach; the princess, too,
most beautiful. I prayed her to assist me,
and her good sense was perfect; one could hope
for no behavior like it from the young,
thoughtless as they most often are. But she   315
gave me good provender and good red wine,
a river bath, and finally this clothing.
There is the bitter tale. These are the facts."

But in reply Alkínoös observed:

"Friend, my child's good judgment failed in this—   320
not to have brought you in her company home.
Once you approached her, you became her charge."

To this Odysseus tactfully replied:

"Sir, as to that, you should not blame the princess.
She did tell me to follow with her maids,   325
but I would not. I felt abashed, and feared
the sight would somehow ruffle or offend you.
All of us on this earth are plagued by jealousy."

Alkínoös' answer was a declaration:

"Friend, I am not a man for trivial anger: 330
better a sense of measure in everything.
No anger here. I say that if it should please
our father Zeus, Athena, and Apollo—
seeing the man you are, seeing your thoughts
are my own thoughts—my daughter should be yours   335
and you my son-in-law, if you remained.
A home, lands, riches you should have from me
if you could be contented here. If not,
by Father Zeus, let none of our men hold you!
On the contrary, I can assure you now   340
of passage late tomorrow: while you sleep
my men will row you through the tranquil night
to your own land and home or where you please.
It may be, even, far beyond Euboia—[6]
called most remote by seamen of our isle   345

6. The long island which hugs the coast of Attica. *Rhadamanthos* was the son of Zeus by the mortal Europa, and brother to King Minos of Krete. *Tityos* was a giant who tried to rape Leto, the mother, by Zeus, of Apollo and Artemis. Later on (Book XI), Odysseus sees him in the Underworld, eternally punished for his crime. Why Rhadamanthos went to see Tityos we have no idea.

who landed there, conveying Rhadamanthos
when he sought Títyos, the son of Gaia.
They put about, with neither pause nor rest,
and entered their home port the selfsame day.
But this you, too, will see: what ships I have,   350
how my young oarsmen send the foam a-scudding!"

Now joy welled up in the patient Lord Odysseus
who said devoutly in the warmest tones:

"O Father Zeus, let all this be fulfilled
as spoken by Alkínoös! Earth of harvests   355
remember him! Return me to my homeland!"

In this manner they conversed with one another;
but the great lady called her maids, and sent them
to make a kingly bed, with purple rugs
piled up, and sheets outspread, and fleecy   360
coverlets, in an eastern colonnade.
The girls went out with torches in their hands,
swift at their work of bedmaking; returning
they whispered at the lord Odysseus' shoulder:

"Sir, you may come; your bed has been prepared."   365

How welcome the word "bed" came to his ears!
Now, then, Odysseus laid him down and slept
in luxury under the Porch of Morning,
while in his inner chamber Alkínoös
retired to rest where his dear consort lay.   370

BOOK VIII

The Songs of the Harper

Under the opening fingers of the dawn
Alkínoös, the sacred prince, arose,
and then arose Odysseus, raider of cities.
As the king willed, they went down by the shipways
to the assembly ground of the Phaiákians.   5
Side by side the two men took their ease there
on smooth stone benches. Meanwhile Pallas Athena
roamed through the byways of the town, contriving
Odysseus' voyage home—in voice and feature
the crier of the king Alkínoös   10
who stopped and passed the word to every man:

"Phaiákian lords and counselors, this way!
Come to assembly: learn about the stranger,

the new guest at the palace of Alkínoös—
a man the sea drove, but a comely man;   15
the gods' own light is on him."

                                        She aroused them,
and soon the assembly ground and seats were filled
with curious men, a throng who peered and saw
the master mind of war, Laërtês' son.
Athena now poured out her grace upon him,   20
head and shoulders, height and mass—a splendor
awesome to the eyes of the Phaiákians;
she put him in a fettle to win the day,
mastering every trial they set to test him.
When all the crowd sat marshalled, quieted,   25
Alkínoös addressed the full assembly:

"Hear me, lords and captains of the Phaiákians!
Hear what my heart would have me say!
Our guest and new friend—nameless to me still—
comes to my house after long wandering   30
in Dawn lands, or among the Sunset races.
Now he appeals to me for conveyance home.
As in the past, therefore, let us provide
passage, and quickly, for no guest of mine
languishes here for lack of it. Look to it: 35
get a black ship afloat on the noble sea,
and pick our fastest sailer; draft a crew
of two and fifty from our younger townsmen—
men who have made their names at sea. Loop oars
well to your tholepins, lads, then leave the ship,   40
come to our house, fall to, and take your supper:
we'll furnish out a feast for every crewman.
These are your orders. As for my older peers
and princes of the realm, let them foregather
in festival for our friend in my great hall;   45
and let no man refuse. Call in our minstrel,
Demódokos, whom God made lord of song,
heart-easing, sing upon what theme he will."

He turned, led the procession, and those princes
followed, while his herald sought the minstrel.   50
Young oarsmen from the assembly chose a crew
of two and fifty, as the king commanded,
and these filed off along the waterside
to where the ship lay, poised above open water.
They hauled the black hull down to ride the sea,   55
rigging a mast and spar in the black ship,

with oars at trail from corded rawhide, all
seamanly; then tried the white sail, hoisting,
and moored her off the beach. Then going ashore
the crew went up to the great house of Alkínoös.   60
Here the enclosures, entrance ways, and rooms
were filled with men, young men and old, for whom
Alkínoös had put twelve sheep to sacrifice,
eight tuskers and a pair of shambling oxen.
These, now, they flayed and dressed to make their banquet.   65
The crier soon came, leading that man of song
whom the Muse cherished; by her gift he knew
the good of life, and evil—
for she who lent him sweetness made him blind.
Pontónoös fixed a studded chair for him   70
hard by a pillar amid the banqueters,
hanging the taut harp from a peg above him,
and guided up his hands upon the strings;
placed a bread basket at his side, and poured
wine in a cup, that he might drink his fill.   75
Now each man's hand went out upon the banquet.

In time, when hunger and thirst were turned away,
the Muse brought to the minstrel's mind a song
of heroes whose great fame rang under heaven:
the clash between Odysseus and Akhilleus,   80
how one time they contended at the godfeast
raging, and the marshal, Agamémnon,
felt inward joy over his captains' quarrel;
for such had been foretold him by Apollo
at Pytho[7]—hallowed height—when the Akhaian   85
crossed that portal of rock to ask a sign—
in the old days when grim war lay ahead
for Trojans and Danaans, by God's will.
So ran the tale the minstrel sang. Odysseus
with massive hand drew his rich mantle down   90
over his brow, cloaking his face with it,
to make the Phaiákians miss the secret tears
that started to his eyes. How skillfully
he dried them when the song came to a pause!
threw back his mantle, spilt his gout of wine!   95
But soon the minstrel plucked his note once more
to please the Phaiákian lords, who loved the song;
then in his cloak Odysseus wept again.
His tears flowed in the mantle unperceived;
only Alkínoös, at his elbow, saw them,   100

---

7. The oracular shrine of Apollo at Delphi, high up on the mountain side.

and caught the low groan in the man's breathing.
At once he spoke to all the seafolk round him:

"Hear me, lords and captains of the Phaiákians.
Our meat is shared, our hearts are full of pleasure
from the clear harp tone that accords with feasting;   105
now for the field and track; we shall have trials
in the pentathlon. Let our guest go home
and tell his friends what champions we are
at boxing, wrestling, broadjump and foot racing."

On this he led the way and all went after.   110
The crier unslung and pegged the shining harp
and, taking Demódokos's hand,
led him along with all the rest—Phaiákian
peers, gay amateurs of the great games.
They gained the common, where a crowd was forming,   115
and many a young athlete now came forward
with seaside names like Tipmast, Tiderace, Sparwood,
Hullman, Sternman, Beacher and Pullerman,
Bluewater, Shearwater, Runningwake, Boardalee,
Seabelt, son of Grandfleet Shipwrightson;   120
Seareach stepped up, son of the Launching Master,
rugged as Arês,[8] bane of men: his build
excelled all but the Prince Laódamas;
and Laódamas made entry with his brothers,
Halios and Klytóneus, sons of the king.   125
The runners, first, must have their quarter mile.
All lined up tense; then Go! and down the track
they raised the dust in a flying bunch, strung out
longer and longer behind Prince Klytóneus.
By just so far as a mule team, breaking ground,   130
will distance oxen, he left all behind
and came up to the crowd, an easy winner.
Then they made room for wrestling—grinding bouts
that Seareach won, pinning the strongest men;
then the broadjump; first place went to Seabelt;   135
Sparwood gave the discus the mightiest fling,
and Prince Laódamas outboxed them all.
Now it was he, the son of Alkínoös,
who said when they had run through these diversions:

"Look here, friends, we ought to ask the stranger   140
if he competes in something. He's no cripple;
look at his leg muscles and his forearms.
Neck like a bollard; strong as a bull, he seems;

8. The Greek war-god.

and not old, though he may have gone stale under
the rough times he had. Nothing like the sea   145
for wearing out the toughest man alive."

Then Seareach took him up at once, and said:

"Laódamas, you're right, by all the powers.
Go up to him, yourself, and put the question."

At this, Alkínoös' tall son advanced   150
to the center ground, and there addressed Odysseus:

"Friend, Excellency, come join our competition,
if you are practiced, as you seem to be.
While a man lives he wins no greater honor
than footwork and the skill of hands can bring him.   155
Enter our games, then; ease your heart of trouble.
Your journey home is not far off, remember;
the ship is launched, the crew all primed for sea."

Odysseus, canniest of men, replied:

"Laódamas, why do you young chaps challenge me?   160
I have more on my mind than track and field—
hard days, and many, have I seen, and suffered.
I sit here at your field meet, yes; but only
as one who begs your king to send him home."

Now Seareach put his word in, and contentiously: 165

"The reason being, as I see it, friend,
you never learned a sport, and have no skill
in any of the contests of fighting men.
You must have been the skipper of some tramp
that crawled from one port to the next, jam full   170
of chaffering hands: a tallier of cargoes,
itching for gold—not, by your looks, an athlete."

Odysseus frowned, and eyed him coldly, saying:

"That was uncalled for, friend, you talk like a fool.
The gods deal out no gift, this one or any—   175
birth, brains, or speech—to every man alike.
In looks a man may be a shade, a specter,
and yet be master of speech so crowned with beauty
that people gaze at him with pleasure. Courteous,
sure of himself, he can command assemblies,   180
and when he comes to town, the crowds gather.
A handsome man, contrariwise, may lack

grace and good sense in everything he says.
You now, for instance, with your fine physique—
a god's, indeed—you have an empty noddle.   185
I find my heart inside my ribs aroused
by your impertinence. I am no stranger
to contests, as you fancy. I rated well
when I could count on youth and my two hands.
Now pain has cramped me, and my years of combat   190
hacking through ranks in war, and the bitter sea.
Aye. Even so I'll give your games a trial.
You spoke heart-wounding words. You shall be answered."

He leapt out, cloaked as he was, and picked a discus,
a rounded stone, more ponderous than those   195
already used by the Phaiákian throwers,
and, whirling, let it fly from his great hand
with a low hum. The crowd went flat on the ground—
all those oar-pulling, seafaring Phaiákians—
under the rushing noise. The spinning disk   200
soared out, light as a bird, beyond all others.
Disguised now as a Phaiákian, Athena
staked it and called out:

                    "Even a blind man,
friend, could judge this, finding with his fingers
one discus, quite alone, beyond the cluster.   205
Congratulations; this event is yours;
not a man here can beat you or come near you."

That was a cheering hail, Odysseus thought,
seeing one friend there on the emulous field,
so, in relief, he turned among the Phaiákians   210
and said:

                    "Now come alongside that one, lads.
The next I'll send as far, I think, or farther.
Anyone else on edge for competition
try me now. By heaven, you angered me.
Racing, wrestling, boxing—I bar nothing   215
with any man except Laódamas,
for he's my host. Who quarrels with his host?
Only a madman—or no man at all—
would challenge his protector among strangers,
cutting the ground away under his feet.   220
Here are no others I will not engage,
none but I hope to know what he is made of.
Inept at combat, am I? Not entirely.
Give me a smooth bow; I can handle it,

and I might well be first to hit my man   225
amid a swarm of enemies, though archers
in company around me drew together.
Philoktêtês[9] alone, at Troy, when we
Akhaians took the bow, used to outshoot me.
Of men who now eat bread upon the earth   230
I hold myself the best hand with a bow—
conceding mastery to the men of old,
Heraklês, or Eurýtos of Oikhalía,[1]
heroes who vied with gods in bowmanship.
Eurýtos came to grief, it's true; old age   235
never crept over him in his long hall;
Apollo took his challenge ill, and killed him.
What then, the spear? I'll plant it like an arrow.
Only in sprinting, I'm afraid, I may
be passed by someone. Roll of the sea waves   240
wearied me, and the victuals in my ship
ran low; my legs are flabby."

                    When he finished,
the rest were silent, but Alkínoös answered:

"Friend, we take your challenge in good part,
for this man angered and affronted you   245
here at our peaceful games. You'd have us note
the prowess that is in you, and so clearly,
no man of sense would ever cry it down!
Come, turn your mind, now, on a thing to tell
among your peers when you are home again,   250
dining in hall, beside your wife and children:
I mean our prowess, as you may remember it,
for we, too, have our skills, given by Zeus,
and practiced from our father's time to this—
not in the boxing ring nor the palestra[2]   255
conspicuous, but in racing, land or sea;
and all our days we set great store by feasting,
harpers, and the grace of dancing choirs,
changes of dress, warm baths, and downy beds.
O master dancers of the Phaiákians!   260
Perform now: let our guest on his return
tell his companions we excel the world
in dance and song, as in our ships and running.
Someone go find the gittern[3] harp in hall
and bring it quickly to Demódokos!"   265

9. He inherited the bow of Herakles, which never missed its mark.   1. Eurýtos of Oikhalía (in central
Greece) challenged Apollo (also an archer) and was killed by the god. Eurýtos' bow was given to Odysseus
by his son Iphitos and it is with that bow that Odysseus will kill the suitors in Book XXII.   2. Wrestling
ground.   3. Shaped like a guitar.

At the serene king's word, a squire ran
to bring the polished harp out of the palace,
and place was given to nine referees—
peers of the realm, masters of ceremony—
who cleared a space and smoothed a dancing floor.   270
The squire brought down, and gave Demódokos,
the clear-toned harp; and centering on the minstrel
magical young dancers formed a circle
with a light beat, and stamp of feet. Beholding,
Odysseus marvelled at the flashing ring.   275

Now to his harp the blinded minstrel sang
of Arês' dalliance with Aphroditê:
how hidden in Hephaistos' house they played
at love together, and the gifts of Arês,
dishonoring Hephaistos' bed—and how   280
the word that wounds the heart came to the master
from Hélios,[4] who had seen the two embrace;
and when he learned it, Lord Hephaistos went
with baleful calculation to his forge.
There mightily he armed his anvil block   285
and hammered out a chain whose tempered links
could not be sprung or bent; he meant that they should hold.
Those shackles fashioned, hot in wrath Hephaistos
climbed to the bower and the bed of love,
pooled all his net of chain around the bed posts   290
and swung it from the rafters overhead—
light as a cobweb even gods in bliss
could not perceive, so wonderful his cunning.
Seeing his bed now made a snare, he feigned
a journey to the trim stronghold of Lemnos,[5]   295
the dearest of earth's towns to him. And Arês?
Ah, golden Arês' watch had its reward
when he beheld the great smith leaving home.
How promptly to the famous door he came,
intent on pleasure with sweet Kythereia![6]   300
She, who had left her father's side but now,
sat in her chamber when her lover entered;
and tenderly he pressed her hand and said:

"Come and lie down, my darling, and be happy!
Hephaistos is no longer here, but gone   305
to see his grunting[7] Sintian friends on Lemnos."

---

4. The sun, who sees everything.   5. An island off the coast of Asia Minor, the "dearest of earth's towns" to Hephaistos because when Zeus threw him off Olympus (*Iliad*, I.714ff) he landed on Lemnos and the inhabitants took care of him.   6. A title of Aphrodite.   7. The Sintians, the inhabitants of Lemnos, do not speak Greek.

As she, too, thought repose would be most welcome,
the pair went in to bed—into a shower
of clever chains, the netting of Hephaistos.
So trussed, they could not move apart, nor rise,   310
at last they knew there could be no escape,
they were to see the glorious cripple now—
for Hêlios had spied for him, and told him;
so he turned back this side of Lemnos Isle,
sick at heart, making his way homeward.   315
Now in the doorway of the room he stood
while deadly rage took hold of him; his voice,
hoarse and terrible, reached all the gods:

"O Father Zeus, O gods in bliss forever,
here is indecorous entertainment for you,   320
Aphroditê, Zeus's daughter,
caught in the act, cheating me, her cripple,
with Arês—devastating Arês.
Cleanlimbed beauty is her joy, not these
bandylegs I came into the world with: 325
no one to blame but the two gods who bred me![8]
Come see this pair entwining here
in my own bed! How hot it makes me burn!
I think they may not care to lie much longer,
pressing on one another, passionate lovers;   330
they'll have enough of bed together soon.
And yet the chain that bagged them holds them down
till Father sends me back my wedding gifts—
all that I poured out for his damned pigeon,
so lovely, and so wanton."

                      All the others   335
were crowding in, now, to the brazen house—
Poseidon who embraces earth, and Hermês
the runner, and Apollo, lord of Distance.
The goddesses stayed home for shame; but these
munificences ranged there in the doorway,   340
and irrepressible among them all
arose the laughter of the happy gods.
Gazing hard at Hephaistos' handiwork
the gods in turn remarked among themselves:

"No dash in adultery now."

                      "The tortoise tags the hare—   345
Hephaistos catches Arês—and Arês outran the wind."

8. Zeus and Hera.

"The lame god's craft has pinned him. Now shall he
pay what is due from gods taken in cuckoldry."

They made these improving remarks to one another,
but Apollo leaned aside to say to Hermês: 350

"Son of Zeus, beneficent Wayfinder,
would you accept a coverlet of chain, if only
you lay by Aphroditê's golden side?"

To this the Wayfinder replied, shining:

"Would I not, though, Apollo of distances!   355
Wrap me in chains three times the weight of these,
come goddesses and gods to see the fun;
only let me lie beside the pale-golden one!"

The gods gave way again to peals of laughter,
all but Poseidon, and he never smiled,   360
but urged Hephaistos to unpinion Arês,
saying emphatically, in a loud voice:

                    "Free him;
you will be paid, I swear; ask what you will;
he pays up every jot the gods decree."

To this the Great Gamelegs replied:

                    "Poseidon,   365
lord of the earth-surrounding sea, I should not
swear to a scoundrel's honor. What have I
as surety from you, if Arês leaves me
empty-handed, with my empty chain?"

The Earth-shaker for answer urged again: 370

"Hephaistos, let us grant he goes, and leaves
the fine unpaid; I swear, then, I shall pay it."

Then said the Great Gamelegs at last:

                    "No more;
you offer terms I cannot well refuse."

And down the strong god bent to set them free,   375
till disencumbered of their bond, the chain,
the lovers leapt away—he into Thrace,[9]
while Aphroditê, laughter's darling, fled

---

9. The non-Greek territory to the North, where the war-god was supposed to be at home.

to Kypros[1] Isle and Paphos, to her meadow
and altar dim with incense. There the Graces   380
bathed and anointed her with golden oil—
a bloom that clings upon immortal flesh alone—
and let her folds of mantle fall in glory.

So ran the song the minstrel sang.

                                        Odysseus,
listening, found sweet pleasure in the tale,   385
among the Phaiákian mariners and oarsmen.
And next Alkínoös called upon his sons,
Halios and Laódamas, to show
the dance no one could do as well as they—
handling a purple ball carven by Pólybos.   390
One made it shoot up under the shadowing clouds
as he leaned backward; bounding high in air
the other cut its flight far off the ground—
and neither missed a step as the ball soared.
The next turn was to keep it low, and shuttling   395
hard between them, while the ring of boys
gave them a steady stamping beat.
Odysseus now addressed Alkínoös:

"O majesty, model of all your folk,
your promise was to show me peerless dancers;   400
here is the promise kept. I am all wonder."

At this Alkínoös in his might rejoicing
said to the seafarers of Phaiákia:

"Attend me now, Phaiákian lords and captains:
our guest appears a clear-eyed man and wise.   405
Come, let him feel our bounty as he should.
Here are twelve princes of the kingdom—lords
paramount, and I who make thirteen;
let each one bring a laundered cloak and tunic,
and add one bar of honorable gold.   410
Heap all our gifts together; load his arms;
let him go joyous to our evening feast!
As for Seareach—why, man to man
he'll make amends, and handsomely; he blundered."

Now all as one acclaimed the king's good pleasure,   415
and each one sent a squire to bring his gifts.
Meanwhile Seareach found speech again, saying:

1. Cyprus, where Aphrodite had a famous shrine at Paphos.

"My lord and model of us all, Alkínoös,
as you require of me, in satisfaction,
this broadsword of clear bronze goes to our guest.   420
Its hilt is silver, and the ringed sheath
of new-sawn ivory—a costly weapon."

He turned to give the broadsword to Odysseus,
facing him, saying blithely:

                    "Sir, my best
wishes, my respects; if I offended,   425
I hope the seawinds blow it out of mind.
God send you see your lady and your homeland
soon again, after the pain of exile."

Odysseus, the great tactician, answered:

"My hand, friend; may the gods award you fortune.   430
I hope no pressing need comes on you ever
for this fine blade you give me in amends."

He slung it, glinting silver, from his shoulder,
as the light shone from sundown. Messengers
were bearing gifts and treasure to the palace,   435
where the king's sons received them all, and made
a glittering pile at their grave mother's side;
then, as Alkínoös took his throne of power,
each went to his own high-backed chair in turn,
and said Alkínoös to Arêtê: 440

"Lady, bring here a chest, the finest one;
a clean cloak and tunic; stow these things;
and warm a cauldron for him. Let him bathe,
when he has seen the gifts of the Phaiákians,
and so dine happily to a running song.   445
My own wine-cup of gold intaglio
I'll give him, too; through all the days to come,
tipping his wine to Zeus or other gods
in his great hall, he shall remember me."

Then said Arêtê to her maids:

                    "The tripod: 450
stand the great tripod legs about the fire."

They swung the cauldron on the fire's heart,
poured water in, and fed the blaze beneath
until the basin simmered, cupped in flame.
The queen set out a rich chest from her chamber   455
and folded in the gifts—clothing and gold

given Odysseus by the Phaiákians;
then she put in the royal cloak and tunic,
briskly saying to her guest:

          "Now here, sir,
look to the lid yourself, and tie it down   460
against light fingers, if there be any,
on the black ship tonight while you are sleeping."

Noble Odysseus, expert in adversity,
battened the lid down with a lightning knot
learned, once, long ago, from the Lady Kirkê.[2]   465
And soon a call came from the Bathing Mistress
who led him to a hip-bath, warm and clear—
a happy sight, and rare in his immersions
after he left Kalypso's home—where, surely,
the luxuries of a god were ever his.   470
When the bath maids had washed him, rubbed him down,
put a fresh tunic and a cloak around him,
he left the bathing place to join the men
at wine in hall.

          The princess Nausikaa,
exquisite figure, as of heaven's shaping,   475
waited beside a pillar as he passed
and said swiftly, with wonder in her look:

"Fare well, stranger; in your land remember me
who met and saved you. It is worth your thought."

The man of all occasions now met this: 480

"Daughter of great Alkínoös, Nausikaa,
may Zeus the lord of thunder, Hera's consort,
grant me daybreak again in my own country!
But there and all my days until I die
may I invoke you as I would a goddess,   485
princess, to whom I owe my life."

                He left her
and went to take his place beside the king.

Now when the roasts were cut, the winebowls full,
a herald led the minstrel down the room
amid the deference of the crowd, and paused   490
to seat him near a pillar in the center—

2. Or Circe. A divine sorceress on whose island Odysseus had spent some time during his travels (see
Book XII).

whereupon that resourceful man, Odysseus,
carved out a quarter from his chine of pork,
crisp with fat, and called the blind man's guide:

"Herald! here, take this to Demódokos: 495
let him feast and be merry, with my compliments.
All men owe honor to the poets—honor
and awe, for they are dearest to the Muse
who puts upon their lips the ways of life."

Gentle Demódokos took the proffered gift   500
and inwardly rejoiced. When all were served,
every man's hand went out upon the banquet,
repelling hunger and thirst, until at length
Odysseus spoke again to the blind minstrel:

"Demódokos, accept my utmost praise.   505
The Muse, daughter of Zeus in radiance,
or else Apollo gave you skill to shape
with such great style your songs of the Akhaians—
their hard lot, how they fought and suffered war.
You shared it, one would say, or heard it all.   510
Now shift your theme, and sing that wooden horse
Epeios built, inspired by Athena—
the ambuscade Odysseus filled with fighters
and sent to take the inner town of Troy.
Sing only this for me, sing me this well,   515
and I shall say at once before the world
the grace of heaven has given us a song."

The minstrel stirred, murmuring to the god, and soon
clear words and notes came one by one, a vision
of the Akhaians in their graceful ships   520
drawing away from shore: the torches flung
and shelters flaring: Argive soldiers crouched
in the close dark around Odysseus: and
the horse, tall on the assembly ground of Troy.
For when the Trojans pulled it in, themselves,   525
up to the citadel, they sat nearby
with long-drawn-out and hapless argument—
favoring, in the end, one course of three:
either to stave the vault with brazen axes,
or haul it to a cliff and pitch it down,   530
or else to save it for the gods, a votive glory—
the plan that could not but prevail.
For Troy must perish, as ordained, that day
she harbored the great horse of timber; hidden
the flower of Akhaia lay, and bore   535

slaughter and death upon the men of Troy.
He sang, then, of the town sacked by Akhaians
pouring down from the horse's hollow cave,
this way and that way raping the steep city,
and how Odysseus came like Arês to   540
the door of Deïphobos, with Meneláos,
and braved the desperate fight there—
conquering once more by Athena's power.

The splendid minstrel sang it.

                              And Odysseus
let the bright molten tears run down his cheeks,   545
weeping the way a wife mourns for her lord
on the lost field where he has gone down fighting
the day of wrath that came upon his children.
At sight of the man panting and dying there,
she slips down to enfold him, crying out;   550
then feels the spears, prodding her back and shoulders,
and goes bound into slavery and grief.
Piteous weeping wears away her cheeks:
but no more piteous than Odysseus' tears,
cloaked as they were, now, from the company.   555
Only Alkínoös, at his elbow, knew—
hearing the low sob in the man's breathing—
and when he knew, he spoke:

"Hear me, lords and captains of Phaiákia!
And let Demódokos touch his harp no more.   560
His theme has not been pleasing to all here.
During the feast, since our fine poet sang,
our guest has never left off weeping. Grief
seems fixed upon his heart. Break off the song!
Let everyone be easy, host and guest;   565
there's more decorum in a smiling banquet!
We had prepared here, on our friend's behalf,
safe conduct in a ship, and gifts to cheer him,
holding that any man with a grain of wit
will treat a decent suppliant like a brother.   570
Now by the same rule, friend, you must not be
secretive any longer! Come, in fairness,
tell me the name you bore in that far country;
how were you known to family, and neighbors?
No man is nameless—no man, good or bad,   575
but gets a name in his first infancy,
none being born, unless a mother bears him!
Tell me your native land, your coast and city—
sailing directions for the ships, you know—

for those Phaiákian ships of ours   580
that have no steersman, and no steering oar,
divining the crew's wishes, as they do,
and knowing, as they do, the ports of call
about the world. Hidden in mist or cloud
they scud the open sea, with never a thought   585
of being in distress or going down.
There is, however, something I once heard
Nausíthoös, my father, say: Poseidon
holds it against us that our deep sea ships
are sure conveyance for all passengers.   590
My father said, some day one of our cutters
homeward bound over the cloudy sea
would be wrecked by the god, and a range of hills
thrown round our city. So, in his age, he said,
and let it be, or not, as the god please.   595
But come, now, put it for me clearly, tell me
the sea ways that you wandered, and the shores
you touched; the cities, and the men therein,
uncivilized, if such there were, and hostile,
and those godfearing who had kindly manners.   600
Tell me why you should grieve so terribly
over the Argives and the fall of Troy.
That was all gods' work, weaving ruin there
so it should make a song for men to come!
Some kin of yours, then, died at Ilion,   605
some first rate man, by marriage near to you,
next your own blood most dear?
Or some companion of congenial mind
and valor? True it is, a wise friend
can take a brother's place in our affection."   610

BOOK IX

New Coasts and Poseidon's Son

Now this was the reply Odysseus made:

"Alkínoös, king and admiration of men,
how beautiful this is, to hear a minstrel
gifted as yours: a god he might be, singing!
There is no boon in life more sweet, I say,   5
then when a summer joy holds all the realm,
and banqueters sit listening to a harper
in a great hall, by rows of tables heaped
with bread and roast meat, while a steward goes
to dip up wine and brim your cups again.   10
Here is the flower of life, it seems to me!

But now you wish to know my cause for sorrow—
and thereby give me cause for more.
                           What shall I
say first? What shall I keep until the end?
The gods have tried me in a thousand ways.   15
But first my name: let that be known to you,
and if I pull away from pitiless death,
friendship will bind us, though my land lies far.

I am Laërtês' son, Odysseus.
                        Men hold me
formidable for guile in peace and war: 20
this fame has gone abroad to the sky's rim.
My home is on the peaked sea-mark of Ithaka
under Mount Neion's wind-blown robe of leaves,
in sight of other islands—Doulíkhion,
Samê, wooded Zakynthos—Ithaka   25
being most lofty in that coastal sea,
and northwest, while the rest lie east and south.
A rocky isle, but good for a boy's training;
I shall not see on earth a place more dear,
though I have been detained long by Kalypso,   30
loveliest among goddesses, who held me
in her smooth caves, to be her heart's delight,
as Kirkê of Aiaia, the enchantress,
desired me, and detained me in her hall.
But in my heart I never gave consent.   35
Where shall a man find sweetness to surpass
his own home and his parents? In far lands
he shall not, though he find a house of gold.

What of my sailing, then, from Troy?
                        What of those years
of rough adventure, weathered under Zeus?   40
The wind that carried west from Ilion
brought me to Ísmaros, on the far shore,
a strongpoint on the coast of the Kikonês.[3]
I stormed that place and killed the men who fought.
Plunder we took, and we enslaved the women,   45
to make division, equal shares to all—
but on the spot I told them: 'Back, and quickly!
Out to sea again!' My men were mutinous,
fools, on stores of wine. Sheep after sheep

---

3. Allies of the Trojans, but Odysseus does not even mention this fact to excuse the piratical raid; he did not think any excuse was needed.

they butchered by the surf, and shambling cattle,   50
feasting,—while fugitives went inland, running
to call to arms the main force of Kikonês.
This was an army, trained to fight on horseback
or, where the ground required, on foot. They came
with dawn over that terrain like the leaves   55
and blades of spring. So doom appeared to us,
dark word of Zeus for us, our evil days.
My men stood up and made a fight of it—
backed on the ships, with lances kept in play,
from bright morning through the blaze of noon   60
holding our beach, although so far outnumbered;
but when the sun passed toward unyoking time,
then the Akhaians, one by one, gave way.
Six benches were left empty in every ship
that evening when we pulled away from death.   65
And this new grief we bore with us to sea:
our precious lives we had, but not our friends.
No ship made sail next day until some shipmate
had raised a cry, three times, for each poor ghost
unfleshed by the Kikonês on that field.   70

Now Zeus the lord of cloud roused in the north
a storm against the ships, and driving veils
of squall moved down like night on land and sea.
The bows went plunging at the gust; sails
cracked and lashed out strips in the big wind.   75
We saw death in that fury, dropped the yards,
unshipped the oars, and pulled for the nearest lee:
then two long days and nights we lay offshore
worn out and sick at heart, tasting our grief,
until a third Dawn came with ringlets shining.   80
Then we put up our masts, hauled sail, and rested,
letting the steersmen and the breeze take over.

I might have made it safely home, that time,
but as I came round Malea[4] the current
took me out to sea, and from the north   85
a fresh gale drove me on, past Kythera.
Nine days I drifted on the teeming sea
before dangerous high winds. Upon the tenth
we came to the coastline of the Lotos Eaters,[5]
who live upon that flower. We landed there   90

---

4. The southeastern tip of the Peloponnese. *Kythera*: a large island off the headland.   5. It is generally
thought that this story contains some memory of early Greek contact with North Africa; the north wind
Odysseus describes would have taken him to the area of Cyrenaica, modern Libya. Modern identifications
of the lotos range from dates to hashish.

to take on water. All ships' companies
mustered alongside for the mid-day meal.
Then I sent out two picked men and a runner
to learn what race of men that land sustained.
They fell in, soon enough, with Lotos Eaters,   95
who showed no will to do us harm, only
offering the sweet Lotos to our friends—
but those who ate this honeyed plant, the Lotos,
never cared to report, nor to return:
they longed to stay forever, browsing on   100
that native bloom, forgetful of their homeland.
I drove them, all three wailing, to the ships,
tied them down under their rowing benches,
and called the rest: 'All hands aboard;
come, clear the beach and no one taste   105
the Lotos, or you lose your hope of home.'
Filing in to their places by the rowlocks
my oarsmen dipped their long oars in the surf,
and we moved out again on our sea faring.

In the next land[6] we found were Kyklopês,   110
giants, louts, without a law to bless them.
In ignorance leaving the fruitage of the earth in mystery
to the immortal gods, they neither plow
nor sow by hand, nor till the ground, though grain—
wild wheat and barley—grows untended, and   115
wine-grapes, in clusters, ripen in heaven's rain.
Kyklopês have no muster and no meeting,
no consultation or old tribal ways,
but each one dwells in his own mountain cave
dealing out rough justice to wife and child,   120
indifferent to what the others do.
                        Well, then:
across the wide bay from the mainland
there lies a desert island, not far out,
but still not close inshore. Wild goats in hundreds
breed there; and no human being comes   125
upon the isle to startle them—no hunter
of all who ever tracked with hounds through forests
or had rough going over mountain trails.
The isle, unplanted and untilled, a wilderness,
pastures goats alone. And this is why: 130
good ships like ours with cheekpaint[7] at the bows
are far beyond the Kyklopês. No shipwright

6. According to ancient tradition the Kyklopês lived in Sicily.   7. On a Greek ship an emblem (often shown as a huge eye on vase-paintings) was painted on the bows.

toils among them, shaping and building up
symmetrical trim hulls to cross the sea
and visit all the seaboard towns, as men do   135
who go and come in commerce over water.
This isle—seagoing folk would have annexed it
and built their homesteads on it: all good land,
fertile for every crop in season: lush
well-watered meads along the shore, vines in profusion,   140
prairie, clear for the plow, where grain would grow
chin high by harvest time, and rich sub-soil.
The island cove is landlocked, so you need
no hawsers out astern, bow-stones[8] or mooring:
run in and ride there till the day your crews   145
chafe to be under sail, and a fair wind blows.
You'll find good water flowing from a cavern
through dusky poplars into the upper bay.
Here we made harbor. Some god guided us
that night, for we could barely see our bows   150
in the dense fog around us, and no moonlight
filtered through the overcast. No look-out,
nobody saw the island dead ahead,
nor even the great landward rolling billow
that took us in: we found ourselves in shallows,   155
keels grazing shore: so furled our sails
and disembarked where the low ripples broke.
There on the beach we lay, and slept till morning.

When Dawn spread out her finger tips of rose
we turned out marvelling, to tour the isle,   160
while Zeus's shy nymph daughters flushed wild goats
down from the heights—a breakfast for my men.
We ran to fetch our hunting bows and long-shanked
lances from the ships, and in three companies
we took our shots. Heaven gave us game a-plenty: 165
for every one of twelve ships in my squadron
nine goats fell to be shared; my lot was ten.
So there all day, until the sun went down,
we made our feast on meat galore, and wine—
wine from the ship, for our supply held out,   170
so many jars were filled at Ísmaros
from stores of the Kikonês that we plundered.
We gazed, too, at Kyklopês Land, so near,
we saw their smoke, heard bleating from their flocks.
But after sundown, in the gathering dusk,   175
we slept again above the wash of ripples.

8. A primitive anchor made up of a stone attached to a rope.

When the young Dawn with finger tips of rose
came in the east, I called my men together
and made a speech to them:

                    'Old shipmates, friends,
the rest of you stand by; I'll make the crossing   180
in my own ship, with my own company,
and find out what the mainland natives are—
for they may be wild savages, and lawless,
or hospitable and god-fearing men.'

At this I went aboard, and gave the word   185
to cast off by the stern. My oarsmen followed,
filing in to their benches by the rowlocks,
and all in line dipped oars in the grey sea.

As we rowed on, and nearer to the mainland,
at one end of the bay, we saw a cavern   190
yawning above the water, screened with laurel,
and many rams and goats about the place
inside a sheepfold—made from slabs of stone
earthfast between tall trunks of pine and rugged
towering oak trees.
              A prodigious man   195
slept in this cave alone, and took his flocks
to graze afield—remote from all companions,
knowing none but savage ways, a brute
so huge, he seemed no man at all of those
who eat good wheaten bread; but he seemed rather   200
a shaggy mountain reared in solitude.
We beached there, and I told the crew
to stand by and keep watch over the ship;
as for myself I took my twelve best fighters
and went ahead. I had a goatskin full   205
of that sweet liquor that Euanthês' son,
Maron, had given me. He kept Apollo's
holy grove at Ísmaros; for kindness
we showed him there, and showed his wife and child,
he gave me seven shining golden talents[9]   210
perfectly formed, a solid silver winebowl,
and then this liquor—twelve two-handled jars
of brandy, pure and fiery. Not a slave
in Maron's household knew this drink; only
he, his wife and the storeroom mistress knew;   215
and they would put one cupful—ruby-colored,
honey-smooth—in twenty more of water,

9. Ingots of gold; the talent was a standard weight.

but still the sweet scent hovered like a fume
over the winebowl. No man turned away
when cups of this came round.
                              A wineskin full   220
I brought along, and victuals in a bag,
for in my bones I knew some towering brute
would be upon us soon—all outward power,
a wild man, ignorant of civility.

We climbed, then, briskly to the cave. But Kyklops   225
had gone afield, to pasture his fat sheep,
so we looked round at everything inside:
a drying rack that sagged with cheeses, pens
crowded with lambs and kids, each in its class:
firstlings apart from middlings, and the 'dewdrops,'   230
or newborn lambkins, penned apart from both.
And vessels full of whey were brimming there—
bowls of earthenware and pails of milking.
My men came pressing round me, pleading:

                              'Why not
take these cheeses, get them stowed, come back,   235
throw open all the pens, and make a run for it?
We'll drive the kids and lambs aboard. We say
put out again on good salt water!'

                              Ah,
how sound that was! Yet I refused, I wished
to see the caveman, what he had to offer—   240
no pretty sight, it turned out, for my friends.
We lit a fire, burnt an offering,
and took some cheese to eat; then sat in silence
around the embers, waiting. When he came
he had a load of dry boughs on his shoulder   245
to stoke his fire at suppertime. He dumped it
with a great crash into that hollow cave,
and we all scattered fast to the far wall.
Then over the broad cavern floor he ushered
the ewes he meant to milk. He left his rams   250
and he-goats in the yard outside, and swung
high overhead a slab of solid rock
to close the cave. Two dozen four-wheeled wagons,
with heaving wagon teams, could not have stirred
the tonnage of that rock from where he wedged it   255
over the doorsill. Next he took his seat
and milked his bleating ewes. A practiced job
he made of it, giving each ewe her suckling;
thickened his milk, then, into curds and whey,

sieved out the curds to drip in withy baskets,   260
and poured the whey to stand in bowls
cooling until he drank it for his supper.
When all these chores were done, he poked the fire,
heaping on brushwood. In the glare he saw us.

'Strangers,' he said, 'who are you? And where from?   265
What brings you here by sea ways—a fair traffic?
Or are you wandering rogues, who cast your lives
like dice, and ravage other folk by sea?'

We felt a pressure on our hearts, in dread
of that deep rumble and that mighty man.   270
But all the same I spoke up in reply:

'We are from Troy, Akhaians, blown off course
by shifting gales on the Great South Sea;
homeward bound, but taking routes and ways
uncommon; so the will of Zeus would have it.   275
We served under Agamémnon, son of Atreus—
the whole world knows what city
he laid waste, what armies he destroyed.
It was our luck to come here; here we stand,
beholden for your help, or any gifts   280
you give[1]—as custom is to honor strangers.
We would entreat you, great Sir, have a care
for the gods' courtesy; Zeus will avenge
the unoffending guest.'

                    He answered this
from his brute chest, unmoved:

                              'You are a ninny,   285
or else you come from the other end of nowhere,
telling me, mind the gods! We Kyklopês
care not a whistle for your thundering Zeus
or all the gods in bliss; we have more force by far.
I would not let you go for fear of Zeus—   290
you or your friends—unless I had a whim to.
Tell me, where was it, now, you left your ship—
around the point, or down the shore, I wonder?'

He thought he'd find out, but I saw through this,
and answered with a ready lie:

                              'My ship?   295
Poseidon Lord, who sets the earth a-tremble,

---

1. It is the mark of civilized men in the *Odyssey*, like Meneláos and Alkínoös, that they welcome the stranger and send him on his way with gifts.

broke it up on the rocks at your land's end.
A wind from seaward served him, drove us there.
We are survivors, these good men and I.'

Neither reply nor pity came from him,   300
but in one stride he clutched at my companions
and caught two in his hands like squirming puppies
to beat their brains out, spattering the floor.
Then he dismembered them and made his meal,
gaping and crunching like a mountain lion—   305
everything: innards, flesh, and marrow bones.
We cried aloud, lifting our hands to Zeus,
powerless, looking on at this, appalled;
but Kyklops went on filling up his belly
with manflesh and great gulps of whey,   310
then lay down like a mast among his sheep.
My heart beat high now at the chance of action,
and drawing the sharp sword from my hip I went
along his flank to stab him where the midriff
holds the liver. I had touched the spot   315
when sudden fear stayed me: if I killed him
we perished there as well, for we could never
move his ponderous doorway slab aside.
So we were left to groan and wait for morning.

When the young Dawn with finger tips of rose   320
lit up the world, the Kyklops built a fire
and milked his handsome ewes, all in due order,
putting the sucklings to the mothers. Then,
his chores being all dispatched, he caught
another brace of men to make his breakfast,   325
and whisked away his great door slab
to let his sheep go through—but he, behind,
reset the stone as one would cap a quiver.
There was a din of whistling as the Kyklops
rounded his flock to higher ground, then stillness.   330
And now I pondered how to hurt him worst,
if but Athena granted what I prayed for.
Here are the means I thought would serve my turn:

a club, or staff, lay there along the fold—
an olive tree, felled green and left to season   335
for Kyklops' hand. And it was like a mast
a lugger of twenty oars, broad in the beam—
a deep-sea going craft—might carry:
so long, so big around, it seemed. Now I

chopped out a six foot section of this pole   340
and set it down before my men, who scraped it;
and when they had it smooth, I hewed again
to make a stake with pointed end. I held this
in the fire's heart and turned it, toughening it,
then hid it, well back in the cavern, under   345
one of the dung piles in profusion there.
Now came the time to toss for it: who ventured
along with me? whose hand could bear to thrust
and grind that spike in Kyklops' eye, when mild
sleep had mastered him? As luck would have it,   350
the men I would have chosen won the toss—
four strong men, and I made five as captain.

At evening came the shepherd with his flock,
his woolly flock. The rams as well, this time,
entered the cave: by some sheep-herding whim—   355
or a god's bidding—none were left outside.
He hefted his great boulder into place
and sat him down to milk the bleating ewes
in proper order, put the lambs to suck,
and swiftly ran through all his evening chores.   360
Then he caught two more men and feasted on them.
My moment was at hand, and I went forward
holding an ivy bowl of my dark drink,
looking up, saying:

        'Kyklops, try some wine.
Here's liquor to wash down your scraps of men.   365
Taste it, and see the kind of drink we carried
under our planks. I meant it for an offering
if you would help us home. But you are mad,
unbearable, a bloody monster! After this,
will any other traveller come to see you?'   370

He seized and drained the bowl, and it went down
so fiery and smooth he called for more:

'Give me another, thank you kindly. Tell me,
how are you called? I'll make a gift will please you.
Even Kyklopês know the wine-grapes grow   375
out of grassland and loam in heaven's rain,
but here's a bit of nectar and ambrosia!'

Three bowls I brought him, and he poured them down.
I saw the fuddle and flush come over him,
then I sang out in cordial tones:

'Kyklops,   380
you ask my honorable name? Remember
the gift you promised me, and I shall tell you.
My name is Nohbdy: mother, father, and friends,
everyone calls me Nohbdy.'

And he said:

'Nohbdy's my meat, then, after I eat his friends.   385
Others come first. There's a noble gift, now.'

Even as he spoke, he reeled and tumbled backward,
his great head lolling to one side: and sleep
took him like any creature. Drunk, hiccuping,
he dribbled streams of liquor and bits of men.   390

Now, by the gods, I drove my big hand spike
deep in the embers, charring it again,
and cheered my men along with battle talk
to keep their courage up: no quitting now.
The pike of olive, green though it had been,   395
reddened and glowed as if about to catch.
I drew it from the coals and my four fellows
gave me a hand, lugging it near the Kyklops
as more than natural force nerved them; straight
forward they sprinted, lifted it, and rammed it   400
deep in his crater eye, and I leaned on it
turning it as a shipwright turns a drill
in planking, having men below to swing
the two-handled strap that spins it in the groove.
So with our brand we bored that great eye socket   405
while blood ran out around the red hot bar.
Eyelid and lash were seared; the pierced ball
hissed broiling, and the roots popped.

In a smithy
one sees a white-hot axehead or an adze
plunged and wrung in a cold tub, screeching steam—   410
the way they make soft iron hale and hard—:
just so that eyeball hissed around the spike.
The Kyklops bellowed and the rock roared round him,
and we fell back in fear. Clawing his face
he tugged the bloody spike out of his eye,   415
threw it away, and his wild hands went groping;
then he set up a howl for Kyklopês
who lived in caves on windy peaks nearby.
Some heard him; and they came by divers ways
to clump around outside and call:

                                    'What ails you,   420
Polyphêmos? Why do you cry so sore
in the starry night? You will not let us sleep.
Sure no man's driving off your flock? No man
has tricked you, ruined you?'

                              Out of the cave
the mammoth Polyphêmos roared in answer: 425

'Nohbdy, Nohbdy's tricked me, Nohbdy's ruined me!'

To this rough shout they made a sage reply:

'Ah well, if nobody has played you foul
there in your lonely bed, we are no use in pain
given by great Zeus. Let it be your father,   430
Poseidon Lord, to whom you pray.'

                                    So saying
they trailed away. And I was filled with laughter
to see how like a charm the name deceived them.
Now Kyklops, wheezing as the pain came on him,
fumbled to wrench away the great doorstone   435
and squatted in the breach with arms thrown wide
for any silly beast or man who bolted—
hoping somehow I might be such a fool.
But I kept thinking how to win the game:
death sat there huge; how could we slip away?   440
I drew on all my wits, and ran through tactics,
reasoning as a man will for dear life,
until a trick came—and it pleased me well.
The Kyklops' rams were handsome, fat, with heavy
fleeces, a dark violet.
                          Three abreast   445
I tied them silently together, twining
cords of willow from the ogre's bed;
then slung a man under each middle one
to ride there safely, shielded left and right.
So three sheep could convey each man. I took   450
the woolliest ram, the choicest of the flock,
and hung myself under his kinky belly,
pulled up tight, with fingers twisted deep
in sheepskin ringlets for an iron grip.
So, breathing hard, we waited until morning.   455

When Dawn spread out her finger tips of rose
the rams began to stir, moving for pasture,
and peals of bleating echoed round the pens

where dams with udders full called for a milking.
Blinded, and sick with pain from his head wound,   460
the master stroked each ram, then let it pass,
but my men riding on the pectoral fleece
the giant's blind hands blundering never found.
Last of them all my ram, the leader, came,
weighted by wool and me with my meditations.   465
The Kyklops patted him, and then he said:

'Sweet cousin ram, why lag behind the rest
in the night cave? You never linger so,
but graze before them all, and go afar
to crop sweet grass, and take your stately way   470
leading along the streams, until at evening
you run to be the first one in the fold.
Why, now, so far behind? Can you be grieving
over your Master's eye? That carrion rogue
and his accurst companions burnt it out   475
when he had conquered all my wits with wine.
Nohbdy will not get out alive, I swear.
Oh, had you brain and voice to tell
where he may be now, dodging all my fury!
Bashed by this hand and bashed on this rock wall   480
his brains would strew the floor, and I should have
rest from the outrage Nohbdy worked upon me.'

He sent us into the open, then. Close by,
I dropped and rolled clear of the ram's belly,
going this way and that to untie the men.   485
With many glances back, we rounded up
his fat, stiff-legged sheep to take aboard,
and drove them down to where the good ship lay.
We saw, as we came near, our fellows' faces
shining; then we saw them turn to grief   490
tallying those who had not fled from death.
I hushed them, jerking head and eyebrows up,
and in a low voice told them: 'Load this herd;
move fast, and put the ship's head toward the breakers.'
They all pitched in at loading, then embarked   495
and struck their oars into the sea. Far out,
as far off shore as shouted words would carry,
I sent a few back to the adversary:

'O Kyklops! Would you feast on my companions?
Puny, am I, in a Caveman's hands?   500
How do you like the beating that we gave you,
you damned cannibal? Eater of guests
under your roof! Zeus and the gods have paid you!'

The blind thing in his doubled fury broke
a hilltop in his hands and heaved it after us.   505
Ahead of our black prow it struck and sank
whelmed in a spuming geyser, a giant wave
that washed the ship stern foremost back to shore.
I got the longest boathook out and stood
fending us off, with furious nods to all   510
to put their backs into a racing stroke—
row, row, or perish. So the long oars bent
kicking the foam sternward, making head
until we drew away, and twice as far.
Now when I cupped my hands I heard the crew   515
in low voices protesting:

                              'Godsake, Captain!
Why bait the beast again? Let him alone!'

'That tidal wave he made on the first throw
all but beached us.'

                    'All but stove us in!'

'Give him our bearing with your trumpeting,   520
he'll get the range and lob a boulder.'

                                  'Aye
He'll smash our timbers and our heads together!'

I would not heed them in my glorying spirit,
but let my anger flare and yelled:

                                  'Kyklops,
if ever mortal man inquire   525
how you were put to shame and blinded, tell him
Odysseus, raider of cities, took your eye:
Laërtês' son, whose home's on Ithaka!'

At this he gave a mighty sob and rumbled:

'Now comes the weird[2] upon me, spoken of old.   530
A wizard, grand and wondrous, lived here—Télemos,
a son of Eurymos; great length of days
he had in wizardry among the Kyklopês,
and these things he foretold for time to come:
my great eye lost, and at Odysseus' hands.   535
Always I had in mind some giant, armed
in giant force, would come against me here.
But this, but you—small, pitiful and twiggy—
you put me down with wine, you blinded me.

2. Fate, destiny.

Come back, Odysseus, and I'll treat you well,   540
praying the god of earthquake to befriend you—
his son I am, for he by his avowal
fathered me, and, if he will, he may
heal me of this black wound—he and no other
of all the happy gods or mortal men.'   545

Few words I shouted in reply to him:

'If I could take your life I would and take
your time away, and hurl you down to hell!
The god of earthquake could not heal you there!'

At this he stretched his hands out in his darkness   550
toward the sky of stars, and prayed Poseidon:

'O hear me, lord, blue girdler of the islands,
if I am thine indeed, and thou art father:
grant that Odysseus, raider of cities, never
see his home: Laërtês' son, I mean,   555
who kept his hall on Ithaka. Should destiny
intend that he shall see his roof again
among his family in his father land,
far be that day, and dark the years between.
Let him lose all companions, and return   560
under strange sail to bitter days at home.'

In these words he prayed, and the god heard him.
Now he laid hands upon a bigger stone
and wheeled around, titanic for the cast,
to let it fly in the black-prowed vessel's track.   565
But it fell short, just aft the steering oar,
and whelming seas rose giant above the stone
to bear us onward toward the island.
                                        There
as we ran in we saw the squadron waiting,
the trim ships drawn up side by side, and all   570
our troubled friends who waited, looking seaward.
We beached her, grinding keel in the soft sand,
and waded in, ourselves, on the sandy beach.
Then we unloaded all the Kyklops' flock
to make division, share and share alike,   575
only my fighters voted that my ram,
the prize of all, should go to me. I slew him
by the sea side and burnt his long thighbones
to Zeus beyond the stormcloud, Kronos' son,
who rules the world. But Zeus disdained my offering;   580
destruction for my ships he had in store

and death for those who sailed them, my companions.
Now all day long until the sun went down
we made our feast on mutton and sweet wine,
till after sunset in the gathering dark   585
we went to sleep above the wash of ripples.

When the young Dawn with finger tips of rose
touched the world, I roused the men, gave orders
to man the ships, cast off the mooring lines;
and filing in to sit beside the rowlocks   590
oarsmen in line dipped oars in the grey sea.
So we moved out, sad in the vast offing,
having our precious lives, but not our friends.

BOOK X

The Grace of the Witch

We made our landfall on Aiolia Island,[3]
domain of Aiolos Hippotadês,
the wind king dear to the gods who never die—
an isle adrift upon the sea, ringed round
with brazen ramparts on a sheer cliffside.   5
Twelve children had old Aiolos at home—
six daughters and six lusty sons—and he
gave girls to boys to be their gentle brides;
now those lords, in their parents' company,
sup every day in hall—a royal feast   10
with fumes of sacrifice and winds that pipe
'round hollow courts; and all the night they sleep
on beds of filigree beside their ladies.
Here we put in, lodged in the town and palace,
while Aiolos played host to me. He kept me   15
one full month to hear the tale of Troy,
the ships and the return of the Akhaians,
all which I told him point by point in order.
When in return I asked his leave to sail
and asked provisioning, he stinted nothing,   20
adding a bull's hide sewn from neck to tail
into a mighty bag, bottling storm winds;
for Zeus had long ago made Aiolos
warden of winds, to rouse or calm at will.
He wedged this bag under my afterdeck,   25
lashing the neck with shining silver wire

3. A moving island, the home of the king of the winds (whose name in Greek means "shifting, changeable"). It has been located by modern geographers in the Lipari Islands of the Sicilian coast. The great
ancient geographer Eratosthenes was not so confident. He once said that we would know exactly where
Odysseus wandered after we had traced the leatherworker who made the bag in which the winds were
contained.

so not a breath got through; only the west wind
he lofted for me in a quartering breeze
to take my squadron spanking home.
                                No luck:
the fair wind failed us when our prudence failed.   30

Nine days and nights we sailed without event,
till on the tenth we raised our land. We neared it,
and saw men building fires along the shore;
but now, being weary to the bone, I fell
into deep slumber; I had worked the sheet   35
nine days alone, and given it to no one,
wishing to spill no wind on the homeward run.
But while I slept, the crew began to parley:
silver and gold, they guessed, were in that bag
bestowed on me by Aiolos' great heart;   40
and one would glance at his benchmate and say:
'It never fails. He's welcome everywhere:
hail to the captain when he goes ashore!
He brought along so many presents, plunder
out of Troy, that's it. How about ourselves—   45
his shipmates all the way. Nigh home we are
with empty hands. And who has gifts from Aiolos?
He has. I say we ought to crack that bag,
there's gold and silver, plenty, in that bag!'

Temptation had its way with my companions,   50
and they untied the bag.
                        Then every wind
roared into hurricane; the ships went pitching
west with many cries; our land was lost.
Roused up, despairing in that gloom, I thought:
"Should I go overside for a quick finish   55
or clench my teeth and stay among the living?'
Down in the bilge I lay, pulling my sea cloak
over my head, while the rough gale blew the ships
and rueful crews clear back to Aiolia.

We put ashore for water; then all hands   60
gathered alongside for a mid-day meal.
When we had taken bread and drink, I picked
one soldier, and one herald, to go with me
and called again on Aiolos. I found him
at meat with his young princes and his lady,   65
but there beside the pillars, in his portico,
we sat down silent at the open door.
The sight amazed them, and they all exclaimed:

'Why back again, Odysseus?'

                              'What sea fiend
rose in your path?'

                    'Did we not launch you well   70
for home, or for whatever land you chose?'

Out of my melancholy I replied:

'Mischief aboard and nodding at the tiller—
a damned drowse—did for me. Make good my loss,
dear friends! You have the power!'

                              Gently I pleaded,   75
but they turned cold and still. Said Father Aiolos:

'Take yourself out of this island, creeping thing—
no law, no wisdom, lays it on me now
to help a man the blessed gods detest—
out! Your voyage here was cursed by heaven!'   80

He drove me from the place, groan as I would,
and comfortless we went again to sea,
days of it, till the men flagged at the oars—
no breeze, no help in sight, by our own folly—
six indistinguishable nights and days   85
before we raised the Laistrygonian height
and far stronghold of Lamos.[4] In that land
the daybreak follows dusk, and so the shepherd
homing calls to the cowherd setting out;
and he who never slept could earn two wages,   90
tending oxen, pasturing silvery flocks,
where the low night path of the sun is near
the sun's path by day.[5] Here, then, we found
a curious bay with mountain walls of stone
to left and right, and reaching far inland,—   95
a narrow entrance opening from the sea
where cliffs converged as though to touch and close.
All of my squadron sheltered here, inside
the cavern of this bay.

                    Black prow by prow
those hulls were made fast in a limpid calm   100
without a ripple stillness all around them.
My own black ship I chose to moor alone
on the sea side, using a rock for bollard;
and climbed a rocky point to get my bearings.

4. Presumably the founder of the city of the Laistrygonians, a race of man-eating giants.   5. Generally
thought to be a confused reference to the short summer nights of the far north.

No farms, no cultivated land appeared,   105
but puffs of smoke rose in the wilderness;
so I sent out two picked men and a herald
to learn what race of men this land sustained.

My party found a track—a wagon road
for bringing wood down from the heights to town;   110
and near the settlement they met a daughter
of Antiphatês the Laistrygon—a stalwart
young girl taking her pail to Artakía,
the fountain where these people go for water.
My fellows hailed her, put their questions to her: 115
who might the king be? ruling over whom?
She waved her hand, showing her father's lodge,
so they approached it. In its gloom they saw
a woman like a mountain crag, the queen—
and loathed the sight of her. But she, for greeting,   120
called from the meeting ground her lord and master,
Antiphatês, who came to drink their blood.
He seized one man and tore him on the spot,
making a meal of him; the other two
leaped out of doors and ran to join the ships.   125
Behind, he raised the whole tribe howling, countless
Laistrygonês—and more than men they seemed,
gigantic when they gathered on the sky line
to shoot great boulders down from slings; and hell's own
crashing rose, and crying from the ships,   130
as planks and men were smashed to bits—poor gobbets
the wildmen speared like fish and bore away.
But long before it ended in the anchorage—
havoc and slaughter—I had drawn my sword
and cut my own ship's cable. 'Men,' I shouted,   135
'man the oars and pull till your hearts break
if you would put this butchery behind!'
The oarsmen rent the sea in mortal fear
and my ship spurted out of range, far out
from that deep canyon where the rest were lost.   140
So we fared onward and death fell behind,
and we took breath to grieve for our companions.

Our next landfall was on Aiaia, island
of Kirkê, dire beauty and divine,
sister of baleful Aiêtês, like him   145
fathered by Hêlios the light of mortals
on Persê, child of the Ocean stream.
                                              We came
washed in our silent ship upon her shore,

and found a cove, a haven for the ship—
some god, invisible, conned us in. We landed,   150
to lie down in that place two days and nights,
worn out and sick at heart, tasting our grief.
But when Dawn set another day a-shining
I took my spear and broadsword and I climbed
a rocky point above the ship, for sight   155
or sound of human labor. Gazing out
from that high place over a land of thicket,
oaks and wide watercourses, I could see
a smoke wisp from the woodland hall of Kirkê.
So I took counsel with myself: should I   160
go inland scouting out that reddish smoke?
No: better not, I thought, but first return
to waterside and ship, and give the men
breakfast before I sent them to explore.
Now as I went down quite alone, and came   165
a bowshot from the ship, some god's compassion
set a big buck in motion to cross my path—
a stag with noble antlers, pacing down
from pasture in the woods to the riverside,
as long thirst and the power of sun constrained him.   170
He started from the bush and wheeled: I hit him
square in the spine midway along his back
and the bronze point broke through it. In the dust
he fell and whinnied as life bled away.
I set one foot against him, pulling hard   175
to wrench my weapon from the wound, then left it,
butt-end on the ground. I plucked some withies
and twined a double strand into a rope—
enough to tie the hocks of my huge trophy;
then pickaback I lugged him to the ship,   180
leaning on my long spearshaft; I could not
haul that mighty carcass on one shoulder.
Beside the ship I let him drop, and spoke
gently and low to each man standing near:

'Come, friends, though hard beset, we'll not go down   185
into the House of Death before our time.
As long as food and drink remain aboard
let us rely on it, not die of hunger.'

At this those faces, cloaked in desolation
upon the waste sea beach, were bared;   190
their eyes turned toward me and the mighty trophy,
lighting, foreseeing pleasure, one by one.
So hands were washed to take what heaven sent us.

And all that day until the sun went down
we had our fill of venison and wine,   195
till after sunset in the gathering dusk
we slept at last above the line of breakers.
When the young Dawn with finger tips of rose
made heaven bright, I called them round and said:

'Shipmates, companions in disastrous time,   200
O my dear friends, where Dawn lies, and the West,
and where the great Sun, light of men, may go
under the earth by night, and where he rises—
of these things we know nothing.[6] Do we know
any least thing to serve us now? I wonder.   205
All that I saw when I went up the rock
was one more island in the boundless main,
a low landscape, covered with woods and scrub,
and puffs of smoke ascending in mid-forest.'

They were all silent, but their hearts contracted,   210
remembering Antiphatês the Laistrygon
and that prodigious cannibal, the Kyklops.
They cried out, and the salt tears wet their eyes.
But seeing our time for action lost in weeping,
I mustered those Akhaians under arms,   215
counting them off in two platoons, myself
and my godlike Eurýlokhos commanding.
We shook lots in a soldier's dogskin cap
and his came bounding out—valiant Eurýlokhos!—
So off he went, with twenty-two companions   220
weeping, as mine wept, too, who stayed behind.

In the wild wood they found an open glade,
around a smooth stone house—the hall of Kirkê—
and wolves and mountain lions lay there, mild
in her soft spell, fed on her drug of evil.   225
None would attack—oh, it was strange, I tell you—
but switching their long tails they faced our men
like hounds, who look up when their master comes
with tidbits for them—as he will—from table.
Humbly those wolves and lions with mighty paws   230
fawned on our men—who met their yellow eyes
and feared them.
            In the entrance way they stayed
to listen there: inside her quiet house
they heard the goddess Kirkê.

6. In view of the immediately preceding lines, this can hardly be taken literally. It is possibly a sailor's
metaphorical way of saying, "We don't know where we are."

                        Low she sang
in her beguiling voice, while on her loom   235
she wove ambrosial fabric sheer and bright,
by that craft known to the goddesses of heaven.
No one would speak, until Politês—most
faithful and likable of my officers, said:

'Dear friends, no need for stealth: here's a young weaver   240
singing a pretty song to set the air
a-tingle on these lawns and paven courts.
Goddess she is, or lady. Shall we greet her?'

So reassured, they all cried out together,
and she came swiftly to the shining doors   245
to call them in. All but Eurýlokhos—
who feared a snare—the innocents went after her.
On thrones she seated them, and lounging chairs,
while she prepared a meal of cheese and barley
and amber honey mixed with Pramnian wine,[7]   250
adding her own vile pinch, to make them lose
desire or thought of our dear father land.
Scarce had they drunk when she flew after them
with her long stick and shut them in a pigsty—
bodies, voices, heads, and bristles, all   255
swinish now, though minds were still unchanged.
So, squealing, in they went. And Kirkê tossed them
acorns, mast, and cornel berries—fodder
for hogs who rut and slumber on the earth.

Down to the ship Eurýlokhos came running   260
to cry alarm, foul magic doomed his men!
But working with dry lips to speak a word
he could not, being so shaken; blinding tears
welled in his eyes; foreboding filled his heart.
When we were frantic questioning him, at last   265
we heard the tale: our friends were gone. Said he:

'We went up through the oak scrub where you sent us,
Odysseus, glory of commanders,
until we found a palace in a glade,
a marble house on open ground, and someone   270
singing before her loom a chill, sweet song—
goddess or girl, we could not tell. They hailed her,
and then she stepped through shining doors and said,
"Come, come in!" Like sheep they followed her,
but I saw cruel deceit, and stayed behind.   275

---

7. A harsh, dark wine.

Then all our fellows vanished. Not a sound,
and nothing stirred, although I watched for hours.'

When I heard this I slung my silver-hilted
broadsword on, and shouldered my long bow,
and said, 'Come, take me back the way you came.'   280
But he put both his hands around my knees
in desperate woe, and said in supplication:

'Not back there, O my lord! Oh, leave me here!
You, even you, cannot return, I know it,
I know you cannot bring away our shipmates;   285
better make sail with these men, quickly too,
and save ourselves from horror while we may.'

But I replied:

           'By heaven, Eurýlokhos,
rest here then; take food and wine;
stay in the black hull's shelter. Let me go,   290
as I see nothing for it but to go.'

I turned and left him, left the shore and ship,
and went up through the woodland hushed and shady
to find the subtle witch in her long hall.
But Hermês met me, with his golden wand,   295
barring the way—a boy whose lip was downy
in the first bloom of manhood, so he seemed.
He took my hand and spoke as though he knew me:[8]

'Why take the inland path alone,
poor seafarer, by hill and dale   300
upon this island all unknown?
Your friends are locked in Kirkê's pale;
all are become like swine to see;
and if you go to set them free
you go to stay, and never more make sail   305
for your old home upon Thaki.

But I can tell you what to do
to come unchanged from Kirkê's power
and disenthrall your fighting crew:
take with you to her bower   310
as amulet, this plant I know—
it will defeat her horrid show,
so pure and potent is the flower;
no mortal herb was ever so.

8. The four rhymed stanzas which follow are a translator's license; in the original there is no change of
meter and, of course, no rhyme. *Thaki*, below: Ithaka.

Your cup with numbing drops of night   315
and evil, stilled of all remorse,
she will infuse to charm your sight;
but this great herb with holy force
will keep your mind and senses clear:
when she turns cruel, coming near   320
with her long stick to whip you out of doors,
then let your cutting blade appear,

Let instant death upon it shine,
and she will cower and yield her bed—
a pleasure you must not decline,   325
so may her lust and fear bestead
you and your friends, and break her spell;
but make her swear by heaven and hell
no witches' tricks, or else, your harness shed,
you'll be unmanned by her as well.'   330

He bent down glittering for the magic plant
and pulled it up, black root and milky flower—
a *molü* in the language of the gods—
fatigue and pain for mortals to uproot;
but gods do this, and everything, with ease.   335

Then toward Olympos through the island trees
Hermês departed, and I sought out Kirkê,
my heart high with excitement, beating hard.
Before her mansion in the porch I stood
to call her, all being still. Quick as a cat   340
she opened her bright doors and sighed a welcome;
then I strode after her with heavy heart
down the long hall, and took the chair she gave me,
silver-studded, intricately carved,
made with a low footrest. The lady Kirkê   345
mixed me a golden cup of honeyed wine,
adding in mischief her unholy drug.
I drank, and the drink failed. But she came forward
aiming a stroke with her long stick, and whispered:

'Down in the sty and snore among the rest!'   350

Without a word, I drew my sharpened sword
and in one bound held it against her throat.
She cried out, then slid under to take my knees,
catching her breath to say, in her distress:

'What champion, of what country, can you be?   355
Where are your kinsmen and your city?

Are you not sluggish with my wine? Ah, wonder!
Never a mortal man that drank this cup
but when it passed his lips he had succumbed.
Hale must your heart be and your tempered will.   360
Odysseus then you are, O great contender,
of whom the glittering god with golden wand[9]
spoke to me ever, and foretold
the black swift ship would carry you from Troy.
Put up your weapon in the sheath. We two   365
shall mingle and make love upon our bed.
So mutual trust may come of play and love.'

To this I said:

            'Kirkê, am I a boy,
that you should make me soft and doting now?
Here in this house you turned my men to swine;   370
now it is I myself you hold, enticing
into your chamber, to your dangerous bed,
to take my manhood when you have me stripped.
I mount no bed of love with you upon it.
Or swear me first a great oath, if I do,   375
you'll work no more enchantment to my harm.'

She swore at once, outright, as I demanded,
and after she had sworn, and bound herself,
I entered Kirkê's flawless bed of love.

Presently in the hall her maids were busy,   380
the nymphs who waited upon Kirkê: four,
whose cradles were in fountains, under boughs,
or in the glassy seaward-gliding streams.
One came with richly colored rugs to throw
on seat and chairback, over linen covers;   385
a second pulled the tables out, all silver,
and loaded them with baskets all of gold;
a third mixed wine as tawny-mild as honey
in a bright bowl, and set out golden cups.
The fourth came bearing water, and lit a blaze   390
under a cauldron. By and by it bubbled,
and when the dazzling brazen vessel seethed
she filled a bathtub to my waist, and bathed me,
pouring a soothing blend on head and shoulders,
warming the soreness of my joints away.   395
When she had done, and smoothed me with sweet oil,

9. Hermes.

she put a tunic and a cloak around me
and took me to a silver-studded chair
with footrest, all elaborately carven.
Now came a maid to tip a golden jug   400
of water into a silver finger bowl,
and draw a polished table to my side.
The larder mistress brought her tray of loaves
with many savory slices, and she gave
the best, to tempt me. But no pleasure came;   405
I huddled with my mind elsewhere, oppressed.

Kirkê regarded me, as there I sat
disconsolate, and never touched a crust.
Then she stood over me and chided me:

'Why sit at table mute, Odysseus?   410
Are you mistrustful of my bread and drink?
Can it be treachery that you fear again,
after the gods' great oath I swore for you?'

I turned to her at once, and said:

                              'Kirkê,
where is the captain who could bear to touch   415
this banquet, in my place? A decent man
would see his company before him first.
Put heart in me to eat and drink—you may,
by freeing my companions. I must see them.'

But Kirkê had already turned away.   420
Her long staff in her hand, she left the hall
and opened up the sty, I saw her enter,
driving those men turned swine to stand before me.
She stroked them, each in turn, with some new chrism;
and then, behold! their bristles fell away,   425
the coarse pelt grown upon them by her drug
melted away, and they were men again,
younger, more handsome, taller than before.
Their eyes upon me, each one took my hands,
and wild regret and longing pierced them through,   430
so the room rang with sobs, and even Kirkê
pitied that transformation. Exquisite
the goddess looked as she stood near me, saying:

'Son of Laërtês and the gods of old,
Odysseus, master mariner and soldier,   435
go to the sea beach and sea-breasting ship;
drag it ashore, full length upon the land;

stow gear and stores in rock-holes under cover;
return; be quick; bring all your dear companions.'

Now, being a man, I could not help consenting.   440
So I went down to the sea beach and the ship,
where I found all my other men on board,
weeping, in despair along the benches.
Sometimes in farmyards when the cows return
well fed from pasture to the barn, one sees   445
the pens give way before the calves in tumult,
breaking through to cluster about mothers,
bumping together, bawling. Just that way
my crew poured round me when they saw me come—
their faces wet with tears as if they saw   450
their homeland, and the crags of Ithaka,
even the very town where they were born.
And weeping still they all cried out in greeting:

'Prince, what joy this is, your safe return!
Now Ithaka seems here, and we in Ithaka!   455
But tell us now, what death befell our friends?'

And, speaking gently, I replied:

'First we must get the ship high on the shingle,
and stow our gear and stores in clefts of rock
for cover. Then come follow me, to see   460
your shipmates in the magic house of Kirkê
eating and drinking, endlessly regaled.'

They turned back, as commanded, to this work;
only one lagged, and tried to hold the others;
Eurýlokhos it was, who blurted out: 465

'Where now, poor remnants? is it devil's work
you long for? Will you go to Kirkê's hall?
Swine, wolves, and lions she will make us all,
beasts of her courtyard, bound by her enchantment.
Remember those the Kyklops held, remember   470
shipmates who made that visit with Odysseus!
The daring man! They died for his foolishness!'

When I heard this I had a mind to draw
the blade that swung against my side and chop him,
bowling his head upon the ground—kinsman[1]   475
or no kinsman, close to me though he was.
But others came between, saying, to stop me,

1. Eurýlokhos was related to Odysseus by marriage.

'Prince, we can leave him, if you say the word;
let him stay here on guard. As for ourselves,
show us the way to Kirkê's magic hall.'   480

So all turned inland, leaving shore and ship,
and Eurýlokhos—he, too, came on behind,
fearing the rough edge of my tongue. Meanwhile
at Kirkê's hands the rest were gently bathed,
anointed with sweet oil, and dressed afresh   485
in tunics and new cloaks with fleecy linings.
We found them all at supper when we came.
But greeting their old friends once more, the crew
could not hold back their tears; and now again
the rooms rang with sobs. Then Kirkê, loveliest   490
of all immortals, came to counsel me:

'Son of Laërtês and the gods of old.
Odysseus, master mariner and soldier,
enough of weeping fits. I know—I, too—
what you endured upon the inhuman sea,   495
what odds you met on land from hostile men.
Remain with me, and share my meat and wine;
restore behind your ribs those gallant hearts
that served you in the old days, when you sailed
from stony Ithaka. Now parched and spent,   500
your cruel wandering is all you think of,
never of joy, after so many blows.'

As we were men we could not help consenting.
So day by day we lingered, feasting long
on roasts and wine, until a year grew fat.   505
But when the passing months and wheeling seasons
brought the long summery days, the pause of summer,
my shipmates one day summoned me and said:

'Captain, shake off this trance, and think of home—
if home indeed awaits us,
                      if we shall ever see   510
your own well-timbered hall on Ithaka.'

They made me feel a pang, and I agreed.
That day, and all day long, from dawn to sundown,
we feasted on roast meat and ruddy wine,
and after sunset when the dusk came on   515
my men slept in the shadowy hall, but I
went through the dark to Kirkê's flawless bed
and took the goddess' knees in supplication,
urging, as she bent to hear:

'O Kirkê,
now you must keep your promise; it is time.   520
Help me make sail for home. Day after day
my longing quickens, and my company
give me no peace, but wear my heart away
pleading when you are not at hand to hear.'

The loveliest of goddesses replied: 525

'Son of Laërtês and the gods of old,
Odysseus, master mariner and soldier,
you shall not stay here longer against your will;
but home you may not go
unless you take a strange way round and come   530
to the cold homes of Death and pale Perséphonê.[2]
You shall hear prophecy from the rapt shade
of blind Teirêsias of Thebes,[3] forever
charged with reason even among the dead;
to him alone, of all the flitting ghosts,   535
Perséphonê has given a mind undarkened.'

At this I felt a weight like stone within me,
and, moaning, pressed my length against the bed,
with no desire to see the daylight more.
But when I had wept and tossed and had my fill   540
of this despair, at last I answered her:

'Kirkê, who pilots me upon this journey?
No man has ever sailed to the land of Death.'

That loveliest of goddesses replied:

'Son of Laërtês and the gods of old,   545
Odysseus, master of land ways and sea ways,
feel no dismay because you lack a pilot;
only set up your mast and haul your canvas
to the fresh blowing North; sit down and steer,
and hold that wind, even to the bourne of Ocean,   550
Perséphonê's deserted stand and grove,
dusky with poplars and the drooping willow.
Run through the tide-rip, bring your ship to shore,
land there, and find the crumbling homes of Death.
Here, toward the Sorrowing Water, run the streams   555
of Wailing, out of Styx, and quenchless Burning[4]—
torrents that join in thunder at the Rock.
Here then, great soldier, setting foot obey me:

2. Queen of the underworld.   3. A blind prophet who figures prominently in the legends of Thebes (he is a character in Sophocles' *Oedipus the King*).   4. Pyriphlegethon, a river of the underworld, as are the Sorrowing Water (Acheron), the stream of Wailing (Cocytus), and the Styx.

dig a well shaft a forearm square; pour out
libations round it to the unnumbered dead: 560
sweet milk and honey, then sweet wine, and last
clear water, scattering handfuls of white barley.
Pray now, with all your heart, to the faint dead;
swear you will sacrifice your finest heifer,
at home in Ithaka, and burn for them   565
her tenderest parts in sacrifice; and vow
to the lord Teirêsias, apart from all,
a black lamb, handsomest of all your flock—
thus to appease the nations of the dead.
Then slash a black ewe's throat, and a black ram,   570
facing the gloom of Erebos;[5] but turn
your head away toward Ocean. You shall see, now
souls of the buried dead in shadowy hosts,
and now you must call out to your companions
to flay those sheep the bronze knife has cut down,   575
for offerings, burnt flesh to those below,
to sovereign Death and pale Perséphonê.
Meanwhile draw sword from hip, crouch down, ward off
the surging phantoms from the bloody pit
until you know the presence of Teirêsias.   580
He will come soon, great captain; be it he
who gives you course and distance for your sailing
homeward across the cold fish-breeding sea.'

As the goddess ended, Dawn came stitched in gold.
Now Kirkê dressed me in my shirt and cloak,   585
put on a gown of subtle tissue, silvery,
then wound a golden belt about her waist
and veiled her head in linen,
while I went through the hall to rouse my crew.

I bent above each one, and gently said: 590

'Wake from your sleep; no more sweet slumber. Come,
we sail: the Lady Kirkê so ordains it.'

They were soon up, and ready at that word;
but I was not to take my men unharmed
from this place, even from this. Among them all   595
the youngest was Elpênor—
no mainstay in a fight nor very clever—
and this one, having climbed on Kirkê's roof[6]
to taste the cool night, fell asleep with wine.

---

5. The darkest region of the underworld, usually imagined as below the underworld itself but here to the
west.   6. A flat roof, and the coolest place to sleep.

Waked by our morning voices, and the tramp   600
of men below, he started up, but missed
his footing on the long steep backward ladder
and fell that height headlong. The blow smashed
the nape cord, and his ghost fled to the dark.
But I was outside, walking with the rest,   605
saying:

       'Homeward you think we must be sailing
to our own land; no, elsewhere is the voyage
Kirkê has laid upon me. We must go
to the cold homes of Death and pale Perséphonê
to hear Teirêsias tell of time to come.'   610

They felt so stricken, upon hearing this,
they sat down wailing loud, and tore their hair.
But nothing came of giving way to grief.
Down to the shore and ship at last we went,
bowed with anguish, cheeks all wet with tears,   615
to find that Kirkê had been there before us
and tied nearby a black ewe and a ram:
she had gone by like air.
For who could see the passage of a goddess
unless she wished his mortal eyes aware?   620

BOOK XI

A *Gathering of Shades*

We bore down on the ship at the sea's edge
and launched her on the salt immortal sea,
stepping our mast and spar in the black ship;
embarked the ram and ewe and went aboard
in tears, with bitter and sore dread upon us.   5
But now a breeze came up for us astern—
a canvas-bellying landbreeze, hale shipmate
sent by the singing nymph with sun-bright hair;
so we made fast the braces, took our thwarts,
and let the wind and steersman work the ship   10
with full sail spread all day above our coursing,
till the sun dipped, and all the ways grew dark
upon the fathomless unresting sea.
              By night
our ship ran onward toward the Ocean's bourne,
the realm and region of the Men of Winter,[7]   15

---

7. Although Homer usually places Hades below the earth, here he puts it across a great expanse of sea, apparently in the far north.

hidden in mist and cloud. Never the flaming
eye of Hêlios lights on those men
at morning, when he climbs the sky of stars,
nor in descending earthward out of heaven;
ruinous night being rove[8] over those wretches.   20
We made the land, put ram and ewe ashore,
and took our way along the Ocean stream
to find the place foretold for us by Kirkê.
There Perimêdês and Eurýlokhos
pinioned the sacred beasts. With my drawn blade   25
I spaded up the votive pit, and poured
libations round it to the unnumbered dead:
sweet milk and honey, then sweet wine, and last
clear water; and I scattered barley down.
Then I addressed the blurred and breathless dead,   30
vowing to slaughter my best heifer for them
before she calved, at home in Ithaka,
and burn the choice bits on the altar fire;
as for Teirêsias, I swore to sacrifice
a black lamb, handsomest of all our flock.   35
Thus to assuage the nations of the dead
I pledged these rites, then slashed the lamb and ewe,
letting their black blood stream into the wellpit.
Now the souls gathered, stirring out of Erebos,
brides and young men, and men grown old in pain,   40
and tender girls whose hearts were new to grief;
many were there, too, torn by brazen lanceheads,
battle-slain, bearing still their bloody gear.
From every side they came and sought the pit
with rustling cries; and I grew sick with fear.   45
But presently I gave command to my officers
to flay those sheep the bronze cut down, and make
burnt offerings of flesh to the gods below—
to sovereign Death, to pale Perséphonê.
Meanwhile I crouched with my drawn sword to keep   50
the surging phantoms from the bloody pit
till I should know the presence of Teirêsias.

One shade came first—Elpênor, of our company,
who lay unburied still on the wide earth
as we had left him—dead in Kirkê's hall,   55
untouched, unmourned, when other cares compelled us.
Now when I saw him there I wept for pity
and called out to him:

8. Stretched or spread.

'How is this, Elpênor,
how could you journey to the western gloom
swifter afoot than I in the black lugger?'   60

He sighed, and answered:

'Son of great Laërtês,
Odysseus, master mariner and soldier,
bad luck shadowed me, and no kindly power;
ignoble death I drank with so much wine.
I slept on Kirkê's roof, then could not see   65
the long steep backward ladder, coming down,
and fell that height. My neck bone, buckled under,
snapped, and my spirit found this well of dark.
Now hear the grace I pray for, in the name
of those back in the world, not here—your wife   70
and father, he who gave you bread in childhood,
and your own child, your only son, Telémakhos,
long ago left at home.
                              When you make sail
and put these lodgings of dim Death behind,
you will moor ship, I know, upon Aiaia Island;   75
there, O my lord, remember me, I pray,
do not abandon me unwept, unburied,
to tempt the gods' wrath, while you sail for home;
but fire my corpse, and all the gear I had,
and build a cairn for me above the breakers—   80
an unknown sailor's mark for men to come.
Heap up the mound there, and implant upon it
the oar I pulled in life with my companions.'

He ceased, and I replied:

'Unhappy spirit,
I promise you the barrow and the burial.'   85

So we conversed, and grimly, at a distance,
with my long sword between, guarding the blood,
while the faint image of the lad spoke on.
Now came the soul of Antikleía, dead,
my mother, daughter of Autólykos,   90
dead now, though living still when I took ship
for holy Troy. Seeing this ghost I grieved,
but held her off, through pang on pang of tears,
till I should know the presence of Teirêsias.
Soon from the dark that prince of Thebes came forward   95
bearing a golden staff; and he addressd me:

'Son of Laërtês and the gods of old,
Odysseus, master of land ways and sea ways,
why leave the blazing sun, O man of woe,
to see the cold dead and the joyless region?   100
Stand clear, put up your sword;
let me but taste of blood, I shall speak true.'

At this I stepped aside, and in the scabbard
let my long sword ring home to the pommel silver,
as he bent down to the sombre blood. Then spoke   105
the prince of those with gift of speech:[9]

                              'Great captain,
a fair wind and the honey lights of home
are all you seek. But anguish lies ahead;
the god who thunders on the land prepares it,
not to be shaken from your track, implacable,   110
in rancor for the son whose eye you blinded.
One narrow strait may take you through his blows:
denial of yourself, restraint of shipmates.
When you make landfall on Thrinakia first
and quit the violet sea, dark on the land   115
you'll find the grazing herds of Hêlios
by whom all things are seen, all speech is known.
Avoid those kine, hold fast to your intent,
and hard seafaring brings you all to Ithaka.
But if you raid the beeves, I see destruction   120
for ship and crew. Though you survive alone,
bereft of all companions, lost for years,
under strange sail shall you come home, to find
your own house filled with trouble: insolent men
eating your livestock as they court your lady.   125
Aye, you shall make those men atone in blood!
But after you have dealt out death—in open
combat or by stealth—to all the suitors,
go overland on foot, and take an oar,
until one day you come where men have lived   130
with meat unsalted, never known the sea,
nor seen seagoing ships, with crimson bows
and oars that fledge light hulls for dipping flight.
The spot will soon be plain to you, and I
can tell you how: some passerby will say,   135
"What winnowing fan is that upon your shoulder?"

9. Tiresias here predicts the future of Odysseus. Like many Greek prophecies, it contains alternatives.
The second (l. 120ff.) is what happens. The journey inland to find a people who have never seen the sea
(and so mistake an oar for a winnowing-fan—l. 136) does not take place within the *Odyssey* itself.

Halt, and implant your smooth oar in the turf
and make fair sacrifice to Lord Poseidon:
a ram, a bull, a great buck boar; turn back,
and carry out pure hekatombs at home   140
to all wide heaven's lords, the undying gods,
to each in order. Then a seaborne death
soft as this hand of mist will come upon you
when you are wearied out with rich old age,
your country folk in blessed peace around you.   145
And all this shall be just as I foretell.'

When he had done, I said at once,

                          'Teirêsias,
my life runs on then as the gods have spun it.
But come, now, tell me this; make this thing clear:
I see my mother's ghost among the dead   150
sitting in silence near the blood. Not once
has she glanced this way toward her son, nor spoken.
Tell me, my lord,
may she in some way come to know my presence?'

To this he answered:

                    'I shall make it clear   155
in a few words and simply. Any dead man
whom you allow to enter where the blood is
will speak to you, and speak the truth; but those
deprived will grow remote again and fade.'

When he had prophesied, Teirêsias' shade   160
retired lordly to the halls of Death;
but I stood fast until my mother stirred,
moving to sip the black blood; then she knew me
and called out sorrowfully to me:

                        'Child,
how could you cross alive into this gloom   165
at the world's end?—No sight for living eyes;
great currents run between, desolate waters,
the Ocean first, where no man goes a journey
without ship's timber under him.

                        Say, now,
is it from Troy, still wandering, after years,   170
that you come here with ship and company?
Have you not gone at all to Ithaka?
Have you not seen your lady in your hall?'

She put these questions, and I answered her:

'Mother, I came here, driven to the land of death   175
in want of prophecy from Teirêsias' shade;
nor have I yet coasted Akhaia's hills
nor touched my own land, but have had hard roving
since first I joined Lord Agamémnon's host
by sea for Ilion, the wild horse country,   180
to fight the men of Troy.
But come now, tell me this, and tell me clearly,
what was the bane that pinned you down in Death?
Some ravaging long illness, or mild arrows
a-flying down one day from Artemis?   185
Tell me of Father, tell me of the son
I left behind me; have they still my place,
my honors, or have other men assumed them?
Do they not say that I shall come no more?
And tell me of my wife: how runs her thought,   190
still with her child, still keeping our domains,
or bride again to the best of the Akhaians?'

To this my noble mother quickly answered:

'Still with her child indeed she is, poor heart,
still in your palace hall. Forlorn her nights   195
and days go by, her life used up in weeping.
But no man takes your honored place. Telémakhos
has care of all your garden plots and fields,
and holds the public honor of a magistrate,
feasting and being feasted. But your father   200
is country bound and comes to town no more.
He owns no bedding, rugs, or fleecy mantles,
but lies down, winter nights, among the slaves,
rolled in old cloaks for cover, near the embers.
Or when the heat comes at the end of summer,   205
the fallen leaves, all round his vineyard plot,
heaped into windrows, make his lowly bed.
He lies now even so, with aching heart,
and longs for your return, while age comes on him.
So I, too, pined away, so doom befell me,   210
not that the keen-eyed huntress[1] with her shafts
had marked me down and shot to kill me; not
that illness overtook me—no true illness
wasting the body to undo the spirit;
only my loneliness for you, Odysseus,   215
for your kind heart and counsel, gentle Odysseus,
took my own life away.'

1. Artemis.

                         I bit my lip,
rising perplexed, with longing to embrace her,
and tried three times, putting my arms around her,
but she went sifting through my hands, impalpable   220
as shadows are, and wavering like a dream.
Now this embittered all the pain I bore,
and I cried in the darkness:

                                    'O my mother,
will you not stay, be still, here in my arms,
may we not, in this place of Death, as well,   225
hold one another, touch with love, and taste
salt tears' relief, the twinge of welling tears?
Or is this all hallucination, sent
against me by the iron queen, Perséphonê,
to make me groan again?'

                         My noble mother   230
answered quickly:

                    'O my child—alas,
most sorely tried of men—great Zeus's daughter,
Perséphonê, knits no illusion for you.
All mortals meet this judgment when they die.
No flesh and bone are here, none bound by sinew,   235
since the bright-hearted pyre consumed them down—
the white bones long exanimate—to ash;
dreamlike the soul flies, insubstantial.

You must crave sunlight soon.
                         Note all things strange
seen here, to tell your lady in after days.'   240

So went our talk; then other shadows came,
ladies in company, sent by Perséphonê—
consorts or daughters of illustrious men—
crowding about the black blood.
                         I took thought
how best to separate and question them,   245
and saw no help for it, but drew once more
the long bright edge of broadsword from my hip,
that none should sip the blood in company
but one by one, in order; so it fell
that each declared her lineage and name.   250

Here was great loveliness of ghosts![2] I saw
before them all, that princess of great ladies,

---

2. There follows a "catalogue of women," a list of famous and beautiful women of former times.

Tyro,[3] Salmoneus' daughter, as she told me,
and queen to Krêtheus, a son of Aiolos.
She had gone daft for the river Enipeus,[4]   255
most graceful of all running streams, and ranged
all day by Enipeus' limpid side,
whose form the foaming girdler of the islands,
the god who makes earth tremble, took and so
lay down with her where he went flooding seaward,   260
their bower a purple billow, arching round
to hide them in a sea-vale, god and lady.
Now when his pleasure was complete, the god
spoke to her softly, holding fast her hand:

'Dear mortal, go in joy! At the turn of seasons,   265
winter to summer, you shall bear me sons;
no lovemaking of gods can be in vain.
Nurse our sweet children tenderly, and rear them.
Home with you now, and hold your tongue, and tell
no one your lover's name—though I am yours,   270
Poseidon, lord of surf that makes earth tremble.'

He plunged away into the deep sea swell,
and she grew big with Pelias and Neleus,[5]
powerful vassals, in their time, of Zeus.
Pelias lived on broad Iolkos seaboard   275
rich in flocks, and Neleus at Pylos.
As for the sons borne by that queen of women
to Krêtheus, their names were Aison,[6] Pherês,
and Amytháon, expert charioteer.

Next after her I saw Antiopê,   280
daughter of Ásopos.[7] She too could boast
a god for lover, having lain with Zeus
and borne two sons to him: Amphion and
Zêthos, who founded Thebes, the upper city,
and built the ancient citadel. They sheltered   285
no life upon that plain, for all their power,
without a fortress wall.

                    And next I saw
Amphitrion's true wife, Alkmênê, mother,
as all men know, of lionish Heraklês,
conceived when she lay close in Zeus's arms;   290

---

3. A queen of Thessaly; among her famous descendants were Nestor and Jason.   4. A river of Thessaly.
Tyro had fallen in love with the rivergod; Poseidon, the "god who makes earth tremble," assumed his
shape.   5. Father of Nestor of Pylos.   6. Father of Jason, the Argonaut.   7. A river in Boeotia, the
territory of Thebes.

and Megarê, high-hearted Kreon's daughter,
wife of Amphitrion's unwearying son.

I saw the mother of Oidipous, Epikastê,[8]
whose great unwitting deed it was
to marry her own son. He took that prize   295
from a slain father; presently the gods
brought all to light that made the famous story.
But by their fearsome wills he kept his throne
in dearest Thebes, all through his evil days,
while she descended to the place of Death,   300
god of the locked and iron door. Steep down
from a high rafter, throttled in her noose,
she swung, carried away by pain, and left him
endless agony from a mother's Furies.

And I saw Khloris, that most lovely lady,   305
whom for her beauty in the olden time
Neleus wooed with countless gifts, and married.
She was the youngest daughter of Amphion,
son of Iasos. In those days he[9] held
power at Orkhómenos, over the Minyai.   310
At Pylos then as queen she bore her children—
Nestor, Khromios, Periklýmenos,
and Pêro, too, who turned the heads of men
with her magnificence. A host of princes
from nearby lands came courting her; but Neleus   315
would hear of no one, not unless the suitor
could drive the steers of giant Iphiklos
from Phylakê—longhorns, broad in the brow,
so fierce that one man only, a diviner,[1]
offered to round them up. But bitter fate   320
saw him bound hand and foot by savage herdsmen.
Then days and months grew full and waned, the year
went wheeling round, the seasons came again,
before at last the power of Íphiklos,
relenting, freed the prisoner, who foretold   325
all things to him. So Zeus's will was done.

And I saw Lêda,[2] wife of Tyndareus,
upon whom Tyndareus had sired twins
indomitable: Kastor, tamer of horses,
and Polydeukês, best in the boxing ring.   330
Those two live still, though life-creating earth

---

8. Usually known as Jocasta. *Oidipous*: Oedipus.   9. Amphion (not the same Amphion who founded
Thebes, l. 284).   1. Named Melampus.   2. She bore Helen to Zeus; to her husband Tyndareus, she
bore the two sons, Castor and Polydeuces, and Clytemnestra, who was to be the wife of Agamemnon.

embraces them: even in the underworld
honored as gods by Zeus, each day in turn[3]
one comes alive, the other dies again.

Then after Lêda to my vision came   335
the wife of Aloeus, Iphimedeia,
proud that she once had held the flowing sea[4]
and borne him sons, thunderers for a day,
the world-renowned Otos and Ephialtês.
Never were men on such a scale   340
bred on the plowlands and the grainlands, never
so magnificent any, after Orion.[5]
At nine years old they towered nine fathoms tall,
nine cubits in the shoulders, and they promised
furor upon Olympos, heaven broken by battle cries,   345
the day they met the gods in arms.
                               With Ossa's
mountain peak[6] they meant to crown Olympos
and over Ossa Pelion's forest pile
for footholds up the sky. As giants grown
they might have done it, but the bright son of Zeus[7]   350
by Lêto of the smooth braid shot them down
while they were boys unbearded; no dark curls
clustered yet from temples to the chin.

Then I saw Phaidra,[8] Prokris; and Ariadnê,
daughter of Minos,[9] the grim king. Theseus took her   355
aboard with him from Krete for the terraced land
of ancient Athens; but he had no joy of her.
Artemis killed her on the Isle of Dia
at a word from Dionysos.[1]
                        Maira, then,
and Klymênê, and that detested queen,   360
Eríphylê,[2] who betrayed her lord for gold . . .
but how name all the women I beheld there,
daughters and wives of kings? The starry night
wanes long before I close.

3. They shared, as it were, one immortality between them.   4. Poseidon.   5. The hunter who was,
according to later legend, transformed into the constellation which still bears his name; in Homer he is in
the underworld after his death (ll. 643ff.).   6. Ossa and Pelion are mountains near Olympus in Thessaly.
7. Apollo, son of Zeus and Lêto.   8. The Cretan wife of Theseus of Athens, who fell in love with her
stepson Hippolytus. Prokris: the unfaithful wife of Cephalus, king of Athens. Ariadnê: sister of Phaedra;
she helped Theseus slay the Minotaur on Crete and escaped with him, only to die on the island of Dia.
9. King of Crete, father of Phaedra and Ariadnê.   1. We have no other account of this version of the
episode which explains why Dionysus wanted Ariadnê killed; the prevalent version of the story in later
times is that Dionysus carried Ariadnê off to be his bride. Maira: a nymph of Artemis who broke her vow
of chastity and was killed by the goddess.   2. Bribed with a golden necklace by Polynices, son of Oedipus, she persuaded her husband Amphiaraus to take part in the attack on Thebes, where he was killed.
Klymênê: some story must have been attached to this name, but we do not know what it was.

                    Here, or aboard ship,
amid the crew, the hour for sleep has come.   365
Our sailing is the gods' affair and yours."[3]

Then he fell silent. Down the shadowy hall
the enchanted banqueters were still. Only
the queen with ivory pale arms, Arêtê, spoke,
saying to all the silent men:

                    "Phaiákians,   370
how does he stand, now, in your eyes, this captain,
the look and bulk of him, the inward poise?
He is my guest, but each one shares that honor.
Be in no haste to send him on his way
or scant your bounty in his need. Remember   375
how rich, by heaven's will, your possessions are."

Then Ekhenêos, the old soldier, eldest
of all Phaiákians, added his word:

"Friends, here was nothing but our own thought spoken,
the mark hit square. Our duties to her majesty.   380
For what is to be said and done,
we wait upon Alkínoös' command."

At this the king's voice rang:

                    "I so command—
as sure as it is I who, while I live,
rule the sea rovers of Phaiákia. Our friend   385
longs to put out for home, but let him be
content to rest here one more day, until
I see all gifts bestowed. And every man
will take thought for his launching and his voyage,
I most of all, for I am master here."   390

Odysseus, the great tactician, answered:

"Alkínoös, king and admiration of men,
even a year's delay, if you should urge it,
in loading gifts and furnishing for sea—
I too could wish it; better far that I   395
return with some largesse of wealth about me—
I shall be thought more worthy of love and courtesy
by every man who greets me home in Ithaka."

The king said:

3. Odysseus breaks off the story of his wanderings, and we are transported back to the scene of the banqueting hall of the Phaiákians.

"As to that, one word, Odysseus:
from all we see, we take you for no swindler—   400
though the dark earth be patient of so many,
scattered everywhere, baiting their traps with lies
of old times and of places no one knows.
You speak with art, but your intent is honest.
The Argive troubles, and your own troubles,   405
you told as a poet would, a man who knows the world.
But now come tell me this: among the dead
did you meet any of your peers, companions
who sailed with you and met their doom at Troy?
Here's a long night—an endless night—before us,   410
and no time yet for sleep, not in this hall.
Recall the past deeds and the strange adventures.
I could stay up until the sacred Dawn
as long as you might wish to tell your story."

Odysseus the great tactician answered: 415

"Alkínoös, king and admiration of men,
there is a time for story telling; there is
also a time for sleep. But even so,
if, indeed, listening be still your pleasure,
I must not grudge my part. Other and sadder   420
tales there are to tell, of my companions,
of some who came through all the Trojan spears,
clangor and groan of war,
only to find a brutal death at home—
and a bad wife behind it.

               After Perséphonê,   425
icy and pale, dispersed the shades of women,
the soul of Agamémnon, son of Atreus,
came before me, sombre in the gloom,
and others gathered round, all who were with him
when death and doom struck in Aegísthos' hall.   430
Sipping the black blood, the tall shade perceived me,
and cried out sharply, breaking into tears;
then tried to stretch his hands toward me, but could not,
being bereft of all the reach and power
he once felt in the great torque of his arms.   435
Gazing at him, and stirred, I wept for pity,
and spoke across to him:

               'O son of Atreus,
illustrious Lord Marshal, Agamémnon,
what was the doom that brought you low in death?
Were you at sea, aboard ship, and Poseidon   440
blew up a wicked squall to send you under,

or were you cattle-raiding on the mainland
or in a fight for some strongpoint, or women,
when the foe hit you to your mortal hurt?'

But he replied at once:

              'Son of Laërtês,   445
Odysseus, master of land ways and sea ways,
neither did I go down with some good ship
in any gale Poseidon blew, nor die
upon the mainland, hurt by foes in battle.
It was Aigísthos who designed my death,   450
he and my heartless wife, and killed me, after
feeding me, like an ox felled at the trough.
That was my miserable end—and with me
my fellows butchered, like so many swine
killed for some troop, or feast, or wedding banquet   455
in a great landholder's household. In your day
you have seen men, and hundreds, die in war,
in the bloody press, or downed in single combat,
but these were murders you would catch your breath at:
think of us fallen, all our throats cut, winebowl   460
brimming, tables laden on every side,
while blood ran smoking over the whole floor.
In my extremity I heard Kassandra,[4]
Priam's daughter, piteously crying
as the traitress Klytaimnéstra made to kill her   465
along with me. I heaved up from the ground
and got my hands around the blade, but she
eluded me, that whore. Nor would she close
my two eyes[5] as my soul swam to the underworld
or shut my lips. There is no being more fell,   470
more bestial than a wife in such an action,
and what an action that one planned!
The murder of her husband and her lord.
Great god, I thought my children and my slaves
at least would give me welcome. But that woman,   475
plotting a thing so low, defiled herself
and all her sex, all women yet to come,
even those few who may be virtuous.'

He paused then, and I answered:

              'Foul and dreadful.
That was the way that Zeus who views the wide world   480

---

4. She was part of Agamémnon's share of the booty at Troy.   5. I.e., give me a proper burial.

vented his hatred on the sons of Atreus—
intrigues of women, even from the start.
Myriads
died by Helen's fault, and Klytaimnéstra
plotted against you half the world away.'

And he at once said:

'Let it be a warning   485
even to you. Indulge a woman never,
and never tell her all you know. Some things
a man may tell, some he should cover up.
Not that I see a risk for you, Odysseus,
of death at your wife's hands. She is too wise,   490
too clear-eyed, sees alternatives too well,
Penélopê, Ikários' daughter—
that young bride whom we left behind—think of it!—
when we sailed off to war. The baby boy
still cradled at her breast—now he must be   495
a grown man, and a lucky one. By heaven,
you'll see him yet, and he'll embrace his father
with old fashioned respect, and rightly.
My own
lady never let me glut my eyes
on my own son, but bled me to death first.   500
One thing I will advise, on second thought;
stow it away and ponder it.
Land your ship
in secret on your island; give no warning.
The day of faithful wives is gone forever.

But tell me, have you any word at all   505
about my son's life? Gone to Orkhómenos
or sandy Pylos, can he be? Or waiting
with Meneláos in the plain of Sparta?
Death on earth has not yet taken Orestês.'

But I could only answer:

'Son of Atreus,   510
why do you ask these questions of me? Neither
news of home have I, nor news of him,
alive or dead. And empty words are evil.'

So we exchanged our speech, in bitterness,
weighed down by grief, and tears welled in our eyes,   515
when there appeared the spirit of Akhilleus,

son of Peleus; then Patróklos' shade,
and then Antílokhos,[6] and then Aias,
first among all the Danaans in strength
and bodily beauty, next to prince Akhilleus.   520
Now that great runner, grandson of Aíakhos,[7]
recognized me and called across to me:

'Son of Laërtês and the gods of old,
Odysseus, master mariner and soldier,
old knife, what next? What greater feat remains   525
for you to put your mind on, after this?
How did you find your way down to the dark
where these dimwitted dead are camped forever,
the after images of used-up men?'

                                I answered:

'Akhilleus, Peleus' son, strongest of all   530
among the Akhaians, I had need of foresight
such as Teirêsias alone could give
to help me, homeward bound for the crags of Ithaka.
I have not yet coasted Akhaia, not yet
touched my land; my life is all adversity.   535
But was there ever a man more blest by fortune
than you, Akhilleus? Can there ever be?
We ranked you with immortals in your lifetime,
we Argives did, and here your power is royal
among the dead men's shades. Think, then, Akhilleus: 540
you need not be so pained by death.'
                                To this
he answered swiftly:
                        'Let me hear no smooth talk
of death from you, Odysseus, light of councils.
Better, I say, to break sod as a farm hand
for some poor country man, on iron rations,   545
than lord it over all the exhausted dead.
Tell me, what news of the prince my son:[8] did he
come after me to make a name in battle
or could it be he did not? Do you know
if rank and honor still belong to Peleus   550
in the towns of the Myrmidons? Or now, may be,
Hellas and Phthia spurn him, seeing old age
fetters him, hand and foot. I cannot help him
under the sun's rays, cannot be that man
I was on Troy's wide seaboard, in those days   555
when I made bastion for the Argives

6. Son of Nestor.   7. Akhilleus.   8. Neoptólemos (the name means "new war").

and put an army's best men in the dust.
Were I but whole again, could I go now
to my father's house, one hour would do to make
my passion and my hands no man could hold   560
hateful to any who shoulder him aside.'

Now when he paused I answered:

                                'Of all that—
of Peleus' life, that is—I know nothing;
but happily I can tell you the whole story
of Neoptólemos, as you require.   565
In my own ship I brought him out from Skyros[9]
to join the Akhaians under arms.
                              And I can tell you,
in every council before Troy thereafter
your son spoke first and always to the point;
no one but Nestor and I could out-debate him.   570
And when we formed against the Trojan line
he never hung back in the mass, but ranged
far forward of his troops—no man could touch him
for gallantry. Aye, scores went down before him
in hard fights man to man. I shall not tell   575
all about each, or name them all—the long
roster of enemies he put out of action,
taking the shock of charges on the Argives.
But what a champion his lance ran through
in Eurýpulos[1] the son of Télephos! Keteians   580
in throngs around that captain also died—
all because Priam's gifts had won his mother
to send the lad to battle; and I thought
Memnon[2] alone in splendor ever outshone him.

But one fact more: while our picked Argive crew   585
still rode that hollow horse Epeios built,
and when the whole thing lay with me, to open
the trapdoor of the ambuscade or not,
at that point our Danaan lords and soldiers
wiped their eyes, and their knees began to quake,   590
all but Neoptólemos. I never saw
his tanned cheek change color or his hand
brush one tear away. Rather he prayed me,
hand on hilt, to sortie, and he gripped
his tough spear, bent on havoc for the Trojans.   595

9. The Greeks were told by a prophet that Troy would fall only to the son of Akhilleus, who was living
on the rocky island of Skyros.   1. He came to the aid of the Trojans with a fresh army. *Keteians:* The
people of Eurýpulos, from Asia Minor.   2. Son of the dawn goddess, King of the Ethiopians, and a
Trojan ally.

And when we had pierced and sacked Priam's tall city
he loaded his choice plunder and embarked
with no scar on him; not a spear had grazed him
nor the sword's edge in close work—common wounds
one gets in war. Arês in his mad fits   600
knows no favorites.'

      But I said no more,
for he had gone off striding the field of asphodel,
the ghost of our great runner, Akhilleus Aíákidês,[3]
glorying in what I told him of his son.

Now other souls of mournful dead stood by,   605
each with his troubled questioning, but one
remained alone, apart: the son of Télamon,
Aîas, it was—the great shade burning still
because I had won favor on the beachhead
in rivalry over Akhilleus' arms.[4]   610
The Lady Thetis, mother of Akhilleus,
laid out for us the dead man's battle gear,
and Trojan children, with Athena,
named the Danaan fittest to own them. Would
god I had not borne the palm that day!   615
For earth took Aîas then to hold forever,
the handsomest and, in all feats of war,
noblest of the Danaans after Akhilleus.
Gently therefore I called across to him:

'Aîas, dear son of royal Télamon,   620
you would not then forget, even in death,
your fury with me over those accurst
calamitous arms?—and so they were, a bane
sent by the gods upon the Argive host.
For when you died by your own hand we lost   625
a tower, formidable in war. All we Akhaians
mourn you forever, as we do Akhilleus;
and no one bears the blame but Zeus.
He fixed that doom for you because he frowned
on the whole expedition of our spearmen.   630
My lord, come nearer, listen to our story!
Conquer your indignation and your pride.'

But he gave no reply, and turned away,
following other ghosts toward Erebos.

3. Akhilleus is the son of Peleus, whose father was Aiakos.   4. After Akhilleus was killed by the Trojan
Paris, his mother Thetis offered his weapons as a prize to the Greek who had done most harm to the
Trojans. They were awarded to Odysseus. Ajax, after an attempt to kill Odysseus and the two kings,
Meneláos and Agamémnon, committed suicide.

Who knows if in that darkness he might still   635
have spoken, and I answered?
                       But my heart
longed, after this, to see the dead elsewhere.
And now there came before my eyes Minos,
the son of Zeus, enthroned, holding a golden staff,
dealing out justice among ghostly pleaders   640
arrayed about the broad doorways of Death.

And then I glimpsed Orion, the huge hunter,
gripping his club, studded with bronze, unbreakable,
with wild beasts he had overpowered in life
on lonely mountainsides, now brought to bay   645
on fields of asphodel.
                And I saw Títyos,
the son of Gaia, lying
abandoned over nine square rods of plain.
Vultures, hunched above him, left and right,
rifling his belly, stabbed into the liver,   650
and he could never push them off.
                    This hulk
had once committed rape of Zeus's mistress,
Léto, in her glory, when she crossed
the open grass of Panopeus toward Pytho.

Then I saw Tántalos[5] put to the torture: 655
in a cool pond he stood, lapped round by water
clear to the chin, and being athirst he burned
to slake his dry weasand with drink, though drink
he would not ever again. For when the old man
put his lips down to the sheet of water   660
it vanished round his feet, gulped underground,
and black mud baked there in a wind from hell.
Boughs, too, drooped low above him, big with fruit,
pear trees, pomegranates, brilliant apples,
luscious figs, and olives ripe and dark;   665
but if he stretched his hand for one, the wind
under the dark sky tossed the bough beyond him.

Then Sísyphos[6] in torment I beheld
being roustabout to a tremendous boulder.
Leaning with both arms braced and legs driving,   670
he heaved it toward a height, and almost over,
but then a Power spun him round and sent

5. King of Lydia. He was the confidant of the gods and ate at their table, but he betrayed their secrets.
6. King of Corinth, the archetype of the liar and trickster. We do not know what misdeed he is being punished for in this passage.

the cruel boulder bounding again to the plain.
Whereon the man bent down again to toil,
dripping sweat, and the dust rose overhead.   675
Next I saw manifest the power of Heraklês—
a phantom, this, for he himself has gone
feasting amid the gods, reclining soft
with Hêbê of the ravishing pale ankles,
daughter of Zeus and Hêra, shod in gold.   680
But, in my vision, all the dead around him
cried like affrighted birds; like Night itself
he loomed with naked bow and nocked arrow
and glances terrible as continual archery.
My hackles rose at the gold swordbelt he wore   685
sweeping across him: gorgeous intaglio
of savage bears, boars, lions with wildfire eyes,
swordfights, battle, slaughter, and sudden death—
the smith who had that belt in him, I hope
he never made, and never will make, another.   690
The eyes of the vast figure rested on me,
and of a sudden he said in kindly tones:

'Son of Laërtês and the gods of old,
Odysseus, master mariner and soldier,
under a cloud, you too? Destined to grinding   695
labors like my own in the sunny world?
Son of Kroníon Zeus or not, how many
days I sweated out, being bound in servitude
to a man far worse than I, a rough master!⁷
He made me hunt this place one time   700
to get the watchdog of the dead: no more
perilous task, he thought, could be; but I
brought back that beast, up from the underworld;
Hermês and grey-eyed Athena showed the way.'

And Heraklês, down the vistas of the dead,   705
faded from sight; but I stood fast, awaiting
other great souls who perished in times past.
I should have met, then, god-begotten Theseus⁸
and Peirithoös, whom both I longed to see,
but first came shades in thousands, rustling   710
in a pandemonium of whispers, blown together,
and the horror took me that Perséphonê
had brought from darker hell some saurian death's head.

7. Heraklês, son of Zeus, was made subject to the orders of Eurýstheus of Argos who ordered him to perform the twelve famous labors. One of them was to bring back from Hades the dog which guarded the gate.   8. After his adventures in Krete, he went with his friend Perithoös to Hades to kidnap Perséphonê; the venture failed, and the two heroes, imprisoned in Hades, were rescued by Heraklês.

I whirled then, made for the ship, shouted to crewmen
to get aboard and cast off the stern hawsers,   715
an order soon obeyed. They took their thwarts,
and the ship went leaping toward the stream of Ocean
first under oars, then with a following wind.

BOOK XII

Sea Perils and Defeat

The ship sailed on, out of the Ocean Stream,
riding a long swell on the open sea
for the Island of Aiaia.
              Summering Dawn
has dancing grounds there, and the Sun his rising;[9]
but still by night we beached on a sand shelf   5
and waded in beyond the line of breakers
to fall asleep, awaiting the Day Star.

When the young Dawn with finger tips of rose
made heaven bright, I sent shipmates to bring
Elpênor's body from the house of Kirkê.   10
We others cut down timber on the foreland,
on a high point, and built his pyre of logs,
then stood by weeping while the flame burnt through
corse and equipment.
              Then we heaped his barrow,
lifting a gravestone on the mound, and fixed   15
his light but unwarped oar against the sky.
These were our rites in memory of him. Soon, then,
knowing us back from the Dark Land, Kirkê came
freshly adorned for us, with handmaids bearing
loaves, roast meats, and ruby-colored wine.   20
She stood among us in immortal beauty
jesting:

      'Hearts of oak, did you go down
alive into the homes of Death? One visit
finishes all men but yourselves, twice mortal!
Come, here is meat and wine, enjoy your feasting   25
for one whole day; and in the dawn tomorrow
you shall put out to sea. Sailing directions,
landmarks, perils, I shall sketch for you, to keep you
from being caught by land or water
in some black sack of trouble.'

9. This places Kirkê's island in the east, whereas Odysseus' ship, when it was blown past Cape Malea, was
headed west. It is one more indication that Odyssean geography is highly imaginative.

In high humor   30
and ready for carousal, we agreed;
so all that day until the sun went down
we feasted on roast meat and good red wine,
till after sunset, at the fall of night,
the men dropped off to sleep by the stern hawsers.   35
She took my hand then, silent in that hush,
drew me apart, made me sit down, and lay
beside me, softly questioning, as I told
all I had seen, from first to last.
Then said the Lady Kirkê:

'So: all those trials are over.
Listen with care   40
to this, now, and a god will arm your mind.
Square in your ship's path are Seirênês,[1] crying
beauty to bewitch men coasting by;
woe to the innocent who hears that sound!
He will not see his lady nor his children   45
in joy, crowding about him, home from sea;
the Seirênês will sing his mind away
on their sweet meadow lolling. There are bones
of dead men rotting in a pile beside them
and flayed skins shrivel around the spot.
Steer wide;   50
keep well to seaward; plug your oarsmen's ears
with beeswax kneaded soft; none of the rest
should hear that song.
But if you wish to listen,
let the men tie you in the lugger, hand
and foot, back to the mast, lashed to the mast,   55
so you may hear those harpies' thrilling voices;
shout as you will, begging to be untied,
your crew must only twist more line around you
and keep their stroke up, till the singers fade.
What then? One of two courses you may take,   60
and you yourself must weigh them. I shall not
plan the whole action for you now, but only
tell you of both.
Ahead are beetling rocks
and dark blue glancing Amphitritê,[2] surging,
roars around them. Prowling Rocks,[3] or Drifters,   65
the gods in bliss have named them—named them well.

1. Sirens.   2. I.e., the sea.   3. Homer does not precisely identify them with the Symplegades, the
Clashing Rocks which came together and crushed whatever tried to pass between them. They were thought
of as located at the entrance to the Black Sea; the Argo passed safely through them on its way to the land
of the golden fleece. Homer's Prowling Rocks seem to be located, like Scylla and Charybdis, near the
straits between Sicily and Italy.

Not even birds can pass them by, not even
the timorous doves that bear ambrosia
to Father Zeus; caught by downdrafts, they die
on rockwall smooth as ice.
                    Each time, the Father   70
wafts a new courier to make up his crew.

Still less can ships get searoom of these Drifters,
whose boiling surf, under high fiery winds,
carries tossing wreckage of ships and men.
Only one ocean-going craft, the far-famed   75
Argo, made it, sailing from Aiêta;
but she, too, would have crashed on the big rocks
if Hêra had not pulled her through, for love
of Iêson, her captain.
                    A second course
lies between headlands. One is a sharp mountain   80
piercing the sky, with stormcloud round the peak
dissolving never, not in the brightest summer,
to show heaven's azure there, nor in the fall.
No mortal man could scale it, nor so much
as land there, not with twenty hands and feet,   85
so sheer the cliffs are—as of polished stone.
Midway that height, a cavern full of mist
opens toward Erebos and evening.[4] Skirting
this in the lugger, great Odysseus,
your master bowman, shooting from the deck,   90
would come short of the cavemouth with his shaft;
but that is the den of Skylla, where she yaps
abominably, a newborn whelp's cry,
though she is huge and monstrous. God or man,
no one could look on her in joy. Her legs—   95
and there are twelve—are like great tentacles,
unjointed, and upon her serpent necks
are borne six heads like nightmares of ferocity,
with triple serried rows of fangs and deep
gullets of black death. Half her length, she sways   100
her heads in air, outside her horrid cleft,
hunting the sea around that promontory
for dolphins, dogfish, or what bigger game
thundering Amphitritê feeds in thousands.
And no ship's company can claim   105
to have passed her without loss and grief; she takes,
from every ship, one man for every gullet.

4. I.e., northwest.

The opposite point seems more a tongue of land
you'd touch with a good bowshot, at the narrows.
A great wild fig, a shaggy mass of leaves,   110
grows on it, and Kharybdis lurks below
to swallow down the dark sea tide. Three times
from dawn to dusk she spews it up
and sucks it down again three times, a whirling
maelstrom; if you come upon her then   115
the god who makes earth tremble could not save you.
No, hug the cliff of Skylla, take your ship
through on a racing stroke. Better to mourn
six men than lose them all, and the ship, too.'

So her advice ran; but I faced her, saying: 120

'Only instruct me, goddess, if you will,
how, if possible, can I pass Kharybdis,
or fight off Skylla when she raids my crew?'

Swiftly that loveliest goddess answered me:

'Must you have battle in your heart forever?   125
The bloody toil of combat? Old contender,
will you not yield to the immortal gods?
That nightmare cannot die, being eternal
evil itself—horror, and pain, and chaos;
there is no fighting her, no power can fight her,   130
all that avails is flight.
                          Lose headway there
along that rockface while you break out arms,
and she'll swoop over you, I fear, once more,
taking one man again for every gullet.
No, no, put all your backs into it, row on;   135
invoke Blind Force, that bore this scourge of men,
to keep her from a second strike against you.

Then you will coast Thrinákia,[5] the island
where Hêlios' cattle graze, fine herds, and flocks
of goodly sheep. The herds and flocks are seven,   140
with fifty beasts in each.
                          No lambs are dropped,
or calves, and these fat cattle never die.
Immortal, too, their cowherds are—their shepherds—
Phaëthousa and Lampetía, sweetly braided
nymphs that divine Neaira bore   145
to the overlord of high noon, Hêlios.

5. Later Greeks identified this island as Sicily.

These nymphs their gentle mother bred and placed
upon Thrinákia, the distant land,
in care of flocks and cattle for their father.

Now give those kine a wide berth, keep your thoughts   150
intent upon your course for home,
and hard seafaring brings you all to Ithaka.
But if you raid the beeves, I see destruction
for ship and crew.
            Rough years then lie between
you and your homecoming, alone and old,   155
the one survivor, all companions lost.'

As Kirkê spoke, Dawn mounted her golden throne,
and on the first rays Kirkê left me, taking
her way like a great goddess up the island.
I made straight for the ship, roused up the men   160
to get aboard and cast off at the stern.
They scrambled to their places by the rowlocks
and all in line dipped oars in the grey sea.
But soon an off-shore breeze blew to our liking—
a canvas-bellying breeze, a lusty shipmate   165
sent by the singing nymph with sunbright hair.
So we made fast the braces, and we rested,
letting the wind and steersman work the ship.
The crew being now silent before me, I
addressed them, sore at heart:
                        'Dear friends,   170
more than one man, or two, should know those things
Kirkê foresaw for us and shared with me,
so let me tell her forecast: then we die
with our eyes open, if we are going to die,
or know what death we baffle if we can. Seirênês   175
weaving a haunting song over the sea
we are to shun, she said, and their green shore
all sweet with clover; yet she urged that I
alone should listen to their song. Therefore
you are to tie me up, tight as a splint,   180
erect along the mast, lashed to the mast,
and if I shout and beg to be untied,
take more turns of the rope to muffle me.'

I rather dwelt on this part of the forecast,
while our good ship made time, bound outward down   185
the wind for the strange island of Seirênês.
Then all at once the wind fell, and a calm

came over all the sea, as though some power
lulled the swell.
          The crew were on their feet
briskly, to furl the sail, and stow it; then,   190
each in place, they poised the smooth oar blades
and sent the white foam scudding by. I carved
a massive cake of beeswax into bits
and rolled them in my hands until they softened—
no long task, for a burning heat came down   195
from Hêlios, lord of high noon. Going forward
I carried wax along the line, and laid it
thick on their ears. They tied me up, then, plumb
amidships, back to the mast, lashed to the mast,
and took themselves again to rowing. Soon,   200
as we came smartly within hailing distance,
the two Seirênês, noting our fast ship
off their point, made ready, and they sang:

> *This way, oh turn your bows,*[6]
> *Akhaia's glory,*   205
> *As all the world allows—*
> *Moor and be merry.*
>
> *Sweet coupled airs we sing.*
> *No lonely seafarer*
> *Holds clear of entering*   210
> *Our green mirror.*
>
> *Pleased by each purling note*
> *Like honey twining*
> *From her throat and my throat,*
> *Who lies a-pining?*   215
>
> *Sea rovers here take joy*
> *Voyaging onward,*
> *As from our song of Troy*
> *Greybeard and rower-boy*
> *Goeth more learnèd.*   220
>
> *All feats on that great field*
> *In the long warfare,*
> *Dark days the bright gods willed,*
> *Wounds you bore there,*

6. Fitzgerald has turned the eight unrhymed lines of the original into a lyric poem. Here is a prose version of the Greek: "Draw near, illustrious Odysseus, flower of Akhaian chivalry, and bring your ship to rest so that you may hear our voices. No seaman ever sailed his black ship past this spot without listening to the sweet tones that flow from our lips, and none that has listened has not been delighted and gone on a wiser man. For we know all that the Argives and Trojans suffered on the broad plain of Troy by the will of the gods, and we have foreknowledge of all that is going to happen on this fruitful earth."

Argos' old soldiery   225
On Troy beach teeming,
Charmed out of time we see.
No life on earth can be
Hid from our dreaming.

The lovely voices in ardor appealing over the water   230
made me crave to listen, and I tried to say
'Untie me!' to the crew, jerking my brows;
but they bent steady to the oars. Then Perimêdês
got to his feet, he and Eurýlokhos,
and passed more line about, to hold me still.   235
So all rowed on, until the Seirênês
dropped under the sea rim, and their singing
dwindled away.

        My faithful company
rested on their oars now, peeling off
the wax that I had laid thick on their ears;   240
then set me free.

        But scarcely had that island
faded in blue air than I saw smoke
and white water, with sound of waves in tumult—
a sound the men heard, and it terrified them.
Oars flew from their hands; the blades went knocking   245
wild alongside till the ship lost way,
with no oarblades to drive her through the water.

Well, I walked up and down from bow to stern,
trying to put heart into them, standing over
every oarsman, saying gently,

               'Friends,   250
have we never been in danger before this?
More fearsome, is it now, than when the Kyklops
penned us in his cave? What power he had!
Did I not keep my nerve, and use my wits
to find a way out for us?

        Now I say   255
by hook or crook this peril too shall be
something that we remember.

            Heads up, lads!
We must obey the orders as I give them.
Get the oarshafts in your hands, and lay back
hard on your benches; hit these breaking seas.   260
Zeus help us pull away before we founder.
You at the tiller, listen, and take in
all that I say—the rudders are your duty;

keep her out of the combers and the smoke;
steer for that headland; watch the drift, or we
fetch up in the smother, and you drown us.' 265

That was all, and it brought them round to action.
But as I sent them on toward Skylla, I
told them nothing, as they could do nothing.
They would have dropped their oars again, in panic, 270
to roll for cover under the decking. Kirkê's
bidding against arms had slipped my mind,
so I tied on my cuirass and took up
two heavy spears, then made my way along
to the foredeck—thinking to see her first from there, 275
the monster of the grey rock, harboring
torment for my friends. I strained my eyes
upon that cliffside veiled in cloud, but nowhere
could I catch sight of her.
                          And all this time,
in travail, sobbing, gaining on the current, 280
we rowed into the strait—Skylla to port
and on our starboard beam Kharybdis, dire
gorge of the salt sea tide. By heaven! when she
vomited, all the sea was like a cauldron
seething over intense fire, when the mixture 285
suddenly heaves and rises.
                          The shot spume
soared to the landside heights, and fell like rain.

But when she swallowed the sea water down
we saw the funnel of the maelstrom, heard
the rock bellowing all around, and dark 290
sand raged on the bottom far below.
My men all blanched against the gloom, our eyes
were fixed upon that yawning mouth in fear
of being devoured.
                  Then Skylla made her strike,
whisking six of my best men from the ship. 295
I happened to glance aft at ship and oarsmen
and caught sight of their arms and legs, dangling
high overhead. Voices came down to me
in anguish, calling my name for the last time.

A man surfcasting on a point of rock 300
for bass or mackerel, whipping his long rod
to drop the sinker and the bait far out,
will hook a fish and rip it from the surface
to dangle wriggling through the air:

                         so these
were borne aloft in spasms toward the cliff.   305

She ate them as they shrieked there, in her den,
in the dire grapple, reaching still for me—
and deathly pity ran me through
at that sight—far the worst I ever suffered,
questing the passes of the strange sea.
                              We rowed on.   310
The Rocks were now behind; Kharybdis, too,
and Skylla dropped astern.
                         Then we were coasting
the noble island of the god, where grazed
those cattle with wide brows, and bounteous flocks
of Hêlios, lord of noon, who rides high heaven.   315

From the black ship, far still at sea, I heard
the lowing of the cattle winding home
and sheep bleating; and heard, too, in my heart
the words of blind Teirêsias of Thebes
and Kirkê of Aiaia: both forbade me   320
the island of the world's delight, the Sun.
So I spoke out in gloom to my companions:

'Shipmates, grieving and weary though you are,
listen: I had forewarning from Teirêsias
and Kirkê, too; both told me I must shun   325
this island of the Sun, the world's delight.
Nothing but fatal trouble shall we find here.
Pull away, then, and put the land astern.'

That strained them to the breaking point, and, cursing,
Eurýlokhos cried out in bitterness: 330

'Are you flesh and blood, Odysseus, to endure
more than a man can? Do you never tire?
God, look at you, iron is what you're made of.
Here we all are, half dead with weariness,
falling asleep over the oars, and you   335
say "No landing"—no firm island earth
where we could make a quiet supper. No:
pull out to sea, you say, with night upon us—
just as before, but wandering now, and lost.
Sudden storms can rise at night and swamp   340
ships without a trace.
                    Where is your shelter
if some stiff gale blows up from south or west—
the winds that break up shipping every time

when seamen flout the lord gods' will? I say
do as the hour demands and go ashore   345
before black night comes down.
                              We'll make our supper
alongside, and at dawn put out to sea.'

Now when the rest said 'Aye' to this, I saw
the power of destiny devising ill.
Sharply I answered, without hesitation: 350

'Eurýlokhos, they are with you to a man.
I am alone, outmatched.
                        Let this whole company
swear me a great oath: Any herd of cattle
or flock of sheep here found shall go unharmed;
no one shall slaughter out of wantonness   355
ram or heifer; all shall be content
with what the goddess Kirkê put aboard.'

They fell at once to swearing as I ordered,
and when the round of oaths had ceased, we found
a halfmoon bay to beach and moor the ship in,   360
with a fresh spring nearby. All hands ashore
went about skillfully getting up a meal.
Then, after thirst and hunger, those besiegers,
were turned away, they mourned for their companions
plucked from the ship by Skylla and devoured,   365
and sleep came soft upon them as they mourned.

In the small hours of the third watch, when stars
that shone out in the first dusk of evening
had gone down to their setting, a giant wind
blew from heaven, and clouds driven by Zeus   370
shrouded land and sea in a night of storm;
so, just as Dawn with finger tips of rose
touched the windy world, we dragged our ship
to cover in a grotto, a sea cave
where nymphs had chairs of rock and sanded floors.   375
I mustered all the crew and said:

                              'Old shipmates,
our stores are in the ship's hold, food and drink;
the cattle here are not for our provision,
or we pay dearly for it.
                        Fierce the god is
who cherishes these heifers and these sheep: 380
Hêlios; and no man avoids his eye.'

To this my fighters nodded. Yes. But now
we had a month of onshore gales, blowing
day in, day out—south winds, or south by east.
As long as bread and good red wine remained   385
to keep the men up, and appease their craving,
they would not touch the cattle. But in the end,
when all the barley in the ship was gone,
hunger drove them to scour the wild shore
with angling hooks, for fishes and sea fowl,   390
whatever fell into their hands; and lean days
wore their bellies thin.

                The storms continued.
So one day I withdrew to the interior
to pray the gods in solitude, for hope
that one might show me some way of salvation.   395
Slipping away, I struck across the island
to a sheltered spot, out of the driving gale.
I washed my hands there, and made supplication
to the gods who own Olympos, all the gods—
but they, for answer, only closed my eyes   400
under slow drops of sleep.
                Now on the shore Eurýlokhos
made his insidious plea:

                'Comrades,' he said,
'You've gone through everything; listen to what I say.
All deaths are hateful to us, mortal wretches,
but famine is the most pitiful, the worst   405
end that a man can come to.
                Will you fight it?
Come, we'll cut out the noblest of these cattle
for sacrifice to the gods who own the sky;
and once at home, in the old country of Ithaka,
if ever that day comes—   410
we'll build a costly temple and adorn it
with every beauty for the Lord of Noon.
But if he flares up over his heifers lost,
wishing our ship destroyed, and if the gods
make cause with him, why, then I say: Better   415
open your lungs to a big sea once for all
than waste to skin and bones on a lonely island!'

Thus Eurýlokhos; and they murmured 'Aye!'
trooping away at once to round up heifers.
Now, that day tranquil cattle with broad brows   420

were grazing near, and soon the men drew up
around their chosen beasts in ceremony.
They plucked the leaves that shone on a tall oak—
having no barley meal—to strew the victims,
performed the prayers and ritual, knifed the kine   425
and flayed each carcass, cutting thighbones free
to wrap in double folds of fat. These offerings,
with strips of meat, were laid upon the fire.
Then, as they had no wine, they made libation
with clear spring water, broiling the entrails first;   430
and when the bones were burnt and tripes shared,
they spitted the carved meat.

                          Just then my slumber
left me in a rush, my eyes opened,
and I went down the seaward path. No sooner
had I caught sight of our black hull, than savory   435
odors of burnt fat eddied around me;
grief took hold of me, and I cried aloud:

'O Father Zeus and gods in bliss forever,
you made me sleep away this day of mischief!
O cruel drowsing, in the evil hour!   440
Here they sat, and a great work they contrived.'

Lampetía in her long gown meanwhile
had borne swift word to the Overlord of Noon:

'They have killed your kine.'

                    And the Lord Hêlios
burst into angry speech amid the immortals: 445

'O Father Zeus and gods in bliss forever,
punish Odysseus' men! So overweening,
now they have killed my peaceful kine, my joy
at morning when I climbed the sky of stars,
and evening, when I bore westward from heaven.   450
Restitution or penalty they shall pay—
and pay in full—or I go down forever
to light the dead men in the underworld.'

Then Zeus who drives the stormcloud made reply:

'Peace, Hêlios: shine on among the gods,   455
shine over mortals in the fields of grain.
Let me throw down one white-hot bolt, and make
splinters of their ship in the winedark sea.'

—Kalypso later told me of this exchange,
as she declared that Hermês had told her.   460
Well, when I reached the sea cave and the ship,
I faced each man, and had it out; but where
could any remedy be found? There was none.
The silken beeves of Hêlios were dead.
The gods, moreover, made queer signs appear: 465
cowhides began to crawl, and beef, both raw
and roasted, lowed like kine upon the spits.

Now six full days my gallant crew could feast
upon the prime beef they had marked for slaughter
from Hêlios' herd; and Zeus, the son of Kronos,   470
added one fine morning.
                    All the gales
had ceased, blown out, and with an offshore breeze
we launched again, stepping the mast and sail,
to make for the open sea. Astern of us
the island coastline faded, and no land   475
showed anywhere, but only sea and heaven,
when Zeus Kroníon piled a thunderhead
above the ship, while gloom spread on the ocean.
We held our course, but briefly. Then the squall
struck whining from the west, with gale force, breaking   480
both forestays, and the mast came toppling aft
along the ship's length, so the running rigging
showered into the bilge.
                    On the after deck
the mast had hit the steersman a slant blow
bashing the skull in, knocking him overside,   485
as the brave soul fled the body, like a diver.
With crack on crack of thunder, Zeus let fly
a bolt against the ship, a direct hit,
so that she bucked, in reeking fumes of sulphur,
and all the men were flung into the sea.   490
They came up 'round the wreck, bobbing a while
like petrels on the waves.
                    No more seafaring
homeward for these, no sweet day of return;
the god had turned his face from them.
                             I clambered
fore and aft my hulk until a comber   495
split her, keel from ribs, and the big timber
floated free; the mast, too, broke away.
A backstay floated dangling from it, stout
rawhide rope, and I used this for lashing

mast and keel together. These I straddled,   500
riding the frightful storm.
                Nor had I yet
seen the worst of it: for now the west wind
dropped, and a southeast gale came on—one more
twist of the knife—taking me north again,
straight for Kharybdis. All that night I drifted,   505
and in the sunrise, sure enough, I lay
off Skylla mountain and Kharybdis deep.
There, as the whirlpool drank the tide, a billow
tossed me, and I sprang for the great fig tree,
catching on like a bat under a bough.   510
Nowhere had I to stand, no way of climbing,
the root and bole being far below, and far
above my head the branches and their leaves,
massed, overshadowing Kharybdis' pool.
But I clung grimly, thinking my mast and keel   515
would come back to the surface when she spouted.
And ah! how long, with what desire, I waited!
till, at the twilight hour, when one who hears
and judges pleas in the marketplace all day
between contentious men, goes home to supper,   520
the long poles at last reared from the sea.

Now I let go with hands and feet, plunging
straight into the foam beside the timbers,
pulled astride, and rowed hard with my hands
to pass by Skylla. Never could I have passed her   525
had not the Father of gods and men, this time,
kept me from her eyes. Once through the strait,
nine days I drifted in the open sea
before I made shore, buoyed up by the gods,
upon Ogýgia Isle. The dangerous nymph   530
Kalypso lives and sings there, in her beauty,
and she received me, loved me.
                But why tell
the same tale that I told last night in hall
to you and to your lady? Those adventures
made a long evening, and I do not hold   535
with tiresome repetition of a story."

BOOK XIII

One More Strange Island

He ended it, and no one stirred or sighed
in the shadowy hall, spellbound as they all were,
until Alkínoös answered:

"When you came
here to my strong home, Odysseus, under
my tall roof, headwinds were left behind you.   5
Clear sailing shall you have now, homeward now,
however painful all the past.
                                My lords,
ever my company, sharing the wine of Council,
the songs of the blind harper, hear me further:
garments are folded for our guest and friend   10
in the smooth chest, and gold
in various shaping of adornment lies
with other gifts, and many, brought by our peers;
let each man add his tripod and deep-bellied
cauldron: we'll make levy upon the realm   15
to pay us for the loss each bears in this."

Alkínoös had voiced their own hearts' wish.
All gave assent, then home they went to rest;
but young Dawn's finger tips of rose, touching
the world, roused them to make haste to the ship,   20
each with his gift of noble bronze. Alkínoös,
their ardent king, stepping aboard himself,
directed the stowing under the cross planks,
not to cramp the long pull of the oarsmen.
Going then to the great hall, lords and crew   25
prepared for feasting.
                        As the gods' anointed,
Alkínoös made offering on their behalf—an ox
to Zeus beyond the stormcloud, Kronos' son,
who rules the world. They burnt the great thighbones
and feasted at their ease on fresh roast meat,   30
as in their midst the godlike harper sang—
Demódokos, honored by all that realm.
                                Only Odysseus
time and again turned craning toward the sun,
impatient for day's end, for the open sea.
Just as a farmer's hunger grows, behind   35
the bolted plow and share, all day afield,
drawn by his team of winedark oxen: sundown
is benison for him, sending him homeward
stiff in the knees from weariness, to dine;
just so, the light on the sea rim gladdened Odysseus,   40
and as it dipped he stood among the Phaiákians,
turned to Alkínoös, and said:

"O king and admiration of your people,
give me fare well, and stain the ground with wine;

my blessings on you all! This hour brings   45
fulfillment to the longing of my heart:
a ship for home, and gifts the gods of heaven
make so precious and so bountiful.
                                    After this voyage
god grant I find my own wife in my hall
with everyone I love best, safe and sound!   50
And may you, settled in your land, give joy
to wives and children; may the gods reward you
every way, and your realm be free of woe."

Then all the voices rang out, "Be it so!"
and "Well spoken!" and "Let our friend make sail!"   55

Whereon Alkínoös gave command to his crier:

"Fill the winebowl, Pontónoös: mix and serve:
go the whole round, so may this company
invoke our Father Zeus, and bless our friend,
seaborne tonight and bound for his own country."   60

Pontónoös mixed the honey-hearted wine
and went from chair to chair, filling the cups;
then each man where he sat poured out his offering
to the gods in bliss who own the sweep of heaven.
With gentle bearing Odysseus rose, and placed   65
his double goblet in Arêtê's hands,
saying:

        "Great Queen, farewell;
be blest through all your days till age comes on you,
and death, last end for mortals, after age.
Now I must go my way. Live in felicity,   70
and make this palace lovely for your children,
your countrymen, and your king, Alkínoös."

Royal Odysseus turned and crossed the door sill,
a herald at his right hand, sent by Alkínoös
to lead him to the sea beach and the ship.   75
Arêtê, too, sent maids in waiting after him,
one with a laundered great cloak and a tunic,
a second balancing the crammed sea chest,
a third one bearing loaves and good red wine.
As soon as they arrived alongside, crewmen   80
took these things for stowage under the planks,
their victualling and drink; then spread a rug
and linen cover on the after deck,
where Lord Odysseus might sleep in peace.

Now he himself embarked, lay down, lay still,   85
while oarsmen took their places at the rowlocks
all in order. They untied their hawser,
passing it through a drilled stone ring; then bent
forward at the oars and caught the sea
as one man, stroking.
                      Slumber, soft and deep   90
like the still sleep of death, weighed on his eyes
as the ship hove seaward.
                         How a four horse team
whipped into a run on a straightaway
consumes the road, surging and surging over it!
So ran that craft and showed her heels to the swell,   95
her bow wave riding after, and her wake
on the purple night-sea foaming.
                               Hour by hour
she held her pace; not even a falcon wheeling
downwind, swiftest bird, could stay abreast of her
in that most arrowy flight through open water,   100
with her great passenger—godlike in counsel,
he that in twenty years had borne such blows
in his deep heart, breaking through ranks in war
and waves on the bitter sea.
                           This night at last
he slept serene, his long-tried mind at rest.   105

When on the East the sheer bright star arose
that tells of coming Dawn, the ship made landfall
and came up islandward in the dim of night.
Phorkys, the old sea baron, has a cove
here in the realm of Ithaka; two points   110
of high rock, breaking sharply, hunch around it,
making a haven from the plunging surf
that gales at sea roll shoreward. Deep inside,
at mooring range, good ships can ride unmoored.
There, on the inmost shore, an olive tree   115
throws wide its boughs over the bay; nearby
a cave of dusky light is hidden
for those immortal girls, the Naiadês.[7]
Within are winebowls hollowed in the rock
and amphorai; bees bring their honey here;   120
and there are looms of stone, great looms, whereon
the weaving nymphs make tissues, richly dyed
as the deep sea is; and clear springs in the cavern
flow forever. Of two entrances,

7. Nymphs of lake, river, and stream.

one on the north allows descent of mortals,   125
but beings out of light alone, the undying,
can pass by the south slit; no men come there.

This cove the sailors knew. Here they drew in,
and the ship ran half her keel's length up the shore,
she had such way on her from those great oarsmen.   130
Then from their benches forward on dry ground
they disembarked. They hoisted up Odysseus
unruffled on his bed, under his cover,
handing him overside still fast asleep,
to lay him on the sand; and they unloaded   135
all those gifts the princes of Phaiákia
gave him, when by Athena's heart and will
he won his passage home. They bore this treasure
off the beach, and piled it close around
the roots of the olive tree, that no one passing   140
should steal Odysseus' gear before he woke.
That done, they pulled away on the homeward track.

But now the god that shakes the islands, brooding
over old threats of his against Odysseus,
approached Lord Zeus to learn his will. Said he: 145

"Father of gods, will the bright immortals ever
pay me respect again, if mortals do not?—
Phaiákians, too, my own blood kin?
                              I thought
Odysseus should in time regain his homeland;
I had no mind to rob him of that day—   150
no, no; you promised it, being so inclined;
only I thought he should be made to suffer
all the way.
              But now these islanders
have shipped him homeward, sleeping soft, and put him
on Ithaka, with gifts untold   155
of bronze and gold, and fine cloth to his shoulder.
Never from Troy had he borne off such booty
if he had got home safe with all his share."

Then Zeus who drives the stormcloud answered, sighing:

"God of horizons, making earth's underbeam   160
tremble, why do you grumble so?
The immortal gods show you no less esteem,
and the rough consequence would make them slow
to let barbs fly at their eldest and most noble.
But if some mortal captain, overcome   165

by his own pride of strength, cuts or defies you,
are you not always free to take reprisal?
Act as your wrath requires and as you will."

Now said Poseidon, god of earthquake:

                                        "Aye,
god of the stormy sky, I should have taken   170
vengeance, as you say, and on my own;
but I respect, and would avoid, your anger.
The sleek Phaiákian cutter, even now,
has carried out her mission and glides home
over the misty sea. Let me impale her,   175
end her voyage, and end all ocean-crossing
with passengers, then heave a mass of mountain
in a ring around the city."

Now Zeus who drives the stormcloud said benignly:

"Here is how I should do it, little brother: 180
when all who watch upon the wall have caught
sight of the ship, let her be turned to stone—
an island like a ship, just off the bay.
Mortals may gape at that for generations!
But throw no mountain round the sea port city."[8]   185

When he heard this, Poseidon, god of earthquake,
departed for Skhería, where the Phaiákians
are born and dwell. Their ocean-going ship
he saw already near, heading for harbor;
so up behind her swam the island-shaker   190
and struck her into stone, rooted in stone, at one
blow of his palm,
                    then took to the open sea.
Those famous ship handlers, the Phaiákians,
gazed at each other, murmuring in wonder;
you could have heard one say:

                        "Now who in thunder   195
has anchored, moored that ship in the seaway,
when everyone could see her making harbor?"

The god had wrought a charm beyond their thought.
But soon Alkínoös made them hush, and told them:

8. This translates a correction of the text made in antiquity by the Alexandrian scholar Aristophanes of
Byzantium. But another great Alexandrian scholar, Aristarchus, defended the original text, which means
"and throw a big mountain round." Zeus, in other words, approved of Poseidon's intention to cut the
Phaiákians off from the sea altogether, and adds the proposal to turn the ship into a rock. It is a difficult
question to decide, since Homer does not tell us what happened to the Phaiákians in the end.

"This present doom upon the ship—on me— 200
my father prophesied in the olden time.
If we gave safe conveyance to all passengers
we should incur Poseidon's wrath, he said,
whereby one day a fair ship, manned by Phaiákians,
would come to grief at the god's hands; and great 205
mountains would hide our city from the sea.
So my old father forecast.
                              Use your eyes:
these things are even now being brought to pass.
Let all here abide by my decree:
                                  We make
an end henceforth of taking, in our ships, 210
castaways who may land upon Skhería;
and twelve choice bulls we dedicate at once
to Lord Poseidon, praying him of his mercy
not to heave up a mountain round our city."

In fearful awe they led the bulls to sacrifice 215
and stood about the altar stone, those captains,
peers of Phaiákia, led by their king in prayer
to Lord Poseidon.

                  Meanwhile, on his island,
his father's shore, that kingly man, Odysseus,
awoke, but could not tell what land it was 220
after so many years away; moreover,
Pallas Athena, Zeus's daughter, poured
a grey mist all around him, hiding him
from common sight—for she had things to tell him
and wished no one to know him, wife or townsmen, 225
before the suitors paid up for their crimes.

The landscape then looked strange, unearthly strange
to the Lord Odysseus: paths by hill and shore,
glimpses of harbors, cliffs, and summer trees.
He stood up, rubbed his eyes, gazed at his homeland, 230
and swore, slapping his thighs with both his palms,
then cried aloud:

                  "What am I in for now?
Whose country have I come to this time? Rough
savages and outlaws, are they, or
godfearing people, friendly to castaways? 235
Where shall I take these things? Where take myself,
with no guide, no directions? These should be

still in Phaiákian hands, and I uncumbered,
free to find some other openhearted
prince who might be kind and give me passage.   240
I have no notion where to store this treasure;
first-comer's trove it is, if I leave it here.

My lords and captains of Phaiákia
were not those decent men they seemed, not honorable,
landing me in this unknown country—no,   245
by god, they swore to take me home to Ithaka
and did not! Zeus attend to their reward,
Zeus, patron of petitioners, who holds
all other mortals under his eye; he takes
payment from betrayers!
                              I'll be busy.   250
I can look through my gear. I shouldn't wonder
if they pulled out with part of it on board."

He made a tally of his shining pile—
tripods, cauldrons, cloaks, and gold—and found
he lacked nothing at all.
                              And then he wept,   255
despairing, for his own land, trudging down
beside the endless wash of the wide, wide sea,
weary and desolate as the sea. But soon
Athena came to him from the nearby air,
putting a young man's figure on—a shepherd,   260
like a king's son, all delicately made.
She wore a cloak, in two folds off her shoulders,
and sandals bound upon her shining feet.
A hunting lance lay in her hands.
                              At sight of her
Odysseus took heart, and he went forward   265
to greet the lad, speaking out fair and clear:

"Friend, you are the first man I've laid eyes on
here in this cove. Greetings. Do not feel
alarmed or hostile, coming across me; only
receive me into safety with my stores.   270
Touching your knees I ask it, as I might
ask grace of a god.
                              O sir, advise me,
what is this land and realm, who are the people?
Is it an island all distinct, or part
of the fertile mainland, sloping to the sea?"   275

To this grey-eyed Athena answered:

"Stranger,
you must come from the other end of nowhere,
else you are a great booby, having to ask
what place this is. It is no nameless country.
Why, everyone has heard of it, the nations   280
over on the dawn side, toward the sun,
and westerners in cloudy lands of evening.
No one would use this ground for training horses,
it is too broken, has no breadth of meadow;
but there is nothing meager about the soil,   285
the yield of grain is wondrous, and wine, too,
with drenching rains and dewfall.
     There's good pasture
for oxen and for goats, all kinds of timber,
and water all year long in the cattle ponds.
For these blessings, friend, the name of Ithaka   290
has made its way even as far as Troy—
and they say Troy lies far beyond Akhaia."

Now Lord Odysseus, the long-enduring,
laughed in his heart, hearing his land described
by Pallas Athena, daughter of Zeus who rules   295
the veering stormwind; and he answered her
with ready speech—not that he told the truth,
but, just as she did, held back what he knew,
weighing within himself at every step
what he made up to serve his turn.

       Said he: 300

"Far away in Krete I learned of Ithaka—
in that broad island over the great ocean.
And here I am now, come myself to Ithaka!
Here is my fortune with me. I left my sons
an equal part, when I shipped out. I killed   305
Orsílokhos, the courier, son of Idómeneus.
This man could beat the best cross country runners
in Krete, but he desired to take away
my Trojan plunder, all I had fought and bled for,
cutting through ranks in war and the cruel sea.   310
Confiscation is what he planned; he knew
I had not cared to win his father's favor
as a staff officer in the field at Troy,
but led my own command.
      I acted: I
hit him with a spearcast from a roadside   315
as he came down from the open country. Murky

night shrouded all heaven and the stars.
I made that ambush with one man at arms.
We were unseen. I took his life in secret,
finished him off with my sharp sword. That night   320
I found asylum on a ship off shore
skippered by gentlemen of Phoinikia;[9] I gave
all they could wish, out of my store of plunder,
for passage, and for landing me at Pylos
or Elis Town,[1] where the Epeioi are in power.   325
Contrary winds carried them willy-nilly
past that coast; they had no wish to cheat me,
but we were blown off course.
                          Here, then, by night
we came, and made this haven by hard rowing.
All famished, but too tired to think of food,   330
each man dropped in his tracks after the landing,
and I slept hard, being wearied out. Before
I woke today, they put my things ashore
on the sand here beside me where I lay,
then reimbarked for Sidon, that great city.   335
Now they are far at sea, while I am left
forsaken here."

          At this the grey-eyed goddess
Athena smiled, and gave him a caress,
her looks being changed now, so she seemed a woman,
tall and beautiful and no doubt skilled   340
at weaving splendid things. She answered briskly:

"Whoever gets around you must be sharp
and guileful as a snake; even a god
might bow to you in ways of dissimulation.
You! You chameleon!   345
Bottomless bag of tricks! Here in your own country
would you not give your stratagems a rest
or stop spellbinding for an instant?

You play a part as if it were your own tough skin.

No more of this, though. Two of a kind, we are,   350
contrivers, both. Of all men now alive
you are the best in plots and story telling.
My own fame is for wisdom among the gods—
deceptions, too.
          Would even you have guessed
that I am Pallas Athena, daughter of Zeus,   355

9. Phoenicia.   1. In the Western Peloponnese. *Epeioi:* The local tribe.

I that am always with you in times of trial,
a shield to you in battle, I who made
the Phaiákians befriend you, to a man?
Now I am here again to counsel with you—
but first to put away those gifts the Phaiákians   360
gave you at departure—I planned it so.
Then I can tell you of the gall and wormwood
it is your lot to drink in your own hall.
Patience, iron patience, you must show;
so give it out to neither man nor woman   365
that you are back from wandering. Be silent
under all injuries, even blows from men."

His mind ranging far, Odysseus answered:

"Can mortal man be sure of you on sight,
even a sage, O mistress of disguises?   370
Once you were fond of me—I am sure of that—
years ago, when we Akhaians made
war, in our generation, upon Troy.
But after we had sacked the shrines of Priam
and put to sea, God scattered the Akhaians;   375
I never saw you after that, never
knew you aboard with me, to act as shield
in grievous times—not till you gave me comfort
in the rich hinterland of the Phaiákians
and were yourself my guide into that city.   380

Hear me now in your father's name, for I
cannot believe that I have come to Ithaka.
It is some other land. You made that speech
only to mock me, and to take me in.
Have I come back in truth to my home island?"   385

To this the grey-eyed goddess Athena answered:

"Always the same detachment! That is why
I cannot fail you, in your evil fortune,
coolheaded, quick, well-spoken as you are!
Would not another wandering man, in joy,   390
make haste home to his wife and children? Not
you, not yet. Before you hear their story
you will have proof about your wife.
                    I tell you,
she still sits where you left her, and her days
and nights go by forlorn, in lonely weeping.   395
For my part, never had I despaired; I felt
sure of your coming home, though all your men

should perish; but I never cared to fight
Poseidon, Father's brother, in his baleful
rage with you for taking his son's eye.   400

Now I shall make you see the shape of Ithaka.
Here is the cove the sea lord Phorkys owns,
there is the olive spreading out her leaves
over the inner bay, and there the cavern
dusky and lovely, hallowed by the feet   405
of those immortal girls, the Naiadês—
the same wide cave under whose vault you came
to honor them with hekatombs—and there
Mount Neion, with his forest on his back!"

She had dispelled the mist, so all the island   410
stood out clearly. Then indeed Odysseus'
heart stirred with joy. He kissed the earth,
and lifting up his hands he prayed to the nymphs:

"O slim shy Naiadês, young maids of Zeus,
I had not thought to see you ever again!
                              O listen smiling   415
to my gentle prayers, and we'll make offering
plentiful as in the old time, granted I
live, granted my son grows tall, by favor
of great Athena, Zeus's daughter,
who gives the winning fighter his reward!"   420

The grey-eyed goddess said directly:

                              "Courage;
and let the future trouble you no more.
We go to make a cache now, in the cave,
to keep your treasure hid. Then we'll consider
how best the present action may unfold."   425

The goddess turned and entered the dim cave,
exploring it for crannies, while Odysseus
carried up all the gold, the fire-hard bronze,
and well-made clothing the Phaiákians gave him.
Pallas Athena, daughter of Zeus the storm king,   430
placed them, and shut the cave mouth with a stone,
and under the old grey olive tree those two
sat down to work the suitors death and woe.
Grey-eyed Athena was the first to speak, saying:

"Son of Laërtês and the gods of old,   435
Odysseus, master of land ways and sea ways,
put your mind on a way to reach and strike
a crowd of brazen upstarts.

                              Three long years
they have played master in your house: three years
trying to win your lovely lady, making   440
gifts as though betrothed. And she? Forever
grieving for you, missing your return,
she has allowed them all to hope, and sent
messengers with promises to each—
though her true thoughts are fixed elsewhere."

                                        At this   445
the man of ranging mind, Odysseus, cried:

"So hard beset! An end like Agamémnon's
might very likely have been mine, a bad end,
bleeding to death in my own hall. You forestalled it,
goddess, by telling me how the land lies.   450
Weave me a way to pay them back! And you, too,
take your place with me, breathe valor in me
the way you did that night when we Akhaians
unbound the bright veil from the brow of Troy!
O grey-eyed one, fire my heart and brace me!   455
I'll take on fighting men three hundred strong
if you fight at my back, immortal lady!"

The grey-eyed goddess Athena answered him:

"No fear but I shall be there; you'll go forward
under my arm when the crux comes at last.   460
And I foresee your vast floor stained with blood,
spattered with brains of this or that tall suitor
who fed upon your cattle.
                              Now, for a while,
I shall transform you; not a soul will know you,
the clear skin of your arms and legs shriveled,   465
your chestnut hair all gone, your body dressed
in sacking that a man would gag to see,
and the two eyes, that were so brilliant, dirtied—
contemptible, you shall seem to your enemies,
as to the wife and son you left behind.   470

But join the swineherd first—the overseer
of all your swine, a good soul now as ever,
devoted to Penélopê and your son.
He will be found near Raven's Rock and the well
of Arethousa, where the swine are pastured,   475
rooting for acorns to their hearts' content,
drinking the dark still water. Boarflesh grows
pink and fat on that fresh diet. There

stay with him and question him, while I
am off to the great beauty's land of Sparta,   480
to call your son Telémakhos home again—
for you should know, he went to the wide land
of Lakedaimon, Meneláos' country,
to learn if there were news of you abroad."

Odysseus answered:

           "Why not tell him, knowing   485
my whole history, as you do? Must he
traverse the barren sea, he too, and live
in pain, while others feed on what is his?"

At this the grey-eyed goddess Athena said:

"No need for anguish on that lad's account.   490
I sent him off myself, to make his name
in foreign parts—no hardship in the bargain,
taking his ease in Meneláos' mansion,
lapped in gold.
          The young bucks here, I know,
lie in wait for him in a cutter, bent   495
on murdering him before he reaches home.
I rather doubt they will. Cold earth instead
will take in her embrace a man or two
of those who fed so long on what is his."

Speaking no more, she touched him with her wand,   500
shriveled the clear skin of his arms and legs,
made all his hair fall out, cast over him
the wrinkled hide of an old man, and bleared
both his eyes, that were so bright. Then she
clapped an old tunic, a foul cloak, upon him,   505
tattered, filthy, stained by greasy smoke,
and over that a mangy big buck skin.
A staff she gave him, and a leaky knapsack
with no strap but a loop of string.
                Now then,
their colloquy at an end, they went their ways—   510
Athena toward illustrious Lakedaimon
far over sea, to join Odysseus' son.

BOOK XIV

Hospitality in the Forest

He went up from the cove through wooded ground,
taking a stony trail into the high hills, where

the swineherd lived, according to Athena.
Of all Odysseus' field hands in the old days
this forester cared most for the estate;   5
and now Odysseus found him
in a remote clearing, sitting inside the gate
of a stockade he built to keep the swine
while his great lord was gone.
                    Working alone,
far from Penélopê and old Laërtês,   10
he had put up a fieldstone hut and timbered it
with wild pear wood. Dark hearts of oak he split
and trimmed for a high palisade around it,
and built twelve sties adjoining in this yard
to hold the livestock. Fifty sows with farrows   15
were penned in each, bedded upon the earth,
while the boars lay outside—fewer by far,
as those well-fatted were for the suitors' table,
fine pork, sent by the swineherd every day.
Three hundred sixty now lay there at night,   20
guarded by dogs—four dogs like wolves, one each
for the four lads the swineherd reared and kept
as under-herdsmen.
                    When Odysseus came,
the good servant sat shaping to his feet
oxhide for sandals, cutting the well-cured leather.   25
Three of his young men were afield, pasturing
herds in other woods; one he had sent
with a fat boar for tribute into town,
the boy to serve while the suitors got their fill.

The watch dogs, when they caught sight of Odysseus,   30
faced him, a snarling troop, and pelted out
viciously after him. Like a tricky beggar
he sat down plump, and dropped his stick. No use.
They would have rolled him in the dust and torn him
there by his own steading if the swineherd   35
had not sprung up and flung his leather down,
making a beeline for the open. Shouting,
throwing stone after stone,
he made them scatter; then turned to his lord
and said:

          "You might have got a ripping, man!   40
Two shakes more and a pretty mess for me
you could have called it, if you had the breath.
As though I had not trouble enough already,
given me by the gods, my master gone,

true king that he was. I hang on here,   45
still mourning for him, raising pigs of his
to feed foreigners, and who knows where the man is,
in some far country among strangers! Aye—
if he is living still, if he still sees the light of day.

Come to the cabin. You're a wanderer too.   50
You must eat something, drink some wine, and tell me
where you are from and the hard times you've seen."

The forester now led him to his hut
and made a couch for him, with tips of fir
piled for a mattress under a wild goat skin,   55
shaggy and thick, his own bed covering.
                                  Odysseus,
in pleasure at this courtesy, gently said:

"May Zeus and all the gods give you your heart's desire
for taking me in so kindly, friend."

                                  Eumaios—
O my swineherd![2]—answered him:

                                  "Tush, friend,   60
rudeness to a stranger is not decency,
poor though he may be, poorer than you.
                                  All wanderers
and beggars come from Zeus. What we can give
is slight but well-meant—all we dare. You know
that is the way of slaves, who live in dread   65
of masters—new ones like our own.
                                  I told you
the gods, long ago, hindered our lord's return.
He had a fondness for me, would have pensioned me
with acres of my own, a house, a wife
that other men admired and courted; all   70
gifts good-hearted kings bestow for service,
for a life work the bounty of god has prospered—
for it does prosper here, this work I do.
Had he grown old in his own house, my master
would have rewarded me. But the man's gone.   75
God curse the race of Helen and cut it down,
that wrung the strength out of the knees of many!
And he went, too—for the honor of Agamémnon

2. This direct address by the poet to one of his characters is confined to Eumaios; it occurs frequently in
connection with his name through Books XIV–XVII. A medieval commentator suggested that it showed
a special affection for Eumaios on Homer's part, but since in the *Iliad* a similar form of address is used for
five different characters (among them the god Apollo and the obscure Melanippos) this seems unlikely. In
the case of Eumaios it may have been a formula devised to avoid hiatus (clashing vowels).

he took ship overseas for the wild horse country
of Troy, to fight the Trojans."

          This being told,   80
he tucked his long shirt up inside his belt
and strode into the pens for two young porkers.
He slaughtered them and singed them at the fire,
flayed and quartered them, and skewered the meat
to broil it all; then gave it to Odysseus   85
hot on the spits. He shook out barley meal,
took a winebowl of ivy wood and filled it,
and sat down facing him, with a gesture, saying:

"There is your dinner, friend, the pork of slaves.
Our fat shoats are all eaten by the suitors,   90
cold-hearted men, who never spare a thought
for how they stand in the sight of Zeus. The gods
living in bliss are fond of no wrongdoing,
but honor discipline and right behavior.
Even the outcasts of the earth, who bring   95
piracy from the sea, and bear off plunder
given by Zeus in shiploads—even those men
deep in their hearts tremble for heaven's eye.
But the suitors, now, have heard some word, some oracle
of my lord's death, being so unconcerned   100
to pay court properly or to go about their business.
All they want is to prey on his estate,
proud dogs: they stop at nothing. Not a day
goes by, and not a night comes under Zeus,
but they make butchery of our beeves and swine—   105
not one or two beasts at a time, either.
As for swilling down wine, they drink us dry.
Only a great domain like his could stand it—
greater than any on the dusky mainland
or here in Ithaka. Not twenty heroes   110
in the whole world were as rich as he. I know:
I could count it all up: twelve herds in Elis,
as many flocks, as many herds of swine,
and twelve wide ranging herds of goats, as well,
attended by his own men or by others—   115
out at the end of the island, eleven herds
are scattered now, with good men looking after them,
and every herdsman, every day, picks out
a prize ram to hand over to those fellows.
I too as overseer, keeper of swine,   120
must go through all my boars and send the best."

While he ran on, Odysseus with zeal
applied himself to the meat and wine, but inwardly
his thought shaped woe and ruin for the suitors.
When he had eaten all that he desired   125
and the cup he drank from had been filled again
with wine—a welcome sight—,
he spoke, and the words came light upon the air:

"Who is this lord who once acquired you,
so rich, so powerful, as you describe him?   130
You think he died for Agamémnon's honor.
Tell me his name: I may have met someone
of that description in my time. Who knows?
Perhaps only the immortal gods could say
if I should claim to have seen him: I have roamed   135
about the world so long."

                    The swineherd answered
as one who held a place of trust:

                              "Well, man,
his lady and his son will put no stock
in any news of him brought by a rover.
Wandering men tell lies for a night's lodging,   140
for fresh clothing; truth doesn't interest them.
Every time some traveller comes ashore
he has to tell my mistress his pretty tale,
and she receives him kindly, questions him,
remembering her prince, while the tears run   145
down her cheeks—and that is as it should be
when a woman's husband has been lost abroad.
I suppose you, too, can work your story up
at a moment's notice, given a shirt or cloak.
No: long ago wild dogs and carrion   150
birds, most like, laid bare his ribs on land
where life had left him. Or it may be, quick fishes
picked him clean in the deep sea, and his bones
lie mounded over in sand upon some shore.
One way or another, far from home he died,   155
a bitter loss, and pain, for everyone,
certainly for me. Never again shall I
have for my lot a master mild as he was
anywhere—not even with my parents
at home, where I was born and bred. I miss them   160
less than I do him—though a longing comes
to set my eyes on them in the old country.
No, it is the lost man I ache to think of—

Odysseus. And I speak the name respectfully,
even if he is not here. He loved me, cared for me.   165
I call him dear my lord, far though he be."

Now royal Odysseus, who had borne the long war,
spoke again:

          "Friend, as you are so dead sure
he will not come—and so mistrustful, too—
let me not merely talk, as others talk,   170
but swear to it: your lord is now at hand.
And I expect a gift for this good news
when he enters his own hall. Till then I would not
take a rag, no matter what my need.
I hate as I hate Hell's own gate that weakness   175
that makes a poor man into a flatterer.
Zeus be my witness, and the table garnished
for true friends, and Odysseus' own hearth—
by heaven, all I say will come to pass!
He will return, and he will be avenged   180
on any who dishonor his wife and son."

Eumaios—O my swineherd!—answered him:

"I take you at your word, then: you shall have
no good news gift from me. Nor will Odysseus   185
enter his hall. But peace! drink up your wine.
Let us talk now of other things. No more
imaginings. It makes me heavy-hearted
when someone brings my master back to mind—
my own true master.
                    No, by heaven,   190
let us have no oaths! But if Odysseus
can come again god send he may! My wish
is that of Penélopê and old Laërtês
and Prince Telémakhos.
                    Ah, he's another
to be distressed about—Odysseus' child,   195
Telémakhos! By the gods' grace he grew
like a tough sapling, and I thought he'd be
no less a man than his great father—strong
and admirably made; but then someone,
god or man, upset him, made him rash,   200
so that he sailed away to sandy Pylos
to hear news of his father. Now the suitors
lie in ambush on his homeward track,

ready to cut away the last shoot of Arkêsios'[3]
line, the royal stock of Ithaka.
                                    No good   205
dwelling on it. Either he'll be caught
or else Kroníon's[4] hand will take him through.

Tell me, now, of your own trials and troubles.
And tell me truly first, for I should know,
who are you, where do you hail from, where's your home   210
and family? What kind of ship was yours,
and what course brought you here? Who are your sailors?
I don't suppose you walked here on the sea."

To this the master of improvisation answered:

"I'll tell you all that, clearly as I may.   215
If we could sit here long enough, with meat
and good sweet wine, warm here, in peace and quiet
within doors, while the work of the world goes on—
I might take all this year to tell my story
and never end the tale of misadventures   220
that wore my heart out, by the gods' will.

My native land is the wide seaboard of Krete
where I grew up. I had a wealthy father,
and many other sons were born to him
of his true lady. My mother was a slave,   225
his concubine; but Kastor Hylákidês,
my father, treated me as a true born son.
High honor came to him in that part of Krete
for wealth and ease, and sons born for renown,
before the death-bearing Kêrês drew him down   230
to the underworld. His avid sons thereafter
dividing up the property by lot
gave me a wretched portion, a poor house.
But my ability won me a wife
of rich family. Fool I was never called,   235
nor turn-tail in a fight.
                            My strength's all gone,
but from the husk you may divine the ear
that stood tall in the old days. Misery owns me
now, but then great Arês and Athena
gave me valor and man-breaking power,   240
whenever I made choice of men-at-arms
to set a trap with me for my enemies.

3. Father of Laërtês, grandfather of Odysseus.   4. Zeus, son of Kronos.

Never, as I am a man, did I fear Death
ahead, but went in foremost in the charge,
putting a spear through any man whose legs   245
were not as fast as mine. That was my element,
war and battle. Farming I never cared for,
nor life at home, nor fathering fair children.
I reveled in long ships with oars; I loved
polished lances, arrows in the skirmish,   250
the shapes of doom that others shake to see.
Carnage suited me; heaven put those things
in me somehow. Each to his own pleasure!
Before we young Akhaians shipped for Troy
I led men on nine cruises in corsairs   255
to raid strange coasts, and had great luck, taking
rich spoils on the spot, and even more
in the division. So my house grew prosperous,
my standing therefore high among the Kretans.
Then came the day when Zeus who views the wide world   260
drew men's eyes upon that way accurst
that wrung the manhood from the knees of many!
Everyone pressed me, pressed King Idómeneus
to take command of ships for Ilion.
No way out; the country rang with talk of it.   265
So we Akhaians had nine years of war.
In the tenth year we sacked the inner city,
Priam's town, and sailed for home; but heaven
dispersed the Akhaians. Evil days for me
were stored up in the hidden mind of Zeus.   270
One month, no more, I stayed at home in joy
with children, wife, and treasure. Lust for action
drove me to go to sea then, in command
of ships and gallant seamen bound for Egypt.
Nine ships I fitted out; my men signed on   275
and came to feast with me, as good shipmates,
for six full days. Many a beast I slaughtered
in the gods' honor, for my friends to eat.
Embarking on the seventh, we hauled sail
and filled away from Krete on a fresh north wind   280
effortlessly, as boats will glide down stream.
All rigging whole and all hands well, we rested,
letting the wind and steersmen work the ships,
for five days; on the fifth we made the delta.[5]
I brought my squadron in to the river bank   285
with one turn of the sweeps. There, heaven knows,
I told the men to wait and guard the ships

5. Of the Nile.

while I sent out patrols to rising ground.
But reckless greed carried them all away
to plunder the rich bottomlands; they bore off   290
wives and children, killed what men they found.

When this news reached the city, all who heard it
came at dawn. On foot they came, and horsemen,
filling the river plain with dazzle of bronze;
and Zeus lord of lightning   295
threw my men into blind panic: no one dared
stand against that host closing around us.
Their scything weapons left our dead in piles,
but some they took alive, into forced labor.
And I—ah, how I wish that I had died   300
in Egypt, on that field! So many blows
awaited me!— Well, Zeus himself inspired me;
I wrenched my dogskin helmet off my head,
dropped my spear, dodged out of my long shield,
ran for the king's chariot and swung on   305
to embrace and kiss his knees. He pulled me up,
took pity on me, placed me on the footboards,
and drove home with me crouching there in tears.
Aye—for the troops, in battle fury still,
made one pass at me after another, pricking me   310
with spears, hoping to kill me. But he saved me,
for fear of the great wrath of Zeus that comes
when men who ask asylum are given death.

Seven years, then, my sojourn lasted there,
and I amassed a fortune, going about   315
among the openhanded Egyptians.
But when the eighth came round, a certain
Phoinikian adventurer came too,
a plausible rat, who had already done
plenty of devilry in the world.

                              This fellow   320
took me in completely with his schemes,
and led me with him to Phoinikia,
where he had land and houses. One full year
I stayed there with him, to the month and day,
and when fair weather came around again   325
he took me in a deepsea ship for Libya,
pretending I could help in the cargo trade;
he meant, in fact, to trade me off, and get
a high price for me. I could guess the game
but had to follow him aboard. One day   330

on course due west, off central Krete, the ship
caught a fresh norther, and we ran southward
before the wind while Zeus piled ruin ahead.
When Krete was out of sight astern, no land
anywhere to be seen, but sky and ocean,   335
Kroníon put a dark cloud in the zenith
over the ship, and gloom spread on the sea.
With crack on crack of thunder, he let fly
a bolt against the ship, a direct hit,
so that she bucked, in sacred fumes of sulphur,   340
and all the men were flung into the water.
They came up round the wreck, bobbing a while
like petrels on the waves. No homecoming
for these, from whom the god had turned his face!
Stunned in the smother as I was, yet Zeus   345
put into my hands the great mast of the ship—
a way to keep from drowning. So I twined
my arms and legs around it in the gale
and stayed afloat nine days. On the tenth night,
a big surf cast me up in Thesprotia.[6]   350
Pheidon the king there gave me refuge, nobly,
with no talk of reward. His son discovered me
exhausted and half dead with cold, and gave me
a hand to bear me up till he reached home
where he could clothe me in a shirt and cloak.   355
In that king's house I heard news of Odysseus,
who lately was a guest there, passing by
on his way home, the king said; and he showed me
the treasure that Odysseus had brought:
bronze, gold, and iron wrought with heavy labor—   360
in that great room I saw enough to last
Odysseus' heirs for ten long generations.
The man himself had gone up to Dodona[7]
to ask the spelling leaves of the old oak
the will of God: how to return, that is,   365
to the rich realm of Ithaka, after so long
an absence—openly, or on the quiet.
And, tipping wine out, Pheidon swore to me
the ship was launched, the seamen standing by
to take Odysseus to his land at last.   370
But he had passage first for me: Thesprotians
were sailing, as luck had it, for Doulíkhion,[8]
the grain-growing island; there, he said,
they were to bring me to the king, Akastos.

6. On the west coast of the Greek mainland, north of Ithaka.   7. An oracle of Zeus. The message of
the god was supposed to come from the sacred oak, perhaps from the rushing of the leaves in the wind.
8. An island off the west coast of Greece.

Instead, that company saw fit to plot   375
foul play against me; in my wretched life
there was to be more suffering.
                                  At sea, then,
when land lay far astern, they sprang their trap.
They'd make a slave of me that day, stripping
cloak and tunic off me, throwing around me   380
the dirty rags you see before you now.
At evening, off the fields of Ithaka,
they bound me, lashed me down under the decking
with stout ship's rope, while they all went ashore
in haste to make their supper on the beach.   385
The gods helped me to pry the lashing loose
until it fell away. I wound my rags
in a bundle round my head and eased myself
down the smooth lading plank into the water,
up to the chin, then swam an easy breast stroke   390
out and around, putting that crew behind,
and went ashore in underbrush, a thicket,
where I lay still, making myself small.
They raised a bitter yelling, and passed by
several times. When further groping seemed   395
useless to them, back to the ship they went
and out to sea again. The gods were with me,
keeping me hid; and with me when they brought me
here to the door of one who knows the world.
My destiny is yet to live awhile."   400

The swineherd bowed and said:

                            "Ah well, poor drifter,
you've made me sad for you, going back over it,
all your hard life and wandering. That tale
about Odysseus, though, you might have spared me;
you will not make me believe that.   405
Why must you lie, being the man you are,
and all for nothing?
                I can see so well
what happened to my master, sailing home!
Surely the gods turned on him, to refuse him
death in the field, or in his friends' arms   410
after he wound up the great war at Troy.
They would have made a tomb for him, the Akhaians,
and paid all honor to his son thereafter. No,
stormwinds made off with him. No glory came to him.

I moved here to the mountain with my swine.   415
Never, now, do I go down to town

unless I am sent for by Penélopê
when news of some sort comes. But those who sit
around her go on asking the old questions—
a few who miss their master still,   420
and those who eat his house up, and go free.
For my part, I have had no heart for inquiry
since one year an Aitolian[9] made a fool of me.
Exiled from land to land after some killing,
he turned up at my door; I took him in.   425
My master he had seen in Krete, he said,
lodged with Idómeneus, while the long ships,
leaky from gales, were laid up for repairs.
But they were all to sail, he said, that summer,
or the first days of fall—hulls laden deep   430
with treasure, manned by crews of heroes.
                                          This time
you are the derelict the Powers bring.
Well, give up trying to win me with false news
or flattery. If I receive and shelter you,
it is not for your tales but for your trouble,   435
and with an eye to Zeus, who guards a guest."

Then said that sly and guileful man, Odysseus:

"A black suspicious heart beats in you surely;
the man you are, not even an oath could change you.
Come then, we'll make a compact; let the gods   440
witness it from Olympos, where they dwell.
Upon your lord's homecoming, if he comes
here to this very hut, and soon—
then give me a new outfit, shirt and cloak,
and ship me to Doulíkhion—I thought it   445
a pleasant island. But if Odysseus
fails to appear as I predict, then Swish!
let the slaves pitch me down from some high rock,
so the next poor man who comes will watch his tongue."

The forester gave a snort and answered:

                                          "Friend,   450
if I agreed to that, a great name
I should acquire in the world for goodness—
at one stroke and forever: your kind host
who gave you shelter and the hand of friendship,
only to take your life next day!   455

9. Aitolia is on the mainland, east of Ithaka.

How confidently, after that, should I
address my prayers to Zeus, the son of Kronos!

It is time now for supper. My young herdsmen
should be arriving soon to set about it.
We'll make a quiet feast here at our hearth."   460

At this point in their talk the swine had come
up to the clearing, and the drovers followed
to pen them for the night—the porkers squealing
to high heaven, milling around the yard.
The swineherd then gave orders to his men: 465

"Bring in our best pig for a stranger's dinner.
A feast will do our hearts good, too; we know
grief and pain, hard scrabbling with our swine,
while the outsiders live on our labor."

                          Bronze
axe in hand, he turned to split up kindling,   470
while they drove in a tall boar, prime and fat,
planting him square before the fire. The gods,
as ever, had their due in the swineherd's thought,
for he it was who tossed the forehead bristles
as a first offering on the flames, calling   475
upon the immortal gods to let Odysseus
reach his home once more.
                    Then he stood up
and brained the boar with split oak from the woodpile.
Life ebbed from the beast; they slaughtered him,
singed the carcass, and cut out the joints.   480
Eumaios, taking flesh from every quarter,
put lean strips on the fat of sacrifice,
floured each one with barley meal, and cast it
into the blaze. The rest they sliced and skewered,
roasted with care, then took it off the fire   485
and heaped it up on platters. Now their chief,
who knew best the amenities, rose to serve,
dividing all that meat in seven portions—
one to be set aside, with proper prayers,
for the wood nymphs and Hermês, Maia's son;   490
the others for the company. Odysseus
he honored with long slices from the chine—
warming the master's heart. Odysseus looked at him
and said:

            "May you be dear to Zeus
as you are dear to me for this, Eumaios,   495
favoring with choice cuts a man like me."

And—O my swineherd!—you replied, Eumaios:
"Bless you, stranger, fall to and enjoy it
for what it is. Zeus grants us this or that,
or else refrains from granting, as he wills;   500
all things are in his power."

                    He cut and burnt
a morsel for the gods who are young forever,
tipped out some wine, then put it in the hands
of Odysseus, the old soldier, raider of cities,
who sat at ease now with his meat before him.   505
As for the loaves, Mesaúlios dealt them out,
a yard boy, bought by the swineherd on his own,
unaided by his mistress or Laërtês,
from Taphians, while Odysseus was away.
Now all hands reached for that array of supper,   510
until, when hunger and thirst were turned away
Mesaúlios removed the bread and, heavy
with food and drink, they settled back to rest.

Now night had come on, rough, with no moon,
but a nightlong downpour setting in, the rainwind   515
blowing hard from the west. Odysseus
began to talk, to test the swineherd, trying
to put it in his head to take his cloak off
and lend it, or else urge the others to.
He knew the man's compassion.
                        "Listen," he said,   520
"Eumaios, and you others, here's a wishful
tale that I shall tell. The wine's behind it,
vaporing wine, that makes a serious man
break down and sing, kick up his heels and clown,
or tell some story that were best untold.   525
But now I'm launched, I can't stop now.
                                Would god I felt
the hot blood in me that I had at Troy!
Laying an ambush near the walls one time,
Odysseus and Meneláos were commanders
and I ranked third. I went at their request.   530
We worked in toward the bluffs and battlements
and, circling the town, got into canebreaks,
thick and high, a marsh where we took cover,
hunched under arms.
                    The northwind dropped, and night
came black and wintry. A fine sleet descending   535
whitened the cane like hoarfrost, and clear ice

grew dense upon our shields. The other men,
all wrapt in blanket cloaks as well as tunics,
rested well, in shields up to their shoulder,
but I had left my cloak with friends in camp,   540
foolhardy as I was. No chance of freezing hard,
I thought, so I wore kilts and a shield only.
But in the small hours of the third watch, when stars
that rise at evening go down to their setting,
I nudged Odysseus, who lay close beside me;   545
he was alert then, listening, and I said:

'Son of Laërtês and the gods of old,
Odysseus, master mariner and soldier,
I cannot hold on long among the living.
The cold is making a corpse of me. Some god   550
inveigled me to come without a cloak.
No help for it now; too late.'

                Next thing I knew
he had a scheme all ready in his mind—
and what a man he was for schemes and battles!
Speaking under his breath to me, he murmured: 555

'Quiet; none of the rest should hear you.'

                   Then,
propping his head on his forearm, he said:

'Listen, lads, I had an ominous dream,
the point being how far forward from our ships
and lines we've come. Someone should volunteer   560
to tell the corps commander, Agamémnon;
he may reinforce us from the base.'

             At this,
Thoas jumped up, the young son of Andraimon,
put down his crimson cloak and headed off,
running shoreward.

          Wrapped in that man's cloak   565
how gratefully I lay in the bitter dark
until the dawn came stitched in gold! I wish
I had that sap and fiber in me now!"

Then—O my swineherd!—you replied, Eumaios:

"That was a fine story, and well told,   570
not a word out of place, not a pointless word.
No, you'll not sleep cold for lack of cover,
or any other comfort one should give

to a needy guest. However, in the morning,
you must go flapping in the same old clothes.   575
Shirts and cloaks are few here; every man
has one change only. When our prince arrives,
the son of Odysseus, he will make you gifts—
cloak, tunic, everything—and grant you passage
wherever you care to go."

> On this he rose   580
and placed the bed of balsam near the fire,
strewing sheepskins on top, and skins of goats.
Odysseus lay down. His host threw over him
a heavy blanket cloak, his own reserve
against the winter wind when it came wild.   585
So there Odysseus dropped off to sleep,
while herdsmen slept nearby. But not the swineherd:
not in the hut could he lie down in peace,
but now equipped himself for the night outside;
and this rejoiced Odysseus' heart, to see him   590
care for the herd so, while his lord was gone.
He hung a sharp sword from his shoulder, gathered
a great cloak round him, close, to break the wind,
and pulled a shaggy goatskin on his head.
Then, to keep at a distance dogs or men,   595
he took a sharpened lance, and went to rest
under a hollow rock where swine were sleeping
out of the wind and rain.

BOOK XV

How They Came to Ithaka

> South into Lakedaimon
into the land where greens are wide for dancing
Athena went, to put in mind of home
her great-hearted hero's honored son,
rousing him to return.

> And there she found him   5
with Nestor's lad in the late night at rest
under the portico of Meneláos,
the famous king. Stilled by the power of slumber
the son of Nestor lay, but honeyed sleep
had not yet taken in her arms Telémakhos.   10
All through the starlit night, with open eyes,
he pondered what he had heard about his father,
until at his bedside grey-eyed Athena
towered and said:

"The brave thing now, Telémakhos,
would be to end this journey far from home.   15
All that you own you left behind
with men so lost to honor in your house
they may devour it all, shared out among them.
How will your journey save you then?
                              Go quickly
to the lord of the great war cry, Meneláos;   20
press him to send you back. You may yet find
the queen your mother in her rooms alone.
It seems her father and her kinsmen say
Eurýmakhos is the man for her to marry.
He has outdone the suitors, all the rest,   25
in gifts to her, and made his pledges double.
Check him, or he will have your lands and chattels[1]
in spite of you.
              You know a woman's pride
at bringing riches to the man she marries.
As to her girlhood husband, her first children,   30
he is forgotten, being dead—and they
no longer worry her.
                   So act alone.
Go back; entrust your riches to the servant
worthiest in your eyes, until the gods
make known what beauty you yourself shall marry.   35

This too I have to tell you: now take heed:
the suitors' ringleaders are hot for murder,
waiting in the channel between Ithaka
and Samê's rocky side; they mean to kill you
before you can set foot ashore. I doubt   40
they'll bring it off. Dark earth instead
may take to her cold bed a few brave suitors
who preyed upon your cattle.
                          Bear well out
in your good ship, to eastward of the islands,
and sail again by night. Someone immortal   45
who cares for you will make a fair wind blow.
Touch at the first beach, go ashore, and send
your ship and crew around to port by sea,
while you go inland to the forester,
your old friend, loyal keeper of the swine.   50

1. The Greek could also mean: "Be careful she (Penélopê) doesn't carry off, against your will, some of
your property," i.e., for her new husband. This would explain why Athena tells Telémakhos, in the
following lines, to turn the property over to the maids he has most confidence in. The suggestion that
Penélopê is planning to marry Eurýmakhos and take Telémakhos' property with her is not to be taken
seriously; Athena uses it to get Telémakhos moving.

Remain that night with him; send him to town
to tell your watchful mother Penélopê
that you are back from Pylos safe and sound."

With this Athena left him for Olympos.
He swung his foot across and gave a kick   55
and said to the son of Nestor:

                                        "Open your eyes,
Peisístratos. Get our team into harness.
We have a long day's journey."

                            Nestor's son
turned over and answered him:

                                        "It is still night,
and no moon. Can we drive now? We can not,   60
itch as we may for the road home. Dawn is near.
Allow the captain of spearmen, Meneláos,
time to pack our car with gifts and time
to speak a gracious word, sending us off.
A guest remembers all his days   65
that host who makes provision for him kindly."

The Dawn soon took her throne of gold, and Lord
Meneláos, clarion in battle,
rose from where he lay beside the beauty
of Helen with her shining hair. He strode   70
into the hall nearby.
                        Hearing him come,
Odysseus' son pulled on his snowy tunic
over the skin, gathered his long cape
about his breadth of shoulder like a captain,
the heir of King Odysseus. At the door   75
he stood and said:

                    "Lord Marshal, Meneláos,
send me home now to my own dear country:
longing has come upon me to go home."

The lord of the great war cry said at once:

"If you are longing to go home, Telémakhos,   80
I would not keep you for the world, not I.
I'd think myself or any other host
as ill-mannered for over-friendliness
as for hostility.
                    Measure is best in everything.
To send a guest packing, or cling to him   85

when he's in haste—one sin equals the other.
'Good entertaining ends with no detaining.'
Only let me load your car with gifts
and fine ones, you shall see.
                          I'll bid the women
set out breakfast from the larder stores;   90
honor and appetite—we'll attend to both
before a long day's journey overland.
Or would you care to try the Argive midlands
and Hellas, in my company? I'll harness
my own team, and take you through the towns.   95
Guests like ourselves no lord will turn away;
each one will make one gift, at least,
to carry home with us: tripod or cauldron
wrought in bronze, mule team, or golden cup."

Clearheaded Telémakhos replied:
                          "Lord Marshal   100
Meneláos, royal son of Atreus,
I must return to my own hearth. I left
no one behind as guardian of my property.
This going abroad for news of a great father—
heaven forbid it be my own undoing,   105
or any precious thing be lost at home."

At this the tall king, clarion in battle,
called to his lady and her waiting women
to give them breakfast from the larder stores.
Eteóneus, the son of Boethoös, came   110
straight from bed, from where he lodged nearby,
and Meneláos ordered a fire lit
for broiling mutton. The king's man obeyed.
Then down to the cedar chamber Meneláos
walked with Helen and Prince Megapénthês.   115
Amid the gold he had in that place lying
the son of Atreus picked a wine cup, wrought
with handles left and right, and told his son
to take a silver winebowl.
                          Helen lingered
near the deep coffers filled with gowns, her own   120
handiwork.
          Tall goddess among women,
she lifted out one robe of state so royal,
adorned and brilliant with embroidery,
deep in the chest it shimmered like a star.
Now all three turned back to the door to greet   125

Telémakhos. And red-haired Meneláos
cried out to him:

          "O prince Telémakhos,
may Hêra's Lord of Thunder see you home
and bring you to the welcome you desire!
Here are your gifts—perfect and precious things   130
I wish to make your own, out of my treasure."

And gently the great captain, son of Atreus,
handed him the goblet. Megapénthês
carried the winebowl glinting silvery
to set before him, and the Lady Helen   135
drew near, so that he saw her cheek's pure line.
She held the gown and murmured:

         "I, too,
bring you a gift, dear child, and here it is;
remember Helen's hands by this; keep it   140
for your own bride, your joyful wedding day;
let your dear mother guard it in her chamber.
My blessing: may you come soon to your island,
home to your timbered hall."

                  So she bestowed it,
and happily he took it. These fine things   145
Peisístratos packed well in the wicker carrier,
admiring every one. Then Meneláos
led the two guests in to take their seats
on thrones and easy chairs in the great hall.
Now came a maid to tip a golden jug   150
of water over a silver finger bowl,
and drew the polished tables up beside them;
the larder mistress brought her tray of loaves,
with many savories to lavish on them;
viands were served by Eteóneus, and wine   155
by Meneláos' son. Then every hand
reached out upon good meat and drink to take them,
driving away hunger and thirst. At last,
Telémakhos and Nestor's son led out
their team to harness, mounted their bright car,   160
and drove down under the echoing entrance way,
while red-haired Meneláos, Atreus' son,
walked alongside with a golden cup—
wine for the wayfarers to spill at parting.
Then by the tugging team he stood, and spoke   165
over the horses' heads:

"Farewell, my lads.
Homage to Nestor, the benevolent king;
in my time he was fatherly to me,
when the flower of Akhaia warred on Troy."

Telémakhos made this reply: 170
                "No fear
but we shall bear at least as far as Nestor
your messages, great king. How I could wish
to bring them home to Ithaka! If only
Odysseus were there, if he could hear me tell   175
of all the courtesy I have had from you,
returning with your finery and your treasure."

Even as he spoke, a beat of wings went skyward
off to the right—a mountain eagle, grappling
a white goose in his talons, heavy prey   180
hooked from a farmyard. Women and men-at-arms
made hubbub, running up, as he flew over,
but then he wheeled hard right before the horses—
a sight that made the whole crowd cheer, with hearts
lifting in joy. Peisístratos called out: 185

"Read us the sign, O Meneláos, Lord
Marshal of armies! Was the god revealing
something thus to you, or to ourselves?"

At this the old friend of the god of battle
groped in his mind for the right thing to say,   190
but regal Helen put in quickly:

"Listen:
I can tell you—tell what the omen means,
as light is given me, and as I see it
point by point fulfilled. The beaked eagle   195
flew from the wild mountain of his fathers
to take for prey the tame house bird. Just so,
Odysseus, back from his hard trials and wandering,
will soon come down in fury on his house.
He may be there today, and a black hour   200
he brings upon the suitors."

                Telémakhos
gazed and said:

           "May Zeus, the lord of Hêra,
make it so! In far-off Ithaka, all my life,
I shall invoke you as a goddess, lady."

He let the whip fall, and the restive mares   205
broke forward at a canter through the town
into the open country.
            All that day
they kept their harness shaking, side by side,
until at sundown when the roads grew dim
they made a halt at Pherai. There Dióklês   210
son of Ortílokhos whom Alpheios fathered,
welcomed the young men, and they slept the night.
Up when the young Dawn's finger tips of rose
opened in the east, they hitched the team
once more to the painted car   215
and steered out westward through the echoing gate,
whipping their fresh horses into a run.
Approaching Pylos Height at that day's end,
Telémakhos appealed to the son of Nestor:

"Could you, I wonder, do a thing I'll tell you,   220
supposing you agree?
We take ourselves to be true friends—in age
alike, and bound by ties between our fathers,
and now by partnership in this adventure.
Prince, do not take me roundabout,   225
but leave me at the ship, else the old king
your father will detain me overnight
for love of guests, when I should be at sea."

The son of Nestor nodded, thinking swiftly
how best he could oblige his friend.   230
Here was his choice: to pull the team hard over
along the beach till he could rein them in
beside the ship. Unloading Meneláos'
royal keepsakes into the stern sheets,
he sang out:

         "Now for action! Get aboard,   235
and call your men, before I break the news
at home in hall to father. Who knows better
the old man's heart than I? If you delay,
he will not let you go, but he'll descend on you
in person and imperious; no turning   240
back with empty hands for him, believe me,
once his blood is up."

         He shook the reins
to the lovely mares with long manes in the wind,
guiding them full tilt toward his father's hall.
Telémakhos called in the crew, and told them: 245

"Get everything shipshape aboard this craft;
we pull out now, and put sea miles behind us."

The listening men obeyed him, climbing in
to settle on their benches by the rowlocks,
while he stood watchful by the stern. He poured out   250
offerings there, and prayers to Athena.

Now a strange man came up to him, an easterner
fresh from spilling blood in distant Argos,
a hunted man. Gifted in prophecy,
he had as forebear that Melampous, wizard   255
who lived of old in Pylos, mother city
of western flocks.
                    Melampous, a rich lord, [2]
had owned a house unmatched among the Pylians,
until the day came when king Neleus, noblest
in that age, drove him from his native land.   260
And Neleus for a year's term sequestered
Melampous' fields and flocks, while he lay bound
hand and foot in the keep of Phylakos.
Beauty of Neleus' daughter put him there
and sombre folly the inbreaking Fury   265
thrust upon him. But he gave the slip
to death, and drove the bellowing herd of Iphiklos
from Phylakê to Pylos, there to claim
the bride that ordeal won him from the king.
He led her to his brother's house, and went on   270
eastward into another land, the bluegrass
plain of Argos. Destiny held for him
rule over many Argives. Here he married,
built a great manor house, fathered Antíphatês
and Mantios, commanders both, of whom   275
Antíphatês begot Oikleiês
and Oikleiês the firebrand Amphiaraos.

2. The complicated story which follows (obscure in some of its details) gives us the genealogical background of the young man who comes up to Telémakhos. His name, as we learn only at the end of the genealogy, is Theoklýmenos, and he has an important role to play in the last part of the Odyssey. He is a prophet, one who can interpret signs, foretell the future. This gift is hereditary: his ancestor Melampous had it (and so did another descendant of Melampous, Amphiaraos). The brother of Melampous (who lived in Pylos under King Neleus, Nestor's father) asked for the hand of Neleus' daughter: Neleus demanded as bride-price the herds of cattle of a neighboring lord, Phylakos. Melampous tried to steal the cattle for his brother, was caught and imprisoned. In prison he heard the worms in the roofbeams announce that the wood was almost eaten through and predicted the collapse of the roof. Phylakos, impressed, released him, with the cattle; his brother was given the bride. Melampous then left for Argos where he settled and prospered: one of his great-grandsons was the prophet Amphiaraos who foresaw that if he joined the champions who went to besiege Thebes (The Seven against Thebes) he would lose his life. But his wife persuaded him to go: she had been bribed with a golden necklace by Polyneicês, son of Oedipus, who was preparing to attack his brother, Eteoclês, now King of Thebes. Amphiaraos was the grandson of Melampous' son Antíphatês; the other son of Melampous, Mantios, had a son called Polypheidês (also a prophet) who moved to Hypereia (in the vicinity of Argos); his son Theoklýmenos now begs Telémakhos for a place in his ship, so that he can escape the relatives of a man he has killed.

This champion the lord of stormcloud, Zeus,
and strong Apollo loved; nor had he ever
to cross the doorsill into dim old age.   280
A woman, bought by trinkets, gave him over
to be cut down in the assault on Thebes.
His sons were Alkmáon and Amphílokhos.
In the meantime Lord Mantios begot
Polypheidês, the prophet, and   285
Kleitos—famous name! For Dawn in silks
of gold carried off Kleitos for his beauty
to live among the gods. But Polypheidês,
high-hearted and exalted by Apollo
above all men for prophecy, withdrew   290
to Hyperesia when his father angered him.
He lived on there, foretelling to the world
the shape of things to come.
                              His son it was,
Theoklýmenos, who came upon Telémakhos
as he poured out the red wine in the sand   295
near his trim ship, with prayer to Athena;
and he called out, approaching:

                              "Friend, well met
here at libation before going to sea.
I pray you by the wine you spend, and by
your god, your own life, and your company;   300
enlighten me, and let the truth be known.
Who are you? Of what city and what parents?"

Telémakhos turned to him and replied:

"Stranger, as truly as may be, I'll tell you.
I am from Ithaka, where I was born;   305
my father is, or he once was, Odysseus.
But he's a long time gone, and dead, may be;
and that is what I took ship with my friends
to find out—for he left long years ago."

Said Theoklýmenos in reply: 310

"I too
have had to leave my home. I killed a cousin.
In the wide grazing lands of Argos live
many kinsmen of his and friends in power,
great among the Akhaians. These I fled.   315
Death and vengeance at my back, as Fate
has turned now, I came wandering overland.

Give me a plank aboard your ship, I beg,
or they will kill me. They are on my track."

Telémakhos made answer:

                                    "No two ways   320
about it. Will I pry you from our gunnel
when you are desperate to get to sea?
Come aboard; share what we have, and welcome."

He took the bronze-shod lance from the man's hand
and laid it down full-length on deck; then swung   325
his own weight after it aboard the cutter,
taking position aft, making a place
for Theoklýmenos near him. The stern lines
were slacked off, and Telémakhos commanded:

"Rig the mast; make sail!" Nimbly they ran   330
to push the fir pole high and step it firm
amidships in the box, make fast the forestays,
and hoist aloft the white sail on its halyards.
A following wind came down from grey-eyed Athena,
blowing brisk through heaven, and so steady   335
the cutter lapped up miles of salt blue sea,
passing Krounoi abeam and Khalkis estuary[3]
at sundown when the sea ways all grew dark.
Then, by Athena's wind borne on, the ship
rounded Pheai by night and coasted Elis,   340
the green domain of the Epeioi; thence
he put her head north toward the running pack
of islets, wondering if by sailing wide
he sheered off Death, or would be caught.

                              That night
Odysseus and the swineherd supped again   345
with herdsmen in their mountain hut. At ease
when appetite and thirst were turned away,
Odysseus, while he talked, observed the swineherd
to see if he were hospitable still—
if yet again the man would make him stay   350
under his roof, or send him off to town.

"Listen," he said, "Eumaios; listen, lads.
At daybreak I must go and try my luck
around the port. I burden you too long.

3. The precise location of these places is disputed but the mention of Elis in line 340 shows that they are
all on the west coast of the Peloponnese, south of the Gulf of Corinth.

Direct me, put me on the road with someone.   355
Nothing else for it but to play the beggar
in populous parts. I'll get a cup or loaf,
maybe, from some householder. If I go
as far as the great hall of King Odysseus
I might tell Queen Penélopê my news.   360
Or I can drift inside among the suitors
to see what alms they give, rich as they are.
If they have whims, I'm deft in ways of service—
that I can say, and you may know for sure.
By grace of Hermês the Wayfinder, patron   365
of mortal tasks, the god who honors toil,
no man can do a chore better than I can.
Set me to build a fire, or chop wood,
cook or carve, mix wine and serve—or anything
inferior men attend to for the gentry."   370

Now you were furious at this, Eumaios,
and answered—O my swineherd!—

                    "Friend, friend,
how could this fantasy take hold of you?
You dally with your life, and nothing less,
if you feel drawn to mingle in that company—   375
reckless, violent, and famous for it
out to the rim of heaven. Slaves
they have, but not like you. No—theirs are boys
in fresh cloaks and tunics, with pomade
ever on their sleek heads, and pretty faces.   380
These are their minions, while their tables gleam
and groan under big roasts, with loaves and wine.
Stay with us here. No one is burdened by you,
neither myself nor any of my hands.
Wait here until Odysseus' son returns.   385
You shall have clothing from him, cloak and tunic,
and passage where your heart desires to go."

The noble and enduring man replied:

"May you be dear to Zeus for this, Eumaios,
even as you are to me. Respite from pain   390
you give me—and from homelessness. In life
there's nothing worse than knocking about the world,
no bitterness we vagabonds are spared
when the curst belly rages! Well, you master it
and me, making me wait for the king's son.   395
But now, come, tell me:
what of Odysseus' mother, and his father

whom he took leave of on the sill of age?
Are they under the sun's rays, living still,
or gone down long ago to lodge with Death?"   400

To this the rugged herdsman answered:

                                        "Aye,
that I can tell you; it is briefly told.
Laërtês lives, but daily in his hall
prays for the end of life and soul's delivery,   405
heartbroken as he is for a son long gone
and for his lady. Sorrow, when she died,
aged and enfeebled him like a green tree stricken;
but pining for her son, her brilliant son,
wore out her life.
                    Would god no death so sad   410
might come to benefactors dear as she!
I loved always to ask and hear about her
while she lived, although she lived in sorrow.
For she had brought me up with her own daughter,
Princess Ktimenê, her youngest child.   415
We were alike in age and nursed as equals
nearly, till in the flower of our years
they gave her, married her, to a Samian prince,[4]
taking his many gifts. For my own portion
her mother gave new clothing, cloak and sandals,   420
and sent me to the woodland. Well she loved me.
Ah, how I miss that family! It is true
the blissful gods prosper my work; I have
meat and drink to spare for those I prize;
but so removed I am, I have no speech   425
with my sweet mistress, now that evil days
and overbearing men darken her house.
Tenants all hanker for good talk and gossip
around their lady, and a snack in hall,
a cup or two before they take the road   430
to their home acres, each one bearing home
some gift to cheer his heart."

                        The great tactician
answered:

            "You were still a child, I see,
when exiled somehow from your parents' land.
Tell me, had it been sacked in war, the city   435
of spacious ways in which they made their home,

_____
4. From Same, a nearby island or town.

your father and your gentle mother? Or
were you kidnapped alone, brought here by sea
huddled with sheep in some foul pirate squadron,
to this landowner's hall? He paid your ransom?"   440

The master of the woodland answered:

                              "Friend,
now that you show an interest in that matter,
attend me quietly, be at your ease,
and drink your wine. These autumn nights are long,
ample for story-telling and for sleep.   445
You need not go to bed before the hour;
sleeping from dusk to dawn's a dull affair.
Let any other here who wishes, though,
retire to rest. At daybreak let him breakfast
and take the king's own swine into the wilderness.   450
Here's a tight roof; we'll drink on, you and I,
and ease our hearts of hardships we remember,
sharing old times. In later days a man
can find a charm in old adversity,
exile and pain. As to your question, now: 455

A certain island, Syriê by name—
you may have heard the name—lies off Ortýgia⁵
due west, and holds the sunsets of the year.
Not very populous, but good for grazing
sheep and kine; rich too in wine and grain.   460
No dearth is ever known there, no disease
wars on the folk, of ills that plague mankind;
but when the townsmen reach old age, Apollo
with his longbow of silver comes, and Artemis,
showering arrows of mild death.
                              Two towns   465
divide the farmlands of that whole domain,
and both were ruled by Ktêsios, my father,
Orménos' heir, and a great godlike man.

Now one day some of those renowned seafaring
men, sea-dogs, Phoinikians, came ashore   470
with bags of gauds for trading. Father had
in our household a woman of Phoinikia,
a handsome one, and highly skilled. Well, she
gave in to the seductions of those rovers.

5. Another name for Delos, the central island of the Cyclades, but also the name of the central island of
the city of Syracuse in Sicily. However, the fact that on Syrie there is no disease and that everyone there
dies painlessly suggests that it is not located in this world at all—like Phaiákia, it is in Fairyland.

One of them found her washing near the mooring   475
and lay with her, making such love to her
as women in their frailty are confused by,
even the best of them.
                     In due course, then,
he asked her who she was and where she hailed from:
and nodding toward my father's roof, she said: 480

'I am of Sidon town, smithy of bronze
for all the East. Arubas Pasha's daughter.
Taphian pirates caught me in a byway
and sold me into slavery overseas
in this man's home. He could afford my ransom.'   485

The sailor who had lain with her replied:

'Why not ship out with us on the run homeward,
and see your father's high-roofed hall again,
your father and your mother? Still in Sidon
and still rich, they are said to be.'

                          She answered: 490

'It could be done, that, if you sailors take
oath I'll be given passage home unharmed.'

Well, soon she had them swearing it all pat
as she desired, repeating every syllable,
whereupon she warned them:
                          'Not a word   495
about our meeting here! Never call out to me
when any of you see me in the lane
or at the well. Some visitor might bear
tales to the old man. If he guessed the truth,
I'd be chained up, your lives would be in peril.   500
No: keep it secret. Hurry with your peddling,
and when your hold is filled with livestock, send
a message to me at the manor hall.
Gold I'll bring, whatever comes to hand,
and something else, too, as my passage fee—   505
the master's child, my charge: a boy so high,
bright for his age; he runs with me on errands.
I'd take him with me happily; his price
would be I know not what in sale abroad.'

Her bargain made, she went back to the manor.   510
But they were on the island all that year,
getting by trade a cargo of our cattle;

until, the ship at length being laden full,
ready for sea, they sent a messenger
to the Phoinikian woman. Shrewd he was,   515
this fellow who came round my father's hall,
showing a golden chain all strung with amber,
a necklace. Maids in waiting and my mother
passed it from hand to hand, admiring it,
engaging they would buy it. But that dodger,   520
as soon as he had caught the woman's eye
and nodded, slipped away to join the ship.
She took my hand and led me through the court
into the portico. There by luck she found
winecups and tables still in place—for Father's   525
attendant counselors had dined just now
before they went to the assembly. Quickly
she hid three goblets in her bellying dress
to carry with her while I tagged along
in my bewilderment. The sun went down   530
and all the lanes grew dark as we descended,
skirting the harbor in our haste to where
those traders of Phoinikia held their ship.
All went aboard at once and put to sea,
taking the two of us. A favoring wind   535
blew from the power of heaven. We sailed on
six nights and days without event. Then Zeus
the son of Kronos added one more noon—and sudden
arrows from Artemis pierced the woman's heart.
Stone-dead she dropped   540
into the sloshing bilge the way a tern
plummets; and the sailors heaved her over
as tender pickings for the seals and fish.
Now I was left in dread, alone, while wind
and current bore them on to Ithaka.   545
Laërtês purchased me. That was the way
I first laid eyes upon this land."

                              Odysseus,
the kingly man, replied:

                    "You rouse my pity,
telling what you endured when you were young.
But surely Zeus put good alongside ill: 550
torn from your own far home, you had the luck
to come into a kind man's service, generous
with food and drink. And a good life you lead,
unlike my own, all spent in barren roaming
from one country to the next, till now."   555

So the two men talked on, into the night,
leaving few hours for sleep before the Dawn
stepped up to her bright chair.
                              The ship now drifting
under the island lee, Telémakhos'
companions took in sail and mast, unshipped   560
the oars and rowed ashore. They moored her stern
by the stout hawser lines, tossed out the bow stones,
and waded in beyond the wash of ripples
to mix their wine and cook their morning meal.
When they had turned back hunger and thirst, Telémakhos   565
arose to give the order of the day.

"Pull for the town," he said, "and berth our ship,
while I go inland across country. Later,
this evening, after looking at my farms,
I'll join you in the city. When day comes   570
I hope to celebrate our crossing, feasting
everyone on good red meat and wine."

His noble passenger, Theoklýmenos,
now asked:

              "What as to me, my dear young fellow,
where shall I go? Will I find lodging here   575
with some one of the lords of stony Ithaka?
Or go straight to your mother's hall and yours?"

Telémakhos turned round to him and said:

"I should myself invite you to our hall
if things were otherwise; there'd be no lack   580
of entertainment for you. As it stands,
no place could be more wretched for a guest
while I'm away. Mother will never see you;
she almost never shows herself at home
to the suitors there, but stays in her high chamber   585
weaving upon her loom. No, let me name
another man for you to go to visit:
Eurýmakhos, the honored son of Pólybos.
In Ithaka they are dazzled by him now—
the strongest of their princes, bent on making   590
mother and all Odysseus' wealth his own.
Zeus on Olympos only knows
if some dark hour for them will intervene."

The words were barely spoken, when a hawk,
Apollo's courier, flew up on the right,   595

clutching a dove and plucking her—so feathers
floated down to the ground between Telémakhos
and the moored cutter. Theoklýmenos
called him apart and gripped his hand, whispering:

"A god spoke in this bird-sign on the right.   600
I knew it when I saw the hawk fly over us.
There is no kinglier house than yours, Telémakhos,
here in the realm of Ithaka. Your family
will be in power forever."

                              The young prince,
clear in spirit, answered:

                              "Be it so,   605
friend, as you say. And may you know as well
the friendship of my house, and many gifts
from me, so everyone may call you fortunate."

He called a trusted crewman named Peiraios,
and said to him:

                    "Peiraios, son of Klýtios,   610
can I rely on you again as ever, most
of all the friends who sailed with me to Pylos?
Take this man home with you, take care of him,
treat him with honor, till I come."

                              To this
Peiraios the good spearman answered: 615

                              "Aye,
stay in the wild country while you will,
I shall be looking after him, Telémakhos.
He will not lack good lodging."

                              Down to the ship
he turned, and boarded her, and called the others   620
to cast off the stern lines and come aboard.
So the men climbed in to sit beside the rowlocks.
Telémakhos now tied his sandals on
and lifted his tough spear from the ship's deck;
hawsers were taken in, and they shoved off   625
to reach the town by way of the open sea
as he commanded them—royal Odysseus'
own dear son, Telémakhos.
                              On foot
and swiftly he went up toward the stockade
where swine were penned in hundreds, and at night   630

the guardian of the swine, the forester,
slept under arms on duty for his masters.

Father and Son

But there were two men in the mountain hut—
Odysseus and the swineherd. At first light
blowing their fire up, they cooked their breakfast
and sent their lads out, driving herds to root
in the tall timber.

       When Telémakhos came,   5
the wolvish troop of watchdogs only fawned on him
as he advanced. Odysseus heard them go
and heard the light crunch of a man's footfall—
at which he turned quickly to say:

                "Eumaios,
here is one of your crew come back, or maybe   10
another friend: the dogs are out there snuffling
belly down; not one has even growled.
I can hear footsteps—"

                But before he finished
his tall son stood at the door.
                The swineherd
rose in surprise, letting a bowl and jug   15
tumble from his fingers. Going forward,
he kissed the young man's head, his shining eyes
and both hands, while his own tears brimmed and fell.
Think of a man whose dear and only son,
born to him in exile, reared with labor,   20
has lived ten years abroad and now returns:
how would that man embrace his son! Just so
the herdsman clapped his arms around Telémakhos
and covered him with kisses—for he knew
the lad had got away from death. He said: 25

"Light of my days, Telémakhos,
you made it back! When you took ship for Pylos
I never thought to see you here again.
Come in, dear child, and let me feast my eyes;
here you are, home from the distant places!   30
How rarely anyway, you visit us,
your own men, and your own woods and pastures!
Always in the town, a man would think
you loved the suitors' company, those dogs!"

Telémakhos with his clear candor said: 35

"I am with you, Uncle. See now, I have come
because I wanted to see you first, to hear from you
if Mother stayed at home—or is she married
off to someone and Odysseus' bed
left empty for some gloomy spider's weaving?"   40

Gently the forester replied to this:

"At home indeed your mother is, poor lady,
still in the women's hall. Her nights and days
are wearied out with grieving."

                                    Stepping back
he took the bronze-shod lance, and the young prince   45
entered the cabin over the worn door stone.
Odysseus moved aside, yielding his couch,
but from across the room Telémakhos checked him:

"Friend, sit down; we'll find another chair
in our own hut. Here is the man to make one!"   50

The swineherd, when the quiet man sank down,
built a new pile of evergreens and fleeces—
a couch for the dear son of great Odysseus—
then gave them trenchers of good meat, left over
from the roast pork of yesterday, and heaped up   55
willow baskets full of bread, and mixed
an ivy bowl of honey-hearted wine.
Then he in turn sat down, facing Odysseus,
their hands went out upon the meat and drink
as they fell to, ridding themselves of hunger,   60
until Telémakhos paused and said:

                              "Oh, Uncle,
what's your friend's home port? How did he come?
Who were the sailors brought him here to Ithaka?
I doubt if he came walking on the sea."

And you replied, Eumaios—O my swineherd—   65

"Son, the truth about him is soon told.
His home land, and a broad land, too, is Krete,
but he has knocked about the world, he says,
for years, as the Powers wove his life. Just now
he broke away from a shipload of Thesprotians   70
to reach my hut. I place him in your hands.
Act as you will. He wishes your protection."

The young man said:

        "Eumaios, my protection!
The notion cuts me to the heart. How can I
receive your friend at home? I am not old enough   75
or trained in arms. Could I defend myself
if someone picked a fight with me?
                       Besides,
mother is in a quandary, whether to stay with me
as mistress of our household, honoring
her lord's bed, and opinion in the town,   80
or take the best Akhaian who comes her way—
the one who offers most.
                I'll undertake,
at all events, to clothe your friend for winter,
now he is with you. Tunic and cloak of wool,
a good broadsword, and sandals—these are his.   85
I can arrange to send him where he likes
or you may keep him in your cabin here.
I shall have bread and wine sent up; you need not
feel any pinch on his behalf.
                  Impossible
to let him stay in hall, among the suitors.   90
They are drunk, drunk on impudence, they might
injure my guest—and how could I bear that?
How could a single man take on those odds?
Not even a hero could.
            The suitors are too strong."

At this the noble and enduring man, Odysseus,   95
addressed his son:

        "Kind prince, it may be fitting
for me to speak a word. All that you say
gives me an inward wound as I sit listening.
I mean this wanton game they play, these fellows,
riding roughshod over you in your own house,   100
admirable as you are. But tell me,
are you resigned to being bled? The townsmen,
stirred up against you, are they, by some oracle?
Your brothers—can you say your brothers fail you?
A man should feel his kin, at least, behind him   105
in any clash, when a real fight is coming.
If my heart were as young as yours, if I were
son of Odysseus, or the man himself,
I'd rather have my head cut from my shoulders
by some slashing adversary, if I   110
brought no hurt upon that crew! Suppose

I went down, being alone, before the lot,
better, I say, to die at home in battle
than see these insupportable things, day after
day the stranger cuffed, the women slaves   115
dragged here and there, shame in the lovely rooms,
the wine drunk up in rivers, sheer waste
of pointless feasting, never at an end!"

Telémakhos replied:

            "Friend, I'll explain to you.
There is no rancor in the town against me,   120
no fault of brothers, whom a man should feel
behind him when a fight is in the making;
no, no—in our family the First Born
of Heaven, Zeus, made single sons the rule.
Arkeísios had but one, Laërtês; he   125
in his turn fathered only one, Odysseus,
who left me in his hall alone, too young
to be of any use to him.
And so you see why enemies fill our house
in these days: all the princes of the islands,   130
Doulíkhion, Samê, wooded Zakýnthos,
Ithaka, too—lords of our island rock—
eating our house up as they court my mother.
She cannot put an end to it; she dare not
bar the marriage that she hates; and they   135
devour all my substance and my cattle,
and who knows when they'll slaughter me as well?
It rests upon the gods' great knees.
                     Uncle,
go down at once and tell the Lady Penélopê
that I am back from Pylos, safe and sound.   140
I stay here meanwhile. You will give your message
and then return. Let none of the Akhaians
hear it; they have a mind to do me harm."

To this, Eumaios, you replied:

             "I know.
But make this clear, now—should I not likewise   145
call on Laërtês with your news? Hard hit
by sorrow though he was, mourning Odysseus,
he used to keep an eye upon his farm.
He had what meals he pleased, with his own folk.
But now no more, not since you sailed for Pylos;   150
he has not taken food or drink, I hear,

sitting all day, blind to the work of harvest,
groaning, while the skin shrinks on his bones."

Telémakhos answered:

"One more misery,
but we had better leave it so.   155
If men could choose, and have their choice, in everything,
we'd have my father home.

Turn back
when you have done your errand, as you must,
not to be caught alone in the countryside.[6]
But wait—you may tell Mother   160
to send our old housekeeper on the quiet
and quickly; she can tell the news to Grandfather."

The swineherd, roused, reached out to get his sandals,
tied them on, and took the road.

Who else
beheld this but Athena? From the air   165
she walked, taking the form of a tall woman,
handsome and clever at her craft, and stood
beyond the gate in plain sight of Odysseus,
unseen, though, by Telémakhos, unguessed,
for not to everyone will gods appear.   170
Odysseus noticed her; so did the dogs,
who cowered whimpering away from her. She only
nodded, signing to him with her brows,
a sign he recognized. Crossing the yard,
he passed out through the gate in the stockade   175
to face the goddess. There she said to him:

"Son of Laërtês and the gods of old,
Odysseus, master of land ways and sea ways,
dissemble to your son no longer now.
The time has come: tell him how you together   180
will bring doom on the suitors in the town.
I shall not be far distant then, for I
myself desire battle."

Saying no more,
she tipped her golden wand upon the man,
making his cloak pure white, and the knit tunic   185
fresh around him. Lithe and young she made him,

6. The Greek says something more like: "and don't go wandering round the countryside after him" (i.e.,
Laërtês).

ruddy with sun, his jawline clean, the beard
no longer grey upon his chin. And she
withdrew when she had done.
                    Then Lord Odysseus
reappeared—and his son was thunderstruck.   190
Fear in his eyes, he looked down and away
as though it were a god, and whispered:

                           "Stranger,
you are no longer what you were just now!
Your cloak is new; even your skin! You are
one of the gods who rule the sweep of heaven!   195
Be kind to us, we'll make you fair oblation
and gifts of hammered gold. Have mercy on us!"

The noble and enduring man replied:

"No god. Why take me for a god? No, no.
I am that father whom your boyhood lacked   200
and suffered pain for lack of. I am he."

Held back too long, the tears ran down his cheeks
as he embraced his son.
                  Only Telémakhos,
uncomprehending, wild
with incredulity, cried out:

                    "You cannot   205
be my father Odysseus! Meddling spirits
conceived this trick to twist the knife in me!
No man of woman born could work these wonders
by his own craft, unless a god came into it
with ease to turn him young or old at will.   210
I swear you were in rags and old,
and here you stand like one of the immortals!"

Odysseus brought his ranging mind to bear
and said:

             "This is not princely, to be swept
away by wonder at your father's presence.   215
No other Odysseus will ever come,
for he and I are one, the same; his bitter
fortune and his wanderings are mine.
Twenty years gone, and I am back again
on my own island.
               As for my change of skin,   220

that is a charm Athena, Hope of Soldiers,[7]
uses as she will; she has the knack
to make me seem a beggar man sometimes
and sometimes young, with finer clothes about me.
It is no hard thing for the gods of heaven   225
to glorify a man or bring him low."

When he had spoken, down he sat.
                              Then, throwing
his arms around this marvel of a father
Telémakhos began to weep. Salt tears
rose from the wells of longing in both men,   230
and cries burst from both as keen and fluttering
as those of the great taloned hawk,
whose nestlings farmers take before they fly.
So helplessly they cried, pouring out tears,
and might have gone on weeping so till sundown,   235
had not Telémakhos said:

                    "Dear father! Tell me
what kind of vessel put you here ashore
on Ithaka? Your sailors, who were they?
I doubt you made it, walking on the sea!"

Then said Odysseus, who had borne the barren sea: 240

"Only plain truth shall I tell you, child.
Great seafarers, the Phaiákians, gave me passage
as they give other wanderers. By night
over the open ocean, while I slept,
they brought me in their cutter, set me down   245
on Ithaka, with gifts of bronze and gold
and stores of woven things. By the gods' will
these lie all hidden in a cave. I came
to this wild place, directed by Athena,
so that we might lay plans to kill our enemies.   250
Count up the suitors for me, let me know
what men at arms are there, how many men.
I must put all my mind to it, to see
if we two by ourselves can take them on
or if we should look round for help."

                              Telémakhos   255
replied:

7. Athena was a warrior goddess.

"O Father, all my life your fame
as a fighting man has echoed in my ears—
your skill with weapons and the tricks of war—
but what you speak of is a staggering thing,
beyond imagining, for me. How can two men   260
do battle with a houseful in their prime?
For I must tell you this is no affair
of ten or even twice ten men, but scores,
throngs of them. You shall see, here and now.
The number from Doulíkhion alone   265
is fifty-two picked men, with armorers,
a half dozen; twenty-four came from Samê,
twenty from Zakýnthos; our own island
accounts for twelve, high-ranked, and their retainers,
Medôn the crier, and the Master Harper,   270
besides a pair of handymen at feasts.
If we go in against all these
I fear we pay in salt blood for your vengeance.
You must think hard if you would conjure up
the fighting strength to take us through."

                                        Odysseus   275
who had endured the long war and the sea
answered:

          "I'll tell you now.
Suppose Athena's arm is over us, and Zeus
her father's, must I rack my brains for more?"

Clearheaded Telémakhos looked hard and said: 280

"Those two are great defenders, no one doubts it,
but throned in the serene clouds overhead;
other affairs of men and gods they have
to rule over."

          And the hero answered:

"Before long they will stand to right and left of us   285
in combat, in the shouting, when the test comes—
our nerve against the suitors' in my hall.
Here is your part: at break of day tomorrow
home with you, go mingle with our princes.
The swineherd later on will take me down   290
the port-side trail—a beggar, by my looks,
hangdog and old. If they make fun of me
in my own courtyard, let your ribs cage up
your springing heart, no matter what I suffer,

no matter if they pull me by the heels   295
or practice shots at me, to drive me out.
Look on, hold down your anger. You may even
plead with them, by heaven! in gentle terms
to quit their horseplay—not that they will heed you,
rash as they are, facing their day of wrath.   300
Now fix the next step in your mind.
                                   Athena,
counseling me, will give me word, and I
shall signal to you, nodding: at that point
round up all armor, lances, gear of war
left in our hall, and stow the lot away   305
back in the vaulted store room. When the suitors
miss those arms and question you, be soft
in what you say: answer:

                    'I thought I'd move them
out of the smoke. They seemed no longer those
bright arms Odysseus left us years ago   310
when he went off to Troy. Here where the fire's
hot breath came, they had grown black and drear.
One better reason, too, I had from Zeus:
Suppose a brawl starts up when you are drunk,
you might be crazed and bloody one another,   315
and that would stain your feast, your courtship. Tempered
iron can magnetize a man.'
                         Say that.
But put aside two broadswords and two spears
for our own use, two oxhide shields nearby
when we go into action. Pallas Athena   320
and Zeus All Provident will see you through,
bemusing our young friends.
                           Now one thing more.
If son of mine you are and blood of mine,
let no one hear Odysseus is about.
Neither Laërtês, nor the swineherd here,   325
nor any slave, nor even Penélopê.
But you and I alone must learn how far
the women are corrupted; we should know
how to locate good men among our hands,
the loyal and respectful, and the shirkers   330
who take you lightly, as alone and young."

His admirable son replied:

                              "Ah, Father,
even when danger comes I think you'll find
courage in me. I am not scatterbrained.

But as to checking on the field hands now,   335
I see no gain for us in that. Reflect,
you make a long toil, that way, if you care
to look men in the eye at every farm.
while these gay devils in our hall at ease
eat up our flocks and herds, leaving us nothing.   340

As for the maids I say, Yes: make distinction
between good girls and those who shame your house;
all that I shy away from is a scrutiny
of cottagers just now. The time for that
comes later—if in truth you have a sign   345
from Zeus the Stormking."

               So their talk ran on,
while down the coast, and round toward Ithaka,
hove the good ship that had gone out to Pylos
bearing Telémakhos and his companions.
Into the wide bay waters, on to the dark land,   350
they drove her, hauled her up, took out the oars
and canvas for light-hearted squires to carry
homeward—as they carried, too, the gifts
of Meneláos round to Klýtios'[8] house.
But first they sped a runner to Penélopê.   355
They knew that quiet lady must be told
the prince her son had come ashore, and sent
his good ship round to port; not one soft tear
should their sweet queen let fall.
                  Both messengers,
crewman and swineherd—reached the outer gate   360
in the same instant, bearing the same news,
and went in side by side to the king's hall.
He of the ship burst out among the maids:
"Your son's ashore this morning, O my Queen!"

But the swineherd calmly stood near Penélopê   365
whispering what her son had bade him tell
and what he had enjoined on her. No more.
When he had done, he left the place and turned
back to his steading in the hills.

             By now,
sullen confusion weighed upon the suitors.   370
Out of the house, out of the court they went,
beyond the wall and gate, to sit in council.

---

8. The father of Peiraios (XV. 608), the man to whom Telémakhos entrusted his suppliant Theoklýmenos.

Eurýmakhos, the son of Pólybos,
opened discussion:

      "Friends, face up to it;
that young pup, Telémakhos, has done it;   375
he made the round trip, though we said he could not.
Well—now to get the best craft we can find
afloat, with oarsmen who can drench her bows,
and tell those on the island to come home."

He was yet speaking when Amphínomos,   380
craning seaward, spotted the picket ship
already in the roadstead under oars
with canvas brailed up; and this fresh arrival
made him chuckle. Then he told his friends:

"Too late for messages. Look, here they come   385
along the bay. Some god has brought them news,
or else they saw the cutter pass—and could not
overtake her."

      On their feet at once,
the suitors took the road to the sea beach,
where, meeting the black ship, they hauled her in.   390
Oars and gear they left for their light-hearted
squires to carry, and all in company
made off for the assembly ground. All others,
young and old alike, they barred from sitting.
Eupeithês' son, Antínoös, made the speech: 395

"How the gods let our man escape a boarding,
that is the wonder.

      We had lookouts posted
up on the heights all day in the sea wind,
and every hour a fresh pair of eyes;
at night we never slept ashore   400
but after sundown cruised the open water
to the southeast, patrolling until Dawn.
We were prepared to cut him off and catch him,
squelch him for good and all. The power of heaven
steered him the long way home.   405

Well, let this company plan his destruction,
and leave him no way out, this time. I see
our business here unfinished while he lives.
He knows, now, and he's no fool. Besides,
his people are all tired of playing up to us.   410
I say, act now, before he brings the whole

body of Akhaians to assembly—
and he would leave no word unsaid, in righteous
anger speaking out before them all
of how we plotted murder, and then missed him.   415
Will they commend us for that pretty work?
Take action now, or we are in for trouble;
we might be exiled, driven off our lands.
Let the first blow be ours.
If we move first, and get our hands on him   420
far from the city's eye, on path or field,
then stores and livestock will be ours to share;
the house we may confer upon his mother—
and on the man who marries her. Decide
otherwise you may—but if, my friends,   425
you want that boy to live and have his patrimony,
then we should eat no more of his good mutton,
come to this place no more.
                         Let each from his own hall
court her with dower gifts. And let her marry
the destined one, the one who offers most."   430

He ended, and no sound was heard among them,
sitting all hushed, until at last the son
of Nísos Aretíadês arose—
Amphínomos.
                He led the group of suitors
who came from grainlands on Doulíkhion,   435
and he had lightness in his talk that pleased
Penélopê, for he meant no ill.
Now, in concern for them, he spoke:

                          "O Friends
I should not like to kill Telémakhos.
It is a shivery thing to kill a prince   440
of royal blood.
                We should consult the gods.
If Zeus hands down a ruling for that act,
then I shall say, 'Come one, come all,' and go
cut him down with my own hand—
but I say Halt, if gods are contrary."   445

Now this proposal won them, and it carried.
Breaking their session up, away they went
to take their smooth chairs in Odysseus' house.
Meanwhile Penélopê the Wise,
decided, for her part, to make appearance   450
before the valiant young men.

                          She knew now
they plotted her child's death in her own hall,
for once more Medôn, who had heard them, told her.
Into the hall that lovely lady came,
with maids attending, and approached the suitors,   455
till near a pillar of the well-wrought roof
she paused, her shining veil across her cheeks,
and spoke directly to Antínoös:

                          "Infatuate,
steeped in evil! Yet in Ithaka they say
you were the best one of your generation   460
in mind and speech. Not so, you never were.
Madman, why do you keep forever knitting
death for Telémakhos? Have you no pity
toward men dependent on another's mercy?
Before Lord Zeus, no sanction can be found   465
for one such man to plot against another!
Or are you not aware that your own father
fled to us when the realm was up in arms
against him? He had joined the Taphian pirates
in ravaging Thesprotian folk, our friends.   470
Our people would have raided *him*, then—breached
his heart, butchered his herds to feast upon—
only Odysseus took him in, and held
the furious townsmen off. It is Odysseus'
house you now consume, his wife you court,   475
his son you kill, or try to kill. And me
you ravage now, and grieve. I call upon you
to make an end of it!—and your friends too!"

The son of Pólybos it was, Eurýmakhos,
who answered her with ready speech:

                                        "My lady   480
Penélopê, wise daughter of Ikários,
you must shake off these ugly thoughts. I say
that man does not exist, nor will, who dares
lay hands upon your son Telémakhos,
while I live, walk the earth, and use my eyes.   485
The man's life blood, I swear,
will spurt and run out black around my lancehead!
For it is true of me, too, that Odysseus,
raider of cities, took me on his knees
and fed me often—tidbits and red wine.   490
Should not Telémakhos, therefore, be dear to me
above the rest of men? I tell the lad
he must not tremble for his life, at least

alone in the suitors' company. Heaven
deals death no man avoids."
                  Blasphemous lies   495
in earnest tones he told—the one who planned
the lad's destruction!
             Silently the lady
made her way to her glowing upper chamber,
there to weep for her dear lord, Odysseus,
until grey-eyed Athena   500
cast sweet sleep upon her eyes.

                  At fall of dusk
Odysseus and his son heard the approach
of the good forester. They had been standing
over the fire with a spitted pig,
a yearling. And Athena coming near   505
with one rap of her wand made of Odysseus
an old old man again, with rags about him—
for if the swineherd knew his lord were there
he could not hold the news; Penélopê
would hear it from him.
               Now Telémakhos   510
greeted him first:

               "Eumaios, back again!
What was the talk in town? Are the tall suitors
home again, by this time, from their ambush,
or are they still on watch for my return?"

And you replied, Eumaios—O my swineherd: 515

"There was no time to ask or talk of that;
I hurried through the town. Even while I spoke
my message, I felt driven to return.
A runner from your friends turned up, a crier,
who gave the news first to your mother. Ah!   520
One thing I do know; with my own two eyes
I saw it. As I climbed above the town
to where the sky is cut by Hermês' ridge,
I saw a ship bound in for our own bay
with many oarsmen in it, laden down   525
with sea provisioning and two-edged spears,
and I surmised those were the men.
                Who knows?"

Telémakhos, now strong with magic, smiled
across at his own father—but avoided
the swineherd's eye.

> So when the pig was done,   530
the spit no longer to be turned, the table
garnished, everyone sat down to feast
on all the savory flesh he craved. And when
they had put off desire for meat and drink,
they turned to bed and took the gift of sleep.   535

BOOK XVII

The Beggar at the Manor

When the young Dawn came bright into the East
spreading her finger tips of rose, Telémakhos
the king's son, tied on his rawhide sandals
and took the lance that bore his handgrip. Burning
to be away, and on the path to town,   5
he told the swineherd:

> "Uncle, the truth is
I must go down myself into the city.
Mother must see me there, with her own eyes,
or she will weep and feel forsaken still,
and will not set her mind at rest. Your job   10
will be to lead this poor man down to beg.
Some householder may want to dole him out
a loaf and pint. I have my own troubles.
Am I to care for every last man who comes?
And if he takes it badly—well, so much   15
the worse for him. Plain truth is what I favor."

At once Odysseus the great tactician
spoke up briskly:

> "Neither would I myself
care to be kept here, lad. A beggar man
fares better in the town. Let it be said   20
I am not yet so old I must lay up
indoors and mumble, 'Aye, Aye' to a master.
Go on, then. As you say, my friend can lead me
as soon as I have had a bit of fire
and when the sun grows warmer. These old rags   25
could be my death, outside on a frosty morning,
and the town is distant, so they say."

> Telémakhos
with no more words went out, and through the fence,
and down hill, going fast on the steep footing,
nursing woe for the suitors in his heart.   30

Before the manor hall, he leaned his lance
against a great porch pillar and stepped in
across the door stone.
           Old Eurýkleia
saw him first, for that day she was covering
handsome chairs nearby with clean fleeces.   35
She ran to him at once, tears in her eyes;
and other maidservants of the old soldier
Odysseus gathered round to greet their prince,
kissing his head and shoulders.
                 Quickly, then,
Penélopê the Wise, tall in her beauty   40
as Artemis or pale-gold Aphroditê,
appeared from her high chamber and came down
to throw her arms around her son. In tears
she kissed his head, kissed both his shining eyes,
then cried out, and her words flew:

                     "Back with me!   45
Telémakhos, more sweet to me than sunlight!
I thought I should not see you again, ever,
after you took the ship that night to Pylos—
against my will, with not a word! you went
for news of your dear father. Tell me now   50
of everything you saw!"

              But he made answer:

"Mother, not now. You make me weep. My heart
already aches—I came near death at sea.
You must bathe, first of all, and change your dress,
and take your maids to the highest room to pray.   55
Pray, and burn offerings to the gods of heaven,
that Zeus may put his hand to our revenge.

I am off now to bring home from the square
a guest, a passenger I had. I sent him
yesterday with all my crew to town.   60
Peiraios was to care for him, I said,
and keep him well, with honor, till I came."

She caught back the swift words upon her tongue.
Then softly she withdrew
to bathe and dress her body in fresh linen,   65
and make her offerings to the gods of heaven,
praying Almighty Zeus
to put his hand to their revenge.

                    Telémakhos
had left the hall, taken his lance, and gone
with two quick hounds at heel into the town,   70
Athena's grace in his long stride
making the people gaze as he came near.
And suitors gathered, primed with friendly words,
despite the deadly plotting in their hearts—
but these, and all their crowd, he kept away from.   75
Next he saw sitting some way off, apart,
Mentor, with Antiphos and Halithersês,
friends of his father's house in years gone by.
Near these men he sat down, and told his tale
under their questioning.
                    His crewman, young Peiraios,   80
guided through town, meanwhile, into the Square,
the Argive exile, Theoklýmenos.
Telémakhos lost no time in moving toward him;
but first Peiraios had his say:

                    "Telémakhos,
you must send maids to me, at once, and let me   85
turn over to you those gifts from Meneláos!"

The prince had pondered it, and said:

                    "Peiraios,
none of us knows how this affair will end.
Say one day our fine suitors, without warning,
draw upon me, kill me in our hall,   90
and parcel out my patrimony—I wish
you, and no one of them, to have those things.
But if my hour comes, if I can bring down
bloody death on all that crew,
you will rejoice to send my gifts to me—   95
and so will I rejoice!"

                    Then he departed,
leading his guest, the lonely stranger, home.

Over chair-backs in hall they dropped their mantles
and passed in to the polished tubs, where maids
poured out warm baths for them, anointed them,   100
and pulled fresh tunics, fleecy cloaks around them.
Soon they were seated at their ease in hall.
A maid came by to tip a golden jug
over their fingers into a silver bowl
and draw a gleaming table up beside them.   105
The larder mistress brought her tray of loaves
and savories, dispensing each.

In silence
across the hall, beside a pillar, propped
in a long chair, Telémakhos' mother
spun a fine wool yarn.
      The young men's hands   110
went out upon the good things placed before them,
and only when their hunger and thirst were gone
did she look up and say:

          "Telémakhos,
what am I to do now? Return alone
and lie again on my forsaken bed—   115
sodden how often with my weeping
since that day when Odysseus put to sea
to join the Atreidai[9] before Troy?
          Could you not
tell me, before the suitors fill our house,
what news you have of his return?"

          He answered: 120
"Now that you ask a second time, dear Mother,
here is the truth.
      We went ashore at Pylos
to Nestor, lord and guardian of the West,
who gave me welcome in his towering hall.
So kind he was, he might have been my father   125
and I his long-lost son—so truly kind,
taking me in with his own honored sons.
But as to Odysseus' bitter fate,
living or dead, he had no news at all
from anyone on earth, he said. He sent me   130
overland in a strong chariot
to Atreus' son, the captain, Meneláos.
And I saw Helen there, for whom the Argives
fought, and the Trojans fought, as the gods willed.
Then Meneláos of the great war cry   135
asked me my errand in that ancient land
of Lakedaimon. So I told our story,
and in reply he burst out:

          'Intolerable!
That feeble men, unfit as those men are,
should think to lie in that great captain's bed,   140
fawns in the lion's lair! As if a doe
put down her litter of sucklings there, while she

9. The sons of Atreus, Agamémnon and Meneláos.

sniffed at the glen or grazed a grassy hollow.
Ha! Then the lord returns to his own bed
and deals out wretched doom on both alike.   145

So will Odysseus deal out doom on these.
O Father Zeus, Athena, and Apollo!
I pray he comes as once he was, in Lesbos,
when he stood up to wrestle Philomeleidês—
champion and Island King—   150
and smashed him down. How the Akhaians cheered!
If that Odysseus could meet the suitors,
they'd have a quick reply, a stunning dowry!
Now for your questions, let me come to the point.
I would not misreport it for you; let me   155
tell you what the Ancient of the Sea,
that infallible seer, told me.
                    On an island
your father lies and grieves. The Ancient saw him
held by a nymph, Kalypso, in her hall;
no means of sailing home remained to him,   160
no ship with oars, and no ship's company
to pull him on the broad back of the sea.'

I had this from the lord marshal, Meneláos,
and when my errand in that place was done
I left for home. A fair breeze from the gods   165
brought me swiftly back to our dear island."

The boy's tale made her heart stir in her breast,
but this was not all. Mother and son now heard
Theoklýmenos, the diviner, say:

"He does not see it clear—
                    O gentle lady,   170
wife of Odysseus Laërtiadês,
listen to me, I can reveal this thing.
Zeus be my witness, and the table set
for strangers and the hearth to which I've come—
the lord Odysseus, I tell you,   175
is present now, already, on this island!
Quartered somewhere, or going about, he knows
what evil is afoot. He has it in him
to bring a black hour on the suitors. Yesterday,
still at the ship, I saw this in a portent.   180
I read the sign aloud, I told Telémakhos!"

The prudent queen, for her part, said:

                              "Stranger,
if only this came true—
our love would go to you, with many gifts;
aye, every man who passed would call you happy!"   185

So ran the talk between these three.
                              Meanwhile,
swaggering before Odysseus' hall,
the suitors were competing at the discus throw
and javelin, on the level measured field.
But when the dinner hour drew on, and beasts   190
were being driven from the fields to slaughter—
as beasts were, every day—Medôn spoke out:
Medôn, the crier, whom the suitors liked;
he took his meat beside them.

                      "Men," he said,
"each one has had his work-out and his pleasure,   195
come in to Hall now; time to make our feast.
Are discus throws more admirable than a roast
when the proper hour comes?"

                      At this reminder
they all broke up their games, and trailed away
into the gracious, timbered hall. There, first,   200
they dropped their cloaks on chairs; then came their ritual:
putting great rams and fat goats to the knife—
pigs and a cow, too.
                      So they made their feast.

During these hours, Odysseus and the swineherd
were on their way out of the hills to town.   205
The forester had got them started, saying:

"Friend, you have hopes, I know, of your adventure
into the heart of town today. My lord
wishes it so, not I. No, I should rather
you stood by here as guardian of our steading.   210
But I owe reverence to my prince, and fear
he'll make my ears burn later if I fail.
A master's tongue has a rough edge. Off we go.
Part of the day is past; nightfall will be
early, and colder, too."

                      Odysseus,   215
who had it all timed in his head, replied:

"I know, as well as you do. Let's move on.
You lead the way—the whole way. Have you got

a staff, a lopped stick, you could let me use
to put my weight on when I slip? This path   220
is hard going, they said."

                              Over his shoulders
he slung his patched-up knapsack, an old bundle
tied with twine. Eumaios found a stick for him,
the kind he wanted, and the two set out,
leaving the boys and dogs to guard the place.   225
In this way good Eumaios led his lord
down to the city.
                    And it seemed to him
he led an old outcast, a beggar man,
leaning most painfully upon a stick,
his poor cloak, all in tatters, looped about him.   230

Down by the stony trail they made their way
as far as Clearwater, not far from town—
a spring house where the people filled their jars.
Ithakos, Nêritos, and Polýktor[1] built it,
and round it on the humid ground a grove,   235
a circular wood of poplars grew. Ice cold
in runnels from a high rock ran the spring,
and over it there stood an altar stone
to the cool nymphs, where all men going by
laid offerings.
                Well, here the son of Dólios   240
crossed their path—Melánthios.
                                  He was driving
a string of choice goats for the evening meal,
with two goatherds beside him; and no sooner
had he laid eyes upon the wayfarers
than he began to growl and taunt them both   245
so grossly that Odysseus' heart grew hot:

"Here comes one scurvy type leading another!
God pairs them off together, every time.
Swineherd, where are you taking your new pig,
that stinking beggar there, licker of pots?   250
How many doorposts has he rubbed his back on
whining for garbage, where a noble guest
would rate a cauldron or a sword?
                                    Hand him
over to me, I'll make a farmhand of him,
a stall scraper, a fodder carrier! Whey   255

---

1. Presumably the first rulers of Ithaka: Ithakos, who gave the island its name; Nêritos, whose name was
given to the mountain on Ithaka (IX. 22); and Polýktor, whose name may possibly mean "having great
possessions."

for drink will put good muscle on his shank!
No chance: he learned his dodges long ago—
no honest sweat. He'd rather tramp the country
begging, to keep his hoggish belly full.
Well, I can tell you this for sure: 260
in King Odysseus' hall, if he goes there,
footstools will fly around his head—good shots
from strong hands. Back and side, his ribs will catch it
on the way out!"

            And like a drunken fool
he kicked at Odysseus' hip as he passed by.   265
Not even jogged off stride, or off the trail,
the Lord Odysseus walked along, debating
inwardly whether to whirl and beat
the life out of this fellow with his stick,
or toss him, brain him on the stony ground.   270
Then he controlled himself, and bore it quietly.
Not so the swineherd.
                 Seeing the man before him,
he raised his arms and cried:
                 "Nymphs of the spring,
daughters of Zeus, if ever Odysseus
burnt you a thighbone in rich fat—a ram's   275
or kid's thighbone, hear me, grant my prayer:
let our true lord come back, let heaven bring him
to rid the earth of these fine courtly ways
Melánthios picks up around the town—
all wine and wind! Bad shepherds ruin flocks!"   280

Melánthios the goatherd answered:
                        "Bless me!
The dog can snap: how he goes on! Some day
I'll take him in a slave ship overseas
and trade him for a herd!
                 Old Silverbow
Apollo, if he shot clean through Telémakhos   285
in hall today, what luck! Or let the suitors
cut him down!
         Odysseus died at sea;
no coming home for him."
                 He flung this out
and left the two behind to come on slowly,
while he went hurrying to the king's hall.   290
There he slipped in, and sat among the suitors,

beside the one he doted on—Eurýmakhos.
Then working servants helped him to his meat
and the mistress of the larder gave him bread.

Reaching the gate, Odysseus and the forester   295
halted and stood outside, for harp notes came
around them ripping on the air
as Phêmios picked out a song. Odysseus
caught his companion's arm and said:

                              "My friend,
here is the beautiful place—who could mistake it?   300
Here is Odysseus' hall: no hall like this!
See how one chamber grows out of another;
see how the court is tight with wall and coping;
no man at arms could break this gateway down!
Your banqueting young lords are here in force,   305
I gather, from the fumes of mutton roasting
and strum of harping—harping, which the gods
appoint sweet friend of feasts!"

                    And—O my swineherd!
you replied:

              "That was quick recognition;
but you are no numbskull—in this or anything.   310
Now we must plan this action. Will you take
leave of me here, and go ahead alone
to make your entrance now among the suitors?
Or do you choose to wait?—Let me go forward
and go in first.
              Do not delay too long;   315
someone might find you skulking here outside
and take a club to you, or heave a lance.
Bear this in mind, I say."

                    The patient hero
Odysseus answered:

              "Just what I was thinking.
You go in first, and leave me here a little.   320
But as for blows and missiles,
I am no tyro at these things. I learned
to keep my head in hardship—years of war
and years at sea. Let this new trial come.
The cruel belly, can you hide its ache?   325
How many bitter days it brings! Long ships
with good stout planks athwart—would fighters rig them

to ride the barren sea, except for hunger?
Seawolves—woe to their enemies!"

                              While he spoke
an old hound, lying near, pricked up his ears   330
and lifted up his muzzle. This was Argos,
trained as a puppy by Odysseus,
but never taken on a hunt before
his master sailed for Troy. The young men, afterward,
hunted wild goats with him, and hare, and deer,   335
but he had grown old in his master's absence.
Treated as rubbish now, he lay at last
upon a mass of dung before the gates—
manure of mules and cows, piled there until
fieldhands could spread it on the king's estate.   340
Abandoned there, and half destroyed with flies,
old Argos lay.
                    But when he knew he heard
Odysseus' voice nearby, he did his best
to wag his tail, nose down, with flattened ears,
having no strength to move nearer his master.   345
And the man looked away,
wiping a salt tear from his cheek; but he
hid this from Eumaios. Then he said:

"I marvel that they leave this hound to lie
here on the dung pile;   350
he would have been a fine dog, from the look of him,
though I can't say as to his power and speed
when he was young. You find the same good build
in house dogs, table dogs landowners keep
all for style."

                    And you replied, Eumaios: 355

"A hunter owned him—but the man is dead
in some far place. If this old hound could show
the form he had when Lord Odysseus left him,
going to Troy, you'd see him swift and strong.
He never shrank from any savage thing   360
he'd brought to bay in the deep woods; on the scent
no other dog kept up with him. Now misery
has him in leash. His owner died abroad,
and here the women slaves will take no care of him.
You know how servants are: without a master   365
they have no will to labor, or excel.
For Zeus who views the wide world takes away

half the manhood of a man, that day
he goes into captivity and slavery."

Eumaios crossed the court and went straight forward   370
into the mégaron² among the suitors;
but death and darkness in that instant closed
the eyes of Argos, who had seen his master,
Odysseus, after twenty years.

                        Long before anyone else
Telémakhos caught sight of the grey woodsman   375
coming from the door, and called him over
with a quick jerk of his head. Eumaios'
narrowed eyes made out an empty bench
beside the one the carver used—that servant
who had no respite, carving for the suitors.   380
This bench he took possession of, and placed it
across the table from Telémakhos
for his own use. Then the two men were served
cuts from a roast and bread from a bread basket.

At no long interval, Odysseus came   385
through his own doorway as a mendicant,
humped like a bundle of rags over his stick.
He settled on the inner ash wood sill,
leaning against the door jamb—cypress timber
the skilled carpenter planed years ago   390
and set up with a plumbline.

                   Now Telémakhos
took an entire loaf and a double handful
of roast meat; then he said to the forester:

"Give these to the stranger there. But tell him
to go among the suitors, on his own;   395
he may beg all he wants. This hanging back
is no asset to a hungry man."

The swineherd rose at once, crossed to the door,
and halted by Odysseus.

                "Friend," he said,
"Telémakhos is pleased to give you these,   400
but he commands you to approach the suitors;

2. The great hall.

you may ask all you want from them. He adds,
your shyness is no asset to a beggar."

The great tactician, lifting up his eyes,
cried:

    "Zeus aloft! A blessing on Telémakhos!   405
Let all things come to pass as he desires!"

Palms held out, in the beggar's gesture, he
received the bread and meat and put it down
before him on his knapsack—lowly table!—
then he fell to, devouring it. Meanwhile   410
the harper in the great room sang a song.
Not till the man was fed did the sweet harper
end his singing—whereupon the company
made the walls ring again with talk.

                    Unseen,
Athena took her place beside Odysseus   415
whispering in his ear:

             "Yes, try the suitors.
You may collect a few more loaves, and learn
who are the decent lads, and who are vicious—
although not one can be excused from death!"

So he appealed to them, one after another,   420
going from left to right, with open palm,
as though his life time had been spent in beggary.
And they gave bread, for pity—wondering, though,
at the strange man. Who could this beggar be,
where did he come from? each would ask his neighbor;   425
till in their midst the goatherd, Melánthios,
raised his voice:

         "Hear just a word from me,
my lords who court our illustrious queen!
                 This man,
this foreigner, I saw him on the road;
the swineherd, here was leading him this way;   430
who, what, or whence he claims to be, I could not
say for sure."
        At this, Antínoös
turned on the swineherd brutally, saying:
                 "You famous
breeder of pigs, why bring this fellow here?

Are we not plagued enough with beggars,   435
foragers and such rats?
                    You find the company
too slow at eating up your lord's estate—
is that it? So you call this scarecrow in?"

The forester replied:

                    "Antínoös,
well born you are, but that was not well said.   440
Who would call in a foreigner?—unless
an artisan with skill to serve the realm,
a healer, or a prophet, or a builder,
or one whose harp and song might give us joy.
All these are sought for on the endless earth,   445
but when have beggars come by invitation?
Who puts a field mouse in his granary? My lord,
you are a hard man, and you always were,
more so than others of this company—hard
on all Odysseus' people and on me.   450
But this I can forget
as long as Penélopê lives on, the wise and tender
mistress of this hall; as long
as Prince Telémakhos—"

                    But he broke off
at a look from Telémakhos, who said:

                    "Be still.   455
Spare me a long-drawn answer to this gentleman.
With his unpleasantness, he will forever make
strife where he can—and goad the others on."

He turned and spoke out clearly to Antínoös:

"What fatherly concern you show me! Frighten   460
this unknown fellow, would you, from my hall
with words that promise blows—may God forbid it!
Give him a loaf. Am I a niggard? No,
I call on you to give. And spare your qualms
as to my mother's loss, or anyone's—   465
not that in truth you have such care at heart:
your heart is all in feeding, not in giving."

Antínoös replied:

                    "What high and mighty
talk, Telémakhos! No holding you!
If every suitor gave what I may give him,   470
he could be kept for months—kept out of sight!"

He reached under the table for the footstool
his shining feet had rested on—and this
he held up so that all could see his gift.

But all the rest gave alms,   475
enough to fill the beggar's pack with bread
and roast meat.
       So it looked as though Odysseus
had had his taste of what these men were like
and could return scot free to his own doorway—
but halting now before Antínoös   480
he made a little speech to him. Said he:

"Give a mite, friend. I would not say, myself,
you are the worst man of the young Akhaians.
The noblest, rather; kingly, by your look;
therefore you'll give more bread than others do.   485
Let me speak well of you as I pass on
over the boundless earth!
       I, too, you know,
had fortune once, lived well, stood well with men,
and gave alms, often, to poor wanderers
like this one that you see—aye, to all sorts,   490
no matter in what dire want. I owned
servants—many, god knows—and all the rest
that goes with being prosperous, as they say.
But Zeus the son of Kronos brought me down.

                        No telling
why he would have it, but he made me go   495
to Egypt with a company of rovers—
a long sail to the south—for my undoing.
Up the broad Nile and in to the river bank
I brought my dipping squadron. There, indeed,
I told the men to stand guard at the ships;   500
I sent patrols out—out to rising ground;
but reckless greed carried my crews away
to plunder the Egyptian farms; they bore off
wives and children, killed what men they found.
The news ran on the wind to the city, a night cry,   505
and sunrise brought both infantry and horsemen,
filling the river plain with dazzle of bronze;
then Zeus lord of lightning
threw my men into a blind panic; no one dared
stand against that host closing around us.   510
Their scything weapons left our dead in piles,
but some they took alive, into forced labor,

myself among them. And they gave me, then,
to one Dmêtor, a traveller, son of Iasos,
who ruled at Kypros.[3] He conveyed me there.   515
From that place, working northward, miserably—"

But here Antínoös broke in, shouting:
                              "God!
What evil wind blew in this pest?
                              Get over,
stand in the passage! Nudge my table, will you?
Egyptian whips are sweet   520
to what you'll come to here, you nosing rat,
making your pitch to everyone!
These men have bread to throw away on you
because it is not theirs. Who cares? Who spares
another's food, when he has more than plenty?"   525

With guile Odysseus drew away, then said:

"A pity that you have more looks than heart.
You'd grudge a pinch of salt from your own larder
to your own handy man. You sit here, fat
on others' meat, and cannot bring yourself   530
to rummage out a crust of bread for me!"

Then anger made Antínoös' heart beat hard,
and, glowering under his brows, he answered:

                              "Now!
You think you'll shuffle off and get away
after that impudence? Oh, no you don't!"   535

The stool he let fly hit the man's right shoulder
on the packed muscle under the shoulder blade—
like solid rock, for all the effect one saw.
Odysseus only shook his head, containing
thoughts of bloody work, as he walked on,   540
then sat, and dropped his loaded bag again
upon the door sill. Facing the whole crowd
he said, and eyed them all:

                              "One word only,
my lords, and suitors of the famous queen.
One thing I have to say.   545
There is no pain, no burden for the heart
when blows come to a man, and he defending
his own cattle—his own cows and lambs.

3. Cyprus.

Here it was otherwise. Antínoös
hit me for being driven on by hunger—   550
how many bitter seas men cross for hunger!
If beggars interest the gods, if there are Furies
pent in the dark to avenge a poor man's wrong, then may
Antínoös meet his death before his wedding day!"

Then said Eupeithês' son, Antínoös:

                                        "Enough.   555
Eat and be quiet where you are, or shamble elsewhere,
unless you want these lads to stop your mouth
pulling you by the heels, or hands and feet,
over the whole floor, till your back is peeled!"

But now the rest were mortified, and someone   560
spoke from the crowd of young bucks to rebuke him:

"A poor show, that—hitting this famished tramp—
bad business, if he happened to be a god.
You know they go in foreign guise, the gods do,
looking like strangers, turning up   565
in towns and settlements to keep an eye
on manners, good or bad."

                                But at this notion
Antínoös only shrugged.
                                Telémakhos,
after the blow his father bore, sat still
without a tear, though his heart felt the blow.   570
Slowly he shook his head from side to side,
containing murderous thoughts.
                                Penélopê
on the higher level of her room had heard
the blow, and knew who gave it. Now she murmured:

"Would god you could be hit yourself, Antínoös—   575
hit by Apollo's bowshot!"

                                And Eurýnomê
her housekeeper, put in:

                                "He and no other?
If all we pray for came to pass, not one
would live till dawn!"

                        Her gentle mistress said:

"Oh, Nan, they are a bad lot; they intend   580
ruin for all of us; but Antínoös
appears a blacker-hearted hound than any.

Here is a poor man come, a wanderer,
driven by want to beg his bread, and everyone
in hall gave bits, to cram his bag—only   585
Antínoös threw a stool, and banged his shoulder!"

So she described it, sitting in her chamber
among her maids—while her true lord was eating.
Then she called in the forester and said:

"Go to that man on my behalf, Eumaios,   590
and send him here, so I can greet and question him.
Abroad in the great world, he may have heard
rumors about Odysseus—may have known him!"

Then you replied—O swineherd!

                              "Ah, my queen,
if these Akhaian sprigs would hush their babble   595
the man could tell you tales to charm your heart.
Three days and nights I kept him in my hut;
he came straight off a ship, you know, to me.
There was no end to what he made me hear
of his hard roving and I listened, eyes   600
upon him, as a man drinks in a tale
a minstrel sings—a minstrel taught by heaven
to touch the hearts of men. At such a song
the listener becomes rapt and still. Just so
I found myself enchanted by this man.   605
He claims an old tie with Odysseus, too—
in his home country, the Minoan land
of Krete. From Krete he came, a rolling stone
washed by the gales of life this way and that
to our own beach.
                    If he can be believed   610
he has news of Odysseus near at hand
alive, in the rich country of Thesprotia,
bringing a mass of treasure home."

Then wise Penélopê said again:

"Go call him, let him come here, let him tell   615
that tale again for my own ears.
                          Our friends
can drink their cups outside or stay in hall,
being so carefree. And why not? Their stores
lie intact in their homes, both food and drink,
with only servants left to take a little.   620
But these men spend their days around our house
killing our beeves, our fat goats and our sheep,

carousing, drinking up our good dark wine;
sparing nothing, squandering everything.
No champion like Odysseus takes our part.   625
Ah, if he comes again, no falcon ever
struck more suddenly than he will, with his son,
to avenge this outrage!"

                The great hall below
at this point rang with a tremendous sneeze—
"kchaou!" from Telémakhos—like an acclamation.   630
And laughter seized Penélopê.
                    Then quickly,
lucidly she went on:

                "Go call the stranger
straight to me. Did you hear that, Eumaios?
My son's thundering sneeze at what I said!
May death come of a sudden so; may death   635
relieve us, clean as that, of all the suitors!
Let me add one thing—do not overlook it—
if I can see this man has told the truth,
I promise him a warm new cloak and tunic."

With all this in his head, the forester   640
went down the hall, and halted near the beggar,
saying aloud:
                "Good father, you are called
by the wise mother of Telémakhos,
Penélopê. The queen, despite her troubles,
is moved by a desire to hear your tales   645
about her lord—and if she finds them true,
she'll see you clothed in what you need, a cloak
and a fresh tunic.
                You may have your belly
full each day you go about this realm
begging. For all may give, and all they wish."   650

Now said Odysseus, the old soldier:

"Friend,
I wish this instant I could tell my facts
to the wise daughter of Ikários, Penélopê—
and I have much to tell about her husband;   655
we went through much together.
                But just now
this hard crowd worries me. They are, you said
infamous to the very rim of heaven

for violent acts: and here, just now, this fellow
gave me a bruise. What had I done to him?   660
But who would lift a hand for me? Telémakhos?
Anyone else?
        No; bid the queen be patient.
Let her remain till sundown in her room,
and then—if she will seat me near the fire—
inquire tonight about her lord's return.   665
My rags are sorry cover; you know that;
I showed my sad condition first to you."

The woodsman heard him out, and then returned;
but the queen met him on her threshold, crying:

"Have you not brought him? Why? What is he thinking?   670
Has he some fear of overstepping? Shy
about these inner rooms? A hangdog beggar?"

To this you answered, friend Eumaios:

"No:
he reasons as another might, and well,   675
not to tempt any swordplay from these drunkards.
Be patient, wait—he says—till darkness falls.
And, O my queen, for you too that is better:
better to be alone with him, and question him,
and hear him out."

        Penélopê replied: 680

"He is no fool; he sees how it could be.
Never were mortal men like these
for bullying and brainless arrogance!"

Thus she accepted what had been proposed,
so he went back into the crowd. He joined   685
Telémakhos, and said at once in whispers—
his head bent, so that no one else might hear:

"Dear prince, I must go home to keep good watch
on hut and swine, and look to my own affairs.
Everything here is in your hands. Consider   690
your own safety before the rest; take care
not to get hurt. Many are dangerous here.
May Zeus destroy them first, before we suffer!"

Telémakhos said:

        "Your wish is mine, Uncle.
Go when your meal is finished. Then come back   695

at dawn, and bring good victims for a slaughter.
Everything here is in my hands indeed—
and in the disposition of the gods."

Taking his seat on the smooth bench again,
Eumaios ate and drank his fill, then rose   700
to climb the mountain trail back to his swine,
leaving the mégaron and court behind him
crowded with banqueters.
                    These had their joy
of dance and song, as day waned into evening.

BOOK XVIII

Blows and a Queen's Beauty

Now a true scavenger came in—a public tramp
who begged around the town of Ithaka,
a by-word for his insatiable swag-belly,
feeding and drinking, dawn to dark. No pith
was in him, and no nerve, huge as he looked.   5
Arnaios, as his gentle mother called him,
he had been nicknamed "Iros" by the young
for being ready to take messages.[4]
                    This fellow
thought he would rout Odysseus from his doorway,
growling at him:

                    "Clear out, grandfather,   10
or else be hauled out by the ankle bone.
See them all giving me the wink? That means,
'Go on and drag him out!' I hate to do it.
Up with you! Or would you like a fist fight?"

Odysseus only frowned and looked him over,   15
taking account of everything, then said:

"Master, I am no trouble to you here.
I offer no remarks. I grudge you nothing.
Take all you get, and welcome. Here is room
for two on this doorslab—or do you own it?   20
You are a tramp, I think, like me. Patience:
a windfall from the gods will come. But drop
that talk of using fists; it could annoy me.
Old as I am, I might just crack a rib
or split a lip for you. My life would go   25

---

4. The goddess Iris often served as messenger for the gods.

even more peacefully, after tomorrow,
looking for no more visits here from you."

Iros the tramp grew red and hooted:

"Ho,
listen to him! The swine can talk your arm off,   30
like an old oven woman! With two punches
I'd knock him snoring, if I had a mind to—
and not a tooth left in his head, the same
as an old sow caught in the corn! Belt up!
And let this company see the way I do it   35
when we square off. Can you fight a fresher man?"

Under the lofty doorway, on the door sill
of wide smooth ash, they held this rough exchange.
And the tall full-blooded suitor, Antínoös,
overhearing, broke into happy laughter.   40
Then he said to the others:

                    "Oh, my friends,
no luck like this ever turned up before!
What a farce heaven has brought this house!
                    The stranger
and Iros have had words, they brag of boxing!
Into the ring they go, and no more talk!"   45

All the young men got on their feet now, laughing,
to crowd around the ragged pair. Antínoös
called out:

                    "Gentlemen, quiet! One more thing:
here are goat stomachs ready on the fire
to stuff with blood and fat, good supper pudding.   50
The man who wins this gallant bout
may step up here and take the one he likes.
And let him feast with us from this day on:
no other beggar will be admitted here
when we are at our wine."

                    This pleased them all.   55
But now that wily man, Odysseus, muttered:

"An old man, an old hulk, has no business
fighting a young man, but my belly nags me;
nothing will do but I must take a beating.
Well, then, let every man here swear an oath   60
not to step in for Iros. No one throw
a punch for luck. I could be whipped that way."

So much the suitors were content to swear,
but after they reeled off their oaths, Telémakhos
put in a word to clinch it, saying:

"Friend,   65
if you will stand and fight, as pride requires,
don't worry about a foul blow from behind.
Whoever hits you will take on the crowd.
You have my word as host; you have the word
of these two kings, Antínoös and Eurýmakhos—   70
a pair of thinking men."

All shouted, "Aye!"
So now Odysseus made his shirt a belt
and roped his rags around his loins, baring
his hurdler's thighs and boxer's breadth of shoulder,
the dense rib-sheath and upper arms. Athena   75
stood nearby to give him bulk and power,
while the young suitors watched with narrowed eyes—
and comments went around:

"By god, old Iros now retires."

"Aye,
he asked for it, he'll get it—bloody, too."   80

"The build this fellow had, under his rags!"

Panic made Iros' heart jump, but the yard-boys
hustled and got him belted by main force,
though all his blubber quivered now with dread.
Antínoös' angry voice rang in his ears: 85

"You sack of guts, you might as well be dead,
might as well never have seen the light of day,
if this man makes you tremble! Chicken-heart,
afraid of an old wreck, far gone in misery!
Well, here is what I say—and what I'll do.   90
If this ragpicker can outfight you, whip you,
I'll ship you out to that king in Epeíros,⁵
Ékhetos—he skins everyone alive.
Let him just cut your nose off and your ears
and pull your privy parts out by the roots   95
to feed raw to his hunting dogs!"

Poor Iros
felt a new fit of shaking take his knees.

5. Epirus, the mainland north of Ithaka. *Ékhetos:* All we know of him is what Homer tells us here.

But the yard-boys pushed him out. Now both contenders
put their hands up. Royal Odysseus
pondered if he should hit him with all he had   100
and drop the man dead on the spot, or only
spar, with force enough to knock him down.
Better that way, he thought—a gentle blow,
else he might give himself away.
                          The two
were at close quarters now, and Iros lunged   105
hitting the shoulder. Then Odysseus hooked him
under the ear and shattered his jaw bone,
so bright red blood came bubbling from his mouth,
as down he pitched into the dust, bleating,
kicking against the ground, his teeth stove in.   110
The suitors whooped and swung their arms, half dead
with pangs of laughter.
                          Then, by the ankle bone,
Odysseus hauled the fallen one outside,
crossing the courtyard to the gate, and piled him
against the wall. In his right hand he stuck   115
his begging staff, and said:

                    "Here, take your post.
Sit here to keep the dogs and pigs away.
You can give up your habit of command
over poor waifs and beggarmen—you swab.
Another time you may not know what hit you."   120

When he had slung his rucksack by the string
over his shoulder, like a wad of rags,
he sat down on the broad door sill again,
as laughing suitors came to flock inside;
and each young buck in passing gave him greeting,   125
saying, maybe,

              "Zeus fill your pouch for this!
May the gods grant your heart's desire!"
                                      "Well done
to put that walking famine out of business."

"We'll ship him out to that king in Epeíros,
Ékhetos—he skins everyone alive."   130

Odysseus found grim cheer in their good wishes—
his work had started well.
                    Now from the fire
his fat blood pudding came, deposited

before him by Antínoös—then, to boot,
two brown loaves from the basket, and some wine   135
in a fine cup of gold. These gifts Amphínomos
gave him. Then he said:

                        "Here's luck, grandfather;
a new day; may the worst be over now."

Odysseus answered, and his mind ranged far:

"Amphínomos, your head is clear, I'd say;   140
so was your father's—or at least I've heard
good things of Nísos the Doulíkhion,
whose son you are, they tell me—an easy man.
And you seem gently bred.
                  In view of that,
I have a word to say to you, so listen.   145

Of mortal creatures, all that breathe and move,
earth bears none frailer than mankind. What man
believes in woe to come, so long as valor
and tough knees are supplied him by the gods?
But when the gods in bliss bring miseries on,   150
then willy-nilly, blindly, he endures.
Our minds are as the days are, dark or bright,
blown over by the father of gods and men.

So I, too, in my time thought to be happy;
but far and rash I ventured, counting on   155
my own right arm, my father, and my kin;
behold me now.
                No man should flout the law,
but keep in peace what gifts the gods may give.

I see you young blades living dangerously,
a household eaten up, a wife dishonored—   160
and yet the master will return, I tell you,
to his own place, and soon; for he is near.
So may some power take you out of this,
homeward, and softly, not to face that man
the hour he sets foot on his native ground.   165
Between him and the suitors I foretell
no quittance, no way out, unless by blood,
once he shall stand beneath his own roof-beam."

Gravely, when he had done, he made libation
and took a sip of honey-hearted wine,   170

giving the cup, then, back into the hands
of the young nobleman. Amphínomos, for his part,
shaking his head, with chill and burdened breast,
turned in the great hall.
                Now his heart foreknew
the wrath to come, but he could not take flight,   175
being by Athena bound there.
                      Death would have him
broken by a spear thrown by Telémakhos.
So he sat down where he had sat before.

And now heart-prompting from the grey-eyed goddess
came to the quiet queen, Penélopê: 180
a wish to show herself before the suitors;
for thus by fanning their desire again
Athena meant to set her beauty high
before her husband's eyes, before her son.
Knowing no reason, laughing confusedly,   185
she said:

         "Eurýnomê, I have a craving
I never had at all—I would be seen
among those ruffians, hateful as they are.
I might well say a word, then, to my son,
for his own good—tell him to shun that crowd;   190
for all their gay talk, they are bent on evil."

Mistress Eurýnomê replied:

                "Well said, child,
now is the time. Go down, and make it clear,
hold nothing back from him.
                But you must bathe
and put a shine upon your cheeks—not this way,   195
streaked under your eyes and stained with tears.
You make it worse, being forever sad,
and now your boy's a bearded man! Remember
you prayed the gods to let you see him so."

Penélopê replied:

         "Eurýnomê,   200
it is a kind thought, but I will not hear it—
to bathe and sleek with perfumed oil. No, no,
the gods forever took my sheen away
when my lord sailed for Troy in the decked ships.
Only tell my Autonoë to come,   205
and Hippodameía; they should be attending me

in hall, if I appear there. I could not
enter alone into that crowd of men."

At this the good old woman left the chamber
to tell the maids her bidding. But now too   210
the grey-eyed goddess had her own designs.
Upon the quiet daughter of Ikários
she let clear drops of slumber fall, until
the queen lay back asleep, her limbs unstrung,
in her long chair. And while she slept the goddess   215
endowed her with immortal grace to hold
the eyes of the Akhaians. With ambrosia
she bathed her cheeks and throat and smoothed her brow—
ambrosia, used by flower-crowned Kythereia[6]
when she would join the rose-lipped Graces dancing.   220
Grandeur she gave her, too, in height and form,
and made her whiter than carved ivory.
Touching her so, the perfect one was gone.
Now came the maids, bare-armed and lovely, voices
breaking into the room. The queen awoke   225
and as she rubbed her cheek she sighed:

                            "Ah, soft
that drowse I lay embraced in, pain forgot!
If only Artemis the Pure would give me
death as mild, and soon! No heart-ache more,
no wearing out my lifetime with desire   230
and sorrow, mindful of my lord, good man
in all ways that he was, best of the Akhaians!"

She rose and left her glowing upper room,
and down the stairs, with her two maids in train,
this beautiful lady went before the suitors.   235
Then by a pillar of the solid roof
she paused, her shining veil across her cheek,
the two girls close to her and still;
and in that instant weakness took those men
in the knee joints, their hearts grew faint with lust;   240
not one but swore to god to lie beside her.
But speaking for her dear son's ears alone
she said:

          "Telémakhos, what has come over you?
Lightminded you were not, in all your boyhood.
Now you are full grown, come of age; a man   245
from foreign parts might take you for the son

6. Aphrodite.

of royalty, to go by your good looks;
and have you no more thoughtfulness or manners?
How could it happen in our hall that you
permit the stranger to be so abused?   250
Here, in our house, a guest, can any man
suffer indignity, come by such injury?
What can this be for you but public shame?"

Telémakhos looked in her eyes and answered,
with his clear head and his discretion: 255

"Mother,
I cannot take it ill that you are angry.
I know the meaning of these actions now,
both good and bad. I had been young and blind.
How can I always keep to what is fair   260
while these sit here to put fear in me?—princes
from near and far whose interest is my ruin;
are any on my side?
                    But you should know
the suitors did not have their way, matching
the stranger here and Iros—for the stranger   265
beat him to the ground.
                        O Father Zeus!
Athena and Apollo! could I see
the suitors whipped like that! Courtyard and hall
strewn with our friends, too weak-kneed to get up,
chapfallen to their collarbones, the way   270
old Iros rolls his head there by the gate
as though he were pig-drunk! No energy
to stagger on his homeward path; no fight
left in his numb legs!"

                        Thus Penélopê
reproached her son, and he replied. Now, interrupting,   275
Eurýmakhos called out to her:

                        "Penélopê,
deep-minded queen, daughter of Ikários,
if all Akhaians in the land of Argos
only saw you now! What hundreds more
would join your suitors here to feast tomorrow!   280
Beauty like yours no woman had before,
or majesty, or mastery."

                    She answered:

"Eurýmakhos, my qualities—I know—
my face, my figure, all were lost or blighted

when the Akhaians crossed the sea to Troy,   285
Odysseus my lord among the rest.
If he returned, if he were here to care for me,
I might be happily renowned!
But grief instead heaven sent me—years of pain.
Can I forget?—the day he left this island,   290
enfolding my right hand and wrist in his,
he said:

      'My lady, the Akhaian troops
will not easily make it home again
full strength, unhurt, from Troy. They say the Trojans
are fighters too; good lances and good bowmen,   295
horsemen, charioteers—and those can be
decisive when a battle hangs in doubt.
So whether God will send me back, or whether
I'll be a captive there, I cannot tell.
Here, then, you must attend to everything.   300
My parents in our house will be a care for you
as they are now, or more, while I am gone.
Wait for the beard to darken our boy's cheek;
then marry whom you will, and move away.'

The years he spoke of are now past; the night   305
comes when a bitter marriage overtakes me,
desolate as I am, deprived by Zeus
of all the sweets of life.
         How galling, too,
to see newfangled manners in my suitors!
Others who go to court a gentlewoman,   310
daughter of a rich house, if they are rivals,
bring their own beeves and sheep along; her friends
ought to be feasted, gifts are due to her;
would any dare to live at her expense?"

Odysseus' heart laughed when he heard all this—   315
her sweet tones charming gifts out of the suitors
with talk of marriage, though she intended none.
Eupeithês' son, Antínoös, now addressed her:

"Ikários' daughter, O deep-minded queen!
If someone cares to make you gifts, accept them!   320
It is no courtesy to turn gifts away.
But we go neither to our homes nor elsewhere
until of all Akhaians here you take
the best man for your lord."

                    Pleased at this answer,
every man sent a squire to fetch a gift—   325
Antínoös, a wide resplendent robe,
embroidered fine, and fastened with twelve brooches,
pins pressed into sheathing tubes of gold;
Eurýmakhos, a necklace, wrought in gold,
with sunray pieces of clear glinting amber.   330
Eurýdamas' men came back with pendants,
ear-drops in triple clusters of warm lights;
and from the hoard of Lord Polýktor's son,
Peisándros, came a band for her white throat,
jewelled adornment. Other wondrous things   335
were brought as gifts from the Akhaian princes.
Penélopê then mounted the stair again,
her maids behind, with treasure in their arms.

And now the suitors gave themselves to dancing,
to harp and haunting song, as night drew on;   340
black night indeed came on them at their pleasure.
But three torch fires were placed in the long hall
to give them light. On hand were stores of fuel,
dry seasoned chips of resinous wood, split up
by the bronze hatchet blade—these were mixed in   345
among the flames to keep them flaring bright;
each housemaid of Odysseus took her turn.

Now he himself, the shrewd and kingly man,
approached and told them:

                    "Housemaids of Odysseus,
your master so long absent in the world,   350
go to the women's chambers, to your queen.
Attend her, make the distaff whirl, divert her,
stay in her room, comb wool for her.
                            I stand here
ready to tend these flares and offer light
to everyone. They cannot tire me out,   355
even if they wish to drink till Dawn.
I am a patient man."

                    But the women giggled,
glancing back and forth—laughed in his face;
and one smooth girl, Melántho, spoke to him
most impudently. She was Dólios' daughter,   360
taken as ward in childhood by Penélopê
who gave her playthings to her heart's content

and raised her as her own. Yet the girl felt
nothing for her mistress, no compunction,
but slept and made love with Eurýmakhos.   365
Her bold voice rang now in Odysseus' ears:

"You must be crazy, punch drunk, you old goat.
Instead of going out to find a smithy
to sleep warm in—or a tavern bench—you stay
putting your oar in, amid all our men.   370
Numbskull, not to be scared! The wine you drank
has clogged your brain, or are you always this way,
boasting like a fool? Or have you lost
your mind because you beat that tramp, that Iros?
Look out, or someone better may get up   375
and give you a good knocking about the ears
to send you out all bloody."

                    But Odysseus
glared at her under his brows and said:

                              "One minute:
let me tell Telémakhos how you talk
in hall, you slut; he'll cut your arms and legs off!"   380

This hard shot took the women's breath away
and drove them quaking to their rooms, as though
knives were behind: they felt he spoke the truth.
So there he stood and kept the firelight high
and looked the suitors over, while his mind   385
roamed far ahead to what must be accomplished.

They, for their part, could not now be still
or drop their mockery—for Athena wished
Odysseus mortified still more.
                    Eurýmakhos,
the son of Pólybos, took up the baiting,   390
angling for a laugh among his friends.

"Suitors of our distinguished queen," he said,
"hear what my heart would have me say.
                              This man
comes with a certain aura of divinity
into Odysseus' hall. He shines.
                              He shines   395
around the noggin, like a flashing light,
having no hair at all to dim his lustre."

Then turning to Odysseus, raider of cities,
he went on:

"Friend, you have a mind to work,
do you? Could I hire you to clear stones   400
from wasteland for me—you'll be paid enough—
collecting boundary walls and planting trees?
I'd give you a bread ration every day,
a cloak to wrap in, sandals for your feet.
Oh no: you learned your dodges long ago—   405
no honest sweat. You'd rather tramp the country
begging, to keep your hoggish belly full."

The master of many crafts replied:

                         "Eurýmakhos,
we two might try our hands against each other
in early summer when the days are long,   410
in meadow grass, with one good scythe for me
and one as good for you: we'd cut our way
down a deep hayfield, fasting to late evening.
Or we could try our hands behind a plow,
driving the best of oxen—fat, well-fed,   415
well-matched for age and pulling power, and say
four strips apiece of loam the share could break:
you'd see then if I cleft you a straight furrow.
Competition in arms? If Zeus Kroníon
roused up a scuffle now, give me a shield,   420
two spears, a dogskin cap with plates of bronze
to fit my temples, and you'd see me go
where the first rank of fighters lock in battle.
There would be no more jeers about my belly.
You thick-skinned menace to all courtesy!   425
You think you are a great man and a champion,
but up against few men, poor stuff, at that.
Just let Odysseus return, those doors
wide open as they are, you'd find too narrow
to suit you on your sudden journey out."   430

Now fury mounted in Eurýmakhos,
who scowled and shot back:

                         "Bundle of rags and lice!
By god, I'll make you suffer for your gall,
your insolent gabble before all our men."

He had his foot-stool out: but now Odysseus   435
took to his haunches by Amphínomos' knees,
fearing Eurýmakhos' missile, as it flew.
It clipped a wine steward on the serving hand,
so that his pitcher dropped with a loud clang
while he fell backward, cursing, in the dust.   440

In the shadowy hall a low sound rose—of suitors
murmuring to one another.

                    "Ai!" they said,
"This vagabond would have done well to perish
somewhere else, and make us no such rumpus.
Here we are, quarreling over tramps; good meat   445
and wine forgotten; good sense gone by the board."

Telémakhos, his young heart high, put in:

"Bright souls, alight with wine, you can no longer
hide the cups you've taken.[7] Aye, some god
is goading you. Why not go home to bed?—   450
I mean when you are moved to. No one jumps
at my command."

                    Struck by his blithe manner,
the young men's teeth grew fixed in their under lips,
but now the son of Nísos, Lord Amphínomos
of Aretíadês, addressed them all: 455

"O friends, no ruffling replies are called for;
that was fair counsel.
                    Hands off the stranger, now,
and hands off any other servant here
in the great house of King Odysseus. Come,
let my own herald wet our cups once more,   460
we'll make an offering, and then to bed.
The stranger can be left behind in hall;
Telémakhos may care for him; he came
to Telémakhos' door, not ours."

                    This won them over.
The soldier Moulios, Doulíkhion herald,   465
comrade in arms of Lord Amphínomos,
mixed the wine and served them all. They tipped out
drops for the blissful gods, and drank the rest,
and when they had drunk their thirst away
they trailed off homeward drowsily to bed.   470

BOOK XIX

Recognitions and a Dream

Now by Athena's side in the quiet hall
studying the ground for slaughter, Lord Odysseus
turned to Telémakhos.

---

7. I.e., you can't hide the fact that you are drunk.

"The arms," he said.
"Harness and weapons must be out of sight
in the inner room. And if the suitors miss them,   5
be mild; just say 'I had a mind to move them
out of the smoke. They seemed no longer
the bright arms that Odysseus left at home
when he went off to Troy. Here where the fire's
hot breath came, they had grown black and drear.   10
One better reason struck me, too:
suppose a brawl starts up when you've been drinking—
you might in madness let each other's blood,
and that would stain your feast, your courtship.
                                                  Iron
itself can draw men's hands.' "

                                    Then he fell silent,   15
and Telémakhos obeyed his father's word.
He called Eurýkleia, the nurse, and told her:

"Nurse, go shut the women in their quarters
while I shift Father's armor back
to the inner rooms—these beautiful arms unburnished,   20
caked with black soot in his years abroad.
I was a child then. Well, I am not now.
I want them shielded from the draught and smoke."

And the old woman answered:

                                    "It is time, child,
you took an interest in such things. I wish   25
you'd put your mind on all your house and chattels.
But who will go along to hold a light?
You said no maids, no torch-bearers."

                                    Telémakhos
looked at her and replied:

                                    "Our friend here.
A man who shares my meat can bear a hand,   30
no matter how far he is from home."

                                    He spoke so soldierly
her own speech halted on her tongue. Straight back
she went to lock the doors of the women's hall.
And now the two men sprang to work—father
and princely son, loaded with round helms   35
and studded bucklers, lifting the long spears,
while in their path Pallas Athena

held up a golden lamp of purest light.
Telémakhos at last burst out:

               "Oh, Father,
here is a marvel! All around I see   40
the walls and roof beams, pedestals and pillars,
lighted as though by white fire blazing near.
One of the gods of heaven is in this place!"

Then said Odysseus, the great tactician,

"Be still: keep still about it: just remember it.   45
The gods who rule Olympos make this light.
You may go off to bed now. Here I stay
to test your mother and her maids again.
Out of her long grief she will question me."

Telémakhos went across the hall and out   50
under the light of torches—crossed the court
to the tower chamber where he had always slept.
Here now again he lay, waiting for dawn,
while in the great hall by Athena's side
Odysseus waited with his mind on slaughter.   55

Presently Penélopê from her chamber
stepped in her thoughtful beauty.
                    So might Artemis
or golden Aphroditê have descended;
and maids drew to the hearth her own smooth chair
inlaid with silver whorls and ivory. The artisan   60
Ikmálios had made it, long before,
with a footrest in a single piece, and soft
upon the seat a heavy fleece was thrown.
Here by the fire the queen sat down. Her maids,
leaving their quarters, came with white arms bare   65
to clear the wine cups and the bread, and move
the trestle boards where men had lingered drinking.
Fiery ashes out of the pine-chip flares
they tossed, and piled on fuel for light and heat.
And now a second time Melántho's voice   70
rang brazen in Odysseus' ears:

                  "Ah, stranger,
are you still here, so creepy, late at night
hanging about, looking the women over?
You old goat, go outside, cuddle your supper;
get out, or a torch may kindle you behind!"   75

At this Odysseus glared under his brows
and said:

"Little devil, why pitch into me again?
Because I go unwashed and wear these rags,
and make the rounds? But so I must, being needy;
that is the way a vagabond must live.   80
And do not overlook this: in my time
I too had luck, lived well, stood well with men,
and gave alms, often, to poor wanderers
like him you see before you—aye, to all sorts,
no matter in what dire want. I owned   85
servants—many, I say—and all the rest
that goes with what men call prosperity.
But Zeus the son of Kronos brought me down.
Mistress, mend your ways, or you may lose
all this vivacity of yours. What if her ladyship   90
were stirred to anger? What if Odysseus came?—
and I can tell you, there is hope of that—
or if the man is done for, still his son
lives to be reckoned with, by Apollo's will.
None of you can go wantoning on the sly   95
and fool him now. He is too old for that."

Penélopê, being near enough to hear him,
spoke out sharply to her maid:

                                    "Oh, shameless,
through and through! And do you think me blind,
blind to your conquest? It will cost your life.   100
You knew I waited—for you heard me say it—
waited to see this man in hall and question him
about my lord; I am so hard beset."

She turned away and said to the housekeeper:

"Eurýnomê, a bench, a spread of sheepskin,   105
to put my guest at ease. Now he shall talk
and listen, and be questioned."

                                    Willing hands
brought a smooth bench, and dropped a fleece upon it.
Here the adventurer and king sat down;
then carefully Penélopê began: 110

"Friend, let me ask you first of all:
who are you, where do you come from, of what nation
and parents were you born?"

                    And he replied:

"My lady, never a man in the wide world
should have a fault to find with you. Your name   115

has gone out under heaven like the sweet
honor of some god-fearing king, who rules
in equity over the strong: his black lands bear
both wheat and barley, fruit trees laden bright,
new lambs at lambing time—and the deep sea   120
gives great hauls of fish by his good strategy,
so that his folk fare well.

     O my dear lady,
this being so, let it suffice to ask me
of other matters—not my blood, my homeland.
Do not enforce me to recall my pain.   125
My heart is sore; but I must not be found
sitting in tears here, in another's house:
it is not well forever to be grieving.
One of the maids might say—or you might think—
I had got maudlin over cups of wine."   130

And Penélopê replied:

     "Stranger, my looks,
my face, my carriage, were soon lost or faded
when the Akhaians crossed the sea to Troy,
Odysseus my lord among the rest.
If he returned, if he were here to care for me,   135
I might be happily renowned!
But grief instead heaven sent me—years of pain.
Sons of the noblest families on the islands,
Doulíkhion, Samê, wooded Zakýnthos,
with native Ithakans, are here to court me,   140
against my wish; and they consume this house.
Can I give proper heed to guest or suppliant
or herald on the realm's affairs?

       How could I?
wasted with longing for Odysseus, while here
they press for marriage.

     Ruses served my turn   145
to draw the time out—first a close-grained web
I had the happy thought to set up weaving
on my big loom in hall. I said, that day:
'Young men—my suitors, now my lord is dead,
let me finish my weaving before I marry,   150
or else my thread will have been spun in vain.
It is a shroud I weave for Lord Laërtês
when cold Death comes to lay him on his bier.
The country wives would hold me in dishonor
if he, with all his fortune, lay unshrouded.'   155
I reached their hearts that way, and they agreed.

So every day I wove on the great loom,
but every night by torchlight I unwove it;
and so for three years I deceived the Akhaians.
But when the seasons brought a fourth year on,   160
as long months waned, and the long days were spent,
through impudent folly in the slinking maids
they caught me—clamored up to me at night;
I had no choice then but to finish it.
And now, as matters stand at last,   165
I have no strength left to evade a marriage,
cannot find any further way; my parents
urge it upon me, and my son
will not stand by while they eat up his property.
He comprehends it, being a man full grown,   170
able to oversee the kind of house
Zeus would endow with honor.
                      But you too
confide in me, tell me your ancestry.
You were not born of mythic oak or stone.″

And the great master of invention answered: 175

″O honorable wife of Lord Odysseus,
must you go on asking about my family?
Then I will tell you, though my pain
be doubled by it: and whose pain would not
if he had been away as long as I have   180
and had hard roving in the world of men?
But I will tell you even so, my lady.

One of the great islands of the world
— in midsea, in the winedark sea, is Krete:
spacious and rich and populous, with ninety   185
cities and a mingling of tongues.
Akhaians there are found, along with Kretan
hillmen of the old stock, and Kydonians,
Dorians in three blood-lines, Pelasgians—
and one among their ninety towns is Knossos.[8]   190
Here lived King Minos whom great Zeus received
every ninth year in private council—Minos,
the father of my father, Deukálion.
Two sons Deukálion had: Idómeneus,
who went to join the Atreidai before Troy   195

8. The site of the great palace discovered by Evans, who called the civilization which produced it Minoan.
It is impossible to extract historical fact from this confused account of the population of Crete: Kydonians
may be the inhabitants of the western end of the island; Dorians were the people who, according to Greek
belief, invaded Greece and destroyed the Mycenean palace-civilizations (but Homer does not mention
them elsewhere); Pelasgians were the pre-Greek inhabitants of the area.

in the beaked ships of war; and then myself,
Aithôn by name—a stripling next my brother.
But I saw with my own eyes at Knossos once
Odysseus.
        Gales had caught him off Cape Malea,
driven him southward on the coast of Krete,   200
when he was bound for Troy. At Ámnisos,
hard by the holy cave of Eileithuía,[9]
he lay to, and dropped anchor, in that open
and rough roadstead riding out the blow.
Meanwhile he came ashore, came inland, asking   205
after Idómeneus: dear friends he said they were;
but now ten mornings had already passed,
ten or eleven, since my brother sailed.
So I played host and took Odysseus home,
saw him well lodged and fed, for we had plenty;   210
then I made requisitions—barley, wine,
and beeves for sacrifice—to give his company
abundant fare along with him.
                      Twelve days
they stayed with us, the Akhaians, while that wind
out of the north shut everyone inside—   215
even on land you could not keep your feet,
such fury was abroad. On the thirteenth,
when the gale dropped, they put to sea."

Now all these lies he made appear so truthful
she wept as she sat listening. The skin   220
of her pale face grew moist the way pure snow
softens and glistens on the mountains, thawed
by Southwind after powdering from the West,
and, as the snow melts, mountain streams run full:
so her white cheeks were wetted by these tears   225
shed for her lord—and he close by her side.
Imagine how his heart ached for his lady,
his wife in tears; and yet he never blinked;
his eyes might have been made of horn or iron
for all that she could see. He had this trick—   230
wept, if he willed to, inwardly.
                    Well, then,
as soon as her relieving tears were shed
she spoke once more:
                "I think that I shall say, friend,
give me some proof, if it is really true
that you were host in that place to my husband   235

9. Goddess of childbirth. Ámnisos: On the coast near Knossos.

with his brave men, as you declare. Come, tell me
the quality of his clothing, how he looked,
and some particular of his company."

Odysseus answered, and his mind ranged far:

"Lady, so long a time now lies between,   240
it is hard to speak of it. Here is the twentieth year
since that man left the island of my father.
But I shall tell what memory calls to mind.
A purple cloak, and fleecy, he had on—
a double thick one. Then, he wore a brooch   245
made of pure gold with twin tubes for the prongs,
and on the face a work of art: a hunting dog
pinning a spotted fawn in agony
between his forepaws—wonderful to see
how being gold, and nothing more, he bit   250
the golden deer convulsed, with wild hooves flying.
Odysseus' shirt I noticed, too—a fine
closefitting tunic like dry onion skin,
so soft it was, and shiny.
                                        Women there,
many of them, would cast their eyes on it.   255
But I might add, for your consideration,
whether he brought these things from home, or whether
a shipmate gave them to him, coming aboard,
I have no notion: some regardful host
in another port perhaps it was. Affection   260
followed him—there were few Akhaians like him.
And I too made him gifts: a good bronze blade,
a cloak with lining and a broidered shirt,
and sent him off in his trim ship with honor.
A herald, somewhat older than himself,   265
he kept beside him; I'll describe this man:
round-shouldered, dusky, woolly-headed;
Eurýbatês, his name was—and Odysseus
gave him preferment over the officers.
He had a shrewd head, like the captain's own."   270

Now hearing these details—minutely true—
she felt more strangely moved, and tears flowed
until she had tasted her salt grief again.
Then she found words to answer:

                                        "Before this
you won my sympathy, but now indeed   275
you shall be our respected guest and friend.
With my own hands I put that cloak and tunic

upon him—took them folded from their place—
and the bright brooch for ornament.
                                        Gone now,
I will not meet the man again   280
returning to his own home fields. Unkind
the fate that sent him young in the long ship
to see that misery at Ilion, unspeakable!"

And the master improviser answered:
                                        "Honorable
wife of Odysseus Laërtiadês,   285
you need not stain your beauty with these tears,
nor wear yourself out grieving for your husband.
Not that I can blame you. Any wife
grieves for the man she married in her girlhood,
lay with in love, bore children to—though he   290
may be no prince like this Odysseus,
whom they compare even to the gods. But listen:
weep no more, and listen:
I have a thing to tell you, something true.
I heard but lately of your lord's return,   295
heard that he is alive, not far away,
among Thesprótians in their green land
amassing fortune to bring home. His company
went down in shipwreck in the winedark sea
off the coast of Thrinákia. Zeus and Hêlios   300
held it against him that his men had killed
the kine of Hêlios. The crew drowned for this.
He rode the ship's keel. Big seas cast him up
on the island of Phaiákians, godlike men
who took him to their hearts. They honored him   305
with many gifts and a safe passage home,
or so they wished. Long since he should have been here,
but he thought better to restore his fortune
playing the vagabond about the world;
and no adventurer could beat Odysseus   310
at living by his wits—no man alive.
I had this from King Phaidôn of Thesprótia;
and, tipping wine out, Phaidôn swore to me
the ship was launched, the seamen standing by
to bring Odysseus to his land at last,   315
but I got out to sea ahead of him
by the king's order—as it chanced a freighter
left port for the grain bins of Doulíkhion.
Phaidôn, however, showed me Odysseus' treasure.
Ten generations of his heirs or more   320

could live on what lay piled in that great room.
The man himself had gone up to Dodona
to ask the spelling leaves of the old oak
what Zeus would have him do—how to return to Ithaka
after so many years—by stealth or openly.   325
You see, then, he is alive and well, and headed
homeward now, no more to be abroad
far from his island, his dear wife and son.
Here is my sworn word for it. Witness this,
god of the zenith, noblest of the gods,   330
and Lord Odysseus' hearthfire, now before me:
I swear these things shall turn out as I say.
Between this present dark and one day's ebb,
after the wane, before the crescent moon,
Odysseus will come."

                    Penélopê,   335
the attentive queen, replied to him:

                        "Ah, stranger,
if what you say could ever happen!
You would soon know our love! Our bounty, too:
men would turn after you to call you blessed.
But my heart tells me what must be.   340
Odysseus will not come to me; no ship
will be prepared for you. We have no master
quick to receive and furnish out a guest
as Lord Odysseus was.
               Or did I dream him?

Maids, maids: come wash him, make a bed for him,   345
bedstead and colored rugs and coverlets
to let him lie warm into the gold of Dawn.
In morning light you'll bathe him and anoint him
so that he'll take his place beside Telémakhos
feasting in hall. If there be one man there   350
to bully or annoy him, that man wins
no further triumph here, burn though he may.
How will you understand me, friend, how find in me,
more than in common women, any courage
or gentleness, if you are kept in rags   355
and filthy at our feast? Men's lives are short.
The hard man and his cruelties will be
cursed behind his back, and mocked in death.
But one whose heart and ways are kind—of him
strangers will bear report to the wide world,   360
and distant men will praise him."

Warily
Odysseus answered:

"Honorable lady,
wife of Odysseus Laërtiadês,
a weight of rugs and cover? Not for me.
I've had none since the day I saw the mountains   365
of Krete, white with snow, low on the sea line
fading behind me as the long oars drove me north.
Let me lie down tonight as I've lain often,
many a night unsleeping, many a time
afield on hard ground waiting for pure Dawn.   370
No: and I have no longing for a footbath
either; none of these maids will touch my feet,
unless there is an old one, old and wise,
one who has lived through suffering as I have:
I would not mind letting my feet be touched   375
by that old servant."

And Penélopê said:

"Dear guest, no foreign man so sympathetic
ever came to my house, no guest more likeable,
so wry and humble are the things you say.
I have an old maidservant ripe with years,   380
one who in her time nursed my lord. She took him
into her arms the hour his mother bore him.
Let her, then, wash your feet, though she is frail.
Come here, stand by me, faithful Eurýkleia,
and bathe—bathe your master, I almost said,   385
for they are of an age, and now Odysseus'
feet and hands would be enseamed like his.
Men grow old soon in hardship."

Hearing this,
the old nurse hid her face between her hands
and wept hot tears, and murmured:

"Oh, my child!   390
I can do nothing for you! How Zeus hated you,
no other man so much! No use, great heart,
O faithful heart, the rich thighbones you burnt
to Zeus who plays in lightning—and no man
ever gave more to Zeus—with all your prayers   395
for a green age, a tall son reared to manhood.
There is no day of homecoming for you.
Stranger, some women in some far off place
perhaps have mocked my lord when he'd be home

as now these strumpets mock you here. No wonder   400
you would keep clear of all their whorishness
and have no bath. But here am I. The queen
Penélopê, Ikários' daughter, bids me;
so let me bathe your feet to serve my lady—
to serve you, too.
                    My heart within me stirs,   405
mindful of something. Listen to what I say:
strangers have come here, many through the years,
but no one ever came, I swear, who seemed
so like Odysseus—body, voice and limbs—
as you do."

            Ready for this, Odysseus answered: 410
"Old woman, that is what they say. All who have seen
the two of us remark how like we are,
as you yourself have said, and rightly, too."

Then he kept still, while the old nurse filled up
her basin glittering in firelight; she poured   415
cold water in, then hot.
                         But Lord Odysseus
whirled suddenly from the fire to face the dark.
The scar: he had forgotten that. She must not
handle his scarred thigh, or the game was up.
But when she bared her lord's leg, bending near,   420
she knew the groove at once.
                             An old wound
a boar's white tusk inflicted, on Parnassos[1]
years ago. He had gone hunting there
in company with his uncles and Autólykos,
his mother's father—a great thief and swindler   425
by Hermês' favor,[2] for Autólykos pleased him
with burnt offerings of sheep and kids. The god
acted as his accomplice. Well, Autólykos
on a trip to Ithaka
arrived just after his daughter's boy was born.   430
In fact, he had no sooner finished supper
than Nurse Eurýkleia put the baby down
in his own lap and said:

                    "It is for you, now,
to choose a name for him, your child's dear baby;
the answer to her prayers."

1. The mountain range above Apollo's oracular shrine at Delphi.   2. Hermes was not only the messenger of the gods and the god who guided the dead down to the lower world, he was also the god of the marketplace and so of trickery and swindling.

Autólykos replied: 435

"My son-in-law, my daughter, call the boy
by the name I tell you. Well you know, my hand
has been against the world of men and women;
odium[3] and distrust I've won. Odysseus
should be his given name. When he grows up,   440
when he comes visiting his mother's home
under Parnassos, where my treasures are,
I'll make him gifts and send him back rejoicing."

Odysseus in due course went for the gifts,
and old Autólykos and his sons embraced him   445
with welcoming sweet words; and Amphithéa,
his mother's mother, held him tight and kissed him,
kissed his head and his fine eyes.
                          The father
called on his noble sons to make a feast,
and going about it briskly they led in   450
an ox of five years, whom they killed and flayed
and cut in bits for roasting on the skewers
with skilled hands, with care; then shared it out.
So all the day until the sun went down
they feasted to their hearts' content. At evening,   455
after the sun was down and dusk had come,
they turned to bed and took the gift of sleep.

When the young Dawn spread in the eastern sky
her finger tips of rose, the men and dogs
went hunting, taking Odysseus. They climbed   460
Parnassos' rugged flank mantled in forest,
entering amid high windy folds at noon
when Hêlios beat upon the valley floor
and on the winding Ocean whence he came.
With hounds questing ahead, in open order,   465
the sons of Autólykos went down a glen,
Odysseus in the lead, behind the dogs,
pointing his long-shadowing spear.
                            Before them
a great boar lay hid in undergrowth,
in a green thicket proof against the wind   470
or sun's blaze, fine soever the needling sunlight,
impervious too to any rain, so dense
that cover was, heaped up with fallen leaves.
Patter of hounds' feet, men's feet, woke the boar

---

3. The translator is reproducing a pun in the original Greek: Autólykos speaks of himself as *odyssamenos*, one who is angry and gives cause for anger.

as they came up—and from his woody ambush   475
with razor back bristling and raging eyes
he trotted and stood at bay. Odysseus,
being on top of him, had the first shot,
lunging to stick him; but the boar
had already charged under the long spear.   480
He hooked aslant with one white tusk and ripped out
flesh above the knee, but missed the bone.
Odysseus' second thrust went home by luck,
his bright spear passing through the shoulder joint;
and the beast fell, moaning as life pulsed away.   485
Autólykos' tall sons took up the wounded,
working skillfully over the Prince Odysseus
to bind his gash, and with a rune[4] they stanched
the dark flow of blood. Then downhill swiftly
they all repaired to the father's house, and there   490
tended him well—so well they soon could send him,
with Grandfather Autólykos' magnificent gifts,
rejoicing, over sea to Ithaka.
His father and the Lady Antikleía
welcomed him, and wanted all the news   495
of how he got his wound; so he spun out
his tale, recalling how the boar's white tusk
caught him when he was hunting on Parnassos.

This was the scar the old nurse recognized;
she traced it under her spread hands, then let go,   500
and into the basin fell the lower leg
making the bronze clang, sloshing the water out.
Then joy and anguish seized her heart; her eyes
filled up with tears; her throat closed, and she whispered,
with hand held out to touch his chin:

                                        "Oh yes!   505
You are Odysseus! Ah, dear child! I could not
see you until now—not till I knew
my master's very body with my hands!"

Her eyes turned to Penélopê with desire
to make her lord, her husband, known—in vain,   510
because Athena had bemused the queen,
so that she took no notice, paid no heed.
At the same time Odysseus' right hand
gripped the old throat; his left hand pulled her near,
and in her ear he said:

4. An incantation, primitive magic to stop the flow of blood.

"Will you destroy me,   515
nurse, who gave me milk at your own breast?
Now with a hard lifetime behind I've come
in the twentieth year home to my father's island.
You found me out, as the chance was given you.
Be quiet; keep it from the others, else   520
I warn you, and I mean it, too,
if by my hand god brings the suitors down
I'll kill you, nurse or not, when the time comes—
when the time comes to kill the other women."

Eurýkleia kept her wits and answered him: 525

"Oh, what mad words are these you let escape you!
Child, you know my blood, my bones are yours;
no one could whip this out of me. I'll be
a woman turned to stone, iron I'll be.
And let me tell you too—mind now—if god   530
cuts down the arrogant suitors by your hand,
I can report to you on all the maids,
those who dishonor you, and the innocent."

But in response the great tactician said:

"Nurse, no need to tell me tales of these.   535
I will have seen them, each one, for myself.
Trust in the gods, be quiet, hold your peace."

Silent, the old nurse went to fetch more water,
her basin being all spilt.
                    When she had washed
and rubbed his feet with golden oil, he turned,   540
dragging his bench again to the fire side
for warmth, and hid the scar under his rags.
Penélopê broke the silence, saying:

                    "Friend,
allow me one brief question more. You know,
the time for bed, sweet rest, is coming soon,   545
if only that warm luxury of slumber
would come to enfold us, in our trouble. But for me
my fate at night is anguish and no rest.
By day being busy, seeing to my work,
I find relief sometimes from loss and sorrow;   550
but when night comes and all the world's abed
I lie in mine alone, my heart thudding,
while bitter thoughts and fears crowd on my grief.

Think how Pandáreos' daughter,[5] pale forever,
sings as the nightingale in the new leaves   555
through those long quiet hours of night,
on some thick-flowering orchard bough in spring;
how she rills out and tilts her note, high now, now low,
mourning for Itylos whom she killed in madness—
her child, and her lord Zêthos' only child.   560
My forlorn thought flows variable as her song,
wondering: shall I stay beside my son
and guard my own things here, my maids, my hall,
to honor my lord's bed and the common talk?
Or had I best join fortunes with a suitor,   565
the noblest one, most lavish in his gifts?
Is it now time for that?
My son being still a callow boy forbade
marriage, or absence from my lord's domain;
but now the child is grown, grown up, a man,   570
he, too, begins to pray for my departure,
aghast at all the suitors gorge on.

                    Listen:
interpret me this dream: From a water's edge
twenty fat geese have come to feed on grain
beside my house. And I delight to see them.   575
But now a mountain eagle with great wings
and crooked beak storms in to break their necks
and strew their bodies here. Away he soars
into the bright sky; and I cry aloud—
all this in dream—I wail and round me gather   580
softly braided Akhaian women mourning
because the eagle killed my geese.
                         Then down
out of the sky he drops to a cornice beam
with mortal voice telling me not to weep.
'Be glad,' says he, 'renowned Ikários' daughter: 585
here is no dream but something real as day,
something about to happen. All those geese
were suitors, and the bird was I. See now,
I am no eagle but your lord come back
to bring inglorious death upon them all!'   590
As he said this, my honeyed slumber left me.

5. The reference is to one of the many Greek legends that explain the song of the nightingale. In this one (for another see note 8, XX. 68) the daughter of Pandáreos, a Cretan King, was married to Zêthos, King of Thebes. She had only one son; her sister-in-law Niobe had many. In a fit of jealousy she tried to kill Niobe's eldest son but by mistake (in the dark) killed her own son, Itylos, instead. Zeus changed her into a nightingale and she sings in mourning for Itylos.

Peering through half-shut eyes, I saw the geese
in hall, still feeding at the self-same trough."

The master of subtle ways and straight replied:

"My dear, how can you choose to read the dream   595
differently? Has not Odysseus himself
shown you what is to come? Death to the suitors,
sure death, too. Not one escapes his doom."

Penélopê shook her head and answered:

                    "Friend,
many and many a dream is mere confusion,   600
a cobweb of no consequence at all.
Two gates for ghostly dreams there are: one gateway
of honest horn, and one of ivory.
Issuing by the ivory gate are dreams
of glimmering illusion, fantasies,   605
but those that come through solid polished horn
may be borne out, if mortals only know them.
I doubt it came by horn, my fearful dream—
too good to be true, that, for my son and me.
But one thing more I wish to tell you: listen   610
carefully. It is a black day, this that comes.
Odysseus' house and I are to be parted.
I shall decree a contest for the day.
We have twelve axe heads. In his time, my lord
could line them up, all twelve, at intervals   615
like a ship's ribbing; then he'd back away
a long way off and whip an arrow through.[6]
Now I'll impose this trial on the suitors.
The one who easily handles and strings the bow
and shoots through all twelve axes I shall marry,   620
whoever he may be—then look my last
on this my first love's beautiful brimming house.
But I'll remember, though I dream it only."

Odysseus said:

             "Dear honorable lady,
wife of Odysseus Laërtiadês,   625
let there be no postponement of the trial.
Odysseus, who knows the shifts of combat,

6. The nature of this archery contest is a puzzle that has never been satisfactorily solved. The axes were probably double-headed; the aperture through which the arrow passed must have been the socket in which the wooden handle fitted. If the twelve axe heads were lined up, fixed in the ground (Telémakhos later digs a trench for them) so that the empty sockets were on a straight line, an archer might be able to shoot through them. (When Odysseus finally does so, he is sitting down, XXI. 441.)

will be here: aye, he'll be here long before
one of these lads can stretch or string that bow
or shoot to thread the iron!"

                    Grave and wise,   630
Penélopê replied:
        "If you were willing
to sit with me and comfort me, my friend,
no tide of sleep would ever close my eyes.
But mortals cannot go forever sleepless.
This the undying gods decree for all   635
who live and die on earth, kind furrowed earth.
Upstairs I go, then, to my single bed,
my sighing bed, wet with so many tears
after my Lord Odysseus took ship
to see that misery at Ilion, unspeakable.   640
Let me rest there, you here. You can stretch out
on the bare floor, or else command a bed."

So she went up to her chamber softly lit,
accompanied by her maids. Once there, she wept
for Odysseus, her husband, till Athena   645
cast sweet sleep upon her eyes.

BOOK XX

Signs and a Vision

Outside in the entry way he made his bed—
raw oxhide spread on level ground, and heaped up
fleeces, left from sheep the Akhaians killed.
And when he had lain down, Eurýnomê
flung out a robe to cover him. Unsleeping   5
the Lord Odysseus lay, and roved in thought
to the undoing of his enemies.
                    Now came a covey of women
laughing as they slipped out, arm in arm,
as many a night before, to the suitors' beds;
and anger took him like a wave to leap   10
into their midst and kill them, every one—
or should he let them all go hot to bed
one final night? His heart cried out within him
the way a brach[7] with whelps between her legs
would howl and bristle at a stranger—so   15
the hackles of his heart rose at that laughter.
Knocking his breast he muttered to himself:

7. An obsolete word meaning "bitch."

"Down; be steady. You've seen worse, that time
the Kyklops like a rockslide ate your men
while you looked on. Nobody, only guile,   20
got you out of that cave alive."

                   His rage,
held hard in leash, submitted to his mind,
while he himself rocked, rolling from side to side,
as a cook turns a sausage, big with blood
and fat, at a scorching blaze, without a pause,   25
to broil it quick: so he rolled left and right,
casting about to see how he, alone,
against the false outrageous crowd of suitors
could press the fight.
                And out of the night sky
Athena came to him; out of the nearby dark   30
in body like a woman; came and stood
over his head to chide him:
                  "Why so wakeful,
most forlorn of men? Here is your home,
there lies your lady; and your son is here,
as fine as one could wish a son to be."   35

Odysseus looked up and answered:

"Aye,
goddess, that much is true; but still
I have some cause to fret in this affair.
I am one man; how can I whip those dogs?   40
They are always here in force. Neither
is that the end of it, there's more to come.
If by the will of Zeus and by your will
I killed them all, where could I go for safety?
Tell me that!"

           And the grey-eyed goddess said: 45

"Your touching faith! Another man would trust
some villainous mortal, with no brains—and what
am I? Your goddess-guardian to the end
in all your trials. Let it be plain as day:
if fifty bands of men surrounded us   50
and every sword sang for your blood,
you could make off still with their cows and sheep.
Now you, too, go to sleep. This all night vigil
wearies the flesh. You'll come out soon enough
on the other side of trouble."

                    Raining soft   55
sleep on his eyes, the beautiful one was gone
back to Olympos. Now at peace, the man
slumbered and lay still, but not his lady.
Wakeful again with all her cares, reclining
in the soft bed, she wept and cried aloud   60
until she had had her fill of tears, then spoke
in prayer first to Artemis:

                    "O gracious
divine lady Artemis, daughter of Zeus,
if you could only make an end now quickly,
let the arrow fly, stop my heart,   65
or if some wind could take me by the hair
up into running cloud, to plunge in tides of Ocean,
as hurricane winds took Pandareos' daughters[8]
when they were left at home alone. The gods
had sapped their parents' lives. But Aphroditê   70
fed those children honey, cheese, and wine,
and Hêra gave them looks and wit, and Artemis,
pure Artemis, gave lovely height, and wise
Athena made them practised in her arts—
till Aphroditê in glory walked on Olympos,   75
begging for each a happy wedding day
from Zeus, the lightning's joyous king, who knows
all fate of mortals, fair and foul—
but even at that hour the cyclone winds
had ravished them away   80
to serve the loathsome Furies.
                     Let me be
blown out by the Olympians! Shot by Artemis,
I still might go and see amid the shades
Odysseus in the rot of underworld.
No coward's eye should light by my consenting!   85
Evil may be endured when our days pass
in mourning, heavy-hearted, hard beset,
if only sleep reign over nighttime, blanketing
the world's good and evil from our eyes.
But not for me: dreams too my demon sends me.   90
Tonight the image of my lord came by
as I remember him with troops. O strange
exultation! I thought him real, and not a dream."

---

8. These are the other daughters of Pendáreos; their fate was different from the one who married Zêthos and became a nightingale (XIX. 564). They paid for the sin of their father who stole a golden image from the temple of Hephaistos. Though the gods showered gifts on them, in the end they were swept away to their deaths by the stormwinds.

Now as the Dawn appeared all stitched in gold,
the queen's cry reached Odysseus at his waking,   95
so that he wondered, half asleep: it seemed
she knew him, and stood near him! Then he woke
and picked his bedding up to stow away
on a chair in the mégaron. The oxhide pad
he took outdoors. There, spreading wide his arms,   100
he prayed:

          "O Father Zeus, if over land and water,
after adversity, you willed to bring me home,
let someone in the waking house give me good augury,
and a sign be shown, too, in the outer world."

He prayed thus, and the mind of Zeus in heaven   105
heard him. He thundered out of bright Olympos
down from above the cloudlands in reply—
a rousing peal for Odysseus. Then a token
came to him from a woman grinding flour
in the court nearby. His own handmills were there,   110
and twelve maids had the job of grinding out
whole grain and barley meal, the pith of men.
Now all the rest, their bushels ground, were sleeping;
one only, frail and slow, kept at it still.
She stopped, stayed her hand, and her lord heard   115
the omen from her lips:

          "Ah, Father Zeus
almighty over gods and men!
A great bang of thunder that was, surely,
out of the starry sky, and not a cloud in sight.
It is your nod to someone. Hear me, then,   120
make what I say come true:
let this day be the last the suitors feed
so dainty in Odysseus' hall!
They've made me work my heart out till I drop,
grinding barley. May they feast no more!"   125

The servant's prayer, after the cloudless thunder
of Zeus, Odysseus heard with lifting heart,
sure in his bones that vengeance was at hand.
Then other servants, wakening, came down
to build and light a fresh fire at the hearth.   130
Telémakhos, clear-eyed as a god, awoke,
put on his shirt and belted on his sword,
bound rawhide sandals under his smooth feet,

and took his bronze-shod lance. He came and stood
on the broad sill of the doorway, calling Eurýkleia: 135

"Nurse, dear Nurse, how did you treat our guest?
Had he a supper and a good bed? Has he lain
uncared for still? My mother is like that,
perverse for all her cleverness:
she'd entertain some riff-raff, and turn out   140
a solid man."

       The old nurse answered him:

"I would not be so quick to accuse her, child.
He sat and drank here while he had a mind to;
food he no longer hungered for, he said—
for she did ask him. When he thought of sleeping,   145
she ordered them to make a bed. Poor soul!
Poor gentleman! So humble and so miserable,
he would accept no bed with rugs to lie on,
but slept on sheepskins and a raw oxhide
in the entry way. We covered him ourselves."   150

Telémakhos left the hall, hefting his lance,
with two swift flickering hounds for company,
to face the island Akhaians in the square;
and gently born Eurýkleia the daughter
of Ops Peisenóridês, called to the maids: 155

"Bestir yourselves! you have your brooms, go sprinkle
the rooms and sweep them, robe the chairs in red,
sponge off the tables till they shine.
Wash out the winebowls and two-handled cups.
You others go fetch water from the spring;   160
no loitering; come straight back. Our company
will be here soon; morning is sure to bring them;
everyone has a holiday today."

The women ran to obey her—twenty girls
off to the spring with jars for dusky water,   165
the rest at work inside. Then tall woodcutters
entered to split up logs for the hearth fire,
the water carriers returned; and on their heels
arrived the swineherd, driving three fat pigs,
chosen among his pens. In the wide court   170
he let them feed, and said to Odysseus kindly:

"Friend, are they more respectful of you now,
or still insulting you?"

Replied Odysseus:

"The young men, yes. And may the gods requite
those insolent puppies for the game they play   175
in a home not their own. They have no decency."

During this talk, Melánthios the goatherd
came in, driving goats for the suitors' feast,
with his two herdsmen. Under the portico
they tied the animals, and Melánthios   180
looked at Odysseus with a sneer. Said he:

                                        "Stranger,
I see you mean to stay and turn our stomachs
begging in this hall. Clear out, why don't you?
Or will you have to taste a bloody beating
before you see the point? Your begging ways   185
nauseate everyone. There are feasts elsewhere."

Odysseus answered not a word, but grimly
shook his head over his murderous heart.
A third man came up now: Philoítios
the cattle foreman, with an ox behind him   190
and fat goats for the suitors. Ferrymen
had brought these from the mainland, as they bring
travellers, too—whoever comes along.
Philoítios tied the beasts under the portico
and joined the swineherd.

                          "Who is this," he said,   195
"Who is the new arrival at the manor?
Akhaian? or what else does he claim to be?
Where are his family and fields of home?
Down on his luck, all right: carries himself like a captain.
How the immortal gods can change and drag us down   200
once they begin to spin dark days for us!—
Kings and commanders, too."

                          Then he stepped over
and took Odysseus by the rght hand, saying:

"Welcome, Sir. May good luck lie ahead
at the next turn. Hard times you're having, surely.   205
O Zeus! no god is more berserk in heaven
if gentle folk, whom you yourself begot,
you plunge in grief and hardship without mercy!
Sir, I began to sweat when I first saw you,
and tears came to my eyes, remembering   210
Odysseus: rags like these he may be wearing

somewhere on his wanderings now—
I mean, if he's alive still under the sun.
But if he's dead and in the house of Death,
I mourn Odysseus. He entrusted cows to me   215
in Kephallênia, when I was knee high,
and now his herds are numberless, no man else
ever had cattle multiply like grain.
But new men tell me I must bring my beeves
to feed them, who care nothing for our prince,   220
fear nothing from the watchful gods. They crave
partition of our lost king's land and wealth.
My own feelings keep going round and round
upon this tether: can I desert the boy
by moving, herds and all, to another country,   225
a new life among strangers? Yet it's worse
to stay here, in my old post, herding cattle
for upstarts.
              I'd have gone long since,
gone, taken service with another king; this shame
is no more to be borne; but I keep thinking   230
my own lord, poor devil, still might come
and make a rout of suitors in his hall."

Odysseus, with his mind on action, answered:

"Herdsman, I make you out to be no coward
and no fool: I can see that for myself.   235
So let me tell you this. I swear by Zeus
all highest, by the table set for friends,
and by your king's hearthstone to which I've come,
Odysseus will return. You'll be on hand
to see, if you care to see it,   240
how those who lord it here will be cut down."

The cowman said:

              "Would god it all came true!
You'd see the fight that's in me!"

                        Then Eumaios
echoed him, and invoked the gods, and prayed
that his great-minded master should return.   245
While these three talked, the suitors in the field
had come together plotting—what but death
for Telémakhos?—when from the left an eagle
crossed high with a rockdove in his claws.

Amphínomos got up. Said he, cutting them short: 250

"Friends, no luck lies in that plan for us,
no luck, knifing the lad. Let's think of feasting."

A grateful thought, they felt, and walking on
entered the great hall of the hero Odysseus,
where they all dropped their cloaks on chairs or couches   255
and made a ritual slaughter, knifing sheep,
fat goats and pigs, knifing the grass-fed steer.
Then tripes were broiled and eaten. Mixing bowls
were filled with wine. The swineherd passed out cups,
Philoítios, chief cowherd, dealt the loaves   260
into the panniers, Melánthios poured wine,
and all their hands went out upon the feast.

Telémakhos placed his father to advantage
just at the door sill of the pillared hall,
setting a stool there and a sawed-off table,   265
gave him a share of tripes, poured out his wine
in a golden cup, and said:
                            "Stay here, sit down
to drink with our young friends. I stand between you
and any cutting word or cuffing hand
from any suitor. Here is no public house   270
but the old home of Odysseus, my inheritance.
Hold your tongues then, gentlemen, and your blows,
and let no wrangling start, no scuffle either."

The others, disconcerted, bit their lips
at the ring in the young man's voice. Antínoös,   275
Eupeithês' son, turned round to them and said:

"It goes against the grain, my lords, but still
I say we take this hectoring by Telémakhos.
You know Zeus balked at it, or else
we might have shut his mouth a long time past,   280
the silvery speaker."

                    But Telémakhos
paid no heed to what Antínoös said.

Now public heralds wound through Ithaka
leading a file of beasts for sacrifice, and islanders
gathered under the shade trees of Apollo,   285
in the precinct of the Archer[9]—while in hall
the suitors roasted mutton and fat beef

---

9. An epithet of Apollo. See *Iliad*, Book I. The trees are in his open-air precinct.

on skewers, pulling off the fragrant cuts;
and those who did the roasting served Odysseus
a portion equal to their own, for so   290
Telémakhos commanded.
            But Athena
had no desire now to let the suitors
restrain themselves from wounding words and acts.
Laërtês' son again must be offended.
There was a scapegrace fellow in the crowd   295
named Ktésippos, a Samian, rich beyond
all measure, arrogant with riches, early
and late a bidder for Odysseus' queen.
Now this one called attention to himself:

"Hear me, my lords, I have a thing to say.   300
Our friend has had his fair share from the start
and that's polite; it would be most improper
if we were cold to guests of Telémakhos—
no matter what tramp turns up. Well then, look here,
let me throw in my own small contribution.   305
He must have prizes to confer, himself,
on some brave bathman or another slave
here in Odysseus' house."

               His hand went backward
and, fishing out a cow's foot from the basket,
he let it fly.
            Odysseus rolled his head   310
to one side softly, ducking the blow, and smiled
a crooked smile with teeth clenched. On the wall
the cow's foot struck and fell. Telémakhos
blazed up:

          "Ktésippos, lucky for you, by heaven,
not to have hit him! He took care of himself,   315
else you'd have had my lance-head in your belly;
no marriage, but a grave instead on Ithaka
for your father's pains.
             You others, let me see
no more contemptible conduct in my house!
I've been awake to it for a long time—by now   320
I know what is honorable and what is not.
Before, I was a child. I can endure it
while sheep are slaughtered, wine drunk up, and bread—
can one man check the greed of a hundred men?—
but I will suffer no more viciousness.   325
Granted you mean at last to cut me down:
I welcome that—better to die than have

humiliation always before my eyes,
the stranger buffeted, and the serving women
dragged about, abused in a noble house."   330

They quieted, grew still, under his lashing,
and after a long silence, Ageláos,
Damástor's son, spoke to them all:

                              "Friends, friends,
I hope no one will answer like a fishwife.
What has been said is true. Hands off this stranger,   335
he is no target, neither is any servant
here in the hall of King Odysseus.
Let me say a word, though, to Telémakhos
and to his mother, if it please them both:
as long as hope remained in you to see   340
Odysseus, that great gifted man, again,
you could not be reproached for obstinacy,
tying the suitors down here; better so,
if still your father fared the great sea homeward.
How plain it is, though, now, he'll come no more!   345
Go sit then by your mother, reason with her,
tell her to take the best man, highest bidder,
and you can have and hold your patrimony,
feed on it, drink it all, while she
adorns another's house."

                              Keeping his head,   350
Telémakhos replied:

                              "By Zeus Almighty,
Ageláos, and by my father's sufferings,
far from Ithaka, whether he's dead or lost,
I make no impediment to Mother's marriage.
'Take whom you wish,' I say, 'I'll add my dowry.'   355
But can I pack her off against her will
from her own home? Heaven forbid!"

                              At this,
Pallas Athena touched off in the suitors
a fit of laughter, uncontrollable.
She drove them into nightmare, till they wheezed   360
and neighed as though with jaws no longer theirs,
while blood defiled their meat, and blurring tears
flooded their eyes, heart-sore with woe to come.
Then said the visionary, Theoklýmenos:

"O lost sad men, what terror is this you suffer?   365
Night shrouds you to the knees, your heads, your faces;

dry retch of death runs round like fire in sticks;
your cheeks are streaming; these fair walls and pedestals
are dripping crimson blood. And thick with shades
is the entry way, the courtyard thick with shades   370
passing athirst toward Érebos, into the dark,
the sun is quenched in heaven, foul mist hems us in . . ."

The young men greeted this with shouts of laughter,
and Eurýmakhos, the son of Pólybos, crowed:

"The mind of our new guest has gone astray.   375
Hustle him out of doors, lads, into the sunlight;
he finds it dark as night inside!"

The man of vision looked at him and said:

"When I need help, I'll ask for it, Eurýmakhos.
I have my eyes and ears, a pair of legs,   380
and a straight mind, still with me. These will do
to take me out. Damnation and black night
I see arriving for yourselves: no shelter,
no defence for any in this crowd—
fools and vipers in the king's own hall."   385

With this he left that handsome room and went
home to Peiraios, who received him kindly.
The suitors made wide eyes at one another
and set to work provoking Telémakhos
with jokes about his friends. One said, for instance: 390

"Telémakhos, no man is a luckier host
when it comes to what the cat dragged in. What burning
eyes your beggar had for bread and wine!
But not for labor, not for a single heave—
he'd be a deadweight on a field. Then comes   395
this other, with his mumbo-jumbo. Boy,
for your own good, I tell you, toss them both
into a slave ship for the Sikels.[1] That would pay you."

Telémakhos ignored the suitors' talk.
He kept his eyes in silence on his father,   400
awaiting the first blow. Meanwhile
the daughter of Ikários, Penélopê,
had placed her chair to look across and down
on father and son at bay; she heard the crowd,
and how they laughed as they resumed their dinner,   405
a fragrant feast, for many beasts were slain—

1. The primitive (pre-Greek) inhabitants of Sicily.

but as for supper, men supped never colder
than these, on what the goddess and the warrior
were even then preparing for the suitors,
whose treachery had filled that house with pain.   410

BOOK XXI

The Test of the Bow

Upon Penélopê, most worn in love and thought,
Athena cast a glance like a grey sea
lifting her. Now to bring the tough bow out and bring
the iron blades. Now try those dogs at archery
to usher bloody slaughter in.
    So moving stairward   5
the queen took up a fine doorhook of bronze,
ivory-hafted, smooth in her clenched hand,
and led her maids down to a distant room,
a storeroom where the master's treasure lay:
bronze, bar gold, black iron forged and wrought.   10
In this place hung the double-torsion bow
and arrows in a quiver, a great sheaf—
quills of groaning.
    In the old time in Lakedaimon
her lord had got these arms from Íphitos,
Eurýtos' son. The two met in Messenia[2]   15
at Ortílokhos' table, on the day
Odysseus claimed a debt owed by that realm—
sheep stolen by Messenians out of Ithaka
in their long ships, three hundred head, and herdsmen.
Seniors of Ithaka and his father sent him   20
on that far embassy when he was young.
But Íphitos had come there tracking strays,
twelve shy mares, with mule colts yet unweaned.
And a fatal chase they led him over prairies
into the hands of Heraklês. That massive   25
son of toil and mortal son of Zeus
murdered his guest[3] at wine in his own house—
inhuman, shameless in the sight of heaven—
to keep the mares and colts in his own grange.
Now Íphitos, when he knew Odysseus, gave him   30
the master bowman's arm; for old Eurýtos
had left it on his deathbed to his son.
In fellowship Odysseus gave a lance
and a sharp sword. But Heraklês killed Íphitos

---

2. A coastal district in the Western Peloponnese. *Íphitos:* Son of Eurýtos, king of Oekhalia in Thessaly. *Ortílokhos:* King of Pherai in Thessaly (see III. 528).   3. I.e., Íphitos.

before one friend could play host to the other.   35
And Lord Odysseus would not take the bow
in the black ships to the great war at Troy.
As a keepsake he put it by:
it served him well at home in Ithaka.

Now the queen reached the storeroom door and halted.   40
Here was an oaken sill, cut long ago
and sanded clean and bedded true. Foursquare
the doorjambs and the shining doors were set
by the careful builder. Penélopê untied the strap
around the curving handle, pushed her hook   45
into the slit, aimed at the bolts inside
and shot them back. Then came a rasping sound
as those bright doors the key had sprung gave way—
a bellow like a bull's vaunt in a meadow—
followed by her light footfall entering   50
over the plank floor. Herb-scented robes
lay there in chests, but the lady's milkwhite arms
went up to lift the bow down from a peg
in its own polished bowcase.
                        Now Penélopê
sank down, holding the weapon on her knees,   55
and drew her husband's great bow out, and sobbed
and bit her lip and let the salt tears flow.
Then back she went to face the crowded hall,
tremendous bow in hand, and on her shoulder hung
the quiver spiked with coughing death. Behind her   60
maids bore a basket full of axeheads, bronze
and iron implements for the master's game.
Thus in her beauty she approached the suitors,
and near a pillar of the solid roof
she paused, her shining veil across her cheeks,   65
her maids on either hand and still,
then spoke to the banqueters:

                        "My lords, hear me:
suitors indeed, you commandeered this house
to feast and drink in, day and night, my husband
being long gone, long out of mind. You found   70
no justification for yourselves—none
except your lust to marry me. Stand up, then:
we now declare a contest for that prize.
Here is my lord Odysseus' hunting bow.
Bend and string it if you can. Who sends an arrow   75
through iron axe-helve sockets, twelve in line?
I join my life with his, and leave this place, my home,

my rich and beautiful bridal house, forever
to be remembered, though I dream it only."

Then to Eumaios:

                  "Carry the bow forward.   80
Carry the blades."

                  Tears came to the swineherd's eyes
as he reached out for the big bow. He laid it
down at the suitors' feet. Across the room
the cowherd sobbed, knowing the master's weapon.
Antínoös growled, with a glance at both:

                          "Clods.   85
They go to pieces over nothing.
                     You two, there,
why are you sniveling? To upset the woman
even more? Has she not pain enough
over her lost husband? *Sit down.*
Get on with dinner quietly, or cry about it   90
outside, if you must. Leave us the bow.
A clean-cut game, it looks to me.
Nobody bends that bowstave easily
in this company. Is there a man here
made like Odysseus? I remember him   95
from childhood: I can see him even now."

That was the way he played it, hoping inwardly
to span the great horn bow with corded gut
and drill the iron with his shot—he, Antínoös,
destined to be the first of all to savor   100
blood from a biting arrow at his throat,
a shaft drawn by the fingers of Odysseus
whom he had mocked and plundered, leading on
the rest, his boon companions. Now they heard
a gay snort of laughter from Telémakhos,   105
who said then brilliantly:

                    "A queer thing, that!
Has Zeus almighty made me a half-wit?
For all her spirit, Mother has given in,
promised to go off with someone—and
is that amusing? What am I cackling for?   110
Step up, my lords, contend now for your prize.
There is no woman like her in Akhaia,
not in old Argos, Pylos, or Mykênê,
neither in Ithaka nor on the mainland,

and you all know it without praise of mine.   115
Come on, no hanging back, no more delay
in getting the bow bent. Who's the winner?
I myself should like to try that bow.
Suppose I bend it and bring off the shot,
my heart will be less heavy, seeing the queen my mother   120
go for the last time from this house and hall,
if I who stay can do my father's feat."

He moved out quickly, dropping his crimson cloak,
and lifted sword and sword belt from his shoulders.
His preparation was to dig a trench,   125
heaping the earth in a long ridge beside it
to hold the blades half-bedded. A taut cord
aligned the socket rings. And no one there
but looked on wondering at his workmanship,
for the boy had never seen it done.
                    He took his stand then   130
on the broad door sill to attempt the bow.
Three times he put his back into it and sprang it,
three times he had to slack off. Still he meant
to string that bow and pull for the needle shot.
A fourth try and he had it all but strung—   135
when a stiffening in Odysseus made him check.
Abruptly then he stopped and turned and said:

"Blast and damn it, must I be a milksop
all my life? Half-grown, all thumbs,
no strength or knack at arms, to defend myself   140
if someone picks a fight with me.
                    Take over,
O my elders and betters, try the bow,
run off the contest."

                    And he stood the weapon
upright against the massy-timbered door
with one arrow across the horn aslant,   145
then went back to his chair. Antínoös
gave the word:

            "Now one man at a time
rise and go forward. Round the room in order;
left to right from where they dip the wine."

As this seemed fair enough, up stood Leódês   150
the son of Oinops. This man used to find
visions for them in the smoke of sacrifice.
He kept his chair well back, retired by the winebowl,

for he alone could not abide their manners
but sat in shame for all the rest. Now it was he   155
who had first to confront the bow,
standing up on the broad door sill. He failed.
The bow unbending made his thin hands yield,
no muscle in them. He gave up and said:

"Friends, I cannot. Let the next man handle it.   160
Here is a bow to break the heart and spirit
of many strong men. Aye. And death is less
bitter than to live on and never have
the beauty that we came here laying siege to
so many days. Resolute, are you still,   165
to win Odysseus' lady Penélopê?
Pit yourselves against the bow, and look
among Akhaians for another's daughter.
Gifts will be enough to court and take her.
Let the best offer win."

                    With this Leódês   170
thrust the bow away from him, and left it
upright against the massy-timbered door,
with one arrow aslant across the horn.
As he went down to his chair he heard Antínoös'
voice rising:

                    "What is that you say?   175
It makes me burn. You cannot string the weapon,
so 'Here is a bow to break the heart and spirit
of many strong men.' Crushing thought!
You were not born—you never had it in you—
to pull that bow or let an arrow fly.   180
But here are men who can and will."

He called out to the goatherd, Melánthios:

"Kindle a fire there, be quick about it,
draw up a big bench with a sheepskin on it,
and bring a cake of lard out of the stores.   185
Contenders from now on will heat and grease the bow.
We'll try it limber, and bring off the shot."

Melánthios darted out to light a blaze,
drew up a bench, threw a big sheepskin over it,
and brought a cake of lard. So one by one   190
the young men warmed and greased the bow for bending,
but not a man could string it. They were whipped.
Antínoös held off; so did Eurýmakhos,
suitors in chief, by far the ablest there.

Two men had meanwhile left the hall: 195
swineherd and cowherd, in companionship,
one downcast as the other. But Odysseus
followed them outdoors, outside the court,
and coming up said gently:

        "You, herdsman,
and you, too, swineherd, I could say a thing to you,   200
or should I keep it dark?
        No, no; speak,
my heart tells me. Would you be men enough
to stand by Odysseus if he came back?
Suppose he dropped out of a clear sky, as I did?
Suppose some god should bring him?   205
Would you bear arms for him, or for the suitors?"

The cowherd said:

        "Ah, let the master come!
Father Zeus, grant our old wish! Some courier
guide him back! Then judge what stuff is in me
and how I manage arms!"

        Likewise Eumaios   210
fell to praying all heaven for his return,
so that Odysseus, sure at least of these,
told them:

        "I am at home, for I am he.
I bore adversities, but in the twentieth year
I am ashore in my own land. I find   215
the two of you, alone among my people,
longed for my coming. Prayers I never heard
except your own that I might come again.
So now what is in store for you I'll tell you:
If Zeus brings down the suitors by my hand   220
I promise marriages to both, and cattle,
and houses built near mine. And you shall be
brothers-in-arms of my Telémakhos.
Here, let me show you something else, a sign
that I am he, that you can trust me, look: 225
this old scar from the tusk wound that I got
boar hunting on Parnassos—
Autólykos' sons and I."

        Shifting his rags
he bared the long gash. Both men looked, and knew,
and threw their arms around the old soldier, weeping,   230

kissing his head and shoulders. He as well
took each man's head and hands to kiss, then said—
to cut it short, else they might weep till dark—

"Break off, no more of this.
Anyone at the door could see and tell them.   235
Drift back in, but separately at intervals
after me.
          Now listen to your orders:
when the time comes, those gentlemen, to a man,
will be dead against giving me bow or quiver.
Defy them. Eumaios, bring the bow   240
and put it in my hands there at the door.
Tell the women to lock their own door tight.
Tell them if someone hears the shock of arms
or groans of men, in hall or court, not one
must show her face, but keep still at her weaving.   245
Philoítios, run to the outer gate and lock it.
Throw the cross bar and lash it."

                              He turned back
into the courtyard and the beautiful house
and took the stool he had before. They followed
one by one, the two hands loyal to him.   250

Eurýmakhos had now picked up the bow.
He turned it round, and turned it round
before the licking flame to warm it up,
but could not, even so, put stress upon it
to jam the loop over the tip
                              though his heart groaned to bursting.   255
Then he said grimly:

                    "Curse this day.
What gloom I feel, not for myself alone,
and not only because we lose that bride.
Women are not lacking in Akhaia,
in other towns, or on Ithaka. No, the worst   260
is humiliation—to be shown up for children
measured against Odysseus—we who cannot
even hitch the string over his bow.
What shame to be repeated of us, after us!"

Antínoös said:

                    "Come to yourself. You know   265
that is not the way this business ends.

Today the islanders held holiday, a holy day,
no day to sweat over a bowstring.
                              Keep your head.
Postpone the bow. I say we leave the axes
planted where they are. No one will take them.   270
No one comes to Odysseus' hall tonight.
Break out good wine and brim our cups again,
we'll keep the crooked bow safe overnight,
order the fattest goats Melánthios has
brought down tomorrow noon, and offer thighbones burning   275
to Apollo, god of archers,
while we try out the bow and make the shot."

As this appealed to everyone, heralds came
pouring fresh water for their hands, and boys
filled up the winebowls. Joints of meat went round,   280
fresh cuts for all, while each man made his offering,
tilting the red wine to the gods, and drank his fill.
Then spoke Odysseus, all craft and gall:

"My lords, contenders for the queen, permit me:
a passion in me moves me to speak out.   285
I put it to Eurýmakhos above all
and to that brilliant prince, Antínoös. Just now
how wise his counsel was, to leave the trial
and turn your thoughts to the immortal gods! Apollo
will give power tomorrow to whom he wills.   290
But let me try my hand at the smooth bow!
Let me test my fingers and my pull
to see if any of the oldtime kick is there,
or if thin fare and roving took it out of me."

Now irritation beyond reason swept them all,   295
since they were nagged by fear that he could string it.
Antínoös answered, coldly and at length:

"You bleary vagabond, no rag of sense is left you.
Are you not coddled here enough, at table
taking meat with gentlemen, your betters,   300
denied nothing, and listening to our talk?
When have we let a tramp hear all our talk?
The sweet goad of wine has made you rave!
Here is the evil wine can do
to those who swig it down. Even the centaur   305
Eurýtion,[4] in Peiríthoös' hall

4. The centaurs were half-horse, half-man. At a wedding in the house of the Lapíthai, their human neighbors, they got drunk and tried to rape the women; a fight ensued. The great pediment at Olympia presents this scene, and individual contests of Lapith and centaur are portrayed on the Parthenon at Athens.

among the Lapíthai, came to a bloody end
because of wine; wine ruined him: it crazed him,
drove him wild for rape in that great house.
The princes cornered him in fury, leaping on him   310
to drag him out and crop his ears and nose.
Drink had destroyed his mind, and so he ended
in that mutilation—fool that he was.
Centaurs and men made war for this,
but the drunkard first brought hurt upon himself.   315

The tale applies to you: I promise you
great trouble if you touch that bow. You'll come by
no indulgence in our house; kicked down
into a ship's bilge, out to sea you go,
and nothing saves you. Drink, but hold your tongue.   320
Make no contention here with younger men."
At this the watchful queen Penélopê
interposed:

        "Antínoös, discourtesy
to a guest of Telémakhos—whatever guest—
that is not handsome. What are you afraid of?   325
Suppose this exile put his back into it
and drew the great bow of Odysseus—
could he then take me home to be his bride?
You know he does not imagine that! No one
need let that prospect weigh upon his dinner!   330
How very, very improbable it seems."

It was Eurýmakhos who answered her:

"Penélopê, O daughter of Ikários,
most subtle queen, we are not given to fantasy.
No, but our ears burn at what men might say   335
and women, too. We hear some jackal whispering:
'How far inferior to the great husband
her suitors are! Can't even budge his bow!
Think of it; and a beggar, out of nowhere,
strung it quick and made the needle shot!'   340
That kind of disrepute we would not care for."

Penélopê replied, steadfast and wary:

"Eurýmakhos, you have no good repute
in this realm, nor the faintest hope of it—
men who abused a prince's house for years,   345
consumed his wine and cattle. Shame enough.

Why hang your heads over a trifle now?
The stranger is a big man, well-compacted,
and claims to be of noble blood.
Ai!   350
Give him the bow, and let us have it out!
What I can promise him I will:
if by the kindness of Apollo he prevails
he shall be clothed well and equipped.
A fine shirt and a cloak I promise him;   355
a lance for keeping dogs at bay, or men;
a broadsword; sandals to protect his feet;
escort, and freedom to go where he will."

Telémakhos now faced her and said sharply:

"Mother, as to the bow and who may handle it   360
or not handle it, no man here
has more authority than I do—not one lord
of our own stony Ithaka nor the islands lying
east toward Elis:[5] no one stops me if I choose
to give these weapons outright to my guest.   365
Return to your own hall. Tend your spindle.
Tend your loom. Direct your maids at work.
This question of the bow will be for men to settle,
most of all for me. I am master here."

She gazed in wonder, turned, and so withdrew,   370
her son's clearheaded bravery in her heart.
But when she had mounted to her rooms again
with all her women, then she fell to weeping
for Odysseus, her husband. Grey-eyed Athena
presently cast a sweet sleep on her eyes.   375

The swineherd had the horned bow in his hands
moving toward Odysseus, when the crowd
in the banquet hall broke into an ugly din,
shouts rising from the flushed young men:

                                        "Ho! Where
do you think you are taking that, you smutty slave?"   380

"What is this dithering?"

                        "We'll toss you back alone
among the pigs, for your own dogs to eat,
if bright Apollo nods and the gods are kind!"

---

5. In the Peloponnese. The Olympic Games were held in its territory.

He faltered, all at once put down the bow, and stood
in panic, buffeted by waves of cries,   385
hearing Telémakhos from another quarter
shout:

"Go on, take him the bow!
                              Do you obey this pack?
You will be stoned back to your hills! Young as I am
my power is over you! I wish to God   390
I had as much the upper hand of these!
There would be suitors pitched like dead rats
through our gate, for the evil plotted here!"

Telémakhos' frenzy struck someone as funny,
and soon the whole room roared with laughter at him,   395
so that all tension passed. Eumaios picked up
bow and quiver, making for the door,
and there he placed them in Odysseus' hands.
Calling Eurýkleia to his side he said:
                                   "Telémakhos
trusts you to take care of the women's doorway.   400
Lock it tight. If anyone inside
should hear the shock of arms or groans of men
in hall or court, not one must show her face,
but go on with her weaving."

                         The old woman
nodded and kept still. She disappeared   405
into the women's hall, bolting the door behind her.
Philoítios left the house now at one bound,
catlike, running to bolt the courtyard gate.
A coil of deck-rope of papyrus fiber[6]
lay in the gateway; this he used for lashing,   410
and ran back to the same stool as before,
fastening his eyes upon Odysseus.
                              And Odysseus took his time,
turning the bow, tapping it, every inch,
for borings that termites might have made
while the master of the weapon was abroad.   415
The suitors were now watching him, and some
jested among themselves:

                    "A bow lover!"

"Dealer in old bows!"

---

6. The fibers of a plant grown in Egypt, used, as here, for rope, later as writing material (paper).

                    "Maybe he has one like it
at home!"

        "Or has an itch to make one for himself."

"See how he handles it, the sly old buzzard!"   420

And one disdainful suitor added this:

"May his fortune grow an inch for every inch he bends it!"

But the man skilled in all ways of contending,
satisfied by the great bow's look and heft,
like a musician, like a harper, when   425
with quiet hand upon his instrument
he draws between his thumb and forefinger
a sweet new string upon a peg: so effortlessly
Odysseus in one motion strung the bow.
Then slid his right hand down the cord and plucked it,   430
so the taut gut vibrating hummed and sang
a swallow's note.
                In the hushed hall it smote the suitors
and all their faces changed. Then Zeus thundered
overhead, one loud crack for a sign.
And Odysseus laughed within him that the son   435
of crooked-minded Kronos had flung that omen down.
He picked one ready arrow from his table
where it lay bare: the rest were waiting still
in the quiver for the young men's turn to come.
He nocked it, let it rest across the handgrip,   440
and drew the string and grooved butt of the arrow,
aiming from where he sat upon the stool.
                                Now flashed
arrow from twanging bow clean as a whistle
through every socket ring, and grazed not one,
to thud with heavy brazen head beyond.
                                Then quietly   445
Odysseus said:

                "Telémakhos, the stranger
you welcomed in your hall has not disgraced you.
I did not miss, neither did I take all day
stringing the bow. My hand and eye are sound,
not so contemptible as the young men say.   450
The hour has come to cook their lordships' mutton—
supper by daylight. Other amusements later,
with song and harping that adorn a feast."

He dropped his eyes and nodded, and the prince
Telémakhos, true son of King Odysseus,   455

belted his sword on, clapped hand to his spear,
and with a clink and glitter of keen bronze
stood by his chair, in the forefront near his father.

BOOK XXII

Death in the Great Hall

Now shrugging off his rags the wiliest fighter of the islands[7]
leapt and stood on the broad door sill, his own bow in his hand.
He poured out at his feet a rain of arrows from the quiver
and spoke to the crowd:

                "So much for that. Your clean-cut game is over.
Now watch me hit a target that no man has hit before,   5
if I can make this shot. Help me, Apollo."

He drew to his fist the cruel head of an arrow for Antínoös
just as the young man leaned to lift his beautiful drinking cup,
embossed, two-handled, golden: the cup was in his fingers:
the wine was even at his lips: and did he dream of death?   10
How could he? In that revelry amid his throng of friends
who would imagine a single foe—though a strong foe indeed—
could dare to bring death's pain on him and darkness on his eyes?
Odysseus' arrow hit him under the chin
and punched up to the feathers through his throat.   15

Backward and down he went, letting the winecup fall
from his shocked hand. Like pipes his nostrils jetted
crimson runnels, a river of mortal red,
and one last kick upset his table
knocking the bread and meat to soak in dusty blood.   20
Now as they craned to see their champion where he lay
the suitors jostled in uproar down the hall,
everyone on his feet. Wildly they turned and scanned
the walls in the long room for arms; but not a shield,
not a good ashen spear was there for a man to take and throw.   25
All they could do was yell in outrage at Odysseus:

"Foul! to shoot at a man! That was your last shot!"

"Your own throat will be slit for this!"

                "Our finest lad is down!
You killed the best on Ithaka."

                "Buzzards will tear your eyes out!"

---

7. In the account of the battle in the hall the translator occasionally, as here, uses a longer line than usual. There is no such variation of length in the original.

For they imagined as they wished—that it was a wild shot,   30
an unintended killing—fools, not to comprehend
they were already in the grip of death.
But glaring under his brows Odysseus answered:

"You yellow dogs, you thought I'd never make it
home from the land of Troy. You took my house to plunder,   35
twisted my maids to serve your beds. You dared
bid for my wife while I was still alive.
Contempt was all you had for the gods who rule wide heaven,
contempt for what men say of you hereafter.
Your last hour has come. You die in blood."   40

As they all took this in, sickly green fear
pulled at their entrails, and their eyes flickered
looking for some hatch or hideaway from death.
Eurýmakhos alone could speak. He said:

"If you are Odysseus of Ithaka come back,   45
all that you say these men have done is true.
Rash actions, many here, more in the countryside.
But here he lies, the man who caused them all.
Antínoös was the ringleader; he whipped us on
to do these things. He cared less for a marriage   50
than for the power Kroníon has denied him
as king of Ithaka. For that
he tried to trap your son and would have killed him.
He is dead now and has his portion. Spare
your own people. As for ourselves, we'll make   55
restitution of wine and meat consumed,
and add, each one, a tithe of twenty oxen
with gifts of bronze and gold to warm your heart.
Meanwhile we cannot blame you for your anger."

Odysseus glowered under his black brows   60
and said:

        "Not for the whole treasure of your fathers,
all you enjoy, lands, flocks, or any gold
put up by others, would I hold my hand.
There will be killing till the score is paid.
You forced yourselves upon this house. Fight your way out,   65
or run for it, if you think you'll escape death.
I doubt one man of you skins by."

They felt their knees fail, and their hearts—but heard
Eurýmakhos for the last time rallying them.

"Friends," he said, "the man is implacable.   70
Now that he's got his hands on bow and quiver
he'll shoot from the big door stone there
until he kills us to the last man.
                    Fight, I say,
let's remember the joy of it. Swords out!
Hold up your tables to deflect his arrows.   75
After me, everyone: rush him where he stands.
If we can budge him from the door, if we can pass
into the town, we'll call out men to chase him.
This fellow with his bow will shoot no more."

He drew his own sword as he spoke, a broadsword of fine bronze,   80
honed like a razor on either edge. Then crying hoarse and loud
he hurled himself at Odysseus. But the kingly man let fly
an arrow at that instant, and the quivering feathered butt
sprang to the nipple of his breast as the barb stuck in his liver.
The bright broadsword clanged down. He lurched and fell aside,   85
pitching across his table. His cup, his bread and meat,
were spilt and scattered far and wide, and his head slammed on the ground.
Revulsion, anguish in his heart, with both feet kicking out,
he downed his chair, while the shrouding wave of mist closed on his eyes.

Amphínomos now came running at Odysseus,   90
broadsword naked in his hand. He thought to make
the great soldier give way at the door.
But with a spear throw from behind Telémakhos hit him
between the shoulders, and the lancehead drove
clear through his chest. He left his feet and fell   95
forward, thudding, forehead against the ground.
Telémakhos swerved around him, leaving the long dark spear
planted in Amphínomos. If he paused to yank it out
someone might jump him from behind or cut him down with a sword
at the moment he bent over. So he ran—ran from the tables   100
to his father's side and halted, panting, saying:

"Father let me bring you a shield and spear,
a pair of spears, a helmet.
I can arm on the run myself; I'll give
outfits to Eumaios and this cowherd.   105
Better to have equipment."

                    Said Odysseus:

"Run then, while I hold them off with arrows
as long as the arrows last. When all are gone
if I'm alone they can dislodge me."

Quick
upon his father's word Telémakhos   110
ran to the room where spears and armor lay.
He caught up four light shields, four pairs of spears,
four helms of war high-plumed with flowing manes,
and ran back, loaded down, to his father's side.
He was the first to pull a helmet on   115
and slide his bare arm in a buckler strap.
The servants armed themselves, and all three took their stand
beside the master of battle.
                   While he had arrows
he aimed and shot, and every shot brought down
one of his huddling enemies.   120
But when all barbs had flown from the bowman's fist,
he leaned his bow in the bright entry way
beside the door, and armed: a four-ply shield
hard on his shoulder, and a crested helm,
horsetailed, nodding stormy upon his head,   125
then took his tough and bronze-shod spears.
                                     The suitors
who held their feet, no longer under bowshot,
could see a window high in a recess of the wall,
a vent, lighting the passage to the storeroom.
This passage had one entry, with a door,   130
at the edge of the great hall's threshold, just outside.

Odysseus told the swineherd to stand over
and guard this door and passage. As he did so,
a suitor named Ageláos asked the others:

"Who will get a leg up on that window   135
and run to alarm the town? One sharp attack
and this fellow will never shoot again."

                              His answer
came from the goatherd, Melánthios:

                              "No chance, my lord.
The exit into the courtyard is too near them,
too narrow. One good man could hold that portal   140
against a crowd. No: let me scale the wall
and bring you arms out of the storage chamber.
Odysseus and his son put them indoors,
I'm sure of it; not outside."

                   The goatish goatherd
clambered up the wall, toes in the chinks,   145

and slipped through to the storeroom. Twelve light shields,
twelve spears he took, and twelve thick-crested helms,
and handed all down quickly to the suitors.
Odysseus, when he saw his adversaries
girded and capped and long spears in their hands   150
shaken at him, felt his knees go slack,
his heart sink, for the fight was turning grim.
He spoke rapidly to his son:

"Telémakhos, one of the serving women
is tipping the scales against us in this fight,   155
or maybe Melánthios."

                    But sharp and clear
Telémakhos said:

                  "It is my own fault, Father,
mine alone. The storeroom door—I left it
wide open. They were more alert than I.
Eumaios, go and lock that door,   160
and bring back word if a woman is doing this
or Melánthios, Dólios' son. More likely he."

Even as they conferred, Melánthios
entered the storeroom for a second load,
and the swineherd at the passage entry saw him.   165
He cried out to his lord:

                "Son of Laërtês,
Odysseus, master mariner and soldier,
there he goes, the monkey, as we thought,
there he goes into the storeroom.
                Let me hear your will:
put a spear through him—I hope I am the stronger—   170
or drag him here to pay for his foul tricks
against your house?"

                Odysseus said:

                    "Telémakhos and I
will keep these gentlemen in hall, for all their urge to leave.
You two go throw him into the storeroom, wrench his arms
and legs behind him, lash his hands and feet   175
to a plank, and hoist him up to the roof beams.
Let him live on there suffering at his leisure."

The two men heard him with appreciation
and ducked into the passage. Melánthios,
rummaging in the chamber, could not hear them   180

as they came up; nor could he see them freeze
like posts on either side the door.
He turned back with a handsome crested helmet
in one hand, in the other an old shield
coated with dust—a shield Laërtês bore   185
soldiering in his youth. It had lain there for years,
and the seams on strap and grip had rotted away.
As Melánthios came out the two men sprang,
jerked him backward by the hair, and threw him.
Hands and feet they tied with a cutting cord   190
behind him, so his bones ground in their sockets,
just as Laërtês' royal son commanded.
Then with a whip of rope they hoisted him
in agony up a pillar to the beams,
and—O my swineherd—you were the one to say: 195

"Watch through the night up there, Melánthios.
An airy bed is what you need.
You'll be awake to see the primrose Dawn
when she goes glowing from the streams of Ocean
to mount her golden throne.
                    No oversleeping   200
the hour for driving goats to feed the suitors."

They stopped for helm and shield and left him there
contorted, in his brutal sling,
and shut the doors, and went to join Odysseus,
whose mind moved through the combat now to come.   205
Breathing deep, and snorting hard, they stood
four at the entry, facing two score men.
But now into the gracious doorway stepped
Zeus's daughter Athena. She wore the guise of Mentor,
and Odysseus appealed to her in joy: 210

"O Mentor, join me in this fight! Remember
how all my life I've been devoted to you,
friend of my youth!"

                    For he guessed it was Athena,
Hope of Soldiers. Cries came from the suitors,
and Ageláos, Damástor's son, called out: 215

"Mentor, don't let Odysseus lead you astray
to fight against us on his side.
Think twice: we are resolved—and we will do it—
after we kill them, father and son,
you too will have your throat slit for your pains   220
if you make trouble for us here. It means your life.

Your life—and cutting throats will not be all.
Whatever wealth you have, at home, or elsewhere,
we'll mingle with Odysseus' wealth. Your sons
will be turned out, your wife and daughters   225
banished from the town of Ithaka."

Athena's anger grew like a storm wind as he spoke
until she flashed out at Odysseus:

                    "Ah, what a falling off!
Where is your valor, where is the iron hand
that fought at Troy for Helen, pearl of kings,   230
no respite and nine years of war? How many foes
your hand brought down in bloody play of spears?
What stratagem but yours took Priam's town?
How is it now that on your own door sill,
before the harriers of your wife, you curse your luck   235
not to be stronger?
                    Come here, cousin, stand by me,
and you'll see action! In the enemies' teeth
learn how Mentor, son of Álkimos,
repays fair dealing!"

                    For all her fighting words
she gave no overpowering aid—not yet;   240
father and son must prove their mettle still.
Into the smoky air under the roof
the goddess merely darted to perch on a blackened beam—
no figure to be seen now but a swallow.

Command of the suitors had fallen to Ageláos.   245
With him were Eurýnomos, Amphímedon,
Demoptólemos, Peisándros, Pólybos,
the best of the lot who stood to fight for their lives
after the streaking arrows downed the rest.
Ageláos rallied them with his plan of battle: 250

"Friends, our killer has come to the end of his rope,
and much good Mentor did him, that blowhard, dropping in.
Look, only four are left to fight, in the light there at the door.
No scattering of shots, men, no throwing away good spears;
we six will aim a volley at Odysseus alone,   255
and may Zeus grant us the glory of a hit.
If he goes down, the others are no problem."

At his command, then, "Ho!" they all let fly
as one man. But Athena spoiled their shots.
One hit the doorpost of the hall, another   260

stuck in the door's thick timbering, still others
rang on the stone wall, shivering hafts of ash.
Seeing his men unscathed, royal Odysseus
gave the word for action.

               "Now I say, friends,
the time is overdue to let them have it.   265
Battlespoil they want from our dead bodies
to add to all they plundered here before."

Taking aim over the steadied lanceheads
they all let fly together. Odysseus killed
Demoptólemos; Telémakhos   270
killed Eurýadês; the swineherd, Élatos;
and Peisándros went down before the cowherd.
As these lay dying, biting the central floor,
their friends gave way and broke for the inner wall.
The four attackers followed up with a rush   275
to take spears from the fallen men.

                     Re-forming,
the suitors threw again with all their strength,
but Athena turned their shots, or all but two.
One hit a doorpost in the hall, another
stuck in the door's thick timbering, still others   280
rang on the stone wall, shivering hafts of ash.
Amphímedon's point bloodied Telémakhos'
wrist, a superficial wound, and Ktésippos'
long spear passing over Eumaios' shield
grazed his shoulder, hurtled on and fell.   285
No matter: with Odysseus the great soldier
the wounded threw again. And Odysseus raider of cities
struck Eurýdamas down. Telémakhos
hit Amphímedon, and the swineherd's shot
killed Pólybos. But Ktésippos, who had last evening thrown   290
a cow's hoof at Odysseus, got the cowherd's heavy cast
full in the chest—and dying heard him say:

"You arrogant joking bastard!
Clown, will you, like a fool, and parade your wit?
Leave jesting to the gods who do it better.   295
This will repay your cow's-foot courtesy
to a great wanderer come home."

                   The master
of the black herds had answered Ktésippos.
Odysseus, lunging at close quarters, put a spear
through Ageláos, Damastor's son. Telémakhos   300

hit Leókritos from behind and pierced him,
kidney to diaphragm. Speared off his feet,
he fell face downward on the ground.

At this moment that unmanning thunder cloud,
the aegis,[8] Athena's shield,   305
took form aloft in the great hall.
                 And the suitors mad with fear
at her great sign stampeded like stung cattle by a river
when the dread shimmering gadfly strikes in summer,
in the flowering season, in the long-drawn days.
After them the attackers wheeled, as terrible as falcons   310
from eyries in the mountains veering over and diving down
with talons wide unsheathed on flights of birds,
who cower down the sky in chutes and bursts along the valley—
but the pouncing falcons grip their prey, no frantic wing avails,
and farmers love to watch those beakèd hunters.   315
So these now fell upon the suitors in that hall,
turning, turning to strike and strike again,
while torn men moaned at death, and blood ran smoking
over the whole floor.
           Now there was one
who turned and threw himself at Odysseus' knees—   320
Leódês, begging for his life:

                   "Mercy,
mercy on a suppliant, Odysseus!
Never by word or act of mine, I swear,
was any woman troubled here. I told the rest
to put an end to it. They would not listen,   325
would not keep their hands from brutishness,
and now they are all dying like dogs for it.
I had no part in what they did: my part
was visionary—reading the smoke of sacrifice.
Scruples go unrewarded if I die."   330

The shrewd fighter frowned over him and said:

"You were diviner to this crowd? How often
you must have prayed my sweet day of return
would never come, or not for years!—and prayed
to have my dear wife, and beget children on her.   335
No plea like yours could save you
from this hard bed of death. Death it shall be!"

---

8. A magical shield (or breastplate) used by Athena and Zeus; it created a panic when displayed.

He picked up Ageláos' broadsword
from where it lay, flung by the slain man,
and gave Leódês' neck a lopping blow   340
so that his head went down to mouth in dust.

One more who had avoided furious death
was the son of Terpis, Phêmios, the minstrel,
singer by compulsion to the suitors.
He stood now with his harp, holy and clear,   345
in the wall's recess, under the window, wondering
if he should flee that way to the courtyard altar,
sanctuary of Zeus, the Enclosure God.[9]
Thighbones in hundreds had been offered there
by Laërtês and Odysseus. No, he thought;   350
the more direct way would be best—to go
humbly to his lord. But first to save
his murmuring instrument he laid it down
carefully between the winebowl and a chair,
then he betook himself to Lord Odysseus,   355
clung hard to his knees, and said:

                              "Mercy,
mercy on a suppliant, Odysseus!
My gift is song for men and for the gods undying.
My death will be remorse for you hereafter.
No one taught me: deep in my mind a god   360
shaped all the various ways of life in song.
And I am fit to make verse in your company
as in the god's. Put aside lust for blood.
Your own dear son Telémakhos can tell you,
never by my own will or for love   365
did I feast here or sing amid the suitors.
They were too strong, too many; they compelled me."

Telémakhos in the elation of battle
heard him. He at once called to his father:

"Wait: that one is innocent: don't hurt him.   370
And we should let our herald live—Medôn;
he cared for me from boyhood. Where is he?
Has he been killed already by Philoítios
or by the swineherd? Else he got an arrow
in that first gale of bowshots down the room."   375

9. Zeus Herkeios, guardian of the inner space of the home.

Now this came to the ears of prudent Medôn
under the chair where he had gone to earth,
pulling a new-flayed bull's hide over him.
Quiet he lay while blinding death passed by.
Now heaving out from under   380
he scrambled for Telémakhos' knees and said:

"Here I am, dear prince; but rest your spear!
Tell your great father not to see in me
a suitor for the sword's edge—one of those
who laughed at you and ruined his property!"   385

The lord of all the tricks of war surveyed
this fugitive and smiled. He said:

"Courage: my son has dug you out and saved you.
Take it to heart, and pass the word along:
fair dealing brings more profit in the end.   390
Now leave this room. Go and sit down outdoors
where there's no carnage, in the court,
you and the poet with his many voices,
while I attend to certain chores inside."

At this the two men stirred and picked their way   395
to the door and out, and sat down at the altar,
looking around with wincing eyes
as though the sword's edge hovered still.
And Odysseus looked around him, narrow-eyed,
for any others who had lain hidden   400
while death's black fury passed.
                                In blood and dust
he saw that crowd all fallen, many and many slain.

Think of a catch that fishermen haul in to a halfmoon bay
in a fine-meshed net from the white-caps of the sea:
how all are poured out on the sand, in throes for the salt sea,   405
twitching their cold lives away in Hêlios' fiery air:
so lay the suitors heaped on one another.

Odysseus at length said to his son:

"Go tell old Nurse I'll have a word with her.
What's to be done now weighs on my mind."   410

Telémakhos knocked at the women's door and called:

"Eurýkleia, come out here! Move, old woman.
You kept your eye on all our servant girls.
Jump, my father is here and wants to see you."

His call brought no reply, only the doors   415
were opened, and she came. Telémakhos
led her forward. In the shadowy hall
full of dead men she found his father
spattered and caked with blood like a mountain lion
when he has gorged upon an ox, his kill—   420
with hot blood glistening over his whole chest,
smeared on his jaws, baleful and terrifying—
even so encrimsoned was Odysseus
up to his thighs and armpits. As she gazed
from all the corpses to the bloody man   425
she raised her head to cry over his triumph,
but felt his grip upon her, checking her.
Said the great soldier then:

               "Rejoice
inwardly. No crowing aloud, old woman.
To glory over slain men is no piety.   430
Destiny and the gods' will vanquished these,
and their own hardness. They respected no one,
good or bad, who came their way.
For this, and folly, a bad end befell them.
Your part is now to tell me of the women,   435
those who dishonored me, and the innocent."

His own old nurse Eurýkleia said:

               "I will, then.
Child, you know you'll have the truth from me.
Fifty all told they are, your female slaves,
trained by your lady and myself in service,   440
wool carding and the rest of it, and taught
to be submissive. Twelve went bad,
flouting me, flouting Penélopê, too.
Telémakhos being barely grown, his mother
would never let him rule the serving women—   445
but you must let me go to her lighted rooms
and tell her. Some god sent her a drift of sleep."

But in reply the great tactician said:

"Not yet. Do not awake her. Tell those women
who were the suitors' harlots to come here."   450

She went back on this mission through his hall.
Then he called Telémakhos to his side
and the two herdsmen. Sharply Odysseus said:

"These dead must be disposed of first of all.
Direct the women. Tables and chairs will be   455

scrubbed with sponges, rinsed and rinsed again.
When our great room is fresh and put in order,
take them outside, these women,
between the roundhouse and the palisade,
and hack them with your swordblades till you cut   460
the life out of them, and every thought of sweet
Aphroditê under the rutting suitors,
when they lay down in secret."

　　　　　　　　　　As he spoke
here came the women in a bunch, all wailing,
soft tears on their cheeks. They fell to work   465
to lug the corpses out into the courtyard
under the gateway, propping one
against another as Odysseus ordered,
for he himself stood over them. In fear
these women bore the cold weight of the dead.   470
The next thing was to scrub off chairs and tables
and rinse them down. Telémakhos and the herdsman
scraped the packed earth floor with hoes, but made
the women carry out all blood and mire.
When the great room was cleaned up once again,   475
at swordpoint they forced them out, between
the roundhouse and the palisade, pell-mell
to huddle in that dead end without exit.
Telémakhos, who knew his mind, said curtly:

"I would not give the clean death of a beast[1]   480
to trulls who made a mockery of my mother
and of me too—you sluts, who lay with suitors."

He tied one end of a hawser to a pillar
and passed the other about the roundhouse top,
taking the slack up, so that no one's toes   485
could touch the ground. They would be hung like doves
or larks in springès triggered in a thicket,
where the birds think to rest—a cruel nesting.
So now in turn each woman thrust her head
into a noose and swung, yanked high in air,   490
to perish there most piteously.
Their feet danced for a little, but not long.

From storeroom to the court they brought Melánthios,
chopped with swords to cut his nose and ears off,
pulled off his genitals to feed the dogs   495
and raging hacked his hands and feet away.

---

1. I.e., by sword or spear. Hanging was considered an ignominious way to die.

As their own hands and feet called for a washing,
they went indoors to Odysseus again.
Their work was done. He told Eurýkleia:

                    "Bring me
brimstone and a brazier—medicinal   500
fumes to purify my hall. Then tell
Penélopê to come, and bring her maids.
All servants round the house must be called in."

His own old nurse Eurýkleia replied:

"Aye, surely that is well said, child. But let me   505
find you a good clean shirt and cloak and dress you.
You must not wrap your shoulders' breadth again
in rags in your own hall. That would be shameful."

Odysseus answered:

                    "Let me have the fire.
The first thing is to purify this place."   510

With no more chat Eurýkleia obeyed
and fetched out fire and brimstone. Cleansing fumes
he sent through court and hall and storage chamber.
Then the old woman hurried off again
to the women's quarters to announce her news,   515
and all the servants came now, bearing torches
in twilight, crowding to embrace Odysseus,
taking his hands to kiss, his head and shoulders,
while he stood there, nodding to every one,
and overcome by longing and by tears.   520

BOOK XXIII

The Trunk of the Olive Tree

The old nurse went upstairs exulting,
with knees toiling, and patter of slapping feet,
to tell the mistress of her lord's return,
and cried out by the lady's pillow:

                    "Wake,
wake up, dear child! Penélopê, come down,   5
see with your own eyes what all these years you longed for!
Odysseus is here! Oh, in the end, he came!
And he has killed your suitors, killed them all
who made his house a bordel and ate his cattle
and raised their hands against his son!"

Penélopê said: 10

"Dear nurse . . . the gods have touched you.
They can put chaos into the clearest head
or bring a lunatic down to earth. Good sense
you always had. They've touched you. What is this
mockery you wake me up to tell me,   15
breaking in on my sweet spell of sleep?
I had not dozed away so tranquilly
since my lord went to war, on that ill wind
to Ilion.
            Oh, leave me! Back down stairs!
If any other of my women came in babbling   20
things like these to startle me, I'd see her
flogged out of the house! Your old age spares you that."

Euríkleia said:

"Would I play such a trick on you, dear child?
It is true, true, as I tell you, he has come!   25
That stranger they were baiting was Odysseus.
Telémakhos knew it days ago—
cool head, never to give his father away,
till he paid off those swollen dogs!"

The lady in her heart's joy now sprang up   30
with sudden dazzling tears, and hugged the old one,
crying out:

            "But try to make it clear!
If he came home in secret, as you say,
could he engage them singlehanded? How?
They were all down there, still in the same crowd."   35

To this Euríkleia said:

                "I did not see it,
I knew nothing; only I heard the groans
of men dying. We sat still in the inner rooms
holding our breath, and marvelling, shut in,
until Telémakhos came to the door and called me—   40
your own dear son, sent this time by his father!
So I went out, and found Odysseus
erect, with dead men littering the floor
this way and that. If you had only seen him!
It would have made your heart glow hot!—a lion   45
splashed with mire and blood.
                        But now the cold
corpses are all gathered at the gate,

and he has cleansed his hall with fire and brimstone,
a great blaze. Then he sent me here to you.
Come with me: you may both embark this time   50
for happiness together, after pain,
after long years. Here is your prayer, your passion,
granted: your own lord lives, he is at home,
he found you safe, he found his son. The suitors
abused his house, but he has brought them down."   55

The attentive lady said:

                    "Do not lose yourself
in this rejoicing: wait: you know
how splendid that return would be for us,
how dear to me, dear to his son and mine;
but no, it is not possible, your notion   60
must be wrong.
                    Some god has killed the suitors,
a god, sick of their arrogance and brutal
malice—for they honored no one living,
good or bad, who ever came their way.
Blind young fools, they've tasted death for it.   65
But the true person of Odysseus?
He lost his home, he died far from Akhaia."

The old nurse sighed:

                    "How queer, the way you talk!
Here he is, large as life, by his own fire,
and you deny he ever will get home!   70
Child, you always were mistrustful!
But there is one sure mark that I can tell you:
that scar left by the boar's tusk long ago.
I recognized it when I bathed his feet
and would have told you, but he stopped my mouth,   75
forbade me, in his craftiness.
                    Come down,
I stake my life on it, he's here!
Let me die in agony if I lie!"

                    Penélopê said:

"Nurse dear, though you have your wits about you,
still it is hard not to be taken in   80
by the immortals. Let us join my son, though,
and see the dead and that strange one who killed them."

She turned then to descend the stair, her heart
in tumult. Had she better keep her distance

and question him, her husband? Should she run   85
up to him, take his hands, kiss him now?
Crossing the door sill she sat down at once
in firelight, against the nearest wall,
across the room from the lord Odysseus.
                                            There
leaning against a pillar, sat the man   90
and never lifted up his eyes, but only waited
for what his wife would say when she had seen him.
And she, for a long time, sat deathly still
in wonderment—for sometimes as she gazed
she found him—yes, clearly—like her husband,   95
but sometimes blood and rags were all she saw.
Telémakhos' voice came to her ears:
                          "Mother,
cruel mother, do you feel nothing,
drawing yourself apart this way from Father?
Will you not sit with him and talk and question him?   100
What other woman could remain so cold?
Who shuns her lord, and he come back to her
from wars and wandering, after twenty years?
Your heart is hard as flint and never changes!"

Penélopê answered:
                          "I am stunned, child.   105
I cannot speak to him. I cannot question him.
I cannot keep my eyes upon his face.
If really he is Odysseus, truly home,
beyond all doubt we two shall know each other
better than you or anyone. There are   110
secret signs we know, we two."

                          A smile
came now to the lips of the patient hero, Odysseus,
who turned to Telémakhos and said:

"Peace: let your mother test me at her leisure.
Before long she will see and know me best.   115
These tatters, dirt—all that I'm caked with now—
make her look hard at me and doubt me still.
As to this massacre, we must see the end.
Whoever kills one citizen, you know,
and has no force of armed men at his back,   120
had better take himself abroad by night
and leave his kin. Well, we cut down the flower of Ithaka,
the mainstay of the town. Consider that."

Telémakhos replied respectfully:

"Dear Father,
enough that you yourself study the danger,   125
foresighted in combat as you are,
they say you have no rival.
                    We three stand
ready to follow you and fight. I say
for what our strength avails, we have the courage."

And the great tactician, Odysseus, answered:

"Good.   130
Here is our best maneuver, as I see it:
bathe, you three, and put fresh clothing on,
order the women to adorn themselves,
and let our admirable harper choose a tune
for dancing, some lighthearted air, and strum it.   135
Anyone going by, or any neighbor,
will think it is a wedding feast he hears.
These deaths must not be cried about the town
till we can slip away to our own woods. We'll see
what weapon, then, Zeus puts into our hands."   140

They listened attentively, and did his bidding,
bathed and dressed afresh; and all the maids
adorned themselves. Then Phêmios the harper
took his polished shell and plucked the strings,
moving the company to desire   145
for singing, for the sway and beat of dancing,
until they made the manor hall resound
with gaiety of men and grace of women.
Anyone passing on the road would say:

"Married at last, I see—the queen so many courted.   150
Sly, cattish wife! She would not keep—not she!—
the lord's estate until he came."

                    So travellers'
thoughts might run—but no one guessed the truth.
Greathearted Odysseus, home at last,
was being bathed now by Eurýnomê   155
and rubbed with golden oil, and clothed again
in a fresh tunic and a cloak. Athena
lent him beauty, head to foot. She made him
taller, and massive, too, with crisping hair
in curls like petals of wild hyacinth   160
but all red-golden. Think of gold infused

on silver by a craftsman, whose fine art
Hephaistos taught him, or Athena: one
whose work moves to delight: just so she lavished
beauty over Odysseus' head and shoulders.   165
He sat then in the same chair by the pillar,
facing his silent wife, and said:

                              "Strange woman,
the immortals of Olympos made you hard,
harder than any. Who else in the world
would keep aloof as you do from her husband   170
if he returned to her from years of trouble,
cast on his own land in the twentieth year?

Nurse, make up a bed for me to sleep on.
Her heart is iron in her breast."

                         Penélopê
spoke to Odysseus now. She said:

                              "Strange man,   175
if man you are . . . This is no pride on my part
nor scorn for you—not even wonder, merely.
I know so well how you—how he—appeared
boarding the ship for Troy. But all the same . . .

Make up his bed for him, Eurýkleia.   180
Place it outside the bedchamber my lord
built with his own hands. Pile the big bed
with fleeces, rugs, and sheets of purest linen."

With this she tried him to the breaking point,
and he turned on her in a flash raging: 185

"Woman, by heaven you've stung me now!
Who dared to move my bed?
No builder had the skill for that—unless
a god came down to turn the trick. No mortal
in his best days could budge it with a crowbar.   190
There is our pact and pledge, our secret sign,
built into that bed—my handiwork
and no one else's!
                    An old trunk of olive
grew like a pillar on the building plot,
and I laid out our bedroom round that tree,   195
lined up the stone walls, built the walls and roof,
gave it a doorway and smooth-fitting doors.
Then I lopped off the silvery leaves and branches,

hewed and shaped that stump from the roots up
into a bedpost, drilled it, let it serve   200
as model for the rest. I planed them all,
inlaid them all with silver, gold and ivory,
and stretched a bed between—a pliant web
of oxhide thongs dyed crimson.
                                There's our sign!
I know no more. Could someone's else's hand   205
have sawn that trunk and dragged the frame away?"

Their secret! as she heard it told, her knees
grew tremulous and weak, her heart failed her.
With eyes brimming tears she ran to him,
throwing her arms around his neck, and kissed him,   210
murmuring:

             "Do not rage at me, Odysseus!
No one ever matched your caution! Think
what difficulty the gods gave: they denied us
life together in our prime and flowering years,
kept us from crossing into age together.   215
Forgive me, don't be angry. I could not
welcome you with love on sight! I armed myself
long ago against the frauds of men,
impostors who might come—and all those many
whose underhanded ways bring evil on!   220
Helen of Argos, daughter of Zeus and Leda,
would she have joined the stranger, lain with him,
if she had known her destiny? known the Akhaians
in arms would bring her back to her own country?
Surely a goddess moved her to adultery,   225
her blood unchilled by war and evil coming,
the years, the desolation; ours, too.
But here and now, what sign could be so clear
as this of our own bed?
No other man has ever laid eyes on it—   230
only my own slave, Aktoris, that my father
sent with me as a gift—she kept our door.
You make my stiff heart know that I am yours."

Now from his breast into his eyes the ache
of longing mounted, and he wept at last,   235
his dear wife, clear and faithful, in his arms,
longed for
          as the sunwarmed earth is longed for by a swimmer
spent in rough water where his ship went down
under Poseidon's blows, gale winds and tons of sea.

Few men can keep alive through a big surf   240
to crawl, clotted with brine, on kindly beaches
in joy, in joy, knowing the abyss behind:
and so she too rejoiced, her gaze upon her husband,
her white arms round him pressed as though forever.

The rose Dawn might have found them weeping still   245
had not grey-eyed Athena slowed the night
when night was most profound, and held the Dawn
under the Ocean of the East. That glossy team,
Firebright and Daybright, the Dawn's horses
that draw her heavenward for men—Athena   250
stayed their harnessing.

                Then said Odysseus:

"My dear, we have not won through to the end.
One trial—I do not know how long—is left for me
to see fulfilled. Teirêsias' ghost forewarned me
the night I stood upon the shore of Death, asking   255
about my friends' homecoming and my own.

But now the hour grows late, it is bed time,
rest will be sweet for us; let us lie down."

To this Penélopê replied:

                        "That bed,
that rest is yours whenever desire moves you,   260
now the kind powers have brought you home at last.
But as your thought has dwelt upon it, tell me:
what is the trial you face? I must know soon;
what does it matter if I learn tonight?"

The teller of many stories said:

                        "My strange one,   265
must you again, and even now,
urge me to talk? Here is a plodding tale;
no charm in it, no relish in the telling.
Teirêsias told me I must take an oar
and trudge the mainland, going from town to town,   270
until I discover men who have never known
the salt blue sea, nor flavor of salt meat—
strangers to painted prows, to watercraft
and oars like wings, dipping across the water.
The moment of revelation he foretold   275
was this, for you may share the prophecy:

some traveller falling in with me will say:
'A winnowing fan, that on your shoulder, sir?'
There I must plant my oar, on the very spot,
with burnt offerings to Poseidon of the Waters: 280
a ram, a bull, a great buck boar. Thereafter
when I come home again, I am to slay
full hekatombs to the gods who own broad heaven,
one by one.
      Then death will drift upon me
from seaward, mild as air, mild as your hand,   285
in my well-tended weariness of age,
contented folk around me on our island.
He said all this must come."

             Penélopê said:
"If by the gods' grace age at least is kind,
we have that promise—trials will end in peace."   290

So he confided in her, and she answered.
Meanwhile Eurýnomê and the nurse together
laid soft coverlets on the master's bed,
working in haste by torchlight. Eurýkleia
retired to her quarters for the night,   295
and then Eurýnomê, as maid-in-waiting,
lighted her lord and lady to their chamber
with bright brands.
        She vanished.
           So they came
into that bed so steadfast, loved of old,
opening glad arms to one another.[2]   300
Telémakhos by now had hushed the dancing,
hushed the women. In the darkened hall
he and the cowherd and the swineherd slept.

The royal pair mingled in love again
and afterward lay revelling in stories: 305
hers of the siege her beauty stood at home
from arrogant suitors, crowding on her sight,
and how they fed their courtship on his cattle,
oxen and fat sheep, and drank up rivers
of wine out of the vats.

2. Two great Alexandrian critics said that this line was the "end" of the Odyssey (though one of the words they are said to have used could mean simply "culmination"). Modern critics are divided; some find the rest of the poem banal, unartistic, full of linguistic anomalies, and so on. But if the poem stops here we are left in suspense about many important themes that have been developed and demand a sequel—the question of reprisals for the slaughter in the hall, to mention only one.

Odysseus told 310
of what hard blows he had dealt out to others
and of what blows he had taken—all that story.
She could not close her eyes till all was told.

His raid on the Kikonês, first of all,
then how he visited the Lotos Eaters, 315
and what the Kyklops did, and how those shipmates,
pitilessly devoured, were avenged.
Then of his touching Aiolos's isle
and how that king refitted him for sailing
to Ithaka; all vain: gales blew him back 320
groaning over the fishcold sea. Then how
he reached the Laistrygonians' distant bay
and how they smashed his ships and his companions.
Kirkê, then: of her deceits and magic,
then of his voyage to the wide underworld 325
of dark, the house of Death, and questioning
Teirêsias, Theban spirit.
Dead companions,
many, he saw there, and his mother, too.
Of this he told his wife, and told how later
he heard the choir of maddening Seirênês, 330
coasted the Wandering Rocks, Kharybdis' pool
and the fiend Skylla who takes toll of men.
Then how his shipmates killed Lord Hêlios' cattle
and how Zeus thundering in towering heaven
split their fast ship with his fuming bolt, 335
so all hands perished.
He alone survived,
cast away on Kalypso's isle, Ogýgia.
He told, then, how that nymph detained him there
in her smooth caves, craving him for her husband,
and how in her devoted lust she swore 340
he should not die nor grow old, all his days,
but he held out against her.
Last of all
what sea-toil brought him to the Phaiákians;
their welcome; how they took him to their hearts
and gave him passage to his own dear island 345
with gifts of garments, gold and bronze . . .
Remembering,
he drowsed over the story's end. Sweet sleep
relaxed his limbs and his care-burdened breast.

Other affairs were in Athena's keeping.
Waiting until Odysseus had his pleasure 350

of love and sleep, the grey-eyed one bestirred
the fresh Dawn from her bed of paling Ocean
to bring up daylight to her golden chair,
and from his fleecy bed Odysseus
arose. He said to Penélopê:

              "My lady,   355
what ordeals have we not endured! Here, waiting
you had your grief, while my return dragged out—
my hard adventures, pitting myself against
the gods' will, and Zeus, who pinned me down
far from home. But now our life resumes: 360
we've come together to our longed-for bed.
Take care of what is left me in our house;
as to the flocks that pack of wolves laid waste
they'll be replenished: scores I'll get on raids
and other scores our island friends will give me   365
till all the folds are full again.
                     This day
I'm off up country to the orchards. I must see
my noble father, for he missed me sorely.
And here is my command for you—a strict one,
though you may need none, clever as you are.   370
Word will get about as the sun goes higher
of how I killed those lads. Go to your rooms
on the upper floor, and take your women. Stay there
with never a glance outside or a word to anyone."

Fitting cuirass and swordbelt to his shoulders,   375
he woke his herdsmen, woke Telémakhos,
ordering all in arms. They dressed quickly,
and all in war gear sallied from the gate,
led by Odysseus.
                Now it was broad day
but these three men Athena hid in darkness,   380
going before them swiftly from the town.

BOOK XXIV

Warriors, Farewell

Meanwhile the suitors' ghosts were called away
by Hermês of Kyllênê,[3] bearing the golden wand
with which he charms the eyes of men or wakens
whom he wills.
             He waved them on, all squeaking
as bats will in a cavern's underworld,   5

---

3. Hermês was born on Mount Kyllênê in Arcadia.

all flitting, flitting criss-cross in the dark
if one falls and the rock-hung chain is broken.
So with faint cries the shades trailed after Hermês,
pure Deliverer.

        He led them down dank ways,
over grey Ocean tides, the Snowy Rock,   10
past shores of Dream and narrows of the sunset,
in swift flight to where the Dead inhabit
wastes of asphodel at the world's end.

Crossing the plain they met Akhilleus' ghost,
Patróklos and Antílokhos, then Aias,   15
noblest of Danaans after Akhilleus
in strength and beauty. Here the newly dead
drifted together, whispering. Then came
the soul of Agamémnon, son of Atreus,
in black pain forever, surrounded by men-at-arms   20
who perished with him in Aigísthos' hall.

Akhilleus greeted him:

                "My lord Atreidês,
we held that Zeus who loves the play of lightning
would give you length of glory, you were king
over so great a host of soldiery   25
before Troy, where we suffered, we Akhaians.
But in the morning of your life
you met that doom that no man born avoids.
It should have found you in your day of victory,
marshal of the army, in Troy country;   30
then all Akhaia would have heaped your tomb
and saved your honor for your son. Instead
piteous death awaited you at home."

And Atreus' son replied:

                "Fortunate hero,
son of Pêleus, godlike and glorious,   35
at Troy you died, across the sea from Argos,
and round you Trojan and Akhaian peers
fought for your corpse and died. A dustcloud wrought
by a whirlwind hid the greatness of you slain,
minding no more the mastery of horses.   40
All that day we might have toiled in battle
had not a storm from Zeus broken it off.
We carried you out of the field of war
down to the ships and bathed your comely body
with warm water and scented oil. We laid you   45

upon your long bed, and our officers
wept hot tears like rain and cropped their hair.
Then hearing of it in the sea, your mother, Thetis,
came with nereids of the grey wave crying
unearthly lamentation over the water,   50
and trembling gripped the Akhaians to the bone.
They would have boarded ship that night and fled
except for one man's wisdom—venerable
Nestor, proven counselor in the past.
He stood and spoke to allay their fear: 'Hold fast,   55
sons of the Akhaians, lads of Argos.
His mother it must be, with nymphs her sisters,
come from the sea to mourn her son in death.'

Veteran hearts at this contained their dread
while at your side the daughters of the ancient   60
seagod wailed and wrapped ambrosial shrouding
around you.
              Then we heard the Muses sing
a threnody in nine immortal voices.
No Argive there but wept, such keening rose
from that one Muse who led the song.
                                    Now seven   65
days and ten, seven nights and ten, we mourned you,
we mortal men, with nymphs who know no death,
before we gave you to the flame, slaughtering
longhorned steers and fat sheep on your pyre.

Dressed by the nereids and embalmed with honey,   70
honey and unguent in the seething blaze,
you turned to ash. And past the pyre Akhaia's
captains paraded in review, in arms,
clattering chariot teams and infantry.
Like a forest fire the flame roared on, and burned   75
your flesh away. Next day at dawn, Akhilleus,
we picked your pale bones from the char to keep
in wine and oil. A golden amphora
your mother gave for this—Hephaistos' work,
a gift from Dionysos.[4] In that vase,   80
Akhilleus, hero, lie your pale bones mixed
with mild Patróklos' bones, who died before you,
and nearby lie the bones of Antílokhos,
the one you cared for most of all companions
after Patróklos.

---

4. A god of the countryside especially associated with wine. Rarely mentioned in Homer, he later presides,
at the Athenian festivals, over tragedy and comedy.

We of the Old Army,   85
we who were spearmen, heaped a tomb for these
upon a foreland over Hellê's waters,[5]
to be a mark against the sky for voyagers
in this generation and those to come.
Your mother sought from the gods magnificent trophies   90
and set them down midfield for our champions. Often
at funeral games after the death of kings
when you yourself contended, you've seen athletes
cinch their belts when trophies went on view.
But these things would have made you stare—the treasures   95
Thetis on her silver-slippered feet
brought to your games—for the gods held you dear.
You perished, but your name will never die.
It lives to keep all men in mind of honor
forever, Akhilleus.
                         As for myself, what joy   100
is this, to have brought off the war? Foul death
Zeus held in store for me at my coming home;
Aigísthos and my vixen cut me down."

While they conversed, the Wayfinder came near,
leading the shades of suitors overthrown   105
by Lord Odysseus. The two souls of heroes
advanced together, scrutinizing these.
Then Agamémnon recognized Amphímedon,
son of Meláneus—friends of his on Ithaka—
and called out to him:

                         "Amphímedon,   110
what ruin brought you into this undergloom?
All in a body, picked men, and so young?
One could not better choose the kingdom's pride.
Were you at sea, aboard ship, and Poseidon
blew up a dire wind and foundering waves,   115
or cattle-raiding, were you, on the mainland,
or in a fight for some stronghold, or women,
when the foe hit you to your mortal hurt?
Tell me, answer my question. Guest and friend
I say I am of yours—or do you not remember   120
I visited your family there? I came
with Prince Meneláos, urging Odysseus
to join us in the great sea raid on Troy.
One solid month we beat our way, breasting
south sea and west, resolved to bring him round,   125
the wily raider of cities."

5. I.e., the Hellespont, the strait separating Asia Minor from Europe, visible from Troy.

The new shade said:

"O glory of commanders, Agamémnon,
all that you bring to mind I remember well.
As for the sudden manner of our death
I'll tell you of it clearly, first to last.   130
After Odysseus had been gone for years
we were all suitors of his queen. She never
quite refused, nor went through with a marriage,
hating it, ever bent on our defeat.
Here is one of her tricks: she placed her loom,   135
her big loom, out for weaving in her hall,
and the fine warp of some vast fabric on it.
We were attending her, and she said to us:
'Young men, my suitors, now my lord is dead,
let me finish my weaving before I marry,   140
or else my thread will have been spun in vain.
This is a shroud I weave for Lord Laërtês
when cold Death comes to lay him on his bier.
The country wives would hold me in dishonor
if he, with all his fortune, lay unshrouded.'   145
We had men's hearts; she touched them; we agreed.
So every day she wove on the great loom—
but every night by torchlight she unwove it,
and so for three years she deceived the Akhaians.
But when the seasons brought the fourth around,   150
as long months waned, and the slow days were spent,
one of her maids, who knew the secret, told us.
We found her unraveling the splendid shroud,
and then she had to finish, willy nilly—
finish, and show the big loom woven tight   155
from beam to beam with cloth. She washed the shrouding
clean as sun or moonlight.
                        Then, heaven knows
from what quarter of the world, fatality
brought in Odysseus to the swineherd's wood
far up the island. There his son went too   160
when the black ship put him ashore from Pylos.
The two together planned our death-trap. Down
they came to the famous town—Telémakhos
long in advance: we had to wait for Odysseus.
The swineherd led him to the manor later   165
in rags like a foul beggar, old and broken,
propped on a stick. These tatters that he wore
hid him so well that none of us could know him
when he turned up, not even the older men.
We jeered at him, took potshots at him, cursed him.   170

Daylight and evening in his own great hall
he bore it, patient as a stone. That night
the mind of Zeus beyond the stormcloud stirred him
with Telémakhos at hand to shift his arms
from mégaron to storage room and lock it. 175
Then he assigned his wife her part: next day
she brought his bow and iron axeheads out
to make a contest. Contest there was none;
that move doomed us to slaughter. Not a man
could bend the stiff bow to his will or string it, 180
until it reached Odysseus. We shouted,
'Keep the royal bow from the beggar's hands
no matter how he begs!' Only Telémakhos
would not be denied.
             So the great soldier
took his bow and bent it for the bowstring 185
effortlessly. He drilled the axeheads clean,
sprang, and decanted arrows on the door sill,
glared, and drew again. This time he killed
Antínoös.
             There facing us he crouched
and shot his bolts of groaning at us, brought us 190
down like sheep. Then some god, his familiar,
went into action with him round the hall,
after us in a massacre. Men lay groaning,
mortally wounded, and the floor smoked with blood.

That was the way our death came, Agamémnon. 195
Now in Odysseus' hall untended still
our bodies lie, unknown to friends or kinsmen
who should have laid us out and washed our wounds
free of the clotted blood, and mourned our passing.
So much is due the dead."

             But Agamémnon's 200
tall shade when he heard this cried aloud:
"O fortunate Odysseus, master mariner
and soldier, blessed son of old Laërtês!
The girl you brought home made a valiant wife!
True to her husband's honor and her own, 205
Penélopê, Ikários' faithful daughter!
The very gods themselves will sing her story
for men on earth—mistress of her own heart,
Penélopê!
Tyndáreus' daughter waited, too—how differently! 210
Klytaimnéstra, the adulteress,

waited to stab her lord and king. That song
will be forever hateful. A bad name
she gave to womankind, even the best."

These were the things they said to one another   215
under the rim of earth where Death is lord.

Leaving the town, Odysseus and his men
that morning reached Laërtês garden lands,
long since won by his toil from wilderness—
his homestead, and the row of huts around it   220
where fieldhands rested, ate and slept. Indoors
he had an old slave woman, a Sikel, keeping
house for him in his secluded age.

Odysseus here took leave of his companions.

"Go make yourselves at home inside," he said.   225
"Roast the best porker and prepare a meal.
I'll go to try my father. Will he know me?
Can he imagine it, after twenty years?"

He handed spear and shield to the two herdsmen,
and in they went, Telémakhos too. Alone   230
Odysseus walked the orchard rows and vines.
He found no trace of Dólios and his sons
nor the other slaves—all being gone that day
to clear a distant field, and drag the stones
for a boundary wall.
                    But on a well-banked plot   235
Odysseus found his father in solitude
spading the earth around a young fruit tree.

He wore a tunic, patched and soiled, and leggings—
oxhide patches, bound below his knees
against the brambles; gauntlets on his hands   240
and on his head a goatskin cowl of sorrow.
This was the figure Prince Odysseus found—
wasted by years, racked, bowed under grief.
The son paused by a tall pear tree and wept,
then inwardly debated: should he run   245
forward and kiss his father, and pour out
his tale of war, adventure, and return,
or should he first interrogate him, test him?
Better that way, he thought—
first draw him out with sharp words, trouble him.   250
His mind made up, he walked ahead. Laërtês

went on digging, head down, by the sapling,
stamping the spade in. At his elbow then
his son spoke out:

          "Old man, the orchard keeper
you work for is no townsman. A good eye   255
for growing things he has; there's not a nurseling,
fig tree, vine stock, olive tree or pear tree
or garden bed uncared for on this farm.
But I might add—don't take offense—your own
appearance could be tidier. Old age   260
yes—but why the squalor, and rags to boot?
It would not be for sloth, now, that your master
leaves you in this condition; neither at all
because there's any baseness in your self.
No, by your features, by the frame you have,   265
a man might call you kingly,
one who should bathe warm, sup well, and rest easy
in age's privilege. But tell me:
who are your masters? whose fruit trees are these
you tend here? Tell me if it's true this island   270
is Ithaka, as that fellow I fell in with
told me on the road just now? He had
a peg loose, that one: couldn't say a word
or listen when I asked about my friend,
my Ithakan friend. I asked if he were alive   275
or gone long since into the underworld.
I can describe him if you care to hear it:
I entertained the man in my own land
when he turned up there on a journey; never
had I a guest more welcome in my house.   280
He claimed his stock was Ithakan: Laërtês
Arkeísiadês, he said his father was.
I took him home, treated him well, grew fond of him—
though we had many guests—and gave him
gifts in keeping with his quality: seven   285
bars of measured gold, a silver winebowl
filigreed with flowers, twelve light cloaks,
twelve rugs, robes and tunics—not to mention
his own choice of women trained in service,
the four well-favored ones he wished to take."   290

His father's eyes had filled with tears. He said:

"You've come to that man's island, right enough,
but dangerous men and fools hold power now.
You gave your gifts in vain. If you could find him
here in Ithaka alive, he'd make   295

return of gifts and hospitality,
as custom is, when someone has been generous.
But tell me accurately—how many years
have now gone by since that man was your guest?
your guest, my son—if he indeed existed—   300
born to ill fortune as he was. Ah, far
from those who loved him, far from his native land,
in some sea-dingle fish have picked his bones,
or else he made the vultures and wild beasts
a trove ashore! His mother at his bier   305
never bewailed him, nor did I, his father,
nor did his admirable wife, Penélopê,
who should have closed her husband's eyes in death
and cried aloud upon him as he lay.
So much is due the dead.
                        But speak out, tell me further: 310
who are you, of what city and family?
where have you moored the ship that brought you here,
where is your admirable crew? Are you a peddler
put ashore by the foreign ship you came on?"

Again Odysseus had a fable ready.   315

"Yes," he said, "I can tell you all those things.
I come from Rover's Passage where my home is,
and I'm King Allwoes' only son. My name
is Quarrelman.
                Heaven's power in the westwind
drove me this way from Sikania,[6]   320
off my course. My ship lies in a barren
cove beyond the town there. As for Odysseus,
now is the fifth year since he put to sea
and left my homeland—bound for death, you say.
Yet landbirds flying from starboard crossed his bow—   325
a lucky augury. So we parted joyously,
in hope of friendly days and gifts to come."

A cloud of pain had fallen on Laërtês.
Scooping up handfuls of the sunburnt dust
he sifted it over his grey head, and groaned,   330
and the groan went to the son's heart. A twinge
prickling up through his nostrils warned Odysseus
he could not watch this any longer.
He leaped and threw his arms around his father,
kissed him, and said:

6. Another name for Sicily.

"Oh, Father, I am he!   335
Twenty years gone, and here I've come again
to my own land!
              Hold back your tears! No grieving!
I bring good news—though still we cannot rest.
I killed the suitors to the last man!
Outrage and injury have been avenged!"   340

Laërtês turned and found his voice to murmur:

"If you are Odysseus, my son, come back,
give me some proof, a sign to make me sure."

His son replied:

              "The scar then, first of all.
Look, here the wild boar's flashing tusk   345
wounded me on Parnassos; do you see it?
You and my mother made me go, that time,
to visit Lord Autólykos, her father,
for gifts he promised years before on Ithaka.
Again—more proof—let's say the trees you gave me   350
on this revetted plot of orchard once.
I was a small boy at your heels, wheedling
amid the young trees, while you named each one.
You gave me thirteen pear, ten apple trees,
and forty fig trees. Fifty rows of vines   355
were promised too, each one to bear in turn.
Bunches of every hue would hang there ripening,
weighed down by the god of summer days."

The old man's knees failed him, his heart grew faint,
recalling all that Odysseus calmly told.   360
He clutched his son. Odysseus held him swooning
until he got his breath back and his spirit
and spoke again:

              "Zeus, Father! Gods above!—
you still hold pure Olympos, if the suitors
paid for their crimes indeed, and paid in blood!   365
But now the fear is in me that all Ithaka
will be upon us. They'll send messengers
to stir up every city of the islands."

Odysseus the great tactician answered:

"Courage, and leave the worrying to me.   370
We'll turn back to your homestead by the orchard.

I sent the cowherd, swineherd, and Telémakhos
ahead to make our noonday meal."

                              Conversing
in this vein they went home, the two together,
into the stone farmhouse. There Telémakhos   375
and the two herdsmen were already carving
roast young pork, and mixing amber wine.
During these preparations the Sikel woman
bathed Laërtês and anointed him,
and dressed him in a new cloak. Then Athena,   380
standing by, filled out his limbs again,
gave girth and stature to the old field captain
fresh from the bathing place. His son looked on
in wonder at the godlike bloom upon him,
and called out happily:

                    "Oh, Father,   385
surely one of the gods who are young forever
has made you magnificent before my eyes!"

Clearheaded Laërtês faced him, saying:

"By Father Zeus, Athena and Apollo,
I wish I could be now as once I was,   390
commander of Kephallenians, when I took
the walled town, Nérikos,[7] on the promontory!
Would god I had been young again last night
with armor on me, standing in our hall
to fight the suitors at your side! How many   395
knees I could have crumpled, to your joy!"

While son and father spoke, cowherd and swineherd
attended, waiting, for the meal was ready.
Soon they were all seated, and their hands
picked up the meat and bread.

                    But now old Dólios   400
appeared in the bright doorway with his sons,
work-stained from the field. Laërtês' housekeeper,
who reared the boys and tended Dólios
in his bent age, had gone to fetch them in.
When it came over them who the stranger was   405
they halted in astonishment. Odysseus
hit an easy tone with them. Said he:

---

7. On the mainland; its exact location is unknown.

"Sit down and help yourselves. Shake off your wonder.
Here we've been waiting for you all this time,
and our mouths watering for good roast pig!"   410

But Dólios came forward, arms outstretched,
and kissed Odysseus' hand at the wrist bone,
crying out:

              "Dear master, you returned!
You came to us again! How we had missed you!
We thought you lost. The gods themselves have brought you!   415
Welcome, welcome; health and blessings on you!
And tell me, now, just one thing more: Penélopê,
does she know yet that you are on the island?
or should we send a messenger?"

Odysseus gruffly said,
                    "Old man, she knows.   420
Is it for you to think of her?"

                    So Dólios
quietly took a smooth bench at the table
and in their turn his sons welcomed Odysseus,
kissing his hands; then each went to his chair
beside his father. Thus our friends   425
were occupied in Laërtês' house at noon.

Meanwhile to the four quarters of the town
the news ran: bloody death had caught the suitors;
and men and women in a murmuring crowd
gathered before Odysseus' hall. They gave   430
burial to the piteous dead, or bore
the bodies of young men from other islands
down to the port, thence to be ferried home.
Then all the men went grieving to assembly
and being seated, rank by rank, grew still,   435
as old Eupeithês rose to address them. Pain
lay in him like a brand for Antínoös,
the first man that Odysseus brought down,
and tears flowed for his son as he began:

"Heroic feats that fellow did for us   440
Akhaians, friends! Good spearmen by the shipload
he led to war and lost—lost ships and men,
and once ashore again killed these, who were
the islands' pride.
              Up with you! After him!—
before he can take flight to Pylos town   445

or hide at Elis, under Epeian law!
We'd be disgraced forever! Mocked for generations
if we cannot avenge our sons' blood, and our brothers'!
Life would turn to ashes—at least for me;
rather be dead and join the dead!
           I say   450
we ought to follow now, or they'll gain time
and make the crossing."

              His appeal, his tears,
moved all the gentry listening there;
but now they saw the crier and the minstrel
come from Odysseus' hall, where they had slept.   455
The two men stood before the curious crowd,
and Medôn said:

          "Now hear me, men of Ithaka.
When these hard deeds were done by Lord Odysseus
the immortal gods were not far off. I saw
with my own eyes someone divine who fought   460
beside him, in the shape and dress of Mentor;
it was a god who shone before Odysseus,
a god who swept the suitors down the hall
dying in droves."

          At this pale fear assailed them,
and next they heard again the old forecaster,   465
Halithérsês Mastóridês. Alone
he saw the field of time, past and to come.
In his anxiety for them he said:

"Ithakans, now listen to what I say.
Friends, by your own fault these deaths came to pass.   470
You would not heed me nor the captain, Mentor;
would not put down the riot of your sons.
Heroic feats they did!—all wantonly
raiding a great man's flocks, dishonoring
his queen, because they thought he'd come no more.   475
Let matters rest; do as I urge; no chase,
or he who wants a bloody end will find it."

The greater number stood up shouting "Aye!"
But many held fast, sitting all together
in no mind to agree with him. Eupeithês   480
had won them to his side. They ran for arms,
clapped on their bronze, and mustered
under Eupeithês at the town gate
for his mad foray.

Vengeance would be his,
he thought, for his son's murder; but that day   485
held bloody death for him and no return.

At this point, querying Zeus, Athena said:

"O Father of us all and king of kings,
enlighten me. What is your secret will?
War and battle, worse and more of it,   490
or can you not impose a pact on both?"

The summoner of cloud replied:
                                    "My child,
why this formality of inquiry?
Did you not plan that action by yourself—
see to it that Odysseus, on his homecoming,   495
should have their blood?
                         Conclude it as you will.
There is one proper way, if I may say so:
Odysseus' honor being satisfied,
let him be king by a sworn pact forever,
and we, for our part, will blot out the memory   500
of sons and brothers slain. As in the old time
let men of Ithaka henceforth be friends;
prosperity enough, and peace attend them."

Athena needed no command, but down
in one spring she descended from Olympos   505
just as the company of Odysseus finished
wheat crust and honeyed wine, and heard him say:

"Go out, someone, and see if they are coming."

One of the boys went to the door as ordered
and saw the townsmen in the lane. He turned   510
swiftly to Odysseus.

                      "Here they come,"
he said, "best arm ourselves, and quickly."

All up at once, the men took helm and shield—
four fighting men, counting Odysseus,
with Dólios' half dozen sons. Laërtês   515
armed as well, and so did Dólios—
greybeards, they could be fighters in a pinch.
Fitting their plated helmets on their heads
they sallied out, Odysseus in the lead.

Now from the air Athena, Zeus's daughter,   520
appeared in Mentor's guise, with Mentor's voice,
making Odysseus' heart grow light. He said
to put cheer in his son:

               "Telémakhos,
you are going into battle against pikemen
where hearts of men are tried. I count on you   525
to bring no shame upon your forefathers.
In fighting power we have excelled this lot
in every generation."

               Said his son:
"If you are curious, Father, watch and see
the stuff that's in me. No more talk of shame."   530

And old Laërtês cried aloud:

"Ah, what a day for me, dear gods!
to see my son and grandson vie in courage!"

Athena halted near him, and her eyes
shone like the sea. She said:

               "Arkeísiadês,   535
dearest of all my old brothers-in-arms,
invoke the grey-eyed one and Zeus her father,
heft your spear and make your throw."

Power flowed into him from Pallas Athena,
whom he invoked as Zeus's virgin child,   540
and he let fly his heavy spear.
               It struck
Eupeithês on the cheek plate of his helmet,
and undeflected the bronze head punched through.
He toppled, and his armor clanged upon him.
Odysseus and his son now furiously   545
closed, laying on with broadswords, hand to hand,
and pikes: they would have cut the enemy down
to the last man, leaving not one survivor,
had not Athena raised a shout
that stopped all fighters in their tracks.

               "Now hold!"   550
she cried, "Break off this bitter skirmish;
end your bloodshed, Ithakans, and make peace."

Their faces paled with dread before Athena,
and swords dropped from their hands unnerved, to lie
strewing the ground, at the great voice of the goddess.   555
Those from the town turned fleeing for their lives.
But with a cry to freeze their hearts
and ruffling like an eagle on the pounce,
the lord Odysseus reared himself to follow—
at which the son of Kronos dropped a thunderbolt   560
smoking at his daughter's feet.
                        Athena
cast a grey glance at her friend and said:

"Son of Laërtês and the gods of old,
Odysseus, master of land ways and sea ways,
command yourself. Call off this battle now,   565
or Zeus who views the wide world may be angry."

He yielded to her, and his heart was glad.
Both parties later swore to terms of peace
set by their arbiter, Athena, daughter
of Zeus who bears the stormcloud as a shield—   570
though still she kept the form and voice of Mentor.

SAPPHO OF LESBOS
born ca. 630 B.C.

About Sappho's life we know very little: she was born about 630 B.C. on the fertile
island of Lesbos off the coast of Asia Minor and spent most of her life there; she
was married and had a daughter. Her lyric poems (i.e., poems sung to the accompaniment of the lyre) were so admired in the ancient world that a later poet called
her the tenth Muse. In the third century B.C. scholars at the great library in Alexandria arranged her poems in nine books, of which the first contained over a thousand lines. But what we have now is a pitiful remnant: one (or possibly two) complete
short poems, and a collection of quotations from her work by ancient writers,
supplemented by bits and pieces written on ancient scraps of papyrus found in
excavations in Egypt. Yet these remnants fully justify the enthusiasm of the ancient
critics; Sappho's poems (insofar as we can guess at their nature from the fragments)
give us the most vivid evocation of the joys and sorrows of love in all Greek literature.

Her themes are those of a Greek woman's world—girlhood, marriage, and love,
especially the love of young women for each other and the poignancy of their
parting as they leave to assume the responsibilities of a wife. About the social
context of these songs we can only guess; all that can be said is that they reflect a
world in which women, at least women of the aristocracy, lived an intense communal life of their own, one of female occasions, functions, and festivities, in
which their young passionate natures were fully engaged with each other; to most

of them, presumably, this was a stage preliminary to their later career in that world as wife and mother.

The first two poems in our selection were quoted in their entirety by ancient critics (though it is possible that there was another stanza at the end of the second); their text is not a problem. But the important recent additions to our knowledge of Sappho's poetry, the pieces of ancient books found in Egypt, are difficult to read and usually full of gaps. Our third selection, in fact, comes from the municipal rubbish heap of the Egyptian village of Oxyrhyncos. Most of the gaps in the text are due to holes or tears in the papyrus and can easily be filled in from our knowledge of Sappho's dialect and the strict meter in which she wrote, but the end of the third stanza and the whole of the fourth are imaginative reconstructions by the translator. The papyrus, for instance, tells us only that someone or something led Helen astray; Lattimore's "Queen of Cyprus" (i.e., the love goddess Aphrodite) may well be right but is not certain. In the next stanza all that we have is part of a word that means something like "flexible" (Lattimore's "hearts that can be persuaded"), an adverb "lightly" and "remembering Anaktoria who is not here." As a matter of fact we don't have that all-important "not" but the sense demands it. Fortunately, the final stanza, with its telling echo of the opening theme, is almost intact.

The most recent short survey of Sappho's poetry (by David A. Campbell) is to be found in *The Cambridge History of Classical Literature Vol. I* (1985). For a fuller treatment see C. M. Bowra, *Greek Lyric Poetry* (1961). Worth consulting also is A. Lesky, *A History of Greek Literature* (1966).

"Throned in splendor, deathless, O Aphrodite"[1]

Throned in splendor, deathless, O Aphrodite,
child of Zeus, charm-fashioner, I entreat you
not with griefs and bitternesses to break my
    spirit, O goddess:

standing by me rather, if once before now   5
far away you heard, when I called upon you,
left your father's dwelling place and descended,
    yoking the golden

chariot to sparrows,[2] who fairly drew you
down in speed aslant the black world, the bright air   10
trembling at the heart to the pulse of countless
    fluttering wingbeats.

Swiftly then they came, and you, blessed lady,
smiling on me out of immortal beauty,
asked me what affliction was on me, why I   15
    called thus upon you,

what beyond all else I would have befall my
tortured heart: "Whom then would you have Persuasion

---

1. A prayer to the goddess of love, Aphrodite. The translator, Richmond Lattimore, has skillfully reproduced the metrical form of the Greek, the "Sapphic" stanza.   2. Aphrodite's sacred birds.

force to serve desire in your heart? Who is it,
    Sappho, that hurt you?   20

Though she now escape, she soon will follow;
though she take not gifts from you, she will give them:
though she love not, yet she will surely love you
    even unwilling."

In such guise come even again and set me   25
free from doubt and sorrow; accomplish all those
things my heart desires to be done; appear and
    stand at my shoulder.

"Like the very gods in my sight is he"

Like the very gods in my sight is he who
sits where he can look in your eyes, who listens
close to you, to hear the soft voice, its sweetness
    murmur in love and

laughter, all for him. But it breaks my spirit;   5
underneath my breast all the heart is shaken.
Let me only glance where you are, the voice dies,
    I can say nothing,

but my lips are stricken to silence, underneath my skin the tenuous flame suffuses;   10
nothing shows in front of my eyes, my ears are
    muted in thunder.

And the sweat breaks running upon me, fever
shakes my body, paler I turn than grass is;
I can feel that I have been changed, I feel that   15
    death has come near me.

"Some there are who say that the fairest things seen"

Some there are who say that the fairest thing seen
on the black earth is an array of horsemen;
some, men marching; some would say ships; but I say
    she whom one loves best

is the loveliest. Light were the work to make this   5
plain to all, since she, who surpassed in beauty
all mortality, Helen, once forsaking
    her lordly husband,

fled away to Troy-land across the water.
Not the thought of child nor beloved parents   10

was remembered, after the Queen of Cyprus[3]
    won her at first sight.

Since young brides have hearts that can be persuaded
easily, light things, palpitant to passion
as am I, remembering Anaktória   15
    who has gone from me

and whose lovely walk and the shining pallor
of her face I would rather see before my
eyes than Lydia's chariots in all their glory
    armored for battle.   20

AESCHYLUS
524?–456 B.C.

The earliest documents in the history of the Western theater are the seven plays of
Aeschylus which have come down to us through the more than two thousand years
since his death. When he produced his first play in the opening years of the fifth
century B.C., the performance that we know as drama was still less than half a
century old, still open to innovation—and Aeschylus, in fact, made such significant contributions to its development that he has been called "the creator of tragedy."

    The origins of the theatrical contests in Athens are obscure; they were a puzzle
even for Aristotle who in the fourth century B.C. wrote a famous treatise on tragedy.
All that we know for certain is that the drama began as a religious celebration which
took the form of song and dance.

    Such ceremonies are of course to be found in the communal life of many early
cultures, but it was in Athens, and in Athens alone, that the ceremony gave rise to
what we know as tragedy and comedy and produced dramatic masterpieces that are
still admired, read, and performed.

    At some time in the late sixth century B.C. the Athenians converted what seems
to have been a rural celebration of Dionysus, a vegetation deity especially associated with the vine, into an annual city festival at which dancing choruses, competing for prizes, sang hymns of praise to the god. It was from this choral performance
that tragedy and comedy developed. Some unknown innovator (his name was
probably Thespis) combined the choral song with the speech of a masked actor,
who, playing a god or hero, engaged the chorus in dialogue. It was Aeschylus who
added a second actor and so created the possibility of conflict and the prototype of
the drama as we know it.

    After the defeat of the Persian invaders (480–479 B.C.), as Athens with its fleets
and empire moved toward supremacy in the Greek world, this spring festival became
a splendid occasion. The Dionysia, as it was now called, lasted for four days, during
which public business (except in emergencies) was suspended and prisoners were
released on bail for the duration of the festival. In an open-air theater that could
seat 14,000 spectators, tragic and comic poets competed for the prizes offered by

3. Aphrodite.

by the city. Three poets in each genre had been selected by the magistrates for the year. After an opening day devoted to the traditional choral hymns, a tragic poet with three plays and a comic poet with one provided the program for each of the three remaining days.

The three tragedies could deal with quite separate stories or, as in the case of Aeschylus' *Oresteia*, with the successive stages of one extended action. By the time this trilogy was produced (458 B.C.) the number of actors had been raised to three; the spoken part of the performance became steadily more important. In the *Oresteia* an equilibrium between the two elements of the performance has been established. The actors, with their speeches, create the dramatic situation and its movement, the plot; the chorus, while contributing to dramatic suspense and illusion, ranges free of the immediate situation in its odes, which extend and amplify the significance of the action.

In 458 B.C. Aeschylus was at the end of a great career; he was to die, two years later, in the Greek city of Gela, in Sicily. He had begun his career as a dramatist before the Persian Wars, in the first days of the new Athenian democracy. He fought against the Persians at Marathon (where his brother was killed) and almost certainly also in the great sea fight at Salamis in 480 (his play, the *Persians*, produced in 472 B.C., contains what sounds like an eyewitness account of that battle). Only seven of his plays survive (we know that he produced 90); besides the *Persians* and the three plays of the *Oresteia*, we have the text of *Suppliants* (sometime in the 460s) and a famous and influential play, the *Prometheus Bound* (date unknown).

The *Oresteia* is a trilogy: the first play, *Agamemnon*, was followed at its performance by two more plays, the *Libation Bearers* and the *Eumenides*, which carried on its story and its theme to a conclusion. The theme of the trilogy is justice, and its story, like that of almost all Greek tragedies, is a legend that was already well known to the audience that saw the first performance of the play. This particular legend, the story of the house of Atreus, was rich in dramatic potential, for it deals with a series of retributive murders that stained the hands of three generations of a royal family, and it has also a larger significance, social and historical, of which Aeschylus took full advantage. The legend preserves the memory of an important historical process through which the Greeks had passed: the transition from tribal institutions of justice to communal justice, from a tradition that demanded that a murdered man's next of kin avenge his death to a system requiring settlement of the private quarrel by a court of law, the typical institution of the city-state which replaced the primitive tribe. When Agamemnon returns victorious from Troy, he is killed by his wife, Clytemnestra, and her lover, Aegisthus, who is Agamemnon's cousin. Clytemnestra kills her husband to avenge her daughter Iphigenia, whom Agamemnon sacrificed to the goddess Artemis when he had to choose between his daughter's life and his ambition to conquer Troy. Aegisthus avenges the crime of a previous generation, the hideous murder of his brothers by Agamemnon's father, Atreus. The killing of Agamemnon is, by the standards of the old system, justice; but it is the nature of this justice that the process can never be arrested, that one act of violence must give rise to another. Agamemnon's murder must be avenged too, as it is in the second play of the trilogy by Orestes, his son, who kills both Aegisthus and his own mother, Clytemnestra. Orestes has acted justly according to the code of tribal society based on blood relationship, but in doing so he has violated the most sacred blood relationship of all, the bond between mother and son. The old system of justice has produced an insoluble dilemma.

At the end of the *Libation Bearers*, Orestes sees a vision of the Furies. They are

serpent-haired female hunters, the avengers of blood. Agamemnon had a son to
avenge him, but for Clytemnestra there was no one to exact payment. This task is
taken up by the Furies, who are the guardians of the ancient tribal sanctities; they
enforce the old dispensation when no earthly agent is at hand to do so. Female
themselves, they assert the claim of the mother against the son who killed her to
avenge his father. At the end of the second play they are only a vision in Orestes'
mind—"You can't see them," he says to the chorus. "I can; they drive me on. I
must move on." But in the final play we see them too; they are the chorus, and
they have pursued Orestes to the great shrine of Apollo at Delphi where he has
come to seek refuge.

Apollo can save him from immediate destruction at the Furies' hands but he
cannot resolve the dilemma; Orestes must go to Athens, where Athena, the patron
goddess of the city, will set up the first court of law to try his case. At Athens,
before the ancient court of the Areopagus, the Furies argue eloquently but Apollo
himself arrives to testify that he ordered Orestes to act. Athena instructs the judges
in Orestes' favor and Orestes, acquitted, goes home to Argos. The Furies threaten
to turn their dreadful wrath against Athens itself but the goddess persuades them to
accept a home deep in Athenian earth, to act as protectors of the court and of the
land.

More important than the arguments employed in the trial and the decision reached
by the judges is the fact of the court's establishment. This is the end of an old era
and the beginning of a new. The existence of the court is a guarantee that the
tragic series of events that drove Orestes to the murder of his mother will never be
repeated. The system of communal justice, which allows consideration of circumstance and motive, and which punishes impersonally, has at last replaced the
inconclusive anarchy of individual revenge.

But the play is concerned with much more than the history of human institutions—with more even than the general problem of violence between man and
man for which the particular instances of the trilogy stand. It is also a religious
statement. The whole sequence of events, stretching over many generations, is
presented as the working out of the will of Zeus. The tragic action of the *Iliad* was
also the expression of the will of Zeus (though it is characteristic of Homer that
Achilles was at least equally responsible), but for Aeschylus the will of Zeus means
something new. In this trilogy the working out of Zeus' will proceeds intricately
through three generations of bloodshed to the creation of a human institution that
will prevent any repetition of the cycle of murder that produced it. Agamemnon
dies, and Clytemnestra dies in her turn, and Orestes is hounded over land and sea
to his trial, but out of all this suffering comes an important advance in human
understanding and civilization. The chorus of the *Agamemnon*, celebrating the
power of Zeus, tells us that he

> . . . has led us on to know,
> that Helmsman lays it down as law
> that we must suffer, suffer into truth.

From the suffering comes knowledge of the truth, whereas in the *Iliad* nothing at
all comes out of the suffering, except the certainty of more. "Far from the land of
my fathers," says Achilles to Priam, "I sit here in Troy, and bring nothing but
sorrow to you and your children." But his last words to Priam are a reminder that
this interval of sympathy is only temporary. After Hector's burial the war will go
on as before. This is Zeus' will; Homer does not attempt to explain it. But the

Aeschylean trilogy is nothing less than an attempt to justify the ways of God to man. The suffering is shown to us as the fulfillment of a purpose we can understand, a purpose beneficent to man.

The full scope of Zeus' will is apparent only to the audience, which follows the pattern of its execution through the three plays of the trilogy. As in the Book of Job, the characters who act and suffer are in the dark. They claim a knowledge of Zeus' will and boast that their actions are its fulfillment (it is in these terms that Agamemnon speaks of the sack of Troy, and Clytemnestra of Agamemnon's murder), and they are, of course, in one sense, right. But their knowledge is limited: Agamemnon does not realize that Zeus' will includes his death at the hands of Clytemnestra, nor Clytemnestra that it demands her death at the hands of her son. The chorus has, at times, a deeper understanding. In its opening ode it announces the law of Zeus, that men must learn by suffering, and at the end it recognizes the responsibility of Zeus in the death of Agamemnon—"all through the will of Zeus, the cause of all, the one who works it all." But the chorus cannot interpret the event in any way it can accept, for it can see no further than the immediate present. Its knowledge of Zeus' law is an abstraction that it cannot relate to the terrible fact.

In this murky atmosphere (made all the more terrible by the beacon fire of the opening lines, which brings not light, but deeper darkness), one human being sees clear; she possesses the concrete vision of the future which complements the chorus's abstract knowledge of the law. This is the prophet Cassandra, Priam's daughter, brought from Troy as Agamemnon's share of the spoils. She has been given the power of true prophecy by the god Apollo, but the gift is nullified by the condition that her prophecies will never be believed. Like the Hebrew prophets, she sees reality—past, present, and future—so clearly that she is cut off from ordinary human beings by the clarity of her vision and the terrible burden of her knowledge. Like them she expresses herself in poetic figures, and like them she is rejected by her hearers. To the everyday world, represented by the chorus, she appears to be mad, the fate of prophets in all ages. And it is only as she goes into the palace to the death she foresees that the old men of the chorus begin to accept, fearfully and hesitantly, the truth that she has been telling them.

The great scene in which she mouths her hysterical prophecies at them delays the action for which everything has been prepared—the death of Agamemnon. Before we hear his famous cry offstage, Cassandra presents us with a mysterious vision in which she combines cause, effect, and result: the murders that have led to this terrible moment, the death of Agamemnon (which will not take place until she leaves the stage), and the murders that will follow. We do not see Agamemnon's death—we see much more. The past, present, and future of Clytemnestra's action and Agamemnon's suffering are fused into a timeless unity in Cassandra's great lines, an unearthly unity that is dissolved only when Agamemnon, in the real world of time and space, screams in mortal agony.

The tremendous statement of the trilogy is made in a style that for magnificence and richness of suggestion can be compared only with the style of Shakespeare at the height of his poetic power, the Shakespeare of *King Lear* and *Antony and Cleopatra*. The language of the *Oresteia* is an Oriental carpet of imagery in which combinations of metaphor, which at first seem bombastic in their violence, take their place in the ordered pattern of the poem as a whole. An image, once introduced, recurs, and reappears again, to run its course verbally and visually through the whole length of the trilogy, richer in meaning with each fresh appearance. In the second choral ode, for example, the chorus, welcoming the news of Agamemnon's victory at Troy, sings of the net that Zeus and Night threw over the city, trapping the inhabitants like animals. The net is here an image of Zeus' justice, a retributive justice, since Troy is paying for the crime of taking Helen, and the image identifies Zeus' justice with Agamemnon's action in sacking the city. This image occurs again, with a different emphasis, in the hypocritical speech of welcome that Clytemnestra makes to her husband on his return. She tells how she feared for his safety at Troy, how she trembled at the rumors of his death:

> and the rumors spread and fester,
> a runner comes with something dreadful,
> close on his heels the next and his news worse,
> and they shout it out and the whole house can hear;
> and wounds—if he took one wound for each report
> to penetrate these walls, he's gashed like a dragnet . . . .

This vision of Agamemnon dead she speaks of as her fear, but we know that it represents her deepest desire, and more, the purpose that she is now preparing to execute. When, later, she stands in triumph over her husband's corpse, she uses the same image to describe the robe that she threw over his limbs to blind and baffle him before she stabbed him—"Inextricable like a net for fishes / I cast about him a vicious wealth of raiment"—and this time the image materializes into an object visible on stage. We can see the net, the gashed robe still folded round Agamemnon's body. We shall see it again, for in the second play Orestes, standing over his mother's body as she now stands over his father's, will display the robe before us, with its holes and bloodstains, as a justification for what he has just done. Elsewhere in the *Agamemnon* the chorus compares Cassandra to a wild animal caught in the net, and later Aegisthus exults to see Agamemnon's body lying "in the nets of Justice." For each speaker the image has a different meaning, but not one realizes the terrible sense in which it applies to them all. They are all caught in the net, the system of justice by vengeance which only binds tighter the more its captives struggle to free themselves. Clytemnestra attempts to escape, to arrest the process of the chain of murders and the working out of the will of Zeus. "But I will swear a pact with the spirit born within us," she says, but Agamemnon's body and the net she threw over him are there on the stage to remind us that her appeal will not be heard; one more generation must act and suffer before the net will vanish, never to be seen again.

Richmond Lattimore, *Aeschylus, Oresteia* (1953), contains a valuable introduction aimed at the general reader. D. J. Conacher, *Aeschylus' Oresteia: A Literary Commentary* (1987) is a scene-by-scene (and sometimes line-by-line) commentary that combines literary analysis and philological discussion; it is addressed as much to Greekless readers as to classical scholars. James Hogan, *A Commentary on the Complete Greek Tragedies: Aeschylus* (1987) contains a line-by-line commentary on Richmond Lattimore's translation of the *Oresteia*. Hugh Lloyd-Jones's three volumes, *Agamemnon, The Libation Bearers*, and *The Eumenides* (1970), provide helpful introductions, a precise prose translation, and a valuable running commentary at the bottom of the page. John Herington, *Aeschylus* (1986), deals with the political and religious background of the tragedies and provides a perceptive discussion of the plays (*Oresteia*, pp. 111–56).

The Oresteia[1]

Agamemnon

Characters

WATCHMAN

CLYTAEMNESTRA

HERALD

AGAMEMNON

CASSANDRA

AEGISTHUS

CHORUS, *the Old Men of Argos and
their* LEADER

*Attendants of Clytaemnestra and of
Agamemnon, bodyguard of
Aegisthus*

[TIME AND SCENE: *A night in the tenth and final autumn of the Trojan
war. The house of Atreus in Argos. Before it, an altar stands unlit; a watchman on the high roofs fights to stay awake.*]

WATCHMAN: Dear gods, set me free from all the pain,
    the long watch I keep, one whole year awake . . .
    propped on my arms, crouched on the roofs of Atreus
    like a dog.
            I know the stars by heart,
    the armies of the night, and there in the lead   5
    the ones that bring us snow or the crops of summer,
    bring us all we have—
    our great blazing kings of the sky,
    I know them, when they rise and when they fall . . .
    and now I watch for the light, the signal-fire[2]   10
    breaking out of Troy, shouting Troy is taken.
    So she commands, full of her high hopes.
    That woman[3]—she maneuvers like a man.

    And when I keep to my bed, soaked in dew,
    and the thoughts go groping through the night   15
    and the good dreams that used to guard my sleep . . .
    not here, it's the old comrade, terror, at my neck.
    I mustn't sleep, no—
        [*Shaking himself awake.*]
                        Look alive, sentry.
    And I try to pick out tunes, I hum a little,
    a good cure for sleep, and the tears start,   20
    I cry for the hard times come to the house,
    no longer run like the great place of old.

    Oh for a blessed end to all our pain,
    some godsend burning through the dark—
        [*Light appears slowly in the east; he struggles to his feet and scans it.*]

1. Translated by Robert Fagles.   2. The fire the watchman waits to see is the bonfire nearest to Argos,
the last in a chain extending all the way to Troy, each one visible, when fired at night, from the next.
3. Clytaemnestra.

                                    I salute you!
You dawn of the darkness, you turn night to day—   25
I see the light at last.
They'll be dancing in the streets of Argos[4]
thanks to you, thanks to this new stroke of—
                                    Aieeeeee!
There's your signal clear and true, my queen!
Rise up from bed—hurry, lift a cry of triumph   30
through the house, praise the gods for the beacon,
if they've taken Troy . . .
                              But there it burns,
fire all the way. I'm for the morning dances.
Master's luck is mine. A throw of the torch
has brought us triple-sixes[5]—we have won!   35
My move now—
        [*Beginning to dance, then breaking off, lost in thought.*]
                    Just bring him home. My king,
I'll take your loving hand in mine and then . . .
the rest is silence. The ox is on my tongue.[6]
Aye, but the house and these old stones,
give them a voice and what a tale they'd tell.   40
And so would I, gladly . . .
I speak to those who know; to those who don't
my mind's a blank. I never say a word.
        [*He climbs down from the roof and disappears into the palace through
        a side entrance. A* CHORUS, *the old men of Argos who have not learned
        the news of victory, enters and marches round the altar.*]
CHORUS: Ten years gone, ten to the day
our great avenger went for Priam—   45
        Menelaus and lord Agamemnon,[7]
two kings with the power of Zeus,
the twin throne, twin sceptre,
Atreus' sturdy yoke of sons
launched Greece in a thousand ships,   50
armadas cutting loose from the land,
armies massed for the cause, the rescue—
        [*From within the palace* CLYTAEMNESTRA *raises a cry of triumph.*]
the heart within them screamed for all-out war!
Like vultures robbed of their young,

---

4. In Homer, Agamemnon, son of Atreus, is King of Mycenae. Later Greek poets, however, referred to
his kingdom as Argos or Mycenae, perhaps because the Achaeans in Homer are sometimes called Argives.
In 463 B.C., just five years before the production of the play, Argos had defeated Mycenae in battle and
put an end to the city, displacing the inhabitants or selling them into slavery. Soon after, Argos and Athens
entered into an alliance, aimed, of course, at Sparta. Since in the last play of the trilogy this alliance will
be alluded to, it is important for Aeschylus to establish the un-Homeric location of the action right at the
beginning.   5. The highest throw in the ancient Greek dice game.   6. A proverbial phrase for enforced
silence.   7. Sons of Atreus, kings of Argos, commanders of the Greek expedition against Troy. *Priam:*
King of Troy. His son Paris abducted (or seduced) Menelaus' wife, Helen.

the agony sends them frenzied,   55
soaring high from the nest, round and
round they wheel, they row their wings,
stroke upon churning thrashing stroke,
but all the labor, the bed of pain,
  the young are lost forever.   60
Yet someone hears on high—Apollo,
Pan or Zeus[8]—the piercing wail
these guests of heaven raise,
and drives at the outlaws, late
but true to revenge, a stabbing Fury![9]   65
  [CLYTAEMNESTRA *appears at the doors and pauses with her entou-*
  rage.[1]]
So towering Zeus the god of guests[2]
drives Atreus' sons at Paris,
all for a woman manned by many
the generations wrestle, knees
grinding the dust, the manhood drains,   70
the spear snaps in the first blood rites
  that marry Greece and Troy.
And now it goes as it goes
and where it ends is Fate.
And neither by singeing flesh   75
nor tipping cups of wine[3]
nor shedding burning tears can you
enchant away the rigid Fury.
  [CLYTAEMNESTRA *lights the altar-fires.*]
We are the old, dishonoured ones,[4]
the broken husks of men.
Even then they cast us off,   80
the rescue mission left us here
to prop a child's strength upon a stick.
What if the new sap rises in his chest?
He has no soldiery in him,   85
  no more than we,
and we are aged past aging,
gloss of the leaf shriveled,
three legs[5] at a time we falter on.

8. Pan as a god of the wild places; Zeus because eagles and vultures were symbolic of his power; Apollo perhaps as a prophetic god: the movements of birds are regarded as prophetic signs.   9. The Greek word is *Erinyes*. This is the first mention of these avenging spirits who will actually appear on stage as the chorus of the final play.   1. There are no stage directions on the manuscript copies of the plays which have come down to us. Here the translator has the queen enter so that she will be visible on stage when the chorus addresses her by name in 94. Other scholars, pointing out that in Greek tragedy characters who are off stage are often addressed, disagree, and bring Clytaemnestra on stage only at 256.   2. Zeus was thought to be particularly interested in punishing those who violated the code of hospitality. Paris, a guest in Menelaus' house, had run away with his wife, Helen.   3. Neither by burnt sacrifice nor by pouring libations.   4. The general sense of the passage is that only two classes of the male population are left in Argos, those who are too young to fight and those who, like the chorus, are too old.   5. Because they walk with a stick to support them.

Old men are children once again,   90
   a dream that sways and wavers
into the hard light of day.
                        But you,
daughter of Leda, queen Clytaemnestra,
what now, what news, what message
drives you through the citadel   95
   burning victims?[6] Look,
the city gods, the gods of Olympus,
gods of the earth and public markets—
all the altars blazing with your gifts!
   Argos blazes! Torches   100
race the sunrise up her skies—
drugged by the lulling holy oils,
   unadulterated,
run from the dark vaults of kings.
   Tell us the news!   105
What you can, what is right—
Heal us, soothe our fears!
Now the darkness comes to the fore,
now the hope glows through your victims,
beating back this raw, relentless anguish   110
   gnawing at the heart.

   [CLYTAEMNESTRA *ignores them and pursues her rituals; they assemble*
   for the opening chorus.]

O but I still have power to sound the god's command at the roads
that launched the kings. The gods breathe power through my song,
   my fighting strength, Persuasion grows with the years—
I sing how the flight of fury hurled the twin command,   115
   one will that hurled young Greece
and winged the spear of vengeance straight for Troy!
The kings of birds[7] to kings of the beaking prows, one black,
   one with a blaze of silver
      skimmed the palace spearhand right   120
      and swooping lower, all could see,
         plunged their claws in a hare, a mother
bursting with unborn young—the babies spilling,
quick spurts of blood—cut off the race just dashing into life!
Cry, cry for death, but good win out in glory in the end.   125
But the loyal seer[8] of the armies studied Atreus' sons,
two sons with warring hearts—he saw two eagle-kings
   devour the hare and spoke the things to come,[9]

---

6. Clytaemnestra is sacrificing in thanksgiving for the news of Troy's fall; the chorus does not know that
the news has come via the signalfires.   7. Eagles. The chorus proceeds to describe the omen which
accompanied the departure of the army for Troy ten years before. Two eagles seized and tore a pregnant
hare; this was interpreted by the prophet Calchas as meaning that the two kings would destroy the city of
Troy, thus killing not only the living Trojans but the Trojan generations yet unborn.   8. Calchas.
9. The seer identified the two eagles as symbolic of the two kings, their action as a symbolic prophecy of
the destruction of Troy.

"Years pass, and the long hunt nets the city of Priam,
      the flocks beyond the walls,   130
a kingdom's life and soul—Fate stamps them out.
Just let no curse of the gods lour on us first,
      shatter our giant armor
            forged to strangle Troy. I see
                  pure Artemis bristle in pity[1]—   135
            yes, the flying hounds[2] of the Father
slaughter for armies . . . their own victim . . . a woman
trembling young, all born to die—She[3] loathes the eagles' feast!"
Cry, cry for death, but good win out in glory in the end.

      "Artemis, lovely Artemis, so kind   140
to the ravening lion's tender, helpless cubs,
the suckling young of beasts that stalk the wilds—
      bring this sign for all its fortune,
            all its brutal torment home to birth![4]
I beg you, Healing Apollo, soothe her before   145
her crosswinds hold us down and moor the ships too long,[5]
pressing us on to another victim . . .
      nothing sacred, no
            no feast to be eaten[6]
                  the architect of vengeance   150
[Turning to the palace.]
            growing strong in the house
      with no fear of the husband
here she waits
the terror raging back and back in the future
      the stealth, the law of the hearth, the mother—   155
            Memory womb of Fury child-avenging Fury!"
So as the eagles wheeled at the crossroads,
Calchas clashed out the great good blessings mixed with doom
      for the halls of kings, and singing with our fate
we cry, cry for death, but good win out in glory in the end.   160

                  Zeus, great nameless all in all,
                        if that name will gain his favor,[7]
                        I will call him Zeus.

1. Artemis, a virgin goddess, patron of hunting and the protectress of wild life, is angry that the eagles have destroyed a pregnant animal. The prophet fears that she may turn her wrath against the kings whom the eagles represent.   2. The eagles.   3. Artemis. A *woman trembling young*: Just as the eagles kill the hare, the kings will kill Agamemnon's daughter Iphigenia. The Greek text refers only to the hare but the translator has made the allusion clear.   4. Calchas prays that in spite of its bad aspects, the omen will be truly prophetic, i.e., that the Achaeans will capture Troy. He goes on to anticipate and try to avert some of the evils it portends.   5. He foresees the future. Artemis will send unfavorable winds to prevent the sailing of the Greek expedition from Aulis, the port of embarkation. She will demand the sacrifice of Agamemnon's daughter Iphigenia as the price of the fleet's release.   6. At an ordinary sacrifice the celebrants gave the gods their due portion and then feasted on the animal's flesh. The word "sacrifice" comes to have the connotation of "feast." There will be no feast at this sacrifice, since the victim will be a human being. The ominous phrase reminds us of a feast of human flesh which has already taken place, Thyestes' feasting on his own children.   7. It was important, in prayer, to address the divinity by his or her right name: here the chorus uses an inclusive formula—they call on Zeus by whatever name pleases him.

I have no words to do him justice,
  weighing all in the balance,   165
all I have is Zeus, Zeus—
lift this weight, this torment from my spirit,
  cast it once for all.

He who was so mighty once,[8]
storming for the wars of heaven,   170
  he has had his day.
And then his son[9] who came to power
met his match in the third fall
  and he is gone. Zeus, Zeus—
raise your cries and sing him Zeus the Victor!   175
  You will reach the truth:

Zeus has led us on to know,
  the Helmsman lays it down as law
that we must suffer, suffer into truth.
We cannot sleep, and drop by drop at the heart   180
  the pain of pain remembered comes again,
and we resist, but ripeness comes as well.
From the gods enthroned on the awesome rowing-bench[1]
  there comes a violent love.

So it was that day the king,   185
  the steersman at the helm of Greece,
would never blame a word the prophet said—
swept away by the wrenching winds of fortune
he conspired! Weatherbound we could not sail,
our stores exhausted, fighting strength hard-pressed,   190
and the squadrons rode in the shallows off Chalkis[2]
  where the riptide crashes, drags,

and winds from the north pinned down our hulls at Aulis,
port of anguish . . . head winds starving,
sheets and the cables snapped   195
  and the men's minds strayed,
    the pride, the bloom of Greece
  was raked as time ground on,
ground down, and then the cure for the storm
and it was harsher—Calchas cried,   200
"My captains, Artemis must have blood!"—
so harsh the sons of Atreus
  dashed their scepters on the rocks,
could not hold back the tears,

---

8. Uranus, father of Cronos, grandfather of Zeus, the first lord of heaven. This whole passage refers to a primitive legend which told how Uranus was violently supplanted by his son, Cronos, who was in his turn overthrown by his son, Zeus. This legend is made to bear new meaning by Aeschylus, for he suggests that it is not a meaningless series of acts of violence, but a progression to the rule of Zeus, who stands for order and justice. Thus the law of human life which Zeus proclaims and administers, that wisdom comes through suffering, has its counterpart in the history of the establishment of the divine rule. 9. Cronos. 1. The bench of the ship where the helmsman sat. 2. The unruly water of the narrows between Aulis on the mainland and Chalkis on the island of Euboea.

and I still can hear the older warlord saying, 205
"Obey, obey, or a heavy doom will crush me!—
Oh but doom *will* crush me
    once I rend my child,
        the glory of my house—
    a father's hands are stained, 210
blood of a young girl streaks the altar.
Pain both ways and what is worse?
Desert the fleets, fail the alliance?
    No, but stop the winds with a virgin's blood,
        feed their lust, their fury?—feed their fury!— 215
    Law is law!—
            Let all go well."

And once he slipped his neck in the strap of Fate,
his spirit veering black, impure, unholy,
once he turned he stopped at nothing,
        seized with the frenzy 220
            blinding driving to outrage—
wretched frenzy, cause of all our grief!
Yes, he had the heart
        to sacrifice his daughter!—
    to bless the war that avenged a woman's loss, 225
    a bridal rite that sped the men-of-war.

"My father, father!"—she might pray to the winds;
no innocence moves her judges mad for war.
Her father called his henchmen on,
        on with a prayer, 230
        "Hoist her over the altar
like a yearling, give it all your strength!
She's fainting—lift her,
    sweep her robes around her,
but slip this strap in her gentle curving lips . . . 235
    here, gag her hard, a sound will curse the house"—

and the bridle chokes her voice . . . her saffron robes
pouring over the sand
                her glance like arrows showering
wounding every murderer through with pity
        clear as a picture, live, 240
she strains to call their names . . .
I remember often the days with father's guests
when over the feast her voice unbroken,
    pure as the hymn her loving father
bearing third libations,[3] sang to Saving Zeus— 245

---

3. At the banquet three libations (offerings of wine) were poured, the third and last to Zeus the Savior. The last libation was accompanied by a hymn of praise.

transfixed with joy, Atreus' offspring
   throbbing out their love.

What comes next? I cannot see it, cannot say.
The strong techniques of Calchas do their work.[4]
But Justice turns the balance scales,   250
   sees that we suffer
and we suffer and we learn.
And we will know the future when it comes.
Greet it too early, weep too soon.
   It all comes clear in the light of day.   255
Let all go well today, well as she could want,
   [*Turning to* CLYTAEMNESTRA.]
our midnight watch, our lone defender,
   single-minded queen.

LEADER: We've come,
Clytaemnestra. We respect your power.
Right it is to honor the warlord's woman   260
once he leaves the throne.
                      But why these fires?
Good news, or more good hopes? We're loyal,
we want to hear, but never blame your silence.

CLYTAEMNESTRA: Let the new day shine, as the proverb says,
   glorious from the womb of Mother Night.   265
   [*Lost in prayer, then turning to the* CHORUS.]
You will hear a joy beyond your hopes.
Priam's citadel—the Greeks have taken Troy!

LEADER: No, what do you mean? I can't believe it.

CLYTAEMNESTRA: Troy is ours. Is that clear enough?

LEADER: The joy of it,
stealing over me, calling up my tears—   270

CLYTAEMNESTRA: Yes, your eyes expose your loyal hearts.

LEADER: And you have proof?

CLYTAEMNESTRA: I do,
I must. Unless the god is lying.

LEADER: That,
or a phantom spirit sends you into raptures.

CLYTAEMNESTRA: No one takes me in with visions—senseless dreams.   275

LEADER: Or giddy rumor, you haven't indulged yourself—

CLYTAEMNESTRA: You treat me like a child, you mock me?

LEADER: Then when did they storm the city?

CLYTAEMNESTRA: Last night, I say, the mother of this morning.

LEADER: And who on earth could run the news so fast?   280

CLYTAEMNESTRA: The god of fire—rushing fire from Ida![5]

---

4. This seems to refer to the sacrifice of Iphigenia. Some scholars take the Greek words to refer to the fulfillment of Calchas's prophecies.   5. The mountain range near Troy. The names which follow in this speech designate the places where beacon fires flashed the message of Troy's fall to Argos. The chain extends from Ida to Hermes' cliff on the island of Lemnos (off the coast of Asia Minor), to Mount Athos

And beacon to beacon rushed it on to me,
my couriers riding home the torch.
                                    From Troy
to the bare rock of Lemnos, Hermes' Spur,
and the Escort winged the great light west   285
to the Saving Father's face, Mount Athos hurled it
third in the chain and leaping Ocean's back
the blaze went dancing on to ecstasy—pitch-pine
streaming gold like a new-born sun—and brought
the word in flame to Mount Makistos' brow.   290
No time to waste, straining, fighting sleep,
that lookout heaved a torch glowing over
the murderous straits of Euripos to reach
Messapion's watchmen craning for the signal.
Fire for word of fire! tense with the heather   295
withered gray, they stack it, set it ablaze—
the hot force of the beacon never flags,
it springs the Plain of Asôpos, rears
like a harvest moon to hit Kithairon's crest
and drives new men to drive the fire on.   300
That relay pants for the far-flung torch,
they swell its strength outstripping my commands
and the light inflames the marsh, the Gorgon's Eye,
it strikes the peak where the wild goats range—
my laws, my fire whips that camp!   305
They spare nothing, eager to build its heat,
and a huge beard of flame overcomes the headland
beetling down the Saronic Gulf, and flaring south
it brings the dawn to the Black Widow's face—
the watch that looms above your heads—and now   310
the true son of the burning flanks of Ida
crashes on the roofs of Atreus' sons!

(which is situated on a rocky peninsula in north Greece), to Mount Makistos on the island of Euboea (off the coast of central Greece), to Messapion, a mountain of the mainland, to Kithairon, a mountain near Thebes, across Lake Gorgopis (the Gorgon's Eye) to Mount Aegiplanctus (the wild goat's range) on the Isthmus of Corinth, across the sea (the Saronic Gulf) to Mount Arachnaeus (Spider—Black Widow Mountain) in Argive territory. This fire is the one seen by the watchman at the beginning of the play. The speech has often been criticized as discursive, but it has great poetic importance. The image of the light which will dispel the darkness, first introduced by the watchman, is one of the dominant images of the trilogy, and is here developed with magnificent ambiguous effect. For the watchman the light means the safe return of Agamemnon and the restoration of order in the house; for Clytaemnestra it means the return of Agamemnon to his death at her hands. Each swift jump of the racing light is one step nearer home and death for Agamemnon. The light the watchman longs for brings only greater darkness, but eventually it brings darkness for Clytaemnestra too. The final emergence of the true light comes in the glare of the torchlight procession which ends the last play of the trilogy, a procession which symbolizes perfect reconciliation on both the human and the divine levels, and the working out of the will of Zeus in the substitution of justice for vengeance. The conception of the beacons as a chain of descendants (compare "the true son of the burning flanks of Ida," l. 311) is also important; the fire at Argos which announces Agamemnon's imminent death is a direct descendant of the fire on Ida which announces the sack of Troy and Agamemnon's sacrilegious conduct there. The metaphor thus reminds us of the sequence of crimes from generation to generation which is the history of the house of Pelops.

And I ordained it all.
Torch to torch, running for their lives,
one long succession racing home my fire.   315
                                        One,
first in the laps and last,[6] wins out in triumph.
There you have my proof, *my* burning sign, I tell you—
the power my lord passed on from Troy to me!
LEADER: We'll thank the gods, my lady—first this story,
let me lose myself in the wonder of it all!   320
Tell it start to finish, tell us all.
CLYTAEMNESTRA: The city's ours—in our hands this very day!
I can hear the cries in crossfire rock the walls.
Pour oil and wine in the same bowl,
what have you, friendship? A struggle to the end.   325
So with the victors and the victims—outcries,
you can hear them clashing like their fates.

They are kneeling by the bodies of the dead,
embracing men and brothers, infants over
the aged loins that gave them life, and sobbing,   330
as the yoke constricts their last free breath,
for every dear one lost.
                          And the others,
there, plunging breakneck through the night—
the labor of battle sets them down, ravenous;
to breakfast on the last remains of Troy.
Not by rank but the lots of chance they draw,   335
they lodge in the houses captured by the spear,
settling in so soon, released from the open sky,
the frost and dew. Lucky men, off guard at last,
they sleep away their first good night in years.

If only they are revering the city's gods,   340
the shrines of the gods who love the conquered land,
no plunderer will be plundered in return.
Just let no lust, no mad desire[7] seize the armies
to ravish what they must not touch—
overwhelmed by all they've won!
                                The run for home   345
and safety waits, the swerve at the post,[8]
the final lap of the gruelling two-lap race.
And even if the men come back with no offense
to the gods, the avenging dead may never rest—
Oh let no new disaster strike! And here   350
you have it, what a woman has to say.

6. The chain of beacons is compared to a relay race in which the runners carry torches: the last runner (who runs the final lap) comes in first to win.   7. Clytaemnestra, who intends to murder Agamemnon on his return, hopes of course for the opposite of what she here prays for. The audience was familiar with the traditional account, according to which Agamemnon and his army failed signally to respect the gods and temples of Troy.   8. Greek runners turned at the post and came back on a parallel track.

Let the best win out, clear to see.
A small desire but all that I could want.
LEADER: Spoken like a man, my lady, loyal,
full of self-command. I've heard your sign   355
and now your vision.
    [*Reaching towards her as she turns and re-enters the palace.*]
                        Now to praise the gods.
The joy is worth the labor.
CHORUS: O Zeus my king and Night, dear Night,[9]
    queen of the house who covers us with glories,[1]
    you slung your net on the towers of Troy,   360
    neither young nor strong could leap
    the giant dredge net of slavery,
        all-embracing ruin.
I adore you, iron Zeus of the guests
and your revenge—you drew your longbow   365
year by year to a taut full draw
till one bolt, not falling short
or arching over the stars,
    could split the mark of Paris!

The sky stroke of god!—it is all Troy's to tell,   370
but even I can trace it to its cause:
god does as god decrees.
    And still some say
that heaven would never stoop to punish men
who trample the lovely grace of things[2]   375
untouchable. How wrong they are!
    A curse burns bright on crime—[3]
        full-blown, the father's crimes will blossom,
            burst into the son's.
Let there be less suffering . . .   380
give us the sense to live on what we need.

                Bastions of wealth
                are no defense for the man
                who treads the grand altar of Justice
                    down and out of sight.   385

Persuasion, maddening child of Ruin
overpowers him—Ruin plans it all.
And the wound will smolder on,
    there is no cure,

9. Troy fell to a night attack.   1. An obscure expression in the original; the "glories" must be the moon and stars.   2. The language throughout this passage is significantly general. The chorus refers to Paris but everything it says is equally applicable to Agamemnon, who sacrificed his daughter for his ambitions. 3. The original Greek is corrupt (i.e., has been garbled in the hand-written tradition) but seems to proclaim the doctrine that the sins of the fathers are visited on the children. So Paris (and Agamemnon) pay for the misdeeds of their ancestors (as well as their own).

a terrible brilliance kindles on the night.   380
He is bad bronze scraped on a touchstone:
put to the test, the man goes black.[4]
   Like the boy who chases
     a bird on the wing, brands his city,
       brings it down and prays,   395
but the gods are deaf
to the one who turns to crime, they tear him down.

           So Paris learned:
           he came to Atreus' house
           and shamed the tables spread for guests,   400
             he stole away the queen.

And she left her land *chaos*, clanging shields,
companions tramping, bronze prows, men in bronze,
   and she came to Troy with a dowry, death,
strode through the gates   405
     defiant in every stride,
as prophets of the house[5] looked on and wept,
"Oh the halls and the lords of war,
   the bed and the fresh prints of love.
I *see* him, unavenging, unavenged,   410
the stun of his desolation is so clear—
   he longs for the one who lies across the sea
until her phantom seems to sway the house.

           Her curving images,
           her beauty hurts her lord,   415
           the eyes starve and the touch
            of love is gone,

and radiant dreams are passing in the night,
the memories throb with sorrow, joy with pain . . .
   it is pain to dream and see desires   420
slip through the arms,
     a vision lost forever
winging down the moving drifts of sleep."
So he grieves at the royal hearth
   yet others' grief is worse, far worse.   425
All through Greece for those who flocked to war
they are holding back the anguish now,
   you can feel it rising now in every house;
I tell you there is much to tear the heart.

           They knew the men they sent,   430
           but now in place of men

---

4. Inferior bronze, adulterated with lead, turns black with use.   5. The house of Menelaus.

ashes and urns come back
to every hearth.[6]

War, War, the great gold-broker[7] of corpses
holds the balance of the battle on his spear!   435
Home from the pyres he sends them,
    home from Troy to the loved ones,
weighted with tears, the urns brimmed full,
    the heroes return in gold-dust,
dear, light ash for men; and they weep,   440
they praise them, "He had skill in the swordplay,"
    "He went down so tall in the onslaught,"
"All for another's woman." So they mutter
in secret and the rancor steals
toward our staunch defenders, Atreus' sons.   445

> And there they ring the walls, the young,
> the lithe, the handsome hold the graves
> they won in Troy; the enemy earth
>   rides over those who conquered.

The people's voice is heavy with hatred,   450
now the curses of the people must be paid,
and now I wait, I listen . . .
    there—there is something breathing
under the night's shroud. God takes aim
    at the ones who murder many;   455
the swarthy Furies stalk the man
gone rich beyond all rights—with a twist
    of fortune grind him down, dissolve him
into the blurring dead—there is no help.
The reach for power can recoil,   460
the bolt of god can strike you at a glance.

> Make me rich with no man's envy,
> neither a raider of cities,[8] no,
> nor slave come face to face with life
>   overpowered by another.   465

[Speaking singly.]
—Fire comes and the news is good,
    it races through the streets
but is it true? Who knows?
Or just another lie from heaven?

6. This strikes a contemporary note. In Homer the fallen Achaeans are buried at Troy: it was in the Athens of Aeschylus that the dead were cremated on the battlefield and their ashes brought home for burial. 7. The war god is a broker who gives, in exchange for bodies, gold dust, (the word used for "bodies" could mean living bodies or corpses); the "dust" he gives is of course the ashes of the warrior.   8. Later we will see Agamemnon come on stage with the spoils of Troy and Cassandra, his Trojan captive. The chorus, which started out to sing a hymn of praise for the fall of Troy (l. 357) ends in fear and despondency. They now question the truth of Clytaemnestra's announcement: perhaps Troy has not fallen after all (l. 469).

—Show us the man so childish, wonderstruck,   470
  he's fired up with the first torch,
  then when the message shifts
  he's sick at heart.

                —Just like a woman
  to fill with thanks before the truth is clear.

—So gullible. Their stories spread like wildfire,   475
  they fly fast and die faster;
  rumors voiced by women come to nothing.
LEADER: Soon we'll know her fires for what they are,
  her relay race of torches hand-to-hand—
  know if they're real or just a dream,   480
  the hope of a morning here to take our senses.
  I see a herald running from the beach
  and a victor's spray of olive shades his eyes
  and the dust he kicks, twin to the mud of Troy,
  shows he has a voice—no kindling timber   485
  on the cliffs, no signal-fires for him.
  He can shout the news and give us joy,
  or else . . . please, not that.
                          Bring it on,
  good fuel to build the first good fires.
  And if anyone calls down the worst on Argos   490
  let him reap the rotten harvest of his mind.
    [The HERALD rushes in and kneels on the ground.]
HERALD: Good Greek earth, the soil of my fathers!
  Ten years out, and a morning brings me back.
  All hopes snapped but one—I'm home at last.
  Never dreamed I'd die in Greece, assigned   495
  the narrow plot I love the best.
                          And now
  I salute the land, the light of the sun,
  our high lord Zeus and the king of Pytho[9]—
  no more arrows, master, raining on our heads![1]
  At Scamander's banks we took our share,   500
  your longbow brought us down like plague.
  Now come, deliver us, heal us—lord Apollo!
  Gods of the market, here, take my salute.
  And you, my Hermes, Escort,
  loving Herald, the herald's shield and prayer![2]—   505
  And the shining dead[3] of the land who launched the armies,
  warm us home . . . we're all the spear has left.

9. Apollo.   1. Cf. the opening scene of the *Iliad*, Book I where Apollo punishes the Greeks with his arrows (a metaphor for plague).   2. Hermes, the gods' messenger, was the patron deity of heralds.
3. The heroes of past time, buried in the soil of Argos and worshipped.

You halls of the kings, you roofs I cherish,
sacred seats—you gods that catch the sun,
if your glances ever shone on him in the old days,   510
greet him well—so many years are lost.
He comes, he brings us light in the darkness,
free for every comrade, Agamemnon lord of men.

Give him the royal welcome he deserves!
He hoisted the pickax of Zeus who brings revenge,   515
he dug Troy down, he worked her soil down,
the shrines of her gods and the high altars, gone!—
and the seed of her wide earth he ground to bits.
That's the yoke he claps on Troy. The king,
the son of Atreus comes. The man is blest,   520
the one man alive to merit such rewards.

Neither Paris nor Troy, partners to the end,
can say their work outweighs their wages now.
Convicted of rapine, stripped of all his spoils,
and his father's house and the land that gave it life—   525
he's scythed them to the roots. The sons of Priam
pay the price twice over.
LEADER: Welcome home
from the wars, herald, long live your joy.
HERALD: *Our* joy—
now I could die gladly. Say the word, dear gods.
LEADER: Longing for your country left you raw?   530
HERALD: The tears fill my eyes, for joy.
LEADER: You too,
down the sweet disease that kills a man
with kindness . . .
HERALD: Go on, I don't see what you—
LEADER: Love
for the ones who love you—that's what took you.
HERALD: You mean
the land and the armies hungered for each other?   535
LEADER: There were times I thought I'd faint with longing.
HERALD: So anxious for the armies, why?
LEADER: For years now,
only my silence kept me free from harm.
HERALD: What,
with the kings gone did someone threaten you?
LEADER: So much . . .
now as you say,[4] it would be good to die.   540
HERALD: True, we *have* done well.
Think back in the years and what have you?

4. Throughout this dialogue the chorus has been nerving itself to warn the herald that there may be danger for Agamemnon at home; at this point its nerve fails, and it abandons the attempt.

A few runs of luck, a lot that's bad.
Who but a god can go through life unmarked?

A long, hard pull we had, if I would tell it all.   545
The iron rations, penned in the gangways
hock by jowl like sheep. Whatever miseries
break a man, our quota, every sunstarved day.

Then on the beaches it was worse. Dug in
under the enemy ramparts—deadly going.   550
Out of the sky, out of the marshy flats
the dews soaked us, turned the ruts we fought from
into gullies, made our gear, our scalps
crawl with lice.
                    And talk of the cold,
the sleet to freeze the gulls, and the big snows   555
come avalanching down from Ida. Oh but the heat,
the sea and the windless noons, the swells asleep,
dropped to a dead calm . . .

But why weep now?
It's over for us, over for them.   560
The dead can rest and never rise again;
no need to call their muster. We're alive,
do we have to go on raking up old wounds?
Good-by to all that. Glad I am to say it.

For us, the remains of the Greek contingents,   565
the good wins out, no pain can tip the scales,
not now. So shout this boast to the bright sun—
fitting it is—wing it over the seas and rolling earth:

"Once when an Argive expedition captured Troy
they hauled these spoils back to the gods of Greece,   570
they bolted them high across the temple doors,
the glory of the past!"
                       And hearing that,
men will applaud our city and our chiefs,
and Zeus will have the hero's share of fame—
he did the work.
                That's all I have to say.   575
LEADER: I'm convinced, glad that I was wrong.
    Never too old to learn; it keeps me young.
        [CLYTAEMNESTRA *enters with her women.*]
    First the house and the queen, it's their affair,
    but I can taste the riches.
CLYTAEMNESTRA: I cried out long ago!—[5]
    for joy, when the first herald came burning   580

5. As the Watchman had told her to (l. 30).

through the night and told the city's fall.
And there were some who smiled and said,
"A few fires persuade you Troy's in ashes.
Women, women, elated over nothing."

You made me seem deranged.   585
For all that I sacrificed—a woman's way,
you'll say—station to station on the walls
we lifted cries of triumph that resounded
in the temples of the gods. We lulled and blessed
the fires with myrrh and they consumed our victims.   590
    [*Turning to the* HERALD.]
But enough. Why prolong the story?
From the king himself I'll gather all I need.
Now for the best way to welcome home
my lord, my good lord . . .
                    No time to lose!
What dawn can feast a woman's eyes like this?   595
I can see the light, the husband plucked from war
by the Saving God and open wide the gates.

Tell him that, and have him come with speed,
the people's darling—how they long for him.
And for his wife,   600
may he return and find her true at hall,
just as the day he left her, faithful to the last.
A watchdog gentle to him alone,
    [*Glancing towards the palace.*]
                            savage
to those who cross his path. I have not changed.
The strains of time can never break our seal.   605
In love with a new lord, in ill repute I am
as practiced as I am in dyeing bronze.[6]

That is my boast, teeming with the truth.
I am proud, a woman of my nobility—
I'd hurl it from the roofs!   610
    [*She turns sharply, enters the palace.*]
LEADER: She speaks well, but it takes no seer to know
    she only says what's right.
    [*The* HERALD *attempts to leave; the* LEADER *takes him by the arm.*]
                    Wait, one thing.
Menelaus, is he home too, safe with the men?[7]
The power of the land—dear king.

6. She is no more capable of adultery, she claims, than she is of dyeing bronze. But she will later kill Agamemnon with a bronze weapon.   7. The relevance of this question and the following speeches lies in the fact that Menelaus' absence makes Agamemnon's murder easier (his presence might have made it impossible), and in the fact that Menelaus is bringing Helen home; the choral ode which follows shows how much the chorus is obsessed with Helen's guilt—so much that it fails to recognize the true responsibility for the war and the imminence of disaster.

HERALD: I doubt that lies will help my friends,   615
  in the lean months to come.
LEADER: Help us somehow, tell the truth as well.
  But when the two conflict it's hard to hide—
  out with it.
HERALD: He's lost, gone from the fleets![8]
  He and his ship, it's true.
LEADER: After you watched him   620
  pull away from Troy? Or did some storm
  attack you all and tear him off the line?
HERALD: There,
  like a marksman, the whole disaster cut to a word.
LEADER: How do the escorts give him out—dead or alive?
HERALD: No clear report. No one knows . . .   625
  only the wheeling sun that heats the earth to life.
LEADER: But then the storm—how did it reach the ships?
  How did it end? Were the angry gods on hand?
HERALD: This blessed day, ruin it with *them?*
  Better to keep their trophies far apart.   635

When a runner comes, his face in tears,
  saddled with what his city dreaded most,[9]
  the armies routed, two wounds in one,
  one to the city, one to hearth and home . . .
  our best men, droves of them, victims   635
  herded from every house by the two-barb whip
  that Ares[1] likes to crack,
                that charioteer
who packs destruction shaft by shaft,
  careening on with his brace of bloody mares—
When he comes in, I tell you, dragging that much pain,   640
  wail your battle-hymn to the Furies, and high time!
But when he brings salvation home to a city
  singing out her heart—
how can I mix the good with so much bad
  and blurt out this?—
              "Storms swept the Greeks,   645
and not without the anger of the gods!"

Those enemies for ages, fire[2] and water,
  sealed a pact and showed it to the world—
  they crushed our wretched squadrons.
                 Night looming,
  breakers lunging in for the kill   650
and the black gales come brawling out of the north—

---

8. For what happened to Menelaus see his account in *Odyssey,* Book IV.   9. The herald creates a vivid picture of a messenger bringing news of disaster to his city—a role he wishes to avoid.   1. The war god.
2. I.e., lightning.

ships ramming, prow into hooking prow, gored
by the rush-and-buck of hurricane pounding rain
by the cloudburst—
        ships stampeding into the darkness,
lashed and spun by the savage shepherd's hand![3] 655

But when the sun comes up to light the skies
I see the Aegean heaving into a great bloom
of corpses . . . Greeks, the pick of a generation
scattered through the wrecks and broken spars.

But not us, not our ship, our hull untouched. 660
Someone stole us away or begged us off.
No mortal—a god, death grip on the tiller,
or lady luck herself, perched on the helm,
she pulled us through, she saved us. Aye,
we'll never battle the heavy surf at anchor, 665
never shipwreck up some rocky coast.

But once we cleared that sea-hell, not even
trusting luck in the cold light of day,
we battened on our troubles, they were fresh—
the armada punished, bludgeoned into nothing. 670

And now if one of them still has the breath
he's saying we are lost. Why not?
We say the same of him. Well,
here's to the best.
        And Menelaus?
Look to it, he's come back, and yet . . . 675
if a shaft of the sun can track him down,
alive, and his eyes full of the old fire—
thanks to the strategies of Zeus, Zeus
would never tear the house out by the roots—
then there's hope our man will make it home. 680

You've heard it all. Now you have the truth.
[*Rushing out.*]
CHORUS: Who—what power named the name[4] that drove your fate?—
what hidden brain could divine your future,
steer that word to the mark,
to the bride of spears, 685
    the whirlpool churning armies,
        Oh for all the world a Helen!
Hell at the prows, hell at the gates
hell on the men-of-war,

3. The ships were scattered like sheep dispersed by a cruel shepherd. 4. Helen. The name contains a Greek root *hele*—which means "destroy."

from her lair's sheer veils she drifted   690
   launched by the giant western wind,
     and the long tall waves of men in armor,[5]
huntsmen trailing the oar-blades' dying spoor
slipped into her moorings,
   Simois'[6] mouth that chokes with foliage,   695
     bayed for bloody strife,
for Troy's Blood Wedding Day—she drives her word,
her burning will to the birth, the Fury
late but true to the cause,
to the tables shamed   700
   and Zeus who guards the hearth—[7]
     the Fury makes the Trojans pay!
Shouting their hymns, hymns for the bride
hymns for the kinsmen doomed
to the wedding march of Fate.   705
   Troy changed her tune in her late age,
     and I think I hear the dirges mourning
"Paris, born and groomed for the bed of Fate!"
They mourn with their life breath,
   they sing their last, the sons of Priam   710
     born for bloody slaughter.

   So a man once reared
a lion cub at hall, snatched
from the breast, still craving milk
   in the first flush of life.   715
A captivating pet for the young,
and the old men adored it, pampered it
   in their arms, day in, day out,
like an infant just born.
Its eyes on fire, little beggar,   720
fawning for its belly, slave to food.

   But it came of age
and the parent strain broke out
and it paid its breeders back.
   Grateful it was, it went   725
through the flock to prepare a feast,
an illicit orgy—the house swam with blood,
   none could resist that agony—
     massacre vast and raw!
From god there came a priest of ruin,   730
adopted by the house to lend it warmth.

---

5. The Achaean army which came after her, like huntsmen.   6. One of the rivers of Troy.   7. Zeus
in his capacity as protector of host and guest.

And the first sensation Helen brought to Troy . . .
call it a spirit
    shimmer of winds dying
      glory light as gold   735
    shaft of the eyes dissolving, open bloom
that wounds the heart with love.
But veering wild in mid-flight
she whirled her wedding on to a stabbing end,
slashed at the sons of Priam—hearthmate, friend to the death,   740
    sped by Zeus who speeds the guest,
a bride of tears, a Fury.

There's an ancient saying,[8] old as man himself:
men's prosperity
    never will die childless,   745
      once full-grown it breeds.
    Sprung from the great good fortune in the race
comes bloom on bloom of pain—
insatiable wealth. But not I,
I alone say this. Only the reckless act   750
can breed impiety, multiplying crime on crime,
    while the house kept straight and just
is blessed with radiant children.

      But ancient Violence longs to breed,
        new Violence comes   755
    when its fatal hour comes, the demon comes
    to take her toll—no war, no force, no prayer
      can hinder the midnight Fury stamped
    with parent Fury moving through the house.

      But Justice shines in sooty hovels,[9]   760
        loves the decent life.
From proud halls crusted with gilt by filthy hands
    she turns her eyes to find the pure in spirit—
    spurning the wealth stamped counterfeit with praise,
      she steers all things toward their destined end.   765
[AGAMEMNON *enters in his chariot, his plunder borne before him by
his entourage; behind him, half hidden, stands* CASSANDRA. *The old
men press toward him.*]
Come, my king, the scourge of Troy,
    the true son of Atreus—
How to salute you, how to praise you
neither too high nor low, but hit
the note of praise that suits the hour?   770
So many prize some brave display,

8. These lines state the traditional Greek view that immoderate good fortune (or excellence of any kind beyond the average) is itself the cause of disaster. In the lines which follow, the chorus rejects this view and states that only an act of evil produces evil consequences. It later admits by implication (ll. 739ff.) that those who are less prosperous are less likely to commit such an act. 9. The homes of the poor.

they prefer some flaunt of honor
  once they break the bounds.[1]
When a man fails they share his grief,
but the pain can never cut them to the quick.   775
When a man succeeds they share his glory,
torturing their faces into smiles.
But the good shepherd knows his flock.
When the eyes seem to brim with love
  and it is only unction,   780
he will know, better than we can know.
That day you marshaled the armies
all for Helen—no hiding it now—
I drew you in my mind in black;
you seemed a menace at the helm,   785
  sending men to the grave
to bring her home, that hell on earth.
But now from the depths of trust and love
I say Well fought, well won—
  the end is worth the labor!   790
Search, my king, and learn at last
  who stayed at home and kept their faith
    and who betrayed the city.

AGAMEMNON: First,
  with justice I salute my Argos and my gods,
  my accomplices who brought me home and won   795
  my rights from Priam's Troy—the just gods.
  No need to hear our pleas. Once for all
  they consigned their lots to the urn of blood,[2]
  they pitched on death for men, annihilation
  for the city. Hope's hand, hovering   800
  over the urn of mercy, left it empty.
  Look for the smoke—it is the city's seamark,
  building even now.
                    The storms of ruin live!
  Her last dying breath, rising up from the ashes
  sends us gales of incense rich in gold.   805

  For that we must thank the gods with a sacrifice
  our sons will long remember. For their mad outrage
  of a queen we raped their city—we were right.
  The beast of Argos, foals of the wild mare,[3]
  thousands massed in armor rose on the night   810
  the Pleiades went down,[4] and crashing through

---

1. The chorus tries to warn Agamemnon against flatterers and dissemblers, but he misses their drift.
2. In an Athenian law court there were two urns, one for acquittal, one for condemnation, into which the jurors dropped their pebbles. (The audience will see them on stage in the final play of the trilogy.)
3. The wooden horse, the stratagem with which the Greeks captured the city.   4. The setting of the constellation called the Pleiades, late in the fall.

their walls our bloody lion lapped its fill,
gorging on the blood of kings.
                              Our thanks to the gods,
long drawn out, but it is just the prelude.
  [CLYTAEMNESTRA *approaches with her women; they are carrying dark*
  red tapestries. AGAMEMNON *turns to the* LEADER.]
And your concern, old man, is on my mind.   815
I hear you and agree, I will support you.
How rare, men with the character to praise
a friend's success without a trace of envy,
poison to the heart—it deals a double blow.
Your own losses weigh you down but then,   820
look at your neighbor's fortune and you weep.
Well I know. I understand society,
the fawning mirror of the proud.
                              My comrades . . .
they're shadows, I tell you, ghosts of men
who swore they'd die for me. Only Odysseus: 825
I dragged that man to the wars[5] but once in harness
he was a trace-horse, he gave his all for me.
Dead or alive, no matter, I can praise him.

And now this cause involving men and gods.
We must summon the city for a trial,   830
found a national tribunal. Whatever's healthy,
shore it up with law and help it flourish.
Wherever something calls for drastic cures
we make our noblest effort: amputate or wield
the healing iron, burn the cancer at the roots.   835

Now I go to my father's house—
I give the gods my right hand, my first salute.
The ones who sent me forth have brought me home.
  [*He starts down from the chariot, looks at* CLYTAEMNESTRA, *stops, and*
  offers up a prayer.]
Victory, you have sped my way before,
now speed me to the last.
  [CLYTAEMNESTRA *turns from the king to the* CHORUS.]
CLYTAEMNESTRA: Old nobility of Argos   840
gathered here, I am not ashamed to tell you
how I love the man. I am older,
and the fear dies away . . . I am human.
Nothing I say was learned from others.
This is my life, my ordeal, long as the siege   845
he laid at Troy and more demanding.

---

5. Feigning madness in order to escape going to Troy, Odysseus was tricked into demonstrating his sanity.
Agamemnon's remark shows that the truth is far from his mind; he has no thought that his danger comes
from a woman.

First,

when a woman sits at home and the man is gone,
the loneliness is terrible,
unconscionable . . .
and the rumors spread and fester,   850
a runner comes with something dreadful,
close on his heels the next and his news worse,
and they shout it out and the whole house can hear;
and wounds—if he took one wound for each report
to penetrate these walls, he's gashed like a dragnet,   855
more, if he had only died . . .
for each death that swelled his record, he could boast
like a triple-bodied Geryon[6] risen from the grave,
"Three shrouds I dug from the earth, one for every body
that went down!"

The rumors broke like fever,   860

broke and then rose higher. There were times
they cut me down and eased my throat from the noose.
I wavered between the living and the dead.
[*Turning to* AGAMEMNON.]

And so

our child is gone, not standing by our side,
the bond of our dearest pledges, mine and yours;   865
by all rights our child should be here . . .
Orestes. You seem startled.
You needn't be. Our loyal brother-in-arms
will take good care of him, Strophios[7] the Phocian.
He warned from the start we court two griefs in one.   870
You risk all on the wars—and what if the people
rise up howling for the king, and anarchy
should dash our plans?

Men, it is their nature,

trampling on the fighter once he's down.
Our child is gone. That is my self-defense   875
and it is true.

For me, the tears that welled

like springs are dry. I have no tears to spare.
I'd watch till late at night, my eyes still burn,
I sobbed by the torch I lit for you alone.
[*Glancing towards the palace.*]
I never let it die . . . but in my dreams   880
the high thin wail of a gnat would rouse me,
piercing like a trumpet—I could see you

---

6. A monster (eventually killed by Heracles) who had three bodies and three heads.   7. King of Phocis,
a mountainous region near Delphi. His son, Pylades, accompanies Orestes when he returns to avenge
Agamemnon's death.

suffer more than all
the hours that slept with me could ever bear.

I endured it all. And now, free of grief,   885
I would salute that man the watchdog of the fold,
the mainroyal,[8] saving stay of the vessel,
rooted oak that thrusts the roof sky-high,
the father's one true heir.
Land at dawn to the shipwrecked past all hope,   890
light of the morning burning off the night of storm,
the cold clear spring to the parched horseman—
O the ecstasy, to flee the yoke of Fate!

It is right to use the titles he deserves.
Let envy keep her distance. We have suffered   895
long enough.
          [*Reaching toward* AGAMEMNON.]
                    Come to me now, my dearest,
down from the car of war, but never set the foot
that stamped out Troy on earth again, my great one.

Women, why delay? You have your orders.
Pave his way with tapestries.[9]
          [*They begin to spread the crimson tapestries between the king and the
          palace doors.*]
                              Quickly.   900
Let the red stream flow and bear him home
to the home he never hoped to see—Justice,
lead him in!
                    Leave all the rest to me.
The spirit within me never yields to sleep.
We will set things right, with the god's help.   905
We will do whatever Fate requires.
AGAMEMNON: There
is Leda's daughter,[1] the keeper of my house.
And the speech to suit my absence, much too long.
But the praise that does us justice,
let it come from others, then we prize it.
                              This—   910
You treat me like a woman. Groveling, gaping up at me!
What am I, some barbarian[2] peacocking out of Asia?
Never cross my path with robes and draw the lightning.

---

8. Upper section of the mainmast.   9. To walk on those tapestries, wall hangings dyed with the expensive crimson, would be an act of extravagant pride. Pride is the keynote of Agamemnon's character, and it
suits Clytaemnestra's sense of fitness that he should go into his death in godlike state, "trampling royal
crimson," the color of blood.   1. Clytaemnestra and Helen are both daughters of Leda.   2. Foreigner,
especially Asiatic. Aeschylus is thinking of the pomp and servility of the contemporary Persian court.

Never—only the gods deserve the pomps of honor
and the stiff brocades of fame. To walk on them . . .   915
I am human, and it makes my pulses stir
with dread.
            Give me the tributes of a man
and not a god, a little earth to walk on,
not this gorgeous work.
      There is no need to sound my reputation.   920
I have a sense of right and wrong, what's more—
heaven's proudest gift. Call no man blest
until he ends his life in peace, fulfilled.
If I can live by what I say, I have no fear.
CLYTAEMNESTRA: One thing more. Be true to your ideals and tell me— 925
AGAMEMNON: True to my ideals? Once I violate them I am lost.
CLYTAEMNESTRA: Would you have sworn this act to god in a time of terror?
AGAMEMNON: Yes, if a prophet called for a last, drastic rite.
CLYTAEMNESTRA: But Priam—can you see him if he had your success?
AGAMEMNON: Striding on the tapestries of God, I see him now.   930
CLYTAEMNESTRA: And *you* fear the reproach of common men?
AGAMEMNON: The voice of the people—aye, they have enormous power.
CLYTAEMNESTRA: Perhaps, but where's the glory without a little gall?
AGAMEMNON: And where's the woman in all this lust for glory?
CLYTAEMNESTRA: But the great victor—it becomes him to give way.   935
AGAMEMNON: Victory in this . . . war of ours, it means so much to you?
CLYTAEMNESTRA: O give way! The power is yours if you surrender
all of your own free will to me.
AGAMEMNON: Enough.
If you are so determined—
      [*Turning to the women, pointing to his boots.*]
Let someone help me off with these at least.   940
Old slaves, they've stood me well.
                        Hurry,
and while I tread his splendors dyed red in the sea,[3]
may no god watch and strike me down with envy
from on high. I feel such shame—
to tread the life of the house, a kingdom's worth   945
of silver in the weaving.
      [*He steps down from the chariot to the tapestries and reveals* CASSAN-
      DRA, *dressed in the sacred regalia, the fillets, robes and scepter of
      Apollo.*]
                        Done is done.
Escort this stranger[4] in, be gentle.
Conquer with compassion. Then the gods

---

3. The dye was made from shellfish.   4. Cassandra, daughter of Priam, Agamemnon's share of the
human booty of the sack of Troy. She was loved by Apollo and by him given the gift of prophecy; but
when she refused her love to the god he added to his gift the proviso that her prophecies, though true,
should never be believed until it was too late.

shine down upon you, gently. No one chooses
the yoke of slavery, not of one's free will—   950
and she least of all. The gift of the armies,
flower and pride of all the wealth we won,
she follows me from Troy.
                          And now,
since you have brought me down with your insistence,
just this once I enter my father's house,   955
trampling royal crimson as I go.
        [*He takes his first steps and pauses.*]
CLYTAEMNESTRA: There is the sea
and who will drain it dry? Precious as silver,
inexhaustible, ever-new, it breeds the more we reap it—
tides on tides of crimson dye our robes blood-red.
Our lives are based on wealth, my king,   960
the gods have seen to that.
Destitution, our house has never heard the word.
I would have sworn to tread on legacies of robes,
at one command from an oracle, deplete the house—
suffer the worst to bring that dear life back!   965
        [*Encouraged,* AGAMEMNON *strides to the entrance.*]
When the root lives on, the new leaves come back,
spreading a dense shroud of shade across the house
to thwart the Dog Star's fury.[5] So you return
to the father's hearth, you bring us warmth in winter
like the sun—
                          And you are Zeus when Zeus   970
tramples the bitter virgin grape for new wine
and the welcome chill steals through the halls, at last
the master moves among the shadows of his house, fulfilled.
        [AGAMEMNON *goes over the threshold; the women gather up the tapes-
        tries while* CLYTAEMNESTRA *prays.*]
Zeus, Zeus, master of all fullfillment, now fulfill our prayers—
speed our rites to their fulfillment once for all!   975
        [*She enters the palace, the doors close, the old men huddle in terror.*]
CHORUS: Why, why does it rock me, never stops,
this terror beating down my heart,
        this seer that sees it all—
it beats its wings, uncalled unpaid
thrust on the lungs   980
the mercenary song beats on and on
singing a prophet's strain—
        and I can't throw it off
like dreams that make no sense,
and the strength drains   985

5. The appearance of Sirius, the Dog Star, in the summer sky, marked the beginning of the hot season.

that filled the mind with trust,
and the years drift by and the driven sand
    has buried the mooring lines
that churned when the armored squadrons cut for Troy . . .
and now I believe it, I can prove he's home,   990
    my own clear eyes for witness—
                                    Agamemnon!
Still it's chanting, beating deep so deep in the heart
this dirge of the Furies, oh dear god,
not fit for the lyre,[6] its own master
    it kills our spirit   995
kills our hopes
and it's real, true, no fantasy—
        stark terror whirls the brain
        and the end is coming
            Justice comes to birth—   1000
I pray my fears prove false and fall
and die and never come to birth!
Even exultant health, well we know,
    exceeds its limits,[7] comes so near disease
it can breach the wall between them.   1005

Even a man's fate, held true on course,
    in a blinding flash rams some hidden reef;
but if caution only casts the pick of the cargo—[8]
one well-balanced cast—
the house will not go down, not outright;   1010
laboring under its wealth of grief
the ship of state rides on.

Yes, and the great green bounty of god,
sown in the furrows year by year and reaped each fall
can end the plague of famine.   1015

But a man's lifeblood
    is dark and mortal.
Once it wets the earth
what song can sing it back?
Not even the master-healer[9]   1020
    who brought the dead to life—
Zeus stopped the man before he did more harm.

Oh, if only the gods had never forged
    the chain that curbs our excess,

6. The lyre was played on joyful occasions (hence "lyric" poetry): the Furies' song is a dirge.   7. Excess, even in blessings like health, is always dangerous. The chorus fears that Agamemnon's triumphant success may threaten his safety.   8. These lines refer to a traditional Greek belief that the fortunate man could avert the envy of heaven by deliberately getting rid of some precious possession.   9. Asclepius, the great physician who was so skilled that he finally succeeded in restoring a dead man to life. Zeus struck him with a thunderbolt for going too far.

one man's fate curbing the next man's fate,   1025
my heart would outrace my song, I'd pour out all I feel—
     but no, I choke with anguish,
     mutter through the nights.
Never to ravel out a hope in time
and the brain is swarming, burning—   1030
     [CLYTAEMNESTRA *emerges from the palace and goes to* CASSANDRA,
     impassive in the chariot.]
CLYTAEMNESTRA: Won't you come inside? I mean you, Cassandra.
Zeus in all his mercy wants you to share
some victory libations with the house.
The slaves are flocking. Come, lead them
up to the altar of the god who guards   1035
our dearest treasures.
                    Down from the chariot,
no time for pride. Why even Heracles,[1]
they say, was sold into bondage long ago,
he had to endure the bitter bread of slaves.
But if the yoke descends on you, be grateful   1040
for a master born and reared in ancient wealth.
Those who reap a harvest past their hopes
are merciless to their slaves.
                         From us
you will receive what custom says is right.
     [CASSANDRA *remains impassive.*]
LEADER: It's you she is speaking to, it's all too clear.   1045
You're caught in the nets of doom—obey
if you can obey, unless you cannot bear to.
CLYTAEMNESTRA: Unless she's like a swallow, possessed
of her own barbaric song,[2] strange, dark.
I speak directly as I can—she must obey.   1050
LEADER: Go with her. Make the best of it, she's right.
Step down from the seat, obey her.
CLYTAEMNESTRA: Do it *now*—
I have no time to spend outside. Already
the victims crowd the hearth, the Navelstone,[3]
to bless this day of joy I never hoped to see!—   1055
our victims waiting for the fire and the knife,
and you,
if you want to taste our mystic rites, come now.
If my words can't reach you—

---

1. The Greek hero, famous for his twelve labors which rid the earth of monsters, was at one time forced
to be the slave to Omphale, an Eastern queen.   2. The comparison of foreign speech to the twittering
of a swallow was a Greek commonplace.   3. The hearth, which was the religious center of the home,
with an altar of Zeus Herkeios, guardian of the enclosed space.

[*Turning to the* LEADER.]
Give her a sign,
one of her exotic handsigns.
LEADER: I think   1060
the stranger needs an interpreter, someone clear.
She's like a wild creature, fresh caught.
CLYTAEMNESTRA: She's mad,
her evil genius murmuring in her ears.
She comes from a *city* fresh caught.
She must learn to take the cutting bridle   1065
before she foams her spirit off in blood—
and that's the last I waste on her contempt!
[*Wheeling, re-entering the palace. The* LEADER *turns to* CASSANDRA,
who remains transfixed.]
LEADER: Not I, I pity her. I will be gentle.
Come, poor thing. Leave the empty chariot—
Of your own free will try on the yoke of Fate.   1070
CASSANDRA: Aieeeeee! Earth—Mother—
Curse of the Earth—Apollo Apollo!
LEADER: Why cry to Apollo?
He's not the god to call with sounds of mourning.
CASSANDRA: Aieeeeee! Earth—Mother—   1075
Rape of the Earth—Apollo Apollo!
LEADER: Again, it's a bad omen.
She cries for the god who wants no part of grief.[4]
[CASSANDRA *steps from the chariot, looks slowly towards the rooftops
of the palace.*]
CASSANDRA: God of the long road,
Apollo *Apollo* my destroyer—   1080
you destroy me once, destroy me twice—[5]
LEADER: She's about to sense her own ordeal, I think.
Slave that she is, the god lives on inside her.
CASSANDRA: God of the iron marches,
Apollo *Apollo* my destroyer—   1085
where, where have you led[6] me now? what house—
LEADER: The house of Atreus and his sons. Really—
don't you know? It's true, see for yourself.
CASSANDRA: No . . . the house that hates god,
an echoing womb of guilt, kinsmen   1090
torturing kinsmen, severed heads,
slaughterhouse of heroes, soil streaming blood—

---

4. Apollo, and the Olympian gods in general, were not invoked in mourning or lamentation.   5. The
name Apollo suggests the Greek word *(apollumi)* for "destroy." He "destroyed" her the first time when, as
she tells later, he gave her the gift of true prophecy that no one would believe. *God of the long road:* Apollo
Agyieus; this statue, a conical pillar, was set up outside the door of the house; no doubt there was one on
stage.   6. The Greek word for led (a form of the verb *ago*) suggests the god's title Agyieus.

LEADER: A keen hound, this stranger.
　　Trailing murder, and murder she will find.
CASSANDRA: See, my witnesses—   1095
　　　I trust to them, to the babies
　　　　wailing, skewered on the sword,
　　their flesh charred, the father gorging on their parts—[7]
LEADER: We'd heard your fame as a seer,
　　but no one looks for seers in Argos.   1100
CASSANDRA: Oh no, what horror, what new plot,
　　new agony this?—[8]
　　it's growing, massing, deep in the house,
　　　a plot, a monstrous—*thing*
　　　　to crush the loved ones, no,   1105
　　　there is no cure, and rescue's far away[9] and—
LEADER: I can't read these signs; I knew the first,
　　the city rings with them.
CASSANDRA: You, you godforsaken—you'd do *this*?
　　The lord of your bed,   1110
　　you bathe him . . . his body glistens, then—
　　　how to tell the climax?—
　　　　comes so quickly, see,
　　hand over hand shoots out, hauling ropes—
　　　　　　　　　　　　　　　　then lunge!
LEADER: Still lost. Her riddles, her dark words of god—   1115
　　I'm groping, helpless.
CASSANDRA:　　　　　　　No no, look *there!*—
　　what's that? some net flung out of hell—
　　　No, *she* is the snare,
　　the bedmate, deathmate, murder's strong right arm!
　　　Let the insatiate discord in the race   1120
　　rear up and shriek "Avenge the victim—stone them dead!"
LEADER: What Fury is this? Why rouse it, lift its wailing
　　through the house? I hear you and lose hope.
CHORUS: Drop by drop at the heart, the gold of life ebbs out.
　　We are the old soldiers . . . wounds will come   1125
　　with the crushing sunset of our lives.
　　Death is close, and quick.
CASSANDRA:　　　　　　Look out! *look out!*—
　　Ai, drag the great bull from the mate!—
　　　a thrash of robes, she traps him—
　　writhing—   1130
　　　　black horn glints, twists—
　　　　　　　　　　　she gores him through!
　　And now he buckles, look, the bath swirls red—

---

7. The feast of Thyestes.　　8. Cassandra foresees Clytaemnestra's murder of Agamemnon.　　9. A reference to Menelaus (distant in space) and Orestes (distant in time).

There's stealth and murder in the cauldron, do you hear?
LEADER: I'm no judge, I've little skill with the oracles,
    but even I know danger when I hear it.   1135
CHORUS: What good are the oracles to men? Words, more words,
    and the hurt comes on us, endless words
    and a seer's techniques have brought us
    terror and the truth.
CASSANDRA: The agony—O I am breaking!—Fate's so hard,   1140
    and the pain that floods my voice is mine alone.
    Why have you brought me here, tormented as I am?
    Why, unless to die with him, why else?
LEADER AND CHORUS: Mad with the rapture—god speeds you on
    to the song, the deathsong,   1145
    like the nightingale that broods on sorrow,[1]
    mourns her son, her son,
    her life inspired with grief for him,
    she lilts and shrills, dark bird that lives for night.
CASSANDRA: The nightingale—O for a song, a fate like hers!   1150
    The gods gave her a life of ease, swathed her in wings,
    no tears, no wailing. The knife waits for me.
    They'll splay me on the iron's double edge.
LEADER AND CHORUS: Why?—what god hurls you on, stroke on stroke
    to the long dying fall?   1155
    Why the horror clashing through your music,
    terror struck to song?—
    why the anguish, the wild dance?
    Where do your words of god and grief begin?
CASSANDRA: Ai, the wedding, wedding of Paris,   1160
    death to the loved ones. Oh Scamander,[2]
    you nursed my father . . . once at your banks
        I nursed and grew, and now at the banks
    of Acheron,[3] the stream that carries sorrow,
    it seems I'll chant my prophecies too soon.   1165
LEADER AND CHORUS: What are you saying? Wait, it's clear,
    a child could see the truth, it wounds within,
        like a bloody fang it tears—
    I hear your destiny—breaking sobs,
    cries that stab the ears.   1170
CASSANDRA: Oh the grief, the grief of the city
    ripped to oblivion. Oh the victims,
    the flocks my father burned at the wall,
        rich herds in flames . . . no cure for the doom

1. Philomela was raped by Tereus, the husband of her sister Procne. The two sisters avenged themselves by killing Tereus' son, Itys, and serving up his flesh to Tereus to eat. Procne was changed into a nightingale mourning for Itys (the name is an imitation of the sound of the nightingale's song).   2. A Trojan river. 3. One of the rivers of the underworld.

that took the city after all, and I,   1175
her last ember, I go down with her.

LEADER AND CHORUS: You cannot stop, your song goes on—
    some spirit drops from the heights and treads you down
        and the brutal strain grows—
        your death-throes come and come and   1180
        I cannot see the end!

CASSANDRA: Then off with the veils that hid the fresh young
    bride—[4]
we will see the truth.
Flare up once more, my oracle! Clear and sharp   1185
as the wind that blows toward the rising sun,
I can feel a deeper swell now, gathering head
to break at last and bring the dawn of grief.

No more riddles. I will teach you.
Come, bear witness, run and hunt with me.   1190
We trail the old barbaric works of slaughter.

These roofs—look up—there is a dancing troupe
that never leaves. And they have their harmony
but it is harsh, their words are harsh, they drink
beyond the limit. Flushed on the blood of men   1195
their spirit grows and none can turn away
their revel breeding in the veins—the Furies!
They cling to the house for life. They sing,
sing of the frenzy that began it all,
strain rising on strain, showering curses   1200
on the man who tramples on his brother's bed.[5]

There. Have I hit the mark or not? Am I a fraud,
a fortune-teller babbling lies from door to door?
Swear how well I know the ancient crimes
that live within this house.

LEADER: And if I did?   1205
Would an oath bind the wounds and heal us?
But you amaze me. Bred across the sea,
your language strange, and still you sense the truth
as if you had been here.

CASSANDRA: Apollo the Prophet
introduced me to his gift.   1210

LEADER: A *god*—and moved with love?

CASSANDRA: I was ashamed to tell this once,
    but now . . .

---

4. At this point, as the meter indicates, Cassandra changes from lyric song, the medium of emotion, to spoken iambic lines, the medium of rational discourse.   5. Thyestes, who seduced the wife of his brother, Atreus.

LEADER: We spoil ourselves with scruples,
  long as things go well.
CASSANDRA: He came like a wrestler,
  magnificent, took me down and breathed his fire   1215
  through me and—
LEADER: You bore him a child?
CASSANDRA: I yielded,
  then at the climax I recoiled—I deceived Apollo!
LEADER: But the god's skills—they seized you even then?
CASSANDRA: Even then I told my people all the grief to come.
LEADER: And Apollo's anger never touched you?—is it possible?   1220
CASSANDRA: Once I betrayed him I could never be believed.
LEADER: We believe you. Your visions seem so true.
CASSANDRA: Aieeeee!—
  the pain, the terror! the birth-pang of the seer
  who tells the truth—
                  it whirls me, oh,
  the storm comes again, the crashing chords!   1225
  Look, you see them nestling at the threshold?
  Young, young in the darkness like a dream,
  like children really, yes, and their loved ones
  brought them down . . .
                  their hands, they fill their hands
  with their own flesh, they are serving it like food,   1230
  holding out their entrails . . . now it's clear,
  I can see the armfuls of compassion, see the father
  reach to taste and—
                  For so much suffering,
  I tell you, someone plots revenge.
  A lion who lacks a lion's heart,[6]   1235
  he sprawled at home in the royal lair
  and set a trap for the lord on his return.
  My lord . . . I must wear his yoke, I am his slave.
  The lord of the men-of-war, he obliterated Troy—
  he is so blind, so lost to that detestable hellhound   1240
  who pricks her ears and fawns and her tongue draws out
  her glittering words of welcome—
                  No, he cannot see
  the stroke that Fury's hiding, stealth, murder.
  What outrage—the woman kills the man!
                  What to call
  that . . . monster of Greece, and bring my quarry down?   1245
  Viper coiling back and forth?
                  Some sea-witch?—

6. Aegisthus.

Scylla[7] crouched in her rocky nest—nightmare of sailors?
Raging mother of death, storming deathless war against
the ones she loves!
          And how she howled in triumph,
boundless outrage. Just as the tide of battle   1250
broke her way, she seems to rejoice that he
is safe at home from war, saved for her.
Believe me if you will. What will it matter
if you won't? It comes when it comes,
and soon you'll see it face to face   1255
and say the seer was all too true.
You will be moved with pity.
LEADER: Thyestes' feast,
the children's flesh—that I know,
and the fear shudders through me. It's true,
real, no dark signs about it. I hear the rest   1260
but it throws me off the scent.
CASSANDRA: Agamemnon.
You will see him dead.
LEADER: Peace, poor girl!
Put those words to sleep.
CASSANDRA: No use,
the Healer[8] has no hand in this affair.
LEADER: Not if it's true—but god forbid it is!   1265
CASSANDRA: You pray, and they close in to kill!
LEADER: What man prepares this, this dreadful—
CASSANDRA: Man?
You *are* lost, to every word I've said.
LEADER: Yes—
I don't see who can bring the evil off.
CASSANDRA: And yet I know my Greek, too well.   1270
LEADER: So does the Delphic oracle,[9]
but he's hard to understand.
CASSANDRA: His *fire!*—
sears me, sweeps me again—the torture!
Apollo Lord of the Light, you burn,
you blind me—
         Agony!
            She is the lioness,   1275
she rears on her hind legs, she beds with the wolf
when her lion king goes ranging—
            she will kill me—
Ai, the torture!
        She is mixing her drugs,
adding a measure more of hate for me.

7. A man-eating sea monster; see *Odyssey* XII.   8. Apollo.   9. Its replies were celebrated for their obscurity and ambiguity.

She gloats as she whets the sword for him.   1280
He brought me home and we will pay in carnage.

Why mock yourself with these—trappings, the rod,
the god's wreath, his yoke around my throat?
Before I die I'll tread you—
        [*Ripping off her regalia, stamping it into the ground.*]
                        Down, out,
die die die!   1285
Now you're down. I've paid you back.
Look for another victim—I am free at last—
make her rich in all your curse and doom.
        [*Staggering backwards as if wrestling with a spirit tearing at her robes.*]
                                        See,
Apollo himself, his fiery hands—I feel him again,
he's stripping off my robes, the Seer's robes!   1290
And after he looked down and saw me mocked,
even in these, his glories, mortified by friends
I loved, and they hated me, they were so blind
to their own demise—
                        I went from door to door,
I was wild with the god, I heard them call me   1295
"Beggar! Wretch! Starve for bread in hell!"

And I endured it all, and now he will
extort me as his due. A seer for the Seer.
He brings me here to die like this,
not to serve at my father's altar. No,   1300
the block is waiting. The cleaver steams
with my life blood, the first blood drawn
for the king's last rites.
        [*Regaining her composure and moving to the altar.*]
                        We will die,
but not without some honor from the gods.
There will come another to avenge us,[1]   1305
born to kill his mother, born
his father's champion. A wanderer, a fugitive
driven off his native land, he will come home
to cope the stones of hate that menace all he loves.
The gods have sworn a monumental oath: as his father lies   1310
upon the ground he draws him home with power like a prayer.

Then why so pitiful, why so many tears?
I have seen my city faring as she fared,
and those who took her, judged by the gods,
faring as they fare. I must be brave.   1315

─────────
1. Orestes.

It is my turn to die.
   [*Approaching the doors.*]
I address you as the Gates of Death.
I pray it comes with one clear stroke,
no convulsions, the pulses ebbing out
in gentle death. I'll close my eyes and sleep.   1320
LEADER: So much pain, poor girl, and so much truth,
   you've told so much. But if you *see* it coming,
   clearly—how can you go to your own death,
   like a beast to the altar driven on by god,
   and hold your head so high?
CASSANDRA: No escape, my friends,   1325
   not now.
LEADER: But the last hour should be savored.
CASSANDRA: My time has come. Little to gain from flight.
LEADER: You're brave, believe me, full of gallant heart.
CASSANDRA: Only the wretched go with praise like that.
LEADER: But to go nobly lends a man some grace.   1330
CASSANDRA: My noble father—you and your noble children.
   [*She nears the threshold and recoils, groaning in revulsion.*]
LEADER: What now? what terror flings you back?
   Why? Unless some horror in the brain—
CASSANDRA: Murder.
   The house breathes with murder—bloody shambles![2]
LEADER: No, no, only the victims at the hearth.   1335
CASSANDRA: I know that odor. I smell the open grave.
LEADER: But the Syrian myrrh,[3] it fills the halls with splendor,
   can't you sense it?
CASSANDRA: Well, I must go in now,
   mourning Agamemnon's death and mine.
   Enough of life!
   [*Approaching the doors again and crying out.*]
                  Friends—I cried out,   1340
   not from fear like a bird fresh caught,
   but that you will testify to *how* I died.
   When the queen, woman for woman, dies for me,
   and a man falls for the man who married grief.
   That's all I ask, my friends. A stranger's gift   1345
   for one about to die.
LEADER: Poor creature, you
   and the end you see so clearly. I pity you.
CASSANDRA: I'd like a few words more, a kind of dirge,
   it is my own. I pray to the sun,
   the last light I'll see,   1350
   that when the avengers cut the assassins down

---

2. A slaughterhouse.   3. Incense burned at the sacrifice. Another interpretation of this line runs: "What
you speak of [i.e., the smell of the open grave] is no Syrian incense, giving splendor to the palace."

they will avenge me too, a slave who died,
an easy conquest.
               Oh men, your destiny.
When all is well a shadow can overturn it.
When trouble comes a stroke of the wet sponge,   1355
and the picture's blotted out. And that,
I think that breaks the heart.
    [*She goes through the doors.*]
CHORUS: But the lust for power never dies—
    men cannot have enough.
No one will lift a hand to send it   1360
from his door, to give it warning,
"Power, never come again!"
Take this man: the gods in glory
gave him Priam's city to plunder,
brought him home in splendor like a god.   1365
But now if he must pay for the blood
    his fathers shed, and die for the deaths
he brought to pass, and bring more death
to avenge his dying, show us one
    who boasts himself born free   1370
of the raging angel, once he hears—
    [*Cries break out within the palace.*]
AGAMEMNON: Aagh!
Struck deep—the death-blow, deep—
LEADER: Quiet. Cries,
but who? Someone's stabbed—
AGAMEMNON: Aaagh, again . . .
second blow—struck home.
LEADER: The work is done,
you can feel it. The king, and the great cries—   1375
Close ranks now, find the right way out.
    [*But the old men scatter, each speaks singly.*]
CHORUS:—I say send out heralds, muster the guard,
    they'll save the house.

             —And I say rush in now,
catch them red-handed—butchery running on their blades.

—Right with you, do something—now or never!   1380

—Look at them, beating the drum for insurrection.

                  —Yes,
we're wasting time. They rape the name of caution,
their hands will never sleep.

          —Not a plan in sight.
Let men of action do the planning, too.

—I'm helpless. Who can raise the dead with words?   1385

—What, drag out our lives? bow down to the tyrants,
the ruin of the house?

                    —Never, better to die
on your feet than live on your knees.

                              —Wait,
do we take the cries for signs, prophesy like seers
and give him up for dead?

                              —No more suspicions,   1390
not another word till we have proof.

                              —Confusion
on all sides—one thing to do. See how it stands
with Agamemnon, once and for all we'll see—
[*He rushes at the doors. They open and reveal a silver cauldron that
holds the body of* AGAMEMNON *shrouded in bloody robes, with the
body of* CASSANDRA *to his left and* CLYTAEMNESTRA *standing to his
right, sword in hand. She strides towards the* CHORUS.]
CLYTAEMNESTRA: Words, endless words I've said to serve the moment—
Now it makes me proud to tell the truth.   1395
How else to prepare a death for deadly men
who seem to love you? How to rig the nets
of pain so high no man can overleap them?

I brooded on this trial, this ancient blood feud
year by year. At last my hour came.   1400
Here I stand and here I struck
and here my work is done.
I did it all. I don't deny it, no.
He had no way to flee or fight his destiny—
[*Unwinding the robes from* AGAMEMNON's *body, spreading them before
the altar where the old men cluster around them, unified as a chorus
once again.*]
our never-ending, all embracing net, I cast it   1405
wide for the royal haul, I coil him round and round
in the wealth, the robes of doom, and then I strike him
once, twice, and at each stroke he cries in agony—
he buckles at the knees and crashes here!
And when he's down I add the third, last blow,   1410
to the Zeus who saves the dead beneath the ground
I send that third blow[4] home in homage like a prayer.

So he goes down, and the life is bursting out of him—
great sprays of blood, and the murderous shower

_____
4. Like the third libation to Zeus above.

wounds me, dyes me black and I, I revel   1415
like the Earth when the spring rains come down,
the blessed gifts of god, and the new green spear
splits the sheath and rips to birth in glory!

So it stands, elders of Argos gathered here.
Rejoice if you can rejoice—I glory.   1420
And if I'd pour upon his body the libation
it deserves, what wine could match my words?
It is right and more than right. He flooded
the vessel of our proud house with misery,
with the vintage of the curse and now   1425
he drains the dregs. My lord is home at last.

LEADER: You appall me, you, your brazen words—
exulting over your fallen king.

CLYTAEMNESTRA: And you,
you try me like some desperate woman.
My heart is steel, well you know. Praise me,   1430
blame me as you choose. It's all one.
Here is Agamemnon, my husband made a corpse
by this right hand—a masterpiece of Justice.
Done is done.

CHORUS: Woman!—what poison cropped from the soil
or strained from the heaving sea, what nursed you,   1435
drove you insane? You brave the curse of Greece.
    You have cut away and flung away and now
the people cast you off to exile,
broken with our hate.

CLYTAEMNESTRA: And now you sentence me?—
you banish *me* from the city, curses breathing   1440
down my neck? But he—
name one charge you brought against him then.
He thought no more of it than killing a beast,
and his flocks were rich, teeming in their fleece,
but he sacrificed his own child, our daughter,   1445
the agony I labored into love,
to charm away the savage winds of Thrace.[5]

Didn't the law demand you banish him?—
hunt him from the land for all his guilt?
But now you witness what I've done   1450
and you are ruthless judges.
                    Threaten away!
I'll meet you blow for blow. And if I fall
the throne is yours. If god decrees the reverse,
late as it is, old men, you'll learn your place.

---

5. I.e., winds from the North (at Aulis).

CHORUS: Mad with ambition,   1455
    shrilling pride!—some Fury
crazed with the carnage rages through your brain—
    I can see the flecks of blood inflame your eyes!
But vengeance comes—you'll lose your loved ones,
stroke for painful stroke.   1460
CLYTAEMNESTRA: Then learn this, too, the power of my oaths.
By the child's Rights I brought to birth,
by Ruin, by Fury—the three gods to whom
I sacrificed this man—I swear my hopes
will never walk the halls of fear so long   1465
as Aegisthus lights the fire on my hearth.
Loyal to me as always, no small shield
to buttress my defiance.   Here he lies.
He brutalized me. The darling of all
the golden girls[6] who spread the gates of Troy.   1470
And here his spearprize . . . what wonders she beheld!—
the seer of Apollo shared my husband's bed,
his faithful mate who knelt at the rowing-benches,
worked by every hand.   They have their rewards.
He as you know. And she, the swan of the gods   1475
who lived to sing her latest, dying song—
his lover lies beside him.
She brings a fresh, voluptuous relish to my bed!
CHORUS: Oh quickly, let me die—
no bed of labor, no, no wasting illness . . .   1480
bear me off in the sleep that never ends,
    now that he has fallen,
now that our dearest shield lies battered—
    Woman made him suffer,
    woman struck him down.   1485

    Helen the wild, maddening Helen,
    one for the many, the thousand lives
    you murdered under Troy. Now you are crowned
    with this consummate wreath, the blood
    that lives in memory, glistens age to age.   1490
    Once in the halls she walked and she was war,
    angel of war, angel of agony, lighting men to death.

CLYTAEMNESTRA: Pray no more for death, broken
    as you are. And never turn
        your wrath on her, call her   1495
    the scourge of men, the one alone

6. In Greek *Chryseidon*, which recalls the girl in the first book of the *Iliad*, Chryseis, whom Agamemnon said he preferred to Clytaemnestra (*Iliad*, I. 133).

who destroyed a myriad Greek lives—
Helen the grief that never heals.
CHORUS: The *spirit!*—you who tread
   the house and the twinborn sons of Tantalus—[7]   1500
   you empower the sisters, Fury's twins
      whose power tears the heart!
   Perched on the corpse your carrion raven
      glories in her hymn,
         her screaming hymn of pride.   1505
CLYTAEMNESTRA: Now you set your judgment straight,
   you summon *him!* Three generations
      feed the spirit in the race.
   Deep in the veins he feeds our bloodlust—
   aye, before the old wound dies   1510
   it ripens in another flow of blood.
CHORUS: The great curse of the house, the spirit,
      dead weight wrath—and you can praise it!
   Praise the insatiate doom that feeds
   relentless on our future and our sons.   1515
   Oh all through the will of Zeus,
   the cause of all, the one who works it all.
      What comes to birth that is not Zeus?
   Our lives are pain, what part not come from god?

      Oh, my king, my captain,   1520
      how to salute you, how to mourn you?
      What can I say with all my warmth and love?
      Here in the black widow's web you lie,
      gasping out your life
      in a sacrilegious death, dear god,   1525
      reduced to a slave's bed,
      my king of men, yoked by stealth and Fate,
      by the wife's hand that thrust the two-edged sword.

CLYTAEMNESTRA: You claim the work is mine, call me
   Agamemnon's wife—you are so wrong.   1530
   Fleshed in the wife of this dead man,
      the spirit lives within me,
   our savage ancient spirit of revenge.
   In return for Atreus' brutal feast
   he kills his perfect son—for every   1535
   murdered child, a crowning sacrifice.
CHORUS: And *you,* innocent of his murder?
      And who could swear to that? and how? . . .
   and still an avenger could arise,
   bred by the fathers' crimes, and lend a hand.   1540

7. Father of Pelops, grandfather of Atreus. "Sons" here must mean "descendants," i.e., Agamemnon and Menelaus.

He wades in the blood of brothers,
stream on mounting stream—black war erupts
    and where he strides revenge will stride,
clots will mass for the young who were devoured.

    Oh my king, my captain,   1545
    how to salute you, how to mourn you?
    What can I say with all my warmth and love?
    Here in the black widow's web you lie,
    gasping out your life
    in a sacrilegious death, dear god,   1550
    reduced to a slave's bed,
    my king of men, yoked by stealth and Fate,
    by the wife's hand that thrust the two-edged sword.

CLYTAEMNESTRA: No slave's death, I think—
    no stealthier than the death he dealt   1555
    our house and the offspring of our loins,
      Iphigeneia, girl of tears.
    Act for act, wound for wound!
    Never exult in Hades, swordsman,
    here you are repaid. By the sword   1560
    you did your work and by the sword you die.

CHORUS: The mind reels—where to turn?
        All plans dashed, all hope! I cannot think . . .
    the roofs are toppling, I dread the drumbeat thunder
        the heavy rains of blood will crush the house   1565
            the first light rains are over—
        Justice brings new acts of agony, yes,
    on new grindstones Fate is grinding sharp the sword of Justice.
Earth, dear Earth,
    if only you'd drawn me under   1570
    long before I saw him huddled
    in the beaten silver bath.
    Who will bury him, lift his dirge?
    [Turning to CLYTAEMNESTRA.]
    You, can you dare this?
    To kill your lord with your own hand   1575
    then mourn his soul with tributes, terrible tributes—
    do his enormous works a great dishonor.
    This godlike man, this hero. Who at the grave
    will sing his praises, pour the wine of tears?
    Who will labor there with truth of heart?   1580
CLYTAEMNESTRA: This is no concern of yours.
    The hand that bore and cut him down
    will hand him down to Mother Earth.
    This house will never mourn for him.
    Only our daughter Iphigeneia,   1585

by all rights, will rush to meet him
first at the churning straits,[8]
the ferry over tears—
she'll fling her arms around her father,
pierce him with her love.   1590

CHORUS: Each charge meets counter-charge.
                    None can judge between them. Justice.
          The plunderer plundered, the killer pays the price.
          The truth still holds while Zeus still holds the throne:
                    the one who acts must suffer—   1595
               that is law. Who, who can tear from the veins
          the bad seed, the curse? The race is welded to its ruin.

CLYTAEMNESTRA: At last you see the future and the truth!
     But I will swear a pact with the spirit
     born within us. I embrace his works,   1600
     cruel as they are but done at last,
          if he will leave our house
     in the future, bleed another line
     with kinsmen murdering kinsmen.
     Whatever he may ask. A few things   1605
     are all I need, once I have purged
     our fury to destroy each other—
          purged it from our halls.
     [AEGISTHUS *has emerged from the palace with his bodyguard and stands*
     triumphant over the body of AEGISTHUS.]
AEGISTHUS: O what a brilliant day
     it is for vengeance! Now I can say once more
     there are gods in heaven avenging men,   1610
     blazing down on all the crimes of earth.
     Now at last I see this man brought down
     in the Furies' tangling robes. It feasts my eyes—
     he pays for the plot his father's hand contrived.

     Atreus, this man's father, was king of Argos.   1615
     My father, Thyestes—let me make this clear—
     Atreus' brother challenged him for the crown,
     and Atreus drove him out of house and home
     then lured him back, and home Thyestes came,
     poor man, a suppliant to his own hearth,   1620
     to pray that Fate might save him.
                         So it did.
     There was no dying, no staining our native ground
     with *his* blood. Thyestes was the guest,

8. The river of the lower world over which the dead were ferried.

and this man's godless father—
        [*Pointing to* AGAMEMNON.]
the zeal of the host outstripping a brother's love,   1625
made my father a feast that seemed a feast for gods,
a love feast of his children's flesh.
                        He cuts
the extremities, feet and delicate hands
into small pieces, scatters them over the dish
and serves it to Thyestes throned on high.   1630
He picks at the flesh he cannot recognize,
the soul of innocence eating the food of ruin—
look,
        [*Pointing to the bodies at his feet.*]
                that feeds upon the house! And then,
when he sees the monstrous thing he's done, he shrieks,
he reels back head first and vomits up that butchery,   1635
tramples the feast—brings down the curse of Justice:
"Crash to ruin, all the race of Pleisthenes,[9] crash down!"

So you see him, down. And I, the weaver of Justice,
plotted out the kill. Atreus drove us into exile,
my struggling father and I, a babe-in-arms,   1640
his last son, but I became a man
and Justice brought me home. I was abroad
but I reached out and seized my man,
link by link I clamped the fatal scheme
together. Now I could die gladly, even I—   1645
now I see this monster in the nets of Justice.
LEADER: Aegisthus, you revel in pain—you sicken me.
You say you killed the king in cold blood,
singlehanded planned his pitiful death?
I say there's no escape. In the hour of judgment,   1650
trust to this, your head will meet the people's
rocks and curses.
AEGISTHUS: You say! you slaves at the oars—
while the master of the benches cracks the whip?
You'll learn, in your late age, how much it hurts
to teach old bones their place. We have techniques—   1655
chains and the pangs of hunger,
two effective teachers, excellent healers.
They can even cure old men of pride and gall.
Look—can't you see? The more you kick
against the pricks, the more you suffer.   1660
LEADER: You, pathetic—
the king had just returned from battle.

---

9. A name sometimes inserted into the genealogy of the house of Tantalus.

You waited out the war and fouled his lair,
you planned my great commander's fall.
AEGISTHUS: Talk on—
    you'll scream for every word, my little Orpheus.[1]   1665
    We'll see if the world comes dancing to your song,
    your absurd barking—snarl your breath away!
    I'll make you dance, I'll bring you all to heel.
LEADER: You rule Argos? You who schemed his death
    but cringed to cut him down with your own hand?   1670
AEGISTHUS: The treachery was the woman's work, clearly.
    I was a marked man, his enemy for ages.
    But I will use his riches, stop at nothing
    to civilize his people. All but the rebel:
    him I'll yoke and break—   1675
    no cornfed colt, running free in the traces.
    Hunger, ruthless mate of the dark torture-chamber,
    trains her eyes upon him till he drops!
LEADER: Coward, why not kill the man yourself?
    Why did the woman, the corruption of Greece   1680
    and the gods of Greece, have to bring him down?
    Orestes—If he still sees the light of day,
    bring him home, good Fates, home to kill
    this pair at last. Our champion in slaughter!
AEGISTHUS: Bent on insolence? Well, you'll learn, quickly.   1685
    At them, men—you have your work at hand!
    [His men draw swords; the old men take up their sticks.]
LEADER: At them, fist at the hilt, to the last man—
AEGISTHUS: Fist at the hilt, I'm not afraid to die.
LEADER: It's death you want and death you'll have—
    we'll make that word your last.
    [CLYTAEMNESTRA moves between them, restraining AEGISTHUS.]
CLYTAEMNESTRA: No more, my dearest,   1690
    no more grief. We have too much to reap
    right here, our mighty harvest of despair.
    Our lives are based on pain. No bloodshed now.

    Fathers of Argos, turn for home before you act
    and suffer for it. What we did was destiny.   1695
    If we could end the suffering, how we would rejoice.
    The spirit's brutal hoof has struck our heart.
    And that is what a woman has to say.
    Can you accept the truth?
    [CLYTAEMNESTRA turns to leave.]
AEGISTHUS: But these . . . mouths
    that bloom in filth—spitting insults in my teeth.   1700

1. A mythical singer who charmed all nature with his music.

You tempt your fates, you insubordinate dogs—
to hurl abuse at me, your master!
LEADER: No Greek
    worth his salt would grovel at your feet.
AEGISTHUS: I—I'll stalk you all your days!
LEADER: Not if the spirit brings Orestes home.   1705
AEGISTHUS: Exiles feed on hope—well I know.
LEADER: More,
    gorge yourself to bursting—soil justice, while you can.
AEGISTHUS: I promise you, you'll pay, old fools—in good time, too!
LEADER: Strut on your own dunghill, you cock beside your mate.
CLYTAEMNESTRA: Let them howl—they're impotent. You and I have   1710
    power now.
We will set the house in order once for all.
    [*They enter the palace; the great doors close behind them; the old
    men disband and wander off.*]

The Libation Bearers

Characters

ORESTES, *son of Agamemnon and*   CLYTAEMNESTRA
    Clytaemnestra   CILISSA, *Orestes' old nurse*
PYLADES, *his companion*   AEGISTHUS
ELECTRA, *his sister*   A SERVANT *of Aegisthus*
CHORUS *of Slavewomen and their*   *Attendants of Orestes, bodyguard of*
    LEADER   *Aegisthus*

[TIME AND SCENE: *Several years have passed since Agamemnon's death.
At Argos, before the tomb of the king and his fathers, stands an altar;
behind it looms the house of Atreus.* ORESTES *and* PYLADES *enter, dressed
as travelers.* ORESTES *kneels and prays.*[1]]

ORESTES: Hermes, lord of the dead, look down and guard
    the fathers' power. Be my savior, I beg you,
    be my comrade now.
                    I have come home
    to my own soil, an exile home at last.
    Here at the mounded grave I call my father,   5
    Hear me—I am crying out to you . . .
    [*He cuts two locks of hair and lays them on the grave.*]
    There is a lock for Inachos[2] who nursed me
    into manhood, there is one for death.

1. The beginning of the play (perhaps as many as thirty lines) is missing in our manuscripts. Nine lines
have been assembled from other ancient authors who quoted them.   2. The river of Thebes. Greek
youths, on coming to manhood, offered a lock of their hair to the river of their country as thanks for the
nurture it had helped to provide. And locks of hair were offered on the graves of the dead.

I was not here to mourn you when you died,
my father, never gave the last salute   10
when they bore your corpse away.

> [ELECTRA *and a chorus of slave-women enter in procession. They are*
> *dressed in black and bear libations, moving toward* ORESTES *at the*
> *grave.*]

                                   What's this?
Look, a company moving toward us. Women,
robed in black . . . so clear in the early light.

I wonder what they mean, what turn of fate?—
some new wound to the house?   15
Or perhaps they come to honor you, my father,
bearing cups[3] to soothe and still the dead.
That's right, it must be . . .
Electra, I think I see *her* coming, there,
my own sister, worn, radiant in her grief—   20
Dear god, let me avenge my father's murder—
fight beside me now with all your might!

Out of their way, Pylades.[4] I must know
what they mean, these women turning towards us,
what their prayers call forth.   25

> [*They withdraw behind the tomb.*]

CHORUS: Rushed from the house we come
    escorting cups for the dead,
in step with the hands' hard beat,
    our cheeks glistening,
flushed where the nails have raked new furrows running blood;[5]   30
and life beats on, and through it all
we nurse our lives with tears,
to the sound of ripping linen beat our robes in sorrow,
    close to the breast the beats throb
and laughter's gone and fortune throbs and throbs.   35

Aie!—bristling Terror struck—
    Terror the seer of the house,
the nightmare ringing clear
    breathed its wrath in sleep,
in the midnight watch a cry!—the voice of Terror   40
deep in the house, bursting down
on the women's darkened chambers, yes,
and the old ones, skilled at dreams, swore oaths to god and called,

---

3. Libations, drink offerings to pour on the grave.   4. Son of Strophios, who was Orestes' host in his
kingdom of Phocis.   5. This and the following lines list the semiritual actions of mourning for the dead:
scratching the cheek, beating the head and breast, ripping clothes.

"The proud dead stir under earth,
they rage against the ones who took their lives." 45

But the gifts,[6] the empty gifts
    she hopes will ward them off—
good Mother Earth!—that godless woman sends me here . . .
    I dread to say her prayer.
What can redeem the blood that wets the soil? 50
Oh for the hearthfire banked with grief,
    the rampart's down, a fine house down—
dark, dark, and the sun, the life is curst,
    and mist enshrouds the halls
        where the lords of war went down. 55

And the ancient pride no war,
        no storm, no force could tame,
ringing in all men's ears, in all men's hearts is gone.
    They are afraid. Success,
they bow to success, more god than god himself. 60
But justice waits and turns the scales:
    a sudden blow for some at dawn,
for some in the no man's land of dusk
    her torments grow with time,
        and the lethal night takes others. 65

And the blood that Mother Earth consumes
clots hard, it won't seep through, it breeds revenge
    and frenzy goes through the guilty,
seething like infection, swarming through the brain.

For the one who treads a virgin's bed 70
there is no cure. All the streams of the world,
    all channels run into one
to cleanse a man's red hands will swell the bloody tide.[7]

And I . . . Fate and the gods brought down their yoke,
they ringed our city, out of our fathers' halls 75
    they led us here as slaves.[8]
And the will breaks, we kneel at their command—
        our masters right or wrong!
    And we beat the tearing hatred down,
    behind our veils we weep for her, 80
    [*Turning to* ELECTRA.]
her senseless fate.
Sorrow turns the secret heart to ice.

6. Clytaemnestra's nightmare is interpreted by the "old ones, skilled at dreams": the dead are angry with
their killers. The gifts are the libations poured on the grave to appease the wrathful dead. They were a
mixture of honey, oil, wine, milk, and water.   7. Bloodguilt can no more be washed away than virginity
restored.   8. The chorus consists of women enslaved when their city was captured. It is not so stated in
the text but they are probably Trojan captives brought home by Agamemnon.

ELECTRA: Dear women,
you keep the house in order, best you can;
and now you've come to the grave to say a prayer
with me, my escorts. I'll need your help with this.   85
What to say when I pour the cup of sorrow?
[*Lifting her libation cup.*]
What kindness, what prayer can touch my father?
Shall I say I bring him love for love, a woman's
love for husband? My mother, love from her?
I've no taste for that, no words to say   90
as I run the honeyed oil on father's tomb.

Or try the salute we often use at graves?
"A wreath for a wreath. Now bring the givers
gifts to match" . . . no, give them pain for pain.

Or silent, dishonored, just as father died,   95
empty it out for the soil to drink and then
retrace my steps, like a slave sent out with scourings
left from the purging of the halls, and throw
the cup behind me, looking straight ahead.[9]
Help me decide, my friends. Join me here.   100
We nurse a common hatred in the house.
Don't hide your feelings—no, fear no one.
Destiny waits us all,
    [*Looking toward the tomb.*]
                              born free,
or slaves who labor under another's hand.
Speak to me, please. Perhaps you've had   105
a glimpse of something better.
LEADER: I revere
your father's death-mound like an altar.
I'll say a word, now that you ask,
that comes from deep within me.
ELECTRA: Speak on,
with everything you feel for father's grave.   110
LEADER: Say a blessing as you pour, for those who love you.
ELECTRA: And of the loved ones, whom to call my friends?
LEADER: First yourself, then all who hate Aegisthus.
ELECTRA: I and you. I can say a prayer for us
and then for—
LEADER: You know, try to say it.   115
ELECTRA: There is someone else to rally to our side?
LEADER: Remember Orestes, even abroad and gone.
ELECTRA: Well said, the best advice I've had.

---

9. After throwing away refuse, an ancient Greek returned without looking back, as if afraid that the action
might have provoked some hostile powers.

LEADER: Now for the murderers. Remember them and—
ELECTRA: What?
  I'm so unseasoned, teach me what to say.   120
LEADER: Let some god or man come down upon them.
ELECTRA: Judge or avenger, which?
LEADER: Just say "the one who murders in return!"
ELECTRA: How can I ask the gods for that
  and keep my conscience clear?
LEADER: How not,[1]   125
  and pay the enemy back in kind?
      [ELECTRA *kneels at the grave in prayer.*]
ELECTRA: —Herald king
  of the world above and the quiet world below,
  lord of the dead, my Hermes, help me now.
  Tell the spirits underground to hear my prayers,
  and the high watch hovering over father's roofs,   130
  and have her listen too, the Earth herself
  who brings all things to life and makes them strong,
  then gathers in the rising tide once more.

  And I will tip libations to the dead.
  I call out to my father. Pity me,   135
  dear Orestes too.
  Rekindle the light that saves our house!
  We're auctioned off, drift like vagrants now.
  Mother has pawned us for a husband, Aegisthus,
  her partner in her murdering.
                              I go like a slave,   140
  and Orestes driven from his estates while they,
  they roll in the fruits of all your labors,
  magnificent and sleek. O bring Orestes home,
  with a happy twist of fate, my father. Hear me,
  make me far more self-possessed than mother,   145
  make this hand more pure.

  These prayers for us. For our enemies I say,
  Raise up your avenger, into the light, my father—
  kill the killers in return, with justice!
  So in the midst of prayers for good I place   150
  this curse for them.
                      Bring up your blessings,
  up into the air, led by the gods and Earth
  and all the rights that bring us triumph.
      [*Pouring libations on the tomb and turning to the women.*]
  These are my prayers. Over them I pour libations.

---

1. Common Greek morality saw nothing wrong in individual vengeance. But it will lead, in this play, to a son's murder of a mother, and in the last play be superseded by communal justice.

Yours to adorn them with laments, to make them bloom,   155
so custom says—sing out and praise the dead.
CHORUS: Let the tears fall, ring out and die,
     die with the warlord at this bank,
this bulwark of the good, defense against the bad,
the guilt, the curse we ward away   160
with prayer and all we pour. Hear me, majesty, hear me,
     lord of glory, from the darkness of your heart.
                              Ohhhhhh!—
Dear god, let him come! Some man
with a strong spear, born to free the house,
     with the torsion bow of Scythia[2] bent for slaughter,   165
splattering shafts like a god of war—sword in fist
     for the slash-and-hack of battle!
     [ELECTRA *remains at the grave, staring at the ground.*]
ELECTRA: Father,
you have it now, the earth has drunk your wine.
Wait, friends, here's news. Come share it.
LEADER: Speak on,
my heart's a dance of fear.
ELECTRA: A lock of hair,   170
here on the grave . . .
LEADER: Whose? A man's?
A growing girl's?
ELECTRA: And it has the marks,
and anyone would think—
LEADER: What?
We're old. You're young, now you teach us.
ELECTRA: No one could have cut this lock but I and—   175
LEADER: Callous they are, the ones who ought to shear
the hair and mourn.
ELECTRA: Look at the texture, just like—
LEADER: Whose? I want to know.
ELECTRA: Like mine, identical,
can't you see?
LEADER: Orestes . . . he brought a gift
in secret?
ELECTRA: It's *his*—I can see his curls.   180
LEADER: And how could he risk the journey here?
ELECTRA: He sent it, true, a lock to honor father.
LEADER: All the more cause for tears. You mean
he'll never set foot on native ground again.
ELECTRA: Yes!
It's sweeping over me too—anguish   185
like a breaker—a sword ripping through my heart!

_____

2. The Scythians, who lived far to the north and east of Greece, were famous archers.

Tears come like the winter rains that flood the gates—
can't hold them back, when I see this lock of hair.

How could I think another Greek[3] could play
the prince with this?
                        She'd never cut it,   190
the murderess, my mother. She insults the name,
she and her godless spirit preying on her children.

But how, how can I come right out and say it *is*
the glory of the dearest man I know—Orestes?
Stop, I'm fawning on hope.
                        Oh, if only   195
it had a herald's voice, kind and human—
I'm so shaken, torn—and told me clearly
to throw it away, they severed it from a head
that I detest. Or it could sorrow with me
like a brother, aye,   200
this splendor come to honor father's grave.

We call on the gods, and the gods well know
what storms torment us, sailors whirled to nothing.
But if we are to live and reach the haven,
one small seed could grow a mighty tree—   205
Look, tracks.
                A new sign to tell us more.
Footmarks . . . pairs of them, like mine.
Two outlines, two prints, his own, and there,
a fellow traveler's.
        [*Putting her foot into* ORESTES' *print.*]
                        The heel, the curve of the arch
like twins.[4]
        [*While* ORESTES *emerges from behind the grave, she follows cautiously in his steps until they come together.*]
                Step by step, my step in his . . .
                                we meet—   210
Oh the pain, like pangs of labor—this is madness!
ORESTES: Pray for the future. Tell the gods they've brought
        your prayers to birth, and pray that we succeed.
        [ELECTRA *draws back, struggling for composure.*]
ELECTRA: The gods—why now? What have I ever won from them?
ORESTES: The sight you prayed to see for many years.   215
ELECTRA: And you know the one I call?
ORESTES: I know Orestes,
        know he moves you deeply.

---

3. Only a close relative would have done it.   4. Since Greeks wore open sandals they were much more conscious than we are of the shape of each other's feet. Cf. *Odyssey,* IV. 156, where Menelaus sees a resemblance between the feet of Telemachus and Odysseus.

ELECTRA: Yes,
  but now what's come to fill my prayers?
ORESTES: Here I am. Look no further.
  No one loves you more than I.
ELECTRA: No,   220
  it's a trap, stranger . . . a net you tie around me?
ORESTES: Then I tie myself as well.
ELECTRA: But the pain,
  you're laughing at all—
ORESTES: Your pain is mine.
  If I laugh at yours, I only laugh at mine.
ELECTRA: *Orestes*—
  can I call you?—are you really—   225
ORESTES: I am!
  Open your eyes. So slow to learn.
  You saw the lock of hair I cut in mourning.
  You scanned my tracks, you could see my marks,
  your breath leapt, you all but saw me in the flesh—   230
  Look—
    [*Holding the lock to his temple, then to* ELECTRA*'s.*]
      put it where I cut it.
  It's your brother's. Try, it matches yours.
    [*Removing a strip of weaving from his clothing.*]
  Work of your own hand, you tamped the loom,
  look, there are wild creatures in the weaving.
    [*She kneels beside him, weeping; he lifts her to her feet and they
    embrace.*]
  No, no, control yourself—don't lose yourself in joy!   235
  Our loved ones, well I know, would slit our throats.
LEADER: Dearest, the darling of your father's house,
  hope of the seed we nursed with tears—you save us.
  Trust to your power, win your father's house once more!
ELECTRA: You light to my eyes, four loves in one!   240
  I have to call you father, it is fate;
  and I turn to you the love I gave my mother—
  I despise her, she deserves it, yes,
  and the love I gave my sister, sacrificed
  on the cruel sword, I turn to you.   245
  You were my faith, my brother—
  you alone restore my self-respect.
    [*Praying.*]
  Power and Justice, Saving Zeus, Third Zeus,[5]
  almighty all in all, be with us now.
ORESTES: Zeus, Zeus, watch over all we do,   250
  fledglings reft of the noble eagle father.

5. Zeus is called on when the third libation is poured at the feast (see *Agamemnon*, l. 244, and note):
Zeus was third in the succession of the rulers of the gods (see *Agamemnon*, l. 169 note).

He died in the coils, the viper's dark embrace.
We are his orphans worn down with hunger,
weak, too young to haul the father's quarry
home to shelter.
                    Look down on us!   255
I and Electra too, I tell you, children
robbed of our father, both of us bound
in exile from our house.
                    And what a father—
a priest at sacrifice, he showered you
with honors. Put an end to his nestlings now   260
and who will serve you banquets rich as his?
Destroy the eagle's brood, you can never
send a sign that wins all men's belief.
Rot the stock of a proud dynastic tree—
it can never shore your altar steaming   265
with the oxen in the mornings.
                              Tend us—
we seem in ruins now, I know. Up from nothing
rear a house to greatness.

LEADER: Softly, children,
white hopes of your father's hearth. Someone
might hear you, children, charmed with his own voice   270
blurt all this out to the masters. Oh, just once
to see them— live bones crackling in the fire
spitting pitch!

ORESTES: Apollo will never fail me, no,
his tremendous power, his oracle charges me
to see this trial through.
                          I can still hear the god—   275
a high voice ringing with winters of disaster,
piercing the heart within me, warm and strong,
unless I hunt my father's murderers, cut them down
in their own style—they destroyed my birthright.
"Gore them like a bull!" he called, "or pay their debt   280
with your own life, one long career of grief."

He revealed so much about us,
told how the dead take root beneath the soil,
they grow with hate and plague the lives of men.
He told of the leprous boils that ride the flesh,[6]   285
their wild teeth gnawing the mother tissue, aye,
and a white scurf spreads like cancer over these,
and worse, he told how assaults of Furies spring
to life on the father's blood . . .

6. This list of the loathsome afflictions that await the man who fails to avenge his murdered father moves
from disease to social ostracism; the man who fails in his duty dies cut off from society and the gods.

                    You can *see* them—
the eyes burning, grim brows working over you in the dark—   290
the dark sword of the dead—your murdered kinsmen
pleading for revenge. And the madness haunts
the midnight watch, the empty terror shakes you,
harries, drives you on—an exile from your city—
a brazen whip will mutilate your back.   295
For such as us, no share in the winebowl,
no libations poured in love. You never see
your father's wrath but it pulls you from the altars.
There is no refuge, none to take you in.
A pariah, reviled, at long last you die,   300
withered in the grip of all this dying.

Such oracles are persuasive,
don't you think?   And even if I am not convinced,
the rough work of the world is still to do.
So many yearnings meet and urge me on.   305
The god's commands. Mounting sorrow for father.
Besides, the lack of patrimony presses hard;
and my compatriots, the glory of men
who toppled Troy with nerves of singing steel,
go at the beck and call of a brace of women.   310
Womanhearted he is[7]—if not, we'll soon see.
    [*The* LEADER *lights the altar fires.* ORESTES, ELECTRA, *and the* CHORUS
    gather for the invocation at the grave.]
CHORUS: Powers of destiny, mighty queens of Fate!—
    by the will of Zeus your will be done,
    press on to the end now,
        Justice turns the wheel.   315
    "Word for word, curse for curse
    be born now," Justice thunders,
        hungry for retribution,
    "stroke for bloody stroke be paid.
        The one who acts must suffer."   320
    Three generations strong the word resounds.
ORESTES: Dear father, father of dread,
    what can I do or say to reach you now?
        What breath can reach from here
    to the bank where you lie moored at anchor?   325
    What light can match your darkness? None,
    but there is a kind of grace that comes
        when the tears revive a proud old house
    and Atreus' sons, the warlords lost and gone.
LEADER: The ruthless jaws of the fire,   330

─────────

7. I.e., Aegisthus is a coward; Argos is ruled by a "brace of women."

my child, can never tame the dead,
    his rage inflames his sons.
Men die and the voices rise, they light the guilty, true—
cries raised for the fathers, clear and just,
    will hunt their killers harried to the end.   335
ELECTRA: Then hear me now, my father,
    it is my turn, my tears are welling now,
      as child by child we come
to the tomb and raise the dirge, my father.
Your grave receives a girl in prayer   340
and a man in flight, and we are one,
    and the pain is equal, whose is worse?
And who outwrestles death—what third last fall?[8]
CHORUS: But still some god, if he desires,
    may work our strains to a song of joy,   345
from the dirges chanted over the grave
    may lift a hymn in the kings' halls
and warm the loving cup you stir this morning.
ORESTES:[9] If only at Troy
a Lycian[1] cut you down, my father—   350
gone, with an aura left at home behind you,
    children to go their ways
and the eyes look on them bright with awe,
and the tomb you win on headlands seas away
    would buoy up the house . . .   355
LEADER: And loved by the men you loved
    who died in glory, there you'd rule
      beneath the earth—lord, prince,
stern aide to the giant kings who judge the shadows there.
You were a king of kings when you drew breath;   360
    the mace you held could make men kneel or die.
ELECTRA: No, not under Troy!—
    not dead and gone with them, my father,
hordes pierced by the spear Scamander washes down.
    Sooner the killers die   365
as they killed you—at the hands of friends,
and the news of death would come from far away,
    we'd never know this grief.
CHORUS: You are dreaming, children,
    dreams dearer than gold, more blest   370
than the Blest beyond the Northwind's raging.[2]
    Dreams are easy, oh,
but the double lash is striking home.

---

8. There were three falls in a Greek wrestling match.   9. Compare this and the next stanza with the speech of Achilles in Hades (*Odyssey*, XXIV. 22).   1. Allies of the Trojans; their kings were the famous warriors Glaukos and Sarpedon.   2. The land of the Hyperboreans, a legendary race of worshipers of Apollo who lived a paradisal life in the far North.

Now our comrades group underground.
Our masters' reeking hands are doomed—   375
      the children take the day!
ORESTES: That thrills his ear,
      that arrow lands!
      Zeus, Zeus, force up from the earth
destruction, late but true to the mark,   380
to the reckless heart, the killing hand—
      for parents of revenge revenge be done.
LEADER: And the ripping cries of triumph mine
to sing when the man is stabbed,
      the woman dies—[3]   385
      why, why hide what's deep inside me,
black wings beating, storming the spirit's prow—
      hurricane, slashing hatred!
ELECTRA: Both fists at once
      come down, come down—
      Zeus, *crush* their skulls! Kill! kill!   390
Now give the land some faith, I beg you,
from these ancient wrongs bring forth our rights.
      Hear me, Earth, and all you lords of death.
CHORUS: It is the law: when the blood of slaughter
wets the ground it wants more blood.   395
      Slaughter cries for the Fury
of those long dead to bring destruction
on destruction churning in its wake!
ORESTES: Sweet Earth, how long?—great lords of death, look on,
you mighty curses of the dead. Look on   400
the last of Atreus' children, here, the remnant
      helpless, cast from home . . . god, where to turn?
LEADER: And again my pulses race and leap,
      I can feel your sobs, and hope
            becomes despair   405
      and the heart goes dark to hear you—
then the anguish ebbs, I see you stronger,
      hope and the light come on me.
ELECTRA: *What* hope?—what force to summon, what can help?
What but the pain we suffer, bred by her?   410
So let her fawn. She can never soothe her young wolves—
Mother dear, you bred our wolves' raw fury.
LEADER AND CHORUS: I beat and beat the dirge like a Persian mourner,[4]
hands clenched tight and the blows are coming thick and fast,
      you can see the hands shoot out,   415
            now hand over hand and down—the head pulsates,
            blood at the temples pounding to explode!

3. For the first time, the killing of Clytaemnestra is mentioned. 4. Oriental mourning was thought to be even more wild and extravagant than Greek.

ELECTRA: Reckless, brutal mother—oh dear god!—
　　the brutal, cruel cortège,
　　　the warlord stripped of his honor guard   420
　　　　and stripped of mourning rites—
　　you dared entomb your lord unwept, unsung.
ORESTES: Shamed for all the world, you mean—
　　dear god, my father degraded so!
　　Oh she'll pay,   425
　　she'll pay, by the gods and these bare hands—
　　just let me take her life and *die!*[5]
LEADER AND CHORUS: Shamed? *Butchered*, I tell you—hands lopped,
　　strung to shackle his neck and arms!
　　So she worked,   430
　　she buried him, made your life a hell.
　　Your father mutilated[6]—do you hear?
ELECTRA: You tell him of father's death, but I was an outcast,
　　worthless, leashed like a vicious dog in a dark cell.
　　I wept—laughter died that day . . .   435
　　　I wept, pouring out the tears behind my veils.
　　Hear *that*, my brother, carve it on your heart!
LEADER AND CHORUS: Let it ring in your ears
　　but let your heart stand firm.
　　The outrage stands as it stands,   440
　　　you burn to know the end,
　　but first be strong, be steel, then down and fight.
ORESTES: I am calling you, my father—be with all you love!
ELECTRA: I am with you, calling through my tears.
LEADER AND CHORUS: We band together now, the call resounds—   445
　　hear us now, come back into the light.
　　Be with us, battle all you hate.
ORESTES: Now force *clash* with force—right with right!
ELECTRA: Dear gods, be just—win back our rights.
LEADER AND CHORUS: The flesh crawls to hear them pray.   450
　　the hour of doom has waited long . . .
　　pray for it once, and oh my god, it comes.
CHORUS: Oh, the torment bred in the race,
　　the grinding scream of death
　　　and the stroke that hits the vein,   455
　　the hemorrhage none can staunch, the grief,
　　the curse no man can bear.

　　But there is a cure in the house
　　　and not outside it, no,
　　　not from others but from *them*,   460

---

5. This is not, as might appear from the translation, an expression of despair. The Greek phrase is an example of a fairly common formula which has the force: "I'd be willing to *die*, if I could only . . ."
6. This practice was supposed to prevent the dead man from rising from the grave to haunt his murderer.

their bloody strife. We sing to you,
dark gods beneath the earth.

Now hear, you blissful powers underground—
answer the call, send help.
Bless the children, give them triumph now. 465
[*They withdraw, while* ELECTRA *and* ORESTES *come to the altar.*]
ORESTES: Father, king, no royal death you died—
give me the power now to rule our house.
ELECTRA: I need you too, my father.
Help me kill her lover, then go free.
ORESTES: Then men will extend the sacred feast to you. 470
Or else, when the steam and the rich savor burn
for Mother Earth, you will starve for honor.
ELECTRA: And I will pour my birthright out to you—
the wine of the fathers' house, my bridal wine,
and first of all the shrines revere your tomb. 475
ORESTES: O Earth, bring father up to watch me fight.
ELECTRA: O Persephone,[7] give us power—lovely, gorgeous power!
ORESTES: Remember the bath—they stripped away your life, my father.
ELECTRA: Remember the all-embracing net—they made it first for you.
ORESTES: Chained like a beast—chains of hate, not bronze, my father! 480
ELECTRA: Shamed in the schemes, the hoods they slung around you!
ORESTES: Does our taunting wake you, oh my father?
ELECTRA: Do you lift your beloved head?
ORESTES: Send us justice, fight for all you love,
or help us pin them grip for grip. They threw you— 485
don't you long to throw them down in turn?
ELECTRA: One last cry, father. Look at your nestlings
stationed at your tomb—pity
your son and daughter. We are all you have.
ORESTES: Never blot out the seed of Pelops here. 490
Then in the face of death you cannot die.
[*The* LEADER *comes forward again.*]
LEADER: The voices of children—salvation to the dead!
Corks to the net, they rescue the linen meshes
from the depths. This line will never drown!
ELECTRA: Hear us—the long wail we raise is all for you. 495
Honor our call and you will save yourself.
LEADER: And a fine thing it is to lengthen out the dirge;
you adore a grave and fate they never mourned.
But now for action—now you're set on action,
put your stars to proof.
ORESTES: So we will. 500
One thing first, I think it's on the track.
Why did she send libations? What possessed her,

---

7. Queen of the underworld.

so late, to salve a wound past healing?
To the unforgiving dead she sends this sop,
this . . . who am I to appreciate her gifts? 505
They fall so short of all her failings. True,
"pour out your all to atone an act of blood,
you work for nothing." So the saying goes.
I'm ready. Tell me what you know.
LEADER: I know, my boy,
I was there. She had bad dreams. Some terror 510
came groping through the night, it shook her,
and she sent these cups, unholy woman.
ORESTES: And you know the dream, you can tell it clearly?
LEADER: She dreamed she bore a snake, said so herself and . . .
ORESTES: Come to the point—where does the story end? 515
LEADER: . . . she swaddled it like a baby, laid it to rest.
ORESTES: And food, what did the little monster want?
LEADER: She gave it her breast to suck—she was dreaming.
ORESTES: And didn't it tear her nipple, the brute inhuman—
LEADER: Blood curdled the milk with each sharp tug . . . 520
ORESTES: No empty dream. The vision of a man.
LEADER: . . . and she woke with a scream, appalled,
and rows of torches, burning out of the blind dark,
flared across the halls to soothe the queen,
and then she sent the libations for the dead, 525
an easy cure she hopes will cut the pain.
ORESTES: No,
I pray to the Earth and father's grave to bring
that dream to life in me. I'll play the seer—
it all fits together, watch!
If the serpent came from the same place as I, 530
and slept in the bands that swaddled me, and its jaws
spread wide for the breast that nursed me into life
and clots stained the milk, mother's milk,
and she cried in fear and agony—so be it.
As she bred this sign, this violent prodigy, 535
so she dies by violence. I turn serpent,
I kill her. So the vision says.
LEADER: You are the seer for me, I like your reading.
Let it come! But now rehearse your friends.
Say do this, or don't do that— 540
ORESTES: The plan is simple. My sister goes inside.
And I'd have her keep the bond with me a secret.
They killed an honored man by cunning, so
they die by cunning, caught in the same noose.
So he commands, 545
Apollo the Seer who's never lied before.

And I like a stranger, equipped for all events,
go to the outer gates with this man here,
Pylades, a friend, the house's friend-in-arms.
And we both will speak Parnassian, both try   550
for the native tones of Delphi.[8]
                       Now, say none
at the doors will give us a royal welcome
(after all the house is ridden by a curse),
well then we wait . . . till a passer-by will stop
and puzzle and make insinuations at the house,   555
"Aegisthus shuts his door on the man who needs him.
Why, I wonder—does he know? Is he home?"

But once through the gates, across the threshold,
once I find that man on *my* father's throne,
or returning late to meet me face to face,   560
and his eyes shift and fall—
                      I promise you,
before he can ask me, "Stranger, who are you?"—
I drop him dead, a thrust of the sword, and twist!
Our Fury never wants for blood. *His* she drinks unmixed,
our third libation poured to Saving Zeus.   565
    [*Turning to* ELECTRA.]
Keep a close watch inside, dear, be careful.
We must work together step by step.
    [*To the* CHORUS.]
                   And you,
better hold your tongues, religiously.
Silence, friends, or speak when it will help.
    [*Looking towards* PYLADES *and the death-mound and beyond.*]
For the rest, watch over me, I need you—   570
guide my sword through struggle, guide me home!
    [*As* ORESTES, PYLADES, *and* ELECTRA *leave, the women reassemble for*
    the CHORUS.]

CHORUS: Marvels, the Earth breeds many marvels,
               terrible marvels overwhelm us.
     The heaving arms of the sea embrace and swarm
      with savage life. And high in the no man's land of night   575
        torches[9] hang like swords. The hawk on the wing,
           the beast astride the fields
     can tell of the whirlwind's fury roaring strong.

    Oh but a man's high daring spirit,
      who can account for that? Or woman's   580

8. Delphi is on the slopes of Mount Parnassus: the inhabitants of the area spoke a dialect which differed
from that of Argos (and Athens). Of course, the actors playing Orestes and Pylades do not, in fact, switch
to Parnassian dialect. 9. Comets, meteors, etc.

desperate passion daring past all bounds?
She couples with every form of ruin known to mortals.
Woman, frenzied, driven wild with lust,
    twists the dark, warm harness
of wedded love—tortures man and beast!   585

Well you know, you with a sense of truth
    recall Althaia,[1]
the heartless mother
who killed her son,
ai! what a scheme she had—   590
    she rushed his destiny,
        lit the bloody torch
preserved from the day he left her loins with a cry—
        the life of the torch paced his,
burning on till Fate burned out his life.   595

There is one more in the tales of hate:
    remember Scylla,[2]
the girl of slaughter
seduced by foes
to take her father's life.   600
    The gift of Minos,
        a choker forged in gold
turned her head and Nisos' immortal lock she cut
        as he slept away his breath . . .
ruthless bitch, now Hermes takes her down.   605

Now that I call to mind old wounds that never heal—
    Stop, it's time for the wedded love-in-hate,[3]
for the curse of the halls,
    the woman's brazen cunning
        bent on her lord in arms,   610
    her warlord's power—
        Do you respect such things?
I prize the hearthstone warmed by faith,
a woman's temper nothing bends to outrage.

First at the head of legendary crime stands Lemnos.[4]
    People shudder and moan, and can't forget—   615
each new horror that comes

---

1. Mother of the hero Meleager. At his birth she was given a prophecy that his life would be no longer than that of a piece of wood then burning on the fire. She extinguished it and hid it away. But when, now a young man, Meleager killed her brother in a quarrel, she took it and threw it back on the fire, thus ending her son's life.   2. Daughter of Nisos, King of Megara, who had a purple lock of hair which made it impossible for him to die. When Megara was besieged by Minos, King of Crete, Scylla, bribed with a golden necklace, cut off her father's lock of hair. He died, and Scylla was changed into the sea monster of the *Odyssey*.   3. This stanza refers to Clytaemnestra.   4. An island off the coast of Asia Minor. The men of Lemnos brought back slave women from a war in neighboring Thrace: their wives, angry and jealous because of their husbands' affection for these women, massacred all the men on the island.

we call the hells of Lemnos.
       Loathed by the gods for guilt,
     cast off by men, disgraced, their line dies out.
Who could respect what god detests?   620
What of these tales have I not picked with justice?

            The sword's at the lungs!—it stabs deep,
                 the edge cuts through and through
        and Justice drives it—Outrage still lives on,
        not trodden to pieces underfoot, not yet,   625
              though the laws lie trampled down,
                   the majesty of Zeus.

            The anvil of Justice stands fast
              and Fate beats out her sword.
        Tempered for glory, a child will wipe clean   630
        the inveterate stain of blood shed long ago—
              Fury brings him home at last,
                the brooding mother Fury!

[*The women leave.* ORESTES *and* PYLADES *approach the house of*
     Atreus.]
ORESTES: Slave, the slave!—
    where is he? Hear me pounding the gates?
    Is there a man inside the house?   635
    For the third time, come out of the halls!
    If Aegisthus has them welcome friendly guests.
       [*A voice from inside.*]
PORTER: All right, I hear you . . .
    Where do you come from, stranger? Who are you?
ORESTES: Announce me to the masters of the house.   640
    I've come for them, I bring them news.
                            Hurry,
    the chariot of the night is rushing on the dark!
    The hour falls, the traveler casts his anchor
    in an inn where every stranger feels at home.
                            Come out!
    Whoever rules the house. The woman in charge.   645
    No, the man, better that way.
    No scruples then. Say what you mean,
    man to man launch in and prove your point,
    make it clear, strong.
       [CLYTAEMNESTRA *emerges from the palace, attended by* ELECTRA.]
CLYTAEMNESTRA: Strangers, please,
    tell me what you would like and it is yours.   650
    We've all you might expect in a house like ours.
    We have warm baths and beds to charm away your pains
    and the eyes of Justice look on all we do.
    But if you come for higher things, affairs

that touch the state, that is the men's concern   655
and I will stir them on.
ORESTES: I am a stranger,
from Daulis, close to Delphi, I'd just set out,
packing my own burden bound for Argos
(here I'd put my burden down and rest),
when I met a perfect stranger, out of the blue,   660
who asks about my way and tells me his.
                                        Strophios,
a Phocian, so I gathered in conversation.
"Well, my friend," he says, "out for Argos
in any case? Remember to tell the parents
he is dead, Orestes . . .
                              promise me please   665
(it's only right), it will not slip your mind.
Then whatever his people want, to bring him home
or bury him here, an alien, all outcast here
forever, won't you ferry back their wishes?
As it is, a bronze urn is armor to his embers   670
The man's been mourned so well . . ."
                                        I only tell you
what I heard. And am I speaking now
with guardians, kinsmen who will care?
It's hard to say. But a parent ought to know.
CLYTAEMNESTRA: I, I—
your words, you storm us, raze us to the roots,   675
you curse of the house so hard to wrestle down!
How you range—targets at peace, miles away,
and a shaft from your lookout brings them down.
You strip me bare of all I love, destroy me,
now—Orestes.   680

And he was trained so well, we'd been so careful,
kept his footsteps clear of the quicksand of death.
Just now, the hope of the halls, the surgeon to cure
our Furies' lovely revel—he seemed so close,
he's written off the rolls.
ORESTES: If only I were . . .   685
my friends, with hosts as fortunate as you
if only I could be known for better news
and welcomed like a brother. The tie between
the host and stranger, what is kinder?
But what an impiety, so it seemed to me,   690
not to bring this to a head for loved ones.
I was bound by honor, bound by the rights
of hospitality.
CLYTAEMNESTRA: Nothing has changed.

For all that you receive what you deserve,
as welcome in these halls as one of us.   695
Wouldn't another bear the message just as well?
But you must be worn from the long day's journey—
time for your rewards.
    [*To* ELECTRA.]
                Escort him in,
where the men who come are made to feel at home.
He and his retinue, and fellow travelers.   700
Let them taste the bounty of our house.
Do it, as if you depended on his welfare.

And we will rouse the powers in the house
and share the news. We never lack for loved ones,
we will probe this turn of fortune every way.   705
    [ELECTRA *leads* ORESTES, PYLADES, *and their retinue into the halls;*
    CLYTAEMNESTRA *follows, while the* CHORUS *reassembles.*]
LEADER: Oh dear friends who serve the house,
    when can we speak out, when
    can the vigor of our voices serve Orestes?
CHORUS: Queen of the Earth, rich mounded Earth,
    breasting over the lord of ships,   710
    the king's corpse at rest,
    hear us now, now help us,
        now the time is ripe—
    Down to the pit Persuasion goes
    with all her cunning. Hermes of Death,   715
    the great shade patrols the ring
    to guide the struggles, drive the tearing sword.
LEADER: And I think our new friend is at his mischief.
    Look, Orestes' nurse in tears.
    [*Enter* CILISSA.[5]]
    Where now, old-timer, padding along the gates?   720
    With pain a volunteer to go your way.
NURSE: "Aegisthus,"
    your mistress calling, "hurry and meet your guests.
    There's news. It's clearer man to man, you'll see."

And she looks at the maids and pulls that long face
and down deep her eyes are laughing over the work   725
that's done. Well and good for her. For the house
it's the curse all over—the strangers make that plain.
But let *him* hear, he'll revel once he knows.
                      Oh god,
the life is hard. The old griefs, the memories
mixing, cups of pain, so much pain in the halls,   730

---

5. The nurse's name means simply "a woman from Cilicia" (in Asia Minor): she is a slave.

the house of Atreus . . . I suffered, the heart within me
always breaking, oh, but I never shouldered
misery like this. So many blows, good slave,
I took my blows.
                        Now dear Orestes—
the sweetest, dearest plague of all our lives!   735

Red from your mother's womb I took you, reared you . . .
nights, the endless nights I paced, your wailing
kept me moving—led me a life of labor,
all for what?
                        And such care I gave it . . .
baby can't think for itself, poor creature.   740
You have to nurse it, don't you? Read its mind,
little devil's got no words, it's still swaddled.
Maybe it wants a bite or a sip of something,
or its bladder pinches—a baby's soft insides
have a will of their own. I had to be a prophet.   745
Oh I tried, and missed, believe you me, I missed,
and I'd scrub its pretty things until they sparkled.
Washerwoman and wet-nurse shared the shop.
A jack of two trades, that's me,
and an old hand at both . . .
                        and so I nursed Orestes,   750
yes, from his father's arms I took him once,
and now they say he's dead,
I've suffered it all, and now I'll fetch that man,
the ruination of the house—give him the news,
he'll relish every word.

LEADER: She tells him to come,   755
but how, prepared?

NURSE: Prepared, how else?
I don't see . . .

LEADER: With his men, I mean, or all alone?

NURSE: Oh, she says to bring his bodyguard, his cutthroats.

LEADER: No, not now, not if you hate our master—
tell him to come alone.   760
Nothing for him to fear then, when he hears.
Have him come quickly too, rejoicing all the way!
The teller sets the crooked message straight.

NURSE: What,
you're *glad* for the news that's come?

LEADER: Why not,
if Zeus will turn the evil wind to good?   765

NURSE: But how? Orestes, the hope of the house is gone.

LEADER: Not yet. It's a poor seer who'd say so.

NURSE: What are you saying?—something I don't know?

LEADER: Go in with your message. Do as you're told.
May the gods take care of cares that come from them.   770
NURSE: Well, I'm off. Do as I'm told.
And here's to the best . . .
some help, dear gods, some help.
[*Exit.*]
CHORUS: O now bend to my prayer, Father Zeus,
 lord of the gods astride the sky—   775
grant them all good fortune,
the lords of the house who strain to see
 strict discipline return.
Our cry is the cry of Justice,
 Zeus, safeguard it well.

     Zeus,   780
set him against his enemies in the halls!
 Do it, rear him to greatness—two, threefold
 he will repay you freely, gladly.

Look now—watch the colt of a man you loved,
 yoked to the chariot of pain.   785
Now the orphan needs you—
harness his racing, rein him in,
 preserve his stride so we
can watch him surge at the last turn,
 storming for the goal.   790

And you who haunt the vaults[6]
where the gold glows in the darkness,
hear us now, good spirits of the house,
 conspire with us—come,
 and wash old works of blood   795
in the fresh-drawn blood of Justice.
Let the gray retainer, murder, breed no more.

And you, Apollo, lord of the glorious masoned cavern,[7]
 grant that this man's house lift up its head,
 that we may see with loving eyes   800
the light of freedom burst from its dark veil!

 And lend a hand and scheme
for the rights, my Hermes,[8] help us,
sail the action on with all your breath.
 Reveal what's hidden, please,   805
or say a baffling word

---

6. The gods of the house—Hestia (the hearth), Zeus Ktesios (the storeroom), etc. 7. The temple of Apollo at Delphi. It was believed that his prophetess, the Pythia, was inspired by emanations from subterranean caves. 8. In his capacity of god of the marketplace and of thieves: he is the appropriate divinity to steer the murder plan which is based on deceit.

in the night and blind men's eyes—
when the morning comes your word is just as dark.

Soon, at last, in the dawn that frees the house,
  we sea-widows wed to the winds   810
    will beat our mourning looms of song
    and sing, "Our ship's come in!
  Mine, mine is the wealth that swells her holds—
  those I love are home and free of death."

But you, when your turn in the action comes, be strong.   815
  When she cries "Son!" cry out "My *father's* son!"
  Go through with the murder—innocent at last.

Raise up the heart of Perseus[9] in your breast!
  And for all you love under earth
    and all above its rim, now scarf your eyes   820
      against the Gorgon's fury—
  In, go in for the slaughter now!
    [*Enter* AEGISTHUS, *alone.*]
  The butcher comes. Wipe out death with death.
AEGISTHUS: Coming, coming. Yes, I have my summons.
  There's news, I gather, travelers here to tell it.   825
  No joy in the telling, though—Orestes dead.
  Saddle the house with a bloody thing like that
  and it might just collapse. It's still raw
  from the last murders, galled and raw.

But how to take the story, for living truth?   830
  Or work of a woman's panic, gossip starting up
  in the night to flicker out and die?
    [*Turning to the* LEADER.]
                              Do you know?
  Tell me, clear my mind.
LEADER: We've heard a little.
  But get it from the strangers, go inside.
  Messengers have no power. Nothing like   835
  a face-to-face encounter with the source.
AEGISTHUS: —Must see him, test the messenger. Where was he
  when the boy died, standing on the spot?
  Or is he dazed with rumor, mouthing hearsay?
  No, he'll never trap me open-eyed!   840
    [*Striding through the doors.*]
CHORUS: Zeus, Zeus, what can I say?—
  how to begin this prayer, call down
    the gods for help? what words

---

9. The hero who killed the Gorgon, Medusa. Anyone who looked at her face was turned to stone; Perseus used a shield given him by Athena as a mirror.

can reach the depth of all I feel?
Now they swing to the work,   845
the red edge of the cleaver
hacks at flesh and men go down.
Agamemnon's house goes down—
    all-out disaster now,
or a son ignites the torch of freedom,   850
wins the throne, the citadel,
    the fathers' realms of gold.
The last man on the bench, a challenger
must come to grips with two. Up,
like a young god, Orestes, wrestle—   855
    let it be to win.
    [*A scream inside the palace.*]
—Listen!
        —What's happening?
                —The house,
what have they done to the house?
LEADER: Back,
    till the work is over! Stand back—
    they'll count us clean of the dreadful business.   860
    [*The women scatter; a wounded* SERVANT *of* AEGISTHUS *enters.*]
    Look, the die is cast, the battle's done.
SERVANT: Ai,
    Ai, all over, master's dead—Aie,
    a third, last salute. Aegisthus is no more.
    [*Rushing at a side door, struggling to work it open.*]
    Open up, wrench the bolts on the women's doors.
    Faster! A strong young arm it takes,   865
    but not to save him now, he's finished.
    What's the use?
                Look—wake up!
                        No good,
    I call to the deaf, to sleepers . . . a waste of breath.
    Where are you, Clytaemnestra? What are you doing?
LEADER: Her head is ripe for lopping on the block.   870
    She's next, and justice wields the ax.
    [*The door opens, and* CLYTAEMNESTRA *comes forth.*]
CLYTAEMNESTRA: What now?
    Why this shouting up and down the halls?
SERVANT: The dead are killing the living, I tell you!
CLYTAEMNESTRA: Ah, a riddle. I do well at riddles.
    By cunning we die, precisely as we killed.   875
    Hand me the man-ax, someone, hurry!
    [*The* SERVANT *dashes out.*]
    Now we will see. Win all or lose all,
    we have come to this—the crisis of our lives.

[*The main doors open;* ORESTES, *sword in hand, is standing over the body of* AEGISTHUS, *with* PYLADES *close behind him.*]

ORESTES: It's you I want. This one's had enough.

CLYTAEMNESTRA: Gone, my violent one—Aegisthus, very dear.   880

ORESTES: You love your man? Then lie in the same grave.
You can never be unfaithful to the dead.

[*Pulling her towards* AEGISTHUS' *body.*]

CLYTAEMNESTRA: Wait, son—no feeling for this, my child?
The breast you held, drowsing away the hours,
soft gums tugging the milk that made you grow?   885

[ORESTES *turns to* PYLADES.]

ORESTES: What will I do, Pylades?—I dread to kill my mother!

PYLADES: What of the future? What of the Prophet God Apollo,
the Delphic voice, the faith and oaths we swear?
Make all mankind your enemy, not the gods.

ORESTES: O you win me over—good advice.

[*Wheeling on* CLYTAEMNESTRA, *thrusting her towards* AEGISTHUS.]

This way—   890
I want to butcher you—right across his body!
In life you thought he dwarfed my father—*Die!*—
go down with him forever!   You love this man,
the man you should have loved you hated.

CLYTAEMNESTRA: I gave you life. Let me grow old with you.   895

ORESTES: What—kill my father, then you'd live with me?

CLYTAEMNESTRA: Destiny had a hand in that, my child.

ORESTES: This too: destiny is handing you your death.

CLYTAEMNESTRA: You have no fear of a mother's curse, my son?

ORESTES: Mother? You flung me to a life of pain.   900

CLYTAEMNESTRA: Never flung you, placed you in a comrade's house.

ORESTES: —Disgraced me, sold me, a freeborn father's son.

CLYTAEMNESTRA: Oh? then name the price I took for you.

ORESTES: I am ashamed to mention it[1] in public.

CLYTAEMNESTRA: Please, and tell your father's failings, too.   905

ORESTES: Never judge him—he suffered, you sat here at home.

CLYTAEMNESTRA: It hurts women, being kept from men, my son.

ORESTES: Perhaps . . . but the man slaves to keep them safe at home.

CLYTAEMNESTRA: —I see murder in your eyes, my child—mother's murder!

ORESTES: You are the murderer, not I—and you will kill yourself.   910

CLYTAEMNESTRA: Watch out—the hounds of a mother's curse will hunt
you down.

ORESTES: But how to escape a father's if I fail?

CLYTAEMNESTRA: I must be spilling live tears on a tomb of stone.[2]

ORESTES: Yes, my father's destiny—it decrees your death.

CLYTAEMNESTRA: Ai—you are the snake I bore[3]—I gave you life!

1. He means, of course, her adulterous liaison with Aegisthus.   2. This echoes a proverbial expression for futile action—"pleading with a tomb."   3. Clytaemnestra remembers her dream (ll. 514ff.)

ORESTES: *Yes!*   915
   That was the great seer, that terror in your dreams.
   You killed and it was outrage—suffer outrage now.
   [*He draws her over the threshold; the doors close behind them, and
   the* CHORUS *gathers at the altar.*]
LEADER: I even mourn the victims' double fates.
   But Orestes fought, he reached the summit
   of bloodshed here—we'd rather have it so.   920
   The bright eye of the halls must never die.
CHORUS: Justice came at last to the sons of Priam,
   late but crushing vengeance, yes,
   but to Agamemnon's house returned
      the double lion,[4]   925
      the double onslaught
   drove to the hilt—the exile sped by god,
   by Delphi's just command that drove him home.

   Lift the cry of triumph O! the master's house
      wins free of grief, free of the ones   930
   who bled its wealth, the couple stained with murder,
      free of Fate's rough path.

   He came back with a lust for secret combat,
   stealthy, cunning vengeance, yes,
   but his hand was steered in open fight   935
      by god's true daughter,
      Right, Right we call her,
   we and our mortal voices aiming well—
   she breathes her fury, shatters all she hates.

   Lift the cry of triumph O! the master's house   940
      wins free of grief, free of the ones
   who bled its wealth, the couple stained with murder,
      free of Fate's rough path.

      Apollo wills it so!—
   Apollo, clear from the Earth's deep cleft   945
      his voice came shrill, "Now stealth will master stealth!"
   And the pure god came down and healed our ancient wounds,
      the heavens come, somehow, to lift our yoke of grief—
      Now to praise the heavens' just command.

      Look, the light is breaking!   950
   The huge chain that curbed the halls gives way.
      Rise up, proud house, long, too long
   your walls lay fallen, strewn along the earth.

---

4. Orestes and Pylades.

Time brings all to birth—
soon Time will stride through the gates with blessings,   955
    once the hearth burns off corruption, once
the house drives off the Furies. Look, the dice of Fate
    fall well for all to see. We sing how fortune smiles—
    the aliens in the house are routed out at last!

    Look, the light is breaking!   960
The huge chain that curbed the halls gives way.
    Rise up, proud house, long, too long
    your walls lay fallen, strewn along the earth.
[*The doors open. Torches light* PYLADES *and* ORESTES, *sword in hand,
    standing over the bodies of* CLYTAEMNESTRA *and* AEGISTHUS, *as* CLY-
    TAEMNESTRA *stood over the bodies of* AGAMEMNON *and* CASSANDRA.]
ORESTES: Behold the double tyranny of our land!
They killed my father, stormed my fathers' house.   965
They had their power when they held the throne.
Great lovers still, as you may read their fate.
True to their oath, hand in hand they swore
to kill my father, hand in hand to die.
Now they keep their word.
    [*Unwinding from the bodies on the bier the robes that entangled* AGA-
    MEMNON, *he displays them, as* CLYTAEMNESTRA *had displayed them,
    to the chorus at the altar.*]
                          Look once more on this,   970
you who gather here to attend our crimes—
the master-plot that bound my wretched father,
shackled his ankles, manacled his hands.
Spread it out! Stand in a ring around it,
a grand shroud for a man.
                          Here, unfurl it   975
so the Father—no, not mine but the One
who watches over all, the Sun can behold
my mother's godless work. So he may come,
my witness when the day of judgment comes,
that I pursued this bloody death with justice,   980
mother's death.
                          Aegisthus, why mention him?
The adulterer dies. An old custom, justice.[5]

But she who plotted this horror against her husband,
she carried his children, growing in her womb
and she—I loved her once   985
and now I loathe, I have to loathe—
                          what is she?
[*Kneeling by the body of his mother.*]

─────────
5. An Athenian had the right to kill a man taken in adultery with his wife.

Some moray eel, some viper born to rot her mate
with a single touch, no fang to strike him,
just the wrong, the reckless fury in her heart!
   [*Glancing back and forth from* CLYTAEMNESTRA *to the robes.*]
This—how can I dignify this . . . snare for a beast?—   990
sheath for a corpse's feet?
                  This winding-sheet,
this tent for the bath of death!
                      No, a hunting net,
a coiling—what to call—?
                Foot-trap—
woven of robes . . .
why, this is perfect gear for the highwayman   995
who entices guests and robs them blind and plies
the trade of thieves. With a sweet lure like this
he'd hoist a hundred lives and warm his heart.

Live with such a woman, marry *her*? Sooner
the gods destroy me—die without an heir!   1000
CHORUS: Oh the dreadful work . . .
   Death calls and she is gone.
     But oh, for you, the survivor,
suffering is just about to bloom.
ORESTES: Did she do the work or not?—Here, come close—   1005
This shroud's my witness, dyed with Aegisthus' blade—
Look, the blood ran here, conspired with time to blot
the swirling dyes, the handsome old brocade.
   [*Clutching* AGAMEMNON'S *robes, burying his face in them and weeping.*]
Now I can praise you, now I am here to mourn.
You were my father's death, great robe, I hail you!   1010
Even if I must suffer the work and the agony
and all the race of man—
               I embrace you . . . you,
my victory, are my guilt, my curse, and still—
CHORUS: No man can go through life
and reach the end unharmed.   1015
   Aye, trouble is now,
and trouble still to come.
ORESTES: But *still*,
that you may know—
            I see no end in sight,
I am a charioteer—the reins are flying, look,
the mares plunge off the track—
                  my bolting heart,   1020
it beats me down and terror beats the drum,
my dance-and-singing master pitched to fury—

And still, while I still have some self-control,
I say to my friends in public: I killed my mother,
not with a little justice. She was stained   1025
with father's murder, she was cursed by god.
And the magic spells that fired up my daring?
One comes first. The Seer of Delphi who declared,
"Go through with this and you go free of guilt.
Fail and—"
           I can't repeat the punishment.   1030
What bow could hit the crest of so much pain?
    [PYLADES *gives* ORESTES *a branch of olive and invests him in the robes
    of* APOLLO, *the wreath and insignia of suppliants to* DELPHI.]
Now look on me, armed with the branch and wreath,
a suppliant bound for the Navelstone of Earth,
Apollo's sacred heights
where they say the fire of heaven[6] can never die.   1035
    [*Looking at his hand that still retains the sword.*]
I must escape this blood . . . it is my own.
—Must turn toward his hearth,
none but his, the Prophet God decreed.

I ask you, Argos and all my generations,
remember how these brutal things were done.   1040
Be my witness to Menelaus when he comes.
And now I go, an outcast driven off the land,
in life, in death, I leave behind a name for—
LEADER: But you've done well. Don't burden yourself
    with bad omens, lash yourself with guilt.   1045
You've set us free, the whole city of Argos,
lopped the heads of these two serpents once for all.
    [*Staring at the women and beyond,* ORESTES *screams in terror.*]
ORESTES: No, no! Women—look—like Gorgons,
    shrouded in black, their heads wreathed,
    swarming serpents!
             —Cannot stay, I must move on.   1050
LEADER: What dreams can whirl you so? You of all men,
    you have your father's love. Steady,
    nothing to fear with all you've won.
ORESTES: No dreams,
    these torments, not to me, they're clear, real—the hounds
    of mother's hate.
LEADER: The blood's still wet on your hands.   1055
    It puts a kind of frenzy in you . . .
ORESTES: *God Apollo!*

6. A sacred fire was permanently maintained at Delphi: from it other fires, which had gone out through
natural calamities or the sack of a city, could be renewed. *Navelstone:* Delphi claimed to be the center of
the Earth: in the temple was a stone called the "navel."

Here they come, thick and fast,
their eyes dripping hate—
LEADER: One thing
will purge you. Apollo's touch will set you free
from all your . . . torments.
ORESTES: You can't see them—   1060
I can, they drive me on! I must move on—
[He rushes out; PYLADES follows close behind.]
LEADER: Farewell then. God look down on you with kindness,
guard you, grant you fortune.
CHORUS: Here once more, for the third time,
the tempest in the race has struck   1065
the house of kings and run its course.
First the children eaten,
the cause of all our pain, the curse.
And next the kingly man's ordeal,
the bath where the proud commander,   1070
lord of Achaea's armies lost his life.
And now a third has come, but who?
A third like Saving Zeus?
Or should we call him death?
Where will it end?—   1075
where will it sink to sleep and rest,
this murderous hate, this Fury?

The Eumenides

Characters

The PYTHIA, the priestess of Apollo   CHORUS OF FURIES and their LEADER
APOLLO   ATHENA
HERMES   Escorting CHORUS of Athenian
ORESTES   women
THE GHOST OF CLYTAEMNESTRA   Men of the jury, herald, citizens

[TIME AND SCENE: The FURIES have pursued ORESTES to the temple of
APOLLO at Delphi. It is morning. The priestess of the god appears at the
great doors and offers up her prayer.]

PYTHIA: First of the gods I honor in my prayer is Mother Earth,
the first of the gods to prophesy,[1] and next I praise
Tradition, second to hold her Mother's mantic seat,
so legend says, and third by the lots of destiny,
by Tradition's free will—no force to bear her down—   5

1. The Pythia (the priestess of Apollo's oracle) traces the peaceful succession of powers that controlled the
great prophetic site of Delphi. First Mother Earth, then Tradition (Themis in the Greek), then Phoebe,
grandmother of Apollo, who handed it over to him as a birthday gift. This is a succession myth that stresses
orderly, peaceful succession: in other versions Apollo fights and kills a great serpent, Pytho, to gain
possession.

another Titan, child of the Earth, took her seat
and Phoebe passed it on as a birthday gift to Phoebus,
Phoebus a name for clear pure light derived from hers.
Leaving the marsh and razorback of Delos,[2] landing
at Pallas' headlands[3] flocked by ships, here he came   10
to make his home Parnassus and the heights.[4]
And an escort filled with reverence brought him on,
the highway-builders, sons of the god of fire[5] who tamed
the savage country, civilized the wilds—on he marched
and the people lined his way to cover him with praise,   15
led by Delphos, lord, helm of the land, and Zeus
inspired his mind with the prophet's skill, with godhead,
made him fourth in the dynasty of seers to mount this throne,
but it is Zeus that Apollo speaks for, Father Zeus.
These I honor in the prelude of my prayers—these gods.   20
But Athena at the Forefront of the Temple[6] crowns our legends.
I revere the nymphs who keep the Corycian rock's deep hollows,[7]
loving haunt of birds where the spirits drift and hover.
And Great Dionysus[8] rules the land. I never forget that day
he marshaled his wild women in arms—he was all god,   25
he ripped Pentheus[9] down like a hare in the nets of doom.
And the rushing springs of Pleistos,[1] Poseidon's force I call,
and the king of the sky, the king of all fulfillment, Zeus.
Now the prophet goes to take her seat. God speed me—
grant me a vision greater than all my embarkations past!   30
[*Turning to the audience.*]
Where are the Greeks among you? Draw your lots and enter.
It is the custom here. I will tell the future
only as the god will lead the way.
[*She goes through the doors and reappears in a moment, shaken,
thrown to her knees by some terrific force.*]
                    Terrors—
terrors to tell, terrors all can see!—
they send me reeling back from Apollo's house.   35
The strength drains, it's very hard to stand,
crawling on all fours, no spring in the legs . . .
an old woman, gripped by fear, is nothing,
a child, nothing more.
[*Struggling to her feet, trying to compose herself.*]

2. The small rocky island in the Cyclades, where Apollo was born.   **3.** I.e., the coast of Attica.
4. The oracular site is situated on the lower slopes of the Parnassus mountain range (2,457 meters at its summit).   **5.** Athenians, whose legendary ancestor Erechthonios was a son of Hephaestus, the smith-god.   **6.** *Pronaia*, the title of a temple of Athena situated at the entrance to the sacred precinct.   **7.** A capacious cave high above the site of Delphi, sacred to Pan and the nymphs.   **8.** This god, giver of wine and ecstasy, was thought to inhabit Delphi in the winter months, when Apollo left for the land of the Hyperboreans (the happy people who lived, as their name indicates, beyond the North Wind). Dionysiac festivals at which women danced on the hills at night were held at Delphi in historical times.   **9.** A King of Thebes who resisted the establishment of Dionysiac rites in his domains.   **1.** The river (dry in summer) in the bottom of the deep gorge below Delphi.

I'm on my way to the vault,   40
it's green with wreaths, and there at the Navelstone[2]
I see a man—an abomination to god—
he holds the seat where suppliants sit for purging;
his hands dripping blood, and his sword just drawn,
and he holds a branch (it must have topped an olive)   45
wreathed with a fine tuft of wool,[3] all piety,
fleece gleaming white. So far it's clear, I tell you.
But there in a ring around the man, an amazing company—
women, sleeping, nestling against the benches . . .
women? No,   50
Gorgons I'd call them; but then with Gorgons
you'd see the grim, inhuman . . .
                              I saw a picture
years ago, the creatures tearing the feast
away from Phineus—[4]
                      These have no wings,
I looked. But black they are, and so repulsive.   55
Their heavy, rasping breathing makes me cringe.
And their eyes ooze a discharge, sickening,
and what they wear[5]—to flaunt that at the gods,
the idols, sacrilege! even in the homes of men.
The tribe that produced that brood I never saw,   60
or a plot of ground to boast it nursed their kind
without some tears, some pain for all its labor.

Now for the outcome. This is his concern,
Apollo the master of this house, the mighty power.
Healer, prophet, diviner of signs, he purges   65
the halls of others—He must purge his own.
    [*She leaves. The doors of the temple open and reveal* APOLLO *rising
    over* ORESTES; *he kneels in prayer at the Navelstone, surrounded by
    the* FURIES *who are sleeping.* HERMES *waits in the background.*]
APOLLO: No, I will never fail you, through to the end
    your guardian standing by your side or worlds away!
    I will show no mercy to your enemies! Now
    look at these—
        [*Pointing to the* FURIES.]
                      these obscenities!—I've caught them,   70
    beaten them down with sleep.
                          They disgust me.
    These gray, ancient children never touched
    by god, man, or beast—the eternal virgins.

2. A sacred stone that was supposed to mark the navel, i.e., the center of the earth. **3.** Suppliants usually carried a branch of olive, hung with small woolen wreaths. **4.** Whenever he spread the table for a meal, the food was carried off by loathsome creatures—half bird, half woman—called Harpies. The Pythia first thinks the Erinyes are Gorgons, but then rejects that theory (we are not told why); her next guess, Harpies, has to be abandoned because the Erinyes have no wings. **5.** Long black robes.

Born for destruction only, the dark pit,
they range the bowels of Earth, the world of death,   75
loathed by men and the gods who hold Olympus.

Nevertheless keep racing on and never yield.
Deep in the endless heartland they will drive you,
striding horizons, feet pounding the earth forever,
on, on over seas and cities swept by tides!   80
Never surrender, never brood on the labor.
And once you reach the citadel of Pallas,[6] kneel
and embrace her ancient idol in your arms and there,
with judges of your case, with a magic spell—
with words—we will devise the master-stroke   85
that sets you free from torment once for all.
I persuaded you to take your mother's life.
ORESTES: Lord Apollo, you know the rules of justice,
know them well. Now learn compassion, too.
No one doubts your power to do great things.   90
APOLLO: Remember that. No fear will overcome you.
    [*Summoning* HERMES *from the shadows.*]
You, my brother, blood of our common Father,
Hermes, guard him well. Live up to your name,
good Escort. Shepherd him well, he is my suppliant,
and outlaws have their rights that Zeus reveres.   95
Lead him back to the world of men with all good speed.
    [APOLLO *withdraws to his inner sanctuary;* ORESTES *leaves with* HERMES
    in the lead. The GHOST OF CLYTAEMNESTRA *appears at the Navelstone,*
    hovering over the FURIES *as they sleep.*]
THE GHOST OF CLYTAEMNESTRA:[7] You—how can you *sleep?*
Awake, awake—what use are sleepers now?
I go stripped of honor, thanks to you,
alone among the dead. And for those I killed   100
the charges of the dead will never cease, never—
I wander in disgrace, I feel the guilt, I tell you,
withering guilt from all the outraged dead!

But I suffered too, terribly, from dear ones,
and none of my spirits rages to avenge me.   105
I was slaughtered by his matricidal hand.
See these gashes—
    [*Seizing one of the* FURIES *weak with sleep.*]
            Carve them in your heart!

The sleeping brain has eyes that give us light;
we can never see our destiny by day.

6. Athens, city of Pallas (Athena). *Ancient idol:* In a temple on the Acropolis at Athens there was an
ancient wooden statue of Athena.   7. She is not really a ghost. She tells us later what she is: a dream in
the head of the Furies. (l. 121).

And after all my libations . . . how you lapped   110
the honey, the sober offerings poured to soothe you,
awesome midnight feasts[8] I burned at the hearthfire,
your dread hour never shared with gods.
All those rites, I see them trampled down.
And he springs free like a fawn, one light leap   115
at that—he's through the thick of your nets,
he breaks away!
Mocking laughter twists across his face.
Hear me, I am pleading for my life.
Awake, my Furies, goddesses of the Earth!   120
A dream is calling—Clytaemnestra calls you now.
     [*The* FURIES *mutter in their sleep.*]
Mutter on. Your man is gone, fled far away.
My son has friends to defend him, not like mine.
     [*They mutter again.*]
You sleep too much, no pity for my ordeal.
Orestes murdered his mother—he is gone.   125
     [*They begin to moan.*]
Moaning, sleeping—onto your feet, quickly.
What is your work? What but causing pain?
Sleep and toil, the two strong conspirators,
they sap the mother dragon's deadly fury—
     [*The* FURIES *utter a sharp moan and moan again, but they are still
     asleep.*]
FURIES: Get him, get him, get him, get him—   130
    there he goes.
THE GHOST OF CLYTAEMNESTRA: The prey you hunt is just a dream—
    like hounds mad for the sport you bay him on,
    you never leave the kill.
                    But what are you *doing?*
Up! don't yield to the labor, limp with sleep.
Never forget my anguish.   135
Let my charges hurt you, they are just;
deep in the righteous heart they prod like spurs.

You, blast him on with your gory breath,
the fire of your vitals—wither him, after him,
one last foray—waste him, burn him out!
     [*She vanishes. The lead* FURY *urges on the pack.*]
LEADER: Wake up!   140
    I rouse you, you rouse her. Still asleep?
Onto your feet, kick off your stupor.
See if this prelude has some grain of truth.

---

8. Offerings to the Erinyes were made only at night. *Sober offerings:* No wine was included in offerings to
them.

[*The* FURIES *circle, pursuing the scent with hunting calls, and cry out singly when they find* ORESTES *gone.*]

FURIES: —Aieeeeee—no, no, *no*, they do us wrong, dear sisters.

—The miles of pain, the pain I suffer . . .   145
and all for nothing, all for pain, more pain,
    the anguish, oh, the grief too much to bear.

—The quarry's slipped from the nets, our quarry lost and gone.

—Sleep defeats me . . . I have lost the prey.

—You—child of Zeus[9]—*you*, a common thief!   150

—Young god, you have ridden down the powers
proud with age. You worship the suppliant,
    the godless man who tears his parent's heart—

—The matricide, you steal him away, and you a god!

—Guilt both ways, and who can call it justice?   155

—Not I: her charges stalk my dreams,
    yes, the charioteer rides hard,
        her spurs digging the vitals,
            under the heart, under the heaving breast—

        —I can feel the executioner's lash, it's searing   160
            deeper, sharper, the knives of burning ice—

—Such is your triumph, you young gods,
    world dominion past all rights.
        Your throne is streaming blood,
        blood at the foot, blood at the crowning head—   165

—I can see the Navelstone of the Earth, it's bleeding,
    bristling corruption, oh, the guilt it has to bear—

Stains on the hearth! The Prophet stains the vault,
    he cries it on, drives on the crime himself.
        Breaking the god's first law, he rates men first,   170
        destroys the old dominions of the Fates.

He wounds me too, yet *him* he'll never free,
    plunging under the earth, no freedom then:
        curst as he comes for purging, at his neck
        he feels new murder springing from his blood.   175
[APOLLO *strides from his sanctuary in full armor, brandishing his bow and driving back the* FURIES.]

APOLLO: Out, I tell you, out of these halls—fast!—
set the Prophet's chamber free!

___

9. Apollo.

[*Seizing one of the* FURIES, *shaking an arrow across her face.*]
                    Or take
the flash and stab of this, this flying viper
whipped from the golden cord that strings my bow!

Heave in torment, black froth erupting from your lungs,   180
vomit the clots of all the murders you have drained.
But never touch my halls, you have no right.

Go where heads are severed,[1] eyes gouged out,
where Justice and bloody slaughter are the same . . .
castrations, wasted seed, young men's glories butchered,   185
extremities maimed, and huge stones at the chest,
and the victims wail for pity—
spikes inching up the spine, torsos stuck on spikes.
    [*The* FURIES *close in on him.*]
So, you hear your love feast, yearn to have it all?
You revolt the gods. Your look,   190
your whole regalia gives you away—your kind
should infest a lion's cavern reeking blood.
But never rub your filth on the Prophet's shrine.
Out, you flock without a herdsman—out!
No god will ever shepherd you with love.   195
LEADER: Lord Apollo, now it is your turn to listen.
You are no mere accomplice in this crime.
You did it all, and all the guilt is yours.
APOLLO: No, how? Enlarge on that, and only that.
LEADER: You commanded the guest to kill his mother.   200
APOLLO: —Commanded him to avenge his father, what of it?
LEADER: And then you dared embrace him, fresh from bloodshed.
APOLLO: Yes, I ordered him on, to my house, for purging.[2]
LEADER: And we sped him on, and you revile us?
APOLLO: Indeed, you are not fit to approach this house.   205
LEADER: And yet we have our mission and our—
APOLLO: Authority—you? Sound out your splendid power.
LEADER: Matricides: we drive them from their houses.
APOLLO: And what of the wife who strikes her husband down?
LEADER: That murder would not destroy one's flesh and blood.[3]   210
APOLLO: Why, you'd disgrace—obliterate the bonds of Zeus
    and Hera queen of brides! And the queen of love[4]

1. The methods of torture and execution listed by Apollo are what the Greeks saw as typically Eastern
and, indeed, castration and impalement (l. 188) were Persian, not Greek, customs. But Apollo's dismissal
of the Erinyes as non-Greek has no basis in fact: the Erinyes are not only Greek but much older than he
is.   2. For ritual purification.   3. Crimes of blood relations against each other are the most heinous
kind. But husband and wife are, and must be, of different blood. The Furies would have pursued Orestes
if he had not avenged his father, and they pursue him now because he killed his mother, but the killing
of a husband by a wife seems to them a lesser crime. They think and feel in tribal terms, those of a society
that has not yet developed the city-state, the *polis*, in which the institution of marriage (which Apollo
champions in his reply, ll. 215ff.) was the guarantee of the legitimacy of male heirs for the transmittal of
property from generation to generation.   4. Aphrodite. *Hera:* The marriage of Zeus and Hera was the
divine model of earthly marriages and Hera was the goddess who presided over marriage ceremonies.

you'd throw to the winds at a word, disgrace love,
the source of mankind's nearest, dearest ties.
Marriage of man and wife is Fate itself,   215
stronger than oaths, and Justice guards its life.
But if one destroys the other and you relent—
no revenge, not a glance in anger—then
I say your manhunt of Orestes is unjust.
Some things stir your rage, I see. Others,   220
atrocious crimes, lull your will to act.
                           Pallas
will oversee this trial. She is one of us.
LEADER: I will never let that man go free, never.
APOLLO: Hound him then, and multiply your pains.
LEADER: Never try to cut my power with your logic.   225
APOLLO: I'd never touch it, not as a gift—your power.
LEADER: Of course,
   great as you are, they say, throned on high with Zeus.
But blood of the mother draws me on—must hunt
the man for Justice. Now I'm on his trail!
[*Rushing out, with the* FURIES *in full cry.*]
APOLLO: And I will defend my suppliant and save him.   230
A terror to gods and men, the outcast's anger,
once I fail him, all of my own free will.
[APOLLO *leaves. The scene changes to the Acropolis in Athens. Escorted by* HERMES, ORESTES *enters and kneels, exhausted, before the ancient shrine and idol of* ATHENA.]
ORESTES: Queen Athena,
under Apollo's orders I have come.
Receive me kindly. Curst and an outcast,
no suppliant for purging . . . my hands are clean.[5]   235
My murderous edge is blunted now, worn down at last
on the outland homesteads, beaten paths of men.
On and out over seas and dry frontiers,
I kept alive the Prophet's strong commands.
Struggling toward your house, your idol—
[*Taking the knees of* ATHENA's *idol in his arms.*]
                           Goddess,   240
here I keep my watch,
I await the consummation of my trial.
[*The* FURIES *enter in pursuit but cannot find* ORESTES *who is entwined around* ATHENA's *idol. The* LEADER *sees the footprints.*]
LEADER: At last!
The clear trail of the man. After it, silent
but it tracks his guilt to light. He's wounded—[6]

---

5. Orestes has been given ritual purification by Apollo but he also claims that the blood guilt is now "worn down" by his travels and contacts with men (cf. ll. 280–285).   6. The Furies track him down by scent of the blood he shed, as if he were a wounded animal leaving a trace behind him.

go for the fawn, my hounds, the splash of blood,   245
hunt him, rake him down.
                         Oh, the labor,
the man-killing labor. My lungs are bursting . . .
over the wide rolling earth we've ranged in flock,
hurdling the waves in wingless flight and now we come,
all hot pursuit, outracing ships astern—and now   250
he's here, somewhere, cowering like a hare . . .
the reek of human blood—it's laughter to my heart!
    [*Inciting a pair of* FURIES.]
Look, look again, you two,
scour the ground before he escapes—one dodge
and the matricide slips free.
    [*Seeing* ORESTES, *one by one they press around him and* ATHENA'*s
    idol.*]
FURIES: —There he is!   255
Clutching the knees of power[7] once again,
    twined in the deathless goddess' idol, look,
he wants to go on trial for his crimes.

                         —Never . . .
    the mother's blood that wets the ground,
    you can never bring it back, dear god,   260
the Earth drinks, and the running life is gone.

                            —No,
you'll give me blood for blood, you must!
    Out of your living marrow I will drain
    my red libation, out of your veins I suck my food,
    my raw, brutal cups—

                        —Wither you alive,   265
    drag you down and there you pay, agony
for mother-killing agony!

                 —And there you will see them all.
Every mortal who outraged god or guest or loving parent:
each receives the pain his pains exact.

—A mighty god is Hades. There   270
at the last reckoning underneath the earth
    he scans all, he squares all men's accounts
and graves them on the tablets of his mind.
    [ORESTES *remains impassive.*]
ORESTES: I have suffered into truth. Well I know
    the countless arts of purging, where to speak,   275
    where silence is the rule. In this ordeal
a compelling master urges me to speak.

---

7. Orestes is clinging to the statue of the goddess Pallas Athena.

[*Looking at his hands.*]
The blood sleeps, it is fading on my hands,
the stain of mother's murder washing clean.
It was still fresh at the god's hearth. Apollo   280
killed the swine and the purges drove it off.
Mine is a long story
if I'd start with the many hosts I met,
I lived with, and I left them all unharmed.
Time refines all things that age with time.   285

And now with pure, reverent lips I call
the queen of the land. Athena, help me!
Come without your spear—without a battle
you will win myself, my land, the Argive people[8]
true and just, your friends-in-arms for ever.   290
Where are you now? The scorching wilds of Libya,[9]
bathed by the Triton pool where you were born?
Robes shrouding your feet
or shod and on the march to aid allies?
Or striding the Giants' Plain,[1] marshal of armies,   295
hero scanning, flashing through the ranks?
                               Come—
you can hear me from afar, you are a god.
Set me free from this!

LEADER: Never—neither
Apollo's nor Athena's strength can save you.
Down you go, abandoned,   300
searching your soul for joy but joy is gone.
Bled white, gnawed by demons, a husk, a wraith—
[*She breaks off, waiting for reply, but* ORESTES *prays in silence.*]
No reply? you spit my challenge back?
You'll feast me alive, my fatted calf,
not cut on the altar first. Now hear my spell,   305
the chains of song I sing to bind you tight.

FURIES: Come, Furies, dance!—
link arms for the dancing hand-to-hand,
now we long to reveal our art,
our terror, now to declare our right
to steer the lives of men,   310
we all conspire, we dance! we are
the just and upright, we maintain.
Hold out your hands, if they are clean
no fury of ours will stalk you,

---

8. This is the first clear reference to the alliance which Athens had concluded with Argos in 459 B.C., the
year before the production of the trilogy.   9. One of Athena's titles, Tritogeneia, was thought to derive
from Lake Tritonis, in Libya, where some said she was born. There may be a contemporary allusion here;
Athens was backing, with ships and troops, a Libyan ruler, Inaros, who was fighting the Persian rulers of
Egypt.   1. Athena, a warrior-goddess, took a prominent part in the battle between the gods and the
giants, in which Zeus and the Olympians won a decisive victory.

you will go through life unscathed.   315
But show us the guilty—one like this
   who hides his reeking hands,
and up from the outraged dead we rise,
witness bound to avenge their blood
we rise in flames against him to the end!   320

Mother who bore me,
   O dear Mother Night,
to avenge the blinded dead
and those who see by day,
   now hear me! The whelp Apollo   325
spurns my rights, he tears this trembling victim
      from my grasp—the one to bleed,
      to atone away the mother-blood at last.

   Over the victim's burning head
   this chant this frenzy striking frenzy   330
      lightning crazing the mind
         this hymn of Fury
   chaining the senses, ripping cross the lyre, [2]
      withering lives of men!

This, this is our right,
   spun for us by the Fates,   335
the ones who bind the world,
and none can shake our hold.
   Show us the mortals overcome,
insane to murder kin—we track them down
   till they go beneath the earth,   340
and the dead find little freedom in the end.

   Over the victim's burning head
   this chant this frenzy striking frenzy
      lightning crazing the mind
         this hymn of Fury   345
   chaining the senses, ripping cross the lyre,
      withering lives of men!

Even at birth, I say, our rights were so ordained.
   The deathless gods must keep their hands far off—
no god may share our cups, our solemn feasts.   350
We want no part of their pious white robes—
   the Fates who gave us power made us free.

   Mine is the overthrow of houses, yes,
   when warlust reared like a tame beast
      seizes near and dear—   355

2. Not accompanied by the lyre, an instrument associated with joyous occasions.

down on the man we swoop, aie!
　　for all his power black him out!—
for the blood still fresh from slaughter on his hands.

So now, striving to wrench our mandate from the gods,
　　we make ourselves exempt from their control,   360
we brook no trial—no god can be our judge.
　　[*Reaching toward* ORESTES.]
His breed, worthy of loathing, streaked with blood,
Zeus slights, unworthy his contempt.

　　Mine is the overthrow of houses, yes,
　　　　when warlust reared like a tame beast   365
　　　　　seizes near and dear—
　　　　　　down on the man we swoop, aie!
　　　　　　　for all his power black him out!—
for the blood still fresh from slaughter on his hands.

And all men's dreams of grandeur,   370
　　　　tempting the heavens,
all melt down, under earth their pride goes down—
　　　lost in our onslaught, black robes swarming,
　　　　Furies throbbing, dancing out our rage.

Yes! leaping down from the heights,   375
dead weight in the crashing footfall
　　down we hurl on the runner
　　　breakneck for the finish—
cut him down, our fury stamps him down!

Down he goes, sensing nothing,   380
　　blind with defilement . . .
darkness hovers over the man, dark guilt,
　　and a dense pall overhangs his house,
　　　legend tells the story through her tears.

Yes! leaping down from the heights,   385
　　dead weight in the crashing footfall
　　down we hurl on the runner
　　　breakneck for the finish—
cut him down, our fury stamps him down!

　　　　　　So the center holds.   390
　　　　We are the skilled, the masterful,
　　　　　we the great fulfillers,
　　　memories of grief, we awesome spirits
　　　　stern, unappeasable to man,
　　　disgraced, degraded, drive our powers through;   395
　　　banished far from god to a sunless, torchlit dusk,

we drive men through their rugged passage,
blinded dead and those who see by day.

Then where is the man
not stirred with awe, not gripped by fear   400
to hear us tell the law that
Fate ordains, the gods concede the Furies,
absolute till the end of time?
And so it holds, our ancient power still holds.
We are not without our pride, though beneath the earth   405
our strict battalions form their lines,
groping through the mist and sunstarved night.

[*Enter* ATHENA, *armed for combat with her aegis and her spear.*]
ATHENA: From another world I heard a call for help.
I was on the Scamander's banks, just claiming Troy.
The Achaean warlords chose the hero's share   410
of what their spear had won—they decreed that land,
root and branch all mine, for all time to be,
for Theseus' sons[3] a rare, matchless gift.

Home from the wars I come, my pace unflagging,
wingless, flown on the whirring, breasting cape[4]   415
that yokes my racing spirit in her prime.
      [*Unfurling the aegis, seeing* ORESTES *and the* FURIES *at her shrine.*]
And I see some new companions on the land.
Not fear, a sense of wonder fills my eyes.

Who are you? I address you all as one:
you, the stranger seated at my idol,   420
and you, like no one born of the sown seed,
no goddess watched by the gods, no mortal either,
not to judge by your look at least, your features . . .
Wait, I call my neighbors into question.
They've done nothing wrong. It offends the rights,   425
it violates tradition.
LEADER: You will learn it all,
young daughter of Zeus, cut to a few words.
We are the everlasting children of the Night.
Deep in the halls of Earth they call us Curses.
ATHENA: Now I know your birth, your rightful name—   430

---

3. Homer does not mention it, but in later Athenian tradition, the two sons of Theseus, the national hero
who unified the whole of Attica under Athens, fought at Troy. This reference to Athenian participation
in the war may be another reference to contemporary reality; Athenians had won a foothold in the Troad,
the region around Troy, under the tyrant Pisistratus at the end of the sixth century and in Aeschylus' day
cities in and near the Troad, along the vital route for grain of the Black Sea area, were part of the Athenian
empire. But there is another reason for introducing the subject of the Trojan war. In the *Agamemnon* the
audience is given an almost unrelievedly critical view of the war. But now Orestes is to be tried and
acquitted; Agamemnon's good name restored. The war has now to be presented in a favorable light (Cf.
also ll. 469ff.).   4. The *aegis*, a cloak worn by Athena: it has the face of the Gorgon Medusa on it. Here
Athena uses it to fly; at other times it is used as a shield to produce terror as in *Odyssey*, XXII.

LEADER: But not our powers, and you will learn them quickly.

ATHENA: I can accept the facts, just tell them clearly.

LEADER: Destroyers of life: we drive them from their houses.

ATHENA: And the murderer's flight, where does it all end?

LEADER: Where there is no joy, the word is never used.   435

ATHENA: Such flight for him? You shriek him on to that?

LEADER: Yes,
he murdered his mother—called that murder just.

ATHENA: And nothing forced him on, no fear of someone's anger?

LEADER: What spur would force a man to kill his mother?

ATHENA: Two sides are here, and only half is heard.   440

LEADER: But the oath—he will neither take the oath nor give it,
no, his will is set.

ATHENA: And you are set
on the name of justice rather than the act.

LEADER: How? Teach us. You have a genius for refinements.

ATHENA: Injustice, I mean, should never triumph thanks to oaths.   445

LEADER: Then examine him yourself, judge him fairly.

ATHENA: you would turn over responsibility to me,
to reach the final verdict?

LEADER: Certainly.
We respect you. You show us respect.

    [ATHENA *turns to* ORESTES.]

ATHENA: Your turn, stranger. What do you say to this?   450
Tell us your land, your birth, your fortunes.
Then defend yourself against their charge,
if trust in your rights has brought you here to guard
my hearth and idol, a suppliant for purging
like Ixion,[5] sacred. Speak to all this clearly,   455
speak to me.

ORESTES: Queen Athena, first,
the misgiving in your final words is strong.
Let me remove it. I haven't come for purging.
Look, not a stain on the hands that touch your idol.
I have proof for all I say, and it is strong.   460

The law condemns the man of the violent hand
to silence, till a master trained at purging
slits the throat of a young suckling victim,
blood absolves his blood. Long ago
at the halls of others I was fully cleansed   465
in the cleansing springs, the blood of many victims.
Threat of pollution—sweep it from your mind.

Now for my birth. You will know at once.
I am from Argos. My father, well you ask,

5. The Greek Cain, the first murderer. He killed his father-in-law; coming to Zeus as a suppliant, he was purified by the great god himself.

was Agamemnon, sea-lord of the men-of-war,   470
your partisan when you made the city Troy
a city of the dead.
                    What an ignoble death he died
when he came home—Ai! my blackhearted mother
cut him down, enveloped him in her handsome net—
it still attests his murder in the bath.   475
But I came back, my years of exile weathered—
killed the one who bore me, I won't deny it,
killed her in revenge. I loved my father,
fiercely.
        And Apollo shares the guilt—
he spurred me on, he warned of the pains I'd feel   480
unless I acted, brought the guilty down.
But were we just or not? Judge us now.
My fate is in your hands. Stand or fall
I shall accept your verdict.

ATHENA: Too large a matter,
some may think, for mortal men to judge.   485
But by all rights not even I should decide
a case of murder—murder whets the passions.
Above all, the rites have tamed your wildness.
A suppliant, cleansed, you bring my house no harm.
If you are innocent, I'd adopt you for my city.   490
    [Turning to the FURIES.]
But they have their destiny too, hard to dismiss,
and if they fail to win their day in court—
how it will spread, the venom of their pride,
plague everlasting blights our land, our future . . .

So it stands. A crisis either way.   495
    [Looking back and forth from ORESTES to the FURIES.]
Embrace the one? expel the other? It defeats me.

But since the matter comes to rest on us,
I will appoint the judges of manslaughter,
swear them in, and found a tribunal here
for all time to come.[6]
    [To ORESTES and the FURIES.]
                    My contestants,   500
summon your trusted witnesses and proofs,
your defenders under oath to help your cause.
And I will pick the finest men of Athens,
return and decide the issue fairly, truly—
bound to our oaths, our spirits bent on justice.   505
    [ATHENA leaves. The FURIES form their chorus.]

---

6. The Areopagus, which in Aeschylus' lifetime was the court that tried homicide cases.

FURIES: Here, now, is the overthrow
  of every binding law[7]—once his appeal,
    his outrage wins the day,
  his matricide! One act links all mankind,
  hand to desperate hand in bloody license.   510
    Over and over deathstrokes
      dealt by children wait their parents,
    mortal generations still unborn.

    We are the Furies still, yes,
  but now our rage that patrolled the crimes of men,   515
    that stalked their rage dissolves—
  we loose a lethal tide to sweep the world!
  Man to man foresees his neighbor's torments,
    groping to cure his own—
      poor wretch, there is no cure, no use,   520
    the drugs that ease him speed the next attack.

  Now when the sudden blows come down,
  let no one sound the call that once brought help,
  "Justice, hear me—Furies throned in power!"
    Oh I can hear the father now   525
    or the mother sob with pain
      at the pain's onset . . . hopeless now,
    the house of Justice falls.

  There is a time when terror helps,
  the watchman must stand guard upon the heart.   530
  It helps, at times, to suffer into truth.
  Is there a man who knows no fear
  in the brightness of his heart,
    or a man's city, both are one,
    that still reveres the rights?   535

        Neither the life of anarchy
        nor the life enslaved by tyrants, no,
          · worship neither.
      Strike the balance all in all and god will give you power;
        the laws of god may veer from north to south—   540
          we Furies plead for Measure.
      Violence is Impiety's child, true to its roots,
        but the spirit's great good health breeds all we love
          and all our prayers call down,
              prosperity and peace.   545

7. The Furies argue that the acquittal of Orestes will be a precedent for universal crime. Furthermore, they will no longer, in that case, continue to see that vengeance is exacted; appeals to the Furies for justice will be disregarded (ll. 523ff.).

All in all I tell you people,
    bow before the altar of the rights,
        revere it well.
Never trample it underfoot, your eyes set on spoils;
    revenge will hunt the godless day and night—   550
        the destined end awaits.
So honor your parents first with reverence, I say,
    and the stranger guest you welcome to your house,
        turn to attend his needs,
        respect his sacred rights.   555

All of your own free will, all uncompelled,
    be just and you will never want for joy,
you and your kin can never be uprooted from the earth.
    But the reckless one—I warn the marauder
dragging plunder, chaotic, rich beyond all rights: 560
    he'll strike his sails,
        harried at long last,
stunned when the squalls of torment break his spars to bits.

He cries to the deaf, he wrestles walls of sea
sheer whirlpools down, down, with the gods' laughter   565
breaking over the man's hot heart—they see him flailing, crushed.
    The one who boasted never to shipwreck
now will never clear the cape and steer for home;
        who lived for wealth,
        golden his life long—   570
he rams on the reef of law and drowns unwept, unseen.
[*The scene has shifted to the Areopagus, the tribunal on the Crag of
Ares.*[8] ATHENA *enters in procession with a herald and ten Citizens she
has chosen to be judges.*]
ATHENA: Call for order, herald, marshal our good people.
Lift the Etruscan battle-trumpet,[9]
strain it to full pitch with human breath,
crash out a stabbing blast along the ranks.   575
[*The trumpet sounds. The judges take up positions between the audience and the actors.* ATHENA *separates the* FURIES *and* ORESTES, *directing him to the Stone of Outrage and the* LEADER *to the Stone of
Unmercifulness,*[1] *where the* FURIES *form their chorus. Then* ATHENA
takes her stand between two urns that will receive the ballots.]
And while this court of judgment fills, my city,
silence will be best. So that you can learn
my everlasting laws. And you too,
[*To* ORESTES *and the* FURIES.]

<hr>

8. A literal translation of the word *Areopagus.*   9. The Etruscans, a people living in central Italy, were
supposed to have invented the trumpet.   1. Though Aeschylus does not mention them, we know that
there were two stone bases on the Areopagus where prosecutor and defendant took their places for the trial;
naturally the Stone of Unmercifulness was reserved for the prosecutor.

that our verdict may be well observed by all.
[APOLLO *enters suddenly and looms behind* ORESTES.]
Lord Apollo—rule it over your own sphere!   580
What part have you in this? Tell us.[2]
APOLLO: I come
as a witness. This man, according to custom,
this suppliant sought out my house and hearth.
I am the one who purged his bloody hands.
His champion too, I share responsibility   585
for his mother's execution.
                         Bring on the trial.
You know the rules, now turn them into justice.
[ATHENA *turns to the* FURIES.]
ATHENA: The trial begins! Yours is the first word—
the prosecution opens. Start to finish,
set the facts before us, make them clear.   590
LEADER: Numerous as we are, we will be brief.
    [*To* ORESTES.]
Answer count for count, charge for charge.
First, tell us, did you kill your mother?
ORESTES: I killed her. There's no denying that.
LEADER: Three falls[3] in the match. One is ours already.   595
ORESTES: You exult before your man is on his back.
LEADER: But *how* did you kill her? You must tell us that.
ORESTES: I will. I drew my sword—more, I cut her throat.
LEADER: And who persuaded you? who led you on?
ORESTES: This god and his command.
    [*Indicating* APOLLO.]
                                   He bears me witness.   600
LEADER: The Seer? He drove you on to matricide?
ORESTES: Yes,
and to this hour I have no regrets.
LEADER: If the verdict
brings you down, you'll change your story quickly.
ORESTES: I have my trust; my father will help me from the grave.
LEADER: Trust to corpses now! You made your mother one.   605
ORESTES: I do. She had two counts against her, deadly crimes.
LEADER: How? Explain that to your judges.
ORESTES: She killed her husband—killed my father too.
LEADER: But murder set her free, and you live on for trial.
ORESTES: She lived on. You never drove *her* into exile—why?   610
LEADER: The blood of the man she killed was not her own.
ORESTES: And I? Does mother's blood run in my veins?
LEADER: How could she breed you in her body, murderer?
    Disclaim your mother's blood? She gave you life.

2. The manuscripts assign ll. 580–581 to the leader of the chorus; the peremptory tone certainly sounds more suitable to the Furies than to Athena.   3. There were three falls in a Greek wrestling match.

[ORESTES *turns to* APOLLO.]

ORESTES: Bear me witness—show me the way, Apollo!   615
Did I strike her down with justice?
Strike I did, I don't deny it, no.
But how does our bloody work impress you now?—
Just or not? Decide.
I must make my case to them.

APOLLO: [*Looking to the judges.*] *Just,*   620
I say, to you and your high court, Athena.
Seer that I am, I never lie. Not once
from the Prophet's thrones have I declared
a word that bears on man, woman or city
that Zeus did not command, the Olympian Father.   625
This is *his* justice—omnipotent, I warn you.
Bend to the will of Zeus. No oath can match
the power of the Father.

LEADER: Zeus, you say,[4]
gave that command to your oracle? He charged
Orestes here to avenge his father's death   630
and spurn his mother's rights?

APOLLO: —Not the same
for a noble man to die, covered with praise,
his scepter the gift of god—murdered, at that,
by a woman's hand, no arrows whipping in
from a distance as an Amazon would fight.[5]   635
But as you will hear, Athena, and your people
poised to cast their lots and judge the case.

Home from the long campaign he came, more won
than lost on balance, home to her loyal, waiting arms,
the welcome bath . . .

                         he was just emerging at the edge,   640
and there she pitched her tent, her circling shroud—
she shackled her man in robes,
in her gorgeous never-ending web she chopped him down!

Such was the outrage of his death, I tell you,
the lord of the squadrons, that magnificent man.   645
Her I draw to the life to lash your people,
marshaled to reach a verdict.

LEADER: Zeus, you say,
sets more store by a father's death? He shackled

---

4. The chorus wants Apollo to state clearly that Zeus gave him the specific instructions for Orestes to kill his mother. When they have that assurance, they will face Apollo with a flagrant contradiction of his claim that Zeus is the champion of the father's rights (ll. 647–651).   5. The Amazons were a mythical tribe of female warriors, skilled archers, who were thought to have lived in Asia Minor on the Black Sea and to have once invaded Attica.

his own father, Kronos proud with age.
Doesn't that contradict you?   650
      [*To the judges.*]
Mark it well. I call you all to witness.
APOLLO:[6] You grotesque, loathsome—the gods detest you!
Zeus can break chains, we've cures for that,
countless ingenious ways to set us free.
But once the dust drinks down a man's blood,   655
he is gone, once for all. No rising back,
no spell sung over the grave can sing him back—
not even Father can. Though all things else
he can overturn and never strain for breath.
LEADER: So
you'd force this man's acquittal? Behold, Justice!   660
      [*Exhibiting* APOLLO *and* ORESTES.]
Can a son spill his mother's blood on the ground,
then settle into his father's halls in Argos?
Where are the public altars he can use?
Can the kinsmen's holy water touch his hands?
APOLLO: Here is the truth, I tell you—see how right I am.   665
The woman you call the mother of the child[7]
is not the parent, just a nurse to the seed,
the new-sown seed that grows and swells inside her.
The *man* is the source of life—the one who mounts.
She, like a stranger for a stranger, keeps   670
the shoot alive unless god hurts the roots.

I give you proof that all I say is true.
The father can father forth without a mother.
Here she stands, our living witness. Look—
      [*Exhibiting* ATHENA.]
Child sprung full-blown from Olympian Zeus,   675
never bred in the darkness of the womb
but such a stock no goddess could conceive!

And I, Pallas, with all my strong techniques
will rear your host and battlements to glory.
So I dispatched this suppliant to your hearth   680
that he might be your trusted friend[8] forever,
that you might win a new ally, dear goddess.
He and his generations arm-in-arm with yours,
your bonds stand firm for all posterity—

6. Apollo walks into the trap. Zeus only bound Kronos, he did not kill him, says Apollo. But Orestes did
kill his mother.   7. This doctrine, that the woman is not really a parent of the child but merely a sort
of receptacle and nurse, appears elsewhere in Greek literature also; it was a comforting formula for a society
which, like the goddess Athena (752), honored the male. Apollo appeals for confirmation to the birth of
the goddess herself; she had no mother but was born from the head of Zeus.   8. Another reference to
the Athenian alliance with Argos.

ATHENA: Now
  have we heard enough? May I have them cast   685
  their honest lots as conscience may decide?
LEADER: For us, we have shot our arrows, every one.
  I wait to hear how this ordeal will end.
ATHENA: Of course.
  And what can I do to merit your respect?
APOLLO: You have heard what you have heard.   690
  [*To the judges.*]
  Cast your lots, my friends,
  strict to the oath that you have sworn.
ATHENA: And now
  if you would hear my law, you men of Greece,
  you who will judge the first trial of bloodshed.

  Now and forever more, for Aegeus' people[9]   695
  this will be the court where judges reign.
  This is the Crag of Ares, where the Amazons
  pitched their tents when they came marching down
  on Theseus, full tilt in their fury, erecting
  a new city to overarch his city, towers thrust   700
  against his towers—they sacrificed to Ares,
  named this rock from that day onward Ares' Crag.

  Here from the heights, terror and reverence,
  my people's kindred powers
  will hold them from injustice through the day   705
  and through the mild night. Never pollute
  our law with innovations. No, my citizens,
  foul a clear well and you will suffer thirst.

  Neither anarchy nor tyranny,[1] my people.
  Worship the Mean, I urge you,   710
  shore it up with reverence and never
  banish terror from the gates, not outright.
  Where is the righteous man who knows no fear?
  The stronger your fear, your reverence for the just,
  the stronger your country's wall and city's safety,   715
  stronger by far than all men else possess
  in Scythia's rugged steppes[2] or Pelops' level plain.
  Untouched by lust for spoil, this court of law
  majestic, swift to fury, rising above you
  as you sleep, our night watch always wakeful,   720
  guardian of our land—I found it here and now.

9. The Athenians; Aegeus was the father of Theseus.   1. Athena repeats the advice and even the words
of the Furies (ll. 536ff).   2. In S. Russia; *Pelop's level plain* is the Peloponnese—central Greece. The
expression may signify just geographical expanse but there is possibly also an appropriateness in the choice
of the two locations; the Scythians were famous for their good laws and the Peloponnese was the territory
of Sparta, famous for its stable constitution.

So I urge you, Athens. I have drawn this out
to rouse you to your future. You must rise,
each man must cast his lot and judge the case,
reverent to his oath. Now I have finished.   725
    [*The judges come forward, pass between the urns and cast their lots.*]
LEADER: Beware. Our united force can break your land.
    Never wound our pride, I tell you, never.
APOLLO: The oracles, not mine alone but Zeus', too—
    dread them, I warn you, never spoil their fruit.
    [*The* LEADER *turns to* APOLLO.]
LEADER: You dabble in works of blood beyond your depth.   730
    Oracles, your oracles will be stained forever.
APOLLO: Oh, so the Father's judgment faltered when Ixion,
    the first man-slayer, came to him for purging?
LEADER: Talk on, talk on. But if I lose this trial
    I will return in force to crush the land.   735
APOLLO: Never—among the gods, young and old,
    you go disgraced. I will triumph over you!
LEADER: Just as you triumphed in the house of Pheres,[3]
    luring the Fates to set men free from death.
APOLLO: What?—is it a crime to help the pious man,   740
    above all, when his hour of need has come?
LEADER: You brought them down, the oldest realms of order,
    seduced the ancient goddesses with wine.
APOLLO: *You* will fail this trial—in just a moment
    spew your venom and never harm your enemies.   745
LEADER: You'd ride me down, young god, for all my years?
    Well here I stand, waiting to learn the verdict.
    Torn with doubt . . . to rage against the city or—
ATHENA: My work is here, to render the final judgment.
    Orestes,
    [*Raising her arm, her hand clenched as if holding a ballot-stone.*]
        I will cast my lot for you.   750
    No mother gave me birth.
    I honor the male, in all things but marriage.
    Yes, with all my heart I am my Father's child.
    I cannot set more store by the woman's death—
    she killed her husband, guardian of their house.   755
    Even if the vote is equal, Orestes wins.[4]

    Shake the lots from the urns. Quickly,
    you of the jury charged to make the count.

---

3. Father of Admetus, king of Thessaly. Apollo repaid kindness shown him by Admetus by persuading
the fates to let Admetus avoid an early death if he could find someone willing to die in his stead. (His wife
Alcestis was willing; this is the subject of Euripides' famous play *Alcestis*.) According to the Furies (l. 743)
Apollo got the Fates drunk.   **4.** So, in Athenian courts, a split jury meant acquittal. Athena announces
that if the votes are equal, she will give a casting vote for acquittal. (At the real court of the Areopagus, if
the votes were equal, the defendant was declared acquitted by "the vote of Athena.")

[*Judges come forward, empty the urns, and count the ballot-stones.*]
ORESTES: O God of the Light, Apollo, how will the verdict go?
LEADER: O Night, dark mother, are you watching now?   760
ORESTES: Now for the goal—the noose, or the new day!
LEADER: Now we go down, or forge ahead in power.
APOLLO: Shake out the lots and count them fairly, friends.
   Honor Justice. An error in judgment now
   can mean disaster. The cast of a single lot   765
   restores a house to greatness.
      [*Receiving the judges' count,* ATHENA *lifts her arm once more.*]
ATHENA: The man goes free,
   cleared of the charge of blood. The lots are equal.
ORESTES: O Pallas Athena—you, you save my house!
   I was shorn of the fatherland but you
   reclaim it for me. Now any Greek will say,   770
   "He lives again, the man of Argos lives
   on his fathers' great estates. Thanks to Pallas,
   Apollo, and Zeus, the lord of all fulfillment,
   Third, Saving Zeus." He respected father's death,
   looked down on mother's advocates—
      [*Indicating the* FURIES.]
                              he saved me.   775

   And now I journey home. But first I swear
   to you, your land and assembled host, I swear
   by the future years that bring their growing yield
   that no man, no helmsman of Argos wars on Athens,
   spears in the vanguard moving out for conquest.   780
   We ourselves, even if we must rise up from the grave,[5]
   will deal with those who break the oath I take—
   baffle them with disasters, curse their marches,
   send them hawks aloft on the left[6] at every crossing—
   make their pains recoil upon their heads.   785
   But all who keep our oath, who uphold your rights
   and citadel forever, comrades spear to spear,
   we bless with all the kindness of our heart.

   Now farewell, you and the people of your city.
   Good wrestling—a grip no foe can break.   790
   A saving hope, a spear to bring you triumph!
      [*Exit* ORESTES, *followed by* APOLLO. *The* FURIES *reel in wild confusion
      around* ATHENA.]
FURIES: You, you younger gods!—you have ridden down
      the ancient laws, wrenched them from my grasp—
   and I, robbed of my birthright, suffering, great with wrath,
      I loose my poison over the soil, aieee!—   795

5. Orestes will be a "hero" in the Greek sense: a protecting spirit for the land.   6. Birds seen on the left were a portent of an evil to come.

poison to match my grief comes pouring out my heart,
    cursing the land to burn it sterile and now
rising up from its roots a cancer blasting leaf and child,
    now for Justice, Justice!—cross the face of the earth
the bloody tide comes hurling, all mankind destroyed.   800
. . . Moaning, only moaning? What will I do?
  The mockery of it, Oh unbearable,
mortified by Athens,
we the daughters of Night,
our power stripped, cast down.

ATHENA: Yield to me.   805
No more heavy spirits. You were not defeated—
the vote was tied, a verdict fairly reached
with no disgrace to you, no, Zeus brought
luminous proof before us. He who spoke
god's oracle, he bore witness that Orestes   810
did the work but should not suffer harm.

And now you'd vent your anger, hurt the land?
Consider a moment. Calm yourself. Never
render us barren, raining your potent showers
down like spears, consuming every seed.   815
By all my rights I promise you your seat
in the depths of earth, yours by all rights—
stationed at hearths equipped with glistening thrones,
covered with praise! My people will revere you.

FURIES: You, you younger gods!—you have ridden down   820
    the ancient laws, wrenched them from my grasp—
and I, robbed of my birthright, suffering, great with wrath,
  I loose my poison over the soil, aieee!—
poison to match my grief comes pouring out my heart,
    cursing the land to burn it sterile and now   825
rising up from its roots a cancer blasting leaf and child,
    now for Justice, Justice!—cross the face of the earth
the bloody tide comes hurling, all mankind destroyed.
. . . Moaning, only moaning? What will I do?
  The mockery of it, Oh unbearable,   830
mortified by Athens,
we the daughters of Night,
our power stripped, cast down.

ATHENA: You have your power,
you are goddesses—but not to turn
on the world of men and ravage it past cure.   835
I put my trust in Zeus and . . . must I add this?
I am the only god who knows the keys
to the armory where his lightning-bolt is sealed.
No need of that, not here.

Let me persuade you.
The lethal spell of your voice, never cast it   840
down on the land and blight its harvest home.
Lull asleep that salt black wave of anger—
awesome, proud with reverence, live with me.
The land is rich, and more, when its first fruits,
offered for heirs and the marriage rites,[7] are yours   845
to hold forever, you will praise my words.

FURIES: But for me to suffer such disgrace . . . I,
the proud heart of the past, driven under the earth,
condemned, like so much filth,
    and the fury in me breathing hatred—   850
O good Earth,
    what is this stealing under the breast,
what agony racks the spirit? . . . Night, dear Mother Night!
All's lost, our ancient powers torn away by their cunning,
ruthless hands, the gods so hard to wrestle down   855
obliterate us all.

ATHENA: I will bear with your anger.
You are older. The years have taught you more,
much more than I can know. But Zeus, I think,
gave me some insight too, that has its merits.
If you leave for an alien land and alien people,   860
you will come to love this land, I promise you.
As time flows on, the honors flow through all
my citizens, and you, throned in honor
before the house of Erechtheus,[8] will harvest
more from men and women moving in solemn file   865
than you can win throughout the mortal world.

Here in our homeland never cast the stones
that whet our bloodlust. Never waste our youth,
inflaming them with the burning wine of strife.
Never pluck the heart of the battle cock   870
and plant it in our people—intestine war
seething against themselves. Let our wars
rage on abroad,[9] with all their force, to satisfy
our powerful lust for fame. But as for the bird
that fights at home—my curse on civil war.   875

This is the life I offer, it is yours to take.
Do great things, feel greatness, greatly honored.
Share this country cherished by the gods.

---

7. The Erinyes, as spirits of the earth, did in fact receive in Athens offerings for children born and marriages made.   8. The old shrine of Erechtheus on the Acropolis had been destroyed by the Persians in 480 B.C.; in 421 B.C. the Athenians began the construction of the new Erechtheum, which, much damaged, still stands.   9. Athens was at this time at war with Sparta and her forces may still have been engaged in Egypt.

FURIES: But for me to suffer such disgrace . . . I,
    the proud heart of the past, driven under the earth,   880
    condemned, like so much filth,
      and the fury in me breathing hatred—
    O good Earth,
        what is this stealing under the breast,
    what agony racks the spirit? . . . Night, dear Mother Night!   885
    All's lost, our ancient powers torn away by thir cunning,
    ruthless hands, the gods so hard to wrestle down
    obliterate us all.
ATHENA: No, I will never tire
    of telling you your gifts. So that you,
    the older gods, can never say that I,   890
    a young god and the mortals of my city
    drove you outcast, outlawed from the land.

    But if you have any reverence for Persuasion,
    the majesty of Persuasion,
    the spell of my voice that would appease your fury—   895
    Oh please stay . . .
               and if you refuse to stay,
    it would be wrong, unjust to afflict this city
    with wrath, hatred, populations routed. Look,
    it is all yours, a royal share of our land—
    justly entitled, glorified forever.
LEADER: Queen Athena,   900
    where is the home you say is mine to hold?
ATHENA: Where all the pain and anguish end. Accept it.
LEADER: And if I do, what honor waits for me?
ATHENA: No house can thrive without you.
LEADER: You would do that—
    grant me that much power?
ATHENA: Whoever reveres us—   905
    we will raise the fortunes of their lives.
LEADER: And you will pledge me that, for all time to come?
ATHENA: Yes—I must never promise things I cannot do.
LEADER: Your magic is working . . . I can feel the hate,
    the fury slip away.
ATHENA: At last! And now take root   910
    in the land and win yourself new friends.
LEADER: A spell—
    what spell to sing? to bind the land forever? Tell us.
ATHENA: Nothing that strikes a note of brutal conquest. Only peace—
    blessings, rising up from the earth and the heaving sea,
    and down the vaulting sky let the wind-gods breathe   915
    a wash of sunlight streaming through the land,

and the yield of soil and grazing cattle flood
our city's life with power and never flag
with time. Make the seed of men live on,
the more they worship you the more they thrive.   920
I love them as a gardener loves his plants,
these upright men, this breed fought free of grief.
All that is yours to give.
                And I,
in the trials of war where fighters burn for fame,
will never endure the overthrow of Athens—   925
all will praise her, victor city, pride of man.
     [*The* FURIES *assemble, dancing around* ATHENA, *who becomes their
     leader.*]
FURIES: I will embrace
              one home with you, Athena,
                  never fail the city
            you and Zeus almighty, you and Ares   930
           hold as the fortress of the gods, the shield
of the high Greek altars, glory of the powers.
      Spirit of Athens, hear my words, my prayer
         like a prophet's warm and kind,
           that the rare good things of life   935
             come rising crest on crest,
          sprung from the rich black earth and
        gleaming with the bursting flash of sun.
ATHENA: These blessings I bestow on you, my people, gladly.
I enthrone these strong, implacable spirits here   940
and root them in our soil.
                 Theirs,
theirs to rule the lives of men,
   it is their fated power.
But he who has never felt their weight,
or known the blows of life and how they fall,   945
the crimes of his fathers hale him toward their bar,
and there for all his boasts—destruction,
   silent, majestic in anger,
crushes him to dust.
FURIES: Yes and I ban   950
          the winds that rock the olive—
           hear my love, my blessing—
     thwart their scorching heat that blinds the buds,
      hold from our shores the killing icy gales,
and I ban the blight that creeps on fruit and withers—   955
     God of creation, Pan, make flocks increase
        and the ewes drop fine twin lambs
         when the hour of labor falls.

And silver,[1] child of Earth,
    secret treasure of Hermes,   960
come to light and praise the gifts of god.

ATHENA: Blessings—now do you hear, you guards of Athens,
    all that she will do?
Fury the mighty queen, the dread
of the deathless gods and those beneath the earth,   965
deals with mortals clearly, once for all.
She delivers songs to some, to others
    a blinding life of tears—
Fury works her will.

FURIES: And the lightning stroke
    that cuts men down before their prime, I curse,   970
but the lovely girl who finds a mate's embrace,
the deep joy of wedded life—O grant that gift, that prize,
    you gods of wedlock, grant it, goddesses of Fate!
Sisters born of the Night our mother,
        spirits steering law,   975
      sharing at all our hearths,
        at all times bearing down
     to make our lives more just,
all realms exalt you highest of the gods.

ATHENA: Behold, my land, what blessings Fury kindly,   980
    gladly brings to pass—
I am in my glory! Yes, I love Persuasion;
she watched my words, she met their wild refusals.
Thanks to Zeus of the Councils who can turn
dispute to peace—he won the day.   985
[To the FURIES.]
Thanks to our duel for blessings;
we win through it all.

FURIES: And the brutal strife,
    the civil war devouring men, I pray
      that it never rages through our city, no,   990
that the good Greek soil never drinks the blood of Greeks,
    shed in an orgy of reprisal life for life—
      that Fury like a beast will never
      rampage through the land.
      Give joy in return for joy,   995
      one common will for love,
    and hate with one strong heart:
such union heals a thousand ills of man.

ATHENA: Do you *hear* how Fury sounds her blessings forth,
    how Fury finds the way?   1000
Shining out of the terror of their faces

---

1. At Laurion, in SE Attica, silver had been mined for many years when, sometime before 480 B.C., rich new veins were discovered. The Athenians used the money to build the fleet which fought at Salamis.

I can see great gains for you, my people.
Hold them kindly, kind as they are to you.
Exalt them always, you exalt your land,
    your city straight and just—   1005
its light goes through the world.

FURIES: Rejoice,
                rejoice in destined wealth,
                rejoice, Athena's people—
                poised by the side of Zeus,   1010
                loved by the loving virgin girl,
                achieve humanity at last,
                    nestling under Pallas' wings
                and blessed with Father's love.

ATHENA: You too rejoice! and I must lead the way   1015
    to your chambers by the holy light of these,
        your escorts bearing fire.
        [Enter ATHENA's entourage of women, bearing offerings and victims
        and torches still unlit.]
Come, and sped beneath the earth
    by our awesome sacrifices,
keep destruction from the country,   1020
bring prosperity home to Athens,
triumph sailing in its wake.
                        And you,
my people born of the Rock King,[2]
lead on our guests for life, my city—
May they treat you with compassion,   1025
compassionate as you will be to them.

FURIES: Rejoice!—
            rejoice—the joy resounds—
            all those who dwell in Athens,
                spirits and mortals, come,   1030
                govern Athena's city well,
                revere us well, we are your guests;
            you will learn to praise your Furies,
            you will praise the fortunes of your lives.

ATHENA: My thanks! And I will speed your prayers, your blessings—   1035
    lit by the torches breaking into flame
    I send you home, home to the core of Earth,
    escorted by these friends who guard my idol
    duty-bound.
        [ATHENA's entourage comes forward, bearing crimson robes.]
                Bright eye of the land of Theseus,
come forth, my splendid troupe. Girls and mothers,   1040
trains of aged women grave in movement,

2. A legendary ancestor, Cranaos, whose name means "rocky." The soil of Attica is not rich.

dress our Furies now in blood-red robes.[3]
Praise them—let the torch move on!
So the love this family bears toward our land
will bloom in human strength from age to age. 1045
 [*The women invest the* FURIES *and sing the final chorus. Torches
 blaze; a procession forms, including the actors and the judges.* ATHENA
 leads them from the theater and escorts them through the city.]
 ENA *leads them from the theater and escorts them through the city.*]
THE WOMEN OF THE CITY: On, on, good spirits born for glory,
 Daughters of Night, her children always young,
   now under loyal escort—
 Blessings, people of Athens, sing your blessings out.

 Deep, deep in the first dark vaults of Earth, 1050
 sped by the praise and victims we will bring,
   reverence will attend you—
 Blessings now, all people, sing your blessings out.

 You great good Furies, bless the land with kindly hearts,
 you Awesome Spirits,[4] come—exult in the blazing torch, 1055
   exultant in our fires, journey on.
 Cry, cry in triumph, carry on the dancing on and on!

 This peace between Athena's people and their guests
 must never end. All-seeing Zeus and Fate embrace,
   down they come to urge our union on— 1060
 Cry, cry in triumph, carry on the dancing on and on!

SOPHOCLES

ca. 496–406 B.C.

Aeschylus belonged to the generation that fought at Marathon; his manhood and
his old age were passed in the heroic period of the Persian defeat on Greek soil and
the war that Athens fought to liberate her kinsmen in the islands of the Aegean
and on the Asiatic coast. Sophocles, his younger contemporary, lived to see an
Athens that had advanced in power and prosperity far beyond the city that Aeschylus knew. The league of free Greek cities against Persia that Athens had led to
victory in the Aegean had become an empire, in which Athens taxed and coerced
the subject cities that had once been her free allies. Sophocles, born around 496
B.C., played his part—a prominent one—in the city's affairs. In 443 B.C. he served
as one of the treasurers of the imperial league and, with Pericles, as one of the ten
generals elected for the war against the island of Samos which tried to secede from
the Athenian league a few years later. When the Athenian expedition to Sicily
ended in disaster, Sophocles was appointed to a special committee set up in 411

---

3. At the Great Panathenea, the principal festival of Athens, resident aliens as well as full citizens took
part in the procession to the Acropolis. The resident aliens, *metics* as they were called, wore crimson cloaks
on this occasion. The Furies are thus given residential status in Attic soil.   4. *Semnai* in Greek, a
favorable formula for the Furies, like *Eumenides* (Kindly Ones), the title of the play.

B.C. to deal with the emergency. He died in 406, two years before Athens surrendered to Sparta.

His career as a brilliantly successful dramatist began in 468; in that year he won first prize at the Dionysia, competing against Aeschylus. Over the next sixty-two years he produced over a hundred and twenty plays. He won first prize no fewer than twenty-four times and when he was not first, came in second, never third.

Aeschylus had been an actor as well as a playwright and director, but Sophocles, early in his career, gave up acting. It was he who added a third actor to the team; the early Aeschylean plays (*Persians, Seven Against Thebes,* and *Suppliants*) can be played by two actors (who of course can change masks to extend the range of *dramatis personae*). In the *Oresteia*, Aeschylus has taken advantage of the Sophoclean third actor; this makes possible the role of Cassandra, the one three-line speech of Pylades in *Libation Bearers*, and the trial scene in *Eumenides*. But Sophocles used his third actor to create complex triangular scenes like the dialogue between Oedipus and the Corinthian messenger, which reveals to a listening Jocasta the ghastly truth that Oedipus will not discover until the next scene.

We have only seven of his plays, and not many of them can be accurately dated. The *Ajax* (which deals with the suicide of the hero whose shade turns silently away from Odysseus in the *Odyssey*) and the *Trachiniae* (the story of the death of Heracles) are both generally thought to be early productions. *Antigone* is fairly securely fixed in the late 440s, and *Oedipus the King* was probably staged during the early years of the Peloponnesian War, which began in 431 B.C. For *Electra* we have no date, but it is probably later than *Oedipus the King*. *Philoctetes*, a tale of the Trojan War, was staged in 409 B.C. and *Oedipus at Colonus*, which presents Oedipus' strangely triumphant death on Athenian soil, was produced after Sophocles' death.

Most of these plays date from the last half of the fifth century; they were written in and for an Athens that, since the days of Aeschylus, had undergone an intellectual revolution. It was in a time of critical re-evaluation of accepted standards and traditions (see pp. 5–8) that Sophocles, in the early years of the Peloponnesian war (431–404 B.C.), produced his masterpiece, *Oedipus the King*, and the problems of the time are reflected in the play.

OEDIPUS THE KING

This tragedy, which deals with a man of high principles and probing intelligence who follows the prompting of that intelligence to the final consequence of true self-knowledge—which makes him put out his eyes—was as full of significance for Sophocles' contemporaries as it is for us. Unlike a modern dramatist, Sophocles used for his tragedy a story well known to the audience and as old as their own history, a legend told by parent to child, handed down from generation to generation because of its implicit wealth of meaning, learned in childhood and rooted deep in the consciousness of every member of the community. Such a story the Greeks called a *myth*, and the use of it presented Sophocles, as it did Aeschylus in his trilogy, with material which, apart from its great inherent dramatic potential, already possessed the significance and authority that the modern dramatist must create for himself. It had the authority of history, for the history of ages that leave no records is myth—that is to say, the significant event of the past, stripped of irrelevancies and imaginatively shaped by the oral tradition. It had a religious authority, for the Oedipus story, like the story of the house of Atreus, is concerned with the relation between man and god. Lastly, and this is especially true of the Oedipus myth, it had the power, because of its subject matter, to arouse the irrational hopes and fears that lie deep and secret in the human consciousness.

The use of the familiar myth enabled the dramatist to draw on all its wealth of unformulated meaning, but it did not prevent him from striking a contemporary note. Oedipus, in Sophocles' play, is at one and the same time the mysterious figure of the past who broke the most fundamental human taboos and a typical fifth-century Athenian. His character contains all the virtues for which the Athenians were famous and the vices for which they were notorious. The best commentary on Oedipus' character is the speech that Thucydides, the contemporary historian of the Peloponnesian War, attributed to a Corinthian spokesman at Sparta: it is a hostile but admiring assessment of the Athenian genius. "Athenians . . . [are] equally quick in the conception and in the execution of every new plan"—so Oedipus has already sent to Delphi when the priest advises him to do so, and has already sent for Tiresias when the chorus suggests this course of action. "They are bold beyond their strength; they run risks which prudence would condemn"—as Oedipus risked his life to answer the riddle of the Sphinx and later, in spite of the oracle about his marriage, accepted the hand of the queen. "In the midst of misfortune they are full of hope"—so Oedipus, when he is told that he is not the son of Polybus and Merope, and Jocasta has already realized whose son he is, claims that he is the "child of Fortune." "When they do not carry out an intention that they have formed, they seem to have sustained a personal bereavement"—so Oedipus, shamed by Jocasta and the chorus into sparing Creon's life, yields sullenly and petulantly.

The Athenian devotion to the city, which received the main emphasis in Pericles' praise of Athens, is strong in Oedipus; his answer to the priest at the beginning of the play shows that he is a conscientious and patriotic ruler. His sudden unreasoning rage is the characteristic fault of Athenian democracy, which in 406 B.C., to give only one instance, condemned and executed the generals who had failed, in the stress of weather and battle, to pick up the drowned bodies of their own men killed in the naval engagement at Arginusae. Oedipus is like the fifth-century Athenian most of all in his confidence in the human intelligence, especially his own. This confidence takes him in the play through the whole cycle of the critical, rationalist movement of the century, from the piety and orthodoxy he displays in the opening scene, through his taunts at oracles when he hears that Polybus is dead, to the despairing courage with which he accepts the consequences when he sees the abyss opening at his feet. "I'm right at the edge, the horrible truth—I've got to say it!" speaks the herdsman from whom he is dragging the truth. "And I'm right at the edge of hearing horrors, yes," Oedipus replies, "but I must hear!" And hear he does. He learns that the oracle he had first fought against and then laughed at has been fulfilled; that every step his intelligence prompted was one step nearer to disaster; that his knowledge was ignorance, his clear vision blindness. Faced with the reality that his determined probing finally reveals, he puts out his eyes.

The relation of Oedipus' character to the development of the action is the basis of the most famous attempt to define the nature of the tragic process, Aristotle's theory that pity and terror are aroused most effectively by the spectacle of a man who is "not pre-eminent in virtue and justice, and yet on the other hand does not fall into misfortune through vice or depravity, but falls because of some mistake, one among the number of the highly renowned and prosperous, such as Oedipus." Other references by Aristotle to this play make it clear that this influential critical canon is based particularly on Sophocles' masterpiece, and the canon has been universally applied to the play. But the great influence (and validity) of the Aristotelian theory should not be allowed to obscure the fact that Sophocles' *Oedipus the*

King is more highly organized and economical than Aristotle implies. The fact that the critics have differed about the nature of Oedipus' mistake or frailty (his errors are many and his frailties include anger, impiety, and self-confidence) is a clue to the real situation. Oedipus falls not through "some vicious mole of nature" or some "particular fault" (to use Hamlet's terms), but because he is the man he is, because of all aspects of his character, good and bad alike; and the development of the action right through to the catastrophe shows us every aspect of his character at work in the process of self-revelation and self-destruction. His first decision in the play, to hear Creon's message from Delphi in public rather than, as Creon suggests, in private, is evidence of his kingly solicitude for his people and his trust in them, but it makes certain the full publication of the truth. His impetuous proclamation of a curse on the murderer of Laius, an unnecessary step prompted by his civic zeal, makes his final situation worse than it need have been. His anger at Tiresias forces a revelation that drives him on to accuse Creon; this in turn provokes Jocasta's revelations. And throughout the play his confidence in the efficacy of his own action, his hopefulness as the situation darkens, and his passion for discovering the truth, guide the steps of the investigation which is to reveal the detective as the criminal. All aspects of his character, good and bad alike, are equally involved; it is no frailty or error that leads him to the terrible truth, but his total personality.

The character of Oedipus as revealed in the play does something more than explain the present action; it also explains his past. In Oedipus' speeches and actions on stage we can see the man who, given the circumstances in which Oedipus was involved, would inevitably do just what Oedipus has done. Each action on stage shows us the mood in which he committed some action in the past; his angry death sentence on Creon reveals the man who killed Laius because of an insult on the highway; his impulsive proclamation of total excommunication for the unknown murderer shows us the man who, without forethought, accepted the hand of Jocasta; his intelligent, persistent search for the truth shows us the brain and the courage that solved the riddle of the Sphinx. The revelation of his character in the play is at once a re-creation of his past and an interpretation of the oracle that predicted his future.

This organization of the material is what makes it possible for us to accept the story as tragedy at all, for it emphasizes Oedipus' independence of the oracle. When we first see Oedipus, he has already committed the actions for which he is to suffer—actions prophesied, before his birth, by Apollo. But the dramatist's emphasis on Oedipus' character suggests that although Apollo has predicted what Oedipus will do, he does not determine it; Oedipus determines his own conduct, by being the man he is. Milton's explanation of a similar situation, Adam's fall and God's foreknowledge of it, may be applied to Oedipus; foreknowledge had no influence on his fault. The relationship between Apollo's prophecy and Oedipus' actions is not that of cause and effect. It is the relationship of two independent entities that are equated.

This correspondence between his character and his fate removes the obstacle to our full acceptance of the play which an external fate governing his action would set up. Nevertheless, we feel that he suffers more than he deserves. He has served as an example of the inadequacy of the human intellect and a warning that there is a power in the universe that humanity cannot control, or even fully understand, but Oedipus the man still has our sympathy. Sophocles felt this too, and in a later play, his last, the *Oedipus at Colonus,* he dealt with the reward that finally balanced Oedipus' suffering. In *Oedipus the King* itself there is a foreshadowing of this final development; the last scene shows us a man already beginning to recover from the shock of the catastrophe and reasserting a natural superiority.

"I am going—you know on what condition?" he says to Creon when ordered back into the house, and a few lines later Creon has to say bluntly to him: "Still the king, the master of all things? / No more; here your power ends." This renewed imperiousness is the first expression of a feeling on his part that he is not entirely guilty, a beginning of the reconstitution of the magnificent man of the opening scenes; it reaches its fulfillment in the final Oedipus play, the *Oedipus at Colonus*, in which he is a titanic figure, confident of his innocence and more masterful than he has ever been.

ANTIGONE

Though the *Antigone* was almost certainly produced before *Oedipus the King*, it deals with mythological events that, in the story, come after the exposure of Oedipus' identity and his self-blinding. Creon eventually expelled Oedipus from Thebes, to wander as a blind beggar, accompanied only by his daughter Antigone. His sons, Eteocles and Polynices, raised no hand to help him; when he died at Colonus, near Athens, Antigone returned to Thebes. Eteocles and Polynices, who had agreed to rule jointly, soon quarreled; they fought each other for the throne of Thebes. Eteocles expelled his brother, who recruited supporters in Argos; seven champions attacked the seven gates of Thebes. The assault was beaten off; but Polynices and Eteocles killed each other in the battle. The rule of Thebes fell to Creon. His first decision is to forbid burial to the corpse of Polynices, the traitor who brought foreign troops against his own city. Antigone disobeys the decree by scattering dust on the body; captured and brought before Creon, she defies him in the name of the eternal unwritten laws. In the struggle between them it is the king who in the end surrenders; he buries the body of Polynices and orders Antigone's release. But she has already killed herself in her underground prison, thus bringing about the two deaths that crush her enemy, the suicides of his son Haemon and of his wife Eurydice.

Antigone, as a heroine of the resistance to tyrannical power, has deservedly become one of the Western world's great symbolic figures; she is clearly presented, in her famous speech, as a champion of a higher morality against the overriding claims of state necessity, which the Sophist intellectuals of Sophocles' time had begun to formulate in philosophical terms. But Creon, too, is given his due; he is not a mere tyrant of melodrama but a ruler whose action stems from political and religious attitudes which were probably shared by many of the audience. Antigone and Creon clash not only as individuals, shaped with all Sophocles' dramatic genius (the ancient anonymous biography of Sophocles says truly that he could "match the moment with the action so as to create a whole character out of half a line or even a single word"), but also as representatives of two irreconcilable social and religious positions.

Antigone's chief loyalty is clearly to the family. She makes no distinction between the brothers though one was a patriot and the other a traitor, and when her sister Ismene refuses to help her defy the state to bury a brother she harshly disowns her. The denial of burial to Polynices strikes directly at her family loyalty, for it was the immemorial privilege and duty of the women of the house to mourn the dead man in unrestrained sorrow, sing his praises, wash his body, and consign him to the earth. Creon, on the other hand, sees loyalty to the state as the only valid criterion, and in his opening speech expressly repudiates one who "places a friend above the good of his own country" (the Greek word translated "friend" also means "relative"). This inaugural address of Creon repeats many concepts and even phrases that are to be found in the speeches of the democratic leader Pericles; and in fact, there was an ancient antagonism between the new democratic institutions that stressed the equal rights and obligations of all citizens and the old powerful families that through their wide influence had acted as separate factions in the body politic. The nature of Creon's assertion of state against family, refusal of burial to a corpse, is repellent, but the principle behind it was one most Athenians would have accepted as valid.

These opposing social viewpoints have their corresponding religious sanctions. For Antigone, the gods, especially the gods below, demand equality for all the dead, the common inalienable right of burial. But Creon's gods are the gods who protect the city; how, he asks, could those gods have any feeling for Polynices, a traitor who raised and led a foreign army against the city they protect and that contains their temples? Here again, there must have been many in the audience who saw merit in this argument.

But as the action develops, whatever validity Creon's initial position may have had is destroyed, and by Creon himself. For like all holders of absolute power, he proceeds, when challenged, to equate loyalty to the community with loyalty to himself—"the city is the king's—that's the law!" he tells his son Haemon. And in the end the prophet Tiresias tells him plainly that Antigone was right—the gods are on her side. He swallows his pride and surrenders, but too late. Antigone's suicide brings him to disaster in that institution, the family, which he subordinated to reasons of state; his son spits in his face before killing himself, and his wife dies cursing him as the murderer of his son.

Creon is punished, but Antigone is dead. As the play ends, the chorus points a moral: the "mighty blows of fate . . . at long last . . . will teach us wisdom." But the price of wisdom is high: the *Antigone*, like so many of the Shakespearean tragedies, leaves us with a poignant sense of loss.

C. H. Whitman, *Sophocles, A Study in Heroic Humanism* (1951), is a brilliant study, which explores an approach very different from that proposed here. For a short, general survey of Sophoclean drama, see P. E. Easterling in *The Cambridge History of Classical Literature*, vol. 1 (1985), pp. 295–316. B. M. W. Knox, *Oedipus at Thebes* (1957), is a detailed examination of the play in the context of its age; Knox's *The Heroic Temper* (1964) concentrates on the characters of Oedipus, Antigone, Electra, and Philoctetes. Sophocles, *The Three Theban Plays*, translated by R. Fagles, introductions and notes by B. Knox (1982), contains substantial introductions to *Oedipus the King and Antigone*. See also: R. P. Winnington-Ingram, *Sophocles: An Interpretation* (1980), pp. 91–149 (*Antigone*) and pp. 150–204 (*Oedipus the King*). Also Charles Segal, *An Interpretation of Sophocles* (1981), pp. 152–206 (*Antigone*) and pp. 207–48 (*Oedipus the King*).

Oedipus the King[1]

Characters

OEDIPUS, *king of Thebes*

A PRIEST *of Zeus*

CREON, *brother of Jocasta*

A CHORUS *of Theban citizens and*
    their LEADER

TIRESIAS, *a blind prophet*

JOCASTA, *the queen, wife of*
    Oedipus

A MESSENGER *from Corinth*

A SHEPHERD

A MESSENGER *from inside the*
    palace

ANTIGONE, ISMENE, *daughters of*
    Oedipus and Jocasta

GUARDS *and attendants*

PRIESTS *of Thebes*

[TIME AND SCENE: *The royal house of Thebes. Double doors dominate the
façade; a stone altar stands at the center of the stage.*

Many years have passed since OEDIPUS *solved the riddle of the Sphinx
and ascended the throne of Thebes, and now a plague has struck the city.
A procession of priests enters; suppliants, broken and despondent, they
carry branches wound in wool and lay them on the altar.*

The doors open. Guards assemble. OEDIPUS *comes forward, majestic but
for a telltale limp, and slowly views the condition of his people.*]

PROLOGUE

OEDIPUS: Oh my children, the new blood of ancient Thebes,
    why are you here? Huddling at my altar,
    praying before me, your branches wound in wool.[2]
    Our city reeks with the smoke of burning incense,
    rings with cries for the Healer[3] and wailing for the dead.   5
    I thought it wrong, my children, to hear the truth
    from others, messengers. Here I am myself—
    you all know me, the world knows my fame:
    I am Oedipus.
        [*Helping a* PRIEST *to his feet.*]
                        Speak up, old man. Your years,
    your dignity—you should speak for the others.   10
    Why here and kneeling, what preys upon you so?
    Some sudden fear? some strong desire?
    You can trust me. I am ready to help,
    I'll do anything. I would be blind to misery
    not to pity my people kneeling at my feet.   15
PRIEST: Oh Oedipus, king of the land, our greatest power!
    You see us before you now, men of all ages
    clinging to your altars. Here are boys,
    still too weak to fly from the nest,
    and here the old, bowed down with the years,   20
    the holy ones—a priest of Zeus myself—and here

---

1. Translated by Robert Fagles.   2. The insignia of suppliants, laid on the altar and left there until the
suppliant's request was granted. At the end of the scene, when Oedipus promises action, he will tell them
to take the branches away.   3. A title of Apollo.

the picked, unmarried men, the young hope of Thebes.
And all the rest, your great family gathers now,
branches wreathed, massing in the squares,
kneeling before the two temples of queen Athena   25
or the river-shrine where the embers glow and die
and Apollo sees the future in the ashes.[4]
                            Our city—
look around you, see with your own eyes—
our ship pitches wildly, cannot lift her head
from the depths, the red waves of death . . .   30
Thebes is dying. A blight on the fresh crops
and the rich pastures, cattle sicken and die,
and the women die in labor, children stillborn,
and the plague, the fiery god of fever hurls down
on the city, his lightning slashing through us—   35
raging plague in all its vengeance, devastating
the house of Cadmus![5] And black Death luxuriates
in the raw, wailing miseries of Thebes.
Now we pray to you. You cannot equal the gods,
your children know that, bending at your altar.   40
But we do rate you first of men,
both in the common crises of our lives
and face-to-face encounters with the gods.
You freed us from the Sphinx,[6] you came to Thebes
and cut us loose from the bloody tribute[7] we had paid   45
that harsh, brutal singer. We taught you nothing,
no skill, no extra knowledge, still you triumphed.
A god was with you, so they say, and we believe it—
you lifted up our lives.
                        So now again,
Oedipus, king, we bend to you, your power—   50
we implore you, all of us on our knees:
find us strength, rescue! Perhaps you've heard
the voice of a god or something from other men,
Oedipus . . . what do you know?
The man of experience—you see it every day—   55
his plans will work in a crisis, his first of all.

Act now—we beg you, best of men, raise up our city!
Act, defend yourself, your former glory!
Your country calls you savior now

---

4. At a temple of Apollo in Thebes the priests foretold the future according to patterns they saw in the ashes of the burned flesh of sacrificial victims.   5. Mythical founder of Thebes and its first king. 6. The winged female monster that terrorized the city of Thebes until her riddle was finally answered by Oedipus. The riddle was: "What is it that walks on four feet and two feet and three feet and has only one voice; when it walks on most feet, it is weakest?" Oedipus's answer was Man. (He has four feet as a child crawling on "all fours," and three feet in old age when he walks with the aid of a stick.)   7. Many young men of Thebes had tried to answer the riddle, failed, and been killed.

for your zeal, your action years ago.   60
Never let us remember of your reign:
you helped us stand, only to fall once more.
Oh raise up our city, set us on our feet.
The omens were good that day you brought us joy—
be the same man today!   65
Rule our land, you know you have the power,
but rule a land of the living, not a wasteland.
Ship and towered city are nothing, stripped of men
alive within it, living all as one.

OEDIPUS: My children,
I pity you. I see—how could I fail to see   70
what longings bring you here? Well I know
you are sick to death, all of you,
but sick as you are, not one is sick as I.
Your pain strikes each of you alone, each
in the confines of himself, no other. But my spirit   75
grieves for the city, for myself and all of you.
I wasn't asleep, dreaming. You haven't wakened me—
I've wept through the nights, you must know that,
groping, laboring over many paths of thought.
After a painful search I found one cure: 80
I acted at once. I sent Creon,
my wife's own brother, to Delphi[8]—
Apollo the Prophet's oracle—to learn
what I might do or say to save our city.

Today's the day. When I count the days gone by   85
it torments me . . . what is he doing?
Strange, he's late, he's gone too long.
But once he returns, then, then I'll be a traitor
if I do not do all the god makes clear.

PRIEST: Timely words. The men over there   90
are signaling—Creon's just arriving.

OEDIPUS: [*Sighting* CREON, *then turning to the altar.*]
                     Lord Apollo,
let him come with a lucky word of rescue,
shining like his eyes!

PRIEST: Welcome news, I think—he's crowned, look,
and the laurel wreath is bright with berries.[9]   95

OEDIPUS: We'll soon see. He's close enough to hear—
     [*Enter* CREON *from the side; his face is shaded with a wreath.*]
Creon, prince, my kinsman, what do you bring us?
What message from the god?

8. The oracular shrine of Apollo at Delphi, below Mount Parnassus in central Greece.   9. Creon is wearing a crown of laurel as a sign that he brings good news.

CREON: Good news.
I tell you even the hardest things to bear,
if they should turn out well, all would be well.   100
OEDIPUS: Of course, but what were the god's *words?* There's no hope
and nothing to fear in what you've said so far.
CREON: If you want my report in the presence of these . . .
    [*Pointing to the priests while drawing* OEDIPUS *toward the palace.*]
I'm ready now, or we might go inside.
OEDIPUS: Speak out,
speak to us all. I grieve for these, my people,   105
far more than I fear for my own life.
CREON: Very well,
I will tell you what I heard from the god.
Apollo commands us—he was quite clear—
"Drive the corruption from the land,
don't harbor it any longer, past all cure,   110
don't nurse it in your soil—root it out!"
OEDIPUS: How can we cleanse ourselves—what rites?
What's the source of the trouble?
CREON: Banish the man, or pay back blood with blood.
Murder sets the plague-storm on the city.
OEDIPUS: Whose murder?   115
Whose fate does Apollo bring to light?
CREON: Our leader,
my lord, was once a man named Laius,
before you came and put us straight on course.
OEDIPUS: I know—
or so I've heard. I never saw the man myself.
CREON: Well, he was killed, and Apollo commands us now—   120
he could not be more clear,
"Pay the killers back—whoever is responsible."
OEDIPUS: Where on earth are they? Where to find it now,
the trail of the ancient guilt so hard to trace?
CREON: "Here in Thebes," he said.   125
Whatever is sought for can be caught, you know,
whatever is neglected slips away.
OEDIPUS: But where,
in the palace, the fields or foreign soil,
where did Laius meet his bloody death?
CREON: He went to consult an oracle, Apollo said,   130
and he set out and never came home again.
OEDIPUS: No messenger, no fellow-traveler saw what happened?
Someone to cross-examine?
CREON: No,
they were all killed but one. He escaped,
terrified, he could tell us nothing clearly,   135
nothing of what he saw—just one thing.

OEDIPUS: What's that?
one thing could hold the key to it all,
a small beginning give us grounds for hope.
CREON: He said thieves attacked them—a whole band,
not single-handed, cut King Laius down.
OEDIPUS: A thief,   140
so daring, so wild, he'd kill a king? Impossible,
unless conspirators paid him off in Thebes.
CREON: We suspected as much. But with Laius dead
no leader appeared to help us in our troubles.
OEDIPUS: Trouble? Your *king* was murdered—royal blood!   145
What stopped you from tracking down the killer
then and there?
CREON: The singing, riddling Sphinx.
She . . . persuaded us to let the mystery go
and concentrate on what lay at our feet.
OEDIPUS: No,
I'll start again—I'll bring it all to light myself!   150
Apollo is right, and so are you, Creon,
to turn our attention back to the murdered man.
Now you have *me* to fight for you, you'll see:
I am the land's avenger by all rights,
and Apollo's champion too.   155
But not to assist some distant kinsman, no,
for my own sake I'll rid us of this corruption.
Whoever killed the king may decide to kill me too,
with the same violent hand—by avenging Laius
I defend myself.
   [*To the priests.*]
                          Quickly, my children.   160
Up from the steps, take up your branches now.
   [*To the guards.*]
One of you summon the city[1] here before us,
tell them I'll do everything. God help us,
we will see our triumph—or our fall.
   [OEDIPUS *and* CREON *enter the palace, followed by the guards.*]
PRIEST: Rise, my sons. The kindness we came for   165
Oedipus volunteers himself.
Apollo has sent his word, his oracle—
Come down, Apollo, save us, stop the plague.
   [*The priests rise, remove their branches and exit to the side. Enter a*
   CHORUS, *the citizens of Thebes, who have not heard the news that*
   CREON *brings. They march around the altar, chanting.*]
CHORUS: Zeus!
Great welcome voice of Zeus,[2] what do you bring?

1. Represented by the chorus which comes on to the circular dancing floor immediately after this scene.
2. Apollo was his son, and spoke for him.

What word from the gold vaults of Delphi   170
comes to brilliant Thebes? Racked with terror—
       terror shakes my heart
and I cry your wild cries, Apollo, Healer of Delos[3]
I worship you in dread . . . what now, what is your price?
some new sacrifice? some ancient rite from the past   175
come round again each spring?—
       what will you bring to birth?
Tell me, child of golden Hope
       warm voice that never dies!

You are the first I call, daughter of Zeus   180
deathless Athena—I call your sister Artemis,[4]
heart of the market place enthroned in glory,
       guardian of our earth—
I call Apollo, Archer astride the thunderheads of heaven—
O triple shield against death, shine before me now!   185
If ever, once in the past, you stopped some ruin
launched against our walls
       you hurled the flame of pain
far, far from Thebes—you gods
       come now, come down once more!
                              No, no   190
the miseries numberless, grief on grief, no end—
too much to bear, we are all dying
O my people . . .
       Thebes like a great army dying
and there is no sword of thought to save us, no   195
and the fruits of our famous earth, they will not ripen
no and the women cannot scream their pangs to birth—
screams for the Healer, children dead in the womb
       and life on life goes down
              you can watch them go   200
       like seabirds winging west, outracing the day's fire
down the horizon, irresistibly
       streaking on to the shores of Evening
                              Death
so many deaths, numberless deaths on deaths, no end—
Thebes is dying, look, her children   205
stripped of pity . . .
       generations strewn on the ground
unburied, unwept, the dead spreading death
and the young wives and gray-haired mothers with them
cling to the altars, trailing in from all over the city—   210

---

3. Apollo was born on the sacred island of Delos.   4. Sister of Apollo: a goddess associated with hunting, and also a protector of women in childbirth.

Thebes, city of death, one long cortege
   and the suffering rises
      wails for mercy rise
   and the wild hymn for the Healer blazes out
clashing with our sobs our cries of mourning—   215
   O golden daughter of god,[5] send rescue
   radiant as the kindness in your eyes!

Drive him back!—the fever, the god of death
   that raging god of war[6]
not armored in bronze, not shielded now, he burns me,   220
battle cries in the onslaught burning on—
O rout him from our borders!
Sail him, blast him out to the Sea-queen's chamber
   the black Atlantic gulfs
   or the northern harbor, death to all   225
where the Thracian surf[7] comes crashing.
Now what the night spares he comes by day and kills—
the god of death.

         O lord of the stormcloud,
you who twirl the lightning, Zeus, Father,
thunder Death to nothing!   230

Apollo, lord of the light, I beg you—
   whip your longbow's golden cord
showering arrows on our enemies—shafts of power
champions strong before us rushing on!

Artemis, Huntress,   235
torches flaring over the eastern ridges—
   ride Death down in pain!

God of the headdress gleaming gold, I cry to you—
   your name and ours are one, Dionysus—
      come with your face aflame with wine   240
      your raving women's[8] cries
   your army on the march! Come with the lightning
come with torches blazing, eyes ablaze with glory!
Burn that god of death that all gods hate!
   [OEDIPUS *enters from the palace to address the* CHORUS, *as if addressing
   the entire city of Thebes.*]

EPISODE I

OEDIPUS: You pray to the gods? Let me grant your prayers.   245
Come, listen to me—do what the plague demands:
you'll find relief and lift your head from the depths.

---

5. Athena, daughter of Zeus.   6. The plague is identified with Ares, the war god, though he comes now without armor and shield. Ares is not elsewhere connected with plague; this passage may be an allusion to the early years of the Peloponnesian War, when Spartan troops threatened the city from outside and the plague raged inside the walls.   7. Ares was thought to be at home among the savages of Thrace, to the northeast of Greece proper.   8. The Bacchanals, nymphs or human female votaries of the god Dionysus (Bacchus) who celebrated him with wild dancing rites.

I will speak out now as a stranger to the story,
a stranger to the crime. If I'd been present then,
there would have been no mystery, no long hunt   250
without a clue in hand. So now, counted
a native Theban years after the murder,
to all of Thebes I make this proclamation:
if any one of you knows who murdered Laius,
the son of Labdacus, I order him to reveal   255
the whole truth to me. Nothing to fear,
even if he must denounce himself,
let him speak up
and so escape the brunt of the charge—
he will suffer no unbearable punishment,   260
nothing worse than exile, totally unharmed.

[OEDIPUS *pauses, waiting for a reply.*]

                                          Next,
if anyone knows the murderer is a stranger,
a man from alien soil, come, speak up.
I will give him a handsome reward, and lay up
gratitude in my heart for him besides.   265

[*Silence again, no reply.*]

But if you keep silent, if anyone panicking,
trying to shield himself or friend or kin,
rejects my offer, then hear what I will do.
I order you, every citizen of the state
where I hold throne and power: banish this man—   270
whoever he may be—never shelter him, never
speak a word to him, never make him partner
to your prayers, your victims burned to the gods.
Never let the holy water touch his hands
Drive him out, each of you, from every home.   275
He is the plague, the heart of our corruption,
as Apollo's oracle has just revealed to me.
So I honor my obligations:
I fight for the god and for the murdered man.

Now my curse on the murderer. Whoever he is,   280
a lone man unknown in his crime
or one among many, let that man drag out
his life in agony, step by painful step—
I curse myself as well . . . if by any chance
he proves to be an intimate of our house,   285
here at my hearth, with my full knowledge,
may the curse I just called down on him strike me!

These are your orders: perform them to the last.
I command you, for my sake, for Apollo's, for this country
blasted root and branch by the angry heavens.   290

Even if god had never urged you on to act,
how could you leave the crime uncleansed so long?
A man so noble—your king, brought down in blood—
you should have searched. But I am the king now,
I hold the throne that he held then, possess his bed   295
and a wife who shares our seed . . . why, our seed
might be the same, children born of the same mother
might have created blood-bonds between us
if his hope of offspring hadn't met disaster—
but fate swooped at his head and cut him short.   300
So I will fight for him as if he were my father,
stop at nothing, search the world
to lay my hands on the man who shed his blood,
the son of Labdacus descended of Polydorus,
Cadmus of old and Agenor, founder of the line: 305
their power and mine are one.
                                      Oh dear gods,
my curse on those who disobey these orders!
Let no crops grow out of the earth for them—
shrivel their women, kill their sons,
burn them to nothing in this plague   310
that hits us now, or something even worse.
But you, loyal men of Thebes who approve my actions,
may our champion, Justice, may all the gods
be with us, fight beside us to the end!
LEADER: In the grip of your curse, my king, I swear   315
    I'm not the murderer, I cannot point him out.
    As for the search, Apollo pressed it on us—
    he should name the killer.
OEDIPUS: Quite right,
    but to force the gods to act against their will—
    no man has the power.
LEADER: Then if I might mention   320
    the next best thing . . .
OEDIPUS: The third best too—
    don't hold back, say it.
LEADER: I still believe . . .
    Lord Tiresias[9] sees with the eyes of Lord Apollo.
    Anyone searching for the truth, my king,
    might learn it from the prophet, clear as day.   325
OEDIPUS: I've not been slow with that. On Creon's cue
    I sent the escorts, twice, within the hour.
    I'm surprised he isn't here.
LEADER: We need him—
    without him we have nothing but old, useless rumors.

9. The blind prophet of Thebes (whose ghost Odysseus goes to consult in Hades in *Odyssey* XI).

OEDIPUS: Which rumors? I'll search out every word.   330
LEADER: Laius was killed, they say, by certain travelers.
OEDIPUS: I know—but no one can find the murderer.
LEADER: If the man has a trace of fear in him
    he won't stay silent long,
    not with your curses ringing in his ears.   335
OEDIPUS: He didn't flinch at murder,
    he'll never flinch at words.
    [*Enter* TIRESIAS, *the blind prophet, led by a boy with escorts in attendance. He remains at a distance.*]
LEADER: Here is the one who will convict him, look,
    they bring him on at last, the seer, the man of god.
    The truth lives inside him, him alone.
OEDIPUS: O Tiresias,   340
    master of all the mysteries of our life,
    all you teach and all you dare not tell,
    signs in the heavens, signs that walk the earth!
    Blind as you are, you can feel all the more
    what sickness haunts our city. You, my lord,   345
    are the one shield, the one savior we can find.

    We asked Apollo—perhaps the messengers
    haven't told you—he sent his answer back:
    "Relief from the plague can only come one way.
    Uncover the murderers of Laius,   350
    put them to death or drive them into exile."
    So I beg you, grudge us nothing now, no voice,
    no message plucked from the birds, the embers
    or the other mantic ways within your grasp.
    Rescue yourself, your city, rescue me—   355
    rescue everything infected by the dead.
    We are in your hands. For a man to help others
    with all his gifts and native strength:
    that is the noblest work.
TIRESIAS: How terrible—to see the truth
    when the truth is only pain to him who sees!   360
    I knew it well, but I put it from my mind,
    else I never would have come.
OEDIPUS: What's this? Why so grim, so dire?
TIRESIAS: Just send me home. You bear your burdens,
    I'll bear mine. It's better that way,   365
    please believe me.
OEDIPUS: Strange response . . . unlawful,
    unfriendly too to the state that bred and reared you—
    you withhold the word of god.
TIRESIAS: I fail to see
    that your own words are so well-timed.

I'd rather not have the same thing said of me   370
OEDIPUS: For the love of god, don't turn away,
    not if you know something. We beg you,
    all of us on our knees.
TIRESIAS: None of you knows—
    and I will never reveal my dreadful secrets,
    not to say your own.   375
OEDIPUS: What? You know and you won't tell?
    You're bent on betraying us, destroying Thebes?
TIRESIAS: I'd rather not cause pain for you or me.
    So why this . . . useless interrogation?
    You'll get nothing from me.
OEDIPUS: Nothing! You,   380
    you scum of the earth, you'd enrage a heart of stone!
    You won't talk? Nothing moves you?
    Out with it, once and for all!
TIRESIAS: You criticize my temper . . . unaware
    of the one[1] *you* live with, you revile me.   385
OEDIPUS: Who could restrain his anger hearing you?
    What outrage—you spurn the city!
TIRESIAS: What will come will come.
    Even if I shroud it all in silence.
OEDIPUS: What will come? You're bound to *tell* me that.   390
TIRESIAS: I'll say no more. Do as you like, build your anger
    to whatever pitch you please, rage your worst—
OEDIPUS: Oh I'll let loose, I have such fury in me—
    now I see it all. You helped hatch the plot,
    you did the work, yes, short of killing him   395
    with your own hands—and given eyes I'd say
    you did the killing single-handed!
TIRESIAS: Is that so!
    I charge you, then, submit to that decree
    you just laid down: from this day onward
    speak to no one, not these citizens, not myself.   400
    You are the curse, the corruption of the land!
OEDIPUS: You, shameless—
    aren't you appalled to start up such a story?
    You think you can get away with this?
TIRESIAS: I have already.
    The truth with all its power lives inside me.   405
OEDIPUS: Who primed you for this? Not your prophet's trade.
TIRESIAS: You did, you forced me, twisted it out of me.
OEDIPUS: What? Say it again—I'll understand it better.

---

1. In the Greek the veiled reference to Jocasta is more forceful, since the word translated "the one" has a
feminine ending (agreeing with the feminine noun *orgê*—"temper").

TIRESIAS: Didn't you understand, just now?
　　Or are you tempting me to talk?   410
OEDIPUS: No, I can't say I grasped your meaning.
　　Out with it, again!
TIRESIAS: I say you are the murderer you hunt.
OEDIPUS: That obscenity, twice—by god, you'll pay.
TIRESIAS: Shall I say more, so you can really rage?   415
OEDIPUS: Much as you want. Your words are nothing—futile.
TIRESIAS: You cannot imagine . . . I tell you,
　　you and your loved ones live together in infamy,
　　you cannot see how far you've gone in guilt.
OEDIPUS: You think you can keep this up and never suffer?   420
TIRESIAS: Indeed, if the truth has any power.
OEDIPUS: It does
　　but not for you, old man. You've lost your power,
　　stone-blind, stone-deaf—senses, eyes blind as stone!
TIRESIAS: I pity you, flinging at me the very insults
　　each man here will fling at you so soon.
OEDIPUS: Blind,   425
　　lost in the night, endless night that cursed you!
　　You can't hurt me or anyone else who sees the light—
　　you can never touch me.
TIRESIAS: True, it is not your fate
　　to fall at my hands. Apollo is quite enough,
　　and he will take some pains to work this out.   430
OEDIPUS: Creon! Is this conspiracy his or yours?
TIRESIAS: Creon is not your downfall, no, you are your own.
OEDIPUS: O power—
　　wealth and empire, skill outstripping skill
　　in the heady rivalries of life,
　　what envy lurks inside you! Just for this,   435
　　the crown the city gave me—I never sought it,
　　they laid it in my hands—for this alone, Creon,
　　the soul of trust, my loyal friend from the start
　　steals against me . . . so hungry to overthrow me
　　he sets this wizard on me, this scheming quack,   440
　　this fortune-teller peddling lies, eyes peeled
　　for his own profit—seer blind in his craft!

　　Come here, you pious fraud. Tell me,
　　when did you ever prove yourself a prophet?
　　When the Sphinx, that chanting Fury kept her deathwatch here, 445
　　why silent then, not a word to set our people free?
　　There was a riddle, not for some passer-by to solve—
　　it cried out for a prophet. Where were you?
　　Did you rise to the crisis? Not a word,

you and your birds, your gods—nothing.   450
No, but I came by, Oedipus the ignorant,
I stopped the Sphinx! With no help from the birds,
the flight of my own intelligence hit the mark.

And this is the man you'd try to overthrow?
You think you'll stand by Creon when he's king?   455
You and the great mastermind—
you'll pay in tears, I promise you, for this,
this witch-hunt. If you didn't look so senile
the lash would teach you what your scheming means!
LEADER: I would suggest his words were spoken in anger,   460
Oedipus . . . yours too, and it isn't what we need.
The best solution to the oracle, the riddle
posed by god—we should look for that.
TIRESIAS: You are the king no doubt, but in one respect,
at least, I am your equal: the right to reply.   465
I claim that privilege too.
I am not your slave. I serve Apollo.
I don't need Creon to speak for me in public.
                                          So,
you mock my blindness? Let me tell you this.
You with your precious eyes,   470
you're blind to the corruption of your life,
to the house you live in, those you live with—
who *are* your parents? Do you know? All unknowing
you are the scourge of your own flesh and blood,
the dead below the earth and the living here above,   475
and the double lash of your mother and your father's curse
will whip you from this land one day, their footfall
treading you down in terror, darkness shrouding
your eyes that now can see the light!
                                          Soon, soon
you'll scream aloud—what haven won't reverberate?   480
What rock of Cithaeron[2] won't scream back in echo?
That day you learn the truth about your marriage,
the wedding-march that sang you into your halls,
the lusty voyage home to the fatal harbor!
And a crowd of other horrors you'd never dream   485
will level you with yourself and all your children.

There. Now smear us with insults—Creon, myself,
and every word I've said. No man will ever
be rooted from the earth as brutally as you.
OEDIPUS: Enough! Such filth from him? Insufferable—   490
what, still alive? Get out—

---

2. The mountain range near Thebes, on which Oedipus was left to die when an infant.

faster, back where you came from—vanish!
TIRESIAS: I would never have come if you hadn't called me here.
OEDIPUS: If I thought you would blurt out such absurdities,
   you'd have died waiting before I'd had you summoned.   495
TIRESIAS: Absurd, am I! To you, not to your parents:
   the ones who bore you found me sane enough.
OEDIPUS: Parents—who? Wait . . . who is my father?
TIRESIAS: This day will bring your birth and your destruction.
OEDIPUS: Riddles—all you can say are riddles, murk and darkness.   500
TIRESIAS: Ah, but aren't you the best man alive at solving riddles?
OEDIPUS: Mock me for that, go on, and you'll reveal my greatness.
TIRESIAS: Your great good fortune, true, it was your ruin.
OEDIPUS: Not if I saved the city—what do I care?
TIRESIAS: Well then, I'll be going.
   [To his attendant.]
                         Take me home, boy.   505
OEDIPUS: Yes, take him away. You're a nuisance here.
   Out of the way, the irritation's gone.
   [Turning his back on TIRESIAS, moving toward the palace.[3]]
TIRESIAS: I will go,
   once I have said what I came here to say.
   I'll never shrink from the anger in your eyes—
   you can't destroy me. Listen to me closely: 510
   the man you've sought so long, proclaiming,
   cursing up and down, the murderer of Laius—
   he is here. A stranger,
   you may think, who lives among you,
   he soon will be revealed a native Theban   515
   but he will take no joy in the revelation.
   Blind who now has eyes, beggar who now is rich,
   he will grope his way toward a foreign soil,
   a stick tapping before him step by step.
   [OEDIPUS enters the palace.]
   Revealed at last, brother and father both   520
   to the children he embraces, to his mother
   son and husband both—he sowed the loins
   his father sowed, he spilled his father's blood!

   Go in and reflect on that, solve that.
   And if you find I've lied   525
   from this day onward call the prophet blind.
   [TIRESIAS and the boy exit to the side.]
CHORUS: Who—   ODE I
   who is the man the voice of god denounces

---

3. There are no stage directions in our texts. It is suggested here that Oedipus moves off stage and does not hear the critical section of Tiresias's speech (ll. 520ff) which he could hardly fail to connect with the prophecy made to him by Apollo many years ago.

resounding out of the rocky gorge of Delphi?
　The horror too dark to tell,
　whose ruthless bloody hands have done the work?　530
His time has come to fly
　to outrace the stallions of the storm
　　his feet a streak of speed—
Cased in armor, Apollo son of the Father
lunges on him, lightning-bolts afire!　535
And the grim unerring Furies[4]
　closing for the kill.
　　　　Look,
the word of god has just come blazing
flashing off Parnassus'[5] snowy heights!
That man who left no trace—　540
after him, hunt him down with all our strength!
Now under bristling timber
　up through rocks and caves he stalks
　　like the wild mountain bull—
cut off from men, each step an agony, frenzied, racing blind　545
but he cannot outrace the dread voices of Delphi
ringing out of the heart of Earth,
　the dark wings beating around him shrieking doom
　　the doom that never dies, the terror—

The skilled prophet scans the birds and shatters me with terror!　550
I can't accept him, can't deny him, don't know what to say,
I'm lost, and the wings of dark foreboding beating—
I cannot see what's come, what's still to come . . .
and what could breed a blood feud between
Laius' house and the son of Polybus?[6]　555
I know of nothing, not in the past and not now,
no charge to bring against our king, no cause
　to attack his fame that rings throughout Thebes—
　　not without proof—not for the ghost of Laius,
　　not to avenge a murder gone without a trace.　560

Zeus and Apollo know, they know, the great masters
　of all the dark and depth of human life.
But whether a mere man can know the truth,
whether a seer can fathom more than I—
there is no test, no certain proof　565
　though matching skill for skill
a man can outstrip a rival. No, not till I see
these charges proved will I side with his accusers.
We saw him then, when the she-hawk[7] swept against him,

---

4. Avenging spirits who pursued a murderer when no earthly avenger was at hand.   5. A mountain
range in central Greece. The great oracular shrine of Apollo at Delphi was on its lower slopes.   6. King
of Corinth and, so far as anyone except Tiresias knows, the father of Oedipus.   7. The Sphinx.

saw with our own eyes his skill, his brilliant triumph—   570
there was the test—he was the joy of Thebes!
Never will I convict my king, never in my heart.
[*Enter* CREON *from the side.*]

EPISODE 2

CREON: My fellow-citizens, I hear King Oedipus
levels terrible charges at me. I had to come.
I resent it deeply. If, in the present crisis   575
he thinks he suffers any abuse from me,
anything I've done or said that offers him
the slightest injury, why, I've no desire
to linger out this life, my reputation in ruins.
The damage I'd face from such an accusation   580
is nothing simple. No, there's nothing worse:
branded a traitor in the city, a traitor
to all of you and my good friends.

LEADER: True,
but a slur might have been forced out of him,
by anger perhaps, not any firm conviction.   585

CREON: The charge was made in public, wasn't it?
I put the prophet up to spreading lies?

LEADER: Such things were said . . .
I don't know with what intent, if any.

CREON: Was his glance steady, his mind right   590
when the charge was brought against me?

LEADER: I really couldn't say. I never look
to judge the ones in power.
[*The doors open.* OEDIPUS *enters.*]

                                        Wait,
here's Oedipus now.

OEDIPUS: You—here? You have the gall
to show your face before the palace gates?   595
You, plotting to kill me, kill the king—
I see it all, the marauding thief himself
scheming to steal my crown and power!

                                        Tell me,
in god's name, what did you take me for,
coward or fool, when you spun out your plot?   600
Your treachery—you think I'd never detect it
creeping against me in the dark? Or sensing it,
not defend myself? Aren't you the fool,
you and your high adventure. Lacking numbers,
powerful friends, out for the big game of empire—   605
you need riches, armies to bring that quarry down!

CREON: Are you quite finished? It's your turn to listen
for just as long as you've . . . . instructed me.
Hear me out, then judge me on the facts.

OEDIPUS: You've a wicked way with words, Creon,   610

but I'll be slow to learn—from you.
I find you a menace, a great burden to me.
CREON: Just one thing, hear me out in this.
OEDIPUS: Just one thing,
don't tell *me* you're not the enemy, the traitor.
CREON: Look, if you think crude, mindless stubbornness 615
such a gift, you've lost your sense of balance.
OEDIPUS: If you think you can abuse a kinsman,
then escape the penalty, you're insane.
CREON: Fair enough, I grant you. But this injury
you say I've done you, what is it? 620
OEDIPUS: Did you induce me, yes or no,
to send for that sanctimonious prophet?
CREON: I did. And I'd do the same again.
OEDIPUS: All right then, tell me, how long is it now
since Laius . . .
CREON: Laius—what did *he* do?
OEDIPUS: Vanished, 625
swept from sight, murdered in his tracks.
CREON: The count of the years would run you far back . . .
OEDIPUS: And that far back, was the prophet at his trade?
CREON: Skilled as he is today, and just as honored.
OEDIPUS: Did he ever refer to me then, at that time?
CREON: No, 630
never, at least, when I was in his presence.
OEDIPUS: But you did investigate the murder, didn't you?
CREON: We did our best, of course, discovered nothing.
OEDIPUS: But the great seer never accused me then—why not?
CREON: I don't know. And when I don't, *I* keep quiet. 635
OEDIPUS: You do know this, you'd tell it too—
if you had a shred of decency.
CREON: What?
If I know, I won't hold back.
OEDIPUS: Simply this:
if the two of you had never put heads together,
we would never have heard about *my* killing Laius. 640
CREON: If that's what he says . . . well, you know best.
But now I have a right to learn from you
as you just learned from me.
OEDIPUS: Learn your fill,
you never will convict me of the murder.
CREON: Tell me, you're married to my sister, aren't you? 645
OEDIPUS: A genuine discovery—there's no denying that.
CREON: And you rule the land with her, with equal power?
OEDIPUS: She receives from me whatever she desires.
CREON: And I am the third, all of us are equals?

OEDIPUS: Yes, and it's there you show your stripes—   650
    you betray a kinsman.
CREON: Not at all.
    Not if you see things calmly, rationally,
    as I do. Look at it this way first:
    who in his right mind would rather rule
    and live in anxiety than sleep in peace?   655
    Particularly if he enjoys the same authority.
    Not I, I'm not the man to yearn for kingship,
    not with a king's power in my hands. Who would?
    No one with any sense of self-control.
    Now, as it is, you offer me all I need,   660
    not a fear in the world. But if I wore the crown . . .
    there'd be many painful duties to perform,
    hardly to my taste.
                        How could kingship
    please me more than influence, power
    without a qualm? I'm not that deluded yet,   665
    to reach for anything but privilege outright,
    profit free and clear.
    Now all men sing my praises, all salute me,
    now all who request your favors curry mine.
    I am their best hope: success rests in me.   670
    Why give up that, I ask you, and borrow trouble?
    A man of sense, someone who sees things clearly
    would never resort to treason.
    No, I've no lust for conspiracy in me,
    nor could I ever suffer one who does.   675

    Do you want proof? Go to Delphi yourself,
    examine the oracle and see if I've reported
    the message word-for-word. This too:
    if you detect that I and the clairvoyant
    have plotted anything in common, arrest me,   680
    execute me. Not on the strength of one vote,
    two in this case, mine as well as yours.
    But don't convict me on sheer unverified surmise.
    How wrong it is to take the good for bad,
    purely at random, or take the bad for good.   685
    But reject a friend, a kinsman? I would as soon
    tear out the life within us, priceless life itself.
    You'll learn this well, without fail, in time.
    Time alone can bring the just man to light—
    the criminal you can spot in one short day.   690
LEADER: Good advice,
    my lord, for anyone who wants to avoid disaster.

Those who jump to conclusions may go wrong.
OEDIPUS: When my enemy moves against me quickly,
plots in secret, I move quickly too, I must,
I plot and pay him back. Relax my guard a moment,   695
waiting his next move—he wins his objective,
I lose mine.
CREON: What do you want?
You want me banished?
OEDIPUS: No, I want you dead.
CREON: Just to show how ugly a grudge can . . .
OEDIPUS: So,
still stubborn? you don't think I'm serious?   700
CREON: I think you're insane.
OEDIPUS: Quite sane—in my behalf.
CREON: Not just as much in mine?
OEDIPUS: You—my mortal enemy?
CREON: What if you're wholly wrong?
OEDIPUS: No matter—I must rule.
CREON: Not if you rule unjustly.
OEDIPUS: Hear him, Thebes, my city!
CREON: My city too, not yours alone!   705
LEADER: Please, my lords.
    [*Enter* JOCASTA *from the palace.*]
                    Look, Jocasta's coming,
and just in time too. With her help
you must put this fighting of yours to rest.
JOCASTA: Have you no sense? Poor misguided men,
such shouting—why this public outburst?   710
Aren't you ashamed, with the land so sick,
to stir up private quarrels?
    [*To* OEDIPUS.]
Into the palace now. And Creon, you go home.
Why make such a furor over nothing?
CREON: My sister, it's dreadful . . . Oedipus, your husband,   715
he's bent on a choice of punishments for me,
banishment from the fatherland or death.
OEDIPUS: Precisely. I caught him in the act, Jocasta,
plotting, about to stab me in the back.
CREON: Never—curse me, let me die and be damned   720
if I've done you any wrong you charge me with.
JOCASTA: Oh god, believe it, Oedipus,
honor the solemn oath he swears to heaven.
Do it for me, for the sake of all your people.
    [*The* CHORUS *begins to chant.*]
CHORUS: Believe it, be sensible   725
    give way, my king, I beg you!
OEDIPUS: What do you want from me, concessions?

CHORUS: Respect him—he's been no fool in the past
and now he's strong with the oath he swears to god.
OEDIPUS: You know what you're asking?
CHORUS: I do.
OEDIPUS: Then out with it!   730
CHORUS: The man's your friend, your kin, he's under oath—
    don't cast him out, disgraced
    branded with guilt on the strength of hearsay only.
OEDIPUS: Know full well, if that is what you want
    you want me dead or banished from the land.   735
CHORUS: Never—
    no, by the blazing Sun, first god of the heavens!
    Stripped of the gods, stripped of loved ones,
    let me die by inches if that ever crossed my mind.
    But the heart inside me sickens, dies as the land dies
    and now on top of the old griefs you pile this,   740
    your fury—both of you!
OEDIPUS: Then let him go,
    even if it does lead to my ruin, my death
    or my disgrace, driven from Thebes for life.
    It's you, not him I pity—your words move me.
    He, wherever he goes, my hate goes with him.   745
CREON: Look at you, sullen in yielding, brutal in your rage—
    you'll go too far. It's perfect justice:
    natures like yours are hardest on themselves.
OEDIPUS: Then leave me alone—get out!
CREON: I'm going.
    You're wrong, so wrong. These men know I'm right.   750
    [Exit to the side. The CHORUS turns to JOCASTA.]
CHORUS: Why do you hesitate, my lady
    why not help him in?
JOCASTA: Tell me what's happened first.
CHORUS: Loose, ignorant talk started dark suspicions
    and a sense of injustice cut deeply too.   755
JOCASTA: On both sides?
CHORUS: Oh yes.
JOCASTA: What did they say?
CHORUS: Enough, please, enough! The land's so racked already
    or so it seems to me . . .
    End the trouble here, just where they left it.
OEDIPUS: You see what comes of your good intentions now?   760
    And all because you tried to blunt my anger.
CHORUS: My king,
    I've said it once, I'll say it time and again—
    I'd be insane, you know it,
    senseless, ever to turn my back on you.
    You who set our beloved land—storm-tossed, shattered—   765

straight on course. Now again, good helmsman,
steer us through the storm!
   [*The* CHORUS *draws away, leaving* OEDIPUS *and* JOCASTA *side by side.*]
JOCASTA: For the love of god,
Oedipus, tell me too, what is it?
Why this rage? You're so unbending.
OEDIPUS: I will tell you. I respect you, Jocasta,   770
much more than these . . .
   [*Glancing at the* CHORUS.]
Creon's to blame, Creon schemes against me.
JOCASTA: Tell me clearly, how did the quarrel start?
OEDIPUS: He says I murdered Laius—I am guilty.
JOCASTA: How does he know? Some secret knowledge   775
or simple hearsay?
OEDIPUS: Oh, he sent his prophet in
to do his dirty work. You know Creon,
Creon keeps his own lips clean.
JOCASTA: A prophet?
Well then, free yourself of every charge!
Listen to me and learn some peace of mind: 780
no skill in the world,
nothing human can penetrate the future.
Here is proof, quick and to the point.

An oracle came to Laius one fine day
(I won't say from Apollo himself   785
but his underlings, his priests) and it said
that doom would strike him down at the hands of a son,
our son, to be born of our own flesh and blood. But Laius,
so the report goes at least, was killed by strangers,
thieves, at a place where three roads meet . . . my son—   790
he wasn't three days old and the boy's father
fastened his ankles, had a henchman fling him away
on a barren, trackless mountain.
                         There, you see?
Apollo brought neither thing to pass. My baby
no more murdered his father than Laius suffered—   795
his wildest fear—death at his own son's hands.
That's how the seers and all their revelations
mapped out the future. Brush them from your mind.
Whatever the god needs and seeks
he'll bring to light himself, with ease.   800
OEDIPUS: Strange,
hearing you just now . . . my mind wandered,
my thoughts racing back and forth.
JOCASTA: What do you mean? Why so anxious, startled?
OEDIPUS: I thought I heard you say that Laius

was cut down at a place where three roads meet. 805
JOCASTA: That was the story. It hasn't died out yet.
OEDIPUS: Where did this thing happen? Be precise.
JOCASTA: A place called Phocis, where two branching roads,
   one from Daulia, one from Delphi,
   come together—a crossroads. 810
OEDIPUS: When? How long ago?
JOCASTA: The heralds no sooner reported Laius dead
   than you appeared and they hailed you king of Thebes.
OEDIPUS: My god, my god—what have you planned to do to me?
JOCASTA: What, Oedipus? What haunts you so?
OEDIPUS: Not yet. 815
   Laius—how did he look? Describe him.
   Had he reached his prime?
JOCASTA: He was swarthy,
   and the gray had just begun to streak his temples,
   and his build . . . wasn't far from yours.
OEDIPUS: Oh no no,
   I think I've just called down a dreadful curse 820
   upon myself—I simply didn't know!
JOCASTA: What are you saying? I shudder to look at you.
OEDIPUS: I have a terrible fear the blind seer can see.
   I'll know in a moment. One thing more—
JOCASTA: Anything,
   afraid as I am—ask, I'll answer, all I can. 825
OEDIPUS: Did he go with a light or heavy escort,
   several men-at-arms, like a lord, a king?
JOCASTA: There were five in the party, a herald among them,
   and a single wagon carrying Laius.
OEDIPUS: Ai—
   now I can see it all, clear as day. 830
   Who told you all this at the time, Jocasta?
JOCASTA: A servant who reached home, the lone survivor.
OEDIPUS: So, could he still be in the palace—even now?
JOCASTA: No indeed. Soon as he returned from the scene
   and saw you on the throne with Laius dead and gone, 835
   he knelt and clutched my hand, pleading with me
   to send him into the hinterlands, to pasture,
   far as possible, out of sight of Thebes.
   I sent him away. Slave though he was,
   he'd earned that favor—and much more. 840
OEDIPUS: Can we bring him back, quickly?
JOCASTA: Easily. Why do you want him so?
OEDIPUS: I'm afraid,
   Jocasta, I have said too much already.
   That man—I've got to see him.
JOCASTA: Then he'll come.

But even I have a right, I'd like to think,   845
to know what's torturing you, my lord.
OEDIPUS: And so you shall—I can hold nothing back from you,
now I've reached this pitch of dark foreboding.
Who means more to me than you? Tell me,
whom would I turn toward but you   850
as I go through all this?

My father was Polybus, king of Corinth.
My mother, a Dorian, Merope. And I was held
the prince of the realm among the people there,
till something struck me out of nowhere,   855
something strange . . . worth remarking perhaps,
hardly worth the anxiety I gave it.
Some man at a banquet who had drunk too much
shouted out—he was far gone, mind you—
that I am not my father's son. Fighting words!   860
I barely restrained myself that day
but early the next I went to mother and father,
questioned them closely, and they were enraged
at the accusation and the fool who let it fly.
So as for my parents I was satisfied,   865
but still this thing kept gnawing at me,
the slander spread—I had to make my move.
                                    And so,
unknown to mother and father I set out for Delphi,
and the god Apollo spurned me, sent me away
denied the facts I came for,   870
but first he flashed before my eyes a future
great with pain, terror, disaster—I can hear him cry,
"You are fated to couple with your mother, you will bring
a breed of children into the light no man can bear to see—
you will kill your father, the one who gave you life!"   875
I heard all that and ran. I abandoned Corinth,
from that day on I gauged its landfall only
by the stars, running, always running
toward some place where I would never see
the shame of all those oracles come true.   880
And as I fled I reached that very spot
where the great king, you say, met his death.

Now, Jocasta, I will tell you all.
Making my way toward this triple crossroad
I began to see a herald, then a brace of colts   885
drawing a wagon, and mounted on the bench . . . a man,
just as you've described him, coming face-to-face,
and the one in the lead and the old man himself
were about to thrust me off the road—brute force—

and the one shouldering me aside, the driver,   890
I strike him in anger!—and the old man, watching me
coming up along his wheels—he brings down
his prod, two prongs straight at my head!
I paid him back with interest!
Short work, by god—with one blow of the staff   895
in this right hand I knock him out of his high seat,
roll him out of the wagon, sprawling headlong—
I killed them all—every mother's son!

Oh, but if there is any blood-tie
between Laius and this stranger . . .   900
what man alive more miserable than I?
More hated by the gods? I am the man
no alien, no citizen welcomes to his house,
law forbids it—not a word to me in public,
driven out of every hearth and home.   905
And all these curses I—no one but I
brought down these piling curses on myself!
And you, his wife, I've touched your body with these,
the hands that killed your husband cover you with blood.

Wasn't I born for torment? Look me in the eyes!   910
I am abomination—heart and soul!
I must be exiled, and even in exile
never see my parents, never set foot
on native ground again. Else I am doomed
to couple with my mother and cut my father down . . .   915
Polybus who reared me, gave me life.
                              But why, why?
Wouldn't a man of judgment say—and wouldn't he be right—
some savage power has brought this down upon my head?

Oh no, not that, you pure and awesome gods,
never let me see that day! Let me slip   920
from the world of men, vanish without a trace
before I see myself stained with such corruption,
stained to the heart.
LEADER: My lord, you fill our hearts with fear.
But at least until you question the witness,   925
do take hope.
OEDIPUS: Exactly. He is my last hope—
I am waiting for the shepherd. He is crucial.
JOCASTA: And once he appears, what then? Why so urgent?
OEDIPUS: I will tell you. If it turns out that his story
matches yours, I've escaped the worst.   930
JOCASTA: What did I say? What struck you so?
OEDIPUS: You said *thieves*—

he told you a whole band of them murdered Laius.
So, if he still holds to the same number,
I cannot be the killer. One can't equal many.
But if he refers to one man, one alone,   935
clearly the scales come down on me:
I am guilty.
JOCASTA: Impossible. Trust me,
I told you precisely what he said,
and he can't retract it now;
the whole city heard it, not just I.   940
And even if he should vary his first report
by one man more or less, still, my lord,
he could never make the murder of Laius
truly fit the prophecy. Apollo was explicit:
my son was doomed to kill my husband . . . my son,   945
poor defenseless thing, he never had a chance
to kill his father. They destroyed him first.

So much for prophecy. It's neither here nor there.
From this day on, I wouldn't look right or left.
OEDIPUS: True, true. Still, that shepherd,   950
someone fetch him—now!
JOCASTA: I'll send at once. But do let's go inside.
I'd never displease you, least of all in this.
      [OEDIPUS and JOCASTA enter the palace.]
CHORUS: Destiny guide me always
Destiny find me filled with reverence   955
      pure in word and deed.
Great laws tower above us, reared on high
born for the brilliant vault of heaven—
      Olympian Sky their only father,
nothing mortal, no man gave them birth,   960
their memory deathless, never lost in sleep:
within them lives a mighty god, the god does not grow old.

Pride breeds the tyrant
violent pride, gorging, crammed to bursting
      with all that is overripe and rich with ruin—   965
clawing up to the heights, headlong pride
crashes down the abyss—sheer doom!
      No footing helps, all foothold lost and gone.
But the healthy strife that makes the city strong—
I pray that god will never end that wrestling: 970
god, my champion, I will never let you go.

But if any man comes striding, high and mighty
      in all he says and does,
no fear of justice, no reverence

for the temples of the gods—   975
   let a rough doom tear him down,
repay his pride, breakneck, ruinous pride!
If he cannot reap his profits fairly
   cannot restrain himself from outrage—
mad, laying hands on the holy things untouchable!   980

    Can such a man, so desperate, still boast
    he can save his life from the flashing bolts of god?
      If all such violence goes with honor now
        why join the sacred dance?

Never again will I go reverent to Delphi,   985
   the inviolate heart of Earth
or Apollo's ancient oracle at Abae
or Olympia[8] of the fires—
   unless these prophecies all come true
for all mankind to point toward in wonder.   990
King of kings, if you deserve your titles
   Zeus, remember, never forget!
You and your deathless, everlasting reign.

    They are dying, the old oracles sent to Laius,
    now our masters strike them off the rolls.   995
      Nowhere Apollo's golden glory now—
        the gods, the gods go down.

[*Enter* JOCASTA *from the palace, carrying a suppliant's branch wound in wool.*]

JOCASTA: Lords of the realm,[9] it occurred to me,
   just now, to visit the temples of the gods,
so I have my branch in hand and incense too.   1000

Oedipus is beside himself. Racked with anguish,
no longer a man of sense, he won't admit
the latest prophecies are hollow as the old—
he's at the mercy of every passing voice
if the voice tells of terror.   1005
I urge him gently, nothing seems to help,
so I turn to you, Apollo, you are nearest.

[*Placing her branch on the altar, while an old herdsman enters from the side, not the one just summoned by the King but an unexpected* MESSENGER *from Corinth.*]

I come with prayers and offerings . . . I beg you,
cleanse us, set us free of defilement!
Look at us, passengers in the grip of fear,   1010
watching the pilot of the vessel go to pieces.

---

8. Abae was a city in central Greece, and Olympia a site in the western Peloponnese, where there were important oracles of Apollo and Zeus, respectively.   9. She is addressing the chorus.

MESSENGER: [*Approaching* JOCASTA *and the* CHORUS.]
Strangers, please, I wonder if you could lead us
to the palace of the king . . . I think it's Oedipus.
Better, the man himself—you know where he is?
LEADER: This is his palace, stranger. He's inside.   1015
But here is his queen, his wife and mother
of his children.
MESSENGER: Blessings on you, noble queen,
queen of Oedipus crowned with all your family—
blessings on you always!
JOCASTA: And the same to you, stranger, you deserve it . . .   1020
such a greeting. But what have you come for?
Have you brought us news?
MESSENGER: Wonderful news—
for the house, my lady, for your husband too.
JOCASTA: Really, what? Who sent you?
MESSENGER: Corinth.
I'll give you the message in a moment.   1025
You'll be glad of it—how could you help it?—
though it costs a little sorrow in the bargain.
JOCASTA: What can it be, with such a double edge?
MESSENGER: The people there, they want to make your Oedipus
king of Corinth, so they're saying now.   1030
JOCASTA: Why? Isn't old Polybus still in power?
MESSENGER: No more. Death has got him in the tomb.
JOCASTA: What are you saying? Polybus, dead?—dead?
MESSENGER: If not,
if I'm not telling the truth, strike me dead too.
JOCASTA: [*To a servant.*]
Quickly, go to your master, tell him this!   1035
You prophecies of the gods, where are you now?
This is the man that Oedipus feared for years,
he fled him, not to kill him—and now he's dead,
quite by chance, a normal, natural death,
not murdered by his son.   1040
OEDIPUS: [*Emerging from the palace.*]
                    Dearest,
what now? Why call me from the palace?
JOCASTA: [*Bringing the* MESSENGER *closer.*]
Listen to *him*, see for yourself what all
those awful prophecies of god have come to.
OEDIPUS: And who is he? What can he have for me?
JOCASTA: He's from Corinth, he's come to tell you   1045
your father is no more—Polybus—he's dead!
OEDIPUS: [*Wheeling on the* MESSENGER.]
What? Let me have it from your lips.

MESSENGER: Well,
  if that's what you want first, then here it is:
  make no mistake, Polybus is dead and gone.
OEDIPUS: How—murder? sickness?—what? what killed him?   1050
MESSENGER: A light tip of the scales can put old bones to rest.
OEDIPUS: Sickness then—poor man, it wore him down.
MESSENGER: That,
  and the long count of years he'd measured out.
OEDIPUS: So!
  Jocasta, why, why look to the Prophet's hearth,
  the fires of the future? Why scan the birds   1055
  that scream above our heads? They winged me on
  to the murder of my father, did they? That was my doom?
  Well look, he's dead and buried, hidden under the earth,
  and here I am in Thebes, I never put hand to sword—
  unless some longing for me wasted him away,   1060
  then in a sense you'd say I caused his death.
  But now, all those prophecies I feared—Polybus
  packs them off to sleep with him in hell!
  They're nothing, worthless.
JOCASTA: There.
  Didn't I tell you from the start?   1065
OEDIPUS: So you did. I was lost in fear.
JOCASTA: No more, sweep it from your mind forever.
OEDIPUS: But my mother's bed, surely I must fear—
JOCASTA: Fear?
  What should a man fear? It's all chance,
  chance rules our lives. Not a man on earth   1070
  can see a day ahead, groping through the dark.
  Better to live at random, best we can.
  And as for this marriage with your mother—
  have no fear. Many a man before you,
  in his dreams, has shared his mother's bed.   1075
  Take such things for shadows, nothing at all—
  Live, Oedipus,
  as if there's no tomorrow!
OEDIPUS: Brave words,
  and you'd persuade me if mother weren't alive.
  But mother lives, so for all your reassurances   1080
  I live in fear, I must.
JOCASTA: But your father's death,
  that, at least, is a great blessing, joy to the eyes!
OEDIPUS: Great, I know . . . but I fear *her*—she's still alive.
MESSENGER: Wait, who is this woman, makes you so afraid?
OEDIPUS: Merope, old man. The wife of Polybus.   1085
MESSENGER: The queen? What's there to fear in her?

OEDIPUS: A dreadful prophecy, stranger, sent by the gods.

MESSENGER: Tell me, could you? Unless it's forbidden
other ears to hear.

OEDIPUS: Not at all.
Apollo told me once—it is my fate—   1090
I must make love with my own mother,
shed my father's blood with my own hands.
So for years I've given Corinth a wide berth,
and it's been my good fortune too. But still,
to see one's parents and look into their eyes   1095
is the greatest joy I know.

MESSENGER: You're afraid of that?
That kept you out of Corinth?

OEDIPUS: My *father*, old man—
so I wouldn't kill my father.

MESSENGER: So that's it.
Well then, seeing I came with such good will, my king,
why don't I rid you of that old worry now?   1100

OEDIPUS: What a rich reward you'd have for that!

MESSENGER: What do you think I came for, majesty?
So you'd come home and I'd be better off.

OEDIPUS: Never, I will never go near my parents.

MESSENGER: My boy, it's clear, you don't know what you're doing.   1105

OEDIPUS: What do you mean, old man? For god's sake, explain.

MESSENGER: If you ran from *them*, always dodging home . . .

OEDIPUS: Always, terrified Apollo's oracle might come true—

MESSENGER: And you'd be covered with guilt, from both your parents.

OEDIPUS: That's right, old man, that fear is always with me.   1110

MESSENGER: Don't you know? You've really nothing to fear.

OEDIPUS: But why? If I'm their son—Merope, Polybus?

MESSENGER: Polybus was nothing to you, that's why, not in blood.

OEDIPUS: What are you saying—Polybus was not my father?

MESSENGER: No more than I am. He and I are equals.

OEDIPUS: My father—   1115
how can my father equal nothing? You're nothing to me!

MESSENGER: Neither was he, no more your father than I am.

OEDIPUS: Then why did he call me his son?

MESSENGER: You were a gift,
years ago—know for a fact he took you
from my hands.

OEDIPUS: No, from another's hands?   1120
Then how could he love me so? He loved me, deeply . . .

MESSENGER: True, and his early years without a child
made him love you all the more.

OEDIPUS: And you, did you . . .
buy me? find me by accident?

MESSENGER: I stumbled on you,

down the woody flanks of Mount Cithaeron.
OEDIPUS: So close,   1125
what were you doing here, just passing through?
MESSENGER: Watching over my flocks, grazing them on the slopes.
OEDIPUS: A herdsman, were you? A vagabond, scraping for wages?
MESSENGER: Your savior too, my son, in your worst hour.
OEDIPUS: Oh—
when you picked me up, was I in pain? What exactly?   1130
MESSENGER: Your ankles . . . they tell the story. Look at them.
OEDIPUS: Why remind me of that, that old affliction?
MESSENGER: Your ankles were pinned together. I set you free.
OEDIPUS: That dreadful mark—I've had it from the cradle.
MESSENGER: And you got your name[1] from that misfortune too,   1135
the name's still with you.
OEDIPUS: Dear god, who did it?—
mother? father? Tell me.
MESSENGER: I don't know.
The one who gave you to me, he'd know more.
OEDIPUS: What? You took me from someone else?
You didn't find me yourself?
MESSENGER: No sir,   1140
another shepherd passed you on to me.
OEDIPUS: Who? Do you know? Describe him.
MESSENGER: He called himself a servant of . . .
if I remember rightly—Laius.
[JOCASTA *turns sharply.*]
OEDIPUS: The king of the land who ruled here long ago?   1145
MESSENGER: That's the one. That herdsman was *his* man.
OEDIPUS: Is he still alive? Can I see him?
MESSENGER: They'd know best, the people of these parts.
[OEDIPUS *and the* MESSENGER *turn to the* CHORUS.]
OEDIPUS: Does anyone know that herdsman,
the one he mentioned? Anyone seen him   1150
in the fields, in the city? Out with it!
The time has come to reveal this once for all.
LEADER: I think he's the very shepherd you wanted to see,
a moment ago. But the queen, Jocasta,
she's the one to say.
OEDIPUS: Jocasta,   1155
you remember the man we just sent for?
Is *that* the one he means?
JOCASTA: That man . . .
why ask? Old shepherd, talk, empty nonsense,
don't give it another thought, don't even think—
OEDIPUS: What—give up now, with a clue like this?   1160

1. In Greek the name *Oidipous* suggests "swollen foot."

Fail to solve the mystery of my birth?
Not for all the world!
JOCASTA: Stop—in the name of god,
if you love your own life, call off this search!
My suffering is enough.
OEDIPUS: Courage!
Even if my mother turns out to be a slave,   1165
and I a slave, three generations back,
you would not seem common.
JOCASTA: Oh no,
listen to me, I beg you, don't do this.
OEDIPUS: Listen to you? No more. I must know it all,
must see the truth at last.
JOCASTA: No, please—   1170
for your sake—I want the best for you!
OEDIPUS: Your best is more than I can bear.
JOCASTA: You're doomed—
may you never fathom who you are!
OEDIPUS: [*To a servant.*] Hurry, fetch me the herdsman, now!
Leave her to glory in her royal birth.   1175
JOCASTA: Aieeeeee—
                    man of agony—
that is the only name I have for you,
that, no other—ever, ever, ever!
    [*Flinging through the palace doors. A long, tense silence follows.*]
LEADER: Where's she gone, Oedipus?
Rushing off, such wild grief . . .   1180
I'm afraid that from this silence
something monstrous may come bursting forth.
OEDIPUS: Let it burst! Whatever will, whatever must!
I must know my birth, no matter how common
it may be—I must see my origins face-to-face.   1185
She perhaps, she with her woman's pride
may well be mortified by my birth,
but I, I count myself the son of Chance,
the great goddess, giver of all good things—
I'll never see myself disgraced. She is my mother!   1190
And the moons have marked me out, my blood-brothers,
one moon on the wane, the next moon great with power.
That is my blood, my nature—I will never betray it,
never fail to search and learn my birth!
CHORUS: Yes—if I am a true prophet   1195
        if I can grasp the truth,
    by the boundless skies of Olympus,
at the full moon of tomorrow, Mount Cithaeron
you will know how Oedipus glories in you—
you, his birthplace, nurse, his mountain-mother!   1200

And we will sing you, dancing out your praise—
you lift our monarch's heart!
    Apollo, Apollo, god of the wild cry
      may our dancing please you!
                     Oedipus—
    son, dear child, who bore you?   1205
Who of the nymphs who seem to live forever[2]
mated with Pan,[3] the mountain-striding Father?
Who was your mother? who, some bride of Apollo
the god who loves the pastures spreading toward the sun?
    Or was it Hermes, king of the lightning ridges?   1210
Or Dionysus,[4] lord of frenzy, lord of the barren peaks—
did he seize you in his hands, dearest of all his lucky finds?—
    found by the nymphs, their warm eyes dancing, gift
to the lord who loves them dancing out his joy!

[OEDIPUS *strains to see a figure coming from the distance. Attended
by palace guards, an old* SHEPHERD *enters slowly, reluctant to approach
the king.*]

OEDIPUS: I never met the man, my friends . . . still,   1215
    if I had to guess, I'd say that's the shepherd,
    the very one we've looked for all along.
    Brothers in old age, two of a kind,
    he and our guest here. At any rate
    the ones who bring him in are my own men,   1220
    I recognize them.
        [*Turning to the* LEADER.]
                  But you know more than I,
    you should, you've seen the man before.
LEADER: I know him, definitely. One of Laius' men,
    a trusty shepherd, if there ever was one.
OEDIPUS: You, I ask you first, stranger,   1225
    you from Corinth—is this the one you mean?
MESSENGER: You're looking at him. He's your man.
OEDIPUS: [*To the* SHEPHERD.]
    You, old man, come over here—
    look at me. Answer all my questions.
    Did you ever serve King Laius?
SHEPHERD: So I did . . .   1230
    a slave, not bought on the block though,
    born and reared in the palace.
OEDIPUS: Your duties, your kind of work?
SHEPHERD: Herding the flocks, the better part of my life.
OEDIPUS: Where, mostly? Where did you do your grazing?   1235

---

2. Nymphs were not immortal, like the gods, but lived much longer than mortals.   3. A woodland god;
patron of shepherds and flocks.   4. Dionysus like Pan and Hermes haunted the wild country, woods
and mountains. Hermes was born on Mount Kyllene in Arcadia.

SHEPHERD: Well,
  Cithaeron sometimes, or the foothills round about.
OEDIPUS: This man—you know him? ever see him there?
SHEPHERD: [*Confused, glancing from the* MESSENGER *to the King.*]
  Doing what?—what man do you mean?
OEDIPUS: [*Pointing to the* MESSENGER.]
  This one here—ever have dealings with him?
SHEPHERD: Not so I could say, but give me a chance,   1240
  my memory's bad . . .
MESSENGER: No wonder he doesn't know me, master.
  But let me refresh his memory for him.
  I'm sure he recalls old times we had
  on the slopes of Mount Cithaeron;   1245
  he and I, grazing our flocks, he with two
  and I with one—we both struck up together,
  three whole seasons, six months at a stretch
  from spring to the rising of Arcturus in the fall,[5]
  then with winter coming on I'd drive my herds   1250
  to my own pens, and back he'd go with his
  to Laius' folds.
      [*To the* SHEPHERD.]
                    Now that's how it was,
  wasn't it—yes or no?
SHEPHERD: Yes, I suppose . . .
  it's all so long ago.
MESSENGER: Come, tell me,
  you gave me a child back then, a boy, remember?   1255
  A little fellow to rear, my very own.
SHEPHERD: What? Why rake up that again?
MESSENGER: Look, here he is, my fine old friend—
  the same man who was just a baby then.
SHEPHERD: Damn you, shut your mouth—quiet!   1260
OEDIPUS: Don't lash out at him, old man—
  you need lashing more than he does.
SHEPHERD: Why,
  master, majesty—what have I done wrong?
OEDIPUS: You won't answer his question about the boy.
SHEPHERD: He's talking nonsense, wasting his breath.   1265
OEDIPUS: So, you won't talk willingly—
  then you'll talk with pain.
      [*The guards seize the* SHEPHERD.]
SHEPHERD: No, dear god, don't torture an old man!
OEDIPUS: Twist his arms back, quickly!
SHEPHERD: God help us, why?—
  what more do you need to know?   1270

5. Arcturus is the principal star in the constellation Bootes. Its "rising" (i.e., its reappearance in the night sky just before dawn in September) signaled the end of summer.

OEDIPUS: Did you give him that child? He's asking.
SHEPHERD: I did . . . I wish to god I'd died that day.
OEDIPUS: You've got your wish if you don't tell the truth.
SHEPHERD: The more I tell, the worse the death I'll die.
OEDIPUS: Our friend here wants to stretch things out, does he?   1275
    [*Motioning to his men for torture.*]
SHEPHERD: No, no, I gave it to him—I just said so.
OEDIPUS: Where did you get it? Your house? Someone else's?
SHEPHERD: It wasn't mine, no, I got it from . . . someone.
OEDIPUS: Which one of them?
    [*Looking at the citizens.*]
                            Whose house?
SHEPHERD: No—
    god's sake, master, no more questions!   1280
OEDIPUS: You're a dead man if I have to ask again.
SHEPHERD: Then—the child came from the house . . . of Laius.
OEDIPUS: A slave? or born of his own blood?
SHEPHERD: Oh no,
    I'm right at the edge, the horrible truth—I've got to say it!
OEDIPUS: And I'm at the edge of hearing horrors, yes, but I must hear!   1285
SHEPHERD: All right! His son, they said it was—his son!
    But the one inside, your wife,
    she'd tell it best.
OEDIPUS: My wife—
    she gave it to you?   1290
SHEPHERD: Yes, yes, my king.
OEDIPUS: Why, what for?
SHEPHERD: To kill it.
OEDIPUS: Her own child,
    how could she?   1295
SHEPHERD: She was afraid—
    frightening prophecies.
OEDIPUS: What?
SHEPHERD: They said—
    he'd kill his parents.
OEDIPUS: But you gave him to this old man—why?   1300
SHEPHERD: I pitied the little baby, master,
    hoped he'd take him off to his own country,
    far away, but he saved him for this, this fate.
    If you are the man he says you are, believe me,
    you were born for pain.
OEDIPUS: O god—   1305
    all come true, all burst to light!
    O light—now let me look my last on you!
    I stand revealed at last—
    cursed in my birth, cursed in marriage,
    cursed in the lives I cut down with these hands!   1310

[*Rushing through the doors with a great cry. The Corinthian* MESSEN-
GER, *the* SHEPHERD *and attendants exit slowly to the side.*]

ODE 4   CHORUS: O the generations of men
the dying generations—adding the total
of all your lives I find they come to nothing . . .
        does there exist, is there a man on earth
who seizes more joy than just a dream, a vision?   1315
And the vision no sooner dawns than dies
blazing into oblivion.

You are my great example, you, your life
your destiny, Oedipus, man of misery—
I count no man blest.

                You outranged all men!   1320
    Bending your bow to the breaking-point
you captured priceless glory, O dear god,
and the Sphinx came crashing down,
        the virgin, claws hooked
like a bird of omen singing, shrieking death—   1325
like a fortress reared in the face of death
you rose and saved our land.

From that day on we called you king
we crowned you with honors, Oedipus, towering over all—
mighty king of the seven gates of Thebes.   1330

But now to hear your story—is there a man more agonized?
More wed to pain and frenzy? Not a man on earth,
the joy of your life ground down to nothing
O Oedipus, name for the ages—
    one and the same wide harbor served you   1335
        son and father both
son and father came to rest in the same bridal chamber.
How, how could the furrows your father plowed
bear you, your agony, harrowing on
in silence O so long?

                But now for all your power   1340
Time, all-seeing Time has dragged you to the light,
judged your marriage monstrous from the start—
the son and the father tangling, both one—
O child of Laius, would to god
    I'd never seen you, never never!   1345
    Now I weep like a man who wails the dead
and the dirge comes pouring forth with all my heart!
I tell you the truth, you gave me life
my breath leapt up in you
and now you bring down night upon my eyes.   1350

[*Enter a* MESSENGER *from the palace.*]

MESSENGER: Men of Thebes, always first in honor,   *EPISODE 5*
what horrors you will hear, what you will see,
what a heavy weight of sorrow you will shoulder . . .
if you are true to your birth, if you still have
some feeling for the royal house of Thebes.   1355
I tell you neither the waters of the Danube
nor the Nile[6] can wash this palace clean.
Such things it hides, it soon will bring to light—
terrible things, and none done blindly now,
all done with a will. The pains   1360
we inflict upon ourselves hurt most of all.

LEADER: God knows we have pains enough already.
What can you add to them?

MESSENGER: The queen is dead.

LEADER: Poor lady—how?

MESSENGER: By her own hand. But you are spared the worst,   1365
you never had to watch . . . I saw it all,
and with all the memory that's in me
you will learn what that poor woman suffered.

Once she'd broken in through the gates,
dashing past us, frantic, whipped to fury,   1370
ripping her hair out with both hands—
straight to her rooms she rushed, flinging herself
across the bridal-bed, doors slamming behind her—
once inside, she wailed for Laius, dead so long,
remembering how she bore his child long ago,   1375
the life that rose up to destroy him, leaving
its mother to mother living creatures
with the very son she'd borne.
Oh how she wept, mourning the marriage-bed
where she let loose that double brood—monsters—   1380
husband by her husband, children by her child.

                              And then—
but how she died is more than I can say. Suddenly
Oedipus burst in, screaming, he stunned us so
we couldn't watch her agony to the end,
our eyes were fixed on him. Circling   1385
like a maddened beast, stalking, here, there,
crying out to us—
                    Give him a sword![7] His wife,
no wife, his mother, where can he find the mother earth
that cropped two crops at once, himself and all his children?
He was raging—one of the dark powers pointing the way,   1390

---

6. The Greek says Phasis—a river in Asia Minor. The translator has substituted a big river more familiar to modern readers.   7. Presumably so that he could kill himself.

none of us mortals crowding around him, no,
with a great shattering cry—someone, something leading him on—
he hurled at the twin doors and bending the bolts back
out of their sockets, crashed through the chamber.
And there we saw the woman hanging by the neck,   1395
cradled high in a woven noose, spinning,
swinging back and forth. And when he saw her,
giving a low, wrenching sob that broke our hearts,
slipping the halter from her throat, he eased her down,
in a slow embrace he laid her down, poor thing . . .   1400
then, what came next, what horror we beheld!

He rips off her brooches, the long gold pins
holding her robes—and lifting them high,
looking straight up into the points,
he digs them down the sockets of his eyes, crying, "You,   1405
you'll see no more the pain I suffered, all the pain I caused!
Too long you looked on the ones you never should have seen,
blind to the ones you longed to see, to know! Blind
from this hour on! Blind in the darkness—blind!"
His voice like a dirge, rising, over and over   1410
raising the pins, raking them down his eyes.
And at each stroke blood spurts from the roots,
splashing his beard, a swirl of it, nerves and clots—
black hail of blood pulsing, gushing down.

These are the griefs that burst upon them both,   1415
coupling man and woman. The joy they had so lately,
the fortune of their old ancestral house
was deep joy indeed. Now, in this one day,
wailing, madness and doom, death, disgrace,
all the griefs in the world that you can name,   1420
all are theirs forever.
LEADER: Oh poor man, the misery—
has he any rest from pain now?
    [A voice within, in torment.]
MESSENGER: He's shouting,
"Loose the bolts, someone, show me to all of Thebes!
My father's murderer, my mother's—"
No, I can't repeat it, it's unholy.   1425
Now he'll tear himself from his native earth,
not linger, curse the house with his own curse.
But he needs strength, and a guide to lead him on.
This is sickness more than he can bear.
    [The palace doors open.]
                    Look,
he'll show you himself. The great doors are opening—   1430
you are about to see a sight, a horror

even his mortal enemy would pity.
[*Enter* OEDIPUS, *blinded, led by a boy. He stands at the palace steps, as if surveying his people once again.*]
CHORUS: O the terror—
the suffering, for all the world to see,   *ODE 5*
the worst terror that ever met my eyes.
What madness swept over you? What god,   1435
what dark power leapt beyond all bounds,
beyond belief, to crush your wretched life?—
godforsaken, cursed by the gods!
I pity you but I can't bear to look.
I've much to ask, so much to learn,   1440
so much fascinates my eyes,
but you . . . I shudder at the sight.
OEDIPUS: Oh, Ohh—   *EXODOS*
the agony! I am agony—
where am I going? where on earth?
where does all this agony hurl me?   1445
where's my voice?—
winging, swept away on a dark tide—
My destiny, my dark power, what a leap you made!
CHORUS: To the depths of terror, too dark to hear, to see.
OEDIPUS: Dark, horror of darkness   1450
my darkness, drowning, swirling around me
crashing wave on wave—unspeakable, irresistible
headwind, fatal harbor! Oh again,
the misery, all at once, over and over
the stabbing daggers, stab of memory   1455
raking me insane.
CHORUS: No wonder you suffer
twice over, the pain of your wounds,
the lasting grief of pain.
OEDIPUS: Dear friend, still here?
Standing by me, still with a care for me,
the blind man? Such compassion,   1460
loyal to the last. Oh it's you,
I know you're here, dark as it is
I'd know you anywhere, your voice—
it's yours, clearly yours.
CHORUS: Dreadful, what you've done . . .
how could you bear it, gouging out your eyes?   1465
What superhuman power drove you on?
OEDIPUS: Apollo, friends, Apollo—
he ordained my agonies—these, my pains on pains!
But the hand that struck my eyes was mine,
mine alone—no one else—   1470
I did it all myself!

What good were eyes to me?
Nothing I could see could bring me joy.
CHORUS: No, no, exactly as you say.
OEDIPUS: What can I ever see?
    What love, what call of the heart   1475
    can touch my ears with joy? Nothing, friends.
        Take me away, far, far from Thebes,
            quickly, cast me away, my friends—
    this great murderous ruin, this man cursed to heaven,
        the man the deathless gods hate most of all!   1480
CHORUS: Pitiful, you suffer so, you understand so much . . .
    I wish you'd never known.
OEDIPUS: Die, die—
    whoever he was that day in the wilds
    who cut my ankles free of the ruthless pins,
        he pulled me clear of death, he saved my life   1485
    for this, this kindness—
            Curse him, kill him!
    If I'd died then, I'd never have dragged myself,
        my loved ones through such hell.
CHORUS: Oh if only . . . would to god.
OEDIPUS: I'd never have come to this,   1490
    my father's murderer—never been branded
    mother's husband, all men see me now! Now,
        loathed by the gods, son of the mother I defiled
        coupling in my father's bed, spawning lives in the loins
    that spawned my wretched life. What grief can crown this grief?   1495
        It's mine alone, my destiny—I am Oedipus!
CHORUS: How can I say you've chosen for the best?
    Better to die than be alive and blind.
OEDIPUS: What I did was best—don't lecture me,
    no more advice. I, with *my* eyes,   1500
    how could I look my father in the eyes
    when I go down to death? Or mother, so abused . . .
    I have done such things to the two of them,
    crimes too huge for hanging.
                        Worse yet,
    the sight of my children, born as they were born,   1505
    how could I long to look into their eyes?
    No, not with these eyes of mine, never.
    Not this city either, her high towers,
    the sacred glittering images of her gods—
    I am misery! I, her best son, reared   1510
    as no other son of Thebes was ever reared,
    I've stripped myself, I gave the command myself.
    All men must cast away the great blasphemer,

SOLILOQUY

the curse now brought to light by the gods,
the son of Laius—I, my father's son! 1515

Now I've exposed my guilt, horrendous guilt,
could I train a level glance on you, my countrymen?
Impossible! No, if I could just block off my ears,
the springs of hearing, I would stop at nothing—
I'd wall up my loathsome body like a prison, 1520
blind to the sound of life, not just the sight.
Oblivion—what a blessing . . .
for the mind to dwell a world away from pain.

O Cithaeron, why did you give me shelter?
Why didn't you take me, crush my life out on the spot? 1525
I'd never have revealed my birth to all mankind.

O Polybus, Corinth, the old house of my fathers,
so I believed—what a handsome prince you raised—
under the skin, what sickness to the core.
Look at me! Born of outrage, outrage to the core. 1530
O triple roads—it all comes back, the secret,
dark ravine, and the oaks closing in
where the three roads join . . .
You drank my father's blood, my own blood
spilled by my own hands—you still remember me? 1535
What things you saw me do? Then I came here
and did them all once more!
                              Marriages! O marriage,
you gave me birth, and once you brought me into the world
you brought my sperm rising back, springing to light
fathers, brothers, sons—one murderous breed— 1540
brides, wives, mothers. The blackest things
a man can do, I have done them all!
                              No more—
it's wrong to name what's wrong to do. Quickly,
for the love of god, hide me somewhere,
kill me, hurl me into the sea 1545
where you can never look on me again.

[*Beckoning to the* CHORUS *as they shrink away.*]
                              Closer,
it's all right. Touch the man of grief.
Do. Don't be afraid. My troubles are mine
and I am the only man alive who can sustain them.

[*Enter* CREON *from the palace, attended by palace guards.*]
LEADER: Put your requests to Creon. Here he is, 1550
just when we need him. He'll have a plan, he'll act.

Now that he's the sole defense of the country
in your place.
OEDIPUS: Oh no, what can I say to him?
How can I ever hope to win his trust?
I wronged him so, just now, in every way.   1555
You must see that—I was so wrong, so wrong.
CREON: I haven't come to mock you, Oedipus,
or to criticize your former failings.
          [*Turning to the guards.*]
                                  You there,
have you lost all respect for human feelings?
At least revere the Sun, the holy fire   1560
that keeps us all alive. Never expose a thing
of guilt and holy dread so great it appalls
the earth, the rain from heaven, the light of day!
Get him into the halls—quickly as you can.
Piety demands no less. Kindred alone   1565
should see a kinsman's shame. This is obscene.
OEDIPUS: Please, in god's name . . . you wipe my fears away,
coming so generously to me, the worst of men.
Do one thing more, for your sake, not mine.
CREON: What do you want? Why so insistent?   1570
OEDIPUS: Drive me out of the land at once, far from sight,
where I can never hear a human voice.
CREON: I'd have done that already, I promise you.
First I wanted the god to clarify my duties.
OEDIPUS: The god? His command was clear, every word: 1575
death for the father-killer, the curse—
he said destroy me!
CREON: So he did. Still, in such a crisis
it's better to ask precisely what to do.
OEDIPUS: So miserable—
you'd consult the god about a man like me?   1580
CREON: By all means. And this time, I assume,
even you will obey the god's decrees.
OEDIPUS: I will,
I will. And you, I command you—I beg you . . .
the woman inside, bury her as you see fit.
It's the only decent thing,   1585
to give your own the last rites. As for me,
never condemn the city of my fathers
to house my body, not while I'm alive, no,
let me live on the mountains, on Cithaeron,
my favorite haunt, I have made it famous.   1590
Mother and father marked out that rock
to be my everlasting tomb—buried alive.
Let me die there, where they tried to kill me.

Oh but this I know: no sickness can destroy me,
nothing can. I would never have been saved   1595
from death—I have been saved
for something great and terrible, something strange.
Well let my destiny come and take me on its way!
About my children, Creon, the boys at least,
don't burden yourself. They're men,   1600
wherever they go, they'll find the means to live.
But my two daughters, my poor helpless girls,
clustering at our table, never without me
hovering near them . . . whatever I touched,
they always had their share. Take care of them,   1605
I beg you. Wait, better—permit me, would you?
Just to touch them with my hands and take
our fill of tears. Please . . . my king.
Grant it, with all your noble heart.
If I could hold them, just once, I'd think   1610
I had them with me, like the early days
when I could see their eyes.
        [ANTIGONE *and* ISMENE, *two small children, are led in from the palace*
        by a nurse.]
                            What's that
O god! Do I really hear you sobbing?—
my two children. Creon, you've pitied me?
Sent me my darling girls, my own flesh and blood!   1615
Am I right?
CREON: Yes, it's my doing.
I know the joy they gave you all these years,
the joy you must feel now.
OEDIPUS: Bless you, Creon!
May god watch over you for this kindness,
better than he ever guarded me.
                            Children, where are you?   1620
Here, come quickly—
        [*Groping for* ANTIGONE *and* ISMENE, *who approach their father cau-*
        tiously, then embrace him.]
                            Come to these hands of mine,
your brother's hands, your own father's hands
that served his once bright eyes so well—
that made them blind. Seeing nothing, children,
knowing nothing, I became your father,   1625
I fathered you in the soil that gave me life.

How I weep for you—I cannot see you now . . .
just thinking of all your days to come, the bitterness,
the life that rough mankind will thrust upon you.
Where are the public gatherings you can join,   1630

the banquets of the clans? Home you'll come,
in tears, cut off from the sight of it all,
the brilliant rites unfinished.
And when you reach perfection, ripe for marriage,
who will he be, my dear ones? Risking all   1635
to shoulder the curse that weighs down my parents,
yes and you too—that wounds us all together.
What more misery could you want?
Your father killed his father, sowed his mother,
one, one and the selfsame womb sprang you—   1640
he cropped the very roots of his existence.

Such disgrace, and you must bear it all!
Who will marry you then? Not a man on earth.
Your doom is clear: you'll wither away to nothing,
single, without a child.
          [*Turning to* CREON.]
                              Oh Creon,   1645
you are the only father they have now . . .
we who brought them into the world
are gone, both gone at a stroke—
Don't let them go begging, abandoned,
women without men. Your own flesh and blood!   1650
Never bring them down to the level of my pains.
Pity them. Look at them, so young, so vulnerable,
shorn of everything—you're their only hope.
Promise me, noble Creon, touch my hand!
          [*Reaching toward* CREON, *who draws back.*]
You, little ones, if you were old enough   1655
to understand, there is much I'd tell you.
Now, as it is, I'd have you say a prayer.
Pray for life, my children,
live where you are free to grow and season.
Pray god you find a better life than mine,   1660
the father who begot you.
CREON: Enough.
You've wept enough. Into the palace now.
OEDIPUS: I must, but I find it very hard.
CREON: Time is the great healer, you will see.
OEDIPUS: I am going—you know on what condition?   1665
CREON: Tell me. I'm listening.
OEDIPUS: Drive me out of Thebes, in exile.
CREON: Not I. Only the gods can give you that.
OEDIPUS: Surely the gods hate me so much—
CREON: You'll get your wish at once.
OEDIPUS: You consent?   1670
CREON: I try to say what I mean; it's my habit.

OEDIPUS: Then take me away. It's time.
CREON: Come along, let go of the children.
OEDIPUS: No—
  don't take them away from me, not now! No no no!
  [*Clutching his daughters as the guards wrench them loose and take
  them through the palace doors.*]
CREON: Still the king, the master of all things?   1675
  No more: here your power ends.
  None of your power follows you through life.
  [*Exit* OEDIPUS *and* CREON *to the palace. The* CHORUS *comes forward
  to address the audience directly.*]
CHORUS: People of Thebes, my countrymen, look on Oedipus.
  He solved the famous riddle with his brilliance,
  he rose to power, a man beyond all power.   1680
  Who could behold his greatness without envy?
  Now what a black sea of terror has overwhelmed him.
  Now as we keep our watch and wait the final day,
  count no man happy till he dies, free of pain at last.
  [*Exit in procession.*]

Antigone[1]

Characters

ANTIGONE, *daughter of Oedipus and
  Jocasta*
ISMENE, *sister of Antigone*
A CHORUS, *of old Theban citizens
  and their* LEADER
CREON, *king of Thebes, uncle of
  Antigone and Ismene*
A SENTRY

HAEMON, *son of Creon and Euryd-
  ice*
TIRESIAS, *a blind prophet*
A MESSENGER
EURYDICE, *wife of Creon*
Guards, attendants, and a boy

[TIME AND SCENE: *The royal house of Thebes. It is still night, and the
invading armies of Argos have just been driven from the city. Fighting on
opposite sides, the sons of Oedipus, Eteocles and Polynices, have killed
each other in combat. Their uncle,* CREON, *is now king of Thebes.*

  Enter ANTIGONE, *slipping through the central doors of the palace. She
motions to her sister,* ISMENE, *who follows her cautiously toward an altar
at the center of the stage.*]

ANTIGONE: My own flesh and blood—dear sister, dear Ismene,
  how many griefs our father Oedipus handed down!
  Do you know one, I ask you, one grief

1. Translated by Robert Fagles.

that Zeus will not perfect for the two of us
while we still live and breathe? There's nothing,   5
no pain—our lives are pain—no private shame,
no public disgrace, nothing I haven't seen
in your griefs and mine. And now this:
an emergency decree, they say, the Commander[2]
has just now declared for all of Thebes.   10
What, haven't you heard? Don't you see?
The doom reserved for enemies
marches on the ones we love the most.
ISMENE: Not I, I haven't heard a word, Antigone.
Nothing of loved ones,   15
no joy or pain has come my way, not since
the two of us were robbed of our two brothers,
both gone in a day, a double blow—
not since the armies of Argos vanished,
just this very night. I know nothing more,   20
whether our luck's improved or ruin's still to come.
ANTIGONE: I thought so. That's why I brought you out here,
past the gates, so you could hear in private.
ISMENE: What's the matter? Trouble, clearly . . .
you sound so dark, so grim.   25
ANTIGONE: Why not? Our own brothers' burial!
Hasn't Creon graced one with all the rites,
disgraced the other? Eteocles, they say,
has been given full military honors,
rightly so—Creon has laid him in the earth   30
and he goes with glory down among the dead.
But the body of Polynices, who died miserably—
why, a city-wide proclamation, rumor has it,
forbids anyone to bury him, even mourn him.
He's to be left unwept, unburied, a lovely treasure   35
for birds that scan the field and feast to their heart's content.

Such, I hear, is the martial law our good Creon
lays down for you and me—yes, me, I tell you—
and he's coming here to alert the uninformed
in no uncertain terms,   40
and he won't treat the matter lightly. Whoever
disobeys in the least will die, his doom is sealed:
stoning to death inside the city walls!

There you have it. You'll soon show what you are,
worth your breeding, Ismene, or a coward—   45
for all your royal blood.
ISMENE: My poor sister, if things have come to this,

2. Creon. In the original he is given a military title; Antigone will not refer to him as king.

who am I to make or mend them, tell me,
what good am I to you?
ANTIGONE: Decide.
Will you share the labor, share the work?   50
ISMENE: What work, what's the risk? What do you mean?
ANTIGONE: [*Raising her hands.*]
Will you lift up his body with these bare hands
and lower it with me?
ISMENE: What? You'd bury him—
when a law forbids the city?
ANTIGONE: Yes!
He is my brother and—deny it as you will—   55
your brother too.
No one will ever convict me for a traitor.
ISMENE: So desperate, and Creon has expressly—
ANTIGONE: No,
he has no right to keep me from my own.
ISMENE: Oh my sister, think—   60
think how our own father died, hated,[3]
his reputation in ruins, driven on
by the crimes he brought to light himself
to gouge out his eyes with his own hands—
then mother . . . his mother and wife, both in one,   65
mutilating her life in the twisted noose—
and last, our two brothers dead in a single day,
both shedding their own blood, poor suffering boys,
battling out their common destiny hand-to-hand.

Now look at the two of us left so alone . . .   70
think what a death we'll die, the worst of all
if we violate the laws and override
the fixed decree of the throne, its power—
we must be sensible. Remember we are women,
we're not born to contend with men. Then too,   75
we're underlings, ruled by much stronger hands,
so we must submit in this, and things still worse.

I, for one, I'll beg the dead to forgive me—
I'm forced, I have no choice—I must obey
the ones who stand in power. Why rush to extremes?   80
It's madness, madness.
ANTIGONE: I won't insist,
no, even if you should have a change of heart,
I'd never welcome you in the labor, not with me.
So, do as you like, whatever suits you best—

3. This play was written before *Oedipus the King* and *Oedipus at Colonus*, which give us a different picture of Oedipus' end.

I will bury him myself.						85
And even if I die in the act, that death will be a glory.
I will lie with the one I love and loved by him—
an outrage sacred to the gods! I have longer
to please the dead than please the living here:
in the kingdom down below I'll lie forever.			90
Do as you like, dishonor the laws
the gods hold in honor.
ISMENE:					I'd do them no dishonor . . .
but defy the city? I have no strength for that.
ANTIGONE: You have your excuses. I am on my way,
I'll raise a mound for him, for my dear brother.		95
ISMENE: Oh Antigone, you're so rash—I'm so afraid for you!
ANTIGONE: Don't fear for me. Set your own life in order.
ISMENE: Then don't, at least, blurt this out to anyone.
Keep it a secret. I'll join you in that, I promise.
ANTIGONE: Dear god, shout it from the rooftops. I'll hate you		100
all the more for silence—tell the world!
ISMENE: So fiery—and it ought to chill your heart.
ANTIGONE: I know I please where I must please the most.
ISMENE: Yes, if you can, but you're in love with impossibility.
ANTIGONE: Very well then, once my strength gives out		105
I will be done at last.
ISMENE:					You're wrong from the start,
you're off on a hopeless quest.
ANTIGONE: If you say so you will make me hate you,
and the hatred of the dead, by all rights,
will haunt you night and day.				110
But leave me to my own absurdity, leave me
to suffer this—dreadful thing. I will suffer
nothing as great as death without glory.
	[*Exit to the side.*]
ISMENE: Then go if you must, but rest assured,
wild, irrational as you are, my sister,			115
you are truly dear to the ones who love you.
	[*Withdrawing to the palace. Enter a* CHORUS, *the old citizens of Thebes
	chanting as the sun begins to rise.*]
CHORUS:[4] Glory!—great beam of the sun, brightest of all
that ever rose on the seven gates of Thebes,
	you burn through night at last!
	Great eye of the golden day,				120
mounting the Dirce's[5] banks you throw him back—
the enemy out of Argos, the white shield,[6] the man of bronze—
he's flying headlong now
	the bridle of fate stampeding him with pain!

---

4. The chorus of old men celebrates the victory won over the Argive forces and Polynices.   5. A river of the Theban plain.   6. The Argive soldiers' shields were painted white.

And he had driven against our borders,   125
launched by the warring claims of Polynices—
like an eagle screaming, winging havoc
over the land, wings of armor
shielded white as snow,
a huge army massing,   130
crested helmets bristling for assault.

He hovered above our roofs, his vast maw gaping
closing down around our seven gates,
   his spears thirsting for the kill
   but now he's gone, look,   135
before he could glut his jaws with Theban blood
or the god of fire put our crown of towers to the torch.
He grappled the Dragon[7] none can master—Thebes—
   the clang of our arms like thunder at his back!

   Zeus hates with a vengeance all bravado,   140
   the mighty boasts of men. He watched them
   coming on in a rising flood, the pride
   of their golden armor ringing shrill—
   and brandishing his lightning
   blasted the fighter just at the goal,[8]   145
   rushing to shout his triumph from our walls.

Down from the heights he crashed, pounding down on the earth!
And a moment ago, blazing torch in hand—
   mad for attack, ecstatic
he breathed his rage, the storm   150
   of his fury hurling at our heads!
But now his high hopes have laid him low
and down the enemy ranks the iron god of war
   deals his rewards, his stunning blows—Ares[9]
   rapture of battle, our right arm in the crisis.   155

   Seven captains marshaled at seven gates
   seven against their equals, gave
   their brazen trophies[1] up to Zeus
   god of the breaking rout of battle,
   all but two: those blood brothers,   160
   one father, one mother—matched in rage,
   spears matched for the twin conquest—
   clashed and won the common prize of death.

But now for Victory! glorious in the morning,
joy in her eyes to meet our joy   165

---

7. According to legend, the Thebans sprang from the dragon's teeth sown by Cadmus. 8. Capaneus,
the most violent of the Seven against Thebes. He had almost scaled the wall when the lightning of Zeus
threw him down. 9. Not only the god of war but also one of the patron deities of Thebes. 1. The
victors in Greek battle set up a trophy consisting of the armor of one of the enemy dead, fixed to a post
and set up at the place where the enemy turned to run away.

she is winging[2] down to Thebes,
our fleets of chariots wheeling in her wake—
Now let us win oblivion from the wars,
thronging the temples of the gods
in singing, dancing choirs through the night!   170
   Lord Dionysus,[3] god of the dance
   that shakes the land of Thebes, now lead the way!
  [*Enter* CREON *from the palace, attended by his guard.*]

     But look, the king of the realm is coming,
     Creon, the new man for the new day,
     whatever the gods are sending now . . .   175
     what new plan will he launch?
     Why this, this special session?
     Why this sudden call to the old men
     summoned at one command?

CREON: My countrymen,
  the ship of state is safe. The gods who rocked her,   180
  after a long, merciless pounding in the storm,
  have righted her once more.
                 Out of the whole city
  I have called you here alone. Well I know,
  first, your undeviating respect
  for the throne and royal power of King Laius.   185
  Next, while Oedipus steered the land of Thebes,
  and even after he died, your loyalty was unshakable,
  you still stood by their children. Now then,
  since the two sons are dead—two blows of fate
  in the same day, cut down by each other's hands,   190
  both killers, both brothers stained with blood—
  as I am next in kin to the dead,
  I now possess the throne and all its powers.

  Of course you cannot know a man completely,
  his character, his principles, sense of judgment,   195
  not till he's shown his colors, ruling the people,
  making laws. Experience, there's the test.
  As I see it, whoever assumes the task,
  the awesome task of setting the city's course,
  and refuses to adopt the soundest policies   200
  but fearing someone, keeps his lips locked tight,
  he's utterly worthless. So I rate him now,
  I always have. And whoever places a friend
  above the good of his own country, he is nothing:
  I have no use for him. Zeus my witness,   205
  Zeus who sees all things, always—

2. Victory is portrayed in Greek painting and sculpture as a winged young woman.   3. A god of revel,
but also a god born to Zeus and a Theban princess, Semele.

I could never stand by silent, watching destruction
march against our city, putting safety to rout,
nor could I ever make that man a friend of mine
who menaces our country. Remember this: 210
our country *is* our safety.
Only while she voyages true on course
can we establish friendships, truer than blood itself.
Such are my standards. They make our city great.

Closely akin to them I have proclaimed,   215
just now, the following decree to our people
concerning the two sons of Oedipus.
Eteocles, who died fighting for Thebes,
excelling all in arm: he shall be buried,
crowned with a hero's honors, the cups we pour[4]   220
to soak the earth and reach the famous dead.

But as for his blood brother, Polynices,
who returned from exile, home to his father-city
and the gods of his race, consumed with one desire—
to burn them roof to roots—who thirsted to drink   225
his kinsmen's blood and sell the rest to slavery:
that man—a proclamation has forbidden the city
to dignify him with burial, mourn him at all.
No, he must be left unburied, his corpse
carrion for the birds and dogs to tear,   230
an obscenity for the citizens to behold!

These are my principles. Never at my hands
will the traitor be honored above the patriot.
But whoever proves his loyalty to the state—
I'll prize that man in death as well as life.   235
LEADER: If this is your pleasure, Creon, treating
our city's enemy and our friend this way . . .
The power is yours, I suppose, to enforce it
with the laws, both for the dead and all of us,
the living.
CREON: Follow my orders closely then,   240
be on your guard.
LEADER: We're too old.
Lay that burden on younger shoulders.
CREON: No, no,
I don't mean the body—I've posted guards already.
LEADER: What commands for us then? What other service?
CREON: See that you never side with those who break my orders.   245
LEADER: Never. Only a fool could be in love with death.
CREON: Death is the price—you're right. But all too often

---

4. Libations (liquid offerings—wine, honey, etc.) poured on the grave.

the mere hope of money has ruined many men.

[*A* SENTRY *enters from the side.*]

SENTRY: My lord,
   I can't say I'm winded from running, or set out
   with any spring in my legs either—no sir,   250
   I was lost in thought, and it made me stop, often,
   dead in my track, heeling, turning back,
   and all the time a voice inside me muttering,
   "Idiot, why? You're going straight to your death."
   Then muttering, "Stopped again, poor fool?   255
   If somebody gets the news to Creon first,
   what's to save your neck?"
                                 And so,
   mulling it over, on I trudge, dragging my feet,
   you can make a short road take forever . . .
   but at last, look, common sense won out,   260
   I'm here, and I'm all yours,
   and even though I come empty-handed
   I'll tell my story just the same, because
   I've come with a good grip on one hope,
   what will come will come, whatever fate—   265
CREON: Come to the point!
   What's wrong—why so afraid?
SENTRY: First, myself, I've got to tell you,
   I didn't do it, didn't see who did—
   Be fair, don't take it out on me.   270
CREON: You're playing it safe, soldier,
   barricading yourself from any trouble.
   It's obvious, you've something strange to tell.
SENTRY: Dangerous too, and danger makes you delay
   for all you're worth.   275
CREON: Out with it—then dismiss!
SENTRY: All right, here it comes. The body—
   someone's just buried it, then run off . . .
   sprinkled some dry dust on the flesh,[5]
   given it proper rites.
CREON: What?   280
   What man alive would dare—
SENTRY: I've no idea, I swear it.
   There was no mark of a spade, no pickaxe there,
   no earth turned up, the ground packed hard and dry,
   unbroken, no tracks, no wheelruts, nothing,
   the workman left no trace. Just at sunup   285
   the first watch of the day points it out—

5. A symbolic burial, all Antigone could do alone, without Ismene's help.

it was a wonder! We were stunned . . .
a terrific burden too, for all of us, listen:
you can't see the corpse, not that it's buried,
really, just a light cover of road-dust on it,   290
as if someone meant to lay the dead to rest
and keep from getting cursed.
Not a sign in sight that dogs or wild beasts
had worried the body, even torn the skin.

But what came next! Rough talk flew thick and fast,   295
guard grilling guard—we'd have come to blows
at last, nothing to stop it; each man for himself
and each the culprit, no one caught red-handed,
all of us pleading ignorance, dodging the charges,
ready to take up red-hot iron in our fists,   300
go through fire,[6] swear oaths to the gods—
"I didn't do it, I had no hand in it either,
not in the plotting, not the work itself!"

Finally, after all this wrangling came to nothing,
one man spoke out and made us stare at the ground,   305
hanging our heads in fear. No way to counter him,
no way to take his advice and come through
safe and sound. Here's what he said:
"Look, we've got to report the facts to Creon,
we can't keep this hidden." Well, that won out,   310
and the lot fell to me, condemned me,
unlucky as ever, I got the prize. So here I am,
against my will and yours too, well I know—
no one wants the man who brings bad news.
LEADER: My king,
ever since he began I've been debating in my mind,   315
could this possibly be the work of the gods?
CREON: Stop—
before you make me choke with anger—the gods!
You, you're senile, must you be insane?
You say—why it's intolerable—say the gods
could have the slightest concern for the corpse?   320
Tell me, was it for meritorious service
they proceeded to bury him, prized him so? The hero
who came to burn their temples ringed with pillars,
their golden treasures—scorch their hallowed earth
and fling their laws to the winds.   325
Exactly when did you last see the gods
celebrating traitors? Inconceivable!

6. Both traditional assertions of truthfulness, derived perhaps from some primitive ritual of ordeal—only
the liar would get burned.

No, from the first there were certain citizens
who could hardly stand the spirit of my regime,
grumbling against me in the dark, heads together,   330
tossing wildly, never keeping their necks beneath
the yoke, loyally submitting to their king.
These are the instigators, I'm convinced—
they've perverted my own guard, bribed them
to do their work.
                Money! Nothing worse   335
in our lives, so current, rampant, so corrupting.
Money—you demolish cities, rot men from their homes,
you train and twist good minds and set them on
to the most atrocious schemes. No limit,
you make them adept at every kind of outrage,   340
every godless crime—money!
                  Everyone—
the whole crew bribed to commit this crime,
they've made one thing sure at least:
sooner or later they will pay the price.
   [*Wheeling on the* SENTRY.]
                     You—
I swear to Zeus as I still believe in Zeus,   345
if you don't find the man who buried that corpse,
the very man, and produce him before my eyes,
simple death won't be enough for you,
not till we string you up alive
and wring the immorality out of you.   350
Then you can steal the rest of our days,
better informed about where to make a killing.
You'll have learned, at last, it doesn't pay
to itch for rewards from every hand that beckons.
Filthy profits wreck most men, you'll see—   355
they'll never save your life.
SENTRY: Please,
   may I say a word or two, or just turn and go?
CREON: Can't you tell? Everything you say offends me.
SENTRY: Where does it hurt you, in the ears or in the heart?
CREON: And who are you to pinpoint my displeasure?   360
SENTRY: The culprit grates on your feelings,
   I just annoy your ears.
CREON: Still talking?
   You talk too much! a born nuisance—
SENTRY: Maybe so,
   but I never did this thing, so help me!
CREON: Yes you did—
   what's more, you squandered your life for silver!   365

SENTRY: Oh it's terrible when the one who does the judging
    judges things all wrong.
CREON: Well now,
    you just be clever about your judgments—
    if you fail to produce the criminals for me,
    you'll swear your dirty money brought you pain.   370
    [*Turning sharply, reentering the palace.*]
SENTRY: I hope he's found. Best thing by far.
    But caught or not, that's in the lap of fortune:
    I'll never come back, you've seen the last of me.
    I'm saved, even now, and I never thought,
    I never hoped—   375
    dear gods, I owe you all my thanks!
    [*Rushing out.*]
CHORUS: Numberless wonders
    terrible wonders walk the world but none the match for man—
    that great wonder crossing the heaving gray sea,
           driven on by the blasts of winter
    on through breakers crashing left and right,   380
        holds his steady course
    and the oldest of the gods he wears away—
    the Earth, the immortal, the inexhaustible—
    as his powers go back and forth, year in, year out
        with the breed of stallions[7] turning up the furrows.   385

And the blithe, lightheaded race of birds he snares,
    the tribes of savage beasts, the life that swarms the depths—
        with one fling of his nets
    woven and coiled tight, he takes them all,
        man the skilled, the brilliant!   390
He conquers all, taming with his techniques
    the prey that roams the cliffs and wild lairs,
    training the stallion, clamping the yoke across
        his shaggy neck, and the tireless mountain bull.
And speech and thought, quick as the wind   395
    and the mood and mind for law that rules the city—
        all these he has taught himself
    and shelter from the arrows of the frost
    when there's rough lodging under the cold clear sky
    and the shafts of lashing rain—   400
        ready, resourceful man!
            Never without resources
    never an impasse as he marches on the future—
    only Death, from Death alone he will find no rescue
    but from desperate plagues he has plotted his escapes.   405

---

7. Mules, the working animal of a Greek farmer.

Man the master, ingenious past all measure
past all dreams, the skills within his grasp—
   he forges on, now to destruction
now again to greatness. When he weaves in
the laws of the land, and the justice of the gods   410
that binds his oaths together
      he and his city rise high—
        but the city casts out
that man who weds himself to inhumanity
thanks to reckless daring. Never share my hearth   415
never think my thoughts, whoever does such things.

    [*Enter* ANTIGONE *from the side, accompanied by the* SENTRY.]
Here is a dark sign from the gods—
what to make of this? I know her,
how can I deny it? That young girl's Antigone!
Wretched, child of a wretched father,   420
Oedipus. Look, is it possible?
They bring you in like a prisoner—
why? did you break the king's laws?
Did they take you in some act of mad defiance?

SENTRY: She's the one, she did it single-handed—   425
we caught her burying the body. Where's Creon?

    [*Enter* CREON *from the palace.*]

LEADER: Back again, just in time when you need him.

CREON: In time for what? What is it?

SENTRY: My king,
there's nothing you can swear you'll never do—
second thoughts make liars of us all.   430
I could have sworn I wouldn't hurry back
(what with your threats, the buffeting I just took),
but a stroke of luck beyond our wildest hopes,
what a joy, there's nothing like it. So,
back I've come, breaking my oath, who cares?   435
I'm bringing in our prisoner—this young girl—
we took her giving the dead the last rites.
But no casting lots this time; this is *my* luck,
my prize, no one else's.
              Now, my lord,
here she is. Take her, question her,   440
cross-examine her to your heart's content.
But set me free, it's only right—
I'm rid of this dreadful business once for all.

CREON: Prisoner! Her? You took her—where, doing what?

SENTRY: Burying the man. That's the whole story.

CREON: What?   445
You mean what you say, you're telling me the truth?

SENTRY: She's the one. With my own eyes I saw her

bury the body, just what you've forbidden.
There. Is that plain and clear?
CREON: What did you see? Did you catch her in the act?   450
SENTRY: Here's what happened. We went back to our post,
   those threats of yours breathing down our necks—
   we brushed the corpse clean of the dust that covered it,
   stripped it bare . . . it was slimy, going soft,
   and we took to high ground, backs to the wind   455
   so the stink of him couldn't hit us;
   jostling, baiting each other to keep awake,
   shouting back and forth—no napping on the job,
   not this time. And so the hours dragged by
   until the sun stood dead above our heads,   460
   a huge white ball in the noon sky, beating,
   blazing down, and then it happened—
   suddenly, a whirlwind!
   Twisting a great dust-storm up from the earth,
   a black plague of the heavens, filling the plain,   465
   ripping the leaves off every tree in sight,
   choking the air and sky. We squinted hard
   and took our whipping from the gods.

And after the storm passed—it seemed endless—
   there, we saw the girl!   470
   And she cried out a sharp, piercing cry,
   like a bird come back to an empty nest,
   peering into its bed, and all the babies gone . . .
   Just so, when she sees the corpse bare
   she bursts into a long, shattering wail   475
   and calls down withering curses on the heads
   of all who did the work. And she scoops up dry dust,
   handfuls, quickly, and lifting a fine bronze urn,
   lifting it high and pouring, she crowns the dead
   with three full libations.
                          Soon as we saw   480
   we rushed her, closed on the kill like hunters,
   and she, she didn't flinch. We interrogated her,
   charging her with offenses past and present—
   she stood up to it all, denied nothing. I tell you,
   it made me ache and laugh in the same breath.   485
   It's pure joy to escape the worst yourself,
   it hurts a man to bring down his friends.
   But all that, I'm afraid, means less to me
   than my own skin. That's the way I'm made.
CREON: [*Wheeling on* ANTIGONE.]   You,
   with your eyes fixed on the ground—speak up.   490
   Do you deny you did this, yes or no?

ANTIGONE: I did it. I don't deny a thing.

CREON: [To the SENTRY.]

You, get out, wherever you please—
you're clear of a very heavy charge.

[He leaves; CREON turns back to ANTIGONE.]

You, tell me briefly, no long speeches—   495
were you aware a decree had forbidden this?

ANTIGONE: Well aware. How could I avoid it? It was public.

CREON: And still you had the gall to break this law?

ANTIGONE: Of course I did. It wasn't Zeus, not in the least,
who made this proclamation—not to me.   500
Nor did that Justice, dwelling with the gods
beneath the earth, ordain such laws for men.
Nor did I think your edict had such force
that you, a mere mortal, could override the gods,
the great unwritten, unshakable traditions.   505
They are alive, not just today or yesterday:
they live forever, from the first of time,
and no one knows when they first saw the light.

These laws—I was not about to break them,
not out of fear of some man's wounded pride,   510
and face the retribution of the gods.
Die I must, I've known it all my life—
how could I keep from knowing?—even without
your death-sentence ringing in my ears.
And if I am to die before my time   515
I consider that a gain. Who on earth
alive in the midst of so much grief as I,
could fail to find his death a rich reward?
So for me, at least, to meet this doom of yours
is precious little pain. But if I had allowed   520
my own mother's son to rot, an unburied corpse—
that would have been an agony! This is nothing.
And if my present actions strike you as foolish,
let's just say I've been accused of folly
by a fool.

LEADER: Like father like daughter,   525
passionate, wild . . .
she hasn't learned to bend before adversity.

CREON: No? Believe me, the stiffest stubborn wills
fall the hardest; the toughest iron,
tempered strong in the white-hot fire,   530
you'll see it crack and shatter first of all.
And I've known spirited horses you can break
with a light bit—proud, rebellious horses.

There's no room for pride, not in a slave,
not with the lord and master standing by.　535

This girl was an old hand at insolence
when she overrode the edicts we made public.
But once she'd done it—the insolence,
twice over—to glory in it, laughing,
mocking us to our face with what she'd done.　540
I am not the man, not now: she is the man
if this victory goes to her and she goes free.

Never! Sister's child or closer in blood
than all my family clustered at my altar
worshiping Guardian Zeus—she'll never escape,　545
she and her blood sister, the most barbaric death.
Yes, I accuse her sister of an equal part
in scheming this, this burial.
　　[To his attendants.]
　　　　　　　　　　Bring her here!
I just saw her inside, hysterical, gone to pieces.
It never fails: the mind convicts itself　550
in advance, when scoundrels are up to no good,
plotting in the dark. Oh but I hate it more
when a traitor, caught red-handed,
tries to glorify his crimes.
ANTIGONE: Creon, what more do you want　555
than my arrest and execution?
CREON: Nothing. Then I have it all.
ANTIGONE: Then why delay? Your moralizing repels me,
every word you say—pray god it always will.
So naturally all I say repels you too.
　　　　　　　　　　Enough.　560
Give me glory! What greater glory could I win
than to give my own brother decent burial?
These citizens here would all agree,
　　[To the CHORUS.]
they would praise me too
if their lips weren't locked in fear.　565
　　[Pointing to CREON.]
Lucky tyrants—the perquisites of power!
Ruthless power to do and say whatever pleases *them*.
CREON: You alone, of all the people in Thebes,
see things that way.
ANTIGONE:　　　　　They see it just that way
but defer to you and keep their tongues in leash.　570
CREON: And you, aren't you ashamed to differ so from them?
So disloyal!

ANTIGONE: Not ashamed for a moment,
  not to honor my brother, my own flesh and blood.
CREON: Wasn't Eteocles a brother too—cut down, facing him?
ANTIGONE: Brother, yes, by the same mother, the same father.   575
CREON: Then how can you render his enemy such honors,
  such impieties in his eyes?
ANTIGONE: He'll never testify to that,
  Eteocles dead and buried.
CREON: He will—
  if you honor the traitor just as much as him.   580
ANTIGONE: But it was his brother, not some slave that died—
CREON: Ravaging our country!—
  but Eteocles died fighting in our behalf.
ANTIGONE: No matter—Death longs for the same rites for all.
CREON: Never the same for the patriot and the traitor.   585
ANTIGONE: Who, Creon, who on earth can say the ones below
  don't find this pure and uncorrupt?
CREON: Never. Once an enemy, never a friend,
  not even after death.
ANTIGONE: I was born to join in love, not hate—   590
  that is my nature.
CREON: Go down below and love,
  if love you must—love the dead! while I'm alive,
  no woman is going to lord it over me.
    [Enter ISMENE from the palace, under guard.]
CHORUS: Look,
  Ismene's coming, weeping a sister's tears,
  loving sister, under a cloud . . .   595
  her face is flushed, her cheeks streaming.
  Sorrow puts her lovely radiance in the dark.
CREON: You—
  in my own house, you viper, slinking undetected,
  sucking my life-blood! I never knew
  I was breeding twin disasters, the two of you   600
  rising up against my throne. Come, tell me,
  will you confess your part in the crime or not?
  Answer me. Swear to me.
ISMENE: I did it, yes—
  if only she consents—I share the guilt,
  the consequences too.
ANTIGONE: No,   605
  Justice will never suffer that—not you,
  you were unwilling. I never brought you in.
ISMENE: But now you face such dangers . . . I'm not ashamed
  to sail through trouble with you,
  make your troubles mine.
ANTIGONE: Who did the work?   610

Let the dead and the god of death bear witness!
I have no love for a friend who loves in words alone.
ISMENE: Oh no, my sister, don't reject me, please,
    let me die beside you, consecrating
    the dead together.
ANTIGONE: Never share my dying,   615
    don't lay claim to what you never touched.
    My death will be enough.
ISMENE: What do I care for life, cut off from you?
ANTIGONE: Ask Creon. Your concern is all for him.
ISMENE: Why abuse me so? It doesn't help you now.
ANTIGONE: You're right—   620
    if I mock you, I get no pleasure from it,
    only pain.
ISMENE: Tell me, dear one,
    what can I do to help you, even now?
ANTIGONE: Save yourself. I don't grudge you your survival.
ISMENE: Oh no, no, denied my portion in your death?   625
ANTIGONE: You chose to live, I chose to die.
ISMENE: Not, at least,
    without every kind of caution I could voice.
ANTIGONE: Your wisdom appealed to one world—mine, another.
ISMENE: But look, we're both guilty, both condemned to death.
ANTIGONE: Courage! Live your life. I gave myself to death,   630
    long ago, so I might serve the dead.
CREON: They're both mad, I tell you, the two of them.
    One's just shown it, the other's been that way
    since she was born.
ISMENE: True, my king,
    the sense we were born with cannot last forever . . .   635
    commit cruelty on a person long enough
    and the mind begins to go.
CREON: Yours did,
    when you chose to commit your crimes with her.
ISMENE: How can I live alone, without her?
CREON: Her?
    Don't even mention her—she no longer exists.   640
ISMENE: What? You'd kill your own son's bride?
CREON: Absolutely:
    there are other fields for him to plow.
ISMENE: Perhaps,
    but never as true, as close a bond as theirs.
CREON: A worthless woman for my son? It repels me.
ISMENE: Dearest Haemon, your father wrongs you so!   645
CREON: Enough, enough—you and your talk of marriage!
ISMENE: Creon—you're really going to rob your son of Antigone?
CREON: Death will do it for me—break their marriage off.

LEADER: So, it's settled then? Antigone must die?
CREON: Settled, yes—we both know that.   650
    [*To the guards.*]
Stop wasting time. Take them in.
From now on they'll act like women.
Tie them up, no more running loose;
even the bravest will cut and run,
once they see Death coming for their lives.   655
    [*The guards escort* ANTIGONE *and* ISMENE *into the palace.* CREON
    remains while the old citizens form their CHORUS.]
CHORUS: Blest, they are the truly blest who all their lives
have never tasted devastation. For others, once
    the gods have rocked a house to its foundations
    the ruin will never cease, cresting on and on
from one generation on throughout the race—   660
like a great mounting tide
driven on by savage northern gales,
    surging over the dead black depths
rolling up from the bottom dark heaves of sand
and the headlands, taking the storm's onslaught full-force,   665
roar, and the low moaning
                    echoes on and on
                              and now
as in ancient times I see the sorrows of the house,
the living heirs of the old ancestral kings,
piling on the sorrows of the dead
    and one generation cannot free the next—   670
some god will bring them crashing down,
the race finds no release.
And now the light, the hope
    springing up from the late last root
in the house of Oedipus, that hope's cut down in turn   675
by the long, bloody knife swung by the gods of death
by a senseless word
                    by fury at the heart.
                              Zeus,
yours is the power, Zeus, what man on earth
can override it, who can hold it back?
Power that neither Sleep, the all-ensnaring   680
    no, nor the tireless months of heaven
can ever overmaster—young through all time,
mighty lord of power, you hold fast
    the dazzling crystal mansions of Olympus.
And throughout the future, late and soon   685
as through the past, your law prevails:
no towering form of greatness

enters into the lives of mortals
    free and clear of ruin.
                True,
our dreams, our high hopes voyaging far and wide   690
bring sheer delight to many, to many others
    delusion, blithe, mindless lusts
and the fraud steals on one slowly . . . unaware
till he trips and puts his foot into the fire.
    He was a wise old man who coined   695
the famous saying: "Sooner or later
foul is fair, fair is foul
to the man the gods will ruin"—
    He goes his way for a moment only
        free of blinding ruin.   700
    [*Enter* HAEMON *from the palace.*]
    Here's Haemon now, the last of all your sons.
    Does he come in tears for his bride,
    his doomed bride, Antigone—
    bitter at being cheated of their marriage?
CREON: We'll soon know, better than seer could tell us.   705
    [*Turning to* HAEMON.]
    Son, you've heard the final verdict on your bride?
    Are you coming now, raving against your father?
    Or do you love me, no matter what I do?
HAEMON: Father, I'm your *son* . . . you in your wisdom
    set my bearings for me—I obey you.   710
    No marriage could ever mean more to me than you,
    whatever good direction you may offer.
CREON: Fine, Haemon.
    That's how you ought to feel within your heart,
    subordinate to your father's will in every way.
    That's what a man prays for: to produce good sons—   715
    a household full of them, dutiful and attentive,
    so they can pay his enemy back with interest
    and match the respect their father shows his friend.
    But the man who rears a brood of useless children,
    what has he brought into the world, I ask you?   720
    Nothing but trouble for himself, and mockery
    from his enemies laughing in his face.
                    Oh Haemon,
    never lose your sense of judgment over a woman.
    The warmth, the rush of pleasure, it all goes cold
    in your arms, I warn you . . . a worthless woman   725
    in your house, a misery in your bed.
    What wound cuts deeper than a loved one
    turned against you? Spit her out,

like a mortal enemy—let the girl go.
Let her find a husband down among the dead.   730
Imagine it: I caught her in naked rebellion,
the traitor, the only one in the whole city.
I'm not about to prove myself a liar,
not to my people, no, I'm going to kill her!
That's right—so let her cry for mercy, sing her hymns   735
to Zeus who defends all bonds of kindred blood.
Why, if I bring up my own kin to be rebels,
think what I'd suffer from the world at large.
Show me the man who rules his household well:
I'll show you someone fit to rule the state.   740
That good man, my son,
I have every confidence he and he alone
can give commands and take them too. Staunch
in the storm of spears he'll stand his ground,
a loyal, unflinching comrade at your side.   745

But whoever steps out of line, violates the laws
or presumes to hand out orders to his superiors,
he'll win no praise from me. But that man
the city places in authority, his orders
must be obeyed, large and small,   750
right and wrong.
              Anarchy—
show me a greater crime in all the earth!
She, she destroys cities, rips up houses,
breaks the ranks of spearmen into headlong rout.
But the ones who last it out, the great mass of them   755
owe their lives to discipline. Therefore
we must defend the men who live by law,
never let some woman triumph over us.
Better to fall from power, if fall we must,
at the hands of a man—never be rated   760
inferior to a woman, never.
LEADER: To us,
unless old age has robbed us of our wits,
you seem to say what you have to say with sense.
HAEMON: Father, only the gods endow a man with reason,
the finest of all their gifts, a treasure.   765
Far be it from me—I haven't the skill,
and certainly no desire, to tell you when,
if ever, you make a slip in speech . . . though
someone else might have a good suggestion.

Of course it's not for you,   770
in the normal run of things, to watch

whatever men say or do, or find to criticize.
The man in the street, you know, dreads your glance,
he'd never say anything displeasing to your face.
But it's for me to catch the murmurs in the dark,   775
the way the city mourns for this young girl.
"No woman," they say, "ever deserved death less,
and such a brutal death for such a glorious action.
She, with her own dear brother lying in his blood—
she couldn't bear to leave him dead, unburied,   780
food for the wild dogs or wheeling vultures.
Death? She deserves a glowing crown of gold!"
So they say, and the rumor spreads in secret,
darkly . . .
                    I rejoice in your success, father—
nothing more precious to me in the world.   785
What medal of honor brighter to his children
than a father's glowing glory? Or a child's
to his proud father? Now don't, please,
be quite so single-minded, self-involved,
or assume the world is wrong and you are right.   790
Whoever thinks that he alone possesses intelligence,
the gift of eloquence, he and no one else,
and character too . . . such men, I tell you,
spread them open—you will find them empty.
                                        No,
it's no disgrace for a man, even a wise man,   795
to learn many things and not to be too rigid.
You've seen trees by a raging winter torrent,
how many sway with the flood and salvage every twig,
but not the stubborn—they're ripped out, roots and all.
Bend or break. The same when a man is sailing: 800
haul your sheets too taut, never give an inch,
you'll capsize, and go the rest of the voyage
keel up and the rowing-benches under.

Oh give way. Relax your anger—change!
I'm young, I know, but let me offer this: 805
it would be best by far, I admit,
if a man were born infallible, right by nature.
If not—and things don't often go that way,
it's best to learn from those with good advice.
LEADER: You'd do well, my lord, if he's speaking to the point,   810
to learn from him,
        [*Turning to* HAEMON.]
                and you, my boy, from him.
You both are talking sense.

CREON: So,
   men our age, we're to be lectured, are we?—
   schooled by a boy his age?
HAEMON: Only in what is right. But if I seem young,   815
   look less to my years and more to what I do.
CREON: Do? Is admiring rebels an achievement?
HAEMON: I'd never suggest that you admire treason.
CREON: Oh?—
   isn't that just the sickness that's attacked her?
HAEMON: The whole city of Thebes denies it, to a man.   820
CREON: And is Thebes about to tell me how to rule?
HAEMON: Now, you see? Who's talking like a child?
CREON: Am I to rule this land for others—or myself?
HAEMON: It's no city at all, owned by one man alone.
CREON: What? The city *is* the king's—that's the law!   825
HAEMON: What a splendid king you'd make of a desert island—
   you and you alone.
CREON: [*To the* CHORUS.]
   This boy, I do believe,
   is fighting on her side, the woman's side.
HAEMON: If you are a woman, yes—
   my concern is all for you.   830
CREON: Why, you degenerate—bandying accusations,
   threatening me with justice, your own father!
HAEMON: I see my father offending justice—wrong.
CREON: Wrong?
   To protect my royal rights?
HAEMON: Protect your rights?
   When you trample down the honors of the gods?   835
CREON: You, you soul of corruption, rotten through—
   woman's accomplice!
HAEMON: That may be,
   but you'll never find me accomplice to a criminal.
CREON: That's what *she* is,
   and every word you say is a blatant appeal for her—   840
HAEMON: And you, and me, and the gods beneath the earth.
CREON: You will never marry her, not while she's alive.
HAEMON: Then she'll die . . . but her death will kill another.
CREON: What, brazen threats? You go too far!
HAEMON: What threat?
   Combating your empty, mindless judgments with a word?   845
CREON: You'll suffer for your sermons, you and your empty wisdom!
HAEMON: If you weren't my father, I'd say you were insane.
CREON: Don't flatter me with Father—you woman's slave!
HAEMON: You really expect to fling abuse at me
   and not receive the same?
CREON: Is that so!   850

Now, by heaven, I promise you, you'll pay—
taunting, insulting me! Bring her out,
that hateful—she'll die now, here,
in front of his eyes, beside her groom!
HAEMON: No, no, she will never die beside me—   855
don't delude yourself. And you will never
see me, never set eyes on my face again.
Rage your heart out, rage with friends
who can stand the sight of you.
    [Rushing out.]
LEADER: Gone, my king, in a burst of anger.   860
A temper young as his . . . hurt him once,
he may do something violent.
CREON: Let him do—
dream up something desperate, past all human limit!
Good riddance. Rest assured,
he'll never save those two young girls from death.   865
LEADER: Both of them, you really intend to kill them both?
CREON: No, not her, the one whose hands are clean—
you're quite right.
LEADER: But Antigone—
what sort of death do you have in mind for her?
CREON: I'll take her down some wild, desolate path   870
never trod by men, and wall her up alive[8]
in a rocky vault, and set out short rations,[9]
just the measure piety demands
to keep the entire city free of defilement.
There let her pray to the one god she worships: 875
Death—who knows?—may just reprieve her from death.
Or she may learn at last, better late than never,
what a waste of breath it is to worship Death.
    [Exit to the palace.]
CHORUS: Love, never conquered in battle
Love the plunderer laying waste the rich!   880
Love standing the night-watch
    guarding a girl's soft cheek,
you range the seas, the shepherds' steadings off in the wilds—
not even the deathless gods can flee your onset,
nothing human born for a day—   885
whoever feels your grip is driven mad.
                        Love!—
you wrench the minds of the righteous into outrage,

---

8. The penalty originally proclaimed was death by stoning. But this demands the participation of the citizens and it may be that Creon, after listening to Haemon's remarks, is not as sure as he once was of popular support.   9. The penalty proposed by Creon seems to be imprisonment in a tomb with a certain ration of food. Since Antigone would die of starvation but not actually by anyone's hand, Creon seems to think that the city will not be "defiled," i.e., incur blood guilt.

swerve them to their ruin—you have ignited this,
this kindred strife, father and son at war
   and Love alone the victor—   890
warm glance of the bride triumphant, burning with desire!
Throned in power, side-by-side with the mighty laws!
Irresistible Aphrodite,[1] never conquered—
Love, you mock us for your sport.
    [ANTIGONE *is brought from the palace under guard.*]
    But now, even I'd rebel against the king,   895
    I'd break all bounds when I see this—
    I fill with tears, I cannot hold them back,
    not any more . . . I see Antigone make her way
    to the bridal vault where all are laid to rest.
ANTIGONE: Look at me, men of my fatherland,   900
    setting out on the last road
looking into the last light of day
the last I'll ever see . . .
    the god of death who puts us all to bed
takes me down to the banks of Acheron[2] alive—   905
    denied my part in the wedding-songs,
no wedding-song in the dusk has crowned my marriage—
I go to wed the lord of the dark waters.
CHORUS: Not crowned with glory,[3] or with a dirge,
    you leave for the deep pit of the dead.   910
No withering illness laid you low,
    no strokes of the sword—a law to yourself,
alone, no mortal like you, ever, you go down
    to the halls of Death alive and breathing.
ANTIGONE: But think of Niobe[4]—well I know her story—   915
    think what a living death she died,
Tantalus' daughter, stranger queen from the east:
there on the mountain heights, growing stone
binding as ivy, slowly walled her round
and the rains will never cease, the legends say   920
the snows will never leave her . . .
    wasting away, under her brows the tears
showering down her breasting ridge and slopes—
a rocky death like hers puts me to sleep.
CHORUS: But she was a god, born of gods,   925

---

1. Goddess of sexual love.   2. A river of the world of the dead.   3. The usual version of this line is: "crowned with glory. . . ." The Greek word *oukoun* can be negative or positive, depending on the accent, which determines the pronunciation; since these written accents were not yet in use in Sophocles's time, no one will ever know for sure which meaning he intended. The present version is based on the belief that the chorus is expressing pity for Antigone's ignominious and abnormal death; she has no funeral at which her fame and praise are recited, she will not die by either of the usual causes—violence or disease—but by a living death. It is, as they say, her own choice: she is "a law to [herself]" (l. 912).   4. A Phrygian princess married to Amphion, king of Thebes. She boasted that she had borne more children than Leto, mother of Apollo and Artemis; these two killed her children. She returned to Phrygia where she was turned into a rock on Mount Sipylus; the melting of the snow on the mountain caused "tears" to flow down the rock formation which resembled a woman's face.

and we are only mortals born to die.
And yet, of course, it's a great thing
for a dying girl to hear, just to hear
she shares a destiny equal to the gods,
during life and later, once she's dead.

ANTIGONE: O you mock me! 930
Why, in the name of all my fathers' gods
why can't you wait till I am gone—
must you abuse me to my face?
O my city, all your fine rich sons!
And you, you springs of the Dirce, 935
holy grove of Thebes where the chariots gather,
you at least, you'll bear me witness, look,
unmourned by friend and forced by such crude laws
I go to my rockbound prison, strange new tomb—
always a stranger, O dear god, 940
I have no home on earth and none below,
not with the living, not with the breathless dead.

CHORUS: You went too far, the last limits of daring—
smashing against the high throne of Justice!
Your life's in ruins, child—I wonder . . . 945
do you pay for your father's terrible ordeal?

ANTIGONE: There—at last you've touched it, the worst pain
the worst anguish! Raking up the grief for father
three times over, for all the doom
that's struck us down, the brilliant house of Laius. 950
O mother, your marriage-bed
the coiling horrors, the coupling there—
you with your own son, my father—doomstruck mother!
Such, such were my parents, and I their wretched child.
I go to them now, cursed, unwed, to share their home— 955
I am a stranger! O dear brother, doomed
in your marriage—your marriage murders mine,[5]
your dying drags me down to death alive!

[Enter CREON.]

CHORUS: Reverence asks some reverence in return—
but attacks on power never go unchecked, 960
not by the man who holds the reins of power.
Your own blind will, your passion has destroyed you.

ANTIGONE: No one to weep for me, my friends,
no wedding-song—they take me away
in all my pain . . . the road lies open, waiting. 965
Never again, the law forbids me to see
the sacred eye of day. I am agony!
No tears for the destiny that's mine,

5. Polynices had married the daughter of Adrastus of Argos, to seal the alliance that enabled him to march against Thebes.

no loved one mourns my death.
CREON: Can't you see?
If a man could wail his own dirge *before* he dies,   970
he'd never finish.
[*To the guards.*]
                    Take her away, quickly!
Wall her up in the tomb, you have your orders.
Abandon her there, alone, and let her choose—
death or a buried life with a good roof for shelter.
As for myself, my hands are clean. This young girl—   975
dead or alive, she will be stripped of her rights,
her stranger's rights,[6] here in the world above.
ANTIGONE: O tomb, my bridal-bed—my house, my prison
cut in the hollow rock, my everlasting watch!
I'll soon be there, soon embrace my own,   980
the great growing family of our dead
Persephone[7] has received among her ghosts.
                                          I,
the last of them all, the most reviled by far,
go down before my destined time's run out.
But still I go, cherishing one good hope: 985
my arrival may be dear to father,
dear to you, my mother,
dear to you, my loving brother, Eteocles—
When you died I washed you with my hands,
I dressed you all, I poured the sacred cups   990
across your tombs. But now, Polynices,
because I laid your body out as well,
this, this is my reward. Nevertheless
I honored you—the decent will admit it—
well and wisely too.
                    Never, I tell you,   995
if I had been the mother of children
or if my husband died, exposed and rotting—
I'd never have taken this ordeal upon myself,
never defied our people's will. What law,
you ask, do I satisfy with what I say?   1000
A husband dead, there might have been another.
A child by another too, if I had lost the first.
But mother and father both lost in the halls of Death,
no brother could ever spring to light again.[8]

6. The Greek words suggest that he sees her not as a citizen but as a resident alien; by her action she has forfeited citizenship. But now she will be deprived even of that inferior status.   7. Queen of the underworld.   8. This strange justification for her action (ll. 995ff) has been considered unacceptable by many critics and they have suspected that it was an interpolation by some later producer of the play. But Aristotle quotes it in the next century and appears to have no doubt of its authenticity. If genuine, it does mean that Antigone momentarily abandons the laws she championed against Creon—that all men had a right to burial—and sees her motive as exclusive devotion to her dead brother. For someone facing the prospect

For this law alone I held you first in honor.   1005
For this, Creon, the king, judges me a criminal
guilty of dreadful outrage, my dear brother!
And now he leads me off, a captive in his hands,
with no part in the bridal-song, the bridal-bed,
denied all joy of marriage, raising childen—   1010
deserted so by loved ones, struck by fate,
I descend alive to the caverns of the dead.

What law of the mighty gods have I transgressed?
Why look to the heavens any more, tormented as I am?
Whom to call, what comrades now? Just think,   1015
my reverence only brands me for irreverence!
Very well: if this is the pleasure of the gods,
once I suffer I will know that I was wrong.
But if these men are wrong, let them suffer
nothing worse than they mete out to me—   1020
these masters of injustice!
LEADER: Still the same rough winds, the wild passion
raging through the girl.
CREON: [*To the guards.*] Take her away.
You're wasting time—you'll pay for it too.
ANTIGONE: Oh god, the voice of death. Its come, it's here.   1025
CREON: True. Not a word of hope—your doom is sealed.
ANTIGONE: Land of Thebes, city of all my fathers—
O you gods, the first gods of the race!⁹
They drag me away, now, no more delay.
Look on me, you noble sons of Thebes—   1030
the last of a great line of kings,
I alone, see what I suffer now
at the hands of what breed of men—
all for reverence, my reverence for the gods!
[*She leaves under guard: the* CHORUS *gathers.*]
CHORUS: Danaë, Danaë¹—   1035
even she endured a fate like yours,
in all her lovely strength she traded
the light of day for the bolted brazen vault—
buried within her tomb, her bridal-chamber,
wed to the yoke and broken.   1040
But she was of glorious birth
my child, my child
and treasured the seed of Zeus within her womb,

of a slow and hideous death such a self-examination and realization is not impossible. And it makes no difference to the courage and tenacity of her defiance of state power.   9. The Theban royal house traced its ancestry through Harmonia, wife of Cadmus, to Aphrodite and Ares, her parents. Cadmus's daughter Semele was the mother, by Zeus, of the god Dionysus.   1. Daughter of Acrisius, king of Argos. It was prophesied that he would be killed by his daughter's son; so he shut her up in a bronze tower. But Zeus came to her in the form of a golden rainshower and she bore a son, Perseus, who did in the end kill his grandfather.

the cloudburst streaming gold!
    The power of fate is a wonder,   1045
    dark, terrible wonder—
    neither wealth nor armies
    towered walls nor ships
    black hulls lashed by the salt
    can save us from that force.   1050

The yoke tamed him too
    young Lycurgus[2] flaming in anger
    king of Edonia, all for his mad taunts
Dionysus clamped him down, encased
in the chain-mail of rock   1055
    and there his rage
      his terrible flowering rage burst—
sobbing, dying away .. . at last that madman
came to know his god—
      the power he mocked, the power   1060
      he taunted in all his frenzy
      trying to stamp out
      the women strong with the god—
      the torch, the raving sacred cries—
      enraging the Muses who adore the flute.   1065

And far north[3] where the Black Rocks
    cut the sea in half
and murderous straits
split the coast of Thrace
    a forbidding city stands   1070
where once, hard by the walls
the savage Ares thrilled to watch
a king's new queen, a Fury rearing in rage
    against his two royal sons—
      her bloody hands, her dagger-shuttle   1075
stabbing out their eyes—cursed, blinding wounds—
their eyes blind sockets screaming for revenge!

They wailed in agony cries echoing cries
    the princes doomed at birth . . .
and their mother doomed to chains,   1080
walled up in a tomb of stone—[4]

2. The Thracian (Edonian) king. He opposed the introduction of Dionysiac religion into his kingdom and was imprisoned by the god.   3. The whole story is difficult to follow and its application to the case of Antigone obscure. Cleopatra, the daughter of the Athenian princess Orithyia, whom Boreas the North Wind carried off to his home in Thrace, was married to Phineus, the Thracian king, and bore him two sons. He tired of her, abandoned her, and married Eidothea, "a King's new queen" (l. 1073) who put out the eyes of the two sons of Cleopatra. Ares, the god of war, associated with Thrace, watched the savage act.   4. Lines 1080–1081 have no equivalent in the Greek text. They represent a belief that Sophocles's audience knew a version of the legend in which Cleopatra was imprisoned in a stone tomb (which is found

but she traced her own birth back
to a proud Athenian line and the high gods
and off in caverns half the world away,
born of the wild North Wind   1085
she sprang on her father's gales,
    racing stallions up the leaping cliffs—
child of the heavens. But even on her the Fates
the gray everlasting Fates rode hard
my child, my child.

[*Enter* TIRESIAS, *the blind prophet, led by a boy.*]

TIRESIAS: Lord of Thebes,   1090
I and the boy have come together,
hand in hand. Two see with the eyes of one . . .
so the blind must go, with a guide to lead the way.

CREON: What is it, old Tiresias? What news now?

TIRESIAS: I will teach you. And you obey the seer.

CREON: I will,   1095
I've never wavered from your advice before.

TIRESIAS: And so you kept the city straight on course.

CREON: I owe you a great deal, I swear to that.

TIRESIAS: Then reflect, my son: you are poised,
once more, on the razor-edge of fate.   1100

CREON: What is it? I shudder to hear you.

TIRESIAS: You will learn
when you listen to the warnings of my craft.
As I sat on the ancient seat of augury, [5]
in the sanctuary where every bird I know
will hover at my hands—suddenly I hear it,   1105
a strange voice in the wingbeats, unintelligible,
barbaric, a mad scream! Talons flashing, ripping,
they were killing each other—that much I knew—
the murderous fury whirring in those wings
made that much clear!
                        I was afraid,   1110
I turned quickly, tasted the burnt-sacrifice,
ignited the altar at all points—but no fire,
the god in the fire never blazed.
Not from those offerings . . . over the embers
slid a heavy ooze from the long thighbones,   1115
smoking, sputtering out, and the bladder
puffed and burst—spraying gall into the air—
and the fat wrapping the bones slithered off
and left them glistening white. No fire!
The rites failed that might have blazed the future   1120

in a later source). This would give a point of comparison to Antigone (like the mention of prison in the strophes dealing with Danaë and Lycurgus). 5. A place where the birds gathered, and Tiresias watched for omens.

with a sign. So I learned from the boy here:
he is my guide, as I am guide to others.
                            And it is you—
your high resolve that sets this plague on Thebes.
The public altars and sacred hearths are fouled,
one and all, by the birds and dogs with carrion   1125
torn from the corpse, the doomstruck son of Oedipus!
and so the gods are deaf to our prayers, they spurn
the offerings in our hands, the flame of holy flesh.
No birds cry out an omen clear and true—
they're gorged with the murdered victim's blood and fat.   1130

Take these things to heart, my son, I warn you.
All men make mistakes, it is only human.
But once the wrong is done, a man
can turn his back on folly, misfortune too,
if he tries to make amends, however low he's fallen,   1135
and stops his bullnecked ways. Stubbornness
brands you for stupidity—pride is a crime.
No, yield to the dead!
Never stab the fighter when he's down.
Where's the glory, killing the dead twice over?   1140

I mean you well. I give you sound advice.
It's best to learn from a good adviser
when he speaks for your own good:
it's pure gain.
CREON: Old man—all of you! So,
you shoot your arrows at my head like archers at the target—   1145
I even have *him* loosed on me, this fortune-teller.
Oh his ilk has tried to sell me short
and ship me off for years. Well,
drive your bargains, traffic—much as you like—
in the gold of India, silver-gold of Sardis.[6]   1150
You'll never bury that body in the grave,
not even if Zeus' eagles rip the corpse
and wing their rotten pickings off to the throne of god!
Never, not even in fear of such defilement
will I tolerate his burial, that traitor.   1155
Well I know, we can't defile the gods—
no mortal has the power.
                            No,
reverend old Tiresias, all men fall,
it's only human, but the wisest fall obscenely
when they glorify obscene advice with rhetoric—   1160
all for their own gain.

6. In Asia Minor. Electrum, a mixture of gold and silver, was found in a nearby river.

TIRESIAS: Oh god, is there a man alive
  who knows, who actually believes . . .
CREON: What now?
  What earth-shattering truth are you about to utter?
TIRESIAS: . . . just how much a sense of judgment, wisdom   1165
  is the greatest gift we have?
CREON: Just as much, I'd say,
  as a twisted mind is the worst affliction known.
TIRESIAS: You are the one who's sick, Creon, sick to death.
CREON: I am in no mood to trade insults with a seer.
TIRESIAS: You have already, calling my prophecies a lie.
CREON: Why not?   1170
  You and the whole breed of seers are mad for money!
TIRESIAS: And the whole race of tyrants lusts for filthy gain.
CREON: This slander of yours—
  are you aware you're speaking to the king?
TIRESIAS: Well aware. Who helped you save the city?
CREON: You—   1175
  you have your skills, old seer, but you lust for injustice!
TIRESIAS: You will drive me to utter the dreadful secret in my heart.
CREON: Spit it out! Just don't speak it out for profit.
TIRESIAS: Profit? No, not a bit of profit, not for you.
CREON: Know full well, you'll never buy off my resolve.   1180
TIRESIAS: Then know this too, learn this by heart!
  The chariot of the sun will not race through
  so many circuits more, before you have surrendered
  one born of your own loins, your own flesh and blood,
  a corpse for corpses given in return, since you have thrust   1185
  to the world below a child sprung for the world above,
  ruthlessly lodged a living soul within the grave—
  then you've robbed the gods below the earth,
  keeping a dead body here in the bright air,
  unburied, unsung, unhallowed by the rites.   1190

  You, you have no business with the dead,
  nor do the gods above—this is violence
  you have forced upon the heavens.
  And so the avengers, the dark destroyers late
  but true to the mark, now lie in wait for you,   1195
  the Furies sent by the gods and the god of death
  to strike you down with the pains that you perfected!

  There. Reflect on that, tell me I've been bribed.
  The day comes soon, no long test of time, not now,
  when the mourning cries for men and women break   1200
  throughout your halls. Great hatred rises against you—
  cities in tumult, all whose mutilated sons
  the dogs have graced with burial, or the wild beasts

or a wheeling crow that wings the ungodly stench of carrion
back to each city, each warrior's hearth and home.   1205

These arrows for your heart! Since you've raked me
I loose them like an archer in my anger,
arrows deadly true. You'll never escape
their burning, searing force.
     [*Motioning to his escort.*]
Come, boy, take me home.   1210
So he can vent his rage on younger men,
and learn to keep a gentler tongue in his head
and better sense than what he carries now.
     [*Exit to the side.*]
LEADER: The old man's gone, my king—
terrible prophecies. Well I know,   1215
since the hair on this old head went gray,
he's never lied to Thebes.
CREON: I know it myself—I'm shaken, torn.
It's a dreadful thing to yield . . . but resist now?
Lay my pride bare to the blows of ruin?   1220
That's dreadful too.
LEADER: But good advice,
     Creon, take it now, you must.
CREON: What should I do? Tell me . . . I'll obey.
LEADER: Go! Free the girl from the rocky vault
     and raise a mound for the body you exposed.   1225
CREON: That's your advice? You think I should give in?
LEADER: Yes, my king, quickly. Disasters sent by the gods
     cut short our follies in a flash.
CREON: Oh it's hard,
     giving up the heart's desire . . . but I will do it—
     no more fighting a losing battle with necessity.   1230
LEADER: Do it now, go, don't leave it to others.
CREON: Now—I'm on my way! Come, each of you,
     take up axes, make for the high ground,
     over there, quickly! I and my better judgment
     have come round to this—I shackled her,   1235
     I'll set her free myself. I am afraid . . .
     it's best to keep the established laws
     to the very day we die.
          [*Rushing out, followed by his entourage. The* CHORUS *clusters around
          the altar.*]
CHORUS: God of a hundred names!
                         Great Dionysus—
     Son and glory of Semele! Pride of Thebes—   1240
     Child of Zeus whose thunder rocks the clouds—

Lord of the famous lands of evening—
King of the Mysteries!
           King of Eleusis,[7] Demeter's plain
her breasting hills that welcome in the world—
Great Dionysus!
           Bacchus, living in Thebes   1245
the mother-city of all your frenzied women—
                    Bacchus
living along the Ismenus'[8] rippling waters
standing over the field sown with the Dragon's teeth!

You—we have seen you through the flaring smoky fires,
    your torches blazing over the twin peaks[9]   1250
where nymphs of the hallowed cave climb onward
    fired with you, your sacred rage—
we have seen you at Castalia's running spring
and down from the heights of Nysa[1] crowned with ivy
the greening shore rioting vines and grapes   1255
    down you come in your storm of wild women
         ecstatic, mystic cries—
             Dionysus—
down to watch and ward the roads of Thebes!

First of all cities, Thebes you honor first
you and your mother, bride of the lightning—   1260
come, Dionysus! now your people lie
in the iron grip of plague,
come in your racing, healing stride
      down Parnassus' slopes
or across the moaning straits.
              Lord of the dancing—   1265
dance, dance the constellations breathing fire!
Great master of the voices of the night!
Child of Zeus, God's offspring, come, come forth!
Lord, king, dance with your nymphs, swirling, raving
arm-in-arm in frenzy through the night   1270
    they dance you, Iacchus[2]—
             Dance, Dionysus
giver of all good things!
    [*Enter a* MESSENGER *from the side.*]
MESSENGER: Neighbors,
friends of the house of Cadmus and the kings,
there's not a thing in this mortal life of ours

7. Near Athens, the site of the mysteries, the worship of Demeter, the grain and harvest goddess. Dionysus (Bacchus) was among the divinities worshiped by the initiates.   8. A river at Thebes.   9. The two cliffs above Delphi, where Dionysus was thought to reside in the winter months.   1. A mountain associated with Dionysiac worship; there is more than one mountain so named but the reference here is probably to the one on the island of Euboea, off the Attic coast.   2. Dionysus.

I'd praise or blame as settled once for all.   1275
Fortune lifts and Fortune fells the lucky
and unlucky every day. No prophet on earth
can tell a man his fate. Take Creon:
there was a man to rouse your envy once,
as I see it. He saved the realm from enemies,   1280
taking power, he alone, the lord of the fatherland,
he set us true on course—he flourished like a tree
with the noble line of sons he bred and reared . . . .
and now it's lost, all gone.
                              Believe me,
when a man has squandered his true joys,   1285
he's good as dead, I tell you, a living corpse.
Pile up riches in your house, as much as you like—
live like a king with a huge show of pomp,
but if real delight is missing from the lot,
I wouldn't give you a wisp of smoke for it,   1290
not compared with joy.
LEADER: What now?
What new grief do you bring the house of kings?
MESSENGER: Dead, dead—and the living are guilty of their death!
LEADER: Who's the murderer? Who is dead? Tell us.
MESSENGER: Haemon's gone, his blood spilled by the very hand—   1295
LEADER: His father's or his own?
MESSENGER: His own . . .
raging mad with his father for the death—
LEADER: Oh great seer,
you saw it all, you brought your word to birth!
MESSENGER: Those are the facts. Deal with them as you will.
    [As he turns to go, EURYDICE enters from the palace.]
LEADER: Look, Eurydice. Poor woman, Creon's wife,   1300
so close at hand. By chance perhaps,
unless she's heard the news about her son.
EURYDICE: My countrymen,
all of you—I caught the sound of your words
as I was leaving to do my part,
to appeal to queen Athena with my prayers.   1305
I was just loosing the bolts, opening the doors,
when a voice filled with sorrow, family sorrow,
struck my ears, and I fell back, terrified,
into the women's arms—everything went black.
Tell me the news, again, whatever it is . . .   1310
sorrow and I are hardly strangers.
I can bear the worst.
MESSENGER: I—dear lady,
I'll speak as an eye-witness. I was there.
And I won't pass over one word of the truth.

Why should I try to soothe you with a story,   1315
only to prove a liar in a moment?
Truth is always best.
                    So,
I escorted your lord, I guided him
to the edge of the plain where the body lay,
Polynices, torn by the dogs and still unmourned.   1320
And saying a prayer to Hecate of the Crossroads,
Pluto[3] too, to hold their anger and be kind,
we washed the dead in a bath of holy water
and plucking some fresh branches, gathering . . .
what was left of him, we burned them all together   1325
and raised a high mound of native earth, and then
we turned and made for that rocky vault of hers,
the hollow, empty bed of the bride of Death.
And far off one of us heard a voice,
a long wail rising, echoing   1330
out of that unhallowed wedding-chamber,
he ran to alert the master and Creon pressed on,
closer—the strange, inscrutable cry came sharper,
throbbing around him now, and he let loose
a cry of his own, enough to wrench the heart,   1335
"Oh god, am I the prophet now? going down
the darkest road I've ever gone? My son—
it's his dear voice, he greets me! Go, men,
closer, quickly! Go through the gap,
the rocks are dragged back—   1340
right to the tomb's very mouth—and look,
see if it's Haemon's voice I think I hear,
or the gods have robbed me of my senses."

The king was shattered. We took his orders,
went and searched, and there in the deepest,   1345
dark recesses of the tomb we found her . . .
hanged by the neck in a fine linen noose,
strangled in her veils—and the boy,
his arms flung around her waist,
clinging to her, wailing for his bride,   1350
dead and down below, for his father's crimes
and the bed of his marriage blighted by misfortune.
When Creon saw him, he gave a deep sob,
he ran in, shouting, crying out to him,
"Oh my child—what have you done? what seized you,   1355
what insanity? what disaster drove you mad?
Come out, my son! I beg you on my knees!"

3. Divinities of the underworld. Pluto is another name of Hades; Hecate is a goddess associated with darkness and burial grounds. Offerings to her were left at crossroads.

But the boy gave him a wild burning glance,
spat in his face, not a word in reply,
he drew his sword—his father rushed out,   1360
running as Haemon lunged and missed!—
and then, doomed, desperate with himself,
suddenly leaning his full weight on the blade,
he buried it in his body, halfway to the hilt.
And still in his senses, pouring his arms around her,   1365
he embraced the girl and breathing hard,
released a quick rush of blood,
bright red on her cheek glistening white.
And there he lies, body enfolding body . . .
he has won his bride a last, poor boy,   1370
not here but in the houses of the dead.

Creon shows the world that of all the ills
afflicting men the worst is lack of judgment.
    [EURYDICE *turns and reenters the palace.*]
LEADER: What do you make of that? The lady's gone,
    without a word, good or bad.
MESSENGER: I'm alarmed too   1375
    but here's my hope—faced with her son's death
    she finds it unbecoming to mourn in public.
    Inside, under her roof, she'll set her women
    to the task and wail the sorrow of the house.
    She's too discreet. She won't do something rash.   1380
LEADER: I'm not so sure. To me, at least,
    a long heavy silence promises danger,
    just as much as a lot of empty outcries.
MESSENGER: We'll see if she's holding something back,
    hiding some passion in her heart.   1385
    I'm going in. You may be right—who knows?
    Even too much silence has its dangers.
    [*Exit to the palace. Enter* CREON *from the side, escorted by attendants
    carrying* HAEMON*'s body on a bier.*]
LEADER: The king himself! Coming toward us,
    look, holding the boy's head in his hands.
    Clear, damning proof, if it's right to say so—   1390
    proof of his own madness, no one else's,
        no, his own blind wrongs.
CREON: Ohhh,
    so senseless, so insane . . . my crimes,
    my stubborn, deadly—
    Look at us, the killer, the killed,   1395
    father and son, the same blood—the misery!
    My plans, my mad fanatic heart,
    my son, cut off so young!

Ai, dead, lost to the world,
not through your stupidity, no, my own.
LEADER: Too late,   1400
too late, you see what justice means.
CREON: Oh I've learned
through blood and tears! Then, it was then,
when the god came down and struck me—a great weight
shattering, driving me down that wild savage path,
ruining, trampling down my joy. Oh the agony,   1405
the heartbreaking agonies of our lives.
[*Enter the* MESSENGER *from the palace.*]
MESSENGER: Master,
what a hoard of grief you have, and you'll have more.
The grief that lies to hand you've brought yourself—
[*Pointing to* HAEMON'*s body.*]
the rest, in the house, you'll see it all too soon.
CREON: What now? What's worse than this?
MESSENGER: The queen is dead.   1410
The mother of this dead boy . . . mother to the end—
poor thing, her wounds are fresh.
CREON: No, no,
harbor of Death, so choked, so hard to cleanse!—
why me? why are you killing me?
Herald of pain, more words, more grief?   1415
I died once, you kill me again and again!
What's the report, boy . . . some news for me?
My wife dead? O dear god!
Slaughter heaped on slaughter?
[*The doors open; the body of* EURYDICE *is brought out on her bier.*]
MESSENGER: See for yourself:
now they bring her body from the palace.
CREON: Oh no,   1420
another, a second loss to break the heart.
What next, what fate still waits for me?
I just held my son in my arms and now,
look, a new corpse rising before my eyes—
wretched, helpless mother—O my son!   1425
MESSENGER: She stabbed herself at the altar,
then her eyes went dark, after she'd raised
a cry for the noble fate of Megareus,[4] the hero
killed in the first assault, then for Haemon,
then with her dying breath she called down   1430
torments on your head—you killed her sons.
CREON: Oh the dread,
I shudder with dread! Why not kill me too?—

---

4. Another son of Creon and Eurydice; he was killed during the siege of the city.

run me through with a good sharp sword?
Oh god, the misery, anguish—
I, I'm churning with it, going under.   1435
MESSENGER: Yes, and the dead, the woman lying there,
piles the guilt of all their deaths on you.
CREON: How did she end her life, what bloody stroke?
MESSENGER: She drove home to the heart with her own hand,
once she learned her son was dead . . . that agony.   1440
CREON: And the guilt is all mine—
can never be fixed on another man,
no escape for me. I killed you,
I, god help me, I admit it all!
  [To his attendants.]
Take me away, quickly, out of sight.   1445
I don't even exist—I'm no one. Nothing.
LEADER: Good advice, if there's any good in suffering.
Quickest is best when troubles block the way.
CREON: [Kneeling in prayer.]
  Come, let it come—that best of fates for me
that brings the final day, best fate of all.   1450
Oh quickly, now—
so I never have to see another sunrise.
LEADER: That will come when it comes;
we must deal with all that lies before us.
The future rests with the ones who tend the future.   1455
CREON: That prayer—I poured my heart into that prayer!
LEADER: No more prayers now. For mortal men
there is no escape from the doom we must endure.
CREON: Take me away, I beg you, out of sight.
A rash, indiscriminate fool!   1460
I murdered you, my son, against my will—
you too, my wife . . .
           Wailing wreck of a man,
whom to look to? where to lean for support?
  [Desperately turning from HAEMON to EURYDICE on their biers.]
Whatever I touch goes wrong—once more
a crushing fate's come down upon my head!   1465
  [The MESSENGER and attendants lead CREON into the palace.]
CHORUS: Wisdom is by far the greatest part of joy,
and reverence toward the gods must be safeguarded.
The mighty words of the proud are paid in full
with mighty blows of fate, and at long last
those blows will teach us wisdom.   1470
  [The old citizens exit to the side.]

EURIPIDES
480–406 B.C.

Euripides' *Medea*, produced in 431 B.C., the year that brought the beginning of the Peloponnesian War, appeared earlier than the *Oedipus the King* of Sophocles, but it has a bitterness that is more in keeping with the spirit of a later age. If the *Oedipus* is, in one sense, a warning to a generation that has embarked on an intellectual revolution, the *Medea* is the ironic expression of the disillusion that comes after the shipwreck. In this play we are conscious for the first time of an attitude characteristic of modern literature, the artist's feeling of separation from his audience, the isolation of the poet. "Often previously," says Medea to the king,

> Through being considered clever I have suffered much. . . . .
> If you put new ideas before the eyes of fools
> They'll think you foolish and worthless into the bargain;
> And if you are thought superior to those who have
> Some reputation for learning, you will become hated.

The common background of audience and poet is disappearing, the old certainties are being undermined, the city divided. Euripides is the first Greek poet to suffer the fate of so many of the great modern writers: rejected by most of his contemporaries (he rarely won first prize and was the favorite target for the scurrilous humor of the comic poets), he was universally admired and revered by the Greeks of the centuries that followed his death.

It is significant that what little biographical information we have for Euripides makes no mention of military service or political office; unlike Aeschylus, who fought in the ranks at Marathon, and Sophocles, who took an active part in public affairs from youth to advanced old age, Euripides seems to have lived a private, an intellectual life. Younger than Sophocles (though they died in the same year), he was more receptive to the critical theories and the rhetorical techniques offered by the Sophist teachers; his plays often subject received ideas to fundamental questioning, expressed in vivid dramatic debate. His *Medea* is typical of his iconoclastic approach; his choice of subject and of central characters is in itself a challenge to established canons. He still dramatizes myth, but the myth he chooses is exotic and disturbing, and the protagonist is not a man but a woman. Medea is both woman and foreigner; that is to say, in terms of the audience's prejudice and practice she is a representative of the two free-born groups in Athenian society that had almost no rights at all (though the male foreign resident had more rights than the native woman). The tragic hero is no longer a king, "one who is highly renowned and prosperous such as Oedipus," but a woman, who, because she finds no redress for her wrongs in society, is driven by her passion to violate that society's most sacred laws in a rebellion against its typical representative, Jason, her husband. She is not just a woman and a foreigner; she is also a person of great intellectual power. Compared to her the credulous king and her complacent husband are children, and once her mind is made up, she moves them like pawns to their proper places in her barbaric game. The myth is used for new purposes, to shock the members of the audience, attack their deepest prejudices, and shake them out of their complacent pride in the superiority of Greek masculinity.

But the play is more compelling than that. Before it is over, our sympathies have come full circle; the contempt with which we regard the Jason of the opening scenes turns to pity as we feel the measure of his loss and the ferocity of Medea's revenge. Medea's passion has carried her too far; the death of Creon and his daughter we might have accepted, but the murder of the children is too much. It was, of course, meant to be. Euripides' theme, like Homer's, is violence, but this is the unspeakable violence of the oppressed, which is greater than the violence of the oppressor and which, because it has been long pent up, cannot be controlled.

In this, as in the other plays, the gods have their place. In the *Oresteia* the will of Zeus is manifested in every action and implied in every word; in *Oedipus the King* the gods bide their time and watch Oedipus fulfill the truth of their prophecy, but in *Medea*, the divine will, which is revealed at the end, is enigmatic and, far from bringing harmony, concludes the play with a terrifying discord. All through *Medea* the human beings involved call on the gods; two especially are singled out for attention, Earth and Sun. It is by these two gods that Medea makes Aegeus swear to give her refuge in Athens, the chorus invokes them to prevent Medea's violence against her sons, and Jason wonders how Medea can look upon earth and sun after she has killed her own children. These emphatic appeals clearly raise the question of the attitude of the gods, and the answer to the question is a shock. We are not told what Earth does, but Sun sends the magic chariot on which Medea makes her escape. His reason, too, is stated; it is not any concern for justice, but the fact that Medea is his granddaughter. Euripides is here using the letter of the myth for his own purposes. This jarring detail emphasizes the significance of the whole. The play creates a world in which there is no relation whatsoever between the powers that rule the universe and the fundamental laws of human morality. It dramatizes disorder, not just the disorder of the family of Jason and Medea, but the disorder of the universe as a whole. It is the nightmare in which the dream of the fifth century was to end, the senseless fury and degradation of permanent violence. "Flow backward to your sources, sacred rivers," the chorus sings, "And let the world's great order be reversed."

For a short, general survey of Euripidean drama, see B. M. W. Knox in *The Cambridge History of Classical Literature*, vol. 1 (1985), pp. 316–39. Perceptive analyses of *Medea* can be found in Emily A. McDermott, *Euripides' Medea: The Incarnation of Disorder* (1989) and *Euripides, A Collection of Critical Essays*, edited by E. Segal (1968). B. M. W. Knox, "The *Medea* of Euripides," and P. E. Easterling, "The Infanticide in Euripides' *Medea*," both in *Yale Classical Studies* 24 (1977), will also be helpful to students.

Medea[1]

Characters

MEDEA, *princess of Colchis and wife of Jason*
JASON, *son of Aeson, king of Iolcos*
Two CHILDREN *of Medea and Jason*
KREON, *king of Corinth*
AIGEUS, *king of Athens*
NURSE *to Medea*
TUTOR *to Medea's children*
MESSENGER
CHORUS OF CORINTHIAN WOMEN

[SCENE—*In front of Medea's house in Corinth. Enter from the house Medea's* NURSE.]

1. Translated by Rex Warner.

NURSE: How I wish the Argo[2] never had reached the land
Of Colchis, skimming through the blue Symplegades,[3]
Nor ever had fallen in the glades of Pelion[4]
The smitten fir-tree to furnish oars for the hands
Of heroes who in Pelias' name attempted   5
The Golden Fleece![5] For then my mistress Medea
Would not have sailed for the towers of the land of Iolcos,
Her heart on fire with passionate love for Jason;
Nor would she have persuaded the daughters of Pelias
To kill their father,[6] and now be living here   10
In Corinth with her husband and children. She gave
Pleasure to the people of her land of exile,
And she herself helped Jason in every way.
This is indeed the greatest salvation of all,—
For the wife not to stand apart from the husband.   15
But now there's hatred everywhere. Love is diseased.
For, deserting his own children and my mistress,
Jason has taken a royal wife to his bed,
The daughter of the ruler of this land, Kreon.
And poor Medea is slighted, and cries aloud on the   20
Vows they made to each other, the right hands clasped
In eternal promise. She calls upon the gods to witness
What sort of return Jason has made to her love.
She lies without food and gives herself up to suffering,
Wasting away every moment of the day in tears.   25
So it has gone since she knew herself slighted by him.
Not stirring an eye, not moving her face from the ground,
No more than either a rock or surging sea water
She listens when she is given friendly advice.
Except that sometimes she twists back her white neck and   30
Moans to herself, calling out on her father's name,
And her land, and her home betrayed[7] when she came away with
A man who now is determined to dishonor her.
Poor creature, she has discovered by her sufferings
What it means to one not to have lost one's own country.   35
She has turned from the children and does not like to see them.
I am afraid she may think of some dreadful thing,
For her heart is violent. She will never put up with

2. The ship in which Jason and his companions sailed on the quest for the Golden Fleece.   3. Clashing
rocks, which crushed ships endeavoring to pass between them. They were supposed to be located at the
Hellespont, the passage between the Mediterranean and the Black Sea.   4. A mountain in the north of
Greece near Iolcos, the place from which Jason sailed.   5. Pelias seized the kingdom of Iolcos, expelling
Aeson, Jeson's father. When Jason came to claim his rights, Pelias sent him to get the Golden Fleece.
6. After Jason returned to Iolcos with the Fleece and Medea, Pelias's daughters were persuaded by Medea,
who had a reputation as a sorceress, to cut Pelias up and boil the pieces, in order to restore him to youth.
The experiment was, of course, unsuccessful, but the son of Pelias expelled Jason and Medea from the
kingdom, and they took refuge in Corinth on the isthmus between the Peloponnese and Attica. In Euripides's time it was a wealthy trading city, a commercial rival of Athens.   7. Medea, daughter of the king
of Colchis, fell in love with Jason and helped him to take the Golden Fleece away from her own country.

The treatment she is getting. I know and fear her
Lest she may sharpen a sword and thrust to the heart,   40
Stealing into the palace where the bed is made,
Or even kill the king and the new-wedded groom,
And thus bring a greater misfortune on herself.
She's a strange woman. I know it won't be easy
To make an enemy of her and come off best.   45
But here the children come. They have finished playing.
They have no thought at all of their mother's trouble.
Indeed it is not usual for the young to grieve.
   [Enter from the right the slave who is the TUTOR to Medea's two small
   children. The CHILDREN follow him.]
TUTOR: You old retainer of my mistress's household,
   Why are you standing here all alone in front of the   50
   Gates and moaning to yourself over your misfortune?
   Medea could not wish you to leave her alone.
NURSE: Old man, and guardian of the children of Jason,
   If one is a good servant, it's a terrible thing
   When one's master's luck is out; it goes to one's heart.   55
   So I myself have got into such a state of grief
   That a longing stole over me to come outside here
   And tell the earth and air of my mistress's sorrows.
TUTOR: Has the poor lady not yet given up her crying?
NURSE: Given up? She's at the start, not halfway through her tears.   60
TUTOR: Poor fool,—if I may call my mistress such a name,—
   How ignorant she is of trouble more to come.
NURSE: What do you mean, old man? You needn't fear to speak.
TUTOR: Nothing. I take back the words which I used just now.
NURSE: Don't, by your beard, hide this from me, your fellow-servant.   65
   If need be, I'll keep quiet about what you tell me.
TUTOR: I heard a person saying, while I myself seemed
   Not to be paying attention, when I was at the place
   Where the old draught-players[8] sit, by the holy fountain,
   That Kreon, ruler of the land, intends to drive   70
   These children and their mother in exile from Corinth.
   But whether what he said is really true or not
   I do not know. I pray that it may not be true.
NURSE: And will Jason put up with it that his children
   Should suffer so, though he's no friend to their mother?   75
TUTOR: Old ties give place to new ones. As for Jason, he
   No longer has a feeling for this house of ours.
NURSE: It's black indeed for us, when we add new to old
   Sorrows before even the present sky has cleared.
TUTOR: But you be silent, and keep all this to yourself.   80
   It is not the right time to tell our mistress of it.

8. Checker players.

NURSE: Do you hear, children, what a father he is to you?
   I wish he were dead,—but no, he is still my master.
   Yet certainly he has proved unkind to his dear ones.
TUTOR: What's strange in that? Have you only just discovered   85
   That everyone loves himself more than his neighbor?
   Some have good reason, others get something out of it.
   So Jason neglects his children for the new bride.
NURSE: Go indoors, children. That will be the best thing.
   And you, keep them to themselves as much as possible.   90
   Don't bring them near their mother in her angry mood.
   For I've seen her already blazing her eyes at them
   As though she meant some mischief and I am sure that
   She'll not stop raging until she has struck at someone.
   May it be an enemy and not a friend she hurts!   95
   [MEDEA *is heard inside the house.*]
MEDEA: Ah, wretch! Ah, lost in my sufferings,
   I wish, I wish I might die.
NURSE: What did I say, dear children? Your mother
   Frets her heart and frets it to anger.
   Run away quickly into the house,   100
   And keep well out of her sight.
   Don't go anywhere near, but be careful
   Of the wildness and bitter nature
   Of that proud mind.
   Go now! Run quickly indoors.   105
   It is clear that she soon will put lightning
   In that cloud of her cries that is rising
   With a passion increasing. Oh, what will she do,
   Proud-hearted and not to be checked on her course,
   A soul bitten into with wrong?   110
   [*The* TUTOR *takes the children into the house.*]
MEDEA: Ah, I have suffered
   What should be wept for bitterly. I hate you,
   Children of a hateful mother. I curse you
   And your father. Let the whole house crash.
NURSE: Ah, I pity you, you poor creature.   115
   How can your children share in their father's
   Wickedness? Why do you hate them? Oh children,
   How much I fear that something may happen!
   Great people's tempers are terrible, always
   Having their own way, seldom checked,   120
   Dangerous they shift from mood to mood.
   How much better to have been accustomed
   To live on equal terms with one's neighbours.
   I would like to be safe and grow old in a
   Humble way. What is moderate sounds best,   125
   Also in practice *is* best for everyone.

Greatness brings no profit to people.
God indeed, when in anger, brings
Greater ruin to great men's houses.

[*Enter, on the right, a* CHORUS OF CORINTHIAN WOMEN. *They have come to inquire about* MEDEA *and to attempt to console her.*]

CHORUS: I heard the voice, I heard the cry   130
Of Colchis' wretched daughter.
Tell me, mother, is she not yet
At rest? Within the double gates
Of the court I heard her cry. I am sorry
For the sorrow of this home. O, say, what has happened?   135
NURSE: There is no home. It's over and done with.
Her husband holds fast to his royal wedding,
While she, my mistress, cries out her eyes
There in her room, and takes no warmth from
Any word of any friend.   140
MEDEA: Oh, I wish
That lightning from heaven would split my head open.
Oh, what use have I now for life?
I would find my release in death
And leave hateful existence behind me.   145
CHORUS: O God and Earth and Heaven!
Did you hear what a cry was that
Which the sad wife sings?
Poor foolish one, why should you long
For that appalling rest?   150
The final end of death comes fast.
No need to pray for that.
Suppose your man gives honor
To another woman's bed.
It often happens. Don't be hurt.   155
God will be your friend in this.
You must not waste away
Grieving too much for him who shared your bed.
MEDEA: Great Themis, lady Artemis,[9] behold
The things I suffer, though I made him promise,   160
My hateful husband. I pray that I may see him,
Him and his bride and all their palace shattered
For the wrong they dare to do me without cause.
Oh, my father! Oh, my country! In what dishonor
I left you, killing my own brother for it.[1]   165
NURSE: Do you hear what she says, and how she cries
On Themis, the goddess of Promises, and on Zeus,
Whom we believe to be the Keeper of Oaths?
Of this I am sure, that no small thing

---

9. The protector of women in pain and distress. *Themis:* justice.   1. Medea killed him to delay the pursuit when she escaped with Jason.

Will appease my mistress's anger.   170
CHORUS: Will she come into our presence?
    Will she listen when we are speaking
    To the words we say?
    I wish she might relax her rage
    And temper of her heart.   175
    My willingness to help will never
    Be wanting to my friends.
    But go inside and bring her
    Out of the house to us,
    And speak kindly to her: hurry,   180
    Before she wrongs her own.
    This passion of hers moves to something great.
NURSE: I will, but I doubt if I'll manage
    To win my mistress over.
    But still I'll attempt it to please you.   185
    Such a look she will flash on her servants
    If any comes near with a message,
    Like a lioness guarding her cubs.
    It is right, I think, to consider
    Both stupid and lacking in foresight   190
    Those poets of old who wrote songs
    For revels and dinners and banquets,
    Pleasant sounds for men living at ease;
    But none of them all has discovered
    How to put an end with their singing   195
    Or musical instruments grief,
    Bitter grief, from which death and disaster
    Cheat the hopes of a house. Yet how good
    If music could cure men of this! But why raise
    To no purpose the voice at a banquet? For *there* is   200
    Already abundance of pleasure for men
    With a joy of its own.
        [*The* NURSE *goes into the house.*]
CHORUS: I heard a shriek that is laden with sorrow.
    Shrilling out her hard grief she cries out
    Upon him who betrayed both her bed and her marriage.   205
    Wronged, she calls on the gods,
    On the justice of Zeus, the oath sworn,
    Which brought her away
    To the opposite shore of the Greeks
    Through the gloomy salt straits to the gateway   210
    Of the salty unlimited sea.
        [MEDEA, *attended by servants, comes out of the house.*]
MEDEA: Women of Corinth, I have come outside to you
    Lest you should be indignant with me; for I know
    That many people are overproud, some when alone,

And others when in company. And those who live 215
Quietly, as I do, get a bad reputation.
For a just judgment is not evident in the eyes
When a man at first sight hates another, before
Learning his character, being in no way injured;
And a foreigner especially must adapt himself.[2] 220
I'd not approve of even a fellow-countryman
Who by pride and want of manners offends his neighbors.
But on me this thing has fallen so unexpectedly,
It has broken my heart. I am finished. I let go
All my life's joy. My friends, I only want to die. 225
It was everything to me to think well of one man,
And he, my own husband, has turned out wholly vile.

Of all things which are living and can form a judgment
We women are the most unfortunate creatures.[3]
Firstly, with an excess of wealth it is required 230
For us to buy a husband and take for our bodies
A master; for not to take one is even worse.
And now the question is serious whether we take
A good or bad one; for there is no easy escape
For a woman, nor can she say no to her marriage. 235
She arrives among new modes of behaviour and manners,
And needs prophetic power, unless she has learnt at home,
How best to manage him who shares the bed with her.
And if we work out all this well and carefully,
And the husband lives with us and lightly bears his yoke, 240
Then life is enviable. If not, I'd rather die.
A man, when he's tired of the company in his home,
Goes out of the house and puts an end to his boredom
And turns to a friend or companion of his own age.
But we are forced to keep our eyes on one alone. 245
What they say of us is that we have a peaceful time
Living at home, while they do the fighting in war.
How wrong they are! I would very much rather stand
Three times in the front of battle than bear one child.
Yet what applies to me does not apply to you. 250
You have a country. Your family home is here.
You enjoy life and the company of your friends.
But I am deserted, a refugee, thought nothing of
By my husband,—something he won in a foreign land.
I have no mother or brother, nor any relation 255
With whom I can take refuge in this sea of woe.
This much then is the service I would beg from you:

---

2. Foreign residents were encouraged to come to Athens, but were rarely admitted to the rights of full citizenship, which was a jealously guarded privilege.   3. Athenian rights and institutions were made for men; the women had few privileges and almost no legal rights. The following two lines refer to the dowry that had to be provided for the bride.

If I can find the means or devise any scheme
To pay my husband back for what he has done to me,—
Him and his father-in-law and the girl who married him,—   260
Just to keep silent. For in other ways a woman
Is full of fear, defenseless, dreads the sight of cold
Steel; but, when once she is wronged in the matter of love,
No other soul can hold so many thoughts of blood.
CHORUS: This I will promise. You are in the right, Medea,   265
In paying your husband back. I am not surprised at you
For being sad. But look! I see our king Kreon
Approaching. He will tell us of some new plan.
[*Enter, from the right,* KREON, *with attendants.*]
KREON: You, with that angry look, so set against your husband,
Medea, I order you to leave my territories   270
An exile, and take along with you your two children,
And not to waste time doing it. It is my decree,
And I will see it done. I will not return home
Until you are cast from the boundaries of my land.
MEDEA: Oh, this is the end for me. I am utterly lost.   275
Now I am in the full force of the storm of hate
And have no harbor from ruin to reach easily.
Yet still, in spite of it all, I'll ask the question:
What is your reason, Kreon, for banishing me?
KREON: I am afraid of you,—why should I dissemble it?—   280
Afraid that you may injure my daughter mortally.
Many things accumulate to support my feeling.
You are a clever woman, versed in evil arts,
And are angry at having lost your husband's love.
I hear that you are threatening, so they tell me,   285
To do something against my daughter and Jason
And me, too. I shall take my precautions first.
I tell you, I prefer to earn your hatred now
Than to be soft-hearted and afterwards regret it.
MEDEA: This is not the first time, Kreon. Often previously   290
Through being considered clever I have suffered much.
A person of sense ought never to have his children
Brought up to be more clever than the average.
For, apart from cleverness bringing them no profit,
It will make them objects of envy and ill-will.   295
If you put new ideas before the eyes of fools
They'll think you foolish and worthless into the bargain;
And if you are thought superior to those who have
Some reputation for learning, you will become hated.
I have some knowledge myself of how this happens;   300
For being clever, I find that some will envy me,
Others object to me. Yet all my cleverness
Is not so much. Well, then, are you frightened, Kreon,

That I should harm you? There is no need. It is not
My way to transgress the authority of a king.   305
How have you injured me? You gave your daughter away
To the man you wanted. O, certainly I hate
My husband, but you, I think, have acted wisely;
Nor do I grudge it you that your affairs go well.
May the marriage be a lucky one! Only let me   310
Live in this land. For even though I have been wronged,
I will not raise my voice, but submit to my betters.
KREON: What you say sounds gentle enough. Still in my heart
I greatly dread that you are plotting some evil,
And therefore I trust you even less than before.   315
A sharp-tempered woman, or for that matter a man,
Is easier to deal with than the clever type
Who holds her tongue. No. You must go. No need for more
Speeches. The thing is fixed. By no manner of means
Shall you, an enemy of mine, stay in my country.   320
MEDEA: I beg you. By your knees, by your new-wedded girl.
KREON: Your words are wasted. You will never persuade me.
MEDEA: Will you drive me out, and give no heed to my prayers?
KREON: I will, for I love my family more than you.
MEDEA: O my country! How bitterly now I remember you!   325
KREON: I love my country too,—next after my children.
MEDEA: O what an evil to men is passionate love!
KREON: That would depend on the luck that goes along with it.
MEDEA: O God, do not forget who is the cause of this!
KREON: Go. It is no use. Spare me the pain of forcing you.   330
MEDEA: I'm spared no pain. I lack no pain to be spared me.
KREON: Then you'll be removed by force by one of my men.
MEDEA: No, Kreon, not that! But do listen, I beg you.
KREON: Woman, you seem to want to create a disturbance.
MEDEA: I *will* go into exile. *This* is not what I beg for.   335
KREON: Why then this violence and clinging to my hand?
MEDEA: Allow me to remain here just for this one day,
    So I may consider where to live in my exile,
    And look for support for my children, since their father
    Chooses to make no kind of provision for them.   340
    Have pity on them! You have children of your own.
    It is natural for you to look kindly on them.
    For myself I do not mind if I go into exile.
    It is the children being in trouble that I mind.
KREON: There is nothing tyrannical about my nature,   345
    And by showing mercy I have often been the loser.
    Even now I know that I am making a mistake.
    All the same you shall have your will. But this I tell you,
    That if the light of heaven tomorrow shall see you,
    You and your children in the confines of my land,   350
    You die. This word I have spoken is firmly fixed.

But now, if you must stay, stay for this day alone.
For in it you can do none of the things I fear.
  [*Exit* KREON *with his attendants.*]
CHORUS: Oh, unfortunate one! Oh, cruel!
Where will you turn? Who will help you?   355
What house or what land to preserve you
From ill can you find?
Medea, a god has thrown suffering
Upon you in waves of despair.
MEDEA: Things have gone badly every way. No doubt of that.   360
But not these things this far, and don't imagine so.
There are still trials to come for the new-wedded pair,
And for their relations pain that will mean something.
Do you think that I would ever have fawned on that man
Unless I had some end to gain or profit in it?   365
I would not even have spoken or touched him with my hands.
But he has got to such a pitch of foolishness
That, though he could have made nothing of all my plans
By exiling me, he has given me this one day
To stay here, and in this I will make dead bodies   370
Of three of my enemies,—father, the girl and my husband.
I have many ways of death which I might suit to them,
And do not know, friends, which one to take in hand;
Whether to set fire underneath their bridal mansion,
Or sharpen a sword and thrust it to the heart,   375
Stealing into the palace where the bed is made.
There is just one obstacle to this. If I am caught
Breaking into the house and scheming against it,
I shall die, and give my enemies cause for laughter.
It is best to go by the straight road, the one in which   380
I am most skilled, and make away with them by poison.
So be it then.
And now suppose them dead. What town will receive me?
What friend will offer me a refuge in his land,
Or the guarantee of his house and save my own life?   385
There is none. So I must wait a little time yet,
And if some sure defense should then appear for me,
In craft and silence I will set about this murder.
But if my fate should drive me on without help,
Even though death is certain, I will take the sword   390
Myself and kill, and steadfastly advance to crime.
It shall not be,—I swear it by her, my mistress,
Whom most I honor and have chosen as partner,
Hecate,[4] who dwells in the recesses of my hearth,—
That any man shall be glad to have injured me.   395

4. The patron of witchcraft, sometimes identified with Artemis. Medea has a statue and shrine of Hecate in the house.

Bitter I will make their marriage for them and mournful,
Bitter the alliance and the driving me out of the land.
Ah, come, Medea, in your plotting and scheming
Leave nothing untried of all those things which you know.
Go forward to the dreadful act. The test has come   400
For resolution. You see how you are treated. Never
Shall you be mocked by Jason's Corinthian wedding,
Whose father was noble, whose grandfather Helios.[5]
You have the skill. What is more, you were born a woman,
And women, though most helpless in doing good deeds,   405
Are of every evil the cleverest of contrivers.
CHORUS: Flow backward to your sources, sacred rivers,
And let the world's great order be reversed.
It is the thoughts of *men* that are deceitful,
Their pledges that are loose.   410
Story shall now turn my condition to a fair one,
Women are paid their due.
No more shall evil-sounding fame be theirs.

Cease now, you muses of the ancient singers,
To tell the tale of my unfaithfulness;   415
For not on us did Phoebus,[6] lord of music,
Bestow the lyre's divine
Power, for otherwise I should have sung an answer
To the other sex. Long time
Has much to tell of us, and much of them.   420

You sailed away from your father's home,
With a heart on fire you passed
The double rocks of the sea.
And now in a foreign country
You have lost your rest in a widowed bed,   425
And are driven forth, a refugee
In dishonor from the land.

Good faith has gone, and no more remains
In great Greece a sense of shame.
It has flown away to the sky.   430
No father's house for a haven
Is at hand for you now, and another queen
Of your bed has dispossessed you and
Is mistress of your home.
   [*Enter* JASON, *with attendants.*]
JASON: This is not the first occasion that I have noticed   435
How hopeless it is to deal with a stubborn temper.
For, with reasonable submission to our ruler's will,
You might have lived in this land and kept your home.

5. The sun, father of Medea's father, Aeëtes.   6. Apollo.

As it is you are going to be exiled for your loose speaking.
Not that I mind myself. You are free to continue   440
Telling everyone that Jason is a worthless man.
But as to your talk about the king, consider
Yourself most lucky that exile is your punishment.
I, for my part, have always tried to calm down
The anger of the king, and wished you to remain.   445
But you will not give up your folly, continually
Speaking ill of him, and so you are going to be banished.
All the same, and in spite of your conduct, I'll not desert
My friends, but have come to make some provision for you,
So that you and the children may not be penniless   450
Or in need of anything in exile. Certainly
Exile brings many troubles with it. And even
If you hate me, I cannot think badly of you.
MEDEA: O coward in every way,—that is what I call you,
With bitterest reproach for your lack of manliness,   455
You have come, you, my worst enemy, have come to me!
It is not an example of over-confidence
Or of boldness thus to look your friends in the face,
Friends you have injured,—no, it is the worst of all
Human diseases, shamelessness. But you did well   460
To come, for I can speak ill of you and lighten
My heart, and you will suffer while you are listening.
And first I will begin from what happened first.
I saved your life, and every Greek knows I saved it
Who was a ship-mate of yours aboard the Argo,   465
When you were sent to control the bulls that breathed fire[7]
And yoke them, and when you would sow that deadly field.
Also that snake, who encircled with his many folds
The Golden Fleece and guarded it and never slept,
I killed, and so gave you the safety of the light.   470
And I myself betrayed my father and my home,
And came with you to Pelias' land of Iolcos.
And then, showing more willingness to help than wisdom,
I killed him, Pelias, with a most dreadful death
At his own daughters' hands, and took away your fear.   475
This is how I behaved to you, you wretched man,
And you forsook me, took another bride to bed
Though you had children; for, if that had not been,
You would have had an excuse for another wedding.
Faith in your word has gone. Indeed I cannot tell   480
Whether you think the gods whose names you swore by then
Have ceased to rule and that new standards are set up,

---

7. This and the following lines refer to ordeals through which Jason had to pass to win the Fleece, and in which Medea helped him. He had to yoke a team of firebreathing bulls, then sow a field which immediately sprouted armed warriors, then deal with the snake that guarded the Fleece.

Since you must know you have broken your word to me.
O my right hand, and the knees which you often clasped
In supplication, how senselessly I am treated   485
By this bad man, and how my hopes have missed their mark!
Come, I will share my thoughts as though you were a friend,—
You! Can I think that you would ever treat me well?
But I will do it, and these questions will make you
Appear the baser. Where am I to go? To my father's?   490
Him I betrayed and his land when I came with you.
To Pelias' wretched daughters? What a fine welcome
They would prepare for me who murdered their father!
For this is my position,—hated by my friends
At home, I have, in kindness to you, made enemies   495
Of others whom there was no need to have injured.
And how happy among Greek women you have made me
On your side for all this! A distinguished husband
I have,—for breaking promises. When in misery
I am cast out of the land and go into exile,   500
Quite without friends and all alone with my children,
That will be a fine shame for the new-wedded groom,
For his children to wander as beggars and she who saved him.
O God, you have given to mortals a sure method
Of telling the gold that is pure from the counterfeit;   505
Why is there no mark engraved upon men's bodies,
By which we could know the true ones from the false ones?
CHORUS: It is a strange form of anger, difficult to cure
When two friends turn upon each other in hatred.
JASON: As for me, it seems I must be no bad speaker.   510
But, like a man who has a good grip of the tiller,
Reef up his sail, and so run away from under
This mouthing tempest, woman, of your bitter tongue.
Since you insist on building up your kindness to me,
My view is that Cypris[8] was alone responsible   515
Of men and gods for the preserving of my life.
You are clever enough,—but really I need not enter
Into the story of how it was love's inescapable
Power that compelled you to keep my person safe.
On this I will not go into too much detail.   520
In so far as you helped me, you did well enough.
But on this question of saving me, I can prove
You have certainly got from me more than you gave.
Firstly, instead of living among barbarians,
You inhabit a Greek land and understand our ways,   525
How to live by law instead of the sweet will of force.
And all the Greeks considered you a clever woman.

8. Aphrodite, goddess of love.

You were honored for it; while, if you were living at
The ends of the earth, nobody would have heard of you.
For my part, rather than stores of gold in my house   530
Or power to sing even sweeter songs than Orpheus,
I'd choose the fate that made me a distinguished man.
There is my reply to your story of my labors.
Remember it was you who started the argument.
Next for your attack on my wedding with the princess: 535
Here I will prove that, first, it was a clever move,
Secondly, a wise one, and, finally, that I made it
In your best interests and the children's. Please keep calm.
When I arrived here from the land of Iolcos,
Involved, as I was, in every kind of difficulty,   540
What luckier chance could I have come across than this,
An exile to marry the daughter of the king?
It was not,—the point that seems to upset you—that I
Grew tired of your bed and felt the need of a new bride;
Nor with any wish to outdo your number of children.   545
We have enough already. I am quite content.
But,—this was the main reason—that we might live well,
And not be short of anything. I know that all
A man's friends leave him stone-cold if he becomes poor.
Also that I might bring my children up worthy   550
Of my position, and, by producing more of them
To be brothers of yours, we would draw the families
Together and all be happy. You need no children.
And it pays me to do good to those I have now
By having others. Do you think this a bad plan?   555
You wouldn't if the love question hadn't upset you.
But you women have got into such a state of mind
That, if your life at night is good, you think you have
Everything; but, if in that quarter things go wrong,
You will consider your best and truest interests   560
Most hateful. It would have been better far for men
To have got their children in some other way, and women
Not to have existed. Then life would have been good.
CHORUS: Jason, though you have made this speech of yours look well,
  Still I think, even though others do not agree,   565
  You have betrayed your wife and are acting badly.
MEDEA: Surely in many ways I hold different views
  From others, for I think that the plausible speaker
  Who is a villain deserves the greatest punishment.
  Confident in his tongue's power to adorn evil,   570
  He stops at nothing. Yet he is not really wise.
  As in your case. There is no need to put on the airs
  Of a clever speaker, for one word will lay you flat.
  If you were not a coward, you would not have married

Behind my back, but discussed it with me first.   575
JASON: And you, no doubt, would have furthered the proposal,
  If I had told you of it, you who even now
  Are incapable of controlling your bitter temper.
MEDEA: It was not that. No, you thought it was not respectable
  As you got on in years to have a foreign wife.   580
JASON: Make sure of this: it was not because of a woman
  I made the royal alliance in which I now live,
  But, as I said before, I wished to preserve you
  And breed a royal progeny to be brothers
  To the children I have now, a sure defense to us.   585
MEDEA: Let me have no happy fortune that brings pain with it,
  Or prosperity which is upsetting to the mind!
JASON: Change your ideas of what you want, and show more sense.
  Do not consider painful what is good for you,
  Nor, when you are lucky, think yourself unfortunate.   590
MEDEA: You can insult me. You have somewhere to turn to.
  But I shall go from this land into exile, friendless.
JASON: It was what you chose yourself. Don't blame others for it.
MEDEA: And how did I choose it? Did I betray my husband?
JASON: You called down wicked curses on the king's family.   595
MEDEA: A curse, that is what I am become to your house too.
JASON: I do not propose to go into all the rest of it;
  But, if you wish for the children or for yourself
  In exile to have some of my money to help you,
  Say so, for I am prepared to give with open hand,   600
  Or to provide you with introductions to my friends
  Who will treat you well. You are a fool if you do not
  Accept this. Cease your anger and you will profit.
MEDEA: I shall never accept the favors of friends of yours,
  Nor take a thing from you, so you need not offer it.   605
  There is no benefit in the gifts of a bad man.
JASON: Then, in any case, I call the gods to witness that
  I wish to help you and the children in every way,
  But you refuse what is good for you. Obstinately
  You push away your friends. You are sure to suffer for it.   610
MEDEA: Go! No doubt you hanker for your virginal bride,
  And are guilty of lingering too long out of her house.
  Enjoy your wedding. But perhaps,—with the help of God—
  You will make the kind of marriage that you will regret.
  [JASON goes out with his attendants.]
CHORUS: When love is in excess   615
  It brings a man no honor
  Nor any worthiness.
  But if in moderation Cypris comes,
  There is no other power at all so gracious.

O goddess, never on me let loose the unerring   620
Shaft of your bow in the poison of desire.

Let my heart be wise.
It is the gods' best gift.
On me let mighty Cypris
Inflict no wordy wars or restless anger   625
To urge my passion to a different love.
But with discernment may she guide women's weddings,
Honoring most what is peaceful in the bed.

O country and home,
Never, never may I be without you,   630
Living the hopeless life,
Hard to pass through and painful,
Most pitiable of all.
Let death first lay me low and death
Free me from this daylight.   635
There is no sorrow above
The loss of a native land.

I have seen it myself,
Do not tell of a secondhand story.
Neither city nor friend   640
Pitied you when you suffered
The worst of sufferings.
O let him die ungraced whose heart
Will not reward his friends,
Who cannot open an honest mind   645
No friend will he be of mine.

[*Enter* AIGEUS, *king of Athens, an old friend of* MEDEA.]

AIGEUS: Medea, greeting! This is the best introduction
    Of which men know for conversation between friends.
MEDEA: Greeting to you too, Aigeus, son of King Pandion,
    Where have you come from to visit this country's soil?   650
AIGEUS: I have just left the ancient oracle of Phoebus.
MEDEA: And why did you go to earth's prophetic center?
AIGEUS: I went to inquire how children might be born to me.
MEDEA: Is it so? Your life still up to this point childless?
AIGEUS: Yes. By the fate of some power we have no children.   655
MEDEA: Have you a wife, or is there none to share your bed?
AIGEUS: There is. Yes, I am joined to my wife in marriage.
MEDEA: And what did Phoebus say to you about children?
AIGEUS: Words too wise for a mere man to guess their meaning.
MEDEA: Is it proper for me to be told the God's reply?   660
AIGEUS: It is. For sure what is needed is cleverness.
MEDEA: Then what was his message? Tell me, if I may hear.

AIGEUS: I am not to loosen the hanging foot of the wine-skin . . .[9]
MEDEA: Until you have done something, or reached some country?
AIGEUS: Until I return again to my hearth and house. 665
MEDEA: And for what purpose have you journeyed to this land?
AIGEUS: There is a man called Pittheus,[1] king of Troezen.
MEDEA: A son of Pelops, they say, a most righteous man.
AIGEUS: With him I wish to discuss the reply of the god.
MEDEA: Yes. He is wise and experienced in such matters. 670
AIGEUS. And to me also the dearest of all my spear-friends.[2]
MEDEA: Well, I hope you have good luck, and achieve your will.
AIGEUS: But why this downcast eye of yours, and this pale cheek?
MEDEA: O Aigeus, my husband has been the worst of all to me.
AIGEUS: What do you mean? Say clearly what has caused this grief. 675
MEDEA: Jason wrongs me, though I have never injured him.
AIGEUS: What has he done? Tell me about it in clearer words.
MEDEA: He has taken a wife to his house, supplanting me.
AIGEUS: Surely he would not dare to do a thing like that.
MEDEA: Be sure he has. Once dear, I now am slighted by him. 680
AIGEUS: Did he fall in love? Or is he tired of your love?
MEDEA: He was greatly in love, this traitor to his friends.
AIGEUS: Then let him go, if, as you say, he is so bad.
MEDEA: A passionate love,—for an alliance with the king.
AIGEUS: And who gave him his wife? Tell me the rest of it. 685
MEDEA: It was Kreon, he who rules this land of Corinth.
AIGEUS: Indeed, Medea, your grief was understandable.
MEDEA: I am ruined. And there is more to come: I am banished.
AIGEUS: Banished? By whom? Here you tell me of a new wrong.
MEDEA: Kreon drives me an exile from the land of Corinth. 690
AIGEUS: Does Jason consent? I cannot approve of this.
MEDEA: He pretends not to, but he will put up with it.
Ah, Aigeus, I beg and beseech you, by your beard
And by your knees I am making myself your suppliant,
Have pity on me, have pity on your poor friend, 695
And do not let me go into exile desolate,
But receive me in your land and at your very hearth.
So may your love, with God's help, lead to the bearing
Of children, and so may you yourself die happy.
You do not know what a chance you have come on here. 700
I will end your childlessness, and I will make you able
To beget children. The drugs I know can do this.
AIGEUS: For many reasons, woman, I am anxious to do
This favor for you. First, for the sake of the gods,
And then for the birth of children which you promise, 705
For in that respect I am entirely at my wits' end.

9. This cryptic phrase probably means "not to have intercourse." 1. Aigeus's father-in-law. *Troezen:* in the Peloponnese. Corinth was on the way from Delphi to Troezen. 2. Allies in war, companions in fighting.

But this is my position: if you reach my land,
I, being in my rights, will try to befriend you.
But this much I must warn you of beforehand:
I shall not agree to take you out of this country;   710
But if you by yourself can reach my house, then you
Shall stay there safely. To none will I give you up.
But from this land you must make your escape yourself,
For I do not wish to incur blame from my friends.
MEDEA: It shall be so. But, if I might have a pledge from you   715
For this, then I would have from you all I desire.
AIGEUS: Do you not trust me? What is it rankles with you?
MEDEA: I trust you, yes. But the house of Pelias hates me,
And so does Kreon. If you are bound by this oath,
When they try to drag me from your land, you will not   720
Abandon me; but if our pact is only words,
With no oath to the gods, you will be lightly armed,
Unable to resist their summons. I am weak,
While they have wealth to help them and a royal house.
AIGEUS: You show much foresight for such negotiations.   725
Well, if you will have it so, I will not refuse.
For, both on my side this will be the safest way
To have some excuse to put forward to your enemies,
And for you it is more certain. You may name the gods.
MEDEA: Swear by the plain of Earth, and Helios, father   730
Of my father, and name together all the gods. . . .
AIGEUS: That I will act or not act in what way? Speak.
MEDEA: That you yourself will never cast me from your land,
Nor, if any of my enemies should demand me,
Will you, in your life, willingly hand me over.   735
AIGEUS: I swear by the Earth, by the holy light of Helios,
By all the gods, I will abide by this you say.
MEDEA: Enough. And, if you fail, what shall happen to you?
AIGEUS: What comes to those who have no regard for heaven.
MEDEA: Go on your way. Farewell. For I am satisfied,   740
And I will reach your city as soon as I can,
Having done the deed I have to do and gained my end.
     [AIGEUS goes out.]
CHORUS: May Hermes, god of travellers,
Escort you, Aigeus, to your home!
And may you have the things you wish   745
So eagerly; for you
Appear to me to be a generous man.
MEDEA: God, and God's daughter, justice, and light of Helios!
Now, friends, has come the time of my triumph over
My enemies, and now my foot is on the road.   750
Now I am confident they will pay the penalty.
For this man, Aigeus, has been like a harbor to me

In all my plans just where I was most distressed.
To him I can fasten the cable of my safety
When I have reached the town and fortress of Pallas.[3]   755
And now I shall tell to you the whole of my plan.
Listen to these words that are not spoken idly.
I shall send one of my servants to find Jason
And request him to come once more into my sight.
And when he comes, the words I'll say will be soft ones.   760
I'll say that I agree with him, that I approve
The royal wedding he has made, betraying me.
I'll say it was profitable, an excellent idea.
But I shall beg that my children may remain here:
Not that I would leave in a country that hates me   765
Children of mine to feel their enemies' insults,
But that by a trick I may kill the king's daughter.
For I will send the children with gifts in their hands
To carry to the bride, so as not to be banished,—
A finely woven dress and a golden diadem.   770
And if she takes them and wears them upon her skin
She and all who touch the girl will die in agony;
Such poison will I lay upon the gifts I send.
But there, however, I must leave that account paid.
I weep to think of what a deed I have to do   775
Next after that; for I shall kill my own children.
My children, there is none who can give them safety.
And when I have ruined the whole of Jason's house,
I shall leave the land and flee from the murder of my
Dear children, and I shall have done a dreadful deed.   780
For it is not bearable to be mocked by enemies.
So it must happen. What profit have I in life?
I have no land, no home, no refuge from my pain.
My mistake was made the time I left behind me
My father's house, and trusted the words of a Greek,   785
Who, with heaven's help, will pay me the price for that.
For those children he had from me he will never
See alive again, nor will he on his new bride
Beget another child, for she is to be forced
To die a most terrible death by these my poisons.   790
Let no one think me a weak one, feeble-spirited,
A stay-at-home, but rather just the opposite,
One who can hurt my enemies and help my friends;
For the lives of such persons are most remembered.
CHORUS: Since you have shared the knowledge of your plan with us,   795
    I both wish to help you and support the normal
    Ways of mankind, and tell you not to do this thing.

3. Athens, city of Pallas Athene.

MEDEA: I can do no other thing. It is understandable
For you to speak thus. You have not suffered as I have.
CHORUS: But can you have the heart to kill your flesh and blood?   800
MEDEA: Yes, for this is the best way to wound my husband.
CHORUS: And you too. Of women you will be most unhappy.
MEDEA: So it must be. No compromise is possible.
[*She turns to the* NURSE.]
Go, you, at once, and tell Jason to come to me.
You I employ on all affairs of greatest trust.   805
Say nothing of these decisions which I have made,
If you love your mistress, if you were born a woman.
CHORUS: From of old the children of Erechtheus[4] are
Splendid, the sons of blessed gods. They dwell
In Athens' holy and unconquered land,[5]   810
Where famous Wisdom feeds them and they pass gaily
Always through that most brilliant air where once, they say,
That golden Harmony gave birth to the nine
Pure Muses of Pieria.[6]

And beside the sweet flow of Cephisos' stream,[7]   815
Where Cypris sailed, they say, to draw the water,
And mild soft breezes breathed along her path,
And on her hair were flung the sweet-smelling garlands
Of flowers of roses by the Lovers, the companions
Of Wisdom, her escort, the helpers of men   820
In every kind of excellence.

How then can these holy rivers
Or this holy land love you,
Or the city find you a home,
You, who will kill your children,   825
You, not pure with the rest?
O think of the blow at your children
And think of the blood that you shed.
O, over and over I beg you,
By your knees I beg you do not   830
Be the murderess of your babes!

O where will you find the courage
Or the skill of hand and heart,
When you set yourself to attempt
A deed so dreadful to do?   835
How, when you look upon them,

---

4. An early king of Athens, a son of Hephaestus.   5. It was the Athenians' boast that their descent from the original settlers was uninterrupted by an invasion. There is a topical reference here, for the play was produced in 431 B.C., in a time of imminent war.   6. A fountain in Boeotia where the Muses were supposed to live. The sentence means that the fortunate balance ("Harmony") of the elements and the genius of the people produced the cultivation of the arts ("the nine pure Muses").   7. Athenian river. Cypris, mentioned in the next line, is the goddess of love and therefore of the principle of fertility.

Can you tearlessly hold the decision
For murder? You will not be able,
When your children fall down and implore you,
You will not be able to dip   840
Steadfast your hand in their blood.
    [*Enter* JASON *with attendants.*]
JASON: I have come at your request. Indeed, although you are
Bitter against me, this you shall have: I will listen
To what new thing you want, woman, to get from me.
MEDEA: Jason, I beg you to be forgiving towards me   845
For what I said. It is natural for you to bear with
My temper, since we have had much love together.
I have talked with myself about this and I have
Reproached myself. "Fool" I said, "why am I so mad?
Why am I set against those who have planned wisely?   850
Why make myself an enemy of the authorities
And of my husband, who does the best thing for me
By marrying royalty and having children who
Will be as brothers to my own? What is wrong with me?
Let me give up anger, for the gods are kind to me.   855
Have I not children, and do I not know that we
In exile from our country must be short of friends?"
When I considered this I saw that I had shown
Great lack of sense, and that my anger was foolish.
Now I agree with you. I think that you are wise   860
In having this other wife as well as me, and I
Was mad. I should have helped you in these plans of yours,
Have joined in the wedding, stood by the marriage bed,
Have taken pleasure in attendance on your bride.
But we women are what we are,—perhaps a little   865
Worthless; and you men must not be like us in this,
Nor be foolish in return when we are foolish.
Now I give in, and admit that then I was wrong.
I have come to a better understanding now.
    [*She turns towards the house.*]
Children, come here, my children, come outdoors to us!   870
Welcome your father with me, and say goodbye to him,
And with your mother, who just now was his enemy,
Join again in making friends with him who loves us.
    [*Enter the* CHILDREN, *attended by the* TUTOR.]
We have made peace, and all our anger is over.
Take hold of his right hand,—O God, I am thinking   875
Of something which may happen in the secret future.
O children, will you just so, after a long life,
Hold out your loving arms at the grave? O children,
How ready to cry I am, how full of foreboding!
I am ending at last this quarrel with your father,   880

And, look, my soft eyes have suddenly filled with tears.
CHORUS: And the pale tears have started also in my eyes.
O may the trouble not grow worse than now it is!
JASON: I approve of what you say. And I cannot blame you
Even for what you said before. It is natural   885
For a woman to be wild with her husband when he
Goes in for secret love. But now your mind has turned
To better reasoning. In the end you have come to
The right decision, like the clever woman you are.
And of you, children, your father is taking care.   890
He has made, with God's help, ample provision for you.
For I think that a time will come when you will be
The leading people in Corinth with your brothers.
You must grow up. As to the future, your father
And those of the gods who love him will deal with that.   895
I want to see you, when you have become young men,
Healthy and strong, better men than my enemies.
Medea, why are your eyes all wet with pale tears?
Why is your cheek so white and turned away from me?
Are not these words of mine pleasing for you to hear?   900
MEDEA: It is nothing. I was thinking about these children.
JASON: You must be cheerful. I shall look after them well.
MEDEA: I will be. It is not that I distrust your words,
But a woman is a frail thing, prone to crying.
JASON: But why then should you grieve so much for these children?   905
MEDEA: I am their mother. When you prayed that they might live
I felt unhappy to think that these things will be.
But come, I have said something of the things I meant
To say to you, and now I will tell you the rest.
Since it is the king's will to banish me from here,—   910
And for me too I know that this is the best thing,
Not to be in your way by living here or in
The king's way, since they think me ill-disposed to them,—
I then am going into exile from this land;
But do you, so that you may have the care of them,   915
Beg Kreon that the children may not be banished.
JASON: I doubt if I'll succeed, but still I'll attempt it.
MEDEA: Then you must tell your wife to beg from her father
That the children may be reprieved from banishment.
JASON: I will, and with her I shall certainly succeed.   920
MEDEA: If she is like the rest of us women, you will.
And I too will take a hand with you in this business,
For I will send her some gifts which are far fairer,
I am sure of it, than those which now are in fashion,
A finely-woven dress and a golden diadem,   925
And the children shall present them. Quick, let one of you
Servants bring here to me that beautiful dress.

[*One of her attendants goes into the house.*]
She will be happy not in one way, but in a hundred,
Having so fine a man as you to share her bed,
And with this beautiful dress which Helios of old,   930
My father's father, bestowed on his descendants.
[*Enter attendant carrying the poisoned dress and diadem.*]
There, children, take these wedding presents in your hands.
Take them to the royal princess, the happy bride,
And give them to her. She will not think little of them.
JASON: No, don't be foolish, and empty your hands of these.   935
Do you think the palace is short of dresses to wear?
Do you think there is no gold there? Keep them, don't give them
Away. If my wife considers me of any value,
She will think more of me than money, I am sure of it.
MEDEA: No, let me have my way. They say the gods themselves   940
Are moved by gifts, and gold does more with men than words.
Hers is the luck, her fortune that which god blesses;
She is young and a princess; but for my children's reprieve
I would give my very life, and not gold only.
Go children, go together to that rich palace,   945
Be suppliants to the new wife of your father,
My lady, beg her not to let you be banished.
And give her the dress,—for this is of great importance,
That she should take the gift into her hand from yours.
Go, quick as you can. And bring your mother good news   950
By your success of those things which she longs to gain.
[JASON *goes out with his attendants, followed by the* TUTOR *and the*
CHILDREN *carrying the poisoned gifts.*]
CHORUS: Now there is no hope left for the children's lives.
Now there is none. They are walking already to murder.
The bride, poor bride, will accept the curse of the gold,
Will accept the bright diadem.   955
Around her yellow hair she will set that dress
Of death with her own hands.
The grace and the perfume and glow of the golden robe
Will charm her to put them upon her and wear the wreath,
And now her wedding will be with the dead below,   960
Into such a trap she will fall,
Poor thing, into such a fate of death and never
Escape from under that curse.
You too, O wretched bridegroom, making your match with kings,
You do not see that you bring   965
Destruction on your children and on her,
Your wife, a fearful death.
Poor soul, what a fall is yours!

In your grief too I weep, mother of little children,
You who will murder your own,   970

In vengeance for the loss of married love
Which Jason has betrayed
As he lives with another wife.
[*Enter the* TUTOR *with the* CHILDREN.]
TUTOR: Mistress, I tell you that these children are reprieved,
And the royal bride has been pleased to take in her hands 975
Your gifts. In that quarter the children are secure.
But come,
Why do you stand confused when you are fortunate?
Why have you turned round with your cheek away from me?
Are not these words of mine pleasing for you to hear? 980
MEDEA: Oh! I am lost!
TUTOR: That word is not in harmony with my tidings.
MEDEA: I am lost, I am lost!
TUTOR: Am I in ignorance telling you
Of some disaster, and not the good news I thought?
MEDEA: You have told what you have told. I do not blame you. 985
TUTOR: Why then this downcast eye, and this weeping of tears?
MEDEA: Oh, I am forced to weep, old man. The gods and I,
    I in a kind of madness have contrived all this.
TUTOR: Courage! You too will be brought home by your children.
MEDEA: Ah, before that happens I shall bring others home. 990
TUTOR: Others before you have been parted from their children.
    Mortals must bear in resignation their ill luck.
MEDEA: That is what I shall do. But go inside the house,
    And do for the children your usual daily work.
    [*The* TUTOR *goes into the house.* MEDEA *turns to her* CHILDREN.]
    O children, O my children, you have a city, 995
    You have a home, and you can leave me behind you,
    And without your mother you may live there for ever.
    But I am going in exile to another land
    Before I have seen you happy and taken pleasure in you,
    Before I have dressed your brides and made your marriage beds 1000
    And held up the torch at the ceremony of wedding.
    Oh, what a wretch I am in this my self-willed thought!
    What was the purpose, children, for which I reared you?
    For all my travail and wearing myself away?
    They were sterile, those pains I had in the bearing of you. 1005
    O surely once the hopes in you I had, poor me,
    Were high ones: you would look after me in old age,
    And when I died would deck me well with your own hands;
    A thing which all would have done. O but now it is gone,
    That lovely thought. For, once I am left without you, 1010
    Sad will be the life I'll lead and sorrowful for me.
    And you will never see your mother again with
    Your dear eyes, gone to another mode of living.
    Why, children, do you look upon me with your eyes?
    Why do you smile so sweetly that last smile of all? 1015

Oh, Oh, what can I do? My spirit has gone from me,
Friends, when I saw that bright look in the children's eyes.
I cannot bear to do it. I renounce my plans
I had before. I'll take my children away from
This land. Why should I hurt their father with the pain   1020
They feel, and suffer twice as much of pain myself?
No, no, I will not do it. I renounce my plans.
Ah, what is wrong with me? Do I want to let go
My enemies unhurt and be laughed at for it?
I must face this thing. Oh, but what a weak woman   1025
Even to admit to my mind these soft arguments.
Children, go into the house. And he whom law forbids
To stand in attendance at my sacrifices,
Let him see to it. I shall not mar my handiwork.
Oh! Oh!   1030
Do not, O my heart, you must not do these things!
Poor heart, let them go, have pity upon the children.
If they live with you in Athens they will cheer you.
No! By Hell's avenging furies it shall not be,—
This shall never be, that I should suffer my children   1035
To be the prey of my enemies' insolence.
Every way is it fixed. The bride will not escape.
No, the diadem is now upon her head, and she,
The royal princess, is dying in the dress, I know it.
But,—for it is the most dreadful of roads for me   1040
To tread, and them I shall send on a more dreadful still—
I wish to speak to the children.
      [She calls the CHILDREN to her.]
                              Come, children, give
Me your hands, give your mother your hands to kiss them.
O the dear hands, and O how dear are these lips to me,   1045
And the generous eyes and the bearing of my children!
I wish you happiness, but not here in this world.
What is here your father took. O how good to hold you!
How delicate the skin, how sweet the breath of children!
Go, go! I am no longer able, no longer   1050
To look upon you. I am overcome by sorrow.
      [The CHILDREN go into the house.]
I know indeed what evil I intend to do,
But stronger than all my afterthoughts is my fury,
Fury that brings upon mortals the greatest evils.
      [She goes out to the right, towards the royal palace.]
CHORUS: Often before   1055
I have gone through more subtle reasons,
And have come upon questionings greater
Than a woman should strive to search out.
But we too have a goddess to help us

And accompany us into wisdom.   1060
Not all of us. Still you will find
Among many women a few,
And our sex is not without learning.
This I say, that those who have never
Had children, who know nothing of it,   1065
In happiness have the advantage
Over those who are parents.
The childless, who never discover
Whether children turn out as a good thing
Or as something to cause pain, are spared   1070
Many troubles in lacking this knowledge.
And those who have in their homes
The sweet presence of children, I see that their lives
Are all wasted away by their worries.
First they must think how to bring them up well and   1075
How to leave them something to live on.
And then after this whether all their toil
Is for those who will turn out good or bad,
Is still an unanswered question.
And of one more trouble, the last of all,   1080
That is common to mortals I tell.
For suppose you have found them enough for their living,
Suppose that the children have grown into youth
And have turned out good, still, if God so wills it,
Death will away with your children's bodies,   1085
And carry them off into Hades.
What is our profit, then, that for the sake of
Children the gods should pile upon mortals
After all else
This most terrible grief of all?   1090
    [*Enter* MEDEA, *from the spectators' right.*]
MEDEA: Friends, I can tell you that for long I have waited
  For the event. I stare towards the place from where
  The news will come. And now, see one of Jason's servants
  Is on his way here, and that labored breath of his
  Shows he has tidings for us, and evil tidings.   1095
    [*Enter, also from the right, the* MESSENGER.]
MESSENGER: Medea, you who have done such a dreadful thing,
  So outrageous, run for your life, take what you can,
  A ship to bear you hence or chariot on land.
MEDEA: And what is the reason deserves such flight as this?
MESSENGER: She is dead, only just now, the royal princess,   1100
  And Kreon dead too, her father, by your poisons.
MEDEA: The finest words you have spoken. Now and hereafter
  I shall count you among my benefactors and friends.
MESSENGER: What! Are you right in the mind? Are you not mad,

Woman? The house of the king is outraged by you. 1105
Do you enjoy it? Not afraid of such doings?
MEDEA: To what you say I on my side have something too
To say in answer. Do not be in a hurry, friend,
But speak. How did they die? You will delight me twice
As much again if you say they died in agony. 1110
MESSENGER: When those two children, born of you, had entered in,
Their father with them, and passed into the bride's house,
We were pleased, we slaves who were distressed by your wrongs.
All through the house we were talking of but one thing,
How you and your husband had made up your quarrel. 1115
Some kissed the children's hands and some their yellow hair,
And I myself was so full of my joy that I
Followed the children into the women's quarters.
Our mistress, whom we honor now instead of you,
Before she noticed that your two children were there, 1120
Was keeping her eye fixed eagerly on Jason.
Afterwards however she covered up her eyes,
Her cheek paled and she turned herself away from him,
So disgusted was she at the children's coming there.
But your husband tried to end the girl's bad temper, 1125
And said "You must not look unkindly on your friends.
Cease to be angry. Turn your head to me again.
Have as your friends the same ones as your husband has.
And take these gifts, and beg your father to reprieve
These children from their exile. Do it for my sake." 1130
She, when she saw the dress, could not restrain herself.
She agreed with all her husband said, and before
He and the children had gone far from the palace,
She took the gorgeous robe and dressed herself in it,
And put the golden crown around her curly locks, 1135
And arranged the set of the hair in a shining mirror,
And smiled at the lifeless image of herself in it.
Then she rose from her chair and walked about the room,
With her gleaming feet stepping most soft and delicate,
All overjoyed with the present. Often and often 1140
She would stretch her foot out straight and look along it.
But after that it was a fearful thing to see.
The color of her face changed, and she staggered back,
She ran, and her legs trembled, and she only just
Managed to reach a chair without falling flat down. 1145
An aged woman servant who, I take it, thought
This was some seizure of Pan[8] or another god,
Cried out "God bless us," but that was before she saw

8. As the god of wild nature he was supposed to be the source of the sudden, apparently causeless terror which solitude in wild surroundings may produce, and thence of all kinds of sudden madness. (Compare our word "panic.")

The white foam breaking through her lips and her rolling
The pupils of her eyes and her face all bloodless. 1150
Then she raised a different cry from that "God bless us,"
A huge shriek, and the women ran, one to the king,
One to the newly wedded husband to tell him
What had happened to his bride; and with frequent sound
The whole of the palace rang as they went running. 1155
One walking quickly round the course of a race-track
Would now have turned the bend and be close to the goal,
When she, poor girl, opened her shut and speechless eye,
And with a terrible groan she came to herself.
For a two-fold pain was moving up against her. 1160
The wreath of gold that was resting around her head
Let forth a fearful stream of all-devouring fire,
And the finely-woven dress your children gave to her,
Was fastening on the unhappy girl's fine flesh.
She leapt up from the chair, and all on fire she ran, 1165
Shaking her hair now this way and now that, trying
To hurl the diadem away; but fixedly
The gold preserved its grip, and, when she shook her hair,
Then more and twice as fiercely the fire blazed out.
Till, beaten by her fate, she fell down to the ground, 1170
Hard to be recognised except by a parent.
Neither the setting of her eyes was plain to see,
Nor the shapeliness of her face. From the top of
Her head there oozed out blood and fire mixed together.
Like the drops on pine-bark, so the flesh from her bones 1175
Dropped away, torn by the hidden fang of the poison.
It was a fearful sight; and terror held us all
From touching the corpse. We had learned from what had happened.
But her wretched father, knowing nothing of the event,
Came suddenly to the house, and fell upon the corpse, 1180
And at once cried out and folded his arms about her,
And kissed her and spoke to her, saying, "O my poor child,
What heavenly power has so shamefully destroyed you?
And who has set me here like an ancient sepulchre,
Deprived of you? O let me die with you, my child!" 1185
And when he had made an end of his wailing and crying,
Then the old man wished to raise himself to his feet;
But, as the ivy clings to the twigs of the laurel,
So he stuck to the fine dress, and he struggled fearfully.
For he was trying to lift himself to his knee, 1190
And she was pulling him down, and when he tugged hard
He would be ripping his aged flesh from his bones.
At last his life was quenched and the unhappy man
Gave up the ghost, no longer could hold up his head.
There they lie close, the daughter and the old father, 1195

Dead bodies, an event he prayed for in his tears.
As for your interests, I will say nothing of them,
For you will find your own escape from punishment.
Our human life I think and have thought a shadow,
And I do not fear to say that those who are held   1200
Wise amongst men and who search the reasons of things
Are those who bring the most sorrow on themselves.
For of mortals there is no one who is happy.
If wealth flows in upon one, one may be perhaps
Luckier than one's neighbor, but still not happy.   1205
      [*Exit.*]
CHORUS: Heaven, it seems, on this day has fastened many
Evils on Jason, and Jason has deserved them.
Poor girl, the daughter of Kreon, how I pity you
And your misfortunes, you who have gone quite away
To the house of Hades because of marrying Jason.   1210
MEDEA: Women, my task is fixed: as quickly as I may
To kill my children, and start away from this land,
And not, by wasting time, to suffer my children
To be slain by another hand less kindly to them.
Force every way will have it they must die, and since   1215
This must be so, then I, their mother, shall kill them.
O arm yourself in steel, my heart! Do not hang back
From doing this fearful and necessary wrong.
O come, my hand, poor wretched hand, and take the sword,
Take it, step forward to this bitter starting point,   1220
And do not be a coward, do not think of them,
How sweet they are, and how you are their mother. Just for
This one short day be forgetful of your children,
Afterwards weep; for even though you will kill them,
They were very dear,— O, I am an unhappy woman!   1225
      [*With a cry she rushes into the house.*]
CHORUS: O Earth, and the far shining
Ray of the sun, look down, look down upon
This poor lost woman, look, before she raises
The hand of murder against her flesh and blood.
Yours was the golden birth from which   1230
She sprang, and now I fear divine
Blood may be shed by men.
O heavenly light, hold back her hand,
Check her, and drive from out the house
The bloody Fury raised by fiends of Hell.   1235

Vain waste, your care of children;
Was it in vain you bore the babes you loved,
After you passed the inhospitable strait
Between the dark blue rocks, Symplegades?

O wretched one, how has it come,   1240
This heavy anger on your heart,
This cruel bloody mind?
For God from mortals asks a stern
Price for the stain of kindred blood
In like disaster falling on their homes.   1245
    [*A cry from one of the* CHILDREN *is heard.*]
CHORUS: Do you hear the cry, do you hear the children's cry?
    O you hard heart, O woman fated for evil!
ONE OF THE CHILDREN: [*From within.*]
    What can I do and how escape my mother's hands?
ONE OF THE CHILDREN: [*From within.*]
    O my dear brother, I cannot tell.
    We are lost.
CHORUS: Shall I enter the house? O surely I should   1250
    Defend the children from murder.
A CHILD: [*From within.*]
    O help us, in God's name, for now we need your help.
    Now, now we are close to it. We are trapped by the sword.
CHORUS: O your heart must have been made of rock or steel,
    You who can kill   1255
    With your own hand the fruit of your own womb.
    Of one alone I have heard, one woman alone
    Of those of old who laid her hands on her children,
    Ino, sent mad by heaven when the wife of Zeus
    Drove her out from her home and made her wander;   1260
    And because of the wicked shedding of blood
    Of her own children she threw
    Herself, poor wretch, into the sea and stepped away
    Over the sea-cliff to die with her two children.
    What horror more can be? O women's love,   1265
    So full of trouble,
    How many evils have you caused already!
    [*Enter* JASON, *with attendants.*]
JASON: You women, standing close in front of this dwelling,
    Is she, Medea, she who did this dreadful deed,
    Still in the house, or has she run away in flight?   1270
    For she will have to hide herself beneath the earth,
    Or raise herself on wings into the height of air,
    If she wishes to escape the royal vengeance.
    Does she imagine that, having killed our rulers,
    She will herself escape uninjured from this house?   1275
    But I am thinking not so much of her as for
    The children,—her the king's friends will make to suffer
    For what she did. So I have come to save the lives
    Of my boys, in case the royal house should harm them
    While taking vengeance for their mother's wicked deed.   1280

CHORUS: O Jason, if you but knew how deeply you are
  Involved in sorrow, you would not have spoken so.
JASON: What is it? That she is planning to kill me also?
CHORUS: Your children are dead, and by their own mother's hand.
JASON: What! This is it? O woman, you have destroyed me.   1285
CHORUS: You must make up your mind your children are no more.
JASON: Where did she kill them? Was it here or in the house?
CHORUS: Open the gates and there you will see them murdered.
JASON: Quick as you can unlock the doors, men, and undo
  The fastenings and let me see this double evil,   1290
  My children dead and her,—O her I will repay.
    [His attendants rush to the door. MEDEA appears above the house in a
    chariot drawn by dragons. She has the dead bodies of the children
    with her.]
MEDEA: Why do you batter these gates and try to unbar them,
  Seeking the corpses and for me who did the deed?
  You may cease your trouble, and, if you have need of me,
  Speak, if you wish. You will never touch me with your hand,   1295
  Such a chariot has Helios, my father's father,
  Given me to defend me from my enemies.
JASON: You hateful thing, you woman most utterly loathed
  By the gods and me and by all the race of mankind,
  You who have had the heart to raise a sword against   1300
  Your children, you, their mother, and left me childless,—
  You have done this, and do you still look at the sun
  And at the earth, after these most fearful doings?
  I wish you dead. Now I see it plain, though at that time
  I did not, when I took you from your foreign home   1305
  And brought you to a Greek house, you, an evil thing,
  A traitress to your father and your native land.
  The gods hurled the avenging curse of yours on me.
  For your own brother you slew at your own hearthside,
  And then came aboard that beautiful ship, the Argo.   1310
  And that was your beginning. When you were married
  To me, your husband, and had borne children to me,
  For the sake of pleasure in the bed you killed them.
  There is no Greek woman who would have dared such deeds,
  Out of all those whom I passed over and chose you   1315
  To marry instead, a bitter destructive match,
  A monster not a woman, having a nature
  Wilder than that of Scylla⁹ in the Tuscan sea.
  Ah! no, not if I had ten thousand words of shame
  Could I sting you. You are naturally so brazen.   1320
  Go, worker in evil, stained with your children's blood.
  For me remains to cry aloud upon my fate,

9. A monster located in the straits between Italy and Sicily, who snatched sailors off passing ships and
devoured them.

Who will get no pleasure from my newly-wedded love,
And the boys whom I begot and brought up, never
Shall I speak to them alive. Oh, my life is over!   1325
MEDEA: Long would be the answer which I might have made to
These words of yours, if Zeus the father did not know
How I have treated you and what you did to me.
No, it was not to be that you should scorn my love,
And pleasantly live your life through, laughing at me;   1330
Nor would the princess, nor he who offered the match,
Kreon, drive me away without paying for it.
So now you may call me a monster, if you wish,
Or Scylla housed in the caves of the Tuscan sea
I too, as I had to, have taken hold of your heart.   1335
JASON: You feel the pain yourself. You share in my sorrow.
MEDEA: Yes, and my grief is gain when you cannot mock it.
JASON: O children, what a wicked mother she was to you!
MEDEA: They died from a disease they caught from their father.
JASON: I tell you it was not my hand that destroyed them.   1340
MEDEA: But it was your insolence, and your virgin wedding.
JASON: And just for the sake of that you chose to kill them.
MEDEA: Is love so small a pain, do you think, for a woman?
JASON: For a wise one, certainly. But you are wholly evil.
MEDEA: The children are dead. I say this to make you suffer.   1345
JASON: The children, I think, will bring down curses on you.
MEDEA: The gods know who was the author of this sorrow.
JASON: Yes, the gods know indeed, they know your loathsome heart.
MEDEA: Hate me. But I tire of your barking bitterness.
JASON: And I of yours. It is easier to leave you.   1350
MEDEA: How then? What shall I do? I long to leave you too.
JASON: Give me the bodies to bury and to mourn them.
MEDEA: No, that I will not. I will bury them myself,
Bearing them to Hera's temple on the promontory;
So that no enemy may evilly treat them   1355
By tearing up their grave. In this land of Corinth
I shall establish a holy feast and sacrifice[1]
Each year for ever to atone for the blood guilt.
And I myself go to the land of Erechtheus
To dwell in Aigeus' house, the son of Pandion.   1360
While you, as is right, will die without distinction,
Struck on the head by a piece of the Argo's timber,
And you will have seen the bitter end of my love.
JASON: May a Fury for the children's sake destroy you,
And justice, requitor of blood.   1365
MEDEA: What heavenly power lends an ear
To a breaker of oaths, a deceiver?

---

1. Some such ceremony was still performed at Corinth in Euripides' time.

JASON: O, I hate you, murderess of children.
MEDEA: Go to your palace. Bury your bride.
JASON: I go, with two children to mourn for.   1370
MEDEA: Not yet do you feel it. Wait for the future.
JASON: Oh, children I loved!
MEDEA: I loved them, you did not.
JASON: You loved them, and killed them.
MEDEA: To make you feel pain   1375
JASON: Oh, wretch that I am, how I long
    To kiss the dear lips of my children!
MEDEA: Now you would speak to them, now you would kiss them.
    Then you rejected them.
JASON: Let me, I beg you,   1380
    Touch my boys' delicate flesh.
MEDEA: I will not. Your words are all wasted.
JASON: O God, do you hear it, this persecution,
    These my sufferings from this hateful
    Woman, this monster, murderess of children?   1385
    Still what I can do that I will do:
    I will lament and cry upon heaven,
    Calling the gods to bear me witness
    How you have killed my boys and prevent me from
    Touching their bodies or giving them burial.   1390
    I wish I had never begot them to see them
    Afterwards slaughtered by you.
CHORUS: Zeus in Olympus is the overseer
    Of many doings. Many things the gods
    Achieve beyond our judgment. What we thought   1395
    Is not confirmed and what we thought not god
    Contrives. And so it happens in this story.

ARISTOPHANES
450?–385? B.C.

By the fifth century both tragedy and comedy were regularly produced at the winter
festivals of the god Dionysus in Athens. Comedy, like tragedy, employed a chorus,
that is to say, a group of dancers (who also sang) and actors, who wore masks; its
tone was burlesque and parodic, though there was often a serious theme emphasized by the crude clowning and the free play of wit. The only comic poet of the
fifth century whose work has survived is Aristophanes; in his thirteen extant comedies, produced over the years 425–388 B.C., the institutions and personalities of
his time are caricatured and criticized in a brilliant combination of poetry and
obscenity, of farce and wit, which has no parallel in European literature. It can be
described only in terms of itself, by the adjective "Aristophanic."

He was born sometime in the middle of the fifth century and died in the next, around 385 B.C. The earliest of his plays to survive, *The Acharnians*, was produced in 425 B.C. and the bulk of his extant work dates from the years of the Peloponnesian War, 431–404 B.C. The war, in fact, is one of his comic targets; in *The Acharnians*, an Athenian citizen, fed up with the privations caused by the Spartan invasions which shut the Athenians inside their walls, makes a separate peace for himself and his family, defends his decision against an irate chorus of patriots (the Acharnians of the title), and proceeds to enjoy all the benefits of peace while his fellow citizens suffer as before. In the *Peace* (421 B.C.) another Athenian flies up to heaven on a gigantic dung-beetle (a parody of a Euripidean play in which a hero flew up on a winged horse); once arrived, he petitions Zeus to stop the war. Euripides is another favorite target and was held up to ridicule in play after play; and Socrates was the "hero" of a play, the *Clouds* (423 B.C.), which held him up to ridicule as a sophistic charlatan. (Socrates refers to this play in his speech in court, p. 808). In the *Birds* (414 B.C.) two Athenians, tired of the war and taxes, go off to found a new city; they organize the birds, who cut off the smoke of sacrifice which the gods live on, and force Zeus to surrender the government of the universe to the birds. These plays are all excellent fooling; they are also sexually and scatologically explicit. But coarse humor and exquisite wit combine with lyric poetry of a high quality and comic plots of startling audacity to produce a mixture unlike anything that went before or has come after it.

Lysistrata, which is outstanding among the Aristophanic comedies in its coherence of structure and underlying seriousness of theme, was first produced in 411 B.C. In 413 the news of the total destruction of the Athenian fleet in Sicily had reached Athens, and though heroic efforts to carry on the war were under way, the confidence in victory with which Athens had begun the war had gone forever. It is a recurring feature of Aristophanic comedy that the comic hero upsets the *status quo* to produce a series of extraordinary results that are exploited to the full for their comic potential. In this play the Athenian women, who have no political rights, seize the Acropolis and leave the men without women. At the same time similar revolutions take place in all the Greek cities according to a coordinated plan. The men are eventually "starved" into submission and the Spartans come to Athens to end the war.

Aristophanes does not miss a trick in his exploitation of the possibilities for ribald humor inherent in this situation, a female sex-strike against war; Myrrhine's teasing game with her husband Cinesias, for example, is rare fooling and the final appearance of the uncomfortably rigid Spartan ambassadors and their equally tense Athenian hosts is a visual and verbal climax of astonishing brilliance. But underneath all the fooling, real issues are pursued, and they come to the surface with telling effect in the argument between Lysistrata and the magistrate who has been sent to suppress the revolt. Reversing the words of Hector to Andromache, which had become proverbial, Lysistrata claims that "War shall be the concern of Women!"— it is too important a matter to be left to men, for women are its real victims. And when asked what the women will do, she explains that they will treat politics just as they do wool in their household tasks: "when it's confused and snarled . . . draw out a thread here and a thread there . . . we'll unsnarl this war. . . ."

We do not know how the Athenians welcomed the play. All we know is that they were not impressed by its serious undertone; the war continued for seven more exhausting years, until Athens's last fleet was defeated, the city laid open to the enemy, the empire lost.

K. J. Dover, *Aristophanic Comedy* (1972), is a general survey of the whole range of Aristophanic comedy. Jeffrey Henderson, *Aristophanes' Lysistrata* (1987), pp. xv–xli, is a helpful introduction to the play. See also Kenneth J. Rockford, *Aristophanes' Old-and-New Comedy* (1987), pp. 301–11.

Lysistrata[1]

Characters[2]

LYSISTRATA	THREE ATHENIAN WOMEN
CALONICE *Athenian women*	CINESIAS, *an Athenian, husband of*
MYRRHINE	*Myrrhine*
LAMPITO, *a Spartan woman*	SPARTAN HERALD
LEADER *of the Chorus of Old Men*	SPARTAN AMBASSADORS
CHORUS *of Old Men*	ATHENIAN AMBASSADORS
LEADER *of the Chorus of Old*	TWO ATHENIAN CITIZENS
Women	CHORUS *of Athenians*
CHORUS *of Old Women*	CHORUS *of Spartans*
ATHENIAN MAGISTRATE	

[SCENE: *In Athens, beneath the Acropolis. In the center of the stage is the Propylaea, or gate-way to the Acropolis; to one side is a small grotto, sacred to Pan. The Orchestra represents a slope leading up to the gate-way.*
It is early in the morning. LYSISTRATA *is pacing impatiently up and down.*]

LYSISTRATA: If they'd been summoned to worship the God of Wine, or Pan, or to visit the Queen of Love, why, you couldn't have pushed your way through the streets for all the timbrels.[3] But now there's not a single woman here—except my neighbor; here she comes.
[*Enter* CALONICE.]
Good day to you, Calonice.

CALONICE: And to you, Lysistrata. [*Noticing* LYSISTRATA's *impatient air*] But what ails you? Don't scowl, my dear; it's not becoming to you to knit your brows like that.

LYSISTRATA: [*Sadly*] Ah, Calonice, my heart aches; I'm so annoyed at us women. For among men we have a reputation for sly trickery—

CALONICE: And rightly too, on my word!

LYSISTRATA: —but when they were told to meet here to consider a matter of no small importance, they lie abed and don't come.

CALONICE: Oh, they'll come all right, my dear. It's not easy for a woman to get out, you know. One is working on her husband, another is getting up the maid, another has to put the baby to bed, or wash and feed it.

1. Translated by Charles T. Murphy. 2. As is usual in ancient comedy, the leading characters have significant names. *Lysistrata* is "She who disbands the armies"; Lampito is a celebrated Spartan name; *Cinesias*, although a real name in Athens, is chosen to suggest a Greek verb *kinein, to move,* then *to make love, to have intercourse,* and the name of his deme, *Paionidai,* suggests the verb *paiein,* which has about the same significance. 3. These instruments were used in most orgiastic cults, especially in the worship of Dionysus, the "God of Wine."

LYSISTRATA: But after all, there are other matters more important than all that.

CALONICE: My dear Lysistrata, just what is this matter you've summoned us women to consider? What's up? Something big?

LYSISTRATA: Very big.

CALONICE: [*Interested*] Is it stout, too?

LYSISTRATA: [*Smiling*] Yes indeed—both big and stout.

CALONICE: What? And the women still haven't come?

LYSISTRATA: It's not what you suppose; they'd have come soon enough for *that*. But I've worked up something, and for many a sleepless night I've turned it this way and that.

CALONICE: [*In mock disappointment*] Oh, I guess it's pretty fine and slender, if you've turned it this way and that.

LYSISTRATA: So fine that the safety of the whole of Greece lies in us women.

CALONICE: In us women? It depends on a very slender reed then.

LYSISTRATA: Our country's fortunes are in our hands; and whether the Spartans shall perish—

CALONICE: Good! Let them perish, by all means.

LYSISTRATA: —and the Boeotians shall be completely annihilated.

CALONICE: Not completely! Please spare the eels.[4]

LYSISTRATA: As for Athens, I won't use any such unpleasant words. But you understand what I mean. But if the women will meet here—the Spartans, the Boeotians, and we Athenians—then all together we will save Greece.

CALONICE: But what could women do that's clever or distinguished? We just sit around all dolled up in silk robes, looking pretty in our sheer gowns and evening slippers.

LYSISTRATA: These are just the things I hope will save us: these silk robes, perfumes, evening slippers, rouge, and our chiffon blouses.

CALONICE: How so?

LYSISTRATA: So never a man alive will lift a spear against the foe—

CALONICE: I'll get a silk gown at once.

LYSISTRATA: —or take up his shield—

CALONICE: I'll put on my sheerest gown!

LYSISTRATA: —or sword.

CALONICE: I'll buy a pair of evening slippers.

LYSISTRATA: Well then, shouldn't the women have come?

CALONICE: Come? Why, they should have *flown* here.

LYSISTRATA: Well, my dear, just watch: they'll act in true Athenian fashion—everything too late! And now there's not a woman here from the shore or from Salamis.[5]

CALONICE: They're coming. I'm sure; at daybreak they were laying—to their oars to cross the straits.

4. A favorite Athenian delicacy from the Boeotian lakes, eels were then very rare in Athens because of the war.   5. Just across the bay from Piraeus, the port of Athens.

LYSISTRATA: And those I expected would be the first to come—the women of Acharnae[6]—they haven't arrived.

CALONICE: Yet the wife of Theagenes[7] means to come: she consulted Hecate about it. [*Seeing a group of women approaching*] But look! Here come a few. And there are some more over here. Hurrah! Where do they come from?

LYSISTRATA: From Anagyra.[8]

CALONICE: Yes indeed! We've raised up quite a stink from Anagyra anyway.

[*Enter* MYRRHINE *in haste, followed by several other women.*]

MYRRHINE: [*Breathlessly*] Have we come in time, Lysistrata? What do you say? Why so quiet?

LYSISTRATA: I can't say much for you, Myrrhine, coming at this hour on such important business.

MYRRHINE: Why, I had trouble finding my girdle in the dark. But if it's so important, we're here now; tell us.

LYSISTRATA: No. Let's wait a little for the women from Boeotia and the Peloponnesus.

MYRRHINE: That's a much better suggestion. Look! Here comes Lampito now.

[*Enter* LAMPITO *with two other women.*]

LYSISTRATA: Greetings, my dear Spartan friend. How pretty you look, my dear. What a smooth complexion and well-developed figure! You could throttle an ox.

LAMPITO: Faith, yes, I think I could. I take exercises and kick my heels against my bum. [*She demonstrates with a few steps of the Spartan "bottom-kicking" dance.*]

LYSISTRATA: And what splendid breasts you have.

LAMPITO: La! You handle me like a prize steer.

LYSISTRATA: And who is this young lady with you?

LAMPITO: Faith, she's an Ambassadress from Boeotia.

LYSISTRATA: Oh yes, a Boeotian, and blooming like a garden too.

CALONICE: [*Lifting up her skirt*] My word! How neatly her garden's weeded!

LYSISTRATA: And who is the other girl?

LAMPITO: Oh, she's a Corinthian swell.

MYRRHINE: [*After a rapid examination*] Yes indeed. She swells very nicely [*Pointing*] here and here.

LAMPITO: Who has gathered together this company of women?

LYSISTRATA: I have.

LAMPITO: Speak up, then. What do you want?

MYRRHINE: Yes, my dear, tell us what this important matter is.

6. A large village a few miles northwest of Athens.   7. A very superstitious Athenian (perhaps he was sitting in the audience) who never went out without consulting the shrine of Hecate at his doorstep.
8. A district south of Athens. It was also the name of a bad-smelling shrub and the phrase "to stir up the anagyra" was proverbially used to describe people who brought trouble on themselves by interfering.

LYSISTRATA: Very well, I'll tell you. But before I speak, let me ask you a little question.

MYRRHINE: Anything you like.

LYSISTRATA: [*Earnestly*] Tell me: don't you yearn for the fathers of your children, who are away at the wars? I know you all have husbands abroad.

CALONICE: Why, yes; mercy me! my husband's been away for five months in Thrace keeping guard on—Eucrates.[9]

MYRRHINE: And mine for seven whole months in Pylos.[1]

LAMPITO: And mine, as soon as ever he returns from the fray, readjusts his shield and flies out of the house again.

LYSISTRATA: And as for lovers, there's not even a ghost of one left. Since the Milesians revolted from us,[2] I've not even seen an eight-inch dingus to be a leather consolation for us widows. Are you willing, if I can find a way, to help me end the war?

MYRRHINE: Goodness, yes! I'd do it, even if I had to pawn my dress and— get drunk on the spot!

CALONICE: And I, even if I had to let myself be split in two like a flounder.

LAMPITO: I'd climb up Mt. Taygetus[3] if I could catch a glimpse of peace.

LYSISTRATA: I'll tell you, then, in plain and simple words. My friends, if we are going to force our men to make peace, we must do without—

MYRRHINE: Without what? Tell us.

LYSISTRATA: Will you do it?

MYRRHINE: We'll do it, if it kills us.

LYSISTRATA: Well, then we must do without sex altogether. [*General consternation*] Why do you turn away? Where go you? Why turn so pale? Why those tears? Will you do it or not? What means this hesitation?

MYRRHINE: I won't do it! Let the war go on.

CALONICE: Nor I! Let the war go on.

LYSISTRATA: So, my little flounder? Didn't you say just now you'd split yourself in half?

CALONICE: Anything else you like. I'm willing, even if I have to walk through fire. Anything rather than sex. There's nothing like it, my dear.

LYSISTRATA: [*To* MYRRHINE] What about you?

MYRRHINE: [*Sullenly*] I'm willing to walk through fire, too.

LYSISTRATA: Oh vile and cursed breed! No wonder they make tragedies about us: we're naught but "love-affairs and bassinets."[4] But you, my dear Spartan friend, if you alone are with me, our enterprise might yet succeed. Will you vote with me?

LAMPITO: 'Tis cruel hard, by my faith, for a woman to sleep alone without her nooky; but for all that, we certainly do need peace.

LYSISTRATA: O my dearest friend! You're the only real woman here.

9. We have no details on this campaign in Thrace.   1. A point on the west coast of the Peloponnese held by an Athenian garrison.   2. The city of Miletus, an Athenian ally ever since the Persian war, had deserted the Athenian cause in the previous year. The objects Lysistrata speaks of were supposed to be manufactured there.   3. The mountain which towers over Sparta.   4. In the *Tyro* of Sophocles, which had recently been produced, the heroine, who had borne twin sons to the god Poseidon, left them exposed in a bassinet.

CALONICE: [*Wavering*] Well, if we do refrain from—[*Shuddering*] what you say (God forbid!), would that bring peace?

LYSISTRATA: My goodness, yes! If we sit at home all rouged and powdered, dressed in our sheerest gowns, and neatly depilated, our men will get excited and want to take us; but if you don't come to them and keep away, they'll soon make a truce.

LAMPITO: Aye; Menelaus caught sight of Helen's naked breast and dropped his sword, they say.

CALONICE: What if the men give us up?

LYSISTRATA: "Flay a skinned dog,"[5] as Pherecrates says.

CALONICE: Rubbish! These make-shifts are no good. But suppose they grab us and drag us into the bedroom?

LYSISTRATA: Hold on to the door.

CALONICE: And if they beat us?

LYSISTRATA: Give in with a bad grace. There's no pleasure in it for them when they have to use violence. And you must torment them in every possible way. They'll give up soon enough; a man gets no joy if he doesn't get along with his wife.

MYRRHINE: If this is your opinion, we agree.

LAMPITO: As for our own men, we can persuade them to make a just and fair peace; but what about the Athenian rabble? Who will persuade them not to start any more monkey-shines?

LYSISTRATA: Don't worry. We guarantee to convince them.

LAMPITO: Not while their ships are rigged so well and they have that mighty treasure in the temple of Athene.

LYSISTRATA: We've taken good care for that too: we shall seize the Acropolis today. The older women have orders to do this, and while we are making our arrangements, they are to pretend to make a sacrifice and occupy the Acropolis.

LAMPITO: All will be well then. That's a very fine idea.

LYSISTRATA: Let's ratify this, Lampito, with the most solemn oath.

LAMPITO: Tell us what oath we shall swear.

LYSISTRATA: Well said. Where's our Policewoman? [*To a Scythian slave*] What are you gaping at? Set a shield upside-down here in front of me, and give me the sacred meats.

CALONICE: Lysistrata, what sort of an oath are we to take?

LYSISTRATA: What oath? I'm going to slaughter a sheep over the shield, as they do in Aeschylus.[6]

CALONICE: Don't, Lysistrata! No oaths about peace over a shield.

LYSISTRATA: What shall the oath be, then?

CALONICE: How about getting a white horse somewhere and cutting out its entrails for the sacrifice?

LYSISTRATA: White horse indeed!

CALONICE: Well then, how shall we swear?

5. A proverb for useless activity. *Pherecrates*: a fifth-century comic poet.   6. In Aeschylus's *Seven Against Thebes*, the enemy champions are described as swearing loyalty to each other and slaughtering a bull so that the blood flowed into the hollow of a shield.

MYRRHINE: I'll tell you: let's place a large black bowl upside-down and then slaughter—a flask of Thasian wine.[7] And then let's swear—not to pour in a single drop of water.

LAMPITO: Lord! How I like that oath!

LYSISTRATA: Someone bring out a bowl and a flask.

[A slave brings the utensils for the sacrifice.]

CALONICE: Look, my friends! What a big jar! Here's a cup that 'twould give me joy to handle. [She picks up the bowl.]

LYSISTRATA: Set it down and put your hands on our victim. [As CALONICE places her hands on the flask] O Lady of Persuasion and dear Loving Cup, graciously vouchsafe to receive this sacrifice from us women. [She pours the wine into the bowl.]

CALONICE: The blood has a good colour and spurts out nicely.

LAMPITO: Faith, it has a pleasant smell, too.

MYRRHINE: Oh, let me be the first to swear, ladies!

CALONICE: No, by our Lady! Not unless you're allotted the first turn.

LYSISTRATA: Place all your hands on the cup, and one of you repeat on behalf of all what I say. Then all will swear and ratify the oath. I will suffer no man, be he husband or lover,

CALONICE: I will suffer no man, be he husband or lover,

LYSISTRATA: To approach me all hot and horny. [As CALONICE hesitates] Say it!

CALONICE: [Slowly and painfully] To approach me all hot and horny. O Lysistrata, I feel so weak in the knees!

LYSISTRATA: I will remain at home unmated,

CALONICE: I will remain at home unmated,

LYSISTRATA: Wearing my sheerest gown and carefully adorned,

CALONICE: Wearing my sheerest gown and carefully adorned,

LYSISTRATA: That my husband may burn with desire for me.

CALONICE: That my husband may burn with desire for me.

LYSISTRATA: And if he takes me by force against my will,

CALONICE: And if he takes me by force against my will,

LYSISTRATA: I shall do it badly and keep from moving.

CALONICE: I shall do it badly and keep from moving.

LYSISTRATA: I will not stretch my slippers toward the ceiling,

CALONICE: I will not stretch my slippers toward the ceiling,

LYSISTRATA: Nor will I take the posture of the lioness on the knife-handle.

CALONICE: Nor will I take the posture of the lioness on the knife-handle.

LYSISTRATA: If I keep this oath, may I be permitted to drink from this cup,

CALONICE: If I keep this oath, may I be permitted to drink from this cup,

LYSISTRATA: But if I break it, may the cup be filled with water.

CALONICE: But if I break it, may the cup be filled with water.

LYSISTRATA: Do you all swear to this?

ALL: I do, so help me!

---

7. Strong wine from the island of Thasos in the northern Aegean. In Athens the wife was in charge of the household supplies and it is a frequent Aristophanic joke to present her as addicted to the bottle.

LYSISTRATA: Come then, I'll just consummate this offering. [*She takes a long drink from the cup.*]

CALONICE: [*Snatching the cup away*] Shares, my dear! Let's drink to our continued friendship.

[*A shout is heard from off-stage.*]

LAMPITO: What's that shouting?

LYSISTRATA: That's what I was telling you: the women have just seized the Acropolis. Now, Lampito, go home and arrange matters in Sparta; and leave these two ladies here as hostages. We'll enter the Acropolis to join our friends and help them lock the gates.

CALONICE: Don't you suppose the men will come to attack us?

LYSISTRATA: Don't worry about them. Neither threats nor fire will suffice to open the gates, except on the terms we've stated.

CALONICE: I should say not! Else we'd belie our reputation as unmanageable pests.

[LAMPITO *leaves the stage. The other women retire and enter the Acropolis through the Propylaea.*]

[*Enter the* CHORUS OF OLD MEN, *carrying fire-pots and a load of heavy sticks.*]

LEADER OF MEN: Onward, Draces, step by step, though your shoulder's aching.

Cursèd logs of olive-wood, what a load you're making!

FIRST SEMI-CHORUS OF OLD MEN: [*Singing*]

Aye, many surprises await a man who lives to a ripe old age;
For who could suppose, Strymodorus my lad, that the women we've nourished (alas!),
    Who sat at home to vex our days,
    Would seize the holy image here
    And occupy this sacred shrine,
    With bolts and bars, with fell design,
    To lock the Propylaea?

LEADER OF MEN: Come with speed, Philourgus, come! to the temple hast'ning.

There we'll heap these logs about in a circle round them,
And whoever has conspired, raising this rebellion,
Shall be roasted, scorched, and burnt, all without exception,
Doomed by one unanimous vote—but first the wife of Lycon.[8]

SECOND SEMI-CHORUS: [*Singing*]

No, no! by Demeter, while I'm alive, no woman shall mock at me.
Not even the Spartan Cleomenes,[9] our citadel first to seize,
    Got off unscathed; for all his pride

8. The ancient commentaries tell us that she was called Rhodia and was not too careful about her reputation.   9. In 508 B.C., the Athenians expelled the tyrant Hippias and were about to install a democratic regime under the leadership of Cleisthenes when the oligarchic party appealed to Sparta for help. The Spartan king Cleomenes invaded Attica, seized the city, and began a purge of the democrats. A popular uprising, however, forced him into the Acropolis, where he was besieged; after two days he was allowed to withdraw with his troops and Cleisthenes began the reforms that established the democracy.

And haughty Spartan arrogance,
He left his arms and sneaked away,
Stripped to his shirt, unkempt, unshav'd,
With six years' filth still on him.
LEADER OF MEN: I besieged that hero bold, sleeping at my station,
Marshalled at these holy gates sixteen deep against him.
Shall I not these cursèd pests punish for their daring,
Burning these Euripides-and-God-detested women?[1]
Aye! or else may Marathon overturn my trophy.[2]
FIRST SEMI-CHORUS: [Singing]
There remains of my road
Just this brow of the hill;
There I speed on my way.
Drag the logs up the hill, though we're got no ass to help.
(God! my shoulder's bruised and sore!)
Onward still must we go
Blow the fire! Don't let it go out
Now we're near the end of our road.
ALL: [Blowing on the fire-pots]
Whew! Whew! Drat the smoke!
SECOND SEMI-CHORUS: [Singing]
Lord, what smoke rushing forth
From the pot, like a dog
Running mad, bites my eyes!
This must be Lemnos-fire.[3] What a sharp and stinging smoke!
Rushing onward to the shrine
Aid the gods. Once for all
Show your mettle, Laches my boy!
To the rescue hastening all!
ALL: [Blowing on the fire-pots] Whew! Whew! Drat the smoke!
[The chorus has now reached the edge of the Orchestra nearest the
stage, in front of the Propylaea. They begin laying their logs and fire-
pots on the ground.]
LEADER OF MEN: Thank heaven, this fire is still alive. Now let's first put
down these logs here and place our torches in the pots to catch; then
let's make a rush for the gates with a battering-ram. If the women don't
unbar the gate at our summons, we'll have to smoke them out.
Let me put down my load. Ouch! That hurts! [To the audience] Would
any of the generals in Samos[4] like to lend a hand with this log? [Throw-
ing down a log] Well, that won't break my back any more, at any rate.
[Turning to his fire-pot] Your job, my little pot, is to keep those coals
alive and furnish me shortly with a red-hot torch.

1. Euripides is always presented in Aristophanic comedy as a misogynist and hence hated by women in
return. There does not seem to be any foundation for Aristophanes's view, though Euripides's realistic (if
sympathetic) presentation of women may possibly have enraged Athenian society ladies. 2. If the chorus
really fought at Marathon, they are very old men. The trophy was on a high mound that covered the
Athenian dead and is still in place. 3. Lemnos is a volcanic island in the Aegean. 4. At this time,
the headquarters of the Athenian fleet.

O mistress Victory, be my ally and grant me to rout these audacious
women in the Acropolis.
[*While the men are busy with their logs and fires, the* CHORUS OF OLD
WOMEN *enters, carrying pitchers of water.*]
LEADER OF WOMEN: What's this I see? Smoke and flames? Is that a fire
ablazing?
Let's rush upon them. Hurry up! They'll find us women ready.
FIRST SEMI-CHORUS OF OLD WOMEN: [*Singing*]
    With wingèd foot onward I fly,
    Ere the flames consume Neodice;
    Lest Critylla be overwhelmed
By a lawless, accurst herd of old men.
I shudder with fear. Am I too late to aid them?
At break of the day filled we our jars with water
Fresh from the spring, pushing our way straight through the crowds.
Oh, what a din!
    Mid crockery crashing, jostled by slave-girls,
    Sped we to save them, aiding our neighbors,
    Bearing this water to put out the flames.
SECOND SEMI-CHORUS OF OLD WOMEN: [*Singing*]
    Such news I've heard: doddering fools
    Come with logs, like furnace-attendants,
    Loaded down with three hundred pounds,
Breathing many a vain, blustering threat,
That all these abhorred sluts will be burnt to charcoal.
O goddess, I pray never may they be kindled;
Grant them to save Greece and our men; madness and war help them
to end.
    With this as our purpose, golden-plumed Maiden,
    Guardian of Athens, seized we thy precinct.
    Be my ally, Warrior-maiden,
    'Gainst these old men, bearing water with me.
[*The women have now reached their position in the Orchestra, and
their* LEADER *advances toward the* LEADER OF THE MEN.]
LEADER OF WOMEN: Hold on there! What's this, you utter scoundrels? No
decent, God-fearing citizens would act like this.
LEADER OF MEN: Oho! Here's something unexpected: a swarm of women
have come out to attack us.
LEADER OF WOMEN: What, do we frighten you? Surely you don't think
we're too many for you. And yet there are ten thousand times more of
us whom you haven't even seen.
LEADER OF MEN: What say, Phaedria?[5] Shall we let these women wag their
tongues? Shan't we take our sticks and break them over their backs?
LEADER OF WOMEN: Let's set our pitchers on the ground; then if anyone
lays a hand on us, they won't get in our way.

---

5. A man's name; the remark is addressed to another member of the male chorus.

LEADER OF MEN: By God! If someone gave them two or three smacks on
the jaw, like Bupalus,[6] they wouldn't talk so much!

LEADER OF WOMEN: Go on, hit me, somebody! Here's my jaw! But no other
bitch will bite a piece out of you before me.

LEADER OF MEN: Silence! or I'll knock out your—senility!

LEADER OF WOMEN: Just lay one finger on Stratyllis, I dare you!

LEADER OF MEN: Suppose I dust you off with this fist? What will you do?

LEADER OF WOMEN: I'll tear the living guts out of you with my teeth.

LEADER OF MEN: No poet is more clever than Euripides: "There is no beast
so shameless as a woman."

LEADER OF WOMEN: Let's pick up our jars of water, Rhodippe.

LEADER OF MEN: Why have you come here with water, you detestable slut?

LEADER OF WOMEN: And why have you come with fire, you funeral vault?
To cremate yourself?

LEADER OF MEN: To light a fire and singe your friends.

LEADER OF WOMEN: And I've brought water to put out your fire.

LEADER OF MEN: What? You'll put out my fire?

LEADER OF WOMEN: Just try and see!

LEADER OF MEN: I wonder: shall I scorch you with this torch of mine?

LEADER OF WOMEN: If you've got any soap, I'll give you a bath.

LEADER OF MEN: Give *me* a bath, you stinking hag?

LEADER OF WOMEN: Yes—a bridal bath!

LEADER OF MEN: Just listen to her! What crust!

LEADER OF WOMEN: Well, I'm a free citizen.

LEADER OF MEN: I'll put an end to your bawling.

[*The men pick up their torches.*]

LEADER OF WOMEN: You'll never do jury-duty[7] again.

[*The women pick up their pitchers.*]

LEADER OF MEN: Singe her hair for her!

LEADER OF WOMEN: Do your duty, water!

[*The women empty their pitchers on the men.*]

LEADER OF MEN: Ow! Ow! For heaven's sake!

LEADER OF WOMEN: Is it too hot?

LEADER OF MEN: What do you mean "hot"? Stop! What are you doing?

LEADER OF WOMEN: I'm watering you, so you'll be fresh and green.

LEADER OF MEN: But I'm all withered up with shaking.

LEADER OF WOMEN: Well, you've got a fire; why don't you dry yourself?

[*Enter an Athenian* MAGISTRATE, *accompanied by four Scythian
policemen.*[8]]

MAGISTRATE: Have these wanton women flared up again with their timbrels
and their continual worship of Sabazius?[9] Is this another Adonis-dirge[1]

6. A sixth-century sculptor, the target of the poet Hipponax's satirical attacks.   7. Paid attendance at
the courts, the usual source of income for older Athenians.   8. The regular police of Athens. They
carried bows and arrows.   9. The cult of the oriental deity Sabazius had been recently introduced in
Athens. It was considered somewhat disorderly and immoral by religious conservatives.   1. The lament
of the women for Adonis (Tammuz), another oriental cult. When the great expedition to Sicily set sail,
the women were mourning the death of Adonis—a bad omen that proved all too true. Demostratus was
one of the supporters of the expedition (the most prominent was Alcibiades) and he proposed to enroll
heavy armed infantry from the island of Zacynthus, off the west coast of Greece, on the way to Sicily.

upon the roof-tops—which we heard not long ago in the Assembly? That confounded Demostratus was urging us to sail to Sicily, and the whirling women shouted, "Woe for Adonis!" And then Demostratus said we'd best enroll the infantry from Zacynthus, and a tipsy woman on the roof shrieked, "Beat your breasts for Adonis!" And that vile and filthy lunatic forced his measure through. Such license do our women take.

LEADER OF MEN: What if you heard of the insolence of these women here? Besides their other violent acts, they threw water all over us, and we have to shake out our clothes just as if we'd leaked in them.

MAGISTRATE: And rightly, too, by God! For we ourselves lead the women astray and teach them to play the wanton; from these roots such notions blossom forth. A man goes into the jeweler's shop and says, "About that necklace you made for my wife, goldsmith: last night, while she was dancing, the fastening-bolt slipped out of the hole. I have to sail over to Salamis today; if you're free, do come around tonight and fit in a new bolt for her." Another goes to the shoe-maker, a strapping young fellow with manly parts, and says, "See here, cobbler, the sandal-strap chafes my wife's little—toe; it's so tender. Come around during the siesta and stretch it a little, so she'll be more comfortable." Now we see the results of such treatment: here I'm a special Councillor and need money to procure oars for the galleys; and I'm locked out of the Treasury by these women.

But this is no time to stand around. Bring up crow-bars there! I'll put an end to their insolence. [*To one of the policemen*] What are you gaping at, you wretch? What are you staring at? Got an eye out for a tavern, eh? Set your crow-bars here to the gates and force them open. [*Retiring to safe distance*] I'll help from over here.

[*The gates are thrown open and* LYSISTRATA *comes out followed by several other women.*]

LYSISTRATA: Don't force the gates; I'm coming out of my own accord. We don't need crow-bars here; what we need is good sound common-sense.

MAGISTRATE: Is that so, you strumpet? Where's my policeman? Officer, arrest her and tie her arms behind her back.

LYSISTRATA: By Artemis, if he lays a finger on me, he'll pay for it, even if he is a public servant.

[*The policeman retires in terror.*]

MAGISTRATE: You there, are you afraid? Seize her round the waist—and you, too. Tie her up, both of you!

FIRST WOMAN: [*As the second policeman approaches* LYSISTRATA] By Pandrosus,[2] if you but touch her with your hand, I'll kick the stuffings out of you.

[*The second policeman retires in terror.*]

MAGISTRATE: Just listen to that: "kick the stuffings out." Where's another policeman? Tie *her* up first, for her chatter.

2. A mythical Athenian princess.

SECOND WOMAN: By the Goddess of the Light, if you lay the tip of your finger on her, you'll soon need a doctor.

[*The third policeman retires in terror.*]

MAGISTRATE: What's this? Where's my policeman? Seize *her* too. I'll soon stop your sallies.

THIRD WOMAN: By the Goddess of Tauros,[3] if you go near her, I'll tear out your hair until it shrieks with pain.

[*The fourth policeman retires in terror.*]

MAGISTRATE: Oh, damn it all! I've run out of policemen. But women must never defeat us. Officers, let's charge them all together. Close up your ranks!

[*The policemen rally for a mass attack.*]

LYSISTRATA: By heaven, you'll soon find out that we have four companies of warrior-women, all fully equipped within!

MAGISTRATE: [*Advancing*] Twist their arms off, men!

LYSISTRATA: [*Shouting*] To the rescue, my valiant women!
O sellers-of-barley-green-stuffs-and-eggs,
O sellers-of-garlic, ye keepers-of-taverns, and vendors-of-bread,
Grapple! Smite! Smash!
Won't you heap filth on them? Give them a tongue-lashing!

[*The women beat off the policemen.*]

Halt! Withdraw! No looting on the field.

MAGISTRATE: Damn it! My police-force has put up a very poor show.

LYSISTRATA: What did you expect? Did you think you were attacking slaves? Didn't you know that women are filled with passion?

MAGISTRATE: Aye, passion enough—for a good strong drink!

LEADER OF MEN: O chief and leader of this land, why spend your words in vain?
Don't argue with these shameless beasts. You know not how we've fared:
A soapless bath they've given us; our clothes are soundly soaked.

LEADER OF WOMEN: Poor fool! You never should attack or strike a peaceful girl.
But if you do, your eyes must swell. For I am quite content
To sit unmoved, like modest maids, in peace and cause no pain;
But let a man stir up my hive, he'll find me like a wasp.

CHORUS OF MEN: [*Singing*]
O God, whatever shall we do with creatures like Womankind?
This can't be endured by any man alive. Question them!
Let us try to find out what this means.
To what end have they seized on this shrine,
This steep and rugged, high and holy,
Undefiled Acropolis?

LEADER OF MEN: Come, put your questions; don't give in, and probe her every statement.
For base and shameful it would be to leave this plot untested.

3. Artemis.

MAGISTRATE: Well then, first of all I wish to ask her this: for what purpose have you barred us from the Acropolis?

LYSISTRATA: To keep the treasure safe, so you won't make war on account of it.

MAGISTRATE: What? Do we make war on account of the treasure?

LYSISTRATA: Yes, and you cause all our other troubles for it, too. Peisander[4] and those greedy office-seekers keep things stirred up so they can find occasions to steal. Now let them do what they like: they'll never again make off with any of this money.

MAGISTRATE: What will you do?

LYSISTRATA: What a question! We'll administer it ourselves.

MAGISTRATE: You will administer the treasure?

LYSISTRATA: What's so strange in that? Don't we administer the household money for you?

MAGISTRATE: That's different.

LYSISTRATA: How is it different?

MAGISTRATE: We've got to make war with this money.

LYSISTRATA: But that's the very first thing: you mustn't make war.

MAGISTRATE: How else can we be saved?

LYSISTRATA: We'll save you.

MAGISTRATE: You?

LYSISTRATA: Yes, we!

MAGISTRATE: God forbid!

LYSISTRATA: We'll save you, whether you want it or not.

MAGISTRATE: Oh! This is terrible!

LYSISTRATA: You don't like it, but we're going to do it none the less.

MAGISTRATE: Good God! it's illegal!

LYSISTRATA: We *will* save you, my little man!

MAGISTRATE: Suppose I don't want you to?

LYSISTRATA: That's all the more reason.

MAGISTRATE: What business have you with war and peace?

LYSISTRATA: I'll explain.

MAGISTRATE: [*Shaking his fist*] Speak up, or you'll smart for it.

LYSISTRATA: Just listen, and try to keep your hands still.

MAGISTRATE: I can't. I'm so mad I can't stop them.

FIRST WOMAN: Then you'll be the one to smart for it.

MAGISTRATE: Croak to yourself, old hag! [*To* LYSISTRATA] Now then, speak up.

LYSISTRATA: Very well. Formerly we endured the war for a good long time with our usual restraint, no matter what you men did. You wouldn't let us say "boo," although nothing you did suited us. But we watched you well, and though we stayed at home we'd often hear of some terribly stupid measure you'd proposed. Then, though grieving at heart, we'd smile sweetly and say, "What was passed in the Assembly today about

4. A leader of the war party.

writing on the treaty-stone?"[5] "What's that to you?" my husband would
say. "Hold your tongue!" And I held my tongue.

FIRST WOMAN: But I wouldn't have—not I!

MAGISTRATE: You'd have been soundly smacked, if you hadn't kept still.

LYSISTRATA: So I kept still at home. Then we'd hear of some plan still worse
than the first; we'd say, "Husband, how could you pass such a stupid
proposal?" He'd scowl at me and say, "If you don't mind your spinning,
your head will be sore for weeks. War shall be the concern of Men."[6]

MAGISTRATE: And he was right, upon my word!

LYSISTRATA: Why right, you confounded fool, when your proposals were
so stupid and we weren't allowed to make suggestions?
"There's not a man left in the country," says one. "No, not one,"
says another. Therefore all we women have decided in council to make
a common effort to save Greece. How long should we have waited?
Now, if you're willing to listen to our excellent proposals and keep silence
for us in your turn, we still may save you.

MAGISTRATE: We men keep silence for you? That's terrible; I won't endure
it!

LYSISTRATA: Silence!

MAGISTRATE: Silence for you, you wench, when you're wearing a snood?
I'd rather die!

LYSISTRATA: Well, if that's all that bothers you—here! take my snood and
tie it round your head. [During the following words the women dress up
the MAGISTRATE in women's garments.] And now keep quiet! Here, take
this spinning-basket, too, and card your wool with robes tucked up,
munching on beans. War shall be the concern of Women!

LEADER OF WOMEN: Arise and leave your pitchers, girls; no time is this to
falter.
We too must aid our loyal friends; our turn has come for action.

CHORUS OF WOMEN: [Singing]
I'll never tire of aiding them with song and dance; never may
Faintness keep my legs from moving to and fro endlessly.
For I yearn to do all for my friends;
They have charm, they have wit, they have grace,
With courage, brains, and best of virtues—
Patriotic sapience.

LEADER OF WOMEN: Come, child of manliest ancient dames, offspring of
stinging nettles,
Advance with rage unsoftened; for fair breezes speed you onward.

LYSISTRATA: If only sweet Eros and the Cyprian Queen of Love shed charm
over our breasts and limbs and inspire our men with amorous longing
and priapic spasms, I think we may soon be called Peacemakers among
the Greeks.

MAGISTRATE: What will you do?

5. The text of a treaty was inscribed on a stone which was set up in a public place.   6. Hector to
Andromache (Iliad, VI. 528).

LYSISTRATA: First of all, we'll stop those fellows who run madly about the Marketplace in arms.

FIRST WOMAN: Indeed we shall, by the Queen of Paphos.[7]

LYSISTRATA: For now they roam about the market, amid the pots and greenstuffs, armed to the teeth like Corybantes.[8]

MAGISTRATE: That's what manly fellows ought to do!

LYSISTRATA: But it's so silly: a chap with a Gorgon-emblazoned shield buying pickled herring.

FIRST WOMAN: Why, just the other day I saw one of those long-haired dandies who command our cavalry ride up on horseback and pour into his bronze helmet the egg-broth he'd bought from an old dame. And there was a Thracian slinger too, shaking his lance like Tereus;[9] he'd scared the life out of the poor fig-peddler and was gulping down all her ripest fruit.

MAGISTRATE: How can you stop all the confusion in the various states and bring them together?

LYSISTRATA: Very easily.

MAGISTRATE: Tell me how.

LYSISTRATA: Just like a ball of wool, when it's confused and snarled: we take it thus, and draw out a thread here and a thread there with our spindles; thus we'll unsnarl this war, if no one prevents us, and draw together the various states with embassies here and embassies there.

MAGISTRATE: Do you suppose you can stop this dreadful business with balls of wool and spindles, you nit-wits?

LYSISTRATA: Why, if you had any wits, you'd manage all affairs of state like our wool-working.

MAGISTRATE: How so?

LYSISTRATA: First you ought to treat the city as we do when we wash the dirt out of a fleece: stretch it out and pluck and thrash out of the city all those prickly scoundrels; aye, and card out those who conspire and stick together to gain office, pulling off their heads. Then card the wool, all of it, into one fair basket of goodwill, mingling in the aliens residing here, any loyal foreigners, and anyone who's in debt to the Treasury; and consider that all our colonies lie scattered round about like remnants; from all of these collect the wool and gather it together here, wind up a great ball, and then weave a good stout cloak for the democracy.

MAGISTRATE: Dreadful! Talking about thrashing and winding balls of wool, when you haven't the slightest share in the war!

LYSISTRATA: Why, you dirty scoundrel, we bear more than twice as much as you. First, we bear children and send off our sons as soldiers.

MAGISTRATE: Hush! Let bygones be bygones!

LYSISTRATA: Then, when we ought to be happy and enjoy our youth, we sleep alone because of your expeditions abroad. But never mind us married women: I grieve most for the maids who grow old at home unwed.

7. Aphrodite.   8. The armed priests of the goddess Cybele.   9. A mythical king of Thrace. Thracian mercenaries had served in the Athenian ranks during the war.

MAGISTRATE: Don't men grow old, too?

LYSISTRATA: For heaven's sake! That's not the same thing. When a man comes home, no matter how grey he is, he soon finds a girl to marry. But woman's bloom is short and fleeting; if she doesn't grasp her chance, no man is willing to marry her and she sits at home a prey to every fortune-teller.

MAGISTRATE: [*Coarsely*] But if a man can still get it up—

LYSISTRATA: See here, you: what's the matter? Aren't you dead yet? There's plenty of room for you. Buy yourself a shroud and I'll bake you a honey-cake.[1] [*Handing him a copper coin for his passage across the Styx*] Here's your fare! Now get yourself a wreath.

[*During the following dialogue the women dress up the* MAGISTRATE *as a corpse.*]

FIRST WOMAN: Here, take these fillets.

SECOND WOMAN: Here, take this wreath.

LYSISTRATA: What do you want? What's lacking? Get moving; off to the ferry! Charon is calling you; don't keep him from sailing.

MAGISTRATE: Am I to endure these insults? By God! I'm going straight to the magistrates to show them how I've been treated.

LYSISTRATA: Are you grumbling that you haven't been properly laid out? Well, the day after tomorrow we'll send around all the usual offerings early in the morning.

[*The* MAGISTRATE *goes out still wearing his funeral decorations.* LYSISTRATA *and the women retire into the Acropolis.*]

LEADER OF MEN: Wake, ye sons of freedom, wake! 'Tis no time for sleeping. Up and at them, like a man! Let us strip for action.

[*The* CHORUS OF MEN *remove their outer cloaks.*]

CHORUS OF MEN: [*Singing*]
Surely there is something here greater than meets the eye;
For without a doubt I smell Hippias' tyranny.[2]
Dreadful fear assails me lest certain bands of Spartan men,
Meeting here with Cleisthenes,[3] have inspired through treachery
All these god-detested women secretly to seize
Athens' treasure in the temple, and to stop that pay
      Whence I live at my ease.

LEADER OF MEN: Now isn't it terrible for them to advise the state and chatter about shields, being mere women?

And they think to reconcile us with the Spartans—men who hold nothing sacred any more than hungry wolves. Surely this is a web of deceit, my friends, to conceal an attempt at tyranny. But they'll never lord it over me; I'll be on my guard and from now on,
      "The blade I bear   A myrtle spray shall wear."

1. The dead were provided with a honey cake to throw to Cerberus, the three-headed dog which guarded the entry to the underworld. The copper coin was to pay the fare required by Charon, the ferryman over the river Styx.   2. The last tyrant of Athens, driven out in 510 B.C.   3. Not the great reformer who set up the democracy, but a contemporary of Aristophanes, notorious for his effeminacy (and therefore suspect as a fellow-conspirator of the women).

I'll occupy the market under arms and stand next to Aristogeiton.[4]

Thus I'll stand beside him. [*He strikes the pose of the famous statue of the tyrannicides, with one arm raised.*] And here's my chance to take this accurst old hag and—[Striking the LEADER OF WOMEN] smack her on the jaw!

LEADER OF WOMEN: You'll go home in such a state your Ma won't recognize you!

Ladies all, upon the ground let us place these garments.

[*The* CHORUS OF WOMEN *remove their outer garments.*]

CHORUS OF WOMEN: [*Singing*]

Citizens of Athens, hear useful words for the state.

Rightly; for it nurtured me in my youth royally.

As a child of seven years carried I the sacred box;[5]

Then I was a Miller-maid, grinding at Athene's shrine;

Next I wore the saffron robe and played Brauronia's Bear;

And I walked as Basket-bearer, wearing chains of figs,

    As a sweet maiden fair.

LEADER OF WOMEN: Therefore, am I not bound to give good advice to the city? Don't take it ill that I was born a woman, if I contribute something better than our present troubles. I pay my share; for I contribute MEN: But you miserable old fools contribute nothing, and after squandering our ancestral treasure, the fruit of the Persian Wars, you make no contribution in return. And now, all on account of you, we're facing ruin.

What, muttering, are you? If you annoy me, I'll take this hard, rough slipper and—[*Striking the* LEADER OF MEN] smack you on the jaw!

CHORUS OF MEN: [*Singing*]

This is outright insolence! Things go from bad to worse.

If you're men with any guts, prepare to meet the foe.

Let us strip our tunics off! We need the smell of male

Vigor. And we cannot fight all swaddled up in clothes.

[*They strip off their tunics.*]

Come then, my comrades, on to the battle, ye who once to Leipsydrion[6] came;

Then ye were MEN: Now call back your youthful vigor.

    With light, wingèd footstep advance,

    Shaking old age from your frame.

LEADER OF MEN: If any of us give these wenches the slightest hold, they'll stop at nothing: such is their cunning.

They will even build ships and sail against us, like Artemisia.[7] Or if

---

4. One of the two heroes of the democracy who assassinated Hipparchus, the brother of the tyrant Hippias. A drinking song which was frequently heard at Athenian banquets ran: "In a branch of myrtle, I'll hide my sword, like Harmodius and Aristogeiton, who killed the tyrant, and made Athens free."   5. This and the next four lines describe the religious duties of a well-born Athenian girl. The sacred box contained religious objects connected with the worship of Athena in the Erechtheum. The miller-maids ground flour for sacred cakes. At Brauron in Attica, young girls who represented themselves as bears (the saffron robe was a substitute for a more primitive bearskin) worshiped Artemis. In the Panathenaic procession certain selected girls carried baskets on their heads.   6. The base of the aristocratic family of the Almaeonidae (the family of Pericles) in their first attempt to overthrow Hippias.   7. Queen of Halicarnassus in Asia Minor. She played a prominent part in Xerxes's invasion of Greece and her ships fought at Salamis.

they turn to mounting, I count our Knights as done for: a woman's such
a tricky jockey when she gets astraddle, with a good firm seat for trotting.
Just look at those Amazons that Micon[8] painted, fighting on horseback
against men!

But we must throw them all in the pillory—[*Seizing and choking the*
LEADER OF WOMEN] grabbing hold of yonder neck!

CHORUS OF WOMEN: [*Singing*]
'Ware my anger! Like a boar 'twill rush upon you men.
Soon you'll bawl aloud for help, you'll be so soundly trimmed!
Come, my friends, let's strip with speed, and lay aside these robes;
Catch the scent of women's rage. Attack with tooth and nail!

[*They strip off their tunics.*]
Now then, come near me, you miserable man! you'll never eat garlic or
black beans again.
And if you utter a single hard word, in rage I will "nurse" you as once
      The beetle[9] requited her foe.

LEADER OF WOMEN: For you don't worry me; no, not so long as my Lampito
lives and our Theban friend, the noble Ismenia.

You can't do anything, not even if you pass a dozen—decrees! You
miserable fool, all our neighbours hate you. Why, just the other day
when I was holding a festival for Hecate, I invited as playmate from our
neighbours the Boeotians a charming, well-bred Copaic—eel. But they
refused to send me one on account of your decrees.

And you'll never stop passing decrees until I grab your foot and—
[*Tripping up the* LEADER OF MEN] toss you down and break your neck!

[*Here an interval of five days is supposed to elapse.* LYSISTRATA *comes
out from the Acropolis.*]

LEADER OF WOMEN: [*Dramatically*] Empress[1] of this great emprise and
undertaking,
Why come you forth, I pray, with frowning brow?

LYSISTRATA: Ah, these cursèd women! Their deeds and female notions make
me pace up and down in utter despair.

LEADER OF WOMEN: Ah, what sayest thou?

LYSISTRATA: The truth, alas! the truth.

LEADER OF WOMEN: What dreadful tale hast thou to tell thy friends?

LYSISTRATA: 'Tis shame to speak, and not to speak is hard.

LEADER OF WOMEN: Hide not from me whatever woes we suffer.

LYSISTRATA: Well then, to put it briefly, we want—laying!

LEADER OF WOMEN: O Zeus, Zeus!

LYSISTRATA: Why call on Zeus? That's the way things are. I can no longer
keep them away from the men, and they're all deserting. I caught one
wriggling through a hole near the grotto of Pan, another sliding down a
rope, another deserting her post; and yesterday I found one getting on a

8. A painter who had lately decorated several public buildings with frescos. The battles of the Greeks and
Amazons were favorite subjects of sculptors and painters all through the fifth century.   9. In a fable of
Aesop the beetle revenges itself on the eagle by breaking its eggs.   1. The tone of the following passage
is mock-tragic.

sparrow's back to fly off to Orsilochus,[2] and had to pull her back by the
hair. They're digging up all sorts of excuses to get home. Look, here
comes one of them now. [*A woman comes hastily out of the Acropolis.*]
Here you! Where are you off to in such a hurry?

FIRST WOMAN: I want to go home. My very best wool is being devoured by
moths.

LYSISTRATA: Moths? Nonsense! Go back inside.

FIRST WOMAN: I'll come right back; I swear it. I just want to lay it out on
the bed.

LYSISTRATA: Well, you won't lay it out, and you won't go home, either.

FIRST WOMAN: Shall I let my wool be ruined?

LYSISTRATA: If necessary, yes. [*Another woman comes out.*]

SECOND WOMAN: Oh dear! Oh dear! My precious flax! I left it at home all
unpeeled.

LYSISTRATA: Here's another one, going home for her "flax." Come back
here!

SECOND WOMAN: But I just want to work it up a little and then I'll be right
back.

LYSISTRATA: No indeed! If you start this, all the other women will want to
do the same. [*A third woman comes out.*]

THIRD WOMAN: O Eilithyia, goddess of travail, stop my labor till I come to
a lawful spot![3]

LYSISTRATA: What's this nonsense?

THIRD WOMAN: I'm going to have a baby—right now!

LYSISTRATA: But you weren't even pregnant yesterday.

THIRD WOMAN: Well, I am today. O Lysistrata, do send me home to see a
midwife, right away.

LYSISTRATA: What are you talking about? [*Putting her hand on her stomach*] What's this hard lump here?

THIRD WOMAN: A little boy.

LYSISTRATA: My goodness, what have you got there? It seems hollow; I'll
just find out. [*Pulling aside her robe*] Why, you silly goose, you've got
Athene's sacred helmet there. And you said you were having a baby!

THIRD WOMAN: Well, I *am* having one, I swear!

LYSISTRATA: Then what's this helmet for?

THIRD WOMAN: If the baby starts coming while I'm still in the Acropolis,
I'll creep into this like a pigeon and give birth to it there.

LYSISTRATA: Stuff and nonsense! It's plain enough what you're up to. You
just wait here for the christening of this—helmet.

THIRD WOMAN: But I can't sleep in the Acropolis since I saw the sacred
snake.[4]

FIRST WOMAN: And I'm dying for lack of sleep: the hooting of the owls[5]
keeps me awake.

LYSISTRATA: Enough of these shams, you wretched creatures. You want

2. The sparrow, Aphrodite's bird, pulled her chariot. *Orsilochus* ran a house of ill repute.   3. The
Acropolis was holy ground, and would be polluted by either birth or death.   4. A snake was kept in the
Erechtheum.   5. The sacred bird of Athene.

your husbands, I suppose. Well, don't you think they want us? I'm sure they're spending miserable nights. Hold out, my friends, and endure for just a little while. There's an oracle that we shall conquer, if we don't split up. [*Producing a roll of paper*] Here it is.

FIRST WOMAN: Tell us what it says.

LYSISTRATA: Listen.

"When in the length of time the Swallows shall gather together,
Fleeing the Hoopoe's amorous flight and the Cockatoo shunning,
Then shall your woes be ended and Zeus who thunders in heaven
Set what's below on top—"

FIRST WOMAN: What? Are we going to be on top?

LYSISTRATA: "But if the Swallows rebel and flutter away from the temple,
Never a bird in the world shall seem more wanton and worthless."

FIRST WOMAN: That's clear enough, upon my word!

LYSISTRATA: By all that's holy, let's not give up the struggle now. Let's go back inside. It would be a shame, my dear friends, to disobey the oracle.

[*The women all retire to the Acropolis again.*]

CHORUS OF MEN: [*Singing*]
  I have a tale to tell,
  Which I know full well.
    It was told me
    In the nursery.

  Once there was a likely lad,
    Melanion they name him;
  The thought of marriage made him mad,
    For which I cannot blame him.[6]

  So off he went to mountains fair;
    (No women to upbraid him!)
  A mighty hunter of the hare,
    He had a dog to aid him.

  He never came back home to see
    Detested women's faces.
  He showed a shrewd mentality.
    With him I'd fain change places!

ONE OF THE MEN: [*To one of the women*] Come here, old dame, give me a kiss.

WOMAN: You'll ne'er eat garlic, if you dare!

MAN: I want to kick you—just like this!

WOMAN: Oh, there's a leg with bushy hair!

MAN: Myronides and Phormio[7]
  Were hairy—and they thrashed the foe.

CHORUS OF WOMEN: [*Singing*]

6. The chorus of men here recasts a well-known myth for its own purposes. In the myth it was Atalanta who avoided marriage, challenging her suitors to a foot race which she always won; Melanion threw a golden apple in front of her; when she stopped to pick it up, she lost the race to him.　7. Successful Athenian generals.

I have another tale,
With which to assail
    Your contention
    'Bout Melanion.

Once upon a time a man
Named Timon[8] left our city,
To live in some deserted land.
    (We thought him rather witty.)

He dwelt alone amidst the thorn;
    In solitude he brooded.
From some grim Fury he was born:
    Such hatred he exuded.

He cursed you men, as scoundrels through
    And through, till life he ended.
He couldn't stand the sight of YOU!
    But women he befriended.

WOMAN: [*To one of the men*] I'll smash your face in, if you like.
MAN: Oh no, please don't! You frighten me.
WOMAN: I'll lift my foot—and thus I'll strike.
MAN: Aha! Look there! What's that I see?
WOMAN: Whate'er you see, you cannot say
    That I'm not neatly trimmed today.
    [LYSISTRATA *appears on the wall of the Acropolis.*]
LYSISTRATA: Hello! Hello! Girls, come here quick!
    [*Several women appear beside her.*]
WOMAN: What is it? Why are you calling?
LYSISTRATA: I see a man coming: he's in a dreadful state. He's mad with passion. O Queen of Cyprus, Cythera, and Paphos, just keep on this way!
WOMAN. Where is the fellow?
LYSISTRATA: There, beside the shrine of Demeter.
WOMAN: Oh yes, so he is. Who is he?
LYSISTRATA: Let's see. Do any of you know him?
MYRRHINE: Yes indeed. That's my husband, Cinesias.
LYSISTRATA: It's up to you, now: roast him, rack him, fool him, love him—and leave him! Do everything, except what our oath forbids.
MYRRHINE: Don't worry; I'll do it.
LYSISTRATA: I'll stay here to tease him and warm him up a bit. Off with you.
    [*The other women retire from the wall. Enter* CINESIAS *followed by a slave carrying a baby.* CINESIAS *is obviously in great pain and distress.*]
CINESIAS: [*Groaning*] Oh-h! Oh-h-h! This is killing me! O God, what tortures I'm suffering!

8. The famous misanthrope, the subject of Shakespeare's play. There is no evidence that he "befriended" women; his hatred seems to have been directed at the whole human race.

LYSISTRATA: [*From the wall*] Who's that within our lines?

CINESIAS: Me.

LYSISTRATA: A *man?*

CINESIAS: [*Pointing*] A *man*, indeed!

LYSISTRATA: Well, go away!

CINESIAS: Who are you to send me away?

LYSISTRATA: The captain of the guard.

CINESIAS: Oh, for heaven's sake, call out Myrrhine for me.

LYSISTRATA: Call Myrrhine? Nonsense! Who are you?

CINESIAS: Her husband, Cinesias of Paionidai.

LYSISTRATA: [*Appearing much impressed*] Oh, greetings, friend. Your name is not without honor here among us. Your wife is always talking about you, and whenever she takes an egg or an apple, she says, "Here's to my dear Cinesias!"

CINESIAS: [*Quivering with excitement*] Oh, ye gods in heaven!

LYSISTRATA: Indeed she does! And whenever our conversations turn to men, your wife immediately says, "All others are mere rubbish compared with Cinesias."

CINESIAS: [*Groaning*] Oh! Do call her for me.

LYSISTRATA: Why should I? What will you give me?

CINESIAS: Whatever you want. All I have is yours—and you see what I've got.

LYSISTRATA: Well then, I'll go down and call her. [*She descends.*]

CINESIAS: And hurry up! I've had no joy of life ever since she left home. When I go in the house, I feel awful: everything seems so empty and I can't enjoy my dinner. I'm in such a state all the time!

MYRRHINE: [*From behind the wall*] I *do* love him so. But he won't let me love him. No, no! Don't ask me to see him!

CINESIAS: O my darling, O Myrrhine honey, why do you do this to me? [*MYRRHINE appears on the wall.*] Come down here!

MYRRHINE: No, I won't come down.

CINESIAS: Won't you come, Myrrhine, when *I* call you?

MYRRHINE: No; you don't want me.

CINESIAS: *Don't want you?* I'm in agony!

MYRRHINE: I'm going now.

CINESIAS: Please don't! At least, listen to your baby. [*To the baby*] Here you, call your mamma! [*Pinching the baby*]

BABY: Ma-ma! Ma-ma! Ma-ma!

CINESIAS: [*To* MYRRHINE] What's the matter with you? Have you no pity for your child, who hasn't been washed or fed for five whole days?

MYRRHINE: Oh, poor child; your father pays no attention to you.

CINESIAS: Come down then, you heartless wretch, for the baby's sake.

MYRRHINE: Oh, what it is to be a mother! I've got to come down, I suppose. [*She leaves the wall and shortly reappears at the gate.*]

CINESIAS: [*To himself*] She seems much younger, and she has such a sweet look about her. Oh, the way she teases me! And her pretty, provoking ways make me burn with longing

MYRRHINE: [*Coming out of the gate and taking the baby*] O my sweet little angel. Naughty papa! Here, let Mummy kiss you, Mamma's little sweetheart! [*She fondles the baby lovingly.*]

CINESIAS: [*In despair*] You heartless creature, why do you do this? Why follow these other women and make both of us suffer so? [*He tries to embrace her.*]

MYRRHINE: Don't touch me!

CINESIAS: You're letting all our things at home go to wrack and ruin.

MYRRHINE: I don't care.

CINESIAS: You don't care that your wool is being plucked to pieces by the chickens?

MYRRHINE: Not in the least.

CINESIAS: And you haven't celebrated the rites of Aphrodite for ever so long. Won't you come home?

MYRRHINE: Not on your life, unless you men make a truce and stop the war.

CINESIAS: Well then, if that pleases you, we'll do it.

MYRRHINE: Well then, if that pleases *you*, I'll come home—afterwards! Right now I'm on oath not to.

CINESIAS: Then just lie down here with me for a moment.

MYRRHINE: No—[*In a teasing voice*] and yet, I won't say I don't love you.

CINESIAS: You love me? Oh, do lie down here, Myrrhine dear!

MYRRHINE: What, you silly fool! in front of the baby?

CINESIAS: [*Hastily thrusting the baby at the slave*] Of course not. Here—home! Take him, Manes! [*The slave goes off with the baby.*] See, the baby's out of the way. Now won't you lie down?

MYRRHINE: But where, my dear?

CINESIAS: Where? The grotto of Pan's a lovely spot.

MYRRHINE: How could I purify myself before returning to the shrine?

CINESIAS: Easily: just wash here in the Clepsydra.[9]

MYRRHINE: And then, shall I go back on my oath?

CINESIAS: On my head be it! Don't worry about the oath.

MYRRHINE: All right, then. Just let me bring out a bed.

CINESIAS: No, don't. The ground's all right.

MYRRHINE: Heavens, no! Bad as you are, I won't let you lie on the bare ground. [*She goes into the Acropolis.*]

CINESIAS: Why, she really loves me; it's plain to see.

MYRRHINE: [*Returning with a bed*] There! Now hurry up and lie down. I'll just slip off this dress. But—let's see: oh yes, I must fetch a mattress.

CINESIAS: Nonsense! No mattress for me.

MYRRHINE: Yes indeed! It's not nice on the bare springs.

CINESIAS: Give me a kiss.

MYRRHINE: [*Giving him a hasty kiss*] There! [*She goes.*]

CINESIAS: [*In mingled distress and delight*] Oh-h! Hurry back!

MYRRHINE: [*Returning with a mattress*] Here's the mattress; lie down on it.

9. A spring on the Acropolis.

I'm taking my things off now—but—let's see: you have no pillow.

CINESIAS: I don't *want* a pillow!

MYRRHINE: But I do. [*She goes.*]

CINESIAS: Cheated again, just like Heracles and his dinner![1]

MYRRHINE: [*Returning with a pillow*] Here, lift your head. [*To herself, wondering how else to tease him*] Is that all?

CINESIAS: Surely that's all! Do come here, precious!

MYRRHINE: I'm taking off my girdle. But remember: don't go back on your promise about the truce.

CINESIAS: Hope to die, if I do.

MYRRHINE: You don't have a blanket.

CINESIAS: [*Shouting in exasperation*] I don't want one! I want to—

MYRRHINE: Sh-h! There, there, I'll be back in a minute. [*She goes.*]

CINESIAS: She'll be the death of me with these bed-clothes.

MYRRHINE: [*Returning with a blanket*] Here, get up.

CINESIAS: I've got *this* up!

MYRRHINE: Would you like some perfume?

CINESIAS: Good heavens, no! I won't have it!

MYRRHINE: Yes, you shall, whether you want it or not. [*She goes.*]

CINESIAS: O lord! Confound all perfumes anyway!

MYRRHINE: [*Returning with a flask*] Stretch out your hand and put some on.

CINESIAS: [*Suspiciously*] By God, I don't much like this perfume. It smells of shilly-shallying, and has no scent of the marriage-bed.

MYRRHINE: Oh dear! This is Rhodian perfume I've brought.

CINESIAS: It's quite all right dear. Never mind.

MYRRHINE: Don't be silly! [*She goes out with the flask.*]

CINESIAS: Damn the man who first concocted perfumes!

MYRRHINE: [*Returning with another flask*] Here, try this flask.

CINESIAS: I've got another one all ready for you. Come, you wretch, lie down and stop bringing me things.

MYRRHINE: All right; I'm taking off my shoes. But, my dear, see that you vote for peace.

CINESIAS: [*Absently*] I'll consider it. [MYRRHINE *runs away to the Acropolis.*] I'm ruined! The wretch has skinned me and run away! [*Chanting, in tragic style*] Alas! Alas! Deceived, deserted by this fairest of women, whom shall I—lay? Ah, my poor little child, how shall I nurture thee? Where's Cynalopex?[2] I needs must hire a nurse!

LEADER OF MEN: [*Chanting*] Ah, wretched man, in dreadful wise beguiled, bewrayed, thy soul is sore distressed. I pity thee, alas! alas! What soul, what loins, what liver could stand this strain? How firm and unyielding he stands, with naught to aid him of a morning.

CINESIAS: O lord! O Zeus! What tortures I endure!

LEADER OF MEN: This is the way she's treated you, that vile and cursèd wanton.

1. The point of this proverb seems to be that the hero is such a glutton that his hosts are never quick enough with their entertainment.   2. A local brothel-keeper.

LEADER OF WOMEN: Nay, not vile and cursèd, but sweet and dear.

LEADER OF MEN: Sweet, you say? Nay, hateful, hateful!

CINESIAS: Hateful indeed! O Zeus, Zeus!
  Seize her and snatch her away,
  Like a handful of dust, in a mighty,
  Fiery tempest! Whirl her aloft, then let her drop
  Down to the earth, with a crash, as she falls—
  On the point of this waiting
  Thingummybob! [*He goes out.*]
    [*Enter a Spartan* HERALD, *in an obvious state of excitement, which he
    is doing his best to conceal.*]

HERALD: Where can I find the Senate or the Prytanes?[3] I've got an important message.
    [*The Athenian* MAGISTRATE *enters.*]

MAGISTRATE: Say there, are you a man or Priapus?[4]

HERALD: [*In annoyance*] I'm a herald, you lout! I've come from Sparta about the truce.

MAGISTRATE: Is that a spear you've got under your cloak?

HERALD: No, of course not!

MAGISTRATE: Why do you twist and turn so? Why hold your cloak in front of you? Did you rupture yourself on the trip?

HERALD: By gum, the fellow's an old fool.

MAGISTRATE: [*Pointing*] Why, you dirty rascal, you're all excited.

HERALD: Not at all. Stop this tom-foolery.

MAGISTRATE: Well, what's that I see?

HERALD: A Spartan message-staff.[5]

MAGISTRATE: Oh, certainly! That's just the kind of message-staff I've got. But tell me the honest truth: How are things going in Sparta?

HERALD: All the land of Sparta is up in arms—and our allies are up, too. We need Pellene.[6]

MAGISTRATE: What brought this trouble on you? A sudden Panic?

HERALD: No, Lampito started it and then all the other women in Sparta with one account chased their husbands out of their beds.

MAGISTRATE: How do you feel?

HERALD: Terrible. We walk around the city bent over like men lighting matches in a wind. For our women won't let us touch them until we all agree and make peace throughout Greece.

MAGISTRATE: This is a general conspiracy of the women; I see it now. Well, hurry back and tell the Spartans to send ambassadors here with full powers to arrange a truce. And I'll go tell the Council to choose ambassadors from here; I've got a little something here that will soon persuade them!

---

3. The permanent committee of the Council (Senate).   4. A god whose grossly phallic statue was set to guard orchards and gardens.   5. An encoding device. The papyrus was wrapped around the staff on a spiral and the message could be read only when the papyrus was wound around an exactly similar staff. 6. A city held by the Athenians and claimed by the Spartans; also the name of a famous Athenian prostitute.

HERALD: I'll fly there; for you've made an excellent suggestion.

[*The* HERALD *and the* MAGISTRATE *depart on opposite sides of the stage.*]

LEADER OF MEN: No beast or fire is harder than womankind to tame.

Nor is the spotted leopard so devoid of shame.

LEADER OF WOMEN: Knowing this, you dare provoke us to attack?

I'd be your steady friend, if you'd but take us back.

LEADER OF MEN: I'll never cease my hatred keen of womankind.

LEADER OF WOMEN: Just as you will. But now just let me help you find

That cloak you threw aside. You look so silly there

Without your clothes. Here, put it on and don't go bare.

LEADER OF MEN: That's very kind, and shows you're not entirely bad.

But I threw off my things when I was good and mad.

LEADER OF WOMEN: At last you seem a man, and won't be mocked, my
lad.

If you'd been nice to me, I'd take this little gnat

That's in your eye and pluck it out for you, like that.

LEADER OF MEN: So that's what's bothered me and bit my eye so long!

Please dig it out for me. I own that I've been wrong.

LEADER OF WOMEN: I'll do so, though you've been a most ill-natured brat.

Ye gods! See here! A huge and monstrous little gnat!

LEADER OF MEN: Oh, how that helps! For it was digging wells in me.

And now it's out, my tears can roll down hard and free.

LEADER OF WOMEN: Here, let me wipe them off, although you're such a
knave,

And kiss me.

LEADER OF MEN: No!

LEADER OF WOMEN: Whate'er you say, a kiss I'll have. [*She kisses him.*]

LEADER OF MEN: Oh, confound these women! They've a coaxing way about
them.

He was wise and never spoke a truer word, who said,

"We can't live with women, but we cannot live without them."

Now I'll make a truce with you. We'll fight no more: instead,

I will not injure you if you do me no wrong.

And now let's join our ranks and then begin a song.

COMBINED CHORUS: [*Singing*]

Athenians, we're not prepared,

To say a single ugly word

About our fellow-citizens.

Quite the contrary: we desire but to say and to do

Naught but good. Quite enough are the ills now on hand.

Men and women, be advised:

If anyone requires

Money—minae two or three—

We've got what he desires.

My purse is yours, on easy terms:

When Peace shall reappear,

Whate'er you've borrowed will be due.
  So speak up without fear.

You needn't pay me back, you see,
  If you can get a cent from me!

We're about to entertain
  Some foreign gentlemen;
We've soup and tender, fresh-killed pork.
  Come round to dine at ten.

Come early; wash and dress with care,
  And bring the children, too.
Then step right in, no "by your leave."
  We'll be expecting you.

Walk in as if you owned the place.
  You'll find the door—shut in your face!

[Enter a group of Spartan Ambassadors; they are in the same desperate condition as the Herald in the previous scene.]

LEADER OF CHORUS: Here come the envoys from Sparta, sprouting long beards and looking for all the world as if they were carrying pig-pens in front of them.
  Greetings, gentlemen of Sparta. Tell me, in what state have you come?

SPARTAN: Why waste words? You can plainly see what state we're come in!

LEADER OF CHORUS: Wow! You're in a pretty high-strung condition, and it seems to be getting worse.

SPARTAN: It's indescribable. Won't someone please arrange a peace for us— in any way you like.

LEADER OF CHORUS: Here come our own, native ambassadors, crouching like wrestlers and holding their clothes in front of them; this seems an athletic kind of malady.

[Enter several Athenian Ambassadors.]

ATHENIAN: Can anyone tell us where Lysistrata is? You see our condition.

LEADER OF CHORUS: Here's another case of the same complaint. Tell me, are the attacks worse in the morning?

ATHENIAN: No, we're always afflicted this way. If someone doesn't soon arrange this truce, you'd better not let me get my hands on—Cleisthenes!

LEADER OF CHORUS: If you're smart, you'll arrange your cloaks so none of the fellows who smashed the Hermae[7] can see you.

SPARTAN: Right you are; a very good suggestion.

ATHENIAN: Greetings, Spartan. We've suffered dreadful things.

SPARTAN: My dear fellow, we'd have suffered still worse if one of those fellows had seen us in this condition.

---

7. Small statues of the god Hermes equipped with phalluses, which stood at the door of most Athenian houses. Just before the great expedition left for Sicily, rioters (probably oligarchic conspirators opposed to the expedition) smashed many of these statues.

ATHENIAN: Well, gentlemen, we must get down to business. What's your errand here?

SPARTAN: We're ambassadors about peace.

ATHENIAN: Excellent; so are we. Only Lysistrata can arrange things for us; shall we summon her?

SPARTAN: Aye, and Lysistratus too, if you like.

LEADER OF CHORUS: No need to summon her, it seems. She's coming out of her own accord.

[*Enter* LYSISTRATA *accompanied by a statue of a nude female figure, which represents Reconciliation.*]

Hail, noblest of women; now must thou be
A judge shrewd and subtle, mild and severe,
Be sweet yet majestic: all manners employ.
The leaders of Hellas, caught by thy love-charms
Have come to thy judgment, their charges submitting.

LYSISTRATA: This is no difficult task, if one catch them still in amorous passion, before they've resorted to each other. But I'll soon find out. Where's Reconciliation? Go, first bring the Spartans here, and don't seize them rudely and violently, as our tactless husbands used to do, but as befits a woman, like an old, familiar friend; if they won't give you their hands, take them however you can. Then go fetch these Athenians here, taking hold of whatever they offer you. Now then, men of Sparta, stand here beside me, and you Athenians on the other side, and listen to my words.

I am a woman, it is true, but I have a mind; I'm not badly off in native wit, and by listening to my father and my elders, I've had a decent schooling.

Now I intend to give you a scolding which you both deserve. With one common font you worship at the same altars, just like brothers, at Olympia, at Thermopylae, at Delphi—how many more might I name, if time permitted;—and the Barbarians stand by waiting with their armies; yet you are destroying the men and towns of Greece.

ATHENIAN: Oh, this tension is killing me!

LYSISTRATA: And now, men of Sparta,—to turn to you—don't you remember how the Spartan Pericleidas came here once as a suppliant, and sitting at our altar, all pale with fear in his crimson cloak, begged us for an army?[8] For all Messene had attacked you and the god sent an earthquake too? Then Cimon went forth with four thousand hoplites and saved all Lacedaemon. Such was the aid you received from Athens, and now you lay waste the country which once treated you so well.

ATHENIAN: [*Hotly*] They're in the wrong, Lysistrata, upon my word, they are!

SPARTAN: [*Absently, looking at the statue of Reconciliation*] We're in the wrong. What hips! How lovely they are!

8. After a disastrous earthquake the Spartans were in great danger as a result of a rebellion of their serfs, the Helots. The Athenians under Cimon sent a large force of soldiers to help them (464 B.C.).

LYSISTRATA: Don't think I'm going to let you Athenians off. Don't you
remember how the Spartans came in arms when you were wearing the
rough, sheepskin cloak of slaves and slew the host of Thessalians, the
comrades and allies of Hippias?[9] Fighting with you on that day, alone
of all the Greeks, they set you free and instead of a sheepskin gave your
folk a handsome robe to wear.

SPARTAN: [*Looking at* LYSISTRATA] I've never seen a more distinguished
woman.

ATHENIAN: [*Looking at Reconciliation*] I've never seen a more voluptuous
body!

LYSISTRATA: Why then, with these many noble deeds to think of, do you
fight each other? Why don't you stop this villainy? Why not make peace?
Tell me, what prevents it?

SPARTAN: [*Waving vaguely at Reconciliation*] We're willing, if you're willing to give up your position on yonder flank.

LYSISTRATA: What position, my good man?

SPARTAN: Pylos; we've been panting for it for ever so long.

ATHENIAN: No, by God! You shan't have it!

LYSISTRATA: Let them have it, my friend.

ATHENIAN: Then, what shall we have to rouse things up?

LYSISTRATA: Ask for another place in exchange.

ATHENIAN: Well, let's see: first of all [*Pointing to various parts of Reconciliation's anatomy*] give us Echinus[1] here, this Maliac Inlet in back there,
and these two Megarian legs.

SPARTAN: No, by heavens! You can't have *everything*, you crazy fool!

LYSISTRATA: Let it go. Don't fight over a pair of legs.

ATHENIAN: [*Taking off his cloak*] I think I'll strip and do a little planting
now.

SPARTAN: [*Following suit*] And I'll just do a little fertilizing, by gosh!

LYSISTRATA: Wait until the truce is concluded. Now if you've decided on
this course, hold a conference and discuss the matter with your allies.

ATHENIAN: Allies? Don't be ridiculous! They're in the same state we are.
Won't all our allies want the same thing we do—to jump in bed with
their women?

SPARTAN: Ours will, I know.

ATHENIAN: Especially the Carystians,[2] by God!

LYSISTRATA: Very well. Now purify yourselves, that your wives may feast
and entertain you in the Acropolis; we've provisions by the basketful.
Exchange your oaths and pledges there, and then each of you may take
his wife and go home.

ATHENIAN: Let's go at once.

SPARTAN: Come on, where you will.

9. Hippias the tyrant had allowed exiled democrats to return to Attica but they had to stay outside the city
and wear sheepskins so that they could readily be identified. With the help of Spartan soldiers the exiles
and the people of Attica finally defeated the Thessalian troops of Hippias.   1. Like Pylos (on the "flank"
of the Peloponnese), these names are all double-barrelled references to territories in dispute in the war and
salient portions of the anatomy of Reconciliation.   2. The people of Carystus on the island of Euboea
were supposed to be of pre-Hellenic stock and therefore primitive and savage.

ATHENIAN: For God's sake, let's hurry!
  [*They all go into the Acropolis.*]
CHORUS: [*Singing.*]
    Whate'er I have of coverlets
      And robes of varied hue
    And golden trinkets,—without stint
      I offer them to you.

    Take what you will and bear it home,
      Your children to delight,
    Or if your girl's a Basket-maid;
      Just choose whate'er's in sight.

    There's naught within so well secured
      You cannot break the seal
    And bear it off; just help yourselves;
      No hesitation feel.

    But you'll see nothing, though you try,
      Unless you've sharper eyes than I!

    If anyone needs bread to feed
      A growing family,
    I've lots of wheat and full-grown loaves;
      So just apply to me.

    Let every poor man who desires
      Come round and bring a sack
    To fetch the grain; my slave is there
      To load it on his back.

    But don't come near my door, I say.
    Beware the dog, and stay away!
  [*An* ATHENIAN *enters carrying a torch; he knocks at the gate.*]
ATHENIAN: Open the door! [*To the* CHORUS, *which is clustered around the gate*] Make way, won't you! What are you hanging around for? Want me to singe you with this torch? [*To himself*] No; it's a stale trick, I won't do it! [*To the audience*] Still, if I've got to do it to please *you*, I suppose I'll have to take the trouble.
  [*A* SECOND ATHENIAN *comes out of the gate.*]
SECOND ATHENIAN: And I'll help you.
FIRST ATHENIAN: [*Waving his torch at the* CHORUS] Get out! Go bawl your heads off! Move on there, so the Spartans can leave in peace when the banquet's over.
  [*They brandish their torches until the* CHORUS *leaves the Orchestra.*]
SECOND ATHENIAN: I've never seen such a pleasant banquet: the Spartans are charming fellows, indeed they are! And we Athenians are very witty in our cups.
FIRST ATHENIAN: Naturally: for when we're sober we're never at our best. If the Athenians would listen to me, we'd always get a little tipsy on our

embassies. As things are now, we go to Sparta when we're sober and look around to stir up trouble. And then we don't hear what they say—and as for what they *don't* say, we have all sorts of suspicions. And then we bring back varying reports about the mission. But this time everything is pleasant; even if a man should sing the Telamon-song when he ought to sing "Cleitagoras,"[3] we'd praise him and swear it was excellent.

[*The two* CHORUSES *return, as a* CHORUS OF ATHENIANS *and a* CHORUS OF SPARTANS.]

Here they come back again. Go to the devil, you scoundrels!

SECOND ATHENIAN: Get out, I say! They're coming out from the feast.

[*Enter the Spartan and Athenian envoys, followed by* LYSISTRATA *and all the women.*]

SPARTAN: [*To one of his fellow-envoys*] My good fellow, take up your pipes; I want to do a fancy two-step and sing a jolly song for the Athenians.

ATHENIAN: Yes, do take your pipes, by all means. I'd love to see you dance.

SPARTAN: [*Singing and dancing with the* CHORUS OF SPARTANS]

These youths inspire
To song and dance, O Memory;
Stir up my Muse, to tell how we
And Athens' men, in our galleys clashing
At Artemisium,[4] 'gainst foemen dashing
    In godlike ire,
Conquered the Persian and set Greece free.

    Leonidas
Led on his valiant warriors
Whetting their teeth like angry boars.
Abundant foam on their lips was flow'ring,
A stream of sweat from their limbs was show'ring.
    The Persian was
Numberless as the sand on the shores.

O Huntress[5] who slayest the beasts in the glade,
O Virgin divine, hither come to our truce,
Unite us in bonds which all time will not loose.
Grant us to find in this treaty, we pray,
An unfailing source of true friendship today,
And all of our days, helping us to refrain
From weaseling tricks which bring war in their train.
    Then hither, come hither! O huntress maid.

LYSISTRATA: Come then, since all is fairly done, men of Sparta, lead away your wives, and you, Athenians, take yours. Let every man stand beside his wife, and every wife beside her man, and then, to celebrate our fortune, let's dance. And in the future, let's take care to avoid these misunderstandings.

---

3. At an Athenian banquet each guest in turn, when the time came to sing, was supposed to cap the singer before him by choosing an appropriate drinking song.   4. The indecisive naval battle that took place off the coast while Leonidas held the pass at Thermopylae.   5. Artemis.

CHORUS OF ATHENIANS: [*Singing and dancing*]
 Lead on the dances, your graces revealing.
 Call Artemis hither, call Artemis' twin,
 Leader of dances, Apollo the Healing,
 Kindly God—hither! let's summon him in!

 Nysian Bacchus call,
 Who with his Maenads, his eyes flashing fire,
 Dances, and last of all
 Zeus of the thunderbolt flaming, the Sire.
 And Hera in majesty,
 Queen of prosperity.

 Come, ye Powers who dwell above
 Unforgetting, our witnesses be
 Of Peace with bonds of harmonious love—
 The Peace which Cypris[6] has wrought for me.
 Alleluia! Io Paean!
 Leap in joy—hurrah! hurrah!
 'Tis victory—hurrah! hurrah!
 Euoi! Euoi! Euai! Euai!

LYSISTRATA: [*To the Spartans*] Come now, sing a new song to cap ours.
CHORUS OF SPARTANS: [*Singing and dancing*]
 Leaving Taygetus fair and renown'd,
 Muse of Laconia,[7] hither come:
 Amyclae's god in hymns resound,
 Athene of the Brazen Home,[8]
 And Castor and Pollux, Tyndareus' sons,
 Who sport where Eurotas[9] murmuring runs.

  On with the dance! Heia! Ho!
   All leaping along,
  Mantles a-swinging as we go!
  Of Sparta our song.

 There the holy chorus ever gladdens,
 There the beat of stamping feet,
 As our winsome fillies, lovely maidens,
 Dance, beside Eurotas' banks a-skipping,—
  Nimbly go to and fro
 Hast'ning, leaping feet in measures tripping,
 Like the Bacchae's revels, hair a-streaming.
 Leda's child,[1] divine and mild,
 Leads the holy dance, her fair face beaming.

  On with the dance! as your hand
   Presses the hair

6. Aphrodite. 7. The Spartan region. *Amyclae:* Part of Sparta. 8. The bronze-plated temple of Athena in Sparta. 9. The river of Sparta. 1. Helen (later of Troy).

         Streaming away unconfined.
            Leap in the air
          Light as the deer; footsteps resound
          Aiding our dance, beating the ground.

         Praise Athene, Maid divine, unrivalled in her might,
         Dweller in the Brazen Home, unconquered in the fight.
        [*All go out singing and dancing.*]

PLATO

429–347 B.C.

Socrates himself (see pp. 7–8) wrote nothing; we know what we do about him mainly from the writings of his pupil Plato, a philosophical and literary genius of the first rank. It is very difficult to distinguish between what Socrates actually said and what Plato put into his mouth, but there is general agreement that the *Apology*, which Plato wrote as a representation of what Socrates said at his trial, is the clearest picture we have of the historical Socrates. He is on trial for impiety and "corrupting the youth." He deals with these charges, but he also takes the opportunity to present a defense and explanation of the mission to which his life has been devoted.

The *Apology* is a defiant speech; Socrates rides roughshod over legal forms and seems to neglect no opportunity of outraging his listeners. But this defiance is not stupidity (as he hints himself, he could, if he had wished, have made a speech to please the court), nor is it a deliberate courting of martyrdom. It is the only course possible for him in the circumstances if he is not to betray his life's work, for Socrates knows as well as his accusers that what the Athenians really want is to silence him without having to take his life. What Socrates is making clear is that there is no such easy way out; he will have no part of any compromise that would restrict his freedom of speech or undermine his moral position. The speech is a sample of what the Athenians will have to put up with if they allow him to live; he will continue to be the gadfly that stings the sluggish horse. He will go on persuading them not to be concerned for their persons or their property, but first and chiefly to care about the improvement of the soul. He has spent his life denying the validity of worldly standards, and he will not accept them now.

He was declared guilty, and condemned to death. Though influential friends offered means of escape (and there is reason to think the Athenians would have been glad to see him go), Socrates refused to disobey the laws: in any case he had already, in his court speech, rejected the possibility of living in some foreign city.

The sentence was duly carried out. And in Plato's account of the execution we can see the calmness and kindness of a man who has led a useful life and who is secure in his faith that, contrary to appearances, "no evil can happen to a good man, either in life or after death."

The form of the *Apology* is dramatic: Plato re-creates the personality of his beloved teacher by presenting him as speaking directly to the reader. In most of the many books that he wrote in the course of a long life (429–347 B.C.) he continued to feature Socrates as the principal speaker in philosophical dialogues that explored the ethical and political problems of the age. These dialogues (the *Republic* the most famous) were preserved in their entirety and have exerted an enormous influence on Western thought ever since. Plato also founded a philosophical school, the Academy, in 385 B.C., and it remained active as a center of philosophical training and research until it was suppressed by the Roman emperor Justinian in A.D. 529. Plato came from an aristocratic Athenian family and as a young man thought of a political career; the execution of Socrates by the courts of democratic Athens disgusted him with politics and prompted his famous remark that there was no hope for the cities until the rulers became philosophers or the philosophers rulers. His attempts, however, to influence real rulers—the tyrant Dionysius of Syracuse in Sicily and, later, his son—ended in failure.

A. E. Taylor, *Plato, The Man and His Work* (1927), is a detailed analysis of the whole corpus of Platonic dialogues. G. M. A. Grube, *Plato's Thought* (1935), studies six principal themes of Platonic philosophy. R. S. Brumbaugh, *Plato for the Modern Age* (1962), presents a general introduction with stress on the historical background and an emphasis on the scientific and mathematical aspects of Plato's thought. On the importance of Socrates, see W. K. C. Guthrie, *A History of Greek Philosophy*, vol. 3 (1969), pp. 378–567.

The Apology of Socrates[1]

How you, O Athenians, have been affected by my accusers, I cannot tell; but I know that they almost made me forget who I was—so persuasively did they speak; and yet they have hardly uttered a word of truth. But of the many falsehoods told by them, there was one which quite amazed me;—I mean when they said that you should be upon your guard and not allow yourselves to be deceived by the force of my eloquence. To say this, when they were certain to be detected as soon as I opened my lips and proved myself to be anything but a great speaker, did indeed appear to me most shameless—unless by the force of eloquence they mean the force of truth; for if such is their meaning, I admit that I am eloquent. But in how different a way from theirs! Well, as I was saying, they have scarcely spoken the truth at all; but from me you shall hear the whole truth: not, however, delivered after their manner in a set oration duly ornamented with words and phrases. No, by heaven! but I shall use the words and arguments which occur to me at the moment; for I am confident in the justice of my cause: at my time of life I ought not to be appearing before you, O men of Athens, in the character of a juvenile orator—let no one expect it of me. And I must beg of you to grant me a favour:—If I defend myself in my accustomed manner, and you hear me using the words which I have been in the habit of using in the agora,[2] at the tables of the money-changers, or anywhere else, I would ask you not to be surprised, and not to interrupt me on this account. For I am more than seventy years of age, and appearing now for the first time in a court of law, I am quite a stranger to the language of the place; and therefore I would have you regard me as if I were really a stranger, whom you would excuse if he spoke in his native

1. Translated by Benjamin Jowett. "Apology" means "defense."   2. The marketplace.

tongue, and after the fashion of his country:—Am I making an unfair request of you? Never mind the manner, which may or may not be good; but think only of the truth of my words, and give heed to that: let the speaker speak truly and the judge decide justly.

And first, I have to reply to the older charges[3] and to my first accusers, and then I will go on to the later ones. For of old I have had many accusers, who have accused me falsely to you during many years; and I am more afraid of them than of Anytus and his associates, who are dangerous, too, in their own way. But far more dangerous are the others, who began when you were children, and took possession of your minds with their falsehoods, telling of one Socrates, a wise man, who speculated about the heaven above, and searched into the earth beneath, and made the worse appear the better cause.[4] The disseminators of this tale are the accusers whom I dread; for their hearers are apt to fancy that such enquirers do not believe in the existence of the gods. And they are many, and their charges against me are of ancient date, and they were made by them in the days when you were more impressible than you are now—in childhood, or it may have been in youth—and the cause when heard went by default, for there was none to answer. And hardest of all, I do not know and cannot tell the names of my accusers; unless in the chance case of a Comic poet.[5] All who from envy and malice have persuaded you—some of them having first convinced themselves—all this class of men are most difficult to deal with; for I cannot have them up here, and cross-examine them, and therefore I must simply fight with shadows in my own defence, and argue when there is no one who answers. I will ask you then to assume with me, as I was saying, that my opponents are of two kinds; one recent, the other ancient: and I hope that you will see the propriety[6] of my answering the latter first, for these accusations you heard long before the others, and much oftener.

Well, then, I must make my defence, and endeavor to clear away, in a short time, a slander which has lasted a long time. May I succeed, if to succeed be for my good and yours, or likely to avail me in my cause! The task is not an easy one; I quite understand the nature of it. And so leaving the event with God, in obedience to the law I will now make my defence.

I will begin at the beginning, and ask what is the accusation which has given rise to the slander of me, and in fact has encouraged Meletus to prefer this charge against me. Well, what do the slanderers say? They shall

---

3. Socrates had been the object of much criticism and satire for many years before the trial. He here disregards legal forms and announces that he will deal first with the prejudices that lie behind the formal charge that has been brought against him.   4. He was accused by some of his enemies of being a materialist philosopher who speculated about the physical nature of the universe, and by others of being one of the Sophists, professional teachers of rhetoric and other subjects, many of whom taught methods that were more effective than honest.   5. He is referring to the poet Aristophanes, whose play *The Clouds* (produced in 423 B.C.) is a broad satire on Socrates and his associates, and a good example of the prejudice Socrates is dealing with, for it presents him propounding fantastic theories about matter and religion, and teaching students how to avoid payment of debts.   6. He says this with his tongue in his cheek, for he is actually paying no attention to legal propriety. This becomes clearer below, where he goes so far as to paraphrase the actual terms of the indictment and put into the mouths of his accusers the prejudice he claims is the basis of their action.

be my prosecutors, and I will sum up their words in an affidavit: 'Socrates is an evil-doer, and a curious person, who searches into things under the earth, and in heaven, and he makes the worse appear the better cause; and he teaches the aforesaid doctrines to others.' Such is the nature of the accusation: it is just what you have yourselves seen in the comedy of Aristophanes, who has introduced a man whom he calls Socrates, going about and saying that he walks in air,[7] and talking a deal of nonsense concerning matters of which I do not pretend to know either much or little—not that I mean to speak disparagingly of any one who is a student of natural philosophy. I should be very sorry if Meletus could bring so grave a charge against me. But the simple truth is, O Athenians, that I have nothing to do with physical speculations. Very many of those here present are witnesses to the truth of this, and to them I appeal. Speak then, you who have heard me, and tell your neighbours whether any of you have ever known me hold forth in few words or in many upon such matters. . . . You hear their answer. And from what they say of this part of the charge you will be able to judge of the truth of the rest.

As little foundation is there for the report that I am a teacher, and take money;[8] this accusation has no more truth in it than the other. Although, if a man were really able to instruct mankind, to receive money for giving instruction would, in my opinion, be an honour to him. There is Gorgias of Leontium, and Prodicus of Ceos, and Hippias of Elis,[9] who go the round of the cities, and are able to persuade the young men to leave their own citizens by whom they might be taught for nothing, and come to them whom they not only pay, but are thankful if they may be allowed to pay them. There is at this time a Parian philosopher[1] residing in Athens, of whom I have heard; and I came to hear of him in this way:—I came across a man who has spent a world of money on the Sophists, Callias, the son of Hipponicus, and knowing that he had sons, I asked him: 'Callias,' I said, 'if your two sons were foals or calves, there would be no difficulty in finding some one to put over them; we should hire a trainer of horses, or a farmer probably, who would improve and perfect them in their own proper virtue and excellence; but as they are human beings, whom are you thinking of placing over them? Is there any one who understands human and political virtue? You must have thought about the matter, for you have sons; is there any one?' 'There is,' he said. 'Who is he?' said I; 'and of what country? and what does he charge?' 'Evenus the Parian,' he replied; 'he is the man, and his charge is five minae.'[2] Happy is Evenus, I said to myself;

---

7. In the comedy of Aristophanes Socrates first appears suspended in a basket, and when asked what he is doing replies, "I walk in air and contemplate the sun." He explains that only by suspending his intelligence can he investigate celestial matters.   8. Unlike Socrates, who beggared himself in the quest for truth, the professional teachers made great fortunes. The wealth of Protagoras, the first of the Sophists who demanded fees, was proverbial.   9. From Elis, in the Peloponnese; he claimed to be able to teach any and all subjects, including handicrafts. *Gorgias:* From Leontium in Sicily; he was famous as the originator of an antithetical, ornate prose style which had great influence. *Prodicus:* From Ceos, an island in the Aegean; he taught rhetoric and was well known for his pioneering grammatical studies.   1. From Paros, a small island in the Aegean.   2. A relatively moderate sum; Protagoras is said to have charged a hundred minae for a course of instruction.

if he really has this wisdom, and teaches at such a moderate charge. Had I the same, I should have been very proud and conceited; but the truth is that I have no knowledge of the kind.

I dare say, Athenians, that some one among you will reply, 'Yes, Socrates, but what is the origin of these accusations which are brought against you; there must have been something strange which you have been doing? All these rumours and this talk about you would never have arisen if you had been like other men: tell us, then, what is the cause of them, for we should be sorry to judge hastily of you.' Now I regard this as a fair challenge, and I will endeavour to explain to you the reason why I am called wise and have such an evil fame. Please to attend then. And although some of you may think that I am joking, I declare that I will tell you the entire truth. Men of Athens, this reputation of mine has come of a certain sort of wisdom which I possess. If you ask me what kind of wisdom, I reply, wisdom such as may perhaps be attained by man, for to that extent I am inclined to believe that I am wise; whereas the persons of whom I was speaking have a superhuman wisdom, which I may fail to describe, because I have it not myself; and he who says that I have, speaks falsely, and is taking away my character. And here, O men of Athens, I must beg you not to interrupt me, even if I seem to say something extravagant. For the word which I will speak is not mine. I will refer you to a witness who is worthy of credit; that witness shall be the God of Delphi[3]—he will tell you about my wisdom, if I have any, and of what sort it is. You must have known Chaerephon; he was early a friend of mine, and also a friend of yours, for he shared in the recent exile of the people, and returned with you.[4] Well, Chaerephon, as you know, was very impetuous in all his doings, and he went to Delphi and boldly asked the oracle to tell him whether— as I was saying, I must beg you not to interrupt—he asked the oracle to tell him whether any one was wiser than I was, and the Pythian prophetess answered, that there was no man wiser. Chaerephon is dead himself; but his brother, who is in court, will confirm the truth of what I am saying.

Why do I mention this? Because I am going to explain to you why I have such an evil name. When I heard the answer, I said to myself, What can the god mean? and what is the interpretation of his riddle? for I know that I have no wisdom, small or great. What then can he mean when he says that I am the wisest of men? And yet he is a god, and cannot lie; that would be against his nature. After long consideration, I thought of a method of trying the question. I reflected that if I could only find a man wiser than myself, then I might go to the god with a refutation in my hand. I should say to him, 'Here is a man who is wiser than I am; but you said that I was the wisest.' Accordingly I went to one who had the reputation of wisdom, and observed him—his name I need not mention; he was a politician whom I selected for examination—and the result was as follows: When I

3. The oracle of Apollo at Delphi.   4. One of Socrates's closest associates; he appears in Aristophanes's comedy. Chaerephon was an enthusiastic enough partisan of the democratic regime to have to go into exile in 404 B.C. when the Thirty Tyrants carried on an oligarchic reign of terror. The phrase "the recent exile of the people" refers to the exile into which all known champions of democracy were forced until the democracy was restored.

began to talk with him, I could not help thinking that he was not really wise, although he was thought wise by many, and still wiser by himself; and thereupon I tried to explain to him that he thought himself wise, but was not really wise; and the consequence was that he hated me, and his enmity was shared by several who were present and heard me. So I left him, saying to myself, as I went away: Well, although I do not suppose that either of us knows anything really beautiful and good, I am better off than he is,—for he knows nothing, and thinks that he knows; I neither know nor think that I know. In this latter particular, then, I seem to have slightly the advantage of him. Then I went to another who had still higher pretensions to wisdom, and my conclusion was exactly the same. Whereupon I made another enemy of him, and of many others besides him.

Then I went to one man after another, being not unconscious of the enmity which I provoked, and I lamented and feared this: But necessity was laid upon me,—the word of God, I thought, ought to be considered first. And I said to myself, Go I must to all who appear to know, and find out the meaning of the oracle. And I swear to you, Athenians, by the dog I swear![5]—for I must tell you the truth—the result of my mission was just this: I found that the men most in repute were all but the most foolish; and that others less esteemed were really wiser and better. I will tell you the tale of my wanderings and of the 'Herculean' labours, as I may call them, which I endured only to find at last the oracle irrefutable. After the politicians, I went to the poets; tragic, dithyrambic,[6] and all sorts. And there, I said to myself, you will be instantly detected; now you will find out that you are more ignorant than they are. Accordingly, I took them some of the most elaborate passages in their own writings, and asked what was the meaning of them—thinking that they would teach me something. Will you believe me? I am almost ashamed to confess the truth, but I must say that there is hardly a person present who would not have talked better about their poetry than they did themselves. Then I knew that not by wisdom do poets write poetry, but by a sort of genius and inspiration; they are like diviners or soothsayers who also say many fine things, but do not understand the meaning of them.[7] The poets appeared to me to be much in the same case; and I further observed that upon the strength of their poetry they believed themselves to be the wisest of men in other things in which they were not wise. So I departed, conceiving myself to be superior to them for the same reason that I was superior to the politicians.

At last I went to the artisans, for I was conscious that I knew nothing at all, as I may say, and I was sure that they knew many fine things; and here I was not mistaken, for they did know many things of which I was ignorant, and in this they certainly were wiser than I was. But I observed that even the good artisans fell into the same error as the poets;—because they were good workmen they thought that they also knew all sorts of high matters, and this defect in them overshadowed their wisdom; and therefore I asked

5. A euphemistic oath (compare, "by George").   6. The dithyramb was a short performance by a chorus, produced, like tragedy, at state expense and at a public festival.   7. For a fuller exposition of this famous theory of poetic inspiration see Plato's *Ion*.

myself on behalf of the oracle, whether I would like to be as I was, neither having their knowledge nor their ignorance, or like them in both; and I made answer to myself and to the oracle that I was better off as I was.

This inquisition has led to my having many enemies of the worst and most dangerous kind, and has given occasion also to many calumnies. And I am called wise, for my hearers always imagine that I myself possess the wisdom which I find wanting in others: but the truth is, O men of Athens, that God only is wise; and by his answer he intends to show that the wisdom of men is worth little or nothing; he is not speaking of Socrates, he is only using my name by way of illustration, as if he said, He, O men, is the wisest, who, like Socrates, knows that his wisdom is in truth worth nothing. And so I go about the world, obedient to the god, and search and make enquiry into the wisdom of any one, whether citizen or stranger, who appears to be wise; and if he is not wise, then in vindication of the oracle I show him that he is not wise; and my occupation quite absorbs me, and I have no time to give either to any public matter of interest or to any concern of my own, but I am in utter poverty by reason of my devotion to the god.

There is another thing:—young men of the richer classes, who have not much to do, come about me of their own accord; they like to hear the pretenders examined, and they often imitate me, and proceed to examine others; there are plenty of persons, as they quickly discover, who think that they know something, but really know little or nothing; and then those who are examined by them instead of being angry with themselves are angry with me: This confounded Socrates, they say; this villainous misleader of youth!—and then if somebody asks them, Why, what evil does he practice or teach? they do not know, and cannot tell; but in order that they may not appear to be at a loss, they repeat the ready-made charges which are used against all philosophers about teaching things up in the clouds and under the earth, and having no gods, and making the worse appear the better cause; for they do not like to confess that their pretence of knowledge has been detected—which is the truth; and as they are numerous and ambitious and energetic, and are drawn up in battle array and have persuasive tongues, they have filled your ears with their loud and inveterate calumnies. And this is the reason why my three accusers, Meletus and Anytus and Lycon, have set upon me; Meletus, who has a quarrel with me on behalf of the poets; Anytus, on behalf of the craftsmen and politicians; Lycon, on behalf of the rhetoricians[8]: and as I said at the beginning, I cannot expect to get rid of such a mass of calumny all in a moment. And this, O men of Athens, is the truth and the whole truth; I have concealed nothing, I have dissembled nothing. And yet, I know that my plainness of speech makes them hate me, and what is their hatred but a proof that I am speaking the truth?—Hence has arisen the prejudice against me; and this is the reason of it, as you will find out either in this or in any future enquiry.

---

8. The three accusers. Anytus was a prominent politician; the connection of Meletus with poetry and of Lycon with rhetoric is known only from this passage.

I have said enough in my defence against the first class of my accusers; I turn to the second class. They are headed by Meletus, that good man and true lover of his country, as he calls himself. Against these, too, I must try to make a defence:—Let their affidavit be read: it contains something of this kind: It says that Socrates is a doer of evil, who corrupts the youth; and who does not believe in the gods of the state, but has other new divinities of his own.[9] Such is the charge; and now let us examine the particular counts. He says that I am a doer of evil, and corrupt the youth; but I say, O men of Athens, that Meletus is a doer of evil, in that he pretends to be in earnest when he is only in jest, and is so eager to bring men to trial from a pretended zeal and interest about matters in which he really never had the smallest interest. And the truth of this I will endeavour to prove to you.

Come hither, Meletus, and let me ask a question of you.[1] You think a great deal about the improvement of youth?

Yes, I do.

Tell the judges, then, who is their improver; for you must know, as you have taken the pains to discover their corrupter, and are citing and accusing me before them. Speak, then, and tell the judges who their improver is.—Observe, Meletus, that you are silent, and have nothing to say. But is not this rather disgraceful, and a very considerable proof of what I was saying, that you have no interest in the matter? Speak up, friend, and tell us who their improver is.

The laws.

But that, my good sir, is not my meaning. I want to know who the person is, who, in the first place, knows the laws.

The judges,[2] Socrates, who are present in court.

What, do you mean to say, Meletus, that they are able to instruct and improve youth?

Certainly they are.

What, all of them, or some only and not others?

All of them.

By the goddess Here,[3] that is good news! There are plenty of improvers, then. And what do you say of the audience,—do they improve them?

Yes, they do.

And the senators?[4]

Yes, the senators improve them.

9. The precise meaning of the charge is not clear. As this translation indicates, the Greek words may mean "new divinities," with a reference to Socrates's famous inner voice, which from time to time warned him against action on which he had decided. Or the words may mean "practicing strange rites," though this charge is difficult to understand. In any case, the importance of the phrase is that it implies religious belief of some sort and can later be used against Meletus when he loses his head and accuses Socrates of atheism. 1. Socrates avails himself of his right to interrogate the accuser. He is, of course, a master in this type of examination, for he has spent his life in the practice of puncturing inflated pretensions and exposing logical contradictions in the arguments of his adversaries. He is here fulfilling his earlier promise to defend himself in the manner to which he has been accustomed and use the words which he has been in the habit of using in the agora (p. 807). 2. The jury. There was no judge in the Athenian law court. The Athenian jury was large; in this trial it probably consisted of five hundred citizens. In the following questions Socrates forces Meletus to extend the capacity to improve the youth to successively greater numbers, until it appears that the entire citizen body is a good influence and Socrates the only bad one. Meletus is caught in the trap of his own demagogic appeal. 3. Hera. 4. The members of the standing council of the assembly, five hundred in number.

But perhaps the members of the assembly[5] corrupt them?— or do they too improve them?

They improve them.

Then every Athenian improves and elevates them; all with the exception of myself; and I alone am their corrupter? Is that what you affirm?

That is what I stoutly affirm.

I am very unfortunate if you are right. But suppose I ask you a question: How about horses?[6] Does one man do them harm and all the world good? Is not the exact opposite the truth? One man is able to do them good, or at least not many;—the trainer of horses, that is to say, does them good, and others who have to do with them rather injure them? Is not that true, Meletus, of horses, or any other animals? Most assuredly it is; whether you and Anytus say yes or no. Happy indeed would be the condition of youth if they had one corrupter only, and all the rest of the world were their improvers. But you, Meletus, have sufficiently shown that you never had a thought about the young: your carelessness is seen in your not caring about the very things which you bring against me.

And now, Meletus, I will ask you another question—by Zeus I will: Which is better, to live among bad citizens, or among good ones? Answer, friend, I say; the question is one which may be easily answered. Do not the good do their neighbours good, and the bad do them evil?

Certainly.

And is there any one who would rather be injured than benefited by those who live with him? Answer, my good friend, the law requires you to answer—does any one like to be injured?

Certainly not.

And when you accuse me of corrupting and deteriorating the youth, do you allege that I corrupt them intentionally or unintentionally?

Intentionally, I say.

But you have just admitted that the good do their neighbours good, and evil do them evil. Now, is that a truth which your superior wisdom has recognized thus early in life, and am I, at my age, in such darkness and ignorance as not to know that if a man with whom I have to live is corrupted by me, I am very likely to be harmed by him; and yet I corrupt him, and intentionally, too—so you say, although neither I nor any other human being is ever likely to be convinced by you. But either I do not corrupt them, or I corrupt them unintentionally; and on either view of the case you lie. If my offence is unintentional, the law has no cognizance of unintentional offences: you ought to have taken me privately, and warned and admonished me; for if I had been better advised, I should have left off doing what I only did unintentionally—no doubt I should; but you would have nothing to say to me and refused to teach me. And now you bring me up in this court, which is not a place of instruction, but of punishment.

It will be very clear to you, Athenians, as I was saying, that Meletus has

---

5. The sovereign body in the Athenian constitution, theoretically an assembly of the whole citizen body.
6. This simple analogy is typical of the Socratic method; he is still defending himself in his accustomed manner.

no care at all, great or small, about the matter. But still I should like to know, Meletus, in what I am affirmed to corrupt the young. I suppose you mean, as I infer from your indictment, that I teach them not to acknowledge the gods which the state acknowledges, but some other new divinities or spiritual agencies in their stead. These are the lessons by which I corrupt the youth, as you say.

Yes, that I say emphatically.

Then, by the gods, Meletus, of whom we are speaking, tell me and the court, in somewhat plainer terms, what you mean! for I do not as yet understand whether you affirm that I teach other men to acknowledge some gods, and therefore that I do believe in gods, and am not an entire atheist—this you do not lay to my charge,—but only you say that they are not the same gods which the city recognizes—the charge is that they are different gods. Or, do you mean that I am an atheist simply, and a teacher of atheism?

I mean the latter—that you are a complete atheist.[7]

What an extraordinary statement! Why do you think so, Meletus? Do you mean that I do not believe in the godhead of the sun or moon, like other men?

I assure you, judges, that he does not: for he says that the sun is stone, and the moon earth.[8]

Friend Meletus, you think that you are accusing Anaxagoras: and you have but a bad opinion of the judges, if you fancy them illiterate to such a degree as not to know that these doctrines are found in the books of Anaxagoras the Clazomenian,[9] which are full of them. And so, forsooth, the youth are said to be taught them by Socrates, when [they can buy the book in the theater district for one drachma at most][1] and laugh at Socrates if he pretends to father these extraordinary views. And so, Meletus, you really think that I do not believe in any god?

I swear by Zeus that you believe absolutely in none at all.

Nobody will believe you, Meletus, and I am pretty sure that you do not believe yourself. I cannot help thinking, men of Athens, that Meletus is reckless and impudent, and that he has written this indictment in a spirit of mere wantonness and youthful bravado. Has he not compounded a riddle, thinking to try me? He said to himself:—I shall see whether the wise Socrates will discover my facetious contradiction, or whether I shall be able to deceive him and the rest of them. For he certainly does appear to me to contradict himself in the indictment as much as if he said that Socrates is guilty of not believing in the gods, and yet of believing in them— but this is not like a person who is in earnest.

7. Meletus jumps at the most damaging charge, and falls into the trap.   8. Meletus falls back on the old prejudices which Socrates claims are the real indictment against him.   9. A fifth-century philosopher from Clazomenae in Asia Minor. He was an intimate friend of Pericles, but this did not save him from indictment for impiety. He was condemned, and forced to leave Athens. He is famous for his doctrine that matter was set in motion and ordered by Intelligence (Nous), which, however, did not create it. He also declared that the sun was a mass of red-hot metal larger than the Peloponnese, and that there were hills and ravines on the moon.   1. The translator took this to mean that the doctrines of Anaxagoras were reflected in the works of the tragic poets; the bracketed passage reflects what is now the generally accepted interpretation.

I should like you, O men of Athens, to join me in examining what I conceive to be his inconsistency; and do you, Meletus, answer. And I must remind the audience of my request that they would not make a disturbance[2] if I speak in my accustomed manner:

Did ever man, Meletus, believe in the existence of human things, and not of human beings? . . . I wish, men of Athens, that he would answer, and not be always trying to get up an interruption. Did ever any man believe in horsemanship, and not in horses? or in flute-playing, and not in flute-players? No, my friend; I will answer to you and to the court, as you refuse to answer for yourself. There is no man who ever did. But now please to answer the next question: Can a man believe in spiritual and divine agencies, and not in spirits or demigods?

He cannot.

How lucky I am to have extracted that answer, by the assistance of the court! But then you swear in the indictment that I teach and believe in divine or spiritual agencies (new or old, no matter for that); at any rate, I believe in spiritual agencies,—so you say and swear in the affidavit; and yet if I believe in divine beings, how can I help believing in spirits or demigods;—must I not? To be sure I must; and therefore I may assume that your silence gives consent. Now what are spirits or demigods? are they not either gods or the sons of gods?

Certainly they are.

But this is what I call the facetious riddle invented by you: the demigods or spirits are gods, and you say first that I do not believe in gods, and then again that I do believe in gods; that is, if I believe in demigods. For if the demigods are the illegitimate sons of gods, whether by the nymphs or by any other mothers, of whom they are said to be the sons—what human being will ever believe that there are no gods if they are the sons of gods? You might as well affirm the existence of mules, and deny that of horses and asses. Such nonsense, Meletus, could only have been intended by you to make trial of me. You have put this into the indictment because you had nothing real of which to accuse me. But no one who has a particle of understanding will ever be convinced by you that the same men can believe in divine and superhuman things, and yet not believe that there are gods and demigods and heroes.

I have said enough in answer to the charge of Meletus: any elaborate defence is unnecessary; but I know only too well how many are the enmities which I have incurred, and this is what will be my destruction if I am destroyed;—not Meletus, nor yet Anytus, but the envy and detraction of the world, which has been the death of many good men, and will probably be the death of many more; there is no danger of my being the last of them.

Some one will say: And are you not ashamed, Socrates, of a course of life which is likely to bring you to an untimely end? To him I may fairly

---

2. The disturbance is presumably due to the frustration of the enemies of Socrates, who see him assuming complete control of the proceedings and turning them into a street-corner argument of the type in which he is invincible.

answer: There you are mistaken: a man who is good for anything ought not to calculate the chance of living or dying; he ought only to consider whether in doing anything he is doing right or wrong—acting the part of a good man or of a bad. Whereas, upon your view, the heroes who fell at Troy were not good for much, and the son of Thetis[3] above all, who altogether despised danger in comparison with disgrace; and when he was so eager to slay Hector, his goddess mother said to him, that if he avenged his companion Patroclus, and slew Hector, he would die himself—'Fate,' she said, in these or the like words, 'waits for you next after Hector'; he, receiving this warning, utterly despised danger and death, and instead of fearing them, feared rather to live in dishonour, and not to avenge his friend. 'Let me die forthwith,' he replies, 'and be avenged of my enemy, rather than abide here by the beaked ships, a laughing-stock and a burden of the earth.' Had Achilles any thought of death and danger? For wherever a man's place is, whether the place which he has chosen or that in which he has been placed by a commander, there he ought to remain in hour of danger; he should not think of death or of anything but of disgrace. And this, O men of Athens, is a true saying.

Strange, indeed, would be my conduct, O men of Athens, if I who, when I was ordered by the generals whom you chose to command me at Potidaea and Amphipolis and Delium,[4] remained where they placed me, like any other man, facing death—if now, when, as I conceive and imagine, God orders me to fulfil the philosopher's mission of searching into myself and other men, I were to desert my post through fear of death, or any other fear; that would indeed be strange, and I might justly be arraigned in court for denying the existence of the gods, if I disobeyed the oracle because I was afraid of death, fancying that I was wise when I was not wise. For the fear of death is indeed the pretence of wisdom, and not real wisdom, being a pretence of knowing the unknown; and no one knows whether death, which men in their fear apprehend to be the greatest evil, may not be the greatest good. Is not this ignorance of a disgraceful sort, the ignorance which is the conceit that man knows what he does not know? And in this respect only I believe myself to differ from men in general, and may perhaps claim to be wiser than they are:—that whereas I know but little of the world below,[5] I do not suppose that I know: but I do know that injustice and disobedience to a better, whether God or man, is evil and dishonourable, and I will never fear or avoid a possible good rather than a certain evil. And therefore if you let me go now, and are not convinced by Anytus, who said that since I had been prosecuted I must be put to death (or if not that I ought never to have been prosecuted at all); and that if I escape now, your sons will all be utterly ruined by listening to my words—if you say to me, Socrates, this time we will not mind Anytus, and you shall be let off, but upon one condition, that you are not to enquire and speculate in this

3. Achilles. See the *Iliad*, XVIII. 110ff.   4. Three of the battles in the Peloponnesian War in which Socrates had fought as an infantryman. The battle at Potidaea (in northern Greece) occurred in 432 B.C. (For a fuller account of Socrates' conduct there see Plato's *Symposium*.) The date of the battle at Amphipolis (in northern Greece) is uncertain. The battle at Delium (in central Greece) took place in 424 B.C.
    5. The next world. The dead were supposed to carry on a sort of existence below the earth.

way any more, and that if you are caught doing so again you shall die:—if this was the condition on which you let me go, I should reply: Men of Athens, I honour and love you; but I shall obey God rather than you, and while I have life and strength I shall never cease from the practice and teaching of philosophy, exhorting any one whom I meet and saying to him after my manner: You, my friend,—a citizen of the great and mighty and wise city of Athens,—are you not ashamed of heaping up the greatest amount of money and honour and reputation, and caring so little about wisdom and truth and the greatest improvement of the soul, which you never regard or heed at all? And if the person with whom I am arguing, says: Yes, but I do care; then I do not leave him or let him go at once; but I proceed to interrogate and examine and cross-examine him, and if I think that he has no virtue in him, but only says that he has, I reproach him with undervaluing the greater, and overvaluing the less. And I shall repeat the same words to every one whom I meet, young and old, citizen and alien, but especially to the citizens, inasmuch as they are my brethren. For know that this is the command of God; and I believe that no greater good has ever happened in the state than my service to the God. For I do nothing but go about persuading you all, old and young alike, not to take thought for your persons or your properties, but first and chiefly to care about the greatest improvement of the soul. I tell you that virtue is not given by money, but that from virtue comes money and every other good of man, public as well as private. This is my teaching, and if this is the doctrine which corrupts the youth, I am a mischievous person. But if any one says that this is not my teaching, he is speaking an untruth. Wherefore, O men of Athens, I say to you, do as Anytus bids or not as Anytus bids, and either acquit me or not; but whichever you do, understand that I shall never alter my ways, not even if I have to die many times.

Men of Athens, do not interrupt,[6] but hear me; there was an understanding between us that you should hear me to the end: I have something more to say, at which you may be inclined to cry out; but I believe that to hear me will be good for you, and therefore I beg that you will not cry out. I would have you know, that if you kill such an one as I am, you will injure yourselves more than you will injure me. Nothing will injure me, not Meletus nor yet Anytus—they cannot, for a bad man is not permitted to injure a better than himself. I do not deny that Anytus may, perhaps, kill him, or drive him into exile, or deprive him of civil rights; and he may imagine, and others may imagine, that he is inflicting a great injury upon him: but there I do not agree. For the evil of doing as he is doing—the evil of unjustly taking away the life of another—is greater far.

And now, Athenians, I am not going to argue for my own sake, as you may think, but for yours, that you may not sin against the God by condemning me, who am his gift to you. For if you kill me you will not easily find a successor to me, who, if I may use such a ludicrous figure of speech, am a sort of gadfly, given to the state by God; and the state is a great and

---

6. The disturbance this time is presumably more general, for Socrates is defying the court and the people.

noble steed who is tardy in his motions owing to his very size, and requires to be stirred into life. I am that gadfly which God has attached to the state, and all day long and in all places am always fastening upon you, arousing and persuading and reproaching you. You will not easily find another like me, and therefore I would advise you to spare me. I dare say that you may feel out of temper (like a person who is suddenly awakened from sleep), and you think that you might easily strike me dead as Anytus advises, and then you would sleep on for the remainder of your lives, unless God in his care of you sent you another gadfly. When I say that I am given to you by God, the proof of my mission is this:—if I had been like other men, I should not have neglected all my own concerns or patiently seen the neglect of them during all these years, and have been doing yours, coming to you individually like a father or elder brother, exhorting you to regard virtue; such conduct, I say, would be unlike human nature. If I had gained anything, or if my exhortations had been paid, there would have been some sense in my doing so; but now, as you will perceive, not even the impudence of my accusers dares to say that I have ever exacted or sought pay of any one; of that they have no witness. And I have a sufficient witness to the truth of what I say—my poverty.

Some one may wonder why I go about in private giving advice and busying myself with the concerns of others, but do not venture to come forward in public and advise the state. I will tell you why. You have heard me speak at sundry times and in divers places of an oracle or sign which comes to me, and is the divinity which Meletus ridicules in the indictment. This sign, which is a kind of voice, first began to come to me when I was a child; it always forbids but never commands me to do anything which I am going to do. This is what deters me from being a politician. And rightly, as I think. For I am certain, O men of Athens, that if I had engaged in politics, I should have perished long ago, and done no good either to you or to myself. And do not be offended at my telling you the truth: for the truth is, that no man who goes to war with you or any other multitude, honestly striving against the many lawless and unrighteous deeds which are done in a state, will save his life; he who will fight for the right, if he would live even for a brief space, must have a private station and not a public one.

I can give you convincing evidence of what I say, not words only, but what you value far more—actions. Let me relate to you a passage of my own life which will prove to you that I should never have yielded to injustice from any fear of death, and that 'as I should have refused to yield' I must have died at once. I will tell you a tale of the courts, not very interesting perhaps, but nevertheless true. The only office of state which I ever held, O men of Athens, was that of senator: the tribe Antiochis,[7] which is my tribe, had the presidency at the trial of the generals who had not taken

---

7. The Council of the Five Hundred consisted of fifty members of each of the ten tribes into which the population was divided. (Socrates' tribe, like the other nine, was named after a mythical hero, in this case Antiochus.) Each tribal delegation acted as a standing committee of the whole body for a part of the year. The members of this standing committee were called Prytanes. In acting as a member of the council Socrates was not "engaging in politics" but simply fulfilling his duty as a citizen when called upon.

up the bodies of the slain after the battle of Arginusae;[8] and you proposed to try them in a body, contrary to law, as you all thought afterwards; but at the time I was the only one of the Prytanes who was opposed to the illegality, and I gave my vote against you; and when the orators threatened to impeach and arrest me, and you called and shouted, I made up my mind that I would run the risk, having law and justice with me, rather than take part in your injustice because I feared imprisonment and death. This happened in the days of the democracy.[9] But when the oligarchy of the Thirty was in power,[1] they sent for me and four others into the rotunda, and bade us bring Leon the Salaminian from Salamis,[2] as they wanted to put him to death. This was a specimen of the sort of commands which they were always giving with the view of implicating as many as possible in their crimes; and then I showed, not in word only but in deed, that, if I may be allowed to use such an expression, I cared not a straw for death, and that my great and only care was lest I should do an unrighteous or unholy thing. For the strong arm of that oppressive power did not frighten me into doing wrong; and when we came out of the rotunda the other four went to Salamis and fetched Leon, but I went quietly home. For which I might have lost my life, had not the power of the Thirty shortly afterwards come to an end. And many will witness to my words.

Now do you really imagine that I could have survived all these years, if I had led a public life, supposing that like a good man I had always maintained the right and had made justice, as I ought, the first thing? No indeed, men of Athens, neither I nor any other man. But I have been always the same in all my actions, public as well as private, and never have I yielded any base compliance to those who are slanderously termed my disciples, or to any other. Not that I have any regular disciples. But if any one likes to come and hear me while I am pursuing my mission, whether he be young or old, he is not excluded. Nor do I converse only with those who pay; but any one, whether he be rich or poor, may ask and answer me and listen to my words; and whether he turns out to be a bad man or a good one, neither result can be justly imputed to me; for I never taught or professed to teach him anything. And if any one says that he has ever learned or heard anything from me in private which all the world has not heard, let me tell you that he is lying.

But I shall be asked, Why do people delight in continually conversing with you? I have told you already, Athenians, the whole truth about this matter: they like to hear the cross-examination of the pretenders to wisdom; there is amusement in it. Now this duty of cross-examining other men has

---

8. An Athenian naval victory over Sparta, in 406 B.C. The Athenian commanders failed to pick up the bodies of a large number of Athenians whose ships had been destroyed. Whether they were prevented from doing so by the wind or simply neglected this duty in the excitement of victory is not known; in any case, the Athenian population suspected the worst and put all ten generals on trial, not in a court of law but before the assembly. The generals were tried not individually, but in a group, and condemned to death. The six who had returned to Athens were executed, among them a son of Pericles.   9. Socrates gives two instances of his political actions, one under the democracy and one under the Thirty Tyrants. In both cases, he was in opposition to the government.   1. In 404 B.C., with Spartan backing the Thirty Tyrants (as they were known to their enemies) ruled for eight months over a defeated Athens. Prominent among them was Critias, who had been one of the rich young men who listened eagerly to Socrates.   2. Athenian territory, an island off Piraeus, the port of Athens. *Rotunda:* The circular building in which the Prytanes held their meetings.

been imposed upon me by God; and has been signified to me by oracles, visions, and in every way in which the will of divine power was ever intimated to any one. This is true, O Athenians; or, if not true, would be soon refuted. If I am or have been corrupting the youth, those of them who are now grown up and become sensible that I gave them bad advice in the days of their youth should come forward as accusers, and take their revenge; or if they do not like to come themselves, some of their relatives, fathers, brothers, or other kinsmen, should say what evil their families have suffered at my hands. Now is their time. Many of them I see in the court. There is Crito,[3] who is of the same age and of the same deme with myself, and there is Critobulus his son, whom I also see. Then again there is Lysanias of Sphettus, who is the father of Aeschines—he is present; and also there is Antiphon of Cephisus, who is the father of Epigenes; and there are the brothers of several who have associated with me. There is Nicostratus the son of Theosdotides, and the brother of Theodotus (now Theodotus himself is dead, and therefore he, at any rate, will not seek to stop him); and there is Paralus the son of Demodocus, who had a brother Theages; and Adeimantus the son of Ariston, whose brother Plato[4] is present; and Aeantodorus, who is the brother of Apollodorus, whom I also see. I might mention a great many others, some of whom Meletus should have produced as witnesses in the course of his speech; and let him still produce them, if he has forgotten—I will make way for him. And let him say, if he has any testimony of the sort which he can produce. Nay, Athenians, the very opposite is the truth. For all these are ready to witness on behalf of the corrupter, of the injurer of their kindred, as Meletus and Anytus call me; not the corrupted youth only—there might have been a motive for that—but their uncorrupted elder relatives. Why should they too support me with their testimony? Why, indeed, except for the sake of truth and justice, and because they know that I am speaking the truth, and that Meletus is a liar.

Well, Athenians, this and the like of this is all the defence which I have to offer. Yet a word more. Perhaps there may be some one who is offended at me, when he calls to mind how he himself on a similar, or even a less serious occasion, prayed and entreated the judges with many tears, and how he produced his children in court, which was a moving spectacle, together with a host of relations and friends;[5] whereas I, who am probably in danger of my life, will do none of these things. The contrast may occur to his mind, and he may be set against me, and vote in anger because he is displeased at me on this account. Now if there be such a person among you,—mind, I do not say that there is,—to him I may fairly reply: My friend, I am a man, and like other men, a creature of flesh and blood, and not 'of wood or stone,' as Homer says;[6] and I have a family, yes, and sons, O Athenians, three in number, one almost a man, and two others who are

3. A friend of Socrates who later tried to persuade him to escape from prison. *Deme:* Precinct; the local unit of Athenian administration.   4. The writer of the *Apology.*   5. The accepted ending of the speech for the defense was an unrestrained appeal to the pity of the jury. Socrates' refusal to make it is another shock for the prejudices of the audience.   6. In the *Odyssey,* XIX. 162–163, Penelope says to her husband Odysseus (who is disguised as a beggar), "Tell me of your family and where you come from. For you did not spring from an oak or a rock, as the old saying goes."

still young; and yet I will not bring any of them hither in order to petition you for an acquittal. And why not? Not from any self-assertion or want of respect for you. Whether I am or am not afraid of death is another question, of which I will not now speak. But, having regard to public opinion, I feel that such conduct would be discreditable to myself, and to you, and to the whole state. One who has reached my years, and who has a name for wisdom, ought not to demean himself. Whether this opinion of me be deserved or not, at any rate the world has decided that Socrates is in some way superior to other men. And if those among you who are said to be superior in wisdom and courage, and any other virtue, demean themselves in this way, how shameful is their conduct! I have seen men of reputation, when they have been condemned, behaving in the strangest manner: they seemed to fancy that they were going to suffer something dreadful if they died, and that they could be immortal if you only allowed them to live; and I think that such are a dishonour to the state, and that any stranger coming in would have said of them that the most eminent men of Athens, to whom the Athenians themselves give honour and command, are no better than women. And I say that these things ought not to be done by those of us who have a reputation; and if they are done, you ought not to permit them; you ought rather to show that you are far more disposed to condemn the man who gets up a doleful scene and makes the city ridiculous, than him who holds his peace.

But, setting aside the question of public opinion, there seems to be something wrong in asking a favour of a judge, and thus procuring an acquittal, instead of informing and convincing him. For his duty is, not to make a present of justice, but to give judgment; and he has sworn that he will judge according to the laws, and not according to his own good pleasure; and we ought not to encourage you, nor should you allow yourself to be encouraged, in this habit of perjury—there can be no piety in that. Do not then require me to do what I consider dishonourable and impious and wrong, especially now, when I am being tried for impiety on the indictment of Meletus. For if, O men of Athens, by force of persuasion and entreaty I could overpower your oaths, then I should be teaching you to believe that there are no gods, and in defending should simply convict myself of the charge of not believing in them. But that is not so—far otherwise. For I do believe that there are gods, and in a sense higher than that in which any of my accusers believe in them. And to you and to God I commit my cause, to be determined by you as is best for you and me.[7]

There are many reasons why I am not grieved, O men of Athens, at the vote of condemnation. I expected it, and am only surprised that the votes are so nearly equal; for I had thought that the majority against me would

---

7. The jury reaches a verdict of guilty. It appears from what Socrates says later that the jury was split, 280 for this verdict and 220 against it. The penalty is to be settled by the jury's choice between the penalty proposed by the prosecution and that offered by the defense. The jury itself cannot propose a penalty. Meletus demands death. Socrates must propose the lightest sentence he thinks he can get away with, but one heavy enough to satisfy the majority of the jury who voted him guilty. The prosecution probably expects him to propose exile from Athens, but Socrates surprises them.

have been far larger; but now, had thirty votes gone over to the other side, I should have been acquitted. And I may say, I think, that I have escaped Meletus. I may say more; for without the assistance of Anytus and Lycon, any one may see that he would not have had a fifth part of the votes,[8] as the law requires, in which case he would have incurred a fine of a thousand drachmae.

And so he proposes death as the penalty. And what shall I propose on my part, O men of Athens? Clearly that which is my due. And what is my due? What return shall be made to the man who has never had the wit to be idle during his whole life; but has been careless of what the many care for—wealth, and family interests, and military offices, and speaking in the assembly, and magistracies, and plots, and parties. Reflecting that I was really too honest a man to be a politician and live, I did not go where I could do no good to you or to myself; but where I could do the greatest good privately to every one of you, thither I went, and sought to persuade every man among you that he must look to himself, and seek virtue and wisdom before he looks to his private interests, and look to the state before he looks to the interests of the state; and that this should be the order which he observes in all his actions. What shall be done to such an one? Doubtless some good thing, O men of Athens, if he has his reward; and the good should be of a kind suitable to him. What would be a reward suitable to a poor man who is your benefactor, and who desires leisure that he may instruct you? There can be no reward so fitting as maintenance in the Prytaneum,[9] O men of Athens, a reward which he deserves far more than the citizen who has won the prize at Olympia in the horse or chariot race, whether the chariots were drawn by two horses or by many. For I am in want, and he has enough; and he only gives you the appearance of happiness, and I give you the reality. And if I am to estimate the penalty fairly, I should say that maintenance in the Prytaneum is the just return.

Perhaps you think that I am braving you in what I am saying now, as in what I said before about the tears and prayers. But this is not so. I speak rather because I am convinced that I never intentionally wronged any one, although I cannot convince you—the time has been too short; if there were a law at Athens, as there is in other cities, that a capital cause should not be decided in one day,[1] then I believe that I should have convinced you. But I cannot in a moment refute great slander; and, as I am convinced that I never wronged another, I will assuredly not wrong myself. I will not say of myself that I deserve any evil, or propose any penalty. Why should I? Because I am afraid of the penalty of death which Meletus proposes? When I do not know whether death is a good or an evil, why should I propose a penalty which would certainly be an evil? Shall I say imprisonment? And why should I live in prison, and be the slave of the magistrates of the year—of the Eleven?[2] Or shall the penalty be a fine, and imprisonment

8. Socrates jokingly divides the votes against him into three parts, one for each of his three accusers, and points out that Meletus's votes fall below the minimum necessary to justify the trial.   9. The place in which the Prytanes, as representatives of the city, entertained distinguished visitors and winners at the athletic contests at Olympia.   1. There was such a law in Sparta.   2. A committee that had charge of prisons and of public executions.

until the fine is paid? There is the same objection. I should have to lie in prison, for money I have none, and cannot pay. And if I say exile (and this may possibly be the penalty which you will affix), I must indeed be blinded by the love of life, if I am so irrational as to expect that when you, who are my own citizens, cannot endure my discourses and words, and have found them so grievous and odious that you will have no more of them, others are likely to endure me. No indeed, men of Athens, that is not very likely. And what a life should I lead, at my age, wandering from city to city, ever changing my place of exile, and always being driven out! For I am quite sure that wherever I go, there, as here, the young men will flock to me; and if I drive them away, their elders will drive me out at their request; and if I let them come, their fathers and friends will drive me out for their sakes.

Some one will say: Yes, Socrates, but cannot you hold your tongue, and then you may go into a foreign city, and no one will interfere with you? Now I have great difficulty in making you understand my answer to this. For if I tell you that to do as you say would be a disobedience to the God, and therefore that I cannot hold my tongue, you will not believe that I am serious; and if I say again that daily to discourse about virtue, and of those other things about which you hear me examining myself and others, is the greatest good of man, and that the unexamined life is not worth living, you are still less likely to believe me. Yet I say what is true, although a thing of which it is hard for me to persuade you. Also, I have never been accustomed to think that I deserve to suffer any harm. Had I money I might have estimated the offence at what I was able to pay, and not have been much the worse. But I have none, and therefore I must ask you to proportion the fine to my means. Well, perhaps I could afford a mina,[3] and therefore I propose that penalty: Plato, Crito, Critobulus, and Apollodorus, my friends here, bid me say thirty minae, and they will be the sureties. Let thirty minae be the penalty; for which sum they will be ample security to you.[4]

Not much time will be gained, O Athenians, in return for the evil name which you will get from the detractors of the city, who will say that you killed Socrates, a wise man; for they will call me wise, even although I am not wise, when they want to reproach you. If you had waited a little while, your desire would have been fulfilled in the course of nature. For I am far advanced in years, as you may perceive, and not far from death. I am speaking now not to all of you, but only to those who have condemned me to death. And I have another thing to say to them: You think that I was convicted because I had no words of the sort which would have procured my acquittal—I mean, if I had thought fit to leave nothing undone or unsaid. Not so; the deficiency which led to my conviction was not of words—

3. It is almost impossible to express the value of ancient money in modern terms. A mina was a considerable sum; in Aristotle's time (fourth century B.C.) one mina was recognized as a fair ransom for a prisoner of war. 4. The jury decides for death (according to a much later source, the vote this time was 300 to 200). The decision is not surprising in view of Socrates's intransigence. Socrates now makes a final statement to the court.

certainly not. But I had not the boldness or impudence or inclination to address you as you would have liked me to do, weeping and wailing and lamenting, and saying and doing many things which you have been accustomed to hear from others, and which, as I maintain, are unworthy of me. I thought at the time that I ought not to do anything common or mean when in danger: nor do I now repent of the style of my defence; I would rather die having spoken after my manner, than speak in your manner and live. For neither in war nor yet at law ought I or any man to use every way of escaping death. Often in battle there can be no doubt that if a man will throw away his arms, and fall on his knees before his pursuers, he may escape death; and in other dangers there are other ways of escaping death, if a man is willing to say and do anything. The difficulty, my friends, is not to avoid death, but to avoid unrighteousness; for that runs faster than death. I am old and move slowly, and the slower runner has overtaken me, and my accusers are keen and quick, and the faster runner, who is unrighteousness, has overtaken them. And now I depart hence condemned by you to suffer the penalty of death,—they too go their ways condemned by the truth to suffer the penalty of villainy and wrong; and I must abide by my award—let them abide by theirs. I suppose that these things may be regarded as fated,—and I think that they are well.

And now, O men who have condemned me, I would fain prophesy to you; for I am about to die, and in the hour of death men are gifted with prophetic power.[5] And I prophesy to you who are my murderers, that immediately after my departure punishment far heavier than you have inflicted on me will surely await you. Me you have killed because you wanted to escape the accuser, and not to give an account of your lives. But that will not be as you suppose: far otherwise. For I say that there will be more accusers of you than there are now;[6] accusers whom hitherto I have restrained: and as they are younger they will be more inconsiderate with you, and you will be more offended at them. If you think that by killing men you can prevent some one from censuring your evil lives, you are mistaken; that is not a way of escape which is either possible or honourable; the easiest and the noblest way is not to be disabling others, but to be improving yourselves. This is the prophecy which I utter before my departure to the judges who have condemned me.

Friends, who would have acquitted me, I would like also to talk with you about the thing which has come to pass, while the magistrates are busy, and before I go to the place at which I must die. Stay then a little, for we may as well talk with one another while there is time. You are my friends, and I should like to show you the meaning of this event which has happened to me. O my judges—for you I may truly call judges—I should like to tell you of a wonderful circumstance. Hitherto the divine faculty of which the internal oracle is the source has constantly been in the habit of opposing me even about trifles, if I was going to make a slip or error in any

5. As the dying Hector foretells the death of Achilles; see the *Iliad*, XXII. 418–424.   6. Socrates' prophecy was fulfilled, for all of the many different philosophical schools of the early fourth century claimed descent from Socrates and developed one or another aspect of his teachings.

matter; and now as you see there has come upon me that which may be thought, and is generally believed to be, the last and worst evil. But the oracle made no sign of opposition, either when I was leaving my house in the morning, or when I was on my way to the court, or while I was speaking, at anything which I was going to say; and yet I have often been stopped in the middle of a speech, but now in nothing I either said or did touching the matter in hand has the oracle opposed me. What do I take to be the explanation of this silence? I will tell you. It is an intimation that what has happened to me is a good, and that those of us who think that death is an evil are in error. For the customary sign would surely have opposed me had I been going to evil and not to good.

Let us reflect in another way, and we shall see that there is great reason to hope that death is a good; for one of two things—either death is a state of nothingness and utter unconsciousness, or, as men say, there is a change and migration of the soul from this world to another. Now if you suppose that there is no consciousness, but a sleep like the sleep of him who is undisturbed even by dreams, death will be an unspeakable gain. For if a person were to select the night in which his sleep was undisturbed even by dreams, and were to compare with this the other days and nights of his life, and then were to tell us how many days and nights he had passed in the course of his life better and more pleasantly than this one, I think that any man, I will not say a private man, but even the great king will not find many such days or nights, when compared with the others. Now if death be of such a nature, I say that to die is gain; for eternity is then only a single night. But if death is the journey to another place, and there, as men say, all the dead abide, what good, O my friends and judges, can be greater than this? If indeed when the pilgrim arrives in the world below, he is delivered from the professors of justice in this world, and finds the true judges who are said to give judgment there, Minos and Rhadamanthus and Aeacus and Triptolemus,[7] and other sons of God who were righteous in their own life, that pilgrimage will be worth making. What would not a man give if he might converse with Orpheus and Musaeus[8] and Hesiod and Homer? Nay, if this be true, let me die again and again. I myself, too, shall have a wonderful interest in there meeting and conversing with Palamedes, and Ajax the son of Telamon,[9] and any other ancient hero who has suffered death through an unjust judgment; and there will be no small pleasure, as I think, in comparing my own sufferings with theirs. Above all, I shall then be able to continue my search into true and false knowledge; as in this world, so also in the next and I shall find out who is wise, and who pretends to be wise, and is not. What would not a

7. Minos appears as a judge of the dead in Homer's *Odyssey*, Book XI; Rhadamanthus and Aeacus, like Minos, were models of just judges in life and after death; Triptolemus, the mythical inventor of agriculture, is associated with judgment in the next world only in this passage. The first three are sons of Zeus.
8. Legendary poets and religious teachers. *Hesiod:* Early Greek poet (eighth century B.C.?) who wrote *The Works and Days*, a didactic poem containing precepts for the farmer.   9. Both victims of unjust trials. Palamedes, one of the Greek chieftains at Troy, was unjustly executed for treason on the false evidence of his enemy Odysseus, and Ajax committed suicide after the arms of the dead Achilles were adjudged to his enemy Odysseus as the bravest warrior on the Greek side.

man give, O judges, to be able to examine the leader of the great Trojan expedition; or Odysseus or Sisyphus,[1] or numberless others, men and women too! What infinite delight would there be in conversing with them and asking them questions! In another world they do not put a man to death for asking questions: assuredly not. For besides being happier than we are, they will be immortal, if what is said is true.

Wherefore, O judges, be of good cheer about death, and know of a certainty, that no evil can happen to a good man, either in life or after death. He and his are not neglected by the gods; nor has my own approaching end happened by mere chance. But I see clearly that the time had arrived when it was better for me to die and be released from trouble; wherefore the oracle gave no sign. For which reason, also, I am not angry with my condemners, or with my accusers; they have done me no harm, although they did not mean to do me any good; and for this I may gently blame them.

Still I have a favour to ask of them. When my sons are grown up, I would ask you, O my friends, to punish them; and I would have you trouble them, as I have troubled you, if they seem to care about riches, or anything more than about virtue; or if they pretend to be something when they are really nothing,—then reprove them, as I have reproved you, for not caring about that for which they ought to care, and thinking that they are something when they are really nothing. And if you do this, both I and my sons will have received justice at your hands.

The hour of departure has arrived, and we go our ways—I to die, and you to live. Which is better God only knows.

Phaedo[2]

[The Death of Socrates]

[The narrator, Phaedo, who was present at the execution of Socrates, gives his friend Echecrates an account of Socrates' last hours. Many of his friends were with him on that day, among them Crito and two Theban philosophers, Simmias and Cebes. These two engaged him in an argument about the immortality of the soul, which Socrates succeeded in proving to their satisfaction. He concluded with an account of the next world, describing the place of reward for the virtuous and of punishment for the wicked. The opening words of the following selection are his conclusion of the argument.]

A man of sense ought not to say, nor will I be very confident, that the description which I have given of the soul and her mansions is exactly true. But I do say that, inasmuch as the soul is shown to be immortal, he

1. Odysseus was the most cunning of the Greek chieftains at Troy, the hero of Homer's *Odyssey*; Sisyphus was famous for his unscrupulousness and cunning. Each is presumably an example of the man who "pretends to be wise and is not." 2. Translated by Benjamin Jowett.

may venture to think, not improperly or unworthily, that something of the kind is true. The venture is a glorious one, and he ought to comfort himself with words like these, which is the reason why I lengthen out the tale. Wherefore, I say, let a man be of good cheer about his soul, who having cast away the pleasures and ornaments of the body as alien to him and working harm rather than good, has sought after the pleasures of knowledge; and has arrayed the soul, not in some foreign attire, but in her own proper jewels, temperance, and justice, and courage, and nobility, and truth—in these adorned she is ready to go on her journey to the world below, when her hour comes. You, Simmias and Cebes, and all other men, will depart at some time or other. Me already, as a tragic poet would say, the voice of fate calls. Soon I must drink the poison;[3] and I think that I had better repair to the bath first, in order that the women may not have the trouble of washing my body after I am dead.

When he had done speaking, Crito said: And have you any commands for us, Socrates—anything to say about your children, or any other matter in which we can serve you?

Nothing particular, Crito, he replied: only, as I have always told you, take care of yourselves; that is a service which you may be ever rendering to me and mine and to all of us, whether you promise to do so or not. But if you have no thought for yourselves, and care not to walk according to the rule which I have prescribed for you, not now for the first time, however much you may profess or promise at the moment, it will be of no avail.

We will do our best, said Crito: And in what way shall we bury you?

In any way that you like; but you must get hold of me, and take care that I do not run away from you. Then he turned to us, and added with a smile:—I cannot make Crito believe that I am the same Socrates who has been talking and conducting the argument; he fancies that I am the other Socrates whom he will soon see, a dead body—and he asks, How shall he bury me? And though I have spoken many words in the endeavour to show that when I have drunk the poison I shall leave you and go to the joys of the blessed,—these words of mine, with which I was comforting you and myself, have had, as I perceive, no effect upon Crito. And therefore I want you to be surety for me to him now, as at the trial he was surety to the judges for me: but let the promise be of another sort; for he was surety for me to the judges that I would remain, and you must be my surety to him that I shall not remain, but go away and depart; and then he will suffer less at my death, and not be grieved when he sees my body being burned or buried. I would not have him sorrow at my hard lot, or say at the burial, Thus we lay out Socrates, or, Thus we follow him to the grave or bury him; for false words are not only evil in themselves, but they inflict the soul with evil. Be of good cheer then, my dear Crito, and say that you are

---

3. Hemlock. This was the regular method of execution at Athens. The action of the poison is described below.

burying my body only, and do with that whatever is usual, and what you think best.

When he had spoken these words, he arose and went into a chamber to bathe; Crito followed him and told us to wait. So we remained behind, talking and thinking of the subject of discourse, and also of the greatness of our sorrow; he was like a father of whom we were being bereaved, and we were about to pass the rest of our lives as orphans. When he had taken the bath his children were brought to him (he had two young sons and an elder one); and the women of his family also came, and he talked to them and gave them a few directions in the presence of Crito; then he dismissed them and returned to us.

Now the hour of sunset was near, for a good deal of time had passed while he was within. When he came out, he sat down with us again after his bath, but not much was said. Soon the jailer, who was the servant of the Eleven, entered and stood by him, saying:—To you, Socrates, whom I know to be the noblest and gentlest and best of all who ever came to this place, I will not impute the angry feeling of other men, who rage and swear at me, when, in obedience to the authorities, I bid them drink the poison—indeed, I am sure that you will not be angry with me; for others, as you are aware, and not I, are to blame. And so fare you well, and try to bear lightly what must needs be—you know my errand. Then bursting into tears he turned away and went out.

Socrates looked at him and said: I return your good wishes, and will do as you bid. Then turning to us, he said, How charming the man is: since I have been in prison he has always been coming to see me, and at times he would talk to me, and was as good to me as could be, and now see how generously he sorrows on my account. We must do as he says, Crito; and therefore let the cup be brought, if the poison is prepared: if not, let the attendant prepare some.

Yet, said Crito, the sun is still upon the hill-tops, and I know that many a one has taken the draught late, and after the announcement has been made to him, he has eaten and drunk, and enjoyed the society of his beloved: do not hurry—there is time enough.

Socrates said: Yes, Crito, and they of whom you speak are right in so acting, for they think that they will be gainers by the delay; but I am right in not following their example, for I do not think that I should gain anything by drinking the poison a little later; I should only be ridiculous in my own eyes for sparing and saving a life which is already forfeit. Please then to do as I say, and not to refuse me.

Crito made a sign to the servant, who was standing by; and he went out, and having been absent for some time, returned with the jailer carrying the cup of poison. Socrates said: You, my good friend, who are experienced in these matters, shall give me directions how I am to proceed. The man answered: You have only to walk about until your legs are heavy, and then to lie down, and the poison will act. At the same time he handed the cup to Socrates, who in the easiest and gentlest manner, without the least fear or change of colour or feature, looking at the man with all his eyes,[4] Echecrates, as his manner was, took the cup and said: What do you say about making a libation[5] out of this cup to any god? May I, or not? The man answered: We only prepare, Socrates, just so much as we deem enough. I understand, he said: but I may and must ask the gods to prosper my journey from this to the other world—even so— and so be it according to my prayer. Then raising the cup to his lips, quite readily and cheerfully he drank off the poison. And hitherto most of us had been able to control our sorrow; but now when we saw him drinking, and saw too that he had finished the draught, we could no longer forbear, and in spite of myself my own tears were flowing fast; so that I covered my face and wept, not for him, but at the thought of my own calamity in having to part from such a friend. Nor was I the first; for Crito, when he found himself unable to restrain his tears, had got up, and I followed; and at that moment, Apollodorus, who had been weeping all the time, broke out in a loud and passionate cry which made cowards of us all. Socrates alone retained his calmness: What is this strange outcry? he said. I sent away the women mainly in order that they might not misbehave in this way, for I have been told that a man should die in peace. Be quiet then, and have patience. When we heard his words we were ashamed, and refrained our tears; and he walked about until, as he said, his legs began to fail, and then he lay on his back, according to directions, and the man who gave him the poison now and then looked at his feet and legs; and after a while he pressed his foot hard, and asked him if he could feel; and he said, No; and then his leg, and so upwards and upwards, and showed us that he was cold and stiff. And he felt them himself, and said: When the poison reaches the heart, that will be the end. He was beginning to grow cold about the groin, when he uncovered his face, for he had covered himself up, and said— they were his last words—he said: Crito, I owe a cock to Asclepius;[6] will you remember to pay the debt? The debt shall be paid, said Crito; is there anything else? There was no answer to this question; but in a minute or two a movement was heard, and the attendants uncovered him; his eyes were set, and Crito closed his eyes and mouth.

Such was the end, Echecrates, of our friend; concerning whom I may truly say, that of all men of his time whom I have known, he was the wisest and justest and best.

---

4. Socrates was famous for his projecting eyes and his intent stare.   **5.** He asks if he may pour a little of it out in honor of the gods, as if it were wine.   **6.** A sacrifice to the god of healing, perhaps as a thank offering for the painlessness of his death.

ARISTOTLE

384–322 B.C.

One member of Plato's Academy, Aristotle (384–322 B.C.), was to become as celebrated and influential as his teacher.

He was not, like Plato, a native Athenian; he was born in the north of Greece, at Stagira, close to the kingdom of Macedonia, which was eventually to become the dominant power in the Greek world. Aristotle entered the Academy at the age of 17 but left it when Plato died (348). He carried on his researches (he was especially interested in zoology) at various places on the Aegean, served as tutor to the young Alexander, son of Philip II of Macedon, and returned to Athens in 355, to found his own philosophical school, the Lyceum. Here he established the world's first research library and at the Lyceum he and his pupils carried on research in zoology, botany, biology, physics, political science, ethics, logic, music, and mathematics. He left Athens when Alexander died in Babylon (323 B.C.) and the Athenians, for a while, were able to demonstrate their hatred of Macedon and everything connected with it; he died a year later.

The scope of his written work, philosophical and scientific, is immense; he is represented here by some excerpts from the *Poetics*, the first systematic work of literary criticism in our tradition.

Aristotle's Poetics, translated, with an introduction and notes by James Hutton (1982), is the best source for the student.

From Poetics[1]

. . . Thus, Tragedy is an imitation of an action that is serious, complete, and possessing magnitude; in embellished language, each kind of which is used separately in the different parts; in the mode of action and not narrated; and effecting through pity and fear [what we call] the *catharsis*[2] of such emotions. By "embellished language" I mean language having rhythm and melody, and by "separately in different parts" I mean that some parts of a play are carried on solely in metrical speech while others again are sung.

The constituent parts of tragedy. Since the imitation is carried out in the dramatic mode by the personages themselves, it necessarily follows, first, that the arrangement of Spectacle will be a part of tragedy, and next, that Melody and Language will be parts, since these are the media in which

---

1. Selected passages. Translated by James Hutton. (Bracketed material has been added for clarity.)
2. This is probably the most disputed passage in the Western critical tradition. There are two main schools of interpretation; they differ in their understanding of the metaphor implied in the word *katharsis*. Some critics take the word to mean "purification," implying a metaphor from the religious process of purification from guilt; the passions are "purified" by the tragic performance since the excitement of these passions by the performance weakens them and reduces them to just proportions in the individual. (This theory was supported by the German critic Lessing.) Others take the metaphor to be medical, reading the word as "purging" and interpreting the phrase to mean that the tragic performance excites the emotions only to allay them, thus ridding the spectator of the disquieting emotions from which he suffers in everyday life; tragedy thus has a therapeutic effect.

they effect the imitation. By "language" I mean precisely the composition of the verses, by "melody" only that which is perfectly obvious. And since tragedy is the imitation of an action and is enacted by men in action, these persons must necessarily possess certain qualities of Character and Thought, since these are the basis for our ascribing qualities to the actions them-selves—character and thought are two natural causes of actions—and it is in their actions that men universally meet with success or failure. The imitation of the action is the Plot. By plot I here mean the combination of the events; Character is that in virtue of which we say that the personages are of such and such a quality; and Thought is present in everything in their utterances that aims to prove a point or that expresses an opinion. Necessarily, therefore, there are in tragedy as a whole, considered as a special form, six constituent elements, viz. Plot, Character, Language, Thought, Spectacle, and Melody. Of these elements, two [Language and Melody] are the *media* in which they effect the imitation, one [Spectacle] is the *manner*, and three [Plot, Character, Thought] are the *objects* they imitate; and besides these there are no other parts. So then they employ these six forms, not just some of them so to speak; for every drama has spectacle, character, plot, language, melody, and thought in the same sense, but the most important of them is the organization of the events [the plot].

Plot and character. For tragedy is not an imitation of men but of actions and of life. It is in action that happiness and unhappiness are found, and the end[3] we aim at is a kind of activity, not a quality; in accordance with their characters men are of such and such a quality, in accordance with their actions they are fortunate or the reverse. Consequently, it is not for the purpose of presenting their characters that the agents engage in action, but rather it is for the sake of their actions that they take on the characters they have. Thus, what happens—that is, the plot—is the end for which a tragedy exists, and the end or purpose is the most important thing of all. What is more, without action there could not be a tragedy, but there could be without characterization. . . .

Now that the parts are established, let us next discuss what qualities the plot should have, since plot is the primary and most important part of tragedy. I have posited that tragedy is an imitation of an action that is a whole and complete in itself and of a certain magnitude—for a thing may be a whole, and yet have no magnitude to speak of. Now a thing is a whole if it has a beginning, a middle, and an end. A beginning is that which does not come necessarily after something else, but after which it is natural for another thing to exist or come to be. An end, on the contrary, is that which naturally comes after something else, either as its necessary sequel or as its usual [and hence probable] sequel, but itself has nothing after it. A middle is that which both comes after something else and has another thing fol-lowing it. A well-constructed plot, therefore, will neither begin at some

_____

3. Purpose.

chance point nor end at some chance point, but will observe the principles here stated. . . .

Contrary to what some people think, a plot is not ipso facto a unity if it revolves about one man. Many things, indeed an endless number of things, happen to any one man some of which do not go together to form a unity, and similarly among the actions one man performs there are many that do not go together to produce a single unified action. Those poets seem all to have erred, therefore, who have composed a *Heracleid*, a *Theseid*, and other such poems, it being their idea evidently that since Heracles was one man, their plot was bound to be unified. . . .

From what has already been said, it will be evident that the poet's function is not to report things that have happened, but rather to tell of such things as might happen, things that are possibilities by virtue of being in themselves inevitable or probable. Thus the difference between the historian and the poet is not that the historian employs prose and the poet verse—the work of Herodotus[4] could be put into verse, and it would be no less a history with verses than without them; rather the difference is that the one tells of things that have been and the other of such things as might be. Poetry, therefore, is a more philosophical and a higher thing than history, in that poetry tends rather to express the universal, history rather the particular fact. A universal is: The sort of thing that (in the circumstances) a certain kind of person will say or do either probably or necessarily, which in fact is the universal that poetry aims for (with the addition of names for the persons); a particular, on the other hand is: What Alcibiades[5] did or had done to him. . . .

Among plots and actions of the simple type, the episodic form is the worst. I call episodic a plot in which the episodes follow one another in no probable or inevitable sequence. Plots of this kind are constructed by bad poets on their own account, and by good poets on account of the actors; since they are composing entries for a competitive exhibition, they stretch the plot beyond what it can bear and are often compelled, therefore, to dislocate the natural order. . . .

Some plots are simple, others complex; indeed the actions of which the plots are imitation are at once so differentiated to begin with. Assuming the action to be continuous and unified, as already defined, I call that action simple in which the change of fortune takes place without a reversal or recognition, and that action complex in which the change of fortune involves a recognition or a reversal or both. These events [recognitions and reversals] ought to be so rooted in the very structure of the plot that they follow from the preceding events as their inevitable or probable outcome; for there is a vast difference between following from and merely following after. . . .

Reversal (Peripety) is, as aforesaid, a change from one state of affairs to its exact opposite, and this, too, as I say, should be in conformance with probability or necessity. For example, in *Oedipus*, the messenger[6] comes

---

4. The historian of the Persian wars, a contemporary of Sophocles.   5. A brilliant but unscrupulous Athenian statesman of the fifth century B.C.   6. The Corinthian herdsman.

to cheer Oedipus by relieving him of fear with regard to his mother, but by revealing his true identity, does just the opposite of this. . . .

Recognition, as the word itself indicates, is a change from ignorance to knowledge, leading either to friendship or to hostility on the part of those persons who are marked for good fortune or bad. The best form of recognition is that which is accompanied by a reversal, as in the example from *Oedipus*. . . .

Next in order after the points I have just dealt with, it would seem necessary to specify what one should aim at and what avoid in the construction of plots, and what it is that will produce the effect proper to tragedy.

Now since in the finest kind of tragedy the structure should be complex and not simple, and since it should also be a representation of terrible and piteous events (that being the special mark of this type of imitation), in the first place, it is evident that good men ought not to be shown passing from prosperity to misfortune, for this does not inspire either pity or fear, but only revulsion; nor evil men rising from ill fortune to prosperity, for this is the most untragic plot of all—it lacks every requirement, in that it neither elicits human sympathy nor stirs pity or fear. And again, neither should an extremely wicked man be seen falling from prosperity into misfortune, for a plot so constructed might indeed call forth human sympathy, but would not excite pity or fear, since the first is felt for a person whose misfortune is undeserved and the second for someone like ourselves—pity for the man suffering undeservedly, fear for the man like ourselves—and hence neither pity nor fear would be aroused in this case. We are left with the man whose place is between these extremes. Such is the man who on the one hand is not pre-eminent in virtue and justice, and yet on the other hand does not fall into misfortune through vice or depravity, but falls because of some mistake;[7] one among the number of the highly renowned and prosperous, such as Oedipus and Thyestes and other famous men from families like theirs.

It follows that the plot which achieves excellence will necessarily be single in outcome and not, as some contend, double, and will consist in a change of fortune, not from misfortune to prosperity, but the opposite from prosperity to misfortune, occasioned not by depravity, but by some great mistake on the part of one who is either such as I have described or better than this rather than worse. (What actually has taken place confirms this; for though at first the poets accepted whatever myths came to hand, today the finest tragedies are founded upon the stories of only a few houses, being concerned, for example, with Alcmeon, Oedipus, Orestes, Meleager, Thyestes, Telephus, and such others as have chanced to suffer terrible things or to do them.) So, then, tragedy having this construction is the finest kind of tragedy from an artistic point of view. And consequently, those persons fall into the same error who bring it as a charge against

---

7. The Greek word is *hamartia*. It has sometimes been translated as "flaw" (hence the expression "tragic flaw") and thought of as a moral defect, but comparison with Aristotle's use of the word in other contexts suggests strongly that he means by it "mistake" or "error" (of judgment).

Euripides that this is what he does in his tragedies and that most of his plays have unhappy endings. For this is in fact the right procedure, as I have said; and the best proof is that on the stage and in the dramatic contests, plays of this kind seem the most tragic, provided they are successfully worked out, and Euripides, even if in everything else his management is faulty, seems at any rate the most tragic of the poets. . . .

In the characters and the plot construction alike, one must strive for that which is either necessary or probable, so that whatever a character of any kind says or does may be the sort of thing such a character will inevitably or probably say or do and the events of the plot may follow one after another either inevitably or with probability. (Obviously, then, the denouement of the plot should arise from the plot itself and not be brought about "from the machine,"[8] as it is in *Medea* and in the embarkation scene in the *Iliad*.[9] The machine is to be used for matters lying outside the drama, either antecedents of the action which a human being cannot know, or things subsequent to the action that have to be prophesied and announced; for we accept it that the gods see everything. Within the events of the plot itself, however, there should be nothing unreasonable, or if there is, it should be kept outside the play proper, as is done in the *Oedipus* of Sophocles.) . . .

The chorus in tragedy. The chorus ought to be regarded as one of the actors, and as being part of the whole and integrated into performance, not in Euripides' way but in that of Sophocles. In the other poets, the choral songs have no more relevance to the plot than if they belonged to some other play. And so nowadays, following the practice introduced by Agathon,[1] the chorus merely sings interludes. But what difference is there between the singing of interludes and taking a speech or even an entire episode from one play and inserting it into another?

CATULLUS
84?–54? B.C.

Gaius Valerius Catullus, born in the North Italian city of Verona around 84 B.C., lived out his short life of some thirty years in the last violent century of the Roman republic—a time of political upheaval that broke out more than once into civil war and culminated in the establishment of imperial authority by Augustus (see the general introduction, p. 10). The one hundred and sixteen of his poems that have come down to us present a rich variety: imitations of Greek poets (including a brilliant translation of one of Sappho's most passionate lyrics—number two in our

8. Literally the machine that was employed in the theater to show the gods flying in space. It has come to mean any implausible way of solving the complications of the plot. Medea escapes from Corinth "on the machine" in her magic chariot. 9. Aristotle refers to an incident in the second book of the *Iliad*; an attempt of the Greek rank and file to return home and abandon the siege is arrested by the intervention of Athena. (If it were a drama she would appear "on the machine.") 1. A younger contemporary of Euripides; most of his plays were produced in the fourth century B.C.

selection, p. 542) and long poems on Greek mythological themes as well as scurrilous personal attacks on contemporary politicians and private individuals, lighthearted verses designed to amuse his friends, a magnificent marriage hymn, and, above all, a series of poems (our selection represents them) which deal with his love affair, at first ecstatically happy, then despairing, with a Roman lady he calls Lesbia but who was probably Clodia, the enchanting but viciously corrupt sister of one of Rome's most cynical and violent aristocrats turned political gangster. These poems present all the phases of the liaison, from the unalloyed happiness of the first encounters through doubt and hesitation to despair and virulent accusation, ending in heartbroken resignation to the bitter fact. They express both the joy of passionate love requited and the torment of betrayal in language so direct and simple, so charged with ecstasy and fury, that they have been the despair of translators ever since.

For a sensitive appreciation of Catullus's poetry see E. A. Havelock, *The Lyric Genius of Catullus* (1932, reprinted 1967). For a brief but masterly assessment see J. W. Mackail, *Latin Literature* (1895, reprinted 1962).

1^1

Come, Lesbia, let us live and love,
    nor give a damn what sour old men say.
The sun that sets may rise again
but when our light has sunk into the earth,
    it is gone forever.   5
        Give me a thousand kisses,
    then a hundred, another thousand,
    another hundred
        and in one breath
still kiss another thousand,   10
another hundred.
        O then with lips and bodies joined
many deep thousands;
        confuse
their number,   15
        so that poor fools and cuckolds (envious
even now) shall never
learn our wealth and curse us
with their
    evil eyes.   20

2

There are many who think of Quintia in terms of beauty,
    but to me she is merely tall and golden white, erect,
    and I admit each of these separate distinctions in her favour,
    yet I object, deny,

---

1. Our selection (15 poems out of 116) are translated by Horace Gregory. The numbers of the poems in the original text are: 5, 86, 87, 107, 109, 83, 70, 72, 60, 85, 75, 8, 58, 11, 76.

that the word "beauty" describes her person;   5
for she has no charm, not even a grain of salt in her whole body
to give you appetite—
now Lesbia has beauty, she is everything
that's handsome, glorious,
and she has captured all that Venus has to offer   10
in ways of love.

3

No woman, if she is honest, can say that she's
been blessed with greater love, my Lesbia,
than I have given you;
nor has any man held to a contract made
with more fidelity   5
than I have shown, my dear,
in loving you.

4

When at last after long despair, our hopes ring true again
and long-starved desire eats, O then the mind leaps in the sunlight—Lesbia
so it was with me when you returned. Here was a treasure
more valuable than gold; you, whom I love beyond hope, giving yourself
to me again. That hour, a year of holidays, radiant,   5
where is the man more fortunate than I,
where can he find anything in life more glorious
than the sight of all his wealth restored?

5

My life, my love, you say our love will last forever;
O gods remember
her pledge, convert the words of her avowal into a prophecy.
Now let her blood speak, let sincerity govern each syllable fallen
from her lips, so that the long years of our lives shall be   5
a contract of true love inviolate
against time itself, s symbol of eternity.

6

Lesbia speaks evil of me with her husband near and he (damned idiot)
        loves to hear her.
Chuckling, the fool is happy, seeing nothing, understanding nothing.
If she forgetting me fell silent, her heart would be his alone, content and
        peaceful;
but she raves, spitting hatred upon me, all of which carries this meaning:

I am never out of her mind, and what is more, she rises in fury against
me   5
with words that make her burn, her blood passionate for me.

7

My woman says that she would rather wear the wedding-veil for me
than anyone: even if Jupiter himself came storming after her;
that's what she says, but when a woman talks to a hungry,
ravenous lover, her words should be written upon the wind
and engraved in rapid waters.   5

8

There was a time, O Lesbia, when you said Catullus was the only man on
    earth who could understand you,
who could twine his arms round you, even Jove himself less welcome.
And when I thought of you, my dear, you were not the mere flesh and
the means by which a lover finds momentary rapture.
My love was half paternal, as a father greets his son or   5
smiles at his daughter's husband.

Although I know you well (too well), my love now turns to fire
and you are small and shallow.
Is this a miracle? Your wounds in love's own battle
have made me your companion, perhaps, a greater lover,   10
but O, my dear, I'll never be
the modest boy who saw you as a lady, delicate and sweet,
a paragon of virtue.

9

Were you born of a lioness in the Libyan Mountains,
or that half-woman monster, Scylla,[2]
screaming in the lowest chambers of her womb,
sent forth already merciless and hard,
one who could never hear the cries of a man, even in his mortal agony, 5
O heart made bitter and cruel beyond all measure.

10

I hate and love.
    And if you ask me why,
        I have no answer, but I discern,
            can feel, my senses rooted in eternal torture.

2. A sea monster who snatched sailors from their ships and devoured them. She was woman above the
waist and a pack of ravenous hounds below.

11

You are the cause of this destruction, Lesbia,
that has fallen upon my mind;
this mind that has ruined itself
by fatal constancy.
And now it cannot rise from its own misery   5
to wish that you become
best of women, nor can it fail
to love you even though all is lost and you destroy
all hope.

12

Poor damned Catullus, here's no time for nonsense,
open your eyes, O idiot, innocent boy, look at what has happened:
once there were sunlit days when you followed after
where ever a girl would go, she loved with greater
love than any woman knew.   5
Then you took your pleasure
and the girl was not unwilling. Those were the bright days, gone;
now she's no longer yielding; you must be, poor idiot,
more like a man! not running after
her your mind all tears; stand firm, insensitive.   10
Say with a smile, voice steady, "Good-bye, my girl," Catullus
strong and manly no longer follows you, nor comes when you are calling
him at night and you shall need him.
You whore! Where's your man to cling to, who will praise your beauty,
where's the man that you love and who will call you his,   15
and when you fall to kissing, whose lips will you devour?
But always, your Catullus will be as firm as rock is.

13

Caelius, my Lesbia, that one, that only Lesbia,
Lesbia whom Catullus loved more than himself and all things
he ever owned or treasured.
Now her body's given up in alley-ways,
on highroads to these fine Roman gentlemen,   5
fathered centuries ago by the noble Remus.[3]

14

Furius, Aurelius, bound to Catullus
though he marches piercing farthest India

---

3. Brother of Romulus, founder of Rome.

where echoing waves of the Eastern Oceans
    break up the shores:
Under Caspian seas, to mild Arabia,   5
east of Parthia, dark with savage bowmen,
or where the Nile, sevenfold and uprising,
    stains its leveled sands,—

Even though he marches over Alps to gaze on
great Caesar's monuments:[4] the Gallic Rhine and   10
Britons who live beyond torn seas, remotest
    men of distant lands—

Friends who defy with me all things, whatever
gods may send us, go now, friends, deliver
these words to my lady, nor sweet—flattering,   15
    nor kind nor gentle:

Live well and sleep with adulterous lovers,
three hundred men between your thighs, embracing
all love turned false, again, again, and breaking
    their strength, now sterile.   20

She will not find my love (once hers) returning;
she it was who caused love, this lonely flower,
tossed aside, to fall by the plough dividing
    blossoming meadows.

15

If man can find rich consolation, remembering his good deeds and all he
    has done,
if he remembers his loyalty to others, nor abuses his religion by heartless
    betrayal
of friends to the anger of powerful gods,
then, my Catullus, the long years before you shall not sink in darkness
    with all hope gone,
wandering, dismayed, through the ruins of love.   5
All the devotion that man gives to man, you have given, Catullus,
your heart and your brain flowed into a love that was desolate, wasted, nor
    can it return.
But why, why do you crucify love and yourself through the years?
Take what the gods have to offer and standing serene, rise forth as a rock
    against darkening skies;
and yet you do nothing but grieve, sunken deep in your sorrow, Catullus,
for it is hard, hard to throw aside years lived in poisonous love that has
    tainted your brain
and must end.

4. Julius Caesar began the conquest of Gaul in 58 B.C. and in 55 B.C. made an expedition to Britain.

If this seems impossible now, you must rise

to salvation. O gods of pity and mercy, descend and witness my sorrow, if
    ever

you have looked upon man in his hour of death, see me now in despair. 15

Tear this loathsome disease from my brain. Look, a subtle corruption has
    entered my bones,

no longer shall happiness flow through my veins like a river.

    No longer I pray

that she love me again, that her body be chaste, mine forever.

Cleanse my soul of this sickness of love, give me power to rise, resurrected,
    to thrust love aside,   20

I have given my heart to the gods, O hear me, omnipotent heaven,

and ease me of love and its pain.

VIRGIL

70–19 B.C.

Publius Virgilius Maro was born in 70 B.C. in the north of Italy. Very little is
known about his life. The earliest work which is certainly his is the *Bucolics*, a
collection of poems in the pastoral genre which have had enormous influence.
These were followed by the *Georgics*, a didactic poem on farming, in four books,
which many critics consider his finest work. The *Aeneid*, the Roman epic, was left
unfinished at his early death in 19 B.C.

Like all the Latin poets, Virgil built on the solid foundations of his Greek predecessors. The story of Aeneas, the Trojan prince who came to Italy and whose
descendants founded Rome, combines the themes of the *Odyssey* (the wanderer in
search of home) and the *Iliad* (the hero in battle). Virgil borrows Homeric turns of
phrase, similes, sentiments, whole incidents: his Aeneas, like Achilles, sacrifices
prisoners to the shade of a friend and, like Odysseus, descends alive to the world of
the dead. But unlike Achilles, Aeneas does not satisfy the great passion of his life,
nor, like Odysseus, does he find a home and peace. The personal objectives of
both of Homer's heroes are sacrificed by Aeneas for a greater objective. There is
something greater than himself. His mission, imposed on him by the gods, is to
found a city, from which, in the fullness of time, will spring the Roman state.

Homer presents us in the *Iliad* with the tragic pattern of the individual will,
Achilles' wrath. But Aeneas is more than an individual. He is the prototype of the
ideal Roman ruler; his qualities are the devotion to duty and the seriousness of
purpose that were to give the Mediterranean world two centuries of ordered government. Aeneas' mission begins in disorder in the burning city of Troy, but he
leaves it carrying his father on his shoulders and leading his little son by the hand.
This famous picture emphasizes the fact that, unlike Achilles, he is securely set in
a continuity of generations, the immortality of the family group, just as his mission
to found a city, a home for the gods of Troy whose statues he carries with him,
places him in a political and religious continuity. Achilles has no future. When
he mentions his father and son, neither of whom he will see again, he emphasizes
for us the loneliness of his short career; the brilliance of his life is that of a meteor
that burns itself out to darkness. Odysseus has a father, wife, and son, and his

heroic efforts are directed toward re-establishing himself in his proper context, that home in which he will be no longer a man in a world of magic and terror, but a man in an organized and continuous community. But he fights for himself. Aeneas, on the other hand, suffers and fights, not for himself but for the future; his own life is unhappy and his death miserable. Yet he can console himself with the glory of his sons to come, the pageant of Roman achievement which he is shown by his father in the world below and which he carries on his shield. Aeneas' future is Virgil's present; the consolidation of the Roman peace under Augustus is the reward of Aeneas' unhappy life of effort and suffering.

Summarized like this, the *Aeneid* sounds like propaganda, which, in one sense of the word, it is. What saves it from the besetting fault of even the best propaganda—the partial concealment of the truth—is the fact that Virgil maintains an independence of the power that he is celebrating and sees his hero in the round. He knows that the Roman ideal of devotion to duty has another side, the suppression of many aspects of the personality; that the man who wins and uses power must sacrifice much of himself, must live a life that, compared with that of Achilles or Odysseus, is constricted. In Virgil's poem Aeneas betrays the great passion of his life, his love for Dido, queen of Carthage. He does it reluctantly, but nevertheless he leaves her, and the full realization of what he has lost comes to him only when he meets her ghost in the world below. He weeps (as he did not at Carthage) and he pleads, in stronger terms than he did then, the overriding power that forced him to depart: "I left your land against my will, my queen." She leaves him without a word, her silence as impervious to pleas and tears as his at Carthage once, and he follows her weeping as she goes back to join her first love, her husband Sychaeus. He has sacrificed his love to something greater, but this does not insulate him from unhappiness. The limitations upon the dedicated man are emphasized by the contrasting figure of Dido, who follows her own impulse always, even in death. By her death, Virgil tells us expressly, she forestalls fate, breaks loose from the pattern in which Aeneas remains to the bitter end.

The angry reactions that this part of the poem has produced in many critics are the true measure of Virgil's success. Aeneas does act in such a way that he forfeits much of our sympathy, but this is surely exactly what Virgil intended. The Dido episode is not, as many critics have supposed, a flaw in the great design, a case of Virgil's sympathy outrunning his admiration for Aeneas; it is Virgil's emphatic statement of the sacrifice that the Roman ideal of duty demands. Aeneas' sacrifice is so great that few of us could make it ourselves, and none of us can contemplate it in another without a feeling of loss. It is an expression of the famous Virgilian sadness that informs every line of the *Aeneid* and that makes a poem that was in its historical context a command performance into the great epic that has dominated Western literature ever since.

W. A. Camps, *An Introduction to Virgil's Aeneid* (1969), is a short and simply written discussion of all aspects of the poem. *Virgil: A Collection of Critical Essays*, edited by Steele Commager (1966), contains essays by various hands, ten of them on the *Aeneid*. Jasper Griffin, *Virgil* (1986), is a splendid introduction to the world and work of the poet. See also R. D. Williams, "The *Aeneid*," in *The Cambridge History of Classical Literature*, vol. 2 (1982), pp. 333–69.

VIRGIL IN LATIN

Conticuere omnes intentique ora tenebant;
inde toro pater Aeneas sic orsus ab alto:
    Infandum, regina, iubes renovare dolorem,
Troianas ut opes et lamentabile regnum
eruerint Danai, quaeque ipse miserrima uidi
et quorum pars magna fui. quis talia fando
Myrmidonum Dolopomue aut duri miles Ulixi
temperet a lacrimis? et iam nox umida caelo
praecipitat suadentque cadentia sidera somnos.
sed si tantus amor casus cognoscere nostros
et breviter Troiae supremum audire laborem,
quamquam animus meminisse horret luctuque refugit,
incipiam.

This is the beginning of Book II of the *Aeneid*; Aeneas, at the banquet in Carthage, tells the story of the fall of Troy. The long lines do not employ rhyme but they have a regular rhythmic pattern based not on stress, as in English verse, but on length of syllable, i.e., the time taken to pronounce it. Some vowels are naturally long and others naturally short; but a short vowel may be made long by position (i.e., if it is followed by two consonants it takes just as much time to pronounce as if it were naturally long). The line consists of six feet, either dactyl (–∪∪) or spondee (– –). In the first four feet various combinations are employed, but the last two feet, except in cases where a special effect is sought, are always dactyl plus spondee.

This hexameter (six foot) line is capable of great variety, contained always in the formal pattern. Unfortunately, attempts to reproduce its disciplined variety in English stressed verse (Longfellow's "This is the forest primeval . . ." for example) have not proved successful and our translator has used a modern adaptation of the basic English line, the iambic pentameter of Shakespeare and Milton.

The subtle variation of the rhythm is not the only problem faced by the translator; he must also try to compensate for the loss of effects that depend on the flexibility of Latin word order. In English, syntactical relationship is determined by that order: "man bites dog" means the opposite of "dog bites man." In Latin since the terminations of the nouns show who does what to whom, "man bites dog" is *vir mordet canem* and "dog bites man" *canis mordet virum*. Consequently the words can be arranged in any order with no change of meaning. *Virum canis mordet*, *canis virum mordet*, and any other combination of these three elements all mean the same thing: "dog bites man." But the word order is not without its force: it can indicate emphasis. Normal order—subject, object, verb (for the Latin verb tends towards the end of the sentence)—would be *canis virum mordet*. But putting *virum*, the object, first—*virum canis mordet*—would draw attention to the word: "it was a *man* the dog bit."

This is a simple example; much more complicated effects are available to a poet in extended sentences. Line 3 of the passage quoted above, for example—*Infandum, regina, iubes renovare dolorem*—uses the flexibility of word order not only for emphasis but also to explore the possibilities of ambiguity and surprise offered by a highly inflected language. *Infandum*—"unspeakable, something that cannot be said"—is the first word and we do not know from its termination whether it is subject or object nor whether it is to be understood as a noun—"an unspeakable thing"—or an adjective for which a noun will be supplied later. *Regina* ("queen") could, according to is termination, be the subject of the sentence, but the context, Aeneas' reply to the Queen's request for his story, suggests strongly that it is a form of address: "Unspeakable, oh Queen. . . ." The subject comes with the next word, the verb *iubes*; its termination shows that this is the second person, the "you" form—"you command." She has commanded something unspeakable. Is the reader being prepared for a refusal on the part of Aeneas to tell his story? *Renovare* defines the Queen's order—"to renew"—and *dolorem* tells us what he is to renew—"sorrow." And the termination of this word suggests that the first word of the line, *infandum*, is in fact an adjective defining *dolorem*. The line, at this last word, reforms itself into an unexpected pattern: "Unspeakable, oh Queen, is the sorrow you command me to renew." The line is enclosed between the two most important words in Aeneas' statement, *infandum* and *dolorem*; its last word imposes upon us a slight change in our understanding of its first and so redirects attention to that solemn opening word of Aeneas' evocation of the fall of Troy, three long syllables heavy with grief for the lost splendor of a city that is now ash and rubble.

The Aeneid[1]

From BOOK I

I sing of warfare and a man at war.[2]
From the sea-coast of Troy in early days
He came to Italy by destiny,
To our Lavinian western shore,[3]
A fugitive, this captain, buffeted   5
Cruelly on land as on the sea
By blows from powers of the air—behind them
Baleful Juno[4] in her sleepless rage.
And cruel losses were his lot in war,
Till he could found a city and bring home   10
His gods to Latium,[5] land of the Latin race,
The Alban lords,[6] and the high walls of Rome.
Tell me the causes now, O Muse, how galled
In her divine pride, and how sore at heart
From her old wound, the queen of gods compelled him—   15
A man apart, devoted to his mission—
To undergo so many perilous days
And enter on so many trials. Can anger
Black as this prey on the minds of heaven?
Tyrian[7] settlers in that ancient time   20

1. Abridged. Translated by Robert Fitzgerald.   2. Aeneas, one of the Trojan champions in the fight for Troy, son of Aphrodite (Venus) and Anchises, a member of the royal house of Troy. Aeneas survived the fall of the city and set off in search of another home. After years of wandering he settled in Italy, and from his line sprang, in the fullness of time, the founders of Rome.   3. The west coast of Italy in the vicinity of Rome, named after the nearby city of Lavinium. Lavinia is the name of the Italian princess whom Aeneas is eventually to marry.   4. The Latin equivalent of Hera, wife of the ruler of the gods. As in the *Iliad*, she is a bitter enemy of the Trojans.   5. The coastal plain on which Rome is situated.   6. The city of Alba Longa was to be founded by Aeneas's son Ascanius, and from it were to come Romulus and Remus, the builders of Rome.   7. From Tyre, the principal city of the Phoenicians, a seafaring people, located on the coast of Palestine.

Held Carthage,[8] on the far shore of the sea,
Set against Italy and Tiber's[9] mouth,
A rich new town, warlike and trained for war.
And Juno, we are told, cared more for Carthage
Than for any walled city of the earth,   25
More than for Samos,[1] even. There her armor
And chariot were kept, and, fate permitting,
Carthage would be the ruler of the world.
So she intended, and so nursed that power.
But she had heard long since   30
That generations born of Trojan blood
Would one day overthrow her Tyrian walls,
And from that blood a race would come in time
With ample kingdoms, arrogant in war,
For Libya's ruin: so the Parcae[2] spun.   35
In fear of this, and holding in memory
The old war she had carried on at Troy
For Argos'[3] sake (the origins of that anger,
That suffering, still rankled: deep within her,
Hidden away, the judgment Paris gave,[4]   40
Snubbing her loveliness; the race she hated;
The honors given ravished Ganymede),
Saturnian Juno,[5] burning for it all,
Buffeted on the waste of sea those Trojans
Left by the Greeks and pitiless Achilles,   45
Keeping them far from Latium. For years
They wandered as their destiny drove them on
From one sea to the next: so hard and huge
A task it was to found the Roman people.

(Aeneas Arrives in Carthage)

[The story opens with a storm, provoked by Juno's agency, which scatters Aeneas' fleet off Sicily and separates him from his companions. He lands on the African coast near Carthage. Setting out with his friend Achates to explore the country, he meets his mother, Venus (Aphrodite), who tells him that the rest of his ships are safe and directs him to the city just founded

---

8. On the coast of North Africa, opposite Sicily. Originally a Tyrian colony, it became a rich commercial center, controlling traffic in the Western Mediterranean. In the third and second centuries B.C. Carthage fought a series of bitter wars against Rome for the domination of the area. Carthage was captured and destroyed by the Romans in 146 B.C.   9. The river that flows through Rome.   1. A large island off the coast of Asia Minor, famous for its cult of Hera (Juno).   2. The Fates, who were imagined as female divinities, who spun human destinies. *Libya*: An inclusive name for the North African coast.   3. Home city of the Achaean Kings Agamemnon and Menelaus; Menelaus's wife Helen ran off to Troy with Paris and the Achaeans laid siege to Troy. The goddess Hera (Juno) supported the Achaean side.   4. Paris, son to King Priam of Troy, was chosen to judge which was the most beautiful goddess—Hera, Aphrodite, or Athena. All three attempted to bribe him, but Aphrodite's promise, the love of Helen, prevailed and he awarded her the prize.   5. Juno's father was Saturn (Greek Kronos). *Ganymede*: A beautiful Trojan boy taken up into heaven by Jupiter.

by Dido, the queen of Carthage. Venus surrounds Aeneas and Achates
with a cloud so that they can see without being seen.]

Meanwhile
The two men pressed on where the pathway led,
Soon climbing a long ridge that gave a view
Down over the city and facing towers.
Aeneas found, where lately huts had been,   5
Marvelous buildings, gateways, cobbled ways,
And din of wagons. There the Teucrians[6]
Were hard at work: laying courses for walls,
Rolling up stones to build the citadel,
While others picked out building sites and plowed   10
A boundary furrow. Laws were being enacted,
Magistrates and a sacred senate chosen.
Here men were dredging harbors, there they laid
The deep foundation of a theater,
And quarried massive pillars to enhance   15
The future stage—as bees in early summer
In sunlight in the flowering fields
Hum at their work, and bring along the young
Full-grown to beehood; as they cram their combs
With honey, brimming all the cells with nectar,   20
Or take newcomers' plunder, or like troops
Alerted, drive away the lazy drones,
And labor thrives and sweet thyme scents the honey.
Aeneas said: "How fortunate these are
Whose city walls are rising here and now!"   25

He looked up at the roofs, for he had entered,
Swathed in cloud—strange to relate—among them,
Mingling with men, yet visible to none.
In mid-town stood a grove that cast sweet shade
Where the Phoenicians, shaken by wind and sea,   30
Had first dug up that symbol Juno showed them,
A proud warhorse's head: this meant for Carthage
Prowess in war and ease[7] of life through ages.
Here being built by the Sidonian[8] queen
Was a great temple planned in Juno's honor,   35
Rich in offerings and the godhead there.
Steps led up to a sill of bronze, with brazen
Lintel, and bronze doors on groaning pins.
Here in this grove new things that met his eyes
Calmed Aeneas' fear for the first time.   40
Here for the first time he took heart to hope

6. Another name for Trojans.   7. Because they would have a land fertile enough to support horses.
8. From Sidon, another city of the Phoenicians.

For safety, and to trust his destiny more
Even in affliction. It was while he walked
From one to another wall of the great temple
And waited for the queen, staring amazed   45
At Carthaginian promise, at the handiwork
Of artificers and the toil they spent upon it:
He found before his eyes the Trojan battles
In the old war, now known throughout the world—
The great Atridae, Priam, and Achilles,[9]   50
Fierce in his rage at both sides. Here Aeneas
Halted, and tears came.
                    "What spot on earth,"
He said, "what region of the earth, Achatës,
Is not full of the story of our sorrow?
Look, here is Priam. Even so far away   55
Great valor has due honor; they weep here
For how the world goes, and our life that passes
Touches their hearts. Throw off your fear. This fame
Insures some kind of refuge."
                            He broke off
To feast his eyes and mind on a mere image,   60
Sighing often, cheeks grown wet with tears,
To see again how, fighting around Troy,
The Greeks broke here, and ran before the Trojans,
And there the Phrygians[1] ran, as plumed Achilles
Harried them in his warcar. Nearby, then,   65
He recognized the snowy canvas tents
Of Rhesus,[2] and more tears came: these, betrayed
In first sleep, Diomedes devastated,
Swording many, till he reeked with blood,
Then turned the mettlesome horses toward the beachhead   70
Before they tasted Trojan grass or drank
At Xanthus ford.
                    And on another panel
Troilus,[3] without his armor, luckless boy,
No match for his antagonist, Achilles,
Appeared pulled onward by his team: he clung   75
To his warcar, though fallen backward, hanging
On to the reins still, head dragged on the ground,
His javelin scribbling S's in the dust.
Meanwhile to hostile Pallas'[4] shrine
The Trojan women walked with hair unbound,   80

---

9. The greatest warrior on the Achaean side; he quarreled with Agamemnon (hence "rage at both sides").
Atridae: Sons of Atreus: Agamemnon and Menelaus.   1. Trojans.   2. King of Thrace, who came to
the help of Troy just before the end of the war. An oracle proclaimed that if his horses ate Trojan grass
and drank the water of the river Xanthus, Troy would not fall. Odysseus and Diomedes went into the
Trojan lines at night, killed the king, and stole the horses.   3. A young son of Priam, killed by Achilles.
4. Athena (cf. Iliad, VI. 297 ff.).

Bearing the robe of offering, in sorrow,
Entreating her, beating their breasts. But she,
Her face averted, would not raise her eyes.
And there was Hector, dragged around Troy walls
Three times, and there for gold Achilles sold him,   85
Bloodless and lifeless. Now indeed Aeneas
Heaved a mighty sigh from deep within him,
Seeing the spoils, the chariot, and the corpse
Of his great friend, and Priam, all unarmed,
Stretching his hands out.
                              He himself he saw   90
In combat with the first of the Achaeans,
And saw the ranks of Dawn, black Memnon's[5] arms;
Then, leading the battalion of Amazons
With half-moon shields, he saw Penthesilëa[6]
Fiery amid her host, buckling a golden   95
Girdle beneath her bare and arrogant breast,
A girl who dared fight men, a warrior queen.
Now, while these wonders were being surveyed
By Aeneas of Dardania,[7] while he stood
Enthralled, devouring all in one long gaze,   100
The queen paced toward the temple in her beauty,
Dido, with a throng of men behind.

As on Eurotas bank or Cynthus[8] ridge
Diana trains her dancers, and behind her
On every hand the mountain nymphs appear,   105
A myriad converging; with her quiver
Slung on her shoulders, in her stride she seems
The tallest, taller by a head than any,
And joy pervades Latona's[9] quiet heart:
So Dido seemed, in such delight she moved   110
Amid her people, cheering on the toil
Of a kingdom in the making. At the door
Of the goddess' shrine, under the temple dome,
All hedged about with guards on her high throne,
She took her seat. Then she began to give them   115
Judgments and rulings, to apportion work
With fairness, or assign some tasks by lot,
When suddenly Aeneas saw approaching,
Accompanied by a crowd, Antheus and Sergestus
And brave Cloanthus,[1] with a few companions,   120
Whom the black hurricane had driven far

---

5. King of the Aethiopians, who fought on the Trojan side. *Achaeans:* Greeks.   6. Queen of the Amazons, killed by Achilles.   7. Another name for the kingdom of Troy.   8. A mountain on the island of Delos, birthplace of Diana (Artemis), virgin goddess of the hunt. *Eurotas:* A river near Sparta where Artemis was worshipped.   9. Leto, mother of Diana.   1. Ship captains of Aeneas' fleet from whom he had been separated in the storm.

Over the sea and brought to other coasts.
He was astounded, and Achatës too
Felt thrilled by joy and fear: both of them longed
To take their friends' hands, but uncertainty   125
Hampered them. So, in their cloudy mantle,
They hid their eagerness, waiting to learn
What luck these men had had, where on the coast
They left their ships, and why they came. It seemed
Spokesmen for all the ships were now arriving,   130
Entering the hall, calling for leave to speak.
When all were in, and full permission given
To make their plea before the queen, their eldest,
Ilioneus, with composure said:
                              "Your majesty,
Granted by great Jupiter freedom to found   135
Your new town here and govern fighting tribes
With justice—we poor Trojans, worn by winds
On every sea, entreat you: keep away
Calamity of fire from our ships!
Let a godfearing people live, and look   140
More closely at our troubles. Not to ravage
Libyan hearths or turn with plunder seaward
Have we come; that force and that audacity
Are not for beaten men.
                        There is a country
Called by the Greeks Hesperia,[2] very old,   145
Potent in warfare and in wealth of earth;
Oenotrians[3] farmed it; younger settlers now,
The tale goes, call it by their chief's[4] name, Italy.
We laid our course for this.
But stormy Orion[5] and a high sea rising   150
Deflected us on shoals and drove us far,
With winds against us, into whelming waters,
Unchanneled reefs. We kept afloat, we few,
To reach your coast. What race of men is this?
What primitive state could sanction this behavior?   155
Even on beaches we are denied a landing,
Harried by outcry and attack, forbidden
To set foot on the outskirts of your country.
If you care nothing for humanity
And merely mortal arms, respect the gods   160
Who are mindful of good actions and of evil!

We had a king, Aeneas—none more just,
More zealous, greater in warfare and in arms.

2. Italy, literally "the western country." 3. The original inhabitants of Italy. 4. Italus. 5. The setting of this constellation in November signaled the onset of stormy weather at sea

If fate preserves him, if he does not yet
Lie spent amid the insensible shades but still   165
Takes nourishment of air, we need fear nothing;
Neither need you repent of being first
In courtesy, to outdo us. Sicily too
Has towns and plowlands and a famous king
Of Trojan blood, Acestës.[6] May we be   170
Permitted here to beach our damaged ships,
Hew timbers in your forest, cut new oars,
And either sail again for Latium, happily,
If we recover shipmates and our king,
Or else, if that security is lost,   175
If Libyan waters hold you, Lord Aeneas,
Best of Trojans, hope of Iulus[7] gone,
We may at least cross over to Sicily
From which we came, to homesteads ready there,
And take Acestës for our king."
                    Ilioneus   180
Finished, and all the sons of Dardanus[8]
Murmured assent. Dido with eyes downcast
Replied in a brief speech:
                  "Cast off your fear,
You Teucrians, put anxiety aside.
Severe conditions and the kingdom's youth   185
Constrain me to these measures, to protect
Our long frontiers with guards.
             Who has not heard
Of the people of Aeneas, of Troy city,
Her valors and her heroes, and the fires
Of the great war? We are not so oblivious,   190
We Phoenicians. The sun yokes his team
Within our range[9] at Carthage. Whether you choose
Hesperia Magna and the land of Saturn
Or Eryx[1] in the west and King Acestës,
I shall dispatch you safely with an escort,   195
Provisioned from my stores. Or would you care
To join us in this realm on equal terms?
The city I build is yours; haul up your ships;
Trojan and Tyrian will be all one to me.
If only he were here, your king himself,   200
Caught by the same easterly, Aeneas!

6. A Sicilian king. His mother was a Trojan and he had offered Aeneas and his men a home in his dominions.   7. Ascanius, Aeneas' son.   8. Ancestor of the Trojans.   9. This sentence seems to mean: "we are not outside the circuit of the sun, we are part of the civilized world and hear the news." 1. On the West coast of Sicily. *Hesperia Magna:* 'Great' Westland, i.e., Italy as opposed to Sicily. *Land of Saturn:* An old legend connected Italy with Saturn (Cronos), the father of Jupiter (Zeus). The "age of Saturn" was the Golden Age.

Indeed, let me send out trustworthy men
Along the coast, with orders to comb it all
From one end of Libya to the other,
In case the sea cast the man up and now   205
He wanders lost, in town or wilderness."

Elated at Dido's words, both staunch Achatës
And father Aeneas had by this time longed
To break out of the cloud. Achatës spoke
With urgency:
            "My lord, born to the goddess,   210
What do you feel, what is your judgment now?
You see all safe, our ships and friends recovered.
One is lost;[2] we saw that one go down
Ourselves, amid the waves. Everything else
Bears out your mother's own account of it."   215

He barely finished when the cloud around them
Parted suddenly and thinned away
Into transparent air. Princely Aeneas
Stood and shone in the bright light, head and shoulders
Noble as a god's. For she who bore him[3]   220
Breathed upon him beauty of hair and bloom
Of youth and kindled brilliance in his eyes,
As an artist's hand gives style to ivory,
Or sets pure silver, or white stone of Paros,[4]
In framing yellow gold. Then to the queen   225
He spoke as suddenly as, to them all,
He had just appeared:
                    "Before your eyes I stand,
Aeneas the Trojan, that same one you look for,
Saved from the sea off Libya.
                            You alone,
Moved by the untold ordeals of old Troy,   230
Seeing us few whom the Greeks left alive,
Worn out by faring ill on land and sea,
Needy of everything—you'd give these few
A home and city, allied with yourselves.
Fit thanks for this are not within our power,   235
Not to be had from Trojans anywhere
Dispersed in the great world.
                            May the gods—
And surely there are powers that care for goodness,
Surely somewhere justice counts—may they
And your own consciousness of acting well   240
Reward you as they should. What age so happy

2. One ship, captained by Orontes, was sunk in the storm in sight of Aeneas.   3. Venus (Aphrodite).
4. The marble of the island of Paros was famous.

Brought you to birth? How splendid were your parents
To have conceived a being like yourself!
So long as brooks flow seaward, and the shadows
Play over mountain slopes, and highest heaven   245
Feeds the stars, your name and your distinction
Go with me, whatever lands may call me."

With this he gave his right hand to his friend
Ilioneus, greeting Serestus with his left,
Then took the hands of those brave men, Cloanthus,   250
Gyas, and the rest.
    Sidonian Dido
Stood in astonishment, first at the sight
Of such a captain, then at his misfortune,
Presently saying:
     "Born of an immortal
Mother though you are, what adverse destiny   255
Dogs you through these many kinds of danger?
What rough power brings you from sea to land
In savage places? Are you truly he,
Aeneas, whom kind Venus bore
To the Dardanian, the young Anchisës,
Near to the stream of Phrygian[5] Simoïs?   260
I remember the Greek, Teucer,[6] came to Sidon,
Exiled, and in search of a new kingdom.
Belus, my father, helped him. In those days
Belus campaigned with fire and sword on Cyprus
And won that island's wealth. Since then, the fall   265
Of Troy, your name, and the Pelasgian[7] kings
Have been familiar to me. Teucer, your enemy,
Spoke often with admiration of the Teucrians[8]
And traced his own descent from Teucrian stock.
Come, then, soldiers, be our guests. My life   270
Was one of hardship and forced wandering
Like your own, till in this land at length
Fortune would have me rest. Through pain I've learned
To comfort suffering men."
     She led Aeneas
Into the royal house, but not before   275
Declaring a festal day in the gods' temples.
As for the ships' companies, she sent
Twenty bulls to the shore, a hundred swine,
Huge ones, with bristling backs, and fatted lambs,
A hundred of them, and their mother ewes—   280
All gifts for happy feasting on that day.

---

5. Trojan. 6. A Greek warrior who fought at Troy and afterward was exiled from his home. He founded
a city on the island of Cyprus. (Not to be confused with the Trojan king, Teucer.) 7. Greek.
8. Trojans.

Now the queen's household made her great hall glow
As they prepared a banquet in the kitchens.
Embroidered table cloths, proud crimson-dyed,
Were spread, and set with massive silver plate,   285
Or gold, engraved with brave deeds of her fathers,
A sequence carried down through many captains
In a long line from the founding of the race.

[At the banquet which Dido gives for Aeneas, he relates, at her request,
the story of the fall of Troy.]

BOOK II

How They Took the City

The room fell silent, and all eyes were on him,
As Father Aeneas from his high couch began:

"Sorrow too deep to tell, your majesty,
You order me to feel and tell once more:
How the Danaans[9] leveled in the dust   5
The splendor of our mourned-forever kingdom—
Heartbreaking things I saw with my own eyes
And was myself a part of. Who could tell them,
Even a Myrmidon or Dolopian[1]
Or ruffian of Ulysses, without tears?   10
Now, too, the night is well along, with dewfall
Out of heaven, and setting stars weigh down
Our heads toward sleep. But if so great desire
Moves you to hear the tale of our disasters,
Briefly recalled, the final throes of Troy,   15
However I may shudder at the memory
And shrink again in grief, let me begin.

Knowing their strength broken in warfare, turned
Back by the fates, and years—so many years—
Already slipped away, the Danaan captains   20
By the divine handicraft of Pallas built
A horse of timber, tall as a hill,
And sheathed its ribs with planking of cut pine.
This they gave out to be an offering
For a safe return by sea, and the word went round.   25
But on the sly they shut inside a company
Chosen from their picked soldiery by lot,
Crowding the vaulted caverns in the dark—
The horse's belly—with men fully armed.

9. Greeks.   1. Soldiers of Achilles. *Ulysses:* Odysseus.

Offshore there's a long island, Tenedos, 30
Famous and rich while Priam's kingdom lasted,
A treacherous anchorage now, and nothing more.
They crossed to this and hid their ships behind it
On the bare shore beyond. We thought they'd gone,
Sailing home to Mycenae before the wind, 35
So Teucer's town is freed of her long anguish,
Gates thrown wide! And out we go in joy
To see the Dorian[2] campsites, all deserted,
The beach they left behind. Here the Dolopians
Pitched their tents, here cruel Achilles lodged, 40
There lay the ships, and there, formed up in ranks,
They came inland to fight us. Of our men
One group stood marveling, gaping up to see
The dire gift of the cold unbedded goddess,[3]
The sheer mass of the horse.

                  Thymoetes shouts 45
It should be hauled inside the walls and moored
High on the citadel—whether by treason
Or just because Troy's fate went that way now.
Capys opposed him; so did the wiser heads:
'Into the sea with it,' they said, 'or burn it, 50
Build up a bonfire under it,
This trick of the Greeks, a gift no one can trust,
Or cut it open, search the hollow belly!'

Contrary notions pulled the crowd apart.
Next thing we knew, in front of everyone, 55
Laocoön with a great company
Came furiously running from the Height,[4]
And still far off cried out: 'O my poor people,
Men of Troy, what madness has come over you?
Can you believe the enemy truly gone? 60
A gift from the Danaans, and no ruse?
Is that Ulysses' way, as you have known him?
Achaeans must be hiding in this timber,
Or it was built to butt against our walls,
Peer over them into our houses, pelt 65
The city from the sky. Some crookedness
Is in this thing. Have no faith in the horse!
Whatever it is, even when Greeks bring gifts
I fear them, gifts and all.'

                He broke off then
And rifled his big spear with all his might 70
Against the horse's flank, the curve of belly.

---

2. Another name for the Greeks. 3. Athena (Minerva) was a virgin goddess. 4. The citadel, the
acropolis.

It stuck there trembling, and the rounded hull
Reverberated groaning at the blow.
If the gods' will had not been sinister,
If our own minds had not been crazed,   75
He would have made us foul that Argive den
With bloody steel, and Troy would stand today—
O citadel of Priam, towering still!

But now look: hillmen, shepherds of Dardania,
Raising a shout, dragged in before the king   80
An unknown fellow with hands tied behind—
This all as he himself had planned,
Volunteering, letting them come across him,
So he could open Troy to the Achaeans.
Sure of himself this man was, braced for it   85
Either way, to work his trick or die.
From every quarter Trojans run to see him,
Ring the prisoner round, and make a game
Of jeering at him. Be instructed now
In Greek deceptive arts: one barefaced deed   90
Can tell you of them all.
As the man stood there, shaken and defenceless,
Looking around at ranks of Phrygians,
'Oh god,' he said, 'what land on earth, what seas
Can take me in? What's left me in the end,   95
Outcast that I am from the Danaans,
Now the Dardanians will have my blood?'

The whimpering speech brought us up short; we felt
A twinge for him. Let him speak up, we said,
Tell us where he was born, what news he brought,   100
What he could hope for as a prisoner.
Taking his time, slow to discard his fright,
He said:
        'I'll tell you the whole truth, my lord,
No matter what may come of it. Argive
I am by birth, and will not say I'm not.   105
That first of all: Fortune has made a derelict
Of Sinon, but the bitch
Won't make an empty liar of him, too.
Report of Palamedes[5] may have reached you,
Scion of Belus' line, a famous man   110
Who gave commands against the war. For this,
On a trumped-up charge, on perjured testimony,
The Greeks put him to death—but now they mourn him,
Now he has lost the light. Being kin to him,

5. A Greek warrior who advised Agamemnon to abandon the war against Troy; his downfall was engi-
neered by Ulysses (Odysseus), who planted forged proofs of dealings with the enemy in his tent.

In my first years I joined him as companion,   115
Sent by my poor old father on this campaign,
And while he held high rank and influence
In royal councils, we did well, with honor.
Then by the guile and envy of Ulysses—
Nothing unheard of there!—he left this world,   120
And I lived on, but under a cloud, in sorrow,
Raging for my blameless friend's downfall.
Demented, too, I could not hold my peace
But said if I had luck, if I won through
Again to Argos, I'd avenge him there.   125
And I roused hatred with my talk; I fell
Afoul now of that man. From that time on,
Day in, day out, Ulysses
Found new ways to bait and terrify me,
Putting out shady rumors among the troops,   130
Looking for weapons he could use against me.
He could not rest till Calchas⁶ served his turn—
But why go on? The tale's unwelcome, useless,
If Achaeans are all one,
And it's enough I'm called Achaean, then   135
Exact the punishment, long overdue;
The Ithacan⁷ desires it; the Atridae
Would pay well for it.'
                     Burning with curiosity,
We questioned him, called on him to explain—
Unable to conceive such a performance,   140
The art of the Pelasgian. He went on,
Atremble, as though he feared us:
                                  'Many times
The Danaans wished to organize retreat,
To leave Troy and the long war, tired out.
If only they had done it! Heavy weather   145
At sea closed down on them, or a fresh gale
From the Southwest would keep them from embarking,
Most of all after this figure here,
This horse they put together with maple beams,
Reached its full height. Then wind and thunderstorms   150
Rumbled in heaven. So in our quandary
We sent Eurypylus to Phoebus'⁸ oracle,
And he brought back this grim reply:

'Blood and a virgin slain⁹
You gave to appease the winds, for your first voyage   155
Troyward, O Danaans. Blood again
And Argive blood, one life, wins your return.'

6. The prophet of the Greek army.   7. Ulysses.   8. Apollo. *Eurypylus:* A minor Greek chieftain.
9. Iphigenia, Agamemnon's daughter.

When this got round among the soldiers, gloom
Came over them, and a cold chill that ran
To the very marrow. Who had death in store?   160
Whom did Apollo call for? Now the man
Of Ithaca haled Calchas out among us
In tumult, calling on the seer to tell
The true will of the gods. Ah, there were many
Able to divine the crookedness   165
And cruelty afoot for me, but they
Looked on in silence. For ten days the seer
Kept still, kept under cover, would not speak
Of anyone, or name a man for death,
Till driven to it at last by Ulysses' cries—   170
By prearrangement—he broke silence, barely
Enough to designate me for the altar.
Every last man agreed. The torments each
Had feared for himself, now shifted to another,
All could endure. And the infamous day came,   175
The ritual, the salted meal,[1] the fillets . . .
I broke free, I confess it, broke my chains,
Hid myself all night in a muddy marsh,
Concealed by reeds, waiting for them to sail
If they were going to.
     Now no hope is left me   180
Of seeing my home country ever again,
My sweet children, my father, missed for years.
Perhaps the army will demand they pay
For my escape, my crime here, and their death,
Poor things, will be my punishment. Ah, sir,   185
I beg you by the gods above, the powers
In whom truth lives, and by what faith remains
Uncontaminated to men, take pity
On pain so great and so unmerited!'

For tears we gave him life, and pity, too.   190
Priam himself ordered the gyves removed
And the tight chain between. In kindness then
He said to him:
     'Whoever you may be,
The Greeks are gone; forget them from now on;
You shall be ours. And answer me these questions: 195
Who put this huge thing up, this horse?
Who designed it? What do they want with it?
Is it religious or a means of war?'

These were his questions. Then the captive, trained
In trickery, in the stagecraft of Achaea,   200

---

1. The paraphernalia of animal sacrifice. *Fillets* are tufts of wool attached to the victim.

Lifted his hands unfettered to the stars.
'Eternal fires of heaven,' he began,
'Powers inviolable, I swear by thee,
As by the altars and blaspheming swords
I got away from, and the gods' white bands[2]   205
I wore as one chosen for sacrifice,
This is justice, I am justified
In dropping all allegiance to the Greeks—
As I had cause to hate them; I may bring
Into the open what they would keep dark.   210
No laws of my own country bind me now.
Only be sure you keep your promises
And keep faith, Troy, as you are kept from harm
If what I say proves true, if what I give
Is great and valuable.
                          The whole hope   215
Of the Danaans, and their confidence
In the war they started, rested all along
In help from Pallas. Then the night came
When Diomedes and that criminal,
Ulysses, dared to raid her holy shrine.   220
They killed the guards on the high citadel
And ripped away the statue, the Palladium,[3]
Desecrating with bloody hands the virginal
Chaplets of the goddess. After that,
Danaan hopes waned and were undermined,   225
Ebbing away, their strength in battle broken,
The goddess now against them. This she made
Evident to them all with signs and portents.
Just as they set her statue up in camp,
The eyes, cast upward, glowed with crackling flames,   230
And salty sweat ran down the body. Then—
I say it in awe—three times, up from the ground,
The apparition of the goddess rose
In a lightning flash, with shield and spear atremble.
Calchas divined at once that the sea crossing   235
Must be attempted in retreat—that Pergamum[4]
Cannot be torn apart by Argive swords
Unless at Argos first they beg new omens,
Carrying homeward the divine power
Brought overseas in ships. Now they are gone   240
Before the wind to the fatherland, Mycenae,
Gone to enlist new troops and gods. They'll cross
The water again and be here, unforeseen.

2. Fillets.   3. A statue of Pallas, kept in her shrine at Troy. There was an oracle which stated that Troy
could not be captured as long as it remained in place.   4. The name of the citadel of Troy.

So Calchas read the portents. Warned by him,
They set this figure up in reparation   245
For the Palladium stolen, to appease
The offended power and expiate the crime.
Enormous, though, he made them build the thing
With timber braces, towering to the sky,
Too big for the gates, not to be hauled inside   250
And give the people back their ancient guardian.
If any hand here violates this gift
To great Minerva, then extinction waits,
Not for one only—would god it were so—
But for the realm of Priam and all Phrygians.   255
If this proud offering, drawn by your hands,
Should mount into your city, then so far
As the walls of Pelops' town[5] the tide of Asia
Surges in war: that doom awaits our children.'

This fraud of Sinon, his accomplished lying,   260
Won us over; a tall tale and fake tears
Had captured us, whom neither Diomedes
Nor Larisaean Achilles[6] overpowered,
Nor ten long years, nor all their thousand ships.

And now another sign, more fearful still,   265
Broke on our blind miserable people,
Filling us all with dread. Laocoön,
Acting as Neptune's[7] priest that day by lot,
Was on the point of putting to the knife
A massive bull before the appointed altar,   270
When ah—look there!
From Tenedos, on the calm sea, twin snakes—
I shiver to recall it—endlessly
Coiling, uncoiling, swam abreast for shore,
Their underbellies showing as their crests   275
Reared red as blood above the swell; behind
They glided with great undulating backs.
Now came the sound of thrashed seawater foaming;
Now they were on dry land, and we could see
Their burning eyes, fiery and suffused with blood,   280
Their tongues a-flicker out of hissing maws.
We scattered, pale with fright. But straight ahead
They slid until they reached Laocoön.
Each snake enveloped one of his two boys,
Twining about and feeding on the body.   285
Next they ensnared the man as he ran up
With weapons: coils like cables looped and bound him

5. Argos. Pelops was the father of Atreus.   6. So called after Larissa, a town in his homeland of
Thessaly.   7. Poseidon.

Twice round the middle; twice about his throat
They whipped their back-scales, and their heads towered,
While with both hands he fought to break the knots,   290
Drenched in slime, his head-bands black with venom,
Sending to heaven his appalling cries
Like a slashed bull escaping from an altar,
The fumbled axe shrugged off. The pair of snakes
Now flowed away and made for the highest shrines,   295
The citadel of pitiless Minerva,
Where coiling they took cover at her feet
Under the rondure of her shield. New terrors
Ran in the shaken crowd: the word went round
Laocoön had paid, and rightfully,   300
For profanation of the sacred hulk
With his offending spear hurled at its flank.

'The offering must be hauled to its true home,'
They clamored. 'Votive prayers to the goddess
Must be said there!'
                    So we breached the walls   305
And laid the city open. Everyone
Pitched in to get the figure underpinned
With rollers, hempen lines around the neck.
Deadly, pregnant with enemies, the horse
Crawled upward to the breach. And boys and girls   310
Sang hymns around the towrope as for joy
They touched it. Rolling on, it cast a shadow
Over the city's heart. O Fatherland,
O Ilium, home of gods! Defensive wall
Renowned in war for Dardanus's people!   315
There on the very threshold of the breach
It jarred to a halt four times, four times the arms
In the belly thrown together made a sound—
Yet on we strove unmindful, deaf and blind,
To place the monster on our blessed height.   320
Then, even then, Cassandra's[8] lips unsealed
The doom to come: lips by a god's command
Never believed or heeded by the Trojans.
So pitiably we, for whom that day
Would be the last, made all our temples green   325
With leafy festal boughs throughout the city.

As heaven turned, Night from the Ocean stream
Came on, profound in gloom on earth and sky
And Myrmidons in hiding. In their homes
The Teucrians lay silent, wearied out,   330

---

8. A prophetess, daughter of Priam, King of Troy. She foretold the future correctly, but no one believed what she said (cf. Aeschylus, *Agamemnon*, ll. 1206ff).

And sleep enfolded them. The Argive fleet,
Drawn up in line abreast, left Tenedos
Through the aloof moon's friendly stillnesses
And made for the familiar shore. Flame signals
Shone from the command ship. Sinon, favored   335
By what the gods unjustly had decreed,
Stole out to tap the pine walls and set free
The Danaans in the belly. Opened wide,
The horse emitted men; gladly they dropped
Out of the cavern, captains first, Thessandrus,   340
Sthenelus and the man of iron, Ulysses;
Hand over hand upon the rope, Acamas, Thoas,
Neoptolemus[9] and Prince Machaon,
Menelaus and then the master builder,
Epeos, who designed the horse decoy.   345
Into the darkened city, buried deep
In sleep and wine, they made their way,
Cut the few sentries down,
Let in their fellow soldiers at the gate,
And joined their combat companies as planned.   350

That time of night it was when the first sleep,
Gift of the gods, begins for ill mankind,
Arriving gradually, delicious rest.
In sleep, in dream, Hector appeared to me,
Gaunt with sorrow, streaming tears, all torn—   355
As by the violent car on his death day—
And black with bloody dust,
His puffed-out feet cut by the rawhide thongs.
Ah god, the look of him! How changed
From that proud Hector who returned to Troy   360
Wearing Achilles' armor,[1] or that one
Who pitched the torches on Danaan ships;
His beard all filth, his hair matted with blood,
Showing the wounds, the many wounds, received
Outside his father's city walls. I seemed   365
Myself to weep and call upon the man
In grieving speech, brought from the depth of me:

'Light of Dardania, best hope of Troy,
What kept you from us for so long, and where?
From what far place, O Hector, have you come,   370
Long, long awaited? After so many deaths
Of friends and brothers, after a world of pain
For all our folk and all our town, at last,

---

9. Son of Achilles.   1. He stripped it from the corpse of Patroclus, Achilles' close friend, whom Hector
killed in battle. Achilles revenged Patroclus by killing Hector.

Boneweary, we behold you! What has happened
To ravage your serene face? Why these wounds?'   375

He wasted no reply on my poor questions
But heaved a great sigh from his chest and said:
'Ai! Give up and go, child of the goddess,
Save yourself, out of these flames. The enemy
Holds the city walls, and from her height   380
Troy falls in ruin. Fatherland and Priam
Have their due; if by one hand our towers
Could be defended, by this hand, my own,
They would have been. Her holy things, her gods
Of hearth and household[2] Troy commends to you.   385
Accept them as companions of your days;
Go find for them the great walls that one day
You'll dedicate, when you have roamed the sea.'

As he said this, he brought out from the sanctuary
Chaplets and Vesta, Lady of the Hearth,   390
With her eternal fire.[3]
                            While I dreamed,
The turmoil rose, with anguish, in the city.
More and more, although Anchises'[4] house
Lay in seclusion, muffled among trees,
The din at the grim onset grew; and now   395
I shook off sleep, I climbed to the roof top
To cup my ears and listen. And the sound
Was like the sound a grassfire makes in grain,
Whipped by a Southwind, or a torrent foaming
Out of a mountainside to strew in ruin   400
Fields, happy crops, the yield of plowing teams,
Or woodlands borne off in the flood; in wonder
The shepherd listens on a rocky peak.
I knew then what our trust had won for us,
Knew the Danaan fraud: Deïphobus'[5]   405
Great house in flames, already caving in
Under the overpowering god of fire;
Ucalegon's already caught nearby;
The glare lighting the straits beyond Sigeum;[6]
The cries of men, the wild calls of the trumpets.   410

To arm was my first maddened impulse—not
That anyone had a fighting chance in arms;
Only I burned to gather up some force
For combat, and to man some high redoubt.

2. The Romans kept images of household gods, the Penates, in a shrine in the home. The custom is here
transferred, unhistorically, to Troy.   3. Vesta was the goddess of the hearth and fire, which, in the
temple, was never allowed to go out.   4. Aeneas's father.   5. A son of Priam.   6. A promontory
overlooking the straits which connect the Aegean with the Black Sea.

So fury drove me, and it came to me   415
That meeting death was beautiful in arms.
Then here, eluding the Achaean spears,
Came Panthus, Orthrys' son, priest of Apollo,
Carrying holy things, our conquered gods,
And pulling a small grandchild along: he ran   420
Despairing to my doorway.
                    'Where's the crux,
Panthus,' I said. 'What strongpoint shall we hold?'

Before I could say more, he groaned and answered:
'The last day for Dardania has come,
The hour not to be fought off any longer.   425
Trojans we have been; Ilium has been;
The glory of the Teucrians is no more;
Black Jupiter has passed it on to Argos.
Greeks are the masters in our burning city.
Tall as a cliff, set in the heart of town,   430
Their horse pours out armed men. The conqueror,
Gloating Sinon, brews new conflagrations.
Troops hold the gates—as many thousand men
As ever came from great Mycenae; others
Block the lanes with crossed spears; glittering   435
In a combat line, swordblades are drawn for slaughter.
Even the first guards at the gates can barely
Offer battle, or blindly make a stand.'

Impelled by these words, by the powers of heaven,
Into the flames I go, into the fight,   440
Where the harsh Fury, and the din and shouting,
Skyward rising, calls. Crossing my path
In moonlight, five fell in with me, companions:
Ripheus, and Epytus, a great soldier,
Hypanis, Dymas, cleaving to my side   445
With young Coroebus, Mygdon's son. It happened
That in those very days this man had come
To Troy, aflame with passion for Cassandra,
Bringing to Priam and the Phrygians
A son-in-law's right hand. Unlucky one,   450
To have been deaf to what his bride foretold!
Now when I saw them grouped, on edge for battle,
I took it all in and said briefly,
                              'Soldiers,
Brave as you are to no end, if you crave
To face the last fight with me, and no doubt of it,   455
How matters stand for us each one can see.
The gods by whom this kingdom stood are gone,
Gone from the shrines and altars. You defend

A city lost in flames. Come, let us die,
We'll make a rush into the thick of it.   460
The conquered have one safety: hope for none.'

The desperate odds doubled their fighting spirit:
From that time on, like predatory wolves
In fog and darkness, when a savage hunger
Drives them blindly on, and cubs in lairs   465
Lie waiting with dry famished jaws—just so
Through arrow flights and enemies we ran
Toward our sure death, straight for the city's heart,
Cavernous black night over and around us.
Who can describe the havoc of that night   470
Or tell the deaths, or tally wounds with tears?
The ancient city falls, after dominion
Many long years. In windows, on the streets,
In homes, on solemn porches of the gods,
Dead bodies lie. And not alone the Trojans   475
Pay the price with their heart's blood; at times
Manhood returns to fire even the conquered
And Danaan conquerors fall. Grief everywhere,
Everywhere terror, and all shapes of death.

Androgeos was the first to cross our path   480
Leading a crowd of Greeks; he took for granted
That we were friends, and hailed us cheerfully:

'Men, get a move on! Are you made of lead
To be so late and slow? The rest are busy
Carrying plunder from the fires and towers.   485
Are you just landed from the ships?'
                                        His words
Were barely out, and no reply forthcoming
Credible to him, when he knew himself
Fallen among enemies. Thunderstruck,
He halted, foot and voice, and then recoiled   490
Like one who steps down on a lurking snake
In a briar patch and jerks back, terrified,
As the angry thing rears up, all puffed and blue.
So backward went Androgeos in panic.
We were all over them in a moment, cut   495
And thrust, and as they fought on unknown ground,
Startled, unnerved, we killed them everywhere.
So Fortune filled our sails at first. Coroebus,
Elated at our feat and his own courage,
Said:
          'Friends, come follow Fortune. She has shown   500
The way to safety, shown she's on our side.

We'll take their shields and put on their insignia!
Trickery, bravery: who asks, in war?
The enemy will arm us.'
                              He put on
The plumed helm of Androgeos, took the shield   505
With blazon and the Greek sword to his side.
Ripheus, Dymas—all were pleased to do it,
Making the still fresh trophies our equipment.
Then we went on, passing among the Greeks,
Protected by our own gods now no longer;   510
Many a combat, hand to hand, we fought
In the black night, and many a Greek we sent
To Orcus.[7] There were some who turned and ran
Back to the ships and shore; some shamefully
Clambered again into the horse, to hide   515
In the familiar paunch.
                       When gods are contrary
They stand by no one. Here before us came
Cassandra, Priam's virgin daughter, dragged
By her long hair out of Minerva's shrine,
Lifting her brilliant eyes in vain to heaven—   520
Her eyes alone, as her white hands were bound.
Coroebus, infuriated, could not bear it,
But plunged into the midst to find his death.
We all went after him, our swords at play,
But here, here first, from the temple gable's height,   525
We met a hail of missiles from our friends,
Pitiful execution, by their error,
Who thought us Greek from our Greek plumes and shields.
Then with a groan of anger, seeing the virgin
Wrested from them, Danaans from all sides   530
Rallied and attacked us: fiery Ajax,[8]
Atreus' sons, Dolopians in a mass—
As, when a cyclone breaks, conflicting winds
Will come together, Westwind, Southwind, Eastwind
Riding high out of the Dawnland; forests   535
Bend and roar, and raging all in spume
Nereus[9] with his trident churns the deep.
Then some whom we had taken by surprise
Under cover of night throughout the city
And driven off, came back again: they knew   540
Our shields and arms for liars now, our speech
Alien to their own. They overwhelmed us.

7. The abode of the dead.   8. Not the great Ajax, son of Telamon (who had killed himself before Troy
fell—see *Odyssey*, Book XI), but the lesser Ajax, son of Oileus. His rape of Cassandra after dragging her
away from Athena's temple was eventually punished: he was drowned on his way home.   9. An old sea
god, father of the sea nymphs, the Nereids.

Coroebus fell at the warrior goddess' altar,
Killed by Peneleus; and Ripheus fell,
A man uniquely just among the Trojans,   545
The soul of equity; but the gods would have it
Differently. Hypanis, Dymas died,
Shot down by friends; nor did your piety,
Panthus, nor Apollo's fillets shield you
As you went down.
             Ashes of Ilium!   550
Flames that consumed my people! Here I swear
That in your downfall I did not avoid
One weapon, one exchange with the Danaans,
And if it had been fated, my own hand
Had earned my death. But we were torn away   555
From that place—Iphitus and Pelias too,
One slow with age, one wounded by Ulysses,
Called by a clamor at the hall of Priam.
Truly we found here a prodigious fight,
As though there were none elsewhere, not a death   560
In the whole city: Mars[1] gone berserk, Danaans
In a rush to scale the roof; the gate besieged
By a tortoise shell of overlapping shields.[2]
Ladders clung to the wall, and men strove upward
Before the very doorposts, on the rungs,   565
Left hand putting the shield up, and the right
Reaching for the cornice. The defenders
Wrenched out upperworks and rooftiles: these
For missiles, as they saw the end, preparing
To fight back even on the edge of death.   570
And gilded beams, ancestral ornaments,
They rolled down on the heads below. In hall
Others with swords drawn held the entrance way,
Packed there, waiting. Now we plucked up heart
To help the royal house, to give our men   575
A respite, and to add our strength to theirs,
Though all were beaten. And we had for entrance
A rear door, secret, giving on a passage
Between the palace halls; in other days
Andromachë, poor lady, often used it,   580
Going alone to see her husband's parents
Or taking Astyanax[3] to his grandfather.
I climbed high on the roof, where hopeless men
Were picking up and throwing futile missiles.
Here was a tower like a promontory   585

---

1. The Roman war god (Ares).   2. Roman soldiers, when attacking a walled position, shielded their
heads from missiles from above by a roof of interlocking shields—like the plates of a tortoise shell.
3. Son of Hector and Andromache.

Rising toward the stars above the roof:
All Troy, the Danaan ships, the Achaean camp,
Were visible from this. Now close beside it
With crowbars, where the flooring made loose joints,
We pried it from its bed and pushed it over.   590
Down with a rending crash in sudden ruin
Wide over the Danaan lines it fell;
But fresh troops moved up, and the rain of stones
With every kind of missile never ceased.

Just at the outer doors of the vestibule   595
Sprang Pyrrhus,[4] all in bronze and glittering,
As a serpent, hidden swollen underground
By a cold winter, writhes into the light,
On vile grass fed, his old skin cast away,
Renewed and glossy, rolling slippery coils,   600
With lifted underbelly rearing sunward
And triple tongue a-flicker. Close beside him
Giant Periphas and Automedon,
His armor-bearer, once Achilles' driver,
Besieged the place with all the young of Scyros,[5]   605
Hurling their torches at the palace roof.
Pyrrhus shouldering forward with an axe
Broke down the stony threshold, forced apart
Hinges and brazen door-jambs, and chopped through
One panel of the door, splitting the oak,   610
To make a window, a great breach. And there
Before their eyes the inner halls lay open,
The courts of Priam and the ancient kings,
With men-at-arms ranked in the vestibule.
From the interior came sounds of weeping,   615
Pitiful commotion, wails of women
High-pitched, rising in the formal chambers
To ring against the silent golden stars;
And, through the palace, mothers wild with fright
Ran to and fro or clung to doors and kissed them.   620
Pyrrhus with his father's brawn stormed on,
No bolts or bars or men availed to stop him:
Under his battering the double doors
Were torn out of their sockets and fell inward.
Sheer force cleared the way: the Greeks broke through   625
Into the vestibule, cut down the guards,
And made the wide hall seethe with men-at-arms—
A tumult greater than when dykes are burst
And a foaming river, swirling out in flood,

4. Another name of Neoptolemus, the son of Achilles.   5. Island in the North Aegean where Neoptolemus grew up.

Whelms every parapet and races on 630
Through fields and over all the lowland plains,
Bearing off pens and cattle. I myself
Saw Neoptolemus furious with blood
In the entrance way, and saw the two Atridae;
Hecuba[6] I saw, and her hundred daughters, 635
Priam before the altars, with his blood
Drenching the fires that he himself had blessed.
Those fifty bridal chambers, hope of a line
So flourishing; those doorways high and proud,
Adorned with takings of barbaric gold, 640
Were all brought low: fire had them, or the Greeks.

What was the fate of Priam, you may ask.
Seeing his city captive, seeing his own
Royal portals rent apart, his enemies
In the inner rooms, the old man uselessly 645
Put on his shoulders, shaking with old age,
Armor unused for years, belted a sword on,
And made for the massed enemy to die.
Under the open sky in a central court
Stood a big altar; near it, a laurel tree 650
Of great age, leaning over, in deep shade
Embowered the Penatës.[7] At this altar
Hecuba and her daughters, like white doves
Blown down in a black storm, clung together,
Enfolding holy images in their arms. 655
Now, seeing Priam in a young man's gear,
She called out:
                    'My poor husband, what mad thought
Drove you to buckle on these weapons?
Where are you trying to go? The time is past
For help like this, for this kind of defending, 660
Even if my own Hector could be here.
Come to me now: the altar will protect us,
Or else you'll die with us.'
                    She drew him close,
Heavy with years, and made a place for him
To rest on the consecrated stone.
                    Now see 665
Politès, one of Priam's sons, escaped
From Pyrrhus' butchery and on the run
Through enemies and spears, down colonnades,
Through empty courtyards, wounded. Close behind
Comes Pyrrhus burning for the death-stroke: has him, 670
Catches him now, and lunges with the spear.

6. Wife of Priam and mother of Hector.   7. The (Roman) gods of the household.

The boy has reached his parents, and before them
Goes down, pouring out his life with blood.
Now Priam, in the very midst of death,
Would neither hold his peace nor spare his anger.   675

'For what you've done, for what you've dared,' he said,
'If there is care in heaven for atrocity,
May the gods render fitting thanks, reward you
As you deserve. You forced me to look on
At the destruction of my son: defiled   680
A father's eyes with death. That great Achilles
You claim to be the son of—and you lie—
Was not like you to Priam, his enemy;
To me who threw myself upon his mercy
He showed compunction, gave me back for burial   685
The bloodless corpse of Hector, and returned me
To my own realm.'
                    The old man threw his spear
With feeble impact; blocked by the ringing bronze,
It hung there harmless from the jutting boss.
Then Pyrrhus answered:
                    'You'll report the news   690
To Pelidës,[8] my father; don't forget
My sad behavior, the degeneracy
Of Neoptolemus. Now die.'
                    With this,
To the altar step itself he dragged him trembling,
Slipping in the pooled blood of his son,   695
And took him by the hair with his left hand.
The sword flashed in his right; up to the hilt
He thrust it in his body.
                    That was the end
Of Priam's age, the doom that took him off,
With Troy in flames before his eyes, his towers   700
Headlong fallen—he that in other days
Had ruled in pride so many lands and peoples,
The power of Asia.
                    On the distant shore
The vast trunk headless lies without a name.

For the first time that night, inhuman shuddering   705
Took me, head to foot. I stood unmanned,
And my dear father's image came to mind
As our king, just his age, mortally wounded,
Gasped his life away before my eyes.
Creusa[9] came to mind, too, left alone;   710

8. Achilles, son of Peleus.   9. Aeneas's wife. *Iulus:* his son, also known as Ascanius.

The house plundered; danger to little Iulus.
I looked around to take stock of my men,
But all had left me, utterly played out,
Giving their beaten bodies to the fire
Or plunging from the roof.
                              It came to this,   715
That I stood there alone. And then I saw
Lurking beyond the doorsill of the Vesta,
In hiding, silent, in that place reserved,
The daughter of Tyndareus.[1] Glare of fires
Lighted my steps this way and that, my eyes   720
Glancing over the whole scene, everywhere.
That woman, terrified of the Trojans' hate
For the city overthrown, terrified too
Of Danaan vengeance, her abandoned husband's
Anger after years—Helen, that Fury   725
Both to her own homeland and Troy, had gone
To earth, a hated thing, before the altars.
Now fires blazed up in my own spirit—
A passion to avenge my fallen town
And punish Helen's whorishness.
                         'Shall this one   730
Look untouched on Sparta and Mycenae
After her triumph, going like a queen,
And see her home and husband, kin and children,
With Trojan girls for escort, Phrygian slaves?
Must Priam perish by the sword for this?   735
Troy burn, for this? Dardania's littoral
Be soaked in blood, so many times, for this?
Not by my leave. I know
No glory comes of punishing a woman,
The feat can bring no honor. Still, I'll be   740
Approved for snuffing out a monstrous life,
For a just sentence carried out. My heart
Will teem with joy in this avenging fire,
And the ashes of my kin will be appeased.'

So ran my thoughts. I turned wildly upon her,   745
But at that moment, clear, before my eyes—
Never before so clear—in a pure light
Stepping before me, radiant through the night,
My loving mother[2] came: immortal, tall,
And lovely as the lords of heaven know her.   750
Catching me by the hand, she held me back,
Then with her rose-red mouth reproved me:

1. Helen.   2. Venus (Aphrodite).

                                        'Son,
Why let such suffering goad you on to fury
Past control? Where is your thoughtfulness
For me, for us? Will you not first revisit   755
The place you left your father, worn and old,
Or find out if your wife, Creusa, lives,
And the young boy, Ascanius—all these
Cut off by Greek troops foraging everywhere?
Had I not cared for them, fire would by now   760
Have taken them, their blood glutted the sword.
You must not hold the woman of Laconia,[3]
That hated face, the cause of this, nor Paris.
The harsh will of the gods it is, the gods,
That overthrows the splendor of this place   765
And brings Troy from her height into the dust.
Look over there: I'll tear away the cloud
That curtains you, and films your mortal sight,
The fog around you.—Have no fear of doing
Your mother's will, or balk at obeying her.—   770
Look: where you see high masonry thrown down,
Stone torn from stone, with billowing smoke and dust,
Neptune is shaking from their beds the walls
That his great trident pried up, undermining,
Toppling the whole city down. And look: 775
Juno in all her savagery holds
The Scaean Gates,[4] and raging in steel armor
Calls her allied army from the ships.
Up on the citadel—turn, look—Pallas Tritonia[5]
Couched in a stormcloud, lightening, with her Gorgon![6]   780
The Father himself empowers the Danaans,
Urges assaulting gods on the defenders.
Away, child; put an end to toiling so.
I shall be near, to see you safely home.'

She hid herself in the deep gloom of night,   785
And now the dire forms appeared to me
Of great immortals, enemies of Troy.
I knew the end then: Ilium was going down
In fire, the Troy of Neptune[7] going down,
As in high mountains when the countrymen   790
Have notched an ancient ash, then make their axes
Ring with might and main, chopping away
To fell the tree—ever on the point of falling,

3. Sparta; she means Helen.   4. One of the principal entrances to Troy.   5. Athena (Minerva). The
significance of the adjective Tritonia is not known; perhaps a reference to her birthplace, Lake Tritonis,
in North Africa. (But the birthplace legend may have been invented to explain the title.)   6. Monster
whose appearance turned men to stone. Athena had a Gorgon face on her shield.   7. Although Neptune
(Poseidon) is now one of the powers hostile to Troy, he helped to build it.

Shaken through all its foliage, and the treetop
Nodding; bit by bit the strokes prevail   795
Until it gives a final groan at last
And crashes down in ruin from the height.

Now I descended where the goddess guided,
Clear of the flames, and clear of enemies,
For both retired; so gained my father's door,   800
My ancient home. I looked for him at once,
My first wish being to help him to the mountains;
But with Troy gone he set his face against it,
Not to prolong his life, or suffer exile.

'The rest of you, all in your prime,' he said,   805
'Make your escape; you are still hale and strong.
If heaven's lords had wished me a longer span
They would have saved this home for me. I call it
More than enough that once before I saw
My city taken and wrecked,[8] and went on living.   810
Here is my death bed, here. Take leave of me.
Depart now. I'll find death with my sword arm.
The enemy will oblige; they'll come for spoils.
Burial can be dispensed with. All these years
I've lingered in my impotence,[9] at odds   815
With heaven, since the Father of gods and men
Breathed high winds of thunderbolt upon me
And touched me with his fire.'
                              He spoke on
In the same vein, inflexible. The rest of us,
Creusa and Ascanius and the servants,   820
Begged him in tears not to pull down with him
Our lives as well, adding his own dead weight
To the fates' pressure. But he would not budge,
He held to his resolve and to his chair.
I felt swept off again to fight, in misery   825
Longing for death. What choices now were open,
What chance had I?
                   'Did you suppose, my father,
That I could tear myself away and leave you?
Unthinkable; how could a father say it?
Now if it please the powers above that nothing   830
Stand of this great city; if your heart
Is set on adding your own death and ours
To that of Troy, the door's wide open for it:
Pyrrhus will be here, splashed with Priam's blood;

---

8. Troy had been captured and sacked once before, by the hero Heracles. 9. Anchises was punished
by Jupiter (Zeus) for being the lover of Venus (Aphrodite), the mother of his son Aeneas. Anchises was
struck by a thunderbolt and crippled.

He kills the son before his father's eyes,   835
The father at the altars.
                              My dear mother,
Was it for this, through spears and fire, you brought me,
To see the enemy deep in my house,
To see my son, Ascanius, my father,
And near them both, Creusa,   840
Butchered in one another's blood? My gear,
Men, bring my gear. The last light calls the conquered.
Give me back to the Greeks. Let me take up
The combat once again. We shall not all
Die this day unavenged.'
                          I buckled on   845
Swordbelt and blade and slid my left forearm
Into the shield-strap, turning to go out,
But at the door Creusa hugged my knees,
Then held up little Iulus to his father.

'If you are going out to die, take us   850
To face the whole thing with you. If experience
Leads you to put some hope in weaponry
Such as you now take, guard your own house here.
When you have gone, to whom is Iulus left?
Your father? Wife?—one called that long ago.'   855

She went on, and her wailing filled the house,
But then a sudden portent came, a marvel:
Amid his parents' hands and their sad faces
A point on Iulus' head seemed to cast light,
A tongue of flame that touched but did not burn him,   860
Licking his fine hair, playing round his temples.
We, in panic, beat at the flaming hair
And put the sacred fire out with water;
Father Anchises lifted his eyes to heaven
And lifted up his hands, his voice, in joy: 865

'Omnipotent Jupiter, if prayers affect you,
Look down upon us, that is all I ask,
If by devotion to the gods we earn it,
Grant us a new sign, and confirm this portent!'
The old man barely finished when it thundered   870
A loud crack on the left. Out of the sky
Through depths of night a star fell trailing flame
And glided on, turning the night to day.
We watched it pass above the roof and go
To hide its glare, its trace, in Ida's[1] wood;   875
But still, behind, the luminous furrow shone

1. The mountain range near Troy.

And wide zones fumed with sulphur.
                    Now indeed
My father, overcome, addressed the gods,
And rose in worship of the blessed star.

'Now, now, no more delay. I'll follow you.   880
Where you conduct me, there I'll be.
                    Gods of my fathers,
Preserve this house, preserve my grandson. Yours
This portent was. Troy's life is in your power.
I yield. I go as your companion, son.'
Then he was still. We heard the blazing town   885
Crackle more loudly, felt the scorching heat.

'Then come, dear father. Arms around my neck:
I'll take you on my shoulders, no great weight.
Whatever happens, both will face one danger,
Find one safety. Iulus will come with me,   890
My wife at a good interval behind.
Servants, give your attention to what I say.
At the gate inland there's a funeral mound
And an old shrine of Ceres the Bereft;[2]
Near it an ancient cypress, kept alive   895
For many years by our fathers' piety.
By various routes we'll come to that one place.
Father, carry our hearthgods, our Penatës.
It would be wrong for me to handle them—
Just come from such hard fighting, bloody work—   900
Until I wash myself in running water.'

When I had said this, over my breadth of shoulder
And bent neck, I spread out a lion skin
For tawny cloak and stooped to take his weight.
Then little Iulus put his hand in mine   905
And came with shorter steps beside his father.
My wife fell in behind. Through shadowed places
On we went, and I, lately unmoved
By any spears thrown, any squads of Greeks,
Felt terror now at every eddy of wind,   910
Alarm at every sound, alert and worried
Alike for my companion and my burden.
I had got near the gate, and now I thought
We had made it all the way, when suddenly
A noise of running feet came near at hand,   915
And peering through the gloom ahead, my father
Cried out:
                    'Run, boy; here they come; I see

2. Ceres (Demeter) mourning the loss of her daughter Proserpina (Persephone).

Flame light on shields, bronze shining.'
                                    I took fright,
And some unfriendly power, I know not what,
Stole all my addled wits—for as I turned   920
Aside from the known way, entering a maze
Of pathless places on the run—
                            Alas,
Creusa, taken from us by grim fate, did she
Linger, or stray, or sink in weariness?
There is no telling. Never would she be   925
Restored to us. Never did I look back
Or think to look for her, lost as she was,
Until we reached the funeral mound and shrine
Of venerable Ceres. Here at last
All came together, but she was not there;   930
She alone failed[3] her friends, her child, her husband.
Out of my mind, whom did I not accuse,
What man or god? What crueller loss had I
Beheld, that night the city fell? Ascanius,
My father, and the Teucrian Penatës,   935
I left in my friends' charge, and hid them well
In a hollow valley.
                    I turned back alone
Into the city, cinching my bright harness.
Nothing for it but to run the risks
Again, go back again, comb all of Troy,
And put my life in danger as before: 940
First by the town wall, then the gate, all gloom,
Through which I had come out—and so on backward,
Tracing my own footsteps through the night;
And everywhere my heart misgave me: even
Stillness had its terror. Then to our house,   945
Thinking she might, just might, have wandered there.
Danaans had got in and filled the place,
And at that instant fire they had set,
Consuming it, went roofward in a blast;
Flames leaped and seethed in heat to the night sky.   950
I pressed on, to see Priam's hall and tower.
In the bare colonnades of Juno's shrine
Two chosen guards, Phoenix and hard Ulysses,
Kept watch over the plunder. Piled up here
Were treasures of old Troy from every quarter,   955
Torn out of burning temples: altar tables,
Robes, and golden bowls. Drawn up around them,
Boys and frightened mothers stood in line.

3. The original Latin does not imply fault and is better read "was not to be found" (literally, "was lacking to").

I even dared to call out in the night;
I filled the streets with calling; in my grief 960
Time after time I groaned and called Creusa,
Frantic, in endless quest from door to door.
Then to my vision her sad wraith appeared—
Creusa's ghost, larger than life, before me.
Chilled to the marrow, I could feel the hair 965
On my head rise, the voice clot in my throat;
But she spoke out to ease me of my fear:

'What's to be gained by giving way to grief
So madly, my sweet husband? Nothing here
Has come to pass except as heaven willed. 970
You may not take Creusa with you now;
It was not so ordained, nor does the lord
Of high Olympus give you leave. For you
Long exile waits, and long sea miles to plough.
You shall make landfall on Hesperia 975
Where Lydian Tiber⁴ flows, with gentle pace,
Between rich farmlands, and the years will bear
Glad peace, a kingdom, and a queen for you.
Dismiss these tears for your beloved Creusa.
I shall not see the proud homelands of Myrmidons 980
Or of Dolopians, or go to serve
Greek ladies, Dardan lady that I am
And daughter-in-law of Venus the divine.
No: the great mother of the gods⁵ detains me
Here on these shores. Farewell now; cherish still 985
Your son and mine.'
          With this she left me weeping,
Wishing that I could say so many things,
And faded on the tenuous air. Three times
I tried to put my arms around her neck,
Three times enfolded nothing, as the wraith 990
Slipped through my fingers, bodiless as wind,
Or like a flitting dream.
          So in the end
As night waned I rejoined my company.
And there to my astonishment I found
New refugees in a great crowd: men and women 995
Gathered for exile, young—pitiful people
Coming from every quarter, minds made up,
With their belongings, for whatever lands
I'd lead them to by sea.
          The morning star

4. The Tiber River was the center of many Etruscan settlements and the Etruscans were supposed to be immigrants from Lydia, in Asia Minor.   5. Cybele, an Asiatic mother-goddess worshiped (according to Virgil) at Troy.

Now rose on Ida's ridges, bringing day.   1000
Greeks had secured the city gates. No help
Or hope of help existed.
So I resigned myself, picked up my father,
And turned my face toward the mountain range."

[Aeneas goes on to tell the story of his wanderings in search of a new home.
By the end of the evening, Dido, already falling in love with him before
the banquet (through the intervention of Venus and Juno, who both promote the affair, each for different reasons), now feels the full force of her
passion for Aeneas.]

BOOK IV

The Passion of the Queen

The queen, for her part, all that evening ached
With longing that her heart's blood fed, a wound
Or inward fire eating her away.
The manhood of the man, his pride of birth,
Came home to her time and again; his looks,   5
His words remained with her to haunt her mind,
And desire for him gave her no rest.
                    When Dawn
Swept earth with Phoebus' torch and burned away
Night-gloom and damp, this queen, far gone and ill,
Confided to the sister of her heart:
"My sister Anna, quandaries and dreams   10
Have come to frighten me—such dreams!
                    Think what a stranger
Yesterday found lodging in our house:
How princely, how courageous, what a soldier.
I can believe him in the line of gods,
And this is no delusion. Tell-tale fear   15
Betrays inferior souls. What scenes of war
Fought to the bitter end he pictured for us!
What buffetings awaited him at sea!
Had I not set my face against remarriage
After my first love died[6] and failed me, left me   20
Barren and bereaved—and sick to death
At the mere thought of torch and bridal bed—
I could perhaps give way in this one case
To frailty. I shall say it: since that time
Sychaeus, my poor husband, met his fate,   25
And blood my brother shed stained our hearth gods,
This man alone has wrought upon me so

---

6. Her first husband, Sychaeus, was murdered by Pygmalion, king of Tyre, Dido's brother. Her husband's
ghost warned her in a dream to leave Tyre and seek a new home.

And moved my soul to yield. I recognize
The signs of the old flame, of old desire.
But O chaste life, before I break your laws,   30
I pray that Earth may open, gape for me
Down to its depth, or the omnipotent
With one stroke blast me to the shades, pale shades
Of Erebus[7] and the deep world of night!
That man who took me to himself in youth   35
Has taken all my love; may that man keep it,
Hold it forever with him in the tomb."

At this she wept and wet her breast with tears.
But Anna answered:
                    "Dearer to your sister
Than daylight is, will you wear out your life,   40
Young as you are, in solitary mourning,
Never to know sweet children, or the crown
Of joy that Venus brings? Do you believe
This matters to the dust, to ghosts in tombs?
Granted no suitors up to now have moved you,   45
Neither in Libya nor before, in Tyre—
Iarbas[8] you rejected, and the others,
Chieftains bred by the land of Africa
Their triumphs have enriched—will you contend
Even against a welcome love? Have you   50
Considered in whose lands you settled here?
On one frontier the Gaetulans,[9] their cities,
People invincible in war—with wild
Numidian[1] horsemen, and the offshore banks,
The Syrtës; on the other, desert sands,   55
Bone-dry, where fierce Barcaean nomads[2] range.
Or need I speak of future wars brought on
From Tyre, and the menace of your brother?[3]
Surely by dispensation of the gods
And backed by Juno's will, the ships from Ilium   60
Held their course this way on the wind.
                                        Sister,
What a great city you'll see rising here,
And what a kingdom, from this royal match!
With Trojan soldiers as companions in arms
By what exploits will Punic[4] glory grow!   65
Only ask the indulgence of the gods,
Win them with offerings, give your guests ease,
And contrive reasons for delay, while winter

---

7. The lower depths of Hades.   8. The most prominent of Dido's African suitors.   9. A savage African people living southwest of Carthage.   1. The most powerful of the local tribes. *Syrtes:* on the coast
to the west.   2. To the East.   3. Pygmalion.   4. Carthaginian.

Gales rage, drenched Orion storms at sea,
And their ships, damaged still, face iron skies."   70

This counsel fanned the flame, already kindled,
Giving her hesitant sister hope, and set her
Free of scruple. Visiting the shrines
They begged for grace at every altar first,
Then put choice rams and ewes to ritual death   75
For Ceres Giver of Laws,[5] Father Lyaeus,
Phoebus, and for Juno most of all
Who has the bonds of marriage in her keeping.
Dido herself, splendidly beautiful,
Holding a shallow cup, tips out the wine   80
On a white shining heifer, between the horns,
Or gravely in the shadow of the gods
Approaches opulent altars. Through the day
She brings new gifts, and when the breasts are opened
Pores over organs,[6] living still, for signs.   85
Alas, what darkened minds have soothsayers!
What good are shrines and vows to maddened lovers?
The inward fire eats the soft marrow away,
And the internal wound bleeds on in silence.

Unlucky Dido, burning, in her madness   90
Roamed through all the city, like a doe
Hit by an arrow shot from far away
By a shepherd hunting in the Cretan woods—
Hit by surprise, nor could the hunter see
His flying steel had fixed itself in her;   95
But though she runs for life through copse and glade
The fatal shaft clings to her side.
                         Now Dido
Took Aeneas with her among her buildings,
Showed her Sidonian[7] wealth, her walls prepared,
And tried to speak, but in mid-speech grew still.   100
When the day waned she wanted to repeat
The banquet as before, to hear once more
In her wild need the throes of Ilium,
And once more hung on the narrator's words.
Afterward, when all the guests were gone,   105
And the dim moon in turn had quenched her light,

---

5. Ceres (Demeter) the goddess who guarantees the growth of crops, Lyaeus (Dionysus-Bacchus) the wine god, and Phoebus (Apollo) are selected as deities especially connected with the founding of cities; one of Apollo's titles is "Founder," and Ceres and Dionysus (Bacchus) control the essential crops that will enable the colonists to live. Dido prays to these gods at the moment when she is about to abandon her responsibilities as founder of a city; a similar irony is present in her prayer to Juno, whose "business" is the marriage bond, at the moment when she is about to break her long fidelity to the memory of Sychaeus.   6. An Etruscan and Roman practice was to inspect the entrails of the sacrificial victim and interpret irregular or unusual features as signs of what the future held in store.   7. Sidon is the Phoenician city from which Dido fled, to found Carthage.

And setting stars weighed weariness to sleep,
Alone she mourned in the great empty hall
And pressed her body on the couch he left:
She heard him still, though absent—heard and saw him.   110
Or she would hold Ascanius in her lap,
Enthralled by him, the image of his father,
As though by this ruse to appease a love
Beyond all telling.
                    Towers, half-built, rose
No farther; men no longer trained in arms   115
Or toiled to make harbors and battlements
Impregnable. Projects were broken off,
Laid over, and the menacing huge walls
With cranes unmoving stood against the sky.

As soon as Jove's dear consort saw the lady   120
Prey to such illness, and her reputation
Standing no longer in the way of passion,
Saturn's daughter said to Venus:
                                    "Wondrous!
Covered yourself with glory, have you not,
You and your boy, and won such prizes, too.   125
Divine power is something to remember
If by collusion of two gods one mortal
Woman is brought low.
                        I am not blind.
Your fear of our new walls has not escaped me,
Fear and mistrust of Carthage at her height.   130
But how far will it go? What do you hope for,
Being so contentious? Why do we not
Arrange eternal peace and formal marriage?
You have your heart's desire: Dido in love,
Dido consumed with passion to her core.   135
Why not, then, rule this people side by side
With equal authority? And let the queen
Wait on her Phrygian lord, let her consign
Into your hand her Tyrians as a dowry."

Now Venus knew this talk was all pretence,   140
All to divert the future power from Italy
To Libya; and she answered:
                                "Who would be
So mad, so foolish as to shun that prospect
Or prefer war with you? That is, provided
Fortune is on the side of your proposal.   145
The fates here are perplexing: would one city
Satisfy Jupiter's will for Tyrians
And Trojan exiles? Does he approve

A union and a mingling of these races?
You are his consort: you have every right   150
To sound him out. Go on, and I'll come, too."

But regal Juno pointedly replied:
"That task will rest with me. Just now, as to
The need of the moment and the way to meet it,
Listen, and I'll explain in a few words.   155
Aeneas and Dido in her misery
Plan hunting in the forest, when the Titan
Sun comes up with rays to light the world.
While beaters in excitement ring the glens
My gift will be a black raincloud, and hail,   160
A downpour, and I'll shake heaven with thunder.
The company will scatter, lost in gloom,
As Dido and the Trojan captain come
To one same cavern. I shall be on hand,
And if I can be certain you are willing,   165
There I shall marry them and call her his.
A wedding, this will be."
                    Then Cytherëa,[8]
Not disinclined, nodded to Juno's plea,
And smiled at the stratagem now given away.

Dawn came up meanwhile from the Ocean stream,   170
And in the early sunshine from the gates
Picked huntsmen issued: wide-meshed nets and snares,
Broad spearheads for big game, Massylian[9] horsemen
Trooping with hounds in packs keen on the scent.
But Dido lingered in her hall, as Punic   175
Nobles waited, and her mettlesome hunter
Stood nearby, cavorting in gold and scarlet,
Champing his foam-flecked bridle. At long last
The queen appeared with courtiers in a crowd,
A short Sidonian cloak edged in embroidery   180
Caught about her, at her back a quiver
Sheathed in gold, her hair tied up in gold,
And a brooch of gold pinning her scarlet dress.
Phrygians came in her company as well,
And Iulus, joyous at the scene. Resplendent   185
Above the rest, Aeneas walked to meet her,
To join his retinue with hers. He seemed—
Think of the lord Apollo in the spring
When he leaves wintering in Lycia
By Xanthus torrent, for his mother's isle   190
Of Delos, to renew the festival;

8. Venus   9. Massilia is now Marseilles, in the south of France.

Around his altars Cretans, Dryopës,
And painted Agathyrsans[1] raise a shout,
But the god walks the Cynthian[2] ridge alone
And smooths his hair, binds it in fronded laurel,   195
Braids it in gold; and shafts ring on his shoulders.
So elated and swift, Aeneas walked
With sunlit grace upon him.
                            Soon the hunters,
Riding in company to high pathless hills,
Saw mountain goats shoot down from a rocky peak   200
And scamper on the ridges; toward the plain
Deer left the slopes, herding in clouds of dust
In flight across the open lands. Alone,
The boy Ascanius,[3] delightedly riding
His eager horse amid the lowland vales,   205
Outran both goats and deer. Could he only meet
Amid the harmless game some foaming boar,
Or a tawny lion down from the mountainside!

Meanwhile in heaven began a rolling thunder,
And soon the storm broke, pouring rain and hail.   210
Then Tyrians and Trojans in alarm—
With Venus' Dardan grandson[4]—ran for cover
Here and there in the wilderness, as freshets
Coursed from the high hills.
                        Now to the self-same cave
Came Dido and the captain of the Trojans.   215
Primal Earth herself and Nuptial Juno
Opened the ritual, torches of lightning blazed,
High Heaven became witness to the marriage,
And nymphs cried out wild hymns from a mountain top.
    That day was the first cause of death, and first   220
Of sorrow. Dido had no further qualms
As to impressions given and set abroad;
She thought no longer of a secret love
But called it marriage. Thus, under that name,
She hid her fault.
                Now in no time at all   225
Through all the African cities Rumor goes—
Nimble as quicksilver among evils. Rumor
Thrives on motion, stronger for the running,
Lowly at first through fear, then rearing high,
She treads the land and hides her head in cloud.   230
As people fable it, the Earth, her mother,
Furious against the gods, bore a late sister

---

1. I.e., pilgrims from various regions.   2. Cynthus is a mountain in Apollo's native Delos.   3. Aeneas's
son.   4. Iulus (Ascanius).

To the giants Coeus and Enceladus,
Giving her speed on foot and on the wing:
Monstrous, deformed, titanic. Pinioned, with   235
An eye beneath for every body feather,
And, strange to say, as many tongues and buzzing
Mouths as eyes, as many pricked-up ears,
By night she flies between the earth and heaven
Shrieking through darkness, and she never turns   240
Her eye-lids down to sleep. By day she broods,
On the alert, on rooftops or on towers,
Bringing great cities fear, harping on lies
And slander evenhandedly with truth.
In those days Rumor took an evil joy   245
At filling countrysides with whispers, whispers,
Gossip of what was done, and never done:
How this Aeneas landed, Trojan born,
How Dido in her beauty graced his company,
Then how they reveled all the winter long   250
Unmindful of the realm, prisoners of lust.

These tales the scabrous goddess put about
On men's lips everywhere. Her twisting course
Took her to King Iarbas, whom she set
Ablaze with anger piled on top of anger.   255
Son of Jupiter Hammon by a nymph,
A ravished Garamantean, this prince
Had built the god a hundred giant shrines,
A hundred altars, each with holy fires.
Alight by night and day, sentries on watch,   260
The ground enriched by victims' blood, the doors
Festooned with flowering wreaths. Before his altars
King Iarbas, crazed by the raw story,
Stood, they say, amid the Presences,
With supplicating hands, pouring out prayer: 265

"All powerful Jove, to whom the feasting Moors
At ease on colored couches tip their wine,
Do you see this? Are we then fools to fear you
Throwing down your bolts? Those dazzling fires
Of lightning, are they aimless in the clouds   270
And rumbling thunder meaningless? This woman
Who turned up in our country and laid down
A tiny city at a price, to whom
I gave a beach to plow—and on my terms—
After refusing to marry me has taken   275
Aeneas to be master in her realm.
And now Sir Paris with his men, half-men,
His chin and perfumed hair tied up

In a Maeonian bonnet, takes possession.
As for ourselves, here we are bringing gifts   280
Into these shrines—supposedly your shrines—
Hugging that empty fable."
                Pleas like this
From the man clinging to his altars reached
The ears of the Almighty. Now he turned   285
His eyes upon the queen's town and the lovers
Careless of their good name; then spoke to Mercury,[5]
Assigning him a mission:
                "Son, bestir yourself,
Call up the Zephyrs,[6] take to your wings and glide.
Approach the Dardan captain where he tarries   290
Rapt in Tyrian Carthage, losing sight
Of future towns the fates ordain. Correct him,
Carry my speech to him on the running winds:
No son like this did his enchanting mother
Promise to us, nor such did she deliver   295
Twice from peril at the hands of Greeks.
He was to be the ruler of Italy,
Potential empire, armorer of war;
To father men from Teucer's[7] noble blood
And bring the whole world under law's dominion.   300
If glories to be won by deeds like these
Cannot arouse him, if he will not strive
For his own honor, does he begrudge his son,
Ascanius, the high strongholds of Rome?
What has he in mind? What hope, to make him stay   305
Amid a hostile race, and lose from view
Ausonian[8] progeny, Lavinian lands?
The man should sail: that is the whole point.
Let this be what you tell him, as from me."

He finished and fell silent. Mercury   310
Made ready to obey the great command
Of his great father, and he first tied on
The golden sandals, winged, that high in air
Transport him over seas or over land
Abreast of gale winds; then he took the wand   315
With which he summons pale souls out of Orcus
And ushers others to the underzloom,
Lulls men to slumber or awakens them,
And opens dead men's eyes. This wand in hand,
He can drive winds before him, swimming down   320

5. The Latin equivalent of the Greek Hermes, the divine messenger.   6. The west winds.   7. First
of the Trojan Kings.   8. Italian. *Lavinian lands:* the dowry of Lavinia, daughter of Latinus, who gives
her in marriage to Aeneas.

Along the stormcloud. Now aloft, he saw
The craggy flanks and crown of patient Atlas,[9]
Giant Atlas, balancing the sky
Upon his peak—his pine-forested head
In vapor cowled, beaten by wind and rain.   325
Snow lay upon his shoulders, rills cascaded
Down his ancient chin and beard a-bristle,
Caked with ice. Here Mercury of Cyllenë[1]
Hovered first on even wings, then down
He plummeted to sea-level and flew on   330
Like a low-flying gull that skims the shallows
And rocky coasts where fish ply close inshore.
So, like a gull between the earth and sky,
The progeny of Cyllenë, on the wing
From his maternal grandsire, split the winds   335
To the sand bars of Libya.
                          Alighting tiptoe
On the first hutments, there he found Aeneas
Laying foundations for new towers and homes.
He noted well the swordhilt the man wore,
Adorned with yellow jasper; and the cloak   340
Aglow with Tyrian dye upon his shoulders—
Gifts of the wealthy queen, who had inwoven
Gold thread in the fabric. Mercury
Took him to task at once:
                          "Is it for you
To lay the stones for Carthage's high walls,   345
Tame husband that you are, and build their city?
Oblivious of your own world, your own kingdom!
From bright Olympus he that rules the gods
And turns the earth and heaven by his power—
He and no other sent me to you, told me   350
To bring this message on the running winds:
What have you in mind? What hope, wasting your days
In Libya? If future history's glories
Do not affect you, if you will not strive
For your own honor, think of Ascanius,   355
Think of the expectations of your heir,
Iulus, to whom the Italian realm, the land
Of Rome, are due."
                          And Mercury, as he spoke,
Departed from the visual field of mortals
To a great distance, ebbed in subtle air.   360

---

9. A high mountain range in western North Africa. Virgil is referring, by the personification of the mountain, to the legend that the Titan Atlas was punished for his part in the revolt against Zeus (Jupiter) by being made to hold up the sky on his shoulders.   1. A mountain in Arcadia, birthplace of Hermes-Mercury.

Amazed, and shocked to the bottom of his soul
By what his eyes had seen, Aeneas felt
His hackles rise, his voice choke in his throat.
As the sharp admonition and command
From heaven had shaken him awake, he now   365
Burned only to be gone, to leave that land
Of the sweet life behind. What can he do? How tell
The impassioned queen and hope to win her over?
What opening shall he choose? This way and that
He let his mind dart, testing alternatives,   370
Running through every one. And as he pondered
This seemed the better tactic: he called in
Mnestheus, Sergestus and stalwart Serestus,
Telling them:
                    "Get the fleet ready for sea,
But quietly, and collect the men on shore.   375
Lay in ship stores and gear."
                                As to the cause
For a change of plan, they were to keep it secret,
Seeing the excellent Dido had no notion,
No warning that such love could be cut short;
He would himself look for the right occasion,   380
The easiest time to speak, the way to do it.
The Trojans to a man gladly obeyed.

The queen, for her part, felt some plot afoot
Quite soon—for who deceives a woman in love?
She caught wind of a change, being in fear   385
Of what had seemed her safety. Evil Rumor,[2]
Shameless as before, brought word to her
In her distracted state of ships being rigged
In trim for sailing. Furious, at her wits' end,
She traversed the whole city, all aflame   390
With rage, like a Bacchanté[3] driven wild
By emblems shaken, when the mountain revels
Of the odd year possess her, when the cry
Of Bacchus rises and Cithaeron[4] calls
All through the shouting night. Thus it turned out   395
She was the first to speak and charge Aeneas:

"You even hoped to keep me in the dark
As to this outrage, did you, two-faced man,
And slip away in silence? Can our love
Not hold you, can the pledge we gave not hold you,   400

2. Earlier, Rumor (personified as a semi-divine being) had spread the report of Dido's "marriage," which
had incited Iarbas to make his indignant prayer to Jupiter.   3. A female devotee of the god Dionysus
(Bacchus), in an ecstatic trance at the Dionysian festival, held every other year.   4. Mountain near
Thebes, sacred to Dionysus.

Can Dido not, now sure to die in pain?
Even in winter weather must you toil
With ships, and fret to launch against high winds
For the open sea? Oh, heartless!
                            Tell me now,
If you were not in search of alien lands   405
And new strange homes, if ancient Troy remained,
Would ships put out for Troy on these big seas?
Do you go to get away from me? I beg you,
By these tears, by your own right hand,⁵ since I
Have left my wretched self nothing but that—   410
Yes, by the marriage that we entered on,
If ever I did well and you were grateful
Or found some sweetness in a gift from me,
Have pity now on a declining house!
Put this plan by, I beg you, if a prayer   415
Is not yet out of place.
Because of you, Libyans and nomad kings
Detest me, my own Tyrians are hostile;
Because of you, I lost my integrity
And that admired name by which alone   420
I made my way once toward the stars.
                            To whom
Do you abandon me, a dying woman,
Guest that you are—the only name now left
From that of husband? Why do I live on?
Shall I, until my brother Pygmalion comes   425
To pull my walls down? Or the Gaetulan
Iarbas leads me captive? If at least
There were a child by you for me to care for,
A little one to play in my courtyard
And give me back Aeneas, in spite of all,   430
I should not feel so utterly defeated,
Utterly bereft."
                    She ended there.
The man by Jove's command held fast his eyes
And fought down the emotion in his heart.
At length he answered:
                    "As for myself, be sure   435
I never shall deny all you can say,
Your majesty, of what you meant to me.
Never will the memory of Elissa⁶
Stale for me, while I can still remember
My own life, and the spirit rules my body.   440
As to the event, a few words. Do not think

5. The handclasp with which he pledged his love and which Dido takes as an earnest of marriage.
6. Another name of Dido.

I meant to be deceitful and slip away.
I never held the torches of a bridegroom,
Never entered upon the pact of marriage.
If Fate permitted me to spend my days   445
By my own lights, and make the best of things
According to my wishes, first of all
I should look after Troy and the loved relics
Left me of my people. Priam's great hall
Should stand again; I should have restored the tower   450
Of Pergamum for Trojans in defeat.
But now it is the rich Italian land
Apollo tells me I must make for: Italy,
Named by his oracles. There is my love;
There is my country. If, as a Phoenician,   455
You are so given to the charms of Carthage,
Libyan city that it is, then tell me,
Why begrudge the Teucrian new lands
For homesteads in Ausonia? Are we not
Entitled, too, to look for realms abroad?   460
Night never veils the earth in damp and darkness,
Fiery stars never ascend the east,
But in my dreams my father's troubled ghost[7]
Admonishes and frightens me. Then, too,
Each night thoughts come of young Ascanius,   465
My dear boy wronged, defrauded of his kingdom,
Hesperian lands of destiny. And now
The gods' interpreter, sent by Jove himself—
I swear it by your head and mine—has brought
Commands down through the racing winds! I say   470
With my own eyes in full daylight I saw him
Entering the building! With my very ears
I drank his message in! So please, no more
Of these appeals that set us both afire.
I sail for Italy not of my own free will."   475

During all this she had been watching him
With face averted, looking him up and down
In silence, and she burst out raging now:

"No goddess was your mother. Dardanus
Was not the founder of your family.   480
Liar and cheat! Some rough Caucasian[8] cliff
Begot you on flint. Hyrcanian tigresses
Tendered their teats to you. Why should I palter?

---

7. Anchises had died in Sicily just before Aeneas, leaving for Italy, was blown by the storm winds to
Carthage.   8. The Caucasus is a mountain range near the Caspian Sea. It had connotations of outlan-
dishness and of cruelty. *Hyrcanian:* from the same general areas as the Caucasus.

Why still hold back for more indignity?
Sigh, did he, while I wept? Or look at me?   485
Or yield a tear, or pity her who loved him?
What shall I say first, with so much to say?
The time is past when either supreme Juno
Or the Saturnian father⁹ viewed these things
With justice. Faith can never be secure.   490
I took the man in, thrown up on this coast
In dire need, and in my madness then
Contrived a place for him in my domain,
Rescued his lost fleet, saved his shipmates' lives.
Oh, I am swept away burning by furies!   495
Now the prophet Apollo, now his oracles,
Now the gods' interpreter, if you please,
Sent down by Jove¹ himself, brings through the air
His formidable commands! What fit employment
For heaven's high powers! What anxieties   500
To plague serene immortals!² I shall not
Detain you or dispute your story. Go,
Go after Italy on the sailing winds,
Look for your kingdom, cross the deepsea swell!
If divine justice counts for anything,   505
I hope and pray that on some grinding reef
Midway at sea you'll drink your punishment
And call and call on Dido's name!
From far away I shall come after you
With my black fires, and when cold death has parted   510
Body from soul I shall be everywhere
A shade to haunt you! You will pay for this,
Unconscionable! I shall hear! The news will reach me
Even among the lowest of the dead!"

At this abruptly she broke off and ran   515
In sickness from his sight and the light of day,
Leaving him at a loss, alarmed, and mute
With all he meant to say. The maids in waiting
Caught her as she swooned and carried her
To bed in her marble chamber.
                                   Duty-bound,   520
Aeneas, though he struggled with desire
To calm and comfort her in all her pain,
To speak to her and turn her mind from grief,
And though he sighed his heart out, shaken still
With love of her, yet took the course heaven gave him   525
And went back to the fleet. Then with a will

---

9. Jupiter (son of Saturn).   1. Jupiter.   2. Dido is referring to the Epicurean idea that the gods are
unaffected by human events.

The Teucrians fell to work and launched ships
Along the whole shore: slick with tar each hull
Took to the water. Eager to get away,
The sailors brought oar-boughs out of the woods   530
With leaves still on, and oaken logs unhewn.
Now you could see them issuing from the town
To the water's edge in streams, as when, aware
Of winter, ants will pillage a mound of spelt
To store it in their granary; over fields   535
The black battalion moves, and through the grass
On a narrow trail they carry off the spoil;
Some put their shoulders to the enormous weight
Of a trundled grain, while some pull stragglers in
And castigate delay; their to-and-fro   540
Of labor makes the whole track come alive.
At that sight, what were your emotions, Dido?
Sighing how deeply, looking out and down
From your high tower on the seething shore
Where all the harbor filled before your eyes   545
With bustle and shouts! Unconscionable Love,
To what extremes will you not drive our hearts!
She now felt driven to weep again, again
To move him, if she could, by supplication,
Humbling her pride before her love— to leave   550
Nothing untried, not to die needlessly.

"Anna, you see the arc of waterfront
All in commotion: they come crowding in
From everywhere. Spread canvas calls for wind,
The happy crews have garlanded the sterns.   555
If I could brace myself for this great sorrow,
Sister, I can endure it, too. One favor,
Even so, you may perform for me.
Since that deserter chose you for his friend
And trusted you, even with private thoughts,   560
Since you alone know when he may be reached,
Go, intercede with our proud enemy.
Remind him that I took no oath at Aulis[3]
With Danaans to destroy the Trojan race;
I sent no ship to Pergamum. Never did I   565
Profane his father Anchises' dust and shade.
Why will he not allow my prayers to fall
On his unpitying ears? Where is he racing?
Let him bestow one last gift on his mistress:
This, to await fair winds and easier flight.   570
Now I no longer plead the bond he broke

3. Alluding to Agamemnon's oath when departing from Aulis for Troy.

Of our old marriage, nor do I ask that he
Should live without his dear love, Latium,
Or yield his kingdom. Time is all I beg,
Mere time, a respite and a breathing space   575
For madness to subside in, while my fortune
Teaches me how to take defeat and grieve.
Pity your sister. This is the end, this favor—
To be repaid with interest when I die."

She pleaded in such terms, and such, in tears,   580
Her sorrowing sister brought him, time and again.
But no tears moved him, no one's voice would he
Attend to tractably. The fates opposed it;
God's will blocked the man's once kindly ears.
And just as when the north winds from the Alps   585
This way and that contend among themselves
To tear away an oaktree hale with age,
The wind and tree cry, and the buffeted trunk
Showers high foliage to earth, but holds
On bedrock, for the roots go down as far   590
Into the underworld as cresting boughs
Go up in heaven's air: just so this captain,
Buffeted by a gale of pleas
This way and that way, dinned all the day long,
Felt their moving power in his great heart,   595
And yet his will stood fast; tears fell in vain.

On Dido in her desolation now
Terror grew at her fate. She prayed for death,
Being heartsick at the mere sight of heaven.
That she more surely would perform the act   600
And leave the daylight, now she saw before her
A thing one shudders to recall: on altars
Fuming with incense where she placed her gifts,
The holy water blackened, the spilt wine
Turned into blood and mire. Of this she spoke   605
To no one, not to her sister even. Then, too,
Within the palace was a marble shrine
Devoted to her onetime lord, a place
She held in wondrous honor, all festooned
With snowy fleeces and green festive boughs.   610
From this she now thought voices could be heard
And words could be made out, her husband's words,
Calling her, when midnight hushed the earth;
And lonely on the rooftops the night owl
Seemed to lament, in melancholy notes,   615
Prolonged to a doleful cry. And then, besides,
The riddling words of seers in ancient days,

Foreboding sayings, made her thrill with fear.
In nightmare, fevered, she was hunted down
By pitiless Aeneas, and she seemed   620
Deserted always, uncompanioned always,
On a long journey, looking for her Tyrians
In desolate landscapes—
                         as Pentheus[4] gone mad
Sees the oncoming Eumenidës and sees
A double sun and double Thebes appear,   625
Or as when, hounded on the stage, Orestës[5]
Runs from a mother armed with burning brands,
With serpents hellish black,
And in the doorway squat the Avenging Ones.

So broken in mind by suffering, Dido caught   630
Her fatal madness and resolved to die.
She pondered time and means, then visiting
Her mournful sister, covered up her plan
With a calm look, a clear and hopeful brow.

"Sister, be glad for me! I've found a way   635
To bring him back or free me of desire.
Near to the Ocean boundary, near sundown,
The Aethiops' farthest territory lies,
Where giant Atlas turns the sphere of heaven
Studded with burning stars. From there   640
A priestess of Massylian[6] stock has come;
She had been pointed out to me: custodian
Of that shrine named for daughters of the west,
Hesperidës;[7] and it is she who fed
The dragon, guarding well the holy boughs   645
With honey dripping slow and drowsy poppy.
Chanting her spells she undertakes to free
What hearts she wills, but to inflict on others
Duress of sad desires; to arrest
The flow of rivers, make the stars move backward,   650
Call up the spirits of deep Night. You'll see
Earth shift and rumble underfoot and ash trees
Walk down mountainsides. Dearest, I swear
Before the gods and by your own sweet self,
It is against my will that I resort   655

4. King of Thebes. He persecuted the worshipers of the new god Dionysus and imprisoned the god himself. He was later mocked by the god, who inspired him with the Dionysiac spirit (and perhaps with wine) so that he saw double. In this state he was led off to his death on Cithaeron. These events are dramatized in Euripides' play *The Bacchanals (Bacchae)* but the Eumenides (Furies) are not mentioned there. Perhaps Virgil is using them simply as a symbol for madness.   5. Another reference to Greek tragedy. In the *Choephoroe* (The Libation Bearers) of Aeschylus, Orestes kills his mother, Clytemnestra, and is pursued by the Furies. In other tragic contexts he is represented as pursued by the ghost of his mother.   6. From the African tribe.   7. The daughters of Hesperus, in the west, who lived in a garden that contained golden apples, guarded by a dragon.

For weaponry to magic powers. In secret
Build up a pyre in the inner court
Under the open sky, and place upon it
The arms that faithless man left in my chamber,
All his clothing, and the marriage bed   660
On which I came to grief—solace for me
To annihilate all vestige of the man,
Vile as he is: my priestess shows me this."

While she was speaking, cheek and brow grew pale.
But Anna could not think her sister cloaked   665
A suicide in these unheard-of rites;
She failed to see how great her madness was
And feared no consequence more grave
Than at Sychaeus' death. So, as commanded,
She made the preparations. For her part,   670
The queen, seeing the pyre in her inmost court
Erected huge with pitch-pine and sawn ilex,
Hung all the place under the sky with wreaths
And crowned it with funereal cypress boughs.
On the pyre's top she put a sword he left   675
With clothing, and an effigy on a couch,
Her mind fixed now ahead on what would come.
Around the pyre stood altars, and the priestess,
Hair unbound, called in a voice of thunder
Upon three hundred gods, on Erebus,[8]   680
On Chaos, and on triple Hecatë,
Three-faced Diana. Then she sprinkled drops
Purportedly from the fountain of Avernus.[9]
Rare herbs were brought out, reaped at the new moon
By scythes of bronze, and juicy with a milk   685
Of dusky venom; then the rare love-charm
Or caul torn from the brow of a birthing foal
And snatched away before the mother found it.
Dido herself with consecrated grain
In her pure hands, as she went near the altars,   690
Freed one foot from sandal straps, let fall
Her dress ungirdled, and, now sworn to death,
Called on the gods and stars that knew her fate.
She prayed then to whatever power may care
In comprehending justice for the grief   695
Of lovers bound unequally by love.

The night had come, and weary in every land
Men's bodies took the boon of peaceful sleep.

---

8. The lowest depth of the underworld. *Chaos:* Greek personification of the disorder that preceded the creation of the universe. *Hecatë:* Title of Diana as goddess of sorcery; she is Hecatë, the moon, and Diana the virgin huntress.   9. A lake in southern Italy that was supposed to be the entrance to the lower world.

The woods and the wild seas had quieted
At that hour when the stars are in mid-course   700
And every field is still; cattle and birds
With vivid wings that haunt the limpid lakes
Or nest in thickets in the country places
All were asleep under the silent night.
Not, though, the agonized Phoenician queen: 705
She never slackened into sleep and never
Allowed the tranquil night to rest
Upon her eyelids or within her heart.
Her pain redoubled; love came on again,
Devouring her, and on her bed she tossed   710
In a great surge of anger.
                                        So awake,
She pressed these questions, musing to herself:

"Look now, what can I do? Turn once again
To the old suitors, only to be laughed at—
Begging a marriage with Numidians   715
Whom I disdained so often? Then what? Trail
The Ilian ships and follow like a slave
Commands of Trojans? Seeing them so agreeable,
In view of past assistance and relief,
So thoughtful their unshaken gratitude?   720
Suppose I wished it, who permits or takes
Aboard their proud ships one they so dislike?
Poor lost soul, do you not yet grasp or feel
The treachery of the line of Laömedon?[1]
What then? Am I to go alone, companion   725
Of the exultant sailors in their flight?
Or shall I set out in their wake, with Tyrians,
With all my crew close at my side, and send
The men I barely tore away from Tyre
To sea again, making them hoist their sails   730
To more sea-winds? No: die as you deserve,
Give pain quietus with a steel blade.
                                        Sister,
You are the one who gave way to my tears
In the beginning, burdened a mad queen
With sufferings, and thrust me on my enemy.   735
It was not given me to lead my life
Without new passion, innocently, the way
Wild creatures live, and not to touch these depths.
The vow I took to the ashes of Sychaeus
Was not kept."
                    So she broke out afresh   740

1. A king of Troy who twice broke his promise, once to Heracles and once to Apollo and Poseidon.

In bitter mourning. On his high stern deck
Aeneas, now quite certain of departure,
Everything ready, took the boon of sleep.
In dream the figure of the god returned
With looks reproachful as before: he seemed   745
Again to warn him, being like Mercury
In every way, in voice, in golden hair,
And in the bloom of youth.
                          "Son of the goddess,
Sleep away this crisis, can you still?
Do you not see the dangers growing round you,   750
Madman, from now on? Can you not hear
The offshore westwind blow? The woman hatches
Plots and drastic actions in her heart,
Resolved on death now, whipping herself on
To heights of anger. Will you not be gone   755
In flight, while flight is still within your power?
Soon you will see the offing boil with ships
And glare with torches; soon again
The waterfront will be alive with fires,
If Dawn comes while you linger in this country.   760
Ha! Come, break the spell! Woman's a thing
Forever fitful and forever changing."

At this he merged into the darkness. Then
As the abrupt phantom filled him with fear,
Aeneas broke from sleep and roused his crewmen: 765
"Up, turn out now! Oarsmen, take your thwarts!
Shake out sail! Look here, for the second time
A god from heaven's high air is goading me
To hasten our break away, to cut the cables.
Holy one, whatever god you are,   770
We go with you, we act on your command
Most happily! Be near, graciously help us,
Make the stars in heaven propitious ones!"

He pulled his sword aflash out of its sheath
And struck at the stern hawser. All the men   775
Were gripped by his excitement to be gone,
And hauled and hustled. Ships cast off their moorings,
And an array of hulls hid inshore water
As oarsmen churned up foam and swept to sea.

Soon early Dawn, quitting the saffron bed   780
Of old Tithonus,[2] cast new light on earth,
And as air grew transparent, from her tower

2. Human consort of Eos-Aurora, the dawn-goddess. He is "old" because although she made him immortal when she took him to her bed, she forgot to obtain for him the gift of eternal youth.

The queen caught sight of ships on the seaward reach
With sails full and the wind astern. She knew
The waterfront now empty, bare of oarsmen.   785
Beating her lovely breast three times, four times,
And tearing her golden hair,
                              "O Jupiter,"
She said, "will this man go, will he have mocked
My kingdom, stranger that he was and is?
Will they not snatch up arms and follow him   790
From every quarter of the town? and dockhands
Tear our ships from moorings? On! Be quick
With torches! Give out arms! Unship the oars!
What am I saying? Where am I? What madness
Takes me out of myself? Dido, poor soul,   795
Your evil doing has come home to you.
Then was the right time, when you offered him
A royal scepter. See the good faith and honor
Of one they say bears with him everywhere
The hearthgods of his country! One who bore   800
His father, spent with age, upon his shoulders!
Could I not then have torn him limb from limb
And flung the pieces on the sea? His company,
Even Ascanius could I not have minced
And served up to his father at a feast?   805
The luck of battle might have been in doubt—
So let it have been! Whom had I to fear,
Being sure to die? I could have carried torches
Into his camp, filled passage ways with flame,
Annihilated father and son and followers   810
And given my own life on top of all!
O Sun, scanning with flame all works of earth,
And thou, O Juno, witness and go-between
Of my long miseries; and Hecatë,
Screeched for at night at crossroads in the cities;   815
And thou, avenging Furies, and all gods
On whom Elissa dying may call: take notice,
Overshadow this hell with your high power,
As I deserve, and hear my prayer!
If by necessity that impious wretch   820
Must find his haven and come safe to land,
If so Jove's destinies require, and this,
His end in view, must stand, yet all the same
When hard beset in war by a brave people,
Forced to go outside his boundaries   825
And torn from Iulus, let him beg assistance,
Let him see the unmerited deaths of those
Around and with him, and accepting peace

On unjust terms, let him not, even so,
Enjoy his kingdom or the life he longs for,   830
But fall in battle before his time and lie
Unburied on the sand![3] This I implore,
This is my last cry, as my last blood flows.
Then, O my Tyrians, besiege with hate
His progeny and all his race to come: 835
Make this your offering to my dust. No love,
No pact must be between our peoples;[4] No,
But rise up from my bones, avenging spirit![5]
Harry with fire and sword the Dardan countrymen
Now, or hereafter, at whatever time   840
The strength will be afforded. Coast with coast
In conflict, I implore, and sea with sea,
And arms with arms: may they contend in war,
Themselves and all the children of their children!"

Now she took thought of one way or another,   845
At the first chance, to end her hated life,
And briefly spoke to Barcë, who had been
Sychaeus' nurse; her own an urn of ash
Long held in her ancient fatherland.
                              "Dear nurse,
Tell Sister Anna to come here, and have her   850
Quickly bedew herself with running water
Before she brings out victims for atonement.
Let her come that way. And you, too, put on
Pure wool around your brows. I have a mind
To carry out that rite to Stygian Jove[6]   855
That I have readied here, and put an end
To my distress, committing to the flames
The pyre of that miserable Dardan."

At this with an old woman's eagerness
Barcë hurried away. And Dido's heart   860
Beat wildly at the enormous thing afoot.
She rolled her bloodshot eyes, her quivering cheeks
Were flecked with red as her sick pallor grew
Before her coming death. Into the court
She burst her way, then at her passion's height   865

3. This prophecy of Dido's, expressed in the form of a wish, is destined to come true. Aeneas meets resistance in Italy; at one point in the war he has to leave Ascanius behind and go to beg aid from an Italian king, Evander. The final peace is made on condition that the name of his people be changed from "Trojans" to "Latins"; and he is eventually drowned in an Italian river. Aeneas' reward for all his struggles is to come not during his life, but in the glory of the generations which succeed him.   **4.** In fact, the Romans and Carthaginians fought three separate wars (called Punic Wars from the Roman word for the Carthaginians). Rome won them all (though she almost lost the second one): after the third, the city of Carthage was razed to the ground.   **5.** Dido foresees the harrying of Italy by the Carthaginian general Hannibal, who in the third century B.C. invaded Italy, defeating the Romans in battle after battle, but failed to capture Rome.   **6.** Jove (Jupiter) as lord of the Underworld, where flowed the river Styx.

She climbed the pyre and bared the Dardan sword—
A gift desired once, for no such need.
Her eyes now on the Trojan clothing there
And the familiar bed, she paused a little,
Weeping a little, mindful, then lay down   870
And spoke her last words:
                          "Remnants dear to me
While god and fate allowed it, take this breath
And give me respite from these agonies.
I lived my life out to the very end
And passed the stages Fortune had appointed.   875
Now my tall shade goes to the under world.
I built a famous town, saw my great walls,
Avenged my husband, made my hostile brother
Pay for his crime. Happy, alas, too happy,
If only the Dardanian keels had never   880
Beached on our coast." And here she kissed the bed.
"I die unavenged," she said, "but let me die.
This way, this way,[7] a blessed relief to go
Into the undergloom. Let the cold Trojan,
Far at sea, drink in this conflagration   885
And take with him the omen of my death!"

Amid these words her household people saw her
Crumpled over the steel blade, and the blade
Aflush with red blood, drenched her hands. A scream
Pierced the high chambers. Now through the shocked city   890
Rumor went rioting, as wails and sobs
With women's outcry echoed in the palace
And heaven's high air gave back the beating din,
As though all Carthage or old Tyre fell
To storming enemies,[8] and, out of hand,   895
Flames billowed on the roofs of men and gods.
Her sister heard the trembling, faint with terror,
Lacerating her face, beating her breast,
Ran through the crowd to call the dying queen:

"It came to this, then, sister? You deceived me?   900
The pyre meant this, altars and fires meant this?
What shall I mourn first, being abandoned? Did you
Scorn your sister's company in death?
You should have called me out to the same fate!
The same blade's edge and hurt, at the same hour,   905
Should have taken us off. With my own hands
Had I to build this pyre, and had I to call
Upon our country's gods, that in the end

7. In Latin sic, sic—the repetition represents the two thrusts of the sword.   8. These lines prefigure the
capture and destruction of Carthage in the Third Punic War (146 B.C.).

With you placed on it there, O heartless one,
I should be absent? You have put to death   910
Yourself and me, the people and the fathers
Bred in Sidon, and your own new city.
Give me fresh water, let me bathe her wound
And catch upon my lips any last breath
Hovering over hers."
              Now she had climbed   915
The topmost steps and took her dying sister
Into her arms to cherish, with a sob,
Using her dress to stanch the dark blood flow.
But Dido trying to lift her heavy eyes
Fainted again. Her chest-wound whistled air.   920
Three times she struggled up on one elbow
And each time fell back on the bed. Her gaze
Went wavering as she looked for heaven's light
And groaned at finding it. Almighty Juno,
Filled with pity for this long ordeal   925
And difficult passage, now sent Iris[9] down
Out of Olympus to set free
The wrestling spirit from the body's hold.
For since she died, not at her fated span
Nor as she merited, but before her time   930
Enflamed and driven mad, Proserpina[1]
Had not yet plucked from her the golden hair,
Delivering her to Orcus of the Styx.
So humid Iris through bright heaven flew
On saffron-yellow wings, and in her train   935
A thousand hues shimmered before the sun.
At Dido's head she came to rest.
              "This token
Sacred to Dis[2] I bear away as bidden
And free you from your body."
               Saying this,
She cut a lock of hair. Along with it   940
Her body's warmth fell into dissolution,
And out into the winds her life withdrew.

[After his hurried departure from Carthage, Aeneas goes to Sicily, to the
kingdom of his friend Acestes. There he organizes funeral games in honor
of his father, Anchises (who had died in Sicily on their first visit there),
and leaves behind those of his following who are unwilling to go on to the

9. As in Homer, a divine messenger. Sometimes identified with the rainbow (hence "humid Iris" l. 771
below).   1. The queen of the underworld. Before an animal was sacrificed, some hair was cut from the
forehead: before a human being died, Proserpina (Persephone) was thought to cut a lock of hair as an
offering to Dis, the god of the underworld. Since Dido by her suicide has anticipated her fated day,
Proserpina cannot cut the lock; Juno sends Iris to do it.   2. Roman name for Greek Hades, god of the
underworld.

uncertainty of a settlement in Italy. Once on Italian soil, Aeneas, obeying instructions from his dead father who had appeared to him in a dream, consults the Sibyl, who guides him down to the world of the dead. There he is to see his father and the vision of his race, which is to be his only reward, for he will die before his people are settled in their new home.]

From BOOK VI

(Aeneas in the Underworld)

Gods who rule the ghosts; all silent shades;
And Chaos and infernal Fiery Stream,[3]
And regions of wide night without a sound,
May it be right to tell what I have heard,
May it be right, and fitting, by your will,   5
That I describe the deep world sunk in darkness
Under the earth.
        Now dim to one another
In desolate night they[4] walked on through the gloom,
Through Dis's homes all void, and empty realms,
As one goes through a wood by a faint moon's   10
Treacherous light, when Jupiter veils the sky
And black night blots the colors of the world.
Before the entrance, in the jaws of Orcus,
Grief and avenging Cares have made their beds,
And pale Diseases and sad Age are there,   15
And Dread, and Hunger that sways men to crime,
And sordid Want—in shapes to affright the eyes—
And Death and Toil and Death's own brother, Sleep,
And the mind's evil joys; on the door sill
Death-bringing War, and iron cubicles   20
Of the Eumenidës, and raving Discord,
Viperish hair bound up in gory bands.
In the courtyard a shadowy giant elm
Spreads ancient boughs, her ancient arms where dreams,
False dreams, the old tale goes, beneath each leaf   25
Cling and are numberless. There, too,
About the doorway forms of monsters crowd—
Centaurs,[5] twiformed Scyllas, hundred-armed
Briareus, and the Lernaean hydra[6]
Hissing horribly, and the Chimaera   30
Breathing dangerous flames, and Gorgons, Harpies,[7]

---

3. A translation of *Phlegethon*, the name of one of the underworld rivers.   4. Aeneas and the Sibyl.
5. Mythical creatures, half man, half horse—a byword for violence. *Scyllas:* Many-headed monsters.
Briareus had fifty heads.   6. Many-headed serpent killed by Heracles. Each time one head was cut off,
two new ones grew in its place. *Chimaera:* One-third lion, one-third goat, one-third snake.   7. Not,
here, the creatures which carried off the food of Phineus' table but spirits of the storm wind which carry
souls off to Hades. *Gorgons:* Monsters whose look could turn people to stone.

Huge Geryon,[8] triple-bodied ghost.
Here, swept by sudden fear, drawing his sword,
Aeneas stood on guard with naked edge
Against them as they came. If his companion,   35
Knowing the truth, had not admonished him
How faint these lives were—empty images
Hovering bodiless—he had attacked
And cut his way through phantoms, empty air.

The path goes on from that place to the waves   40
Of Tartarus's Acheron.[9] Thick with mud,
A whirlpool out of a vast abyss
Boils up and belches all the silt it carries
Into Cocytus.[1] Here the ferryman,
A figure of fright, keeper of waters and streams,   45
Is Charon,[2] foul and terrible, his beard
Grown wild and hoar, his staring eyes all flame,
His sordid cloak hung from a shoulder knot.
Alone he poles his craft and trims the sails
And in his rusty hull ferries the dead,   50
Old now—but old age in the gods is green.

Here a whole crowd came streaming to the banks,
Mothers and men, the forms with all life spent
Of heroes great in valor, boys and girls
Unmarried, and young sons laid on the pyre   55
Before their parents' eyes—as many souls
As leaves that yield their hold on boughs and fall
Through forests in the early frost of autumn,
Or as migrating birds from the open sea
That darken heaven when the cold season comes   60
And drives them overseas to sunlit lands.
There all stood begging to be first across
And reached out longing hands to the far shore.

But the grim boatman now took these aboard,
Now those, waving the rest back from the strand.   65
In wonder at this and touched by the commotion,
Aeneas said:
          "Tell me, Sister, what this means,
The crowd at the stream. Where are the souls bound?
How are they tested, so that these turn back,
While those take oars to cross the dead-black water?"   70

Briefly the ancient priestess answered him:

---

8. A giant with three bodies: an opponent of Heracles.   9. One of the rivers of the underworld. *Tartarus*: The lower depths of the underworld.   1. Another infernal river. The name suggests in Greek, "mourning," "lamentation."   2. The ferryman who took the souls across the river. He is a god, and very old, but age in gods does not affect their vitality or strength ("old age in the gods is green").

"Cocytus is the deep pool that you see,
The swamp of Styx beyond, infernal power
By which the gods take oath and fear to break it.
All in the nearby crowd you notice here   75
Are pauper souls, the souls of the unburied.
Charon's the boatman. Those the water bears
Are souls of buried men. He may not take them
Shore to dread shore on the hoarse currents there
Until their bones rest in the grave, or till   80
They flutter and roam this side a hundred years;
They may have passage then, and may return
To cross the deeps they long for."
                                          Anchises' son
Had halted, pondering on so much, and stood
In pity for the souls' hard lot. Among them   85
He saw two sad ones of unhonored death,
Leucaspis and the Lycian fleet's commander,
Orontës,[3] who had sailed the windy sea
From Troy together, till the Southern gale
Had swamped and whirled them down, both ship and men.   90
Of a sudden he saw his helmsman, Palinurus,
Going by, who but a few nights before
On course from Libya, as he watched the stars,
Had been pitched overboard astern. As soon
As he made sure of the disconsolate one   95
In all the gloom, Aeneas called:
                                "Which god
Took you away from us and put you under,
Palinurus? Tell me. In this one prophecy
Apollo, who had never played me false,
Falsely foretold you'd be unharmed at sea   100
And would arrive at the Ausonian coast.
Is the promise kept?"
                      But the shade said:
                                "Phoebus' caldron[4]
Told you no lie, my captain, and no god
Drowned me at sea. The helm that I hung on to,
Duty bound to keep our ship on course,   105
By some great shock chanced to be torn away,
And I went with it overboard. I swear
By the rough sea, I feared less for myself
Than for your ship: with rudder gone and steersman
Knocked overboard, it might well come to grief   110
In big seas running. Three nights, heavy weather
Out of the South on the vast water tossed me.

3. Trojans lost at sea in the storm which took Aeneas to Carthage.   4. The Pythia, priestess of Apollo
at Delphi, delivered the god's prophecies seated on a tripod, a three-legged shallow caldron.

On the fourth dawn, I sighted Italy
Dimly ahead, as a wave-crest lifted me.
By turns I swam and rested, swam again   115
And got my footing on the beach, but savages
Attacked me as I clutched at a cliff-top,
Weighted down by my wet clothes. Poor fools,
They took me for a prize and ran me through.
Surf has me now, and sea winds, washing me   120
Close inshore.
        By heaven's happy light
And the sweet air, I beg you, by your father,
And by your hopes of Iulus' rising star,
Deliver me from this captivity,
Unconquered friend! Throw earth on me—you can—   125
Put in to Velia[5] port! Or if there be
Some way to do it, if your goddess mother
Shows a way—and I feel sure you pass
These streams and Stygian marsh by heaven's will—
Give this poor soul your hand, take me across,   130
Let me at least in death find quiet haven."
When he had made his plea, the Sibyl said:
"From what source comes this craving, Palinurus?
Would you though still unburied see the Styx
And the grim river of the Eumenidës,   135
Or even the river bank, without a summons?
Abandon hope by prayer to make the gods
Change their decrees. Hold fast to what I say
To comfort your hard lot: neighboring folk
In cities up and down the coast will be   140
Induced by portents to appease your bones,
Building a tomb and making offerings there
On a cape forever named for Palinurus."

The Sibyl's words relieved him, and the pain
Was for a while dispelled from his sad heart,   145
Pleased at the place-name. So the two walked on
Down to the stream. Now from the Stygian water
The boatman, seeing them in the silent wood
And headed for the bank, cried out to them
A rough uncalled-for challenge:
                "Who are you   150
In armor, visiting our rivers? Speak
From where you are, stop there, say why you come.
This is the region of the Shades, and Sleep,
And drowsy Night. It breaks eternal law
For the Stygian craft to carry living bodies.   155

5. South of the Bay of Naples, near Cape Palinuro (which is still named after Aeneas' pilot).

Never did I rejoice, I tell you, letting
Alcidës[6] cross, or Theseus and Pirithous,
Demigods by paternity though they were,
Invincible in power. One forced in chains
From the king's own seat the watchdog of the dead   160
And dragged him away trembling. The other two
Were bent on carrying our lady off
From Dis's chamber."
                    This the prophetess
And servant of Amphrysian Apollo[7]
Briefly answered:
                    "Here are no such plots,   165
So fret no more. These weapons threaten nothing.
Let the great watchdog at the door howl on
Forever terrifying the bloodless shades.
Let chaste Proserpina remain at home
In her uncle's house. The man of Troy, Aeneas,   170
Remarkable for loyalty, great in arms,
Goes through the deepest shades of Erebus
To see his father.
                    If the very image
Of so much goodness moves you not at all,
Here is a bough"[8]—at this she showed the bough   175
That had been hidden, held beneath her dress—
"You'll recognize it."
                    Then his heart, puffed up
With rage, subsided. They had no more words.
His eyes fixed on the ancient gift, the bough,
The destined gift, so long unseen, now seen,   180
He turned his dusky craft and made for shore.
There from the long thwarts where they sat he cleared
The other souls and made the gangway wide,
Letting the massive man step in the bilge.
The leaky coracle groaned at the weight   185
And took a flood of swampy water in.
At length, on the other side, he put ashore
The prophetess and hero in the mire,
A formless ooze amid the grey-green sedge.
Great Cerberus barking with his triple throat   190
Makes all that shoreline ring, as he lies huge
In a facing cave. Seeing his neck begin
To come alive with snakes, the prophetess

6. Heracles. One of his labors was to bring Cerberus, the watchdog of Hades, up from the lower world.
Theseus . . . Pirithoüs: They came to kidnap Proserpina (Persephone): they failed and were imprisoned but
Heracles rescued Theseus.   7. An elaborate learned allusion. Apollo had once served as herdsman to
King Admetus on the banks of the river Amphrysus in Thessaly.   8. The golden bough which Aeneas
had been ordered to take as tribute to Proserpina.

Tossed him a lump of honey and drugged meal
To make him drowse. Three ravenous gullets gaped   195
And he snapped up the sop. Then his great bulk
Subsided and lay down through all the cave.
Now seeing the watchdog deep in sleep, Aeneas
Took the opening: swiftly he turned away
From the river over which no soul returns.   200

Now voices crying loud were heard at once—
The souls of infants wailing. At the door
Of the sweet life they were to have no part in,
Torn from the breast, a black day took them off
And drowned them all in bitter death. Near these   205
Were souls falsely accused, condemned to die.
But not without a judge, or jurymen,
Had these souls got their places: Minos[9] reigned
As the presiding judge, moving the urn,
And called a jury of the silent ones   210
To learn of lives and accusations. Next
Were those sad souls, benighted, who contrived
Their own destruction, and as they hated daylight,
Cast their lives away. How they would wish
In the upper air now to endure the pain   215
Of poverty and toil! But iron law
Stands in the way, since the drear hateful swamp
Has pinned them down here, and the Styx that winds
Nine times around exerts imprisoning power.
Not far away, spreading on every side,   220
The Fields of Mourning came in view, so called
Since here are those whom pitiless love consumed
With cruel wasting, hidden on paths apart
By myrtle woodland growing overhead.
In death itself, pain will not let them be.   225
He saw here Phaedra, Procris, Eriphylë[1]
Sadly showing the wounds her hard son gave;
Evadnë and Pasiphaë, at whose side
Laodamia[2] walked, and Caeneus,[3]
A young man once, a woman now, and turned   230

9. King of Crete, now judge of the dead. *The urn:* The magistrate of a Roman court decided the order in which cases were to be heard by drawing lots from an urn. *Silent ones:* The dead.   1. She betrayed her husband for gold and was killed by her own son. *Phaedra:* Wife of Theseus, king of Athens, who fell in love with Hippolytus, her husband's son by another woman; the result was her death by suicide and Hippolytus's death through his father's curse. *Procris:* Killed by her husband in an accident that was brought about by her own jealousy.   2. She begged to be allowed to talk with her dead husband; the request was granted by the gods and when his time came to return, she went back with him to the land of the dead. *Evadnë:* Threw herself on the pyre of her husband, who was killed by Zeus for impiety. *Pasiphaë:* Wife of Minos of Crete, she conceived a monstrous love for a bull, and gave birth to the Minotaur. 3. Virgil's words in the original are ambiguous (perhaps to reflect the ambiguity of the sex of Caeneus). The usual explanation of the passage is that Caenis (a woman) was changed by Poseidon into a man (Caeneus) but returned to her original sex after death. Since the name occurs here in a catalogue of women, this seems the most likely explanation.

Again by fate into the older form.
Among them, with her fatal wound still fresh,
Phoenician Dido wandered the deep wood.
The Trojan captain paused nearby and knew
Her dim form in the dark, as one who sees,   235
Early in the month, or thinks to have seen, the moon
Rising through cloud, all dim. He wept and spoke
Tenderly to her:
                    "Dido, so forlorn,
The story then that came to me was true,
That you were out of life, had met your end   240
By your own hand. Was I, was I the cause?
I swear by heaven's stars, by the high gods,
By any certainty below the earth,
I left your land against my will, my queen.
The gods' commands drove me to do their will,   245
As now they drive me through this world of shades,
These mouldy waste lands and these depths of night.
And I could not believe that I would hurt you
So terribly by going. Wait a little.
Do not leave my sight.   250
Am I someone to flee from? The last word
Destiny lets me say to you is this."

Aeneas with such pleas tried to placate
The burning soul, savagely glaring back,
And tears came to his eyes. But she had turned   255
With gaze fixed on the ground as he spoke on,
Her face no more affected than if she were
Immobile granite or Marpesian⁴ stone.
At length she flung away from him and fled,
His enemy still, into the shadowy grove   260
Where he whose bride she once had been, Sychaeus,
Joined in her sorrows and returned her love.
Aeneas still gazed after her in tears,
Shaken by her ill fate and pitying her.

[After being shown a pageant of the great Romans who will make Rome
mistress of the world, Aeneas returns to the upper air and begins his settlement in Italy. He is offered the hand of the princess Lavinia by her father
Latinus, but this provokes a war against the Trojans, led by King Turnus
of Laurentum, in the course of which Aeneas is wounded and stops by a
stream to rest. At this point his mother, Venus, comes to him with the
armor made for him by Vulcan (Hephaestus), her husband; on the shield
is carved a representation of the future glories of Rome.]

────────────

4. Marpessa was a marble quarry on the island of Paros.

From BOOK VIII

(The Shield of Aeneas)

          Venus the gleaming goddess,
Bearing her gifts, came down amid high clouds
And far away still, in a vale apart,
Sighted her son beside the ice-cold stream.
Then making her appearance as she willed   5
She said to him:
          "Here are the gifts I promised,
Forged to perfection by my husband's craft,
So that you need not hesitate to challenge
Arrogant Laurentines or savage Turnus,
However soon, in battle."
          As she spoke   10
Cytherëa[5] swept to her son's embrace
And placed the shining arms before his eyes
Under an oak tree. Now the man in joy
At a goddess' gifts, at being so greatly honored,
Could not be satisfied, but scanned each piece   15
In wonder and turned over in his hands
The helmet with its terrifying plumes
And gushing flames, the sword-blade edged with fate,
The cuirass of hard bronze, blood-red and huge—
Like a dark cloud burning with sunset light   20
That sends a glow for miles—the polished greaves[6]
Of gold and silver alloy, the great spear,
And finally the fabric of the shield
Beyond description.
          There the Lord of Fire,
Knowing the prophets, knowing the age to come,   25
Had wrought the future story of Italy,
The triumphs of the Romans: there one found
The generations of Ascanius' heirs,
The wars they fought, each one. Vulcan[7] had made
The mother wolf,[8] lying in Mars' green grotto;   30
Made the twin boys at play about her teats,
Nursing the mother without fear, while she
Bent round her smooth neck fondling them in turn
And shaped their bodies with her tongue.[9]
          Nearby,
Rome had been added by the artisan,   35
And Sabine women[1] roughly carried off

5. A title of Venus, who was born from the sea-foam off the Greek island of Cythera.   6. Leg pieces.
7. Hephaestus, the "Lord of Fire."   8. The twins who were to build Rome, Romulus and Remus, sons
of Mars the war god, were cast out into the woods and there suckled by a she-wolf.   9. See Ovid,
Metamorphoses, XV. 330–333.   1. The newly founded city of Rome consisted almost entirely of men;
the Romans decided to steal the wives of their neighbors, the Sabines. They invited them to an athletic

Out of the audience at the Circus games;
Then suddenly a new war coming on
To pit the sons of Romulus against
Old Tatius[2] and his austere town of Curës.   40
Later the same kings, warfare laid aside,
In arms before Jove's altar stood and held
Libation dishes as they made a pact
With offering of wine. Not far from this
Two four-horse war-cars, whipped on, back to back,   45
Had torn Mettus[3] apart (still, man of Alba,
You should have kept your word) and Roman Tullus
Dragged the liar's rags of flesh away
Through woods where brambles dripped a bloody dew.
There, too, Porsenna[4] stood, ordering Rome   50
To take the exiled Tarquin back, then bringing
The whole city under massive siege.
There for their liberty Aeneas' sons
Threw themselves forward on the enemy spears.
You might have seen Porsenna imaged there   55
To the life, a menacing man, a man in anger
At Roman daring: Cocles[5] who downed the bridge,
Cloelia who broke her bonds and swam the river.

On the shield's upper quarter Manlius,[6]
Guard of the Tarpeian Rock, stood fast   60
Before the temple and held the Capitol,
Where Romulus' house[7] was newly thatched and rough.
Here fluttering through gilded porticos
At night, the silvery goose warned of the Gauls
Approaching: under cover of the darkness   65
Gauls amid the bushes had crept near
And now lay hold upon the citadel.
Golden locks they had and golden dress,
Glimmering with striped cloaks, their milky necks
Entwined with gold. They hefted Alpine spears,   70
Two each, and had long body shields for cover.
Vulcan had fashioned naked Luperci
And Salii[8] leaping there with woolen caps

festival and at a given signal, every Roman carried off a Sabine bride. The war that followed ended in the amalgamation of the Roman and Sabine peoples.   2. A Sabine king.   3. Of Alba. He broke an agreement made during the early wars of Rome and was punished by being torn apart by two chariots moving in opposite directions. *Tullus:* The Roman king who punished Mettus.   4. The Etruscan king who attempted to restore the last of the Roman kings, Tarquin, to the throne from which he had been expelled.   5. Horatius Cocles, who with two companions defended the bridge across the Tiber to give the Romans time to destroy it. *Cloelia:* A Roman hostage held by Porsenna.   6. Consul in 392 B.C.; he was in charge of the citadel ("Tarpeian Rock") at a time when the Gauls from the north held all the rest of the city. They made a night attack on the citadel, but Manlius, awakened by the cackling of the sacred geese, beat it off, and saved Rome.   7. In Virgil's time there was still preserved at Rome a rustic building that was supposed to have been the dwelling place of Romulus.   8. The twelve priests of Mars, who danced in his honor carrying shields that had fallen from heaven. *Luperci:* Priests of Lupercus, a Roman god corresponding to the Greek Pan.

And fallen-from-heaven shields, and put chaste ladies
Riding in cushioned carriages through Rome 75
With sacred images. At a distance then
He pictured the deep hell of Tartarus,
Dis's high gate, crime's punishments, and, yes,
You, Catiline,[9] on a precarious cliff
Hanging and trembling at the Furies' glare. 80
Then, far away from this, were virtuous souls
And Cato[1] giving laws to them. Mid-shield,
The pictured sea flowed surging, all of gold,
As whitecaps foamed on the blue waves, and dolphins
Shining in silver round and round the scene 85
Propelled themselves with flukes and cut through billows.
Vivid in the center were the bronze-beaked
Ships and the fight at sea off Actium.[2]
Here you could see Leucata all alive
With ships maneuvering, sea glowing gold, 90
Augustus Caesar leading into battle
Italians, with both senators and people,
Household gods and great gods: there he stood
High on the stern, and from his blessed brow
Twin flames gushed upward, while his crest revealed 95
His father's star. Apart from him, Agrippa,[3]
Favored by winds and gods, led ships in column,
A towering figure, wearing on his brows
The coronet adorned with warships' beaks,
Highest distinction for command at sea. 100
Then came Antonius with barbaric wealth
And a diversity of arms, victorious
From races of the Dawnlands and Red Sea,
Leading the power of the East, of Egypt,
Even of distant Bactra[4] of the steppes. 105
And in his wake the Egyptian consort came
So shamefully. The ships all kept together
Racing ahead, the water torn by oar-strokes,
Torn by the triple beaks, in spume and foam.
All made for the open sea. You might believe 110
The Cyclades[5] uprooted were afloat
Or mountains running against mountain heights

9. Leader of a conspiracy to overthrow the republic which was halted mainly through the efforts of Cicero, consul in 63 B.C. Catiline is the type of discord, representing the civil war which almost destroyed the Roman state, and to which Augustus later put an end. 1. The noblest of the republicans who had fought Julius Caesar; he stood for honesty and the seriousness that the Romans most admired. He committed suicide in 47 B.C. after Caesar's victory in Africa. Before taking his life he read through Plato's *Phaedo*, a dialogue concerned with the immortality of the soul, which ends with an account of the death of Socrates. 2. On the west coast of Greece. The naval battle fought here in 31 B.C. was the decisive engagement of the civil war. Augustus, the master of the western half of the empire, defeated Antony, who held the eastern half and was supported by Cleopatra, queen of Egypt. *Leucata:* A promontory near Actium; there was a temple of Apollo on it. 3. Augustus' admiral at Actium. 4. On the borders of India. 5. The islands of the southern Aegean Sea.

When seamen in those hulks pressed the attack
Upon the other turreted ships. They hurled
Broadsides of burning flax on flying steel,   115
And fresh blood reddened Neptune's fields. The queen
Amidst the battle called her flotilla on
With a sistrum's[6] beat, a frenzy out of Egypt,
Never turning her head as yet to see
Twin snakes of death behind, while monster forms   120
Of gods of every race, and the dog-god
Anubis[7] barking, held their weapons up
Against our Neptune, Venus, and Minerva.
Mars, engraved in steel, raged in the fight
As from high air the dire Furies came   125
With Discord, taking joy in a torn robe,
And on her heels, with bloody scourge, Bellona.[8]

Overlooking it all, Actian Apollo[9]
Began to pull his bow. Wild at this sight,
All Egypt, Indians, Arabians, all   130
Sabaeans[1] put about in flight, and she,
The queen, appeared crying for winds to shift
Just as she hauled up sail and slackened sheets.
The Lord of Fire had portrayed her there,
Amid the slaughter, pallid with death to come,   135
Then borne by waves and wind from the northwest,
While the great length of mourning Nile awaited her
With open bays, calling the conquered home
To his blue bosom and his hidden streams.
But Caesar then in triple triumph[2] rode   140
Within the walls of Rome, making immortal
Offerings to the gods of Italy—
Three hundred princely shrines throughout the city.
There were the streets, humming with festal joy
And games and cheers, an altar to every shrine,   145
To every one a mothers' choir, and bullocks
Knifed before the altars strewed the ground.
The man himself, enthroned before the snow-white
Threshold of sunny Phoebus, viewed the gifts
The nations of the earth made, and he fitted them   150
To the tall portals. Conquered races passed
In long procession, varied in languages
As in their dress and arms. Here Mulciber,[3]
Divine smith, had portrayed the Nomad tribes

---

6. An Oriental rattle, used in the worship of Isis.   7. The Egyptian death-god, depicted with the head of a jackal.   8. A Roman war-goddess.   9. So called because of his temple at Actium; the temple (and its cult statue) overlooked the sea battle.   1. Arabs from the Yemen.   2. In 29 B.C.: Augustus celebrated a triple triumph for victories in Dalmatia, at Actium, and at Alexandria.   3. Another name of Vulcan.

And Afri with ungirdled flowing robes,   155
Here Leleges and Carians,[4] and here
Gelonians with quivers. Here Euphrates,
Milder in his floods now, there Morini,[5]
Northernmost of men; here bull-horned Rhine,
And there the still unconquered Scythian Dahae;   160
Here, vexed at being bridged, the rough Araxes.[6]
All these images on Vulcan's shield,
His mother's gift, were wonders to Aeneas.
Knowing nothing of the events themselves,
He felt joy in their pictures, taking up   165
Upon his shoulder all the destined acts
And fame of his descendants.

[In the course of the desperate battles which follow, the young Pallas,
entrusted to Aeneas' care by his father, is killed by the Italian champion
Turnus, who takes and wears the belt of Pallas as the spoil of victory. The
fortunes of the war later change in favor of the Trojans, and Aeneas kills
the Etruscan King Mezentius, Turnus' ally. Eventually, as the Italians
prepare to accept the generous peace terms offered by Aeneas, Turnus
forestalls them by accepting Aeneas' challenge to single combat to decide
the issue. But this solution is frustrated by the intervention of Juno, who
foresees Aeneas' victory. She prompts Turnus' sister, the river nymph
Juturna, to intervene in an attempt to save Turnus' life. Juturna stirs up
the Italians who are watching the champions prepare for the duel; the truce
is broken, and in the subsequent fighting Aeneas is wounded by an arrow.
Healed by Venus, he returns to the fight, and the Italians are driven back.
Turnus finally faces his adversary. His sword breaks on the armor forged
by Vulcan, and he runs from Aeneas; he is saved by Juturna, who, assum-
ing the shape of his charioteer, hands him a fresh sword. At this point
Jupiter intervenes to stop the vain attempts of Juno and Juturna to save
Turnus.]

From BOOK XII

(The Death of Turnus)

Omnipotent Olympus' king meanwhile
Had words for Juno, as she watched the combat
Out of a golden cloud. He said:
           "My consort,
What will the end be? What is left for you?
You yourself know, and say you know, Aeneas   5
Born for heaven, tutelary of this land,
By fate to be translated to the stars.[7]

---

4. Peoples of Asia Minor. *Gelonians:* From Scythia (in the Balkans).   5. A Belgian tribe.   6. A turbulent river in Armenia. Augustus built a new bridge over it.   7. Aeneas is destined for immortality:
after his death, he will be worshiped as a local god.

What do you plan? What are you hoping for,
Keeping your seat apart in the cold clouds?
Fitting, was it, that a mortal archer   10
Wound an immortal? That a blade let slip
Should be restored to Turnus, and new force
Accrue to a beaten man? Without your help
What could Juturna do? Come now, at last
Have done, and heed our pleading, and give way.   15
Let yourself no longer be consumed
Without relief by all that inward burning;
Let care and trouble not forever come to me
From your sweet lips. The finish is at hand.
You had the power to harry men of Troy   20
By land and sea, to light the fires of war
Beyond belief, to scar a family
With mourning before marriage.[8] I forbid
Your going further."
                      So spoke Jupiter,
And with a downcast look Juno replied: 25

"Because I know that is your will indeed,
Great Jupiter, I left the earth below,
Though sore at heart, and left the side of Turnus.
Were it not so, you would not see me here
Suffering all that passes, here alone,   30
Resting on air. I should be armed in flames
At the very battle-line, dragging the Trojans
Into a deadly action. I persuaded
Juturna—I confess—to help her brother
In his hard lot, and I approved her daring   35
Greater difficulties to save his life,
But not that she should fight with bow and arrow.
This I swear by Styx' great fountainhead
Inexorable, which high gods hold in awe.
I yield now and for all my hatred leave   40
This battlefield. But one thing not retained
By fate I beg for Latium, for the future
Greatness of your kin: when presently
They crown peace with a happy wedding day—
So let it be—and merge their laws and treaties,   45
Never command the land's own Latin folk
To change their old name, to become new Trojans,
Known as Teucrians; never make them alter
Dialect or dress. Let Latium be.

---

8. A reference not only to the Italian losses but also to the suicide of Amata, wife of King Latinus, who hanged herself when the Trojans assaulted the city just before the duel between Aeneas and Turnus began.

Let there be Alban kings for generations,   50
And let Italian valor be the strength
Of Rome in after times. Once and for all
Troy fell, and with her name let her lie fallen."

The author of men and of the world replied
With a half-smile:
                              "Sister of Jupiter[9]   55
Indeed you are, and Saturn's other child,
To feel such anger, stormy in your breast.
But come, no need; put down this fit of rage.
I grant your wish. I yield, I am won over
Willingly. Ausonian folk will keep   60
Their fathers' language and their way of life,
And, that being so, their name. The Teucrians
Will mingle and be submerged, incorporated.
Rituals and observances of theirs
I'll add, but make them Latin, one in speech.   65
The race to come, mixed with Ausonian blood,
Will outdo men and gods in its devotion,
You shall see—and no nation on earth
Will honor and worship you so faithfully."

To all this Juno nodded in assent   70
And, gladdened by his promise, changed her mind.
Then she withdrew from sky and cloud.
                              That done,
The Father set about a second plan—
To take Juturna from her warring brother.
Stories are told of twin fiends, called the Dirae,[1]   75
Whom, with Hell's Megaera, deep Night bore
In one birth. She entwined their heads with coils
Of snakes and gave them wings to race the wind.
Before Jove's throne, a step from the cruel king,
These twins attend him and give piercing fear   80
To ill mankind, when he who rules the gods
Deals out appalling death and pestilence,
Or war to terrify our wicked cities.
Jove now dispatched one of these, swift from heaven,
Bidding her be an omen to Juturna.   85
Down she flew, in a whirlwind borne to earth,
Just like an arrow driven through a cloud
From a taut string, an arrow armed with gall
Of deadly poison, shot by a Parthian—[2]

---

9. Jupiter and Juno, like their prototypes Zeus and Hera, are brother and sister as well as husband and wife.   1. Literally "dreadful ones" (the termination shows they are female, like the Erinyes). One of them is called Megaera.   2. Parthia was the most dangerous neighbor of the Roman Empire in the east. Parthian mounted archers were famous, as were Cretan archers.

A Parthian or a Cretan—for a wound   90
Immedicable; whizzing unforeseen
It goes through racing shadows: so the spawn
Of Night went diving downward to the earth.

On seeing Trojan troops drawn up in face
Of Turnus' army, she took on at once   95
The shape of that small bird[3] that perches late
At night on tombs or desolate roof-tops
And troubles darkness with a gruesome song.
Shrunk to that form, the fiend in Turnus' face
Went screeching, flitting, flitting to and fro   100
And beating with her wings against his shield.
Unstrung by numbness, faint and strange, he felt
His hackles rise, his voice choke in his throat.
As for Juturna, when she knew the wings,
The shriek to be the fiend's, she tore her hair,   105
Despairing, then she fell upon her cheeks
With nails, upon her breast with clenched hands.

"Turnus, how can your sister help you now?
What action is still open to me, soldierly
Though I have been? Can I by any skill   110
Hold daylight for you? Can I meet and turn
This deathliness away? Now I withdraw,
Now leave this war. Indecent birds, I fear you;
Spare me your terror. Whip-lash of your wings
I recognize, that ghastly sound, and guess   115
Great-hearted Jupiter's high cruel commands.
Returns for my virginity,[4] are they?
He gave me life eternal—to what end?
Why has mortality been taken from me?
Now beyond question I could put a term   120
To all my pain, and go with my poor brother
Into the darkness, his companion there.
Never to die? Will any brook of mine
Without you, brother, still be sweet to me?
If only earth's abyss were wide enough   125
To take me downward, goddess though I am,
To join the shades below!"
                          So she lamented,
Then with a long sigh, covering up her head
In her grey mantle, sank to the river's depth.

Aeneas moved against his enemy   130
And shook his heavy pine-tree spear. He called
From his hot heart:

3. The owl.   4. Jupiter had been the lover of Juturna and had rewarded her with immortality.

"Rearmed now, why so slow?
Why, even now, fall back? The contest here
Is not a race, but fighting to the death
With spear and sword. Take on all shapes there are,   135
Summon up all your nerve and skill, choose any
Footing, fly among the stars, or hide
In caverned earth—"
                          The other shook his head,
Saying:
          "I do not fear your taunting fury,
Arrogant prince. It is the gods I fear   140
And Jove my enemy."
                          He said no more,
But looked around him. Then he saw a stone,
Enormous, ancient, set up there to prevent
Landowners' quarrels. Even a dozen picked men
Such as the earth produces in our day   145
Could barely lift and shoulder it. He swooped
And wrenched it free, in one hand, then rose up
To his heroic height, ran a few steps,
And tried to hurl the stone against his foe—
But as he bent and as he ran   150
And as he hefted and propelled the weight
He did not know himself. His knees gave way,
His blood ran cold and froze. The stone itself,
Tumbling through space, fell short and had no impact.

Just as in dreams when the night-swoon of sleep   155
Weighs on our eyes, it seems we try in vain
To keep on running, try with all our might,
But in the midst of effort faint and fail;
Our tongue is powerless, familiar strength
Will not hold up our body, not a sound   160
Or word will come: just so with Turnus now:
However bravely he made shift to fight
The immortal fiend blocked and frustrated him.
Flurrying images passed through his mind.
He gazed at the Rutulians,[5] and beyond them,   165
Gazed at the city, hesitant, in dread.
He trembled now before the poised spear-shaft
And saw no way to escape; he had no force
With which to close, or reach his foe, no chariot
And no sign of the charioteer, his sister.   170
At a dead loss he stood. Aeneas made
His deadly spear flash in the sun and aimed it,
Narrowing his eyes for a lucky hit.

5. The Italian troops watching the combat between Turnus and Aeneas.

Then, distant still, he put his body's might
Into the cast. Never a stone that soared   175
From a wall-battering catapult went humming
Loud as this, nor with so great a crack
Burst ever a bolt of lightning. It flew on
Like a black whirlwind bringing devastation,
Pierced with a crash the rim of sevenfold shield,   180
Cleared the cuirass' edge, and passed clean through
The middle of Turnus' thigh. Force of the blow
Brought the huge man to earth, his knees buckling,
And a groan swept the Rutulians as they rose,
A groan heard echoing on all sides from all   185
The mountain range, and echoed by the forests.
The man brought down, brought low, lifted his eyes
And held his right hand out to make his plea:

"Clearly I earned this, and I ask no quarter.
Make the most of your good fortune here.   190
If you can feel a father's grief—and you, too,
Had such a father in Anchises—then
Let me bespeak your mercy for old age
In Daunus,[6] and return me, or my body,
Stripped, if you will, of life, to my own kin.   195
You have defeated me. The Ausonians
Have seen me in defeat, spreading my hands.
Lavinia is your bride. But go no further
Out of hatred."
                    Fierce under arms, Aeneas
Looked to and fro, and towered, and stayed his hand   200
Upon the sword-hilt. Moment by moment now
What Turnus said began to bring him round
From indecision. Then to his glance appeared
The accurst swordbelt surmounting Turnus' shoulder,
Shining with its familiar studs—the strap   205
Young Pallas wore when Turnus wounded him
And left him dead upon the field; now Turnus
Bore that enemy token on his shoulder—
Enemy still. For when the sight came home to him,
Aeneas raged at the relic of his anguish   210
Worn by this man as trophy. Blazing up
And terrible in his anger, he called out:

"You in your plunder, torn from one of mine,
Shall I be robbed of you? This wound will come
From Pallas: Pallas makes this offering   215
And from your criminal blood exacts his due."

6. Father of Turnus.

He sank his blade in fury in Turnus' chest.
Then all the body slackened in death's chill,
And with a groan for that indignity
His spirit fled into the gloom below.   220

OVID

43 B.C.–A.D. 17

Virgil had grown to manhood in the years of civil war, when no man's property,
nor even his life, was safe. He knew all too well the horrors that would inevitably
recur if Augustus' attempt to establish stable government should fail; like all his
generation, he knew how precarious the newfound peace was and felt himself
deeply engaged in the Augustan program. But a new generation of poets, who had
not known the time of troubles, took much of what had been achieved for granted,
and turned to new themes. The most brilliant of them, Ovid, was a boy of eleven
when Octavius (later Augustus) defeated Anthony at Actium. The early years of his
manhood, far from being dominated by fear of chaos come again, were marked by
rapid literary and social success in the brilliant society of a capital intent on enjoying the peace and prosperity that had been restored with so much effort.

Ovid was a versifier of genius. "Whatever I tried to say," he wrote, "came out in
verse," and Pope adapted the line for his own case: "I lisped in numbers for the
numbers came." Elegance, wit, and precision remained the hallmarks of Ovid's
poetry throughout his long and productive career; though his themes are often
frivolous, the technical perfection of the medium carries the dazzled reader along.
The *Amores*, unabashed chronicles of a Roman Don Juan, was his first publication;
it was soon followed by the *Art of Love*, a handbook of seduction (originally circulated as Books I and II, for men—Book III, for women, was added by popular
request).

In A.D. 8 Ovid was banished by imperial decree to the town of Tomi, in what is
now Rumania: it was outside the frontiers of the empire. He remained there until
his death in A.D. 17, sending back to Rome poetic epistles, the *Sorrows*, which
asked for pardon but to no effect. The reason for his banishment is not known:
involvement in some scandal concerning Augustus' daughter Julia is a possibility,
but the cynical love poetry may have been a contributing factor. Augustus was
trying hard, by propaganda and legislation, to revive old Roman standards of morality
and Ovid's *Art of Love* was not exactly helpful. His most influential work, the
Metamorphoses, is a treasure house of Greek and Roman mythological stories brilliantly combined in a long narrative and retold with such wit, charm, and surpassing beauty that poets ever since, Chaucer, Shakespeare, and Milton among them,
have used it as a source.

It consists of fifteen books; beginning with the creation of the world, the transformation of matter into living bodies, Ovid regales his readers with tales of human
beings changed into animals, flowers, trees, proceeding through Greek myth to
stories of early Rome and so to his own day—the ascension of the murdered Julius
Caesar to the heavens in the form of a star and the divine promise that Augustus
too, on some day far in the future, will become a god. Our selection contains one
of the best known episodes, Apollo and Daphne, from Book I, and from Book XV,

the long discourse of the philosopher Pythagoras who preaches the doctrine of impermanence, of unceasing change.

H. Fraenkel, *Ovid: A Poet Between Two Worlds* (1945), looks at Ovid as a poet in his historical context. G. K. Galinsky, *Ovid's Metamorphoses: An Introduction to the Basic Aspects* (1975), is a useful guide. Sara Mack, *Ovid* (1988), is an introduction to all the poems of Ovid, intended for the general reader. It is especially illuminating on Ovid's narrative technique; the *Metamorphoses* are discussed on pp. 99–144. See also Brooks Otis, *Ovid as an Epic Poet* (1966, 1970), and E. J. Kenney in *The Cambridge History of Classical Literature*, vol. 2 (1982), pp. 430–41.

Metamorphoses[1]

Book 1

My intention is to tell of bodies changed
To different forms; the gods, who made the changes,
Will help me—or I hope so—with a poem
That runs from the world's beginning to our own days.[2]

THE CREATION

Before the ocean was, or earth, or heaven,   5
Nature was all alike, a shapelessness,
Chaos, so-called, all rude and lumpy matter,
Nothing but bulk, inert, in whose confusion
Discordant atoms warred: there was no sun
To light the universe; there was no moon   10
With slender silver crescents filling slowly;
No earth hung balanced in surrounding air;
No sea reached far along the fringe of shore.
Land, to be sure, there was, and air, and ocean,
But land on which no man could stand, and water   15
No man could swim in, air no man could breathe,
Air without light, substance forever changing,
Forever at war: within a single body
Heat fought with cold, wet fought with dry, the hard
Fought with the soft, things having weight contended   20
With weightless things.
                          Till God, or kindlier Nature,
Settled all argument, and separated
Heaven from earth, water from land, our air
From the high stratosphere, a liberation
So things evolved, and out of blind confusion   25
Found each its place, bound in eternal order.

1. A selection. Translated by Rolfe Humphries.   2. In fact the last metamorphosis in the poem is that of the soul of the murdered dictator Julius Caesar, which is turned into a star. Caesar was murdered in 44 B.C.; Ovid was born in the next year, 43 B.C.

The force of fire, that weightless element,
Leaped up and claimed the highest place[3] in heaven;
Below it, air; and under them the earth
Sank with its grosser portions; and the water,   30
Lowest of all, held up, held in, the land.

Whatever god it was, who out of chaos
Brought order to the universe, and gave it
Division, subdivision, he molded earth,
In the beginning, into a great globe,   35
Even on every side, and bade the waters
To spread and rise, under the rushing winds,
Surrounding earth; he added ponds and marshes,
He banked the river-channels, and the waters
Feed earth or run to sea, and that great flood   40
Washes on shores, not banks. He made the plains
Spread wide, the valleys settle, and the forest
Be dressed in leaves; he made the rocky mountains
Rise to full height, and as the vault of Heaven
Has two zones,[4] left and right, and one between them   45
Hotter than these, the Lord of all Creation
Marked on the earth the same design and pattern.
The torrid zone too hot for men to live in,
The north and south too cold, but in the middle
Varying climate, temperature and season.   50
Above all things the air, lighter than earth,
Lighter than water, heavier than fire,
Towers and spreads; there mist and cloud assemble,
And fearful thunder and lightning and cold winds,
But these, by the Creator's order, held   55
No general dominion; even as it is,
These brothers brawl and quarrel; though each one
Has his own quarter, still, they come near tearing
The universe apart. Eurus is monarch
Of the lands of dawn,[5] the realms of Araby,   60
The Persian ridges under the rays of morning.
Zephyrus holds the west that glows at sunset,
Boreas, who makes men shiver, holds the north,
Warm Auster governs in the misty southland,
And over them all presides the weightless ether,   65
Pure without taint of earth.
                              These boundaries given,
Behold, the stars, long hidden under darkness,
Broke through and shone, all over the spangled heaven,
Their home forever, and the gods lived there,

3. The upper atmosphere, the *aether* as the Greeks called it, was thought of as a fiery element.   4. I.e.,
two zones to the "right" (the north) and two to the "left" (the south).   5. I.e., the sunrise, the east.
Eurus: The east wind.

And shining fish were given the waves for dwelling   70
And beasts the earth, and birds the moving air.

But something else was needed, a finer being,
More capable of mind, a sage, a ruler,
So Man was born, it may be, in God's image,
Or Earth, perhaps, so newly separated   75
From the old fire of Heaven, still retained
Some seed of the celestial force which fashioned
Gods out of living clay and running water.
All other animals look downward; Man,
Alone, erect, can raise his face toward Heaven.   80

THE FOUR AGES[6]

The Golden Age was first, a time that cherished
Of its own will, justice and right; no law,
No punishment, was called for; fearfulness
Was quite unknown, and the bronze tablets held
No legal threatening; no suppliant throng   85
Studied a judge's face; there were no judges,
There did not need to be. Trees had not yet
Been cut and hollowed, to visit other shores.
Men were content at home, and had no towns
With moats and walls around them; and no trumpets   90
Blared out alarums; things like swords and helmets
Had not been heard of. No one needed soldiers.
People were unaggressive, and unanxious;
The years went by in peace. And Earth, untroubled,
Unharried by hoe or plowshare, brought forth all   95
That men had need for, and those men were happy,
Gathering berries from the mountain sides,
Cherries, or blackcaps, and the edible acorns.
Spring was forever, with a west wind blowing
Softly across the flowers no man had planted,   100
And Earth, unplowed, brought forth rich grain; the field,
Unfallowed, whitened with wheat, and there were rivers
Of milk, and rivers of honey, and golden nectar
Dripped from the dark-green oak-trees.
                          After Saturn[7]
Was driven to the shadowy land of death,   105
And the world was under Jove, the Age of Silver
Came in, lower than gold, better than bronze.

---

6. In this myth of the four ages Ovid is following the account of the archaic Greek poet Hesiod (who, however, counted five ages; he interposed the age of the heroes, the wars of Thebes and Troy, between the Bronze and Iron ages).   7. Father of Jove (Jupiter), who, like his counterpart Zeus, overthrew his father's regime.

Jove made the springtime shorter, added winter,
Summer, and autumn, the seasons as we know them.
That was the first time when the burnt air glowed   110
White-hot, or icicles hung down in winter.
And men built houses for themselves; the caverns,
The woodland thickets, and the bark-bound shelters
No longer served; and the seeds of grain were planted
In the long furrows, and the oxen struggled   115
Groaning and laboring under the heavy yoke.

Then came the Age of Bronze, and dispositions
Took on aggressive instincts, quick to arm,
Yet not entirely evil. And last of all
The Iron Age succeeded, whose base vein   120
Let loose all evil: modesty and truth
And righteousness fled earth, and in their place
Came trickery and slyness, plotting, swindling,
Violence and the damned desire of having.
Men spread their sails to winds unknown to sailors,   125
The pines came down their mountain-sides, to revel
And leap in the deep waters, [8] and the ground,
Free, once, to everyone, like air and sunshine,
Was stepped off by surveyors. The rich earth,
Good giver of all the bounty of the harvest,   130
Was asked for more; they dug into her vitals,
Pried out the wealth a kinder lord had hidden
In Stygian shadow, [9] all that precious metal,
The root of evil. They found the guilt of iron,
And gold, more guilty still. And War came forth   135
That uses both to fight with; bloody hands
Brandished the clashing weapons. Men lived on plunder.
Guest was not safe from host, nor brother from brother,
A man would kill his wife, a wife her husband,
Stepmothers, dire and dreadful, stirred their brews   140
With poisonous aconite, and sons would hustle
Fathers to death, and Piety lay vanquished,
And the maiden Justice, last of all immortals,
Fled from the bloody earth.
                         Heaven was no safer.
Giants attacked the very throne of Heaven,   145
Piled Pelion on Ossa, [1] mountain on mountain
Up to the very stars. Jove struck them down
With thunderbolts, and the bulk of those huge bodies
Lay on the earth, and bled, and Mother Earth,
Made pregnant by that blood, brought forth new bodies,   150

8. I.e., after they were made into ships.   9. The Styx is one of the rivers of the underworld.   1. Two
mountains in central Greece, south of Olympus.

And gave them, to recall her older offspring,
The forms of men. And this new stock was also
Contemptuous of gods, and murder-hungry
And violent. You would know they were sons of blood.

JOVE'S INTERVENTION

And Jove was witness from his lofty throne   155
Of all this evil, and groaned as he remembered
The wicked revels of Lycaon's[2] table,
The latest guilt, a story still unknown
To the high gods. In awful indignation
He summoned them to council. No one dawdled.   160
Easily seen when the night skies are clear,
The Milky Way shines white. Along this road
The gods move toward the palace of the Thunderer,
His royal halls, and, right and left, the dwellings
Of other gods are open, and guests come thronging.   165
The lesser gods live in a meaner section,
An area not reserved, as this one is,
For the illustrious Great Wheels of Heaven.
(Their Palatine Hill,[3] if I might call it so.)

They took their places in the marble chamber   170
Where high above them all their king was seated,
Holding his ivory sceptre, shaking out
Thrice, and again, his awful locks, the sign
That made the earth and stars and ocean tremble,
And then he spoke, in outrage: "I was troubled   175
Less for the sovereignty of all the world
In that old time when the snake-footed giants
Laid each his hundred hands on captive Heaven.
Monstrous they were, and hostile, but their warfare
Sprung from one source, one body. Now, wherever   180
The sea-gods roar around the earth, a race
Must be destroyed, the race of men. I swear it!
I swear by all the Stygian rivers gliding
Under the world, I have tried all other measures.
The knife must cut the cancer out, infection   185
Averted while it can be, from our numbers.
Those demigods, those rustic presences,
Nymphs, fauns, and satyrs, wood and mountain dwellers,
We have not yet honored with a place in Heaven,
But they should have some decent place to dwell in,   190
In peace and safety. Safety? Do you reckon
They will be safe, when I, who wield the thunder,

---

2. King of Arcadia, in the Peloponnese.   3. The hill of Rome where the emperor Augustus lived.

Who rule you all as subjects, am subjected
To the plottings of the barbarous Lycaon?"

They burned, they trembled. Who was this Lycaon,   195
Guilty of such rank infamy? They shuddered
In horror, with a fear of sudden ruin,
As the whole world did later, when assassins
Struck Julius Caesar down, and Prince Augustus
Found satisfaction in the great devotion   200
That cried for vengeance, even as Jove took pleasure,
Then, in the gods' response. By word and gesture
He calmed them down, awed them again to silence,
And spoke once more:

THE STORY OF LYCAON

"He has indeed been punished.
On that score have no worry. But what he did,   205
And how he paid, are things that I must tell you.
I had heard the age was desperately wicked,
I had heard, or so I hoped, a lie, a falsehood,
So I came down, as man, from high Olympus,
Wandered about the world. It would take too long   210
To tell you how widespread was all that evil.
All I had heard was grievous understatement!
I had crossed Maenala, a country bristling
With dens of animals, and crossed Cyllene,
And cold Lycaeus' pine woods.[4] Then I came   215
At evening, with the shadows growing longer,
To an Arcadian palace, where the tyrant
Was anything but royal in his welcome.
I gave a sign that a god had come, and people
Began to worship, and Lycaon mocked them,   220
Laughed at their prayers, and said: 'Watch me find out
Whether this fellow is a god or mortal,
I can tell quickly, and no doubt about it.'
He planned, that night, to kill me while I slumbered;
That was his way to test the truth. Moreover,   225
And not content with that, he took hostage,
One sent by the Molossians,[5] cut his throat,
Boiled pieces of his flesh, still warm with life,
Broiled others, and set them before me on the table.
That was enough. I struck, and the bolt of lightning   230
Blasted the household of that guilty monarch.
He fled in terror, reached the silent fields,

---

4. Maenala, Cyllene, and Lycaeus are mountains in Arcadia.   5. A tribe located in Epirus, the northernmost extremity of Greece.

And howled,[6] and tried to speak. No use at all!
Foam dripped from his mouth; bloodthirsty still, he turned
Against the sheep, delighting still in slaughter,   235
And his arms were legs, and his robes were shaggy hair,
Yet he is still Lycaon, the same grayness,
The same fierce face, the same red eyes, a picture
Of bestial savagery. One house has fallen,
But more than one deserves to. Fury reigns   240
Over all the fields of Earth. They are sworn to evil,
Believe it. Let them pay for it, and quickly!
So stands my purpose."
                              Part of them approved
With words and added fuel to his anger,
And part approved with silence, and yet all   245
Were grieving at the loss of humankind,
Were asking what the world would be, bereft
Of mortals: who would bring their altars incense?
Would earth be given the beasts, to spoil and ravage?
Jove told them not to worry; he would give them   250
Another race, unlike the first, created
Out of a miracle; he would see to it.

He was about to hurl his thunderbolts
At the whole world, but halted, fearing Heaven
Would burn from fire so vast, and pole to pole   255
Break out in flame and smoke, and he remembered
The fates had said that some day land and ocean,
The vault of Heaven, the whole world's mighty fortress,
Besieged by fire, would perish. He put aside
The bolts made in Cyclopean[7] workshops; better,   260
He thought, to drown the world by flooding water.

THE FLOOD

So, in the cave of Aeolus,[8] he prisoned
The North-wind, and the West-wind, and such others
As ever banish cloud, and he turned loose
The South-wind, and the South-wind came out streaming   265
With dripping wings, and pitch-black darkness veiling
His terrible countenance. His beard is heavy
With rain-cloud, and his hoary locks a torrent,
Mists are his chaplet, and his wings and garments
Run with the rain. His broad hands squeeze together   270
Low-hanging clouds, and crash and rumble follow

6. The beginning of the first metamorphosis—Lycaon (the first part of whose name is the Greek for "wolf") becomes a wolf.   7. Made by the Cyclopes, one-eyed giants like Polyphemus in the *Odyssey* (Book IX). But unlike Polyphemus and his pastoral relatives, these Cyclopes are metalworkers who forge the thunderbolts of Jupiter (Zeus).   8. King of the winds (cf. *Odyssey* Book X).

Before the cloudburst, and the rainbow, Iris,
Draws water from the teeming earth, and feeds it
Into the clouds again. The crops are ruined,
The farmers' prayers all wasted, all the labor   275
Of a long year, comes to nothing.
                                        And Jove's anger,
Unbounded by his own domain, was given
Help by his dark-blue brother. Neptune[9] called
His rivers all, and told them, very briefly,
To loose their violence, open their houses,   280
Pour over embankments, let the river horses
Run wild as ever they would. And they obeyed him.
His trident struck the shuddering earth; it opened
Way for the rush of waters. The leaping rivers
Flood over the great plains. Not only orchards   285
Are swept away, not only grain and cattle,
Not only men and houses, but altars, temples,
And shrines with holy fires. If any building
Stands firm, the waves keep rising over its roof-top,
Its towers are under water, and land and ocean   290
Are all alike, and everything is ocean,
An ocean with no shore-line.
                                        Some poor fellow
Seizes a hill-top; another, in a dinghy,
Rows where he used to plough, and one goes sailing
Over his fields of grain or over the chimney   295
Of what was once his cottage. Someone catches
Fish in the top of an elmtree, or an anchor
Drags in green meadow-land, or the curved keel brushes
Grape-arbors under water. Ugly sea-cows
Float where the slender she-goats used to nibble   300
The tender grass, and the Nereids[1] come swimming
With curious wonder, looking, under water,
At houses, cities, parks, and groves. The dolphins
Invade the woods and brush against the oak-trees;
The wolf swims with the lamb; lion and tiger   305
Are borne along together; the wild boar
Finds all his strength is useless, and the deer
Cannot outspeed that torrent; wandering birds
Look long, in vain, for landing-place, and tumble,
Exhausted, into the sea. The deep's great license   310
Has buried all the hills and new waves thunder
Against the mountain-tops. The flood has taken
All things, or nearly all, and those whom water,
By chance, has spared, starvation slowly conquers.

9. (Poseidon) the sea god.   1. Sea-nymphs.

DEUCALION AND PYRRHA

Phocis, a fertile land, while there was land,   315
Marked off Oetean from Boeotian[2] fields.
It was ocean now, a plain of sudden waters.
There Mount Parnassus lifts its twin peaks skyward,
High, steep, cloud-piercing. And Deucalion came there
Rowing his wife. There was no other land,   320
The sea had drowned it all. And here they worshipped
First the Corycian nymphs[3] and native powers,
Then Themis, oracle and fate-revealer.
There was no better man than this Deucalion,
No one more fond of right; there was no woman   325
More scrupulously reverent than Pyrrha.
So, when Jove saw the world was one great ocean,
Only one woman left of all those thousands,
And only one man left of all those thousands,
Both innocent and worshipful, he parted   330
The clouds, turned loose the North-wind, swept them off,
Showed earth to heaven again, and sky to land,
And the sea's anger dwindled, and King Neptune
Put down his trident, calmed the waves, and Triton,
Summoned from far down under, with his shoulders   335
Barnacle-strewn, loomed up above the waters,
The blue-green sea-god, whose resounding horn
Is heard from shore to shore. Wet-bearded, Triton
Set lip to that great shell, as Neptune ordered,
Sounding retreat, and all the lands and waters   340
Heard and obeyed. The sea has shores; the rivers,
Still running high, have channels; the floods dwindle,
Hill-tops are seen again; the trees, long buried,
Rise with their leaves still muddy. The world returns.

Deucalion saw that world, all desolation,   345
All emptiness, all silence, and his tears
Rose as he spoke to Pyrrha: "O my wife,
The only woman, now, on all this earth,
My consort and my cousin and my partner
In these immediate dangers, look! Of all the lands   350
To East or West, we two, we two alone,
Are all the population. Ocean holds
Everything else; our foothold, our assurance,
Are small as they can be, the clouds still frightful.
Poor woman—well, we are not all alone—   355
Suppose you had been, how would you bear your fear?

---

2. On the Theban plain. *Phocis:* A district in central Greece, north of the Gulf of Corinth. *Oetean:* Mt.
Oeta is in southern Thessaly.   3. The Corycian cave is high above Delphi, on the upper slopes of
Parnassus. *Themis:* "Tradition" in Greek, one of the predecessors of Apollo at Delphi.

Who would console your grief? My wife, believe me,
Had the sea taken you, I would have followed.
If only I had the power, I would restore
The nations as my father[4] did, bring clay   360
To life with breathing. As it is, we two
Are all the human race, so Heaven has willed it,
Samples of men, mere specimens."
                                  They wept,
and prayed together, and having wept and prayed,
Resolved to make petition to the goddess   365
To seek her aid through oracles. Together
They went to the river-water, the stream Cephisus,
Still far from clear, but flowing down its channel,
And they took river-water, sprinkled foreheads,
Sprinkled their garments, and they turned their steps   370
To the temple of the goddess, where the altars
Stood with the fires gone dead, and ugly moss
Stained pediment and column. At the stairs
They both fell prone, kissed the chill stone in prayer:
"If the gods' anger ever listens   375
To righteous prayers, O Themis, we implore you,
Tell us by what device our wreck and ruin
May be repaired. Bring aid, most gentle goddess,
To sunken circumstance."
                         And Themis heard them,
And gave this oracle: "Go from the temple,   380
Cover your heads, loosen your robes, and throw
Your mother's bones behind you!" Dumb, they stood
In blank amazement, a long silence, broken
By Pyrrha, finally: she would not do it!
With trembling lips she prays whatever pardon   385
Her disobedience might merit, but this outrage
She dare not risk, insult her mother's spirit
By throwing her bones around. In utter darkness
They voice the cryptic saying over and over,
What can it mean? They wonder. At last Deucalion   390
Finds the way out: "I might be wrong, but surely
The holy oracles would never counsel
A guilty act. The earth is our great mother,
And I suppose those bones the goddess mentions
Are the stones of earth; the order means to throw them,   395
The stones, behind us."
                     She was still uncertain,
And he by no means sure, and both distrustful
Of that command from Heaven; but what damage,

---

4. Prometheus. A Greek legend credited him with making the first human beings out of clay.

What harm, would there be in trying? They descended,
Covered their heads, loosened their garments, threw   400
The stones behind them as the goddess ordered.
The stones—who would believe it, had we not
The unimpeachable witness of Tradition?—
Began to lose their hardness, to soften, slowly,
To take on form, to grow in size, a little,   405
Become less rough, to look like human beings,
Or anyway as much like human beings
As statues do, when the sculptor is only starting,
Images half blocked out. The earthy portion,
Damp with some moisture, turned to flesh, the solid   410
Was bone, the veins were as they always had been.
The stones the man had thrown turned into men,
The stones the woman threw turned into women,
Such being the will of God. Hence we derive
The hardness that we have, and our endurance   415
Gives proof of what we have come from.
                                        Other forms
Of life came into being, generated
Out of the earth: the sun burnt off the dampness,
Heat made the slimy marshes swell; as seed
Swells in a mother's womb to shape and substance,   420
So new forms came to life. When the Nile river
Floods and recedes and the mud is warmed by sunshine,
Men, turning over the earth, find living things,
And some not living, but nearly so, imperfect,
On the verge of life,[5] and often the same substance   425
Is part alive, part only clay. When moisture
Unites with heat, life is conceived; all things
Come from this union. Fire may fight with water,
But heat and moisture generate all things,
Their discord being productive. So when earth,   430
After that flood, still muddy, took the heat,
Felt the warm fire of sunlight, she conceived,
Brought forth, after their fashion, all the creatures,
Some old, some strange and monstrous.
                                        One, for instance,
She bore unwanted, a gigantic serpent,[6]   435
Python by name, whom the new people dreaded,
A huge bulk on the mountain-side. Apollo,

---

5. This strange doctrine, the automatic generation of living species in warm river mud, stems from Greek philosophical speculation about the origins of life.   6. Pytho. The following lines are a good example of Ovid's witty and skillful transitions from one story to another: he will vary them like a virtuoso in the course of the fifteen books. From the spontaneous birth of animals in the Nile mud he singles out one, Pytho, killed by Apollo, who instituted games in commemoration of the feat and decreed for the winner a crown of oak. As every one of his readers knew, the crown at the Pythian games was of laurel. But, says Ovid, the laurel did not then exist and this launches him on the story of its origin, the transformation of Daphne (the name means "laurel").

God of the glittering bow, took a long time
To bring him down, with arrow after arrow
He had never used before except in hunting   440
Deer and the skipping goats. Out of the quiver
Sped arrows by the thousand, till the monster,
Dying, poured poisonous blood on those black wounds.
In memory of this, the sacred games,
Called Pythian, were established, and Apollo   445
Ordained for all young winners in the races,
On foot or chariot, for victorious fighters,
The crown of oak. That was before the laurel,
That was before Apollo wreathed his forehead
With garlands from that tree, or any other.   450

APOLLO AND DAPHNE

Now the first girl Apollo loved was Daphne,
Whose father was the river-god Peneus,[7]
And this was no blind chance, but Cupid's malice.
Apollo, with pride and glory still upon him
Over the Python slain, saw Cupid bending   455
His tight-strung little bow. "O silly youngster,"
He said, "What are you doing with such weapons?
Those are for grown-ups! The bow is for my shoulders;
I never fail in wounding beast or mortal,
And not so long ago I slew the Python   460
With countless darts; his bloated body covered
Acre on endless acre, and I slew him!
The torch, my boy, is enough for you to play with,
To get the love-fires burning. Do not meddle
With honors that are mine!" And Cupid answered: 465
"Your bow shoots everything, Apollo—maybe—
But mine will fix you! You are far above
All creatures living, and by just that distance
Your glory less than mine." He shook his wings,
Soared high, came down to the shadows of Parnassus,   470
Drew from his quiver different kinds of arrows,
One causing love, golden and sharp and gleaming,
The other blunt, and tipped with lead, and serving
To drive all love away, and this blunt arrow
He used on Daphne, but he fired the other,   475
The sharp and golden shaft, piercing Apollo
Through bones, through marrow, and at once he loved
And she at once fled from the name of lover,
Rejoicing in the woodland hiding places

7. The main river of Thessaly.

And spoils of beasts which she had taken captive,   480
A rival of Diana, virgin goddess.[8]
She had many suitors, but she scorned them all;
Wanting no part of any man, she travelled
The pathless groves, and had no care whatever
For husband, love, or marriage. Her father often   485
Said, "Daughter, give me a son-in-law!" and "Daughter,
Give me some grandsons!" But the marriage torches
Were something hateful, criminal, to Daphne,
So she would blush, and put her arms around him,
And coax him: "Let me be a virgin always;   490
Diana's father said she might. Dear father!
Dear father—please!" He yielded, but her beauty
Kept arguing against her prayer. Apollo
Loves at first sight; he wants to marry Daphne,
He hopes for what he wants—all wishful thinking!—   495
Is fooled by his own oracles. As stubble
Burns when the grain is harvested, as hedges
Catch fire from torches that a passer-by
Has brought too near, or left behind in the morning,
So the god burned, with all his heart, and burning   500
Nourished that futile love of his by hoping.
He sees the long hair hanging down her neck
Uncared for, says, "But what if it were combed?"
He gazes at her eyes—they shine like stars!
He gazes at her lips, and knows that gazing   505
Is not enough. He marvels at her fingers,
Her hands, her wrists, her arms, bare to the shoulder,
And what he does not see he thinks is better.
But still she flees him, swifter than the wind,
And when he calls she does not even listen: 510
"Don't run away, dear nymph! Daughter of Peneus,
Don't run away! I am no enemy,
Only your follower: don't run away!
The lamb flees from the wolf, the deer the lion,
The dove, on trembling wing, flees from the eagle.   515
All creatures flee their foes. But I, who follow,
Am not a foe at all. Love makes me follow,
Unhappy fellow that I am, and fearful
You may fall down, perhaps, or have the briars
Make scratches on those lovely legs, unworthy   520
To be hurt so, and I would be the reason.
The ground is rough here. Run a little slower,
And I will run, I promise, a little slower.
Or wait a minute: be a little curious

8. I.e., Artemis, a hunting goddess, daughter of Jupiter (Zeus).

Just who it is you charm. I am no shepherd,   525
No mountain-dweller, I am not a ploughboy,
Uncouth and stinking of cattle. You foolish girl,
You don't know who it is you run away from,
That must be why you run. I am lord of Delphi
And Tenedos and Claros and Patara.[9]   530
Jove is my father. I am the revealer
Of present, past and future; through my power
The lyre and song make harmony; my arrow
Is sure in aim—there is only one arrow surer,
The one that wounds my heart. The power of healing   535
Is my discovery; I am called the Healer
Through all the world: all herbs are subject to me.
Alas for me, love is incurable
With any herb; the arts which cure the others
Do me, their lord, no good!"
                              He would have said   540
Much more than this, but Daphne, frightened, left him
With many words unsaid, and she was lovely
Even in flight, her limbs bare in the wind,
Her garments fluttering, and her soft hair streaming,
More beautiful than ever. But Apollo,   545
Too young a god to waste his time in coaxing,
Came following fast. When a hound starts a rabbit
In an open field, one runs for game, one safety,
He has her, or thinks he has, and she is doubtful
Whether she's caught or not, so close the margin,   550
So ran the god and girl, one swift in hope,
The other in terror, but he ran more swiftly,
Borne on the wings of love, gave her no rest,
Shadowed her shoulder, breathed on her streaming hair.
Her strength was gone, worn out by the long effort   555
Of the long flight; she was deathly pale, and seeing
The river of her father, cried "O help me,
If there is any power in the rivers,
Change and destroy the body which has given
Too much delight!" And hardly had she finished,   560
When her limbs grew numb and heavy, her soft breasts
Were closed with delicate bark, her hair was leaves,
Her arms were branches, and her speedy feet
Rooted and held, and her head became a tree top,
Everything gone except her grace, her shining.   565
Apollo loved her still. He placed his hand
Where he had hoped and felt the heart still beating
Under the bark; and he embraced the branches

9. All famous oracular shrines of Apollo.

As if they still were limbs, and kissed the wood,
And the wood shrank from his kisses, and the god   570
Exclaimed: "Since you can never be my bride,
My tree at least you shall be! Let the laurel
Adorn, henceforth, my hair, my lyre, my quiver:
Let Roman victors, in the long procession,
Wear laurel wreaths for triumph and ovation.   575
Beside Augustus' portals let the laurel
Guard and watch over the oak, and as my head
Is always youthful, let the laurel always
Be green and shining!" He said no more. The laurel,
Stirring, seemed to consent, to be saying *Yes.*   580

There is a grove in Thessaly, surrounded
By woodlands with steep slopes; men call it Tempe.
Through this the Peneus River's foamy waters
Rise below Pindus mountain. The cascades
Drive a fine smoky mist along the tree tops,   585
Frail clouds, or so it seems, and the roar of the water
Carries beyond the neighborhood. Here dwells
The mighty god himself,[1] his holy of holies
Is under a hanging rock; it is here he gives
Laws to the nymphs, laws to the very water.   590
And here came first the streams of his own country
Not knowing what to offer, consolation
Or something like rejoicing: crowned with poplars
Sperchios came, and restless Enipeus,
Old Apidanus, Aeas, and Amphrysos[2]   595
The easy-going. And all the other rivers
That take their weary waters into oceans
All over the world, came there, and only one
Was absent, Inachus,[3] hiding in his cavern,
Salting his stream with tears, oh, most unhappy,   600
Mourning a daughter lost. Her name was Io,
Who might, for all he knew, be dead or living,
But since he can not find her anywhere
He thinks she must be nowhere, and his sorrow
Fears for the worst.

JOVE AND IO

Jove had seen Io coming
From the river of her father, and had spoken: 605
"O maiden, worthy of the love of Jove,
And sure to make some lover happy in bed,
Come to the shade of these deep woods" (he showed them)

---

1. The river Peneus.   2. Thessalian rivers.   3. A river near Argos.

"Come to the shade, the sun is hot and burning,
No beasts will hurt you there, I will go with you,   610
If a god is at your side, you will walk safely
In the very deepest woods. I am a god,
And no plebeian godling, either, but the holder
Of Heaven's scepter, hurler of the thunder.
Oh, do not flee me!" She had fled already   615
Leaving Lyrcea's plains, and Lerna's⁴ meadows,
When the god hid the lands in murk and darkness
And stayed her flight, and took her.
                              Meanwhile Juno
Looked down on Argos: what could those clouds be doing
In the bright light of day? They were not mists   620
Rising from rivers or damp ground. She wondered,
Took a quick look around to see her husband,
Or see where he might be—she knew his cheating!
So when she did not find him in the heaven,
She said, "I am either wrong, or being wronged,"   625
Came gliding down from Heaven, stood on earth,
Broke up the clouds. But Jove, ahead of time,
Could tell that she was coming; he changed Io
Into a heifer, white and shining, lovely
Even in altered form, and even Juno   630
Looked on, though hating to, with admiration,
And asked whom she belonged to, from what pasture,
As if she did not know! And Jove, the liar,
To put a stop to questions, said she had sprung
Out of the earth, full-grown. Then Juno asked him,   635
"Could I have her, as a present?" What could he do?
To give his love away was surely cruel,
To keep her most suspicious. Shame on one side
Says *Give her up!* and love says *Don't!* and shame
Might have been beaten by love's argument,   640
But then, if he refused his wife the heifer,
So slight a present—if he should refuse it,
Juno might think perhaps it was no heifer!

Her rival thus disposed of, still the goddess
Did not at once abandon all suspicion.   645
Afraid of Jove, and worried over his cheating,
She turned her over to the keeping of Argus
Who had a hundred eyes; two at a time,
No more than two, would ever close in slumber,
The rest kept watch. No matter how he stood,   650
Which way he turned, he always looked at Io,
Always had Io in sight. He let her graze

4. A marsh in the territory of Argos.

By daylight, but at sundown locked her in,
Hobbled and haltered. She would feed on leaves
And bitter grasses, and her couch, poor creature,   655
Was ground, not always grassy, and the water
She drank was muddy, often. When she wanted
To reach toward Argus her imploring arms,
She had no arms to reach with; when she tried
To plead, she only lowed, and her own voice   660
Filled her with terror. When she came to the river,
Her father's, where she used to play, and saw,
Reflected in the stream, her jaws and horns,
She fled in panic. None of her sisters knew her,
And Inachus, her father, did not know her,   665
But following them, she let them pet and praise her.
Old Inachus pulled grass and gave it to her,
And she licked his hand and tried to give it kisses,
Could not restrain her tears. If she could talk,
She would ask for help, and tell her name and sorrow,   670
But as it was, all she could do was furrow
The dust with one forefoot, and make an I,
And then an O beside it, spelling her name,
Telling the story of her changed condition.
Her father knew her, cried, "Alas for me!"   675
Clung to her horns and snowy neck, poor heifer,
Crying, "Alas for me! I have sought you, daughter,
All over the world, and now that I have found you,
I have found a greater grief. You do not answer,
And what you think is sighing comes out mooing!   680
And all the while I, in my ignorance, counted
On marriage for you, wanting, first, a son,
Then, later, grandsons; now your mate must be
Selected from some herd, your son a bullock.
Not even death can end my heavy sorrow.   685
It hurts to be a god; the door of death,
Shut in my face, prolongs my grief forever."
And both of them were weeping, but their guardian,
Argus the star-eyed, drove her from her father
To different pasture-land, and sat there, watching,   690
Perched on a mountain-top above the valley.
Jove could not bear her sorrows any longer;
He called his son, born of the shining Pleiad,[5]
Told him *Kill Argus!* And Mercury came flying
On winged sandals, wearing the magic helmet,   695
Bearing the sleep-producing wand, and lighted
On earth, and put aside the wings and helmet

5. Maia, daughter of Atlas. She and her six sisters became stars, the Pleiades.

Keeping the wand. With this he plays the shepherd
Across the pathless countryside, a driver
Of goats, collected somewhere, and he goes   700
Playing a little tune on a pipe of reeds,
And this new sound is wonderful to Argus.
"Whoever you are, come here and sit beside me,"
He says, "This rock is in the shade; the grass
Is nowhere any better." And Mercury joins him,   705
Whiling the time away with conversation
And soothing little melodies, and Argus
Has a hard fight with drowsiness; his eyes,
Some of them, close, but some of them stay open.
To keep himself awake by listening,   710
He asks about the pipe of reeds, how was it
This new invention came about?
                           The god
Began the story: "On the mountain slopes
Of cool Arcadia, a woodland nymph
Once lived, with many suitors, and her name   715
Was Syrinx.[6] More than once the satyrs chased her,
And so did other gods of field or woodland,
But always she escaped them, virgin always
As she aspired to be, one like Diana,
Like her in dress and calling, though her bow   720
Was made of horn, not gold, but even so,
She might, sometimes, be taken for the goddess.
Pan,[7] with a wreath of pine around his temples,
Once saw her coming back from Mount Lycaeus,[8]
And said" and Mercury broke off the story   725
And then went on to tell what Pan had told her,
How she said No, and fled, through pathless places,
Until she came to Ladon's river, flowing
Peaceful along the sandy banks, whose water
Halted her flight, and she implored her sisters[9]   730
To change her form, and so, when Pan had caught her
And thought he held a nymph, it was only reeds
That yielded in his arms, and while he sighed,
The soft air stirring in the reeds made also
The echo of a sigh. Touched by this marvel,   735
Charmed by the sweetness of the tone, he murmured
This much I have! and took the reeds, and bound them
With wax, a tall and shorter one together,
And called them Syrinx, still.
                    And Mercury

---

6. The name means "shepherd's pipe." It is made of reeds. *Satyrs:* Woodland creatures, half animal, half man, bald, bearded, and highly sexed.   7. A god of the wild mountain pastures and woods.   8. An Arcadian mountain, sacred to Pan.   9. The water nymphs of the river Ladon.

Might have told more, but all the eyes of Argus,   740
He saw, had closed, and he made the slumber deeper
With movements of the wand, and then he struck
The nodding head just where it joins the shoulder,
Severed it with the curving blade, and sent it
Bloody and rolling over the rocks. So Argus   745
Lay low, and all the light in all those eyes
Went out forever, a hundred eyes, one darkness.
And Juno took the eyes and fastened them
On the feathers of a bird of hers, the peacock,
So that the peacock's tail is spread with jewels,   750
And Juno, very angry, sent a fury
To harass Io, to drive her mad with terror,
In flight all over the world. At last a river
Halted her flight, the Nile, and when she came there
She knelt beside the stream, lifted her head,   755
The only gesture she could make of praying,
And seemed, with groans and tears and mournful lowing,
To voice complaint to Jove, to end her sorrows,
And he was moved to pity; embracing Juno
He begged her: "End this punishment; hereafter   760
Io, I swear, will never cause you anguish,"
And what he swore he called the Styx to witness.
And Juno was appeased. Io became
What once she was, again; the bristles vanish,
The horns are gone, the great round eyes grow smaller,   765
The gaping jaws are narrower, the shoulders
Return, she has hands again, and toes and fingers,
The only sign of the heifer is the whiteness.
She stands erect, a nymph again, still fearful
That speech may still be mooing, but she tries   770
And little by little gains back the use of language.
Now people, robed in linen, pay her homage,
A very goddess, and a son is born,
Named Epaphus, the seed of Jove; his temples
Are found beside his mother's in many cities.[1]   775

Book XV

[By the beginning of Book XV, Ovid has pursued the theme of metamorphosis through all the cycles of Greek mythology and has turned to the
legends of early Rome. After Rome's founder and first king, Romulus the
warrior, came Numa, the peaceful giver of laws and religious rites. Ovid
has him journey to Croton in Southern Italy to listen to the teachings of

---

1. The next line runs: "His boon companion was young Phaethon . . ." It is Ovid's transition to the next
extended narrative, that of Phaethon and the chariot of the sun, which occupies the next 400 lines or so.

the Greek philosopher Pythagoras. The teachings of Pythagoras, in Ovid
at any rate, are an exposition of the theme of metamorphosis from a philosophical and religious standpoint, a striking contrast to the witty and generally amatory treatment of the subject so far.]

THE TEACHINGS OF PYTHAGORAS

There was a man here, Samian born,[2] but he
Had fled from Samos, for he hated tyrants
And chose, instead, an exile's lot. His thought
Reached far aloft, to the great gods in Heaven,
And his imagination looked on visions   5
Beyond his mortal sight. All things he studied
With watchful eager mind, and he brought home
What he had learned and sat among the people
Teaching them what was worthy, and they listened
In silence, wondering at the revelations: 10
How the great world began, the primal cause,
The nature of things, what God is, whence the snows
Come down, where lightning breaks from, whether wind
Or Jove speaks in the thunder from the clouds,
The cause of earthquakes, by what law the stars   15
Wheel in their courses, all the secrets hidden
From man's imperfect knowledge. He was first
To say that animal food should not be eaten,
And learnèd as he was, men did not always
Believe him when he preached "Forbear, O mortals,   20
To spoil your bodies with such impious food!
There is corn for you, apples, whose weight bears down
The bending branches; there are grapes that swell
On the green vines, and pleasant herbs, and greens
Made mellow and soft with cooking; there is milk   25
And clover-honey. Earth is generous
With her provision, and her sustenance
Is very kind; she offers, for your tables,
Food that requires no bloodshed and no slaughter.
Meat is for beasts to feed on, yet not all   30
Are carnivores, for horses, sheep, and cattle
Subsist on grass, but those whose disposition
Is fierce and cruel, tigers, raging lions,
And bears and wolves delight in bloody feasting.
Oh, what a wicked thing it is for flesh   35
To be the tomb of flesh, for the body's craving

2. The historical Pythagoras (sixth century B.C.) was born in Samos, a Greek island off the coast of Asia
Minor, but emigrated to Croton in southern Italy. He founded a philosophical school which seems to
have been more like a religious brotherhood; the Pythagoreans were vegetarians; they believed in the
transmigration of souls from men to animals and vice versa. Consequently, they were opposed to animal
sacrifice. They were noted also for their skill as mathematicians (Pythagoras' theorem).

To fatten on the body of another,
For one live creature to continue living
Through one live creature's death. In all the richness
That Earth, the best of mothers, tenders to us, 　　40
Does nothing please except to chew and mangle
The flesh of slaughtered animals? The Cyclops
Could do no worse! Must you destroy another
To satiate your greedy-gutted cravings?
There was a time, the Golden Age, we call it, 　　45
Happy in fruits and herbs, when no men tainted
Their lips with blood, and birds went flying safely
Through air, and in the fields the rabbits wandered
Unfrightened, and no little fish was ever
Hooked by its own credulity: all things 　　50
Were free from treachery and fear and cunning,
And all was peaceful. But some innovator,
A good-for-nothing, whoever he was, decided,
In envy, that what lions ate was better,
Stuffed meat into his belly like a furnace, 　　55
And paved the way for crime. It may have been
That steel was warmed and dyed with blood through killing
Dangerous beasts, and that could be forgiven
On grounds of self-defense; to kill wild beasts
Is lawful, but they never should be eaten. 　　60

One crime leads to another: first the swine
Were slaughtered, since they rooted up the seeds
And spoiled the season's crop; then goats were punished
On vengeful altars for nibbling at the grape-vines.
These both deserved their fate, but the poor sheep, 　　65
What had they ever done, born for man's service,
But bring us milk, so sweet to drink, and clothe us
With their soft wool, who give us more while living
Than ever they could in death? And what had oxen,
Incapable of fraud or trick or cunning, 　　70
Simple and harmless, born to a life of labor,
What had they ever done? None but an ingrate,
Unworthy of the gift of grain, could ever
Take off the weight of the yoke, and with the axe
Strike at the neck that bore it, kill his fellow 　　75
Who helped him break the soil and raise the harvest.
It is bad enough to do these things; we make
The gods our partners in the abomination,
Saying they love the blood of bulls in Heaven.
So there he stands, the victim at the altars, 　　80
Without a blemish, perfect (and his beauty
Proves his own doom), in sacrificial garlands,

Horns tipped with gold, and hears the priest intoning:
Not knowing what he means, watches the barley
Sprinkled between his horns, the very barley   85
He helped make grow, and then is struck
And with his blood he stains the knife whose flashing
He may have seen reflected in clear water.
Then they tear out his entrails, peer, examine,
Search for the will of Heaven, seeking omens.   90
And then, so great man's appetite for food
Forbidden, then, O human race, you feed,
You feast, upon your kill. Do not do this,
I pray you, but remember: when you taste
The flesh of slaughtered cattle, you are eating   95
Your fellow-workers.
                    "Now, since the god inspires me,
I follow where he leads, to open Delphi,
The very heavens, bring you revelation
Of mysteries, great matters never traced
By any mind before, and matters lost   100
Or hidden and forgotten, these I sing.
There is no greater wonder than to range
The starry heights, to leave the earth's dull regions,
To ride the clouds, to stand on Atlas' shoulders,
And see, far off, far down, the little figures   105
Wandering here and there, devoid of reason,
Anxious, in fear of death, and so advise them,
And so make fate an open book.
                    "O mortals,
Dumb in cold fear of death, why do you tremble
At Stygian rivers, shadows, empty names,   110
The lying stock of poets, and the terrors
Of a false world? I tell you that your bodies
Can never suffer evil, whether fire
Consumes them, or the waste of time. Our souls
Are deathless; always, when they leave our bodies,   115
They find new dwelling-places. I myself,
I well remember, in the Trojan War
Was Panthous' son, Euphorbus, and my breast
Once knew the heavy spear of Menelaus.[3]
Not long ago, in Argos, Abas'[4] city,   120
In Juno's temple, I saw the shield I carried
On my left arm. All things are always changing,
But nothing dies. The spirit comes and goes,
Is housed wherever it wills, shifts residence
From beasts to men, from men to beasts, but always   125

---

3. This claim is found in early, reliable sources.   4. A mythical king of Argos.

It keeps on living. As the pliant wax
Is stamped with new designs, and is no longer
What once it was, but changes form, and still
Is pliant wax, so do I teach that spirit
Is evermore the same, though passing always   130
To ever-changing bodies. So I warn you,
Lest appetite murder brotherhood, I warn you
By all the priesthood in me, do not exile
What may be kindred souls by evil slaughter.
Blood should not nourish blood.

                  "Full sail, I voyage   135
Over the boundless ocean, and I tell you
Nothing is permanent in all the world.
All things are fluent; every image forms,
Wandering through change. Time is itself a river
In constant movement, and the hours flow by   140
Like water, wave on wave, pursued, pursuing,
Forever fugitive, forever new.
That which has been, is not; that which was not,
Begins to be; motion and moment always
In process of renewal. Look, the night,   145
Worn out, aims toward the brightness, and sun's glory
Succeeds the dark. The color of the sky
Is different at midnight, when tired things
Lie all at rest, from what it is at morning
When Lucifer rides his snowy horse, before   150
Aurora paints the sky for Phoebus'[5] coming.
The shield of the god reddens at early morning,
Reddens at evening, but is white at noonday
In purer air, farther from earth's contagion.
And the Moon-goddess changes in the nighttime,   155
Lesser today than yesterday, if waning,
Greater tomorrow than today, when crescent.

Notice the year's four seasons: they resemble
Our lives. Spring is a nursling, a young child,
Tender and young, and the grass shines and buds   160
Swell with new life, not yet full-grown nor hardy,
But promising much to husbandmen, with blossom
Bright in the fertile fields. And then comes summer
When the year is a strong young man, no better time
Than this, no richer, no more passionate vigor.   165
Then comes the prime of Autumn, a little sober,
But ripe and mellow, moderate of mood,
Halfway from youth to age, with just a showing

5. The sun. *Lucifer*: The morning star.

Of gray around the temples. And then Winter,
Tottering, shivering, bald or gray, and agèd.   170

Our bodies also change. What we have been,
What we now are, we shall not be tomorrow.
There was a time when we were only seed,
Only the hope of men, housed in the womb,
Where Nature shaped us, brought us forth, exposed us   175
To the void air, and there in light we lay,
Feeble and infant, and were quadrupeds
Before too long, and after a little wobbled
And pulled ourselves upright, holding a chair,
The side of the crib, and strength grew into us,   180
And swiftness; youth and middle age went swiftly
Down the long hill toward age, and all our vigor
Came to decline, so Milon, the old wrestler,
Weeps when he sees his arms whose bulging muscles
Were once like Hercules', and Helen weeps   185
To see her wrinkles in the looking glass:
Could this old woman ever have been ravished,
Taken twice over?[6] Time devours all things
With envious Age, together. The slow gnawing
Consumes all things, and very, very slowly.   190

Not even the so-called elements are constant.
Listen, and I will tell you of their changes.
There are four of them, and two, the earth and water,
Are heavy, and their own weight bears them downward,
And two, the air and fire (and fire is purer   195
Even than air) are light, rise upward
If nothing holds them down. These elements
Are separate in space, yet all things come
From them and into them, and they can change
Into each other. Earth can be dissolved   200
To flowing water, water can thin to air,
And air can thin to fire, and fire can thicken
To air again, and air condense to water,
And water be compressed to solid earth.
Nothing remains the same: the great renewer,   205
Nature, makes form from form, and, oh, believe me
That nothing ever dies. What we call birth
Is the beginning of a difference,
No more than that, and death is only ceasing
Of what had been before. The parts may vary,   210
Shifting from here to there, hither and yon,
And back again, but the great sum is constant.

6. Once by Theseus, then by Paris.

Nothing, I am convinced, can be the same
Forever. There was once an Age of Gold,
Later, an Age of Iron. Every place   215
Submits to Fortune's wheel. I have seen oceans
That once were solid land, and I have seen
Lands made from ocean. Often sea-shells lie
Far from the beach, and men have found old anchors
On mountain-tops. Plateaus have turned to valleys,   220
Hills washed away, marshes become dry desert,
Deserts made pools. Here Nature brings forth fountains,
There shuts them in; when the earth quakes, new rivers
Are born and old ones sink and dry and vanish.
Lycus,[7] for instance, swallowed by the earth   225
Emerges far away, a different stream,
And Erasinus[8] disappears, goes under
The ground, and comes to light again in Argos,
And Mysus, so the story goes, was tired
Of his old source and banks and went elsewhere   230
And now is called Caicus. The Anigrus[9]
Was good to drink from once, but now rolls down
A flood that you had better leave alone,
Unless the poets lie, because the Centaurs
Used it to wash their wounds from Hercules' arrows.[1]   235
And Hypanis, rising from Scythian mountains,
Once fresh and sweet to the taste, is salty and brackish.

Antissa, Pharos, Tyre,[2] all inland cities,
Were islands once, Leucas and Zancle[3] mainland,
And Helice and Buris,[4] should you seek them,   240
Those old Achaian cities, you would find them
Under the waves, and mariners can show you
The sloping ramps, the buried walls. Near Troezen[5]
Stands a high treeless hill, a level plain
Until the violent winds, penned underground,   245
Stifled in gloomy caverns, struggled long
For freer air to breathe, since that black prison
Had never a chink, made the ground swell to bursting,
The way one blows a bladder or a goatskin,
And where that blister or that bubble grew   250
Out of the ground, the lump remained and hardened
With time, and now it seems a rounded hill-top.

---

7. A river of Asia Minor, as is Mysus, below.   8. A river that ran underground from Lake Stymphalus
to Argos.   9. A river of Elis, in the western Peloponnese.   1. They were poison-tipped. *Hypanis:* A
river in Scythia, running into the Black Sea.   2. A Phoenician trading city on the coast of Lebanon.
Antissa. On the island of Lesbos. *Pharos:* Peninsula connected to the mainland of Alexandria in Egypt.
3. Off the coast of Sicily. *Leucas:* A large island off the west coast of Greece.   4. Coastal cities in
Achaea, which disappeared into the sea in 373 B.C.   5. In the Peloponnese, across from Attica. The
mountain on the peninsula of Methana, north of Troezen, is made of volcanic rock.

Example on example! I could cite you
So many more that I have seen or heard of.
Just a few more. The element of water   255
Gives and receives strange forms. At midday Ammon[6]
Is cold, but warm in the morning and the evening.
The Athamanians[7] set wood on fire
By pouring water on it in the dark of the moon,
And the Ciconian[8] people have a river   260
They never drink, for they would turn to marble.
Crathis and Sybaris,[9] in our own country,
Turn hair the color of platinum or gold,
And there are other streams, more marvelous even,
Whose waters affect the mind as well as body.   265
You have heard about Salmacis;[1] there are lakes
In Ethiopia where a swallow of the water
Will drive you raving mad or hold you rigid
In catatonic lethargy. No man
Who likes his wine should ever drink from Clytor[2]   270
Or he would hate it; something in that water,
It may be, counteracts the heat of wine,
Or possibly, and so the natives tell us,
Melampus,[3] when he cured the maddened daughters
Of Proetus by his herbs and magic singing,   275
Threw in that spring mind-clearing hellebore,[4]
So that a hatred of wine stays in those waters.
Lyncestis[5] river is just the opposite;
Whoever drinks too freely there will stagger
As if he had taken undiluted wine.   280
At Pheneus, in Arcadia, there are springs
Harmless by day, injurious in the nighttime.
As lakes and rivers vary in their virtues,
So lands can change. The little island Delos
Once floated on the waters, but now stands firm,   285
And Jason's Argo, as you well remember,
Dreaded the Clashing Rocks,[6] the high-flung spray,
Immovable now, contemptuous of the winds.
Etna,[7] whose furnaces glow hot with sulphur,
Will not be fiery always in the future,   290
And was not always fiery in the past.

6. The spring at the site of the oracle of Ammon, in Libya.   7. A people of northwestern Greece. This
miraculously hot spring was supposed to have been at Dodona, an oracular shrine in that region.   8. A
Thracian tribe.   9. Rivers in southern Italy.   1. In Book IV, Ovid had already explained that bathing
in the spring of Salmacis (in Caria, a district of Asia Minor) made men soft and weak.   2. In Arcadia.
3. A prophet, who cured the daughters of Proetus, King of Argos. They had been driven mad in punishment for their pride; the madness, inflicted by Juno, made them imagine they were cows.   4. A drug
made from herbs, which was supposed to restore sanity.   5. The Lyncestae were a tribe in Macedonia.
6. Two rocks in the Black Sea which crushed any ship that came between them; after the Argo passed
through them successfully, they remained fixed in place forever.   7. The volcano (still active) in northeast Sicily.

The earth has something animal about it,
Living almost, with many lungs to breathe through,
Sending out flames, but the passages of breathing
Are changeable; some caverns may be closed   295
And new ones open whence the fire can issue.
Deep caves compress the violent winds, which drive
Rock against rock, imprisoning the matter
That holds the seeds of flame, and this bursts blazing
Ignited by the friction, and the caves   300
Cool when the winds are spent. The tars and pitches,
The yellow sulphur with invisible burning,
Are no eternal fuel, so volcanoes,
Starved of their nourishment, devour no longer,
Abandon fire, as they have been abandoned.   305

Far to the north, somewhere around Pallene,[8]
The story goes, there is a lake where men
Who plunge nine times into the chilly waters
Come out with downy feathers over their bodies.
This I do not believe, nor that the women   310
Of Scythia sprinkle their bodies with magic juices
For the same purpose and effect.
                              "However,
There are stranger things that have been tried and tested
And these we must believe. You have seen dead bodies,
Rotten from time or heat, breed smaller creatures.   315
Bury the carcasses of slaughtered bullocks,
Chosen for sacrifice (all men know this),
And from the putrid entrails will come flying
The flower-culling bees,[9] whose actions prove
Their parenthood, for they are fond of meadows,   320
Are fond of toil, and work with hopeful spirit.
The horse, being warlike, after he is buried
Produces hornets. Cut a sea-crab's claws,
Bury the rest of the body, and a scorpion
Comes from the ground. And worms that weave cocoons   325
White on the leaves of the trees, as country people
Know well, turn into moths with death's-head marking.
The mud holds seeds that generate green frogs,
Legless at first, but the legs grow, to swim with,
And take long jumps with, later. And a bear-cub,   330
New-born, is not a bear at all, but only
A lump, hardly alive, whose mother gives it
A licking into shape, herself as model.
The larvae of the honey-bearing bees,

8. A peninsula in Macedonia.   9. Compare the riddle Sampson put to the Philistines, Judges 14–18.

Safe in hexagonal waxen cells, are nothing   335
But wormlike bodies; feet and wings come later.
Who would believe that from an egg would come
Such different wonders as Juno's bird, the peacock,
Jove's eagle, Venus' dove, and all the fliers?
Some people think that when the human spine   340
Has rotted in the narrow tomb, the marrow
Is changed into a serpent.
                            "All these things
Have their beginning in some other creature,
But there is one bird which renews itself
Out of itself. The Assyrians call it the phoenix.   345
It does not live on seeds nor the green grasses,
But on the gum of frankincense and juices
Of cardamon. It lives five centuries,
As you may know, and then it builds itself
A nest in the highest branches of a palm-tree,   350
Using its talons and clean beak to cover
This nest with cassia and spikes of spikenard,
And cinnamon and yellow myrrh, and there
It dies among the fragrance, and from the body
A tiny phoenix springs to birth, whose years   355
Will be as long. The fledgling, gaining strength
To carry burdens, lifts the heavy nest,
His cradle and the old one's tomb, and bears it
Through the thin air to the city of the Sun
And lays it as an offering at the doors   360
Of the Sun-god's holy temple.
                              "Wonders, wonders!
The same hyena can be male or female,
To take or give the seed of life, at pleasure,
And the chameleon, a little creature
Whose food is wind and air, takes on the color   365
Of anything it rests on. India, conquered,
Gave Bacchus,[1] tendril-crowned, the tawny lynxes
Whose urine, when it met the air, was hardened
Becoming stone; so coral also hardens
At the first touch of air, while under water   370
It sways, a pliant weed.
                         "The day will end,
The Sun-god plunge tired horses in the ocean
Before I have the time I need to tell you
All of the things that take new forms. We see
The eras change, nations grow strong, or weaken,   375
Like Troy, magnificent in men and riches,

---

1. The god Dionysus with his army of maenads and satyrs conquered the Indians.

For ten years lavish with her blood, and now
Displaying only ruins and for wealth
The old ancestral tombs. Sparta, Mycenae,
Athens, and Thebes, all flourished once, and now   380
What are they more than names? I hear that Rome
Is rising, out of Trojan blood, established
On strong and deep foundations, where the Tiber
Comes from the Apennines.[2] Rome's form is changing
Growing to greatness, and she will be, some day,   385
Head of the boundless world; so we are told
By oracles and seers. I can remember
When Troy was tottering ruinward, a prophet,
Helenus, son of Priam, told Aeneas
In consolation for his doubts and weeping   390
'O son of Venus, if you bear in mind
My prophecies, Troy shall not wholly perish
While you are living: fire and sword will give you
Safe passage through them; you will carry on
Troy's relics, till a land, more friendly to you   395
Than your own native soil, will give asylum.
I see the destined city for the Trojans
And their sons' sons, none greater in all the ages,
Past, present, or to come. Through long, long eras
Her famous men will bring her power, but one,   400
Sprung from Iulus' blood,[3] will make her empress
Of the whole world, and after earth has used him
The heavens will enjoy him, Heaven will be
His destination.' What Helenus told Aeneas,
I have told you, I remember, and I am happy   405
That for our kin[4] new walls, at last, are rising,
That the Greek victory was to such good purpose.

We must not wander far and wide, forgetting
The goal of our discourse. Remember this:
The heavens and all below them, earth and her creatures,   410
All change, and we, part of creation, also
Must suffer change. We are not bodies only,
But wingèd spirits, with the power to enter
Animal forms, house in the bodies of cattle.
Therefore, we should respect those dwelling-places   415
Which may have given shelter to the spirit
Of fathers, brothers, cousins, human beings
At least, and we should never do them damage,
Not stuff ourselves like the cannibal Thyestes.[5]

2. The mountainous spine of the Italian peninsula. *Tiber:* The river that flows through Rome.
3. Augustus.   4. Pythagoras, who was in a former incarnation Euphorbus (cf. l. 118) speaks here as a
Trojan.   5. His brother Atreus tricked him into eating the flesh of his own children. (Cf. Aeschylus,
Agamemnon.)

An evil habit, impious preparation, 420
Wicked as human bloodshed, to draw the knife
Across the throat of the calf, and hear its anguish
Cry to deaf ears! And who could slay
The little goat whose cry is like a baby's,
Or eat a bird he has himself just fed? 425
One might as well do murder; it is only
The shortest step away. Let the bull plow
And let him owe his death to length of days;
Let the sheep give you armor for rough weather,
The she-goats bring full udders to the milking. 430
Have done with nets and traps and snares and springes,
Bird-lime and forest-beaters, lines and fish-hooks.
Kill, if you must, the beasts that do you harm,
But, even so, let killing be enough;
Let appetite refrain from flesh, take only 435
A gentler nourishment."

THE NEW TESTAMENT

In the last years of Augustus' life, in the Roman province of Judea, there was born to Joseph, a carpenter of Nazareth, and his wife, Mary, a son who was in the tradition of the Hebrew prophets but was also the bearer of a message that was to transform the world. His life on earth was short; it ended in the agony of crucifixion at about his thirty-third year. This event is a point of intersection of the three main lines of development of the ancient world—Hebrew, Greek, and Latin—for this Hebrew prophet was executed by a Roman governor, and his life and teachings were written down in the Greek language. These documents, which eventually, with some additions, constituted what we now know as the New Testament, circulated in the Greek-speaking half of the Roman Empire and later, in a Latin translation, in the West. They became the sacred texts of a church that, at first persecuted by and then triumphantly associated with Roman imperial power, outlasted the destruction of the empire and ruled over a spiritual empire that still exists.

The teaching of Jesus was revolutionary not only in terms of Greek and Roman feeling but also in terms of the Hebrew religious tradition. The Hebrew idea of a personal God who is yet not anthropomorphic, who is omnipotent, omniscient, and infinitely just, was now broadened to include among His attributes an infinite mercy that tempered the justice. Greek and Roman religion was outward and visible, the formal practice of ritual acts in a social context; Christianity was inward and spiritual, the important relationship was that between the individual soul and God. All human beings were on an equal plane in the eyes of their Creator. This idea ran counter to the theory and practice of an institution basic to the economy of the ancient world, slavery. Like the earlier Hebrew prophets, Jesus was rejected by his own people, as prophets have always been, and his death on the cross and resurrection provided his followers and the future converts with an unforgettable symbol of a new dispensation, the son of God in human form suffering to atone for the sins of humanity, the supreme expression of divine mercy. This conception is the basis of the teaching of Paul, the apostle to the gentiles, who in the middle years of the first century A.D. changed Christianity from a Jewish sect to a world-wide movement with flourishing churches all over Asia Minor and Greece—and even in Rome. The burden of his teaching was the frailty and corruption of this life and world, and the certainty of resurrection. "For this corruptible must put on incorruption, and this mortal must put on immortality." To those who had accepted this vision, the secular materialism that was the dominant view in the new era of peace and progress guaranteed by the stabilization of Roman rule was no longer tenable.

Recommended reading is Bruce M. Metzger, *The New Testament, Its Background, Growth, and Content* (1965). For a translation in modern English, with commentary, see *The New Oxford Annotated Bible*, eds. Herbert E. May and Bruce Metzger (1975).

The New Testament[1]

LUKE 2

(The Birth and Youth of Jesus)[2]

2. And it came to pass in those days, that there went out a decree from Cæsar Augustus, that all the world[3] should be taxed. (And this taxing was first made when Cyrenius was governor of Syria.) And all went to be taxed, every one unto his own city. And Joseph also went up from Galilee, out of the city of Nazareth, into Judæa, unto the city of David, which is called Bethlehem; (because he was of the house and lineage of David:) to be taxed with Mary his espoused wife, being great with child. And so it was, that, while they were there, the days were accomplished that she should be delivered. And she brought forth her firstborn son, and wrapped him in swaddling clothes, and laid him in a manger; because there was no room for them in the inn. And there were in the same country shepherds abiding in the field, keeping watch over their flock by night. And, lo, the angel of the Lord came upon them, and the glory of the Lord shone round about them: and they were sore afraid. And the angel said unto them, Fear not: for, behold, I bring you good tidings of great joy, which shall be to all people. For unto you is born this day in the city of David a Saviour, which is Christ[4] the Lord. And this shall be a sign unto you; ye shall find the babe wrapped in swaddling clothes, lying in a manger. And suddenly there was with the angel a multitude of the heavenly host praising God, and saying, Glory to God in the highest, and on earth peace, good will toward men. And it came to pass, as the angels were gone away from them into heaven, the shepherds said one to another, Let us now go even unto Bethlehem, and see this thing which is come to pass, which the Lord hath made known unto us. And they came with haste, and found Mary, and

---

1. The text of these selections is that of the King James, or Authorized, Version.   2. Luke 2:1–52.
3. The Roman Empire.   4. A Greek word meaning "anointed," used of kings, priests, and the Deliverer promised by the Prophets.

Joseph, and the babe lying in a manger. And when they had seen it, they made known abroad the saying which was told them concerning this child. And all they that heard it wondered at those things which were told them by the shepherds. But Mary kept all these things, and pondered them in her heart. And the shepherds returned, glorifying and praising God for all the things that they had heard and seen, as it was told unto them. And when eight days were accomplished for the circumcising of the child, his name was called JESUS,[5] which was so named of the angel[6] before he was conceived in the womb. And when the days of her purification according to the law of Moses were accomplished,[7] they brought him to Jerusalem, to present him to the Lord; (as it is written in the law of the Lord, Every male that openeth the womb[8] shall be called holy to the Lord;) and to offer a sacrifice according to that which is said in the law of the Lord, A pair of turtledoves, or two young pigeons. And, behold, there was a man in Jerusalem, whose name was Simeon; and the same man was just and devout, waiting for the consolation of Israel: and the Holy Ghost was upon him. And it was revealed unto him by the Holy Ghost, that he should not see death, before he had seen the Lord's Christ. And he came by the Spirit into the temple: and when the parents brought in the child Jesus, to do for him after the custom of the law, then took he him up in his arms, and blessed God, and said, Lord, now lettest thou thy servant depart in peace, according to thy word: for mine eyes have seen thy salvation, which thou hast prepared before the face of all people; a light to lighten the Gentiles,[9] and the glory of thy people Israel. And Joseph and his mother marvelled at those things which were spoken of him. And Simeon blessed them, and said unto Mary his mother, Behold, this child is set for the fall and rising again[1] of many in Israel; and for a sign which shall be spoken against; (yea, a sword shall pierce through thy own soul also,) that the thoughts of many hearts may be revealed. And there was one Anna, a prophetess, the daughter of Phanuel, of the tribe of Aser: she was of a great age, and had lived with an husband seven years from her virginity; and she was a widow of about fourscore and four years, which departed not from the temple, but served God with fastings and prayers night and day. And she coming in that instant gave thanks likewise unto the Lord, and spoke of him to all them that looked for redemption in Jerusalem. And when they had performed all things according to the law of the Lord, they returned into Galilee, to their own city Nazareth. And the child grew, and waxed strong in spirit, filled with wisdom: and the grace of God was upon him. Now his parents went to Jerusalem every year at the feast of the passover. And when he was twelve years old, they went up to Jerusalem after the custom of the feast. And when they had fulfilled the days, as they returned, the child Jesus tarried behind in Jerusalem; and Joseph and his mother knew not of it. But they, supposing him to have been in the company, went a day's journey; and they sought him among their kinsfolk and acquaintance. And

---

5. A form of the name Joshua, which means "he shall save."   6. In the Annunciation to Mary. (Luke 1:31.)   7. For the law here referred to, see Leviticus 12.   8. Firstborn son, regarded as belonging to God. See Exodus 13:2.   9. Non-Jews.   1. The Greek word is the one always used of the resurrection of the dead.

when they found him not, they turned back again to Jerusalem, seeking him. And it came to pass that after three days they found him in the temple, sitting in the midst of the doctors,[2] both hearing them, and asking them questions. And all that heard him were astonished at his understanding and answers. And when they saw him, they were amazed: and his mother said unto him, Son, why hast thou thus dealt with us? behold, thy father and I have sought thee sorrowing. And he said unto them, How is it that ye sought me? wist ye not that I must be about my Father's business? And they understood not the saying which he spake unto them. And he went down with them, and came to Nazareth, and was subject unto them: but his mother kept all these sayings in her heart. And Jesus increased in wisdom and stature, and in favour with God and man.

MATTHEW 5-7

(The Teaching of Jesus: The Sermon on the Mount)[3]

5. And seeing the multitudes, he went up into a mountain: and when he was set, his disciples came unto him: and he opened his mouth, and taught them, saying, Blessed are the poor in spirit: for theirs is the kingdom of heaven. Blessed are they that mourn: for they shall be comforted. Blessed are the meek: for they shall inherit the earth. Blessed are they which do hunger and thirst after righteousness: for they shall be filled. Blessed are the merciful: for they shall obtain mercy. Blessed are the pure in heart: for they shall see God. Blessed are the peacemakers: for they shall be called the children of God. Blessed are they which are persecuted for righteousness' sake: for theirs is the kingdom of heaven. Blessed are ye, when men shall revile you, and persecute you, and shall say all manner of evil against you falsely, for my sake. Rejoice, and be exceeding glad: for great is your reward in heaven: for so persecuted they the prophets which were before you.

Ye are the salt of the earth: but if the salt have lost his savour, wherewith shall it be salted?[4] it is thenceforth good for nothing, but to be cast out, and to be trodden under foot of men. Ye are the light of the world. A city that is set on a hill cannot be hid. Neither do men light a candle, and put it under a bushel,[5] but on a candlestick; and it giveth light unto all that are in the house. Let your light so shine before men, that they may see your good works, and glorify your Father which is in heaven.

Think not that I am come to destroy the law, or the prophets: I am not come to destroy, but to fulfil. For verily I say unto you, Till heaven and earth pass, one jot or one tittle shall in no wise pass from the law, till all be fulfilled. Whosoever therefore shall break one of these least commandments, and shall teach men so, he shall be called the least in the kingdom of heaven: but whosoever shall do and teach them, the same shall be called great in the kingdom of heaven. For I say unto you, That except your

2. Teachers, rabbis.   3. Matthew 5:1–7:29.   4. How can it regain its savor?   5. A household vessel with the capacity of a bushel.

righteousness shall exceed the righteousness of the scribes and Pharisees,[6] ye shall in no case enter into the kingdom of heaven.

Ye have heard that it was said by them of old time, Thou shalt not kill; and whosoever shall kill shall be in danger of the judgment: but I say unto you, That whosoever is angry with his brother without a cause shall be in danger of the judgment: and whosoever shall say to his brother, Raca,[7] shall be in danger of the council: but whosoever shall say, Thou fool, shall be in danger of hell fire.[8] Therefore if thou bring thy gift to the altar, and there rememberest that thy brother hath ought against thee; leave there thy gift before the altar, and go thy way; first be reconciled to thy brother, and then come and offer thy gift. Agree with thine adversary quickly, whiles thou art in the way with him; lest at any time the adversary deliver thee to the judge, and the judge deliver thee to the officer, and thou be cast into prison. Verily I say unto thee, Thou shalt by no means come out thence, till thou hast paid the uttermost farthing.

Ye have heard that it was said by them of old time, Thou shalt not commit adultery: but I say unto you, That whosoever looketh on a woman to lust after her hath committed adultery with her already in his heart. And if thy right eye offend thee, pluck it out, and cast it from thee: for it is profitable for thee that one of thy members should perish, and not that thy whole body should be cast into hell. And if thy right hand offend thee, cut it off, and cast it from thee: for it is profitable for thee that one of thy members should perish, and not that thy whole body should be cast into hell. It hath been said, Whosoever shall put away his wife, let him give her a writing of divorcement: but I say unto you, That whosoever shall put away his wife, saving for the cause of fornication, causeth her to commit adultery: and whosoever shall marry her that is divorced committeth adultery.

Again, ye have heard that it hath been said by them of old time, Thou shalt not forswear thyself, but shalt perform unto the Lord thine oaths: but I say unto you, Swear not at all; neither by heaven; for it is God's throne: nor by the earth; for it is his footstool: neither by Jerusalem; for it is the city of the great King. Neither shalt thou swear by thy head, because thou canst not make one hair white or black. But let your communication be, Yea, yea; Nay, nay: for whatsoever is more than these cometh of evil.

Ye have heard that it hath been said, An eye for an eye, and a tooth for a tooth: but I say unto you, That ye resist not evil: but whosoever shall smite thee on thy right cheek, turn to him the other also. And if any man will sue thee at the law, and take away thy coat, let him have thy cloak also. And whosoever shall compel thee to go a mile, go with him twain.

---

6. A sect that insisted on strict observance of the Mosaic law. *Scribes:* The official interpreters of the Sacred Scriptures.   7. The word means "empty."   8. The reference is to Jewish legal institutions. The penalties that might be inflicted for murder (see the opening sentence of this paragraph) were death by the sword (a sentence of a local court, "the judgment"), death by stoning (the sentence of a higher court, "the council"), and lastly the burning of the criminal's body in the place where refuse was thrown, Gehenna, which is hence used as a name for hell. Jesus compares the different degrees of punishment (administered by God) for the new sins which he here lists to the degrees of punishment recognized by Jewish law.

Give to him that asketh thee, and from him that would borrow of thee turn not thou away.

Ye have heard that it hath been said, Thou shalt love thy neighbour, and hate thine enemy. But I say unto you, Love your enemies, bless them that curse you, do good to them that hate you, and pray for them which despitefully use you, and persecute you; that ye may be the children of your Father which is in heaven: for he maketh his sun to rise on the evil and on the good, and sendeth rain on the just and on the unjust. For if ye love them which love you, what reward have ye? do not even the publicans[9] the same? And if ye salute your brethren only, what do ye more than others? do not even the publicans so? Be ye therefore perfect, even as your Father which is in heaven is perfect.

6. Take heed that ye do not your alms before men, to be seen of them: otherwise ye have no reward of your Father which is in heaven. Therefore when thou doest thine alms, do not sound a trumpet before thee, as the hypocrites do in the synagogues and in the streets, that they may have glory of men. Verily I say unto you, They have their reward. But when thou doest alms, let not thy left hand know what thy right hand doeth: that thine alms may be in secret: and thy Father which seeth in secret himself shall reward thee openly.

And when thou prayest, thou shalt not be as the hypocrites are: for they love to pray standing in the synagogues and in the corners of the streets, that they may be seen of men. Verily I say unto you, They have their reward. But thou, when thou prayest, enter into thy closet, and when thou hast shut thy door, pray to thy Father which is in secret; and thy Father which seeth in secret shall reward thee openly. But when ye pray, use not vain repetitions, as the heathen do; for they think that they shall be heard for their much speaking. Be not ye therefore like unto them: for your Father knoweth what things ye have need of, before ye ask him. After this manner therefore pray ye: Our Father which art in heaven, Hallowed be thy name. Thy kingdom come. Thy will be done in earth, as it is in heaven. Give us this day our daily bread. And forgive us our debts, as we forgive our debtors. And lead us not into temptation, but deliver us from evil: For thine is the kingdom, and the power, and the glory, for ever. Amen. For if ye forgive men their trespasses, your heavenly Father will also forgive you: but if ye forgive not men their trespasses, neither will your Father forgive your trespasses.

Moreover when ye fast, be not, as the hypocrites, of a sad countenance: for they disfigure their faces, that they may appear unto men to fast. Verily I say unto you, They have their reward. But thou, when thou fastest, anoint thine head, and wash thy face; that thou appear not unto men to fast, but unto thy Father which is in secret: and thy Father, which seeth in secret shall reward thee openly.

Lay not up for yourselves treasures upon earth, where moth and rust

---

9. The men who collected the taxes for the Roman tax-farming corporations; they were, naturally, universally despised and hated.

doth corrupt, and where thieves break through and steal: but lay up for yourselves treasures in heaven, where neither moth nor rust doth corrupt, and where thieves do not break through nor steal: for where your treasure is, there will your heart be also. The light of the body is the eye: if therefore thine eye be single,[1] thy whole body shall be full of light. But if thine eye be evil, thy whole body shall be full of darkness. If therefore the light that is in thee be darkness, how great is that darkness!

No man can serve two masters: for either he will hate the one, and love the other; or else he will hold to the one, and despise the other. Ye cannot serve God and Mammon. Therefore I say unto you, Take no thought for your life, what ye shall eat, or what ye shall drink; nor yet for your body, what ye shall put on. Is not the life more than meat, and the body than raiment? Behold the fowls of the air: for they sow not, neither do they reap, nor gather into barns; yet your heavenly Father feedeth them. Are ye not much better than they? Which of you by taking thought can add one cubit unto his stature? And why take ye thought for raiment? Consider the lilies of the field, how they grow; they toil not, neither do they spin. And yet I say unto you, That even Solomon in all his glory was not arrayed like one of these. Wherefore, if God so clothe the grass of the field, which to-day is, and tomorrow is cast into the oven, shall he not much more clothe you, O ye of little faith? Therefore take no thought, saying, What shall we eat? or, What shall we drink? or, Wherewithal shall we be clothed? (For after all these things do the Gentiles seek:) for your heavenly Father knoweth that ye have need of all these things. But seek ye first the kingdom of God, and his righteousness; and all these things shall be added unto you. Take therefore no thought for the morrow: for the morrow shall take thought for the things of itself. Sufficient unto the day is the evil thereof.

7. Judge not, that ye be not judged. For with what judgment ye judged, ye shall be judged: and with what measure ye mete, it shall be measured to you again. And why beholdest thou the mote that is in thy brother's eye, but considerest not the beam[2] that is in thine own eye? Or how wilt thou say to thy brother, Let me pull out the mote out of thine eye; and, behold, a beam is in thine own eye? Thou hypocrite, first cast out the beam out of thine own eye; and then shalt thou see clearly to cast out the mote out of thy brother's eye.

Give not that which is holy unto the dogs, neither cast ye your pearls before swine, lest they trample them under their feet, and turn again and rend you.

Ask, and it shall be given you; seek, and ye shall find; knock, and it shall be opened unto you: for every one that asketh receiveth; and he that seeketh findeth; and to him that knocketh it shall be opened. Or what man is there of you, whom if his son ask bread, will he give him a stone? Or if he ask a fish, will he give him a serpent? If ye then, being evil, know how to give good gifts unto your children, how much more shall your Father

1. Clear.   2. A long piece of heavy timber (in contrast to *mote*: a particle or speck).

which is in heaven give good things to them that ask him? Therefore all things whatsoever ye would that men should do to you, do ye even so to them: for this is the law and the prophets.

Enter ye in at the strait gate: for wide is the gate, and broad is the way, that leadeth to destruction, and many there be which go in thereat: because strait is the gate, and narrow is the way, which leadeth unto life, and few there be that find it.

Beware of false prophets, which come to you in sheep's clothing, but inwardly they are ravening wolves. Ye shall know them by their fruits. Do men gather grapes of thorns, or figs of thistles? Even so every good tree bringeth forth good fruit; but a corrupt tree bringeth forth evil fruit. A good tree cannot bring forth evil fruit, neither can a corrupt tree bring forth good fruit. Every tree that bringeth not forth good fruit is hewn down, and cast into the fire. Wherefore by their fruits ye shall know them.

Not every one that saith unto me, Lord, Lord, shall enter into the kingdom of heaven; but he that doeth the will of my Father which is in heaven. Many will say to me in that day, Lord, Lord, have we not prophesied in thy name? and in thy name have cast out devils? and in thy name done many wonderful works? And then will I profess unto them, I never knew you: depart from me, ye that work iniquity.

Therefore whosoever heareth these sayings of mine, and doeth them, I will liken him unto a wise man, which built his house upon a rock; and the rain descended, and the floods came and the winds blew, and beat upon that house; and it fell not: for it was founded upon a rock. And every one that heareth these sayings of mine, and doeth them not, shall be likened unto a foolish man, which built his house upon the sand: and the rain descended, and the floods came, and the winds blew, and beat upon that house; and it fell: and great was the fall of it. And it came to pass, when Jesus had ended these sayings, the people were astonished at his doctrine: for he taught them as one having authority, and not as the scribes.

LUKE 15

(The Teaching of Jesus: Parables)[3]

15. Then drew near unto him all the publicans and sinners for to hear him. And the Pharisees and scribes murmured, saying, This man receiveth sinners, and eateth with them.

And he spoke this parable unto them, saying, What man of you, having a hundred sheep, if he lose one of them, doth not leave the ninety and nine in the wilderness, and go after that which is lost, until he find it? And when he hath found it, he layeth it on his shoulders, rejoicing. And when he cometh home, he calleth together his friends and neighbours, saying unto them, Rejoice with me; for I have found my sheep which was lost. I say unto you that likewise joy shall be in heaven over one sinner that

3. Luke 15:1–32.

repenteth, more than over ninety and nine just persons, which need no repentance.

Either what woman having ten pieces of silver, if she lose one piece, doth not light a candle, and sweep the house, and seek diligently till she find it? And when she hath found it, she calleth her friends and her neighbours together, saying, Rejoice with me; for I have found the piece which I had lost. Likewise, I say unto you, there is joy in the presence of the angels of God over one sinner that repenteth.

And he said, A certain man had two sons: and the younger of them said to his father, Father, give me the portion of goods that falleth to me. And he divided unto them his living. And not many days after the younger son gathered all together, and took his journey into a far country, and there wasted his substance with riotous living. And when he had spent all, there arose a mighty famine in that land; and he began to be in want. And he went and joined himself to a citizen of that country; and he sent him into his fields to feed swine. And he would fain have filled his belly with the husks that the swine did eat: and no man gave unto him. And when he came to himself, he said, How many hired servants of my father's have bread enough and to spare, and I perish with hunger! I will arise and go to my father, and will say unto him, Father, I have sinned against heaven, and before thee, and am no more worthy to be called thy son: make me as one of thy hired servants. And he arose, and came to his father. But when he was yet a great way off, his father saw him, and had compassion, and ran, and fell on his neck, and kissed him. And the son said unto him, Father, I have sinned against heaven, and in thy sight, and am no more worthy to be called thy son. But the father said to his servants, Bring forth the best robe, and put it on him; and put a ring on his hand, and shoes on his feet: and bring hither the fatted calf, and kill it; and let us eat, and be merry: for this my son was dead, and is alive again; he was lost, and is found. And they began to be merry. Now his elder son was in the field: and as he came and drew nigh to the house, he heard musick and dancing. And he called one of the servants, and asked what these things meant. And he said unto him, Thy brother is come; and thy father hath killed the fatted calf, because he hath received him safe and sound. And he was angry, and would not go in: therefore came his father out, and intreated him. And he answering said to his father, Lo, these many years do I serve thee, neither transgressed I at any time thy commandment: and yet thou never gavest me a kid, that I might make merry with my friends: but as soon as this thy son was come, which hath devoured thy living with harlots, thou hast killed for him the fatted calf. And he said unto him, Son, thou art ever with me, and all that I have is thine. It was meet that we should make merry, and be glad: for this thy brother was dead, and is alive again; and was lost, and is found.

MATTHEW 26

(The Betrayal of Jesus)[4]

26. . . . . Then one of the twelve, called Judas Iscariot, went unto the chief priests, and said unto them, What will ye give me, and I will deliver him unto you? And they covenanted with him for thirty pieces of silver. And from that time he sought opportunity to betray him.

Now the first day of the feast of unleavened bread[5] the disciples came to Jesus, saying unto him, Where wilt thou that we prepare for thee to eat the passover? And he said, Go into the city to such a man, and say unto him, The Master saith, My time is at hand; I will keep the passover at thy house with my disciples. And the disciples did as Jesus had appointed them; and they made ready the passover. Now when the even was come, he sat down with the twelve. And as they did eat, he said, Verily I say unto you, that one of you shall betray me. And they were exceeding sorrowful, and began every one of them to say unto him, Lord, is it I? And he answered and said, He that dippeth his hand with me in the dish, the same shall betray me. The Son of man goeth as it is written of him: but woe unto that man by whom the Son of man is betrayed! it had been good for that man if he had not been born. Then Judas, which betrayed him, answered and said, Master, is it I? He said unto him, Thou hast said.

And as they were eating, Jesus took bread, and blessed it, and brake it, and gave it to the disciples, and said, Take, eat; this is my body. And he took the cup, and gave thanks, and gave it to them, saying, Drink ye all of it; for this is my blood of the new testament,[6] which is shed for many for the remission of sins. But I say unto you, I will not drink henceforth of this fruit of the vine, until that day when I drink it new with you in my Father's kingdom. And when they had sung an hymn, they went out into the mount of Olives. Then saith Jesus unto them, All ye shall be offended[7] because of me this night: for it is written,[8] I will smite the shepherd, and the sheep of the flock shall be scattered abroad. But after I am risen again, I will go before you into Galilee. Peter answered and said unto him, Though all men shall be offended because of thee, yet will I never be offended. Jesus said unto him, Verily I say unto thee, That this night, before the cock crow, thou shalt deny me thrice. Peter said unto him, Though I should die with thee, yet will I not deny thee. Likewise also said all the disciples.

Then cometh Jesus with them unto a place called Gethsemane, and saith unto the disciples, Sit ye here, while I go and pray yonder. And he took with him Peter and the two sons of Zebedee,[9] and began to be sorrowful and very heavy. Then saith he unto them, My soul is exceeding sorrowful, even unto death: tarry ye here, and watch with me.[1] And he went a little farther, and fell on his face, and prayed, saying, O my Father, if it

4. Matthew 26:14–75.   5. Held in remembrance of the delivery of the Jews from captivity in Egypt. See Exodus 12.   6. I.e., of the new covenant, or agreement. Jesus compares himself to the lamb that was killed at the Passover as a sign of the convenant between God and the Jews.   7. The Greek means literally, "you will be made to stumble."   8. See Zechariah 13:7.   9. James and John.   1. Stay awake.

be possible, let this cup pass from me: nevertheless, not as I will, but as thou wilt. And he cometh unto the disciples, and findeth them asleep, and saith unto Peter, What, could ye not watch with me one hour? Watch and pray, that ye enter not into temptation: the spirit indeed is willing, but the flesh is weak. He went away again the second time, and prayed, saying, O my Father, if this cup may not pass away from me, except I drink it, thy will be done. And he came and found them asleep again: for their eyes were heavy. And he left them, and went away again, and prayed the third time, saying the same words. Then cometh he to his disciples, and saith unto them, Sleep on now, and take your rest: behold, the hour is at hand, and the Son of man is betrayed into the hands of sinners. Rise, let us be going: behold, he is at hand that doth betray me.

And while he yet spake, lo, Judas, one of the twelve, came, and with him a great multitude with swords and staves, from the chief priests and elders of the people. Now he that betrayed him gave them a sign, saying, Whomsoever I shall kiss, that same is he: hold him fast. And forthwith he came to Jesus and said, Hail, master; and kissed him. And Jesus said unto him, Friend, wherefore art thou come? Then came they and laid hands on Jesus, and took him. And behold, one of them which were with Jesus[2] stretched out his hand, and drew his sword, and struck a servant of the high priest's, and smote off his ear. Then said Jesus unto him, Put up again thy sword into his place: for all they that take the sword shall perish with the sword. Thinkest thou that I cannot now pray to my Father, and he shall presently give me more than twelve legions of angels?[3] But how then shall the scriptures be fulfilled, that thus it must be? In that same hour said Jesus to the multitudes, Are ye come out as against a thief with swords and staves for to take me? I sat daily with you teaching in the temple, and ye laid no hold on me. But all this was done that the scriptures of the prophets might be fulfilled. Then all the disciples forsook him, and fled.

And they that had laid hold on Jesus led him away to Caiaphas the high priest, where the scribes and the elders were assembled. But Peter followed him afar off unto the high priest's palace, and went in, and sat with the servants, to see the end. Now the chief priests, and elders, and all the council, sought false witness against Jesus, to put him to death; but found none: yea, though many false witnesses came, yet found they none. At the last came two false witnesses, and said, This fellow said, I am able to destroy the temple of God, and to build it in three days. And the high priest arose, and said unto him, Answerest thou nothing? What is it which these witness against thee? But Jesus held his peace. And the high priest answered and said unto him, I adjure thee by the living God, that thou tell us whether thou be the Christ, the Son of God. Jesus saith unto him, Thou hast said: nevertheless I say unto you, Hereafter shall ye see the Son of man sitting on the right hand of power, and coming in the clouds of heaven. Then the high priest rent his clothes, saying, He hath spoken

2. This was Peter.   3. The legion was a Roman military formation; its full complement was six thousand men.

blasphemy; what further need have we of witnesses? behold, now ye have heard his blasphemy. What think ye? They answered and said, He is guilty of death.[4] Then did they spit in his face, and buffeted him; and others smote him with the palms of their hands, saying, Prophesy unto us, thou Christ, Who is he that smote thee?

Now Peter sat without in the palace: and a damsel came unto him, saying, Thou also wast with Jesus of Galilee. But he denied before them all, saying, I know not what thou sayest. And when he was gone out into the porch, another maid saw him and said unto them that were there, This fellow was also with Jesus of Nazareth. And again he denied with an oath, I do not know the man. And after a while came unto him they that stood by, and said to Peter, Surely thou also art one of them; for thy speech betrayeth thee.[5] Then began he to curse and to swear, saying, I know not the man. And immediately the cock crew. And Peter remembered the word of Jesus, which said unto him, Before the cock crow thou shalt deny me thrice. And he went out, and wept bitterly.

MATTHEW 27

(The Trial and Crucifixion of Jesus)[6]

27. When the morning was come, all the chief priests and elders of the people took counsel against Jesus to put him to death: and when they had bound him, they led him away, and delivered him to Pontius Pilate the governor.[7]

Then Judas, which had betrayed him, when he saw that he was condemned, repented himself, and brought again the thirty pieces of silver to the chief priests and elders, saying, I have sinned in that I have betrayed the innocent blood. And they said, What is that to us? see thou to that. And he cast down the pieces of silver in the temple, and departed, and went and hanged himself. And the chief priests took the silver pieces, and said, It is not lawful for to put them into the treasury, because it is the price of blood. And they took counsel, and bought with them the potter's field,[8] to bury strangers in. Wherefore that field was called, The field of blood, unto this day. Then was fulfilled that which was spoken by Jeremy the prophet,[9] saying, And they took the thirty pieces of silver, the price of him that was valued, whom they of the children of Israel did value; and gave them for the potter's field, as the Lord appointed me. And Jesus stood before the governor: and the governor asked him, saying, Art thou the King of the Jews? And Jesus said unto him, Thou sayest.

And when he was accused of the chief priests and elders, he answered nothing. Then said Pilate unto him, Hearest thou not how many things they witness against thee? And he answered him to never a word; insomuch

---

4. Liable to the death penalty.   5. Betrays. Peter's speech revealed his Galilean origin.   6. Matthew 27:1–66.   7. His official title was procurator of the province of Judea. The Roman policy was to allow the Jews as much independence as possible (especially in religious matters), but only the Roman authorities could impose a death sentence.   8. A field which had been dug for potter's clay, and was consequently not worth very much as land.   9. Jeremiah. The prophecy here quoted is a version of Zechariah 11:13.

that the governor marvelled greatly. Now at that feast the governor was wont to release unto the people a prisoner, whom they would. And they had then a notable prisoner, called Barabbas.[1] Therefore when they were gathered together, Pilate said unto them, Whom will ye that I release unto you? Barabbas, or Jesus which is called Christ? For he knew that for envy they had delivered him.[2]

When he was set down on the judgment seat, his wife sent unto him, saying, Have thou nothing to do with that just man: for I have suffered many things this day in a dream because of him. But the chief priests and elders persuaded the multitude that they should ask Barabbas, and destroy Jesus. The governor answered and said unto them, Whether of the twain will ye that I release unto you? They said, Barabbas. Pilate saith unto them, What shall I do then with Jesus which is called Christ? They all say unto him, Let him be crucified.[3] And the governor said, Why, what evil hath he done? But they cried out the more, saying, Let him be crucified.

When Pilate saw that he could prevail nothing, but that rather a tumult was made, he took water, and washed his hands before the multitude, saying, I am innocent of the blood of this just person: see ye to it. Then answered all the people, and said, His blood be on us, and on our children.

Then released he Barabbas unto them: and when he had scourged[4] Jesus, he delivered him to be crucified. Then the soldiers of the governor took Jesus into the common hall, and gathered unto him the whole band of soldiers. And they stripped him, and put on him a scarlet robe.

And when they had platted a crown of thorns, they put it upon his head, and a reed[5] in his right hand: and they bowed the knee before him, and mocked him, saying, Hail, King of the Jews! And they spit upon him, and took the reed, and smote him on the head. And after that they had mocked him, they took the robe off from him, and put his own raiment on him, and led him away to crucify him. And as they came out, they found a man of Cyrene,[6] Simon by name: him they compelled to bear his cross. And when they were come unto a place called Golgotha, that is to say, a place of a skull,

They gave him vinegar to drink mingled with gall:[7] and when he had tasted thereof, he would not drink. And they crucified him, and parted his garments, casting lots: that it might be fulfilled which was spoken by the prophet, They parted my garments among them, and upon my vesture did they cast lots.[8] And sitting down they watched him there; and set up over his head his accusation written, THIS IS JESUS THE KING OF THE JEWS. Then were there two thieves crucified with him, one on the right hand, and another on the left.

And they that passed by reviled him, wagging their heads, and saying,

1. Under sentence of death for sedition and murder. 2. I.e., to the Roman authorities. 3. The regular Roman punishment for sedition. 4. Whipped, a routine part of the punishment. 5. To represent the king's scepter. 6. On the coast of North Africa. 7. The Greek word translated "vinegar" describes a sour wine which was the regular drink of the Roman soldiery. The addition of bitter gall is further mockery. 8. *That it might . . . cast lots*: It is generally agreed that this is a late addition to the text.

Thou that destroyest the temple, and buildest it in three days, save thyself.
If thou be the Son of God, come down from the cross. Likewise also the
chief priests mocking him, with the scribes and elders, said, He saved
others; himself he cannot save. If he be the King of Israel, let him now
come down from the cross, and we will believe him. He trusted in God;
let him deliver him now, if he will have him: for he said, I am the Son of
God. The thieves also, which were crucified with him, cast the same in
his teeth. Now from the sixth hour there was darkness over all the land
unto the ninth hour. And about the ninth hour Jesus cried with a loud
voice, saying, Eli, Eli, lama sabachthani? that is to say, My God, my God,
why hast thou forsaken me?[9] Some of them that stood there, when they
heard that, said, This man calleth for Elias.[1] And straightway one of them
ran, and took a sponge, and filled it with vinegar, and put it on a reed, and
gave him to drink. The rest said, Let be, let us see whether Elias will come
to save him.

Jesus, when he had cried again with a loud voice, yielded up the ghost.
And, behold, the veil of the temple[2] was rent in twain from the top to the
bottom; and the earth did quake, and the rocks rent; and the graves were
opened; and many bodies of the saints which slept arose, and came out of
the graves after his resurrection, and went into the holy city, and appeared
unto many. Now when the centurion,[3] and they that were with him,
watching Jesus, saw the earthquake, and those things that were done, they
feared greatly, saying, Truly this was the Son of God. And many women
were there beholding afar off, which followed Jesus from Galilee, ministering unto him: among which was Mary Magdalene, and Mary the mother
of James and Joseph, and the mother of Zebedee's children. When the
even was come, there came a rich man of Arimathæa, named Joseph, who
also himself was Jesus' disciple. He went to Pilate, and begged the body of
Jesus. Then Pilate commanded the body to be delivered. And when Joseph
had taken the body, he wrapped it in clean linen cloth, and laid it in his
own new tomb, which he had hewn out in the rock: and he rolled a great
stone to the door of the sepulchre, and departed. And there was Mary
Magdalene, and the other Mary, sitting over against the sepulchre.

Now the next day, that followed the day of the preparation, the chief
priests and Pharisees came together unto Pilate, saying, Sir, we remember
that that deceiver said, while he was yet alive, After three days I will rise
again. Command therefore that the sepulchre be made sure[4] until the
third day, lest his disciples come by night, and steal him away, and say
unto the people, He is risen from the dead: so the last error shall be worse
than the first. Pilate said unto them, Ye have a watch:[5] go your way, make
it as sure as ye can. So they went, and made the sepulchre sure, sealing
the stone, and setting a watch.

9. The opening words of Psalm 22. The actual words of Jesus, "Eli, Eli, lama sabachthani?" are Aramaic,
the spoken Hebrew of the period.   1. The prophet Elijah.   2. The curtain that screened off the holy
of holies.   3. The Roman officer in charge of the execution.   4. Guarded.   5. Police force.

MATTHEW 28

(The Resurrection)[6]

28. In the end of the sabbath, as it began to dawn toward the first day of the week, came Mary Magdalene and the other Mary to see the sepulchre. And, behold, there was a great earthquake: for the angel of the Lord descended from heaven, and came and rolled back the stone from the door, and sat upon it. His countenance was like lightning, and his raiment white as snow: and for fear of him the keepers did shake, and became as dead men. And the angel answered and said unto the women, Fear not ye: for I know that ye seek Jesus, which was crucified. He is not here: for he is risen, as he said. Come, see the place where the Lord lay. And go quickly, and tell his disciples that he is risen from the dead; and, behold, he goeth before you into Galilee; there shall ye see him: lo, I have told you. And they departed quickly from the sepulchre with fear and great joy; and did run to bring his disciples word.

And as they went to tell his disciples, behold, Jesus met them, saying, All hail! And they came and held him by the feet, and worshipped him. Then said Jesus unto them, Be not afraid: go tell my brethren that they go into Galilee, and there shall they see me.

Now when they were going, behold, some of the watch came into the city, and shewed unto the chief priests all the things that were done. And when they were assembled with the elders, and had taken counsel, they gave large money unto the soldiers, saying, Say ye, His disciples came by night, and stole him away while we slept. And if this come to the governor's ears, we will persuade him, and secure you. So they took the money, and did as they were taught: and this saying is commonly reported among the Jews until this day.

Then the eleven disciples went away into Galilee, unto a mountain where Jesus had appointed them. And when they saw him, they worshipped him: but some doubted. And Jesus came and spake unto them, saying, All power is given unto me in heaven and in earth.

Go ye therefore, and teach all nations, baptizing them in the name of the Father, and of the Son, and of the Holy Ghost: teaching them to observe all things whatsoever I have commanded you: and, lo, I am with you always, even unto the end of the world. Amen.

PETRONIUS
died A.D. 65

It is not certain that Titus Petronius (Arbiter) was the author of the *Satyricon*, but he is the best candidate. A friend of Nero's, he committed suicide at the imperial order after becoming involved in the Pisonian conspiracy against the emperor in

6. Matthew 28:1–20.

A.D. 65. A brilliant account of Petronius' character and death is given by Tacitus in the eighteenth and nineteenth chapters of Book XVI of the *Annals*.

It is in the satiric masterpiece of this Roman aristocrat that the pragmatic, materialistic attitude Christianity was to supplant is most clearly displayed. It was probably written during the principate of Nero (A.D. 54–68), a period in which the material benefits and the spiritual weakness of the new order had already become apparent. The *Satyricon* itself has survived only in fragments; we know nothing certain about the scope of the work as a whole, but from the fragments it is clear that this book is the work of a satiric genius, perhaps the most original genius of Latin literature.

"Dinner with Trimalchio," one of the longer fragments, selections from which are included here, shows us a tradesman's world. The narrator, a student of literature, and his cronies may have an aristocratic disdain for the businessmen at whose tables they eat, but they know that Trimalchio and his kind have inherited the earth. Trimalchio began life as a foreign slave, but he is now a multimillionaire. The representative of culture, Agamemnon the teacher, drinks his wine and praises his fatuous remarks; he is content to be the court jester, the butt of Trimalchio's witticisms. Trimalchio knows no god but Mercury, the patron of business operations, but the gold bracelet, a percentage of his income which he has dedicated to Mercury, he wears on his own arm. He identifies himself with the god, and worships himself, the living embodiment of the power of money. The conversation at his table is a sardonic revelation of the temper of a whole civilization. Written in brilliantly humorous and colloquial style it exposes mercilessly a blindness to spiritual values of any kind, a distrust of the intellect, and a ferocious preoccupation with the art of cheating one's neighbor. The point is made more effective by the conscious evocation of the epic tradition throughout the work. The names alone of the teacher, Agamemnon, and his assistant in instruction, Menelaus; the wall paintings that show "the Iliad and the Odyssey and the gladiator's show given by Laenas"; Trimalchio's exhibition of monstrous ignorance of Homer (which nobody dares to correct); the Nestorian tone of Ganymedes, who regrets the old days when men were men (he is talking of the time when Safinius forced the bakers to lower the price of bread)—one touch after another reminds us that these figures are the final product of a tradition that began with Achilles and Odysseus.

The satire is witty, but it is nonetheless profound. All of them live for the moment, in material enjoyment, but they know that it cannot last. "Let us remember the living" is their watchword, but they cannot forget the dead. And as the banquet goes on, the thought of death, suppressed beneath the debased Epicureanism of Trimalchio and his associates, emerges slowly to the surface of their consciousness and comes to dominate it completely. The last arrival at the banquet is Habinnas the undertaker, and his coming coincides with the last stage of Trimalchio's drunkenness, the maudlin exhibition of his funeral clothes and the description of his tomb. "I would that I were dead," says the Sibyl in the story Trimalchio tells early in the evening; at its end he himself acts out his own funeral, complete with ointment, robes, wine, and trumpet players. The fact of death, the one fact that the practical materialism of Trimalchio and his circle can neither deny nor assimilate, asserts itself triumphantly as the supreme fact in the emptiness of Trimalchio's mind.

The introduction to *Petronius: The Satyricon*, translated by J. P. Sullivan (1977), will be helpful to the student, as will William Arrowsmith's introduction to his *The Satyricon of Petronius* (1959), pp. vii–xxii. J. P. Sullivan, *The 'Satyricon' of Petronius: A Literary Study* (1969), is a full-length critical discussion of the work.

Dinner with Trimalchio[1]

[The narrator, Encolpius, is a penniless vagabond who is a student of rhetoric under a master named Agamemnon. His close associates are Ascyltus, a fellow student, and Giton, a handsome boy who has no particular occupation. After some disreputable and very tiring adventures they are invited, as pupils of Agamemnon, to a banquet. The scene of the story is an unidentified city in southern Italy, the time probably about A.D. 50.]

The next day but one finally arrived. But we were so knocked about that we wanted to run rather than rest. We were mournfully discussing how to avoid the approaching storm,[2] when one of Agamemnon's slaves broke in on our frantic debate.

"Here," said he, "don't you know who's your host today? It's Trimalchio—he's terribly elegant. . . . He has a clock[3] in the dining-room and a trumpeter[4] all dressed up to tell him how much longer he's got to live."

This made us forget all our troubles. We dressed carefully and told Giton, who was very kindly acting as our servant, to attend us at the baths.[5]

We did not take our clothes off but began wandering around, or rather exchanging jokes while circulating among the little groups. Suddenly we saw a bald old man in a reddish shirt, playing ball with some long-haired boys. It was not so much the boys that made us watch, although they alone were worth the trouble, but the old gentleman himself. He was taking his exercise in slippers and throwing a green ball around. But he didn't pick it up if it touched the ground; instead there was a slave holding a bagful, and he supplied them to the players. We noticed other novelties. Two eunuchs stood around at different points: one of them carried a silver chamber pot, the other counted the balls, not those flying from hand to hand according to the rules, but those that fell to the ground. We were still admiring these elegant arrangements when Menelaus[6] hurried up to us.

"This is the man you'll be dining with," he said. "In fact, you are now watching the beginning of the dinner."

No sooner had Menelaus spoken than Trimalchio snapped his fingers. At the signal the eunuch brought up the chamber pot for him, while he went on playing. With the weight off his bladder, he demanded water for his hands, splashed a few drops on his fingers and wiped them on a boy's head.

It would take too long to pick out isolated incidents. Anyway, we entered the baths where we began sweating at once and we went immediately into the cold water. Trimalchio had been smothered in perfume and was already being rubbed down, not with linen towels, but with bath-robes of the finest wool. As this was going on, three masseurs sat drinking Falernian[7] in front of him. Through quarreling they spilled most of it and Trimalchio said

---

1. Translated by J. P. Sullivan.   2. A repetition of the unsavory incidents they have just experienced.
3. At this period a rare and expensive article. *Trimalchio:* The name suggests "triply blessed" or "triply powerful."   4. To sound off every hour on the hour.   5. A public institution. They were magnificent buildings, containing not only baths of many types and temperatures, but places for conversation and games and even libraries.   6. Appropriately enough, Agamemnon's assistant in instruction.   7. A famous wine from Campania south of Rome.

they were drinking his health.[8] Wrapped in thick scarlet felt he was put into a litter. Four couriers with lots of medals went in front, as well as a go-cart in which his favourite boy was riding—a wizened, bleary-eyed youngster, uglier than his master. As he was carried off, a musician with a tiny set of pipes took his place by Trimalchio's head and whispered a tune in his ear the whole way.

We followed on, choking with amazement by now, and arrived at the door with Agamemnon at our side. On the doorpost a notice was fastened which read:

> ANY SLAVE LEAVING THE HOUSE WITHOUT HIS MASTER'S
> PERMISSION WILL RECEIVE ONE HUNDRED LASHES

Just at the entrance stood the hall-porter, dressed in a green uniform with a belt of cherry red. He was shelling peas into a silver basin. Over the doorway hung—of all things—a golden cage from which a spotted magpie greeted visitors.

As I was gaping at all this, I almost fell over backwards and broke a leg. There on the left as one entered, not far from the porter's cubbyhole, was a huge dog with a chain round its neck. It was painted on the wall and over it, in big capitals, was written:

> BEWARE OF THE DOG

My colleagues laughed at me, but when I got my breath back I went to examine the whole wall. There was a mural of a slave market, price tags and all. Then Trimalchio himself, holding a wand of Mercury and being led into Rome by Minerva.[9] After this a picture of how he learned accounting and, finally how he became a steward. The painstaking artist had drawn it all in great detail with descriptions underneath. Just where the colonnade ended Mercury hauled him up by the chin and rushed him to a high platform. . . .

I began asking the porter what were the pictures they had in the middle. "The *Iliad*, and *Odyssey*, and the gladiatorial show given by Laenas," he told me.

Time did not allow us to look at many things there . . . by now we had reached the dining-room. . . .

Finally we took our places. Boys from Alexandria poured iced water over our hands. Others followed them and attended to our feet, removing any hangnails with great skill. But they were not quiet even during this troublesome operation: they sang away at their work. I wanted to find out if the whole staff were singers, so I asked for a drink. In a flash a boy was there, singing in a shrill voice while he attended to me—and anyone else who was asked to bring something did the same. It was more like a musical comedy than a respectable dinner party.

---

8. He claims they are pouring a libation.   9. Athena, patron goddess of arts and skills. *Mercury* (Hermes): As a trickster, the patron god of thieves and businessmen.

Some extremely elegant hors d'oeuvre were served at this point—by now everyone had taken his place with the exception of Trimalchio, for whom, strangely enough, the place at the top was reserved. The dishes for the first course included an ass of Corinthian bronze with two panniers, white olives on one side and black on the other. Over the ass were two pieces of plate, with Trimalchio's name and the weight of the silver inscribed on the rims. There were some small iron frames shaped like bridges supporting dormice sprinkled with honey and poppy seed. There were steaming hot sausages too, on a silver gridiron with damsons and pomegranate seeds underneath.

We were in the middle of these elegant dishes when Trimalchio himself was carried in to the sound of music and set down on a pile of tightly stuffed cushions. The sight of him drew an astonished laugh from the guests. His cropped head stuck out from a scarlet coat; his neck was well muffled up and he had put round it a napkin with a broad purple stripe and tassels dangling here and there. On the little finger of his left hand he wore a heavy gilt ring and a smaller one on the last joint of the next finger. This I thought was solid gold, but actually it was studded with little iron stars. And to show off even more of his jewellery, he had his right arm bare and set off by a gold armlet and an ivory circlet fastened with a gleaming metal plate.

After picking his teeth with a silver toothpick, he began: "My friends, I wasn't keen to come into the dining room yet. But if I stayed away any more, I would have kept you back, so I've deprived myself of all my little pleasures for you. However, you'll allow me to finish my game."

A boy was at his heels with a board of terebinth wood[1] with glass squares, and I noticed the very last word in luxury—instead of white and black pieces he had gold and silver coins. While he was swearing away like a trooper over his game and we were still on the hors d'oeuvre, a tray was brought in with a basket on it. There sat a wooden hen, its wings spread round it the way hens are when they are broody. Two slaves hurried up and as the orchestra played a tune they began searching through the straw and dug out peahens' eggs, which they distributed to the guests.

Trimalchio turned to look at this little scene and said: "My friends, I gave orders for that bird to sit on some peahens' eggs. I hope to goodness they are not starting to hatch. However, let's try them and see if they are still soft."

We took up our spoons (weighing at least half a pound each) and cracked the eggs, which were made of rich pastry. To tell the truth, I nearly threw away my share, as the chicken seemed already formed. But I heard a guest who was an old hand say: "There should be something good here." So I searched the shell with my fingers and found the plumpest little figpecker, all covered with yolk and seasoned with pepper.

At this point Trimalchio became tired of his game and demanded that all the previous dishes be brought to him. He gave permission in a loud

---

1. A very hard wood which takes a high polish and is very expensive (like everything Trimalchio has).

voice for any of us to have another glass of mead if we wanted it. Suddenly there was a crash from the orchestra and a troop of waiters—still singing—snatched away the hors d'oeuvre. However in the confusion one of the side-dishes happened to fall and a slave picked it up from the floor. Trimalchio noticed this, had the boy's ears boxed and told him to throw it down again. A cleaner came in with a broom and began to sweep up the silver plate along with the rest of the rubbish. Two long-haired Ethiopians followed him, carrying small skin bottles like those they use for scattering sand in the circus, and they poured wine over our hands—no one ever offered us water.

Our host was complimented on these elegant arrangements. "You've got to fight fair," he replied. "That is why I gave orders for each guest to have his own table. At the same time these smelly slaves won't crowd so."

Carefully sealed wine bottles were immediately brought, their necks labelled:

FALERNIAN
CONSUL OPIMIUS
ONE HUNDRED YEARS OLD[2]

While we were examining the labels, Trimalchio clapped his hands and said with a sigh:

"Wine has a longer life than us poor folks. So let's wet our whistles. Wine is life. I'm giving you real Opimian. I didn't put out such good stuff yesterday, though the company was much better class."

Naturally we drank and missed no opportunity of admiring his elegant hospitality. In the middle of this a slave brought in a silver skeleton, put together in such a way that its joints and backbone could be pulled out and twisted in all directions. After he had flung it about on the table once or twice, its flexible joints falling into various postures, Trimalchio recited:

"Man's life alas! is but a span,
So let us live it while we can,
We'll be like this when dead."

After our applause the next course was brought in. Actually it was not as grand as we expected, but it was so novel that everyone stared. It was a deep circular tray with the twelve signs of the Zodiac arranged round the edge. . . .

After this course Trimalchio got up and went to the toilet. Free of his domineering presence, we began to strike up a general conversation. Dama[3] started off by calling for bigger glasses.

"The day's nothin'," he said, "It's night 'fore y'can turn around. So the best thing's get out of bed and go straight to dinner. Lovely cold weather we've had too. M'bath hardly thawed me out. Still, a hot drink's as good

2. The wine was labeled with the name of the man who was consul in the year it was bottled. Opimius was consul in 121 B.C. Since it was in this year that the custom of dating the wine by the consul's name began, Trimalchio's wine was the oldest possible. If genuine, it would have been undrinkable.   3. One of Trimalchio's friends. Like those of Seleucus and Phileros who join the conversation later, his name is Greek.

as an overcoat. I've been throwin' it back neat, and I'm pretty tight—the wine's gone to m'head."

This started Seleucus off.

"Me now," he said, "I don't have a bath every day. It's like gettin' rubbed with fuller's[4] earth, havin' a bath. The water bites into you, and as the days go by, your heart turns to water. But when I've knocked back a hot glass of wine and honey, kiss-my-arse I say to the cold weather. Mind you, I couldn't have a bath—I was at a funeral today. Poor old Chrysanthus has just given up the ghost—nice man he was! It was only the other day he stopped me in the street. I still seem to hear his voice. Dear, dear! We're just so many walking bags of wind. We're worse than flies—at least flies have got some strength in them, but we're no more than empty bubbles.

"And what would he have been like if he hadn't been on a diet? For five days he didn't take a drop of water or a crumb of bread into his mouth. But he's gone to join the majority. The doctors finished him—well, hard luck, more like. After all, a doctor is just to put your mind at rest. Still, he got a good sendoff—he had a bier and all beautifully draped. His mourners—several of his slaves were left their freedom—did him proud, even though his widow was a bit mean with her tears. Suppose now he hadn't been so good to her! But women as a sex are real vultures. It's no good doing them a favour, you might as well throw it down a well. An old passion is just an ulcer."

He was being a bore and Phileros said loudly:

"Let's think of the living. He's got what he deserved. He lived an honest life and he died an honest death. What has he got to complain about? He started out in life with just a penny and he was ready to pick up less than that from a muck-heap, if he had to use his teeth. He went up in the world. He got bigger and bigger till he got where you see, like a honeycomb. I honestly think he left a solid hundred thousand and he had the lot in hard cash. But I'll be honest about it—seeing I'm a bit of a cynic— he had a foul mouth and too much lip. He wasn't a man, he was just murder.

"Now his brother was a fine man, a real friend to his friends, always ready with a helping hand or a decent meal.

"Chrysanthus had bad luck at first, but the first vintage set him on his feet. He fixed his own price when he sold the wine. And what properly kept his head above water was a legacy he came in for, when he pocketed more than was left to him. And the blockhead, when he had a quarrel with his brother, cut him out of his will in favour of some sod we've never heard of. You're leaving a lot behind when you leave your own flesh and blood. But he took advice from his slaves and they really fixed him. It's never right to believe all you're told, especially for a business man. But it's true he enjoyed himself while he lived. You got it, you keep it. He was certainly Fortune's favourite—lead turned to gold in his hand. Mind you, it's easy when everything runs smoothly.

4. *Fuller:* A cleaner (of woollen cloaks). They used very strong solvents.

"And how old do you think he was? Seventy or more! But he was hard as nails and carried his age well. His hair was black as a raven's wing. I knew the man for ages and ages and he was still an old lecher. I honestly don't think he left the dog alone. What's more, he liked little boys—he could turn his hand to anything. Well, I don't blame him—after all, he couldn't take anything else with him."

This was Phileros, then Ganymedes said:

"You're all talking about things that don't concern heaven or earth. Meanwhile, no one gives a damn the way we're hit by the corn situation. Honest to God, I couldn't get hold of a mouthful of bread today. And look how there's still no rain. It's been absolute starvation for a whole year now. To hell with the food officers! They're in with the bakers—'You be nice to me and I'll be nice to you.' So the little man suffers, while those grinders of the poor never stop celebrating. Oh, if only we still had the sort of men I found here when I first arrived from Asia. Like lions they were. That was the life! Come one, come all! If white flour was inferior to the very finest, they'd thrash those bogeymen till they thought God Almighty was after them.

"I remember Safinius—he used to live by the old arch then; I was a boy at the time. He wasn't a man, he was all pepper. He used to scorch the ground wherever he went. But he was dead straight—don't let him down and he wouldn't let you down. You'd be ready to play *morra*[5] with him in the dark. But on the city council, how he used to wade into some of them—no beating about the bush, straight from the shoulder! And when he was in court, his voice got louder and louder like a trumpet. He never sweated or spat—I think there was a touch of the old acid about him. And very affable he was when you met him, calling everyone by name just like one of us. Naturally at the time corn was dirt cheap. You could buy a penny loaf that two of you couldn't get through. Today—I've seen bigger bull's-eyes.

"Ah me! It's getting worse every day. This place is going down like a calf's tail. But why do we have a third-rate food officer who wouldn't lose a penny to save our lives? He sits at home laughing and rakes in more money a day than anyone else's whole fortune. I happen to know he's just made a thousand in gold. But if we had any balls at all, he wouldn't be feeling so pleased with himself. People today are lions at home and foxes outside.

"Take me, I've already sold the rags off my back for food and if this shortage continues, I'll be selling my bit of a house. What's going to happen to this place if neither god nor man will help us? As I hope to go home tonight, I'm sure all this is heaven's doing.

"Nobody believes in heaven, see, nobody fasts, nobody gives a damn for the Almighty. No, people only bow their heads to count their money. In the old days high-class ladies used to climb up the hill barefoot, their hair loose and their hearts pure, and ask God for rain. And he'd send it down

---

5. A game (still played in southern Italy) which requires the players to match the number of fingers held out by the opponent.

in bucketfuls right away—it was then or never—and everyone went home like drowned rats. Since we've given up religion the gods nowadays keep their feet well wrapped up. The fields just lie . . . ."

"Please, please," broke in Echion the rag merchant, "be a bit more cheerful. 'First it's one thing, then another,' as the yokel said when he lost his spotted pig. What we haven't got today, we'll have tomorrow. That's the way life goes. Believe me, you couldn't name a better country, if it had the people. As things are, I admit, it's having a hard time, but it isn't the only place. We mustn't be soft. The sky don't get no nearer wherever you are. If you were somewhere else, you'd be talking about the pigs walking round ready roasted back here.

"And another thing, we'll be having a holiday with a three-day show that's the best ever—and not just a hack troupe of gladiators but freedmen for the most part. My old friend Titus has a big heart and a hot head. Maybe this, maybe that, but something at all events. I'm a close friend of his and he does nothing by halves. He'll give us cold steel, no quarter and the slaughterhouse right in the middle where all the stands can see it. And he's got the wherewithal—he was left thirty million when his poor father died. Even if he spent four hundred thousand, his pocket won't feel it and he'll go down in history. He's got some big brutes already, and a woman who fights in a chariot and Glyco's steward,[6] who was caught having fun with his mistress. You'll see quite a quarrel in the crowd between jealous husbands and romantic lovers. But that half-pint Glyco threw his steward to the lions, which is just giving himself away. How is it the servant's fault when he's forced into it? It's that old pisspot who really deserves to be tossed by a bull. But if you can't beat the ass you beat the saddle. But how did Glyco imagine the poisonous daughter of Hermogenes[7] would ever turn out well? The old man could cut the claws off a flying kite, and a snake don't hatch old rope. Glyco—well, Glyco's got his. He's branded for as long as he lives and only the grave will get rid ot it. But everyone pays for their mistakes.

"But I can almost smell the dinner Mammaea is going to give us[8]—two denarii apiece for me and the family. If he really does it, he'll make off with all Norbanus's votes, I tell you he'll win at a canter. After all, what good has Nobanus done us? He put on some half-pint gladiators, so done in already that they'd have dropped if you blew at them. I've seen animal-killers[9] fight better. As for the horsemen killed, he got them off a lamp[1]—they ran round like cocks in a backyard. One was just a carthorse, the other couldn't stand up, and the reserve was just one corpse instead of another—he was practically hamstrung. One boy did have a bit of spirit—he was in Thracian armour,[2] and even he didn't show any initiative. In fact, they were all flogged afterwards, there were so many shouts of 'Give

6. A household slave. His master was permitted by law to punish him by forcing him to fight wild beasts in the arena.   7. Presumably the father of Glyco's wife.   8. A public banquet, given by Mammaea as part of his electoral campaign. His rival Norbanus has been giving gladiatorial shows.   9. Professional fighters of wild animals, considered inferior to gladiators.   1. They were as small as the horsemen depicted on a lamp.   2. Light armor, such as that worn by soldiers from Thrace, a savage country northeast of Greece.

'em what for!' from the crowd. Pure yellow, that's all. " 'Well, I've put on
a show for you,' he says. 'And I'm clapping you,' says I. 'Reckon it up—
I'm giving more than I got. So we're quits.'

"Hey, Agamemnon! I suppose you're saying 'What is that bore going on
and on about?' It's because a good talker like you don't talk. You're a cut
above us, and so you laugh at what us poor people say. We all know you're
off your head with all that reading. But never mind! Some day I'll get you
to come down to my place in the country and have a look at our little
cottage. We'll find something to eat—a chicken, some eggs. It'll be nice,
even though the unreliable weather this year has made off with everything.
Anyway, we'll find enough to fill our bellies.

"And my kid is growing up to be a pupil of yours. He can divide by four
already. If God spares him, you'll have him ready to do anything for you.
In his spare time, he won't take his head out of his exercise book. He's
clever and there's good stuff in him, even if he is crazy about birds. Only
yesterday I killed his three goldfinches and told him a weasel ate them.
But he's found some other silly hobbies, and he's having a fine time painting. Still, he's already well ahead with his Greek, and he's starting to take
to his Latin, though his tutor is too pleased with himself and unreliable—
he just comes and goes. He knows his stuff but doesn't want to work. There
is another one as well, not so clever but he is conscientious—he teaches
the boy more than he knows himself. In fact, he makes a habit of coming
around on holidays, and whatever you give him, he's happy.

"Anyway, I've just bought the boy some law books, as I want him to
pick up some legal training for home use. There's a living in that sort of
thing. He's done enough dabbling in poetry and such like. If he objects,
I've decided he'll learn a trade—barber, auctioneer, or at least a barrister—
something he can't lose till he dies. Well, yesterday I gave it to him straight:
'Believe me, my lad, any studying you do will be for your own good. You
see Phileros the solicitor—if he hadn't studied, he'd be starving today. It's
not so long since he was humping round loads on his back. Now he can
even look Norbanus in the face. An education is an investment, and a
proper profession never goes dead on you.' "

This was the sort of conversation flying round when Trimalchio came
in, dabbed his forehead and washed his hands in perfume. There was a
short pause, then he said:

"Excuse me, dear people, my inside has not been answering the call for
several days now. The doctors are puzzled. But some pomegranate rind
and resin in vinegar has done me good. But I hope now it will be back on
its good behaviour. Otherwise my stomach rumbles like a bull. So if any
of you wants to go out, there's no need for him to be embarrassed. None
of us was born solid. I think there's nothing so tormenting as holding
yourself in. This is the one thing even God Almighty can't object to. Yes,
laugh, Fortunata,[3] but you generally keep me up all night with this sort of
thing.

3. Trimalchio's wife.

"Anyway, I don't object to people doing what suits them even in the middle of dinner—and the doctors forbid you to hold yourself in. Even if it's a longer business, everything is there just outside—water, bowls, and all the other little comforts. Believe me, if the wind goes to your brain it starts flooding your whole body too. I've known a lot of people die from this because they wouldn't be honest with themselves."

We thanked him for being so generous and considerate and promptly proceeded to bury our amusement in our glasses. Up to this point we'd not realized we were only in mid-stream, as you might say.

The orchestra played, the tables were cleared, and then three white pigs were brought into the dining-room, all decked out in muzzles and bells. The first, the master of ceremonies announced, was two years old, the second three, and the third six. I was under the impression that some acrobats were on their way in and the pigs were going to do some tricks, the way they do in street shows. But Trimalchio dispelled this impression by asking:

"Which of these would you like for the next course? Any clodhopper can do you a barnyard cock or a stew and trifles like that, but my cooks are used to boiling whole calves."

He immediately sent for the chef and without waiting for us to choose he told him to kill the oldest pig.

He then said to the man in a loud voice:

"Which division are you from?"

When he replied he was from number forty, Trimalchio asked:

"Were you bought or were you born here?"

"Neither," said the chef, "I was left to you in Pansa's will."

"Well, then," said Trimalchio, "see you serve it up carefully—otherwise I'll have you thrown into the messenger's division."

So the chef, duly reminded of his master's magnificence, went back to his kitchen, the next course leading the way.

Trimalchio looked around at us with a gentle smile: "If you don't like the wine, I'll have it changed. It is up to you to do it justice. I don't buy it, thank heaven. In fact, whatever wine really tickles your palate this evening, it comes from an estate of mine which as yet I haven't seen. It's said to join my estates at Tarracina and Tarentum. What I'd like to do now is add Sicily to my little bit of land, so that when I want to go to Africa, I could sail there without leaving my own property.

"But tell me, Agamemnon, what was your debate about today? Even though I don't go in for the law, still I've picked up enough education for home consumption. And don't you think I turn my nose up at studying, because I have two libraries, one Greek, one Latin. So tell us, just as a favour, what was the topic of your debate?"

Agamemnon was just beginning, "A poor man and a rich man were enemies . . ." when Trimalchio said: "What's a poor man?" "Oh, witty!" said Agamemnon, and then told us about some fictitious case or other. Like lightning Trimalchio said: "If this happened, it's not a fictitious case— if it didn't happen, then it's nothing at all."

We greeted this witticism and several more like it with the greatest
enthusiasm.

"Tell me, my dear Agamemnon," continued Trimalchio, "do you
remember the twelve labours of Hercules and the story of Ulysses—how
the Cyclops tore out his thumb with a pair of pincers.[4] I used to read about
them in Homer, when I was a boy. In fact, I actually saw the Sibyl at
Cumae with my own eyes dangling in a bottle, and when the children
asked her in Greek: 'What do you want, Sybil?' she used to answer: 'I want
to die.' "

[Presents for the guests are distributed with a slave announcing the nature
of each gift and making in each case an atrocious pun on the name of the
guest.]

We laughed for ages. There were hundreds of things like this but they've
slipped my mind now.

Ascyltus, with his usual lack of restraint, found everything extremely
funny, lifting up his hands and laughing till the tears came. Eventually
one of Trimalchio's freedman[5] friends flared up at him—the one sitting
above me, in fact.

"You with the sheep's eyes," he said, "what's so funny? Isn't our host
elegant enough for you? You're better off, I suppose, and used to a bigger
dinner. Holy guardian here preserve me! If I was sitting by him, I'd make
him bleat! A fine pippin he is to be laughing at other people! Some fly-by-
night from god knows where—not worth his own piss. In fact, if I pissed
round him, he wouldn't know where to turn.

"By god, it takes a lot to make me boil, but if you're too soft, worms like
this only come to the top. Look at him laughing! What's he got to laugh
at? Did his father pay cash for him? You're a Roman knight,[6] are you?
Well, my father was a king.

" 'Why are you only a freedman?' did you say? Because I went into
service voluntarily. I wanted to be a Roman citizen, not a subject with
taxes to pay. And today, I hope no one can laugh at the way I live. I'm a
man among men, and I walk with my head up. I don't owe anybody a
penny—there's never been a court-order out for me. No one's said 'Pay
up!' to me in the street.

"I've bought a bit of land and some tiny pieces of plate. I've twenty
bellies to feed, as well as a dog. I bought my old woman's freedom so
nobody could wipe his dirty hands on her hair. Four thousand I paid for
myself. I was elected to the Augustan College[7] and it cost me nothing. I
hope when I die I won't have to blush in my coffin.

"But you now, you're such a busybody you don't look behind you. You
see a louse on somebody else, but not the fleas on your own back. You're
the only one who finds us funny. Look at the professor now—he's an older

---

4. Trimalchio refers to Odysseus's adventures in the cave of the Cyclops (*Odyssey*, IX). In spite of what
he goes on to say, he has obviously not read Homer.   5. A former slave who had bought his freedom.
6. A Roman class including all who had property above a certain amount.   7. The state religion was
the worship of Augustus, the emperor. The office of priest might be sold or conferred.

man than you and we get along with him. But you're still wet from your
mother's milk and not up to your ABC yet. Just a crackpot—you're like a
piece of wash-leather in soak, softer but no better! You're grander than
us—well, have two dinners and two suppers! I'd rather have my good name
than any amount of money. When all's said and done, who's ever asked
me for money twice? For forty years I slaved but nobody ever knew if I was
a slave or a free man. I came to this colony when I was a lad with long
hair—the town-hall hadn't been built then. But I worked hard to please
my master—there was a real gentleman, with more in his little finger-nail
than there is in your whole body. And I had people in the house who tried
to trip me up one way or another, but still—thanks be to his guardian
spirit!—I kept my head above water. That's real success: being born free is
as easy as all get-out. Now what are you gawping at, like a goat in a vetch
field?"

At this remark, Giton, who was waiting on me, could not suppress his
laughter and let out a filthy guffaw, which did not pass unnoticed by Ascyltus's opponent. He turned his abuse on the boy.

"So!" he said, "you're amused too, are you, you curly-headed onion? A
merry Saturnalia[8] to you! Is it December, I'd like to know? When did *you*
pay your liberation tax?[9] Look, he doesn't know what to do, the gallow's
bird, the crow's meat.

"God's curse on you, and your master too, for not keeping you under
control! As sure as I get my bellyful, it's only because of Trimalchio that I
don't take it out of you here and now. He's a freedman like myself. We're
doing all right, but those good-for-nothings, well—. It's easy to see, like
master, like man. I can hardly hold myself back, and I'm not naturally
hot-headed—but once I start, I don't give a penny for my own mother.

"All right! I'll see you when we get outside, you rat, you excrescence.
I'll knock your master in the dirt before I'm an inch taller or shorter. And
I won't let you off either, by heaven, even if you scream down God Almighty.
Your cheap curls and your no-good master won't be much use to you
then—I'll see to that. I'll get my teeth into you, all right. Either I'm much
mistaken about myself or you won't be laughing at us behind your golden
beard. Athena's curse on you and the man who first made you such a
forward brat.

"I didn't learn no geometry or criticism and such silly rubbish, but I can
read the letters on a notice board and I can do my percentages in metal,
weights, and money. In fact, if you like, we'll have a bet. Come on, here's
my cash. Now you'll see how your father wasted his money, even though
you do know how to make a speech.

"Try this:

> Something we all have.
> Long I come, broad I come. What am I?

8. A December festival in honor of an ancient Italian deity at which the normal order of everyday life was
reversed and the slaves and children made fun of their masters.   9. The freed slave had to pay 5 percent
of his value to the treasury.

"I'll give you it: something we all have that runs and doesn't move from its place: something we all have that grows and gets smaller.[1]

"You're running round in circles, you've had enough, like the mouse in the pisspot. So either keep quiet or keep out of the way of your betters, they don't even know you're alive—unless you think I care about your boxwood rings that you swiped from your girl friend! Lord make me lucky! Let's go into town and borrow some money. You'll soon see they trust this iron one.

"Pah! a drownded fox makes a nice sight, I must say. As I hope to make my pile and die so famous that people swear by my dead body, I'll hound you to death. And he's a nice thing too—the one who taught you all these tricks—a muttonhead, not a master. We learned different. Our teacher used to say: 'Are your things in order? Go straight home. No looking around. And be polite to your elders.' Nowadays it's all an absolute muck-heap. They turn out nobody worth a penny. I'm like you see me and I thank God for the way I was learnt." . . .

In the middle of all this, a lictor[2] knocked at the double doors and a drunken guest entered wearing white, followed by a large crowd of people. I was terrified by this lordly apparition and thought it was the chief magistrate arriving. So I tried to rise and get my bare feet on the floor. Agamemnon laughed at this panic and said:

"Get hold of yourself, you silly fool. This is Habinnas—Augustan College and monumental mason."

Relieved by this information I resumed my position and watched Habinnas' entry with huge admiration. Being already drunk, he had his hands on his wife's shoulders; loaded with several garlands, oil pouring down his forehead and into his eyes, he settled himself into the place of honour and immediately demanded some wine and hot water. Trimalchio, delighted by these high spirits, demanded a larger cup for himself and asked how he had enjoyed it all.

"The only thing we missed," replied Habinnas, "was yourself—the apple of my eye was here. Still, it was damn good. Scissa was giving a ninth-day dinner[3] in honour of a poor slave of hers she'd freed on his death-bed. And I think she'll have a pretty penny to pay in liberation tax because they reckon he was worth fifty thousand. Still, it was pleasant enough, even if we did have to pour half our drinks over his wretched bones."

"Well," said Trimalchio, "what did you have for dinner?"

"I'll tell you if I can—I've such a good memory that I often forget my own name. For the first course we had a pig crowned with sausages and served with blood-puddings and very nicely done giblets, and of course beetroot and pure wholemeal bread—which I prefer to white myself: it's very strengthening and I don't regret it when I do my business. The next course was cold tart and a concoction of first-class Spanish wine poured

---

1. There is no agreement about the correct answer to these riddles. Suggested answers are, to the first, the foot; the second, the eye; the third, the hair.   2. A magistrate's attendant.   3. On the last day of the mourning period.

over hot honey. I didn't eat anything at all of the actual tart, but I dived right into the honey. Scattered round were chickpeas, lupines, a choice of nuts and an apple apiece—though I took two. And look, I've got them tied up in a napkin, because if I don't take something in the way of a present to my youngster, I'll have a row on my hands.

"Oh, yes, my good lady reminds me. We had a hunk of bearmeat set before us, which Scintilla was foolish enough to try, and she practically spewed up her guts; but I ate more than a pound of it, as it tasted like real wild-boar. And I say if bears can eat us poor people, it's all the more reason why us poor people should eat bears.

"To finish up with, we had some cheese basted with new wine, snails all round, chitterlings, plates of liver, eggs in pastry hoods, turnips, mustard, and some filthy concoction—good riddance to that. There were pickled cumin seeds too, passed round in a bowl and some people were that bad-mannered they took three handfuls. You see, we sent the ham away.

"But tell me something, Gaius, now I ask—why isn't Fortunata at the table?"

"You know her," replied Trimalchio, "unless she's put the silver away and shared out the left-overs among the slaves, she won't put a drop of water to her mouth."

"All the same," retorted Habinnas, "unless she sits down, I'm shagging off."

And he was starting to get up, when at a given signal all the servants shouted "*Fortunata*" four or five times. So in she came with her skirt tucked up under a yellow sash to show her cerise petticoat underneath, as well as her twisted anklets and gold-embroidered slippers. Wiping her hands on a handkerchief which she carried round her neck, she took her place on the couch where Habbinas' wife was reclining. She kissed her. "Is it really you?" she said, clapping her hands together.

It soon got to the point where Fortunata took the bracelets from her great fat arms and showed them to the admiring Scintilla. In the end she even undid her anklets and her gold hair net, which she said was pure gold. Trimalchio noticed this and had it all brought to him and commented:

"A woman's chains, you see. This is the way us poor fools get robbed. She must have six and a half pounds on her. Still, I've got a bracelet myself, made up from one-tenth per cent to Mercury[4]—and it weighs not an ounce less than ten pounds."

Finally, for fear he looked like a liar, he even had some scales brought in and had them passed round to test the weight.

Scintilla was no better. From round her neck she took a little gold locket, which she called her "lucky box." From it she extracted two earrings and in her turn gave them to Fortunata to look at.

"A present from my good husband," she said, "and no one has a finer set."

---

4. Trimalchio sets aside a percentage of his profits to offer to his patron deity.

"Hey!" said Habinnas, "you cleaned me out to buy you a glass bean. Honestly, if I had a daughter, I'd cut her little ears off. If there weren't any women, everything would be dirt cheap. As it is, we've got to drink cold water and piss it out hot."

Meanwhile, the women giggled tipsily between themselves and kissed each other drunkenly, one crying up her merits as a housewife, the other crying about her husband's demerits and boy friends. While they had their heads together like this, Habinnas rose stealthily and taking Fortunata's feet, flung them up over the couch.

"Oh, oh!" she shrieked, as her underskirt wandered up over her knees. So she settled herself in Scintilla's lap and hid her disgusting red face in her handkerchief.

Then came an interval, after which Trimalchio called for dessert. . . .

Fortunata was now wanting to dance, and Scintilla was doing more clapping than talking, when Trimalchio said:

"Philargyrus—even though you are such a terrible fan of the Greens[5]— you have my permission to join us. And tell your dear Menophila to sit down as well."

Need I say more? We were almost thrown out of our places, so completely did the household fill the dining-room. I even noticed that the chef was actually given a place above me, and he was reeking of pickles and sauce. And he wasn't satisfied with just having a place, but he had to start straight off on an imitation of the tragedian Ephesus, and then challenge his master to bet against the Greens winning at the next races.

Trimalchio became expansive after this argument.

"My dear people," he said, "slaves are human beings too. They drink the same milk as anybody else, even though luck's been agin 'em. Still, if nothing happens to me, they'll have their taste of freedom soon. In fact, I'm setting them all free in my will. I'm giving Philargyrus a farm, what's more, and the woman he lives with. As for Cario, I'm leaving him a block of flats, his five per cent manumission tax, and a bed with all the trimmings. I'm making Fortunata my heir, and I want all my friends to look after her.

"The reason I'm telling everyone all this is so my household will love me now as much as if I was dead."

Everyone began thanking his lordship for his kindness, when he became very serious and had a copy of his will brought in. Amid the sobs of his household he read out the whole thing from beginning to end.

Then looking at Habinnas, he said:

"What have you to say, my dear old friend? Are you building my monument the way I told you? I particularly want you to keep a place at the foot of my statue and put a picture of my pup there, as well as paintings of wreaths, scent-bottles, and all the contests of Petraites,[6] and thanks to you I'll be able to live on after I'm dead. And another thing! See that it's a hundred feet facing the road and two hundred back into the field. I want

5. One of the teams in the chariot races.   6. A popular gladiator.

all the various sorts of fruit round my ashes and lots and lots of vines. After all, it's a big mistake to have nice houses just for when you're alive and not worry about the one we have to live in for much longer. And that's why I want this written up before anything else:

THIS MONUMENT DOES NOT GO TO THE HEIR

"But I'll make sure in my will that I don't get done down once I'm dead. I'll put one of my freedmen in charge of my tomb to look after it and not let people run up and shit on my monument. I'd like you to put some ships there too, sailing under full canvas, and me sitting on a high platform in my robes of office, wearing five gold rings and pouring out a bagful of money for the people. You know I gave them all a dinner and two denarii apiece. Let's have in a banqueting hall as well, if you think it's a good idea, and show the whole town having a good time. Put up a statue of Fortunata on my right, holding a dove, and have her leading her little dog tied to her belt—and this dear little chap as well, and great big wine jars sealed up so the wine won't spill. And perhaps you could carve me a broken wine jar and boy crying over it. A clock in the middle, so that anybody who looks at the time, like it or not, has got to read my name. As for the inscription now, take a good look and see if this seems suitable enough:

HERE SLEEPS
GAIUS POMPEIUS TRIMALCHIO
MAECENATIANUS
ELECTED TO THE AUGUSTAN COLLEGE IN HIS ABSENCE
HE COULD HAVE BEEN ON EVERY BOARD IN ROME
BUT HE REFUSED
GOD-FEARING BRAVE AND TRUE
A SELF-MADE MAN
HE LEFT AN ESTATE OF 30,000,000
AND HE NEVER HEARD A PHILOSOPHER
FAREWELL
AND YOU FARE WELL, TRIMALCHIO."

[After a visit to the baths, where Encolpius and his friends made an unsuccessful attempt to escape, the dinner is resumed.]

After this dish Trimalchio looked at the servants and said:
"Why haven't you had dinner yet? Off you go and let some others come on duty."
Up came another squad and as the first set called out: "Good night, Gaius!" the new arrivals shouted: "Good evening, Gaius!"
This led to the first incident that damped the general high spirits. Not a bad-looking boy entered with the newcomers and Trimalchio jumped at him and began kissing him at some length. Fortunata, asserting her just and legal rights, began hurling insults at Trimalchio, calling him a low scum and a disgrace, who couldn't control his beastly desires. "You dirty dog!" she finally added.

Trimalchio took offence at this abuse and flung his glass into Fortunata's face. She screamed as though she'd lost an eye and put her trembling hands across her face. Scintilla was terrified too and hugged the quaking woman to her breast. An obliging slave pressed a little jug of cold water to her cheek, while Fortunata rested her head on it and began weeping. Trimalchio just said:

"Well, well, forgotten her chorus days, has she? She doesn't remember, but she was bought and sold, and I took her away from it all and made her as good as the next. Yet she puffs herself up like a frog and doesn't even spit for luck. Just a great hunk, not a woman. But those as are born over a shop don't dream of a house. May I never have a day's good luck again, if I don't teach that Cassandra in clogs some manners!

"There was I, not worth twopence, and I could have had ten million. And you know I'm not lying about it. Agatho, who ran a perfume shop for the lady next door, he took me on one side and said: 'You don't want to let your family die out, you know!' But me, trying to do the right thing and not wanting to look changeable, I cut my own throat.

"All right! I'll make you want to dig me up with your bare nails. Just so you'll know on the spot what you've done for yourself—Habinnas! I don't want you to put her statue on my tomb, so at least when I'm dead I won't have any more squabbles. And another thing! just to show I can get my own back—when I'm dead I don't want her to kiss me."

After this thunderbolt, Habinnas began asking him to calm down: "None of us are without faults," he said, "we're not gods, we're human!" Scintilla said the same, calling him Gaius, and she began asking him, in the name of his guardian spirit, to give in.

Trimalchio held back his tears no longer. "I ask you, Habinnas," he said, "as you hope to enjoy your bit of savings—if I did anything wrong, spit in my face. I kissed this very careful little fellow, not for his pretty face, but because he's careful with money—he says his ten times table, he reads a book at sight, he's got himself some Thracian kit out of his daily allowance, and he's bought himself an easy chair and two cups out of his own pocket. Doesn't he deserve to be the apple of my eye? But Fortunata won't have it.

"Is that the way you feel, high heels? I'll give you a piece of advice: don't let your good luck turn your head, you kite, and don't make me show my teeth, my little darling—otherwise you'll feel my temper. You know me: once I've decided on something, it's fixed with a twelve-inch nail.

"But to come back to earth—I want you to enjoy yourselves, my dear people. After all, I was once like you are, but being the right sort, I got where I am. It's the old headpiece that makes a man, the rest is all rubbish. 'Buy right—sell right!'—that's me! Different people will give you a different line. I'm just on top of the world, I'm that lucky.

"But you, you snoring thing, are you still moaning? I'll give you something to moan about in a minute.

"However, as I'd started to say, it was my shrewd way with money that got me to my present position. I came from Asia as big as this candlestick.

In fact, every day I used to measure myself against it, and to get some whiskers round my beak quicker, I used to oil my lips from the lamp. Still, for fourteen years I was the old boy's fancy. And there's nothing wrong if the boss wants it. But I did all right by the old girl too. You know what I mean—I don't say anything because I'm not the boasting sort.

"Well, as heaven will have it, I became boss in the house, and the old boy, you see, couldn't think of anything but me. That's about it—he made me co-heir with the Emperor[7] and I got a senator's fortune. But nobody gets enough, never. I wanted to go into business. Not to make a long story of it, I built five ships, I loaded them with wine—it was absolute gold at the time—and I sent them to Rome. You'd have thought I ordered it— every single ship was wrecked. That's fact, not fable! In one single day Neptune swallowed up thirty million. Do you think I gave up? This loss honestly wasn't more than a flea-bite to me—it was as if nothing had happened. I built more boats, bigger and better and luckier, so nobody could say I wasn't a man of courage. You know, the greater the ship, the greater the confidence. I loaded them again—with wine, bacon, beans, perfumes and slaves. At this point Fortunata did the decent thing, because she sold off all her gold trinkets, all her clothes, and put ten thousand in gold pieces in my hand. This was the yeast my fortune needed to rise. What heaven wants, soon happens. In one voyage I carved out a round ten million. I immediately bought back all my old master's estates. I built a house, I invested in slaves, and I bought up the horse trade. Whatever I touched grew like a honeycomb. Once I had more than the whole country, then down tools! I retired from business and began advancing loans through freedmen.

"Actually I was tired of trading on my own account, but it was an astrologer who convinced me. He happened to come to our colony, a sort of Greek, Serapa by name, and he could have told heaven itself what to do. He even told me things I'd forgotten. He went through everything for me from A to Z. He knew me inside out—the only thing he didn't tell me was what I ate for dinner the day before. You'd have thought he'd never left my side.

"Wasn't there that thing, Habinnas?—I think you were there: 'You got your lady wife out of those *certain circumstances.* You are not lucky in your friends. Nobody thanks you enough for your trouble. You have large estates. You are nursing a viper in your bosom.'

"And he said—though I shouldn't tell you—I have thirty years, four months, two days to live. What's more, I shall soon receive a legacy. My horoscope tells me this. If I'm allowed to join my estates to Apulia,[8] I'll have lived enough.

"Meantime, under the protection of Mercury, I built this house. As you know, it was still a shack, now it's a shrine. It has four dining-rooms, twenty bedrooms, two marble colonnades, a row of boxrooms up above, a

---

7. An honor which Trimalchio shared with many others, for it was customary (as a prudent measure, to avoid confiscation on some pretext or other) to include a bequest to the emperor in one's will.   8. The southeastern extremity of Italy.

bedroom where I sleep myself, a nest for this viper, and a really good lodge for the porter. The guest apartment takes a hundred guests. In fact, when Scaurus[9] came here, he didn't want to stay anywhere else, even though he's got his father's guest house down by the sea. And there are a lot of other things I'll show you in a second.

"Believe me: have a penny, and you're worth a penny. You got something, you'll be thought something. Like your old friend—first a frog, now a king.

"Meantime, Stichus, bring out the shroud and the things I want to be buried in. Bring some cosmetic cream too, and a sample from that jar of wine I want my bones washed in."

Stichus did not delay over it, but brought his white shroud and his formal dress into the dining-room . . . . Trimalchio told us to examine them and see if they were made of good wool. Then he said with a smile:

"Now you, Stichus, see no mice or moths get at those—otherwise I'll burn you alive. I want to be buried in style, so the whole town will pray for my rest."

He opened a bottle of nard on the spot, rubbed some on all of us and said:

"I hope this'll be as nice when I'm dead as when I'm alive." The wine he had poured into a big decanter and he said:

"I want you to think you've been invited to my wake."

The thing was becoming absolutely sickening, when Trimalchio, showing the effects of his disgusting drunkenness, had a fresh entertainment brought into the dining-room, some cornet players. Propped up on a lot of cushions, he stretched out along the edge of the couch and said: "Pretend I'm dead and say something nice."

The cornet players struck up a dead march. One man in particular, the slave of his undertaker (who was the most respectable person present) blew so loudly that he roused the neighbourhood. As a result, the fire brigade, thinking Trimalchio's house was on fire, suddenly broke down the front door and began kicking up their own sort of din with their water and axes.

Seizing this perfect chance, we gave Agamemnon the slip and escaped as rapidly as if there really were a fire.

ST. AUGUSTINE
A.D. 354–430

Aurelius Augustinus was born in 354 A.D. at Tagaste, in North Africa. He was baptized as a Christian in 387 A.D. and ordained bishop of Hippo, in North Africa, in 395 A.D. When he died there in 430 A.D., the city was besieged by Gothic invaders. Besides the *Confessions* (begun in 397 A.D.) he wrote *The City of God* (finished in 426 A.D.) and many polemical works against schismatics and heretics.

9. Unknown. The name is aristocratic but our translator suggests Trimalchio may be referring to a well-known manufacturer of fish sauce from Pompeii.

He was born into a world that no longer enjoyed the "Roman peace." Invading barbarians had pierced the empire's defenses and were increasing their pressure every year. The economic basis of the empire was cracking under the strain of the enormous taxation needed to support the army; the land was exhausted. The empire was Christian, but the Church was split, beset by heresies and organized heretical sects. The empire was on the verge of ruin, and there was every prospect that the Church would go down with it.

Augustine, one of the men responsible for the consolidation of the Church in the West, especially for the systematization of its doctrine and policy, was not converted to Christianity until he had reached middle life. "Late have I loved Thee, O Beauty so ancient and so new," he says in his *Confessions*, written long after his conversion. The lateness of his conversion and his regret for his wasted youth were among the sources of the energy that drove him to assume the intellectual leadership of the Western Church and to guarantee, by combating heresy on the one hand and laying new ideological foundations for Christianity on the other, the Church's survival through the dark centuries to come. Augustine had been brought up in the literary and philosophical tradition of the classical world, and it is partly because of his assimilation of classical literature and method to Christian training and teaching that the literature of the ancient world survived at all when Roman power collapsed in a welter of bloodshed and destruction that lasted for generations.

In his *Confessions* he set down, for the benefit of others, the story of his early life and his conversion to Christianity. This is, as far as we know, the first authentic ancient autobiography, and that fact itself is a significant expression of the Christian spirit, which proclaims the value of the individual soul and the importance of its relation with God. Throughout the *Confessions* Augustine talks directly to God, in humility, yet conscious that God is concerned for him personally. At the same time he comes to an understanding of his own feelings and development as a human being which marks his *Confessions* as one of the great literary documents of the Western world. His description of his childhood is the only detailed account of the childhood of a great man that antiquity has left us, and his accurate observation and keen perception are informed by the Hebrew and Christian idea of the sense of sin. "So small a boy and so great a sinner"—from the beginning of his narrative to the end Augustine sees man not as the Greek at his most optimistic tended to see him, the center and potential master of the universe, but as a child, wandering in ignorance, capable of reclamation only through the divine mercy which waits eternally for him to turn to it.

In Augustine are combined the intellectual tradition of the ancient world and the religious feeling that was characteristic of the Middle Ages. The transition from the old world to the new can be seen in his pages; his analytical intellect pursues its Odyssey through strange and scattered islands—the mysticism of the Manichees, the skepticism of the Academic philosophers, the fatalism of the astrologers—until he finds his home in the Church, to which he was to render such great service. His account of his conversion in the garden at Milan records the true moment of transition from the ancient to the medieval world. The innumerable defeats and victories, the burning towns and ravaged farms, the bloodshed, dates, and statistics of the end of an era are all illuminated and ordered by this moment in the history of the human spirit. Here is the point of change itself.

For criticism and biography, see P. Brown, *Augustine of Hippo* (1967), an authoritative and engrossing account of his whole career.

Confessions[1]

From BOOK I

(Childhood)

What have I to say to Thee, God, save that I know not where I came from, when I came into this life-in-death—or should I call it death-in-life? I do not know. I only know that the gifts Your mercy had provided sustained me from the first moment: not that I remember it but so I have heard from the parents of my flesh, the father from whom, and the mother in whom, You fashioned me in time.

Thus for my sustenance and my delight I had woman's milk: yet it was not my mother or my nurses who stored their breasts for me: it was Yourself, using them to give me the food of my infancy, according to Your ordinance and the riches set by You at every level of creation. It was by Your gift that I desired what You gave and no more, by Your gift that those who suckled me willed to give me what You had given them: for it was by the love implanted in them by You that they gave so willingly that milk which by Your gift flowed in the breasts. It was a good for them that I received good from them, though I received it not *from* them but only through them: since all good things are from You, O God, and *from God is all my health.*[2] But this I have learnt since: You have made it abundantly clear by all that I have seen You give, within me and about me. For at that time I knew how to suck, to lie quiet when I was content, to cry when I was in pain: and that was all I knew.

Later I added smiling to the things I could do, first in sleep, then awake. This again I have on the word of others, for naturally I do not remember; in any event, I believe it, for I have seen other infants do the same. And gradually I began to notice where I was, and the will grew in me to make my wants known to those who might satisfy them; but I could not, for my wants were within me and those others were outside: nor had they any faculty enabling them to enter into my mind. So I would fling my arms and legs about and utter sounds, making the few gestures in my power— these being as apt to express my wishes as I could make them: but they were not very apt. And when I did not get what I wanted, either because my wishes were not clear or the things not good for me, I was in a rage— with my parents as though I had a right to their submission, with free human beings as though they had been bound to serve me; and I took my revenge in screams. That infants are like this, I have learnt from watching other infants; and that I was like it myself I have learnt more clearly from these other infants, who did not know me, than from my nurses who did.

*   *   *

1. Abridged. Translated by F. J. Sheed.   2. Throughout the *Confessions*, Augustine quotes liberally from the Bible; this citation, set off like the others in italics, has no special significance, but where a quotation alludes to a passage which bears more directly on Augustine's situation, it is glossed.

From infancy I came to boyhood, or rather it came to me, taking the place of infancy. Yet infancy did not go: for where was it to go to? Simply it was no longer there. For now I was not an infant, without speech, but a boy, speaking. This I remember; and I have since discovered by observation how I learned to speak. I did not learn by elders teaching me words in any systematic way, as I was soon after taught to read and write. But of my own motion, using the mind which You, my God, gave me, I strove with cries and various sounds and much moving of my limbs to utter the feelings of my heart—all this in order to get my own way. Now I did not always manage to express the right meanings to the right people. So I began to reflect [I observed that][3] my elders would make some particular sound, and as they made it would point at or move towards some particular thing: and from this I came to realize that the thing was called by the sound they made when they wished to draw my attention to it. That they intended this was clear from the motions of their body, by a kind of natural language common to all races which consists in facial expressions, glances of the eye, gestures, and the tones by which the voice expresses the mind's state— for example whether things are to be sought, kept, thrown away, or avoided. So, as I heard the same words again and again properly used in different phrases, I came gradually to grasp what things they signified; and forcing my mouth to the same sounds, I began to use them to express my own wishes. Thus I learnt to convey what I meant to those about me; and so took another long step along the stormy way of human life in society, while I was still subject to the authority of my parents and at the beck and call of my elders.

O God, my God, what emptiness and mockeries did I now experience: for it was impressed upon me as right and proper in a boy to obey those who taught me, that I might get on in the world and excel in the handling of words[4] to gain honor among men and deceitful riches. I, poor wretch, could not see the use of the things I was sent to school to learn; but if I proved idle in learning, I was soundly beaten. For this procedure seemed wise to our ancestors: and many, passing the same way in days past, had built a sorrowful road by which we too must go, with multiplication of grief and toil upon the sons of Adam.

Yet, Lord, I observed men praying to You: and I learnt to do likewise, thinking of You (to the best of my understanding) as some great being who, though unseen, could hear and help me. As a boy I fell into the way of calling upon You, my Help and my Refuge; and in those prayers I broke the strings of my tongue—praying to You, small as I was but with no small energy, that I might not be beaten at school.[5] And when You did not hear me (*not as giving me over to folly*), my elders and even my parents, who certainly wished me no harm, treated my stripes as a huge joke, which

3. Words in brackets are the translator's own.   4. The study of rhetoric, which was the passport to eminence in public life.   5. Augustine recognizes the necessity of this rigorous training; that he never forgot its harshness is clear from his remark in the *City of God*, Book XXI, Section 14: "If a choice were given him between suffering death and living his early years over again, who would not shudder and choose death?"

they were very far from being to me. Surely, Lord, there is no one so steeled in mind or cleaving to You so close—or even so insensitive, for that might have the same effect—as to make light of the racks and hooks and other torture instruments[6] (from which in all lands men pray so fervently to be saved) while truly loving those who are in such bitter fear of them. Yet my parents seemed to be amused at the torments inflicted upon me as a boy by my masters, though I was no less afraid of my punishments or zealous in my prayers to You for deliverance. But in spite of my terrors I still did wrong, by writing or reading or studying less than my set tasks. It was not, Lord, that I lacked mind or memory, for You had given me as much of these as my age required; but the one thing I revelled in was play; and for this I was punished by men who after all were doing exactly the same things themselves. But the idling of men is called business; the idling of boys, though exactly like, is punished by those same men: and no one pities either boys or men. Perhaps an unbiased observer would hold that I was rightly punished as a boy for playing with a ball: because this hindered my progress in studies—studies which would give me the opportunity as a man to play at things more degraded. And what difference was there between me and the master who flogged me? For if on some trifling point he had the worst of the argument with some fellow-master, he was more torn with angry vanity than I when I was beaten in a game of ball.

*   *   *

But to continue with my boyhood, which was in less peril of sin than my adolescence. I disliked learning and hated to be forced to it. But I *was* forced to it, so that good was done to me though it was not my doing. Short of being driven to it, I certainly would not have learned. But no one does well against his will, even if the thing he does is a good thing to do. Nor did those who forced me do well: it was by You, O God, that well was done. Those others had no deeper vision of the use to which I might put all they forced me to learn, but to sate the insatiable desire of man for wealth that is but penury and glory that is but shame. But You, Lord, *by Whom the very hairs of our head are numbered,*[7] used for my good the error of those who urged me to study; but my own error, in that I had no will to learn, you used for my punishment—a punishment richly deserved by one so small a boy and so great a sinner. Thus, You brought good for me out of those who did ill, and justly punished me for the ill I did myself. So You have ordained and so it is: that every disorder of the soul is its own punishment.

To this day I do not quite see why I so hated the Greek tongue[8] that I was made to learn as a small boy. For I really liked Latin—not the rudiments that we got from our first teachers but the literature that we came to

6. The instruments of public execution.   7. Who knows and attends to the smallest detail of each life. [Matthew 10:30.]   8. Important not only for gaining knowledge of Greek literature but also because it was the official language of the Eastern half of the Roman Empire. Augustine never really mastered Greek, though his remark elsewhere, that he had acquired so little Greek that it amounted to practically none, is overmodest.

be taught later. For the rudiments—reading and writing and figuring—I found as hard and hateful as Greek. Yet this too could come only from sin and the vanity of life, because *I was flesh, and a wind that goes away and returns not.* For those first lessons were the surer. I acquired the power I still have to read what I find written and to write what I want to express; whereas in the studies that came later I was forced to memorize the wanderings of Aeneas[9]—whoever *he* was—while forgetting my own wanderings; and to weep for the death of Dido who killed herself for love,[1] while bearing dry-eyed my own pitiful state, in that among these studies I was becoming dead to You, O God, my life.

Nothing could be more pitiful than a pitiable creature who does not see to pity himself, and weeps for the death that Dido suffered through love of Aeneas and not for the death he suffers himself through not loving You, O God, Light of my heart, Bread of my soul, Power wedded to my mind and the depths of my thought. I did not love You and I went away from You in fornication:[2] and all around me in my fornication echoed applauding cries "Well done! Well done!" *For the friendship of this world is fornication against Thee:* and the world cries "Well done" so loudly that one is ashamed of unmanliness not to do it. And for this I did not grieve; but I grieved for Dido, slain as she sought by the sword an end to her woe, while I too followed after the lowest of Your creatures, forsaking You, earth going unto earth. And if I were kept from reading, I grieved at not reading the tales that caused me such grief. This sort of folly is held nobler and richer than the studies by which we learn to read and write!

But now let my God cry aloud in my soul, and let Your truth assure me that it is not so: the earlier study is the better. I would more willingly forget the wanderings of Aeneas and all such things than how to write and read. Over the entrance of these grammar schools hangs a curtain:[3] but this should be seen not as lending honor to the mysteries, but as a cloak to the errors taught within. Let not those masters—who have now lost their terrors for me—cry out against me, because I confess to You, my God, the desire of my soul, and find soul's rest in blaming my evil ways that I may love Your holy ways. Let not the buyers or sellers of book-learning cry out against me. If I ask them whether it is true, as the poet says, that Aeneas ever went to Carthage, the more ignorant will have to answer that they do not know, the more scholarly that he certainly did not. But if I ask with what letters the name Aeneas is spelt, all whose schooling has gone so far will answer correctly, according to the convention men have agreed upon for the use of letters. Or again, were I to ask which loss would be more damaging to human life—the loss from men's memory of reading and writing or the loss of these poetic imaginings—there can be no question what anyone would answer who had not lost his own memory. Therefore as a boy I did wrong in liking the empty studies more than the useful—or rather in loving the empty and hating the useful. For one and one make

9. Virgil's *Aeneid*, Book III.   1. *Aeneid*, Book IV.   2. Metaphorically in this instance.   3. School was often held in a building open on one side and curtained off from the street.

two, two and two make four, I found a loathsome refrain; but such empty unrealities as the Wooden Horse with its armed men, and Troy on fire, and Creusa's Ghost, were sheer delight.[4]

Give me leave, O my God, to speak of my mind, Your gift, and of the follies in which I wasted it. It chanced that a task was set me, a task which I did not like but had to do. There was the promise of glory if I won, the fear of ignominy, and a flogging as well, if I lost. It was to declaim the words uttered by Juno in her rage and grief when she could not keep the Trojan prince from coming to Italy.[5] I had learnt that Juno had never said these words, but we were compelled to err in the footsteps of the poet who had invented them: and it was our duty to paraphrase in prose what he had said in verse. In this exercise that boy won most applause in whom the passions of grief and rage were expressed most powerfully and in the language most adequate to the majesty of the personage represented.

What could all this mean to me, O My true Life, My God? Why was there more applause for the performance I gave than for so many classmates of my own age? Was not the whole business so much smoke and wind? Surely some other matter could have been found to exercise mind and tongue. Thy praises, Lord, might have upheld the fresh young shoot of my heart, so that it might not have been whirled away by empty trifles, defiled, a prey to the spirits of the air. For there is more than one way of sacrificing to the fallen angels.

*   *   *

From BOOK II

(The Pear Tree)

I propose now to set down my past wickedness and the carnal corruptions of my soul, not for love of them but that I may love Thee, O my God. I do it for love of Thy love, passing again in the bitterness of remembrance over my most evil ways that Thou mayest thereby grow ever lovelier to me, O Loveliness that dost not deceive, Loveliness happy and abiding: and I collect my self out of that broken state in which my very being was torn asunder because I was turned away from Thee, the One, and wasted myself upon the many.

Arrived now at adolescence I burned for all the satisfactions of hell, and I sank to the animal in a succession of dark lusts: *my beauty consumed away*, and I stank in Thine eyes, yet was pleasing in my own and anxious to please the eyes of men.

My one delight was to love and to be loved. But in this I did not keep the measure of mind to mind, which is the luminous line of friendship;

---

4. *Aeneid*, Book II.   5. Augustine was assigned the task of delivering a prose paraphrase of Juno's angry speech in the *Aeneid*, Book I. (She complains that her enemies, the Trojans under Aeneas, are on their way to their destined goal in Italy in spite of her resolution to prevent them.) Rhetorical exercises such as this were common in the schools, since they served the double purpose of teaching literature and rhetorical composition at the same time.

but from the muddy concupiscence of the flesh and the hot imagination of puberty mists steamed up to becloud and darken my heart so that I could not distinguish the white light of love from the fog of lust. Both love and lust boiled within me, and swept my youthful immaturity over the precipice of evil desires to leave me half drowned in a whirlpool of abominable sins. Your wrath had grown mighty against me and I knew it not. I had grown deaf from the clanking of the chain of my mortality, the punishment for the pride of my soul: and I departed further from You, and You left me to myself: and I was tossed about and wasted and poured out and boiling over in my fornications: and You were silent, O my late-won Joy. You were silent, and I, arrogant and depressed, weary and restless, wandered further and further from You into more and more sins which could bear no fruit save sorrows.

*   *   *

Where then was I, and how far from the delights of Your house, in that sixteenth year of my life in this world, when the madness of lust—needing no licence from human shamelessness, receiving no licence from Your laws—took complete control of me, and I surrendered wholly to it? My family took no care to save me from this moral destruction by marriage: their only concern was that I should learn to make as fine and persuasive speeches as possible.

*   *   *

Your law, O Lord, punishes theft; and this law is so written in the hearts of men that not even the breaking of it blots it out: for no thief bears calmly being stolen from—not even if he is rich and the other steals through want. Yet I chose to steal, and not because want drove me to it—unless a want of justice and contempt for it and an excess for iniquity. For I stole things which I already had in plenty and of better quality. Nor had I any desire to enjoy the things I stole, but only the stealing of them and the sin. There was a pear tree near our vineyard, heavy with fruit, but fruit that was not particularly tempting either to look at or to taste. A group of young blackguards, and I among them, went out to knock down the pears and carry them off late one night, for it was our bad habit to carry on our games in the streets till very late. We carried off an immense load of pears, not to eat—for we barely tasted them before throwing them to the hogs. Our only pleasure in doing it was that it was forbidden. Such was my heart, O God, such was my heart: yet in the depth of the abyss You had pity on it. Let that heart now tell You what it sought when I was thus evil for no object, having no cause for wrongdoing save my wrongness. The malice of the act was base and I loved it—that is to say I loved my own undoing, I loved the evil in me—not the thing for which I did the evil, simply the evil: my soul was depraved, and hurled itself down from security in You into utter destruction, seeking no profit from wickedness but only to be wicked.

*   *   *

From BOOK III

(Student at Carthage)

I came to Carthage[6] where a cauldron of illicit loves leapt and boiled about me. I was not yet in love, but I was in love with love, and from the very depth of my need hated myself for not more keenly feeling the need. I sought some object to love, since I was thus in love with loving; and I hated security and a life with no snares for my feet. For within I was hungry, all for the want of that spiritual food which is Thyself, my God; yet [though I was hungry for want of it] I did not hunger for it: I had no desire whatever for incorruptible food, not because I had it in abundance but the emptier I was, the more I hated the thought of it. Because of all this my soul was sick, and broke out in sores, whose itch I agonized to scratch with the rub of carnal things—carnal, yet if there were no soul in them, they would not be objects of love. My longing then was to love and to be loved, but most when I obtained the enjoyment of the body of the person who loved me.

Thus I polluted the stream of friendship with the filth of unclean desire and sullied its limpidity with the hell of lust. And vile and unclean as I was, so great was my vanity that I was bent upon passing for clean and courtly. And I did fall in love, simply from wanting to. O my God, my Mercy, with how much bitterness didst Thou in Thy goodness sprinkle the delights of that time! I was loved, and our love came to the bond of con-summation: I wore my chains with bliss but with torment too, for I was scourged with the red hot rods of jealousy, with suspicions and fears and tempers and quarrels.

I developed a passion for stage plays, with the mirror they held up to my own miseries and the fuel they poured on my flame. How is it that a man wants to be made sad by the sight of tragic sufferings that he could not bear in his own person? Yet the spectator does want to feel sorrow, and it is actually his feeling of sorrow that he enjoys. Surely this is the most wretched lunacy? For the more a man feels such sufferings in himself, the more he is moved by the sight of them on the stage. Now when a man suffers himself, it is called misery; when he suffers in the suffering of another, it is called pity. But how can the unreal sufferings of the stage possibly move pity? The spectator is not moved to aid the sufferer but merely to be sorry for him; and the more the author of these fictions makes the audience grieve, the better they like him. If the tragic sorrows of the characters— whether historical or entirely fictitious—be so poorly represented that the spectator is not moved to tears, he leaves the theatre unsatisfied and full of complaints; if he *is* moved to tears, he stays to the end, fascinated and revelling in it.

*   *   *

6. The capital city of the province, where Augustine went to study rhetoric.

Those of my occupations at that time which were held as reputable[7] were directed towards the study of the law, in which I meant to excel—and the less honest I was, the more famous I should be. The very limit of human blindness is to glory in being blind. By this time I was a leader in the School of Rhetoric and I enjoyed this high station and was arrogant and swollen with importance: though You know, O Lord, that I was far quieter in my behavior and had no share in the riotousness of the *eversores*—the Overturners[8]—for this blackguardly diabolical name they wore as the very badge of sophistication. Yet I was much in their company and much ashamed of the sense of shame that kept me from being like them. I was with them and I did for the most part enjoy their companionship, though I abominated the acts that were their specialty—as when they made a butt of some hapless newcomer, assailing him with really cruel mockery for no reason whatever, save the malicious pleasure they got from it. There was something very like the action of devils in their behavior. They were rightly called Overturners, since they had themselves been first overturned and perverted, tricked by those same devils who were secretly mocking them in the very acts by which they amused themselves in mocking and making fools of others.

With these men as companions of my immaturity, I was studying the books of eloquence; for in eloquence it was my ambition to shine, all from a damnable vaingloriousness and for the satisfaction of human vanity. Following the normal order of study I had come to a book of one Cicero, whose tongue[9] practically everyone admires, though not his heart. That particular book is called *Hortensius*[1] and contains an exhortation to philosophy. Quite definitely it changed the direction of my mind, altered my prayers to You, O Lord, and gave me a new purpose and ambition. Suddenly all the vanity I had hoped in I saw as worthless, and with an incredible intensity of desire I longed after immortal wisdom. I had begun that journey upwards by which I was to return to You. My father was now dead two years; I was eighteen and was receiving money from my mother for the continuance of my study of eloquence. But I used that book not for the sharpening of my tongue; what won me in it was what it said, not the excellence of its phrasing.

*   *   *

So I resolved to make some study of the Sacred Scriptures and find what kind of books they were. But what I came upon was something not grasped by the proud, not revealed either to children, something utterly humble in the hearing but sublime in the doing, and shrouded deep in mystery. And I was not of the nature to enter into it or bend my neck to follow it. When I first read those Scriptures, I did not feel in the least what I have

---

7. I.e. his rhetorical studies.   8. A group of students who prided themselves on their wild actions and indiscipline; *eversores* is the Latin word that means "Overturners."   9. Style.   1. Only fragments of this dialogue remain. In it Cicero replies to an opponent of philosophy with an impassioned defense of the intellectual life.

just said; they seemed to me unworthy to be compared with the majesty of
Cicero. My conceit was repelled by their simplicity, and I had not the
mind to penetrate into their depths. They were indeed of a nature to grow
in Your little ones.[2] But I could not bear to be a little one; I was only
swollen with pride, but to myself I seemed a very big man.

*   *   *

From BOOK VI

(Worldly Ambitions)

By this time my mother had come to me, following me over sea and
land with the courage of piety and relying upon You in all perils. For they
were in danger from a storm, and she reassured even the sailors—by whom
travelers newly ventured upon the deep are ordinarily reassured—promising them safe arrival because thus You had promised her in a vision. She
found me in a perilous state through my deep despair of ever discovering
the truth. But even when I told her that if I was not yet a Catholic Christian, I was no longer a Manichean,[3] she was not greatly exultant as at some
unlooked-for good news, because she had already received assurance upon
that part of my misery; she bewailed me as one dead certainly, but certainly
to be raised again by You, offering me in her mind as one stretched out
dead, that You might say to the widow's son: *"Young man, I say to thee
arise"*:[4] and he should sit up and begin to speak and You should give him
to his mother.

*   *   *

Nor did I then groan in prayer for Your help. My mind was intent upon
inquiry and unquiet for argumentation. I regarded Ambrose[5] as a lucky
man by worldly standards to be held in honor by such important people:
only his celibacy seemed to me a heavy burden. I had no means of guess-
ing, and no experience of my own to learn from, what hope he bore within
him, what struggles he might have against the temptations that went with
his high place, what was his consolation in adversity, and on what joys of
Your bread the hidden mouth of his heart fed. Nor did he know how I was
inflamed nor the depth of my peril. I could not ask of him what I wished
as I wished, for I was kept from any face to face conversation with him by
the throng of men with their own troubles, whose infirmities he served.
The very little time he was not with these he was refreshing either his body

---

2. Refers not only to the rhetorical simplicity of Jesus' teachings but his interest in teaching children, "for
to such belongs the kingdom of heaven." [Matthew 19:14.]   3. Augustine had for nine years been a
member of this religious sect, which followed the teaching of the Babylonian mystic Mani (216–77). The
Manicheans believed that the world was a battleground for the forces of good and evil: redemption in a
future life would come to the Elect, who renounced worldly occupations and possessions and practiced a
severe asceticism (including abstention from meat). Augustine's mother, Monica, was a Christian, and
lamented her son's Manichean beliefs.   4. Luke 7:14, recounting one of Christ's miracles.   5. The
leading personality among the Christians of the West. Not many years after this he defied the power of the
emperor Theodosius, and forced him to beg for God's pardon in the church at Milan for having put the
inhabitants of Thessalonica to the sword.

with necessary food or his mind with reading. When he read, his eyes traveled across the page and his heart sought into the sense, but voice and tongue were silent. No one was forbidden to approach him nor was it his custom to require that visitors should be announced: but when we came into him we often saw him reading and always to himself; and after we had sat long in silence, unwilling to interrupt a work on which he was so intent, we would depart again. We guessed that in the small time he could find for the refreshment of his mind, he would wish to be free from the distraction of other men's affairs and not called away from what he was doing. Perhaps he was on his guard lest [if he read aloud] someone listening should be troubled and want an explanation if the author he was reading expressed some idea over-obscurely, and it might be necessary to expound or discuss some of the more difficult questions. And if he had to spend time on this, he would get through less reading than he wished. Or it may be that his real reason for reading to himself was to preserve his voice, which did in fact readily grow tired. But whatever his reason for doing it, that man certainly had a good reason.

*   *   *

I was all hot for honors, money, marriage: and You made mock of my hotness. In my pursuit of these, I suffered most bitter disappointments, but in this You were good to me since I was thus prevented from taking delight in anything not Yourself. Look now into my heart, Lord, by whose will I remember all this and confess it to You. Let my soul cleave to You now that You have freed it from the tenacious hold of death. At that time my soul was in misery, and You pricked the soreness of its wound, that leaving all things it might turn to You, who are over all and without whom all would return to nothing, that it might turn to You and be healed. I was in utter misery and there was one day especially on which You acted to bring home to me the realization of my misery. I was preparing an oration in praise of the Emperor[6] in which I was to utter any number of lies to win the applause of people who knew they were lies. My heart was much wrought upon by the shame of this and inflamed with the fever of the thoughts that consumed it. I was passing along a certain street in Milan when I noticed a beggar. He was jesting and laughing and I imagine more than a little drunk. I fell into gloom and spoke to the friends who were with me about the endless sorrows that our own insanity brings us: for here was I striving away, dragging the load of my unhappiness under the spurring of my desires, and making it worse by dragging it: and with all our striving, our one aim was to arrive at some sort of happiness without care: the beggar had reached the same goal before us, and we might quite well never reach it at all. The very thing that he had attained by means of a few pennies begged from passers-by—namely the pleasure of a temporary happiness—I was plotting for with so many a weary twist and turn.

Certainly his joy was no true joy; but the joy I sought in my ambition

6. Probably the young Valentinian, whose court was at Milan.

was emptier still. In any event he was cheerful and I worried, he had no cares and I nothing but cares. Now if anyone had asked me whether I would rather be cheerful or fearful, I would answer: "Cheerful"; but if he had gone on to ask whether I would rather be like that beggar or as I actually was, I would certainly have chosen my own state though so troubled and anxious. Now this was surely absurd. It could not be for any true reason. I ought not to have preferred my own state rather than his merely because I was the more learned, since I got no joy from my learning, but sought only to please men by it—not even to teach them, only to please them. Therefore did You break my bones with the rod of Your discipline.

✻   ✻   ✻

Great effort was made to get me married. I proposed, the girl was promised me. My mother played a great part in the matter for she wanted to have me married and then cleansed with the saving waters of baptism,[7] rejoicing to see me grow every day more fitted for baptism and feeling that her prayers and Your promises were to be fulfilled in my faith. By my request and her own desire she begged You daily with the uttermost intensity of her heart to show her in a vision something of my future marriage, but You would never do it. She did indeed see certain vain fantasies, under the pressure of her mind's preoccupation with the matter; and she told them to me, not, however, with the confidence she always had when You had shown things to her, but as if she set small store by them; for she said that there was a certain unanalyzable savor, not to be expressed in words, by which she could distinguish between what You revealed and the dreams of her own spirit. Still she pushed on with the matter of my marriage, and the girl was asked for. She was still two years short of the age for marriage[8] but I liked her and agreed to wait.

There was a group of us friends who had much serious discussion together, concerning the cares and troubles of human life which we found so hard to endure. We had almost decided to seek a life of peace, away from the throng of men. This peace we hoped to attain by putting together whatever we could manage to get, and making one common household for all of us: so that in the clear trust of friendship, things should not belong to this or that individual, but one thing should be made of all our possessions, and belong wholly to each one of us, and everybody own everything. It seemed that there might be perhaps ten men in this fellowship. Among us there were some very rich men, especially Romanianus, our fellow townsman, who had been a close friend of mine from childhood and had been brought to the court in Milan by the press of some very urgent business. He was strongest of all for the idea and he had considerable influence in persuasion because his wealth was much greater than anyone else's. We agreed that two officers should be chosen every year to handle the details of our life together, leaving the rest undisturbed. But then we began to wonder whether

7. He could not be baptized while living in sin with his mistress, a liaison that resulted in the birth of a son, Adeodatus, who later accompanied Augustine to Italy.   8. The legal age was twelve years. Augustus was in his early thirties.

our wives would agree, for some of us already had wives and I meant to have one. So the whole plan, which we had built up so neatly, fell to pieces in our hands and was simply dropped. We returned to our old sighing and groaning and treading of this world's broad and beaten ways:[9] for many thoughts were in our hearts, but *Thy counsel standeth forever.* And out of Thy counsel didst Thou deride ours and didst prepare Thine own things for us, meaning to *give us meat in due season and to open Thy hands and fill our souls with Thy blessing.*

Meanwhile my sins were multiplied. She with whom I had lived so long was torn from my side as a hindrance to my forthcoming marriage. My heart which had held her very dear was broken and wounded and shed blood. She went back to Africa, swearing that she would never know another man, and left with me the natural son I had had of her. But I in my unhappiness could not, for all my manhood, imitate her resolve. I was unable to bear the delay of two years which must pass before I was to get the girl I had asked for in marriage. In fact it was not really marriage that I wanted. I was simply a slave to lust. So I took another woman, not of course as a wife; and thus my soul's disease was nourished and kept alive as vigorously as ever, indeed worse than ever, that it might reach the realm of matrimony in the company of its ancient habit. Nor was the wound healed that had been made by the cutting off of my former mistress. For there was first burning and bitter grief; and after that it festered, and as the pain grew duller it only grew more hopeless.

*   *   *

From BOOK VIII

(Conversion)

*   *   *

Thus I was sick at heart and in torment, accusing myself with a new intensity of bitterness, twisting and turning in my chain in the hope that it might be utterly broken, for what held me was so small a thing! But it still held me. And You stood in the secret places of my soul, O Lord, in the harshness of Your mercy redoubling the scourges of fear and shame lest I should give way again and that small slight tie which remained should not be broken but should grow again to full strength and bind me closer even than before. For I kept saying within myself: "Let it be now, let it be now," and by the mere words I had begun to move toward the resolution. I almost made it, yet I did not quite make it. But I did not fall back into my original state, but as it were stood near to get my breath. And I tried again and I was almost there, and now I could all but touch it and hold it: yet I was not quite there, I did not touch it or hold it. I still shrank from dying unto death and living unto life. The lower condition which had grown habitual was more powerful than the better condition which I had not tried. The

9. Cf. Matthew 7:13: "Broad is the way that leadeth to destruction," that is, to damnation.

nearer the point of time came in which I was to become different, the more it struck me with horror; but it did not force me utterly back nor turn me utterly away, but held me there between the two.

Those trifles of all trifles, and vanities of vanities, my one-time mistresses, held me back, plucking at my garment of flesh and murmuring softly: "Are you sending us away?" And "From this moment shall we not be with you, now or forever?" And "From this moment shall this or that not be allowed you, now or forever?" What were they suggesting to me in the phrase I have written "this or that," what were they suggesting to me, O my God? Do you in your mercy keep from the soul of Your servant the vileness and uncleanness they were suggesting. And now I began to hear them not half so loud; they no longer stood against me face to face, but were softly muttering behind my back and, as I tried to depart, plucking stealthily at me to make me look behind. Yet even that was enough, so hesitating was I, to keep me from snatching myself free, from shaking them off and leaping upwards on the way I was called: for the strong force of habit said to me: "Do you think you can live without them?"

But by this time its voice was growing fainter. In the direction toward which I had turned my face and was quivering in fear of going, I could see the austere beauty of Continence, serene and indeed joyous but not evilly, honorably soliciting me to come to her and not linger, stretching forth loving hands to receive and embrace me, hands full of multitudes of good examples. With her I saw such hosts of young men and maidens, a multitude of youth and of every age, gray widows and women grown old in virginity, and in them all Continence herself, not barren but the fruitful mother of children, her joys, by You, Lord, her Spouse. And she smiled upon me and her smile gave courage as if she were saying: "Can you not do what these men have done, what these women have done? Or could men or women have done such in themselves, and not in the Lord their God? The Lord their God gave me to them. Why do you stand upon yourself and so not stand at all? Cast yourself upon Him and be not afraid; He will not draw away and let you fall. Cast yourself without fear, He will receive you and heal you."

Yet I was still ashamed, for I could still hear the murmuring of those vanities, and I still hung hesitant. And again it was as if she said: "Stop your ears against your unclean members, that they may be mortified. They tell you of delights, but not of such delights as the law of the Lord your God tells." This was the controversy raging in my heart, a controversy about myself against myself. And Alypius[1] stayed by my side and awaited in silence the issue of such agitation as he had never seen in me.

When my most searching scrutiny had drawn up all my vileness from the secret depths of my soul and heaped it in my heart's sight, a mighty storm arose in me, bringing a mighty rain of tears. That I might give way to my tears and lamentations, I rose from Alypius: for it struck me that

---

1. A student of Augustine's at Carthage; he had joined the Manichees with Augustine, followed him to Rome and Milan, and now shared his desires and doubts. Alypius finally became a bishop in North Africa.

solitude was more suited to the business of weeping. I went far enough from him to prevent his presence from being an embarrassment to me. So I felt, and he realized it. I suppose I had said something and the sound of my voice was heavy with tears. I arose, but he remained where we had been sitting, still in utter amazement. I flung myself down somehow under a certain fig tree and no longer tried to check my tears, which poured forth from my eyes in a flood, *an acceptable sacrifice to Thee.* And much I said not in these words but to this effect: *"And Thou, O Lord, how long? How long, Lord; wilt Thou be angry forever? Remember not our former iniquities."*[2] For I felt that I was still bound by them. And I continued my miserable complaining: "How long, how long shall I go on saying tomorrow and again tomorrow? Why not now, why not have an end to my uncleanness this very hour?"

Such things I said, weeping in the most bitter sorrow of my heart. And suddenly I heard a voice from some nearby house, a boy's voice or a girl's voice, I do not know: but it was a sort of singsong, repeated again and again. "Take and read, take and read." I ceased weeping and immediately began to search my mind most carefully as to whether children were accustomed to chant these words in any kind of game, and I could not remember that I had ever heard any such thing. Damming back the flood of my tears I arose, interpreting the incident as quite certainly a divine command to open my book of Scripture and read the passage at which I should open. For it was part of what I had been told about Anthony,[3] that from the Gospel which he happened to be reading he had felt that he was being admonished as though what he read was spoken directly to himself: *Go, sell what thou hast and give to the poor and thou shalt have treasure in heaven; and come follow Me.*[4] By this experience he had been in that instant converted to You. So I was moved to return to the place where Alypius was sitting, for I had put down the Apostle's[5] book there when I arose. I snatched it up, opened it and in silence read the passage upon which my eyes first fell: *Not in rioting and drunkenness, not in chambering and impurities, not in contention and envy, but put ye on the Lord Jesus Christ and make not provision for the flesh in its concupiscences.* [Romans xiii, 13.] I had no wish to read further, and no need. For in that instant, with the very ending of the sentence, it was as though a light of utter confidence shone in all my heart, and all the darkness of uncertainty vanished away. Then leaving my finger in the place or marking it by some other sign, I closed the book and in complete calm told the whole thing to Alypius and he similarly told me what had been going on in himself, of which I knew nothing. He asked to see what I had read. I showed him, and he looked further than I had read. I had not known what followed. And this is what followed: *"Now him that is weak in faith, take unto you."* He applied this to himself and told me so. And he was confirmed by this message, and with no troubled wavering gave himself to God's goodwill

2. The quotation is from Psalm 79; Augustine compares his spiritual despair with that of captive and subjected Israel.   3. The Egyptian saint whose abstinence and self-control are still proverbial; he was one of the founders of the system of monastic life.   4. Luke 18:22.   5. Paul.

and purpose—a purpose indeed most suited to his character, for in these matters he had been immeasurably better than I.

Then we went in to my mother and told her, to her great joy. We related how it had come about: she was filled with triumphant exultation, and praised You who are mighty beyond what we ask or conceive: for she saw that You had given her more than with all her pitiful weeping she had ever asked. For You converted me to Yourself so that I no longer sought a wife nor any of this world's promises, but stood upon that same rule of faith in which You had shown me to her so many years before.[6] Thus You changed her mourning into joy, a joy far richer than she had thought to wish, a joy much dearer and purer than she had thought to find in grandchildren of my flesh.

From BOOK IX

(Death of His Mother)

*   *   *

And I thought it would be good in Your sight if I did not dramatically snatch my tongue's service from the speech-market but quietly withdrew; but that in any event withdraw I must, so that youths—not students of Your law or Your peace but of lying follies and the conflicts of the law— should no longer buy at my mouth the tools of their madness. Fortunately it happened that there were only a few days left before the Vintage Vacation,[7] and I decided to endure them so that I might leave with due deliberation, seeing that I had been redeemed by You and was not going to put myself up for sale again. Our purpose therefore was known to You, but not to men other than our own friends. We had agreed among ourselves not to spread the news abroad at all, although, in our ascent from *the valley of tears and our singing of the song of degrees*, You had given us *sharp arrows* and *burning coals* against *cunning tongues* that might argue against us with pretended care for our interest, might destroy us saying that they loved us: as men consume food saying that they love it.

*   *   *

Furthermore that very summer, under the too heavy labor of teaching, my lungs had begun to give way and I breathed with difficulty,[8] the pain in my breast showed that they were affected and they no longer let me talk with any strength for too long at a time. At first this had disturbed me, because it made it practically a matter of necessity that I should lay down the burden of teaching, or at least give it up for the time if I was to be cured and grow well again. But when the full purpose of giving myself leisure to meditate on how You are the Lord arose in me and became a

6. At Carthage, when Augustine was still a Manichee, Monica had dreamed that she was standing on a wooden ruler weeping for her son, and then saw that he was standing on the same ruler as herself. 7. This grape-harvesting and wine-making holiday lasted from the end of August to the middle of October. 8. Since he not only lectured but also read aloud, as is suggested by his comments on Ambrose's silent reading (Book VI).

settled resolve—as you know, O my God—I actually found myself glad to have this perfectly truthful excuse to offer parents who might be offended and for their children's sake would never willingly have let me give up teaching. So I was full of joy, and I put up with the space of time that still had to run—I fancy it was about twenty days. But to bear the time took considerable fortitude. Desire for money, which formerly had helped me to bear the heavy labor of teaching, was quite gone; so that I should have [had nothing to help me bear it and so] found it altogether crushing if patience had not taken the place of covetousness. Some of Your servants, my brethren, may think that I sinned in this, since having enrolled with all my heart in Your service, I allowed myself to sit for so much as an hour in the chair of untruthfulness. It may be so. But, most merciful Lord, have You not pardoned and remitted this sin, along with others most horrible and deadly, in the holy water of baptism?

*   *   *

And now the day was come on which I was to be set free from the teaching of Rhetoric in fact, as I was already free in mind. And so it came about. You delivered my tongue as You had already delivered my heart, and I rejoiced and praised You, and so went off with my friends to the country-house.[9] The amount of writing I did there—the writing was now in your service but during this breathing-space still smacked of the school of pride—my books[1] exist to witness, with the record they give of discussions either with my friends there present or with Yourself when I was alone with You; and there are my letters to show what correspondence I had with Nebridius[2] while he was away.

*   *   *

When the Vintage Vacation was over I gave the people of Milan notice that they must find someone else to sell the art of words to their students, because I had chosen to serve You, and because owing to my difficulty in breathing and the pain in my lungs I could not continue my teaching. And in a letter I told Your bishop, the holy Ambrose, of my past errors and my present purpose, that he might advise me which of Your Scriptures I should especially read to prepare me and make me more fit to receive so great a grace. He told me to read Isaiah the prophet, I imagine because he more clearly foretells the gospel and the calling of the gentiles[3] than the other Old Testament writers; but I did not understand the first part of this book, and thinking that it would be all of the same kind, put it aside meaning to return to it when I should be more practised in the Lord's way of speech.

9. At Cassiciacum, in the country, placed at his disposal by a friend.   1. While at Cassiciacum, Augustine wrote a book attacking the Academic philosophers, a book on the happy life, and another entitled *De ordine*, a treatise on divine providence.   2. Nebridius came from Carthage to Milan with Augustine, shared his spiritual pilgrimage through the pagan philosophies and Manichean doctrines to become a Christian, and returned to Africa where he died. Augustine's letters to Nebridius are still extant.   3. The appeal of Christ's apostles to peoples outside the Hebrew nation: "I am sought of them that asked not for me: I am found of them that sought me not." [Isaiah 65:1ff.]

When the time had come to give in my name for baptism, we left the country and returned to Milan. Alypius had decided to be born again in You at the same time, for he was already endowed with the humility that Your sacraments require, and had brought his body so powerfully under control that he could tread the icy soil of Italy with bare feet, which required unusual fortitude. We also took with us the boy Adeodatus, carnally begotten by me in my sin. You had made him well. He was barely fifteen, yet he was more intelligent than many a grave and learned man. In this I am but acknowledging to You Your own gifts, O Lord my God, Creator of all and powerful to reshape our shapelessness: for I had no part in that boy but the sin. That he had been brought up by us in Your way was because You had inspired us, no other. I do but acknowledge to You Your own gifts. There is a book of mine called *De Magistro*:[4] it is a dialogue between him and me. You know, O God, that all the ideas which are put into the mouth of the other party to the dialogue were truly his, though he was but sixteen. I had experience of many other remarkable qualities in him. His great intelligence filled me with a kind of awe: and who but You could be the maker of things so wonderful? But You took him early from this earth, and I think of him utterly without anxiety, for there is nothing in his boyhood or youth or anywhere in him to cause me to fear. We took him along with us, the same age as ourselves in Your grace, to be brought up in Your discipline: and we were baptized, and all anxiety as to our past life fled away. The days were not long enough as I meditated, and found wonderful delight in meditating, upon the depth of Your design for the salvation of the human race. I wept at the beauty of Your hymns and canticles, and was powerfully moved at the sweet sound of Your Church's singing. Those sounds flowed into my ears, and the truth streamed into my heart: so that my feeling of devotion overflowed, and the tears ran from my eyes, and I was happy in them.

It was only a little while before that the church of Milan had begun to practice this kind of consolation and exultation, to the great joy of the brethen singing together with heart and voice. For it was only about a year, or not much more, since Justina, the mother of the boy emperor Valentinian, was persecuting Your servant Ambrose in the interests of her own heresy: for she had been seduced by the Arians.[5] The devoted people had stayed day and night in the church, ready to die with their bishop, Your servant. And my mother, Your handmaid, bearing a great part of the trouble and vigil, had lived in prayer. I also, though still not warmed by the fire of Your Spirit, was stirred to excitement by the disturbed and wrought-up state of the city. It was at this time that the practice was instituted of singing hymns and psalms after the manner of the Eastern churches,[6] to

4. *The Teacher*, written at Tagaste in Africa two years after Augustine's baptism and shortly after his return from Italy. The subject is teaching and the thesis that only God is the cause for man's acquisition of learning and truth.   5. Members of a heretical sect who followed the doctrine of Arius (A.D. 250?–336) that the Son had not existed from all eternity and was therefore inferior to the Father. At the Council of Nicaea (A.D. 325) Arius and his followers were declared heretical, but the Arian heresy remained a serious problem for the Church for many years. Justina demanded that Ambrose allow the Arians to hold public services inside the walls of Milan.   6. The Greek-speaking churches of the Eastern half of the empire. They split off from the Catholic Church in the ninth century.

keep the people from being altogether worn out with anxiety and want of sleep. The custom has been retained from that day to this, and has been imitated by many, indeed in almost all congregations throughout the world.

At this time You revealed to Your bishop Ambrose in a vision the place where the bodies of the martyrs Protasius and Gervasius[7] lay hid, which You had for so many years kept incorrupt in the treasury of Your secret knowledge that You might bring them forth at the proper moment to check a woman's fury—the woman being the ruler of the Empire![8] For when they were discovered and dug up and with due honor brought to Ambrose's basilica, not only were people cured who had been tormented by evil spirits—and the devils themselves forced to confess it—but also there was a man, a citizen well known to the city, who had been blind for many years: he asked what was the cause of the tumultuous joy of the people, and when he heard, he sprang up and asked his guide to lead him into the place. When he arrived there he asked to be allowed to touch with his handkerchief the place on which lay the saints, whose death is precious in Your sight. He did so, put the handkerchief to his eyes, and immediately they were opened. The news spread abroad, Your praises glowed and shone, and if the mind of that angry woman was not brought to the sanity of belief, it was at least brought back from the madness of persecution. Thanks be to my God! From what and towards what have You led my memory, that it should confess to You these great things which I had altogether forgotten? Yet even then, *when the odor of Thy ointments was so sweet smelling*, I did *not run after Thee*: and for this I wept all the more now when I heard Your hymns and canticles, as one who had then sighed for You and now breathed in You, breathed so far as the air allows in this our house of grass.[9]

You, Lord, who make men of one mind to dwell in one house brought to our company a young man of our own town, Evodius. He had held office in the civil service, had been converted and baptized before us, had resigned from the state's service, and given himself to Yours. We kept together, meaning to live together in our devout purpose. We thought deeply as to the place in which we might serve You most usefully. As a result we started back for Africa. And when we had come as far as Ostia[1] on the Tiber, my mother died. I pass over many things, for I must make haste. Do You, O my God, accept my confessions and my gratitude for countless things of which I say nothing. But I will not omit anything my mind brings forth concerning her, Your servant, who brought me forth— brought me forth in the flesh to this temporal light, and in her heart to light eternal. Not of her gifts do I speak but of Your gifts in her. For she did not bring herself into the world or educate herself in the world: it was You who created her, nor did her father or mother know what kind of being was to come forth from them. It was the scepter of Your Christ, the

7. Two beheaded skeletons discovered by St. Ambrose at Milan were identified as the relics of these saints: nothing certain is known about them, but they were said to have been martyred in the second century A.D.   8. Justina.   9. "All flesh is grass. . . . The grass withers, the flower fades, but the word of our God will stand forever." [Isaiah 40:6–8.]   1. A port on the southwest coast of Italy; it was the port of Rome and the point of departure for Africa.

discipline of your Only-Begotten, that brought her up in holy fear, in a
Catholic family which was a worthy member of Your church. Yet it was
not the devotion of her mother in her upbringing that she talked most of,
but of a certain aged servant, who had indeed carried my mother's father
on her back when he was a baby, as little ones are accustomed to be carried
on the backs of older girls. Because of this, because also of her age and her
admirable character, she was very much respected by her master and mistress in their Christian household. As a result she was given charge of her
master's daughters. This charge she fulfilled most conscientiously, checking them sharply when necessary with holy severity and teaching them
soberly and prudently. Thus, except at the times when they ate—and that
most temperately—at their parents' table, she would not let them even
drink water, no matter how tormenting their thirst. By this she prevented
the forming of a bad habit, and she used to remark very sensibly: "Now
you drink water because you are not allowed to have wine: but when you
are married, and thus mistresses of food-stores and wine-cellars, you will
despise water, but the habit of drinking will still remain." By this kind of
teaching and the authority of her commands she moderated the greediness
that goes with childhood and brought the little girls' thirst to such a control
that they no longer wanted what they ought not to have.

Yet, as Your servant told me, her son, there did steal upon my mother
an inclination to wine. For when, in the usual way, she was sent by her
parents, as a well-behaved child, to draw wine from the barrel, she would
dip the cup in, but before pouring the wine from the cup into the flagon,
she would sip a little with the very tip of her lips, only a little because she
did not yet like the taste sufficiently to take more. Indeed she did it not out
of any craving for wine, but rather from the excess of childhood's high
spirits, which tend to boil over in absurdities, and are usually kept in check
by the authority of elders. And so, adding to that daily drop a little more
from day to day—for he that despises small things, falls little by little—she
fell into the habit, so that she would drink off greedily cups almost full of
wine. Where then was that wise old woman with her forceful prohibitions?
Could anything avail against the evil in us, unless Your healing, O Lord,
watched over us? When our father and mother and nurses are absent, You
are present, who created us, who call us, who can use those placed over
us for some good unto the salvation of our souls. What did You do then,
O my God? How did You cure her, and bring her to health? From another
soul you drew a harsh and cutting sarcasm, as though bringing forth a
surgeon's knife from Your secret store, and with one blow amputated that
sore place. A maidservant with whom she was accustomed to go to the
cellar, one day fell into a quarrel with her small mistress when no one else
chanced to be about, and hurled at her the most biting insult possible,
calling her a drunkard. My mother was pierced to the quick, saw her fault
in its true wickedness, and instantly condemned it and gave it up. Just as
the flattery of a friend can pervert, so the insult of an enemy can sometimes
correct. Nor do You, O God, reward men according to what You do by
means of them, but according to what they themselves intended. For the

girl being in a temper wanted to enrage her young mistress, not to amend her, for she did it when no one else was there, either because the time and place happened to be thus when the quarrel arose, or because she was afraid that elders[2] would be angry because she had not told it sooner. But You, O Lord, Ruler of heavenly things and earthly, who turn to Your own purposes the very depths of rivers as they run and order the turbulence of the flow of time, did by the folly of one mind bring sanity to another; thus reminding us not to attribute it to our own power if another is amended by our word, even if we meant to amend him.

My mother, then, was modestly and soberly brought up, being rather made obedient to her parents by You than to You by her parents. When she reached the age for marriage, and was bestowed upon a husband, she served him as her lord. She used all her effort to win him to You, preaching You to him by her character, by which You made her beautiful to her husband, respected and loved by him and admirable in his sight. For she bore his acts of unfaithfulness quietly, and never had any jealous scene with her husband about them. She awaited Your mercy upon him, that he might grow chaste through faith in You. And as a matter of fact, though generous beyond measure, he had a very hot temper. But she knew that a woman must not resist a husband in anger, by deed or even by word. Only, when she saw him calm again and quiet, she would take the opportunity to give him an explanation of her actions, if it happened that he had been roused to anger unreasonably. The result was that whereas many matrons with much milder husbands carried the marks of blows to disfigure their faces, and would all get together to complain of the way their husbands behaved, my mother—talking lightly but meaning it seriously—advised them against their tongues: saying that from the day they heard the matrimonial contract read to them they should regard it as an instrument by which they became servants; and from that time they should be mindful of their condition and not set themselves up against their masters. And they often expressed amazement—for they knew how violent a husband she had to live with—that it had never been heard, and there was no mark to show, that Patricius[3] had beaten his wife or that there had been any family quarrel between them for so much as a single day. And when her friends asked her the reason, she taught them her rule, which was as I have just said. Those who followed it, found it good and thanked her; those who did not, went on being bullied and beaten.

Her mother-in-law began by being angry with her because of the whispers of malicious servants. But my mother won her completely by the respect she showed, and her unfailing patience and mildness. She ended by going to her son, telling him of the tales the servants had bandied about to the destruction of peace in the family between herself and her daughter-in-law, and asking him to punish them for it. So he, out of obedience to his mother and in the interests of order in the household and peace among his womenfolk, had the servants beaten whose names he had been given,

2. Leaders of the church.   3. Augustine's father.

as she had asked when giving them. To which she added the promise that anyone must expect a similar reward from her own hands who should think to please her by speaking ill of her daughter-in-law. And as no one had the courage to do so, they lived together with the most notable degree of kindness and harmony.

This great gift also, O my God, my Mercy, You gave to Your good servant, in whose womb You created me, that she showed herself, wherever possible, a peacemaker between people quarreling and minds at discord. For swelling and undigested discord often belches forth bitter words when in the venom of intimate conversation with a present friend hatred at its rawest is breathed out upon an absent enemy. But when my mother heard bitter things said by each of the other, she never said anything to either about the other save what would help to reconcile them. This might seem a small virtue, if I had not had the sorrow of seeing for myself so many people who—as if by some horrible widespreading infection of sin— not only tell angry people the things their enemies said in anger, but even add things that were never said at all. Whereas, on the contrary, ordinary humanity would seem to require not merely that we refrain from exciting or increasing wrath among men by evil speaking, but that we study to extinguish wrath by kind speaking. Such a one was she: and You were the master who taught her most secretly in the school of her heart.

The upshot was that toward the very end of his life she won her husband to You; and once he was a Christian she no longer had to complain of the things she had had to bear with before he was a Christian. Further, she was a servant of Your servants. Such of them as knew her praised and honored and loved You, O God, in her; for they felt Your presence in her heart, showing itself in the fruit of her holy conversation. She had been *the wife of one husband, had requited her parents, had governed her house* piously, *was well reported of for good works. She had brought up her children,* [4] being in labor of them as often as she saw them swerving away from You. Finally of all of us Your servants, O Lord—since by Your gift You suffer us to speak—who before her death were living together [5] after receiving the grace of baptism, she took as much care as if she had been the mother of us all, and served us as if she had been the daughter of us all.

When the day was approaching on which she was to depart this life—a day that You knew though we did not—it came about, as I believe by Your secret arrangement, that she and I stood alone leaning in a window, which looked inwards to the garden within the house where we were staying, at Ostia on the Tiber; for there we were away from everybody, resting for the sea voyage from the weariness of our long journey by land. There we talked together, she and I alone, in deep joy; and *forgetting the things that were behind and looking forward to those that were before,* we were discussing in the presence of Truth, which You are, what the eternal life of the saints could be like, *which eye has not seen nor ear heard, nor has it entered into*

---

4. Augustine is quoting Paul's description of the duties of a widow. [I Timothy 5.]   5. Augustine and his fellow converts.

the heart of man. But with the mouth of our heart we panted for the high waters of Your fountain, the fountain of the life which is with You: that being sprinkled from that fountain according to our capacity, we might in some sense meditate upon so great a matter.

And our conversation had brought us to this point, that any pleasure whatsoever of the bodily senses, in any brightness whatsoever of corporeal light, seemed to us not worthy of comparison with the pleasure of that eternal Light, not worthy even of mention. Rising as our love flamed upward towards that Selfsame,[6] we passed in review the various levels of bodily things, up to the heavens themselves, whence sun and moon and stars shine upon this earth. And higher still we soared, thinking in our minds and speaking and marveling at Your works: and so we came to our own souls, and went beyond them to come at last to that region of richness unending, where You feed Israel forever with the food of truth: and there life is that Wisdom by which all things are made, both the things that have been and the things that are yet to be. But this Wisdom itself is not made: it is as it has ever been, and so it shall be forever: indeed "has ever been" and "shall be forever" have no place in it, but it simply is, for it is eternal: whereas "to have been" and "to be going to be" are not eternal. And while we were thus talking of His Wisdom and panting for it, with all the effort of our heart we did for one instant attain to touch it; then sighing, and leaving the first fruits of our spirit bound to it, we returned to the sound of our own tongue, in which a word has both beginning and ending. For what is like to your Word, Our Lord, who abides in Himself forever, yet grows not old and makes all things new!

So we said: If to any man the tumult of the flesh grew silent, silent the images of earth and sea and air: and if the heavens grew silent, and the very soul grew silent to herself and by not thinking of self mounted beyond self: if all dreams and imagined visions grew silent, and every tongue and every sign and whatsoever is transient—for indeed if any man could hear them, he should hear them saying with one voice: We did not make our- selves, but He made us who abides forever: but if, having uttered this and so set us to listening to Him who made them, they all grew silent, and in their silence He alone spoke to us, not by them but by Himself: so that we should hear His word, not by any tongue of flesh nor the voice of an angel nor the sound of thunder nor in the darkness of a parable,[7] but that we should hear Himself whom in all these things we love, should hear Him- self and not them: just as we two had but now reached forth and in a flash of the mind attained to touch the eternal Wisdom which abides over all: and if this could continue, and all other visions so different be quite taken away, and this one should so ravish and absorb and wrap the beholder in inward joys that his life should eternally be such as that one moment of understanding for which we had been sighing—would not this be: *Enter*

---

6. Reality, the divine principle. This ecstasy of Augustine and Monica is throughout described in philo- sophical terms, in which God is Wisdom.   7. Alludes to Luke 8:10: "To you [the disciples of Jesus] it has been given to know the secrets of the kingdom of God; but for others they are in parables, so that seeing they may not see, and hearing they may not understand."

Thou into the joy of Thy Lord? But when shall it be? Shall it be when *we shall all rise again* and *shall not all be changed?*[8]

Such thoughts I uttered, though not in that order or in those actual words; but You know, O Lord, that on that day when we talked of these things the world with all its delights seemed cheap to us in comparison with what we talked of. And my mother said: "Son, for my own part I no longer find joy in anything in this world. What I am still to do here and why I am here I know not, now that I no longer hope for anything from this world. One thing there was, for which I desired to remain still a little longer in this life, that I should see you a Catholic Christian before I died. This God has granted me in superabundance, in that I now see you His servant to the contempt of all worldly happiness. What then am I doing here?"

What answer I made, I do not clearly remember; within five days or not much longer she fell into a fever. And in her sickness, she one day fainted away and for the moment lost consciousness. We ran to her but she quickly returned to consciousness, and seeing my brother and me standing by her she said as one wondering: "Where was I?" Then looking closely upon us as we stood wordless in our grief, she said: "Here you will bury your mother." I stayed silent and checked my weeping. But my brother said something to the effect that he would be happier if she were to die in her own land and not in a strange country. But as she heard this she looked at him anxiously, restraining him with her eye because he savored of earthly things, and then she looked at me and said: "See the way he talks." And then she said to us both: "Lay this body wherever it may be. Let no care of it disturb you: this only I ask of you that you should remember me at the altar of the Lord wherever you may be." And when she had uttered this wish in such words as she could manage, she fell silent as her sickness took hold of her more strongly.

But as I considered Your gifts, O unseen God, which You send into the hearts of Your faithful to the springing up of such wonderful fruits, I was glad and gave thanks to You, remembering what I had previously known of the care as to her burial which had always troubled her: for she had arranged to be buried by the body of her husband. Because they had lived together in such harmony, she had wished—so little is the human mind capable of rising to the divine—that it should be granted her, as an addition to her happiness and as something to be spoken of among men, that after her pilgrimage beyond the sea the earthly part of man and wife should lie together under the same earth. Just when this vain desire had begun to vanish from her heart through the fullness of Your goodness, I did not know; but I was pleased and surprised that it had now so clearly vanished: though indeed in the conversation we had had together at the window, when she said: "What am I still doing here?" there had appeared no desire to die in her own land. Further I heard afterwards that in the time we were

---

8. Refers to the Last Judgment, when "the trumpet shall sound, and the dead shall be raised incorruptible, and we shall be changed." [1 Corinthians 15:52.]

at Ostia, she had talked one day to some of my friends, as a mother talking to her children, of the contempt of this life and of the attraction of death. I was not there at the time. They marveled at such courage in a woman—but it was You who had given it to her—and asked if she was not afraid to leave her body so far from her own city. But she said: "Nothing is far from God, and I have no fear that He will not know at the end of the world from what place He is to raise me up." And so on the ninth day of her illness, in the fifty-sixth year of her life and the thirty-third of mine, that devout and holy soul was released from the body.

I closed her eyes; and an immeasurable sorrow flowed into my heart and would have overflowed in tears. But my eyes under the mind's strong constraint held back their flow and I stood dry-eyed. In that struggle it went very ill with me. As she breathed her last, the child Adeodatus broke out into lamentation and we all checked him and brought him to silence. But in this very fact the childish element in me, which was breaking out into tears, was checked and brought to silence by the manlier voice of my mind. For we felt that it was not fitting that her funeral should be solemnized with moaning and weeping and lamentation, for so it is normal to weep when death is seen as sheer misery or as complete extinction. But she had not died miserably, nor did she wholly die. Of the one thing we were sure by reason of her character, of the other by the reality of our faith.

What then was it that grieved my heart so deeply? Only the newness of the wound, in finding the custom I had so loved of living with her suddenly snapped short. It was a joy to me to have this one testimony from her: when her illness was close to its end, meeting with expressions of endearment such services as I rendered, she called me a dutiful loving son, and said in the great affection of her love that she had never heard from my mouth any harsh or reproachful word addressed to herself. But what possible comparison was there, O my God who made us, between the honor I showed her and the service she had rendered me?

Because I had now lost the great comfort of her, my soul was wounded and my very life torn asunder, for it had been one life made of hers and mine together. When the boy had been quieted and ceased weeping, Evodius took up the psalter and began to chant—with the whole house making the responses—the psalm *Mercy and judgment I will sing to Thee, O Lord.*[9] And when they heard what was being done, many of the brethren and religious women came to us; those whose office it was were making arrangement for the burial, while, in another part of the house where it could properly be done I discoursed, with friends who did not wish to leave me by myself, upon matters suitable for that time. Thus I used truth as a kind of fomentation[1] to bring relief to my torment, a torment known to You, but not known to those others: so that listening closely to me they thought that I lacked all feeling of grief. But in Your ears, where none of them could hear, I accused the emotion in me as weakness; and I held in the flood of my grief. It was for the moment a little diminished, but returned

9. The opening words of Psalm 101.   1. Soothing dressing for a wound.

with fresh violence, not with any pouring of tears or change of countenance: but I knew what I was crushing down in my heart. I was very much ashamed that these human emotions could have such power over me—though it belongs to the due order and the lot of our earthly condition that they should come to us—and I felt a new grief at my grief and so was afflicted with a twofold sorrow.

When the body was taken to burial, I went and returned without tears. During the prayers which we poured forth to you when the sacrifice of our redemption[2] was offered for her—while the body, as the custom there is, lay by the grave before it was actually buried—during those prayers I did not weep. Yet all that day I was heavy with grief within and in the trouble of my mind I begged of You in my own fashion to heal my pain; but You would not—I imagine because You meant to impress upon my memory by this proof how strongly the bond of habit holds the mind even when it no longer feeds upon deception. The idea came to me to go and bathe, for I had heard that the bath—which the Greeks call βαλανειον— is so called because it drives anxiety from the mind.[3] And this also I acknowledge to Your mercy, O Father of orphans, that I bathed and was the same man after as before. The bitterness of grief had not sweated out of my heart. Then I fell asleep, and woke again to find my grief not a little relieved. And as I was in bed and no one about, I said over those true verses that Your servant Ambrose wrote of You:

> Deus creator omnium
> polique rector vestiens
> diem decoro lumine,
> noctem sopora gratia,
>
> artus solutos ut quies
> reddat laboris usui
> mentesque fessas allevet
> luctusque solvat anxios.[4]

And then little by little I began to recover my former feeling about Your handmaid, remembering how loving and devout was her conversation with You, how pleasant and considerate her conversation with me, of which I was thus suddenly deprived. And I found solace in weeping in Your sight both about her and for her, about myself and for myself. I no longer tried to check my tears, but let them flow as they would, making them a pillow for my heart: and it rested upon them, for it was Your ears that heard my weeping, and not the ears of a man, who would have misunderstood my tears and despised them. But now, O Lord, I confess it to You in writing, let him read it who will and interpret it as he will: and if he sees it as sin that for so small a portion of an hour I wept for my mother, now dead and

---

2. Perhaps a communion service. 3. Augustine evidently derives *balaneion*, the Greek word for "bath," from the words *ballo* and *ania*, which mean "cast away" and "sorrow" respectively. 4. "God, the creator of all things and ruler of the heavens, / you who clothe the day with the glory of light / and the night with the gift of sleep, / so that rest may relax the limbs / and restore them for the day's work, / relieve the fatigue of the mind / and dispel anxiety and grief."

departed from my sight, who had wept so many years for me that I should live ever in Your sight—let him not scorn me but rather, if he is a man of great charity, let him weep for my sins to You, the Father of all the brethren of Your Christ.

Now that my heart is healed of that wound, in which there was perhaps too much of earthly affection, I pour forth to You, O our God, tears of a very different sort for Your handmaid—tears that flow from a spirit shaken by the thought of the perils there are for every soul that dies in Adam. [5] For though she had been made alive in Christ, and while still in the body had so lived that Your name was glorified in her faith and her character, yet I dare not say that from the moment of her regeneration in baptism no word issued from her mouth contrary to Your Command. Your Son, who is Truth, has said: *Whosoever shall say to his brother, Thou fool, shall be in danger of hell fire;*[6] and it would go ill with the most praiseworthy life lived by men, if You were to examine it with Your mercy laid aside! But because You do not enquire too fiercely into our sins, we have hope and confidence of a place with You. Yet if a man reckons up before You the merits he truly has, what is he reckoning except Your own gifts? If only men would know themselves to be but men, so that he that glories would glory in the Lord!

Thus, my Glory and my Life, God of my heart, leaving aside for this time her good deeds, for which I give thanks to Thee in joy, I now pray to Thee for my mother's sins. Grant my prayer through the true Medicine of our wounds,[7] who hung upon the cross and who now sitting at Thy right hand makes intercession for us. I know that she dealt mercifully, and from her heart forgave those who trespassed against her: do Thou also forgive such trespasses as she may have been guilty of in all the years since her baptism, forgive them, Lord, forgive them, I beseech Thee: enter not into judgment with her. Let Thy mercy be exalted above Thy justice for Thy words are true and Thou hast promised that the merciful shall obtain mercy. That they should be merciful is Thy gift who *hast mercy on whom Thou wilt, and wilt have compassion on whom Thou wilt.*

And I believe that Thou hast already done what I am now asking; but be not offended, Lord, at the things my mouth would utter. For on that day when her death was so close, she was not concerned that her body should be sumptuously wrapped or embalmed with spices, nor with any thought of choosing a monument or even for burial in her own country. Of such things she gave us no command, but only desired to be remembered at Thy altar, which she had served without ever missing so much as a day, on which she knew that the holy Victim was offered; *by whom the handwriting is blotted out of the decree that was contrary to us,*[8] by which offering too the enemy was overcome who, reckoning our sins and seeking what may be laid to our charge, found nothing in Him, in whom we are

5. That is, with the curse of Adam not nullified through baptism in Jesus Christ and conformity with his teachings.   6. From Jesus' Sermon on the Mount. He is preaching a more severe moral code than the traditional one that whoever kills shall be liable to judgment.   7. I.e., Jesus Christ.   8. Alludes to Christ's redemption of humanity from the curse of Adam through the Crucifixion.

conquerors. Who shall restore to Him his innocent blood? Who shall give Him back the price by which He purchased us and so take us from Him? To this sacrament of our redemption Thy handmaid had bound her soul by the bond of faith. Let none wrest her from Thy protection; let neither the lion nor the dragon[9] bar her way by force or craft. For she will not answer that she owes nothing, lest she should be contradicted and confuted by that cunning accuser: but she will answer that her debts have been remitted by Him, to whom no one can hand back the price which He paid for us, though He owed it not.

So let her rest in peace, together with her husband, for she had no other before nor after him, but served him, in patience bringing forth fruit for Thee, and winning him likewise for Thee. And inspire, O my Lord my God, inspire Thy servants my brethren, Thy sons my masters, whom I serve with heart and voice and pen, that as many of them as read this may remember at Thy altar Thy servant Monica, with Patricius, her husband, by whose bodies Thou didst bring me into this life, though how I know not.[1] May they with loving mind remember these who were my parents in this transitory light, my brethren who serve Thee as our Father in our Catholic mother, and those who are to be fellow citizens with me in the eternal Jerusalem,[2] which Thy people sigh for in their pilgrimage from birth until they come there: so that what my mother at her end asked of me may be fulfilled more richly in the prayers of so many gained for her by my Confessions than by my prayers alone.

*   *   *

9. Psalm 91:13 invokes God's protection of the godly: "Thou shalt tread upon the lion and the adder; the young lion and the dragon shalt thou trample under feet."   1. I.e., Augustine does not understand the seemingly miraculous process by which the fetus grows in the womb.   2. Heaven.

Masterpieces of the
Middle Ages

The period of the Middle Ages—approximately A.D. 500–1500—encompasses a thousand years of European history distinguished by the unique fusion of a Heroic-Age society with Greco-Roman culture and Christian religion. The era is fairly well marked off by the emergence and disappearance of certain massive forces. It begins with the collapse of the Roman Empire in Western Europe, a development coincident with and partly occasioned by the settlement of Germanic peoples within the territory of the empire. It ends with the discovery of the Western Hemisphere, the invention of the printing press, the consolidation of strong national states, the break in religious unity brought about by the Protestant Reformation, and the renewal—after a lapse of nearly a thousand years—of direct contact with Greek art, thought, and literature. This renewal was mediated by Christian Europe's neighbor to the east and south, Islam, another civilization that had schooled itself on Greek learning. Starting in the ninth century, Islam translated much of Greek science and philosophy into Arabic, preserving and enriching this tradition at the very time that it was in decline in Europe. It was at Muslim universities and centers of learning in Spain and Sicily that European scholars were first able both to regain access to the Greek originals and to study their Muslim commentators. The medieval centuries bequeathed to us such institutional patterns as the Christian church; the monarchical state; the town and village; the traditional European social order—combining church-power and state-power in the "lords spiritual," the "lords temporal," along with the hierarchy of nobility and gentry ranging from duke to knight, and the third, or bourgeois, estate; the university; the system and logical method of Scholastic philosophy; Romanesque and Gothic architecture; and a rich variety of literary forms, many in the *native* languages of various European peoples.

The literature of the earlier Middle Ages reflects directly and clearly (as did the *Iliad*) the life and civilization of a Heroic Age. The dominant figure is the fighting king or chieftain; the favorite pursuit is war, either against one's Christian neighbors or the heathen Saracens (Muslims); the characteristic goals are power, wealth, and glory; and the primary virtues, accordingly, are valor and loyalty. The literary pattern is based on actuality, of which it presents a kind of idealization. In early Germanic and Celtic society the king ruled a small, essentially tribal nation; he and his companions in battle constituted a formal or informal noble class controlling the life of the people. The poems of such a society naturally tell chiefly of the battles of great champions, though also of the druids or other counselors who advised them and of the minstrels who entertained them. The proportions and the emphases are much the same in the literature of the Irish, the Scandinavians, the French of the twelfth century, the Germans of the thirteenth. The hero of the *Song of Roland*, a twelfth-century French work, combines the fighting chieftain, serving his king, with the devout Crusader; and Archbishop Turpin is both spiritual adviser and fighting champion.

In the literature of the fourteenth century, the warrior plays a smaller role and is assimilated to the more extensive pattern of later medieval civilization. Thus in Dante's Paradise only one of the nine celestial spheres—Mars—is occupied by great men-at-arms, all devout Christians, of course. Chaucer's Knight and Squire are only two among twenty-nine pilgrims on their way to Canterbury. The Knight, who has proved himself as a warrior in the Crusades, is devoted to truth and honor, generosity, and courteous conduct, while his son, along with other virtues appropriate to a young soldier, possesses those of a courtly lover. The fighting champion of the Heroic Age has become the "officer and gentleman" of the modern world.

This gradual assimilation of the Celtic and Germanic hero to a civilization in which Christianity ordered the Greco-Roman culture to new ends was made possible by the religious unity and authority of Western Europe. The medieval millennium was indeed an age of faith, though it was far from being an age of religious passivity or inertia. The first half of the period was occupied in winning the new peoples of Europe to Christianity. When this had been accomplished, the Crusades began—a series of holy wars initiated by Pope Urban II in 1095 and intended both to rescue Palestine from the control of Muslim rulers and to expel the Muslims from Spain. Although it was initially successful, the Crusader presence in the Levant ended after two centuries, and the impact of the Crusades was far greater on Europe than on Islam. Moreover, the Greek and Arabic learning that Muslim scholars introduced into Europe in the twelfth and thirteenth centuries helped stimulate a profound transformation of European culture. The sharpness of the Crusader's sword had to be matched by the acumen of the Scholastic philosopher; one of the chief works of St. Thomas Aquinas is a summation of principles in defense of Christianity "against the pagans" (his *summa contra Gentiles*). Medieval Christianity could never afford to take itself for granted. For the first four centuries of the Christian era the new religion was aggressively on the defensive; thereafter it had to be actively on the offensive in both the practical and the ideological spheres. Nevertheless, in Western Europe itself the combination of theological unity and ecclesiastical authority was a phenomenon unmatched either before or after the Middle Ages. The Roman Empire had provided political unity, law, and order, to assure the success of secular pursuits. Beyond that, it had left moral and spiritual problems to be handled by the individual, singly or in voluntary or ethnic groups. In medieval Europe political disunity was at something like a maximum; but under the leadership and direction of the Church there was achieved a remarkable unanimity of spiritual, moral, and intellectual attitudes and ideals.

The community of European culture in this period was such that the productions of individual countries look like regional manifestations of a central nuclear force. Generally speaking, students and scholars moved freely from land to land; monks, abbots, and bishops might be sent from the country of their birth to serve or preside in distant places; artists and poets wandered widely either in the train of or in search of patrons. Besides the native tongue, an educated man or woman might be expected to speak and write the common "standard" language of Europe— Latin. In an age when the political state was relatively weak, a person's strongest loyalties were to an individual, a feudal lord, for example; or a code, such as the code of chivalry; or an order, of monks or friars or nuns.

These ties—except for the feudal, and sometimes including that also—were *international* in nature. In such a cultural atmosphere the themes and subjects and techniques of art and literature circulated freely throughout Europe. The *Gothic* architecture of a building is a more central aspect of it than the fact that it was designed and built by an English, a French, a German, or an Italian school of builders. Christianity itself furnished a common subject matter for painters, sculptors, and countless others skilled in the graphic and plastic arts; the biblical stories and scenes had the same meaning in every country. The stories of Charlemagne, Roland, and Arthur, of Aeneas, of Troy and Thebes, were European literary property. They were handled and rehandled, copied, translated, adapted, expanded, condensed, and in general appropriated by innumerable authors, writing in various languages, with no thought of property rights or misgivings about plagiarism. There were no copyright regulations and no author's royalties to motivate insistence on individuality of authorship; there was comparatively little concern about the identity of the artist. Many medieval poems and tales are anonymous, including some of the greatest.

The submergence of the artist in his work is accounted for in part, at least, by the medieval system of human values. The dominant hierarchy of values—we have seen that it did not dominate universally, especially in the literature of northern Europe—was based on the Christian view of humanity. Men and women, in this conception, are creatures of God, toward whom they are inevitably oriented but from whom they are separated by the world in which they must live their earthly, mortal lives. Civilization under Christian direction may be regarded as ideally designed—even if not actually so functioning—to assist all people on their way to union with God. This is the criterion acccording to which the institutions of society and the patterns of its culture should ultimately be evaluated. Hence derive the scale, the order, the hierarchical categories of medieval life and thought. Since the spiritual side of humanity transcends the material, the saint becomes the ideal. The saint is one whose life is most fully subdued, assimilated, and ordered to the spiritual. On earth he or she may be a hermit, like Cuthbert; an abbess, like Hilda; a reformer of monasteries, like Bernard; a philosopher and a theologian, like Aquinas; a mystic, like Catharine of Siena; a king, like Louis IX of France; or a humble citizen in private life. As a whole, medieval literature is a study in human life judged according to this scale of values. The scale is represented clearly in Dante's *Divine Comedy*. Secular-value patterns may be assimilated to it, as in the *Song of Roland*; or it may be taken for granted without much emphasis, as in the works of Chaucer. For the modern reader it supplies a focus for the adequate reading and understanding of most of the literature of the Middle Ages.

FURTHER READING

Robert S. Hoyt, *Europe in the Middle Ages* (1957), is a general historical survey. For a view of medieval thought and culture as a whole, the standard older work is H. O. Taylor, *The Mediaeval Mind*, 2 vols., 4th ed. (1925). E. K. Rand, *Founders of the Middle Ages* (1928), vividly portrays central figures from Ambrose and Jerome to Augustine. R. L. Fox, *Pagans and Christians* (1987), traces in full and lively detail the struggle between the religious orientations of the contending parties. C. S. Lewis, *The Discarded Image* (1964), offers an illuminating survey of the basic assumptions and outlook of medieval people. C. W. Previté-Orton, *Shorter Cambridge Medieval History*, 2 vols. (1952), is an authoritative account of the period as a whole. Norman Daniel, *The Arabs and Medieval Europe* (1975), is a good introduction to Muslim influences on European thought and culture.

THE KORAN

For Muslims the Koran is something greater than prophetic revelation. It is an earthly duplicate of a divine Koran that exists in Paradise engraved with figures of gold on tablets of marble. Like God, it was not created, but exists for all eternity—a complete and sufficient guide to our conduct on earth. It is God's final revelation to humanity, and was sent by Him to complete and correct all prior revelations. Since God chose to make this last revelation in the Arabic language, it cannot be translated in any true sense. Interpretive renderings into other languages have been made and used for teaching purposes since the earliest period of Islam, but Muslims do not accept them as the Koran in the sense that Christians accept the Bible in English (or in any other language than the one in which it was first revealed) as the Bible.

The Koran is composed of the revelations which Muhammad (ca. 570–632), known to Muslims as the Prophet of God, received during the last two decades of his life—from roughly 610, when the angel Gabriel first appeared to him, to his death on June 8, 632. During his lifetime these revelations were recorded by various of his followers, but they were only gathered together into a comprehensive volume after his death. The title given this collection is "the Koran" (al-qur'ân), or "the Recitation." The revelations came to Muhammad in verses (âya) of varying length and number. These were gathered into larger divisions, or suras, that were organized roughly by subject, although there are abrupt transitions from subject to subject in the longer suras, and only the shortest are thematically unified. The suras were then arranged by length with the longer suras preceding the shorter. Each sura was given a name taken from some striking image or theme that appears in it. They are also identified as having been received in either Mecca or Medina, the two communities (in present-day Saudi Arabia) in which Muhammad lived. It is an article of faith with Muslims that the Koran we now have is a complete and accurate record of God's revelations to Muhammad.

God is the speaker throughout the Koran, usually referring to Himself as "We." He often speaks to Muhammad directly in a dramatic dialogue, addressing a series of rhetorical questions to him, or commanding him to give his community a particular message, or to "Recite!" Although the Koran was revealed over a relatively brief period, its style varies enormously. The earliest and shortest suras sound like charms or incantations, the later and longer ones like legal prescriptions. And many, perhaps most, have the quality of sermons delivered in a highly charged and poetic language, and often enriched by parables and brief narratives. The style of the individual suras reflects in general terms the moments in Muhammad's life when they were revealed. In the early, Meccan period of his mission (610–619), his concerns were those of an embattled prophet exhorting his community to believe in God and fear Him, and defending himself against the hostility and skepticism of those who doubted both him and his God. The suras from this period are filled with fierce and eloquent exhortations promising Paradise to those who believe in God, and eternal damnation to those who deny Him. These suras are also marked by calls for social justice, expressed principally in concern for the plight of widows and orphans. It was in Mecca, too, that the accounts of earlier prophets from Noah (Nuh) to Jesus (Isâ) who like Muhammad had had to defend themselves against a hostile and unbelieving community were revealed to him.

Eventually, Muhammad's success in converting people to his beliefs made him so unwelcome in his home that he and his followers were forced to emigrate to the nearby oasis of Medina. There, in 622, he established his community among the tribes already settled around the oasis. While Muhammad continued to be the prophet of Islam, he now had to turn his attention to the legal and political demands of his community as well. He was also obliged to cope with the growing number of believers who flocked to him, and to lead them in a series of battles that ended with the Muslim domination of the whole of the Arabian peninsula. (Within a century of his death Arab Muslim armies would go on to conquer Iran and Central Asia, Mesopotamia, Egypt and North Africa, and Spain to the Pyrenees.) The suras revealed in Medina reflect these concerns in setting forth an extensive and detailed legal code that addresses the demands of the day-to-day life of the community as well as its spiritual needs.

References to Christians and Christianity in the Koran—which are somewhat overrepresented in the selections to follow—indicate a familiarity with some parts of the Gospels, but not with the later writings of the New Testament. The Koran's relation to the Old Testament is an important and problematic one. While the Koran does not explicitly refer to these earlier revelations, it seems—to Christians and Jews at least—to assume some awareness of them on the part of its audience. Of all the prophetic tales, only Joseph's is told in a single, continuous narrative. More commonly they appear as illustrations in a number of suras, but piecemeal and allusively. The scattered fragments are not gathered into independent narratives as they are in the Old Testament. Nor is there much concern for historical sequence. A retelling of the story of Jesus and Mary may immediately precede a brief excerpt from the story of Abraham. There is little concern to connect the prophets through genealogy.

These stylistic differences point up an obvious distinction between the two texts. The essence of the Koran is exhortation and guidance. It is not held together by a narrative thread. The Koran's coherence as a work is a product of the themes that are reiterated throughout its many suras. Nor does it trace the history of a single nation. For all the importance it gives to one language, its message is a more general one. The story of Joseph (Yusuf) in the Koranic version does not emphasize his role as a divinely sent leader of his people, but as a man who prospered by trusting in God. The several references to Moses (Musa) exemplify how even an ordinary, flawed man may be chosen by God to be His prophet, and make virtually nothing of his leading his people out of Egypt. The meaning of the Koran, as it often asserts, is for all humanity.

The most informative general introduction to the Koran is Bell's Introduction to the Qur'ân, revised and enlarged by W. Montgomery Watt (1970). Michael Cook has written and excellent brief biography of the Prophet of Islam, Muhammad (1983). Fazlur Rahman, Major Themes of the Qur'ân (1980), is a good presentation of the principal beliefs of Islam as they appear in the Koran.

From The Koran[1]

1. THE EXORDIUM

[Mecca]

IN THE NAME OF GOD
THE COMPASSIONATE
THE MERCIFUL[2]

Praise be to God, Lord of the Creation,
The Compassionate, the Merciful,
King of the Last Judgement!
You alone we worship, and to You alone
we pray for help.
Guide us to the straight path,
The path of those whom You have favoured,
Not of those who have incurred Your wrath,
Nor of those who have gone astray.

4. WOMEN

[Medina]

In the Name of God, the Compassionate, the Merciful

Men, have fear of your Lord, who created you from a single soul. From that soul He created its mate, and through them He bestrewed the earth with countless men and women.

Fear God, in whose name you plead with one another, and honour the mothers who bore you. God is ever watching over you.

Give orphans the property which belongs to them. Do not exchange their valuables for worthless things or cheat them of their possessions; for this would surely be a great sin. If you fear that you cannot treat orphans[3] with fairness, then you may marry other women who seem good to you: two, three, or four of them. But if you fear that you cannot maintain equality among them, marry one only or any slavegirls you may own. This will make it easier for you to avoid injustice.

Give women their dowry as a free gift; but if they choose to make over to you a part of it, you may regard it as lawfully yours.

Do not give the feeble-minded the property with which God has entrusted you for their support; but maintain and clothe them with its proceeds, and give them good advice.

Put orphans to the test until they reach a marriageable age. If you find them capable of sound judgement, hand over to them their property, and do not deprive them of it by squandering it before they come of age.

Let not the rich guardian touch the property of his orphan ward; and let him who is poor use no more than a fair portion of it for his own advantage.

1. Translated by N.J. Dawood.   2. According to Islamic law, this phrase, spoken or written, must precede all written work; it is also used by Muslims at the beginning of most formal tasks.   3. Orphan girls.

When you hand over to them their property, call in some witnesses; sufficient is God's accounting of your actions.

Men shall have a share in what their parents and kinsmen leave; and women shall have a share in what their parents and kinsmen leave: whether it be little or much, they shall be legally entitled to their share.

If relatives, orphans, or needy men are present at the division of an inheritance, give them, too, a share of it, and speak to them kind words.

Let those who are solicitous about the welfare of their young children after their own death take care not to wrong orphans. Let them fear God and speak for justice.

Those that devour the property of orphans unjustly, swallow fire into their bellies; they shall burn in a mighty conflagration.

God has thus enjoined you concerning your children:

A male shall inherit twice as much as a female. If there be more than two girls, they shall have two-thirds of the inheritance; but if there be one only, she shall inherit the half. Parents shall inherit a sixth each, if the deceased have a child; but if he leave no child and his parents be his heirs, his mother shall have a third. If he have brothers, his mother shall have a sixth after payment of any legacy he may have bequeathed or any debt he may have owed.

You may wonder whether your parents or your children are more beneficial to you. But this is the law of God; God is all-knowing and wise.

You shall inherit the half of your wives' estate if they die childless. If they leave children, a quarter of their estate shall be yours after payment of any legacies they may have bequeathed or any debt they may have owed.

Your wives shall inherit one quarter of your estate if you die childless. If you leave children, they shall inherit one-eighth, after payment of any legacies you may have bequeathed or any debts you may have owed.

If a man or a woman leave neither children nor parents and have a brother or a sister, they shall each inherit one-sixth. If there be more, they shall equally share the third of the estate, after payment of any legacy that he may have bequeathed or any debt he may have owed, without prejudice to the rights of the heirs. That is a commandment from God. God is all-knowing and gracious.

Such are the bounds set by God. He that obeys God and His apostle shall dwell for ever in gardens watered by running streams. That is the supreme triumph. But he that defies God and His apostle and transgresses His bounds, shall be cast into a fire wherein he will abide for ever. A shameful punishment awaits him.

If any of your women commit fornication, call in four witnesses from among yourselves against them; if they testify to their guilt confine them to their houses till death overtakes them or till God finds another way for them.

If two men among you commit indecency punish them both. If they repent and mend their ways, let them be. God is forgiving and merciful.

God forgives those who commit evil in ignorance and then quickly turn to Him in repentance. God will pardon them. God is wise and all-knowing. But He will not forgive those who do evil and, when death comes to them, say: 'Now we repent!' Nor those who die unbelievers: for them We have prepared a woeful scourge.

Believers, it is unlawful for you to inherit the women of your deceased kinsmen against their will, or to bar them from re-marrying, in order that you may force them to give up a part of what you have given them, unless they be guilty of a proven crime. Treat them with kindness; for even if you dislike them, it may well be that you may dislike a thing which God has meant for your own abundant good.

If you wish to (replace a wife with) another, do not take from her the dowry you have given her even if it be a talent of gold. That would be improper and grossly unjust; for how can you take it back when you have lain with each other and entered into a firm contract?

You shall not marry the women whom your fathers married. That was an evil practice, indecent and abominable.

Forbidden to you are your mothers, your daughters, your sisters, your paternal and maternal aunts, the daughters of your brothers and sisters, your foster-mothers, your foster sisters, the mothers of your wives, your step-daughters who are in your charge, born of the wives with whom you have lain (it is no offence for you to marry your step-daughters if you have not consummated your marriage with their mothers), and the wives of your own begotten sons. You are also forbidden to take in marriage two sisters at one and the same time: all previous such marriages excepted. God is forgiving and merciful.

Also married women, except those whom you own as slaves. Such is the decree of God. All women other than these are lawful to you, provided you seek them with your wealth in modest conduct, not in fornication. Give them their dowry for the enjoyment you have had of them as a duty; but it shall be no offence for you to make any other agreement among yourselves after you have fulfilled your duty. God is all-knowing and wise.

If any one of you cannot afford to marry a free believing woman, let him marry a slave-girl who is a believer (God best knows your faith: you are born one of another). Marry them with the permission of their masters and give them their dowry in all justice, provided they are honourable and chaste and have not entertained other men. If after marriage they commit adultery, they shall suffer half the penalty inflicted upon free adulteresses. Such is the law for those of you who fear to commit sin: but if you abstain, it will be better for you. God is forgiving and merciful.

God desires to make this known to you and to guide you along the paths of those who have gone before you, and to turn to you in mercy. God is all-knowing and wise.

God wishes to forgive you, but those who follow their own appetites wish to see you far astray. God wishes to lighten your burdens, for man was created weak.

Believers, do not consume your wealth among yourselves in vanity, but rather trade with it by mutual consent.

Do not destroy yourselves. God is merciful to you, but he that does that through wickedness and injustice shall be burned in fire. That is easy enough for God.

If you avoid the enormities you are forbidden, We shall pardon your misdeeds and usher you in with all honour. Do not covet the favours by which God has exalted some of you above others. Men shall be rewarded according to their deeds, and women shall be rewarded according to their deeds. Rather implore God to bestow on you His gifts. God has knowledge of all things.

To every parent and kinsman We have appointed heirs who will inherit from him. As for those with whom you have entered into agreements, let them, too, have their due. God bears witness to all things.

Men have authority over women because God has made the one superior to the other, and because they spend their wealth to maintain them. Good women are obedient. They guard their unseen parts because God has guarded them. As for those from whom you fear disobedience, admonish them and send them to beds apart and beat them. Then if they obey you, take no further action against them. God is high, supreme.

If you fear a breach between a man and his wife, appoint an arbiter from his people and another from hers. If they wish to be reconciled God will bring them together again. God is all-knowing and wise.

Serve God and associate none with Him. Show kindness to your parents and your kindred, to orphans and to the helpless, to near and distant neighbours, to those that keep company with you, to the traveller in need, and to the slaves whom you own. God does not love arrogant and boastful men, who are themselves niggardly and enjoin others to be niggardly; who conceal the riches which God of His bounty has bestowed upon them (We have prepared a shameful punishment for the unbelievers); and who spend their wealth for the sake of ostentation, believing neither in God nor in the Last Day. He that chooses Satan for his friend, an evil friend has he.

*   *   *

5. THE TABLE

[Medina]
In the Name of God, the Compassionate, the Merciful

Believers, be true to your obligations. It is lawful for you to eat the flesh of all beasts other than that which is hereby announced to you. Game is forbidden while you are on pilgrimage. God decrees what He will.

Believers, do not violate the rites of God, or the sacred month, or the offerings or their ornaments, or those that repair to the Sacred House seeking God's grace and pleasure. Once your pilgrimage is ended, you shall be free to go hunting.

Do not allow your hatred for those who would debar you from the Holy Mosque to lead you into sin. Help one another in what is good and pious, not in what is wicked and sinful. Have fear of God, for He is stern in retribution.

You are forbidden carrion, blood, and the flesh of swine; also any flesh dedicated to any other than God. You are forbidden the flesh of strangled animals and of those beaten or gored to death; of those killed by a fall or mangled by beasts of prey (unless you make it clean by giving the death-stroke yourselves); also of animals sacrificed to idols.

You are forbidden to settle disputes by consulting the Arrows.[4] That is a pernicious practice.

The unbelievers have this day abandoned all hope of vanquishing your religion. Have no fear of them: fear Me.

This day I have perfected your religion for you and completed My favour to you. I have chosen Islam to be your faith.

He that is constrained by hunger to eat of what is forbidden, not intending to commit sin, will find God forgiving and merciful.

They ask you what is lawful to them. Say: "All good things are lawful to you, as well as that which you have taught the birds and beasts of prey to catch, training them as God has taught you. Eat of what they catch for you, pronouncing upon it the name of God. And have fear of God: swift is God's reckoning."

All good things have this day been made lawful to you. The food of those to whom the Book was given[5] is lawful to you, and yours to them.

Lawful to you are the believing women and the free women from among those who were given the Book before you, provided that you give them their dowries and live in honour with them, neither committing fornication nor taking them as mistresses.

He that denies the Faith shall gain nothing from his labours. In the world to come he shall have much to lose.

Believers, when you rise to pray wash your faces and your hands as far as the elbow, and wipe your heads and your feet to the ankle. If you are polluted cleanse yourselves. But if you are sick or travelling the road; or if, when you have just relieved yourselves or had intercourse with women, you can find no water, take some clean sand and rub your hands and faces with it. God does not wish to burden you; He seeks only to purify you and to perfect His favour to you, so that you may give thanks.

Remember God's favour to you, and the covenant with which He bound you when you said: "We hear and obey." Have fear of God. God knows the innermost thoughts of men.

Believers, fulfil your duties to God and bear true witness. Do not allow your hatred for other men to turn you away from justice. Deal justly; that is nearer to true piety. Have fear of God; God is cognizant of all your actions.

God has promised those that have faith and do good works forgiveness and a rich reward. As for those who disbelieve and deny Our revelations, they are the heirs of Hell.

Believers, remember the favour which God bestowed upon you when

4. A form of casting lots.   5. The Jews (but not the Christians).

He restrained the hands of those who sought to harm you. Have fear of God. In God let the faithful put their trust.

God made a covenant with the Israelites and raised among them twelve chieftains. God said: "I shall be with you. If you attend to your prayers and render the alms levy; if you believe in My apostles and assist them and give God a generous loan, I shall forgive you your sins and admit you to gardens watered by running streams. But he that hereafter denies Me shall stray from the right path."

But because they broke their covenant We laid on them Our curse and hardened their hearts. They have tampered with words out of their context and forgotten much of what they were enjoined. You will ever find them deceitful, except for a few of them. But pardon them and bear with them. God loves those who do good.

With those who said they were Christians We made a covenant also, but they too have forgotten much of what they were enjoined. Therefore We stirred among them enmity and hatred, which shall endure till the Day of Resurrection, when God will declare to them all that they have done.

People of the Book![6] Our aspostle has come to reveal to you much of what you have hidden of the Scriptures, and to forgive you much. A light has come to you from God and a glorious Book, with which God will guide to the paths of peace those that seek to please Him; He will lead them by His will from darkness to the light; He will guide them to a straight path.

Unbelievers are those who declare: "God is the Messiah, the son of Mary." Say: "Who could prevent God, if He so willed, from destroying the Messiah, the son of Mary, his mother, and all the people of the earth? God has sovereignty over the heavens and the earth and all that lies between them. He creates what He will and God has power over all things."

The Jews and the Christians say: "We are the children of God and His loved ones." Say: "Why then does He punish you for your sins? Surely you are mortals of His own creation. He forgives whom He will and punishes whom He pleases. God has sovereignty over the heavens and the earth and all that lies between them. All shall return to Him."

People of the Book! Our apostle has come to you with revelations after an interval during which there were no apostles, lest you say: "No one has come to give us good news or to warn us." Now someone has come to give you good news and to warn you. God has power over all things.

Bear in mind the words of Moses to his people. He said: "Remember, my people, the favours which God has bestowed upon you. He has raised up prophets among you, made you kings, and given you that which He has given to no other nation. Enter, my people, the holy land which God has assigned for you. Do not turn back, or you shall be ruined."

"Moses," they replied, "a race of giants dwells in this land. We will not

6. Jews and Christians.

set foot in it till they are gone. As soon as they are gone we will enter."

Thereupon two God-fearing men whom God had favoured, said: "Go in to them through the gates, and when you have entered you shall surely be victorious. In God put your trust, if you are true believers."

But they replied: "Moses, we will not go in so long as *they* are in it. Go, you and your Lord, and fight. Here we will stay."

"Lord," cried Moses, "I have none but myself and my brother. Do not confound us with these wicked people."

He replied: "They shall be forbidden this land for forty years, during which time they shall wander homeless on the earth. Do not grieve for these wicked people."

Recount to them in all truth the story of Adam's two sons: how they each made an offering, and how the offering of the one was accepted while that of the other was not. One said: "I will surely kill you." The other replied: "God accepts offerings only from the righteous. If you stretch your hand to kill me, I shall not lift mine to slay you; for I fear God, Lord of the Universe. I would rather you should add your sin against me to your other sins and thus become an inmate of the Fire. Such is the reward of the wicked."

His soul prompted him to slay his brother; he slew him and thus became one of the lost. Then God sent down a raven, which dug the earth to show him how to bury the naked corpse of his brother. "Alas!" he cried. "Have I not strength enough to do as this raven has done and so bury my brother's naked corpse?" And he repented.

That was why We laid it down for the Israelites that whoever killed a human being, except as a punishment for murder or other villainy in the land, shall be looked upon as though he had killed all mankind; and that whoever saved a human life should be regarded as though he had saved all mankind.

Our apostles brought them veritable proofs: yet it was not long before many of them committed great evils in the land.

Those that make war against God and His apostle and spread disorder in the land shall be put to death or crucified or have their hands and feet cut off on alternate sides, or be banished from the country. They shall be held up to shame in this world and sternly punished in the hereafter: except those that repent before you reduce them. For you must know that God is forgiving and merciful.

Believers, have fear of God and seek the right path to Him. Fight valiantly for His cause, so that you may triumph.

As for the unbelievers, if they offered all that the earth contains and as much besides to redeem themselves from the torment of the Day of Resurrection, it shall not be accepted from them. Theirs shall be a woeful punishment.

They will strive to get out of Hell, but they shall not: theirs shall be a lasting punishment.

As for the man or woman who is guilty of theft, cut off their hands to punish them for their crimes. That is the punishment enjoined by God.

God is mighty and wise. But whoever repents after committing evil, and mends his ways, shall be pardoned by God. God is forgiving and merciful.

Do you not know that God has sovereignty over the heavens and the earth? He punishes whom He will and forgives whom He pleases. God has power over all things.

Apostle, do not grieve for those who plunge headlong into unbelief; those who say with their tongues: "We believe," but have no faith in their hearts, and those Jews who listen to the lies of others and pay no heed to you. They tamper with the words out of their context and say: "If this be given you, accept it; if not, then beware!"

You cannot help a man if God seeks to confound him. Those whose hearts He does not please to purify shall be rewarded with disgrace in this world and a grievous punishment in the hereafter.

They listen to falsehoods and practise what is unlawful. If they come to you, give them your judgement or avoid them. If you avoid them they can in no way harm you; but if you do act as their judge, judge them with fairness. God loves those that deal justly.

But how will they come to you for judgement, when they already have the Torah which enshrines God's own judgement? Soon after, they will turn their backs: they are no true believers.

We have revealed the Torah, in which there is guidance and light. By it the prophets who surrendered themselves judged the Jews, and so did the rabbis and the divines, according to God's Book which had been committed to their keeping and to which they themselves were witnesses.

Have no fear of man; fear Me, and do not sell My revelations for a paltry end. Unbelievers are those who do not judge according to God's revelations.

We decreed for them a life for a life, an eye for an eye, a nose for a nose, an ear for an ear, a tooth for a tooth, and a wound for a wound. But if a man charitably forbears from retaliation, his remission shall atone for him. Transgressors are those that do not judge according to God's revelations.

After them We sent forth Jesus, the son of Mary, confirming the Torah already revealed, and gave him the Gospel, in which there is guidance and light, corroborating what was revealed before it in the Torah, a guide and an admonition to the righteous. Therefore let the followers of the Gospel judge according to what God has revealed therein. Evil-doers are those that do not base their judgements on God's revelations.

And to you We have revealed the Book with the truth. It confirms the Scriptures which came before it and stands as a guardian over them. Therefore give judgement among men according to God's revelations and do not yield to their fancies or swerve from the truth made known to you.

We have ordained a law and assigned a path for each of you. Had God pleased, He could have made you one nation: but it is His wish to prove you by that which He has bestowed upon you. Vie with each other in good works, for to God you shall all return and He will resolve for you your differences.

Pronounce judgement among them according to God's revelations and do not be led by their desires. Take heed lest they should turn you away from a part of that which God has revealed to you. If they reject your judgement, know that it is God's wish to scourge them for their sins. A great many of mankind are evil-doers.

Is it pagan laws that they wish to be judged by? Who is a better judge than God for men whose faith is firm?

Believers, take neither Jews nor Christians for your friends. They are friends with one another. Whoever of you seeks their friendship shall become one of their number. God does not guide the wrongdoers.

You see the faint-hearted hastening to woo them. They say: "We fear lest a change of fortune should befall us." But when God grants you victory or makes known His will, they shall regret their secret plans. Then will the faithful say: "Are these the men who solemnly swore by God that they would stand with you?" Their works will come to nothing and they will lose all.

Believers, if any of you renounce the faith, God will replace them by others who love Him and are loved by Him, who are humble towards the faithful and stern towards the unbelievers, zealous for God's cause and fearless of man's censure. Such is the grace of God: He bestows it on whom He will. God is munificent and all-knowing.

Your only protectors are God, His apostle, and the faithful: those who attend to their prayers, render the alms levy, and kneel down in worship. Those who seek the protection of God, His apostle, and the faithful must know that God's followers are sure to triumph.

Believers, do not seek the friendship of the infidels and those who were given the Book before you, who have made of your religion a jest and a pastime. Have fear of God, if you are true believers. When you call them to pray, they treat their prayers as a jest and a pastime. This is because they are devoid of understanding.

Say: "People of the Book, is it not that you hate us only because we believe in God and in what has been revealed to us and to others before us, and that most of you are evil-doers?"

Say: "Shall I tell you who will receive the worse reward from God? Those whom God has cursed and with whom He has been angry, transforming them into apes and swine, and those who serve the devil. Worse is the plight of these, and they have strayed farther from the right path."

When they came to you they said: "We are believers." Indeed, infidels they came and infidels they departed. God knew best what they concealed.

You see many among them vie with one another in sin and wickedness and practice what is unlawful. Evil is what they do.

Why do their rabbis and divines not forbid them to blaspheme or to practise what is unlawful? Evil indeed are their doings.

The Jews say: "God's hand is chained." May their own hands be chained! May they be cursed for what they say! By no means. His hands are both outstretched: He bestows as He will.

That which is revealed to you from your Lord will surely increase the wickedness and unbelief of many of them. We have stirred among them enmity and hatred, which will endure till the Day of Resurrection. Whenever they kindle the fire of war, God puts it out. They spread evil in the land, but God does not love the evil-doers.

If the People of the Book accept the true faith and keep from evil, We will pardon them their sins and admit them to the gardens of delight. If they observe the Torah and the Gospel and what is revealed to them from their Lord, they shall enjoy abundance from above and from beneath.

There are some among them who are righteous men; but many among them who do nothing but evil.

Apostle, proclaim what is revealed to you from your Lord; if you do not, you will surely fail to convey His message. God will protect you from all men. He does not guide the unbelievers.

Say: "People of the Book, you will attain nothing until you observe the Torah and the Gospel and that which is revealed to you from your Lord."

That which is revealed to you from your Lord will surely increase the wickedness and unbelief of many of them. But do not grieve for the unbelievers.

Believers, Jews, Sabaeans, or Christians—whoever believes in God and the Last Day and does what is right—shall have nothing to fear or to regret.

We made a convenant with the Israelites and sent forth apostles among them. But whenever an apostle came to them with a message that did not suit their fancies, some they accused of lying and some they put to death. They thought no harm would come to them: they were blind and deaf. God turned to them in mercy, but many of them again became blind and deaf. God is ever watching over their actions.

Unbelievers are those that say: "God is the Messiah, the son of Mary." For the Messiah himself said: "Children of Israel, serve God, my Lord and your Lord." He that worships other gods besides God, God will deny him Paradise and Hell shall be his home. None shall help the evil-doers.

Unbelievers are those that say: "God is one of three." There is but one God. If they do not desist from so saying, those of them that disbelieve shall be sternly punished.

Will they not turn to God in repentance and seek forgiveness of Him? He is forgiving and merciful.

The Messiah, the son of Mary, was no more than an apostle: other apostles passed away before him. His mother was a saintly woman. They both ate earthly food.

See how We make plain to them Our revelations. See how they ignore the truth.

Say: "Will you serve instead of God that which can neither harm nor help you? God hears all and knows all."

Say: "People of the Book! Do not transgress the bounds of truth in your religion. Do not yield to the desires of those who have erred before; who have led many astray and have themselves strayed from the even path."

Those of the Israelites who disbelieved were cursed by David and Jesus, the son of Mary: they cursed them because they rebelled and committed evil. Nor did they censure themselves for any wrong they did. Evil were their deeds.

You see many of them making friends with unbelievers. Evil is that to which their souls prompt them. They have incurred the wrath of God and shall endure eternal torment. Had they believed in God and the Prophet and that which is revealed to him, they would not have befriended them. But many of them are evil-doers.

You will find that the most implacable of men in their enmity to the faithful are the Jews and the pagans, and that the nearest in affection to them are those who say: "We are Christians." That is because there are priests and monks among them; and because they are free from pride.

When they listen to that which was revealed to the Apostle, you will see their eyes fill with tears as they recognize its truth. They say: "Lord, we believe. Count us among Your witnesses. Why should we not believe in God and in the truth that has come down to us? Why should we not hope our Lord will admit us among the righteous?" And for their words God has rewarded them with gardens watered by running streams, where they shall dwell for ever. Such is the recompense of the righteous. But those that disbelieve and deny Our revelations shall be the inmates of Hell.

Believers, do not forbid the wholesome things which God has made lawful to you. Do not transgress; God does not love the transgressors. Eat of the lawful and wholesome things which God has given you. Have fear of God, in whom you believe.

God will not punish you for that which is inadvertent in your oaths. But He will take you to task for the oaths which you solemnly swear. The penalty for a broken oath is the feeding of ten needy men with such food as you normally offer to your own people; or the clothing of ten needy men; or the freeing of one slave. He that cannot afford any of these must fast three days. In this way you shall expiate your broken oaths. Therefore be true to that which you have sworn. Thus God makes plain to you His revelations, so that you may give thanks.

Believers, wine and games of chance, idols and divining arrows, are abominations devised by Satan. Avoid them, so that you may prosper. Satan seeks to stir up enmity and hatred among you by means of wine and gambling, and to keep you from the remembrance of God and from your prayers. Will you not abstain from them?

Obey God, and obey the Apostle. Beware; if you give no heed, know that Our apostle's duty is only to give plain warning.

No blame shall be attached to those that have embraced the faith and done good works in regard to any food they may have eaten, so long as they fear God and believe in Him and do good works; so long as they fear God and believe in Him; so long as they fear God and do good works. God loves the charitable.

Believers, God will put you to the proof by means of the game which you can catch with your hands or with your spears, so that He may know those who fear Him in their hearts. He that transgresses hereafter shall be sternly punished.

Believers, kill no game whilst on pilgrimage. He that kills game by design, shall present, as an offering to the Ka'ba, an animal equivalent to that which he has killed, to be determined by two just men among you; or he shall, in expiation, either feed the poor or fast, so that he may taste the evil consequences of his deed. God has forgiven what is past; but if any one relapses into wrongdoing He will avenge Himself on him: He is mighty and capable of revenge.

Lawful to you is what you catch from the sea and the sustenance it provides; a wholesome food for you and for the seafarer. But you are forbidden the game of the land while you are on pilgrimage. Have fear of God, before whom you shall all be assembled.

God has made the Ka'ba, the Sacred House, the sacred month, and the sacrificial offerings with their ornaments, eternal values for mankind; so that you may know that God has knowledge of all that the heavens and the earth contain; that God has knowledge of all things.

Know that God is stern in retribution, and that God is forgiving and merciful.

The duty of the Apostle is only to give warning. God knows all that you hide and all that you reveal.

Say: "Good and evil are not alike, even though the abundance of evil may tempt you. Have fear of God, you men of understanding, so that you may triumph."

Believers, do not ask questions about things which, if made known to you, would only pain you; but if you ask them when the Koran is being revealed, they shall be made plain to you. God will pardon you for this; God is forgiving and gracious. Other men inquired about them before you, only to disbelieve them afterwards.

God demands neither a *bahirah*, nor a *saibah*, nor a *wasilah*, nor a *hami*.[7] The unbelievers invent falsehoods about God. Most of them are lacking in judgement.

When it is said to them: "Come to that which God has revealed, and to the Apostle," they reply: "Sufficient for us is the faith we have inherited from our fathers," even though their fathers knew nothing and were not rightly guided.

Believers, you are accountable for none but yourselves; he that goes astray cannot harm you if you are on the right path. To God you shall all return, and He will declare to you what you have done.

Believers, when death approaches you, let two just men from among you act as witnesses when you make your testaments; or two men from another tribe if the calamity of death overtakes you while you are travelling the land. Detain them after prayers, and if you doubt their honesty ask them to swear by God: "We will not sell our testimony for any price even to a kinsman. We will not hide the testimony of God; for we should then be evil-doers." If both prove dishonest, replace them by another pair from among those immediately concerned, and let them both swear by God,

---

7. Names given by pagan Arabs to sacred animals offered at the Ka'ba.

saying: "Our testimony is truer than theirs. We have told no lies, for we should then be wrongdoers." Thus they will be more likely to bear true witness or to fear that the oaths of others may contradict theirs. Have fear of God and be obedient. God does not guide the evil-doers.

One day God will gather all the apostles and ask them: "How were you received?" They will reply: "We have no knowledge. You alone know what is hidden." God will say: "Jesus, son of Mary, remember the favour I have bestowed on you and on your mother: how I strengthened you with the Holy Spirit, so that you preached to men in your cradle and in the prime of manhood; how I instructed you in the Book and in wisdom, in the Torah and in the Gospel; how by My leave you fashioned from clay the likeness of a bird and breathed into it so that, by My leave, it became a living bird; how, by My leave, you healed the blind man and the leper, and by My leave restored the dead to life; how I protected you from the Israelites when you had come to them with clear signs: when those of them who disbelieved declared: 'This is but plain sorcery'; how when I enjoined the disciples to believe in Me and in My apostle they replied: 'We believe; bear witness that we submit.'"

"Jesus, son of Mary," said the disciples, "can your Lord send down to us from heaven a table spread with food?"

He replied: "Have fear of God, if you are true believers."

"We wish to eat of it," they said, "so that we may reassure our hearts and know that what you said to us is true, and that we may be witnesses of it."

"Lord," said Jesus, the son of Mary, "send to us from heaven a table spread with food, that it may mark a feast for us and for those that will come after us: a sign from You. Give us our sustenance; You are the best Giver."

God replied: "I am sending one to you. But whoever of you disbelieves hereafter shall be punished as no man has ever been punished."

Then God will say: "Jesus, son of Mary, did you ever say to mankind: 'Worship me and my mother as gods beside God?'"

"Glory to You," he will answer, "how could I ever say that to which I have no right? If I had ever said so, You would have surely known it. You know what is in my mind, but I know not what is in Yours. You alone know what is hidden. I told them only what You bade me. I said: 'Serve God, my Lord and your Lord.' I watched over them while living in their midst, and ever since You took me to Yourself, You have been watching over them. You are the witness of all things. If You punish them, they surely are Your servants; and if You forgive them, surely You are mighty and wise."

God will say: "This is the day when their truthfulness will benefit the truthful. They shall for ever dwell in gardens watered by running streams. God is pleased with them and they are pleased with Him. That is the supreme triumph."

God has sovereignty over the heavens and the earth and all that they contain. He has power over all things.

10. JONAH

[Mecca]
In the Name of God, the Compassionate, the Merciful

Alif lām rā.[8] These are the verses of the Wise Book: Does it seem strange to mankind that We revealed Our will to a mortal from among themselves, saying: "Give warning to mankind, and tell the faithful their endeavours shall be rewarded by their Lord?"

The unbelievers say: "This man[9] is a skilled enchanter." Yet your Lord is God, who in six days created the heavens and the earth and then ascended His throne, ordaining all things. None has power to intercede for you except him who has received His sanction. Such is God, your Lord: therefore serve Him. Will you not take heed?

To Him you shall all return: God's promise shall be fulfilled. He gives being to all His creatures, and in the end He will bring them back to life, so that He may justly reward those who have believed in Him and done good works. As for the unbelievers, they shall drink scalding water and be sternly punished for their unbelief.

It was He that gave the sun his brightness and the moon her light, ordaining her phases that you may learn to compute the seasons and the years. God created them only to manifest the truth. He makes plain His revelations to men of understanding.

In the alternation of night and day, and in all that God has created in the heavens and the earth, there are signs for righteous men.

Those who entertain no hope of meeting Us, being pleased and contented with the life of this world, and those who give no heed to Our revelations, shall have the Fire as their home in requital for their deeds.

As for those that believe and do good works, God will guide them through their faith. Rivers will run at their feet in the Gardens of Delight. Their prayer will be: "Glory to You, Lord!" and their greeting: "Peace!" "Praise be to God, Lord of the Universe," will be the burthen of their plea.

Had God hastened the punishment of men as they would hasten their reward, their fate would have been sealed. Therefore We let those who entertain no hope of meeting Us blunder about in their wrongdoing.

When misfortune befalls man, he prays to Us lying on his side, standing, or sitting down. But as soon as We relieve his affliction he pursues his former ways, as though he never prayed for Our help. Thus their foul deeds seem fair to the transgressors.

We destroyed generations before your time on account of the wrongs they did; their apostles came to them with veritable signs, but they would not believe. Thus shall the guilty be rewarded. Then We made you their successors in the land, so that We might observe how you would conduct yourselves.

When Our clear revelations are recited to them, those who entertain no

8. A number of suras begin with several letters of the Arabic alphabet; the meaning is unclear.
9. Muhammad.

hope of meeting Us say to you: "Give us a different Koran, or make some changes in it."

Say:[1] "It is not for me to change it. I follow only what is revealed to me. I cannot disobey my Lord, for I fear the punishment of a fateful day."

Say: "Had God pleased, I would never have recited it to you, nor would He have given you any knowledge of it. A whole life-time I dwelt amongst you before it was revealed. Will you not understand?'

Who is more wicked than the man who invents a falsehood about God or denies His revelations? Truly, the evil-doers shall not triumph.

They worship idols that can neither harm nor help them, and say: "These will intercede for us with God."

Say: "Do you presume to tell God of what He knows to be neither in the heavens nor in the earth? Glory to Him! Exalted be He above the gods they serve beside Him!"

There was a time when men followed but one religion. Then they disagreed among themselves: and but for a word from your Lord, long since decreed, their differences would have been firmly resolved.

And they ask: "Why has no sign been given him by his Lord?"

Say: "God alone has knowledge of what is hidden. Wait if you will: I too am waiting!"

No sooner do We show mercy to a people after some misfortune has afflicted them than they begin to scheme against Our revelations. Say: "More swift is God's scheming. Our angels are recording your intrigues."

It is He who guides them by land and sea. They embark: and as the ships set sail, rejoicing in a favouring wind, a raging tempest overtakes them. Billows surge upon them from every side and they fear that they are encompassed by death. They pray to God with all fervour, saying: "Deliver us from this peril and we will be truly thankful."

Yet when He does deliver them, they commit evil in the land and act unjustly.

Men, it is your own souls that you are corrupting. Take your enjoyment in this life: to Us you shall in the end return, and We will declare to you all that you have done.

This present life is like the rich garment with which the earth adorns itself when watered by the rain we send down from the sky. Crops, sustaining man and beast, grow luxuriantly: but as its hopeful tenants prepare themselves for the rich harvest, down comes Our scourge upon it, by night or in broad day, laying it waste, even though it did not blossom but yesterday. Thus do We make plain Our revelations to thoughtful men.

God invites you to the Home of Peace. He guides whom He will to a straight path. Those that do good works shall have a good reward and more besides. Neither blackness nor misery shall overcast their faces. They are the heirs of Paradise: in it they shall abide for ever.

As for those that have earned evil, evil shall be rewarded with like evil.

1. God's instruction to Muhammad.

Misery will oppress them (they shall have none to defend them from God), as though patches of the night's own darkness veiled their faces. They are the heirs of Hell: in it they shall abide for ever.

On the day when We assemble them all together, We shall say to the idolaters: "Keep to your places, you and your idols!" We will separate them one from another, and then their idols will say to them: "It was not us that you worshipped, God is our all-sufficient witness. Nor were we aware of your worship."

Thereupon each soul will know what it has done. They shall be sent back to God, their true Lord, and the idols they invented will forsake them.

Say: "Who provides for you from heaven and earth? Who has endowed you with sight and hearing? Who brings forth the living from the dead, and the dead from the living? Who ordains all things?"

They will reply: "God."

Say: "Will you not take heed, then? Such is God, your true Lord. That which is not true must needs be false. How then can you turn away from Him?"

Thus is the word of your Lord made good. The evil-doers have no faith.

Say: "Can any of your idols conceive Creation, then renew it? God conceives Creation, then renews it. How is it that you are so misled?"

Say: "Can any of your idols guide you to the truth? God can guide you to the truth. Who is more worthy to be followed: He that can guide to the truth or he that cannot and is himself in need of guidance? What has come over you that you so judge?'

Most of them follow nothing but mere conjecture. But conjecture is in no way a substitute for Truth. God is cognizant of all their actions.

This Koran could not have been devised by any but God. It confirms what was revealed before it and fully explains the Scriptures. It is beyond doubt from the Lord of the Universe.

If they say: "He invented it himself," say: "Bring me one chapter like it. Call on whom you may besides God to help you, if what you say be true!"

Indeed, they disbelieve what they cannot grasp, for they have not yet seen its prophecy fulfilled. Likewise did those who passed before them disbelieve. But see what was the end of the wrong-doers.

Some believe in it, while others do not. But your Lord best knows the evil-doers.

If they disbelieve you, say: "My deeds are mine and your deeds are yours. You are not accountable for my actions, nor am I accountable for what you do."

Some of them listen to you. But can you make the deaf hear you, incapable as they are of understanding?

Some of them look upon you. But can you show the way to the blind, bereft as they are of sight?

Indeed, in no way does God wrong mankind, but men wrong themselves.

The day will come when He will gather them all together, as though

they had sojourned in this world but for an hour. They will acquaint themselves with each other. Lost shall be those that disbelieved in meeting and
did not follow the right path.

Whether We let you glimpse in some measure the scourge with which
We threaten them, or cause you to die before we smite them, to Us they
shall return. God is searching over all their actions.

An apostle is sent to every nation. When their apostle comes, justice is
done among them; they are not wronged.

They ask: "When will this promise be fulfilled, if what you say be true?"
Say: "I have no control over any harm or benefit to myself, except by
the will of God. A space of time is fixed for every nation; when their hour
is come, not for one hour shall they delay: nor can they go before it."

Say: "Do but consider. Should His scourge fall upon you by night or by
the light of day, what punishment would the guilty hasten? Will you believe
in it when it does overtake you, although it was your wish to hurry it on?"

Then it shall be said to the wrongdoers: "Feel the everlasting torment!
Shall you not be rewarded according to your deeds?"

They ask you if it is true. Say: "Yes, by the Lord, it is true! And you
shall not be immune."

To redeem himself then, each sinner would gladly give all that the earth
contains if he possessed it. When they behold the scourge, they will repent
in secret. But judgement shall be fairly passed upon them; they shall not
be wronged.

To God belongs all that the heavens and the earth contain. The promise
of God is true, though most of them may not know it. It is He who ordains
life and death, and to Him you shall all return.

Men, an admonition has come to you from your Lord, a cure for the
mind, a guide and a blessing to true believers.

Say: "In the grace and mercy of God let them rejoice, for these are better
than the worldly riches they amass."

Say: "Do but consider the things that God has given you. Some you
pronounced unlawful and others lawful." Say: "Was it God who gave you
His leave, or do you invent falsehoods about God?"

What will they think, those who invent falsehoods about God, on the
Day of Resurrection? God is bountiful to men: yet most of them do not
give thanks.

You shall engage in no affair, you shall recite no verse from the Koran,
you shall commit no act, but We will witness it. Not an atom's weight in
earth or heaven escapes your Lord, nor is there any object smaller or greater,
but is recorded in a glorious book.

The servants of God have nothing to fear or to regret. Those that have
faith and keep from evil shall rejoice both in this world and in the hereafter: the word of God shall never change. That is the supreme triumph.

Let their words not grieve you. All glory belongs to God. He alone hears
all and knows all.

To God belong all who dwell on earth and in heaven. Those that worship gods beside God follow nothing but idle fancies and preach nothing but falsehoods.

He it is who has ordained the night for your rest and given the day its light. Surely in this there are signs for prudent men.

They say: "God has begotten a son." God forbid! Self-sufficient is He. His is all that the heavens and the earth contain. Surely for this you have no sanction. Would you say of God what you do not know?

Say: "Those that invent falsehoods about God shall not prosper. They may take their ease in this life, but to Us they shall in the end return, and We shall make them taste a grievous torment for their unbelief."

Recount to them the tale of Noah. He said to his people: "If it offends you that I should dwell in your midst and preach to you God's revelations (for in Him I have put my trust), muster all your idols and decide your course of action. Do not intrigue in secret. Execute your judgement and give me no respite. If you turn away from me, remember I demand of you no recompense. Only God will reward me. I am commanded to be one of those who shall submit to Him."

But they disbelieved him. Therefore We saved Noah and those who were with him in the Ark, so that they survived, and drowned the others who denied Our revelations. Consider the fate of those who were forewarned.

After that we sent apostles to their descendants. They showed them veritable signs, but they persisted in their unbelief. Thus do We seal up the hearts of the transgressors.

Then We sent forth Moses and Aaron with Our signs to Pharaoh and his nobles. But they rejected them with scorn, for they were wicked men. When the truth had come to them from Us, they declared: "This is but plain sorcery."

Moses replied: "Is this what you say of the Truth when it has come to you? Is this sorcery? Sorcerers shall never prosper."

They said: "Have you come to turn us away from the faith of our fathers, so that you two may lord it over the land? We will never believe in you."

Then Pharaoh said: "Bring every learned sorcerer to my presence."

And when the sorcerers attended Moses said to them: "Cast down what you wish to cast." And when they had thrown, he said "The sorcery that you have wrought God will surely bring to nothing. He does not bless the work of those who do evil. By His words He vindicates the truth, much as the guilty may dislike it."

Few of his[2] people believed in Moses, for they feared the persecution of Pharaoh and his nobles. Pharaoh was a tyrant in the land, an evil-doer.

Moses said: "If you believe in God, my people, and have surrendered yourselves to Him, in Him alone then put your trust."

They replied: "In God we have put our trust. Lord, do not let us suffer

---

2. Pharaoh's.

at the hands of wicked men. Deliver us, through Your mercy, from the unbelievers."

We revealed Our will to Moses and his brother, saying: "Build houses in Egypt for your people and make your homes places of worship. Conduct prayers and give good news to the faithful."

"Lord," said Moses. "You have bestowed on Pharaoh and his princes splendour and riches in this life, so that they might stray from your path. Lord, destroy their riches and harden their hearts, so that they shall persist in unbelief until they face the woeful scourge."

God replied: "Your prayer shall be answered. Follow the right path and do not walk in the footsteps of ignorant men."

We led the Israelites across the sea, and Pharaoh and his legions pursued them with wickedness and hate. But as he was drowning, Pharaoh cried: "Now I believe no god exists except the God in whom the Israelites believe. To Him I give up myself."

"Only now! But before this you were a rebel and a wrongdoer. We shall save your body this day, so that you may become a sign to all posterity: for a great many of mankind do not heed Our signs."

We settled the Israelites in a blessed land and provided them with good things. Nor did they disagree among themselves until knowledge was given them. Your Lord will judge their differences on the Day of Resurrection.

If you doubt what We have revealed to you, ask those who have read the Scriptures before you. The truth has come to you from your Lord: therefore do not doubt it. Nor shall you deny the revelations of God, for then you shall be lost.

Those for whom the word of your Lord shall be fulfilled will not have faith, even if they be given every sign, until they face the woeful scourge. Were it otherwise, every nation, had it believed, would have profited from its faith. But it was so only with Jonah's people. When they believed, We spared them the penalty of disgrace in this life and gave them comfort for a while. Had your Lord pleased, all the people of the earth would have believed in Him, one and all. Would you then force people to have faith?

None can have faith except by the will of God. He will visit His scourge upon the senseless.

Say: "Behold what the heavens and the earth contain!" But neither signs nor warnings will avail the unbelievers.

What can they wait for but the fate of those who have gone before them? Say: "Wait if you will; I too am waiting."

We shall save Our apostles and the true believers. It is but just that We should save the faithful.

Say: "Men! Doubt my religion if you will, but never will I worship those that you worship besides God. I worship God, to whom you shall all return: for I am commanded to be one of the faithful, I was bidden: 'Dedicate yourself to the Faith in all uprightness and serve none besides God. You shall not pray to idols which can neither help nor harm you, for if you do, you will become a wrongdoer. If God afflicts you with a misfortune none can remove it but He; and if He bestows on you a favour, none can withhold His bounty. He is bountiful to whom He will. He is the Forgiving One, the Merciful.' "

Say: "Men! The truth has come to you from your Lord. He that follows the right path follows it to his own good, and he that goes astray does so at his own peril. I am not your keeper."

Observe what is revealed to you, and have patience till God makes known his judgement. He is the best of judges.

12. JOSEPH

[Mecca]
In the Name of God, the Compassionate, the Merciful

Alif lām rā. These are the verses of the Glorious Book. We have revealed the Koran in the Arabic tongue so that you may grow in understanding.

In revealing this Koran We will recount to you the best of narratives, though before it you were heedless.

Joseph said to his father: "Father, I dreamt of eleven stars and the sun and the moon; I saw them prostrate themselves before me."

"My son," he replied, "say nothing of this dream to your brothers, lest they plot evil against you: Satan is the sworn enemy of man. You shall be chosen by your Lord. He will teach you to interpret visions, and will perfect His favour to you and to the house of Jacob, as He perfected it to your forefathers Abraham and Isaac before you. Your Lord is wise and all-knowing."

Surely in Joseph and his brothers there are signs for doubting men.

They said to each other: "Joseph and his brother are dearer to our father than ourselves, though we are many. Truly, our father is much mistaken. Let us slay Joseph, or cast him away in some far-off land, so that we may have no rivals in our father's love, and after that be honourable men."

One of them said: "Do not slay Joseph; but if you must, rather cast him into a dark pit. Some caravan will take him up."

They said to their father: "Why do you not trust us with Joseph? Surely we wish him well. Send him with us tomorrow, that he may play and enjoy himself. We will take good care of him."

He replied: "It would much grieve me to let him go with you; for I fear lest the wolf should eat him when you are off your guard."

They said: "If the wolf could eat him despite our numbers, then we should surely be lost!"

And when they took Joseph with them, they decided to cast him into a dark pit. We revealed to him, saying: "You shall tell them of all this when they will not know you."

At nightfall they returned weeping to their father. They said: "We went off to compete together and left Joseph with our packs. The wolf devoured him. But you will not believe us, though we speak the truth." And they showed him their brother's shirt, stained with false blood.

"No!" he cried. "Your souls have tempted you to evil. Sweet patience! God alone can help me bear the loss you speak of."

And a caravan passed by, who sent their water-bearer to the pit. And when he had let down his pail, he cried: "Rejoice! A boy!"

They concealed him as part of their merchandise. But God knew what they did. They sold him for a trifling price, for a few pieces of silver. They cared nothing for him.

The Egyptian who bought him said to his wife:[3] "Be kind to him. He may prove useful to us, or we may adopt him as our son."

Thus We established Joseph in the land, and taught him to interpret dreams. God has power over all things, though most men may not know it. And when he reached maturity We bestowed on him wisdom and knowledge. Thus We reward the righteous.

His master's wife sought to seduce him. She bolted the doors and said: "Come!"

"God forbid!" he replied. "My lord has treated me with kindness. Wrongdoers never prosper."

She made for him, and he himself would have succumbed to her had he not been shown a sign from his Lord. Thus did We shield him from wantonness, for he was one of Our faithful servants.

They both rushed to the door. She tore his shirt from behind. And at the door they met her husband.

She cried: "Shall not the man who wished to violate your wife be thrown into prison or sternly punished?"

Joseph said: "It was she who attempted to seduce me."

"If his shirt is torn from the front," said one of her people, "she is speaking the truth and he is lying. If it is torn from behind, then he is speaking the truth and she is lying."

And when her husband saw Joseph's shirt rent from behind, he said to her: "This is but one of your tricks. Your cunning is great indeed! Joseph, say no more about this. Woman, ask pardon for your sin. You have done wrong."

In the city women were saying: "The Prince's wife has sought to seduce her servant. She has conceived a passion for him. It is clear that she has gone astray."

When she heard of their intrigues, she invited them to a banquet at her house. To each she gave a knife, and ordered Joseph to present himself before them. When they saw him, they were amazed at him and cut their hands, exclaiming: "God preserve us! This is no mortal, but a gracious angel."

"This is the man," she said, "on whose account you blamed me. I sought to seduce him, but he was unyielding. If he declines to do my bidding, he shall be thrown into prison and shall be held in scorn."

"Lord," said Joseph, "sooner would I go to prison than give in to their advances. Shield me from their cunning, or I shall yield to them and lapse into folly."

---

3. Traditionally given the name Zuleikha.

His Lord heard his prayer and warded off their wiles from him. He hears all and knows all.

Yet for all the evidence they had seen, they thought it right to jail him for a time.

Two young men entered the prison with him. One of them said: "I dreamt that I was pressing grapes." And the other said: "I dreamt that I was carrying a loaf upon my head, and that the birds came and ate of it. Tell us the meaning of these dreams, for we can see you are a virtuous man."

Joseph replied: "I can interpret them long before they are fulfilled. Whatever food you are provided with, I can divine for you its meaning, even before it reaches you. This knowledge my Lord has given me, for I have left the faith of those that disbelieve in God and deny the life to come. I follow the faith of my forefathers, Abraham, Isaac, and Jacob. We will serve no idols besides God. Such is the grace which God has bestowed on us and on all mankind. Yet most men do not give thanks.

"Fellow-prisoners! Are sundry gods better than God, the One, the One who conquers all? Those you serve besides Him are nothing but names which you and your fathers have devised and for which God has revealed no sanction. Judgement rests only with God. He has commanded you to worship none but Him. That is the true faith: yet most men do not know it.

"Fellow-prisoners, one of you will serve his lord with wine. The other will be crucified, and the birds will peck at his head. This is the answer to your question."

And Joseph said to the prisoner who he knew would be freed: "Remember me in the presence of your lord."

But Satan made him forget to mention Joseph to his lord, so that he stayed in prison for several years.

The king said: "I saw seven fatted cows which seven lean ones devoured; also seven green ears of corn and seven others dry. Tell me the meaning of this vision, my nobles, if you can interpret visions."

They replied: "It is but a medley of dream; nor are we skilled in the interpretation of dreams."

Thereupon the man who had been freed remembered Joseph after all that time. He said: "I shall tell you what it means. Give me leave to go."

He said to Joseph: "Tell us, man of truth, of the seven fatted cows which seven lean ones devoured; also of the seven green ears of corn and the other seven which were dry: so that I may go back to my masters and inform them."

He replied: "You shall sow for seven consecutive years. Leave in the ear the corn you reap, except a little which you may eat. Then there shall follow seven hungry years which will consume all but little of what you have stored. Then there will come a year of abundant rain, in which the people will press the grape."

The king said: "Bring this man before me."

But when the envoy came to him, Joseph said: "Go back to your master and ask him about the women who cut their hands. My master knows their cunning."

The king questioned the women, saying: "What made you attempt to seduce Joseph?"

"God forbid!" they replied. "We know no evil of him."

"Now the truth must come to light," said the Prince's wife. "It was I who sought to seduce him. He has told the truth."

"From this," said Joseph, "my lord will know that I did not betray him in his absence, and that God does not guide the work of the treacherous. Not that I am free from sin: man's soul is prone to evil, except his to whom God has shown mercy. My Lord is forgiving and merciful."

The king said: "Bring him before me. I will choose him for my own."

And when he had spoken with him, the king said: "You shall henceforth dwell with us, honoured and trusted."

Joseph said: "Give me charge of the granaries of the realm. I shall husband them wisely."

Thus did We establish Joseph in the land, and he dwelt there as he pleased. We bestow Our mercy on whom We will, and never deny the righteous their reward. Better is the reward of the life to come for those who believe in God and keep from evil.

Joseph's brothers arrived and presented themselves before him. He recognized them, but they knew him not. And when he had given them their provisions, he said: "Bring me your other brother from your father. Do you not see that I give just measure and am the best of hosts? If you do not bring him, you shall have no corn, nor shall you come near me again."

They replied: "We will endeavour to fetch him from his father. This we will surely do."

Joseph said to his servants: "Put their money into their packs, so that they may find it when they return to their people. Perchance they will come back."

When they returned to their father, they said: "Father, corn is henceforth denied us. Send our brother with us and we shall have our measure. We will take good care of him."

He replied: "Am I to trust you with him as I once trusted you with his brother? But God is the best of guardians: and of all those that show mercy He is the most merciful."

When they opened their packs, they discovered that their money had been returned to them. "Father," they said, "what more can we desire? Here is our money paid back to us. We will buy provisions for our people and take good care of our brother. We shall receive an extra camel-load; a camel-load should be easy enough."

He replied: "I will not let him go with you until you promise in God's name to bring him back to me, unless the worst befall you."

And when they had given him their pledge, he said: "God is the witness of your oath. My sons, enter the town by different gates. If you do wrong, I cannot ward off from you the wrath of God: judgement is His alone. In Him I have put my trust. In Him alone let the faithful put their trust."

And when they entered as their father had bade them, his counsel availed them nothing against the decree of God. It was but a wish in Jacob's soul which he had thus fulfilled. He was possessed of knowledge which We had given him, though most men have no knowledge.

When they went in to Joseph, he embraced his brother, and said: "I am your brother. Do not grieve at what they did."

And when he had given them their provisions, he hid a drinking-cup in his brother's pack.

Then a crier called out after them: "Travellers, you are thieves!"

They turned back and asked: "What have you lost?"

"We miss the king's drinking-cup," he replied. "He that brings it shall have a camel-load of corn. I pledge my word for it."

"In God's name," they cried, "you know we did not come to do evil in this land. We are no thieves."

The Egyptians said: "What penalty shall be his who stole it, if you prove to be lying?"

They replied: "He in whose pack the cup is found shall be your bondsman. Thus we punish the wrongdoers."

Joseph searched their bags before his brother's, and then took out the cup from his brother's bag.

Thus We directed Joseph. By the king's law he had no right to seize his brother: but God willed otherwise. We exalt in knowledge whom We will: but above those that have knowledge there is One more knowing.

They said: "If he has stolen—know then that a brother of his has committed theft before him."[4]

But Joseph kept his secret and revealed nothing to them. He said: "Your deed was worse. God best knows the things you speak of."

They said: "Noble prince, this boy has an aged father. Take one of us, instead of him. We can see you are a generous man."

He replied: "God forbid that we should take any but the man with whom our property was found: for then we should be unjust."

When they despaired of him, they went aside to confer in private. The eldest said: "Have you forgotten that your father took from you a pledge in God's name, and that long ago you did your worst with Joseph. I will not stir from this land until my father gives me leave or God makes known to me His judgement: He is the best of judges. Return to your father and say to him: 'Father, your son has committed a theft. We testify only to what we know. How could we guard against the unforeseen? Inquire at the city where we lodged, and from the caravan with which we travelled. We speak the truth.' "

"No!" cried their father. "Your souls have tempted you to evil. But I will have sweet patience. God may bring them all to me. He alone is all-knowing and wise." And he turned away from them, crying: "Alas for Joseph!" His eyes went white with grief and he was oppressed with silent sorrow.

---

4. Commentators say that Joseph had stolen an idol of his maternal grandfather's and broken it, so that he might not worship it.

His sons exclaimed: "In God's name, will you not cease to think of Joseph until you ruin your health and die?"

He replied: "I complain to God of my sorrow and sadness. He has made known to me things that you know not. Go, my sons, and seek news of Joseph and his brother. Do not despair of God's spirit; none but unbelievers despair of God's spirit."

And when they went in to him, they said: "Noble prince, we and our people are scourged with famine. We have brought but little money. Give us some corn, and be charitable to us: God rewards the charitable."

"Do you know," he replied, "what you did to Joseph and his brother? You are surely unaware."

They cried: "Can you indeed be Joseph?"

"I am Joseph," he answered, "and this is my brother. God has been gracious to us. Those that keep from evil and endure with fortitude, God will not deny them their reward."

"By the Lord," they said, "God has exalted you above us all. We have indeed been guilty."

He replied: "None shall reproach you this day. May God forgive you: Of all those who show mercy, He is the most merciful. Take this shirt of mine and throw it over my father's face: he will recover his sight. Then return to me with all your people."

When the caravan departed their father said: "I feel the breath of Joseph, though you will not believe me."

"In God's name," said those who heard him, "it is but your old illusion."

And when the bearer of good news arrived, he threw Joseph's shirt over the old man's face, and he regained his sight. He said: "Did I not tell you that God has made known to me what you know not?"

His sons said: "Father, implore forgiveness for our sins. We have indeed done wrong."

He replied: "I shall implore my Lord to forgive you. He is forgiving and merciful."

And when they went in to Joseph, he embraced his parents and said: "Welcome to Egypt, safe, if God wills!"

He helped his parents to a couch, and they all fell on their knees and prostrated themselves before him.

"This," said Joseph to his father, "is the meaning of my old vision: my Lord has fulfilled it. He has been gracious to me. He has released me from prison and brought you out of the desert after Satan had stirred up strife between me and my brothers. My lord is gracious to whom He will. He alone is all-knowing and wise.

"Lord, You have given me authority and taught me to interpret dreams. Creator of the heavens and the earth, my Guardian in this world and in the hereafter. Allow me to die in submission, and admit me among the righteous."

That which We have now revealed to you[5] is a tale of the unknown.

5. Muhammad.

You were not present when Joseph's brothers conceived their plans and schemed against him. Yet strive as you may, most men will not believe. You shall demand of them no recompense for this. It is an admonition to all mankind.

Many are the marvels of the heavens and the earth; yet they pass them by and pay no heed to them. The greater part of them believe in God only if they can worship other gods besides Him.

Are they confident that God's scourge will not fall upon them, or that the Hour of Doom will not overtake them unawares, without warning? Say: "This is my path. With sure knowledge I call on you to have faith in God, I and all my followers. Glory be to God! I am no idolater."

Nor were the apostles whom We sent before you other than mortals inspired by Our will and chosen from among their people.

Have they not travelled in the land and seen what was the end of those who disbelieved before them? Better is the world to come for those that keep from evil. Can you not understand?

And when at length Our apostles despaired and thought they were denied, Our help came down to them, delivering whom We pleased. The evil-doers could not be saved from Our scourge. Their annals point to a moral to men of understanding.

This[6] is no invented tale, but a confirmation of previous scriptures, an explanation of all things, a guide and a blessing to true believers.

19. MARY

[Mecca]
In the Name of God, the Compassionate, the Merciful

Kaf hā' yā' 'ain sād. An account of your Lord's goodness to His servant Zacharias:

He invoked Him in secret, saying: "My bones are enfeebled, and my head grows silver with age. Yet never, Lord, have I prayed to You in vain. I now fear my kinsmen who will succeed me, for my wife is barren. Grant me a son who will be my heir and an heir to the house of Jacob, and who will find grace in Your sight."

"Rejoice, Zacharias," came the answer. "You shall be given a son, and he shall be called John; a name no man has borne before him."

"How shall I have a son, Lord," asked Zacharias, "when my wife is barren and I am well-advanced in years?"

He replied: "Such is the will of your Lord. It shall be no difficult task for Me, for I brought you into being when you were nothing before."

"Lord," said Zacharias, "give me a sign."

"Your sign is that for three days and three nights," He replied, "you shall be bereft of speech, though otherwise sound in body."

Then Zacharias came out from the Shrine and exhorted his people to give glory to their Lord morning and evening.

To John We said: "Observe the Scriptures with a firm resolve." We

6. The Koran.

bestowed on him wisdom, grace, and purity while yet a child, and he grew
up a righteous man; honouring his father and mother, and neither arrogant
nor rebellious. Blessed was he on the day he was born and the day of his
death; and may peace be on him when he is raised to life.

And you shall recount in the Book the story of Mary: how she left her
people and betook herself to a solitary place to the east.

We sent to her Our spirit in the semblance of a full-grown man. And
when she saw him she said: "May the Merciful defend me from you! If
you fear the Lord, leave me and go your way."

"I am the messenger of your Lord," he replied, "and have come to give
you a holy son."

"How shall I bear a child," she answered, "when I am a virgin, untouched
by man?"

"Such is the will of your Lord," he replied. "That is no difficult thing
for Him. 'He shall be a sign to mankind,' says the Lord, 'and a blessing
from Ourself. This is Our decree.' "

Thereupon she conceived him, and retired to a far-off place. And when
she felt the throes of childbirth she lay down by the trunk of a palm-tree
crying: "Oh, would that I had died and passed into oblivion!"

But a voice from below cried out to her: "Do not despair. Your Lord has
provided a brook that runs at your feet, and if you shake the trunk of this
palm-tree it will drop fresh ripe dates in your lap. Therefore eat and drink
and rejoice; and should you meet any mortal say to him: 'I have vowed a
fast to the Merciful and will not speak with any man today.' "

Carrying the child, she came to her people, who said to her: "This is
indeed a strange thing! Sister of Aaron,[7] your father was never a whore-
monger, nor was your mother a harlot."

She made a sign to them, pointing to the child. But they replied: "How
can we speak with a babe in the cradle?"

Whereupon he spoke and said: "I am the servant of God. He has given
me the Book and ordained me a prophet. His blessing is upon me wherever
I go, and He has commanded me to be steadfast in prayer and to give alms
to the poor as long as I shall live. He has exhorted me to honour my
mother and has purged me of vanity and wickedness. I was blessed on the
day I was born, and blessed I shall be on the day of my death; and may
peace be upon me on the day when I shall be raised to life."

Such was Jesus, the son of Mary. That is the whole truth, which they
still doubt. God forbid that He Himself should beget a son! When He
decrees a thing He need only say: "Be," and it is.

God is my Lord and your Lord: therefore serve Him. That is the right
path.

Yet the Sects are divided concerning Jesus. But when the fateful day
arrives, woe to the unbelievers! Their sight and being shall be sharpened

---

7. Muslim commentators deny the charge that there is confusion here between Miriam, Aaron's sister,
and Maryam (Mary), mother of Jesus. "Sister of Aaron," they argue, simply means "virtuous woman" in
this context.

on the day when they appear before Us. Truly, the unbelievers are in the grossest error.

Forewarn them of that woeful day, when Our decrees shall be fulfilled whilst they heedlessly persist in unbelief. For We shall inherit the earth and all who dwell upon it. To Us they shall return.

You shall also recount in the Book the story of Abraham: He was a saintly man and a prophet. He said to his father: "How can you serve a worthless idol, a thing that can neither see nor hear?

"Father, things you know nothing of have come to my knowledge: therefore follow me, that I may guide you along an even path.

"Father, do not worship Satan; for he has rebelled against the Lord of Mercy.

"Father, I fear that a scourge will fall upon you from the Merciful, and you will become one of Satan's minions."

He replied: "Do you dare renounce my gods, Abraham? Desist from this folly or I shall stone you. Begone from my house this instant!"

"Peace be with you," said Abraham. "I shall implore my Lord to forgive you: for to me He has been gracious. But I will not live with you or with your idols. I will call on my Lord, and trust that my prayers will not be ignored."

And when Abraham had cast off his people and the idols which they worshipped, We gave him Isaac and Jacob. Each of them We made a prophet, and We bestowed on them gracious gifts and high renown.

In the Book tell also of Moses, who was a chosen man, an apostle, and a prophet.

We called out to him from the right side of the Mountain, and when he came near We communed with him in secret. We gave him, of Our mercy, his brother Aaron, himself a prophet.

And in the Book you shall tell of Ishmael: he, too, was a man of his word, an apostle, and a prophet.

He enjoined prayer and almsgiving on his people, and his Lord was pleased with him.

And of Idris[8]: he, too, was a saint and a prophet, whom We honoured and exalted.

These are the men to whom God has been gracious: the prophets from among the descendants of Adam and of those whom We carried in the Ark with Noah; the descendants of Abraham, of Israel, and of those whom We have guided and chosen. For when the revelations of the Merciful were recited to them they fell down on their knees in tears and adoration.

But the generations who succeeded them neglected their prayers and succumbed to their desires. These shall assuredly be lost. But those that repent and embrace the Faith and do what is right shall be admitted to Paradise and shall in no way be wronged. They shall enter the gardens of Eden, which the Merciful has promised His servants in reward for their faith. His promise shall be fulfilled.

8. Enoch.

There they shall hear no idle talk, but only the voice of peace. And their sustenance shall be given them morning and evening. Such is the Paradise which We shall give the righteous to inherit.

We do not descend from Heaven save at the bidding of your Lord.[9] To Him belongs what is before us and behind us, and all that lies between. Your Lord does not forget. He is the Lord of the heavens and the earth and all that is between them. Worship Him, then, and be patient in His service; for do you know any other worthy of His name?

"What!" says man. "When I am once dead, shall I be raised to life?" Does man forget that We created him out of the void? By the Lord, We will call them to account in company with all the devils and set them on their knees around the fire of Hell: from every sect We will carry off its stoutest rebels against the Lord of Mercy. We know best who deserves most to be burnt therein.

There is not one of you who shall not pass through it: such is the absolute decree of your Lord. We will deliver those who fear Us, but the wrongdoers shall be left there on their knees.

When Our clear revelations are recited to them the unbelievers say to the faithful: "Which of us two will have a finer dwelling and better companions?"

How many generations have We destroyed before them, far greater in riches and in splendour!

Say: "The Merciful will bear long with those in error, until they witness the fulfilment of His threats: be it a worldly scourge or the Hour of Doom. Then shall they know whose is the worse plight and whose the smaller following."

God will add guidance to those that are rightly guided. Deeds of lasting merit shall earn you a better reward in His sight and a more auspicious end.

Mark the words of him who denies Our signs and who yet boasts: "I shall surely be given wealth and children!" he boasts.

Has the future been revealed to him? Or has the Merciful made him such a promise?

By no means! We will record his words and make his punishment long and terrible. All he speaks of he shall leave behind and come before us all alone.

They have chosen other gods to help them. But in the end they will renounce their worship and turn against them.

Know that We send down to the unbelievers devils who incite them to evil. Therefore have patience: their days are numbered. The day will surely come when We will gather the righteous in multitudes before the Lord of Mercy, and drive the sinful in great hordes into Hell. None has power to intercede for them save him who has received the sanction of the Merciful.

Those who say: "The Lord of Mercy has begotten a son," preach a monstrous falsehood, at which the very heavens might crack, the earth

9. Commentators say that these are the words of the Angel Gabriel, in reply to Muhammad's complaint of long intervals elapsing between periods of revelation.

break asunder, and the mountains crumble to dust. That they should ascribe a son to the Merciful, when it does not become the Lord of Mercy to beget one!

There is none in the heavens or the earth but shall return to the Merciful in utter submission. He has kept strict count of all His creatures, and one by one they shall approach Him on the Day of Resurrection. He will cherish those who accepted the true faith and were charitable in their lifetime.

We have revealed to you the Koran in your own tongue that you may thereby proclaim good tidings to the upright and give warning to a contentious nation.

How many generations have We destroyed before them! Can you find one of them still alive, or hear so much as a whisper from them?

55. THE MERCIFUL[1]

[Mecca]
In the Name of God, the Compassionate, the Merciful

It is the Merciful who has taught the Koran.

He created man and taught him articulate speech. The sun and the moon pursue their ordered course. The plants and the trees bow down in adoration.

He raised the heaven on high and set the balance of all things, that you might not transgress that balance. Give just weight and full measure.

He laid the earth for His creatures, with all its fruits and blossom-bearing palm, chaff-covered grain and scented herbs. Which of your Lord's blessings would you deny?

He created man from potter's clay and the jinn from smokeless fire.[2] Which of your Lord's blessings would you deny?

The Lord of the two easts[3] is He, and the Lord of the two wests. Which of your Lord's blessings would you deny?

He has let loose the two oceans:[4] they meet one another. Yet between them stands a barrier which they cannot overrun. Which of your Lord's blessings would you deny?

Pearls and corals come from both. Which of your Lord's blessings would you deny?

His are the ships that sail like mountains upon the ocean. Which of your Lord's blessings would you deny?

All that lives on earth is doomed to die. But the face of your Lord will abide for ever, in all its majesty and glory. Which of your Lord's blessings would you deny?

All who dwell in heaven and earth entreat Him. Each day some mighty task engages Him. Which of your Lord's blessings would you deny?

---

1. Compare this chapter with Psalm 136 of the Old Testament. 2. The jinns are a separate order of creation from humans. The question that follows is addressed to humans and the jinn. 3. The points at which the sun rises in summer and winter. 4. Salt water and fresh water; more specifically, a reference to fresh water springs in the ocean floor.

Mankind and jinn, We shall surely find the time to judge you! Which of your Lord's blessings would you deny?

Mankind and jinn, if you have power to penetrate the confines of heaven and earth, then penetrate them! But this you shall not do except with Our own authority. Which of your Lord's blessings would you deny?

Flames of fire shall be lashed at you, and molten brass. There shall be none to help you. Which of your Lord's blessings would you deny?

When the sky splits asunder and reddens like a rose or stainéd leather (which of your Lord's blessings would you deny?), on that day neither man nor jinnee shall be asked about his sins. Which of your Lord's blessings would you deny?

The wrongdoers shall be known by their looks; they shall be seized by their forelocks and their feet. Which of your Lord's blessings would you deny?

That is the Hell which the sinners deny. They shall wander between fire and water fiercely seething. Which of your Lord's blessings would you deny?

But for those that fear the majesty of their Lord there are two gardens (which of your Lord's blessings would you deny?) planted with shady trees. Which of your Lord's blessings would you deny?

Each is watered by a flowing spring. Which of your Lord's blessings would you deny?

Each bears every kind of fruit in pairs. Which of your Lord's blessings would you deny?

They shall recline on couches lined with thick brocade, and within their reach will hang the fruits of both gardens. Which of your Lord's blessings would you deny?

They shall dwell with bashful virgins whom neither man nor jinnee will have touched before. Which of your Lord's blessings would you deny?

Virgins as fair as corals and rubies. Which of your Lord's blessings would you deny?

Shall the reward of goodness be anything but good? Which of your Lord's blessings would you deny?

And beside these there shall be two other gardens (which of your Lord's blessings would you deny?) of darkest green. Which of your Lord's blessings would you deny?

A gushing fountain shall flow in each. Which of your Lord's blessings would you deny?

Each planted with fruit-trees, the palm and the promegranate. Which of your Lord's blessings would you deny?

In each there shall be virgins chaste and fair. Which of your Lord's blessings would you deny?

Dark-eyed virgins sheltered in their tents (which of your Lord's blessings would you deny?) whom neither man nor jinnee will have touched before. Which of your Lord's blessings would you deny?

They shall recline on green cushions and rich carpets. Which of your Lord's blessings would you deny?

Blessed be the name of your Lord, the lord of majesty and glory!

62. FRIDAY, OR THE DAY OF CONGREGATION

[Medinah]
In the Name of God, the Compassionate, the Merciful

All that is in heaven and earth gives glory to God, the Sovereign Lord, the Holy One, the Almighty, the Wise One.

It is He that has sent forth among the gentiles an apostle of their own to recite to them His revelations, to purify them, and to instruct them in the Book and in wisdom though they have hitherto been in gross error, together with others of their own kin who have not yet followed them. He is the Mighty, the Wise One.

Such is the grace of God: He bestows it on whom He will. His grace is infinite.

Those to whom the burden of the Torah was entrusted and yet refused to bear it are like a donkey laden with books. Wretched is the example of those who deny God's revelations. God does not guide the wrongdoers.

Say to the Jews: "If your claim be true that of all men you alone are God's friends, then you should wish for death, if what you say be true!" But, because of what their hands have done, they will never wish for death. God knows the wrongdoers.

Say: "The death from which you shrink is sure to overtake you. Then you shall be sent back to Him who knows the unknown and the manifest, and He will declare to you all that you have done."

Believers, when you are summoned to Friday prayers hasten to the remembrance of God and cease your trading. That would be best for you, if you but knew it. Then, when the prayers are ended, disperse and go in quest of God's bounty. Remember God always, so that you may prosper.

Yet no sooner do they see some commerce or merriment than they flock to it eagerly, leaving you standing all alone.

Say: "That which God has in store is far better than any commerce or merriment. God is the Most Munificent Giver."

71. NOAH

[Mecca]
In the Name of God, the Compassionate, the Merciful

We sent forth Noah to his people, saying: "Give warning to your people before a woeful scourge overtakes them."

He said: "My people, I come to warn you plainly. Serve God and fear Him, and obey me. He will forgive you your sins and give you respite for an appointed time. When God's time arrives, none shall put it back. Would that you understood this!"

"Lord," said Noah, "day and night I have pleaded with my people, but my pleas have only added to their aversion. Each time I call on them to seek Your pardon, they thrust their fingers in their ears and draw their cloaks over their heads, persisting in sin and bearing themselves with insolent pride. I called out loud to them, and appealed to them in public and in private. 'Seek forgiveness of your Lord,' I said. 'He is ever ready to forgive you. He sends down for you abundant rain from heaven and bestows upon you wealth and children. He has provided you with gardens and with running brooks. Why do you deny the greatness of God when He has made you in gradual stages? Can you not see how He created the seven heavens one above the other, placing in them the moon for a light and the sun for a lantern? God has brought you forth from the earth like a plant, and to the earth He will restore you. Then He will bring you back afresh. He has made the earth a vast expanse for you, so that you may roam in spacious paths.' "

And Noah said: "Lord, my people disobey me and follow those whose wealth and offspring will only hasten their perdition. They have devised an outrageous plot, and said to each other: 'Do not renounce your gods. Do not forsake Wadd or Suwā' or Yaghuth or Ya'uq or Nasr.'[5] They have led numerous men astray. You surely drive the wrongdoers to further error."

And because of their sins they were overwhelmed by the Flood and cast into the Fire. They found none besides God to help them.

And Noah said: "Lord, do not leave a single unbeliever in the land. If you spare them they will mislead Your servants and beget none but sinners and unbelievers. Forgive me, Lord, and forgive my parents and every true believer who seeks refuge in my house. Forgive all the faithful, men and women, and hasten the destruction of the wrongdoers."

76. MAN

[Mecca]
In the Name of God, the Compassionate, the Merciful

Does there not pass over man a space of time when his life is a blank?[6] We have created man from the union of the two sexes so that We may put him to the proof. We have endowed him with hearing and sight and, be he thankful or oblivious of Our favours, We have shown him the right path.

For the unbelievers We have prepared fetters and chains, and a blazing Fire. But the righteous shall drink of a cup tempered at the Camphor Fountain, a gushing spring at which the servants of God will refresh themselves: they who keep their vows and dread the far-spread terrors of Judgement-day; who, though they hold it dear, give sustenance to the poor man, the orphan, and the captive, saying: "We feed you for God's sake only; we seek of you neither recompense nor thanks: for we fear from God a day of anguish and of woe."

God will deliver them from the evil of that day and make their faces shine with joy. He will reward them for their steadfastness with robes of silk and the delights of Paradise. Reclining there upon soft couches, they shall feel neither the scorching heat nor the biting cold. Trees will spread their shade around them, and fruits will hang in clusters over them.

They shall be served with silver dishes, and beakers as large as goblets;

5. Names of idols that were worshiped in Mecca before Muhammad had them destroyed. 6. In the womb.

silver goblets which they themselves shall measure: and cups brim-full with ginger-flavoured water from the Fount of Salsabīl. They shall be attended by boys graced with eternal youth, who to the beholder's eyes will seem like sprinkled pearls. When you gaze upon that scene you will behold a kingdom blissful and glorious.

They shall be arrayed in garments of fine green silk and rich brocade, and adorned with bracelets of silver. Their Lord will give them pure nectar to drink.

Thus you shall be rewarded; your high endeavours are gratifying to God.

We have made known to you the Koran by gradual revelation; therefore wait with patience the judgement of your Lord and do not yield to the wicked and the unbelieving. Remember the name of your Lord morning and evening; in the nighttime worship Him: praise Him all night long.

The unbelievers love this fleeting life too well, and thus prepare for themselves a heavy day of doom. We created them, and endowed their limbs and joints with strength; but if We please We can replace them by other men.

This is indeed an admonition. Let him that will, take the right path to his Lord. Yet you cannot will, except by the will of God. God is wise and all-knowing.

He is merciful to whom He will: but for the wrongdoers He has prepared a woeful punishment.

BEOWULF

In the sense that Greek literature begins with Homer, English literature begins with *Beowulf*. The Greek epics, the *Iliad* and the *Odyssey*, were undoubtedly preceded by centuries of oral poetry, tales in verse not written but recited for an audience. What the epic poet did was to organize a large body of this material and focus it—in the *Iliad* on the "wrath of Achilles," in the *Odyssey* on the struggle of Odysseus to return to his homeland after the Trojan War. In much the same way, the hero Beowulf is the focus of the poem that bears his name.

Beowulf divides readily into two parts, although not thus noted in the text itself. The first part, after a brief sketch of the Danish rulers from Shild to Hrothgar, relates Beowulf's killing of two monsters, Grendel and his mother (lines 1–2199). The second part tells how Beowulf, who has now been king of the Geats for fifty years, kills a dragon but is also mortally wounded in the fight (lines 2200–3182). The poem is in Old English—that is, the form of the language in use from the Anglo-Saxon settlement in Britain down to the eleventh century—and has come down to us in a single manuscript. The poet has surrounded the supernatural plot (or plots) with a rich context of realistic narrative and description. This background comes from the Scandinavian and other West Germanic tribal kingdoms of the fifth and sixth centuries A.D. At least one event in the narrative is corroborated historically: the expedition of Higlac, king of the Geats, against a Frankish tribal kingdom (see the footnote at line 1214), which occurred in the year 521 or shortly thereafter. According to the poem, Beowulf, Higlac's nephew and thane, accompanied his king in this campaign; after Higlac was killed, Beowulf returned to Geatland.

Many, perhaps most, of the figures we find in the allusions, brief narratives, or longer "digressions" in *Beowulf* can be found also in the West Germanic heroic tradition, especially the Scandinavian. But since neither history, myth, nor legend tells us anything about a hero named Beowulf, he is likely a fictional creation of the poet. What sort of person was this anonymous poet? What was his (or perhaps her) purpose and intention in composing the poem? A number of inferences can be made from the poem itself—although it is undated and undatable. (Most scholars would probably place it between the mid-eighth and mid-tenth centuries.) For one thing, the poet is thoroughly familiar with the pattern and style of the (secular) short narrative poem as a genre in favor virtually everywhere in the West Germanic nations—and found in the poems of the Norse *Elder Edda*, the German *Hildebrandslied*, the Old English *Battle of Brunanburh* and *The Fight at Finnsburg*, to name only a few. Although these poems are never more than a few hundred lines in length, in contrast to the "epic" length of *Beowulf*, fundamentally—if one considers the treatment of any single incident—*Beowulf* employs the same style. As a result, the poem presents us with an enhancement of a traditional form of poetic composition, though the scope is wider, individual scenes are more detailed, and there is a greater range of mood and feeling. There are also clear indications of the poet's fondness for traditional verse forms and themes. Surely no poem of comparable stature is more richly allusive. Incident after incident reminds the author of another story—either through similarity or striking contrast. And the several banquets described in *Beowulf* provide further occasions for the recital of tales of heroism, conflict, and disaster.

The poem's religious stance—its view of good and evil in human life—is more problematic. The poet was a devout Christian; this is clear from the strong condemnation of the Danes' resorting to heathen gods in the face of Grendel's attacks. But of course the Scandinavians of the sixth century were still pagan, as were most of the German nations as well. With this in mind the poet is careful not to impute an unhistorical Christianity to them. On the other hand, it would be distasteful for a Christian at that time to depict or celebrate the Germanic gods and goddesses in the manner of the poems of the *Elder Edda*. Hence the *Beowulf* poet appears to offer a tacit compromise. Belief in a single, all-powerful God, just and benevolent, is attributed to "good" characters, chiefly Hrothgar and Beowulf; but there is no treatment of Christian theology or saints' legends. As for a warrior's conduct, the poet fits his hero generally into the pre-Christian ethical code. A principal aspect of this code is the manner in which a man (or woman, doubtless—the evidence is not abundant) speaks about him- or herself. Like Odysseus and other Homeric characters, the traditional Germanic hero was not reticent about abilities and accomplishments. This was approved in a society in which repute and social esteem were of paramount importance.

Beowulf seems to share this attitude wholeheartedly. To be sure, his claim to a record of giant killing, made in his first speech to Hrothgar at the Danish court, may strike us as natural enough for a visiting foreigner. He is presenting his credentials as a champion worthy to face Grendel. Later at the same banquet, Unferth taunts Beowulf in a speech of twenty-three lines: Brecca, another Geat, had bested Beowulf in a foolish swimming contest on the high seas, and Grendel is likely to have the upper hand if Beowulf dares challenge him. The poet here gives his hero a chance to defend himself, which he exploits in some seventy-odd lines: Beowulf and Brecca were not contestants but friends sharing a youthful adventure; Brecca could never outswim his friend, and Beowulf had no wish to desert Brecca; but they were driven apart by the wild sea, after which Beowulf slew some nine water monsters before returning home. In the latter part of his speech Beowulf makes a counterattack against Unferth: not only can he claim no such feats as Beowulf; he is actually guilty of murdering his brothers; and if he were really as great a warrior as he thinks he is, Grendel would have been disposed of long ago. Now the Geatish company will deal with him this night. (The episode occupies lines 499–610.) The taunt is a motif found elsewhere in heroic tradition; the refutation by the hero is an obvious means of enhancing his reputation. When the travel-weary Odysseus declines an offer to participate in the games and contests of the Phaeacians, someone insults him and implies that he is no gentleman-athlete but a lower class of person altogether. Of course, Odysseus promptly refutes the accusation in both deed and word (see the note at line 499).

The desire for fame is no less a feature of Beowulf's character in old age. When death is imminent, he directs his kinsman Wiglaf to have the Geats build a memorial mound on the spit of land nearby; it will serve as his tomb and will be called Beowulf's Barrow ("tower" in our translation) (lines 2801–8). This attitude, if we understand it fully, may clear up some circumstances surrounding Beowulf's fight with the dragon. In his last speech to his companions he says:

> Wait for me close by, my friends.
> . . . No one else could do
> What I mean to, here, no man but me
> Could hope to defeat this monster. No one
> Could try. And this dragon's treasure, his gold
> And everything hidden in that tower, will be mine
> Or war will sweep me to a bitter death!
> (2529, 2532–37)

The old hero does not ask his small band to help him kill the dragon; he expects to do the whole job himself, just as he did with Grendel and Grendel's mother. Indeed, he claims a proprietary interest in the combat. The band of Geats—like those long ago in Heorot when he awaited Grendel—are there primarily as witnesses. To be sure, it is their duty to come to the aid of their king if the need should arise, and Wiglaf rightly rebukes them for failing to do so; but this does not affect Beowulf's anticipation.

The obligation to take revenge, important in Germanic tradition, is another aspect of this concern for personal reputation. Regarded after the conversion to Christianity as a form of "wild justice," revenge could not be suppressed entirely; in some areas it was expressly integrated into the legal system. It is wholeheartedly endorsed by Beowulf as he comforts King Hrothgar, whose friend and counselor Esher has been slain by Grendel's mother:

> Let your sorrow end! It is better for us all
> To avenge our friends, not mourn them forever.
> Each of us will come to the end of this life
> On earth; he who can earn it should fight
> For the glory of his name; fame after death
> Is the noblest of goals.
> (1384–89)

Beowulf's killing of Dagref, the slayer of Higlac during the expedition against the Franks, is also considered revenge, since Higlac was Beowulf's king and kinsman.

Also relevant here is the gift giving that is a conspicuous feature of the world depicted in the poem; we often hear of arm rings, neck rings, swords, coats of mail, etc., either offered or received. A gift was important both for its intrinsic value and as a token of esteem; it conferred status on the recipient.

Another feature of the poem's many-sided portrayal of life in the old Germanic world is the role of women in the narrative. As queens, they preside at banquets alongside their royal husbands and participate in the exchange of gifts referred to above. They may also influence the control of the nation in various ways. Welthow, wife of King Hrothgar, is the central figure among the Danes in Herot at the dinner celebrating Beowulf's triumph over Grendel. In two speeches, "wearing her bright crown," she offers toasts, first to the king and then to Beowulf, to whom she presents noble gifts. But she goes beyond that, taking advantage of this ceremonial occasion to enlist Beowulf's support and protection for her young sons, Hrethric and Hrothmund. A skilful diplomat, she says that she is sure of the good will of Hrothulf, their uncle—but it is clear from the repetitions in her speeches that her actual feeling is one of anxiety and apprehension. (This anxiety is apparently well based; tradition implies that Hrothulf later usurped the crown.) When Beowulf returns from his expedition at the Danish court, he finds Queen Higd, the wife of King Higlac, likewise serving ale to the Geats. Years later, when Higlac has been killed, Higd offers the kingship to Beowulf, believing her young son not yet strong enough for the responsibility. What is notable about this is that Higd is evidently in a position to offer the crown to anyone. (Beowulf declines the offer but promises to help and protect the young prince.)

These events take place within the direct narrative of the poem, but women are prominent also in the incorporated tales. Thus in the story of Hnaf, the Dane, and Finn, the Frisian, a Danish princess, the sister of Hnaf (her name is not given in the translation, but it is Hildeburh in the Old English text), has been married to Finn in the hope of ending strife between the two nations. But the effort comes to naught some years later and, in the renewed conflict both Finn and Hnaf, as well as a young son of the queen, are killed. The anguish of her desolation is vividly described in the account of the funeral pyre. The similar tale of Ingeld (a Heatho-Bard prince), and Freaw, daughter of Hrothgar, the Danish king, is ingeniously put in the form of a prediction or prophecy: the intended match is news that Beowulf brings back to Geatland from the Danish court. But the probability, Beowulf suggests, is that the reconciliation will be short-lived indeed; and he shows just how strife may be renewed at the wedding itself. (The chronology that the poet was following probably accounts for his presenting the story as a future rather than a past event.) Then there is the description of Thrith, the shrew, who may represent a traditional character type. Finally, there is the "gnarled old woman," not named, who mourns at Beowulf's funeral and utters a prophecy of evils to descend upon the nation. She is also a traditional figure; seeresses, women endowed with foreknowledge, are a feature of early Germanic (and Celtic) culture.

The two parts of the poem differ significantly in mood and tone. The first is filled with strange and powerful creatures and the equally mysterious landscape they occupy. There is danger and terror but also enthusiasm, confidence, and victory after great struggle—followed by banquets, praise of the hero, and gift giving. The hero is young, though not in his earliest youth, and the overall outlook is optimistic. The second part presents a marked contrast. The now aged Beowulf is perplexed; he does not understand why his people have been afflicted by the dragon. Nevertheless, he feels it his duty to combat the monster; indeed, he hopes to win new glory and new treasure. But the poet—and hence the reader—know from the outset that Beowulf will not survive the battle. The tension thus created is sustained throughout the narrative, or until the hero's death, not far from the end of the poem. Instead of banquets and revelry, we have solitude and mourning for departed happiness. This is the mood of the last survivor of a once flourishing family when he commits the treasure (later discovered by the dragon) to the earth. And an even more bitter anguish is expressed in the verses in which Beowulf himself describes the grief of a man whose son has been hanged for an offense against a king. (The first passage is at line 2247, the second at 2444.) The poet here adopts the mood and diction found in independent elegiac poems.

Starting from a pair of folk-tale plots the *Beowulf* poet thus presents us with something altogether different, whatever one chooses to call it. Enlarging the typical pattern of folk tales, he makes the monsters into creatures whom the reader must understand in human terms. More important, he convinces the reader that these monsters have brought about a crisis in the life of the nations that they attack and threaten. He then relates how diverse individuals and groups respond to this danger; and he further extends the poem's scope through the incorporated short narratives. One of the poet's central interests is the portrayal of the good ruler (his examples include Hrothgar and various kings of earlier generations) in contrast to the bad ruler; the negative example (Hermod) is a favorite target. But there is no doubt that Beowulf himself is the poet's exemplary creation: the good man who also becomes a good king. As a young Geat, he comes to the Danish court to deal with Grendel; this is an act of benevolence (as well as pursuit of fame). He avenges his king, Higlac, whom he had always faithfully served. He declines Queen Higd's offer of the kingship but protects and supports her young son, the natural heir to the throne. At the end of his life he fights the dragon—once again both to save the nation from disaster and to enhance his fame. And in the closing verses of the poem, his people say that, of all kings in the world, he was the kindest to his people, the mildest, and the most eager to be worthy of praise.

It has become widely known that Alcuin, an eighth-century bishop of York, in England, rebuked the monks in some contemporary monasteries for listening to Germanic legends of the kind we have observed in *Beowulf*. Alcuin asked, "What has Ingeld to do with Christ?" Whether or not *Beowulf* can be seen as one poet's answer to Alcuin's rhetorical question, it is, at any rate, the portrait of a man who can live energetically according to the mores of a preconversion Germanic society and also practice the ethical teachings of Christianity in the conduct of his life.

The translator has produced a bright, vivid, and exciting poem in Modern English. His rendering occupies the same number of lines as the Old English original (3182), an extraordinary feat, indeed. This is not a literal translation, but we believe it is always faithful to the spirit of the original. The abundant alliteration reflects the more regular and systematic—though flexible—pattern of the Old English.

E. B. Irving, Jr., *Introduction to Beowulf* (1969) remains the best single study for readers coming to the poem for the first time. One of the most recent surveys of the backgrounds of the poem is Fred C. Robinson, "History, Religion, Culture," in Jess B. Bessinger, Jr., and Robert F. Yeager, *Approaches to Teaching Beowulf* (1984). A wide range of views will be found in Donald K. Fry, ed., *The Beowulf Poet: A Collection of Critical Essays* (1968) and in Lewis E. Nicholson, ed., *An Anthology of Beowulf Criticism* (1963). John C. Gardner offers an interesting novelistic treatment in *Grendel* (1971).

Beowulf[1]

Prologue

Hear me! We've heard of Danish heroes,
Ancient kings and the glory they cut
For themselves, swinging mighty swords!
How Shild[2] made slaves of soldiers from every
Land, crowds of captives he'd beaten   5
Into terror; he'd traveled to Denmark alone,
An abandoned child, but changed his own fate,
Lived to be rich and much honored. He ruled
Lands on all sides: wherever the sea
Would take them his soldiers sailed, returned   10
With tribute and obedience. There was a brave
King! And he gave them more than his glory,
Conceived a son for the Danes, a new leader
Allowed them by the grace of God. They had lived,
Before his coming, kingless and miserable;   15
Now the Lord of all life, Ruler
Of glory, blessed them with a prince, Beo,
Whose power and fame soon spread through the world.
Shild's strong son was the glory of Denmark;
His father's warriors were wound round his heart   20
With golden rings, bound to their prince
By his father's treasure. So young men build
The future, wisely open-handed in peace,
Protected in war; so warriors earn
Their fame, and wealth is shaped with a sword,   25
    When his time was come the old king died,
Still strong but called to the Lord's hands.
His comrades carried him down to the shore,
Bore him as their leader had asked, their lord
And companion, while words could move on his tongue.   30
Shild's reign had been long; he'd ruled them well.
There in the harbor was a ring-prowed fighting
Ship,[3] its timbers icy, waiting,
And there they brought the belovèd body
Of their ring-giving lord, and laid him near   35
The mast. Next to that noble corpse
They heaped up treasures, jeweled helmets,
Hooked swords and coats of mail, armor
Carried from the ends of the earth: no ship
Had ever sailed so brightly fitted,   40

1. Translated by Burton Raffel.   2. A mythological Danish king, Beo's father, Healfdane's grandfather, and Hrothgar's great grandfather.   3. For a description of the objects found in the excavation of a ship-burial in 1939 in England, see L. S. Bruce-Mitford, *The Sutton Ho Ship-Burial: A Provisional Guide* (1956) and later publications of the same author.

No king sent forth more deeply mourned.
Forced to set him adrift, floating
As far as the tide might run, they refused
To give him less from their hoards of gold
Than those who'd shipped him away, an orphan   45
And a beggar, to cross the waves alone.
High up over his head they flew
His shining banner, then sadly let
The water pull at the ship, watched it
Slowly sliding to where neither rulers   50
Nor heroes nor anyone can say whose hands
Opened to take that motionless cargo.

1

Then Beo was king in that Danish castle,
Shild's son ruling as long as his father
And as loved, a famous lord of men.   55
And he in turn gave his people a son,
The great Healfdane, a fierce fighter
Who led the Danes to the end of his long
Life and left them four children,
Three princes to guide them in battle, Hergar   60
And Hrothgar and Halga the Good, and one daughter,
Yrs, who was given to Onela, king
Of the Swedes, and became his wife and their queen.
    Then Hrothgar, taking the throne, led
The Danes to such glory that comrades and kinsmen   65
Swore by his sword, and young men swelled
His armies, and he thought of greatness and resolved
To build a hall that would hold his mighty
Band and reach higher toward Heaven than anything
That had ever been known to the sons of men.   70
And in that hall he'd divide the spoils
Of their victories, to old and young what they'd earned
In battle, but leaving the common pastures
Untouched, and taking no lives. The work
Was ordered, the timbers tied and shaped   75
By the hosts that Hrothgar ruled. It was quickly
Ready, that most beautiful of dwellings, built
As he'd wanted, and then he whose word was obeyed
All over the earth named it Herot.
His boast come true he commanded a banquet,   80
Opened out his treasure-full hands.
That towering place, gabled and huge,
Stood waiting for time to pass, for war
To begin, for flames to leap as high

As the feud that would light them, and for Herot to burn.   85
   A powerful monster, living down
In the darkness, growled in pain, impatient
As day after day the music rang
Loud in that hall, the harp's rejoicing
Call and the poet's clear songs, sung   90
Of the ancient beginnings of us all, recalling
The Almighty making the earth, shaping
These beautiful plains marked off by oceans,
Then proudly setting the sun and moon
To glow across the land and light it;   95
The corners of the earth were made lovely with trees
And leaves, made quick with life, with each
Of the nations who now move on its face. And then
As now warriors sang of their pleasure:
So Hrothgar's men lived happy in his hall   100
Till the monster stirred, that demon, that fiend,
Grendel, who haunted the moors, the wild
Marshes, and made his home in a hell
Not hell but earth. He was spawned in that slime,
Conceived by a pair of those monsters born   105
Of Cain, murderous creatures banished
By God, punished forever for the crime
Of Abel's death.[4] The Almighty drove
Those demons out, and their exile was bitter,
Shut away from men; they split   110
Into a thousand forms of evil—spirits
And fiends, goblins, monsters, giants,
A brood forever opposing the Lord's
Will, and again and again defeated.

2

   Then, when darkness had dropped, Grendel   115
Went up to Herot, wondering what the warriors
Would do in that hall when their drinking was done.
He found them sprawled in sleep, suspecting
Nothing, their dreams undisturbed. The monster's
Thoughts were as quick as his greed or his claws: 120
He slipped through the door and there in the silence
Snatched up thirty men, smashed them
Unknowing in their beds and ran out with their bodies,
The blood dripping behind him, back
To his lair, delighted with his night's slaughter.   125
   At daybreak, with the sun's first light, they saw

4. Genesis 4. In some post-biblical traditions, Cain was regarded as the ancestor of monsters and evil spirits of various kinds.

How well he had worked, and in that gray morning
Broke their long feast with tears and laments
For the dead. Hrothgar, their lord, sat joyless
In Herot, a mighty prince mourning   130
The fate of his lost friends and companions,
Knowing by its tracks that some demon had torn
His followers apart. He wept, fearing
The beginning might not be the end. And that night
Grendel came again, so set   135
On murder that no crime could ever be enough,
No savage assault quench his lust
For evil. Then each warrior tried
To escape him, searched for rest in different
Beds, as far from Herot as they could find,   140
Seeing how Grendel hunted when they slept.
Distance was safety; the only survivors
Were those who fled him. Hate had triumphed.

    So Grendel ruled, fought with the righteous,
One against many, and won; so Herot   145
Stood empty, and stayed deserted for years,
Twelve winters of grief for Hrothgar, king
Of the Danes, sorrow heaped at his door
By hell-forged hands. His misery leaped
The seas, was told and sung in all   150
Men's ears: how Grendel's hatred began,
How the monster relished his savage war
On the Danes, keeping the bloody feud
Alive, seeking no peace, offering
No truce, accepting no settlement, no price   155
In gold or land, and paying the living
For one crime only with another. No one
Waited for reparation from his plundering claws:
That shadow of death hunted in the darkness,
Stalked Hrothgar's warriors, old   160
And young, lying in waiting, hidden
In mist, invisibly following them from the edge
Of the marsh, always there, unseen.

    So mankind's enemy continued his crimes,
Killing as often as he could, coming   165
Alone, bloodthirsty and horrible. Though he lived
In Herot, when the night hid him, he never
Dared to touch king Hrothgar's glorious
Throne, protected by God—God,
Whose love Grendel could not know. But Hrothgar's   170
Heart was bent. The best and most noble
Of his council debated remedies, sat
In secret sessions, talking of terror

And wondering what the bravest of warriors could do.
And sometimes they sacrificed to the old stone gods,   175
Made heathen vows, hoping for Hell's
Support, the Devil's guidance in driving
Their affliction off.[5] That was their way,
And the heathen's only hope, Hell
Always in their hearts, knowing neither God   180
Nor His passing as He walks through our world, the Lord
Of Heaven and earth; their ears could not hear
His praise nor know His glory. Let them
Beware, those who are thrust into danger,
Clutched at by trouble, yet can carry no solace   185
In their hearts, cannot hope to be better! Hail
To those who will rise to God, drop off
Their dead bodies and seek our Father's peace!

3

    So the living sorrow of Healfdane's son
Simmered, bitter and fresh, and no wisdom   190
Or strength could break it: that agony hung
On king and people alike, harsh
And unending, violent and cruel, and evil.
    In his far-off home Beowulf, Higlac's[6]
Follower and the strongest of the Geats—greater   195
And stronger than anyone anywhere in this world—
Heard how Grendel filled nights with horror
And quickly commanded a boat fitted out,
Proclaiming that he'd go to that famous king,
Would sail across the sea to Hrothgar,   200
Now when help was needed. None
Of the wise ones regretted his going, much
As he was loved by the Geats: the omens were good,
And they urged the adventure on. So Beowulf
Chose the mightiest men he could find,   205
The bravest and best of the Geats, fourteen
In all, and led them down to their boat;
He knew the sea, would point the prow
Straight to that distant Danish shore.
    Then they sailed, set their ship   210
Out on the waves, under the cliffs.
Ready for what came they wound through the currents,
The seas beating at the sand, and were borne
In the lap of their shining ship, lined

---

5. As Christianity was regarded as the only true and valid religion, all other religions and gods were ultimately traceable to the enemy of God, the Devil.   6. King of the Geats, a people of southern Sweden. Higlac is both Beowulf's feudal lord and his uncle.

With gleaming armor, going safely   215
In that oak-hard boat to where their hearts took them.
The wind hurried them over the waves,
The ship foamed through the sea like a bird
Until, in the time they had known it would take,
Standing in the round-curled prow they could see   220
Sparkling hills, high and green,
Jutting up over the shore, and rejoicing
In those rock-steep cliffs they quietly ended
Their voyage. Jumping to the ground, the Geats
Pushed their boat to the sand and tied it   225
In place, mail shirts and armor rattling
As they swiftly moored their ship. And then
They gave thanks to God for their easy crossing.
    High on a wall a Danish watcher
Patrolling along the cliffs saw   230
The travelers crossing to the shore, their shields
Raised and shining; he came riding down,
Hrothgar's lieutenant, spurring his horse,
Needing to know why they'd landed, these men
In armor. Shaking his heavy spear   235
In their faces he spoke:
                        "Whose soldiers are you,
You who've been carried in your deep-keeled ship
Across the sea-road to this country of mine?
Listen! I've stood on these cliffs longer   240
Than you know, keeping our coast free
Of pirates, raiders sneaking ashore
From their ships, seeking our lives and our gold.
None have ever come more openly—
And yet you've offered no password, no sign   245
From my prince, no permission from my people for your landing
Here. Nor have I ever seen,
Out of all the men on earth, one greater
Than has come with you; no commoner carries
Such weapons, unless his appearance, and his beauty,   250
Are both lies. You! Tell me your name,
And your father's; no spies go further onto Danish
Soil than you've come already. Strangers,
From wherever it was you sailed, tell it,
And tell it quickly, the quicker the better,   255
I say, for us all. Speak, say
Exactly who you are, and from where, and why."

4

Their leader answered him, Beowulf unlocking
Words from deep in his breast:
                              "We are Geats,   260
Men who follow Higlac. My father
Was a famous soldier, known far and wide
As a leader of men. His name was Edgetho.
His life lasted many winters;
Wise men all over the earth surely   265
Remember him still. And we have come seeking
Your prince, Healfdane's son, protector
Of this people, only in friendship: instruct us,
Watchman, help us with your words! Our errand
Is a great one, our business with the glorious king   270
Of the Danes no secret; there's nothing dark
Or hidden in our coming. You know (if we've heard
The truth, and been told honestly) that your country
Is cursed with some strange, vicious creature
That hunts only at night and that no one   275
Has seen. It's said, watchman, that he has slaughtered
Your people, brought terror to the darkness. Perhaps
Hrothgar can hunt, here in my heart,
For some way to drive this devil out—
If anything will ever end the evils   280
Afflicting your wise and famous lord.
Here he can cool his burning sorrow.
Or else he may see his suffering go on
Forever, for as long as Herot towers
High on your hills."   285
                    The mounted officer
Answered him bluntly, the brave watchman:
    "A soldier should know the difference between words
And deeds, and keep that knowledge clear
In his brain. I believe your words, I trust in   290
Your friendship. Go forward, weapons and armor
And all, on into Denmark. I'll guide you
Myself—and my men will guard your ship,
Keep it safe here on our shores,
Your fresh-tarred boat, watch it well,   295
Until that curving prow carries
Across the sea to Geatland a chosen
Warrior who bravely does battle with the creature
Haunting our people, who survives that horror
Unhurt, and goes home bearing our love."   300
    Then they moved on. Their boat lay moored,

Tied tight to its anchor. Glittering at the top
Of their golden helmets wild boar heads gleamed,
Shining decorations, swinging as they marched,
Erect like guards, like sentinels, as though ready   305
To fight. They marched, Beowulf and his men
And their guide, until they could see the gables
Of Herot, covered with hammered gold
And glowing in the sun—that most famous of all dwellings,
Towering majestic, its glittering roofs   310
Visible far across the land.
Their guide reined in his horse, pointing
To that hall, built by Hrothgar for the best
And bravest of his men; the path was plain,
They could see their way. And then he spoke: 315
    "Now I must leave you; may the Lord our God
Protect your coming and going! The sea
Is my job, keeping these coasts free
Of invaders, bands of pirates: I must go back."

5

    The path he'd shown them was paved, cobbled   320
Like a Roman road. They arrived with their mail shirts
Glittering, silver-shining links
Clanking an iron song as they came.
Sea-weary still, they set their broad,
Battle-hardened shields in rows   325
Along the wall, then stretched themselves
On Herot's benches. Their armor rang;
Their ash-wood spears stood in a line,
Gray-tipped and straight: the Geats' war-gear
Were honored weapons.   330
                        A Danish warrior
Asked who they were, their names and their fathers':
    "Where have you carried these gold-carved shields from,
These silvery shirts and helmets, and those spears
Set out in long lines? I am Hrothgar's   335
Herald and captain. Strangers have come here
Before, but never so freely, so bold.
And you come too proudly to be exiles: not poverty
But your hearts' high courage has brought you to Hrothgar."
    He was answered by a famous soldier, the Geats'   340
Proud prince:
                "We follow Higlac, break bread
At his side. I am Beowulf. My errand
Is for Healfdane's great son to hear, your glorious

Lord; if he chooses to receive us we will greet him,   345
Salute the chief of the Danes and speak out
Our message."
         Wulfgar replied—a prince
Born to the Swedes, famous for both strength
And wisdom: 350
         "Our warmhearted lord will be told
Of your coming; I shall tell our king, our giver
Of bright rings, and hurry back with his word,
And speak it here, however he answers
Your request."   355
         He went quickly to where Hrothgar sat,
Gray and old, in the middle of his men,
And knowing the custom of that court walked straight
To the king's great chair, stood waiting to be heard,
Then spoke: 360
         "There are Geats who have come sailing the open
Ocean to our land, come far over
The high waves, led by a warrior
Called Beowulf. They wait on your word, bring messages
For your ears alone. My lord, grant them   365
A gracious answer, see them and hear
What they've come for! Their weapons and armor are nobly
Worked—these men are no beggars. And Beowulf
Their prince, who showed them the way to our shores,
Is a mighty warrior, powerful and wise."   370

6

     The Danes' high prince and protector answered:
     "I knew Beowulf as a boy. His father
Was Edgetho, who was given Hrethel's one daughter
—Hrethel, Higlac's father. Now Edgetho's
Brave son is here, come visiting a friendly   375
King. And I've heard that when seamen came,
Bringing their gifts and presents to the Geats,
They wrestled and ran together, and Higlac's
Young prince showed them a mighty battle-grip,
Hands that moved with thirty men's strength,   380
And courage to match. Our Holy Father
Has sent him as a sign of His grace, a mark
Of His favor, to help us defeat Grendel
And end that terror. I shall greet him with treasures,
Gifts to reward his courage in coming to us.   385
Quickly, order them all to come to me
Together, Beowulf and his band of Geats.
And tell them, too, how welcome we will make them!"

Then Wulfgar went to the door and addressed
The waiting seafarers with soldier's words: 390
    "My lord, the great king of the Danes, commands me
To tell you that he knows of your noble birth
And that having come to him from over the open
Sea you have come bravely and are welcome.
Now go to him as you are, in your armor and helmets,   395
But leave your battle-shields here, and your spears,
Let them lie waiting for the promises your words
May make."
                    Beowulf arose, with his men
Around him, ordering a few to remain   400
With their weapons, leading the others quickly
Along under Herot's steep roof into Hrothgar's
Presence. Standing on that prince's own hearth,
Helmeted, the silvery metal of his mail shirt
Gleaming with a smith's high art, he greeted   405
The Danes' great lord:
                    "Hail, Hrothgar!
Higlac is my cousin and my king; the days
Of my youth have been filled with glory. Now Grendel's
Name has echoed in our land: sailors   410
Have brought us stories of Herot, the best
Of all mead-halls, deserted and useless when the moon
Hangs in skies the sun had lit,
Light and life fleeing together.
My people have said, the wisest, most knowing   415
And best of them, that my duty was to go to the Danes'
Great king. They have seen my strength for themselves,
Have watched me rise from the darkness of war,
Dripping with my enemies' blood. I drove
Five great giants into chains, chased   420
All of that race from the earth. I swam
In the blackness of night, hunting monsters
Out of the ocean, and killing them one
By one; death was my errand and the fate
They had earned. Now Grendel and I are called   425
Together, and I've come. Grant me, then,
Lord and protector of this noble place,
A single request! I have come so far,
Oh shelterer of warriors and your people's loved friend,
That this one favor you should not refuse me—   430
That I, alone and with the help of my men,
May purge all evil from this hall. I have heard,
Too, that the monster's scorn of men
Is so great that he needs no weapons and fears none.
Nor will I. My lord Higlac   435

Might think less of me if I let my sword
Go where my feet were afraid to, if I hid
Behind some broad linden shield: my hands
Alone shall fight for me, struggle for life
Against the monster. God must decide   440
Who will be given to death's cold grip.
Grendel's plan, I think, will be
What it has been before, to invade this hall
And gorge his belly with our bodies. If he can,
If he can. And I think, if my time will have come,   445
There'll be nothing to mourn over, no corpse to prepare
For its grave: Grendel will carry our bloody
Flesh to the moors, crunch on our bones
And smear torn scraps of our skin on the walls
Of his den. No, I expect no Danes   450
Will fret about sewing our shrouds, if he wins.
And if death does take me, send the hammered
Mail of my armor to Higlac, return
The inheritance I had from Hrethel, and he
From Wayland.[7] Fate will unwind as it must!"   455

                            7

   Hrothgar replied, protector of the Danes:
   "Beowulf, you've come to us in friendship, and because
Of the reception your father found at our court.
Edgetho had begun a bitter feud,
Killing Hathlaf, a Wulfing warrior: 460
Your father's countrymen were afraid of war,
If he returned to his home, and they turned him away.
Then he traveled across the curving waves
To the land of the Danes. I was new to the throne,
Then, a young man ruling this wide   465
Kingdom and its golden city: Hergar,
My older brother, a far better man
Than I, had died and dying made me,
Second among Healfdane's sons, first
In this nation. I bought the end of Edgetho's   470
Quarrel, sent ancient treasures through the ocean's
Furrows to the Wulfings; your father swore
He'd keep that peace. My tongue grows heavy,
And my heart, when I try to tell you what Grendel
Has brought us, the damage he's done, here   475
In this hall. You see for yourself how much smaller
Our ranks have become, and can guess what we've lost

---

7. Or *Weland*: a mythological blacksmith, known for his gifted hammer and wonderful workmanship.

To his terror. Surely the Lord Almighty
Could stop his madness, smother his lust!
How many times have my men, glowing   480
With courage drawn from too many cups
Of ale, sworn to stay after dark
And stem that horror with a sweep of their swords.
And then, in the morning, this mead-hall glittering
With new light would be drenched with blood, the benches   485
Stained red, the floors, all wet from that fiend's
Savage assault—and my soldiers would be fewer
Still, death taking more and more.
But to table, Beowulf, a banquet in your honor:
Let us toast your victories, and talk of the future."   490
    Then Hrothgar's men gave places to the Geats,
Yielded benches to the brave visitors
And led them to the feast. The keeper of the mead
Came carrying out the carved flasks,
And poured that bright sweetness. A poet   495
Sang, from time to time, in a clear
Pure voice. Danes and visiting Geats
Celebrated as one, drank and rejoiced.

8

Unferth[8] spoke, Ecglaf's son,
Who sat at Hrothgar's feet, spoke harshly   500
And sharp (vexed by Beowulf's adventure,
By their visitor's courage, and angry that anyone
In Denmark or anywhere on earth had ever
Acquired glory and fame greater
Than his own):   505
          "You're Beowulf, are you—the same
Boastful fool who fought a swimming
Match with Brecca,[9] both of you daring
And young and proud, exploring the deepest
Seas, risking your lives for no reason   510
But the danger? All older and wiser heads warned you
Not to, but no one could check such pride.
With Brecca at your side you swam along
The sea-paths, your swift-moving hands pulling you
Over the ocean's face. Then winter   515
Churned through the water, the waves ran you
As they willed, and you struggled seven long nights
To survive. And at the end victory was his,
Not yours. The sea carried him close

8. One of Hrothgar's courtiers, skillful with words.   9. A contemporary and young companion of Beowulf.

To his home, to southern Norway, near 520
The land of the Brondings, where he ruled and was loved,
Where his treasure was piled and his strength protected
His towns and his people. He'd promised to outswim you:
Bonstan's son made that boast ring true.
You've been lucky in your battles, Beowulf, but I think 525
Your luck may change if you challenge Grendel,
Staying a whole night through in this hall,
Waiting where that fiercest of demons can find you."
    Beowulf answered, Edgetho's great son:
    "Ah! Unferth, my friend, your face 530
Is hot with ale, and your tongue has tried
To tell us about Brecca's doings. But the truth
Is simple: no man swims in the sea
As I can, no strength is a match for mine.
As boys, Brecca and I had boasted— 535
We were both too young to know better—that we'd risk
Our lives far out at sea, and so
We did. Each of us carried a naked
Sword, prepared for whales or the swift
Sharp teeth and beaks of needlefish. 540
He could never leave me behind, swim faster
Across the waves than I could, and I
Had chosen to remain close to his side.
I remained near him for five long nights,
Until a flood swept us apart; 545
The frozen sea surged around me,
It grew dark, the wind turned bitter, blowing
From the north, and the waves were savage. Creatures
Who sleep deep in the sea were stirred
Into life—and the iron hammered links 550
Of my mail shirt, these shining bits of metal
Woven across my breast, saved me
From death. A monster seized me, drew me
Swiftly toward the bottom, swimming with its claws
Tight in my flesh. But fate let me 555
Find its heart with my sword, hack myself
Free; I fought that beast's last battle,
Left it floating lifeless in the sea.

9

    "Other monsters crowded around me,
Continually attacking. I treated them politely, 560
Offering the edge of my razor-sharp sword.
But the feast, I think, did not please them, filled
Their evil bellies with no banquet-rich food,

Thrashing there at the bottom of the sea;
By morning they'd decided to sleep on the shore,   565
Lying on their backs, their blood spilled out
On the sand. Afterwards, sailors could cross
That sea-road and feel no fear; nothing
Would stop their passing. Then God's bright beacon
Appeared in the east, the water lay still,   570
And at last I could see the land, wind-swept
Cliff-walls at the edge of the coast. Fate saves
The living when they drive away death by themselves!
Lucky or not, nine was the number
Of sea-huge monsters I killed. What man,   575
Anywhere under Heaven's high arch, has fought
In such darkness, endured more misery or been harder
Pressed? Yet I survived the sea, smashed
The monsters' hot jaws, swam home from my journey.
The swift-flowing waters swept me along   580
And I landed on Finnish soil. I've heard
No tales of you, Unferth, telling
Of such clashing terror, such contests in the night!
Brecca's battles were never so bold;
Neither he nor you can match me—and I mean   585
No boast, have announced no more than I know
To be true. And there's more: you murdered your brothers,
Your own close kin. Words and bright wit
Won't help your soul; you'll suffer hell's fires,
Unferth, forever tormented. Ecglaf's   590
Proud son, if your hands were as hard, your heart
As fierce as you think it, no fool would dare
To raid your hall, ruin Herot
And oppress its prince, as Grendel has done.
But he's learned that terror is his alone,   595
Discovered he can come for your people with no fear
Of reprisal; he's found no fighting, here,
But only food, only delight.
He murders as he likes, with no mercy, gorges
And feasts on your flesh, and expects no trouble,   600
No quarrel from the quiet Danes. Now
The Geats will show him courage, soon
He can test his strength in battle. And when the sun
Comes up again, opening another
Bright day from the south, anyone in Denmark   605
May enter this hall: that evil will be gone!"
    Hrothgar, gray-haired and brave, sat happily
Listening, the famous ring-giver sure,
At last, that Grendel could be killed; he believed
In Beowulf's bold strength and the firmness of his spirit.   610

There was the sound of laughter, and the cheerful clanking
Of cups, and pleasant words. Then Welthow,
Hrothgar's gold-ringed queen, greeted
The warriors; a noble woman who knew
What was right, she raised a flowing cup   615
To Hrothgar first, holding it high
For the lord of the Danes to drink, wishing him
Joy in that feast. The famous king
Drank with pleasure and blessed their banquet.
Then Welthow went from warrior to warrior,   620
Pouring a portion from the jeweled cup
For each, till the bracelet-wearing queen
Had carried the mead-cup among them and it was Beowulf's
Turn to be served. She saluted the Geats'
Great prince, thanked God for answering her prayers,   625
For allowing her hands the happy duty
Of offering mead to a hero who would help
Her afflicted people. He drank what she poured,
Edgetho's brave son, then assured the Danish
Queen that his heart was firm and his hands   630
Ready:
        "When we crossed the sea, my comrades
And I, I already knew that all
My purpose was this: to win the good will
Of your people or die in battle, pressed   635
In Grendel's fierce grip. Let me live in greatness
And courage, or here in this hall welcome
My death!"
        Welthow was pleased with his words,
His bright-tongued boasts; she carried them back   640
To her lord, walked nobly across to his side.
     The feast went on, laughter and music
And the brave words of warriors celebrating
Their delight. Then Hrothgar rose, Healfdane's
Son, heavy with sleep; as soon   645
As the sun had gone, he knew that Grendel
Would come to Herot, would visit that hall
When night had covered the earth with its net
And the shapes of darkness moved black and silent
Through the world. Hrothgar's warriors rose with him.   650
     He went to Beowulf, embraced the Geats'
Brave prince, wished him well, and hoped
That Herot would be his to command. And then
He declared:
        "No one strange to this land   655
Has ever been granted what I've given you,
No one in all the years of my rule.

Make this best of all mead-halls yours, and then
Keep it free of evil, fight
With glory in your heart! Purge Herot   660
And your ship will sail home with its treasure-holds full."

10

Then Hrothgar left that hall, the Danes'
Great protector, followed by his court; the queen
Had preceded him and he went to lie at her side,
Seek sleep near his wife. It was said that God   665
Himself had set a sentinel in Herot,
Brought Beowulf as a guard against Grendel and a shield
Behind whom the king could safely rest.
And Beowulf was ready, firm with our Lord's
High favor and his own bold courage and strength.   670
   He stripped off his mail shirt, his helmet, his sword
Hammered from the hardest iron, and handed
All his weapons and armor to a servant,
Ordered his war-gear guarded till morning.
And then, standing beside his bed,   675
He exclaimed:
               "Grendel is no braver, no stronger
Than I am! I could kill him with my sword; I shall not,
Easy as it would be. This fiend is a bold
And famous fighter, but his claws and teeth   680
Scratching at my shield, his clumsy fists
Beating at my sword blade, would be helpless. I will meet him
With my hands empty—unless his heart
Fails him, seeing a soldier waiting
Weaponless, unafraid. Let God in His wisdom   685
Extend His hand where He wills, reward
Whom He chooses!"
               Then the Geats' great chief dropped
His head to his pillow, and around him, as ready
As they could be, lay the soldiers who had crossed the sea   690
At his side, each of them sure that he was lost
To the home he loved, to the high-walled towns
And the friends he had left behind where both he
And they had been raised. Each thought of the Danes
Murdered by Grendel in a hall where Geats   695
And not Danes now slept. But God's dread loom
Was woven with defeat for the monster, good fortune
For the Geats; help against Grendel was with them,
And through the might of a single man
They would win. Who doubts that God in His wisdom   700
And strength holds the earth forever

In His hands? Out in the darkness the monster
Began to walk. The warriors slept
In that gabled hall where they hoped that He
Would keep them safe from evil, guard them   705
From death till the end of their days was determined
And the thread should be broken. But Beowulf lay wakeful,
Watching, waiting, eager to meet
His enemy, and angry at the thought of his coming.

11

Out from the marsh, from the foot of misty   710
Hills and bogs, bearing God's hatred,
Grendel came, hoping to kill
Anyone he could trap on this trip to high Herot.
He moved quickly through the cloudy night,
Up from his swampland, sliding silently   715
Toward that gold-shining hall. He had visited Hrothgar's
Home before, knew the way—
But never, before nor after that night,
Found Herot defended so firmly, his reception
So harsh. He journeyed, forever joyless,   720
Straight to the door, then snapped it open,
Tore its iron fasteners with a touch
And rushed angrily over the threshold.
He strode quickly across the inlaid
Floor, snarling and fierce: his eyes   725
Gleamed in the darkness, burned with a gruesome
Light. Then he stopped, seeing the hall
Crowded with sleeping warriors, stuffed
With rows of young soldiers resting together.
And his heart laughed, he relished the sight,   730
Intended to tear the life from those bodies
By morning; the monster's mind was hot
With the thought of food and the feasting his belly
Would soon know. But fate, that night, intended
Grendel to gnaw the broken bones   735
Of his last human supper. Human
Eyes were watching his evil steps,
Waiting to see his swift hard claws.
Grendel snatched at the first Geat[1]
He came to, ripped him apart, cut   740
His body to bits with powerful jaws,
Drank the blood from his veins and bolted
Him down, hands and feet; death

---

1. Hondshew. The name is given at line 2076, in Beowulf's report of the entire expedition to Higlac.

And Grendel's great teeth came together,
Snapping life shut. Then he stepped to another   745
Still body, clutched at Beowulf with his claws,
Grasped at a strong-hearted wakeful sleeper
—And was instantly seized himself, claws
Bent back as Beowulf leaned up on one arm.
   That shepherd of evil, guardian of crime,   750
Knew at once that nowhere on earth
Had he met a man whose hands were harder;
His mind was flooded with fear—but nothing
Could take his talons and himself from that tight
Hard grip. Grendel's one thought was to run   755
From Beowulf, flee back to his marsh and hide there:
This was a different Herot than the hall he had emptied.
But Higlac's follower remembered his final
Boast and, standing erect, stopped
The monster's flight, fastened those claws   760
In his fists till they cracked, clutched Grendel
Closer. The infamous killer fought
For his freedom, wanting no flesh but retreat,
Desiring nothing but escape; his claws
Had been caught, he was trapped. That trip to Herot   765
Was a miserable journey for the writhing monster!
   The high hall rang, its roof boards swayed,
And Danes shook with terror. Down
The aisles the battle swept, angry
And wild. Herot trembled, wonderfully   770
Built to withstand the blows, the struggling
Great bodies beating at its beautiful walls;
Shaped and fastened with iron, inside
And out, artfully worked, the building
Stood firm. Its benches rattled, fell   775
To the floor, gold-covered boards grating
As Grendel and Beowulf battled across them.
Hrothgar's wise men had fashioned Herot
To stand forever; only fire,
They had planned, could shatter what such skill had put   780
Together, swallow in hot flames such splendor
Of ivory and iron and wood. Suddenly
The sounds changed, the Danes started
In new terror, cowering in their beds as the terrible
Screams of the Almighty's enemy sang   785
In the darkness, the horrible shrieks of pain
And defeat, the tears torn out of Grendel's
Taut throat, hell's captive caught in the arms
Of him who of all the men on earth
Was the strongest.   790

12

That mighty protector of men
Meant to hold the monster till its life
Leaped out, knowing the fiend was no use
To anyone in Denmark. All of Beowulf's
Band had jumped from their beds, ancestral   795
Swords raised and ready, determined
To protect their prince if they could. Their courage
Was great but all wasted: they could hack at Grendel
From every side, trying to open
A path for his evil soul, but their points   800
Could not hurt him, the sharpest and hardest iron
Could not scratch at his skin, for that sin-stained demon
Had bewitched all men's weapons, laid spells
That blunted every mortal man's blade.
And yet his time had come, his days   805
Were over, his death near; down
To hell he would go, swept groaning and helpless
To the waiting hands of still worse fiends.
Now he discovered—once the afflictor
Of men, tormentor of their days—what it meant   810
To feud with Almighty God: Grendel
Saw that his strength was deserting him, his claws
Bound fast, Higlac's brave follower tearing at
His hands. The monster's hatred rose higher,
But his power had gone. He twisted in pain,   815
And the bleeding sinews deep in his shoulder
Snapped, muscle and bone split
And broke. The battle was over, Beowulf
Had been granted new glory: Grendel escaped,
But wounded as he was could flee to his den,   820
His miserable hole at the bottom of the marsh,
Only to die, to wait for the end
Of all his days. And after that bloody
Combat the Danes laughed with delight.
He who had come to them from across the sea,   825
Bold and strong-minded, had driven affliction
Off, purged Herot clean. He was happy,
Now, with that night's fierce work; the Danes
Had been served as he'd boasted he'd serve them; Beowulf,
A prince of the Geats, had killed Grendel,   830
Ended the grief, the sorrow, the suffering
Forced on Hrothgar's helpless people
By a bloodthirsty fiend. No Dane doubted
The victory, for the proof, hanging high
From the rafters where Beowulf had hung it, was the monster's   835
Arm, claw and shoulder and all.

13

And then, in the morning, crowds surrounded
Herot, warriors coming to that hall
From faraway lands, princes and leaders
Of men hurrying to behold the monster's   840
Great staggering tracks. They gaped with no sense
Of sorrow, felt no regret for his suffering,
Went tracing his bloody footprints, his beaten
And lonely flight, to the edge of the lake
Where he'd dragged his corpselike way, doomed   845
And already weary of his vanishing life.
The water was bloody, steaming and boiling
In horrible pounding waves, heat
Sucked from his magic veins; but the swirling
Surf had covered his death, hidden   850
Deep in murky darkness his miserable
End, as hell opened to receive him.
    Then old and young rejoiced, turned back
From that happy pilgrimage, mounted their hard-hooved
Horses, high-spirited stallions, and rode them   855
Slowly toward Herot again, retelling
Beowulf's bravery as they jogged along.
And over and over they swore that nowhere
On earth or under the spreading sky
Or between the seas, neither south nor north,   860
Was there a warrior worthier to rule over men.
(But no one meant Beowulf's praise to belittle
Hrothgar, their kind and gracious king!)
    And sometimes, when the path ran straight and clear,
They would let their horses race, red   865
And brown and pale yellow backs streaming
Down the road. And sometimes a proud old soldier
Who had heard songs of the ancient heroes
And could sing them all through, story after story,
Would weave a net of words for Beowulf's   870
Victory, tying the knot of his verses
Smoothly, swiftly, into place with a poet's
Quick skill, singing his new song aloud
While he shaped it, and the old songs as well—Siegmund's[2]
Adventures, familiar battles fought   875
By that glorious son of Vels. And struggles,
Too, against evil and treachery that no one
Had ever heard of, that no one knew

---

2. In Germanic tradition, Siegmund was known both as a heroic warrior against human foes and as a dragon slayer. For the former, see the Old Norse *Volsungasaga*, chapters 3–8. In later tradition—for example, the German *Nibelungenlied*—the dragon-slayer is Siegmund's son, Sigurd. V*els*: Siegmund's father. *Fitla*: Son (and nephew) of Siegmund.

Except Fitla, who had fought at his uncle's side,
A brave young comrade carefully listening   880
When Siegmund's tongue unwound the wonders
He had worked, confiding in his closest friend.
There were tales of giants wiped from the earth
By Siegmund's might—and forever remembered,
Fame that would last him beyond life and death,   885
His daring battle with a treasure-rich dragon.
Heaving a hoary gray rock aside
Siegmund had gone down to the dragon alone,
Entered the hole where it hid and swung
His sword so savagely that it slit the creature   890
Through, pierced its flesh and pinned it
To a wall, hung it where his bright blade rested.
His courage and strength had earned him a king-like
Treasure, brought gold and rich rings to his glorious
Hands. He loaded that precious hoard   895
On his ship and sailed off with a shining cargo.
And the dragon dissolved in its own fierce blood.
    No prince, no protector of his warriors, knew power
And fame and glory like Siegmund's; his name
And his treasures grew great. Hermod could have hoped   900
For at least as much; he was once the mightiest
Of men. But pride and defeat and betrayal
Sent him into exile with the Jutes, and he ended
His life on their swords. That life had been misery
After misery, and he spread sorrow as long   905
As he lived it, heaped troubles on his unhappy people's
Heads, ignored all wise men's warnings,
Ruled only with courage. A king
Born, entrusted with ancient treasures
And cities full of stronghearted soldiers,   910
His vanity swelled him so vile and rank
That he could hear no voices but his own. He deserved
To suffer and die. But Beowulf was a prince
Well-loved, followed in friendship, not fear;
Hermod's heart had been hollowed by sin.   915
    The horses ran, when they could, on the gravel
Path. Morning slid past and was gone.
The whole brave company came riding to Herot,
Anxious to celebrate Beowulf's success
And stare at that arm. And Hrothgar rose   920
From beside his wife and came with his courtiers
Crowded around him. And Welthow rose
And joined him, his wife and queen with her women,
All of them walking to that wonderful hall.

14

Hrothgar stood at the top of the stairway   925
And stared at Grendel's great claw, swinging
High from that gold-shining roof. Then he cried:
"Let God be thanked! Grendel's terrible
Anger hung over our heads too long,
Dropping down misery; but the Almighty makes miracles   930
When He pleases, wonder after wonder, and this world
Rests in His hands. I had given up hope,
Exhausted prayer, expected nothing
But misfortune forever. Herot was empty,
Bloody; the wisest and best of our people   935
Despaired as deeply, found hope no easier,
Knew nothing, no way to end this unequal
War of men and devils, warriors
And monstrous fiends. One man found it,
Came to Denmark and with the Lord's help   940
Did what none of the Danes could do,
Our wisdom, our strength, worthless without him.
The woman who bore him, whoever, wherever,
Alive now, or dead, knew the grace of the God
Of our fathers, was granted a son for her glory   945
And His. Beowulf, best of soldiers,
Let me take you to my heart, make you my son too,
And love you: preserve this passionate peace
Between us. And take, in return, whatever
You may want from whatever I own. Warriors   950
Deserving far less have been granted as much,
Given gifts and honored, though they fought
No enemy like yours. Glory is now yours
Forever and ever, your courage has earned it,
And your strength. May God be as good to you forever   955
As He has been to you here!"
                    Then Beowulf answered:
"What we did was what our hearts helped
Our hands to perform; we came to fight
With Grendel, our strength against his. I wish   960
I could show you, here in Herot, his corpse
Stretched on this floor! I twisted my fingers
Around his claw, ripped and tore at it
As hard as I could: I meant to kill him
Right here, hold him so tightly that his heart   965
Would stop, would break, his life spill
On this floor. But God's will was against me,
As hard as I held him he still pulled free
And ran, escaped from this hall with the strength

Fear had given him. But he offered me his arm   970
And his claw, saved his life yet left me
That prize. And paying even so willingly
For his freedom he still fled with nothing
But the end of his evil days, ran
With death pressing at his back, pain   975
Splitting his panicked heart, pulling him
Step by step into hell. Let him burn
In torment, lying and trembling, waiting
For the brightness of God to bring him his reward."
    Unferth grew quiet, gave up quarreling over   980
Beowulf's old battles, stopped all his boasting
Once everyone saw proof of that prince's strength,
Grendel's huge claw swinging high
From Hrothgar's mead-hall roof, the fingers
Of that loathsome hand ending in nails   985
As hard as bright steel—so hard, they all said,
That not even the sharpest of swords could have cut
It through, broken it off the monster's
Arm and ended its life, as Beowulf
Had done armed with only his bare hands.   990

15

    Then the king ordered Herot cleaned
And hung with decorations: hundreds of hands,
Men and women, hurried to make
The great hall ready. Golden tapestries
Were lined along the walls, for a host   995
Of visitors to see and take pleasure in. But that glorious
Building was bent and broken, its iron
Hinges cracked and sprung from their corners
All around the hall. Only
Its roof was undamaged when the blood-stained demon   1000
Burst out of Herot, desperately breaking
Beowulf's grip, running wildly
From what no one escapes, struggle and writhe
As he will. Wanting to stay we go,
All beings here on God's earth, wherever   1005
It is written that we go, taking our bodies
From death's cold bed to the unbroken sleep
That follows life's feast.
                    Then Hrothgar made his way
To the hall; it was time, and his heart drew him   1010
To the banquet. No victory was celebrated better,
By more or by better men and their king.
A mighty host, and famous, they lined

The benches, rejoicing; the king and Hrothulf,
His nephew, toasted each other, raised mead-cups   1015
High under Herot's great roof, their speech
Courteous and warm. King and people
Were one; none of the Danes was plotting,
Then, no treachery hid in their smiles.
    Healfdane's son gave Beowulf a golden   1020
Banner, a fitting flag to signal
His victory, and gave him, as well, a helmet,
And a coat of mail, and an ancient sword;
They were brought to him while the warriors watched. Beowulf
Drank to those presents, not ashamed to be praised,   1025
Richly rewarded in front of them all.
No ring-giver has given four such gifts,
Passed such treasures through his hands, with the grace
And warmth that Hrothgar showed. The helmet's
Brim was wound with bands of metal,   1030
Rounded ridges to protect whoever
Wore it from swords swung in the fiercest
Battles, shining iron edges
In hostile hands. And then the protector
Of warriors, lord of the Danes, ordered   1035
Eight horses led to the hall, and into it,
Eight steeds with golden bridles. One stood
With a jeweled saddle on its back, carved
Like the king's war-seat it was; it had carried
Hrothgar when that great son of Healfdane rode   1040
To war—and each time carried him wherever
The fighting was most fierce, and his followers had fallen.
Then Beowulf had been honored by both the gifts
Hrothgar could have given him, horses and weapons:
The king commanded him to use them well.   1045
Thus that guardian of Denmark's treasures
Had repaid a battle fought for his people
By giving noble gifts, had earned praise
For himself from those who try to know truth.

16

    And more: the lord of Herot ordered   1050
Treasure-gifts for each of the Geats
Who'd sailed with Beowulf and still sat beside him,
Ancient armor and swords—and for the one
Murdered by Grendel gold was carefully
Paid.[3] The monster would have murdered again   1055

3. Known as *wergild*, "payment for a man." When an injury—and consequent obligation—was recognized but personal vengeance was not feasible, it was often used as an alternative.

And again had not God, and the hero's courage,
Turned fate aside. Then and now
Men must lie in their Maker's holy
Hands, moved only as He wills:
Our hearts must seek out that will. The world,   1060
And its long days full of labor, brings good
And evil; all who remain here meet both.

    Hrothgar's hall resounded with the harp's
High call, with songs and laughter and the telling
Of tales, stories sung by the court   1065
Poet as the joyful Danes drank
And listened, seated along their mead-benches.[4]
He told them of Finn's people, attacking
Hnaf with no warning, half wiping out
That Danish tribe, and killing its king.   1070
Finn's wife, Hnaf's sister, learned what good faith
Was worth to her husband: his honeyed words
And treachery cost her two belovèd lives,
Her son and her brother, both falling on spears
Guided by fate's hand. How she wept!   1075
And when morning came she had reason to mourn,
To weep for her dead, her slaughtered son
And the bloody corpse of his uncle—both
The men she most dearly loved, and whose love
She could trust to protect her. But Finn's troops, too   1080
Had fallen to Danish spears: too few
Were left to drive the Danes to their death,
To force Hnaf's follower, Hengest, to flee
The hall where they'd fought and he'd stayed. Finn offered them,
Instead of more war, words of peace: 1085
There would be no victory, they'd divide the hall
And the throne, half to the Danes, half
To Finn's followers. When gifts were given
Finn would give Hengest and his soldiers half,
Share shining rings, silver   1090
And gold, with the Danes, both sides equal,
All of them richer, all of their purses
Heavy, every man's heart warm
With the comfort of gold.
                      Both sides accepted   1095
Peace and agreed to keep it. Finn
Swore it with solemn oaths: what wise men
Had written was his word as well as theirs.

---

4. What follows is the longest and most nearly complete of the stories that the poet has incorporated in
Beowulf. It is a tale of Danish-Frisian conflict with two episodes separated by a truce that lasts through a
winter. (There is a fragmentary Old English poem of 48 lines, dealing with the first part and usually called
The Fight at Finnsburg. Anonymous and of unknown date, it seems to be wholly independent of the
account in *Beowulf*.)

He and the brave Hengest would live
Like brothers; neither leader nor led would break 1100
The truce, would not talk of evil things,
Remind the Danes that the man they served
Killed Hnaf, their lord. They had no king,
And no choice. And he swore that his sword would silence
Wagging tongues if Frisian warriors 1105
Stirred up hatred, brought back the past.
    A funeral pyre was prepared, and gold
Was brought; Hnaf's dead body was dressed
For burning, and the others with him. Bloody
Mail shirts could be seen, and golden helmets, 1110
Some carved with boar-heads, all battle-hard
And as useless, now, as the corpses that still wore them,
Soldier after soldier! Then Hnaf's sister,
Finn's sad wife, gave her son's body
To be burned in that fire; the flames charring 1115
His uncle would consume both kinsmen at once.
Then she wept again, and weeping sang
The dead's last praise. The Danish king
Was lifted into place, smoke went curling
Up, logs roared, open 1120
Wounds split and burst, skulls
Melted, blood came bubbling down,
And the greedy fire-demons drank flesh and bones
From the dead of both sides, until nothing was left.

17

    Finn released a few of his soldiers, 1125
Allowed them to return to their distant towns
And estates. Hengest lived the whole stormy
Winter through, there with Finn
Whom he hated. But his heart lived in Denmark—
Which he and the other survivors could not visit, 1130
Could not sail to, as long as the wind-whipped sea
Crashed and whirled, or while winter's cold hands
Froze the water hard, tied it
In icy knots. They would wait for the new year,
For spring to come following the sun, melting 1135
The old year away and reopening the ocean.
Winter was over, the earth grew lovely,
And Hengest dreamed of his home—but revenge
Came first, settling his bitter feud
With Finn, whose bloody sword he could never 1140
Forget. He planned, he waited, wove plans
And waited. Then a Danish warrior dropped

A sword in his lap, a weapon Finn
And his men remembered and feared, and the time
Had come, and Hengest rose, hearing   1145
The Danes' murmur, and drove his new sword
Into Finn's belly, butchering that king
Under his own roof. And the Danes rose,
Their hearts full of Finn's treachery,
And the misery he'd brought them, their sword arms restless   1150
And eager. The hall they'd shared with their enemies
Ran red with enemy blood and bodies
Rolled on the floor beside Finn. They took
The queen, looted everything they could find
That belonged to her dead husband, loaded   1155
Their ship with rings, necklaces, shining
Jewels wonderfully worked, and sailed
Bringing treasure and a willing captive to the land
She'd left and had longed for, alone no longer.
      The singer finished his song; his listeners   1160
Laughed and drank, their pleasure loud
In that hall. The cup-bearers hurried with their sparkling
Vessels. And then the queen, Welthow, wearing her bright crown,
Appeared among them, came to Hrothgar and Hrothulf, his nephew,
Seated peacefully together, their friendship and Hrothulf's good faith
      still unbroken.   1165
And Unferth sat at Hrothgar's feet; everyone trusted him,
Believed in his courage, although he'd spilled his relatives' blood.
Then Welthow spoke:
                  "Accept this cup,
My lord and king! May happiness come   1170
To the Danes' great ring-giver; may the Geats receive
Mild words from your mouth, words they have earned!
Let gifts flow freely from your open hands,
Treasures your armies have brought you from all over
The world. I have heard that the greatest of the Geats   1175
Now rests in your heart like a son. Herot
Stands purged, restored by his strength: celebrate
His courage, rejoice and be generous while a kingdom
Sits in your palm, a people and power
That death will steal. But your sons will be safe,   1180
Sheltered in Hrothulf's gracious protection,
If fate takes their father while Hrothulf is alive;
I know your nephew's kindness, I know
He'll repay in kind the goodness you have shown him,
Support your two young sons as you   1185
And I sustained him in his own early days,
His father dead and he but a boy."
      Then she walked to the bench where Hrethric and Hrothmund,

Her two sons, sat together; Beowulf,
Prince of the Geats, was seated between them; 1190
Crossing the hall she sat quietly at their side.

18

They brought a foaming cup and offered it
To Beowulf; it was taken and given in friendship.
And he was given a mail shirt, and golden arm-bands,
And the most beautiful necklace known to men: 1195
Nowhere in any treasure-hoard anywhere
On earth was there anything like it, not since
Hama carried the Brosings' necklace
Home to his glorious city, saved
Its tight-carved jewels, and his skin, and his soul 1200
From Ermric's treachery, and then came to God.
Higlac had it next, Swerting's
Grandson; defending the golden hoard
His battle-hard hands had won for him, the Geats'
Proud king lost it, was carried away 1205
By fate when too much pride made him feud
With the Frisians. He had asked for misery; it was granted him.
He'd borne those precious stones on a ship's
Broad back; he fell beneath his shield.
His body, and his shining coat of mail, 1210
And that necklace, all lay for Franks to pluck,
For jackal warriors to find when they walked through
The rows of corpses; Geats, and their king,
Lay slaughtered wherever the robbers looked.[5]
The warriors shouted. And Welthow spoke: 1215
"Wear these bright jewels, belovèd Beowulf;
Enjoy them, and the rings, and the gold, oh fortunate young
Warrior; grow richer, let your fame and your strength
Go hand in hand; and lend these two boys
Your wise and gentle heart! I'll remember your 1220
Kindness. Your glory is too great to forget:
It will last forever, wherever the earth
Is surrounded by the sea, the winds' home,
And waves lap at its walls. Be happy
For as long as you live! Your good fortune warms 1225
My soul. Spread your blessèd protection
Across my son, and my king's son!
All men speak softly, here, speak mildly

---

5. The only narrative in *Beowulf* that is confirmed by reliable history; it is found in the Latin *Historia Francorum* ("History of the Franks"), written around the middle of the sixth century by Gregory, Archbishop of Tours. Other (partial) accounts appear at *Beowulf*, lines 2354–72, lines 2500–08, and lines 2910–21.

And trust their neighbors, protect their lord,
Are loyal followers who would fight as joyfully   1230
As they drink. May your heart help you do as I ask!"
   She returned to her seat. The soldiers ate
And drank like kings. The savage fate
Decreed for them hung dark and unknown, what would follow
After nightfall, when Hrothgar withdrew from the hall,   1235
Sought his bed and left his soldiers
To theirs. Herot would house a host
Of men, that night, as it had been meant to do.
They stacked away the benches, spread out
Blankets and pillows. But those beer-drinking sleepers   1240
Lay down with death beside their beds.
They slept with their shining shields at the edge
Of their pillows; the hall was filled with helmets
Hanging near motionless heads; spears
Stood by their hands, their hammered mail shirts   1245
Covered their chests. It was the Danes' custom
To be ready for war, wherever they rested,
At home or in foreign lands, at their lord's
Quick call if he needed them, if trouble came
To their king. They knew how soldiers must live!   1250

19

   They sank into sleep. The price of that evening's
Rest was too high for the Dane who bought it
With his life, paying as others had paid
When Grendel inhabited Herot, the hall
His till his crimes pulled him into hell.   1255
And now it was known that a monster had died
But a monster still lived, and meant revenge.
She'd brooded on her loss, misery had brewed
In her heart, that female horror, Grendel's
Mother, living in the murky cold lake   1260
Assigned her since Cain had killed his only
Brother, slain his father's son
With an angry sword. God drove him off,
Outlawed him to the dry and barren desert,
And branded him with a murderer's mark. And he bore   1265
A race of fiends accursed like their father;
So Grendel was drawn to Herot, an outcast
Come to meet the man who awaited him.
He'd snatched at Beowulf's arm, but that prince
Remembered God's grace and the strength He'd given him   1270
And relied on the Lord for all the help,
The comfort and support he would need. He killed

The monster, as God had meant him to do,
Tore the fiend apart and forced him
To run as rapidly as he could toward death's   1275
Cold waiting hands. His mother's sad heart,
And her greed, drove her from her den on the dangerous
Pathway of revenge. So she reached Herot,
Where the Danes slept as though already dead;   1280
Her visit ended their good fortune, reversed
The bright vane of their luck. No female, no matter
How fierce, could have come with a man's strength,
Fought with the power and courage men fight with,
Smashing their shining swords, their bloody,   1285
Hammer-forged blades onto boar-headed helmets,
Slashing and stabbing with the sharpest of points.
The soldiers raised their shields and drew
Those gleaming swords, swung them above
The piled-up benches, leaving their mail shirts   1290
And their helmets where they'd lain when the terror took hold of them.
To save her life she moved still faster,
Took a single victim and fled from the hall,
Running to the moors, discovered, but her supper
Assured, sheltered in her dripping claws.   1295
She'd taken Hrothgar's closest friend,
The man he most loved of all men on earth;[6]
She'd killed a glorious soldier, cut
A noble life short. No Geat could have stopped her:
Beowulf and his band had been given better   1300
Beds; sleep had come to them in a different
Hall. Then all Herot burst into shouts:
She had carried off Grendel's claw. Sorrow
Had returned to Denmark. They'd traded deaths,
Danes and monsters, and no one had won,   1305
Both had lost!
           The wise old king
Trembled in anger and grief, his dearest
Friend and adviser dead. Beowulf
Was sent for at once: a messenger went swiftly   1310
To his rooms and brought him. He came, his band
About him, as dawn was breaking through,
The best of all warriors, walking to where Hrothgar
Sat waiting, the gray-haired king wondering
If God would ever end this misery.   1315
The Geats tramped quickly through the hall; their steps

6. Esher, a Danish nobleman.

Beat and echoed in the silence. Beowulf
Rehearsed the words he would want with Hrothgar;
He'd ask the Danes' great lord if all
Were at peace, if the night had passed quietly.   1320

20

Hrothgar answered him, protector of his people:
"There's no happiness to ask about! Anguish has descended
On the Danes. Esher is dead, Ermlaf's
Older brother and my own most trusted
Counselor and friend, my comrade, when we went   1325
Into battle, who'd beaten back enemy swords,
Standing at my side. All my soldiers
Should be as he was, their hearts as brave
And as wise! Another wandering fiend
Has found him in Herot, murdered him, fled   1330
With his corpse: he'll be eaten, his flesh become
A horrible feast—and who knows where
The beast may be hiding, its belly stuffed full?
She's taking revenge for your victory over Grendel,
For your strength, your mighty grip, and that monster's   1335
Death. For years he'd been preying on my people;
You came, he was dead in a single day,
And now there's another one, a second hungry
Fiend, determined to avenge the first,
A monster willing and more than able   1340
To bring us more sorrow—or so it must seem
To the many men mourning that noble
Treasure-giver, for all men were treated
Nobly by those hands now forever closed.
        "I've heard that my people, peasants working   1345
In the fields, have seen a pair of such fiends
Wandering in the moors and marshes, giant
Monsters living in those desert lands.
And they've said to my wise men that, as well as they could see,
One of the devils was a female creature.   1350
The other, they say, walked through the wilderness
Like a man—but mightier than any man.
They were frightened, and they fled, hoping to find help
In Herot. They named the huge one Grendel:
If he had a father no one knew him,   1355
Or whether there'd been others before these two,
Hidden evil before hidden evil.
They live in secret places, windy
Cliffs, wolf-dens where water pours
From the rocks, then runs underground, where mist   1360

Steams like black clouds, and the groves of trees
Growing out over their lake are all covered
With frozen spray, and wind down snakelike
Roots that reach as far as the water
And help keep it dark. At night that lake   1365
Burns like a torch. No one knows its bottom,
No wisdom reaches such depths. A deer,
Hunted through the woods by packs of hounds,
A stag with great horns, though driven through the forest
From faraway places, prefers to die   1370
On those shores, refuses to save its life
In that water. It isn't far, nor is it
A pleasant spot! When the wind stirs
And storms, waves splash toward the sky,
As dark as the air, as black as the rain   1375
That the heavens weep. Our only help,
Again, lies with you. Grendel's mother
Is hidden in her terrible home, in a place
You've not seen. Seek it, if you dare! Save us,
Once more, and again twisted gold,   1380
Heaped-up ancient treasure, will reward you
For the battle you win!"

                            21

                        Beowulf spoke:
    "Let your sorrow end! It is better for us all
To avenge our friends, not mourn them forever.   1385
Each of us will come to the end of this life
On earth; he who can earn it should fight
For the glory of his name; fame after death
Is the noblest of goals. Arise, guardian
Of this kingdom, let us go, as quickly as we can,   1390
And have a look at this lady monster.
I promise you this: she'll find no shelter,
No hole in the ground, no towering tree,
No deep bottom of a lake, where her sins can hide.
Be patient for one more day of misery;   1395
I ask for no longer."
                    The old king leaped
To his feet, gave thanks to God for such words.
Then Hrothgar's horse was brought, saddled
And bridled. The Danes' wise ruler rode,   1400
Stately and splendid; shield-bearing soldiers
Marched at his side. The monster's tracks
Led them through the forest; they followed her heavy
Feet, that had swept straight across

The shadowy waste land, her burden the lifeless   1405
Body of the best of Hrothgar's men.
The trail took them up towering, rocky
Hills, and over narrow, winding
Paths they had never seen, down steep
And slippery cliffs where creatures from deep   1410
In the earth hid in their holes. Hrothgar
Rode in front, with a few of his most knowing
Men, to find their way. Then suddenly,
Where clumps of trees bent across
Cold gray stones, they came to a dismal   1415
Wood; below them was the lake, its water
Bloody and bubbling. And the Danes shivered,
Miserable, mighty men tormented
By grief, seeing, there on that cliff
Above the water, Esher's bloody   1420
Head. They looked down at the lake, felt
How its heat rose up, watched the waves'
Blood-stained swirling. Their battle horns sounded,
Then sounded again. Then they set down their weapons.
   They could see the water crawling with snakes,   1425
Fantastic serpents swimming in the boiling
Lake, and sea beasts lying on the rocks
—The kind that infest the ocean, in the early
Dawn, often ending some ship's
Journey with their wild jaws. They rushed   1430
Angrily out of sight, when the battle horns blew.
Beowulf aimed an arrow at one
Of the beasts, swimming sluggishly away,
And the point pierced its hide, stabbed
To its heart; its life leaked out, death   1435
Swept it off. Quickly, before
The dying monster could escape, they hooked
Its thrashing body with their curved boar-spears,
Fought it to land, drew it up on the bluff,
Then stood and stared at the incredible wave-roamer,   1440
Covered with strange scales and horrible. Then Beowulf
Began to fasten on his armor,
Not afraid for his life but knowing the woven
Mail, with its hammered links, could save
That life when he lowered himself into the lake,   1445
Keep slimy monsters' claws from snatching at
His heart, preserve him for the battle he was sent
To fight. Hrothgar's helmet would defend him;
That ancient, shining treasure, encircled
With hard-rolled metal, set there by some smith's   1450
Long dead hand, would block all battle

Swords, stop all blades from cutting at him
When he'd swum toward the bottom, gone down in the surging
Water, deep toward the swirling sands.
And Unferth helped him, Hrothgar's courtier   1455
Lent him a famous weapon, a fine,
Hilted old sword named Hrunting; it had
An iron blade, etched and shining
And hardened in blood. No one who'd worn it
Into battle, swung it in dangerous places,   1460
Daring and brave, had ever been deserted—
Nor was Beowulf's journey the first time it was taken
To an enemy's camp, or asked to support
Some hero's courage and win him glory.
Unferth had tried to forget his greeting   1465
To Beowulf, his drunken speech of welcome;
A mighty warrior, he lent his weapon
To a better one. Only Beowulf would risk
His life in that lake; Unferth was afraid,
Gave up that chance to work wonders, win glory   1470
And a hero's fame. But Beowulf and fear
Were strangers; he stood ready to dive into battle.

                              22

   Then Edgetho's brave son[7] spoke:
                          "Remember,
Hrothgar, Oh knowing king, now   1475
When my danger is near, the warm words we uttered,
And if your enemy should end my life
Then be, oh generous prince, forever
The father and protector of all whom I leave
Behind me, here in your hands, my belovèd   1480
Comrades left with no leader, their leader
Dead. And the precious gifts you gave me,
My friend, send them to Higlac. May he see
In their golden brightness, the Geats' great lord
Gazing at your treasure, that here in Denmark   1485
I found a noble protector, a giver
Of rings whose rewards I won and briefly
Relished. And you, Unferth, let
My famous old sword stay in your hands:
I shall shape glory with Hrunting, or death   1490
Will hurry me from this earth!"
                          As his words ended
He leaped into the lake, would not wait for anyone's

7. Beowulf.

Answer; the heaving water covered him
Over. For hours he sank through the waves;   1495
At last he saw the mud of the bottom.
And all at once the greedy she-wolf
Who'd ruled those waters for half a hundred
Years discovered him, saw that a creature
From above had come to explore the bottom   1500
Of her wet world. She welcomed him in her claws,
Clutched at him savagely but could not harm him,
Tried to work her fingers through the tight
Ring-woven mail on his breast, but tore
And scratched in vain. Then she carried him, armor   1505
And sword and all, to her home; he struggled
To free his weapon, and failed. The fight
Brought other monsters swimming to see
Her catch, a host of sea beasts who beat at
His mail shirt, stabbing with tusks and teeth   1510
As they followed along. Then he realized, suddenly,
That she'd brought him into someone's battle-hall,
And there the water's heat could not hurt him,
Nor anything in the lake attack him through
The building's high-arching roof. A brilliant   1515
Light burned all around him, the lake
Itself like a fiery flame.
                         Then he saw
The mighty water witch, and swung his sword,
His ring-marked blade, straight at her head;   1520
The iron sang its fierce song,
Sang Beowulf's strength. But her guest
Discovered that no sword could slice her evil
Skin, that Hrunting could not hurt her, was useless
Now when he needed it. They wrestled, she ripped   1525
And tore and clawed at him, bit holes in his helmet,
And that too failed him; for the first time in years
Of being worn to war it would earn no glory;
It was the last time anyone would wear it. But Beowulf
Longed only for fame, leaped back   1530
Into battle. He tossed his sword aside,
Angry; the steel-edged blade lay where
He'd dropped it. If weapons were useless he'd use
His hands, the strength in his fingers. So fame
Comes to men who mean to win it   1535
And care about nothing else! He raised
His arms and seized her by the shoulder; anger
Doubled his strength, he threw her to the floor.
She fell, Grendel's fierce mother, and the Geats'
Proud prince was ready to leap on her. But she rose   1540

At once and repaid him with her clutching claws,
Wildly tearing at him. He was weary, that best
And strongest of soldiers; his feet stumbled
And in an instant she had him down, held helpless.
Squatting with her weight on his stomach, she drew   1545
A dagger, brown with dried blood, and prepared
To avenge her only son. But he was stretched
On his back, and her stabbing blade was blunted
By the woven mail shirt he wore on his chest.
The hammered links held; the point   1550
Could not touch him. He'd have traveled to the bottom of the earth,
Edgetho's son, and died there, if that shining
Woven metal had not helped—and Holy
God, who sent him victory, gave judgment
For truth and right, Ruler of the Heavens,   1555
Once Beowulf was back on his feet and fighting.

                            23

    Then he saw, hanging on the wall, a heavy
Sword, hammered by giants, strong
And blessed with their magic, the best of all weapons
But so massive that no ordinary man could lift   1560
Its carved and decorated length. He drew it
From its scabbard, broke the chain on its hilt,
And then, savage, now, angry
And desperate, lifted it high over his head
And struck with all the strength he had left,   1565
Caught her in the neck and cut it through,
Broke bones and all. Her body fell
To the floor, lifeless, the sword was wet
With her blood, and Beowulf rejoiced at the sight.
    The brilliant light shone, suddenly,   1570
As though burning in that hall, and as bright as Heaven's
Own candle, lit in the sky. He looked
At her home, then following along the wall
Went walking, his hands tight on the sword,
His heart still angry. He was hunting another   1575
Dead monster, and took his weapon with him
For final revenge against Grendel's vicious
Attacks, his nighttime raids, over
And over, coming to Herot when Hrothgar's
Men slept, killing them in their beds,   1580
Eating some on the spot, fifteen
Or more, and running to his loathsome moor
With another such sickening meal waiting
In his pouch. But Beowulf repaid him for those visits,

Found him lying dead in his corner, 1585
Armless, exactly as that fierce fighter
Had sent him out from Herot, then struck off
His head with a single swift blow. The body
Jerked for the last time, then lay still.

   The wise old warriors who surrounded Hrothgar, 1590
Like him staring into the monsters' lake,
Saw the waves surging and blood
Spurting through. They spoke about Beowulf,
All the graybeards, whispered together
And said that hope was gone, that the hero 1595
Had lost fame and his life at once, and would never
Return to the living, come back as triumphant
As he had left; almost all agreed that Grendel's
Mighty mother, the she-wolf, had killed him.
The sun slid over past noon, went further 1600
Down. The Danes gave up, left
The lake and went home, Hrothgar with them.
The Geats stayed, sat sadly, watching,
Imagining they saw their lord but not believing
They would ever see him again.
                   —Then the sword 1605
Melted, blood-soaked, dripping down
Like water, disappearing like ice when the world's
Eternal Lord loosens invisible
Fetters and unwinds icicles and frost
As only He can, He who rules 1610
Time and seasons, He who is truly
God. The monsters' hall was full of
Rich treasures, but all that Beowulf took
Was Grendel's head and the hilt of the giants'
Jeweled sword; the rest of that ring-marked 1615
Blade had dissolved in Grendel's steaming
Blood, boiling even after his death.
And then the battle's only survivor
Swam up and away from those silent corpses;
The water was calm and clean, the whole 1620
Huge lake peaceful once the demons who'd lived in it
Were dead.
           Then that noble protector of all seamen
Swam to land, rejoicing in the heavy
Burdens he was bringing with him. He 1625
And all his glorious band of Geats
Thanked God that their leader had come back unharmed;
They left the lake together. The Geats
Carried Beowulf's helmet, and his mail shirt.
Behind them the water slowly thickened 1630

As the monsters' blood came seeping up.
They walked quickly, happily, across
Roads all of them remembered, left
The lake and the cliffs alongside it, brave men
Staggering under the weight of Grendel's skull,   1635
Too heavy for fewer than four of them to handle—
Two on each side of the spear jammed through it—
Yet proud of their ugly load and determined
That the Danes, seated in Herot, should see it.
Soon, fourteen Geats arrived   1640
At the hall, bold and warlike, and with Beowulf,
Their lord and leader, they walked on the mead-hall
Green. Then the Geats' brave prince entered
Herot, covered with glory for the daring
Battles he had fought; he sought Hrothgar   1645
To salute him and show Grendel's head.
He carried that terrible trophy by the hair,
Brought it straight to where the Danes sat,
Drinking, the queen among them. It was a weird
And wonderful sight, and the warriors stared.   1650

                            24

    Beowulf spoke:
                "Hrothgar! Behold,
Great Healfdane's son, this glorious sign
Of victory, brought you by joyful Geats.
My life was almost lost, fighting for it,   1655
Struggling under water: I'd have been dead at once,
And the fight finished, the she-devil victorious,
If our Father in Heaven had not helped me. Hrunting,
Unferth's noble weapon, could do nothing,
Nor could I, until the Ruler of the world   1660
Showed me, hanging shining and beautiful
On a wall, a mighty old sword—so God
Gives guidance to those who can find it from no one
Else. I used the weapon He had offered me,
Drew it and, when I could, swung it, killed   1665
The monstrous hag in her own home.
Then the ring-marked blade burned away,
As that boiling blood spilled out. I carried
Off all that was left, this hilt.
I've avenged their crimes, and the Danes they've killed.   1670
And I promise you that whoever sleeps in Herot
—You, your brave soldiers, anyone
Of all the people in Denmark, old
Or young—they, and you, may now sleep·

Without fear of either monster, mother 1675
Or son."
     Then he gave the golden sword hilt
To Hrothgar, who held it in his wrinkled hands
And stared at what giants had made, and monsters
Owned; it was his, an ancient weapon 1680
Shaped by wonderful smiths, now that Grendel
And his evil mother had been driven from the earth,
God's enemies scattered and dead. That best
Of swords belonged to the best of Denmark's
Rulers, the wisest ring-giver Danish 1685
Warriors had ever known. The old king
Bent close to the handle of the ancient relic,
And saw written there the story of ancient wars
Between good and evil, the opening of the waters,
The Flood sweeping giants away, how they suffered 1690
And died, that race who hated the Ruler
Of us all and received judgment from His hands,
Surging waves that found them wherever
They fled. And Hrothgar saw runic letters
Clearly carved in that shining hilt, 1695
Spelling its original owner's name,
He for whom it was made, with its twisted
Handle and snakelike carvings. Then he spoke,
Healfdane's son, and everyone was silent.
    "What I say, speaking from a full memory 1700
And after a life spent in seeking
What was right for my people, is this: this prince
Of the Geats, Beowulf, was born a better
Man! Your fame is everywhere, my friend,
Reaches to the ends of the earth, and you hold it in your heart
    wisely, 1705
Patient with your strength and our weakness. What I said I will do, I
    will do,
In the name of the friendship we've sworn. Your strength must solace your
    people,
Now, and mine no longer.
               "Be not
As Hermod[8] once was to my people, too proud 1710
To care what their hearts hid, bringing them
Only destruction and slaughter. In his mad
Rages he killed them himself, comrades
And followers who ate at his table. At the end
He was alone, knew none of the joys of life 1715

8. An archetypal but partly historical Danish king, of great military prowess combined with the lowest possible character.

With other men, a famous ruler
Granted greater strength than anyone
Alive in his day but dark and bloodthirsty
In spirit. He shared out no treasure, showed
His soldiers no road to riches and fame.   1720
And then that affliction on his people's face
Suffered horribly for his sins. Be taught
By his lesson, learn what a king must be:
I tell his tale, old as I am,
Only for you.   1725
         "Our eternal Lord
Grants some men wisdom, some wealth, makes others
Great. The world is God's, He allows
A man to grow famous, and his family rich,
Gives him land and towns to rule   1730
And delight in, lets his kingdom reach
As far as the world runs—and who
In human unwisdom, in the middle of such power,
Remembers that it all will end, and too soon?
Prosperity, prosperity, prosperity: nothing   1735
Troubles him, no sickness, not passing time,
No sorrows, no sudden war breaking
Out of nowhere, but all the world turns
When he spins it. How can he know when he sins?

                              24
"And then pride grows in his heart, planted   1740
Quietly but flourishing. And while the keeper of his soul
Sleeps on, while conscience rests and the world
Turns faster a murderer creeps closer, comes carrying
A tight-strung bow with terrible arrows.
And those sharp points strike home, are shot   1745
In his breast, under his helmet. He's helpless.
And so the Devil's dark urgings wound him, for he can't
Remember how he clung to the rotting wealth
Of this world, how he clawed to keep it, how he earned
No honor, no glory, in giving golden   1750
Rings, how he forgot the future glory
God gave him at his birth, and forgetting did not care.
And finally his body fails him, these bones
And flesh quickened by God fall
And die—and some other soul inherits   1755
His place in Heaven, some open-handed
Giver of old treasures, who takes no delight
In mere gold. Guard against such wickedness,
Belovèd Beowulf, best of warriors,

And choose, instead, eternal happiness;   1760
Push away pride! Your strength, your power,
Are yours for how many years? Soon
You'll return them where they came from, sickness or a sword's edge
Will end them, or a grasping fire, or the flight
Of a spear, or surging waves, or a knife's   1765
Bite, or the terror of old age, or your eyes
Darkening over. It will come, death
Comes faster than you think, no one can flee it.
     "So I have led the Danes for half
A hundred years, protected them from all peoples   1770
On this earth, my sword and my spear so ready
That no one anywhere under God's high sun
Was eager to wage war here in Denmark.
And here, here too the change has come,
And we wept for our dead when Grendel invaded   1775
Herot, my enemy raided this hall;
My sorrow, my grief, was as great and lasting
As it was helpless. Then thanks be given to God,
Eternal Lord of us all: you came
And that endless misery was over and I lived,   1780
Now, to behold this bloody head!
Go in, go in: feast, be as happy
As your fame deserves. When morning shines
We shall each have owned more of my treasures."
     Beowulf obeyed him, entered Herot   1785
Cheerfully and took his place at the table.
And once again Danes and Geats
Feasted together, a host of famous
Warriors in a single hall.—Then the web
Of darkness fell and it was night. They rose;   1790
Hrothgar, the gray-haired old Dane, was heavy
With sleep. And Beowulf was glad that a bed
Was waiting, the bravest of warriors exhausted
With the work he'd done. A Danish servant
Showed him the road to that far-off, quiet   1795
Country where sleep would come and take him
And his followers; Hrothgar's visitors were well
Cared for, whatever they needed was theirs.
     Then Beowulf rested; Herot rose high
Above him, gleaming in the darkness; the Geats   1800
Slept till a black-feathered raven sang
His cheerful song and the shining sun
Burned away shadows. And those seafarers hurried
From their beds, anxious to begin the voyage
Home, ready to start, their hearts   1805
Already sailing on a ship's swift back.

Then Unferth came, with Hrunting, his famous
Sword, and offered it to Beowulf, asked him
To accept a precious gift. The prince
Took it, thanked him, and declared the weapon   1810
One he was proud to own; his words
Blamed it for nothing, were spoken like the hero
He was! The war-gear was ready, the Geats
Were armored and eager to be gone. Quickly,
Beowulf sought Hrothgar's throne, where the king   1815
Sat waiting for his famous visitor's farewell.

                                    26
Beowulf spoke:
                    "We crossed the sea
To come here; it is time to return, to go back
To our belovèd lord, Higlac. Denmark   1820
Was a gracious host; you welcomed us warmly.
Anything I can do, here on this earth,
To earn your love, oh great king, anything
More than I have done, battles I can fight
In your honor, summon me, I will come as I came   1825
Once before. If I hear, from across the ocean,
That your neighbors have threatened you with war, or oppressed you
As enemies once oppressed you, here, I will bring
A thousand warriors, a thousand armed Geats
To protect your throne. I trust Higlac: 1830
Our king is young, but if I need his help
To better help you, to lend you our strength,
Our battle-sharp spears, to shield you and honor you
As you deserve, I know his words and his deeds
Will support me. And someday, if your oldest son,   1835
Hrethric, comes visiting our court, he will find
A host of good friends among the Geats:
No one who goes visiting far-off lands
Is more welcome than a strong and noble warrior."
Hrothgar replied: 1840
                    "All-knowing God
Must have sent you such words; nothing so wise
From a warrior so young has ever reached
These ancient ears. Your hands are strong,
Your heart and your lips are knowing! If your lord,   1845
Hrethel's son, is slain by a spear,
Or falls sick and dies, or is killed by a sword,
And you have survived whatever battle
Sweeps him off, I say that the Geats

Could do no better, find no man better   1850
Suited to be king, keeper of warriors
And their treasure, than you—if you take the throne
They will surely offer you. Belovèd Beowulf,
You please me more the longer I can keep you
Here in Denmark. You've turned Danes   1855
And Geats into brothers, brought peace where once
There was war, and sealed friendship with affection.
This will last as long as I live, and am king here:
We will share our treasures, greeting travelers
From across the sea with outstretched hands;   1860
Ring-prowed ships will carry our gifts
And the tokens of our love. Your people live
By the old ways, their hearts, like ours, are forever
Open to their friends, but firmly closed
Against their enemies."   1865
            Then he gave the Geats'
Prince a dozen new gifts, prayed
For his safety, commanded him to seek his people,
Yet not to delay too long in visiting
Hrothgar once more. The old king kissed him,   1870
Held that best of all warriors by the shoulder
And wept, unable to hold back his tears.
Gray and wise, he knew how slim
Were his chances of ever greeting Beowulf
Again, but seeing his face he was forced   1875
To hope. His love was too warm to be hidden,
His tears came running too quickly to be checked;
His very blood burned with longing.
And then Beowulf left him, left Herot, walked
Across the green in his golden armor,   1880
Exulting in the treasures heaped high in his arms.
His ship was at anchor; he had it ready to sail.
And so Hrothgar's rich treasures would leave him, travel
Far from that perfect king, without fault
Or blame until winter had followed winter   1885
And age had stolen his strength, spirited it
Off, as it steals from many men.

27

    Then the band of Geats, young and brave,
Marching in their ring-locked armor, reached
The shore. The coast-guard saw them coming   1890
And about to go, as he'd seen them before;
He hurried down the hillside, whipping
His horse, but this time shouted no challenge,

Told them only how the Geats would be watching
Too, and would welcome such warriors in shining   1895
Mail. Their broad-beamed ship lay bobbing
At the edge of the sand: they loaded it high
With armor and horses and all the rich treasure
It could hold. The mast stood high and straight
Over heaped-up wealth—Hrothgar's, and now theirs.   1900
Beowulf rewarded the boat's watchman,
Who had stayed behind, with a sword that had hammered
Gold wound on its handle: the weapon
Brought him honor. Then the ship left shore, left Denmark,
Traveled through deep water. Deck timbers creaked,   1905
And the wind billowing through the sail stretched
From the mast, tied tight with ropes, did not hold them
Back, did not keep the ring-prowed ship
From foaming swiftly through the waves, the sea
Currents, across the wide ocean until   1910
They could see familiar headlands, cliffs
That sprang out of Geatish soil. Driven
By the wind the ship rammed high on the shore.
Harbor guards came running to greet them,
Men who for days had waited and watched   1915
For their belovèd comrades to come crossing the waves;
They anchored the high-bowed ship, moored it
Close to the shore, where the booming sea
Could not pull it loose and lead it away.
Then they carried up the golden armor,   1920
The ancient swords, the jewels, brought them
To Higlac's home, their ring-giver's hall
Near the sea, where he lived surrounded
By his followers.
      He was a famous king, with a fitting   1925
High hall and a wife, Higd, young
But wise and knowing beyond her years.
She was Hareth's daughter, a noble queen
With none of the niggardly ways of women
Like Thrith.[9] Higd gave the Geats gifts   1930
With open hands. But Thrith was too proud,
An imperious princess with a vicious tongue
And so fierce and wild that her father's followers
Averted their eyes as she passed, knowing
That if anyone but their king watched where she walked   1935
Her hands would shape a noose to fit
Their necks. She would lie, her father's lieutenants
Would write out her warrants, and he who had stared

9. The wife of Offa, a king of the Angles, who "tames" and gentles her.

Would end his life on the edge of an ancient
Sword. And how great a sin for a woman,   1940
Whether fair or black, to create fear
And destruction, for a woman, who should walk in the ways
Of peace, to kill with pretended insults.
But Hemming's kinsman tamed her: his hall-guests
Told a different story, spread the news   1945
That Thrith had forgotten her gory tricks
Once her wise father had sent her to a wedding
With Offa, married her to that brave young soldier,
Sent her across the yellow-green sea
To that gold-adorned champion, a fierce fighter   1950
In war or peace. They praised her, now,
For her generous heart, and her goodness, and the high
And most noble paths she walked, filled
With adoring love for that leader of warriors,
Her husband; he was a man as brave and strong   1955
And good, it is said, as anyone on this earth,
A spear-bold soldier who knew no fear,
Exalted with gifts, victorious in war,
A king who ruled his native land
Wisely and well. Emer was his son,   1960
Hemming's kinsman, Garmund's grandson,
A powerful swordsman and his warriors' shield.

28

    Then Beowulf and his men went walking along
The shore, down the broad strip of sand.
The world's bright candle shone, hurrying   1965
Up from the south. It was a short journey
From their ship to Higlac's home, to the hall
Where their king, Ongentho's killer, lived
With his warriors and gave treasures away. They walked
Quickly. The young king knew   1970
They were back, Beowulf and his handful of brave
Men, come safely home; he sat,
Now, waiting to see them, to greet
His battle-comrades when they arrived at his court.
    They came. And when Beowulf had bowed to his lord,   1975
And standing in front of the throne had solemnly
Spoken loyal words, Higlac
Ordered him to sit at his side—he
Who had survived, sailed home victorious, next to
His kinsman and king. Mead cups were filled   1980
And Hareth's daughter took them through the hall,
Carried ale to her husband's comrades.

Higlac, unable to stay silent, anxious
To know how Beowulf's adventure had gone,
Began to question him, courteous but eager   1985
To be told everything.

                        "Belovèd Beowulf,
Tell us what your trip to far-off places
Brought you, your sudden expedition on the salty
Waves, your search for war in Herot?   1990
Did you end Hrothgar's hopeless misery,
Could you help that glorious king? Grendel's
Savagery lay heavy on my heart but I was afraid
To let you go to him; for a long time
I held you here, kept you safe,   1995
Forced you to make the Danes fight
Their own battles. God be praised
That my eyes have beheld you once more, unharmed!"
    Beowulf spoke, Edgetho's brave son:
"My lord Higlac, my meeting with Grendel   2000
And the nighttime battle we fought are known
To everyone in Denmark, where the monster was once
The uncrowned ruler, murdering and eating
Hrothgar's people, forever bringing them
Misery. I ended his reign, avenged   2005
His crimes so completely in the crashing darkness
That not even the oldest of his evil kind
Will ever boast, lying in sin
And deceit, that the monster beat me. I sought out
Hrothgar, first, came to him in his hall;   2010
When Healfdane's famous son heard
That I'd come to challenge Grendel, he gave me
A seat of honor alongside his son.
His followers were drinking; I joined their feast,
Sat with that band, as bright and loud-tongued   2015
As any I've ever seen. His famous
Queen went back and forth, hurrying
The cup-bearing boys, giving bracelets
And rings to her husband's warriors. I heard
The oldest soldiers of all calling   2020
For ale from Hrothgar's daughter's hands,
And Freaw was the way they greeted her when she gave them
The golden cups. And Hrothgar will give her
To Ingeld, gracious Froda's son;
She and that ripening soldier will be married,   2025
The Danes' great lord and protector has declared,
Hoping that his quarrel with the Hathobards can be settled
By a woman. He's wrong: how many wars
Have been put to rest in a prince's bed?

Few. A bride can bring a little   2030
Peace, make spears silent for a time,
But not long. Ingeld and all his men
Will be drinking in the hall, when the wedding is done
And Freaw is his wife; the Danes will be wearing
Gleaming armor and ring-marked old swords;   2035
And the prince and his people will remember those treasures,
Will remember that their fathers once wore them, fell
With those helmets on their heads, those swords in their hands.

29

"And seeing their ancestral armor and weapons
Ingeld and his followers will be angry. And one   2040
Of his soldiers, sitting with ale in his cup
And bitterness heavy in his heart, will remember
War and death, and while he sits and drinks
His sharp old tongue will begin to tempt
Some younger warrior, pushing and probing   2045
For a new war:
                " 'That sword, that precious old blade
Over there, I think you know it, friend.
Your father carried it, fought with it the last time
He could swing a sword; the Danes killed him   2050
—And many more of our men—and stripped
The dead bodies: the brave, bold Danes!
One of the princess' people, here,
Now, might be the murderer's son,
Boasting about his treasures, his ancient   2055
Armor—which ought to be yours, by right.'
    "Bitter words will work in a hot-tempered
Brain, pushing up thoughts of the past,
And then, when he can, calling his father's
Name, the youngster will kill some innocent   2060
Dane, a servant—and bloody sword
In hand will run from the hall, knowing
His way through the woods. But war will begin
As he runs, to the sound of broken oaths,
And its heat will dry up Ingeld's heart,   2065
Leave him indifferent to his Danish bride.
Hrothgar may think the Hathobards love him,
Loving Freaw, but the friendship can't last,
The vows are worthless.
                        "But of Grendel: you need to   2070
Know more to know everything; I ought to
Go on. It was early in the evening, Heaven's
Jewel had slid to its rest, and the jealous

Monster, planning murder, came seeking us
Out, stalking us as we guarded Hrothgar's   2075
Hall. Hondshew, sleeping in his armor,
Was the first Geat he reached: Grendel
Seized him, tore him apart, swallowed him
Down, feet and all, as fate
Had decreed—a glorious young soldier, killed   2080
In his prime. Yet Grendel had only begun
His bloody work, meant to leave us
With his belly and his pouch both full, and Herot
Half-empty. Then he tested his strength against mine,
Hand to hand. His pouch hung   2085
At his side, a huge bag sewn
From a dragon's skin, worked with a devil's
Skill; it was closed by a marvelous clasp.
The monster intended to take me, put me
Inside, save me for another meal.   2090
He was bold and strong, but once I stood
On my feet his strength was useless, and it failed him.

                              30

"The whole tale of how I killed him,
Repaid him in kind for all the evil
He'd done, would take too long: your people,   2095
My prince, were honored in the doing. He escaped,
Found a few minutes of life, but his hand,
His whole right arm, stayed in Herot;
The miserable creature crept away,
Dropped to the bottom of his lake, half dead   2100
As he fell. When the sun had returned, the Danes'
Great king poured out treasure, repaid me
In hammered gold for the bloody battle
I'd fought in his name. He ordered a feast;
There were songs, and the telling of tales. One ancient   2105
Dane told of long-dead times,
And sometimes Hrothgar himself, with the harp
In his lap, stroked its silvery strings
And told wonderful stories, a brave king
Reciting unhappy truths about good   2110
And evil—and sometimes he wove his stories
On the mournful thread of old age, remembering
Buried strength and the battles it had won.
He would weep, the old king, wise with many
Winters, remembering what he'd done, once,   2115
What he'd seen, what he knew. And so we sat
The day away, feasting. Then darkness

Fell again, and Grendel's mother
Was waiting, ready for revenge, hating
The Danes for her son's death. The monstrous   2120
Hag succeeded, burst boldly into Herot
And killed Esher, one of the king's oldest
And wisest soldiers. But when the sun shone
Once more the death-weary Danes could not build
A pyre and burn his belovèd body,   2125
Lay him on flaming logs, return ashes
To dust: she'd carried away his corpse,
Brought it to her den deep in the water.
Hrothgar had wept for many of his men,
But this time his heart melted, this   2130
Was the worst. He begged me, in your name, half-weeping
As he spoke, to seek still greater glory
Deep in the swirling waves, to win
Still higher fame, and the gifts he would give me.
Down in that surging lake I sought   2135
And found her, the horrible hag, fierce
And wild; we fought, clutching and grasping;
The water ran red with blood and at last,
With a mighty sword that had hung on the wall,
I cut off her head. I had barely escaped   2140
With my life, my death was not written. And the Danes'
Protector, Healfdane's great son, heaped up
Treasures and precious jewels to reward me.

31

    "He lived his life as a good king must:
I lost nothing, none of the gifts   2145
My strength could have earned me. He opened his store
Of gems and armor, let me choose as I liked,
So I could bring his riches to you, my ruler,
And prove his friendship, and my love. Your favor
Still governs my life: I have almost no family,   2150
Higlac, almost no one, now, but you."
    Then Beowulf ordered them to bring in the boar-head
Banner, the towering helmet, the ancient,
Silvery armor, and the gold-carved sword:
    "This war-gear was Hrothgar's reward, my gift   2155
From his wise old hands. He wanted me to tell you,
First, whose treasures these were. Hergar
Had owned them, his older brother, who was king
Of Denmark until death gave Hrothgar the throne:
But Hergar kept them, would not give them to Herward,   2160
His brave young son, though the boy had proved

His loyalty. These are yours: may they serve you well!"
And after the gleaming armor four horses
Were led in, four bays, swift and all
Alike. Beowulf had brought his king   2165
Horses and treasure—as a man must,
Not weaving nets of malice for his comrades,
Preparing their death in the dark, with secret,
Cunning tricks. Higlac trusted
His nephew, leaned on his strength, in war,   2170
Each of them intent on the other's joy.
And Beowulf gave Welthow's gift, her wonderful
Necklace, to Higd, Higlac's queen,
And gave her, also, three supple, graceful,
Saddle-bright horses; she received his presents,   2175
Then wore that wonderful jewel on her breast.
    So Edgetho's son proved himself,
Did as a famous soldier must do
If glory is what he seeks: not killing his comrades
In drunken rages, his heart not savage,   2180
But guarding God's gracious gift, his strength,
Using it only in war, and then using it
Bravely. And yet as a boy he was scorned;
The Geats considered him worthless. When he sat
In their mead-hall, and their lord was making men rich,   2185
He held no claim on the king's good will.
They were sure he was lazy, noble but slow.
The world spun round, he was a warrior more famous
Than any, and all the insults were wiped out.
    Then Higlac, protector of his people, brought in   2190
His father's—Beowulf's grandfather's—great sword,
Worked in gold; none of the Geats
Could boast of a better weapon. He laid it
In Beowulf's lap, then gave him seven
Thousand hides of land, houses   2195
And ground and all. Geatland was home
For both king and prince; their fathers had left them
Buildings and fields—but Higlac's inheritance
Stretched further, it was he who was king, and was followed.

    Afterwards,[1] in the time when Higlac was dead   2200
And Herdred, his son, who'd ruled the Geats
After his father, had followed him into darkness—
Killed in battle with the Swedes, who smashed
His shield, cut through the soldiers surrounding
Their king—then, when Higd's one son   2205
Was gone, Beowulf ruled in Geatland,

1. I.e., many years later. (Beowulf has been king for fifty years.)

Took the throne he'd refused, once,
And held it long and well. He was old
With years and wisdom, fifty winters
A king, when a dragon awoke from its darkness   2210
And dreams and brought terror to his people. The beast
Had slept in a huge stone tower, with a hidden
Path beneath; a man stumbled on
The entrance, went in, discovered the ancient
Treasure, the pagan jewels and gold   2215
The dragon had been guarding, and dazzled and greedy
Stole a gem-studded cup, and fled.
But now the dragon hid nothing, neither
The theft nor itself; it swept through the darkness,
And all Geatland knew its anger.   2220

32

But the thief had not come to steal; he stole,
And roused the dragon, not from desire
But need. He was someone's slave, had been beaten
By his masters, had run from all men's sight,
But with no place to hide; then he found the hidden   2225
Path, and used it. And once inside,
Seeing the sleeping beast, staring as it
Yawned and stretched, not wanting to wake it,
Terror-struck, he turned and ran for his life,
Taking the jeweled cup.   2230
             That tower
Was heaped high with hidden treasure, stored there
Years before by the last survivor
Of a noble race, ancient riches
Left in the darkness as the end of a dynasty   2235
Came. Death had taken them, one
By one, and the warrior who watched over all
That remained mourned their fate, expecting,
Soon, the same for himself, knowing
The gold and jewels he had guarded so long   2240
Could not bring him pleasure much longer. He brought
The precious cups, the armor and the ancient
Swords, to a stone tower built
Near the sea, below a cliff, a sealed
Fortress with no windows, no doors, waves   2245
In front of it, rocks behind. Then he spoke:
    "Take these treasures, earth, now that no one
Living can enjoy them. They were yours, in the beginning;
Allow them to return. War and terror
Have swept away my people, shut   2250

Their eyes to delight and to living, closed
The door to all gladness. No one is left
To lift these swords, polish these jeweled
Cups: no one leads, no one follows. These hammered
Helmets, worked with gold, will tarnish   2255
And crack; the hands that should clean and polish them
Are still forever. And these mail shirts, worn
In battle, once, while swords crashed
And blades bit into shields and men,
Will rust away like the warriors who owned them.   2260
None of these treasures will travel to distant
Lands, following their lords. The harp's
Bright song, the hawk crossing through the hall
On its swift wings, the stallion tramping
In the courtyard—all gone, creatures of every   2265
Kind, and their masters, hurled to the grave!"
     And so he spoke, sadly, of those
Long dead, and lived from day to day,
Joyless, until, at last, death touched
His heart and took him too. And a stalker   2270
In the night, a flaming dragon, found
The treasure unguarded; he whom men fear
Came flying through the darkness, wrapped in fire,
Seeking caves and stone-split ruins
But finding gold. Then it stayed, buried   2275
Itself with heathen silver and jewels
It could neither use nor ever abandon.
     So mankind's enemy, the mighty beast,
Slept in those stone walls for hundreds
Of years; a runaway slave roused it,   2280
Stole a jeweled cup and bought
His master's forgiveness, begged for mercy
And was pardoned when his delighted lord took the present
He bore, turned it in his hands and stared
At the ancient carvings. The cup brought peace   2285
To a slave, pleased his master, but stirred
A dragon's anger. It turned, hunting
The thief's tracks, and found them, saw
Where its visitor had come and gone. He'd survived,
Had come close enough to touch its scaly   2290
Head and yet lived, as it lifted its cavernous
Jaws, through the grace of almighty God
And a pair of quiet, quick-moving feet.
The dragon followed his steps, anxious
To find the man who had robbed it of silver   2295
And sleep; it circled around and around
The tower, determined to catch him, but could not,

He had run too fast, the wilderness was empty.
The beast went back to its treasure, planning
A bloody revenge, and found what was missing,   2300
Saw what thieving hands had stolen.
Then it crouched on the stones, counting off
The hours till the Almighty's candle went out,
And evening came, and wild with anger
It could fly burning across the land, killing   2305
And destroying with its breath. Then the sun was gone,
And its heart was glad: glowing with rage
It left the tower, impatient to repay
Its enemies. The people suffered, everyone
Lived in terror, but when Beowulf had learned   2310
Of their trouble his fate was worse, and came quickly.

33

      Vomiting fire and smoke, the dragon
Burned down their homes. They watched in horror
As the flames rose up: the angry monster
Meant to leave nothing alive. And the signs   2315
Of its anger flickered and glowed in the darkness,
Visible for miles, tokens of its hate
And its cruelty, spread like a warning to the Geats
Who had broken its rest. Then it hurried back
To its tower, to its hidden treasure, before dawn   2320
Could come. It had wrapped its flames around
The Geats; now it trusted in stone
Walls, and its strength, to protect it. But they would not.
      Then they came to Beowulf, their king, and announced
That his hall, his throne, the best of buildings,   2325
Had melted away in the dragon's burning
Breath. Their words brought misery, Beowulf's
Sorrow beat at his heart: he accused
Himself of breaking God's law, of bringing
The Almighty's anger down on his people.   2330
Reproach pounded in his breast, gloomy
And dark, and the world seemed a different place.
But the hall was gone, the dragon's molten
Breath had licked across it, burned it
To ashes, near the shore it had guarded. The Geats   2335
Deserved revenge; Beowulf, their leader
And lord, began to plan it, ordered
A battle-shield shaped of iron, knowing that
Wood would be useless, that no linden shield
Could help him, protect him, in the flaming heat   2340
Of the beast's breath. That noble prince

Would end his days on earth, soon,
Would leave this brief life, but would take the dragon
With him, tear it from the heaped-up treasure
It had guarded so long. And he'd go to it alone,   2345
Scorning to lead soldiers against such
An enemy: he saw nothing to fear, thought nothing
Of the beast's claws, or wings, or flaming
Jaws—he had fought, before, against worse
Odds, had survived, been victorious, in harsher   2350
Battles, beginning in Herot, Hrothgar's
Unlucky hall. He'd killed Grendel
And his mother, swept that murdering tribe
Away. And he'd fought in Higlac's war
With the Frisians, fought at his lord's side   2355
Till a sword reached out and drank Higlac's
Blood, till a blade swung in the rush
Of battle killed the Geats' great king.
Then Beowulf escaped, broke through Frisian
Shields and swam to freedom, saving   2360
Thirty sets of armor from the scavenging
Franks, river people who robbed
The dead as they floated by. Beowulf
Offered them only his sword, ended
So many jackal lives that the few   2365
Who were able skulked silently home, glad
To leave him. So Beowulf swam sadly back
To Geatland, almost the only survivor
Of a foolish war. Higlac's widow
Brought him the crown, offered him the kingdom,   2370
Not trusting Herdred, her son and Higlac's,
To beat off foreign invaders. But Beowulf
Refused to rule when his lord's own son
Was alive, and the leaderless Geats could choose
A rightful king. He gave Herdred   2375
All his support, offering an open
Heart where Higlac's young son could see
Wisdom he still lacked himself: warmth
And good will were what Beowulf brought his new king.
    But Swedish exiles came, seeking   2380
Protection; they were rebels against Onela,
Healfdane's son-in-law and the best ring-giver
His people had ever known. And Onela
Came too, a mighty king, marched
On Geatland with a huge army; Herdred   2385
Had given his word and now he gave
His life, shielding the Swedish strangers.
Onela wanted nothing more:

When Herdred had fallen that famous warrior
Went back to Sweden, let Beowulf rule!²   2390

34

But Beowulf remembered how his king had been killed.
As soon as he could he lent the last
Of the Swedish rebels soldiers and gold,
Helped him to a bitter battle across
The wide sea, where victory, and revenge, and the Swedish   2395
Throne were won, and Onela was slain.
So Edgetho's son survived, no matter
What dangers he met, what battles he fought,
Brave and forever triumphant, till the day
Fate sent him to the dragon and sent him death.   2400
A dozen warriors walked with their angry
King, when he was brought to the beast; Beowulf
Knew, by then, what had woken the monster,
And enraged it. The cup had come to him, traveled
From dragon to slave, to master, to king,   2405
And the slave was their guide, had begun the Geats'
Affliction, and now, afraid of both beast
And men, was forced to lead them to the monster's
Hidden home. He showed them the huge
Stones, set deep in the ground, with the sea   2410
Beating on the rocks close by. Beowulf
Stared, listening to stories of the gold
And riches heaped inside. Hidden,
But wakeful, now, the dragon waited,
Ready to greet him. Gold and hammered   2415
Armor have been buried in pleasanter places!
The battle-brave king rested on the shore,
While his soldiers wished him well, urged him
On. But Beowulf's heart was heavy:
His soul sensed how close fate   2420
Had come, felt something, not fear but knowledge
Of old age. His armor was strong, but his arm
Hung like his heart. Body and soul
Might part, here; his blood might be spilled,
His spirit torn from his flesh. Then he spoke: 2425
"My early days were full of war,
And I survived it all; I can remember everything.
I was seven years old when Hrethel opened
His home and his heart for me, when my king and lord

2. These are incidents of the intermittent strife between Danes and Swedes in the period before Beowulf
was old enough to participate; the same is true of the passage (ll. 2472ff.) dealing with wars between Geats
and Swedes.

Took me from my father and kept me, taught me   2430
Gave me gold and pleasure, glad that I sat
At his knee. And he never loved me less
Than any of his sons—Herbald, the oldest
Of all, or Hathcyn, or Higlac, my lord.
Herbald died a horrible death,   2435
Killed while hunting: Hathcyn, his brother,
Stretched his horn-tipped bow, sent
An arrow flying, but missed his mark
And hit Herbald instead, found him
With a bloody point and pierced him through.   2440
The crime was great, the guilt was plain,
But nothing could be done, no vengeance, no death
To repay that death, no punishment, nothing.
    "So with the graybeard whose son sins
Against the king, and is hanged: he stands   2445
Watching his child swing on the gallows,
Lamenting, helpless, while his flesh and blood
Hangs for the raven to pluck. He can raise
His voice in sorrow, but revenge is impossible.
And every morning he remembers how his son   2450
Died, and despairs; no son to come
Matters, no future heir, to a father
Forced to live through such misery. The place
Where his son once dwelled, before death compelled him
To journey away, is a windy wasteland,   2455
Empty, cheerless; the childless father
Shudders, seeing it. So riders and ridden
Sleep in the ground; pleasure is gone,
The harp is silent, and hope is forgotten.

                        35

    "And then, crying his sorrow, he crawls   2460
To his bed: the world, and his home, hurt him
With their emptiness. And so it seemed to Hrethel,
When Herbald was dead, and his heart swelled
With grief. The murderer lived; he felt
No love for him, now, but nothing could help,   2465
Word nor hand nor sharp-honed blade,
War nor hate, battle or blood
Or law. The pain could find no relief,
He could only live with it, or leave grief and life
Together. When he'd gone to his grave Hathcyn   2470
And Higlac, his sons, inherited everything.
    "And then there was war between Geats and Swedes,
Bitter battles carried across

The broad sea, when the mighty Hrethel slept
And Ongentho's sons thought Sweden could safely   2475
Attack, saw no use to pretending friendship
But raided and burned, and near old Rennsburg
Slaughtered Geats with their thieving swords.
My people repaid them, death for death,
Battle for battle, though one of the brothers   2480
Bought that revenge with his life—Hathcyn,
King of the Geats, killed by a Swedish
Sword. But when dawn came the slayer
Was slain, and Higlac's soldiers avenged
Everything with the edge of their blades. Efor   2485
Caught the Swedish king, cracked
His helmet, split his skull, dropped him,
Pale and bleeding, to the ground, then put him
To death with a swift stroke, shouting
His joy.   2490
         "The gifts that Higlac gave me,
And the land, I earned with my sword, as fate
Allowed: he never needed Danes
Or Goths or Swedes, soldiers and allies
Bought with gold, bribed to his side.   2495
My sword was better, and always his.
In every battle my place was in front;
Alone, and so it shall be forever,
As long as this sword lasts, serves me
In the future as it has served me before. So   2500
I killed Dagref, the Frank, who brought death
To Higlac, and who looted his corpse: Higd's
Necklace, Welthow's treasure, never
Came to Dagref's king. The thief
Fell in battle, but not on my blade.   2505
He was brave and strong, but I swept him in my arms,
Ground him against me till his bones broke,
Till his blood burst out.[3] And now I shall fight
For this treasure, fight with both hand and sword."
   And Beowulf uttered his final boast: 2510
"I've never known fear; as a youth I fought
In endless battles. I am old, now,
But I will fight again, seek fame still,
If the dragon hiding in his tower dares
To face me."   2515
         Then he said farewell to his followers,
Each in his turn, for the last time:
   "I'd use no sword, no weapon, if this beast

3. This occurred in Higlac's expedition against the Franks (ll. 1202–13).

Could be killed without it, crushed to death
Like Grendel, gripped in my hands and torn   2520
Limb from limb. But his breath will be burning
Hot, poison will pour from his tongue.
I feel no shame, with shield and sword
And armor, against this monster: when he comes to me
I mean to stand, not run from his shooting   2525
Flames, stand till fate decides
Which of us wins. My heart is firm,
My hands calm: I need no hot
Words. Wait for me close by, my friends.
We shall see, soon, who will survive   2530
This bloody battle, stand when the fighting
Is done. No one else could do
What I mean to, here, no man but me
Could hope to defeat this monster. No one
Could try. And this dragon's treasure, his gold   2535
And everything hidden in that tower, will be mine
Or war will sweep me to a bitter death!"
     Then Beowulf rose, still brave, still strong,
And with his shield at his side, and a mail shirt on his breast,
Strode calmly, confidently, toward the tower, under   2540
The rocky cliffs: no coward could have walked there!
And then he who'd endured dozens of desperate
Battles, who'd stood boldly while swords and shields
Clashed, the best of kings, saw
Huge stone arches and felt the heat   2545
Of the dragon's breath, flooding down
Through the hidden entrance, too hot for anyone
To stand, a streaming current of fire
And smoke that blocked all passage. And the Geats'
Lord and leader, angry, lowered   2550
His sword and roared out a battle cry,
A call so loud and clear that it reached through
The hoary rock, hung in the dragon's
Ear. The beast rose, angry,
Knowing a man had come—and then nothing   2555
But war could have followed. Its breath came first,
A steaming cloud pouring from the stone,
Then the earth itself shook. Beowulf
Swung his shield into place, held it
In front of him, facing the entrance. The dragon   2560
Coiled and uncoiled, its heart urging it
Into battle. Beowulf's ancient sword
Was waiting, unsheathed, his sharp and gleaming
Blade. The beast came closer; both of them
Were ready, each set on slaughter. The Geats'   2565

Great prince stood firm, unmoving, prepared
Behind his high shield, waiting in his shining
Armor. The monster came quickly toward him,
Pouring out fire and smoke, hurrying
To its fate. Flames beat at the iron   2570
Shield, and for a time it held, protected
Beowulf as he'd planned; then it began to melt,
And for the first time in his life that famous prince
Fought with fate against him, with glory
Denied him. He knew it, but he raised his sword   2575
And struck at the dragon's scaly hide.
The ancient blade broke, bit into
The monster's skin, drew blood, but cracked
And failed him before it went deep enough, helped him
Less than he needed. The dragon leaped   2580
With pain, thrashed and beat at him, spouting
Murderous flames, spreading them everywhere.
And the Geats' ring-giver did not boast of glorious
Victories in other wars: his weapon
Had failed him, deserted him, now when he needed it   2585
Most, that excellent sword. Edgetho's
Famous son stared at death,
Unwilling to leave this world, to exchange it
For a dwelling in some distant place—a journey
Into darkness that all men must make, as death   2590
Ends their few brief hours on earth.
    Quickly, the dragon came at him, encouraged
As Beowulf fell back; its breath flared,
And he suffered, wrapped around in swirling
Flames—a king, before, but now   2595
A beaten warrior. None of his comrades
Came to him, helped him, his brave and noble
Followers; they ran for their lives, fled
Deep in a wood. And only one of them
Remained, stood there, miserable, remembering,   2600
As a good man must, what kinship should mean.

36

    His name was Wiglaf, he was Wexstan's son
And a good soldier; his family had been Swedish,
Once. Watching Beowulf, he could see
How his king was suffering, burning. Remembering   2605
Everything his lord and cousin had given him,
Armor and gold and the great estates
Wexstan's family enjoyed, Wiglaf's
Mind was made up; he raised his yellow

Shield and drew his sword—an ancient 2610
Weapon that had once belonged to Onela's
Nephew, and that Wexstan had won, killing
The prince when he fled from Sweden, sought safety
With Herdred, and found death. And Wiglaf's father
Had carried the dead man's armor, and his sword, 2615
To Onela, and the king had said nothing, only
Given him armor and sword and all,
Everything his rebel nephew had owned
And lost when he left this life. And Wexstan
Had kept those shining gifts, held them 2620
For years, waiting for his son to use them,
Wear them as honorably and well as once
His father had done; then Wexstan died
And Wiglaf was his heir, inherited treasures
And weapons and land. He'd never worn 2625
That armor, fought with that sword, until Beowulf
Called him to his side, led him into war.
But his soul did not melt, his sword was strong;
The dragon discovered his courage, and his weapon,
When the rush of battle brought them together. 2630
    And Wiglaf, his heart heavy, uttered
The kind of words his comrades deserved:
    "I remember how we sat in the mead-hall, drinking
And boasting of how brave we'd be when Beowulf
Needed us, he who gave us these swords 2635
And armor: all of us swore to repay him,
When the time came, kindness for kindness
—With our lives, if he needed them. He allowed us to join him,
Chose us from all his great army, thinking
Our boasting words had some weight, believing 2640
Our promises, trusting our swords. He took us
For soldiers, for men. He meant to kill
This monster himself, our mighty king,
Fight this battle alone and unaided,
As in the days when his strength and daring dazzled 2645
Men's eyes. But those days are over and gone
And now our lord must lean on younger
Arms. And we must go to him, while angry
Flames burn at his flesh, help
Our glorious king! By almighty God, 2650
I'd rather burn myself than see
Flames swirling around my lord.
And who are we to carry home
Our shields before we've slain his enemy
And ours, to run back to our homes with Beowulf 2655
So hard-pressed here? I swear that nothing

He ever did deserved an end
Like this, dying miserably and alone,
Butchered by this savage beast: we swore
That these swords and armor were each for us all!"   2660
    Then he ran to his king, crying encouragement
As he dove through the dragon's deadly fumes:
    "Belovèd Beowulf, remember how you boasted,
Once, that nothing in the world would ever
Destroy your fame: fight to keep it,   2665
Now, be strong and brave, my noble
King, protecting life and fame
Together. My sword will fight at your side!"
    The dragon heard him, the man-hating monster,
And was angry; shining with surging flames   2670
It came for him, anxious to return his visit.
Waves of fire swept at his shield
And the edge began to burn. His mail shirt
Could not help him, but before his hands dropped
The blazing wood Wiglaf jumped   2675
Behind Beowulf's shield; his own was burned
To ashes. Then the famous old hero, remembering
Days of glory, lifted what was left
Of Nagling, his ancient sword, and swung it
With all his strength, smashed the gray   2680
Blade into the beast's head. But then Nagling
Broke to pieces, as iron always
Had in Beowulf's hands. His arms
Were too strong, the hardest blade could not help him,
The most wonderfully worked. He carried them to war   2685
But fate had decreed that the Geats' great king
Would be no better for any weapon.
    Then the monster charged again, vomiting
Fire, wild with pain, rushed out
Fierce and dreadful, its fear forgotten.   2690
Watching for its chance it drove its tusks
Into Beowulf's neck; he staggered, the blood
Came flooding forth, fell like rain.

37

    And then when Beowulf needed him most
Wiglaf showed his courage, his strength   2695
And skill, and the boldness he was born with. Ignoring
The dragon's head, he helped his lord
By striking lower down. The sword
Sank in; his hand was burned, but the shining
Blade had done its work, the dragon's   2700

Belching flames began to flicker
And die away. And Beowulf drew
His battle-sharp dagger: the blood-stained old king
Still knew what he was doing. Quickly, he cut
The beast in half, slit it apart.   2705
It fell, their courage had killed it, two noble
Cousins had joined in the dragon's death.
Yet what they did all men must do
When the time comes! But the triumph was the last
Beowulf would ever earn, the end   2710
Of greatness and life together. The wound
In his neck began to swell and grow;
He could feel something stirring, burning
In his veins, a stinging venom, and knew
The beast's fangs had left it. He fumbled   2715
Along the wall, found a slab
Of stone, and dropped down; above him he saw
Huge stone arches and heavy posts,
Holding up the roof of that giant hall.
Then Wiglaf's gentle hands bathed   2720
The blood-stained prince, his glorious lord,
Weary of war, and loosened his helmet.
   Beowulf spoke, in spite of the swollen,
Livid wound, knowing he'd unwound
His string of days on earth, seen   2725
As much as God would grant him; all worldly
Pleasure was gone, as life would go,
Soon:
          "I'd leave my armor to my son,
Now, if God had given me an heir,   2730
A child born of my body, his life
Created from mine. I've worn this crown
For fifty winters: no neighboring people
Have tried to threaten the Geats, sent soldiers
Against us or talked of terror. My days   2735
Have gone by as fate willed, waiting
For its word to be spoken, ruling as well
As I knew how, swearing no unholy oaths,
Seeking no lying wars. I can leave
This life happy; I can die, here,   2740
Knowing the Lord of all life has never
Watched me wash my sword in blood
Born of my own family. Belovèd
Wiglaf, go, quickly, find
The dragon's treasure: we've taken its life,   2745
But its gold is ours, too. Hurry,
Bring me ancient silver, precious

Jewels, shining armor and gems,
Before I die. Death will be softer,
Leaving life and this people I've ruled   2750
So long, if I look at this last of all prizes."

38

    Then Wexstan's son went in, as quickly
As he could, did as the dying Beowulf
Asked, entered the inner darkness
Of the tower, went with his mail shirt and his sword.   2755
Flushed with victory he groped his way,
A brave young warrior, and suddenly saw
Piles of gleaming gold, precious
Gems, scattered on the floor, cups
And bracelets, rusty old helmets, beautifully   2760
Made but rotting with no hands to rub
And polish them. They lay where the dragon left them;
It had flown in the darkness, once, before fighting
Its final battle. (So gold can easily
Triumph, defeat the strongest of men,   2765
No matter how deep it is hidden!) And he saw,
Hanging high above, a golden
Banner, woven by the best of weavers
And beautiful. And over everything he saw
A strange light, shining everywhere,   2770
On walls and floor and treasure. Nothing
Moved, no other monsters appeared;
He took what he wanted, all the treasures
That pleased his eye, heavy plates
And golden cups and the glorious banner,   2775
Loaded his arms with all they could hold.
Beowulf's dagger, his iron blade,
Had finished the fire-spitting terror
That once protected tower and treasures
Alike; the gray-bearded lord of the Geats   2780
Had ended those flying, burning raids
Forever.
        Then Wiglaf went back, anxious
To return while Beowulf was alive, to bring him
Treasure they'd won together. He ran,   2785
Hoping his wounded king, weak
And dying, had not left the world too soon.
Then he brought their treasure to Beowulf, and found
His famous king bloody, gasping
For breath. But Wiglaf sprinkled water   2790
Over his lord, until the words

Deep in his breast broke through and were heard.
Beholding the treasure he spoke, haltingly:
"For this, this gold, these jewels, I thank
Our Father in Heaven, Ruler of the Earth—   2795
For all of this, that His grace has given me,
Allowed me to bring to my people while breath
Still came to my lips. I sold my life
For this treasure, and I sold it well. Take
What I leave, Wiglaf, lead my people,   2800
Help them; my time is gone. Have
The brave Geats build me a tomb,
When the funeral flames have burned me, and build it
Here, at the water's edge, high
On this spit of land, so sailors can see   2805
This tower, and remember my name, and call it
Beowulf's tower, and boats in the darkness
And mist, crossing the sea, will know it."
    Then that brave king gave the golden
Necklace from around his throat to Wiglaf,   2810
Gave him his gold-covered helmet, and his rings,
And his mail shirt, and ordered him to use them well:
"You're the last of all our far-flung family.
Fate has swept our race away,
Taken warriors in their strength and led them   2815
To the death that was waiting. And now I follow them."
    The old man's mouth was silent, spoke
No more, had said as much as it could;
He would sleep in the fire, soon. His soul
Left his flesh, flew to glory.[4]   2820

39

    And then Wiglaf was left, a young warrior
Sadly watching his belovèd king,
Seeing him stretched on the ground, left guarding
A torn and bloody corpse. But Beowulf's
Killer was dead, too, the coiled   2825
Dragon, cut in half, cold
And motionless: men, and their swords, had swept it
From the earth, left it lying in front of
Its tower, won its treasure when it fell
Crashing to the ground, cut it apart   2830
With their hammered blades, driven them deep in
Its belly. It would never fly through the night,
Glowing in the dark sky, glorying

4. The Old English text says, "[His] soul went to seek the judgment of the righteous," relevant in connection with the poem's Christian ethic.

In its riches, burning and raiding: two warriors
Had shown it their strength, slain it with their swords.   2835
Not many men, no matter how strong,
No matter how daring, how bold, had done
As well, rushing at its venomous fangs,
Or even quietly entering its tower,
Intending to steal but finding the treasure's   2840
Guardian awake, watching and ready
To greet them. Beowulf had gotten its gold,
Bought it with blood; dragon and king
Had ended each other's days on earth.
    And when the battle was over Beowulf's followers   2845
Came out of the wood, cowards and traitors,
Knowing the dragon was dead. Afraid,
While it spit its fires, to fight in their lord's
Defense, to throw their javelins and spears,
They came like shamefaced jackals, their shields   2850
In their hands, to the place where the prince lay dead,
And waited for Wiglaf to speak. He was sitting
Near Beowulf's body, wearily sprinkling
Water in the dead man's face, trying
To stir him. He could not. No one could have kept   2855
Life in their lord's body, or turned
Aside the Lord's will: world
And men and all move as He orders,
And always have, and always will.
    Then Wiglaf turned and angrily told them   2860
What men without courage must hear.
Wexstan's brave son stared at the traitors,
His heart sorrowful, and said what he had to:
    "I say what anyone who speaks the truth
Must say. Your lord gave you gifts,   2865
Swords and the armor you stand in now;
You sat on the mead-hall benches, prince
And followers, and he gave you, with open hands,
Helmets and mail shirts, hunted across
The world for the best of weapons. War   2870
Came and you ran like cowards, dropped
Your swords as soon as the danger was real.
Should Beowulf have boasted of your help, rejoiced
In your loyal strength? With God's good grace
He helped himself, swung his sword   2875
Alone, won his own revenge.
The help I gave him was nothing, but all
I was able to give; I went to him, knowing
That nothing but Beowulf's strength could save us,
And my sword was lucky, found some vital   2880

Place and bled the burning flames
Away. Too few of his warriors remembered
To come, when our lord faced death, alone.
And now the giving of swords, of golden
Rings and rich estates, is over,   2885
Ended for you and everyone who shares
Your blood: when the brave Geats hear
How you bolted and ran none of your race
Will have anything left but their lives. And death
Would be better for them all, and for you, than the kind   2890
Of life you can lead, branded with disgrace!"

40

      Then Wiglaf ordered a messenger to ride
Across the cliff, to the Geats who'd waited
The morning away, sadly wondering
If their belovèd king would return, or be killed,   2895
A troop of soldiers sitting in silence
And hoping for the best. Whipping his horse
The herald came to them; they crowded around,
And he told them everything, present and past:
      "Our lord is dead, leader of this people.   2900
The dragon killed him, but the beast is dead,
Too, cut in half by a dagger;
Beowulf's enemy sleeps in its blood.
No sword could pierce its skin, wound
That monster. Wiglaf is sitting in mourning,   2905
Close to Beowulf's body, Wexstan's
Weary son, silent and sad,
Keeping watch for our king, there
Where Beowulf and the beast that killed him lie dead.
      "And this people can expect fighting, once   2910
The Franks, and the Frisians, have heard that our king
Lies dead. The news will spread quickly.
Higlac began our bitter quarrel
With the Franks, raiding along their river
Rhine with ships and soldiers, until   2915
They attacked him with a huge army, and Higlac
Was killed, the king and many of our men,
Mailed warriors defeated in war,
Beaten by numbers. He brought no treasure
To the mead-hall, after that battle. And ever   2920
After we knew no friendship with the Franks.
      "Nor can we expect peace from the Swedes.
Everyone knows how their old king,
Ongentho, killed Hathcyn, caught him

Near a wood when our young lord went   2925
To war too soon, dared too much.
The wise old Swede, always terrible
In war, allowed the Geats to land
And begin to loot, then broke them with a lightning
Attack, taking back treasure and his kidnaped   2930
Queen, and taking our king's life.
And then he followed his beaten enemies,
Drove them in front of Swedish swords
Until darkness dropped, and weary, lordless,
They could hide in the wood. But he waited, Ongentho 2935
With his mass of soldiers, circled around
The Geats who'd survived, who'd escaped him, calling
Threats and boasts at that wretched band
The whole night through. In the morning he'd hang
A few, he promised, to amuse the birds,   2940
Then slaughter the rest. But the sun rose
To the sound of Higlac's horns and trumpets,
Light and that battle cry coming together
And turning sadhearted Geats into soldiers.
Higlac had followed his people, and found them.   2945

41

    "Then blood was everywhere, two bands of Geats
Falling on the Swedes, men fighting
On all sides, butchering each other.
Sadly, Ongentho ordered his soldiers
Back, to the high ground where he'd built   2950
A fortress; he'd heard of Higlac, knew
His boldness and strength. Out in the open
He could never resist such a soldier, defend
Hard-won treasure, Swedish wives
And children, against the Geats' new king.   2955
Brave but wise, he fled, sought safety
Behind earthen walls. Eagerly, the Geats
Followed, sweeping across the field,
Smashing through the walls, waving Higlac's
Banners as they came. Then the gray-haired old king[5] 2960
Was brought to bay, bright sword-blades
Forcing the lord of the Swedes to take
Judgment at Efor's hands. Efor's
Brother, Wulf,[6] raised his weapon
First, swung it angrily at the fierce   2965
Old king, cracked his helmet; blood

5. Ongentho.   6. Efor and Wulf are Geats.

Seeped through his hair. But the brave old Swede
Felt no fear: he quickly returned
A better blow than he'd gotten, faced
Toward Wulf and struck him savagely. And Efor's   2970
Bold brother was staggered, half raised his sword
But only dropped it to the ground. Ongentho's
Blade had cut through his helmet, his head
Spouted blood, and slowly he fell.
The wound was deep, but death was not due   2975
So soon; fate let him recover, live
On. But Efor, his brave brother,
Seeing Wulf fall, came forward with his broad-bladed
Sword, hammered by giants, and swung it
So hard that Ongentho's shield shattered   2980
And he sank to the earth, his life ended.
Then, with the battlefield theirs, the Geats
Rushed to Wulf's side, raised him up
And bound his wound. Wulf's brother
Stripped the old Swede, took   2985
His iron mail shirt, his hilted sword
And his helmet, and all his ancient war-gear,
And brought them to Higlac, his new lord.
The king welcomed him, warmly thanked him
For his gifts and promised, there where everyone   2990
Could hear, that as soon as he sat in his mead-hall
Again Efor and Wulf would have treasure
Heaped in their battle-hard hands; he'd repay them
Their bravery with wealth, give them gold
And lands and silver rings, rich rewards for the glorious   2995
Deeds they'd done with their swords. The Geats agreed. And to prove
Efor's grace in his eyes, Higlac
Swore he'd give him his only daughter.
    "These are the quarrels, the hatreds, the feuds,
That will bring us battles, force us into war   3000
With the Swedes, as soon as they've learned how our lord
Is dead, know that the Geats are leaderless,
Have lost the best of kings, Beowulf—
He who held our enemies away,
Kept land and treasure intact, who saved   3005
Hrothgar and the Danes—he who lived
All his long life bravely. Then let us
Go to him, hurry to our glorious lord,
Behold him lifeless, and quickly carry him
To the flames. The fire must melt more   3010
Than his bones, more than his share of treasure:
Give it all of this golden pile,
This terrible, uncounted heap of cups

And rings, bought with his blood. Burn it
To ashes, to nothingness. No one living   3015
Should enjoy these jewels; no beautiful women
Wear them, gleaming and golden, from their necks,
But walk, instead, sad and alone
In a hundred foreign lands, their laughter
Gone forever, as Beowulf's has gone,   3020
His pleasure and his joy. Spears shall be lifted,
Many cold mornings, lifted and thrown,
And warriors shall waken to no harp's bright call
But the croak of the dark-black raven, ready
To welcome the dead, anxious to tell   3025
The eagle how he stuffed his craw with corpses,
Filled his belly even faster than the wolves."
    And so the messenger spoke, a brave
Man on an ugly errand, telling
Only the truth. Then the warriors rose,   3030
Walked slowly down from the cliff, stared
At those wonderful sights, stood weeping as they saw
Beowulf dead on the sand, their bold
Ring-giver resting in his last bed;
He'd reached the end of his days, their mighty   3035
War-king, the great lord of the Geats,
Gone to a glorious death. But they saw
The dragon first, stretched in front
Of its tower, a strange, scaly beast
Gleaming a dozen colors dulled and   3040
Scorched in its own heat. From end
To end fifty feet, it had flown
In the silent darkness, a swift traveler
Tasting the air, then gliding down
To its den. Death held it in his hands;   3045
It would guard no caves, no towers, keep
No treasures like the cups, the precious plates
Spread where it lay, silver and brass
Encrusted and rotting, eaten away
As though buried in the earth for a thousand winters.   3050
And all this ancient hoard, huge
And golden, was wound around with a spell:
No man could enter the tower, open
Hidden doors, unless the Lord
Of Victories, He who watches over men,   3055
Almighty God Himself, was moved
To let him enter, and him alone.

42

Hiding that treasure deep in its tower,
As the dragon had done, broke God's law
And brought it no good. Guarding its stolen   3060
Wealth it killed Wiglaf's king,
But was punished with death. Who knows when princes
And their soldiers, the bravest and strongest of men,
Are destined to die, their time ended,
Their homes, their halls empty and still?   3065
So Beowulf sought out the dragon, dared it
Into battle, but could never know what God
Had decreed, or that death would come to him, or why.
So the spell was solemnly laid, by men
Long dead; it was meant to last till the day   3070
Of judgment. Whoever stole their jewels,
Their gold, would be cursed with the flames of hell,
Heaped high with sin and guilt, if greed
Was what brought him: God alone could break
Their magic, open His grace to man.   3075
   Then Wiglaf spoke, Wexstan's son:
"How often an entire country suffers
On one man's account! That time has come to us:
We tried to counsel our belovèd king,
Our shield and protection, show him danger,   3080
Urge him to leave the dragon in the dark
Tower it had lain in so long, live there
Till the end of the world. Fate, and his will,
Were too strong. Everyone knows the treasure
His life bought: but Beowulf was worth   3085
More than this gold, and the gift is a harsh one.
I've seen it all, been in the tower
Where the jewels and armor were hidden, allowed
To behold them once war and its terror were done.
I gathered them up, gold and silver,   3090
Filled my arms as full as I could
And quickly carried them back to my king.
He lay right here, still alive,
Still sure in mind and tongue. He spoke
Sadly, said I should greet you, asked   3095
That after you'd burned his body you bring
His ashes here, make this the tallest
Of towers and his tomb—as great and lasting
As his fame, when Beowulf himself walked
The earth and no man living could match him.   3100
Come, let us enter the tower, see
The dragon's marvelous treasure one

Last time: I'll lead the way, take you
Close to that heap of curious jewels,
And rings, and gold. Let the pyre be ready   3105
And high: as soon as we've seen the dragon's
Hoard we will carry our belovèd king,
Our leader and lord, where he'll lie forever
In God's keeping."
                         Then Wiglaf commanded   3110
The wealthiest Geats, brave warriors
And owners of land, leaders of his people,
To bring wood for Beowulf's funeral:
    "Now the fire must feed on his body,
Flames grow heavy and black with him   3115
Who endured arrows falling in iron
Showers, feathered shafts, barbed
And sharp, shot through linden shields,[6]
Storms of eager arrowheads dropping."
    And Wexstan's wise son took seven   3120
Of the noblest Geats, led them together
Down the tunnel, deep into the dragon's
Tower; the one in front had a torch,
Held it high in his hands. The best
Of Beowulf's followers entered behind   3125
That gleaming flame: seeing gold
And silver rotting on the ground, with no one
To guard it, the Geats were not troubled with scruples
Or fears, but quickly gathered up
Treasure and carried it out of the tower.   3130
And they rolled the dragon down to the cliff
And dropped it over, let the ocean take it,
The tide sweep it away. Then silver
And gold and precious jewels were put
On a wagon, with Beowulf's body, and brought   3135
Down the jutting sand, where the pyre waited.

43

    A huge heap of wood was ready,
Hung around with helmets, and battle
Shields, and shining mail shirts, all
As Beowulf had asked. The bearers brought   3140
Their belovèd lord, their glorious king,
A weeping laid him high on the wood.
Then the warriors began to kindle that greatest
Of funeral fires; smoke rose

7. Shields made of linden wood.

Above the flames, black and thick,   3145
And while the wind blew and the fire
Roared they wept, and Beowulf's body
Crumbled and was gone. The Geats stayed,
Moaning their sorrow, lamenting their lord:
A gnarled old woman, hair wound   3150
Tight and gray on her head, groaned
A song of misery, of infinite sadness
And days of mourning, of fear and sorrow
To come, slaughter and terror and captivity.
And Heaven swallowed the billowing smoke.   3155
    Then the Geats built the tower, as Beowulf
Had asked, strong and tall, so sailors
Could find it from far and wide; working
For ten long days they made his monument,
Sealed his ashes in walls as straight   3160
And high as wise and willing hands
Could raise them. And the riches he and Wiglaf
Had won from the dragon, rings, necklaces,
Ancient, hammered armor—all
The treasures they'd taken were left there, too,   3165
Silver and jewels buried in the sandy
Ground, back in the earth, again
And forever hidden and useless to men.
And then twelve of the bravest Geats
Rode their horses around the tower,   3170
Telling their sorrow, telling stories
Of their dead king and his greatness, his glory,
Praising him for heroic deeds, for a life
As noble as his name. So should all men
Raise up words for their lords, warm   3175
With love, when their shield and protector leaves
His body behind, sends his soul
On high. And so Beowulf's followers
Rode, mourning their belovèd leader,
Crying that no better king had ever   3180
Lived, no prince so mild, no man
So open to his people, so deserving of praise.

THE WANDERER

This anonymous poem of the eighth or ninth century A.D. offers us a vivid reflection not only of Old English but of Germanic life generally in its time and long
before. The opening and the closing lines provide a framework of devout Christian
faith for the soliloquy or dramatic monologue spoken by the "wanderer," a solitary

or lonely man. The speaker has been the liegeman of a beloved, generous chieftain, a lord who has long given him both affection and a home. Now that his lord is dead, he must go in search of another. Meanwhile he gives utterance in soliloquy to the deep emotions that his stoic code forbids him to disclose to other men. The geography of the poem is that of the British islands and northern coasts, the landscape more of a seascape, with its rough winds and wild seabirds. The wanderer feels keenly the contrast between these wintry scenes and the happiness and warmth of his lost lord's hall. He is thus led to a pessimistic view of the course of the world and the lot of the people in it; like many poets before and since, he sorrowfully asks, "Where have the good friends and good things gone?" The poet's concluding reliance on "the heavenly Father, our Fortress and Strength" is the typical attitude of the medieval Christian. But the poem has a convincing reality not dependent on religious faith.

Our translator (like Auden in his rendering of the Icelandic *Song of The Seeress*) uses an alliterative pattern broadly similar to that of the Old English original. Thus each line of verse contains two or more stressed syllables with the same sound; for example, "Oft to the Wanderer, weary of exile" shows alliteration with the consonant *w*. Further, any vowel or diphthong may alliterate with any other, as in "Earneth no help. Men eager for honor."

For historical background and English life in the Old English period (c. 500–1100), Dorothy Whitelock, *The Beginnings of English Society* (1952), is excellent and highly readable. For Old English literature in general, see S. B. Greenfield, *A Critical History of Old English Literature* (1965) and C. L. Wrenn, A *Study of Old English Literature* (1966). Scholarly editions of *The Wanderer* include R. A. Leslie, *The Wanderer* (1965) and T. P. Dunning and A. J. Bliss, *The Wanderer* (1969).

The Wanderer[1]

Oft to the Wanderer, weary of exile,
Cometh God's pity, compassionate love,
Though woefully toiling on wintry seas
With churning oar in the icy wave,
Homeless and helpless he fled from Fate.   5
Thus saith the Wanderer mindful of misery,
Grievous disasters, and death of kin:
"Oft when the day broke, oft at the dawning,
Lonely and wretched I wailed my woe.
No man is living, no comrade left,   10
To whom I dare fully unlock my heart.
I have learned truly the mark of a man
Is keeping his counsel and locking his lips,
Let him think what he will! For, woe of heart
Withstandeth not Fate; a failing spirit   15
Earneth no help. Men eager for honor
Bury their sorrow deep in the breast.

1. Translated by Charles W. Kennedy.

So have I also, often, in wretchedness
Fettered my feelings, far from my kin,
Homeless and hapless, since days of old,   20
When the dark earth covered my dear lord's face,
And I sailed away with sorrowful heart,
Over wintry seas, seeking a gold-lord,
If far or near lived one to befriend me
With gift in the mead-hall[2] and comfort for grief.   25
Who bears it, knows what a bitter companion,
Shoulder to shoulder, sorrow can be,
When friends are no more. His fortune is exile,
Not gifts of fine gold; a heart that is frozen,
Earth's winsomeness dead. And he dreams of the hallmen,   30
The dealing of treasure, the days of his youth,
When his lord bade welcome to wassail and feast.
But gone is that gladness, and never again
Shall come the loved counsel of comrade and king.
Even in slumber his sorrow assaileth,   35
And, dreaming, he claspeth his dear lord again,
Head on knee, hand on knee, loyally laying,
Pledging his liege as in days long past.
Then from his slumber he starts lonely-hearted,
Beholding gray stretches of tossing sea,   40
Sea-birds bathing, with wings outspread,
While hail-storms darken, and driving snow.
Bitterer then is the bane of his wretchedness,
The longing for loved one: his grief is renewed.
The forms of his kinsmen take shape in the silence;   45
In rapture he greets them; in gladness he scans
Old comrades remembered. But they melt into air
With no word of greeting to gladden his heart.
Then again surges his sorrow upon him;
And grimly he spurs on his weary soul   50
Once more to the toil of the tossing sea.
No wonder therefore, in all the world,
If a shadow darkens upon my spirit
When I reflect on the fates of men—
How one by one proud warriors vanish   55
From the halls that knew them, and day by day
All this earth ages and droops unto death.
No man may know wisdom till many a winter
Has been his portion. A wise man is patient,
Not swift to anger, nor hasty of speech,   60
Neither too weak, nor too reckless, in war,
Neither fearful nor fain, nor too wishful of wealth,

2. The large public room where a king or chieftain dispensed food and drink to the warriors who served him. Mead is a fermented beverage with a honey base.

Nor too eager in vow—ere he know the event.
A brave man must bide when he speaketh his boast
Until he know surely the goal of his spirit. 65
A wise man will ponder how dread is that doom
When all this world's wealth shall be scattered and waste—
As now, over all, through the regions of earth,
Walls stand rime-covered and swept by the winds.
The battlements crumble, the wine-halls decay; 70
Joyless and silent the heroes are sleeping
Where the proud host fell by the wall they defended.
Some battle launched on their long, last journey;
One a bird bore o'er the billowing sea;
One the gray wolf slew; one a grieving earl 75
Sadly gave to the grave's embrace.
The Warden of men hath wasted this world
Till the sound of music and revel is stilled,
And these giant-built structures stand empty of life.
He who shall muse on these mouldering ruins, 80
And deeply ponder this darkling life,
Must brood on old legends of battle and bloodshed,
And heavy the mood that troubles his heart:
'Where now is the warrior? Where is the war-horse?
Bestowal of treasure, and sharing of feast? 85
Alas! the bright ale-cup, the byrny-clad[3] warrior,
The prince in his splendor—those days are long sped
In the night of the past, as if they never had been!'
And now remains only, for warriors' memorial,
A wall wondrous high with serpent shapes carved. 90
Storms of ash-spears have smitten the earls,
Carnage of weapon, and conquering Fate.
Storms now batter these ramparts of stone;
Blowing snow and the blast of winter
Enfold the earth; night-shadows fall 95
Darkly lowering, from the north driving
Raging hail in wrath upon men.
Wretchedness fills the realm of earth,
And Fate's decrees transform the world.
Here wealth is fleeting, friends are fleeting, 100
Man is fleeting, maid is fleeting;
All the foundation of earth shall fail!"
Thus spake the sage in solitude pondering.
Good man is he who guardeth his faith.
He must never too quickly unburden his breast 105
Of its sorrow, but eagerly strive for redress;

3. Wearing a coat of iron mail.

And happy the man who seeketh for mercy
From his heavenly Father, our Fortress and Strength.

THE STORY OF DEIRDRE

Like the Greeks, the Germanic and Celtic peoples had a Heroic Age. For some centuries after about 1000 B.C., the Celts were the dominant people in Europe north of the Mediterranean and south of Scandinavia; their settlements extended from western Asia (Galatia) to Ireland. In medieval and modern times they are represented by the ethnic groups and languages known as Irish, Scottish Gaelic, Manx, Welsh, Cornish, and Breton. As with the epics of Homer, early Irish literature reflects the civilization and culture of *their* Heroic Age, from approximately the second century B.C. to the fourth century A.D. It was an era of kings not of all Ireland but of each of the four or five provinces, such as Ulaid [oo-lid] (modern Ulster) and Connachta [Con-nak-ta] (modern Connaught, in the west); below these were the kings of the many small tribal nations. There were no cities; the political and social capital was the king's court, a compound of wooden buildings dominated by a large hall or room in which the ruler sat in state (more or less), surrounded by liegemen who, along with the women, slept on beds or on the floor at night. Warriors traveled and fought in two-wheeled chariots drawn by a pair of horses and driven by a charioteer. In this preliterate time learning was the prerogative of the druids, a quasi-professional, perhaps quasi-priestly class who transmitted knowledge orally from one generation to the next. According to the early literature, the kings often looked to them for advice, and they were believed to have the gift of prophecy.

Attached to the royal court there was also apt to be a more or less official storyteller (*scelaige*, [skay-lig-eh] in Irish), who entertained the company with traditional tales (*scela*) [skay-lah] of great men and women and their notable deeds. There was a hierarchy of competence among these professional entertainers; a person holding the highest rank, that of *ollave* [ol-lav], was expected, according to one account, to have a repertory of 350 stories. Probably he called on his memory of outlines of the plots, while depending on his creative imagination for narrative detail. This may account for the brevity of some of the early texts, such as *The Story of Deirdre*. The ordinary use of writing—as distinct from Ogham inscriptions using notches scratched originally on stone or wood or horn—came in with the conversion to Christianity, beginning in the fifth century. The oldest texts of the tales of the Ulster Cycle, as they are called, were written in the eighth and ninth centuries (the extant manuscripts date from the twelfth century and later). The writers—and copiers—were, of course, Christian; this, along with the time interval, explains the paucity of information in the stories about the religion of the Irish before the conversion. Besides, the principal characters may originally have been figures of regeneration or fertility myths, and thus gods, or supernatural beings, who in later, Christian tradition became human. This is doubtless why the heroes and heroines are so often supermen and women. What would be miracles wrought by saints in Christian legend are reported as powers of magic attributed to superhuman heroes. We can recognize this in the prowess of Noisiu [Noy-shu] and his two brothers in the Deirdre story—together, "they could hold off the entire province of Ulaid," and they were as swift as hunting dogs. And the strength and skills of Cuchulainn [Cu-húl-in] the central figure of the *Cattle Raid of Cooley*, greatest and longest work of the Ulster cycle, are clearly supernatural. But his character and personality, like those of Deirdre and Noisiu, are fully and attractively human.

The traditional Irish title of our story was *The Exile of the Sons of Uisliu* [Wees-li-u], in allusion to their flight from the court of Conchobur (Con-co-vor] and subsequent sojourn and travel in Scotland and elsewhere. The prose narrative is brief and bare, yet extraordinarily vivid and moving. The poems in clear images bring before us the (partly) happy life of the exiles as they camp in the open forest, and thus vary the deep mood of fatalistic prophecy at the beginning of the story and, later, the unalloyed pathos of Deirdre's grief for the slain Noisiu. Deirdre and Noisiu are as star-crossed lovers as ever were Juliet and Romeo. Their love, indeed, does not begin in the manner of courtly romance; instead, Noisiu must choose between disobedience to Conchobur and the disgrace that will fall upon him if he refuses Deirdre's challenge. But once the choice is made, the commitment and the devotion of the pair are total and unswerving; and, like Shakespeare's Juliet, Deirdre is the stronger and the more articulate character.

Deirdre has been called the Irish Helen, in allusion to the wife of the Argive king Meneleus, whose abduction by the prince Paris led to the Trojan War. The fatal beauty of one woman caused the destruction of Troy; that of the other woman caused the burning of Emuin Machae [Ev-in Mah-ka], King Conchobur's capital. For more than a millennium Deirdre has haunted the memory and imagination of Irish poets. Among the works of modern Anglo-Irish authors are Synge's *Deirdre of the Sorrows*, a three-act play first produced in 1910 at the Abbey Theatre in Dublin, shorter dramas by Yeats and AE (George William Russell), and a novelistic treatment by James Stephens.

Our ancient narrative begins with the birth of Deirdre at the court of Conchobur, king of the Ulaid, as the people of Ulster were then called. The scene may remind us of situations in Homer; for instance, the company surrounding King Alcinous when Odysseus is invited to tell his story were also eating and drinking. The Greek minstrel has his counterpart in the Irish storyteller; the setting, simpler and cruder than that in Phaeacia, has more ominous elements of wonder and awe. By marvel and by prophecy alike Deirdre is destined for no ordinary life. As in Greek epic and tragedy, the portrayal of major figures may vary from story to story. Creon in *Oedipus the King* is a patient, benign person, unlike the rigid ruler of *Antigone*. In most Irish narratives Conchubur is favorably shown as a beneficent king of the Ulaid and protector of the great Cuchulainn, his nephew. But in the Deirdre story he is the relentless and unscrupulous enemy of the lovers. After promising them a safe return to his court, he plots the assassination of Noisiu and his brothers. They had sworn to eat no food after landing in Ireland until they reached Conchubur's capital. Hence Conchubur first detaches Fergus, the principal "guarantor" on whom Noisiu and Deirdre rely for their safety, from the party of returning travelers. To do this he makes use of a peculiar Irish custom, known as the *geis* [gaysh]—a kind of taboo to which a person might be subject. Now Fergus has a *geis* that requires him never to refuse an invitation to food or drink. He is thus obliged to remain behind while Noisiu and most of the entourage go on—and fall into the power of Conchubur. Later, Fergus will take spectacular revenge; but by then, of course, the sons of Uisliu have been slain and Deirdre made a helpless captive of the king.

An excellent translation of the *Cattle Raid of Cooley* is available in Thomas

Kinsella, *The Táin*, translated from the Irish Epic *Táin Bó Cúailnge* [Tawn Bo Koo-ling-e] (1970). Several shorter tales of the Ulster cycle are admirably translated in Jeffrey Gantz, *Early Irish Myths and Sagas* (1981). Kenneth H. Jackson, *The Oldest Irish Tradition: A Window on the Iron Age* (1964), is the best brief account of Heroic Age civilization and literature in Ireland, (55 pp.). Proinsias Mac Cana, *Celtic Mythology* (1970), is clear, brief, and handsomely illustrated. The largest collection of Old and Middle Irish stories in English translation is T. P. Cross and C. H. Slover, *Ancient Irish Tales* (1936), reprinted with C. W. Dunn as editor (1969). Myles Dillon, *Early Irish Literature* (1948) is an attractive, brief account of the several "cycles" into which the large body of stories has been traditionally divided; it includes representative examples from each cycle (in English translation). Myles Dillon and Nora Chadwick, *The Celtic Realms* (1967) is a comprehensive account of early Celtic culture. Stuart Piggott, *The Druids* (1968), reprinted in the Penguin series (1974), deals with this difficult and controversial subject. P. L. Henry, *The Early English and Celtic Lyric* (1966) is interesting in connection with *The Wanderer* and the poems in *The Story of Deirdre*.

The Story of Deirdre[1]

The Ulaid were drinking at the house of Fedilmid[2] son of Dall, Conchubur's storyteller, and Fedilmid's wife was standing over them and serving, even though she was with child. Drinking horns and portions of food went round, and the house was filled with drunken shouting. When it came time to sleep, Fedilmid's wife rose to go to her bed, but as she crossed the house the child in her womb screamed so that it was heard throughout the court. At that scream the men all rose, and they were standing chin to chin, but Senchae[3] son of Ailill quieted them, saying 'Do not disturb each other! Let the woman be brought to us that we might learn what caused that noise.' So the woman was brought to them, and her husband asked her:

> What is this violent noise that resounds,
> that rages in your roaring womb?
> The outcry between your two sides—mighty its sound—
> crushes the ears of those who hear it.
> My heart is terribly wounded:
> a great fear has seized it.

Then Fedilmid's wife spoke to Cathub,[4] for he was a wise man:

> Listen to Cathub, fair of face,
> a handsome prince, great and powerful his crown,
> exalted by his druid wisdom.
> I myself do not have the white[5] words
> through which my husband might obtain
> an answer to his question,
> for, though it cried out in the cradle of my body,

---

1. Translated by Jeffrey Gantz. 2. [Fay-dil-mid]. 3. [Shen-kay]: A wise counselor at the court of King Conchubur. *Ailill* [Al-il]: This is not the same man as Ailill, king of Connachta. 4. A seer or druid endowed with the gift of prophecy. 5. I.e., true, wise.

> no woman knows
> what her womb bears.

And Cathub replied:

> In the cradle of your womb there cried out
> a woman with twisted yellow hair
> and beautiful grey green eyes.
> Foxglove her purple pink cheeks,
> the colour of snow her flawless teeth,
> brilliant her Parthian-red[6] lips.
> A woman over whom there will be great slaughter
> among the chariot-warriors of Ulaid.
> There screams in your roaring womb
> a tall, beautiful, long-haired woman
> whom champions will contest,
> whom high kings will woo;
> and to the west of Conchubur's province
> there will be a rich harvest of fighting men.
> Parthian-red lips will frame
> those flawless teeth;
> high queens will envy her
> her matchless, faultless form.

Then Cathub placed his hand on the woman's womb, and the child
murmured, and he said 'Indeed, it is a girl, and her name will be Derdriu,[7]
and there will be trouble on her account.' After the girl had been born,
Cathub said:

> Though you may have fame and beauty,
> Derdriu, you will destroy much;
> Ulaid will suffer on your account,
> fair daughter of Fedilmid.

> And after that there will be still more deaths
> because of you, woman like a flame.
> In your lifetime—hear this—
> the three sons of Uisliu will be exiled.

> In your lifetime a violent deed
> will be done at Emuin;
> repented thereafter will be the treachery
> that violated the guarantee of mighty Fergus.

> Because of you, woman of fate,
> Fergus will be exiled from Ulaid,
> and—a deed that will cause much weeping—
> Conchubur's son Fiachnae[8] will be slain.

> Because of you, woman of fate,
> Gerrce[9] son of Illadán will be slain,

6. A deep, rich color, traditionally associated with the Eastern country of Parthia.   7. [Der-dri-oo]: The
nominative case form of the name in Irish.   8. [Fee-ak-nay]: He will be killed in revenge for the treacherous attack on Noísiu, as the narrative tells.   9. [Ger-kay]: Nothing further is told of him. *Illadán:* [Il-
lah-don]

and—a crime no less awful—
Éogan[1] son of Durthacht will be destroyed.

You will do a frightful fierce deed[2]
out of anger at Ulaid's high king;
your grave will be everywhere[3]—
yours will be a famous tale, Derdriu.

'Let the child be slain!' said the young warriors. 'No,' said Conchubur, 'I will take her away tomorrow, and I will rear her as I see fit, and she will be my companion.' And none of the Ulaid dared oppose him. Derdriu was reared by Conchubur until she was by far the most beautiful woman in Ériu.[4] She was reared in a court apart, lest any of the Ulaid see her before she was to sleep with Conchubur, and no one was allowed into that court save her foster-father and her foster-mother[5] and a woman named Lebarcham who was a satirist[6] and could not be barred.

One day, in winter, Derdriu's foster-father was outside, in the snow, flaying a weaned calf for her. Derdriu saw a raven drinking the blood on the snow, and she said to Lebarcham 'I could love a man with those three colours: hair like a raven, cheeks like blood and body like snow.' 'Then luck and good fortune are with you,' answered Lebarcham, 'for such a man is not far off. In fact, he is quite near: Noísiu son of Uisliu.' Derdriu replied 'I will be ill, then, until I see him.'[7]

It happened one day that Noísiu was standing alone on the rampart of the stronghold of Emuin, and he was singing. The singing of the sons of Uisliu was very melodious: every cow that heard it gave two thirds more milk, and every man who heard it grew peaceful and sated with music. The sons of Uisliu were also good fighters: when they stood back to back, they could hold off the entire province of Ulaid. Moreover, they were as swift as hunting hounds and could overtake and kill wild animals.

When Noísiu was outside alone, then, Derdriu stole out to him and made as if to go past, and he did not recognize her. 'A fine heifer[8] that that is going by,' he said. 'The heifers are bound to be fine where there are no bulls,' she answered. 'You have the bull of the province: the king of Ulaid,' Noísiu said. 'Between the two of you, I would choose a young bull like yourself,' Derdriu replied. 'No! There is Cathub's prophecy,' said Noísiu. 'Are you rejecting me, then?' she asked. 'I am, indeed,' he answered. At that, Derdriu leapt at him and seized him by the ears, saying 'Two ears of shame and mockery these unless you take me with you!' 'Away from me, woman!' Noísiu said. 'Too late!'[9] answered Derdriu.

1. [Yóg-an]. *Durthacht* [Door-thakt]: Éogan will be the actual slayer of Noísiu. The narrative does not tell us how Éogan met death.   2. Perhaps a reference to Deirdre's violent suicide.   3. Many places in Ireland will claim to be Deirdre's grave—an indication of her fame.   4. [A-ri-oo]: The usual name of Ireland in the Irish language.   5. Children of the higher classes were often brought up by foster parents; here the names are not given.   6. Satirists—often female—were a prominent feature of early Irish society and literature. It was believed that their invectives could inflict physical injury (through the magical power of words). *Lebarcham*: [Lay-vor-kam].   7. Besides love at first sight, familiar elsewhere in the world, love *before* first sight is frequent in early Irish literature—inspired, as here, by report. 8. No disrespect is intended; rather, admiration. Cattle were a principal form of wealth in the Irish Heroic Age. And one might compare our use of "lamb" or "chick" or "fox" to refer to an attractive young person.   9. The challenge ("two ears of shame and mockery") has already been uttered (and is irreversible).

With that, Noísiu began to sing.[1] When the Ulaid heard his singing they rose up against each other, but the other sons of Uisliu[2] went out to restrain their brother. 'What are you doing?' they asked. 'The Ulaid will be coming to blows on your account.' Then Noísiu told his brothers what had happened. 'Evil will come of this,' they said. 'Even so, you will not be disgraced while we are alive. We will all take her to another land— there is not in Ériu a king who will turn us away.' That was their advice. They departed that night: three fifties of warriors and three fifties of women and three fifties of hounds and three fifties of servants and Derdriu mingled in with them.

For a long time, the brothers found protection with kings throughout Ériu, though through his snares and treacheries Conchubur often attempted to destroy them, from Ess Rúaid[3] to the south-west and then back north-east to Bend Étair. Finally, the Ulaid drove them out of Ériu and into Albu;[4] there, they settled in the wilderness, and, when the game of the mountains ran out, they helped themselves to cattle. One day, the men of Albu gathered to destroy them, so they went to the king of Albu, and he took them into his entourage; they became mercenaries and erected their dwellings on the green. Because of Derdriu, they built their houses so that no one could see her, for they feared there might be killing on her account.

Early one morning, however, the king's steward went out round the house of Derdriu and Noísiu, and he saw the lovers sleeping. At once, he went and awakened the king, saying 'Until now, we have not found a woman worthy of you. But there is with Noísiu son of Uisliu a woman worthy of the king of the western world. Let Noísiu be slain that the woman might sleep with you.' 'No,' replied the king, 'but go to her each day in secret and woo her for me.'

The steward did that, but everything he said to Derdriu she told Noísiu the same night. Since nothing could be got from her, the sons of Uisliu were sent into battles and hazards and dangerous situations that they might be killed, but they were so hardy that every attempt failed. So the men of Albu gathered to kill them; they told Derdriu, and she told Noísiu, saying 'Depart! Unless you leave tonight, you will be slain tomorrow.' That night, Derdriu and the sons of Uisliu departed and went to an island in the sea.

This news reached the Ulaid, and they said to Conchubur, 'A pity that the sons of Uisliu should die in a strange land because of a bad woman. Better that you should be lenient and not slay them—let them return and take them in.' 'Let them come, then,' said Conchubur, 'or let guarantors[5] be sent to them.' That message was taken to Noísiu and his brothers, and they replied, 'A welcome message that. We will come; we ask for Fergus as a guarantor, and Dubthach,[6] and Conchubur's son Cormac.'

So these men went to Albu and accompanied Derdriu and the sons of

---

1. The reticent author does not say whether in exultation or dismay; at any rate, the Ulaid are apparently upset by the loudness of the song.   2. Aindle [End-lay] and Arddán [Ard-dahn]; their names are given in a stanza below.   3. [Es-roo-a]: The modern Asseroe, in the county Donegal. *Bend Étair* [A-tare]: the Hill of Howth, in Dublin Bay.   4. Probably Scotland.   5. Men who would pledge themselves to assure the safety of Noisiu and the rest of the exiles. The guarantors are named a few lines below. 6. [Doov-thak].

Uisliu back to Ériu. On Conchubur's orders, however, the Ulaid all strove to invite Fergus to feasts[7] and banquets, for the sons of Uisliu had sworn that the first food they touched in Ériu would be Conchubur's. Thus, Fergus and Dubthach remained behind, while Fergus's son Fíachu[8] went on with Derdriu and the sons of Uisliu until they reached the green of Emuin Machae. Meanwhile, Éogan son of Durthacht, the king of Fernmag,[9] had made up with Conchubur—the two had long been at odds— and had been charged to kill the sons of Uisliu, who would be kept from Conchubur by the king of Ulaid's mercenaries.

The sons of Uisliu were waiting in the centre of the green; the women of Emuin were sitting along the ramparts; Éogan was crossing the green with his troops. Fíachu came up to join Noísiu. Éogan, however, greeted Noísiu with the point of his spear and broke his back. At that, Fíachu put his arms round Noísiu and pulled him down and covered him, so that thereafter Noísiu was struck from above through the son of Fergus. The sons of Uisliu were then hunted from one end of the green to the other, and no one escaped save by point of spear and edge of sword. Derdriu was taken to stand beside Conchubur, her hands tied behind her.

This news reached Fergus and Dubthach and Cormac, and at once they went to Emuin and performed great deeds. Dubthach killed Conchubur's son Mane[1] and dispatched Fíachnae, the son of Conchubur's daughter Fedelm,[2] with a single blow; Fergus killed Traigthrén[3] son of Traiglethan and his brother. Conchubur was outraged, and a battle ensued: in one day, three hundred Ulaid fell, and Dubthach slew the young women of the province, and Fergus fired Emuin. Afterwards, Fergus and Dubthach and Cormac and their followers went to Connachta, for they knew that Ailill and Medb[4] would maintain them, though Connachta was no refuge of love for men from Ulaid. Three thousand was the number of the exiles, and, for sixteen years, these people saw that there was weeping and trembling in Ulaid every night.

Derdriu spent the year following Noísiu's death with Conchubur, and, during that time, she neither laughed nor smiled, nor did she ever have her fill of food or sleep. She never lifted her head from her knee, and, whenever musicians were brought to her, she recited this poem:

> Fair to you the ardent warriors
> who march into Emuin after an expedition;
> more nobly did they march to their dwelling,
> the three very heroic sons of Uisliu.

> Noísiu with fine hazel mead
> (I would wash him by the fire),
> Arddán with a stag or fine pig,
> Tall Aindle with a load on his back.

7. Conchubur's strategy is explained on p. 1128.   8. [Fee-ah-koo].   9. [Fern-moy].   1. [Mahnay].   2. [Fay-delm].   3. [Trayg-thrayn]. *Traiglethan* [Trayg-leth-an].   4. [Mayv]. Ailill and Medb were the king and queen of the province of Connachta.

Sweet to you the fine mead
that battle-glorious Conchubur drinks;
but often I had before me, across the ocean,
food that was sweeter.

When modest Noísiu spread out
the cooking hearth on the wild forest floor,
sweeter than any honeyed food
was what the son of Uisliu prepared.

Melodious always to you
your pipers and trumpeters;
yet today I tell you
I have heard music that was sweeter.

Melodious to Conchubur, your king,
his pipers and trumpeters;
sweeter to me—fame of hosts—
the singing of the sons of Uisliu.

A wave the sound of Noísiu's voice—
his singing was always sweet;
Arddán's baritone was good,
and Aindle's tenor from his hunting lodge.

Noísiu's grave has now been made,
and the accompaniment was mournful.
For him I poured out—hero of heroes—
the deadly drink that killed him.[5]

Dear his short shining hair,
a handsome man, even very beautiful;
sad that I cannot await him today,
cannot expect the son of Uisliu.

Dear his desire, right and proper,
dear this modest noble warrior;
after his going to the forest's edge,
dear his company in the early morning.

Dear the grey eyes that women loved;
fierce they were to foes.
After a circuit of the forest—a noble union—
dear his tenor through the great dark wood.

I do not sleep now,
nor do I brighten my nails:
there is no joy for me
since the son of Tindell[6] will not come.

I do not sleep
but lie awake half the night;
my thoughts flee from these hosts,
I neither eat nor smile.

5. A figurative expression—she was the cause of his death.   6. The mother of Noísiu and his brothers.

I have today no cause for joy
in the assembly of Emuin—throng of chieftains—
no peace, no delight, no comfort,
no great house, no fine adornments.

And when Conchubur tried to comfort her, she would recite this poem
to him:

Conchubur, be quiet!
You have brought me grief upon sorrow;
as long as I live, surely,
your love will be of no concern to me.

You have taken from me—a great crime—
the one I thought most beautiful on earth,
the one I loved most.
I will not see him again until I die.

His absence is my despair,
the absence of the son of Uisliu.
A jet black cairn over his white body
once so well known among men.

Brighter than a river meadow his glistening cheeks,
red his lips, beetle-black his brows;
the noble colour of snow
his shining, pearly teeth.

Well known his bright garb
among the warriors of Albu;
fair and brilliant his mantle—a noble union—
with its fringe of red gold.

A true treasure his satin tunic
with its hundred gems—a gentle number—
and for decoration, clear and shining,
fifty ounces of white gold.

A gold-hilted sword in his hand,
two steely spears with javelin points;
a shield with a rim of yellow gold
and a boss of silver.

Fair Fergus betrayed us[7]
after bringing us across the great sea;
he sold his honour for beer,
his great deeds are no more.

Although the Ulaid might gather
about Conchubur upon the plain,
I would forsake them all, openly,
for the company of Noísiu son of Uisliu.

7. Deirdre may have been unaware of the dilemma in which Fergus was caught; see p. 1128.

Break no more my heart today—
I will reach my early grave soon enough.
Sorrow is stronger than the sea
if you are wise, Conchubur.

'What do you hate most that you see?' asked Conchubur. 'Yourself, surely, and Éogan son of Durthacht,' she replied. 'Then you will spend a year with Éogan,' Conchubur said. He took her to Éogan. The following day they went to a fair at Emuin Machae, Derdriu standing behind Éogan in his chariot. She had sworn that she would never see her two companions together in the same place. 'Well, Derdriu,' said Conchubur, 'it is the eye of a ewe between two rams you make between myself and Éogan.' There was a great boulder before Derdriu. She let her head be driven against it, and the boulder made fragments of her head, and she died.

THE SONG OF THE SEERESS

People originally from the Scandinavian countries played an important part in the history of northwestern Europe between the eighth and the eleventh centuries A.D. These Danes, Norwegians, and Swedes form a northern group of the Germanic branch of the Indo-European–speaking nations. First as raiders and then as permanent settlers, they occupied the coasts of Ireland, most of England except the southwest, and the peninsula of France hence called Normandy. In the late ninth century they—chiefly the Norwegians—settled Iceland, which continued as an independent country until nearly the middle of the thirteenth century. Like the Celts, these Norse had a rich "oral literature"; for them also the ordinary use of writing began with the conversion to Christianity in the eleventh century. What is notable about the Norse, among the Germanic nations, is the transmission or composition of an abundant pagan mythology. The English, the Germans, and the Dutch in later times kept little of their pre-Christian religious heritage except the names of four of the days of the week. Thus Tuesday preserves the memory of Tiu (Norse Tyr); Wednesday is the day of Woden (Norse Odin); Thursday belongs to Thor; and Friday is the day of the goddess of love and fertility, Freya. But the Norse, and especially the Icelanders, have left us some twenty or twenty-five narrative poems about the gods and the earliest Germanic heroes. In these we hear of Thor's fights against the Giants and the Midgard Serpent, a dragon who lives in the ocean surrounding all the lands; of Odin's contests with elves and his numerous adventures in pursuit of hidden knowledge; and of his dealings with Brunhild, Sigurd (the German Siegfried), Sigmund, and others. From this as ultimate source come the figures and part of the plot framework of Wagner's operatic sequence the *Ring of the Nibelung*. The English and the Germans retained a vivid memory of the demigod Wayland, the marvelous smith; but to understand the allusions to him in their traditions we must turn to the Norse *Völundarkvitha* for the full story.

Although *The Song of the Seeress* incorporates or builds on many of the myths of the gods, it is well-nigh unique—cast in the form of a dialogue between Odin and Heidi, the seeress. (He has called her from the dead to answer his questions.)

In this way the poet presents a vision of the universe: in the beginning, nothing but a primordial giant and empty space, "a yawning gap"; then the shaping of a world order from the body of the giant; then the emergence of the divine figures and the appearance of men and women; the continual confrontation of the gods and the monsters who seek to reduce the cosmos to chaos; and the Armageddon-like end in reciprocal destruction—and a final vision of benevolence and order restored. The poet is often concise and allusive; he was speaking to an audience familiar with myths beyond our knowledge; we cannot always be sure that we are reading him fully or correctly. The *Song* was probably composed near the end of the pagan period (Iceland accepted Christianity in the year 1000); the last section apparently shows influence from Christian ideas about "a new heaven and earth." It is impossible to say how many of the myths in the *Song* and in the other poems of this group (the *Elder Edda*) were a common Germanic heritage and how many were known only among the Scandinavians, or some of them. In any case, our own "nuclear" age should not find it difficult to understand the pervading concep-tion of the *Song*: civilization and life itself are constantly threatened; the gods meanwhile carry on war of sorts to keep them at bay for as long as possible. Many readers will find the portrayal of this struggle not unlike that in J. R. R. Tolkien's *The Lord of the Rings*. To some degree, indeed, the modern author has borrowed the mood and tone of the poem, as well as some proper names; strophe 15 has a number of names used or adapted by Tolkien. And the translators' dedication acknowledges *their* relationship—"For J. R. R. Tolkien."

In his translation the poet W. H. Auden uses a verse form similar to the Norse original. Each line or verse contains at least two, sometimes three alliterating, stressed syllables; thus, in the first line of the poem, "Heidi men call me when their homes I visit," "Heidi" and "homes" alliterate, that is, begin with the same sound, the consonant *h*. The fourth line has three alliterating syllables: "To wicked women welcome always." Further, any vowel or diphthong may alliterate with any other; thus in line 11, "Odin, I know where your eye is concealed," the required alliteration is provided by "Odin" and "eye," while "I" may offer a third syllable if it is stressed in reading.

For translations of the poems in the *Elder Edda* (besides Taylor and Auden), see Henry Adams Bellows, *The Poetic Edda* (1923; and later printings) and L. M. Hollander, *The Poetic Edda* (1962). For the background see E. O. G. Turville-Petre, *Myth and Religion of the North* (1964), as well as his *Origins of Icelandic Literature* (1953).

The Song of the Seeress[1]

1

Heidi men call me when their homes I visit,
A far-seeing witch, wise in talismans,
Caster of spells, cunning in magic,
To wicked women welcome[2] always.

1. Translated by Paul B. Taylor and W. H. Auden.   2. Witches and seeresses had a bad reputation generally in Scandinavia—despite their recognized knowledge.

2

Arm-rings and necklaces, Odin, you gave me   5
To learn my lore, to learn my magic:
Wider and wider through all worlds[3] I see.

3

Outside I sat by myself when you came,
Terror of the Gods, and gazed in my eyes.
What do you ask of me? Why tempt me?   10
Odin, I know where your eye is concealed,[4]
Hidden away in the Well of Mimir:
Mimir each morning his mead drinks
From Valfather's Pledge. *Well, would you know more?*[5]

4

Of Heimdal,[6] too, and his horn I know,   15
Hidden under the holy tree;
Down on it pours a precious stream
From Valfather's Pledge. *Well, would you know more?*

5

Silence I ask of the Sacred Folk,[7]
Silence of the kith and kin of Heimdal:
At your will, Valfather, I shall well relate   20
The old songs of men I remember best.

6

I tell of giants from times forgotten,
Those who fed me in former days:
Nine Worlds I can reckon, nine roots of the Tree,   25
The wonderful Ash, way under the ground.

7

When Ymir[8] lived long ago
Was no sand or sea, no surging waves,

3. The divisions of the universe in which, severally, lived gods, elves, dwarfs, etc.   4. At some time in
the past Odin had given Mimir one of his eyes in return for secret knowledge (hence Odin is regularly
represented with one eye). As the poem says, Mimir (a supernatural being) used the eye as a drinking cup.
Valfather: An epithet of Odin—"Father (i.e., ruler or protector) of the slain." 5. This question, repeated
several times in the poem, dramatizes the tension between the seeress and Odin. Although she boasts of
her knowledge, she would like to be released as soon as possible.   6. Watchman of the gods, whose
horn can summon or warn. *The holy tree*: The World-Ash; see strophe 6 below.   7. The assembly of
gods who, apparently, will hear her along with Odin.   8. The primeval giant from whom the universe
was shaped.

Nowhere was there earth nor heaven above,
But a grinning gap and grass nowhere.   30

8

The Sons of Bur[9] then built up the lands,
Molded in magnificence Middle Earth:[1]
Sun stared from the south on the stones of their hall,
From the ground there sprouted green leeks.

9

Sun turned from the south, Sister of Moon,   35
Her right arm rested on the rim of Heaven;
She had no inkling where her hall was,
Nor Moon a notion of what might be had,
The planets knew not where their places were.[2]

10

The High Gods gathered in council   40
In their Hall of Judgment, all the rulers:
To Night and to Nightfall their names gave,
The Morning they named and the Mid-Day,
Mid-Winter, Mid-Summer, for the assigning of years.

11

At Idavale the Aesir[3] met: 45
Temple and altar they timbered and raised,
Set up a forge to smithy treasures,
Tongs they fashioned and tools wrought;

12

Played chess[4] in the court and cheerful were;
Gold they lacked not, the gleaming metal.   50
Then came Three, the Thurse Maidens,[5]
Rejoicing in their strength, from Gianthome.

---

9. Odin and his brothers Ve and Vili.   1. In the newly ordered world, Asgard, the realm of the gods, was at the center; next was the earth; farthest out was Utgard, including the realms of the giants and other creatures. Earth was in the middle, hence Middle Earth. A similar arrangement in the Tolkien books. 2. At first the sun, moon, and planets had no regular orbits; the gods ordained the regularity we know, and hence the boundaries of day and night, the seasons, etc., as the following strophe sets forth. 3. Aesir is a plural noun; it designates the principal family of the gods. *Idavale:* We are never told where this was, perhaps in the general realm of Asgard.   4. More likely a game such as backgammon. 5. Giantesses; but they appear out of place at this point in the poem.

13

The High Gods gathered in council
In their Hall of Judgment: Who of the dwarves
Should mold man by mastercraft   55
From Brimir's blood and Bláin's limbs?[6]

14

Mótsognir was their mighty ruler,
Greatest of dwarves, and Durin after him:
The dwarves did as Durin directed,
Many man-forms made from the earth.   60

15

Nýi and Nídi, Nordri, Sundri,
Austri and Vestri, Althjóf, Dvalin,
Bívor, Bávor, Bömbur, Nóri,
An and Ánar, Óinn, Mjödvitnir,
Veig and Gandálf, Vindálf, Thorin,   65
Thrór and Thráin, Thekkur, Littur,
Vitur, Nyr and Nýrádur,
Fíli, Kíli, Fundin, Náli,
Hefti, Víli, Hanar, Svíur,
Billing, Brúni, Bíldur, and Buri,   70
Frár, Hornbori, Fraegur, Lóni,
Aurvangur, Jari, Eikinskjaldi:
(All Durin's folk I have duly named.)

16

I must tell of the dwarves in Dvalin's[7] host
Like lions they were in Lokar's time: 75
In Juravale's marsh they made their dwelling,
From their stone hall set out on journeys.

17

There was Draupnir and Dólgthrasir,
Hár, Haugspori, Hlévangur, Glói,
Dori, Ori, Dufur, Andvari,   80
Skirfir, Virfir, Skáfidur, Ái,

---

6. These may be other names for the primeval giant Ymir or, possibly, intermediate members of the Giant family. The "man" of strophe 13 would seem actually to refer to the dwarfs, which were of human shape. At any rate, the following passage is concerned with dwarfs, not men and women.   7. A chief of dwarfs, as probably were also Lokar and Lofar. *Juravale*: Not identified.

Álf and Yngvi, Eikinskjaldi,
Fjalar and Frosti, Finn and Ginnar:
Men will remember while men live
The long line of Lofar's forebears.   85

18

Then from the host Three[8] came,
Great, merciful, from the god's home:
Ash and *Elm* on earth they found,
Faint, feeble, with no fate assigned them.

19

Breath they had not, nor blood nor senses,   90
Nor language possessed, nor life-hue:
Odin gave them breath, Haenir senses,
Blood and life-hue Lodur gave.

20

I know an ash-tree, named Yggdrasil:[9]
Sparkling showers are shed on its leaves   95
That drip dew into the dales below.
By Urd's Well it waves evergreen,
Stands over that still pool,
Near it a bower whence now there come
The Fate Maidens, first Urd.   100
Skuld second, scorer of runes,[1]
Then Verdandi, third of the Norns:
The laws that determine the lives of men
They fixed forever and their fate sealed.

21

The first war in the world I well remember,   105
When Gullveg[2] was spitted on spear points
And burned in the hall of the High God:
Thrice burned, thrice reborn
Often laid low, she lives yet.

8. The gods Odin, Haenir, and Lodur, as explained below. *Ash and Elm:* The first man and woman.
9. The name of the tree; literally, the "steed of Ygg," another name of Odin. Odin hanged himself on the
tree in order to gain secret knowledge.   1. She used the runic alphabet to inscribe prophecies (on wood
or stone). *Urd:* That which has come about—the Past; *Skuld:* That which is destined—the Future; *Verdandi:* That which is becoming—the Present. *Norns:* Fates.   2. The mysterious Gullveg was somehow
connected, apparently, with the conflict between two families of gods, the Aesir and the Vanes (Frey and
Freya, god and goddess of love and fertility). The myth probably reflects first war, then reconciliation
between peoples who had different deities.

22

The gods hastened to their Hall of Judgment, 110
Sat in council to decide whether
To endure great loss in loud strife
Or let both command men's worship.

23

At the host Odin hurled his spear
In the first world-battle; broken was the plankwall 115
Of the god's fortress: the fierce Vanes
Caused war to occur in the fields.

24

The gods hastened to their Hall of Judgment,
Sat in council to discover who
Had tainted all the air with corruption 120
And Odin's Maid offered to the giants.[3]

25

One Thor felled[4] in his fierce rage;
Seldom he sits when of such he hears:
Oaths were broken, binding vows,
Solemn agreements sworn between them. 125

26

Valkyries[5] I saw, coming from afar,
Eagerly riding to aid the Goths;
Skuld bore one shield, Skögul another,
Gunn, Hild, Göngul and Spearskögul:
Duly have I named the Daughters of Odin, 130
The valiant riders, the Valkyries.

27

Baldur I saw, the bleeding god,
His fate still hidden, Odin's son:
Tall on the plain a plant grew,
A slender marvel, the mistletoe. 135

3. This was Loki, a clever but (usually) malevolent figure who often sits with the gods but is actually an ally of the giants and monsters. He contracted with the giants to give them Freya ("Odin's Maid")—and the sun and moon—in payment for building the citadel Asgard, and the gods were committed to the bargain. 4. Thor slew one of the giants. *Oaths were broken:* When the gods finally realized the enormity of the bargain they broke the contract. 5. Literally, "choosers of the slain" in battles, in obedience to Odin, their father. (One of the operas in Wagner's *Ring* is *The Valkyries.*) *Goths:* I.e., men.

28

From that fair shrub, shot by Hödur,
Flew the fatal dart that felled the God,[6]
But Baldur's Brother was born soon after:
Though one night old, Odin's Son
Took a vow to avenge that death.   140

29

His hands he washed not nor his hair combed
Till Baldur's Bane[7] was borne to the pyre:
Deadly the bow drawn by Vali,
The strong string of stretched gut,
But Frigg[8] wept in Fensalir   145
For the woe of Valhalla. *Well, would you know more?*

30

I see one in bonds by the boiling springs;[9]
Like Loki he looks, loathsome to view:
There Sigyn sits, sad by her husband,
In woe by her man. *Well, would you know more?*   150

31

From the east through Venom Valley runs
Over jagged rocks the River Gruesome.

32

North, in Darkdale, stands the dwelling place
Of Sindri's kin,[1] covered with gold;
A hall also in Everfrost,   155
The banquet hall of Brimir the Giant.

33

A third I see, that no sunlight reaches,
On Dead Man's Shore: the doors face northward,
Through its smoke vent venom drips,
Serpent skins enskein that hall.   160

6. Loki induced the blind god Hödur to cast a spear made of mistletoe at Baldur, who was invulnerable to any other material.   7. Baldur's slayer, Hödur, was slain in turn by Vali, a son of Odin. The line refers to cremation on a funeral pyre.   8. The wife of Odin and mother of Baldur; Fensalir is the name of her dwelling. *Valhalla:* Odin's great hall.   9. Loki has been captured by the gods and placed in bonds. Sigyn is Loki's wife.   1. The dwarves.

34

Men wade there,[2] tormented by the stream,
Vile murderers, men forsworn,
And artful seducers of other men's wives:
Nidhógg[3] sucks blood from the bodies of the dead,
The Wolf rends them. *Well, would you know more?*   165

35

In the east dwells a crone,[4] in Ironwood:
The brood of Fenris are bred there,
Wolf-monsters, one of whom
Eventually shall devour the sun.

36

The giant's Watchman, joyful Eggthur,   170
Sits on his howe and harps well:
The red cock,[5] called All-Knower
Boldly crows from Birdwood.

37

Goldencomb to the Gods crows,
Who wakes the warriors in Valhalla: 175
A soot-red hen also calls
From Hel's Hall, deep under the ground.

38

Loud howls Garm before Gnipahellir,[6]
Bursting his fetters, Fenris runs:
Further in the future, afar I behold   180
The Twilight of the gods[7] who gave victory.

39

Brother shall strike brother and both fall,
Sisters' sons slay each other,

2. The river is in Hel, a cold, dark area, the abode of the dead, where crimes committed in life are punished.   3. A dragon; he also gnaws at the roots of the World-Ash. *The Wolf:* It is uncertain whether this is one of the family of Fenris (strophe 35) or another wolf.   4. The mother of two wolves; one, Skoll, will swallow the sun at the end of the world-order; the other, Hati, will swallow the moon. *Ironwood* and *Birdwood* are not precisely located by the poet.   5. The red cock in the Giants' realm, Goldencomb in Valhalla, the hall of Odin, and the "red hen" in Hel form a series. *Howe:* A mound or a low hill. 6. The entrance to Hel, guarded by the monstrous dog Garm.   7. "Twilight" corresponds to the term used in Wagner's opera *Götterdämmerung*, but the Norse term almost certainly means "the destruction of the gods."

Evil be on earth, an Age of Whoredom,
Of sharp sword-play and shields' clashing,   185
A Wind-Age, a Wolf-Age, till the world ruins:
No man to another shall mercy show.

40

The waters are troubled, the waves surge up:
Announcing now the knell of Fate,
Heimdal winds his horn aloft,[8]   190
On Hel's Road all men tremble.

41

Yggdrasil trembles, the towering Ash
Groans in woe; the Wolf is loose:
Odin speaks with the Head of Mimir
Before he is swallowed by Surt's kin.[9]   195

42

From the east drives Hrym,[1] lifts up his shield,
The squamous serpent squirms with rage,
The Great Worm with the waves contending,
The pale-beaked eagle pecks at the dead,
Shouting for joy: the ship Naglfar[2]   200

43

Sails out from the east, at its helm Loki,
With the children of darkness, the doom-bringers,
Offspring of monsters, allies of the Wolf,
All who Byleist's Brother[3] follow.

44

What of the gods? What of the elves?   205
Gianthome groans, the gods are in council,
The dwarves grieve before their door of stone,
Masters of walls. *Well, would you know more?*

8. As a warning signal that the monsters are approaching Asgard, the capital of the gods.   9. Fenris,
the wolf who will finally swallow Odin. Surt was a giant whose weapon was fire (hence the name—Surtsey,
Surt's island—given to the island formed by the volcanic eruption off the south coast of Iceland in 1963).
1. The leader of the Giants in the final assault. *The squamous serpent . . . the Great Worm:* Both terms
refer to the Midgard serpent or dragon who lies in the ocean.   2. A ship made of dead men's
fingernails.   3. Loki.

45

Surt with the bane-of-branches[4] comes
From the south, on his sword the sun of the Valgods,   210
Crags topple, the crone falls headlong,
Men tread Hel's Road, the Heavens split open.

46

A further woe falls upon Hlín[5]
As Odin comes forth to fight the Wolf;
The killer of Beli[6] battles with Surt: 215
Now shall fall Frigg's beloved.

47

Now valiant comes Valfather's Son,
Vidar, to vie with Valdyr[7] in battle,
Plunges his sword into the Son of Hvedrung,
Avenging his father with a fell thrust.   220

48

Now the Son of Hlödyn and Odin[8] comes
To fight with Fenris; fiercest of warriors,
He mauls in his rage all Middle Earth;
Men in fear all flee their homesteads;
Nine paces back steps Bur's Son,[9]   225
Retreats from the Worm, of taunts unafraid.

49

Now death is the portion of doomed men,
Red with blood the buildings of gods,
The sun turns black in the summer after,
Winds whine. *Well, would you know more?*   230

50

Earth sinks in the sea, the sun turns black,
Cast down from Heaven are the hot stars,

---

4. An epithet of fire, which destroys the limbs of trees. *Sun of the Valgods:* More literally, the sun is reflected from the sword of the Battle-gods. *The Crone:* The mother of two wolves who will swallow the sun and moon.   5. Another name of Frigg, wife of Odin.   6. The god Frey; Beli was a giant. *Frigg's beloved:* Her husband, Odin.   7. The wolf Fenris, who is also the "Son of Hvethrung."   8. Thor, who destroys the Midgard Serpent but is himself mortally injured by the poison of the Serpent. The Icelandic text is not clear, but Fenris must be incorrect here, for he has already been slain.   9. Thor.

Fumes reek, into flames burst,
The sky itself is scorched with fire.

51

I see Earth rising a second time   235
Out of the foam, fair and green;
Down from the fells, fish to capture,
Wings the eagle; waters flow.

52

At Idavale the Aesir meet:
They remember the Worm of Middle Earth,   240
Ponder again the Great Twilight
And the ancient runes of the High God.

53

Boards shall be found of a beauty to wonder at,
Boards of gold in the grass long after,
The chess boards they owned in the olden days.   245

54

Unsown acres shall harvests bear,
Evil be abolished, Baldur return
And Hropt's[1] Hall with Hödur rebuild,
Wise gods. *Well, would you know more?*

55

Haenir shall wield the wand of prophecy,   250
The sons of two brothers[2] set up their dwelling
In wide Windhome. *Well, would you know more?*

56

Fairer than sunlight, I see a hall,
A hall thatched with gold in Gimlé:[3]
Kind lords shall live there in delight for ever.   255

---

1. Hropt was another name for Odin.   2. Perhaps the sons of Ve and Vili, brothers of Odin.
3. Apparently "meadow of gems"—a name for a kind of earthly paradise.

57

Now rides the Strong One[4] to Rainbow Door,
Powerful from heaven, the All-Ruler:
From the depths below a drake comes flying,
The Dark Dragon[5] from Darkfell,
Bears on his pinions the bodies of men,   260
Soars overhead. I sink now.[6]

THORSTEIN THE STAFF-STRUCK

Medieval Iceland produced not only a unique and highly interesting body of poetry but also some of the finest prose narratives in European literature. Some of these, like the *Saga of the Volsungs*, deal with figures of early Germanic tradition. But some thirty or forty, called sagas of Icelanders, are about men and women who lived in Iceland (and often in Norway in their youth) from the late ninth to the early eleventh centuries. Written mostly in the thirteenth century, they may remind us a bit of the historical novels of a later time. But in the historical novel, usually, the major characters are fictional, products of the author's invention, while those well known to history serve as framework or background. In the Icelandic saga the converse is true: the principal figures were actual people attested by documents and other evidence, as were also most of the events and acts attributed to them. Oral tradition bridged the interval between the tenth century and the thirteenth. Thus the author of an extant saga was free to shape characterization, motivation, mood, and tone as he saw fit. It is now believed that the milieu of thirteenth-century Iceland may have influenced features of some of these narratives. A few may have been entirely fictional, except for the use of the names of actual persons. Like the Eddic poems, the sagas are nearly always anonymous. Some of the most notable are of novel length, like the *Saga of the Laxdalers* or the Grettir saga, or the *Saga of Burnt Njal*, greatest of all.

As must be evident, the story of Thorstein the Staff-Struck is very short; in fact, it was not called a saga but a *tháttr*, literally, a "thread." Nevertheless, it shows the characteristic features of a family saga. Although the action is "strong," to use a modern term—people kill and are killed—violence is not included for its own sake; instead, it interests the narrator chiefly as an expression of personality and character. The incidents of the story are conducted in such a way as to distinguish sharply nearly all of the participants; these are all members of one or the other of two families or households who live in northeast Iceland. The "fierce," now aged but still irascible Thorarin is contrasted with his husky and confident but even-tempered son Thorstein; only when the insolent Thord wilfully insults him does Thorstein take action. In prosecuting Thorstein for manslaughter, Bjarni, Thord's employer and also the district chieftain, fullfils a more or less automatic obligation. However, when Thorstein ignores the sentence of exile, Bjarni (whose responsibility it was to attack Thorstein) takes no action. We learn that he is unwilling to deprive the

---

4. Apparently a benevolent deity, but the name is uncertain. The Rainbow Door is probably the earth; in Norse mythology the rainbow was a bridge reaching from heaven to earth.   5. Neither his identity nor his role is clear.   6. The seeress ends her discourse; she will now return to the realm of the dead.

infirm, nearly blind Thorarin of his son's support. Nevertheless, when Bjarni over-hears the malicious gossip of Thorhall and Thorvald, he sends them out with instructions to kill Thorstein. We are not told what he expected would happen, but when he learns that Thorstein has slain the two brothers, once again he does nothing; when his wife Rannveig goads him, he remarks that "Thorstein has never killed anyone without a good reason." All the same, when she tells him of the taunts in circulation about him, he decides that he cannot avoid a confrontation with Thorstein.

Although the circumstances are different, Bjarni's motive in his (reluctant) chal-lenge of Thorstein is the same as the latter's when he (at last) challenges Thord. Each man considers the respect of the community essential to his self-respect; hence they act as the code requires, regardless of their personal inclination or of the intrinsic merits of the case. The thirteenth-century Christian author faithfully presents this pre-Christian pattern; the ethical dilemma, unacknowledged by the protagonists, is implicit in the narration. Hence in the final encounter Bjarni and Thorstein carry out the *form* of conduct that tradition makes obligatory, while the *manner* in which they do so insures a morally satisfactory result.

Readers will enjoy this succinct narrative best if they ask themselves such ques-tions—among others—as: What purposes are served by the dialogue? What is Thorarin's motive for each of his acts? How does the author make use of the two female characters?

A concise general account of the family sagas is Peter Hallberg, translated by Paul Schach, *The Icelandic Saga* (1962). A critical study of structure and organi-zation, with plot summaries, is Theodore M. Anderson, *The Icelandic Family Saga* (1967). Admirable translations of several of the principal sagas are available in the Penguin paperback series. Jesse Byock, *Feud in the Icelandic Sage* (1982) is a recent scholarly study. Jacqueline Simpson, *Icelandic Folktales and Legends* (1972), paperback printing (1979), provides a modern translation of short narratives (not sagas) collected especially from oral sources.

Thorstein the Staff-Struck[1]

There was a man called Thorarin who lived at Sunnudale; he was old and nearly blind. He had been a fierce viking in his younger years, and even in his old age he was very hard to deal with. He had an only son, Thor-stein, who was a tall man, powerful but even-tempered; he worked so hard on his father's farm that three other men could hardly have done any better. Thorarin had little money, but a good many weapons. He and his son owned some breeding horses and that was their main source of income, for the young colts they sold never failed in spirit or strength.

Bjarni of Hof[2] had a servant called Thord who looked after his riding horses and was considered very good at the job. Thord was an arrogant man and would never let anyone forget the fact that he was in the service of a chieftain. But this didn't make him a better man and added nothing

---

1. Translated, with footnotes, by Hermann Pálsson.   2. Bjarni of Hof was the local chieftain, and the wealthiest and most powerful farmer in the district.

to his popularity. Bjarni also had two brothers working for him who were called Thorhall and Thorvald, both great scandalmongers about any gossip they heard in the district.

Thorstein and Thord arranged a horse-fight for their young stallions.[3] During the fight, Thord's horse started giving way, and when Thord realized he was losing, he struck Thorstein's horse a hard blow on the jaw. Thorstein saw this and hit back with an even heavier blow at Thord's horse, forcing it to back away. This got the spectators shouting with excitement. Then Thord aimed a blow at Thornstein with his horse-goad, hitting him so hard on the eye-brow that the skin broke and the lid fell hanging down over the eye. Thorstein tore a piece off his shirt and bandaged his head. He said nothing about what had happened, apart from asking people to keep this from his father. That should have been the end of the incident, but Thorvald and Thorhall kept jeering at Thorstein and gave him the nickname Staff-Struck.

One morning that winter just before Christmas, when the women at Sunnudale were getting up for their work, Thorstein went out to feed the cattle. He soon came back and lay down on a bench. His father, old Thorarin, came into the room and asked who was lying there. Thorstein told him.

'Why are you up so early, son?' said Thorarin.

Thorstein answered, 'It seems to me there aren't many men about to share the work with me.'

'Have you got a head-ache, son?' said Thorarin.

'Not that I've noticed,' said Thorstein.

'What can you tell me about the horse-fight last summer, son?' said Thorarin. 'Weren't you beaten senseless like a dog?'

'It's no credit to me if you call it a deliberate blow, not an accident,' said Thorstein.

Thorarin said, 'I'd never have thought I could have a coward for a son.'

'Father,' said Thorstein, 'Don't say anything now that you'll live to regret later.'

'I'm not going to say as much as I've a mind to,' said Thorarin.

Thorstein got to his feet, seized his weapons and set off. He came to the stable where Thord was grooming Bjarni's horses, and when he saw Thord he said, 'I'd like to know, friend Thord, whether it was accidental when you hit me in the horse-fight last summer, or deliberate. If it was deliberate, you'll be willing to pay me compensation.'

'If only you were double-tongued,' said Thord, 'then you could easily speak with two voices and call the blow accidental with one and deliberate with the other. That's all the compensation you're getting from me.'

'In that case don't expect me to make this claim a second time,' said Thorstein.

With that he rushed at Thord and dealt him his death-blow. Then he

---

3. Horse-fights used to be a favourite sport in Iceland. Two stallions were pitted against one another, and behind each of them there was a man equipped with a goad to prod them on. At these horse fights tempers would often run high.

went up to the house at Hof where he saw a woman standing outside the door. 'Tell Bjarni that a bull has gored Thord, his horse-boy,' he said to her, 'and also that Thord will be waiting for him at the stable.'

'Go back home, man,' she said. 'I'll tell Bjarni in my own good time.' Thorstein went back home, and the woman carried on with her work.

After Bjarni had got up that morning and was sitting at table, he asked where Thord could be, and was told he had gone to see to the horses.

'I'd have thought he'd be back by now, unless something has happened to him,' said Bjarni.

The woman Thorstein had spoken to broke in. 'It's true what we women are often told, we're not very clever. Thorstein the Staff-Struck came here this morning and he said Thord had been gored by a bull and couldn't look after himself. I didn't want to wake you, and then I forgot all about it.'

Bjarni left the table, went over to the stable and found Thord lying there, dead. Bjarni had him buried, then brought a court action against Thorstein and had him sentenced to outlawry for manslaughter. But Thorstein stayed on at Sunnudale and worked for his father, and Bjarni did nothing more about it.

One day in the autumn when the men of Hof were busy singeing sheep's heads[4], Bjarni lay down on top of the kitchen wall to listen to their talk. Now the brothers Thorhall and Thorvald started gossiping; 'It never occurred to us when we came to live here with Killer-Bjarni[5] that we'd be singeing lambs' heads while his outlaw Thorstein is singeing the heads of wethers. It would have been better for Bjarni to have been more lenient with his kinsmen at Bodvarsdale and not to let his outlaw at Sunnudale act just like his own equal. But "A wounded coward lies low," and it's not likely that he'll ever wipe away this stain on his honour.'

One of the men said, 'Those words were better left unsaid, the trolls must have twisted your tongue. I think Bjarni simply isn't prepared to take the only breadwinner at Sunnudale away from Thorstein's blind father and other dependents there. I'll be more than surprised if you singe many more lambs' heads here, or tattle on much longer about the fight at Bodvarsdale.'

Then they went inside to have their meal, and after that to bed. Bjarni gave no sign that he had heard anything of what had been said. But early next morning he roused Thorhall and Thorvald and told them to ride over to Sunnudale and bring him Thorstein's severed head before mid-morning. 'I think you're more likely than anyone else to wipe away that stain from my honour, since I haven't the courage to do it for myself,' he said.

The brothers realized they had said too much, but they set off and went over to Sunnudale. Thorstein was standing in the doorway, sharpening a short sword. He asked them where they were going, and they told him they

---

4. In Iceland, as in some other sheep-raising countries, sheep's heads were (and still are) considered a great delicacy. The heads are singed over a fire to remove all traces of wool before they are cleaned and cooked.   5. The name Killer-Bjarni is an allusion to the fact that Bjarni fought and killed some of his own kinsmen in the battle of Bodvarsdale which is mentioned in the following sentence.

were looking for some horses. Thorstein said they didn't have very far to go. 'The horses are down by the fence.'

'We're not sure we'll be able to find them unless you tell us more precisely,' they said.

Thorstein came outside, and as they were walking together across the meadow, Thorvald raised his axe and rushed at him. But Thorstein pushed him back so hard that he fell, then ran him through with the short sword. Thorhall tried to attack Thorstein and went the same way as his brother. Thorstein tied them to their saddles, fixed the reins to the horses' manes, and drove them off.

The horses went back to Hof. Some of the servants there were out of doors and went inside to tell Bjarni that Thorvald and Thorhall had come back and their journey hadn't been wasted. Bjarni went outside and saw what had happened. He said nothing and had the two men buried. Then everything was quiet till after Christmas.

One evening after Bjarni and his wife Rannveig had gone to bed, she said to him, 'What do you think everyone in the district is talking about these days?'

'I couldn't say,' said Bjarni. 'In my opinion most people talk a lot of rubbish.'

'This is what people are mainly talking about now,' she continued: 'They're wondering how far Thorstein the Staff-Struck can go before you bother to take revenge. He's killed three of your servants, and your supporters are beginning to doubt whether you can protect them, seeing that you've failed to avenge this. You often take action when you shouldn't and hold back when you should.'

'It's the same old story,' said Bjarni, 'no one seems willing to learn from another man's lesson. Thorstein has never killed anyone without a good reason—but still, I'll think about your suggestion.'

With that they dropped the subject and slept through the night. In the morning Rannveig woke up as Bjarni was taking down his sword and shield. She asked him where he was going.

'The time has come for me to settle that matter of honour between Thorstein of Sunnudale and myself,' he said.

'How many men are you taking with you?' she asked.

'I'm not taking a whole army to attack Thorstein,' he said. 'I'm going alone.'

'You mustn't do that,' she said, 'risking your life against the weapons of that killer.'

'You're a typical woman,' said Bjarni, 'arguing against the very thing you were urging just a few hours ago! There's a limit to my patience, I can only stand so much taunting from you and others. And once my mind's made up, there's no point in trying to hold me back.'

Bjarni went over to Sunnudale. He saw Thorstein standing in the doorway, and they exchanged some words.

'You'll fight me in single combat,' said Bjarni, 'on that hillock over there in the home-meadow.'

'I'm in no way good enough to fight you,' said Thorstein. 'I give you my promise to leave the country with the first ship that sails abroad. I know a generous man like you will provide my father with labour to run the farm if I go away.'

'You can't talk yourself out of this now,' said Bjarni.

'You'll surely let me go and see my father first,' said Thorstein.

'Certainly,' said Bjarni.

Thorstein went inside and told his father that Bjarni had come and challenged him to a duel.

The old man said, 'Anybody who offends a more powerful man in his own district can hardly expect to wear out many more new shirts. In my opinion your offences are so serious, I can't find any excuse for you. So you'd better take your weapons and defend yourself the best you can. In my younger days I'd never have given way before someone like Bjarni, great fighting-man though he may be. I'd much rather lose you than have a coward for a son.'

Thorstein went outside and walked with Bjarni up the hillock. They started fighting with determination and destroyed each other's shield. When they had been fighting for a long time, Bjarni said to Thorstein, 'I'm getting very thirsty now, I'm not so used to hard work as you are.'

'Go down to the stream then and drink,' said Thorstein.

Bjarni did so, and laid the sword down beside him. Thorstein picked it up, examined it and said, 'You can't have been using this sword at Bodvarsdale.'

Bjarni said nothing, and they went back to the hillock. After they'd been fighting for a time, it became obvious to Bjarni that Thorstein was a highly skilled fighter, and the outcome seemed less certain than he'd expected.

'Everything seems to go wrong for me today,' he said. 'Now my shoethong's loose.'

'Tie it up then,' said Thorstein.

When Bjarni bent down to tie it, Thorstein went into the house and brought back two shields and a sword. He joined Bjarni on the hillock and said, 'Here's a sword and shield my father sends you. The sword shouldn't get so easily blunted as the one you've been using. And I don't want to stand here any longer with no shield to protect me against your blows. I'd very much like us to stop this game now, for I'm afraid your good luck will prove stronger than my bad luck. Every man wants to save his life, and I would too, if I could.'

'There's no point in your trying to talk yourself out of this,' said Bjarni. 'The fight must go on.'

'I wouldn't like to be the first to strike,' said Thorstein.

Then Bjarni struck at Thorstein, destroying his shield, and Thorstein hacked down Bjarni's shield in return.

'That was a blow,' said Bjarni.

Thorstein replied, 'Yours wasn't any lighter.'

Bjarni said, 'Your sword seems to be biting much better now than it was earlier.'

'I want to save myself from the foulest of luck if I possibly can,' said Thorstein. 'It scares me to have to fight you, so I want you yourself to settle the matter between us.'

It was Bjarni's turn to strike. Both men had lost their shields. Bjarni said, 'It would be a great mistake in one stroke both to throw away good fortune and do wrong. In my opinion I'd be fully paid for my three servants if you took their place and served me faithfully.'

Thorstein said, 'I've had plenty of opportunity today to take advantage of you, if my bad luck had been stronger than your good luck. I'll never deceive you.'

'Now I can see what a remarkable man you must be,' said Bjarni. 'You'll allow me to go inside to see your father and tell him about this in my own words?'

'You can go if you want as far as I'm concerned,' said Thorstein, 'but be on your guard.'

Bjarni went up to the bed-closet where Old Thorarin was lying. Thorarin asked who was there, and Bjarni told him.

'What's your news, friend Bjarni?' said Thorarin.

'The killing of Thorstein, your son,' said Bjarni.

'Did he put up any defence at all?' asked Thorarin.

'I don't think there's ever been a better fighter than your son, Thorarin,' said Bjarni.

'It's no wonder your opponents at Bodvarsdale found you so hard to deal with,' said Thorarin, 'seeing that you've overcome my son.'

Bjarni said, 'I want to invite you to come over to Hof and take the seat of honour there for the rest of your life. I'll be just like a son to you.'

'I'm in the same position now as any other pauper,' said Thorarin. 'Only a fool accepts a promise gladly, and promises of chieftains like yourself aren't usually honoured for more than a month after the event, while you're trying to console us. After that we're treated as ordinary paupers, though our grief doesn't grow any the less for that. Still, anyone who shakes hands on a bargain with a man of your character should be satisfied, in spite of other men's lessons. So I'd like to shake hands with you, and you'd better come into the bed-closet to me. Come closer now, for I'm an old man and trembling on my feet because of ill-health and old age. And I must admit, the loss of my son has upset me a bit.'

Bjarni went into the bed-closet and shook Thorarin by the hand. Then he realized the old man was groping for a short sword with the idea of thrusting it at him. Bjarni pulled back his hand and said, 'You merciless old rascal! I can promise you now you'll get what you deserve. Your son Thorstein is alive and well, and he'll come with me over to Hof, but you'll be given slaves to run the farm for you, and never suffer any want for the rest of your life.'

Thorstein went with Bjarni over to Hof, and stayed in his service for the rest of his life. He was considered a man of great courage and integrity. Bjarni kept his standing and became better-liked and more self-controlled the older he grew. He was a very trustworthy man. In the last years of his life he became a devout Christian and went to Rome on pilgrimage. He died on that journey, and is buried at a town called Sutri,[6] just north of Rome.[7]

THE SONG OF ROLAND

With some literal inaccuracy, but with substantial truth, it has been said that French literature begins with the *Song of Roland*. Certainly it is the first great narrative poem in that language. Of unknown authorship and date, it was apparently composed in the decade or decades after the year 1100. Imbued with the spirit of the First Crusade, it seems to reproduce some details of the campaigns and expeditions to capture and hold the Holy Land for Christendom. The story it tells was developed from a historical incident in the career of Charlemagne (Charles the Great). As the Emperor was returning from a successful war in northern Spain, the Gascons attacked his baggage train and rearguard in the mountain passes of the Pyrenees. The rearguard perished, including Roland, the prefect of the Breton March. These events occurred in the year 778. Our poet of the twelfth century has transformed them—somewhat as Geoffrey of Monmouth, Chrétien de Troyes, and Malory transformed incidents involving the (probably also historical) Arthur, his exploits, and the deeds of his warriors. The Charles of the *Roland*, a magnificent figure, is white-haired and venerable, and not without a touch of the miraculous: though still valiant in fight, he is reputed among the enemy to be two hundred years old, or more. He is served especially by a choice band of leaders, the twelve peers, of whom the chief is Roland, his nephew—a relationship that in Heroic narrative intensifies either loyalty or disloyalty. The enemy, too, has been changed. Not a few border Gascons or Basques, but enormous Saracen armies fight against Roland and the Emperor. Thus we have a holy war; all the motives of a Crusade are invoked in this struggle of Christians against Mohammedans. Keeping the Emperor as the central *background* figure, the poet has concentrated his efforts on Roland as the hero, the central *foreground* character. Close beside him stand Oliver, the wise and faithful friend, and Ganelon, whose hatred of Roland leads him to treason against Charles.

The world of the poem is an idealization of feudal society in the early twelfth century. This society was headed by proud barons—a hereditary nobility—whose independent spirit found liberal scope in valiant action, fierce devotion, and bitter personal antagonism. A man was esteemed for his prowess in battle, for his loyalty to his king or other feudal chief, and for his wisdom, as the portrait of Oliver reminds us. The action of the poem is infused with a warm glow of patriotic feeling—not the flag-waving variety, but a cherishing love of the homeland, "sweet France." It might be called regional rather than political patriotism, for in a feudal regime a man's binding obligations are to his lord rather than to the country as a whole. Yet the larger issue enters, in a special way: in the second half of the poem, Ganelon is finally condemned and punished because in compassing the destruc-

---

6. The MSS have Vateri, which is probably a scribal error. The town Sutri is mentioned elsewhere in early Icelandic records.   7. The story concludes with a long account of Bjarni's descendants, extending into the thirteenth century. [Editor's note.]

tion of Roland he has injured the king and the French nation; the poet denies
Ganelon's claim that these are separable things.

The present volume includes only the first half of the poem, but this portion has
a satisfactory completeness. We see the anger of Ganelon at Roland, out of which
grows his treachery and the attack of the Saracens; the valor of Roland, and the
rest, in battle; and their heroic death. The second half of the poem relates the
vengeance taken by Charles against the Saracens—in two separate battles—and the
trial and execution of Ganelon. Although the *Song of Roland* was the work, and
probably the *written* work, of a well-educated man, during the period immediately
following its composition it was sung or chanted. It is divided into strophes aver-
aging fourteen lines, each of ten (or eleven) syllables.

It is easy to see why modern French readers and critics assign the *Roland* a high
place in their national literature. Inherent in its structure and texture are the qualities especially esteemed in the French literary tradition—clarity of focus, lucidity
in exposition and narration, definite design, and mastery of technical detail. In the
poem as a whole—even in our abridgment of a part—scale and proportion are
evident. The succession of quarrels, treachery, and battles is only the raw material
out of which the poet has built a highly wrought work of art. The emphasis on
action—on what Roland, Ganelon, and Oliver do and say—has been recognized
since Aristotle as the right method for a poet. But mere action is the formula of the
adventure story. The great-literature standard requires that the action have significance—which the author of the *Roland* has provided in rich and ordered variety.
The acts of the hero, of his friend, and of his foe are presented as part of the total
character of each; they grow out of the whole man, including his temperament
and personality. But they are also presented against an ethical and social background. Every act, every decision, bears a relation to the feudal code of conduct,
of right and wrong, and hence is an indication of human good or evil. Courage
rather than cowardice, loyalty rather than treachery, judgment rather than folly—
a belief in these criteria is implicit or explicit in the presentation of each action.
And they apply to the outermost frame within which the poet has placed the specific events of the narrative—the contest between Christianity and paganism. For
to the author and his audience the Christian cause is just, the Saracen, unjust.
Roland, fighting for the crusading Emperor, is *right*; Ganelon, aiding the heathen
enemy against his brother-in-arms, is doubly *wrong*.

The man who brings about the death of Roland and twenty thousand Franks is
no mean and petty villain. The husband of the Emperor's sister and the stepfather
of Roland, he holds a very high place in Charles's council. Nor does he lack the
ability or the personality to sustain this position. He has no hesitation in speaking
against Roland in the first discussion of the Saracen proposals; his nomination as
envoy to King Marsile is readily accepted by Charles; and his success in his treachery is a brilliant feat. For in order to accomplish it he must first provoke the now
peacefully inclined Marsile to wrath and then turn this anger against Roland. To
this end he takes a calculated risk for the sake of a calculated—but far from guaranteed—result. Insulting Marsile deliberately, in the name of the Emperor, he
makes himself the first target of the Saracen king's fury and certainly endangers his
own life. Luckily for him, the king's hand is stayed; and the Saracen nobles applaud
Ganelon's magnificent courage. The rest is comparatively easy—though everything
now depends on Ganelon's success in getting Roland placed in command of the
rear guard. That he succeeds is the more credible because it was Roland who
previously nominated Ganelon for the embassy: Roland and Charles may be expected
to act, as in fact they do, on the principle that turn about is fair play.

To the twelfth-century poet and his audience of proud knights the question of motive in Ganelon's hatred of Roland doubtless presented little difficulty. Indeed, if Ganelon had not resorted to treason, a tenable defense of his attitude could be established. For it may well be that he is honestly opposed to the policy of relentless war against the Saracens. His speech at the first council, urging acceptance of Marsile's proposals, wins the support of the wise counselor Naimes, and carries the day. An advocate of peace would obviously regard the uncompromising spokesman of the war party—Roland—as his opponent. Later, talking with the Saracen envoy Blancandrin, Ganelon plausibly represents Roland as the chief obstacle to pacific relations between the two peoples. To be sure, Ganelon is now plotting against Roland; but that should not blind us to the possibility that he honestly differs with Roland about this question of the Emperor's foreign policy. When we have said this, and when we have recognized the faults in Roland's personality that might normally vex another powerful, but less powerful, courtier, we have said all that can be said in defense of Ganelon. His acts put him quite beyond the possibility of moral justification. But justifying him is one thing; understanding him is quite another, and this the author has enabled us to do.

In Roland the poet has created one of the great heroes of European literature. Like Achilles, Aeneas, and Hamlet, he is the embodiment of a definite ideal of humanity. The ideal that Roland incarnates is that of feudal chivalry. Roland exhibits in superlative degree the traits and attitudes that feudal society and institutions sought to produce in a whole class. He is a supremely valiant fighter, a completely faithful vassal, and a warmly affectionate friend; and, since his creator lived in the early twelfth century, his fervent Christianity bears the Crusader's stamp. His words to his friend Oliver before the battle epitomize his vocation as he sees it:

> A man must bear some hardships for his lord,
> stand everything, the great heat, the great cold,
> lose the hide and hair on him for his good lord.
> Now let each man make sure to strike hard here:
> let them not sing a bad song about us!
> Pagans are wrong and Christians are right!
> They'll make no bad example of me this day!

This is the code of a man of action, of one to whom action appears as duty. Neither here nor elsewhere in the poem is Roland touched by any sense of the "doubtful doom of human kind" that haunts Aeneas. Nor is he ever plagued by Hamlet's doubts. In assurance and self-reliance he is much closer to Achilles, except that Achilles fought essentially for himself—certainly not for Agamemnon! In Roland the man is wholly assimilated to the vassal. The ceiling above him is lower, the pattern he follows is more limited, than those of Achilles, Aeneas, and Hamlet; yet within his pattern Roland achieves perfection, as they do in theirs.

Roland's feats in battle require no analysis; they are bright and glorious; they outshine the great deeds of his noble comrades. This superiority is no more than the poet has led us to expect. It is the hero's weakness—weakness counterpoised to his greatness—that gives the poem depth and produces the tension that commands our interest. Roland's defect has been called the excess of his special virtue—confidence, courage, bravery; if assurance outstrips prudence, then bravery becomes recklessness, which can bring disaster upon the hero and those for whom he is responsible. The author carefully shows us that Roland has no habit or instinct of caution to match his marvelous courage. Charles notes the vindictive manner in which Ganelon proposes Roland for the rear guard, and though at a loss to divine its meaning, is moved to assign half his entire army to Roland. But Roland either has not noticed the gleam of triumph in Ganelon's eye, or, if he has, loftily disregards it and firmly refuses to take more than twenty thousand men, a relatively small force.

So far Roland has done nothing definitely wrong, though he has revealed a certain lack of perception and of intuitive prudence. But he does do wrong when, surprised by an army of a hundred thousand Saracens, he refuses to blow the horn that would summon Charles to the rescue. The error is emphasized by the repetition in Oliver's effort to persuade him, and the relationship between Roland's refusal and his rashness of character is made apparent both through his answers and through the contrast with Oliver. Roland fears that asking for help would make him look foolish among the Franks—instead, he will slay the foe himself; he will not leave his kin at home open to reproach because of him; if, as Oliver says, the rearguard is hopelessly outnumbered, then death is better than disgrace. Actually, Roland is confident of victory despite the odds. His judgment is not equal to his daring. As the poet summarizes, "Roland is fierce and Oliver wise."

The result is catastrophe. But it is catastrophe redeemed by glorious heroism, as well as self-sacrificing penitence. When, despite tremendous exploits of the Franks, especially by Roland, all but a handful of the rearguard have been slain, Roland wishes to sound the horn to let the Emperor know what has happened. But now Oliver dissents on the ground of honor: Roland had refused to summon Charles to a rescue, and it would be shameful to summon him only to witness a disaster. The repetitions in this scene balance those of the earlier one. Though the question is decided by Archbishop Turpin, the argument has embittered Oliver against Roland. Hence it is that when, blinded by his own blood, Oliver later strikes Roland, his comrade has to ask whether the blow was intentional. Roland's humility here is a part of his penitence, a penitence never put into words but sublimely revealed in deeds. Exhausted by battle as he is, his superhuman and repeated blasts on the horn burst his temples. The angels and archangels who receive his soul in Paradise are functional symbols of his final triumph in defeat. The poet does not remit the penalty of Roland's error, which is paid by his death. But his victory combines an epic with a tragic conclusion; atonement and redemption, not merely death, is the end, as it is in another profoundly Christian poem of action, Milton's *Samson Agonistes*.

The best summary in English of information about the origin and nature of the poem is contained in the introduction to the edition by T. A. Jenkins, *La Chanson de Roland* (1924). For discussion against the background of the *chanson de geste* in general, see Urban Tigner Holmes, *A History of Old French Literature* (1938). P. le Gentil, *The "Chanson de Roland"* (1969), provides technical information in the first half and a more general commentary in the second. J. J. Duggan, *The Song of Roland*, makes the strongest case for it as the work of an oral poet. Frederick Goldin, *The Song of Roland* (1978) contains a valuable introduction. Another excellent book for the general reader is Eugene Vance, *Reading the Song of Roland* (1970). The most comprehensive and detailed recent scholarly work is Gerald S. Brault, *The Song of Roland: An Analytical Edition*, two volumes (1978).

From The Song of Roland[1]

1

Charles the King, our Emperor, the Great,
has been in Spain for seven full years,
has conquered the high land down to the sea.
There is no castle that stands against him now,
no wall, no citadel left to break down—   5
except Saragossa, high on a mountain.[2]
King Marsilion holds it, who does not love God,
who serves Mahumet and prays to Apollin.[3]
He cannot save himself: his ruin will find him there. AOI.[4]

2

King Marsilion was in Saragossa.   10
He has gone forth into a grove, beneath its shade,
and he lies down on a block of blue marble,
twenty thousand men, and more, all around him.
He calls aloud to his dukes and his counts:
"Listen, my lords, to the troubles we have.   15
The Emperor Charles of the sweet land of France
has come into this country to destroy us.
I have no army able to give him battle,
I do not have the force to break his force.
Now act like my wise men: give me counsel,   20
save me, save me from death, save me from shame!"
No pagan there has one word to say to him
except Blancandrin, of the castle of Valfunde.

3

One of the wisest pagans was Blancandrin,
brave and loyal, a great mounted warrior,   25
a useful man, the man to aid his lord;
said to the King: "Do not give way to panic.
Do this: send Charles, that wild, terrible man,
tokens of loyal service and great friendship:
you will give him bears and lions and dogs,   30
seven hundred camels, a thousand molted hawks,
four hundred mules weighed down with gold and silver,
and fifty carts, to cart it all away:

---

1. Translated, with footnotes, by Frederick Goldin. Additional notes provided by the editor.   2. Saragossa,
in northeastern Spain, is not actually on a mountaintop. The poet's geography is not always accurate.
3. The Greek god Apollo; but the poet is mistaken, for these people worship only one god, Allah. *Mahumet:* A variation of Muhammed, the founder of the Islamic religion.   4. These three mysterious letters
appear at certain moments throughout the text, 180 times in all. No one has ever adequately explained
them, though every reader feels their effect.

he'll have good wages for his men who fight for pay.
Say he's made war long enough in this land: 35
let him go home, to France, to Aix,[5] at last—
come Michaelmas you will follow him there,
say you will take their faith, become a Christian,
and be his man with honor, with all you have.
If he wants hostages, why, you'll send them,   40
ten, or twenty, to give him security.
Let us send him the sons our wives have borne.
I'll send my son with all the others named to die.
It is better that they should lose their heads[6]
than that we, Lord, should lose our dignity   45
and our honors—and be turned into beggars!" AOI.

                                    4

Said Blancandrin: "By this right hand of mine
and by this beard that flutters on my chest,
you will soon see the French army disband,
the Franks will go to their own land, to France.   50
When each of them is in his dearest home,
King Charles will be in Aix, in his chapel.
At Michaelmas he will hold a great feast—
that day will come, and then our time runs out,
he'll hear no news, he'll get no word from us.   55
This King is wild, the heart in him is cruel:
he'll take the heads of the hostages we gave.
It is better, Lord, that they lose their heads
than that we lose our bright, our beautiful Spain—
and nothing more for us but misery and pain!"   60
The pagans say: "It may be as he says."

                                    5

King Marsilion brought his counsel to end,
then he summoned Clarin of Balaguét,
Estramarin and Eudropin, his peer,
And Priamun, Guarlan, that bearded one,   65
and Machiner and his uncle Maheu,
and Joüner, Malbien from over-sea,
and Blancandrin, to tell what was proposed.
From the worst of criminals he called these ten.
"Barons, my lords, you're to go to Charlemagne;   70
he's at the siege of Cordres,[7] the citadel.

---

5. Aachen (Aix-la-Chapelle), capital of Charlemagne's empire. *Michaelmas:* The feast of Saint Michael,
September 29.   6. The speaker expects that the hostages will be killed by the French when the deception
becomes clear. Sometime before, hostages sent by the French had been similarly slain; see ll. 207–09
below.   7. Córdoba, in southern Spain.

Olive branches are to be in your hands—
that signifies peace and humility.
If you've the skill to get me an agreement,
I will give you a mass of gold and silver   75
and lands and fiefs, as much as you could want."
Say the pagans: "We'll benefit from this!" AOI.

6

Marsilion brought his council to an end,
said to his men: "Lords, you will go on now,
and remember: olive branches in your hands;   80
and in my name tell Charlemagne the King
for his god's sake to have pity on me—
he will not see a month from this day pass
before I come with a thousand faithful;
say I will take that Christian religion   85
and be his man in love and loyalty.
If he wants hostages, why, he'll have them."
Said Blancandrin: "Now you will get good terms." AOI.

7

King Marsilion had ten white mules led out,
sent to him once by the King of Suatilie,[8]   90
with golden bits and saddles wrought with silver.
The men are mounted, the men who brought the message,
and in their hands they carry olive branches.
They came to Charles, who has France in his keeping.
He cannot prevent it: they will fool him. AOI.   95

8

The Emperor is secure and jubilant:
he has taken Cordres, broken the walls,
knocked down the towers with his catapults.
And what tremendous spoils his knights have won—
gold and silver, precious arms, equipment.   100
In the city not one pagan remained
who is not killed or turned into a Christian.
The Emperor is in an ample grove,
Roland and Oliver are with him there,
Samson the Duke and Ansëis the fierce,   105
Geoffrey d'Anjou, the King's own standard-bearer;
and Gerin and Gerer, these two together always,

8. A subordinate king, owing allegiance to Marsilion.

and the others, the simple knights, in force:
fifteen thousand from the sweet land of France.
The warriors sit on bright brocaded silk;   110
they are playing at tables to pass the time,
the old and the wisest men sitting at chess,
the young light-footed men fencing with swords.
Beneath a pine, beside a wild sweet-briar,
there was a throne, every inch of pure gold.   115
There sits the King, who rules over sweet France.
His beard is white, his hair flowering white.
That lordly body! the proud fierce look of him!—
If someone should come here asking for him,
      there'd be no need to point out the King of France.
The messengers dismounted, and on their feet   120
they greeted him in all love and good faith.

9

Blancandrin spoke, he was the first to speak,
said to the King: "Greetings, and God save you,
that glorious God whom we all must adore.
Here is the word of the great king Marsilion: 125
he has looked into this law of salvation,
wants to give you a great part of his wealth,
bears and lions and hunting dogs on chains,
seven hundred camels, a thousand molted hawks,
four hundred mules packed tight with gold and silver,   130
and fifty carts, to cart it all away;
and there will be so many fine gold bezants,[9]
you'll have good wages for the men in your pay.
You have stayed long—long enough!—in this land,
it is time to go home, to France, to Aix.   135
My master swears he will follow you there."
The Emperor holds out his hands toward God,
bows down his head, begins to meditate. AOI.

10

The Emperor held his head bowed down;
never was he too hasty with his words: 140
his custom is to speak in his good time.
When his head rises, how fierce the look of him;
he said to them: "You have spoken quite well.
King Marsilion is my great enemy.

9. Gold coins; the name is derived from Byzantium.

Now all these words that you have spoken here—   145
how far can I trust them? How can I be sure?"
The Saracen: "He wants to give you hostages.
How many will you want? ten? fifteen? twenty?
I'll put my son with the others named to die.[1]
You will get some, I think, still better born.   150
When you are at home in your high royal palace,
at the great feast of Saint Michael-in-Peril,[2]
the lord who nurtures me will follow you,
and in those baths[3]—the baths God made for you—
my lord will come and want to be made Christian."   155
King Charles replies: "He may yet save his soul." AOI.

11

Late in the day it was fair, the sun was bright.
Charles has them put the ten mules into stables.
The King commands a tent pitched in the broad grove,
and there he has the ten messengers lodged;   160
twelve serving men took splendid care of them.
There they remained that night till the bright day.
The Emperor rose early in the morning,
the King of France, and heard the mass and matins.
And then the King went forth beneath a pine,   165
calls for his barons to complete his council:
he will proceed only with the men of France. AOI.

12

The Emperor goes forth beneath a pine,
calls for his barons to complete his council:
Ogier the Duke, and Archbishop Turpin,
Richard the Old, and his nephew Henri;   170
from Gascony, the brave Count Acelin,
Thibaut of Reims, and his cousin Milun;
and Gerer and Gerin, they were both there,
and there was Count Roland, he came with them,   175
and Oliver, the valiant and well-born;
a thousand Franks of France, and more, were there.
Ganelon came, who committed the treason.[4]
Now here begins the council that went wrong. AOI.

---

1. That is, if the promise is broken. *Saracen:* The usual term for the enemy.   2. The epithet "in peril
of the sea" was applied to the famous sanctuary of Saint Michael on the Normandy coast because it could
only be reached on foot at low tide, and pilgrims were endangered by the incoming tide; eventually the
phrase was applied to the saint himself.   3. Famous healing springs at Aix.   4. The poet anticipates
the treason that Ganelon will commit. The next line represents a similar anticipation: the plan adopted at
the council will prove to be a mistake.

13

"Barons, my lords," said Charles the Emperor,   180
"King Marsilion has sent me messengers,
wants to give me a great mass of his wealth,
bears and lions and hunting dogs on chains,
seven hundred camels, a thousand molting hawks,
four hundred mules packed with gold of Araby,   185
and with all that, more than fifty great carts;
but also asks that I go back to France:
he'll follow me to Aix, my residence,
and take our faith, the one redeeming faith,
become a Christian, hold his march[5] lands from me.   190
But what lies in his heart? I do not know."
And the French say: "We must be on our guard!" AOI.

14

The Emperor has told them what was proposed.
Roland the Count will never assent to that,
gets to his feet, comes forth to speak against it;   195
says to the King: "Trust Marsilion—and suffer!
We came to Spain seven long years ago,
I won Noples for you, I won Commibles,
I took Valterne and all the land of Pine,
and Balaguer and Tudela and Seville.   200
And then this king, Marsilion, played the traitor:
he sent you men, fifteen of his pagans—
and sure enough, each held an olive branch;
and they recited just these same words to you.
You took counsel with all your men of France;   205
they counseled you to a bit of madness:
you sent two Counts across to the Pagans,
one was Basan, the other was Basile.
On the hills below Haltille, he took their heads.
They were your men. Fight the war you came to fight!   210
Lead the army you summoned on to Saragossa!
Lay siege to it all the rest of your life!
Avenge the men that this criminal murdered!" AOI.

15

The Emperor held his head bowed down with this,
and stroked his beard, and smoothed his mustache down,   215

---

5. A frontier province or territory.

and speaks no word, good or bad, to his nephew.
The French keep still, all except Ganelon:
he gets to his feet and, come before King Charles,
how fierce he is as he begins his speech;
said to the King: "Believe a fool—me or   220
another—and suffer! Protect your interest!
When Marsilion the King sends you his word
that he will join his hands[6] and be your man,
and hold all Spain as a gift from your hands
and then receive the faith that we uphold—   225
whoever urges that we refuse this peace,
that man does not care, Lord, what death we die.
That wild man's counsel must not win the day here—
let us leave fools, let us hold with wise men!" AOI.

16

And after that there came Naimon the Duke—   230
no greater vassal in that court than Naimon—
said to the King: "You've heard it clearly now,
Count Ganelon has given you your answer:
let it be heeded, there is wisdom in it.
King Marsilion is beaten in this war,   235
you have taken every one of his castles,
broken his walls with your catapults,
burnt his cities and defeated his men.
Now when he sends to ask you to have mercy,
it would be a sin to do still more to him.   240
Since he'll give you hostages as guarantee,
this great war must not go on, it is not right."
And the French say: "The Duke has spoken well." AOI.

17

"Barons, my lords, whom shall we send down there,
to Saragossa, to King Marsilion?"   245
Naimon replies, "I'll go, if you grant it!
At once, my lord! give me the glove and the staff."[7]
The King replies: "You're a man of great wisdom:
now by my beard, now by this mustache of mine,
you will not go so far from me this year; or ever.   250
Go take your seat when no one calls on you."

---

6. Part of the gesture of homage; the lord enclosed the joined hands of his vassal with his own hands.
7. Symbols of his commission from the Emperor Charles.

18

"Barons, my lords, whom can we send down there,
to this Saracen who holds Saragossa?"
Roland replies: "I can go there! No trouble!"
"No, no, not you!" said Oliver the Count,   255
"that heart in you is wild, spoils for a fight,
how I would worry—you'd fight with them, I know.
Now I myself could go, if the King wishes."
The King replies: "Be still, the two of you!
Not you, not he—neither will set foot there.   260
Now by this beard, as sure as you see white,
let no man here name one of the Twelve Peers!"
The French keep still, see how he silenced them.

19

Turpin of Reims has come forth from the ranks,
said to the King: "Let your Franks have a rest.   265
You have been in this land for seven years,
the many pains, the struggles they've endured!
I'm the one, Lord, give me the glove and the staff,
and I'll go down to this Saracen of Spain
and then I'll see what kind of man we have."   270
The Emperor replies to him in anger:
"Now you go back and sit on that white silk
and say no more unless I command it!" AOI.

20

"My noble knights," said the Emperor Charles,
"choose me one man: a baron from my march,   275
to bring my message to King Marsilion."[8]
And Roland said: "Ganelon, my stepfather."
The French respond: "Why, that's the very man!
pass this man by and you won't send a wiser."
And hearing this Count Ganelon began to choke,   280
pulls from his neck the great furs of marten
and stands there now, in his silken tunic,
eyes full of lights, the look on him of fury,
he has the body, the great chest of a lord;
stood there so fair, all his peers gazed on him;   285
said to Roland: "Madman, what makes you rave?
Every man knows I am your stepfather,
yet you named me to go to Marsilion.

8. Charlemagne wants them to choose a baron from an outlying region and not one of the Twelve Peers,
the circle of his dearest men.

Now if God grants that I come back from there,
you will have trouble: I'll start a feud with you,   290
it will go on till the end of your life."
Roland replies: "What wild words—all that blustering!
Every man knows that threats don't worry me.
But we need a wise man to bring the message:
if the King wills, I'll gladly go in your place."   295

21

Ganelon answers: "You will not go for me. AOI.
You're not my man, and I am not your lord.
Charles commands me to perform this service:
I'll go to Marsilion in Saragossa.
And I tell you, I'll play a few wild tricks   300
before I cool the anger in me now."
When he heard that, Roland began to laugh. AOI.

22

Ganelon sees: *Roland laughing at him!*
and feels such pain he almost bursts with rage,
needs little more to go out of his mind;   305
says to the Count: "I have no love for you,
you *made* this choice fall on me, and that was wrong.
Just Emperor, here I am, before you.
I have one will: to fulfill your command."

23

"I know now I must go to Saragossa. AOI.   310
Any man who goes there cannot return.
And there is this: I am your sister's husband,
have a son by her, the finest boy there can be,
Baldewin," says he, "who will be a good man.
To him I leave my honors, fiefs, and lands.   315
Protect my son: these eyes will never see him."
Charles answers him: "That tender heart of yours!
You have to go, I have commanded it."

24

And the King said: "Ganelon, come forward, AOI.
come and receive the staff and the glove.   320
You have heard it: the Franks have chosen you."
Said Ganelon: "Lord, it's Roland who did this.
In all my days I'll have no love for him,

or Oliver, because he's his companion,
or the Twelve Peers, because they love him so.   325
I defy them, here in your presence, Lord."
And the King said: "What hate there is in you!
You will go there, for I command you to."
"I can go there, but I'll have no protector. AOI.
Basile had none, nor did Basan his brother."   330

25

The Emperor offers him his right glove.
But Ganelon would have liked not to be there.
When he had to take it, it fell to the ground.
"God!" say the French, "What's that going to mean?
What disaster will this message bring us!"   335
Said Ganelon: "Lords, you'll be hearing news."

26

Said Ganelon: "Lord, give me leave to go,
since go I must, there's no reason to linger."
And the King said: "In Jesus' name and mine,"
absolved him and blessed him with his right hand.   340
Then he gave him the letter and the staff.

27

Count Ganelon goes away to his camp.
He chooses, with great care, his battle-gear,
picks the most precious arms that he can find.
The spurs he fastened on were golden spurs;   345
he girds his sword, Murgleis, upon his side;
he has mounted Tachebrun, his battle horse,
his uncle, Guinemer, held the stirrup.
And there you would have seen brave men in tears,
his men, who say: "Baron, what bad luck for you!   350
All your long years in the court of the King,
always proclaimed a great and noble vassal!
Whoever it was doomed you to go down there—
Charlemagne himself will not protect that man.
Roland the Count should not have thought of this—   355
and you the living issue of a mighty line!"
And then they say: "Lord, take us there with you!"
Ganelon answers: "May the Lord God forbid!
It is better that I alone should die
      than so many good men and noble knights.
You will be going back, Lords, to sweet France: 360

go to my wife and greet her in my name,
and Pinabel, my dear friend and peer,
and Baldewin, my son, whom you all know:
give him your aid, and hold him as your lord."
And he starts down the road; he is on his way. AOI.   365

28

Ganelon rides to a tall olive tree,
there he has joined the pagan messengers.
And here is Blancandrin, who slows down for him:
and what great art they speak to one another.
Said Blancandrin: "An amazing man, Charles!   370
conquered Apulia, conquered all of Calabria,
crossed the salt sea on his way into England,
won its tribute,[9] got Peter's pence for Rome:
what does he want from us here in our march?"
Ganelon answers: "That is the heart in him.   375
There'll never be a man the like of him." AOI.

29

Said Blancandrin: "The Franks are a great people.
Now what great harm all those dukes and counts do
to their own lord when they give him such counsel:
they torment him, they'll destroy him, and others."   380
Ganelon answers: "Well, now, I know no such man
except Roland, who'll suffer for it yet.
One day the Emperor was sitting in the shade:
his nephew came, still wearing his hauberk,
he had gone plundering near Carcassonne;   385
and in his hand he held a bright red apple:
'Dear Lord, here, take,' said Roland to his uncle;
'I offer you the crowns of all earth's kings.'
Yes, Lord, that pride of his will destroy him,
for every day he goes riding at death.   390
And *should* someone kill him, we would have peace." AOI.

30

Said Blancandrin: "A wild man, this Roland!
wants to make every nation beg for his mercy
and claims a right to every land on earth!
But what men support him, if that is his aim?"   395

9. Although begun perhaps as early as the eighth century, it was not due to any effort of Charlemagne, who did not in fact visit England. Peter's pence: A tribute of one penny per house "for the use of Saint Peter," that is, for the Pope in Rome.

Ganelon answers: "Why, Lord, the men of France.
They love him so, they will never fail him.
He gives them gifts, masses of gold and silver,
mules, battle horses, brocaded silks, supplies.
And it is all as the Emperor desires: 400
he'll win the lands from here to the Orient." AOI.

31

Ganelon and Blancandrin rode on until
each pledged his faith to the other and swore
they'd find a way to have Count Roland killed.
They rode along the paths and ways until,   405
in Saragossa, they dismount beneath a yew.
There was a throne in the shade of a pine,
covered with silk from Alexandria.
There sat the king who held the land of Spain,
and around him twenty thousand Saracens.   410
There is no man who speaks or breathes a word,
poised for the news that all would like to hear.
Now here they are: Ganelon and Blancandrin.

32

Blancandrin came before Marsilion,
his hand around the fist of Ganelon,   415
said to the King: "May Mahumet save you,
and Apollin, whose sacred laws we keep!
We delivered your message to Charlemagne:
when we finished, he raised up both his hands
and praised his god. He made no other answer.   420
Here he sends you one of his noble barons,
a man of France, and very powerful.
You'll learn from him whether or not you'll have peace."
"Let him speak, we shall hear him," Marsilion answers. AOI.

33

But Ganelon had it all well thought out.   425
With what great art he commences his speech,
a man who knows his way about these things;
said to the King: "May the Lord God save you,
that glorious God, whom we must all adore.
Here is the word of Charlemagne the King: 430
you are to take the holy Christian faith;
he will give you one half of Spain in fief.
If you refuse, if you reject this peace,

you will be taken by force, put into chains,
and then led forth to the King's seat at Aix;   435
you will be tried; you will be put to death:
you will die there, in shame, vilely, degraded."
King Marsilion, hearing this, was much shaken.
In his hand was a spear, with golden feathers.
He would have struck, had they not held him back. AOI.   440

34

Marsilion the King—his color changed!
He shook his spear, waved the shaft to and fro.
When he saw that, Ganelon laid hand to sword,
he drew it out two fingers from its sheath;
and spoke to it: "How beautiful and bright!   445
How long did I bear you in the King's court
before I died! The Emperor will not say
I died alone in that foreign country:
they'll buy you first, with the best men they have!"
The pagans say: "Let us break up this quarrel!"   450

35

The pagan chiefs pleaded with Marsilion
till he sat down once again on his throne.
The Caliph[1] spoke: "You did us harm just now,
served us badly, trying to strike this Frenchman.
You should have listened, you should have heard him out."   455
Said Ganelon: "Lord, I must endure it.
I shall not fail, for all the gold God made,
for all the wealth there may be in this land,
to tell him, as long as I have breath, all
that Charlemagne—that great and mighty King!—   460
has sent through me to his mortal enemy."
He is buckled in a great cloak of sable,
covered with silk from Alexandria:
he throws it down. Blancandrin picks it up.
But his great sword he will never throw down!   465
In his right fist he grasps its golden pommel.
Say the pagans: "That's a great man! A noble!" AOI.

36

Now Ganelon drew closer to the King
and said to him: "You are wrong to get angry,

1. A high official of King Marsilion.

for Charles, who rules all France, sends you this word: 470
you are to take the Christian people's faith;
he will give you one half of Spain in fief,
the other half goes to his nephew: Roland—
quite a partner you will be getting there!
If you refuse, if you reject this peace,   475
he will come and lay siege to Saragossa;
you will be taken by force, put into chains,
and brought straight on to Aix, the capital.
No saddle horse, no war horse for you then,
no he-mule, no she-mule for you to ride: 480
you will be thrown on some miserable dray;
you will be tried, and you will lose your head.
Our Emperor sends you this letter."
He put the letter in the pagan's right fist.

37

Marsilion turned white; he was enraged;   485
he breaks the seal, he's knocked away the wax,
runs through the letter, sees what is written there:
"Charles sends me word, this king who rules in France:
I'm to think of his anger and his grief—
he means Basan and his brother Basile,   490
I took their heads in the hills below Haltille;
if I want to redeem the life of my body,
I must send him my uncle: the Algalife.[2]
And otherwise he'll have no love for me."
Then his son came and spoke to Marsilion,   495
said to the King: 'Ganelon has spoken madness.
He crossed the line, he has no right to live.
Give him to me, I will do justice on him."
When he heard that, Ganelon brandished his sword;
he runs to the pine, set his back against the trunk.   500

38

King Marsilion went forth into the orchard,
he takes with him the greatest of his men;
Blancandrin came, that gray-haired counselor,
and Jurfaleu, Marsilion's son and heir,
the Algalife, uncle and faithful friend.   505
Said Blancandrin: "Lord, call the Frenchman back.
He swore to me to keep faith with our cause."
And the King said: "Go, bring him back here, then."

2. The Caliph.

He took Ganelon's right hand by the fingers,
leads him into the orchard before the King.   510
And there they plotted that criminal treason. AOI.

39

Said Marsilion: "My dear Lord Ganelon,
that was foolish, what I just did to you,
I showed my anger, even tried to strike you.
Here's a pledge of good faith, these sable furs,   515
the gold alone worth over five hundred pounds:
I'll make it all up before tomorrow night."
Ganelon answers: "I will not refuse it.
May it please God to reward you for it." AOI.

40

Said Marsilion: "I tell you, Ganelon,   520
I have a great desire to love you dearly.
I want to hear you speak of Charlemagne.
He is so old, he's used up all his time—
from what I hear, he is past two hundred!
He has pushed his old body through so many lands,   525
taken so many blows on his buckled shield,
made beggars of so many mighty kings:
when will he lose the heart for making war?"
Ganelon answers: "Charles is not one to lose heart.
No man sees him, no man learns to know him   530
who does not say: the Emperor is great.
I do not know how to praise him so highly
that his great merit would not surpass my praise.
Who could recount his glory and his valor?
God put the light in him of such lordliness,   535
he would choose death before he failed his barons."

41

Said the pagan: "I have reason to marvel
at Charlemagne, a man so old and gray—
he's two hundred years old, I hear, and more;
he has tortured his body through so many lands,   540
and borne so many blows from lance and spear,
made beggars of so many mighty kings:
when will he lose the heart for making war?"
"Never," said Ganelon, "while his nephew lives,
he's a fighter, there's no vassal like him
    under the vault of heaven. And he has friends.   545

There's Oliver, a good man, his companion.
And the Twelve Peers, whom Charles holds very dear,
form the vanguard, with twenty thousand knights.
Charles is secure, he fears no man on earth." AOI.

42

Said the pagan: "Truly, how I must marvel   550
at Charlemagne, who is so gray and white—
over two hundred years, from what I hear;
gone through so many lands a conqueror,
and borne so many blows from strong sharp spears,
killed and conquered so many mighty kings: 555
when will he lose the heart for making war?"
"Never," said Ganelon, "while one man lives: Roland!
no man like him from here to the Orient!
There's his companion, Oliver, a brave man.
And the Twelve Peers, whom Charles holds very dear,   560
form the vanguard, with twenty thousand Franks.
Charles is secure, he fears no man alive." AOI.

43

"Dear Lord Ganelon," said Marsilion the King,
"I have my army, you won't find one more handsome:
I can muster four hundred thousand knights!   565
With this host, now, can I fight Charles and the French?"
Ganelon answers: "No, no, don't try that now,
you'd take a loss: thousands of your pagans!
Forget such foolishness, listen to wisdom:
send the Emperor so many gifts   570
there'll be no Frenchman there who does not marvel.
For twenty hostages—those you'll be sending—
he will go home: home again to sweet France!
And he will leave his rear-guard behind him.
There will be Roland, I do believe, his nephew,   575
and Oliver, brave man, born to the court.
These Counts are dead, if anyone trusts me.
Then Charles will see that great pride of his go down,
he'll have no heart to make war on you again." AOI.

44

"Dear Lord Ganelon," said Marsilion the King,   580
"What must I do to kill Roland the Count?"
Ganelon answers: "Now I can tell you that.

The King will be at Cize,[3] in the great passes,
he will have placed his rear-guard at his back:
there'll be his nephew, Count Roland, that great man,   585
and Oliver, in whom he puts such faith,
and twenty thousand Franks in their company.
Now send one hundred thousand of your pagans
against the French—let them give the first battle.
The French army will be hit hard and shaken.   590
I must tell you: your men will be martyred.
Give them a second battle, then, like the first.
One will get him, Roland will not escape.
Then you'll have done a deed, a noble deed,
and no more war for the rest of your life!" AOI.   595

45

"If someone can bring about the death of Roland,
then Charles would lose the right arm of his body,
that marvelous army would disappear—
never again could Charles gather such forces.
Then peace at last for the Land of Fathers!"[4]   600
When Marsilion heard that, he kissed his neck.
Then he begins to open up his treasures. AOI.

46

Marsilion said, "Why talk. . . .
No plan has any worth which one. . . .[5]
Now swear to me that you will betray Roland."   605
Ganelon answers: "Let it be as you wish."
On the relics in his great sword Murgleis
he swore treason and became a criminal. AOI.

47

There stood a throne made all of ivory.
Marsilion commands them bring forth a book: 610
it was the law of Mahum and Tervagant.[6]
This is the vow sworn by the Saracen of Spain:
if he shall find Roland in the rear-guard,
he shall fight him, all his men shall fight him,
and once he finds Roland, Roland will die.   615
Says Ganelon: "May it be as you will." AOI.

---

3. The pass through the Pyrenees.   4. *Tere Major*, in the text, can mean either "the great land," or
"the land of fathers, ancestors." It always refers to France.   5. Parts of lines 603–4 are unintelligible in
the manuscript.   6. A fictitious deity whom the poet mistakenly says the Saracens worshipped.

48

And now there came a pagan, Valdabrun,
he was the man who raised Marsilion.
And, all bright smiles, he said to Ganelon:
"You take my sword, there's no man has one better: 620
a thousand coins, and more, are in the hilt.
It is a gift, dear lord, made in friendship,
only help us to Roland, that great baron,
let us find him standing in the rear-guard."
"It shall be done," replies Count Ganelon.   625
And then they kissed, on the face, on the chin.

49

And there came then a pagan, Climborin,
and, all bright smiles, he said to Ganelon:
"You take my helmet, I never saw one better,
only help us to Roland, lord of the march,   630
show us the way to put Roland to shame."
"It shall be done," replied Count Ganelon.
And then they kissed, on the face, on the mouth. AOI.

50

And then there came the Queen, Bramimunde;
said to the Count: "Lord, I love you well,   635
for my lord and all his men esteem you so.
I wish to send your wife two necklaces,
they are all gold, jacinths, and amethysts,
they are worth more than all the wealth of Rome.
Your Emperor has never seen their like."   640
He has taken them, thrusts them into his boot. AOI.

51

The King calls for Malduit, his treasurer:
"The gifts for Charles—is everything prepared?"
And he replies: "Yes, Lord, and well prepared:
seven hundred camels, packed with gold and silver,   645
and twenty hostages, the noblest under heaven." AOI.

52

Marsilion took Ganelon by the shoulder
and said to him: "You're a brave man, a wise man.
Now by that faith you think will save your soul,

take care you do not turn your heart from us.   650
I will give you a great mass of my wealth,
ten mules weighed down with fine Arabian gold;
and come each year, I'll do the same again.
Now you take these, the keys to this vast city:
present King Charles with all of its great treasure;   655
then get me Roland picked for the rear-guard.
Let me find him in some defile or pass,
I will fight him, a battle to the death."
Ganelon answers: "It's high time that I go."
Now he is mounted, and he is on his way. AOI.   660

53

The Emperor moves homeward, he's drawing near.
Now he has reached the city of Valterne:
Roland had stormed it, destroyed it, and it stood
from that day forth a hundred years laid waste.
Charles is waiting for news of Ganelon   665
and the tribute from Spain, from that great land.
In the morning, at dawn, with the first light,
Count Ganelon came to the Christian camp. AOI.

54

The Emperor rose early in the morning,
the King of France, and has heard mass and matins.   670
On the green grass he stood before his tent.
Roland was there, and Oliver, brave man,
Naimon the Duke, and many other knights.
Ganelon came, the traitor, the foresworn.
With what great cunning he commences his speech;   675
said to the King: "May the Lord God save you!
Here I bring you the keys to Saragossa.
And I bring you great treasure from that city,
and twenty hostages, have them well guarded.
And good King Marsilion sends you this word: 680
Do not blame him concerning the Algalife:
I saw it all myself, with my own eyes:
        four hundred thousand men, and all in arms,
their hauberks on, some with their helms laced on,
swords on their belts, the hilts enameled gold,
who went with him to the edge of the sea.   685
They are in flight: it is the Christian faith—
they do not want it, they will not keep its law.
They had not sailed four full leagues out to sea
when a high wind, a tempest swept them up.

They were all drowned; you will never see them;   690
if he were still alive, I'd have brought him.
As for the pagan King, Lord, believe this:
before you see one month from this day pass,
he'll follow you to the Kingdom of France
and take the faith—he will take your faith, Lord,   695
and join his hands and become your vassal.
He will hold Spain as a fief from your hand."
Then the King said: "May God be thanked for this.
You have done well, you will be well rewarded."
Throughout the host they sound a thousand trumpets.   700
The French break camp, strap their gear on their pack-horses.
They take the road to the sweet land of France. AOI.

55

King Charlemagne laid waste the land of Spain,
stormed its castles, ravaged its citadels.
The King declares his war is at an end.   705
The Emperor rides toward the land of sweet France.
Roland the Count affixed the gonfanon,[7]
raised it toward heaven on the height of a hill;
the men of France make camp across that country.
Pagans are riding up through these great valleys,   710
their hauberks on, their tunics of double mail,
their helms laced on, their swords fixed on their belts,
shields on their necks, lances trimmed with their banners.
In a forest high in the hills they gathered:
four hundred thousand men waiting for dawn.   715
God, the pity of it! the French do not know! AOI.

56

The day goes by; now the darkness of night.
Charlemagne sleeps, the mighty Emperor.
He dreamt he was at Cize, in the great passes,
and in his fists held his great ashen lance.   720
Count Ganelon tore it away from him
and brandished it, shook it with such fury
the splinters of the shaft fly up toward heaven.
Charlemagne sleeps, his dream does not wake him.

57

And after that he dreamed another vision: 725
he was in France, in his chapel at Aix,

7. Pennant.

a cruel wild boar was biting his right arm;
saw coming at him—from the Ardennes—a leopard,
it attacked him, fell wildly on his body.
And a swift hound running down from the hall   730
came galloping, bounding over to Charles,
tore the right ear off that first beast, the boar,
turns, in fury, to fight against the leopard.
And the French say: It is a mighty battle,
but cannot tell which one of them will win.   735
Charlemagne sleeps, his dream does not wake him. AOI.

58

The day goes by, and the bright dawn arises.
Throughout that host. . . .[8]
The Emperor rides forth with such fierce pride.
"Barons, my lords," said the Emperor Charles,   740
"look at those passes, at those narrow defiles—
pick me a man to command the rear-guard."
Ganelon answers: "Roland, here, my stepson.
You have no baron as great and brave as Roland."
When he hears that, the King stares at him in fury;   745
and said to him: "You are the living devil,
a mad dog—the murderous rage in you!
And who will precede me, in the vanguard?"
Ganelon answers, "Why, Ogier of Denmark,
you have no baron who could lead it so well."   750

59

Roland the Count, when he heard himself named,
knew what to say, and spoke as a knight must speak:
"Lord Stepfather, I have to cherish you!
You have had the rear-guard assigned to me.
Charles will not lose, this great King who rules France,   755
I swear it now, one palfrey, one war horse—
    while I'm alive and know what's happening—
one he-mule, one she-mule that he might ride,
Charles will not lose one sumpter, not one pack horse
that has not first been bought and paid for with swords."
Ganelon answers: "You speak the truth, I know." AOI.   760

60

When Roland hears he will lead the rear-guard,
he spoke in great fury to his stepfather:

8. Second hemistich unintelligible in the manuscript.

"Hah! you nobody, you base-born little fellow,
and did you think the glove would fall from my hands
as the staff fell from yours before King Charles?"[9] AOI.   765

61

"Just Emperor," said Roland, that great man,
"give me the bow that you hold in your hand.
And no man here, I think, will say in reproach
I let it drop, as Ganelon let the staff drop
from his right hand, when he should have taken it."   770
The Emperor bowed down his head with this,
he pulled his beard, he twisted his mustache,
cannot hold back, tears fill his eyes, he weeps.

62

And after that there came Naimon the Duke,
no greater vassal in the court than Naimon,   775
said to the King: "You've heard it clearly now:
it is Count Roland. How furious he is.
He is the one to whom the rear-guard falls,
no baron here can ever change that now.
Give him the bow that you have stretched and bent,   780
and then find him good men to stand with him."
The King gives him the bow; Roland has it now.

63

The Emperor calls forth Roland the Count:
"My lord, my dear nephew, of course you know
I will give you half my men, they are yours.   785
Let them serve you, it is your salvation."
"None of that!" said the Count. "May God strike me
if I discredit the history of my line.
I'll keep twenty thousand Franks—they are good men.
Go your way through the passes, you will be safe.   790
You must not fear any man while I live."

64

Roland the Count mounted his battle horse. AOI.
Oliver came to him, his companion.
And Gerin came, and the brave Count Gerer,

---

9. Ganelon had let fall a glove, not a staff (l. 333). For this and other less objective reasons, some editors
have questioned the authenticity of this *laisse*. In the following *laisse*, at line 769, a reviser tried to make
the text more consistent by adding the reference to the staff.

and Aton came, and there came Berenger,   795
and Astor came, and Anseïs, fierce and proud,
and the old man Gerard of Roussillon,
and Gaifier, that great and mighty duke.
Said the Archbishop: "I'm going, by my head!"
"And I with you," said Gautier the Count,   800
"I am Count Roland's man and must not fail him."
And together they choose twenty thousand men. AOI.

65

Roland the Count summons Gautier de l'Hum:
"Now take a thousand Franks from our land, France,
and occupy those passes and the heights there.   805
The Emperor must not lose a single man." AOI.
Gautier replies: "Lord, I'll fight well for you."
And with a thousand French of France, their land,
Gautier rides out to the hills and defiles;
will not come down, for all the bad news, again,   810
till seven hundred swords have been drawn out.
King Almaris of the Kingdom of Belferne
gave them battle that day, and it was bitter.

66

High are the hills, the valleys tenebrous,
the cliffs are dark, the defiles mysterious.   815
That day, and with much pain, the French passed through.
For fifteen leagues around one heard their clamor.
When they reach Tere Majur, the Land of Fathers,
they beheld Gascony, their lord's domain.
Then they remembered: their fiefs, their realms, their honors,   820
remembered their young girls, their gentle wives:
not one who does not weep for what he feels.
Beyond these others King Charles is in bad straits:
his nephew left in the defiles of Spain!
feels the pity of it; tears break through. AOI.   825

67

And the Twelve Peers are left behind in Spain,
and twenty thousand Franks are left with them.
They have no fear, they have no dread of death.
The Emperor is going home to France.
Beneath his cloak, his face shows all he feels.   830
Naimon the Duke is riding beside him;
and he said to the King: "What is this grief?"

And Charles replies: "Whoever asks me, wrongs me.
I feel such pain, I cannot keep from wailing.
France will be destroyed by Ganelon.   835
Last night I saw a vision brought by angels:
the one who named my nephew for the rear-guard
shattered the lance between my fists to pieces.
I have left him in a march among strangers.
If I lose him, God! I won't find his like." AOI.   840

                              68

King Charles the Great cannot keep from weeping.
A hundred thousand Franks feel pity for him;
and for Roland, an amazing fear.
Ganelon the criminal has betrayed him;
got gifts for it from the pagan king,   845
gold and silver, cloths of silk, gold brocade,
mules and horses and camels and lions.
Marsilion sends for the barons of Spain,
counts and viscounts and dukes and almaçurs,
and the emirs,[1] and the sons of great lords: 850
four hundred thousand assembled in three days.
In Saragossa he has them beat the drums,
they raise Mahumet upon the highest tower:
no pagan now who does not worship him
and adore him. Then they ride, racing each other,   855
search through the land, the valleys, the mountains;
and then they saw the banners of the French.
The rear-guard of the Twelve Companions
will not fail now, they'll give the pagans battle.

                              69

Marsilion's nephew has come forward   860
riding a mule that he goads with a stick;
said—a warrior's laugh on him—to his uncle:
"Dear Lord and King, how long I have served you,
and all the troubles, the pains I have endured,
so many battles fought and won on the field   865
Give me a fief, the first blow at Roland.
I will kill him, here's the spear I'll do it with.
If Mahumet will only stand by me,
I will set free every strip of land in Spain,
from the passes of Aspre to Durestant.   870
Charles will be weary, his Franks will give it up:

---

1. *Almaçurs . . . emirs:* Lords of high rank.

and no more war for the rest of your life!"
King Marsilion gave him his glove, as sign. AOI.

70

The King's nephew holds the glove in his fist,
speaks these proud words to Marsilion his uncle: 875
"You've given me, dear Lord, King, a great gift!
Choose me twelve men, twelve of your noble barons,
and I will fight against the Twelve Companions."
And Falsaron was the first to respond—
he was the brother of King Marsilion: 880
"Dear Lord, Nephew, it's you and I together!
We'll fight, that's sure! We'll battle the rear-guard
of Charlemagne's grand army! We are the ones!
We have been chosen. We'll kill them all! It is fated." AOI.

71

And now again: there comes King Corsablis,   885
a Berber, a bad man, a man of cunning;
and now he spoke as a brave vassal speaks:
for all God's gold he would not be a coward.
Now rushing up: Malprimis de Brigal,
faster on his two feet than any horse;   890
and cries great-voiced before Marsilion:
"I'm on my way to Rencesvals to fight!
Let me find Roland, I won't stop till I kill him!"

[Lines 894–993 continue the roll call of volunteers.]

79

They arm themselves in Saracen hauberks,
all but a few are lined with triple mail;   995
they lace on their good helms of Saragossa,
gird on their swords, the steel forged in Vienne;
they have rich shields, spears of Valencia,
and gonfanons of white and blue and red.
They leave the mules and riding horses now,   1000
mount their war horses and ride in close array.
The day was fair, the sun was shining bright,
all their armor was aflame with the light;
a thousand trumpets blow: that was to make it finer.
That made a great noise, and the men of France heard.   1005
Said Oliver: "Companion, I believe
we may yet have a battle with the pagans."

Roland replies: "Now may God grant us that.
We know our duty: to stand here for our King.
A man must bear some hardships for his lord,   1010
stand everything, the great heat, the great cold,
lose the hide and hair on him for his good lord.
Now let each man make sure to strike hard here:
let them not sing a bad song about us!
Pagans are wrong and Christians are right!   1015
They'll make no bad example of me this day!" AOI.

80

Oliver climbs to the top of a hill,
looks to his right, across a grassy vale,
sees the pagan army on its way there;
and called down to Roland, his companion: 1020
"That way, toward Spain: the uproar I see coming!
All their hauberks, all blazing, helmets like flames!
It will be a bitter thing for our French.
Ganelon knew, that criminal, that traitor,
when he marked us out before the Emperor."   1025
"Be still, Oliver," Roland the Count replies.
"He is my stepfather—my stepfather.
    I won't have you speak one word against him."

81

Oliver has gone up upon a hill,
sees clearly now: the kingdom of Spain,
and the Saracens assembled in such numbers: 1030
helmets blazing, bedecked with gems in gold,
those shields of theirs, those hauberks sewn with brass,
and all their spears, the gonfanons affixed;
cannot begin to count their battle corps,
there are too many, he cannot take their number.   1035
And he is deeply troubled by what he sees.
He made his way quickly down from the hill,
came to the French, told them all he had seen.

82

Said Oliver: "I saw the Saracens,
no man on earth ever saw more of them—   1040
one hundred thousand, with their shields, up in front,
helmets laced on, hauberks blazing on them,
the shafts straight up, the iron heads like flames—
you'll get a battle, nothing like it before.

My lords, my French, may God give you the strength.   1045
Hold your ground now! Let them not defeat us!"
And the French say: "God hate the man who runs!
We may die here, but no man will fail you." AOI.

83

Said Oliver: "The pagan force is great;
from what I see, our French here are too few.   1050
Roland, my companion, sound your horn then,
Charles will hear it, the army will come back."
Roland replies: "I'd be a fool to do it.
I would lose my good name all through sweet France.
I will strike now, I'll strike with Durendal,   1055
the blade will be bloody to the gold from striking!
These pagan traitors came to these passes doomed!
I promise you, they are marked men, they'll die." AOI.

84

"Roland, Companion, now sound the olifant,[2]
Charles will hear it, he will bring the army back,   1060
the King will come with all his barons to help us."
Roland replies: "May it never please God
that my kin should be shamed because of me,
or that sweet France should fall into disgrace.
Never! Never! I'll strike with Durendal,   1065
I'll strike with this good sword strapped to my side,
you'll see this blade running its whole length with blood.
These pagan traitors have gathered here to die.
I promise you, they are all bound for death." AOI.

85

"Roland, Companion, sound your olifant now,   1070
Charles will hear it, marching through those passes.
I promise you, the Franks will come at once."
Roland replies: "May it never please God
that any man alive should come to say
that pagans—pagans!—once made me sound this horn: 1075
no kin of mine will ever bear that shame.
Once I enter this great battle coming
and strike my thousand seven hundred blows,
you'll see the bloody steel of Durendal.

2. The word (which is a form of "elephant") means (a) "ivory," (b) "a horn made of ivory," and is used specifically, almost as a proper name, to denote Roland's horn, made of an elephant's tusk, and adorned with gold and jewels about the rim.

These French are good—they will strike like brave men.   1080
Nothing can save the men of Spain from death."

86

Said Oliver: "I see no blame in it—
I watched the Saracens coming from Spain,
the valleys and mountains covered with them,
every hillside and every plain all covered,   1085
hosts and hosts everywhere of those strange men—
and here we have a little company."
Roland replies: "That whets my appetite.
May it not please God and his angels and saints
to let France lose its glory because of me—   1090
let me not end in shame, let me die first.
The Emperor loves us when we fight well."

87

Roland is good, and Oliver is wise,
both these vassals men of amazing courage:
once they are armed and mounted on their horses,   1095
they will not run, though they die for it, from battle.
Good men, these Counts, and their words full of spirit.
Traitor pagans are riding up in fury.
Said Oliver: "Roland, look—the first ones,
on top of us—and Charles is far away.   1100
You did not think it right to sound your olifant:
if the King were here, we'd come out without losses.
Now look up there, toward the passes of Aspre—
you can see the rear-guard: it will suffer.
No man in that detail will be in another."   1105
Roland replies: "Don't speak such foolishness—
shame on the heart gone coward in the chest.
We'll hold our ground, we'll stand firm—we're the ones!
We'll fight with spears, we'll fight them hand to hand!" AOI.

88

When Roland sees that there will be a battle,   1110
it makes him fiercer than a lion or leopard;
shouts to the French, calls out to Oliver:
"Lord, companion: friend, do not say such things.
The Emperor, who left us these good French,
had set apart these twenty thousand men: 1115
he knew there was no coward in their ranks.
A man must meet great troubles for his lord,

stand up to the great heat and the great cold,
give up some flesh and blood—it is his duty.
Strike with the lance, I'll strike with Durendal—   1120
it was the King who gave me this good sword!
If I die here, the man who gets it can say:
it was a noble's, a vassal's, a good man's sword."

89

And now there comes the Archbishop Turpin.
He spurs his horse, goes up into a mountain,   1125
summons the French; and he preached them a sermon:
"Barons, my lords, Charles left us in this place.
We know our duty: to die like good men for our King.
Fight to defend the holy Christian faith.
Now you will have a battle, you know it now,   1130
you see the Saracens with your own eyes.
Confess your sins, pray to the Lord for mercy.
I will absolve you all, to save your souls.
If you die here, you will stand up holy martyrs,
you will have seats in highest Paradise."   1135
The French dismount, cast themselves on the ground;
the Archbishop blesses them in God's name.
He commands them to do one penance: strike.

90

The French arise, stand on their feet again;
they are absolved, released from all their sins: 1140
the Archbishop has blessed them in God's name.
Now they are mounted on their swift battle horses,
bearing their arms like faithful warriors;
and every man stands ready for the battle.
Roland the Count calls out to Oliver: 1145
"Lord, Companion, you knew it, you were right,
Ganelon watched for his chance to betray us,
got gold for it, got goods for it, and money.
The Emperor will have to avenge us now.
King Marsilion made a bargain for our lives,   1150
but still must pay, and that must be with swords." AOI.

91

Roland went forth into the Spanish passes
on Veillantif, his good swift-running horse.
He bears his arms—how they become this man!—
grips his lance now, hefting it, working it,   1155

now swings the iron point up toward the sky,
the gonfanon all white laced on above—
the golden streamers beat down upon his hands:
a noble's body, the face aglow and smiling.
Close behind him his good companion follows;   1160
the men of France hail him: their protector!
He looks wildly toward the Saracens,
and humbly and gently to the men of France;
and spoke a word to them, in all courtesy:
"Barons, my lords, easy now, keep at a walk.   1165
These pagans are searching for martyrdom.
We'll get good spoils before this day is over,
no king of France ever got such treasure!"
And with these words, the hosts are at each other. AOI.

92

Said Oliver: "I will waste no more words.   1170
You did not think it right to sound your olifant,
there'll be no Charles coming to your aid now.
He knows nothing, brave man, he's done no wrong;
those men down there—they have no blame in this.
Well, then, ride now, and ride with all your might!   1175
Lords, you brave men, stand your ground, hold the field!
Make up your minds, I beg you in God's name,
to strike some blows, take them and give them back!
Here we must not forget Charlemagne's war cry."
And with that word the men of France cried out.   1180
A man who heard that shout: Munjoie! Munjoie!³
would always remember what manhood is.
Then they ride, God! Look at their pride and spirit!
and they spur hard, to ride with all their speed,
come on to strike—what else would these men do?   1185
The Saracens kept coming, never fearing them.
Franks and pagans, here they are, at each other.

93

Marsilion's nephew is named Aëlroth.
He rides in front, at the head of the army,
comes on shouting insults against our French: 1190
"French criminals, today you fight our men.
One man should have saved you: he betrayed you.

---

3. A mountjoy (montjoie) was (according to Littré) a mound or cairn of stones set up to mark the site of a victory. The old French war cry, "Montjoie St.-Denis!" or, briefly, "Montjoie!" derived from the cairn set up at St.-Denis on the site of the saint's martyrdom (his spiritual victory). Others derive "Montjoie" from the Hill of Rama, called "Mons Gaudii," from which pilgrims obtained their first view of Jerusalem.

A fool, your King, to leave you in these passes.
This is the day sweet France will lose its name,
and Charlemagne the right arm of his body."   1195
When he hears that—God!—Roland is outraged!
He spurs his horse, gives Veillantif its head.
The Count comes on to strike with all his might,
smashes his shield, breaks his hauberk apart,
and drives: rips through his chest, shatters the bones,   1200
knocks the whole backbone out of his back,
casts out the soul of Aëlroth with his lance;
which he thrusts deep, makes the whole body shake,
throws him down dead, lance straight out,[4] from his horse;
he has broken his neck; broken it in two.   1205
There is something, he says, he must tell him:
"Clown! Nobody! Now you know Charles is no fool,
he never was the man to love treason.
It took his valor to leave us in these passes!
France will not lose its name, sweet France! today.   1210
Brave men of France, strike hard! The first blow is ours!
We're in the right, and these swine in the wrong!" AOI.

94

A duke is there whose name is Falsaron,
he was the brother of King Marsilion,
held the wild land of Dathan and Abiram;[5]   1215
under heaven, no criminal more vile;
a tremendous forehead between his eyes—
a good half-foot long, if you had measured it.
His pain is bitter to see his nephew dead;
rides out alone, baits the foe with his body,   1220
and riding shouts the war cry of the pagans,
full of hate and insults against the French:
"This is the day sweet France will lose its honor!"
Oliver hears, and it fills him with fury,
digs with his golden spurs into his horse,   1225
comes on to strike the blow a baron strikes,
smashes his shield, breaks his hauberk apart,
thrusts into him the long streamers of his gonfalon,
knocks him down, dead, lance straight out, from the saddle;
looks to the ground and sees the swine stretched out,   1230
and spoke these words—proud words, terrible words:
"You nobody, what are your threats to me!

---

4. The lance is held, not thrown, and used to knock the enemy from his horse. To throw one's weapons
is savage and ignoble. Note *laisses* 154 and 160, and the outlandish names of the things the pagans throw
at Roland, Gautier, and Turpin.   5. See Numbers 16:1–35.

Men of France, strike! Strike and we will beat them!"
Munjoie! he shouts—the war cry of King Charles. AOI.

95

A king is there whose name is Corsablis,   1235
a Berber, come from that far country.
He spoke these words to all his Saracens:
"Now here's one battle we'll have no trouble with,
look at that little troop of Frenchmen there,
a few odd men—they're not worth noticing!   1240
King Charles won't save a single one of them.
Their day has come, they must all die today."
And Archbishop Turpin heard every word:
no man on earth he wants so much to hate!
digs with spurs of fine gold into his horse,   1245
comes on to strike with all his awful might;
smashed through his shield, burst the rings of his hauberk,
sent his great lance into the body's center,
drove it in deep, he made the dead man shake,
knocked him down, dead, lance straight out, on the road;   1250
looks to the ground and sees the swine stretched out;
there is something, he says, he must tell him:
"You pagan! You nobody! You told lies there:
King Charles my lord is our safeguard forever!
Our men of France have no heart for running.   1255
As for your companions—we'll nail them to the ground;
and then you must all die the second death.[6]
At them, you French! No man forget what he is!
Thanks be to God, now the first blow is ours";
and shouts Munjoie! Munjoie! to hold the field.   1260

[Lines 1261–1319 narrate a series of single combats, many of them quite
    similar.]

104

The battle is fearful and wonderful   1320
and everywhere. Roland never spares himself,
strikes with his lance as long as the wood lasts:
the fifteenth blow he struck, it broke, was lost.
Then he draws Durendal, his good sword, bare,
and spurs his horse, comes on to strike Chernuble,   1325
smashes his helmet, carbuncles shed their light,

---

6. The death of the soul, eternal damnation. See Revelation 20:11–15; 21:8.

cuts through the coif, through the hair on his head,
cut through his eyes, through his face, through that look,
the bright, shining hauberk with its fine rings,
down through the trunk to the fork of his legs, 　　　　1330
through the saddle, adorned with beaten gold,
into the horse; and the sword came to rest:
cut through the spine, never felt for the joint;
knocks him down, dead, on the rich grass of the meadow;
then said to him: "You were doomed when you started, 　　　　1335
Clown! Nobody! Let Mahum help you now.
No pagan swine will win this field today."

105

Roland the Count comes riding through the field,
holds Durendal, that sword! it carves its way!
and brings terrible slaughter down on the pagans. 　　　　1340
To have seen him cast one man dead on another,
the bright red blood pouring out on the ground,
his hauberk, his two arms, running with blood,
his good horse—neck and shoulders running with blood!
And Oliver does not linger, he strikes! 　　　　1345
and the Twelve Peers, no man could reproach them;
and the brave French, they fight with lance and sword.
The pagans die, some simply faint away!
Said the Archbishop: "Bless our band of brave men!"
Munjoie! he shouts—the war cry of King Charles. AOI. 　　　　1350

106

Oliver rides into that battle-storm,
his lance is broken, he holds only the stump;
comes on to strike a pagan, Malsarun;
and he smashes his shield, all flowers and gold,
sends his two eyes flying out of his head, 　　　　1355
and his brains come pouring down to his feet;
casts him down, dead, with seven hundred others.
Now he has killed Turgis and Esturguz,
and the shaft bursts, shivers down to his fists.
Count Roland said: "Companion, what are you doing? 　　　　1360
Why bother with a stick in such a battle?
Iron and steel will do much better work!
Where is your sword, your Halteclere—that name!
Where is that crystal hilt, that golden guard?"
"Haven't had any time to draw it out, 　　　　1365
been so busy fighting," said Oliver. AOI.

107

Lord Oliver has drawn out his good sword—
that sword his companion had longed to see—
and showed him how a good man uses it:
strikes a pagan, Justin of Val Ferrée,   1370
and comes down through his head, cuts through the center,
through his body, his hauberk sewn with brass,
the good saddle beset with gems in gold,
into the horse, the backbone cut in two;
knocks him down, dead, before him on the meadow.   1375
Count Roland said: "Now I know it's you, Brother.
The Emperor loves us for blows like that."
Munjoie! that cry! goes up on every side. AOI.

108

Gerin the Count sits on his bay Sorél
and Gerer his companion on Passe-Cerf;   1380
and they ride, spurring hard, let loose their reins,
come on to strike a pagan, Timozel,
one on his shield, the other on his hauberk.
They broke their two lances in his body;
turn him over, dead, in a fallow field.   1385
I do not know and have never heard tell
which of these two was swifter, though both were swift.
Esperveris: he was the son of Borel
and now struck dead by Engeler of Bordeaux.
Turpin the Archbishop killed Siglorel,   1390
the enchanter, who had been in Hell before:
Jupiter brought him there, with that strange magic.
Then Turpin said: "That swine owed us his life!
Roland replies: "And now the scoundrel's dead.
Oliver, Brother, those were blows! I approve!"   1395

109

In the meantime, the fighting grew bitter.
Franks and pagans, the fearful blows they strike—
those who attack, those who defend themselves;
so many lances broken, running with blood,
the gonfanons in shreds, the ensigns torn,   1400
so many good French fallen, their young lives lost:
they will not see their mothers or wives again,
or the men of France who wait for them at the passes. AOI.
Charlemagne waits and weeps and wails for them.
What does that matter? They'll get no help from him.   1405

Ganelon served him ill that day he sold,
in Saragossa, the barons of his house.
He lost his life and limbs for what he did:
was doomed to hang in the great trial at Aix,
and thirty of his kin were doomed with him,   1410
who never expected to die that death. AOI.

110

The battle is fearful and full of grief.
Oliver and Roland strike like good men,
the Archbishop, more than a thousand blows,
and the Twelve Peers do not hang back, they strike!   1415
the French fight side by side, all as one man.
The pagans die by hundreds, by thousands:
whoever does not flee finds no refuge from death,
like it or not, there he ends all his days.
And there the men of France lose their greatest arms;   1420
they will not see their fathers, their kin again,
or Charlemagne, who looks for them in the passes.
Tremendous torment now comes forth in France,
a mighty whirlwind, tempests of wind and thunder,
rains and hailstones, great and immeasurable,   1425
bolts of lightning hurtling and hurtling down:
it is, in truth, a trembling of the earth.
From Saint Michael-in-Peril to the Saints,
from Besançon to the port of Wissant,
there is no house whose veil of walls does not crumble.   1430
A great darkness at noon falls on the land,
there is no light but when the heavens crack.
No man sees this who is not terrified,
and many say: "The Last Day! Judgment Day!
The end! The end of the world is upon us!"   1435
They do not know, they do not speak the truth:
it is the worldwide grief for the death of Roland.

111

The French have fought with all their hearts and strength,
pagans are dead by the thousands, in droves:
of one hundred thousand, not two are saved.   1440
Said the Archbishop: "Our men! What valiant fighters!
No king under heaven could have better.
It is written in the Gesta Francorum:[7]
our Emperor's vassals were all good men."

---

7. "The deeds of the French." The reference is to a Latin account of these events; it has not survived.

They walk over the field to seek their dead,   1445
they weep, tears fill their eyes, in grief and pity
for their kindred, with love, with all their hearts.
Marsilion the King, with all his men
    in that great host, rises up before them. AOI.

112

King Marsilion comes along a valley
with all his men, the great host he assembled: 1450
twenty divisions, formed and numbered by the King,
helmets ablaze with gems beset in gold,
and those bright shields, those hauberks sewn with brass.
Seven thousand clarions sound the pursuit,
and the great noise resounds across that country.   1455
Said Roland then: "Oliver, Companion, Brother,
that traitor Ganelon has sworn our deaths:
it is treason, it cannot stay hidden,
the Emperor will take his terrible revenge.
We have this battle now, it will be bitter,   1460
no man has ever seen the like of it.
I will fight here with Durendal, this sword,
and you, my companion, with Halteclere—
we've fought with them before, in many lands!
how many battles have we won with these two!   1465
Let no one sing a bad song of our swords." AOI.

113

When the French see the pagans so numerous,
the fields swarming with them on every side,
they call the names of Oliver, and Roland,
and the Twelve Peers: protect them, be their warranter.   1470
The Archbishop told them how he saw things:
"Barons, my lords, do not think shameful thoughts,
do not, I beg you all in God's name, run.
Let no brave man sing shameful songs of us:
let us all die here fighting: that is far better.   1475
We are promised: we shall soon find our deaths,
after today we won't be living here.
But here's one thing, and I am your witness:
Holy Paradise lies open to you,
you will take seats among the Innocents."[8]   1480
And with these words the Franks are filled with joy,
there is no man who does not shout Munjoie! AOI.

8. The infants slain by King Herod; see Matthew 2:13–18.

114

A Saracen was there of Saragossa,
half that city was in this pagan's keeping,
this Climborin, who fled before no man,   1485
who took the word of Ganelon the Count,
kissed in friendship the mouth that spoke that word,
gave him a gift: his helmet and its carbuncle.
Now he will shame, says he, the Land of Fathers,
he will tear off the crown of the Emperor;   1490
sits on the horse that he calls Barbamusche,
swifter than the sparrowhawk, than the swallow;
digs in his spurs, gives that war horse its head,
comes on to strike Engeler of Gascony,
whose shield and fine hauberk cannot save him;   1495
gets the head of his spear into his body,
drives it in deep, gets all the iron through,
throws him back, dead, lance straight out, on the field.
And then he cries: "It's good to kill these swine!
At them, Pagans! At them and break their ranks!"   1500
"God!" say the French, "the loss of that good man!" AOI.

115

Roland the Count calls out to Oliver:
"Lord, Companion, there is Engeler dead,
we never had a braver man on horse."
The Count replies: "God let me avenge him";   1505
and digs with golden spurs into his horse,
grips—the steel running with blood—Halteclere,
comes on to strike with all his mighty power:
the blow comes flashing down; the pagan falls.
Devils take away the soul of Climborin.   1510
And then he killed Alphaïen the duke,
cut off the head of Escababi,
struck from their horses seven great Arrabites:
they'll be no use for fighting any more!
And Roland said: "My companion is enraged!   1515
Why, he compares with me! he earns his praise!
Fighting like that makes us dearer to Charles";
lifts up his voice and shouts: "Strike! you are warriors!" AOI.

[Lines 1519–1627 narrate another series of single combats.]

125

Marsilion sees his people's martyrdom.
He commands them: sound his horns and trumpets;

and he rides now with the great host he has gathered.   1630
At their head rides the Saracen Abisme:
no worse criminal rides in that company,
stained with the marks of his crimes and great treasons,
lacking the faith in God, Saint Mary's son.
And he is black, as black as melted pitch,   1635
a man who loves murder and treason more
than all the gold of rich Galicia,
no living man ever saw him play or laugh;
a great fighter, a wild man, mad with pride,
and therefore dear to that criminal king;   1640
holds high his dragon,[9] where all his people gather.
The Archbishop will never love that man,
no sooner saw than wanted to strike him;
considered quietly, said to himself:
"That Saracen—a heretic, I'll wager.   1645
Now let me die if I do not kill him—
I never loved cowards or cowards' ways." AOI.

                              126

Turpin the Archbishop begins the battle.
He rides the horse that he took from Grossaille,
who was a king this priest once killed in Denmark.   1650
Now this war horse is quick and spirited,
his hooves high-arched, the quick legs long and flat,
short in the thigh, wide in the rump, long in the flanks,
and the backbone so high, a battle horse!
and that white tail, the yellow mane on him,   1655
the little ears on him, the tawny head!
No beast on earth could ever run with him.
The Archbishop—that valiant man!—spurs hard,
he will attack Abisme, he will not falter,
strikes on his shield, a miraculous blow: 1660
a shield of stones, of amethysts, topazes,
esterminals,[1] carbuncles all on fire—
a gift from a devil, in Val Metas,
sent on to him by the Amiral Galafre.
There Turpin strikes, he does not treat it gently—   1665
after that blow, I'd not give one cent for it;
cut through his body, from one side to the other,
and casts him down dead in a barren place.
And the French say: "A fighter, that Archbishop!
Look at him there, saving souls with that crozier!"   1670

9. Banner.   1. Precious ornaments.

127

Roland the Count calls out to Oliver:
"Lord, Companion, now you have to agree
the Archbishop is a good man on horse,
there's none better on earth or under heaven,
he knows his way with a lance and a spear."   1675
The Count replies: "Right! Let us help him then."
And with these words the Franks began anew,
the blows strike hard, and the fighting is bitter;
there is a painful loss of Christian men.
To have seen them, Roland and Oliver,   1680
these fighting men, striking down with their swords,
the Archbishop with them, striking with his lance!
One can recount the number these three killed:
it is written—in charters, in documents;
the Geste tells it: it was more than four thousand.   1685
Through four assaults all went well with our men;
then comes the fifth, and that one crushes them.
They are all killed, all these warriors of France,
all but sixty, whom the Lord God has spared:
they will die too, but first sell themselves dear. AOI.   1690

128

Count Roland sees the great loss of his men,
calls on his companion, on Oliver:
"Lord, Companion, in God's name, what would you do?
All these good men you see stretched on the ground.
We can mourn for sweet France, fair land of France!   1695
a desert now, stripped of such great vassals.
Oh King, and friend, if only you were here!
Oliver, Brother, how shall we manage it?
What shall we do to get word to the King?"
Said Oliver: "I don't see any way.   1700
I would rather die now than hear us shamed." AOI.

129

And Roland said: "I'll sound the olifant,
Charles will hear it, drawing through the passes,
I promise you, the Franks will return at once."
Said Oliver: "That would be a great disgrace,   1705
a dishonor and reproach to all your kin,
the shame of it would last them all their lives.
When I urged it, you would not hear of it;

you will not do it now with my consent.
It is not acting bravely to sound it now—   1710
look at your arms, they are covered with blood."
The Count replies: "I've fought here like a lord."[2] AOI.

130

And Roland says: "We are in a rough battle.
I'll sound the olifant, Charles will hear it."
Said Oliver: "No good vassal would do it.   1715
When I urged it, friend, you did not think it right.
If Charles were here, we'd come out with no losses.
Those men down there—no blame can fall on them."
Oliver said: "Now by this beard of mine,
If I can see my noble sister, Aude,   1720
once more, you will never lie in her arms!"[3] AOI.

131

And Roland said: "Why are you angry at me?"
Oliver answers: "Companion, it is your doing.
I will tell you what makes a vassal good:
    it is judgment, it is never madness;
restraint is worth more than the raw nerve of a fool.   1725
Frenchmen are dead because of your wildness.
And what service will Charles ever have from us?
If you had trusted me, my lord would be here,
we would have fought this battle through to the end,
Marsilion would be dead, or our prisoner.   1730
Roland, your prowess—had we never seen it!
    And now, dear friend, we've seen the last of it.
No more aid from us now for Charlemagne,
a man without equal till Judgment Day,
you will die here, and your death will shame France.
We kept faith, you and I, we were companions;
    and everything we were will end today.   1735
We part before evening, and it will be hard." AOI.

132

Turpin the Archbishop hears their bitter words,
digs hard into his horse with golden spurs
and rides to them; begins to set them right:

2. Some have found lines 1710–12 difficult. Oliver means: We have fought this far—look at the enemy's
blood on your arms: It is too late, it would be a disgrace to summon help when there is no longer any
chance of being saved. And Roland thinks that that is the one time when it is not a disgrace.   3. Aude
had been betrothed to Roland.

"You, Lord Roland, and you, Lord Oliver,   1740
I beg you in God's name do not quarrel.
To sound the horn could not help us now, true,
but still it is far better that you do it:
let the King come, he can avenge us then—
these men of Spain must not go home exulting!   1745
Our French will come, they'll get down on their feet,
and find us here—we'll be dead, cut to pieces.
They will lift us into coffins on the backs of mules,
and weep for us, in rage and pain and grief,
and bury us in the courts of churches;   1750
and we will not be eaten by wolves or pigs or dogs."
Roland replies, "Lord, you have spoken well." AOI.

133

Roland has put the olifant to his mouth,
he sets it well, sounds it with all his strength.
The hills are high, and that voice ranges far,   1755
they heard it echo thirty great leagues away.
King Charles heard it, and all his faithful men.
And the King says: "Our men are in a battle."
And Ganelon disputed him and said:
"Had someone else said that, I'd call him liar!" AOI.   1760

134

And now the mighty effort of Roland the Count:
he sounds his olifant; his pain is great,
and from his mouth the bright blood comes leaping out,
and the temple bursts in his forehead.
That horn, in Roland's hands, has a mighty voice: 1765
King Charles hears it drawing through the passes.
Naimon heard it, the Franks listen to it.
And the King said: "I hear Count Roland's horn;
he'd never sound it unless he had a battle."
Says Ganelon: "Now no more talk of battles!   1770
You are old now, your hair is white as snow,
the things you say make you sound like a child.
You know Roland and that wild pride of his—
what a wonder God has suffered it so long!
Remember? he took Noples without your command: 1775
the Saracens rode out, to break the siege;
they fought with him, the great vassal Roland.
Afterwards he used the streams to wash the blood
from the meadows: so that nothing would show.
He blasts his horn all day to catch a rabbit,   1780

he's strutting now before his peers and bragging—
who under heaven would dare meet him on the field?
So now: ride on! Why do you keep on stopping?
The Land of Fathers lies far ahead of us." AOI.

135

The blood leaping from Count Roland's mouth,   1785
the temple broken with effort in his forehead,
he sounds his horn in great travail and pain.
King Charles heard it, and his French listen hard.
And the King said: "That horn has a long breath!"
Naimon answers: "It is a baron's breath.   1790
There is a battle there, I know there is.
He betrayed him! and now asks you to fail him!
Put on your armor! Lord, shout your battle cry,
and save the noble barons of your house!
You hear Roland's call. He is in trouble."   1795

136

The Emperor commanded the horns to sound,
the French dismount, and they put on their armor:
their hauberks, their helmets, their gold-dressed swords,
their handsome shields; and take up their great lances,
the gonfalons of white and red and blue.   1800
The barons of that host mount their war horses
and spur them hard the whole length of the pass;
and every man of them says to the other:
"If only we find Roland before he's killed,
we'll stand with him, and then we'll do some fighting!"   1805
What does it matter what they say? They are too late.

137

It is the end of day, and full of light,
arms and armor are ablaze in the sun,
and fire flashes from hauberks and helmets,
and from those shields, painted fair with flowers,
and from those lances, those gold-dressed gonfanons.   1810
The Emperor rides on in rage and sorrow,
the men of France indignant and full of grief.
There is no man of them who does not weep,
they are in fear for the life of Roland.
The King commands: seize Ganelon the Count!   1815
and gave him over to the cooks of his house;
summons the master cook, their chief, Besgun:

"Guard him for me like the traitor he is:
he has betrayed the barons of my house."   1820
Besgun takes him, sets his kitchen comrades,
a hundred men, the best, the worst, on him;
and they tear out his beard and his mustache,
each one strikes him four good blows with his fist;
and they lay into him with cudgels and sticks,   1825
put an iron collar around his neck
and chain him up, as they would chain a bear;
dumped him, in dishonor, on a packhorse,
and guard him well till they give him back to Charles.

138

High are the hills, and tenebrous, and vast, AOI.   1830
the valleys deep, the raging waters swift;
to the rear, to the front, the trumpets sound:
they answer the lone voice of the olifant.
The Emperor rides on, rides on in fury,
the men of France in grief and indignation.   1835
There is no man who does not weep and wail,
and they pray God: protect the life of Roland
till they come, one great host, into the field
and fight at Roland's side like true men all.
What does it matter what they pray? It does no good.   1840
They are too late, they cannot come in time. AOI.

139

King Charles the Great rides on, a man in wrath,
his great white beard spread out upon his hauberk.[4]
All the barons of France ride spurring hard,
there is no man who does not wail, furious   1845
not to be with Roland, the captain count,
who stands and fights the Saracens of Spain,
so set upon, I cannot think his soul abides.
God! those sixty men who stand with him, what men!
No king, no captain ever stood with better. AOI.   1850

140

Roland looks up on the mountains and slopes,
sees the French dead, so many good men fallen,
and weeps for them, as a great warrior weeps:
"Barons, my lords, may God give you his grace,

---

4. The beard spread out upon the hauberk is a gesture of defiance toward the enemy.

may he grant Paradise to all your souls,   1855
make them lie down among the holy flowers.
I never saw better vassals than you.
All the years you've served me, and all the times,
the mighty lands you conquered for Charles our King!
The Emperor raised you for this terrible hour!   1860
Land of France, how sweet you are, native land,
laid waste this day, ravaged, made a desert.
Barons of France, I see you die for me,
and I, your lord—I cannot protect you.
May God come to your aid, that God who never failed.   1865
Oliver, brother, now I will not fail you.
I will die here—of grief, if no man kills me.
Lord, Companion, let us return and fight."

141

Roland returned to his place on the field,
strikes—a brave man keeping faith—with Durendal,   1870
struck through Faldrun de Pui, cut him to pieces,
and twenty-four of the men they valued most;
no man will ever want his vengeance more!
As when the deer turns tail before the dogs,
so the pagans flee before Roland the Count.   1875
Said the Archbishop: "You! Roland! What a fighter!
Now that's what every knight must have in him
who carries arms and rides on a fine horse:
he must be strong, a savage, when he's in battle;
for otherwise, what's he worth? Not four cents!   1880
Let that four-cent man be a monk in some minster,
and he can pray all day long for our sins."
Roland replies: "Attack, do not spare them!"
And with that word the Franks began again.
There was a heavy loss of Christian men.   1885

142

When a man knows there'll be no prisoners,
what will that man not do to defend himself!
And so the Franks fight with the fury of lions.
Now Marsilion, the image of a baron,
mounted on that war horse he calls Gaignun,   1890
digs in his spurs, comes on to strike Bevon,
who was the lord of Beaune and of Dijon;
smashes his shield, rips apart his hauberk,
knocks him down, dead, no need to wound him more.
And then he killed Yvorie and Yvon,   1895

and more: he killed Gerard of Rousillon.
Roland the Count is not far away now,
said to the pagan: "The Lord God's curse on you!
You kill my companions, how you wrong me!
You'll feel the pain of it before we part,   1900
you will learn my sword's name by heart today";
comes on to strike—the image of a baron.
He has cut off Marsilion's right fist;
now takes the head of Jurfaleu the blond—
the head of Jurfaleu! Marsilion's son.   1905
The pagans cry: "Help, Mahumet! Help us!
Vengeance, our gods, on Charles! the man who set
these criminals on us in our own land,
they will not quit the field, they'll stand and die!"
And one said to the other: "Let *us* run then."   1910
And with that word, some hundred thousand flee.
Now try to call them back: they won't return. AOI.

143

What does it matter? If Marsilion has fled,
his uncle has remained: the Algalife,[5]
who holds Carthage, Alfrere, and Garmalie,   1915
and Ethiopia: a land accursed;
holds its immense black race under his power,
the huge noses, the enormous ears on them;
and they number more than fifty thousand.
These are the men who come riding in fury,   1920
and now they shout that pagan battle cry.
And Roland said: "Here comes our martyrdom;
I see it now: we have not long to live.
But let the world call any man a traitor
        who does not make them pay before he dies!
My lords, attack! Use those bright shining swords!   1925
Fight a good fight for your deaths and your lives,
let no shame touch sweet France because of us!
When Charles my lord comes to this battlefield
and sees how well we punished these Saracens,
finds fifteen of their dead for one of ours,   1930
I'll tell you what he will do: he will bless us." AOI.

144

When Roland sees that unbelieving race,
those hordes and hordes blacker than blackest ink—

5. The Caliph, Marsilion's uncle, whom Ganelon lied about to Charlemagne. See lines 680–91 (also ll.
453, 493, 505).

no shred of white on them except their teeth—
then said the Count: "I see it clearly now,   1935
we die today: it is there before us.
Men of France, strike! I will start it once more."
Said Oliver: "God curse the slowest man."
And with that word, the French strike into battle.

145

The Saracens, when they saw these few French,   1940
looked at each other, took courage, and presumed,
telling themselves: "The Emperor is wrong!"
The Algalife rides a great sorrel horse,
digs into it with his spurs of fine gold,
strikes Oliver, from behind, in the back,   1945
shattered the white hauberk upon his flesh,
drove his spear through the middle of his chest;
and speaks to him: "Now you feel you've been struck!
Your great Charles doomed you when he left you in this pass.
That man wronged us, he must not boast of it.   1950
I've avenged all our dead in you alone!"

146

Oliver feels: he has been struck to death;
grips Halteclere, that steel blade shining, strikes
on the gold-dressed pointed helm of the Algalife,
sends jewels and flowers crackling down to the earth,   1955
into the head, into the little teeth;
draws up his flashing sword, casts him down, dead,
and then he says: "Pagan, a curse on you!
If only I could say Charles has lost nothing—
but no woman, no lady you ever knew   1960
will hear you boast, in the land you came from,
that you could take one thing worth a cent from me,
or do me harm, or do any man harm";
then cries out to Roland to come to his aid. AOI.

147

Oliver feels he is wounded to death,   1965
will never have his fill of vengeance, strikes,
as a baron strikes, where they are thickest,
cuts through their lances, cuts through those buckled shields,
through feet, through fists, through saddles, and through flanks.
Had you seen him, cutting the pagans limb   1970
from limb, casting one corpse down on another,

you would remember a brave man keeping faith.
Never would he forget Charles' battle-cry,
Munjoie! he shouts, that mighty voice ringing;
calls to Roland, to his friend and his peer: 1975
"Lord, Companion, come stand beside me now.
We must part from each other in pain today." AOI.

148

Roland looks hard into Oliver's face,
it is ashen, all its color is gone,
the bright red blood streams down upon his body,   1980
Oliver's blood spattering on the earth.
"God!" said the Count, "I don't know what to do,
Lord, Companion, your fight is finished now.
There'll never be a man the like of you.
Sweet land of France, today you will be stripped   1985
of good vassals, laid low, a fallen land!
The Emperor will suffer the great loss";
faints with that word, mounted upon his horse. AOI.

149

Here is Roland, lords, fainted on his horse,
and Oliver the Count, wounded to death: 1990
he has lost so much blood, his eyes are darkened—
he cannot see, near or far, well enough
to recognize a friend or enemy:
struck when he came upon his companion,
strikes on his helm, adorned with gems in gold,   1995
cuts down straight through, from the point to the nasal,[6]
but never harmed him, he never touched his head.
Under this blow, Count Roland looked at him;
and gently, softly now, he asks of him:
"Lord, Companion, do you mean to do this?   2000
It is Roland, who always loved you greatly.
You never declared that we were enemies."
Said Oliver: "Now I hear it is you—
I don't see you, may the Lord God see you.
Was it you that I struck? Forgive me then."   2005
Roland replies: "I am not harmed, not harmed,
I forgive you, Friend, here and before God."
And with that word, each bowed to the other.
And this is the love, lords, in which they parted.

---

6. The nosepiece protruding down from the cone-shaped helmet.

150

Oliver feels: death pressing hard on him;   2010
his two eyes turn, roll up into his head,
all hearing is lost now, all sight is gone;
gets down on foot, stretches out on the ground,
cries out now and again: *mea culpa!*[7]
his two hands joined, raised aloft toward heaven,   2015
he prays to God: grant him His Paradise;
and blesses Charles, and the sweet land of France,
his companion, Roland, above all men.
The heart fails him, his helmet falls away,
the great body settles upon the earth.   2020
The Count is dead, he stands with us no longer.
Roland, brave man, weeps for him, mourns for him,
you will not hear a man of greater sorrow.

151

Roland the Count, when he sees his friend dead,
lying stretched out, his face against the earth,   2025
softly, gently, begins to speak the regret:[8]
"Lord, Companion, you were brave and died for it.
We have stood side by side through days and years,
you never caused me harm, I never wronged you;
when you are dead, to be alive pains me."   2030
And with that word the lord of marches faints
upon his horse, which he calls Veillantif.
He is held firm by his spurs of fine gold,
whichever way he leans, he cannot fall.

152

Before Roland could recover his senses   2035
and come out of his faint, and be aware,
a great disaster had come forth before him:
the French are dead, he has lost every man
except the Archbishop, and Gautier de l'Hum,
who has come back, down from that high mountain: 2040
he has fought well, he fought those men of Spain.
His men are dead, the pagans finished them;
flees now down to these valleys, he has no choice,
and calls on Count Roland to come to his aid:
"My noble Count, my brave lord, where are you?   2045
I never feared whenever you were there.

---

7. "My guilt." A formula used in the confession of one's sins.   8. What follows is a formal and customary lament for the dead.

It is Walter: I conquered Maëlgut,
my uncle is Droün, old and gray: your Walter
and always dear to you for the way I fought;
and I have fought this time: my lance is shattered,   2050
my good shield pierced, my hauberk's meshes broken;
and I am wounded, a lance struck through my body.
I will die soon, but I sold myself dear."
And with that word, Count Roland has heard him,
he spurs his horse, rides spurring to his man. AOI.   2055

153

Roland in pain, maddened with grief and rage:
rushes where they are thickest and strikes again,
strikes twenty men of Spain, strikes twenty dead,
and Walter six, and the Archbishop five.
The pagans say: "Look at those criminals!   2060
Now take care, Lords, they don't get out alive,
only a traitor will not attack them now!
Only a coward will let them save their skins!"
And then they raise their hue and cry once more,
rush in on them, once more, from every side. AOI.   2065

154

Count Roland was always a noble warrior,
Gautier de l'Hum is a fine mounted man,
the Archbishop, a good man tried and proved:
not one of them will ever leave the others;
strike, where they are thickest, at the pagans.   2070
A thousand Saracens get down on foot,
and forty thousand more are on their mounts:
and I tell you, not one will dare come close,
they throw, and from afar, lances and spears,
wigars and darts, mizraks, javelins, pikes.   2075
With the first blows they killed Gautier de l'Hum
and struck Turpin of Reims, pierced through his shield,
broke the helmet on him, wounded his head;
ripped his hauberk, shattered its rings of mail,
and pierced him with four spears in his body,   2080
the war horse killed under him; and now there comes
great pain and rage when the Archbishop falls. AOI.

155

Turpin of Reims, when he feels he is unhorsed,
struck to the earth with four spears in his body,

quickly, brave man, leaps to his feet again;   2085
his eyes find Roland now, he runs to him
and says one word: "See! I'm not finished yet!
What good vassal ever gives up alive!";
and draws Almace, his sword, that shining steel!
and strikes, where they are thickest, a thousand blows, and more.   2090
Later, Charles said: Turpin had spared no one;
he found four hundred men prostrate around him,
some of them wounded, some pierced from front to back,
some with their heads hacked off. So says the Geste,
and so says one who was there, on that field,   2095
the baron Saint Gilles,[9] for whom God performs miracles,
who made the charter setting forth these great things
        in the Church of Laon. Now any man
who does not know this much understands nothing.

156

Roland the Count fights well and with great skill,
but he is hot, his body soaked with sweat;   2100
has a great wound in his head, and much pain,
his temple broken because he blew the horn.
But he must know whether King Charles will come;
draws out the olifant, sounds it, so feebly.
The Emperor drew to a halt, listened.   2105
"Seigneurs," he said, "it goes badly for us—
My nephew Roland falls from our ranks today.
I hear it in the horn's voice: he hasn't long.
Let every man who wants to be with Roland
ride fast! Sound trumpets! Every trumpet in this host!"   2110
Sixty thousand, on these words, sound, so high
the mountains sound, and the valleys resound.
The pagans hear: it is no joke to them;
cry to each other: "We're getting Charles on us!"

157

The pagans say: "The Emperor is coming, AOI.   2115
listen to their trumpets—it is the French!
If Charles comes back, it's all over for us,
if Roland lives, this war begins again
and we have lost our land, we have lost Spain."
Some four hundred, helmets laced on, assemble,   2120

9. Saint Gilles of Provence: These lines explain how the story of Rencesvals could be told after all who had fought there died.

some of the best, as they think, on that field.
They storm Roland, in one fierce, bitter attack.
And now Count Roland has some work on his hands. AOI.

158

Roland the Count, when he sees them coming,
how strong and fierce and alert he becomes!   2125
He will not yield to them, not while he lives.
He rides the horse they call Veillantif, spurs,
digs into it with his spurs of fine gold,
and rushes at them all where they are thickest,
the Archbishop—that Turpin!—at his side.   2130
Said one man to the other: "Go at it, friend.
The horns we heard were the horns of the French,
King Charles is coming back with all his strength."[1]

159

Roland the Count never loved a coward,
a blusterer, an evil-natured man,   2135
a man on horse who was not a good vassal.
And now he called to Archbishop Turpin:
"You are on foot, Lord, and here I am mounted,
and so, here I take my stand: for love of you.
We'll take whatever comes, the good and bad,   2140
together, Lord: no one can make me leave you.
They will learn our swords' names today in battle,
the name of Almace, the name of Durendal!"
Said the Archbishop: "Let us strike or be shamed!
Charles is returning, and he brings our revenge."   2145

160

Say the pagans: "We were all born unlucky!
The evil day that dawned for us today!
We have lost our lords and peers, and now comes Charles—
that Charlemagne!—with his great host. Those trumpets!
that shrill sound on us—the trumpets of the French!   2150
And the loud roar of that Munjoie! This Roland
is a wild man, he is too great a fighter—
What man of flesh and blood can ever hope
to bring him down? Let us cast at him, and leave him there."
And so they did: arrows, wigars, darts,   2155

---

1. Lines 2131–33 could be spoken either by Roland and the Archbishop or by the pagans.

lances and spears, javelots dressed with feathers;
struck Roland's shield, pierced it, broke it to pieces,
ripped his hauberk, shattered its rings of mail,
but never touched his body, never his flesh.
They wounded Veillantif in thirty places,   2160
struck him dead, from afar, under the Count.
The pagans flee, they leave the field to him.
Roland the Count stood alone, on his feet. AOI.

161

The pagans flee, in bitterness and rage,
strain every nerve running headlong toward Spain,   2165
and Count Roland has no way to chase them,
he has lost Veillantif, his battle horse;
he has no choice, left alone there on foot.
He went to the aid of Archbishop Turpin,
unlaced the gold-dressed helmet, raised it from his head,   2170
lifted away his bright, light coat of mail,
cut his under tunic into some lengths,
stilled his great wounds with thrusting on the strips;
then held him in his arms, against his chest,
and laid him down, gently, on the green grass;   2175
and softly now Roland entreated him:
"My noble lord, I beg you, give me leave:
our companions, whom we have loved so dearly,
are all dead now, we must not abandon them.
I want to look for them, know them once more,   2180
and set them in ranks, side by side, before you."
Said the Archbishop: "Go then, go and come back.
The field is ours, thanks be to God, yours and mine."

162

So Roland leaves him, walks the field all alone,
seeks in the valleys, and seeks in the mountains.   2185
He found Gerin, and Gerer his companion,
and then he found Berenger and Otun,
Anseïs and Sansun, and on that field
he found Gerard the old of Roussillon;
and carried them, brave man, all, one by one,   2190
came back to the Archbishop with these French dead,
and set them down in ranks before his knees.
The Archbishop cannot keep from weeping,
raises his hand and makes his benediction;
and said: "Lords, Lords, it was your terrible hour.   2195

May the Glorious God set all your souls
among the holy flowers of Paradise!
Here is my own death, Lords, pressing on me,
I shall not see our mighty Emperor."

163

And Roland leaves, seeks in the field again;   2200
he has found Oliver, his companion,
held him tight in his arms against his chest;
came back to the Archbishop, laid Oliver
down on a shield among the other dead.
The Archbishop absolved him, signed him with the Cross.   2205
And pity now and rage and grief increase;
and Roland says: "Oliver, dear companion,
you were the son of the great duke Renier,
who held the march of the vale of Runers.
Lord, for shattering lances, for breaking shields,   2210
for making men great with presumption weak with fright,
for giving life and counsel to good men,
for striking fear in that unbelieving race,
no warrior on earth surpasses you."

164

Roland the Count, when he sees his peers dead,   2215
and Oliver, whom he had good cause to love,
felt such grief and pity, he begins to weep;
and his face lost its color with what he felt:
a pain so great he cannot keep on standing,
he has no choice, falls fainting to the ground.   2220
Said the Archbishop: "Baron, what grief for you."

165

The Archbishop, when he saw Roland faint,
felt such pain then as he had never felt;
stretched out his hand and grasped the olifant.
At Rencesvals there is a running stream: 2225
he will go there and fetch some water for Roland;
and turns that way, with small steps, staggering;
he is too weak, he cannot go ahead,
he has no strength: all the blood he has lost.
In less time than a man takes to cross a little field   2230
that great heart fails, he falls forward, falls down;
and Turpin's death comes crushing down on him.

166

Roland the Count recovers from his faint,
gets to his feet, but stands with pain and grief;
looks down the valley, looks up the mountain, sees: 2235
on the green grass, beyond his companions,
that great and noble man down on the ground,
the Archbishop, whom God sent in His name;
who confesses his sins, lifts up his eyes,
holds up his hands joined together to heaven,   2240
and prays to God: grant him that Paradise.
Turpin is dead, King Charles' good warrior.
In great battles, in beautiful sermons
he was ever a champion against the pagans.
Now God grant Turpin's soul His holy blessing. AOI.   2245

167

Roland the Count sees the Archbishop down,
sees the bowels fallen out of his body,
and the brain boiling down from his forehead.
Turpin has crossed his hands upon his chest
beneath the collarbone, those fine white hands.   2250
Roland speaks the lament, after the custom
followed in his land: aloud, with all his heart:
"My noble lord, you great and well-born warrior,
I commend you today to the God of Glory,
whom none will ever serve with a sweeter will.   2255
Since the Apostles no prophet the like of you[2]
arose to keep the faith and draw men to it.
May your soul know no suffering or want,
and behold the gate open to Paradise."

168

Now Roland feels that death is very near.   2260
His brain comes spilling out through his two ears;
prays to God for his peers: let them be called;
and for himself, to the angel Gabriel;
took the olifant: there must be no reproach!
took Durendal his sword in his other hand,   2265
and farther than a crossbow's farthest shot
he walks toward Spain, into a fallow land,
and climbs a hill: there beneath two fine trees
stand four great blocks of stone, all are of marble;

2. Compare Deuteronomy 34:10, on the death of Moses.

and he fell back, to earth, on the green grass,   2270
has fainted there, for death is very near.

169

High are the hills, and high, high are the trees;
there stand four blocks of stone, gleaming of marble.
Count Roland falls fainting on the green grass,
and is watched, all this time, by a Saracen: 2275
who has feigned death and lies now with the others,
has smeared blood on his face and on his body;
and quickly now gets to his feet and runs—
a handsome man, strong, brave, and so crazed with pride
that he does something mad and dies for it: 2280
laid hands on Roland, and on the arms of Roland,
and cried: "Conquered! Charles's nephew conquered!
I'll carry this sword home to Arabia!"
As he draws it, the Count begins to come round.

170

Now Roland feels: *someone taking his sword!*   2285
opened his eyes, and had one word for him:
"I don't know you, you aren't one of ours";
grasps that olifant that he will never lose,
strikes on the helm beset with gems in gold,
shatters the steel, and the head, and the bones,   2290
sent his two eyes flying out of his head,
dumped him over stretched out at his feet dead;
and said: "You nobody! how could you dare
lay hands on me—rightly or wrongly: how?
Who'll hear of this and not call you a fool?   2295
Ah! the bell-mouth of the olifant is smashed,
the crystal and the gold fallen away."

171

Now Roland the Count feels: his sight is gone;
gets on his feet, draws on his final strength,
the color on his face lost now for good.   2300
Before him stands a rock; and on that dark rock
in rage and bitterness he strikes ten blows:
the steel blade grates, it will not break, it stands unmarked.
"Ah!" said the Count, "Blessed Mary, your help!
Ah Durendal, good sword, your unlucky day,   2305
for I am lost and cannot keep you in my care.
The battles I have won, fighting with you,

the mighty lands that holding you I conquered,
that Charles rules now, our King, whose beard is white!
Now you fall to another: it must not be
        a man who'd run before another man!   2310
For a long while a good vassal held you:
there'll never be the like in France's holy land."

172

Roland strikes down on that rock of Cerritania:
the steel blade grates, will not break, stands unmarked.
Now when he sees he can never break that sword,   2315
Roland speaks the lament, in his own presence:
"Ah Durendal, how beautiful and bright!
so full of light, all on fire in the sun!
King Charles was in the vales of Moriane
when God sent his angel and commanded him,   2320
from heaven, to give you to a captain count.
That great and noble King girded it on me.
And with this sword I won Anjou and Brittany,
I won Poitou, I won Le Maine for Charles,
and Normandy, that land where men are free,   2325
I won Provence and Aquitaine with this,
and Lombardy, and every field of Romagna,
I won Bavaria, and all of Flanders,
all of Poland, and Bulgaria, for Charles,
Constantinople, which pledged him loyalty,   2330
and Saxony, where he does as he wills;
and with this sword I won Scotland and Ireland,
and England, his chamber, his own domain—
the lands, the nations I conquered with this sword,
for Charles, who rules them now, whose beard is white!   2335
Now, for this sword, I am pained with grief and rage:
Let it not fall to pagans! Let me die first!
Our Father God, save France from that dishonor."

173

Roland the Count strikes down on a dark rock,
and the rock breaks, breaks more than I can tell,   2340
and the blade grates, but Durendal will not break,
the sword leaped up, rebounded toward the sky.
The Count, when he sees that sword will not be broken,
softly, in his own presence, speaks the lament:
"Ah Durendal, beautiful, and most sacred,   2345
the holy relics in this golden pommel!
Saint Peter's tooth and blood of Saint Basile,

a lock of hair of my lord Saint Denis,
and a fragment of blessed Mary's robe:
your power must not fall to the pagans,   2350
you must be served by Christian warriors.
May no coward ever come to hold you!
It was with you I conquered those great lands
that Charles has in his keeping, whose beard is white,
the Emperor's lands, that make him rich and strong."   2355

174

Now Roland feels: death coming over him,
death descending from his temples to his heart.
He came running underneath a pine tree
and there stretched out, face down, on the green grass,
lays beneath him his sword and the olifant.   2360
He turned his head toward the Saracen hosts,
and this is why: with all his heart he wants
King Charles the Great and all his men to say,
he died, that noble Count, a conqueror;
makes confession, beats his breast often, so feebly,   2365
offers his glove, for all his sins, to God. AOI.

175

Now Roland feels that his time has run out;
he lies on a steep hill, his face toward Spain;
and with one of his hands he beat his breast:
"Almighty God, *mea culpa* in thy sight,[3]   2370
forgive my sins, both the great and the small,
sins I committed from the hour I was born
until this day, in which I lie struck down."
And then he held his right glove out to God.
Angels descend from heaven and stand by him. AOI.   2375

176

Count Roland lay stretched out beneath a pine;
he turned his face toward the land of Spain,
began to remember many things now:
how many lands, brave man, he had conquered;
and he remembered: sweet France, the men of his line,   2380
remembered Charles, his lord, who fostered him:
cannot keep, remembering, from weeping, sighing;
but would not be unmindful of himself:

3. See Psalm 51:4.

he confesses his sins, prays God for mercy:
"Loyal Father, you who never failed us,   2385
who resurrected Saint Lazarus from the dead,
and saved your servant Daniel from the lions:[4]
now save the soul of me from every peril
for the sins I committed while I still lived."
Then he held out his right glove to his Lord: 2390
Saint Gabriel took the glove from his hand.
He held his head bowed down upon his arm,
he is gone, his two hands joined, to his end.
Then God sent him his angel Cherubin[5]
and Saint Michael, angel of the sea's Peril;   2395
and with these two there came Saint Gabriel:
they bear Count Roland's soul to Paradise.

*   *   *

MARIE DE FRANCE

The first woman known to write poetry in French was Marie de France, who lived in the last third of the twelfth century. As often with medieval authors, the name does not identify her with any specific historical figure; but it indicates that she was a French native. Her works show that she was associated in some way with the court of King Henry II of England, husband of the famous Queen Eleanor of Aquitaine. Marie was probably familiar with English as well as Latin and French. A versatile writer, she produced works in three varieties of literature: fables, visions of purgatory, and *lais*. She may or may not have been the first author of Breton *lais* and thus have given a designation to the genre. These were comparatively short narratives based in varying degrees on a story or song circulated by traveling entertainers (*jongleurs*) from the northwestern province of France known as Brittany. They were presumably in Breton, originally the Celtic language of Brittany, but none have come down to us. For French and English poets, a Breton *lai* was a narrative of moderate length recounting an event remarkable in some way, often associated with the magical or miraculous; most often, the "adventure" involves what we should call romantic love. Thus *Eliduc*, the longest of Marie's dozen *lais*, has been called a story of a man with two wives. In that respect it recalls the better-known story of Tristan and the two Isoldes. As Marie rightly says, her tale centers on the two women; it's a pity that her change of the title to *Guildelüec and Guilliadun* has not prevailed in literary history.

Marie's handling of the plot precludes any dismissal of Eliduc as a mere villain, an exploiter of women. The reader's sympathy is engaged by his loyalty to the lord in his home country (where he suffers baseless slander) whom Eliduc returns to help in a time of need—and also by his faithful service to the lord of the country to which he goes. He is an honorable knight, exceptionally able and dependable.

4. See Daniel 6:12–23. For the raising of Lazarus, see the Gospel of St. John 11:1–44.   5. The poet seems to have regarded this as the name of a single angel.

There is nothing said to his discredit about his relationship to Guildelüec, his wife in his home country, before he goes into exile. And there is no doubt about the reality or strength of his love for Guilliadun in the new country. This is made quite clear in the narrtive—by his clandestine return in order to take her with him to his homeland and by his inconsolable grief when he believes her dead—to say nothing of their later long and happy life together. On the other hand, it is a selfish affection, and it leads to dishonesty in his treatment of both the princess and her father. He does not tell her that he already has a wife in his home country, and in taking her away secretly he betrays the trust that her father has clearly placed in him. We are told that these considerations disturb Eliduc—but they do not deter him. The penalty is not long delayed: the storm at sea, the harsh revelation of Eliduc's marital state by the sailor on the ship, and Guilliadun's apparent death from shock.

In Guilliadun, the author presents a young, inexperienced, and rather naïve woman—but one determined to have what she wants. From the beginning she is obsessed by her love of Eliduc. It is she who makes all the advances, she who begs, "Take me with you," at the decisive moment. (This may serve to mitigate our judgment of Eliduc's conduct, though it does not, in the end, justify it.) Guilliadun seems undisturbed by her violation of the trust of an apparently affectionate father; he might or might not have forbidden the alliance, but she gives him no chance to say. As we have seen, retribution strikes the lovers together, but its impact is more drastic for Guilliadun than for Eliduc. She suffers two shocks at once: the news that Eliduc already has a wife and the sailor's proposal to throw her overboard as a means of calming the storm. (In the stress of the moment she cannot know whether this is a real danger or not.) The combined effect of the two is overwhelming; no wonder that it seems fatal—and a miracle is necessary to restore her to life.

In Eliduc and Guilliadun the author examines the moral or ethical defects of an exclusive, self-regarding love; in Guildelüec she presents a contrast to that kind of love—a paragon of "good" love. Guildelüec's affection for Eliduc is genuine and strong. She grieves at his going into exile; her life in his absence is flawless, but she is distressed when his coldness on his first return might suggest otherwise and offers to answer any possible accusations. Later, on his second return, she seeks to understand his grief and sorrow in order to relieve them if she can. This love is never in conflict with other claims on her loyalty; it never leads her into unjust treatment of other people. That is, she has it under control, as the others do not have theirs. When, through her own assiduity, she comes to understand the relationship that has developed between Eliduc and Guilliadun, she does all she can to promote their happiness. With the help of the weasel's miraculous flower she restores Guilliadun from apparent death to life, reassures her of Eliduc's devotion, organizes a search for him, and finally reunites the pair. Then, so that they can be married and live in accord with the laws of God and man, she voluntarily renounces her status as Eliduc's wife and becomes a nun. Thus she does not allow "sexual" love to undermine or preclude the love that is traditionally known as *charity*—that is, devotion to the welfare of others. It might also be said that here the two are combined: she loves Eliduc enough to renounce him.

Robert Hanning and Joan Ferrante, *The Lais of Marie de France* (1982) contains translations of all the twelve *lais*, with a lengthy introduction and an excellent bibliography. A convenient edition of the twelfth-century French text is Jeanne Lods, *Les Lais de Marie de France* (1959), in the series *Les Classiques Français du moyen âge*.

Eliduc[1]

I am going to give you the full story of a very old Celtic tale, at least as I've been able to understand the truth of it.

In Brittany there was once a knight called Eliduc. He was a model of his type, one of the bravest men in the country, and he had a wife of excellent and influential family, as finely bred as she was faithful to him. They lived happily for several years, since it was a marriage of truth and love. But then a war broke out and he went away to join the fighting. There he fell in love with a girl, a ravishingly pretty princess called Guilliadun. The Celtic name of the wife who stayed at home was Guildelüec, and so the story is called *Guildelüec and Guilliadun* after their names. Its original title was *Eliduc*, but it was changed because it's really about the two women. Now I'll tell you exactly how it all happened.

Eliduc's overlord was the king of Brittany, who was very fond of the knight and looked after his interests. Eliduc served him faithfully—whenever the king had to go abroad, Eliduc was left in charge of his territories, and kept them safe by his military skills. He got many favors in return. He was allowed to hunt in the royal forests. No gamekeeper, even the most resolute, dared stand in his way or complain about him. But other people's envy of his good luck did its usual work. He was slandered and traduced, and brought into bad relations with the king. Finally he was dismissed from the court without any reason. Left in the dark, Eliduc repeatedly asked to be allowed to defend himself before the king—the slanders were lies, he had served the king well, and happily so. But no answer came from the court. Convinced he would never get a hearing, Eliduc decided to go into exile. So he went home and called together all his friends. He told them how things lay with the king, of the anger toward him. Eliduc had done the best he could and there was no justice in the royal resentment. When the plowman gets the rough edge of his master's tongue, the peasants have a proverb: *Never trust a great man's love*. If someone in Eliduc's position is sensible, he puts more trust in the love of his neighbors. So now he says[2] he's sick of Brittany, he'll cross the sea to England and amuse himself there for a while. He'll leave his wife at home; have his servants take care of her, along with his friends.

Once it was made, he kept to this decision. He fitted himself—and the ten horsemen he took with him—out handsomely for the journey. His friends were very sad to see him go, and as for his wife . . . she accompanied him for the first part of the journey, in tears that she was losing him. But he swore solemnly that he would stay true to her. Then he says goodbye and rides straight on to the sea. There he takes ship, crosses successfully and arrives at the port of Totnes.[3]

There were several kings in that part of England, and they were at war. Toward Exeter in this country there lived a very powerful old man. He

---

1. Translated by John Fowles. The punctuation ". . ." does not indicate omissions from this text.
2. The shifts to the narrative present (like those into dialogue) are all in the original. [Translator's note.]
3. On the southern coast of England.

had no male heir, simply an unmarried daughter. This explained the present war: because he had refused her hand to an equal from another dynasty, the other king was putting all his land to the sack. He had trapped the old king in one of his fortified cities.[4] No one there had the courage to go out and join combat, general or single, with the invader. Eliduc heard about all this and decided that since there was war he would stay in those parts instead of going on. He wanted to help the besieged king, who was getting into worse and worse trouble and faced with ruin and disaster. He would hire himself out as a mercenary.[5]

He sent messengers to the king, explaining in a letter that he had left his own country and had come to help him; but he was at the king's disposal and if he didn't want Eliduc's services, then Eliduc asked only for safe-conduct through his lands, so that he could go and offer his fighting abilities somewhere else. When the king saw the messengers, he was delighted and welcomed them warmly. He summoned the castle commander and ordered that an escort be provided immediately for Eliduc and that he should be brought to him. Then the king had lodgings arranged. All that was necessary for a month's stay was also provided.

The escort were armed and horsed and sent to fetch Eliduc. He was received with great honor, having made the journey without trouble. His lodging was with a rich townsman, a decent and well-mannered man who gave up his tapestry-hung best room to the knight. Eliduc had a good meal prepared and invited to it all the other anxious knights[6] who were quartered in the city. He forbade his own men, even the most grabbing, to accept any gift or wages for the first forty days.

On his third day at Exeter the cry ran through the city that the enemy had arrived and were all over the surrounding countryside—and already preparing an attack on the city gates. Eliduc heard the uproar from the panicking townspeople and immediately donned armor. His companions did the same. There were fourteen other knights capable of fighting in the town, the rest being wounded, or captured. Seeing Eliduc mount his horse, they go to their lodgings and put on their own armor as well. They won't wait to be called, they'll go out of the gates with him.

"We'll ride with you, sir," they now say. "And whatever you do, we'll do the same."

Eliduc answers. "My thanks. Is there anyone here who knows an ambush place? A defile? Somewhere where we might catch them hopping? If we wait here, we'll get a good fight. But we have no advantage. Has anyone a better plan?"

"There's a narrow cart road, sir. Beside that wood by the flax field over there. When they've got enough loot, they'll return by it. They ride back

4. The text says "in a castle," but it seems clear that Exeter, then a walled city, is meant. Marie would have known of its importance in West Saxon times and of William the Conqueror's siege of 1068. [Translator's note.] 5. . . . *en soudees remaner*. The knight *soudoyer* has to be understood (at least in romance) in a far more honorable—and honor driven—sense than in the contemporary or even the Renaissance use of "mercenary." Perhaps the Japanese samurai is the best equivalent. [Translator's note.] Similarly, the Knight of Chaucer's *Canterbury Tales* was an honorable mercenary; see the General Prologue, ll. 46–65.
6. Anxious because of their precarious or uncertain status.

carelessly from such work, as a rule. Like that they're asking for a quick death."

It could be over in a flash; and much damage done.

"My friends," said Eliduc, "one thing for certain. Nothing venture, even when things look hopeless, then nothing gain—either in war or reputation. You're all the king's men, you owe him complete loyalty. So follow me, wherever I go, and do as I do. I promise you there won't be setbacks if I can help it. We may not get any loot. But we'll never be forgotten if we beat the enemy today."

His confidence spread to the other knights and they led him to the wood. There they hid by the road and waited for the enemy to return from their raid. Eliduc had planned everything, showed them how they should charge at the gallop and what to cry. When the enemy reached the narrow place, Eliduc shouted the battle challenge, then cried to his friends to fight well. They struck hard, and gave no quarter. Taken by surprise, the enemy were soon broken and put to flight. The engagement was brief. They captured the officer in command and many other knights, whom they entrust to their squires. Eliduc's side had had twenty-five men, and they took thirty of the enemy. They also took a great deal of armor, and a quantity of other valuable things. Now they return triumphantly to the city, full of this splendid victory. The king was there on a tower, desperately anxious for his men. He complained bitterly, having convinced himself that Eliduc was a traitor and had lost him all his knights.

They come in a crowd, some laden, others bound—many more on the return than at the going out, which was why the king was misled and stayed in doubt and suspense. He orders the city gates closed and the people up on the walls, bows and other weapons at the ready. But they have no need of them. Eliduc's party had sent a squire galloping on ahead to explain what had happened. The man told the king about the Breton mercenary, how he had driven the enemy away, how well he had conducted himself. There was never a better handler of arms on horseback. He had personally captured the enemy commander and taken twenty-nine prisoners, besides wounding and killing many others.

When the king hears the good news, he's beside himself with joy. He came down from the tower and went to meet Eliduc; then thanked him for all he had done and gave him all the prisoners for ransoming. Eliduc shared out the armor among the other knights, keeping no more for his own men than three horses that had been allocated to them. He distributed everything else, even his own rightful part as well, among the prisoners and the other people.

After this exploit the king made Eliduc his favorite. He retained him and his companions for a whole year and Eliduc gave his oath of faithful service. He then became the protector of the king's lands.

The king's young daughter heard all about Eliduc and his splendid actions—how good-looking he was, such a proud knight, how civilized and openhanded. She sent one of her personal pages to request, to *beg*

Eliduc to come and amuse her. They must talk, get to know each other, and she would be very hurt if he didn't come. Eliduc replies: of course he'll come, he looks forward very much to meeting her. He got on his horse; and taking a servant with him, he goes to chat with the girl. When he's at the door of her room, he sends the page ahead. He doesn't barge in, but waits a little, till the page comes back. Then with gentle expression, sincere face and perfect good manners he addressed the young lady formally and thanked her for having invited him to visit her. Guilliadun was very pretty, and she took him by the hand and led him to a couch, where they sat and talked of this and that. She kept stealing looks at him . . . his face, his body, his every expression . . . and said to herself how attractive he was, how close to her ideal man. Love fires his arrow, she falls headlong in love. She goes pale, she sighs, but she can't declare herself, in case he despises her for it.

Eliduc stayed a long time, but in the end took his leave and went away. Guilliadun was very unwilling to let him go, but there it was. He returned to his lodgings, unsmiling and very thoughtful. The girl alarmed him, since she was the king's daughter and he the king's servant. She had seemed so shy, yet subtly accused him of something. He feels badly done by[7]—to have been so long in the country, yet not to have seen her once till now. Yet when he said that to himself, he felt ashamed. He remembered his wife, and how he had promised to behave as a husband should.

Now she had met him, the girl wanted to make Eliduc her lover. She had never liked a man more—if only she can, if only he'll agree. All night she was awake thinking of him, and had neither rest nor sleep. The next morning she got up at dawn and went to a window and called down to her page. Then she revealed everything to him.

"Dear God," she says, "I'm in such a state, I've fallen into such a trap. I love the new mercenary. Eliduc. Who's fought so brilliantly. I haven't slept a wink all night, my eyes just wouldn't shut. If he's really in love with me, if he'll only show he's serious, I'll do anything he likes. And there's so much to hope for—he could be king here one day. I'm mad about him. He's so intelligent, so easy-mannered. If he doesn't love me, I'll die of despair."

When he'd heard all she had to say, the young page gave her good advice: no need to give up hope so soon.

"My lady, if you're in love with him, then let him know it. Send him a belt or a ribbon—or a ring. To see if it pleases him. If he's happy to accept the gift, looks glad to have heard from you, then you're in! He loves you. And show me an emperor who wouldn't dance for joy if he knew you fancied him."

The girl mulled over this advice.

"But how shall I know just by a gift whether he really wants me? You don't realize. A gentleman has to accept, whether he likes the sender or

---

7. The Old French is less specific: it is too bad it turned out they hadn't met.

not. One has to take such things with good grace. I should loathe it if he
made fun of me. But perhaps you could learn something from his expression. So get ready. Quickly. And go."

"I am ready."

"Take him this gold ring. And here, give him my belt. And be very
warm when you greet him for me."

The page turned away, leaving her in such a state that she very nearly
calls him back. Nevertheless she lets him go—and then begins to rave to
herself.

"Oh God, I've fallen in love with a foreigner! I don't even know if he's
of good family. Whether he won't suddenly disappear. I shall be left in
despair. I'm insane to have made it all so obvious. I'd never even spoken
with him before yesterday, and now I'm throwing myself at him. I think
he'll just despise me. No he won't, if he's nice he'll like me for it. It's all
in the lap of the gods now. If he doesn't care for me at all, I shall feel such
a fool. I'll never be happy again, as long as I live."

Meanwhile, as she agonized on like that, the page rode fast on his way.
He found Eliduc and gave him in private the kind of greetings the girl had
asked. Then he handed him the little ring and the belt. The knight had
thanked him, then put the ring on his finger and fastened the belt[8] around
his waist. But he said nothing else to the page, asked him nothing—except
that he offered him his own ring and belt in return. But the page didn't
accept them and went away back to his young mistress. He found her in
her room; then passed on Eliduc's return of greetings and thanks.

"For pity's sake, don't hide the truth. Does he really love me?"

"I think so. He wouldn't deceive you. In my opinion he's playing polite
and being shrewd—he knows how to hide his feelings. I said hallo to him
for you and gave him the presents. He put the belt on himself, and was
rather careful to get it right. Then the ring on his finger. I didn't say
anything else to him. Or he to me."

"But did he realize what it meant? Because if he didn't, I'm lost!"

"I honestly don't know. But if you must have my solemn opinion, then,
well, since he didn't turn up his nose at what you sent, he doesn't exactly
. . . hate you?"

"Stop teasing me, you cheeky boy! I'm perfectly well aware he doesn't
hate me. How could I ever hurt him? Except by loving him so much. But
if he does, he deserves to die. Until I've spoken with him myself, I won't
have anything to do with him. Either through you or anyone else. I'll show
him myself how wanting him tears me apart. But if only I knew how long
he was staying here!"

"Lady, the king has him under contract for a year. That ought to be
time enough to show him how you feel?"

When she heard Eliduc wasn't going away, Guilliadun was in ecstasy:
how wonderful that he must stay! What she didn't know was the torment
Eliduc had been in from the moment he set eyes on her. Fear had dealt

8. The fashionable belt of the Middle Ages had links, with a hook at one end. It was fastened with a free
end left hanging at the side.

him a cruel hand—that promise to his wife when he left home, that he'd never look at another woman. Now his heart was in a vise. He wanted to stay faithful. But nothing could hide the fact that he had hopelessly fallen for Guilliadun and her prettiness. To see her again and talk with her, kiss her and hold her in his arms . . . yet he could never show her this longing, which would disgrace him—on the one hand for breaking his promise to his wife, on the other because of his relationship with the king. He was torn in two; then mounted his horse, and wavered no more. He calls his friends to him, then goes to the castle to speak to the king. If it can be managed, he will see the girl—and that is why he hurries so.

The king has just risen from table and gone to his daughter's rooms, and now he's begun to play chess with a knight from overseas. On the other side of the chessboard, his daughter had to show the moves. Eliduc came forward. The king greeted him kindly and made Eliduc sit beside him. He spoke to his daughter.

"My dear, you must get to know this gentleman. And pay him every honor. There's no finer knight in the country."

The girl was delighted to hear this command from her father. She stands up, invites Eliduc to sit with her well away from the others. Both are struck dumb with love. She dared not explain herself to him, and he was afraid to speak as well . . . except to thank her for the presents she had sent him: he had never liked a present so much. She tells him she is pleased that he is pleased. Then suddenly why she sent him the ring, and her belt as well—that her body was his, she couldn't resist, she loved him to madness, she gave herself to his every wish. If she couldn't have him, he knew, he must know it was true, no other man would ever have her.

Now it was Eliduc's turn.

"Princess, I'm so happy that you love me. All joy. That you should like me so much—how could I feel otherwise? I shan't ever forget it. You know I'm promised to your father for a year, under oath that I shan't leave till the war's ended. Then I shall go home. Provided you'll let me. I don't want to stay here."

"Eliduc, I'm so grateful for your frankness. You're so honest, you know such a lot. Long before you go you'll have decided what to do with me. I love you, I trust you more than anything else in the world."

They knew now that they were sure of each other; and on that occasion no more was said.

Eliduc goes back to his lodgings, enchanted at how well things have turned out. He can talk as often as he likes with Guilliadun, they're wildly in love.

He now occupied himself so well with the war that he captured the enemy king, and liberated the old king's country. His military reputation grew, as did that of his ingenuity and public generosity. On this side of his life everything went very well.

But during this same time the king of Brittany had sent three messengers over the sea to find Eliduc. Things at home were in a very bad way, and getting worse. All his strong points were under siege, his lands being put to the sword. With increasing bitterness, the king regretted having driven Eliduc away. His judgment had been distorted by the malicious advice he had listened to. Already he had thrown the treacherous clique who had blackened Eliduc and intrigued against him into permanent exile. Now, in his hour of great need, he commanded, he summoned, he begged Eliduc—in the name of the trust that had existed between them ever since the knight first paid homage to him—to come and save the situation. He was in the direst straits.

Eliduc read this news. It distressed him deeply. He thought of Guilliadun. He loved her now to the anguished depths of his being, and she felt the same for him. But there had been no madness between them—nothing improper, theirs was no casual affair. Caressing and talking, giving each other lovely presents—the passionate feeling between them hadn't gone beyond that. She kept it so on purpose, because of what she hoped. She thought he'd be entirely hers, and hers alone, if she played her cards right. She did not know there was a wife.

"Alas," thinks Eliduc to himself, "I've gone astray. I've stayed too long here. It was cursed, the day I first set eyes on this country. I've fallen head over heels in love. And she with me. If I have to say farewell to her now, one of us will die. Perhaps both. And yet I must go, the king of Brittany's letter commands it, and there's my promise to him. To say nothing of the one I swore my wife. I must pull myself together. I can't stay any longer, I have no alternative. If I were to marry Guilliadun, the Church would never stand for it. In all ways it's a mess. And oh God, to think of never seeing her again! I must be open with her, whatever the cost. I'll do whatever she wants, whichever way she sees it. Her father has got a decent peace, no one wants war with him anymore. I'll plead the king of Brittany's need and ask for permission to leave before the day's out. It was what was agreed—I'd go to him as soon as we had peace here. I'll see Guilliadun and explain the whole business. Then she can tell me what she wants, and I'll do my best to make it come true."

Without further delay, Eliduc went to the king to seek leave. He explained the situation in Brittany and showed him the letter the king there had sent him—the cry for help. The old king reads the command and realizes he will lose Eliduc. He is very upset and worried. He offered him a share of his possessions, a third of his heritage, his treasury—if he'll only stay, he'll do so much for him that Eliduc will be eternally grateful.

But Eliduc stayed firm.

"At this juncture, since my king's in danger and he's taken such trouble to find me, I must go to his assistance. Nothing would make me stop here. But if you ever need my services again, I'll willingly return—and bring plenty of other knights with me."

At that the king thanked him and gave him leave to go without further argument. He puts all his household possessions at Eliduc's disposal—gold and silver, hounds and horses and beautiful silk. Eliduc took no more than he needed. Then he politely told the king that he would like very much to speak with his daughter, if it were allowed.

"Consent is a pleasure," said the king.

Eliduc sends a young lady ahead to open the door of Guilliandun's room. Then he goes in to speak with her. When she saw him, she cried out his name and passionately clung to him. Then they discussed his problem, and he explained briefly the necessity for his journey. But when he had made it all clear, and yet pointedly still not asked for her permission to leave, for his freedom, she nearly fainted with the shock. Her face went white. When Eliduc sees the agony she is in, he begins to go mad. He keeps kissing her mouth and begins to cry in sympathy. At last he takes her in his arms and holds her until she recovers.

"You sweetest thing, oh God, listen—you're life and death to me, you're my whole existence. That's why I've come. So that we can talk about it, and trust each other. I must go home. I've got your father's permission. But I'll do whatever you want. Whatever may happen to me."

"Then take me with you, if you don't want to stay! If you don't, I'll kill myself. Nothing good or happy will ever happen to me again."

Gently Eliduc tells her how much he loves her; how beautiful she is. "But I've solemnly sworn to obey your father. If I take you away with me I'll be breaking my oath to him before its term is over. I swear, I promise you with all my heart that if you'll let me leave you now for a while, but name a day on which I must come back, then nothing on earth will stop me doing so—as long as I'm alive and in good health. My life's entirely in your hands."

She loved him so much. So she gave him a final date, a day by which he must return and take her away. They parted in tears and misery, exchanging their gold rings and tenderly kissing each other.

Eliduc rode to the sea. The wind was good and the crossing quick. When he gets home, the king of Brittany is overjoyed, and so are Eliduc's relations and friends and everyone else—and especially his wife, who remained as attractive and worthy of him as ever. But all the time Eliduc stayed turned in on himself, because of the shock of his love affair in England. Nothing he saw gave him any pleasure, he wouldn't smile—he'll never be happy till he sees Guilliadun again. His wife was very depressed by his secretive behavior, since she had no idea what caused it. She felt sorry for herself; kept asking if he hadn't heard from someone that she'd misbehaved while he was abroad. She'll willingly defend herself before the world, whenever he wants.

"My lady, no one's accused you of anything bad. But I've solemnly sworn to the king in the country where I've been that I shall return to him. He has great need of me. I told him I'd be on my way within a week, as soon as the king of Brittany had peace. I've got a huge task ahead of me before I can return. I can't take pleasure in anything at all until I've got back there. I *will* not break promises."

And that was all he told his wife. He went to join the king of Brittany and helped him greatly. The king adopted his strategy and saved his kingdom. But when the date approached that Guilliadun had named, Eliduc intervened to make peace. He agreed to all the terms the enemy wanted,[9]

9. The Old French says that he reconciled the enemy (to the king).

then he got ready to travel and picked his companions—two nephews he was fond of and one of his pages, a boy who had known what was going on and had carried messages between Eliduc and Guilliadun. Besides them, only his squires; he didn't want anyone else. He made these companions swear to keep the secret.

He waits no longer, puts to sea and soon arrives in Totnes. At last he was back where he was so longed for. Eliduc was very cunning. He found an inn well away from the harbor, since he was very anxious not to be seen . . . traced and recognized. He got his page ready and sent him to Guilliadun to tell her he had returned and kept strictly to his promise. By night, when darkness had fallen, she must slip out of the city; the page would escort her and Eliduc come to meet her. The boy changed into a disguise and went all the way on foot straight to Exeter. He cleverly found a way to get into her private apartments; then greeted the princess and told her her lover had come back. He found her sad and hopeless, but when she hears the news she breaks down and begins to cry, then kisses and kisses the page. He told her she must leave with him that evening; and they spent the whole day planning their escape in every detail.

When night had come, they stole cautiously out of the city alone together. They were terrified someone might see them. She wore a silk dress delicately embroidered in gold and a short cloak.

About a bowshot from the city gate there was a copse enclosed in a fine garden. Eliduc, who had come to fetch her, waited under the hedge. The page led her to the place. Eliduc sprang down from his horse and kissed her: such joy to meet again. He helped her onto a horse, then mounted his own and took her bridle. They rode quickly away, back to the port of Totnes, and boarded the ship at once: no other passengers but Eliduc's men and his beloved Guilliadun. They had favorable winds and settled weather, but when they came near the coast of Brittany they ran into a storm. A contrary wind drove them out away from the harbor. Then the mast split and broke, and they lost all the sails. They prayed in despair— to God, to St. Nicholas and St. Clement—to Our Lady, that she might invoke Christ's protection for them, save them from drowning and bring them to land. Backward and forward they were driven along the coast, the storm raging around them. One of the sailors began to shout.

"What are we doing? My lord, it's the girl you've brought aboard who's going to drown us all. We'll never reach land. You have a proper wife at home. But now you want another woman. It's against God and the law. Against all decency and religion. So let's throw her in the sea, and save our skins."

Eliduc hears what the man cries, and nearly goes berserk.

"You son of a whore, you fiend, you rat—shut your mouth! If she goes into the sea, I'll make you pay for it!"

He held Guilliadun in his arms, gave her what comfort he could. She was seasick, and riven by what she'd just heard: that her lover had a wife at home. She fainted and fell to the deck, deathly pale; and stayed like that, without breath or sign of consciousness. Eliduc knew she was only there because of him, and sincerely thought she was dead. He was in agony. He stood up and rushed at the sailor and struck him down with an oar. The man collapsed to the deck and Eliduc kicked the body over the side, where the waves took it away. As soon as he had done that, he went to the helm. There he steered and held the ship so well that they came to the harbor and land. When they were safely in, he cast anchor and had the gangway let down. Still Guilliadun lay unconscious, her only appearance that of death. Eliduc wept without stop—if he had had his way, he would have been dead with her. He asked his companions their advice, where he could carry her. He refused to leave her side until she was buried with every honor and full ritual, and laid to rest in holy ground. She was a king's daughter, it was her due. But his men were at a loss and could suggest nothing. Eliduc began to think for himself. His own house was not far from the sea, not a day's ride away. There was a forest around it, some thirty miles across. A saintly hermit had lived there for forty years and had a chapel. Eliduc had often spoken with him.

I'll take her there, Eliduc said to himself, I'll bury her in his chapel. Then bestow land and found an abbey or a monastery. Nuns or canons, who can pray for her every day, may God have mercy on her soul.

He had horses brought and ordered everyone to mount, then made them promise they would never betray him. He carried Guilliadun's body in front of him, on his own horse. They took the most direct road and soon entered the forest. At last they came to the chapel, and called and knocked. But no voice answered and the door stayed closed. Eliduc made one of his men climb in and open it. They found a fresh tomb: the pure and saintly hermit had died that previous week. They stood there sad and dismayed. The men wanted to prepare the grave in which Eliduc must leave Guilliadun forever, but he made them withdraw outside the chapel.

"This isn't right. I need advice first from the experts on how I can glorify this place with an abbey or a convent. For now we'll lay Guilliadun before the altar and leave her in God's care."

He had bedding brought and they quickly made a resting place for the girl; then laid her there, and left her for dead. But when Eliduc came to leave the chapel, he thought he would die of pain. He kissed her eyes, her face.

"Darling heart, may it please God I'll never bear arms again or live in the outer world. I damn the day you ever saw me. Dear gentle thing, why did you come with me? Not even a queen could have loved me more trustingly. More deeply. My heart breaks for you. On the day I bury you, I'll enter a monastery. Then come here every day and weep all my desolation out on your tomb."

Abruptly then he turned from the girl's body and closed the chapel door.

He had sent a messenger on ahead to tell his wife he was coming, but tired and worn. Full of happiness at the news, she dressed to meet him; and welcomed him back affectionately. But she had little joy of it. Eliduc gave her not a single smile or a kind word. No one dared to ask why. He stayed like that for a couple of days—each early morning, having heard mass, he took the road to the forest and the chapel where Guilliadun lay . . . still unconscious, without breathing, no sign of life. Yet something greatly puzzled him: she had hardly lost color, her skin stayed pink and white, only very faintly pale. In profound despair, Eliduc wept and prayed for her soul. Then having done that, he returned home.

The following day, when he came out of the church after mass, there was a spy—a young servant his wife had promised horses and arms to if he could follow at a distance and see which way his master went. The lad did as she ordered. He rides into the forest after Eliduc without being seen. He watched well, saw how Eliduc went into the chapel, and heard the state he was in. As soon as Eliduc came out, the servant went home and told his mistress everything—all the sounds of anguish her husband had made inside the chapel. From being resentful, she now felt touched.

"We'll go there as soon as possible and search the place. Your master must be off soon to court, to confer with the king. The hermit died some time ago. I know Eliduc was very fond of him, but that wouldn't make him behave like this. Not show such grief."

Thus for the time being she left the mystery.

That very same afternoon Eliduc set off to speak with the king of Brittany. His wife took the servant with her and he led her to the hermitage chapel. As soon as she went in she saw the bed and the girl lying on it, as fresh as a first rose. She pulled back the covering and revealed the slender body, the slim arms, the white hands with their long and delicately smooth-skinned fingers. She knew the truth at once—why Eliduc had his tragic face. She called the servant forward and showed him the miraculous corpse.

"Do you see this girl? She's as lovely as a jewel. She's my husband's mistress. That's why he's so miserable. Somehow it doesn't shock me. So pretty . . . to have died so young. I feel only pity for her. And I still love him. It's a tragedy for us all."

She began to cry, in sympathy for Guilliadun. But as she sat by the deathbed with tears in her eyes a weasel darts out from beneath the altar. The servant struck at it with a stick to stop it running over the corpse. He killed it, then threw the small body into the middle of the chancel floor. It had not been there long when its mate appeared and saw where it lay. The living animal ran around the dead one's head and touched it several times with a foot. But when this failed, it seemed distressed. Suddenly it ran out of the chapel into the forest grass. There it picked a deep red flower with its teeth, then carried it quickly back and placed it in the mouth of the weasel the servant had killed. Instantly the animal came back to life. The wife had watched all this, and now she cried out to the servant.

"Catch it! Throw, boy! Don't let it escape!"

He hurled his stick and hit the weasel. The blossom fell from between its teeth. Eliduc's wife went and picked it up, then returned and placed the exquisite red flower in Guilliadun's mouth. For a second or two nothing happened, but then the girl stirred, sighed, and opened her eyes.[1]

1. Abundant parallels from folklore represent an animal as having the gift of immortality—or being able to restore life after apparent death.

"Good lord," she murmured, "how long I've slept!"

When the wife heard her speak, she thanked heaven. Then she asked Guilliadun who she was.

"My lady, I'm British born, the daughter of a king there. I fell hopelessly in love with a knight, a brave mercenary called Eliduc. He eloped with me. But he was wicked, he deceived me. He had a wife all the time. He never told me, never gave me the least hint. When I heard the truth, I fainted with the agony of it. Now he's brutally left me helpless here in a foreign country. He tricked me, I don't know what will become of me. Women are mad to trust in men."

"My dear," said the lady, "he's been quite inconsolable. I can assure you of that. He thinks you're dead, he's been mad with grief. He's come here to look at you every day. But obviously you've always been unconscious. I'm his real wife, and I'm deeply sorry for him. He was so unhappy . . . I wanted to find out where he was disappearing to, so I had him followed, and that's how I found you. And now I'm glad you're alive after all. I'm going to take you away with me. And give you back to him. I'll tell the world he's not to blame for anything. Then I shall take the veil."

She spoke so comfortingly that Guilliadun went home with her. The wife made the servant get ready and sent him after Eliduc. He rode hard and soon came up with him. The lad greeted Eliduc respectfully, then tells him the whole story. Eliduc leaps on a horse, without waiting for his friends. That same night he was home, and found Guilliadun restored to life. He gently thanks his wife, he's in his seventh heaven, he's never known such happiness. He can't stop kissing Guilliadun; and she keeps kissing him shyly back. They can't hide their joy at being reunited. When Eliduc's wife saw how things stood, she told her husband her plans. She asked his formal permission for a separation, she wished to become a nun and serve God. He must give her some of his land and she would found an abbey on it. And then he must marry the girl he loved so much, since it was neither decent nor proper, besides being against the law, to live with two wives. Eliduc did not try to argue with her; he'll do exactly as she wants and give her the land.

In the same woodlands near the castle that held the hermitage chapel he had a church built, and all the other offices of a nunnery. Then he settled a great deal of property and other possessions on it. When everything was ready, his wife took the veil, along with thirty other nuns. Thus she established her order and her new way of life.

Eliduc married Guilliadun. The wedding was celebrated with great pomp and circumstance, and for a long time they lived happily together in a perfect harmony of love. They gave a great deal away and performed many good deeds, so much so that in the end they also turned religious. After great deliberation and forethought, Eliduc had a church built on the other side of his castle and endowed it with all his money and the greater part of his estate. He appointed servants and other religious people to look after the order and its buildings. When all was ready, he delays no more: he surrenders himself with his servants to omnipotent God. And Guilliadun, whom he loved so much, he sent to join his first wife. Guildelüec received her as if she were her own sister and did her great honor, teaching her how to serve God and live the religious life of the order. They prayed for the salvation of Eliduc's soul, and in his turn he prayed for both of them. He found out by messengers how they were, how they comforted each other. All three tried in their own ways to love God with true faith; and in the end, by the mercy of God in whom all truth reposes, each died a peaceful death.

The noble Celts composed this story long ago to enshrine the strange adventure of these three. May it never be forgotten!

AUCASSIN AND NICOLETTE

Some readers of *Aucassin and Nicolette* consider it the most charming literary work of the entire Middle Ages. Its author is unknown, but it is written in the language of northern France in the thirteenth century. The alternation of prose and verse is somewhat unusual, but there are other examples of it. One is the fifth-century *Consolation of Philosophy* of Boethius, in Latin. Another is the *New Life (Vita Nuova)*, a youthful work of Dante, in Italian, in the late thirteenth century. But, unlike these, *Aucassin and Nicolette* was intended for performance, with one actor speaking the prose parts and the other singing those in verse. It may have been presented in places somewhat like the castle of Count Garin de Beaucaire, father of Aucassin in the story.

The remarkable achievement of *Aucassin* is the masterly use of familiar elements of diverse kinds to produce a unique result. A wide variety of incidents, motifs, and themes has been woven into a unified pattern designed and sustained with precision. It *partly* resembles several of the recognized types of narrative: the folk tale, the romance, the adventure story, and it recalls a number of familiar themes: the love of prince and pauper, the child of royalty in disguise, the conversion of the heathen. The repetition of statements in nearly identical phrasing, especially in the dialogue of the early prose sections, offers the assurance and the emphasis that repetition provides in the fairy tale. And the beauty of Nicolette is so surpassing that we may be tempted to suspect that she is a supernatural creature—until we find the ignorant shepherds making exactly that mistake. The escapes, the traveling to strange lands, the separation by capture and shipwreck, the hardships, all these are the materials of the *romans d'aventure* (tales of adventure). But here they are handled with a brevity and deftness that make them incidental to the central theme; vivid or comic, strange or poignant, none of them delays us long. Nor do the other motifs, mentioned above, ever dominate the narrative or determine the real structure of the work.

Aucassin and Nicolette is, of course, a love story. But the treatment differs considerably from that customary in the *romans d'amour* (tales of love). In these the lady is often hostile, at least ostensibly, or, at best, unaware of her lover's pangs. She has to be won; frequently she is capricious and gives her knight a hard time— he must conquer the lady's affection as well as the numerous and wearying external obstacles that keep them apart. But Nicolette is as much in love as Aucassin, and more ingenious and enterprising; both are utterly candid, direct, and steadily devoted to each other. The specific dangers and the devices employed to elude them, the castles, dungeons, escapes by a window into a garden and through a moat—these are traditional. But the atmosphere in which they are related is not: the warm night of early summer, saturated with moonlight and nightingales, the lyric joy of the two lovers. The work is built, by rigid selection, from elements of the real life of the time, a time when there actually were moats, dungeons, sentinels, parental authority, chattel slaves, fierce counts carrying on private wars—not to insist on Saracens or uncouth shepherds in the woodland. Hence, perhaps, the freshness and spontaneity, the naturally springing gaiety and joy. Hence, too, the stress, without impairment of tone, on the picturesque and the humorous in a world from which the processes of moral judgment have been largely expunged. Action is straightforward and decisive. At one point Aucassin is taken prisoner by his father's enemies before he realizes what has happened; when he becomes aware of his situation, he lays about him manfully, captures the enemy count, and so puts an end to a twenty years' war! The same directness is expressed in Aucassin's famous reply to the viscount of the town, who warns him that he may be sent to hell for loving Nicolette. He wants to go there, says Aucassin, along with the lively knights, the gay, sweet ladies, and the musicians and poets; that is, he belongs with those who take delight in the joys and beauties of human life. A heaven filled with the ugly, the weak, the miserable, and those who deny nature in the name of religion would not suit him at all. This is exuberance, of course, not atheism; the extravagance of Aucassin's words is a part of his character and a feature of his world.

The work is a kind of gospel of the religion of love, a religion that exacts a complete devotion and bestows a complete happiness. Yet there is some question about the tone that the *author* intended to give it for his/or her day and generation. Precisely because motivation and action are so absolute, so neat, some modern students of medieval French literature believe that it is a parody or satire. They may well be correct. But the modern reader, unburdened by lengthy metrical romances of chivalric adventure and courtly love conducted by means of stereotyped characters and formula situations, need not worry too much about the question. *Aucassin and Nicolette* is a delight whether regarded simply as a story or as a vehicle for literary satire.

For a statement of the little that is known about the background of *Aucassin and Nicolette (Aucassin et Nicolete)*, see the English introduction to the edition by F. W. Bourdillon (1919); and Urban Tigner Holmes, *A History of Old French Literature* (1938). Henry Adams devotes a chapter to it in *Mont-Saint-Michel and Chartres* (1913). An excellent edition of the medieval French text and an accurate translation will be found in Volume 47, Series A, of the Garland Library of Medieval Literature: *The Pilgrimage of Charlemagne* [and] *Aucassin and Nicolette* (1988), which also contains a scholarly introduction and a generous bibliography.

Aucassin and Nicolette[1]

I

If anyone should wish to hear good verse
About the old man's[2] pleasure,
And about two lovely little children,

---

1. Translated by Glyn S. Burgess.   2. The identity of the "old man" is uncertain. The lines may refer to the author or perhaps to one of the actors who recited the story.

Nicolette and Aucassin,
About the great suffering he endured   5
And the acts of prowess he performed
For his friend with countenance so fair,
The melody is sweet, the poem fair,
Courtly and well ordered.
No man can be so perplexed,   10
In such sorrow or discomfort,
So terribly ill,
That, if he hears it, he cannot be cured,
And infused with joy,
   So sweet is the song.   15

II

Now they say and recount and relate that Count Bougar of Valence was
waging war on Count Garin of Beaucaire so great and so marvellous and
so mortal that not a single day dawned without his being at the gates, the
walls, and the barriers of the city with one hundred knights and ten thousand soldiers on foot or on horseback, and he was burning his land and
devastating his territory and killing his men.

Count Garin of Beaucaire was old and frail and he had outlived his span
of life. He had no heir, son or daughter, except for one young boy; he was
such as I shall describe him to you. Aucassin was the youth's name. He
was handsome and noble and tall and his legs, feet, body, and arms were
well formed. He had blond hair with little curls and sparkling, laughing
eyes, a fair, oval face with a high, well-positioned nose; he was endowed
with so many good qualities that he had no bad qualities, only good ones.
But he was so smitten by Love, which overcomes everything, that he did
not wish to become a knight, or to take up arms, or to go to tournaments,
or to do anything he ought to do. His father and mother said to him:

"Son, take up your arms, mount your horse, defend your land and help
your vassals: if they see you amongst them, they will then be better able to
defend themselves and their possessions, and your land and mine."

"Father," says Aucassin, "what are you talking about now? May God
never give me anything I ask of Him, if I ever become a knight or mount
a horse or enter combat or battle, where I would strike a knight or be struck
by other knights, if you do not give me Nicolette, my sweet friend whom
I love so much."

"Son," said the father, "that is impossible. Leave Nicolette be, for she
is a slave girl who was brought from a foreign land, and the viscount of
this town purchased her from the Saracens, brought her to this town, raised
her at the font, baptized her and made her his godchild, and one of these
days he will give her a young man who will earn bread for her honourably;
this is no concern of yours. If you wish to have a wife, I shall give you the
daughter of a king or a count. No man in France is so rich that, if you
wanted his daughter, you could not have her."

"Come now, father," said Aucassin, "where on this earth does there exist such a high honour that, if Nicolette, my very sweet friend, had it, it would not be enhanced by her? If she were empress of Constantinople or Germany, or queen of France or England, even this would be little enough for her, so worthy and courtly and noble is she, and so well endowed with every quality."

Now it is sung.

III

Aucassin was from Beaucaire,
From a castle of fair repose.
No one could make him give up
Nicolette, the well formed,
Whom his father would not let him have,   5
And his mother threatened him:
"Come now, foolish boy, what are your intentions?"
"Nicolette is elegant and gracious."
"She was taken by force from Carthage[3]
And bought from a Saracen.   10
If you want to take a wife,
Marry a woman of high lineage."
"Mother, I can do nothing about it:
Nicolette is well born;
Her noble body, her face,   15
And her beauty soothe my heart.
It is quite right for me to have her love,
    As she is so sweet."

Now they say and recount and relate.

IV

When Count Garin of Beaucaire saw he could not prevent his son from loving Nicolette, he made his way to the viscount of the town, who was his vassal, and addressed him:

"Count, get rid of your goddaughter Nicolette: cursed be the land from which she was brought to this country, because through her I am losing Aucassin, since he refuses to become a knight or to do anything he ought to do; and I'll have you know that, if I could catch her, I should burn her at the stake, and you yourself would have reason to fear for your life."

"Lord," said the viscount, "it grieves me that he comes and goes and talks to her. I bought her with my own money and raised her at the font and baptized her and made her my goddaughter, and I intended to give

---

3. Either the city in North Africa (Tunis) or Cartagena, a city in southwestern Spain.

her a bachelor who would earn bread for her honourably: this would have
been no concern of your son Aucassin. But since it is your will and desire,
I shall send her away to a land and a country such that he will never again
set eyes on her."

"Mind you do," said Count Garin. "Great harm could come to you
because of this."

Then they parted. The viscount was a very rich man and he possessed a
rich palace with an adjoining garden. He had Nicolette placed in a chamber on an upper floor and with her an old woman to keep her company,
and he gave them a supply of bread, meat, wine, and everything they
needed. Then he had the door sealed so that no one could enter or leave
from any side, leaving just a very small window overlooking the garden to
let in a little air.

Now it is sung.

V

Nicolette is in prison,
In a vaulted chamber,
Constructed with great care
And marvellously decorated.
At the marble window   5
The girl leaned out.
Her hair was blond,
Her brows well fashioned,
Her face fair and slim:
You never saw a more beautiful girl.   10
She looked out over the woodland
And saw the roses in bloom
And heard the song of the birds;
This made her bewail her fate.
"Alas! Woe is me! Wretched one!   15
Why am I in prison?
Aucassin, my young lord,
I am your friend,
And you do not hate me.
For you I have been imprisoned   20
In this vaulted room,
Where I lead a life of woe.
But, by Christ, the son of Mary,
I shall not remain here long,
If I can help it."   25

Now they say and recount and relate.

VI

Nicolette was, as you have heard, imprisoned in the chamber. The cry and the rumour spread throughout the country and over the entire region that she was lost. Some said she had fled the country, others that Count Garin of Beaucaire had murdered her. If anyone else rejoiced at this, Aucassin was not at all happy, so he made his way to the viscount of the town and addressed him:

"Lord viscount, what have you done with Nicolette, my very sweet friend whom I loved more than anything in the whole world? Have you stolen her from me or taken her away? I'll have you know that, if this ends in my death, vengeance will be exacted from you, and rightly so, because you will have killed me with your own two hands, for you have stolen the thing I loved most in all the world."

"Lord," said the count, "let this be. Nicolette is a captive whom I brought from a foreign land, and I purchased her from Saracens[4] with my own money and raised her at the font and baptized her and made her my god-child, and brought her up, and one of these days I would have given her a young man who would earn bread for her honourably; this is no concern of yours. You should take the daughter of a king or a count. Besides, what do you expect to have gained by making her your mistress and putting her in your bed? You would have gained very little, as your soul would remain in Hell for the rest of time, since you would never enter Paradise."

"Why should I be interested in Paradise? I have no wish to go there, unless I have with me Nicolette, my very sweet friend whom I love so much; because the only people who go to Paradise are these. That is where old priests go, and old cripples, and the maimed who grovel day and night in front of altars and in old crypts, and there are those clad in old, thread-bare cloaks, and old rags, naked, barefoot, and in tatters, dying of hunger, thirst, cold, and misery. They go to Paradise: I don't want anything to do with them. What I want is to go to Hell, for Hell is where handsome clerics go, and handsome knights who have died in tournaments and rich wars, and brave men-at-arms and noblemen: I want to go with them. That is where beautiful courtly ladies go, because they have two or three lovers as well as their husbands, and the gold and silver goes there, and all the fine furs, and the harpists and jongleurs and the kings of the lay world. I want to go with them, provided I have with me Nicolette, my very sweet friend."

"Certainly," said the viscount, "your words are in vain, for you will never see her again. If you spoke to her and your father found out, he would burn me and her at the stake and you yourself would have reason to fear for your life."

"This distresses me," said Aucassin, and disconsolately he left the vis-count.

Now it is sung.

4. Arabs and other non-Christian peoples in the Middle East.

VII

Aucassin turned away,
Distressed and anguished:
Because of his friend with countenance so fair
No one could comfort him
Or give him good counsel.   5
He made his way to the palace,
Climbed the steps
And entered a chamber,
Where he began to cry
And give vent to his grief   10
And mourn his beloved:
"Nicolette, how sweet it is to be with you,
How sweet to see you come and go,
How sweet the pleasure which you give, how sweet your words,
How sweet your smile, how sweet your laughter,   15
How sweet your kisses and embraces.
Because of you I am beset with grief
And in a plight so dreadful
That I doubt I can escape alive,
My dear, sweet friend."   20

                             Now they say and recount and relate.

VIII

    Whilst Aucassin was in the chamber mourning his beloved Nicolette,
Count Bougar of Valence, who had his war to wage, did not neglect his
duty; he summoned his foot soldiers and his horsemen and approached
the castle to attack it. And there arose a great outcry and clamour, and the
knights and men-at-arms donned their armour and ran to the gates and the
walls to defend the castle and the burghers climbed on to the ramparts and
hurled down bricks and sharp pikes. Whilst the assault was at its height,
Count Garin of Beaucaire went into the chamber where Aucassin was
lamenting and mourning Nicolette, his very sweet friend whom he loved
so dearly.
    "Ah son," said the count, "what an unhappy and wretched state you are
in, when you see this attack on your finest and sturdiest castle! You must
realize that, if you lose it, you have nothing to inherit. Son, take up your
arms and mount your horse, defend your land, help your men and go into
battle. Even though you may not strike anyone or be struck by anyone
else, if they see you amongst them, they will then defend their possessions,
and themselves and your land and mine. You are so tall and strong that
you can easily do this, and it is your duty to do it."
    "Father," said Aucassin, "what are you talking about now? May God
never give me anything I ask of Him, if I become a knight or mount a

horse, or enter battle, where I would strike a knight or be struck by other knights, if you do not give me Nicolette, my sweet friend whom I love so much."

"Son," said the father, "that is impossible. I should rather be disinherited and lose everything I have than let you have her as your wife or spouse."

He turned away. And when Aucassin saw him leave, he called him back.

"Father," said Aucassin, "come back: I shall make a bargain with you."

"What will that be, my son?"

"I shall take up arms and enter battle, on condition that, if God brings me back safe and sound, you will allow me to see my sweet friend Nicolette long enough to be able to say two or three words to her and give her just one kiss."

"Agreed," said the father. He gave his word and Aucassin was filled with joy.

Now it is sung.

IX

Aucassin heard of the kiss
He would have on his return:
A hundred thousand marks of pure gold
Could not have made him more joyful.
He demanded costly armour   5
And it was made ready for him:
He donned a double-linked coat of mail
And fixed a helmet upon his head,
Girded on the sword with its pommel of pure gold
And then mounted his horse,   10
Taking the shield and lance.
He looked down at his feet,
Which were well fixed in their stirrups:
He was very pleased with his appearance.
He thought of his friend   15
And spurred on his steed;
Off it went most willingly,
Heading straight for the gate
    And into battle.

Now they tell and relate.

X

Aucassin sat upon his horse fully armed, as you have heard. God, how his shield around his neck suited him and the helmet on his head and his sword belt on his left hip! He was a tall, strong youth, handsome, noble and well-built, and the horse on which he sat was swift and fleet and the young man rode it straight through the gate.

Now do not think that he was intent on catching oxen, cows, or goats, or on striking knights or being struck by them. Not a bit of it. Such a thing never occurred to him; for his mind was so firmly fixed on Nicolette, his sweet friend, that he neglected his reins and everything he was supposed to be doing. And the horse, feeling the spurs, carried him right into the throng and launched itself into the midst of his enemies; and they flung out their arms on all sides and seized him, dispossessed him of his shield and lance and carried him off as a captive; and, as they departed, they were already discussing the means by which he would be put to death. And when Aucassin heard this, he said:

"Oh God, sweet Lord! Are these my mortal enemies who are taking me away and intending to cut off my head? Once I have lost my head, I shall never again speak to Nicolette, my sweet friend whom I love so much. I still have here a good sword and I am seated on a good, fresh horse; if I do not now defend myself for her sake, may God never again be of any help to her, if she should ever love me!"

The youth was tall and strong, and the horse he was riding was mettlesome: and he took hold of his sword and began to strike right and left and to cut off helmets, nose-pieces, hands, and arms, and to cause mayhem around him, just like a wild boar assailed by dogs in the forest, and he unhorsed ten knights and wounded seven, and forcing his way out of the throng he came galloping back, sword in hand.

Count Bougar of Valence, having heard that Aucassin his enemy was to be hung, was on his way over. Aucassin did not fail to spot him: he held his sword in his hand and struck him across the helmet, forcing it down over his head. He was so stunned that he fell to the ground; and Aucassin stretched out his hand, seized him and led him away by the nose-piece of his helmet and handed him over to his father.

"Father," said Aucassin, "here is your enemy who has waged war against you for so long and done you so much harm. This war has already lasted for twenty years and no one could manage to end it."

"My son," said the father, "this is just the sort of act a young man should be performing, rather than indulging in idle dreaming."

"Father," said Aucassin, "no sermons, just keep your bargain."

"Bah! What bargain, my son?"

"Come now, father, have you forgotten? By my head, if anyone else forgets, I certainly shall not. It is very important to me. Did you not have an agreement with me that, if I took up arms and entered battle and God brought me back safe and sound, you would let me see my sweet friend Nicolette long enough to have a word or two with her, and did you not agree that I could give her one kiss? I want this bargain kept."

"I?" said the father. "May God never be of help to me, if I ever keep a bargain with you. And, if she were here, I should burn her at the stake and you yourself would have reason to fear for your life."

"Is that your last word?" said Aucassin.

"So help me God," said the father, "yes."

"Certainly," said Aucassin, "I am very distressed when a man of your age lies. Count of Valence," said Aucassin, "have I taken you prisoner?"

"That is true, Lord, indeed," said the Count.

"Give me your hand," said Aucassin.

"Willingly, Lord."

He put his hand in his.

"Promise me," said Aucassin, "that as long as you live you will not neglect any opportunity to shame or discomfort my father in respect of his body or his property."

"Lord," he said, "in God's name, do not mock me; just demand a ransom for me. No matter how much gold or silver you ask of me, how many horses or palfreys, furs or dogs or fowl, I shall give them to you."

"What," said Aucassin, "do you not realize that I have taken you prisoner?"

"Yes, Lord," said Count Bougar.

"May God never be of help to me," said Aucassin, "if I do not send your head flying, unless you promise me this."

"In God's name," he said, "I promise you whatever you wish."

He made his promise; and Aucassin made him mount one horse and he mounted another and led him to safety.

                                                        Now it is sung.

XI

Now that Count Garin saw
That he would not turn
His son Aucassin away
From Nicolette with countenance so fair,
He imprisoned him   5
In an underground room,
Made of dark-hued marble.
When he arrived there,
He was distressed as never before;
He began to bewail his fate,   10
As you can hear:
"Nicolette, lily flower,
Sweet beloved with countenance so fair,
You are sweeter than a grape
Or than a sop dipped in wine.   15
The other day I saw a pilgrim,
Born in Limousin,
Who was suffering from madness
And lying in bed
In great discomfort,   20
And terribly ill.
You passed by his bed

And lifted up your train
And your ermine cloak,
And your white linen shift,   25
Far enough for him to see your leg.
The pilgrim was cured
And as well as he had ever been.
He left his bed
And returned to his homeland,   30
Safe and sound, completely cured.
Sweet beloved, lily flower,
How sweet to see you come and go,
How sweet your laughter and your smile,
How sweet your words, what sweet delight you cause,   35
How sweet your kisses and embraces.
No one could hate you.
Because of you I am in prison,
In this underground room,
Where I am coming to a sad end.   40
Now I must die,
     For you, friend."

           Now they say and recount and relate.

XII

Aucassin had been put in prison, as you have heard, and Nicolette was still in her chamber. It was summer in the month of May, with warm days, long and fair, and nights which were tranquil and serene. Nicolette lay in bed one night and saw the moon shining clearly through a window and heard the song of the nightingale in the garden, and she thought of Aucassin, her friend whom she loved so much. Her mind turned to Count Garin who had a mortal hatred for her, and she decided she would remain there no longer, because, if she were accused and Count Garin found out, he would subject her to a painful death. She realized that the old woman who lived with her was asleep. So she rose, put on a very fine silk tunic which she possessed, took sheets and towels, knotted them together to make as long a rope as possible, and tied it to a pillar at the window. She climbed down into the garden, held her dress at the front with one hand and at the back with the other, and pulled up the hem because she saw how heavy was the dew which lay on the grass, and she made her way down the garden.

She had blond hair with little curls and sparkling, laughing eyes, and an oval face with a high, well-positioned nose, and tiny lips which were redder than a cherry or a rose in summer. Her teeth were white and close fitting, and her small, hard breasts pushed out her dress as if they were two large walnuts; and around her waist she was so slim that one could encircle her with two hands, and the daisies which she crushed with her toes, as they came up over her insteps, were quite black in comparison with her feet and legs, so white was the young girl.

She reached the gate, opened it and went out into the streets of Beaucaire through the shadows, for the moon was shining very brightly; she made her way to the tower where her friend was. The tower was cracked in several places: and she pressed herself up close to one of the pillars, wrapped herself in her coat and put her head through a crack in the tower, which was old and ancient, and within she could hear Aucassin weeping and bewailing his fate and mourning his sweet friend whom he loved so much. And when she had listened to him for a time, she began to speak.

Now it is sung.

XIII

Nicolette with countenance so fair
Leaned against a pillar
And heard Aucassin weeping,
And bewailing his friend.
Then she spoke and revealed her thoughts: 5
"Aucassin, noble and brave,
Fine, honourable young man,
What use is it to lament,
To mourn or to weep,
When you can never enjoy me?   10
For your father hates me,
As does your entire family.
For you I shall cross the sea
And go to another kingdom."
She cut off a lock of hair   15
And tossed it inside to him.
Aucassin, the brave, took it,
Honoured it greatly, then
Kissed and embraced it.
He stuffed it close to his breast   20
And began to weep again,
All for his beloved.

Then they say and recount and relate.

XIV

When Aucassin heard Nicolette say that she intended to go to another country, he could only feel grief.

"Fair, sweet friend," he said, "you must not go, for then you would kill me. And the first man who saw you and could manage it would immediately take you and put you in his bed and make you his mistress. When you have lain in any man's bed other than mine, do not think that I should wait long enough to find a knife to plunge into my heart and kill myself. Not at all, I should not wait so long; rather would I hurl myself against the first wall or block of granite I could find, and I should strike my head so hard that my eyes and all my brains would fly out. I should prefer such a death to the knowledge that you had lain in another man's bed rather than mine."

"Aucassin," she said, "I do not think you love me as much as you say, but I love you more than you love me."

"Come now," said Aucassin, "fair, sweet friend. It is not possible that you love me as much as I love you. A woman cannot love a man as much as a man loves a woman. For a woman's love is in her eye and in the nipple of her breast and in her big toe; but a man's love is planted in his heart, whence it cannot escape."

Whilst Aucassin and Nicolette were talking together, the city's watchmen were making their way along one of the streets; their swords were drawn beneath their capes, for Count Garin had ordered them to kill her, if they could capture her. And the sentinel on the tower saw them approaching and heard them discussing Nicolette and threatening to kill her.

"God!" he said, "what a great loss such a beautiful girl would be, if they killed her! It would be an act of kindness if I could warn her, in such a way that they do not find out and so that she can watch out for them; for, if they kill her, Aucassin, my young lord, will also die, which will be a great loss."

Now it is sung.

XV

The watchman was a most worthy man,
Brave and courtly and wise.
He began to sing
A fine and charming song:
"Oh, maiden with heart so noble,   5
Body so fair and comely,
Hair so blond and lovely,
Sparkling eyes and face so full of fun.
From your appearance I can see
That you have spoken to your beloved   10
Who is wasting away because of you.
I say to you and you should listen:
Beware the traitors
Who are out looking for you
With naked swords beneath their capes;   15
Great are the threats they direct at you,

They will soon do you harm,
Unless you pay heed."[5]

Now they say and recount and relate.

XVI

"Oh," said Nicolette, "may the soul of your father and your mother have blessed repose, now that you have told me this in such a fair and kindly way. If it pleases God, I shall pay heed, and may God protect me!" She wrapped her coat around her and hid in the shadow of the pillar, until they had passed by, and she took leave of Aucassin and made her way to the wall of the castle. The wall had been damaged and patched up with wattle and she climbed up and managed to get between the wall and the moat. She looked down and saw the depth and the steepness of the moat and was terrified.

"Oh God," she said, "sweet Lord! If I fall, I shall break my neck and if I remain here I shall be caught tomorrow and burnt at the stake. Yet I would rather die here than have everyone stare at me tomorrow."

She crossed herself and let herself slip down into the moat, and when she reached the bottom, her beautiful hands and feet, which had never been accustomed to such treatment, were scratched and torn, so that blood poured out in a good dozen places, yet she felt no pain or hurt because she was so frightened. And if she found it difficult to get in, getting out was more difficult still. She realized that no good could come from tarrying, so finding a sharp pike which the inhabitants had thrown down as a means of defending the castle, she put one foot before the other and managed with the greatest difficulty to reach the top. Now just two bowshots away was the forest, thirty leagues long and thirty broad, and full of wild beasts and snakes. She was afraid of being killed by them, if she entered, then remembered that, if she was discovered here, she would be taken back to the town to be burnt.

Now it is sung.

XVII

Nicolette with countenance so fair,
Now atop the moat,
Began to mourn her fate
And to call upon Jesus Christ:
"Father, king of majesty,   5
I do not know which way to go.
If I go into the dense forest,

5. The watchman's song is modeled on the *alba*, or "dawn song," traditionally used to awaken (and warn) lovers.

I shall be eaten
By the wolves, the lions, and the boars,
Of which there are so many;   10
And if I wait until dawn,
When I might be discovered,
The fire will be lit
To consume my body.
But, by God in his majesty,   15
I much prefer
To be eaten by the wolves,
The lions, and the boars,
Than to enter the town;
     I shall not do so."   20

Now they say and recount and relate.

XVIII

Nicolette lamented greatly, as you have heard. She commended herself
to God and made her way into the forest. She did not dare go in too far
for fear of the wild beasts and the snakes; so she squatted in a thick bush
and began to feel sleepy. She fell asleep and dozed until past prime,[6] when
the shepherds left the town, driving their flock between the woods and the
river over towards a very beautiful spring to one side, right at the edge of
the forest, where they spread out a cape on which they placed their bread.
Whilst they were eating, Nicolette was woken up by the noise of the birds
and the shepherds, and she hurried towards them.

"My children," she said, "may God help you."

"And may God bless you," said one who was more talkative than the
others.

"My children," she said, "do you know Aucassin, son of Count Garin
of Beaucaire?"

"Yes, we know him well."

"So help you God, my children," she said. "Tell him there is a beast in
this forest and that he should come in search of it; and, if he could catch
it, he would not give up one of its limbs for one hundred marks of gold,
for five hundred, or for any money at all."

They looked at her and were all astounded at how beautiful she was.

"What! Tell him?" said the one who was more talkative than the others.
"Cursed be anyone who speaks to him of this, or who tells him! What you
are saying is pure fantasy; there is no such valuable beast in this forest, no
stag, lion or boar, one of whose limbs is worth more than two deniers,[7] or
three at the most, and you speak of such great wealth! A curse on anyone

---

6. The first hour of daylight.   7. A coin of little value. A sou (below) had greater value.

who believes you or who tells him! You are a fairy and we have no desire
for your company; be on your way."

"Oh, my children," she said, "do tell him. The beast has such healing
powers that Aucassin will be cured of his ills. And I have five sous here in
my purse: take them and tell him. He must hunt the animal within three
days, and, if he fails to find it within three days, he will never be cured of
his ills."

"Upon my word," he said, "we shall take the money, and if he comes
by, we shall tell him, but we shall not go looking for him."

"So be it," she said. Then she took leave of the shepherds and departed.

Now it is sung.

XIX

Nicolette with countenance so fair
Left the shepherds;
She set off on her way,
Straight through the dense wood
Along an old and ancient path,   5
Until she reached a road
Which forked into seven ways
Leading to different parts of the region.
Then she began to think up
A test for her beloved,   10
To reveal whether he loved her as he said.
She took lily flowers
And herbs from the moor,
And leaves too,
To create a beautiful bower,   15
The fairest ever seen.
She swears to the ever truthful God
That, if Aucassin came that way
Without resting there a while,
Because of his love for her,   20
Never would he be her friend,
Nor she his.

Now they say and recount and relate.

XX

Nicolette had made the bower, as you have heard, very fine and pleasing, and she had skilfully woven flowers and leaves inside and out; then
she lay down to rest beside the bower, in a thick bush, to see what Aucassin
would do.

The cry and the rumour spread throughout the country and over the entire region that Nicolette was lost. Some said she had fled, others that Count Garin had murdered her. If anyone else rejoiced at this, Aucassin was not at all happy; and Count Garin, his father, released him from prison and summoned knights and maidens from his land, and prepared a very costly celebration, thinking it would be a comfort to his son Aucassin.

Whilst the celebration was at its height, Aucassin was leaning against a balustrade, plunged into grief and sadness: others may have been rejoicing, but Aucassin had no desire to do so, as he saw no sign of the one he loved. A knight looked at him, came up to him and spoke thus:

"Aucassin," he said, "I have experienced the very same ill which besets you. I shall give you some good advice, if you will trust me."

"Lord," said Aucassin, "many thanks; I should appreciate some good advice."

"Mount a horse," he said, "and ride off gaily into the forest; you will see the flowers and the herbs, hear the birds singing and perhaps hear something to cheer you up."

"Lord," said Aucassin, "many thanks; this I shall do."

He left the hall, went down the steps and entered the stable where his horse stood. He had it saddled and bridled; then he placed his foot on the stirrup, mounted, and left the castle. He rode until he reached the forest and continued as far as the spring where he came across the shepherds at the ninth hour of the day, and they had spread a cape on the grass and were eating their bread and enjoying themselves greatly.

Now it is sung.

XXI

Now the young shepherds are together,
Esmeret and Martinet,
Fruelin and Johanet,
Robeçon and Aubriet.
One said: "Fair companions,   5
May God help young Aucassin,
Yes, indeed, that fair, young boy;
And the maid with body so slim,
Hair so blond,
Face so fair, and eyes so sparkling,   10
Who gave us pennies
To buy little cakes,
Sheaths and knives,
Little flutes and horns,
Clubs and pipes: 15
      May God protect her!"

Now they say and recount and relate.

XXII

When Aucassin heard the shepherds, he remembered Nicolette, his very sweet friend whom he loved so much, and he realized that she had been there; he spurred on his horse and came up to the shepherds:

"My children, may God help you."

"May God bless you," said the one who was more talkative than the others.

"My children," he said, "repeat the song you were singing just now."

"We shall not repeat it," said the one who was more talkative than the others. "A curse on anyone who sings it for you, fair Lord!"

"My children," said Aucassin, "do you know who I am?"

"Yes, we know that you are our young Lord, Aucassin, but we are not your men; we belong to the count."

"My children, do sing it, I beg you."

"Look here, by God incarnate!" he said, "why should I sing it for you, if it does not suit me, when there is no one in this land, however rich, with the exception of Count Garin himself, who, if he found my oxen or my cows or my sheep in his fields or in his wheat, would be foolhardy enough, with the risk of having his eyes put out, to dare to drive them out? Why should I sing it or you, if it does not suit me?"

"May God help you, my children, do sing it; take these ten sous which I have here in my purse."

"Lord, we shall take the money, but I shall not sing it for you, as I have sworn not to do so. But I shall relate the story to you, if you wish."

"In God's name," said Aucassin, "that is better than nothing."

"Lord, we were here between prime and terce,[8] eating our bread at this fountain, as we are doing now; and a maiden came here, the loveliest on earth, so lovely that we thought she was a fairy, and the whole wood was illuminated by her; she was so generous with her money that we struck a bargain with her, that, if you came here, we would tell you that you should go hunting in this forest, where there is a beast which, should you capture it, is such that you would not give up one of its limbs for five hundred marks of silver or for any amount of money: because the beast has such healing powers that, if you can catch it, you will be cured of your ill. You must catch it within three days, and if you have not done so, you will never find it. Now go in search of it, if you wish, and, if you wish, forget it; for I have fulfilled my promise to her."

"My children," said Aucassin, "you have said enough, and may God let me find it."

Now it is sung.

XXIII

Aucassin heard these words
Of his beloved, so fair of form,

8. 9:00 A.M.

And they affected him profoundly.
At once he left the shepherds
And entered the heart of the wood;   5
The horse took him swiftly away,
Galloping along with him.
Now he spoke and said three words:
"Nicolette, so fair of body,
For you I have come into this wood.   10
I am not hunting stags or boars,
But following tracks because of you.
Your sparkling eyes and noble form,
Your lovely smile and words so sweet,
Have caused a mortal wound in my heart.   15
If God, the almighty father, pleases,
I shall see you again,
        Dear, sweet friend."

                              Now they say and recount and relate.

                              XXIV

Aucassin made his way through the forest from path to path, and the
horse carried him swiftly along. Do not think that the thorns and the brambles spared him: not at all! In fact they tore his clothing in such a way that
one could scarcely have tied a gold crown in the largest section left, and
the blood flowed from his arms and sides and legs in forty places or thirty,
so that one could have followed the trail of blood he left behind him on
the grass. But so deeply was he thinking of Nicolette, his sweet friend, that
he felt no pain or ill. The whole day long he rode through the forest
without hearing any news of her; and when he saw that evening was
approaching, he began to cry because he could not find her.

He was riding along a grassy path, and looking ahead saw in the middle
of his path a young man such as I shall describe to you. He was tall and
strange, ugly and hideous; he had a large head, blacker than a piece of
coal, and there was more than a palm's breadth between his two eyes, and
he had large cheeks and a huge flat nose and thick lips, redder than grilled
meat, and huge, ugly, yellow teeth; he was dressed in leggings and shoes
made of ox-hide held up, above the knee, with lime-bark, and he was
muffled up in a cape with two wrong sides, and leaning on a huge club.
Aucassin came upon him suddenly and was frightened when he saw him.

"My brother, God protect you."

"God bless you!" said the other.

"God protect you, what are you doing here?"

"What business is it of yours?" he said.

"None," said Aucassin, "I am only passing the time of day."

"But why are you weeping," he said, "and making such a fuss? Certainly, if I were as rich as you, nothing on earth would make me weep."

"Huh! Do you know who I am?" said Aucassin.

"Yes, I know that you are Aucassin, the count's son; and if you tell me why you are weeping, I shall tell you what I am doing here."

"Certainly," said Aucassin, "I shall be happy to tell you. This morning I came hunting in the forest and had with me a white hound, the finest on earth, and I have lost it: that is why I am weeping."

"Listen!" he said, "by the heart which our Lord had in his body, why are you crying for a stinking dog? A curse on anyone who ever esteems you! For there is no one in this land, however rich, who, if your father asked him for ten, fifteen, or twenty dogs, would not let him have them very willingly and be only too pleased about it. But I am the one who should weep and lament."

"Why is this, brother?"

"Lord, I shall tell you. I was hired out to a rich peasant and was driving his team with four oxen. Now three days ago a great disaster overtook me, for I lost the best of my oxen, Roget, the finest in the team; I am looking for him. I have not eaten or drunk for three days now and dare not go into town, as I should be put in prison, for I have no money to pay for it. All I have in the world is what you see on me. I had a poor mother, who owned nothing more valuable than a mattress and that was dragged from under her and she is lying on straw. I am concerned about that much more than about myself; for money comes and goes: if I have lost on this occasion, I shall win some other time, and I shall pay for my ox when I can, and I am not going to cry over it. And you are crying for a dunghill dog! A curse on anyone who ever esteems you!"

"You are certainly a great comfort, my brother; a blessing on you! What was your ox worth?"

"Lord, they are asking twenty sous for it; I cannot get a single penny knocked off."

"Look," said Aucassin, "I have twenty here in my purse, so pay for your ox."

"Lord," he said, "many thanks, and may God let you find what you are seeking!"

He left him and Aucassin rode on. The night was fine and still, and he went on until he reached .... and there .... Nicolette ....[9] flowers inside and out, on top and in front, and it was as lovely as could be. When Aucassin noticed it, he stopped immediately and the moonlight fell onto it.

"Oh God," said Aucassin, "Nicolette, my sweet friend, was here and she made this with her beautiful hands. Because she is so sweet and because I love her so much, I shall dismount right now and rest here for the night."

He placed his foot on the stirrup to dismount and the horse was big and tall. His mind was so firmly fixed on Nicolette, his very sweet friend, that he fell so hard on to a stone that his shoulder was dislocated. He realized he was seriously injured, but he strove with all his might and tied his horse

9. The manuscript is badly damaged here and in section XXV, but evidently Aucassin finds the bower that Nicolette had made (described at XIX and XX above).

to a bush with the other hand and turned on to his side until he reached the bower on his back. Through a hole in the bower he could see the stars in the sky and saw that one was clearer than the others and he began to recite:

                                                              Now it is sung.

XXV

"Little star, I see you,
Drawn towards the moon.
Nicolette is with you,
My little, blond-haired friend.
I think God wants her   5
For the light of the evening
. . . .
. . . .
. . . .
Even at the risk of falling,   10
That I were up there with you.
I should hold you in tight embrace;
If I were a king's son,
You would be a perfect match for me,
    Sweet beloved."   15

                    Now they say and recount and relate.

XXVI

When Nicolette heard Aucassin, she came to him, for she was not far away; she entered the bower, threw her arms around his neck and kissed and embraced him.
"Sweet friend, how good to see you!"
"And it is good to see you too, sweet friend!"
They kissed and embraced and great was their rejoicing.
"Ah! sweet friend," said Aucassin, "I have been severely wounded in my shoulder and now I feel no pain or ill, because I have you."
She took hold of him and discovered that his shoulder was dislocated: she manipulated it with her white hands, as God, who loves lovers, desired, until it went back into place; then she took flowers and fresh grass and green leaves and tied them on with the hem of her smock and he was completely cured.
"Aucassin," she said, "my sweet friend, give some thought to what you are going to do. If your father were to have the forest searched tomorrow and found me, whatever happened to you, I should be killed."

"Certainly, my sweet friend, that would distress me greatly: but, if I can help it, they will not lay hands on you."

He mounted his horse and placed his beloved in front of him, kissing and embracing her, and they entered the open meadows.

Now it is sung.

XXVII

Aucassin, the fair, the blond,
The noble, the lover,
Left the deep wood,
In his arms his love
Before him on the saddle-bows.   5
He kissed her eyes and brow,
Her mouth and chin.
She addressed him:
"Aucassin, my sweet friend,
For which land are we heading?"   10
"My beloved, how do I know?
I do not care where we are going,
To forest or barren waste,
Providing you are with me."
They passed valleys and mountains,   15
Cities and towns;
At dawn they reached the sea,
And dismounted on the strand,
Beside the shore.

Now they say and recount and relate.

XXVIII

Aucassin and his beloved dismounted, as you have heard. He held his horse by the reins and his beloved by the hand and they began to walk along the shore . . .[1]

He hailed them and they came up to him, and he succeeded in persuading them to let them aboard their ship. And when they were on the high seas, a huge and terrible storm arose which took them from land to land, until they reached a foreign country and entered the port belonging to the castle of Torelore.[2] Then they asked what land this was and they were told that it was the King of Torelore's land. Then he asked what sort of man he was and whether there was a war on, and he was told:

"Yes, a mighty one."

---

1. A few lines are illegible in the manuscript. Evidently the lovers talk with the crew or passengers of a ship. 2. A fictional country where the men alternately bear children and fight wars.

He left the merchants and entrusted them to God. He mounted his horse, his sword girt about him and his beloved in front of him, and rode up to the castle. He asked where the king was and was told that he was lying in childbed.

"Where is his wife, then?" He was told that she was away fighting and had taken with her all the country's inhabitants; Aucassin heard this and thought how remarkable it was. He came to the palace where he and his beloved dismounted; she held his horse and he went up the palace steps, his sword girt about him, and made his way up to the bedroom where the king was lying.

                                                        Now it is sung.

                              XXIX

Into the bedroom went Aucassin,
The courtly, the noble.
He approached the bed
In which the king lay;
He stopped before him   5
And spoke, hear what he said:
"Come now, you fool, what are you doing here?"
The king said: "I am in childbed.
When my month is up
And I am in good health,   10
Then I shall go to mass,
As my ancestor did,
And return with great vigour
To the war against my enemies:
    Nothing will stop me."   15

                    Now they say and recount and relate.

                              XXX

When Aucassin heard what the king said, he pulled off the sheets covering him and flung them to the far end of the room; he saw behind him a stick, took it and turned round and struck him, beating him almost to death:

"Oh! Lord," said the king, "what do you want from me? Have you gone out of your mind, beating me in my own house?"

"By God incarnate," said Aucassin, "wretched son of a whore, I shall kill you, unless you promise me that never again will any man in your land lie in childbed."

He promised, and when he had done so:

"Lord," said Aucassin, "now take me to your wife on the battlefield."

"Willingly, Lord," said the king. He mounted a horse and Aucassin mounted his, and Nicolette remained in the queen's bedchamber. The king and Aucassin rode until they came to where the queen was and discovered that the battle was being fought with rotten crab-apples, eggs and fresh cheeses; and Aucassin began to look at them with great surprise.

Now it is sung.

XXXI

Aucassin came to a halt,
And, leaning on his saddle-bows,
Started to survey the entire battlefield.
Everyone had brought
A supply of fresh cheeses,   5
Rotten crab-apples
And large mushrooms from the fields.
He who was best at disturbing the fords
Was acknowledged as lord.
Aucassin, the brave, the worthy,   10
Began to look at them
And started to laugh.

Now they say and recount and relate.

XXXII

When Aucassin saw this marvel, he came to the king and addressed him:
"Lord," said Aucassin, "are these your enemies?"
"Yes, Lord," said the king.
"Do you want me to avenge you?"
"Yes," he said, "willingly."
And Aucassin grasped his sword and dashed into their midst, beginning to strike right and left, killing many of them. When the king saw he was killing them, he took him by the bridle and said:
"Come, Lord, do not kill people like this."
"What?" said Aucassin, "you do want me to avenge you, don't you?"
"Lord," said the king, "you have done too well. It is not our custom to kill each other."
The enemy fled; and the king and Aucassin returned to the castle of Torelore. The inhabitants of the region told the king to throw Aucassin out of his land and keep Nicolette for his son, as she appeared to be a woman of noble birth. Nicolette heard this and it did not please her, so she began to speak:

Now it is sung.

XXXIII

"Lord King of Torelore,"
Said the beautiful Nicolette,
"Your people think I am a fool.
When my sweet friend embraces me
And feels how plump and soft I am,   5
It gives me such pleasure that
No dance or jig or round,
No harp, fiddle or violin,
No game or pastime
Would be worth so much."   10

Now they say and recount and relate.

XXXIV

Aucassin was at the castle of Torelore with his beloved Nicolette, full of
joy and happiness because he had with him Nicolette, his sweet friend
whom he loved so much. But whilst he was enjoying such joy and happiness, a Saracen pirate ship arrived by sea and attacked the castle and took
it by force. They seized money and possessions and took men and women
away as prisoners; they captured Nicolette and Aucassin, bound Aucassin
hand and foot, and threw him on to one ship and Nicolette on to another;
and a storm arose at sea which separated them.

The ship containing Aucassin remained at sea until it reached the castle
of Beaucaire; and the local inhabitants came running out in search of
flotsam and found Aucassin, whom they recognized. When the people of
Beaucaire saw their lord, they were filled with joy, for Aucassin had been
at the castle of Torelore a full three years, and his father and mother were
dead. They took him to the castle of Beaucaire and all became his vassals,
and he held his land in peace.

Now it is sung.

XXXV

Aucassin returned
To Beaucaire, his city;
He held the country and the region
In a state of peace.
He swore to God on high   5
That he was far more concerned
About Nicolette with countenance so fair
Than about the members of his family,
If they had all died.

"Sweet friend with countenance so fair,   10
I know not where to seek you;
God never made the kingdom,
On land or at sea,
Where, if I thought I could find you,
I would not seek you."   15

Now they say and recount and relate.

XXXVI

Now we shall leave Aucassin and speak of Nicolette. The ship in which
Nicolette was a captive belonged to the king of Carthage, and he was her
father; and she had twelve brothers, all princes or kings. When they[3] saw
how beautiful she was, they honoured her greatly and there was much
rejoicing over her. They asked her repeatedly who she was, for it was obvious
that she was a most noble woman of high lineage. But she could not tell
them who she was, because she had been taken away as a small child.

They sailed on until they arrived beneath the city of Carthage. And
when Nicolette saw the walls of the castle and the surrounding area, she
realized who she was and that she had been raised there and taken away as
a small child; but she had not been too young to be well aware that she
was the daughter of the King of Carthage and that she had been raised in
that city.

Now it is sung.

XXXVII

Nicolette, the worthy and wise,
Reached the shore.
She saw the walls and the dwellings,
The palaces and the halls,
And bewailed her misfortune;   5
"How sad to be of noble birth,
Daughter of the King of Carthage,
Cousin of the Emir!
Enemies have brought me here.
Aucassin, the noble and the wise,   10
Fine and honourable young man,
Your sweet love goads me on,
Stimulates and torments me.
May God in whom we hope
Allow me to hold you in my arms again   15

---

3. The crew of the ship.

> And let you kiss my face,
> My mouth, my countenance,
> O noble lord!"

Now they say and recount and relate.

XXXVIII

When the King of Carthage heard Nicolette utter these words, he flung his arms around her neck.

"Fair, sweet friend," he said, "tell me who you are; do not be afraid of me."

"Lord," she said, "I am the daughter of the King of Carthage and I was taken away as a young child, a good fifteen years ago."

When they heard her utter these words, they knew she was telling the truth and rejoiced greatly over her, taking her to the palace with great honour, as befitted a king's daughter. They wanted to give her a pagan king as husband, but she had no desire to marry.

She was there a full three or four days. She gave some thought to the means by which she could seek out Aucassin. She got hold of a viol and learned to play it, until one day they wanted to marry her off to a rich pagan king; so she stole away at night, made her way to the port, took lodgings with a poor woman on the seashore, took a herb and rubbed her head and face with it until she was completely black and swarthy. She had a smock, cloak, shirt, and breeches made, and disguised herself as a jongleur; she took her viol and approached a sailor whom she managed to persuade to take her on board. They set off and sailed over the high seas until they reached the land of Provence. Nicolette disembarked, took her viol and played it throughout the land until she arrived at the castle of Beaucaire, where Aucassin was.

Now it is sung.

XXXIX

> In Beaucaire, beneath the tower,
> Was Aucassin one day;
> There he sat on a block of stone,
> His noble barons all around.
> He saw the herbs and the flowers,   5
> And heard the song of the birds;
> He remembered his love
> For Nicolette the worthy,
> Whom he had loved for so long;
> He sighed and wept.   10
> Lo and behold, Nicolette was before him.

She took out her viol and her bow,
Then spoke, uttering these words:
"Listen to me, noble barons,
Wherever you are, far or near,   15
Would you like to hear a song
About Aucassin, a noble baron,
And about Nicolette the worthy?
So long did their love last
That he sought her deep in the forest.   20
In the keep of Torelore
Pagans captured them one day.
Of Aucassin we know nothing,
But Nicolette the worthy
Is in the keep of Carthage,   25
For her father loves her dearly,
And he is lord of that kingdom.
They want to marry her off
To a treacherous pagan king.
Nicolette has no desire for this,   30
For she loves a youth
Whose name is Aucassin;
In the name of God she swears
She will take no husband
Except her beloved   35
For whom she longs."

                         Now they say and recount and relate.

                              XL

When Aucassin heard Nicolette speak these words, he was full of joy
and took her to one side and asked her:

"My friend," said Aucassin, "do you know anything of this Nicolette of
whom you have just sung?"

"Yes, Lord: I know her to be the finest, noblest, wisest creature ever
born. She is daughter of the King of Carthage, who captured her where
Aucassin was captured; and he took her to the city of Carthage, until he
discovered she was his daughter, and then rejoiced greatly over her and
every day they want to marry her off to one of the most powerful kings in
all Spain. But she would rather be hanged or burnt than take any of them,
however powerful."

"Oh! my fair friend," said Count Aucassin, "if you would like to return
there and tell her to come and talk to me, I should give you as much of
my wealth as you dared to ask for or take away. I must tell you that because
of my love for her I do not wish to marry any woman, however well born
she may be, but I am waiting for her and shall marry no one but her; and

if I had known where to find her, I should not have to look for her now."

"Lord," she said, "if you were to do this, I should go and fetch her, for your sake and for hers, as I love her so much."

He promised and then gave her twenty pounds. She left and he wept because Nicolette was so sweet. And when she saw his tears:

"Lord," she said, "do not be upset, as I shall soon have brought her to you in this town, so that you will see her."

And when Aucassin heard these words, he was filled with joy. And she left and made her way to the home of the viscountess in the town (for the viscount, her godfather, had died). She stayed there and in the course of conversation told her the whole story, so that the viscountess recognized her and realized that she was Nicolette whom she had brought up. She washed and bathed her and had her stay for a full week.

She took a herb called celandine[4] and rubbed it on her and she was just as beautiful as she had ever been at any time; she dressed in garments of costly silk, of which the lady had plenty, and sat in the bedroom on a silken counterpane and called the lady and told her to go and fetch Aucassin, her beloved. This she did; and when she reached the palace, she found Aucassin weeping and bewailing Nicolette, his beloved, because she was so long coming. And the lady called to him and said:

"Aucassin, do not be distressed any longer, but come with me, and I shall show you the thing you love most in the world: for it is Nicolette, your sweet friend, who has come for you from afar."

And Aucassin was filled with joy.

Now it is sung.

XLI

When Aucassin heard
Of his beloved with countenance so fair,
That she had arrived in this land,
Then he was filled with joy, as never before,
He set off with the lady   5
And went straight to her house,
They entered the bed chamber
Where Nicolette was sitting.
When she saw her beloved,
She was full of joy, as never before.   10
She jumped up to greet him;
When Aucassin saw her,
He held out both his arms,
And welcomed her tenderly
Kissing her eyes and her face.   15
That night they left it at that,
Until the next morning

---

4. Known as a medicinal plant but not a restorer of beauty, as here.

When Aucassin married her:
He made her Lady of Beaucaire.
Then they lived for many a long day
And took their fill of pleasure.
Now Aucassin knew true joy
And Nicolette as well.
Our cante-fable[5] ends:
I know no more.

MEDIEVAL LATIN LYRIC POETRY

Latin, the language of republican and imperial Rome, did not perish with the collapse of the Empire. Throughout the Middle Ages, and well into the Renaissance, it continued to be a principal medium of expression and communication. It was the primary language of the Church, of government, of philosophy and science. Indeed, it extended its domain in the medieval centuries, becoming a second language for educated people everywhere in western Europe. As a consequence, much of the best poetry of this long period was written in Latin.

Anicius Manlius Severinus Boethius lived in Italy from A.D. 480 to about 524. Deeply versed in Plato and Aristotle, but probably (though not quite certainly) a Christian, he is a fine example of the transition from the ancient to the medieval world. A modern scholar has called him one of the "founders" of the Middle Ages, chiefly on the basis of the *Consolation of Philosophy*, which was translated into English by King Alfred (in the ninth century) and Chaucer, and by others into most of the medieval languages. The *Consolation* was written while Boethius was what would now be called a political prisoner and consists of alternating poems and passages of prose. The first poem in our book, "He who has made his reckoning with life," expresses a fortitude equally Stoic and Christian in the face of adversity and injustice. Then "O Maker of the starry world" proclaims the universal power of God the Creator—and at the same time asks Him to intervene in human affairs and set things right. The short poem "O Father, give the spirit power to climb," nobly states the aspiration of the soul to a place of rest in God. "He that hath set his headlong heart" asserts the futility of ambition for fame; the group of verses beginning "Tell me where is Brutus laid" anticipates Villon's later (rhetorical) question about Thais and Heloise.

Saint Venantius Fortunatus (ca. 530–609), a prototype of the medieval wandering scholar and cleric, finally settled at Poitiers in the south of France, where he became a bishop. His processional hymn, "The Standards of the King go forth," written in honor of the reception in Poitiers of a fragment of the cross on which Christ was crucified, was a marching song, five hundred years later, for crusaders. The other poem, "If 'twere the time of lilies," addressed to Queen Radegunde, a nun and abbess, expresses a delicate devotion.

Alcuin (ca. 735–804), born an Englishman and educated at York, had his major career in the service of the emperor Charlemagne. Besides conducting a palace school for the emperor's court, he was charged with duties regarding the administration of other schools. In this poem, ostensibly about a cuckoo, he evinces a deep concern and affection for a pupil who has apparently wandered far away.

5. The author's term for a story partly sung and partly recited—a work in verse and prose.

Sedulius Scottus (Scottus means "Irishman"), of insular origin like Alcuin, was active as poet and cleric on the Continent during the middle decades of the ninth century. His witty "begging" poem, addressed to his patron bishop, is an early example of a kind of poetry that would become frequent in later centuries.

The anonymous "Come, sweetheart, come," from the tenth century, besides being a charming piece in itself, illustrates the direct, frank speech of medieval Latin love poetry.

"Low in thy grave with thee" is from a collection of hymns written by Peter Abélard (1079–1142), famous as a philosopher and as the lover of Heloise. In this poem, David, the Old Testament hero, laments the death of his close friend Jonathan, slain in battle.

"Seething over inwardly" is the best known of some ten poems ascribed to a wandering scholar who came to be known as the Archpoet and who apparently died in 1165. Written in the form of a "confession" addressed to his bishop—who was also apparently his patron and his judge—it expresses with great poignancy the inner struggle between the flesh and the spirit. The poet alternates between acknowledgment and defense of his failings—failings associated with wine, women, and song. Some stanzas of the medieval poem have become famous as a drinking song—especially those beginning "For on this my heart is set" (in the original Latin, "Mihi est propositum in taberna mori"). The Archpoet found many kindred spirits in his own and later centuries, among them the anonymous authors of the poems in the *Carmina Burana*, a thirteenth-century collection. "Let's away with study" is one of these; "O happy hour" is another.

Like Alcuin and Abélard, the great philosopher Saint Thomas Aquinas (ca. 1225–1274) reminds us of the versatility of the medieval intellectual—he could write poetry as well as philosophy. "The Word went forth" is a hymn, later adopted as a part of the Roman *Breviary*. Its conciseness and succinctness are the same qualities found in the author's philosophcal works.

Helen Waddell, *Mediaeval Latin Lyrics* (1929, 1948), is perhaps the best known collection, with Latin originals and English translations; by the same author, *More Latin Lyrics, from Virgil to Milton* (1977). On origin and development, Peter Dronke, *The Medieval Lyric* (1968, 1977) is a basic book. For an account of some of the people who produced these poems, see Helen Waddell, *The Wandering Scholars* (1928). The Dronke book contains an extensive bibliography arranged under the several languages.

ANICIUS MANLIUS
SEVERINUS BOETHIUS[1]
(480—ca. 524)

The Consolation of Philosophy

"He who has made his reckoning with life"

He who has made his reckoning with life
Hath haughty fate beneath his feet,

---

1. All selections translated by Helen Waddell.

And gazing straight at fortune, good or ill,
Can hold a high indomitable head.
The rage and menace of the sea   5
With its deep boiling surge,
Vesuvius' moving slope and smoking fires
Burst from the dungeon forge,
These cannot rack
Nor the bright track   10
Of lightning when it strikes high towers.

Why do unhappy folk eye with such awe
Fierce tyrants with no sinews in their rage?
Have done with hope and fear,
And you've disarmed him: he is impotent.   15
But he who trembles with desire or dread,
Because he hath no stay,
Is not in his own power.
He hath thrown away his shield, and given ground:
Himself hath locked the chain   20
Wherewith they'll drag him.

"O Maker of the starry world"

O Maker of the starry world
Who, resting on thy everlasting throne,
Turnst heaven like a spindle
And hast the stars brought under law,
So that the moon, now shining at the full,   5
Straight in the pathway of her brother's flame,
Blots out the lesser stars:
Now with her crescent dim
Draws near the sun and loses all her light:
And Hesperus, in the first hour of eve,   10
Awakens the cold welling of the stars,
And then as Lucifer[2]
Grows pallid in the rising of the sun.
It is thy power tempers the changing year
So that the leaves the North Wind swept away   15
The West Wind brings again.
Arcturus watched the sowing of the seed
That Sirius parches in the standing grain.[3]
Naught is there that escapes the ancient law,
Or leaves the work of its appointed ward.   20
Thou guidest all things to their certain goal,
All but the ways of men:
Keep them in check Thou wilt not.
O Ruler of the world, Thou hast spat them out.
Why should the noxious consequence of sin   25
Take hold upon the sinless?
The pervert sits enthroned,

2. Hesperus and Lucifer are the planet Venus, first as evening and then as morning star.   3. Arcturus
and Sirius are two of the highest stars in the sky.

And ruffians set their heel on the neck of saints.
Bright goodness lurks unknown, hid in the dark,
The just man bears the guilt of the unjust.   30
No perjury,
No fraud tricked out with gaudy lies
Can damage evil men:
And when they have a mind to use their power,
They take delight in subjugating kings   35
That kept the world in awe.
O Thou, whoe'er Thou art,
Thou who dost bind all things in covenant,
Now, now look down on these unhappy lands.
We are not the vilest part of thy creation,   40
Great though it be—men tossed on bitter seas.
Rein in the surge of wild rushing waters,
And Thou that rulest heaven's immensity,
By that same covenant, steady the earth.

"O Father, give the spirit power to climb"

O Father, give the spirit power to climb
To the fountain of all light, and be purified.
Break through the mists of earth, the weight of the clod,
Shine forth in splendour, Thou that art calm weather,
And quiet resting place for faithful souls.   5
To see Thee is the end and the beginning,
Thou carriest us, and Thou dost go before,
Thou art the journey, and the journey's end.

"He that hath set his headlong heart"

He that hath set his headlong heart
     On ultimate renown,
Let him lift up his eyes to the vast fields of air
     And then look down
On this cramped earth that crouches here.   5
     How shall he not think shame
     Of that poor fame,
That cannot even fill so brief horizon?
     Why do men strain
     To lift the yoke of man's mortality   10
     From their proud necks in vain?
Your name has gone the rounds
Of foreign lands, spoken by foreign tongue,
Your house is starry with historic blazon.
     But Death despises glory.   15
Wraps in his grave-clothes humble head and proud,
Rich man and poor man level in their shroud.

Tell me, where is Brutus laid?
Where stern Cato burièd?

Fabricius that defended Rome?[4]   20
  A ghostly fame
  Lives after them,
  Writes on a page or two
  An empty name.
But though we know the names of famous men,   25
What know we of the men who carried them?
Lie down to die, and straight you are unknown,
Fame can no knowledge give of any man.
Think not the echo of a mortal name
Shall lengthen life beyond your span.   30
  The twilight of our day
  Shall steal this too away.
    To die to Fame
    Is to die once again.

SAINT VENANTIUS FORTUNATUS

(ca. 530–609)

"The standards of the King go forth"

The standards of the King go forth,
  Shines out the blazoned mystery,
The Cross whereon the Lord of men
  As man was hung.

Where he was wounded by a thrust,   5
  The edge of that sharp lance,
That he might wash us from guilt;
  Water and blood flowed down.

Fulfilled are now the prophecies
  That David[5] sang of, long ago,   10
Saying, The nations of the earth
  God ruleth from a tree.

O Tree of beauty and of light,
  With royal purple dyed,
Well wert thou chosen then to bear   15
  The sacred load.

Blessed, that on thy branches hung
  The ransom of the world,
The balance of his holy flesh,
  And hell despoiled.   20

---

4. Brutus, Cato, and Fabricius are heroic figures from ancient Roman history.   5. King David was
regarded as the author of the Old Testament Psalms.

To the Lady Radegunde, with Violets

If 'twere the time of lilies,
　Or of the crimson rose,
I'd pluck them in the fields for you,
　Or my poor garden close:
Small gift for you so rare.　　　　　　　　5

But I can find no lilies,
　Green herbs are all I bring.
Yet love makes vetches roses,
　And in their shadowing
Hide violets as fair.　　　　　　　　　10

For royal is their purple,
　And fragrant is their breath,
And to one sweet and royal,
　Their fragrance witnesseth
Beauty abiding there.　　　　　　　　15

ALCUIN

(ca. 735–804)

Lament for the Cuckoo

O cuckoo that sang to us and art fled,
　Where'er thou wanderest, on whatever shore
Thou lingerest now, all men bewail thee dead,
　They say our cuckoo will return no more.
Ah, let him come again, he must not die,　　　　5
　Let him return with the returning spring,
And waken all the songs he used to sing.
　But will he come again? I Know not, I.

I fear the dark sea breaks above his head.
　Caught in the whirlpool, dead beneath the waves.　　10
Sorrow for me, if that ill god of wine
　Hath drowned him deep where young things find their graves.
But if he lives yet, surely he will come,
　Back to the kindly nest, from the fierce crows.
Cuckoo, what took you from the nesting place?　　　15
　But will he come again? That no man knows.

If you love songs, cuckoo, then come again,
　Come again, come again, quick, pray you come.
Cuckoo, delay not, hasten thee home again,
　Daphnis[6] who loveth thee longs for his own.　　　20

---

6. Shepherd of Greek myth.

Now spring is here again, wake from thy sleeping,
　Alcuin the old man thinks long for thee.
Through the green meadows go the oxen grazing;
　Only the cuckoo is not. Where is he?

Wail for the cuckoo, everywhere bewail him, 25
　Joyous he left us: shall he grieving come?
Let him come grieving, if he will but come again,
　Yea, we shall weep with him, moan for his moan.
Unless a rock begat thee, thou wilt weep with us.
　How canst thou not, thyself remembering? 30
Shall not the father weep the son he lost him,
　Brother for brother still be sorrowing?

Once were we three, with but one heart among us.
　Scarce are we two, now that the third is fled.
Fled is he, fled is he, but the grief remaineth; 35
　Bitter the weeping, for so dear a head.
Send a song after him, send a song of sorrow,
　Songs bring the cuckoo home, or so they tell.
Yet be thou happy, wheresoe'er thou wanderest.
　Sometimes remember us. Love, fare you well. 40

SEDULIUS SCOTTUS
(ninth century)

He Complains to Bishop Hartgar of Thirst

The standing corn is green, the wild in flower,
　The vines are swelling, 'tis the sweet o' the year,
Bright-winged the birds, and heaven shrill with song,
　And laughing sea and earth and every star.

But with it all, there's never a drink for me, 5
　No wine, nor mead, nor even a drop of beer.
Ah, how hath failed that substance manifold,
　Born of the kind earth and the dewy air!

I am a writer, I, a musician, Orpheus[7] the second,
　And the ox that treads out the corn, and your well-wisher I, 10
I am your champion armed with the weapons of wisdom and logic,
　Muse, tell my lord bishop and father his servant is dry.

7. The musician of Greek myth, whose singing and playing could tame even wild beasts.

MSS. OF SALZBURG, CANTERBURY,
AND LIMOGES
(tenth century)

"Come, sweetheart, come"

Come, sweetheart, come,
  Dear as my heart to me,
Come to the room
  I have made fine for thee.

Here there be couches spread,   5
  Tapestry tented,
Flowers for thee to tread,
  Green herbs sweet scented.

Here is the table spread,
  Love, to invite thee,   10
Clear is the wine and red,
  Love, to delight thee.

Sweet sounds the viol,
  Shriller the flute,
A lad and a maiden   15
  Sing to the lute.

He'll touch the harp for thee,
  She'll sing the air,
They will bring wine for thee,
  Choice wine and rare.   20

Yet for this care not I,
  'Tis what comes after,
Not all this lavishness,
  But thy dear laughter.

Mistress mine, come to me,   25
  Dearest of all,
Light of mine eyes to me,
  Half of my soul.

Alone in the wood
  I have loved hidden places,   30
Fled from the tumult,
  And crowding of faces.

Now the snow's melting,
  Out the leaves start,
The nightingale's singing,   35
  Love's in the heart.

Dearest, delay not,
  Ours love to learn,

I love not without thee,
  Love's hour is come. 40

What boots delay, Love,
  Since love must be?
Make no more stay, Love,
  I wait for thee.

PIERRE ABÉLARD
(1079–1142)

David's Lament for Jonathan

Low in thy grave with thee
  Happy to lie,
Since there's no greater thing left Love to do;
  And to live after thee
    Is but to die, 5
For with but half a soul what can Life do?

So share thy victory,
  Or else thy grave,
Either to rescue thee, or with thee lie:
    Ending that life for thee, 10
    That thou didst save,[8]
So Death that sundereth might bring more nigh.

Peace, O my stricken lute!
  Thy strings are sleeping.
Would that my heart could still 15
  Its bitter weeping!

THE ARCHPOET
(d. 1165?)

His Confession

Seething over inwardly
  With fierce indignation,
In my bitterness of soul,
  Hear my declaration.
I am of one element, 5
  Levity my matter,
Like enough a withered leaf
  For the winds to scatter.

8. Jonathan had helped David escape the wrath of King Saul.

Since it is the property
     Of the sapient   10
To sit firm upon a rock,
     It is evident
That I am a fool, since I
     Am a flowing river,
Never under the same sky,   15
     Transient for ever.

Hither, thither, masterless
     Ship upon the sea,
Wandering through the ways of air,
     Go the birds like me.   20
Bound am I by ne'er a bond,
     Prisoner to no key,
Questing go I for my kind,
     Find depravity.

Never yet could I endure   25
     Soberness and sadness,
Jests I love and sweeter than
     Honey find I gladness.
Whatsoever Venus bids
     Is a joy excelling,   30
Never in an evil heart
     Did she make her dwelling.

Down the broad way do I go,
     Young and unregretting,
Wrap me in my vices up,   35
     Virtue all forgetting,
Greedier for all delight
     Than heaven to enter in:
Since the soul in me is dead,
     Better save the skin.   40

Pardon, pray you, good my lord,
     Master of discretion,
But this death I die is sweet,
     Most delicious poison.
Wounded to the quick am I   45
     By a young girl's beauty:
She's beyond my touching? Well,
     Can't the mind do duty?

Hard beyond all hardness, this
     Mastering of Nature: 50
Who shall say his heart is clean,
     Near so fair a creature?
Young are we, so hard a law,
     How should we obey it?
And our bodies, they are young,   55
     Shall they have no say in't?

Sit you down amid the fire,
  Will the fire not burn you?
To Pavia[9] come, will you
  Just as chaste return you?   60
Pavia, where Beauty draws
  Youth with finger-tips,
Youth entangled in her eyes,
  Ravished with her lips.

Let you bring Hippolytus,[1]   65
  In Pavia dine him,
Never more Hippolytus
  Will the morning find him.
In Pavia not a road
  But leads to venery,   70
Nor among its crowding towers
  One to chastity.

Yet a second charge they bring:
  I'm for ever gaming.
Yea, the dice hath many a time   75
  Stripped me to my shaming.
What an if the body's cold,
  If the mind is burning,
On the anvil hammering,
  Rhymes and verses turning?   80

Look again upon your list.
  Is the tavern on it?
Yea, and never have I scorned,
  Never shall I scorn it,
Till the holy angels come,   85
  And my eyes discern them,
Singing for the dying soul,
  Requiem aeternam.[2]

For on this my heart is set:
  When the hour is nigh me,   90
Let me in the tavern die,
  With a tankard by me,
While the angels looking down
  Joyously sing o'er me,
Deus sit propitius   95
  Huic potatori.[3]

'Tis the fire that's in the cup
  Kindles the soul's torches,
'Tis the heart that drenched in wine
  Flies to heaven's porches.   100
Sweeter tastes the wine to me
  In a tavern tankard

9. Italian city then known for its wild life.   1. Legendary figure of ancient Greece, noted for his vehement opposition to the pleasures of the flesh.   2. "Eternal rest," the opening words of the Catholic mass for the dead.   3. "May God be gracious to this drinker."

Than the watered stuff my Lord
    Bishop hath decanted.

Let them fast and water drink,   105
    All the poets' chorus,
Fly the market and the crowd
    Racketing uproarious:
Sit in quiet spots and think,
    Shun the tavern's portal,   110
Write, and never having lived,
    Die to be immortal.

Never hath the spirit of
    Poetry descended,
Till with food and drink my lean   115
    Belly was distended,
But when Bacchus lords it in
    My cerebral story,
Comes Apollo with a rush,
    Fills me with his glory.   120

Unto every man his gift.
    Mine was not for fasting.
Never could I find a rhyme
    With my stomach wasting.
As the wine is, so the verse: 125
    'Tis a better chorus
When the landlord hath a good
    Vintage set before us.

Good my lord, the case is heard,
    I myself betray me,
And affirm myself to be   130
    All my fellows say me.
See, they in thy presence are:
    Let whoe'er hath known
His own heart and found it clean,   135
    Cast at me the stone.

CARMINA BURANA
(thirteenth century)

"Let's away with study"

Let's away with study,
    Folly's sweet.
Treasure all the pleasure
    Of our youth:
Time enough for age   5
    To think on Truth.

So short a day,
And life so quickly hasting,
And in study wasting
    Youth that would be gay!   10

'Tis our spring that's slipping,
    Winter draweth near,
Life itself we're losing,
    And this sorry cheer
Dries the blood and chills the heart,   15
    Shrivels all delight.
Age and all its crowd of ills
    Terrifies our sight.
So short a day,
And life so quickly hasting,   20
And in study wasting
    Youth that would be gay!

Let us as the gods do,
    'Tis the wiser part:
Leisure and love's pleasure
    Seek the young in heart
Follow the old fashion,
    Down into the street!
Down among the maidens,
    And the dancing feet!   30
So short a day,
And life so quickly hasting,
And in study wasting
    Youth that would be gay!

There for the seeing   35
    Is all loveliness,
White limbs moving
    Light in wantonness.
Gay go the dancers,
    I stand and see,   40
Gaze, till their glances
    Steal myself from me.
So short a day,
And life so quickly hasting,
And in study wasting   45
    Youth that would be gay!

"O happy hour"

O happy hour
When one so debonair
Took life upon her,
So gay, so fine, so rare.
O shining hair,   5
Hair of gold!

Naught that is base
Could that heart ever hold.
There is none like her, none.
That forehead with its crown of hair,   10
And that dark brow
Arched after Iris'[4] bow.

Snow white,
Rose red,
Her like   15
Not among a thousand shall you find her.
Full lips aglow
White teeth a-sparkle
Voice soft and slow
Slender hands and slender side   20
Throat, all beauty else beside,
So the gods designed her.

A spark of living fire
Down flying from her
Whom above all other   25
I most desire
Kindled my heart that now in ashes lies.
  O thou that Beauty's handmaid art,
    If thou wilt have no pity on my smart
  A living man now dies.   30
  O tender Phyllis,
If thou wilt have no care
For my despair,
Never shall my heart be still
    For never shall I rest   35
Till my lips close on thy lips are laid
  My head upon thy breast.

THOMAS AQUINAS
(1225?–1274)
"The Word went forth"

The Word[5] went forth,
  Yet from his Father never went away.
Came to his work on earth,
  And laboured till the twilight of his day.

Men envied him: He went to death,   5
  By his own man[6] betrayed,
Yet first to his own men himself had given
  In wine and broken bread.[7]

4. The rainbow; also a messenger of the gods.   5. Jesus Christ.   6. Judas Iscariot.   7. The Eucharist or Last Supper.

In birth he gave himself a friend to men,
  At meat, their holy bread: 10
Dying, he gave himself their ransoming:
  Reigning, their high reward.

O Victim slain for us and our salvation,
  Opening the doors of light,
The warring hosts are set on our damnation,   15
  Give us the strength to fight.

DANTE ALIGHIERI

1265–1321

The greatest poem of the Middle Ages, called by its author a comedy and desig-
nated in later centuries *The Divine Comedy (La divina commedia)*, was written in
the early fourteenth century. The poet, Dante Alighieri, was born in late May
1265, in Florence, Italy. In 1291 he married Gemma Donati, by whom he had
two sons and one or two daughters. In 1295 he was a member of the "people's
council" of Florence, and in 1300 served for two months, the usual term, as one
of the six priors, or magistrates, of Florence. In 1302 the Blacks, opponents of the
Whites (a political group with which Dante was affiliated), seized power in Florence, and he, with other White leaders, was exiled. Dante had gone to Rome on
a mission to Pope Boniface in 1301, and as the decree of banishment was soon
coupled with a condemnation to execution by fire (on false charges of corruption
in office), he never returned to his native city. The last twenty years of his life,
from 1301 to 1321, were spent in exile in various parts of Italy and possibly elsewhere. He died at Ravenna in September 1321.

The New Life *(Vita Nuova)* was probably written about 1292. It consists of sonnets and odes with a prose account and running commentary by the poet; the
poems were mostly inspired by Beatrice Portinari (1266–1290), Dante's first love,
who appears in the *Commedia* as a heavenly guide whose name signifies blessedness or salvation. *The Banquet*, of uncertain date, unfinished, is a work of encyclopedic scope in the form of a prose commentary on a series of the poet's odes
(canzoni). On the Vernacular Language, in Latin prose, of uncertain date, unfinished, is an essay on language and poetry, especially on the dialects of Italy and
Provence; it is of great linguistic and literary interest. *On Single Government*, in
Latin prose, of uncertain date, presents a closely reasoned defense of world government, together with an attempt to demonstrate the independent status of the Holy
Roman Empire and the Papacy.

The Divine Comedy, date of beginning uncertain, was apparently finished shortly
before Dante's death in 1321. The poem is in many ways both the supreme and
the centrally representative expression of the medieval mind in imaginative literature. But to appreciate the poem adequately in this light a reader must know it in
its entirety, since it is an organic whole designed with the utmost symmetry. The
present volume contains the entire *Inferno* and several cantos from the other two
divisions. It will be best to look rapidly at the general plan and then concentrate
on the part included in this book.

The three great divisions of the poem, *Hell (Inferno)*, *Purgatory (Purgatorio)*,
and *Paradise (Paradiso)*, are of identical length; each of the last two has thirty-three

cantos, and the first, the *Inferno*, has thirty-four; but the opening canto is a prologue to the entire poem. The total, one hundred, is the square of ten, regarded in
the thought of the time as a perfect number. The three divisions correspond in
number to the Trinity. Nine, the square of three, figures centrally in the interior
structure of each of the three divisions. In Hell, the lost souls are arranged in three
main groups, and occupy nine circles. Most of the circles are themselves subdivided. Hell itself is a funnel-shaped opening in the earth extending from the surface
to the center. Dante's journey thus takes him steadily downward through the nine
concentric circles. The progression is from the least to the greatest types of evil; all
the souls are irrevocably condemned, but all are not intrinsically equal in the
degree or nature of their sin. Thus, as we follow Dante in his descent, we find first
an ante-Hell, the abode of those who refused to choose between right and wrong;
then the boundary river, Acheron; then a circle for virtuous pagans who did not
know Christ; and then a series of circles occupied by those guilty of sins of self-
indulgence, or Incontinence, of all kinds. These include the illicit lovers, the
gluttons, the hoarders and spendthrifts, and those of violent or sullen disposition.
Comparable classes and subclasses are found within the other two main groups of
sinners, those guilty respectively of Violence and of Fraud, the latter including
treachery and treason. At the bottom is the fallen angel, Satan, or Lucifer.

Purgatory is situated on a lofty mountain rising on an island in the sea. It is
divided into the ante-Purgatory, which is the lower half of the mountain; Purgatory
proper, just above; and the Earthly Paradise, or Garden of Eden, at the summit.
Purgatory proper is arranged in a series of seven ledges encircling the mountain,
each devoted to the purification of souls from particular kinds of sinful disposition—Pride, Envy, Anger, Sloth, Avarice, Gluttony, and Illicit Love. These seven
divisions, plus the ante-Purgatory and the Earthly Paradise, make a total of nine.

The *Paradise* takes us, in ascending order, through the circles of the seven planets
of medieval astronomy, the moon, Mercury, Venus, the sun, Mars, Jupiter, and
Saturn; then through the circles of the fixed stars and the *primum mobile*, or outermost circle, which moves the others; and finally to the Empyrean, or Heaven
itself, the abode of God, the angels, and the redeemed souls. Again we have nine
circles, besides the Empyrean, inclusion of which would give a total of ten. Such
is the vast design and scope of *The Divine Comedy* as a whole.

INFERNO

The poem itself begins with action, not outline; explanations appear in suitable
places; they are part of the traveler's experience. We shall do well to follow the
hint. The incidents recounted in Canto I of the *Inferno* are concrete and definite;
their literal meaning is perfectly plain. As critics have often said, Dante is a highly
visual poet; he gives us clear pictures or images. Beginning with a man lost in a
wood, hindered by three beasts from escape by his own effort, the canto might well
be the start of a tale of unusual but quite earthly adventures. But when the stranger
Dante meets identifies himself as the shade of the poet Virgil and offers to conduct
him through realms that, though not named, can only be Hell and Purgatory, we
realize that there is a meaning beyond the one that appears on the surface. We
recognize that the wood, the mountain, the sun, and the three beasts, though
casually introduced, are not casual features of the scene. They represent something
other than themselves; they are symbols. In the light of the entire poem, it is
usually possible to determine, at least in a general sense, what they signify, and in
this volume the headnotes and footnotes identify them. Occasionally, however,
there is doubt. What do the three beasts stand for? A lack of certainty is not a

serious disadvantage to readers; they should regard it as a challenge to reach a decision for themselves. Indeed, if they go on to read the entire poem, they may arrive at an identification that seems sounder and more consistent with the work as a whole than those proposed. Meanwhile, there is no ambiguity about the animals themselves; they are the satisfying and specific images of poetry.

The simple style of this first canto may surprise readers who have been told that *The Divine Comedy* is one of the five or six great poems of European literature, especially if they assume that it will sound like an epic. For Dante begins with neither the splendor of Homer nor the stateliness of Virgil nor the grandeur of Milton. Indeed, except for the use of verse, Canto I seems more like a narrative by Daniel Defoe or Jonathan Swift, particularly at the outset. It is quiet, factual, economical; it convinces us by its air of serious simplicity. Dante called the poem a comedy, in accordance with the use of the term in his day, not only because it began in misery and ended in happiness, but also because in that literary form a sustained loftiness of style was not requisite. In other words, he is free to use the whole range of style, from the humblest, including the colloquial and the humorous, to the highest. There is, indeed, a great variety of tone in the poem. Yet readers will doubtless eventually agree that Dante strikes the right note *for him* at the beginning. Variation will result chiefly from change in intensity, achieved by differing degrees of concentration and repetition—rather than from a shift to the "grand style." This unpretentious manner is, we see, most suitable to a prolonged work of serious fiction in which the author is the central character. For *The Divine Comedy* is not primarily a Cook's tour of the world of the dead; it is an account of the effect of such a journey on the man who takes it—Dante. It is a record of his moral and spiritual experience of illumination, regeneration, and beatitude. We are interested partly because of the unique and individual character of the traveler—Dante as the man he was, the man revealed in the poem—and partly because the experience of the author is imaginatively available and meaningful to all of us.

In Canto IV we come to the first of the nine concentric circles of Hell. Here are the noble heroes, wise philosophers, and inspired poets of the ancient—and medieval—pagan world. They are excluded from Heaven because they knew nothing of Christ and his religion. This fate may seem harsh to us, but the orthodox view recognized only one gate to Heaven. These spirits suffer no punishment, Virgil (who is one of them) tells Dante, only "without hope, we live on in desire." Here Dante's fervent pity and sympathy at once nourish and mirror the reader's; but there is no rebellion against God's decree. Further explanation, and thereby justification, in Dante's view, will come as the poem progresses toward its goal.

With Canto V we reach the second circle, the first of those containing souls guilty of active sin unrepented at the time of death. Here, therefore, is found the contemptuous and monstrous judge Minos, another figure taken from classical myth and freely adapted to Dante's purposes. The souls assigned to the second circle are those guilty of unlawful love. The poet's method here, as throughout the journey, is first to point out a number of prominent figures who would be familiar to his fourteenth-century readers, and then to concentrate attention on a very few, one or two in each circle, telling more about them and eliciting their stories. In general, Dante lets the place and condition in which the sinners are found serve as a minimum essential of information. For the penalties in the various circles are of many different kinds. Their fundamental characteristic is appropriateness to the particular sin; this is one of the principal differences between the punishments in Dante's Hell and the miscellaneous and arbitrary horrors of many accounts of the place. In Dante the penalties symbolize the sin. Thus the illicit lovers of the second circle are continually blown about by storm winds, for their sin consisted in the surrender of reason to lawless passions.

Here we find Paolo and Francesca, the best-known figures of the entire *Divine Comedy*. Like all the human beings presented in the poem, they actually existed. They lived in Italy about the time of Dante's childhood and early youth, and were slain by Francesca's husband, a brother of Paolo. Dante's method, it is hence clear, is not to build up an allegorical cast of personified abstractions. Instead of, say, Passion and Rebellion, he portrays Paolo and Francesca. They represent, or symbolize, sinful love by example. They show how an intrinsically noble emotion, love, if contrary to God's law, can bring two essentially fine persons to damnation and spiritual ruin. The tenderness and the sympathy with which the story is told are famous. But its pathos, and Dante's personal response of overwhelming pity, should not blind us to the *justice* of the penalty. The poet who describes himself as fainting at the end of Francesca's recital is the same man who consigned her to Hell. His purpose is partly to portray the attractiveness of sin, an especially congenial theme when *this* is the sin involved—both for Dante and for most readers. But although Dante allows the lovers the bitter sweetness of inseparability in Hell, the modern "romantic" idea that union anywhere is sufficient happiness for lovers does not even occur to him. Paolo and Francesca indeed have their love; but they have lost God and thus corrupted their personalities—their inmost selves—from order into anarchy; they can hardly be considered happy. In a sense, they have what they wanted; they continue in the lawless condition that they chose on earth. But that condition, seen from the point of view of eternity, is not bliss.

In Canto X we are among the heretics in their flaming tomb in the sixth circle. Situated within the walled city of Dis—the capital, as it were, of Hell—this circle is a kind of border between the upper Hell (devoted to punishments for Incontinence) and the lower (concerned with Violence and Fraud). Here Dante portrays the proud aristocrat Farinata and his associate, the elder Cavalcante, father of Dante's closest friend. Their crime is heresy, a flagrant aspect of intellectual pride. But there is a nobility in Farinata's pride; Dante, like the reader, admires the splendid self-sufficiency of a man who, in this situation, can seem "to hold all Hell in disrespect." And the essence of the aristocratic nature is distilled in his address to Dante as "the great soul stared almost contemptuously, / before he asked: 'Of what line do you come?' " and in his abrupt resumption of the conversation interrupted by Cavalcante. Alongside the haughtiness of Farinata, Dante sets the pathetic—and mistaken—grief of Cavalcante for his son; each portrait gains in effect by the extreme contrast.

Canto XIII shows us one group of those guilty of Violence; for the suicides have been violent against themselves. Here they are turned into monstrous trees, their misery finding expression when a bough is torn or plucked. In the eyes of the Church, suicide was murder, in no way diminished by the fact that the slayer and the victim were the same. By representing in Pier delle Vigne a man who had every human motive to end his life, Dante achieves the deepest pathos and evokes our shuddering pity. As Francesca displays in her dramatic monologue the charm and the potential weakness of her character, as Farinata's manner of speech reveals his nature, so Pier delle Vigne by his exact and legal-sounding language lets us see the careful, methodical counselor whose sense of logic and sense of justice were so outraged that he saw no point in enduring life any longer. His judgment is still unimpaired; he does not reproach his king, only the jealous courtiers who misled him. The Wood of the Suicides is one of the greatest—among many admirable—examples of landscape in Hell assimilated to theme and situation.

Canto XV describes the meeting of Dante and his venerable teacher and adviser, the scholar Brunetto Latini. We are in another ring of the seventh circle, among more of those who have sinned through Violence. The impact of this scene results from the contrast between the dignity of the man and the indignity of his condition in hell, and by the tact with which both he and Dante ignore it for the moment. Brunetto, with the others guilty of homosexual "vice," must move continually along a sandy desert under a rain of fire. Dante accords him the utmost respect and expresses his gratitude in the warmest terms; and something like their earthly relationship of teacher and pupil is re-enacted, for Brunetto is keenly interested in Dante's prospects in life. In the final image of Brunetto running, not like the loser, but like the winner of a race, Dante extracts dignity and victory out of indignity itself.

The presence of such people as these will remind the reader that Hell is not reserved exclusively for arrant scoundrels. They are there, of course; but so are many charming, and some noble and great, men and women. These are in Hell because they preferred something else—no matter what—to God; at the moment of death they were therefore in rebellion against Him. God and Heaven would not be congenial to them, *as they are and as He is*; and there is no acceptable repentance after death. Hence they go on unchanged—only now experiencing the harsher aspects of the sin in which they chose to live.

In Canto XVII the travelers are carried on the back of the flying monster Geryon down the deep descent from the seventh to the eighth circle. With the face of a just man and the body of a serpent, Geryon symbolizes Fraud. He is one of the most exciting figures in Hell. In an age before ferris wheels and airplanes, he gives our poets a ride that anticipates some of the terrifying thrill that a young child may feel in an airplane journey. The eighth circle is subdivided into ten chasms or trenches (Malebolge), each with its own kind of sinners: seducers and panderers; flatterers; simoniacs (buyers and sellers of appointments in the Church), sorcerers, grafters, hypocrites, thieves, evil counselors, troublemakers, forgers, and impostors.

Most readers will agree that the punishments fit the crimes of the eighth circle. It is a long catalogue of iniquity; much, but not all, is sordid. Dante has avoided monotony not only by the vividness and intensity of the separate scenes but also by their ingenious variety and by the frequent changes of pace in the narrative. The satirical situation and fierce denunciation of the simoniacs is followed by the quiet horror of the sorcerers with twisted necks. The hilarious episode of the grafters precedes the encounter with the solemn, slow-walking hypocrites; and these are succeeded by the macabre serpent-transformations of the thieves. Nevertheless, our slow descent in hell gradually produces a sense of oppressiveness. This is appropriate and deliberate; it is a part of Dante's total design. But he recognizes the need of momentary relief, a breath of fresh air, a reminder of the world above. These he provides, for example, in the long simile describing the shipyard in Venice (the opening of Canto XXI) or the picture of the peasant and his two sallies outside on a winter morning (the opening of Canto XXIV).

The episode of the grafters (Cantos XXI and XXII) probably has biographical relevance for Dante. During his absence from Florence on business of state, the opposing political party seized power and sentenced Dante to death if he should return to Florence. The quite unfounded charge against him was misappropriation of public funds. In these cantos Dante cuts a ludicrous figure: fearful, cowering, in constant danger from the demons. He escapes their clutches, first by a distraction and then by belated vigilance. The whole sequence affords an oblique and amusing view of an actual episode. It is worth noting also that here, and here only, in the poem, we find ourselves in the kind of hell known in popular lore and anecdote, with winged devils playing rough jokes on their human prey. Scenes, style, and language alike here show one extreme of the range of the poem—the "low" comic. Dante very unobtrusively indicates his awareness of this by the contrasting allusions found in Canto XX, line 113 and Canto XXI, line 2.

Cantos XXVI and XXVII take us among the wicked counselors, who occupy the eighth chasm, or subdivision, of the eighth circle. Appearing at a distance like fireflies in a summer valley, these souls are wrapped in individual, or occasionally twin, flames. Fire is a fit punishment for those who used the flame of intellect to accomplish evil. When the two poets approach more closely, Virgil identifies one flame as that of Ulysses (Odysseus) and Diomede, who burn together. Among the deceptions devised by Ulysses was the wooden horse, which made possible the capture of Troy. It will strike the reader as strange that a man should suffer for his powers as a military tactician. But the Greeks were enemies of the Trojans, whom the Romans and later most of the nations of Western Europe regarded as their ancestors. Ulysses was on the wrong side, and was responsible for his deeds; but Dante mingles with his condemnation an admiration of the man's mental powers. Ulysses remains aloof; he does not converse with Dante, like most of the souls we have met. Instead, as Dorothy Sayers puts it in the notes to her translation of the poem, Virgil conjures the flame into monologue. Thus we are told how Ulysses determined not to return home after the Trojan War but to explore the western ocean instead. In this narrative, apparently invented by Dante, Ulysses becomes the type of the adventuring and searching spirit of man; the voyage is an act of the mind and soul as well as the body. When he has sailed within sight of a mountainous island, his ship is wrecked by a storm and he perishes. Since, as other parts of the poem indicate, this is the island of Purgatory, the episode clearly has symbolic significance. On this island is the Earthly Paradise, or Garden of Eden, lost to man by the sin of Adam. Man, unassisted by divine grace—pagan man, represented by Ulysses—cannot regain it by his own intelligence, although the effort toward that end is noble in itself.

The other evil counselor, Guido da Montefeltro, speaks fluently in Canto XXVII; he shows a quite earthly eagerness for news, crafty, garrulous old intriguer that he is. It is a neat irony that, in spite of Guido's deserved reputation for cleverness, Dante shows him twice deceived: first on earth, as he himself relates, and now in Hell—he does not want his story known and is convinced that Dante will never return to earth to tell it. He sketches in detail, with recollective acidity, the steps by which the pope led him, an aging and reformed man, to return for a moment to his old ways. He even includes the contest of St. Francis and the devil for his soul at his death, along with the devil's bitter witticism: you didn't think I was a logician, perhaps!

In Cantos XXXII and XXXIII the poet reaches the ninth and last circle, where the traitors are immersed in ice that symbolizes their unfeeling hearts. At the end of one canto we are shown the horror of Ugolino gnawing the skull of his enemy Ruggieri, both partly fastened in the ice. Dante does not concentrate on the acts that have put either man in Hell. Instead he lets Ugolino tell us, in the next canto, why his hatred of Ruggieri is so implacable. The fearful pathos, the power, and at the same time the restraint and compression of this narrative make it one of the finest episodes in the poem.

The last canto, Canto XXXIV, shows us the enormous shape of the fallen angel, Satan, fixed at the bottom of Hell; where the motion of his wings freezes the ice in which we have found the traitors immersed. In one of his three mouths he holds Judas Iscariot, who betrayed Christ; in the other two are Brutus and Cassius, who plotted the assassination of Julius Caesar. Dante did not regard them, as we generally do today, as perhaps misguided patriots; to him they were the destroyers of a providentially ordained ruler. Readers who remember John Milton's *Paradise Lost* may be surprised at the absence of any interior presentation of Satan. One critic regrets that his suffering is not shown as different from that of the other inhabitants of Hell. But the fact is that his suffering is not presented at all; he is not a person, to Dante, but an object, a part of the machinery and geography of Hell. For *The Divine Comedy* is occupied exclusively with human sin, human redemption, and human beatitude.

PURGATORY

At the beginning of the *Purgatory*, Dante and Virgil have once more reached the surface of the earth and can look up and see the sky and the stars. Their long climb from the bottom of Hell, where they left Satan, has brought them out on the shore of the mountain-island of Purgatory. The scene and the situation are presented by Dante with a bold and happy use of imaginative symbols. Guided by Reason in the person of Virgil, Dante, a man still in the earthly life, has looked closely at sin and evil—in Hell—and turned away from them, and is now in search of the means of self-correction and purification. He arrives on the island shore, just before dawn, to find the reverend figure of Cato acting as guardian of the mountain. The austerely glorious figure of Cato, his face illumined by rays from stars representing the pagan virtues of Prudence, Temperance, Fortitude, and Justice, embodies the highest moral and ethical ideal available to man without divine revelation, pre- or post-Christian. Dante meets him, appropriately, before dawn—before the sun of God's illumination has risen. These elements in the situation, together with the reference to his sojourn with Marcia, his wife, in the circle of virtuous pagans in Hell, make Cato a remarkable transition or border symbol, standing both between Hell and Purgatory and between Greco-Roman philosophy and ethics and the dispensation of the Old and New Testaments.

These opening cantos admirably set quite a new tone in the second great division of the poem. They show us joy and brightness, cheer and hope, contrasting totally with the darkness and misery of Hell. They show us an angel arriving with a cargo of souls, all joyfully singing. They accustom us to a different set of attitudes, a different kind of people, and especially, they portray the naïveté, the almost child-like lack of intellectual and moral sophistication, the need of orientation, which characterize the penitent soul at this point in its progress to perfection. As yet uninstructed and spiritually immature, it looks back, seeking to carry on the harmless but no longer suitable delights of earthly life. Dante—and Virgil—share this simplicity to the full.

Cantos III–XVIII, not included in this book, take the reader along the slopes of the lower half of the mountain—the ante-Purgatory, where some of the souls must wait for varying periods of time (and for different reasons) before entering Purgatory itself—and through four of the seven terraces, those devoted to purgation from Pride, Envy, Anger, and Sloth. In Canto XIX we go on to the fifth of the ledges encircling the mountain, that in which the souls are purified of Avarice. There we meet Pope Adrian, one of Dante's most vivid illustrations of the anguish of purification. Concisely he sketches for Dante the poignant story of his late conversion (to the reality of the Christian life), his repentance, and his present hard penance. Only when, after a life of self-seeking, he had attained the pinnacle of the papacy did disillusionment come—and spiritual discovery: "I saw no heart's rest there, nor ease from strife." Now he recognizes the equity of the reforming penalty:

> We would not raise our eyes to the shining spheres
> but kept them turned to mundane things: so Justice
> bends them to earth here in this place of tears.

Dante, on learning from Adrian's words that he was a pope, has knelt down in respect. But Adrian, perceiving this without lifting his eyes from the ground, peremptorily corrects Dante: there are no popes here. All the hierarchies and social orders of earth are annihilated in Purgatory—and, we may add, the hierarchy of Heaven is not that of earth. Having answered Dante's questions, Adrian bids him go on—he hinders the task of penitence. Finally, remembering that Dante had offered to carry news of him to those possibly dear to him on earth—which might lead to helpful prayers—the old man adds that he has only a niece there who, if not corrupted by the bad example of his family, could possibly help him. But for this soul, absorbed in his penance, the earth has receded far away, and Heaven is not yet attained; he is essentially alone with his suffering.

The remaining parts of the *Purgatory* included in this book, Cantos XXVII, XXX, and XXXI, add a dimension to Dante's role in the poem. He is, as has been said, the protagonist throughout; the journey and all its disclosures are carried out for his benefit. In Hell, to be sure, he could do little except look and learn; yet his emotional education through the revelation of perfected evil was a large and positive achievement. As a candidate for salvation, he has learned to abhor sin more completely in proportion as he has been shown its real nature; while, as a man of flesh and blood, he has felt alternate pity and hate for the sinners. Along the penitential ledges of Purgatory he has partially assimilated himself to the penitents; he has felt humility while among those purging themselves of Pride, and generosity among those seeking to root out Envy from their natures. On the seventh terrace, he has recognized an even closer kinship with those engaged in refining their love by fire. But now this same fire, it develops, is the boundary between Purgatory and the Earthly Paradise at the top of the mountain. To reach that goal, Dante must go through the fire. Remembering "human bodies / I once saw burned," he is overcome by a terrible fear. The encouraging words of the angel guardian of the ledge, the assurances of Virgil, who reminds him of perils safely passed— neither avail to move him until he is told that Beatrice is beyond the wall of flame. Then his resistance melts and he perseveres through the frightful but harmless fire. It is now nearly sunset, when all ascent ceases, but next morning Dante takes the few last steps to the Earthly Paradise. Here Virgil, who has guided him through Hell and Purgatory, gives him a farewell benediction. Dante, says Virgil, has explored evil in its final effects (Hell) and the means of correcting the human inclinations that produce it (in Purgatory). His regenerated will is now truly free, and he may fearlessly follow its direction. He no longer needs the guidance of a teacher of morality (Virgil) or a political structure ("crown") or an ecclesiastical institution ("mitre"). In short, he has regained the condition of man before the Fall.

These words apply to Dante in his role as a kind of Everyman, representing whoever has fully discerned the nature of evil and wholly freed himself from the impulses to sin. They apply to every soul when it completes the experience of Purgatory; if they did not, the soul would not be ready to go to Heaven, to enter the presence of God. But obviously they cannot apply, actually and practically, to any man still living on earth. That they were not meant as a literal description of Dante the Italian poet and political exile from Florence is clear enough from the events of Cantos XXX and XXXI. For if Dante has already perfected himself by penance, why should he now, in the scenes with Beatrice, repeat the painful experience of rebuke, confession, and satisfaction? It is this latter series of incidents that constitutes Dante's personal, individual experience of correction and purification.

In the midst of the celestial pageant that moves before Dante in the Earthly Paradise appears a lady whom he instantly recognizes as one who was the object of his idealizing love when she lived as a woman on earth. Turning excitedly to confide this to Virgil, he cannot find him anywhere, and is stricken with grief. Presently the Lady names herself as Beatrice—whom the reader will remember for two reasons: she sent Virgil to guide her endangered servant, Dante, through Hell and Purgatory; and to see her Dante forced himself to go through the barrier of fire. There is no cause to doubt that, like the other human beings in the poem, Beatrice is an actual person transformed by the shaping imagination of the poet. What she was to Dante in her earthly life he tells us in the *New Life*, written not long after her death in 1290. She was an incarnation of beauty and virtue; simply by existing, she engrossed the young Dante's ardent but remote devotion; her smile or greeting left him in trembling rapture. This was the full extent of the relationship between them. But the poems in the *New Life* are mostly inspired by the thought of her, whether on earth or in heaven. In short, she was a real woman who, even in this world, was an ideal for Dante, and after death became an even more glorious image of goodness and divine wisdom. The last section of the *New Life* records Dante's resolution to devote a great work to her, when he shall be qualified to achieve it; *The Divine Comedy* is that work. We have seen that he makes her the instigator of the imaginary journey through two realms of the life after death and the motive for his endurance of the fire. Now, as successor to Virgil, she comes to guide him herself through the heavenly paradise. In the same way that Virgil is Reason without ceasing to be Virgil, Beatrice fulfills the role of Divine Revelation without ceasing to be Beatrice.

It is in this dual character, part beloved woman and part the voice of divine wisdom, that Beatrice, in Canto XXXI, unsparingly rebukes Dante. He had loved her mortal beauty as an image of the immortal; when death destroyed it, his devotion ought thenceforth to have fixed itself on the immortal and indestructible virtue of which that beauty had been the image. Instead, he turned aside to the lure of material things. Dante accepts the reproach with the utmost contrition. It is quite probable that this episode is based on some actual lapse, in Dante's life, from his highest moral ideal. These passages, then, recount his own personal experience of purgation, the autobiographical analogue of the penitence and purification portrayed on the mountain as a whole.

PARADISE

Like the invocations of *Paradise Lost*, that with which Dante begins the third division of his poem expresses his sense of the loftiness of the theme. Like Milton, he is venturing things unattempted hitherto in prose or verse. The three invocations of *The Divine Comedy* are incremental; the first (in Canto II of the *Hell*) is brief and unobtrusive, the second (in Canto I of the *Purgatory*) more extended, and the third (in Canto I of the *Paradise*) by its earnestness and solemnity indicates the epic stature, though not epic form, that he expects the poem to attain. The *Paradise* offers us an imagined experience of the entire celestial universe as it was charted by medieval astronomy. In that cosmology, the sun, the moon, and the rest, though immensely distant, have not retreated from the earth according to the scale established by modern knowledge. Dante's world is geocentric; the planetary circles, including those of the sun and moon, revolve about the earth, as does the circle of the stars—as does, in fact, everything except the "real" Heaven, or Empyrean, the abode of God and the saints and angels. The *Paradise* is the chronicle of an ascent from planet to planet, until finally Dante is in the Empyrean itself. In each planet a group of redeemed and perfected souls, come from their proper dwelling in the Empyrean, are present to converse with Dante and his guide, Beatrice. Their successive discussions set forth the essentials of Christian doctrine, along with the fundamental scientific concepts of the time; and they themselves exemplify various kinds and degrees of beatitude. For Dante—and the reader—the experience is educational, morally edifying, and spiritually preparatory for the vision with which the poem ends. In Canto III Dante learns of the hierarchy of souls in Heaven; not all are equal, indeed, no two are identical in bliss; yet each is completely satisfied, fulfilled, and happy—"in His will is our peace." Piccarda, the not wholly blameless nun who speaks these words, is among the souls encountered in the moon, the group of lowest rank in Heaven. From these we rise to higher and higher kinds of blessed souls, each rejoicing wholly in God in its predestined way and in accordance with its capacity.

When all the cycles of the cosmos have been traversed, we come, in Canto XXXI, to Heaven itself, the real home of the blessed. Here the souls are arranged in the form of a great white rose; God is at the center—an ineffable brightness—and the souls have the aspect of rows of petals. Here Beatrice, who has set forth the truths of Divine Revelation throughout the journey, goes back to her place in Heaven, and St. Bernard, the great mystic of the twelfth century, becomes Dante's guide, or rather sponsor. For what remains is that Dante should be vouchsafed a vision in which, for an instant, he may see God as He really is—in so far as his human capacity enables him to do so. The last canto, Canto XXXIII, opens with Bernard's prayer to the Virgin Mary for intercession in Dante's behalf. There is no religious lyric poetry of greater depth or simplicity or beauty than this prayer; its intimacy, tenderness, and humility are consummate.

To obtain, to endure, such a vision is just within the limit of Dante's powers. It transports him into an utterly different kind of being; it leaves him with the memory of an overpowering but indescribable experience. For of course no mystic can ever reveal the content of his vision; it does not belong to the order of reportable things. Dante can only tell us that he discerned with direct but momentary certitude the identity of God as inclusive of man and of universal love, and that he knew himself to be at that instant one with Him.

The Divine Comedy thus ends both quietly and climactically. For this union with God was the purpose of the entire long and arduous journey. This is the good that St. Thomas Aquinas, and Boethius before him, pointed out as the goal of man, as of the entire creation. But what the philosophers attempt to prove, Dante experiences, imaginatively. And we reach both center and summit of the medieval structure of human life in proportion as we can follow the record of that experience.

DANTE IN ITALIAN

This book presents the *Inferno* complete, together with several cantos of the *Purgatorio* and *Paradiso*, in English translation. Our translator is the American poet John Ciardi. As with some other poems in the book, the reader may find it interesting to have a brief look at the Italian text, so here are the opening lines of the *Inferno* in the original language.

Nel mezzo del cammin di nostra vita
mi retrovai per una selva oscura
ché la diritta via era smarrita.

Ah, quanto a dir qual era è cosa dura
esta selva selvaggia e aspra e forte
che nel pensier rinova la paura!

Tant'è amara che poco è più morte;
ma per trattar del ben ch'io vi trovai,
dirò dell'altre cose ch'i' v'ho scorte.

Io non so ben ridir com'io v'entrai,
tant'era pieno di sonno a quel punto
che la verace via abbandonai.

The individual lines are metrically similar to most lines in Chaucer or Shakespeare; they regularly have five metrical feet, each consisting of an unstressed syllable followed by a stressed one, or vice versa, with the possibility of an additional unstressed syllable or two somewhere within the line. But the most notable metrical feature of the *Divine Comedy* is the pattern of rhymes, or the *terza rima*. Thus the lines form groups of three: *vita* in the first line above rhymes with the last two syllables of *smarrita* in the third line, while *oscura* in the second line rhymes with *dura* in the first line and *paura* in the third line of the next group. The groups are independent units interlocked by the sequence of rhymes. This overall structure reminds the reader of the Christian Trinity: God the Father, Son, and Holy Spirit; it is one expression of the poet's religious devotion. In his translation Ciardi maintains the separation into groups of three lines: *astray* in the first line rhymes with *I say* in the third. But he does not keep the interlocking rhyme scheme: *myself* in line two of the first group does not rhyme with *drear* and *fear* in the second group. The sound structure of the Italian language makes Dante's rhyme patterns easier than this arrangement would be in an English poem. Attempts to reproduce it entirely have not been very successful in our language.

For biographical information, the general reader will find Michele Barbi, *Life of Dante*, translated by Paul G. Ruggiers (1954), readable and convenient. Also helpful for background is Dorothy Sayers, *Introductory Papers on Dante* (1954); as well as her *Further Papers on Dante* (1957). T. G. Bergin, *Dante's* Divine Comedy (1971) is a valuable overall account. The series of *Dante Studies* by Charles S. Singleton (1956) is intensive and demanding (1. *Commedia: Elements of Structure*. 2. *Journey to Beatrice; et al.*). Important studies of particular topics are Erich Auerbach, *Dante, Poet of the Secular World*, translated by Ralph Manheim (1961); Francis Fergusson, *Dante's Drama of the Mind: A Modern Reading of the Purgatorio* (1953, reprinted 1968); and John Freccero, ed., *Dante: A Collection of Critical Essays* (1965). Freccero is also the author of a recent book of distinction: *Dante, The Poetics of Conversion*, edited by Rachel Jacoff (1986).

A broader context of study and interpretation is attempted in K. Vossler, *Medieval Culture: An Introduction to Dante and his Times* (1929) and E. R. Curtius, *European Literature and the Latin Middle Ages* (1953). A still broader context can be found in George Santayana, "Dante," in *Three Philosophical Poets* (1910) and T. S. Eliot, "Dante," in his *Selected Essays* (1932).

The Slope of Hell

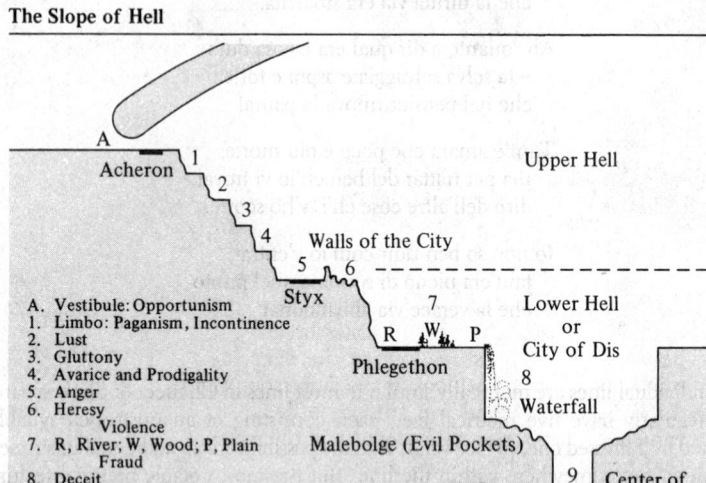

A

Acheron   1   Upper Hell

2

3

4   Walls of the City

5   6

A. Vestibule: Opportunism   Styx   Lower Hell
1. Limbo: Paganism, Incontinence   7   or
2. Lust   R   W   P   City of Dis
3. Gluttony
4. Avarice and Prodigality   Phlegethon
5. Anger   8
6. Heresy   Waterfall
     Violence
7. R, River; W, Wood; P, Plain   Malebolge (Evil Pockets)
     Fraud
8. Deceit   9   Center of
9. Treachery   Cocytus   the Earth

The Heavenly Spheres

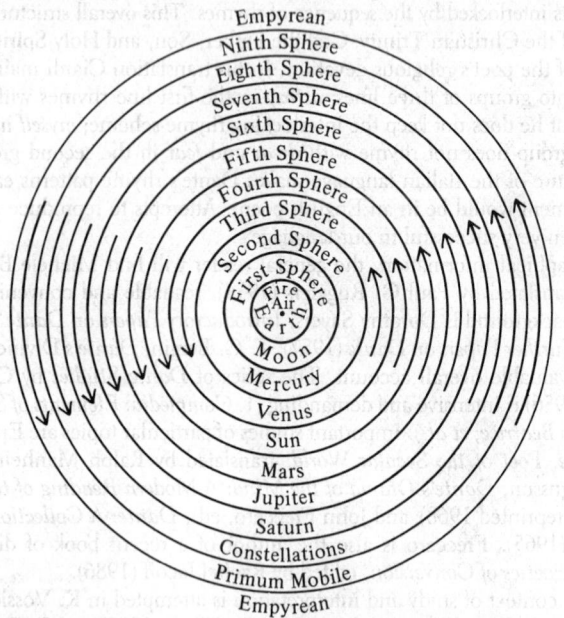

Empyrean
Ninth Sphere
Eighth Sphere
Seventh Sphere
Sixth Sphere
Fifth Sphere
Fourth Sphere
Third Sphere
Second Sphere
First Sphere
Fire
Air
Water
Earth
Moon
Mercury
Venus
Sun
Mars
Jupiter
Saturn
Constellations
Primum Mobile
Empyrean

The diagrams are intended to represent the stages of Dante's journey through each of the three realms, Hell, Purgatory, and Heaven. (1) Hell is entirely below the surface of the earth; Dante moves steadily downward until he reaches its center at the bottom of Hell. There is a corresponding gradation or hierarchy of evil— from bad to worse and worst. (2) On the mountain of Purgatory this arrangement

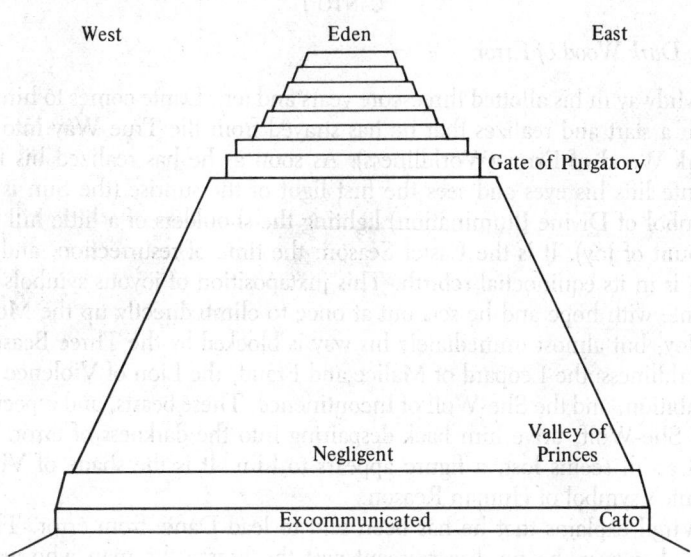

Island of Purgatory

West   Eden   East

Gate of Purgatory

Valley of Princes

Negligent

Excommunicated   Cato

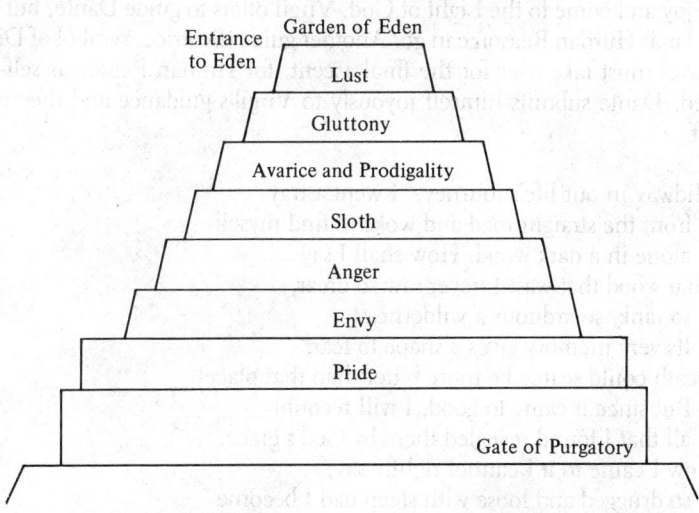

Eden and Purgatory

Entrance to Eden   Garden of Eden

Lust

Gluttony

Avarice and Prodigality

Sloth

Anger

Envy

Pride

Gate of Purgatory

is reversed; Dante moves steadily *upward* to the Garden of Eden at the top (where Adam and Eve lived before the Fall). (3) Retaining the hierarchical plan, the heavenly spheres represent various levels of spiritual blessedness or perfection. In Dante's time the earth was believed to be the center of the cosmos, or world; all the planets then known—including the sun—revolved around the earth.

The Divine Comedy[1]

Inferno

CANTO I

The Dark Wood of Error

Midway in his allotted threescore years and ten, Dante comes to himself
with a start and realizes that he has strayed from the True Way into the
Dark Wood of Error (Worldliness). As soon as he has realized his loss,
Dante lifts his eyes and sees the first light of the sunrise (the Sun is the
Symbol of Divine Illumination) lighting the shoulders of a little hill (the
Mount of Joy). It is the Easter Season, the time of resurrection, and the
sun is in its equinoctial rebirth. This juxtaposition of joyous symbols fills
Dante with hope and he sets out at once to climb directly up the Mount
of Joy, but almost immediately his way is blocked by the Three Beasts of
Worldliness: the Leopard of Malice and Fraud, the Lion of Violence and
Ambition, and the She-Wolf of Incontinence. These beasts, and especially
the She-Wolf, drive him back despairing into the darkness of error. But
just as all seems lost, a figure appears to him. It is the shade of Virgil,
Dante's symbol of Human Reason.

Virgil explains that he has been sent to lead Dante from error. There
can, however, be no direct ascent past the beasts: the man who would
escape them must go a longer and harder way. First he must descend
through Hell (the Recognition of Sin), then he must ascend through Purgatory (the Renunciation of Sin), and only then may he reach the pinnacle
of joy and come to the Light of God. Virgil offers to guide Dante, but only
as far as Human Reason can go. Another guide (Beatrice, symbol of Divine
Love) must take over for the final ascent, for Human Reason is self-lim-
ited. Dante submits himself joyously to Virgil's guidance and they move
off.

Midway in our life's journey,[2] I went astray
   from the straight road and woke to find myself
   alone in a dark wood. How shall I say
what wood that was! I never saw so drear,
   so rank, so arduous a wilderness!   5
   Its very memory gives a shape to fear.
Death could scarce be more bitter than that place!
   But since it came to good, I will recount
   all that I found revealed there by God's grace.
How I came to it I cannot rightly say,   10
   so drugged and loose with sleep had I become
   when I first wandered there from the True Way.

---

1. The *Inferno* complete, with selections from the *Purgatorio* and *Paradiso*. Translated, with notes and
commentary, by John Ciardi.   2. The Biblical life span is three-score years and ten (seventy years). The
action opens in Dante's thirty-fifth year, i.e., A.D. 1300.

But at the far end of that valley of evil
  whose maze had sapped my very heart with fear,
  I found myself before a little hill   15
and lifted up my eyes. Its shoulders glowed
  already with the sweet rays of that planet[3]
  whose virtue leads men straight on every road,
and the shining strengthened me against the fright
  whose agony had wracked the lake of my heart   20
  through all the terrors of that piteous night.
Just as a swimmer, who with his last breath
  flounders ashore from perilous seas, might turn
  to memorize the wide water of his death—
so did I turn, my soul still fugitive   25
  from death's surviving image, to stare down
  that pass that none had ever left alive.
And there I lay to rest from my heart's race
  till calm and breath returned to me. Then rose
  and pushed up that dead slope at such a pace   30
each footfall rose above the last.[4] And lo!
  almost at the beginning of the rise
  I faced a spotted Leopard, all tremor and flow
and gaudy pelt. And it would not pass, but stood
  so blocking my every turn that time and again   35
  I was on the verge of turning back to the wood.
This fell at the first widening of the dawn
  as the sun was climbing Aries with those stars
  that rode with him to light the new creation.[5]
Thus the holy hour and the sweet season   40
  of commemoration did much to arm my fear
  of that bright murderous beast with their good omen.
Yet not so much but what I shook with dread
  at sight of a great Lion that broke upon me
  raging with hunger, its enormous head   45
held high as if to strike a mortal terror
  into the very air. And down his track,
  a She-Wolf drove upon me, a starved horror

---

3. The sun. Ptolemaic astronomers considered it a planet. It is also symbolic of God as He who lights the way.   4. The literal rendering would be: "So that the fixed foot was ever the lower." "Fixed" has often been translated "right" and an ingenious reasoning can support that reading, but a simpler explanation offers itself and seems more competent: Dante is saying that he climbed with such zeal and haste that every footfall carried him above the last despite the steepness of the climb. At a slow pace, on the other hand, the rear foot might be brought up only as far as the forward foot.   5. The medieval tradition had it that the sun was in Aries at the time of the Creation. The significance of the astronomical and religious conjunction is an important part of Dante's intended allegory. It is just before dawn of Good Friday A.D. 1300 when he awakens in the Dark Wood. Thus his new life begins under Aries, the sign of creation, at dawn (rebirth) and in the Easter season (resurrection). Moreover the moon is full and the sun is in the equinox, conditions that did not fall together on any Friday of 1300. Dante is obviously constructing poetically the perfect Easter as a symbol of his new awakening.

ravening and wasted beyond all belief.[6]
She seemed a rack for avarice, gaunt and craving.   50
Oh many the souls she has brought to endless grief!
She brought such heaviness upon my spirit
   at sight of her savagery and desperation,
   I died from every hope of that high summit.
And like a miser—eager in acquisition   55
   but desperate in self-reproach when Fortune's wheel
   turns to the hour of his loss—all tears and attrition
I wavered back; and still the beast pursued,
   forcing herself against me bit by bit
   till I slid back into the sunless wood.   60
And as I fell to my soul's ruin, a presence
   gathered before me on the discolored air,
   the figure of one who seemed hoarse from long silence.
At sight of him in that friendless waste I cried:
   "Have pity on me, whatever thing you are,   65
   whether shade or living man." And it replied:
"Not man, though man I once was, and my blood
   was Lombard, both my parents Mantuan.
I was born, though late, sub Julio,[7] and bred
   in Rome under Augustus in the noon   70
   of the false and lying gods. I was a poet
and sang of old Anchises' noble son[8]
   who came to Rome after the burning of Troy.
But you—why do you return to these distresses
   instead of climbing that shining Mount of Joy   75
   which is the seat and first cause of man's bliss?"
"And are you then that Virgil and that fountain
   of purest speech?" My voice grew tremulous:
"Glory and light of poets! now may that zeal
   and love's apprenticeship that I poured out   80
   on your heroic verses serve me well!
For you are my true master and first author,
   the sole maker from whom I drew the breath
   of that sweet style whose measures have brought me honor.
See there, immortal sage, the beast I flee.   85
   For my soul's salvation, I beg you, guard me from her,
   for she has struck a mortal tremor through me."
And he replied, seeing my soul in tears:
   "He must go by another way who would escape
   this wilderness, for that mad beast that fleers   90

6. These three beasts undoubtedly are taken from Jeremiah 5:6. Many additional and incidental interpretations have been advanced for them, but the central interpretation must remain as noted. They foreshadow the three divisions of Hell (incontinence, violence, and fraud) which Virgil explains at length in Canto XI. 16–111.   7. In the reign of Julius Caesar.   8. Aeneas.

before you there, suffers no man to pass.
  She tracks down all, kills all, and knows no glut,
  but, feeding, she grows hungrier than she was.
  She mates with any beast, and will mate with more
  before the Greyhound[9] comes to hunt her down.   95
  He will not feed on lands nor loot, but honor
and love and wisdom will make straight his way.
  He will rise between Feltro and Feltro, and in him
  shall be the resurrection and new day
of that sad Italy for which Nisus died,   100
  and Turnus, and Euryalus, and the maid Camilla.[1]
  He shall hunt her through every nation of sick pride
till she is driven back forever to Hell
  whence Envy first released her on the world.
  Therefore, for your own good, I think it well   105
you follow me and I will be your guide
  and lead you forth through an eternal place.
  There you shall see the ancient spirits tried
in endless pain, and hear their lamentation
  as each bemoans the second death[2] of souls.   110
  Next you shall see upon a burning mountain
souls in fire and yet content in fire,
  knowing that whensoever it may be
  they yet will mount into the blessed choir.
To which, if it is still your wish to climb,   115
  a worthier spirit shall be sent to guide you.
  With her shall I leave you, for the King of Time,
who reigns on high, forbids me to come there
  since, living, I rebelled against his law.[3]
  He rules the waters and the land and air   120
and there holds court, his city and his throne.
  Oh blessed are they he chooses!" And I to him:
  "Poet, by that God to you unknown,
lead me this way. Beyond this present ill
  and worse to dread, lead me to Peter's gate[4]   125

9. Almost certainly refers to Can Grande della Scala (1290–1329), great Italian leader born in Verona, which lies between the towns of Feltre and Montefeltro.   1. All were killed in the war between the Trojans and the Latians when, according to legend, Aeneas led the survivors of Troy into Italy. Nisus and Euryalus (*Aeneid* IX) were Trojan comrades-in-arms who died together. Camilla (*Aeneid* XI) was the daughter of the Latian king and one of the warrior women. She was killed in a horse charge against the Trojans after displaying great gallantry. Turnus (*Aeneid* XII) was killed by Aeneas in a duel.   2. Damnation. "This is the second death, even the lake of fire." (Revelation 20:14)   3. Salvation is only through Christ in Dante's theology. Virgil lived and died before the establishment of Christ's teachings in Rome, and cannot therefore enter Heaven.   4. The gate of Purgatory. (See *Purgatorio* IX. 76ff.) The gate is guarded by an angel with a gleaming sword. The angel is Peter's vicar (Peter, the first Pope, symbolized all Popes; i.e., Christ's vicar on earth) and is entrusted with the two great keys. Some commentators argue that this is the gate of Paradise, but Dante mentions no gate beyond this one in his ascent to Heaven. It should be remembered, too, that those who pass the gate of Purgatory have effectively entered Heaven.

and be my guide through the sad halls of Hell."
And he then: "Follow." And he moved ahead
in silence, and I followed where he led.

CANTO II

The Descent

It is evening of the first day (Friday). Dante is following Virgil and finds himself tired and despairing. How can he be worthy of such a vision as Virgil has described? He hesitates and seems about to abandon his first purpose.

To comfort him Virgil explains how Beatrice descended to him in Limbo and told him of her concern for Dante. It is she, the symbol of Divine Love, who sends Virgil to lead Dante from error. She has come into Hell itself on this errand, for Dante cannot come to Divine Love unaided; Reason must lead him. Moreover Beatrice has been sent with the prayers of the Virgin Mary (Compassion), and of Saint Lucia (Divine Light). Rachel (the Contemplative Life) also figures in the heavenly scene which Virgil recounts.

Virgil explains all this and reproaches Dante: how can he hesitate longer when such heavenly powers are concerned for him, and Virgil himself has promised to lead him safely?

Dante understands at once that such forces cannot fail him, and his spirits rise in joyous anticipation.

The light was departing. The brown air drew down
  all the earth's creatures, calling them to rest
  from their day-roving, as I, one man alone,
prepared myself to face the double war
  of the journey and the pity, which memory   5
  shall here set down, nor hesitate, nor err.
O Muses! O High Genius! Be my aid!
  O Memory, recorder of the vision,
  here shall your true nobility be displayed!
Thus I began: "Poet, you who must guide me,   10
  before you trust me to that arduous passage,
  look to me and look through me—can I be worthy?
You sang how the father of Sylvius,[5] while still

5. Aeneas. Lines 13–30 are a fair example of the way in which Dante absorbed pagan themes into his Catholicism. According to Virgil, Aeneas is the son of mortal Anchises and of Venus. Venus, in her son's interest, secures a prophecy and a promise from Jove to the effect that Aeneas is to found a royal line that shall rule the world. After the burning of Troy, Aeneas is directed by various signs to sail for the Latian lands (Italy) where his destiny awaits him. After many misadventures, he is compelled (like Dante) to descend to the underworld of the dead. There he finds his father's shade, and there he is shown the shades of the great kings that are to stem from him (Aeneid VI. 921ff.). Among them are Romulus, Julius Caesar, and Augustus Caesar. The full glory of the Roman Empire is also foreshadowed to him. Dante, however, continues the Virgilian theme and includes in the predestination not only the Roman Empire but the

in corruptible flesh won to that other world,
crossing with mortal sense the immortal sill.   15
But if the Adversary of all Evil
weighing his consequence and who and what
should issue from him, treated him so well—
that cannot seem unfitting to thinking men,
since he was chosen father of Mother Rome   20
and of her Empire by God's will and token.
Both, to speak strictly, were founded and foreknown
as the established Seat of Holiness
for the successors of Great Peter's throne.
In that quest, which your verses celebrate,   25
he learned those mysteries from which arose
his victory and Rome's apostolate.
There later came the chosen vessel, Paul,
bearing the confirmation of that Faith
which is the one true door to life eternal.   30
But I—how should I dare? By whose permission?
I am not Aeneas. I am not Paul.
Who could believe me worthy of the vision?
How, then, may I presume to this high quest
and not fear my own brashness? You are wise   35
and will grasp what my poor words can but suggest."
As one who unwills what he wills, will stay
strong purposes with feeble second thoughts
until he spells all his first zeal away—
so I hung back and balked on that dim coast   40
till thinking had worn out my enterprise,
so stout at starting and so early lost.
"I understand from your words and the look in your eyes,"
that shadow of magnificence answered me,
"your soul is sunken in that cowardice   45
that bears down many men, turning their course
and resolution by imagined perils,
as his own shadow turns the frightened horse.
To free you of this dread I will tell you all
of why I came to you and what I heard   50
when first I pitied you. I was a soul
among the souls of Limbo,[6] when a Lady
so blessed and so beautiful, I prayed her
to order and command my will, called to me.
Her eyes were kindled from the lamps of Heaven.   55
Her voice reached through me, tender, sweet, and low.

Holy Roman Empire and its Church. Thus what Virgil presented as an arrangement of Jove, a concession
to the son of Venus, becomes part of the divine scheme of the Catholic God, and Aeneas is cast as a direct
forerunner of Peter and Paul.   6. See Canto IV, lines 31–45, where Virgil explains his state in Hell.

An angel's voice, a music of its own:
'O gracious Mantuan whose melodies
   live in earth's memory and shall live on
   till the last motion ceases in the skies,   60
my dearest friend, and fortune's foe, has strayed
   onto a friendless shore and stands beset
   by such distresses that he turns afraid
from the True Way, and news of him in Heaven
   rumors my dread he is already lost.   65
   I come, afraid that I am too-late risen.
Fly to him and with your high counsel, pity,
   and with whatever need be for his good
   and soul's salvation, help him, and solace me.
It is I, Beatrice, who send you to him.   70
   I come from the blessed height for which I yearn.
   Love called me here. When amid Seraphim
I stand again before my Lord, your praises
   shall sound in Heaven.' She paused, and I began:
   'O Lady of that only grace that raises   75
feeble mankind within its mortal cycle
   above all other works God's will has placed
   within the heaven of the smallest circle;[7]
so welcome is your command that to my sense,
   were it already fulfilled, it would yet seem tardy.   80
   I understand, and am all obedience.
But tell me how you dare to venture thus
   so far from the wide heaven of your joy
   to which your thoughts yearn back from this abyss.'
'Since what you ask,' she answered me, 'probes near   85
   the root of all, I will say briefly only
   how I have come through Hell's pit without fear.
Know then, O waiting and compassionate soul,
   that is to fear which has the power to harm,
   and nothing else is fearful even in Hell.   90
I am so made by God's all-seeing mercy
   your anguish does not touch me, and the flame
   of this great burning has no power upon me.
There is a Lady in Heaven so concerned
   for him I send you to, that for her sake   95

7. The moon. "Heaven" here is used in its astronomical sense. All within that circle is the earth. According to the Ptolemaic system the earth was the center of creation and was surrounded by nine heavenly spheres (nine heavens) concentrically placed around it. The moon was the first of these, and therefore the smallest. A cross section of this universe could be represented by drawing nine concentric circles (at varying distances about the earth as a center). Going outward from the center these circles would indicate, in order, the spheres of: the Moon, Mercury, Venus, the Sun, Mars, Jupiter, Saturn, the Fixed Stars, and the Primum Mobile. Beyond the Primum Mobile lies the Empyrean. (See diagram on p. 284.)

the strict decree is broken. She has turned
and called Lucia[8] to her wish and mercy
saying: 'Thy faithful one is sorely pressed;
in his distresses I commend him to thee.'
Lucia, that soul of light and foe of all   100
cruelty, rose and came to me at once
where I was sitting with the ancient Rachel,[9]
saying to me: 'Beatrice, true praise of God,
why dost thou not help him who loved thee so
that for thy sake he left the vulgar crowd?   105
Dost thou not hear his cries? Canst thou not see
the death he wrestles with beside that river
no ocean can surpass for rage and fury?'
No soul of earth was ever as rapt to seek
its good or flee its injury as I was—   110
when I had heard my sweet Lucia speak—
to descend from Heaven and my blessed seat
to you, laying my trust in that high speech
that honors you and all who honor it.'
She spoke and turned away to hide a tear   115
that, shining, urged me faster. So I came
and freed you from the beast that drove you there,
blocking the near way to the Heavenly Height.
And now what ails you? Why do you lag? Why
this heartsick hesitation and pale fright   120
when three such blessed Ladies lean from Heaven
in their concern for you and my own pledge
of the great good that waits you has been given?"
As flowerlets drooped and puckered in the night
turn up to the returning sun and spread   125
their petals wide on his new warmth and light—
just so my wilted spirits rose again
and such a heat of zeal surged through my veins
that I was born anew. Thus I began:
"Blessèd be that Lady of infinite pity,   130
and blessèd be thy taxed and courteous spirit
that came so promptly on the word she gave thee.
Thy words have moved my heart to its first purpose.
My Guide! My Lord! My Master! Now lead on:
one will shall serve the two of us in this."   135
He turned when I had spoken, and at his back
I entered on that hard and perilous track.

8. Allegorically she represents Divine Light. Her name in Italian inevitably suggests *luce* (light), and she is the patron saint of eyesight.   9. Represents the Contemplative Life.

CANTO III

The Vestibule of Hell   The Opportunists

   The Poets pass the Gate of Hell and are immediately assailed by cries of
anguish. Dante sees the first of the souls in torment. They are the Opportunists, those souls who in life were neither for good nor evil but only for
themselves. Mixed with them are those outcasts who took no sides in the
Rebellion of the Angels. They are neither in Hell nor out of it. Eternally
unclassified, they race round and round pursuing a wavering banner that
runs forever before them through the dirty air; and as they run they are
pursued by swarms of wasps and hornets, who sting them and produce a
constant flow of blood and putrid matter which trickles down the bodies of
the sinners and is feasted upon by loathsome worms and maggots who coat
the ground.
   The law of Dante's Hell is the law of symbolic retribution. As they
sinned so are they punished. They took no sides, therefore they are given
no place. As they pursued the ever-shifting illusion of their own advantage,
changing their courses with every changing wind, so they pursue eternally
an elusive, ever-shifting banner. As their sin was a darkness, so they move
in darkness. As their own guilty conscience pursued them, so they are
pursued by swarms of wasps and hornets. And as their actions were a moral
filth, so they run eternally through the filth of worms and maggots which
they themselves feed.
   Dante recognizes several, among them Pope Celestine V, but without
delaying to speak to any of these souls, the Poets move on to Acheron, the
first of the rivers of Hell. Here the newly-arrived souls of the damned
gather and wait for monstrous Charon to ferry them over to punishment.
Charon recognizes Dante as a living man and angrily refuses him passage.
Virgil forces Charon to serve them, but Dante swoons with terror, and
does not reawaken until he is on the other side.

I AM THE WAY INTO THE CITY OF WOE.
   I AM THE WAY TO A FORSAKEN PEOPLE.
   I AM THE WAY INTO ETERNAL SORROW.
SACRED JUSTICE MOVED MY ARCHITECT.
   I WAS RAISED HERE BY DIVINE OMNIPOTENCE,   5
   PRIMORDIAL LOVE AND ULTIMATE INTELLECT.
ONLY THOSE ELEMENTS TIME CANNOT WEAR[1]
   WERE MADE BEFORE ME, AND BEYOND TIME I STAND.[2]
   ABANDON ALL HOPE YE WHO ENTER HERE.[3]
These mysteries I read cut into stone   10

---

1. The Angels, the Empyrean, and the First Matter are the elements time cannot wear, for they will last
to all time. Man, however, in his mortal state, is not eternal. The Gate of Hell, therefore, was created
before man.   2. So odious is sin to God that there can be no end to its just punishment.   3. The
admonition, of course, is to the damned and not to those who come on Heaven-sent errands.

above a gate. And turning I said: "Master,
  what is the meaning of this harsh inscription?"
And he then as initiate to novice:
  "Here must you put by all division of spirit
  and gather your soul against all cowardice.   15
This is the place I told you to expect.
  Here you shall pass among the fallen people,
  souls who have lost the good of intellect."
So saying, he put forth his hand to me,
  and with a gentle and encouraging smile   20
  he led me through the gate of mystery.
Here sighs and cries and wails coiled and recoiled
  on the starless air, spilling my soul to tears.
  A confusion of tongues and monstrous accents toiled
in pain and anger. Voices hoarse and shrill   25
  and sounds of blows, all intermingled, raised
  tumult and pandemonium that still
whirls on the air forever dirty with it
  as if a whirlwind sucked at sand. And I,
  holding my head in horror, cried: "Sweet Spirit,   30
what souls are these who run through this black haze?"
  And he to me: "These are the nearly soulless
  whose lives concluded neither blame nor praise.
They are mixed here with that despicable corps
  of angels who were neither for God nor Satan,   35
  but only for themselves. The High Creator
scourged them from Heaven for its perfect beauty,
  and Hell will not receive them since the wicked
  might feel some glory over them." And I:
"Master, what gnaws at them so hideously   40
  their lamentation stuns the very air?"
  "They have no hope of death," he answered me,
"and in their blind and unattaining state
  their miserable lives have sunk so low
  that they must envy every other fate.   45
No word of them survives their living season.
  Mercy and Justice deny them even a name.
  Let us not speak of them: look, and pass on."
I saw a banner there upon the mist.
  Circling and circling, it seemed to scorn all pause.   50
  So it ran on, and still behind it pressed
a never-ending rout of souls in pain.
  I had not thought death had undone so many
  as passed before me in that mournful train.
And some I knew among them; last of all   55
  I recognized the shadow of that soul

who, in his cowardice, made the Great Denial.[4]
At once I understood for certain: these
  were of that retrograde and faithless crew
  hateful to God and to His enemies.   60
These wretches never born and never dead
  ran naked in a swarm of wasps and hornets
  that goaded them the more the more they fled,
and made their faces stream with bloody gouts
  of pus and tears that dribbled to their feet   65
  to be swallowed there by loathsome worms and maggots.
Then looking onward I made out a throng
  assembled on the beach of a wide river,
  whereupon I turned to him: "Master, I long
to know what souls these are, and what strange usage   70
  makes them as eager to cross as they seem to be
  in this infected light." At which the Sage:
"All this shall be made known to you when we stand
  on the joyless beach of Acheron." And I
  cast down my eyes, sensing a reprimand   75
in what he said, and so walked at his side
  in silence and ashamed until we came
  through the dead cavern to that sunless tide.
There, steering toward us in an ancient ferry
  came an old man[5] with a white bush of hair,   80
  bellowing: "Woe to you depraved souls! Bury
here and forever all hope of Paradise:
  I come to lead you to the other shore,
  into eternal dark, into fire and ice.
And you who are living yet, I say begone   85
  from these who are dead." But when he saw me stand
  against his violence he began again:
"By other windings and by other steerage
  shall you cross to that other shore. Not here! Not here!
  A lighter craft than mine must give you passage."[6]   90
And my Guide to him: "Charon, bite back your spleen:
  this has been willed where what is willed must be,
  and is not yours to ask what it may mean."

---

4. This is almost certainly intended to be Celestine V, who became Pope in 1294. He was a man of saintly life, but allowed himself to be convinced by a priest named Benedetto that his soul was in danger since no man could live in the world without being damned. In fear for his soul he withdrew from all worldly affairs and renounced the papacy. Benedetto promptly assumed the mantle himself and became Boniface VIII, a Pope who became for Dante a symbol of all the worst corruptions of the church. Dante also blamed Boniface and his intrigues for many of the evils that befell Florence. We shall learn in Canto XIX that the fires of Hell are waiting for Boniface in the pit of the Simoniacs, and we shall be given further evidence of his corruption in Canto XXVII. Celestine's great guilt is that his cowardice (in selfish terror for his own welfare) served as the door through which so much evil entered the church.   5. Charon. He is the ferryman of dead souls across the Acheron in all classical mythology.   6. Charon recognizes Dante not only as a living man but as a soul in grace, and knows, therefore, that the Internal Ferry was not intended for him. He is probably referring to the fact that souls destined for Purgatory and Heaven assemble not at his ferry point, but on the banks of the Tiber, from which they are transported by an Angel.

The steersman of that marsh of ruined souls,
  who wore a wheel of flame around each eye,   95
  stifled the rage that shook his woolly jowls.
But those unmanned and naked spirits there
  turned pale with fear and their teeth began to chatter
  at sound of his crude bellow. In despair
they blasphemed God,[7] their parents, their time on earth,   100
  the race of Adam, and the day and the hour
  and the place and the seed and the womb that gave them birth.
But all together they drew to that grim shore
  where all must come who lose the fear of God.
  Weeping and cursing they come for evermore,   105
and demon Charon with eyes like burning coals
  herds them in, and with a whistling oar
  flails on the stragglers to his wake of souls.
As leaves in autumn loosen and stream down
  until the branch stands bare above its tatters   110
  spread on the rustling ground, so one by one
the evil seed of Adam in its Fall
  cast themselves, at his signal, from the shore
  and streamed away like birds who hear their call.
So they are gone over that shadowy water,   115
  and always before they reach the other shore
  a new noise stirs on this, and new throngs gather.
"My son," the courteous Master said to me,
  "all who die in the shadow of God's wrath
  converge to this from every clime and country.   120
And all pass over eagerly, for here
  Divine Justice transforms and spurs them so
  their dread turns wish: they yearn for what they fear.[8]
No soul in Grace comes ever to this crossing;
  therefore if Charon rages at your presence   125
  you will understand the reason for his cursing."
When he had spoken, all the twilight country
  shook so violently, the terror of it
  bathes me with sweat even in memory:
the tear-soaked ground gave out a sigh of wind   130
  that spewed itself in flame on a red sky,
  and all my shuttered senses left me. Blind,
like one whom sleep comes over in a swoon,
I stumbled into darkness and went down.[9]

---

7. The souls of the damned are not permitted to repent, for repentance is a divine grace.   8. Hell
(allegorically Sin) is what the souls of the damned really wish for. Hell is their actual and deliberate choice,
for divine grace is denied to none who wish for it in their hearts. The damned must, in fact, deliberately
harden their hearts to God in order to become damned. Christ's grace is sufficient to save all who wish for
it.   9. This device (repeated at the end of Canto V) serves a double purpose. The first is technical: Dante
uses it to cover a transition. We are never told how he crossed Acheron, for that would involve certain
narrative matters he can better deal with when he crosses Styx in Canto VII. The second is to provide a
point of departure for a theme that is carried through the entire descent: the theme of Dante's emotional

CANTO IV

Circle One: Limbo   The Virtuous Pagans

Dante wakes to find himself across Acheron. The Poets are now on the
brink of Hell itself, which Dante conceives as a great funnel-shaped cave
lying below the northern hemisphere with its bottom point at the earth's
center. Around this great circular depression runs a series of ledges, each
of which Dante calls a Circle. Each circle is assigned to the punishment
of one category of sin.

As soon as Dante's strength returns, the Poets begin to cross the First
Circle. Here they find the Virtuous Pagans. They were born without the
light of Christ's revelation, and, therefore, they cannot come into the light
of God, but they are not tormented. Their only pain is that they have no
hope.

Ahead of them Dante sights a great dome of light, and a voice trumpets
through the darkness welcoming Virgil back, for this is his eternal place in
Hell. Immediately the great Poets of all time appear—Homer, Horace,
Ovid, and Lucan. They greet Virgil, and they make Dante a sixth in their
company.

With them Dante enters the Citadel of Human Reason and sees before
his eyes the Master Souls of Pagan Antiquity gathered on a green, and
illuminated by the radiance of Human Reason. This is the highest state
man can achieve without God, and the glory of it dazzles Dante, but he
knows also that it is nothing compared to the glory of God.

A monstrous clap of thunder broke apart
   the swoon that stuffed my head; like one awakened
   by violent hands, I leaped up with a start.
And having risen; rested and renewed,
   I studied out the landmarks of the gloom   5
   to find my bearings there as best I could.
And I found I stood on the very brink of the valley
   called the Dolorous Abyss, the desolate chasm
   where rolls the thunder of Hell's eternal cry,
so depthless-deep and nebulous and dim   10
   that stare as I might into its frightful pit
   it gave me back no feature and no bottom.
Death-pale,[1] the Poet spoke: "Now let us go
   into the blind world waiting here below us.
   I will lead the way and you shall follow."   15
And I, sick with alarm at his new pallor,
   cried out, "How can I go this way when you

reaction to Hell. These two swoons early in the descent show him most susceptible to the grief about him.
As he descends, pity leaves him, and he even goes so far as to add to the torments of one sinner. The
allegory is clear: we must harden ourselves against every sympathy for sin. 1. Virgil is most likely
affected here by the return to his own place in Hell. "The pain of these below" then (l. 19) would be the
pain of his own group in Limbo (the Virtuous Pagans) rather than the total of Hell's suffering.

who are my strength in doubt turn pale with terror?"
And he: "The pain of these below us here,
　drains the color from my face for pity,   20
　and leaves this pallor you mistake for fear.
Now let us go, for a long road awaits us."
　So he entered and so he led me in
　to the first circle and ledge of the abyss.
No tortured wailing rose to greet us here   25
　but sounds of sighing rose from every side,
　sending a tremor through the timeless air,
a grief breathed out of untormented sadness,
　the passive state of those who dwelled apart,
　men, women, children—a dim and endless congress.   30
And the Master said to me: "You do not question
　what souls these are that suffer here before you?
　I wish you to know before you travel on
that these were sinless. And still their merits fail,
　for they lacked Baptism's grace, which is the door   35
　of the true faith *you* were born to. Their birth fell
before the age of the Christian mysteries,
　and so they did not worship God's Trinity
　in fullest duty. I am one of these.
For such defects are we lost, though spared the fire   40
　and suffering Hell in one affliction only:
　that without hope we live on in desire."
I thought how many worthy souls there were
　suspended in that Limbo, and a weight
　closed on my heart for what the noblest suffer.   45
"Instruct me, Master and most noble Sir,"
　I prayed him then, "better to understand
　the perfect creed that conquers every error:
has any, by his own or another's merit,
　gone ever from this place to blessedness?"   50
　He sensed my inner question and answered it:
"I was still new to this estate of tears
　when a Mighty One[2] descended here among us,
　crowned with the sign of His victorious years.
He took from us the shade of our first parent,[3]   55
　of Abel, his pure son, of ancient Noah,
　of Moses, the bringer of law, the obedient.
Father Abraham, David the King,
　Israel[4] with his father and his children,
　Rachel,[5] the holy vessel of His blessing,   60

2. Christ. His name is never directly uttered in Hell. *Descended here:* The legend of the Harrowing of Hell is apocryphal. It is based on I Peter 3:19: "He went and preached unto the spirits in prison." The legend is that Christ in the glory of His resurrection descended into Limbo and took with Him to Heaven the first human souls to be saved. The event would, accordingly, have occurred in A.D. 33 or 34. Virgil died in 19 B.C.   3. Adam.   4. Another name for Jacob; his father was Isaac.   5. Wife of Jacob.

and many more He chose for elevation
   among the elect. And before these, you must know,
   no human soul had ever won salvation."
We had not paused as he spoke, but held our road
   and passed meanwhile beyond a press of souls   65
   crowded about like trees in a thick wood.
And we had not traveled far from where I woke
   when I made out a radiance before us
   that struck away a hemisphere of dark.
We were still some distance back in the long night,   70
   yet near enough that I half-saw, half-sensed,
   what quality of souls lived in that light.
"O ornament of wisdom and of art,
   what souls are these whose merit lights their way
   even in Hell. What joy sets them apart?"   75
And he to me: "The signature of honor
   they left on earth is recognized in Heaven
   and wins them ease in Hell out of God's favor."
And as he spoke a voice rang on the air:
   "Honor the Prince of Poets; the soul and glory   80
   that went from us returns. He is here! He is here!"
The cry ceased and the echo passed from hearing;
   I saw four mighty presences come toward us
   with neither joy nor sorrow in their bearing.
"Note well," my Master said as they came on,   85
   "that soul that leads the rest with sword in hand
   as if he were their captain and champion.
It is Homer, singing master of the earth.
   Next after him is Horace, the satirist,
   Ovid is third, and Lucan is the fourth.   90
Since all of these have part in the high name
   the voice proclaimed, calling me Prince of Poets,
   the honor that they do me honors them."
So I saw gathered at the edge of light
   the masters of that highest school whose song   95
   outsoars all others like an eagle's flight.
And after they had talked together a while,
   they turned and welcomed me most graciously,
   at which I saw my approving Master smile.
And they honored me far beyond courtesy,   100
   for they included me in their own number,
   making me sixth in that high company.
So we moved toward the light, and as we passed
   we spoke of things as well omitted here
   as it was sweet to touch on there. At last   105
we reached the base of a great Citadel
   circled by seven towering battlements

and by a sweet brook flowing round them all.[6]
This we passed over as if it were firm ground.[7]
Through seven gates I entered with those sages   110
and came to a green meadow blooming round.
There with a solemn and majestic poise
stood many people gathered in the light,
speaking infrequently and with muted voice.
Past that enameled green we six withdrew   115
into a luminous and open height
from which each soul among them stood in view.
And there directly before me on the green
the master souls of time were shown to me.
I glory in the glory I have seen![8]   120
Electra stood in a great company
among whom I saw Hector and Aeneas
and Caesar in armor with his falcon's eye.
I saw Camilla, and the Queen Amazon
across the field. I saw the Latian King   125
seated there with his daughter by his throne.
And the good Brutus who overthrew the Tarquin:
Lucrezia, Julia, Marcia, and Cornelia;
and, by himself apart, the Saladin.
And raising my eyes a little I saw on high   130
Aristotle, the master of those who know,

6. The most likely allegory is that the Citadel represents philosophy (that is, human reason without the light of God) surrounded by seven walls that represent the seven liberal arts, or the seven sciences, or the seven virtues. Note that Human Reason makes a light of its own, but that it is a light in darkness and forever separated from the glory of God's light. The *sweet brook flowing* round them all has been interpreted in many ways. Clearly fundamental, however, is the fact that it divides those in the Citadel (those who wish to know) from those in the outer darkness.   7. Since Dante still has his body, and since all others in Hell are incorporeal shades, there is a recurring narrative problem in the *Inferno* (and through the rest of the *Commedia*): how does flesh act in contact with spirit? In the *Purgatorio* Dante attempts to embrace the spirit of Casella and his arms pass through him as if he were empty air. In the Third Circle, below (Canto VI. 34–36), Dante steps on some of the spirits lying in the slush and his foot passes right through them. (The original lines offer several possible readings of which I have preferred this one.) And at other times Virgil, also a spirit, picks Dante up and carries him bodily. It is clear, too, that Dante means the spirits of Hell to be weightless. When Virgil steps into Phlegyas' bark (Canto VIII) it does not settle into the water, but it does when Dante's living body steps aboard. There is no narrative reason why Dante should not sink into the waters of this stream and Dante follows no fixed rule in dealing with such phenomena, often suiting the physical action to the allegorical need. Here, the moat probably symbolizes some requirement (The Will to Know) which he and the other poets meet without difficulty.   8. The inhabitants of the citadel fall into three main groups: 1. *The heroes and heroines:* All of these it must be noted were associated with the Trojans and their Roman descendants. The Electra Dante mentions here is not the sister of Orestes (see Euripides' *Electra*) but the daughter of Atlas and the mother of Dardanus, the founder of Troy. 2. *The philosophers:* Most of this group is made up of philosophers whose teachings were, at least in part, acceptable to church scholarship. Democritus, however, "who ascribed the world to chance," would clearly be an exception. The group is best interpreted, therefore, as representing the highest achievements of Human Reason unaided by Divine Love. *Plato and Aristotle:* Through a considerable part of the Middle Ages Plato was held to be the fountainhead of all scholarship, but in Dante's time practically all learning was based on Aristotelian theory as interpreted through the many commentaries. *Linus:* the Italian is "Lino" and for it some commentators read "Livio" (Livy). 3. *The naturalists:* They are less well known today. In Dante's time their place in scholarship more or less corresponded to the role of the theoretician and historian of science in our universities. Avicenna (his major work was in the eleventh century) and Averrhoës (twelfth century) were Arabian philosophers and physicians especially famous in Dante's time for their commentaries on Aristotle. *Great Commentary:* has the force of a title, i.e., The Great Commentary as distinguished from many lesser commentaries. *The Saladin:* This is the famous Saladin who was defeated by Richard the Lion-Heart, and whose great qualities as a ruler became a legend in medieval Europe.

ringed by the great souls of philosophy.
All wait upon him for their honor and his.
I saw Socrates and Plato at his side
before all others there. Democritus   135
who ascribes the world to chance, Diogenes,
and with him there Thales, Anaxagoras,
Zeno, Heraclitus, Empedocles.
And I saw the wise collector and analyst—
Dioscorides I mean. I saw Orpheus there,   140
Tully, Linus, Seneca the moralist,
Euclid the geometer, and Ptolemy,
Hippocrates, Galen, Avicenna,
and Averrhoës of the Great Commentary.
I cannot count so much nobility;   145
my longer theme pursues me so that often
the word falls short of the reality.
The company of six is reduced by four.
My Master leads me by another road
out of that serenity to the roar   150
and trembling air of Hell. I pass from light
into the kingdom of eternal night.

CANTO V

Circle Two   The Carnal

   The Poets leave Limbo and enter the Second Circle. Here begin the
torments of Hell proper, and here, blocking the way, sits Minos, the dread
and semi-bestial judge of the damned who assigns to each soul its eternal
torment. He orders the Poets back; but Virgil silences him as he earlier
silenced Charon, and the Poets move on.
   They find themselves on a dark ledge swept by a great whirlwind, which
spins within it the souls of the Carnal, those who betrayed reason to their
appetites. Their sin was to abandon themselves to the tempest of their
passions: so they are swept forever in the tempest of Hell, forever denied
the light of reason and of God. Virgil identifies many among them. Semiramis is there, and Dido, Cleopatra, Helen, Achilles, Paris, and Tristan.
Dante sees Paolo and Francesca swept together, and in the name of love
he calls to them to tell their sad story. They pause from their eternal flight
to come to him, and Francesca tells their history while Paolo weeps at her
side. Dante is so stricken by compassion at their tragic tale that he swoons
once again.

So we went down to the second ledge alone;
   a smaller circle[9] of so much greater pain
   the voice of the damned rose in a bestial moan.

---

9. The pit of Hell tapers like a funnel. The circles of ledges accordingly grow smaller as they descend.

There Minos[1] sits, grinning, grotesque, and hale.
He examines each lost soul as it arrives   5
and delivers his verdict with his coiling tail.
That is to say, when the ill-fated soul
appears before him it confesses all,
and that grim sorter of the dark and foul
decides which place in Hell shall be its end,   10
then wraps his twitching tail about himself
one coil for each degree it must descend.
The soul descends and others take its place:
each crowds in its turn to judgment, each confesses,
each hears its doom and falls away through space.   15
"O you who come into this camp of woe,"
cried Minos when he saw me turn away
without awaiting his judgment, "watch where you go
once you have entered here, and to whom you turn!
Do not be misled by that wide and easy passage!"   20
And my Guide to him: "That is not your concern;
it is his fate to enter every door.
This has been willed where what is willed must be,
and is not yours to question. Say no more."
Now the choir of anguish, like a wound,   25
strikes through the tortured air. Now I have come
to Hell's full lamentation, sound beyond sound.
I came to a place stripped bare of every light
and roaring on the naked dark like seas
wracked by a war of winds. Their hellish flight   30
of storm and counterstorm through time foregone,
sweeps the souls of the damned before its charge.
Whirling and battering it drives them on,
and when they pass the ruined gap of Hell[2]
through which we had come, their shrieks begin anew.   35
There they blaspheme the power of God eternal.
And this, I learned, was the never ending flight
of those who sinned in the flesh, the carnal and lusty
who betrayed reason to their appetite.
As the wings of wintering starlings bear them on   40
in their great wheeling flights, just so the blast
wherries these evil souls through time foregone.

1. The son of Europa and of Zeus who descended to her in the form of a bull. Minos became a mythological king of Crete, so famous for his wisdom and justice that after death his soul was made judge of
the dead. Virgil presents him fulfilling the same office at Aeneas's descent to the underworld. Dante,
however, transforms him into an irate and hideous monster with a tail. The transformation may have been
suggested by the form Zeus assumed for the rape of Europa—the monster is certainly bullish enough
here—but the obvious purpose of the brutalization is to present a figure symbolic of the guilty conscience
of the wretches who come before it to make their confessions.   2. See note to Canto IV. 53. At the time
of the Harrowing of Hell a great earthquake shook the underworld, shattering rocks and cliffs. Ruins
resulting from the same shock are noted in Canto XII. 34, and Canto XXI. 112ff. At the beginning of
Canto XXIV, the Poets leave the bolgia of the Hypocrites by climbing the ruined slabs of a bridge that was
shattered by this earthquake.

Here, there, up, down, they whirl and, whirling, strain
  with never a hope of hope to comfort them,
  not of release, but even of less pain.   45
As cranes go over sounding their harsh cry,
  leaving the long streak of their flight in air,
  so come these spirits, wailing as they fly.
And watching their shadows lashed by wind, I cried:
  "Master, what souls are these the very air   50
  lashes with its black whips from side to side?"
"The first of these whose history you would know,"
  he answered me, "was Empress of many tongues.[3]
  Mad sensuality corrupted her so
that to hide the guilt of her debauchery   55
  she licensed all depravity alike,
  and lust and law were one in her decree.
She is Semiramis of whom the tale is told
  how she married Ninus and succeeded him
  to the throne of that wide land the Sultans hold.   60
The other is Dido;[4] faithless to the ashes
  of Sichaeus, she killed herself for love.
The next whom the eternal tempest lashes
is sense-drugged Cleopatra. See Helen[5] there,
  from whom such ill arose. And great Achilles,[6]   65
  who fought at last with love in the house of prayer.
And Paris. And Tristan." As they whirled above
  he pointed out more than a thousand shades
  of those torn from the mortal life by love.
I stood there while my Teacher one by one   70
  named the great knights and ladies of dim time;
  and I was swept by pity and confusion.
At last I spoke: "Poet, I should be glad
  to speak a word with those two swept together
  so lightly on the wind and still so sad."[7]   75

3. Semiramis, a legendary queen of Assyria who assumed full power at the death of her husband, Ninus.
4. Queen and founder of Carthage. She had vowed to remain faithful to her husband, Sichaeus, but she fell in love with Aeneas. When Aeneas abandoned her she stabbed herself on a funeral pyre she had had prepared.
    According to Dante's own system of punishments, she should be in the Seventh Circle (Canto XIII) with the suicides. The only clue Dante gives to the tempering of her punishment is his statement that "she killed herself for love." Dante always seems readiest to forgive in that name.   5. She was held responsible for the Trojan War; the wife of King Menelaus of Sparta, she ran away with the visiting prince Paris from Troy.   6. He is placed among this company because of his passion for Polyxena, the daughter of Priam. For love of her, he agreed to desert the Greeks and to join the Trojans, but when he went to the temple for the wedding (according to the legend Dante has followed) he was killed by Paris.   7. Paolo and Francesca. In 1275 Giovanni Malatesta of Rimini, called Giovanni the Lame, a somewhat deformed but brave and powerful warrior, made a political marriage with Francesca, daughter of Guido da Polenta of Ravenna. Francesca came to Rimini and there an amour grew between her and Giovanni's younger brother Paolo. Despite the fact that Paolo had married in 1269 and had become the father of two daughters by 1275, his affair with Francesca continued for many years. It was sometime between 1283 and 1286 that Giovanni surprised them in Francesca's bedroom and killed both of them. Around these facts the legend has grown that Paolo was sent by Giovanni as his proxy to the marriage, that Francesca thought he was her real bridegroom and accordingly gave him her heart irrevocably at first sight. The legend obviously increases the pathos, but nothing in Dante gives it support.

And he to me: "Watch them. When next they pass,
     call to them in the name of love that drives
     and damns them here. In that name they will pause."
Thus, as soon as the wind in its wild course
     brought them around, I called: "O wearied souls!   80
     if none forbid it, pause and speak to us."
As mating doves that love calls to their nest
     glide through the air with motionless raised wings,
     borne by the sweet desire that fills each breast—
Just so those spirits turned on the torn sky   85
     from the band where Dido whirls across the air;
     such was the power of pity in my cry.
"O living creature, gracious, kind, and good,
     going this pilgrimage through the sick night,
     visiting us who stained the earth with blood,   90
were the King of Time our friend, we would pray His peace
     on you who have pitied us. As long as the wind
     will let us pause, ask of us what you please.
The town where I was born lies by the shore
     where the Po descends into its ocean rest   95
     with its attendant streams in one long murmur.
Love, which in gentlest hearts will soonest bloom
     seized my lover with passion for that sweet body
     from which I was torn unshriven to my doom.
Love, which permits no loved one not to love,   100
     took me so strongly with delight in him
     that we are one in Hell, as we were above.⁸
Love led us to one death. In the depths of Hell
     Caïna waits for him⁹ who took our lives."
     This was the piteous tale they stopped to tell.   105
And when I had heard those world-offended lovers
     I bowed my head. At last the Poet spoke:
     "What painful thoughts are these your lowered brow covers?"
When at length I answered, I began: "Alas!
     What sweetest thoughts, what green and young desire   110
     led these two lovers to this sorry pass."
Then turning to those spirits once again,
     I said: "Francesca, what you suffer here
     melts me to tears of pity and of pain.
But tell me: in the time of your sweet sighs   115
     by what appearances found love the way

---

8. At many points of the *Inferno* Dante makes clear the principle that the souls of the damned are locked so blindly into their own guilt that none can feel sympathy for another, or find any pleasure in the presence of another. The temptation of many readers is to interpret this line romantically: i.e., that the love of Paolo and Francesca survives Hell itself. The more Dantean interpretation, however, is that they add to one another's anguish (a) as mutual reminders of their sin, and (b) as insubstantial shades of the bodies for which they once felt such great passion.   9. Giovanni Malatesta was still alive at the writing. His fate is already decided, however, and upon his death, his soul will fall to Caïna, the first ring of the last circle (Canto XXXII), where lie those who performed acts of treachery against their kin.

to lure you to his perilous paradise?"
And she: "The double grief of a lost bliss
   is to recall its happy hour in pain.
   Your Guide and Teacher knows the truth of this.   120
But if there is indeed a soul in Hell
   to ask of the beginning of our love
   out of his pity, I will weep and tell:
On a day for dalliance we read the rhyme
   of Lancelot,[1] how love had mastered him.   125
   We were alone with innocence and dim time.[2]
Pause after pause that high old story drew
   our eyes together while we blushed and paled;
   but it was one soft passage overthrew
our caution and our hearts. For when we read   130
   how her fond smile was kissed by such a lover,
   he who is one with me alive and dead
breathed on my lips the tremor of his kiss.
   That book, and he who wrote it, was a pander.[3]
   That day we read no further." As she said this,   135
the other spirit, who stood by her, wept
   so piteously, I felt my senses reel
   and faint away with anguish. I was swept
by such a swoon as death is, and I fell,
   as a corpse might fall, to the dead floor of Hell.   140

CANTO VI

Circle Three   The Gluttons

   Dante recovers from his swoon and finds himself in the Third Circle. A
great storm of putrefaction falls incessantly, a mixture of stinking snow and
freezing rain, which forms into a vile slush underfoot. Everything about
this Circle suggests a gigantic garbage dump. The souls of the damned lie
in the icy paste, swollen and obscene, and Cerberus, the ravenous three-
headed dog of Hell, stands guard over them, ripping and tearing them with
his claws and teeth.
   These are the Gluttons. In life they made no higher use of the gifts of
God than to wallow in food and drink, producers of nothing but garbage
and offal. Here they lie through all eternity, themselves like garbage, half-
buried in fetid slush, while Cerberus slavers over them as they in life slav-
ered over their food.
   As the Poets pass, one of the speakers sits up and addresses Dante. He is

---

   1. The story of Lancelot and Guinevere (of Arthurian legend) exists in many forms. The details Dante
makes use of are from an Old French version.   2. The original simply reads "We were alone, suspecting
nothing." "Dim time" is rhyme-forced, but not wholly outside the legitimate implications of the original,
I hope. The old courtly romance may well be thought of as happening in the dim ancient days. The
apology, of course, comes after the fact: one does the possible then argues for justification, and there
probably is none.   3. "Galeotto," the Italian word for "pander," is also the Italian rendering of the name
of Gallehault, who in the French Romance Dante refers to here, urged Lancelot and Guinevere on to
love.

Ciacco, the Hog, a citizen of Dante's own Florence. He recognizes Dante and asks eagerly for news of what is happening there. With the foreknowledge of the damned, Ciacco then utters the first of the political prophecies that are to become a recurring theme of the *Inferno*. The poets then move on toward the next Circle, at the edge of which they encounter the monster Plutus.

My senses had reeled from me out of pity
　for the sorrow of those kinsmen and lost lovers.
　Now they return, and waking gradually,
I see new torments and new souls in pain
　about me everywhere. Wherever I turn   5
　away from grief I turn to grief again.
I am in the Third Circle of the torments.
　Here to all time with neither pause nor change
　the frozen rain of Hell descends in torrents.
Huge hailstones, dirty water, and black snow   10
　pour from the dismal air to putrefy
　the putrid slush that waits for them below.
Here monstrous Cerberus,[4] the ravening beast,
　howls through his triple throats like a mad dog
　over the spirits sunk in that foul paste.   15
His eyes are red, his beard is greased with phlegm,
　his belly is swollen, and his hands are claws
　to rip the wretches and flay and mangle them.
And they, too, howl like dogs in the freezing storm,
　turning and turning from it as if they thought   20
　one naked side could keep the other warm.
When Cerberus discovered us in that swill
　his dragon-jaws yawned wide, his lips drew back
　in a grin of fangs. No limb of him was still.
My Guide bent down and seized in either fist   25
　a clod of the stinking dirt that festered there
　and flung them down the gullet of the beast.
As a hungry cur will set the echoes raving
　and then fall still when he is thrown a bone,
　all of his clamor being in his craving,   30
so the three ugly heads of Cerberus,
　whose yowling at those wretches deafened them,
　choked on their putrid sops and stopped their fuss.
We made our way across the sodden mess
　of souls the rain beat down, and when our steps   35
　fell on a body, they sank through emptiness.

4. In classical mythology Cerberus appears as a three-headed dog. His master was Pluto, king of the Underworld. Cerberus was placed at the Gate of the Underworld to allow all to enter, but none to escape. His three heads and his ravenous disposition make him an apt symbol of gluttony. *Like a mad dog*: Dante seems clearly to have visualized him as a half-human monster. The beard (l. 16) suggests that at least one of his three heads is human, and many illuminated manuscripts so represent him.

All those illusions of being seemed to lie
  drowned in the slush; until one wraith among them
  sat up abruptly and called as I passed by:
"O you who are led this journey through the shade 40
  of Hell's abyss, do you recall this face?
  You had been made before I was unmade."[5]
And I: "Perhaps the pain you suffer here
  distorts your image from my recollection.
  I do not know you as you now appear." 45
And he to me: "Your own city, so rife
  with hatred that the bitter cup flows over
  was mine too in that other, clearer life.
Your citizens nicknamed me Ciacco, The Hog:
  gluttony was my offense, and for it 50
  I lie here rotting like a swollen log.
Nor am I lost in this alone; all these
  you see about you in this painful death
  have wallowed in the same indecencies."
I answered him: "Ciacco, your agony 55
  weighs on my heart and calls my soul to tears;
  But tell me, if you can, what is to be
for the citizens of that divided state,
  and whether there are honest men among them,
  and for what reasons we are torn by hate." 60
And he then: "After many words given and taken
  it shall come to blood; White shall rise over Black
  and rout the dark lord's force, battered and shaken.
Then it shall come to pass within three suns
  that the fallen shall arise, and by the power 65
  of one now gripped by many hesitations
Black shall ride on White for many years,
  loading it down with burdens and oppressions
  and humbling of proud names and helpless tears.
Two are honest, but none will heed them. There, 70
  pride, avarice, and envy are the tongues
  men know and heed, a Babel of despair."[6]

5. That is, "you were born before I died." The further implication is that they must have seen one another in Florence, a city one can still walk across in twenty minutes, and around in a very few hours. Dante certainly would have known everyone in Florence. 6. This is the first of the political prophecies that are to become a recurring theme of the *Inferno*. (It is the second if we include the political symbolism of the Greyhound in Canto I.) Dante is, of course, writing after these events have all taken place. At Easter time of 1300, however, the events were in the future.
    The Whites and the Blacks of Ciacco's prophecy should not be confused with the Guelphs and the Ghibellines. The internal strife between the Guelphs and the Ghibellines ended with the total defeat of the Ghibellines. By the end of the thirteenth century that strife had passed. But very shortly a new feud began in Florence between White Guelphs and Black Guelphs. A rather gruesome murder perpetrated by Focaccio de' Cancellieri became the cause of new strife between two branches of the Cancellieri family. On May 1 of 1300 the White Guelphs (Dante's party) drove the Black Guelphs from Florence in bloody fighting. Two years later, however ("within three suns"), the Blacks, aided by Dante's detested Boniface VIII, returned and expelled most of the prominent Whites, among them Dante; for he had been a member of the Priorate (City Council) that issued a decree banishing the leaders of both sides. This was the beginning of Dante's long exile from Florence.

Here he broke off his mournful prophecy.
And I to him: "Still let me urge you on
to speak a little further and instruct me: 75
Farinata and Tegghiaio, men of good blood,
   Jacopo Rusticucci, Arrigo, Mosca,[7]
and the others who set their hearts on doing good—
where are they now whose high deeds might be-gem
   the crown of kings? I long to know their fate.   80
Does Heaven soothe or Hell envenom them?"
And he: "They lie below in a blacker lair.
   A heavier guilt draws them to greater pain.
If you descend so far you may see them there.
But when you move again among the living,   85
   oh speak my name to the memory of men![8]
Having answered all, I say no more." And giving
his head a shake, he looked up at my face
   cross-eyed, then bowed his head and fell away
among the other blind souls of that place.   90
And my Guide to me: "He will not wake again
until the angel trumpet sounds the day
   on which the host shall come to judge all men.
Then shall each soul before the seat of Mercy
   return to its sad grave and flesh and form   95
to hear the edict of Eternity."
So we picked our slow way among the shades
   and the filthy rain, speaking of life to come.
"Master," I said, "when the great clarion fades
into the voice of thundering Omniscience,   100
   what of these agonies? Will they be the same,
or more, or less, after the final sentence?"
And he to me: "Look to your science[9] again
   where it is written: the more a thing is perfect
the more it feels of pleasure and of pain.   105
As for these souls, though they can never soar
to true perfection, still in the new time
   they will be nearer it than they were before."
And so we walked the rim of the great ledge
   speaking of pain and joy, and of much more   110
that I will not repeat, and reached the edge

---

7. Farinata will appear in Canto X among the Heretics: Tegghiaio and Jacopo Rusticucci, in Canto XVI with the homosexuals, Mosca in Canto XXVIII with the sowers of discord. Arrigo does not appear again and he has not been positively identified. Dante probably refers here to Arrigo (or Oderigo) dei Fifanti, one of those who took part in the murder of Buondelmonte (Canto XXVIII. 106, note).   8. Excepting those shades in the lowest depths of Hell whose sins are so shameful that they wish only to be forgotten, all of the damned are eager to be remembered on earth. The concept of the family name and of its survival in the memories of men were matters of first importance among Italians of Dante's time, and expressions of essentially the same attitude are common in Italy today.   9. "Science" to those of Dante's time meant specifically "the writings of Aristotle and the commentaries upon them."

where the descent begins. There, suddenly,
we came on Plutus, the great enemy.

CANTO VII

Circle Four   The Hoarders and the Wasters
Circle Five   The Wrathful and the Sullen

Plutus menaces the Poets, but once more Virgil shows himself more powerful than the rages of Hell's monsters. The Poets enter the Fourth Circle and find what seems to be a war in progress.

The sinners are divided into two raging mobs, each soul among them straining madly at a great boulder-like weight. The two mobs meet, clashing their weights against one another, after which they separate, pushing the great weights apart, and begin over again.

One mob is made up of the Hoarders, the other of the Wasters. In life, they lacked all moderation in regulating their expenses; they destroyed the light of God within themselves by thinking of nothing but money. Thus in death, their souls are encumbered by dead weights (mundanity) and one excess serves to punish the other. Their souls, moreover, have become so dimmed and awry in their fruitless rages that there is no hope of recognizing any among them.

The Poets pass on while Virgil explains the function of Dame Fortune in the Divine Scheme. As he finishes (it is past midnight now of Good Friday) they reach the inner edge of the ledge and come to a Black Spring which bubbles murkily over the rocks to form the Marsh of Styx, which is the Fifth Circle, the last station of the Upper Hell.

Across the marsh they see countless souls attacking one another in the foul slime. These are the Wrathful and the symbolism of their punishment is obvious. Virgil also points out to Dante certain bubbles rising from the slime and informs him that below that mud lie entombed the souls of the Sullen. In life they refused to welcome the sweet light of the Sun (Divine Illumination) and in death they are buried forever below the stinking waters of the Styx, gargling the words of an endless chant in a grotesque parody of singing a hymn.

"Papa Satán, Papa Satán, aleppy,"[1]
Plutus[2] clucked and stuttered in his rage;
and my all-knowing Guide, to comfort me:

---

1. Virgil, the all-knowing, may understand these words, but no one familiar with merely human languages has deciphered them. In Canto XXXI the monster Nimrod utters a similar meaningless jargon, and Virgil there cites it as evidence of the dimness of his mind. Gibberish is certainly a characteristic appropriate to monsters, and since Dante takes pains to make the reference to Satan apparent in the gibberish, it is obviously infernal and debased, and that is almost certainly all he intended. The word "papa" as used here probably means "Pope" rather than "father." "Il papa santo" is the Pope. "Papa Satán" would be his opposite. In the original the last word is "aleppe." On the assumption that jargon translates jargon I have twisted it a bit to rhyme with "me."   2. In Greek mythology, Plutus was the God of Wealth. Many commentators suggest that Dante confused him with Pluto, the son of Saturn and God of the Underworld. But in that case, Plutus would be identical with Lucifer himself and would require a central place in Hell, whereas the classical function of Plutus as God of Material Wealth makes him the ideal overseer of the miserly and the prodigal.

"Do not be startled, for no power of his,
    however he may lord it over the damned,   5
    may hinder your descent through this abyss."
And turning to that carnival of bloat
    cried: "Peace, you wolf of Hell. Choke back your bile
    and let its venom blister your own throat.
Our passage through this pit is willed on high   10
    by that same Throne that loosed the angel wrath
    of Michael on ambition and mutiny."
As puffed out sails fall when the mast gives way
    and flutter to a self-convulsing heap—
    so collapsed Plutus into that dead clay.   15
Thus we descended the dark scarp of Hell
    to which all the evil of the Universe
    comes home at last, into the Fourth Great Circle
and ledge of the abyss. O Holy Justice,
    who could relate the agonies I saw!   20
    What guilt is man that he can come to this?
Just as the surge Charybdis[3] hurls to sea
    crashes and breaks upon its countersurge,
    so these shades dance and crash eternally.
Here, too, I saw a nation of lost souls,   25
    far more than were above: they strained their chests
    against enormous weights, and with mad howls
rolled them at one another. Then in haste
    they rolled them back, one party shouting out:
    "Why do you hoard?" and the other: "Why do you waste?"   30
So back around that ring they puff and blow,
    each faction to its course, until they reach
    opposite sides, and screaming as they go
the madmen turn and start their weights again
    to crash against the maniacs. And I,   35
    watching, felt my heart contract with pain.
"Master," I said, "what people can these be?
    And all those tonsured ones there on our left—
    is it possible they all were of the clergy?"
And he: "In the first life beneath the sun   40
    they were so skewed and squinteyed in their minds
    their misering or extravagance mocked all reason.
The voice of each clamors its own excess
    when lust meets lust at the two points of the circle
    where opposite guilts meet in their wretchedness.   45
These tonsured wraiths of greed were priests indeed,
    and popes and cardinals, for it is in these
    the weed of avarice sows its rankest seed."

3. A famous whirlpool in the Straits of Sicily.

And I to him: "Master, among this crew
  surely I should be able to make out   50
  the fallen image of some soul I knew."
And he to me: "This is a lost ambition.
  In their sordid lives they labored to be blind,
  and now their souls have dimmed past recognition.
All their eternity is to butt and bray: 55
  one crew will stand tight-fisted, the other stripped
  of its very hair at the bar of Judgment Day.
Hoarding and squandering wasted all their light
  and brought them screaming to this brawl of wraiths.
  You need no words of mine to grasp their plight.   60
Now may you see the fleeting vanity
  of the goods of Fortune for which men tear down
  all that they are, to build a mockery.
Not all the gold that is or ever was
  under the sky could buy for one of these   65
  exhausted souls the fraction of a pause."
"Master," I said, "tell me—now that you touch
  on this Dame Fortune[4]—what *is* she, that she holds
  the good things of the world within her clutch?"
And he to me: "O credulous mankind,   70
  is there one error that has wooed and lost you?
  Now listen, and strike error from your mind:
That king whose perfect wisdom transcends all,
  made the heavens and posted angels on them
  to guide the eternal light that it might fall   75
from every sphere to every sphere the same.
  He made earth's splendors by a like decree
  and posted as their minister this high Dame,
the Lady of Permutations. All earth's gear
  she changes from nation to nation, from house to house,   80
  in changeless change through every turning year.
No mortal power may stay her spinning wheel.
  The nations rise and fall by her decree.
  None may foresee where she will set her heel:[5]
she passes, and things pass. Man's mortal reason   85
  cannot encompass her. She rules her sphere
  as the other gods[6] rule theirs. Season by season
her changes change her changes endlessly,
  and those whose turn has come press on her so,

---

4. A central figure in medieval mythology. She is almost invariably represented as a female figure holding an ever-revolving wheel symbolic of Chance. Dante incorporates her into his scheme of the Universe, ranking her among the angels, and giving her a special office in the service of the Catholic God.   5. A literal translation of the original would be "She is hidden like a snake in the grass." To avoid the comic overtone of that figure in English, I have substituted another figure which I believe expresses Dante's intent without destroying his tone.   6. Dante can only mean here "the other angels and ministers of God."

she must be swift by hard necessity.   90
And this is she so railed at and reviled
  that even her debtors in the joys of time
  blaspheme her name. Their oaths are bitter and wild,
but she in her beatitude does not hear.
  Among the Primal Beings of God's joy   95
  she breathes her blessedness and wheels her sphere.
But the stars that marked our starting fall away.[7]
  We must go deeper into greater pain,
  for it is not permitted that we stay."
And crossing over to the chasm's edge   100
  we came to a spring[8] that boiled and overflowed
  through a great crevice worn into the ledge.
By that foul water, black from its very source,
  we found a nightmare path among the rocks
  and followed the dark stream along its course.   105
Beyond its rocky race and wild descent
  the river floods and forms a marsh called Styx,[9]
  a dreary swampland, vaporous and malignant.
And I, intent on all our passage touched,
  made out a swarm of spirits in that bog   110
  savage with anger, naked, slime-besmutched.
They thumped at one another in that slime
  with hands and feet, and they butted, and they bit
  as if each would tear the other limb from limb.
And my kind Sage: "My son, behold the souls   115
  of those who lived in wrath. And do you see
  the broken surfaces of those water-holes
on every hand, boiling as if in pain?
  There are souls beneath that water. Fixed in slime
  they speak their piece, end it, and start again: 120
'Sullen were we in the air made sweet by the Sun;
  in the glory of his shining our hearts poured
  a bitter smoke. Sullen were we begun;
sullen we lie forever in this ditch.'
  This litany they gargle in their throats   125
  as if they sang, but lacked the words and pitch."
Then circling on along that filthy wallow,
  we picked our way between the bank and fen,
  keeping our eyes on those foul souls that swallow

---

7. It is now past midnight of Good Friday.   8. All the waters of Hell derive from one source (see Canto
XIV. 12ff). This black spring must therefore be the waters of Acheron boiling out of some subterranean
passage.   9. The river Styx figures variously in classic mythology, but usually (and in later myths always)
as a river of the Underworld. Dante, to heighten his symbolism, makes it a filthy marsh. This marsh marks
the first great division of Hell. Between Acheron and Styx are punished the sins of Incontinence (the Sins
of the She-Wolf). This is the Upper Hell. Beyond Styx rise the flaming walls of the infernal city of Dis,
within which are punished Violence and Fraud (the sins of the Lion, and the Sins of the Leopard).

the slime of Hell. And so at last we came   130
to foot of a Great Tower that has no name.[1]

CANTO VIII

Circle Five: Styx   The Wrathful, Phlegyas
Circle Six: Dis   The Fallen Angels

The Poets stand at the edge of the swamp, and a mysterious signal flames
from the great tower. It is answered from the darkness of the other side,
and almost immediately the Poets see Phlegyas, the Boatman of Styx, racing toward them across the water, fast as a flying arrow. He comes avidly,
thinking to find new souls for torment, and he howls with rage when he
discovers the Poets. Once again, however, Virgil conquers wrath with a
word and Phlegyas reluctantly gives them passage.

As they are crossing, a muddy soul rises before them. It is Filippo Argenti,
one of the Wrathful. Dante recognizes him despite the filth with which he
is covered, and he berates him soundly, even wishing to see him tormented
further. Virgil approves Dante's disdain and, as if in answer to Dante's
wrath, Argenti is suddenly set upon by all the other sinners present, who
fall upon him and rip him to pieces.

The boat meanwhile has sped on, and before Argenti's screams have
died away, Dante sees the flaming red towers of Dis, the Capital of Hell.
The great walls of the iron city block the way to the Lower Hell. Properly
speaking, all the rest of Hell lies within the city walls, which separate the
Upper and the Lower Hell.

Phlegyas deposits them at a great Iron Gate which they find to be guarded
by the Rebellious Angels. These creatures of Ultimate Evil, rebels against
God Himself, refuse to let the Poets pass. Even Virgil is powerless against
them, for Human Reason by itself cannot cope with the essence of Evil.
Only Divine Aid can bring hope. Virgil accordingly sends up a prayer for
assistance and waits anxiously for a Heavenly Messenger to appear.

Returning to my theme,[2] I say we came
   to the foot of a Great Tower; but long before
   we reached it through the marsh, two horns of flame
flared from the summit, one from either side,
   and then, far off, so far we scarce could see it   5
   across the mist, another flame replied.
I turned to that sea of all intelligence
   saying: "What is this signal and counter-signal?
   Who is it speaks with fire across this distance?"
And he then: "Look across the filthy slew: 10

---

1. No special significance need be attributed to the Tower. It serves as a signaling point for calling the
ferryman from Dis.   2. There is evidence that Dante stopped writing for a longer or shorter period
between the seventh and eighth Cantos. None of the evidence is conclusive but it is quite clear that the
plan of the *Inferno* changes from here on. Up to this point the Circles have been described in one canto
apiece. If this was Dante's original plan, Hell would have been concluded in five more cantos, since there
are only nine Circles in all. But in the later journey the Eighth Circle alone occupies thirteen Cantos.
Dante's phrase may be simply transitional, but it certainly marks a change in the plan of the poem.

you may already see the one they summon,
if the swamp vapors do not hide him from you."
No twanging bowspring ever shot an arrow
    that bored the air it rode dead to the mark
    more swiftly than the flying skiff whose prow   15
shot toward us over the polluted channel
    with a single steersman at the helm who called:
    "So, do I have you at last, you whelp of Hell?"
"Phlegyas, Phlegyas,"[3] said my Lord and Guide,
    "this time you waste your breath: you have us only   20
for the time it takes to cross to the other side."
Phlegyas, the madman, blew his rage among
    those muddy marshes like a cheat deceived,
    or like a fool at some imagined wrong.
My Guide, whom all the fiend's noise could not nettle,   25
    boarded the skiff, motioning me to follow:
    and not till I stepped aboard did it seem to settle[4]
into the water. At once we left the shore,
    that ancient hull riding more heavily
    than it had ridden in all of time before   30
And as we ran on that dead swamp, the slime
    rose before me, and from it a voice cried:
    "Who are you that come here before your time?"
And I replied: "If I come, I do not remain.
    But you, who are you, so fallen and so foul?"   35
And he: "I am one who weeps." And I then:
"May you weep and wail to all eternity,
    for I know you, hell-dog, filthy as you are."[5]
Then he stretched both hands to the boat, but warily
the Master shoved him back, crying, "Down! Down!   40
with the other dogs!" Then he embraced me saying:
"Indignant spirit, I kiss you as you frown.
Blessed be she who bore you.[6] In world and time
    this one was haughtier yet. Not one unbending
    graces his memory. Here is his shadow in slime.   45

3. Mythological King of Boeotia. He was the son of Ares (Mars) by a human mother. Angry at Apollo, who had seduced his daughter (Aesculapius was born of this union), he set fire to Apollo's temple at Delphi. For this offense, the God killed him and threw his soul into Hades under sentence of eternal torment. Dante's choice of a ferryman is especially apt. Phlegyas is the link between the Wrathful (to whom his paternity relates him) and the Rebellious Angels who menaced God (as he menaced Apollo). 4. Because of his living weight.   5. Filippo Argenti was one of the Adimari family, who were bitter political enemies of Dante. Dante's savagery toward him was probably intended in part as an insult to the family. He pays them off again in the Paradiso when he has Cacciaguida call them "The insolent gang that makes itself a dragon to chase those who run away, but is sweet as a lamb to any who show their teeth—or their purse."   6. These were Luke's words to Christ. To have Virgil apply them to Dante after such violence seems shocking, even though the expression is reasonably common in Italian. But Dante does not use such devices lightly. The Commedia, it must be remembered, is a vision of the progress of man's soul toward perfection. In being contemptuous of Wrath, Dante is purging it from his soul. He is thereby growing nearer to perfection, and Virgil, who has said nothing in the past when Dante showed pity for other sinners (though Virgil will later take him to task for daring to pity those whom God has shut off from pity), welcomes this sign of relentless rejection. Only by a ruthless enmity toward evil may the soul be purified.

How many living now, chancellors of wrath,
    shall come to lie here in this pigmire,
    leaving a curse to be their aftermath!"
And I: "Master, it would suit my whim
    to see the wretch scrubbed down into the swill   50
    before we leave this stinking sink and him."
And he to me: "Before the other side
    shows through the mist, you shall have all you ask.
    This is a wish that should be gratified."
And shortly after, I saw the loathsome spirit   55
    so mangled by a swarm of muddy wraiths
    that to this day I praise and thank God for it.
"After Filippo Argenti!" all cried together.
    The maddog Florentine wheeled at their cry
    and bit himself for rage. I saw them gather.   60
And there we left him. And I say no more.
    But such a wailing beat upon my ears,
    I strained my eyes ahead to the far shore.
"My son," the Master said, "the City called Dis⁷
    lies just ahead, the heavy citizens,   65
    the swarming crowds of Hell's metropolis."
And I then: "Master, I already see
    the glow of its red mosques,⁸ as if they came
    hot from the forge to smolder in this valley."
And my all-knowing Guide: "They are eternal   70
    flues to eternal fire that rages in them
    and makes them glow across this lower Hell."
And as he spoke we entered the vast moat
    of the sepulchre. Its wall seemed made of iron
    and towered above us in our little boat.   75
We circled through what seemed an endless distance
    before the boatman ran his prow ashore
    crying: "Out! Out! Get out! This is the entrance."
Above the gates more than a thousand shades
    of spirits purged from Heaven⁹ for its glory   80
    cried angrily: "Who is it that invades
Death's Kingdom in his life?" My Lord and Guide
    advanced a step before me with a sign
    that he wished to speak to some of them aside.
They quieted somewhat, and one called, "Come,   85
    but come alone. And tell that other one,
    who thought to walk so blithely through death's kingdom,
he may go back along the same fool's way

---

7. Pluto, King of the Underworld of ancient mythology, was sometimes called Dis. This, then, is his city, the metropolis of Satan.   8. To a European of Dante's time a mosque would seem the perversion of a church, the impious counterpart of the House of God, just as Satan is God's impious counterpart. 9. The Rebellious Angels. We have already seen, on the other side of Acheron, the Angels who sinned by refusing to take sides.

he came by. Let him try his living luck.
You who are dead can come only to stay."   90
Reader, judge for yourself, how each black word
     fell on my ears to sink into my heart:
     I lost hope of returning to the world.
"O my beloved Master, my Guide in peril,
     who time and time again[1] have seen me safely   95
     along this way, and turned the power of evil,
stand by me now," I cried, "in my heart's fright.
     And if the dead forbid our journey to them,
     let us go back together toward the light."
My Guide then, in the greatness of his spirit: 100
"Take heart. Nothing can take our passage from us
     when such a power has given warrant for it.
Wait here and feed your soul while I am gone
     on comfort and good hope; I will not leave you
     to wander in this underworld alone."   105
So the sweet Guide and Father leaves[2] me here,
     and I stay on in doubt with yes and no
     dividing all my heart to hope and fear.
I could not hear my Lord's words, but the pack
     that gathered round him suddenly broke away   110
     howling and jostling and went pouring back,
slamming the towering gate hard in his face.
     That great Soul stood alone outside the wall.
     Then he came back; his pain showed in his pace.
His eyes were fixed upon the ground, his brow   115
     had sagged from its assurance. He sighed aloud:
     "Who has forbidden me the halls of sorrow?"
And to me he said: "You need not be cast down
     by my vexation, for whatever plot
     these fiends may lay against us, we will go on.   120
This insolence of theirs is nothing new:
     they showed it once at a less secret gate[3]
     that still stands open for all that they could do—
the same gate where you read the dead inscription;
     and through it at this moment a Great One[4] comes.   125
     Already he has passed it and moves down
ledge by dark ledge. He is one who needs no guide,
     and at his touch all gates must spring aside."

1. A literal translation of the original would read "more than seven times." "Seven" is used here as an
indeterminate number indicating simply "quite a number of times." Italian makes rather free use of such
numbers.   2. Dante shifts tenses more freely than English readers are accustomed to.   3. The Gate
of Hell. According to an early medieval tradition, these demons gathered at the outer gate to oppose the
descent of Christ into Limbo at the time of the Harrowing of Hell, but Christ broke the door open and it
has remained so ever since. The service of the Mass for Holy Saturday still sings *Hodie portas mortis et
seras pariter Salvator noster disrupit*. (On this day our Saviour broke open the door of the dead and its lock
as well.)   4. A Messenger of Heaven. He is described in the next Canto.

CANTO IX

Circle Six   The Heretics

At the Gate of Dis the Poets wait in dread. Virgil tries to hide his anxiety from Dante, but both realize that without Divine Aid they will surely be lost. To add to their terrors Three Infernal Furies, symbols of Eternal Remorse, appear on a near-by tower, from which they threaten the Poets and call for Medusa to come and change them to stone. Virgil at once commands Dante to turn and shut his eyes. To make doubly sure, Virgil himself places his hands over Dante's eyes, for there is an Evil upon which man must not look if he is to be saved.

But at the moment of greatest anxiety a storm shakes the dirty air of Hell and the sinners in the marsh begin to scatter like frightened Frogs. The Heavenly Messenger is approaching. He appears walking majestically through Hell, looking neither to right nor to left. With a touch he throws open the Gate of Dis while his words scatter the Rebellious Angels. Then he returns as he came.

The Poets now enter the gate unopposed and find themselves in the Sixth Circle. Here they find a countryside like a vast cemetery. Tombs of every size stretch out before them, each with its lid lying beside it, and each wrapped in flames. Cries of anguish sound endlessly from the entombed dead.

This is the torment of the Heretics of every cult. By Heretic, Dante means specifically those who did violence to God by denying immortality. Since they taught that the soul dies with the body, so their punishment is an eternal grave in the fiery morgue of God's wrath.

My face had paled to a mask of cowardice
    when I saw my Guide turn back. The sight of it
    the sooner brought the color back to his.
He stood apart like one who strains to hear
    what he cannot see, for the eye could not reach far   5
    across the vapors of that midnight air.
"Yet surely we were meant to pass these tombs,"
    he said aloud. "If not . . . so much was promised . . .
    Oh how time hangs and drags till our aid comes!"
I saw too well how the words with which he ended   10
    covered his start, and even perhaps I drew
    a worse conclusion from that than he intended.
"Tell me, Master, does anyone ever come
    from the first ledge,[5] whose only punishment
    is hope cut off, into this dreary bottom?"   15
I put this question to him, still in fear
    of what his broken speech might mean; and he:
    "Rarely do any of us enter here.

5. Limbo.

Once before, it is true, I crossed through Hell
  conjured by cruel Erichtho[6] who recalled   20
  the spirits to their bodies. Her dark spell
forced me, newly stripped of my mortal part,
  to enter through this gate and summon out
  a spirit from Judaïca.[7] Take heart,
That is the last depth and the darkest lair   25
  and the farthest from Heaven which encircles all,
  and at that time I came back even from there.
The marsh from which the stinking gasses bubble
  lies all about this capital of sorrow
  whose gates we may not pass now without trouble."   30
All this and more he expounded; but the rest
  was lost on me, for suddenly my attention
  was drawn to the turret with the fiery crest
where all at once three hellish and inhuman
  Furies[8] sprang to view, bloodstained and wild.   35
  Their limbs and gestures hinted they were women.
Belts of greenest hydras wound and wound
  about their waists, and snakes and horned serpents
  grew from their heads like matted hair and bound
their horrid brows. My Master, who well knew   40
  the handmaids of the Queen of Woe,[9] cried: "Look:
  the terrible Erinyes of Hecate's crew.
That is Megaera to the left of the tower.
  Alecto is the one who raves on the right.
  Tisiphone stands between." And he said no more.   45
With their palms they beat their brows, with their nails they clawed
  their bleeding breasts. And such mad wails broke from them
  that I drew close to the Poet, overawed.
And all together screamed, looking down at me:
  "Call Medusa that we may change him to stone!   50
  Too lightly we let Theseus go free."[1]
"Turn your back and keep your eyes shut tight;
  for should the Gorgon come and you look at her,
  never again would you return to the light."
This was my Guide's command. And he turned me about   55

6. A sorceress drawn from Lucan (*Pharsalia* VI. 508ff). 7. Judaïca (or Judecca) is the final pit of Hell.
Erichtho called up the spirit in order to foretell the outcome of the campaign between Pompey and Caesar.
There is no trace of the legend in which Virgil is chosen for the descent; Virgil, in fact, was still alive at
the time of the battle of Pharsalia.   8. Or Erinyes. In classical mythology they were especially malignant
spirits who pursued and tormented those who had violated fundamental taboos (desecration of temples,
murder of kin, etc.). They are apt symbols of the guilty conscience of the damned.   9. Proserpine (or
Hecate) was the wife of Pluto, and therefore Queen of the Underworld.   1. Theseus and Pirithous tried
to kidnap Hecate. Pirithous was killed in the attempt and Theseus was punished by being chained to a
great rock. He was later set free by Hercules, who descended to his rescue in defiance of all the powers of
Hell. The meaning of the Furies' cry is that Dante must be made an example of. Had they punished
Theseus properly, men would have acquired more respect for their powers and would not still be attempting to invade the Underworld. *The Gorgon*: She turned to stone whoever looked at her.

himself, and would not trust my hands alone,
but, with his placed on mine, held my eyes shut.
Men of sound intellect and probity,
  weigh with good understanding what lies hidden
  behind the veil of my strange allegory!²   60
Suddenly there broke on the dirty swell
  of the dark marsh a squall of terrible sound
  that sent a tremor through both shores of Hell;
a sound as if two continents of air,
  one frigid and one scorching, clashed head on   65
  in a war of winds that stripped the forests bare,
ripped off whole boughs and blew them helter skelter
  along the range of dust it raised before it
  making the beasts and shepherds run for shelter.
The Master freed my eyes. "Now turn," he said,   70
  "and fix your nerve of vision on the foam
  there where the smoke is thickest and most acrid."
As frogs before the snake that hunts them down
  churn up their pond in flight, until the last
  squats on the bottom as if turned to stone—   75
so I saw more than a thousand ruined souls
  scatter away from one who crossed dry-shod
  the Stygian marsh into Hell's burning bowels.
With his left hand he fanned away the dreary
  vapors of that sink as he approached;   80
  and only of that annoyance did he seem weary.
Clearly he was a Messenger from God's Throne,
  and I turned to my Guide; but he made me a sign
  that I should keep my silence and bow down.
Ah, what scorn breathed from that Angel-presence!   85
  He reached the gate of Dis and with a wand
  he waved it open, for there was no resistance.
"Outcasts of Heaven, you twice-loathsome crew,"
  he cried upon that terrible sill of Hell,
  "how does this insolence still live in you?   90
Why do you set yourselves against that Throne
  whose Will none can deny, and which, times past,
  has added to your pain for each rebellion?
Why do you butt against Fate's ordinance?
  Your Cerberus, if you recall, still wears   95
  his throat and chin peeled for such arrogance."³
Then he turned back through the same filthy tide
  by which he had come. He did not speak to us,

2. Most commentators take this to mean the allegory of the Three Furies, but the lines apply as aptly to the allegory that follows. Dante probably meant both. Almost certainly, too, "my strange allegory" refers to the whole *Commedia*.   3. When Cerberus opposed the fated entrance of Hercules into Hell, Hercules threw a chain about his neck and dragged him to the upperworld. Cerberus' throat, according to Dante, is still peeled raw from it.

but went his way like one preoccupied
by other presences than those before him.   100
And we moved toward the city, fearing nothing
after his holy words. Straight through the dim
and open gate we entered unopposed.

And I, eager to learn what new estate
of Hell those burning fortress walls enclosed,   105
began to look about the very moment
we were inside, and I saw on every hand
a countryside of sorrow and new torment.

As at Arles where the Rhone sinks into stagnant marshes,
as at Pola[4] by the Quarnaro Gulf, whose waters   110
close Italy and wash her farthest reaches,
the uneven tombs cover the even plain—
such fields I saw here, spread in all directions,
except that here the tombs were chests of pain:
for, in a ring around each tomb, great fires   115
raised every wall to a red heat. No smith
works hotter iron in his forge. The biers
stood with their lids upraised, and from their pits
an anguished moaning rose on the dead air
from the desolation of tormented spirits.   120
And I: "Master, what shades are these who lie
buried in these chests and fill the air
with such a painful and unending cry?"
"These are the arch-heretics of all cults,
with all their followers," he replied. "Far more   125
than you would think lie stuffed into these vaults.
Like lies with like in every heresy,
and the monuments are fired, some more, some less;
to each depravity its own degree."
He turned then, and I followed through that night   130
between the wall and the torments, bearing right.[5]

CANTO X

Circle Six   The Heretics

As the Poets pass on, one of the damned hears Dante speaking, recognizes him as a Tuscan, and calls to him from one of the fiery tombs. A moment later he appears. He is Farinata degli Uberti, a great war-chief of the Tuscan Ghibellines. The majesty and power of his bearing seem to diminish Hell itself. He asks Dante's lineage and recognizes him as an

4. *Arles . . . Pola:* Situated as indicated on the Rhone and the Quarnaro Gulf respectively, these cities were the sites of great cemeteries dating back to the time of Rome. The Quarnaro Gulf is the body of water on which Fiume is situated.   5. Through all of Hell the Poets bear left in their descent with only two exceptions, the first in their approach to the Heretics, the second in their approach to Geryon, the monster of fraud (see Canto XVII. 29, below). Note that both these exceptions occur at a major division of the *Inferno.* There is no satisfactory explanation of Dante's allegorical intent in making these exceptions.

enemy. They begin to talk politics, but are interrupted by another shade, who rises from the same tomb. This one is Cavalcante dei Cavalcanti, father of Guido Cavalcanti, a contemporary poet. If it is genius that leads Dante on his great journey, the shade asks, why is Guido not with him? Can Dante presume to a greater genius than Guido's? Dante replies that he comes this way only with the aid of powers Guido has not sought. His reply is a classic example of many-leveled symbolism as well as an overt criticism of a rival poet. The senior Cavalcanti mistakenly infers from Dante's reply that Guido is dead, and swoons back into the flames.

Farinata, who has not deigned to notice his fellow-sinner, continues from the exact point at which he had been interrupted. It is as if he refuses to recognize the flames in which he is shrouded. He proceeds to prophesy Dante's banishment from Florence, he defends his part in Florentine politics, and then, in answer to Dante's question, he explains how it is that the damned can foresee the future but have no knowledge of the present. He then names others who share his tomb, and Dante takes his leave with considerable respect for his great enemy, pausing only long enough to leave word for Cavalcanti that Guido is still alive.

We go by a secret path along the rim
    of the dark city, between the wall and the torments.
    My Master leads me and I follow him.
"Supreme Virtue, who through this impious land
    wheel me at will down these dark gyres," I said,   5
    "speak to me, for I wish to understand.
Tell me, Master, is it permitted to see
    the souls within these tombs? The lids are raised,
    and no one stands on guard." And he to me:
"All shall be sealed forever on the day   10
    these souls return here from Jehosaphat[6]
    with the bodies they have given once to clay.
In this dark corner of the morgue of wrath
    lie Epicurus[7] and his followers,
    who make the soul share in the body's death.   15
And here you shall be granted presently
    not only your spoken wish, but that other as well,[8]
    which you had thought perhaps to hide from me."
And I: "Except to speak my thoughts in few
    and modest words, as I learned from your example,   20
    dear Guide, I do not hide my heart from you."

6. A valley outside Jerusalem. The popular belief that it would serve as the scene of the Last Judgment was based on Joel 3:2, 12.   7. The Greek philosopher. The central aim of his philosophy was to achieve happiness, which he defined as the absence of pain. For Dante this doctrine meant the denial of the Eternal life, since the whole aim of the Epicurean was temporal happiness.   8. "All knowing" Virgil is frequently presented as being able to read into Dante's mind. The "other wish" is almost certainly Dante's desire to speak to someone from Florence with whom he could discuss politics. Many prominent Florentines were Epicureans.

"O Tuscan, who go living through this place
  speaking so decorously,[9] may it please you pause
  a moment on your way, for by the grace
of that high speech in which I hear your birth,   25
  I know you for a son of that noble city
  which perhaps I vexed too much in my time on earth."
These words broke without warning from inside
  one of the burning arks. Caught by surprise,
  I turned in fear and drew close to my Guide.   30
And he: "Turn around. What are you doing? Look there:
  it is Farinata[1] rising from the flames.
  From the waist up his shade will be made clear."
My eyes were fixed on him already. Erect,
  he rose above the flame, great chest, great brow;   35
  he seemed to hold all Hell in disrespect.
My Guide's prompt hands urged me among the dim
  and smoking sepulchres to that great figure,
  and he said to me: "Mind how you speak to him."
And when I stood alone at the foot of the tomb,   40
  the great soul stared almost contemptuously,
  before he asked: "Of what line do you come?"
Because I wished to obey, I did not hide
  anything from him: whereupon, as he listened,
  he raised his brows a little, then replied: 45
"Bitter enemies were they to me,
  to my fathers, and to my party, so that twice
  I sent them scattering from high Italy."
"If they were scattered, still from every part
  they formed again and returned both times," I answered,   50
  "but yours have not yet wholly learned that art."
At this another shade[2] rose gradually,
  visible to the chin. It had raised itself,
  I think, upon its knees, and it looked around me
as if it expected to find through that black air   55
  that blew about me, another traveler.

9. Florence lies in the province of Tuscany. Italian, to an extent unknown in America, is a language of dialects, all of them readily identifiable even when they are not well understood by the hearer. Dante's native Tuscan has become the main source of modern official Italian. Two very common sayings still current in Italy are: "*Lingua toscana, lingua di Dio*" (the Tuscan tongue is the language of God) and—to express the perfection of Italian speech—"*Lingua toscana in bocca romana* (the Tuscan tongue in a Roman mouth).   1. Farinata degli Uberti was head of the ancient noble house of the Uberti. He became leader of the Ghibellines of Florence in 1239, and played a large part in expelling the Guelphs in 1248. The Guelphs returned in 1251, but Farinata remained. His arrogant desire to rule singlehandedly led to difficulties, however, and he was expelled in 1258. With the aid of the Manfredi of Siena, he gathered a large force and defeated the Guelphs at Montaperti on the River Arbia in 1260. Reentering Florence in triumph, he again expelled the Guelphs, but at the Diet of Empoli, held by the victors after the battle of Montaperti, he alone rose in open counsel to resist the general sentiment that Florence should be razed. He died in Florence in 1264. In 1266 the Guelphs once more returned and crushed forever the power of the Uberti, destroying their palaces and issuing special decrees against persons of the Uberti line. In 1283 a decree of heresy was published against Farinata.   2. Cavalcante dei Cavalcanti was a famous Epicurean ("like lies with like"). He was the father of Guido Cavalcanti, a poet and friend of Dante. Guido was also Farinata's son-in-law.

And weeping when it found no other there,
turned back. "And if," it cried, "you travel through
this dungeon of the blind by power of genius,
where is my son? why is he not with you?"   60
And I to him: "Not by myself[3] am I borne
this terrible way. I am led by him who waits there,
and whom perhaps your Guido held in scorn."
For by his words and the manner of his torment
I knew his name already, and could, therefore,   65
answer both what he asked and what he meant.
Instantly he rose to his full height:
"He *held*? What is it you say? Is he dead, then?
Do his eyes no longer fill with that sweet light?"
And when he saw that I delayed a bit   70
in answering his question, he fell backwards
into the flame, and rose no more from it.
But that majestic spirit at whose call
I had first paused there, did not change expression,
nor so much as turn his face to watch him fall.   75
"And if," going on from his last words, he said,
"men of my line have yet to learn that art,
that burns me deeper than this flaming bed.
But the face of her who reigns in Hell[4] shall not
be fifty times rekindled in its course   80
before you learn what griefs attend that art.
And as you hope to find the world again,
tell me: why is that populace[5] so savage
in the edicts they pronounce against my strain?"
And I to him: "The havoc and the carnage   85
that dyed the Arbia red at Montaperti
have caused these angry cries in our assemblage."
He sighed and shook his head. "I was not alone
in that affair," he said, "nor certainly
would I have joined the rest without good reason.   90
But I *was* alone at that time when every other
consented to the death of Florence; I
alone with open face defended her."
"Ah, so may your soul sometime have rest,"
I begged him, "solve the riddle that pursues me   95
through this dark place and leaves my mind perplexed:
you seem to see in advance all time's intent,
if I have heard and understood correctly;

---

3. Cavalcanti assumes that the resources of human genius are all that are necessary for such a journey. (It is an assumption that well fits his character as an Epicurean.) Dante replies as a man of religion that other aid is necessary.   4. Hecate or Proserpine. She is also the moon goddess. The sense of this prophecy, therefore, is that Dante will be exiled within fifty full moons. Dante was banished from Florence in 1302, well within the fifty months of the prophecy.   5. The Florentines.

but you seem to lack all knowledge of the present."
"We see asquint, like those whose twisted sight   100
    can make out only the far-off," he said,
    "for the King of All still grants us that much light.
When things draw near, or happen, we perceive
    nothing of them. Except what others bring us
    we have no news of those who are alive.   105
So may you understand that all we know
    will be dead forever from that day and hour
    when the Portal of the Future is swung to."
Then, as if stricken by regret, I said:
    "Now, therefore, will you tell that fallen one   110
    who asked about his son, that he is not dead,
and that, if I did not reply more quickly,
    it was because my mind was occupied
    with this confusion you have solved for me."
And now my Guide was calling me. In haste,   115
    therefore, I begged that mighty shade to name
    the others who lay with him in that chest.
And he: "More than a thousand cram this tomb.
    The second Frederick[6] is here, and the Cardinal
    of the Ubaldini.[7] Of the rest let us be dumb."   120
And he disappeared without more said, and I
    turned back and made my way to the ancient Poet,
    pondering the words of the dark prophecy.
He moved along, and then, when we had started,
    he turned and said to me, "What troubles you?   125
    Why do you look so vacant and downhearted?"
And I told him. And he replied: "Well may you bear
    those words in mind." Then, pausing, raised a finger:
    "Now pay attention to what I tell you here:
when finally you stand before the ray   130
    of that Sweet Lady[8] whose bright eye sees all,
    from her you will learn the turnings of your way."
So saying, he bore left, turning his back
    on the flaming walls, and we passed deeper yet
    into the city of pain, along a track   135
that plunged down like a scar into a sink
which sickened us already with its stink.

---

6. The Emperor Frederick II. In Canto XIII Dante has Pier delle Vigne speak of him as one worthy of
honor, but he was commonly reputed to be an Epicurean.   7. In the original Dante refers to him simply
as "il Cardinale." Ottaviano degli Ubaldini (b. ca. 1209, d. 1273) became a Cardinal in 1245, but his
energies seem to have been directed exclusively to money and political intrigue. When he was refused an
important loan by the Ghibellines, he is reported by many historians as having remarked: "I may say that
if I have a soul, I have lost it in the cause of the Ghibellines, and no one of them will help me now." The
words "If I have a soul" would be enough to make him guilty in Dante's eyes of the charge of heresy.
8. Beatrice.

Circle Six   The Heretics

The Poets reach the inner edge of the Sixth Circle and find a great jumble of rocks that had once been a cliff, but which has fallen into rubble as the result of the great earthquake that shook Hell when Christ died. Below them lies the Seventh Circle, and so fetid is the air that arises from it that the Poets cower for shelter behind a great tomb until their breaths can grow accustomed to the stench.

Dante finds an inscription on the lid of the tomb labeling it as the place in Hell of Pope Anastasius.

Virgil takes advantage of the delay to outline in detail the Division of the Lower Hell, a theological discourse based on *The Ethics* and *The Physics* of Aristotle with subsequent medieval interpretations. Virgil explains also why it is that the Incontinent are not punished within the walls of Dis, and rather ingeniously sets forth the reasons why Usury is an act of Violence against Art, which is the child of Nature and hence the Grandchild of God. (By "Art," Dante means the arts and crafts by which man draws from nature, i.e., Industry.)

As he concludes he rises and urges Dante on. By means known only to Virgil, he is aware of the motion of the stars and from them he sees that it is about two hours before Sunrise of Holy Saturday.

We came to the edge of an enormous sink
rimmed by a circle of great broken boulders.[9]
Here we found ghastlier gangs. And here the stink
thrown up by the abyss so overpowered us
    that we drew back, cowering behind the wall   5
    of one of the great tombs; and standing thus,
I saw an inscription in the stone, and read:
    "I guard Anastasius, once Pope,
    he whom Photinus[1] led from the straight road."
"Before we travel on to that blind pit   10
    we must delay until our sense grows used
    to its foul breath, and then we will not mind it,"
my Master said. And I then: "Let us find
    some compensation for the time of waiting."
And he: "You shall see I have just that in mind.   15
My son," he began, "there are below this wall
    three smaller circles,[2] each in its degree

9. These boulders were broken from the earthquake that shook Hell at the death of Christ.   1. Anastasius II was Pope from 496 to 498. This was the time of schism between the Eastern (Greek) and Western (Roman) churches. Photinus, deacon of Thessalonica, was of the Greek church and held to the Acacian heresy, which denied the divine paternity of Christ. Dante follows the report that Anastasius gave communion to Photinus, thereby countenancing his heresy. Dante's sources, however, had probably confused Anastasius II, the Pope, with Anastasius I, who was Emperor from 491 to 518. It was the Emperor Anastasius who was persuaded by Photinus to accept the Acacian heresy.   2. The Poets are now at the cliff that bounds the Sixth Circle. Below them lie Circles Seven, Eight, and Nine. They are smaller in circum-

like those you are about to leave, and all
are crammed with God's accurst. Accordingly,
    that you may understand their sins at sight,   20
I will explain how each is prisoned, and why.
Malice is the sin most hated by God.
    And the aim of malice is to injure others
    whether by fraud or violence. But since fraud
is the vice of which man alone is capable,   25
God loathes it most. Therefore, the fraudulent
    are placed below, and their torment is more painful.
The first below are the violent. But as violence
    sins in three persons, so is that circle formed
    of three descending rounds of crueler torments.   30
Against God, self, and neighbor is violence shown.
    Against their persons and their goods, I say,
    as you shall hear set forth with open reason.
Murder and mayhem are the violation
    of the person of one's neighbor: and of his goods;   35
    harassment, plunder, arson, and extortion.
Therefore, homicides, and those who strike
    in malice—destroyers and plunderers—all lie
    in that first round, and like suffers with like.
A man may lay violent hands upon his own   40
    person and substance; so in that second round
    eternally in vain repentance moan
the suicides and all who gamble away
    and waste the good and substance of their lives
    and weep in that sweet time when they should be gay.   45
Violence may be offered the deity
    in the heart that blasphemes and refuses Him
    and scorns the gifts of Nature, her beauty and bounty.
Therefore, the smallest round brands with its mark
    both Sodom and Cahors,[3] and all who rail   50
    at God and His commands in their hearts' dark.
Fraud, which is a canker to every conscience,
    may be practiced by a man on those who trust him,
    and on those who have reposed no confidence.
The latter mode seems only to deny   55
    the bond of love which all men have from Nature;
    therefore within the second circle lie
simoniacs, sycophants, and hypocrites,
    falsifiers, thieves, and sorcerers,
    grafters, pimps, and all such filthy cheats.   60

---

ference, being closer to the center, but they are all intricately subdivided, and will be treated at much
greater length than were the Circles of Upper Hell.   3. Both these cities are used as symbols for the sins
that are said to have flourished within them. Sodom (Genesis 19) is, of course, identified with unnatural
sex practices. Cahors, a city in southern France, was notorious in the Middle Ages for its usurers.

The former mode of fraud not only denies
    the bond of Nature, but the special trust
    added by bonds of friendship or blood-ties.
Hence, at the center point of all creation,[4]
    in the smallest circle, on which Dis is founded,   65
    the traitors lie in endless expiation."
"Master," I said, "the clarity of your mind
    impresses all you touch; I see quite clearly
    the orders of this dark pit of the blind.
But tell me: those who lie in the swamp's bowels,   70
    those the wind blows about, those the rain beats,
    and those who meet and clash with such mad howls[5]—
why are *they* not punished in the rust-red city[6]
    if God's wrath be upon them? and if it is not,
    why must they grieve through all eternity?"   75
And he: "Why does your understanding stray
    so far from its own habit? or can it be
    your thoughts are turned along some other way?
Have you forgotten that your *Ethics*[7] states
    the three main dispositions of the soul   80
    that lead to those offenses Heaven hates—
incontinence, malice, and bestiality?
    and how incontinence offends God least
    and earns least blame from Justice and Charity?
Now if you weigh this doctrine and recall   85
    exactly who they are whose punishment
    lies in that upper Hell outside the wall,
you will understand at once why they are confined
    apart from these fierce wraiths, and why less anger
    beats down on them from the Eternal Mind."   90
"O sun which clears all mists from troubled sight,
    such joy attends your rising that I feel
    as grateful to the dark as to the light.
Go back a little further," I said, "to where
    you spoke of usury as an offense   95
    against God's goodness. How is that made clear?"
"Philosophy makes plain by many reasons,"
    he answered me, "to those who heed her teachings,
    how all of Nature,—her laws, her fruits, her seasons,—
springs from the Ultimate Intellect and Its art: 100
    and if you read your *Physics*[8] with due care,
    you will note, not many pages from the start,
that Art strives after her by imitation,
    as the disciple imitates the master;

---

4. In the Ptolemaic system the earth was the center of the Universe. In Dante's geography, the bottom of
Hell is the center of the earth.   5. These are, of course, the sinners of the Upper Hell.   6. Dis. All
of Lower Hell is within the city walls.   7. *The Ethics* of Aristotle.   8. *The Physics* of Aristotle.

Art, as it were, is the Grandchild of Creation.   105
By this, recalling the Old Testament
    near the beginning of Genesis, you will see
    that in the will of Providence, man was meant
to labor and to prosper. But usurers,
    by seeking their increase in other ways,   110
    scorn Nature in herself and her followers.
But come, for it is my wish now to go on:
    the wheel turns and the Wain lies over Caurus,[9]
    the Fish are quivering low on the horizon,
and there beyond us runs the road we go   115
down the dark scarp into the depths below."

CANTO XII

Circle Seven: Round One   The Violent Against Neighbors

The Poets begin the descent of the fallen rock wall, having first to evade
the Minotaur, who menaces them. Virgil tricks him and the Poets hurry
by.

Below them they see the River of Blood, which marks the First Round
of the Seventh Circle as detailed in the previous Canto. Here are punished
the Violent Against Their Neighbors, great war-makers, cruel tyrants,
highwaymen—all who shed the blood of their fellowmen. As they wallowed in blood during their lives, so they are immersed in the boiling
blood forever, each according to the degree of his guilt, while fierce Centaurs patrol the banks, ready to shoot with their arrows any sinner who
raises himself out of the boiling blood beyond the limits permitted him.
Alexander the Great is here, up to his lashes in the blood, and with him
Attila, the Scourge of God. They are immersed in the deepest part of the
river, which grows shallower as it circles to the other side of the ledge, then
deepens again.

The Poets are challenged by the Centaurs, but Virgil wins a safe conduct
from Chiron, their chief, who assigns Nessus to guide them and to bear
them across the shallows of the boiling blood. Nessus carries them across
at the point where it is only ankle deep and immediately leaves them and
returns to his patrol.

The scene that opened from the edge of the pit
    was mountainous, and such a desolation
    that every eye would shun the sight of it:

---

9. The Wain is the constellation of the Great Bear. Caurus was the northwest wind in classical mythology.
Hence the constellation of the Great Bear now lies in the northwest. The Fish is the constellation and
zodiacal sign of Pisces. It is just appearing over the horizon. The next sign of the zodiac is Aries. We know
from Canto I that the sun is in Aries, and since the twelve signs of the zodiac each cover two hours of the
day, it must now be about two hours before dawn. It is, therefore, approximately 4:00 A.M. of Holy
Saturday. The stars are not visible in Hell, but throughout the *Inferno* Virgil reads them by some special
power which Dante does not explain.

a ruin like the Slides of Mark[1] near Trent
   on the bank of the Adige, the result of an earthquake   5
   or of some massive fault in the escarpment—
for, from the point on the peak where the mountain split
   to the plain below, the rock is so badly shattered
   a man at the top might make a rough stair of it.[2]
Such was the passage down the steep, and there   10
   at the very top, at the edge of the broken cleft,
   lay spread the Infamy of Crete,[3] the heir
of bestiality and the lecherous queen
   who hid in a wooden cow. And when he saw us,
   he gnawed his own flesh in a fit of spleen.   15
And my Master mocked: "How you do pump your breath!
   Do you think, perhaps, it is the Duke of Athens,
   who in the world above served up your death?
Off with you, monster; this one does not come
   instructed by your sister, but of himself   20
   to observe your punishment in the lost kingdom."
As a bull that breaks its chains just when the knife
   has struck its death-blow, cannot stand nor run
   but leaps from side to side with its last life—
so danced the Minotaur, and my shrewd Guide   25
   cried out: "Run now! While he is blind with rage!
   Into the pass, quick, and get over the side!"
So we went down across the shale and slate
   of that ruined rock, which often slid and shifted
   under me at the touch of living weight.   30
I moved on, deep in thought; and my Guide to me:
   "You are wondering perhaps about this ruin
   which is guarded by the beast upon whose fury
I played just now. I should tell you that when last
   I came this dark way to the depths of Hell,   35
   this rock had not yet felt the ruinous blast.[4]
But certainly, if I am not mistaken,
   it was just before the coming of Him who took

---

1. *Li Slavoni di Marco* are about two miles from Rovereto (between Verona and Trent) on the left bank
of the River Adige.   **2.** I am defeated in all attempts to convey Dante's emphasis in any sort of a verse
line. The sense of the original: "It might provide some sort of a way down for one who started at the top,
but (by implication) would not be climbable from below."   **3.** This is the infamous Minotaur of classical
mythology. His mother was Pasiphaë, wife of Minos, the King of Crete. She conceived an unnatural
passion for a bull, and in order to mate with it, she crept into a wooden cow. From this union the Minotaur
was born, half-man, half-beast. King Minos kept him in an ingenious labyrinth from which he could not
escape. When Androgeos, the son of King Minos, was killed by the Athenians, Minos exacted an annual
tribute of seven maidens and seven youths. These were annually turned into the labyrinth and there were
devoured by the Minotaur. The monster was finally killed by Theseus, Duke of Athens. He was aided by
Ariadne, daughter of Minos (and half-sister of the monster). She gave Theseus a ball of cord to unwind as
he entered the labyrinth and a sword with which to kill the Minotaur.   **4.** According to Matthew 27:51,
an earthquake shook the earth at the moment of Christ's death. These stones, Dante lets us know, were
broken off in that earthquake. We shall find other effects of the same shock in the Eighth Circle. It is
worth noting also that both the Upper (See Canto V. 34) and the Lower Hell begin with evidences of this
ruin. For details of Virgil's first descent see notes to Canto IX.

the souls from Limbo, that all Hell was shaken
so that I thought the universe felt love   40
and all its elements moved toward harmony,
    whereby the world of matter, as some believe,
has often plunged to chaos.[5] It was then,
    that here and elsewhere in the pits of Hell,
    the ancient rock was stricken and broke open.   45
But turn your eyes to the valley; there we shall find
    the river of boiling blood[6] in which are steeped
    all who struck down their fellow men." Oh blind!
Oh ignorant, self-seeking cupidity
    which spurs us so in the short mortal life   50
    and steeps us so through all eternity!
I saw an arching fosse that was the bed
    of a winding river circling through the plain
    exactly as my Guide and Lord had said.
A file of Centaurs[7] galloped in the space   55
    between the bank and the cliff, well armed with arrows,
    riding as once on earth they rode to the chase.
And seeing us descend, that straggling band
    halted, and three of them moved out toward us,
    their long bows and their shafts already in hand.   60
And one of them cried out while still below:
    "To what pain are you sent down that dark coast?
    Answer from where you stand, or I draw the bow!"
"Chiron[8] is standing there hard by your side;
    our answer will be to him. This wrath of yours   65
    was always your own worst fate," my Guide replied.
And to me he said: "That is Nessus, who died in the wood
    for insulting Dejanira.[9] At his death
    he plotted his revenge in his own blood.
The one in the middle staring at his chest   70
    is the mighty Chiron, he who nursed Achilles:
    the other is Pholus,[1] fiercer than all the rest.

---

5. The Greek philosopher Empedocles taught that the universe existed by the counterbalance (discord or mutual repulsion) of its elements. Should the elemental matter feel harmony (love or mutual attraction) all would fly together into chaos.   6. Phlegethon, the river that circles through the First Round of the Seventh Circle, then sluices through the wood of the suicides (the Second Round) and the burning sands (Third Round) to spew over the Great Cliff into the Eighth Circle, and so, eventually, to the bottom of Hell (Cocytus).   7. Creatures of classical mythology, half-horse, half-men. They were skilled and savage hunters, creatures of passion and violence. Like the Minotaur, they are symbols of the bestial-human, and as such, they are fittingly chosen as the tormentors of these sinners.   8. The son of Saturn and of the nymph Philira. He was the wisest and most just of the Centaurs and reputedly was the teacher of Achilles and of other Greek heroes to whom he imparted great skill in bearing arms, medicine, astronomy, music, and augury. Dante places him far down in Hell with the others of his kind, but though he draws Chiron's coarseness, he also grants him a kind of majestic understanding.   9. Nessus carried travelers across the River Evenus for hire. He was hired to ferry Dejanira, the wife of Hercules, and tried to abduct her, but Hercules killed him with a poisoned arrow. While Nessus was dying, he whispered to Dejanira that a shirt stained with his poisoned blood would act as a love charm should Hercules' affections stray. When Hercules fell in love with Iole, Dejanira sent him a shirt stained with the Centaur's blood. The shirt poisoned Hercules and he died in agony.   1. A number of classical poets mention Pholus but very little else is known of him.

They run by that stream in thousands, snapping their bows
    at any wraith who dares to raise himself
    out of the blood more than his guilt allows."   75
We drew near those swift beasts. In a thoughtful pause
    Chiron drew an arrow, and with its notch
    he pushed his great beard back along his jaws.
And when he had thus uncovered the huge pouches
    of his lips, he said to his fellows: "Have you noticed   80
    how the one who walks behind moves what he touches?
That is not how the dead go." My good Guide,
    already standing by the monstrous breast
    in which the two mixed natures joined, replied:
"It is true he lives; in his necessity   85
    I alone must lead him through this valley.
    Fate brings him here, not curiosity.
From singing Alleluia the sublime
    spirit[2] who sends me came. He is no bandit.
    Nor am I one who ever stooped to crime.   90
But in the name of the Power by which I go
    this sunken way across the floor of Hell,
    assign us one of your troop whom we may follow,
that he may guide us to the ford, and there
    carry across on his back the one I lead,   95
    for he is not a spirit to move through air."
Chiron turned his head on his right breast[3]
    and said to Nessus: "Go with them, and guide them,
    and turn back any others that would contest
their passage." So we moved beside our guide   100
    along the bank of the scalding purple river
    in which the shrieking wraiths were boiled and dyed.
Some stood up to their lashes in that torrent,
    and as we passed them the huge Centaur said:
    "These were the kings of bloodshed and despoilment.   105
Here they pay for their ferocity.
    Here is Alexander.[4] And Dionysius,
    who brought long years of grief to Sicily.
That brow you see with the hair as black as night
    is Azzolino;[5] and that beside him, the blonde,   110
    is Opizzo da Esti,[6] who had his mortal light
blown out by his own stepson." I turned then
    to speak to the Poet but he raised a hand:

2. Beatrice.   3. The right is the side of virtue and honor. In Chiron it probably signifies his human
side as opposed to his bestial side.   4. Alexander the Great. *Dionysius:* Dionysius I (d. 367 B.C.) and his
son, Dionysius II (d. 343), were tyrants of Sicily. Both were infamous as prototypes of the bloodthirsty and
exorbitant ruler. Dante may intend either or both.   5. Ezzelino da Romano, Count of Onora (1194–
1259). The cruelest of the Ghibelline tyrants. In 1236 Frederick II appointed Ezzelino his vicar in Padua.
Ezzelino became especially infamous for his bloody treatment of the Paduans, whom he slaughtered in
great numbers.   6. Marquis of Ferrara (1264–1293). The account of his life is confused. One must
accept Dante's facts as given.

"Let him be the teacher now, and I will listen."
Further on, the Centaur stopped beside   115
   a group of spirits steeped as far as the throat
   in the race of boiling blood, and there our guide
pointed out a sinner who stood alone:
   "That one before God's altar pierced a heart
   still honored on the Thames."[7] And he passed on.   120
We came in sight of some who were allowed
   to raise the head and all the chest from the river,
   and I recognized many there. Thus, as we followed
along the stream of blood, its level fell
   until it cooked no more than the feet of the damned.   125
   And here we crossed the ford to deeper Hell.
"Just as you see the boiling stream grow shallow
   along this side," the Centaur said to us
   when we stood on the other bank, "I would have you know
that on the other, the bottom sinks anew   130
   more and more, until it comes again
   full circle to the place where the tyrants stew.
It is there that Holy Justice spends its wrath
   on Sextus[8] and Pyrrhus through eternity,
   and on Attila,[9] who was a scourge on earth: 135
and everlastingly milks out the tears
   of Rinier da Corento and Rinier Pazzo,[1]
   those two assassins who for many years
stalked the highways, bloody and abhorred."
And with that he started back across the ford.   140

CANTO XIII

Circle Seven: Round Two   The Violent Against Themselves

   Nessus carries the Poets across the river of boiling blood and leaves them
in the Second Round of the Seventh Circle, the Wood of the Suicides.
Here are punished those who destroyed their own lives and those who
destroyed their substance.
   The souls of the Suicides are encased in thorny trees whose leaves are
eaten by the odious Harpies, the overseers of these damned. When the
Harpies feed upon them, damaging their leaves and limbs, the wound
bleeds. Only as long as the blood flows are the souls of the trees able to

7. The sinner indicated is Guy de Montfort. His father, Simon de Montfort, was a leader of the barons
who rebelled against Henry III and was killed at the battle of Evesham (1265) by Prince Edward (later
Edward I). In 1271, Guy (then Vicar General of Tuscany) avenged his father's death by murdering Henry's
nephew (who was also named Henry). The crime was openly committed in a church at Viterbo. The
murdered Henry's heart was sealed in a casket and sent to London, where it was accorded various
honors.   8. Probably the younger son of Pompey the Great. His piracy is mentioned in Lucan (*Pharsalia*
VI. 420–422). *Pyrrhus:* Pyrrhus, the son of Achilles, was especially bloodthirsty at the sack of Troy.
Pyrrhus, King of Epirus (319–372 B.C.), waged relentless and bloody war against the Greeks and Romans.
Either may be intended.   9. King of the Huns from 433 to 453. He was called the Scourge of God.
1. Both were especially bloodthirsty robber-barons of the thirteenth century.

speak. Thus, they who destroyed their own bodies are denied a human form; and just as the supreme expression of their lives was self-destruction, so they are permitted to speak only through that which tears and destroys them. Only through their own blood do they find voice. And to add one more dimension to the symbolism, it is the Harpies—defilers of all they touch—who give them their eternally recurring wounds.

The Poets pause before one tree and speak with the soul of Pier delle Vigne. In the same wood they see Jacomo da Sant' Andrea, and Lano da Siena, two famous Squanderers and Destroyers of Goods pursued by a pack of savage hounds. The hounds overtake Sant' Andrea, tear him to pieces and go off carrying his limbs in their teeth, a self-evident symbolic retribution for the violence with which these sinners destroyed their substance in the world. After this scene of horror, Dante speaks to an Unknown Florentine Suicide whose soul is inside the bush which was torn by the hound pack when it leaped upon Sant' Andrea.

Nessus had not yet reached the other shore
   when we moved on into a pathless wood
   that twisted upward from Hell's broken floor.
Its foliage was not verdant, but nearly black.
   The unhealthy branches, gnarled and warped and tangled,   5
   bore poison thorns instead of fruit. The track
of those wild beasts that shun the open spaces
   men till between Cecina and Corneto
   runs through no rougher nor more tangled places.[2]
Here nest the odious Harpies[3] of whom my Master   10
   wrote how they drove Aeneas and his companions
   from the Strophades with prophecies of disaster.
Their wings are wide, their feet clawed, their huge bellies
   covered with feathers, their necks and faces human.
   They croak eternally in the unnatural trees.   15
"Before going on, I would have you understand,"
   my Guide began, "we are in the second round
   and shall be till we reach the burning sand.[4]
Therefore look carefully and you will see
   things in this wood, which, if I told them to you   20
   would shake the confidence you have placed in me."
I heard cries of lamentation rise and spill
   on every hand, but saw no souls in pain
   in all that waste; and, puzzled, I stood still.

2. The reference here is to the Maremma district of Tuscany which lies between the mountains and the sea. The river Cecina is the northern boundary of this district; Corneto is on the river Marta, which forms the southern boundary. It is a wild district of marsh and forest. 3. These hideous birds with the faces of malign women were often associated with the Erinyes (Furies). Their original function in mythology was to snatch away the souls of men at the command of the Gods. Later, they were portrayed as defilers of food, and, by extension, of everything they touched. The islands of the Strophades were their legendary abode. Aeneas and his men landed there and fought with the Harpies, who drove them back and pronounced a prophecy of unbearable famine upon them. 4. The Third Round of this Circle.

I think perhaps he thought that I was thinking[5]   25
    those cries rose from among the twisted roots
    through which the spirits of the damned were slinking
to hide from us. Therefore my Master said:
    "If you break off a twig, what you will learn
    will drive what you are thinking from your head."   30
Puzzled, I raised my hand a bit and slowly
    broke off a branchlet from an enormous thorn:
    and the great trunk of it cried: "Why do you break me?"
And after blood had darkened all the bowl
    of the wound, it cried again: "Why do you tear me?   35
    Is there no pity left in any soul?
Men we were, and now we are changed to sticks;
    well might your hand have been more merciful
    were we no more than souls of lice and ticks."
As a green branch with one end all aflame   40
    will hiss and sputter sap out of the other
    as the air escapes—so from that trunk there came
words and blood together, gout by gout.
    Startled, I dropped the branch that I was holding
    and stood transfixed by fear, half turned about   45
to my Master, who replied: "O wounded soul,
    could he have believed before what he has seen
    in my verses only,[6] you would yet be whole,
for his hand would never have been raised against you.
    But knowing this truth could never be believed   50
    till it was seen, I urged him on to do
what grieves me now; and I beg to know your name,
    that to make you some amends in the sweet world
    when he returns, he may refresh your fame."
And the trunk: "So sweet those words to me that I   55
    cannot be still, and may it not annoy you
    if I seem somewhat lengthy in reply.
I am he who held both keys to Frederick's heart,[7]

---

5. The original is *"Cred' io ch'ei credette ch'io credesse."* This sort of word play was considered quite elegant by medieval rhetoricians and by the ornate Sicilian School of poetry. Dante's style is based on a rejection of all such devices in favor of a sparse and direct diction. The best explanation of this unusual instance seems to be that Dante is anticipating his talk with Pier delle Vigne, a rhetorician who, as we shall see, delights in this sort of locution.   6. The *Aeneid*, Book III, describes a similar bleeding plant. There, Aeneas pulls at a myrtle growing on a Thracian hillside. It bleeds where he breaks it and a voice cries out of the ground. It is the voice of Polydorus, son of Priam and friend of Aeneas. He had been treacherously murdered by the Thracian king.   7. Pier delle Vigne (1190–1249). A famous and once-powerful minister of Emperor Frederick II. He enjoyed Frederick's whole confidence until 1247 when he was accused of treachery and was imprisoned and blinded. He committed suicide to escape further torture. (For Frederick see Canto X.) Pier delle Vigne was famous for his eloquence and for his mastery of the ornate Provençal-inspired Sicilian School of Italian Poetry, and Dante styles his speech accordingly. It is worth noting, however, that the style changes abruptly in the middle of line 72. There, his courtly preamble finished, delle Vigne speaks from the heart, simply and passionately. *Who held both keys:* The phrasing unmistakably suggests the Papal keys; delle Vigne may be suggesting that he was to Frederick as the Pope is to God.

    locking, unlocking with so deft a touch
    that scarce another soul had any part   60
in his most secret thoughts. Through every strife
    I was so faithful to my glorious office
    that for it I gave up both sleep and life.
That harlot, Envy, who on Caesar's[8] face
    keeps fixed forever her adulterous stare,   65
    the common plague and vice of court and palace,
inflamed all minds against me. These inflamed
    so inflamed him that all my happy honors
    were changed to mourning. Then, unjustly blamed,
my soul, in scorn, and thinking to be free   70
    of scorn in death, made me at last, though just,
    unjust to myself. By the new roots[9] of this tree
I swear to you that never in word or spirit
    did I break faith to my lord and emperor
    who was so worthy of honor in his merit.   75
If either of you return to the world, speak for me,
    to vindicate in the memory of men
    one who lies prostrate from the blows of Envy."
The Poet stood. Then turned. "Since he is silent,"
    he said to me, "do not you waste this hour,   80
    if you wish to ask about his life or torment."
And I replied: "Question him for my part,
    on whatever you think I would do well to hear;
    I could not, such compassion chokes my heart."
The Poet began again: "That this man may   85
    with all his heart do for you what your words
    entreat him to, imprisoned spirit, I pray,
tell us how the soul is bound and bent
    into these knots, and whether any ever
    frees itself from such imprisonment."   90
At that the trunk blew powerfully, and then
    the wind became a voice that spoke these words:
    "Briefly is the answer given: when
out of the flesh from which it tore itself,
    the violent spirit comes to punishment,   95
    Minos assigns it to the seventh shelf.
It falls into the wood, and landing there,
    wherever fortune flings it,[1] it strikes root,
    and there it sprouts, lusty as any tare,
shoots up a sapling, and becomes a tree.   100

8. Frederick II was of course Caesar of the Roman Empire, but in this generalized context "Caesar" seems to be used as a generic term for any great ruler, i.e., "The harlot, Envy, never turns her attention from those in power."   9. Pier delle Vigne had only been in Hell fifty-one years, a short enough time on the scale of eternity.   1. Just as the soul of the suicide refused to accept divine regulation of its mortal life span, so eternal justice takes no special heed of where the soul falls.

The Harpies, feeding on its leaves then, give it
  pain and pain's outlet simultaneously.[2]
Like the rest, we shall go for our husks on Judgment Day,
  but not that we may wear them, for it is not just
  that a man be given what he throws away.   105
Here shall we drag them and in this mournful glade
  our bodies will dangle to the end of time,
  each on the thorns of its tormented shade."
We waited by the trunk, but it said no more;
  and waiting, we were startled by a noise   110
  that grew through all the wood. Just such a roar
and trembling as one feels when the boar and chase
  approach his stand, the beasts and branches crashing
  and clashing in the heat of the fierce race.
And there on the left, running so violently   115
  they broke off every twig in the dark wood,
  two torn and naked wraiths went plunging by me.
The leader cried, "Come now, O Death! Come now!"
  And the other, seeing that he was outrun,
  cried out: "Your legs were not so ready, Lano,[3]   120
in the jousts at the Toppo." And suddenly in his rush,
  perhaps because his breath was failing him,
  he hid himself inside a thorny bush
and cowered among its leaves. Then at his back,
  the wood leaped with black bitches, swift as greyhounds   125
  escaping from their leash, and all the pack
sprang on him; with their fangs they opened him
  and tore him savagely, and then withdrew,
  carrying his body with them, limb by limb.
Then, taking me by the hand across the wood,   130
  my Master led me toward the bush. Lamenting,
  all its fractures blew out words and blood:
"O Jacomo da Sant' Andrea!"[4] it said,
  "what have you gained in making me your screen?
  What part had I in the foul life you led?"   135
And when my Master had drawn up to it
  he said: "Who were you, who through all your wounds
  blow out your blood with your lament, sad spirit?"
And he to us: "You who have come to see
  how the outrageous mangling of these hounds   140
  has torn my boughs and stripped my leaves from me,

2. Suicide also gives pain and its outlet simultaneously.   3. Lano da Siena, a famous squanderer. He
died at the ford of the river Toppo near Arezzo in 1287 in a battle against the Aretines. Boccaccio writes
that he deliberately courted death having squandered all his great wealth and being unwilling to live on in
poverty. Thus his companion's jeer probably means: "You were not so ready to run then, Lano: why are
you running now?"   4. A Paduan with an infamous lust for laying waste his own goods and those of his
neighbors; arson was his favorite prank. On one occasion, to celebrate the arrival of certain noble guests,
he set fire to all the workers' huts and outbuildings of his estate. He was murdered in 1239, probably by
assassins hired by Ezzolino (for whom see Canto XII).

O heap them round my ruin! I was born
　　in the city that tore down Mars and raised the Baptist.[5]
On that account the God of War has sworn
her sorrow shall not end. And were it not　　　　　　　　　　145
　　that something of his image still survives
　　on the bridge across the Arno, some have thought
those citizens who of their love and pain
　　afterwards rebuilt it from the ashes
　　left by Attila,[6] would have worked in vain.　　　　　　150
I am one who has no tale to tell:
I made myself a gibbet of my own lintel."

CANTO XIV

Circle Seven: Round Three　The Violent Against God, Nature, and Art

　　Dante, in pity, restores the torn leaves to the soul of his countryman
and the Poets move on to the next round, a great Plain of Burning Sand
upon which there descends an eternal slow Rain of Fire. Here, scorched
by fire from above and below, are three classes of sinners suffering differing
degrees of exposure to the fire. The Blasphemers (the Violent Against
God) are stretched supine upon the sand, the Sodomites (the Violent
Against Nature) run in endless circles, and the Usurers (the Violent Against
Art, which is the Grandchild of God) huddle on the sands.

　　The Poets find Capaneus stretched out on the sands, the chief sinner of
that place. He is still blaspheming God. They continue along the edge of
the Wood of the Suicides and come to a blood-red rill which flows boiling
from the Wood and crosses the burning plain. Virgil explains the miraculous power of its waters and discourses on the Old Man of Crete and the
origin of all the rivers of Hell.

　　The symbolism of the burning plain is obviously centered in sterility
(the desert image) and wrath (the fire image). Blasphemy, sodomy, and
usury are all unnatural and sterile actions: thus the unbearing desert is the
eternity of these sinners; and thus the rain, which in nature should be
fertile and cool, descends as fire. Capaneus, moreover, is subjected not to
the wrath of nature (the sands below) and the wrath of God (the fire from
above), but is tortured most by his own inner violence, which is the root
of blasphemy.

Love of that land that was our common source
　　moved me to tears; I gathered up the leaves

5. Florence. Mars was the first patron of the city and when the Florentines were converted to Christianity
they pulled down his equestrian statue and built a church on the site of his temple. The statue of Mars
was placed on a tower beside the Arno. When Totila (see note to line 150, following) destroyed Florence
the tower fell into the Arno and the statue with it. Legend has it that Florence could never have been
rebuilt had not the mutilated statue been rescued. It was placed on the Ponte Vecchio but was carried
away in the flood of 1333.　6. Dante confuses Attila with Totila, King of the Ostrogoths (d. 552). He
destroyed Florence in 542. Attila (d. 453), King of the Huns, destroyed many cities of northern Italy, but
not Florence.

and gave them back. He was already hoarse.
We came to the edge of the forest where one goes
    from the second round to the third, and there we saw   5
    what fearful arts the hand of Justice knows.
To make these new things wholly clear, I say
    we came to a plain whose soil repels all roots.
    The wood of misery rings it the same way
the wood itself is ringed by the red fosse.   10
    We paused at its edge: the ground was burning sand,
    just such a waste as Cato marched across.[7]
O endless wrath of God: how utterly
    thou shouldst become a terror to all men
    who read the frightful truths revealed to me!   15
Enormous herds of naked souls I saw,
    lamenting till their eyes were burned of tears;
    they seemed condemned by an unequal law,
for some were stretched supine upon the ground,
    some squatted with their arms about themselves,   20
    and others without pause roamed round and round.
Most numerous were those that roamed the plain.
    Far fewer were the souls stretched on the sand,
    but moved to louder cries by greater pain.
And over all that sand on which they lay   25
    or crouched or roamed, great flakes of flame fell slowly
    as snow falls in the Alps on a windless day.
Like those Alexander met in the hot regions
    of India, flames raining from the sky
    to fall still unextinguished on his legions: 30
whereat he formed his ranks, and at their head
    set the example, trampling the hot ground
    for fear the tongues of fire might join and spread—[8]
just so in Hell descended the long rain
    upon the damned, kindling the sand like tinder   35
    under a flint and steel, doubling the pain.
In a never-ending fit upon those sands,
    the arms of the damned twitched all about their bodies,
    now here, now there, brushing away the brands.
"Poet," I said, "master of every dread   40
    we have encountered, other than those fiends
    who sallied from the last gate of the dead—
who is that wraith who lies along the rim
    and sets his face against the fire in scorn,
    so that the rain seems not to mellow him?"   45

7. In 47 B.C., Cato of Utica led an army across the Libyan desert. Lucan described the march in *Pharsalia* IX. 587ff.   8. This incident of Alexander the Great's campaign in India is described in *De Meteoris* of Albertus Magnus and was taken by him with considerable alteration from a letter reputedly sent to Aristotle by Alexander.

And he himself,[9] hearing what I had said
  to my Guide and Lord concerning him, replied:
  "What I was living, the same am I now, dead.
Though Jupiter wear out his sooty smith
  from whom on my last day he snatched in anger   50
  the jagged thunderbolt he pierced me with;
though he wear out the others one by one
  who labor at the forge at Mongibello[1]
  crying again 'Help! Help! Help me, good Vulcan!'
as he did at Phlegra[2] and hurl down endlessly   55
  with all the power of Heaven in his arm,
  small satisfaction would he win from me."
At this my Guide spoke with such vehemence
  as I had not heard from him in all of Hell:
  "O Capaneus, by your insolence   60
you are made to suffer as much fire inside
  as falls upon you. Only your own rage
  could be fit torment for your sullen pride."
Then he turned to me more gently. "That," he said,
  "was one of the Seven who laid siege to Thebes.   65
Living, he scorned God, and among the dead
he scorns Him yet. He thinks he may detest
  God's power too easily, but as I told him,
  his slobber is a fit badge for his breast.
Now follow me; and mind for your own good   70
  you do not step upon the burning sand,
  but keep well back along the edge of the wood."
We walked in silence then till we reached a rill
  that gushes from the wood;[3] it ran so red
  the memory sends a shudder through me still.   75
As from the Bulicame[4] springs the stream
  the sinful women keep to their own use;
  so down the sand the rill flowed out in steam.
The bed and both its banks were petrified,
  as were its margins; thus I knew at once   80
  our passage through the sand lay by its side.
"Among all other wonders I have shown you
  since we came through the gate denied to none,

9. Capaneus, one of the seven captains who warred on Thebes. As he scaled the walls of Thebes, Capaneus defied Jove to protect them. Jove replied with a thunderbolt that killed the blasphemer with his
blasphemy still on his lips. (Statius, *Thebiad* X. 845ff.)   1. Mt. Etna. Vulcan was believed to have his
smithy inside the volcano.   2. At the battle of Phlegra in Thessaly the Titans tried to storm Olympus.
Jove drove them back with the help of the thunderbolts Vulcan forged for him.   3. The rill, still blood-
red and still boiling, is the overflow of Phlegethon which descends across the Wood of the Suicides and
the Burning Plain to plunge over the Great Cliff into the Eighth Circle. It is clearly a water of marvels,
for it not only petrifies the sands over which it flows, but its clouds of steam quench all the flames above
its course.   4. A hot sulphur spring near Viterbo. The choice is strikingly apt, for the waters of the
Bulicame not only boil and steam but have a distinctly reddish tint as a consequence of their mineral
content. A part of the Bulicame flows out through what was once a quarter reserved to prostitutes; and
they were given special rights to the water, since they were not permitted to use the public baths.

nothing your eyes have seen is equal to
the marvel of the rill by which we stand,   85
for it stifles all the flames above its course
as it flows out across the burning sand."
So spoke my Guide across the flickering light,
    and I begged him to bestow on me the food
    for which he had given me the appetite.   90
"In the middle of the sea, and gone to waste,
    there lies a country known as Crete," he said,
    "under whose king the ancient world was chaste.
Once Rhea[5] chose it as the secret crypt
    and cradle of her son; and better to hide him,   95
    her Corybantes raised a din when he wept.
An ancient giant[6] stands in the mountain's core.
    He keeps his shoulder turned toward Damietta,
    and looks toward Rome as if it were his mirror.
His head is made of gold; of silverwork   100
    his breast and both his arms, of polished brass
    the rest of his great torso to the fork.
He is of chosen iron from there down,
    except that his right foot is terra cotta;
    it is this foot he rests more weight upon.   105
Every part except the gold is split
    by a great fissure from which endless tears
    drip down and hollow out the mountain's pit.
Their course sinks to this pit from stone to stone,
    becoming Acheron, Phlegethon, and Styx.   110
    Then by this narrow sluice they hurtle down
to the end of all descent, and disappear
    into Cocytus.[7] You shall see what sink that is
    with your own eyes. I pass it in silence here."
And I to him: "But if these waters flow   115
    from the world above, why is this rill met only

5. Wife of Saturn (Cronos) and mother of Jove (Zeus). It had been prophesied to Saturn that one of his
own children would dethrone him. To nullify the prophecy Saturn devoured each of his children at birth.
On the birth of Jove, Rhea duped Saturn by letting him bolt down a stone wrapped in baby clothes. After
this tribute to her husband's appetite she hid the infant on Mount Ida in Crete. There she posted her
Corybantes (or Bacchantes) as guards and instructed them to set up a great din whenever the baby cried.
Thus Saturn would not hear him. The Corybantic dances of the ancient Greeks were based on the frenzied
shouting and clashing of swords on shields with which the Corybantes protected the infant Jove.   6. This
is the Old Man of Crete. The original of this figure occurs in Daniel 2:32–34, where it is told by Daniel
as Nebuchadnezzar's dream. Dante follows the details of the original closely but adds a few of his own and
a totally different interpretation. In Dante each metal represents one of the ages of humanity, each deteriorating from the Golden Age of Innocence. The left foot, terminating the Age of Iron, is the Holy Roman
Empire. The right foot, of terra cotta, is the Roman Catholic Church, a more fragile base than the left,
but the one upon which the greater weight descends. The tears of the woes of humanity are a Dantean
detail: they flow down the great fissure that defaces all but the Golden Age. Thus, starting in woe, they
flow through humanity's decline, into the hollow of the mountain and become the waters of all Hell.
Dante's other major addition is the site and position of the figure: equidistant from the three continents,
the Old Man stands at a sort of center of Time, with his back turned to Damietta in Egypt (here symbolizing
the East, the past, the birth of religion) and fixes his gaze upon Rome (the West, the future, the Catholic
Church). It is certainly the most elaborately worked single symbol in the *Inferno*.   7. The frozen lake
that lies at the bottom of Hell. (See Cantos XXXII–XXXIV.)

along this shelf?" And he to me: "You know
the place is round, and though you have come deep
    into the valley through the many circles,
    always bearing left along the steep,   120
you have not traveled any circle through
    its total round; hence when new things appear
    from time to time, that hardly should surprise you."
And I: "Where shall we find Phlegethon's course?
    And Lethe's? One you omit, and of the other   125
    you only say the tear-flood is its source."
"In all you ask of me you please me truly,"
    he answered, "but the red and boiling water
    should answer the first question you put to me,
and you shall stand by Lethe, but far hence: 130
    there, where the spirits go to wash themselves
    when their guilt has been removed by penitence."
And then he said: "Now it is time to quit
    this edge of shade: follow close after me
    along the rill, and do not stray from it;   135
for the unburning margins form a lane,
    and by them we may cross the burning plain."

CANTO XV

Circle Seven: Round Three   The Violent Against Nature

Protected by the marvelous powers of the boiling rill, the Poets walk
along its banks across the burning plain. The Wood of the Suicides is
behind them; the Great Cliff at whose foot lies the Eighth Circle is before
them.

They pass one of the roving bands of Sodomites. One of the sinners
stops Dante, and with great difficulty the Poet recognizes him under his
baked features as Ser Brunetto Latino. This is a reunion with a dearly loved
man and writer, one who had considerably influenced Dante's own development, and Dante addresses him with great and sorrowful affection, paying him the highest tribute offered to any sinner in the *Inferno*. Brunetto
prophesies Dante's sufferings at the hands of the Florentines, gives an account
of the souls that move with him through the fire, and finally, under Divine
Compulsion, races off across the plain.

We go by one of the stone margins now
    and the steam of the rivulet makes a shade above it,
    guarding the stream and banks from the flaming snow.
As the Flemings in the lowland between Bruges
    and Wissant, under constant threat of the sea,   5
    erect their great dikes to hold back the deluge;[8]

8. Dante compares the banks of the rill of Phlegethon to the dikes built by the Flemings to hold back the
sea, and to those built by the Paduans to hold back the spring floods of the river Brent. Chiarentana (Latin:
Clarentana) was a Duchy in the Middle Ages. Its territory included the headwaters of the Brent (Brenta).

as the Paduans along the shores of the Brent
  build levees to protect their towns and castles
  lest Chiarentana drown in the spring torrent—
to the same plan, though not so wide nor high,[9]   10
  did the engineer, whoever he may have been,
  design the margin we were crossing by.
Already we were so far from the wood
  that even had I turned to look at it,
  I could not have made it out from where I stood,   15
when a company of shades came into sight
  walking beside the bank. They stared at us
  as men at evening by the new moon's light
stare at one another when they pass by
  on a dark road, pointing their eyebrows toward us   20
  as an old tailor squints at his needle's eye.
Stared at so closely by that ghostly crew,
  I was recognized by one who seized the hem
  of my skirt and said: "Wonder of wonders! You?"
And I, when he stretched out his arm to me,   25
  searched his baked features closely, till at last
  I traced his image from my memory
in spite of the burnt crust, and bending near
  to put my face closer to his, at last
  I answered: "Ser Brunetto,[1] are you here?"   30
"O my son! may it not displease you," he cried,
  "if Brunetto Latino leave his company
  and turn and walk a little by your side."
And I to him: "With all my soul I ask it.
  Or let us sit together, if it please him   35
  who is my Guide and leads me through this pit."
"My son!" he said, "whoever of this train
  pauses a moment, must lie a hundred years
  forbidden to brush off the burning rain.
Therefore, go on; I will walk at your hem,[2]   40
  and then rejoin my company, which goes
  mourning eternal loss in eternal flame."
I did not dare descend to his own level
  but kept my head inclined, as one who walks
  in reverence meditating good and evil.   45
"What brings you here before your own last day?

9. Their width is never precisely specified, but we shall see when Dante walks along speaking to Ser Brunetto (l. 40) that their height is about that of a man.   1. A prominent Florentine Guelph (1212?– 1294) who held, among many other posts, that of notary, whence the title Ser (sometimes Sere). He was not Dante's schoolmaster as many have supposed—he was much too busy and important a man for that. Dante's use of the word "master" is to indicate spiritual indebtedness to Brunetto and his works. It is worth noting that Dante addresses him in Italian as "voi" instead of using the less respectful "tu" form. Farinata is the only other sinner so addressed in the Inferno. Brunetto's two principal books, both of which Dante admires, were the prose Livre dou Tresor (The Book of the Treasure) and the poetic Tesoretta (The Little Treasure). Dante learned a number of his devices from the allegorical journey which forms the Tesoretto. 2. Dante is standing on the dike at approximately the level of Brunetto's head and he cannot descend because of the rain of fire and the burning sands.

What fortune or what destiny?" he began.
"And who is he that leads you this dark way?"
"Up there in the happy life I went astray
   in a valley," I replied, "before I had reached   50
   the fullness of my years. Only yesterday
at dawn I turned from it. This spirit showed
   himself to me as I was turning back,
   and guides me home again along this road."
And he: "Follow your star, for if in all   55
   of the sweet life I saw one truth shine clearly,
   you cannot miss your glorious arrival.
And had I lived to do what I meant to do,
   I would have cheered and seconded your work,
   observing Heaven so well disposed toward you.   60
But that ungrateful and malignant stock
   that came down from Fiesole of old
   and still smacks of the mountain and the rock,
for your good works will be your enemy.[3]
   And there is cause: the sweet fig is not meant   65
   to bear its fruit beside the bitter sorb-tree.[4]
Even the old adage calls them blind,[5]
   an envious, proud, and avaricious people:
   see that you root their customs from your mind.
It is written in your stars, and will come to pass,   70
   that your honours shall make both sides hunger for you:[6]
   but the goat shall never reach to crop that grass.
Let the beasts of Fiesole[7] devour their get
   like sows, but never let them touch the plant,
   if among their rankness any springs up yet,   75
in which is born again the holy seed
   of the Romans who remained among their rabble
   when Florence made a new nest for their greed."
"Ah, had I all my wish," I answered then,
   "you would not yet be banished from the world   80
   in which you were a radiance among men,
for that sweet image, gentle and paternal,
   you were to me in the world when hour by hour
   you taught me how man makes himself eternal,
lives in my mind, and now strikes to my heart;   85
   and while I live, the gratitude I owe it

3. The ancient Etruscan city of Fiesole was situated on a hill about three miles north of the present site
of Florence. According to legend, Fiesole had taken the side of Catiline in his war with Julius Caesar.
Caesar destroyed the town and set up a new city called Florence on the Arno, peopling it with Romans
and Fiesolans. The Romans were the aristocracy of the new city, but the Fiesolans were a majority. Dante
ascribes the endless bloody conflicts of Florence largely to the internal strife between these two strains. His
scorn of the Fiesolans is obvious in this passage. Dante proudly proclaimed his descent from the Roman
strain.   4. A species of tart apple.   5. The source of this proverbial expression, "Blind as a Florentine," can no longer be traced with any assurance, though many incidents from Florentine history suggest
possible sources.   6. Brunetto can scarcely mean that both sides will hunger to welcome the support of
a man of Dante's distinction. Rather, that both sides will hunger to destroy him. (See also lines 94–95.
Dante obviously accepts this as another dark prophecy.)   7. The Fiesolans themselves.

will speak to men out of my life and art.
What you have told me of my course, I write
    by another text I save to show a Lady[8]
    who will judge these matters, if I reach her height.   90
This much I would have you know: so long, I say,
    as nothing in my conscience troubles me
    I am prepared for Fortune, come what may.
Twice already in the eternal shade
    I have heard this prophecy;[9] but let Fortune turn   95
    her wheel as she please, and the countryman his spade."
My guiding spirit paused at my last word
    and, turning right about, stood eye to eye
    to say to me: "Well heeded is well heard."
But I did not reply to him, going on   100
    with Ser Brunetto to ask him who was with him
    in the hot sands, the best-born and best known.
And he to me: "Of some who share this walk
    it is good to know; of the rest let us say nothing,
    for the time would be too short for so much talk.   105
In brief, we all were clerks and men of worth,
    great men of letters, scholars of renown;
    all by the one same crime defiled on earth.
Priscian[1] moves there along the wearisome
    sad way, and Francesco d'Accorso,[2] and also there,   110
    if you had any longing for such scum,
you might have seen that one the Servant of Servants[3]
    sent from the Arno to the Bacchiglione
    where he left his unnatural organ[4] wrapped in cerements.
I would say more, but there across the sand   115
    a new smoke rises and new people come,
    and I must run to be with my own band.
Remember my *Treasure*, in which I still live on:
    I ask no more." He turned then, and he seemed,
    across that plain, like one of those who run   120
for the green cloth at Verona;[5] and of those,
    more like the one who wins, than those who lose.

8. Beatrice.   9. The prophecies of Ciacco (Canto VI) and of Farinata (Canto X) are the other two places at which Dante's exile and suffering are foretold. Dante replies that come what may he will remain true to his purpose through all affliction; and Virgil turns to look proudly at his pupil, uttering a proverb: "*Bene ascolta chi la nota*," i.e., "Well heeded is well heard."   1. Latin grammarian and poet of the first half of the sixth century.   2. Florentine scholar. He served as a professor at Bologna and, from 1273 to 1280, at Oxford. He died in Bologna in 1294.   3. Dante's old enemy, Boniface VIII (d. 1303). *Servus servorum* is technically a correct papal title, but there is certainly a touch of irony in Dante's application of it in this context. In 1295 Boniface transferred Bishop Andrea de'Mozzi from the Bishopric of Florence (on the Arno) to that of Vicenza (on the Bacchiglione). The transference was reputedly brought about at the request of the Bishop's brother, Tommaso de' Mozzi of Florence, who wished to remove from his sight the spectacle of his brother's stupidity and unnatural vices.   4. The original, *mal protesi nervi*, contains an untranslatable word-play. *Nervi* may be taken as "the male organ" and *protesi* for "erected"; thus the organ aroused to passion for unnatural purposes (*mal*). Or *nervi* may be taken as "nerves" and *mal protesi* for "dissolute." Taken in context, the first rendering strikes me as more Dantean.   5. On the first Sunday of Lent all the young men of Verona ran a race for the prize of green cloth. The last runner in was given a live rooster and was required to carry it through the town.

CANTO XVI

Circle Seven: Round Three   The Violent Against Nature and Art

The Poets arrive within hearing of the waterfall that plunges over the Great Cliff into the Eighth Circle. The sound is still a distant throbbing when three wraiths, recognizing Dante's Florentine dress, detach themselves from their band and come running toward him. They are Jacopo Rusticucci, Guido Guerra, and Tegghiaio Aldobrandi, all of them Florentines whose policies and personalities Dante admired. Rusticucci and Tegghiaio have already been mentioned in a highly complimentary way in Dante's talk with Ciacco (Canto VI).

The sinners ask for news of Florence, and Dante replies with a passionate lament for her present degradation. The three wraiths return to their band and the Poets continue to the top of the falls. Here, at Virgil's command, Dante removes a Cord from about his waist and Virgil drops it over the edge of the abyss. As if in answer to a signal, a great distorted shape comes swimming up through the dirty air of the pit.

We could already hear the rumbling drive
    of the waterfall in its plunge to the next circle,
    a murmur like the throbbing of a hive,
when three shades turned together on the plain,
    breaking toward us from a company   5
    that went its way to torture in that rain.
They cried with one voice as they ran toward me:
    "Wait, oh wait, for by your dress you seem
    a voyager from our own tainted country."
Ah! what wounds I saw, some new, some old,   10
    branded upon their bodies! Even now
    the pain of it in memory turns me cold.
My Teacher heard their cries, and turning-to,
    stood face to face. "Do as they ask," he said,
    "for these are souls to whom respect is due;   15
and were it not for the darting flames that hem
    our narrow passage in, I should have said
    it were more fitting you ran after them."
We paused, and they began their ancient wail
    over again, and when they stood below us   20
    they formed themselves into a moving wheel.
As naked and anointed champions do
    in feeling out their grasp and their advantage
    before they close in for the thrust or blow—
so circling, each one stared up at my height,   25
    and as their feet moved left around the circle,
    their necks kept turning backward to the right.
"If the misery of this place, and our unkempt
    and scorched appearance," one of them began,

"bring us and what we pray into contempt,   30
still may our earthly fame move you to tell
  who and what you are, who so securely
  set your live feet to the dead dusts of Hell.
This peeled and naked soul who runs before me
  around this wheel, was higher than you think   35
  there in the world, in honor and degree.
Guido Guerra[6] was the name he bore,
  the good Gualdrada's[7] grandson. In his life
  he won great fame in counsel and in war.
The other who behind me treads this sand   40
  was Tegghiaio Aldobrandi,[8] whose good counsels
  the world would have done well to understand.
And I who share their torment, in my life
  was Jacopo Rusticucci;[9] above all
  I owe my sorrows to a savage wife."   45
I would have thrown myself to the plain below
  had I been sheltered from the falling fire;
  and I think my Teacher would have let me go.
But seeing I should be burned and cooked, my fear
  overcame the first impulse of my heart   50
  to leap down and embrace them then and there.
"Not contempt," I said, "but the compassion
  that seizes on my soul and memory
  at the thought of you tormented in this fashion—
it was grief that choked my speech when through the scorching   55
  air of this pit my Lord announced to me
  that such men as you are might be approaching.
I am of your own land, and I have always
  heard with affection and rehearsed with honor
  your name and the good deeds of your happier days.   60
Led by my Guide and his truth, I leave the gall
  and go for the sweet apples of delight.

6. (ca. 1220–1272). A valiant leader of the Guelphs (hence his name, which signifies Guido of War)
despite his Ghibelline origin as one of the counts of Guidi. It is a curious fact, considering the prominence
of Guido, that Dante is the only writer to label him a sodomite.   7. The legend of "the good Gualdrada," Guido Guerra's grandmother, is a typical example of the medieval talent for embroidery. She was
the daughter of Bellincione Berti de' Ravignana. The legend is that Emperor Otto IV saw her in church
and, attracted by her beauty, asked who she was. Bellincione replied that she was the daughter of one
whose soul would be made glad to have the Emperor salute her with a kiss. The young-lady-of-all-virtues,
hearing her father's words, declared that no man might kiss her unless he were her husband. Otto was so
impressed by the modesty and propriety of this remark that he married her to one of his noblemen and
settled a large estate upon the couple. It was from this marriage that the counts Guidi de Modigliano
(among them Guido Guerra) were said to descend. Unfortunately for the legend, Otto's first visit to Italy
was in 1209, and surviving records show that Count Guido had already had two children by his wife
Gualdrada as early as 1202.   8. Date of birth unknown. He died shortly before 1266. A valiant knight
of the family degli Adimari of the Guelph nobles. With Guido Guerra he advised the Florentines not to
move against the Sienese at the disastrous battle of Montaperti (See Farinata, Canto X), knowing that the
Sienese had been heavily reinforced by mercenaries. It is probably these good counsels that "the world
would have done well to understand." This is another case in which Dante is the only writer to bring the
charge of sodomy.   9. Dates of birth and death unknown, but mention of him exists in Florentine
records of 1235, 1236, 1254, and 1266. A rich and respected Florentine knight. Dante's account of his
sin and of its cause is the only record and it remains unsupported: no details of his life are known.

But first I must descend to the center of all."
"So may your soul and body long continue
together on the way you go," he answered,   65
"and the honor of your days shine after you—
tell me if courtesy and valor raise
their banners in our city as of old,
or has the glory faded from its days?
For Borsiere,[1] who is newly come among us   70
and yonder goes with our companions in pain,
taunts us with such reports, and his words have stung us."
"O Florence! your sudden wealth and your upstart
rabble, dissolute and overweening,
already set you weeping in your heart!"   75
I cried with face upraised, and on the sand
those three sad spirits looked at one another
like men who hear the truth and understand.
"If this be your manner of speaking, and if you can
satisfy others with such ease and grace,"   80
they said as one, "we hail a happy man.
Therefore, if you win through this gloomy pass
and climb again to see the heaven of stars;
when it rejoices you to say 'I was',
speak of us to the living." They parted then,   85
breaking their turning wheel, and as they vanished
over the plain, their legs seemed wings. "Amen"
could not have been pronounced between their start
and their disappearance over the rim of sand.
And then it pleased my Master to depart.   90
A little way beyond we felt the quiver
and roar of the cascade, so close that speech
would have been drowned in thunder. As that river—[2]
the first one on the left of the Apennines
to have a path of its own from Monte Veso   95
to the Adriatic Sea—which, as it twines
is called the Acquacheta from its source
until it nears Forli, and then is known
as the Montone in its further course—
resounds from the mountain in a single leap   100
there above San Benedetto dell'Alpe
where a thousand falls might fit into the steep;
so down from a sheer bank, in one enormous

1. "Borsiere" in Italian means "pursemaker," and the legend has grown without verification or likelihood that this was his origin. He was a courtier, a peacemaker, and an arranger of marriages. Boccaccio speaks of him in highly honorable terms in the Eighth Tale of the First Day of the *Decameron*.   2. The water course described by Dante and made up of the Acquacheta and the Montone flows directly into the sea without draining via the Po. The placement of it as "first on the left of the Apennines" has been shown by Casella to result from the peculiar orientation of the maps of Dante's time. The "river" has its source and course along a line running almost exactly northwest from Florence. San Benedetto dell' Alpe is a small monastery situated on that line about twenty-five miles from Florence.

plunge, the tainted water roared so loud
a little longer there would have deafened us.   105
I had a cord bound round me like a belt[3]
which I had once thought I might put to use
to snare the leopard with the gaudy pelt.
When at my Guide's command I had unbound
its loops from about my habit, I gathered it   110
and held it out to him all coiled and wound.
He bent far back to his right, and throwing it
out from the edge, sent it in a long arc
into the bottomless darkness of the pit.
"Now surely some unusual event,"   115
I said to myself, "must follow this new signal
upon which my good Guide is so intent."
Ah, how cautiously a man should breathe
near those who see not only what we do,
but have the sense which reads the mind beneath!   120
He said to me: "You will soon see arise
what I await, and what you wonder at;
soon you will see the thing before your eyes."
To the truth which will seem falsehood every man
who would not be called a liar while speaking fact   125
should learn to seal his lips as best he can.
But here I cannot be still: Reader, I swear
by the lines of my Comedy—so may it live—
that I saw swimming up through that foul air
a shape to astonish the most doughty soul,   130
a shape like one returning through the sea
from working loose an anchor run afoul
of something on the bottom—so it rose,
its arms spread upward and its feet drawn close.

CANTO XVII

Circle Seven: Round Three   The Violent Against Art. Geryon

The monstrous shape lands on the brink and Virgil salutes it ironically.
It is Geryon, the Monster of Fraud. Virgil announces that they must fly
down from the cliff on the back of this monster. While Virgil negotiates
for their passage, Dante is sent to examine the Usurers (the Violent Against
Art).

These sinners sit in a crouch along the edge of the burning plain that
approaches the cliff. Each of them has a leather purse around his neck,

3. As might be expected, many ingenious explanations have been advanced to account for the sudden
appearance of this cord. It is frequently claimed, but without proof, that Dante had been a minor friar of
the Franciscans but had left without taking vows. The explanation continues that he had clung to the
habit of wearing the white cord of the Franciscans, which he now produces with the information that he
had once intended to use it to snare the Leopard. One invention is probably as good as another. What
seems obvious is that the narrative required some sort of device for signaling the monster, and that to meet
his narrative need, Dante suddenly invented the business of the cord.

and each purse is blazoned with a coat of arms. Their eyes, gushing with tears, are forever fixed on these purses. Dante recognizes none of these sinners, but their coats of arms are unmistakably those of well-known Florentine families.

Having understood who they are and the reason for their present condition, Dante cuts short his excursion and returns to find Virgil mounted on the back of Geryon. Dante joins his Master and they fly down from the great cliff.

Their flight carries them from the Hell of the Violent and the Bestial (the Sins of the Lion) into the Hell of the Fraudulent and Malicious (the Sins of the Leopard).

> "Now see the sharp-tailed beast that mounts the brink.
> He passes mountains, breaks through walls and weapons.
> Behold the beast that makes the whole world stink."[4]
> These were the words my Master spoke to me;
> then signaled the weird beast to come to ground   5
> close to the sheer end of our rocky levee.
> The filthy prototype of Fraud drew near
> and settled his head and breast upon the edge
> of the dark cliff, but let his tail hang clear.
> His face was innocent of every guile,   10
> benign and just in feature and expression;
> and under it his body was half reptile.
> His two great paws were hairy to the armpits;
> all his back and breast and both his flanks
> were figured with bright knots and subtle circlets: 15
> never was such a tapestry of bloom
> woven on earth by Tartar or by Turk,[5]
> nor by Arachne[6] at her flowering loom.
> As a ferry sometimes lies along the strand,
> part beached and part afloat; and as the beaver,[7]   20
> up yonder in the guzzling Germans' land,
> squats halfway up the bank when a fight is on—
> just so lay that most ravenous of beasts
> on the rim which bounds the burning sand with stone.
> His tail twitched in the void beyond that lip,   25

---

4. Geryon, a mythical king of Spain represented as a giant with three heads and three bodies. He was killed by Hercules, who coveted the king's cattle. A later tradition represents him as killing and robbing strangers whom he lured into his realm. It is probably on this account that Dante chose him as the prototype of fraud, though in a radically altered bodily form. Some of the details of Dante's Geryon may be drawn from Revelation 9:9–20, but most of them are almost certainly his own invention: a monster with the general shape of a dragon but with the tail of a scorpion, hairy arms, a gaudily-marked reptilian body, and the face of a just and honest man.   5. These were the most skilled weavers of Dante's time. 6. She was so famous as a spinner and weaver that she challenged Minerva to a weaving contest. There are various accounts of what happened in the contest, but all of them end with the goddess so moved to anger that she changed Arachne into a spider.   7. Dante's description of the beaver is probably drawn from some old bestiary or natural history. It may be based on the medieval belief that the beaver fished by crouching on the bank, scooping the fish out with its tail. *The guzzling Germans:* The heavy drinking of the Germans was proverbial in the Middle Ages and far back into antiquity.

thrashing, and twisting up the envenomed fork
which, like a scorpion's stinger, armed the tip.
My Guide said: "It is time now we drew near
     that monster." And descending on the right[8]
we moved ten paces outward to be clear   30
of sand and flames. And when we were beside him,
     I saw upon the sand a bit beyond us
     some people crouching close beside the brim.[9]
The Master paused. "That you may take with you
     the full experience of this round," he said,   35
     "go now and see the last state of that crew.
But let your talk be brief, and I will stay
     and reason with this beast till you return,
     that his strong back may serve us on our way."
So further yet along the outer edge   40
     of the seventh circle I moved on alone.
     And came to the sad people of the ledge.
Their eyes burst with their grief; their smoking hands
     jerked about their bodies, warding off
     now the flames and now the burning sands.   45
Dogs in summer bit by fleas and gadflies,
     jerking their snouts about, twitching their paws
     now here, now there, behave no otherwise.
I examined several faces there among
     that sooty throng, and I saw none I knew;   50
     but I observed that from each neck there hung
an enormous purse, each marked with its own beast
     and its own colors like a coat of arms.
     On these their streaming eyes appeared to feast.
Looking about, I saw one purse display   55
     azure on or, a kind of lion;[1] another,
     on a blood red field, a goose whiter than whey.[2]
And one that bore a huge and swollen sow
     azure on field argent[3] said to me:
     "What are you doing in this pit of sorrow?   60
Leave us alone! And since you have not yet died,
     I'll have you know my neighbor Vitaliano[4]
     has a place reserved for him here at my side.

8. The Poets had crossed on the right bank of the rill. In the course of Geryon's flight they will be carried to the other side of the falls, thus continuing their course to the left. It should be noted that inside the walls of Dis, approaching the second great division of Hell (as here the third) they also moved to the right. No satisfactory reason can be given for these exceptions.   9. The Usurers. Virgil explains in Canto XI why they sin against Art, which is the Grandchild of God. They are the third and final category of the Violent against God and His works.   1. The arms of the Gianfigliazzi of Florence were a lion azure on a field of gold. The sinner bearing this purse must be Catello di Rosso Gianfigliazzi, who set up as a usurer in France and was made a knight on his return to Florence.   2. A white goose on a red field was the arms of the noble Ghibelline family of the Ubriachi, or Ebriachi, of Florence. The wearer is probably Ciappo Ubriachi, a notorious usurer.   3. These are the arms of the Scrovegni of Padua. The bearer is probably Reginaldo Scrovegni.   4. Vitaliano di Iacopo Vitaliani, another Paduan.

A Paduan among Florentines, I sit here
    while hour by hour they nearly deafen me   65
    shouting: 'Send us the sovereign cavalier
with the purse of the three goats!' "[5] He half arose,
    twisted his mouth, and darted out his tongue
    for all the world like an ox licking its nose.
And I, afraid that any longer stay   70
    would anger him who had warned me to be brief,
    left those exhausted souls without delay.
Returned, I found my Guide already mounted
    upon the rump of that monstrosity.
He said to me: "Now must you be undaunted: 75
this beast must be our stairway to the pit:
    mount it in front, and I will ride between
    you and the tail, lest you be poisoned by it."
Like one so close to the quartanary chill[6]
    that his nails are already pale and his flesh trembles   80
    at the very sight of shade or a cool rill—
so did I tremble at each frightful word.
    But his scolding filled me with that shame that makes
    the servant brave in the presence of his lord.
I mounted the great shoulders of that freak   85
    and tried to say "Now help me to hold on!"
    But my voice clicked in my throat and I could not speak.
But no sooner had I settled where he placed me
    than he, my stay, my comfort, and my courage
    in other perils, gathered and embraced me.   90
Then he called out: "Now, Geryon, we are ready:
    bear well in mind that his is living weight
    and make your circles wide and your flight steady."
As a small ship slides from a beaching or its pier,
    backward, backward—so that monster slipped   95
    back from the rim. And when he had drawn clear
he swung about, and stretching out his tail
    he worked it like an eel, and with his paws
    he gathered in the air, while I turned pale.
I think there was no greater fear the day   100
    Phaeton[7] let loose the reins and burned the sky
    along the great scar of the Milky Way,

5. Giovanni di Buiamonte was esteemed in Florence as "the sovereign cavalier" and was chosen for many high offices. He was a usurer and a gambler who lost great sums at play. Dante's intent is clearly to bewail the decay of standards which permits Florence to honor so highly a man for whom Hell is waiting so dismally. Buiamonte was of the Becchi family whose arms were three black goats on a gold field. "Becchi" in Italian is the plural form of the word for "goat."   6. Quartan fever is an ague that runs a four-day cycle with symptoms roughly like those of malaria. At the approach of the chill, Dante intends his figure to say, any thought of coolness strikes terror into the shivering victim.   7. Son of Apollo who drove the chariot of the sun. Phaeton begged his father for a chance to drive the chariot himself but he lost control of the horses and Zeus killed him with a thunderbolt for fear the whole earth would catch fire. The scar left in the sky by the runaway horses is marked by the Milky Way.

nor when Icarus, too close to the sun's track
   felt the wax melt, unfeathering his loins,
   and heard his father cry "Turn back! Turn back!"—[8]   105
than I felt when I found myself in air,
   afloat in space with nothing visible
   but the enormous beast that bore me there.
Slowly, slowly, he swims on through space,
   wheels and descends, but I can sense it only   110
   by the way the wind blows upward past my face.
Already on the right I heard the swell
   and thunder of the whirlpool. Looking down
   I leaned my head out and stared into Hell.
I trembled again at the prospect of dismounting   115
   and cowered in on myself, for I saw fires
   on every hand, and I heard a long lamenting.
And then I saw—till then I had but felt it—
   the course of our down-spiral to the horrors
   that rose to us from all sides of the pit.   120
As a flight-worn falcon sinks down wearily
   though neither bird nor lure has signalled it,[9]
   the falconer crying out: "What! spent already!"—
then turns and in a hundred spinning gyres
   sulks from her master's call, sullen and proud—   125
   so to that bottom lit by endless fires
the monster Geryon circled and fell,
   setting us down at the foot of the precipice
   of ragged rock on the eighth shelf of Hell.
And once freed of our weight, he shot from there   130
into the dark like an arrow into air.

CANTO XVIII

Circle Eight (Malebolge)   The Fraudulent and Malicious
Bolgia One   The Panderers and Seducers
Bolgia Two   The Flatterers

   Dismounted from Geryon, the Poets find themselves in the Eighth Circle, called Malebolge (the Evil Ditches). This is the upper half of the Hell of the Fraudulent and Malicious. Malebolge is a great circle of stone that slopes like an amphitheater. The slopes are divided into ten concentric ditches; and within these ditches, each with his own kind, are punished those guilty of Simple Fraud.

   A series of stone dikes runs like spokes from the edge of the great cliff face to the center of the place, and these serve as bridges.

8. Daedalus, the father of Icarus, made wings for himself and his son and they flew into the sky, but Icarus, ignoring his father's commands, flew too close to the sun. The heat melted the wax with which the wings were fastened and Icarus fell into the Aegean and was drowned.   9. Falcons, when sent aloft, were trained to circle until sighting a bird, or until signaled back by the lure (a stuffed bird). Flight-weary, Dante's metaphoric falcon sinks bit by bit, rebelling against his training and sulking away from his master in wide slow circles.

The Poets bear left toward the first ditch, and Dante observes below him and to his right the sinners of the first bolgia, the Panderers and Seducers. These make two files, one along either bank of the ditch, and are driven at an endless fast walk by horned demons who hurry them along with great lashes. In life these sinners goaded others on to serve their own foul purposes; so in Hell are they driven in their turn. The horned demons who drive them symbolize the sinners' own vicious natures, embodiments of their own guilty consciences. Dante may or may not have intended the horns of the demons to symbolize cuckoldry and adultery.

The Poets see Venedico Caccianemico and Jason in the first pit, and pass on to the second, where they find the souls of the Flatterers sunk in excrement, the true equivalent of their false flatteries on earth. They observe Alessio Interminelli and Thaïs, and pass on.

There is in Hell a vast and sloping ground
   called Malebolge,[1] a lost place of stone
   as black as the great cliff that seals it round.
Precisely in the center of that space
   there yawns a well extremely wide and deep.[2]   5
   I shall discuss it in its proper place.
The border that remains between the well-pit
   and the great cliff forms an enormous circle,
   and ten descending troughs are cut in it,
offering a general prospect like the ground   10
   that lies around one of those ancient castles
   whose walls are girded many times around
by concentric moats. And just as, from the portal,
   the castle's bridges run from moat to moat
   to the last bank; so from the great rock wall   15
across the embankments and the ditches, high
   and narrow cliffs run to the central well,
   which cuts and gathers them like radii.
Here, shaken from the back of Geryon,
   we found ourselves. My Guide kept to the left   20
   and I walked after him. So we moved on.
Below, on my right, and filling the first ditch
   along both banks, new souls in pain appeared,
   new torments, and new devils black as pitch.
All of these sinners were naked; on our side   25
   of the middle they walked toward us; on the other,
   in our direction, but with swifter stride.
Just so the Romans, because of the great throng

1. *Bolgia* in Italian equals "ditch" or "pouch." That combination of meanings is not possible in a single English word, but it is well to bear in mind that Dante intended both meanings: not only a ditch of evil, but a pouch full of it, a filthy treasure of ill-gotten souls.   2. This is the final pit of Hell, and in it are punished the Treacherous (those Guilty of Compound Fraud). Cantos XXIX–XXXIV will deal with this part of Hell.

in the year of the Jubilee, divide the bridge[3]
in order that the crowds may pass along,   30
so that all face the Castle as they go
on one side toward St. Peter's, while on the other,
all move along facing toward Mount Giordano.
And everywhere along that hideous track
  I saw horned demons with enormous lashes   35
  move through those souls, scourging them on the back.
Ah, how the stragglers of that long rout stirred
  their legs quick-march at the first crack of the lash!
  Certainly no one waited a second, or third!
As we went on, one face in that procession   40
  caught my eye and I said: "That sinner there:
  It is certainly not the first time I've seen that one."
I stopped, therefore, to study him, and my Guide
  out of his kindness waited, and even allowed me
  to walk back a few steps at the sinner's side.   45
And that flayed spirit, seeing me turn around,
  thought to hide his face, but I called to him:
  "You there, that walk along with your eyes on the ground—
if those are not false features, then I know you
  as Venedico Caccianemico of Bologna:[4]   50
  what brings you here among this pretty crew?"
And he replied: "I speak unwillingly,
  but something in your living voice, in which
  I hear the world again, stirs and compels me.
It was I who brought the fair Ghisola 'round   55
  to serve the will and lust of the Marquis,
  however sordid that old tale may sound.
There are many more from Bologna who weep away
  eternity in this ditch; we fill it so
  there are not as many tongues that are taught to say   60
'sipa'[5] in all the land that lies between
  the Reno and the Saveno, as you must know
  from the many tales of our avarice and spleen."
And as he spoke, one of those lashes fell
  across his back, and a demon cried, "Move on,   65
  you pimp, there are no women here to sell."
Turning away then, I rejoined my Guide.
  We came in a few steps to a raised ridge

3. Boniface VIII had proclaimed 1300 a Jubilee Year, and consequently throngs of pilgrims had come to
Rome. Since the date of the vision is also 1300, the Roman throngs are moving back and forth across the
Tiber via Ponte Castello Sant' Angelo at the very time Dante is watching the sinners in Hell.   4. To
win the favor of the Marquis Obbizo da Este of Ferrara, Caccianemico acted as the procurer of his own
sister Ghisola, called "la bella" or "Ghisolabella."   5. Bolognese dialect for sì, i.e., "yes." Bologna lies
between the Savena and the Reno. This is a master taunt at Bologna as a city of panderers and seducers,
for it clearly means that the Bolognese then living on earth were fewer in number than the Bolognese dead
who had been assigned to this bolgia.

that made a passage to the other side.
This we climbed easily, and turning right 70
    along the jagged crest, we left behind
    the eternal circling of those souls in flight.
And when we reached the part at which the stone
    was tunneled for the passage of the scourged,
    my Guide said, "Stop a minute and look down 75
on these other misbegotten wraiths of sin.
    You have not seen their faces, for they moved
    in the same direction we were headed in."
So from that bridge we looked down on the throng
    that hurried toward us on the other side. 80
    Here, too, the whiplash hurried them along.
And the good Master, studying that train,
    said: "Look there, at that great soul that approaches
    and seems to shed no tears for all his pain—
what kingliness moves with him even in Hell! 85
    It is Jason,[6] who by courage and good advice
    made off with the Colchian Ram. Later it fell
that he passed Lemnos, where the women of wrath,
    enraged by Venus' curse that drove their lovers
    out of their arms, put all their males to death. 90
There with his honeyed tongue and his dishonest
    lover's wiles, he gulled Hypsipyle,
    who, in the slaughter, had gulled all the rest.
And there he left her, pregnant and forsaken.
    Such guilt condemns him to such punishment; 95
    and also for Medea is vengenace taken.
All seducers march here to the whip.
    And let us say no more about this valley
    and those it closes in its stony grip."
We had already come to where the walk 100
    crosses the second bank, from which it lifts
    another arch, spanning from rock to rock.
Here we heard people whine in the next chasm,
    and knock and thump themselves with open palms,
    and blubber through their snouts as if in a spasm. 105
Steaming from that pit, a vapour rose
    over the banks, crusting them with a slime
    that sickened my eyes and hammered at my nose.
That chasm sinks so deep we could not sight

6. Leader of the Argonauts. He carried off the Colchian Ram (i.e., The Golden Fleece). "The good advice" that helped him win the fleece was given by Medea, daughter of the King of Colchis, whom Jason took with him and later abandoned for Creusa ("Also for Medea is vengeance taken.") In the course of his very Grecian life, Jason had previously seduced Hypsipyle and deserted her to continue his voyage after the fleece. She was one of the women of Lemnos whom Aphrodite, because they no longer worshiped her, cursed with a foul smell which made them unbearable to their husbands and lovers. The women took their epic revenge by banding together to kill all their males, but Hypsipyle managed to save her father, King Thoas, by pretending to the women that she had already killed him.

its bottom anywhere until we climbed   110
along the rock arch to its greatest height.
Once there, I peered down; and I saw long lines
of people in a river of excrement
that seemed the overflow of the world's latrines.
I saw among the felons of that pit   115
one wraith who might or might not have been tonsured—
one could not tell, he was so smeared with shit.
He bellowed: "You there, why do you stare at me
more than at all the others in this stew?"
And I to him: "Because if memory   120
serves me, I knew you when your hair was dry.
You are Alessio Interminelli da Lucca.[7]
That's why I pick you from this filthy fry."
And he then, beating himself on his clown's head:
"Down to this have the flatteries I sold   125
the living sunk me here among the dead."
And my Guide prompted then: "Lean forward a bit
and look beyond him, there—do you see that one
scratching herself with dungy nails, the strumpet
who fidgets to her feet, then to a crouch?   130
It is the whore Thaïs[8] who told her lover
when he sent to ask her, 'Do you thank me much?'
'Much? Nay, past all believing!' And with this
let us turn from the sight of this abyss."

CANTO XIX

Circle Eight: Bolgia Three   The Simoniacs

Dante comes upon the Simoniacs (sellers of ecclesiastic favors and offices)
and his heart overflows with the wrath he feels against those who corrupt
the things of God. This *bolgia* is lined with round tube-like holes and the
sinners are placed in them upside down with the soles of their feet ablaze.
The heat of the blaze is proportioned to their guilt.

The holes in which these sinners are placed are debased equivalents of
the baptismal fonts common in the cities of Northern Italy and the sinners'
confinement in them is temporary: as new sinners arrive, the souls drop
through the bottom of their holes and disappear eternally into the crevices
of the rock.

As always, the punishment is a symbolic retribution. Just as the Simoniacs made a mock of holy office, so are they turned upside down in a
mockery of the baptismal font. Just as they made a mockery of the holy

---

7. One of the noble family of the Interminelli or Interminei, a prominent White family of Lucca. About
all that is known of Alessio is the fact that he was still alive in 1295.   8. The flattery uttered by Thaïs is
put into her mouth by Terence in his *Eunuchus* (act 2, sc. 1, ll. 1–2). Thaïs' lover had sent her a slave,
and later sent a servant to ask if she thanked him much. *Magnas vero agere gratias Thais mihi?* The servant
reported her as answering *Ingentes!* Cicero later commented on the passage as an example of immoderate
flattery, and Dante's conception of Thaïs probably springs from this source. (*De Amicitia*, 26.)

water of baptism, so is their hellish baptism by fire, after which they are wholly immersed in the crevices below. The oily fire that licks at their soles may also suggest a travesty on the oil used in Extreme Unction (last rites for the dying).

Virgil carries Dante down an almost sheer ledge and lets him speak to one who is the chief sinner of that place, Pope Nicholas III. Dante delivers himself of another stirring denunciation of those who have corrupted church office, and Virgil carries him back up the steep ledge toward the Fourth Bolgia.

O Simon Magus![9] O you wretched crew
　who follow him, pandering for silver and gold
　the things of God which should be wedded to
love and righteousness! O thieves for hire,
　now must the trump of judgment sound your doom　5
　here in the third fosse of the rim of fire!
We had already made our way across
　to the next grave, and to that part of the bridge[1]
　which hangs above the mid-point of the fosse.
O Sovereign Wisdom, how Thine art doth shine　10
　in Heaven, on Earth, and in the Evil World![2]
　How justly doth Thy power judge and assign!
I saw along the walls and on the ground
　long rows of holes cut in the livid stone;
　all were cut to a size, and all were round.　15
They seemed to be exactly the same size
　as those in the font of my beautiful San Giovanni,
　built to protect the priests who come to baptize;[3]
(one of which, not so long since, I broke open
　to rescue a boy who was wedged and drowning in it.　20
　Be this enough to undeceive all men.)[4]
From every mouth a sinner's legs stuck out
　as far as the calf. The soles were all ablaze
　and the joints of the legs quivered and writhed about.
Withes and tethers would have snapped in their throes.　25
　As oiled things blaze upon the surface only,
　so did they burn from the heels to the points of their toes.
"Master," I said, "who is that one in the fire

9. Simon the Samarian magician (cf. Acts 8:9–24) from whom the word "Simony" derives. Upon his conversion to Christianity he offered to buy the power to administer the Holy Ghost and was severely rebuked by Peter.　1. The Center point, obviously the best observation point. The next grave: The next bolgia.　2. Hell.　3. It was the custom in Dante's time to baptize only on Holy Saturday and on Pentecost. These occasions were naturally thronged, therefore, and to protect the priests a special font was built in the Baptistry of San Giovanni with marble stands for the priests, who were thus protected from both the crowds and the water in which they immersed those to be baptized. The Baptistry is still standing, but the font is no longer in it. A similar font still exists, however, in the Baptistry at Pisa.　4. In these lines Dante is replying to a charge of sacrilege that had been rumored against him. One day a boy playing in the baptismal font became jammed in the marble tube and could not be extricated. To save the boy from drowning, Dante took it upon himself to smash the tube.

who writhes and quivers more than all the others?[5]
From him the ruddy flames seem to leap higher."   30
And he to me: "If you wish me to carry you down
    along that lower bank, you may learn from him
    who he is, and the evil he has done."
And I: "What you will, I will. You are my lord
    and know I depart in nothing from your wish;   35
    and you know my mind beyond my spoken word."
We moved to the fourth ridge, and turning left
    my Guide descended by a jagged path
    into the strait and perforated cleft.
Thus the good Master bore me down the dim   40
    and rocky slope, and did not put me down
    till we reached the one whose legs did penance for him.
"Whoever you are, sad spirit," I began,
    "who lie here with your head below your heels
    and planted like a stake—speak if you can."   45
I stood like a friar who gives the sacrament
    to a hired assassin, who, fixed in the hole,
    recalls him, and delays his death a moment.[6]
"Are you there already, Boniface?[7] Are you there
    already?" he cried. "By several years the writ   50
    has lied. And all that gold, and all that care—
are you already sated with the treasure
    for which you dared to turn on the Sweet Lady
    and trick and pluck and bleed her at your pleasure?"
I stood like one caught in some raillery,   55
    not understanding what is said to him,
    lost for an answer to such mockery.
Then Virgil said. "Say to him: 'I am not he,
    I am not who you think.' " And I replied
    as my good Master had instructed me.   60
The sinner's feet jerked madly; then again
    his voice rose, this time choked with sighs and tears,
    and said at last: "What do you want of me then?
If to know who I am drives you so fearfully
    that you descend the bank to ask it, know   65
    that the Great Mantle[8] was once hung upon me.

---

5. The fire is proportioned to the guilt of the sinner. These are obviously the feet of the chief sinner of this *bolgia*. In a moment we shall discover that he is Pope Nicholas III.   6. Persons convicted of murdering for hire were sometimes executed by being buried alive upside down. If the friar were called back at the last moment, he should have to bend over the hole in which the man is fixed upside down awaiting the first shovelful of earth.   7. The speaker is Pope Nicholas III, Giovanni Gaetano degli Orsini, Pope from 1277–1280. His presence here is self-explanatory. He is awaiting the arrival of his successor, Boniface VIII, who will take his place in the stone tube and who will in turn be replaced by Clement V, a Pope even more corrupt than Boniface. With the foresight of the damned he had read the date of Boniface's death (1303) in the Book of Fate. Mistaking Dante for Boniface, he thinks his foresight has erred by three years, since it is now 1300.   8. Of the Papacy.

And in truth I was a son of the She-Bear,[9]
so sly and eager to push my whelps ahead,
that I pursed wealth above, and myself here.[1]
Beneath my head are dragged all who have gone   70
before me in buying and selling holy office;
there they cower in fissures of the stone.
I too shall be plunged down when that great cheat
for whom I took you comes here in his turn.
Longer already have I baked my feet   75
and been planted upside-down, than he shall be
before the west sends down a lawless Shepherd[2]
of uglier deeds to cover him and me.
He will be a new Jason of the Maccabees;
and just as that king bent to his high priests' will,   80
so shall the French king do as this one please."
Maybe—I cannot say—I grew too brash
at this point, for when he had finished speaking
I said: "Indeed! Now tell me how much cash
our Lord required of Peter in guarantee   85
before he put the keys into his keeping?
Surely he asked nothing but 'Follow me!'
Nor did Peter, nor the others, ask silver or gold
of Matthew when they chose him for the place
the despicable and damned apostle sold.[3]   90
Therefore stay as you are; this hole well fits you—
and keep a good guard on the ill-won wealth
that once made you so bold toward Charles of Anjou.[4]
And were it not that I am still constrained
by the reverence I owe to the Great Keys[5]   95
you held in life, I should not have refrained
from using other words and sharper still;
for this avarice of yours grieves all the world,
tramples the virtuous, and exalts the evil.
Of such as you was the Evangelist's[6] vision   100

9. Nicholas's family name, degli Orsini, means in Italian "of the bear cubs."   1. A play on the second meaning of *bolgia* (i.e., "purse"). "Just as I put wealth in my purse when alive, so am I put in this foul purse now that I am dead."   2. Clement V, Pope from 1305 to 1314. He came from Gascony (the West) and was involved in many intrigues with the King of France. It was Clement V who moved the Papal See to Avignon where it remained until 1377. He is compared to Jason (see Maccabees 4:7ff.) who bought an appointment as High Priest of the Jews from King Antiochus and thereupon introduced pagan and venal practices into the office in much the same way as Clement used his influence with Philip of France to secure and corrupt his high office. Clement will succeed Boniface in Hell because Boniface's successor, Benedictus XI (1303–1304), was a good and holy man.   3. Upon the expulsion of Judas from the band of Apostles, Matthias was chosen in his place.   4. The seventh son of Louis VIII of France. Charles became King of Naples and of Sicily largely through the good offices of Pope Urban IV and later of Clement IV. Nicholas III withdrew the high favor his predecessors had shown Charles, but the exact nature and extent of his opposition are open to dispute. Dante probably believed, as did many of his contemporaries, that Nicholas instigated the massacre called the Sicilian Vespers, in which the Sicilians overthrew the rule of Charles and held a general slaughter of the French who had been their masters. The Sicilian Vespers, however, was a popular and spontaneous uprising, and it did not occur until Nicholas had been dead for two years.   5. Of the Papacy.   6. St. John the Evangelist. His vision of She who sits upon the waters is set forth in Revelation 17. The Evangelist intended it as a vision of Pagan Rome,

when he saw She who Sits upon the Waters
   locked with the Kings of earth in fornication.
She was born with seven heads and ten enormous
   and shining horns strengthened and made her glad
   as long as love and virtue pleased her spouse.   105
Gold and silver are the gods you adore!
   In what are you different from the idolater,
   save that he worships one, and you a score?
Ah Constantine, what evil marked the hour—
   not of your conversion, but of the fee   110
   the first rich Father[7] took from you in dower!"
And as I sang him this tune, he began to twitch
   and kick both feet out wildly, as if in rage
   or gnawed by conscience—little matter which.
And I think, indeed, it pleased my Guide: his look   115
   was all approval as he stood beside me
   intent upon each word of truth I spoke.
He approached, and with both arms he lifted me,
   and when he had gathered me against his breast,
   remounted the rocky path out of the valley,   120
nor did he tire of holding me clasped to him,
   until we reached the topmost point of the arch
   which crosses from the fourth to the fifth rim
of the pits of woe. Arrived upon the bridge,
   he tenderly set down the heavy burden   125
   he had been pleased to carry up that ledge
which would have been hard climbing for a goat.
Here I looked down on still another moat.

CANTO XX

Circle Eight: Bolgia Four   The Fortune Tellers and Diviners

Dante stands in the middle of the bridge over the Fourth Bolgia and
looks down at the souls of the Fortune Tellers and Diviners. Here are the
souls of all those who attempted by forbidden arts to look into the future.
Among these damned are: Amphiareus, Tiresias, Aruns, Manto, Eurypylus, Michael Scott, Guido Bonatti, and Asdente.

Characteristically, the sin of these wretches is reversed upon them: their
punishment is to have their heads turned backwards on their bodies and to
be compelled to walk backwards through all eternity, their eyes blinded
with tears. Thus, those who sought to penetrate the future cannot even see
in front of themselves; they attempted to move themselves forward in time,

but Dante interprets it as a vision of the Roman Church in its simoniacal corruption. The seven heads are
the seven sacraments; the ten horns, the ten commandments.   7. Silvester (Pope from 314 to 355).
Before him the Popes possessed nothing, but when Constantine was converted and Catholicism became
the official religion of the Empire, the church began to acquire wealth. Dante and the scholars of his time
believed, according to a document called "The Donation of Constantine," that the Emperor had moved
his Empire to the East in order to leave sovereignty of the West to the Church. The document was not
shown to be a forgery until the fifteenth century.

so must they go backwards through all eternity; and as the arts of sorcery
are a distortion of God's law, so are their bodies distorted in Hell.

No more need be said of them: Dante names them, and passes on to fill
the Canto with a lengthy account of the founding of Virgil's native city of
Mantua.

Now must I sing new griefs, and my verses strain
   to form the matter of the Twentieth Canto
   of Canticle One,[8] the Canticle of Pain.
My vantage point[9] permitted a clear view
   of the depths of the pit below: a desolation   5
   bathed with the tears of its tormented crew,
who moved about the circle of the pit
   at about the pace of a litany procession.[1]
   Silent and weeping, they wound round and round it.
And when I looked down from their faces,[2] I saw   10
   that each of them was hideously distorted
   between the top of the chest and the lines of the jaw;
for the face was reversed on the neck, and they came on
   backwards, staring backwards at their loins,[3]
   for to look before them was forbidden. Someone,   15
sometime, in the grip of a palsy may have been
   distorted so, but never to my knowledge;
   nor do I believe the like was ever seen.
Reader, so may God grant you to understand
   my poem and profit from it, ask yourself   20
   how I could check my tears, when near at hand
I saw the image of our humanity
   distorted so that the tears that burst from their eyes
   ran down the cleft of their buttocks. Certainly
I wept. I leaned against the jagged face   25
   of a rock and wept so that my Guide said: "Still?
   Still like the other fools? There is no place
for pity here. Who is more arrogant
   within his soul, who is more impious
   than one who dares to sorrow at God's judgment?   30
Lift up your eyes, lift up your eyes and see
   him the earth swallowed before all the Thebans,
   at which they cried out: 'Whither do you flee,

8. The *Inferno*. The other Canticles are, of course, the *Purgatorio* and the *Paradiso*.   9. Virgil, it will
be recalled, had set Dante down on the bridge across the Fourth Bolgia.   1. The litanies are chanted
not only in church (before the mass), but sometimes in procession, the priest chanting the prayers and the
marchers the response. As one might gather from the context, the processions move very slowly.   2. A
typically Dantean conception. Dante often writes as if the eye pin-pointed on one feature of a figure seen
at a distance. The pin-point must then be deliberately shifted before the next feature can be observed. As
far as I know, this stylistic device is peculiar to Dante.   3. General usage seems to have lost sight of the
fact that the first meaning of "loin" is "that part of a human being or quadruped on either side of the spinal
column between the hipbone and the false ribs." (Webster.)

Amphiareus?[4] Why do you leave the field?'
  And he fell headlong through the gaping earth   35
  to the feet of Minos, where all sin must yield.
Observe how he has made a breast of his back.
  In life he wished to see too far before him,
  and now he must crab backwards round this track.
And see Tiresias,[5] who by his arts   40
  succeeded in changing himself from man to woman,
  transforming all his limbs and all his parts;
later he had to strike the two twined serpents
  once again with his conjurer's wand before
  he could resume his manly lineaments.   45
And there is Aruns,[6] his back to that one's belly,
  the same who in the mountains of the Luni
  tilled by the people of Carrara's valley,
made a white marble cave his den, and there
  with unobstructed view observed the sea   50
  and the turning constellations year by year.
And she whose unbound hair flows back to hide
  her breasts—which you cannot see—and who also wears
  all of her hairy parts on that other side,
was Manto, who searched countries far and near,   55
  then settled where I was born.[7] In that connection
  there is a story I would have you hear.
Tiresias was her sire. After his death,
  Thebes, the city of Bacchus, became enslaved,
  and for many years she roamed about the earth.   60
High in sweet Italy, under the Alps that shut
  the Tyrolean gate of Germany, there lies
  a lake known as Benacus[8] roundabout.
Through endless falls, more than a thousand and one,
  Mount Appennine from Garda to Val Cammonica   65
  is freshened by the waters that flow down
into that lake. At its center is a place
  where the Bishops of Brescia, Trentine, and Verona
  might all give benediction with equal grace.
Peschiera, the beautiful fortress, strong in war   70

---

4. Another of the seven Captains who fought against Thebes (v. Capaneus, Canto XIV). Statius (*Thebaid* VII. 690ff. and VIII. 8ff.) tells how he foresaw his own death in this war, and attempted to run away from it, but was swallowed in his flight by an earthquake. I have Romanized his name from "Amphiaraus." **5.** A Theban diviner and magician. Ovid (*Metamorphoses* III) tells how he came on two twined serpents, struck them apart with his stick, and was thereupon transformed into a woman. Seven years later he came on two serpents similarly entwined, struck them apart, and was changed back.   **6.** An Etruscan sooth-sayer (see Lucan, *Pharsalia* I. 580ff.). He foretold the war between Pompey and Julius Caesar, and also that it would end with Caesar's victory and Pompey's death. *Luni*: Also *Luna*. An ancient Etruscan city. *Carrara's valley*: The Carrarese valley is famous for its white (Carrara) marble.   **7.** Dante's version of the founding of Mantua is based on a reference in the *Aeneid* X. 198–200.   **8.** The ancient name for the famous Lago di Garda, which lies a short distance north of Mantua. The other places named in this passage lie around Lago di Garda. On an island in the lake the three dioceses mentioned in line 68 conjoined. All three bishops, therefore, had jurisdiction on the island.

against the Brescians and the Bergamese,
sits at the lowest point along that shore.
There, the waters Benacus cannot hold
within its bosom, spill and form a river
that winds away through pastures green and gold.   75
But once the water gathers its full flow,
it is called Mincius rather than Benacus
from there to Governo, where it joins the Po.
Still near its source, it strikes a plain, and there
it slows and spreads, forming an ancient marsh   80
which in the summer heats pollutes the air.
The terrible virgin, passing there by chance,
saw dry land at the center of the mire,
untilled, devoid of all inhabitants.
There, shunning all communion with mankind,   85
she settled with the ministers of her arts,
and there she lived, and there she left behind
her vacant corpse. Later the scattered men
who lived nearby assembled on that spot
since it was well defended by the fen.   90
Over those whited bones they raised the city,
and for her who had chosen the place before all others
they named it—with no further augury—
Mantua. Far more people lived there once—
before sheer madness prompted Casalodi   95
to let Pinamonte play him for a dunce.⁹
Therefore, I charge you, should you ever hear
other accounts of this, to let no falsehood
confuse the truth which I have just made clear."
And I to him: "Master, within my soul   100
your word is certainty, and any other
would seem like the dead lumps of burned out coal.
But tell me of those people moving down
to join the rest. Are any worth my noting?
For my mind keeps coming back to that alone."   105
And he: "That one whose beard spreads like a fleece
over his swarthy shoulders, was an augur
in the days when so few males remained in Greece
that even the cradles were all but empty of sons.
He chose the time for cutting the cable at Aulis,   110
and Calchas joined him in those divinations.
He is Eurypylus.¹ I sing him somewhere

9. Albert, Count of Casalodi and Lord of Mantua, let himself be persuaded by Pinamonte de Buonaccorsi
to banish the nobles from Mantua as a source of danger to his rule. Once the nobles had departed,
Pinamonte headed a rebellion against the weakened lord and took over the city himself.   1. According
to Greek custom an augur was summoned before each voyage to choose the exact propitious moment for
departure (cutting the cables). Dante has Virgil imply that Eurypylus and Calchas were selected to choose
the moment for Agamemnon's departure from Aulis to Troy. Actually, according to the *Aeneid*, Eurypylus

in my High Tragedy; you will know the place
who know the whole of it. The other there,
the one beside him with the skinny shanks   115
was Michael Scott,[2] who mastered every trick
of magic fraud, a prince of mountebanks.

See Guido Bonatti[3] there; and see Asdente,
who now would be wishing he had stuck to his last,
but repents too late, though he repents aplenty.   120

And see on every hand the wretched hags
who left their spinning and sewing for soothsaying
and casting of spells with herbs, and dolls, and rags.

But come: Cain with his bush of thorns[4] appears
already on the wave below Seville,   125
above the boundary of the hemispheres;
and the moon was full already yesternight.

as you must well remember from the wood,
for it certainly did not harm you when its light
shone down upon your way before the dawn."   130
And as he spoke to me, we traveled on.

CANTO XXI

Circle Eight: Bolgia Five   The Grafters

The Poets move on, talking as they go, and arrive at the Fifth Bolgia.
Here the Grafters are sunk in boiling pitch and guarded by Demons, who
tear them to pieces with claws and grappling hooks if they catch them
above the surface of the pitch.

The sticky pitch is symbolic of the sticky fingers of the Grafters. It serves
also to hide them from sight, as their sinful dealings on earth were hidden
from men's eyes. The demons, too, suggest symbolic possibilities, for they
are armed with grappling hooks and are forever ready to rend and tear all
they can get their hands on.

The Poets watch a demon arrive with a grafting Senator of Lucca and
fling him into the pitch where the demons set upon him.

To protect Dante from their wrath, Virgil hides him behind some jagged
rocks and goes ahead alone to negotiate with the demons. They set upon
him like a pack of mastiffs, but Virgil secures a safe-conduct from their
leader, Malacoda. Thereupon Virgil calls Dante from hiding, and they are

was not at Aulis. The *Aeneid* (II. 110ff.) tells how Eurypylus and Calchas were both consulted in choosing
the moment for the departure from Troy. Dante seems to have confused the two incidents. *Even the
cradles were all but empty of sons:* At the time of the Trojan Wars, Greece was said to be so empty of males
that scarcely any were to be found even in the cradles.   2. An Irish scholar of the first half of the
thirteenth century. His studies were largely in the occult. Sir Walter Scott refers to him in *The Lay of the
Last Minstrel.*   3. A thirteenth-century astrologer of Forli. He was court astrologer to Guido da Montefeltro (see Canto XXVII) advising him in his wars. *Asdente:* A shoemaker of Parma who turned diviner
and won wide fame for his forecastings in the last half of the thirteenth century.   4. The Moon. Cain
with a bush of thorns was the medieval equivalent of our Man in the Moon. Dante seems to mean by
"Seville" the whole area of Spain and the Straits of Gibraltar (Pillars of Hercules), which were believed to
be the western limit of the world. The moon is setting (i.e., it appears on the western waves) on the
morning of Holy Saturday, 1300.

about to set off when they discover that the Bridge Across the Sixth Bolgia
lies shattered. Malacoda tells them there is another further on and sends a
squad of demons to escort them. Their adventures with the demons continue through the next Canto.
    These two Cantos may conveniently be remembered as the Gargoyle
Cantos. If the total *Commedia* is built like a cathedral (as so many critics
have suggested), it is here certainly that Dante attaches his grotesqueries.
At no other point in the *Commedia* does Dante give such free rein to his
coarsest style.

Thus talking of things which my Comedy does not care
    to sing, we passed from one arch to the next
    until we stood upon its summit. There
we checked our steps to study the next fosse
    and the next vain lamentations of Malebolge;   5
    awesomely dark and desolate it was.
As in the Venetian arsenal,[5] the winter through
    there boils the sticky pitch to caulk the seams
    of the sea-battered bottoms when no crew
can put to sea—instead of which, one starts   10
    to build its ship anew, one plugs the planks
    which have been sprung in many foreign parts;
some hammer at a mast, some at a rib;
    some make new oars, some braid and coil new lines;
    one patches up the mainsail, one the jib—   15
so, but by Art Divine and not by fire,
    a viscid pitch boiled in the fosse below
    and coated all the bank with gluey mire.
I saw the pitch; but I saw nothing in it
    except the enormous bubbles of its boiling,   20
    which swelled and sank, like breathing, through all the pit.
And as I stood and stared into that sink,
    my Master cried, "Take care!" and drew me back
    from my exposed position on the brink.
I turned like one who cannot wait to see   25
    the thing he dreads, and who, in sudden fright,
    runs while he looks, his curiosity
competing with his terror—and at my back
    I saw a figure that came running toward us
    across the ridge, a Demon huge and black.   30
Ah what a face he had, all hate and wildness!
    Galloping so, with his great wings outspread
    he seemed the embodiment of all bitterness.
Across each high-hunched shoulder he had thrown
    one haunch of a sinner, whom he held in place   35

5. The arsenal was not only an arms manufactory but a great center of shipbuilding and repairing.

with a great talon round each ankle bone.
"Blacktalons[6] of our bridge," he began to roar,
"I bring you one of Santa Zita's[7] Elders!

Scrub him down while I go back for more:
I planted a harvest of them in that city: 40
everyone there is a grafter except Bonturo.[8]

There 'Yes' is 'No' and 'No' is 'Yes' for a fee."
Down the sinner plunged, and at once the Demon
spun from the cliff; no mastiff ever sprang

more eager from the leash to chase a felon.   45
Down plunged the sinner and sank to reappear
with his backside arched and his face and both his feet

glued to the pitch, almost as if in prayer.
But the Demons under the bridge, who guard that place
and the sinners who are thrown to them, bawled out: 50

"You're out of bounds here for the Sacred Face:[9]
this is no dip in the Serchio: take your look
and then get down in the pitch. And stay below

unless you want a taste of a grappling hook."
Then they raked him with more than a hundred hooks   55
bellowing: "Here you dance below the covers.

Graft all you can there: no one checks your books."
They dipped him down into that pitch exactly
as a chef makes scullery boys dip meat in a boiler,

holding it with their hooks from floating free.   60
And the Master said: "You had best not be seen[1]
by these Fiends till I am ready. Crouch down here.

One of these rocks will serve you as a screen.
And whatever violence you see done to me,
you have no cause to fear. I know these matters: 65

I have been through this once and come back safely."
With that, he walked on past the end of the bridge;
and it wanted all his courage to look calm

from the moment he arrived on the sixth ridge.
With that same storm and fury that arouses   70
all the house when the hounds leap at a tramp

who suddenly falls to pleading where he pauses—

6. The original is Malebranche, i.e., "Evil Claws."   7. The patron saint of the city of Lucca. "One of
Santa Zita's Elders" would therefore equal "One of Lucca's Senators" (i.e., Aldermen). Commentators
have searched the records of Luccan Aldermen who died on Holy Saturday of 1300, and one Martino
Bottaio has been suggested as the newcomer, but there is no evidence that Dante had a specific man in
mind. More probably he meant simply to underscore the fact that Lucca was a city of grafters, just as
Bologna was represented as a city of panderers and seducers.   8. Bonturo Dati, a politician of Lucca.
The phrase is ironic: Bonturo was the most avid grafter of them all.   9. Il volto santo was an ancient
wooden image of Christ venerated by the Luccanese. These ironies and the grotesqueness of the Elder's
appearance mark the beginning of the gargoyle dance that swells and rolls through this Canto and the
next. Serchio: A river near Lucca.   1. It is only in the passage through this Bolgia, out of the total
journey, that Dante presents himself as being in physical danger. Since his dismissal from office and his
exile from Florence (on pain of death if he return) was based on a false charge of grafting, the reference is
pointedly autobiographical.

so rushed those Fiends from below, and all the pack
    pointed their gleaming pitchforks at my Guide.
    But he stood fast and cried to them: "Stand back!   75
Before those hooks and grapples make too free,
    send up one of your crew to hear me out,
    then ask yourselves if you still care to rip me."
All cried as one: "Let Malacoda² go."
    So the pack stood and one of them came forward,   80
    saying: "What good does he think *this* will do?"
"Do you think, Malacoda," my good Master said,
    "you would see me here, having arrived this far
    already, safe from you and every dread,
without Divine Will and propitious Fate?   85
    Let me pass on, for it is willed in Heaven
    that I must show another this dread state."
The Demon stood there on the flinty brim,
    so taken aback he let his pitchfork drop;
    then said to the others: "Take care not to harm him!"   90
"O you crouched like a cat," my Guide called to me,
    "among the jagged rock piles of the bridge,
    come down to me, for now you may come safely."
Hearing him, I hurried down the ledge;
    and the Demons all pressed forward when I appeared,   95
    so that I feared they might not keep their pledge.
So once I saw the Pisan infantry
    march out under truce from the fortress at Caprona,
    staring in fright at the ranks of the enemy.³
I pressed the whole of my body against my Guide,   100
    and not for an instant did I take my eyes
    from those black fiends who scowled on every side.
They swung their forks saying to one another:
    "Shall I give him a touch in the rump?" and answering:
    "Sure; give him a taste to pay him for his bother."   105
But the Demon who was talking to my Guide
    turned round and cried to him: "At ease there, Snatcher!"
And then to us: "There's no road on this side:
    the arch lies all in pieces in the pit.
If you *must* go on, follow along this ridge;   110
    there's another cliff to cross by just beyond it.⁴

---

2. The name equals "Bad Tail," or "Evil Tail." He is the captain of these grim and semi-military police.
I have not translated his name as I have those of the other fiends, since I cannot see that it offers any real
difficulty to an English reader.   3. A Tuscan army attacked the fortress of Caprona near Pisa in 1289
and after fierce fighting the Pisan defenders were promised a safe-conduct if they would surrender. Dante
was probably serving with the Tuscans (the opening lines of the next Canto certainly suggest that he had
seen military service). In some accounts it is reported that the Tuscans massacred the Pisans despite their
promised safe-conduct—an ominous analogy if true. In any case the emerging Pisans would be sufficiently
familiar with the treacheries of Italian politics to feel profoundly uneasy at being surrounded by their
enemies under such conditions.   4. Malacoda is lying, as the Poets will discover: all the bridges across
the Sixth Bolgia have fallen as a result of the earthquake that shook Hell at the death of Christ.

In just five hours it will be, since the bridge fell,
    a thousand two hundred sixty-six years and a day;[5]
    that was the time the big quake shook all Hell.
I'll send a squad of my boys along that way   115
    to see if anyone's airing himself below:
    you can go with them: there will be no foul play.
Front and center here, Grizzly and Hellken,"
    he began to order them. "You too, Deaddog.
Curlybeard, take charge of a squad of ten.   120
Take Grafter and Dragontooth along with you.
    Pigtusk, Catclaw, Cramper, and Crazyred.
    Keep a sharp lookout on the boiling glue
as you move along, and see that these gentlemen
    are not molested until they reach the crag   125
    where they can find a way across the den."
"In the name of heaven, Master," I cried, "what sort
    of guides are these? Let us go on alone
    if you know the way. Who can trust such an escort!
If you are as wary as you used to be   130
    you surely see them grind their teeth at us,
    and knot their beetle brows so threateningly."
And he: "I do not like this fear in you.
    Let them gnash and knot as they please; they menace only
    the sticky wretches simmering in that stew."   135
They turned along the left bank in a line;
    but not before they formed a single rank
    had stuck their pointed tongues out as a sign
to their Captain that they wished permission to pass,
    and he had made a trumpet of his ass.   140

CANTO XXII

Circle Eight: Bolgia Five   The Grafters

   The poets set off with their escorts of demons. Dante sees the Grafters
lying in the pitch like frogs in water with only their muzzles out. They
disappear as soon as they sight the demons and only a ripple on the surface
betrays their presence.
   One of the Grafters, an Unidentified Navarrese, ducks too late and is
seized by the demons who are about to claw him, but Curlybeard holds
them back while Virgil questions him. The wretch speaks of his fellow
sinners, Friar Gomita and Michel Zanche, while the uncontrollable demons
rake him from time to time with their hooks.

---

5. Christ died on Good Friday of the year 34, and it is now Holy Saturday of the year 1300, five hours
before the hour of death. Many commentators (and Dante himself in the *Convivio*) place the hour of
Christ's death at exactly noon. Accordingly, it would now be 7:00 A.M. of Holy Saturday—exactly eight
minutes since the Poets left the bridge over the Fourth Bolgia (at moonset). In the gospels of Matthew,
Mark, and Luke, however, the hour of Christ's death is precisely stated as 3:00 P.M. Dante would certainly
be familiar with the Synoptic Gospels, and on that authority it would now be 10:00 A.M.

The Navarrese offers to lure some of his fellow sufferers into the hands
of the demons, and when his plan is accepted he plunges into the pitch
and escapes. Hellken and Grizzly fly after him, but too late. They start a
brawl in mid-air and fall into the pitch themselves. Curlybeard immediately organizes a rescue party and the Poets, fearing the bad temper of the
frustrated demons, take advantage of the confusion to slip away.

I have seen horsemen breaking camp. I have seen
    the beginning of the assault, the march and muster,
    and at times the retreat and riot. I have been
where chargers trampled your land, O Aretines![6]
    I have seen columns of foragers, shocks of tourney,   5
    and running of tilts.[7] I have seen the endless lines
march to bells,[8] drums, trumpets, from far and near.
    I have seen them march on signals from a castle.[9]
    I have seen them march with native and foreign gear.
But never yet have I seen horse or foot,   10
    nor ship in range of land nor sight of star,
    take its direction from so low a toot.
We went with the ten Fiends—ah, savage crew!—
    but "In church with saints; with stewpots in the tavern,"
    as the old proverb wisely bids us do.   15
All my attention was fixed upon the pitch:
    to observe the people who were boiling in it,
    and the customs and the punishments of that ditch.
As dolphins surface and begin to flip
    their arched backs from the sea, warning the sailors   20
    to fall-to and begin to secure ship—[1]
So now and then, some soul, to ease his pain.
    showed us a glimpse of his back above the pitch
    and quick as lightning disappeared again.
And as, at the edge of a ditch, frogs squat about   25
    hiding their feet and bodies in the water,
    leaving only their muzzles sticking out—
so stood the sinners in that dismal ditch;
    but as Curlybeard approached, only a ripple
    showed where they had ducked back into the pitch.   30
I saw—the dread of it haunts me to this day—
    one linger a bit too long, as it sometimes happens
    one frog remains when another spurts away;

6. The people of Arezzo. In 1289 the Guelphs of Florence and Lucca defeated the Ghibellines of Arrezo
at Campaldino. Dante was present with the Guelphs, though probably as an observer and not as a
warrior.   7. A tourney was contested by groups of knights in a field; a tilt by individuals who tried to
unhorse one another across a barrier.   8. The army of each town was equipped with a chariot on which
bells were mounted. Signals could be given by the bells and special decorations made the chariot stand
out in battle. It served therefore as a rallying point.   9. When troops were in sight of their castle their
movements could be directed from the towers—by banners in daytime and by fires at night, much as some
naval signals are still given today.   1. It was a common belief that when dolphins began to leap around
a ship they were warning the sailors of an approaching storm.

and Catclaw, who was nearest, ran a hook
   through the sinner's pitchy hair and hauled him in.   35
   He looked like an otter dripping from the brook.
I knew the names of all the Fiends by then;
   I had made a note of them at the first muster,
   and, marching, had listened and checked them over again.
"Hey, Crazyred," the crew of Demons cried   40
   all together, "give him a taste of your claws.
   Dig him open a little. Off with his hide."
And I then: "Master, can you find out, please,
   the name and history of that luckless one
   who has fallen into the hands of his enemies?"   45
My Guide approached that wraith from the hot tar
   and asked him whence he came. The wretch replied:
   "I was born and raised in the Kingdom of Navarre.
My mother placed me in service to a knight;
   for she had borne me to a squanderer   50
   who killed himself when he ran through his birthright.
Then I became a domestic in the service
   of good King Thibault.[2] There I began to graft,
   and I account for it in this hot crevice."
And Pigtusk, who at the ends of his lower lip   55
   shot forth two teeth more terrible than a boar's,
   made the wretch feel how one of them could rip.
The mouse had come among bad cats, but here
   Curlybeard locked arms around him crying:
   "While I've got hold of him the rest stand clear!"   60
And turning his face to my Guide: "If you want to ask him
   anything else," he added, "ask away
   before the others tear him limb from limb."
And my Guide to the sinner; "I should like to know
   if among the other souls beneath the pitch   65
   are any Italians?"[3] And the wretch: "Just now
I left a shade who came from parts near by.
   Would I were still in the pitch with him, for then
   these hooks would not be giving me cause to cry."
And suddenly Grafter bellowed in great heat: 70
   "We've stood enough!" And he hooked the sinner's arm
   and, raking it, ripped off a chunk of meat.
Then Dragontooth wanted to play, too, reaching down
   for a catch at the sinner's legs; but Curlybeard
   wheeled round and round with a terrifying frown,   75
and when the Fiends had somewhat given ground

---

2. Thibault II was King of Navarre, a realm that lay in what is now northern Spain. 3. Dante uses the term *Latino* strictly speaking, a person from the area of ancient Latium, now (roughly) Lazio, the province in which Rome is located. It was against the Latians that Aeneas fought on coming to Italy. More generally, Dante uses the term for any southern Italian. Here, however, the usage seems precise, since the sinner refers to "points near by" and means Sardinia. Rome is the point in Italy closest to Sardinia.

and calmed a little, my Guide, without delay,
  asked the wretch, who was staring at his wound:
"Who was the sinner from whom you say you made
  your evil-starred departure to come ashore   80
  among these Fiends?" And the wretch: "It was the shade
of Friar Gomita of Gallura,[4] the crooked stem
  of every Fraud: when his master's enemies
  were in his hands, he won high praise from them.
He took their money without case or docket,   85
  and let them go. He was in all his dealings
  no petty bursar, but a kingly pocket.
With him, his endless crony in the fosse,
  is Don Michel Zanche of Logodoro;[5]
  they babble about Sardinia without pause.   90
But look! See that fiend grinning at your side!
  There is much more that I should like to tell you,
  but oh, I think he means to grate my hide!"
But their grim sergeant wheeled, sensing foul play,
  and turning on Cramper, who seemed set to strike,   95
  ordered: "Clear off, you buzzard. Clear off, I say!"
"If either of you would like to see and hear
  Tuscans or Lombards," the pale sinner said,
  "I can lure them out of hiding if you'll stand clear
and let me sit here at the edge of the ditch,   100
  and get all these Blacktalons out of sight;
  for while they're here, no one will leave the pitch.
In exchange for myself, I can fish you up as pretty
  a mess of souls as you like. I have only to whistle
  the way we do when one of us gets free."   105
Deaddog raised his snout as he listened to him;
  then, shaking his head, said, "Listen to the grafter
  spinning his tricks so he can jump from the brim!"
And the sticky wretch, who was all treachery:
  "Oh I am more than tricky when there's a chance   110
  to see my friends in greater misery."
Hellken, against the will of all the crew,
  could hold no longer. "If you jump," he said
  to the scheming wretch, "I won't come after you
at a gallop, but like a hawk after a mouse.   115
  We'll clear the edge and hide behind the bank:
  let's see if you're trickster enough for all of us."
Reader, here is new game! The Fiends withdrew

4. In 1300 Sardinia was a Pisan possession, and was divided into four districts, of which Gallura was the
northeast. Friar Gomita administered Gallura for his own considerable profit. He was hanged by the Pisan
governor when he was found guilty of taking bribes to let prisoners escape.   5. He was made Vicar of
Logodoro when the King of Sardinia went off to war. The King was captured and did not return. Michel
maneuvered a divorce for the Queen and married her himself. About 1290 he was murdered by his son-
in-law, Branca d'Oria (see Canto XXXIII).

from the bank's edge, and Deaddog, who at first
was most against it, led the savage crew.   120
The Navarrese chose his moment carefully:
and planting both his feet against the ground,
he leaped, and in an instant he was free.
The Fiends were stung with shame, and of the lot
Hellken most, who had been the cause of it.   125
He leaped out madly bellowing: "You're caught!"
but little good it did him; terror pressed
harder than wings; the sinner dove from sight
and the Fiend in full flight had to raise his breast.
A duck, when the falcon dives, will disappear   130
exactly so, all in a flash, while he
returns defeated and weary up the air.
Grizzly, in a rage at the sinner's flight,
flew after Hellken, hoping the wraith would escape,
so he might find an excuse to start a fight.   135
And as soon as the grafter sank below the pitch,
Grizzly turned his talons against Hellken,
locked with him claw to claw above the ditch.
But Hellken was sparrowhawk enough for two
and clawed him well; and ripping one another,   140
they plunged together into the hot stew.
The heat broke up the brawl immediately,
but their wings were smeared with pitch and they could not rise.
Curlybeard, upset as his company,
commanded four to fly to the other coast   145
at once with all their grapples. At top speed
the Fiends divided, each one to his post.
Some on the near edge, some along the far,
they stretched their hooks out to the clotted pair
who were already cooked deep through the scar   150
of their first burn. And turning to one side
we slipped off, leaving them thus occupied.

CANTO XXIII

Circle Eight: Bolgia Six   The Hypocrites

The Poets are pursued by the Fiends and escape them by sliding down
the sloping bank of the next pit. They are now in the Sixth Bolgia. Here
the Hypocrites, weighted down by great leaden robes, walk eternally round
and round a narrow track. The robes are brilliantly gilded on the outside
and are shaped like a monk's habit, for the hypocrite's outward appearance
shines brightly and passes for holiness, but under that show lies the terrible
weight of his deceit which the soul must bear through all eternity.

The Poets talk to Two Jovial Friars and come upon Caiaphas, the chief
sinner of that place. Caiaphas was the High Priest of the Jews who coun-

seled the Pharisees to crucify Jesus in the name of public expedience. He is punished by being himself crucified to the floor of Hell by three great stakes, and in such a position that every passing sinner must walk upon him. Thus he must suffer upon his own body the weight of all the world's hypocrisy, as Christ suffered upon his body the pain of all the world's sins.

The Jovial Friars tell Virgil how he may climb from the pit, and Virgil discovers that Malacoda lied to him about the bridges over the Sixth Bolgia.

Silent, apart, and unattended we went
     as Minor Friars go when they walk abroad,
     one following the other. The incident
recalled the fable of the Mouse and the Frog
     that Aesop tells.[6] For compared attentively   5
     point by point, "pig" is no closer to "hog"
than the one case to the other. And as one thought
     springs from another, so the comparison
     gave birth to a new concern, at which I caught
my breath in fear. This thought ran through my mind: 10
     "These Fiends, through us, have been made ridiculous,
     and have suffered insult and injury of a kind
to make them smart. Unless we take good care—
     now rage is added to their natural spleen—
     they will hunt us down as greyhounds hunt the hare."   15
Already I felt my scalp grow tight with fear.
     I was staring back in terror as I said:
     "Master, unless we find concealment here
and soon, I dread the rage of the Fiends: already
     they are yelping on our trail: I imagine them   20
     so vividly I can hear them now." And he:
"Were I a pane of leaded glass,[7] I could not
     summon your outward look more instantly
     into myself, than I do your inner thought.
Your fears were mixed already with my own   25
     with the same suggestion and the same dark look;
     so that of both I form one resolution:
the right bank may be sloping: in that case
     we may find some way down to the next pit
     and so escape from the imagined chase."   30
He had not finished answering me thus
     when, not far off, their giant wings outspread,

6. The fable was not by Aesop, but was attributed to him in Dante's time: A mouse comes to a body of water and wonders how to cross. A frog, thinking to drown the mouse, offers to ferry him, but the mouse is afraid he will fall off. The frog thereupon suggests that the mouse tie himself to one of the frog's feet. In this way they start across, but in the middle the frog dives from under the mouse, who struggles desperately to stay afloat while the frog tries to pull him under. A hawk sees the mouse struggling and swoops down and seizes him; but since the frog is tied to the mouse, it too is carried away, and so both of them are devoured. The mouse would be the Navarrese Grafter. The frog would be the two fiends, Grizzly and Hellken. By seeking to harm the Navarrese they came to grief themselves.   7. A mirror. Mirrors were backed with lead in Dante's time.

I saw the Fiends come charging after us.
Seizing me instantly in his arms, my Guide—
   like a mother wakened by a midnight noise   35
   to find a wall of flame at her bedside
(who takes her child and runs, and more concerned
   for him than for herself, does not pause even
   to throw a wrap about her) raised me, turned,
and down the rugged bank from the high summit   40
   flung himself down supine onto the slope
   which walls the upper side of the next pit.
Water that turns the great wheel of a land-mill
   never ran faster through the end of a sluice
   at the point nearest the paddles[8]—as down that hill   45
my Guide and Master bore me on his breast,
   as if I were not a companion, but a son.
And the soles of his feet had hardly come to rest
   on the bed of the depth below, when on the height
   we had just left, the Fiends beat their great wings.   50
But now they gave my Guide no cause for fright;
   for the Providence that gave them the fifth pit
   to govern as the ministers of Its will,
takes from their souls the power of leaving it.
About us now in the depth of the pit we found   55
   a painted people, weary and defeated.
   Slowly, in pain, they paced it round and round.
All wore great cloaks cut to as ample a size
   as those worn by the Benedictines of Cluny.[9]
   The enormous hoods were drawn over their eyes.   60
The outside is all dazzle, golden and fair;
   the inside, lead, so heavy that Frederick's capes,[1]
   compared to these, would seem as light as air.
O weary mantle for eternity!
   We turned to the left again along their course,   65
   listening to their moans of misery,
but they moved so slowly down that barren strip,
   tired by their burden, that our company
   was changed at every movement of the hip.
And walking thus, I said: "As we go on,   70
   may it please you to look about among these people
   for any whose name or history may be known."
And one who understood Tuscan cried to us there

8. The sharp drop of the sluice makes the water run faster at the point at which it hits the wheel. *Land-mill*: As distinguished from the floating mills common in Dante's time and up to the advent of the steam engine. These were built on rafts that were anchored in the swift-flowing rivers of Northern Italy. 9. The habit of these monks was especially ample and elegant. St. Bernard once wrote ironically to a nephew who had entered this monastery: "If length of sleeves and amplitude of hood made for holiness, what could hold me back from following [your lead]." 1. Frederick II executed persons found guilty of treason by fastening them into a sort of leaden shell. The doomed man was then placed in a cauldron over a fire and the lead was melted around him.

as we hurried past: "I pray you check your speed.
 you who run so fast through the sick air: 75
it may be I am one who will fit your case."
And at his words my Master turned and said:
"Wait now, then go with him at his own pace."
I waited there, and saw along that track
    two souls who seemed in haste to be with me;   80
    but the narrow way and their burden held them back.
When they had reached me down that narrow way
    they stared at me in silence and amazement,
    then turned to one another. I heard one say:
"This one seems, by the motion of his throat,   85
    to be alive; and if they are dead, how is it
    they are allowed to shed the leaden coat?"
And then to me: "O Tuscan, come so far
    to the college of the sorry hypocrites,
    do not disdain to tell us who you are."   90
And I: "I was born and raised a Florentine
    on the green and lovely banks of Arno's waters,
    I go with the body that was always mine.
But who are *you*, who sighing as you go
    distill in floods of tears that drown your cheeks?   95
    What punishment is this that glitters so?"
"These burnished robes are of thick lead," said one,
    "and are hung on us like counterweights, so heavy
    that we, their weary fulcrums, creak and groan.
Jovial Friars[2] and Bolognese were we.   100
    We were chosen jointly by your Florentines
    to keep the peace,[3] an office usually
held by a single man; near the Gardingo[4]
    one still may see the sort of peace we kept.
    I was called Catalano, he, Loderingo."   105
I began: "O Friars, your evil . . . ."—and then I saw
    a figure crucified upon the ground[5]
    by three great stakes, and I fell still in awe.
When he saw me there, he began to puff great sighs

---

2. A nickname given to the military monks of the order of the Glorious Virgin Mary founded at Bologna
in 1261. Their original aim was to serve as peacemakers, enforcers of order, and protectors of the weak,
but their observance of their rules became so scandalously lax, and their management of worldly affairs so
self-seeking, that the order was disbanded by Papal decree.   3. Catalano dei Malavolti (ca. 1210–1285),
a Guelph, and Loderingo degli Andolo (ca. 1210–1293), a Ghibelline, were both Bolognese and, as
brothers of the Jovial Friars, both had served as *podestà* (the chief officer charged with keeping the peace)
of many cities for varying terms. In 1266 they were jointly appointed to the office of *podestà* of Florence
on the theory that a bipartisan administration by men of God would bring peace to the city. Their tenure
of office was marked by great violence, however; and they were forced to leave in a matter of months.
Modern scholarship has established the fact that they served as instruments of Clement IV's policy in
Florence, working at his orders to overthrow the Ghibellines under the guise of an impartial
administration.   4. The site of the palace of the Ghibelline family degli Uberti. In the riots resulting
from the maladministration of the two Jovial Friars, the Ghibellines were forced out of the city and the
Uberti palace was razed.   5. Caiaphas. His words were: "It is expedient that one man shall die for the
people and that the whole nation perish not." (John 11:50).

into his beard, convulsing all his body;   110
    and Friar Catalano, following my eyes,
said to me: "That one nailed across the road
    counselled the Pharisees that it was fitting
    one man be tortured for the public good.
Naked he lies fixed there, as you see,   115
    in the path of all who pass; there he must feel
    the weight of all through all eternity.
His father-in-law[6] and the others of the Council
    which was a seed of wrath to all the Jews,
    are similarly staked for the same evil."   120
Then I saw Virgil marvel[7] for a while
    over that soul so ignominiously
    stretched on the cross in Hell's eternal exile.
Then, turning, he asked the Friar: "If your law permit,
    can you tell us if somewhere along the right   125
    there is some gap in the stone wall of the pit
through which we two may climb to the next brink
    without the need of summoning the Black Angels
    and forcing them to raise us from this sink?"
He: "Nearer than you hope, there is a bridge   130
    that runs from the great circle of the scarp
    and crosses every ditch from ridge to ridge,
except that in this it is broken; but with care
    you can mount the ruins which lie along the slope
    and make a heap on the bottom." My Guide stood there   135
motionless for a while with a dark look.
    At last he said: "He[8] lied about this business,
    who spears the sinners yonder with his hook."
And the Friar: "Once at Bologna I heard the wise
    discussing the Devil's sins; among them I heard   140
    that he is a liar and the father of lies."
When the sinner had finished speaking, I saw the face
    of my sweet Master darken a bit with anger:
    he set off at a great stride from that place,
and I turned from that weighted hypocrite   145
to follow in the prints of his dear feet.

CANTO XXIV

Circle Eight: Bolgia Seven   The Thieves

    The Poets climb the right bank laboriously, cross the bridge of the Sev-
enth Bolgia and descend the far bank to observe the Thieves. They find
the pit full of monstrous reptiles who curl themselves about the sinners

6. Annas, father-in-law of Caiaphas, was the first before whom Jesus was led upon his arrest. (John 18:13).
He had Jesus bound and delivered to Caiaphas.   7. Caiaphas had not been there on Virgil's first descent
into Hell.   8. Malacoda.

like living coils of rope, binding each sinner's hands behind his back, and knotting themselves through the loins. Other reptiles dart about the place, and the Poets see one of them fly through the air and pierce the jugular vein of one sinner who immediately bursts into flames until only ashes remain. From the ashes the sinner re-forms painfully.

These are Dante's first observations of the Thieves and will be carried further in the next Canto, but the first allegorical retribution is immediately apparent. Thievery is reptilian in its secrecy; therefore it is punished by reptiles. The hands of the thieves are the agents of their crimes; therefore they are bound forever. And as the thief destroys his fellow men by making their substance disappear, so is he painfully destroyed and made to disappear, not once but over and over again.

The sinner who has risen from his own ashes reluctantly identifies himself as Vanni Fucci. He tells his story, and to revenge himself for having been forced to reveal his identity he utters a dark prophecy against Dante.

In the turning season of the youthful year,
     when the sun is warming his rays beneath Aquarius[9]
     and the days and nights already begin to near
their perfect balance; the hoar-frost copies then
     the image of his white sister on the ground,   5
     but the first sun wipes away the work of his pen.[1]
The peasants who lack fodder then arise
     and look about and see the fields all white,
     and hear their lambs bleat; then they smite their thighs,[2]
go back into the house, walk here and there,   10
     pacing, fretting, wondering what to do,
     then come out doors again, and there, despair
falls from them when they see how the earth's face
     has changed in so little time, and they take their staffs
     and drive their lambs to feed—so in that place   15
when I saw my Guide and Master's eyebrows lower,
     my spirits fell and I was sorely vexed;
     and as quickly came the plaster to the sore:
for when he had reached the ruined bridge, he stood
     and turned on me that sweet and open look   20
     with which he had greeted me in the dark wood.
When he had paused and studied carefully
     the heap of stones, he seemed to reach some plan,
     for he turned and opened his arms and lifted me.
Like one who works and calculates ahead,   25
     and is always ready for what happens next—
     so, raising me above that dismal bed

9. The zodiacal sign for the period from January 21 to February 21. The sun is moving north then to approach the vernal equinox (March 21), at which point the days and the nights are equal. The Italian spring comes early, and the first warm days would normally occur under Aquarius.   1. The hoar-frost looks like snow but melts away as soon as the sun strikes it.   2. A common Italian gesture of vexation, about equivalent to smiting the forehead with the palm of the hand.

to the top of one great slab of the fallen slate,
   he chose another saying: "Climb here, but first
   test it to see if it will hold your weight."   30
It was no climb for a lead-hung hypocrite:
   for scarcely we—he light and I assisted—
   could crawl handhold by handhold from the pit;
and were it not that the bank along this side
   was lower than the one down which we had slid,   35
   I at least—I will not speak for my Guide—
would have turned back. But as all of the vast rim
   of Malebolge leans toward the lowest well,
   so each succeeding valley and each brim
is lower than the last. We climbed the face   40
   and arrived by great exertion to the point
   where the last rock had fallen from its place.
My lungs were pumping as if they could not stop;
   I thought I could not go on, and I sat exhausted
   the instant I had clambered to the top.   45
"Up on your feet! This is no time to tire!"
   my Master cried. "The man who lies asleep
   will never waken fame, and his desire
and all his life drift past him like a dream,
   and the traces of his memory fade from time   50
   like smoke in air, or ripples on a stream.
Now, therefore, rise. Control your breath, and call
   upon the strength of soul that wins all battles
   unless it sink in the gross body's fall.
There is a longer ladder yet to climb: 55
   this much is not enough. If you understand me,
   show that you mean to profit from your time."
I rose and made my breath appear more steady
   than it really was, and I replied: "Lead on
   as it pleases you to go: I am strong and ready."   60
We picked our way up the cliff, a painful climb,[3]
   for it was narrower, steeper, and more jagged
   than any we had crossed up to that time.
I moved along, talking to hide my faintness,
   when a voice that seemed unable to form words   65
   rose from the depths of the next chasm's darkness.
I do not know what it said, though by then the Sage
   had led me to the top of the next arch;
   but the speaker seemed in a tremendous rage.
I was bending over the brim, but living eyes   70
   could not plumb to the bottom of that dark;
   therefore I said, "Master, let me advise

3. The "top" Dante mentions in line 45 must obviously have been the top of the fallen stone that was once the bridge. There remains the difficult climb up the remainder of the cliff.

that we cross over and climb down the wall:
　　for just as I hear the voice without understanding,
　　so I look down and make out nothing at all." 75
"I make no other answer than the act,
　　the Master said: "the only fit reply
　　to a fit request is silence and the fact."
So we moved down the bridge to the stone pier
　　that shores the end of the arch on the eighth bank, 80
　　and there I saw the chasm's depths made clear;
and there great coils of serpents met my sight,
　　so hideous a mass that even now
　　the memory makes my blood run cold with fright.
Let Libya[4] boast no longer, for though its sands 85
　　breed chelidrids, jaculi, and phareans,
　　cenchriads, and two-headed amphisbands,
it never bred such a variety
　　of vipers, no, not with all Ethiopia
　　and all the lands that lie by the Red Sea. 90
Amid that swarm, naked and without hope,
　　people ran terrified, not even dreaming
　　of a hole to hide in, or of heliotrope.[5]
Their hands were bound behind by coils of serpents
　　which thrust their heads and tails between the loins 95
　　and bunched in front, a mass of knotted torments.
One of the damned came racing round a boulder,
　　and as he passed us, a great snake shot up
　　and bit him where the neck joins with the shoulder.
No mortal pen—however fast it flash 100
　　over the page—could write down *o* or *i*
　　as quickly as he flamed and fell in ash;
and when he was dissolved into a heap
　　upon the ground, the dust rose of itself
　　and immediately resumed its former shape. 105
Precisely so, philosophers declare,
　　the Phoenix dies and then is born again
　　when it approaches its five hundredth year.[6]
It lives on tears of balsam and of incense;
　　in all its life it eats no herb or grain, 110
　　and nard and precious myrrh sweeten its cerements.

---

4. *Libya . . . Ethiopia . . . lands that lie by the Red Sea:* The desert areas of the Mediterranean shores. Lucan's *Pharsalia* describes the assortment of monsters listed here by Dante. I have rendered their names from Latin to English jabberwocky to avoid problems of pronunciation. In Lucan *chelydri* make their trails smoke and burn, they are amphibious; *jaculi* fly through the air like darts piercing what they hit; *pharese* plow the ground with their tails; *cenchri* waver from side to side when they move; and *amphisboenae* have a head at each end.　　5. Not the flower, but the bloodstone, a spotted chalcedony. It was believed to make the wearer invisible.　　6. The fabulous Phoenix of Arabia was the only one of its kind in the world. Every five hundred years it built a nest of spices and incense which took fire from the heat of the sun and the beating of the Phoenix's wings. The Phoenix was thereupon cremated and was then re-born from its ashes.

And as a person fallen in a fit,
  possessed by a Demon or some other seizure
  that fetters him without his knowing it,
struggles up to his feet and blinks his eyes   115
  (still stupefied by the great agony
  he has just passed), and, looking round him, sighs—
such was the sinner when at last he rose.
  O Power of God! How dreadful is Thy will
  which in its vengeance rains such fearful blows.   120
Then my Guide asked him who he was. And he
  answered reluctantly: "Not long ago
  I rained into this gullet from Tuscany.
I am Vanni Fucci,[7] the beast. A mule among men,
  I chose the bestial life above the human.   125
  Savage Pistoia was my fitting den."
And I to my Guide: "Detain him a bit longer
  and ask what crime it was that sent him here;
  I knew him as a man of blood and anger."[8]
The sinner, hearing me, seemed discomforted,   130
  but he turned and fixed his eyes upon my face
  with a look of dismal shame; at length he said:
"That you have found me out among the strife
  and misery of this place, grieves my heart more
  than did the day that cut me from my life.   135
But I am forced to answer truthfully:
  I am put down so low because it was I
  who stole the treasure from the Sacristy,
for which others once were blamed. But that you may
  find less to gloat about if you escape here,   140
  prick up your ears and listen to what I say:
First Pistoia is emptied of the Black,
  then Florence changes her party and her laws.
From Valdimagra the God of War brings back
a fiery vapor wrapped in turbid air: 145
  then in a storm of battle at Piceno
  the vapor breaks apart the mist, and there
every White shall feel his wounds anew.
And I have told you this that it may grieve you."[9]

7. The bastard son of Fuccio de Lazzeri, a nobleman (Black) of Pistoia. In 1293 with two accomplices he stole the treasure of San Jacopo in the Duomo of San Zeno. Others were accused, and one man spent a year in jail on this charge before the guilty persons were discovered. Vanni Fucci had escaped from Pistoia by then, but his accomplices were convicted.   8. Dante (the traveler within the narrative rather than Dante the author) claims that he did not know Fucci was a thief, but only that he was a man of blood and violence. He should therefore be punished in the Seventh Circle.   9. In May of 1301 the Whites of Florence joined with the Whites of Pistoia to expel the Pistoian Blacks and destroy their houses. The ejected Blacks fled to Florence and joined forces with the Florentine Blacks. On November 1st of the same year, Charles of Valois took Florence and helped the Blacks drive out the Whites. Piceno was the scene of a battle in which the Blacks of Florence and Lucca combined in 1302 to capture Serravalle, a White strong point near Pistoia.

CANTO XXV

Circle Eight: Bolgia Seven   The Thieves

Vanni's rage mounts to the point where he hurls an ultimate obscenity at God, and the serpents immediately swarm over him, driving him off in great pain. The Centaur, Cacus, his back covered with serpents and a fire-eating dragon, also gives chase to punish the wretch.

Dante then meets Five Noble Thieves of Florence and sees the further retribution visited upon the sinners. Some of the thieves appear first in human form, others as reptiles. All but one of them suffer a painful transformation before Dante's eyes. Agnello appears in human form and is merged with Cianfa, who appears as a six-legged lizard. Buoso appears as a man and changes form with Francesco, who first appears as a tiny reptile. Only Puccio Sciancato remains unchanged, though we are made to understand that his turn will come.

For endless and painful transformation is the final state of the thieves. In life they took the substance of others, transforming it into their own. So in Hell their very bodies are constantly being taken from them, and they are left to steal back a human form from some other sinner. Thus they waver constantly between man and reptile, and no sinner knows what to call his own.

When he had finished, the thief—to his disgrace—
    raised his hands with both fists making figs,[1]
    and cried: "Here, God! I throw them in your face!"
Thereat the snakes became my friends, for one
    coiled itself about the wretch's neck   5
    as if it were saying: "You shall not go on!"
and another tied his arms behind him again,
    knotting its head and tail between his loins
    so tight he could not move a finger in pain.
Pistoia! Pistoia! why have you not decreed   10
    to turn yourself to ashes and end your days,
    rather than spread the evil of your seed!
In all of Hell's corrupt and sunken halls
    I found no shade so arrogant toward God,
    not even him who fell from the Theban walls!   15
Without another word, he fled; and there
    I saw a furious Centaur race up, roaring:
    "Where is the insolent blasphemer? Where?"
I do not think as many serpents swarm
    in all the Maremma as he bore on his back   20
    from the haunch to the first sign of our human form.

1. An obscene gesture made by closing the hand into a fist with the thumb protruding between the first and second fingers. The fig is an ancient symbol for the vulva, and the protruding thumb is an obvious phallic symbol. The gesture is still current in Italy and has lost none of its obscene significance since Dante's time.

Upon his shoulders, just behind his head
   a snorting dragon whose hot breath set fire
   to all it touched, lay with its wings outspread.
My Guide said: "That is Cacus.[2] Time and again   25
   in the shadow of Mount Aventine he made
   a lake of blood upon the Roman plain.
He does not go with his kin by the blood-red fosse
   because of the cunning fraud with which he stole
   the cattle of Hercules. And thus it was   30
his thieving stopped, for Hercules found his den
   and gave him perhaps a hundred blows with his club,
   and of them he did not feel the first ten."
Meanwhile, the Centaur passed along his way,
   and three wraiths came. Neither my Guide nor I   35
   knew they were there until we heard them say:
"You there—who are you?" There our talk fell still
   and we turned to stare at them. I did not know them,
   but by chance it happened, as it often will,
one named another. "Where is Cianfa?" he cried;   40
   "Why has he fallen back?" I placed a finger
   across my lips as a signal to my Guide.
Reader, should you doubt what next I tell,
   it will be no wonder, for though I saw it happen,
   I can scarce believe it possible, even in Hell.   45
For suddenly, as I watched, I saw a lizard
   come darting forward on six great taloned feet
   and fasten itself to a sinner from crotch to gizzard.
Its middle feet sank in the sweat and grime
   of the wretch's paunch, its forefeet clamped his arms,   50
   its teeth bit through both cheeks. At the same time
its hind feet fastened on the sinner's thighs:
   its tail thrust through his legs and closed its coil
   over his loins. I saw it with my own eyes!
No ivy ever grew about a tree   55
   as tightly as that monster wove itself
   limb by limb about the sinner's body;
they fused like hot wax, and their colors ran
   together until neither wretch nor monster
   appeared what he had been when he began: 60
just so, before the running edge of the heat
   on a burning page, a brown discoloration
   changes to black as the white dies from the sheet.

2. The son of Vulcan. He lived in a cave at the foot of Mount Aventine, from which he raided the herds
of the cattle of Hercules, which pastured on the Roman plain. Hercules clubbed him to death for his
thievery, beating him in rage long after he was dead. Cacus is condemned to the lower pit for his greater
crime, instead of guarding Phlegethon with his brother centaurs. Virgil, however, did not describe him as
a centaur (*Aeneid* VIII. 193–267). Dante's interpretation of him is probably based on the fact that Virgil
referred to him as "half-human."

The other two cried out as they looked on:
  "Alas! Alas! Agnello, how you change!
  Already you are neither two nor one!"   65
The two heads had already blurred and blended;
  now two new semblances appeared and faded,
  one face where neither face began nor ended.
From the four upper limbs of man and beast   70
  two arms were made, then members never seen
  grew from the thighs and legs, belly and breast.
Their former likenesses mottled and sank
  to something that was both of them and neither;
  and so transformed, it slowly left our bank.   75
As lizards at high noon of a hot day
  dart out from hedge to hedge, from shade to shade,
  and flash like lightning when they cross the way,
so toward the bowels of the other two,
  shot a small monster; livid, furious,   80
  and black as a pepper corn. Its lunge bit through
that part[3] of one of them from which man receives
  his earliest nourishment; then it fell back
  and lay sprawled out in front of the two thieves.
Its victim stared at it but did not speak: 85
  indeed, he stood there like a post, and yawned
  as if lack of sleep, or a fever, had left him weak.
The reptile stared at him, he at the reptile;
  from the wound of one and from the other's mouth
  two smokes poured out and mingled, dark and vile.   90
Now let Lucan be still with his history
  of poor Sabellus and Nassidius,[4]
  and wait to hear what next appeared to me.
Of Cadmus and Arethusa be Ovid silent.
  I have no need to envy him those verses   95
  where he makes one a fountain, and one a serpent:
for he never transformed two beings face to face
  in such a way that both their natures yielded
  their elements each to each, as in this case.
Responding sympathetically to each other,   100
  the reptile cleft his tail into a fork,
  and the wounded sinner drew his feet together.
The sinner's legs and thighs began to join:
  they grew together so, that soon no trace
  of juncture could be seen from toe to loin.   105

3. The navel.   4. In *Pharsalia* (IX. 761ff.) Lucan relates how Sabellus and Nassidius, two soldiers of the army Cato led across the Libyan desert, were bitten by monsters. Sabellus melted into a puddle and Nassidius swelled until he popped his coat of mail. In his *Metamorphoses*, Ovid wrote how Cadmus was changed into a serpent (IV. 562–603) and how Arethusa was changed into a fountain (V. 572–661).

Point by point the reptile's cloven tail
    grew to the form of what the sinner lost;
    one skin began to soften, one to scale.
The armpits swallowed the arms, and the short shank
    of the reptile's forefeet simultaneously   110
    lengthened by as much as the man's arms shrank.
Its hind feet twisted round themselves and grew
    the member man conceals; meanwhile the wretch
    from his one member generated two.
The smoke swelled up about them all the while: 115
    it tanned one skin and bleached the other; it stripped
    the hair from the man and grew it on the reptile.
While one fell to his belly, the other rose
    without once shifting the locked evil eyes
    below which they changed snouts as they changed pose.   120
The face of the standing one drew up and in
    toward the temples, and from the excess matter
    that gathered there, ears grew from the smooth skin;
while of the matter left below the eyes
    the excess became a nose, at the same time   125
    forming the lips to an appropriate size.
Here the face of the prostrate felon slips,
    sharpens into a snout, and withdraws its ears
    as a snail pulls in its horns. Between its lips
the tongue, once formed for speech, thrusts out a fork;   130
    the forked tongue of the other heals and draws
    into his mouth. The smoke has done its work.
The soul that had become a beast went flitting
    and hissing over the stones, and after it
    the other walked along talking and spitting.   135
Then turning his new shoulders, said to the one
    that still remained: "It is Buoso's turn to go
    crawling along this road as I have done."
Thus did the ballast of the seventh hold
    shift and reshift; and may the strangeness of it   140
    excuse my pen if the tale is strangely told.
And though all this confused me, they did not flee
    so cunningly but what I was aware
    that it was Puccio Sciancato alone of the three
that first appeared, who kept his old form still.   145
The other was he for whom you weep, Gaville.[5]

---

5. Francesco dei Cavalcanti. He was killed by the people of Gaville (a village in the Valley of the Arno).
His kin rallied immediately to avenge his death, and many of the townspeople of Gaville were killed in
the resulting feud.

CANTO XXVI

Circle Eight: Bolgia Eight   The Evil Counselors

Dante turns from the Thieves toward the Evil Counselors of the next Bolgia, and between the two he addresses a passionate lament to Florence prophesying the griefs that will befall her from these two sins. At the purported time of the Vision, it will be recalled, Dante was a Chief Magistrate of Florence and was forced into exile by men he had reason to consider both thieves and evil counselors. He seems prompted, in fact, to say much more on this score, but he restrains himself when he comes in sight of the sinners of the next Bolgia, for they are a moral symbolism, all men of gift who abused their genius, perverting it to wiles and stratagems. Seeing them in Hell he knows his must be another road: his way shall not be by deception.

So the Poets move on and Dante observes the Eighth Bolgia in detail. Here the Evil Counselors move about endlessly, hidden from view inside great flames. Their sin was to abuse the gifts of the Almighty, to steal his virtues for low purposes. And as they stole from God in their lives and worked by hidden ways, so are they stolen from sight and hidden in the great flames which are their own guilty consciences. And as, in most instances at least, they sinned by glibness of tongue, so are the flames made into a fiery travesty of tongues.

Among the others, the Poets see a great doubleheaded flame, and discover that Ulysses and Diomede are punished together within it. Virgil addresses the flame, and through its wavering tongue Ulysses narrates an unforgettable tale of his last voyage and death.

Joy to you, Florence, that your banners swell,
    beating their proud wings over land and sea,
    and that your name expands through all of Hell!
Among the thieves I found five who had been
    your citizens, to my shame; nor yet shall you   5
    mount to great honor peopling such a den!
But if the truth is dreamed of toward the morning,[6]
    you soon shall feel what Prato[7] and the others
    wish for you. And were that day of mourning
already come it would not be too soon.   10
    So may it come, since it must! for it will weigh
    more heavily on me as I pass my noon.
We left that place. My Guide climbed stone by stone
    the natural stair by which we had descended

6. A semi-proverbial expression. It was a common belief that those dreams that occur just before waking foretell the future. "Morning" here would equal both "the rude awakening" and the potential "dawn of a new day."   7. Not the neighboring town (which was on good terms with Florence) but Cardinal Niccolò da Prato, papal legate from Benedict XI to Florence. In 1304 he tried to reconcile the warring factions, but found that neither side would accept mediation. Since none would be blessed, he cursed all impartially and laid the city under an interdict (i.e., forbade the offering of the sacraments). Shortly after this rejection by the Church, a bridge collapsed in Florence, and later a great fire broke out. Both disasters cost many lives, and both were promptly attributed to the Papal curse.

and drew me after him. So we passed on,   15
and going our lonely way through that dead land
    among the crags and crevices of the cliff,
    the foot could make no way without the hand.
I mourned among those rocks, and I mourn again
    when memory returns to what I saw: 20
    and more than usually I curb the strain
of my genius, lest it stray from Virtue's course;
    so if some star, or a better thing, grant me merit,
    may I not find the gift cause for remorse.
As many fireflies as the peasant sees   25
    when he rests on a hill and looks into the valley
    (where he tills or gathers grapes or prunes his trees)
in that sweet season when the face of him
    who lights the world rides north, and at the hour
    when the fly yields to the gnat and the air grows dim—   30
such myriads of flames I saw shine through
    the gloom of the eighth abyss when I arrived
    at the rim from which its bed comes into view.
As he the bears avenged[8] so fearfully
    beheld Elijah's chariot depart—   35
    the horses rise toward heaven—but could not see
more than the flame, a cloudlet in the sky,
    once it had risen—so within the fosse
    only those flames, forever passing by
were visible, ahead, to right, to left;   40
    for though each steals a sinner's soul from view
    not one among them leaves a trace of the theft.
I stood on the bridge, and leaned out from the edge;
    so far, that but for a jut of rock I held to
    I should have been sent hurtling from the ledge   45
without being pushed. And seeing me so intent,
    my Guide said: "There are souls within those flames;
    each sinner swathes himself in his own torment."
"Master," I said, "your words make me more sure,
    but I had seen already that it was so   50
    and meant to ask what spirit must endure
the pains of that great flame which splits away
    in two great horns, as if it rose from the pyre
    where Eteocles and Polynices lay?"[9]

---

8. Elisha saw Elijah transported to Heaven in a fiery chariot. Later he was mocked by some children, who called out tauntingly that he should "Go up" as Elijah had. Elisha cursed the children in the name of the Lord, and bears came suddenly upon the children and devoured them. (2 Kings 2:11–24.)   9. Eteocles and Polynices, sons of Oedipus, succeeded jointly to the throne of Thebes, and came to an agreement whereby each one would rule separately for a year at a time. Eteocles ruled the first year and when he refused to surrender the throne at the appointed time, Polynices led the Seven against Thebes in a bloody war. In single combat the two brothers killed one another. Statius (Thebaid XII. 429ff.) wrote that their mutual hatred was so great that when they were placed on the same funeral pyre the very flame of their burning drew apart in two great raging horns.

He answered me: "Forever round this path   55
   Ulysses and Diomede[1] move in such dress,
   united in pain as once they were in wrath;
there they lament the ambush of the Horse
   which was the door through which the noble seed
   of the Romans issued from its holy source;   60
there they mourn that for Achilles slain
   sweet Deidamia weeps even in death;
   there they recall the Palladium in their pain."
"Master," I cried, "I pray you and repray
   till my prayer becomes a thousand—if these souls   65
   can still speak from the fire, oh let me stay
until the flame draws near! Do not deny me:
   You see how fervently I long for it!"
   And he to me: "Since what you ask is worthy,
it shall be. But be still and let me speak;   70
   for I know your mind already, and they perhaps
   might scorn your manner of speaking, since they were Greek."
And when the flame had come where time and place
   seemed fitting to my Guide, I heard him say
   these words to it: "O you two souls who pace   75
together in one flame!—if my days above
   won favor in your eyes, if I have earned
   however much or little of your love
in writing my High Verses, do not pass by,
   but let one of you[2] be pleased to tell where he,   80
   having disappeared from the known world, went to die."
As if it fought the wind, the greater prong
   of the ancient flame began to quiver and hum;
   then moving its tip as if it were the tongue
that spoke, gave out a voice above the roar.   85
"When I left Circe,"[3] it said, "who more than a year
   detained me near Gaëta long before
Aeneas came and gave the place that name,
   not fondness for my son, nor reverence
   for my aged father, nor Penelope's[4] claim   90
to the joys of love, could drive out of my mind

---

1. They suffer here for their joint guilt in counseling and carrying out many stratagems which Dante considered evil, though a narrator who was less passionately a partisan of the Trojans might have thought their actions justifiable methods of warfare. Their first sin was the stratagem of the Wooden Horse, as a result of which Troy fell and Aeneas went forth to found the Roman line. The second evil occurred at Scyros. There Ulysses discovered Achilles in female disguise, hidden by his mother, Thetis, so that he would not be taken off to the war. Deidamia was in love with Achilles and had borne him a son. When Ulysses persuaded her lover to sail for Troy, she died of grief. The third count is Ulysses' theft of the sacred statue of Pallas from the Palladium. Upon the statue, it was believed, depended the fate of Troy. Its theft, therefore, would result in Troy's downfall.   2. Ulysses. He is the figure in the larger horn of the flame (which symbolizes that his guilt, as leader, is greater than that of Diomede). His memorable account of his last voyage and death is purely Dante's invention.   3. She changed Ulysses' men to swine and kept him a prisoner, though with rather exceptional accommodations. *Gaëta:* Southeastern Italian coastal town. According to Virgil (*Aeneid* VII. 1ff.) it was earlier named Caieta by Aeneas in honor of his aged nurse.   4. Ulysses' wife.

the lust to experience the far-flung world
and the failings and felicities of mankind.
I put out on the high and open sea
  with a single ship and only those few souls   95
  who stayed true when the rest deserted me.
As far as Morocco and as far as Spain
  I saw both shores;[5] and I saw Sardinia
  and the other islands of the open main.
I and my men were stiff and slow with age   100
  when we sailed at last into the narrow pass[6]
  where, warning all men back from further voyage,
Hercules' Pillars rose upon our sight.
  Already I had left Ceuta on the left;
  Seville[7] now sank behind me on the right.   105
'Shipmates,' I said, 'who through a hundred thousand
  perils have reached the West, do not deny
  to the brief remaining watch our senses stand
experience of the world beyond the sun.
  Greeks! You were not born to live like brutes,   110
  but to press on toward manhood and recognition!
With this brief exhortation I made my crew
  so eager for the voyage I could hardly
  have held them back from it when I was through;
and turning our stern toward morning, our bow toward night,   115
  we bore southwest out of the world of man;
  we made wings of our oars for our fool's flight.
That night we raised the other pole ahead
  with all its stars, and ours had so declined
  it did not rise out of its ocean bed.[8]   120
Five times since we had dipped our bending oars
  beyond the world, the light beneath the moon
  had waxed and waned, when dead upon our course
we sighted, dark in space, a peak so tall
  I doubted any man had seen the like.[9]   125
  Our cheers were hardly sounded, when a squall
broke hard upon our bow from the new land:
  three times it sucked the ship and the sea about
  as it pleased Another to order and command.
At the fourth, the poop rose and the bow went down   130
till the sea closed over us and the light was gone."

---

5. Of the Mediterranean.   6. The straits of Gilbraltar, formerly called the Pillars of Hercules. They
were presumed to be the Western limit beyond which no man could navigate.   7. In Dante's time this
was the name given to the general region of Spain. Having passed through the Straits, the men are now
in the Atlantic. *Ceuta:* In Africa, opposite Gibraltar.   8. They drove south across the equator, observed
the southern stars, and found that the North Star had sunk below the horizon.   9. Purgatory. They sight
it after five months of passage. According to Dante's geography, the Northern hemisphere is land and the
Southern is all water except for the Mountain of Purgatory which rises above the surface at a point directly
opposite Jerusalem.

CANTO XXVII

Circle Eight: Bolgia Eight   The Evil Counselors

The double flame departs at a word from Virgil and behind it appears another which contains the soul of Count Guido da Montefeltro, a Lord of Romagna. He had overheard Virgil speaking Italian, and the entire flame in which his soul is wrapped quivers with his eagerness to hear recent news of his wartorn country. (As Farinata has already explained, the spirits of the damned have prophetic powers, but lose all track of events as they approach.)

Dante replies with a stately and tragic summary of how things stand in the cities of Romagna. When he has finished, he asks Guido for his story, and Guido recounts his life, and how Boniface VIII persuaded him to sin.

When it had finished speaking, the great flame
　　stood tall and shook no more. Now, as it left us
　　with the sweet Poet's license, another[1] came
along that track and our attention turned
　　to the new flame: a strange and muffled roar   5
　　rose from the single tip to which it burned.
As the Sicilian bull[2]—that brazen spit
　　which bellowed first (and properly enough)
　　with the lament of him whose file had tuned it—
was made to bellow by its victim's cries   10
　　in such a way, that though it was of brass,
　　it seemed itself to howl and agonize:
so lacking any way through or around
　　the fire that sealed them in, the mournful words
　　were changed into its language. When they found   15
their way up the tip, imparting to it
　　the same vibration given them in their passage
　　over the tongue of the concealed sad spirit,
we heard it say: "O you at whom I aim
　　my voice, and who were speaking Lombard, saying: 20
　　'Go now, I ask no more,'[3] just as I came—
though I may come a bit late to my turn,
　　may it not annoy you to pause and speak a while:
　　you see it does not annoy me—and I burn.
If you have fallen only recently   25
　　to this blind world from that sweet Italy
　　where I acquired my guilt, I pray you, tell me:

---

1. Guido da Montefeltro (1223–1298). As head of the Ghibellines of Romagna, he was reputed the wisest and cunningest man in Italy.   2. In the sixth century B.C. Perillus of Athens constructed for Phalaris, Tyrant of Sicily, a metal bull to be used as an instrument of torture. When victims were placed inside it and roasted to death, their screams passed through certain tuned pipes and emerged as a burlesque bellowing of the bull. Phalaris accepted delivery and showed his gratitude by appointing the inventor the bull's first victim. Later Phalaris was overthrown, and he, too, took his turn inside the bull.   3. These are the words with which Virgil dismisses Ulysses and Diomede, his "license."

is there peace or war in Romagna? for on earth
  I too was of those hills between Urbino
  and the fold from which the Tiber springs to birth."[4]   30
I was still staring at it from the dim
  edge of the pit when my Guide nudged me, saying:
  "This one is Italian; *you* speak to him."
My answer was framed already; without pause
  I spoke these words to it: "O hidden soul,   35
  your sad Romagna is not and never was
without war in her tyrants' raging blood;
  but none flared openly when I left just now.
Ravenna's fortunes stand as they have stood
these many years: Polenta's eagles brood   40
  over her walls, and their pinions cover Cervia.[5]
The city that so valiantly withstood
the French, and raised a mountain of their dead,
  feels the Green Claws again.[6] Still in Verrucchio
the Aged Mastiff and his Pup, who shed   45
Montagna's blood, raven in their old ranges.[7]
  The cities of Lamone and Santerno
  are led by the white den's Lion, he who changes
his politics with the compass.[8] And as the city
  the Savio washes[9] lies between plain and mountain,   50
  so it lives between freedom and tyranny.
Now, I beg you, let us know your name;
  do not be harder than one has been to you;
  so, too, you will preserve your earthly fame."
And when the flame had roared a while beneath   55
  the ledge on which we stood, it swayed its tip
  to and fro, and then gave forth this breath:
"If I believed that my reply were made
  to one who could ever climb to the world again,
  this flame would shake no more. But since no shade   60
ever returned—if what I am told is true—
  from this blind world into the living light,
  without fear of dishonor I answer you.
I was a man of arms: then took the rope

---

4. Romagna is the district that runs south from the Po along the east side of the Apennines. Urbino is due east of Florence and roughly south of Rimini. Between Urbino and Florence rise the Coronaro Mountains which contain the headwaters of the Tiber.   5. In 1300 Ravenna was ruled by Guido Vecchio da Polenta, father of Francesca da Rimini. His arms bore an eagle and his domain included the small city of Cervia about twelve miles south of Ravenna.   6. The city is Forlì. In 1282 Guido da Montefeltro defended Forli from the French, but in 1300 it was under the despotic rule of Sinibaldo degli Ordelaffi, whose arms were a green lion.   7. Verrucchio was the castle of Malatesta and his son Malatestino, Lords of Rimini, whom Dante calls dogs for their cruelty. Montagna de' Parcitati, the leader of Rimini's Ghibellines, was captured by Malatesta in 1295 and murdered in captivity by Malatestino.   8. Maginardo de' Pagani (d. 1302) ruled Faenza, on the River Lamone, and Imola, close by the River Santerno. His arms were a blue lion on a white field (hence "the Lion from the white den"). He supported the Ghibellines in the north, but the Guelphs in the south (Florence), changing his politics according to the direction in which he was facing.   9. Cesena. It ruled itself for a number of years, but was taken over by Malatestino in 1314. It lies between Forlì and Rimini.

of the Franciscans, hoping to make amends: 65
and surely I should have won to all my hope
but for the Great Priest[1]—may he rot in Hell!—
who brought me back to all my earlier sins;
and how and why it happened I wish to tell
in my own words: while I was still encased   70
in the pulp and bone my mother bore, my deeds
were not of the lion but of the fox: I raced
through tangled ways; all wiles were mine from birth,
and I won to such advantage with my arts
that rumor of me reached the ends of the earth.   75
But when I saw before me all the signs
of the time of life that cautions every man
to lower his sail and gather in his lines,
that which had pleased me once, troubled my spirit,
and penitent and confessed, I became a monk.   80
Alas! What joy I might have had of it!
It was then the Prince of the New Pharisees[2] drew
his sword and marched upon the Lateran—
and not against the Saracen or the Jew,
for every man that stood against his hand   85
was a Christian soul: not one had warred on Acre,
nor been a trader in the Sultan's land.[3]
It was he abused his sacred vows and mine:
his Office and the Cord I wore, which once
made those it girded leaner. As Constantine   90
sent for Silvestro to cure his leprosy,[4]
seeking him out among Soracte's cells;
so this one from his great throne sent for me
to cure the fever of pride that burned his blood.
He demanded my advice, and I kept silent   95
for his words seemed drunken to me. So it stood
until he said: 'Your soul need fear no wound;
I absolve your guilt beforehand; and now teach me
how to smash Penestrino to the ground.
The Gates of Heaven, as you know, are mine   100
to open and shut, for I hold the two Great Keys
so easily let go by Celestine.'[5]
His weighty arguments led me to fear

---

1. Boniface VIII, so called as Pope.   2. Also Boniface. *Marched upon the Lateran:* Boniface had had a long-standing feud with the Colonna family. In 1297 the Colonna walled themselves in a castle twenty-five miles east of Rome at Penestrino (now called Palestrina) in the Lateran. On Guido's advice the Pope offered a fair-sounding amnesty which he had no intention of observing. When the Colonna accepted the terms and left the castle, the Pope destroyed it, leaving the Colonna without a refuge.   3. It was the Saracens who opposed the Christians at Acre, the Jews who traded in the Sultan's land.   4. In the persecutions of the Christians by the Emperor Constantine, Pope Sylvester I took refuge in the caves of Mount Soracte near Rome. (It is now called Santo Oreste.) Later, according to legend, Constantine was stricken by leprosy and sent for Sylvester, who cured him and converted him to Christianity, in return for which the Emperor was believed to have made the famous "Donation of Constantine." (See Canto XIX.)   5. Celestine V under the persuasion of Boniface abdicated the Papacy. (See Canto III notes.)

silence was worse than sin. Therefore, I said:
'Holy Father, since you clean me here   105
of the guilt into which I fall, let it be done:
long promise and short observance[6] is the road
that leads to the sure triumph of your throne.'
Later, when I was dead, St. Francis came
to claim my soul,[7] but one of the Black Angels   110
said: 'Leave him. Do not wrong me. This one's name
went into my book the moment he resolved
to give false counsel. Since then he has been mine,
for who does not repent cannot be absolved;
nor can we admit the possibility   115
of repenting a thing at the same time it is willed,
for the two acts are contradictory.'
Miserable me! with what contrition
I shuddered when he lifted me, saying: 'Perhaps
you hadn't heard that I was a logician.'   120
He carried me to Minos: eight times round
his scabby back the monster coiled his tail,
then biting it in rage he pawed the ground
and cried: 'This one is for the thievish fire!'
And, as you see, I am lost accordingly,   125
grieving in heart as I go in this attire."
His story told, the flame began to toss
and writhe its horn. And so it left, and we
crossed over to the arch of the next fosse
where from the iron treasury of the Lord   130
the fee of wrath is paid the Sowers of Discord.[8]

CANTO XXVIII

Circle Eight: Bolgia Nine   The Sowers of Discord

The Poets come to the edge of the Ninth Bolgia and look down at a
parade of hideously mutilated souls. These are the Sowers of Discord, and
just as their sin was to rend asunder what God had meant to be united, so
are they hacked and torn through all eternity by a great demon with a
bloody sword. After each mutilation the souls are compelled to drag their
broken bodies around the pit and to return to the demon, for in the course
of the circuit their wounds knit in time to be inflicted anew. Thus is the
law of retribution observed, each sinner suffering according to his degree.

Among them Dante distinguishes three classes with varying degrees of
guilt within each class. First come the Sowers of Religious Discord. Mahomet
is chief among them, and appears first, cleft from crotch to chin, with his
internal organs dangling between his legs. His son-in-law, Ali, drags on

---

6. This is the advice upon which Boniface acted in trapping the Colonna with his hypocritical amnesty.
7. To gather in the soul of one of his monks. *Black Angel:* A devil.   8. I have taken liberties with these
lines in the hope of achieving a reasonably tonic final couplet. The literal reading is: "In which the fee is
paid to those who, sowing discord, acquire weight (of guilt and pain)."

ahead of him, cleft from topknot to chin. These reciprocal wounds symbolize Dante's judgment that, between them, these two sum up the total schism between Christianity and Mohammedanism. The revolting details of Mahomet's condition clearly imply Dante's opinon of that doctrine. Mahomet issues an ironic warning to another schismatic, Fra Dolcino.

Next come the Sowers of Political Discord, among them Pier da Medicina, the Tribune Curio, and Mosca dei Lamberti, each mutilated according to the nature of his sin.

Last of all is Bertrand de Born, Sower of Discord Between Kinsmen. He separated father from son, and for that offense carries his head separated from his body, holding it with one hand by the hair, and swinging it as if it were a lantern to light his dark and endless way. The image of Bertrand raising his head at arm's length in order that it might speak more clearly to the Poets on the ridge is one of the most memorable in the *Inferno*. For some reason that cannot be ascertained, Dante makes these sinners quite eager to be remembered in the world, despite the fact that many who lie above them in Hell were unwilling to be recognized.

> Who could describe, even in words set free
>   of metric and rhyme and a thousand times retold,
>   the blood and wounds that now were shown to me!
> At grief so deep the tongue must wag in vain;
>   the language of our sense and memory   5
>   lacks the vocabulary of such pain.
> If one could gather all those who have stood
>   through all of time on Puglia's[9] fateful soil
>   and wept for the red running of their blood
> in the war of the Trojans;[1] and in that long war   10
>   which left so vast a spoil of golden rings,
>   as we find written in Livy, who does not err;[2]
> along with those whose bodies felt the wet
>   and gaping wounds of Robert Guiscard's lances;[3]
>   with all the rest whose bones are gathered yet   15
> at Ceperano where every last Pugliese
>   turned traitor;[4] and with those from Tagliacozzo
>   where Alardo won without weapons[5]—if all these

9. I have used the modern name but some of the events Dante narrates took place in the ancient province of Apulia. The southeastern area of Italy is the scene of all the fighting Dante mentions in the following passage. It is certainly a bloody total of slaughter that Dante calls upon to illustrate his scene.   1. The Romans (descended from the Trojans) fought the native Samnites in a long series of raids and skirmishes from 343–290 B.C.   2. The Punic Wars (264–146 B.C.). Livy writes that in the battle of Cannae (216 B.C.) so many Romans fell that Hannibal gathered three bushels of gold rings from the fingers of the dead and produced them before the Senate at Carthage.   3. Dante places Guiscard (1015–1085) in the *Paradiso* among the Warriors of God. He fought the Greeks and Saracens in their attempted invasion of Italy.   4. In 1266 the Pugliese under Manfred, King of Sicily, were charged with holding the pass at Ceperano against Charles of Anjou. The Pugliese, probably under Papal pressure, allowed the French free passage, and Charles went on to defeat Manfred at Benevento. Manfred himself was killed in that battle. 5. At Tagliacozzo (1268) in a continuation of the same strife, Charles of Anjou used a stratagem suggested to him by Alard de Valéry and defeated Conradin, nephew of Manfred. "Won without weapons" is certainly an overstatement: what Alardo suggested was a simple but effective concealment of reserve troops. When Conradin seemed to have carried the day and was driving his foes before him, the reserve troops broke on his flank and rear, and defeated Conradin's out-positioned forces.

were gathered, and one showed his limbs run through,
    another his lopped off, that could not equal   20
    the mutilations of the ninth pit's crew.
A wine tun when a stave or cant-bar starts
    does not split open as wide as one I saw
    split from his chin to the mouth with which man farts.
Between his legs all of his red guts hung   25
    with the heart, the lungs, the liver, the gall bladder,
    and the shriveled sac that passes shit to the bung.
I stood and stared at him from the stone shelf;
    he noticed me and opening his own breast
    with both hands cried: "See how I rip myself!   30
See how Mahomet's mangled and split open!
    Ahead of me walks Ali[6] in his tears,
    his head cleft from the top-knot to the chin.
And all the other souls that bleed and mourn
    along this ditch were sowers of scandal and schism: 35
    as they tore others apart, so are they torn.
Behind us, warden of our mangled horde,
    the devil who butchers us and sends us marching
    waits to renew our wounds with his long sword
when we have made the circuit of the pit;   40
    for by the time we stand again before him
    all the wounds he gave us last have knit.
But who are you that gawk down from that sill—
    probably to put off your own descent
    to the pit you are sentenced to for your own evil?"   45
"Death has not come for him, guilt does not drive
    his soul to torment," my sweet Guide replied.
    "That he may experience all while yet alive
I, who am dead, must lead him through the drear
    and darkened halls of Hell, from round to round: 50
    and this is true as my own standing here."
More than a hundred wraiths who were marching under
    the sill on which we stood, paused at his words
    and stared at me, forgetting pain in wonder.
"And if you do indeed return to see   55
    the sun again, and soon, tell Fra Dolcino[7]
    unless he longs to come and march with me
he would do well to check his groceries

---

6. Ali succeeded Mahomet to the Caliphate, but not until three of the disciples had preceded him. Mahomet died in 632, and Ali did not assume the Caliphate until 656.   7. In 1300 Fra Dolcino took over the reformist order called the Apostolic Brothers, who preached, among other things, the community of property and of women. Clement V declared them heretical and ordered a crusade against them. The brotherhood retired with its women to an impregnable position in the hills between Novara and Vercelli, but their supplies gave out in the course of a year-long siege, and they were finally starved out in March of 1307. Dolcino and Margaret of Trent, his "Sister in Christ," were burned at the stake at Vercelli the following June.

before the winter drives him from the hills
    and gives the victory to the Novarese."   60
Mahomet, one foot raised, had paused to say
    these words to me. When he had finished speaking
    he stretched it out and down, and moved away.
Another—he had his throat slit, and his nose
    slashed off as far as the eyebrows, and a wound   65
    where one of his ears had been—standing with those
who stared at me in wonder from the pit,
    opened the grinning wound of his red gullet
    as if it were a mouth, and said through it:
"O soul unforfeited to misery   70
    and whom—unless I take you for another—
    I have seen above in our sweet Italy;
if ever again you see the gentle plain
    that slopes down from Vercelli to Marcabò,[8]
    remember Pier da Medicina in pain,   75
and announce this warning to the noblest two
    of Fano, Messers Guido and Angiolello:
    that unless our foresight sees what is not true
they shall be thrown from their ships into the sea
    and drown in the raging tides near La Cattolica   80
    to satisfy a tyrant's treachery.[9]
Neptune never saw so gross a crime
    in all the seas from Cyprus to Majorca,
    not even in pirate raids, nor the Argive time.[1]
The one-eyed traitor,[2] lord of the demesne   85
    whose hill and streams one who walks here beside me
    will wish eternally he had never seen,
will call them to a parley, but behind
    sweet invitations he will work it so
    they need not pray against Focara's wind."   90
And I to him: "If you would have me bear
    your name to time, show me the one who found
    the sight of that land so harsh, and let me hear
his story and his name." He touched the cheek
    of one nearby, forcing the jaws apart,   95
    and said: "This is the one; he cannot speak.
This outcast settled Caesar's doubts that day
    beside the Rubicon by telling him:
    'A man prepared is a man hurt by delay.' "

8. Vercelli is the most western town in Lombardy. Marcabò stands near the mouth of the Po.
9. Malatestino da Rimini (see preceding Canto), in a move to annex the city of Fano, invited Guido del
Cassero and Angioletto da Carignano, leading citizens of Fano, to a conference at La Cattolica, a point
on the Adriatic midway between Fano and Rimini. At Malatestino's orders the two were thrown overboard
off Focara, a headland swept by such dangerous currents that approaching sailors used to offer prayers for
a safe crossing. 1. The Greeks were raiders and pirates. *Cyprus . . . Majorca:* These islands are at
opposite ends of the Mediterranean. 2. Malatestino.

Ah, how wretched Curio[3] seemed to me   100
with a bloody stump in his throat in place of the tongue
which once had dared to speak so recklessly!
And one among them with both arms hacked through
cried out, raising his stumps on the foul air
while the blood bedaubed his face: "Remember, too,   105
Mosca dei Lamberti,[4] alas, who said
'A thing done has an end!' and with those words
planted the fields of war with Tuscan dead."
"And brought about the death of all your clan!"
I said, and he, stung by new pain on pain,   110
ran off; and in his grief he seemed a madman.
I stayed to watch those broken instruments,
and I saw a thing so strange I should not dare
to mention it without more evidence
but that my own clear conscience strengthens me,   115
that good companion that upholds a man
within the armor of his purity.
I saw it there; I seem to see it still—
a body without a head, that moved along
like all the others in that spew and spill.   120
It held the severed head by its own hair,
swinging it like a lantern in its hand;
and the head looked at us and wept in its despair.
It made itself a lamp of its own head,
and they were two in one and one in two;   125
how this can be, He knows who so commanded.
And when it stood directly under us
it raised the head at arm's length toward our bridge
the better to be heard, and swaying thus
it cried: "O living soul in this abyss,   130
see what a sentence has been passed upon me,
and search all Hell for one to equal this!
When you return to the world, remember me:
I am Bertrand de Born,[5] and it was I
who set the young king on to mutiny,   135
son against father, father against son
as Achitophel[6] set Absalom and David;

3. This is the Roman Tribune Curio, who was banished from Rome by Pompey and joined Caesar's forces, advising him to cross the Rubicon, which was then the boundary between Gaul and the Roman Republic. The crossing constituted invasion, and thus began the Roman Civil War. The Rubicon flows near Rimini. 4. Dante had asked Ciacco (Canto VI) for news of Mosca as a man of good works. Now he finds him, his merit canceled by his greater sin. Buondelmonte dei Buondelmonti had insulted the honor of the Amidei by breaking off his engagement to a daughter of that line in favor of a girl of the Donati. When the Amidei met to discuss what should be done, Mosca spoke for the death of Buondelmonte. The Amidei acted upon his advice and from that murder sprang the bloody feud between the Guelphs and Ghibellines of Florence. 5. (1140–1215), a great knight and master of the troubadours of Provence. He is said to have instigated a quarrel between Henry II of England and his son Prince Henry, called "The Young King" because he was crowned within his father's lifetime. 6. One of David's counselors, who deserted him to assist the rebellious Absalom. (II Samuel 15–17.)

and since I parted those who should be one
in duty and in love, I bear my brain
divided from its source within this trunk;   140
and walk here where my evil turns to pain,
an eye for an eye to all eternity:
thus is the law of Hell observed in me."

CANTO XXIX

Circle Eight: Bolgia Ten   The Falsifiers (Class I, Alchemists)

  Dante lingers on the edge of the Ninth Bolgia expecting to see one of
his kinsmen, Geri del Bello, among the Sowers of Discord. Virgil, however, hurries him on, since time is short, and as they cross the bridge over
the Tenth Bolgia, Virgil explains that he had a glimpse of Geri among the
crowd near the bridge and that he had been making threatening gestures
at Dante.
  The Poets now look into the last Bolgia of the Eighth Circle and see the
Falsifiers. They are punished by afflictions of every sense: by darkness,
stench, thirst, filth, loathsome diseases, and a shrieking din. Some of them,
moreover, run ravening through the pit, tearing others to pieces. Just as in
life they corrupted society by their falsifications, so in death these sinners
are subjected to a sum of corruptions. In one sense they figure forth what
society would be if all falsifiers succeeded—a place where the senses are
an affliction (since falsification deceives the senses) rather than a guide,
where even the body has no honesty, and where some lie prostrate while
others run ravening to prey upon them.
  Not all of these details are made clear until the next Canto, for Dante
distinguishes four classes of Falsifiers, and in the present Canto we meet
only the first class, the Alchemists, the Falsifiers of Things. Of this class
are Griffolino D'Arezzo and Capocchio, with both of whom Dante speaks.

The sight of that parade of broken dead
  had left my eyes so sotted with their tears
  I longed to stay and weep, but Virgil said:
"What are you waiting for? Why do you stare
  as if you could not tear your eyes away   5
  from the mutilated shadows passing there?
You did not act so in the other pits.
  Consider—if you mean perhaps to count them—
  this valley and its train of dismal spirits.
winds twenty-two miles round.[7] The moon already   10
  is under our feet;[8] the time we have is short,
  and there is much that you have yet to see."
"Had you known what I was seeking," I replied,

---

7. Another instance of "poetic" rather than "literal" detail. Dante's measurements cannot be made to fit
together on any scale map.   8. If the moon, nearly at full, is under their feet, the sun must be overhead.
It is therefore approximately noon of Holy Saturday.

"you might perhaps have given me permission
to stay on longer." (As I spoke, my Guide   15
had started off already, and I in turn
had moved along behind him; thus, I answered
as we moved along the cliff.) "Within that cavern
upon whose brim I stood so long to stare,
    I think a spirit of my own blood mourns   20
    the guilt that sinners find so costly there."
And the Master then: "Hereafter let your mind
    turn its attention to more worthy matters
    and leave him to his fate among the blind;
for by the bridge and among that shapeless crew   25
    I saw him point to you with threatening gestures,
    and I heard him called Geri del Bello.[9] You
were occupied at the time with that headless one
    who in his life was master of Altaforte,[1]
    and did not look that way; so he moved on."   30
"O my sweet Guide," I answered, "his death came
    by violence and is not yet avenged
    by those who share his blood, and, thus, his shame.
For this he surely hates his kin, and, therefore,
    as I suppose, he would not speak to me;   35
    and in that he makes me pity him the more."
We spoke of this until we reached the edge
    from which, had there been light, we could have seen
    the floor of the next pit. Out from that ledge
Malebolge's final cloister lay outspread,   40
    and all of its lay brethren might have been
    in sight but for the murk; and from those dead
such shrieks and strangled agonies shrilled through me
    like shafts, but barbed with pity, that my hands
    flew to my ears. If all the misery   45
that crams the hospitals of pestilence
    in Maremma, Valdichiano, and Sardinia[2]
    in the summer months when death sits like a presence
on the marsh air, were dumped into one trench—
    that might suggest their pain. And through the screams, 50
    putrid flesh spread up its sickening stench.
Still bearing left we passed from the long sill
    to the last bridge of Malebolge. There
    the reeking bottom was more visible.
There, High Justice, sacred ministress   55
    of the First Father, reigns eternally

9. A cousin of Dante's father. He became embroiled in a quarrel with the Sacchetti of Florence and was
murdered. At the time of the writing he had not been avenged by his kinsmen in accord with the clan
code of a life for a life.   1. Bertrand de Born was Lord of Hautefort.   2. Malarial plague areas. Val-
dichiano and Maremma were swamp areas of eastern and western Tuscany.

over the falsifiers in their distress.
I doubt it could have been such pain to bear
    the sight of the Aeginian people dying[3]
    that time when such malignance rode the air   60
that every beast down to the smallest worm
    shriveled and died (it was after that great plague
    that the Ancient People, as the poets affirm,
were reborn from the ants)—as it was to see
    the spirits lying heaped on one another   65
    in the dank bottom of that fetid valley.
One lay gasping on another's shoulder,
    one on another's belly; and some were crawling
    on hands and knees among the broken boulders.
Silent, slow step by step, we moved ahead   70
    looking at and listening to those souls
    too weak to raise themselves from their stone bed.
I saw two there like pans that are put
    one against the other to hold their warmth.
    They were covered with great scabs from head to foot.   75
No stable boy in a hurry to go home,[4]
    or for whom his master waits impatiently,
    ever scrubbed harder with his currycomb
than those two spirits of the stinking ditch
    scrubbed at themselves with their own bloody claws   80
    to ease the furious burning of the itch.
And as they scrubbed and clawed themselves, their nails
    drew down the scabs the way a knife scrapes bream
    or some other fish with even larger scales.
"O you," my Guide called out to one, "you there   85
    who rip your scabby mail as if your fingers
    were claws and pincers; tell us if this lair
counts any Italians among those who lurk
    in its dark depths; so may your busy nails
    eternally suffice you for your work."   90
"We both are Italian whose unending loss
    you see before you," he replied in tears.
    "But who are you who come to question us?"
"I am a shade," my Guide and Master said,
    "who leads this living man from pit to pit   95
    to show him Hell as I have been commanded."
The sinners broke apart as he replied

3. Juno, incensed that the nymph Aegina let Jove possess her, set a plague upon the island that bore her
name. Every animal and every human died until only Aeacus, the son born to Aegina of Jove, was left.
He prayed to his father for aid and Jove repopulated the island by transforming the ants at his son's feet
into men. The Aeginians have since been called Myrmidons, from the Greek word for ant (Ovid, *Metamorphoses* VII. 523–660).   4. The literal text would be confusing here. I have translated one possible
interpretation of it as offered by Giuseppe Vandelli. The original line is *"ne da colui che mal volentier
vegghia"* ("nor by one who unwillingly stays awake," or less literally, but with better force: "nor by one
who fights off sleep").

and turned convulsively to look at me,
as others did who overheard my Guide.
My Master, then, ever concerned for me,   100
turned and said: "Ask them whatever you wish."
And I said to those two wraiths of misery:
"So may the memory of your names and actions
not die forever from the minds of men
in that first world, but live for many suns,   105
tell me who you are and of what city;
  do not be shamed by your nauseous punishment
  into concealing your identity."
"I was a man of Arezzo,"⁵ one replied,
  "and Albert of Siena had me burned;   110
but I am not here for the deed for which I died.
It is true that jokingly I said to him once:
  'I know how to raise myself and fly through air';
  and he—with all the eagerness of a dunce—
wanted to learn. Because I could not make   115
  a Daedalus of him—for no other reason—
  he had his father burn me at the stake.
But Minos, the infallible, had me hurled
  here to the final bolgia of the ten
  for the alchemy I practiced in the world."   120
And I to the Poet: "Was there ever a race
  more vain than the Sienese? Even the French,
  compared to them, seem full of modest grace."
And the other leper answered mockingly:
  "Excepting Stricca, who by careful planning   125
  managed to live and spend so moderately;
and Niccolò, who in his time above
  was first of all the shoots in that rank garden
  to discover the costly uses of the clove;
and excepting the brilliant company of talents   130
  in which Caccia squandered his vineyards and his woods,
  and Abbagliato displayed his intelligence.⁶
But if you wish to know who joins your cry
  against the Sienese, study my face
  with care and let it make its own reply.   135
So you will see I am the suffering shadow
  of Capocchio,⁷ who, by practicing alchemy,

<hr>

5. Griffolino D'arezzo, an alchemist who extracted large sums of money from Alberto da Siena on the
promise of teaching him to fly like Daedalus. When the Sienese oaf finally discovered he had been tricked,
he had his "father," the Bishop of Siena, burn Griffolino as a sorcerer. Griffolino, however, is not punished for sorcery, but for falsification of silver and gold through alchemy.   6. *Stricca . . . Niccolò . . .
Caccia . . . Abbagliato:* All of these Sienese noblemen were members of the Spendthrift Brigade and
wasted their substance in competitions of riotous living. Lano (Canto XIII) was also of this company.
Niccolò dei Salimbeni discovered some recipe (details unknown) prepared with fabulously expensive
spices.   7. Reputedly a Florentine friend of Dante's student days. For practicing alchemy he was burned
at the stake at Siena in 1293.

falsified the metals, and you must know,
unless my mortal recollection strays
how good an ape I was of Nature's ways."   140

CANTO XXX

Circle Eight: Bolgia Ten   The Falsifiers (The Remaining Three Classes:
Evil Impersonators, Counterfeiters, False Witnesses)

Just as Capocchio finishes speaking, two ravenous spirits come racing
through the pit; and one of them, sinking his tusks into Capocchio's neck,
drags him away like prey. Capocchio's companion, Griffolino, identifies
the two as Gianni Schicchi and Myrrha, who run ravening through the
pit through all eternity, snatching at other souls and rending them. These
are the Evil Impersonators, Falsifiers of Persons. In life they seized upon
the appearance of others, and in death they must run with never a pause,
seizing upon the infernal apparition of these souls, while they in turn are
preyed upon by their own furies.

Next the Poets encounter Master Adam, a sinner of the third class, a
Falsifier of Money, i.e., a Counterfeiter. Like the alchemists, he is punished by a loathsome disease and he cannot move from where he lies, but
his disease is compounded by other afflictions, including an eternity of
unbearable thirst. Master Adam identifies two spirits lying beside him as
Potiphar's Wife and Sinon the Greek, sinners of the fourth class, the False
Witnesses, i.e., Falsifiers of Words.

Sinon, angered by Master Adam's identification of him, strikes him across
the belly with the one arm he is able to move. Master Adam replies in
kind, and Dante, fascinated by their continuing exchange of abuse, stands
staring at them until Virgil turns on him in great anger, for "The wish to
hear such baseness is degrading." Dante burns with shame, and Virgil
immediately forgives him because of his great and genuine repentance.

At the time when Juno took her furious
    revenge for Semele, striking in rage
    again and again at the Theban royal house, [8]
King Athamas, by her contrivance, grew
    so mad, that seeing his wife out for an airing   5
    with his two sons, he cried to his retinue:
"Out with the nets there! Nets across the pass!
    for I will take this lioness and her cubs!"
    And spread his talons, mad and merciless,
and seizing his son Learchus, whirled him round   10
    and brained him on a rock; at which the mother
    leaped into the sea with her other son and drowned.
And when the Wheel of Fortune spun about

---

8. As in the case of the Aeginians, Jove begot a son (Bacchus) upon a mortal (Semele, daughter of the
King Cadmus of Thebes); and Juno, who obviously could not cope with her husband's excursions directly,
turned her fury upon the mortals in a number of godlike ways, among them inducing the madness of King
Athamas (Semele's brother-in-law) which Ovid recounts in *Metamorphoses* IV. 512ff.

to humble the all-daring Trojan's pride
so that both king and kingdom were wiped out;   15
Hecuba[9]—mourning, wretched, and a slave—
having seen Polyxena sacrificed,
and Polydorus dead without a grave;
lost and alone, beside an alien sea,
began to bark and growl like a dog   20
in the mad seizure of her misery.
But never in Thebes nor Troy were Furies seen
to strike at man or beast in such mad rage
as two I saw, pale, naked, and unclean,
who suddenly came running toward us then,   25
snapping their teeth as they ran, like hungry swine
let out to feed after a night in the pen.
One of them sank his tusks so savagely
into Capocchio's neck, that when he dragged him,
the ditch's rocky bottom tore his belly.   30
And the Aretine,[1] left trembling by me, said:
"That incubus, in life, was Gianni Schicchi;[2]
here he runs rabid, mangling the other dead."
"So!" I answered, "and so may the other one
not sink its teeth in you, be pleased to tell us   35
what shade it is before it races on."
And he: "That ancient shade in time above
was Myrrha,[3] vicious daughter of Cinyras
who loved her father with more than rightful love.
She falsified another's form and came   40
disguised to sin with him just as that other
who runs with her, in order that he might claim
the fabulous lead-mare, lay under disguise
on Buoso Donati's death bed and dictated
a spurious testament to the notaries."   45
And when the rabid pair had passed from sight,
I turned to observe the other misbegotten
spirits that lay about to left and right.
And there I saw another husk of sin,
who, had his legs been trimmed away at the groin,   50
would have looked for all the world like a mandolin.

9. Wife of King Priam. When Troy fell she was taken to Greece as a slave. En route she was forced to
witness the sacrifice of her daughter and to look upon her son lying murdered and unburied. She went
mad in her affliction and fell to howling like a dog. Ovid (Metamorphoses XIII. 568ff.) describes her
anguish but does not say she was changed into a dog.   1. Capocchio's companion, Griffolino.   2. Of
the Cavalcanti of Florence. When Buoso di Donati (see Canto XXV) died, his son, Simone, persuaded
Schicchi to impersonate the dead man and to dictate a will in Simone's favor. Buoso was removed from
the death bed, Schicchi took his place in disguise, and the will was dictated to a notary as if Buoso were
still alive. Schicchi took advantage of the occasion to make several bequests to himself, including one of a
famous and highly prized mare.   3. Moved by an incestuous passion for her father, the King of Cyprus,
she disguised herself and slipped into his bed. After he had mated with her, the king discovered who she
was and threatened to kill her but she ran away and was changed into a myrtle. Adonis was born from her
trunk. (Ovid, Metamorphoses X. 298ff.)

The dropsy's heavy humors, which so bunch
   and spread the limbs, had disproportioned him
   till his face seemed much too small for his swollen paunch.
He strained his lips apart and thrust them forward   55
   the way a sick man, feverish with thirst,
   curls one lip toward the chin and the other upward.
"O you exempt from every punishment
   of this grim world (I know not why)," he cried,
   "look well upon the misery and debasement   60
of him who was Master Adam.[4] In my first
   life's time, I had enough to please me: here,
   I lack a drop of water for my thirst.
The rivulets that run from the green flanks
   of Casentino[5] to the Arno's flood,   65
   spreading their cool sweet moisture through their banks,
run constantly before me, and their plash
   and ripple in imagination dries me
   more than the disease that eats my flesh.
Inflexible Justice that has forked and spread   70
   my soul like hay, to search it the more closely,
   finds in the country where my guilt was bred
this increase of my grief; for there I learned,
   there in Romena, to stamp the Baptist's image[6]
   on alloyed gold—till I was bound and burned.   75
But could I see the soul of Guido here,
   or of Alessandro, or of their filthy brother,[7]
   I would not trade that sight for all the clear
cool flow of Branda's fountain.[8] One of the three—
   if those wild wraiths who run here are not lying—   80
   is here already.[9] But small good it does me
when my legs are useless! Were I light enough
   to move as much as an inch in a hundred years,
   long before this I would have started off
to cull him from the freaks that fill this fosse,   85
   although it winds on for eleven miles
   and is no less than half a mile across.
Because of them I lie here in this pig-pen;
   it was they persuaded me to stamp the florins
   with three carats of alloy." And I then: 90
"Who are those wretched two sprawled alongside
   your right-hand borders, and who seem to smoke
   as a washed hand smokes in winter?" He replied:

4. Of Brescia. Under the orders of the Counts Guidi of Romena, he counterfeited Florentine florins of twenty-one rather than twenty-four carat gold, and on such a scale that a currency crisis arose in Northern Italy. He was burned at the stake by the Florentines in 1281.   5. A mountainous district in which the Arno rises.   6. John the Baptist's. As patron of Florence, his image was stamped on the florins. 7. The Counts Guidi.   8. A spring near Romena. The famous fountain of Branda is in Siena, but Adam is speaking of his home country and must mean the spring.   9. Guido died before 1300.

"They were here when I first rained into this gully,
    and have not changed position since, nor may they,   95
    as I believe, to all eternity.
One is the liar who charged young Joseph wrongly:[1]
    the other, Sinon,[2] the false Greek from Troy.
    A burning fever makes them reek so strongly."
And one of the false pair, perhaps offended   100
    by the manner of Master Adam's presentation,
    punched him in the rigid and distended
belly—it thundered like a drum—and he
    retorted with an arm blow to the face
    that seemed delivered no whit less politely,   105
saying to him: "Although I cannot stir
    my swollen legs, I still have a free arm
    to use at times when nothing else will answer."
And the other wretch said: "It was not so free
    on your last walk to the stake, free as it was   110
    when you were coining." And he of the dropsy:
"That's true enough, but there was less truth in you
    when they questioned you at Troy." And Sinon then:
    "For every word I uttered that was not true
you uttered enough false coins to fill a bushel: 115
    I am put down here for a single crime,
    but you for more than any Fiend in Hell."[3]
"Think of the Horse," replied the swollen shade,
    "and may it torture you, perjurer, to recall
    that all the world knows the foul part you played."   120
"And to you the torture of the thirst that fries
    and cracks your tongue," said the Greek, "and of the water
    that swells your gut like a hedge before your eyes."
And the coiner: "So is your own mouth clogged
    with the filth that stuffs and sickens it as always;   125
    if I am parched while my paunch is waterlogged,
you have the fever and your cankered brain;
    and were you asked to lap Narcissus' mirror[4]
    you would not wait to be invited again."
I was still standing, fixed upon those two   130
    when the Master said to me: "Now keep on looking
    a little longer and I quarrel with you."
When I heard my Master raise his voice to me,
    I wheeled about with such a start of shame
    that I grow pale yet at the memory.   135
As one trapped in a nightmare that has caught

1. Potiphar's wife bore false witness against Joseph (Genesis 39:6–23).   2. The Greek who glibly talked the Trojans into taking the Horse inside the city walls (Aeneid II. 57–194.)   3. Dante must reckon each false florin as a separate sin.   4. A pool of water. Ovid (Metamorphoses III. 407–510) tells how the young Narcissus fell in love with his own reflection in a pool. He remained bent over the reflection till he wasted away and was changed into a flower.

his sleeping mind, wishes within the dream
that it were all a dream, as if it were not—
such I became: my voice could not win through
my shame to ask his pardon; while my shame   140
already won more pardon than I knew.
"Less shame," my Guide said, ever just and kind,
"would wash away a greater fault than yours.
Therefore, put back all sorrow from your mind;
and never forget that I am always by you   145
should it occur again, as we walk on,
that we find ourselves where others of this crew
fall to such petty wrangling and upbraiding.
The wish to hear such baseness is degrading."

CANTO XXXI

The Central Pit of Malebolge   The Giants

Dante's spirits rise again as the Poets approach the Central Pit, a great
well, at the bottom of which lies Cocytus, the Ninth and final circle of
Hell. Through the darkness Dante sees what appears to be a city of great
towers, but as he draws near he discovers that the great shapes he has seen
are the Giants and Titans who stand perpetual guard inside the well-pit
with the upper halves of their bodies rising above the rim.

Among the Giants, Virgil identifies Nimrod, builder of the Tower of
Babel; Ephialtes and Briareus, who warred against the Gods; and Tityos
and Typhon, who insulted Jupiter. Also here, but for no specific offense,
is Antaeus, and his presence makes it clear that the Giants are placed here
less for their particular sins than for their general natures.

These are the sons of earth, embodiments of elemental forces unbal-
anced by love, desire without restraint and without acknowledgment of
moral and theological law. They are symbols of the earth-trace that every
devout man must clear from his soul, the unchecked passions of the beast.
Raised from the earth, they make the very gods tremble. Now they are
returned to the darkness of their origins, guardians of earth's last depth.

At Virgil's persuasion, Antaeus takes the Poets in his huge palm and
lowers them gently to the final floor of Hell.

One and the same tongue had first wounded me
so that the blood came rushing to my cheeks,
and then supplied the soothing remedy.
Just so, as I have heard, the magic steel
of the lance that was Achilles' and his father's   5
could wound at a touch, and, at another, heal.[5]
We turned our backs on the valley and climbed from it

5. Peleus, father of Achilles, left this magic lance to his son. (Ovid, *Metamorphoses* XIII. 171ff.) Sonne-
teers of Dante's time made frequent metaphoric use of this lance: just as the lance could wound and then
heal, so could the lady's look destroy with love and her kiss make whole.

to the top of the stony bank that walls it round,
crossing in silence to the central pit.
Here it was less than night and less than day;   10
my eyes could make out little through the gloom,
but I heard the shrill note of a trumpet bray
louder than any thunder. As if by force,
it drew my eyes; I stared into the gloom
along the path of the sound back to its source.   15
After the bloody rout when Charlemagne
had lost the band of Holy Knights, Roland[6]
blew no more terribly for all his pain.
And as I stared through that obscurity,
I saw what seemed a cluster of great towers,   20
whereat I cried: "Master, what is this city?"
And he: "You are still too far back in the dark
to make out clearly what you think you see;
it is natural that you should miss the mark:
you will see clearly when you reach that place   25
how much your eyes mislead you at a distance;
I urge you, therefore, to increase your pace."
Then taking my hand in his, my Master said:
"The better to prepare you for strange truth,
let me explain those shapes you see ahead: 30
they are not towers but giants. They stand in the well
from the navel down; and stationed round its bank
they mount guard on the final pit of Hell."
Just as a man in a fog that starts to clear
begins little by little to piece together   35
the shapes the vapor crowded from the air—
so, when those shapes grew clearer as I drew
across the darkness to the central brink,
error fled from me; and my terror grew.
For just as at Montereggione[7] the great towers   40
crown the encircling wall; so the grim giants
whom Jove still threatens when the thunder roars
raised from the rim of stone about that well
the upper halves of their bodies, which loomed up
like turrets through the murky air of Hell.   45
I had drawn close enough to one already
to make out the great arms along his sides,

6. Nephew of Charlemagne, hero of the French epic poem, the *Song of Roland*. He protected the rear of Charlemagne's column on the return march through the Pyrenees from a war against the Saracens. When he was attacked he was too proud to blow his horn as a signal for help, but as he was dying he blew so prodigious a blast that it was heard by Charlemagne eight miles away. *Band of Holy Knights:* The original is *"la santa gesta,"* which may be interpreted as "the holy undertaking." *"Gesta,"* however, can also mean "a sworn band or fellowship of men at arms" (such as the Knights of the Round Table), and since it was his Knights, rather than his undertaking, that Charlemagne lost, the second rendering seems more apt in context.   7. A castle in Val d'Elsa near Siena built in 1213. Its walls had a circumference of more than half a kilometer and were crowned by fourteen great towers, most of which are now destroyed.

the face, the shoulders, the breast, and most of the belly.
Nature, when she destroyed the last exemplars
   on which she formed those beasts, surely did well   50
   to take such executioners from Mars.
And if she has not repented the creation
   of whales and elephants, the thinking man
   will see in that her justice and discretion:
for where the instrument of intelligence   55
   is added to brute power and evil will,
   mankind is powerless in its own defense.
His face, it seemed to me, was quite as high
   and wide as the bronze pine cone in St. Peter's[8]
   with the rest of him proportioned accordingly: 60
so that the bank, which made an apron for him
   from the waist down, still left so much exposed
   that three Frieslanders[9] standing on the rim,
one on another, could not have reached his hair;
   for to that point at which men's capes are buckled,   65
   thirty good hand-spans[1] of brute bulk rose clear.
"Rafel mahee amek zabi almit,"[2]
   began a bellowed chant from the brute mouth
   for which no sweeter psalmody was fit.
And my Guide in his direction: "Babbling fool,   70
   stick to your horn and vent yourself with it
   when rage or passion stir your stupid soul.
Feel there around your neck, you muddle-head,
   and find the cord; and there's the horn itself,
   there on your overgrown chest." To me he said: 75
"His very babbling testifies the wrong
   he did on earth: he is Nimrod,[3] through whose evil
   mankind no longer speaks a common tongue.
Waste no words on him: it would be foolish.
   To him all speech is meaningless; as his own,   80
   which no one understands, is simply gibberish."
We moved on, bearing left along the pit,
   and a crossbow-shot away we found the next one,
   an even huger and more savage spirit.
What master could have bound so gross a beast   85
   I cannot say, but he had his right arm pinned
   behind his back, and the left across his breast
by an enormous chain that wound about him

---

8. Originally a part of a fountain. In Dante's time it stood in front of the Basilica of St. Peter. It is now inside the Vatican. It stands about thirteen feet high (Scartazzini-Vandelli give the height as four meters) but shows signs of mutilation that indicate it was once higher.   9. The men of Friesland were reputed to be the tallest in Europe.   1. Dante uses the word "palma," which in Italian signifies the spread of the open hand.   2. This line, as Virgil explains below, is Nimrod's gibberish.   3. The first king of Babylon, supposed to have built the Tower of Babel, for which he is punished, in part, by the confusion of his own tongue and understanding. Nothing in the Biblical reference portrays him as one of the earth-giants.

from the neck down, completing five great turns
before it spiraled down below the rim.   90
"This piece of arrogance," said my Guide to me,
"dared try his strength against the power of Jove;
for which he is rewarded as you see.
He is Ephialtes,[4] who made the great endeavour
with the other giants who alarmed the Gods;   95
the arms he raised then, now are bound forever."
"Were it possible, I should like to take with me,"
I said to him, "the memory of seeing
the immeasurable Briareus."[5] And he:
"Nearer to hand, you may observe Antaeus[6]   100
who is able to speak to us, and is not bound.
It is he will set us down in Cocytus,[7]
the bottom of all guilt. The other hulk
stands far beyond our road. He too, is bound
and looks like this one, but with a fiercer sulk."   105
No earthquake in the fury of its shock
ever seized a tower more violently,
than Ephialtes, hearing, began to rock.
Then I dreaded death as never before;
and I think I could have died for very fear   110
had I not seen what manacles he wore.
We left the monster, and not far from him
we reached Antaeus, who to his shoulders alone
soared up a good five ells above the rim.
"O soul who once in Zama's fateful vale—   115
where Scipio became the heir of glory
when Hannibal and all his troops turned tail—
took more than a thousand lions for your prey;
and in whose memory many still believe
the sons of earth would yet have won the day   120
had you joined with them against High Olympus—
do not disdain to do us a small service,
but set us down where the cold grips Cocytus.
Would you have us go to Tityos or Typhon?[8]—
this man can give you what is longed for here: 125
therefore do not refuse him, but bend down.

---

4. Son of Neptune (the sea) and Iphimedia. With his brother, Otus, he warred against the Gods striving
to pile Mt. Ossa on Mt. Olympus, and Mt. Pelion on Mt. Ossa. Apollo restored good order by killing the
two brothers.   5. Another of the giants who rose against the Olympian Gods. Virgil speaks of him as
having a hundred arms and fifty hands (*Aeneid* X. 565–568), but Dante has need only of his size, and of
his sin, which he seems to view as a kind of revolt of the angels, just as the action of Ephialtes and Otus
may be read as a pagan distortion of the Tower of Babel legend. He was the son of Uranus and Tellus.
6. The son of Neptune and Tellus (the earth). In battle, his strength grew every time he touched the earth,
his mother. He was accordingly invincible until Hercules killed him by lifting him over his head and
strangling him in mid-air. Lucan (*Pharsalia* IV. 595–660) describes Antaeus's great lion-hunting feat in
the valley of Zama where, in a later era, Scipio defeated Hannibal. Antaeus did not join in the rebellion
against the Gods and therefore he is not chained.   7. The final pit of Hell.   8. Also sons of Tellus.
They offended Jupiter, who had them hurled into the crater of Etna, below which the Lake Tartarus was
supposed to lie.

For he can still make new your memory:
    he lives, and awaits long life, unless Grace call him
    before his time to his felicity."
Thus my Master to that Tower of Pride;   130
    and the giant without delay reached out the hands
    which Hercules had felt, and raised my Guide.
Virgil, when he felt himself so grasped,
    called to me: "Come, and I will hold you safe."
And he took me in his arms and held me clasped.   135
The way the Carisenda[9] seems to one
    who looks up from the leaning side when clouds
    are going over it from that direction,
making the whole tower seem to topple—so
    Antaeus seemed to me in the fraught moment   140
    when I stood clinging, watching from below
as he bent down; while I with heart and soul
    wished we had gone some other way, but gently
    he set us down inside the final hole
whose ice holds Judas and Lucifer in its grip.   145
Then straightened like a mast above a ship.

CANTO XXXII

Circle Nine: Cocytus   Compound Fraud
Round One: Caïna   The Treacherous to Kin
Round Two: Antenora   The Treacherous to Country

At the bottom of the well Dante finds himself on a huge frozen lake.
This is Cocytus, the Ninth Circle, the fourth and last great water of Hell,
and here, fixed in the ice, each according to his guilt, are punished sinners
guilty of Treachery Against Those to Whom They Were Bound by Special
Ties. The ice is divided into four concentric rings marked only by the
different positions of the damned within the ice.

This is Dante's symbolic equivalent of the final guilt. The treacheries of
these souls were denials of love (which is God) and of all human warmth.
Only the remorseless dead center of the ice will serve to express their natures.
As they denied God's love, so are they furthest removed from the light and
warmth of His Sun. As they denied all human ties, so are they bound only
by the unyielding ice.

The first round is Caïna, named for Cain. Here lie those who were
treacherous against blood ties. They have their necks and heads out of the
ice and are permitted to bow their heads—a double boon since it allows
them some protection from the freezing gale and, further, allows their tears
to fall without freezing their eyes shut. Here Dante sees Alessandro and
Napoleone degli Alberti, and he speaks to Camicion, who identifies other
sinners of this round.

The second round is Antenora, named for Antenor, the Trojan who was

9. A leaning tower of Bologna.

believed to have betrayed his city to the Greeks. Here lie those guilty of
Treachery to Country. They, too, have their heads above the ice, but they
cannot bend their necks, which are gripped by the ice. Here Dante accidentally kicks the head of Bocca Degli Abbati and then proceeds to treat
him with a savagery he had shown to no other soul in Hell. Bocca names
some of his fellow traitors, and the Poets pass on to discover two heads
frozen together in one hole. One of them is gnawing the nape of the other's
neck.

If I had rhymes as harsh and horrible
   as the hard fact of that final dismal hole
   which bears the weight of all the steeps of Hell,
I might more fully press the sap and substance
   from my conception; but since I must do   5
   without them, I begin with some reluctance.
For it is no easy undertaking, I say,
   to describe the bottom of the Universe;
   nor is it for tongues that only babble child's play.
But may those Ladies of the Heavenly Spring[1]   10
   who helped Amphion wall Thebes, assist my verse,
   that the word may be the mirror of the thing.
O most miscreant rabble, you who keep
   the stations of that place whose name is pain,
   better had you been born as goats or sheep!   15
We stood now in the dark pit of the well,
   far down the slope below the Giant's feet,
   and while I still stared up at the great wall,
I heard a voice cry: "Watch which way you turn:
   take care you do not trample on the heads   20
   of the forworn and miserable brethren."
Whereat I turned and saw beneath my feet
   and stretching out ahead, a lake so frozen
   it seemed to be made of glass. So thick a sheet
never yet hid the Danube's winter course,   25
   nor, far away beneath the frigid sky,
   locked the Don up in its frozen source:
for were Tanbernick and the enormous peak
   of Pietrapana[2] to crash down on it,
   not even the edges would so much as creak.   30
The way frogs sit to croak, their muzzles leaning
   out of the water, at the time and season
   when the peasant woman dreams of her day's gleaning—[3]
Just so the livid dead are sealed in place

---

1. The Muses. They so inspired Amphion's hand upon the lyre that the music charmed blocks of stone
out of Mount Cithaeron, and the blocks formed themselves into the walls of Thebes.   2. There is no
agreement on the location of the mountain Dante called Tanbernick. Pietrapana, today known as *la
Pania*, is in Tuscany.   3. The summer.

up to the part at which they blushed for shame,   35
and they beat their teeth like storks. Each holds his face
bowed toward the ice, each of them testifies
   to the cold with his chattering mouth, to his heart's grief
   with tears that flood forever from his eyes.
When I had stared about me, I looked down   40
   and at my feet I saw two clamped together
   so tightly that the hair of their heads had grown
together. "Who are you," I said, "who lie
   so tightly breast to breast?" They strained their necks,
   and when they had raised their heads as if to reply,   45
the tears their eyes had managed to contain
   up to that time gushed out, and the cold froze them
   between the lids, sealing them shut again
tighter than any clamp grips wood to wood,
   and mad with pain, they fell to butting heads   50
   like billy-goats in a sudden savage mood.
And a wraith who lay to one side and below,
   and who had lost both ears to frostbite, said,
   his head still bowed: "Why do you watch us so?
If you wish to know who they are[4] who share one doom,   55
   they owned the Bisenzio's valley with their father,
   whose name was Albert. They spring from one womb,
and you may search through all Caïna's crew
   without discovering in all this waste
   a squab more fit for the aspic than these two;   60
not him whose breast and shadow a single blow
   of the great lance of King Arthur pierced with light;[5]
   nor yet Focaccia[6] nor this one fastened so
into the ice that his head is all I see,
   and whom, if you are Tuscan, you know well—   65
   his name on the earth was Sassol Mascheroni.[7]
And I—to tell you all and so be through—
   was Camicion de' Pazzi.[8] I wait for Carlin
   beside whose guilt my sins will shine like virtue."
And leaving him,[9] I saw a thousand faces   70

---

4. Alessandro and Napoleone, Counts of Mangona. Among other holdings, they inherited a castle in the Val di Bisenzio. They seemed to have been at odds on all things and finally killed one another in a squabble over their inheritance and their politics (Alessandro was a Guelph and Napoleone a Ghibelline).   5. Mordred, King Arthur's traitorous nephew. He tried to kill Arthur, but the king struck him a single blow of his lance, and when it was withdrawn, a shaft of light passed through the gaping wound and split the shadow of the falling traitor.   6. Of the Cancellieri of Pistoia. He murdered his cousin (among others) and may have been the principal cause of a great feud that divided the Cancellieri, and split the Guelphs into the White and Black parties.   7. Of the Toschi of Florence. He was appointed guardian of one of his nephews and murdered him to get the inheritance for himself.   8. Alberto Camicion de' Pazzi of Valdarno. He murdered a kinsman. *Carlin:* Carlino de' Pazzi, relative of Alberto. He was charged with defending for the Whites the castle of Piantravigne in Valdarno but surrendered it for a bribe. He belongs therefore in the next lower circle, Antenora, as a traitor to his country, and when he arrives there his greater sin will make Alberto seem almost virtuous by comparison.   9. These words mark the departure from Caïna to Antenora.

discolored so by cold, I shudder yet
and always will when I think of those frozen places.
As we approached the center of all weight,
   where I went shivering in eternal shade,
   whether it was my will, or chance, or fate,   75
I cannot say, but as I trailed my Guide
   among those heads, my foot struck violently
   against the face of one.[1] Weeping, it cried:
"Why do you kick me? If you were not sent
   to wreak a further vengeance for Montaperti,   80
   why do you add this to my other torment?"
"Master," I said, "grant me a moment's pause
   to rid myself of a doubt concerning this one;
   then you may hurry me at your own pace."
The Master stopped at once, and through the volley   85
   of foul abuse the wretch poured out, I said:
   "Who are you who curse others so?" And he:
"And who are *you* who go through the dead larder
   of Antenora kicking the cheeks of others
   so hard, that were you alive, you could not kick harder?"   90
"I *am* alive," I said, "and if you seek fame,
   it may be precious to you above all else
   that my notes on this descent include your name."
"Exactly the opposite is my wish and hope,"
   he answered. "Let me be; for it's little you know   95
   of how to flatter on this icy slope."
I grabbed the hair of his dog's-ruff and I said:
   "Either you tell me truly who you are,
   or you won't have a hair left on your head."
And he: "Not though you snatch me bald. I swear   100
   I will not tell my name nor show my face.
   Not though you rip until my brain lies bare."
I had a good grip on his hair; already
   I had yanked out more than one fistful of it,
   while the wretch yelped, but kept his face turned from me;   105
when another said: "Bocca, what is it ails you?
   What the Hell's wrong?[2] Isn't it bad enough
   to hear you bang your jaws? Must you bark too?"
"Now filthy traitor, say no more!" I cried,
   "for to your shame, be sure I shall bear back   110
   a true report of you." The wretch replied:
"Say anything you please but go away.
   And if you *do* get back, don't overlook

---

1. Bocca degli Abbati, a traitorous Florentine. At the battle of Montaperti (cf. Farinata, Canto X) he hacked off the hand of the Florentine standard bearer. The cavalry, lacking a standard around which it could rally, was soon routed.   2. In the circumstances, a monstrous pun. The original is *"qual diavolo ti tocca?"* (what devil touches, or molests, you?) a standard colloquialism for "what's the matter with you?" A similar pun occurs in line 117: "kept crisp (cool) on ice." Colloquially *"stare fresco"* (to be or to remain cool) equals "to be left out in the cold," i.e., to be out of luck.

that pretty one who had so much to say
just now. Here he laments the Frenchman's price.   115
'I saw Buoso da Duera,'[3] you can report,
'where the bad salad is kept crisp on ice.'
And if you're asked who else was wintering here,
Beccheria,[4] whose throat was slit by Florence,
is there beside you. Gianni de' Soldanier[5]   120
is further down, I think, with Ganelon,[6]
and Tebaldello,[7] who opened the gates of Faenza
and let Bologna steal in with the dawn."
Leaving him then, I saw two souls together
in a single hole, and so pinched in by the ice   125
that one head made a helmet for the other.
As a famished man chews crusts—so the one sinner
sank his teeth into the other's nape
at the base of the skull, gnawing his loathsome dinner.
Tydeus in his final raging hour   130
gnawed Menalippus' head[8] with no more fury
than this one gnawed at skull and dripping gore.
"You there," I said, "who show so odiously
your hatred for that other, tell me why
on this condition: that if in what you tell me   135
you seem to have a reasonable complaint
against him you devour with such foul relish,
I, knowing who you are, and his soul's taint,
may speak your cause to living memory,
God willing the power of speech be left to me."   140

CANTO XXXIII

Circle Nine: Cocytus   Compound Fraud
Round Two: Antenora   The Treacherous to Country
Round Three: Ptolomea   The Treacherous to Guests and Hosts

   In reply to Dante's exhortation, the sinner who is gnawing his companion's head looks up, wipes his bloody mouth on his victim's hair, and tells
his harrowing story. He is Count Ugolino and the wretch he gnaws is
Archbishop Ruggieri. Both are in Antenora for treason. In life they had

---

3. Of Cremona. In 1265 Charles of Anjou marched against Manfred and Naples (see Canto XIX), and
Buoso da Duera was sent out in charge of a Ghibelline army to oppose the passage of one of Charles'
armies, but accepted a bribe and let the French pass unopposed. The event took place near Parma.
4. Tesauro dei Beccheria of Pavia, Abbot of Vallombrosa and Papal Legate (of Alexander IV) in Tuscany.
The Florentine Guelphs cut off his head in 1258 for plotting with the expelled Ghibellines.   5. A
Florentine Ghibelline of ancient and noble family. In 1265, however, during the riots that occurred under
the Two Jovial Friars, he deserted his party and became a leader of the commoners (Guelphs). In placing
him in Antenora, Dante makes no distinction between turning on one's country and turning on one's
political party, not at least if the end is simply for power.   6. It was Ganelon who betrayed Roland to
the Saracens. (See Canto XXXI, and above, p. 0000.)   7. Tebaldello de' Zambrasi of Faenza. At dawn
on November 13, 1280, he opened the city gates and delivered Faenza to the Bolognese Guelphs in order
to revenge himself on the Ghibelline family of the Lambertazzi who, in 1274, had fled from Bologna to
take refuge in Faenza.   8. Statius recounts in the *Thebaid* that Tydeus killed Menalippus in battle but
fell himself mortally wounded. As he lay dying he had Menalippus' head brought to him and fell to
gnawing it in his dying rage.

once plotted together. Then Ruggieri betrayed his fellow-plotter and caused
his death, by starvation, along with his four "sons." In the most pathetic
and dramatic passage of the *Inferno*, Ugolino details how their prison was
sealed and how his "sons" dropped dead before him one by one, weeping
for food. His terrible tale serves only to renew his grief and hatred, and he
has hardly finished it before he begins to gnaw Ruggieri again with renewed
fury. In the immutable Law of Hell, the killer-by-starvation becomes the
food of his victim.

The Poets leave Ugolino and enter Ptolomea, so named for the Ptolo-
maeus of Maccabees, who murdered his father-in-law at a banquet. Here
are punished those who were Treacherous Against the Ties of Hospitality.
They lie with only half their faces above the ice and their tears freeze in
their eye sockets, sealing them with little crystal visors. Thus even the
comfort of tears is denied them. Here Dante finds Friar Alberigo and Branca
D'Oria, and discovers the terrible power of Ptolomea: so great is its sin that
the souls of the guilty fall to its torments even before they die, leaving their
bodies still on earth, inhabited by Demons.

The sinner raised his mouth from his grim repast
    and wiped it on the hair of the bloody head
    whose nape he had all but eaten away. At last
he began to speak: "You ask me to renew
    a grief so desperate that the very thought   5
    of speaking of it tears my heart in two.
But if my words may be a seed that bears
    the fruit of infamy for him I gnaw,
    I shall weep, but tell my story through my tears.
Who you may be, and by what powers you reach   10
    into this underworld, I cannot guess,
    but you seem to me a Florentine by your speech.
I was Count Ugolino,[9] I must explain;
    this reverend grace is the Archbishop Ruggieri:
    now I will tell you why I gnaw his brain.   15
That I, who trusted him, had to undergo
    imprisonment and death through his treachery,
    you will know already.[1] What you cannot know—
that is, the lingering inhumanity
    of the death I suffered—you shall hear in full: 20
    then judge for yourself if he has injured me.
A narrow window in that coop[2] of stone

9. Count of Donoratico and a member of the Guelph family della Gherardesca. He and his nephew,
Nino de' Visconti, led the two Guelph factions of Pisa. In 1288 Ugolino intrigued with Archbishop
Ruggieri degli Ubaldini, leader of the Ghibellines, to get rid of Visconti and to take over the command of
all the Pisan Guelphs. The plan worked, but in the consequent weakening of the Guelphs, Ruggieri saw
his chance and betrayed Ugolino, throwing him into prison with his sons and his grandsons. In the
following year the prison was sealed up and they were left to starve to death. 1. News of Ugolino's
imprisonment and death would certainly have reached Florence. *What you cannot know:* No living man
could know what happened after Ugolino and his sons were sealed in the prison and abandoned.
2. Dante uses the word *muda*, in Italian signifying a stone tower in which falcons were kept in the dark
to moult. From the time of Ugolino's death it became known as The Tower of Hunger.

now called the Tower of Hunger for my sake
(within which others yet must pace alone)
had shown me several waning moons already[3]   25
between its bars, when I slept the evil sleep
in which the veil of the future parted for me.
This beast[4] appeared as master of a hunt
chasing the wolf and his whelps across the mountain
that hides Lucca from Pisa.[5] Out in front   30
of the starved and shrewd and avid pack he had placed
Gualandi and Sismondi and Lanfranchi[6]
to point his prey. The father and sons had raced
a brief course only when they failed of breath
and seemed to weaken; then I thought I saw   35
their flanks ripped open by the hounds' fierce teeth.
Before the dawn, the dream still in my head,
I woke and heard my sons,[7] who were there with me,
cry from their troubled sleep, asking for bread.
You are cruelty itself if you can keep   40
your tears back at the thought of what foreboding
stirred in my heart; and if you do not weep,
at what are you used to weeping?—The hour when food
used to be brought, drew near. They were now awake,
and each was anxious from his dream's dark mood.   45
And from the base of that horrible tower I heard
the sound of hammers nailing up the gates:
I stared at my sons' faces without a word.
I did not weep: I had turned stone inside.
They wept. 'What ails you, Father, you look so strange,'   50
my little Anselm, youngest of them, cried.
But I did not speak a word nor shed a tear:
not all that day nor all that endless night,
until I saw another sun appear.
When a tiny ray leaked into that dark prison   55
and I saw staring back from their four faces
the terror and the wasting of my own,
I bit my hands in helpless grief. And they,
thinking I chewed myself for hunger, rose
suddenly together. I heard them say: 60
'Father, it would give us much less pain
if you ate us: it was you who put upon us
this sorry flesh; now strip it off again.'
I calmed myself to spare them. Ah! hard earth,

3. Ugolino was jailed late in 1288. He was sealed in to starve early in 1289.   4. Ruggieri.   5. These
two cities would be in view of one another were it not for Monte San Giuliano.   6. Three Pisan nobles,
Ghibellines and friends of the Archbishop.   7. Actually two of the boys were grandsons and all were
considerably older than one would gather from Dante's account. Anselm, the younger grandson, was
fifteen. The others were really young men and were certainly old enough for guilt despite Dante's charge
in line 90.

why did you not yawn open? All that day   65
and the next we sat in silence. On the fourth,
Gaddo, the eldest, fell before me and cried,
    stretched at my feet upon that prison floor:
    'Father, why don't you help me?' There he died.
And just as you see me, I saw them fall   70
    one by one on the fifth day and the sixth.
Then, already blind, I began to crawl
from body to body shaking them frantically.
Two days I called their names, and they were dead.
Then fasting overcame my grief and me."[8]   75
His eyes narrowed to slits when he was done,
    and he seized the skull again between his teeth
    grinding it as a mastiff grinds a bone.
Ah, Pisa! foulest blemish on the land
    where "si" sounds sweet and clear,[9] since those nearby you   80
    are slow to blast the ground on which you stand,
may Caprara and Gorgona[1] drift from place
    and dam the flooding Arno at its mouth
    until it drowns the last of your foul race!
For if to Ugolino falls the censure   85
    for having betrayed your castles,[2] you for your part
    should not have put his sons to such a torture:
you modern Thebes![3] those tender lives you spilt—
    Brigata, Uguccione, and the others
    I mentioned earlier—were too young for guilt!   90
We passed on further,[4] where the frozen mine
    entombs another crew in greater pain;
    these wraiths are not bent over, but lie supine.
Their very weeping closes up their eyes;
    and the grief that finds no outlet for its tears   95
    turns inward to increase their agonies:
for the first tears that they shed knot instantly
    in their eye-sockets, and as they freeze they form
    a crystal visor above the cavity.
And despite the fact that standing in that place   100
    I had become as numb as any callus,
    and all sensation had faded from my face,

---

8. I.e., he died. Some interpret the line to mean that Ugolino's hunger drove him to cannibalism. Ugolino's present occupation in Hell would certainly support that interpretation but the fact is that cannibalism is the one major sin Dante does not assign a place to in Hell. So monstrous would it have seemed to him that he must certainly have established a special punishment for it. Certainly he could hardly have relegated it to an ambiguity. Moreover, it would be a sin of bestiality rather than of fraud, and as such it would be punished in the Seventh Circle.   9. Italy.   1. These two islands near the mouth of the Arno were Pisan possessions in 1300.   2. In 1284, Ugolino gave up certain castles to Lucca and Florence. He was at war with Genoa at the time and it is quite likely that he ceded the castles to buy the neutrality of these two cities, for they were technically allied with Genoa. Dante, however, must certainly consider the action as treasonable, for otherwise Ugolino would be in Caïna for his treachery to Visconti.   3. Thebes, as a number of the foregoing notes will already have made clear, was the site of some of the most hideous crimes of antiquity.   4. Marks the passage into Ptolomea.

somehow I felt a wind begin to blow,
whereat I said: "Master, what stirs this wind?
Is not all heat extinguished here below?"[5]   105
And the Master said to me: "Soon you will be
where your own eyes will see the source and cause
and give you their own answer to the mystery."
And one of those locked in that icy mall
cried out to us as we passed: "O souls so cruel   110
that you are sent to the last post of all,
relieve me for a little from the pain
of this hard veil; let my heart weep a while
before the weeping freeze my eyes again."
And I to him: "If you would have my service,   115
tell me your name; then if I do not help you
may I descend to the last rim of the ice."[6]
"I am Friar Alberigo,"[7] he answered therefore,
"the same who called for the fruits from the bad garden.
Here I am given dates for figs full store."   120
"What! Are you dead already?" I said to him.
And he then: "How my body stands in the world
I do not know. So privileged is this rim
of Ptolomea, that often souls fall to it
before dark Atropos[8] has cut their thread.   125
And that you may more willingly free my spirit
of this glaze of frozen tears that shrouds my face,
I will tell you this: when a soul betrays as I did,
it falls from flesh, and a demon takes its place,
ruling the body till its time is spent.   130
The ruined soul rains down into this cistern.
So, I believe, there is still evident
in the world above, all that is fair and mortal
of this black shade who winters here behind me.
If you have only recently crossed the portal   135
from that sweet world, you surely must have known
his body: Branca D'Oria[9] is its name,
and many years have passed since he rained down."
"I think you are trying to take me in," I said,
"Ser Branca D'Oria is a living man;   140

---

5. Dante believed (rather accurately, by chance) that all winds resulted from "exhalations of heat." Cocytus, however, is conceived as wholly devoid of heat, a metaphysical absolute zero. The source of the wind,
as we discover in the next Canto, is Satan himself.   6. Dante is not taking any chances; he has to go on
to the last rim in any case. The sinner, however, believes him to be another damned soul and would
interpret the oath quite otherwise than as Dante meant it.   7. Of the Manfredi of Faenza. He was
another Jovial Friar. In 1284 his brother Manfred struck him in the course of an argument. Alberigo
pretended to let it pass, but in 1285 he invited Manfred and his son to a banquet and had them murdered.
The signal to the assassins was the words: "Bring in the fruit." "Friar Alberigo's bad fruit" became a
proverbial saying.   8. The Fate who cuts the thread of life.   9. A Genoese Ghibelline. His sin is
identical in kind to that of Friar Alberigo. In 1275 he invited his father-in-law, Michel Zanche (see Canto
XXII), to a banquet and had him and his companions cut to pieces. He was assisted in the butchery by his
nephew.

he eats, he drinks, he fills his clothes and his bed."
"Michel Zanche had not yet reached the ditch
    of the Black Talons," the frozen wraith replied,
    "there where the sinners thicken in hot pitch,
when this one left his body to a devil,   145
    as did his nephew and second in treachery,
    and plumbed like lead through space to this dead level.
But now reach out your hand, and let me cry."
    And I did not keep the promise I had made,
    for to be rude to him was courtesy.   150
Ah, men of Genoa! souls of little worth,
    corrupted from all custom of righteousness,
    why have you not been driven from the earth?
For there beside the blackest soul of all
    Romagna's evil plain, lies one of yours   155
    bathing his filthy soul in the eternal
glacier of Cocytus for his foul crime,
while he seems yet alive in world and time!

CANTO XXXIV

Ninth Circle: Cocytus   Compound Fraud
Round Four: Judecca   The Treacherous to Their Masters
The Center: Satan

"On march the banners of the King," Virgil begins as the Poets face the
last depth. He is quoting a medieval hymn, and to it he adds the distortion
and perversion of all that lies about him. "On march the banners of the
King—of Hell." And there before them, in an infernal parody of Godhead,
they see Satan in the distance, his great wings beating like a windmill. It
is their beating that is the source of the icy wind of Cocytus, the exhalation
of all evil.

All about him in the ice are strewn the sinners of the last round, Judecca,
named for Judas Iscariot. These are the Treacherous to Their Masters.
They lie completely sealed in the ice, twisted and distorted into every con-
ceivable posture. It is impossible to speak to them, and the Poets move on
to observe Satan.

He is fixed into the ice at the center to which flow all the rivers of guilt;
and as he beats his great wings as if to escape, their icy wind only freezes
him more surely into the polluted ice. In a grotesque parody of the Trinity,
he has three faces, each a different color, and in each mouth he clamps a
sinner whom he rips eternally with his teeth. Judas Iscariot is in the central
mouth: Brutus and Cassius in the mouths on either side.

Having seen all, the Poets now climb through the center, grappling
hand over hand down the hairy flank of Satan himself—a last supremely
symbolic action—and at last, when they have passed the center of all gravity, they emerge from Hell. A long climb from the earth's center to the
Mount of Purgatory awaits them, and they push on without rest, ascending

along the sides of the river Lethe, till they emerge once more to see the stars of Heaven, just before dawn on Easter Sunday.

"On march the banners of the King of Hell,"[1]
my Master said. "Toward us. Look straight ahead:
can you make him out at the core of the frozen shell?"
Like a whirling windmill seen afar at twilight,
    or when a mist has risen from the ground— 5
    just such an engine rose upon my sight
stirring up such a wild and bitter wind
    I cowered for shelter at my Master's back,
    there being no other windbreak I could find.
I stood now where the souls of the last class 10
    (with fear my verses tell it) were covered wholly;
    they shone below the ice like straws in glass.
Some lie stretched out; others are fixed in place
    upright, some on their heads, some on their soles;
    another, like a bow, bends foot to face. 15
When we had gone so far across the ice
    that it pleased my Guide to show me the foul creature[2]
    which once had worn the grace of Paradise,
he made me stop, and, stepping aside, he said:
    "Now see the face of Dis! This is the place 20
    where you must arm your soul against all dread."
Do not ask, Reader, how my blood ran cold
    and my voice choked up with fear. I cannot write it:
    this is a terror that cannot be told.
I did not die, and yet I lost life's breath: 25
    imagine for youself what I became,
    deprived at once of both my life and death.
The Emperor of the Universe of Pain
    jutted his upper chest above the ice;
    and I am closer in size to the great mountain 30
the Titans make around the central pit,
    than they to his arms. Now, starting from this part,
    imagine the whole that corresponds to it!
If he was once as beautiful as now
    he is hideous, and still turned on his Maker, 35
    well may he be the source of every woe!
With what a sense of awe I saw his head
    towering above me! for it had three faces:
    one was in front, and it was fiery red;
the other two, as weirdly wonderful, 40
    merged with it from the middle of each shoulder

---

1. The hymn (Vexilla regis prodeunt) was written in the sixth century by Venantius Fortunatus, Bishop of Poitiers. The original celebrates the Holy Cross, and is part of the service for Good Friday to be sung at the moment of uncovering the cross.   2. Satan.

to the point where all converged at the top of the skull;
the right was something between white and bile;
   the left was about the color that one finds
   on those who live along the banks of the Nile.   45
Under each head two wings rose terribly,
   their span proportioned to so gross a bird:
   I never saw such sails upon the sea.
They were not feathers—their texture and their form
   were like a bat's wings—and he beat them so   50
   that three winds blew from him in one great storm:
   it is these winds that freeze all Cocytus.
He wept from his six eyes, and down three chins
   the tears ran mixed with bloody froth and pus.[3]
In every mouth he worked a broken sinner   55
   between his rake-like teeth. Thus he kept three
   in eternal pain at his eternal dinner.
For the one in front the biting seemed to play
   no part at all compared to the ripping: at times
   the whole skin of his back was flayed away.   60
"That soul that suffers most," explained my Guide,
   "is Judas Iscariot, he who kicks his legs
   on the fiery chin and has his head inside.
Of the other two, who have their heads thrust forward,
   the one who dangles down from the black face   65
   is Brutus: note how he writhes without a word.
And there, with the huge and sinewy arms,[4] is the soul
   of Cassius.—But the night is coming on[5]
   and we must go, for we have seen the whole."
Then, as he bade, I clasped his neck, and he,   70
   watching for a moment when the wings
   were opened wide, reached over dexterously
and seized the shaggy coat of the king demon;
   then grappling matted hair and frozen crusts
   from one tuft to another, clambered down.   75
When we had reached the joint where the great thigh
   merges into the swelling of the haunch,
   my Guide and Master, straining terribly,
turned his head to where his feet had been
   and began to grip the hair as if he were climbing;   80
   so that I thought we moved toward Hell again.
"Hold fast!" my Guide said, and his breath came shrill[6]
   with labor and exhaustion. "There is no way
   but by such stairs to rise above such evil."

---

3. The gore of the sinners he chews which is mixed with his slaver.   4. The Cassius who betrayed
Caesar was more generally described in terms of Shakespeare's "lean and hungry look." Another Cassius
is described by Cicero (Catiline III) as huge and sinewy. Dante probably confused the two.   5. It is now
Saturday evening.   6. Cf. Canto XXIII. 85, where the fact that Dante breathes indicates to the Hypocrites that he is alive. Virgil's breathing is certainly a contradiction.

At last he climbed out through an opening   85
in the central rock, and he seated me on the rim;
then joined me with a nimble backward spring.
I looked up, thinking to see Lucifer
as I had left him, and I saw instead
his legs projecting high into the air.   90
Now let all those whose dull minds are still vexed
by failure to understand what point it was
I had passed through, judge if I was perplexed.
"Get up. Up on your feet," my Master said.
"The sun already mounts to middle tierce,[7]   95
and a long road and hard climbing lie ahead."
It was no hall of state we had found there,
but a natural animal pit hollowed from rock
with a broken floor and a close and sunless air.
"Before I tear myself from the Abyss,"   100
I said when I had risen, "O my Master,
explain to me my error in all this:
where is the ice? and Lucifer—how has he
been turned from top to bottom: and how can the sun
have gone from night to day so suddenly?"   105
And he to me: "You imagine you are still
on the other side of the center where I grasped
the shaggy flank of the Great Worm of Evil
which bores through the world—you were while I climbed down,
but when I turned myself about, you passed   110
the point to which all gravities are drawn.
You are under the other hemisphere where you stand;
the sky above us is the half opposed
to that which canopies the great dry land.
Under the mid-point of that other sky   115
the Man who was born sinless and who lived
beyond all blemish, came to suffer and die.
You have your feet upon a little sphere
which forms the other face of the Judecca.
There it is evening when it is morning here.   120
And this gross Fiend and Image of all Evil
who made a stairway for us with his hide
is pinched and prisoned in the ice-pack still.
On this side he plunged down from heaven's height,
and the land that spread here once hid in the sea   125
and fled North to our hemisphere for fright;
and it may be that moved by that same fear,
the one peak[8] that still rises on this side

---

7. In the canonical day tierce is the period from about six to nine A.M. Middle tierce, therefore, is seven-thirty. In going through the center point, they have gone from night to day. They have moved ahead twelve hours.   8. The Mount of Purgatory.

fled upward leaving this great cavern here.
Down there, beginning at the further bound   130
  of Beelzebub's dim tomb, there is a space
  not known by sight, but only by the sound
of a little stream[9] descending through the hollow
  it has eroded from the massive stone
  in its endlessly entwining lazy flow.   135
My Guide and I crossed over and began
  to mount that little known and lightless road
  to ascend into the shining world again.
He first, I second, without thought of rest
  we climbed the dark until we reached the point   140
  where a round opening brought in sight the blest
and beauteous shining of the Heavenly cars.
And we walked out once more beneath the Stars.[1]

Purgatorio

CANTO I

Ante-Purgatory:
The Shore of the Island   Cato of Utica

The Poets emerge from Hell just before dawn of Easter Sunday (April
10, 1300), and Dante revels in the sight of the rediscovered heavens. As
he looks eagerly about at the stars, he sees nearby an old man of impressive
bearing. The ancient is Cato of Utica, guardian of the shores of Purgatory.
Cato challenges the Poets as fugitives from Hell, but Virgil, after first
instructing Dante to kneel in reverence, explains Dante's mission and Beatrice's command. Cato then gives them instructions for proceeding.
    The Poets have emerged at a point a short way up the slope of Purgatory.
It is essential, therefore, that they descend to the lowest point and begin
from there, an allegory of Humility. Cato, accordingly, orders Virgil to
lead Dante to the shore, to wet his hands in the dew of the new morning,
and to wash the stains of Hell from Dante's face and the film of Hell's
vapors from Dante's eyes. Virgil is then to bind about Dante's waist one of
the pliant reeds (symbolizing Humility) that grow in the soft mud of the
shore.
    Having so commanded, Cato disappears. Dante arises in silence and
stands waiting, eager to begin. His look is all the communication that is
necessary. Virgil leads him to the shore and performs all that Cato has
commanded, Dante's first purification is marked by a miracle: when Virgil

9. Lethe. In classical mythology, the river of forgetfulness, from which souls drank before being born. In
Dante's symbolism it flows down from Purgatory, where it has washed away the memory of sin from the
souls who are undergoing purification. That memory it delivers to Hell, which draws all sin to itself.
1. Dante ends each of the three divisions of the Commedia with this word. Every conclusion of the upward
soul is toward the stars, God's shining symbols of hope and virtue. It is just before dawn of Easter Sunday
that the Poets emerge.

breaks off a reed, the stalk immediately regenerates a new reed, restoring
itself exactly as it had been.

For better waters now the little bark
  of my indwelling powers raises her sails,
  and leaves behind that sea so cruel and dark.
Now shall I sing that second kingdom[2] given
  the soul of man wherein to purge its guilt   5
  and so grow worthy to ascend to Heaven.
Yours am I, sacred Muses! To you I pray.
Here let dead poetry[3] rise once more to life,
  and here let sweet Calliope[4] rise and play
some far accompaniment in that high strain   10
  whose power the wretched Pierides once felt
  so terribly they dared not hope again.
Sweet azure of the sapphire of the east
  was gathering on the serene horizon
  its pure and perfect radiance—a feast   15
to my glad eyes, reborn to their delight,
  as soon as I had passed from the dead air[5]
  which had oppressed my soul and dimmed my sight.
The planet whose sweet influence strengthens love[6]
  was making all the east laugh with her rays,   20
  veiling the Fishes, which she swam above.
I turned then to my right and set my mind
  on the other pole, and there I saw four stars[7]
  unseen by mortals since the first mankind.[8]
The heavens seemed to revel in their light.   25
O widowed Northern Hemisphere, bereft
  forever of the glory of that sight!
As I broke off my gazing, my eyes veered
  a little to the left, to the other pole[9]

2. Purgatory.   3. The verses that sang of Hell. Dante may equally have meant that poetry as an art has
long been surpassed by history as the medium for great subjects. Here poetry will return to its classic
state.   4. Muse of Epic Poetry. Dante exhorts Calliope to fill him with the strains of the music she
played in the defeat of the Pierides, the nine daughters of Pierius, King of Thessaly. They presumed to
challenge the Muses to a contest of song. After their defeat they were changed into magpies for their
presumption. Ovid (*Metamorphoses*, V. 294–340 and 662–678) retells the myth in detail.   5. Of Hell.
6. Venus. Here, as morning star, Venus is described as rising in Pisces, the Fishes, the zodiacal sign
immediately preceding Aries. In Canto I of the *Inferno* Dante has made it clear that the Sun is in Aries.
Hence it is about to rise.   7. Modern readers are always tempted to identify these four stars as the
Southern Cross, but it is almost certain that Dante did not know about that formation. In VIII. 89, Dante
mentions three other stars as emphatically as he does these four and no one has been tempted to identify
them on the star-chart. Both constellations are best taken as allegorical. The four stars represent the Four
Cardinal Virtues: Prudence, Justice, Fortitude, and Temperance. Dante will encounter them again in the
form of nymphs when he achieves the Earthly Paradise.   8. *The first mankind*: Adam and Eve. In
Dante's geography, the Garden of Eden (the Earthly paradise) was at the top of the Mount of Purgatory,
which was the only land in the Southern Hemisphere. All of what were called "the southern continents"
were believed to lie north of the equator. When Adam and Eve were driven from the Garden, therefore,
they were driven into the Northern Hemisphere, and no living soul since had been far enough south to
see those stars. Ulysses and his men (*Inferno*, XXVII) had come within sight of the Mount of Purgatory,
but Ulysses mentioned nothing of having seen these stars.   9. The North Pole. The Wain (Ursa Major,
i.e., the Big Dipper) is below the horizon.

from which, by then, the Wain had disappeared.   30
I saw, nearby, an ancient man, alone.[1]
His bearing filled me with such reverence,
no father could ask more from his best son.
His beard was long and touched with strands of white,
as was his hair, of which two tresses fell   35
over his breast. Rays of the holy light
that fell from the four stars made his face glow
with such a radiance that he looked to me
as if he faced the sun. And standing so,
he moved his venerable plumes and said: 40
"Who are you two who climb by the dark stream
to escape the eternal prison of the dead?
Who led you? or what served you as a light
in your dark flight from the eternal valley,
which lies forever blind in darkest night?   45
Are the laws of the pit so broken? Or is new counsel
published in Heaven that the damned may wander
onto my rocks from the abyss of Hell?"
At that my Master laid his hands upon me,
instructing me by word and touch and gesture   50
to show my reverence in brow and knee,
then answered him: "I do not come this way
of my own will or powers. A Heavenly Lady
sent me to this man's aid in his dark day.
But since your will is to know more, my will   55
cannot deny you; I will tell you truly
why we have come and how. This man has still
to see his final hour, though in the burning
of his own madness he had drawn so near it
his time was perilously short for turning.   60
As I have told you, I was sent to show
the way his soul must take for its salvation;
and there is none but this by which I go.
I have shown him the guilty people. Now I mean
to lead him through the spirits in your keeping,   65
to show him those whose suffering makes them clean.
By what means I have led him to this strand
to see and hear you, takes too long to tell:

---

1. Marcus Porcious Cato, the younger, 95–46 B.C. In the name of freedom, Cato opposed the policies of
both Caesar and Pompey, but because he saw Caesar as the greater evil joined forces with Pompey. After
the defeat of his cause at the Battle of Thapsus, Cato killed himself with his own sword rather than lose
his freedom. Virgil lauds him in the *Aeneid* as a symbol of perfect devotion to liberty, and all writers of
Roman antiquity have given Cato a similar high place. Dante spends the highest praises on him both in
De Monarchia and *Il Convivio*. Why Cato should be so signally chosen by God as the special guardian of
Purgatory has been much disputed. Cato may be taken as representative of supreme virtue short of godliness. He has accomplished everything but the purifying total surrender of his will to God. As such he
serves as an apt transitional symbol, being the highest rung on the ladder of natural virtue, but the lowest
on the ladder of those godly virtues to which Purgatory is the ascent.

from Heaven is the power and the command.
Now may his coming please you, for he goes   70
   to win his freedom; and how dear that is
   the man who gives his life for it best knows.
You know it, who in that cause found death sweet
   in Utica where you put off that flesh
   which shall rise radiant at the Judgment Seat.   75
We do not break the Laws: this man lives yet,
   and I am of that Round not ruled by Minos,[2]
   with your own Marcia,[3] whose chaste eyes seem set
in endless prayers to you. O blessed breast
   to hold her yet your own! for love of her   80
   grant us permission to pursue our quest
across your seven kingdoms.[4] When I go
   back to her side I shall bear thanks of you,
   if you will let me speak your name below."
"Marcia was so pleasing in my eyes   85
   there on the other side," he answered then
   "that all she asked, I did. Now that she lies
beyond the evil river, no word or prayer
   of hers may move me. Such was the Decree
   pronounced upon us when I rose from there.   90
But if, as you have said, a Heavenly Dame
   orders your way, there is no need to flatter:
   you need but ask it of me in her name.
Go then, and lead this man, but first see to it
   you bind a smooth green reed about his waist   95
   and clean his face of all trace of the pit
For it would not be right that one with eyes
   still filmed by mist should go before the angel
   who guards the gate: he is from Paradise.
All round the wave-wracked shore-line, there below,   100
   reeds grow in the soft mud. Along that edge
   no foliate nor woody plant could grow,
for what lives in that buffeting must bend.
   Do not come back this way: the rising sun
   will light an easier way you may ascend."   105
With that he disappeared; and silently
   I rose and moved back till I faced my Guide,
   my eyes upon him, waiting. He said to me:
"Follow my steps and let us turn again:

2. The Judge of the Damned. The round in Hell not ruled by Minos is Limbo, the final resting place of
the Virtuous Pagans. Minos (see *Inferno*, V) is stationed at the entrance to the second circle of Hell. The
souls in Limbo (the first circle) have never had to pass before him to be judged.   3. The daughter of the
consul Philippus and Cato's second wife, bearing his three children. In 56 B.C., in an unusual transaction
approved by her father, Cato released her in order that she might marry his friend Hortensius. (Hence line
87: "that all she asked I did.") After the death of Hortensius, Cato took her back.   4. The main divisions
of Purgatory according to the seven cardinal or deadly sins: Pride, Envy, Anger, Sloth, Avarice, Gluttony,
and Lust.

along this side there is a gentle slope   110
  that leads to the low boundaries of the plain."
The dawn, in triumph, made the day-breeze flee
  before its coming, so that from afar
  I recognized the trembling of the sea.
We strode across that lonely plain like men   115
  who seek the road they strayed from and who count
  the time lost till they find it once again.
When we had reached a place along the way
  where the cool morning breeze shielded the dew
  against the first heat of the gathering day,   120
with gentle graces my Sweet Master bent
  and laid both outspread palms upon the grass.
Then I, being well aware of his intent,
lifted my tear-stained cheeks to him, and there
  he made me clean, revealing my true color   125
  under the residues of Hell's black air.
We moved on then to the deserted strand
  which never yet has seen upon its waters
  a man who found his way back to dry land.
There, as it pleased another, he girded me.   130
  Wonder of wonders! when he plucked a reed
  another took its place there instantly,
arising from the humble stalk he tore
so that it grew exactly as before.

CANTO II

Ante-Purgatory:
The Shore of the Island   The Angel Boatman, Casella, Cato of Utica

It is dawn. Dante, washed, and girded by the reed, is standing by the
shore when he sees a light approaching at enormous speed across the sea.
The light grows and becomes visible as the Angel Boatman who ferries the
souls of the elect from their gathering place at the Mouth of the Tiber to
the shore of Purgatory.

The newly arrived souls debark and, taking the Poets as familiars of the
place, ask directions. Virgil explains that he and Dante are new arrivals
but that they have come by the dark road through Hell. The newly arrived
souls see by his breathing that Dante is alive and crowd about him. One
of the new souls is Casella, a musician who seems to have been a dear
friend of Dante's. Dante tries three times to clasp him to his bosom, but
each time his arms pass through empty air. Casella explains the function
of the Angel Boatman and then, at Dante's request, strikes up a song, one
of Dante's own canzone that Casella had set to music. Instantly, Cato
descends upon the group, berating them, and they break like startled pigeons
up the slope toward the mountain.

The sun already burned at the horizon,
  while the high point of its meridian circle
  covered Jerusalem, and in opposition
equal Night revolved above the Ganges
  bearing the Scales that fall out of her hand   5
  as she grows longer with the season's changes:
thus, where I was, Aurora in her passage
  was losing the pale blushes from her cheeks
  which turned to orange with increasing age.⁵
We were still standing by the sea's new day   10
  like travelers pondering the road ahead
  who send their souls on while their bones delay;
when low above the ocean's western rim,
  as Mars, at times, observed through the thick vapors
  that form before the dawn, burns red and slim;   15
just so—so may I hope to see it again!—
  a light appeared, moving above the sea
  faster than any flight. A moment then
I turned my eyes to question my sweet Guide,
  and when I looked back to that unknown body   20
  I found its mass and brightness magnified.
Then from each side of it came into view
  an unknown something-white; and from beneath it,
  bit by bit, another whiteness grew.
We watched till the white objects at each side   25
  took shape as wings, and Virgil spoke no word.
  But when he saw what wings they were, he cried:
"Down on your knees! It is God's angel comes!
  Down! Fold your hands! From now on you shall see
  many such ministers in the high kingdoms.   30
See how he scorns man's tools: he needs no oars
  nor any other sail than his own wings
  to carry him between such distant shores.
See how his pinions tower upon the air,
  pointing to Heaven: they are eternal plumes   35
  and do not moult like feathers or human hair."
Then as that bird of heaven closed the distance
  between us, he grew brighter and yet brighter
  until I could no longer bear the radiance,
and bowed my head. He steered straight for the shore,   40
  his ship so light and swift it drew no water;
  it did not seem to sail so much as soar.
Astern stood the great pilot of the Lord,
  so fair his blessedness seemed written on him;
  and more than a hundred souls were seated forward,   45

5. The bit of erudite affectation in which Dante indulges in lines 1–9 means simply, "It was dawn."

singing as if they raised a single voice
   in exitu Israel de Aegypto.[6]
   Verse after verse they made the air rejoice.
The angel made the sign of the cross, and they
   cast themselves, at his signal, to the shore.[7]   50
   Then, swiftly as he had come, he went away.
The throng he left seemed not to understand
   what place it was, but stood and stared about
   like men who see the first of a new land.
The Sun, who with an arrow in each ray   55
   had chased the Goat[8] out of the height of Heaven,
   on every hand was shooting forth the day,
when those new souls looked up to where my Guide
   and I stood, saying to us, "If you know it,
   show us the road that climbs the mountainside."   60
Virgil replied: "You think perhaps we two
   have had some long experience of this place,
   but we are also pilgrims, come before you
only by very little, though by a way
   so steep, so broken, and so tortuous   65
   the climb ahead of us will seem like play."
The throng of souls, observing by my breath
   I was still in the body I was born to,
   stared in amazement and grew pale as death.
As a crowd, eager for news, will all but smother   70
   a messenger who bears the olive branch,[9]
   and not care how they trample one another—
so these, each one of them a soul elect,
   pushed close to stare at me, well-nigh forgetting
   the way to go to make their beauty perfect.   75
One came forward to embrace me, and his face
   shone with such joyous love that, seeing it,
   I moved to greet him with a like embrace.
O solid seeming shadows! Three times there
   I clasped my hands behind him, and three times   80
   I drew them to my breast through empty air.
Amazed, I must have lost all color then,
   for he smiled tenderly and drew away,
   and I lunged forward as if to try again.
In a voice as gentle as a melody   85
   he bade me pause; and by his voice I knew him,
   and begged him stay a while and speak to me.
He answered: "As I loved you in the clay
   of my mortal body, so do I love you freed:

---

6. "When Israel out of Egypt came." (Psalm 113).   7. Note that this is exactly what Dante says of the sinners leaving Charon's ferry in *Inferno* III. 113.   8. Capricorn.   9. In Dante's time couriers bore the olive branch to indicate not only peace but good news in general.

therefore I pause. But what brings you this way?"   90
"Casella[1] mine, I go the way I do
   in the hope I may return here," I replied.
"But why has so much time been taken from you?"
And he: "I am not wronged if he whose usage
   accepts the soul at his own time and pleasure   95
   has many times refused to give me passage:
his will moves in the image and perfection
   of a Just Will; indeed, for three months now
   he has taken all who asked,[2] without exception.
And so it was that in my turn I stood   100
   upon that shore where Tiber's stream grows salt,
   and there was gathered to my present good.
It is back to the Tiber's mouth he has just flown,
   for there forever is the gathering place
   of all who do not sink to Acheron."   105
"If no new law has stripped you of your skill
   or of the memory of those songs of love
   that once could calm all passion from my will,"
I said to him, "Oh sound a verse once more
   to soothe my soul which, with its weight of flesh   110
   and the long journey, sinks distressed and sore."
"Love that speaks its reasons in my heart,"
   he sang then, and such grace flowed on the air
   that even now I hear that music start.
My Guide and I and all those souls of bliss   115
   stood tranced in song; when suddenly we heard
   the Noble Elder cry: "What's this! What's this!
Negligence! Loitering! O laggard crew
   run to the mountain and strip off the scurf
   that lets not God be manifest in you!"   120
Exactly as a flock of pigeons gleaning
   a field of stubble, pecking busily,
   forgetting all their primping and their preening,
will rise as one and scatter through the air,
   leaving their feast without another thought   125
   when they are taken by a sudden scare—
so that new band, all thought of pleasure gone,
   broke from the feast of music with a start

---

1. *Casella:* Practically all that is known about Casella has been drawn from the text itself. He seems to have died several months before Dante began his journey, hence early in 1300 or late in 1299. There is no explanation of his delay in reaching Purgatory (the time that has been taken from him). Dante later meets several classes of sinners who must spend a certain period of waiting before they can begin their purification. Clearly it is Dante's conception that the souls bound for Purgatory do not always proceed instantly to their destination, but may be required to expiate by a delay at their gathering point by the mouth of the Tiber (line 101). Casella was a musician and is known to have set some of Dante's *canzone* to music. The song he strikes up (line 112) is such a *canzone.*   2. Boniface VIII decreed a Jubilee Year from Christmas 1299 to Christmas 1300. (Cf. *Inferno* XVIII. 28–33 and note.) His decree extended special indulgences even to the dead. Hence the Angel's permissiveness.

and scattered for the mountainside like one
who leaps and does not look where he will land.   130
Nor were my Guide and I inclined to stand.

*   *   *

CANTO XIX

The Fourth Cornice   The Slothful
Dante's Dream of Sirena
The Ascent   The Angel of Zeal
The Fifth Cornice   The Hoarders and Wasters (The Avaricious)

Just before morning (when the truth is dreamed) Dante dreams of the
Siren that lures the souls of men to incontinent worldliness. Hideous in
her true form, the Siren grows irresistible in men's eyes as they look upon
her. A Heavenly Lady races in upon the dream and calls to Virgil who,
thus summoned, strips the Siren, exposing her filthy body. Such a stench
rises from her, so exposed, that Dante wakens shuddering, to find Virgil
calling him to resume the journey.

The Angel of Zeal shows them the passage, and when his wings have
fanned the Poets, Dante casts off his depression and lethargy, and rushes
up the remaining length of the passage.

Arrived at the Fifth Cornice, Virgil inquires the way of one of the souls
of the Hoarders and Wasters, who lie motionless and outstretched, bound
hand and foot, with their faces in the dust.

The soul of Pope Adrian V replies that, if they have incurred no guilt
by hoarding or wasting, they may pass on to the right. Dante kneels in
reverence to Adrian and is scolded for doing so. Adrian then dismisses
Dante in order to resume his purification. Adrian's last request is that his
niece, Alagia, be asked to pray for his soul.

At the hour when the heat of the day is overcome
   by Earth, or at times by Saturn, and can no longer
   temper the cold of the moon;[3] when on the dome
of the eastern sky the geomancers sight
   Fortuna Major[4] rising on a course   5
   on which, and soon, it will be drowned in light;
there came to me in a dream a stuttering crone,
   squint-eyed, clubfooted, both her hands deformed,
   and her complexion like a whitewashed stone.
I stared at her; and just as the new sun   10
   breathes life to night-chilled limbs, just so my look

3. An intricate passage based on the medieval belief that sunlight reflected from earth to the moon produced warmth on the moon, whereas sunlight reflected from the moon to the earth produced cold on the
earth. *At the hour:* Before dawn. The accumulated heat of the day would have been dissipated through
the long night and could no longer temper the cold of the moon. *Overcome by Earth:* The last heat of the
day is overcome by the night-chilled earth. *Or at times by Saturn:* The times would be those in which
Saturn draws close to the horizon. Saturn was believed to be a cold planet, as opposed to Mars, a hot
planet.   4. A conjunction of the last stars of Aquarius and the first of Pisces, supposed to signify great
good fortune. In this season these stars would be rising just before dawn, hence the sun is coming up
behind them and their course will soon be drowned in light.

began to free her tongue, and one by one
drew straight all her deformities, and warmed
    her dead face, till it bloomed as love would wish it
    for its delight. When she was thus transformed,   15
her tongue thus loosened, she began to sing
    in such a voice that only with great pain
    could I have turned from her soliciting.
"I am," she sang, "Sirena.[5] I am she
    whose voice is honeyed with such sweet enticements   20
    it trances sailing men far out to sea.
I turned Ulysses from his wanderer's way[6]
    with my charmed song, and few indeed who taste
    how well I satisfy would think to stray."
Her mouth had not yet shut when at my side   25
    appeared a saintly lady,[7] poised and eager
    to heap confusion on the Siren's pride.
"O Virgil, Virgil! Who," she cried, "is this?"
    Roused by her indignation, Virgil came:
    his eyes did not once leave that soul of bliss.   30
He seized the witch, and with one rip laid bare
    all of her front, her loins and her foul belly:
    I woke sick with the stench that rose from there.
I turned then, and my Virgil said to me:
    "I have called at least three times now. Rise and come   35
    and let us find your entrance." Willingly
I rose to my feet. Already the high day
    lit all the circles of the holy mountain.
    The sun was at our backs as we took our way.
I followed in his steps, my brow as drawn   40
    as is a man's so bowed with thought he bends
    like half an arch of a bridge. And moving on,
I heard the words: "Come. This is where you climb"[8]
    pronounced in such a soft and loving voice
    as is not heard here in our mortal time.   45
With swanlike wings outspread, he who had spoken
    summoned us up between the walls of rock.
    He fanned us with his shining pinions then,
affirming over us as we went by
    "Blessed are they that mourn"[9]—for they shall have   50
    their consolation given them on high.

5. The Sirens were mythological creatures, usually of great beauty, and with the power of singing so
entrancingly that they charmed the souls of men. They were usually presented as luring sailors at sea to
their destruction. Dante's Sirena is a Christian adaptation.   6. In the Homeric version Ulysses escapes
the Siren's blandishments by stuffing his ears with wax and having himself lashed to the mast of his ship.
Dante may, perhaps, be following another version of the myth, but more probably he means to portray
the Siren as a liar.   7. She may be Beatrice, or she may be Provenient Grace, but any identification is
speculative.   8. Spoken by the Angel of Zeal.   9. The Fourth Beatitude. "Blessed are they that mourn:
for they shall be comforted." (Matthew 4:5).

"What ails you?" said my Guide. "What heavy mood
    makes you stare at the ground?" (We were by then
    above the point at which the Angel stood.)
And I: "An apparition clouds my spirit,   55
    a vision from a dream so strange and dreadful
    I cannot seem to leave off thinking of it."
"Did you see that ageless witch," he said, "for whom
    —and for no other—those above us weep?
    And did you see how men escape her doom?   60
Let it teach your heels to scorn the earth, your eyes
    to turn to the high lure the Eternal King
    spins with his mighty spheres across the skies."
As falcons stare at their feet until they hear
    the wished-for call, then leap with wings outspread   65
    in eagerness for the meat that waits them there;
so did I move: filled with desire, I ran
    up the remaining length of the rock passage
    to the point at which the next great Round began.
When I stood on the fifth ledge and looked around,   70
    I saw a weeping people everywhere
    lying outstretched and face-down on the ground.
"My soul cleaves to the dust,"[1] I heard them cry
    over and over as we stood among them;
    and every word was swallowed by a sigh.   75
"O Chosen of God, spirits whose mournful rites
    both Hope and Justice make less hard to bear,
    show us the passage to the further heights."
"If you have not been sentenced to lie prone
    in the bitter dust, and seek the nearest way,   80
    keep the rim to your right as you go on."
So spoke the Poet, and so a voice replied
    from the ground in front of us. I took good note
    of what its way of speaking did not hide.[2]
I turned my eyes to Virgil then, and he   85
    gave me a happy sign of his permission
    to do what my eyes asked. Being thus free
to act according to my own intention,
    I moved ahead and stood above that soul
    whose speaking had attracted my attention,   90
saying: "O Soul in whom these tears prepare
    that without which no soul can turn to God,
    put off a while, I beg, your greater care,
to tell me who you were, why you lie prone,
    and if there is some way that I may serve you   95

1. Psalm 119.   2. The soul has said, "If you have not been sentenced to lie prone in the bitter dust."
The implication is—and it is the first time the point has emerged clearly—that souls may pass through
some of the Cornices without delay, if they are free of the taint of sin there punished.

---

in the world I left while still in flesh and bone."
"Why Heaven makes us turn our backs shall be
   made known to you," the spirit said, "but first
   scias quod ego fui successor Petri.[3]
Between Sestri and Chiaveri, flowing on   100
   through a fair land, there is a pleasant river[4]
   from which the title of my line is drawn.
A single month, a month and some few days
   I came to know on my own weary body
   how heavily the Papal Mantle weighs   105
upon the wearer who would take good care
   to keep it from the mire; compared to that
   all other burdens are as light as air.
My conversion, alas, came late; for only when
   I had been chosen Pastor of Holy Rome   110
   did I see the falseness in the lives of men.
I saw no heart's rest there, nor ease from strife,
   nor any height the flesh-bound soul might climb,
   and so I came to love this other life.
My soul was lost to God until that moment,   115
   and wholly given over to avarice;
   such was my sin, such is my punishment.
The nature of avarice is here made plain
   in the nature of its penalty; there is not
   a harsher forfeit paid on the whole mountain.   120
We would not raise our eyes to the shining spheres
   but kept them turned to mundane things: so Justice
   bends them to earth here in this place of tears.
As Avarice, there, quenched all our souls' delight
   in the good without which all our works are lost, 125
   so, here, the hand of Justice clamps us tight.
Taken and bound here hand and foot, we lie
   outstretched and motionless; and here we stay
   at the just pleasure of the Father on High."
I had knelt to him. Now I spoke once more.   130
   That spirit sensed at once my voice was nearer
   and guessed my reverence. "Why do you lower
your knees into the dust?" he said to me.
   And I: "My conscience troubled me for standing
   in the presence of your rank and dignity."   135
"Straighten your legs, my brother! Rise from error!"
   he said. "I am, like you and all the others,
   a fellow servant of one Emperor.

---

3. "Know that I was Peter's successor." The speaker is Pope Adrian V. He died in 1276 after having been Pope for thirty-eight days.   4. The Lavagna. It flows between Sestri and Chiaveri, small coastal towns near Genoa. Adrian, born Ottobuono de' Fieschi, was of the line of the Counts of Lavagna.

It is written in holy scripture *Neque nubent;*[5]
    if ever you understood that sacred text,   140
    my reason for speaking will be evident.
Now go your way. I wish to be alone.
    Your presence here distracts me from the tears
    that make me ready. And to your last question:
I have a niece, Alagia,[6] still on earth.   145
    If she can but avoid the bad example
    those of our line have set, her native worth
will lead her yet the way the blessed go.
And she alone remains to me below."

*   *   *

CANTO XXVII

The Seventh Cornice   The Angel of Chastity
The Wall of Fire
The Earthly Paradise   The Angel Guardian

A little before sunset of the third day on the Mountain the Poets come
to the further limit of the Seventh Cornice and are greeted by the Angel of
Chastity, who tells them they must pass through the wall of fire. Dante
recoils in terror, but Virgil persuades him to enter in Beatrice's name.

They are guided through the fire by a chant they hear coming from the
other side. Emerging, they find it is sung by the Angel Guardian of the
Earthly Paradise, who stands in a light so brilliant that Dante cannot see
him.

The Angel hurries them toward the ascent, but night overtakes them,
and the Poets lie down to sleep, each on the step on which he finds himself. (For Statius it will be the last sleep, since there is no night in Heaven.)
There, just before dawn, Dante has a prophetic dream of Leah and Rachel,
which foreshadows the appearance, above, of Matilda and Beatrice.

Day arrives; the Poets rise and race up the rest of the ascent until they
come in sight of the Earthly Paradise. Here Virgil speaks his last words,
for the Poets have now come to the limit of Reason, and Dante is now free
to follow his every impulse, since all will to sin in him has been purged
away.

As the day stands when the Sun begins to glow
    over the land where his Maker's blood was shed,
    and the scales of Libra ride above the Ebro,

---

5. ". . . They neither marry [nor are given in marriage but are as the angels of God in heaven]" (Matthew
22:30). These were Christ's words when asked to which husband a remarried widow would belong in
Heaven. Adrian obviously extends the meaning to include the cancellation of all earthly contracts, fealties,
and honors.   6. Daughter of Niccolò di Tedisio di Ugone de' Fieschi and wife of Moroello Malaspina,
Marquis of Giovagallo. Dante had been well received by Malaspina and knew and admired his wife for
her good works.

while Ganges' waters steam in the noonday glare—[7]
    so it stood, the light being nearly faded,   5
    when we met God's glad Angel[8] standing there
on the rocky ledge beyond the reach of the fire,
    and caroling *"Beati mundo corde"*[9]
    in a voice to which no mortal could aspire.
Then: "Blessèd ones, till by flame purified   10
    no soul may pass this point. Enter the fire
    and heed the singing from the other side."
These were his words to us when we had come
    near as we could, and hearing them, I froze
    as motionless as one laid in his tomb.   15
I lean forward over my clasped hands and stare
    into the fire, thinking of human bodies
    I once saw burned,[1] and once more see them there.
My kindly escorts heard me catch my breath
    and turned, and Virgil said: "Within that flame   20
    there may be torment, but there is no death.
Think well, my son, what dark ways we have trod . . .
    I guided you unharmed on Geryon:[2]
    shall I do less now we are nearer God?
Believe this past all doubt: were you to stay   25
    within that womb of flame a thousand years,
    it would not burn a single hair away.
And if you still doubt my sincerity,
    but reach the hem of your robe into the flame:
    your hands and eyes will be your guarantee.   30
My son, my son, turn here with whole assurance.
    Put by your fears and enter to your peace."
And I stood fixed, at war with my own conscience.
And seeing me still stubborn, rooted fast,
    he said, a little troubled: "Think, my son,   35
    you shall see Beatrice when this wall is past."
As Pyramus, but one breath from the dead,
    opened his eyes when he heard Thisbe's name,[3]
    and looked at her, when the mulberry turned red—
just so my hard paralysis melted from me,   40

7. It is shortly before sunset of the third day on the Mountain. Dante's details here are the reverse of those given at the opening of II, which see. *The land where his Maker's blood was shed:* Jerusalem. *The Ebro:* For Spain.   8. The Angel of Chastity. He is standing on the narrow rocky path outside the wall of fire.   9. "Blessed are the pure in heart [for they shall see God]." (Matthew 5:8.)   1. Dante must mean as a witness at an execution. Burnings at the stake generally took place in public squares. They were a rather common spectacle. Dante's sentence of exile, it is relevant to note, decreed that he was to be burned if taken on Florentine territory.   2. *Geryon:* The Monster of Fraud. See *Inferno*, XVII.   3. Famous tragic lovers of Babylon. Ovid (*Metamorphoses*, IV. 55–166) tells their story. At a tryst by a mulberry (which in those days bore white fruit) Thisbe was frightened by a lion and ran off, dropping her veil. The lion, his jaws bloody from a recent kill, tore at the veil, staining it with blood. Pyramus, arriving later, saw the stained veil, concluded that Thisbe was dead, and stabbed himself. Thisbe, returning, found him and cried to him to open his eyes for his Thisbe. At that name Pyramus opened his eyes, looked at her, and died. Thisbe, invoking the tree to darken in their memory, thereupon stabbed herself. (Cf. Shakespeare's *A Midsummer Night's Dream*.) The mulberry roots drank their blood and the fruit turned red ever after.

and I turned to my Leader at that name
  which wells forever in my memory;
at which he wagged his head, as at a child
won over by an apple. Then he said:
  "Well, then, what are we waiting for?" and smiled.   45
He turned then and went first into the fire,
  requesting Statius, who for some time now
  had walked between us, to bring up the rear.
Once in the flame, I gladly would have cast
  my body into boiling glass to cool it   50
  against the measureless fury of the blast.
My gentle father, ever kind and wise,
  strengthened me in my dread with talk of Beatrice,
  saying: "I seem already to see her eyes."
From the other side, to guide us, rose a paean,   55
  and moving toward it, mindless of all else,
  we emerged at last where the ascent began.
There I beheld a light[4] that burned so brightly
  I had to look away; and from it rang:
  "Venite benedicti patris mei."[5]   60
"Night falls," it added, "the sun sinks to rest;
  do not delay but hurry toward the height
  while the last brightness lingers in the west."
Straight up through the great rock-wall lay the way
  on such a line that, as I followed it,   65
  my body blocked the sun's last level ray.
We had only climbed the first few stairs as yet
  when I and my two sages saw my shadow[6]
  fade from me; and we knew the sun had set.
Before the vast sweep of the limned horizon   70
  could fade into one hue and night win all
  the immeasurable air to its dominion,
each made the step on which he stood his bed,
  for the nature of the Mount not only stopped us
  but killed our wish to climb, once day had fled.   75
As goats on a rocky hill will dance and leap,
  nimble and gay, till they find grass, and then,
  while they are grazing, grow as tame as sheep
at ease in the green shade when the sun is high
  and the shepherd stands by, leaning on his staff,   80
  and at his ease covers them with his eye—
and as the herdsman beds down on the ground,
  keeping his quiet night watch by his flock
  lest it be scattered by a wolf or hound;
just so we lay there, each on his stone block,   85

4. This is the Angel Guardian of the Earthly Paradise.   5. "Come ye blessèd of my Father." (Matthew
25:34.)   6. Virgil and Statius, of course, cast none.

I as the goat, they as my guardians,
   shut in on either side by walls of rock.
I could see little ahead—rock blocked the way—
   but through that little I saw the stars grow larger,
   brighter than mankind sees them. And as I lay,   90
staring and lost in thought, a sleep came on me—
   the sleep that oftentimes presents the fact
   before the event, a sleep of prophecy.
At the hour, I think, when Venus, first returning
   out of the east, shone down upon the mountain—[7]   95
   she who with fires of love comes ever-burning—
I dreamed I saw a maiden innocent
   and beautiful, who walked a sunny field
   gathering flowers, and caroling as she went:
"Say I am Leah if any ask my name,   100
   and my white hands weave garlands wreath on wreath
   to please me when I stand before the frame
of my bright glass. For this my fingers play
   among these blooms. But my sweet sister Rachel[8]
   sits at her mirror motionless all day.   105
To stare into her own eyes endlessly
   is all her joy, as mine is in my weaving.
   She looks, I do. Thus live we joyously."
Now eastward the new day rayed Heaven's dome
   (the sweeter to the returning wanderer   110
   who wakes from each night's lodging nearer home),
and the shadows fled on every side as I
   stirred from my sleep and leaped upon my feet,
   seeing my Lords already standing by.
"This is the day your hungry soul shall be   115
   fed on the golden apples men have sought
   on many different boughs so ardently."
These were the very words which, at the start,
   my Virgil spoke to me, and there have never
   been gifts as dear as these were to my heart.   120
Such waves of yearning to achieve the height
   swept through my soul, that at each step I took
   I felt my feathers growing for the flight.
When we had climbed the stairway to the rise
   of the topmost step, there with a father's love   125
   Virgil turned and fixed me with his eyes.
"My son," he said, "you now have seen the torment

7. It is the hour before dawn, in which the truth is dreamed.   8. Leah and Rachel were, respectively,
the first- and second-born daughters of Laban and the first and second wives of Jacob. Many authors before
Dante had interpreted them as representing the Active and the Contemplative Life of the Soul. Leah's
white hands (le belle mani) symbolize the Active Life, as Rachel's eyes (ll. 104–108) symbolize the Contemplative Life.

of the temporal and the eternal fires;
here, now, is the limit of my discernment.
I have led you here by grace of mind and art;   130
now let your own good pleasure be your guide;
you are past the steep ways, past the narrow part.
See there the sun that shines upon your brow,
the sweet new grass, the flowers, the fruited vines
which spring up without need of seed or plow.   135
Until those eyes come gladdened which in pain
moved me to come to you and lead your way,
sit there at ease or wander through the plain.
Expect no more of me in word or deed:
here your will is upright, free, and whole,   140
and you would be in error not to heed
whatever your own impulse prompts you to:
lord of yourself I crown and mitre you."9

*   *   *

CANTO XXX

The Earthly Paradise   Beatrice
Virgil Vanishes

The procession [of the Heavenly Pageant] halts and the Prophets turn to
the chariot and sing "Come, my bride, from Lebanon." They are summoning Beatrice, who appears on the left side of the chariot, half -hidden
from view by showers of blossoms poured from above by a hundred angels.
Dante, stirred by the sight, turns to Virgil to express his overflowing emotions, and discovers that Virgil has vanished.

Because he bursts into tears at losing Virgil, Dante is reprimanded by
Beatrice. The Angel Choir overhead immediately breaks into a Psalm of
Compassion, but Beatrice, still severe, answers by detailing Dante's offenses
in not making proper use of his great gifts. It would violate the ordering of
the Divine Decree, she argues, to let Dante drink the waters of Lethe,
thereby washing all memory of sin from his soul, before he had shed the
tears of a real repentance.

When the Septentrion of the First Heaven, 1
which does not rise nor set, and which has never
been veiled from sight by any mist but sin,
and which made every soul in that high court
know its true course (just as the lower Seven   5
direct the helmsman to his earthly port),

9. Crown as king of your physical self and mitre (as a bishop) as lord of your soul.   1. The Septentrion
is the seven stars of the Big Dipper. Here Dante means the seven candelabra [of the Heavenly Pageant].
They are the Septentrion of the First Heaven (the empyrean) as distinct from the seven stars of the dipper
which occur lower down in the Sphere of the Fixed Stars.

had stopped; the holy prophets,[2] who till then
   had walked between the Griffon and those lights,
   turned to the car like souls who cry "Amen."
And one among them[3] who seemed sent from Heaven   10
   clarioned: "*Veni, sponsa, de Libano,*"[4]
   three times, with all the others joining in.
As, at the last trump every saint shall rise
   out of the grave, ready with voice new-fleshed
   to carol *Alleluliah* to the skies;   15
just so, above the chariot, at the voice
   of such an elder, rose a hundred Powers
   and Principals[5] of the Eternal Joys,
all saying together: "*Benedictus qui venis*";[6]
   then, scattering flowers about on every side: 20
   "*Manibus o date lilia plenis.*"[7]
Time and again at daybreak I have seen
   the eastern sky glow with a wash of rose
   while all the rest hung limpid and serene,
and the Sun's face rise tempered from its rest   25
   so veiled by vapors that the naked eye
   could look at it for minutes undistressed.
Exactly so, within a cloud of flowers
   that rose like fountains from the angels' hands
   and fell about the chariot in showers,   30
a lady[8] came in view: an olive crown
   wreathed her immaculate veil, her cloak was green,
   the colors of live flame played on her gown.
My soul—such years had passed since last it saw[9]
   that lady and stood trembling in her presence,   35
   stupefied by the power of holy awe—
now, by some power that shone from her above
   the reach and witness of my mortal eyes,
   felt the full mastery of enduring love.
The instant I was smitten by the force,   40
   which had already once transfixed my soul
   before my boyhood years had run their course,
I turned left with the same assured belief
   that makes a child run to its mother's arms
   when it is frightened or has come to grief,   45
to say to Virgil: "There is not within me

2. The twenty-four elders who represent the books of the Old Testament. *Griffon*: A mythical figure with the fore parts of an eagle and the hind parts of a lion, here meant to represent the dual role of Christ as God and Man.   3. *The Song of Songs.*   4. "Come [with me] from Lebanon, my spouse." Song of Songs, 4:8. This cry, reechoed by choirs of angels, summons Beatrice.   5. Angels.   6. "Blessed is he who cometh." (Matthew 21:9.)   7. "Oh, give lilies with full hands." These are the words of Anchises in honor of Marcellus (*Aeneid* VI. 883). Thus they are not only apt to the occasion but their choice is a sweetly conceived last literary compliment to Virgil before he vanishes.   8. Beatrice. She is dressed in the colors of Faith (white), Hope (green), and Caritas (red).   9. Beatrice died in 1290. Thus Dante has passed ten years without sight of her.

one drop of blood unstirred. I recognize
the tokens of the ancient flame." But he,
he had taken his light from us. He had gone.
Virgil had gone. Virgil, the gentle Father   50
to whom I gave my soul for its salvation!
Not all that sight of Eden lost to view
by our First Mother could hold back the tears
that stained my cheeks so lately washed with dew.[1]
"Dante,[2] do not weep yet, though Virgil goes.   55
Do not weep yet, for soon another wound
shall make you weep far hotter tears than those!"
As an admiral takes his place at stern or bow
to observe the handling of his other ships
and spur all hands to do their best—so now,   60
on the chariot's left side, I saw appear
when I turned at the sound of my own name
(which, necessarily, is recorded here),
that lady who had been half-veiled from view
by the flowers of the angel-revels. Now her eyes   65
fixed me across the stream, piercing me through.
And though the veil she still wore, held in place
by the wreathed flowers of wise Minerva's leaves,[3]
let me see only glimpses of her face,
her stern and regal bearing made me dread   70
her next words, for she spoke as one who saves
the heaviest charge till all the rest are read.
"Look at me well. I am she. I am Beatrice.
How dared you make your way to this high mountain?
Did you not know that here man lives in bliss?"   75
I lowered my head and looked down at the stream.
But when I saw myself reflected there,
I fixed my eyes upon the grass for shame.
I shrank as a wayward child in his distress
shrinks from his mother's sternness, for the taste   80
of love grown wrathful is a bitterness.
She paused. At once the angel chorus sang
the blessed psalm: "*In te, Domine, speravi.*"
As far as "*pedes meos*" their voices rang.[4]
As on the spine of Italy the snow   85
lies frozen hard among the living rafters[5]
in winter when the northeast tempests blow;
then, melting if so much as a breath stir

---

1. By Virgil. I. 124.   2. This is the only point in the *Commedia* at which Dante mentions his own name.   3. The olive crown.   4. In mercy the angel chorus sings Psalm 31:1–8, beginning "In thee, O Lord, do I put my trust" and continuing as far as "thou hast set my feet in a large room."   5. The trees. *The spine of Italy:* The Apennines.

from the land of shadowless noon,[6] flows through itself
    like hot wax trickling down a lighted taper—   90
just so I froze, too cold for sighs or tears
    until I heard that choir whose notes are tuned
    to the eternal music of the spheres.
But when I heard the voice of their compassion
    plead for me more than if they had cried out: 95
    "Lady, why do you treat him in this fashion?";
the ice, which hard about my heart had pressed,
    turned into breath and water, and flowed out
    through eyes and throat in anguish from my breast.
Still standing at the chariot's left side,   100
    she turned to those compassionate essences
    whose song had sought to move her, and replied:
"You keep your vigil in the Eternal Day
    where neither night nor sleep obscures from you
    a single step the world takes on its way;   105
but I must speak with greater care that he
    who weeps on that far bank may understand
    and feel a grief to match his guilt. Not only
by the workings of the spheres that bring each seed
    to its fit end according to the stars   110
    that ride above it, but by gifts decreed
in the largesse of overflowing Grace,
    whose rain has such high vapors for its source
    our eyes cannot mount to their dwelling place;
this man, potentially was so endowed   115
    from early youth that marvelous increase
    should have come forth from every good he sowed.
But richest soil the soonest will grow wild
    with bad seed and neglect. For a while I stayed him
    with glimpses of my face. Turning my mild   120
and youthful eyes into his very soul,
    I let him see their shining, and I led him
    by the straight way, his face to the right goal.
The instant I had come upon the sill
    of my second age,[7] and crossed and changed my life,   125
    he left me and let others shape his will.
When I rose from the flesh into the spirit,
    to greater beauty and to greater virtue,
    he found less pleasure in me and less merit.
He turned his steps aside from the True Way,   130

---

6. Africa. In equatorial regions the noonday sun is at the zenith over each point twice a year. Its rays then
fall straight down and objects cast no shadows.   7. Beatrice's womanhood. When she had reached the
full bloom of youth Dante turned from her and wrote to his *donna gentile*. [The *donna gentile* (noble or
gentle lady) is not identified by name.] Allegorically, he turned from divine "sciences" to an overreliance
upon philosophy (the human "sciences"). For this sin he must suffer.

pursuing the false images of good
that promise what they never wholly pay.
Not all the inspiration I won by prayer
and brought to him in dreams and meditations
could call him back, so little did he care.   135
He fell so far from every hope of bliss
that every means of saving him had failed
except to let him see the damned. For this
I visited the portals of the dead
and poured my tears and prayers before that spirit   140
by whom his steps have, up to now, been led.
The seal Almighty God's decree has placed
on the rounds of His creation would be broken
were he to come past Lethe and to taste
the water that wipes out the guilty years   145
without some scot of penitential tears!"[8]

CANTO XXXI

The Earthly Paradise   Lethe; Beatrice, Matilda

Beatrice continues her reprimand, forcing Dante to confess his faults
until he swoons with grief and pain at the thought of his sin. He wakes to
find himself in Lethe, held in the arms of Matilda, who leads him to the
other side of the stream and there immerses him that he may drink the
waters that wipe out all memory of sin.

Matilda then leads him to the Four Cardinal Virtues, who dance about
him and lead him before the Griffon where he may look into the eyes of
Beatrice. In them Dante sees, in a First Beatific Vision, the radiant reflection of the Griffon, who appears now in his human and now in his godly
nature.

The Three Theological Virtues now approach and beg that Dante may
behold the smile of Beatrice. Beatrice removes her veil, and in a Second
Beatific Vision, Dante beholds the splendor of the unveiled shining of
Divine Love.

"You, there, who stand upon the other side—"[9]
(turning to me now, who had thought the edge
of her discourse was sharp, the point) she cried
without pause in her flow of eloquence,
"Speak up! Speak up! Is it true? To such a charge   5
your own confession must give evidence."
I stood as if my spirit had turned numb:
the organ of my speech moved, but my voice
died in my throat before a word could come.

8. In passing Lethe and drinking its waters, the soul loses all memory of guilt. This, therefore, is Dante's
last opportunity to do penance. *Scot:* payment.   9. Of Lethe. But also the other side of the immortal
life, i.e., still living.

Briefly she paused, then cried impatiently: 10
  "What are you thinking? Speak up, for the waters[1]
  have yet to purge sin from your memory."
Confusion joined to terror forced a broken
  "yes" from my throat, so weak that only one
  who read my lips would know that I had spoken.   15
As an arbalest will snap when string and bow
  are drawn too tight by the bowman, and the bolt
  will strike the target a diminished blow—[2]
so did I shatter, strengthless and unstrung,
  under her charge, pouring out floods of tears,   20
  while my voice died in me on the way to my tongue.
And she: "Filled as you were with the desire
  I taught you for That Good beyond which nothing
  exists on earth to which man may aspire,
what yawning moats or what stretched chain-lengths[3] lay   25
  across your path to force you to abandon
  all hope of pressing further on your way?
What increase or allurement seemed to show
  in the brows of others that you walked before them
  as a lover walks below his lady's window?"   30
My breath dragged from me in a bitter sigh;
  I barely found a voice to answer with;
  my lips had trouble forming a reply.
In tears I said: "The things of the world's day,
  false pleasures and enticements, turned my steps   35
  as soon as you had ceased to light my way."
And she: "Had you been silent, or denied
  what you confess, your guilt would still be known
  to Him from Whom no guilt may hope to hide.
But here, before our court, when souls upbraid   40
  themselves for their own guilt in true remorse,
  the grindstone is turned back against the blade.[4]
In any case that you may know your crime
  truly and with true shame and so be stronger
  against the Siren's song another time,   45
control your tears and listen with your soul
  to learn how my departure from the flesh
  ought to have spurred you to the higher goal.
Nothing in Art or Nature could call forth
  such joy from you, as sight of that fair body   50

1. Of Lethe.   2. The figure is a bit confusing. Dante seems to say that the bolt (corresponding to an arrow) of a crossbow strikes the target with less force when the bow snaps. He does not stop to consider that the bolt may miss the target entirely. Nevertheless, the intent of his figure is clear enough.   3. These were, of course, defensive military measures. The moats guarded castles. The chains were strung to block roads, bridges, and gates.   4. Turning the grindstone away from the blade sharpens it. Turning it back against the blade dulls it. Thus Beatrice is saying that when a soul openly confesses in true repentance what could not in any case be hidden from God, the sword of Justice is blunted, i.e., no longer cuts as deeply.

which clothed me once and now sifts back to earth.
And if my dying turned that highest pleasure
  to very dust, what joy could still remain
  in mortal things for you to seek and treasure?
At the first blow you took from such vain things   55
  your every thought should have been raised to follow
  my flight above decay. Nor should your wings
have been weighed down by any joy below—
  love of a maid,[5] or any other fleeting
  and useless thing—to wait a second blow.   60
The fledgling waits a second shaft, a third;
  but nets[6] are spread and the arrow sped in vain
  in sight or hearing of the full-grown bird."
As a scolded child, tongue tied for shame, will stand
  and recognize his fault, and weep for it,   65
  bowing his head to a just reprimand,
so did I stand. And she said: "If to hear me
  grieves you, now raise your beard and let your eyes
  show you a greater cause for misery."[7]
The blast that blows from Libya's hot sand,   70
  or the Alpine gale, overcomes less resistance
  uprooting oaks than I, at her command,
overcame then in lifting up my face;
  for when she had referred to it as my "beard"
  I sensed too well the venom of her phrase.   75
When I had raised my eyes with so much pain,
  I saw those Primal Beings, now at rest,
  who had strewn blossoms round her thick as rain;
and with my tear-blurred and uncertain vision
  I saw Her turned to face that beast which is   80
  one person in two natures without division.[8]
Even veiled and across the river from me
  her face outshone its first-self[9] by as much
  as she outshone all mortals formerly.
And the thorns of my repentance pricked me so   85
  that all the use and substance of the world
  I most had loved, now most appeared my foe.
Such guilty recognition gnawed my heart
  I swooned for pain; and what I then became
  she best knows who most gave me cause to smart.   90
When I returned to consciousness at last
  I found the lady who had walked alone[1]

5. Dante mentions another maiden in some of his songs but in an indefinite way. No specific reference can be attached to these words.   6. Sometimes used for trapping birds.   7. The sight of her accompanied by the guilty knowledge that he had turned away from so much beauty and perfection.   8. The Griffon. He is the masque of Christ and represents His two aspects as man and God.   9. Her mortal self.   1. Matilda, who appears in Canto XXVIII, having been foreshadowed by Leah in Dante's dream (XXVII). She may be taken to symbolize the Active Life of the Soul.

bent over me. "Hold fast!" she said, "Hold fast!"
She had drawn me into the stream up to my throat,
and pulling me behind her, she sped on   95
over the water, light as any boat.
Nearing the sacred bank, I heard her say
in tones so sweet I cannot call them back,
much less describe them here: "*Asperges me.*"[2]
Then the sweet lady took my head between   100
her open arms, and embracing me, she dipped me
and made me drink the waters that make clean.
Then raising me in my new purity
she led me to the dance of the Four Maidens;[3]
each raised an arm and so joined hands above me.   105
"Here we are nymphs; stars are we in the skies.
Ere Beatrice went to earth we were ordained
her handmaids. We will lead you to her eyes;
but that your own may see what joyous light
shines in them, yonder Three,[4] who see more deeply,   110
will sharpen and instruct your mortal sight."
Thus they sang, then led me to the Griffon.
Behind him, Beatrice waited. And when I stood
at the Griffon's breast, they said in unison:
"Look deep, look well, however your eyes may smart.   115
We have led you now before those emeralds[5]
from which Love shot his arrows through your heart."
A thousand burning passions, every one
hotter than any flame, held my eyes fixed
to the lucent eyes she held fixed on the Griffon.   120
Like sunlight in a glass the twofold creature
shone from the deep reflection of her eyes,
now in the one, now in the other nature.
Judge, reader, if I found it passing strange
to see the thing unaltered in itself   125
yet in its image working change on change.
And while my soul in wonder and delight
was savoring that food which in itself
both satisfies and quickens appetite,[6]
the other Three, whose bearing made it clear   130
they were of higher rank, came toward me dancing

---

2. *Asperges me hyssopo, et mundabor; lavabis me, et super nivem dealbabor.* ("Purge me with hyssop, and I shall be clean; wash me, and I shall be whiter than snow.") Psalm 51:7. These are the words the priest utters when he sprinkles holy water over the confessed sinner to absolve him.   3. The Four Cardinal Virtues: Justice, Prudence, Fortitude, and Temperance. In their present manifestation they are nymphs. In another manifestation they are the four stars Dante saw above him when he arrived at the base of the mountain. (Canto I. 23, note.)   4. The Theological Virtues: Faith, Hope, and Charity (i.e., *Caritas*). 5. The eyes of Beatrice. Dante may have intended to describe them as green (hazel) but more likely his choice of words here is meant only to signify "jewel bright." Green is, of course, the color of Hope, and an allegorical significance may be implied in that.   6. "They that eat me shall yet be hungry, and they that drink me shall yet be thirsty." (Ecclesiasticus 24:21.)

to the measure of their own angelic air.
"Turn, Beatrice, oh turn the eyes of grace,"
was their refrain, "upon your faithful one
who comes so far to look upon your face.   135
Grant us this favor of your grace: reveal
your mouth to him, and let his eyes behold
the Second Beauty,[7] which your veils conceal."
O splendor of the eternal living light!
who that has drunk deep of Parnassus' waters,[8]   140
or grown pale in the shadow of its height,
would not, still, feel his burdened genius fail
attempting to describe in any tongue
how you appeared when you put by your veil
in that free air open to heaven and earth   145
whose harmony is your shining shadowed forth!

Paradiso

CANTO I

The Earthly Paradise   The Invocation
Ascent to Heaven   The Sphere of Fire, The Music of the Spheres

Dante states his supreme theme as Paradise itself and invokes the aid not
only of the Muses but of Apollo.

Dante and Beatrice are in the Earthly Paradise, the Sun is at the Vernal
Equinox, it is noon at Purgatory and midnight at Jerusalem when Dante
sees Beatrice turn her eyes to stare straight into the sun and reflexively
imitates her gesture. At once it is as if a second sun had been created, its
light dazzling his senses, and Dante feels the ineffable change of his mortal
soul into Godliness.

These phenomena are more than his senses can grasp, and Beatrice
must explain to him what he himself has not realized: that he and Beatrice
are soaring toward the height of Heaven at an incalculable speed.

Thus Dante climaxes the master metaphor in which purification is equated
to weightlessness. Having purged all dross from his soul he mounts effortlessly, without even being aware of it at first, to his natural goal in the
Godhead. So they pass through the Sphere of Fire, and so Dante first hears
the Music of the Spheres.

The glory of Him who moves all things rays forth
    through all the universe, and is reflected

---

7. The smile of Beatrice (Divine Love). Dante was led to the First Beauty by the Four Cardinal Virtues.
Now the Three Theological Virtues, as higher beings, lead him to the second, and higher, beauty, which
is the joy of Divine Love in receiving the purified soul.   8. The fountain of Castalia. To drink from it
is to receive poetic gifts. To grow pale in the shadow of Parnassus signifies to labor at mastering the art of
poetry.

from each thing in proportion to its worth.
I have been in that Heaven of His most light,
   and what I saw, those who descend from there   5
   lack both the knowledge and the power to write.
For as our intellect draws near its goal
   it opens to such depths of understanding
   as memory cannot plumb within the soul.
Nevertheless, whatever portion time   10
   still leaves me of the treasure of that kingdom
   shall now become the subject of my rhyme.
O good Apollo,[9] for this last task, I pray
   you make me such a vessel of your powers
   as you deem worthy to be crowned with bay.[1]   15
One peak of cleft Parnassus heretofore
   has served my need, now must I summon both[2]
   on entering the arena one time more.
Enter my breast, I pray you, and there breathe
   as high a strain as conquered Marsyas   20
   that time you drew his body from its sheath.[3]
O power divine, but lend to my high strain
   so much as will make clear even the shadow
   of that High Kingdom stamped upon my brain,
and you shall see me come to your dear grove[4]   25
   to crown myself with those green leaves which you
   and my high theme shall make me worthy of.
So seldom are they gathered, Holy Sire,
   to crown an emperor's or a poet's triumph
   (oh fault and shame of mortal man's desire!)   30
that the glad Delphic god must surely find
   increase of joy in the Peneian frond[5]
   when any man thirsts for it in his mind.
Great flames are kindled where the small sparks fly.
   So after me, perhaps, a better voice   35
   shall raise such prayers that Cyrrha[6] will reply.
The lamp of the world rises to mortal view
   from various stations, but that point which joins
   four circles with three crosses, it soars through

---

9. The God of Poetry, and the father of the Muses. Note, too, that Apollo is identified with the Sun and that Dante has consistently used the Sun as a symbol for God.   1. The laurel wreath awarded to poets and conquerors.   2. Parnassus has two peaks: Nisa, which was sacred to the Muses; and Cyrrha, which was sacred to Apollo. Heretofore Nisa has been enough for Dante's need, but for this last canticle he must summon aid from both peaks (i.e., from all the Muses and from Apollo as well).   3. The satyr Marsyas challenged Apollo to a singing contest and was defeated. Ovid (*Metamorphoses* VI. 382–400) recounts in gory detail how Apollo thereupon punished him by pulling him out of his skin leaving all the uncovered organs still functioning.   4. In which grows the sacred laurel, or bay.   5. The laurel or bay, so called for Daphne, daughter of the river god Peneus. Cupid, to avenge a taunt, fired an arrow of love into Apollo and an arrow of aversion into Daphne. Fleeing from the inflamed Apollo, Daphne prayed to her father and was changed into a laurel tree. *The glad Delphic god*: Apollo.   6. Apollo's sacred peak, here taken for Apollo himself. If Apollo does not heed his prayer, Dante will at least show the way, and perhaps a better poet will come after him and have his prayer answered by Apollo, whereby Paradise will at last be well portrayed.

to a happier course in happier conjunction   40
    wherein it warms and seals the wax of the world
    closer to its own nature and high function.[7]
That glad conjunction had made it evening here
    and morning there; the south was all alight,
    while darkness rode the northern hemisphere;   45
when I saw Beatrice had turned left to raise
    her eyes up to the sun; no eagle ever
    stared at its shining with so fixed a gaze.[8]
And as a ray descending from the sky
    gives rise to another, which climbs back again,   50
    as a pilgrim yearns for home; so through my eye
her action, like a ray into my mind,
    gave rise to mine: I stared into the sun
    so hard that here it would have left me blind;
but much is granted to our senses there,   55
    in that garden made to be man's proper place,
    that is not granted us when we are here.
I had to look away soon, and yet not
    so soon but what I saw him spark and blaze
    like new-tapped iron when it pours white-hot.   60
And suddenly, as it appeared to me,
    day was added to day, as if He who can
    had added a new sun to Heaven's glory.
Beatrice stared at the eternal spheres
    entranced, unmoving; and I looked away   65
    from the sun's height to fix my eyes on hers.
And as I looked, I felt begin within me
    what Glaucus felt eating the herb that made him
    a god among the others in the sea.[9]
How speak trans-human change to human sense?   70
    Let the example speak until God's grace
    grants the pure spirit the experience.
Whether I rose in only the last created
    part of my being,[1] O Love that rulest Heaven
    Thou knowest, by whose lamp I was translated.   75

7. Short of pages of diagrams, there is no way of explaining Dante's astronomical figure in detail. A quick gloss must do: *The lamp:* the sun. *Various stations:* various points on the celestial horizon from which the sun rises at various times of the year. *Four circles with three crosses:* The four circles here intended are: (1) the celestial horizon, (2) the celestial equator, (3) the ecliptic, and (4) equinoxial colure, the great circle drawn through both poles and the two equinoxial points. When the sun is in this position the time is sunrise of the vernal equinox and all four circles meet, each of the other three forming a cross with the celestial horizon. Astrologers took this to be a particularly auspicious conjunction. Its *happier course* (l. 40) brings the brighter and longer days of summer. Its *happier conjunction* (l. 40) with the stars of Aries bring it back to the sign of the first creation (see *Inferno* I. 38–39, note). And certainly the fact that the diagram forms three crosses would weigh it with the good omens of both the cross and trinity. All would once more be in God's shaping hand. So the *wax of the world* (l. 41) is warmed and sealed, in a first sense by the warmth of approaching summer, and in a clearly implicit spiritual sense by the favor of God's will upon His creation.   8. In the Middle Ages men believed that the eagle was able to stare directly into the sun.   9. The fisherman Glaucus, noting how his catch revived and leaped into the sea after being laid upon a certain herb, ate some of it and was transformed into a god (Ovid, *Metamorphoses* XIII. 898–968).   1. The soul, which is created after the body. (See *Purgatorio* XXV. 37–75.) *O Love that rulest Heaven:* God. *Whose lamp:* Beatrice as the reflector of God's love.

When the Great Wheel that spins eternally
  in longing for Thee,[2] captured my attention
  by that harmony attuned and heard by Thee,
I saw ablaze with sun from side to side
  a reach of Heaven:[3] not all the rains and rivers   80
  of all of time could make a sea so wide.
That radiance and that new-heard melody
  fired me with such a yearning for their Cause
  as I had never felt before. And she
who saw my every thought as well as I,   85
  saw my perplexity: before I asked
  my question she had started her reply.
Thus she began: "You dull your own perceptions
  with false imaginings and do not grasp
  what would be clear but for your preconceptions.   90
You think you are still on earth: the lightning's spear
  never fled downward from its natural place
  as rapidly as you are rising there."
I grasped her brief and smiling words and shed
  my first perplexity, but found myself   95
  entangled in another, and I said:
"My mind, already recovered from the surprise
  of the great marvel you have just explained,
  is now amazed anew: how can I rise
in my gross body through such aery substance?"   100
  She sighed in pity and turned as might a mother
  to a delirious child. "The elements
of all things," she began, "whatever their mode,
  observe an inner order. It is this form
  that makes the universe resemble God.   105
In this the higher creatures see the hand
  of the Eternal Worth, which is the goal
  to which these norms conduce, being so planned.
All Being within this order, by the laws
  of its own nature is impelled to find   110
  its proper station round its Primal Cause.
Thus every nature moves across the tide
  of the great sea of being to its own port,
  each with its given instinct as its guide.
This instinct draws the fire about the moon.   115
  It is the mover in the mortal heart.
  It draws the earth together and makes it one.
Not only the brute creatures, but all those

2. Dante says, literally: "The wheel that Thou, in being desired [i.e., loved] by it, makest eternal." The Great Wheel is the Primum Mobile, its motion deriving from the love of God. *That harmony:* The Music of the Spheres.   3. Dante believed that the earth's atmosphere extended as high as the Sphere of the Moon. Beyond the Moon is another atmosphere of fire. This sphere of fire was believed to cause lightning. (See also line 115, "the fire about the moon.")

possessed of intellect and love, this instinct
drives to their mark as a bow shoots forth its arrows.   120
The Providence that makes all things hunger here
satisfies forever with its light
the heaven within which whirls the fastest sphere.[4]
And to it now, as to a place foretold,
are we two soaring, driven by that bow   125
whose every arrow finds a mark of gold.
It is true that oftentimes the form of a thing
does not respond to the intent of the art,
the matter being deaf to summoning—
just so, the creature sometimes travels wide   130
of this true course, for even when so driven
it still retains the power to turn aside
(exactly as we may see the heavens' fire
plunge from a cloud) and its first impulse may
be twisted earthward by a false desire.   135
You should not, as I see it, marvel more
at your ascent than at a river's fall
from a high mountain to the valley floor.
If you, free as you are of every dross,
had settled and had come to rest below,   140
that would indeed have been as marvelous[5]
as a still flame there in the mortal plain."
So saying, she turned her eyes to Heaven again.

*   *   *

CANTO III

The First Sphere: The Moon   The Inconstant Piccarda, Constance

As Dante is about to speak to Beatrice he sees the dim traceries of human
faces and taking them to be reflections, he turns to see what souls are being
so reflected. Beatrice, as ever, explains that these pallid images are the
souls themselves. They are the Inconstant, the souls of those who regis-
tered holy vows in Heaven, but who broke or scanted them.

Among them Piccarda Donati identifies herself, and then identifies the
Empress Constance. Both, according to Dante's beliefs, had taken vows as
nuns but were forced to break them in order to contract a political marriage. Not all the souls about them need have failed in the same vows,
however. Any failure to fulfill a holy vow (of holy orders, to go on a pilgrimage, to offer special services to God) might place the soul in this lowest
class of the blessed.

Piccarda explains that every soul in Heaven rejoices in the entire will of
God and cannot wish for a higher place, for to do so would be to come

---

4. The Primum Mobile.   5. Because then it would be going against the order of the universe. What is
purified must ascend to God as inevitably as earthly waters must flow downhill.

into conflict with the will of God. In the perfect harmony of bliss, everywhere in Heaven is Paradise.

That sun that breathed love's fire into my youth[6]
   had thus resolved for me, feature by feature—
   proving, disproving—the sweet face of truth.
I, raising my eyes to her eyes to announce
   myself resolved of error, and well assured,   5
   was about to speak; but before I could pronounce
my first word, there appeared to me a vision.
   It seized and held me so that I forgot
   to offer her my thanks and my confession.
As in clear glass when it is polished bright,   10
   or in a still and limpid pool whose waters
   are not so deep that the bottom is lost from sight,
a footnote of our lineaments[7] will show,
   so pallid that our pupils could as soon
   make out a pearl upon a milk-white brow—[8]   15
so I saw many faces eager to speak,
   and fell to the error opposite the one
   that kindled love for a pool in the smitten Greek.[9]
And thinking the pale traces I saw there
   were reflected images, I turned around   20
   to face the source—but my eyes met empty air.
I turned around again like one beguiled,
   and took my line of sight from my sweet guide
   whose sacred eyes grew radiant as she smiled.
"Are you surprised that I smile at this childish act   25
   of reasoning?" she said, "since even now
   you dare not trust your sense of the true fact,
but turn, as usual, back to vacancy?
   These are true substances you see before you.
   They are assigned here for inconstancy   30
to holy vows. Greet them. Heed what they say,
   and so believe; for the True Light[1] that fills them
   permits no soul to wander from its ray."
So urged, I spoke to those pale spirits, turning
   to one who seemed most eager, and began   35
   like one whose mind goes almost blank with yearning.
"O well created soul, who in the sun
   of the eternal life drinks in the sweetness
   which, until tasted, is beyond conception;
great would be my joy would you confide   40

6. Beatrice.   7. The figure seems oddly out of context but its intent is clear: Dante is suggesting that
the image is related to the face as a footnote is related to the text.   8. The brow would have to be death-
pale as marble, but perhaps Dante intends these spirits to be chalky-white.   9. Narcissus. His error was
in taking a reflection (his own) to be a real face. Dante's opposite error is in taking real faces to be
reflections.   1. God.

to my eager mind your earthly name and fate."
That soul with smiling eyes, at once replied:
"The love that fills us will no more permit
    hindrance to a just wish than does that Love[2]
    that wills all of Its court to be like It.   45
I was a virgin sister[3] there below,
    and if you search your memory with care,
    despite my greater beauty, you will know
I am Piccarda,[4] and I am placed here
    among these other souls of blessedness   50
    to find my blessedness in the slowest sphere.
Our wishes, which can have no wish to be
    but in the pleasure of the Holy Ghost,
    rejoice in being formed to His decree.
And this low-seeming post which we are given   55
    is ours because we broke, or, in some part,
    slighted the vows we offered up to Heaven."
And I then: "Something inexpressibly
    divine shines in your face, subliming you
    beyond your image in my memory: 60
therefore I found you difficult to place;
    but now, with the assistance of your words,
    I find the memory easier to retrace.[5]
But tell me, please: do you who are happy here
    have any wish to rise to higher station,   65
    to see more, or to make yourselves more dear?"[6]
She smiled, as did the spirits at her side;
    then, turning to me with such joy she seemed
    to burn with the first fire of love, replied:
"Brother, the power of love, which is our bliss,   70
    calms all our will. What we desire, we have.
    There is in us no other thirst than this.
Were we to wish for any higher sphere,
    then our desires would not be in accord
    with the high will of Him who wills us here;   75
and if love is our whole being, and if you weigh
    love's nature well, then you will see that discord
    can have no place among these circles. Nay,
the essence of this blessèd state of being

---

2. God, as the essence of *Caritas*.   3. A nun.   4. Piccarda Donati was the daughter of Simone Donati (*Inferno* XXV. 32) and sister of Forese (*Purgatorio* XXIII. 48) and of the war leader, Corso (*Purgatorio*
XXIV. 82ff.). Forese was Dante's friend. Dante was married to Gemma Donati, who also had a brother
named Forese, but Piccarda's family was grander than Dante's in-laws. Piccarda was already a nun and
living in her convent when her brother Corso, needing to establish a political alliance, forced her to marry
Rossellino della Tossa of Florence. Various commentators report that Piccarda sickened and soon died as
a consequence of having been so forced against her will and vows.   5. A desperate simplification of
Dante's untranslatable "*m'è più latino*" (literally: "it is more Latin to me"). Learned men of Dante's time
used Latin naturally and gracefully. Thus to make a thing "more Latin" was to facilitate it. An opposite
form of a similar idiom is our still current "It's Greek to me."   6. More dear to God.

is to hold all our will within His will,   80
whereby our wills are one and all-agreeing.
And so the posts we stand from sill to sill
    throughout this realm, please all the realm as much
    as they please Him who wills us to His will.
In His will is our peace. It is that sea   85
    to which all moves, all that Itself creates
    and Nature bears through all Eternity."
Then was it clear to me that everywhere
    in Heaven is Paradise, though the Perfect Grace
    does not rain down alike on all souls there.   90
But as at times when we have had our fill
    of one food and still hunger for another,
    we put this by with gratitude, while still
asking for that—just so I begged to know,
    by word and sign, through what warp she had not   95
    entirely passed the shuttle[7] of her vow.
"The perfection of her life and her great worth
    enshrine a lady[8] hereabove," she said,
    "in whose rule some go cloaked and veiled on earth,
that till their death they may live day and night   100
    with that sweet Bridegroom[9] who accepts of love
    all vows it makes that add to His delight.[1]
As a girl, I fled the world to walk the way
    she walked, and closed myself into her habit,
    pledged to her sisterhood till my last day.   105
Then men came, men more used to hate than love.
    They tore me away by force from the sweet cloister.
    What my life then became is known above.
This other splendor who lets herself appear[2]
    here to my right to please you, shining full   110
    of every blessedness that lights this sphere,
understands in herself all that I say.
    She, too, was a nun. From her head as from mine
    the shadow of the veil was ripped away.
Against her will and all propriety   115
    she was forced back to the world. Yet even there
    her heart was ever veiled in sanctity.
She is the radiance of the Empress Constance,[3]

---

7. The vertical strings of a loom are the warp. Across them the shuttle draws the woof. Not to draw the
shuttle entirely through is to leave the weaving unfinished, hence her vow unfulfilled.   8. Saint Clara
of Assisi (1194–1253). Born Chiara Sciffi, she became a disciple of St. Francis and, under his influence,
founded in 1212 an order of nuns. *Hereabove:* Higher in Heaven. Probably in the Empyrean, but Dante
does not mention her again.   9. Christ. He is so called several times in the New Testament.   1. Only
those vows that conform to His love are acceptable. A vow to perform a trivial or an evil action would
have no standing.   2. Dante says, "who shows herself to you." Clearly, the souls in Paradise can make
themselves visible or invisible at will (i.e., Heaven reveals itself of its own love). At the end of the conversation the whole company withdraws from sight.   3. (1154–1198.) As the last of the line of Norman
kings who took southern Italy in the eleventh century, she was Empress of the Two Sicilies (Sicily and
Naples). She married the Emperor Henry VI in 1185 and became the mother of Frederick II. Dante

who by the second blast of Swabia
conceived and bore its third and final puissance."[4]   120
She finished, and at once began to sing
Ave Maria, and singing, sank from view
like a weight into deep water, plummeting
out of my sight, which followed while it could,
and then, having lost her, turned about once more   125
to the target of its greater wish and good,
and wholly gave itself to the delight
of the sweet vision of Beatrice. But she
flashed so radiantly upon my sight
that I, at first, was blinded, and thus was slow   130
to ask of her what I most wished to know.

CANTO XXXI

*The Empyrean   The Mystic Rose, The Angel Host, Beatrice Leaves
Dante, St. Bernard*

The Second Soldiery of the Church Triumphant is the Angel Host, and
Dante now receives a vision of them as a swarm of bees in eternal transit
between God and the Rose.

Dante turns from that rapturous vision to speak to Beatrice and finds in
her place a reverend elder. It is St. Bernard, who will serve as Dante's
guide to the ultimate vision of God. Bernard shows Dante his last vision
of Beatrice, who has resumed her throne among the blessed. Across the
vastness of Paradise, Dante sends his soul's prayer of thanks to her. Beatrice
smiles down at Dante a last time, then turns her eyes forever to the eternal
Fountain of God.

Bernard, the most faithful of the worshippers of the Virgin, promises
Dante the final vision of God through the Virgin's intercession. Accordingly, he instructs Dante to raise his eyes to her throne. Dante obeys and
burns with bliss at the vision of her splendor.

Then, in the form of a white rose, the host
of the sacred soldiery[5] appeared to me,
all those whom Christ in his own blood espoused.

follows a legend, for which there was no basis in fact, that she had become a nun and was forced to leave
her convent to marry Henry.   4. The three blasts of Swabia are the three great princes whose origins
were in Swabia (in Germany). Frederick Barbarossa was the first. His son, Henry VI, was the second. To
Henry, Constance bore the third, Frederick II.   5. In XXX. 43, Beatrice promised that Dante would
see both hosts of Paradise. The first host is of the sacred soldiery, those who were once mortal and who
were redeemed by Christ. They are seated upon the thrones of the Mystic Rose in which are gathered
eternally the essences of all those heavenly souls that manifested themselves to Dante in the various spheres
below, moved by caritas to reveal themselves to Dante at the various levels of his developing understanding. How these souls could be eternally within the Rose while yet manifesting themselves to Dante in the
various spheres is, of course, one of the mysteries to be grasped only by revelation. The essential point is
that Dante becomes better able to see; the vision of Heaven unfolds to him ever more clearly and ever
more profoundly. The second soldiery is of the angels who never left heaven. They soar above the Rose
like Heavenly bees, in constant motion between the Rose and the radiance of God. Unlike earthly bees,
however, it is from God, the mystical hive of grace, that they bring the sweetness to the flower, bearing
back to God, of course, the bliss of the souls of Heaven. (See lines 16–18). The first host is more emphatically centered on the aspect of God as the Son; the second, on the aspect of God as the Father.

But the other host (who soar, singing and seeing
His glory, who to will them to his love   5
made them so many in such blissful being,
like a swarm of bees who in one motion dive
into the flowers, and in the next return
the sweetness of their labors to the hive)
flew ceaselessly to the many-petaled rose   10
and ceaselessly returned into that light
in which their ceaseless love has its repose.
Like living flame their faces seemed to glow.[6]
Their wings were gold. And all their bodies shone[7]
more dazzling white than any earthly snow.   15
On entering the great flower they spread about them,
from tier to tier, the ardor and the peace
they had acquired in flying close to Him.
Nor did so great a multitude in flight
between the white rose and what lies above it   20
block in the least the glory of that light;
for throughout all the universe God's ray
enters all things according to their merit,
and nothing has the power to block its way.
This realm of ancient bliss shone, soul on soul,   25
with new and ancient beings, and every eye
and every love was fixed upon one goal.
O Threefold Light which, blazoned in one star,
can so content their vision with your shining,
look down upon us in the storm we are!   30
If the barbarians (coming from that zone
above which Helice[8] travels every day
wheeling in heaven with her belovèd son)
looking at Rome, were stupefied to see
her works in those days when the Lateran[9]   35
outshone all else built by humanity;
What did I feel on reaching such a goal
from human to blest, from time to eternity,
from Florence to a people just and whole—[1]
by what amazement was I overcome?   40
Between my stupor and my new-found joy
my bliss was to hear nothing and be dumb.

6. See the vision of God and Heaven in Ezekiel 1:14ff.   7. See the similar vision in Daniel 10:4ff.
8. The nymph Helice (I am afraid the reader will have to Anglicize her name as HELees) attracted Zeus
and was turned into a bear by jealous Hera. Zeus translated his nymph to heaven as Ursa Major, the
constellation of the Great Bear which contains the Big Dipper. Arcas, her son by Zeus, was translated to
Ursa Minor, within which he forms the Little Dipper. The two dippers, being near the pole, are always
above the horizon in the northland, the zone from which the barbarians came.   9. Today a section of
old Rome. Here Dante uses it to signify Rome in general.   1. This is Dante's last mention of Florence.
Note that Florence has not improved but that on the universal scale it has become too insignificant for the
sort of denunciation he once heaped upon it.

And as a pilgrim at the shrine of his vow
  stares, feels himself reborn, and thinks already
  how he may later describe it[2]—just so now   45
I stood and let my eyes go wandering out
  into that radiance from rank to rank,
  now up, now down, now sweeping round about.
I saw faces that compelled love's charity
  lit by Another's lamp and their own smiles,   50
  and gestures graced by every dignity.
Without having fixed on any part, my eyes
  already had taken in and understood
  the form and general plan of Paradise:
and—my desire rekindled—I wheeled about   55
  to question my sweet lady on certain matters
  concerning which my mind was still in doubt.
One thing I expected; another greeted me:
  I thought to find Beatrice there; I found instead
  an elder[3] in the robes of those in glory.   60
His eyes and cheeks were bathed in the holy glow
  of loving bliss; his gestures, pious grace.
  He seemed a tender father standing so.
"She—where is she?" I cried in sudden dread.
  "To lead you to the goal of all your wish   65
  Beatrice called me from my place," he said;
"And if you raise your eyes you still may find her
  in the third circle down[4] from the highest rank
  upon the throne her merit has assigned her."
Without reply I looked up to that height   70
  and saw her draw an aureole round herself
  as she reflected the Eternal Light.
No mortal eye, though plunged to the last bounds
  of the deepest sea, has ever been so far
  from the topmost heaven to which the thunder sounds 75
as I was then from Beatrice; but there
  the distance did not matter, for her image
  reached me unblurred by any atmosphere.
"O lady in whom my hope shall ever soar

---

2. It was a custom of the pious, as thanks for an answered prayer, to win forgiveness of sins, or as a testimony of faith, to vow a journey to a stated shrine or temple. Such pilgrimages were often dangerous. Travel was rare in the Middle Ages, and the pilgrim returned from far shrines was much sought after for the hopefully miraculous, and in any case rare, news he brought back. How could Dante, having traveled to the Infinite Summit, fail to think ahead to the way he would speak his vision to mankind?   3. St. Bernard (1090–1153), the famous Abbot of Clairvaux, a contemplative mystic and author. Under him the Cistercian Order (a branch of the Benedictines with a stricter rule than the original order) flourished and spread. All Cistercian monasteries are especially dedicated to the Virgin, and St. Bernard is particularly identified with her worship.   4. In the Mystic Rose, Mary sits in the topmost tier, Eve directly below her, Rachel (the Contemplative Life) below Eve. Beatrice sits to the right of Rachel. In Dante, of course, every mention of three must suggest trinity, but the reader is left to decide for himself the significance of the Mary-Eve-Rachel trinity.

and who for my salvation suffered even   80
  to set your feet upon Hell's broken floor;[5]
through your power and your excellence alone
  have I recognized the goodness and the grace
  inherent in the things I have been shown.
You have led me from my bondage and set me free   85
  by all those roads, by all those loving means
  that lay within your power and charity.
Grant me your magnificence that my soul,
  which you have healed, may please you when it slips
  the bonds of flesh and rises to its goal."   90
Such was my prayer, and she—far up a mountain,
  as it appeared to me—looked down and smiled.
  Then she turned back to the Eternal Fountain.
And the holy Elder said: "I have been sent
  by prayer and sacred love to help you reach   95
  the perfect consummation of your ascent.
Look round this garden, therefore, that you may
  by gazing at its radiance, be prepared
  to lift your eyes up to the Trinal Ray.
The Queen of Heaven, for whom in whole devotion   100
  I burn with love, will grant us every grace
  because I am Bernard, her faithful one."
As a stranger afar—a Croat,[6] if you will—
  comes to see our Veronica,[7] and awed
  by its ancient fame, can never look his fill,   105
but says to himself as long as it is displayed:
  "My Lord, Jesus Christ, true God, and is this then
  the likeness of thy living flesh portrayed?"—
just so did I gaze on the living love
  of him who in this world, through contemplation,   110
  tasted the peace which ever dwells above.[8]
"Dear son of Grace," he said, "you cannot know
  this state of bliss while you yet keep your eyes
  fixed only on those things that lie below;
rather, let your eyes mount to the last round   115
  where you shall see the Queen to whom this realm
  is subject and devoted, throned and crowned."
I looked up: by as much as the horizon

---

5. As she did when she descended to Limbo (as, of course, a manifestation) to summon Virgil.   6. Probably used here in a generic sense to signify the native of any far-off Christian land, but Croatia, aside from lying at one of the outer limits of Christianity, was also known for the ardor of its religious belief.
7. From *vera icon*, the true image. Certainly the most famous relic in St. Peter's, the Veronica was the handkerchief of the faithful follower ever after known as St. Veronica. She gave it to Jesus to wipe the blood from his face on the road to Calvary, and what was believed to be the true likeness of Jesus was believed to have appeared on what was believed to be the cloth in what was believed to be His own blood.   8. According to legend, Bernard was rewarded for his holiness by being permitted a vision of Heaven's blessedness while he was yet on earth.

to eastward in the glory of full dawn
outshines the point at which the sun went down;[9]   120
by so much did one region on the height
to which I raised my eyes out of the valley
outshine the rays of every other light.
And as the sky is brightest in that region
where we on earth expect to see the shaft   125
of the chariot so badly steered by Phaeton,
while to one side and the other it grows dim—
just so that peaceful oriflamme lit the center
and faded equally along either rim.[1]
And in the center, great wings spread apart,   130
more than a thousand festive angels shone,
each one distinct in radiance and in art.[2]
I saw there, smiling at this song and sport,
her whose beauty entered like a bliss
into the eyes of all that sainted court.   135
And even could my speech match my conception,
yet I would not dare make the least attempt
to draw her delectation and perfection.
Bernard, seeing my eyes so fixed and burning
with passion on his passion, turned his own   140
up to that height with so much love and yearning
that the example of his ardor sent
new fire through me, making my gaze more ardent.

CANTO XXXII

The Empyrean   St. Bernard, The Virgin Mary, The Thrones of the
Blessed

His eyes fixed blissfully on the vision of the Virgin Mary, Bernard recites
the orders of the Mystic Rose, identifying the thrones of the most blessed.
Mary's Throne is on the topmost tier of the Heavenly Stadium. Directly
across from it rises the Throne of John the Baptist. From her throne to the
central arena (the Yellow of the Rose) descends a Line of Christian Saints.
These two radii form a diameter that divides the stadium. On one side are
throned Those Who Believe in Christ to Come; on the other, Those who
Believed in Christ Descended. The lower half of the Rose contains, on

9. The comparison is not, as careless readers sometimes take it to be, between a dawn and a sunset (whose
brightnesses would be approximately equal) but between the eastern and western horizons at dawn. Bright
as Heaven is, Mary outshines it as the east outshines the west at daybreak.   1. The shaft of the chariot
of the Sun would project ahead of the horses. It would, therefore, be the first point of light of the new
dawn, that moment when light glows on the eastern rim while the horizon to north and south is still dark.
Thus Mary not only outshines all heaven as the east at daybreak outshines the west, but even at the
uppermost tier of the blessed, those radiances at either side of her are dim by comparison.   2. Motion.
No two angel beings are exactly equal in their brightness, nor in the speed of their flight. These festive
angels are, of course, another manifestation of the Angel Hierarchy.

one side, the Pre-Christian Children Saved by Love, and on the other, the
Christian Children saved by Baptism.

Through all these explanations, Bernard has kept his eyes fixed in adoration upon the Virgin. Having finished his preliminary instruction of Dante,
Bernard now calls on him to join in a prayer to the Virgin.

Still rapt in contemplation,[3] the sainted seer
    assumed the vacant office of instruction,
    beginning with these words I still can hear:
"The wound that Mary healed with balm so sweet
    was first dealt and then deepened by that being   5
    who sits in such great beauty at her feet.[4]
Below her, in the circle sanctified
    by the third rank of loves, Rachel is throned
    with Beatrice, as you see, there at her side.
Sarah[5] and Rebecca and Judith and she[6]   10
    who was the great-grandmother of the singer
    who for his sins cried, 'Lord, have mercy on me!'—
as I go down the great ranks tier by tier,
    naming them for you in descending order,
    petal by petal, you shall see them clear.   15
And down from the seventh, continuing from those
    in the first six tiers, a line of Hebrew women
    forms a part in the tresses of the rose.[7]
Arranged to form a wall thus, they divide
    all ranks according to the view of Christ   20
    that marked the faith of those on either side.
On this side, where the flower is in full bloom[8]
    to its last petal, are arranged all those
    whose faith was founded upon Christ to Come;
on that, where the half circles show the unblended   25
    gaps of empty seats, are seated those
    whose living faith was fixed on Christ Descended.
And as, on this side, the resplendent throne
    of Heaven's Lady, with the thrones below it,
    establishes the line of that division;   30

3. Of the Virgin. His eyes have not left her. Nor do they turn again to Dante. The vacant office of
instruction: Formerly held by Beatrice. I still can hear: A rhyme-forced addition, not in Dante's text.
4. Mary, Mother of God, sits in the uppermost tier. At her feet in the second tier sits Eve, Mother of
Man. The wound: Original sin. Balm so sweet: Jesus. Dealt: The first fault, Eve's disobedience. Deepened:
Her seduction of Adam, thus spreading sin to all mankind. In such great beauty: Eve, having been created
directly by God, was perfect in her beauty.   5. Wife of Abraham. Hebrews, 11:11–14, cites her as the
mother (by miraculous fertility in her old age) of the Jews who foresaw Christ's coming and believed in
him. Rebecca: Wife of Isaac. Judith: She killed Holofernes and freed the Jews.   6. Ruth: great-grand-
mother of David ("that singer.") Who for his sins: His lust for Bathsheba, wife of Uriah. In order to marry
Bathsheba, David sent Uriah to his death in the first line of battle. David's lament is in Psalm 50.
7. As if the rose were a head of hair and that vertical row of Hebrew women formed a part in it. In the
next line the part becomes a wall.   8. That half of the rose-stadium that holds the pre-Christian believers
would naturally be completely filled. On the other side there are thrones waiting for those who have yet
to win salvation through Christ Descended. Dante, in fact, is laboring to earn one of them for himself.
The Day of Judgment will be upon mankind when the last throne is filled, for Heaven will then be
complete.

so, facing hers, does the throned blessedness
  of the Great John[9] who, ever holy, bore
  the desert, martyrdom, and Hell's distress;
and under him, forming that line are found
  Francis, Benedict, Augustine,[1] and others   35
  descending to this center round by round.
Now marvel at all-foreseeing profundity:
  this garden shall be complete when the two aspects
  of the one faith have filled it equally.
And know that below that tier that cuts the two   40
  dividing walls at their centerpoint, no being
  has won his seat of glory by his own virtue,
but by another's, under strict condition;
  for all of these were spirits loosed from flesh
  before they had matured to true volition.[2]   45
You can yourself make out their infant graces:
  you need no more than listen to their treble
  and look attentively into their faces.
You do not speak now: many doubts confound you.[3]
  Therefore, to set you free I shall untie   50
  the cords in which your subtle thoughts have bound you.
Infinite order rules in this domain.
  Mere accidence can no more enter in
  than hunger can, or thirst, or grief, or pain.
All you see here is fixed by the decree   55
  of the eternal law, and is so made
  that the ring goes on the finger perfectly.
These, it follows, who had so short a pause
  in the lower life are not ranked higher or lower
  among themselves without sufficient cause.   60
The king in whom this realm abides unchanging
  in so much love and bliss that none dares will
  increase of joy, creating and arranging
the minds of all in the glad Paradise
  of His own sight, grants them degrees of grace   65
  as He sees fit. Here let the effect suffice.[4]
Holy Scripture clearly and expressly
  notes this effect upon those twins who fought
  while still within their mother.[5] So we see

9. The Baptist. He denounced Herod Antipos and was beheaded two years before the Crucifixion. He had to wait in Limbo for two years, therefore, till Christ came for him at the Resurrection.   1. St. Francis of Assisi (1181?–1226), founder of the Franciscan order; St. Benedict (ca. 480–ca.547), founder of the Benedictine Order; St. Augustine (354–430).   2. The lower half of the rose-stadium contains the blessed infants, the souls of those who died before they had achieved the true volition of reason and faith. Salvation is granted them not directly through belief in Christ but through the faith and prayers of their parents, relatives, and others of the faithful who interceded for them.   3. The infants are ranked in tiers that indicate degrees of heavenly merit. But if they were saved through no merit of their own, how can one be more worthy than the other? Such is Dante's doubt, which Bernard goes on to set at rest by telling him, in essence, that God knows what He is doing.   4. The cause is buried in God's mind. The effect must speak for itself.   5. Jacob and Esau. According to Genesis, 25:21ff., they were at odds while still in their

how the Supreme light fittingly makes fair   70
   its aureole by granting them their graces
   according to the color of their hair.[6]
Thus through no merit of their works and days
   they are assigned their varying degrees
   by variance only in original grace.   75
In the first centuries of man's creation
   their innocence and the true faith of their parents
   was all they needed to achieve salvation.
When the first age of man had run its course,
   then circumcision was required of males,   80
   to give their innocent wings sufficient force.
But when the age of grace came to mankind
   then, unless perfectly baptized in Christ,
   such innocents went down among the blind.[7]
Look now on her who most resembles Christ,[8]   85
   for only the great glory of her shining
   can purify your eyes to look on Christ."
I saw such joy rain down upon that face—[9]
   borne to it by those blest Intelligences
   created thus to span those heights of space—   90
that through all else on the long road I trod
   nothing had held my soul so fixed in awe,
   nor shown me such resemblances to God.
The self-same Love that to her first descended[1]
   singing "*Ave Maria, gratia plena*"   95
   stood before her with its wings extended.
Thus rang the holy chant to Heaven's Queen
   and all the blessèd court joined in the song,
   and singing, every face grew more serene.
"O holy Father, who endures for me   100
   the loss of being far from the sweet place
   where fate has raised your throne eternally,
who is that angel who with such desire
   gazes into the eyes of our sweet Queen,
   so rapt in love he seems to be afire?"   105
Thus did I seek instruction from that Great One
   who drew the beauty of his light from Mary
   as the morning star draws beauty from the sun.
And he: "As much as angel or soul can know

---

mother's womb. (Cf. the legend of Polyneices and Eteocles, twin sons of Oedipus and Jocasta.) Dante
follows St. Paul (Romans 9:11–13) in interpreting the division between Jacob and Esau as a working of
God's unfathomable will. "Even as it is written, Jacob I loved, but Esau I hated." Man can note the will
of God in such matters ("the effect") but cannot plumb its causes.   6. For what may seem to be superficial reasons. Esau (Genesis 25:25) was red-headed.   7. Among the souls of Hell. Such infants were
assigned to Limbo.   8. The Virgin Mary.   9. Mary's.   1. The archangel Gabriel, the Angel of the
Annunciation. Dante seems to conceive of Gabriel suspended in air before her, repeating the blissful
chant of the Annunciation as he had first hymned it in Nazareth.

of exultation, gallantry, and poise   110
    there is in him; and we would have it so,
for it was he who brought the victory[2]
    to Mary when the Son of God had willed
    to bear the weight of human misery.
But let your eyes go where my words point out   115
    among this court, and note the mighty peers
    of the empire of the just and the devout.
Those two whose bliss it is to sit so close
    to the radiance of the Empress of All Joy
    are the two eternal roots of this our rose:[3]   120
The one just to the left of her blessedness
    is the father whose unruly appetite
    left man the taste for so much bitterness;
and on her right, that ancient one you see
    is the father of Holy Church to whom Christ gave   125
    the twin keys to this flower of timeless beauty.
And that one who in his prophetic sight
    foretold the evil days of the Sweet Bride
    won by the spear and nails,[4] sits on his right.
While by the other father and first man   130
    sits the great leader to whom manna fell
    to feed an ingrate and rebellious clan.[5]
Across the circle from Peter, behold Anna.[6]
    She feels such bliss in looking at her daughter
    she does not move her eyes to sing 'Hosanna!'   135
And opposite the father of us all
    sits Lucy,[7] who first urged your lady to you
    when you were blindly bent toward your own fall.
But the time allowed for this dream vision flies.
    As a tailor must cut the gown from what cloth is given,   140
    just so must we move on, turning our eyes
to the Primal Love, that as your powers advance
    with looking toward him, you may penetrate
    as deep as may be through His radiance.
But lest you should fall backward when you flare   145
    your mortal wings, intending to mount higher,
    remember grace must be acquired through prayer.
Therefore I will pray that blessèd one[8]
    who has the power to aid you in your need.

2. (Dante says "the palm.") Of God's election, that she bear the promised Messiah.   3. Adam and St.
Peter. Adam as Father of Mankind, Peter as Father of the Church. Note that Peter has the place of honor
on the right.   4. St. John the Evangelist. His *Apocalypse* was received as the prophetic book in which
the entire history of the Church is foretold. He sits on Peter's right.   5. Moses.   6. Ste. Anna, Ste.
Anne, mother of the Virgin. Her position directly across the circle from Peter's puts her to the right
of John the Baptist. *Does not move her eyes to sing 'Hosanna!'*: Like all the other heavenly beings,
she constantly sings the praise of God. All others, naturally when they sing up as they sing. She, however,
is so filled with bliss by the sight of Mary that she does not turn her eyes from her blessed daughter.
7. See *Inferno* II. 97–100. It was she who first sent Beatrice to rescue Dante from the Dark Wood of
Error. She sits opposite Adam. She would, accordingly, be to the left of John the Baptist.   8. Mary.

See that you follow me with such devotion   150
your heart adheres to every word I say."
And with those words the saint began to pray.

CANTO XXXIII

The Empyrean   St. Bernard, Prayer to the Virgin, The Vision of God

St. Bernard offers a lofty prayer to the Virgin, asking her to intercede in
Dante's behalf, and in answer Dante feels his soul swell with new power
and grow calm in rapture as his eyes are permitted the direct vision of God.
There can be no measure of how long the vision endures. It passes, and
Dante is once more mortal and fallible. Raised by God's presence, he had
looked into the Mystery and had begun to understand its power and majesty. Returned to himself, there is no power in him capable of speaking
the truth of what he saw. Yet the impress of the truth is stamped upon his
soul, which he now knows will return to be one with God's love.

"Virgin Mother, daughter of thy son;
    humble beyond all creatures and more exalted;
    predestined turning point of God's intention;
thy merit so ennobled human nature
    that its divine Creator did not scorn   5
    to make Himself the creature of His creature.
The Love that was rekindled in Thy womb
    sends forth the warmth of the eternal peace
    within whose ray this flower has come to bloom.
Here, to us, thou art the noon and scope   10
    of Love revealed; and among mortal men,
    the living fountain of eternal hope.
Lady, thou art so near God's reckonings
    that who seeks grace and does not first seek thee
    would have his wish fly upward without wings.   15
Not only does thy sweet benignity
    flow out to all who beg, but oftentimes
    thy charity arrives before the plea.
In thee is pity, in thee munificence,
    in thee the tenderest heart, in thee unites   20
    all that creation knows of excellence!
Now comes this man who from the final pit
    of the universe up to this height has seen,
    one by one, the three lives of the spirit.
He prays to thee in fervent supplication   25
    for grace and strength, that he may raise his eyes
    to the all-healing final revelation.
And I, who never more desired to see
    the vision myself than I do that he may see It,
    add my own prayer, and pray that it may be   30

enough to move you to dispel the trace
   of every mortal shadow by thy prayers
   and let him see revealed the Sum of Grace.
I pray thee further, all-persuading Queen,
   keep whole the natural bent of his affections[9]   35
   and of his powers after his eyes have seen.
Protect him from the stirrings of man's clay;[1]
   see how Beatrice and the blessèd host
   clasp reverent hands to join me as I pray."
The eyes[2] that God reveres and loves the best   40
   glowed on the speaker, making clear the joy
   with which true prayer is heard by the most blest.
Those eyes turned then to the Eternal Ray,
   through which, we must indeed believe, the eyes
   of others do not find such ready way.   45
And I, who neared the goal of all my nature,
   felt my soul, at the climax of its yearning,
   suddenly, as it ought, grow calm with rapture.
Bernard then, smiling sweetly, gestured to me
   to look up, but I had already become
   within myself all he would have me be.[3]   50
Little by little as my vision grew
   it penetrated further through the aura
   of the high lamp which in Itself is true.[4]
What then I saw is more than tongue can say.   55
   Our human speech is dark before the vision.
   The ravished memory swoons and falls away.
As one who sees in dreams and wakes to find
   the emotional impression of his vision
   still powerful while its parts fade from his mind—   60
just such am I, having lost nearly all
   the vision itself, while in my heart I feel
   the sweetness of it yet distill and fall.
So, in the sun, the footprints fade from snow.
   On the wild wind that bore the tumbling leaves   65
   the Sybil's oracles were scattered so.[5]
O Light Supreme who doth Thyself withdraw
   so far above man's mortal understanding,

9. Bernard is asking Mary to protect Dante lest the intensity of the vision overpower his faculties.
1. Protect him from the stirrings of base human impulse, especially from pride, for Dante is about to receive a grace never before granted to any man and the thought of such glory might well move a mere mortal to a hubris that would turn glory to sinfulness.   2. Of Mary.   3. I.e., "But I had already fixed my entire attention upon the vision of God." But if so, how could Dante have seen Bernard's smile and gesture? Eager students like to believe they catch Dante in a contradiction here. Let them bear in mind that Dante is looking directly at God, as do the souls of Heaven, who thereby acquire—insofar as they are able to contain it—God's own knowledge. As a first stirring of that heavenly power, therefore, Dante is sharing God's knowledge of St. Bernard.   4. The light of God is the one light whose source is Itself. All others are a reflection of this.   5. The Cumean Sybil (Virgil describes her in *Aeneid* III. 441ff.) wrote her oracles on leaves, one letter to a leaf, then sent her message scattering on the wind. Presumably, the truth was all contained in that strew, could one only gather all the leaves and put the letters in the right order.

lend me again some glimpse of what I saw;
make Thou my tongue so eloquent it may   70
of all Thy glory speak a single clue
to those who follow me in the world's day;
for by returning to my memory
somewhat, and somewhat sounding in these verses,
Thou shalt show man more of Thy victory.   75
So dazzling was the splendor of that Ray,
that I must certainly have lost my senses
had I, but for an instant, turned away.[6]
And so it was, as I recall, I could
the better bear to look, until at last   80
my vision made one with the Eternal Good.
Oh grace abounding that had made me fit
to fix my eyes on the eternal light
until my vision was consumed in it!
I saw within Its depth how It conceives   85
all things in a single volume bound by Love,
of which the universe is the scattered leaves;
substance,[7] accident, and their relation
so fused that all I say could do no more
than yield a glimpse of that bright revelation.   90
I think I saw the universal form
that binds these things,[8] for as I speak these words
I feel my joy swell and my spirits warm.
Twenty-five centuries since Neptune saw
the Argo's keel have not moved all mankind,   95
recalling that adventure, to such awe
as I felt in an instant. My tranced being
stared fixed and motionless upon that vision,
ever more fervent to see in the act of seeing.
Experiencing that Radiance, the spirit   100
is so indrawn it is impossible
even to think of ever turning from It.
For the good which is the will's ultimate object
is all subsumed in It; and, being removed,
all is defective which in It is perfect.   105
Now in my recollection of the rest
I have less power to speak than any infant
wetting its tongue yet at its mother's breast;
and not because that Living Radiance bore
more than one semblance, for It is unchanging   110

---

6. How can a light be so dazzling that the beholder would swoon if he looked away for an instant? Would
it not be, rather, in looking at, not away from, the overpowering vision that the viewer's senses would be
overcome? So it would be on earth. But now Dante, with the help of all heaven's prayers, is in the presence
of God and strengthened by all he sees. It is by being so strengthened that he can see yet more.
7. Matter, all that exists in itself. *Accident:* All that exists as a phase of matter.   8. Substance and
accident.

and is forever as it was before;
rather, as I grew worthier to see,
   the more I looked, the more unchanging semblance
   appeared to change with every change in me.
Within the depthless deep and clear existence   115
   of that abyss of light three circles shown—
   three in color, one in circumference:
the second from the first, rainbow from rainbow;
   the third, an exhalation of pure fire
   equally breathed forth by the other two.   120
But oh how much my words miss my conception,
   which is itself so far from what I saw
   that to call it feeble would be rank deception!
O Light Eternal fixed in Itself alone,
   by Itself alone understood, which from Itself   125
   loves and glows, self-knowing and self-known;
that second aureole which shone forth in Thee,
   conceived as a reflection of the first—
   or which appeared so to my scrutiny—
seemed in Itself of Its own coloration   130
   to be painted with man's image. I fixed my eyes
   on that alone in rapturous contemplation.
Like a geometer wholly dedicated
   to squaring the circle, but who cannot find,
   think as he may, the principle indicated—   135
so did I study the supernal face.
   I yearned to know just how our image merges
   into that circle, and how it there finds place;
but mine were not the wings for such a flight.
Yet, as I wished, the truth I wished for came   140
   cleaving my mind in a great flash of light.
Here my powers rest from their high fantasy,
   but already I could feel my being turned—
   instinct and intellect balanced equally
as in a wheel whose motion nothing jars—   145
by the Love that moves the Sun and the other stars.

GIOVANNI BOCCACCIO

1313–1375

The tales of Boccaccio's *Decameron* (completed about 1353) constitute the greatest achievement of prose fiction in a vernacular language of southern Europe during the medieval period. In his hundred stories the Italian author presents a great variety of people and situations, aptly and often acutely characterized, and abundant dialogue of great liveliness and realism.

Born in 1313 in Paris, Giovanni Boccaccio was the son of a Florentine businessman and a Frenchwoman. He was apparently taken to Italy in infancy, and in 1328 was sent to Naples to learn commerce in the office of his father's partner; but after six years, bored with business, he turned to the study of canon law. In 1336 Boccaccio saw Maria d'Aquino in a church at Naples; she is represented as Fiammetta in several of his works, including the *Decameron*. A romantic affair ended in Maria's desertion of her lover, and finally in her death in the plague of 1348. In 1341 Boccaccio returned to Florence. After 1351 he was greatly influenced by Petrarch, and turned in his writing from Italian poetry and prose fiction to Latin works of a scholarly nature. He sheltered Leon Pilatus, inducing him to make the first translation of Homer from Greek. Unlike Petrarch, Boccaccio was devoted to the study of Dante, of whom he wrote a biography; in 1373 he was appointed to a Dante chair or lectureship in Florence. He died in 1375.

Like Chaucer, who wrote his *Canterbury Tales* several decades later, Boccaccio provides a dramatic framework for his narrations. But his storytellers are not miscellaneous pilgrims traveling to a famous shrine; they are seven young ladies and three young gentlemen who have withdrawn from Florence to the countryside, to escape the Black Death, or plague, of 1348.* They engage in gay banter and good-natured raillery; but, as they are all refined and cultivated young people with no occupational bias or ingrained prejudices, their relationships are polite rather than boisterous and lack the force and depth and vitality of those portrayed in *The Canterbury Tales*. They agree on a plan of storytelling—and adhere to it (with slight changes). Here there is no drunken miller, such as interrupts Chaucer's pilgrims, to upset the seemly orderliness acceptable to gentlefolk, for there are no other folk present. Each member of the company is to tell a tale each day; on some days a general topic is assigned, on others each narrator follows his own taste and judgment.

The story about Brother Alberto and his impersonation of the angel Gabriel, a bawdy tale of amorous intrigue and deception, exemplifies what most modern readers regard as typical of the *Decameron*. Like Chaucer's *Miller's Tale*, it presents a (moderately) clever person successfully deceiving a very foolish one, but eventually punished for his trickery. In the present story, the man is the trickster and the woman is the foolish dupe, but these roles are often reversed in other stories of the *Decameron*; indeed, Boccaccio digresses during the introduction to the fourth day to assert his devotion to women—the Muses, after all, were women—and, indeed, the women storytellers outnumber the men. He nonetheless knew that some women are foolish, just as he knew, though he was a devout Christian, that some priests and friars fall short of their vocation. Like other authors of his time, he saw nothing wrong in acknowledging these facts and turning them to artistic use.

If reduced to the bare essentials of its plot, this tale could be told far more briefly, as a mere anecdote, a joke. Indeed, it may well have been in circulation as an anecdote both before and after Boccaccio. But he gives it literary value by the way he handles it. He makes the reader see the successive scenes in vivid detail, he creates memorable and amusing characters, and he relates the incidents of the narrative closely to the personalities of those characters. Lisetta is not only credulous but also inordinately vain—her credulity derives from her vanity—and it is because of these qualities that she can be taken in by Brother Alberto's preposterous account of the angel's interest in her. The reader also notices the tacit perception of Lisetta's woman friend, who at once sees through the friar's scheme but, instead of disabusing her foolish friend, leads her on and then gleefully reveals the whole story to the outside world. And Alberto, though clever, is not as cautious as he should be. Otherwise, once warned, he would not have exposed himself to discovery and disgrace.

The story of Federigo and his falcon is told on a day devoted to accounts of love that turns out happily after difficulties on the way. It presents the courtly-love relationship—or one of the possible relationships—in a remarkable combination of realism and nobility. Federigo's conduct perfectly fulfills the code; he devotes himself completely to Monna Giovanna, and his failure to receive anything in return in no way disturbs the pattern of that devotion. He never repines or complains; his lady's married or widowed condition is all one to him; and, having spent his fortune in the futile effort to attract her, he lives with resignation on his tiny estate. But Federigo is genuinely high-minded and noble; he has absorbed the ideals and not merely the etiquette of courtly love. His declaration, when Giovanna comes to call, that he has gained and not lost by his service to her, might be politeness learned out of a book—a romance, for example. But his sacrifice of the falcon to provide her with a good meal is a splendid and magnificent folly that could come only from an almost unbelievably generous heart. His grief at the outcome is probably sharper than Giovanna's, despite the painful disappointment that it produces for her.

Giovanna's dignity and charm and sensitivity are as clear to us as they evidently are to Federigo. Unwilling, whether as wife or widow, to have a romance with Federigo, she does not encourage him. Yet she knows that he loves her and that he has squandered his wealth on her account. We see her distress at having to ask him for anything, let alone the falcon, his most cherished possession. But when love for her young son, mortally ill, forces her to it, she acts with grace and decorum. And with something more; for she has discerned the nobleness of temper in Federigo through his consistently courteous behavior. It is that to which she appeals, not to any obligation of a courtly lover to please his lady. Later, when her brothers convince her that she should remarry, she also shows both generosity and independence of character. She gives Federigo his reward by marrying him—and seeing that his new fortune is not wasted! The happy ending is agreeable; but the notable achievement of the story is the brief but complete and poignant depiction of the dilemmas faced by the two against a background of preliminary characterization which gives their decision full significance.

Two good biographies are T. C. Chubb, *The Life of Giovanni Boccaccio* (1930), and Edward Hutton, *Giovanni Boccaccio* (1910). Interesting and sensitive criticism is to be found in Charles G. Osgood, *Boccaccio on Poetry* (1930). John Addington Symonds, *Giovanni Boccaccio* (1895), has been reissued (1968). A. D. Scaglione, *Nature and Love in the Middle Ages* (1963), is a useful discussion of the *Decameron*. Twenty-one of the tales from the *Decameron* can be found in Mark Musa and Peter E. Bondanella, *Giovanni Boccaccio: The Decameron, A New Translation* (1977).

The Decameron[1]

THE FIRST DAY

Thirteen hundred and forty-eight years had already passed after the fruitful Incarnation of the Son of God when into the distinguished city of Florence, more noble than any other Italian city, there came the deadly pestilence. It started in the East, either because of the influence of heavenly bodies or because of God's just wrath as a punishment to mortals for our wicked deeds, and it killed an infinite number of people. Without pause it spread from one place and it stretched its miserable length over the West. And against this pestilence no human wisdom or foresight was of any avail; quantities of filth were removed from the city by officials charged with this task; the entry of any sick person into the city was prohibited; and many directives were issued concerning the maintenance of good health. Nor were the humble supplications, rendered not once but many times to God by pious people, through public processions or by other means, efficacious; for almost at the beginning of springtime of the year in question the plague began to show its sorrowful effects in an extraordinary manner. It did not act as it had done in the East, where bleeding from the nose was a manifest sign of inevitable death, but it began in both men and women with certain swellings either in the groin or under the armpits, some of which grew to the size of a normal apple and others to the size of an egg (more or less), and the people called them buboes. And from the two parts of the body already mentioned, within a brief space of time, the said deadly buboes began to spread indiscriminately over every part of the body; and after this, the symptoms of the illness changed to black or livid spots appearing on the arms and thighs, and on every part of the body, some large ones and sometimes many little ones scattered all around. And just as the buboes were originally, and still are, a very certain indication of impending death, in like manner these spots came to mean the same thing for whoever had them. Neither a doctor's advice nor the strength of medicine could do anything to cure this illness; on the contrary, either the nature of the illness was such that it afforded no cure, or else the doctors were so ignorant that they did not recognize its cause and, as a result, could not prescribe the proper remedy (in fact, the number of doctors, other than the well-trained, was increased by a large number of men and women who had never had any medical training); at any rate, few of the sick were ever cured, and almost all died after the third day of the appearance of the previously described symptoms (some sooner, others later), and most of them died without fever or any other side effects.

This pestilence was so powerful that it was communicated to the healthy by contact with the sick, the way a fire close to dry or oily things will set them aflame. And the evil of the plague went even further: not only did talking to or being around the sick bring infection and a common death, but also touching the clothes of the sick or anything touched or used by

1. These selections translated by Mark Musa and Peter E. Bondanella.

them seemed to communicate this very disease to the person involved. What I am about to say is incredible to hear, and if I and others had not witnessed it with our own eyes, I should not dare believe it (let alone write about it), no matter how trustworthy a person I might have heard it from. Let me say, then, that the power of the plague described here was of such virulence in spreading from one person to another that not only did it pass from one man to the next, but, what's more, it was often transmitted from the garments of a sick or dead man to animals that not only became contaminated by the disease, but also died within a brief period of time. My own eyes, as I said earlier, witnessed such a thing one day: when the rags of a poor man who died of this disease were thrown into the public street, two pigs came upon them, as they are wont to do, and first with their snouts and then with their teeth they took the rags and shook them around; and within a short time, after a number of convulsions, both pigs fell dead upon the ill-fated rags, as if they had been poisoned. From these and many similar or worse occurrences there came about such fear and such fantastic notions among those who remained alive that almost all of them took a very cruel attitude in the matter; that is, they completely avoided the sick and their possessions; and in so doing, each one believed that he was protecting his good health.

There were some people who thought that living moderately and avoiding all superfluity might help a great deal in resisting this disease, and so, they gathered in small groups and lived entirely apart from everyone else. They shut themselves up in those houses where there were no sick people and where one could live well by eating the most delicate of foods and drinking the finest of wines (doing so always in moderation), allowing no one to speak about or listen to anything said about the sick and the dead outside; these people lived, spending their time with music and other pleasures that they could arrange. Others thought the opposite: they believed that drinking too much, enjoying life, going about singing and celebrating, satisfying in every way the appetites as best one could, laughing, and making light of everything that happened was the best medicine for such a disease; so they practiced to the fullest what they believed by going from one tavern to another all day and night, drinking to excess; and often they would make merry in private homes, doing everything that pleased or amused them the most. This they were able to do easily, for everyone felt he was doomed to die and, as a result, abandoned his property, so that most of the houses had become common property, and any stranger who came upon them used them as if he were their rightful owner. In addition to this bestial behavior, they always managed to avoid the sick as best they could. And in this great affliction and misery of our city the revered authority of the laws, both divine and human, had fallen and almost completely disappeared, for, like other men, the ministers and executors of the laws were either dead or sick or so short of help that it was impossible for them to fulfill their duties; as a result, everybody was free to do as he pleased.

Many others adopted a middle course between the two attitudes just described: neither did they restrict their food or drink so much as the first group nor did they fall into such dissoluteness and drunkenness as the second; rather, they satisfied their appetites to a moderate degree. They did not shut themselves up, but went around carrying in their hands flowers, or sweet-smelling herbs, or various kinds of spices; and often they would put these things to their noses, believing that such smells were a wonderful means of purifying the brain, for all the air seemed infected with the stench of dead bodies, sickness, and medicines.

Others were of a crueler opinion (though it was, perhaps, a safer one): they maintained that there was no better medicine against the plague than to flee from it; and convinced of this reasoning, not caring about anything but themselves, men and women in great numbers abandoned their city, their houses, their farms, their relatives, and their possessions and sought other places, and they went at least as far away as the Florentine country-side—as if the wrath of God could not pursue them with this pestilence wherever they went but would only strike those it found within the walls of the city! Or perhaps they thought that Florence's last hour had come and that no one in the city would remain alive.

And not all those who adopted these diverse opinions died, nor did they all escape with their lives; on the contrary, many of those who thought this way were falling sick everywhere, and since they had given, when they were healthy, the bad example of avoiding the sick, they, in turn, were abandoned and left to languish away without care. The fact was that one citizen avoided another, that almost no one cared for his neighbor, and that relatives rarely or hardly ever visited each other—they stayed far apart. This disaster had struck such fear into the hearts of men and women that brother abandoned brother, uncle abandoned nephew, sister left brother, and very often wife abandoned husband, and—even worse, almost unbe-lievable—fathers and mothers neglected to tend and care for their chil-dren, as if they were not their own.

Thus, for the countless multitude of men and women who fell sick, there remained no support except the charity of their friends (and these were few) or the avarice of servants, who worked for inflated salaries and indecent periods of time and who, in spite of this, were few and far between; and those few were men or women of little wit (most of them not trained for such service) who did little else but hand different things to the sick when requested to do so or watch over them while they died, and in this service, they very often lost their own lives and their profits. And since the sick were abandoned by their neighbors, their parents, and their friends and there was a scarcity of servants, a practice that was almost unheard of before spread through the city: when a woman fell sick, no matter how attractive or beautiful or noble she might be, she did not mind having a manservant (whoever he might be, no matter how young or old he was), and she had no shame whatsoever in revealing any part of her body to him—the way she would have done to a woman—when the necessity of her sickness required her to do so. This practice was, perhaps, in the days that followed the pestilence, the cause of looser morals in the women who survived the plague. And so, many people died who, by chance, might

have survived if they had been attended to. Between the lack of competent
attendants, which the sick were unable to obtain, and the violence of the
pestilence, there were so many, many people who died in the city both
day and night that it was incredible just to hear this described, not to
mention seeing it! Therefore, out of sheer necessity, there arose among
those who remained alive customs which were contrary to the established
practices of the time.

It was the custom, as it is again today, for the women, relatives, and
neighbors to gather together in the house of a dead person and there to
mourn with the women who had been dearest to him; on the other hand,
in front of the deceased's home, his male relatives would gather together
with his male neighbors and other citizens, and the clergy also came (many
of them, or sometimes just a few) depending upon the social class of the
dead man. Then, upon the shoulders of his equals, he was carried to the
church chosen by him before death with the funeral pomp of candles and
chants. With the fury of the pestilence increasing, this custom, for the
most part, died out and other practices took its place. And so, not only did
people die without having a number of women around them, but there
were many who passed away without even having a single witness present,
and very few were granted the piteous laments and bitter tears of their
relatives; on the contrary, most relatives were somewhere else, laughing,
joking, and amusing themselves; even the women learned this practice too
well, having put aside, for the most part, their womanly compassion for
their own safety. Very few were the dead whose bodies were accompanied
to the church by more than ten or twelve of their neighbors, and these
dead bodies were not even carried on the shoulders of honored and reputable citizens but rather by gravediggers from the lower classes that were
called *becchini*. Working for pay, they would pick up the bier and hurry it
off, not to the church the dead man had chosen before his death but, in
most cases, to the church closest by, accompanied by four or six churchmen with just a few candles, and often none at all. With the help of these
becchini, the churchmen would place the body as fast as they could in
whatever unoccupied grave they could find, without going to the trouble
of saying long or solemn burial services.

The plight of the lower class and, perhaps, a large part of the middle
class, was even more pathetic: most of them stayed in their homes or
neighborhoods either because of their poverty or their hopes for remaining
safe, and every day they fell sick by the thousands; and not having servants
or attendants of any kind, they almost always died. Many ended their lives
in the public streets, during the day or at night, while many others who
died in their homes were discovered dead by their neighbors only by the
smell of their decomposing bodies. The city was full of corpses. The dead
were usually given the same treatment by their neighbors, who were moved
more by the fear that the decomposing corpses would contaminate them
than by any charity they might have felt towards the deceased: either by
themselves or with the assistance of porters (when they were available),
they would drag the corpse out of the home and place it in front of the

doorstep where, usually in the morning, quantities of dead bodies could be seen by any passerby; then, they were laid out on biers, or for lack of biers, on a plank. Nor did a bier carry only one corpse; sometimes it was used for two or three at a time. More than once, a single bier would serve for a wife and husband, two or three brothers, a father or son, or other relatives, all at the same time. And countless times it happened that two priests, each with a cross, would be on their way to bury someone, when porters carrying three or four biers would just follow along behind them; and where these priests thought they had just one dead man to bury, they had, in fact, six or eight and sometimes more. Moreover, the dead were honored with no tears or candles or funeral mourners but worse: things had reached such a point that the people who died were cared for as we care for goats today. Thus, it became quite obvious that what the wise had not been able to endure with patience through the few calamities of every-day life now became a matter of indifference to even the most simple-minded people as a result of this colossal misfortune.

So many corpses would arrive in front of a church every day and at every hour that the amount of holy ground for burials was certainly insufficient for the ancient custom of giving each body its individual place; when all the graves were full, huge trenches were dug in all of the cemeteries of the churches and into them the new arrivals were dumped by the hundreds; and they were packed in there with dirt, one on top of another, like a ship's cargo, until the trench was filled.

But instead of going over every detail of the past miseries which befell our city, let me say that the same unfriendly weather there did not, because of this, spare the surrounding countryside any evil; there, not to speak of the towns which, on a smaller scale, were like the city, in the scattered villages and in the fields the poor, miserable peasants and their families, without any medical assistance or aid of servants, died on the roads and in their fields and in their homes, as many by day as by night, and they died not like men but more like wild animals. Because of this they, like the city dwellers, became careless in their ways and did not look after their posses-sions or their businesses; furthermore, when they saw that death was upon them, completely neglecting the future fruits of their past labors, their livestock, their property, they did their best to consume what they already had at hand. So, it came about that oxen, donkeys, sheep, pigs, chickens and even dogs, man's most faithful companion, were driven from their homes into the fields, where the wheat was left not only unharvested but also unreaped, and they were allowed to roam where they wished; and many of these animals, almost as if they were rational beings, returned at night to their homes without any guidance from a shepherd, satiated after a good day's meal.

Leaving the countryside and returning to the city, what more can one say, except that so great was the cruelty of Heaven, and, perhaps, also that of man, that from March to July of the same year, between the fury of the pestiferous sickness and the fact that many of the sick were badly treated or abandoned in need because of the fear that the healthy had, more than one hundred thousand human beings are believed to have lost their lives for certain inside the walls of the city of Florence whereas, before the deadly plague, one would not have estimated that there were actually that many people dwelling in that city.

Oh, how many great palaces, beautiful homes, and noble dwellings, once filled with families, gentlemen, and ladies, were now emptied, down to the last servant! How many notable families, vast domains, and famous fortunes remained without legitimate heir! How many valiant men, beautiful women, and charming young men, who might have been pronounced very healthy by Galen, Hippocrates, and Aesculapius[2] (not to mention lesser physicians), dined in the morning with their relatives, companions, and friends and then in the evening took supper with their ancestors in the other world!

Reflecting upon so many miseries makes me very sad; therefore, since I wish to pass over as many as I can, let me say that as our city was in this condition, almost emptied of inhabitants, it happened (as I heard it later from a person worthy of trust) that one Tuesday morning in the venerable church of Santa Maria Novella there was hardly any congregation there to hear the holy services except for seven young women, all dressed in garments of mourning as the times demanded, each of whom was a friend, neighbor, or relative of the other, and none of whom had passed her twenty-eighth year, nor was any of them younger than eighteen; all were educated and of noble birth and beautiful to look at, well-mannered and gracefully modest. I would tell you their real names, if I did not have a good reason for not doing so, which is this: I do not wish any of them to be embarrassed in the future because of the things that they said to each other and what they listened to—all of which I shall later recount. Today the laws regarding pleasure are again strict, more so than at that time (for the reasons mentioned above when they were very lax), not only for women of their age but even for those who were older; nor would I wish to give an opportunity to the envious, who are always ready to attack every praiseworthy life, to diminish in any way with their indecent talk the dignity of these worthy ladies. But, so that you may understand clearly what each of them had to say, I intend to call them by names which are either completely or in part appropriate to their personalities. We shall call the first and the oldest Pampinea and the second Fiammetta, the third Filomena, and the fourth Emilia, and we shall name the fifth Lauretta and the sixth Neifile, and the last, not without reason, we shall call Elissa.[3] Not by prior agreement, but purely by chance, they gathered together in one part of the church and were seated almost in a circle, saying their rosaries; after many sighs, they began to discuss among themselves various matters concerning the nature of the times, and after a while, as the others fell silent, Pampinea began to speak in this manner:

2. Roman god of medicine and healing, often identified with Asclepius, Apollo's son, who was the Greek god of medicine. *Galen*: Greek anatomist and physician (A.D. 130?–201?). *Hippocrates*: Greek physician (460?–377? B.C.), to whom the Hippocratic oath, administered to new physicians, is attributed.   3. Perhaps the reason is that, like her namesake, the Carthaginian queen, who is better known as Dido, Boccaccio's Elissa is dominated by a violent passion.

"My dear ladies, you have often heard, as I have, how a proper use of one's reason does harm to no one. It is only natural for everyone born on this earth to aid, preserve, and defend his own life to the best of his ability; this is a right so taken for granted that it has, at times, permitted men to kill each other without blame in order to defend their own lives. And if the laws dealing with the welfare of every human being permit such a thing, how much more lawful, and with no harm to anyone, is it for us, or anyone else, to take all possible precautions to preserve our own lives! When I consider what we have been doing this morning and in the past days and what we have spoken about, I understand, and you must understand too, that each one of us is afraid for her life; nor does this surprise me in the least—rather I am greatly amazed that since each of us has the natural feelings of a woman, we do not find some remedy for ourselves to cure what each one of us dreads. We live in the city, in my opinion, for no other reason than to bear witness to the number of dead bodies that are carried to burial, or to listen whether the friars (whose number has been reduced to almost nothing) chant their offices at the prescribed hours, or to demonstrate to anyone who comes here the quality and the quantity of our miseries by our garments of mourning. And if we leave the church, either we see dead or sick bodies being carried all about, or we see those who were once condemned to exile for their crimes by the authority of the public laws making sport of these laws, running about wildly through the city, because they know that the executors of these laws are either dead or dying; or we see the scum of our city, avid for our blood, who call themselves *becchini* and who ride about on horseback torturing us by deriding everything, making our losses more bitter with their disgusting songs. Nor do we hear anything but 'So-and-so is dead,' and 'So-and-so is dying'; and if there were anyone left to mourn, we should hear nothing but piteous laments everywhere. I do not know if what happens to me also happens to you in your homes, but when I go home I find no one there except my maid, and I become so afraid that my hair stands on end, and wherever I go or sit in my house, I seem to see the shadows of those who have passed away, not with the faces that I remember, but with horrible expressions that terrify me. For these reasons, I am uncomfortable here, outside, and in my home, and the more so since it appears that no one like ourselves, who is well off and who has some other place to go, has remained here except us. And if there are any who remain, according to what I hear and see, they do whatever their hearts desire, making no distinction between what is proper and what is not, whether they are alone or with others, by day or by night; and not only laymen but also those who are cloistered in convents have broken their vows of obedience and have given themselves over to carnal pleasures, for they have made themselves believe that these things are permissible for them and are improper for others, and thinking that they will escape with their lives in this fashion, they have become wanton and dissolute.

"If this is the case, and plainly it is, what are we doing here? What are we waiting for? What are we dreaming about? Why are we slower to protect our health than all the rest of the citizens? Do we hold ourselves less dear than all the others? Or do we believe that our own lives are tied by stronger chains to our bodies than those of others and, therefore, that we need not worry about anything which might have the power to harm them? We are mistaken and deceived, and we are mad if we believe it. We shall have clear proof of this if we just call to mind how many young men and ladies have been struck down by this cruel pestilence. I do not know if you agree with me, but I think that, in order not to fall prey, out of laziness or presumption, to what we might well avoid, it might be a good idea for all of us to leave this city, just as many others before us have done and are still doing. Let us avoid like death itself the ugly examples of others, and go to live in a more dignified fashion in our country houses (of which we all have several) and there let us take what enjoyment, what happiness, and what pleasure we can, without going beyond the rules of reason in any way. There we can hear the birds sing, and we can see the hills and the pastures turning green, the wheat fields moving like the sea, and a thousand kinds of trees; and we shall be able to see the heavens more clearly which, though they still may be cruel, nonetheless will not deny to us their eternal beauties, which are much more pleasing to look at than the empty walls of our city. Besides all this, there in the country the air is much fresher, and the necessities for living in such times as these are plentiful there, and there are just fewer troubles in general; though the peasants are dying there even as the townspeople here, the displeasure is the less in that there are fewer houses and inhabitants than in the city. Here on the other hand, if I judge correctly, we would not be abandoning anyone; on the contrary, we can honestly say it is we ourselves that have been abandoned, for our loved ones are either dead or have fled and have left us alone in such affliction as though we did not belong to them. No reproach, therefore, can come to us if we follow this course of action, whereas sorrow, worry, and perhaps even death can come if we do not follow this course. So, whenever you like, I think it would be well to take our servants, have all our necessary things sent after us, and go from one place one day to another the next, enjoying what happiness and merriment these times permit; let us live in this manner (unless we are overtaken first by death) until we see what ending Heaven has reserved for these horrible times. And remember that it is no more forbidden for us to go away virtuously than it is for most other women to remain here dishonorably."

When they had listened to what Pampinea had said, the other women not only praised her advice but were so anxious to follow it that they had already begun discussing among themselves the details, as if they were going to leave that very instant. But Filomena, who was most discerning, said:

"Ladies, regardless of how convincing Pampinea's arguments are, that is no reason to rush into things, as you seem to wish to do. Remember that we are all women, and any young girl can tell you that women do not know how to reason in a group when they are without the guidance of some man who knows how to control them. We are changeable, quarrelsome, suspicious, timid, and fearful, because of which I suspect that this company will soon break up without honor to any of us if we do not take a guide other than ourselves. We would do well to resolve this matter before we depart."

Then Elissa said:

"Men are truly the leaders of women, and without their guidance, our actions rarely end successfully. But how are we to find any men? We all know that the majority of our relatives are dead and those who remain alive are scattered here and there in various groups, not knowing where we are (they, too, are fleeing precisely what we seek to avoid), and since taking up with strangers would be unbecoming to us, we must, if we wish to leave for the sake of our health, find a means of arranging it so that while going for our own pleasure and repose, no trouble or scandal follow us."

While the ladies were discussing this, three young men came into the church, none of whom was less than twenty-five years of age. Neither the perversity of the times nor the loss of friends or parents, nor fear for their own lives had been able to cool, much less extinguish, the love those lovers bore in their hearts. One of them was called Panfilo, another Filostrato, and the last Dioneo, each one very charming and well-bred; and in those turbulent times they sought their greatest consolation in the sight of the ladies they loved, all three of whom happened to be among the seven ladies previously mentioned, while the others were close relatives of one or the other of the three men. No sooner had they sighted the ladies than they were seen by them, whereupon Pampinea smiled and said:

"See how Fortune favors our plans and has provided us with these discreet and virtuous young men, who would gladly be our guides and servants if we do not hesitate to accept them for such service."

Then Neifile's face blushed out of embarrassment, for she was one of those who was loved by one of the young men, and she said:

"Pampinea, for the love of God, be careful what you say! I realize very well that nothing but good can be said of any of them, and I believe that they are capable of doing much more than that task and, likewise, that their good and worthy company would be fitting not only for us but for ladies much more beautiful and attractive than we are, but it is quite obvious that some of them are in love with some of us who are here present, and I fear that if we take them with us, slander and disapproval will follow, through no fault of ours or of theirs."

Then Filomena said:

"That does not matter at all; as long as I live with dignity and have no remorse of conscience about anything, let anyone who wishes say what he likes to the contrary: God and Truth will take up arms in my defense. Now, if they were just prepared to come with us, as Pampinea says, we could truly say that Fortune was favorable to our departure."

When the others heard her speak in such a manner, the argument was ended, and they all agreed that the young men should be called over, told about their intentions, and asked if they would be so kind as to accompany the ladies on such a journey. Without further discussion, then, Pampinea, who was related to one of the men, rose to her feet and made her way to where they stood gazing at the ladies, and she greeted them with a cheerful expression, outlined their plan to them, and begged them, in everyone's name, to keep them company in the spirit of pure and brotherly affection. At first the young men thought they were being mocked, but when they saw that the lady was speaking seriously, they gladly consented; and in order to start without delay and put the plan into action, before leaving the church they agreed upon what preparations must be made for their departure. And when everything had been arranged and word had been sent on to the place they intended to go, the following morning (that is, Wednesday) at the break of dawn the ladies with some of their servants and the three young men with three of their servants left the city and set out on their way; they had traveled no further than two short miles when they arrived at the first stop they had agreed upon.

The place was somewhere on a little mountain, at some distance away from our roads, full of various shrubs and plants with rich, green foliage— most pleasant to look at; at the top there was a country mansion with a beautiful large inner courtyard with open collonades, halls, and bedrooms, all of them beautiful in themselves and decorated with cheerful and interesting paintings; it was surrounded by meadows and marvelous gardens, with wells of fresh water and cellars full of the most precious wines, the likes of which were more suitable for expert drinkers than for sober and dignified ladies. And the group discovered, to their delight, that the entire palace had been cleaned and the beds made in the bedchambers, and that fresh flowers and rushes had been strewn everywhere. Soon after they arrived and were resting, Dioneo, who was more attractive and wittier than either of the other young men, said:

"Ladies, more than our preparations, it was your intelligence that guided us here. I do not know what you intend to do with your thoughts, but I left mine inside the city walls when I passed through them in your company a little while ago; and so, you must either make up your minds to enjoy yourselves and laugh and sing with me (as much, let me say, as your dignity permits), or you must give me leave to return to my worries and to remain in our troubled city."

To this Pampinea, who had driven away her sad thoughts in the same way, replied happily:

"Dioneo, you speak very well: let us live happily, for after all it was unhappiness that made us flee the city. But when things are not organized they cannot long endure, and since I began the discussions which brought this fine company together, and since I desire the continuation of our happiness, I think it is necessary that we choose a leader from among us, whom we shall honor and obey as our superior and whose every thought shall be to keep us living happily. And in order that each one of us may feel the weight of this responsibility together with the pleasure of its authority, so that no one of us who has not experienced it can envy the others, let me say that both the weight and the honor should be granted to each one of us in turn for a day; the first will be chosen by election; the others that follow will be whomever he or she that will have the rule for that day chooses as the hour of vespers[4] approaches; this ruler, as long as his reign endures, will organize and arrange the place and the manner in which we will spend our time."

These words greatly pleased everyone, and they unanimously elected Pampinea queen for the first day; Filomena quickly ran to a laurel bush, whose leaves she had always heard were worthy of praise and bestowed great honor upon those crowned with them; she plucked several branches from it and wove them into a handsome garland of honor. And when it would be placed upon the head of any one of them, it was to be to all in the group a clear symbol of royal rule and authority over the rest of them for as long as their company stayed together.

After she had been chosen queen, Pampinea ordered everyone to refrain from talking; then, she sent for the four servants of the ladies and for those of the three young men, and as they stood before her in silence, she said:

"Since I must set the first example for you all in order that it may be bettered and thus allow our company to live in order and in pleasure, and without any shame, and so that it may last as long as we wish, I first appoint Parmeno, Dioneo's servant, as my steward, and I commit to his care and management all our household and everything which pertains to the services of the dining hall. I wish Sirisco, the servant of Panfilo, to act as our buyer and treasurer and follow the orders of Parmeno. Tindaro, who is in the service of Filostrato, shall wait on Filostrato and Dioneo and Panfilo in their bedchambers when the other two are occupied with their other duties and cannot do so. Misia, my servant, and Licisca, Filomena's, will be occupied in the kitchen and will prepare those dishes which are ordered by Parmeno. Chimera, Lauretta's servant, and Stratilia, Fiammetta's servant, will take care of the bedchambers of the ladies and the cleaning of those places we use. And in general, we desire and command each of you, if you value our favor and good graces, to be sure—no matter where you go or come from, no matter what you hear or see—to bring us back nothing but pleasant news."

And when these orders, praised by all present, were delivered, Pampinea rose happily to her feet and said:

"Here there are gardens and meadows and many other pleasant places, which all of us can wander about in and enjoy as we like; but at the hour of tierce[5] let everyone be here so that we can eat in the cool of the morning."

After the merry group had been given the new queen's permission, the young men, together with the beautiful ladies, set off slowly through a garden, discussing pleasant matters, making themselves beautiful garlands of various leaves and singing love songs. After the time granted them by the queen had elapsed, they returned home and found Parmeno busy car-

---

4. Late afternoon; the sixth of the seven times of day set aside for prayer by canon law.   5. The third canonical hour, 9 A.M.

rying out the duties of his task; for as they entered a hall on the ground floor, they saw the tables set with the whitest of linens and with glasses that shone like silver and everything decorated with broom blossoms; then, they washed their hands and, at the queen's command, they all sat down in the places assigned them by Parmeno. The delicately cooked foods were brought in and very fine wines were served; the three servants in silence served the tables. Everyone was delighted to see everything so beautiful and well arranged, and they ate merrily and with pleasant conversation. Since all the ladies and young men knew how to dance (and some of them even knew how to play and sing very well), when the tables had been cleared, the queen ordered that instruments be brought, and on her command, Dioneo took a lute and Fiammetta a viola, and they began softly playing a dance tune. After the queen had sent the servants off to eat, she began to dance together with the other ladies and two of the young men; and when that was over, they all began to sing carefree and gay songs. In this manner they continued until the queen felt that it was time to retire; therefore, at the queen's request, the three young men went off to their chambers (which were separate from those of the ladies), where they found their beds prepared and the rooms as full of flowers as the halls; the ladies, too, discovered their chambers decorated in like fashion. Then they all undressed and fell asleep.

Not long after the hour of nones,[6] the queen arose and had the other ladies and young men awakened, stating that too much sleep in the daytime was harmful; then they went out onto a lawn of thick, green grass, where no ray of the sun could penetrate; and there, with a gentle breeze caressing them, they all sat in a circle upon the green grass, as was the wish of their queen. Then she spoke to them in this manner:

"As you see, the sun is high, the heat is great, and nothing can be heard except the cicadas in the olive groves; therefore, to wander about at this hour would be, indeed, foolish. Here it is cool and fresh and, as you see, there are games and chessboards with which all of you can amuse yourselves to your liking. But if you take my advice in this matter, I suggest we spend this hot part of the day not in playing games (a pastime which of necessity disturbs the player who loses without providing much pleasure either for his opponents or for those who watch) but rather in telling stories, for this way one person, by telling a story, can provide amusement for the entire company. In the time it takes for the sun to set and the heat to become less oppressive, you will each have told a little story, and then we can go wherever we like to amuse ourselves; so, if what I say pleases you (and in this I am willing to follow your pleasure), then, let us do it; if not, then let everyone do as he pleases until the hour of vespers."

The entire group of men and women liked the idea of telling stories.

"Then," said the queen, "if this is your wish, for this first day I order each of you to tell a story about any subject he likes."

6. That is, they rested during the early afternoon taking a *siesta. Nones:* The fifth canonical hour, 3 P.M.

And turning to Panfilo, who sat on her right, she ordered him in a gracious manner to begin with one of his tales; whereupon, hearing her command, Panfilo, while everyone listened, began at once as follows:

THE SECOND TALE OF THE FOURTH DAY[7]

Gracious ladies, there was once in Imola a man of wicked and corrupt ways named Berto della Massa, whose evil deeds were so well known by the people of Imola that nobody there would believe him when he told the truth, not to mention when he lied. Realizing that his tricks would no longer work there, in desperation he moved to Venice, that receptacle of all forms of wickedness, thinking that he would adopt a different style of trickery there from what he had used anywhere else before. And almost as if his conscience were struck with remorse for his evil deeds committed in the past, he gave every sign of a man who had become truly humble and most religious; in fact, he went and turned himself into a minor friar, taking the name of Brother Alberto da Imola; and in this disguise he pretended to lead an ascetic life, praising repentance and abstinence, and never eating meat nor drinking wine unless they were of a quality good enough for him.

Never before had such a thief, pimp, forger, and murderer become so great a preacher without having abandoned these vices, even while he may have been practicing them in secret. And besides this, after he became a priest, whenever he celebrated the mass at the altar, in view of all the congregation, he would weep when it came to the Passion of Our Savior, for he was a man to whom tears cost very little when they were called for. And in short, between his sermons and his tears, he managed to beguile the Venetians to such an extent that he was almost always made the trustee and guardian of every will that was made, the keeper of many people's money, and confessor and advisor to the majority of men and women; and acting in this way, he changed from a wolf into a shepherd, and his reputation for sanctity in those parts was far greater than St. Francis's was in Assisi.

Now it happened that there was a foolish and silly young woman named Madonna Lisetta da Ca' Quirino (the wife of a great merchant who had gone with his galleys to Flanders) who, along with other ladies, went to be confessed by this holy friar. She was kneeling at his feet and, being a Venetian (and, as such, a gossip like all of them), she was asked by Brother Alberto halfway through her confession if she had a lover. To this question she crossly replied:

"What, my dear brother, don't you have eyes in your head? Do my charms appear to you to be like all those of other women? I could have even more lovers than I want, but my beauty is not to be enjoyed by just anyone. How many ladies do you know who possess such charms as mine, charms which would make me beautiful even in paradise?"

7. Told by Pampinea. On the fourth day, in Filostrato's reign, the friends were to tell love stories with unhappy endings.

And then she kept on saying so many things about her beauty that it became boring to listen to her. Brother Alberto realized immediately that she was a simpleton, and since he thought she was just the right terrain for plowing, he fell passionately in love with her right then and there; but putting aside his flatteries for a more appropriate time, and reassuming his saintly manner, he began to reproach her and to tell her that her attitude was vainglorious and other such things; and so the lady told him that he was a beast and that he did not know one beauty from another; and because he did not want to upset her too much, Brother Alberto, after having confessed her, let her go off with the other women.

After a few days, he went with a trusted companion to Madonna Lisetta's home and taking her into a room where they could be seen by no one, he threw himself on his knees before her and said:

"My lady, I beg you in God's name to forgive me for speaking to you as I did last Sunday about your beauty, for I was so soundly punished the following night that I have not been able to get up until today."

"And who punished you in this way?" asked Lady Halfwit.

"I shall tell you," replied Brother Alberto. "As I was praying that night in my cell, as I always do, I suddenly saw a glowing light, and before I was able to turn around to see what it was, I saw a very beautiful young man with a large stick in his hand who took me by the collar, dragged me to my feet, and gave me so many blows that he broke practically everything in my body. I asked him why he had done this and he replied:

'Because yesterday you presumed to reproach the celestial beauty of Madonna Lisetta whom I love more than anything else except God.'

"And then I asked: 'Who are you?'

"He replied that he was the angel Gabriel.

" 'Oh My Lord,' I said, 'I beg you to forgive me.'

" 'I shall forgive you on one condition,' he said, 'that you go to her as soon as you are able and beg her forgiveness; and if she does not pardon you, I shall return here and beat you so soundly that you will be sorry for the rest of your life.' "

Lady Lighthead, who was as smart as salt is sweet, enjoyed hearing all these words and believed them all, and after a moment she said:

"I told you, Brother Alberto, that my charms were heavenly; but, God help me, I feel sorry for you, and from now on, in order to spare you more harm, I forgive you on condition that you tell me what the angel said next."

Brother Alberto said: "My lady, since you have forgiven me, I shall gladly tell you, but I remind you of one thing: you must not tell what I tell you to anyone in the world, otherwise you will spoil everything, you who are the most fortunate woman in the world today. The angel Gabriel told me that I was to tell you that you are so pleasing to him that often he would have come to pass the night with you if he had not thought it might frighten you. Now he sends me here with a message that he would like to come to you one night and spend some time with you; but since he is an angel and you would not be able to touch him in the form of an angel, he says that for your pleasure he would like to come as a human being, and he asks when you would have him come and in whose shape should he come, and he will come; therefore you, more than any other woman alive, should consider yourself blessed."

Lady Silly then said that it pleased her very much that the angel Gabriel was in love with her, for she loved him as well and never failed to light a cheap candle in his honor whenever she found a painting of him in church; and whenever he wished to come to her, he would be very welcome, and he would find her all alone in her room, and he could come on the condition that he would not leave her for the Virgin Mary, whom, it was said, he loved very much, and it was obviously true, because everywhere she saw him, he was always on his knees before her;[8] and besides this, she said that he could appear in whatever shape or form he wished—she would not be afraid.

"My Lady," Brother Alberto then said, "you speak wisely, and I shall arrange everything with him as you have said. And you could do me a great favor which will cost you nothing; and the favor is this: that you allow him to come to you in my body. Let me tell you how you would be doing me a favor: he will take my soul from my body and place it in paradise, and he will enter my body, and as long as he is with you my soul will be in paradise."

Then Lady Dimwit replied: "That pleases me; I wish you to have this consolation for the beating he gave you on my account."

Brother Alberto then said: "Now arrange for him to find the door of your house open tonight so that he can come inside; since he will be arriving in the form of a man, he cannot enter unless he uses the door."

The lady replied that it would be done. Brother Alberto departed, and she was so delighted by the whole affair that, jumping for joy, she could hardly keep her skirts over her ass, and it seemed like a thousand years to her waiting for the angel Gabriel to come. Brother Alberto, who was thinking more about getting in the saddle than of being an angel that evening, began to fortify himself with sweetmeats and other delicacies so that he would not be easily thrown from his horse; and then he got permission to stay out that night and, as soon as it was dark, he went with a trusted companion to the house of a lady friend of his, which on other occasions he had used as his point of departure whenever he went to ride the mares; and from there, when the time seemed ripe to him, he went in disguise to the lady's house, and went inside; and, having changed himself into an angel with the different odds and ends he brought with him, he climbed the stairs, and entered the lady's bedroom.

When she saw this white object approaching, she threw herself on her knees in front of him, and the angel blessed her and raised her to her feet, and made a sign for her to get into bed; and she, most anxious to obey, did so immediately, and the angel lay down alongside his devout worshipper. Brother Alberto was a handsome young man with a robust, well-built body;

8. Gabriel told the Virgin Mary that she was to bear the Son of God, and so the two are invariably shown together in paintings of the Annunciation, which Lisetta would often have seen in church.

Lady Lisetta was all fresh and soft, and she discovered that his ride was altogether different from that of her husband. He flew many times that night without his wings, which caused the lady to cry aloud with delight and, in addition, he told her many things about the glory of heaven. Then as day broke, having made another appointment to meet her, he gathered his equipment and returned to his companion, who had struck up a friendly relationship with the good woman of the house so that she would not be afraid of sleeping alone.

When the lady had finished breakfast, she went with one of her attendants to Brother Alberto's and told him the story of the angel Gabriel and of what she had heard from him about the glory of the eternal life and of how he looked, adding all sorts of incredible tales to her story. To this Brother Alberto said:

"My lady, I do not know how you were with him; I only know that last night, when he came to me and I delivered your message to him, in an instant he transported my soul to a place where there were more flowers and roses than I have ever seen before, and he left my soul in this most delightful spot until this morning at the hour of early prayer. What happened to my body I know not."

"But did I not tell you?" replied the lady. "Your body passed the entire night in my arms with the angel Gabriel inside it; and if you do not believe me, look under your left nipple, where I gave the angel such a passionate kiss that he will carry its mark for some days!"

Then Brother Alberto said: "Today I shall perform an act that I have not done for some time—I shall undress myself to see if what you say is true."

And after much more chatter, the lady returned home; and Brother Alberto, without the slightest problem, often went to visit her, disguised as an angel. One day, however, Madonna Lisetta was discussing the nature of beauty with one of her neighbors, and she, showing off and being the silly goose she was, said: "You would not talk about any other women if you knew who it is that loves my beauty."

Her neighbor, anxious to hear more about this and knowing very well the kind of woman Lisetta was, replied: "Madame, you may be right; but as I do not know to whom you are referring, I cannot change my opinion so easily."

"Neighbor," replied Madonna Lisetta, who was easily excited, "he does not want it to be known, but my lover is the angel Gabriel, and he loves me more than himself, and he tells me that this is because I am the most beautiful woman that there is in the world or even in the Maremma."[9]

Her neighbor had the urge to break into laughter right then, but she held herself back in order to make her friend continue talking, and she said: "God's faith, Madame, if the angel Gabriel is your lover and he tells you this, it must really be so; but I did not realize that angels did such things."

"Neighbor," replied the lady, "that is where you are wrong; by God's

9. A small, marshy region of Tuscany.

wounds, he does it better than my husband, and he tells me that they do it up there as well; but since he thinks I am more beautiful than anyone in heaven, he fell in love with me and comes to be with me very often. Now do you see?"

When the neighbor had left Madonna Lisetta, it seemed to her as if a thousand years had passed before she was able to repeat what she had learned; and at a large gathering of women, she told them the whole story. These women told it to their husbands and to other women, who passed it on to others, and thus in less than two days it was the talk of all Venice. But among those whom this story reached were also the woman's in-laws, and they decided, without telling her a word, to find this angel and to see if he knew how to fly; and they kept watch for him for several nights. It just happened that some hint of this got back to Brother Alberto, so he went there one night to reprove the lady, and no sooner was he undressed than her in-laws, who had seen him arrive, were at the door of the bedroom ready to open it. When Brother Alberto heard this and realized what was going on, he jumped up, and seeing no other means of escape, he flung open a window which looked out on the Grand Canal and threw himself into the water.

The water was deep there, but he knew how to swim well, and so he did not hurt himself; after he swam to the other side of the canal, he immediately entered a home that was opened to him and begged the good man inside, for the love of God, to save his life, as he made up a story to explain why he was there at that hour and in the nude. The good man, moved to pity, gave him his own bed, since he had some affairs of his own to attend to, and he told him to remain there until he returned; and having locked him in, he went about his business.

When the lady's in-laws opened the door to her bedroom and entered, they found that the angel Gabriel had flown away, leaving his wings behind him; they abused the lady no end and finally, leaving her alone, all distressed, they returned to their home with the angel's equipment. In the meanwhile, at daybreak, while the good man was on the Rialto, he heard talk about how the angel Gabriel had gone to bed that night with Madonna Lisetta and had been discovered there by her in-laws, and how he had thrown himself into the canal out of fear, and how no one knew what had happened to him; immediately he realized that the man in his house was the man in question. Returning home and identifying him, after much discussion, he came to an agreement with the friar: he would not give him over to the in-laws if he would pay him fifty ducats; and this was done.

When Brother Alberto wished to leave the place, the good man told him:

"There is only one way out, if you agree to it. Today we are celebrating a festival in which men are led around dressed as bears, others dressed as wild men, and others in one costume or another, and a hunt is put on in St. Mark's Square, and with that the festival is ended; then everyone goes away, with whomever he led there, to wherever they please; and if you wish, so that no one will discover you, I am willing to lead you to wherever you like; otherwise, I don't see any way for you to escape from here without being recognized; and the in-laws of the lady, knowing that you have hidden yourself somewhere around here, have posted guards everywhere to trap you."

Though it seemed rough to Brother Alberto to have to go in such a disguise, his fear of the lady's relatives induced him to agree, and he told the man where he would like to go and that in whatever way he might choose to lead him there, he would be happy. The man smeared him completely with honey, covered him up with feathers, put a chain around his neck and a mask on his head; in one of his hands he put a large club and in the other two great dogs which he had brought from the butcher; at the same time he sent someone to the Rialto to announce that whoever wished to see the angel Gabriel should go to St. Mark's Square. And this is what they call good old Venetian honesty!

And when this was done, he took the friar outside and had him take the lead, holding him by a chain from behind; and many bystanders kept asking: "Who is it? What is it?" Thus he led him up to the piazza where, between those who had followed him and those who had heard the announcement and had come from the Rialto, a huge crowd gathered. When he arrived there, he tied his wild man up to a column in a conspicuous and elevated spot, pretending to wait for the hunt; meanwhile, the flies and horseflies were giving Brother Alberto a great deal of trouble, for he was covered with honey. But when the good man saw that the piazza was full, pretending to unchain his wild man, he tore the mask from his face and announced:

"Ladies and gentlemen, since the pig has not come to the hunt, and since there is no hunt, I would not want you to have come in vain; therefore I should like you to see the angel Gabriel, who descends from heaven to earth to console the Venetian women by night."

When his mask was removed, Brother Alberto was instantly recognized by everybody, and everyone cried out against him and shouted the most insulting words that were ever directed at a scoundrel; besides this, one by one they all started throwing garbage in his face, keeping him occupied this way for a long time until, by chance, the news reached his brother friars; six of them came, and throwing a cloak over him, they unchained him, and in the midst of a great commotion, they led him back to their monastery, where he was locked up, and after a miserable life he is believed to have died there.

Thus a man who was thought to be good and who acted evilly, not recognized for what he really was, dared to turn himself into the angel Gabriel, and instead was converted into a wild man, and, finally, was cursed at as he deserved and made to lament in vain for the sins he had committed. May it please God that the same thing happen to all others like him!

*   *   *

There was once in Florence a young man named Federigo, the son of Messer Filippo Alberighi, renowned above all other men in Tuscany for his prowess in arms and for his courtliness. As often happens to most gentlemen, he fell in love with a lady named Monna Giovanna, in her day considered to be one of the most beautiful and one of the most charming women that ever there was in Florence; and in order to win her love, he participated in jousts and tournaments, organized and gave feasts, and spent his money without restraint; but she, no less virtuous than beautiful, cared little for these things done on her behalf, nor did she care for him who did them. Now, as Federigo was spending far beyond his means and was taking nothing in, as easily happens he lost his wealth and became poor, with nothing but his little farm to his name (from whose revenues he lived very meagerly) and one falcon which was among the best in the world.

More in love than ever, but knowing that he would never be able to live the way he wished to in the city, he went to live at Campi, where his farm was. There he passed his time hawking whenever he could, asked nothing of anyone, and endured his poverty patiently. Now, during the time that Federigo was reduced to dire need, it happened that the husband of Monna Giovanna fell ill, and realizing death was near, he made his last will: he was very rich, and he made his son, who was growing up, his heir, and, since he had loved Monna Giovanna very much, he made her his heir should his son die without a legitimate heir; and then he died.

Monna Giovanna was now a widow, and as is the custom among our women, she went to the country with her son to spend a year on one of her possessions very close by to Federigo's farm, and it happened that this young boy became friends with Federigo and began to enjoy birds and hunting dogs; and after he had seen Federigo's falcon fly many times, it pleased him so much that he very much wished it were his own, but he did not dare to ask for it, for he could see how dear it was to Federigo. And during this time, it happened that the young boy took ill, and his mother was much grieved, for he was her only child and she loved him enormously; she would spend the entire day by his side, never ceasing to comfort him, and often asking him if there was anything he desired, begging him to tell her what it might be, for if it were possible to obtain it, she would certainly do everything possible to get it. After the young boy had heard her make this offer many times, he said:

"Mother, if you can arrange for me to have Federigo's falcon, I think I would be well very soon."

When the lady heard this, she was taken aback for a moment, and she began to think what she should do. She knew that Federigo had loved her for a long while, in spite of the fact that he never received a single glance from her, and so, she said to herself:

1. Told by Dioneo. On the fifth day, in Fiammetta's reign, the friends were to tell love stories which end happily after a period of misfortune.

"How can I send or go and ask for this falcon of his which is, as I have heard tell, the best that ever flew, and besides this, his only means of support? And how can I be so insensitive as to wish to take away from this gentleman the only pleasure which is left to him?"

And involved in these thoughts, knowing that she was certain to have the bird if she asked for it, but not knowing what to say to her son, she stood there without answering him. Finally the love she bore her son persuaded her that she should make him happy, and no matter what the consequences might be, she would not send for the bird, but rather go herself for it and bring it back to him; so she answered her son:

"My son, take comfort and think only of getting well, for I promise you that the first thing I shall do tomorrow morning is to go for it and bring it back to you."

The child was so happy that he showed some improvement that very day. The following morning, the lady, accompanied by another woman, as if going for a stroll, went to Federigo's modest house and asked for him. Since it was not the season for it, Federigo had not been hawking for some days and was in his orchard, attending to certain tasks; when he heard that Monna Giovanna was asking for him at the door, he was very surprised and happy to run there; as she saw him coming, she greeted him with feminine charm, and once Federigo had welcomed her courteously, she said:

"Greetings, Federigo!" Then she continued: "I have come to compensate you for the harm you have suffered on my account by loving me more than you needed to; and the compensation is this: I, along with this companion of mine, intend to dine with you—a simple meal—this very day."

To this Federigo humbly replied: "Madonna, I never remember having suffered any harm because of you; on the contrary: so much good have I received from you that if ever I have been worth anything, it has been because of your merit and the love I bore for you; and your generous visit is certainly so dear to me that I would spend all over again that which I spent in the past; but you have come to a poor host."

And having said this, he received her into his home humbly, and from there he led her into his garden, and since he had no one there to keep her company, he said:

"My lady, since there is no one else, this good woman here, the wife of this workman, will keep you company while I go to set the table."

Though he was very poor, Federigo, until now, had never before realized to what extent he had wasted his wealth; but this morning, the fact that he found nothing with which he could honor the lady for the love of whom he had once entertained countless men in the past gave him cause to reflect: in great anguish, he cursed himself and his fortune and, like a man beside himself, he started running here and there, but could find neither money nor a pawnable object. The hour was late and his desire to honor the gracious lady was great, but not wishing to turn for help to others (not even to his own workman), he set his eyes upon his good falcon, perched in a small room; and since he had nowhere else to turn, he took the bird, and finding it plump, he decided that it would be a worthy food for such a lady. So, without further thought, he wrung its neck and quickly gave it to his servant girl to pluck, prepare, and place on a spit to be roasted with care; and when he had set the table with the whitest of tablecloths (a few of which he still had left), he returned, with a cheerful face, to the lady in his garden, saying that the meal he was able to prepare for her was ready.

The lady and her companion rose, went to the table together with Federigo, who waited upon them with the greatest devotion, and they ate the good falcon without knowing what it was they were eating. And having left the table and spent some time in pleasant conversation, the lady thought it time now to say what she had come to say, and so she spoke these kind words to Federigo:

"Federigo, if you recall your past life and my virtue, which you perhaps mistook for harshness and cruelty, I do not doubt at all that you will be amazed by my presumption when you hear what my main reason for coming here is; but if you had children, through whom you might have experienced the power of parental love, it seems certain to me that you would, at least in part, forgive me. But, just as you have no child, I do have one, and I cannot escape the common laws of other mothers; the force of such laws compels me to follow them, against my own will and against good manners and duty, and to ask of you a gift which I know is most precious to you; and it is naturally so, since your extreme condition has left you no other delight, no other pleasure, no other consolation; and this gift is your falcon, which my son is so taken by that if I do not bring it to him, I fear his sickness will grow so much worse that I may lose him. And therefore I beg you, not because of the love that you bear for me, which does not oblige you in the least, but because of your own nobility, which you have shown to be greater than that of all others in practicing courtliness, that you be pleased to give it to me, so that I may say that I have saved the life of my son by means of this gift, and because of it I have placed him in your debt forever."

When he heard what the lady requested and knew that he could not oblige her since he had given her the falcon to eat, Federigo began to weep in her presence, for he could not utter a word in reply. The lady, at first, thought his tears were caused more by the sorrow of having to part with the good falcon than by anything else, and she was on the verge of telling him she no longer wished it, but she held back and waited for Federigo's reply after he stopped weeping. And he said:

"My lady, ever since it pleased God for me to place my love in you, I have felt that Fortune has been hostile to me in many things, and I have complained of her, but all this is nothing compared to what she has just done to me, and I must never be at peace with her again, thinking about how you have come here to my poor home where, while it was rich, you never deigned to come, and you requested a small gift, and Fortune worked to make it impossible for me to give it to you; and why this is so I shall tell you briefly. When I heard that you, out of your kindness, wished to dine with me, I considered it fitting and right, taking into account your excellence and your worthiness, that I should honor you, according to my possibilities, with a more precious food than that which I usually serve to other people; therefore, remembering the falcon that you requested and its value, I judged it a food worthy of you, and this very day you had it roasted and served to you as best I could; but seeing now that you desired it in another way, my sorrow in not being able to serve you is so great that I shall never be able to console myself again."

And after he had said this, he laid the feathers, the feet, and the beak of the bird before her as proof. When the lady heard and saw this, she first reproached him for having killed such a falcon to serve as a meal to a woman; but then to herself she commended the greatness of his spirit, which no poverty was able or would be able to diminish; then, having lost all hope of getting the falcon and, perhaps because of this, of improving the health of her son as well, she thanked Federigo both for the honor paid to her and for his good will, and she left in grief, and returned to her son. To his mother's extreme sorrow, either because of his disappointment that he could not have the falcon, or because his illness must have necessarily led to it, the boy passed from this life only a few days later.

After the period of her mourning and bitterness had passed, the lady was repeatedly urged by her brothers to remarry, since she was very rich and was still young; and although she did not wish to do so, they became so insistent that she remembered the merits of Federigo and his last act of generosity—that is, to have killed such a falcon to do her honor—and she said to her brothers:

"I would prefer to remain a widow, if that would please you; but if you wish me to take a husband, you may rest assured that I shall take no man but Federigo degli Alberighi."

In answer to this, making fun of her, her brothers replied:

"You foolish woman, what are you saying? How can you want him; he hasn't a penny to his name?"

To this she replied: "My brothers, I am well aware of what you say, but I would rather have a man who needs money than money that needs a man."

Her brothers, seeing that she was determined and knowing Federigo to be of noble birth, no matter how poor he was, accepted her wishes and gave her in marriage to him with all her riches; when he found himself the husband of such a great lady, whom he had loved so much and who was so wealthy besides, he managed his financial affairs with more prudence than in the past and lived with her happily the rest of his days.

*   *   *

SIR GAWAIN AND THE GREEN KNIGHT

Sir Gawain and the Green Knight is the best English example of the Medieval romance, a narrative poem presenting, usually, knightly adventures and "courtly" love. The adventures typically involve the hero in fighting or jousting with other knights, and often also in encounters with giants or monsters. No medieval reader or listener would be surprised by the frequent occurrence of magical or supernatural elements. *Courtly love* is the modern term for the relationship between men and women usually depicted in medieval romances. Here the woman—or, rather, the lady—is sovereign; the man (the knight—but never her husband) is the humble suppliant or petitioner for her favors. (In this situation, with the woman on a pedestal but effectively immobilized, and the man looking up to her but with both feet firmly on the ground, may be found an early version of a classic sexual stereotype; it is probably more noticeable in this summary than in the poem itself.) The relationship, though usually adulterous, is carried on with careful regard for the conventions and manners of aristocratic ("courtly") society.

The poem's first audience, men and women of the late fourteenth century, might well have recognized both of the main plots of the story, the "Beheading Game" and the "Temptation," which also appear in earlier romances. This would more have pleased than troubled them, as originality *per se* was not so important then as now—indeed, the anonymous poet himself claims only to be repeating the story "As I heard it in hall." But many members of that first audience, as they listened or read, would also have noticed some of the original features of the poem that intrigue us as well.

To begin with, the hero, Gawain, must prove his courage not by fighting or jousting in the usual way but by accepting an exchange of blows that seems almost certain to kill him. Then, at Bercilak's castle, by another inversion, it is the lady who takes the initiative and woos; and the knight, because of his unusual situation, must resist. Thus Gawain, traditionally the model of the knightly warrior and courtly lover, cannot show his prowess in the traditional way. Indeed, he is tested in the most extreme way, for his fears and desires must be dealt with not in action but by strength of spirit alone. He is prevented, moreover, by the overall design of the double plot from knowing what is really going on until the very end of the story.

The structure of the *Gawain* narrative is also far tighter and more symmetrical than that of most romances. The story begins at King Arthur's court during a Christmas holiday and ends, almost exactly a year later, in the same place. At Bercilak's castle, the three days of hunting are matched by the three visits of the lady to Gawain's bedroom; each day follows the same pattern, beginning with the start of a hunt, continuing with a wooing scene, returning to the hunt, and concluding with evening festivities. The hunting and wooing are also bound together by the agreement between Bercilak and Gawain to exchange winnings at the end of each day.

Mood and atmosphere depend in large part on the premise that it is all a Christmas *game* (a word that recurs often in the poem). The Green Knight declares that he comes in peace, that he asks not for battle but for sport. But, as all realize, it is a grim and dangerous sport, for the Green Knight is clearly a magical being, and behind his apparently absurd challenge lie two threats: death to anyone who accepts it, disgrace to anyone who does not. Gawain's devotion to King Arthur and to the honor of the court compel him to offer himself for the deadly game, and later his high sense of personal obligation leads him to journey through many perils to find the Green Knight and receive the return stroke of the axe. His faithfulness to his word, his honor, are also at stake in the exchange of gifts at Bercilak's castle. A story that began as a Christmas entertainment has become a series of tests of knightly and Christian virtues.

Keeping to the spirit of the game, we might better appreciate the skill of the author if we try to answer some questions about the poem. What is the significance of the many parallels in it? For example, is there any broad similarity between Bercilak's third hunt—of the fox—and the lady's third visit to Gawain? Turning to the conclusion of the poem, what *is* Gawain's fault? Of what does he accuse himself in the final talk with Bercilak? Why are his chagrin and self-disgust so intense? What is Bercilak's view of the matter? Does the poet agree with Gawain or with Bercilak, or can their attitudes be reconciled?

A word about the language of the poem and our Modern English version of it: it was originally written by a contemporary of Chaucer but in a very different dialect than his, that of the English Midlands near the site of modern Birmingham. Further, except at the end of each stanza, the form depends not on rhyme but on the older device of alliteration: two or more words of every line begin with the same sound. The translation reproduces this pattern with great skill and fidelity. One result of this is the occasional use of unusual words or of ordinary words in slightly unaccustomed senses; some of these have been glossed, while the meanings of others may be surmised from the context or, if necessary, found in a dictionary.

The standard edition of the original poem (in Middle English) is by J. R. R. Tolkien and E. V. Gordon, revised by Norman Davis (1967). A few of the recent interpretations are M. Boroff, *Sir Gawain and the Green Knight, A Stylistic and Metrical Study* (1962); Larry D. Benson, *Art and Tradition in Sir Gawain and the Green Knight* (1965); and J. A. Burrow, *A Reading of Sir Gawain and the Green Knight* (1965). Donald R. Howard and Christian K. Zacher, editors, *Critical Studies of Sir Gawain and the Green Knight* (1968), is an excellent collection.

Sir Gawain and the Green Knight[1]

Part I

Since the siege and the assault was ceased at Troy,
The walls breached and burnt down to brands and ashes,
The knight that had knotted the nets of deceit
Was impeached for his perfidy,[2] proven most true,
It was high-born Aeneas and his haughty race   5
That since prevailed over provinces, and proudly reigned
Over well-nigh all the wealth of the West Isles.[3]
Great Romulus[4] to Rome repairs in haste;
With boast and with bravery builds he that city

---

1. Translated by Marie Borroff. Many of the notes are by E. Talbot Donaldson.   2. The treacherous knight is either Aeneas himself or Antenor, both of whom were, according to medieval tradition, traitors to their city Troy; but Aeneas was actually tried ("impeached") by the Greeks for his refusal to hand over to them his sister Polyxena.   3. Perhaps western Europe.   4. The legendary founder of Rome is here given Trojan ancestry, like Aeneas.

And names it with his own name, that it now bears.   10
Ticius to Tuscany,[5] and towers raises,
Langobard[6] in Lombardy lays out homes,
And far over the French Sea,[7] Felix Brutus
On many broad hills and high Britain he sets,[8]
> most fair.   15
> Where war and wrack and wonder
> By shifts have sojourned there,
> And bliss by turns with blunder
> In that land's lot had share.

And since this Britain was built by this baron great,   20
Bold boys bred there, in broils delighting,
That did in their day many a deed most dire.
More marvels have happened in this merry land
Than in any other I know, since that olden time,
But of those that here built, of British kings,   25
King Arthur was counted most courteous of all,
Wherefore an adventure I aim to unfold,
That a marvel of might some men think it,
And one unmatched among Arthur's wonders.
If you will listen to my lay but a little while,   30
As I heard it in hall, I shall hasten to tell
> anew,
> As it was fashioned featly
> In tale of derring-do,
> And linked in measures meetly[9]   35
> By letters tried and true.

This king lay at Camelot[1] at Christmastide;
Many good knights and gay his guests were there,
Arrayed of the Round Table rightful brothers,[2]
With feasting and fellowship and carefree mirth.   40
There true men contended in tournaments many,
Joined there in jousting these gentle knights,
Then came to the court for carol-dancing,
For the feast was in force full fifteen days,
With all the meat and the mirth that men could devise,   45
Such gaiety and glee, glorious to hear,
Brave din by day, dancing by night.
High were their hearts in halls and chambers,
These lords and these ladies, for life was sweet.

5. A region north of Rome; modern Florence is located in it. *Ticius*: Not otherwise known.   6. The reputed founder of Lombardy, a region in the north centered on modern Milan.   7. The North Sea, including the English Channel. *Felix Brutus*: Great-grandson of Aeneas and legendary founder of Britain; not elsewhere given the name Felix (Latin "happy").   8. Establishes.   9. Suitably.   1. Capital of Arthur's kingdom, presumably located in southwest England or southern Wales.   2. According to legend, the Round Table was made by Merlin, the wise magician who had helped Arthur become King, after a dispute broke out among Arthur's knights about precedence: it seated 100 knights. The table described in the poem is not round.

In peerless pleasures passed they their days,   50
The most noble knights known under Christ,
And the loveliest ladies that lived on earth ever,
And he the comeliest king, that that court holds,
For all this fair folk in their first age
                    were still.   55
          Happiest of mortal kind,
          King noblest famed of will;
          You would now go far to find
          So hardy a host on hill.

While the New Year was new, but yesternight come,   60
This fair folk at feast two-fold was served,
When the king and his company were come in together,
The chanting in chapel achieved and ended.
Clerics and all the court acclaimed the glad season,
Cried Noel anew, good news to men;   65
Then gallants gather gaily, hand-gifts to make,
Called them out clearly, claimed them by hand,
Bickered long and busily about those gifts.
Ladies laughed aloud, though losers they were,
And he that won was not angered, as well you will know.[3]   70
All this mirth they made until meat was served;
When they had washed them worthily, they went to their seats,
The best seated above, as best it beseemed,
Guenevere the goodly queen gay in the midst
On a dais well-decked and duly arrayed   75
With costly silk curtains, a canopy over,
Of Toulouse and Turkestan tapestries rich,
All broidered and bordered with the best gems
Ever brought into Britain, with bright pennies
                  to pay.   80
          Fair queen, without a flaw,
          She glanced with eyes of grey.
          A seemlier[4] that once he saw,
          In truth, no man could say.

But Arthur would not eat till all were served;   85
So light was his lordly heart, and a little boyish;
His life he liked lively—the less he cared
To be lying for long, or long to sit,
So busy his young blood, his brain so wild.
And also a point of pride pricked him in heart,   90
For he nobly had willed, he would never eat
On so high a holiday, till he had heard first
Of some fair feat or fray, some far-borne tale,

3. The dispensing of New Year's gifts seems to have involved kissing.   4. More suitable and pleasing
(queen).

Of some marvel of might, that he might trust,
By champions of chivalry achieved in arms,   95
Or some suppliant came seeking some single knight
To join with him in jousting, in jeopardy each
To lay life for life, and leave it to fortune
To afford him on field fair hap[5] or other.
Such is the king's custom, when his court he holds   100
At each far-famed feast amid his fair host
                    so dear.
            The stout king stands in state
            Till a wonder shall appear;
            He leads, with heart elate,   105
            High mirth in the New Year.

So he stands there in state, the stout young king,
Talking before the high table[6] of trifles fair.
There Gawain the good knight by Guenevere sits,
With Agravain à la dure main[7] on her other side,   110
Both knights of renown, and nephews of the king.
Bishop Baldwin above begins the table,
And Yvain, son of Urien, ate with him there.
These few with the fair queen were fittingly served;
At the side-tables sat many stalwart knights.   115
Then the first course comes, with clamor of trumpets
That were bravely bedecked with bannerets bright,
With noise of new drums and the noble pipes.
Wild were the warbles that wakened that day
In strains that stirred many strong men's hearts.   120
There dainties were dealt out, dishes rare,
Choice fare to choose, on chargers so many
That scarce was there space to set before the people
The service of silver, with sundry meats,
                    on cloth.   125
            Each fair guest freely there
            Partakes, and nothing loth;[8]
            Twelve dishes before each pair;
            Good beer and bright wine both.

Of the service itself I need say no more,   130
For well you will know no tittle was wanting.
Another noise and a new was well-nigh at hand,
That the lord might have leave his life to nourish;
For scarce were the sweet strains still in the hall,
And the first course come to that company fair,   135
There hurtles in at the hall-door an unknown rider,
One the greatest on ground in growth of his frame:

5. Good luck.   6. The high table is on a dais; the side tables (l. 115) are on the main floor and run
along the walls at a right angle to the high table.   7. Of the hard hand.   8. Not unwillingly.

From broad neck to buttocks so bulky and thick,
And his loins and his legs so long and so great,
Half a giant on earth I hold him to be,   140
But believe him no less than the largest of men,
And that the seemliest in his stature to see, as he rides,
For in back and in breast though his body was grim,
His waist in its width was worthily small,
And formed with every feature in fair accord   145
                              was he.
              Great wonder grew in hall
              At his hue most strange to see,
              For man and gear and all
              Were green as green could be.   150

And in guise all of green, the gear and the man:
A coat cut close, that clung to his sides,
And a mantle to match, made with a lining
Of furs cut and fitted—the fabric was noble,
Embellished all with ermine, and his hood beside,   155
That was loosed from his locks, and laid on his shoulders.
With trim hose and tight, the same tint of green,
His great calves were girt, and gold spurs under
He bore on silk bands that embellished his heels,
And footgear well-fashioned, for riding most fit.   160
And all his vesture verily was verdant green;
Both the bosses[9] on his belt and other bright gems
That were richly ranged on his raiment noble
About himself and his saddle, set upon silk,
That to tell half the trifles would tax my wits,   165
The butterflies and birds embroidered thereon
In green of the gayest, with many a gold thread.
The pendants of the breast-band, the princely crupper,[1]
And the bars of the bit were brightly enameled;
The stout stirrups were green, that steadied his feet,   170
And the bows of the saddle and the side-panels both,
That gleamed all and glinted with green gems about.
The steed he bestrides of that same green
                              so bright.
              A green horse great and thick;   175
              A headstrong steed of might;
              In broidered bridle quick,
              Mount matched man aright.

Gay was this goodly man in guise all of green,
And the hair of his head to his horse suited;   180
Fair flowing tresses enfold his shoulders;

9. Ornamental knobs.   1. *Breast-band . . . crupper*: Parts of the horse's harness.

A beard big as a bush on his breast hangs,
That with his heavy hair, that from his head falls,
Was evened all about above both his elbows,
That half his arms thereunder were hid in the fashion   185
Of a king's cap-à-dos,[2] that covers his throat.
The mane of that mighty horse much to it like,
Well curled and becombed, and cunningly knotted
With filaments of fine gold amid the fair green,
Here a strand of the hair, here one of gold;   190
His tail and his foretop twin in their hue,
And bound both with a band of a bright green
That was decked adown the dock[3] with dazzling stones
And tied tight at the top with a triple knot
Where many bells well burnished rang bright and clear.   195
Such a mount in his might, nor man on him riding,
None had seen, I dare swear, with sight in that hall
             so grand.
        As lightning quick and light
        He looked to all at hand;   200
        It seemed that no man might
        His deadly dints withstand.

Yet had he no helm, nor hauberk[4] neither,
Nor plate, nor appurtenance appending to arms,
Nor shaft pointed sharp, nor shield for defense,   205
But in his one hand he had a holly bob
That is goodliest in green when groves are bare,
And an ax in his other, a huge and immense,
A wicked piece of work in words to expound:
The head on its haft was an ell[5] long;   210
The spike of green steel, resplendent with gold;
The blade burnished bright, with a broad edge,
As well shaped to shear as a sharp razor;
Stout was the stave in the strong man's gripe,
That was wound all with iron to the weapon's end,   215
With engravings in green of goodliest work.
A lace lightly about, that led to a knot,
Was looped in by lengths along the fair haft,
And tassels thereto attached in a row,
With buttons of bright green, brave to behold.   220
This horseman hurtles in, and the hall enters;
Riding to the high dais, recked he no danger;
Not a greeting he gave as the guests he o'erlooked,
Nor wasted his words, but "Where is," he said,

2. Or *capados*, interpreted by the translator as a garment covering its wearer "from head to back."
3. The solid part of the tail.   4. Tunic of chain mail.   5. Three or four feet long.

"The captain of this crowd? Keenly I wish   225
To see that sire with sight, and to himself say
                    my say."
              He swaggered all about
              To scan the host so gay;
              He halted, as if in doubt   230
              Who in that hall held sway.

There were stares on all sides as the stranger spoke,
For much did they marvel what it might mean
That a horseman and a horse should have such a hue,
Grow green as the grass, and greener, it seemed,   235
Than green fused on gold more glorious by far.
All the onlookers eyed him, and edged nearer,
And awaited in wonder what he would do,
For many sights had they seen, but such a one never,
So that phantom and faerie the folk there deemed it,   240
Therefore chary of answer was many a champion bold,
And stunned at his strong words stone-still they sat
In a swooning silence in the stately hall.
As all were slipped into sleep, so slackened their speech
                    apace   245
              Not all, I think, for dread,
              But some of courteous grace
              Let him who was their head
              Be spokesman in that place.

Then Arthur before the high dais that entrance beholds,   250
And hailed him, as behooved, for he had no fear,
And said "Fellow, in faith you have found fair welcome;
The head of this hostelry Arthur am I;
Leap lightly down, and linger, I pray,
And the tale of your intent you shall tell us after."   255
"Nay, so help me," said the other, "He that on high sits,
To tarry here any time, 'twas not mine errand;
But as the praise of you, prince, is puffed up so high,
And your court and your company are counted the best,
Stoutest under steel-gear on steeds to ride,   260
Worthiest of their works the wide world over,
And peerless to prove in passages of arms,
And courtesy here is carried to its height,
And so at this season I have sought you out.
You may be certain by the branch that I bear in hand   265
That I pass here in peace, and would part friends,
For had I come to this court on combat bent,
I have a hauberk at home, and a helm beside,
A shield and a sharp spear, shining bright,

And other weapons to wield, I ween[6] well, to boot,   270
But as I willed no war, I wore no metal.
But if you be so bold as all men believe,
You will graciously grant the game that I ask
by right."
Arthur answer gave   275
And said, "Sir courteous knight,
If contest here you crave,
You shall not fail to fight."

"Nay, to fight, in good faith, is far from my thought;
There are about on these benches but beardless children,   280
Were I here in full arms on a haughty steed,
For measured against mine, their might is puny.
And so I call in this court for a Christmas game,
For 'tis Yule and New Year, and many young bloods about;
If any in this house such hardihood claims,   285
Be so bold in his blood, his brain so wild,
As stoutly to strike one stroke for another,
I shall give him as my gift this gisarme[7] noble,
This ax, that is heavy enough, to handle as he likes,
And I shall bide[8] the first blow, as bare as I sit.   290
If there be one so wilful my words to assay,
Let him leap hither lightly, lay hold of this weapon;
I quitclaim it forever, keep it[9] as his own,
And I shall stand him a stroke, steady on this floor,
So you grant me the guerdon[1] to give him another,   295
sans[2] blame.
In a twelvemonth and a day
He shall have of me the same;
Now be it seen straightway
Who dares take up the game."   300

If he astonished them at first, stiller were then
All that household in hall, the high and the low;
The stranger on his green steed stirred in the saddle,
And roisterously his red eyes he rolled all about,
Bent his bristling brows, that were bright green,   305
Wagged his beard as he watched who would arise.
When the court kept its counsel he coughed aloud,
And cleared his throat coolly, the clearer to speak:
"What, is this Arthur's house," said that horseman then,
"Whose fame is so fair in far realms and wide?   310
Where is now your arrogance and your awesome deeds,
Your valor and your victories and your vaunting words?
Now are the revel and renown of the Round Table

6. Believe.   7. Weapon.   8. Endure.   9. I.e., let him keep it.   1. Reward.   2. Without.

Overwhelmed with a word of one man's speech,
For all cower and quake, and no cut felt!"   315
With this he laughs so loud that the lord grieved;
The blood for sheer shame shot to his face,
                                       and pride.
              With rage his face flushed red,
              And so did all beside.   320
              Then the king as bold man bred
              Toward the stranger took a stride.

And said "Sir, now we see you will say but folly,
Which whoso has sought, it suits that he find.
No guest here is aghast of your great words.   325
Give to me your gisarme, in God's own name,
And the boon you have begged shall straight be granted."
He leaps to him lightly, lays hold of his weapon;
The green fellow on foot fiercely alights.
Now has Arthur his ax, and the haft grips,   330
And sternly stirs it about, on striking bent.
The stranger before him stood there erect,
Higher than any in the house by a head and more;
With stern look as he stood, he stroked his beard,
And with undaunted countenance drew down his coat,   335
No more moved nor dismayed for his mighty dints
Than any bold man on bench had brought him a drink
                                       of wine.
              Gawain by Guenevere
              Toward the king doth now incline: 340
              "I beseech, before all here,
              That this melee may be mine."

"Would you grant me the grace," said Gawain to the king,
"To be gone from this bench and stand by you there,
If I without discourtesy might quit this board,   345
And if my liege lady[3] misliked it not,
I would come to your counsel before your court noble.
For I find it not fit, as in faith it is known,
When such a boon is begged before all these knights,
Though you be tempted thereto, to take it on yourself   350
While so bold men about upon benches sit,
That no host under heaven is hardier of will,
Nor better brothers-in-arms where battle is joined;
I am the weakest, well I know, and of wit feeblest;
And the loss of my life would be least of any;   355
That I have you for uncle is my only praise;
My body, but for your blood, is barren of worth;

3. Lady entitled to the knight's feudal service.

And for that this folly befits not a king,
And 'tis I that have asked it, it ought to be mine,
And if my claim be not comely let all this court judge,   360
       in sight."
       The court assays the claim,
       And in counsel all unite
       To give Gawain the game
       And release the king outright.   365

Then the king called the knight to come to his side,
And he rose up readily, and reached him with speed,
Bows low to his lord, lays hold of the weapon,
And he releases it lightly, and lifts up his hand,
And gives him God's blessing, and graciously prays   370
That his heart and his hand may be hardy both.
"Keep, cousin," said the king, "what you cut with this day,
And if you rule it aright, then readily, I know,
You shall stand the stroke it will strike after."
Gawain goes to the guest with gisarme in hand,   375
And boldly he bides there, abashed not a whit.
Then hails he Sir Gawain, the horseman in green:
"Recount we our contract, ere you come further.
First I ask and adjure you, how you are called
That you tell me true, so that trust it I may."   380
"In good faith," said the good knight, "Gawain am I
Whose buffet befalls you, whate'er betide after,
And at this time twelvemonth take from you another
With what weapon you will, and with no man else
       alive."   385
       The other nods assent:
       "Sir Gawain, as I may thrive,
       I am wondrous well content
       That you this dint shall drive."

"Sir Gawain," said the Green Knight, "By God, I rejoice   390
That your fist shall fetch this favor I seek,
And you have readily rehearsed, and in right terms,
Each clause of my covenant with the king your lord,
Save that you shall assure me, sir, upon oath,
That you shall seek me yourself, wheresoever you deem   395
My lodgings may lie, and look for such wages
As you have offered me here before all this host."
"What is the way there?" said Gawain, "Where do you dwell?
I heard never of your house, by Him that made me,
Nor I know you not, knight, your name nor your court.   400
But tell me truly thereof, and teach me your name,
And I shall fare forth to find you, so far as I may,
And this I say in good certain, and swear upon oath."

"That is enough in New Year, you need say no more,"
Said the knight in the green to Gawain the noble,   405
"If I tell you true, when I have taken your knock,
And if you handily have hit, you shall hear straightway
Of my house and my home and my own name;
Then follow in my footsteps by faithful accord.
And if I spend no speech, you shall speed the better: 410
You can feast with your friends, nor further trace
                my tracks.
       Now hold your grim tool steady
       And show us how it hacks."
       "Gladly, sir; all ready,"   415
       Says Gawain; he strokes the ax.

The Green Knight upon ground girds him with care:
Bows a bit with his head, and bares his flesh:
His long lovely locks he laid over his crown,
Let the naked nape for the need be shown.   420
Gawain grips to his ax and gathers it aloft—
The left foot on the floor before him he set—
Brought it down deftly upon the bare neck,
That the shock of the sharp blow shivered the bones
And cut the flesh cleanly and clove it in twain,   425
That the blade of bright steel bit into the ground.
The head was hewn off and fell to the floor;
Many found it at their feet, as forth it rolled;
The blood gushed from the body, bright on the green,
Yet fell not the fellow, nor faltered a whit,   430
But stoutly he starts forth upon stiff shanks,
And as all stood staring he stretched forth his hand,
Laid hold of his head and heaved it aloft,
Then goes to the green steed, grasps the bridle,
Steps into the stirrup, bestrides his mount,   435
And his head by the hair in his hand holds,
And as steady he sits in the stately saddle
As he had met with no mishap, nor missing were
                his head.
       His bulk about he haled,[4]   440
       That fearsome body that bled;
       There were many in the court that quailed
       Before all his say was said.

For the head in his hand he holds right up;
Toward the first on the dais directs he the face,   445
And it lifted up its lids, and looked with wide eyes,
And said as much with its mouth as now you may hear:

4. Hauled.

"Sir Gawain, forget not to go as agreed,
And cease not to seek till me, sir, you find,
As you promised in the presence of these proud knights.   450
To the Green Chapel come, I charge you, to take
Such a dint as you have dealt—you have well deserved
That your neck should have a knock on New Year's morn.
The Knight of the Green Chapel I am well-known to many,
Wherefore you cannot fail to find me at last;   455
Therefore come, or be counted a recreant[5] knight."
With a roisterous rush he flings round the reins,
Hurtles out at the hall-door, his head in his hand,
That the flint-fire flew from the flashing hooves.
Which way he went, not one of them knew   460
Nor whence he was come in the wide world
　　　　　　so fair.
　　　　The king and Gawain gay
　　　　Make game of the Green Knight there,
　　　　Yet all who saw it say   465
　　　　'Twas a wonder past compare.

Though high-born Arthur at heart had wonder,
He let no sign be seen, but said aloud
To the comely queen, with courteous speech,
"Dear dame, on this day dismay you no whit;   470
Such crafts are becoming at Christmastide,
Laughing at interludes, light songs and mirth,
Amid dancing of damsels with doughty knights.
Nevertheless of my meat now let me partake,
For I have met with a marvel, I may not deny."   475
He glanced at Sir Gawain, and gaily he said,
"Now, sir, hang up your ax, that has hewn enough,"
And over the high dais it was hung on the wall
That men in amazement might on it look,
And tell in true terms the tale of the wonder.   480
Then they turned toward the table, these two together,
The good king and Gawain, and made great feast,
With all dainties double, dishes rare,
With all manner of meat and minstrelsy both,
Such happiness wholly had they that day   485
　　　　　　in hold.
　　　　　Now take care, Sir Gawain,
　　　　　That your courage wax not cold
　　　　　When you must turn again
　　　　　To your enterprise foretold.   490

5. Cowardly.

Part II

This adventure had Arthur of handsels[6] first
When young was the year, for he yearned to hear tales;
Though they wanted for words when they went to sup,
Now are fierce deeds to follow, their fists stuffed full.
Gawain was glad to begin those games in hall,   495
But if the end be harsher, hold it no wonder,
For though men are merry in mind after much drink,
A year passes apace, and proves ever new:
First things and final conform but seldom.
And so this Yule to the young year yielded place,   500
And each season ensued at its set time;
After Christmas there came the cold cheer of Lent,
When with fish and plainer fare our flesh we reprove;
But then the world's weather with winter contends:
The keen cold lessens, the low clouds lift;   505
Fresh falls the rain in fostering showers
On the face of the fields; flowers appear.
The ground and the groves wear gowns of green;
Birds build their nests, and blithely sing
That solace of all sorrow with summer comes   510
            ere long.
        And blossoms day by day
        Bloom rich and rife in throng;
        Then every grove so gay
        Of the greenwood rings with song.   515

And then the season of summer with the soft winds,
When Zephyr sighs low over seeds and shoots;
Glad is the green plant growing abroad,
When the dew at dawn drops from the leaves,
To get a gracious glance from the golden sun.   520
But harvest with harsher winds follows hard after,
Warns him to ripen well ere winter comes;
Drives forth the dust in the droughty season,
From the face of the fields to fly high in air.
Wroth winds in the welkin[7] wrestle with the sun,   525
The leaves launch from the linden and light on the ground,
And the grass turns to gray, that once grew green.
Then all ripens and rots that rose up at first,
And so the year moves on in yesterdays many,
And winter once more, by the world's law,   530
            draws nigh.
        At Michaelmas[8] the moon

6. Gifts to mark the New Year.   7. The heavens.   8. September 29.

Hangs wintry pale in sky;
Sir Gawain girds him soon
For travails yet to try.   535

Till All-Hallows' Day[9] with Arthur he dwells,
And he held a high feast to honor that knight
With great revels and rich, of the Round Table.
Then ladies lovely and lords debonair
With sorrow for Sir Gawain were sore at heart;   540
Yet they covered their care with countenance glad:
Many a mournful man made mirth for his sake.
So after supper soberly he speaks to his uncle
Of the hard hour at hand, and openly says,
"Now, liege lord of my life, my leave I take;   545
The terms of this task too well you know—
To count the cost over concerns me nothing.
But I am bound forth betimes[1] to bear a stroke
From the grim man in green, as God may direct."
Then the first and foremost came forth in throng: 550
Yvain and Eric and others of note,
Sir Dodinal le Sauvage, the Duke of Clarence,
Lionel and Lancelot and Lucan the good,
Sir Bors and Sir Bedivere, big men both,
And many manly knights more, with Mador de la Porte.   555
All this courtly company comes to the king
To counsel their comrade, with care in their hearts;
There was much secret sorrow suffered that day
That one so good as Gawain must go in such wise
To bear a bitter blow, and his bright sword   560
          lay by.
          He said, "Why should I tarry?"
          And smiled with tranquil eye;
          "In destinies sad or merry,
          True men can but try."   565

He dwelt there all that day, and dressed in the morning;
Asked early for his arms, and all were brought.
First a carpet of rare cost was cast on the floor
Where much goodly gear gleamed golden bright;
He takes his place promptly and picks up the steel,   570
Attired in a tight coat of Turkestan silk
And a kingly cap-à-dos, closed at the throat,
That was lavishly lined with a lustrous fur.
Then they set the steel shoes on his sturdy feet
And clad his calves about with comely greaves,   575

9. November 1.   1. Soon.

And plate well-polished protected his knees,
Affixed with fastenings of the finest gold.
Fair cuisses enclosed, that were cunningly wrought,
His thick-thewed thighs, with thongs bound fast,
And massy chain-mail of many a steel ring   580
He bore on his body, above the best cloth,
With brace burnished bright upon both his arms,
Good couters² and gay, and gloves of plate,
And all the goodly gear to grace him well
                          that tide.   585
            His surcoat³ blazoned bold;
            Sharp spurs to prick with pride;
            And a brave silk band to hold
            The broadsword at his side.

When he had on his arms, his harness was rich,   590
The least latchet or loop laden with gold;
So armored as he was, he heard a mass,
Honored God humbly at the high altar.
Then he comes to the king and his comrades-in-arms,
Takes his leave at last of lords and ladies,   595
And they clasped and kissed him, commending him to Christ.
By then Gringolet⁴ was girt with a great saddle
That was gaily agleam with fine gilt fringe,
New-furbished for the need with nail-heads bright;
The bridle and the bars bedecked all with gold;   600
The breast-plate, the saddlebow, the side-panels both,
The caparison and the crupper accorded in hue,
And all ranged on the red the resplendent studs
That glittered and glowed like the glorious sun.
His helm now he holds up and hastily kisses,   605
Well-closed with iron clinches, and cushioned within;
It was high on his head, with a hasp behind,
And a covering of cloth to encase the visor,
All bound and embroidered with the best gems
On broad bands of silk, and bordered with birds,   610
Parrots and popinjays preening their wings,
Lovebirds and love-knots as lavishly wrought
As many women had worked seven winters thereon,
                          entire.
            The diadem costlier yet   615
            That crowned that comely sire,
            With diamonds richly set,
            That flashed as if on fire.

---

2. Armor for the elbows.   3. Cloth tunic worn over the armor.   4. Gawain's horse.

Then they showed forth the shield, that shone all red,
With the pentangle[5] portrayed in purest gold.   620
About his broad neck by the baldric[6] he casts it,
That was meet for the man, and matched him well.
And why the pentangle is proper to that peerless prince
I intend now to tell, though detain me it must.
It is a sign by Solomon sagely devised   625
To be a token of truth, by its title of old,
For it is a figure formed of five points,
And each line is linked and locked with the next
For ever and ever, and hence it is called
In all England, as I hear, the endless knot.   630
And well may he wear it on his worthy arms,
For ever faithful five-fold in five-fold fashion
Was Gawain in good works, as gold unalloyed,
Devoid of all villainy, with virtues adorned
                    in sight.   635
          On shield and coat in view
          He bore that emblem bright,
          As to his word most true
          And in speech most courteous knight.

And first, he was faultless in his five senses,   640
Nor found ever to fail in his five fingers,
And all his fealty was fixed upon the five wounds
That Christ got on the cross, as the creed tells;
And wherever this man in melee took part,
His one thought was of this, past all things else,   645
That all his force was founded on the five joys[7]
That the high Queen of heaven had in her child.
And therefore, as I find, he fittingly had
On the inner part of his shield her image portrayed,
That when his look on it lighted, he never lost heart.   650
The fifth of the five fives followed by this knight
Were beneficence boundless and brotherly love
And pure mind and manners, that none might impeach,
And compassion most precious—these peerless five
Were forged and made fast in him, foremost of men.   655
Now all these five fives were confirmed in this knight,
And each linked in other, that end there was none,
And fixed to five points, whose force never failed,
Nor assembled all on a side, nor asunder either,

5. A five-pointed star, formed by five lines which are drawn without lifting the pen, supposed to have mystical significance; as Solomon's sign (l. 625), it was enclosed in a circle.   6. Belt worn diagonally across the chest.   7. These were the annunciation to Mary that she was to bear the Son of God, Christ's nativity, resurrection, and ascension into heaven, and the "assumption" or bodily taking up of Mary into heaven to join Him.

Nor anywhere at an end, but whole and entire   660
However the pattern proceeded or played out its course.
And so on his shining shield shaped was the knot
Royally in red gold against red gules,[8]
That is the peerless pentangle, prized of old
                      in lore.   665
          Now armed is Gawain gay,
          And bears his lance before,
          And soberly said good day,
          He thought forevermore.

He struck his steed with the spurs and sped on his way   670
So fast that the flint-fire flashed from the stones.
When they saw him set forth they were sore aggrieved,
And all sighed softly, and said to each other,
Fearing for their fellow, "Ill fortune it is
That you, man, must be marred, that most are worthy!   675
His equal on this earth can hardly be found;
To have dealt more discreetly had done less harm,
And have dubbed him a duke, with all due honor.
A great leader of lords he was like to become,
And better so to have been than battered to bits,   680
Beheaded by an elf-man,[9] for empty pride!
Who would credit that a king could be counseled so,
And caught in a cavil in a Christmas game?"
Many were the warm tears they wept from their eyes
When goodly Sir Gawain was gone from the court   685
                    that day.
          No longer he abode,
          But speedily went his way
          Over many a wandering road,
          As I heard my author say.   690

Now he rides in his array through the realm of Logres,[1]
Sir Gawain, God knows, though it gave him small joy!
All alone must he lodge through many a long night
Where the food that he fancied was far from his plate;
He had no mate but his mount, over mountain and plain,   695
Nor man to say his mind to but almighty God,
Till he had wandered well-nigh into North Wales.
All the islands of Anglesey he holds on his left,
And follows, as he fares, the fords by the coast,
Comes over at Holy Head, and enters next   700
The Wilderness of Wirral[2]—few were within

---

8. Background (gules is the heraldic name for red).   9. Supernatural being, in this case obviously not small.   1. Another name for Arthur's kingdom.   2. *North Wales . . . Wirral:* Gawain went from Camelot north to the northern coast of Wales, opposite the islands of Anglesey; there he turned east across the River Dee to the forest of Wirral, near what is now Liverpool.

That had great good will toward God or man.
And earnestly he asked of each mortal he met
If he had ever heard aught of a knight all green,
Or of a Green Chapel, on ground thereabouts,   705
And all said the same, and solemnly swore
They saw no such knight all solely green
                in hue.
        Over country wild and strange
        The knight sets off anew;   710
        Often his course must change
        Ere the Chapel comes in view.

Many a cliff must he climb in country wild;
Far off from all his friends, forlorn must he ride;
At each strand or stream where the stalwart passed   715
'Twere a marvel if he met not some monstrous foe,
And that so fierce and forbidding that fight he must.
So many were the wonders he wandered among
That to tell but the tenth part would tax my wits.
Now with serpents he wars, now with savage wolves,   720
Now with wild men of the woods, that watched from the rocks,
Both with bulls and with bears, and with boars besides,
And giants that came gibbering from the jagged steeps.
Had he not borne himself bravely, and been on God's side,   725
He had met with many mishaps and mortal harms.
And if the wars were unwelcome, the winter was worse,
When the cold clear rains rushed from the clouds
And froze before they could fall to the frosty earth.
Near slain by the sleet he sleeps in his irons
More nights than enough, among naked rocks,   730
Where clattering from the crest the cold stream ran
And hung in hard icicles high overhead.
Thus in peril and pain and predicaments dire
He rides across country till Christmas Eve,
                our knight.   735
        And at that holy tide
        He prays with all his might
        That Mary may be his guide
        Till a dwelling comes in sight.

By a mountain next morning he makes his way   740
Into a forest fastness, fearsome and wild;
High hills on either hand, with hoar woods below,
Oaks old and huge by the hundred together.
The hazel and the hawthorn were all intertwined
With rough raveled moss, that raggedly hung,   745
With many birds unblithe upon bare twigs
That peeped most piteously for pain of the cold.

The good knight on Gringolet glides thereunder
Through many a marsh and mire, a man all alone;
He feared for his default, should he fail to see
The service of that Sire that on that same night   750
Was born of a bright maid, to bring us His peace.
And therefore sighing he said, "I beseech of Thee, Lord,
And Mary, thou mildest mother so dear,
Some harborage where haply I might hear mass   755
And Thy matins tomorrow—meekly I ask it,
And thereto proffer and pray my pater and ave[3]
                         and creed."
              He said his prayer with sighs,
              Lamenting his misdeed;   760
              He crosses himself, and cries
              On Christ in his great need.

No sooner had Sir Gawain signed himself[4] thrice
Than he was ware, in the wood, of a wondrous dwelling,
Within a moat, on a mound, bright amid boughs   765
Of many a tree great of girth that grew by the water—
A castle as comely as a knight could own,
On grounds fair and green, in a goodly park
With a palisade of palings planted about
For two miles and more, round many a fair tree.   770
The stout knight stared at that stronghold great
As it shimmered and shone amid shining leaves,
Then with helmet in hand he offers his thanks
To Jesus and Saint Julian,[5] that are gentle both,
That in courteous accord had inclined to his prayer;   775
"Now fair harbor," said he, "I humbly beseech!"
Then he pricks his proud steed with the plated spurs,
And by chance he has chosen the chief path
That brought the bold knight to the bridge's end
                         in haste.   780
              The bridge hung high in air;
              The gates were bolted fast;
              The walls well-framed to bear
              The fury of the blast.

The man on his mount remained on the bank   785
Of the deep double moat that defended the place.
The wall went in the water wondrous deep,
And a long way aloft it loomed overhead.
It was built of stone blocks to the battlements' height,
With corbels under cornices[6] in comeliest style;   790

---

3. Two prayers, the Pater Noster ("Our Father," the Lord's Prayer) and Ave Maria ("Hail, Mary").
4. Made the sign of the cross over his own chest.   5. Patron saint of hospitality.   6. Ornamental projections supporting the top courses of stone.

Watch-towers trusty protected the gate,
With many a lean loophole, to look from within:
A better-made barbican the knight beheld never.
And behind it there hoved[7] a great hall and fair:
Turrets rising in tiers, with tines at their tops,   795
Spires set beside them, splendidly long,
With finials well-fashioned, as filigree fine.
Chalk-white chimneys over chambers high
Gleamed in gay array upon gables and roofs;
The pinnacles in panoply, pointing in air,   800
So vied there for his view that verily it seemed
A castle cut of paper for a king's feast.
The good knight on Gringolet thought it great luck
If he could but contrive to come there within
To keep the Christmas feast in that castle fair   805
                              and bright.
                    There answered to his call
                    A porter most polite;
                    From his station on the wall
                    He greets the errant knight.   810

"Good sir," said Gawain, "Wouldst go to inquire
If your lord would allow me to lodge here a space?"
"Peter!"[8] said the porter, "For my part, I think
So noble a knight will not want for a welcome!"
Then he bustles off briskly, and comes back straight,   815
And many servants beside, to receive him the better.
They let down the drawbridge and duly went forth
And kneeled down on their knees on the naked earth
To welcome this warrior as best they were able.
They proffered him passage—the portals stood wide—   820
And he beckoned them to rise, and rode over the bridge.
Men steadied his saddle as he stepped to the ground,
And there stabled his steed many stalwart folk.
Now come the knights and the noble squires
To bring him with bliss into the bright hall.   825
When his high helm was off, there hied forth a throng
Of attendants to take it, and see to its care;
They bore away his brand[9] and his blazoned shield;
Then graciously he greeted those gallants each one,
And many a noble drew near, to do the knight honor.   830
All in his armor into hall he was led,
Where fire on a fair hearth fiercely blazed.
And soon the lord himself descends from his chamber
To meet with good manners the man on his floor.
He said, "To this house you are heartily welcome: 835

7. Arose. *Tines:* sharp points.   8. I.e., "By Saint Peter!"   9. Sword.

What is here is wholly yours, to have in your power
                              and sway."
   "Many thanks," said Sir Gawain;
   "May Christ your pains repay!"
   The two embrace amain   840
   As men well met that day.

Gawain gazed on the host that greeted him there,
And a lusty fellow he looked, the lord of that place:
A man of massive mold, and of middle age;
Broad, bright was his beard, of a beaver's hue,   845
Strong, steady his stance, upon stalwart shanks,
His face fierce as fire, fair-spoken withal,
And well-suited he seemed in Sir Gawain's sight
To be a master of men in a mighty keep.
They pass into a parlor, where promptly the host   850
Has a servant assigned him to see to his needs,
And there came upon his call many courteous folk
That brought him to a bower where bedding was noble,
With heavy silk hangings hemmed all in gold,
Coverlets and counterpanes curiously wrought,   855
A canopy over the couch, clad all with fur,
Curtains running on cords, caught to gold rings,
Woven rugs on the walls of eastern work,
And the floor, under foot, well-furnished with the same.
With light talk and laughter they loosed from him then   860
His war-dress of weight and his worthy clothes.
Robes richly wrought they brought him right soon,
To change there in chamber and choose what he would.
When he had found one he fancied, and flung it about,
Well-fashioned for his frame, with flowing skirts,   865
His face fair and fresh as the flowers of spring,
All the good folk agreed, that gazed on him then,
His limbs arrayed royally in radiant hues,
That so comely a mortal never Christ made
                              as he.   870
          Whatever his place of birth,
          It seemed he well might be
          Without a peer on earth
          In martial rivalry.

A couch before the fire, where fresh coals burned,   875
They spread for Sir Gawain splendidly now
With quilts quaintly stitched, and cushions beside,
And then a costly cloak they cast on his shoulders
Of bright silk, embroidered on borders and hems,
With furs of the finest well-furnished within,   880
And bound about with ermine, both mantle and hood;

And he sat at that fireside in sumptuous estate
And warmed himself well, and soon he waxed merry.
Then attendants set a table upon trestles broad,
And lustrous white linen they laid thereupon,   885
A saltcellar of silver, spoons of the same.
He washed himself well and went to his place,
Men set his fare before him in fashion most fit.
There were soups of all sorts, seasoned with skill,
Double-sized servings, and sundry fish,   890
Some baked, some breaded, some broiled on the coals,
Some simmered, some in stews, steaming with spice,
And with sauces to sup that suited his taste.
He confesses it a feast with free words and fair;
They requite him as kindly with courteous jests,   895
               well-sped.
        "Tonight you fast and pray;
        Tomorrow we'll see you fed."
        The knight grows wondrous gay
        As the wine goes to his head.   900

Then at times and by turns, as at table he sat,
They questioned him quietly, with queries discreet,
And he courteously confessed that he comes from the court,
And owns him of the brotherhood of high-famed Arthur,
The right royal ruler of the Round Table,   905
And the guest by their fireside is Gawain himself,
Who has happened on their house at that holy feast.
When the name of the knight was made known to the lord,
Then loudly he laughed, so elated he was,
And the men in that household made haste with joy   910
To appear in his presence promptly that day,
That of courage ever-constant, and customs pure,
Is pattern and paragon, and praised without end:
Of all knights on earth most honored is he.
Each said solemnly aside to his brother,   915
"Now displays of deportment shall dazzle our eyes
And the polished pearls of impeccable speech;
The high art of eloquence is ours to pursue
Since the father of fine manners is found in our midst.
Great is God's grace, and goodly indeed,   920
That a guest such as Gawain he guides to us here
When men sit and sing of their Savior's birth
               in view.
        With command of manners pure
        He shall each heart imbue;   925
        Who shares his converse, sure,
        Shall learn love's language true."

When the knight had done dining and duly arose,
The dark was drawing on; the day nigh ended.
Chaplains in chapels and churches about   930
Rang the bells aright, reminding all men
Of the holy evensong of the high feast.
The lord attends alone; his fair lady sits
In a comely closet, secluded from sight.
Gawain in gay attire goes thither soon;   935
The lord catches his coat, and calls him by name,
And has him sit beside him, and says in good faith
No guest on God's earth would he gladlier greet.
For that Gawain thanked him; the two then embraced
And sat together soberly the service through.   940
Then the lady, that longed to look on the knight,
Came forth from her closet with her comely maids.
The fair hues of her flesh, her face and her hair
And her body and her bearing were beyond praise,
And excelled the queen herself, as Sir Gawain thought.   945
He goes forth to greet her with gracious intent;
Another lady led her by the left hand
That was older than she—an ancient, it seemed,
And held in high honor by all men about.
But unlike to look upon, those ladies were,   950
For if the one was fresh, the other was faded:
Bedecked in bright red was the body of one;
Flesh hung in folds on the face of the other;
On one a high headdress, hung all with pearls;
Her bright throat and bosom fair to behold,   955
Fresh as the first snow fallen upon hills;
A wimple[1] the other one wore round her throat;
Her swart chin well swaddled, swathed all in white;
Her forehead enfolded in flounces of silk
That framed a fair fillet,[2] of fashion ornate,   960
And nothing bare beneath save the black brows,
The two eyes and the nose, the naked lips,
And they unsightly to see, and sorrily bleared.
A beldame, by God, she may well be deemed,
                            of pride!   965
          She was short and thick of waist,
          Her buttocks round and wide;
          More toothsome, to his taste,
          Was the beauty by her side.

When Gawain had gazed on that gay lady,   970
With leave of her lord, he politely approached;

1. A garment covering the neck and sides of the head.   2. Ornamental ribbon or headband.

To the elder in homage he humbly bows;
The lovelier he salutes with a light embrace.
He claims a comely kiss, and courteously he speaks;
They welcome him warmly, and straightway he asks   975
To be received as their servant, if they so desire.
They take him between them; with talking they bring him
Beside a bright fire; bade then that spices
Be freely fetched forth, to refresh them the better,
And the good wine therewith, to warm their hearts.   980
The lord leaps about in light-hearted mood;
Contrives entertainments and timely sports;
Takes his hood from his head and hangs it on a spear,
And offers him openly the honor thereof
Who should promote the most mirth at that Christmas feast;   985
"And I shall try for it, trust me—contend with the best,
Ere I go without my headgear by grace of my friends!"
Thus with light talk and laughter the lord makes merry
To gladden the guest he had greeted in hall
                  that day.   990
       At the last he called for light
       The company to convey;
       Gawain says goodnight
       And retires to bed straightway.

On the morn when each man is mindful in heart   995
That God's son was sent down to suffer our death,
No household but is blithe for His blessed sake;
So was it there on that day, with many delights.
Both at larger meals and less they were lavishly served
By doughty lads on dais, with delicate fare;   1000
The old ancient lady, highest she sits;
The lord at her left hand leaned, as I hear;
Sir Gawain in the center, beside the gay lady,
Where the food was brought first to that festive board,
And thence throughout the hall, as they held most fit,   1005
To each man was offered in order of rank.
There was meat, there was mirth, there was much joy,
That to tell all the tale would tax my wits,
Though I pained me, perchance, to paint it with care;
But yet I know that our knight and the noble lady   1010
Were accorded so closely in company there,
With the seemly solace of their secret words,
With speeches well-sped, spotless and pure,
That each prince's pastime their pleasures far
                  outshone.   1015
       Sweet pipes beguile their cares,
       And the trumpet of martial tone;

> Each tends his affairs
> And those two tend their own.

That day and all the next, their disport was noble,   1020
And the third day, I think, pleased them no less;
The joys of St. John's Day³ were justly praised,
And were the last of their like for those lords and ladies;
Then guests were to go in the gray morning,
Wherefore they whiled the night away with wine and with mirth,   1025
Moved to the measures of many a blithe carol;
At last, when it was late, took leave of each other,
Each one of those worthies, to wend his way.
Gawain bids goodbye to his goodly host
Who brings him to his chamber, the chimney beside,   1030
And detains him in talk, and tenders his thanks
And holds it an honor to him and his people
That he has harbored in his house at that holy time
And embellished his abode with his inborn grace.
"As long as I may live, my luck is the better   1035
That Gawain was my guest at God's own feast!"
"Noble sir," said the knight, "I cannot but think
All the honor is your own—may heaven requite it!
And your man to command I account myself here
As I am bound and beholden, and shall be, come   1040
> what may."
> The lord with all his might
> Entreats his guest to stay;
> Brief answer makes the knight:
> Next morning he must away.   1045

Then the lord of that land politely inquired
What dire affair had forced him, at that festive time,
So far from the king's court to fare forth alone
Ere the holidays wholly had ended in hall.
"In good faith," said Gawain, "you have guessed the truth: 1050
On a high errand and urgent I hastened away,
For I am summoned by myself to seek for a place—
I would I knew whither, or where it might be!
Far rather would I find it before the New Year
Than own the land of Logres, so help me our Lord!   1055
Wherefore, sir, in friendship this favor I ask,
That you say in sober earnest, if something you know
Of the Green Chapel, on ground far or near,
Or the lone knight that lives there, of like hue of green.
A certain day was set by assent of us both   1060

3. December 27.

To meet at that landmark, if I might last,
And from now to the New Year is nothing too long,
And I would greet the Green Knight there, would God but allow,
More gladly, by God's Son, than gain the world's wealth!
And I must set forth to search, as soon as I may;   1065
To be about the business I have but three days
And would as soon sink down dead as desist from my errand."
Then smiling said the lord, "Your search, sir, is done,
For we shall see you to that site by the set time.
Let Gawain grieve no more over the Green Chapel;   1070
You shall be in your own bed, in blissful ease,
All the forenoon, and fare forth the first of the year,
And make the goal by midmorn, to mind your affairs,
                    no fear!
        Tarry till the fourth day   1075
        And ride on the first of the year.
        We shall set you on your way;
        It is not two miles from here."

Then Gawain was glad, and gleefully he laughed:
"Now I thank you for this, past all things else!   1080
Now my goal is here at hand! With a glad heart I shall
Both tarry, and undertake any task you devise."
Then the host seized his arm and seated him there;
Let the ladies be brought, to delight them the better,
And in fellowship fair by the fireside they sit;   1085
So gay waxed the good host, so giddy his words,
All waited in wonder what next he would say.
Then he stares on the stout knight, and sternly he speaks:
"You have bound yourself boldly my bidding to do—
Will you stand by that boast, and obey me this once?"   1090
"I shall do so indeed," said the doughty knight;
"While I lie in your lodging, your laws will I follow."
"As you have had," said the host, "many hardships abroad
And little sleep of late, you are lacking, I judge,
Both in nourishment needful and nightly rest;   1095
You shall lie abed late in your lofty chamber
Tomorrow until mass, and meet then to dine
When you will, with my wife, who will sit by your side
And talk with you at table, the better to cheer
                    our guest.   1100
        A-hunting I will go
        While you lie late and rest."
        The knight, inclining low,
        Assents to each behest.

"And Gawain," said the good host, "agree now to this: 1105
Whatever I win in the woods I will give you at eve,
And all you have earned you must offer to me;

Swear now, sweet friend, to swap as I say,
Whether hands, in the end, be empty or better."
"By God," said Sir Gawain, "I grant it forthwith!   1110
If you find the game good, I shall gladly take part."
"Let the bright wine be brought, and our bargain is done,"
Said the lord of that land—the two laughed together.
Then they drank and they dallied and doffed all constraint,
These lords and these ladies, as late as they chose,   1115
And then with gaiety and gallantries and graceful adieux
They talked in low tones, and tarried at parting.
With compliments comely they kiss at the last;
There were brisk lads about with blazing torches
To see them safe to bed, for soft repose   1120
          long due.
          Their covenants, yet awhile,
          They repeat, and pledge anew;
          That lord could well beguile
          Men's hearts, with mirth in view.   1125

Part III

Long before daylight they left their beds;
Guests that wished to go gave word to their grooms,
And they set about briskly to bind on saddles,
Tend to their tackle, tie up trunks.
The proud lords appear, appareled to ride,   1130
Leap lightly astride, lay hold of their bridles,
Each one on his way to his worthy house.
The liege lord of the land was not the last
Arrayed there to ride, with retainers many;
He had a bite to eat when he had heard mass;   1135
With horn to the hills he hastens amain.
By the dawn of that day over the dim earth,
Master and men were mounted and ready.
Then they harnessed in couples the keen-scented hounds,
Cast wide the kennel-door and called them forth,   1140
Blew upon their bugles bold blasts three;
The dogs began to bay with a deafening din,
And they quieted them quickly and called them to heel,
A hundred brave huntsmen, as I have heard tell,
          together.   1145
          Men at stations meet;
          From the hounds they slip the tether;
          The echoing horns repeat,
          Clear in the merry weather.

At the clamor of the quest, the quarry trembled;   1150
Deer dashed through the dale, dazed with dread;
Hastened to the high ground, only to be

Turned back by the beaters, who boldly shouted.
They harmed not the harts, with their high heads,
Let the bucks go by, with their broad antlers,   1155
For it was counted a crime, in the close[4] season,
If a man of that demesne should molest the male deer.
The hinds were headed up, with "Hey!" and "Ware!"
The does with great din were driven to the valleys.
Then you were ware, as they went, of the whistling of arrows;   1160
At each bend under boughs the bright shafts flew
That tore the tawny hide with their tapered heads.
Ah! They bray and they bleed, on banks they die,
And ever the pack pell-mell comes panting behind;
Hunters with shrill horns hot on their heels—   1165
Like the cracking of cliffs their cries resounded.
What game got away from the gallant archers
Was promptly picked off at the posts below
When they were harried on the heights and herded to the streams:
The watchers were so wary at the waiting-stations,   1170
And the greyhounds so huge, that eagerly snatched,
And finished them off as fast as folk could see
                          with sight.
            The lord, now here, now there,
            Spurs forth in sheer delight.   1175
            And drives, with pleasures rare,
            The day to the dark night.

So the lord in the linden-wood leads the hunt
And Gawain the good knight in gay bed lies,
Lingered late alone, till daylight gleamed,   1180
Under coverlet costly, curtained about.
And as he slips into slumber, slyly there comes
A little din at his door, and the latch lifted,
And he holds up his heavy head out of the clothes;
A corner of the curtain he caught back a little   1185
And waited there warily, to see what befell.
Lo! it was the lady, loveliest to behold,
That drew the door behind her deftly and still
And was bound for his bed—abashed was the knight,
And laid his head low again in likeness of sleep;   1190
And she stepped stealthily, and stole to his bed,
Cast aside the curtain and came within,
And set herself softly on the bedside there,
And lingered at her leisure, to look on his waking.
The fair knight lay feigning for a long while,   1195
Conning in his conscience what his case might
Mean or amount to—a marvel he thought it.

4. Or closed.

But yet he said within himself, "More seemly it were
To try her intent by talking a little."
So he started and stretched, as startled from sleep,   1200
Lifts wide his lids in likeness of wonder,
And signs himself swiftly, as safer to be,
                              with art.
          Sweetly does she speak
          And kindling glances dart,   1205
          Blent white and red on cheek
          And laughing lips apart.

"Good morning, Sir Gawain," said that gay lady,
"A slack sleeper you are, to let one slip in!
Now you are taken in a trice—a truce we must make,   1210
Or I shall bind you in your bed, of that be assured."
Thus laughing lightly that lady jested.
"Good morning, good lady," said Gawain the blithe,
"Be it with me as you will; I am well content!
For I surrender myself, and sue for your grace,   1215
And that is best, I believe, and behooves me now."
Thus jested in answer that gentle knight.
"But if, lovely lady, you misliked it not,
And were pleased to permit your prisoner to rise,
I should quit this couch and accoutre me better,   1220
And be clad in more comfort for converse here."
"Nay, not so, sweet sir," said the smiling lady;
"You shall not rise from your bed; I direct you better:
I shall hem and hold you on either hand,
And keep company awhile with my captive knight.   1225
For as certain as I sit here, Sir Gawain you are,
Whom all the world worships, whereso you ride;
Your honor, your courtesy are highest acclaimed
By lords and by ladies, by all living men;
And lo! we are alone here, and left to ourselves: 1230
My lord and his liegemen are long departed,
The household asleep, my handmaids too,
The door drawn, and held by a well-driven bolt,
And since I have in this house him whom all love,
I shall while the time away with mirthful speech   1235
                              at will.
          My body is here at hand,
          Your each wish to fulfill;
          Your servant to command
          I am, and shall be still."   1240

"In good faith," said Gawain, "my gain is the greater,
Though I am not he of whom you have heard;
To arrive at such reverence as you recount here

I am one all unworthy, and well do I know it.
By heaven, I would hold me the happiest of men   1245
If by word or by work I once might aspire
To the prize of your praise—'twere a pure joy!"
"In good faith, Sir Gawain," said that gay lady,
"The well-proven prowess that pleases all others,
Did I scant or scout[5] it, 'twere scarce becoming.   1250
But there are ladies, believe me, that had liefer far[6]
Have thee here in their hold, as I have today,
To pass an hour in pastime with pleasant words,
Assuage all their sorrows and solace their hearts,
Than much of the goodly gems and gold they possess.   1255
But laud be to the Lord of the lofty skies,
For here in my hands all hearts' desire
                              doth lie."
              Great welcome got he there
              From the lady who sat him by;   1260
              With fitting speech and fair
              The good knight makes reply.

"Madame," said the merry man, "Mary reward you!
For in good faith, I find your beneficence noble.
And the fame of fair deeds runs far and wide,   1265
But the praise you report pertains not to me,
But comes of your courtesy and kindness of heart."
"By the high Queen of heaven" (said she) "I count it not so,
For were I worth all the women in this world alive,
And all wealth and all worship were in my hands,   1270
And I should hunt high and low, a husband to take,
For the nurture I have noted in thee, knight, here,
The comeliness and courtesies and courtly mirth—
And so I had ever heard, and now hold it true—
No other on this earth should have me for wife."   1275
"You are bound to a better man," the bold knight said,
"Yet I prize the praise you have proffered me here,
And soberly your servant, my sovereign I hold you,
And acknowledge me your knight, in the name of Christ."
So they talked of this and that until 'twas nigh noon,   1280
And ever the lady languishing in likeness of love.
With feat[7] words and fair he framed his defence,
For were she never so winsome, the warrior had
The less will to woo, for the wound that his bane
                              must be.   1285
              He must bear the blinding blow,
              For such is fate's decree;

5. Mock.   6. Would much rather.   7. Fitting.

> The lady asks leave to go;
> He grants it full and free.

Then she gaily said goodbye, and glanced at him, laughing,   1290
And as she stood, she astonished him with a stern speech:
"Now may the Giver of all good words these glad hours repay!
But our guest is not Gawain—forgot is that thought."
"How so?" said the other, and asks in some haste,
For he feared he had been at fault in the forms of his speech.   1295
But she held up her hand, and made answer thus:
"So good a knight as Gawain is given out to be,
And the model of fair demeanor and manners pure,
Had he lain so long at a lady's side,
Would have claimed a kiss, by his courtesy,   1300
Through some touch or trick of phrase at some tale's end."
Said Gawain, "Good lady, I grant it at once!
I shall kiss at your command, as becomes a knight,
And more, lest you mislike, so let be, I pray."
With that she turns toward him, takes him in her arms,   1305
Leans down her lovely head, and lo! he is kissed.
They commend each other to Christ with comely words,
He sees her forth safely, in silence they part,
And then he lies no later in his lofty bed,
But calls to his chamberlain, chooses his clothes,   1310
Goes in those garments gladly to mass,
Then takes his way to table, where attendants wait,
And made merry all day, till the moon rose
> in view
> Was never knight beset   1315
> 'Twixt worthier ladies two:
> The crone and the coquette;
> Fair pastimes they pursue.

And the lord of the land rides late and long,
Hunting the barren hind[8] over the broad heath.   1320
He had slain such a sum, when the sun sank low,
Of does and other deer, as would dizzy one's wits.
Then they trooped in together in triumph at last,
And the count of the quarry quickly they take.
The lords lent a hand with their liegemen many,   1325
Picked out the plumpest and put them together
And duly dressed the deer, as the deed requires.
Some were assigned the assay of the fat:
Two fingers'-width fully they found on the leanest.
Then they slit the slot[9] open and searched out the paunch,   1330

8. Female deer that are not pregnant.   9. The hollow above the breastbone.

Trimmed it with trencher-knives and tied it up tight.
They flayed the fair hide from the legs and trunk,
Then broke open the belly and laid bare the bowels,
Deftly detaching and drawing them forth.
And next at the neck they neatly parted   1335
The weasand[1] from the windpipe, and cast away the guts.
At the shoulders with sharp blades they showed their skill,
Boning them from beneath, lest the sides be marred;
They breached the broad breast and broke it in twain,
And again at the gullet they begin with their knives,   1340
Cleave down the carcass clear to the breach;
Two tender morsels they take from the throat,
Then round the inner ribs they rid off a layer
And carve out the kidney-fat, close to the spine,
Hewing down to the haunch, that all hung together,   1345
And held it up whole, and hacked it free,
And this they named the numbles,[2] that knew such terms
                                      of art.
                    They divide the crotch in two,
                    And straightway then they start   1350
                    To cut the backbone through
                    And cleave the trunk apart.

With hard strokes they hewed off the head and the neck,
Then swiftly from the sides they severed the chine,
And the corbie's bone[3] they cast on a branch.   1355
Then they pierced the plump sides, impaled either one
With the hock of the hind foot, and hung it aloft,
To each person his portion most proper and fit.
On a hide of a hind the hounds they fed
With the liver and the lights,[4] the leathery paunches,   1360
And bread soaked in blood well blended therewith.
High horns and shrill set hounds a-baying,
Then merrily with their meat they make their way home,
Blowing on their bugles many a brave blast.
Ere dark had descended, that doughty band   1365
Was come within the walls where Gawain waits
                                      at leisure.
                    Bliss and hearth-fire bright
                    Await the master's pleasure;
                    When the two men met that night,   1370
                    Joy surpassed all measure.

Then the host in the hall his household assembles,
With the dames of high degree and their damsels fair.
In the presence of the people, a party he sends

---

1. Esophagus.   2. Other internal organs.   3. A bit of gristle for the ravens ("corbies").   4. Lungs.

To convey him his venison in view of the knight.   1375
And in high good-humor he hails him then,
Counts over the kill, the cuts on the tallies,[5]
Holds high the hewn ribs, heavy with fat.
"What think you, sir, of this? Have I thriven well?
Have I won with my woodcraft a worthy prize?"   1380
"In good earnest," said Gawain, "this game is the finest
I have seen in seven years in the season of winter."
"And I give it to you, Gawain," said the goodly host,
"For according to our covenant, you claim it as your own."
"That is so," said Sir Gawain, "the same say I: 1385
What I worthily have won within these fair walls,
Herewith I as willingly award it to you."
He embraces his broad neck with both his arms,
And confers on him a kiss in the comeliest style.
"Have here my profit, it proved no better;   1390
Ungrudging do I grant it, were it greater far."
"Such a gift," said the good host, "I gladly accept—
Yet it might be all the better, would you but say
Where you won this same award, by your wits alone."
"That was no part of the pact; press me no further,   1395
For you have had what behooves; all other claims
                            forbear."
                    With jest and compliment
                    They conversed, and cast off care;
                    To the table soon they went;   1400
                    Fresh dainties wait them there.

And then by the chimney-side they chat at their ease;
The best wine was brought them, and bounteously served;
And after in their jesting they jointly accord
To do on the second day the deeds of the first: 1405
That the two men should trade, betide as it may,
What each had taken in, at eve when they met.
They seal the pact solemnly in sight of the court;
Their cups were filled afresh to confirm the jest;
Then at last they took their leave, for late was the hour,   1410
Each to his own bed hastening away.
Before the barnyard cock had crowed but thrice
The lord had leapt from his rest, his liegemen as well.
Both of mass and their meal they made short work:
By the dim light of dawn they were deep in the woods   1415
                            away.
                    With huntsmen and with horns
                    Over plains they pass that day;

5. Notched sticks were used to count the animals taken in the hunt.

They release, amid the thorns,
Swift hounds that run and bay.   1420

Soon some were on a scent by the side of a marsh;
When the hounds opened cry, the head of the hunt
Rallied them with rough words, raised a great noise.
The hounds that had heard it came hurrying straight
And followed along with their fellows, forty together.   1425
Then such a clamor and cry of coursing hounds
Arose, that the rocks resounded again.
Hunters exhorted them with horn and with voice;
Then all in a body bore off together
Between a mere[6] in the marsh and a menacing crag,   1430
To a rise where the rock stood rugged and steep,
And boulders lay about, that blocked their approach.
Then the company in consort closed on their prey:
They surrounded the rise and the rocks both,
For well they were aware that it waited within,   1435
The beast that the bloodhounds boldly proclaimed.
Then they beat on the bushes and bade him appear,
And he made a murderous rush in the midst of them all;
The best of all boars broke from his cover,
That had ranged long unrivaled, a renegade old,   1440
For of tough-brawned boars he was biggest far,
Most grim when he grunted—then grieved were many,
For three at the first thrust he threw to the earth,
And dashed away at once without more damage.
With "Hi!" "Hi!" and "Hey!" "Hey!" the others followed,   1445
Had horns at their lips, blew high and clear.
Merry was the music of men and of hounds
That were bound after this boar, his bloodthirsty heart
                              to quell.
          Often he stands at bay,   1450
          Then scatters the pack pell-mell;
          He hurts the hounds, and they
          Most dolefully yowl and yell.

Men then with mighty bows moved in to shoot,
Aimed at him with their arrows and often hit,   1455
But the points had no power to pierce through his hide,
And the barbs were brushed aside by his bristly brow;
Though the shank of the shaft shivered in pieces,
The head hopped away, wheresoever it struck.
But when their stubborn strokes had stung him at last,   1460
Then, foaming in his frenzy, fiercely he charges,

6. Pool.

Hies at them headlong that hindered his flight,
And many feared for their lives, and fell back a little.
But the lord on a lively horse leads the chase;
As a high-mettled huntsman his horn he blows;   1465
He sounds the assembly and sweeps through the brush,
Pursuing this wild swine till the sunlight slanted.
All day with this deed they drive forth the time
While our lone knight so lovesome lies in his bed,
Sir Gawain safe at home, in silken bower   1470
        so gay.
     The lady, with guile in heart,
     Came early where he lay;
     She was at him with all her art
     To turn his mind her way.   1475

She comes to the curtain and coyly peeps in;
Gawain thought it good to greet her at once,
And she richly repays him with her ready words,
Settles softly at his side, and suddenly she laughs,
And with a gracious glance, she begins on him thus: 1480
"Sir, if you be Gawain, it seems a great wonder—
A man so well-meaning, and mannerly disposed,
And cannot act in company as courtesy bids,
And if one takes the trouble to teach him, 'tis all in vain.
That lesson learned lately is lightly forgot,   1485
Though I painted it as plain as my poor wit allowed."
"What lesson, dear lady?" he asked all alarmed;
"I have been much to blame, if your story be true."
"Yet my counsel was of kissing," came her answer then,
"Where favor has been found, freely to claim   1490
As accords with the conduct of courteous knights."
"My dear," said the doughty man, "dismiss that thought;
Such freedom, I fear, might offend you much;
It were rude to request if the right were denied."
"But none can deny you," said the noble dame,   1495
"You are stout enough to constrain with strength, if you choose,
Were any so ungracious as to grudge you aught."
"By heaven," said he, "you have answered well,
But threats never throve among those of my land,
Nor any gift not freely given, good though it be.   1500
I am yours to command, to kiss when you please;
You may lay on as you like, and leave off at will."
        With this,
     The lady lightly bends
     And graciously gives him a kiss;   1505
     The two converse as friends
     Of true love's trials and bliss.

"I should like, by your leave," said the lovely lady,
"If it did not annoy you, to know for what cause
So brisk and so bold a young blood as you,   1510
And acclaimed for all courtesies becoming a knight—
And name what knight you will, they are noblest esteemed
For loyal faith in love, in life as in story;
For to tell the tribulations of these true hearts,
Why, 'tis the very title and text of their deeds,   1515
How bold knights for beauty have braved many a foe,
Suffered heavy sorrows out of secret love,
And then valorously avenged them on villainous churls
And made happy ever after the hearts of their ladies.
And you are the noblest knight known in your time;   1520
No household under heaven but has heard of your fame,
And here by your side I have sat for two days
Yet never has a fair phrase fallen from your lips
Of the language of love, not one little word!
And you, that with sweet vows sway women's hearts,   1525
Should show your winsome ways, and woo a young thing,
And teach by some tokens the craft of true love.
How! are you artless, whom all men praise?
Or do you deem me so dull, or deaf to such words?
            Fie! Fie!   1530
        In hope of pastimes new
        I have come where none can spy;
        Instruct me a little, do,
        While my husband is not nearby."

"God love you, gracious lady!" said Gawain then;   1535
"It is a pleasure surpassing, and a peerless joy,
That one so worthy as you would willingly come
And take the time and trouble to talk with your knight
And content you with his company—it comforts my heart.
But to take to myself the task of telling of love,   1540
And touch upon its texts, and treat of its themes
To one that, I know well, wields more power
In that art, by a half, than a hundred such
As I am where I live, or am like to become,
It were folly, fair dame, in the first degree!   1545
In all that I am able, my aim is to please,
As in honor behooves me, and am evermore
Your servant heart and soul, so save me our Lord!"
Thus she tested his temper and tried many a time,
Whatever her true intent, to entice him to sin,   1550
But so fair was his defense that no fault appeared,
Nor evil on either hand, but only bliss

they knew.
They linger and laugh awhile;
She kisses the knight so true,   1555
Takes leave in comeliest style
And departs without more ado.

Then he rose from his rest and made ready for mass,
And then a meal was set and served, in sumptuous style;
He dallied at home all day with the dear ladies,   1560
But the lord lingered late at his lusty sport;
Pursued his sorry swine, that swerved as he fled,
And bit asunder the backs of the best of his hounds
When they brought him to bay, till the bowmen appeared
And soon forced him forth, though he fought for dear life,   1565
So sharp were the shafts they shot at him there.
But yet the boldest drew back from his battering head,
Till at last he was so tired he could travel no more,
But in as much haste as he might, he makes his retreat
To a rise on rocky ground, by a rushing stream.   1570
With the bank at his back he scrapes the bare earth,
The froth foams at his jaws, frightful to see.
He whets his white tusks—then weary were all
Those hunters so hardy that hoved[7] round about
Of aiming from afar, but ever they mistrust   1575
                    his mood.
          He had hurt so many by then
          That none had hardihood
          To be torn by his tusks again,
          That was brainsick, and out for blood.   1580

Till the lord came at last on his lofty steed,
Beheld him there at bay before all his folk;
Lightly he leaps down, leaves his courser,
Bares his bright sword, and boldly advances;
Straight into the stream he strides towards his foe.   1585
The wild thing was wary of weapon and man;
His hackles rose high; so hotly he snorts
That many watched with alarm, lest the worst befall.
The boar makes for the man with a mighty bound
So that he and his hunter came headlong together   1590
Where the water ran wildest—the worse for the beast,
For the man, when they first met, marked him with care,
Sights well the slot, slips in the blade,
Shoves it home to the hilt, and the heart shattered,
And he falls in his fury and floats down the water,   1595

7. Hovered.

ill-sped.
Hounds hasten by the score
To maul him, hide and head;
Men drag him in to shore
And dogs pronounce him dead.   1600

With many a brave blast they boast of their prize,
All hallooed in high glee, that had their wind;
The hounds bayed their best, as the bold men bade
That were charged with chief rank in that chase of renown.
Then one wise in woodcraft, and worthily skilled,   1605
Began to dress the boar in becoming style:
He severs the savage head and sets it aloft,
Then rends the body roughly right down the spine;
Takes the bowels from the belly, broils them on coals,
Blends them well with bread to bestow on the hounds.   1610
Then he breaks out the brawn in fair broad flitches,
And the innards to be eaten in order he takes.
The two sides, attached to each other all whole,
He suspended from a spar that was springy and tough;
And so with this swine they set out for home;   1615
The boar's head was borne before the same man
That had stabbed him in the stream with his strong arm,
right through.
He thought it long indeed
Till he had the knight in view;   1620
At his call, he comes with speed
To claim his payment due.

The lord laughed aloud, with many a light word,
When he greeted Sir Gawain—with good cheer he speaks.
They fetch the fair dames and the folk of the house;   1625
He brings forth the brawn, and begins the tale
Of the great length and girth, the grim rage as well,
Of the battle of the boar they beset in the wood.
The other men meetly commended his deeds
And praised well the prize of his princely sport,   1630
For the brawn of that boar, the bold knight said,
And the sides of that swine surpassed all others.
Then they handled the huge head; he owns it a wonder,
And eyes it with abhorrence, to heighten his praise.
"Now, Gawain," said the good man, "this game becomes yours 1635
By those fair terms we fixed, as you know full well."
"That is true," returned the knight, "and trust me, fair friend,
All my gains, as agreed, I shall give you forthwith."
He clasps him and kisses him in courteous style,
Then serves him with the same fare a second time.   1640
"Now we are even," said he, "at this evening feast,

And clear is every claim incurred here to date,
                    and debt."
            "By Saint Giles!" the host replies,
            "You're the best I ever met!   1645
            If your profits are all this size,
            We'll see you wealthy yet!"

Then attendants set tables on trestles about,
And laid them with linen; light shone forth,
Wakened along the walls in waxen torches.   1650
The service was set and the supper brought;
Royal were the revels that rose then in hall
At that feast by the fire, with many fair sports:
Amid the meal and after, melody sweet,
Carol-dances comely and Christmas songs,   1655
With all the mannerly mirth my tongue may describe.
And ever our gallant knight beside the gay lady;
So uncommonly kind and complaisant was she,
With sweet stolen glances, that stirred his stout heart,
That he was at his wits' end, and wondrous vexed;   1660
But he could not in conscience her courtship repay,
Yet took pains to please her, though the plan might
                    go wrong.
            When they to heart's delight
            Had reveled there in throng,   1665
            To his chamber he calls the knight,
            And thither they go along.

And there they dallied and drank, and deemed it good sport
To enact their play anew on New Year's Eve,
But Gawain asked again to go on the morrow,   1670
For the time until his tryst was not two days.
The host hindered that, and urged him to stay,
And said, "On my honor, my oath here I take
That you shall get to the Green Chapel to begin your chores
By dawn on New Year's Day, if you so desire.   1675
Wherefore lie at your leisure in your lofty bed,
And I shall hunt hereabouts, and hold to our terms,
And we shall trade winnings when once more we meet,
For I have tested you twice, and true have I found you;
Now think this tomorrow: the third pays for all;   1680
Be we merry while we may, and mindful of joy,
For heaviness of heart can be had for the asking."
This is gravely agreed on and Gawain will stay.
They drink a last draught and with torches depart
                    to rest.   1685
            To bed Sir Gawain went;
            His sleep was of the best;

The lord, on his craft intent,
Was early up and dressed.

After mass, with his men, a morsel he takes;   1690
Clear and crisp the morning; he calls for his mount;
The folk that were to follow him afield that day
Were high astride their horses before the hall gates.
Wondrous fair were the fields, for the frost was light;
The sun rises red amid radiant clouds,   1695
Sails into the sky, and sends forth his beams.
They let loose the hounds by a leafy wood;
The rocks all around re-echo to their horns;
Soon some have set off in pursuit of the fox,
Cast about with craft for a clearer scent;   1700
A young dog yaps, and is yelled at in turn;
His fellows fall to sniffing, and follow his lead,
Running in a rabble on the right track,
And he scampers all before; they discover him soon,
And when they see him with sight they pursue him the faster,   1705
Railing at him rudely with a wrathful din.
Often he reverses over rough terrain,
Or loops back to listen in the lee of a hedge;
At last, by a little ditch, he leaps over the brush,
Comes into a clearing at a cautious pace,   1710
Then he thought through his wiles to have thrown off the hounds
Till he was ware, as he went, of a waiting-station
Where three athwart his path threatened him at once,
                    all gray.
          Quick as a flash he wheels   1715
          And darts off in dismay;
          With hard luck at his heels
          He is off to the wood away.

Then it was heaven on earth to hark to the hounds
When they had come on their quarry, coursing together!   1720
Such harsh cries and howls they hurled at his head
As all the cliffs with a crash had come down at once.
Here he was hailed, when huntsmen met him;
Yonder they yelled at him, yapping and snarling;
There they cried "Thief!" and threatened his life,   1725
And ever the harriers at his heels, that he had no rest.
Often he was menaced when he made for the open,
And often rushed in again, for Reynard was wily;
And so he leads them a merry chase, the lord and his men,
In this manner on the mountains, till midday or near,   1730
While our hero lies at home in wholesome sleep
Within the comely curtains on the cold morning.
But the lady, as love would allow her no rest,

And pursuing ever the purpose that pricked her heart,
Was awake with the dawn, and went to his chamber   1735
In a fair flowing mantle that fell to the earth,
All edged and embellished with ermines fine;
No hood on her head, but heavy with gems
Were her fillet and the fret[8] that confined her tresses;
Her face and her fair throat freely displayed;   1740
Her bosom all but bare, and her back as well.
She comes in at the chamber-door, and closes it with care,
Throws wide a window—then waits no longer,
But hails him thus airily with her artful words,
                                 with cheer: 1745
          "Ah, man, how can you sleep?
          The morning is so clear!"
          Though dreams have drowned him deep,
          He cannot choose but hear.

Deep in his dreams he darkly mutters   1750
As a man may that mourns, with many grim thoughts
Of that day when destiny shall deal him his doom
When he greets his grim host at the Green Chapel
And must bow to his buffet, bating all strife.
But when he sees her at his side he summons his wits,   1755
Breaks from the black dreams, and blithely answers.
That lovely lady comes laughing sweet,
Sinks down at his side, and salutes him with a kiss.
He accords her fair welcome in courtliest style;
He sees her so glorious, so gaily attired,   1760
So faultless her features, so fair and so bright,
His heart swelled swiftly with surging joys.
They melt into mirth with many a fond smile,
And there was bliss beyond telling between those two,
                                 at height.   1765
          Good were their words of greeting;
          Each joyed in other's sight;
          Great peril attends that meeting
          Should Mary forget her knight.

For that high-born beauty so hemmed him about,   1770
Made so plain her meaning, the man must needs
Either take her tendered love or distastefully refuse.
His courtesy concerned him, lest crass he appear,
But more his soul's mischief, should he commit sin
And belie his loyal oath to the lord of that house.   1775
"God forbid!" said the bold knight, "That shall not befall!"
With a little fond laughter he lightly let pass

8. Ornamental net.

All the words of special weight that were sped his way;
"I find you much at fault," the fair one said,
"Who can be cold toward a creature so close by your side,   1780
Of all women in this world most wounded in heart,
Unless you have a sweetheart, one you hold dearer,
And allegiance to that lady so loyally knit
That you will never love another, as now I believe.
And, sir, if it be so, then say it, I beg you;   1785
By all your heart holds dear, hide it no longer
                              with guile."
                    "Lady, by Saint John,"
                    He answers with a smile,
                    "Lover have I none,   1790
                    Nor will have, yet awhile."

"Those words," said the woman, "are the worst of all,
But I have had my answer, and hard do I find it!
Kiss me now kindly; I can but go hence
To lament my life long like a maid lovelorn."   1795
She inclines her head quickly and kisses the knight,
Then straightens with a sigh, and says as she stands,
"Now, dear, ere I depart, do me this pleasure:
Give me some little gift, your glove or the like,
That I may think on you, man, and mourn the less."   1800
"Now by heaven," said he, "I wish I had here
My most precious possession, to put it in your hands,
For your deeds, beyond doubt, have often deserved
A repayment far passing my power to bestow.
But a love-token, lady, were of little avail;   1805
It is not to your honor to have at this time
A glove as a guerdon from Gawain's hand,
And I am here on an errand in unknown realms
And have no bearers with baggage with becoming gifts,
Which distresses me, madame, for your dear sake.   1810
A man must keep within his compass: account it neither grief
                              nor slight."
                    "Nay, noblest knight alive,"
                    Said that beauty of body white,
                    "Though you be loath to give,   1815
                    Yet you shall take, by right."

She reached out a rich ring, wrought all of gold,
With a splendid stone displayed on the band
That flashed before his eyes like a fiery sun;
It was worth a king's wealth, you may well believe.   1820
But he waved it away with these ready words:
"Before God, good lady, I forego all gifts;
None have I to offer, nor any will I take."

And she urged it on him eagerly, and ever he refused,
And vowed in very earnest, prevail she would not.   1825
And she sad to find it so, and said to him then,
"If my ring is refused for its rich cost—
You would not be my debtor for so dear a thing—
I shall give you my girdle;[9] you gain less thereby."
She released a knot lightly, and loosened a belt   1830
That was caught about her kirtle, the bright cloak beneath,
Of a gay green silk, with gold overwrought,
And the borders all bound with embroidery fine,
And this she presses upon him, and pleads with a smile,
Unworthy though it were, that it would not be scorned.   1835
But the man still maintains that he means to accept
Neither gold nor any gift, till by God's grace
The fate that lay before him was fully achieved.
"And be not offended, fair lady, I beg,
And give over your offer, for ever I must   1840
              decline.
        I am grateful for favor shown
        Past all deserts of mine,
        And ever shall be your own
        True servant, rain or shine."   1845

"Now does my present displease you," she promptly inquired,
"Because it seems in your sight so simple a thing?
And belike, as it is little, it is less to praise,
But if the virtue that invests it were verily known,
It would be held, I hope, in higher esteem.   1850
For the man that possesses this piece of silk,
If he bore it on his body, belted about,
There is no hand under heaven that could hew him down,
For he could not be killed by any craft on earth."
Then the man began to muse, and mainly he thought   1855
It was a pearl for his plight, the peril to come
When he gains the Green Chapel to get his reward:
Could he escape unscathed, the scheme were noble!
Then he bore with her words and withstood them no more,
And she repeated her petition and pleaded anew,   1860
And he granted it, and gladly she gave him the belt,
And besought him for her sake to conceal it well,
Lest the noble lord should know—and the knight agrees
That not a soul save themselves shall see it thenceforth
              with sight.   1865
        He thanked her with fervent heart,
        As often as ever he might;

9. Belt.

> Three times, before they part,
> She has kissed the stalwart knight.

Then the lady took her leave, and left him there,   1870
For more mirth with that man she might not have.
When she was gone, Sir Gawain got from his bed,
Arose and arrayed him in his rich attire;
Tucked away the token the temptress had left,
Laid it reliably where he looked for it after.   1875
And then with good cheer to the chapel he goes,
Approached a priest in private, and prayed to be taught
To lead a better life and lift up his mind,
Lest he be among the lost when he must leave this world.
And shamefaced at shrift[1] he showed his misdeeds   1880
From the largest to the least, and asked the Lord's mercy,
And called on his confessor to cleanse his soul,
And he absolved him of his sins as safe and as clean
As if the dread Day of Judgment should dawn on the morrow.
And then he made merry amid the fine ladies   1885
With deft-footed dances and dalliance light,
As never until now, while the afternoon wore
>   away.
>   He delighted all around him,
>   And all agreed, that day,   1890
>   They never before had found him
>   So gracious and so gay.

Now peaceful be his pasture, and love play him fair!
The host is on horseback, hunting afield;
He has finished off this fox that he followed so long: 1895
As he leapt a low hedge to look for the villain
Where he heard all the hounds in hot pursuit,
Reynard comes racing out of a rough thicket,
And all the rabble in a rush, right at his heels.
The man beholds the beast, and bides his time,   1900
And bares his bright sword, and brings it down hard,
And he blenches from the blade, and backward he starts;
A hound hurries up and hinders that move,
And before the horse's feet they fell on him at once
And ripped the rascal's throat with a wrathful din.   1905
The lord soon alighted and lifted him free,
Swiftly snatched him up from the snapping jaws,
Holds him over his head, halloos with a will,
And the dogs bayed the dirge, that had done him to death.
Hunters hastened thither with horns at their lips,   1910

---

1. Confession.

Sounding the assembly till they saw him at last.
When that comely company was come in together,
All that bore bugles blew them at once,
And the others all hallooed, that had no horns.
It was the merriest medley that ever a man heard,   1915
The racket that they raised for Sir Reynard's soul
                    that died.
          Their hounds they praised and fed,
          Fondling their heads with pride,
          And they took Reynard the Red   1920
          And stripped away his hide.

And then they headed homeward, for evening had come,
Blowing many a blast on their bugles bright.
The lord at long last alights at his house,
Finds fire on the hearth where the fair knight waits,   1925
Sir Gawain the good, that was glad in heart.
With the ladies, that loved him, he lingered at ease;
He wore a rich robe of blue, that reached to the earth
And a surcoat lined softly with sumptuous furs;
A hood of the same hue hung on his shoulders;   1930
With bands of bright ermine embellished were both.
He comes to meet the man amid all the folk,
And greets him good-humoredly, and gaily he says,
"I shall follow forthwith the form of our pledge
That we framed to good effect amid fresh-filled cups."   1935
He clasps him accordingly and kisses him thrice,
As amiably and as earnestly as ever he could.
"By heaven," said the host, "you have had some luck
Since you took up this trade, if the terms were good."
"Never trouble about the terms," he returned at once,   1940
"Since all that I owe here is openly paid."
"Marry!" said the other man, "mine is much less,
For I have hunted all day, and nought have I got
But this foul fox pelt, the fiend take the goods!
Which but poorly repays those precious things   1945
That you have cordially conferred, those kisses three
                  so good."
          "Enough!" said Sir Gawain;
          "I thank you, by the rood!"[2]
          And how the fox was slain
          He told him, as they stood.   1950

With minstrelsy and mirth, with all manner of meats,
They made as much merriment as any men might

2. Cross.

(Amid laughing of ladies and light-hearted girls,
So gay grew Sir Gawain and the goodly host)   1955
Unless they had been besotted, or brainless fools.
The knight joined in jesting with that joyous folk,
Until at last it was late; ere long they must part,
And be off to their beds, as behooved them each one.
Then politely his leave of the lord of the house   1960
Our noble knight takes, and renews his thanks:
"The courtesies countless accorded me here,
Your kindness at this Christmas, may heaven's King repay!
Henceforth, if you will have me, I hold you my liege,
And so, as I have said, I must set forth tomorrow,   1965
If I may take some trusty man to teach, as you promised,
The way to the Green Chapel, that as God allows
I shall see my fate fulfilled on the first of the year."
"In good faith," said the good man, "with a good will
Every promise on my part shall be fully performed."   1970
He assigns him a servant to set him on the path,
To see him safe and sound over the snowy hills,
To follow the fastest way through forest green
                and grove.
         Gawain thanks him again,   1975
         So kind his favors prove,
         And of the ladies then
         He takes his leave, with love.

Courteously he kissed them, with care in his heart,
And often wished them well, with warmest thanks,   1980
Which they for their part were prompt to repay.
They commend him to Christ with disconsolate sighs;
And then in that hall with the household he parts—
Each man that he met, he remembered to thank
or his deeds of devotion and diligent pains,   1985
And the trouble he had taken to tend to his needs;
And each one as woeful, that watched him depart,
As he had lived with him loyally all his life long.
By lads bearing lights he was led to his chamber
And blithely brought to his bed, to be at his rest.   1990
How soundly he slept, I presume not to say,
For there were matters of moment his thoughts might well
                pursue.
         Let him lie and wait;
         He has little more to do,   1995
         Then listen, while I relate
         How they kept their rendezvous.

Part IV

Now the New Year draws near, and the night passes,
The day dispels the dark, by the Lord's decree;
But wild weather awoke in the world without: 2000
The clouds in the cold sky cast down their snow
With great gusts from the north, grievous to bear.
Sleet showered aslant upon shivering beasts;
The wind warbled wild as it whipped from aloft,
And drove the drifts deep in the dales below.   2005
Long and well he listens, that lies in his bed;
Though he lifts not his eyelids, little he sleeps;
Each crow of the cock he counts without fail.
Readily from his rest he rose before dawn,
For a lamp had been left him, that lighted his chamber.   2010
He called to his chamberlain, who quickly appeared,
And bade him get him his gear, and gird his good steed,
And he sets about briskly to bring in his arms,
And makes ready his master in manner most fit.
First he clad him in his clothes, to keep out the cold,   2015
And then his other harness, made handsome anew,
His plate-armor of proof, polished with pains,
The rings of his rich mail rid of their rust,
And all was fresh as at first, and for this he gave thanks
                              indeed.   2020
          With pride he wears each piece,
          New-furbished for his need:
          No gayer from here to Greece;
          He bids them bring his steed.

In his richest raiment he robed himself then: 2025
His crested coat-armor, close-stitched with craft,
With stones of strange virtue on silk velvet set;
All bound with embroidery on borders and seams
And lined warmly and well with furs of the best.
Yet he left not his love-gift, the lady's girdle;   2030
Gawain, for his own good, forgot not that:
When the bright sword was belted and bound on his haunches,
Then twice with that token he twined him about.
Sweetly did he swathe him in that swatch of silk,
That girdle of green so goodly to see,   2035
That against the gay red showed gorgeous bright.
Yet he wore not for its wealth that wondrous girdle,
Nor pride in its pendants, though polished they were,
Though glittering gold gleamed at the tips,
But to keep himself safe when consent he must   2040
To endure a deadly dint, and all defense

denied.
And now the bold knight came
Into the courtyard wide;
That folk of worthy fame 2045
He thanks on every side.

Then was Gringolet girt, that was great and huge,
And had sojourned safe and sound, and savored his fare;
He pawed the earth in his pride, that princely steed.
The good knight draws near him and notes well his look, 2050
And says sagely to himself, and soberly swears,
"Here is a household in hall that upholds the right!
The man that maintains it, may happiness be his!
Likewise the dear lady, may love betide her!
If thus they in charity cherish a guest 2055
That are honored here on earth, may they have His reward
That reigns high in heaven—and also you all;
And were I to live in this land but a little while,
I should willingly reward you, and well, if I might."
Then he steps into the stirrup and bestrides his mount; 2060
His shield is shown forth; on his shoulder he casts it;
Strikes the side of his steed with his steel spurs,
And he starts across the stones, nor stands any longer
to prance.
On horseback was the swain 2065
That bore his spear and lance;
"May Christ this house maintain
And guard it from mischance!"

The bridge was brought down, and the broad gates
Unbarred and carried back upon both sides; 2070
He commended him[3] to Christ, and crossed over the planks;
Praised the noble porter, who prayed on his knees
That God save Sir Gawain, and bade him good day,
And went on his way alone with the man
That was to lead him ere long to that luckless place 2075
Where the dolorous dint must be dealt him at last.
Under bare boughs they ride, where steep banks rise,
Over high cliffs they climb, where cold snow clings;
The heavens held aloof, but heavy thereunder
Mist mantled the moors, moved on the slopes. 2080
Each hill had a hat, a huge cape of cloud;
Brooks bubbled and broke over broken rocks,
Flashing in freshets that waterfalls fed.
Roundabout was the road that ran through the wood
Till the sun at that season was soon to rise, 2085

3. I.e., himself.

that day.
They were on a hilltop high;
The white snow round them lay;
The man that rode nearby
Now bade his master stay.   2090

"For I have seen you here safe at the set time,
And now you are not far from that notable place
That you have sought for so long with such special pains.
But this I say for certain, since I know you, sir knight,
And have your good at heart, and hold you dear—   2095
Would you heed well my words, it were worth your while—
You are rushing into risks that you reck not of:
There is a villain in yon valley, the veriest on earth,
For he is rugged and rude, and ready with fists,
And most immense in his mold of mortals alive,   2100
And his body bigger than the best four
That are in Arthur's house, Hector[4] or any.
He gets his grim way at the Green Chapel;
None passes by that place so proud in his arms
That he does not dash him down with his deadly blows,   2105
For he is heartless wholly, and heedless of right,
For be it chaplain or churl that by the Chapel rides,
Monk or mass-priest or any man else,
He would as soon strike him dead as stand on two feet.
Wherefore I say, just as certain as you sit there astride, 2110
You cannot but be killed, if his counsel holds,
For he would trounce you in a trice, had you twenty lives
                    for sale.
        He has lived long in this land
        And dealt out deadly bale;   2115
        Against his heavy hand
        Your power cannot prevail.

"And so, good Sir Gawain, let the grim man be;
Go off by some other road, in God's own name!
Leave by some other land, for the love of Christ,   2120
And I shall get me home again, and give you my word
That I shall swear by God's self and the saints above,
By heaven and by my halidom[5] and other oaths more,
To conceal this day's deed, nor say to a soul
That ever you fled for fear from any that I knew."   2125
"Many thanks!" said the other man—and demurring he speaks—
"Fair fortune befall you for your friendly words!
And conceal this day's deed I doubt not you would,
But though you never told the tale, if I turned back now,

---

4. Either the Trojan hero or one of Arthur's knights.   5. Holiness or, more likely, patron saints.

Forsook this place for fear, and fled, as you say,   2130
I were a caitiff[6] coward; I could not be excused.
But I must to the Chapel to chance my luck
And say to that same man such words as I please,
Befall what may befall through Fortune's will
                              or whim.   2135
        Though he be a quarrelsome knave
        With a cudgel great and grim,
        The Lord is strong to save:
        His servants trust in Him."

"Marry," said the man, "since you tell me so much,   2140
And I see you are set to seek your own harm,
If you crave a quick death, let me keep you no longer!
Put your helm on your head, your hand on your lance,
And ride the narrow road down yon rocky slope
Till it brings you to the bottom of the broad valley.   2145
Then look a little ahead, on your left hand,
And you will soon see before you that self-same Chapel,
And the man of great might that is master there.
Now goodbye in God's name, Gawain the noble!
For all the world's wealth I would not stay here,   2150
Or go with you in this wood one footstep further!"
He tarried no more to talk, but turned his bridle,
Hit his horse with his heels as hard as he might,
Leaves the knight alone, and off like the wind
                          goes leaping.   2155
        "By God," said Gawain then,
        "I shall not give way to weeping;
        God's will be done, amen!
        I commend me to His keeping."

He puts his heels to his horse, and picks up the path;   2160
Goes in beside a grove where the ground is steep,
Rides down the rough slope right to the valley;
And then he looked a little about him—the landscape was wild,
And not a soul to be seen, nor sign of a dwelling,
But high banks on either hand hemmed it about,   2165
With many a ragged rock and rough-hewn crag;
The skies seemed scored by the scowling peaks.
Then he halted his horse, and hoved there a space,
And sought on every side for a sight of the Chapel,
But no such place appeared, which puzzled him sore,   2170
Yet he saw some way off what seemed like a mound,
A hillock high and broad, hard by the water,
Where the stream fell in foam down the face of the steep

6. Despicable.

And bubbled as if it boiled on its bed below.
The knight urges his horse, and heads for the knoll;   2175
Leaps lightly to earth; loops well the rein
Of his steed to a stout branch, and stations him there.
He strides straight to the mound, and strolls all about,
Much wondering what it was, but no whit the wiser;
It had a hole at one end, and on either side,   2180
And was covered with coarse grass in clumps all without,
And hollow all within, like some old cave,
Or a crevice of an old crag—he could not discern
                              aright.
            "Can this be the Chapel Green?   2185
            Alack!" said the man, "Here might
            The devil himself be seen
            Saying matins[7] at black midnight!"

"Now by heaven," said he, "it is bleak hereabouts;
This prayer-house is hideous, half-covered with grass!   2190
Well may the grim man mantled in green
Hold here his orisons, in hell's own style!
Now I feel it is the Fiend, in my five wits,
That has tempted me to this tryst, to take my life;
This is a Chapel of mischance, may the mischief take it!   2195
As accursed a country church as I came upon ever!"
With his helm on his head, his lance in his hand,
He stalks toward the steep wall of that strange house.
Then he heard, on the hill, behind a hard rock,
Beyond the brook, from the bank, a most barbarous din: 2200
Lord! it clattered in the cliff fit to cleave it in two,
As one upon a grindstone ground a great scythe!
Lord! it whirred like a mill-wheel whirling about!
Lord! it echoed loud and long, lamentable to hear!
Then "By heaven," said the bold knight, "That business up there   2205
Is arranged for my arrival, or else I am much
                              misled.
            Let God work! Ah me!
            All hope of help has fled!
            Forfeit my life may be   2210
            But noise I do not dread."

Then he listened no longer, but loudly he called,
"Who has power in this place, high parley to hold?
For none greets Sir Gawain, or gives him good day;
If any would a word with him, let him walk forth   2215
And speak now or never, to speed his affairs."
"Abide," said one on the bank above over his head,

---

7. Morning prayers.

"And what I promised you once shall straightway be given."
Yet he stayed not his grindstone, nor stinted its noise,
But worked awhile at his whetting before he would rest,   2220
And then he comes around a crag, from a cave in the rocks,
Hurtling out of hiding with a hateful weapon,
A Danish ax devised for that day's deed,
With a broad blade and bright, bent in a curve,
Filed to a fine edge—four feet it measured   2225
By the length of the lace that was looped round the haft.
And in form as at first, the fellow all green,
His lordly face and his legs, his locks and his beard,
Save that firm upon two feet forward he strides,
Sets a hand on the ax-head, the haft to the earth;   2230
When he came to the cold stream, and cared not to wade,
He vaults over on his ax, and advances amain
On a broad bank of snow, overbearing and brisk
             of mood.
        Little did the knight incline   2235
        When face to face they stood;
        Said the other man, "Friend mine,
        It seems your word holds good!"

"God love you, Sir Gawain!" said the Green Knight then,
"And well met this morning, man, at my place!   2240
And you have followed me faithfully and found me betimes,[8]
And on the business between us we both are agreed:
Twelve months ago today you took what was yours,
And you at this New Year must yield me the same.
And we have met in these mountains, remote from all eyes: 2245
There is none here to halt us or hinder our sport;
Unhasp your high helm, and have here your wages;
Make no more demur than I did myself
When you hacked off my head with one hard blow."
"No, by God," said Sir Gawain, "that granted me life,   2250
I shall grudge not the guerdon, grim though it prove;
Bestow but one stroke, and I shall stand still,
And you may lay on as you like till the last of my part
             be paid."
        He proffered, with good grace,   2255
        His bare neck to the blade,
        And feigned a cheerful face:
        He scorned to seem afraid.

Then the grim man in green gathers his strength,
Heaves high the heavy ax to hit him the blow.   2260

---

8. In good time.

With all the force in his frame he fetches it aloft,
With a grimace as grim as he would grind him to bits;
Had the blow he bestowed been as big as he threatened,
A good knight and gallant had gone to his grave.
But Gawain at the great ax glanced up aside   2265
As down it descended with death-dealing force,
And his shoulders shrank a little from the sharp iron.
Abruptly the brawny man breaks off the stroke,
And then reproved with proud words that prince among knights.
"You are not Gawain the glorious," the green man said,   2270
"That never fell back on field in the face of the foe,
And now you flee for fear, and have felt no harm:
Such news of that knight I never heard yet!
I moved not a muscle when you made to strike,
Nor caviled at the cut in King Arthur's house;   2275
My head fell to my feet, yet steadfast I stood,
And you, all unharmed, are wholly dismayed—
Wherefore the better man I, by all odds,
                         must be."
                         Said Gawain, "Strike once more;   2280
                         I shall neither flinch nor flee;
                         But if my head falls to the floor
                         There is no mending me!

"But go on, man, in God's name, and get to the point!
Deliver me my destiny, and do it out of hand,   2285
For I shall stand to the stroke and stir not an inch
Till your ax has hit home—on my honor I swear it!"
"Have at thee then!" said the other, and heaves it aloft,
And glares down as grimly as he had gone mad.
He made a mighty feint, but marred not his hide;   2290
Withdrew the ax adroitly before it did damage.
Gawain gave no ground, nor glanced up aside,
But stood still as a stone, or else a stout stump
That is held in hard earth by a hundred roots.
Then merrily does he mock him, the man all in green: 2295
"So now you have your nerve again, I needs must strike;
Uphold the high knighthood that Arthur bestowed,
And keep your neck-bone clear, if this cut allows!"
Then was Gawain gripped with rage, and grimly he said,
"Why, thrash away, tyrant, I tire of your threats;   2300
You make such a scene, you must frighten yourself."
Said the green fellow, "In faith, so fiercely you speak
That I shall finish this affair, nor further grace
                         allow."
                         He stands prepared to strike   2305
                         And scowls with both lip and brow;

No marvel if the man mislike
Who can hope no rescue now.

He gathered up the grim ax and guided it well:
Let the barb at the blade's end brush the bare throat;   2310
He hammered down hard, yet harmed him no whit
Save a scratch on one side, that severed the skin;
The end of the hooked edge entered the flesh,
And a little blood lightly leapt to the earth.
And when the man beheld his own blood bright on the snow,   2315
He sprang a spear's length with feet spread wide,
Seized his high helm, and set it on his head,
Shoved before his shoulders the shield at his back,
Bares his trusty blade, and boldly he speaks—
Not since he was a babe born of his mother   2320
Was he once in this world one-half so blithe—
"Have done with your hacking—harry me no more!
I have borne, as behooved, one blow in this place;
If you make another move I shall meet it midway
And promptly, I promise you, pay back each blow   2325
                    with brand.
          One stroke acquits me here;
          So did our covenant stand
          In Arthur's court last year—
          Wherefore, sir, hold your hand!"   2330

He lowers the long ax and leans on it there,
Sets his arms on the head, the haft on the earth,
And beholds the bold knight that bides there afoot,
How he faces him fearless, fierce in full arms,
And plies him with proud words—it pleases him well.   2335
Then once again gaily to Gawain he calls,
And in a loud voice and lusty, delivers these words:
"Bold fellow, on this field your anger forbear!
No man has made demands here in manner uncouth,
Nor done, save as duly determined at court.   2340
I owed you a hit and you have it; be happy therewith!
The rest of my rights here I freely resign.
Had I been a bit busier, a buffet, perhaps,
I could have dealt more directly, and done you some harm.
First I flourished with a feint, in frolicsome mood,   2345
And left your hide unhurt—and here I did well
By the fair terms we fixed on the first night;
And fully and faithfully you followed accord:
Gave over all your gains as a good man should.
A second feint, sir, I assigned for the morning   2350
You kissed my comely wife—each kiss you restored.
For both of these there behooved but two feigned blows

by right.
True men pay what they owe;
No danger then in sight.   2355
You failed at the third throw,
So take my tap, sir knight.

"For that is my belt about you, that same braided girdle,
My wife it was that wore it; I know well the tale,
And the count of your kisses and your conduct too,   2360
And the wooing of my wife—it was all my scheme!
She made trial of a man most faultless by far
Of all that ever walked over the wide earth;
As pearls to white peas, more precious and prized,
So is Gawain, in good faith, to other gay knights.   2365
Yet you lacked, sir, a little in loyalty there,
But the cause was not cunning, nor courtship either,
But that you loved your own life; the less, then, to blame."
The other stout knight in a study stood a long while,
So gripped with grim rage that his great heart shook.   2370
All the blood of his body burned in his face
As he shrank back in shame from the man's sharp speech.
The first words that fell from the fair knight's lips:
"Accursed be a cowardly and covetous heart!
In you is villainy and vice, and virtue laid low!"   2375
Then he grasps the green girdle and lets go the knot,
Hands it over in haste, and hotly he says:
"Behold there my falsehood, ill hap betide it!
Your cut taught me cowardice, care for my life,
And coveting came after, contrary both   2380
To largesse and loyalty belonging to knights.
Now am I faulty and false, that fearful was ever
Of disloyalty and lies, bad luck to them both!
                    and greed.
          I confess, knight, in this place,   2385
          Most dire is my misdeed;
          Let me gain back your good grace,
          And thereafter I shall take heed."

Then the other laughed aloud, and lightly he said,
"Such harm as I have had, I hold it quite healed.   2390
You are so fully confessed, your failings made known,
And bear the plain penance of the point of my blade,
I hold you polished as a pearl, as pure and as bright
As you had lived free of fault since first you were born.
And I give you, sir, this girdle that is gold-hemmed   2395
And green as my garments, that, Gawain, you may
Be mindful of this meeting when you mingle in throng
With nobles of renown—and known by this token

How it chanced at the Green Chapel, to chivalrous knights.
And you shall in this New Year come yet again   2400
And we shall finish out our feast in my fair hall,
                  with cheer."
         He urged the knight to stay,
         And said, "With my wife so dear
         We shall see you friends this day,   2405
         Whose enmity touched you near."

"Indeed," said the doughty knight, and doffed his high helm,
And held it in his hands as he offered his thanks,
"I have lingered long enough—may good luck be yours,
And He reward you well that all worship bestows!   2410
And commend me to that comely one, your courteous wife,
Both herself and that other, my honoured ladies,
That have trapped their true knight in their trammels so quaint.
But if a dullard should dote, deem it no wonder,
And through the wiles of a woman be wooed into sorrow,   2415
For so was Adam by one, when the world began,
And Solomon by many more, and Samson the mighty—
Delilah was his doom, and David thereafter
Was beguiled by Bathsheba, and bore much distress;
Now these were vexed by their devices—'twere a very joy   2420
Could one but learn to love, and believe them not.
For these were proud princes, most prosperous of old,
Past all lovers lucky, that languished under heaven,
                  bemused.
         And one and all fell prey   2425
         To women that they had used;
         If I be led astray,
         Methinks I may be excused.

"But your girdle, God love you! I gladly shall take
And be pleased to possess, not for the pure gold,   2430
Nor the bright belt itself, nor the beauteous pendants,
Nor for wealth, nor worldly state, nor workmanship fine,
But a sign of excess it shall seem oftentimes
When I ride in renown, and remember with shame
The faults and the frailty of the flesh perverse,   2435
How its tenderness entices the foul taint of sin;
And so when praise and high prowess have pleased my heart,
A look at this love-lace will lower my pride.
But one thing would I learn, if you were not loath,
Since you are lord of yonder land where I have long sojourned   2440
With honor in your house—may you have His reward
That upholds all the heavens, highest on throne!
How runs your right name?—and let the rest go."
"That shall I give you gladly," said the Green Knight then;

"Bercilak de Hautdesert this barony I hold,   2445
Through the might of Morgan le Fay,[9] that lodges at my house,
By subtleties of science and sorcerers' arts,
The mistress of Merlin, she has caught many a man,
For sweet love in secret she shared sometime
With that wizard, that knows well each one of your knights   2450
            and you.
      Morgan the Goddess, she,
      So styled by title true;
      None holds so high degree
      That her arts cannot subdue.   2455

"She guided me in this guise to your glorious hall,
To assay, if such it were, the surfeit of pride
That is rumored of the retinue of the Round Table.
She put this shape upon me to puzzle your wits,
To afflict the fair queen, and frighten her to death   2460
With awe of that elvish man that eerily spoke
With his head in his hand before the high table.
She was with my wife at home, that old withered lady,
Your own aunt is she,[1] Arthur's half-sister,
The Duchess' daughter of Tintagel, that dear King Uther   2465
Got Arthur on after, that honored is now.
And therefore, good friend, come feast with your aunt;
Make merry in my house; my men hold you dear,
And I wish you as well, sir, with all my heart,
As any mortal man, for your matchless faith."   2470
But the knight said him nay, that he might by no means.
They clasped then and kissed, and commended each other
To the Prince of Paradise, and parted with one
            assent.
      Gawain sets out anew;   2475
      Toward the court his course is bent;
      And the knight all green in hue,
      Wheresoever he wished, he went.

Wild ways in the world our worthy knight rides
On Gringolet, that by grace had been granted his life.   2480
He harbored often in houses, and often abroad,
And with many valiant adventures verily he met
That I shall not take time to tell in this story.
The hurt was whole that he had had in his neck,
And the bright green belt on his body he bore,   2485
Oblique, like a baldric, bound at his side,
Below his left shoulder, laced in a knot,

---

9. Arthur's half-sister, an enchantress ("Faye," fairy) who sometimes abetted him, sometimes made trouble for him.   1. Morgan was the daughter of Igraine, Duchess of Tintagel, and her husband, the Duke. Igraine conceived Arthur when his father, Uther, lay with her through one of Merlin's trickeries.

In betokening of the blame he had borne for his fault;
And so to court in due course he comes safe and sound.
Bliss abounded in hall when the high-born heard   2490
That good Gawain was come; glad tidings they thought it.
The king kisses the knight, and the queen as well,
And many a comrade came to clasp him in arms,
And eagerly they asked, and awesomely he told,
Confessed all his cares and discomfitures many,   2495
How it chanced at the Chapel, what cheer made the knight,
The love of the lady, the green lace at last.
The nick on his neck he naked displayed
That he got in his disgrace at the Green Knight's hands,
                                        alone.   2500
            With rage in heart he speaks,
            And grieves with many a groan;
            The blood burns in his cheeks
            For shame at what must be shown.

"Behold, sir," said he, and handles the belt,   2505
"This is the blazon of the blemish that I bear on my neck;
This is the sign of sore loss that I have suffered there
For the cowardice and coveting that I came to there;
This is the badge of false faith that I was found in there,
And I must bear it on my body till I breathe my last.   2510
For one may keep a deed dark, but undo it no whit,
For where a fault is made fast, it is fixed evermore."
The king comforts the knight, and the court all together
Agree with gay laughter and gracious intent
That the lords and the ladies belonging to the Table,   2515
Each brother of that band, a baldric should have,
A belt borne oblique, of a bright green,
To be worn with one accord for that worthy's sake.
So that was taken as a token by the Table Round,
And he honored that had it, evermore after,   2520
As the best book of knighthood bids it be known.
In the old days of Arthur this happening befell;
The books of Brutus' deeds bear witness thereto
Since Brutus, the bold knight, embarked for this land
After the siege ceased at Troy and the city fared   2525
                                        amiss.
            Many such, ere we were born,
            Have befallen here, ere this.
            May He that was crowned with thorn
            Bring all men to His bliss! Amen.   2530

GEOFFREY CHAUCER

1340?–1400

Although the French produced the richest and most influential body of vernacular literature in the Middle Ages, the greatest writers of the period were an Italian, Dante, and an Englishman, Chaucer. The Florentine poet and the Londoner both wrote their most important works in the fourteenth century, the former in its early decades, the latter in its latest. In origin and background, both represent the point of view of the upper middle class or the lesser gentry, groups which were not sharply separated in the urban life of Italy and of London in the later medieval centuries. Both were active in public affairs; both on occasion were envoys of their respective governments. Dante was once responsible for widening a street in Florence, and Chaucer for a time held a post comparable to that of an under-secretary of the interior in the cabinet of the United States. If Dante had sharper political convictions and a greater theoretical interest in the philosophy of government, Chaucer held a wider variety of offices—and held them longer.

Geoffrey Chaucer was born in 1340 or a few years later, the son of a London wine merchant. In 1357 he apparently became a page in the household of the Countess of Ulster, wife of Lionel, a son of King Edward III. In 1359, in military service with the English in France, he was captured by the French and ransomed with royal funds. Between 1368 and 1378 Chaucer made several journeys to France and Italy as the king's envoy or courier. In 1374 he received a pension from John of Gaunt, a son of Edward III, and became comptroller of customs in the port of London; about 1385 he moved to Kent, where he was elected knight of the shire in 1386, and sat in Parliament for one term. In 1389 he became Clerk of the King's Works (under Richard II), in 1391 deputy forester of the royal forest of North Petherton in Somerset, and in 1399 pensioner of King Henry IV. He died in 1400.

Chaucer's early works include *The Romance of the Rose*, a translation (probably never finished) of the *Roman de la Rose*; the *Book of the Duchess*; the *House of Fame*; and the *Parliament of Fowls*—all in English verse. He also translated *A Treatise on the Astrolabe* and Boethius' *Consolation of Philosophy* into English prose. His major works are *Troilus and Criseyde*, completed about 1385, and *The Canterbury Tales*, composed largely in the 1390s but with some use of earlier material.

Both Dante and Chaucer probably lived out their lives as laymen; their view of the world is free from the bias of a clerical vocation. Yet both were orthodox in religion and theology. Dante was severe with heretics and schismatics, and Chaucer was neither a Wycliffite nor a sympathizer with the Peasants' Revolt. With the partial exception of Dante's insistence on the equal status of the Holy Roman Empire and the Papacy, alike providentially sponsored, it may be said that both poets found themselves in harmony with the traditional institutions and patterns of medieval civilization. Both were keenly aware of injustices resulting from abuses of the system; each exposed scoundrels and frauds with enthusiasm—Dante with bitterness, Chaucer with amusement. But their denunciation of wicked rulers and their satire directed against the worldliness of bishops and abbots and the corruptness of friars and pardoners do not show either writer to be a rebel against the established institutions of Church or State. The background against which abuses are portrayed is always, implicitly or explicitly, the ideal pattern for the king or priest or monk—not some utopian or revolutionary social order that would dispense with or radically alter the patterns themselves.

On the ultimate issues of human life, as in these questions of the structure of civilization, the two greatest literary geniuses of the Middle Ages were in agreement with each other and with their contemporaries. For each, God was the center of the universe, as humanity and our earth were the center of the cosmic order. Our life's goal was union with God; if we attained it—after this short earthly life—we would spend eternity in heaven; if we missed it, then hell awaited us. For our direction and guidance toward the good in this life and the next, there were the divinely ordained religion and its Church, and the divinely approved hierarchy of society on earth. As men of independent intelligence, of education—and of essentially middle-class origin—both Dante and Chaucer insisted that true nobility depends on intrinsic character, not the accident of birth. But the modern conceptions of political, social, and economic equality, and complete religious freedom, would have appeared to them as anarchy. They had fundamental faith in the quite different patterns of institutional hierarchy and authority.

If Dante chose the life after death as the theme of the greatest medieval poem, Chaucer chose a religious pilgrimage as the framework of the richest portrayal of medieval men and women in the earthly scene. Chaucer's pilgrims are very much alive; they are on their way to thank St. Thomas of Canterbury for his help in keeping them that way! Yet the twenty-nine travelers, including those described in the course of the pilgrimage, are not incomparable in number or vividness to the characters presented with similar fullness in *The Divine Comedy*. Both poets— when they wish—make the individual stand out clearly and distinctly; both—when they choose—present fully the background, the milieu, the occupational or moral setting from which the individual emerges and in terms of which he or she is to be estimated. Both poets sketch the portraits with extraordinary insight, discrimination, and perception of the subtle mixture of good and bad in humanity. It would be interesting to attempt the assignment of Chaucer's pilgrims to their proper places in *The Divine Comedy*—assuming that each of them dies in the condition described in the Prologue.

With the Knight, the Parson, his brother the Plowman, the Clerk of Oxford, and the Nun's Priest (who is characterized in the course of the journey) we should have no trouble. Though thoroughly human, flesh-and-blood people, these are all wholly excellent and admirable men. Moral and ethical nobility is a part of their personal and vocational perfection. They embody—not merely personify as abstractions—the ideal characteristics of men in their several stations in life; they are models as well as individuals. But these individuals are living men on earth. We recognize in the portrait of the Clerk, for instance, an ingredient of tacit humor hardly duplicated in Dante's presentation of the blessed. The Clerk's unique traits of temperament and taste—the concise habit of speech, the aloofness, the ardent book-collecting—might be a little irrelevant in Heaven, while eminently suited to his portrait in this world.

The scoundrels, likewise, would be easy to deal with. The Friar, the Pardoner, the Summoner—and perhaps also the Shipman, the Reeve, the Manciple, and the Miller—would easily find their respective niches in the circles of Hell—most of them in the ten subdivisions of the eighth circle, in which those guilty of various kinds of fraud are punished. Dante might have made each of them tell his story in much the same terms as Chaucer used. He would have done it with as much gusto; indeed, his work includes parallels to most of them. But denunciation and contempt would have replaced Chaucer's detached delight in the cleverness and success of their rascality. Again, the vantage point dictates an appropriate difference of treatment; time and our earth are a different background from eternity and Hell. Both Dante's and Chaucer's portraits achieve symmetry. But Dante's are more decisive, more limited, more exclusively concentrated on ethical definition; Chaucer's have room for more mundane, personal, and morally neutral detail.

We should have great difficulty in classifying some of the other pilgrims. The exquisite Prioress is doubtless destined for Heaven. But should we expect to find her, fairly soon, among the blessed in one of the three lowest spheres—the moon, Mercury, or Venus? Is she, like Piccarda, a soul whose unquestionably genuine devotion is linked with an intrinsically limited spiritual capacity—limited in a way suggested by her unmonastic fondness for pet dogs, nice clothes, and fashionable manners? Or is her sensibility an outward sign of great spiritual endowment, so that, after some time on the terraces of Purgatory, she will be found among the higher spheres of the celestial hierarchy? Dante had to decide such questions concerning his characters, and his portraits naturally show how they fit the classifications. Chaucer did not have to decide; his pilgrims still belong to the earth, and some of their portraits are executed without conclusive moral definition. The worldly, hunting Monk—will he take his place among the avaricious or the hypocrites in Hell? Or will he purge his worldliness, like Pope Adrian, on the fifth ledge of the mountain?

In general, Chaucer shows a large "middle" group of people, confirmed perhaps in neither wickedness nor holiness, but absorbed in the things of this world. Such an absorption exposes the professed cleric, secular or monastic, to ironical satire; for the religious vocation involves renunciation of the world. This is why many of the pilgrims connected with the Church are obvious targets. But laymen also run the risk of ridicule if their absorption in worldly matters leads to excessive egotism or affectation or limitation of perspective. Thus the Sergeant of the Law, whose days are, in fact, full, *seems* even busier than he is; the Merchant apparently talks entirely about profits; and the Physician's financial astuteness is not unmixed with complacency. The Franklin's pride in his hospitality and fine table is a more attractive form of egotism—although one might hesitate to become his cook! Traits such as these, casually mentioned in the Prologue, would be valuable hints as to where on the terraces of Purgatory the several pilgrims might be expected to spend some time. Meanwhile, it is just such qualities, the weaknesses, foibles, excesses, and limitations, that endow them with distinctness and poignancy in this world—in short, with individuality and personality.

It is often said that the characters in the Prologue are delineated in terms of the superlative—each of the pilgrims is the best, or worst, representative of his particular kind. To some degree this is true. Yet it is also true that Chaucer finds far less to say about some than about others. He is, in fact, interested in them in different ways. Thus the Knight is described at length; occupationally, ethically, and otherwise he emerges as an individual member of a class. His son, the young Squire, is presented primarily as a fine but standard specimen of his type, the fashionable young warrior and politely cultivated "lover." And in their servant, the Yeoman, we see a yet smaller segment of the whole character: he is simply an expert woodsman. Other pilgrims, like the five Guildsmen, receive only a collective portrait; they all share in the pride of their crafts and their organized "fraternity," in the garb of which they are handsomely turned out. A few of the company are not described at all in the Prologue.

Evidently Chaucer has allowed himself a margin of freedom in his account of this imaginary company as they present themselves to the imaginary observer and fellow traveler, the poet. With the future possibilities of the pilgrimage in mind, he readily leaves a few members of the group undeveloped; one of these, the Nun's Priest, does emerge in full characterization as the tales proceed. But in the Prologue itself Chaucer gives us the fullest, the most varied, and the liveliest, panorama of men and women in medieval literature. The portraits are usually fairly complete and satisfying in themselves, though, as we have noted, some are miniatures and some large canvases, some are full face, some profile, and a few quarter face. Yet the portraits are not merely lively in themselves; they are dynamic; they prepare us for the highly dramatic relationships that develop among the pilgrims in the course of the journey.

THE MILLER'S TALE

At the end of the General Prologue we are told that the Knight will tell the first tale. This narrative, not included in our book, is a fine example of medieval metrical romance—with important variations from the standard types. As we learn from the Words between the Host and the Miller, the latter, now drunk, refuses to follow the decorous order preferred by the Host; he insists on matching the Knight right now with his tale. When he goes on to say that it will be a story of an old carpenter, his wife, and her student lover, we anticipate, rightly, that it will be the opposite of the Knight's courtly romance. Like the medieval reader, we expect a tale of amorous intrigue and trickery involving people of considerably less than noble rank, in short, a fabliau. But the carpenter's wife, Alison, has not only a husband, John, and a lover, Nicholas; there is also a would-be lover, the parish clerk, Absalom. There is thus a double triangle plot, with Alison at the apex of both triangles; and the denouement comes when one triangle crashes down on the other.

This addition to the traditional fabliau plot is one part of Chaucer's vast enrichment of what must have been a fairly stereotyped narrative. In mediocre tales of this sort, the plot is almost everything; they are comic anecdotes. But Chaucer has lavished as much effort on characterization and depiction of scenes as one expects in the best serious literature. We get to know the clever, opportunistic, cynical Nicholas very well indeed. His rival, Absalom, is a complete contrast. He is theatrical, sentimental, and silly; his "love" songs are an amusing parody of the poetic pleas of chivalric suitors. (Nicholas is much too practical and hardheaded to go in for amorous complaints; he keeps his eye on the main chance—and he is right; he knows how to get what he wants, as Absalom does not.)

The vivid, detailed description of Alison, rich in comparisons and fresh images, would remind the medieval reader of traditional portraits of ladies in romances—by difference rather than similarity. Instead of the standard noble lady, looking out placidly from a castle window, we have Alison, painted in a series of modest similes: "a coin," "a swallow," a "mouth . . . as sweet as honey-ale," "skittish as an untrained colt." The personality of John, the carpenter, is similarly altered. Here the prototype was an old husband married to a young wife; he was jealous and suspicious. Chaucer's John is a great deal more than this. He is genuinely devoted to his wife—he dotes on her; he is fond of Nicholas, his student lodger, though he also believes in the common-sense advantages of the ordinary man (himself) over the scholar; and he is attractively gullible—he embraces the plan for dealing with the flood with great gusto.

The denouement of the Miller's Tale does not satisfy the requirements of poetic justice; it does not reward the good and punish the wicked, at least not consistently. Instead, it penalizes stupidity and vindicates cleverness. Moreover, characterization and plot reinforce each other: the various individuals do the kinds of things that we are willing to believe these kinds of people would do. And there is room for variation within the basic pattern: The ingenuity of Nicholas is duly rewarded, but when overconfidence leads him to overreach himself a bit (both metaphorically and literally), he suffers in the end. Alison's cleverness is not flawed by such excess—and she escapes.

The Pardoner is one of the liveliest rascals on the Canterbury pilgrimage. His crookedness is so complete that it may be difficult for us to realize just what a pardoner was properly or ideally like in the fourteenth century. For one thing, a legitimate pardoner did not go about "pardoning" people for their sins. Many such men were not—and were not expected to be—priests, in the proper sense of the term, at all. Many doubtless were in what is called minor orders, extending up to subdeacon. Such men were not qualified or authorized to hear confession or grant absolution. The legitimate activity of a pardoner consisted in making available to devout persons a certificate of ecclesiastical "indulgence." The charge made for this constituted a gift or offering to God and the Church. The purchase was therefore considered a worthy act in the sight of God that might benefit the soul of the purchaser (as well as relatives or friends if they were doing penance in purgatory, but *not* if they had been sent to hell).

No doubt there were many perfectly honest and worthy pardoners in medieval Europe. But the opportunities for personal profit are evident, and there must have been some who exploited these opportunities unscrupulously. Besides distributing indulgences of doubtful validity, Chaucer's Pardoner preaches in country churches, intimidating the congregation so that they will not fail to put money in the collection plate; and he makes a good profit out of fake relics. Far from being ashamed of these vices, he is proud of his skill in dishonesty. He tells us all about it in the Prologue to his tale.

The Pardoner's Tale itself is a sample of his preaching. The text of the sermon is his favorite: Covetousness is the root of evil. It is ironical, of course, that such a man should preach so regularly and strenuously against his own greatest sin. His sermon, as Chaucer presents it, is really a very old and simple story about three men who went in search of Death and found him unexpectedly. The Pardoner dramatizes the narrative with great energy and imagination. In addition, he embroiders it with brief anecdotes which are really digressions. Before he has really entered into the story, moreover, he takes time out for a ringing denunciation of gluttony (including drunkenness), gambling, and swearing—complete with examples of each.

The tale of Chanticleer and Dame Partlet is Chaucer at his best. Since the basic story of a cock, a hen, and a fox is rich in human implications and applications and in intrinsic humor, it must have been especially congenial to the imaginative comic spirit of the mature Chaucer—and it apparently does belong to a late period in the composition of *The Canterbury Tales*. For its narrator the poet chose the genial Priest who rode with the two nuns on the pilgrimage; his good taste and inexhaustible sense of humor have been ripened by years of reading and observation of life.

The setting of the tale in the Canterbury pilgrimage contributes to its total effect. The Knight, seconded by the Host, has suddenly interrupted the Monk, who was retailing an apparently endless series of "tragedies," or tales of misfortune. This has become unendurably gloomy and dull, they protest; they demand something more cheerful and entertaining. When the Monk has nothing else to offer, the Host turns to Sir John, the Priest, and bids him "Tell us a thing to make our spirits glad. / Be cheerful, though the jade you ride is bad."

Thus launched, the Priest gives us a remarkable version of one of the favorite stories of the Middle Ages. For of course Chaucer did not invent the plot itself. The popular literature of Europe had long included tales of the cock's capture through his weakness for flattery, and his escape through the fox's overweening pride. The narrative can be condensed in a paragraph or spun out to indeterminate length, according to the inclination of the narrator. The Priest, without losing sight of its identity as a moral fable, makes it many other things as well.

First, with leisurely detail and humor, he gives the cock and hen a human background. The quiet, realistic description of the circumstances of the poor widow—her narrow cottage with a small yard surrounded by a wooden fence, her three cows, three hogs, and one sheep, named Moll—reads like the beginning of a skill-fully told modern short story. The implicit contrast with a great house or castle is cumulatively comic; it evokes a smile rather than a guffaw.

Then we are brought to the description of Chanticleer and his seven wives—they are part of the widow's household, indoors and outdoors. The account of the cock is at first simply "superlative," like the characterization of the Canterbury pilgrims themselves; he is initially the best imaginable cock. His regular crowing, exactly on the hour, doubtless appeared less extraordinary to Chaucer's audience than it does to us, for apparently this accuracy was commonly attributed to roosters during the medieval period. But the detailed description of his features and color-ing is done in the manner of the literary portraits of heroes in romances; and the cock's comb, scalloped "like a crenelated castle wall," is a first touch of the mock-heroic. Partlet too has the virtues of highborn ladies in romances; she is courtly, discreet, and debonair. And she has held Chanticleer's firm affection since she was seven nights old!

Having thus acquainted us with the general capacities of these unusual chickens, the Priest moves us on to the first incident in the story itself—Chanticleer's dream. The tone here is that of ordinary, commonplace domesticity: a husband is awak-ened from a nightmare, which he then relates to his wife. Their further conversa-tion is in the same vein, Partlet combining in her character both the wife who measures her husband, reproachfully, against a standard of heroic perfection and the more prosaic wife who confidently diagnoses her husband's indisposition and energetically tells him what to take for it. The line "Have you no man's heart, when you have a beard?" indicates how completely the cock and hen have become a human pair.

In the matrimonial argument about the nature and significance of dreams Chau-cer employs the two principal medieval theories on the subject. He assigns the physiological explanation to Partlet; women were thought to be more realistic and practical than men. Both of their speeches poke fun at the method of proof by citing authorities. But Chanticleer's extended monologue has a further purpose: it is structural in the development of the plot and evokes the comic irony which is at the center of the tale. For the very act of vigorously refuting Partlet and proving that dreams do portend danger has the effect of reassuring him. Having won the argument—to his own satisfaction and because Partlet offers no rebuttal—Chanti-cleer is no longer disturbed about the dream. His thoughts turn exuberantly to love, and the climax of the plot is reached when he declares: "I am then so full of pure felicity / That I defy whatever sort of dream!"

Having fully established this mood in Chanticleer—having in fact characterized him in heroic terms—Chaucer tells us that a cunning fox has made it through the hedge during the night and is now hiding in a bed of herbs in the yard, lying in wait for Chanticleer. This leads to a citation of traitors and deceivers from epic literature and an elaborate raising of the question of predestination, foreknowledge, and free will.

Next it is pointed out that Chanticleer unfortunately took his wife's advice about the dream ("Woman have many times, as wise men hold, / Offered advice that left men in the cold"), and Adam's loss of Paradise is immediately cited as a parallel. Thus we see finally that the whole situation has been presented as a kind of parody of the Fall, with Chanticleer as Adam, Partlet as Eve, and the fox, now lurking but later to speak with persuasive and successful flattery, as the Serpent.

The rest of the tale is carried out in the same vein of elaborate mockery, complete with allusions, exclamations, and comparisons. The fox displays consummate diplomacy, Chanticleer is as naïve and susceptible as possible, and Partlet's grief is epic. Perhaps the finest passage, among many excellent, is the picture of the utter confusion and uproar of men, women, beasts, and fowls when the alarm is given. At last—to provide the happy ending demanded by the Knight and the Host as well as to conform to the familiar plot of the story—comes the second reversal, when Chanticleer escapes. And in conclusion Sir John, who, for all his wit and humor, is a deeply and wholesomely religious man, reminds us:

> Such is it to be reckless and unheedful
> And trust in flattery. . . .
> Think twice, and take the moral, my good men!

CHAUCER IN MIDDLE ENGLISH

Chaucer is presented here in a Modern English version by Theodore Morrison, which is remarkably clear, accurate, and easy to read. But, in order to get some idea of Chaucer's original language, we may profitably compare the first eighteen lines of the *General Prologue* in the two forms. It will be possible to point out only a few of the changes that have occurred in pronunciation, in grammatical forms, and sometimes in the use and meaning of words.

> Whan that Aprille with his shoures sote
> The droghte of Marche hath perced to the rote,
> And bathed every veyne in swich licour,
> Of which vertu engendred is the flour;
> When Zephirus eek with his swete breeth   5
> Inspired hath in every holt and heeth
> The tendre croppes, and the yonge sonne
> Hath in the Ram his halfe cours y-ronne,
> And smale fowles maken melodye,
> That slepen al the night with open yë,   10
> So priketh hem nature in hir corages:
> Than longen folk to goon on pilgrimages
> And palmers for to seken straunge strandes
> To ferne halwes, couthe in sondry landes;
> And specially, from every shires ende   15

Of Engeland, to Caunterbury they wende,
The holy blisful martir for to seke,
That hem hath holpen, whan that they were seke.

In Middle English of the late fourteenth century, the letters representing the stressed vowels were pronounced about as they are in Spanish or Italian in our time. Thus the A of *Aprille* sounded like *a* in our *father;* the first *e* in *swete* (line 5) was like the *a* in Modern English *late;* and the second *i* in *Inspired* (line 6) was like *i* in our *machine.* In verbs, the third person singular ended in -*th,* not -*s,* as in *hath* (line 2); and the plural ending, either -*en* or -*e,* formed a separate syllable, as in *maken* (line 9), *slepen* (line 10), and *wende* (line 16). Among the pronouns and pronominal adjectives, Chaucer's language did not have our *its, their,* or *them.* Instead, the corresponding forms were, respectively, *his* (line 1), *hir(e)* (line 11), and *hem* (line 18). Changes in the meaning or use of words may compel a substitution. Thus Chaucer's *couthe* (line 14) has become obsolete and hence the translation has *renowned* instead; so also *corages* (line 11) becomes *hearts,* and *ferne halwes* (line 14) becomes *foreign shrines.*

It will be noted that both the original and the translation have lines regularly rhyming in couplets. Sometimes the translator has been able to keep the same rhyming words (with some difference of pronunciation) as in lines 7 and 8 and lines 13 and 14. In other places he has found it necessary to substitute a new rhyming pair of his own, as in lines 1 and 2 and lines 17 and 18—although in the first instance the translator keeps one of the original rhyming words but not the other.

The standard edition of Chaucer's works is *The Riverside Chaucer, Third Edition,* general editor Larry D. Benson (1987). This book provides a fully annotated text in the original Middle English, with a glossary, ample introductions,and other apparatus. For the treatment of the *Prologue* and the *Canterbury Tales,* see pp. 3622.

Among the large number of good books about Chaucer, here are a few that may be especially helpful to our readers. For an overall view, G. L. Kittredge, *Chaucer and his Poetry* 91915), is still important. The artistic development of the poet is traced in Derek S. Brewer, *Chaucer* (1953). A survey of critical problems is presented in Derek A. Pearsall, *The Canterbury Tales* (1985). A variety of topics and points of view will be found in Edward Wagenknecht, ed., *Chaucer: Modern Essays in Criticism* (1959).

The Canterbury Tales[1]

GENERAL PROLOGUE

As soon as April pierces to the root
The drought of March, and bathes each bud and shoot
Through every vein of sap with gentle showers
From whose engendering liquor spring the flowers;
When zephyrs[2] have breathed softly all about   5
Inspiring every wood and field to sprout,
And in the zodiac the youthful sun

1. Selections. Translated and edited by Theodore Morrison.   2. The west wind.

His journey halfway through the Ram[3] has run;
When little birds are busy with their song
Who sleep with open eyes the whole night long   10
Life stirs their hearts and tingles in them so,
Then off as pilgrims people long to go,
And palmers[4] to set out for distant strands
And foreign shrines renowned in many lands.
And specially in England people ride   15
To Canterbury from every countryside
To visit there the blessed martyred saint[5]
Who gave them strength when they were sick and faint.

   In Southwark at the Tabard[6] one spring day
It happened, as I stopped there on my way,   20
Myself a pilgrim with a heart devout
Ready for Canterbury to set out,
At night came all of twenty-nine assorted
Travelers, and to that same inn resorted,
Who by a turn of fortune chanced to fall   25
In fellowship together, and they were all
Pilgrims who had it in their minds to ride
Toward Canterbury. The stable doors were wide,
The rooms were large, and we enjoyed the best,
And shortly, when the sun had gone to rest,   30
I had so talked with each that presently
I was a member of their company
And promised to rise early the next day
To start, as I shall show, upon our way.

   But none the less, while I have time and space,   35
Before this tale has gone a further pace,
I should in reason tell you the condition
Of each of them, his rank and his position,
And also what array they all were in;
And so then, with a knight I will begin.   40

   A Knight was with us, and an excellent man,
Who from the earliest moment he began
To follow his career loved chivalry,
Truth, openhandedness, and courtesy.
He was a stout man in the king's campaigns   45
And in that cause had gripped his horse's reins
In Christian lands and pagan through the earth,
None farther, and always honored for his worth.
He was on hand at Alexandria's fall.[7]

---

3. A sign of the Zodiac (Aries); the sun is in the Ram from March 12 to April 11.   4. Pilgrims, who, originally, brought back palm leaves from the Holy Land.   5. St. Thomas à Becket, slain in Canterbury cathedral in 1170.   6. An inn at Southwark, across the river Thames from London.   7. In Egypt, captured in 1365 by King Peter of Cyprus.

He had often sat in precedence to all   50
The nations at the banquet board in Prussia.
He had fought in Lithuania and in Russia,
No Christian knight more often; he had been
In Moorish Africa at Benmarin,
At the siege of Algeciras in Granada,   55
And sailed in many a glorious armada
In the Mediterranean, and fought as well
At Ayas and Attalia when they fell
In Armenia and on Asia Minor's coast.
Of fifteen deadly battles he could boast,   60
And in Algeria, at Tremessen,
Fought for the faith and killed three separate men
In single combat. He had done good work
Joining against another pagan Turk
With the king of Palathia. And he was wise,   65
Despite his prowess, honored in men's eyes,
Meek as a girl and gentle in his ways.
He had never spoken ignobly all his days
To any man by even a rude inflection.
He was a knight in all things to perfection.   70
He rode a good horse, but his gear was plain,
For he had lately served on a campaign.
His tunic was still spattered by the rust
Left by his coat of mail, for he had just
Returned and set out on his pilgrimage.   75
    His son was with him, a young Squire, in age
Some twenty years as near as I could guess.
His hair curled as if taken from a press.
He was a lover and would become a knight.
In stature he was of a moderate height   80
But powerful and wonderfully quick.
He had been in Flanders, riding in the thick
Of forays in Artois and Picardy,
And bore up well for one so young as he,
Still hoping by his exploits in such places   85
To stand the better in his lady's graces.
He wore embroidered flowers, red and white,
And blazed like a spring meadow to the sight.
He sang or played his flute the livelong day.
He was as lusty as the month of May.   90
His coat was short, its sleeves were long and wide.
He sat his horse well, and knew how to ride,
And how to make a song and use his lance,
And he could write and draw well, too, and dance.
So hot his love that when the moon rose pale   95
He got no more sleep than a nightingale.

He was modest, and helped whomever he was able,
And carved as his father's squire at the table.
   But one more servant had the Knight beside,
Choosing thus simply for the time to ride: 100
A Yeoman, in a coat and hood of green.
His peacock-feathered arrows, bright and keen,
He carried under his belt in tidy fashion.
For well-kept gear he had a yeoman's passion,
No draggled feather might his arrows show, 105
And in his hand he held a mighty bow.
He kept his hair close-cropped, his face was brown.
He knew the lore of woodcraft up and down.
His arm was guarded from the bowstring's whip
By a bracer, gaily trimmed. He had at hip 110
A sword and buckler, and at his other side
A dagger whose fine mounting was his pride,
Sharp-pointed as a spear. His horn he bore
In a sling of green, and on his chest he wore
A silver image of St. Christopher, 115
His patron, since he was a forester.
   There was also a Nun, a Prioress,
Whose smile was gentle and full of guilelessness.
"By St. Loy!"[8] was the worst oath she would say.
She sang mass well, in a becoming way, 120
Intoning through her nose the words divine,
And she was known as Madame Eglantine.
She spoke good French, as taught at Stratford-Bow[9]
For the Parisian French she did not know.
She was schooled to eat so primly and so well 125
That from her lips no morsel ever fell.
She wet her fingers lightly in the dish
Of sauce, for courtesy was her first wish.
With every bite she did her skillful best
To see that no drop fell upon her breast. 130
She always wiped her upper lip so clean
That in her cup was never to be seen
A hint of grease when she had drunk her share.
She reached out for her meat with comely air.
She was a great delight, and always tried 135
To imitate court ways, and had her pride,
Both amiable and gracious in her dealings.
As for her charity and tender feelings,
She melted at whatever was piteous.
She would weep if she but came upon a mouse 140
Caught in a trap, if it were dead or bleeding.

8. Perhaps St. Eligius, apparently a popular saint at this time.   9. In Middlesex, near London, where
there was a nunnery.

Some little dogs that she took pleasure feeding
On roasted meat or milk or good wheat bread
She had, but how she wept to find one dead
Or yelping from a blow that made it smart,   145
And all was sympathy and loving heart.
Neat was her wimple in its every plait,
Her nose well formed, her eyes as gray as slate.
Her mouth was very small and soft and red.
She had so wide a brow I think her head   150
Was nearly a span broad, for certainly
She was not undergrown, as all could see.
She wore her cloak with dignity and charm,
And had her rosary about her arm,
The small beads coral and the larger green,   155
And from them hung a brooch of golden sheen,
On it a large A and a crown above;
Beneath, "All things are subject unto love."
    A Priest accompanied her toward Canterbury,
And an attendant Nun, her secretary.   160
    There was a Monk, and nowhere was his peer,
A hunter, and a roving overseer.
He was a manly man, and fully able
To be an abbot. He kept a hunting stable,
And when he rode the neighborhood could hear   165
His bridle jingling in the wind as clear
And loud as if it were a chapel bell.
Wherever he was master of a cell
The principles of good St. Benedict,[1]
For being a little old and somewhat strict,   170
Were honored in the breach, as past their prime.
He lived by the fashion of a newer time.
He would have swapped that text for a plucked hen
Which says that hunters are not holy men,
Or a monk outside his discipline and rule   175
Is too much like a fish outside his pool;
That is to say, a monk outside his cloister.
But such a text he deemed not worth an oyster.
I told him his opinion made me glad.
Why should he study always and go mad,   180
Mewed in his cell with only a book for neighbor?
Or why, as Augustine commanded, labor
And sweat his hands? How shall the world be served?
To Augustine be all such toil reserved!
And so he hunted, as was only right.   185
He had greyhounds as swift as birds in flight.

---

1. Monastic rules, authored by St. Maurus and St. Benedict in the sixth century A.D.

His taste was all for tracking down the hare,
And what his sport might cost he did not care.
His sleeves I noticed, where they met his hand,
Trimmed with gray fur, the finest in the land. 190
His hood was fastened with a curious pin
Made of wrought gold and clasped beneath his chin,
A love knot at the tip. His head might pass,
Bald as it was, for a lump of shining glass,
And his face was glistening as if anointed. 195
Fat as a lord he was, and well appointed.
His eyes were large, and rolled inside his head
As if they gleamed from a furnace of hot lead.
His boots were supple, his horse superbly kept.
He was a prelate to dream of while you slept. 200
He was not pale nor peaked like a ghost.
He relished a plump swan as his favorite roast.
He rode a palfrey brown as a ripe berry.
    A Friar was with us, a gay dog and a merry,
Who begged his district with a jolly air. 205
No friar in all four orders could compare
With him for gallantry; his tongue was wooing.
Many a girl was married by his doing,
And at his own cost it was often done.
He was a pillar, and a noble one, 210
To his whole order. In his neighborhood
Rich franklins[2] knew him well, who served good food,
And worthy women welcomed him to town;
For the license that his order handed down,
He said himself, conferred on him possession 215
Of more than a curate's power of confession.
Sweetly the list of frailties he heard,
Assigning penance with a pleasant word.
He was an easy man for absolution
Where he looked forward to a contribution, 220
For if to a poor order a man has given
It signifies that he has been well shriven,
And if a sinner let his purse be dented
The Friar would stake his oath he had repented.
For many men become so hard of heart 225
They cannot weep, though conscience makes them smart.
Instead of tears and prayers, then, let the sinner
Supply the poor friars with the price of dinner.
For pretty women he had more than shrift.
His cape was stuffed with many a little gift, 230
As knives and pins and suchlike. He could sing

2. Landowners or country squires, not belonging to the nobility.

A merry note, and pluck a tender string,
And had no rival at all in balladry.
His neck was whiter than a fleur-de-lis,[3]
And yet he could have knocked a strong man down.   235
He knew the taverns well in every town.
The barmaids and innkeepers pleased his mind
Better than beggars and lepers and their kind.
In his position it was unbecoming
Among the wretched lepers to go slumming.   240
It mocks all decency, it sews no stitch
To deal with such riffraff, but with the rich,
With sellers of victuals, that's another thing.
Wherever he saw some hope of profiting,
None so polite, so humble. He was good,   245
The champion beggar of his brotherhood.
Should a woman have no shoes against the snow,
So pleasant was his "In principio"[4]
He would have her widow's mite before he went.
He took in far more than he paid in rent   250
For his right of begging within certain bounds.
None of his brethren trespassed on his grounds!
He loved as freely as a half-grown whelp.
On arbitration-days[5] he gave great help,
For his cloak was never shiny nor threadbare   255
Like a poor cloistered scholar's. He had an air
As if he were a doctor or a pope.
It took stout wool to make his semicope[6]
That plumped out like a bell for portliness.
He lisped a little in his rakishness   260
To make his English sweeter on his tongue,
And twanging his harp to end some song he'd sung
His eyes would twinkle in his head as bright
As the stars twinkle on a frosty night.
Hubert this gallant Friar was by name.   265
    Among the rest a Merchant also came.
He wore a forked beard and a beaver hat
From Flanders. High up in the saddle he sat,
In figured cloth, his boots clasped handsomely,
Delivering his opinions pompously,   270
Always on how his gains might be increased.
At all costs he desired the sea policed
From Middleburg in Holland to Orwell.[7]
He knew the exchange rates, and the time to sell

---

3. Lily.   4. "In the beginning"—the opening phrase of a famous passage in the New Testament (John 1:1–16), which the friar recites in Latin as a devotional exercise to awe the ignorant and extract their alms.   5. Days appointed for the adjustment of disputes.   6. A short cape.   7. He desired protection from piracy between Middleburg in Holland and Orwell, an English port near Harwich.

French currency, and there was never yet   275
A man who could have told he was in debt
So grave he seemed and hid so well his feelings
With all his shrewd engagements and close dealings.
You'd find no better man at any turn;
But what his name was I could never learn.   280

There was an Oxford Student too, it chanced,
Already in his logic well advanced.
He rode a mount as skinny as a rake,
And he was hardly fat. For learning's sake
He let himself look hollow and sober enough.   285
He wore an outer coat of threadbare stuff,
For he had no benefice for his enjoyment
And was too unworldly for some lay employment.
He much preferred to have beside his bed
His twenty volumes bound in black or red   290
All packed with Aristotle from end to middle
Than a sumptuous wardrobe or a merry fiddle.
For though he knew what learning had to offer
There was little coin to jingle in his coffer.
Whatever he got by touching up a friend   295
On books and learning he would promptly spend
And busily pray for the soul of anybody
Who furnished him the wherewithal for study.
His scholarship was what he truly heeded.
He never spoke a word more than was needed,   300
And that was said with dignity and force,
And quick and brief. He was of grave discourse
Giving new weight to virtue by his speech,
And gladly would he learn and gladly teach.

There was a Lawyer, cunning and discreet,   305
Who had often been to St. Paul's porch[8] to meet
His clients. He was a Sergeant of the Law,
A man deserving to be held in awe,
Or so he seemed, his manner was so wise.
He had often served as Justice of Assize   310
By the king's appointment, with a broad commission,
For his knowledge and his eminent position.
He had many a handsome gift by way of fee.
There was no buyer of land as shrewd as he.
All ownership to him became fee simple.[9]   315
His titles were never faulty by a pimple.
None was so busy as he with case and cause,
And yet he seemed much busier than he was.
In all cases and decisions he was schooled

---

8. A meeting place for lawyers and their clients.   9. Owned outright without legal impediments.

That were of record since King William[1] ruled.   320
No one could pick a loophole or a flaw
In any lease or contract he might draw.
Each statute on the books he knew by rote.
He traveled in a plain, silk-belted coat.
    A Franklin traveled in his company.   325
Whiter could never daisy petal[2] be
Than was his beard. His ruddy face gave sign
He liked his morning sop of toast in wine.
He lived in comfort, as he would assure us,
For he was a true son of Epicurus[3]   330
Who held the opinion that the only measure
Of perfect happiness was simply pleasure.
Such hospitality did he provide,
He was St. Julian[4] to his countryside.
His bread and ale were always up to scratch.   335
He had a cellar none on earth could match.
There was no lack of pasties in his house,
Both fish and flesh, and that so plenteous
That where he lived it snowed of meat and drink.
With every dish of which a man can think,   340
After the various seasons of the year,
He changed his diet for his better cheer.
He had coops of partridges as fat as cream,
He had a fishpond stocked with pike and bream.
Woe to his cook for an unready pot   345
Or a sauce that wasn't seasoned and spiced hot!
A table in his hall stood on display
Prepared and covered through the livelong day.
He presided at court sessions for his bounty
And sat in Parliament often for his county.   350
A well-wrought dagger and a purse of silk
Hung at his belt, as white as morning milk.
He had been a sheriff and county auditor.
On earth was no such rich proprietor!
    There were five Guildsmen, in the livery   355
Of one august and great fraternity,
A Weaver, a Dyer, and a Carpenter,
A Tapestry-maker and a Haberdasher.
Their gear was furbished new and clean as glass.
The mountings of their knives were not of brass   360
But silver. Their pouches were well made and neat,
And each of them, it seemed, deserved a seat
On the platform at the Guildhall, for each one

1. The conqueror, reigned 1066–1087.   2. The English daisy, a small white flower; not the same as the American.   3. The Greek philosopher whose teaching (presented here in a somewhat debased form) is believed to make pleasure the goal of life.   4. Patron saint of hospitality.

Was likely timber to make an alderman.
They had goods enough, and money to be spent,   365
Also their wives would willingly consent
And would have been at fault if they had not.
For to be "Madamed" is a pleasant lot,
And to march in first at feasts for being well married,
And royally to have their mantles carried.   370
   For the pilgrimage these Guildsmen brought their own
Cook to boil their chicken and marrow bone
With seasoning powder and capers and sharp spice.
In judging London ale his taste was nice.
He well knew how to roast and broil and fry,   375
To mix a stew, and bake a good meat pie,
Or capon creamed with almond, rice, and egg.
Pity he had an ulcer on his leg!
   A Skipper was with us, his home far in the west.
He came from the port of Dartmouth, as I guessed.   380
He sat his carthorse pretty much at sea
In a coarse smock that joggled on his knee.
From his neck a dagger on a string hung down
Under his arm. His face was burnished brown
By the summer sun. He was a true good fellow.   385
Many a time he had tapped a wine cask mellow
Sailing from Bordeaux while the owner slept.
Too nice a point of honor he never kept.
In a sea fight, if he got the upper hand,
Drowned prisoners floated home to every land.   390
But in navigation, whether reckoning tides,
Currents, or what might threaten him besides,
Harborage, pilotage, or the moon's demeanor,
None was his like from Hull to Cartagena.⁵
He knew each harbor and the anchorage there   395
From Gotland to the Cape of Finisterre⁶
And every creek in Brittany and Spain,
And he had called his ship the *Madeleine.*
   With us came also an astute Physician.
There was none like him for a disquisition   400
On the art of medicine or surgery,
For he was grounded in astrology.
He kept his patient long in observation,
Choosing the proper hour for application
Of charms and images by intuition   405
Of magic, and the planets' best position.
For he was one who understood the laws
That rule the humors, and could tell the cause

---

5. A Spanish port. *Hull:* In England.   6. On the Spanish coast. *Gotland:* A Swedish island.

That brought on every human malady,
Whether of hot or cold, or moist or dry.   410
He was a perfect medico, for sure.
The cause once known, he would prescribe the cure
For he had his druggists ready at a motion
To provide the sick man with some pill or potion—
A game of mutual aid, with each one winning.   415
Their partnership was hardly just beginning!
He was well versed in his authorities,
Old Aesculapius, Dioscorides,
Rufus, and old Hippocrates, and Galen,
Haly, and Rhazes, and Serapion,   420
Averroës, Bernard, Johannes Damascenus,
Avicenna, Gilbert, Gaddesden, Constantinus.[7]
He urged a moderate fare on principle,
But rich in nourishment, digestible;
Of nothing in excess would he admit.   425
He gave but little heed to Holy Writ.
His clothes were lined with taffeta; their hue
Was all of blood red and of Persian blue,
Yet he was far from careless of expense.
He saved his fees from times of pestilence,   430
For gold is a cordial, as physicians hold,
And so he had a special love for gold.

    A worthy woman there was from near the city
Of Bath,[8] but somewhat deaf, and more's the pity.
For weaving she possessed so great a bent   435
She outdid the people of Ypres and of Ghent.[9]
No other woman dreamed of such a thing
As to precede her at the offering,
Or if any did, she fell in such a wrath
She dried up all the charity in Bath.   440
She wore fine kerchiefs of old-fashioned air,
And on a Sunday morning, I could swear,
She had ten pounds of linen on her head.
Her stockings were of finest scarlet-red,
Laced tightly, and her shoes were soft and new.   445
Bold was her face, and fair, and red in hue.
She had been an excellent woman all her life
Five men in turn had taken her to wife,
Omitting other youthful company—
But let that pass for now! Over the sea   450
She had traveled freely; many a distant stream
She crossed, and visited Jerusalem

---

7. A list of eminent medical authorities from ancient Greece, ancient and medieval Arabic civilization, and England in the thirteenth and fourteenth centuries.   8. A town in the southwest of England.
9. Towns in Flanders famous for their cloth.

Three times. She had been at Rome and at Boulogne,
At the shrine of Compostella, and at Cologne.[1]
She had wandered by the way through many a scene.   455
Her teeth were set with little gaps between.[2]
Easily on her ambling horse she sat.
She was well wimpled, and she wore a hat
As wide in circuit as a shield or targe.[3]
A skirt swathed up her hips, and they were large.   460
Upon her feet she wore sharp-roweled spurs.
She was a good fellow; a ready tongue was hers.
All remedies of love she knew by name,[4]
For she had all the tricks of that old game.

    There was a good man of the priests' vocation,   465
A poor town Parson of true consecration,
But he was rich in holy thought and work.
Learned he was, in the truest sense a clerk
Who meant Christ's gospel faithfully to preach
And truly his parishioners to teach.   470
He was a kind man, full of industry,
Many times tested by adversity
And always patient. If tithes[5] were in arrears,
He was loth to threaten any man with fears
Of excommunication; past a doubt   475
He would rather spread his offering about
To his poor flock, or spend his property.
To him a little meant sufficiency.
Wide was his parish, with houses far asunder,
But he would not be kept by rain or thunder,   480
If any had suffered a sickness or a blow,
From visiting the farthest, high or low
Plodding his way on foot, his staff in hand.
He was a model his flock could understand,
For first he did and afterward he taught.   485
That precept from the Gospel he had caught,
And he added as a metaphor thereto,
"If the gold rusts, what will the iron do?"
For if a priest is foul, in whom we trust,
No wonder a layman shows a little rust.   490
A priest should take to heart the shameful scene
Of shepherds filthy while the sheep are clean.
By his own purity a priest should give
The example to his sheep, how they should live.
He did not rent his benefice for hire,[6]   495

1. Sites of shrines much visited by pilgrims.   2. I.e., gap-toothed; in a woman considered a sign of sexual prowess.   3. A small shield.   4. Chaucer has Ovid's *Love Cures* (*Remedia Amoris*) in mind.
5. Payments due to the priest, usually a tenth of annual income.   6. I.e., rent out his appointment to a substitute.

Leaving his flock to flounder in the mire,
And run to London, happiest of goals,
To sing paid masses in St. Paul's for souls,
Or as chaplain from some rich guild take his keep,
But dwelt at home and guarded well his sheep   500
So that no wolf should make his flock miscarry.
He was a shepherd, and not a mercenary.
And though himself a man of strict vocation
He was not harsh to weak souls in temptation,
Not overbearing nor haughty in his speech,   505
But wise and kind in all he tried to teach.
By good example and just words to turn
Sinners to heaven was his whole concern.
But should a man in truth prove obstinate,
Whoever he was, of rich or mean estate,   510
The Parson would give him a snub to meet the case.
I doubt there was a priest in any place
His better. He did not stand on dignity
Nor affect in conscience too much nicety,
But Christ's and his disciples' words he sought   515
To teach, and first he followed what he taught.
     There was a Plowman with him on the road,
His brother, who had forked up many a load
Of good manure. A hearty worker he,
Living in peace and perfect charity.   520
Whether his fortune made him smart or smile,
He loved God with his whole heart all the while
And his neighbor as himself. He would undertake,
For every luckless poor man, for the sake
Of Christ to thresh and ditch and dig by the hour   525
And with no wage, if it was in his power.
His tithes on goods and earnings he paid fair.
He wore a coarse, rough coat and rode a mare.
     There also were a Manciple, a Miller,
A Reeve, a Summoner, and a Pardoner,[7]   530
And I—this makes our company complete.
     As tough a yokel as you care to meet
The Miller was. His big-beefed arms and thighs
Took many a ram put up as wrestling prize.
He was a thick, squat-shouldered lump of sins.   535
No door but he could heave it off its pins
Or break it running at it with his head.
His beard was broader than a shovel, and red
As a fat sow or fox. A wart stood clear

---

7. *Manciple:* A steward. *Reeve:* Farm overseer. *Summoner:* He summoned people to appear before the church court (presided over by the archdeacon), and in general acted as a kind of deputy sheriff of the court. *Pardoner:* Dispenser of papal pardons.

Atop his nose, and red as a pig's ear   540
A tuft of bristles on it. Black and wide
His nostrils were. He carried at his side
A sword and buckler. His mouth would open out
Like a great furnace, and he would sing and shout
His ballads and jokes of harlotries and crimes.   545
He could steal corn and charge for it three times,
And yet was honest enough, as millers come,
For a miller, as they say, has a golden thumb.
In white coat and blue hood this lusty clown,
Blowing his bagpipes, brought us out of town.   550
    The Manciple was of a lawyers' college,
And other buyers might have used his knowledge
How to be shrewd provisioners, for whether
He bought on cash or credit, altogether
He managed that the end should be the same: 555
He came out more than even with the game.
Now isn't it an instance of God's grace
How a man of little knowledge can keep pace
In wit with a whole school of learned men?
He had masters to the number of three times ten   560
Who knew each twist of equity and tort;
A dozen in that very Inn of Court
Were worthy to be steward of the estate
To any of England's lords, however great,
And keep him to his income well confined   565
And free from debt, unless he lost his mind,
Or let him scrimp, if he were mean in bounty;
They could have given help to a whole county
In any sort of case that might befall;
And yet this Manciple could cheat them all!   570
    The Reeve was a slender, fiery-tempered man.
He shaved as closely as a razor can.
His hair was cropped about his ears, and shorn
Above his forehead as a priest's is worn.
His legs were very long and very lean.   575
No calf on his lank spindles could be seen.
But he knew how to keep a barn or bin,
He could play the game with auditors and win.
He knew well how to judge by drought and rain
The harvest of his seed and of his grain.   580
His master's cattle, swine, and poultry flock,
Horses and sheep and dairy, all his stock,
Were altogether in this Reeve's control.
And by agreement, he had given the sole
Accounting since his lord reached twenty years.   585
No man could ever catch him in arrears.

There wasn't a bailiff, shepherd, or farmer working
But the Reeve knew all his tricks of cheating and shirking.
He would not let him draw an easy breath.
They feared him as they feared the very death.   590
He lived in a good house on an open space,
Well shaded by green trees, a pleasant place.
He was shrewder in acquisition than his lord.
With private riches he was amply stored.
He had learned a good trade young by work and will.   595
He was a carpenter of first-rate skill.
On a fine mount, a stallion, dappled gray.
Whose name was Scot, he rode along the way.
He wore a long blue coat hitched up and tied
As if it were a friar's, and at his side   600
A sword with rusty blade was hanging down.
He came from Norfolk, from nearby the town
That men call Bawdswell. As we rode the while,
The Reeve kept always hindmost in our file.
    A Summoner in our company had his place.   605
Red as the fiery cherubim[8] his face.
He was pocked and pimpled, and his eyes were narrow.
He was lecherous and hot as a cock sparrow.
His brows were scabby and black, and thin his beard.
His was a face that little children feared.   610
Brimstone or litharge bought in any quarter,
Quicksilver, ceruse, borax, oil of tartar,
No salve nor ointment that will cleanse or bite
Could cure him of his blotches, livid white,
Or the nobs and nubbins sitting on his cheeks.   615
He loved his garlic, his onions, and his leeks.
He loved to drink the strong wine down blood-red.
Then would he bellow as if he had lost his head.
And when he had drunk enough to parch his drouth,
Nothing but Latin issued from his mouth.   620
He had smattered up a few terms, two or three,
That he had gathered out of some decree—
No wonder; he heard law Latin all the day,
And everyone knows a parrot or a jay
Can cry out "Wat" or "Poll" as well as the pope;   625
But give him a strange term, he began to grope.
His little store of learning was paid out,
So "Questio quod juris"[9] he would shout.
He was a goodhearted bastard and a kind one.
If there were better, it was hard to find one.   630
He would let a good fellow, for a quart of wine,

---

8. An order of angels; represented with red faces in medieval art.   9. "The question is, what (part) of the law (applies)."

The whole year round enjoy his concubine
Scot-free from summons, hearing, fine, or bail,
And on the sly he too could flush a quail.
If he liked a scoundrel, no matter for church law.   635
He would teach him that he need not stand in awe
If the archdeacon threatened with his curse—
That is, unless his soul was in his purse,
For in his purse he would be punished well.
"The purse," he said, "is the archdeacon's hell."   640
Of course I know he lied in what he said.
There is nothing a guilty man should so much dread
As the curse that damns his soul, when, without fail,
The church can save him, or send him off to jail.[1]
He had the young men and girls in his control   645
Throughout the diocese; he knew the soul
Of youth, and heard their every last design.
A garland big enough to be the sign
Above an alehouse balanced on his head,
And he made a shield of a great round loaf of bread.   650
    There was a Pardoner of Rouncivalle[2]
With him, of the blessed Mary's hospital,
But now come straight from Rome (or so said he).
Loudly he sang, "Come hither, love, to me,"
While the Summoner's counterbass trolled out profound—   655
No trumpet blew with half so vast a sound.
This Pardoner had hair as yellow as wax,
But it hung as smoothly as a hank of flax.
His locks trailed down in bunches from his head,
And he let the ends about his shoulders spread,   660
But in thin clusters, lying one by one.
Of hood, for rakishness, he would have none,
For in his wallet he kept it safely stowed.
He traveled, as he thought, in the latest mode,
Disheveled. Save for his cap, his head was bare,   665
And in his eyes he glittered like a hare.
A Veronica[3] was stitched upon his cap
His wallet lay before him in his lap
Brimful of pardons from the very seat
In Rome. He had a voice like a goat's bleat.   670
He was beardless and would never have a beard.
His cheek was always smooth as if just sheared.

1. Lines 643–44 attempt to render the sense and tone of a passage in which Chaucer says literally that a guilty man should be in dread "because a curse will slay just as absolution saves, and he should also beware of a Significavit." This word, according to Robinson, was the first word of a writ remanding an excommunicated person to prison. [Translator's note.]   2. A religious house near Charing Cross, now part of London.   3. A reproduction of the handkerchief bearing the miraculous impression of Christ's face, said to have been impressed on the handkerchief that St. Veronica gave him to wipe his face with on the way to his crucifixion.

I think he was a gelding or a mare;
But in this trade, from Berwick down to Ware,
No pardoner could beat him in the race, 675
For in his wallet he had a pillow case
Which he represented as Our Lady's veil;
He said he had a piece of the very sail
St. Peter, when he fished in Galilee
Before Christ caught him, used upon the sea. 680
He had a latten[4] cross embossed with stones
And in a glass he carried some pig's bones,
And with these holy relics, when he found
Some village parson grubbing his poor ground,
He would get more money in a single day 685
Than in two months would come the parson's way.
Thus with his flattery and his trumped-up stock
He made dupes of the parson and his flock.
But though his conscience was a little plastic
He was in church a noble ecclesiastic. 690
Well could he read the Scripture or saint's story,
But best of all he sang the offertory,
For he understood that when this song was sung,
Then he must preach, and sharpen up his tongue
To rake in cash, as well he knew the art, 695
And so he sang out gaily, with full heart.
Now I have set down briefly, as it was,
Our rank, our dress, our number, and the cause
That many our sundry fellowship begin
In Southwark, at this hospitable inn 700
Known as the Tabard, nor far from the Bell.
But what we did that night I ought to tell,
And after that our journey, stage by stage,
And the whole story of our pilgrimage.
But first, in justice, do not look askance 705
I plead, nor lay it to my ignorance
If in this matter I should use plain speech
And tell you just the words and style of each,
Reporting all their language faithfully.
For it must be known to you as well as me 710
That whoever tells a story after a man
Must follow him as closely as he can.
If he takes the tale in charge, he must be true
To every word, unless he would find new
Or else invent a thing or falsify. 715
Better some breadth of language than a lie!
He may not spare the truth to save his brother.

4. An alloy of copper and zinc made to resemble brass.

He might as well use one word as another.
In Holy Writ Christ spoke in a broad sense
And surely his word is without offense.   720
Plato, if his pages you can read,
Says let the word be cousin to the deed.
So I petition your indulgence for it
If I have cut the cloth just as men wore it,
Here in this tale, and shown its very weave.   725
My wits are none too sharp, you must believe.
    Our Host gave each of us a cheerful greeting
And promptly of our supper had us eating.
The victuals that he served us were his best.
The wine was potent, and we drank with zest.   730
Our Host cut such a figure, all in all,
He might have been a marshal in a hall.
He was a big man, and his eyes bulged wide.
No sturdier citizen lived in all Cheapside, [5]
Lacking no trace of manhood, bold in speech,   735
Prudent, and well versed in what life can teach,
And with all this he was a jovial man.
And so when supper ended he began
To jolly us, when all our debts were clear.
"Welcome," he said. "I have not seen this year   740
So merry a company in this tavern as now,
And I would give you pleasure if I knew how.
And just this very minute a plan has crossed
My mind that might amuse you at no cost.
    "You go to Canterbury—may the Lord   745
Speed you, and may the martyred saint reward
Your journey! And to while the time away
You mean to talk and pass the time of day,
For you would be as cheerful all alone
As riding on your journey dumb as stone.   750
Therefore, if you'll abide by what I say,
Tomorrow, when you ride off on your way,
Now, by my father's soul, and he is dead,
If you don't enjoy yourselves, cut off my head!
Hold up your hands, if you accept my speech."   755
    Our counsel did not take us long to reach.
We bade him give his orders at his will.
"Well, sirs," he said, "then do not take it ill,
But hear me in good part, and for your sport.
Each one of you, to make our journey short,   760
Shall tell two stories, as we ride, I mean,
Toward Canterbury; and coming home again

5. A London street.

Shall tell two other tales he may have heard
Of happenings that some time have occurred.
And the one of you whose stories please us most,   765
Here in this tavern, sitting by this post
Shall sup at our expense while we make merry
When we come riding home from Canterbury.
And to cheer you still the more, I too will ride
With you at my own cost, and be your guide.   770
And if anyone my judgment shall gainsay
He must pay for all we spend along the way.
If you agree, no need to stand and reason.
Tell me, and I'll be stirring in good season."
    This thing was granted, and we swore our pledge   775
To take his judgment on our pilgrimage,
His verdict on our tales, and his advice.
He was to plan a supper at a price
Agreed upon; and so we all assented
To his command, and we were well contented.   780
The wine was fetched; we drank, and went to rest.
    Next morning, when the dawn was in the east,
Up spring our Host, who acted as our cock,
And gathered us together in a flock,
And off we rode, till presently our pace   785
Had brought us to St. Thomas' watering place.
And there our Host began to check his horse.
"Good sirs," he said, "you know your promise, of course.
Shall I remind you what it was about?
If evensong and matins don't fall out,   790
We'll soon find who shall tell us the first tale.
But as I hope to drink my wine and ale,
Whoever won't accept what I decide
Pays everything we spend along the ride.
Draw lots, before we're farther from the Inn.   795
Whoever draws the shortest shall begin.
Sir Knight," said he, "my master, choose your straw.
Come here, my lady Prioress, and draw,
And you, Sir Scholar, don't look thoughtful, man!
Pitch in now, everyone!" So all began   800
To draw the lots, and as the luck would fall
The draw went to the Knight, which pleased us all.
And when this excellent man saw how it stood,
Ready to keep his promise, he said, "Good!
Since it appears that I must start the game,   805
Why then, the draw is welcome, in God's name.
Now let's ride on, and listen, what I say."
And with that word we rode forth on our way,

And he, with his courteous manner and good cheer,
Began to tell his tale, as you shall hear.   810

PROLOGUE TO THE MILLER'S TALE

When the Knight had finished,[6] no one, young or old,
In the whole company, but said he had told
A noble story, one that ought to be
Preserved and kept alive in memory,
Especially the gentlefolk, each one.   5
Our good Host laughed, and swore, "The game's begun,
The ball is rolling! This is going well.
Let's see who has another tale to tell.
Come, match the Knight's tale if you can, Sir Monk!"
    The Miller, who by this time was so drunk   10
He looked quite bloodless, and who hardly sat
His horse, he was never one to doff his hat
Or stand on courtesy for any man.
Like Pilate in the Church plays[7] he began
To bellow. "Arms and blood and bones," he swore,   15
"I know a yarn that will even up the score,
A noble one, I'll pay off the Knight's tale!"
    Our Host could see that he was drunk on ale.
"Robin," he said, "hold on a minute, brother.
Some better man shall come first with another.   20
Let's do this right. You tell yours by and by."
    "God's soul," the Miller told him, "that won't I!
Either I'll speak, or go on my own way."
    "The devil with you! Say what you have to say,"
Answered our Host. "You are a fool. Your head   25
Is overpowered."
                    "Now," the Miller said,
"Everyone listen! But first I will propound
That I am drunk, I know it by my sound.
If I can't get my words out, put the blame   30
On Southwark ale, I ask you, in God's name!
For I'll tell a golden legend and a life
Both of a carpenter and of his wife,
How a student put horns on the fellow's head."
    "Shut up and stop your racket," the Reeve said.   35
"Forget your ignorant drunken bawdiness.
It is a sin and a great foolishness
To injure any man by defamation

---

6. The Knight's Tale is the first told, immediately following the General Prologue.   7. Miracle plays
represented Pilate as a braggart and loudmouth. His lines were marked by frequent alliteration.

And to give women such a reputation.
Tell us of other things; you'll find no lack." 40
    Promptly this drunken Miller answered back:
"Oswald, my brother, true as babes are suckled,
The man who has no wife, he is no cuckold.
I don't say for this reason that you are.
There are plenty of faithful wives, both near and far, 45
Always a thousand good for every bad,
And you know this yourself, unless you're mad.
I see you are angry with my tale, but why?
You have a wife; no less, by God, do I.
But I wouldn't, for the oxen in my plow, 50
Shoulder more than I need by thinking how
I may myself, for aught I know, be one.
I'll certainly believe that I am none.
A husband mustn't be curious, for his life,
About God's secrets or about his wife. 55
If she gives him plenty and he's in the clover,
No need to worry about what's left over."
    The Miller, to make the best of it I can,
Refused to hold his tongue for any man,
But told his tale like any low-born clown. 60
I am sorry that I have to set it down,
And all you people, for God's love, I pray,
Whose taste is higher, do not think I say
A word with evil purpose; I must rehearse
Their stories one and all, both better and worse, 65
Or play false with my matter, that is clear.
Whoever, therefore, may not wish to hear,
Turn over the page and choose another tale;
For small and great, he'll find enough, no fail,
Of things from history, touching courtliness, 70
And virtue too, and also holiness.
If you choose wrong, don't lay it on my head.
You know the Miller couldn't be called well bred.
So with the Reeve, and many more as well,
And both of them had bawdy tales to tell. 75
Reflect a little, and don't hold me to blame.
There's no sense making earnest out of game.

THE MILLER'S TALE

There used to be a rich old oaf who made
His home at Oxford, a carpenter by trade,
And took in boarders. With him used to dwell
A student who had done his studies well,
But he was poor; for all that he had learned, 5

It was toward astrology his fancy turned.
He knew a number of figures and constructions
By which he could supply men with deductions
If they should ask him at a given hour
Whether to look for sunshine or for shower,   10
Or want to know whatever might befall,
Events of all sorts, I can't count them all.
  He was known as handy Nicholas,[8] this student.
Well versed in love, he knew how to be prudent,
Going about unnoticed, sly, and sure.   15
In looks no girl was ever more demure.
Lodged at this carpenter's, he lived alone;
He had a room there that he made his own,
Festooned with herbs, and he was sweet himself
As licorice or ginger. On a shelf   20
Above his bed's head, neatly stowed apart,
He kept the trappings that went with his art,
His astrolabe, his books—among the rest,
Thick ones and thin ones, lay his *Almagest*—[9]
And the counters for his abacus as well.   25
Over his cupboard a red curtain fell
And up above a pretty zither lay
On which at night so sweetly would he play
That with the music the whole room would ring.
"Angelus to the Virgin" he would sing   30
And then the song that's known as "The King's Note."
Blessings were called down on his merry throat!
So this sweet scholar passed his time, his end
Being to eat and live upon his friend.
  This carpenter had newly wed a wife   35
And loved her better than he loved his life.
He was jealous, for she was eighteen in age;
He tried to keep her close as in a cage,
For she was wild and young, and old was he
And guessed that he might smack of cuckoldry.   40
His ignorant wits had never chanced to strike
On Cato's word,[1] that man should wed his like;
Men ought to wed where their conditions point,
For youth and age are often out of joint.
But now, since he had fallen in the snare,   45
He must, like other men, endure his care.
  Fair this young woman was, her body trim
As any mink, so graceful and so slim.

8. Chaucer's word is hendë, implying, I take it, both *ready to hand* and *ingratiating*. Nicholas was a Johnny-on-the-spot and also had a way with him. [Translator's note.]   9. Second-century treatise by Ptolemy, an astronomy textbook.   1. Dionysius Cato, the supposed author of a book of maxims employed in elementary education.

She wore a striped belt that was all of silk;
A piece-work apron, white as morning milk, 50
About her loins and down her lap she wore.
White was her smock, her collar both before
And on the back embroidered all about
In coal-black silk, inside as well as out.
And like her collar, her white-laundered bonnet 55
Had ribbons of the same embroidery on it.
Wide was her silken fillet, worn up high,
And for a fact she had a willing eye.
She plucked each brow into a little bow,
And each one was as black as any sloe. 60
She was a prettier sight to see by far
Than the blossoms of the early pear tree are,
And softer than the wool of an old wether.
Down from her belt there hung a purse of leather
With silken tassels and with studs of brass. 65
No man so wise, wherever people pass,
Who could imagine in this world at all
A wench like her, the pretty little doll!
Far brighter was the dazzle of her hue
Than a coin struck in the Tower,[2] fresh and new. 70
As for her song, it twittered from her head
Sharp as a swallow perching on a shed.
And she could skip and sport as a young ram
Or calf will gambol, following his dam.
Her mouth was sweet as honey-ale or mead 75
Or apples in the hay, stored up for need.
She was as skittish as an untrained colt,
Slim as a mast and straighter than a bolt.
On her simple collar she wore a big brooch-pin
Wide as a shield's boss underneath her chin. 80
High up along her legs she laced her shoes.
She was a pigsney, she was a primrose
For any lord to tumble in his bed
Or a good yeoman honestly to wed.
    Now sir, and again sir, this is how it was: 85
A day came round when handy Nicholas,
While her husband was at Oseney,[3] well away,
Began to fool with this young wife, and play.
These students always have a wily head.
He caught her in between the legs, and said, 90
"Sweetheart, unless I have my will with you
I'll die for stifled love, by all that's true,"
And held her by the haunches, hard. "I vow

2. The Tower of London.   3. A town near Oxford.

I'll die unless you love me here and now,
Sure as my soul," he said, "is God's to save."   95
    She shied just as a colt does in the trave,[4]
And turned her head hard from him, this young wife,
And said, "I will not kiss you, on my life.
Why, stop it now," she said, "stop, Nicholas,
Or I will cry out 'Help, help,' and 'Alas!'   100
Be good enough to take your hands away."
    "Mercy," this Nicholas began to pray,
And spoke so well and poured it on so fast
She promised she would be his love at last,
And swore by Thomas à Becket, saint of Kent,   105
That she would serve him when she could invent
Or spy out some good opportunity.
"My husband is so full of jealousy
You must be watchful and take care," she said,
"Or well I know I'll be as good as dead.   110
You must go secretly about this business."
    "Don't give a thought to that," said Nicholas.
"A student has been wasting time at school
If he can't make a carpenter a fool."
And so they were agreed, these two, and swore   115
To watch their chance, as I have said before.
When Nicholas had spanked her haunches neatly
And done all I have spoken of, he sweetly
Gave her a kiss, and then he took his zither
And loudly played, and sang his music with her.   120
    Now in her Christian duty, one saint's day,
To the parish church this good wife made her way,
And as she went her forehead cast a glow
As bright as noon, for she had washed it so
It glistened when she finished with her work.   125
    Serving this church there was a parish clerk
Whose name was Absolom, a ruddy man
With goose-gray eyes and curls like a great fan
That shone like gold on his neatly parted head.
His tunic was light blue and his nose red,   130
And he had patterns that had been cut through
Like the windows of St. Paul's in either shoe.
He wore above his tunic, fresh and gay,
A surplice white as a blossom on a spray.
A merry devil, as true as God can save,   135
He knew how to let blood, trim hair, and shave,
Or write a deed of land in proper phrase,
And he could dance in twenty different ways

4. A wooden frame confining a horse being shod.

In the Oxford fashion, and sometimes he would sing
A loud falsetto to his fiddle string   140
Or his guitar. No tavern anywhere
But he had furnished entertainment there.
Yet his speech was delicate, and for his part
He was a little squeamish toward a fart.
This Absolom, so jolly and so gay,   145
With a censer went about on the saint's day
Censing the parish women one and all.
Many the doting look that he let fall,
And specially on this carpenter's young wife.
To look at her, he thought, was a good life,   150
She was so trim, so sweetly lecherous.
I dare say that if she had been a mouse
And he a cat, he would have made short work
Of catching her. This jolly parish clerk
Had such a heartful of love-hankerings   155
He would not take the women's offerings;
No, no, he said, it would not be polite.
    The moon, when darkness fell, shone full and bright
And Absolom was ready for love's sake
With his guitar to be up and awake,   160
And toward the carpenter's, brisk and amorous,
He made his way until he reached the house
A little after the cocks began to crow.
Under a casement he sang sweet and low,
"Dear lady, by your will, be kind to me,"   165
And strummed on his guitar in harmony.
This lovelorn singing woke the carpenter
Who said to his wife, "What, Alison, don't you hear
Absolom singing under our bedroom wall?"
    "Yes, God knows, John," she answered, "I hear it all."   170
    What would you like? In this way things went on
Till jolly Absolom was woebegone
For wooing her, awake all night and day.
He combed his curls and made himself look gay.
He swore to be her slave and used all means   175
To court her with his gifts and go-betweens.
He sang and quavered like a nightingale.
He sent her sweet spiced wine and seasoned ale,
Cakes that were piping hot, mead sweet with honey,
And since she was town-bred, he proffered money.   180
For some are won by wealth, and some no less
By blows, and others yet by gentleness.
    Sometimes, to keep his talents in her gaze,
He acted Herod[5] in the mystery plays

---

5. A role traditionally played as a bully in the Miracle plays.

High on the stage. But what can help his case?   185
For she so loves this handy Nicholas
That Absolom is living in a bubble.
He has nothing but a laugh for all his trouble.
She leaves his earnestness for scorn to cool
And makes this Absolom her proper fool.   190
For this is a true proverb, and no lie;
"It always happens that the nigh and sly
Will let the absent suffer." So 'tis said,
And Absolom may rage or lose his head
But just because he was farther from her sight   195
This nearby Nicholas got in his light.
　　Now hold your chin up, handy Nicholas,
For Absolom may wail and sing "Alas!"
One Saturday when the carpenter had gone
To Oseney, Nicholas and Alison   200
Agreed that he should use his wit and guile
This simple jealous husband to beguile.
And if it happened that the game went right
She would sleep in his arms the livelong night,
For this was his desire and hers as well.   205
At once, with no more words, this Nicholas fell
To working out his plan. He would not tarry,
But quietly to his room began to carry
Both food and drink to last him out a day,
Or more than one, and told her what to say   210
If her husband asked her about Nicholas.
She must say she had no notion where he was;
She hadn't laid eyes on him all day long;
He must be sick, or something must be wrong;
No matter how her maid had called and cried   215
He wouldn't answer, whatever might betide.
　　This was the plan, and Nicholas kept away,
Shut in his room, for that whole Saturday.
He ate and slept or did as he thought best
Till Sunday, when the sun was going to rest,   220
This carpenter began to wonder greatly
Where Nicholas was and what might ail him lately,
"Now, by St. Thomas, I begin to dread
All isn't right with Nicholas," he said.
"He hasn't, God forbid, died suddenly!   225
The world is ticklish these days, certainly.
Today I saw a corpse to church go past,
A man that I saw working Monday last!
Go up," he told his chore-boy, "call and shout,
Knock with a stone, find what it's all about   230
And let me know."
　　　　　　The boy went up and pounded

And yelled as if his wits had been confounded.
"What, how, what's doing, Master Nicholas?
How can you sleep all day?" But all his fuss   235
Was wasted, for he could not hear a word.
He noticed at the bottom of a board
A hole the cat used when she wished to creep
Into the room, and through it looked in deep
And finally of Nicholas caught sight.   240
This Nicholas sat gaping there upright
As though his wits were addled by the moon
When it was new. The boy went down, and soon
Had told his master how he had seen the man.
    The carpenter, when he heard this news, began   245
To cross himself. "Help us, St. Frideswide!
Little can we foresee what may betide!
The man's astronomy has turned his wit,
Or else he's in some agonizing fit.
I always knew that it would turn out so.   250
What God has hidden is not for men to know.
Aye, blessed is the ignorant man indeed,
Blessed is he that only knows his creed!
So fared another scholar of the sky,
For walking in the meadows once to spy   255
Upon the stars and what they might foretell,
Down in a clay-pit suddenly he fell!
He overlooked that! By St. Thomas, though,
I'm sorry for handy Nicholas. I'll go
And scold him roundly for his studying   260
If so I may, by Jesus, heaven's king!
Give me a staff, I'll pry up from the floor
While you, Robin, are heaving at the door.
He'll quit his books, I think."
                              He took his stand   265
Outside the room. The boy had a strong hand
And by the hasp he heaved it off at once.
The door fell flat. With gaping countenance
This Nicholas sat studying the air
As still as stone. He was in black despair,   270
The carpenter believed, and hard about
The shoulders caught and shook him, and cried out
Rudely, "What, how! What is it? Look down at us!
Wake up, think of Christ's passion, Nicholas!
I'll sign you with the cross to keep away   275
These elves and things!" And he began to say,
Facing the quarters of the house, each side,
And on the threshold of the door outside,
The night-spell: "Jesu and St. Benedict

From every wicked thing this house protect . . ."   280
   Choosing his time, this handy Nicholas
Produced a dreadful sigh, and said, "Alas,
This world, must it be all destroyed straightway?"
   "What," asked the carpenter, "what's that you say?
Do as we do, we working men, and think   285
Of God."
      Nicholas answered, "Get me a drink,
And afterwards I'll tell you privately
Of something that concerns us, you and me.
I'll tell you only, you among all men."   290
   This carpenter went down and came again
With a draught of mighty ale, a generous quart.
As soon as each of them had drunk his part
Nicholas shut the door and made it fast
And sat down by the carpenter at last   295
And spoke to him. "My host," he said, "John dear,
You must swear by all that you hold sacred here
That not to any man will you betray
My confidence. What I'm about to say
Is Christ's own secret. If you tell a soul   300
You are undone, and this will be the toll:
If you betray me, you shall go stark mad."
   "Now Christ forbid it, by His holy blood,"
Answered this simple man. "I don't go blabbing.
If I say it myself, I have no taste for gabbing.   305
Speak up just as you like, I'll never tell,
Not wife nor child, by Him that harrowed hell."[6]
   "Now, John," said Nicholas, "this is no lie.
I have discovered through astrology,
And studying the moon that shines so bright   310
That Monday next, a quarter through the night,
A rain will fall, and such a mad, wild spate
That Noah's flood was never half so great.
This world," he said, "in less time than an hour
Shall drown entirely in that hideous shower.   315
Yes, every man shall drown and lose his life."
   "Alas," the carpenter answered, "for my wife!
Alas, my Alison! And shall she drown?"
For grief at this he nearly tumbled down,
And said, "But is there nothing to be done?"   320
   "Why, happily there is, for anyone
Who will take advice," this handy Nicholas said.
"You mustn't expect to follow your own head.

6. I.e., Christ, who descended into Hell and led away Adam, Eve, the Patriarchs, John the Baptist, and others, redeeming and releasing them. It was the subject of a number of Miracle plays. The original story comes from the Apocryphal New Testament.

For what said Solomon, whose words were true?
'Proceed by counsel, and you'll never rue.'   325
If you will act on good advice, no fail,
I'll promise, and without a mast or sail,
To see that she's preserved, and you and I.
Haven't you heard how Noah was kept dry
When, warned by Christ beforehand, he discovered   330
That the whole earth with water should be covered?"
     "Yes," said the carpenter, "long, long ago."
     "And then again," said Nicholas, "don't you know
The grief they all had trying to embark
Till Noah could get his wife into the Ark?[7]   335
That was a time when Noah, I dare say,
Would gladly have given his best black wethers away
If she could have had a ship herself alone.
And therefore do you know what must be done?
This demands haste, and with a hasty thing   340
People can't stop for talk and tarrying.
     "Start out and get into the house right off
For each of us a tub or kneading-trough,
Above all making sure that they are large,
In which we'll float away as in a barge.   345
And put in food enough to last a day.
Beyond won't matter; the flood will fall away
Early next morning. Take care not to spill
A word to your boy Robin, nor to Jill
Your maid. I cannot save her, don't ask why.   350
I will not tell God's secrets, no, not I.
Let it be enough, unless your wits are mad,
To have as good a grace as Noah had.
I'll save your wife for certain, never doubt it.
Now go along, and make good time about it.   355
     "But when you have, for her and you and me,
Brought to the house these kneading-tubs, all three,
Then you must hang them under the roof, up high,
To keep our plans from any watchful eye.
When you have done exactly as I've said,   360
And put in snug our victuals and our bread,
Also an ax to cut the ropes apart
So when the rain comes we can make our start,
And when you've broken a hole high in the gable
Facing the garden plot, above the stable,   365
To give us a free passage out, each one,
Then, soon as the great fall of rain is done,
You'll swim as merrily, I undertake,

7. A stock comedy scene in the mystery plays, of which the carpenter would have been an avid spectator.
[Translator's note.]

As the white duck paddles along behind her drake.
Then I shall call, 'How, Alison! How, John!   370
Be cheerful, for the flood will soon be gone.'
And 'Master Nicholas, what ho!' you'll say.
'Good morning, I see you clearly, for it's day.'
Then we shall lord it for the rest of life
Over the world, like Noah and his wife.   375
   "But one thing I must warn you of downright.
Use every care that on that selfsame night
When we have taken ship and climbed aboard,
No one of us must speak a single word,
Nor call, nor cry, but pray with all his heart.   380
It is God's will. You must hang far apart,
You and your wife, for there must be no sin
Between you, no more in a look than in
The very deed. Go now, the plans are drawn.
Go, set to work, and may God spur you on!   385
Tomorrow night when all men are asleep
Into our kneading-troughs we three shall creep
And sit there waiting, and abide God's grace.
Go along now, this isn't the time or place
For me to talk at length or sermonize.   390
The proverb says, 'Don't waste words on the wise.'
You are so wise there is no need to teach you.
Go, save our lives—that's all that I beseech you!"
   This simple carpenter went on his way.
Many a time he said, "Alack the day,"   395
And to his wife he laid the secret bare.
She knew it better than he; she was aware
What this quaint bargain was designed to buy.
She carried on as if about to die,
And said, "Alas, go get this business done.   400
Help us escape, or we are dead, each one.
I am your true, your faithful wedded wife.
Go, my dear husband, save us, limb and life!"
   Great things, in all truth, can the emotions be!
A man can perish through credulity   405
So deep the print imagination makes.
This simple carpenter, he quails and quakes.
He really sees, according to his notion,
Noah's flood come wallowing like an ocean
To drown his Alison, his pet, his dear.   410
He weeps and wails, and gone is his good cheer,
And wretchedly he sighs. But he goes off
And gets himself a tub, a kneading-trough,
Another tub, and has them on the sly
Sent home, and there in secret hangs them high   415

Beneath the roof. He made three ladders, these
With his own hands, and stowed in bread and cheese
And a jug of good ale, plenty for a day.
Before all this was done, he sent away
His chore-boy Robin and his wench likewise   420
To London on some trumped-up enterprise,
And so on Monday, when it drew toward night,
He shut the door without a candlelight
And saw that all was just as it should be,
And shortly they went clambering up, all three.   425
They sat there still, and let a moment pass.
    "Now then, 'Our Father,' mum!" said Nicholas,
And "Mum!" said John, and "Mum!" said Alison,
And piously this carpenter went on
Saying his prayers. He sat there still and straining,   430
Trying to make out whether he heard it raining.
    The dead of sleep, for very weariness,
Fell on this carpenter, as I should guess,
At about curfew time, or little more.
His head was twisted, and that made him snore.   435
His spirit groaned in its uneasiness.
Down from his ladder slipped this Nicholas,
And Alison too, downward she softly sped
And without further word they went to bed
Where the carpenter himself slept other nights.   440
There were the revels, there were the delights!
And so this Alison and Nicholas lay
Busy about their solace and their play
Until the bell for lauds began to ring
And in the chancel friars began to sing.   445
    Now on this Monday, woebegone and glum
For love, this parish clerk, this Absolom
Was with some friends at Oseney, and while there
Inquired after John the carpenter.
A member of the cloister drew him away   450
Out of the church, and told him, "I can't say.
I haven't seen him working hereabout
Since Saturday. The abbot sent him out
For timber, I suppose. He'll often go
And stay at the granary a day or so.   455
Or else he's at his own house, possibly.
I can't for certain say where he may be."
    Absolom at once felt jolly and light,
And thought, "Time now to be awake all night,
For certainly I haven't seen him making   460
A stir about his door since day was breaking.
Don't call me a man if when I hear the cock

Begin to crow I don't slip up and knock
On the low window by his bedroom wall.
To Alison at last I'll pour out all   465
My love-pangs, for at this point I can't miss,
Whatever happens, at the least a kiss.
Some comfort, by my word, will come my way.
I've felt my mouth itch the whole livelong day,
And that's a sign of kissing at the least.   470
I dreamed all night that I was at a feast.
So now I'll go and sleep an hour or two,
And then I'll wake and play the whole night through."
    When the first cockcrow through the dark had come
Up rose this jolly lover Absolom   475
And dressed up smartly. He was not remiss
About the least point. He chewed licorice
And cardamom to smell sweet, even before
He combed his hair. Beneath his tongue he bore
A sprig of Paris[8] like a truelove knot.   480
He strolled off to the carpenter's house, and got
Beneath the window. It came so near the ground
It reached his chest. Softly, with half a sound,
He coughed, "My honeycomb, sweet Alison,
What are you doing, my sweet cinnamon?   485
Awake, my sweetheart and my pretty bird,
Awake, and give me from your lips a word!
Little enough you care for all my woe,
How for your love I sweat wherever I go!
No wonder I sweat and faint and cannot eat   490
More than a girl; as a lamb does for the teat
I pine. Yes, truly, I so long for love
I mourn as if I were a turtledove."
    Said she, "You jack-fool, get away from here!
So help me God, I won't sing 'Kiss me, dear!'   495
I love another more than you. Get on,
For Christ's sake, Absolom, or I'll throw a stone.
The devil with you! Go and let me sleep."
    "Ah, that true love should ever have to reap
So evil a fortune," Absolom said. "A kiss,   500
At least, if it can be no more than this,
Give me, for love of Jesus and of me."
    "And will you go away for that?" said she.
    "Yes, truly, sweetheart," answered Absolom.
    "Get ready then," she said, "for here I come,"   505
And softly said to Nicholas, "Keep still,
And in a minute you can laugh your fill."

---

8. A cloverlike plant.

This Absolom got down upon his knee
And said, "I am a lord of pure degree,
For after this, I hope, comes more to savor.   510
Sweetheart, your grace, and pretty bird, your favor!"
    She undid the window quickly. "That will do,"
She said. "Be quick about it, and get through,
For fear the neighbors will look out and spy."
    Absolom wiped his mouth to make it dry.   515
The night was pitch dark, coal-black all about.
Her rear end through the window she thrust out.
He got no better or worse, did Absolom,
Than to kiss her with his mouth on the bare bum
Before he had caught on, a smacking kiss.   520
    He jumped back, thinking something was amiss.
A woman had no beard, he was well aware,
But what he felt was rough and had long hair.
    "Alas," he cried, "what have you made me do?"
    "Te-hee!" she said, and banged the window to.   525
Absolom backed away a sorry pace.
    "You've bearded him!" said handy Nicholas.
"God's body, this is going fair and fit!"
    This luckless Absolom heard every bit,
And gnawed his mouth, so angry he became.   530
He said to himself, "I'll square you, all the same."
    But who now scrubs and rubs, who chafes his lips
With dust, with sand, with straw, with cloth and chips
If not this Absolom? "The devil," says he,
"Welcome my soul if I wouldn't rather be   535
Revenged than have the whole town in a sack!
Alas," he cries, "if only I'd held back!"
His hot love had become all cold and ashen.
He didn't have a curse to spare for passion
From the moment when he kissed her on the ass.   540
That was the cure to make his sickness pass!
He cried as a child does after being whipped;
He railed at love. Then quietly he slipped
Across the street to a smith who was forging out
Parts that the farmers needed round about.   545
He was busy sharpening colter[9] and plowshare
When Absolom knocked as though without a care.
    "Undo the door, Jervice, and let me come."
    "What? Who are you?"
                         "It is I, Absolom."   550
    "Absolom, is it! By Christ's precious tree,
Why are you up so early? Lord bless me,

9. A turf cutter on a plow.

What's ailing you? Some gay girl has the power
To bring you out, God knows, at such an hour!
Yes, by St. Neot, you know well what I mean!"   555
    Absolom thought his jokes not worth a bean.
Without a word he let them all go by.
He had another kind of fish to fry
Than Jervice guessed. "Lend me this colter here
That's hot in the chimney, friend," he said. "Don't fear,   560
I'll bring it back right off when I am through.
I need it for a job I have to do."
    "Of course," said Jervice. "Why, if it were gold
Or coins in a sack, uncounted and untold,
As I'm a rightful smith, I wouldn't refuse it.   565
But, Christ's foot! how on earth do you mean to use it?"
    "Let that," said Absolom, "be as it may.
I'll let you know tomorrow or next day,"
And took the colter where the steel was cold
And slipped out with it safely in his hold   570
And softly over to the carpenter's wall.
He coughed and then he rapped the window, all
As he had done before.
                            "Who's knocking there?"
Said Alison. "It is a thief, I swear."   575
    "No, no," said he. "God knows, my sugarplum,
My bird, my darling, it's your Absolom.
I've brought a golden ring my mother gave me,
Fine and well cut, as I hope that God will save me.
It's yours, if you will let me have a kiss."   580
    Nicholas had got up to take a piss
And thought he would improve the whole affair.
This clerk, before he got away from there,
Should give *his* ass a smack; and hastily
He opened the window, and thrust out quietly,   585
Buttocks and haunches, all the way, his bum.
Up spoke this clerk, this jolly Absolom:
"Speak, for I don't know where you are, sweetheart."
    Nicholas promptly let fly with a fart
As loud as if a clap of thunder broke,   590
So great he was nearly blinded by the stroke,
And ready with his hot iron to make a pass,
Absolom caught him fairly on the ass.
    Off flew the skin, a good handbreadth of fat
Lay bare, the iron so scorched him where he sat.   595
As for the pain, he thought that he would die,
And like a madman he began to cry.
"Help! Water! Water! Help, for God's own heart!"
    At this the carpenter came to with a start.

He heard a man cry "Water!" as if mad.　　　　　600
"It's coming now," was the first thought he had.
"It's Noah's flood, alas, God be our hope!"
He sat up with his ax and chopped the rope
And down at once the whole contraption fell.
He didn't take time out to buy or sell　　　　　605
Till he hit the floor and lay there in a swoon.
　Then up jumped Nicholas and Alison
And in the street began to cry, "Help, ho!"
The neighbors all came running, high and low,
And poured into the house to see the sight.　　　　　610
The man still lay there, passed out cold and white,
For in his tumble he had broken an arm.
But he himself brought on his greatest harm,
For when he spoke he was at once outdone
By handy Nicholas and Alison　　　　　615
Who told them one and all that he was mad.
So great a fear of Noah's flood he had,
By some delusion, that in his vanity
He had bought himself these kneading-troughs, all three.
And hung them from the roof there, up above,　　　　　620
And he had pleaded with them, for God's love,
To sit there in the loft for company.
　The neighbors laughed at such a fantasy,
And round the loft began to pry and poke
And turned his whole disaster to a joke.　　　　　625
He found it was no use to say a word.
Whatever reason he offered, no one heard.
With oaths and curses people swore him down
Until he passed for mad in the whole town.
Wit, clerk, and student all stood by each other.　　　　　630
They said, "It's clear the man is crazy, brother."
Everyone had his laugh about this feud.
So Alison, the carpenter's wife, got screwed
For all the jealous watching he could try,
And Absolom, he kissed her nether eye,　　　　　635
And Nicholas got his bottom roasted well.
God save this troop! That's all I have to tell.

PROLOGUE TO THE PARDONER'S TALE

"In churches," said the Pardoner, "when I preach,
I use, milords, a lofty style of speech
And ring it out as roundly as a bell,
Knowing by rote all that I have to tell.
My text is ever the same, and ever was:　　　　　5

Radix malorum est cupiditas.[1]

   "First I inform them whence I come; that done,
I then display my papal bulls, each one.
I show my license first, my body's warrant,
Sealed by the bishop, for it would be abhorrent   10
If any man made bold, though priest or clerk,
To interrupt me in Christ's holy work.
And after that I give myself full scope.
Bulls in the name of cardinal and pope,
Of bishops and of patriarchs I show.   15
I say in Latin some few words or so
To spice my sermon; it flavors my appeal
And stirs my listeners to greater zeal.
Then I display my cases made of glass
Crammed to the top with rags and bones. They pass   20
For relics with all the people in the place.
I have a shoulder bone in a metal case,
Part of a sheep owned by a holy Jew.
'Good men,' I say, 'heed what I'm telling you:
Just let this bone be dipped in any well   25
And if cow, calf, or sheep, or ox should swell
From eating a worm, or by a worm be stung,
Take water from this well and wash its tongue
And it is healed at once. And furthermore
Of scab and ulcers and of every sore   30
Shall every sheep be cured, and that straightway,
That drinks from the same well. Heed what I say:
If the good man who owns the beasts will go,
Fasting, each week, and drink before cockcrow
Out of this well, his cattle shall be brought   35
To multiply—that holy Jew so taught
Our elders—and his property increase.
   " 'Moreover, sirs, this bone cures jealousies.
Though into a jealous madness a man fell,
Let him cook his soup in water from this well,   40
He'll never, though for truth he knew her sin,
Suspect his wife again, though she took in
A priest, or even two of them or three.
   " 'Now here's a mitten that you all can see.
Whoever puts his hand in it shall gain,   45
When he sows his land, increasing crops of grain,
Be it wheat or oats, provided that he bring
His penny or so to make his offering.
   " 'There is one word of warning I must say,

---

1. "The root of evil is greed."

Good men and women. If any here today   50
Has done a sin so horrible to name
He daren't be shriven of it for the shame,
Or if any woman, young or old, is here
Who has cuckolded her husband, be it clear
They may not make an offering in that case   55
To these my relics; they have no power nor grace.
But any who is free of such dire blame,
Let him come up and offer in God's name
And I'll absolve him through the authority
That by the pope's bull has been granted me.'   60
    "By such hornswoggling I've won, year by year,
A hundred marks[2] since being a pardoner.
I stand in my pulpit like a true divine,
And when the people sit I preach my line
To ignorant souls, as you have heard before,   65
And tell skullduggeries by the hundred more.
Then I take care to stretch my neck well out
And over the people I nod and peer about
Just like a pigeon perching on a shed.
My hands fly and my tongue wags in my head   70
So busily that to watch me is a joy.
Avarice is the theme that I employ
In all my sermons, to make the people free
In giving pennies—especially to me.
My mind is fixed on what I stand to win   75
And not at all upon correcting sin.
I do not care, when they are in the grave,
If souls go berry-picking that I could save.
Truth is that evil purposes determine,
And many a time, the origin of a sermon: 80
Some to please people and by flattery
To gain advancement through hypocrisy,
Some for vainglory, some again for hate.
For when I daren't fight otherwise, I wait
And give him a tongue-lashing when I preach.   85
No man escapes or gets beyond the reach
Of my defaming tongue, supposing he
Has done a wrong to my brethren or to me.
For though I do not tell his proper name,
People will recognize him all the same.   90
By sign and circumstance I let them learn.
Thus I serve those who have done us an ill turn.
Thus I spit out my venom under hue
Of sanctity, and seem devout and true!

2. Probably the equivalent of several thousand dollars.

"But to put my purpose briefly, I confess   95
I preach for nothing but for covetousness.
That's why my text is still and ever was
Radix malorum est cupiditas.
For by this text I can denounce, indeed,
The very vice I practice, which is greed.   100
But though that sin is lodged in my own heart,
I am able to make other people part
From avarice, and sorely to repent,
Though that is not my principal intent.
    "Then I bring in examples, many a one,   105
And tell them many a tale of days long done.
Plain folk love tales that come down from of old.
Such things their minds can well report and hold.
Do you think that while I have the power to preach
And take in silver and gold for what I teach   110
I shall ever live in willful poverty?
No, no, that never was my thought, certainly.
I mean to preach and beg in sundry lands.
I won't do any labor with my hands,
Nor live by making baskets. I don't intend   115
To beg for nothing; that is not my end.
I won't ape the apostles; I must eat,
I must have money, wool, and cheese, and wheat,
Though I took it from the meanest wretch's tillage
Or from the poorest widow in a village,   120
Yes, though her children starved for want. In fine,
I mean to drink the liquor of the vine
And have a jolly wench in every town.
But, in conclusion, lords, I will get down
To business: you would have me tell a tale.   125
Now that I've had a drink of corny ale,
By God, I hope the thing I'm going to tell
Is one that you'll have reason to like well.
For though myself a very sinful man,
I can tell a moral tale, indeed I can,   130
One that I use to bring the profits in
While preaching. Now be still, and I'll begin."

THE PARDONER'S TALE

There was a company of young folk living
One time in Flanders, who were bent on giving
Their lives to follies and extravagances,
Brothels and taverns, where they held their dances
With lutes, harps, and guitars, diced at all hours,   5
And also ate and drank beyond their powers,

Through which they paid the devil sacrifice
In the devil's temple with their drink and dice,
Their abominable excess and dissipation.
They swore oaths that were worthy of damnation;   10
It was grisly to be listening when they swore.
The blessed body of our Lord they tore—
The Jews, it seemed to them, had failed to rend
His body enough—and each laughed at his friend
And fellow in sin. To encourage their pursuits   15
Came comely dancing girls, peddlers of fruits,
Singers with harps, bawds and confectioners
Who are the very devil's officers
To kindle and blow the fire of lechery
That is the follower of gluttony.   20
    Witness the Bible, if licentiousness
Does not reside in wine and drunkenness!
Recall how drunken Lot, unnaturally,
With his two daughters lay unwittingly,
So drunk he had no notion what he did.[3]   25
    Herod, the stories tell us, God forbid,
When full of liquor at his banquet board
Right at his very table gave the word
To kill the Baptist, John, though guiltless he.[4]
    Seneca says a good word, certainly.   30
He says there is no difference he can find
Between a man who has gone out of his mind
And one who carries drinking to excess,
Only that madness outlasts drunkenness.[5]
O gluttony, first cause of mankind's fall,[6]   35
Of our damnation the cursed original
Until Christ bought us with his blood again!
How dearly paid for by the race of men
Was this detestable iniquity!
This whole world was destroyed through gluttony.   40
    Adam our father and his wife also
From paradise to labor and to woe
Were driven for that selfsame vice, indeed.
As long as Adam fasted—so I read—
He was in heaven; but as soon as he   45
Devoured the fruit of that forbidden tree
Then he was driven out in sorrow and pain.
Of gluttony well ought we to complain!
Could a man know how many maladies
Follow indulgences and gluttonies   50
He would keep his diet under stricter measure

3. Genesis 19:33–35.   4. Matthew 14:1–11; Mark 6:14–28.   5. Seneca's *Epistles*, Epistle 83.
6. Since the Fall was caused by eating the forbidden fruit.

And sit at table with more temperate pleasure.
The throat is short and tender is the mouth,
And hence men toil east, west, and north, and south,
In earth, and air, and water—alas to think—   55
Fetching a glutton dainty meat and drink.
   This is a theme, O Paul, that you well treat:
"Meat unto belly, and belly unto meat,
God shall destroy them both," as Paul has said.[7]
When a man drinks the white wine and the red—   60
This is a foul word, by my soul, to say,
And fouler is the deed in every way—
He makes his throat his privy through excess.
   The Apostle says, weeping for piteousness,
"There are many of whom I told you—at a loss   65
I say it, weeping—enemies of Christ's cross,
Whose belly is their god; their end is death."[8]
O cursed belly! Sack of stinking breath
In which corruption lodges, dung abounds!
At either end of you come forth foul sounds.   70
Great cost it is to fill you, and great pain!
These cooks, how they must grind and pound and strain
And transform substance into accident[9]
To please your cravings, though exorbitant!
From the hard bones they knock the marrow out.   75
They'll find a use for everything, past doubt,
That down the gullet sweet and soft will glide.
The spiceries of leaf and root provide
Sauces that are concocted for delight,
To give a man a second appetite.   80
But truly, he whom gluttonies entice
Is dead, while he continues in that vice.
   O drunken man, disfigured is your face,
Sour is your breath, foul are you to embrace!
You seem to mutter through your drunken nose   85
The sound of "Samson, Samson," yet God knows
That Samson never indulged himself in wine.[1]
Your tongue is lost, you fall like a stuck swine,
And all the self-respect that you possess
Is gone, for of man's judgment, drunkenness   90
Is the very sepulcher and annihilation.
A man whom drink has under domination
Can never keep a secret in his head.
Now steer away from both the white and red,
And most of all from that white wine keep wide   95

7. I Corinthians 6:13.   8. Philippians 3:18–19.   9. A distinction was made in philosophy between "substance," the real nature of a thing, and "accident," its merely sensory qualities, such as flavor. 1. Judges 13:4.

That comes from Lepe.[2] They sell it in Cheapside
And Fish Street. It's a Spanish wine, and sly
To creep in other wines that grow nearby,
And such a vapor it has that with three drinks
It takes a man to Spain; although he thinks   100
He is home in Cheapside, he is far away
At Lepe. Then "Samson, Samson" will he say!
    By God himself, who is omnipotent,
All the great exploits in the Old Testament
Were done in abstinence, I say, and prayer.   105
Look in the Bible, you may learn it there.
    Attila,[3] conqueror of many a place,
Died in his sleep in shame and in disgrace
Bleeding out of his nose in drunkenness.
A captain ought to live in temperateness!   110
And more than this, I say, remember well
The injunction that was laid on Lemuel—[4]
Not Samuel, but Lemuel, I say!
Read in the Bible; in the plainest way
Wine is forbidden to judges and to kings.   115
This will suffice; no more upon these things.
    Now that I've shown what gluttony will do,
Now I will warn you against gambling, too;
Gambling, the very mother of low scheming,
Of lying and forswearing and blaspheming   120
Against Christ's name, of murder and waste as well
Alike of goods and time; and, truth to tell,
With honor and renown it cannot suit
To be held a common gambler by repute.
The higher a gambler stands in power and place,   125
The more his name is lowered in disgrace.
If a prince gambles, whatever his kingdom be,
In his whole government and policy
He is, in all the general estimation,
Considered so much less in reputation.   130
    Stilbon, who was a wise ambassador,
From Lacedaemon once to Corinth bore
A mission of alliance. When he came
It happened that he found there at a game
Of hazard all the great ones of the land,   135
And so, as quickly as it could be planned,
He stole back, saying, "I will not lose my name
Nor have my reputation put to shame
Allying you with gamblers. You may send
Other wise emissaries to gain your end,   140

---

2. A town in Spain noted for strong wines.   3. Leader of the Hun invasion of Europe, fifth century
A.D.   4. Proverbs 31:4–7.

For by my honor, rather than ally
My countrymen to gamblers, I will die.
For you that are so gloriously renowned
Shall never with this gambling race be bound
By will of mine or treaty I prepare."   145
Thus did this wise philosopher declare.
    Remember also how the Parthians' lord
Sent King Demetrius, as the books record,
A pair of golden dice, by this proclaiming
His scorn, because that king was known for gaming,   150
And the king of Parthia therefore held his crown
Devoid of glory, value, or renown.
Lords can discover other means of play
More suitable to while the time away.
    Now about oaths I'll say a word or two,   155
Great oaths and false oaths, as the old books do.
Great swearing is a thing abominable,
And false oaths yet more reprehensible.
Almighty God forbade swearing at all,
Matthew be witness;[5] but specially I call   160
The holy Jeremiah on this head.
"Swear thine oaths truly, do not lie," he said.
"Swear under judgment, and in righteousness."[6]
But idle swearing is a great wickedness.
Consult and see, and he that understands   165
In the first table of the Lord's commands
Will find the second of his commandments this:
"Take not the Lord's name idly or amiss."
If a man's oaths and curses are extreme,
Vengeance shall find his house, both roof and beam.   170
"By the precious heart of God," and "By his nails"—
"My chance is seven,[7] by Christ's blood at Hailes,
Yours five and three." "Cheat me, and if you do,
By God's arms, with this knife I'll run you through!"—
Such fruit comes from the bones,[8] that pair of bitches: 175
Oaths broken, treachery, murder. For the riches
Of Christ's love, give up curses, without fail,
Both great and small!—Now, sirs, I'll tell my tale.
    These three young roisterers of whom I tell
Long before prime had rung from any bell   180
Were seated in a tavern at their drinking,
And as they sat, they heard a bell go clinking
Before a corpse being carried to his grave.
One of these roisterers, when he heard it, gave
An order to his boy: "Go out and try   185

5. Matthew 5:34.   6. Jeremiah 4:2.   7. My lucky number is seven. *Hailes:* An abbey in Gloucestershire, where some of Christ's blood was believed to be preserved.   8. Dice.

To learn whose corpse is being carried by.
Get me his name, and get it right. Take heed."
  "Sir," said the boy, "there isn't any need.
I learned before you came here, by two hours.
He was, it happens, an old friend of yours,   190
And all at once, there on his bench upright
As he was sitting drunk, he was killed last night.
A sly thief, Death men call him, who deprives
All the people in this country of their lives,
Came with his spear and smiting his heart in two   195
Went on his business with no more ado.
A thousand have been slaughtered by his hand
During this plague. And, sir, before you stand
Within his presence, it should be necessary,
It seems to me, to know your adversary.   200
Be evermore prepared to meet this foe.
My mother taught me thus; that's all I know."
  "Now by St. Mary," said the innkeeper,
"This child speaks truth. Man, woman, laborer,
Servant, and child the thief has slain this year   205
In a big village a mile or more from here.
I think it is his place of habitation.
It would be wise to make some preparation
Before he brought a man into disgrace."
  "God's arms!" this roisterer said. "So that's the case! 210
Is it so dangerous with this thief to meet?
I'll look for him by every path and street,
I vow it, by God's holy bones! Hear me,
Fellows of mine, we are all one, we three.
Let each of us hold up his hand to the other   215
And each of us become his fellow's brother.
We'll slay this Death, who slaughters and betrays.
He shall be slain whose hand so many slays,
By the dignity of God, before tonight!"
  The three together set about to plight   220
Their oaths to live and die each for the other
Just as though each had been to each born brother,
And in their drunken frenzy up they get
And toward the village off at once they set
Which the innkeeper had spoken of before,   225
And many were the grisly oaths they swore.
They rent Christ's precious body limb from limb—
Death shall be dead, if they lay hands on him!
  When they had hardly gone the first half mile,
Just as they were about to cross a stile,   230
An old man, poor and humble, met them there.
The old man greeted them with a meek air

And said, "God bless you, lords, and be your guide."
"What's this?" the proudest of the three replied.
"Old beggar, I hope you meet with evil grace!   235
Why are you all wrapped up except your face?
What are you doing alive so many a year?"
    The old man at these words began to peer
Into this gambler's face. "Because I can,
Though I should walk to India, find no man,"   240
He said, "in any village or any town,
Who for my age is willing to lay down
His youth. So I must keep my old age still
For as long a time as it may be God's will.
Nor will Death take my life from me, alas!   245
Thus like a restless prisoner I pass
And on the ground, which is my mother's gate,
I walk and with my staff both early and late
I knock and say, 'Dear mother, let me in!
See how I vanish, flesh, and blood, and skin!   250
Alas, when shall my bones be laid to rest?
I would exchange with you my clothing chest,
Mother, that in my chamber long has been
For an old haircloth rag to wrap me in.'
And yet she still refuses me that grace.   255
All white, therefore, and withered is my face.
    "But, sirs, you do yourselves no courtesy
To speak to an old man so churlishly
Unless he had wronged you either in word or deed.
As you yourselves in Holy Writ may read,   260
'Before an aged man whose head is hoar
Men ought to rise.'[9] I counsel you, therefore,
No harm nor wrong here to an old man do,
No more than you would have men do to you
In your old age, if you so long abide.   265
And God be with you, whether you walk or ride!
I must go yonder where I have to go."
    "No, you old beggar, by St. John, not so,"
Said another of these gamblers. "As for me,
By God, you won't get off so easily!   270
You spoke just now of that false traitor, Death,
Who in this land robs all our friends of breath.
Tell where he is, since you must be his spy,
Or you will suffer for it, so say I
By God and by the holy sacrament.   275
You are in league with him, false thief, and bent
On killing us young folk, that's clear to my mind."

9. Leviticus 19:32.

"If you are so impatient, sirs, to find
Death," he replied, "turn up this crooked way,
For in that grove I left him, truth to say,   280
Beneath a tree, and there he will abide.
No boast of yours will make him run and hide.
Do you see that oak tree? Just there you will find
This Death, and God, who bought again mankind,
Save and amend you!" So said this old man;   285
And promptly each of these three gamblers ran
Until he reached the tree, and there they found
Florins of fine gold, minted bright and round,
Nearly eight bushels of them, as they thought.
And after Death no longer then they sought.   290
Each of them was so ravished at the sight,
So fair the florins glittered and so bright,
That down they sat beside the precious hoard.
The worst of them, he uttered the first word.
    "Brothers," he told them, "listen to what I say.   295
My head is sharp, for all I joke and play.
Fortune has given us this pile of treasure
To set us up in lives of ease and pleasure.
Lightly it comes, lightly we'll make it go.
God's precious dignity! Who was to know   300
We'd ever tumble on such luck today?
If we could only carry this gold away,
Home to my house, or either one of yours—
For well you know that all this gold is ours—
We'd touch the summit of felicity.   305
But still, by daylight that can hardly be.
People would call us thieves, too bold for stealth,
And they would have us hanged for our own wealth.
It must be done by night, that's our best plan,
As prudently and slyly as we can.   310
Hence my proposal is that we should all
Draw lots, and let's see where the lot will fall,
And the one of us who draws the shortest stick
Shall run back to the town, and make it quick,
And bring us bread and wine here on the sly,   315
And two of us will keep a watchful eye
Over this gold; and if he doesn't stay
Too long in town, we'll carry this gold away
By night, wherever we all agree it's best."
    One of them held the cut out in his fist   320
And had them draw to see where it would fall,
And the cut fell on the youngest of them all.
At once he set off on his way to town,
And the very moment after he was gone

The one who urged this plan said to the other: 325
"You know that by sworn oath you are my brother.
I'll tell you something you can profit by.
Our friend has gone, that's clear to any eye,
And here is gold, abundant as can be,
That we propose to share alike, we three.   330
But if I worked it out, as I could do,
So that it could be shared between us two,
Wouldn't that be a favor, a friendly one?"
      The other answered, "How that can be done,
I don't quite see. He knows we have the gold.   335
What shall we do, or what shall he be told?"
      "Will you keep the secret tucked inside your head?
And in a few words," the first scoundrel said,
"I'll tell you how to bring this end about."
      "Granted," the other told him. "Never doubt,   340
I won't betray you, that you can believe."
      "Now," said the first, "we are two, as you perceive,
And two of us must have more strength than one.
When he sits down, get up as if in fun
And wrestle with him. While you play this game   345
I'll run him through the ribs. You do the same
With your dagger there, and then this gold shall be
Divided, dear friend, between you and me.
Then all that we desire we can fulfill,
And both of us can roll the dice at will."   350
Thus in agreement these two scoundrels fell
To slay the third, as you have heard me tell.
      The youngest, who had started off to town,
Within his heart kept rolling up and down
The beauty of those florins, new and bright.   355
"O Lord," he thought, "were there some way I might
Have all this treasure to myself alone,
There isn't a man who dwells beneath God's throne
Could live a life as merry as mine should be!"
And so at last the fiend, our enemy,   360
Put in his head that he could gain his ends
If he bought poison to kill off his friends.
Finding his life in such a sinful state,
The devil was allowed to seal his fate.
For it was altogether his intent   365
To kill his friends, and never to repent.
So off he set, no longer would he tarry,
Into the town, to an apothecary,
And begged for poison; he wanted it because
He meant to kill his rats; besides, there was   370
A polecat living in his hedge, he said,

Who killed his capons; and when he went to bed
He wanted to take vengeance, if he might,
On vermin that devoured him by night.
   The apothecary answered, "You shall have   375
A drug that as I hope the Lord will save
My soul, no living thing in all creation,
Eating or drinking of this preparation
A dose no bigger than a grain of wheat,
But promptly with his death-stroke he shall meet.   380
Die, that he will, and in a briefer while
Than you can walk the distance of a mile,
This poison is so strong and virulent."
   Taking the poison, off the scoundrel went,
Holding it in a box, and next he ran   385
To the neighboring street, and borrowed from a man
Three generous flagons. He emptied out his drug
In two of them, and kept the other jug
For his own drink; he let no poison lurk
In that! And so all night he meant to work   390
Carrying off the gold. Such was his plan,
And when he had filled them, this accursed man
Retraced his path, still following his design,
Back to his friends with his three jugs of wine.
   But why dilate upon it any more?   395
For just as they had planned his death before,
Just so they killed him, and with no delay.
When it was finished, one spoke up to say:
"Now let's sit down and drink, and we can bury
His body later on. First we'll be merry,"   400
And as he said the words, he took the jug
That, as it happened, held the poisonous drug,
And drank, and gave his friend a drink as well,
And promptly they both died. But truth to tell,
In all that Avicenna[1] ever wrote   405
He never described in chapter, rule, or note
More marvelous signs of poisoning, I suppose,
Than appeared in these two wretches at the close.
Thus they both perished for their homicide,
And thus the traitorous poisoner also died.   410
   O sin accursed above all cursedness,
O treacherous murder, O foul wickedness,
O gambling, lustfulness, and gluttony,
Traducer of Christ's name by blasphemy
And monstrous oaths, through habit and through pride!   415
Alas, mankind! Ah, how may it betide

---

1. An Arabic physician.

That you to your Creator, he that wrought you
And even with his precious heart's blood bought you,
So falsely and ungratefully can live?
    And now, good men, your sins may God forgive   420
And keep you specially from avarice!
My holy pardon will avail in this,
For it can heal each one of you that brings
His pennies, silver brooches, spoons, or rings.
Come, bow your head under this holy bull!   425
You wives, come offer up your cloth or wool!
I write your names here in my roll, just so.
Into the bliss of heaven you shall go!
I will absolve you here by my high power,
You that will offer, as clean as in the hour   430
When you were born.—Sirs, thus I preach. And now
Christ Jesus, our souls' healer, show you how
Within his pardon evermore to rest,
For that, I will not lie to you, is best.
    But in my tale, sirs, I forgot one thing.   435
The relics and the pardons that I bring
Here in my pouch, no man in the whole land
Has finer, given me by the pope's own hand.
If any of you devoutly wants to offer
And have my absolution, come and proffer   440
Whatever you have to give. Kneel down right here,
Humbly, and take my pardon, full and clear,
Or have a new, fresh pardon if you like
At the end of every mile of road we strike,
As long as you keep offering ever newly   445
Good coins, not counterfeit, but minted truly.
Indeed it is an honor I confer
On each of you, an authentic pardoner
Going along to absolve you as you ride.
For in the country mishaps may betide—   450
One or another of you in due course
May break his neck by falling from his horse.
Think what security it gives you all
That in this company I chanced to fall
Who can absolve you each, both low and high,   455
When the soul, alas, shall from the body fly!
By my advice, our Host here shall begin,
For he's the man enveloped most by sin.
Come, offer first, Sir Host, and once that's done,
Then you shall kiss the relics, every one,   460
Yes, for a penny! Come, undo your purse!
    "No, no," said he. "Then I should have Christ's curse!
I'll do nothing of the sort, for love or riches!

You'd make me kiss a piece of your old britches
And for a saintly relic make it pass   465
Although it had the tincture of your ass.
By the cross St. Helen[2] found in the Holy Land,
I wish I had your balls here in my hand
For relics! Cut 'em off, and I'll be bound
If I don't help you carry them around.   470
I'll have the things enshrined in a hog's turd!"
   The Pardoner did not answer; not a word,
He was so angry, could he find to say.
   "Now," said our Host, "I will not try to play
With you, nor any other angry man."   475
   Immediately the worthy Knight began,
When he saw that all the people laughed, "No more,
This has gone far enough. Now as before,
Sir Pardoner, be gay, look cheerfully,
And you, Sir Host, who are so dear to me,   480
Come, kiss the Pardoner, I beg of you,
And Pardoner, draw near, and let us do
As we've been doing, let us laugh and play."
And so they kissed, and rode along their way.

(THE KNIGHT'S INTERRUPTION OF THE MONK'S TALE)

   "Stop!" cried the Knight. "No more of this, good sir!
You have said plenty, and much more, for sure,
For only a little such lugubriousness
Is plenty for a lot of folk, I guess.
I say for me it is a great displeasure,   5
When men have wealth and comfort in good measure,
To hear how they have tumbled down the slope,
And the opposite is a solace and a hope,
As when a man begins in low estate
And climbs the ladder and grows fortunate,   10
And stands there firm in his prosperity.
That is a welcome thing, it seems to me,
And of such things it would be good to tell."
   "Well said," our Host declared. "By St. Paul's bell,
You speak the truth; this Monk's tongue is too loud.   15
He told how fortune covered with a cloud—
I don't know what-all; and of tragedy
You heard just now, and it's no remedy,
When things are over and done with, to complain.
Besides, as you have said, it is a pain   20
To hear of misery; it is distressing.

---

2. Mother of Constantine the Great; believed to have found the True Cross.

Sir Monk, no more, as you would have God's blessing.
This company is all one weary sigh.
Such talking isn't worth a butterfly,
For where's the amusement in it, or the game?   25
And so, Sir Monk, or Don Pierce by your name,
I beg you heartily, tell us something else.
Truly, but for the jingling of your bells
That from your bridle hang on every side,
By Heaven's King, who was born for us and died,   30
I should long since have tumbled down in sleep,
Although the mud had never been so deep,
And then you would have told your tale in vain;
For certainly, as these learned men explain,
When his audience have turned their backs away,   35
It doesn't matter what a man may say.
I know well I shall have the essence of it
If anything is told here for our profit.
A tale of hunting, sir, pray share with us."
    "No," said the Monk, "I'll not be frivolous.   40
Let another tell a tale, as I have told."
    Then spoke our Host, with a rude voice and bold,
And said to the Nun's Priest, "Come over here,
You priest, come hither, you Sir John, draw near!
Tell us a thing to make our spirits glad.   45
Be cheerful, though the jade you ride is bad.
What if your horse is miserable and lean?
If he will carry you, don't care a bean!
Keep up a joyful heart, and look alive."
    "Yes, Host," he answered, "as I hope to thrive,   50
If I weren't merry, I know I'd be reproached."
And with no more ado his tale he broached,
And this is what he told us, every one,
This precious priest, this goodly man, Sir John.

THE NUN'S PRIEST'S TALE

Once a poor widow, aging year by year,
Lived in a tiny cottage that stood near
A clump of shade trees rising in a dale.
This widow, of whom I tell you in my tale,
Since the last day that she had been a wife   5
Had led a very patient, simple life.
She had but few possessions to content her.
By thrift and husbandry of what God sent her
She and two daughters found the means to dine.
She had no more than three well-fattened swine,   10
As many cows, and one sheep, Moll by name.

Her bower and hall were black from the hearth-flame
Where she had eaten many a slender meal.
No dainty morsel did her palate feel
And no sharp sauce was needed with her pottage.   15
Her table was in keeping with her cottage.
Excess had never given her disquiet.
Her only doctor was a moderate diet,
And exercise, and a heart that was contented.
If she did not dance, at least no gout prevented;   20
No apoplexy had destroyed her head.
She never drank wine, whether white or red.
She served brown bread and milk, loaves white or black,
Singed bacon, all this with no sense of lack,
And now and then an egg or two. In short,   25
She was a dairy woman of a sort.
     She had a yard, on the inside fenced about
With hedges, and an empty ditch without,
In which she kept a cock, called Chanticleer.
In all the realm of crowing he had no peer.   30
His voice was merrier than the merry sound
Of the church organ grumbling out its ground
Upon a saint's day. Stouter was this cock
In crowing than the loudest abbey clock.
Of astronomy instinctively aware,   35
He kept the sun's hours with celestial care,
For when through each fifteen degrees it moved,
He crowed so that it couldn't be improved.
His comb, like a crenelated castle wall,
Red as fine coral, stood up proud and tall.   40
His bill was black; like polished jet it glowed,
And he was azure-legged and azure-toed.
As lilies were his nails, they were so white;
Like burnished gold his hue, it shone so bright.
This cock had in his princely sway and measure   45
Seven hens to satisfy his every pleasure,
Who were his sisters and his sweethearts true,
Each wonderfully like him in her hue,
Of whom the fairest-feathered throat to see
Was fair Dame Partlet. Courteous was she,   50
Discreet, and always acted debonairly.
She was sociable, and bore herself so fairly,
Since the very time that she was seven nights old,
The heart of Chanticleer was in her hold
As if she had him locked up, every limb.   55
He loved her so that all was well with him.
It was a joy, when up the sun would spring,
To hear them both together sweetly sing,

"My love has gone to the country, far away!"
For as I understand it, in that day   60
The animals and birds could sing and speak.
   Now as this cock, one morning at daybreak,
With each of the seven hens that he called spouse,
Sat on his perch inside the widow's house,
And next him fair Dame Partlet, in his throat   65
This Chanticleer produced a hideous note
And groaned like a man who is having a bad dream;
And Partlet, when she heard her husband scream,
Was all aghast, and said, "Soul of my passion,
What ails you that you groan in such a fashion?   70
You are always a sound sleeper. Fie, for shame!"
   And Chanticleer awoke and answered, "Dame,
Take no offense, I beg you, on this score.
I dreamt, by God, I was in a plight so sore
Just now, my heart still quivers from the fright.   75
Now God see that my dream turns out all right
And keep my flesh and body from foul seizure!
I dreamed I was strutting in our yard at leisure
When there I saw, among the weeds and vines,
A beast, he was like a hound, and had designs   80
Upon my person, and would have killed me dead.
His coat was not quite yellow, not quite red,
And both his ears and tail were tipped with black
Unlike the fur along his sides and back.
He had a small snout and a fiery eye.   85
His look for fear still makes me almost die.
This is what made me groan, I have no doubt."
   "For shame! Fie on you, faint heart!" she burst out.
"Alas," she said, "by the great God above,
Now you have lost my heart and all my love!   90
I cannot love a coward, as I'm blest!
Whatever any woman may protest,
We all want, could it be so, for our part,
Husbands who are wise and stout of heart,
No blabber, and no niggard, and no fool,   95
Nor afraid of every weapon or sharp tool,
No braggart either, by the God above!
How dare you say, for shame, to your true love
That there is anything you ever feared?
Have you no man's heart, when you have a beard?   100
Alas, and can a nightmare set you screaming?
God knows there's only vanity in dreaming!
Dreams are produced by such unseemly capers
As overeating; they come from stomach vapors
When a man's humors aren't behaving right   105

From some excess. This dream you had tonight,
It comes straight from the superfluity
Of your red choler,[3] certain as can be,
That causes people terror in their dreams
Of darts and arrows, and fire in red streams,   110
And of red beasts, for fear that they will bite,
Of little dogs, or of being in a fight;
As in the humor of melancholy[4] lies
The reason why so many a sleeper cries
For fear of a black bull or a black bear   115
Or that black devils have him by the hair.
Through other humors also I could go
That visit many a sleeping man with woe,
But I will finish as quickly as I can.
  "Cato, that has been thought so wise a man,   120
Didn't he tell us, 'Put no stock in dreams'?
Now, sir," she said, "when we fly down from our beams,
For God's sake, go and take a laxative!
On my salvation, as I hope to live,
I give you good advice, and no mere folly: 125
Purge both your choler and your melancholy!
You mustn't wait or let yourself bog down,
And since there is no druggist in this town
I shall myself prescribe for what disturbs
Your humors, and instruct you in the herbs   130
That will be good for you. For I shall find
Here in our yard herbs of the proper kind
For purging you both under and above.
Don't let this slip your mind, for God's own love!
Yours is a very choleric complexion.   135
When the sun is in the ascendant, my direction
Is to beware those humors that are hot.
Avoid excess of them; if you should not,
I'll bet a penny, as a true believer,
You'll die of ague, or a tertian[5] fever.   140
A day or so, if you do as I am urging,
You shall have worm-digestives, before purging
With fumitory or with hellebore
Or other herbs that grow here by the score;
With caper-spurge, or with the goat-tree berry   145
Or the ground-ivy, found in your yard so merry.
Peck 'em up just as they grow, and eat 'em in!
Be cheerful, husband, by your father's kin!
Don't worry about a dream. I say no more."
  "Madame," he answered, "thanks for all your lore.   150

3. One of the four humors, or fluids, composing the body, according to ancient medical theory.
4. Black bile, another of the four humors.   5. Recurring every third day.

But still, to speak of Cato,[6] though his name
For wisdom has enjoyed so great a fame,
And though he counseled us there was no need
To be afraid of dreams, by God, men read
Of many a man of more authority   155
Than this Don Cato could pretend to be
Who in old books declare the opposite,
And by experience they have settled it,
That dreams are omens and prefigurations
Both of good fortune and of tribulations   160
That life and its vicissitudes present.
This question leaves no room for argument.
The very upshot makes it plain, indeed.
    "One of the greatest authors that men read
Informs us that two fellow travelers went,   165
Once on a time, and with the best intent,
Upon a pilgrimage, and it fell out
They reached a town where there was such a rout
Of people, and so little lodging space,
They could not find even the smallest place   170
Where they could both put up. So, for that night,
These pilgrims had to do as best they might,
And since they must, they parted company.
Each of them went off to his hostelry
And took his lodging as his luck might fall.   175
Among plow oxen in a farmyard stall
One of them found a place, though it was rough.
His friend and fellow was lodged well enough
As his luck would have it, or his destiny
That governs all us creatures equally.   180
And so it happened, long before the day,
He had a dream as in his bed he lay.
He dreamed that his parted friend began to call
And said, 'Alas, for in an ox's stall
This night I shall be murdered where I lie.   185
Come to my aid, dear brother, or I die.
Come to me quickly, come in haste!' he said.
He started from his sleep, this man, for dread,
But when he had wakened, he rolled back once more
And on this dream of his he set no store.   190
As a vain thing he dismissed it, unconcerned.
Twice as he slept that night the dream returned,
And still another and third time his friend
Came in a dream and said, 'I have met my end!
Look on my wounds! They are bloody, deep, and wide.   195

6. In refuting Cato, Chanticleer gives a long account of authorities who have pronounced in favor of the truth of dreams.

Now rise up early in the morningtide
And at the west gate of the town,' said he,
'A wagon with a load of dung you'll see.
Have it arrested boldly. Do as bidden,
For underneath you'll find my body hidden.　　200
My money caused my murder, truth to tell,'
And told him each detail of how he fell,
With piteous face, and with a bloodless hue.
And do not doubt it, he found the dream was true,
For on the morrow, as soon as it was day,　　205
To the place where his friend had lodged he made his way,
And no sooner did he reach this ox's stall
Than for his fellow he began to call.
　　"Promptly the stableman replied, and said,
'Your friend is gone, sir. He got out of bed　　210
And left the town as soon as day began.'
　　"At last suspicion overtook this man.
Remembering his dreams, he would not wait,
But quickly went and found at the west gate,
Being driven to manure a farmer's land　　215
As it might seem, a dung cart close at hand
That answered the description every way,
As you yourself have heard the dead man say.
And he began to shout courageously
For law and vengeance on this felony.　　220
'My friend was killed this very night! He lies
Flat in this load of dung, with staring eyes.
I call on those who should keep rule and head,
The magistrates and governors here,' he said.
'Alas! Here lies my fellow, done to death!'　　225
　　"Why on this tale should I waste further breath?
The people sprang and flung the cart to ground
And in the middle of the dung they found
The dead man, while his murder was still new.
　　"O blessed God, thou art so just and true,　　230
Murder, though secret, ever thou wilt betray!
Murder will out, we see it day by day.
Murder so loathsome and abominable
To God is, who is just and reasonable,
That he will never suffer it to be　　235
Concealed, though it hide a year, or two, or three.
Murder will out; to this point it comes down.
　　"Promptly the magistrates who ruled that town
Have seized the driver, and put him to such pain.
And the stableman as well, that under strain　　240
Of torture they were both led to confess
And hanged by the neck-bone for their wickedness.

"Here's proof enough that dreams are things to dread!
And in the same book I have also read,
In the very chapter that comes right after this—   245
I don't speak idly, by my hope of bliss—
Two travelers who for some reason planned
To cross the ocean to a distant land
Found that the wind, by an opposing fate,
Blew contrary, and forced them both to wait   250
In a fair city by a harborside.
But one day the wind changed, toward eventide,
And blew just as it suited them instead.
Cheerfully these travelers went to bed
And planned to sail the first thing in the morning.   255
But to one of them befell a strange forewarning
And a great marvel. While asleep he lay,
He dreamed a curious dream along toward day.
He dreamed that a man appeared at his bedside
And told him not to sail, but wait and bide.   260
'Tomorrow,' he told the man, 'if you set sail,
You shall be drowned. I have told you my whole tale.'
He woke, and of this warning he had met
He told his friend, and begged him to forget
His voyage, and to wait that day and bide.   265
His friend, who was lying close at his bedside,
Began to laugh, and told him in derision,
'I am not so flabbergasted by a vision
As to put off my business for such cause.
I do not think your dream is worth two straws!   270
For dreams are but a vain absurdity.
Of apes and owls and many a mystery
People are always dreaming, in a maze
Of things that never were seen in all their days
And never shall be. But I see it's clear   275
You mean to waste your time by waiting here.
I'm sorry for that, God knows; and so good day.'
With this he took his leave and went his way.
But not the half his course had this man sailed—
I don't know why, nor what it was that failed—   280
When by an accident the hull was rent
And ship and man under the water went
In full view of the vessels alongside
That had put out with them on the same tide.
Now then, fair Partlet, whom I love so well,   285
From old examples such as these I tell
You may see that none should give too little heed
To dreams; for I say seriously, indeed,
That many a dream is too well worth our dread.

"Yes, in St. Kenelm's life I have also read—   290
He was the son of Cynewulf, the king
Of Mercia—how this Kenelm dreamed a thing.
One day, as the time when he was killed drew near,
He saw his murder in a dream appear.
His nurse explained his dream in each detail,   295
And warned him to be wary without fail
Of treason; yet he was but seven years old,
And therefore any dream he could but hold
Of little weight, in heart he was so pure.
I'd give my shirt, by God, you may be sure,   300
If you had read his story through like me!

   "Moreover, Partlet, I tell you truthfully,
Macrobius writes—and by his book we know
The African vision of great Scipio—
Confirming dreams, and holds that they may be   305
Forewarnings of events that men shall see.
Again, I beg, look well at what is meant
By the Book of Daniel in the Old Testament,
Whether *he* held that dreams are vanity!
Read also about Joseph. You shall see   310
That dreams, or some of them—I don't say all—
Warn us of things that afterward befall.
Think of the king of Egypt, Don Pharaoh;
Of his butler and his baker think also,
Whether they found that dreams have no result.   315
Whoever will search through kingdoms and consult
Their histories reads many a wondrous thing
Of dreams. What about Croesus, Lydian king—
Didn't he dream he was sitting on a tree,
Which meant he would be hanged? Andromache,   320
The woman who was once great Hector's wife,
On the day that Hector was to lose his life,
The very night before his blood was spilled
She dreamed of how her husband would be killed
If he went out to battle on that day.   325
She warned him; but he would not heed nor stay.
In spite of her he rode out on the plain,
And by Achilles he was promptly slain.
But all that story is too long to tell,
And it is nearly day. I must not dwell   330
Upon this matter. Briefly, in conclusion,
I say this dream will bring me to confusion
And mischief of some sort. And furthermore,
On laxatives, I say, I set no store,
For they are poisonous, I'm sure of it.   335
I do not trust them! I like them not one bit!

"Now let's talk cheerfully, and forget all this.
My pretty Partlet, by my hope of bliss,
In one thing God has sent me ample grace,
For when I see the beauty of your face,   340
You are so scarlet-red about the eye,
It is enough to make my terrors die.
For just as true as *In principio*
Mulier est hominis confusio—[7]
And Madame, what this Latin means is this: 345
'Woman is man's whole comfort and true bliss'—
When I feel you soft at night, and I beside you,
Although it's true, alas, I cannot ride you
Because our perch is built so narrowly,
I am then so full of pure felicity   350
That I defy whatever sort of dream!"
    And day being come, he flew down from the beam,
And with him his hens fluttered, one and all;
And with a "cluck, cluck" he began to call
His wives to where a kernel had been tossed.   355
He was a prince, his fears entirely lost.
The morning had not passed the hour of prime
When he treaded Partlet for the twentieth time.
Grim as a lion he strolled to and fro,
And strutted only on his either toe.   360
He would not deign to set foot on the ground.
"Cluck, cluck," he said, whenever he had found
A kernel, and his wives came running all.
Thus royal as a monarch in his hall
I leave to his delights this Chanticleer,   365
And presently the sequel you shall hear.
    After the month in which the world began,
The month of March, when God created man,[8]
Had passed, and when the season had run through
Since March began just thirty days and two,   370
It happened that Chanticleer, in all his pride,
While his seven hens were walking by his side,
Lifted his eyes, beholding the bright sun,
Which in the sign of Taurus had then run
Twenty and one degrees and somewhat more,   375
And knew by instinct, not by learned lore,
It was the hour of prime.[9] He raised his head
And crowed with lordly voice. "The sun," he said,
"Forty and one degrees and more in height
Has climbed the sky. Partlet, my world's delight,   380
Hear all these birds, how happily they sing,

---

7. As sure as gospel, woman is man's ruin.   8. Man was thought to have been created at the time of
the spring equinox.   9. Nine.

And see the pretty flowers, how they spring.
With solace and with joy my spirits dance!"
But suddenly he met a sore mischance,
For in the end joys ever turn to woes. 385
Quickly the joys of earth are gone, God knows,
And could a rhetorician's art indite it,
He would be on solid ground if he should write it,
In a chronicle, as true notoriously!
Now every wise man, listen well to me. 390
This story is as true, I undertake,
As the very book of Lancelot of the Lake
On which the women set so great a store.
Now to my matter I will turn once more.
    A sly iniquitous fox, with black-tipped ears, 395
Who had lived in the neighboring wood for some three years,
His fated fancy swollen to a height,
Had broken through the hedges that same night
Into the yard where in his pride sublime
Chanticleer with his seven wives passed the time. 400
Quietly in a bed of herbs he lay
Till it was past the middle of the day,
Waiting his hour on Chanticleer to fall
As gladly do these murderers, one and all,
Who lie in wait, concealed, to murder men. 405
O murderer, lurking traitorous in your den!
O new Iscariot, second Ganelon,
False hypocrite, Greek Sinon,[1] who brought on
The utter woe of Troy and all her sorrow!
O Chanticleer, accursed be that morrow 410
When to the yard you flew down from the beams!
That day, as you were well warned in your dreams,
Would threaten you with dire catastrophe.
But that which God foresees must come to be,
As there are certain scholars who aver. 415
Bear witness, any true philosopher,
That in the schools there has been great altercation
Upon this question, and much disputation
By a hundred thousand scholars, man for man.
I cannot sift it down to the pure bran 420
As can the sacred Doctor, Augustine,
Or Boëthius, or Bishop Bradwardine,[2]
Whether God's high foreknowledge so enchains me
I needs must do a thing as it constrains me—

---

1. Traitor at Troy. *Ganelon:* Traitor in the *Song of Roland.*   2. *Augustine:* St. Augustine (354–430), the great Church Father. *Boëthius:* Author of the *Consolation of Philosophy* (*De consolatione philosophiae*), one of the most popular works of the Middle Ages (see pp. 1260–63). *Bradwardine:* Archbishop of Canterbury in Chaucer's childhood.

"Needs must"—that is, by plain necessity;   425
Or whether a free choice is granted me
To do it or not do it, either one,
Though God must know all things before they are done;
Or whether his foresight nowise can constrain
Except contingently, as some explain;   430
I will not labor such a high concern.
My tale is of a cock, as you shall learn,
Who took his wife's advice, to his own sorrow,
And walked out in the yard that fatal morrow.
Women have many times, as wise men hold,   435
Offered advice that left men in the cold.
A woman's counsel brought us first to woe
And out of Paradise made Adam go
Where he lived a merry life and one of ease.
But since I don't know whom I may displease   440
By giving women's words an ill report,
Pass over it; I only spoke in sport.
There are books about it you can read or skim in,
And you'll discover what they say of women.
I'm telling you the cock's words, and not mine.   445
Harm in no woman at all can I divine.

   Merrily bathing where the sand was dry
Lay Partlet, with her sisters all near by,
And Chanticleer, as regal as could be,
Sang merrily as the mermaid in the sea;   450
For the *Physiologus*[3] itself declares
That they know how to sing the merriest airs.
And so it happened that as he fixed his eye
Among the herbs upon a butterfly,
He caught sight of this fox who crouched there low.   455
He felt no impulse then to strut or crow,
But cried "cucock!" and gave a fearful start
Like a man who has been frightened to the heart.
For instinctively, if he should chance to see
His opposite, a beast desires to flee,   460
Even the first time that it meets his eye.

   This Chanticleer, no sooner did he spy
The fox than promptly enough he would have fled.
But "Where are you going, kind sir?" the fox said.
"Are you afraid of me, who am your friend?   465
Truly, I'd be a devil from end to end
If I meant you any harm or villainy.
I have not come to invade your privacy.
In truth, the only reason that could bring

---

3. A collection of nature lore.

This visit of mine was just to hear you sing.   470
Beyond a doubt, you have as fine a voice
As any angel who makes heaven rejoice.
Also you have more feeling in your note
Than Boëthius,[4] or any tuneful throat.
Milord your father once—and may God bless   475
His soul—your noble mother too, no less,
Have been inside my house, to my great ease.
And verily sir, I should be glad to please
You also. But for singing, I declare,
As I enjoy my eyes, that precious pair,   480
Save you, I never heard a man so sing
As your father did when night was on the wing.
Straight from the heart, in truth, came all his song,
And to make his voice more resonant and strong
He would strain until he shut his either eye,   485
So loud and lordly would he make his cry,
And stand up on his tiptoes therewithal
And stretch his neck till it grew long and small.
He had such excellent discretion, too,
That whether his singing, all the region through,   490
Or his wisdom, there was no one to surpass.
I read in that old book, *Don Burnel the Ass*,[5]
Among his verses once about a cock
Hit on the leg by a priest who threw a rock
When he was young and foolish; and for this   495
He caused the priest to lose his benefice.[6]
But no comparison, in all truth, lies
Between your father, so prudent and so wise,
And this other cock, for all his subtlety.
Sing, sir! Show me, for holy charity,   500
Can you imitate your father, that wise man?"
    Blind to all treachery, Chanticleer began
To beat his wings, like one who cannot see
The traitor, ravished by his flattery.
    Alas, you lords, about your court there slips   505
Many a flatterer with deceiving lips
Who can please you more abundantly, I fear,
Than he who speaks the plain truth to your ear.
Read in *Ecclesiastes*,[7] you will see
What flatterers are. Lords, heed their treachery!   510
    This Chanticleer stood tiptoe at full height.
He stretched his neck, he shut his eyelids tight,
And he began to crow a lordly note.

---

4. He was also author of a treatise on music.   5. A twelfth-century Latin work by the Englishman Nigel
Wireker.   6. By failing to wake him with his crowing.   7. This should apparently be Ecclesiasticus
(a book of the Old Testament Apocrypha) 12:10ff; 27:26.

The fox, Don Russell, seized him by the throat
At once, and on his back bore Chanticleer   515
Off toward his den that in the grove stood near,
For no one yet had threatened to pursue.
O destiny, that no man may eschew!
Alas, that he left his safe perch on the beams!
Alas, that Partlet took no stock in dreams!   520
And on a Friday happened this mischance!
   Venus, whose pleasures make the whole world dance,
Since Chanticleer was ever your true servant,
And of your rites with all his power observant
For pleasure rather than to multiply,   525
Would you on Friday suffer him to die?
   Geoffrey,[8] dear master of the poet's art,
Who when your Richard perished by a dart
Made for your king an elegy so burning,
Why have I not your eloquence and learning   530
To chide, as you did, with a heart so filled,
Fridays? For on a Friday he was killed.
Then should I show you how I could complain
For Chanticleer in all his fright and pain!
   In truth, no lamentation ever rose,   535
No shriek of ladies when before its foes
Ilium fell, and Pyrrhus with drawn blade
Had seized King Priam by the beard and made
An end of him— the *Aeneid* tells the tale—[9]
Such as the hens made with their piteous wail   540
In their enclosure, seeing the dread sight
Of Chanticleer. But at the shrillest height
Shrieked Partlet. She shrieked louder than the wife
Of Hasdrubal,[1] when her husband lost his life
And the Romans burned down Carthage; for her state   545
Of torment and of frenzy was so great
She willfully chose the fire for her part,
Leaped in, and burned herself with steadfast heart.
   Unhappy hens, you shrieked as when for pity,
While the tyrant Nero put to flames the city   550
Of Rome, rang out the shriek of senators' wives
Because their husbands had all lost their lives;
This Nero put to death these innocent men.
But I will come back to my tale again.
   Now this good widow and her two daughters heard   555
These woeful hens shriek when the crime occurred,
And sprang outdoors as quickly as they could
And saw the fox, who was making for the wood

8. Geoffrey de Vinsauf, author of a treatise on poetry, with specimens, among them an elegy on Richard
I.   9. Book II, ll. 550 ff.   1. King of Carthage (second century B.C.).

Bearing this Chanticleer across his back.
"Help, help!" they cried. They cried, "Alas! Alack!   560
The fox, the fox!" and after him they ran,
And armed with clubs came running many a man.
Ran Coll the dog, and led a yelping band;
Ran Malkyn, with a distaff in her hand;
Ran cow and calf, and even the very hogs,   565
By the yelping and the barking of the dogs
And men's and women's shouts so terrified
They ran till it seemed their hearts would burst inside;
They squealed like fiends in the pit, with none to still them.
The ducks quacked as if men were going to kill them.   570
The geese for very fear flew over the trees.
Out of the beehive came the swarm of bees.
Ah! Bless my soul, the noise, by all that's true,
So hideous was that Jack Straw's[2] retinue
Made never a hubbub that was half so shrill   575
Over a Fleming they were going to kill
As the clamor made that day over the fox.
They brought brass trumpets, and trumpets made of box,
Of horn, of bone, on which they blew and squeaked,
And those who were not blowing whooped and shrieked.   580
It seemed as if the very heavens would fall!
    Now hear me, you good people, one and all!
Fortune, I say, will suddenly override
Her enemy in his very hope and pride!
This cock, as on the fox's back he lay,   585
Plucked up his courage to speak to him and say.
"God be my help, sir, but I'd tell them all,
That is, if I were you, 'Plague on you fall!
Go back, proud fools! Now that I've reached the wood,
I'll eat the cock at once, for all the good   590
Your noise can do. Here Chanticleer shall stay.' "
    "Fine!" said the fox. "I'll do just what you say."
But the cock, as he was speaking, suddenly
Out of his jaws lurched expeditiously,
And flew at once high up into a tree.   595
And when the fox saw that the cock was free,
"Alas," he said, "alas, O Chanticleer!
Inasmuch as I have given you cause for fear
By seizing you and bearing you away,
I have done you wrong, I am prepared to say.   600
But, sir, I did it with no ill intent.
Come down, and I shall tell you what I meant.
So help me God, it's truth I'll offer you!"

2. Leader of the Peasants' Revolt of 1381, caused in part by the competition in labor of immigrating
Flemings.

"No, no," said he. "We're both fools, through and through.
But curse my blood and bones for the chief dunce   605
If you deceive me oftener than once!
You shall never again by flattery persuade me
To sing and wink my eyes, by him that made me.
For he that willfully winks when he should see,
God never bless him with prosperity!"   610
    "Ah," said the fox, "with mischief may God greet
The man ungoverned, rash, and indiscreet
Who babbles when to hold his tongue were needful!"
    Such is it to be reckless and unheedful
And trust in flattery. But you who hold   615
That this is a mere trifle I have told,
Concerning only a fox, or a cock and hen,
Think twice, and take the moral, my good men!
For truly, of whatever is written, all
Is written for our doctrine, says St. Paul.[3]   620
Then take the fruit, and let the chaff lie still.
Now, gracious God, if it should be your will,
As my Lord teaches, make us all good men
And bring us to your holy bliss! Amen.

FRANÇOIS VILLON

1431–?

François Villon is the poet of the fifteenth century who evokes perhaps the deepest
response from a modern reader. Born in Paris in 1431, well educated at the Sorbonne, he led an irregular life and was often an associate of criminals. In 1455 he
was charged with killing a priest but acquitted on the ground of self-defense. Involved
with others in a theft from the College of Navarre, he left Paris for several years of
wandering. During this period he visited the court of Charles d'Orléans, who was
a poet and a patron of poets. In 1461 he was imprisoned at Meung-sur-Loire,
apparently on a serious charge the nature of which is not known. Liberated later
that year by the new king Louis XI (in a coronation amnesty), Villon returned to
Paris and soon was once more in difficulty with the law. A death sentence was in
January 1463 commuted to banishment from Paris, and from this time on nothing
is known of him.

    Villon wrote poems in a variety of short forms, especially the *lai* and the *ballade*,
and some of these are incorporated in his major work, the *Testament*. Our selection contains one independent *ballade* and a considerable portion of the *Testament*.

    The "Ballade of the Hanged" shows us "five, six" skeletons of criminals who
have been executed long before, and are now twisting slowly in the wind. The
gruesome imagery, the changes wrought by rain and sun—these are starkly realis-

3. Romans 15:4.

tic. The poem asserts both the distance of the hanged men from the rest of mankind
and their affinity with it—"brother humans."

The *Testament* employs a well-established literary form, that of a last will, in
which the author makes various bequests, some actual, some fictitious or facetious
or satirical, and also expresses views about a variety of more or less extraneous
matters. In Villon's poem autobiographical elements are prominent. We see his
resentment against Bishop Thibault, who was responsible for his harsh life in prison,
and his gratitude to King Louis, who released him. In a way that reminds us a bit
of the "Confessions" of the Archpoet, Villon often acknowledges his misdeeds and
at the same time offers a defense, as in the story of Alexander and Diomedes. A
recurrent theme is the inevitability and universality of death, and this leads easily
into the best-known stanzas of the *Testament*, in which the poet asks where now
are the great men and beautiful women of the past—and where are the snows of
last winter? This, too, was a favorite topic of poets; we see it in Boethius. So is the
lament of the once beautiful Helmet-seller, now old and decrepit, for her lost
youth. The details are unsparing and the language uninhibited; these are qualities
more attractive to our generation of readers than to those of many of the intervening centuries. In another vein, Villon moves us by his gratitude toward his fatherly
protector and by his affection for his mother, now old and poor, for whom he
composes a prayer. At the end of the *Testament* the author is again the central
figure: his general misery, his ill-spent life, his need of God's mercy.

For the French original and for further information about Villon, see Galway
Kinnell, *The Poems of François Villon* (1977). A more detailed account can be
found in Henry de Vere Stacpoole, *François Villon: His Life and Times* (1916). A
good critical study is John Fox, *The Poetry of Villon* (1962).

Ballade[1]

Brother humans who live on after us
Don't let your hearts harden against us
For if you have pity on wretches like us
More likely God will show mercy to you
You see us five, six, hanging here   5

As for the flesh we loved too well
A while ago it was eaten and has rotted away
And we the bones turn to ashes and dust
Let no one make us the butt of jokes
But pray God that he absolve us all.   10

Don't be insulted that we call you
Brothers, even if it was by Justice
We were put to death, for you understand
Not every person has the same good sense
Speak up for us, since we can't ourselves   15

Before the son of the virgin Mary
That his mercy toward us shall keep flowing
Which is what keeps us from hellfire

---

1. Translated by Galway Kinnell.

We are dead, may no one taunt us
But pray God that he absolve us all.   20

The rain has rinsed and washed us
The sun dried us and turned us black
Magpies and ravens have pecked out our eyes
And plucked our beards and eyebrows
Never ever can we stand still   25

Now here, now there, as the wind shifts
At its whim it keeps swinging us
Pocked by birds worse than a sewing thimble
Therefore don't join in our brotherhood
But pray God that he absolve us all.   30

Prince Jesus, master over all
Don't let us fall into hell's dominion
We've nothing to do or settle down there
Men, there's nothing here to laugh at
But pray God that he absolve us all.   35

From The Testament[2]

In my thirtieth year of life
When I had drunk down all my disgrace
Neither altogether a fool nor altogether wise
Despite the many blows I had
Every one of which I took   5
At Thibault d'Aussigny's[3] hand
Bishop he may be as he signs the cross
Through the streets, but I deny he is mine.

And he's no more my lord than my bishop
I hold from him nothing but waste   10
I owe him neither fealty nor homage
I am not his serf or his doe
He fed me on a small loaf
And cold water a whole summer long
Open-handed or mean he was stingy with me   15
God be to him as he's been to me.

If someone wants to object
And say I'm cursing the man
I'm not if you see my meaning
I don't speak ill of him at all   20
Here's the sum of my abuse
If he's shown me any mercy
Let Jesus king of paradise
Show him as much to soul and body.

2. Translated by Galway Kinnell, whose notes are adapted for use here.   3. Bishop of Orléans from
1452 to 1473.

And if he has misused me   25
Even worse than I can tell here
All I ask is that the eternal God
Be unto him accordingly
"But the Church asks and expects us
To pray for our enemies"   30
I'll reply "I'm wrong and ashamed
Whatever he did being in God's hands."

So I'll pray for him gladly
And for the soul of the late Cotart[4]
But how? It will be by heart   35
I'm too lazy to read it out
And it will be the way the Picards pray[5]
In case he doesn't know it he should go learn
Before too late if he values my advice
At Douai or at Lille in Flanders.   40

But if he wants a prayer he can hear
By the faith I owe from baptism
Though I won't bandy it about
I'll be sure he gets his wish
From my psalter when I have the time   45
Bound neither in calf nor red leather
I'll recite him the verse set down as seventh
Of the psalm *Deus laudem*.[6]

And now I turn to God's blessed son
On whom I call in times of need   50
And ask that this poor prayer be heard
By him from whom I hold body and soul
Who has shielded me from many trials
And delivered me from iron rule
Praise be to him and our Lady   55
And Louis the good king of France[7]

To whom God grant Jacob's luck[8]
And Solomon's honor and glory
As for prowess he has plenty
And authority too, by my soul   60
And so that his memory may last
In this fleeting world
Such as it has of length and breadth
Let him live as long as Methuselah[9]

4. Jean Cotart, the prayer for whose soul occurs later in the *Testament*. 5. The Picards were a heretical sect that did not believe in prayer. Their headquarters were in Douai and Lille in northwestern France. 6. Psalm 108 (*Deus laudem meam*, "God of my praise") verse 8 (in some editions verse 7) has the prayer *Fiant dies eius pauci et episcopateum eius accipiat alter* ("Let his days be few and let another take his office"). 7. Louis XI (1423–1483), crowned king of France in August 1461, passed through Meung-sur-Loire in October 1461. While there, he freed Villon and the other prisoners being kept by Bishop Thibault. 8. Jacob obtained his older brother Esau's inheritance in exchange for a meal (Genesis 25–27). *Solomon:* King of Israel in the tenth century B.C. famous for his wealth and wisdom; also the reputed author of the Biblical books of Proverbs, The Song of Songs, and Ecclesiastes. 9. The longest-lived of the sons of Adam (Genesis 5), he lived for 969 years.

And see twelve fine children all sons   65
Born of his precious royal blood
Conceived in the marriage bed
Doughty as the great Charles[1]
And good as Saint Martial
May it turn out so for the ex-dauphin[2]   70
I wish him no further trouble
And then paradise at the last.

Because I'm feeling poor
In goods far more than in health
And still have my wits about me   75
At least the few God lent me
For I haven't borrowed from anyone else
I've drawn up this true and authentic
Testament of my last will
Once and for all, irrevocable.   80

Written in the year sixty-one
When the good king set me free
From the hard prison at Meung
And gave me back my life
For which while my heart beats I'm bound   85
To humble myself before him
And so it shall be until he dies
A good act must not be forgotten.

*   *   *

I am a sinner I know it well
And yet God doesn't want me to die   105
But to repent and live right
And so with all others bitten by sin
Though in my sin I may be dead
Yet God and his mercy live
If my conscience gnaws   110
He in his grace forgives me.

*   *   *

In the time when Alexander[3] reigned
A man by the name of Diomedes   130
Was brought into his presence
With screws on his thumbs and fingers
Life a thief, for he was one
Of those freebooters who cruise the seas
That's how he was dragged before this chief   135
To hear his death sentence.

The emperor harangued him thus
"Why are you a robber on the high seas?"

1. Possibly Charlemagne (742–814), founder of the Holy Roman Empire in western Europe. *Saint Martial*: Kinsman of Saint Peter, amiable and effective missionary to the heathen Gauls, also bishop of Limoges.   2. Louis XI. *Dauphin* is the title of the heir apparent to the French throne.   3. Alexander the Great (356–323 B.C.), ruler of Greece, Persia, and Egypt through military conquest and occupation.

To which the other answered
"Why do you call me a robber?   140
Because I'm seen marauding about
In a tiny little skiff?
If I could arm myself like you
Like you I'd be an emperor.

"But what can one expect? Fortune   145
Whom I'm helpless against
Who deals me such bad luck
Sets the course of life I've taken
Take this as some excuse
And know that in great poverty   150
It's said often enough
There lies no great honesty."

When the emperor had mulled over
What Diomedes had said he told him
"I'll have your fortune changed   155
From bad to good" and so he did
After that he never so much as spoke ill
Of anyone again and was a respected man
This is vouched for by Valerian[4]
Who was called "The Great" in Rome.   160

If only God had let me meet
Another merciful Alexander
Who'd put me in line for good luck
After that if I'd been caught
Stooping to crime I'd have sentenced myself   165
With my own voice to the burning stake
Necessity makes people err
And hunger drives wolf from woods.

                 *   *   *

Ah God if only I had studied
In the days of my heedless youth
And set myself in good ways
I'd have a house now and soft bed
But I ran from that school   205
Like some good-for-nothing child
As I write these words
My heart is nearly breaking.

I credited Solomon's words
Far too much (only I am to blame)   210
When he says "Rejoice my son
In the time of your youth"[5] and yet
He dishes it out differently elsewhere

---

4. Valerius Maximus (1st century A.D.), Roman writer and politician; but Villon probably took the story from the *Policraticus*, a work on diplomacy and courtly behavior by the twelfth-century church leader and classical scholar John of Salisbury.   5. Quoted from Ecclesiastes 11:9–10.

For he also says "Childhood and youth"
These his very words no less no more   215
"Are ignorance and error."

My days have fled away
Just as Job says the threads do[6]
On a cloth when the weaver
Takes burning straw in his hand   220
Then if a stray end sticks out
He razes it in a flash
So I no longer fear what ills may come
For everything finishes in death.

Where are the happy young men   225
I ran with in the old days
Who sang so well, who spoke so well
So excellent in word and deed?
Some are stiffened in death
And of those there's nothing left   230
May they find rest in paradise
And my God save those who remain.

And others, God be praised
Are now great lords and masters
And others go begging naked   235
And see white bread only in shop windows
And still others have entered the cloisters
Of the Celestines and Carthusians[7]
Booted and gaitered like oystermen
See how differently they've come out   240

                    *   *   *

I am not, I'm perfectly aware
An angel's son wearing a crown
Of stars or other heavenly bodies
My father is dead, God keep his soul   300
And his body lies under a stone
And my mother will die I realize
And she knows it well poor woman
And the son will not lag behind.

I know that the poor and the rich   305
The wise and the foolish, the priests and the laymen
The nobles, the serfs, the generous, the mean
Small and great, handsome and ugly
Ladies in upturned collars
No matter what their rank   310
Whether in kerchiefs or *bourrelets*[8]
Death seizes them without exception.

6. Job 7–6, "My days are swifter than a weaver's shuttle."   7. Orders of monks.   8. Homely padded
caps.

Be it Paris or Helen[9] who dies
Whoever dies dies in such pain
The wind is knocked out of him   315
His gall breaks on his heart
And he sweats God knows what sweat
And no one can lighten his pain
He hasn't child, brother, or sister
Willing to stand in for him then.   320

Death makes him shudder and blanch
Makes the nose curve, the veins tighten
The neck puff, the flesh go limp
The joints and sinews swell and stretch
Body of woman so tender   325
So polished, so smooth, so dearly loved
Must you too come to these agonies?
Yes or rise in the flesh up to heaven.

Tell me where, in what country
Is Flora[1] the beautiful Roman   330
Archipiada or Thaïs[2]
Who was first cousin[3] to her once
Echo who speaks when there's a sound
Over pond or river
Whose beauty was more than human?   335
But where are the snows of last winter?

Where is the learned Heloïse
For whom they castrated Pierre Abélard
And monked him at Saint Denis?
For his love he suffered this outrage   340
Also where is the queen[4]
Who had Buridan tied in a sack
And dumped into the Seine?
But where are the snows of last winter?

That queen white as a lily[5]   345
Who sang with a siren's voice
And big-footed Berte,[6] Beatrice, Alice
Haremburgis[7] who held Maine
And Jeanne the good maid of Lorraine[8]
Whom the English burned at Rouen, where   350
Where are they sovereign Virgin?
But where are the snows of last winter?

---

9. Helen's elopement with the Trojan prince Paris was a cause of the Trojan War. Paris was killed during the Greek capture of Troy; Helen's death is not recorded.   1. A courtesan of ancient Rome.   2. Mistress of Alexander the Great. *Archipiada*: Alcibiades (ca. 450–404 B.C.), Athenian general and politician. Because of his reputed beauty he was sometimes regarded as a woman in the Middle Ages.   3. Or "counterpart."   4. Of uncertain identification. There was a story that she took lovers from among students at Paris and then had them thrown out a window into the Seine. Buridan was a professor at the University of Paris.   5. Probably Blanche of Castille, mother of the French king Louis XIX.   6. Bertha (Berte *au grand pied*) was the mother of Charlemagne. Beatrice and Alice are figures in the medieval narrative poem *Hervi de Metz*.   7. Erembourg, daughter and heiress of Count Hélie de la Flèche, ruler of the French province of Maine.   8. Joan of Arc.

Prince you may not ask this week
Where they are nor this year
That I won't tell you back the refrain   355
But where are the snows of last winter?

*   *   *

For be it his holiness the Pope   385
Wearing his alb and amice
Who puts on his holy stole
With which to strangle the devil
All flaming with evil power
He dies exactly as his servant   390
Swept off from this life
So much blows away on the wind.

Yet or be it the emperor
Of Constantinople[9] of the golden fist
Or that most noble king of France[1]   395
Singled out above all kings
To build churches and monasteries
To the greater glory of God
If he was honored in his day
So much blows away on the wind.   400

Or be it the dauphin brave and wise
Of Vienne and Grenoble[2]
Or the great men and their eldest sons
Of Dijon, Salins, and Dole[3]
Or the same number of their servants   405
Heralds, trumpeters, men-at-arms
Didn't they happily stuff their faces?
So much blows away on the wind.

Princes are destined to die
And so are all others who live   410
Whether they rage at this or tremble
So much blows away on the wind.

Since popes, kings, and kings' sons
Conceived in wombs of queens
Lie dead and cold under the ground   415
And their reigns pass into other hands
I a poor packman out of Rennes[4]
Won't I also die? Yes, God willing
But as long as I've sown my wild oats
I won't mind an honest death.   420

The world won't last forever
Whatever the robber baron may think

9. Probably refers to a Count of Eu. Villon may have seen his tombstone at Saint-Denis, according to which he was son of a Sir Jehan de Bayne, who was known as emperor of Constantinople. 1. Louis IX, later canonized as Saint Louis.   2. In modern French, *le dauphin* (that is, prince) *du Viennois*.   3. Areas in the domain of the Duke of Burgundy.   4. A city in the French province of Brittany.

The mortal knife hands over us all
A thought which comforts the old-timer
Who was well known in his day   425
For the gaiety of his wit
Who'd be thought a slob, a dirty old man
If in old age he tried to poke fun.

Not he's got to go begging
Necessity obliges it   430
Day after day he longs to die
Sadness so works on his heart
Often but for the fear of God
He'd commit a horrible act
And it may yet happen he breaks God's law   435
And does away with himself.

For if he was amusing once
Now nothing he says gets a laugh
An old monkey is always unpleasant
And every face it makes is ugly   440
If trying to please he keeps quiet
Everybody thinks he's senile
If he speaks they tell him "Pipe down
That plum didn't grown on your tree."

The same with the poor shrunken women   445
Who've grown old and haven't a penny
When they see the young girls
Squeezing them out on the sly
They demand of God why is it
By what right were they born so early?   450
Our Lord keeps quiet and says nothing
For against such bickering he would lose.

Now I think I hear the laments
Of the once-beautiful Helmet-seller
Wishing she were a girl again   455
And saying something like this
"Ah, cruel, arrogant old age
Why have you beaten me down so soon?
What holds me back from striking myself
From killing myself with a blow?   460

"You have taken from me the high hand
That I had by right of beauty
Over clerics, merchants, men of the Church
For then there wasn't a man born
Who wouldn't have given me all he owned   465
Repent though he might later on
If I'd just have let him have
What now tramps won't take for free.

"To many a man I refused it
Which wasn't exactly good sense   470

For the love of a smooth operator
Whom I gave free play with it
And what if I did fool around
I swear I loved him truly
But he just gave me a hard time   475
And loved me for my money.

"He could wipe the floor with me
Or kick me I loved him still
And even if he's broken my back
He could just ask for a kiss   480
And I'd forget my misery
The rascal rotten right through
Would take me in his arms (a lot I got for it)
What's left? The shame and sin.

"Dead he's been these thirty years   485
And here I am old and grizzled
When I think alas of the happy times
What I was, what I've become
When I look at myself naked
And see how I've changed so much   490
Poor, dried-up, lean and bony
I nearly go off my head.

"What's become of the smooth forehead
The yellow hair, the arching eyebrows
The wide-set eyes, the fair gaze   495
That took in all the cleverest men
The straight nose neither large nor small
The little flattened ears
The dimpled chin, the bright rounded cheeks
And the lips beautiful and red?   500

"The delicate little shoulders
The long arms and slender hands
The small breasts, the full buttocks
High, broad, perfectly built
For holding the jousts of love   505
The wide loins and the sweet quim
Set over thick firm thighs
In its own little garden?

"The forehead lined, the hair gray
The eyebrows all fallen out, the eyes clouded   510
Which threw those bright glances
That felled many a poor devil
The nose hooked far from beauty
The ears hairy and lopping down
The cheeks washed out, dead and pasty   515
The chin furrowed, the lips just skin.

"This is what human beauty comes to
The arms short, the hands shriveled

The shoulders all hunched up
The breasts? Shrunk in again   520
The buttocks gone the way of the tits
The quim? aagh! As for the thighs
They aren't thighs now but sticks
Speckled all over like sausages.

"This is how we lament the good old days   525
Among ourselves, poor silly crones
Dumped down on our hunkers
In little heaps like so many skeins
Around a tiny hempstalk fire
That's soon lit and soon gone out   530
And once we were so adorable
So it goes for men and women.

"Now look here pretty Glover
Who used to study under me
And you too Blanche the Shoe-fitter   535
It's time you got it straight
Take what you can right and left
Don't spare a man I beg you
For there's no run on old crones
No more than cried-down money.   540

"And you sweet Sausage-filler
Such a born dancer
And Guillemette the Tapester[5]
Don't fall out with your man
Soon you'll have to close up shop   545
When you've gotten old and flabby
And good for no one but an old priest
No more than cried-down money.

"Jeanneton the Bonnet-maker
Don't let that one lover tie you down   550
And Catherine the Purse-seller
Stop putting men out to pasture
She who's lost her looks can ask them
To come back, she can flash her smile
But ugly old age can't buy love   555
No more than cried-down money.

"Girls, stop a moment
And let it sink in why I weep and cry
I can't get back in circulation
No more than cried-down money."   560

                    *   *   *

So fall in love all you want   625
Go to the dances and festivals

---

5. Properly a maker or seller of rugs; her shop may have been headquarters for a prostitute.

Come home empty-handed
With nothing cracked but your skulls
Love makes beasts of us all
It made an idolater of Solomon[6]
And that's why Samson lost his eyes[7]
Lucky the man who has no part in it.

Love made the sweet minstrel Orpheus[8]
Playing his flutes and bagpipes
Risk death from the murderous   635
Dog four-headed Cerberus
It made the fair-haired boy Narcissus[9]
Drown himself down in a well
For love of his lovelies
Lucky the man who has no part in it.   640

It made the brave knight Sardana[1]
Who subdued the whole kingdom of Crete
Try to turn into a woman
So he could join the virgins at spinning
And made King David the wise prophet   645
Forget all his fear of God
When he saw shapely thighs being washed[2]
Lucky the man who has no part in it.

It made Ammon[3] want to dishonor
While pretending to be eating tarts   650
His sister Tamar and deflower her
Which was wicked incest
Herod and this isn't a joke
Cut off John the Baptist's head
For dances, leaps, and love songs[4]   655
Lucky the man who has no part in it.

Of my poor self let me say
I was pummeled like laundry is an stream
Stark naked no need to hide it
Who forced me to eat this sour mash   660
But Katherine de Vausselles?[5]
Noël[6] was the third one there
At his wedding may he be beaten the same
Lucky the man who has no part in it.

6. King Solomon built temples for heathen deities worshipped by some of his wives (1 Kings 11:3–8.)
7. The Israelite hero was captured and blinded by the Philistines when he told the beautiful seductress
Delilah the secret of his strength. (Judges 13–14.)   8. The musician of Greek myth, who descended to
the underworld to bring his wife Eurydice back to life. Cerberus was the guardian of the way to the
underworld.   9. In Greek myth, a handsome youth who mistook his own reflection in the water for
another person, plunged in and was drowned.   1. Perhaps Sardanapalus, a notorious king of ancient
Assyria, apparently identified with a reputed conqueror of Crete.   2. He saw Bathsheba bathing and fell
in love with her, though she was a married woman (2 Samuel 11).   3. A son of King David; infatuated
with his (half-) sister Tamar, he induced her to serve him a meal in his apartment, whereupon he forced
her. He was later slain at the instigation of Absalom (2 Samuel 13).   4. After his stepdaughter Salome
danced for him, Herod acceded to her demand that the prophet John the Baptist be beheaded. (Matthew
14:3–12).   5. Nothing is known of her. By tradition she is classed as one of Villon's "serious" loves.
6. Perhaps Noël Jolis, who later in the Testament receives a whipping as his bequest.

But will this young bachelor   665
Give up the single girls?
No not even if he has to burn for it
Like a rider of broomsticks
Girls are sweeter to him than civet
But this fool gets taken every time   670
Be they blondes or brunettes
Lucky the man who has no part in it.

✳   ✳   ✳

First I confer my poor soul
On the glorious Trinity
And commend it to our Lady   835
Dwelling place of divinity
And petition all the charity
Of the nine Orders of Heaven[7]
That they may carry this gift
Before the precious throne.   840

Item I bequeath and give my body
To our great mother the Earth
The worms won't find much fat on it
Too long did hunger wage its hard war
Let her receive it straight away   845
From earth it came, to earth it returns
All things unless they stray too far
Long to go back to their own place.

Item to my more than father
Master Guillaume de Villon[8]   850
Who has been gentler to me than mother
To child just out of swaddling clothes
He has saved me from many a tight spot
And isn't exactly enjoying this one
Down on my knees I beg him   855
To leave all the joy of it to me,

I give him my library
Including "The Tale of the Devil's Fart"[9]
Which that truthful fellow
Master Guy Tabarie[1] clear-copied   860
It's in notebooks under a table
Although the style may be crude
The matter itself is so potent
It makes up for the defects.

Item I give my poor mother   865
When suffered bitterly over me
God knows, and had many sorrows

7. The hierarchy of angels.   8. Villon's benefactor.   9. A lost early work by Villon or, more probably, a title Villon made up as a joke. Its subject would be the story of how a group of students as a prank
removed the stone landmark known as "The Devil's Fart" from in front of the hotel of that name.
1. Being questioned by police after the robbery of the chapel of the College of Navarre, Tabarie told the
whole truth, incriminating Villon.

These words to give to our Lady
I've no other castle or fortress
Where I can find refuge body and soul   870
When evil times come upon me
And my mother hasn't either, poor woman.

Lady of heaven, regent of earth
Empress over the swamps of hell
Receive me your humble Christian   875
Let me be counted among your elect
Even though I'm without any worth
My lady and mistress your merits
Are greater by far then my sinfulness
And without them no soul could deserve   880
Or enter heaven, I'm not acting
In this faith I want to live and die.

Tell your son I belong to him
May he wash away my sins
And forgive me as he did the Egyptian woman[2]   885
Or Theophilus the priest[3]
Who with your help was acquitted and absolved
Though he'd made a pact with the devil
Keep me from ever doing that
Virgin who bore with unbroken hymen   890
The sacrament we celebrate at Mass
In this faith I want to live and die.

I'm just a poor old woman
Who knows nothing and can't read
On the walls of my parish church I see   895
A paradise painted with harps and lutes
And a hell where they boil the damned
One gives me a fright, one great bliss and joy
Let me have the good place, mother of God
To whom sinners all must turn   900
Filled with faith, sincere and eager
In this faith I want to live and die.

Virgin so worthy, princess, you bore
Jesus who reigns without end or limit
Lord Almighty who took on our weakness   905
Left heaven and came down to save us
Offering his precious youth to death
Now such is our Lord, such I acknowledge him
In this faith I want to live and die.

                    *   *   *

Item I leave my barber
Name of Colin Galerne[4]

---

2. Saint Mary the Egyptian.   3. Feudal lord, representative in temporal affairs of the Church of Adana in Cilicie. The legend of how he dealt with the devil so as to keep his job is treated often in medieval writings.   4. Barber and churchwarden of Saint-Germain-le-Vieux.

Close neighbor to the herb-dealer Angelot[5]
A large block of ice (From where? The Marne[6])   1665
In order to winter comfortably
He's to press it firmly to his gut
If he does this faithfully all winter
Next summer he won't feel too hot.

*   *   *

Item I order my sepulcher
At Sainte-Avoye[7] and nowhere else
And so everyone may see me   1870
Not in the flesh but in painting
Have my full-length portrait done
In ink if there's money for that
A tombstone? No, forget it
It would break through the floor.   1875

Item around my pit I want
The following words and no others
Inscribed in rather large letters
Lacking something to write with
Use charcoal or a lump of coal   1880
Though watch you don't scratch the plaster
So that at least there'll be some memory left
Such as may be of a wayward one.

Here lies and sleeps in this garret
One love's arrow struck down   1885
A poor obscure scholar
Who was known as François Villon
He never owned a furrow on earth
He parceled it all out, everyone knows
Tables, chairs, bread, basket   1890
Say *Amen* with this *rondeau*.[8]

Rest eternal grant him
Lord and everlasting light[9]
He didn't have the money for a plate or bowl
Or for a sprig of parsley   1895
They shaved him, head, beard, and eyebrows
Like some turnip you scrape or peel
Rest eternal *etc.*

Harsh law exiled him
And whacked him on the ass with a shovel   1900
Even though he cried out "I appeal!"
Which isn't too subtle a phrase
Rest eternal *etc.*

*   *   *

5. Parishioner at Saint-German le-Vieux.   6. River in eastern France.   7. An Augustinian convent
on the rue du Temple in Sainte-Avoie.   8. Verse form of 12 lines, divided into stanzas of 7 and 5 lines,
each ending with the refrain, as in the following passage.   9. Cf. the Mass for the Dead: "Rest eternal
give them, O Lord, and let everlasting light shine upon them."

Here ends and finishes
The testament of poor Villon
Come to his burial
When you hear the bell ringing
Dressed in red vermilion   2000
For he died a martyr to love
This he swore on his testicle
As he made his way out of this world.

And I think it wasn't a lie
For he was chased like a scullion   2005
By his loves so spitefully
From here to Roussilon[1]
There isn't a bush or a shrub
That didn't get, he speaks truly
A shred from his back   2010
As he made his way out of this world.

It was like this, so that
By the time he died he had only a rag
What's worse, as he died, sorely
The spur of love pricked into him   2015
Sharper than the buckle-tongue
Of a baldric he could feel it
And this is what we marvel at
As he made his way out of this world.

Prince graceful as a merlin   2020
Hear what he did as he left
He took a long swig of dead-black wine
As he made his way out of this world.

EVERYMAN

Drama scarcely attained the status of a dominant literary form in the Middle Ages although in the later centuries of the period it was popular, fairly abundant, and varied in character. It began with the impersonation or dramatization of passages from the liturgy of the Resurrection and the Nativity of Christ. Produced at first in the Latin language and inside a church, it was later moved outside and Latin was replaced with vernacular languages of several European peoples. By the fourteenth century, if not earlier, whole "cycles" of short plays were performed on certain feast days of the Church, especially Corpus Christi. A complete sequence began with the revolt of Satan and his followers against God and ended with the Last Judgment; inside these limits, some forty "one-act" pieces presented the important events in the divine plan for human history. The content of these plays was based very closely on the narrative of the Bible, hence the name *miracle* plays.

About the time when the miracle plays had reached their fullest development, another kind of dramatic composition emerged, also religious in nature and pur-

1. A town in south central France.

pose. As the miracle plays dramatize the liturgy and certain Biblical events, so the *morality* plays dramatize the content of a typical homily or sermon. By common consent, *Everyman* is regarded as the best of this kind of drama. We do not know the author's name, but the play belongs to the fifteenth century; it may owe something to a Dutch piece on the same theme. Whereas miracle plays were produced in a long sequence, with "amateur" casts drawn from more or less suitable craft guilds (for example, the carpenters might present the building of Noah's ark and the subsequent flood), morality plays may have been acted by professional or semi-professional companies. Nothing is actually known about the original productions of *Everyman*; it is well suited, however, to outdoor performance. Its comparative length, along with the large part of the title character, favors the possibility of some degree of professionalism in the cast.

The modern reader may find it profitable to compare *Everyman* with such different kinds of drama as Greek tragedy, Marlowe's *Doctor Faustus*, or MacLeish's modern play, *J.B.* In its brevity, simplicity, and concentration on a single theme and situation, it recalls especially the shorter plays of the ancient Greeks. Its topic has much in common with that of Marlowe's play—a man facing death in the light of his past life—but the decisive choice and consequent ending are different. The role assigned to deity is both like and unlike that in MacLeish's adaptation of the story of Job in his play.

As in most morality plays, the characters are personifications of more abstract concepts. Everyman himself of course represents all humanity. But we should not assume in advance that "abstract" characters make a dull play. In the first place, dramatizing the characters gives them actuality; the actors must be flesh and blood. Then, in *Everyman*, the situations, the speech, and the behavior of the various characters are thoroughly realistic as well as representative of their generalized significance. For example, Good Fellowship does and says what a single boon companion would be likely to say and do under the same circumstances. Good Deeds is not a static figure: we see her first bound to the earth (the floor of the stage) by Everyman's sins; when he scourges himself in penance, she rises joyfully to accompany him. The author's ingenuity is notable in the character Goods (Riches): Goods is offstage when Everyman calls him; the audience hears but does not see him at first as he explains that he lies there in corners, trussed and piled up, locked in chests, stuffed in bags! Surely he must have got a laugh when he did come on stage. And of course God, who instigates the action by sending Death to call Everyman to his account, is no abstraction. He was probably a voice offstage rather than an actor—but a very effective character nonetheless.

Together with the lean and rapidly moving plot, it is the rightness of its words that makes *Everyman* a success. God speaks with an unfailing simplicity and directness:

> Charyte they do all clene forgete.
> I hoped well that every man
> In my glory shulde make his mansyon;
> And thereto I had them all electe. . . .
> They be so combred with worldly ryches
> That nedes on them I must do iustyce. . . .

Nor is humor absent from the play. Cousin, asked by Everyman to go with him at the summons of Death, exclaims: "No, by Our Lady! I have the crampe in my to[e]"; and later, Beauty replies to the same effect: "I crosse out all this! Adewe, by Saynt Iohan! / I take my cap in my lappe, and am gone." There is irony in Good Fellowship's farewell verse: "For you I wyll remember that partynge is mournynge." Best of all, perhaps, are the short speeches, scattered throughout the earlier parts of the play especially, which express Everyman's disappointment in his friends and consequent disillusion. One example must suffice. After a long colloquy with Goods, that character asks Everyman, "What! wenest thou that I am thyne?" Reversal, the necessary prelude to reorientation, is condensed in Everyman's brief reply: "I had weened [believed] so."

A good selection of miracle plays, morality plays, and other medieval drama is contained in Joseph Quincy Adams, *Chief Pre-Shakespearean Dramas* (1924). On the medieval theater and staging see Richard Southern, *The Medieval Theatre in the Round; A Study of the Staging of the Castle of Perseverance and Other Matters* (1957). For a recent survey of the whole matter, see Hardin Craig, *English Religious Drama of the Middle Ages* (1955). For an interesting fresh approach, see the chapter on "The Mystery Cycle" in John Speirs, *Medieval English Poetry: The Non-Chaucerian Tradition* (1958). Glynne Wickham, *Shakespeare's Dramatic Heritage* (1969), describes a *modern* production of *Everyman*. W. Roy MacKenzie, *The English Moralities from the Point of View of Allegory* (1966), gives special attention to the play.

Everyman[1]

Dramatis Personae

MESSENGER	KNOWLEDGE
GOD	CONFESSION
DEATH	BEAUTY
EVERYMAN	STRENGTH
FELLOWSHIP	DISCRETION
KINDRED	FIVE-WITS
COUSIN	ANGEL
GOODS	DOCTOR
GOOD DEEDS	

*Here Beginneth a Treatise How the High Father of
Heaven Sendeth Death to Summon Every Creature
to Come and Give Account of Their Lives in This
World, and is in Manner of a Moral Play*

[*Enter* MESSENGER.]

MESSENGER: I pray you all give your audience,
And hear this matter with reverence,
By figure[2] a moral play,
The Summoning of Everyman called it is,
That of our lives and ending shows   5
How transitory we be all day.[3]
The matter is wonder precious,
But the intent of it is more gracious

---

1. Modernized text and notes by E. Talbot Donaldson.   2. In form.   3. Always.

And sweet to bear away.
The story saith: Man, in the beginning 10
Look well, and take good heed to the ending,
Be you never so gay.
You think sin in the beginning full sweet,
Which in the end causeth the soul to weep,
When the body lieth in clay. 15
Here shall you see how fellowship and jollity,
Both strength, pleasure, and beauty,
Will fade from thee as flower in May.
For ye shall hear how our Heaven-King
Calleth Everyman to a general reckoning. 20
Give audience and hear what he doth say.
    [*Exit* MESSENGER.—*Enter* GOD.]
GOD: I perceive, here in my majesty,
How that all creatures be to me unkind,[4]
Living without dread in worldly prosperity.
Of ghostly[5] sight the people be so blind, 25
Drowned in sin, they know me not for their God.
In worldly riches is all their mind:
They fear not of my righteousness the sharp rod;
My law that I showed when I for them died
They forget clean, and shedding of my blood red. 30
I hanged between two,[6] it cannot be denied:
To get them life I suffered to be dead.
I healed their feet, with thorns hurt was my head.
I could do no more than I did, truly—
And now I see the people do clean forsake me. 35
They use the seven deadly sins damnable,
As pride, coveitise,[7] wrath, and lechery
Now in the world be made commendable.
And thus they leave of angels the heavenly company.
Every man liveth so after his own pleasure, 40
And yet of their life they be nothing sure.
I see the more that I them forbear,
The worse they be from year to year:
All that liveth appaireth[8] fast.
Therefore I will, in all the haste, 45
Have a reckoning of every man's person.
For, and[9] I leave the people thus alone
In their life and wicked tempests,
Verily they will become much worse than beasts;
For now one would by envy another up eat. 50
Charity do they all clean forgeet.

---

4. Thoughtless.   5. Spiritual.   6. The two thieves between whom Christ was crucified.
7. Avarice.   8. Degenerates.   9. If.

I hoped well that every man
In my glory should make his mansion,
And thereto I had them all elect.[1]
But now I see, like traitors deject,[2]   55
They thank me not for the pleasure that I to them meant,
Nor yet for their being that I them have lent.
I proffered the people great multitude of mercy,
And few there be that asketh it heartily.
They be so cumbered with worldly riches   60
That needs on them I must do justice—
On every man living without fear.
Where art thou, Death, thou mighty messenger?
    [*Enter* DEATH.]
DEATH: Almighty God, I am here at your will,
    Your commandment to fulfill.   65
GOD: Go thou to Everyman,
    And show him, in my name,
    A pilgrimage he must on him take,
    Which he in no wise may escape;
    And that he bring with him a sure reckoning   70
    Without delay or any tarrying.
DEATH: Lord, I will in the world go run over all,
    And cruelly out-search both great and small.
        [*Exit* GOD.]
    Everyman will I beset that liveth beastly
    Out of God's laws, and dreadeth not folly.   75
    He that loveth riches I will strike with my dart,
    His sight to blind, and from heaven to depart—[3]
    Except that Almsdeeds be his good friend—
    In hell for to dwell, world without end.
    Lo, yonder I see Everyman walking: 80
    Full little he thinketh on my coming;
    His mind is on fleshly lusts and his treasure,
    And great pain it shall cause him to endure
    Before the Lord, Heaven-King.
        [*Enter* EVERYMAN.]
    Everyman, stand still! Whither art thou going   85
    Thus gaily? Hast thou thy Maker forgeet?
EVERYMAN: Why askest thou?
    Why wouldest thou weet?[4]
DEATH: Yea, sir, I will show you:
    In great haste I am sent to thee   90
    From God out of his majesty.
EVERYMAN: What! sent to me?
DEATH: Yea, certainly.

1. Chosen. 2. Abased. 3. Separate. 4. Know.

Though thou have forgot him here,
He thinketh on thee in the heavenly sphere,   95
As, ere we depart, thou shalt know.
EVERYMAN: What desireth God of me?
DEATH: That shall I show thee:
A reckoning he will needs have
Without any longer respite.   100
EVERYMAN: To give a reckoning longer leisure I crave.
This blind[5] matter troubleth my wit.
DEATH: On thee thou must take a long journay:
Therefore thy book of count with thee thou bring,
For turn again thou cannot by no way.   105
And look thou be sure of thy reckoning,
For before God thou shalt answer and shew
Thy many bad deeds and good but a few—
How thou hast spent thy life and in what wise,
Before the Chief Lord of Paradise.   110
Have ado that we were in that way,[6]
For weet thou well thou shalt make none attornay.[7]
EVERYMAN: Full unready I am such reckoning to give.
I know thee not. What messenger art thou?
DEATH: I am Death that no man dreadeth,[8]   115
For every man I 'rest, and no man spareth;
For it is God's commandment
That all to me should be obedient.
EVERYMAN: O Death, thou comest when I had thee least in mind.
In thy power it lieth me to save: 120
Yet of my good will I give thee, if thou will be kind,
Yea, a thousand pound shalt thou have—
And defer this matter till another day.
DEATH: Everyman, it may not be, by no way.
I set nought by gold, silver, nor riches,   125
Nor by pope, emperor, king, duke, nor princes,
For, and I would receive gifts great,
All the world I might get.
But my custom is clean contrary:
I give thee no respite. Come hence and not tarry!   130
EVERYMAN: Alas, shall I have no longer respite?
I may say Death giveth no warning.
To think on thee it maketh my heart sick,
For all unready is my book of reckoning.
But twelve year and I might have a biding,[9]   135
My counting-book I would make so clear
That my reckoning I should not need to fear.

---

5. Unexpected.   6. Let's get started at once.   7. None to appear in your stead.   8. That fears nobody.
9. If I might have a delay for just twelve years.

Wherefore, Death, I pray thee, for God's mercy,
Spare me till I be provided of remedy.
DEATH: Thee availeth not to cry, weep, and pray;   140
But haste thee lightly[1] that thou were gone that journay,
And prove thy friends, if thou can.
For weet thou well the tide abideth no man,
And in the world each living creature
For Adam's sin must die of nature.[2]   145
EVERYMAN: Death, if I should this pilgrimage take
And my reckoning surely make,
Show me, for saint[3] charity,
Should I not come again shortly?
DEATH: No, Everyman. And thou be once there,   150
Thou mayst never more come here,
Trust me verily.
EVERYMAN: O gracious God in the high seat celestial,
Have mercy on me in this most need!
Shall I have no company from this vale terrestrial   155
Of mine acquaintance that way me to lead?
DEATH: Yea, if any be so hardy
That would go with thee and bear thee company.
Hie thee that thou were gone to God's magnificence,
Thy reckoning to give before his presence.   160
What, weenest[4] thou thy life is given thee,
And thy worldly goods also?
EVERYMAN: I had weened so, verily.
DEATH: Nay, nay, it was but lent thee.
For as soon as thou art go,   165
Another a while shall have it and then go therefro,
Even as thou hast done.
Everyman, thou art mad! Thou hast thy wits[5] five,
And here on earth will not amend thy life!
For suddenly I do come.   170
EVERYMAN: O wretched caitiff! Whither shall I flee
That I might 'scape this endless sorrow?
Now, gentle Death, spare me till tomorrow,
That I may amend me
With good advisement.[6]   175
DEATH: Nay, thereto I will not consent,
Nor no man will I respite,
But to the heart suddenly I shall smite,
Without any advisement.
And now out of thy sight I will me hie: 180
See thou make thee ready shortly,
For thou mayst say this is the day

---

1. Quickly.   2. Naturally.   3. Holy.   4. Suppose.   5. Senses.   6. Preparation.

That no man living may 'scape away.
[*Exit* DEATH.]
EVERYMAN: Alas, I may well weep with sighs deep:
Now have I no manner of company   185
To help me in my journey and me to keep.
And also my writing[7] is full unready—
How shall I do now for to excuse me?
I would to God I had never be geet![8]
To my soul a full great profit it had be.   190
For now I fear pains huge and great.
The time passeth: Lord, help, that all wrought!
For though I mourn, it availeth nought.
The day passeth and is almost ago:
I wot[9] not well what for to do.   195
To whom were I best my complaint to make?
What and I to Fellowship thereof spake,
And showed him of this sudden chance?
For in him is all mine affiance,[1]
We have in the world so many a day   200
Be good friends in sport and play.
I see him yonder, certainly.
I trust that he will bear me company.
Therefore to him will I speak to ease my sorrow.
[*Enter* FELLOWSHIP.]
Well met, good Fellowship, and good morrow!   205
FELLOWSHIP: Everyman, good morrow, by this day!
Sir, why lookest thou so piteously?
If anything be amiss, I pray thee me say,
That I may help to remedy.
EVERYMAN: Yea, good Fellowship, yea: 210
I am in great jeopardy.
FELLOWSHIP: My true friend, show to me your mind.
I will not forsake thee to my life's end
In the way of good company.
EVERYMAN: That was well spoken, and lovingly!   215
FELLOWSHIP: Sir, I must needs know your heaviness.
I have pity to see you in any distress.
If any have you wronged, ye shall revenged be,
Though I on the ground be slain for thee,
Though that I know before that I should die.   220
EVERYMAN: Verily, Fellowship, gramercy.[2]
FELLOWSHIP: Tush! by thy thanks I set not a stree.[3]
Show me your grief and say no more.
EVERYMAN: If I my heart should to you break,[4]
And then you to turn your mind fro me,   225

7. Ledger.   8. Been begotten.   9. Know.   1. Trust.   2. Many thanks.   3. Straw.   4. Disclose.

And would not me comfort when ye hear me speak,
Then should I ten times sorrier be.
FELLOWSHIP: Sir, I say as I will do, indeed.
EVERYMAN: Then be you a good friend at need.
I have found you true herebefore.   230
FELLOWSHIP: And so ye shall evermore.
For, in faith, and thou go to hell,
I will not forsake thee by the way.
EVERYMAN: Ye speak like a good friend. I believe you well.
I shall deserve[5] it, and I may.   235
FELLOWSHIP: I speak of no deserving, by this day!
For he that will say and nothing do
Is not worthy with good company to go.
Therefore show me the grief of your mind,
As to your friend most loving and kind.   240
EVERYMAN: I shall show you how it is:
Commanded I am to go a journay,
A long way, hard and dangerous,
And give a strait[6] count, without delay,
Before the high judge Adonai.[7]   245
Wherefore I pray you bear me company,
As ye have promised, in this journay.
FELLOWSHIP: This is matter indeed! Promise is duty—
But, and I should take such a voyage on me,
I know it well, it should be to my pain.   250
Also it maketh me afeard, certain.
But let us take counsel here, as well as we can—
For your words would fear a strong man.
EVERYMAN: Why, ye said if I had need,
Ye would me never forsake, quick ne dead,   255
Though it were to hell, truly.
FELLOWSHIP: So I said, certainly.
But such pleasures[8] be set aside, the sooth to say.
And also, if we took such a journay,
When should we again come?   260
EVERYMAN: Nay, never again, till the day of doom.
FELLOWSHIP: In faith, then will not I come there!
Who hath you these tidings brought?
EVERYMAN: Indeed, Death was with me here.
FELLOWSHIP: Now by God that all hath bought,[9]   265
If Death were the messenger,
For no man that is living today
I will not go that loath journay—
Not for the father that begat me!
EVERYMAN: Ye promised otherwise, pardie.[1]   270

5. Repay.   6. Strict.   7. God.   8. Jokes.   9. Redeemed.   1. By God.

FELLOWSHIP: I wot well I said so, truly.
   And yet, if thou wilt eat and drink and make good cheer,
   Or haunt to women the lusty company,
   I would not forsake you while the day is clear,
   Trust me verily!   275
EVERYMAN: Yea, thereto ye would be ready—
   To go to mirth, solace,[2] and play:
   Your mind to folly will sooner apply
   Than to bear me company in my long journay.
FELLOWSHIP: Now in good faith, I will not that way.   280
   But, and thou will murder or any man kill,
   In that I will help thee with a good will.
EVERYMAN: O that is simple[3] advice, indeed!
   Gentle fellow, help me in my necessity:
   We have loved long, and now I need—   285
   And now, gentle Fellowship, remember me!
FELLOWSHIP: Whether ye have loved me or no,
   By Saint John, I will not with thee go!
EVERYMAN: Yet I pray thee take the labor and do so much for me,
   To bring me forward,[4] for saint charity,   290
   And comfort me till I come without the town.
FELLOWSHIP: Nay, and thou would give me a new gown,
   I will not a foot with thee go.
   But, and thou had tarried, I would not have left thee so.
   And as now, God speed thee in thy journey!   295
   For from thee I will depart as fast as I may.
EVERYMAN: Whither away, Fellowship? Will thou forsake me?
FELLOWSHIP: Yea, by my fay! To God I betake[5] thee.
EVERYMAN: Farewell, good Fellowship! For thee my heart is sore.
   Adieu forever—I shall see thee no more   300
FELLOWSHIP: In faith, Everyman, farewell now at the ending:
   For you I will remember that parting is mourning.
     [*Exit* FELLOWSHIP.]
EVERYMAN: Alack, shall we thus depart[6] indeed—
   Ah, Lady, help!—without any more comfort?
   Lo, Fellowship forsaketh me in my most need!   305
   For help in this world whither shall I resort?
   Fellowship herebefore with me would merry make,
   And now little sorrow for me doth he take.
   It is said, "In prosperity men friends may find
   Which in adversity be full unkind."   310
   Now whither for succor shall I flee,
   Sith[7] that Fellowship hath forsaken me?
   To my kinsmen I will, truly,
   Praying them to help me in my necessity.

2. Pleasure.   3. Foolish.   4. Escort me.   5. Commend.   6. Part.   7. Since.

I believe that they will do so,   315
For kind will creep where it may not go.[8]
I will go 'say[9]—for yonder I see them—
Where[1] be ye now my friends and kinsmen.
[*Enter* KINDRED *and* COUSIN.]
KINDRED: Here be we now at your commandment:
Cousin, I pray you show us your intent   320
In any wise, and not spare.
COUSIN: Yea, Everyman, and to us declare
If ye be disposed to go anywhither.
For, weet you well, we will live and die togither.
KINDRED: In wealth and woe we will with you hold,   325
For over his kin a man may be bold.
EVERYMAN: Gramercy, my friends and kinsmen kind.
Now shall I show you the grief of my mind.
I was commanded by a messenger
That is a high king's chief officer: 330
He bade me go a pilgrimage, to my pain—
And I know well I shall never come again.
Also I must give a reckoning strait,
For I have a great enemy that hath me in wait,[2]
Which intendeth me to hinder.   335
KINDRED: What account is that which ye must render?
That would I know.
EVERYMAN: Of all my works I must show
How I have lived and my days spent;
Also of ill deeds that I have used   340
In my time sith life was me lent,
And of all virtues that I have refused.
Therefore I pray you go thither with me
To help me make mine account, for saint charity.
COUSIN: What, to go thither? Is that the matter?   345
Nay, Everyman, I had liefer fast[3] bread and water
All this five year and more!
EVERYMAN: Alas, that ever I was bore!
For now shall I never be merry
If that you forsake me.   350
KINDRED: Ah, sir, what? Ye be a merry man:
Take good heart to you and make no moan.
But one thing I warn you, by Saint Anne,
As for me, ye shall go alone.
EVERYMAN: My Cousin, will you not with me go?   355
COUSIN: No, by Our Lady! I have the cramp in my toe:
Trust not to me. For, so God me speed,
I will deceive you in your most need.

8. For kinship will creep where it cannot walk (i.e., kinsmen will suffer hardship for one another).
9. Assay.   1. Whether.   2. Satan lies in ambush for me.   3. Rather fast on.

KINDRED: It availeth you not us to 'tice.[4]
   Ye shall have my maid with all my heart: 360
   She loveth to go to feasts, there to be nice,[5]
   And to dance, and abroad to start.[6]
   I will give her leave to help you in that journey,
   If that you and she may agree.
EVERYMAN: Now show me the very effect of your mind: 365
   Will you go with me or abide behind?
KINDRED: Abide behind? Yea, that will I and I may!
   Therefore farewell till another day.
     [*Exit* KINDRED.]
EVERYMAN: How should I be merry or glad?
   For fair promises men to me make,   370
   But when I have most need they me forsake.
   I am deceived. That maketh me sad.
COUSIN: Cousin Everyman, farewell now,
   For verily I will not go with you;
   Also of mine own an unready reckoning   375
   I have to account—therefore I make tarrying.
   Now God keep thee, for now I go.
     [*Exit* COUSIN.]
EVERYMAN: Ah, Jesus, is all come hereto?
   Lo, fair words maketh fools fain:[7]
   They promise and nothing will do, certain.   380
   My kinsmen promised me faithfully
   For to abide with me steadfastly,
   And now fast away do they flee.
   Even so Fellowship promised me.
   What friend were best me of to provide?   385
   I lose my time here longer to abide.
   Yet in my mind a thing there is:
   All my life I have loved riches;
   If that my Good[8] now help me might,
   He would make my heart full light.   390
   I will speak to him in this distress.
   Where art thou, my Goods and riches?
GOODS: [*Within.*] Who calleth me? Everyman? What, hast thou haste?
   I lie here in corners, trussed and piled so high,
   And in chests I am locked so fast—   395
   Also sacked in bags—thou mayst see with thine eye
   I cannot stir, in packs low where I lie.
   What would ye have? Lightly[9] me say.
EVERYMAN: Come hither, Good, in all the haste thou may,
   For of counsel I must desire thee.   400
     [*Enter* GOODS.]

---

4. Entice.   5. Wanton.   6. To go gadding about.   7. Glad.   8. Goods.   9. Quickly.

GOODS: Sir, and ye in the world have sorrow or adversity,
    That can I help you to remedy shortly.
EVERYMAN: It is another disease[1] that grieveth me:
    In this world it is not, I tell thee so.
    I am sent for another way to go,   405
    To give a strait count general
    Before the highest Jupiter of all.
    And all my life I have had joy and pleasure in thee:
    Therefore I pray thee go with me,
    For peradventure, thou mayst before God Almighty   410
    My reckoning help to clean and purify.
    For it is said ever among[2]
    That money maketh all right that is wrong.
GOODS: Nay, Everyman, I sing another song:
    I follow no man in such voyages.   415
    For, and I went with thee,
    Thou shouldest fare much the worse for me;
    For because on me thou did set thy mind,
    Thy reckoning I have made blotted and blind,[3]
    That thine account thou cannot make truly—   420
    And that hast thou for the love of me.
EVERYMAN: That would grieve me full sore,
    When I should come to that fearful answer.
    Up, let us go thither together.
GOODS: Nay, not so, I am too brittle, I may not endure.   425
    I will follow no man one foot, be ye sure.
EVERYMAN: Alas, I have thee loved and had great pleasure
    All my life-days on good and treasure.
GOODS: That is to thy damnation, without leasing,[4]
    For my love is contrary to the love everlasting.   430
    But if thou had me loved moderately during,
    As to the poor to give part of me,
    Then shouldest thou not in this dolor be,
    Nor in this great sorrow and care.
EVERYMAN: Lo, now was I deceived ere I was ware,   435
    And all I may wite[5] misspending of time.
GOODS: What, weenest[6] thou that I am thine?
EVERYMAN: I had weened so.
GOODS: Nay, Everyman, I say no.
    As for a while I was lent thee;   440
    A season thou hast had me in prosperity.
    My condition is man's soul to kill;
    If I save one, a thousand I do spill.
    Weenest thou that I will follow thee?
    Nay, from this world, not verily.   445

1. Distress. 2. Now and then. 3. Illegible. 4. Lie. 5. Blame on. 6. Suppose.

EVERYMAN: I had weened otherwise.

GOODS: Therefore to thy soul Good is a thief;
   For when thou art dead, this is my guise—[7]
   Another to deceive in the same wise
   As I have done thee, and all to his soul's repreef.[8]   450

EVERYMAN: O false Good, cursed thou be,
   Thou traitor to God, that hast deceived me
   And caught me in thy snare!

GOODS: Marry, thou brought thyself in care,[9]
   Whereof I am glad;   455
   I must needs laugh, I cannot be sad.

EVERYMAN: Ah, Good, thou hast had long my heartly[1] love;
   I gave thee that which should be the Lord's above.
   But wilt thou not go with me, indeed?
   I pray thee truth to say.   460

GOODS: No, so God me speed!
   Therefore farewell and have good day.
   [*Exit* GOODS.]

EVERYMAN: Oh, to whom shall I make my moan
   For to go with me in that heavy journay?
   First Fellowship said he would with me gone: 465
   His words were very pleasant and gay,
   But afterward he left me alone.
   Then spake I to my kinsmen, all in despair,
   And also they gave me words fair—
   They lacked no fair speaking,   470
   But all forsake me in the ending.
   Then went I to my Goods that I loved best,
   In hope to have comfort; but there had I least,
   For my Goods sharply did me tell
   That he bringeth many into hell.   475
   Then of myself I was ashamed,
   And so I am worthy to be blamed:
   Thus may I well myself hate.
   Of whom shall I now counsel take?
   I think that I shall never speed   480
   Till that I go to my Good Deed.
   But alas, she is so weak
   That she can neither go[2] nor speak.
   Yet will I venture[3] on her now.
   My Good Deeds, where be you?   485

GOOD DEEDS: [*Speaking from the ground.*] Here I lie, cold in the ground:
   Thy sins hath me sore bound
   That I cannot stear.[4]

EVERYMAN: O Good Deeds, I stand in fear:

---

7. Custom.   8. Shame.   9. Sorrow.   1. Sincere.   2. Walk.   3. Gamble.   4. Stir.

I must you pray of counsel,   490
For help now should come right well.
GOOD DEEDS: Everyman, I have understanding
That ye be summoned, account to make,
Before Messiah of Jer'salem King.
And you do by me, that journey with you will I take.   495
EVERYMAN: Therefore I come to you my moan to make.
I pray you that ye will go with me.
GOOD DEEDS: I would full fain, but I cannot stand, verily.
EVERYMAN: Why, is there anything on you fall?
GOOD DEEDS: Yea, sir, I may thank you of all: 500
If ye had perfectly cheered me,
Your book of count full ready had be.
    [GOOD DEEDS shows him the account book.]
Look, the books of your works and deeds eke,[5]
As how they lie under the feet,
To your soul's heaviness.   505
EVERYMAN: Our Lord Jesus help me!
For one letter here I cannot see.
GOOD DEEDS: There is a blind reckoning in time of distress!
EVERYMAN: Good Deeds, I pray you help me in this need,
Or else I am forever damned indeed.   510
Therefore help me to make reckoning
Before the Redeemer of all thing
That King is and was and ever shall.
GOOD DEEDS: Everyman, I am sorry of your fall
And fain would help you and I were able.   515
EVERYMAN: Good Deeds, your counsel I pray you give me.
GOOD DEEDS: That shall I do verily,
Though that on my feet I may not go;
I have a sister that shall with you also,
Called Knowledge, which shall with you abide   520
To help you to make that dreadful reckoning.
    [Enter KNOWLEDGE.]
KNOWLEDGE: Everyman, I will go with thee and be thy guide,
In thy most need to go by thy side.
EVERYMAN: In good condition I am now in everything,
And am whole content with this good thing,   525
Thanked be God my Creator.
GOOD DEEDS: And when she hath brought you there
Where thou shalt heal thee of thy smart,[6]
Then go you with your reckoning and your Good Deeds together
For to make you joyful at heart   530
Before the blessed Trinity.
EVERYMAN: My Good Deeds, gramercy!

5. Also.   6. Pain.

I am well content, certainly,
With your words sweet.
KNOWLEDGE: Now go we together lovingly   535
To Confession, that cleansing river.
EVERYMAN: For joy I weep—I would we were there!
But I pray you give me cognition,
Where dwelleth that holy man Confession?
KNOWLEDGE: In the House of Salvation: 540
We shall find him in that place
That shall us comfort, by God's grace.
    [KNOWLEDGE *leads* EVERYMAN *to* CONFESSION.]
Lo, this is Confession: kneel down and ask mercy,
For he is in good conceit[7] with God Almighty.
EVERYMAN: [*Kneeling.*] O glorious fountain that all uncleanness doth
    clarify,[8]   545
Wash from me the spots of vice unclean,
That on me no sin may be seen.
I come with Knowledge for my redemption,
Redempt with heart and full contrition,
For I am commanded a pilgrimage to take   550
And great accounts before God to make.
Now I pray you, Shrift, mother of Salvation,
Help my Good Deeds for my piteous exclamation.
CONFESSION: I know your sorrow well, Everyman:
Because with Knowledge ye come to me,   555
I will you comfort as well as I can,
And a precious jewel I will give thee,
Called Penance, voider of adversity.
Therewith shall your body chastised be—
With abstinence and perseverance in God's service.   560
Here shall you receive that scourge of me,
Which is penance strong that ye must endure,
To remember thy Saviour was scourged for thee
With sharp scourges, and suffered it patiently.
So must thou ere thou 'scape that painful pilgrimage.   565
Knowledge, keep him in this voyage,
And by that time Good Deeds will be with thee.
But in any wise be secure of mercy—
For your time draweth fast—and ye will saved be.
Ask God mercy and he will grant, truly.   570
When with the scourge of penance man doth him bind,
The oil of forgiveness then shall he find.
EVERYMAN: Thanked be God for his gracious work,
For now I will my penance begin.
This hath rejoiced and lighted my heart,   575

7. Esteem.   8. Purify.

Though the knots[9] be painful and hard within.
KNOWLEDGE: Everyman, look your penance that ye fulfill,
What pain that ever it to you be;
And Knowledge shall give you counsel at will
How your account ye shall make clearly.   580
EVERYMAN: O eternal God, O heavenly figure,
O way of righteousness, O goodly vision,
Which descended down in a virgin pure
Because he would every man redeem,
Which Adam forfeited by his disobedience;   585
O blessed Godhead, elect and high Divine,
Forgive my grievous offense!
Here I cry thee mercy in this presence:
O ghostly Treasure, O Ransomer and Redeemer,
Of all the world Hope and Conduiter,[1]   590
Mirror of joy, Foundator of mercy,
Which enlumineth heaven and earth thereby,
Hear my clamorous complaint, though it late be;
Receive my prayers, of thy benignity.
Though I be a sinner most abominable,   595
Yet let my name be written in Moses' table.[2]
O Mary, pray to the Maker of all thing
Me for to help at my ending,
And save me from the power of my enemy,
For Death assaileth me strongly.   600
And Lady, that I may by mean of thy prayer
Of your Son's glory to be partner—
By the means of his passion I it crave.
I beseech you help my soul to save.
Knowledge, give me the scourge of penance: 605
My flesh therewith shall give acquittance.[3]
I will now begin, if God give me grace.
KNOWLEDGE: Everyman, God give you time and space![4]
Thus I bequeath you in the hands of our Saviour:
Now may you make your reckoning sure.   610
EVERYMAN: In the name of the Holy Trinity
My body sore punished shall be:
Take this, body, for the sin of the flesh!
Also[5] thou delightest to go gay and fresh,
And in the way of damnation thou did me bring,   615
Therefore suffer now strokes of punishing!
Now of penance I will wade the water clear,
To save me from purgatory, that sharp fire.
GOOD DEEDS: I thank God, now can I walk and go,

9. Knots on the scourge (whip) of penance. *Within:* To my senses. 1. Guide. 2. Tablet on which are recorded those who have been baptized and have done penance. 3. Satisfaction for sins. 4. Opportunity. 5. As.

And am delivered of my sickness and woe.　　　　　620
Therefore with Everyman I will go, and not spare:
His good works I will help him to declare.
KNOWLEDGE: Now Everyman, be merry and glad:
Your Good Deeds cometh now, ye may not be sad.
Now is your Good Deeds whole and sound,　　　　625
Going upright upon the ground.
EVERYMAN: My heart is light, and shall be evermore.
Now will I smite faster than I did before.
GOOD DEEDS: Everyman, pilgrim, my special friend,
Blessed be thou without end!　　　　　　　　　630
For thee is preparate the eternal glory.
Ye have me made whole and sound
Therefore I will bide by thee in every stound.[6]
EVERYMAN: Welcome, my Good Deeds! Now I hear thy voice,
I weep for very sweetness of love.　　　　　　635
KNOWLEDGE: Be no more sad, but ever rejoice:
God seeth thy living in his throne above.
Put on this garment to thy behove,[7]
Which is wet with your tears—
Or else before God you may it miss　　　　　640
When ye to your journey's end come shall.
EVERYMAN: Gentle Knowledge, what do ye it call?
KNOWLEDGE: It is a garment of sorrow;
From pain it will you borrow:[8]
Contrition it is　　　　　　　　　　　　　645
That getteth forgiveness;
It pleaseth God passing[9] well.
GOOD DEEDS: Everyman, will you wear it for your heal?[1]
EVERYMAN: Now blessed be Jesu, Mary's son,
For now have I on true contrition.　　　　　650
And let us go now without tarrying.
Good Deeds, have we clear our reckoning?
GOOD DEEDS: Yea, indeed, I have it here.
EVERYMAN: Then I trust we need not fear.
Now friends, let us not part in twain.　　　　655
KNOWLEDGE: Nay, Everyman, that will we not, certain.
GOOD DEEDS: Yet must thou lead with thee
Three persons of great might.
EVERYMAN: Who should they be?
GOOD DEEDS: Discretion and Strength they hight,[2]　　660
And thy Beauty may not abide behind.
KNOWLEDGE: Also ye must call to mind
Your Five-Wits as for your counselors.
GOOD DEEDS: You must have them ready at all hours.

6. Trial.　7. Advantage.　8. Redeem.　9. Surpassingly.　1. Welfare.　2. Are called.

EVERYMAN: How shall I get them hither? 665
KNOWLEDGE: You must call them all togither,
And they will be here incontinent.³
EVERYMAN: My friends, come hither and be present,
Discretion, Strength, my Five-Wits, and Beauty!
[*They enter.*]
BEAUTY: Here at your will we be all ready. 670
What will ye that we should do?
GOOD DEEDS: That ye would with Everyman go
And help him in his pilgrimage.
Advise you: will ye with him or not in that voyage?
STRENGTH: We will bring him all thither, 675
To his help and comfort, ye may believe me.
DISCRETION: So will we go with him all togither.
EVERYMAN: Almighty God, loved might thou be!
I give thee laud that I have hither brought
Strength, Discretion, Beauty, and Five-Wits—lack I nought— 680
And my Good Deeds, with Knowledge clear,
All be in my company at my will here:
I desire no more to my business.
STRENGTH: And I, Strength, will by you stand in distress,
Though thou would in battle fight on the ground. 685
FIVE-WITS: And though it were through the world round,
We will not depart for sweet ne sour.
BEAUTY: No more will I, until death's hour,
Whatsoever thereof befall.
DISCRETION: Everyman, advise you first of all: 690
Go with a good advisement⁴ and deliberation.
We all give you virtuous monition⁵
That all shall be well.
EVERYMAN: My friends, hearken what I will tell;
I pray God reward you in his heaven-sphere; 695
Now hearken all that be here,
For I will make my testament,
Here before you all present:
In alms half my good I will give with my hands twain,
In the way of charity with good intent; 700
And the other half, still⁶ shall remain,
I 'queath to be returned there it ought to be.
This I do in despite of the fiend of hell,
To go quit out of his perel,⁷
Ever after and this day. 705
KNOWLEDGE: Everyman, hearken what I say:
Go to Priesthood, I you advise,
And receive of him, in any wise,

3. At once. 4. Preparation. 5. Confident prediction. 6. Which still. 7. In order to go free from danger from him.

The holy sacrament and ointment[8] togither;
Then shortly see ye turn again hither: 710
We will all abide you here.
FIVE-WITS: Yea, Everyman, hie you that ye ready were.
There is no emperor, king, duke, ne baron,
That of God hath commission
As hath the least priest in the world being: 715
For of the blessed sacraments pure and bening[9]
He beareth the keys, and thereof hath the cure[1]
For man's redemption—it is ever sure—
Which God for our souls' medicine
Gave us out of his heart with great pine,[2]   720
Here in this transitory life for thee and me.
The blessed sacraments seven there be:
Baptism, confirmation, with priesthood[3] good,
And the sacrament of God's precious flesh and blood,
Marriage, the holy extreme unction, and penance: 725
These seven be good to have in remembrance,
Gracious sacraments of high divinity.
EVERYMAN: Fain would I receive that holy body,
And meekly to my ghostly[4] father I will go.
FIVE-WITS: Everyman, that is the best that ye can do: 730
God will you to salvation bring.
For priesthood exceedeth all other thing:
To us Holy Scripture they do teach,
And converteth man from sin, heaven to reach;
God hath to them more power given   735
Than to any angel that is in heaven.
With five words[5] he may consecrate
God's body in flesh and blood to make,
And handleth his Maker between his hands.
The priest bindeth and unbindeth all bands,[6]   740
Both in earth and in heaven.
Thou ministers[7] all the sacraments seven;
Though we kiss thy feet, thou were worthy;
Thou art surgeon that cureth sin deadly;
No remedy we find under God   745
But all only priesthood.[8]
Everyman, God gave priests that dignity
And setteth them in his stead among us to be.
Thus be they above angels in degree.
    [*Exit* EVERYMAN.]
KNOWLEDGE: If priests be good, it is so, surely.   750

8. Extreme unction. 9. Benign. 1. Care. 2. Torment. 3. Ordination. 4. Spiritual. 5. "For
this is my body," spoken by the priest when he offers the wafer at communion. 6. A reference to the
power of the keys, inherited by the priesthood from St. Peter, who received it from Christ (Matthew 16:
19) with the promise that whatever St. Peter bound or loosed on earth would be bound or loosed in
heaven. 7. Administers. 8. Except from priesthood alone.

But when Jesu hanged on the cross with great smart,[9]
There he gave out of his blessed heart
The same sacrament in great torment,
He sold them not to us, that Lord omnipotent:
Therefore Saint Peter the Apostle doth say   755
That Jesu's curse hath all they
Which God their Saviour do buy or sell,[1]
Or they for any money do take or tell.[2]
Sinful priests giveth the sinners example bad:
Their children sitteth by other men's fires, I have heard;   760
And some haunteth women's company
With unclean life, as lusts of lechery.
These be with sin made blind.
FIVE-WITS: I trust to God no such may we find.
Therefore let us priesthood honor,   765
And follow their doctrine for our souls' succor.
We be their sheep and they shepherds be
By whom we all be kept in surety.
Peace, for yonder I see Everyman come,
Which hath made true satisfaction.   770
GOOD DEEDS: Methink it is he indeed.
       [Re-enter EVERYMAN.]
EVERYMAN: Now Jesu be your alder speed![3]
I have received the sacrament for my redemption,
And then mine extreme unction.
Blessed be all they that counseled me to take it!   775
And now, friends, let us go without longer respite.
I thank God that ye have tarried so long.
Now set each of you on this rood[4] your hond
And shortly follow me:
I go before there[5] I would be. God be our guide!   780
STRENGTH: Everyman, we will not from you go
Till ye have done this voyage long.
DISCRETION: I, Discretion, will bide by you also.
KNOWLEDGE: And though this pilgrimage be never so strong,
I will never part you fro.   785
STRENGTH: Everyman, I will be as sure by thee
As ever I did by Judas Maccabee.[6]
EVERYMAN: Alas, I am so faint I may not stand—
My limbs under me doth fold!
Friends, let us not turn again to this land,   790
Not for all the world's gold.
For into this cave must I creep

---

9. Pain.   1. To give or receive money for the sacraments is simony, named after Simon, who wished
to buy the gift of the Holy Ghost and was cursed by St. Peter.   2. Or who, for any sacrament, take or
count out money.   3. The prosperer of you all.   4. Cross.   5. Where.   6. Judas Maccabaeus
was an enormously powerful warrior in the defense of Israel against the Syrians in late Old Testament
times.

And turn to earth, and there to sleep.
BEAUTY: What, into this grave, alas?
EVERYMAN: Yea, there shall ye consume, more and lass.[7]   795
BEAUTY: And what, should I smother here?
EVERYMAN: Yea, by my faith, and nevermore appear.
  In this world live no more we shall,
  But in heaven before the highest Lord of all.
BEAUTY: I cross out all this! Adieu, by Saint John—   800
  I take my tape in my lap and am gone.[8]
EVERYMAN: What, Beauty, whither will ye?
BEAUTY: Peace, I am deaf—I look not behind me,
  Not and thou wouldest give me all the gold in thy chest.
  [Exit BEAUTY.]
EVERYMAN: Alas, whereto may I trust?   805
  Beauty goeth fast away fro me—
  She promised with me to live and die!
STRENGTH: Everyman, I will thee also forsake and deny.
  Thy game liketh me not at all.
EVERYMAN: Why then, ye will forsake me all?   810
  Sweet Strength, tarry a little space.
STRENGTH: Nay, sir, by the rood of grace,
  I will hie me from thee fast,
  Though thou weep till thy heart tobrast.[9]
EVERYMAN: Ye would ever bide by me, ye said.   815
STRENGTH: Yea, I have you far enough conveyed!
  Ye be old enough, I understand,
  Your pilgrimage to take on hand:
  I repent me that I hither came.
EVERYMAN: Strength, you to displease I am to blame,   820
  Yet promise is debt, this ye well wot.[1]
STRENGTH: In faith, I care not:
  Thou art but a fool to complain;
  You spend your speech and waste your brain.
  Go, thrust thee into the ground.   825
  [Exit STRENGTH.]
EVERYMAN: I had weened[2] surer I should you have found.
  He that trusteth in his Strength
  She him deceiveth at the length.
  Both Strength and Beauty forsaketh me—
  Yet they promised me fair and lovingly.   830
DISCRETION: Everyman, I will after Strength be gone:
  As for me, I will leave you alone.
EVERYMAN: Why Discretion, will ye forsake me?
DISCRETION: Yea, in faith, I will go from thee.
  For when Strength goeth before,   835
  I follow after evermore.

7. Decay, all of you. 8. I tuck my skirts in my belt and am off. 9. Break. 1. Know.
2. Supposed.

EVERYMAN: Yet I pray thee, for the love of the Trinity,
Look in my grave once piteously.
DISCRETION: Nay, so nigh will I not come.
Farewell everyone! 840
[*Exit* DISCRETION.]
EVERYMAN: Of all thing faileth save God alone—
Beauty, Strength, and Discretion.
For when Death bloweth his blast
They all run fro me full fast.
FIVE-WITS: Everyman, my leave now of thee I take. 845
I will follow the other, for here I thee forsake.
EVERYMAN: Alas, then may I wail and weep,
For I took you for my best friend.
FIVE-WITS: I will no longer thee keep.
Now farewell, and there an end! 850
[*Exit* FIVE-WITS.]
EVERYMAN: O Jesu, help, all hath forsaken me!
GOOD DEEDS: Nay, Everyman, I will bide with thee:
I will not forsake thee indeed;
Thou shalt find me a good friend at need.
EVERYMAN: Gramercy, Good Deeds! Now may I true friends see. 855
They have forsaken me every one—
I loved them better than my Good Deeds alone.
Knowledge, will ye forsake me also?
KNOWLEDGE: Yea, Everyman, when ye to Death shall go,
But not yet, for no manner of danger. 860
EVERYMAN: Gramercy, Knowledge, with all my heart!
KNOWLEDGE: Nay, yet will I not from hence depart
Till I see where ye shall become.
EVERYMAN: Methink, alas, that I must be gone
To make my reckoning and my debts pay, 865
For I see my time is nigh spent away.
Take example, all ye that this do hear or see,
How they that I best loved do forsake me,
Except my Good Deeds that bideth truly.
GOOD DEEDS: All earthly things is but vanity. 870
Beauty, Strength, and Discretion do man forsake,
Foolish friends and kinsmen that fair spake—
All fleeth save Good Deeds, and that am I.
EVERYMAN: Have mercy on me, God most mighty,
And stand by me, thou mother and maid, holy Mary! 875
GOOD DEEDS: Fear not: I will speak for thee.
EVERYMAN: Here I cry God mercy!
GOOD DEEDS: Short our end, and 'minish our pain.[3]
Let us go, and never come again.
EVERYMAN: Into thy hands, Lord, my soul I commend: 880

---

3. Make our dying quick and diminish our pain.

Receive it, Lord, that it be not lost.
As thou me boughtest,[4] so me defend,
And save me from the fiend's boast,
That I may appear with that blessed host
That shall be saved at the day of doom.   885
In manus tuas, of mights most,
Forever *commendo spiritum meum.*[5]
    [EVERYMAN *and* GOOD DEEDS *descend into the grave.*]
KNOWLEDGE: Now hath he suffered that we all shall endure,
    The Good Deeds shall make all sure.
    Now hath he made ending,   890
    Methinketh that I hear angels sing
    And make great joy and melody
    Where Everyman's soul received shall be.
ANGEL: [*Within.*] Come, excellent elect spouse to Jesu![6]
    Here above thou shalt go   895
    Because of thy singular virtue.
    Now the soul is taken the body fro,
    Thy reckoning is crystal clear:
    Now shalt thou into the heavenly sphere—
    Unto the which all ye shall come   900
    That liveth well before the day of doom.
    [*Enter* DOCTOR.[7]]
DOCTOR: This memorial men may have in mind:
    Ye hearers, take it of worth, old and young,
    And forsake Pride, for he deceiveth you in the end.
    And remember Beauty, Five-Wits, Strength, and Discretion,   905
    They all at the last do Everyman forsake,
    Save his Good Deeds there doth he take—
    But beware, for and they be small,
    Before God he hath no help at all—
    None excuse may be there for Everyman.   910
    Alas, how shall he do than?[8]
    For after death amends may no man make,
    For then mercy and pity doth him forsake.
    If his reckoning be not clear when he doth come,
    God will say, "*Ite, maledicti, in ignem eternum!*"[9]   915
    And he that hath his account whole and sound,
    High in heaven he shall be crowned,
    Unto which place God bring us all thither,
    That we may live body and soul togither.
    Thereto help, the Trinity!   920
    Amen, say ye, for saint charity.

---

4. Redeemed.   5. "Into thy hands, O greatest of powers, I commend my spirit forever."   6. The soul
is often referred to as the bride of Jesus.   7. The learned theologian who explains the meaning of the
play. *Memorial:* Reminder.   8. Then.   9. "Depart, ye cursed, into everlasting fire."

Masterpieces of the
Renaissance

We meet in Renaissance literature some of the most resonant, thought-provoking characters that literary genius has ever produced: Marlowe's Dr. Faustus, Shakespeare's Hamlet, Rabelais's Gargantua, Cervantes's Quixote, Milton's Adam and Eve. These characters no longer move, as most of Chaucer's do, through a life conceived as pilgrimage within a world of ideas and feelings for the most part firmly structured by religious, feudal, and chivalric values. Renaissance characters tend to be more like us: baffled as to exactly what *is* the structure that contains them (if any), seeking sometimes to feel it out (like Hamlet), sometimes, if they think they already know, rebelling against it (like Faustus or Adam and Eve), and sometimes (like Gargantua) happy to replace it with a giantized image of fleshly freedoms, or (like Quixote) with an idiosyncratic view of things uncontestably their own. Chaucer's populous and well-worn route between the Tabard Inn and Canterbury Cathedral gives way to a crisscross of dimly sensed paths.

As with other terms that have currency in cultural history (for instance, *Romanticism*), the usefulness of the term *Renaissance* depends on its keeping a certain degree of elasticity. The literal meaning of the word—"rebirth"—suggests that one impulse toward the great intellectual and artistic achievements of the period came from the example of ancient culture, or even better, from a certain vision that the artists and intellectuals of the Renaissance possessed of the world of antiquity which was "reborn" through their work. Especially in the more mature phase of the Renaissance, these individuals were aware of having brought about a vigorous renewal, which they openly associated with the cult of antiquity. The restoration of ancient canons was regarded as a glorious achievement to be set beside the thrilling discoveries of their own age. "For now," Rabelais writes through his Gargantua,

> all courses of study have been restored, and the acquisition of languages has become supremely honorable: Greek, without which it is shameful for any man to be called a scholar; Hebrew; Chaldean; and Latin. And in my time we have learned how to produce wonderfully elegant and accurate printed books, just as, on the other hand, we have also learned (by diabolic suggestion) how to make cannon and other such fearful weapons.

Machiavelli, whose infatuation with antiquity is as typical a trait as his better-advertised political realism, suggests in the opening of his *Discourses on the First Ten Books of Livy* (1513–21) that rulers should be as keen on the imitation of ancient "virtues" as are artists, lawyers, and the scientists: "The civil laws are nothing but decisions given by the ancient jurisconsults. . . . And what is the science of medicine, but the experience of ancient physicians, which their successors have taken for their guide?"

Elasticity should likewise be maintained in regard to the chronological span of the Renaissance as a "movement" extending through varying periods of years, and as including phases and traits of the epoch that is otherwise known as the Middle Ages (and vice versa). The peak of the Renaissance can be shown to have occurred at different times in different countries, the "movement" having had its inception in Italy, where its impact was at first most remarkable in the visual arts, while in England, for instance, it developed later and its main achievements were in literature, particularly the drama. The meaning of the term has also, in the course of time, widened considerably. Nowadays it conveys, to say the least, a general notion of artistic creativity, of extraordinary zest for life and knowledge, of sensory delight in opulence and magnificence, of spectacular individual achievement, thus extending far beyond the literal meaning of rebirth and the strict idea of a revival and imitation of antiquity.

Even in its stricter sense, however, the term continues to have its function. The degree to which European intellectuals of the period possessed and were possessed by the writings of the ancient world is difficult for the average modern reader to realize. For these writers references to classical mythology, philosophy, and literature are not ornaments or affectations. Along with references to the Scriptures they are part, and a major part, of their mental equipment and way of thinking. When Erasmus through his *The Praise of Folly* speaks in a cluster of classical allusions, or when Machiavelli writes to a friend: "I will get up before daylight, prepare my birdlime, and go out with a bundle of cages on my back, so that I look like Geta when he came back from the harbor with the books of Amphitryo" (p. 1705, n. 3), the words have by no means the sound of erudite self-gratification that they might have nowadays. They are wholly natural, familiar, unassuming.

When we are overcome by sudden emotion, our first exclamations are likely to be in the language most familiar to us—our dialect, if we happen to have one. Montaigne relates of himself that when once his father unexpectedly fell back in his arms in a swoon, the first words he uttered under the emotion of that experience were in Latin. Similarly Benvenuto Cellini, the Italian sculptor, goldsmith, and autobiographer, talking to his patron and expressing admiration of a Greek statue, establishes with the ancient artist an immediate contact, a proud familiarity:

> I cried to the Duke: "My lord, this is a statue in Greek marble, and it is a miracle of beauty. . . . If your Excellency permits, I should like to restore it—head and arms and feet. . . . It is certainly not my business to patch up statues, that being the trade of botchers, who do it in all conscience villainously ill; yet the art displayed by this great master of antiquity cries out to me to help him."

The men who, starting at about the middle of the fourteenth century, gave new impulse to this emulation of the classics are often referred to as humanists. The word in that sense is related to what we call the humanities, and the humanities at that time were Latin and Greek. Every cultivated person wrote and spoke Latin, with the result that a Western community of intellectuals could exist, a spiritual "republic of letters" above individual nations. There was also a considerable amount of individual contact among humanists. In glancing at the biographies of the authors included in this section, the extensiveness of their travels may strike us as a remarkable or even surprising fact, considering the hardships and slowness of traveling during those centuries.

The archetype of literature as a vocation is often said to be Petrarch—the first author in this section—who anticipated certain ideals of the high Renaissance: a lofty conception of the literary art, a taste for the good life, a basic pacifism, and a strong sense of the memories and glories of antiquity. In this last respect, what should be emphasized is the imaginative quality, the visionary impulse with which the writers of the period looked at those memories—the same vision and imagination with which they regarded such contemporary heroes as the great navigators and astronomers. The Renaissance view of the cultural monuments of antiquity was far from being that of the philologist and the antiquarian; indeed, familiarity was facilitated by the very lack of a scientific sense of history. We find the visionary and imaginative element not only in the creations of poets and dramatists (Shakespeare's Romans, to give an obvious example) but also in the works of political writers: as when Machiavelli describes himself entering, through his reading, the

> ancient courts of ancient men, where, being lovingly received, I feed on that food which alone is mine, and which I was born for; I am not ashamed to speak with them and to ask the reasons for their actions, and they courteously answer me. For . . . hours I feel no boredom and forget every worry; I do not fear poverty, and death does not terrify me. I give myself completely over to the ancients.

Imitation of antiquity acquires, in Machiavelli and many others, a special quality; between mere "academic" imitation and the Renaissance approach there is as much difference as between the impulse to learn and the impulse to *be*.

The vision of an ancient age of glorious intellectual achievement which is "now" brought to life again, implies of course, however roughly, the idea of an intervening "middle" time, by comparison ignorant and dark. The hackneyed notion that the "light" of the Renaissance broke through a long "night" of the Middle Ages may be vastly inaccurate. Yet it is inevitable to remember that this view was not devised by subsequent "enlightened" centuries; it was held by the men of the Renaissance themselves. In his genealogy of giants from Grangousier to Gargantua to Pantagruel, Rabelais conveniently represents the generations of modern learning with their varying degrees of enlightenment. Thus Gargantua writes to his son:

> Though my late father of worthy memory, Grandgousier, devoted all his energy to those things of which I might take the fullest advantage, and from which I might acquire the most sensible knowledge, and though my own effort matched his—or even surpassed it—still, as you know very well, it was neither so fit nor so right a time for learning as exists today, nor was there an abundance of such teachers as you have had. It was still a murky, dark time, oppressed by the misery, unhappiness, and disasters of the Goths, who destroyed all worthwhile literature of every sort. But divine goodness has let me live to see light and dignity returned to humanistic studies, and to see such an improvement, indeed, that it would be hard for me to qualify for the very first class of little schoolboys—I who, in my prime, had the reputation (and not in error) of the most learned man of my day.

Definitions of the Renaissance must also take account of the period's preoccupation with this life rather than with the life beyond. The contrast of an ideal Medieval man or woman, whose mode of action is basically oriented toward the thought of the afterlife—and who therefore conceives of life on earth as transient and preparatory—with an ideal Renaissance man or woman, possessing and cherishing earthly interests so concrete and self-sufficient that the very realization of the ephemeral quality of life is to him or her nothing but an added spur to its immediate enjoyment—this is a useful contrast even though it represents an enormous oversimplification of the facts.

The same emphasis on the immediate and tangible is reflected in the earthly, amoral, and esthetic character of what we may call the Renaissance code of behavior. According to this "code," human action is judged not in terms of right and wrong, of good and evil (as it is judged when life is viewed as a moral "test," with reward or punishment in the afterlife), but in terms of its present concrete validity and effectiveness, of the delight it affords, of its memorability and its beauty. In that sense a good deal that is typical of the Renaissance, from architecture to poetry, from sculpture to rhetoric, may be related to a taste for the harmonious and the memorable, for the spectacular effect, for the successful striking of a pose. Individual human action, seeking as it were in itself its own reward, finds justification in its formal appropriateness; in its being a well-rounded achievement, perfect of its kind; in the zest and gusto with which it is, here and now, performed; and, finally, in its proving worthy of remaining as a testimony to the performer's power on earth.

A convenient way to illustrate this emphasis is to consider certain words especially expressive of the interests of the period—"virtue," "fame," "glory." "Virtue," particularly in its Italian form, *virtù*, is to be understood in a wide sense. As we may see even now in some relics of its older meanings, the word (from the Latin *vir*, "man") connotes active power—the intrinsic force and ability of a person or thing (the "virtue" of a law or of a medicine)—and hence, also, technical skill (the capacity of the "virtuoso"). The Machiavellian prince's "virtues," therefore, are not necessarily goodness, temperance, clemency, and the like; they are whatever forces and skills may help him in the efficient management and preservation of his princely powers. The idealistic, intangible part of the prince's success is consigned to such concepts as "fame" and "glory," but even in this case the dimension within which human action is considered is still an earthly one. These concepts connote the hero's success and reputation with his contemporaries, or look forward to splendid recognition from posterity, on earth.

In this sense (though completely pure examples of such an attitude are rare) the purpose of life is the unrestrained and self-sufficient practice of one's "virtue," the competent and delighted exercise of one's skill. At the same time, there is no reason to forget that such virtues and skills are God's gift. The world view of even some of the most clearly earthbound Renaissance writers was hardly godless; Machiavelli, Rabelais, Cellini take for granted the presence of God in their own and in their heroes' lives:

> . . . we have before our eyes extraordinary and unexampled means prepared by God. The sea has been divided. A cloud has guided you on your way. The rock has given forth water. Manna has fallen. Everything has united to make you great. The rest is for you to do. God does not intend to do everything, lest he deprive us of our free will and the share of glory that belongs to us. (Machiavelli.)

> And then Gargantua and Powerbrain would briefly recapitulate, according to the Pythagorean fashion, everything Gargantua had read and seen and understood, everything he had done and heard, all day long.
> They would both pray to God their Creator, worshiping, reaffirming their faith, glorifying Him for His immense goodness and thanking Him for all they had been given, and forever placing themselves in His hands.
> And then they would go to sleep. (Rabelais.)

> I found that all the bronze my furnace contained had been exhausted in the head of this figure [of the statue of Perseus]. It was a miracle to observe that not one fragment remained in the orifice of the channel, and that nothing was wanting to the statue. In my great astonishment I seemed to see in this the hand of God arranging and controlling all. (Cellini.)

Yet if we compare the attitudes of these authors with the view of the world and of the value of human action that emerges from the major literary work of the Middle Ages, the *Divine Comedy*, and with the manner in which human action is there seen within a grand extratemporal design, the presence of God in the Renaissance writers cited above appears marginal and perfunctory.

In any attempt to discuss the religious temper of the Renaissance, we should not lose sight of certain basic historical facts: the Papacy was not only a spiritual power, but a political and military one as well; furthermore, the European Renaissance was a period of violent religious strife. The consequences of the Protestant Reformation (Lutheranism, Zwinglianism, Calvinism) were not only theological and ideological debates, but also armed conflict and bloodshed, as is apparent from the biographies of several of the writers presented here (Erasmus, Rabelais, Montaigne). It is also apparent that the position of the intellectual generally was not one of militant partisanship or, conversely, of retreat to an "ivory tower," but was characterized by wisdom and attempts at conciliation.

Much about the religious temper of the age is expressed in its art, particularly in Italian painting, where Renaissance Madonnas often make it difficult, as the saying goes, to recite a properly devout Hail Mary—serving as celebrations of earthly beauty rather than exhortations to contrite thoughts and mystical hopes of salvation. Castiglione in the first pages of the *Courtier* pays homage to the memory of the late lord of Montefeltro, in whose palace at Urbino the book's personages hold their lofty debate on the idea of a perfect gentleman (an earlier Montefeltro appears in Dante's Hell, another in Dante's Purgatory); but Castiglione praises him only for his achievements as a man of arms and a promoter of the arts. There is no thought of either the salvation or the damnation of his soul (though the general tone of the work would seem to imply his salvation); he is exalted instead for military victories, and even more warmly, for having built a splendid palace—the tangible symbol of his earthly glory, for it is both the mark of political and social power and a work of art.

Thus the popular view that associates the idea of the Renaissance especially with the flourishing of the arts is correct. The leaders of the period saw in a work of art the clearest instance of beautiful, harmonious, and self-justified performance. To create such a work became the valuable occupation par excellence, the most satisfactory display of *virtù*. The Renaissance view of antiquity exemplifies this attitude. The artists and intellectuals of the period not only drew on antiquity for certain practices and forms but also found there a recognition of the place of the arts among outstanding modes of human action. In this way, the concepts of "fame" and "glory" became particularly associated with the art of poetry because the Renaissance drew from antiquity the idea of the poet as celebrator of high deeds, the "dispenser of glory."[*]

There is, then, an important part of the Renaissance mind that sees terrestrial life as positive fulfillment. This is especially clear where there is a close association between the practical and the intellectual, as in the exercise of political power, the act of scientific discovery, the creation of works of art. The Renaissance assumption is that there are things highly worth doing, within a strictly temporal pattern. By doing them, humanity proves its privileged position in Creation and therefore incidentally follows God's intent. The often cited phrase "the dignity of man" describes

[*] And of course, a typical guarantee of memorability was having oneself portrayed—perhaps at various stages in life—by some of the magnificent and highly honored painters of the period.

this positive, strongly affirmed awareness of the intellectual and physical "virtues" of the human being, and of the individual's place in Creation.

It is important, however, to see this fact about the Renaissance in the light of another phenomenon. Where there is a singularly high capacity for feeling the delight of earthly achievement, there is a possibility that its ultimate worth will also be questioned profoundly. What (the Renaissance mind usually seems to ask at some point) is the purpose of all this activity? What meaningful relation does it bear to any all-inclusive, cosmic pattern? The Renaissance coincided with, and perhaps to some extent occasioned, a loss of firm belief in the final unity and the final intelligibility of the universe, such belief as underlies, for example, the *Divine Comedy*, enabling Dante to say in Paradise:

> I saw within Its depth how It conceives
> all things in a single volume bound by Love,
> of which the universe is the scattered leaves;
> substance, accident, and their relation
> so fused that all I say could do no more
> than yield a glimpse of that bright revelation.

Once the notion of this grand unity of design has lost its authority, certainty about the final value of human actions is no longer to be found. For some minds, indeed, the sense of void becomes so strong as to paralyze all aspiration to power or thirst for knowledge or delight in beauty; the resulting attitude we may call Renaissance melancholy, whether it be openly shown (as by some characters in Elizabethan drama) or provide an undercurrent of sadness, or incite to ironical forms of compromise, to some sort of wise adjustment (as in Erasmus or Montaigne.) The legend of Faust—"Doctor" Faustus—a great amasser of knowledge doomed to frustration by his perception of the vanity of science, for which he finds at one point desperate substitutes in pseudoscience and the devil's arts, is one illustration of this sense of vanity. Shakespeare's *Hamlet* is another, a play in which the very word "thought" seems to acquire a troubled connotation: "the pale cast of thought," "thought and affliction, passion, hell itself." In these instances, the intellectual excitement of understanding, the zest and pride of achievement through what chiefly constitutes human "dignity," the intellect, seem not so much lost as directly inverted.

Thus while on one, and perhaps the better-known, side of the picture human intellect in Renaissance literature enthusiastically expatiates over the realms of knowledge and unveils the mysteries of the universe, on the other it is beset by puzzling doubts and a profound mistrust of its own powers. Our moral nature is seen as only a little lower than the angels', but also scarcely above the beasts'. Earthly power—a favorite theme because Renaissance literature was so largely produced in the courts or with a vivid sense of courtly ideas—is the crown of human aspirations ("How sweet a thing it is to wear a crown, / Within whose circuit is Elysium") but it is also the death's head ("Imperious Caesar, dead and turn'd to clay, / Might stop a hole to keep the wind away").

Much of Renaissance literature takes its character and strength from the tensions generated by this simultaneous exaltation and pessimism about the human condition.

FURTHER READING

Richard L. DeMolen, ed., *The Meaning of Renaissance and Reformation* (1974), is a collection of essays by experts on the Renaissance and Reformation, with maps and illustrations. Paul Oskar Kristeller's lecture series on the Renaissance is now a paperback, *Renaissance Thought: The Classic, Scholastic, and Humanist Strains* (1961). A solid, well-written general historical and cultural presentation is Eugene F. Rice, Jr., *The Foundations of Early Modern Europe, 1460–1559* (1970), with illustrations, facsimiles, maps, bibliographic references. Lewis W. Spitz gives a reliable historical presentation of the period, taking into account literary and artistic trends in *The Renaissance and Reformation Movements* (1971).

On English literature of the Renaissance, see C. S. Lewis, *English Literature in the Sixteenth Century Excluding Drama* (1954) and D. Bush, *English Literature in the Earlier Seventeenth Century 1600–1660* (1962). On Italian literature of the Renaissance, see the appropriate chapters in Eugenio Donadoni, *A History of Italian Literature* (English translation by Richard Monges, 1969), a standard, reliable work widely used as a textbook in Italian schools, and Ernest Hatch Wilkins, *History of Italian Literature* (revised by Thomas G. Bergin, 1974), one of the best of the few histories of Italian literature written in English. Américo Castro, *An Idea of History: Selected Essays of Américo Castro* (English translation by Stephen Gilman, 1977), includes a chapter on "The Problem of the Renaissance in Spain." On French literature of the Renaissance, see John Cruickshank, ed., *French Literature and Its Background* (1968), particularly vol. 1, *The Sixteenth Century.*

FRANCIS PETRARCH

1304–1374

Francesco Petrarca (forty years younger than Dante) was born at Arezzo on July 13, 1304. His father, like Dante, was exiled from Florence for political reasons and in 1312 moved with his family to Avignon with hopes of employment at the Papal court, which had been transferred there in 1309 by a Pope of French nationality—Clement V (Bertrand de Got). Following his father's wish, Petrarch studied law at Montpellier and Bologna for a brief period. A highly cultivated man of the world, on his return to Avignon he was well received by the brilliant and refined society that moved around the Papal court. It was in Avignon, in the church of St. Clare, on April 6, 1327, that he saw for the first time Laura, who would become the object and image of his love poetry. Soon after this momentous event, he began to travel widely (France, Flanders, Germany), not only on diplomatic missions but also, and perhaps more relevantly, as a man of letters and humanist in search of manuscripts from classical antiquity.

In 1338 he made his first trip to Rome, a twofold spiritual capital for him as a classical scholar and as a Christian. Later that same year, at his home in Vaucluse near Avignon, Petrarch attempted to revive the ancient ideal of spiritually active relaxation, or *otium*. He was so imbued with the idea of a renovation of classical antiquity that he expected his major glory as a poet from the work he began at this time—*Africa*, an epic poem in Latin hexameters which has for its central figure Scipio Africanus, conceived by the poet as the model of the valiant and pious Roman hero. No less characteristic of his devotion to classical ideals is the fact that when in 1340 he received invitations from both Paris and Rome to be crowned poet laureate, he chose Rome, and received the crown in the Capitol.

There was in his life, as in Dante's, a pattern of moral dissipation followed by spiritual conflict and repentance. This conflict, which is reflected in Petrarch's autobiographical treatise in Latin, *Secretum*, may have been enhanced by his brother Gherardo's decision to enter a monastery and by the news of Laura's death by plague, which he received in 1348 while traveling in Italy. She died on April 6, the very day of the month on which he had first seen her, and the day of Christ's passion as well. Thus Laura remained an image of exclusively spiritual love, in contrast to Petrarch's more earthly attachments, evidenced by the birth of two illegitimate children, Giovanni, in 1337, and Francesca, in 1343.

As a pilgrim on his way to Rome for the Papal Jubilee of 1350, Petrarch stopped at Florence as a guest of Boccaccio, the great Florentine storyteller and fellow humanist. Most of the years between 1353 and 1361 he spent in Milan, where he was entrusted by the ruling Visconti family with various diplomatic missions (to Venice, to Prague, to the king of France). He alternated such duties with intense literary work, including a complete edition of his lyric poetry in Italian, letters and treatises in Latin, and progress on his great unfinished *terza rima* allegory, *The Triumphs*. To avoid the plague, in 1361 he moved to Padua, spending much of his time in a nearby country house in the Euganean hills at Arquà, now called Arquà Petrarca. He died there in 1374, on the eve of his seventieth birthday, working until the very end on the refinement and ordering of his work and on the careful creation of what we would call today his "public image," polishing for posterity with exquisite care his poems and letters (the letter was then an established literary form). Even accidental events in his life seem to have been inspired by his taste for the harmonious and well-rounded gesture. He came within a few hours of reaching the "perfect" life span, three score and ten, and frequently used April 6, as in sonnet 3, to symbolize his own drama of passion.

If we compare Petrarch to the standard image of the Medieval character, what first strikes us as new is the self-centered quality of his work. A comparison between him and Dante points to this quality, and the contrast is made sharper by certain analogies in their situations. Both illustrate the same basic motif, the quest for salvation. But while Dante as hero of the quest focused dramatically on himself only on a few enormously effective and severe occasions (his first exchange with Beatrice in *Purgatory* XXX, for example), Petrarch was continuously at work on his personal drama, its lights and shades, its subtle modulations of feeling.

A different way of getting at the distinction between the Renaissance and Medieval characters may be found in Petrarch's conception of the literary profession and the status of the poet. His attitude toward classical antiquity makes him "the first writer of the Renaissance," rather than a writer of the Middle Ages. As a self-aware man of letters he modeled his work on classical examples—the texts that, as a humanistic scholar, he had sometimes helped rediscover and bring back to life. In 1333 at Liège, for example, he found a manuscript of Cicero's oration *Pro Archia*, a Roman "defense of poetry," celebrating the role of artist and thinker as creators of value, legislators of virtuous behavior, and dispensers of fame: the program to which Petrarch was to devote his life. It would be difficult to overestimate his importance for European culture in establishing that model of the poet, scholar, and member of the "republic of letters" which remains today an ideal of Western civilization.

But however important this aspect of his work may have been, the prevailing Petrarchan image in literary history is the drama of his love for Laura, both in life and in death. Of course there would be no drama in that love without an element of the tragic—his sense of its sinfulness and vanity. Thus he sounds a "medieval" note, but in a new context: that of the ever-changing, ambiguous attractions of mortal beauty and earthly values. One even surmises that these values might have been less attractive to him had they not kept the taint of vanity, for without it they would have afforded a less rich and complex life. Thus he sings in sonnet 61, "Blest Be the Day," of his first encounter with Laura, the source of his torment. Even though calling him a romantic may stretch the meaning of the term to the point of uselessness, we can say that his definition of love as sorrow has had a yet wider influence than those striking verbal inventions that inspired European poetry for a century and more before degenerating into "Petrarchism," the arsenal of conceits, witticisms, and hyperboles on which much popular twentieth-century songwriting still draws.

Another essential part of Petrarch's drama is the death of his lady and her role as mediator between the penitent poet and Divine Grace. Here again, the inevitable comparison with Dante makes the differences between the two poets stand clear. The shift in tone between Petrarch's poems for Laura "in life" and the ones for her "in death" is less relevant than the similarity of the two sections of the *Canzoniere* (*Song Book*). A sensuous quality pervades both groups of poems, suggesting an earthly relationship even when the beloved lady is dead. Thus the poet, in sonnet 300, envies the earth "folding her in invisible embrace," and in sonnet 292, also written after Laura's death, the larger part of the octave is devoted to the living lady's physical appearance. In other sonnets Laura herself, in heaven, refers to her mortal body as her "beautiful veil." In sonnet 333 the poet implores her to come to him at the moment of his death and guide him to "the blessed place." His poetry has made the world know and love her, and the implication is that he has thus become worthy of her succor. Hence Petrarch is not only a repentant sinner, but also a literary master turning autobiography and confession into art. However strong his sense of the vanity and fallaciousness of human attachments, he seems to have no doubt about the validity of one particular manifestation of *virtù*: the sensuous, expert handling of words, the poetic art itself.

A thorough account of Petrarch's life with many quotations from his writing may be found in Morris Bishop, *Petrarch and His World* (1963). Peter Hainsworth, *Petrarch the Poet: An Introduction to the Rerum Vulgarium Fragmenta* (1988), provides "critical and historical interpretation" of Petrarch's major work in Italian. Nicholas Mann's *Petrarch* (1984) is a clear, cogent analysis of Petrarch's life and works. Two other worthwhile biographical studies are J. H. Whitfield, *Petrarch and the Renaissance* (1943; 1966) and Ernest Hatch Wilkins, *Life of Petrarch* (1961).

Letter to Dionisio da Borgo San Sepolcro[1]

(The Ascent of Mount Ventoux)

To-day[2] I made the ascent of the highest mountain in the region, which is not improperly called Ventosum.[3] My only motive was the wish to see what so great an elevation had to offer. I have had the expedition in mind for many years; for as you know, I have lived in this region from infancy, having been cast here by that fate which determines the affairs of men. Consequently the mountain, which is visible from a great distance, was ever before my eyes, and I conceived the plan of some time doing what I have at last accomplished to-day. The idea took hold upon me with especial force when, in re-reading Livy's *History of Rome*, yesterday, I happened upon the place where Philip of Macedon, the same who waged war against the Romans, ascended Mount Haemus in Thessaly, from whose summit he was able, it is said, to see two seas, the Adriatic and the Euxine.[4] Whether this be true or false I have not been able to determine, for the mountain is too far away, and writers disagree. Pomponius Mela, the cosmographer—not to mention others who have spoken of this occurrence—admits its truth without hesitation[5]; Titus Livius, on the other hand, considers it false. I, assuredly, should not have left the question long in doubt, had that mountain been as easy to explore as this one. Let us leave this matter to one side, however, and return to my mountain here,—it seems to me that a young man in private life may well be excused for attempting what an aged king could undertake without arousing criticism.

When I came to look about for a companion I found, strangely enough,

1. Letter IV, i, from a group of letters entitled *De Rebus Familiaribus*. Translated by James Harvey Robinson and Henry Winchester Rolfe. Dionisio, or Dionigi, da Borgo San Sepolcro was an Augustinian monk whom Petrarch had probably met in Paris in 1333. A learned theologian, he taught at Paris and in 1339 was appointed bishop of Monopoli. He spent the last part of his life in Naples at the court of the learned king Robert d'Anjou and died there in 1342 (Petrarch wrote a verse epistle on his death). 2. April 26. From internal evidence the year should be 1336, ten years after Petrarch left Bologna, but the letter was probably revised and made into an "allegory" at a later date (*cf.* note 8 below). 3. *Ventosum:* windy. Mount Ventoux (elev. 6,000 feet) is near Malaucène, not far from Petrarch's place of retirement in Vaucluse. 4. Cf. Livy, *Roman History*, XL, 21, 2. 5. Pomponius Mela, Roman geographer of Spanish birth, wrote toward the middle of the first century A.D.; the passage referred to in his *Corographia* is II, 17.

that hardly one among my friends seemed suitable, so rarely do we meet with just the right combination of personal tastes and characteristics, even among those who are dearest to us. This one was too apathetic, that one over-anxious; this one too slow, that one too hasty; one was too sad, another over-cheerful; one more simple, another more sagacious, then I desired. I feared this one's taciturnity and that one's loquacity. The heavy delibera-tion of some repelled me as much as the lean incapacity of others. I rejected those who were likely to irritate me by a cold want of interest, as well as those who might weary me by their excessive enthusiasm. Such defects, however grave, could be borne with at home, for charity suffereth all things, and friendship accepts any burden; but it is quite otherwise on a journey, where every weakness becomes much more serious. So, as I was bent upon pleasure and anxious that my enjoyment should be unalloyed, I looked about me with unusual care, balanced against one another the various characteristics of my friends, and without committing any breach of friendship I silently condemned every trait which might prove disagreeable on the way. And—would you believe it?—I finally turned homeward for aid, and proposed the ascent to my only brother, who is younger than I, and with whom you are well acquainted.[6] He was delighted and gratified beyond measure by the thought of holding the place of a friend as well as of a brother.

At the time fixed we left the house, and by evening reached Malaucène, which lies at the foot of the mountain, to the north. Having rested there a day, we finally made the ascent this morning, with no companions except two servants; and a most difficult task it was. The mountain is a very steep and almost inaccessible mass of stony soil. But, as the poet[7] has well said, "Remorseless toil conquers all." It was a long day, the air fine. We enjoyed the advantages of vigour of mind and strength and agility of body, and everything else essential to those engaged in such an undertaking, and so had no other difficulties to face than those of the region itself. We found an old shepherd in one of the mountain dales, who tried, at great length, to dissuade us from the ascent, saying that some fifty years before he had, in the same ardour of youth, reached the summit, but had gotten for his pains nothing except fatigue and regret, and clothes and body torn by the rocks and briars. No one, so far as he or his companions knew, had ever tried the ascent before or after him. But his counsels increased rather than diminished our desire to proceed, since youth is suspicious of warnings. So the old man, finding that his efforts were in vain, went a little way with us, and pointed out a rough path among the rocks, uttering many admo-nitions, which he continued to send after us even after we had left him behind. Surrendering to him all such garments or other possessions as might prove burdensome to us, we made ready for the ascent, and started off at a good pace. But, as usually happens, fatigue quickly followed upon our excessive exertion, and we soon came to a halt at the top of a certain cliff. Upon starting on again we went more slowly, and I especially advanced

6. Gherardo, probably about three years younger than the poet.   7. Virgil in *Georgics*, I, 145–146.

along the rocky way with a more deliberate step. While my brother chose a direct path straight up the ridge,[8] I weakly took an easier one which really descended. When I was called back, and the right road was shown me, I replied that I hoped to find a better way round on the other side, and that I did not mind going farther if the path were only less steep. This was just an excuse for my laziness; and when the others had already reached a considerable height I was still wandering in the valleys. I had failed to find an easier path, and had only increased the distance and difficulty of the ascent. At last I became disgusted with the intricate way I had chosen, and resolved to ascend without more ado. When I reached my brother, who, while waiting for me, had had ample opportunity for rest, I was tired and irritated. We walked along together for a time, but hardly had we passed the first spur when I forgot about the circuitous route which I had just tried, and took a lower one again. Once more I followed an easy, round-about path through winding valleys, only to find myself soon in my old difficulty. I was simply trying to avoid the exertion of the ascent; but no human ingenuity can alter the nature of things, or cause anything to reach a height by going down. Suffice it to say that, much to my vexation and my brother's amusement, I made this same mistake three times or more during a few hours.

After being frequently misled in this way, I finally sat down in a valley and transferred my winged thoughts from things corporeal to the immaterial, addressing myself as follows:—"What thou hast repeatedly experienced to-day in the ascent of this mountain, happens to thee, as to many, in the journey toward the blessed life. But this is not so readily perceived by men, since the motions of the body are obvious and external while those of the soul are invisible and hidden. Yes, the life which we call blessed is to be sought for on a high eminence, and strait is the way that leads to it. Many, also, are the hills that lie between, and we must ascend, by a glorious stairway, from strength to strength. At the top is at once the end of our struggles and the goal for which we are bound. All wish to reach this goal, but, as Ovid says, 'To wish is little; we must long with the utmost eagerness to gain our end.'[9] Thou certainly dost ardently desire, as well as simply wish, unless thou deceivest thyself in this matter, as in so many others. What, then, doth hold thee back? Nothing, assuredly, except that thou wouldst take a path which seems, at first thought, more easy, leading through low and worldly pleasures. But nevertheless in the end, after long wanderings, thou must perforce either climb the steeper path, under the burden of tasks foolishly deferred, to its blessed culmination, or lie down in the valley of thy sins, and (I shudder to think of it!), if the shadow of death overtake thee, spend an eternal night amid constant torments." These thoughts stimulated both body and mind in a wonderful degree for facing the difficulties which yet remained. Oh, that I might traverse in spirit that other road for which I long day and night, even as to-day I overcame

8. In the allegorical reading of the letter, this could be an allusion to Gherardo achieving God and salvation more directly (he became a monk in 1342, retiring into the monastery of Montrieux).   9. Ovid, *Ex Ponto*, III, i, 35.

material obstacles by my bodily exertions! And I know not why it should not be far easier, since the swift immortal soul can reach its goal in the twinkling of an eye, without passing through space, while my progress to-day was necessarily slow, dependent as I was upon a failing body weighed down by heavy members.

One peak of the mountain, the highest of all, the country people call "Sonny," why, I do not know, unless by antiphrasis,[1] as I have sometimes suspected in other instances; for the peak in question would seem to be the father of all the surrounding ones. On its top is a little level place, and here we could at least rest our tired bodies.

Now, my father, since you have followed the thoughts that spurred me on in my ascent, listen to the rest of the story, and devote one hour, I pray you, to reviewing the experiences of my entire day. At first, owing to the unaccustomed quality of the air and the effect of the great sweep of view spread out before me, I stood like one dazed. I beheld the clouds under our feet, and what I had read of Athos and Olympus seemed less incredible as I myself witnessed the same things from a mountain of less fame. I turned my eyes toward Italy, wither my heart most inclined. The Alps, rugged and snow-capped, seemed to rise close by, although they were really at a great distance; the very same Alps through which that fierce enemy of the Roman name once made his way, bursting the rocks, if we may believe the report, by the application of vinegar. I sighed, I must confess, for the skies of Italy, which I beheld rather with my mind than with my eyes. An inexpressible longing came over me to see once more my friend and my country. At the sane time I reproached myself for this double weakness, springing, as it did, from a soul not yet steeled to manly resistance. And yet there were excuses for both of these cravings, and a number of distinguished writers might be summoned to support me.

Then a new idea took possession of me, and I shifted my thoughts to a consideration of time rather than place. "To-day it is ten years since, having completed thy youthful studies, thou didst leave Bologna. Eternal God! In the name of immutable wisdom, think what alterations in thy character this intervening period has beheld! I pass over a thousand instances. I am not yet in a safe harbour where I can calmly recall past storms. The time may come when I can review in due order all the experiences of the past, saying with St. Augustine, 'I desire to recall my foul actions and the carnal corruption of my soul, not because I love them, but that I may the more love thee, O my God.'[2] Much that is doubtful and evil still clings to me, but what I once loved, that I love no longer. And yet what am I saying? I still love it, but with shame, but with heaviness of heart. Now, at last, I have confessed the truth. So it is. I love, but love what I would not love, what I would that I might hate. Though loath to do so, though constrained, though sad and sorrowing, still I do love, and I feel in my miserable self the truth of the well known words, 'I will hate if I can; if not, I will love against my will.[3] Three years have not yet passed since that per-

1. The rhetorical use of a word in a sense opposite to its actual meaning.   2. St. Augustine, *Confessions*, II, i, 1.   3. Ovid, *Amores*, III, ii, 35.

verse and wicked passion which had a firm grasp upon me and held undisputed sway in my heart began to discover a rebellious opponent, who was unwilling longer to yield obedience. These two adversaries have joined in close combat for the supremacy, and for a long time now a harassing and doubtful war has been waged in the field of my thoughts."

Thus I turned over the last ten years in my mind, and then, fixing my anxious gaze on the future, I asked myself, "If, perchance, thou shouldst prolong this uncertain life of thine for yet two lustres, and shouldst make an advance toward virtue proportionate to the distance to which thou hast departed from thine original infatuation during the past two years, since the new longing first encountered the old, couldst thou, on reaching thy fortieth year, face death, if not with complete assurance, at least with hopefulness, calmly dismissing from thy thoughts the residuum of life as it faded into old age?"

These and similar reflections occurred to me, my father. I rejoiced in my progress, mourned my weaknesses, and commiserated the universal instability of human conduct. I had well-nigh forgotten where I was and our object in coming; but at last I dismissed my anxieties, which were better suited to other surroundings, and resolved to look about me and see what we had come to see. The sinking sun and the lengthening shadows of the mountain were already warning us that the time was near at hand when we must go. As if suddenly wakened from sleep, I turned about and gazed toward the west. I was unable to discern the summits of the Pyrenees, which form the barrier between France and Spain; not because of any intervening obstacle that I know of but owing simply to the insufficiency of our mortal vision. But I could see with the utmost clearness, off to the right, the mountains of the region about Lyons, and to the left the bay of Marseilles and the waters that lash the shores of Aigues Mortes, altho' all these places were so distant that it would require a journey of several days to reach them. Under our very eyes flowed the Rhone.

While I was thus dividing my thoughts, now turning my attention to some terrestial object that lay before me, now raising my soul, as I had done my body, to higher planes, it occurred to me to look into my copy of St. Augustine's *Confessions*, a gift that I owe to your love, and that I always have about me, in memory of both the author and the giver. I opened the compact little volume, small indeed in size, but of infinite charm, with the intention of reading whatever came to hand, for I could happen upon nothing that would be otherwise than edifying and devout. Now it chanced that the tenth book presented itself. My brother, waiting to hear something of St. Augustine's from my lips, stood attentively by. I call him, and God too, to witness that where I first fixed my eyes it was written: "And men go about to wonder at the heights of the mountains, and the mighty waves of the sea, and the wide sweep of rivers, and the circuit of the ocean, and the revolution of the stars, but themselves they consider not."[4] I was abashed,

---

4. Augustine, *Confessions*, X, viii, 15.

and asking my brother (who was anxious to hear more), not to annoy me, I closed the book, angry with myself that I should still be admiring earthly things who might long ago have learned from even the pagan philosophers that nothing is wonderful but the soul, which, when great itself, finds nothing great outside itself. Then, in truth, I was satisfied that I had seen enough of the mountain; I turned my inward eye upon myself, and from that time not a syllable fell from my lips until we had reached the bottom again. Those words had given me occupation enough, for I could not believe that it was by a mere accident that I happened upon them. What I had there read I believed to be addressed to me and to no other, remembering that St. Augustine had once suspected the same thing in his own case, when, on opening the book of the Apostle, as he himself tells us,[5] the first words that he saw there were, "Not in rioting and drunkenness, not in chambering and wantonness, not in strife and envying. But put ye on the Lord Jesus Christ, and make not provision for the flesh, to fulfil the lusts thereof."[6]

The same thing happened earlier to St. Anthony, when he was listening to the Gospel where it is written, "If thou wilt be perfect, go and sell that thou hast, and give to the poor, and thou shalt have treasure in heaven: and come and follow me."[7] Believing this scripture to have been read for his especial benefit, as his biographer Athanasius says,[8] he guided himself by its aid to the Kingdom of Heaven. And as Anthony on hearing these words waited for nothing more, and as Augustine upon reading the Apostle's admonition sought no farther, so I concluded my reading in the few words which I have given. I thought in silence of the lack of good counsel in us mortals, who neglect what is noblest in ourselves, scatter our energies in all directions, and waste ourselves in a vain show, because we look about us for what is to be found only within. I wondered at the natural nobility of our soul, save when it debases itself of its own free will, and deserts its original estate, turning what God has given it for its honour into dishonour. How many times, think you, did I turn back that day, to glance at the summit of the mountain, which seemed scarcely a cubit high compared with the range of human contemplation,—when it is not immersed in the foul mire of earth? With every downward step I asked myself this: If we are ready to endure a little nearer heaven, how can a soul struggling toward God, up the steeps of human pride and human destiny, fear any cross or prison or sting of fortune? How few, I thought, but are diverted from their path by the fear of difficulties or the love of ease! How happy the lot of those few, if any such there be! It is to them, assuredly, that the poet was thinking, when he wrote:

> Happy the man who is skilled to understand
> Nature's hid causes; who beneath his feet
> All terrors casts, and death's relentless doom,
> And the loud roar of greedy Acheron.[9]

5. Ibid., VIII, xii, 29.   6. Romans 13:13–14.   7. Matthew, 19:21.   8. Saint Athanasius, Doctor of the Church (ca. 295–373), in his *Vita Antonii*, II.   9. Virgil, *Georgics*, II, 490–492.

How earnestly should we strive, not to stand on mountain-tops, but to trample beneath us those appetites which spring from earthy impulses.

With no consciousness of the difficulties of the way, amidst these preoccupations which I have so frankly revealed, we came, long after dark, but with the full moon lending us its friendly light, to the little inn which we had left that morning before dawn. The time during which the servants have been occupied in preparing our supper, I have spent in a secluded part of the house, hurriedly jotting down these experiences on the spur of the moment, lest, in case my task were postponed, my mood should change on leaving the place, and so my interest in writing flag.

You will see, my dearest father, that I wish nothing to be concealed from you, for I am careful to describe to you not only my life in general but even my individual reflections. And I beseech you, in turn, to pray that these vague and wandering thoughts of mine may some time become firmly fixed, and, after having been vainly tossed about from one interest to another, may direct themselves at last toward the single, true, certain, and everlasting good.

MALAUCÈNE, April 26.

It Was the Morning[1]

It was the morning of that blessèd day[2]
Whereon the Sun in pity veiled his glare
For the Lord's agony, that, unaware,
I fell a captive, Lady, to the sway

Of your swift eyes: that seemed no time to stay   5
The strokes of Love: I stepped into the snare
Secure, with no suspicion: then, and there
I found my cue in man's most tragic play.

Love caught me naked to his shaft, his sheaf,
The entrance for his ambush and surprise   10
Against the heart wide open through the eyes,[3]

The constant gate and fountain of my grief:
How craven so to strike me stricken so,[4]
Yet from you fully armed conceal his bow!

---

1. *Era 'l giorno ch'al sol si scoloraro*, sonnet 3. Translated by Joseph Auslander.   **2.** Elsewhere (sonnet 211) Petrarch gives the date as April 6, 1327, a Monday. Here too the day is apparently intended to be the day of Christ's death (April 6) rather than Good Friday, 1327.   **3.** The image of the eyes as the gateway to the heart had been a poetic commonplace since pre-Dante days.   **4.** With grief on commemorating Christ's Passion.

Blest Be the Day[5]

Blest be the day, and blest the month and year,
Season[6] and hour and very moment blest,
The lovely land and place[7] where first possessed
By two pure eyes I found me prisoner;

And blest the first sweet pain, the first most dear,   5
Which burnt my heart when Love came in as guest;
And blest the bow, the shafts which shook my breast,
And even the wounds which Love delivered there.

Blest be the words and voices which filled grove
And glen with echoes of my lady's name;   10
The sighs, the tears, the fierce despair of love;

And blest the sonnet-sources of my fame;
And blest that thought of thoughts which is her own,
Of her, her only, of herself alone!

Father in Heaven[8]

Father in heaven, after each lost day,
Each night spent raving with that fierce desire
Which in my heart has kindled into fire
Seeing your acts adorned for my dismay;

Grant henceforth that I turn, within your light[9]   5
To another life and deeds more truly fair,
So having spread to no avail the snare
My bitter foe[1] might hold it in despite.

The eleventh year,[2] my Lord, has now come round
Since I was yoked beneath the heavy trace   10
That on the meekest weighs most cruelly.

Pity the abject plight where I am found;
Return my straying thoughts to a nobler place;
Show them this day you were on Calvary.

She Used to Let Her Golden Hair Fly Free[3]

She used to let her golden hair fly free
For the wind to toy and tangle and molest;

---

5. *Benedetto sia 'l giorno e 'l mese e l'anno,* sonnet 61. Translated by Joseph Auslander.   6. Spring.
Hour: "Upon the first hour" (sonnet 211), sunrise.   7. The Church of Saint Clare at Avignon.
8. *Padre del ciel, dopo i perduti giorni,* sonnet 62. Translated by Bernard Bergonzi.   9. The light of
grace.   1. The Devil, not Love as some commentators have thought.   2. 1338.   3. *Erano i capei
d'oro a l'aura sparsi,* sonnet 90. Tr011sated by Morris Bishop.

Her eyes were brighter than the radiant west.
(Seldom they shine so now.) I used to see

Pity look out of those deep eyes on me.   5
("It was false pity," you would now protest.)
I had love's tinder heaped within my breast;
What wonder that the flame burned furiously?

She did not walk in any mortal way,
But with angelic progress; when she spoke,   10
Unearthly voices sang in unison.

She seemed divine among the dreary folk
Of earth. You say she is not so today?
Well, though the bow's unbent, the wound bleeds on.

The Eyes That Drew from Me[4]

The eyes that drew from me such fervent praise,
The arms and hands and feet and countenance
Which made me a stranger in my own romance
And set me apart from the well-trodden ways;

The gleaming golden curly hair, the rays   5
Flashing from a smiling angel's glance
Which moved the world in paradisal dance,
Are grains of dust, insensibilities.

And I live on, but in grief and self-contempt,
Left here without the light I loved so much,   10
In a great tempest and with shrouds unkempt.

No more love songs, then, I have done with such;
My old skill now runs thin at each attempt,
And tears are heard within the harp I touch.[5]

Great Is My Envy of You[6]

Great is my envy of you, earth, in your greed
Folding her in invisible embrace,
Denying me the look of the sweet face
Where I found peace from all my strife at need!
Great is my envy of heaven which can lead   5
And lock within itself in avarice
That spirit from its lovely biding-place
And leave so many others here to bleed!

4. *Gli occhi di ch'io parlai sì caldamente*, sonnet 292. Translated by Edwin Morgan. All the poems in the canon from number 267 on were written to commemorate Laura. She died at Avignon on April 6, 1348.
5. Cf. Job 30:31.   6. *Quanta invidia io ti porto, avara terra*, sonnet 300. Translated by Edwin Morgan.

Great is my envy of those souls whose reward
Is the gentle heaven of her company, 10
Which I so fiercely sought beneath these skies!

Great is my envy of death whose curt hard sword
Carried her whom I called my life away;
Me he disdains, and mocks me from her eyes!

Go, Grieving Rimes of Mine[7]

Go, grieving rimes of mine, to that hard stone
Whereunder lies my darling, lies my dear,
And cry to her to speak from heaven's sphere.
Her mortal part with grass is overgrown.

Tell her, I'm sick of living; that I'm blown 5
By winds of grief from the course I ought to steer,
That praise of her is all my purpose here
And all my business; that of her alone

Do I go telling, that how she lived and died
And lives again in immortality, 10
All men may know, and love my Laura's grace.

Oh, may she deign to stand at my bedside
When I come to die; and may she call to me
And draw me to her in the blessèd place!

DESIDERIUS ERASMUS
1466–1536

Erasmus was born around 1466, apparently in Rotterdam, to a physician's daughter
and a father who later became a priest; in any event, he later referred to himself as
Desiderius Erasmus Roterodamus. He received his early schooling under humanistic tutors who fostered his love of good literature. After both his parents died,
Erasmus's guardians sent him to the Augustinian canons at Steyn, although his
desire had been to enter a university. He was ordained a priest on April 25, 1492.
Erasmus's humanistic aspirations found an outlet in 1494 when he became Latin
secretary to Henry of Bergen, bishop of Cambrai, through whose help he entered
the college of Montaigu at the University of Paris in 1495. College discipline was
very strict, but in the following year, with lodgings in town, he received pupils.
One of his pupils, William Blount, Baron Mountjoy, accompanied him on his
first trip to England in 1499–1500, where he met Thomas More and the English
theologian John Colet; the latter encouraged him toward serious religious study
and a direct scholarly approach to the early Church Fathers.

7. *Ite, rime dolenti, al duro sasso*, sonnet 333. Translated by Morris Bishop.

In the following years Erasmus traveled on the continent. His first collection of *Adages* (short sayings from classical authors) appeared in Paris in 1500, and his *Handbook of the Christian Knight*, a plea for a return to primitive Christian simplicity, was published at Antwerp in 1504. After a second visit to England in 1505–06, during which he met Warham, the archbishop of Canterbury, a chance to act as tutor to the son of Henry VII's physician, Boeri, enabled him to fulfill the humanist's aspiration to visit Italy. He spent time at the universities of Turin (where he received a doctorate of theology) and Bologna, visited Padua and Florence, and conversed with high church dignitaries in Rome. In Venice, the great humanistic printer Aldus Manutius became a friend and published an enlarged collection of *Adages*. In 1509 Erasmus returned to England, where in the same year he wrote *The Praise of Folly*. During this third and longest stay in England (until 1514) he lectured in Greek and divinity at Cambridge. Erasmus offers the highest illustration of the learned cosmopolitan humanist endeavoring to conciliate humanistic learning and religious piety. After leaving England in 1514, he continued to travel on the continent, finally making his most permanent home in Basel, a center whose cultural importance cannot be overestimated, especially as the seat of the printing house of Frobenius, whose general editor Erasmus became. In 1529 religious disturbances and the victories of the Swiss Protestants caused him to move to Freiburg in the Breisgau, the German university town in the Black Forest. His attitude toward the Protestant reformers (Luther in Germany, Zwingli in Switzerland) was typical: having tried to promote an impartial arbitration of the question between Luther and the Roman church, he was alienated by excesses on both sides. The shattering news of Thomas More's execution in England in 1535 reached him in Freiburg. He returned to Basel that same year and died there in July 1536.

Though his literary works and pamphlets, his editions of the Church Fathers, his Latin edition of the New Testament (based on the Greek), and especially his letters (about three thousand of them) gave an important perspective on the cultural life of the period, Erasmus's most famous work remains *The Praise of Folly*. Its popularity is partly due to its dramatic and elegant literary form, partly to the fact that it deals in a wise, temperate way with perennial concerns, as pressing now as they were then: the power (and arrogance) of the human intellect, the worth (and futility) of knowledge, and above all the folly (and wisdom) of human behavior.

To present these issues concretely, Erasmus uses an oratorical and theatrical approach. He takes for his speaker a feminine figure, Folly, placing her in front of an audience of whom she herself makes us aware: "as soon as I began to speak to this great audience, all faces suddenly brightened." We see her gesture, point to her public, call for their attention: "I am almost out of breath." "But why not speak to you more openly . . . ?" "You applaud! I was sure that you were not so wise, or rather so foolish—no, so wise." The general tone of speech balances between the jocose and the serious, the erudite and the foolish. In this way, she also throws light upon the audience—a congenial one, we feel, made up of people to whom the cultured allusions with which her speech is studded are so familiar that they appreciate the comic twists performed upon them, as they appreciate, more generally, the satire on conventional oratory which her monologue contains. "I see that you are expecting a peroration," she admits in the end, "but you are certainly foolish if you think that I can remember any part of such a hodgepodge of words as I have poured out." Her attitude toward her audience is thus not adversary but convivial. The butts of her polemic—the passionless Stoics—constitute a third party, and rather than address such people, she enlists her audience's support in rejecting them: "I ask you, if it were put to a vote, what city would choose such a person as mayor?"

This is the "play" as it is presented to us. But of course it is actually a "play within a play," performed for Erasmus and *his* audience, i.e., ourselves. From his vantage point backstage, he uses Folly as an ambiguous mouthpiece. In fact, by showing her to be foolish, light-headed, and rambling, he throws into sharper focus the truths she expresses; he secures the advantage of her directness and "innocence" while granting her the full support of his own erudition and wit. The apparent surface frivolity calls on us to expect an undercover depth and complexity, to read between the lines, and we may best measure that complexity by asking, What does Folly stand for? Does she stand for carefree living? for a way of life not hostile to the passions? for foolishness? for self-abandonment? for naïveté? for imagination? Is she simply the lighthearted creation of a great scholar in a frivolous moment, deploring the vanity of intellectual knowledge and the scholar's austere and solitary life in favor of instinct, intuition, good fellowship, "innocence"? Or does she embody a paradoxical "wisdom" to be found at the end of a long and perhaps finally frustrating accumulation of learning? Our answer to such questions must be at least as equivocal as the attitude of the work itself.

Clearly, the issue of knowledge versus ignorance underlies *The Praise of Folly*. What "Folly" says may often seem to be a debunking of the former in favor of the latter, but—and this is the function of the "play"—the attitude ultimately suggested is one neither of "barbaric" rebellion nor of unrelieved satiety and desperation. Erasmus's position, whether overtly or between the lines, is that of noble and wise compromise: a serene acceptance of the limitations of knowledge rather than a "melancholic" rejection of its value followed by a desperate gesture of rebellion. The attitude proposed, in other words, is a far cry from that of a dissatisfied intellectual who finds the mind has not provided satisfactory answers and who therefore embraces folly as Faust embraces the diabolical. On the other hand, the author's "praise" of folly is certainly not feigned or *mainly* ironical. His point of view is not that of the sophisticate who takes a frivolous delight in masquerading, let us say, as a shepherd. When Erasmus implies that possibly fools are really wiser than we are (an implication that underlies many a passage in the book), his attitude toward the "fool" includes understanding, affection, and a real question about value. The balance of irony is maintained in both directions; the wisdom of compromise and the wise person's sense of limits guide the performance from backstage.

What has been said about the value of knowledge can be extended to the value of life: the world is a stage, and the forces ruling its actors may be irrational or incomprehensible, but it is in accordance with nature that we should go on playing our roles. Folly is imagination, inventiveness, and therefore make-believe; "everything is pretense." But at the same time, "this play is performed in no other way"; "true prudence . . . consists in not desiring more wisdom than is proper to mortals." This is "to act the play of life."

Acceptance of life as a play, as a pageant, opens a vision of true human reality, Erasmus feels, whereas the wisdom of the Stoics (who stand for pure intellectualism) produces "a marble imitation of a man" from which one shudders away "as from a ghost." Folly's far preferable prescription is "a timely mixture of ignorance, thoughtlessness, forgetfulness of evil, hope of good, and a dash of delight."

A good introduction to Erasmus is Richard L. DeMolen, ed., *Erasmus of Rotterdam. A Quincentennial Symposium* (1971), with brief essays by leading scholars, notes, selected bibliography, and a brief chronology of Erasmus's life. Of more specialized interest are T. A. Dorey, ed., *Erasmus* (1970); Arthur F. Kinney, *"Sante Socrates, ora pro nobis:* the *Encomium Moriae* and the Poetics of Wordplay," chapter 2 of his *Continental Humanist Poetics: Studies in Erasmus, Castiglione, Marguerite de Navarre, Rabelais, and Cervantes* (1989); and Zoja Pavlovskis, *The Praise of Folly: Structure and Irony* (1983), emphasizing "the skill with which Erasmus employs that bewildering literary device, irony." George Faludy's modern biography, *Erasmus of Rotterdam* (1970), is intended for the general reader. Kathleen Williams, ed., *Twentieth Century Interpretations of "The Praise of Folly": A Collection of Critical Essays* (1969) is recommended.

The Praise of Folly[1]

I. FOLLY HERSELF

Folly Speaks:
   No matter what is ordinarily said about me (and I am not ignorant of how bad the name of Folly sounds, even to the biggest fools), I am still the one, the only one I may say, whose influence makes Gods and men cheerful. A convincing proof of this is that as soon as I began to speak to this great audience, all faces suddenly brightened with a new and unusual gaiety, all frowns disappeared, and you applauded hilariously. Now you seem intoxicated with nectar, and also with nepenthe,[2] like the gods of Homer; whereas a moment ago you were sad and careworn, as if you had just come out of the cave of Trophonius.[3] Just as a new and youthful color reappears everywhere when the sun first shows its beautiful, golden face to the earth, or when spring breathes softly after a hard winter, so your faces changed at the sight of me. And thus what great orators can hardly accomplish with long and elaborate speeches, namely the banishment of care, I have done with my appearance alone.
   . . . Since my ancestry is not known to many, I will undertake to describe it, with the Muses' kind assistance. My father was neither Chaos, Orcus, Saturn, Japetus, nor any other of that obsolete and senile set of gods; on the contrary he was Plutus,[4] the real father of men and gods, despite the opinion of Hesiod,[5] Homer, and Jove himself. Now, as always, one nod from Plutus turns everything sacred or profane upside down. By his decision wars, peace, empires, plans, judgments, assemblies, marriages, treaties, pacts, laws, arts, sports, solemnities (I am almost out of breath)—in short, all public and private affairs are governed. Without his help, all the poets' multitude of gods, even, I may boldly say, the chief ones, either would not exist or would have to live leanly at home. Not even Pallas can help the person who arouses Plutus' anger, but with his favor one can laugh at Jove's thunderbolts. What a magnificent father! He did not beget me out of his head, as Jupiter did that grim and gloomy Pallas, but from

---

1. Abridged. Translated by Leonard F. Dean.   2. Legendary drug causing oblivion.   3. Seat of a particularly awesome oracle.   4. God of wealth and abundance. In Aristophanes' play by that name, to which Erasmus refers later in the paragraph, he is shown in decrepit age; ordinarily he is represented as a boy with a cornucopia.   5. Greek didactic poet of the eighth century B.C., cited here because he was author of the *Theogony* (about the generation and genealogy of the gods).

Youth, the best-looking as well as the gayest of all the nymphs. Nor was this done dully in wedlock, in the way that lame blacksmith[6] was conceived, but more pleasantly in passion, as old Homer puts it. It should also be clearly understood that I was not born of Aristophanes' worn-out and weak-eyed Plutus, but of the unimpaired Plutus, hot with youth and still hotter with nectar which by chance he had drunk straight and freely at a party of the gods.

Next, if you want to know the place of my birth (since the place where one first squalled is nowadays considered a mark of nobility), I was born neither in wandering Delos,[7] nor on the foaming sea,[8] nor "in deep caves," but in the Fortunate Isles themselves, where all things grow "without plowing or planting." There where there is no labor, no old age, and no sickness; where not a daffodil, mallow, onion, bean, or any other ordinary thing is to be seen; but where nose and eyes are equally delighted by moly, panacea, nepenthes, sweet marjoram, ambrosia, lotus, rose, violet, hyacinth, and the gardens of Adonis. Being born amidst these pleasant things, I did not begin life crying, but from the first laughed good-naturedly at my mother. I certainly need not envy Jove for being suckled by a she-goat, for I was nursed at the breasts of two charming nymphs—Drunkenness, offspring of Bacchus, and Ignorance, daughter of Pan. Both of them you see here with my other attendants and followers. If you ask the names of the others, I must answer in Greek. The haughty one over there is Philantia (Self-love). The one with laughing eyes who is clapping her hands is Kolakia (Flattery). This drowsy one is Lethe (Forgetfulness). She leaning on her elbows with folded hands is Misoponia (Laziness). She with the perfume and wreath of roses is Hedone (Pleasure). This wild-eyed one is Anoia (Madness). The smooth-skinned and shapely one is Tryphe (Sensuality). And you see those two gods playing with the girls; well, one is Comus (Intemperance) and the other is Negretos Hypnos (Sound Sleep). With the help of these faithful servants I gain control of all things, even dictating to dictators.

II. THE POWERS AND PLEASURES OF FOLLY

. . . Now, that it may not seem that I call myself a goddess without good cause, let me tell you of the range of my influence and of my benefits to men and gods. If to be a god is simply to aid men, as someone has wisely said, and if they have been deservedly deified who have shown mankind the uses of wine or grain, why am I not justly called the Alpha[9] of gods, I who have all alone given all things to all men.

First, what is more dear and precious than life itself? And by whose aid but mine is life conceived? It is not the spear of "potently-sired" Pallas nor the shield of "cloud-controlling" Jove that propagates and multiplies man-

---

6. Hephaestus (Vulcan), born to Zeus (Jove) and his wife Hera (Juno).   7. In Greek myth, a floating island until fixed to the sea bottom to be the birthplace of Apollo.   8. From which Venus emerged. *"In deep caves"*: A Homeric expression. *Fortunate Isles:* The mythical and remote islands where, according to Greek tradition, some favorites of the gods dwelt in immortality and bliss.   9. First letter of the Greek alphabet; hence, "beginning," "origin."

kind. Even the father of gods and the king of men, he who shakes Olympus with a nod, must lay aside the three-pronged thunderer and that Titanic manner with which when he pleases he terrifies the gods, and like a poor actor assume another character, if he wishes to do what he is forever doing, namely, begetting children. The Stoics[1] assert that they are almost godlike. But give me one who is three, four, or six hundred times a Stoic, and if on this occasion he does not remove his beard, the sign of wisdom (in common with goats), at least he will shed his gravity, stop frowning, abandon his rock-bound principles and for a while be a silly fool. In short, the wise man must send for me if he wants to be a father. But why not speak to you more openly, as I usually do? I ask whether the head, the face, the breast, the hand, or the ear—each an honorable part—creates gods and men? I think not, but instead the job is done by that foolish, even ridiculous part which cannot be named without laughter. This is the sacred fountain from which all things rise, more certainly than from the Pythagorean tetrad.[2]

What man, I ask you, would stick his head into the halter of marriage if, following the practice of the wise, he first weighed the inconveniences of that life? Or what woman would ever embrace her husband if she foresaw or considered the dangers of childbirth and the drudgery of motherhood? Now since you owe your life to the marriage-bed, and marriage itself to my follower Madness, you can see how completely indebted you are to me. Moreover, would a woman who had experienced that travail once ever repeat it without the influence of my Forgetfulness? And Venus herself, no matter what Lucretius says,[3] cannot deny that her work would be weak and inconclusive without my help. Hence from my ridiculous and crazy game are produced supercilious philosophers, their present-day successors, vulgarly called monks, kings in purple robes, pious priests, thrice-holy popes, and finally all the gods invented by the poets, so numerous that spacious Olympus is crowded.

That the conception of life is due to me is a small matter when I can show you that I am responsible for everything agreeable. Would life without pleasure be life at all? You applaud! I was sure that you were not so wise, or rather so foolish—no, so wise, as to think otherwise. As a matter of fact, even the Stoics do not really dislike pleasure; they carefully pretend to and they loudly denounce it in public, but only in order to deter others and thus have it all to themselves. Just let them explain to me what part of life is not sad, troublesome, graceless, flat, and distressing without a dash of pleasure, or in other words, folly. This is very adequately proved by

1. Stoicism originated in the Stoa Poikile ("painted porch"), a building in the marketplace in Athens where the philosopher Zeno lectured in the fourth century B.C., and later was perhaps the main type of philosophy of the Roman elite. It became known during the Renaissance especially through Seneca. Erasmus here makes the Stoics the butts of Folly's irony on account of their supposedly godlike disregard of the passions.   2. According to the numerical conception of the universe of Pythagoras (sixth century B.C.) and his followers, the first four numbers (the "tetrad"—one, two, three, and four, adding up to the ideal number, ten) signified the root of all being.   3. In the opening lines of his poem On the Nature of Things, Lucretius (99?–55 B.C.) invokes Venus because "all living things" are conceived through her.

Sophocles,[4] a person insufficiently appreciated, who has left this pretty eulogy of me: "Ignorance is bliss." . . .

If someone should unmask the actors in the middle of a scene on the stage and show their real faces to the audience, would he not spoil the whole play? And would not everyone think he deserved to be driven out of the theater with brickbats as a crazy man? For at once a new order of things would suddenly arise. He who played the woman is now seen to be a man; the juvenile is revealed to be old; he who a little before was a king is suddenly a slave; and he who was a god now appears as a little man. Truly, to destroy the illusion is to upset the whole play. The masks and costumes are precisely what hold the eyes of the spectators. Now what else is our whole life but a kind of stage play through which men pass in various disguises, each one going on to play his part until he is led off by the director? And often the same actor is ordered back in a different costume, so that he who played the king in purple, now acts the slave in rags. Thus everything is pretense; yet this play is performed in no other way.

What if some wise man, dropped from heaven, should suddenly confront me at this point and exclaim that the person whom everyone has looked up to as a god and ruler is not even a man, because he is led sheeplike by his passions; that he is the meanest slave because he voluntarily serves so many and such foul masters? Or what if this wise man should instruct someone mourning his parent's death to laugh, on the grounds that the parent had at last really begun to live—our life here being in one way nothing but a kind of death? And what if he should entitle another who was glorying in ancestry, ignoble and illegitimate, because he was so far from virtue, the only source of nobility? And what if he should speak of all others in the same way? What, I ask, would he gain by it except to be regarded as dangerously insane by everyone? Just as nothing is more foolish than unseasonable wisdom, so nothing is more imprudent than bull-headed prudence. And he is indeed perverse who does not accommodate himself to the way of the world, who will not follow the crowd, who does not at least remember the rule of good fellowship, drink or begone, and who demands that the play shall no longer be a play. True prudence, on the contrary, consists in not desiring more wisdom than is proper to mortals, and in being willing to wink at the doings of the crowd or to go along with it sociably. But that, they say, is folly itself. I shall certainly not deny it; yet they must in turn admit that it is also to act the play of life.

I hesitate to speak about the next point. But why should I be silent about what is truer than truth? For so great an undertaking, however, it would probably be wise to call the Muses from Helicon;[5] the poets usually invoke them on the slightest pretext. Therefore, stand by for a moment, daughters of Jove, while I show that one cannot acquire that widely advertised wisdom, which the wise call the secret of happiness, unless one follows the leadership of Folly. First, everyone admits that all the emotions belong to

4. See his *Ajax*, ll. 554–555: ". . . life is sweetest before the feelings are awake—until one learns to know joy and pain."   5. Mythical mountain, home of the Muses.

folly. Indeed a fool and a wise man are distinguished by the fact that emotions control the former, and reason the latter. Now the Stoics would purge the wise man of all strong emotions, as if they were diseases; yet these emotions serve not only as a guide and teacher to those who are hastening toward the portal of wisdom, but also as a stimulus in all virtuous actions, as exhorters to good deeds. Of course that superstoic, Seneca, strongly denies this and strips the wise of absolutely every emotion; yet in so doing he leaves something that is not a man at all, but rather a new kind of god or sub-god who never existed and never will. To put it bluntly, he makes a marble imitation of a man, stupid, and altogether alien to every human feeling.

If this is the way they want it, let them keep their wise man. They can love him without any rivals and live with him in Plato's republic or, if they prefer, in the realm of Ideas, or in the gardens of Tantalus.[6] Who would not shudder at such a man and flee from him as from a ghost? He would be insensible to every natural feeling, no more moved by love or pity than if he were solid flint or Marpesian stone.[7] Nothing escapes him; he never makes a mistake; like another Lynceus[8] he sees all; he evaluates everything rigidly; he excuses nothing; he alone is satisfied with himself as the only one who is really rich, sane, royal, free—in short, unique in everything, but only so in his own opinion. Desiring no friend, he is himself the friend of none. He does not hesitate to bid the gods go hang themselves. All that life holds he condemns and scorns as folly. And this animal is the perfect wise man. I ask you, if it were put to a vote, what city would choose such a person as mayor? What army would want such a general? What woman such a husband? What host such a guest? What servant such a master? Who would not rather have any man at all from the rank and file of fools? Now such a choice, being a fool, would be able to command or obey fools. He would be able to please those like himself—or nearly everyone; he would be kind to his wife, a jolly friend, a gay companion, a polished guest; finally, he would consider nothing human to be alien to him.[9] But this wise man has been boring me for some time; let us turn to other instructive topics.

Imagine, then, that a man should look down from a great height, as the poets say that Jove does. What calamities would he see in man's life. How miserable, how vile, man's birth. How laborious his education. His childhood is subject to injuries; his youth is painful; his age a burden; his death a hard necessity. He is attacked by a host of diseases, threatened by accidents, and assaulted by misfortunes; there is nothing without some gall. There are also the multitude of evils that man does to man. Here are poverty, imprisonment, infamy, shame, tortures, plots, treachery, slander, lawsuits, fraud. But this is plainly to count the grains of sand. It is not

6. Plato's republic, his celestial realm of pure Ideas (i.e., the ideal models of which real things are only imperfect realizations), and the mythical garden of Tantalus in Hades (where rich fruit always evades Tantalus's grasp) are all mentioned because they are characterized by the presence of abstractions and figments.   7. From Marpessos, a mountain on the island of Paros famous for its marble.   8. A mythical figure whose eyesight was proverbially supposed to penetrate even solid objects.   9. From a proverbial phrase in Terence's Self-Tormentor, l. 77: "I am a man: nothing human do I consider alien to me."

proper for me at the moment to suggest for what offenses men have deserved these misfortunes, nor what angry god caused them to be born to such miseries. Yet will not anyone who considers these things approve the example of the Milesian virgins,[1] pitiable as it is? Recall, however, what kind of people have committed suicide because they were tired of life. Have they not been the wise or near-wise? Among them, besides Diogenes, Xenocrates, Cato, Cassius, and Brutus, there was Chiron,[2] who chose death rather than immortality. Now you begin to see, I believe, what would happen if all men became wise: there would be need for new clay and another potter like Prometheus.[3]

But by a timely mixture of ignorance, thoughtlessness, forgetfulness of evil, hope of good, and a dash of delight, I bring relief from troubles; so that men are unwilling to relinquish their lives even when their lives are ready to relinquish them. They are so far from being weary of existence, that the less reason they have for living, the more they enjoy life. Clearly it is because of my good work that you everywhere see old fellows of Nestor's[4] age, scarcely recognizable as members of the human race, babbling, silly, toothless, white-haired, bald—or better let me describe them in the words of Aristophanes: "dirty, stooped, wrinkled, bald, toothless, and toolless."[5] And yet they are so in love with life and so eager to be young that one of them dyes his white hair, another hides his baldness with a wig, another obtains false teeth from heaven knows where, another is infatuated with some young girl and is a sillier lover than any adolescent. Nowadays for one of these old sticks, these drybones, to marry a juicy young wife, and one without a dowry and sure to be enjoyed by others, is becoming the usual and proper thing. But it is even more entertaining to observe the old women, long since half-dead with age, so cadaverous that they seem to have returned from the grave; yet always saying, "It's good to be alive." They, too, are always in heat, and hire young men at a handsome fee. They carefully paint their faces, and constantly inspect themselves in the mirror; they pluck out hairs from the strangest places; they display their withered and flabby breasts; with a quavering love-song they stir a worn-out desire; they drink and go around with girls; they write love-letters. Everyone laughs at all this, and very properly, since it is the greatest folly in the world; yet the old ladies are well pleased with themselves. They are perfectly happy solely because of me. Moreover, those who scorn this kind of behavior might consider whether it is not better to lead a life of pleasant folly than to look for a rafter and a rope. Anyway, it is nothing to my fools that their actions are scorned; they either feel no shame, or shrug it off easily. If a rock falls on your head, that is clearly painful; but shame, disgrace, and curses hurt only so far as they are felt. What isn't noticed isn't troublesome. So long as you applaud yourself, what harm are the hisses of the world? And folly is the only key to this happiness.

1. Of the city of Miletus, in Asia Minor. There is an ancient tale that most of them, seemingly gone insane, hanged themselves.   2. The centaur (half man, half horse); incurably wounded and suffering great pain, he asked Zeus for relief from his own immortality.   3. He supposedly molded the human race out of clay.   4. The old, eloquent sage in the Homeric epic.   5. See Aristophanes, *Plutus*, ll. 266–267.

I seem to hear the philosophers disagreeing. This is really unhappiness, they say, this life of folly, error, and ignorance. No, indeed; this is to be human. I cannot see why they should call this unhappiness when it is the common lot of all to be thus born, brought up, and constituted. Nothing can be unhappy if it expresses its true nature. Or do you argue that man is to be pitied because he cannot fly with the birds, and cannot run on four legs with the animals, and is not armed with horns like a bull? It can be argued equally well that the finest horse is unhappy because it is not a grammarian and a gourmet, or that a bull is miserable because it is found wanting at the minuet. A foolish man is no more unhappy than an illiterate horse: both are true to themselves.

The casuists argue next that men are naturally imperfect, and support and strengthen themselves by the peculiarly human device of study. As if it were possible that nature should be so careful in making a midge, a flower, or an herb, and then should have dozed in making man! And with the result that the sciences are needed! They were really invented by Theuth,[6] the evil genius of the human race, for the hurt of mankind. Instead of promoting man's happiness, they hinder it. They were probably even discovered for that purpose, just as letters were, according to the admirable argument of Plato's wise king.[7] In this way, studies crept in with the other trials of life, and from the same devilish source. This is shown by their name: "daemons," which means "those who know."

The people of the golden age lived without the advantages of learning, being guided by instinct and nature alone. What was the need of grammar when all spoke the same language, and spoke only to be understood? What use for dialectic when there was no conflict of opinion? What place for rhetoric when no one wished to get the better of another? What need for legal skill before the time of those evil acts which called forth our good laws? Furthermore, they were then too religious to pry impiously into nature's secrets, to measure the size, motion, and influence of the stars, or to seek the hidden causes of things. They considered it a sacrilege for man to know more than he should. They were free from the insane desire to discover what may lie beyond the stars. But as men fell slowly from the innocence of the golden age, the arts were invented, and by evil spirits, as I have said. At first they were few in number and were accepted by a few people. Later, hundreds more were added by the superstition of the Chaldeans and by the idle speculation of the Greeks. This was a needless vexation of the spirit, when one considers that a single grammatical system is perfectly adequate for a lifetime of torture.

Of course the arts which are nearest to common sense, that is, to folly, are most highly esteemed. Theologians are starved, scientists are given the cold shoulder, astrologers are laughed at, and logicians are ignored. The doctor alone, as they say, is worth all the rest put together. And a doctor is honored, especially among nobles, to the degree that he is ignorant and

---

6. In Plato's *Phaedrus*, the name of an Egyptian god who brought the art of writing to King Thamus.
7. King Thamus argued that the invention of writing would produce only false wisdom and destroy the power of man's memory.

impudent. Medicine, as now generally practiced, is a branch of the art of flattery just as much as rhetoric is. Lawyers rank next to doctors. Perhaps they should be placed first, but I hesitate to join the philosophers, who unanimously laugh at lawyers as being so many asses. Nevertheless, all affairs, both great and small, are arbitrated by these asses. Their lands increase; while the theologian, who has mastered a trunkful of manuscripts, lives on beans, and wages a gallant war against lice and fleas. As those arts are more successful which have the greatest proportion of folly, so those people are happiest who have nothing to do with learning and follow nature as their only guide. She is in no way wanting, except as a man wishes to go beyond what is proper for him. Nature hates counterfeits; the less the art, the greater the happiness.

Isn't it true that the happiest creatures are those which are least artificial and most natural? What could be happier than the bees, or more wonderful? They lack some of the senses, but what architect has equalled their constructive skill, or what philosopher has framed a republic to match theirs? Now the horse, who does have some of the human senses and who travels around with men, suffers also from human ills. He feels ashamed if he loses a race. While seeking military glory, he is run through and bites the dust along with his rider. Think, too, of the hard bit, the sharp spurs, the prison-like stable, the whips, sticks, and straps, the rider himself—in short, all the tragedy of servitude to which he exposes himself when he imitates men of honor and zealously seeks vengeance against the enemy. How much more desirable except for the interference of men, is the lot of flies and birds, who live for the moment and by the light of nature. Everyone has noticed how a bird loses its natural beauty when it is shut up in a cage and taught to speak. In every sphere, what is natural is happier than what is falsified by art.

For these reasons I can never sufficiently praise that cock (really Pythagoras)[8] who had been all things—philosopher, man, woman, king, subject, fish, horse, frog, perhaps even a sponge—and who concluded that none is as miserable as man. All the others are content with their natural limitations; man alone is vainly ambitious. Among men, furthermore, the fools are in many respects superior to the learned and the great. Gryllus,[9] for example, proved to be considerably wiser than wise Ulysses when he chose to grunt in a sty rather than to expose himself to the dangers of a further odyssey. Homer, the father of fiction, seems to agree with this: he often observes that men are wretched, and he still oftener describes Ulysses, the pattern of wisdom, as miserable, but he never speaks in this way of Paris, Ajax, or Achilles. Obviously Ulysses was unhappy because that tricky and artful fellow never did anything without consulting the goddess of wisdom. Wouldn't you say that he was over-educated, and that he had got too far away from nature? The seekers after wisdom are the farthest from happiness. They are fools twice over: forgetting the human station to

---

8. In the dialogue *The Dream, or the Cock*, written in the second century A.D. by the Greek satirist Lucian, the cock upholds the Pythagorean notion of transmigration of souls from one body to another by claiming that he is Pythagoras.   9. Character in a dialogue by Plutarch, changed into a pig by Circe.

which they were born, they grasp at divinity, and imitating the Giants,[1] they use their arts as engines with which to attack nature. It follows that the least unhappy are those who approximate the naïveté of the beasts and who never attempt what is beyond men.

There is no need to argue this like a Stoic logician, however, when we can prove it with a plain example. Is anyone happier than those we commonly call morons, fools, nitwits, and naturals—the most beautiful of names? This may sound absurd at first, but it is profoundly true. In the first place, these fools are free from the fear of death—and that fear is not an insignificant evil. They are free from the pangs of conscience. They are not terrified by ghosts and hobgoblins. They are not filled with vain worries and hopes. In short, they are not troubled by the thousand cares to which this life is subject. Shame, fear, ambition, envy, and love are not for them. If they were just a little dumber and more animal-like they would not even sin—or so the theologians say. Count your cares, you stupid intellectuals, and then you will begin to appreciate what I do for my followers. Remember also that they are always merry; wherever they go they bring pleasure, as if they were mercifully created by the gods to lighten the sadness of human life.

In a world where men are mostly at odds, all are as one in their attitude toward these innocents. They are sought out and sheltered; everyone permits them to do and say what they wish with impunity. Even the wild beasts perceive their harmlessness and do not attack them. They are sacred to the gods, and especially to me; therefore do all men properly honor them. Kings cannot eat or travel or spend an hour without their fools, in whom they take the greatest delight. In fact they rather prefer them to their crabbed counsellors, whom they nevertheless support for the sake of appearances. This royal preference is easily explained, I think. Counsellors, confident in their wisdom and forced to speak the unpleasant truth, bring only problems to princes; but fools bring what rulers are always looking for—jokes and laughter.

Fools have another not insignificant virtue: they alone are candid and truthful. What is more admirable than truth? I know that Alcibiades thought that only drunkards and children speak the truth;[2] nevertheless, the merit is really mine, as is proved by a line from Euripides: A fool speaks folly.[3] Whatever a fool has in his heart is all over his face and in his speech. Now wise men have two tongues, as Euripides also remarks,[4] one for speaking the truth, and the other for saying whatever is expedient at the moment. They turn black into white, and blow hot and cold with the same breath; their words are far from what is in their hearts. Kings are unhappiest at this point it seems to me, since in the midst of their prosperity they can find no one to tell them the truth, and are obliged to have flatterers for friends. You may say that kings hate to hear the truth and avoid wise counsellors for fear that one more daring than the others will speak what is true rather

---

1. Following the example of the Giants, or Titans, of Greek mythology who, inspired by their wronged mother Gaea (Earth), fought the Olympian gods and were defeated.   2. See Plato's *Symposium*.   3. *The Bacchanals (Bacchae)*, 1. 369.   4. The source of this reference is uncertain.

than what is pleasant. By and large this is so. It is remarkable, therefore, that kings will take the truth, and a sharp truth too, from my fools. A statement which would cost a wise man his head is received from a fool with the greatest delight. Truth that is free from offensiveness does give genuine pleasure, and only fools have the power to speak it. It is for these reasons, too, that fools are taken up by women, who are naturally inclined to pleasure and frivolity. Moreover, they can explain away whatever games they indulge in with fools, even when the sport becomes serious, as good clean fun—for the sex is ingenious, especially at covering up its own lapses.

Now let's return to the subject of the happiness of fools. After a life of jollity, and with no fear of death, or sense of it, they go straight to the Elysian fields, where they entertain the pious and leisurely shades. Compare the life of a wise man with that of a fool. Put up against a fool some model of wisdom, one who lost his boyhood and youth in the classroom, who dissipated the best part of his life in continual worry and study, and who never tasted a particle of pleasure thereafter. He is always abstemious, poor, unhappy, and crabbed; he is harsh and unjust to himself, grim and mean to others; he is pale, emaciated, sickly, sore-eyed, prematurely old and white-haired, dying before his time. Of course it really makes little difference when such a man dies. He has never lived. Well, there is your wise man for you.

Here the Stoics croak at me again. Nothing, they say, is more lamentable than madness, and pure folly is either very near madness, or more likely is the same thing. What is madness but a wandering of the wits? (But the Stoics wander the whole way.) With the Muses' help we will explode this line of reasoning. The argument is plausible, but our opponents should remember the practice of Socrates in splitting Cupids and Venuses,[5] and distinguish one kind of madness from another—at least they should if they wish to be considered sane themselves. To begin with, not every kind of madness is a calamity. Otherwise Horace would not have said, "A pleasant madness inspires me."[6] Nor would Plato have ranked the frenzy of poets, prophets, and lovers among the chief blessings of life. And the oracle would not have called the labors of Aeneas, insane.[7] Madness is really of two kinds. The first is sent up from hell by the vengeful Furies. Unloosing their snaky locks, they assault the hearts of men with hot desire for war, with insatiable greed and shameful lust, with parricide, incest, sacrilege, or any other evil of that sort. At other times the Furies pursue the guilty and conscience-stricken soul with terror and the fire of wrath. The second kind of madness is far different from this. It comes from me and is to be desired above all things. It arises whenever a cheerful confusion of the mind frees the spirit from care and at the same time anoints it with many-sided delight. It is the state of mind that Cicero desired as a defense against the evils of his age. The Greek in Horace[8] also had the right idea. He was just sufficiently mad to sit alone in the theater all day, laughing and

5. Distinguishing different types of love.   6. Horace, *Odes*, Book III, Ode iv, ll. 5–6.   7. *Aeneid*, Book VI, l. 135.   8. What follows is a paraphrase of a passage in Horace's *Epistles*, Book II, Epistle ii, ll. 128–140.

applauding at a bare stage, because he thought that tragedies were being enacted there. Otherwise he was sane enough—pleasant with his friends, kind to his wife, and indulgent to his servants, who could uncork a bottle without his getting angry. When the care of family and physician had freed him of his disease, he protested that he had been killed rather than cured, that they had taken away his pleasures and destroyed his delightful delusions. And he was perfectly right. They were the mad ones themselves, and needed the medicine more than he did. What sense is there in regarding a fortunate delusion like his as a disease to be purged with drugs?

It is not certain that every delusion and vagary ought to be called madness. A short-sighted man who thinks a mule is an ass is not commonly considered insane, nor is one who judges popular music to be great poetry. However, we must grant that a man is pretty nearly mad if he is continually and extraordinarily deluded by both his senses and his judgment. Take, for example, a person who thinks he is listening to a symphony orchestra whenever an ass brays, or a beggar who believes himself to be Croesus. Nevertheless, when this extreme madness gives pleasure, as it usually does, it is remarkably delightful both to those who are possessed by it, and to those who look on and are not mad in exactly the same way. Indeed this kind of madness is much more common than the ordinary person realizes. One madman laughs at another; they take turns entertaining each other. And the maddest one gets the biggest laugh.

If Folly is any judge, the happiest man is the one who is the most thoroughly deluded. May he maintain that ecstasy. It comes only from me, and is so widespread that I doubt if there is one man anywhere who is consistently wise and untouched by some madness. It may be only a tendency to think a gourd is a woman; but since very few see eye to eye with him on this, he will be called mad. When a man foolishly maintains that his wife (whom he shares with many others) is a pluperfect Penelope, however, nobody calls him mad, because they see that this is a plight common to other husbands.

To this latter class belong those who sacrifice everything for hunting. They swear that the sound of the horn and the baying of the hounds fill them with indescribable joy. I understand that even the dung of the dogs smells like cinnamon to them. And what is so delightful as an animal being butchered? Bulls and oxen are of course slaughtered by commoners, but it is a crime for anyone except a gentleman to touch wild game. Bareheaded and kneeling, he performs the ceremony with a special knife (no other can be used), cutting certain parts in approved order. The silent company stands as if spellbound by some novelty, although it has seen the spectacle a thousand times. If one of them is given a piece to taste, he feels that he has risen somewhat in the ranks of nobility. They think they are living royally, whereas they are really gaining nothing from this butchering and eating of animals, except to degenerate into animals themselves.

A similar class is those who are afire with a tremendous enthusiasm for building. They change round structures into square ones, and then back into round ones again. There is no end to this, until, having built themselves into poverty, they have no house to live in, and nothing to eat. What of it? In the meantime, they have been happy.

Next to these, I believe, are those who with new and secret arts labor to transmute the forms of things and who ransack earth and sea for a fifth essence.[9] Lured on by hope, and begrudging neither pain nor cost, they contrive, with marvelous ingenuity, their own delightful deception. Finally, they have spent all their money and can't afford another furnace.[1] Even then, however, they dream on pleasantly, urging others to experience the same happiness. When absolutely all hope is gone, they find much comfort in this last thought, "In great things, it is enough to have tried." They complain that life is too short for the magnitude of their undertaking.

I am not sure that gamblers should be admitted to our fellowship, and yet some of these addicts are a foolish and ridiculous sight. At the sound of the dice their hearts beat faster. The hope of winning always lures them on, until their means are gone, until their ship is split on the gaming table, which is a more deadly promontory than Malea.[2] Now, when they have lost their shirt, they will cheat anyone except the winner, in order to preserve their word and honor. Think, also, of the old and half-blind fellows, who have to wear glasses to play. When well-earned gout has tied their joints in knots, they hire a proxy to put the dice in the box for them. A delightful affair, were it not that the game usually degenerates into a brawl, and so belongs to the Furies rather than to me.

A group that does belong with us beyond any doubt is made up of those who enjoy telling and hearing monstrous lies and tall tales. They never get enough of ghosts and goblins and the like. They are most pleased by stories that are farthest from the truth. Such wonders are a diversion from boredom, and they may also be very profitable, especially for priests and pardoners.[3]

Closely related are those who have reached the foolish but comforting belief that if they gaze on a picture of Polyphemus-Christopher,[4] they will not die that day; or that whoever speaks the right words to an image of Barbara[5] will return unharmed from battle; or that a novena[6] to Erasmus, with proper prayers and candles, will shortly make one rich. In St. George they have turned up another Hercules or Hippolytus.[7] They all but adore his horse, which is piously studded and ornamented, and they ingratiate themselves by small gifts. To swear by St. George's brass helmets is an oath for a king. Then, what shall I say of those who happily delude themselves with forged pardons for their sins? They calculate the time to be spent in Purgatory down to the year, month, day, and hour, as if from a fool-proof mathematical table. There are also those who propose to get everything they desire by relying on magical charms and prayers devised by some pious impostor for the sake of his soul, or for profit. They will have wealth,

9. A substance (in addition to the four traditional elements—earth, water, air, and fire) of which the heavenly bodies were believed to be composed.   1. For alchemical experiments.   2. A proverbially dangerous promontory in Greece.   3. Cf. above, pp. 1592–1606.   4. Polyphemus is the Cyclops (one-eyed giant) in Homer's *Odyssey*; St. Christopher is also represented with only one eye.   5. St. Barbara, supposed to protect her worshipers against fire and artillery.   6. A nine days' devotion. 7. In Greco-Roman mythology, both fought against monsters.

honor, pleasure, plenty, good health, long life, a vigorous old age, and at last, a place next to Christ in heaven. However they don't want that seat of honor until the very last minute; celestial pleasures may come only when worldly pleasures, hung on to with tooth and nail, finally depart.

I picture a business man, a soldier, or a judge taking from all his loot one small coin as a proper expiation for the infinite evil of his life. He thinks it possible to buy up, like notes, so many perjuries, rapes, debauches, fights, murders, frauds, lies and treacheries. Having done this, he feels free to start with a clean slate on a new round of sin. How foolish also—and how happy—are those who expect something more than the highest happiness if they repeat daily the seven verses of the Psalms. These are the verses believed to have been pointed out to St. Bernard by the devil. He was a merry fellow but not very shrewd, since his tongue was loosened by the saint's trick.[8] Things like that are so foolish that I am almost ashamed of them myself; yet they are accepted not only by the laity but by the professors of theology themselves. The same thing on a larger scale occurs when sections of the country set up regional saints, and assign peculiar rites and powers to each one. One gives relief from toothache, another aids women in labor, a third recovers stolen goods, a fourth succors the shipwrecked, and still another watches over the sheep—the list is too long to finish. Some are helpful in a number of difficulties, especially the Virgin Mother, whom the common people honor more than they do the Son.

Do men ask anything but folly from these saints? Among all the gifts hanging from the walls and even from the ceilings of churches, have you ever seen one in payment for an escape from folly, or for making the giver wiser? One person has escaped from drowning. Another has lived after being run through. This fellow had the good luck or the nerve to leave the battlefield, allowing the others to fight. Another was delivered from the shadow of the gallows by the patron saint of thieves so that he could continue to relieve those who are burdened with too much wealth. This one escaped from jail. That one crossed up his doctor by surviving a fever. This man was saved by a poisoned drink, which loosened his bowels instead of killing him. His wife was not exactly pleased, since she lost both her labor and expense. Another's wagon was overturned, but he drove his horses home unharmed. That fellow's house fell on him and he lived. This one sneaked out safely when he was surprised by a husband. No one, however, gives thanks for warding off folly. It is so pleasant not to be wise that men will seek to avoid anything rather than folly.

Why should I go farther on this sea of superstition? "If I had a hundred tongues, a hundred mouths, a voice of brass, I could not describe all the forms of folly, or list all its names."[9] The life of Christians everywhere runs over with such nonsense. Superstitions are allowed and even promoted by the priests; they do not regret anything so profitable. Imagine, in the midst

---

8. A devil had told St. Bernard that repeating seven particular verses of the Psalms would bring him the certainty of salvation; "the saint's trick" was that of proposing to recite all of the Psalms.   9. A variation on a passage in the *Aeneid*, Book VI, ll. 625–627, in which, however, Virgil is talking of "forms of crime" rather than of "folly."

of this, some insolent wise men speaking the real truth: "You will not die badly if you live well. Your sins are redeemed if to the payment of money you add tears, vigils, prayers, fastings, and hatred of evil, and if you change your whole way of living. The saints will favor you if you imitate them." A wise man who snarled out things like that would throw the world into turmoil and deprive it of happiness!

Also of our fellowship are those who while still living make elaborate funeral arrangements, even prescribing the number of candles, mourners, singers, and hired pall-bearers. They must think that their sight will be returned to them after they are dead, or that their corpses will feel ashamed at not being buried grandly. They labor as if they were planning a civic entertainment.

I must not pass over those nobodies who take enormous pride in empty titles of nobility. One will trace his family back to Aeneas, another to Brutus,[1] and a third to King Arthur. They are surrounded by busts and portraits of their ancestors. They name over their grandfathers and great-grandfathers, and have the old titles by heart. At the same time, they are not far from being senseless statues themselves, and are probably worth less than the ones they show off. My follower, Self-love, enables them to live happily, however; and there are always other fools who regard monsters like these as gods.

Of course Self-love brings joy to others too. This ape-like fellow here seems handsome enough to himself. That one drawing circles over there thinks he is another Euclid. The man with the rooster's voice considers himself a great musician. The happiest fool, however, is the dolt who glories in some talent which is really made possible by his followers. Seneca tells[2] of that double-happy rich man, for example, who had servants on hand to refresh his memory whenever he told stories. He was so weak he could hardly stand, but he was a great fighter—with the support of hired thugs.

Artists are notoriously conceited. They would rather lose the family homestead than any part of their talent. This is especially true of actors, singers, orators, and poets. The worse they are, the more insolent, push-ing, and conceited they become. And the more applause they receive. The worst always please the most, because the majority of people, as I have remarked, are fools. If the poorer artist is most pleased with himself and is admired by the largest number, why should he wish to have true skill? It will cost him more; it will make him self-conscious and critical; and it will please far fewer of his audience.

I observe that races and cities are also attended by self-love. The English pride themselves on their good looks, their music, and their fine food, among other things. Noble or royal lineage is the claim of all Scots, together with argumentative skill. The French are the masters of courtesy; and the Parisians, in addition, are the only ones who understand theology.[3] The Italians have a monopoly on literature and eloquence, and they are pleased

---

1. The legendary founder of Britain.   2. The reference has not been traced.   3. The Sorbonne, the theological faculty in Paris, was the center of theological studies in Europe.

to admit that they alone are not barbarians. Happiest in this delusion are the Romans, who dream pleasantly of their ancient glories. The Venetians are content with their own nobility. The Greeks, of course, discovered the arts and possess the heroes of antiquity. Christian superstitions entertain the Turks and the other actual barbarians, who boast of their own religions. Better yet, the Jews steadfastly await the Messiah, and still hold grimly to Moses. The Spaniards scorn all other soldiers; and the Germans pride themselves on their great size and their knowledge of magic. I believe this is sufficient to convince you that the happiness of men, individually and collectively, springs from self-love.

Another source of pleasure is flattery, an extension of self-love. Instead of admiring yourself, you simply admire someone else. Nowadays flattery is condemned, but only among those who confuse the names of things with the things themselves. They think that flattery is necessarily insincere. The example of dumb animals should show them how wrong they are. What is more fawning than a dog? And yet, what is more faithful and a better friend to man? Or perhaps you prefer fierce lions, tigers, and leopards? Of course there is a harmful kind of flattery, the kind with which traitors and mockers destroy their victims; but my kind springs from kindliness and candor. It is much closer to virtue than is its opposite, surliness—or what Horace calls a heavy and awkward rudeness.[4] It raises the spirits and dispels grief; it stimulates the faint, enlivens the dull, and eases the suffering; it brings lovers together and keeps them together. It entices boys to study literature; it inspires the old. Disguised as praise, it warns and instructs princes without offense. In short, it makes everyone more pleased with himself—which is the chief part of happiness. What is more courteous than the way two mules scratch each other? There is no need to point out that flattery is important in the admired art of oratory, that it is a great part of medicine, and that it is a still greater part of poetry. It is nothing less than the sugar and spice of all human intercourse.

Still, it is a sad thing, they say, to be deceived. No; the saddest thing is not to be deceived. The notion that happiness comes from a knowledge of things as they really are is wrong. Happiness resides in opinion. Human affairs are so obscure and various that nothing can be clearly known. This was the sound conclusion of the Academics,[5] who were the least surly of the philosophers. At least if something can be truly known, it is rarely anything that adds to the pleasure of life. Anyway, man's mind is much more taken with appearances than with reality. This can be easily and surely tested by going to church. When anything serious is being said, the congregation dozes or squirms. But if the ranter—I mean the reverend— begins some old wives' tale, as often happens, everyone wakes up and strains to hear. You will also see more devotion being paid to such fabulous and poetic saints as George, Christopher, or Barbara than to Peter or Paul or even to Christ Himself. But these examples belong elsewhere.

The price of this kind of happiness is very low. Much more must be

---

4. Horace, *Epistles*, Book I, Epistle xviii, l. 508.   5. Philosophers of Plato's school, the Academy, which later became a school of skeptics.

paid for substantial things, even for the least of them—grammar, for instance. It is easy enough to acquire mere opinions; nevertheless they bring greater happiness than knowledge does. The satisfaction of a man who thinks rotten kippers taste and smell like ambrosia is not affected by the fact that his neighbor cannot abide their odor. On the other hand, if the finest fish turn your stomach, their quality has no bearing on your happiness. A man who thinks his extremely ugly wife is another Venus is as well off as if she really were beautiful. Here's a person who gazes admiringly at a picture made of red lead and mud which he believes is by Apelles or Zeuxis. Isn't he happier than someone who has paid a high price for an authentic masterpiece, but who gets little pleasure from it? I know a man by my name,[6] a practical joker, who gave his new wife some imitation jewels and persuaded her that they were genuine and very valuable. Now what difference did it make to the girl? She was delighted with the glass trinkets and kept them locked in a secret place. In the meantime, the husband had saved money, had enjoyed fooling his wife, and had won her devotion as well as he would have by a more expensive present.

What difference do you see between the self-satisfied inhabitants of Plato's cave[7] who contentedly admire the shadows of things, and the wise man who emerges from the cave and sees reality? If Lucian's Micyllus[8] could have dreamed forever his rich and golden dream, there would have been no reason for him to desire any other kind of happiness. Evidently, then, there is either no difference between a fool and a wise man, or if there is a difference, a fool has the better of it. A fool's happiness costs least—no more than a bit of illusion. In addition, it is enjoyed in the company of a great many others. The good things of life must be shared to be delightful; and who has not heard of the scarcity of wise men, if indeed any exist at all. The Greeks listed seven all told;[9] a more accurate census would do well to turn up one-half or one-third of a wise man.

Of course drink will drown your sorrows, but only for a time. The next morning they come galloping back, riding four white horses, as the saying is. Folly, on the other hand, is a spree that never ends. Its effect is complete and immediate. Without requiring any bothersome preparations, it fills the heart with joy. It is available to all, rather than to a chosen few, as with other gifts of the gods. Vintage wine is not made everywhere; beauty comes to few, and eloquence to fewer still. Not many are rich, and not many can be kings. Mars often favors neither side; Neptune drowns more than he saves. The majority are turned away from wisdom. Jove himself thunders, and the anti-Joves—Pluto, Ate, Poena, Febris,[1] and the others—are executioners rather than gods. Only I, great-hearted Folly, embrace all men equally. Nor do I come only when prayed for. If some devotion is

6. Sir Thomas More, who was a close friend of Erasmus's and on whose name Erasmus puns with *moria* (Latin for "folly").   7. The reference is to Plato's allegory in the *Republic*, Book VII, where he compares the soul in the body to a prisoner chained in a cave, his back against the light, able to see only the shadows of things outside.   8. A character in Lucian's *The Dream, or the Cock* who dreams that he has taken the place of a rich man.   9. The Seven Sages listed were philosophers of the sixth century B.C., among them Thales and Solon.   1. Pluto was god of the underworld; Ate, goddess of revenge and discord; Poena, goddess of punishment; Febris, goddess of fever.

neglected, I don't grow testy and demand expiation. I don't upset heaven and earth if I have been left at home and not invited along with the other gods to smell the sacrifices. In fact, the other gods are so hard to please that it is safer and wiser not to try to worship them, but rather to avoid them altogether. Men are sometimes like that; so thin-skinned and irritable that hands off is the best policy.

Even though all this is so, I understand that no one sacrifices to Folly or builds a temple for her. Such ingratitude, I repeat, is amazing. At the same time, I good-naturedly persuade myself that respect is not really lacking. What need have I for incense, meal, a he-goat, or a she-hog, so long as men everywhere whole-heartedly worship me in the way that preachers tell us is best? Let Diana have her human sacrifices! I am not envious when I consider that all men honor me in the truest way, that is, by taking me to their hearts and manifesting me in their lives and actions. This kind of worship of the saints is not exactly customary among Christians. Plenty of them burn little candles to the Virgin, and in the middle of the day, when it does no good; but how few of them burn with zeal to imitate her in chastity, temperance, and love of heavenly things! That, after all, is the true worship, and it is by far the most pleasing to those above. Besides, why should I desire a temple, when the whole world, if I am not mistaken, is a handsome shrine to me? Nor are priests lacking—except where men are lacking. As for stone and painted images, I am not so foolish as to demand what stands in the way of worship. The stupid adore such substitutes in place of the saints themselves, who are finally crowded out altogether. The same thing would happen to me. One might say, of course, that there are as many statues to me as there are people who look foolish, even unintentionally so. What do I care if other gods are worshipped in certain places on stated days—Phoebus at Rhodes, Venus at Cyprus, Juno at Argos, Minerva at Athens, Jupiter at Olympus, Neptune at Tarentum, Priapus[2] at Lampsacus? Why should I envy them when all men eagerly offer greater sacrifices to me?

[The third section deals with "The Followers of Folly," and includes among them, in lively and paradoxical descriptions, all categories of people, from merchants to poets, from scholars to popes and cardinals; in fact, Folly concludes: "My real point has been that no man can live happily unless he has been admitted into my mysteries and enjoys my favor."]

IV. THE CHRISTIAN FOOL

. . . There is really no need for me to marshal proof[3] with so much care, when in the mystical psalms Christ himself, speaking to the Father, says perfectly plainly, "Thou knowest my foolishness."[4] It is not hard to see why fools are greatly pleasing to God. We know that great princes look with suspicion on men who are too clever, and hate them. Julius Caesar,

2. A god of procreation, son of Dionysus and Aphrodite. 3. Of the relationship between "Folly" and Christianity. 4. The quotation is from Psalm 69:5, where the speaker is not Christ, but the Psalmist.

for instance, suspected and hated Brutus and Cassius, while he did not fear the drunken Antony at all. Nero, likewise, was suspicious of Seneca, and Dionysius[5] of Plato; but all princes take pleasure in duller and simpler souls. In the same way, Christ always hates and condemns those who rely on their own wisdom. Paul testifies to this clearly enough when he says, "God has chosen the foolish things of the world,"[6] and when he says, "It has pleased God to save the world by foolishness,"[7] since it could never be redeemed by wisdom. God himself indicates this plainly when he proclaims through the mouth of the prophet, "I will destroy the wisdom of the wise and I will reject the prudence of the prudent."[8] Christ also gave thanks that God had concealed the mystery of salvation from the wise, but had revealed it to babes, that is, to fools.[9] The Greek for "babes" is νηπιοις, which is the opposite of σοφοις, "the wise." Equally pertinent is the fact that in the Gospels Christ often attacks the scribes and Pharisees and doctors of laws, whereas he faithfully defends the ignorant multitude. What is "Woe unto you, scribes and Pharisees,"[1] except "Woe unto you that are wise"? Little children, women, and fishermen seem to delight Him most. Even among animals, those pleased Christ best which had the least slyness. He preferred to ride upon a donkey, though had He chosen He could safely have ridden upon a lion. The Holy Spirit descended in the likeness of a dove, not of an eagle or a hawk; and the Gospels frequently mention harts, fawns, and lambs. Those who are chosen for eternal life are called "sheep." No animal is more foolish, as is shown by the proverbial phrase in Aristotle, "sheepish character," which was suggested by the stupidity of the animal and is commonly used as a taunt against dull and foolish men. Nevertheless, Christ declares himself the shepherd of his flock, and even takes delight in the name of "the Lamb," as when John pointed Him out, "Behold the Lamb of God."[2] The expression also appears frequently in the book of *Revelation*.

What do these things declare except that all men, even the pious, are fools? And that Christ himself, although He possessed the wisdom of the Father,[3] became something like a fool in order to cure the folly of mankind, when He assumed the nature and being of a mortal? And that He was made "to be sin"[4] in order to redeem sinners? He did not wish to redeem them by any way except by the foolishness of the Cross, and by weak and simple apostles. These He taught to practice folly and to avoid wisdom. He incited them by the example of children, lilies, mustard-seed, and sparrows,[5] all of them foolish things, living without art or care, by the light of nature alone. Furthermore, He forbade the apostles to be con-

---

5. Dionysius the Younger, tyrant of Syracuse, in Sicily, in the fourth century B.C.   6. "But God hath chosen the foolish things of the world to confound the wise." (I Corinthians 1:27.)   7. "For after that in the wisdom of God the world by wisdom knew not God, it pleased God by the foolishness of preaching to save them that believe."   8. ". . . for the wisdom of their wise men shall perish, and the understanding of their prudent men shall be hid."   9. "I thank thee, O Father, Lord of heaven and earth, because thou hast hid these things from the wise and prudent, and hast revealed them unto babes." (Matthew 11:25.)   1. Luke 11:44.   2. John 1:29, 36.   3. "But unto them which are called, both Jews and Greeks, Christ the power of God, and the wisdom of God." (I Corinthians 1:24.)   4. "For he hath made him to be sin for us, who knew no sin." (II Corinthians 5:21.)   5. For the reference to *children*, see Luke 18:17; for *lilies*, see Matthew 6:28; for *mustard-seed*, see Luke, 17:6; for *sparrows*, see Matthew 10:29.

cerned about how they should answer the charges of the magistrates, and He forbade them to pry into the times and seasons. They should not rely on their own wisdom, but should wholly depend upon Him. We know, likewise, that the Creator commanded men not to eat of the Tree of Knowledge, just as if knowledge were the destroyer of happiness. Paul roundly condemns knowledge as that which puffs up[6] and works harm. St. Bernard is following him, I believe, when he explains that the mountain wherein Lucifer established his headquarters was "the Mount of Knowledge."

Surely we should not overlook this argument, that folly is so pleasing to the heavenly powers that forgiveness of its errors is certain; whereas nothing is forgiven to wisdom. And so it comes about that when the prudent pray to be forgiven, although they were clever enough when they sinned, they use the excuse and defense of having acted foolishly. This was the argument that Aaron used in the book of *Numbers*, if I remember correctly, to excuse his sister from punishment: "I beseech, my master, that you lay not this sin, which we have committed foolishly, to our charge."[7] Saul asked forgiveness of David by saying, "It is apparent that I have done foolishly."[8] David, in turn, speaks placatingly to the Lord: "I beseech Thee, do away the iniquity of thy servant, for I have done very foolishly."[9] It is as if he could not obtain grace by praying unless he pleaded folly and ignorance. Much stronger proof is the fact that Christ when he prayed on the Cross for His enemies, "Father, forgive them," pleaded no other excuse than ignorance, saying, "for they know not what they do."[1] In the same manner, Paul wrote to Timothy: "But therefore I have obtained the mercy of the Lord, because I acted ignorantly in unbelief."[2] What is "I acted ignorantly" except "I acted foolishly, not maliciously"? What is "But therefore I have obtained the mercy of the Lord" except "I should not have obtained it if I had not been supported by the excuse of folly"? The mystical psalmist, whom I failed to recall at the proper place, aids us: "Remember not the sins of my youth and my ignorances."[3]

Let me stop pursuing the infinite and try to summarize. The Christian religion on the whole seems to have some kinship with folly, while it has none at all with wisdom. If you want proof of this, observe first that children, old people, women, and fools take more delight than anyone else in holy and religious things; and that they are therefore ever nearest the altars, led no doubt solely by instinct. Next, you will notice that the founders of religion have prized simplicity exceedingly, and have been the bitterest foes of learning. Finally, no people seem to act more foolishly than those who have been truly possessed with Christian piety. They give away whatever is theirs; they overlook injuries, allow themselves to be cheated, make no distinction between friends and enemies, shun pleasure, and feast on

---

6. "Knowledge puffeth up, but charity edifieth." (I Corinthians 8:1.)   7. "And Aaron said unto Moses, Alas, my lord, I beseech thee, lay not the sin upon us, wherein we have done foolishly, and wherein we have sinned." (Numbers 12:11.)   8. ". . . behold, I have played the fool, and have erred exceedingly." (I Samuel 26:21.)   9. I Chronicles 21:8.   1. Luke 23:34.   2. ". . . but I obtained mercy, because I did it ignorantly in unbelief." (I Timothy 1:13.)   3. "Remember not the sins of my youth, nor my transgressions." (Psalms 25:7.)

hunger, vigils, tears, labors, and scorn. They disdain life, and utterly prefer death; in short, they seem to have become altogether indifferent to ordinary interests, quite as if their souls lived elsewhere and not in their bodies. What is this, if not to be mad? Considering this, we should not find it very strange that the apostles appeared to be drunk on new wine, and that Paul, in the eyes of Festus, his judge, looked as if he had gone mad.[4]

. . . . Since the pious and the vulgar are so radically different, it comes about that each appears to the other to be mad. It is obvious to me, however, that the word is more correctly applied to the pious rather than to the others. This will become clearer if I briefly demonstrate, as I promised to do, that their *summum bonum* is nothing but a kind of insanity. First, let us assume that Plato was dreaming of approximately the same thing when he wrote that "the madness of lovers is the highest kind of happiness."[5] He who loves intensely no longer lives in himself but in whatever he loves, and the more he can leave himself and enter into the other, the happier he is. Now when a soul is eager to leave the body, and does not use its bodily organs normally, you call it madness and rightly so. Isn't this what is meant by the common sayings: "there's nobody home," and "to come to," and "he is himself again"? Furthermore, as the love becomes more nearly complete, the madness is greater and more delightful. What is that heavenly life, then, towards which the truly religious aspire with such devotion? Very certainly the stronger and victorious spirit will absorb the body, and it will do this the more easily because now it is in its own realm, and also because during life it has cleansed and contracted the body in preparation for this change. Then the soul will itself be marvellously absorbed by that supreme spirit, which is greater than its infinite parts. And so at last the whole man will be outside of himself; nor will he be happy for any other reason than that, being outside of himself, he shall have some ineffable portion of that supreme good which draws all things unto itself. Although this happiness becomes complete only when the soul has recovered its original body by being clothed with immortality; yet since the life of pious folk is a contemplation and a shadowing forth of that other life, they feel a glow and a foretaste of the reward to come. This is only a drop, of course, in comparison with the fountain of eternal happiness, but it far surpasses all physical pleasures, even all mortal delights rolled into one. By so much does the spiritual exceed the bodily, the invisible exceed the visible. This surely is what the prophet has promised: "Eye hath not seen, nor ear heard, neither have entered into the heart of man, the things which God hath prepared for them that love Him."[6] And this is that portion of folly which will not be taken away by the transformation of life, but will be perfected.

Those who are permitted to have a foretaste of this—and it comes to very few—experience something very like madness. They say things that are not quite coherent or conventional, sounds without meaning, and their expressions change suddenly. They are exuberant and melancholy, crying,

---

4. ". . . Festus said with a loud voice, Paul, thou art beside thyself; much learning doth make thee mad." (Acts 26:25–26.)   5. See Plato, *Phaedrus*, 245   6. I Corinthians 2:9.

laughing, and sighing by turns; in brief, they are truly beside themselves. When presently they return to themselves, they say that they do not know where they have been, whether in the body or out of it, waking or sleeping. They do not remember what they have heard, seen, said, or done; and yet mistily as in a dream, they know that they were happiest when they were out of their minds. So they are sorry to come to themselves again, and they desire nothing more than to be mad always with this kind of madness. And this is only the slightest taste of the happiness hereafter.

But indeed I have long since forgotten who I am and have run out of bounds. If anything I have said seems sharp or gossipy, remember that it is Folly and a woman who has spoken. At the same time remember the Greek proverb, "Even a foolish man will often speak a word in season." Or perhaps you think that does not hold for women? I see that you are expecting a peroration, but you are certainly foolish if you think that I can remember any part of such a hodgepodge of words as I have poured out. There is an old saying, "I hate a drinking companion with a memory." Here is a new one, "I hate an audience that remembers anything."

And so farewell. Applaud, live, drink, most distinguished worshippers of Folly.

NICCOLÒ MACHIAVELLI
1469–1527

The most famous and controversial political writer and theorist of his time—indeed, possibly of all time—Niccolò Machiavelli was born in Florence on May 3, 1469. Little is known of his schooling, but it is obvious from his works that he knew the Latin and Italian writers well. He entered public life in 1494 as a clerk and from 1498 to 1512 was secretary to the second chancery of the commune of Florence, whose magistrates were in charge of internal and war affairs. During the conflict between Florence and Pisa, he dealt with military problems first-hand. Thus he had a direct experience of war and likewise of diplomacy; he was entrusted with many missions—among others, to King Louis XII of France in 1500 and in 1502 to Cesare Borgia, duke of Valentinois or "il duca Valentino," the favorite son of Pope Alexander VI. The latter's ruthless methods in crushing a conspiracy during his conquest of the Romagna region Machiavelli described in a terse booklet *Of the Method Followed by Duke Valentino in Killing Vitellozzo Vitelli . . .* which already shows direct insight into the type of the amoral and technically efficient "prince." In 1506 Machiavelli went on a mission to Pope Julius II, whose expedition into Romagna (an old name for North-central Italy) he followed closely. From this and other missions—to Emperor Maximilian (1508) and again to the king of France (1509)—Machiavelli drew his two books of observations or *Portraits* of the affairs of those territories, written in 1508 and 1510.

Preeminently a student of politics and an acute observer of historical events, Machiavelli endeavored to apply his experience of other states to the strengthening of his own, the Florentine Republic, and busied himself in 1507 with the establishment of a Florentine militia, encountering great difficulties. When the republican regime came to an end, he lost his post and was exiled from the city proper, though forbidden to leave Florentine territory. The new regime of the Medici accused him unjustly of conspiracy, and he was released only after a period of imprisonment and torture. To the period of his exile (spent near San Casciano, a few miles from Florence, where he retired with his wife, Marietta Corsini, and his five children), we owe his major works: the *Discourses on the First Ten Books of Livy* (1513–21) and *The Prince*, written in 1513 with the hope of obtaining public office from the Medici. In 1520 Machiavelli was commissioned to write a history of Florence, which he presented in 1525 to Pope Clement VII (Giulio de' Medici). The following year, conscious of imminent dangers, he took part in the work to improve the military fortifications of Florence. The fate of the city at this point depended on the outcome of the larger struggle between Francis I of France and the Holy Roman Emperor, Charles V. Pope Clement's siding with the king of France led to the disastrous "Sack of Rome" by Charles V in 1527, and the result for Florence was the collapse of Medici domination. Machiavelli's hopes, briefly raised by the re-establishment of the republic, came to naught because he was now regarded as a Medici sympathizer. This last disappointment may have accelerated his end. He died on June 22, 1527, and was buried in the church of Santa Croce.

Though Machiavelli has a place in literary history for a short novel and two plays, one of which, *La mandragola*, first performed in the early 1520s, belongs in the upper rank of Italian comedies of intrigue, his world reputation is based on *The Prince*. This "handbook" on how to obtain and keep political power consists of twenty-six chapters. The first eleven deal with different types of dominions and the ways in which they are acquired and preserved—the early title of the whole book, in Latin, was *De principatibus* (*Of Princedoms*)—and the twelfth to fourteenth focus particularly on problems of military power. The book's astounding fame, however, is based on the final part (from chapter fifteen to the end), which deals primarily with the attributes and "virtues" of the prince himself. In other words, despite its reputation for cool, precise realism, the work presents a hypothetical type, the idealized portrait of a certain kind of person.

Manuals of this sort may be classified, in one sense, as pedagogical literature. While for their merits of form and of vivid, if stylized, characterization they can be considered works of art, their overt purpose is to codify a certain set of manners and rules of conduct; the author therefore presents himself as especially wise, an expert in the field, the "mind" offering advice to the executive "arm." Machiavelli is a clear example of this approach. His fervor, the dramatic, oratorical way he confronts his reader, the wealth and pertinence of his illustrations are all essential qualities of his pedagogical *persona*: "Either you are already a prince, or you are on the way to become one. In the first case liberality is dangerous; in the second it is very necessary to be thought liberal. Caesar was one of those. . . . Somebody may answer . . . I answer . . ." Relying on his direct knowledge of politics, he uses examples he can personally vouch for:

> Men are so simple and so subject to present needs that he who deceives in this way will always find those who will let themselves be deceived. I do not wish to keep still about one of the recent instances. Alexander VI did nothing else than deceive men, and had no other intention. . . .

The implied tone of *I know, I have seen such things myself* adds a special immediacy to Machiavelli's prose. His view of the practical world may have been an especially startling one; but the sensation caused by his work would have been far less without the rhetorical power, the drama of argumentation, which make *The Prince* a unique example of "the art of persuasion."

The view of humanity in Machiavelli is not at all cheerful. Indeed, the pessimistic notion that humanity is evil is not so much Machiavelli's conclusion about human nature as his premise; it is the point of departure of all subsequent reasoning upon the course for a ruler to follow. The very fact of its being given as a premise, however, tends to qualify it; it is not a firm philosophical judgment, but a stratagem, dictated by the facts as they are seen by a lucid observer of the here and now. The author is committed to his view of the human being not as a philosopher or as a religious man but as a practical politician. He indicates the rules of the game as his experience shows it must, under the circumstances, be played.

> A prudent . . . ruler cannot and should not observe faith when such observance is to his disadvantage and the causes that made him give his promise have vanished. If men were all good, this advice would not be good, but since men are wicked and do not keep their promises to you, you likewise do not have to keep yours to them.

A basic question in the study of Machiavelli, therefore, is: How much of a realist is he? His picture of the perfectly efficient ruler has something of the quality of an abstraction; it shows, though much less clearly than Castiglione's portrayal of the courtier, the well-known Renaissance tendency toward "perfected" form. Machiavelli's abandonment of complex actualities in favor of an ideal vision is shown most clearly at the conclusion of the book, particularly in the last chapter. This is where he offers what amounts to the greatest of his illustrations as the prince's preceptor and counselor: the ideal ruler, now technically equipped by his pedagogue, is to undertake a mission—the liberation of Machiavelli's Italy. If we regard the last chapter of *The Prince* as a culmination of Machiavelli's discussion rather than as a dissonant addition to it, we are likely to feel at that point not only that Machiavelli's realistic method is ultimately directed toward an ideal task, but also that his conception of that task, far from being based on immediate realities, is founded on cultural and poetic myths. Machiavelli's method here becomes imaginative rather than scientific. His exhortation to liberate Italy, and his final prophecy, belong to the tradition of poetic visions in which a present state of decay is lamented, and a hope of future redemption is expressed (as in Dante, *Purgatory*, Canto VI). And a very significant part of this hope is presented not in terms of technical political considerations (choice of the opportune moment, evaluation of military power), but in terms of a poetic justice for which precedents are sought in religious and ancient history and in mythology:

> . . . if it was necessary to make clear the ability of Moses that the people of Israel should be enslaved in Egypt, and to reveal Cyrus' greatness of mind that the Persians should be oppressed by the Medes, and to demonstrate the excellence of Theseus that the Athenians should be scattered, so at the present time. . . . Everything is now fully disposed for the work . . . if only your House adopts the methods of those I have set forth as examples. Moreover, we have before our eyes extraordinary and unexampled means prepared by God. The sea has been divided. . . . Manna has fallen.

Machiavelli's Italy, as he observed in the preceding chapter, is now a country "without dykes and without any wall of defence." It has suffered from "deluges," and its present rule, a "barbarian" one, "stinks in every nostril." Something is rotten in it, in short, as in Hamlet's Denmark. And we become more and more detached even from the particular example, Italy, as we recognize in the situation a pattern frequently exemplified in tragedy: the desire for communal regeneration, for the cleansing of the city-state, the *polis*. Of this cleansing, Italy on the one side and the imaginary prince on the other may be taken as symbols. The envisaged redemption is identified with antiquity and Roman virtue, while the realism of the political observer is here drowned out by the cry of the humanist dreaming of ancient glories.

Peter E. Bondanella focuses on the literary aspects of Machiavelli's works in *Machiavelli and the Art of Renaissance History* (1973). Sebastian De Grazia, *Machiavelli in Hell* (1989), on politics in *The Prince*, contains indexes and a bibliography. J. R. Hale's biography, *Machiavelli and Renaissance Italy* (1972), places Machiavelli in a historical perspective. A political analysis is provided by Anthony Parel in *The Political Calculus. Essays on Machiavelli's Political Philosophy* (1972). Roberto Ridolfi, *The Life of Niccolò Machiavelli*, translated by Cecil Grayson (1963) is still considered the best and most accurate biography. Silvia Ruffo-Fiore, *Niccolò Machiavelli* (1982) is a useful comprehensive guide for the beginning student.

Letter to Francesco Vettori[1]

["That Food Which Alone Is Mine"]

I am living on my farm, and since my last troubles[2] I have not been in Florence twenty days, putting them all together. Up to now I have been setting snares for thrushes with my own hands; I get up before daylight, prepare my birdlime, and go out with a bundle of cages on my back, so that I look like Geta when he came back from the harbor with the books of Amphitryo,[3] and catch at the least two thrushes and at the most six. So I did all of September; then this trifling diversion, despicable and strange as it is, to my regret failed. What my life is now I shall tell you.

In the morning I get up with the sun and go out into a grove that I am having cut; there I remain a couple of hours to look over the work of the past day and kill some time with the woodmen, who always have on hand some dispute either among themselves or among their neighbors. . . .

When I leave the grove, I go to a spring, and from there into my aviary. I have a book in my pocket, either Dante or Petrarch or one of the minor poets, as Tibullus,[4] Ovid, and the like. I read about their tender passions and their loves, remember mine, and take pleasure for a while in thinking about them. Then I go along the road to the inn, talk with those who pass by, ask the news of their villages, learn various things, and note the varied tastes and different fancies of men. It gets to be dinner time, and with my troop I eat what food my poor farm and my little property permit. After dinner, I return to the inn; there I usually find the host, a butcher, a

---

1. From a letter of December 10, 1513, to Vettori, Florentine Ambassador at Rome. Translated by Allan H. Gilbert.   2. Machiavelli had been suspected of participation in a conspiracy led by two young friends of his, and had been imprisoned and subjected to torture before his innocence was recognized.   3. Allusion to a popular tale in which Amphitryo, returning to Thebes after having studied at Athens, sends forward from the harbor his servant Geta to announce his arrival to his wife Alcmene, and loads him with his books.   4. Albius Tibullus, Roman elegiac poet of the first century B.C.

miller, and two furnace-tenders. With these fellows I sink into vulgarity for the rest of the day, playing at *cricca* and *tricche-trach*;[5] from these games come a thousand quarrels and numberless offensive and insulting words; we often dispute over a penny, and all the same are heard shouting as far as San Casciano.[6] So, involved in these trifles, I keep my brain from getting mouldy, and express the perversity of Fate, for I am willing to have her drive me along this path, to see if she will be ashamed of it.

In the evening, I return to my house, and go into my study. At the door I take off the clothes I have worn all day, mud spotted and dirty, and put on regal and courtly garments. Thus appropriately clothed, I enter into the ancient courts of ancient men,[7] where, being lovingly received, I feed on that food which alone is mine, and which I was born for; I am not ashamed to speak with them and to ask the reasons for their actions, and they courteously answer me. For four hours I feel no boredom and forget every worry; I do not fear poverty, and death does not terrify me. I give myself completely over to the ancients. And because Dante says that there is no knowledge unless one retains what one has read,[8] I have written down the profit I have gained from their conversation, and composed a little book *De principatibus*,[9] in which I go as deep as I can into reflections on this subject, debating what a principate is, what the species are, how they are gained, how they are kept, and why they are lost. If ever any of my trifles can please you, this one should not displease you; and to a prince, and especially a new prince, it ought to be welcome.

The Prince[1]
(Princely Virtues)[2]

ON THE THINGS FOR WHICH MEN, AND ESPECIALLY PRINCES, ARE PRAISED OR CENSURED

. . . Because I know that many have written on this topic, I fear that when I too write I shall be thought presumptuous, because, in discussing it, I break away completely from the principles laid down by my predecessors. But since it is my purpose to write something useful to an attentive reader, I think it more effective to go back to the practical truth of the subject than to depend on my fancies about it. And many have imagined republics and principalities that never have been seen or known to exist in reality. For there is such a difference between the way men live and the way they ought to live, that anybody who abandons what is for what ought to be will learn something that will ruin rather than preserve him, because anyone who determines to act in all circumstances the part of a good man

5. Two popular games, the first played with cards, the second with dice thrown to regulate the movements of pawns on a chessboard.   6. Nearby village; in the region around Florence.   7. Machiavelli here refers figuratively to his study of ancient history.   8. ". . . for knowledge none can vaunt / Who retains not, although he have understood." (*Paradiso*, Canto V, ll. 41–42.)   9. *Of Princedoms*; the Latin title of *The Prince*. All chapter headings are also in Latin in the original.   1. Translated by Allan H. Gilbert.   2. From Chapters 15–18.

must come to ruin among so many who are not good. Hence, if a prince wishes to maintain himself, he must learn how to be not good, and to use that ability or not as is required.

Leaving out of account, then, things about an imaginary prince, and considering things that are true, I say that all men, when they are spoken of, and especially princes, because they are set higher, are marked with some of the qualities that bring them either blame or praise. To wit, one man is thought liberal, another stingy (using a Tuscan word, because *avaricious* in our language is still applied to one who desires to get things through violence, but *stingy* we apply to him who refrains too much from using his own property); one is thought open-handed, another grasping; one cruel, the other compassionate; one is a breaker of faith, the other reliable; one is effeminate and cowardly, the other vigorous and spirited; one is philanthropic, the other egotistic; one is lascivious, the other chaste; one is straight-forward, the other crafty; one hard, the other easy to deal with; one is firm, the other unsettled; one is religious, the other unbelieving; and so on.

And I know that everybody will admit that it would be very praiseworthy for a prince to possess all of the above-mentioned qualities that are considered good. But since he is not able to have them or to observe them completely, because human conditions do not allow him to, it is necessary that he be prudent enough to understand how to avoid getting a bad name because he is given to those vices that will deprive him of his position. He should also, if he can, guard himself from those vices that will not take his place away from him, but if he cannot do it, he can with less anxiety let them go. Moreover, he should not be troubled if he gets a bad name because of vices without which it will be difficult for him to preserve his position. I say this because, if everything is considered, it will be seen that some things seem to be virtuous, but if they are put into practice will be ruinous to him; other things seem to be vices, yet if put into practice will bring the prince security and well-being.

ON LIBERALITY AND PARSIMONY

Beginning, then, with the first of the above-mentioned qualities, I assert that it is good to be thought liberal.[3] Yet liberality, practiced in such a way that you get a reputation for it, is damaging to you, for the following reasons: If you use it wisely and as it ought to be used, it will not become known, and you will not escape being censured for the opposite vice. Hence, if you wish to have men call you liberal, it is necessary not to omit any sort of lavishness. A prince who does this will always be obliged to use up all his property in lavish actions; he will then, if he wishes to keep the name of liberal, be forced to lay heavy taxes on his people and exact money from them, and do everything he can to raise money. This will begin to make his subjects hate him, and as he grows poor he will be little esteemed

3. Generous, openhanded.

by anybody. So it comes about that because of this liberality of his, with which he has damaged a large number and been of advantage to but a few, he is affected by every petty annoyance and is in peril from every slight danger. If he recognizes this and wishes to draw back, he quickly gets a bad name for stinginess.

Since, then, a prince cannot without harming himself practice this virtue of liberality to such an extent that it will be recognized, he will, if he is prudent, not care about being called stingy. As time goes on he will be thought more and more liberal, for the people will see that because of his economy his income is enough for him, that he can defend himself from those who make war against him, and that he can enter upon undertakings without burdening his people. Such a prince is in the end liberal to all those from whom he takes nothing, and they are numerous; he is stingy to those to whom he does not give, and they are few. In our times we have seen big things done only by those who have been looked on as stingy; the others have utterly failed. Pope Julius II,[4] though he made use of a reputation for liberality to attain the papacy, did not then try to maintain it, because he wished to be able to make war. The present King of France[5] has carried on great wars without laying unusually heavy taxes on his people, merely because his long economy has made provision for heavy expenditures. The present King of Spain,[6] if he had continued liberal, would not have carried on or completed so many undertakings.

Therefore a prince ought to care little about getting called stingy, if as a result he does not have to rob his subjects, is able to defend himself, does not become poor and contemptible, and is not obliged to become grasping. For this vice of stinginess is one of those that enables him to rule. Somebody may say: Caesar, by means of his liberality became emperor, and many others have come to high positions because they have been liberal and have been thought so. I answer: Either you are already prince, or you are on the way to become one. In the first case liberality is dangerous; in the second it is very necessary to be thought liberal. Caesar was one of those who wished to attain dominion over Rome. But if, when he had attained it, he had lived for a long time and had not moderated his expenses, he would have destroyed his authority. Somebody may answer: Many who have been thought very liberal have been princes and done great things with their armies. I answer: The prince spends either his own property and that of his subjects or that of others. In the first case he ought to be frugal; in the second he ought to abstain from no sort of liberality. When he marches with his army and lives on plunder, loot, and ransom, a prince controls the property of others. To him liberality is essential, for without it his soldiers would not follow him. You can be a free giver of what does not belong to you or your subjects, as were Cyrus, Caesar, and Alexander, because to spend the money of others does not decrease your reputation

---

4. Giuliano della Róvere, elected to the papacy in 1503 at the death of Pius III, who had been successor to Alexander VI (Rodrigo Borgia). Alexander VI is discussed in the chapter "In What Way Faith Should Be Kept by Princes"; for Machiavelli's view of the character of Julius II, see the chapter "The Power of Fortune in Human Affairs . . ."   5. Louis XII.   6. Ferdinand II, "the Catholic."

but adds to it. It is only the spending of your own money that hurts you. There is nothing that eats itself up as fast as does liberality, for when you practice it you lose the power to practice it, and become poor and contemptible, or else to escape poverty you become rapacious and therefore are hated. And of all the things against which a prince must guard himself, the first is being an object of contempt and hatred. Liberality leads you to both of these. Hence there is more wisdom in keeping a name for stinginess, which produces a bad reputation without hatred, than in striving for the name of liberal, only to be forced to get the name of rapacious, which brings forth both bad reputation and hatred.

ON CRUELTY AND PITY, AND WHETHER IT IS BETTER TO BE LOVED OR TO BE FEARED, AND VICE VERSA

Coming then to the other qualities already mentioned, I say that every prince should wish to be thought compassionate and not cruel; still, he should be careful not to make a bad use of the pity he feels. Cesare Borgia[7] was considered cruel, yet this cruelty of his pacified the Romagna, united it, and changed its condition to that of peace and loyalty. If the matter is well considered, it will be seen that Cesare was much more compassionate than the people of Florence, for in order to escape the name of cruel they allowed Pistoia to be destroyed.[8] Hence a prince ought not to be troubled by the stigma of cruelty, acquired in keeping his subjects united and faithful. By giving a very few examples of cruelty he can be more truly compassionate than those who through too much compassion allow disturbances to continue, from which arise murders or acts of plunder. Lawless acts are injurious to a large group, but the executions ordered by the prince injure a single person. The new prince, above all other princes, cannot possibly avoid the name of cruel, because new states are full of perils. Dido in Vergil puts it thus: "Hard circumstances and the newness of my realm force me to do such things, and to keep watch and ward over all my lands."[9]

All the same, he should be slow in believing and acting, and should make no one afraid of him; his procedure should be so tempered with prudence and humanity that too much confidence does not make him incautious, and too much suspicion does not make him unbearable.

All this gives rise to a question for debate: Is it better to be loved than to be feared, or the reverse? I answer that a prince should wish for both. But because it is difficult to reconcile them, I hold that it is much more secure to be feared than to be loved, if one of them must be given up. The reason for my answer is that one must say of men generally that they are ungrateful, mutable, pretenders and dissemblers, prone to avoid danger, thirsty for gain. So long as you benefit them they are all yours; as I said above, they offer you their blood, their property, their lives, their children, when

7. Son of Pope Alexander VI, and duke of Valentinois and Romagna. His skillful and merciless subjugation of the local lords of Romagna occurred during the years between 1499 and 1502.   8. By internal dissensions because the Florentines, Machiavelli contends, failed to treat the leaders of the dissenting parties with an iron hand.   9. *Aeneid* I. 563–564.

the need for such things is remote. But when need comes upon you, they turn around. So if a prince has relied wholly on their words, and is lacking in other preparations, he falls. For friendships that are gained with money, and not with greatness and nobility of spirit, are deserved but not possessed, and in the nick of time one cannot avail himself of them. Men hesitate less to injure a man who makes himself loved than to injure one who makes himself feared, for their love is held by a chain of obligation, which, because of men's wickedness, is broken on every occasion for the sake of selfish profit; but their fear is secured by a dread of punishment which never fails you.

Nevertheless the prince should make himself feared in such a way that, if he does not win love, he escapes hatred. This is possible, for to be feared and not to be hated can easily coexist. In fact it is always possible, if the ruler abstains from the property of his citizens and subjects, and from their women. And if, as sometimes happens, he finds that he must inflict the penalty of death, he should do it when he has proper justification and evident reason. But above all he must refrain from taking property, for men forget the death of a father more quickly than the loss of their patrimony. Further, causes for taking property are never lacking, and he who begins to live on plunder is always finding cause to seize what belongs to others. But on the contrary, reasons for taking life are rare and fail sooner.

But when a prince is with his army and has a great number of soldiers under his command, then above all he must pay no heed to being called cruel, because if he does not have that name he cannot keep his army united or ready for duty. It should be numbered among the wonderful feats of Hannibal that he led to war in foreign lands a large army, made up of countless types of men, yet never suffered from dissension, either among the soldiers or against the general, in either bad or good fortune. His success resulted from nothing else than his inhuman cruelty, which, when added to his numerous other strong qualities, made him respected and terrible in the sight of his soldiers. Yet without his cruelty his other qualities would not have been adequate. So it seems that those writers have not thought very deeply who on one side admire his accomplishment and on the other condemn the chief cause for it.

The truth that his other qualities alone would not have been adequate may be learned from Scipio,[1] a man of the most unusual powers not only in his own times but in all ages we know of. When he was in Spain his armies mutinied. This resulted from nothing other than his compassion, which had allowed his soldiers more license than befits military discipline. This fault was censured before the Senate by Fabius Maximus, and Scipio was called by him the corrupter of the Roman soldiery. The Locrians[2] were destroyed by a lieutenant of Scipio's, yet he did not avenge them or punish the disobedience of that lieutenant. This all came from his easy nature, which was so well understood that one who wished to excuse him in the Senate said there were many men who knew better how not to err

1. Publius Cornelius Scipio Africanus the Elder (235–183 B.C.). The episode of the mutiny occurred in 206 B.C.   2. Citizens of Locri, in Sicily.

than how to punish errors. This easy nature would in time have over-thrown the fame and glory of Scipio if, in spite of this weakness, he had kept on in independent command. But since he was under the orders of the Senate, this bad quality was not merely concealed but was a glory to him.

Returning, then, to the debate on being loved and feared, I conclude that since men love as they please and fear as the prince pleases, a wise prince will evidently rely on what is in his own power and not on what is in the power of another. As I have said, he need only take pains to avoid hatred.

IN WHAT WAY FAITH SHOULD BE KEPT BY PRINCES

Everybody knows how laudable it is in a prince to keep his faith and to be an honest man and not a trickster. Nevertheless, the experience of our times shows that the princes who have done great things are the ones who have taken little account of their promises and who have known how to addle the brains of men with craft. In the end they have conquered those who have put their reliance on good faith.

You must realize, then, that there are two ways to fight. In one kind the laws are used, in the other, force. The first is suitable to man, the second to animals. But because the first often falls short, one has to turn to the second. Hence a prince must know perfectly how to act like a beast and like a man. This truth was covertly taught to princes by ancient authors, who write that Achilles and many other ancient princes were turned over for their up-bringing to Chiron the centaur,[3] that he might keep them under his tuition. To have as teacher one who is half beast and half man means nothing else than that a prince needs to know how to use the qual-ities of both creatures. The one without the other will not last long.

Since, then, it is necessary for a prince to understand how to make good use of the conduct of the animals, he should select among them the fox and the lion, because the lion cannot protect himself from traps, and the fox cannot protect himself from the wolves. So the prince needs to be a fox that he may know how to deal with traps, and a lion that he may frighten the wolves. Those who act like the lion alone do not understand their business. A prudent ruler, therefore, cannot and should not observe faith when such observance is to his disadvantage and the causes that made him give his promise have vanished. If men were all good, this advice would not be good, but since men are wicked and do not keep their prom-ises to you, you likewise do not have to keep yours to them. Lawful reasons to excuse his failure to keep them will never be lacking to a prince. It would be possible to give innumerable modern examples of this and to show many treaties and promises that have been made null and void by the faithlessness of princes. And the prince who has best known how to act as a fox has come out best. But one who has this capacity must understand

---

3. Reputed in myth to be the educator of many heroes, among them Achilles, Theseus, Jason, and Hercules.

how to keep it covered, and be a skilful pretender and dissembler. Men are so simple and so subject to present needs that he who deceives in this way will always find those who will let themselves be deceived.

I do not wish to keep still about one of the recent instances. Alexander VI[4] did nothing else than deceive men, and had no other intention; yet he always found a subject to work on. There never was a man more effective in swearing that things were true, and the greater the oaths with which he made a promise, the less he observed it. Nonetheless his deceptions always succeeded to his wish, because he thoroughly understood this aspect of the world.

It is not necessary, then, for a prince really to have all the virtues mentioned above, but it is very necessary to seem to have them. I will even venture to say that they damage a prince who possesses them and always observes them, but if he seems to have them they are useful. I mean that he should seem compassionate, trustworthy, humane, honest, and religious, and actually be so; but yet he should have his mind so trained that, when it is necessary not to practice these virtues, he can change to the opposite, and do it skilfully. It is to be understood that a prince, especially a new prince, cannot observe all the things because of which men are considered good, because he is often obliged, if he wishes to maintain his government, to act contrary to faith, contrary to charity, contrary to humanity, contrary to religion. It is therefore necessary that he have a mind capable of turning in whatever direction the winds of Fortune and the variations of affairs require, and, as I said above, that he should not depart from what is morally right, if he can observe it, but should know how to adopt what is bad, when he is obliged to.

A prince, then, should be very careful that there does not issue from his mouth anything that is not full of the above-mentioned five qualities. To those who see and hear him he should seem all compassion, all faith, all honesty, all humanity, all religion. There is nothing more necessary to make a show of possessing than this last quality. For men in general judge more by their eyes than by their hands; everybody is fitted to see, few to understand. Everybody sees what you appear to be; few make out what you really are. And these few do not dare to oppose the opinion of the many, who have the majesty of the state to confirm their view. In the actions of all men, and especially those of princes, where there is no court to which to appeal, people think of the outcome. A prince needs only to conquer and to maintain his position. The means he has used will always be judged honorable and will be praised by everybody, because the crowd is always caught by appearance and by the outcome of events, and the crowd is all there is in the world; there is no place for the few when the many have room enough. A certain prince of the present day,[5] whom it is not good to name, preaches nothing else than peace and faith, and is wholly opposed

---

4. Rodrigo Borgia, father of Cesare Borgia; he was pope from 1492 to 1503.   5. Ferdinand II, "the Catholic," king of Spain. In refraining from mentioning him, Machiavelli apparently had in mind the good relations existing between Spain and the house of Medici.

to both of them, and both of them, if he had observed them, would many times have taken from him either his reputation or his throne.

["*Fortune Is a Woman*"][6]

THE POWER OF FORTUNE IN HUMAN AFFAIRS, AND TO WHAT EXTENT SHE SHOULD BE RELIED ON

It is not unknown to me that many have been and still are of the opinion that the affairs of this world are so under the direction of Fortune and of God that man's prudence cannot control them; in fact, that man has no resource against them. For this reason many think there is no use in sweating much over such matters, but that one might as well let Chance take control. This opinion has been the more accepted in our times, because of the great changes in the state of the world that have been and now are seen every day, beyond all human surmise. And I myself, when thinking on these things, have now and then in some measure inclined to their view. Nevertheless, because the freedom of the will should not be wholly annulled, I think it may be true that Fortune is arbiter of half of our actions, but that she still leaves the control of the other half, or about that, to us.

I liken her to one of those raging streams that, when they go mad, flood the plains, ruin the trees and the buildings, and take away the fields from one bank and put them down on the other. Everybody flees before them; everybody yields to their onrush without being able to resist anywhere. And though this is their nature, it does not cease to be true that, in calm weather, men can make some provisions against them with walls and dykes, so that, when the streams swell, their waters will go off through a canal, or their currents will not be so wild and do so much damage. The same is true of Fortune. She shows her power where there is no wise preparation for resisting her, and turns her fury where she knows that no walls and dykes have been made to hold her in. And if you consider Italy—the place where these variations occur and the cause that has set them in motion—you will see that she is a country without dykes and without any wall of defence. If, like Germany, Spain, and France, she had had a sufficient bulwark of military vigor, this flood would not have made the great changes it has, or would not have come at all.

And this, I think, is all I need to say on opposing oneself to Fortune, in general. But limiting myself more to particulars, I say that a prince may be seen prospering today and falling in ruin tomorrow, though it does not appear that he has changed in his nature or any of his qualities. I believe this comes, in the first place, from the causes that have been discussed at length in preceding chapters. That is, if a prince bases himself entirely on Fortune, he will fall when she varies. I also believe that a ruler will be successful who adapts his mode of procedure to the quality of the times,

6. Chapter 25.

and likewise that he will be unsuccessful if the times are out of accord with his procedure. Because it may be seen that in things leading to the end each has before him, namely glory and riches, men proceed differently. One acts with caution, another rashly; one with violence, another with skill; one with patience, another with its opposite; yet with these different methods each one attains his end. Still further, two cautious men will be seen, of whom one comes to his goal, the other does not. Likewise you will see two who succeed with two different methods, one of them being cautious and the other rash. These results are caused by nothing else than the nature of the times, which is or is not in harmony with the procedure of men. It also accounts for what I have mentioned, namely, that two persons, working differently, chance to arrive at the same result; and that of two who work in the same way, one attains his end, but the other does not.

On the nature of the times also depends the variability of the best method. If a man conducts himself with caution and patience, times and affairs may come around in such a way that his procedure is good, and he goes on successfully. But if times and circumstances change, he is ruined, because he does not change his method of action. There is no man so prudent as to understand how to fit himself to this condition, either because he is unable to deviate from the course to which nature inclines him, or because, having always prospered by walking in one path, he cannot persuade himself to leave it. So the cautious man, when the time comes to go at a reckless pace, does not know how to do it. Hence he comes to ruin. Yet if he could change his nature with the times and with circumstances, his fortune would not be altered.

Pope Julius II proceeded rashly in all his actions, and found the times and circumstances so harmonious with his mode of procedure that he was always so lucky as to succeed. Consider the first enterprise he engaged in, that of Bologna, while messer Giovanni Bentivogli[7] was still alive. The Venetians were not pleased with it; the King of Spain felt the same way; the Pope was debating such an enterprise with the King of France. Nevertheless, in his courage and rashness Julius personally undertook that expedition. This movement made the King of Spain and the Venetians stand irresolute and motionless, the latter for fear, and the King because of his wish to recover the entire kingdom of Naples. On the other side, the King of France was dragged behind Julius, because the King, seeing that the Pope had moved and wishing to make him a friend in order to put down the Venetians, judged he could not refuse him soldiers without doing him open injury. Julius, then, with his rash movement, attained what no other pontiff, with the utmost human prudence, would have attained. If he had waited to leave Rome until the agreements were fixed and everything arranged, as any other pontiff would have done, he would never have succeeded, for the King of France would have had a thousand excuses, and the others would have raised a thousand fears. I wish to omit his other

7. Of the ruling family Bentivogli (the prefix *Messer* means "my lord"); the Pope undertook to dislodge him from Bologna, in 1506.

acts, which are all of the same sort, and all succeeded perfectly. The brevity of his life did not allow him to know anything different. Yet if times had come in which it was necessary to act with caution, they would have ruined him, for he would never have deviated from the methods to which nature inclined him.

I conclude, then, that since Fortune is variable and men are set in their ways, they are successful when they are in harmony with Fortune and unsuccessful when they disagree with her. Yet I am of the opinion that it is better to be rash than over-cautious, because Fortune is a woman and, if you wish to keep her down, you must beat her and pound her. It is evident that she allows herself to be overcome by men who treat her in that way rather than by those who proceed coldly. For that reason, like a woman, she is always the friend of young men, because they are less cautious, and more courageous, and command her with more boldness.

[The Roman Dream][8]

AN EXHORTATION TO TAKE HOLD OF ITALY AND RESTORE HER TO LIBERTY FROM THE BARBARIANS

Having considered all the things discussed above, I have been turning over in my own mind whether at present in Italy the time is ripe for a new prince to win prestige, and whether conditions there give a wise and vigorous ruler occasion to introduce methods that will do him honor, and bring good to the mass of the people of the land. It appears to me that so many things unite for the advantage of a new prince, that I do not know of any time that has ever been more suited for this. And, as I said, if it was necessary to make clear the ability of Moses that the people of Israel should be enslaved in Egypt, and to reveal Cyrus's greatness of mind that the Persians should be oppressed by the Medes, and to demonstrate the excellence of Theseus that the Athenians should be scattered, so at the present time, in order to make known the greatness of an Italian soul, Italy had to be brought down to her present position, to be more a slave than the Hebrews, more a servant than the Persians, more scattered than the Athenians; without head, without government; defeated, plundered, torn asunder, overrun; subject to every sort of disaster.

And though before this, certain persons[9] have showed signs from which it could be inferred that they were chosen by God for the redemption of Italy, nevertheless it has afterwards been seen that in the full current of action they have been cast off by Fortune. So Italy remains without life and awaits the man, whoever he may be, who is to heal her wounds, put an end to the plundering of Lombardy and the tribute laid on Tuscany and the kingdom of Naples, and cure her of those sores that have long been suppurating. She may be seen praying God to send some one to redeem her from these cruel and barbarous insults. She is evidently ready

8. Chapter 26.   9. Possibly Cesare Borgia and Francesco Sforza, discussed in an earlier chapter of the book.

and willing to follow a banner, if only some one will raise it. Nor is there at present anyone to be seen in whom she can put more hope than in your illustrious House,[1] because its fortune and vigor, and the favor of God and of the Church, which it now governs,[2] enable it to be the leader in such a redemption. This will not be very difficult, as you will see if you will bring to mind the actions and lives of those I have named above. And though these men were striking exceptions, yet they were men, and each of them had less opportunity than the present gives; their enterprises were not more just than this, nor easier, nor was God their friend more than he is yours. Here justice is complete. "A way is just to those to whom it is necessary, and arms are holy to him who has no hope save in arms."[3] Everything is now fully disposed for the work, and when that is true an undertaking cannot be difficult, if only your House adopts the methods of those I have set forth as examples. Moreover, we have before our eyes extraordinary and unexampled means prepared by God. The sea has been divided. A cloud has guided you on your way. The rock has given forth water. Manna has fallen.[4] Everything has united to make you great. The rest is for you to do. God does not intend to do everything, lest he deprive us of our free will and the share of glory that belongs to us.

It is no wonder if no one of the above-named Italians[5] has been able to do what we hope your illustrious House can. Nor is it strange if in the many revolutions and military enterprises of Italy, the martial vigor of the land always appears to be exhausted. This is because the old military customs were not good, and there has been nobody able to find new ones. Yet nothing brings so much honor to a man who rises to new power, as the new laws and new methods he discovers. These things, when they are well founded and have greatness in them, make him revered and worthy of admiration. And in Italy matter is not lacking on which to impress forms of every sort. There is great vigor in the limbs if only it is not lacking in the heads. You may see that in duels and combats between small numbers, the Italians have been much superior in force, skill, and intelligence. But when it is a matter of armies, Italians cannot be compared with foreigners. All this comes from the weakness of the heads, because those who know are not obeyed, and each man thinks he knows. Nor up to this time has there been a man able to raise himself so high, through both ability and fortune, that the others would yield to him. The result is that for the past twenty years, in all the wars that have been fought when there has been an army entirely Italian, it has always made a bad showing. Proof of this was given first at the Taro, and then at Alessandria, Capua, Genoa, Vailà, Bologna, and Mestri.[6]

If your illustrious House, then, wishes to imitate those excellent men who redeemed their countries, it is necessary, before everything else, to

1. The house of Medici. *The Prince* was first meant for Giuliano de' Medici; after Giuliano's death it was dedicated to his nephew, Lorenzo, later duke of Urbino.   2. Pope Leo X was a Medici (Giovanni de' Medici).   3. Livy, *History*, Book IX, Chapter 1, paragraph 10.   4. See the allusion to Moses in the preceding paragraph.   5. Possibly a further allusion to Cesare Borgia and Francesco Sforza.   6. Sites of battles occurring between the end of the fifteenth century and the year 1513.

furnish yourself with your own army, as the true foundation of every enterprise. You cannot have more faithful, nor truer, nor better soldiers. And though every individual of these may be good, they become better as a body when they see that they are commanded by their prince, and honored and trusted by him. It is necessary, therefore, that your House should be prepared with such forces, in order that it may be able to defend itself against the foreigners with Italian courage.

And though the Swiss and the Spanish infantry are properly estimated as terribly effective, yet both have defects. Hence a third type would be able not merely to oppose them but to feel sure of overcoming them. The fact is that the Spaniards are not able to resist cavalry, and the Swiss have reason to fear infantry, when they meet any as determined in battle as themselves. For this reason it has been seen and will be seen in experience that the Spaniards are unable to resist the French cavalry, and the Swiss are overthrown by Spanish infantry. And though of this last a clear instance has not been observed, yet an approach to it appeared in the battle of Ravenna,[7] when the Spanish infantry met the German battalions, who use the same methods as the Swiss. There the Spanish, through their ability and the assistance given by their shields, got within the points of the spears from below, and slew their enemies in security, while the Germans could find no means of resistance. If the cavalry had not charged the Spanish, they would have annihilated the Germans. It is possible, then, for one who realizes the defects of these two types, to equip infantry in a new manner, so that it can resist cavalry and not be afraid of foot-soldiers; but to gain this end they must have weapons of the right sorts, and adopt varied methods of combat. These are some of the things which, when they are put into service as novelties, give reputation and greatness to a new ruler.[8]

This opportunity, then, should not be allowed to pass, in order that after so long a time Italy may see her redeemer. I am unable to express with what love he would be received in all the provinces that have suffered from these foreign deluges; with what thirst for vengeance, what firm faith, what piety, what tears! What gates would be shut against him? what peoples would deny him obedience? what envy would oppose itself to him? what Italian would refuse to follow him? This barbarian rule stinks in every nostril. May your illustrious House, then, undertake this charge with the spirit and the hope with which all just enterprises are taken up, in order that, beneath its ensign, our native land may be ennobled, and, under its auspices, that saying of Petrarch may come true: "Manhood[9] will take arms against fury, and the combat will be short, because in Italian hearts the ancient valor is not yet dead."

---

7. Between Spaniards and French in April 1512.   8. Machiavelli was subsequently the author of a treatise on the *Art of War* (1521).   9. An etymological translation of the original *virtù* (from the Latin *vir*, "man"). The quotation is from Petrarch's *canzone* "My Italy."

BALDESAR CASTIGLIONE

1487–1529

Castiglione was born in 1487 at Casatico, near Mantua. His father, Cristoforo, was a courtier, and his mother was a Gonzaga, related to the lords of Mantua. In Milan Castiglione received a humanistic education and prepared himself for the career of a courtier. As such, from 1499 to 1503 he was in the service of Francesco Gonzaga, lord of Mantua, and from 1504 to 1513 he was at Urbino in the service of Guido-baldo da Montefeltro, duke of Urbino, and later of Guidobaldo's successor, Francesco Maria della Rovere, commander of the Pope's army, whom he followed on military campaigns. In 1506 he went to England on a mission to the court of Henry VII, from whom he received, on behalf of his lord, the Order of the Garter and to whom he presented a painting by Raphael. In 1511 he took part in the siege of Mirandola under Pope Julius II (Giuliano della Rovere). As a reward for his services, he was made a count. In 1515 he was again with the Gonzagas, who made him their ambassador to Pope Leo X (Giovanni de' Medici). In Rome, his friends included Raphael and Michelangelo, and he saw Renaissance social and intellectual life at its most brilliant. He thus not only codified the ideal of the refined and "virtuous" courtier in his works, but also embodied it in his life. In 1525 Clement VII made him Papal nuncio to the court of Emperor Charles V in Spain. His premature death in Toledo in 1529 was probably caused in part by sorrow at his failure to foresee the emperor's designs as they most dramatically took shape in the storming and plundering of Rome in 1527 (the "Sack of Rome"). *The Book of the Courtier*, in which the court of Urbino is idealized, was written between 1508 and 1516 and published in 1528 in Venice.

Even from these brief data, it appears very likely that as Castiglione advanced in experience of the world, his treatise on the ideal courtly gentleman acquired a nostalgic character. Indeed, in reading selections from *The Book of the Courtier*, it is helpful to consider the description with which the book opens as a "setting," because this approach serves to suggest the theatrical atmosphere that pervades the work. We should not, however, forget that the characters whose highly mannered conversation the book records were all actual members (presented with their own names) of a courtly milieu of which Castiglione himself had been a part. These people, then, were known to him not as objects of adulation or satire (the two extremes with which we are perhaps accustomed to associate literary portrayals of the aristocracy), but rather as equals and companions whose standards were his own. Hence Castiglione's attitude contains neither flattery nor mockery; the theatrical way in which the scene is set and the characters talk (the traditional form of the Platonic dialogue acquires here the tone of what in the Renaissance was called "civil conversation") is simply the expression of a style, "artificial" in no derogatory sense, that both the characters and the author considered ideally appropriate to people of their kind and station. The speakers appear somewhat like ladies and gentlemen who have kindly consented, on some courtly occasion, to take roles in a play, except that it happens that the play is their own; they enact, so to speak, themselves. The strong element of stylization (the elaborate phrasings, the manner of repartee) is not forced by the writer on his material; we feel rather that in his formalizing process he has merely emphasized qualities inherent in the world he portrays. In this sense the book is an ideal vision of Renaissance court society at its most refined and self-conscious; of a society that had a penchant, as was observed

in the general introduction (pp. 1663–64), for the well-finished gesture, the formally perfect act of its kind—a penchant that was applied to all modes and norms
of activity, conversation or dueling, art, courtship, etiquette.

Our selections are from the first of the four books (or evening conversations) into
which the *Courtier* is divided. The purpose of this first book is to arrive, through
the contributions of the obviously experienced speakers, at a description of the
perfect courtly gentleman. Although Machiavelli, in his description of the prince,
also presents something of an idealization of a type, his explicit intention is to come
down to reality and practical motives, in contrast to the abstractions of preceding
authors. Castiglione's attitude is different from the start. He has what we may call
a Platonic turn of mind, in the sense that he intentionally and openly seeks the
ideal and permanent form behind the transient and fragmentary examples. This
point of view in the *Courtier* suggests, among other things, the sense of rule, of
adjustment to correct norms; Castiglione's optimistic assumption is that such norms
exist and can be defined, and that we can educate ourselves to comply with them.
There is even, as the famous passage on "nonchalance" (*sprezzatura*) at the end of
our second selection suggests, a sort of formalization of informality.

Considered against the background of the period, *The Book of the Courtier* per-
sents a healthy corrective to those views of the Renaissance court, especially pop-
ularized by drama, in which that institution is the typical scene of intrigue, corruption,
and violence. Castiglione codifies a moment of perfection and gentle equilibrium.

Julia Cartwright Ady's illustrated biography, *Baldassare Castiglione, the Perfect
Courtier. His Life and Letters*, 2 vols. (1908), is old-fashioned but thorough. Rob-
ert W. Hanning and David Rosand, eds., *Castiglione: The Ideal and the Real in
Renaissance Culture* (1983), offers several views of Castiglione. An essay on *The
Courtier* is found in Joseph Anthony Mazzeo, *Renaissance and Revolution: The
Remaking of European Thought* (1965).

The Book of the Courtier[1]

[The Setting][2]

On the slopes of the Apennines towards the Adriatic sea, almost in the
centre of Italy, there lies (as everyone knows) the little city of Urbino.
Although amid mountains, and less pleasing ones than perhaps some others that we see in many places, it has yet enjoyed such favour of heaven
that the country round about is very fertile and rich in crops; so that besides
the wholesomeness of the air, there is great abundance of everything needful for human life. But among the greatest blessings that can be attributed
to it, this I believe to be the chief, that for a long time it has ever been
ruled by the best of lords; although in the calamities of the universal wars
of Italy, it was for a season deprived of them.[3] But without seeking further,
we can give good proof of this by the the glorious memory of Duke Federico,[4]
who in his day was the light of Italy; nor is there lack of credible and
abundant witnesses, who are still living, to his prudence, humanity, justice, liberality, unconquered courage,—and to his military discipline, which

1. Translated by Leonard E. Opdycke.   2. Book I, Chapters 2–4.   3. For a certain period of time,
when Duke Guidobaldo, described below, had to relinquish the duchy of Urbino to Cesare Borgia, who
occupied it by force.   4. Federico II (1422–1482), of the house of Montefeltro, duke of Urbino.

is conspicuously attested by his numerous victories, his capture of impregnable places, the sudden swiftness of his expeditions, the frequency with which he put to flight large and formidable armies by means of a very small force, and by his loss of no single battle whatever; so that we may not unreasonably compare him to many famous men of old.

Among his other praiseworthy deeds, he built on the rugged site of Urbino a palace regarded by many as the most beautiful to be found in all Italy; and he so well furnished it with everything suitable that it seemed not a palace but a city in the form of a palace; and not merely with what is ordinarily used,—such as silver vases, hangings of richest cloth-of-gold and silk, and other similar things,—but for ornament he added countless antique statutes in marble and bronze, pictures most choice, and musical instruments of every sort, nor would he admit anything there that was not very rare and excellent. Then at very great cost he collected a goodly number of most excellent and rare books in Greek, Latin and Hebrew, all of which he adorned with gold and with silver, esteeming this to be the chiefest excellence of his great palace.

Following then the course of nature, and already sixty-five years old,[5] he died gloriously, as he had lived; and he left as his successor a motherless little boy of ten years, his only son Guidobaldo. Heir to the State, he seemed to be heir also to all his father's virtues, and soon his noble nature gave such promise as seemed not permissible to hope for from mortal man; so that men esteemed none among the notable deeds of Duke Federico to be greater than to have begotten such a son. But envious of so much virtue, fortune thwarted his glorious beginning with all her power; so that before Duke Guido reached the age of twenty years, he fell ill of the gout, which grew upon him with previous pain, and in a short space of time so crippled all his members that he could neither stand upon his feet nor move; and thus one of the fairest and most promising forms in the world was distorted and spoiled in tender youth.

And not content even with this, fortune was so contrary to him in all his purposes, that he could seldom carry into effect anything that he desired; and although he was very wise to counsel and unconquered in spirit, it seemed that what he undertook, both in war and in everything else whether small or great, always ended ill for him. And proof of this is found in his many and diverse calamities, which he ever bore with such strength of mind, that his spirit was never vanquished by fortune; nay, scorning her assaults with unbroken courage, he lived in illness as if in health and in adversity as if fortunate, with perfect dignity and universal esteem; so that although he was thus infirm in body, he fought with most honourable rank[6] in the service of their Serene Highnesses the Kings of Naples, Alfonso and Ferdinand the Younger;[7] later with Pope Alexander VI,[8] and with the Venetian and Florentine signories.

---

5. Actually only sixty.   6. As a mercenary captain or *condottiere*.   7. Alfonso II and Ferdinand II (both of the house of Aragon), kings of Naples in the late fifteenth century.   8. Rodrigo Borgia, pope from 1492 to 1503.

Upon the accession of Julius II[9] to the pontificate, he was made Captain of the Church;[1] at which time, following his accustomed habit, above all else he took care to fill his household with very noble and valiant gentlemen, with whom he lived most familiarly, delighting in their intercourse: wherein the pleasure he gave to others was not less than that he received from others, he being well versed in both the languages,[2] and uniting affability and pleasantness to a knowledge of things without number. And besides this, the greatness of his spirit so set him on, that although he could not practise in person the exercises of chivalry, as he once had done, yet he took the utmost pleasure in witnessing them in others; and by his words, now correcting now praising every man according to desert, he clearly showed his judgment in those matters; wherefore, in jousts and tournaments, in riding, in the handling of every sort of weapon, as well as in pastimes, games, music,—in short, in all the exercises proper to noble cavaliers,—everyone strove so to show himself, as to merit being deemed worthy of such noble fellowship.

Thus all the hours of the day were assigned to honourable and pleasant exercises as well for the body as for the mind; but since my lord Duke was always wont by reason of his infirmity to retire to sleep very early after supper, everyone usually betook himself at that hour to the presence of my lady Duchess, Elisabetta Gonzaga;[3] where also was ever to be found my lady Emilia Pia, who was endowed with such lively wit and judgment that, as you know, it seemed as if she were the Mistress of us all, and as if everyone gained wisdom and worth from her. Here then, gentle discussions and innocent pleasantries were heard, and on the face of everyone a jocund gaiety was seen depicted, so that the house could truly be called the very abode of mirth: nor ever elsewhere, I think, was so relished, as once was here, how great sweetness may flow from dear and cherished companionship; for not to speak of the honour it was to each of us to serve such a lord as he of whom I have just spoken, there was born in the hearts of all a supreme contentment every time we came into the presence of my lady Duchess; and it seemed as if this were a chain that held us all linked in love, so that never was concord of will or cordial love between brothers greater than that which here was between us all.

The same was it among the ladies, with whom there was intercourse most free and honourable; for everyone was permitted to talk, sit, jest and laugh with whom he pleased; but such was the reverence paid to the wish of my lady Duchess, that this same liberty was a very great check; nor was there anyone who did not esteem it the utmost pleasure he could have in the world, to please her, and the utmost pain to displease her. And thus, most decorous manners were here joined with greatest liberty, and games and laughter in her presence were seasoned not only with witty jests, but

9. In 1503.   1. Captain in the pontiff's army.   2. Greek and Latin.   3. Of the ruling family of Mantua, she had married Duke Guidobaldo in 1488. She is the one who presides over this courtly scene. *Emilia Pia*: sister-in-law and companion of the duchess, widow of an illegitimate son of the old duke, Federico, she wittily directs much of the conversation.

with gracious and sober dignity; for that modesty and loftiness which governed all the acts, words and gestures of my lady Duchess, bantering and
laughing, were such that she would have been known for a lady of noblest
rank by anyone who saw her even but once. And impressing herself thus
upon those about her, she seemed to attune us all to her own quality and
tone; accordingly every man strove to follow this pattern, taking as it were
a rule of beautiful behaviour from the presence of so great and virtuous a
lady; whose highest qualities I do not now purpose to recount, they not
being my theme and being well known to all the world, and far more
because I could not express them with either tongue or pen; and those that
perhaps might have been somewhat hid, fortune, as if wondering at such
rare virtue, chose to reveal through many adversities and stings of calamity,
so as to give proof that in the tender breast of woman, in company with
singular beauty, there may abide prudence and strength of soul, and all
those virtues that even among stern men are very rare.

["Everything He May Do or Say Shall Be Stamped with Grace"][4]

"I am of opinion[5] that the principal and true profession of the Courtier
ought to be that of arms; which I would have him follow actively above all
else, and be known among others as bold and strong, and loyal to whomsoever he serves. And he will win a reputation for these good qualities by
exercising them at all times and in all places, since one may never fail in
this without severest censure. And just as among women, their fair fame
once sullied never recovers its first lustre, so that reputation of a gentleman
who bears arms, if once it be in the least tarnished with cowardice or other
disgrace, remains forever infamous before the world and full of ignominy.
Therefore the more our Courtier excels in this art, the more he will be
worthy of praise; and yet I do not deem essential in him that perfect knowledge of things and those other qualities that befit a commander; since this
would be too wide a sea, let us be content, as we have said, with perfect
loyalty and unconquered courage, and that he be always seen to possess
them. For the courageous are often recognized even more in small things
than in great; and frequently in perils of importance and where there are
many spectators, some men are to be found, who, although their hearts be
dead within them, yet, moved by shame or by the presence of others, press
forward almost with their eyes shut, and do their duty God knows how.
While on occasions of little moment, when they think they can avoid
putting themselves in danger without being detected, they are glad to keep
safe. But those who, even when they do not expect to be observed or seen
or recognized by anyone, show their ardour and neglect nothing, however
paltry, that may be laid to their charge,—they have that strength of mind
which we seek in our Courtier.

4. From Book I, Chapters 17–26.   5. The conversational "game" through which the courtiers at Urbino
are attempting to achieve a description of the perfect courtly gentleman is in progress. The speaker at this
point is Count Ludovico da Canossa (1476–1532). A relative of the writer and a friend of the painter
Raphael, he was later a bishop and held many important offices, such as that of papal ambassador to
England.

"Not that we would have him look so fierce, or go about blustering, or say that he has taken his cuirass to wife, or threaten with those grim scowls that we have often seen in Berto[6]; because to such men as this, one might justly say that which a brave lady jestingly said in gentle company to one whom I will not name at present; who, being invited by her out of compliment to dance, refused not only that, but to listen to the music, and many other entertainments proposed to him,—saying always that such silly trifles were not his business; so that at last the lady said, 'What is your business, then?' He replied with a sour look, 'To fight.' Then the lady at once said, 'Now that you are in no war and out of fighting trim, I should think it were a good thing to have yourself well oiled, and to stow yourself with all your battle harness in a closet until you be needed, lest you grow more rusty than you are'; and so, amid much laughter from the bystanders, she left the discomfited fellow to his silly presumption.

"Therefore let the man we are seeking, be very bold, stern, and always among the first, where the enemy are to be seen; and in every other place, gentle, modest, reserved, above all things avoiding ostentation and that impudent self-praise by which men ever excite hatred and disgust in all who hear them."

Then my lord Gaspar[7] replied:

"As for me, I have known few men excellent in anything whatever, who do not praise themselves; and it seems to me that this may well be permitted them; for when anyone who feels himself to be of worth, sees that he is not known to the ignorant by his works, he is offended that his worth should lie buried, and needs must in some way hold it up to view, in order that he may not be cheated of the fame that is the true reward of worthy effort. Thus among the ancient authors, whoever carries weight seldom fails to praise himself. They indeed are insufferable who do this without desert, but such we do not presume our Courtier to be."

The Count then said:

"If you heard what I said, it was impudent and indiscriminate self-praise that I censured: and as you say, we surely ought not to form a bad opinion of a brave man who praises himself modestly, nay we ought rather to regard such praise as better evidence than if it came from the mouth of others. I say, however, that he, who in praising himself runs into no error and incurs no annoyance or envy at the hands of those that heard him, is a very discreet man indeed and merits praise from others in addition to that which he bestows upon himself; because it is a very difficult matter."

Then my lord Gaspar said:

"You must teach us that."

The Count replied:

"Among the ancient authors there is no lack of those who have taught it; but to my thinking, the whole art consists in saying things in such a way that they shall not seem to be said to that end, but let fall so naturally that it was impossible not to say them, and while seeming always to avoid self-

---

6. An otherwise unidentified character.   7. Count Gaspar Pallavicino (1486–1511), a very young member of the court, who died only a few years afterward.

praise, yet to achieve it; but not after the manner of those boasters, who open their mouths and let the words come forth haphazard. Like one of our friends a few days ago, who, being quite run through the thigh with a spear at Pisa, said he thought it was a fly that had stung him; and another man said he kept no mirror in his room because, when angry, he became so terrible to look at, that the sight of himself would have frightened him too much."

Everyone laughed at this, but Messer Cesare Gonzaga[8] added:

"Why do you laugh? Do you not know that Alexander the Great, on hearing the opinion of a philosopher to be that there was an infinite number of worlds, began to weep, and being asked why he wept, replied, 'Because I have not yet conquered one of them'; as if he would fain have vanquished all? Does not this seem to you a greater boast than that about the fly-sting?"

Then the Count said:

"Yes, and Alexander was a greater man than he who made the other speech. But extraordinary men are surely to be pardoned when they assume much; for he who has great things to do must needs have daring to do them, and confidence in himself, and must not be abject or mean in spirit, yet very modest in speech, showing less confidence in himself than he has, lest his self-confidence lead to rashness."

The Count now paused a little, and messer Bernardo Bibbiena[9] said, laughing:

"I remember what you said earlier, that this Courtier of ours must be endowed by nature with beauty of countenance and person, and with a grace that shall make him so agreeable. Grace and beauty of countenance I think I certainly possess, and this is the reason why so many ladies are ardently in love with me, as you know; but I am rather doubtful as to the beauty of my person, especially as regards these legs of mine, which seem to me decidedly less well proportioned than I should wish: as to my bust and other members, however, I am quite content. Pray, now, describe a little more in particular the sort of body that the Courtier is to have, so that I may dismiss this doubt and set my mind at rest."

After some laughter at this, the Count continued:

"Of a certainty that grace of countenance can be truly said to be yours, nor need I cite further example than this to show what manner of thing it is, for we unquestionably perceive your aspect to be most agreeable and pleasing to everyone, albeit the lineaments of it are not very delicate. Still it is of a manly cast and at the same time full of grace; and this characteristic is to be found in many different types of countenance. And of such sort I would have our Courtier's aspect; not so soft and effeminate as is sought by many, who not only curl their hair and pluck their brows, but gloss their faces with all those arts employed by the most wanton and unchaste women in the world; and in their walk, posture and every act, they seem

8. Considered by some the "first gentleman" at the court of Urbino. A cousin of the writer, he was a warrior, a diplomat, and a pastoral poet; he died in 1512, at thirty-seven.   9. Bernardo Dovizi da Bibbiena (1470–1520), author of a play performed at the court of Urbino, patron and friend of the painter Raphael, and later a cardinal.

so limp and languid that their limbs are like to fall apart; and they pronounce their words so mournfully that they appear about to expire upon the spot: and the more they find themselves with men of rank, the more they affect such tricks. Since nature has not made them women, as they seem to wish to appear and be, they should be treated not as good women but as public harlots, and driven not merely from the courts of great lords but from the society of honest men.

"Then coming to the bodily frame, I say it is enough if this be neither extremely short nor tall, for both of these conditions excite a certain contemptuous surprise, and men of either sort are gazed upon in much the same way that we gaze on monsters. Yet if we must offend in one of the two extremes, it is preferable to fall a little short of the just measure of height than to exceed it, for besides often being dull of intellect, men thus huge of body are also unfit for every exercise of agility, which thing I should much wish in the Courtier. And so I would have him well built and shapely of limb, and would have him show strength and lightness and suppleness, and know all bodily exercises that befit a man of war: whereof I think the first should be to handle every sort of weapon well on foot and on horse, to understand the advantages of each, and especially to be familiar with those weapons that are ordinarily used among gentlemen; for besides the use of them in war, where such subtlety in contrivance is perhaps not needful, there frequently arise differences between one gentleman and another, which afterwards result in duels often fought with such weapons as happen at the moment to be within reach: thus knowledge of this kind is a very safe thing. Nor am I one of those who say that skill is forgotten in the hour of need; for he whose skill forsakes him at such a time, indeed gives token that he has already lost heart and head through fear.

"Moreover I deem it very important to know how to wrestle, for it is a great help in the use of all kinds of weapons on foot. Then, both for his own sake and for that of his friends, he must understand the quarrels and differences that may arise, and must be quick to seize an advantage, always showing courage and prudence in all things. Nor should he be too ready to fight except when honour demands it; for besides the great danger that the uncertainty of fate entails, he who rushes into such affairs recklessly and without urgent cause, merits the severest censure even though he be successful. But when he finds himself so far engaged that he cannot withdraw without reproach, he ought to be most deliberate, both in the preliminaries to the duel and in the duel itself, and always show readiness and daring. Nor must he act like some, who fritter the affair away in disputes and controversies, and who, having the choice of weapons, select those that neither cut nor pierce, and arm themselves as if they were expecting a cannonade; and thinking it enough not to be defeated, stand ever on the defensive and retreat,—showing therein their utter cowardice. And thus they make themselves a laughing-stock for boys, like those two men of Ancona who fought at Perugia not long since, and made everyone laugh who saw them."

"And who were they?" asked my lord Gaspar Pallavicino.

"Two cousins," replied messer Cesare.

Then the Count said:

"In their fighting they were as like as two brothers"; and soon continued: "Even in time of peace weapons are often used in various exercises, and gentlemen appear in public shows before the people and ladies and great lords. For this reason I would have our Courtier a perfect horseman in every kind of seat; and besides understanding horses and what pertains to riding, I would have him use all possible care and diligence to lift himself a little beyond the rest in everything, so that he may be ever recognized as eminent above all others. And as we read of Alcibiades that he surpassed all the nations with whom he lived, each in their particular province, so I would have this Courtier of ours excel all others, and each in that which is most their profession. And as it is the especial pride of the Italians to ride well with the rein, to govern wild horses with consummate skill, and to play at tilting and jousting,—in these things let him be among the best of the Italians. In tourneys and in the arts of defence and attack, let him shine among the best in France. In stick-throwing, bull-fighting, and in casting spears and darts, let him excel among the Spaniards. But above everything he should temper all his movements with a certain good judgment and grace, if he wishes to merit that universal favour which is so greatly prized.

"There are also many other exercises, which although not immediately dependent upon arms, yet are closely connected therewith, and greatly foster manly sturdiness; and one of the chief among these seems to me to be the chase, because it bears a certain likeness to war; and truly it is an amusement for great lords and befitting a man at court, and furthermore it is seen to have been much cultivated among the ancients. It is fitting also to know how to swim, to leap, to run, to throw stones, for besides the use that may be made of this in war, a man often has occasion to show what he can do in such matters; whence good esteem is to be won, especially with the multitude, who must be taken into account withal. Another admirable exercise, and one very befitting a man at court, is the game of tennis, in which are well shown the disposition of the body, the quickness and suppleness of every member, and all those qualities that are seen in nearly every other exercise. Nor less highly do I esteem vaulting on horse, which although it be fatiguing and difficult, makes a man very light and dexterous more than any other thing; and besides its utility, if this lightness is accompanied by grace, it is to my thinking a finer show than any of the others.

"Our Courtier having once become more than fairly expert in these exercises, I think he should leave the others on one side: such as turning summersaults, rope-walking, and the like, which savour of the mountebank and little befit a gentleman.

"But since one cannot devote himself to such fatiguing exercises continually, and since repetition becomes very tiresome and abates the admiration felt for what is rare, we must always diversify our life with various occupations. For this reason I would have our Courtier sometimes descend to quieter and more tranquil exercises, and in order to escape envy and to entertain himself agreeably with everyone, let him do whatever others do, yet never departing from praiseworthy deeds, and governing himself with that good judgment which will keep him from all folly; but let him laugh, jest, banter, frolic and dance, yet in such fashion that he shall always appear genial and discreet, and that everything he may do or say shall be stamped with grace."

Then messer Cesare Gonzaga said:

"We certainly ought on no account to hinder the course of this discussion; but if I were to keep silence, I should be neglected both of the right I have to speak and of my desire to know one thing: and let me be pardoned if I ask a question instead of contradicting; for this I think may be permitted me, after the precedent of messer Bernardo here, who in his over desire to be held comely, broke the rules of our game by asking a question instead of contradicting."[1]

Then my lady Duchess said:

"You see how one error begets many. Therefore he who transgresses and sets a bad example, like messer Bernardo, deserves to be punished not only for his own transgression but also for the others'."

Then messer Cesare replied:

"In that case, my Lady, I shall be exempt from penalty, since messer Bernardo is to be punished for his own fault as well as mine."

"Nay," said my lady Duchess, "you both ought to have double punishment: he for his own transgression and for leading you to transgress; you for your own transgression and for imitating him."

"My Lady," replied messer Cesare, "as yet I have not transgressed; so, to leave all this punishment to messer Bernardo alone, I will keep silence."

And indeed he remained silent; when my lady Emilia laughed and said:

"Say whatever you like, for under leave of my lady Duchess I pardon him that has transgressed and him that shall transgress, in so small a degree."

"I consent," continued my lady Duchess. "But take care lest perchance you fall into the mistake of thinking to gain more by being merciful than by being just; for to pardon him too easily that has transgressed is to wrong him that transgresses not. Yet I would not have my severity reproach your indulgence, and thus be the cause of our not hearing this question of messer Cesare."

And so, being given the signal by my lady Duchess and by my lady Emilia, he at once said:

"If I remember rightly, Sir Count, I think you have repeated several times this evening that the Courtier must accompany his actions, gestures, habits, in short his every movement, with grace; and this you seem to regard as an universal seasoning, without which all other properties and good qualities are of little worth. And indeed I think that in this everyone would allow himself to be persuaded easily, since from the very force of the word, it may be said that he who has grace finds grace. But since you

---

1. According to the plan agreed upon at the start, one of the company began a description of the perfect courtier, and the others made their contributions by contradicting the preceding speaker.

said that this is oftentimes the gift of nature and of heaven and, even when not thus perfect, can with care and pains be made much greater,—those men who are born so fortunate and so rich in this treasure as are some we see, seem to me in this to have little need of other master; because that benign favour of heaven almost in despite of themselves leads them higher than they will, and makes them not only pleasing but admirable to all the world. Therefore I do not discuss this, it not being in our power to acquire it of ourselves. But they who have received from nature only so much, that they are capable of becoming graceful by pains, industry and care,— I long to know by what art, by what training, by what method, they can acquire this grace, as well in bodily exercises (in which you esteem it to be so necessary) as also in everything else that they may do or say. Therefore, since by much praise of this quality you have aroused in all of us, I think, an ardent thirst to pursue it, you are further bound, by the charge that my lady Emilia laid upon you, to satisfy that thirst by teaching us how to attain it."

"I am not bound," said the Count, "to teach you how to become graceful, or anything else; but only to show you what manner of man a perfect Courtier ought to be. Nor would I in any case undertake the task of teaching you this perfection; especially having said a little while ago that the Courtier must know how to wrestle, vault, and do many other things, which I am sure you all know quite as well as if I, who have never learned them, were to teach you. For just as a good soldier knows how to tell the smith what fashion, shape and quality his armour ought to have, but cannot show how it is to be made or forged or tempered; so I perhaps may be able to tell you what manner of man a perfect Courtier ought to be, but cannot teach you what you must do to become one.

"Yet to comply with your request as far as is within my power,—although it is almost a proverb that grace is not to be learned,—I say that whoever would acquire grace in bodily exercises (assuming first that he be by nature not incapable), ought to begin early and learn the rudiments from the best masters. And how important this seemed to King Philip of Macedon, may be seen from the fact that he chose Aristotle, the famous philosopher and perhaps the greatest that has ever been in the world, to teach his son Alexander the first elements of letters. And of the men whom we know at the present day, consider how well and how gracefully my lord Galeazzo Sanseverino,[2] Grand Equerry of France, performs all bodily exercises; and this because in addition to the natural aptitude of person that he possesses, he has taken the utmost pains to study with good masters, and always to have about him men who excel and to select from each the best of what they know: for just as in wrestling, vaulting and in the use of many sorts of weapons, he has taken for his guide our friend messer Pietro Monte,[3] who (as you know) is the true and only master of every form of trained strength and ability,—so in riding, jousting and all else, he has ever had before his eyes the most proficient men that were known in those matters.

---

2. Of a famous Neapolitan family, he fought for Louis XII and Francis I of France, and died at the battle of Pavia (1525). 3. Fencing master at the court of Urbino.

"Therefore he who wishes to be a good pupil, besides performing his tasks well, must put forth every effort to resemble his master, and, if it were possible, to transform himself into his master. And when he feels that he has made some progress, it will be very profitable to observe different men of the same calling, and governing himself with that good judgment which must ever be his guide, to go about selecting now this thing from one and that thing from another. And as the bee in the green meadows is ever wont to rob the flowers among the grass, so our Courtier must steal this grace from all who seem to possess it, taking from each that part which shall most be worthy of praise; and not act like a friend of ours whom you all know, who thought he greatly resembled King Ferdinand the Younger of Aragon,[4] and made it his care to imitate the latter in nothing but a certain trick of continually raising the head and twisting one side of the mouth, which the king had contracted from some infirmity. And there are many such, who think they gain a point if only they be like a great man in some thing; and frequently they devote themselves to that which is his only fault.

"But having before now often considered whence this grace springs, laying aside those men who have it by nature, I find one universal rule concerning it, which seems to me worth more in this matter than any other in all things human that are done or said: and that is to avoid affectation to the uttermost and as it were a very sharp and dangerous rock; and, to use possibly a new word, to practise in everything a certain nonchalance[5] that shall conceal design and show that what is done and said is done without effort and almost without thought. From this I believe grace is in large measure derived, because everyone knows the difficulty of those things that are rare and well done, and therefore facility in them excites the highest admiration; while on the other hand, to strive and as the saying is to drag by the hair, is extremely ungraceful, and makes us esteem everything slightly, however great it be.

"Accordingly we may affirm that to be true art which does not appear to be art; nor to anything must we give greater care than to conceal art, for if it is discovered, it quite destroys our credit and brings us into small esteem. And I remember having once read that there were several very excellent orators of antiquity, who among their other devices strove to make everyone believe that they had no knowledge of letters; and hiding their knowledge they pretended that their orations were composed very simply and as if springing rather from nature and truth than from study and art; the which, if it had been detected, would have made men wary of being duped by it.

"Thus you see how the exhibition of art and study so intense destroys the grace in everything. Which of you is there who does not laugh when our friend messer Pierpaolo[6] dances in his peculiar way, with those capers of his,—legs stiff to the toe and head motionless, as if he were a stick, and with such intentness that he actually seems to be counting the steps? What

4. Ferdinand II, king of Naples from 1495 to 1496.   5. *Sprezzatura*, here translated as "nonchalance," is indeed Castiglione's own word, epitomizing the important concept of gentlemanly behavior discussed in this passage.   6. An otherwise unidentified character.

eye so blind as not to see in this the ungracefulness of affectation,—and in many men and women who are here present, the grace of that nonchalant ease (for in the case of bodily movements many call it thus), showing by word or laugh or gesture that they have no care and are thinking more of everything else than of that, to make the onlooker think they can hardly go amiss?"

MARGUERITE DE NAVARRE

1492–1549

In his classic history of French literature Gustave Lanson writes that Marguerite de Navarre "is in her moment the most complete expression of the French Renaissance . . . the accomplished woman, comparable to the best examples offered by Italy." The French "discovery of Italy" had occurred in the latter part of the fifteenth century, both through travel and, starting with the expedition of 1494 under King Charles VIII, through military invasions. It became the ambition of French rulers and aristocrats to transplant and make flourish on the intellectual soil of their vast kingdom the artistic, literary, and social values that had had their decisive assertion in the smaller and more sophisticated Italian city-states (Castiglione's Urbino is one major literary example). In this process, Marguerite de Navarre played a relevant part. One important element in her intellectual makeup is the preoccupation with religious and ethical issues at a time when Christianity was being vivified and made more complex by the Reformation movements and by that "Christian humanism" of which Erasmus, her senior by about twenty-five years, is the major representative.

Marguerite was born at Angoulême on April 11, 1492, the daughter of Charles of Orléans, count of Angoulême, and of Louise of Savoy. Her brother, the future King Francis I, was born two years later; the next year their father died. From her earliest years Marguerite received an exceptionally good education, being instructed in Latin, Italian, Spanish, and German; later in life she also cultivated Greek and Hebrew. Marriages in her class were at the time arrangements between ruling houses, dictated by political and social convenience; thus at seventeen Marguerite was married to Charles, duke of Alençon, a feudal lord who was culturally not her match. A turning point came in 1515 when her brother succeeded Louis XII to the French throne as Francis I; Marguerite became one of the most influential ladies at Francis's court. She gave him advice and received dignitaries and ambassadors as well as eminent men of letters. One of the most memorable facts about the court of Francis I is that some of the most famous artists of the period worked there, such as Leonardo da Vinci and Benvenuto Cellini.

Francis also inherited the military tradition of his predecessors in carrying on the Italian wars, the complicated conflicts fought on Italian soil between his kingdom and the "Holy Roman" Emperor, Charles V of Spain. The defeat of Francis I in the crucial Battle of Pavia (1525) was a double blow for Marguerite: the king her brother was taken to Madrid as a prisoner, and her husband, alleged to have borne a relevant part of the responsibility for the defeat, died upon his return to France that same year. Marguerite went to Madrid to assist her sick brother and played an important part in the negotiations with Emperor Charles V for his release, which was sanctioned by the Treaty of Madrid in 1526.

The following year Marguerite became "Queen of Navarre" by marrying Henri d'Albret, who was king of Navarre in title only, as most of that domain had been annexed by Spain in 1516, limiting the possessions of the d'Albret dynasty to the lower, French section. This region contained important castles at such places as Pau and Nérac; there Marguerite held court and received visiting intellectuals and reformist religious thinkers. Eleven years younger than Marguerite, Henri d'Albret was a dashing, flighty and intellectually rather disappointing husband (generally considered to be the prototype for the character of Hircan in the *Heptameron*). Their only daughter, Jeanne, was born in 1527 and eventually became the mother of the future King Henry IV of France.

Marguerite's involvement in her royal brother's activities continued sporadically, as when she took part in the negotiations that led to the Treaty of Cambrai (1529) and when she cooperated in diplomatic dealings and peace talks in the years 1536–1538. Marguerite's interest, however, was increasingly focused on intellectual and literary pursuits, and on religious meditation and debate. Throughout her life she was a protector of writers and thinkers accused or suspected of Protestant leanings, including Rabelais, who dedicated the third book of *Gargantua and Pantagruel* to her. Not only the Christian humanist Erasmus, but Calvin also, were among her numerous correspondents. These included, on the other hand, also Pope Paul III. Her own first published work, *The Mirror of the Sinful Soul* (1531, eventually used by the eleven-year-old princess, and later queen, Elizabeth of England for an exercise in translation) was found by the theologians of the Sorbonne to contain elements of Protestant "heresy," and its 1533 re-edition, containing an additional "Dialogue in the Form of a Night Vision" written much earlier and dealing with the theological problem of salvation, was condemned; the king had to intervene on behalf of both his sister and her chaplain.

Later it became more difficult for Francis to maintain a lenient and conciliatory stance in the rivalry between Catholics and Protestants, as that was, of course, not only a religious conflict but more relevantly and bloodily a political and military one. Protestants and their sympathizers were persecuted; not a few prominent intellectuals went into prudent exile or were burned at the stake. The position of Marguerite, who seems never to have abandoned Catholicism, is generally recognized as that of a person of high intellectual caliber with strong elements of mysticism in her piety, who envisaged reforms conducted from within the Church itself.

Typical of the last part of Marguerite's life are several periods of retreat in a convent at Tusson in the French region of Poitou; there in April of 1547 she received the news of her brother's death. The year 1547 also marks the publication of her *Marguerite de la Marguerite des Princesses* (with a play on the word *marguerite*, which in French also means "pearl"), a collection of works in different genres, including long devotional poems and theatrical pieces ranging from the sacred allegory to the farce. Both in this collection and in some of her later poems, a recurring theme is that of sorrow at her brother Francis's death, tempered and solaced by religious faith. During the following year Marguerite returned only for short periods to the French court, where her relations with the new king, Henry II, her nephew, were far from ideal. Marguerite's husband was at her side as her health failed. She died in one of their castles in Navarre, at Odos, on December 21, 1549.

In literary history Marguerite's name is preeminently associated with the *Hep-*

tameron, a work consisting of short stories within a "frame," the genre that had had its major example in Boccaccio's *Decameron*. Ten (Greek *deka*) days of story-telling were planned for Marguerite's work as well, but we actually have only seven, (*hepta* in Greek), as the work remained unfinished. Opinions on the attribution of the stories to a single author, Marguerite herself, vary considerably; the question is made practically insoluble by differences existing among early collections, both in manuscript and in book form (a first printed edition came out only in 1558, nine years after Marguerite's death); in any case, it seems clear that Marguerite at the very least must have acted as a sort of general editor and that the stories are a product and a reflection of the intellectual, social, and religious interests and experiences of her milieu.

The "frame" within which the stories are assembled presents similarities with that of Boccaccio, but the differences are relevant too. In both cases the premise is a natural disaster. The gentlemen and ladies in the *Decameron* have taken refuge in an isolated place to avoid the plague; in the *Heptameron* a similar group of ten cultivated people—five men and five women in this case—who have just spent three weeks taking the cure at the spa town of Cauterets in the mountainous Pyrenees region, are impeded on their way back by flooded roads and particularly by the swollen, impassable Gave de Pau River. As narrated in the Prologue, they eventually take refuge in the Abbey of Our Lady at Sarrance, where they come not in one group, but piecemeal, after struggling not only with adverse natural elements but with human beings as well. These range from violent bandits to the abbot himself, described as "not a particularly nice character," and thus exemplifying at the very start Marguerite's often critical presentation of men of the cloth. On receiving the last two arrivals "he did not dare to refuse them board and lodging, for fear of offending the Seigneur de Béarne [i.e., the local feudal lord], who, as he knew perfectly well, was on friendly terms with them. Hypocrite as he was, he put on as pleasant an air as he was able. . . ."

As the river is ever more swollen, the travelers decide to have a bridge built; the construction, however primitive, will take ten or twelve days, which is judged "rather a boring prospect for all of them, men and women alike. However, Parlamente [generally identified with Marguerite herself], the wife of Hircan [identifiable with Marguerite's husband, Henri d'Albret], was not one to let herself become idle or melancholy, and having asked her husband for permission, she spoke to the old lady Oisille" as to the one who occupies "the position of mother in regard to the rest of us women," asking her to "consider some pastime to alleviate the boredom and distress that we shall have to bear during our long stay here."

Lady Oisille had been the first to arrive at the Abbey of Our Lady, having resolved "not to let the treacherous roads frighten her;" she is "a widow, with much experience of life," possibly identifiable with Louise of Savoy, Marguerite's mother. She is characteristically described as "not . . . so superstitious as to believe that the glorious Virgin should leave her seat at her Son's right hand in order to come and take residence in such a desolate spot," a passing remark that may be compared to some of Erasmus's broadsides against Catholic "superstitions." Oisille's prescription for delivering oneself from boredom and sorrow, and for keeping healthy and happy in old age, is in a pure humanistic-evangelical vein: "As soon as I rise in the morning I take the Scriptures and read them . . . whatever the evils of the day, they are to me so many blessings . . . in the evening I ponder in my mind everything I have done during the day, so that I may ask God forgiveness for my sins . . . and this, my children, is the pastime that I long ago adopted."

Hircan's intervention at this point is no less characterizing: after duly stating that all those present are readers of the Holy Scriptures, he proceeds to declare that they have not yet become "so mortified in the flesh that we are not in need of some sort of amusement . . . between dinner and vespers we should choose some pastime, which, while not prejudicial to the soul, will be agreeable to the body." As he cautiously suggests that his choice would fall on a particular pastime if he could be sure that it was "as agreeable to a certain lady among us as it would be to me," his wife Parlamente, "half angrily and half laughing," suggests in her turn that they "leave on one side all pastimes that require only two participants, and concentrate on those which everybody can join in." And being sure that all of them had read the hundred tales of Boccaccio (a translation had been done under Marguerite's auspices, and a plan to produce a French counterpart to the *Decameron* by members of King Francis's court had been abandoned under the pressure of political events), Parlamente suggests that they take advantage of their present confinement and tell one another stories, "each afternoon from midday to four o'clock," the rest of the day being taken up with more normal occupations, including devotional ones.

Certain rules govern the nature and rhetorics of the storytelling. "Each of us will tell a story which he has either witnessed himself, or which he has heard from somebody worthy of belief." Significantly, in the abandoned court project which is now being somehow resumed, the idea was "to get together a party of ten people who were qualified to contribute something, excluding those who studied and were men of letters," for fear that "rhetorical ornament would in part falsify the truth of the account." This is as much as to state what will be obvious to anyone acquainted with the *Decameron* on first approaching the *Heptameron*—that Marguerite is a much less sophisticated literary artist than Boccaccio; her language bears hardly any trace of aesthetic self-consciousness and tends to be factual, informative, unadorned. See the bluntness of some of the openings: "I've often wished, Ladies, that I'd been able to share the good fortune of the man in the story I'm about to tell you. So here it is" (story 3); or of some of the reports on violent action: "he leaned out of the window and shouted orders for him [his sister's husband] to be killed—orders that were instantly carried out, even as they watched" (story 30). It is quite natural that a casually knowledgeable tone should be maintained in handling characters of high birth (e.g., the king and queen of Naples in our first selection); these are stories told for their own amusement by aristocrats who are very much at ease in court life; the recommendation that the anecdotes be authentic signals a taste for a sort of high-society gossip.

As in much fiction and drama at all times, love is a major theme in the *Heptameron*; it is handled here in various keys, ranging from loose and even bizarre indulgence (our first two selections) to spirituality and renunciation (the close of our third selection). The subject of love is closely interrelated with social and religious themes, for this was a strictly classified society and one in which religious conflict and debate were rampant. Both elements are insistently present in the stories as they were in Marguerite's mind; this is perhaps most evident in the handling of situations that involve the social and ethical codes of married life. The "frame" of the *Heptameron* is very relevant in this connection: each story is followed by a discussion among the participating ladies and gentlemen, a device that in some respects may make Marguerite seem closer to Castiglione than to Boccaccio. The debate that follows story 40 (told by Parlamente-Marguerite herself) reflects the views and inner contradictions of a society that was, in turns, free and strict, crude and highly refined, outspoken and hypocritical. As Parlamente describes "the state of matrimony as God and Nature ordain, loving one another virtuously and accepting their parents' wishes," and as the gentlemen present affirm that "they had all been married in this way, and [swear] that they [have] never regretted it," the narrator's typical comment is: "True or not, the ladies concerned were so pleased with this, that, feeling they could wish to hear nothing better, they got up to go and give thanks to God for it." No less typical is the discussion of the Comte de Jossebelin's killing of his brother-in-law (story 40): a violent action dictated by entrenched prejudice is not seen as a brutally senseless deed, but as a relatively justifiable action within the prevailing aristocratic code—a code that seems to aim at some sort of workable coexistence between the carnal and the spiritual, between moral laxity and trust in salvation.

P. A. Chilton's introduction to his translation of *The Heptameron* (1984) is excellent; B. J. Davis, *The Storytellers in Marguerite de Navarre's Heptameron* (1978), is an interesting, detailed study of the ten narrators and of their individual identities and positions. On the collection's "frame" see Glyn P. Norton, "Narrative Function in the *Heptaméron* Frame-story," in *La Nouvelle française à la Renaissance* (1981), pp. 435–447. Samuel Putnam, *Marguerite de Navarre* (1935), is a well-informed and highly readable biography. Marcel Tetel, *Marguerite de Navarre's Heptameron: Themes, Language, and Structure* (1973), is an in-depth literary study for the more advanced student.

The Heptameron[1]

STORY THREE

The Queen of Naples has revenge on her unfaithful husband, King Alfonso, by taking his mistress's husband as her lover, an arrangement that endures to the end of their days, without the King ever suspecting.

I've often wished, Ladies, that I'd been able to share the good fortune of the man in the story I'm about to tell you.[2] So here it is. In the town of Naples in the time of King Alfonso[3] (whose well-known lasciviousness was, one might say, the very sceptre by which he ruled) there lived a nobleman—a handsome, upright and likeable man, a man indeed whose qualities were so excellent that a certain old gentleman granted him the hand of his daughter. In beauty and charm she was in every way her husband's equal, and they lived in deep mutual affection until a carnival, in the course of which the King disguised himself and went round all the houses in the town, where the people vied with one another to give him a good reception. When he came to the house of the gentleman I have referred to, he was entertained more lavishly than in any of the other houses. Preserves, minstrels, music—all were laid before him, but above all there was the presence of the most beautiful lady that the King had ever seen. At the end of the banquet, the lady sang for the King with her husband, and so sweetly did she sing that her beauty was more than ever

---

1. Our selections translated by P. A. Chilton.   2. The narrator is Saffredent, one of the younger members of the party, fond of company and pleasure, and a devoted admirer of Parlamente. He is often identified with an Admiral Bonnivet whom Marguerite knew well and some of whose amorous adventures are the subject of other stories in the *Heptameron*.   3. Alfonso V of Aragon (1396–1458), the cultivated and unfaithful husband of Maria, daughter of King Henry III of Castile.

enhanced. Seeing such physical perfection, the King took less delight in contemplating the gentle harmony that existed between the lady and her husband, than he did in speculating as to how he might go about spoiling it. The great obstacle to his desires was the evident deep mutual love between them, and so, for the time being, he kept his passion hidden and as secret as he could. But in order to obtain at least some relief for his feelings, he held a series of banquets for the lords and ladies of Naples, to which he did not, of course, omit to invite the gentleman and his fair wife.

As everyone knows, men see and believe just what they want to, and the King thought he caught something in the lady's eyes which augured well— if only the husband were not in the way. To find out if his surmise was correct, therefore, he sent the husband off for two or three weeks to attend to some business in Rome. Up till then the wife had never had him out of her sight, and she was heartbroken the moment he walked out of the door. The King took the opportunity to console her as often as possible, showering blandishments and gifts of all kinds upon her, with the result that in the end she felt not only consoled, but even content in her husband's absence. Before the three weeks were up she had fallen so much in love with the King that she was every bit as upset about her husband's imminent return as she had been about his departure. So, in order that she should not be deprived of the King after her husband's return, it was agreed that she would let her royal lover know whenever her husband was going to his estates in the country. He could then come to see her without running any risks, and in complete secrecy, so that her honour and reputation—which gave her more concern than her conscience—could not possibly be damaged in any way.

Dwelling on the prospect of the King's visits with considerable pleasure, the lady gave her husband such an affectionate reception that, although he had heard during his absence that the King had been paying her a lot of attention, he had not the slightest suspicion of how far things had gone. However, the fire of passion cannot be concealed for long, and as time went by its flames began to be somewhat obvious. He naturally began to guess at the truth, and kept a close watch on his wife until there was no longer any room for doubt. But he decided to keep quiet about it, because he was afraid that if he let on that he knew, he might suffer even worse things at the hands of the King than he had already. He considered, in short, that it was better to put up with the affront, than to risk his life for the sake of a woman who apparently no longer loved him. He was, all the same, angry and bitter, and determined to get his own back if at all possible.

Now he was well aware of the fact that bitterness and jealousy can drive women to do things that love alone will never make them do, and that this is particularly true of women with strong feelings and high principles of honour. So one day, while he was conversing with the Queen, he made so bold as to say that he felt very sorry for her when he saw how little the King really loved her. The Queen had heard all about the affair between the King and the gentleman's wife, and merely replied:

"I do not expect to be able to combine both honour and pleasure in my position. I am perfectly well aware that while I receive honour and respect, it is *she* who has all the pleasure. But then, I know too that while she may have the pleasure, she does not receive the honour and respect."

He knew, of course, to whom she was referring, and this was his reply: "Madame, you were born to honour and respect. You are after all of such high birth that, being queen or being empress could scarcely add to your nobility. But you are also beautiful, charming and refined, and you deserve to have your pleasures as well. The woman who is depriving you of those pleasures which are yours by right, is in fact doing herself more harm—because her moment of glory will eventually turn to shame and she will forfeit as much pleasure as she, you or any woman in the Kingdom of Naples could ever have. And if I may say so, Madame, if the King didn't have a crown on his head, he wouldn't have the slightest advantage over me as far as giving pleasure to ladies is concerned. What is more, I'm quite sure that in order to satisfy a refined person such as yourself, he really ought to be wishing he could exchange his constitution for one more like my own!"

The Queen laughed, and said: "The King may have a more delicate constitution than your own. Even so, the love which he bears me gives me so much satisfaction that I prefer it to all else."

"Madame, if that were the case, then I would not feel so sorry for you, because I know that you would derive great happiness from the pure love you feel within you, if it were matched by an equally pure love on the part of the King. But God has denied you this, in order that you should not find in this man the answer to all your wants and so make him your god on earth."

"I admit," said the Queen, "that my love for him is so deep that you will never find its like, wherever you may look."

"Forgive me," said the gentlemen, "but there are hearts whose love you've never sounded. May I be so bold as to tell you that there is a certain person who loves you, and loves you so deeply and so desperately, that in comparison your love for the King is as nothing? And his love grows and goes on growing in proportion as he sees the King's love for you diminishing. So, if it were, Madame, to please you, and you were to receive his love, you would be more than compensated for all that you have lost."

The Queen began to realize, both from what he was saying, and from the expression on his face, that he was speaking from the depths of his heart. She remembered that he had some time ago sought to do her service,[4] and that he had felt so deeply about it that he had become quite melancholy. At the time she had assumed the cause of his mood lay with his wife, but she was now quite convinced that the real reason was his love for her. Love is a powerful force, and will make itself felt whenever it is

4. I.e., become her *serviteur*. "According to the *serviteur*'s practice, as the *Heptameron* presents it, a married aristocratic woman has the right to maintain several devoted knights in her service . . . since it is supposed to be chaste, the *serviteur*'s relationship, this remnant of courtly and chivalrous love, can coexist with faithful marriage . . . nevertheless, there is evidently considerable anxiety about the institution as such." [from the translator's Introduction].

more than mere pretence, and it was this powerful force that now made her certain of what remained hidden from the rest of the world. She looked at him again. He was certainly more attractive than her husband. He had been left by his wife, too, just as she had been left by the King. Tormented by jealousy and bitterness, allured by the gentleman's passion, she sighed, tears came to her eyes, and she began: "Oh God! Must it take the desire for revenge to drive me to do what love alone would never have driven me to?"

Her words were not lost on the gentleman who replied: "Madame, vengeance is sweet indeed, when instead of taking one's enemy's life, one gives life to a lover who is true. It is time, I think, that the truth freed you from this foolish love for a man who certainly has no love for you. It is time that a just and reasonable love banished from you these fears that so ill become one whose spirit is so strong and so virtuous. Why hesitate, Madame? Let us set aside rank and station. Let us look upon ourselves as a man and a woman, as the two most wronged people in the world, as two people who have been betrayed and mocked by those whom we loved with all our hearts. Let us, Madame, take our revenge, not in order to punish them as they deserve, but in order to do justice to our love. My love for you is unbearable. If it is not requited I shall die. Unless your heart is as hard as diamond or as stone, it is impossible that you should not feel some spark from this fire that burns the more fiercely within me the more I try to stifle it. I am dying for love of you! And if that cannot move you to take pity on me and grant me your love, then at least your own love for yourself must surely force you to do so. For you, who are so perfect that you merit the devotion of all the honourable and worthy men in all the world, have been despised and deserted by the very man for whose sake you have disdained all others!"

At this speech the Queen was quite beside herself. Lest her face betray the turmoil of her mind, she took his arm and led him into the garden adjoining her room. For a long time she walked up and down with him saying nothing. But he knew that the conquest was almost complete, and when they reached the end of the path, where no one could see them, he expressed in the clearest possible way the love that for so long he had kept concealed. At last they were of one mind. And so it was, one might say, that together they enacted a Vengeance, having found the Passion too much to bear.[5]

Before they parted they arranged that whenever the husband made his trips to his village, he would, if the King had gone off to the town, go straight to the castle to see the Queen. Thus they would fool the very people who were trying to fool them. Moreover, there would now be four people joining in the fun, instead of just two thinking they had it all to themselves. Once this was settled, the Queen retired to her room and the gentleman went home, both of them now sufficiently cheered up to forget all their previous troubles. No longer did the King's visits to the gentle-

---

5. An allusion to medieval mystery plays: after the Passion and Resurrection, the mystery of Vengeance depicted the punishment of Christ's slayers [translator's note].

man's lady distress either of them. Dread had now turned to desire, and the gentleman started to make trips to his village rather more often than he had in the past. It was, after all, only half a league out of the town. Whenever the King heard that the gentleman had gone to the country, he would make his way straight to his lady. Similarly, whenever the gentleman heard that the King had left his castle, he would wait till nightfall and then go straight to the Queen—to act, so to speak, as the King's viceroy. He managed to do this in such secrecy that no one had the slightest inkling of what was going on. They proceeded in this fashion for quite a while, but the King, being a public person, had much greater difficulty concealing his love-affair sufficiently to prevent anyone at all getting wind of it. In fact, there were a few unpleasant wags who started to make fun of the gentleman, saying he was a cuckold, and putting up their fingers like cuckold's horns whenever his back was turned. Anyone with any decency felt very sorry for the man. He knew what they were saying, of course, but derived a good deal of amusement from it, and reckoned his horns were surely as good as the King's crown.

One day when the King was visiting the gentleman and his wife at their home, he noticed a set of antlers mounted on the wall. He burst out laughing, and could not resist the temptation to remark that the horns went very well with the house. The gentleman was a match for the King, however. He had an inscription placed on the antlers which read as follows:

> Io porto le corna, ciascun lo vede,
> Ma tal le porta, che no lo crede.[6]

Next time the king was in the house, he saw the inscription, and asked what it meant.

The gentleman simply said: "If the King doesn't tell his secrets to his subjects, then there's no reason why his subjects should tell their secrets to the King. And so far as horns are concerned, you should bear in mind that they don't always stick up and push their wearers' hats off. Sometimes they're so soft that you can wear a hat on top of them, without being troubled by them, and even without knowing they're there at all!"

From these words the King realized that the gentleman knew about his affair with his wife. But he never suspected that the gentleman was having an affair with *his* wife. For her part, the Queen was careful to feign displeasure at her husband's behaviour, though secretly she was pleased, and the more she was pleased, the more displeasure she affected. This amicable arrangement permitted the continuation of their amours for many years to come, until at length old age brought them to order.

*   *   *

"Well, Ladies," concluded Saffredent, "let that story be a lesson to you. When your husbands give you little roe-deer horns, make sure that you give them great big stag's antlers!"

---

6. "I am wearing horns, everyone sees that, / But there is one who wears them who doesn't know it."

"Saffredent," said Ennasuite,[7] laughing, "I'm quite sure that if you were still such an ardent lover as you used to be, you wouldn't mind putting up with horns as big as oaks, as long as you could give a pair back when the fancy took you. But you're starting to go grey, you know, and it really is time you began to give your appetites a rest!"

"Mademoiselle," he replied, "even if the lady I love gives me no hope, and even if age has dampened my ardour somewhat, my desires are as strong as ever. But seeing that you object to my harbouring such noble desires, let me invite you to tell the fourth story, and let's see if you can produce an example to refute what I say."[8]

STORY THIRTY[9]

A young nobleman of some fourteen or fifteen years of age, thinking he is sleeping with one of his mother's ladies, has relations with his mother, who nine months later gives birth to a little girl, who twelve or thirteen years later marries the young man, who is entirely unaware that he is her father and her brother, just as she is entirely unaware that she is his daughter and his sister.

During the reign of King Louis XII, at the time when the Legate[1] at Avignon was one of the d'Amboise family, in fact the nephew of Georges d'Amboise, who was Legate of France, there lived in Languedoc[2] a certain lady whose name, for the sake of her family, I shall not reveal. She had an income of more than four thousand ducats, had been widowed at an early age, and had been left with one son. Whether out of sorrow at the loss of her husband or whether out of her love for her child, she had vowed never to remarry. To avoid any situation that might lead to her doing so, she insisted on having nothing to do with anyone except people who were devout. She thought that it is opportunity that leads to sin, and did not realize that it is the reverse: sin manufactures opportunity. This young widow gave herself up entirely to attending divine service. She shunned all worldly gatherings—to such an extent that she even made going to weddings and listening to the organ in church a matter of conscience. When her son was seven years of age, she took on a man of saintly ways as the boy's tutor, so that he might be instructed in all devotion and sanctity. But when he was between fourteen and fifteen years old, Nature, that most secret of teachers, found that this well-grown lad had nothing to occupy him and began to teach him lessons somewhat different from those of his tutor. He began to gaze upon and to desire the things that seemed to him full of beauty. And amongst these things there was a young lady who slept in his mother's room. No one suspected anything, since he was regarded

7. *Enna* may stand for "Anne," and *suite* means "retinue"; so the character is identifiable with Anne de Vivonne, one of the ladies in Marguerite's entourage who collaborated on the *Heptameron* project at court. Her attitude toward men, as shown here, can be bitter and sharply ironical.   8. Ennasuite is, in fact, the teller of the following story 4, intended to prove that "not all men who are rash enough to try their tricks get what they want."   9. The narrator is Hircan, Parlamente's husband, variously described, in the book itself and by its commentators, as brilliant, flighty, sensual, capable of sarcasm and grossness. The name is related to "Hircania," an imaginary and proverbially wild region in classical literature; the root is that of *hircus*, Latin for "goat" (cf. English "hircine": libidinous).   1. The Pope's delegate, representing him in a particular place or country.   2. A region in the south of France.

as no more than a child, and in any case, in that household nothing was heard but godly conversation. Well, the young gallant started making secret advances to the girl, and the girl came to complain to her mistress. The boy's mother loved her son so much and had such a high opinion of him that she thought the girl was making the complaint simply in order to turn her against him. But the girl persisted in her complaints, and in the end her mistress said:

"I will find out if what you say is true, and if what you say is indeed true, I will punish him. But if your accusation is false, it will be you who shall pay the penalty."

In order to establish the truth of the matter, then, she instructed the girl to make an assignation with her son. He was to come at midnight and join her in the bed where she slept alone by the door of her mistress's chamber. The girl dutifully obeyed, but when the evening came, it was the mother who took her place. If the accusation was true, she was resolved to give her son such a chastising that he would never in the whole of his life get in bed with a woman without remembering it. Such were her angry thoughts, when her son appeared and climbed into the bed with her. But, even though he had actually got into the bed, she still could not believe that he would do anything dishonourable. So she did not speak immediately, waiting till he gave some clear sign that his intentions were bad, for she could not believe on such slender evidence that his desires might go as far as anything criminal. She waited to see what he would do. So long did she wait, and so fragile was her nature, that her anger turned to pleasure, a pleasure so abominable, that she forgot she was a mother. Even as the dammed-up torrent flows more impetuously than the freely flowing stream, so it was with this poor lady whose pride and honour had lain in the restraints she had imposed upon her own body. No sooner had she set her foot on the first rung down the ladder of her chastity, than she found herself suddenly swept away to the bottom. That night she became pregnant by the very one whom she had desired to prevent getting others with child. No sooner had the sin been committed than she was seized with the most violent pangs of remorse, remorse so deep that her repentance was to last her whole life long. She rose from her son, who still believed he had lain with the young girl, and in bitter anguish withdrew to a room apart, where, going over in her mind how her good intentions had come to such wicked fruition, she spent the rest of the night in solitary weeping and gnashing of teeth. Yet, instead of humbling herself and recognizing how impossible it is for our flesh to do otherwise than sin unless we have God's help, she tried to give satisfaction for past deeds through her own means, through her tears and through her own prudence, to avoid future evil. Her excuse for her sin was the situation she had been placed in, never evil inclination, for which there can be no remedy but the grace of God. She thought it would be possible in the future to act in such a way as to avoid slipping again into such unfortunate circumstances, and, as if there were but one kind of sin that can damn us, she bent all her efforts to avoiding this one alone. But the root of pride, which external sin should cure, only grew and increased, with the consequence that by avoiding one kind of evil she merely fell in the way of several others. For the very next morning, as soon as day broke, she sent for her son's tutor and said to him:

"My son is growing up now, and it's time he left home. I have a relative who is away beyond the mountains with the Grand-Maître de Chaumont.[3] His name is Captain Montesson, and he will be very pleased to enlist my son. So, take him at once, and to spare me the pain of parting, tell him not to come to bid me farewell."

So saying, she gave him the necessary money for the journey. That very morning the young man departed for the wars, and, having as he believed spent the night with his paramour, there was nothing better that he could have wished for. The lady remained for a long time plunged into a deep sadness and melancholy. Had it not been for her fear of God, there was many a time when she would gladly have wished that the unhappy fruit of her womb should perish. She pretended to be ill, so that she could wear an outer garment to conceal her fault. When the time of her confinement was near, she turned to the one man in whom she could place her trust, a bastard brother, to whom she had in the past given a great deal. She told him what had befallen her, without telling him about her son, and asked him to help her save her honour, which he gladly agreed to do. A few days before she was due to give birth, he came and invited her to have a change of air, saying that it would help her recover her health if she came to stay in his house for a while. So, accompanied by a small group of attendants, she went with him. Waiting for them they found a midwife who had been told it was the brother's wife she was to attend. One night, without the midwife's realizing who she was, the lady was delivered of a beautiful baby girl. Her brother had the child fostered with a wet-nurse, pretending that it was his own child. The lady stayed one month, and then, fully recovered, returned to her own house, where she began to live a more austere life than ever, subjecting herself to fasts and other disciplines.

When the wars in Italy were over, the lady's son, who by this time had grown to full manhood, sent word to his mother, asking if he might return to her house. But she was afraid of falling into the same sin again, and refused to give her permission. The son persisted, until in the end she could no longer find any reason to continue in her refusal. However, she sent a message to him to the effect that he was never to appear before her unless he was married to somebody he loved deeply. It did not matter who she was; her fortune was not important; so long as she was a girl of gentle birth, that would be sufficient. During this time, the lady's bastard brother saw that his adopted daughter had grown up into a beautiful young girl, and decided that she should be placed in a household in some far-off region where she would not be known. On the advice of her mother she was placed with Catherine, the Queen of Navarre.[4] At the age of twelve or thirteen the girl had indeed grown so beautiful and noble in her ways that the Queen came to hold her very dear, and was anxious that she should

---

3. I.e., fighting in the Italian wars under the lord of Chaumont. Captain Montesson distinguished himself as a soldier at the time of Louis XII, Francis I's predecessor.   4. Marguerite's mother-in-law.

be married to someone of high estate. But though the girl had many men to pay her court, because she was poor, she had none to be her husband. One day, however, the noble lord who was her unknown father came back from over the mountains and arrived at the house of the Queen. No sooner had he caught sight of his daughter than he fell in love with her. Having received permission from his mother to marry whom he pleased, all he desired to know about the girl was whether she was of gentle birth, and on hearing that indeed she was, he asked the Queen for her hand. The Queen, who knew that he was rich, and not only rich but handsome, noble and good, gladly gave her consent.

Once the marriage had been consummated, the noble lord wrote to his mother again, saying that she could surely no longer refuse to have him, for now he could bring with him a daughter-in-law as perfect as anyone could ever desire. His mother asked further about the match he had made, and on realizing that her son's wife was their own daughter, she sank into a state of such utter desperation that she thought her end was near. For the harder she tried to place impediments in the way of disaster, the more she became the instrument whereby ever new catastrophes overcame her. Not knowing what else she could do, she went to the Legate at Avignon, confessed the enormity of her sin, and asked for his advice on what she should now do. In order to satisfy her conscience the Legate summoned several doctors of theology, to whom he explained the whole affair, without revealing the names of the persons involved. In the light of their counsel he concluded that the lady should never say anything to her children, for they had acted in ignorance and consequently had not sinned. But she, their mother, was to do penance for the rest of her life without giving the slightest indication of it to them. The poor lady returned to her house, and not long after that her son and her daughter-in-law arrived. They were very much in love. Never was there such love between husband and wife, never were a husband and wife so close. For she was his daughter, his sister, his wife. And he was her father, brother and husband. They endured for ever in this great love, while the poor lady, their mother, in the extremity of her penitence, could not see them show their love but she would withdraw to weep alone.

*   *   *

"There, Ladies, that is what becomes of those women who presume by their own strength and virtue to overcome love and nature and all the powers that God has placed therein. Better were it to recognize one's weakness, better not to try to do battle with such an enemy, but turning to the one true lover, to say with the Psalmist:[5] 'Lord, I am oppressed; answer thou for me.' "

"One could not possibly hear a stranger story than that," said Oisille,[6]

5. Actually Isaiah 38:14. [Translator's note.]   6. The oldest lady of the group. From here on, the conversation obviously echoes current debate on religious education as well as polemical attitudes toward alleged Catholic practices which these men and women of the world regard as naive and / or hypocritical.

"and I think that every man and woman here should bow their heads in the fear of God, to see how, as a result of presuming to do good, so much evil came about."

"Be you assured, the first step man takes trusting in himself alone is a step away from trust in God," said Parlamente.

"He is a wise man," said Geburon,[7] "who recognizes no enemy but himself, and who distrusts his own will and counsel, however good and holy they may appear to be."

"And no matter how good a thing it might appear to be," said Longarine,[8] "nothing should induce a woman to risk sharing a bed with a male relative, however close he may be to her. It's not safe to set a naked flame near tinder."

"Without a doubt she was one of those foolish, vainglorious women who had had her head filled with nonsense by the Franciscans,"[9] said Enna-suite, "and thought she was so saintly that she was incapable of sin, as some of them would persuade us to believe that through our own efforts we actually can be, though this is an extreme error."

"Is it possible, Longarine," said Oisille, "that some of them are so foolish as to believe that view?"

"They do better than that!" replied Longarine. "They even say that it's necessary to habituate themselves to the virtue of chastity, and in order to put their strength to the test, they converse with the most beautiful women they can find, with women whom they particularly like. Then by means of fondling and kissing they test themselves if they have achieved mortification of the flesh. If they find that they are aroused by these little pleasures, they go into solitude and subject themselves to fasts and austere disciplines. And when they have overcome the desires of the flesh to the point where a conversation and a kiss no longer arouse them, they try out the ultimate temptation of going to bed with a woman and embracing her without lustful desire. However, for every one who survived this test, there were many who did not, and the consequences were so unfortunate that the Archbishop of Milan, where these particular religious practices were rife, was obliged to separate the men from the women, putting the women in women's convents and the men in monasteries of their own."

"Really," said Geburon, "it's the extreme of folly to want to put oneself through one's own efforts above sin, and then actually to go looking for situations where a sin may be committed!"

"Some people do the opposite, however," said Saffredent, "and avoid such situations as much as they can—but even then their concupiscence goes with them. The good Saint Jerome, even after he had flagellated himself and hidden himself away in the wilderness, confessed that he could

---

7. One of the older members of the group, notable for his sententious wisdom. Suggested identifications are with a military man, the lord of Burye, a captain in the "Italian wars"; or with Nicolas Bourbon, a tutor of Jeanne d'Albret, Marguerite's daughter.   8. A young and wisely talkative widow, often identified with one of Marguerite's ladies-in-waiting, who among her titles had that of lady of Longrai (hence her name, which is also interpreted as a word play on *langue orine* meaning "tongue of gold").   9. In several of Marguerite's stories, the Franciscans are the object of anticlerical satire and criticism.

not get rid of the fire that burned in the marrow of his bones. So we should commend ourselves to God, for if He does not hold us in His grip, we stumble and take great pleasure in so doing."

"But you're not taking any notice of what I can see!" interrupted Hircan. "While we've been telling our stories, the monks have been listening behind the hedge! They didn't even hear the bell for vespers, but now that we've started talking about God they've run off and they're ringing the second bell!"

"We will do well to follow them," said Oisille, "and go to render thanks to God for having spent this day so happily."

At this, they rose and made their way to the church, where they all devoutly heard vespers. Afterwards, when they went for supper, they discussed the things that had been said during the day and recounted many things that had happened in their time, in order to see which were worthy of note. After passing the evening in this happy way, they all retired peacefully to bed, looking forward to continuing on the next day the pastime which they found so agreeable. And so the third day came to its close.

STORY FORTY[1]

How the sister of the Comte de Jossebelin marries without her brother's knowledge a gentleman; how, in spite of his liking for this gentleman, the brother subsequently has him killed because he is of a different house; and how his widow spends the rest of her days in the austerity of a hermitage.

Rolandine's[2] father, the Comte de Jossebelin, had several sisters, some of whom had made wealthy marriages, and some of whom had entered religious orders. But there was one who stayed at home and never married. She was incomparably more beautiful than the others, and was so loved by her brother that he put her even before his wife and children. Many eligible men sought her hand in marriage, but because of the brother's fear of losing her, and because he was too fond of his money, they were always turned down. Consequently, she remained unmarried for a great part of her life, living respectably in her brother's house. Now in the same house there lived a handsome young gentleman, who had been brought up there since early childhood, and who had grown up to be a person of such handsome appearance and such excellent qualities that he had acquired a certain influence in his master's house. Thus when the Count wished to send messages to his sister, he always did so by means of this young gentleman. He even gave him the authority to visit her alone, with the result that, seeing her morning and evening as he did, the visits blossomed into deep affection. But the young gentleman feared for his life if his master should be offended, and the lady feared likewise for her honour. So their love went no further than words, until the Seigneur de Jossebelin started

---

1. The narrator is Parlamente, generally identified with Marguerite herself.   2. The heroine of a previous story (31), who after early turmoil, and mistreatment by the count her father, attains happiness and riches in married life.

remarking to his sister that he only wished that the young gentleman was from as good a family as she. There was, he said, nobody he would rather have as a brother-in-law. He said this so often that after discussing the matter carefully, the couple thought that if they were to marry, the brother would forgive them. Those blinded by love believe what they wish to believe and, vainly thinking that nothing but good could come of it, they were married, without anyone but the priest and some female companions knowing.

For several years they enjoyed those pleasures that a married man and woman may take together. They were the handsomest couple in Christendom, and the most deeply and perfectly in love. But Fortune, unable to see two people so happy together, became envious, and roused against them an enemy, who spied on the young lady, and who, though ignorant of her marriage, became aware of her happiness. This enemy came to the Seigneur de Jossebelin and told him that the young gentleman whom he trusted so much was going too often to his sister's room, and at times of the day when gentlemen ought not to. At first the Count did not believe this, because of the great confidence he had both in his sister and in the gentleman. But after much persuasion he was induced in the name of his family's honour to ensure that a watch was placed on them, with the result that the poor couple, who suspected nothing, were discovered. One night the Seigneur de Jossebelin was informed that the gentleman was in his sister's room. He went at once and found the poor love-blind couple in bed. He was speechless with rage, and drawing his sword, chased the gentleman out with the intention of killing him. But the gentleman, who was an agile man, got away, still wearing his nightshirt. Unable to escape by the door, he jumped from a window into the garden. The poor lady, who was also still in her night attire, fell on her knees before her brother, saying:

"Spare my husband's life, Monsieur, I am married to him, and if we have done wrong, then punish me alone, for all that he has done was done at my request."

The brother was beside himself with anger and could only reply: "Even if he were a hundred thousand times your husband, still I would punish him as a bad servant and as one who has deceived me!"

So saying, he leaned out of the window and shouted orders for him to be killed—orders that were instantly carried out, even as they watched. Having witnessed this piteous spectacle, the lady addressed her brother like someone bereft of her senses:

"Brother, I have neither mother nor father, and I am old enough to marry as I please. I have chosen to marry a man of whom you have said again and again that you wished I could have married him. And because I have followed your advice in doing something that I could quite legally have done without it, you kill the one man in the world you loved above all others! So since my pleading could not save him from death, I beg you, in the name of all the love you have ever had for me, make me his companion in death, even as I have been his companion in all his fortunes.

So satisfy the demands of your cruel and unjust anger, grant rest to the body and soul of one who will not and cannot live without her spouse!"

Although the brother was overwrought to the point losing his reason, he had pity on his sister, and without either granting or refusing her request, he walked away and left her standing there. After pondering his deed and ascertaining that the dead gentleman had in fact been married to his sister, he wished that he had never committed the murder. Being afraid that his sister would seek revenge or would appeal to law, he had a castle built in the middle of a forest in which he shut her up, forbidding anyone to speak with her.

After a time, in order to appease his conscience, he tried to regain her confidence and even had the subject of marriage raised. But she sent word back that he had already given her such an unpleasant foretaste that she had no desire to feed further on such fare, and that she hoped to live in such a manner that her own brother would not become the murderer of a second husband. For she could hardly believe that, after committing so vicious a crime against the man he loved best in all the world, he was likely to be merciful to someone else. She also said that in spite of being unable in her weakness to avenge herself, she placed her hope in Him who was the true judge, who left no evil unpunished and in whose love she wished to abide in the lonely castle that was now her hermitage. She was true to her word, for there she remained until she died, living a life of such long-suffering and austerity that after her death people from far and wide visited her remains as if she had been a saint. From then on, the brother's family declined until of his six sons only one was left. They all died miserably. In the end it was his daughter Rolandine who remained sole heiress, as you heard in the earlier story, and inherited the prison which had been built for her aunt.

*   *   *

"Ladies, I pray God that you will take note of this example, and that none of you will wish to marry merely for your own pleasure, without the consent of those to whom you owe obedience. For marriage is an estate of long duration, and one which should not be entered into lightly or without the approval of our closest friends and relatives. Even then, however wisely one marries, one is bound to find at least as much pain as pleasure."

"That is indeed true," said Oisille, "and if there were no God or laws to teach girls to behave themselves, Parlamente's example would be enough to make them show more respect for their parents and relatives than to take it into their heads to make marriages of their own choosing."

"But, Madame," said Nomerfide,[3] "if one had only *one* good day in the year, one can't say one is miserable for the *whole* of one's life! She *did* have the pleasure of seeing, and being able to speak to, the one person she loved best in the world. What is more, she was able to enjoy it through

---

3. The youngest member of the group, who generally views life with joyful optimism.

marriage, without having anything on her conscience. I consider that this satisfaction must have been so great that it makes up for the sorrow she had to bear."

"What you mean," said Saffredent, "is that women derive more pleasure from going to bed with their husbands than displeasure from seeing them murdered under their noses?"

"That's *not* what I meant," said Nomerfide; "that would go against what I know of women. What I mean is that an *unusual* pleasure, such as marrying the man one loves most in the world, must be greater than the pain of losing him through death, which is a common occurrence."

"Yes," said Geburon, "but through a natural death, whereas the death in question was excessively cruel. It seems very strange to me that the Seigneur de Jossebelin should dare to go to such extremes of cruelty, seeing that he was neither her husband nor her father, merely her brother, and seeing that she was of an age at which the law allows daughters to marry as they think fit."

"I don't find it strange at all," said Hircan, "since he didn't kill the sister, whom he loved so much, and over whom he had in any case no authority, but punished the gentleman he had brought up as his son and loved as his own brother. He heaped privileges on him, advanced him in his service and then the man goes and seeks the hand of his master's sister in marriage! He had no right at all to do that."

"Quite," said Nomerfide. "It isn't any common, ordinary pleasure, when a lady of such high birth marries for love alone a gentleman of her household. You may have found his death 'strange,' but the pleasure too must have been rare—and all the greater, since it runs counter to the views expressed by all wise men, and has in its favour the fact that a loving heart found satisfaction and that a soul found true repose. For there was nothing in all this to offend God. And as far as his death is concerned, which according to you was so cruel, it seems to me that since death is inevitable, the swifter it is the better. If one thing is certain, it is that we all must pass from this life. I think the fortunate ones are those who do not have to linger on the outskirts of death, and who soar out of the one state in this world that can be called bliss straight into the bliss that is eternal."

"What do you mean by 'lingering on the outskirts of death'?" asked Simontaut.[4]

"I mean those people who suffer torments of the mind," answered Nomerfide, "and those who have been ill a long time, and who, because of the extreme nature of their bodily or mental suffering, no longer fear death, but rather find it slow in coming. I mean those people who have journeyed through the outskirts and can tell you the names of inns where they have wept rather than rested. It was inevitable that the lady in question should at some time lose her husband, but she was, thanks to her brother's vio-

---

4. Identifiable with François de Bourdeille, a nobleman related to the Montaut family; the name permits a pun alluding to masculinity (*monte haut*-rises high). François was married to Anne de Vivonne, hence in the present context he would be the husband of Ennasuite.

lence, spared the experience of seeing her husband suffer from long sickness or distress. Moreover, she could count herself happy indeed in converting the happiness she had enjoyed with her husband to the service of our Lord."

"Do you give no consideration to the humiliation she suffered, and the imprisonment?" said Longarine.

"I believe," said Nomerfide, "that if one loves perfectly, with a love rooted in God's commandments, then one will not experience humiliation or dishonour, provided one does not go astray and fall from the perfection of one's love. For the glory of loving truly knows no shame. And though her body was imprisoned, her heart was free and united with God and her husband, so that I believe she did not experience her solitude as imprisonment but regarded it rather as the highest liberty. For when one can no longer see the person one loves, one's greatest pleasure is to think about that person incessantly. Prison walls are never confining when the mind is allowed to wander as it will."

"Nothing could be more true than what Nomerfide says," said Simontaut, "but the man who is his fury brought about the separation of the couple ought to consider himself miserable indeed, having offended as he did against God, against Love and against Honour."

"In all truth," said Geburon, "I am amazed by the varied nature of women's love. It seems clear to me that women who love most are the most virtuous, but that those who love to a lesser degree cover up what love they have, because they wish to appear virtuous."

"It's quite true," said Parlamente, "that a heart which opens itself virtuously to both God and men is capable of stronger love than a sinful heart, and is not afraid of anyone seeing into its true feelings."

"I've always heard it said," said Simontaut, "that men should not be condemned for pursuing women, since it was God who put love in men's breasts in the first place and gave them the boldness to do the asking, while He made women timid and chaste, so that they would do the refusing. If a man is punished for having used the powers implanted in him, he suffers an injustice."

"But," said Longarine, "it was extraordinary that the brother should have sung the young gentleman's praises over such a long period of time. It seems to me that it's either madness or cruelty if the keeper of a fountain praises the beauty of its waters to someone dying of thirst, only to kill him when he wants to drink from it!"

"Without doubt," said Parlamente, "it was the brother with his fair words who kindled the fire, and he had no right to put it out with his sword."

"It astonishes me," Saffredent said, "that anyone should so disapprove of an ordinary *gentilhomme*, who after all used neither subterfuge nor coercion other than devoted service, merely because he succeeded in marrying a woman of high birth. For all the ancient philosophers assert that the lowliest of men is worth far more than the highest born and most virtuous woman in the world."

"The reason is," said Dagoucin,[5] "that in order to maintain peace in the state, consideration is given only to the rank of families, the seniority of individuals and the provisions of the law, and not to men's love and virtue, in order that the monarchy should not be undermined. Consequently, in marriages between social equals which are contracted according to the human judgement of the family concerned, the partners are often so different in the feelings of the heart and in temperament that far from entering into a state leading to salvation, they frequently find themselves on the outskirts of Hell."

"Equally," said Geburon, "there have been many couples who are extremely close in their feelings and in their temperament, couples who marry for love without considering differences of family and lineage, and who have never stopped regretting it. Great but indiscreet love of this kind frequently turns into violent jealousy."

"In my opinion," said Parlamente, "neither of these kinds of marriages is praiseworthy. If people submit to the will of God, they are concerned neither with glory, greed, nor sensual enjoyment, but wish only to live in the state of matrimony as God and Nature ordain, loving one another virtuously and accepting their parents' wishes. Even though there is no condition in life that is without some tribulation, I have seen couples like this live together with no regrets. Indeed we are not so unfortunate that in our present gathering we have no such couples at all!"

Hircan, Geburon, Simontaut and Saffredent affirmed that they had all been married in this way, and swore that they had never regretted it. True or not, the ladies concerned were so pleased at this, that, feeling they could wish to hear nothing better, they got up to go and give thanks to God for it, and found the monks were ready to say vespers. After the service they all had supper, returning to the subject of their own marriages, with the men going on to talk the whole evening about their experiences when wooing their wives. But they all kept interrupting one another, and it has been impossible to memorize their tales in full, tales which would have been no less delightful to record than the ones they told in the meadow. They enjoyed themselves so much that bedtime arrived without their noticing. Madame Oisille retired, and the others, still in merry mood, followed her. So happy were they all that I think the married couples amongst them did not do quite so much sleeping as the rest—what with talking about their love in the past and demonstrating it in the present. Thus the night passed sweetly till morning broke.

---

5. The most philosophical member of the group, described elsewhere (story 11) as "so wise that he would rather die than say something foolish." He is also the saintliest; our translator indicates that his name is "a fairly obvious pun: *de goûts saints* ('of saintly tastes')."

FRANÇOIS RABELAIS

1495?–1553

The life of François Rabelais, a man of wide humanistic education in the Renaissance tradition, typifies the variety of interests of the period, for he was at various points a law student, a monk, and a practicing physician; and he knew the life of people in cities and on country estates, in monasteries and at court. Born probably about 1494–95 into a middle-class landowning family at La Devinière, near Chinon in the province of Touraine, Rabelais was the son of a successful lawyer. Apparently first drawn to a monastic career, he was trained as a novice in the Franciscan order in the monastery of La Baumette at Angers. Later, as a monk in the Franciscan monastery of Puy-Saint-Martin at Fontenay-le-Comte, he busied himself especially with the "new learning" (Greek and other humanistic studies), which was suspect to conventional theologians. In 1524 he obtained authorization from Pope Clement VII to transfer to the less strict Benedictine order. He maintained close and continuous contacts, both personal and epistolary, with prominent humanists and jurists. He probably studied law at Poitiers. Between 1527 and 1530 he seems to have traveled extensively, and probably to have studied medicine at the University of Paris, a supposition warranted by the fact that when in 1530 he entered the University of Montpellier as a medical student he received the degree of bachelor of medicine in two months. We know that in 1532 he was a physician in the important hospital of the Pont-du-Rhône at Lyon and practiced medicine with success.

Also in 1532, Rabelais published, under the name of Alcofibas Nasier, an anagram of his own name, the volume of *Pantagruel* which now constitutes Book II of *Gargantua and Pantagruel*. The story of Gargantua, the present Book I, appeared in 1534. In that year Rabelais traveled to Rome as personal physician to Jean du Bellay, then bishop of Paris and later a cardinal. In Rome in 1535 Rabelais obtained papal absolution for having discarded the monk's robe without authorization; later in the same year, back in France, his status became that of a lay priest. In 1537 he received his doctorate of medicine at Montpellier and gave lectures there, using the texts of the ancient Greek physicians such as Hippocrates in the original. In the following years he traveled widely and also acquired some standing at court, holding a minor post in the retinue of King Francis I. Court contacts helped him counteract the condemnations of his literary work by the theologians of the Sorbonne. The seriousness of his difficulties—arising out of accusations of heresy and leanings toward the Protestant Reformation—varied according to the protection that the court could grant him and his own success in compromising. After Book III of *Gargantua and Pantagruel* (1546) was banned, Rabelais resided for two years in voluntary exile at Metz in the Alsace. He was again in Rome in 1548, and in 1551 was appointed to the two curacies of Saint-Martin-de-Meudon and Saint-Christophe-de-Jambet, both of which he resigned early in 1553 because of ill health. The tradition is that Rabelais died in Paris, in the Rue des Jardins, probably in April of that same year. Book IV of *Gargantua and Pantagruel*, which had appeared in 1552, had also been banned; a fifth book, of dubious authenticity, appeared in 1562–64. It is evident from the above that Rabelais's life and work are both highly representative of the period in which he lived and yet conspicuously unique.

Rabelais was by no means exclusively a professional writer; indeed, his story of the giants Gargantua and Pantagruel, written piecemeal during his mature years, is not so much a traditional unified work of fiction as a summation of his wide knowledge, of his diverse notions of the world, and of his fantasies. Its peculiar quality may be described in terms of contrasts: the supernatural and realistic in the characters and action; the solemn and comic, lofty and bawdy in the themes; and the erudite and colloquial in the style. Rabelais's heroes, as giants, move in a dimension that is entirely out of proportion to ordinary reality. They belong—with their extraordinary size, power, and longevity—to a tradition known to us through myths, through folk tales, and through biblical narrative. Yet these same fantastic characters express the feelings and attitudes of ordinary people. In fact, they seem to be presented as epitomes of what we, according to Rabelais, ought to be in a reasonable and enjoyable world.

Rabelais's view of the world, we soon realize, is also well reflected in his literary style. High and low, pedantic and farcical, ponderous and mocking, it shows a broad intellectual and moral inclusiveness, an enthusiastic open-mindedness and gusto. As we come across the learned allusion, the solemn Ciceronian phrasing, and the scholastic pedantry, all mingled with the familiar and folksy, we notice that the presence of the colloquial quality by no means destroys the impact of the erudition or necessarily gives it the tone of parody. For Rabelais attends to both with equal delight and blends them with complete success; the resulting mixture is a consistent whole, sustained throughout by the same rich manipulation of words and the same exuberant vitality. Thus Rabelais's style concretely embodies his view of the world and of man. His message, his view of the human condition, are basically cheerful; his work is usually considered to be a major monument of the Renaissance at its most satisfied and affirmative. The basic theme of drinking, the vast thirst of Rabelais's gigantic protagonists, is conveniently taken to symbolize the healthy and all-embracing sensual and intellectual appetites of the period.

A famous contemporary of Rabelais, Benvenuto Cellini (1500–1571), mentioned in our general introduction, can also be regarded as an instance of the affirmative Renaissance spirit little hampered by doubt and melancholy. In fact, Cellini is even too pure and unmeditative, too "innocent" an example. In his fully adjusted way of living, this somewhat bombastic extrovert does not ask himself about value and meaning. Rabelais, at least implicitly, does take an interest in questions of value; and he seems assured, on what may appear to us relatively scant evidence, of the basic goodness and perfectibility of humanity. The selections from Rabelais given here emphasize that assurance, showing, among other things, his faith in a certain type of physical and mental education; they illustrate his conception of the ideal man fit to live in what he considered to be a new age. It will be observed in this connection that although Rabelais was, among Europeans of the period, as responsible as anyone for the popular notion of an intellectual Renaissance following the aridity and bondage of medieval scholasticism and the barbarism of the Gothic "night," his ideal man also possesses certain qualities that seem to us to be survivals of medieval codes. That man remains a kind of knight-at-arms, despite the added emphasis on the intellectual ornaments of humanism. And this is true of other Renaissance writers. For example, in the works of Castiglione, Cervantes, Shakespeare, and Ludovico Ariosto (1474–1533), author of the epic *Orlando Furioso*, the knightly ideal continues to appear, though variously twisted through irony or distorted in other ways. Rabelais's approach is very direct and hopeful; from his pages we receive the impression that a healthy, wise, gallant, and happy type is a concrete possibility. Give the young the right tutoring—Rabelais's implication is—do away with hampering scholasticism, let them take proper care of their bodily functions, and certain values of tolerance, *bonhommie*, and substantial well-being will finally and inevitably triumph. The sophistic, the arrogant, the hypocritical will be exposed and defeated in the most reasonable and enjoyable of worlds.

Nowhere is this pleasant view expressed more clearly than in the conception of Thélème, the supremely good place on earth, the "abbey" of Rabelais's heart and imagination, where all restrictions are banned, not because total anarchy and license are advocated but rather because for such supremely civilized "nuns" and "monks" as those of the Thélèmite order instinctive inclinations will coincide with virtue: "The constitution of this abbey had only a single clause: DO WHAT YOU WILL— because free men and women, wellborn, well taught, finding themselves joined with other respectable people, are instinctively impelled to do virtuous things and avoid vice. They draw this instinct from nature itself, and they name it 'honor.' " Such optimism is qualified, of course, by the very premise of his story. For all its realism, and in spite of the fact that some episodes are mock-heroic versions of actual and even of provincial and domestic events (the Picrochole war that precedes the establishment of the abbey of Thélème), this is still a fable, with giants as its main heroes and fantasy as its normal mode.

Much war, horror, intrigue, and injustice existed in the world as Rabelais knew it. In practical life, he muddled through by his tolerance, wisdom, and capacity for compromise (his temporary sympathy for the Protestant Reformation, in a time of raging religious conflict, stopped "this side of the stake"). But he survived also because with his literary art he invented a world fashioned according to his own aspirations. In that world, the heroes on the side of good and of justice not only win wars but also display an effective and nobly magniloquent clemency toward the vanquished. Its utopian quality again illustrates the tendency of the Renaissance mind to seek a perfect model, an exemplary, ideal form. Some important passages of the book, especially the famous letter (included in our selections) of Gargantua to Pantagruel, dated from Sir Thomas More's ideal land, Utopia, make clear that this chronicle of giants, biblical in its magnitude and in its patriarchal qualities and Renaissance in its aspiration to "achieve mental, moral and technical excellence," symbolized in its serious moments the urge to perpetuate, from generation to generation, our true and noble form and thus idealistically confirm our divine origin, our "dignity."

Mikhail Mikhailovich Bakhtin, *Rabelais and His World*, translated by Helene Iswolsky (1968), views Rabelais's satire in the racy, carnivalesque context of popular culture. Donald M. Frame, *François Rabelais: A Study* (1977), is a solid treatment intended for the general reader. Thomas M. Greene, *Rabelais: A Study in Comic Courage* (1970), gives a brief, comprehensive account of Rabelais's life and work. The general reader will find Brian Masters, *A Student's Guide to Rabelais* (1977), helpful.

Gargantua and Pantagruel[1]

Book I

(Education of a Giant Humanist)

CHAPTER 14

How Gargantua Was Taught Latin by a Terribly Learned Philosopher

This subject disposed of, that good man Grandgousier was ravished with admiration, thinking about the good sense and marvelous comprehension of his son Gargantua. And so he said to his governesses:

"Philip, king of Macedonia, understood the good sense of his son Alexander by his skill in handling a certain horse, which was so terrible, so completely wild, that no one could even get up on its back. He bucked and threw everyone who tried to ride him, breaking the neck of one, the legs of another, cracking one man's skull and shattering another's jawbone. When Alexander went down into the Hippodrome (which was where they trained and exercised their horses) and analyzed the problem, he saw that the horse's desperate fury came, simply enough, from being afraid of his own shadow. Having come to this understanding, he jumped up on the horse's back and forced him to run straight toward the sun, so that his shadow fell behind him, and by this procedure turned the horse gentle and obedient. And that showed his father what divine understanding his son possessed, and he arranged that the boy be thoroughly trained by Aristotle, who was at that time considered the best philosopher in Greece.

"But I tell you that from this one discussion, which my son and I have just had, right here in front of you, I too understand that his understanding has something divine about it—so acute, subtle, profound, and yet serene—and will attain to a singularly lofty degree of wisdom, provided he is well taught. Accordingly, I wish to put him in the hands of some scholarly man who will teach him everything he is capable of learning. And to this end I propose to open my purse as freely as need be."

So they sent for a great philosopher, Maître Tubalcain Holofernes, who taught him the alphabet so well that he could say it backward, by heart, at which point he was five years and three months old. Then he read with the boy a Latin grammar by Donatus, plus a dull and well-meaning treatise on courtesy, and a long book by Bishop Theodulus, in which he proves that ancient mythology is all a heap of nonsense, and finally an exceedingly long poem in dreadfully moral quatrains.[2] All this took thirteen years, six months, and two weeks to accomplish.

Of course, it's also true that he learned to write in Gothic letters, and wrote out all his own books that way, since this was before the art of printing had been invented.

Most of the time he carried a large writing desk, weighing more than thirty tons, with a pencil box as big and heavy as the four great pillars of

---

1. Translated by Burton Raffel.   2. The books mentioned in this chapter were actually part of the educational curriculum that Rabelais is here satirizing.

Saint-Martin d'Ainay, the old church in Lyons. And the inkpot hung down on huge iron chains, capable of supporting barrels and barrels of merchandise.

And then they read *De modis significandi*, "The Methods of Reasoned Analysis," with the commentaries of Broken Biscuithead, Bouncing Rock, Talktoomuch, Galahad, John the Fatted Calf, Balogny, Cuntprober, and a pile of others. And this took more than eighteen years and six months. And by then Gargantua knew it all so well that, if you asked him, he could recite every single line, backward, proving to his mother that he had the whole thing at his fingertips and, most important of all, that *de modis significandi non erat scientia*, the methods of reasoned analysis were neither reasonable nor a science.

Then they read that great book *Calculation*, surely the longest almanac ever compiled: this took another sixteen years and two months. And then, suddenly, his teacher died, being four hundred and twenty years old: it was the pox that carried him off.

So they brought in another old cougher, Maître Blowhard Birdbrain, with whom he read Bishop Huguito of Ferrara, Eberhard de Bethune's *Greekishnessisms*, Alexander de Villedieu's barbarous Latin grammar, Remigius' *Petty Doctrines* and also his *What's What*, a charming discourse set in question-and-answer form, the *Supplement to All Supplements*, a fat glossary of saints' lives and the like, Sulpicius' long, long poem on the psalms and death, Seneca's *De quatuor virtutibus cardinalibus*, The Four Cardinal Virtues (which wasn't by Seneca at all), Passavantus' *Mirror of True Penitence*, and the same author's *Sleep in Peace*, a collection of sermons chosen to make happy days still happier—and he also read other tough birds of the same feather. And in reading all this he became quite as wise as any blackbird ever baked in a pie.

CHAPTER 15
How Gargantua Got to Study with Other Teachers

By that point his father could see that although he was studying as hard as he could, and spending all his time at it, he didn't seem to be learning much and, what's worse, he was becoming distinctly stupid, a real simpleton, all wishy-washy and driveling.

When he complained of this to Don Philippe des Marais, viceroy of Papeligosse,[3] he was told that it would be better for Gargantua to learn nothing at all than to study such books with such teachers, whose learning was nothing but stupidity and whose wisdom was nothing but gloves with no hands in them—empty. They were specialists in ruining good and noble spirits and nipping the flowering of youth in the bud.

"To show you what I mean," he said, "take some modern youngster, who has only been studying for two years. If he doesn't show better judgment, better use of words, better ability to analyze and discuss than your

3. Rabelais probably alludes to some existing person; his method is to take real people and introduce them into his fantastic world.

son, as well as greater ease and courtesy in dealing with the world, then call me a fat-head from Brenne."[4]

Grandgousier was delighted and told him to do exactly that.

That night, at supper, des Marais introduced one of his young pages, a young fellow named Rightway (in Greek, Eudemon), who was from Villegongis, near Saint-Genou. And he was so well-groomed, so beautifully dressed, so clean and neat in every respect, so courteous in his bearing, that he more nearly resembled a little angel than a human being. And des Marais said to Grandgousier:

"See this child? He's only twelve years old. Shall we see, if you care to, what a difference there is between the learning of your bird-chirping old philosophers and modern youngsters like this?"

Grandgousier liked the idea, and told the page to give them a demonstration of what he knew. Then Rightway, after asking his master's permission to proceed, stood on his feet, his hat in his hands, his face open, his lips red, his eyes confident, his glance fixed on Gargantua with a modesty appropriate to his age, and began both to praise and to glorify Grandgousier's son, first for his virtue and his good manners, second for his knowledge, third for his nobility, fourth for his physical beauty, and then, fifth, sweetly urged him always to honor his father, who had taken such pains to have him well brought up, finally begging Gargantua to consider Master Rightway the most insignificant of his servants, for the boy asked no other gift from the heavens but the grace of pleasing Gargantua by some cheerfully rendered service. And all of this was spoken with such extraordinarily tactful gestures, with a pronunciation so clear, a voice so eloquent, and in language so elegant and such good Latin, that he more nearly resembled a kind of ancient Gracchus, or Cicero, or Ennius than a young person of his own time.

But all Gargantua could do was weep like a cow. He hid his face behind his hat, and it was no more possible to draw a word from him than to get a fart from a dead donkey.

All of which made his father so furious that he wanted to kill Maître Blowhard Birdbrain. But des Marais checked him with a well-turned word of warning, so neatly administered that it cooled his anger. But he ordered that Blowhard Birdbrain be paid what he was owed and allowed to guzzle like a philosopher. And when he'd drunk to his heart's content, he was to be told to go to the devil.

"It won't cost me a thing," he said, "not today at least, if he gets so drunk that he dies of it, like an Englishman."

Maître Blowhard Birdbrain left the house. Grandgousier sought des Marais' advice about who might be available to be Gargantua's new teacher, and the two of them decided that Powerbrain (in Greek, Ponocrates), Rightway's teacher, would be the best man for the job. The three of them would then travel to Paris, the better to understand how the young men of France were pursuing their studies.

4. An actual locality. What was said of Rabelais's characters in the preceding footnote applies also to his geography, his local lore, and the like.

CHAPTER 16

How Gargantua Was Sent to Paris, Riding an Enormous Brood Mare, Which Waged War against the Cow Flies of Beauce

Now, at this same time Fayoles, fourth king of Numidia, happened to send Grandgousier, all the way from Africa, the biggest, tallest brood mare anyone had ever seen. And the most monstrous, too (it being well known that Africa always brings forth new things), for it was the size of six elephants and it had toes, like Julius Caesar's horse; its ears hung down like a Languedoc goat, and it had a horn sticking out of its ass. For the rest, it had a kind of burned chestnut hide, mottled with gray. Most impressive of all was its ghastly tail, because—give a pound, take a pound—it was as big as the old ruin of Saint-Mars, near Langeais (which is forty feet high), and every bit as wide, with hair as closely woven as the tassels on an ear of corn.

And if that strikes you as astonishing, what do you think of those amazing Scythian rams, weighing in at more than thirty pounds apiece, and those Syrian sheep, which (if Jean Thenaud is telling the truth) have an ass so heavy, so long and massive, that they have to tie a supporting cart to its rear end so it can get about at all. You haven't got anything like it, you lowland ass bangers!

It came by sea, in three Genoan schooners and a man-of-war, to the port of Les Sables-d'Olonne, in Talmont.

When Grandgousier saw it:

"This is exactly the right thing," he said, "to carry my son to Paris. Now, God be thanked, everything will turn out all right. Someday he'll surely be a great scholar. If it weren't for our friends the animals, we'd all have to live like philosophers."

The next day, but of course only after having drunk their fill, Gargantua, his new teacher Powerbrain, and all his attendants, together with the young page Rightway, took to the road. And because the weather was calm and moderate, his father had them make soft laced boots for Gargantua. (That great bootmaker Babin tells me they go by the name of buskins.)

So they went merrily down the highway, laughing and singing, until they had almost reached Orléans. There they entered a large forest, ninety miles long and forty miles wide. The place swarmed with horrible cow flies, millions of them, and wasps and hornets, too, the sort that were true highway robbers for all poor mares and mules and horses. But Gargantua's mare took an appropriate revenge for all the outrages her species had suffered, playing a trick that those insects had never expected. Suddenly, as they entered the wood and the flies and wasps began their assault, she whipped out her tail and swatted them so vigorously that in fact she knocked down the entire forest. Left, right, here, there, length and width, over and under, she smashed those trees like a mower cutting grass, until finally there were neither any trees nor any insects, but just a nice flat stretch of land, which is all you can see to this day.

Gargantua watched this performance with immense delight. But he didn't want to sound vainglorious, so all he said to his companions was, "This is fine, but I don't want to boast." And ever since that part of the country has been known as Beauce. But all they got to put in their open mouths was their own yawns—in memory of which the gentlemen of Beauce (and everyone knows how poor they've always been) still dine by yawning and opening and closing their empty mouths, which they've grown to like, especially since it helps them spit.

When at last they reached Paris, Gargantua spent two or three days resting and recovering from their journey, drinking and chatting with the townsfolk and asking what scholars happened to be in the city at that time and what wine Parisians liked to drink.

*   *   *

CHAPTER 21

Gargantua's Studies, and His Way of Life, according to His Philosophical Teachers

Some days after the bells had been put back, and in recognition of Gargantua's courtesy in thus restoring them, the citizens of Paris offered to feed and maintain his mare for as long as he might like, an offer which Gargantua found most acceptable. So the mare was put to pasture in Fontainebleau Forest. I don't think she is still there.

Gargantua was absolutely determined to study under Powerbrain. To begin with, however, Powerbrain directed his new pupil to proceed exactly as he always had, the better to understand how, over such a long period of time, his former teachers had turned him into such a fop, such a fool and ignoramus.

Accordingly, Gargantua lived just as he usually did, waking up between eight and nine (whether it was daylight or not), exactly as his old teachers had prescribed. And they cited the words of King David: *Vanum est vobis ante lucem surgere*, It does you no good to wake before day begins.[5]

So he fooled about, swaggering, wallowing away the time in his bed (the better to enliven his animal spirits), and then dressed himself as the season dictated. But what he really liked to put on was a great long gown of heavy wool, lined with fox fur. And then he combed his hair as that great Ockhamist philosopher Jacob Almain always did—that is, with four fingers and a thumb, because his teachers used to say that, in this world of ours, to pay any more attention than that to your hair—or to washing and keeping yourself clean—was simply a waste of time.

Then he shat, pissed, vomited, belched, farted, yawned, spat, coughed, sighed, sneezed, and blew his nose abundantly. Then he put away a good breakfast, the better to protect himself against the dew and the bad morning air: good fried tripe, some nice broiled steak, several cheerful hams, some good grilled beef, and several platters of bread soaked in bouillon.

5. "It is vain for you to rise up early, to sit up late, to eat the bread of sorrows: for so he giveth his beloved sleep." (Psalm 127:2.)

Powerbrain objected, observing that, fresh out of bed and before he'd been exercising, he hardly needed to take in so much refreshment. Gargantua replied:

"What! Haven't I already done enough exercise? I turned over in bed six or seven times before I got up. Isn't that enough? That's exactly what Pope Alexander used to do, and he was following the advice of his great Jewish doctor and astrologer, Bonnet de Lates. And he lived until he died, too, in spite of those who did not wish him well. This is what my prior teachers got me used to doing, saying that breakfast helped you develop your memory: that was why they started drinking at breakfast, too. I think it's marvelous—and it starts me off so well that I eat an even better supper. And Maître Tubalcain Holofernes (who was right at the head of his class, here in Paris) used to say there was no point at all just to running well: the idea was to leave early enough. So true good health for all of us doesn't require, does it, that we gulp it down, cup after cup after cup, like ducks, but certainly that we start to drink in the morning—*unde versus*, as the little poem says:

> To wake up early in the morning isn't the point:
> You've got to wet your whistle and bend that joint."

And so, after a hearty breakfast, he went to church, where they brought him, in a huge basket, a great fat prayer book, all wrapped in velvet, so heavily oiled, with such heavy clasps, and on such luxurious parchment that it must have weighed at least twenty-five hundred pounds. And then they heard twenty-six or maybe thirty masses. And then his private chaplain would come, dressed like a society swell, and with his breath nicely fortified by wine. He and Gargantua would mumble through the litany, thumbing the rosary so carefully that not a single bead ever fell to the ground.

As he walked out of church, they brought in a heavy-wheeled log carrier and delivered for his personal use an entire cask of carved-wood rosaries, each of them as round around as the rim of a man's hat. And as he and his chaplain strolled through the cloister of the church, and its galleries and gardens, they worked at their beads, saying more prayers than sixteen hermits.

Then he put in a scant half-hour of studying, keeping his eyes on his book. But, like the character in Terence's play, his soul was in the kitchen.[6]

Then he pissed his urinal full, sat down to table, and—being naturally of a calm and imperturbable disposition—began his meal with several dozen hams, smoked beef tongues, caviar, fried tripe, and assorted other appetizers.

Meanwhile, four of his servants began to toss into his mouth, one after the other—but never stopping—shovelfuls of mustard, after which he drank an incredibly long draft of white wine, to make things easier for his kid-

6. See Terence's play *The Eunuch*, l. 816.

neys. And then, eating whatever happened to be in season and he happened to like, he stopped only when his belly began to hang down.

His drinking was totally unregulated, without any limits or decorum. As he said, the time to restrict your drinking was only when the cork soles of your slippers absorb enough so they swell half a foot thick.

*   *   *

CHAPTER 23

How Gargantua Was So Well Taught by Powerbrain That He Never Wasted a Single Hour of the Day

Once Powerbrain understood Gargantua's vicious way of life, he began to reflect on other—and better—ways of instructing him in humanistic matters. But for the first few days he did not make any changes, realizing that nature would not allow abrupt shifts without cataclysmic violence.

Accordingly, to begin his work in the best way possible, he sought the advice of a wise physician, Holygift, with whom he discussed how to set Gargantua on a better path. The learned doctor, proceeding according to his profession's canonical rules, first purged the young man with a sovereign remedy for madness, Anticyrian hellebore, which powerful herb quickly cleaned away all the deterioration and perverse habits to which his brain had succumbed. This procedure had the advantage, also, of making Gargantua forget everything he had learned from his early teachers, just as in ancient times Timotheus[7] did with disciples who'd studied under other musicians.

To help in the good work, Powerbrain introduced Gargantua to some of Paris's truly learned scholars. In trying to be like them, he came to understand their spirit, wanting to acquire knowledge and to make something of himself.

And then he got him into such a way of studying that no hour in the day was wasted: all his time was spent in pursuit of humanistic learning and honest knowledge.

Accordingly, Gargantua now woke up at four in the morning. He would be given a massage, while a portion of the holy Scriptures was read aloud to him, in a high, clear voice, with precise and accurate pronunciation. A young page named Reader, a native of Basché, was given this task. The subject, and also the argument, of this lesson often led Gargantua into reverence and adoration of God, the majesty and marvelous wisdom of whom had thus been exhibited to him, and into prayer and supplication.

Then he would go off and, in some private place, permit the natural result of his digestive process to be excreted. While he was thus occupied, his teacher would repeat what had been read to him, clarifying and explaining the more obscure and difficult points.

7. Timotheus of Miletus, famous musician of the time of Alexander the Great.

Coming back, they would examine and reflect on the state of the heavens: was everything as it had been when they'd seen the sky the night before? into what constellations had the sun newly entered, and likewise the moon?

And then he was dressed and combed, his hair was properly done, and he was equipped and perfumed, while all the time the lessons he'd been given the day before were repeated for him. He recited them by heart, showing by some practical and compassionate illustrations that he understood their meaning. This often lasted two or three hours, though ordinarily they stopped when he was fully dressed.

Then he was read to for three solid hours.

After which they went outdoors, always discussing the meaning of what had been read, and went to the park or somewhere near it, where they played various games, especially three-handed palm ball, giving their bodies the same elegant exercise they had earlier given their souls.

Their games were entirely free: they stopped whenever they felt like stopping—usually when they'd worked up a sweat or when they grew tired. Then they had a vigorous massage, and were wiped clean; they'd change their shirts and, walking quietly, would go to see if dinner was ready. And as they waited they'd recite, clearly and eloquently, remembered portions of the lesson.

However, Sir Appetite arrived, and when they could they seated themselves at the table.

Some entertaining story of ancient heroism was read to them, at the start of the meal, until wine was poured in Gargantua's cup.

Then, if they liked the idea, the reading was resumed, or else they'd begin to chat happily. At the beginning of this new regime, they talked about virtue, proper behavior, the nature and effect of everything placed on their table that day: bread, wine, water, salt, meat, fish, fruit, herbs, roots, and about the preparation of these things. In so doing, Gargantua soon learned all the appropriate passages from Pliny, Athenaeus, Dioscorides, Julius Pollux, Galen, Porphyry, Oppian, Polybius, Heliodorus, Aristotle, Claudius Aelian, and others.[8] In order to be sure they had their authorities right, they'd often have the books brought right to the table. And what was said became so clearly and entirely fixed in Gargantua's memory that no doctor alive understood anything like as much as he did.

Then, talking about the lessons read that morning, and finishing their meal with some quinced sweet, Gargantua would clean his teeth with a bit of fresh green mastic twig. He'd wash his hands and his eyes with good fresh water, and give thanks to God with sweet hymns of praise for His munificence and divine kindness. And cards were brought, not for playing games of chance, but to learn a thousand gracious things and new inventions, all founded in arithmetic.

8. Some of the most famous scientific authors of antiquity are listed in Gargantua's new curriculum, which, exacting as it is, reflects a less "medieval" type of learning than was embodied in his earlier course of study. See also the enumeration of authors on p. 1754.

And in this way Gargantua developed a genuine liking for the numerical science. Every day, after both dinner and supper, he passed his time in arithmetical games just as pleasantly as when he'd been in the habit of playing at dice or cards. Indeed, he came to understand both the theory and the practice of arithmetic so well that Cuthbert Tunstal, the Englishman who had written so much on the subject,[9] was obliged to admit that, truly, in comparison to Gargantua, all he understood was a pack of nonsense.

But arithmetic wasn't the end of it, for they went on to other mathematical sciences, like geometry, astronomy, and music. While waiting for their meal to be digested and properly absorbed, they worked out a thousand pleasant geometrical figures, and shaped appropriate instruments, and practiced astronomical laws in the same way.

Later, they had a wonderful good time, singing four- and five-part rounds, and sometimes singing variations on some melody that was a delight to their throats.

As for musical instruments, Gargantua learned to play the lute, the clavier, the harp, the transverse flute as well as the recorder, the viol, and also the trombone.

As this hour passed, digestion was indeed accomplished, and so he proceeded to purge himself of his natural excrement. Then he at once returned to his main studies for three hours or even more, in order to repeat the morning's lesson and also to continue with whatever book had been set for him. And he practiced writing in the Italian and the Gothic alphabets, and also drawing.

And then they'd go back to their rooms, and along with them went a young gentleman from Touraine, Squire Gymnast by name, who was teaching Gargantua the arts of knighthood.

After changing his clothes, Gargantua would mount a battle horse, a traveling steed, a Spanish stallion, an Arabian racehorse, and a light, quick horse, and ride a hundred laps, making his mount fairly fly through the air, jump ditches, leap over fences, make quick circular turns, both to the right and to the left.

Nor did he break his lance, for it is sheer nonsense to say, "I broke ten lances in battle." Any carpenter could do as much. Real glory comes from breaking ten of your enemies' with one of your own. So, with his steel-tipped, solid, firm lance he learned to break down a door, crack open a suit of armor, uproot a tree, strike right through the center of a hoop, knock a knight's saddle right off his horse, and carry away a coat of mail or a pair of armored gloves. And all the time he was himself in armor, from his head right down to his toes.

When it came to marching his horse in rhythm, or making the animal obey his commands, there was simply no one better. Even Cesare Fieschi, the famous equestrian acrobat, seemed no better than a monkey on horseback, in comparison. He was especially good at leaping from one horse to

9. Tunstal was the author of the treatise *The Art of Computation* (*De arte supputandi*, 1522).

another, without ever setting foot on the ground—the horses were known as leapers—and he could do this from either side, lance erect, without stirrups. Without any reins or bridle he could make a horse do anything he wanted it to do. In short, he was accomplished at everything useful in military matters.

Some days he exercised with the battle-ax, which he could wield like a razor, swinging it so powerfully, slicing it around in a circle so deftly, that he was ranked a knight at arms, passing every sort of trial and declared fit for any battle.

And then he'd practice with the pickax, or at wielding the two-handed sword, or with the short sword (so perfect for thrusting and parrying), and the dagger—sometimes wearing armor, sometimes not, or using a shield, or wearing a cape, or carrying a small wrist shield, known as a *rondelle*.

He hunted deer—stag and doe and fallow buck—bears, wild boar, hares, partridge, pheasant, buzzards. He played with the big kickball, making it bound high in the air, sometimes with his foot, sometimes with his fist. He fought and ran and leaped and jumped—but not a mere three-foot hop and leap, or a high jump in the German style—because, as Gymnast said, jumps of that sort were useless and of no good whatever, when it came to real war—but he'd jump great wide ditches, go flying over a hedgerow, climb six paces up a wall, and thus get in through a window as high off the ground as a lance.

He swam in deep water, breaststroke, backstroke, sidestroke, using his entire body or only his legs, or with one hand high in the air and holding a book, crossing the Seine River without getting a page wet. He swam with his cloak in his teeth, as Julius Caesar did (says Plutarch). Then, pulling himself right into a boat with just one hand, he'd throw himself back into the water, head first, going all the way down to the bottom, sinking among the rocks and swimming to great depths, plunging down to all sorts of chasms and deep abysses. Then he'd turn the boat, and steer it, sometimes quickly, sometimes slowly, now downstream, now upstream, sometimes bringing it to a halt by pressing it against a milldam, guiding it with one hand, his other wielding a great oar or raising the sail. He'd climb up the guide ropes, right to the top of the mast, and run out along the spars. He'd adjust the compass, brace the bowlines, tighten the helm.

Leaving the water, he'd go directly up a mountain and then come right down again. He'd climb trees like a cat, jumping from one to the other like a squirrel, tearing down thick branches as if he were another Milo of Croton. With a pair of sharp-pointed daggers and a couple of good marlinespikes, he'd climb to the top of a house exactly like a rat, then leap down so expertly that the drop wouldn't cause him so much as a twinge.

He threw the javelin, and the iron bar, the millstone, the boar spear, the hunting spear, the spiked halberd. He drew the longbow like an archer, pulled crossbows taut (though this was usually done with a winch), sighted a rifle right against his eye (though usually it had to be rested against the shoulder), set up and mounted cannon, centering them right in on target, aimed them so they could knock a stuffed parrot off a pole, pointing them straight up a mountain or right down into a valley, directing their fire up ahead or to the side or, like the ancient Parthians, back behind him.

They would attach a rope cable to some high tower, hanging down to the ground, and he would climb this, hand over hand, then come down so strongly and with such confidence that he might just as well have been strolling along some nice, flat meadow.

They would rig up a long pole, supported on each side by a tree, and he'd hang from it by his hands, going this way and that without his feet ever touching the ground—and at such a speed that, even running on flat ground, it would have been impossible to catch him.

And in order to exercise his chest and lungs, he would shout like all the devils in hell. Once, I heard him call to Rightway, from the Saint Victor Gate all the way across Paris to Montmartre. Even bull-throated Stentor,[1] at the battle of Troy, could not shout so loud.

To toughen his nerves, they made him two huge molded lead weights, cast in the shape of salmon, each just over eighty thousand pounds: he called them his dumbbells. He'd lift one in each hand, starting from the ground, and hold them both high up over his head—and then he'd keep them there, not moving a muscle, for three-quarters of an hour or even more. This was literally unmatchable strength!

No one was stronger, not in barriers or tug-of-war or any of the games. When it was his turn, he stood his ground so firmly that he could afford to let the most adventurous try to move him a single inch from his place, exactly as Milo of Croton used to do—and in imitation of whom he would clasp a pomegranate in his hand and offer it to anyone who could take it from him. Nor would he permit the fruit to be damaged in the attempt.

Having thus spent his time, he'd have another massage, then clean himself and change his clothes, returning with a smile and, strolling through meadows and other grassy spots, he'd turn his attention to trees and plants, examining them in the light of what the ancients wrote—Theophrastus, Dioscorides, Marinus, Pliny, Nicander, Aemilius Macer, and Galen.[2] He and his companions would fill their hands with herbs and roots and flowers, then bring it all back to their lodgings, where a young page, Rootgatherer, was in charge of all such matters, including care of the hoes, picks, rakes, spades, shovels, and everything else needed for the proper care of growing things.

And once they were back at their lodgings, and while waiting for their supper, they would repeat selected passages from what they had read, earlier, and also what they had discussed at table.

Note, please, that although dinner was a sober and even frugal meal, at which Gargantua would eat only just enough to control the growling in his stomach, supper was a great abundant affair. He would consume everything he needed to sustain and properly nourish himself, which is exactly

1. The loud-voiced herald in the *Iliad*, Book V.   2. Greek and Roman scientists.

the sort of diet prescribed by any good, knowing doctor, though there are plenty of medical hacks (in constant dispute, of course, with learned academic philosophers) who advise exactly the opposite.

Gargantua continued his lessons all during supper, or for as long as he felt in the mood. And then he would turn to good solid discussion, literate, informed, useful.

After a final grace had been said, they would turn to music, singing, the harmonious playing of various instruments, or to pleasant card and dice games. And there they would stay, having a fine time, often amusing themselves until it was time to go to bed. And sometimes they would go visiting the houses of learned people, or perhaps those newly returned from foreign countries.

When night had truly arrived, but before they climbed into bed, they would stand in their lodgings, in the spot from which the sky could be most closely observed, and compare notes about any comets they might see, and the configuration of the stars, their location and aspect, their oppositions and conjunctions.

And then Gargantua and Powerbrain would briefly recapitulate, according to the Pythagorean fashion, everything Gargantua had read and seen and understood, everything he had done and heard, all day long.

They would both pray to God their Creator, worshiping, reaffirming their faith, glorifying Him for His immense goodness and thanking Him for all they had been given, and forever placing themselves in His hands.

And then they would go to sleep.

CHAPTER 24

What Gargantua Did When It Was Rainy

When the weather turned rainy and bad, the time before dinner went exactly as usual, except that Gargantua had a good bright fire lit, to help moderate the intemperate air. But after dinner, in place of exercise, they would stay indoors and, according to the best therapeutic approach, amuse themselves by baling hay, sawing and splitting wood, and threshing the grain stored in the barn. Then they would study the art of painting and sculpture, or else (following ancient custom) play knucklebones, an entertainment about which Leonicus Thomaeus[3] has written so well—and a game which Andreas Lascaris,[4] teacher and friend of Erasmus, and my good friend too, has played with such pleasure. And while they played they turned over in their mind all the passages from classical authors in which the game is either mentioned or used as a metaphor.

In the same way, they would either go to watch the work at metal foundries, or the casting of cannon, or go to observe jewelers, goldsmiths, and those who cut precious stones, or else alchemists and coin makers, or tapestry weavers, silk weavers, velvet makers, watchmakers, mirror makers, printers, organ manufacturers, dyers, and other craftsmen of that sort. And

---

3. A Venetian, professor at Padua (d. 1531).   4. André Jean de Lascaris (ca. 1445–ca.1535), librarian to King Francis I and a friend of Rabelais's.

treating all of them to wine, they learned from the mouths of these masters what their various trades and inventions were all about.

They would go to hear public lectures, solemn convocations, and the careful orations, declamations, and pleadings of wellborn lawyers, or the sermons of evangelical preachers.

He went to all the places where swordsmanship was practiced and taught, and tested himself against those who taught it, in every aspect of fencing and with all the sorts of swords and foils known. And he demonstrated to them that he knew as much as they did, and more.

Instead of going off to collect herbs and examine plants and flowers, they would go to drugstores, herb sellers, and other apothecaries, and contemplate with great care the fruits, roots, leaves, gums, seeds, and all the exotic unguents, and then how they were prepared and diluted for more effective use.

He went to see the jugglers and clowns, the magicians and those who peddled wonderful, half-magical remedies, and contemplated their games and tricks, their somersaults and smooth patter, especially those famous mountebanks from Chauny, in Picardy—born with a silver tongue, every one of them, able to sell water to people swimming in a lake or firewood to those who live inside a volcano.

They would return for supper, and eat more sparingly than on other days—in particular, meats that tend to dry and tame the body. This was made necessary by the excessive humidity in the air, which under the circumstances there was no way to avoid. These simple dietary measures corrected that natural imbalance and saved them from being bothered by the loss of their usual exercise.

And this was how Gargantua's life was regulated. He kept to these rules every day, and he benefited—to be sure!—as a young man of his years can, a youth with good sense. All regular exercise, no matter how hard it may at first seem, becomes pleasant and easy and finally great good fun, more like a royal pastime than a scholar's plodding.

In spite of which, and in order to allow him some relief from such a whirlwind way of life, Powerbrain made sure that Gargantua took off at least one day a month, some day of great clarity and calm brightness. They would leave Paris early in the morning and go to one of the pleasant villages beloved of all Parisian students—Gentilly, perhaps, or Boulogne on the Seine, or Montrouge, or Pont-Charenton, or Vanves, or Saint-Cloud. And they would spent the entire day there, just as happily as they could manage, laughing, telling jokes, drinking gaily, playing, singing, dancing, lying on their backs in beautiful meadows, hunting for sparrows' nests, catching quail, and fishing for frogs and crayfish.

But even on this day spent without books and reading, they didn't completely neglect higher matters, because even lying there in the lovely meadows they would recite from memory cheerful verses from Virgil's *Georgics*, from Hesiod, from Politian's *Rusticus* (Farming), or some pleasant Latin epigrams, which they'd then turn into equally pleasant poems in their own language.

And when they feasted they would not simply mix their wine and water. Instead, as Cato advises in his *Country Matters*, and Pliny too, they would use a cup of ivy wood and wash the wine in a full basin of water, then pour it back out with a funnel.[5] And they would pour the water from one glass to another and construct tiny automatic engines that seemed to work of their own accord, like automatons.

(The Abbey of Thélème)

CHAPTER 52

How Gargantua Built the Abbey of Desire (Thélème) for Brother John

The only one still left to be provided for was the monk.[6] Gargantua wanted to make him abbot of Seuilly, but the monk refused. Gargantua also offered him the abbey of Bourgueil or that of Saint-Florent, whichever best pleased him—and said he could have both those rich, old Benedictine cloisters, if he preferred that.[7] But the monk answered him in no uncertain terms: he wanted neither to govern nor to be in charge of other monks:

"And how," he asked, "should I govern others, when I don't know how to govern myself? If you really think I've done something for you, and I might in the future do something to please you, grant me this: establish an abbey according to my plan."

The request pleased Gargantua, so he offered him the whole land of Thélème, alongside the river Loire, two leagues from the great forest of Port-Huault. And the monk then asked Gargantua to establish this abbey's rules and regulations completely differently from all the others.

"Obviously," said Gargantua, "it won't be necessary to build walls all around it, because all the other abbeys are brutally closed in."

"Indeed," said the monk, "and for good reason. Whenever you've got a whole load of stones in front and a whole load of stones in back, you've got a whole lot of grumbling and complaining, and jealousy, and all kinds of conspiracies."

Moreover, since some of the cloisters already built in this world are in the habit, whenever any woman enters them (I speak only of modest, virtuous women), of washing the ground where she walked, it was decreed that if either a monk or a nun happened to enter the abbey of Thélème, they would scrub the blazes out of the places where they'd been. And since everything is completely regulated, in all the other cloistered houses, tied in and bound down, hour by hour, according to a fierce schedule, it was decreed that in Thélème there would not be a single clock, or even a sundial, and that work would be distributed strictly according to what was needed and who was available to do it—because (said Gargantua) the worst waste of time he knew of was counting the hours—what good could pos-

---

5. Both Cato in his book *On Farming* (*De re rustica*), CIX, and Pliny in his *Natural History* Book XVI, Chapter 63, suggest an ivy-wood cup as a means to detect water in wine.   6. Brother John of the Funnels, the muscular and highly unconventional monk who has had a major part in helping the party of Gargantua's father win the mock-heroic war against the arrogant Picrochole.   7. A satiric allusion to the custom of accumulating church livings.

sibly come of it?—and the biggest, fattest nonsense in the whole world was to be ruled by the tolling of a bell rather than by the dictates of common sense and understanding.

Item: because in these times of ours women don't go into convents unless they're blind in one eye, lame, humpbacked, ugly, misshapen, crazy, stupid, deformed, or pox-ridden, and men only if they're tubercular, low born, blessed with an ugly nose, simpletons, or a burden on their parents . . .

("Oh yes," said the monk, "speaking of which: if a woman isn't pretty and she isn't good, what sort of path can she cut for herself?"

"Straight into a convent," said Gargantua.

"To be sure," said the monk, "especially with a scissors and a needle.")

. . . it was decreed that, in Thélème, women would be allowed only if they were beautiful, well formed, and cheerful, and men only if they were handsome, well formed, and cheerful.

Item: since men were not allowed in convents, unless they sneaked in under cover of darkness, it was decreed that in Thélème there would never be any women unless there were men, nor any men unless there were women.

Item: because both men and women, after they'd entered a cloister and served their probationary year, were obliged to spend the entire rest of their lives there, it was decided that men and women who came to Thélème could leave whenever they wanted to, freely and without restriction.

Item: because monks and nuns usually took three vows—chastity, poverty, and obedience—it was decided that in Thélème one could perfectly honorably be married, that anyone could be rich, and that they could all live wherever they wanted to.

As an age limitation, women should be allowed in at any time from ten to fifteen, and men from twelve to eighteen.

CHAPTER 53

How the Abbey of Desire (Thélème) Was Built and Endowed

In order to build and equip the abbey, Gargantua gave two million seven hundred thousand eight hundred and thirty-one gold pieces. Further, until everything had been completed, he assigned the yearly sum of one million six hundred and sixty thousand gold pieces, from the tolls on the river Dive, payable in funds of an unimaginable astrological purity. To endow and perpetually maintain the abbey he gave two million three hundred thousand and sixty-nine English pounds in property rentals, tax-free, fully secured, and payable yearly at the abbey gate, to which effect he had written out all the appropriate deeds and grants.

The building was hexagonal, constructed so that at each angle there was a great round tower sixty feet in diameter, and each of the towers was exactly like all the others. The river Loire was on the north side. One of the towers, called Artice (meaning "Arctic," or "Northern"), ran down almost to the riverbank; another, called Calaer (meaning "Lovely Air"), was just to the east. Then came Anatole (meaning "Oriental," or "Eastern"), and Mesembriné (meaning "Southern"), and then Hesperia (meaning "Occidental," or "Western"), and finally Cryere (meaning "Glacial"). The distance between each of the towers was three hundred and twelve feet. The building had six floors, counting the subterranean cellars as the first. The second or ground floor had a high vault, shaped like a basket handle. The other floors were stuccoed in a circular pattern, the way they do such things in Flanders; the roof was of fine slate, the coping being lead-decorated with small figurines and animals, handsomely colored and gilded; and there were rainspouts jutting out from the walls, between the casement windows, painted all the way to the ground with blue and gold stripes and ending in great pipes which led down to the river, below the building.

This was all a hundred times more magnificent than the grand chateau at Bonnivet, or that at Chambord, or that at Chantilly,[8] because it had nine thousand three hundred and thirty-two suites, each furnished with an antechamber, a private reading room, a dressing room, and a small personal chapel, and also because each and every room adjoined its own huge hall. Between each tower, in the middle of the main building, was a spiral staircase, its stairs made of crystal porphyry and red Numidian marble and green marble struck through with red and white, all exactly twenty-two feet wide and three fingers thick, there being twelve stairs between each landing. Further: each landing had a beautiful double arch, in Greek style, thus allowing light to flood through and also framing an entryway into overhanging private rooms, each of them just as broad as the stairway itself. The stair wound all the way to the roof, ending there in a pavilion. Off the stair, on each side, one could come to a great hall; the stair also led the way to the private suites and rooms.

Between the tower called Artice and that called Cryere were great beautiful reading rooms, well stocked with books in Greek, Latin, Hebrew, French, Italian, and Spanish, carefully divided according to the languages in which they had been written.

In the center of the main building, entered through an arch thirty-six yards across, stood a marvelous circular ramp. It was fashioned so harmoniously, and built so large, that six men-at-arms, their lances at the ready, could ride clear up to the top of the building, side by side.

Between the tower called Anatole and that called Mesembriné were beautiful galleries, large and open, painted with scenes of ancient heroism, episodes drawn from history, and strange and fascinating plants and animals. Here, too, just as on the side facing the river, were a ramp and a gate. And on this gate was written, in large antique letters, the poem which follows:

---

8. Châteaux built in the early and middle years of the sixteenth century. By referring to actual buildings, building materials, and architectural elements, Rabelais as usual mixed realism with his fantasy.

CHAPTER 54

The Inscription on the Great Gate of Thélème

Hypocrites, bigots, stay away!
Old humbugs, puffed-up liars, playful
Religious frauds, worse than Goths
Or Ostrogoths (or other sloths):
No hairshirts, here, no sexy monks,
No healthy beggars, no preaching skunks,
No cynics, bombasts ripe with abuse:
Go peddle them elsewhere, your filthy views.

    Your wicked talk
    Would clutter our walks
    Like clustering flies:
    But flies or lies,
    We've no room for your cries,
    Your wicked talk.

Hungry lawyers, stay away!
People eaters, who grab while praying,
Scribes and assessors, and gouty judges
Who beat good men with the law's thick cudgels
And tie old pots to their tails, like dogs,
We'll hop you up and down like frogs,
We'll hang you high from the nearest tree:
We're decent men, not legal fleas.

    Summons and complaints
    Don't strike us as quaint,
    And we haven't got time
    For your legal whine
    As you hang from the line
    Of your summons and complaints.

Money suckers, stay away!
Greedy gougers, spending your days
Gobbling up men, stuffing your guts
With gold, you black-faced crows, busting
Your butts for another load of change,
Though your cellar's bursting with rotten exchange.
O lazy scum, you'll pile up more,
Till smiling death knocks at your door.

    Inhuman faces
    With ghastly spaces
    That no heart can see,
    Find other places:
    Here you can't be,
    You inhuman faces.

Slobbering old dogs, stay away!
Old bitter faces, old sour ways,
We want you elsewhere—the jealous, the traitors,
The slime who live as danger creators,
Wherever you come from, you're worse than wolves:
Shove it, you mangy, scabby oafs!
None of your stinking, ugly sores:
We've seen enough, we want no more.

> Honor and praise
> Fill all our days:
> We sing delight
> All day, all night:
> These are our ways:
> Honor and praise.

But you, you, you can always come,
Noble knights and gentlemen,
For this is where you belong: there's money
Enough, and pleasure enough: honey
And milk for all, and all as one:
Come be my friends, come join our fun,
O gallants, sportsmen, lovers, friends,
Or better still: come, gentlemen.

> Gentle, noble,
> Serene and subtle,
> Eternally calm;
> Civility's balm
> To live without trouble,
> Gentle, noble.

And welcome, you who know the Word
And preach it wherever the Word should be heard:
Make this place your holy castle
Against the false religious rascals
Who poison the world with filthy lies:
Welcome, you with your eyes on the skies
And faith in your hearts: we can fight to the death
For truth, fight with our every breath.

> For the holy Word
> Can still be heard,
> That Word is not dead:
> It rings in our heads,
> And we rise from our beds
> For that holy Word.

And welcome, ladies of noble birth,
Live freely here, like nowhere on earth!
Flowers of loveliness, with heaven in your faces,
Who walk like angels, the wisdom of ages
In your hearts: welcome, live here in honor,
As the lord who made this refuge wanted:

He built it for you, he gave it gold
To keep it free: Enter, be bold!

Money's a gift
To give, to lift
The souls of others:
It makes men brothers
In eternal bliss:
For money's a gift.

CHAPTER 55

How They Lived at Thélème

In the middle of the inner court was a magnificent fountain of beautiful alabaster. Above it stood the three Graces, holding the symbolic horns of abundance: water gushed from their breasts, mouths, ears, eyes, and every other body opening.

The building which rose above this fountain stood on giant pillars of translucent quartz and porphyry, joined by archways of sweeping classical proportions. And inside there were handsome galleries, long and large, decorated with paintings and hung with antlers and the horns of the unicorn, rhinoceros, hippopotamus, as well as elephant teeth and tusks and other spectacular objects.

The women's quarters ran from the tower called Artice all the way to the gates of the tower called Mesembriné. The rest was for men. Right in front of the women's quarters was a kind of playing field, an arena-like space set just between the two first towers, on the outer side. Here too were the horse-riding circle, a theater, and the swimming pools, with attached baths at three different levels, all provided with everything one could need, as well as with an endless supply of myrtle water.

Next to the river was a beautiful pleasure garden, and in the middle of it stood a handsome labyrinth. Between the other two towers were fields for playing palm ball and tennis. Alongside the tower called Cryere were the orchards, full of fruit trees of every description, carefully arranged in groups of five, staggered by rows of three. At the end was a great stretch of pastures and forest, well stocked with all kinds of wild animals.

Between the third pair of towers were the target ranges for muskets, bows, and crossbows. The offices were in a separate building, only one story high, which stood just beside the tower called Hesperia, and the stables were just beyond there. The falcon house was situated in front of the offices, staffed with thoroughly expert falconers and hawk trainers: every year supplies of every sort of bird imaginable, all perfect specimens of their breed, were sent by the Cretans, the Venetians, and the Sarmatian-Poles: eagles, great falcons, goshawks, herons and cranes and wild geese, partridge, gyrfalcons, sparrow hawks, tiny but fierce merlins, and others, so well trained and domesticated that, when they left the chateau to fly about in the fields, they would catch everything they found and bring everything to their handlers. The kennels were a bit farther away, in the direction of the woods and pastures.

All the rooms in all the suites, as well as all the smaller private rooms, were hung with a wide variety of tapestries, which were regularly changed to suit the changing seasons. The floors were covered with green cloth, the beds with embroidery. Every dressing room had a mirror of Venetian crystal, framed in fine gold, decorated around with pearls, and so exceedingly large that one could in truth see oneself in it, complete and entire. Just outside the doorways, in the ladies' quarters, were perfumers and hairdressers, who also attended to the men who visited. Every morning, too, they brought rosewater to each of the ladies' rooms, and also orange and myrtle water—and brought each lady a stick of precious incense, saturated with all manner of aromatic balms.

CHAPTER 56

How the Men and Women Who Dwelled at Thélème Were Dressed

In the beginning, the ladies dressed themselves as they pleased. Later, of their own free will, they changed and styled themselves all as one, in the following way:

They wore scarlet or yellow stockings, bordered with pretty embroidery and fretwork, which reached exactly three fingers above the knee. Their garters were colored like their bracelets (gold, enameled with black, green, red, and white), fastened both above and below the knee. Their shoes, dancing pumps, and slippers were red or purple velvet, with edges jagged like lobsters' claws.

Over the chemise they wore a handsome corset, woven of rich silk shot through with goat hair. Over this they wore taffeta petticoats, in white, red, tan, gray, and so on, and on top of this petticoat a tunic of silver taffeta embroidered with gold thread, sewn in tight spirals—or if they were in the mood and the weather was right, their tunics might be of satin, or damask, or orange-colored velvet, or perhaps tan, green, mustard gray, blue, clear yellow, red, scarlet, white, gold, or silvered linen, with bordered spirals, or embroidery, according to what holiday was being celebrated.

Their dresses, again according to the season, were of golden linen waved with silver, or red satin decorated with gold thread, or taffeta in white, blue, black, or tan, or silk serge, or that same rich silk shot through with goat hair, or velvet slashed with silver, or silvered linen, or golden, or else velvet or satin laced with gold in a variety of patterns.

Sometimes, in the summer, they wore shorter gowns, more like cloaks, ornamented in the ways I have described, or else full-length capes in the Moorish style, of purple velvet waved with gold and embroidered with thin spirals of silver, or else with heavier gold thread, decorated at the seams with small pearls from India. They were never without beautiful feathers in their hair, colored to match the sleeves of their gowns and always spangled in gold. In the winter they wore taffeta dresses, colored as I have described, lined with lynx fur, or black skunk, or Calabrian marten, or sable, or some other precious pelt.

Their prayer beads, rings, neck chains, and collar pieces were made of fine gems—red garnets, rubies, orange-red spinels, diamonds, sapphires, emeralds, turquoises, garnets, agates, green beryls, pearls, and fat onion pearls of a rare excellence.

They covered their heads, once again, as the season demanded: in winter, in the French style, with a velvet hood hanging down in the back like a pigtail; in spring, in the Spanish style, with a lace veil; in summer, in the Italian mode, with bare ringed hair studded with jewels, except on Sundays and holidays, when they used the French fashion, which seemed to them both more appropriate and more modest.

And the men wore their fashions, too: their stockings were of light linen or serge, colored scarlet, yellow, white, or black; their breeches were velvet, in the same colors (or very nearly), embroidered and patterned however they pleased. Their jackets were of gold or silver cloth, in velvet, satin, damask, taffeta, once again in the same colors, impeccably patterned and decorated and worn. Their shoes were laced to the breeches with silken thread, colored as before, each lace closed with an enameled gold tip. Their undervests and cloaks were of golden cloth or linen, or silver cloth, or velvet embroidered however they liked. Their gowns were as costly and beautiful as the women's, with silk belts, colored to match their breeches. Each of them wore a handsome sword, with a decorated hilt, the scabbard of velvet (the color matching their stockings), its endpiece of gold and heavily worked jewelry—and their daggers were exactly the same. Their hats were of black velvet, thickly garnished with golden berries and buttons, and the feathered plumes were white, delicately spangled in gold rows and fringed with rubies, emeralds, and the like.

But there was such a close fellowship between the men and the women that they were dressed almost exactly alike, day after day. And to make sure that this happened, certain gentlemen were delegated to inform the others, each and every morning, what sort of clothing the women had chosen to wear that day—because of course the real decisions, in this matter, were made by the women.

Although they wore such well-chosen and rich clothing, don't think these women wasted a great deal of time on their gowns and cloaks and jewelry. There were wardrobe men who, each day, had everything prepared in advance, and their ladies' maids were so perfectly trained that everyone could be dressed from head to toe, and beautifully, in the twinkling of an eye. And to make sure that all of this was perpetually in good order, the wood of Thélème was surrounded by a vast block of houses, perhaps half a league long, good bright buildings well stocked and supplied, and here lived goldsmiths, jewelers, embroiderers, tailors, specialists in hammering and filamenting gold and silver, velvet makers, tapestry weavers, and upholsterers, and they all worked at their trades right there alongside Thélème, and only for the men and women who dwelled in that abbey. All their supplies, metals and minerals and cloths, came to them courtesy My Lord Shipmaster (Nausiclète, in Greek), who each year brought in seven boats from the Little Antilles, the Pearl and Cannibal islands, loaded down with gold ingots, raw silk, pearls, and all sorts of gemstones. And any of the fat pearls which began to lose their sparkle and their natural whiteness were restored by feeding them to handsome roosters (as Avicenna recommends), just as we give laxatives to hawks and falcons.

<h2 style="text-align:center">CHAPTER 57</h2>

How the Men and Women of Thélème Governed Their Lives

Their lives were not ordered and governed by laws and statutes and rules, but according to their own free will. They rose from their beds when it seemed to them the right time, drank, ate, worked, and slept when they felt like it. No one woke them or obliged them to drink, or to eat, or to do anything whatever. This was exactly how Gargantua had ordained it. The constitution of this abbey had only a single clause:

<h2 style="text-align:center">DO WHAT YOU WILL</h2>

—because free men and women, wellborn, well taught, finding themselves joined with other respectable people, are instinctively impelled to do virtuous things and avoid vice. They draw this instinct from nature itself, and they name it "honor." Such people, if they are subjected to vile constraints, brought down to a lower moral level, oppressed and enslaved and turned away from that noble passion toward which virtue pulls them, find themselves led by that same passion to throw off and break any such bondage, just as we always seek out forbidden things and long for whatever is denied us.

And their complete freedom set them nobly in competition, all of them seeking to do whatever they saw pleased any one among them. If he or she said, "Let's drink," everyone drank. If he or she said, "Let's play," they all played. If he or she said, "Let's go and have fun in the meadows," there they all went. If they were engaged in falconry or hunting, the women joined in, mounted on their good tame horses, light but proud, delicately sporting heavy leather gloves, a sparrow hawk perched on their wrists, or a small falcon, or a tiny but fierce merlin. (The other birds were carried by men.)

All of them had been so well educated that there wasn't one among them who could not read, write, sing, play on harmonious instruments, speak five or six languages, and write easy poetry and clear prose in any and all of them. There were never knights so courageous, so gallant, so light on their feet, and so easy on their horses, knights more vigorous, agile, or better able to handle any kind of weapon. There were never ladies so well bred, so delicate, less irritable, or better trained with their hands, sewing and doing anything that any free and worthy woman might be asked to do.

And for this reason, when the time came for anyone to leave the abbey, whether because his parents had summoned him or on any other account, he took one of the ladies with him, she having accepted him, and then they were married. And whatever devotion and friendship they had shown one another, when they lived at Thélème, they continued and even exceeded in their marriage, loving each other to the end of their days just as much as they did on the first day after their wedding. . . .

Book II

(Pantagruel: Birth and Education)

CHAPTER 2

The Birth of the Very Formidable Pantagruel

When he was four hundred and ninety-four, plus four more, Gargantua begat his son Pantagruel on his wife, the daughter of the king of the Amaurotes, in Utopia. Her name was Bigmouth, or Babedec,[9] as we say in the provinces, and she died giving birth to the baby: he was so immensely big, and weighed so incredibly much, that it was impossible for him to see the light without snuffing out his mother.

Now, to truly understand how he got his name, which was bestowed on him at the baptismal font, you must be aware that in the year of his birth there had been such a fearful drought, all across the continent of Africa, that it had not rained for more than thirty-six months, three weeks, four days, thirteen hours, and a little bit over, and the sun had been so hot, and so fierce, that the whole earth had dried up. It wasn't any hotter even in the days of the prophet Elijah than in that year, for not a tree on earth had a leaf or a bud. Grass never turned green, rivers dried up, fountains went dry; the poor fish, deprived of their proper element, flopped about on the ground, crying horribly; since there was no dew to make the air dense enough, the birds could not fly; dead animals lay all over the fields and meadows, their mouths gaping wide—wolves, foxes, stags, wild boars, fallow does, hares, rabbits, weasels, martens, badgers, and many, many others. And it was no better for human beings, whose lives became pitiful things. You could see them with their tongues hanging out, like hares that have been running for six solid hours. Some of them threw themselves down into wells; others crawled into a cow's belly, to stay in the shade (Homer calls them *Alibantes*, desiccated people[1]). Everything everywhere stood still, like a ship at anchor. It was painful to see how hard men worked to protect themselves from this ghastly change in nature: it wasn't easy to keep even the holy water in churches from being used up, though the pope and the College of Cardinals expressly ordered that no one should dare to dip from these blessed basins more than once. All the same, when a priest

9. Names taken from Sir Thomas More's *Utopia*. Literally, "no place," the word *Utopia* has become synonymous with "ideal country."   1. The allusion to Homer is apparently mistaken, but "Alibantes"— possibly derived from the name of Alibas, a dry river in hell—is used by other ancient writers with reference to the dead or the very old.

entered his church you'd see dozens and dozens of these poor parched people come crowding around behind him, and if he blessed anyone the mouths would all gape open to snatch up every single drop, letting nothing fall wasted to the ground—just like the tormented rich man in Luke, who begged for the relief of cool water.[2] Oh, the fortunate ones, in that burning year, whose vaults were cool and well stocked!

The Philosopher tells us, asking why seawater is salty, that once, when Phoebus Apollo let his son Phaeton drive his gleaming chariot,[3] the boy had no idea how to manage it, nor any notion how to follow the sun's proper orbit from tropic to tropic, and drove off the right road and came so close to the earth that he dried up all the countries over which he passed, and burned a great swath through heaven, called by the philosophers *Via Lactea*, the Milky Way, but known to drunkards and lazy louts as Saint John's Road. But the fancy-pants poets say it's really where Juno's milk fell, when she suckled Hercules. Then the earth got so hot that it developed an enormous sweat, which proceeded to sweat away the entire ocean, which thus became salty, because sweat is always salty. And you can see for yourself that this is perfectly true, because all you have to do is taste it—or the sweat of pox-ridden people when they're put in steam baths and work up a great sweat. Try whichever you like: it doesn't matter to me.

It was almost exactly like that, in this year of which I write. One Friday, when everyone was saying prayers and making a beautiful procession, and litanies were being said, and psalms chanted, and they were begging omnipotent God to look mercifully down on them in their desolation, they could suddenly see great drops of water coming out of the earth, exactly as if someone were sweating profusely. And the poor people began to rejoice, as if this were something truly useful, some of them saying that since there wasn't a drop of liquid in the air from which one could have expected rain, the very ground itself was making up for what they lacked. Others, more scholarly, said that this was rain from the opposite side of the earth, as Seneca explains in the fourth book of *Questionum naturalium*, in which he speaks of the source and origin of the river Nile. But they were deceived: once the procession was over, and they went back to collect this precious dew and drink down a full glass, they found that it was just pickle brine, even worse to drink, and even saltier, than seawater.

And it was precisely because Pantagruel was born that very day that his father named him as he did: *Panta* in Greek means "all," and *Gruel* in Arabic means "thirsty," thus indicating that at the hour of his birth the whole world was thirsty—and he saw, prophetically, that someday his son would be lord of the thirsty, for this was shown to him at that same time and by a sign even more obvious. For when the child's mother was in labor, and all the midwives were waiting to receive him, the first thing that came out of her womb was sixty-eight mule drivers, each one leading a pack mule loaded with salt by its halter, after which came nine one-humped

2. "And he cried and said, Father Abraham, have mercy on me, and send Lazarus, that he may dip the tip of his finger in water, and cool my tongue; for I am tormented in this flame." (Luke 16:24.) 3. The chariot of the sun.

camels loaded with hams and smoked beef tongue, and then seven two-humped camels loaded with pickled eels, followed by twenty-five carts all loaded with onions, garlic, leeks, and spring onions. The midwives were frightened out of their wits. But some of them said to the others:

"Here's God's plenty. It signifies that we shouldn't either hold back, when we drink, or, on the other hand, pour it down the way the Swiss do. It's a good sign: these are truly wining signs."

And while they were gabbling and cackling about such trivialities, out popped Pantagruel, as hairy as a bear, at which one of them pronounced prophetically:

"He's been born all covered with fur, so he'll do wonderful things, and if he lives he'll live to an immense age."

(Father's Letter from Home)

CHAPTER 8

How Pantagruel, at Paris, Received a Letter from His Father, Gargantua, with a Copy of That Letter

Pantagruel studied hard, of course, and learned a great deal, because his brain was twice normal size and his memory was as capacious as a dozen kegs of olive oil. While he was thus occupied in Paris,[4] one day he received a letter from his father, which read as follows:

"My very dear son,

"Among the gifts, the graces and the prerogatives with which from the very beginning our sovereign Creator and God has blessed and endowed human nature, that which seems to me uniquely wonderful is the power to acquire a kind of immortality while still in this our mortal state—that is, while passing through this transitory life a man may perpetuate both his name and his race, and this we accomplish through the legitimate issue of holy wedlock. And by that means we partially reestablish that which we lost through the sin of our first parents, Adam and Eve, to whom it was declared that, because they had not obeyed the commands of God their Creator, they would know death and in dying would utterly destroy the magnificent form in which mankind had been shaped.

"But this seminal propagation permits what the parents lose to live on in their children, and what dies in the children to live on in the grandchildren, and so it will continue until the hour of the Last Judgment, when Jesus Christ will return to the hands of God the Father His purified and peaceful kingdom, now utterly beyond any possibility or danger of being soiled by sin. And then all the generations and all the corruptions will come to an end, and all the elements will be taken from their endless cycle of transformations, for the peace so devoutly desired will be achieved, and will be perfect, and all things will be brought to their fit and proper ending.

"So I have very fair and just cause to be thankful to God, my preserver, for having permitted me to see my hoary old age blossoming once again in your youth. Whenever, at His pleasure, He who rules and governs all things, my soul leaves this human dwelling place, I will not consider myself entirely

---

4. Like his father before him, Pantagruel has been sent to Paris to study. The following letter, patterned after Ciceronian models of eloquence, summarizes Rabelais's view of an ideal education, and generally illustrates the attitude of the Renaissance intellectual elite toward culture.

dead, but simply transported from one place to another, for in you, and by you, my visible image lives in in this world, wholly alive, able to see and speak to all honorable men, and all my friends, just as I myself was able to do. I confess that my life on this earth, though I have had divine help and divine grace to show me the way, has not been sinless (for indeed we are all sinners and continually beg God to wash away our sins), and yet it has been beyond reproach.

"Just as the image of my flesh lives on in you, so too shine on the ways of my soul, or else no one would think you the true keeper and treasure of our immortal name, and I would take little pleasure in seeing that, because in that case the least part of me, my body, would live on, and the best part, my soul, in which our name lives and is blessed among men, would be decayed and debased. Nor do I say this because I have any doubt about your virtue, which I have long since tested and approved, but simply to encourage you to proceed from good to still better. And the reason I write to you now is not so much to ensure that you follow the pathways of virtue, but rather that you rejoice in thus living and having lived, and find new joys and fresh courage for the future.

"To consummate and perfect that task, it should be enough for you to remember that I have held back nothing, but have given help and assistance as if I had no other treasure in the world but to someday see you, while I still lived, accomplished and established in virtue, integrity, and wisdom, perfected in all noble and honorable learning, and to be able to thus leave you, after my death, as a mirror representing me, your father—perhaps in actual practice not so perfect an image as I might have wished, but certainly exactly that in both intention and desire.

"But though my late father of worthy memory, Grandgousier, devoted all his energy to those things of which I might take the fullest advantage, and from which I might acquire the most sensible knowledge, and though my own effort matched his—or even surpassed it—still, as you know very well, it was neither so fit nor so right a time for learning as exists today, nor was there an abundance of such teachers as you have had. It was still a murky, dark time, oppressed by the misery, unhappiness, and disasters of the Goths, who destroyed all worthwhile literature of every sort. But divine goodness has let me live to see light and dignity returned to humanistic studies, and to see such an improvement, indeed, that it would be hard for me to qualify for the very first class of little schoolboys—I who, in my prime, had the reputation (and not in error) of the most learned man of my day. Nor do I say this as an empty boast, though indeed I could honorably do so in writing to you—for which you have the authority of Cicero in his book *On Old Age*, and also the judgment of Plutarch, in his book *How a Man May Praise Himself without Fear of Reproach*. No, I say these things to make you wish to surpass me.

"For now all courses of study have been restored, and the acquisition of languages has become supremely honorable: Greek, without which it is shameful for any man to be called a scholar; Hebrew; Chaldean; Latin.[5] And in my time we have learned how to produce wonderfully elegant and accurate printed books,[6] just as, on the other hand, we have also learned (by diabolic suggestion) how to make cannon and other such fearful weapons. The world is full of scholars, of learned teachers, of well-stocked libraries, so that in my opinion study has never been easier, not in Plato's time, or Cicero's, or Papinian's.[7] From this day forward no one will dare to appear anywhere, or in any company, who has not been well and properly taught in the wisdom of Minerva.

5. The languages that are the instruments of classical learning are listed along with those useful for the study of the Old Testament.   6. Printing from movable type was independently invented in Europe about the middle of the fifteenth century.   7. Jurisconsult of the time of Emperor Septimius Severus (reigned A.D. 193–211).

Thieves and highwaymen, hangmen and executioners, common foot soldiers, grooms and stableboys, are now more learned than the scholars and preachers of my day. What should I say? Even women and girls have come to aspire to this marvelous, this heavenly manna of solid learning. Old as I am, I have felt obliged to learn Greek, though I had not despised it, as Cato[8] did: I simply had no leisure for it, when I was young. And how exceedingly glad I am, as I await the hour when it may please God, my Creator, to call me to leave this earth, to read Plutarch's *Morals*, Plato's beautiful *Dialogues*, Pausanias' *Monuments*, and Athenaeus' *Antiquities*.[9]

"Which is why, my son, I strongly advise you not to waste your youth, but to make full use of it for the acquisition of knowledge and virtue. You are in Paris, you have your tutor, Epistemon: you can learn from them, by listening and speaking, by all the noble examples held up in front of your eyes.

"It is my clear desire that you learn languages perfectly, first Greek, as Quintilian decreed, and then Latin.[1] And after that Hebrew, for the Holy Bible, and similarly Chaldean and Arabic. I wish you to form your literary style both on the Greek, following Plato, and on the Latin, following Cicero. Let there be nothing in all of history that is not clear and vivid in your mind, a task in which geographical texts will be of much assistance.

"I gave you some awareness of the liberal arts—geometry, arithmetic, and music—when you were still a child of five and six. Follow them further, and learn all the rules of astronomy. Ignore astrology and its prophecies, and all the hunt for the philosopher's stone which occupied Ramon Lully[2]—leave all those errors and vanities alone.

"As for the civil law, I wish you to know by heart all the worthy texts: deal with them and philosophy side by side.

"I wish you to carefully devote yourself to the natural world. Let there be no sea, river, or brook whose fish you do not know. Nothing should be unknown to you—all the birds of the air, each and every tree and bush and shrub in the forests, every plant that grows from the earth, all the metals hidden deep in the abyss, all the gems of the Orient and the Middle East—nothing.

"Then carefully reread all the books of the Greek physicians, and the Arabs and Romans, without turning your back on the talmudic scholars or those who have written on the Cabala. Make free use of anatomical dissection and acquire a perfect knowledge of that other world which is man himself. Spend several hours each day considering the holy Gospels, first the New Testament and the Apostles' letters, in Greek, and then the Old Testament, in Hebrew.

"In short, plumb all knowledge to the very depths, because when you are a grown man you will be obliged to leave the peace and tranquillity of learning, and acquire the arts of chivalry and warfare, in order to defend my house and lands and come to the aid of our friends if in any way they are attacked by evildoers.

"And soon I shall ask you to demonstrate just how much you have learned, which you can do in no better way than by publicly defending, in front of the entire world and against all who may come to question you, a thesis of your own devising. And continue, as you have been doing, to frequent the company of those leaned men who are so numerous in Paris.

"But since, as the wise Solomon says, wisdom can find no way into a malicious heart, and knowledge without self-awareness is nothing but the soul's ruin, you should serve, and love, and fear God. Put all your thought in Him, and all your hopes, and by faith which has been shaped by love unite yourself with Him so firmly that sin will never separate you away. Be ever watchful of

---

8. Plutarch's life of Cato is the source of the notion that he despised Greek.   9. The works of Pausanias and Athenaeus were standard sources of information on ancient geography, art, and everyday life.
1. In his *Institutio oratoria*, Book I, Chapter 1, paragraph 12, he recommends studying Greek before Latin.   2. Raymond Lully, Spanish philosopher of the thirteenth century, who dabbled in magic.

the world's wicked ways. Never put your heart in vanity, for ours is a transitory existence and the Word of God lives forever. Help your neighbors and love them as you love yourself. Honor your teachers. Avoid the company of those you do not desire to imitate; do not take in vain the blessings God has given you. And when, finally, you know that you have learned all that Paris can teach you, return to me, so that I may look on you and, before I die, give you my blessing.

"My son, may the peace and grace of our Lord be with you. Amen.

"Written from Utopia, this seventeenth day of the month of March.

Your father,
GARGANTUA"

After receiving and reading this letter, Pantagruel was filled with new zeal, positively on fire to learn more than ever before—so much so that, had you seen him at his studies, and observed how much he learned, you would have declared that he was to his books like a fire in dry grass, burning with such an intense and consuming flame.

(Adventures of Panurge)

CHAPTER 16

Panurge's Character, and How He Lived[3]

Panurge was of middle height, neither particularly tall nor especially short, and he had a rather aquiline nose—in fact, very like a razor handle. He was thirty-five years old, more or less (to put a little gilding on a lead dagger), dashing looking, except that he was something of a skirt chaser, and also that he was naturally ill with a disease called, in those days,

Short of money, what a sorrow, what a pain

(as students used to sing)—but all the same, he had at least sixty-three ways of finding what he needed, the most honorable (and usual) of which was sly thievery. He was mischievous, a cheat, a drinker, a hobo, a scrounger (as long as he was in Paris), and for the rest, the best son of a bitch in the world, always cooking up something to make trouble for the constables and watchmen.

Once he got together three or four good country fellows and set them to drinking like Templars[4] the whole night long. Then he brought them down in front of the church of Saint Geneviève, or out in front of Navarre College, and just when the watchmen of the guard were coming by—which he made sure of by resting his sword on the pavement, and his ear against his sword, and when he heard the sword shake he knew it was an infallible sign that the guard was coming—he and his friends would take a dung cart and give it a good shove, making it run rapidly down the slope of those streets and knocking the poor guardsmen down like so many pigs ready to

---

3. Panurge (Pan ourgos in Greek, the "all-doer") is the major character in Gargantua and Pantagruel except for the heroes themselves: a magnification of the perennial-student type, Panurge is an imaginative and scandalous pauper, erudite and bawdy, a lover of outrageous pranks. On first meeting Pantagruel he addressed him in thirteen different languages, a couple of them invented, before discovering that they both spoke French. He has since become a permanent fixture of the young lord's retinue.   4. A medieval religious and medical order, suppressed in 1312. The original templiers, not capitalized, suggests a current proverbial expression.

be trussed for roasting. And then they'd run off in the other direction, because in less than two days he'd made it his business to know every street and alley and byway in Paris as well as he knew his grace after meals, *Deus det nobis*, May God grant us. . . .

Another time, knowing exactly where the night guardsmen would be passing, he laid down a train of gunpowder and, just as they came marching by, threw a match into it and proceeded to thoroughly enjoy himself, watching how gracefully they ran, thinking Saint Anthony's fire had grabbed at their legs.

But it was the poor masters of arts, in theology above all, that he truly enjoyed persecuting. Anytime he met one of them in the street, he did them some mischief or other, either sticking a fresh turd in their big broad-brimmed hats, or tying foxtails to the backs of their coats, or maybe rabbit ears, or something unpleasant, it didn't matter what.

One day, when all the theologians had been told to assemble on the Rue de Feurre, so their faith and belief could be properly tested, he cooked up a proper treat, starting with a ton of garlic, and adding *galbanum, assa fetida*, and *castoreum*,[5] three noxious, toxic, vomit-producing flavors, some nice fresh shit (still warm), all of which he soaked in hot pus from good canker sores, and then that morning he did a fine job pouring it all over, anointing the pavement in every direction, so the devil himself couldn't have stood it. All those good folk proceeded to throw up, right in front of everyone, as if they'd been skinning fox hides; ten or twelve of them died of the plague, fourteen got leprosy, eighteen came down with scabies, and more than twenty-seven got the pox, but he didn't give a damn. And he always carried a whip under his gown, so he could whip the devil out of any servants he ran across, fetching wine for their masters, so he could make them go faster.

His overcoat had more than twenty-six little pockets and pouches, which were always filled:

one, with a pair of little dice, well loaded with hidden lead, and a small knife as sharp as a furrier's needle, which he used to cut open purses;

another, with sour wine or vinegar he could throw in people's eyes;

another, with burrs and prickles to which he'd tied little goose or chicken feathers, so he could throw them on the gowns and hats of respectable folk, and often he managed to create first-class horns, which they would then parade all over the city—sometimes for the whole rest of their lives;

another, especially for women, specially fashioned little penises he'd sometimes stick on their hats, or on the back of their gowns;

another, a bunch of horns stuffed with fleas and lice, borrowed from the beggars at Saint Innocent's cemetery, which he threw, with little reeds or writing pens, down the backs of the sweetest-looking ladies he could find, even in church, for he'd never sit high up in the organ loft or where the choir was. He always stayed down in the nave with the women, whether at mass or vespers or when the sermon was being preached;

5. Asafoetida and galbanum are resins extracted from Persian plants; castoreum is a substance obtained from the inguinal region of the beaver; all three produce nauseating smells.

another, a good supply of fishhooks and knitting needles, so whenever there was a crowd he could stick men and women together, and especially when they were wearing thin taffeta dresses, so when they started to walk away they'd rip their gowns to shreds;

another, a good flint stone, and a sufficiency of fuses, matchsticks, and everything else required;

another, two or three magnifying glasses, which he could use to drive both men and women out of their minds and get them to lose all control, even in church; as he used to say, there wasn't anything to choose from, as between a woman who was crazy for religion and a woman whose ass moved like crazy;

and in another, a supply of needles and thread, with which he played a thousand wicked little jokes. Once, at the door to the Justice Building, in the Grand Ballroom, when a Franciscan monk was to say mass for the magistrates, Panurge helped him to dress himself for the occasion. But in getting him properly attired, he stitched the long robe of white linen, which priests wear for mass, both to his monk's robe and to his undershirt, then quietly disappeared when the magistrates came and took their seats. Now, when the poor friar got to the *Ite missa est*, Go forth, the mass has now been said, and tried to take off his white robe, he also took off his monk's robe and his undershirt, all tightly sewn together, and got everything he was wearing rolled up as far as his shoulders, exhibiting his genitals to the whole world—and without any question he was a very well-hung friar. And the more the poor man pulled and tugged, the more he uncovered himself, until one of the magistrates finally said, "What the devil is this? Is the good father offering us his ass to kiss? May it get kissed by Saint Anthony's fire!" And it was decreed that henceforth the poor good monks were not to dress themselves in public, but only in their robing room, especially when there happened to be women present, who might be driven to the sin of desire. And everyone wondered just why these monks were so exceedingly well hung, a problem that Panurge neatly solved, saying:

"What makes donkey's ears so big is that their mothers never get them to wear hoods on their heads, as that noted theological scholar Pierre d'Ailly writes in his book *Conjectures and Assumptions*. By the same logic, what's responsible for the size of these poor blessed monks' equipment is that their breeches never have bottoms, and so it's all free to drop down as far as it feels like going, swinging down to their knees like the big strings of rosary beads women wear at their belt. But the thickness, which is just as notable— that's caused by the bodily essences swinging right down into their genitals, since as we all know shaking and continual motion create attractive impulses."

Item: Panurge's overcoat had another pocket full of powdered alum, a fierce astringent and itching agent which he liked to toss down the backs of haughty women, making them strip down right in public, or else dance like a chicken on a bed of hot coals, or like a stick beating on a drum, or else run wild through the streets, in which case he would go running after them, while for those who stripped off their clothes he'd most graciously offer his cape and drape it over them like the most courteous, kindest gentleman in the world.

Item: in another pocket he had a flask full of used oil, and when he saw a woman, or a man, who was especially handsomely dressed, he'd grease them up and completely ruin all the best parts, under the pretext of touching and admiring them, saying, "What a fine piece of goods this is, ah, what beautiful satin, what lovely taffeta, madame: may God grant you whatever your noble heart desires! You have a new gown and a new friend: may God permit you much joy of them both!" And as he spoke he'd run his hand down over the collar, and the back, and the deep spots he'd make would stay forever—carved so deep into the soul, as the saying goes, stamped so indelibly onto the body, that the devil himself couldn't remove them. And then he'd say, "Madame, do be careful not to fall: there's a great dirty hole right over there."

And another pocket was full of a pungent, bitter drug that sadly disturbs the stomach and the intestines, which he kept finely powdered, and he'd put a fine lace handkerchief in there, one that he'd stolen from a pretty washerwoman at the Justice Building while pulling a louse out of her bodice (which louse he had of course put there himself). When he found himself surrounded with gentlewomen, he'd turn the talk to lacework and put his hand on their breasts, asking, "Now this, was it made in Flanders or in Hainaut?"[6] And then he'd pull out his handkerchief, saying, "See? See? Just look at how *this* was worked! It's from Frontignan—or from Fontarabie," and he'd give it a good shake under their nose, and they'd sneeze for four hours without being able to stop. And then he'd fart like a horse, and the women would laugh and say to him, "What? Is that you farting, Panurge?" "Hardly, madame," he'd say. "That was just a good harmonious counterpoint to the music you're making with your nose."

In another pocket he had a burglar's wrench, a locksmith's jimmy, a hook, and other iron tools: there wasn't a door or a store box he couldn't pry open.

And yet another pocket he kept full of tiny glasses with which he could play all sorts of cunning tricks, because his fingers were as supple as Minerva's or Arachne's.[7] Indeed, he had once been a traveling showman. And when Panurge gave change, you'd have had to be sharper sighted than Master Flim-Flam-Fly himself if, every single time, five or six small coins didn't somehow disappear, right out in the open, under your very nose, but without any sign of wrongdoing, so that all you were aware of was a slight puff of air as they vanished.

6. Famed for their fine lace.   7. In Greek mythology the goddess Athena, being enraged at the Lydian maid Arachne's irreverence and weaving skill, transformed her into a spider.

CHAPTER 21

How Panurge Fell in Love with a Noble Parisian Lady

Because of his success in this disputation against the Englishman,[8] Panurge began to develop a certain reputation in Paris. This made his codpiece an even more valuable instrument, and he festooned it with bits of embroidery (in the Roman style). They sang his praises everywhere, even making up a song about him, which was sung by the little boys going to fetch mustard. And he became so welcome wherever women and girls were gathered, such a glamorous figure, that he began to think about tumbling one of the city's greatest ladies.

Indeed, not bothering with the long prologues and protestations poured forth by the usual whining, moody Lent lovers, who have no affection for flesh and blood, he said to her:

"Madame, the whole country would find it useful, and it would be a delight to you, an honor to your descendants and, for me, a necessity, for you to be bred to my blood: believe me, experience will show you how truthfully I speak."

At these words the lady pushed him more than a hundred yards away, saying:

"You wicked idiot, what makes you think you have the right to talk to me like that? To whom do you think you're speaking? Go! Don't let me ever see you again—indeed, I'm tempted to have your arms and legs chopped off."

"Now," he said, "it would be perfectly agreeable to lose my arms and legs, provided you and I could shake a mattress together, playing the beast with two backs, because"—and here he showed her his long codpiece—"here's Master John Thomas, who's ready to sing you a merry tune, one you'll relish right through the marrow of your bones. He knows the game very well indeed: he knows just how to find all the little hidden places, all the bumps and itchy spots. When he's been sweeping up, you never need a feather duster."

To which the lady answered:

"Go, you wicked man, go! If you say one more word to me, I'll call for help and have you beaten to a pulp."

"Ho!" he said. "You're not as nasty as you say you are—no, or I've been totally taken in by appearances. The earth will float up into the clouds, and the high heavens drop down into the abyss, and all of nature be turned upside down and inside out, before someone of such beauty, such elegance, possesses so much as a drop of bile or malice. It's truly said that you don't often find

A woman who's truly beautiful
Inclined to make herself dutiful

---

8. Thaumastes, who in the previous chapters has long argued with Panurge, using both words and signs, and has been "nonplussed" by the latter's knowledge.

—but then, they say that about vulgar beauties. Yours is a beauty so excellent, so rare and unusual, so celestial, that I believe nature intended you as a model, letting us know what she could do when she wished to use all her power and all her knowledge. Everything about you is honey, is sugar, is heavenly manna.

"It's you to whom Paris should have given the golden apple, not Venus, no, or Juno, or Minerva, for Juno was never so magnificent, Minerva never so wise, or Venus so elegant, as you.

"O celestial gods and goddesses, how happy he will be, whoever you grant the grace of coupling with this woman, of kissing her, of rubbing his bacon against her. By God, it's got to be me, I see it perfectly well, because she already loves me. I see it, I know it, I was destined for this by all the fairies and elves. No more wasting time, push it, pull it, let's get to it!"

And he tried to take her in his arms, but she started toward the window, as if to call in her neighbors. So Panurge left at once, and as he went said to her:

"Wait right here, madame. Don't trouble yourself: I'll fetch them for you."

And so he went off, not terribly concerned about the rebuff he'd experienced, and not particularly unhappy.

The next day he appeared at church right when she came to hear mass. As she entered the church, he sprinkled holy water on her and made her a profound bow, and then, as they were kneeling in prayer, he approached her familiarly and said:

"Madame, understand: I love you so much I can't piss or shit. I don't know what you think—but suppose I fall sick, whose fault will it be?"

"Go away," she said, "go away, I don't care! Leave me alone, let me say my prayers to God."

"Ah," he said, "but think about *To Beaumont le Vicomte*."

"I don't know it," she said.

"Here's what it means," he said. "!A beau con le vit monte, A prick climbs on a beautiful cunt. And pray to God that He grants me what your noble heart longs for. Here, let me have those prayer beads."

"Take them," she said, "and leave me alone."

And she tried to take off her rosary, which was fashioned of scented wood; the large beads were solid gold. But Panurge quickly pulled out one of his knives and neatly cut it for her, and started off to the pawnshop, saying:

"Madame, may I offer you my knife?"

"No, no!" she said.

"But remember," he said, "it's always at your service, body and baggage, guts and bowels."

But losing her rosary beads didn't make the lady very happy, for they were an important part of her appearance in church, and she thought to herself, "This babbler is out of his mind; he must be a foreigner. I'll never get those beads back. What will I say to my husband? He'll be angry at

me. But I'll tell him a thief cut them off while I was in church, and he'll
surely believe me, seeing the end of the ribbon still tied to my belt."

After dinner, Panurge went to see her, carrying hidden in his sleeve a
fat purse, stuffed with tokens used in high-court business. And he began
by saying:

"Who's more in love, me with you, or you with me?"

To which she answered:

"I certainly don't hate you, because as God commands I love the whole
world."

"But more specifically," he said, "don't you love me?"

"I've already told you," she said, "and over and over, that you're not to
say such things to me! If you insist on speaking to me like this, I will show
you, sir, that dishonorable words may be directed at some women, but not
me. Leave—and give me back my rosary beads, in case my husband asks
for them."

"What?" he said. "Your rosary beads, madame? Ah no, I can't do that,
on my honor I can't. But I'd be delighted to give you others. Which would
you prefer? Enameled gold, with large beads, or handsome love knots, or
something truly enormous, with beads as fat as ingots? Or perhaps you'd
prefer ebony wood, or big blue jacinth stones, or well-cut red garnets, and
every tenth stone a gorgeous turquoise, or else maybe a fine topaz, or a
shining sapphire, or maybe all in rubies with a fat diamond every tenth
stone, something cut with twenty or thirty gleaming faces?

"No—no—that's not good enough. I know a beautiful necklace of fine
emeralds, and every tenth stone marked with great round ambergris, and
the clasp set with an oriental pearl as fat as an orange! It costs only twenty-
five thousand gold pieces. I'd love to give you that; I can afford it without
any trouble."

And as he spoke he jiggled the court counters in his sleeve so they rang
like gold pieces.

"Would you like a bolt of bright crimson velvet, striped with green, or
some embroidered satin, or maybe crimson? What would you like—necklaces, gold things, things for your hair, rings? All you have to do is say yes.
Even fifty thousand gold pieces doesn't bother me."

He was making her fairly salivate, but she answered:

"No. Thank you, but I want nothing from you."

"By God," said he, "I damned well want something from you, and it's
something that won't cost you a cent, and once you've given it you'll still
have it, every bit of it. Here"—and he showed her his long codpiece—
"here's my John Thomas, who wants a place to jump into."

And then he tried to take her in his arms, but she began to scream,
although not too loud. So Panurge dropped all pretense and said to her:

"You won't let me have even a little of it, eh? Shit to you! You don't
deserve such a blessing, or such an honor. By God, I'll get the dogs to
screw you."

And then he got out of there as fast as he could, afraid of being beaten—
for he was a terrible coward.

CHAPTER 22

How Panurge Played a Nasty Joke on the Parisian Lady

The next day was the great feast of Corpus Christi, for which all the women wore their very best gowns. And that day this particular Parisian lady wore a beautiful dress of red satin and a very expensive white velvet petticoat.

The day before the feast, Panurge hunted everywhere till he found a bitch in heat, then tied her to his belt and brought her to his rooms, where he fed her extremely well all day long, and that night, too. And then in the morning he killed her and cut out that portion so well known to the ancient Greek magicians and diviners. He cut it into the smallest possible pieces and, taking it with him, well hidden, he went where the lady would be sure to come, as (by custom and tradition) she followed the holy procession. And when she came by, Panurge sprinkled her with holy water, greeted her most courteously, and a little later, after she had said her prayers, went and sat by her on a bench and gave her a poem carefully written out as follows:

> O lovely lady, just this once
> I told my love: you called me dunce
> And drove me off, said "Don't return!"
> Though what I could have done to earn
> Your hate, by word or deed, I'll never
> Know. What trusting lover was ever
> So shamed? Why not just gently sever
> The knot and tell me my passion must burn
>   Uselessly, just this once?
>
> Look in my heart: what your heart hunts
> Is there—not venom, but only chunks
> Of flaming desire, longing that burns
> Like the sun, and all my desire turns
> On my need to stuff your lovely cunt,
>   But just this once.

And as she unfolded the sheet to read this poem, Panurge quickly sprinkled the hidden substance all over her, here, there, and everywhere, even into the folds of her sleeves and her dress. Then he said:

"Madame, unhappy lovers are rarely at peace. As for me, I hope that the hard nights, the pains, and all the anxiety my love for you has given me will be taken into account, when the fires of purgatory are lit for me. At least, pray to God on my behalf, that He may grant me patience in my suffering."

He had barely finished when all the dogs hanging around the church came running at the lady, drawn by the smell of that which he had sprinkled on her. Little ones and big ones, fat ones and thin ones, they all came, penises at the ready, sniffing and snuffing and pissing all over her. It was one of the nastiest scenes you'll ever hope to see.

Panurge chased away a few of them, but the lady fled, and he went into a small chapel, from which he could watch the show. Those wretched dogs completely pissed up her clothes, a huge wolfhound pissing on her head, others on her sleeves, some on her backside, while the littlest ones pissed on her shoes, with the result that the women who gathered around had a hard time saving her.

And Panurge laughed, saying to a Parisian gentleman:

"By God, that lady must be in heat, or else some wolfhound screwed her not too long ago."

And when he saw that the dogs were snarling and growling all around her, exactly as if she'd been a bitch in heat, he ran off in search of Pantagruel.

And on every street where he found dogs, he kicked them, saying, "Why aren't you at the wedding with all the others? Hurry up, hurry up, by the devil! Hurry!" And when he got to their lodgings, he said to Pantagruel:

"Master, I beg you, come see how all the dogs in the whole country are after a woman, the prettiest in the whole city, and trying to screw her."

And Pantagruel was quite happy to come see this sight, this intensely dramatic spectacle, which struck him as most interesting, as well as brandnew.

But the best of it all was the procession, in which you could see more than six hundred thousand and fourteen dogs all around her, making her life miserable in a thousand ways. Everywhere she went, the dogs came running along behind her, pissing on the road wherever her dress had touched it.

Everyone stopped to watch the show, watching the dogs' fabulous tricks, some of them leaping as high as her shoulders. They completely ruined her beautiful clothes, and finally there was no help for it but to run back to her home, dogs running after her. And when she got home she hid herself, while the chambermaids giggled. Still, even when she'd closed the door behind her, all the dogs from half a mile around came running and bepissed the front door so thoroughly that their urine made a stream in which ducks could have swum. And indeed it is this same stream which, today, flows past Saint Victor, and in which the Gobelins dye their red wools,[9] precisely because of the endowment these pissing dogs gave that water, as our beloved Maître Oribus has publicly declared in a sermon. And so—God help you! A mill could have ground corn alongside that torrent, but Bazacle's mills, in Toulouse, do it still better.

---

9. The geography is correct. At the time of Rabelais's writing, the celebrated dye works were still run by the Gobelin family. Mysterious qualities were attributed to the water of the small river Bièvre, and urine was actually used in the industry on account of its ammonia content.

MICHEL DE MONTAIGNE

1533–1592

Like his fellow Frenchman Rabelais, though in a different context and manner, Michel Eyquem de Montaigne was representative of his age and unique at the same time. Though involved in the political and religious conflicts of the day, he yet maintained an unmistakable sense of individuality and a considerable degree of detachment. These same qualities characterize his writing.

Montaigne was born on February 28, 1533, in the castle of Montaigne (in the wine-rich Bordeaux region), from which his family of traders derived their surname. His father, Pierre Eyquem, was for two terms mayor of Bordeaux and had fought in Italy under Francis I. Montaigne's inclination to tolerance and naturalness may have had its origin in his background and early training: his mother, of Spanish-Jewish descent, was a Protestant, as were his brother Beauregard and his sister Jeanne. The third of nine children, Michel himself, like his other brothers and sisters, was raised a Catholic. His father, though no man of learning, had unconventional ideas of upbringing: Michel, who had a peasant nurse and peasant godparents, was awakened in the morning by the sound of music and had Latin taught him as his mother tongue by a German tutor. At six he went to the famous Collège de Guienne at Bordeaux; later he studied law, probably at Toulouse. In his youth he already had first-hand experience of court life. (At the court celebrations at Rouen for the coming of age of Charles IX in 1560, he saw cannibals, brought from Brazil, who became the subject of the famous essay reprinted here.) In 1557 he was a member of the Bordeaux parliament. In 1565 he married Françoise de la Chassaigne, daughter of a colleague in the Bordeaux parliament, and the object of his temperate love. It is possible that disappointed political ambitions contributed to Montaigne's decision to "retire" at the age of thirty-eight to his castle of Montaigne and devote himself to meditation and writing. His stay there, however, had various interruptions. France was split between the Protestants, led by Henry of Navarre, and two Catholic factions: those faithful to the reigning kings of the house of Valois (first Charles IX and then Henry III) and the "leaguers," i.e., the followers of the house of Guise. Though his sympathies went to the unfanatical Navarre, the future founder of the Bourbon dynasty as Henry IV, Montaigne's attitude was balanced and conservative (both Henry III of Valois and Henry of Navarre bestowed honors upon him), and in 1574 Montaigne attempted to mediate an agreement between Henry and the Duke of Guise.

In 1580 he undertook a journey through Switzerland, Germany, and Italy (partly to cure his gallstones); while in Italy he received news that he had been appointed mayor of Bordeaux, an office he held competently for two terms (1581–1585). Toward the end of his life he began an important friendship with the intelligent and ardently devoted Marie de Gournay, who became a kind of adopted daughter and was his literary executrix. When Henry of Navarre, who had visited him twice in his castle, became King Henry IV, Montaigne expressed his joy, though he refused Henry's offers of money; he did not live to witness in Paris, as he probably would have, the entry of the king turned Catholic ("Paris," Henry said, "is well worth a Mass"), for he died on September 13, 1592, and was buried in a church in Bordeaux.

Montaigne's major claim to fame, the *Essays*, were started as a collection of interesting quotations, observations, recordings of remarkable events, and the like, and slowly developed to their large form and bulk. Of the three books, I and II were first published in 1580; III (together with I and II revised and amplified) appeared in 1588. A posthumous edition prepared by Mlle. de Gournay, and containing some further additions, appeared in 1595. A noteworthy early English translation by John Florio was published in 1603.

Although the quality of Montaigne's *Essays* can be fully appreciated only by a direct experience of them, let us attempt to describe this unique genre and place it within the context of its time. If one accepts the common view that in the Renaissance the individual human being was exalted, and therefore a special emphasis was placed on the study of our "virtues" and singularities, it might be appropriate to think of Montaigne as a typical product of that new emphasis. Indeed, of the writers presented in this book, Montaigne is the one who most openly speaks in his own right, clearly and unabashedly as himself. While, for instance, Erasmus adopts the ambiguous mouthpiece of "Folly" to express his views, Montaigne's characteristic and somewhat rambling prose is in the simplest and most quintessential first person. Perhaps at no other time in literature—certainly not in the nineteenth-century age of romanticism, where in spite of widespread notions about the "free" expression of individual feelings writers so often wrapped themselves in an alter ego or a heroic mask—has a writer so thoroughly attempted to present himself without in the least assuming a pose, of falling into a type.

> Authors communicate themselves to the world by some special and extrinsic mark; I am the first to do so by my general being, as Michel de Montaigne, not as a grammarian or a poet or a lawyer. If the world finds fault with me for speaking too much of myself, I find fault with the world for not even thinking of itself.

Yet nothing would be more erroneous than to suppose that Montaigne's focusing on his individual self implies a sense of the extraordinary importance of humanity, of our central place in the world, or of the special power of our understanding. The contrary is true. In the first place, in temperament Montaigne is singularly opposed to assuming an attitude of importance: one of the keynotes of his writing, and one of his premises in undertaking it, is that the subject is average, "mediocre." He declares that he has "but a private and family end in view," and in that sense, in fact, the way he introduces himself to the reader shows a nobly elegant and perhaps vaguely ironic humbleness—not to mention a considerable degree of the artfulness he disclaims! "So, Reader, I am myself the subject of my book; it is not reasonable to expect you to waste your leisure on a matter so frivolous and empty."

But, more importantly, in deciding to probe, to "essay," his own nature, his serious implication is that this is the only subject on which one can speak with any degree of certainty. So this writer whose work is the most acute exposure of an individual personality in the literature of the Renaissance, is at the same time one of the highest illustrations of the ironic awareness of our intellectual limits.

With all this, Montaigne's work remains an outstanding assertion of an individuality, even though it is an assertion of doubt, contradiction, change. As always the quality and novelty of the work should be experienced in the actual text, in terms of "style." Montaigne's style conjoins a solid classical manner, reflected in certain elements of the syntactical structure and in the continous support of classical quotations, with the variety, the apparent disconnectedness, and the dramatic assertiveness of someone who is continuously analyzing a constantly changing subject, and—his modesty notwithstanding—a singularly attractive one.

> Others form man; I describe him, and portray a particular, very ill-made one, who, if I had to fashion him anew, should indeed be very different from what he is. But now it is done. . . . The world is but a perennial see-saw. All things in it are incessantly on the swing, the earth, the rocks of the Caucasus, the Egyptian pyramids. . . . Even fixedness is nothing but a more sluggish motion. I cannot fix my object; it is befogged, and reels with a natural intoxication. . . . I do not portray the thing in itself. I portray the passage. . . .

In spite of what may often seem a leisurely gait, Montaigne is permanently on the alert, listening to the promptings of his thought, his sensibility, his imagination—and recording them.

Montaigne writes about one individual, and with a fairly obvious abhorrence of any sort of classification or description of human types in the manner of conventional moralists; yet a powerfully keen observation of humanity in general emerges from his writings—an observation of our nature, intellectual power, and capacity for coherent action; of our place on earth among other beings; of our place in Creation.

If we keep in mind the broad range of Renaissance literature, poised between positive and negative, enthusiasm and melancholy, we shall probably find that the general temper of Montaigne's assertions of doubt, and his consciousness of vanity, by no means imply an attitude of despair and gloom. His attitude is positive and negative in the same breath; it is a rich and fruitful sense of the relativity of everything. Thus if he examines and "essays" the human capacity to act purposefully and coherently (see the essay "Of the Inconsistency of Our Actions" among our selections), his implicit verdict is not that our action is absolutely futile. Rather, he refuses to attribute to the human personality a coherence it does not possess and that, we may be tempted to surmise, would rather impoverish it. "Our actions are nothing but a patchwork. . . . There is as much difference between us and ourselves, as between us and others." And he sustains his arguments, as usual, with a wealth of examples and anecdotes. Emperor Augustus, to mention one, pleases him because his character has "slipped through the fingers of even the most daring critics."

A sense of relativity and a balanced outlook are apparent also from Montaigne's observation of the individual in relation to his or her fellow human beings. In the famous essay "Of Cannibals," where a comparison is made between the behavioral codes of primitive tribes and those of "ourselves," the basic idea is not a disparagement of our civilization but a relativistic warning, for "each man calls barbarism whatever is not in his own practice." The enlightening sense of relativity—rather than a more extreme and totally paradoxical view of the "nobility" of savages—permits Montaigne to see and admire what he detects as superior elements in the customs of the cannibals—for instance, their conception of valor for valor's sake. ". . . the honor of valor consists in combating, not in beating," Montaigne writes. Acceptance of this notion of pure *virtù*, practiced for no material purposes, may well be, for writers like Montaigne, the way to preserve their admiration for the warrior's code of manly courage and valor in spite of the basically pacifist tendencies of their temperaments and their revulsion from the spectacles of conflict and bloodshed witnessed in their own time.

Naturally, an even larger sense of relativity emerges from Montaigne's writing when he examines our place in a more universal framework, as he does, in an outstanding instance, in some famous passages of the "Apology for Raymond Sebond" (a selection from which is included in this volume). The notion of our privileged position in Creation is eloquently questioned: Who has persuaded him that that admirable motion of the celestial vault, the eternal light of those torches rolling so proudly above his head, the fearful movements of that infinite sea, were established and have lasted so many centuries for his convenience and his service? In many other writers a similar anxiety about our smallness and ignorance casts a light of tragic vanity upon the human condition. Montaigne's acceptance of the situation is—to use some of our other examples as convenient points of reference—more like Erasmus than Hamlet. If he asks questions that involve, to say the very least, the whole Renaissance conception of human "dignity," our impression is never really one of negation and gloom. While our advantages over other beings are quietly evaluated and discredited ("this licence of thought . . . is an advantage sold to him very dearly. . . . For from it springs the principal source of . . . sin, sickness, irresolution, affliction, despair"), Montaigne maintains a balanced and often humorous tone in which even the frivolous aside of the personal essayist is not dissonant, but characteristic: "When I play with my cat, who knows but that she regards me more as a plaything than I do her?" So while his view of the "mediocrity" of the human race among other beings debunks any form of intellectual conceit, on the other hand an all-encompassing sense of natural fellowship presides over his view of our place in Creation as well as over his conception of the moral individual in relation to others. See the end of our final selection, where the practice of goodness—as, in other instances, that of valor—is seen as a beautiful and self-rewarding act of "virtue":

> There is . . . no good deed that does not rejoice a wellborn nature. . . . It is no slight pleasure to feel oneself preserved from the contagion of so depraved an age, and to say to oneself: "If anyone should see right into my soul, still he would not find me guilty either of anyone's affliction or ruin. . . ." These testimonies of conscience give us pleasure; and this natural rejoicing is a great boon to us, and the only payment that never fails us.

In conclusion—and difficult as it is to reduce Montaigne's views to short and abstract statements—we are left with the impression that here Montaigne's vision of humanity, and of the possibility of a good life, is nearer to hopefulness than to despair. Although his attitude is far from Rabelais's optimism and exuberance, it too is based on a balance between the "natural" and the intellectual, between instinct and reason. He belittles, at times even scornfully, the power of the human intellect, and like Erasmus he points to instinctive simplicity of mind as being more conducive to happiness and even to true knowledge; but on the other hand the whole tone of his work, its intellectual sophistication, its very bulk, and the loving manner with which he attended to it, show that his own thought was not something that "sicklied o'er" his life, but something that gave it sustenance and delight. Thus we see in him some of the basic contrasts of the Renaissance mind—the acceptance and the rejection of our intellectual dignity—leading not to disruption but to temperately positive results. In passages like the one cited in the preceding paragraph, some kind of pattern of the truly virtuous individual seems to emerge unobtrusively. And though it is not imposed upon the audience, any reader is free to think that conforming to this pattern would result in better spiritual balance in the individual and a more harmonious and sensible fellowship in society. Montaigne does not preach ("Others form man; I describe him . . .") because his code of conduct is one that cannot be taught but only experienced. He limits himself to exemplifying it in his own wise and unheroic self.

　　Donald M. Frame, *Montaigne: A Biography* (1965), is a modern work by one of the leading modern scholars of French literature. Frame is also author of *Mon-*

taigne's *Essais: A Study* (1969), a brief, clear, cogent account. A classic study is André Gide, *Montaigne: An Essay in Two Parts* (1929). Philip Paul Hallie's *Montaigne and Philosophy as Self-Portraiture* (1966) and Frederick Rider, *The Dialectic of Selfhood in Montaigne* (1973), assess Montaigne's creation of his self-image in the *Essais*.

Essays[1]

OF CANNIBALS[2]

When King Pyrrhus[3] passed over into Italy, after he had reconnoitered the formation of the army that the Romans were sending to meet him, he said: "I do not know what barbarians these are" (for so the Greeks called all foreign nations), "but the formation of this army that I see is not at all barbarous." The Greeks said as much of the army that Flamininus brought into their country, and so did Philip, seeing from a knoll the order and distribution of the Roman camp, in his kingdom, under Publius Sulpicius Galba.[4] Thus we should beware of clinging to vulgar opinions, and judge things by reason's way, not by popular say.

I had with me for a long time a man who had lived for ten or twelve years in that other world which has been discovered in our century, in the place where Villegaignon landed, and which he called Antarctic France.[5] This discovery of a boundless country seems worthy of consideration. I don't know if I can guarantee that some other such discovery will not be made in the future, so many personages greater than ourselves having been mistaken about this one. I am afraid we have eyes bigger than our stomachs, and more curiosity than capacity. We embrace everything, but we clasp only wind.

Plato brings in Solon,[6] telling how he had learned from the priests of the city of Saïs in Egypt that in days of old, before the Flood, there was a great island named Atlantis, right at the mouth of the Strait of Gibraltar, which contained more land than Africa and Asia put together, and that the kings of that country, who not only possessed that island but had stretched out so far on the mainland that they held the breadth of Africa as far as Egypt, and the length of Europe as far as Tuscany, undertook to step over into Asia and subjugate all the nations that border on the Mediterranean, as far as the Black Sea; and for this purpose crossed the Spains, Gaul, Italy, as far as Greece, where the Athenians checked them; but that some time after, both the Athenians and themselves and their island were swallowed up by the Flood.

It is quite likely that that extreme devastation of waters made amazing changes in the habitations of the earth, as people maintain that the sea cut off Sicily from Italy—

---

1. Translated by Donald Frame.   2. Book I, Chapter 31.   3. King of Epirus, in Greece, fought the Romans in Italy in 280 B.C.   4. Both Titus Quinctius Flaminius (mentioned earlier in this sentence) and Publius Sulpicius Galba were Roman statesmen and generals who fought Philip V of Macedon in the early years of the second century B.C.   5. In Brazil. Villegaignon landed there in 1557.   6. In his *Timaeus.*

> 'Tis said an earthquake once asunder tore
> These lands with dreadful havoc, which before
> Formed but one land, one coast
> > VIRGIL[7]

—Cyprus from Syria, the island of Euboea from the mainland of Boeotia; and elsewhere joined lands that were divided, filling the channels between them with sand and mud:

> A sterile marsh, long fit for rowing, now
> Feeds neighbor towns, and feels the heavy plow.
> > HORACE[8]

But there is no great likelihood that that island was the new world which we have just discovered; for it almost touched Spain, and it would be an incredible result of a flood to have forced it away as far as it is, more than twelve hundred leagues; besides, the travels of the moderns have already almost revealed that it is not an island, but a mainland connected with the East Indies on one side, and elsewhere with the lands under the two poles; or, if it is separated from them, it is by so narrow a strait and interval that it does not deserve to be called an island on that account.

It seems that there are movements, some natural, others feverish, in these great bodies, just as in our own. When I consider the inroads that my river, the Dordogne, is making in my lifetime into the right bank in its descent, and that in twenty years it has gained so much ground and stolen away the foundations of several buildings, I clearly see that this is an extraordinary disturbance; for if it had always gone at this rate, or was to do so in the future, the face of the world would be turned topsy-turvy. But rivers are subject to changes: now they overflow in one direction, now in another, now they keep to their course. I am not speaking of the sudden inundations whose causes are manifest. In Médoc, along the seashore, my brother, the sieur d'Arsac, can see an estate of his buried under the sands that the sea spews forth; the tops of some buildings are still visible; his farms and domains have changed into very thin pasturage. The inhabitants say that for some time the sea has been pushing toward them so hard that they have lost four leagues of land. These sands are its harbingers; and we see great dunes of moving sand that march half a league ahead of it and keep conquering land.

The other testimony of antiquity with which some would connect this discovery is in Aristotle, at least if that little book *Of Unheard-of Wonders* is by him. He there relates that certain Carthaginians, after setting out upon the Atlantic Ocean from the Strait of Gibraltar and sailing a long time, at last discovered a great fertile island, all clothed in woods and watered by great deep rivers, far remote from any mainland; and that they, and others since, attracted by the goodness and fertility of the soil, went there with their wives and children, and began to settle there. The lords of Carthage, seeing that their country was gradually becoming depopulated,

---

7. *Aeneid* III. 414ff.   8. *Art of Poetry*, ll. 65ff.

expressly forbade anyone to go there any more, on pain of death, and drove out these new inhabitants, fearing, it is said, that in course of time they might come to multiply so greatly as to supplant their former masters and ruin their state. This story of Aristotle does not fit our new lands any better than the other.

This man I had was a simple, crude fellow—a character fit to bear true witness; for clever people observe more things and more curiously, but they interpret them; and to lend weight and conviction to their interpretation, they cannot help altering history a little. They never show you things as they are, but bend and disguise them according to the way they have seen them; and to give credence to their judgment and attract you to it, they are prone to add something to their matter, to stretch it out and amplify it. We need a man either very honest, or so simple that he has not the stuff to build up false inventions and give them plausibility; and wedded to no theory. Such was my man; and besides this, he at various times brought sailors and merchants, whom he had known on that trip, to see me. So I content myself with his information, without inquiring what the cosmographers say about it.

We ought to have topographers who would give us an exact account of the places where they have been. But because they have over us the advantage of having seen Palestine, they want to enjoy the privilege of telling us news about all the rest of the world. I would like everyone to write what he knows, and as much as he knows, not only in this, but in all other subjects; for a man may have some special knowledge and experience of the nature of a river or a fountain, who in other matters knows only what everybody knows. However, to circulate this little scrap of knowledge, he will undertake to write the whole of physics. From this vice spring many great abuses.

Now, to return to my subject, I think there is nothing barbarous and savage in that nation, from what I have been told, except that each man calls barbarism whatever is not his own practice; for indeed it seems we have no other test of truth and reason than the example and pattern of the opinions and customs of the country we live in. There is always the perfect religion, the perfect government, the perfect and accomplished manners in all things. Those people are wild, just as we call wild the fruits that Nature has produced by herself and in her normal course; whereas really it is those that we have changed artificially and led astray from the common order, that we should rather call wild. The former retain alive and vigorous their genuine, their most useful and natural, virtues and properties, which we have debased in the latter in adapting them to gratify our corrupted taste. And yet for all that, the savor and delicacy of some uncultivated fruits of those countries is quite as excellent, even to our taste, as that of our own. It is not reasonable that art should win the place of honor over our great and powerful mother Nature. We have so overloaded the beauty and richness of her works by our inventions that we have quite smothered her. Yet wherever her purity shines forth, she wonderfully puts to shame our vain and frivolous attempts:

> Ivy comes readier without our care;
> In lonely caves the arbutus grows more fair;
> No art with artless bird song can compare.
>   PROPERTIUS[9]

All our efforts cannot even succeed in reproducing the nest of the tiniest little bird, its contexture, its beauty and convenience; or even the web of the puny spider. All things, says Plato,[1] are produced by nature, by fortune, or by art; the greatest and most beautiful by one or the other of the first two, the least and most imperfect by the last.

These nations, then, seem to me barbarous in this sense, that they have been fashioned very little by the human mind, and are still very close to their original naturalness. The laws of nature still rule them, very little corrupted by ours; and they are in such a state of purity that I am sometimes vexed that they were unknown earlier, in the days when there were men able to judge them better than we. I am sorry that Lycurgus[2] and Plato did not know of them; for it seems to me that what we actually see in these nations surpasses not only all the pictures in which poets have idealized the golden age and all their inventions in imagining a happy state of man, but also the conceptions and the very desire of philosophy. They could not imagine a naturalness so pure and simple as we see by experience; nor could they believe that our society could be maintained with so little artifice and human solder. This is a nation,[3] I should say to Plato, in which there is no sort of traffic, no knowledge of letters, no science of numbers, no name for a magistrate or for political superiority, no custom of servitude, no riches or poverty, no contracts, no successions, no partitions, no occupations but leisure ones, no care for any but common kinship, no clothes, no agriculture, no metal, no use of wine or wheat. The very words that signify lying, treachery, dissimulation, avarice, envy, belittling, pardon—unheard of. How far from this perfection would he find the republic that he imagined: *Men fresh sprung from the gods* [Seneca].

> These manners nature first ordained.
>   VIRGIL[4]

For the rest, they live in a country with a very pleasant and temperate climate, so that according to my witnesses it is rare to see a sick man there; and they have assured me that they never saw one palsied, bleary-eyed, toothless, or bent with age. They are settled along the sea and shut in on the land side by great high mountains, with a stretch about a hundred leagues wide in between. They have a great abundance of fish and flesh which bear no resemblance to ours, and they eat them with no other artifice than cooking. The first man who rode a horse there, though he had had dealings with them on several other trips, so horrified them in this posture that they shot him dead with arrows before they could recognize him.

9. *Elegies.* I, Elegy ii, ll. 10ff.   1. See his *Laws.*   2. The half-legendary Spartan lawgiver (ninth century B.C.).   3. The passage beginning here is always compared with Shakespeare, *The Tempest,* Act 2, Sc.1, ll. 154ff.   4. *Georgics.* II, 20. *Seneca: Epistles,* Epistle 90.

Their buildings are very long, with a capacity of two or three hundred souls; they are covered with the bark of great trees, the strips reaching to the ground at one end and supporting and leaning on one another at the top, in the manner of some of our barns, whose covering hangs down to the ground and acts as a side. They have wood so hard that they cut with it and make of it their swords and grills to cook their food. Their beds are of a cotton weave, hung from the roof like those in our ships, each man having his own; for the wives sleep apart from their husbands.

They get up with the sun, and eat immediately upon rising, to last them through the day; for they take no other meal than that one. Like some other Eastern peoples, of whom Suidas[5] tells us, who drank apart from meals, they do not drink then; but they drink several times a day, and to capacity. Their drink is made of some root, and is of the color of our claret wines. They drink it only lukewarm. This beverage keeps only two or three days; it has a slightly sharp taste, is not at all heady, is good for the stomach, and has a laxative effect upon those who are not used to it; it is a very pleasant drink for anyone who is accustomed to it. In place of bread they use a certain white substance like preserved coriander. I have tried it; it tastes sweet and a little flat.

The whole day is spent in dancing. The younger men go to hunt animals with bows. Some of the women busy themselves meanwhile with warming their drink, which is their chief duty. Some one of the old men, in the morning before they begin to eat, preaches to the whole barnful in common, walking from one end to the other, and repeating one single sentence several times until he has completed the circuit (for the buildings are fully a hundred paces long). He recommends to them only two things: valor against the enemy and love for their wives. And they never fail to point out this obligation, as their refrain, that it is their wives who keep their drink warm and seasoned.

There may be seen in several places, including my own house, specimens of their beds, of their ropes, of their wooden swords and the bracelets with which they cover their wrists in combats, and of the big canes, open at one end, by whose sound they keep time in their dances. They are close shaven all over, and shave themselves much more cleanly than we, with nothing but a wooden or stone razor. They believe that souls are immortal, and that those who have deserved well of the gods are lodged in that part of heaven where the sun rises, and the damned in the west.

They have some sort of priests and prophets, but they rarely appear before the people, having their home in the mountains. On their arrival there is a great feast and solemn assembly of several villages—each barn, as I have described it, makes up a village, and they are about one French league[6] from each other. The prophet speaks to them in public, exhorting them to virtue and their duty; but their whole ethical science contains only these two articles: resoluteness in war and affection for their wives. He prophesies to them things to come and the results they are to expect from

5. A Byzantine lexicographer.   6. About 2.49 miles.

their undertakings, and urges them to war or holds them back from it; but this is on the condition that when he fails to prophesy correctly, and if things turn out otherwise than he has predicted, he is cut into a thousand pieces if they catch him, and condemned as a false prophet. For this reason, the prophet who has once been mistaken is never seen again.

Divination is a gift of God; that is why its abuse should be punished as imposture. Among the Scythians, when the soothsayers failed to hit the mark, they were laid, chained hand and foot, on carts full of heather and drawn by oxen, on which they were burned. Those who handle matters subject to the control of human capacity are excusable if they do the best they can. But these others who come and trick us with assurances of an extraordinary faculty that is beyond our ken, should they not be punished for not making good their promise, and for the temerity of their imposture?

They have their wars with the nations beyond the mountains, further inland, to which they go quite naked, with no other arms than bows or wooden swords ending in a sharp point, in the manner of the tongues of our boar spears. It is astonishing what firmness they show in their combats, which never end but in slaughter and bloodshed; for as to routs and terror, they know nothing of either.

Each man brings back his trophy the head of the enemy he has killed, and sets it up at the entrance to his dwelling. After they have treated their prisoners well for a long time with all the hospitality they can think of, each man who has a prisoner calls a great assembly of his acquaintances. He ties a rope to one of the prisoner's arms, by the end of which he holds him, a few steps away, for fear of being hurt, and gives his dearest friend the other arm to hold in the same way; and these two, in the presence of the whole assembly, kill him with their swords. This done, they roast him and eat him in common and send some pieces to their absent friends. This is not, as people think, for nourishment, as of old the Scythians used to do; it is to betoken an extreme revenge. And the proof of this came when they saw the Portuguese, who had joined forces with their adversaries, inflict a different kind of death on them when they took them prisoner, which was to bury them up to the waist, shoot the rest of their body full of arrows, and afterward hang them. They thought that these people from the other world, being men who had sown the knowledge of many vices among their neighbors and were much greater masters than themselves in every sort of wickedness, did not adopt this sort of vengeance without some reason, and that it must be more painful than their own; so they began to give up their old method and to follow this one.

I am not sorry that we notice the barbarous horror of such acts, but I am heartily sorry that, judging their faults rightly, we should be so blind to our own. I think there is more barbarity in eating a man alive than in eating him dead; and in tearing by tortures and the rack a body still full of feeling, in roasting a man bit by bit, in having him bitten and mangled by dogs and swine (as we have not only read but seen within fresh memory, not among ancient enemies, but among neighbors and fellow citizens, and what is worse, on the pretext of piety and religion),[7] than in roasting and eating him after he is dead.

Indeed, Chrysippus and Zeno, heads of the Stoic sect, thought there was nothing wrong in using our carcasses for any purpose in case of need, and getting nourishment from them; just as our ancestors,[8] when besieged by Caesar in the city of Alésia, resolved to relieve their famine by eating old men, women, and other people useless for fighting.

> The Gascons once, 'tis said, their life renewed
> By eating of such food.
>
> JUVENAL[9]

And physicians do not fear to use human flesh in all sorts of ways for our health, applying it either inwardly or outwardly. But there never was any opinion so disordered as to excuse treachery, disloyalty, tyranny, and cruelty, which are our ordinary vices.

So we may well call these people barbarians, in respect to the rules of reason, but not in respect to ourselves, who surpass them in every kind of barbarity.

Their warfare is wholly noble and generous, and as excusable and beautiful as this human disease can be; its only basis among them is their rivalry in valor. They are not fighting for the conquest of new lands, for they still enjoy that natural abundance that provides them without toil and trouble with all necessary things in such profusion that they have no wish to enlarge their boundaries. They are still in that happy state of desiring only as much as their natural needs demand; anything beyond that is superfluous to them.

They generally call those of the same age, brothers; those who are younger, children; and the old men are fathers to all the others. These leave to their heirs in common the full possession of their property, without division or any other title at all than just the one that Nature gives to her creatures in bringing them into the world.

If their neighbors cross the mountains to attack them and win a victory, the gain of the victor is glory, and the advantage of having proved the master in valor and virtue; for apart from this they have no use for the goods of the vanquished, and they return to their own country, where they lack neither anything necessary nor that great thing, the knowledge of how to enjoy their condition happily and be content with it. These men of ours do the same in their turn. They demand of their prisoners no other ransom than that they confess and acknowledge their defeat. But there is not one in a whole century who does not choose to die rather than to relax a single bit, by word or look, from the grandeur of an invincible courage; not one who would not rather be killed and eaten than so much as ask not to be. They treat them very freely, so that life may be all the dearer to them, and usually entertain them with threats of their coming death, of the torments they will have to suffer, the preparations that are being made for the pur-

---

7. The allusion is to the spectacles of religious warfare which Montaigne himself had witnessed in his time and country.   8. The Gauls.   9. *Satires.* Satire 15, ll. 93ff.

pose, the cutting up of their limbs, and the feast that will be made at their expense. All this is done for the sole purpose of extorting from their lips some weak or base word, or making them want to flee, so as to gain the advantage of having terrified them and broken down their firmness. For indeed, if you take it the right way, it is in this point alone that true victory lies:

> It is no victory
> Unless the vanquished foe admits your mastery.
> CLAUDIAN[1]

The Hungarians, very bellicose fighters, did not in olden times pursue their advantage beyond putting the enemy at their mercy. For having wrung a confession from him to this effect, they let him go unharmed and unransomed, except, at most, for exacting his promise never again to take up arms against them.

We win enough advantages over our enemies that are borrowed advantages, not really our own. It is the quality of a porter, not of valor, to have sturdier arms and legs; agility is a dead and corporeal quality; it is a stroke of luck to make our enemy stumble, or dazzle his eyes by the sunlight; it is a trick of art and technique, which may be found in a worthless coward, to be an able fencer. The worth and value of a man is in his heart and his will; there lies his real honor. Valor is the strength, not of legs and arms, but of heart and soul; it consists not in the worth of our horse or our weapons, but in our own. He who falls obstinate in his courage, *if he has fallen, he fights on his knees* [Seneca].[2] He who relaxes none of his assurance, no matter how great the danger of imminent death; who, giving up his soul, still looks firmly and scornfully at his enemy—he is beaten not by us, but by fortune; he is killed, not conquered.

The most valiant are sometimes the most unfortunate. Thus there are triumphant defeats that rival victories. Nor did those four sister victories, the fairest that the sun ever set eyes on—Salamis, Plataea, Mycale, and Sicily[3]—ever dare match all their combined glory against the glory of the annihilation of King Leonidas and his men at the pass of Thermopylae.[4]

Who ever hastened with more glorious and ambitious desire to win a battle than Captain Ischolas to lose one? Who ever secured his safety more ingeniously and painstakingly than he did his destruction? He was charged to defend a certain pass in the Peloponnesus against the Arcadians. Finding himself wholly incapable of doing this, in view of the nature of the place and the inequality of the forces, he made up his mind that all who confronted the enemy would necessarily have to remain on the field. On the other hand, deeming it unworthy both of his own virtue and magnanimity and of the Lacedaemonian name to fail in his charge, he took a middle course between these two extremes, in this way. The youngest and

---

1. *Of the Sixth Consulate of Honorius,* ll. 248 ff.　2. *Of Providence,* Book II.　3. Montaigne here refers to the famous Greek victories against the Persians and (at Himera, Sicily) against the Carthaginians in or about 480 B.C.　4. The Spartan king Leonidas's defense of the pass at Thermopylae also took place in 480 B.C., during the war against the Persians.

fittest of his band he preserved for the defense and service of their country, and sent them home; and with those whose loss was less important, he determined to hold this pass, and by their death to make the enemy buy their entry as dearly as he could. And so it turned out. For he was presently surrounded on all sides by the Arcadians, and after slaughtering a large number of them, he and his men were all put to the sword. Is there a trophy dedicated to victors that would not be more due to these vanquished? The role of true victory is in fighting, not in coming off safely; and the honor of valor consists in combating, not in beating.

To return to our story. These prisoners are so far from giving in, in spite of all that is done to them, that on the contrary, during the two or three months that they are kept, they wear a gay expression; they urge their captors to hurry and put them to the test; they defy them, insult them, reproach them with their cowardice and the number of battles they have lost to the prisoners' own people.

I have a song composed by a prisoner which contains this challenge, that they should all come boldly and gather to dine off him, for they will be eating at the same time their own fathers and grandfathers, who have served to feed and nourish his body. "These muscles," he says, "this flesh and these veins are your own, poor fools that you are. You do not recognize that the substance of your ancestors' limbs is still contained in them. Savor them well; you will find in them the taste of your own flesh." An idea that certainly does not smack of barbarity. Those that paint these people dying, and who show the execution, portray the prisoner spitting in the face of his slayers and scowling at them. Indeed, to the last gasp they never stop braving and defying their enemies by word and look. Truly here are real savages by our standards; for either they must be thoroughly so, or we must be; there is an amazing distance between their character and ours.

The men there have several wives, and the higher their reputation for valor the more wives they have. It is a remarkably beautiful thing about their marriages that the same jealousy our wives have to keep us from the affection and kindness of other women, theirs have to win this for them. Being more concerned for their husbands' honor than for anything else, they strive and scheme to have as many companions as they can, since that is a sign of their husbands' valor.

Our wives will cry "Miracle!" but it is no miracle. It is a properly matrimonial virtue, but one of the highest order. In the Bible, Leah, Rachel, Sarah, and Jacob's wives gave their beautiful handmaids to their husbands; and Livia seconded the appetites of Augustus to her own disadvantage; and Stratonice, the wife of King Deiotarus,[5] not only lent her husband for his use a very beautiful young chambermaid in her service, but carefully brought up her children, and backed them up to succeed to their father's estates.

And lest it be thought that all this is done through a simple and servile bondage to usage and through the pressure of the authority of their ancient customs, without reasoning or judgment, and because their minds are so

5. Tetrarch of Galatia, in Asia Minor.

stupid that they cannot take any other course, I must cite some examples of their capacity. Besides the warlike song I have just quoted, I have another, a love song, which begins in this vein: "Adder, stay; stay, adder, that from the pattern of your coloring my sister may draw the fashion and the workmanship of a rich girdle that I may give to my love; so may your beauty and your pattern be forever preferred to all other serpents." This first couplet is the refrain of the song. Now I am familiar enough with poetry to be a judge of this: not only is there nothing barbarous in this fancy, but it is altogether Anacreontic.[6] Their language, moreover, is a soft language, with an agreeable sound, somewhat like Greek in its endings.

Three of these men, ignorant of the price they will pay some day, in loss of repose and happiness, for gaining knowledge of the corruptions of this side of the ocean; ignorant also of the fact that of this intercourse will come their ruin (which I suppose is already well advanced: poor wretches, to let themselves be tricked by the desire for new things, and to have left the serenity of their own sky to come and see ours!)—three of these men were at Rouen, at the time the late King Charles IX was there. The king talked to them for a long time; they were shown our ways, our splendor, the aspect of a fine city. After that, someone asked their opinion, and wanted to know what they had found most amazing. They mentioned three things, of which I have forgotten the third, and I am very sorry for it; but I still remember two of them. They said that in the first place they thought it very strange that so many grown men, bearded, strong, and armed, who were around the king (it is likely that they were talking about the Swiss of his guard) should submit to obey a child, and that one of them was not chosen to command instead. Second (they have a way in their language of speaking of men as halves of one another), they had noticed that there were among us men full and gorged with all sorts of good things, and that their other halves were beggars at their doors, emaciated with hunger and poverty; and they thought it strange that these needy halves could endure such an injustice, and did not take the others by the throat, or set fire to their houses.

I had a very long talk with one of them; but I had an interpreter who followed my meaning so badly, and who was so hindered by his stupidity in taking in my ideas, that I could get hardly any satisfaction from the man. When I asked him what profit he gained from his superior position among his people (for he was a captain, and our sailors called him king), he told me that it was to march foremost in war. How many men followed him? He pointed to a piece of ground, to signify as many as such a space could hold; it might have been four or five thousand men. Did all this authority expire with the war? He said that this much remained, that when he visited the villages dependent on him, they made paths for him through the underbrush by which he might pass quite comfortably.

All this is not too bad—but what's the use? They don't wear breeches.

---

6. Worthy of Anacreon (572?–488? B.C.), major Greek writer of amatory lyrics.

OF THE INCONSISTENCY OF OUR ACTIONS[7]

Those who make a practice of comparing human actions are never so perplexed as when they try to see them as a whole and in the same light; for they commonly contradict each other so strangely that it seems impossible that they have come from the same shop. One moment young Marius[8] is a son of Mars, another moment a son of Venus.[9] Pope Boniface VIII, they say, entered office like a fox, behaved in it like a lion, and died like a dog. And who would believe that it was Nero, that living image of cruelty, who said, when they brought him in customary fashion the sentence of a condemned criminal to sign: "Would to God I had never learned to write!" So much his heart was wrung at condemning a man to death!

Everything is so full of such examples—each man, in fact, can supply himself with so many—that I find it strange to see intelligent men sometimes going to great pains to match these pieces; seeing that irresolution seems to me the most common and apparent defect of our nature, as witness that famous line of Publilius, the farce writer:

> Bad is the plan that never can be changed.
> PUBLILIUS SYRUS[1]

There is some justification for basing a judgment of a man on the most ordinary acts of his life; but in view of the natural instability of our conduct and opinions, it has often seemed to me that even good authors are wrong to insist on fashioning a consistent and solid fabric out of us. They choose one general characteristic, and go and arrange and interpret all a man's actions to fit their picture; and if they cannot twist them enough, they go and set them down to dissimulation. Augustus has escaped them; for there is in this man throughout the course of his life such an obvious, abrupt, and continual variety of actions that even the boldest judges have had to let him go, intact and unsolved. Nothing is harder for me than to believe in men's consistency, nothing easier than to believe in their inconsistency. He who would judge them in detail and distinctly, bit by bit, would more often hit upon the truth.

In all antiquity it is hard to pick out a dozen men who set their lives to a certain and constant course, which is the principal goal of wisdom. For, to comprise all wisdom in a word, says an ancient [Seneca], and to embrace all the rules of our life in one, it is "always to will the same things, and always to oppose the same things."[2] I would not deign, he says, to add "provided the will is just"; for if it is not just, it cannot always be whole.

In truth, I once learned that vice is only unruliness and lack of moderation, and that consequently consistency cannot be attributed to it. It is a maxim of Demosthenes, they say, that the beginning of all virtue is consultation and deliberation; and the end and perfection, consistency. If it

7. Book II, Chapter 1.   8. Nephew of the older and better known Marius. Montaigne's source is Plutarch's *Life of Marius*.   9. *Mars . . . Venus:* war and love.   1. *Apothegms (Sententiae)*, l. 362.   2. *Epistles*, Epistle 20.

were by reasoning that we settled on a particular course of action, we
would choose the fairest course—but no one has thought of that:

> He spurns the thing he sought, and seeks anew
> What he just spurned; he seethes, his life's askew.
> HORACE[3]

Our ordinary practice is to follow the inclinations of our appetite, to the
left, to the right, uphill and down, as the wind of circumstance carries us.
We think of what we want only at the moment we want it, and we change
like that animal which takes the color of the place you set it on. What we
have just now planned, we presently change, and presently again we retrace
our steps: nothing but oscillation and inconsistency:

> Like puppets we are moved by outside strings.
> HORACE[4]

We do not go; we are carried away, like floating objects, now gently, now
violently, according as the water is angry or calm:

> Do we not see all humans unaware
> Of what they want, and always searching everywhere,
> And changing place, as if to drop the load they bear?
> LUCRETIUS[5]

Every day a new fancy, and our humors shift with the shifts in the weather:

> Such are the minds of men, as is the fertile light
> That Father Jove himself sends down to make earth bright.
> HOMER[6]

We float between different states of mind; we wish nothing freely, nothing absolutely, nothing constantly. If any man could prescribe and establish definite laws and a definite organization in his head, we should see
shining throughout his life an evenness of habits, an order, and an infallible relation between his principles and his practice.

Empedocles noticed this inconsistency in the Agrigentines, that they
abandoned themselves to pleasures as if they were to die on the morrow,
and built as if they were never to die.[7]

This man would be easy to understand, as is shown by the example of
the younger Cato[8]: he who has touched one chord of him has touched all;
he is a harmony of perfectly concordant sounds, which cannot conflict.
With us, it is the opposite: for so many actions, we need so many individual judgments. The surest thing, in my opinion, would be to trace our
actions to the neighboring circumstances, without getting into any further
research and without drawing from them any other conclusions.

During the disorders of our poor country,[9] I was told that a girl, living
near where I then was, had thrown herself out of a high window to avoid

3. *Epistles*, Book I, Epistle 1, ll. 98ff.   4. *Satires*, Book II, Satire 7, l. 82.   5. *On the Nature of
Things*, Book III, ll. 1057ff.   6. *Odyssey* XVIII. 135.   7. From the life of the fifth-century Greek
philosopher Empedocles, by Diogenes Laertius.   8. The philosopher, Cato "Uticensis" (first century
B.C.); to Montaigne, and also traditionally, he is an epitome of moral and intellectual integrity.   9. See
note 7, page 1799, and the corresponding passage in the text of "Of Cannibals."

the violence of a knavish soldier quartered in her house. Not killed by the fall, she reasserted her purpose by trying to cut her throat with a knife. From this she was prevented, but only after wounding herself gravely. She herself confessed that the soldier had as yet pressed her only with requests, solicitations, and gifts; but she had been afraid, she said, that he would finally resort to force. And all this with such words, such expressions, not to mention the blood that testified to her virtue, as would have become another Lucrece.[1] Now, I learned that as a matter of fact, both before and since, she was a wench not so hard to come to terms with. As the story[2] says: Handsome and gentlemanly as you may be, when you have had no luck, do not promptly conclude that your mistress is inviolably chaste; for all you know, the mule driver may get his will with her.

Antigonus,[3] having taken a liking to one of his soldiers for his virtue and valor, ordered his physicians to treat the man for a persistent internal malady that had long tormented him. After his cure, his master noticed that he was going about his business much less warmly, and asked him what had changed him so and made him such a coward. "You yourself, Sire," he answered, "by delivering me from the ills that made my life indifferent to me." A soldier of Lucullus[4] who had been robbed of everything by the enemy made a bold attack on them to get revenge. When he had retrieved his loss, Lucullus, having formed a good opinion of him, urged him to some dangerous exploit with all the fine expostulations he could think of,

> With words that might have stirred a coward's heart.
> HORACE[5]

"Urge some poor soldier who has been robbed to do it," he replied;

> Though but a rustic lout,
> "That man will go who's lost his money," he called out;
> HORACE[6]

and resolutely refused to go.

We read that Sultan Mohammed outrageously berated Hassan, leader of his Janissaries, because he saw his troops giving way to the Hungarians and Hassan himself behaving like a coward in the fight, Hassan's only reply was to go and hurl himself furiously—alone, just as he was, arms in hand— into the first body of enemies that he met, by whom he was promptly swallowed up; this was perhaps not so much self-justification as a change of mood, nor so much his natural valor as fresh spite.

That man whom you saw so adventurous yesterday, do not think it strange to find him just as cowardly today: either anger, or necessity, or company, or wine, or the sound of a trumpet, had put his heart in his belly. His was a courage formed not by reason, but by one of these circumstances; it is no wonder if he has now been made different by other, contrary circumstances.

1. The legendary, virtuous Roman who stabbed herself after being raped by King Tarquinius Superbus's son.   2. A common folk tale.   3. Macedonian king.   4. Roman general of the first century B.C.   5. *Epistles*, Book II, Epistle 2, l. 36.   6. *Epistles*, Book II, Epistle 2, ll. 39ff.

These supple variations and contradictions that are seen in us have made some imagine that we have two souls, and others that two powers accompany us and drive us, each in its own way, one toward good, the other toward evil; for such sudden diversity cannot well be reconciled with a simple subject.

Not only does the wind of accident move me at will, but, besides, I am moved and disturbed as a result merely of my own unstable posture; and anyone who observes carefully can hardly find himself twice in the same state. I give my soul now one face, now another, according to which direction I turn it. If I speak of myself in different ways, that is because I look at myself in different ways. All contradictions may be found in me by some twist and in some fashion. Bashful, insolent; chaste, lascivious; talkative, taciturn; tough, delicate; clever, stupid; surly, affable; lying, truthful; learned, ignorant; liberal, miserly, and prodigal: all this I see in myself to some extent according to how I turn; and whoever studies himself really attentively finds in himself, yes, even in his judgment, this gyration and discord. I have nothing to say about myself absolutely, simply, and solidly, without confusion and without mixture, or in one word. *Distinguo*[7] is the most universal member of my logic.

Although I am always minded to say good of what is good, and inclined to interpret favorably anything that can be so interpreted, still it is true that the strangeness of our condition makes it happen that we are often driven to do good by vice itself—were it not that doing good is judged by intention alone.

Therefore one courageous deed must not be taken to prove a man valiant; a man who was really valiant would be so always and on all occasions. If valor were a habit of virtue, and not a sally, it would make a man equally resolute in any contingency, the same alone as in company, the same in single combat as in battle; for, whatever they say, there is not one valor for the pavement and another for the camp. As bravely would he bear an illness in his bed as a wound in camp, and he would fear death no more in his home than in an assault. We would not see the same man charging into the breach with brave assurance, and later tormenting himself, like a woman, over the loss of a lawsuit or a son. When, though a coward against infamy, he is firm against poverty; when, though weak against the surgeons' knives, he is steadfast against the enemy's swords, the action is praiseworthy, not the man.

Many Greeks, says Cicero, cannot look at the enemy, and are brave in sickness; the Cimbrians and Celtiberians, just the opposite; *for nothing can be uniform that does not spring from a firm principle* [Cicero].[8]

There is no more extreme valor of its kind than Alexander's; but it is only of one kind, and not complete and universal enough. Incomparable though it is, it still has its blemishes; which is why we see him worry so frantically when he conceives the slightest suspicion that his men are plotting against his life, and why he behaves in such matters with such violent

7. "I distinguish"; I separate into its components.   8. *Tusculan Disputations*, Book II, Chapter 27.

and indiscriminate injustice and with a fear that subverts his natural reason. Also superstition, with which he was so strongly tainted, bears some stamp of pusillanimity. And the excessiveness of the penance he did for the murder of Clytus[9] is also evidence of the unevenness of his temper.

Our actions are nothing but a patchwork—*they despise pleasure, but are too cowardly in pain; they are indifferent to glory, but infamy breaks their spirit* [Cicero][1]—and we want to gain honor under false colors. Virtue will not be followed except for her own sake; and if we sometimes borrow her mask for some other purpose, she promptly snatches it from our face. It is a strong and vivid dye, once the soul is steeped in it, and will not go without taking the fabric with it. That is why, to judge a man, we must follow his traces long and carefully. If he does not maintain consistency for its own sake, *with a way of life that has been well considered and preconcerted* [Cicero][2]; if changing circumstances makes him change his pace (I mean his path, for his pace may be hastened or slowed), let him go: that man goes before the wind, as the motto of our Talbot[3] says.

It is no wonder, says an ancient [Seneca],[4] that chance has so much power over us, since we live by chance. A man who has not directed his life as a whole toward a definite goal cannot possibly set his particular actions in order. A man who does not have a picture of the whole in his head cannot possibly arrange the pieces. What good does it do a man to lay in a supply of paints if he does not know what he is to paint? No one makes a definite plan of his life; we think about it only piecemeal. The archer must first know what he is aiming at, and then set his hand, his bow, his string, his arrow, and his movements for that goal. Our plans go astray because they have no direction and no aim. No wind works for the man who has no port of destination.

I do not agree with the judgment given in favor of Sophocles, on the strength of seeing one of his tragedies, that it proved him competent to manage his domestic affairs, against the accusation of his son. Nor do I think that the conjecture of the Parians sent to reform the Milesians was sufficient ground for the conclusion they drew. Visiting the island, they noticed the best-cultivated lands and the best-run country houses, and noted down the names of their owners. Then they assembled the citizens in the town and appointed these owners the new governors and magistrates, judging that they, who were careful of their private affairs, would be careful of those of the public.

We are all patchwork, and so shapeless and diverse in composition that each bit, each moment, plays its own game. And there is as much difference between us and ourselves as between us and others. *Consider it a great thing to play the part of one single man* [Seneca].[5] Ambition can teach men valor, and temperance, and liberality, and even justice. Greed can implant in the heart of a shop apprentice, brought up in obscurity and

9. Clytus, a commander in Alexander's army, was killed by him during an argument, an act which Alexander immediately and bitterly regretted, as related by Plutarch in his *Life of Alexander*, Chapters 50–52.   1. *Of Duties (De officiis)*, Book I, Chapter 21.   2. *Paradoxes*, Paradox 5.   3. Talbot, an English captain who fought in France and died there in 1453.   4. *Epistles*, Epistle 71.   5. *Epistles*, Epistle 120.

idleness, the confidence to cast himself far from hearth and home, in a frail boat at the mercy of the waves and angry Neptune; it also teaches discretion and wisdom. Venus herself supplies resolution and boldness to boys still subject to discipline and the rod, and arms the tender hearts of virgins who are still in their mothers' laps:

> Furtively passing sleeping guards, with Love as guide,
> Alone by night the girl comes to the young man's side.
> TIBULLUS[6]

In view of this, a sound intellect will refuse to judge men simply by their outward actions; we must probe the inside and discover what springs set men in motion. But since this is an arduous and hazardous undertaking, I wish fewer people would meddle with it.

From APOLOGY FOR RAYMOND SEBOND[7]

("Man's Presumption and Littleness")

What does truth[8] preach to us, when she exhorts us to flee worldly philosophy,[9] when she so often inculcates in us that our wisdom is but folly before God[1]; that of all vanities the vainest is man; that the man who is presumptuous of his knowledge does not yet know what knowledge is[2]; and that man, who is nothing, if he thinks he is something, seduces and deceives himself?[3] These statements of the Holy Spirit express so clearly and so vividly what I wish to maintain, that no other proof would be needed against men who would surrender with all submission and obedience to its authority. But these men[4] insist on being whipped to their own cost and will not allow us to combat their reason except by itself.

Let us then consider for the moment man alone, without outside assistance, armed solely with his own weapons, and deprived of divine grace and knowledge, which is his whole honor, his strength, and the foundation of his being. Let us see how much presence he has in his fine array. Let him help me to understand, by the force of his reason, on what foundations he has built these great advantages that he thinks he has over other creatures. Who has persuaded him that that admirable motion of the celestial vault, the eternal light of those torches rolling so proudly above his head, the fearful movements of that infinite sea, were established and have lasted so many centuries for his convenience and his service? Is it possible to imagine anything so ridiculous as that this miserable and puny creature, who is not even master of himself, exposed to the attacks of all things, should call himself master and emperor of the universe, the least part of which it is not in his power to know, much less to command? And this privilege that he attributes to himself of being the only one in this great

---

6. *Elegies*, Book II, Elegy 1, ll. 75ff.   7. Book II, Chapter 12. A small but significant section of the very long "Apology" is reprinted here.   8. Revealed truth, the Scriptures.   9. Colossians 2:8.   1. I Corinthians 3:19.   2. I Corinthians 8:2.   3. Galatians 6:3. This and the previous passages from St. Paul were among those inscribed on the walls of Montaigne's library.   4. Those who pretend to arrive at certainty through their human means, their reason, alone.

edifice who has the capacity to recognize its beauty and its parts, the only one who can give thanks for it to the architect and keep an account of the receipts and expenses of the world: who has sealed him this privilege? Let him show us his letters patent for this great and splendid charge.

Have they been granted in favor of the wise only? Then they do not touch many people. Are the fools and the wicked worthy of such extraordinary favor, and, being the worst part of the world, of being preferred to all the rest?

Shall we believe this man? *For whom then shall a man say that the world was made? Naturally, for those souls who have the use of reason. These are gods and men, to whom certainly nothing is superior* [Cicero, quoting Balbus].[5] We shall never have flouted enough the impudence of this coupling.

But, poor wight, what has he in himself worthy of such an advantage? When we consider the incorruptible life of the celestial bodies, their beauty, their greatness, their continual motion by so exact a rule;

> When the vaults of heaven meet our sight,
> Infinite worlds above, ether with stars alight;
> And when the course of sun and moon come to our mind;
> > LUCRETIUS[6]

when we consider the dominion and power that those bodies have, not only over our lives and the conditions of our fortune,

> For on the stars men's deeds and lives depend.
> > MANILIUS[7]

but over our very inclinations, our reasonings, our wills, which they govern, drive, and stir at the mercy of their influences, as our reason finds and teaches us;

> He learns that stars remotely seen
> Govern by silent laws, and intervene;
> To move the universe they alternate,
> And rule by certain signs the twists of fate;
> > MANILIUS[8]

when we see that not merely a man, nor a king, but kingdoms, empires, and all this world below move in step with the slightest movements of the heavens;

> How great a change the slightest motion brings:
> So great this kingdom is that governs kings;
> > MANILIUS[9]

if our virtue, our vices, our competence and knowledge, and this very dissertation that we are making about the power of the stars and this com-

---

5. See Cicero's *Of the Nature of the Gods*, Book II, Chapter 53.   6. *On the Nature of Things,* Book V, ll. 1204ff.   7. *Astronomicon*, Book III, l. 58.   8. *Astronomicon*, Book I, ll. 60ff.   9. *Astronomicon,* Book I, l. 57, and Book IV, l. 93.

parison of them to us, comes, as our reason judges, by their medium and
their favor;

> One, in love's delirium,
> Can cross the sea and conquer Ilium;
> Another man is destined laws to build;
> Fathers kill sons, fathers by sons are killed,
> And brother wounds armed brother in the fray.
> This war is not of ours; Fate makes men stray,
> Punish themselves, their members lacerate.

. . . .

> This too is fated, that I write of fate;
>
>   MANILIUS[1]

if we hold by the dispensation of heaven this portion of reason that we
have, how can our reason make us equal to heaven? How subject its essence
and conditions to our knowledge? All that we see in those bodies astonishes
us. *What preparations, what instruments, what levers, what machines,
what workmen performed so great a work?* [Cicero.][2]

Why do we deny them soul, and life, and reason? Have we recognized
in them some inert, insensible stupidity, we who have no dealings with
them except obedience? Shall we say that we have seen in no other creature than man the exercise of a rational soul? Well, have we seen anything
like the sun? Does it fail to exist, because we have seen nothing like it, and
its movements to exist, because there are none like them? If what we have
not seen does not exist, our knowledge is marvelously shrunk: *How narrow
are the limits of our mind!* [Cicero.][3]

Are these not dreams of human vanity, to make the moon a celestial
earth, to imagine mountains and valleys there, like Anaxagoras;[4] to plant
habitations and human dwellings there, and set up colonies for our convenience, as Plato and Plutarch do;[5] and to make our earth a bright star
lighting the moon? *Among other human infirmities is this one also, mental
fog, and not so much the need to err as the love of errors* [Seneca].[6] *The
corruptible body weighs down the soul, and the earthy tabernacle oppresses
the much pondering mind* [The Book of Wisdom, quoted by Saint Augustine.][7]

Presumption is our natural and original malady. The most vulnerable
and frail of all creatures is man, and at the same time the most arrogant.[8]
He feels and sees himself lodged here, amid the mire and dung of the
world, nailed and riveted to the worst, the deadest, and the most stagnant
part of the universe, on the lowest story of the house and the farthest from
the vault of heaven, with the animals of the worst condition of the three;
and in his imagination he goes planting himself above the circle of the
moon, and bringing the sky down beneath his feet. It is by the vanity of
this same imagination that he equals himself to God, attributes to himself

---

1. *Astronomicon*, Book IV, ll. 79ff., and l. 118.   2. *Of the Nature of the Gods*, Book I, Chapter 8.
3. *Of the Nature of the Gods*, Book I, Chapter 31.   4. According to Diogenes Laertius, *Life of Anaxagoras*, Book II, Chapter 8.   5. For the notion that the moon is inhabited, Montaigne refers to Plutarch's
Of the Face of the Moon.   6. *Of Wrath*, Book II, Chapter 9.   7. *City of God*, Book XII, Section 15.
8. The phrase, originally Pliny's, is another of those engraved on the walls of Montaigne's library.

divine characteristics, picks himself out and separates himself from the horde of other creatures, carves out their shares to his fellows and companions the animals, and distributes among them such portions of faculties and powers as he sees fit. How does he know, by the force of his intelligence, the secret internal stirrings of animals? By what comparison between them and us does he infer the stupidity that he attributes to them?

When I play with my cat, who knows if I am not a pastime to her more than she is to me? Plato,[9] in his picture of the golden age under Saturn, counts among the principal advantages of the man of that time the communication he had with the beasts; inquiring of them and learning from them, he knew the true qualities and differences of each one of them; whereby he acquired a very perfect intelligence and prudence, and conducted his life far more happily than we could possibly do. Do we need a better proof to judge man's impudence with regard to the beasts? That great author[1] opined that in most of the bodily form that Nature gave them, she considered solely the use of prognostications that were derived from them in his time.

This defect that hinders communication between them and us, why is it not just as much ours as theirs? It is a matter of guesswork whose fault it is that we do not understand one another; for we do not understand them any more than they do us. By this same reasoning they may consider us beasts, as we consider them. It is no great wonder if we do not understand them; neither do we understand the Basques[2] and the Troglodytes. However, some have boasted of understanding them, like Apollonius of Tyana, Melampus, Tiresias, Thales, and others.[3] And since it is a fact, as the cosmographers say, that there are nations that accept a dog as their king, they must give a definite interpretation to his voice and motions. We must notice the parity there is between us. We have some mediocre understanding of their meaning; so do they of ours, in about the same degree. They flatter us, threaten us, and implore us, and we them.

Furthermore, we discover very evidently that there is full and complete communication between them and that they understand each other, not only those of the same species, but also those of different species.

> Even dumb cattle and the savage beasts
> Varied and different noises do employ
> When they feel fear or pain, or thrill with joy.
> LUCRETIUS[4]

In a certain bark of the dog the horse knows there is anger; at a certain other sound of his he is not frightened. Even in the beasts that have no voice, from the mutual services we see between them we easily infer some other means of communication; their motions converse and discuss:

9. In his *Statesman*. 1. Plato, in the *Timaeus*. 2. Inhabitants of the Pyrenees region on the Bay of Biscay, known for the difficulty and peculiarity of their language. *Troglodytes*: Cave dwellers. 3. A mixture of mythical and historical figures: Apollonius of Tyana, Greek neo-Pythagorean philosopher and magician (first century A.D.); Melampus, mythical physician and sage; Tiresias, mythical blind prophet of Thebes: Thales, regarded as the first Greek philosopher (sixth century B.C.), one of the Seven Sages of Greece. 4. *On the Nature of Things*, Book V, ll. 1058ff.

> Likewise in children, the tongue's speechlessness
> Leads them to gesture what they would express.
>   LUCRETIUS[5]

Why not; just as well as our mutes dispute, argue, and tell stories by signs? I have seen some so supple and versed in this, that in truth they lacked nothing of perfection in being able to make themselves understood. Lovers grow angry, are reconciled, entreat, thank, make assignations, and in fine say everything, with their eyes:

> And silence too records
> Our prayers and our words.
>   TASSO[6]

What of the hands? We beg, we promise, call, dismiss, threaten, pray, entreat, deny, refuse, question, admire, count, confess, repent, fear, blush, doubt, instruct, command, incite, encourage, swear, testify, accuse, condemn, absolve, insult, despise, defy, vex, flatter, applaud, bless, humiliate, mock, reconcile, commend, exalt, entertain, rejoice, complain, grieve, mope, despair, wonder, exclaim, are silent, and what not, with a variation and multiplication that vie with the tongue. With the head: we invite, send away, avow, disavow, give the lie, welcome, honor, venerate, disdain, demand, show out, cheer, lament, caress, scold, submit, brave, exhort, menace, assure, inquire. What of the eyebrows? What of the shoulders? There is no movement that does not speak both a language intelligible without instruction, and a public language; which means, seeing the variety and particular use of other languages, that this one must rather be judged the one proper to human nature. I omit what necessity teaches privately and promptly to those who need it, and the finger alphabets, and the grammars in gestures, and the sciences which are practiced and expressed only by gestures, and the nations which Pliny says have no other language.

An ambassador of the city of Abdera, after speaking at length to King Agis of Sparta, asked him: "Well, Sire, what answer do you wish me to take back to our citizens?" "That I allowed you to say all you wanted, and as much as you wanted, without ever saying a word."[7] Wasn't that an eloquent and thoroughly intelligible silence?

Moreover, what sort of faculty of ours do we not recognize in the actions of the animals? Is there a society regulated with more order, diversified into more charges and functions, and more consistently maintained, than that of the honeybee? Can we imagine so orderly an arrangement of actions and occupations as this to be conducted without reason and foresight?

> Some, by these signs and instances inclined,
> Have said that bees share in the divine mind
> And the ethereal spirit.
>   VIRGIL[8]

---

5. *On the Nature of Things*, Book V, ll. 1029ff.   6. Torquato Tasso, in the pastoral drama *Aminta*, Act II, Scene 3, ll. 35–36.   7. The story is told by Plutarch in *Apothegms of the Lacedaemonians*. 8. *Georgics*, Book IV, ll. 219ff.

Do the swallows that we see on the return of spring ferreting in all the corners of our houses search without judgment, and choose without discrimination, out of a thousand places, the one which is most suitable for them to dwell in? And in that beautiful and admirable texture of their buildings, can birds use a square rather than a round figure, an obtuse rather than a right angle, without knowing their properties and their effects? Do they take now water, now clay, without judging that hardness is softened by moistening? Do they floor their palace with moss or with down, without foreseeing that the tender limbs of their little ones will lie softer and more comfortably on it? Do they shelter themselves from the rainy wind and face their dwelling toward the orient without knowing the different conditions of these winds and considering that one is more salutary to them than the other? Why does the spider thicken her web in one place and slacken it in another, use now this sort of knot, now that one, unless she has the power of reflection, and thought, and inference?

We recognize easily enough, in most of their works, how much superiority the animals have over us and how feeble is our skill to imitate them. We see, however, in our cruder works, the faculties that we use, and that our soul applies itself with all its power; why do we not think the same thing of them? Why do we attribute to some sort of natural and servile inclination these works which surpass all that we can do by nature and by art? Wherein, without realizing it, we grant them a very great advantage over us, by making Nature, with maternal tenderness, accompany them and guide them as by the hand in all the actions and comforts of their life; while us she abandons to chance and to fortune, and to seek by art the things necessary for our preservation, and denies us at the same time the power to attain, by any education and mental straining, the natural resourcefulness of the animals; so that their brutish stupidity surpasses in all conveniences all that our divine intelligence can do.

Truly, by this reckoning, we should be quite right to call her a very unjust stepmother. But this is not so; our organization is not so deformed and disorderly. Nature has universally embraced all her creatures; and there is none that she has not very amply furnished with all powers necessary for the preservation of its being. For these vulgar complaints that I hear men make (as the license of their opinions now raises them above the clouds, and then sinks them to the antipodes) that we are the only animal abandoned naked on the naked earth, tied, bound, having nothing to arm and cover ourselves with except the spoils of others; whereas all other creatures Nature has clothed with shells, husks, bark, hair, wool, spikes, hide, down, feathers, scales, fleece, and silk, according to the need of their being; has armed them with claws, teeth, or horns for attack and defense; and has herself instructed them in what is fit for them—to swim, to run, to fly, to sing—whereas man can neither walk, nor speak, nor eat, nor do anything but cry, without apprenticeship—

> The infant, like a sailor tossed ashore
> By raging seas, lies naked on the earth.

> Speechless, helpless for life, when at his birth
> Nature from out the womb brings him to light.
> He fills the place with wailing, as is right
> For one who through so many woes must pass.
> Yet flocks, herds, savage beasts of every class
> Grow up without the need for any rattle,
> Or for a gentle nurse's soothing prattle;
> They seek no varied clothes against the sky;
> Lastly they need no arms, no ramparts high
> To guard their own—since earth itself and nature
> Amply bring forth all things for every creature
>
> LUCRETIUS[9]

—those complaints are false, there is a greater equality and a more uniform relationship in the organization of the world. Our skin is provided as adequately as theirs with endurance against the assaults of the weather: witness so many nations who have not yet tried the use of any clothes. Our ancient Gauls wore hardly any clothes; nor do the Irish, our neighbors, under so cold a sky. But we may judge this better by ourselves; for all the parts of the body that we see fit to expose to the wind and air are found fit to endure it: face, feet, hands, legs, shoulders, head, according as custom invites us. For if there is a part of us that is tender and that seems as though it should fear the cold, it should be the stomach, where digestion takes place; our fathers left it uncovered, and our ladies, soft and delicate as they are, sometimes go half bare down to the naval. Nor are the bindings and swaddlings of infants necessary either; and the Lacedaemonian mothers raised their children in complete freedom to move their limbs, without wrapping or binding them. Our weeping is common to most of the other animals; and there are scarcely any who are not observed to complain and wail long after their birth, since it is a demeanor most appropriate to the helplessness that they feel. As for the habit of eating, it is, in us as in them, natural and needing no instruction:

> For each one feels his powers and his needs.
>
> LUCRETIUS[1]

Who doubts that a child, having attained the strength to feed himself, would be able to seek his food? And the earth produces and offers him enough of it for his need, with no other cultivation or artifice; and if not in all weather, neither does she for the beasts: witness the provisions we see the ants and others make for the sterile seasons of the year.

These nations that we have just discovered to be so abundantly furnished with food and natural drink, without care or preparation, have now taught us that bread is not our only food, and that without plowing our mother Nature had provided us in plenty with all we needed; indeed, as seems likely, more amply and richly than she does now that we have interpolated our artifice:

9. *On the Nature of Things*, Book V, ll. 222ff. 1. *On the Nature of Things*, Book V, ll. 1033ff.

> At first and of her own accord the earth
> Brought forth sleek fruits and vintages of worth,
> Herself gave harvests sweet and pastures fair,
> Which now scarce grow, despite our toil and care,
> And we exhaust our oxen and our men;
>   LUCRETIUS[2]

the excess and unruliness of our appetite outstripping all the inventions with which we seek to satisfy it.

As for weapons, we have more that are natural than most other animals, and more varied movements of our limbs; and we get more service out of them, naturally and without lessons. Those who are trained to fight naked are seen to throw themselves into dangers like our own men. If some animals surpass us in this advantage, we surpass many others. And the skill to fortify and protect the body by acquired means, we possess by a natural instinct and precept. As proof that this is so, the elephant sharpens and whets the teeth which he uses in war (for he has special ones for this purpose, which he spares, and does not use at all for his other functions). When bulls go into combat, they spread and toss the dust around them; boars whet their tusks, and the ichneumon, when he is to come to grips with the crocodile, arms his body, coats it, and crusts it all over with mud, well pressed and well kneaded, as with a cuirass. Why shall we not say that it is just as natural to arm ourselves with wood and iron?

As for speech, it is certain that if it is not natural, it is not necessary. Nevertheless, I believe that a child who had been brought up in complete solitude, remote from all association (which would be a hard experiment to make), would have some sort of speech to express his ideas. And it is not credible that Nature has denied us this resource that she has given to many other animals: for what is it but speech, this faculty we see in them of complaining, rejoicing, calling to each other for help, inviting each other to love, as they do by the use of their voice? How could they not speak to one another? They certainly speak to us, and we to them. In how many ways do we not speak to our dogs? And they answer us. We talk to them in another language, with other names, than to birds, hogs, oxen, horses; and we change the idiom according to the species:

> So ants amidst their sable-colored band
> Greet one another, and inquire perchance
> The road each follows, and the prize in hand.
>   DANTE[3]

It seems to me that Lactantius attributes to beasts not only speech but also laughter. And the difference of language that is seen between us, according to the difference of countries, is found also in animals of the same species. Aristotle cites in this connection the various calls of partridges according to the place they are situated in,

---

2. *On the Nature of Things*, Book II, ll. 1157ff.   3. *Purgatory*, Canto XXVI, ll. 34ff.

> And various birds . . .
> Utter at different times far different cries . . .
> And some change with the changing of the skies
> Their raucous songs.
>
> LUCRETIUS[4]

But it is yet to be known what language this child would speak; and what is said about it by conjecture has not much appearance of truth. If they allege to me, against this opinion, that men naturally deaf do not speak at all, I reply that it is not only because they could not be taught speech by ear, but rather because the sense of hearing, of which they are deprived, is related to that of speech, and they hold together by a natural tie; so that what we speak we must speak first to ourselves, and make it ring on our own ears inwardly, before we send it to other ears.

I have said all this to maintain this resemblance that exists to human things, and to bring us back and join us to the majority. We are neither above nor below the rest: all that is under heaven, says the sage, incurs the same law and the same fortune,

> All things are bound by their own chains of fate.
>
> LUCRETIUS[5]

There is some difference, there are orders and degrees; but it is under the aspect of one and the same nature:

> And all things go their own way, nor forget
> Distinctions by the law of nature set.
>
> LUCRETIUS[6]

Man must be constrained and forced into line inside the barriers of this order. The poor wretch is in no position really to step outside them; he is fettered and bound, he is subjected to the same obligation as the other creatures of his class, and in a very ordinary condition, without any real and essential prerogative or preeminence. That which he accords himself in his mind and in his fancy has neither body nor taste. And if it is true that he alone of all the animals has this freedom of imagination and this unruliness in thought that represents to him what is, what is not, what he wants, the false and the true, it is an advantage that is sold him very dear, and in which he has little cause to glory, for from it springs the principal source of the ills that oppress him: sin, disease, irresolution, confusion, despair.

OF REPENTANCE[7]

"These Testimonies of a Good Conscience"

Others form man; I tell of him, and portray a particular one, very ill-formed, whom I should really make very different from what he is if I had to fashion him over again. But now it is done.

---

4. *On the Nature of Things*, Book V, ll. 1078ff.   5. *On the Nature of Things*, Book V, l. 874.   6. *On the Nature of Things*, Book V, ll. 921 ff.   7. Book III, Chapter 2. The opening part of the essay is reprinted here.

Now the lines of my painting do not go astray, though they change and vary. The world is but a perennial movement. All things in it are in constant motion—the earth, the rocks of the Caucasus, the pyramids of Egypt—both with the common motion and with their own. Stability itself is nothing but a more languid motion.

I cannot keep my subject still. It goes along befuddled and staggering, with a natural drunkenness. I take it in this condition, just as it is at the moment I give my attention to it. I do not portray being: I portray passing. Not the passing from one age to another, or, as the people say, from seven years to seven years,[8] but from day to day, from minute to minute. My history needs to be adapted to the moment. I may presently change, not only by chance, but also by intention. This is a record of various and changeable occurrences, and of irresolute and, when it so befalls, contradictory ideas: whether I am different myself, or whether I take hold of my subjects in different circumstances and aspects. So, all in all, I may indeed contradict myself now and then; but truth, as Demades[9] said, I do not contradict. If my mind could gain a firm footing, I would not make essays, I would make decisions; but it is always in apprenticeship and on trial.

I set forth a humble and inglorious life; that does not matter. You can tie up all moral philosophy with a common and private life just as well as with a life of richer stuff. Each man bears the entire form of man's estate.

Authors communicate with the people by some special extrinsic mark; I am the first to do so by my entire being, as Michel de Montaigne, not as a grammarian or a poet or a jurist. If the world complains that I speak too much of myself, I complain that it does not even think of itself.

But is it reasonable that I, so fond of privacy in actual life, should aspire to publicity in the knowledge of me? Is it reasonable too that I should set forth to the world, where fashioning and art have so much credit and authority, some crude and simple products of nature, and of a very feeble nature at that? Is it not making a wall without stone, or something like that, to construct books without knowledge and without art? Musical fancies are guided by art, mine by chance.

At least I have one thing according to the rules: that no man ever treated a subject he knew and understood better than I do the subject I have undertaken; and that in this I am the most learned man alive. Secondly, that no man ever penetrated more deeply into his material, or plucked its limbs and consequences cleaner, or reached more accurately and fully the goal he had set for his work. To accomplish it, I need only bring it to fidelity; and that is in it, as sincere and pure as can be found. I speak the truth, not my fill of it, but as much as I dare speak; and I dare to do so a little more as I grow old, for it seems that custom allows old age more freedom to prate and more indiscretion in talking about oneself. It cannot happen here as I see it happening often, that the craftsman and his work contradict each other: "Has a man whose conversation is so good written

8. An allusion to the popular notion that the human body is completely renewed every seven years.
9. Greek orator and politician of the fourth century B.C.

such a stupid book?" or "Have such learned writings come from a man whose conversation is so feeble?"

If a man is commonplace in conversation and rare in writing, that means that his capacity is in the place from which he borrows it, and not in himself. A learned man is not learned in all matters; but the capable man is capable in all matters, even in ignorance.

In this case we go hand in hand and at the same pace, my book and I. In other cases one may commend or blame the work apart from the workman; not so here; he who touches the one, touches the other. He who judges it without knowing it will injure himself more than me; he who has known it will completely satisfy me. Happy beyond my deserts if I have just this share of public approval, that I make men of understanding feel that I was capable of profiting by knowledge, if I had had any, and that I deserved better assistance from my memory.

Let me here excuse what I often say, that I rarely repent and that my conscience is content with itself—not as the conscience of an angel or a horse, but as the conscience of a man; always adding this refrain, not perfunctorily but in sincere and complete submission: that I speak as an ignorant inquirer, referring the decision purely and simply to the common and authorized beliefs. I do not teach, I tell.

There is no vice truly a vice which is not offensive, and which a sound judgement does not condemn; for its ugliness and painfulness is so apparent that perhaps the people are right who say it is chiefly produced by stupidity and ignorance. So hard it is to imagine anyone knowing it without hating it.

Malice sucks up the greater part of its own venom, and poisons itself with it. Vice leaves repentance in the soul, like an ulcer in the flesh, which is always scratching itself and drawing blood. For reason effaces other griefs and sorrows; but it engenders that of repentance, which is all the more grievous because it springs from within, as the cold and heat of fevers is sharper than that which comes from outside. I consider as vices (but each one according to its measure) not only those that reason and nature condemn, but also those that man's opinion has created, even false and erroneous opinion, if it is authorized by laws and customs.

There is likewise no good deed that does not rejoice a wellborn nature. Indeed there is a sort of gratification in doing good which makes us rejoice in ourselves, and a generous pride that accompanies a good conscience. A boldly vicious soul may perhaps arm itself with security, but with this complacency and satisfaction it cannot provide itself. It is no slight pleasure to feel oneself preserved from the contagion of so depraved an age, and to say to oneself: "If anyone should see right into my soul, still he would not find me guilty either of anyone's affliction or ruin, or of vengeance or envy, or of public offense against the laws, or of innovation and disturbance, or of failing in my word; and in spite of what the license of the times allows and teaches each man, still I have not put my hand either upon the property or into the purse of any Frenchman, and have lived only on my own, both in war and in peace; nor have I used any man's work without paying his wages." These testimonies of conscience give us pleasure; and this natural rejoicing is a great boon to us, and the only payment that never fails us.

MIGUEL DE CERVANTES
1547–1616

The author of Don Quixote's extravagant adventures himself had a most unusual and adventurous life. The son of an apothecary, Miguel de Cervantes Saavedra was born in 1547 in Alcalá de Henares, a university town near Madrid. Almost nothing is known of his childhood and early education. Only in 1569 is he mentioned as a favorite pupil by a Madrid humanist, Juan López. Records indicate that by the end of that year he had left Spain and was living in Rome, for a time in the service of Giulio Acquaviva, who later became a cardinal. We know that he enlisted in the Spanish fleet under the command of Don John of Austria and that he took part in the struggle of the allied forces of Christendom against the Turks. He was at the crucial Battle of Lepanto (1571), where in spite of fever he fought valiantly and received three gunshot wounds, one of which permanently impaired the use of his left hand, "for the greater glory of the right." After further military action and garrison duty at Palermo and Naples, he and his brother Rodrigo, bearing testimonials from Don John and from the viceroy of Sicily, began the journey back to Spain, where Miguel hoped to obtain a captaincy. In September 1575 their ship was captured near the Marseille coast by Barbary pirates, and the two brothers were taken as prisoners to Algiers. Cervantes's captors, considering him a person of some consequence, held him as a slave for a high ransom. He repeatedly attempted to escape, and his daring and fortitude excited the admiration of Hassan Pasha, the viceroy of Algiers, who bought him for five hundred crowns after five years of captivity.

Cervantes was freed on September 15, 1580, and reached Madrid in December of that year. There his literary career began rather inauspiciously; he wrote twenty or thirty plays, with little success, and in 1585 published a pastoral romance, *Galatea*. At about this time he had a daughter with Ana Franca de Rojas, and during the same period married Catalina de Salazar, who was eighteen years his junior. Seeking nonliterary employment, he obtained a position in the navy, requisitioning and collecting supplies for the Invincible Armada. Irregularities in his administration, for which he was held responsible if not directly guilty, caused him to spend more time in prison. In 1590 he tried unsuccessfully to obtain colonial employment in the New World. Later he served as tax collector in the province of Granada, but was dismissed from government service in 1597.

The following years of Cervantes's life are the most obscure: there is a legend that *Don Quixote* was first conceived and planned while its author was in prison in Seville. In 1604 he was in Valladolid, then the temporary capital of Spain, living in sordid surroundings with the numerous women of his family (his wife, daughter, niece, and two sisters). It was in Valladolid, in late 1604, that he obtained the official license for the publication of *Don Quixote* (Part I). The book appeared in 1605 and was a popular success. Cervantes followed the Spanish court when it returned to Madrid, where he continued to live poorly in spite of a popularity with readers that quickly made proverbial figures of his heroes. A false sequel to his book appeared, prompting him to write his own continuation, *Don Quixote*, Part II, published in 1615. His *Exemplary Tales* had appeared in 1613. He died on April 23, 1616, and was buried in the convent of the Barefooted Trinitarian nuns. *Persiles and Sigismunda*, his last novel, was published posthumously in 1617.

Although, as we have indicated, *The Ingenious Gentleman Don Quixote de la Mancha* was a popular success from the time Part I was published in 1605, it was only later recognized as an important work of literature. This delay was due partly to the fact that in a period of established and well-defined literary genres such as the epic, the tragedy, and the pastoral romance (Cervantes himself had tried his hand at some of these forms), the unconventional combination of elements in *Don Quixote* resulted in a work of considerable novelty, with the serious aspects hidden under a mocking surface.

The initial and overt purpose of the book was to satirize the romances of chivalry. In those long yarns, which had to do with the Carolingian and Arthurian legends and which were full of supernatural deeds of valor, implausible and complicated adventures, duels, and enchantments, the literature that had expressed the medieval spirit of chivalry and romance had degenerated to the same extent to which, in our day, certain conventions of romantic literature have degenerated in "pulp" fiction and film melodrama. Up to a point, then, what Cervantes set out to do was to produce a parody, a caricature of a literary type. But neither the nature of his genius nor the particular method he chose allowed him to limit himself to such a relatively simple and direct undertaking. The actual method he followed in order to expose the silliness of the romances of chivalry was to show to what extraordinary consequences they would lead a man insanely infatuated with them, once this man set out to live "now" according to their patterns of action and belief.

So what we have is not mere parody or caricature; for there is a great deal of difference between presenting a remote and more or less imaginary world, and presenting an individual deciding to live by the standards of that world in a modern and realistic context. The first consequence is a mingling of genres. On the one hand, much of the book has the color and intonation of the world of medieval chivalry as its poets had portrayed it. The fact that that vision and that tone depend for their existence in the book on the self-deception of the hero makes them no less operative artistically, and adds, in fact, an important element of idealization. On the other hand, the chivalric world is continuously jostled by elements of contemporary life evoked by the narrator—the realities of landscape and speech, peasants and nobles, inns and highways. So the author can draw on two sources, roughly the realistic and the romantic, truth and vision, practical facts and lofty values. In this respect—having found a way to bring together concrete actuality and highly ideal values—Cervantes can be said to have created the modern novel.

The consequences of Cervantes's invention are more apparent when we begin to analyze a little more closely the nature of these worlds, romantic and realistic, and the kind of impact the first exerts on the second. The hero embodying the world of the romances is not, as we know, a cavalier; he is an impoverished country gentleman who embraces that code in the "modern" world. Chivalry is not directly satirized; it is simply placed in a context different from its native one. The result of that new association is a new whole, a new unity. The "code" is renovated; it is put into a different perspective, given another chance.

We should remember at this point that in the process of deterioration which the romances of chivalry had undergone, certain basically attractive ideals had become empty conventions—for instance, the ideal of love as devoted "service." In this connection, it may be especially interesting to observe that the treatment of love, and Don Quixote's conception of it, are not limited to his well-known admiration for his purely fantastic lady Dulcinea, but are also dealt with from a feminine point of view. See, as illustration, Marcela's elaborate, logical, and poetic speech (Part I, chapter 14, reprinted here) which Don Quixote warmly admires; in it the noble shepherdesss defends herself against the accusation of being "a wild beast and a basilisk" for having caused Grisóstomo's death, and proclaims her right to choose her particular kind of freedom in nature, where "these mountain trees are my company, the clear running waters in these brooks are my mirror. . . ."

No less relevant are Quixote's ideals of adventurousness, of loyalty to high concepts of valor and generosity. In the new context those values are re-examined. Cervantes may well have gained a practical sense of them in his own life while still a youth, for instance at the Battle of Lepanto (the great victory of the European coalition against the "infidels"), and as a pirate's captive. Since he began writing *Don Quixote* in his late fifties, a vantage point from which the adventures of his youth must have appeared impossibly remote, a factor of nostalgia—which could hardly have been present in a pure satire—may well have entered into his work. Furthermore, had he undertaken a direct caricature of the romance genre, the serious and noble values of chivalry could not have been made apparent except negatively, whereas in the context devised by him in *Don Quixote* they find a way to assert themselves positively as well.

The book in its development is, to a considerable extent, the story of that assertion—of the impact that Don Quixote's revitalization of the chivalric code has on a contemporary world. We must remember, of course, that there is ambiguity in the way the assertion is made; it works slowly on the reader, as his or her own discovery rather than as the narrator's overt suggestion. Actually, whatever attraction the chivalric world of his hero's vision may have had for Cervantes, he does not openly support Don Quixote at all. He even seems at times to go further in repudiating him than he needs to, for the hero is officially insane, and the narrator never tires of reminding us of this. One critic has described the attitude Cervantes affects toward his creature as "animosity." Nevertheless, by the very magniloquence and, often, the extraordinary coherence and beauty that the narrator allows his hero to display in his speeches in defense of his vision and his code, we are gradually led to discover for ourselves the serious and important elements these contain. For instance, Don Quixote's speech evoking the lost Golden Age and justifying the institution of knight-errantry (in Part I, chapter 11, reprinted here) is described by the narrator—after Don Quixote has delivered it—as a "futile harangue" which "might very well have been dispensed with"; but there it is, in all of its fervor and effectiveness. Thus the narrator's so-called animosity ultimately does nothing but intensify our interest in Don Quixote and our sympathy for him. And in that process we are, as audience, simply repeating the experience many characters have on the "stage" of the book, in their relationships with him.

Generally speaking, the encounters between the ordinary world and Don Quixote are encounters between the world of reality and that of illusion, between reason and imagination, ultimately between the world in which action is prompted by material considerations and interests and a world in which action is prompted by ideal motives. Our selections illustrate these aspects of the experience. Among the first adventures are some that have most contributed to popularize the Don Quixote legend: he sees windmills and decides they are giants; country inns become castles; flocks of sheep, armies. Though the conclusions of such episodes often have the ludicrousness of slapstick comedy, there is a powerfully imposing quality about Don Quixote's insanity: his madness always has method, a commanding persistence and coherence. And there is perhaps an inevitable sense of moral grandeur in the spectacle of anyone remaining so unflinchingly faithful to his or her own vision. The world of "reason" may win in point of fact, but we come to wonder whether from a moral point of view Quixote is not the victor.

Furthermore, we increasingly realize that Quixote's own manner of action has greatness in itself, and not only the greatness of persistence: his purpose is to redress wrongs, to come to the aid of the afflicted, to offer generous help, to challenge danger and practice valor. And we finally feel the impact of the arguments that sustain his action—for example, in the section from Part II (the episode of the lions) in which he expounds "the meaning of valor." The ridiculousness of the situation is counterbalanced by the basic seriousness of Quixote's motives; his notion of courage for its own sake appears, and is recognized, as singularly noble, a sort of generous display of integrity in a world usually ruled by lower standards. Thus the distinction between "reason" and "madness," truth and illusion, becomes, to say the least, ambiguous. The hero's delusions are indeed exposed when they come up against hard facts, but the authority of such facts is seen to be morally questionable.

The effectiveness of Don Quixote's conduct and vision is seen most clearly in his relationship with his "squire" Sancho Panza. It would be a crude oversimplification to say that Don Quixote and Sancho represent illusion and reality, the insane code of knight-errantry versus down-to-earth practicalities. Actually Sancho—though his nature is strongly defined by such elements as his common sense, his earthy speech, his simple phrases studded with proverbs set against the hero's magniloquence—is mainly characterized in his development by the degree to which he believes in his master. He is caught in the snare of Don Quixote's vision; the seeds of the imaginative life are successfully implanted in him.

The impact of Quixote's view of life on Sancho serves therefore to illustrate one of the important qualities of the protagonist and, we may finally say, one of the important aspects of Renaissance literature: the attempt, ultimately frustrated but extremely attractive as long as it lasts, of the individual mind to produce a vision and a system of its own, in a world that often seems to have lost a universal frame of reference and a fully satisfactory sense of the value and meaning of action. What Don Quixote presents is a vision of a world which, for all its aberrant qualities, appears generally to be more colorful and more thrilling, and also, incidentally, to be inspired by more honorable rules of conduct, than the world of ordinary people, "realism," current affairs, private interests, easy jibes, and petty pranks. It is a world in which actions are performed out of a sense of their beauty and excitement, not for the sake of their usefulness. It is, again, the world as stage, animated by "folly"; in this case the lights go out at the end, an end that is "reasonable" and therefore gloomy. Sancho provides the main example of one who is exposed to that vision and absorbs that light while it lasts. How successfully he has done so is seen during Don Quixote's death scene, in which Sancho begs his master not to die but to continue the play, as has been suggested, in a new costume—that of shepherds in an Arcadian setting. But at that final point the hero is "cured" and killed, and Sancho is restored to the petty interests of the world as he can see it by his own lights, after the cord connecting him to his imaginative master is cut by the latter's "repentance" and death.

William Byron, *Cervantes: A Biography* (1978) is very thorough. The more advanced student of *Don Quixote* will find useful Stephen Gilman's *The Novel According to Cervantes* (1989) and Howard Mancing's detailed study, *The Chivalric World of Don Quijote: Style, Structure, and Narrative Technique* (1982). Lowry

Nelson, ed., *Cervantes: A Collection of Critical Essays* (1969), offers the views of
eminent scholars and authors.

Don Quixote[1]

Part I

("I Know Who I Am, and Who I May Be, If I Choose")

CHAPTER 1

Which treats of the station in life and the pursuits of the famous gentleman, Don Quixote de la Mancha.

In a village of La Mancha[2] the name of which I have no desire to recall,
there lived not so long ago one of those gentlemen who always have a
lance in the rack, an ancient buckler, a skinny nag, and a greyhound for
the chase. A stew with more beef than mutton in it, chopped meat for his
evening meal, scraps for a Saturday, lentils on Friday, and a young pigeon
as a special delicacy for Sunday, went to account for three-quarters of his
income. The rest of it he laid out on a broadcloth greatcoat and velvet
stockings for feast days, with slippers to match, while the other days of the
week he cut a figure in a suit of the finest homespun. Living with him
were a housekeeper in her forties, a niece who was not yet twenty, and a
lad of the field and market place who saddled his horse for him and wielded
the pruning knife.

This gentleman of ours was close on to fifty, of a robust constitution but
with little flesh on his bones and a face that was lean and gaunt. He was
noted for his early rising, being very fond of the hunt. They will try to tell
you that his surname was Quijada or Quesada—there is some difference
of opinion among those who have written on the subject—but according
to the most likely conjectures we are to understand that it was really Quejana. But all this means very little so far as our story is concerned, providing that in the telling of it we do not depart one iota from the truth.

You may know, then, that the aforesaid gentleman, on those occasions
when he was at leisure, which was most of the year around, was in the
habit of reading books of chivalry with such pleasure and devotion as to
lead him almost wholly to forget the life of a hunter and even the administration of his estate. So great was his curiosity and infatuation in this
regard that he even sold many acres of tillable land in order to be able to
buy and read the books that he loved, and he would carry home with him
as many of them as he could obtain.

Of all those that he thus devoured none pleased him so well as the ones
that had been composed by the famous Feliciano de Silva,[3] whose lucid
prose style and involved conceits were as precious to him as pearls; espe-

---

1. Abridged. Translated by Samuel Putnam.   2. Efforts at identifying the village have proved inconclusive; La Mancha is a section of Spain south of Madrid.   3. A sixteenth-century author of romances; the
quotation that follows is from his *Don Florisel de Niquea.*

cially when he came to read those tales of love and amorous challenges that are to be met with in many places, such a passage as the following, for example: "The reason of the unreason that afflicts my reason, in such a manner weakens my reason that I with reason lament me of your comeliness." And he was similarly affected when his eyes fell upon such lines as these: ". . . the high Heaven of your divinity divinely fortifies you with the stars and renders you deserving of that desert your greatness doth deserve."

The poor fellow used to lie awake nights in an effort to disentangle the meaning and make sense out of passages such as these, although Aristotle himself would not have been able to understand them, even if he had been resurrected for that sole purpose. He was not at ease in his mind over those wounds that Don Belianís[4] gave and received; for no matter how great the surgeons who treated him, the poor fellow must have been left with his face and his entire body covered with marks and scars. Nevertheless, he was grateful to the author for closing the book with the promise of an interminable adventure to come; many a time he was tempted to take up his pen and literally finish the tale as had been promised, and he undoubtedly would have done so, and would have succeeded at it very well, if his thoughts had not been constantly occupied with other things of greater moment.

He often talked it over with the village curate, who was a learned man, a graduate of Sigüenza,[5] and they would hold long discussions as to who had been the better knight, Palmerin of England or Amadis of Gaul;[6] but Master Nicholas, the barber of the same village, was in the habit of saying that no one could come up to the Knight of Phoebus,[7] and that if anyone *could* compare with him it was Don Galaor, brother of Amadis of Gaul, for Galaor was ready for anything—he was none of your finical knights, who went around whimpering as his brother did, and in point of valor he did not lag behind him.

In short, our gentleman became so immersed in his reading that he spent whole nights from sundown to sunup and his days from dawn to dusk in poring over his books, until, finally, from so little sleeping and so much reading, his brain dried up and he went completely out of his mind. He had filled his imagination with everything that he had read, with enchantments, knightly encounters, battles, challenges, wounds, with tales of love and its torments, and all sorts of impossible things, and as a result had come to believe that all these fictitious happenings were true; they were more real to him than anything else in the world. He would remark that the Cid Ruy Díaz had been a very good knight, but there was no comparison between him and the Knight of the Flaming Sword, who with a single backward stroke had cut in half two fierce and monstrous giants. He preferred Bernardo del Carpio, who at Roncesvalles had slain Roland despite the charm[8] the latter bore, availing himself of the stratagem which

---

4. The allusion is to a romance by Jeronimo Fernández.   5. Ironical, for Sigüenza was the seat of a minor and discredited university.   6. Heroes of two very famous romances of chivalry.   7. Or Knight of the Sun. Heroes of romances customarily adopted emblematic names and also changed them according to circumstances. See in the following paragraph the reference to the Knight of the Flaming Sword.   8. The magic gift of invulnerability.

Hercules employed when he strangled Antaeus, the son of Earth, in his arms.[9]

He had much good to say for Morgante[1] who, though he belonged to the haughty, overbearing race of giants, was of an affable disposition and well brought up. But, above all, he cherished an admiration for Rinaldo of Montalbán,[2] especially as he beheld him sallying forth from his castle to rob all those that crossed his path, or when he thought of him overseas stealing the image of Mohammed which, so the story has it, was all of gold. And he would have liked very well to have had his fill of kicking that traitor Galalón,[3] a privilege for which he would have given his housekeeper with his niece thrown into the bargain.

At last, when his wits were gone beyond repair, he came to conceive the strangest idea that ever occurred to any madman in this world. It now appeared to him fitting and necessary, in order to win a greater amount of honor for himself and serve his country at the same time, to become a knight-errant and roam the world on horseback, in a suit of armor; he would go in quest of adventures, by way of putting into practice all that he had read in his books; he would right every manner of wrong, placing himself in situations of the greatest peril such as would redound to the eternal glory of his name. As a reward for his valor and the might of his arm, the poor fellow could already see himself crowned Emperor of Trebizond at the very least; and so, carried away by the strange pleasure that he found in such thoughts as these, he at once set about putting his plan into effect.

The first thing he did was to burnish up some old pieces of armor, left him by his great-grandfather, which for ages had lain in a corner, moldering and forgotten. He polished and adjusted them as best he could, and then he noticed that one very important thing was lacking: there was no closed helmet, but only a morion, or visorless headpiece, with turned up brim of the kind foot soldiers wore. His ingenuity, however, enabled him to remedy this, and he proceeded to fashion out of cardboard a kind of half-helmet, which, when attached to the morion, gave the appearance of a whole one. True, when he went to see if it was strong enough to withstand a good slashing blow, he was somewhat disappointed; for when he drew his sword and gave it a couple of thrusts, he succeeded only in undoing a whole week's labor. The ease with which he had hewed it to bits disturbed him no little, and he decided to make it over. This time he placed a few strips of iron on the inside, and then, convinced that it was strong enough, refrained from putting it to any further test; instead, he adopted it then and there as the finest helmet ever made.

After this, he went out to have a look at his nag; and although the animal had more *cuartos*, or cracks, in its hoof than there are quarters in a real,[4]

9. The mythological Antaeus was invulnerable as long as he maintained contact with his mother, Earth; Hercules killed him while holding him raised in his arms.   1. In Pulci's *Morgante maggiore*, a comic-epic poem of the Italian Renaissance.   2. In Boiardo's *Roland in Love (Orlando innamorato)* and Ariosto's *Roland Mad (Orlando furioso)*, romantic and comic-epic poems of the Italian Renaissance. Rinaldo is Roland's cousin.   3. Ganelón, the villain in the Charlemagne legend who betrayed the French at Roncesvalles.   4. A coin (about five cents); a *cuarto* was one eighth of a *real*.

and more blemishes than Gonela's steed which *tantum pellis et ossa fuit*,[5] it nonetheless looked to its master like a far better horse than Alexander's Bucephalus or the Babieca of the Cid.[6] He spent all of four days in trying to think up a name for his mount; for—so he told himself—seeing that it belonged to so famous and worthy a knight, there was no reason why it should not have a name of equal renown. The kind of name he wanted was one that would at once indicate what the nag had been before it came to belong to a knight-errant and what its present status was; for it stood to reason that, when the master's worldly condition changed, his horse also ought to have a famous, high-sounding appellation, one suited to the new order of things and the new profession that it was to follow.

After he in his memory and imagination had made up, struck out, and discarded many names, now adding to and now subtracting from the list, he finally hit upon "Rocinante," a name that impressed him as being sonorous and at the same time indicative of what the steed had been when it was but a hack, whereas now it was nothing other than the first and foremost of all the hacks[7] in the world.

Having found a name for his horse that pleased his fancy, he then desired to do as much for himself, and this required another week, and by the end of that period he had made up his mind that he was henceforth to be known as Don Quixote, which, as has been stated, has led the authors of this veracious history to assume that his real name must undoubtedly have been Quijada, and not Quesada as others would have it. But remembering that the valiant Amadis was not content to call himself that and nothing more, but added the name of his kingdom and fatherland that he might make it famous also, and thus came to take the name Amadis of Gaul, so our good knight chose to add his place of origin and become "Don Quixote de la Mancha"; for by this means, as he saw it, he was making very plain his lineage and was conferring honor upon his country by taking its name as his own.

And so, having polished up his armor and made the morion over into a closed helmet, and having given himself and his horse a name, he naturally found but one thing lacking still: he must seek out a lady of whom he could become enamored; for a knight-errant without a lady-love was like a tree without leaves or fruit, a body without a soul.

"If," he said to himself, "as a punishment for my sins or by a stroke of fortune I should come upon some giant hereabouts, a thing that very commonly happens to knights-errant, and if I should slay him in a hand-to-hand encounter or perhaps cut him in two, or, finally, if I should vanquish and subdue him, would it not be well to have someone to whom I may send him as a present, in order that he, if he is living, may come in, fall upon his knees in front of my sweet lady, and say in a humble and submissive tone of voice, 'I, lady, am the giant Caraculiambro, lord of the island Malindrania, who has been overcome in single combat by that knight who never can be praised enough, Don Quixote de la Mancha, the same

5. Was so much skin and bones.   6. "The chief," Ruy Diaz, celebrated hero of the twelfth-century *Poema del Cid*.   7. In Spanish, *rocin*.

who sent me to present myself before your Grace that your Highness may dispose of me as you see fit'?"

Oh, how our good knight reveled in this speech, and more than ever when he came to think of the name that he should give his lady! As the story goes, there was a very good-looking farm girl who lived near by, with whom he had once been smitten, although it is generally believed that she never knew or suspected it. Her name was Aldonza Lorenzo, and it seemed to him that she was the one upon whom he should bestow the title of mistress of his thoughts. For her he wished a name that should not be incongruous with his own and that would convey the suggestion of a princess or a great lady; and, accordingly, he resolved to call her "Dulcinea del Toboso," she being a native of that place. A musical name to his ears, out of the ordinary and significant, like the others he had chosen for himself and his appurtenances.

CHAPTER 2

Which treats of the first sally that the ingenious Don Quixote made from his native heath.

Having, then, made all these preparations, he did not wish to lose any time in putting his plan into effect, for he could not but blame himself for what the world was losing by his delay, so many were the wrongs that were to be righted, the grievances to be redressed, the abuses to be done away with, and the duties to be performed. Accordingly, without informing anyone of his intention and without letting anyone see him, he set out one morning before daybreak on one of those very hot days in July. Donning all his armor, mounting Rocinante, adjusting his ill-contrived helmet, bracing his shield on his arm, and taking up his lance, he sallied forth by the back gate of his stable yard into the open countryside. It was with great contentment and joy that he saw how easily he had made a beginning toward the fulfillment of his desire.

No sooner was he out on the plain, however, than a terrible thought assailed him, one that all but caused him to abandon the enterprise he had undertaken. This occurred when he suddenly remembered that he had never formally been dubbed a knight, and so, in accordance with the law of knighthood, was not permitted to bear arms against one who had a right to that title. And even if he had been, as a novice knight he would have had to wear white armor, without any device on his shield, until he should have earned one by his exploits. These thoughts led him to waver in his purpose, but, madness prevailing over reason, he resolved to have himself knighted by the first person he met, as many others had done if what he had read in those books that he had at home was true. And so far as white armor was concerned, he would scour his own the first chance that offered until it shone whiter than any ermine. With this he became more tranquil and continued on his way, letting his horse take whatever path it chose, for he believed that therein lay the very essence of adventures.

And so we find our newly fledged adventurer jogging along and talking to himself. "Undoubtedly," he is saying, "in the days to come, when the true history of my famous deeds is published, the learned chronicler who records them, when he comes to describe my first sally so early in the morning, will put down something like this: 'No sooner had the rubicund Apollo spread over the face of the broad and spacious earth the gilded filaments of his beauteous locks, and no sooner had the little singing birds of painted plumage greeted with their sweet and mellifluous harmony the coming of the Dawn, who, leaving the soft couch of her jealous spouse, now showed herself to mortals at all the doors and balconies of the horizon that bounds La Mancha—no sooner had this happened than the famous knight, Don Quixote de la Mancha, forsaking his own downy bed and mounting his famous steed, Rocinante, fared forth and began riding over the ancient and famous Campo de Montiel.' "[8]

And this was the truth, for he was indeed riding over that stretch of plain.

"O happy age and happy century," he went on, "in which my famous exploits shall be published, exploits worthy of being engraved in bronze, sculptured in marble, and depicted in paintings for the benefit of posterity. O wise magician, whoever you be, to whom shall fall the task of chronicling this extraordinary history of mine! I beg of you not to forget my good Rocinante, eternal companion of my wayfarings and my wanderings."

Then, as though he really had been in love: "O Princess Dulcinea, lady of this captive heart! Much wrong have you done me in thus sending me forth with your reproaches and sternly commanding me not to appear in your beauteous presence. O lady, deign to be mindful of this your subject who endures so many woes for the love of you."

And so he went on, stringing together absurdities, all of a kind that his books had taught him, imitating insofar as he was able the language of their authors. He rode slowly, and the sun came up so swiftly and with so much heat that it would have been sufficient to melt his brains if he had had any. He had been on the road almost the entire day without anything happening that is worthy of being set down here; and he was on the verge of despair, for he wished to meet someone at once with whom he might try the valor of his good right arm. Certain authors say that his first adventure was that of Puerto Lápice, while others state that it was that of the windmills; but in this particular instance I am in a position to affirm what I have read in the annals of La Mancha; and that is to the effect that he went all that day until nightfall, when he and his hack found themselves tired to death and famished. Gazing all around him to see if he could discover some castle or shepherd's hut where he might take shelter and attend to his pressing needs, he caught sight of an inn not far off the road along which they were traveling, and this to him was like a star guiding him not merely to the gates, but rather, let us say, to the palace of redemption. Quickening his pace, he came up to it just as night was falling.

8. Famous because it had been the scene of a battle in 1369.

By chance there stood in the doorway two lasses of the sort known as "of the district"; they were on their way to Seville in the company of some mule drivers who were spending the night in the inn. Now, everything that this adventurer of ours thought, saw, or imagined seemed to him to be directly out of one of the storybooks he had read, and so, when he caught sight of the inn, it at once became a castle with its four turrets and its pinnacles of gleaming silver, not to speak of the drawbridge and moat and all the other things that are commonly supposed to go with a castle. As he rode up to it, he accordingly reined in Rocinante and sat there waiting for a dwarf to appear upon the battlements and blow his trumpet by way of announcing the arrival of a knight. The dwarf, however, was slow in coming, and as Rocinante was anxious to reach the stable, Don Quixote drew up to the door of the hostelry and surveyed the two merry maidens, who to him were a pair of beauteous damsels or gracious ladies taking their ease at the castle gate.

And then a swineherd came along, engaged in rounding up his drove of hogs—for, without any apology, that is what they were. He gave a blast on his horn to bring them together, and this at once became for Don Quixote just what he wished it to be: some dwarf who was heralding his coming; and so it was with a vast deal of satisfaction that he presented himself before the ladies in question, who, upon beholding a man in full armor like this, with lance and buckler, were filled with fright and made as if to flee indoors. Realizing that they were afraid, Don Quixote raised his pasteboard visor and revealed his withered, dust-covered face.

"Do not flee, your Ladyships," he said to them in a courteous manner and gentle voice. "You need not fear that any wrong will be done you, for it is not in accordance with the order of knighthood which I profess to wrong anyone, much less such highborn damsels as your appearance shows you to be."

The girls looked at him, endeavoring to scan his face, which was half hidden by his ill-made visor. Never having heard women of their profession called damsels before, they were unable to restrain their laughter, at which Don Quixote took offense.

"Modesty," he observed, "well becomes those with the dower of beauty, and, moreover, laughter that has not good cause is a very foolish thing. But I do not say this to be discourteous or to hurt your feelings; my only desire is to serve you."

The ladies did not understand what he was talking about, but felt more than ever like laughing at our knight's unprepossessing figure. This increased his annoyance, and there is no telling what would have happened if at that moment the innkeeper had not come out. He was very fat and very peaceably inclined; but upon sighting this grotesque personage clad in bits of armor that were quite as oddly matched as were his bridle, lance, buckler, and corselet, mine host was not at all indisposed to join the lasses in their merriment. He was suspicious, however, of all this paraphernalia and decided that it would be better to keep a civil tongue in his head.

"If, Sir Knight," he said, "your Grace desires a lodging, aside from a bed—for there is none to be had in this inn—you will find all else that you may want in great abundance."

When Don Quixote saw how humble the governor of the castle was—for he took the innkeeper and his inn to be no less than that—he replied, "For me, Sir Castellan,[9] anything will do, since

> Arms are my only ornament,
> My only rest the fight, etc."

The landlord thought that the knight had called him a castellan because he took him for one of those worthies of Castile, whereas the truth was, he was an Andalusian from the beach of Sanlúcar, no less a thief than Cacus[1] himself, and as full of tricks as a student or a page boy.

"In that case," he said,

> "Your bed will be the solid rock,
> Your sleep: to watch all night.

This being so, you may be assured of finding beneath this roof enough to keep you awake for a whole year, to say nothing of a single night."

With this, he went up to hold the stirrup for Don Quixote, who encountered much difficulty in dismounting, not having broken his fast all day long. The knight then directed his host to take good care of his steed, as it was the best piece of horseflesh in all the world. The innkeeper looked it over, and it did not impress him as being half as good as Don Quixote had said it was. Having stabled the animal, he came back to see what his guest would have and found the latter being relieved of his armor by the damsels, who by now had made their peace with the new arrival. They had already removed his breastplate and backpiece but had no idea how they were going to open his gorget or get his improvised helmet off. That piece of armor had been tied on with green ribbons which it would be necessary to cut, since the knots could not be undone, but he would not hear of this, and so spent all the rest of that night with his headpiece in place, which gave him the weirdest, most laughable appearance that could be imagined.

Don Quixote fancied that these wenches who were assisting him must surely be the chatelaine and other ladies of the castle, and so proceeded to address them very gracefully and with much wit:

> Never was knight so served
> By any noble dame
> As was Don Quixote
> When from his village he came,
> With damsels to wait on his every need
> While princesses cared for his hack . . .

9. The original, *castellano*, means both "castellan" and "Castilian."   1. In Roman mythology he stole some of the cattle of Hercules, concealing the theft by having them walk backward into his cave, but was finally discovered and slain.

"By hack," he explained, "is meant my steed Rocinante, for that is his name, and mine is Don Quixote de la Mancha. I had no intention of revealing my identity until my exploits done in your service should have made me known to you; but the necessity of adapting to present circumstances that old ballad of Lancelot has led to your becoming acquainted with it prematurely. However, the time will come when your Ladyships shall command and I will obey and with the valor of my good right arm show you how eager I am to serve you."

The young women were not used to listening to speeches like this and had not a word to say, but merely asked him if he desired to eat anything.

"I could eat a bite of something, yes," replied Don Quixote. "Indeed, I feel that a little food would go very nicely just now."

He thereupon learned that, since it was Friday, there was nothing to be had in all the inn except a few portions of codfish, which in Castile is called *abadejo*, in Andalusia *bacalao*, in some places *curadillo*, and elsewhere *truchuela* or small trout. Would his Grace, then, have some small trout, seeing that was all there was that they could offer him?

"If there are enough of them," said Don Quixote, "they will take the place of a trout, for it is all one to me whether I am given in change eight reales or one piece of eight. What is more, those small trout may be like veal, which is better than beef, or like kid, which is better than goat. But however that may be, bring them on at once, for the weight and burden of arms is not to be borne without inner sustenance."

Placing the table at the door of the hostelry, in the open air, they brought the guest a portion of badly soaked and worse cooked codfish and a piece of bread as black and moldy as the suit of armor that he wore. It was a mirth-provoking sight to see him eat, for he still had his helmet on with his visor fastened, which made it impossible for him to put anything into his mouth with his hands, and so it was necessary for one of the girls to feed him. As for giving him anything to drink, that would have been out of the question if the innkeeper had not hollowed out a reed, placing one end in Don Quixote's mouth while through the other end he poured the wine. All this the knight bore very patiently rather than have them cut the ribbons of his helmet.

At this point a gelder of pigs approached the inn, announcing his arrival with four or five blasts on his horn, all of which confirmed Don Quixote in the belief that this was indeed a famous castle, for what was this if not music that they were playing for him? The fish was trout, the bread was the finest, the wenches were ladies, and the innkeeper was the castellan. He was convinced that he had been right in his resolve to sally forth and roam the world at large, but there was one thing that still distressed him greatly, and that was the fact that he had not as yet been dubbed a knight; as he saw it, he could not legitimately engage in any adventure until he had received the order of knighthood.

CHAPTER 3

Of the amusing manner in which Don Quixote had himself dubbed a knight.

Wearied of his thoughts, Don Quixote lost no time over the scanty repast which the inn afforded him. When he had finished, he summoned the landlord and, taking him out to the stable, closed the doors and fell on his knees in front of him.

"Never, valiant knight," he said, "shall I arise from here until you have courteously granted me the boon I seek, one which will redound to your praise and to the good of the human race."

Seeing his guest at his feet and hearing him utter such words as these, the innkeeper could only stare at him in bewilderment, not knowing what to say or do. It was in vain that he entreated him to rise, for Don Quixote refused to do so until his request had been granted.

"I expected nothing less of your great magnificence, my lord," the latter then continued, "and so I may tell you that the boon I asked and which you have so generously conceded me is that tomorrow morning you dub me a knight. Until that time, in the chapel of this your castle, I will watch over my armor, and when morning comes, as I have said, that which I so desire shall then be done, in order that I may lawfully go to the four corners of the earth in quest of adventures and to succor the needy, which is the chivalrous duty of all knights-errant such as I who long to engage in deeds of high emprise."

The innkeeper, as we have said, was a sharp fellow. He already had a suspicion that his guest was not quite right in the head, and he was now convinced of it as he listened to such remarks as these. However, just for the sport of it, he determined to humor him; and so he went on to assure Don Quixote that he was fully justified in his request and that such a desire and purpose was only natural on the part of so distinguished a knight as his gallant bearing plainly showed him to be.

He himself, the landlord added, when he was a young man, had followed the same honorable calling. He had gone through various parts of the world seeking adventures, among the places he had visited being the Percheles of Málaga, the Isles of Riarán, the District of Seville, the Little Market Place of Segovia, the Olivera of Valencia, the Rondilla of Granada, the beach of Sanlúcar, the Horse Fountain of Cordova, the Small Taverns of Toledo, and numerous other localities[2] where his nimble feet and light fingers had found much exercise. He had done many wrongs, cheated many widows, ruined many maidens, and swindled not a few minors until he had finally come to be known in almost all the courts and tribunals that are to be found in the whole of Spain.

At last he had retired to his castle here, where he lived upon his own income and the property of others; and here it was that he received all knights-errant of whatever quality and condition, simply out of the great

---

2. All the places mentioned were reputed to be haunts of robbers and rogues.

affection that he bore them and that they might share with him their possessions in payment of his good will. Unfortunately, in this castle there was no chapel where Don Quixote might keep watch over his arms, for the old chapel had been torn down to make way for a new one; but in case of necessity, he felt quite sure that such a vigil could be maintained anywhere, and for the present occasion the courtyard of the castle would do; and then in the morning, please God, the requisite ceremony could be performed and his guest be duly dubbed a knight, as much a knight as anyone ever was.

He then inquired if Don Quixote had any money on his person, and the latter replied that he had not a cent, for in all the storybooks he had never read of knights-errant carrying any. But the innkeeper told him he was mistaken on this point: supposing the authors of those stories had not set down the fact in black and white, that was because they did not deem it necessary to speak of things as indispensable as money and a clean shirt, and one was not to assume for that reason that those knights-errant of whom the books were so full did not have any. He looked upon it as an absolute certainty that they all had well-stuffed purses, that they might be prepared for any emergency; and they also carried shirts and a little box of ointment for healing the wounds that they received.

For when they had been wounded in combat on the plains and in desert places, there was not always someone at hand to treat them, unless they had some skilled enchanter for a friend who then would succor them, bringing to them through the air, upon a cloud, some damsel or dwarf bearing a vial of water of such virtue that one had but to taste a drop of it and at once his wounds were healed and he was as sound as if he had never received any.

But even if this was not the case, knights in times past saw to it that their squires were well provided with money and other necessities, such as lint and ointment for healing purposes; and if they had no squires—which happened very rarely—they themselves carried these objects in a pair of saddlebags very cleverly attached to their horses' croups in such a manner as to be scarcely noticeable, as if they held something of greater importance than that, for among the knights-errant saddlebags as a rule were not favored. Accordingly, he would advise the novice before him, and inasmuch as the latter was soon to be his godson, he might even command him, that henceforth he should not go without money and a supply of those things that have been mentioned, as he would find that they came in useful at a time when he least expected it.

Don Quixote promised to follow his host's advice punctiliously; and so it was arranged that he should watch his armor in a large barnyard at one side of the inn. He gathered up all the pieces, placed them in a horse trough that stood near the well, and, bracing his shield on his arm, took up his lance and with stately demeanor began pacing up and down in front of the trough even as night was closing in.

The innkeeper informed his other guests of what was going on, of Don Quixote's vigil and his expectation of being dubbed a knight; and, marveling greatly at so extraordinary a variety of madness, they all went out to see for themselves and stood there watching from a distance. For a while the knight-to-be, with tranquil mien, would merely walk up and down; then, leaning on his lance, he would pause to survey his armor, gazing fixedly at it for a considerable length of time. As has been said, it was night now, but the brightness of the moon, which well might rival that of Him who lent it, was such that everything the novice knight did was plainly visible to all.

At this point one of the mule drivers who were stopping at the inn came out to water his drove, and in order to do this it was necessary to remove the armor from the trough.

As he saw the man approaching, Don Quixote cried out to him, "O bold knight, whoever you may be, who thus would dare to lay hands upon the accouterments of the most valiant man of arms that ever girded on a sword, look well what you do and desist if you do not wish to pay with your life for your insolence!"

The muleteer gave no heed to these words—it would have been better for his own sake had he done so—but, taking it up by the straps, tossed the armor some distance from him. When he beheld this, Don Quixote rolled his eyes heavenward and with his thoughts apparently upon his Dulcinea exclaimed, "Succor, O lady mine, this vassal heart in this my first encounter; let not your favor and protection fail me in the peril in which for the first time I now find myself."

With these and other similar words, he loosed his buckler, grasped his lance in both his hands, and let the mule driver have such a blow on the head that the man fell to the ground stunned; and had it been followed by another one, he would have had no need of a surgeon to treat him. Having done this, Don Quixote gathered up his armor and resumed his pacing up and down with the same calm manner as before. Not long afterward, without knowing what had happened—for the first muleteer was still lying there unconscious—another came out with the same intention of watering his mules, and he too was about to remove the armor from the trough when the knight, without saying a word or asking favor of anyone, once more adjusted his buckler and raised his lance, and if he did not break the second mule driver's head to bits, he made more than three pieces of it by dividing it into quarters. At the sound of the fracas everybody in the inn came running out, among them the innkeeper; whereupon Don Quixote again lifted his buckler and laid his hand on his sword.

"O lady of beauty," he said, "strength and vigor of this fainting heart of mine! Now is the time to turn the eyes of your greatness upon this captive knight of yours who must face so formidable an adventure."

By this time he had worked himself up to such a pitch of anger that if all the mule drivers in the world had attacked him he would not have taken one step backward. The comrades of the wounded men, seeing the plight those two were in, now began showering stones on Don Quixote, who shielded himself as best he could with his buckler, although he did not dare stir from the trough for fear of leaving his armor unprotected. The landlord, meanwhile, kept calling for them to stop, for he had told them that this was a madman who would be sure to go free even though he killed them all. The knight was shouting louder than ever, calling them knaves and traitors. As for the lord of the castle, who allowed knights-errant to be treated in this fashion, he was a lowborn villain, and if he, Don Quixote, had but received the order of knighthood, he would make him pay for his treachery.

"As for you others, vile and filthy rabble, I take no account of you; you may stone me or come forward and attack me all you like; you shall see what the reward of your folly and insolence will be."

He spoke so vigorously and was so undaunted in bearing as to strike terror in those who would assail him; and for this reason, and owing also to the persuasions of the innkeeper, they ceased stoning him. He then permitted them to carry away the wounded, and went back to watching his armor with the same tranquil, unconcerned air that he had previously displayed.

The landlord was none too well pleased with these mad pranks on the part of his guest and determined to confer upon him that accursed order of knighthood before something else happened. Going up to him, he begged Don Quixote's pardon for the insolence which, without his knowledge, had been shown the knight by those of low degree. They, however, had been well punished for their impudence. As he had said, there was no chapel in this castle, but for that which remained to be done there was no need of any. According to what he had read of the ceremonial of the order, there was nothing to this business of being dubbed a knight except a slap on the neck and one across the shoulder, and that could be performed in the middle of a field as well as anywhere else. All that was required was for the knight-to-be to keep watch over his armor for a couple of hours, and Don Quixote had been at it more than four. The latter believed all this and announced that he was ready to obey and get the matter over with as speedily as possible. Once dubbed a knight, if he were attacked one more time, he did not think that he would leave a single person in the castle alive, save such as he might command be spared, at the bidding of his host and out of respect to him.

Thus warned, and fearful that it might occur, the castellan brought out the book in which he had jotted down the hay and barley for which the mule drivers owed him, and, accompanied by a lad bearing the butt of a candle and the two aforesaid damsels, he came up to where Don Quixote stood and commanded him to kneel. Reading from the account book—as if he had been saying a prayer—he raised his hand and, with the knight's own sword, gave him a good thwack upon the neck and another lusty one upon the shoulder, muttering all the while between his teeth. He then directed one of the ladies to gird on Don Quixote's sword, which she did with much gravity and composure; for it was all they could do to keep from laughing at every point of the ceremony, but the thought of the knight's prowess which they had already witnessed was sufficient to restrain their mirth.

"May God give your Grace much good fortune," said the worthy lady as she attached the blade, "and prosper you in battle."

Don Quixote thereupon inquired her name, for he desired to know to whom it was he was indebted for the favor he had just received, that he might share with her some of the honor which his strong right arm was sure to bring him. She replied very humbly that her name was Tolosa and that she was the daughter of a shoemaker, a native of Toledo who lived in the stalls of Sancho Bicnaya.[3] To this the knight replied that she would do him a very great favor if from then on she would call herself Doña Tolosa, and she promised to do so. The other girl then helped him on with his spurs, and practically the same conversation was repeated. When asked her name, she stated that it was La Molinera and added that she was the daughter of a respectable miller of Antequera. Don Quixote likewise requested her to assume the "don" and become Doña Molinera and offered to render her further services and favors.

These unheard-of ceremonies having been dispatched in great haste, Don Quixote could scarcely wait to be astride his horse and sally forth on his quest for adventures. Saddling and mounting Rocinante, he embraced his host, thanking him for the favor of having dubbed him a knight and saying such strange things that it would be quite impossible to record them here. The innkeeper, who was only too glad to be rid of him, answered with a speech that was no less flowery, though somewhat shorter, and he did not so much as ask him for the price of a lodging, so glad was he to see him go.

CHAPTER 4

Of what happened to our knight when he sallied forth from the inn.

Day was dawning when Don Quixote left the inn, so well satisfied with himself, so gay, so exhilarated, that the very girths of his steed all but burst with joy. But remembering the advice which his host had given him concerning the stock of necessary provisions that he should carry with him, especially money and shirts, he decided to turn back home and supply himself with whatever he needed, and with a squire as well; he had in mind a farmer who was a neighbor of his, a poor man and the father of a family but very well suited to fulfill the duties of squire to a man of arms. With this thought in mind he guided Rocinante toward the village once more, and that animal, realizing that he was homeward bound, began stepping out at so lively a gait that it seemed as if his feet barely touched the ground.

The knight had not gone far when from a hedge on his right hand he heard the sound of faint moans as of someone in distress.

"Thanks be to Heaven," he at once exclaimed, "for the favor it has shown me by providing me so soon with an opportunity to fulfill the obligations that I owe to my profession, a chance to pluck the fruit of my

3. An old square in Toledo.

worthy desires. Those, undoubtedly, are the cries of someone in distress, who stands in need of my favor and assistance."

Turning Rocinante's head, he rode back to the place from which the cries appeared to be coming. Entering the wood, he had gone but a few paces when he saw a mare attached to an oak, while bound to another tree was a lad of fifteen or thereabouts, naked from the waist up. It was he who was uttering the cries, and not without reason, for there in front of him was a lusty farmer with a girdle who was giving him many lashes, each one accompanied by a reproof and a command, "Hold your tongue and keep your eyes open"; and the lad was saying, "I won't do it again, sir; by God's Passion, I won't do it again. I promise you that after this I'll take better care of the flock."

When he saw what was going on, Don Quixote was very angry. "Discourteous knight," he said, "it ill becomes you to strike one who is powerless to defend himself. Mount your steed and take your lance in hand"— for there was a lance leaning against the oak to which the mare was tied— "and I will show you what a coward you are."

The farmer, seeing before him this figure all clad in armor and brandishing a lance, decided that he was as good as done for. "Sir Knight," he said, speaking very mildly, "this lad that I am punishing here is my servant; he tends a flock of sheep which I have in these parts and he is so careless that every day one of them shows up missing. And when I punish him for his carelessness or his roguery, he says it is just because I am a miser and do not want to pay him the wages that I owe him, but I swear to God and upon my soul that he lies."

"It is you who lie, base lout," said Don Quixote, "and in my presence; and by the sun that gives us light, I am minded to run you through with this lance. Pay him and say no more about it, or else, by the God who rules us, I will make an end of you and annihilate you here and now. Release him at once."

The farmer hung his head and without a word untied his servant. Don Quixote then asked the boy how much has master owed him. For nine months' work, the lad told him, at seven reales the month. The knight did a little reckoning and found that this came to sixty-three reales; whereupon he ordered the farmer to pay over the money immediately, as he valued his life. The cowardly bumpkin replied that, facing death as he was and by the oath that he had sworn—he had not sworn any oath as yet—it did not amount to as much as that; for there were three pairs of shoes which he had given the lad that were to be deducted and taken into account, and a real for two blood-lettings when his servant was ill.

"That," said Don Quixote, "is all very well; but let the shoes and the blood-lettings go for the undeserved lashings which you have given him; if he has worn out the leather of the shoes that you paid for, you have taken the hide off his body, and if the barber let a little blood for him when he was sick,[4] you have done the same when he was well; and so far as that goes, he owes you nothing."

4. Barbers were also surgeons.

"But the trouble is, Sir Knight, that I have no money with me. Come along home with me, Andrés, and I will pay you real for real."

"I go home with him!" cried the lad. "Never in the world! No, sir, I would not even think of it; for once he has me alone he'll flay me like a St. Bartholomew."

"He will do nothing of the sort," said Don Quixote. "It is sufficient for me to command, and he out of respect will obey. Since he has sworn to me by the order of knighthood which he has received, I shall let him go free and I will guarantee that you will be paid."

"But look, your Grace," the lad remonstrated, "my master is no knight; he has never received any order of knighthood whatsoever. He is Juan Haldudo, a rich man and a resident of Quintanar."

"That makes little difference," declared Don Quixote, "for there may well be knights among the Haldudos, all the more so in view of the fact that every man is the son of his works."

"That is true enough," said Andrés, "but this master of mine—of what works is he the son, seeing that he refuses me the pay for my sweat and labor?"

"I do not refuse you, brother Andrés," said the farmer. "Do me the favor of coming with me, and I swear to you by all the orders of knighthood that there are in this world to pay you, as I have said, real for real, and per- fumed at that."

"You can dispense with the perfume," said Don Quixote; "just give him the reales and I shall be satisfied. And see to it that you keep your oath, or by the one that I myself have sworn I shall return to seek you out and chastise you, and I shall find you though you be as well hidden as a lizard. In case you would like to know who it is that is giving you this command in order that you may feel the more obliged to comply with it, I may tell you that I am the valorous Don Quixote de la Mancha, righter of wrongs and injustices; and so, God be with you, and do not fail to do as you have promised, under that penalty that I have pronounced."

As he said this, he put spurs to Rocinante and was off. The farmer watched him go, and when he saw that Don Quixote was out of the wood and out of sight, he turned to his servant, Andrés.

"Come here, my son," he said. "I want to pay you what I owe you as that righter of wrongs has commanded me."

"Take my word for it," replied Andrés, "your Grace would do well to observe the command of that good knight—may he live a thousand years; for as he is valorous and a righteous judge, if you don't pay me then, by Rocque,[5] he will come back and do just what he said!"

"And I will give you my word as well," said the farmer; "but seeing that I am so fond of you, I wish to increase the debt, that I may owe you all the more." And with this he seized the lad's arm and bound him to the tree again and flogged him within an inch of his life. "There, Master Andrés, you may call on that righter of wrongs if you like and you will see

5. The origin of the oath is unknown.

whether or not he rights this one. I do not think I have quite finished with you yet, for I have a good mind to flay you alive as you feared."

Finally, however, he unbound him and told him he might go look for that judge of his to carry out the sentence that had been pronounced. Andrés left, rather down in the mouth, swearing that he would indeed go look for the brave Don Quixote de la Mancha; he would relate to him everything that had happened, point by point, and the farmer would have to pay for it seven times over. But for all that, he went away weeping, and his master stood laughing at him.

Such was the manner in which the valorous knight righted this particular wrong. Don Quixote was quite content with the way everything had turned out; it seemed to him that he had made a very fortunate and noble beginning with his deeds of chivalry, and he was very well satisfied with himself as he jogged along in the direction of his native village, talking to himself in a low voice all the while.

"Well may'st thou call thyself fortunate today, above all other women on earth, O fairest of the fair, Dulcinea del Toboso! Seeing that it has fallen to thy lot to hold subject and submissive to thine every wish and pleasure so valiant and renowned a knight as Don Quixote de la Mancha is and shall be, who, as everyone knows, yesterday received the order of knighthood and this day has righted the greatest wrong and grievance that injustice ever conceived or cruelty ever perpetrated, by snatching the lash from the hand of the merciless foeman who was so unreasonably flogging that tender child."

At this point he came to a road that forked off in four directions, and at once he thought of those crossroads where knights-errant would pause to consider which path they should take. By way of imitating them, he halted there for a while; and when he had given the subject much thought, he slackened Rocinante's rein and let the hack follow its inclination. The animal's first impulse was to make straight for its own stable. After they had gone a couple of miles or so Don Quixote caught sight of what appeared to be a great throng of people, who, as was afterward learned, were certain merchants of Toledo on their way to purchase silk at Murcia. There were six of them altogether with their sunshades, accompanied by four attendants on horseback and three mule drivers on foot.

No sooner had he sighted them than Don Quixote imagined that he was on the brink of some fresh adventure. He was eager to imitate those passages at arms of which he had read in his books, and here, so it seemed to him, was one made to order. And so, with bold and knightly bearing, he settled himself firmly in the stirrups, couched his lance, covered himself with his shield, and took up a position in the middle of the road, where he paused to wait for those other knights-errant (for such he took them to be) to come up to him. When they were near enough to see and hear plainly, Don Quixote raised his voice and made a haughty gesture.

"Let everyone," he cried, "stand where he is, unless everyone will confess that there is not in all the world a more beauteous damsel than the Empress of La Mancha, the peerless Dulcinea del Toboso."

Upon hearing these words and beholding the weird figure who uttered them, the merchants stopped short. From the knight's appearance and his speech they knew at once that they had to deal with a madman; but they were curious to know what was meant by that confession that was demanded of them, and one of their number who was somewhat of a jester and a very clever fellow raised his voice.

"Sir Knight," he said, "we do not know who this beauteous lady is of whom you speak. Show her to us, and if she is as beautiful as you say, then we will right willingly and without any compulsion confess the truth as you have asked of us."

"If I were to show her to you," replied Don Quixote, "what merit would there be in your confessing a truth so self-evident? The important thing is for you, without seeing her, to believe, confess, affirm, swear, and defend that truth. Otherwise, monstrous and arrogant creatures that you are, you shall do battle with me. Come on, then, one by one, as the order of knighthood prescribes; or all of you together, if you will have it so, as is the sorry custom of those of your breed. Come on, and I will await you here, for I am confident that my cause is just."

"Sir Knight," responded the merchant, "I beg your Grace, in the name of all the princes here present, in order that we may not have upon our consciences the burden of confessing a thing which we have never seen nor heard, and one, moreover, so prejudicial to the empresses and queens of Alcarria and Estremadura,[6] that your Grace will show us some portrait of this lady, even though it be no larger than a grain of wheat, for by the thread one comes to the ball of yarn; and with this we shall remain satisfied and assured, and your Grace will likewise be content and satisfied. The truth is, I believe that we are already so much of your way of thinking that though it should show her to be blind of one eye and distilling vermilion and brimstone from the other, nevertheless, to please your Grace, we would say in her behalf all that you desire."

"She distills nothing of the sort, infamous rabble!" shouted Don Quixote, for his wrath was kindling now. "I tell you, she does not distill what you say at all, but amber and civet[7] wrapped in cotton; and she is neither one-eyed nor hunchbacked but straighter than a spindle that comes from Guadarrama. You shall pay for the great blasphemy which you have uttered against such a beauty as is my lady!"

Saying this, he came on with lowered lance against the one who had spoken, charging with such wrath and fury that if fortune had not caused Rocinante to stumble and fall in mid-career, things would have gone badly with the merchant and he would have paid for his insolent gibe. As it was, Don Quixote went rolling over the plain for some little distance, and when he tried to get to his feet, found that he was unable to do so, being too encumbered with his lance, shield, spurs, helmet, and the weight of that ancient suit of armor.

6. Ironical, since both were known as particularly backward regions.   7. A musky substance used in perfume, imported from Africa in cotton packings.

"Do not flee, cowardly ones," he cried even as he struggled to rise. "Stay, cravens, for it is not my fault but that of my steed that I am stretched out here."

One of the muleteers, who must have been an ill-natured lad, upon hearing the poor fallen knight speak so arrogantly, could not refrain from giving him an answer in the ribs. Going up to him, he took the knight's lance and broke it into bits, and then with a companion proceeded to belabor him so mercilessly that in spite of his armor they milled him like a hopper of wheat. The merchants called to them not to lay on so hard, saying that was enough and they should desist, but the mule driver by this time had warmed up to the sport and would not stop until he had vented his wrath, and, snatching up the broken pieces of the lance, he began hurling them at the wretched victim as he lay there on the ground. And through all this tempest of sticks that rained upon him Don Quixote never once closed his mouth nor ceased threatening Heaven and earth and these ruffians, for such he took them to be, who were thus mishandling him.

Finally the lad grew tired, and the merchants went their way with a good story to tell about the poor fellow who had had such a cudgeling. Finding himself alone, the knight endeavored to see if he could rise; but if this was a feat that he could not accomplish when he was sound and whole, how was he to achieve it when he had been thrashed and pounded to a pulp? Yet nonetheless he considered himself fortunate; for as he saw it, misfortunes such as this were common to knights-errant, and he put all the blame upon his horse; and if he was unable to rise, that was because his body was so bruised and battered all over.

CHAPTER 5

In which is continued the narrative of the misfortune that befell our knight.

Seeing, then, that he was indeed unable to stir, he decided to fall back upon a favorite remedy of his, which was to think of some passage or other in his books; and as it happened, the one that he in his madness now recalled was the story of Baldwin and the Marquis of Mantua, when Carloto left the former wounded upon the mountainside,[8] a tale that is known to children, not unknown to young men, celebrated and believed in by the old, and, for all of that, not any truer than the miracles of Mohammed. Moreover, it impressed him as being especially suited to the straits in which he found himself; and, accordingly, with a great show of feeling, he began rolling and tossing on the ground as he feebly gasped out the lines which the wounded knight of the wood is supposed to have uttered:

> "Where art thou, lady mine,
> That thou dost not grieve for my woe?
> Either thou art disloyal,
> Or my grief thou dost not know."

8. The allusion is to an old ballad about Charlemagne's son Charlot (Carloto) wounding Baldwin, nephew of the Marquis of Mantua.

He went on reciting the old ballad until he came to the following verses:

> "O noble Marquis of Mantua,
> My uncle and liege lord true!"

He had reached this point when down the road came a farmer of the same village, a neighbor of his, who had been to the mill with a load of wheat. Seeing a man lying there stretched out like that, he went up to him and inquired who he was and what was the trouble that caused him to utter such mournful complaints. Thinking that this must undoubtedly be his uncle, the Marquis of Mantua, Don Quixote did not answer but went on with his recitation of the ballad, giving an account of the Marquis' misfortunes and the amours of his wife and the emperor's son, exactly as the ballad has it.

The farmer was astounded at hearing all these absurdities, and after removing the knight's visor which had been battered to pieces by the blows it had received, the good man bathed the victim's face, only to discover, once the dust was off, that he knew him very well.

"Señor Quejana," he said (for such must have been Don Quixote's real name when he was in his right senses and before he had given up the life of a quiet country gentleman to become a knight-errant), "who is responsible for your Grace's being in such a plight as this?"

But the knight merely went on with his ballad in response to all the questions asked of him. Perceiving that it was impossible to obtain any information from him, the farmer as best he could relieved him of his breastplate and backpiece to see if he had any wounds, but there was no blood and no mark of any sort. He then tried to lift him from the ground, and with a great deal of effort finally managed to get him astride the ass, which appeared to be the easier mount for him. Gathering up the armor, including even the splinters from the lance, he made a bundle and tied it on Rocinante's back, and, taking the horse by the reins and the ass by the halter, he started out for the village. He was worried in his mind at hearing all the foolish things that Don Quixote said, and that individual himself was far from being at ease. Unable by reason of his bruises and his soreness to sit upright on the donkey, our knight-errant kept sighing to Heaven, which led the farmer to ask him once more what it was that ailed him.

It must have been the devil himself who caused him to remember those tales that seemed to fit his own case; for at this point he forgot all about Baldwin and recalled Abindarráez, and how the governor of Antequera, Rodrigo de Narváez, had taken him prisoner and carried him off captive to his castle. Accordingly, when the countryman turned to inquire how he was and what was troubling him, Don Quixote replied with the very same words and phrases that the captive Abindarráez used in answering Rodrigo, just as he had read in the story *Diana* of Jorge de Montemayor,[9] where it is all written down, applying them very aptly to the present circumstances

9. The reference is to the tale of the love of Abindarráez, a captive Moor, for the beautiful Jarifa (mentioned in the following paragraph), contained in the second edition of *Diana*, the pastoral romance by Jorge de Montemayor.

as the farmer went along cursing his luck for having to listen to such a lot of nonsense. Realizing that his neighbor was quite mad, he made haste to reach the village that he might not have to be annoyed any longer by Don Quixote's tiresome harangue.

"Señor Don Rodrigo de Narváez," the knight was saying, "I may inform your Grace that this beautiful Jarifa of whom I speak is not the lovely Dulcinea del Toboso, in whose behalf I have done, am doing, and shall do the most famous deeds of chivalry that ever have been or will be seen in all the world."

"But, sir," replied the farmer, "sinner that I am, cannot your Grace see that I am not Don Rodrigo de Narváez nor the Marquis of Mantua, but Pedro Alonso, your neighbor? And your Grace is neither Baldwin nor Abindarráez but a respectable gentleman by the name of Señor Quijana."

"I know who I am," said Don Quixote, "and who I may be, if I choose: not only those I have mentioned but all the Twelve Peers of France and the Nine Worthies[1] as well; for the exploits of all of them together, or separately, cannot compare with mine."

With such talk as this they reached their destination just as night was falling; but the farmer decided to wait until it was a little darker in order that the badly battered gentleman might not be seen arriving in such a condition and mounted on an ass. When he thought the proper time had come, they entered the village and proceeded to Don Quixote's house, where they found everything in confusion. The curate and the barber were there, for they were great friends of the knight, and the housekeeper was speaking to them.

"Señor Licentiate Pero Pérez," she was saying, for that was the manner in which she addressed the curate, "what does your Grace think could have happened to my master? Three days now, and not a word of him, nor the hack, nor the buckler, nor the lance, nor the suit of armor. Ah, poor me! I am as certain as I am that I was born to die that it is those cursed books of chivalry he is always reading that have turned his head; for now that I recall, I have often heard him muttering to himself that he must become a knight-errant and go through the world in search of adventures. May such books as those be consigned to Satan and Barabbas,[2] for they have sent to perdition the finest mind in all La Mancha."

The niece was of the same opinion. "I may tell you, Señor Master Nicholas," she said, for that was the barber's name, "that many times my uncle would sit reading those impious tales of misadventure for two whole days and nights at a stretch; and when he was through, he would toss the book aside, lay his hand on his sword, and begin slashing at the walls. When he was completely exhausted, he would tell us that he had just killed four giants as big as castle towers, while the sweat that poured off him was blood from the wounds that he had received in battle. He would

---

1. In the French medieval epics the Twelve Peers (Roland, Olivier, and so on) were warriors all equal in rank forming a sort of guard of honor around Charlemagne. The Nine Worthies, in a tradition originating in France, were nine famous figures, three biblical, three classical, and three Christian (David, Hector, Alexander, Charlemagne, and so on).   2. The thief whose release, rather than that of Jesus, the crowd requested when Pilate, conforming to Passover custom, was ready to have one prisoner set free.

then drink a big jug of cold water, after which he would be very calm and peaceful, saying that the water was the most precious liquid which the wise Esquife, a great magician and his friend, had brought to him. But I blame myself for everything. I should have advised your Worships of my uncle's nonsensical actions so that you could have done something about it by burning those damnable books of his before things came to such a pass; for he has many that ought to be burned as if they were heretics."

"I agree with you," said the curate, "and before tomorrow's sun has set there shall be a public *auto da fé*, and those works shall be condemned to the flames that they may not lead some other who reads them to follow the example of my good friend."

Don Quixote and the farmer overheard all this, and it was then that the latter came to understand the nature of his neighbor's affliction.

"Open the door, your Worships," the good man cried. "Open for Sir Baldwin and the Marquis of Mantua, who comes badly wounded, and for Señor Abindarráez the Moor whom the valiant Rodrigo de Narváez, governor of Antequera, brings captive."

At the sound of his voice they all ran out, recognizing at once friend, master, and uncle, who as yet was unable to get down off the donkey's back. They all ran up to embrace him.

"Wait, all of you," said Don Quixote, "for I am sorely wounded through fault of my steed. Bear me to my couch and summon, if it be possible, the wise Urganda to treat and care for my wounds."

"There!" exclaimed the housekeeper. "Plague take it! Did not my heart tell me right as to which foot my master limped on? To bed with your Grace at once, and we will take care of you without sending for that Urganda of yours. A curse, I say, and a hundred other curses, on those books of chivalry that have brought your Grace to this."

And so they carried him off to bed, but when they went to look for his wounds, they found none at all. He told them it was all the result of a great fall he had taken with Rocinante, his horse, while engaged in combating ten giants, the hugest and most insolent that were ever heard of in all the world.

"Tut, tut," said the curate. "So there are giants in the dance now, are there? Then, by the sign of the cross, I'll have them burned before nightfall tomorrow."

They had a thousand questions to put to Don Quixote, but his only answer was that they should give him something to eat and let him sleep, for that was the most important thing of all; so they humored him in this. The curate then interrogated the farmer at great length concerning the conversation he had had with his neighbor. The peasant told him everything, all the absurd things their friend had said when he found him lying there and afterward on the way home, all of which made the licentiate more anxious than ever to do what he did the following day,[3] when he summoned Master Nicholas and went with him to Don Quixote's house.

3. What he and the barber did was to burn most of Don Quixote's library.

(Fighting the Windmills and a Choleric Biscayan)

CHAPTER 7

Of the second sally of our good knight, Don Quixote de la Mancha.

. . . After that he remained at home very tranquilly for a couple of weeks, without giving sign of any desire to repeat his former madness. During that time he had the most pleasant conversations with his two old friends, the curate and the barber, on the point he had raised to the effect that what the world needed most was knights-errant and a revival of chivalry. The curate would occasionally contradict him and again would give in, for it was only by means of this artifice that he could carry on a conversation with him at all.

In the meanwhile Don Quixote was bringing his powers of persuasion to bear upon a farmer who lived near by, a good man—if this title may be applied to one who is poor—but with very few wits in his head. The short of it is, by pleas and promises, he got the hapless rustic to agree to ride forth with him and serve him as his squire. Among other things, Don Quixote told him that he ought to be more than willing to go, because no telling what adventure might occur which would win them an island, and then he (the farmer) would be left to be the governor of it. As a result of these and other similar assurances, Sancho Panza forsook his wife and children and consented to take upon himself the duties of squire to his neighbor.

Next, Don Quixote set out to raise some money, and by selling this thing and pawning that and getting the worst of the bargain always, he finally scraped together a reasonable amount. He also asked a friend of his for the loan of a buckler and patched up his broken helmet as well as he could. He advised his squire, Sancho, of the day and hour when they were to take to the road and told him to see to laying in a supply of those things that were most necessary, and, above all, not to forget the saddlebags. Sancho replied that he would see to all this and added that he was also thinking of taking along with him a very good ass that he had, as he was not much used to going on foot.

With regard to the ass, Don Quixote had to do a little thinking, trying to recall if any knight-errant had ever had a squire thus asininely mounted. He could not think of any, but nevertheless he decided to take Sancho with the intention of providing him with a nobler steed as soon as occasion offered; he had but to appropriate the horse of the first discourteous knight he met. Having furnished himself with shirts and all the other things that the innkeeper had recommended, he and Panza rode forth one night unseen by anyone and without taking leave of wife and children, housekeeper or niece. They went so far that by the time morning came they were safe from discovery had a hunt been started for them.

Mounted on his ass, Sancho Panza rode along like a patriarch, with saddlebags and flask, his mind set upon becoming governor of that island that his master had promised him. Don Quixote determined to take the same route and road over the Campo de Montiel that he had followed on his first journey; but he was not so uncomfortable this time, for it was early morning and the sun's rays fell upon them slantingly and accordingly did not tire them too much.

"Look, Sir Knight-errant," said Sancho, "your Grace should not forget that island you promised me; for no matter how big it is, I'll be able to govern it right enough."

"I would have you know, friend Sancho Panza," replied Don Quixote, "that among the knights-errant of old it was a very common custom to make their squires governors of the islands or the kingdoms that they won, and I am resolved that in my case so pleasing a usage shall not fall into desuetude. I even mean to go them one better; for they very often, perhaps most of the time, waited until their squires were old men who had had their fill of serving their masters during bad days and worse nights, whereupon they would give them the title of count, or marquis at most, of some valley or province more or less. But if you live and I live, it well may be that within a week I shall win some kingdom with others dependent upon it, and it will be the easiest thing in the world to crown you king of one of them. You need not marvel at this, for all sorts of unforeseen things happen to knights like me, and I may readily be able to give you even more than I have promised."

"In that case," said Sancho Panza, "if by one of those miracles of which your Grace was speaking I should become king, I would certainly send for Juana Gutiérrez, my old lady, to come and be my queen, and the young ones could be infantes."

"There is no doubt about it," Don Quixote assured him.

"Well, I doubt it," said Sancho, "for I think that even if God were to rain kingdoms upon the earth, no crown would sit well on the head of Mari Gutiérrez,[4] for I am telling you, sir, as a queen she is not worth two maravedis.[5] She would do better as a countess, God help her."

"Leave everything to God, Sancho," said Don Quixote, "and he will give you whatever is most fitting; but I trust you will not be so pusillanimous as to be content with anything less than the title of viceroy."

"That I will not," said Sancho Panza, "especially seeing that I have in your Grace so illustrious a master who can give me all that is suitable to me and all that I can manage."

CHAPTER 8

Of the good fortune which the valorous Don Quixote had in the terrifying and never-before-imagined adventure of the windmills, along with other events that deserve to be suitably recorded.

At this point they caught sight of thirty or forty windmills which were standing on the plain there, and no sooner had Don Quixote laid eyes upon them than he turned to his squire and said, "Fortune is guiding our

---

4. Sancho's wife; she is called Juana Gutiérrez a few lines earlier.   5. Coin worth one-thirty-fourths of a real.

affairs better than we could have wished; for you see there before you, friend Sancho Panza, some thirty or more lawless giants with whom I mean to do battle. I shall deprive them of their lives, and with the spoils from this encounter we shall begin to enrich ourselves; for this is righteous warfare, and it is a great service to God to remove so accursed a breed from the face of the earth."

"What giants?" said Sancho Panza.

"Those that you see there," replied his master, "those with the long arms some of which are as much as two leagues in length."

"But look, your Grace, those are not giants but windmills, and what appear to be arms are their wings which, when whirled in the breeze, cause the millstone to go."

"It is plain to be seen," said Don Quixote, "that you have had little experience in this matter of adventures. If you are afraid, go off to one side and say your prayers while I am engaging them in fierce, unequal combat."

Saying this, he gave spurs to his steed Rocinante, without paying any heed to Sancho's warning that these were truly windmills and not giants that he was riding forth to attack. Nor even when he was close upon them did he perceive what they really were, but shouted at the top of his lungs, "Do not seek to flee, cowards and vile creatures that you are, for it is but a single knight with whom you have to deal!"

At that moment a little wind came up and the big wings began turning.

"Though you flourish as many arms as did the giant Briareus,"[6] said Don Quixote when he perceived this, "you still shall have to answer to me."

He thereupon commended himself with all his heart to his lady Dulcinea, beseeching her to succor him in this peril; and, being well covered with his shield and with his lance at rest, he bore down upon them at a full gallop and fell upon the first mill that stood in his way, giving a thrust at the wing, which was whirling at such a speed that his lance was broken into bits and both horse and horseman went rolling over the plain, very much battered indeed. Sancho upon his donkey came hurrying to his master's assistance as fast as he could, but when he reached the spot, the knight was unable to move, so great was the shock with which he and Rocinante had hit the ground.

"God help us!" exclaimed Sancho, "did I not tell your Grace to look well, that those were nothing but windmills, a fact which no one could fail to see unless he had other mills of the same sort in his head?"

"Be quiet, friend Sancho," said Don Quixote. "Such are the fortunes of war, which more than any other are subject to constant change. What is more, when I come to think of it, I am sure that this must be the work of that magician Frestón, the one who robbed me of my study and my books,[7] and who has thus changed the giants into windmills in order to deprive me of the glory of overcoming them, so great is the enmity that he bears

6. Mythological giant with a hundred arms.   7. Don Quixote had promptly attributed the ruin of his library, performed by the curate and the barber, to magical intervention.

me; but in the end his evil arts shall not prevail against this trusty sword of mine."

"May God's will be done," was Sancho Panza's response. And with the aid of his squire the knight was once more mounted on Rocinante, who stood there with one shoulder half out of joint. And so, speaking of the adventure that had just befallen them, they continued along the Puerto Lápice highway; for there, Don Quixote said, they could not fail to find many and varied adventures, this being a much traveled thoroughfare. The only thing was, the knight was exceedingly downcast over the loss of his lance.

"I remember," he said to his squire, "having read of a Spanish knight by the name of Diego Pérez de Vargas, who, having broken his sword in battle, tore from an oak a heavy bough or branch and with it did such feats of valor that day, and pounded so many Moors, that he came to be known as Machuca,[8] and he and his descendants from that day forth have been called Vargas y Machuca. I tell you this because I too intend to provide myself with just such a bough as the one he wielded, and with it I propose to do such exploits that you shall deem yourself fortunate to have been found worthy to come with me and behold and witness things that are almost beyond belief."

"God's will be done," said Sancho. "I believe everything that your Grace says; but straighten yourself up in the saddle a little, for you seem to be slipping down on one side, owing, no doubt, to the shaking-up that you received in your fall."

"Ah, that is the truth," replied Don Quixote, "and if I do not speak of my sufferings, it is for the reason that it is not permitted knights-errant to complain of any wound whatsoever, even though their bowels may be dropping out."

"If that is the way it is," said Sancho, "I have nothing more to say; but, God knows, it would suit me better if your Grace did complain when something hurts him. I can assure you that I mean to do so, over the least little thing that ails me—that is, unless the same rule applies to squires as well."

Don Quixote laughed long and heartily over Sancho's simplicity, telling him that he might complain as much as he liked and where and when he liked, whether he had good cause or not; for he had read nothing to the contrary in the ordinances of chivalry. Sancho then called his master's attention to the fact that it was time to eat. The knight replied that he himself had no need of food at the moment, but his squire might eat whenever he chose. Having been granted this permission, Sancho seated himself as best he could upon his beast, and, taking out from his saddle-bags the provisions that he had stored there, he rode along leisurely behind his master, munching his victuals and taking a good, hearty swig now and then at the leather flask in a manner that might well have caused the biggest-bellied tavernkeeper of Málaga to envy him. Between draughts he

8. Machuca, meaning "The Crusher," was the hero of a folk ballad.

gave not so much as a thought to any promise that his master might have made him, nor did he look upon it as any hardship, but rather as good sport, to go in quest of adventures however hazardous they might be.

The short of the matter is, they spent the night under some trees, from one of which Don Quixote tore off a withered bough to serve him as a lance, placing it in the lance head from which he had removed the broken one. He did not sleep all night long for thinking of his lady Dulcinea; for this was in accordance with what he had read in his books, of men of arms in the forest or desert places who kept a wakeful vigil, sustained by the memory of their ladies fair. Not so with Sancho, whose stomach was full, and not with chicory water. He fell into a dreamless slumber, and had not his master called him, he would not have been awakened either by the rays of the sun in his face or by the many birds who greeted the coming of the new day with their merry song.

Upon arising, he had another go at the flask, finding it somewhat more flaccid then it had been the night before, a circumstance which grieved his heart, for he could not see that they were on the way to remedying the deficiency within any very short space of time. Don Quixote did not wish any breakfast; for, as has been said, he was in the habit of nourishing himself on savorous memories. They then set out once more along the road to Puerto Lápice, and around three in the afternoon they came in sight of the pass that bears that name.

"There," said Don Quixote as his eyes fell upon it, "we may plunge our arms up to the elbow in what are known as adventures. But I must warn you that even though you see me in the greatest peril in the world, you are not to lay hand upon your sword to defend me, unless it be that those who attack me are rabble and men of low degree, in which case you may very well come to my aid; but if they be gentlemen, it is in no wise permitted by the laws of chivalry that you should assist me until you yourself shall have been dubbed a knight."

"Most certainly, sir," replied Sancho, "your Grace shall be very well obeyed in this; all the more so for the reason that I myself am of a peaceful disposition and not fond of meddling in the quarrels and feuds of others. However, when it comes to protecting my own person, I shall not take account of those laws of which you speak, seeing that all laws, human and divine, permit each one to defend himself whenever he is attacked."

"I am willing to grant you that," assented Don Quixote, "but in this matter of defending me against gentlemen you must restrain your natural impulses."

"I promise you I shall do so," said Sancho. "I will observe this precept as I would the Sabbath day."

As they were conversing in this manner, there appeared in the road in front of them two friars of the Order of St. Benedict, mounted upon dromedaries—for the she-mules they rode were certainly no smaller than that. The friars wore travelers' spectacles and carried sunshades, and behind them came a coach accompanied by four or five men on horseback and a couple of muleteers on foot. In the coach, as was afterwards learned, was a lady of Biscay, on her way to Seville to bid farewell to her husband, who had been appointed to some high post in the Indies. The religious were not of her company although they were going by the same road.

The instant Don Quixote laid eyes upon them he turned to his squire. "Either I am mistaken or this is going to be the most famous adventure that ever was seen; for those black-clad figures that you behold must be, and without any doubt are, certain enchanters who are bearing with them a captive princess in that coach, and I must do all I can to right this wrong."

"It will be worse than the windmills," declared Sancho. "Look you, sir, those are Benedictine friars and the coach must be that of some travelers. Mark well what I say and what you do, lest the devil lead you astray."

"I have already told you, Sancho," replied Don Quixote, "that you know little where the subject of adventures is concerned. What I am saying to you is the truth, as you shall now see."

With this, he rode forward and took up a position in the middle of the road along which the friars were coming, and as soon as they appeared to be within earshot he cried out to them in a loud voice, "O devilish and monstrous beings, set free at once the highborn princesses whom you bear captive in that coach, or else prepare at once to meet your death as the just punishment of your evil deeds."

The friars drew rein and sat there in astonishment, marveling as much at Don Quixote's appearance as at the words he spoke. "Sir Knight," they answered him, "we are neither devilish nor monstrous but religious of the Order of St. Benedict who are merely going our way. We know nothing of those who are in that coach, nor of any captive princesses either."

"Soft words," said Don Quixote, "have no effect on me. I know you for what you are, lying rabble!" And without waiting for any further parley he gave spur to Rocinante and, with lowered lance, bore down upon the first friar with such fury and intrepidity that, had not the fellow tumbled from his mule of his own accord, he would have been hurled to the ground and either killed or badly wounded. The second religious, seeing how his companion had been treated, dug his legs into his she-mule's flanks and scurried away over the countryside faster than the wind.

Seeing the friar upon the ground, Sancho Panza slipped lightly from his mount and, falling upon him, began stripping him of his habit. The two mule drivers accompanying the religious thereupon came running up and asked Sancho why he was doing this. The latter replied that the friar's garments belonged to him as legitimate spoils of the battle that his master Don Quixote had just won. The muleteers, however, were lads with no sense of humor, nor did they know what all this talk of spoils and battles was about; but, perceiving that Don Quixote had ridden off to one side to converse with those inside the coach, they pounced upon Sancho, threw him to the ground, and proceeded to pull out the hair of his beard and kick him to a pulp, after which they went off and left him stretched out there, bereft at once of breath and sense.

Without losing any time, they then assisted the friar to remount. The good brother was trembling all over from fright, and there was not a speck of color in his face, but when he found himself in the saddle once more, he quickly spurred his beast to where his companion, at some little distance, sat watching and waiting to see what the result of the encounter would be. Having no curiosity as to the final outcome of the fray, the two of them now resumed their journey, making more signs of the cross than the devil would be able to carry upon his back.

Meanwhile Don Quixote, as we have said, was speaking to the lady in the coach.

"Your beauty, my lady, may now dispose of your person as best may please you, for the arrogance of your abductors lies upon the ground, overthrown by this good arm of mine; and in order that you may not pine to know the name of your liberator, I may inform you that I am Don Quixote de la Mancha, knight-errant and adventurer and captive of the peerless and beauteous Doña Dulcinea del Toboso. In payment of the favor which you have received from me, I ask nothing other than that you return to El Toboso and on my behalf pay your respects to this lady, telling her that it was I who set you free."

One of the squires accompanying those in the coach, a Biscayan,[9] was listening to Don Quixote's words, and when he saw that the knight did not propose to let the coach proceed upon its way but was bent upon having it turn back to El Toboso, he promptly went up to him, seized his lance, and said to him in bad Castilian and worse Biscayan, "Go, *caballero*, and bad luck go with you; for by the God that created me, if you do not let this coach pass, me kill you or me no Biscayan."

Don Quixote heard him attentively enough and answered him very mildly, "If you were a *caballero*,[1] which you are not, I should already have chastised you, wretched creature, for your foolhardiness and your impudence."

"Me no *caballero*." cried the Biscayan "Me swear to God, you lie like a Christian. If you will but lay aside your lance and unsheath your sword, you will soon see that you are carrying water to the cat![2] Biscayan on land, gentleman at sea, but a gentleman in spite of the devil, and you lie if you say otherwise."

" 'You shall see as to that presently,' said Agrajes," Don Quixote quoted.[3] He cast his lance to the earth, drew his sword, and, taking his buckler on his arm, attacked the Biscayan with intent to slay him. The latter, when he saw his adversary approaching, would have liked to dismount from his mule, for she was one of the worthless sort that are let for hire and he had no confidence in her; but there was no time for this, and so he had no choice but to draw his own sword in turn and make the best of it. However, he was near enough to the coach to be able to snatch a cushion from it to serve him as a shield; and then they fell upon each other as though they were mortal enemies. The rest of those present sought to make peace between

9. From the Basque region in northeastern Spain.   1. *Caballero* means both "knight" and "gentleman."   2. An inversion of a proverbial phrase, "carrying the cat to the water."   3. Agrajes is a violent character in the romance *Amadis de Gaul*; his challenging phrase is the conventional opener of a fight.

them but did not succeed, for the Biscayan with his disjointed phrases kept muttering that if they did not let him finish the battle then he himself would have to kill his mistress and anyone else who tried to stop him.

The lady inside the carriage, amazed by it all and trembling at what she saw, directed her coachman to drive on a little way; and there from a distance she watched the deadly combat, in the course of which the Biscayan came down with a great blow on Don Quixote's shoulder, over the top of the latter's shield, and had not the knight been clad in armor, it would have split him to the waist.

Feeling the weight of this blow, Don Quixote cried out, "O lady of my soul, Dulcinea, flower of beauty, succor this your champion who out of gratitude for your many favors finds himself in so perilous a plight!" To utter these words, lay hold of his sword, cover himself with his buckler, and attack the Biscayan was but the work of a moment; for he was now resolved to risk everything upon a single stroke.

As he saw Don Quixote approaching with so dauntless a bearing, the Biscayan was well aware of his adversary's courage and forthwith determined to imitate the example thus set him. He kept himself protected with his cushion, but he was unable to get his she-mule to budge to one side or the other, for the beast, out of sheer exhaustion and being, moreover, unused to such childish play, was incapable of taking a single step. And so, then, as has been stated, Don Quixote was approaching the wary Biscayan, his sword raised on high and with the firm resolve of cleaving his enemy in two; and the Biscayan was awaiting the knight in the same posture, cushion in front of him and with uplifted sword. All the bystanders were trembling with suspense at what would happen as a result of the terrible blows that were threatened, and the lady in the coach and her maids were making a thousand vows and offerings to all the images and shrines in Spain, praying that God would save them all and the lady's squire from this great peril that confronted them.

But the unfortunate part of the matter is that at this very point the author of the history breaks off and leaves the battle pending, excusing himself upon the ground that he has been unable to find anything else in writing concerning the exploits of Don Quixote beyond those already set forth. It is true, on the other hand, that the second author[4] of this work could not bring himself to believe that so unusual a chronicle would have been consigned to oblivion, nor that the learned ones of La Mancha were possessed of so little curiosity as not to be able to discover in their archives or registry offices certain papers that have to do with this famous knight. Being convinced of this, he did not despair of coming upon the end of this pleasing story. . . .

CHAPTER 9

In which is concluded and brought to an end the stupendous battle between the gallant Biscayan and the valiant Knight of La Mancha.

---

4. Cervantes himself, adopting here—with tongue in cheek—a device used in the romances of chivalry to create suspense.

. . . we left the valorous Biscayan and the famous Don Quixote with swords unsheathed and raised aloft, about to let fall furious slashing blows which, had they been delivered fairly and squarely, would at the very least have split them in two and laid them wide open from top to bottom like a pomegranate; and it was at this doubtful point that the pleasing chronicle came to a halt and broke off, without the author's informing us as to where the rest of it might be found.

I was deeply grieved by such a circumstance, and the pleasure I had had in reading so slight a portion was turned into annoyance as I thought of how difficult it would be to come upon the greater part which it seemed to me must still be missing. It appeared impossible and contrary to all good precedent that so worthy a knight should not have had some scribe to take upon himself the task of writing an account of these unheard-of exploits; for that was something that had happened to none of the knights-errant who, as the saying has it, had gone forth in quest of adventures, seeing that each of them had one or two chroniclers, as if ready at hand, who not only had set down their deeds, but had depicted their most trivial thoughts and amiable weaknesses, however well concealed they might be. The good knight of La Mancha surely could not have been so unfortunate as to have lacked what Platir and others like him had in abundance. And so I could not bring myself to believe that this gallant history could have remained thus lopped off and mutilated, and I could not but lay the blame upon the malignity of time, that devourer and consumer of all things, which must either have consumed it or kept it hidden.

On the other hand, I reflected that inasmuch as among the knight's books had been found such modern works as *The Disenchantments of Jealousy* and *The Nymphs and Shepherds of Henares*, his story likewise must be modern, and that even though it might not have been written down, it must remain in the memory of the good folk of his village and the surrounding ones. This thought left me somewhat confused and more than ever desirous of knowing the real and true story, the whole story, of the life and wondrous deeds of our famous Spaniard, Don Quixote, light and mirror of the chivalry of La Mancha, the first in our age and in these calamitous times to devote himself to the hardships and exercises of knight-errantry and to go about righting wrongs, succoring widows, and protecting damsels—damsels such as those who, mounted upon their palfreys and with riding-whip in hand, in full possession of their virginity, were in the habit of going from mountain to mountain and from valley to valley; for unless there were some villain, some rustic with an ax and hood, or some monstrous giant to force them, there were in times past maiden ladies who at the end of eighty years, during all which time they had not slept for a single day beneath a roof, would go to their graves as virginal as when their mothers had borne them.

If I speak of these things, it is for the reason that in this and in all other respects our gallant Quixote is deserving of constant memory and praise, and even I am not to be denied my share of it for my diligence and the labor to which I put myself in searching out the conclusion of this agreeable narrative; although if heaven, luck, and circumstance had not aided me, the world would have had to do without the pleasure and the pastime which anyone may enjoy who will read this work attentively for an hour or two. The manner in which it came about was as follows:

I was standing one day in the Alcaná, or market place, of Toledo when a lad came up to sell some old notebooks and other papers to a silk weaver who was there. As I am extremely fond of reading anything, even though it be but the scraps of paper in the streets, I followed my natural inclination and took one of the books, whereupon I at once perceived that it was written in characters which I recognized as Arabic. I recognized them, but reading them was another thing; and so I began looking around to see if there was any Spanish-speaking Moor near by who would be able to read them for me. It was not very hard to find such an interpreter, nor would it have been even if the tongue in question had been an older and a better one.[5] To make a long story short, chance brought a fellow my way; and when I told him what it was I wished and placed the book in his hands, he opened it in the middle and began reading and at once fell to laughing. When I asked him what the cause of his laughter was, he replied that it was a note which had been written in the margin.

I besought him to tell me the content of the note, and he, laughing still, went on, "As I told you, it is something in the margin here: 'This Dulcinea del Toboso, so often referred to, is said to have been the best hand at salting pigs of any woman in all La Mancha.' "

No sooner had I heard the name Dulcinea del Toboso than I was astonished and held in suspense, for at once the thought occurred to me that those notebooks must contain the history of Don Quixote. With this in mind I urged him to read me the title, and he proceeded to do so, turning the Arabic into Castilian upon the spot: *History of Don Quixote de la Mancha, Written by Cid Hamete Benengeli*[6] *Arabic Historian.* It was all I could do to conceal my satisfaction and, snatching them from the silk weaver, I bought from the lad all the papers and notebooks that he had for half a real; but if he had known or suspected how very much I wanted them, he might well have had more than six reales for them.

The Moor and I then betook ourselves to the cathedral cloister, where I requested him to translate for me into the Castilian tongue all the books that had to do with Don Quixote, adding nothing and subtracting nothing; and I offered him whatever payment he desired. He was content with two arrobas of raisins and two fanegas of wheat[7] and promised to translate them well and faithfully and with all dispatch. However, in order to facilitate matters, and also because I did not wish to let such a find as this out of my hands, I took the fellow home with me, where in a little more than a month and a half he translated the whole of the work just as you will find it set down here.

In the first of the books there was a very lifelike picture of the battle

<hr>

5. I.e., the Hebrew language.   6. Citing some ancient chronicle as the author's source and authority is very much in the tradition of the romances. *Benengeli*, incidentally, means "eggplant."   7. About 50 pounds of the first and 3 bushels of the second.

between Don Quixote and the Biscayan, the two being in precisely the same posture as described in the history, their swords upraised, the one covered by his buckler, the other with his cushion. As for the Biscayan's mule, you could see at the distance of a crossbow shot that it was one for hire. Beneath the Biscayan there was a rubric which read: "Don Sancho de Azpeitia," which must undoubtedly have been his name; while beneath the feet of Rocinante was another inscription: "Don Quixote." Rocinante was marvelously portrayed: so long and lank, so lean and flabby, so extremely consumptivelooking that one could well understand the justness and propriety with which the name of "hack" had been bestowed upon him.

Alongside Rocinante stood Sancho Panza, holding the halter of his ass, and below was the legend: "Sancho Zancas." The picture showed him with a big belly, a short body and long shanks, and that must have been where he got the names of Panza y Zancas[8] by which he is a number of times called in the course of the history. There are other small details that might be mentioned, but they are of little importance and have nothing to do with the truth of the story—and no story is bad so long as it is true.

If there is any objection to be raised against the veracity of the present one, it can be only that the author was an Arab, and that nation is known for its lying propensities; but even though they be our enemies, it may readily be understood that they would more likely have detracted from, rather than added to, the chronicle. So it seems to me, at any rate; for whenever he might and should deploy the resources of his pen in praise of so worthy a knight, the author appears to take pains to pass over the matter in silence; all of which in my opinion is ill done and ill conceived, for it should be the duty of historians to be exact, truthful, and dispassionate, and neither interest nor fear nor rancor nor affection should swerve them from the path of truth, whose mother is history, rival of time, depository of deeds, witness of the past, exemplar and adviser to the present, and the future's counselor. In this work, I am sure, will be found all that could be desired in the way of pleasant reading; and if it is lacking in any way, I maintain that this is the fault of that hound of an author rather than of the subject.

But to come to the point, the second part, according to the translation, began as follows:

As the two valorous and enraged combatants stood there, swords upraised and poised on high, it seemed from their bold mien as if they must surely be threatening heaven, earth, and hell itself. The first to let fall a blow was the choleric Biscayan, and he came down with such force and fury that, had not his sword been deflected in mid-air, that single stroke would have sufficed to put an end to this fearful combat and to all our knight's adventures at the same time; but fortune, which was reserving him for greater things, turned aside his adversary's blade in such a manner that, even though it fell upon his left shoulder, it did him no other damage than to strip him completely of his armor on that side, carrying with it a good part

8. I.e., Paunch and Shanks.

the heart of our hero of La Mancha as he saw himself treated in this
fashion? It may merely be said that he once more reared himself in the
stirrups, laid hold of his sword with both hands, and dealt the Biscayan
such a blow, over the cushion and upon the head, that, even so good a
defense proving useless, it was as if a mountain had fallen upon his enemy.
The latter now began bleeding through the mouth, nose, and ears; he
seemed about to fall from his mule, and would have fallen, no doubt, if
he had not grasped the beast about the neck, but at that moment his feet
slipped from the stirrups and his arms let go, and the mule, frightened by
the terrible blow, began running across the plain, hurling its rider to the
earth with a few quick plunges.

Don Quixote stood watching all this very calmly. When he saw his
enemy fall, he leaped from his horse, ran over very nimbly, and thrust the
point of his sword into the Biscayan's eyes, calling upon him at the same
time to surrender or otherwise he would cut off his head. The Biscayan
was so bewildered that he was unable to utter a single word in reply, and
things would have gone badly with him, so blind was Don Quixote in his
rage, if the ladies of the coach, who up to then had watched the struggle
in dismay, had not come up to him at this point and begged him with
many blandishments to do them the very great favor of sparing their squire's
life.

To which Don Quixote replied with much haughtiness and dignity,
"Most certainly, lovely ladies, I shall be very happy to do that which you
ask of me, but upon one conditon and understanding, and that is that this
knight promise me that he will go to El Toboso and present himself in my
behalf before Doña Dulcinea, in order that she may do with him as she
may see fit."

Trembling and disconsolate, the ladies did not pause to discuss Don
Quixote's request, but without so much as inquiring who Dulcinea might
be they promised him that the squire would fulfill that which was commanded of him.

"Very well, then, trusting in your word, I will do him no further harm,
even though he has well deserved it."

CHAPTER 10

*Of the pleasing conversation that took place between Don Quixote and
Sancho Panza, his squire.*

By this time Sancho Panza had got to his feet, somewhat the worse for
wear as the result of the treatment he had received from the friars' lads. He
had been watching the battle attentively and praying God in his heart to
give the victory to his master, Don Quixote, in order that he, Sancho,
might gain some island where he could go to be governor as had been
promised him. Seeing now that the combat was over and the knight was

returning to mount Rocinante once more, he went up to hold the stirrup for him; but first he fell on his knees in front of him and, taking his hand, kissed it and said, "May your Grace be pleased, Señor Don Quixote, to grant me the governorship of that island which you have won in this deadly affray; for however large it may be, I feel that I am indeed capable of governing it as well as any man in this world has ever done."

To which Don Quixote replied, "Be advised, brother Sancho, that this adventure and other similar ones have nothing to do with islands; they are affairs of the crossroads in which one gains nothing more than a broken head or an ear the less. Be patient, for there will be others which will not only make you a governor, but more than that."

Sancho thanked him very much and, kissing his hand again and the skirt of his cuirass, he assisted him up on Rocinante's back, after which the squire bestraddled his own mount and started jogging along behind his master, who was now going at a good clip. Without pausing for any further converse with those in the coach, the knight made for a near-by wood, with Sancho following as fast as his beast could trot; but Rocinante was making such speed that the ass and its rider were left behind, and it was necessary to call out to Don Quixote to pull up and wait for them. He did so, reining in Rocinante until the weary Sancho had drawn abreast of him.

"It strikes me, sir," said the squire as he reached his master's side, "that it would be better for us to take refuge in some church; for in view of the way you have treated that one with whom you were fighting, it would be small wonder if they did not lay the matter before the Holy Brotherhood[9] and have us arrested; and faith, if they do that, we shall have to sweat a-plenty before we come out of jail."

"Be quiet," said Don Quixote. "And where have you ever seen, or read of, a knight being brought to justice no matter how many homicides he might have committed?"

"I know nothing about omecils,"[1] replied Sancho, "nor ever in my life did I bear one to anybody; all I know is that the Holy Brotherhood has something to say about those who go around fighting on the highway, and I want nothing of it."

"Do not let it worry you," said Don Quixote, "for I will rescue you from the hands of the Chaldeans, not to speak of the Brotherhood. But answer me upon your life: have you ever seen a more valorous knight than I on all the known face of the earth? Have you ever read in the histories of any other who had more mettle in the attack, more perseverance in sustaining it, more dexterity in wounding his enemy, or more skill in overthrowing him?"

"The truth is," said Sancho, "I have never read any history whatsoever, for I do not know how to read or write; but what I would wager is that in all the days of my life I have never served a more courageous master than your Grace; I only hope your courage is not paid for in the place that I

---

9. A tribunal instituted by Ferdinand and Isabella at the end of the fifteenth century to punish highway robbers.   1. In the original, a word play on *homecidio-omecillo*. Not to bear an *omecillo* to anybody means not to bear a grudge; and good-natured Sancho does not.

have mentioned. What I would suggest is that your Grace allow me to do something for that ear, for there is much blood coming from it, and I have here in my saddlebags some lint and a little white ointment."

"We could well dispense with all that," said Don Quixote, "if only I had remembered to bring along a vial of Fierabrás's[2] balm, a single drop of which saves time and medicines."

"What vial and what balm is that?" inquired Sancho Panza.

"It is a balm the receipt[3] for which I know by heart; with it one need have no fear of death nor think of dying from any wound. I shall make some of it and give it to you; and thereafter, whenever in any battle you see my body cut in two—as very often happens—all that is necessary is for you to take the part that lies on the ground, before the blood has congealed, and fit it very neatly and with great nicety upon the other part that remains in the saddle, taking care to adjust it evenly and exactly. Then you will give me but a couple of swallows of the balm of which I have told you, and you will see me sounder than an apple in no time at all."

"If that is so," said Panza, "I herewith renounce the governorship of the island you promised me and ask nothing other in payment of my many and faithful services than that your Grace give me the receipt for this wonderful potion, for I am sure that it would be worth more than two reales the ounce anywhere, and that is all I need for a life of ease and honor. But may I be so bold as to ask how much it costs to make it?"

"For less than three reales you can make something like six quarts," Don Quixote told him.

"Sinner that I am!" exclaimed Sancho. "Then why does your Grace not make some at once and teach me also?"

"Hush, my friend," said the knight, "I mean to teach you greater secrets than that and do you greater favors; but, for the present, let us look after this ear of mine, for it is hurting me more than I like."

Sancho thereupon took the lint and the ointment from his saddlebags; but when Don Quixote caught a glimpse of his helmet, he almost went out of his mind and, laying his hand upon his sword and lifting his eyes heavenward, he cried, "I make a vow to the Creator of all things and to the four holy Gospels in all their fullness of meaning that I will lead from now on the life that the great Marquis of Mantua did after he had sworn to avenge the death of his nephew Baldwin: not to eat bread of a tablecloth, not to embrace his wife, and other things which, although I am unable to recall them, we will look upon as understood—all this until I shall have wreaked an utter vengeance upon the one who has perpetrated such an outrage upon me."

"But let me remind your Grace," said Sancho when he heard these words, "that if the knight fulfills that which was commanded of him, by going to present himself before my lady Dulcinea del Toboso, then he will have paid his debt to you and merits no further punishment at your hands, unless it be for some fresh offense."

---

2. Fierabrás is a giant Saracen healer in the medieval epics of the Twelve Peers (cf. note 1, p. 1843).
3. Recipe.

"You have spoken very well and to the point," said Don Quixote, "and so I annul the vow I have just made insofar as it has to do with any further vengeance, but I make it and confirm it anew so far as leading the life of which I have spoken is concerned, until such time as I shall have obtained by force of arms from some other knight another headpiece as good as this. And do not think, Sancho, that I am making smoke out of straw; there is one whom I well may imitate in this matter, for the same thing happened in all literalness in the case of Mambrino's helmet which cost Sacripante so dear."[4]

"I wish," said Sancho, "that your Grace would send all such oaths to the devil, for they are very bad for the health and harmful for the conscience as well. Tell me, please; supposing that for many days to come we meet no man wearing a helmet, then what are we to do? Must you still keep your vow in spite of all the inconveniences and discomforts, such as sleeping with your clothes on, not sleeping in any town, and a thousand other penances contained in the oath of that old madman of a Marquis of Mantua, an oath which you would now revive? Mark you, sir, along all these roads you meet no men of arms but only muleteers and carters, who not only do not wear helmets but quite likely have never heard tell of them in all their livelong days."

"In that you are wrong," said Don Quixote, "for we shall not be at these crossroads for the space of two hours before we shall see more men of arms than came to Albraca to win the fair Angélica."[5] "Very well, then," said Sancho, "so be it, and pray God that all turns out for the best so that I may at last win that island that is costing me so dearly, and then let me die."

"I have already told you, Sancho, that you are to give no thought to that; should the island fail, there is the kingdom of Denmark or that of Sobradisa,[6] which would fit you like a ring on your finger, and you ought, moreover, to be happy to be on *terra firma*.[7] But let us leave all this for some other time, while you look and see if you have something in those saddlebags for us to eat, after which we will go in search of some castle where we may lodge for the night and prepare that balm of which I was telling you, for I swear to God that my ear is paining me greatly."

"I have here an onion, a little cheese, and a few crusts of bread," said Sancho, "but they are not victuals fit for a valiant knight like your grace."

"How little you know about it!" replied Don Quixote. "I would inform you, Sancho, that it is a point of honor with knights-errant to go for a month at a time without eating, and when they do eat, it is whatever may be at hand. You would certainly know that if you had read the histories as I have. There are many of them, and in none have I found any mention of knights eating unless it was by chance or at some sumptuous banquet that was tendered them; on other days they fasted. And even though it is

4. The enchanted helmet of Mambrino, a Moorish king, is stolen by Rinaldo in the fifteenth-century epic poem *Orlando Innamorato* ("Roland in Love") by Matteo Maria Boiardo.   5. Also an allusion to an episode in Boiardo's poem.   6. A nonexistent realm.   7. *Solid earth*, here also *Firm Island*, an imaginary final destination for the squires of knights-errant.

well understood that, being men like us, they could not go without food entirely, any more than they could fail to satisfy the other necessities of nature, nevertheless, since they spent the greater part of their lives in forest and desert places without any cook to prepare their meals, their diet ordinarily consisted of rustic viands such as those that you now offer me. And so, Sancho my friend, do not be grieved at that which pleases me, nor seek to make the world over, nor to unhinge the institution of knight-errantry."

"Pardon me, your Grace," said Sancho, "but seeing that, as I have told you I do not know how to read or write, I am consequently not familiar with the rules of the knightly calling. Hereafter, I will stuff my saddlebags with all manner of dried fruit for your Grace, but inasmuch as I am not a knight, I shall lay in for myself a stock of fowls and other more substantial fare."

"I am not saying, Sancho, that it is incumbent upon knights-errant to eat only those fruits of which you speak; what I am saying is that their ordinary sustenance should consist of fruit and a few herbs such as are to be found in the fields and with which they are well acquainted, as am I myself."

"It is a good thing," said Sancho, "to know those herbs, for, so far as I can see, we are going to have need of that knowledge one of these days."

With this, he brought out the articles he had mentioned, and the two of them ate in peace, and most companionably. Being desirous, however, of seeking a lodging for the night, they did not tarry long over their humble and unsavory repast. They then mounted and made what haste they could that they might arrive at a shelter before nightfall but the sun failed them, and with it went the hope of attaining their wish. As the day ended they found themselves beside some goatherds' huts, and they accordingly decided to spend the night there. Sancho was as much disappointed at their not having reached a town as his master was content with sleeping under the open sky; for it seemed to Don Quixote that every time this happened it merely provided him with yet another opportunity to establish his claim to the title of knight-errant.

(Of Goatherds, Roaming Shepherdesses, and Unrequited Loves)

CHAPTER 11

Of what happened to Don Quixote in the company of certain goatherds.

He was received by the herders with good grace, and Sancho having looked after Rocinante and the ass to the best of his ability, the knight, drawn by the aroma, went up to where some pieces of goat's meat were simmering in a pot over the fire. He would have liked then and there to see if they were done well enough to be transferred from pot to stomach, but he refrained in view of the fact that his hosts were already taking them off the fire. Spreading a few sheepskins on the ground, they hastily laid their rustic board and invited the strangers to share what there was of it. There were six of them altogether who belonged to that fold, and after they had urged Don Quixote, with rude politeness, to seat himself upon a small trough which they had turned upside down for the purpose, they took their own places upon the sheep hides round about. While his master sat there, Sancho remained standing to serve him the cup, which was made of horn. When the knight perceived this, he addressed his squire as follows:

"In order, Sancho, that you may see the good that there is in knight-errantry and how speedily those who follow the profession, no matter what the nature of their service may be, come to be honored and esteemed in the eyes of the world, I would have you here in the company of these good folk seat yourself at my side, that you may be even as I who am your master and natural lord, and eat from my plate and drink from where I drink; for of knight-errantry one may say the same as of love: that it makes all things equal."

"Many thanks!" said Sancho, "but if it is all the same to your Grace, providing there is enough to go around, I can eat just as well, or better, standing up and alone as I can seated beside an emperor. And if the truth must be told, I enjoy much more that which I eat in my own corner without any bowings and scrapings, even though it be only bread and onions, than I do a meal of roast turkey where I have to chew slowly, drink little, be always wiping my mouth, and can neither sneeze nor cough if I feel like it, nor do any of those other things that you can when you are free and alone.

"And so, my master," he went on, "these honors that your Grace would confer upon me as your servant and a follower of knight-errantry—which I am, being your Grace's squire—I would have you convert, if you will, into other things that will be of more profit and advantage to me; for though I hereby acknowledge them as duly received, I renounce them from this time forth to the end of the world."

"But for all that," said Don Quixote, "you must sit down; for whosoever humbleth himself, him God will exalt." And, laying hold of his squire's arm, he compelled him to take a seat beside him.

The goatherds did not understand all this jargon about squires and knights-errant; they did nothing but eat, keep silent, and study their guests, who very dexterously and with much appetite were stowing away chunks of meat as big as your fist. When the meat course was finished, they laid out upon the sheepskins a great quantity of dried acorns and half a cheese, which was harder than if it had been made of mortar. The drinking horn all this while was not idle but went the rounds so often—now full, now empty, like the bucket of a water wheel—that they soon drained one of the two wine bags that were on hand. After Don Quixote had well satisfied his stomach, he took up a handful of acorns and, gazing at them attentively, fell into a soliloquy.

"Happy the age and happy those centuries to which the ancients gave the name of golden, and not because gold, which is so esteemed in this iron age of ours, was then to be had without toil, but because those who lived in that time did not know the meaning of the words 'thine' and 'mine.' In that blessed year all things were held in common, and to gain his daily sustenance no labor was required of any man save to reach forth his hand and take it from the sturdy oaks that stood liberally inviting him with their sweet and seasoned fruit. The clear-running fountains and rivers in magnificent abundance offered him palatable and transparent water for his thirst; while in the clefts of the rocks and the hollows of the trees the wise and busy honey-makers set up their republic so that any hand whatever might avail itself, fully and freely, of the fertile harvest which their fragrant toil had produced. The vigorous cork trees of their own free will and grace, without the asking, shed their broad, light bark with which men began to cover their dwellings, erected upon rude stakes merely as a protection against the inclemency of the heavens.

"All then was peace, all was concord and friendship; the crooked plowshare had not as yet grievously laid open and pried into the merciful bowels of our first mother, who without any forcing on man's part yielded her spacious fertile bosom on every hand for the satisfaction, sustenance, and delight of her first sons. Then it was that lovely and unspoiled young shepherdesses, with locks that were sometimes braided, sometimes flowing, went roaming from valley to valley and hillock to hillock with no more garments than were needed to cover decently that which modesty requires and always had required should remain covered. Nor were their adornments such as those in use today—of Tyrian purple and silk worked up in tortured patterns; a few green leaves of burdock or of ivy, and they were as splendidly and as becomingly clad as our ladies of the court with all the rare and exotic tricks of fashion that idle curiosity has taught them.

"Thoughts of love, also, in those days were set forth as simply as the simple hearts that conceived them, without any roundabout and artificial play of words by way of ornament. Fraud, deceit, and malice had not yet come to mingle with truth and plain-speaking. Justice kept its own domain, where favor and self-interest dared not trespass, dared not impair her rights, becloud, and persecute her as they now do. There was no such thing then as arbitrary judgments, for the reason that there was no one to judge or be judged. Maidens in all their modesty, as I have said, went where they would and unattended; whereas in this hateful age of ours none is safe, even though she go to hide and shut herself up in some new labyrinth like that of Crete; for in spite of all her seclusion, through chinks and crevices or borne upon the air, the amorous plague with all its cursed importunities will find her out and lead her to her ruin.

"It was for the safety of such as these, as time went on and depravity increased, that the order of knights-errant was instituted, for the protection of damsels, the aid of widows and orphans, and the succoring of the needy. It is to this order that I belong, my brothers, and I thank you for the welcome and the kindly treatment that you have accorded to me and my squire. By natural law, all living men are obliged to show favor to knights-errant, yet without being aware of this you have received and entertained me; and so it is with all possible good will that I acknowledge your own good will to me."

This long harangue on the part of our knight—it might very well have been dispensed with—was all due to the acorns they had given him, which had brought back to memory the age of gold; whereupon the whim had seized him to indulge in this futile harangue with the goatherds as his auditors. They listened in open-mouthed wonderment, saying not a word, and Sancho himself kept quiet and went on munching acorns, taking occasion very frequently to pay a visit to the second wine bag, which they had suspended from a cork tree to keep it cool.

It took Don Quixote much longer to finish his speech than it did to put away his supper; and when he was through, one of the goatherds addressed him.

"In order that your Grace may say with more truth that we have received you with readiness and good will, we desire to give you solace and contentment by having one of our comrades, who will be here soon, sing for you. He is a very bright young fellow and deeply in love, and what is more, you could not ask for anything better than to hear him play the three-stringed lute."

Scarcely had he done saying this when the sound of a rebec was heard, and shortly afterward the one who played it appeared. He was a goodlooking youth, around twenty-two years of age. His companions asked him if he had had his supper, and when he replied that he had, the one who had spoken to Don Quixote said to him, "Well, then, Antonio, you can give us the pleasure of hearing you sing, in order that this gentleman whom we have as our guest may see that we of the woods and mountains also know something about music. We have been telling him how clever you are, and now we want you to show him that we were speaking the truth. And so I beg you by all means to sit down and sing us that lovesong of yours that your uncle the prebendary composed for you and which the villagers liked so well."

"With great pleasure," the lad replied, and without any urging he seated himself on the stump of an oak that had been felled and, tuning up his rebec, soon began singing, very prettily, the following ballad:

The Ballad That Antonio Sang

I know well that thou dost love me,
My Olalla, even though
Eyes of thine have never spoken—
Love's mute tongues—to tell me so.
    Since I know thou knowest my passion,
Of thy love I am more sure:
No love ever was unhappy
When it was both frank and pure.
    True it is, Olalla, sometimes
Thou a heart of bronze hast shown,
And it seemed to me that bosom,
White and fair, was made of stone.
    Yet in spite of all repulses

And a chastity so cold,
It appeared that I Hope's garment
By the hem did clutch and hold.

For my faith I ever cherished;
It would rise to meet the bait;
Spurned, it never did diminish;
Favored, it preferred to wait.

Love, they say, hath gentle manners:
Thus it is it shows its face;
Then may I take hope, Olalla,
Trust to win a longed for grace.

If devotion hath the power
Hearts to move and make them kind,
Let the loyalty I've shown thee
Plead my cause, be kept in mind.

For if thou didst note my costume,
More than once thou must have seen,
Worn upon a simple Monday
Sunday's garb so bright and clean.

Love and brightness go together.
Dost thou ask the reason why
I thus deck myself on Monday?
It is but to catch thine eye.

I say nothing of the dances
I have danced for thy sweet sake;
Nor the serenades I've sung thee
Till the first cock did awake.

Nor will I repeat my praises
Of that beauty all can see;
True my words but oft unwelcome—
Certain lasses hated me.

One girl there is, I well remember—
She's Teresa on the hill—
Said, "You think you love an angel,
But she is a monkey still.

"Thanks to all her many trinkets
And her artificial hair
And her many aids to beauty,
Love's own self she would ensnare."

She was lying, I was angry,
And her cousin, very bold,
Challenged me upon my honor;
What ensued need not be told.

Highflown words do not become me;
I'm a plain and simple man.
Pure the love that I would offer,
Serving thee as best I can.

> Silken are the bonds of marriage,
>   When two hearts do intertwine;
>   Mother Church the yoke will fasten;
>   Bow your neck and I'll bow mine.
>   Or if not, my word I'll give thee,
>   From these mountains I'll come down—
>   Saint most holy be my witness—
>   Wearing a Capuchin gown.

With this the goatherd brought his song to a close, and although Don Quixote begged him to sing some more, Sancho Panza would not hear of this as he was too sleepy for any more ballads.

"Your Grace," he said to his master, "would do well to find out at once where his bed is to be, for the labor that these good men have to perform all day long does not permit them to stay up all night singing."

"I understand, Sancho," replied Don Quixote. "I perceive that those visits to the wine bag call for sleep rather than music as a recompense."

"It tastes well enough to all of us, God be praised," said Sancho.

"I am not denying that," said his master; "but go ahead and settle yourself down wherever you like. As for men of my profession, they prefer to keep vigil. But all the same, Sancho, perhaps you had better look after this ear, for it is paining me more than I like."

Sancho started to do as he was commanded, but one of the goatherds, when he saw the wound, told him not to bother, that he would place a remedy upon it that would heal it in no time. Taking a few leaves of rosemary, of which there was a great deal growing thereabouts, he mashed them in his mouth and, mixing them with a little salt, laid them on the ear, with the assurance that no other medicine was needed; and this proved to be the truth.

CHAPTER 12

Of the story that one of the goatherds told to Don Quixote and the others.

Just then, another lad came up, one of those who brought the goatherds their provisions from the village.

"Do you know what's happening down there, my friends?" he said.

"How should we know?" one of the men answered him.

"In that case," the lad went on, "I must tell you that the famous student and shepherd known as Grisóstomo died this morning, muttering that the cause of his death was the love he had for that bewitched lass of a Marcela, daughter of the wealthy Guillermo—you know, the one who's been going around in these parts dressed like a shepherdess."

"For love of Marcela, you say?" one of the herders spoke up.

"That is what I'm telling you," replied the other lad. "And the best part of it is that he left directions in his will that he was to be buried in the field, as if he were a Moor, and that his grave was to be at the foot of the cliff where the Cork Tree Spring is; for, according to report, and he is supposed to have said so himself, that is the place where he saw her for the first time. There were other provisions, which the clergy of the village say cannot be carried out, nor would it be proper to fulfill them, seeing that they savor of heathen practices. But Grisóstomo's good friend, the student Ambrosio, who also dresses like a shepherd, insists that everything must be done to the letter, and as a result there is great excitement in the village.

"Nevertheless, from all I can hear, they will end by doing as Ambrosio and Grisóstomo's other friends desire, and tomorrow they will bury him with great ceremony in the place that I have mentioned. I believe it is going to be something worth seeing; at any rate, I mean to see it, even though it is too far for me to be able to return to the village before nightfall."

"We will all do the same," said the other goatherds. "We will cast lots to see who stays to watch the goats."

"That is right, Pedro," said one of their number, "but it will not be necessary to go to the trouble of casting lots. I will take care of the flocks for all of us; and do not think that I am being generous or that I am not as curious as the rest of you; it is simply that I cannot walk on account of the splinter I picked up in this foot the other day."

"Well, we thank you just the same," said Pedro.

Don Quixote then asked Pedro to tell him more about the dead man and the shepherd lass; to which the latter replied that all he knew was that Grisóstomo was a rich gentleman who had lived in a near-by village. He had been a student for many years at Salamanca and then had returned to his birthplace with the reputation of being very learned and well read; he was especially noted for his knowledge of the science of the stars and what the sun and moon were doing up there in the heavens, "for he would promptly tell us when their clips was to come."

"*Eclipse,* my friend, not *clips,*" said Don Quixote, "is the name applied to the darkening-over of those major luminaries."

But Pedro, not pausing for any trifles, went on with his story. "He could also tell when the year was going to be plentiful or estil—"

"*Sterile,* you mean to say, friend—"

"*Sterile* or *estil,*" said Pedro, "it all comes out the same in the end. But I can tell you one thing, that his father and his friends, who believed in him, did just as he advised them and they became rich; for he would say to them, 'This year, sow barley and not wheat'; and again, 'Sow chickpeas and not barley'; or, 'This season there will be a good crop of oil[8] but the three following ones you will not get a drop.' "

"That science," Don Quixote explained, "is known as astrology."

"I don't know what it's called," said Pedro, "but he knew all this and more yet. Finally, not many months after he returned from Salamanca, he appeared one day dressed like a shepherd with crook and sheepskin jacket; for he had resolved to lay aside the long gown that he wore as a

8. Olive oil.

scholar, and in this he was joined by Ambrosio, a dear friend of his and the companion of his studies. I forgot to tell you that Grisóstomo was a great one for composing verses; he even wrote the carols for Christmas Eve and the plays that were performed at Corpus Christi by the lads of our village, and everyone said that they were the best ever.

"When the villagers saw the two scholars coming out dressed like shepherds, they were amazed and could not imagine what was the reason for such strange conduct on their part. It was about that time that Grisóstomo's father died and left him the heir to a large fortune, consisting of land and chattels, no small quantity of cattle, and a considerable sum of money, of all of which the young man was absolute master; and, to tell the truth, he deserved it, for he was very sociable and charitably inclined, a friend to all worthy folk, and he had a face that was like a benediction. Afterward it was learned that if he had changed his garments like this, it was only that he might be able to wander over the wastelands on the trail of that shepherdess Marcela of whom our friend was speaking, for the poor fellow had fallen in love with her. And now I should like to tell you, for it is well that you should know, just who this lass is; for it may be—indeed, there is no maybe about it—you will never hear the like in all the days of your life, though you live to be older than Sarna."

"You should say *Sarah*," Don Quixote corrected him; for he could not bear hearing the goatherd using the wrong words all the time.[9]

"The itch," said Pedro, "lives long enough; and if, sir, you go on interrupting me at every word, we'll never be through in a year."

"Pardon me, friend," said Don Quixote, "it was only because there is so great a difference between Sarna and Sarah that I pointed it out to you; but you have given me a very good answer, for the itch does live longer than Sarah; and so go on with your story, and I will not contradict you any more."

"I was about to say, then, my dear sir," the goatherd went on, "that in our village there was a farmer who was richer still than Grisóstomo's father. His name was Guillermo, and, over and above his great wealth, God gave him a daughter whose mother, the most highly respected woman in these parts, died in bearing her. It seems to me I can see the good lady now, with that face that rivaled the sun and moon; and I remember, above all, what a friend she was to the poor, for which reason I believe that her soul at this very moment must be enjoying God's presence in the other world.

"Grieving for the loss of so excellent a wife, Guillermo himself died, leaving his daughter Marcela, now a rich young woman, in the custody of one of her uncles, a priest who holds a benefice in our village. The girl grew up with such beauty as to remind us of her mother, beautiful as that lady had been. By the time she was fourteen or fifteen no one looked at her without giving thanks to God who had created such comeliness, and almost all were hopelessly in love with her. Her uncle kept her very closely shut up, but, for all of that, word of her great beauty spread to such an

---

9. Actually in this case the goatherd is not really wrong, for *sarna* means "itch" and "older than the itch" was a proverbial expression.

extent that by reason of it, as much as on account of the girl's wealth, her uncle found himself besought and importuned not only by the young men of our village, but by those for leagues around who desired to have her for a wife.

"But he, an upright Christian, although he wished to marry her off as soon as she was of age, had no desire to do so without her consent, not that he had any eye to the gain and profit which the custody of his niece's property brought him while her marriage was deferred. Indeed, this much was said in praise of the good priest in more than one circle of the village; for I would have you know, Sir Knight, that in these little places everything is discussed and becomes a subject of gossip; and you may rest assured, as I am for my part, that a priest must be more than ordinarily good if his parishioners feel bound to speak well of him, especially in the small towns."

"That is true," said Don Quixote, "but go on. I like your story very much, and you, good Pedro, tell it with very good grace."

"May the Lord's grace never fail me, for that is what counts. But to go on: Although the uncle set forth to his niece the qualities of each one in particular of the many who sought her hand, begging her to choose and marry whichever one she pleased, she never gave him any answer other than this: that she did not wish to marry at all, since being but a young girl she did not feel that she was equal to bearing the burdens of matrimony. As her reasons appeared to be proper and just, the uncle did not insist but thought he would wait until she was a little older, when she would be capable of selecting someone to her taste. For, he said, and quite right he was, parents ought not to impose a way of life upon their children against the latters' will. And then, one fine day, lo and behold, there was the finical Marcela turned shepherdess; and without paying any attention to her uncle or all those of the village who advised against it, she set out to wander through the fields with the other lasses, guarding flocks as they did.

"Well, the moment she appeared in public and her beauty was uncovered for all to see, I really cannot tell you how many rich young bachelors, gentlemen, and farmers proceeded to don a shepherd's garb and go to make love to her in the meadows. One of her suitors, as I have told you, was our deceased friend, and it is said that he did not love but adored her. But you must not think that because Marcela chose so free and easy a life, and one that offers little or no privacy, that she was thereby giving the faintest semblance of encouragement to those who would disparage her modesty and prudence; rather, so great was the vigilance with which she looked after her honor that of all those who waited upon her and solicited her favors, none could truly say that she had given him the slightest hope of attaining his desire.

"For although she does not flee nor shun the company and conversation of the shepherds, treating them in courteous and friendly fashion, the moment she discovers any intentions on their part, even though it be the just and holy one of matrimony, she hurls them from her like a catapult. As a result, she is doing more damage in this land than if a plague had fallen upon it; for her beauty and graciousness win the hearts of all who would serve her, but her disdain and the disillusionment it brings lead them in the end to despair, and then they can only call her cruel and ungrateful, along with other similar epithets that reveal all too plainly the state of mind that prompts them. If you were to stay here some time, sir, you would hear these uplands and valleys echo with the laments of those who have followed her only to be deceived.

"Not far from here is a place where there are a couple of dozen tall beeches, and there is not a one of them on whose smooth bark Marcela's name has not been engraved; and above some of these inscriptions you will find a crown, as if by this her lover meant to indicate that she deserved to wear the garland of beauty above all the women on the earth. Here a shepherd sighs and there another voices his lament. Now are to be heard amorous ballads, and again despairing ditties. One will spend all the hours of the night seated at the foot of some oak or rock without once closing his tearful eyes, and the morning sun will find him there, stupefied and lost in thought. Another, without giving truce or respite to his sighs, will lie stretched upon the burning sands in the full heat of the most exhausting summer noontide, sending up his complaint to merciful Heaven.

"And, meanwhile, over this one and that one, over one and all, the beauteous Marcela triumphs and goes her own way, free and unconcerned. All those of us who know her are waiting to see how far her pride will carry her, and who will be the fortunate man who will succeed in taming this terrible creature and thus come into possession of a beauty so matchless as hers. Knowing all this that I have told you to be undoubtedly true, I can readily believe this lad's story about the cause of Grisóstomo's death. And so I advise you, sir, not to fail to be present tomorrow at his burial; it will be well worth seeing, for he has many friends, and the place is not half a league from here."

"I will make a point of it," said Don Quixote, "and I thank you for the pleasure you have given me by telling me so delightful a tale."

"Oh," said the goatherd, "I do not know the half of the things that have happened to Marcela's lovers; but it is possible that tomorrow we may meet along the way some shepherd who will tell us more. And now it would be well for you to go and sleep under cover, for the night air may not be good for your wound, though with the remedy that has been put on it there is not much to fear."

Sancho Panza, who had been sending the goatherd to the devil for talking so much, now put in a word with his master, urging him to come and sleep in Pedro's hut. Don Quixote did so; and all the rest of the night was spent by him in thinking of his lady Dulcinea, in imitation of Marcela's lovers. As for Sancho, he made himself comfortable between Rocinante and the ass and at once dropped off to sleep, not like a lovelorn swain but, rather, like a man who has had a sound kicking that day.

CHAPTER 13

In which is brought to a close the story of the shepherdess Marcela, along with other events.

Day had barely begun to appear upon the balconies of the east when five or six goatherds arose and went to awaken Don Quixote and tell him that if he was still of a mind to go see Grisóstomo's famous burial they would keep him company. The knight, desiring nothing better, ordered Sancho to saddle at once, which was done with much dispatch, and then they all set out forthwith.

They had not gone more than a quarter of a league when, upon crossing a footpath, they saw coming toward them six shepherds clad in black sheepskins and with garlands of cypress and bitter rosebay on their heads. Each of them carried a thick staff made of the wood of the holly, and with them came two gentlemen on horseback in handsome traveling attire, accompanied by three lads on foot. As the two parties met they greeted each other courteously, each inquiring as to the other's destination, whereupon they learned that they were all going to the burial, and so continued to ride along together.

Speaking to his companion, one of them said, "I think, Señor Vivaldo, that we are going to be well repaid for the delay it will cost us to see this famous funeral; for famous it must surely be, judging by the strange things that these shepherds have told us of the dead man and the homicidal shepherdess."

"I think so too," agreed Vivaldo. "I should be willing to delay our journey not one day, but four, for the sake of seeing it."

Don Quixote then asked them what it was they had heard of Marcela and Grisóstomo. The traveler replied that on that very morning they had fallen in with those shepherds and, seeing them so mournfully trigged out, had asked them what the occasion for it was. One of the fellows had then told them of the beauty and strange demeanor of a shepherdess by the name of Marcela, her many suitors, and the death of this Grisóstomo, to whose funeral they were bound. He related, in short, the entire story as Don Quixote had heard it from Pedro.

Changing the subject, the gentleman called Vivaldo inquired of Don Quixote what it was that led him to go armed in that manner in a land that was so peaceful.

"The calling that I profess," replied Don Quixote, "does not permit me to do otherwise. An easy pace, pleasure, and repose—those things were invented for delicate courtiers; but toil, anxiety, and arms—they are for those whom the world knows as knights-errant, of whom I, though unworthy, am the very least."

No sooner had they heard this than all of them immediately took him for a madman. By way of assuring himself further and seeing what kind of madness it was of which Don Quixote was possessed, Vivaldo now asked him what was meant by the term knights-errant.

"Have not your Worships read the annals and the histories of England that treat of the famous exploits of King Arthur, who in our Castilian balladry is always called King Artús? According to a very old tradition that is common throughout the entire realm of Great Britain, this king did not die, but by an act of enchantment was changed into a raven; and in due course of time he is to return and reign once more, recovering his kingdom and his scepter; for which reason, from that day to this, no Englishman is known to have killed one of those birds. It was, moreover, in the time of that good king that the famous order of the Knights of the Round Table was instituted; and as for the love of Sir Lancelot of the Lake and Queen Guinevere, everything took place exactly as the story has it, their confidante and go-between being the honored matron Quintañona; whence comes that charming ballad that is such a favorite with us Spaniards:

> Never was there a knight
> So served by maid and dame
> As the one they call Sir Lancelot
> When from Britain he came—

to carry on the gentle, pleasing course of his loves and noble deeds.

"From that time forth, the order of chivalry was passed on and propagated from one individual to another until it had spread through many and various parts of the world. Among those famed for their exploits was the valiant Amadis of Gaul, with all his sons and grandsons to the fifth generation; and there was also the brave Felixmarte of Hircania, and the never sufficiently praised Tirant lo Blanch; and in view of the fact that he lived in our own day, almost, we came near to seeing, hearing, and conversing with that other courageous knight, Don Belianís of Greece.

"And that, gentlemen, is what it means to be a knight-errant, and what I have been telling you of is the order of chivalry which such a knight professes, an order to which, as I have already informed you, I, although a sinner, have the honor of belonging; for I have made the same profession as have those other knights. That is why it is you find me in these wild and lonely places, riding in quest of adventure, being resolved to offer my arm and my person in the most dangerous undertaking fate may have in store for me, that I may be of aid to the weak and needy."

Listening to this speech, the travelers had some while since come to the conclusion that Don Quixote was out of his mind, and were likewise able to perceive the peculiar nature of his madness, and they wondered at it quite as much as did all those who encountered it for the first time. Being endowed with a ready wit and a merry disposition and thinking to pass the time until they reached the end of the short journey which, so he was told, awaited them before they should arrive at the mountain where the burial was to take place, Vivaldo decided to give him a further opportunity of displaying his absurdities.

"It strikes me, Sir Knight-errant," he said, "that your Grace has espoused one of the most austere professions to be found anywhere on earth—even more austere, if I am not mistaken, than that of the Carthusian monks."

"Theirs may be as austere as ours," Don Quixote replied, "but that it is as necessary I am very much inclined to doubt. For if the truth be told, the soldier who carries out his captain's order does no less than the captain who gives the order. By that I mean to say that the religious, in all peace and tranquility, pray to Heaven for earth's good, but we soldiers and knights put their prayers into execution by defending with the might of our good right arms and at the edge of the sword those things for which they pray; and we do this not under cover of a roof but under the open sky, beneath the insufferable rays of the summer sun and the biting cold of winter. Thus we become the ministers of God on earth, and our arms the means by which He executes His decrees. And just as war and all the things that have to do with it are impossible without toil, sweat, and anxiety, it follows that those who have taken upon themselves such a profession must unquestionably labor harder than do those who in peace and tranquility and at their ease pray God to favor the ones who can do little in their own behalf.

"I do not mean to say—I should not think of saying—that the state of knight-errant is as holy as that of the cloistered monk; I merely would imply, from what I myself endure, that ours is beyond a doubt the more laborious and arduous calling, more beset by hunger and thirst, more wretched, ragged, and ridden with lice. It is an absolute certainty that the knights-errant of old experienced much misfortune in the course of their lives; and if some by their might and valor came to be emperors, you may take my word for it, it cost them dearly in blood and sweat, and if those who rose to such a rank had lacked enchanters and magicians to aid them, they surely would have been cheated of their desires, deceived in their hopes and expectations."

"I agree with you on that," said the traveler, "but there is one thing among others that gives me a very bad impression of the knights-errant, and that is the fact that when they are about to enter upon some great and perilous adventure in which they are in danger of losing their lives, they never at that moment think of commending themselves to God as every good Christian is obliged to do under similar circumstances, but, rather, commend themselves to their ladies with as much fervor and devotion as if their mistresses were God himself; all of which to me smacks somewhat of paganism."

"Sir," Don Quixote answered him, "it could not by any means be otherwise; the knight-errant who did not do so would fall into disgrace, for it is the usage and custom of chivalry that the knight, before engaging in some great feat of arms, shall behold his lady in front of him and shall turn his eyes toward her, gently and lovingly, as if beseeching her favor and protection in the hazardous encounter that awaits him, and even though no one hears him, he is obliged to utter certain words between his teeth, commending himself to her with all his heart; and of this we have numerous examples in the histories. Nor is it to be assumed that he does not commend himself to God also, but the time and place for that is in the course of the undertaking."

"All the same," said the traveler, "I am not wholly clear in this matter; for I have often read of two knights-errant exchanging words until, one word leading to another, their wrath is kindled; whereupon, turning their steeds and taking a good run up the field, they whirl about and bear down upon each other at full speed, commending themselves to their ladies in the midst of it all. What commonly happens then is that one of the two topples from his horse's flanks and is run through and through with the other's lance; and his adversary would also fall to the ground if he did not cling to his horse's mane. What I do not understand is how the dead man would have had time to commend himself to God in the course of this accelerated combat. It would be better if the words he wasted in calling upon his lady as he ran toward the other knight had been spent in paying the debt that he owed as a Christian. Moreover, it is my personal opinion that not all knights-errant have ladies to whom to commend themselves, for not all of them are in love."

"That," said Don Quixote, "is impossible. I assert there can be no knight-errant without a lady; for it is as natural and proper for them to be in love as it is for the heavens to have stars, and I am quite sure that no one ever read a story in which a loveless man of arms was to be met with, for the simple reason that such a one would not be looked upon as a legitimate knight but as a bastard one who had entered the fortress of chivalry not by the main gate, but over the walls, like a robber and a thief."

"Nevertheless," said the traveler, "if my memory serves me right, I have read that Don Galaor, brother of the valorous Amadis of Gaul, never had a special lady to whom he prayed, yet he was not held in any the less esteem for that but was a very brave and famous knight."

Once again, our Don Quixote had an answer. "Sir, one swallow does not make a summer. And in any event, I happen to know that this knight was secretly very much in love. As for his habit of paying court to all the ladies that caught his fancy, that was a natural propensity on his part and one that he was unable to resist. There was, however, one particular lady whom he had made the mistress of his will and to whom he did commend himself very frequently and privately; for he prided himself upon being a reticent knight."

"Well, then," said the traveler, "if it is essential that every knight-errant be in love, it is to be presumed that your Grace is also, since you are of the profession. And unless it be that you pride yourself upon your reticence as much as did Don Galaor, then I truly, on my own behalf and in the name of all this company, beseech your Grace to tell us your lady's name, the name of the country where she resides, what her rank is, and something of the beauty of her person, that she may esteem herself fortunate in having all the world know that she is loved and served by such a knight as your Grace appears to me to be."

At this, Don Quixote heaved a deep sigh. "I cannot say," he began, "as to whether or not my sweet enemy would be pleased that all the world should know I serve her. I can only tell you, in response to the question which you have so politely put to me, that her name is Dulcinea, her place of residence El Toboso, a village of La Mancha. As to her rank, she should be at the very least a princess, seeing that she is my lady and my queen. Her beauty is superhuman, for in it are realized all the impossible and chimerical attributes that poets are accustomed to give their fair ones. Her locks are golden, her brow the Elysian Fields, her eyebrows rainbows, her eyes suns, her cheeks roses, her lips coral, her teeth pearls, her neck alabaster, her bosom marble, her hands ivory, her complexion snow-white. As for those parts which modesty keeps covered from the human sight, it is my opinion that, discreetly considered, they are only to be extolled and not compared to any other."

"We should like," said Vivaldo, "to know something as well of her lineage, her race and ancestry."

"She is not," said Don Quixote, "of the ancient Roman Curtii, Caii, or Scipios, nor of the modern Colonnas and Orsini, nor of the Moncades and Requesenses of Catalonia, nor is she of the Rebellas and Villanovas of Valencia, or the Palafoxes, Nuzas, Rocabertis, Corellas, Lunas, Alagones, Urreas, or Gurreas of Aragon, the Cerdas, Manriques, Mendozas, or Guzmanes of Castile, the Alencastros, Pallas, or Menezes of Portugal; but she is of the Tobosos of La Mancha, and although the line is a modern one, it well may give rise to the most illustrious families of the centuries to come. And let none dispute this with me, unless it be under the conditions which Zerbino has set forth in the inscription beneath Orlando's arms:

> *These let none move*
> *Who dares not with Orlando his valor prove.*"[1]

"Although my own line," replied the traveler, "is that of the Gachupins of Laredo, I should not venture to compare it with the Tobosos of La Mancha, in view of the fact that, to tell you the truth, I have never heard the name before."

"How does it come that you have never heard it!" exclaimed Don Quixote.

The others were listening most attentively to the conversation of these two, and even the goatherds and shepherds were by now aware that our knight of La Mancha was more than a little insane. Sancho Panza alone thought that all his master said was the truth, for he was well acquainted with him, having known him since birth. The only doubt in his mind had to do with the beauteous Dulcinea del Toboso, for he knew of no such princess and the name was strange to his ears, although he lived not far from that place.

They were continuing on their way, conversing in this manner, when they caught sight of some twenty shepherds coming through the gap between two high mountains, all of them clad in black woolen garments and with

---

1. From Lodovico Ariosto's *Orlando Furioso*, canto XXIV, stanza 57.

wreaths on their heads, some of the garlands, as was afterward learned, being of cypress, others of yew. Six of them were carrying a bier covered with a great variety of flowers and boughs.

"There they come with Grisóstomo's body," said one of the goatherds, "and the foot of the mountain yonder is where he wished to be buried."

They accordingly quickened their pace and arrived just as those carrying the bier had set it down on the ground. Four of the shepherds with sharpened picks were engaged in digging a grave alongside the barren rock. After a courteous exchange of greetings, Don Quixote and his companions turned to look at the bier. Upon it lay a corpse covered with flowers, the body of a man dressed like a shepherd and around thirty years of age. Even in death it could be seen that he had had a handsome face and had been of a jovial disposition. Round about him upon the bier were a number of books and many papers, open and folded.

Meanwhile, those who stood gazing at the dead man and those who were digging the grave—everyone present, in fact—preserved an awed silence, until one of the pallbearers said to another, "Look well, Ambrosio, and make sure that this is the place that Grisóstomo had in mind, since you are bent upon carrying out to the letter the provisions of his will."

"This is it," replied Ambrosio; "for many times my unfortunate friend told me the story of his misadventure. He told me that it was here that he first laid eyes upon that mortal enemy of the human race, and it was here, also, that he first revealed to her his passion, for he was as honorable as he was lovelorn; and it was here, finally, at their last meeting, that she shattered his illusions and showed him her disdain, thus bringing to an end the tragedy of his wretched life. And here, in memory of his great misfortune, he wished to be laid in the bowels of eternal oblivion."

Then, turning to Don Quixote and the travelers, he went on, "This body, gentlemen, on which you now look with pitying eyes was the depository of a soul which heaven had endowed with a vast share of its riches. This is the body of Grisóstomo, who was unrivaled in wit, unequaled in courtesy, supreme in gentleness of bearing, a model of friendship, generous without stint, grave without conceit, merry without being vulgar—in short, first in all that is good and second to none in the matter of misfortunes. He loved well and was hated, he adored and was disdained; he wooed a wild beast, importuned a piece of marble, ran after the wind, cried out to loneliness, waited upon ingratitude, and his reward was to be the spoils of death midway in his life's course—a life that was brought to an end by a shepherdess whom he sought to immortalize that she might live on in the memory of mankind, as those papers that you see there would very plainly show if he had not commanded me to consign them to the flames even as his body is given to the earth."

"You," said Vivaldo, "would treat them with greater harshness and cruelty than their owner himself, for it is neither just nor fitting to carry out the will of one who commands what is contrary to all reason. It would not have been a good thing for Augustus Caesar to consent to have them execute the behests of the divine Mantuan in his last testament.[2] And so, Señor Ambrosio, while you may give the body of your friend to the earth, you ought not to give his writings to oblivion. If out of bitterness he left such an order, that does not mean that you are to obey it without using your own discretion. Rather, by granting life to these papers, you permit Marcela's cruelheartedness to live forever and serve as an example to the others in the days that are to come in order that they may flee and avoid such pitfalls as these.

"I and those that have come with me know the story of this lovesick and despairing friend of yours; we know the affection that was between you, and what the occasion of his death was, and the things that he commanded be done as his life drew to a close. And from this lamentable tale anyone may see how great was Marcela's cruelty; they may behold Grisóstomo's love, the loyalty that lay in your friendship, and the end that awaits those who run headlong, with unbridled passion, down the path that doting love opens before their gaze. Last night we heard of your friend's death and learned that he was to be buried here, and out of pity and curiosity we turned aside from our journey and resolved to come see with our own eyes that which had aroused so much compassion when it was told to us. And in requital of that compassion, and the desire that has been born in us to prevent if we can a recurrence of such tragic circumstances, we beg you, O prudent Ambrosio!—or, at least, I for my part implore you—to give up your intention of burning these papers and let me carry some of them away with me."

Without waiting for the shepherd to reply he put out his hand and took a few of those that were nearest him.

"Out of courtesy, sir," said Ambrosio when he saw this, "I will consent for you to keep those that you have taken; but it is vain to think that I will refrain from burning the others."

Vivaldo, who was anxious to find out what was in the papers, opened one of them and perceived that it bore the title "Song of Despair."

Hearing this, Ambrosio said, "That is the last thing the poor fellow wrote; and in order, sir, that you may see the end to which his misfortunes brought him, read it aloud if you will, for we shall have time for it while they are digging the grave."

"That I will very willingly do," said Vivaldo.

And since all the bystanders had the same desire, they gathered around as he in a loud clear voice read the following poem.

2. Virgil (born near Mantua) had left instructions that his Roman epic, the *Aeneid*, should be burned.

CHAPTER 14

*In which are set down the despairing verses of the deceased shepherd,
with other unlooked-for happenings.*

Grisóstomo's Song

    Since thou desirest that thy cruelty
Be spread from tongue to tongue and land to land,
The unrelenting sternness of thy heart
Shall turn my bosom's hell to minstrelsy
That all men everywhere may understand
The nature of my grief and what thou art.
And as I seek my sorrows to impart,
Telling of all the things that thou hast done,
My very entrails shall speak out to brand
Thy heartlessness, thy soul to reprimand,
Where no compassion ever have I won.
Then listen well, lend an attentive ear;
This ballad that thou art about to hear
Is not contrived by art; 'tis a simple song
Such as shepherds sing each day throughout the year—
Surcease of pain for me, for thee a prong.
    Then let the roar of lion, fierce wolf's cry,
The horrid hissing of the scaly snake,
The terrifying sound of monsters strange,
Ill-omened call of crow against the sky,
The howling of the wind as it doth shake
The tossing sea where all is constant change,
Bellow of vanquished bull that cannot range
As it was wont to do, the piteous sob
Of the widowed dove as if its heart would break,
Hoot of the envied owl,[3] ever awake,
From hell's own choir the deep and mournful throb—
Let all these sounds come forth and mingle now.
For if I'm to tell my woes, why then, I vow,
I must new measures find, new modes invent,
With sound confusing sense, I may somehow
Portray the inferno where my days are spent.
    The mournful echoes of my murmurous plaint
Father Tagus[4] shall not hear as he rolls his sand,
Nor olive-bordered Betis; my lament shall be
To the tall and barren rock as I acquaint
The caves with my sorrow; the far and lonely strand
No human foot has trod shall hear from me
The story of thine inhumanity

---

3. Envied by other birds as the only one that witnessed the Crucifixion.   4. The river Tagus. *Betis:* the Guadalquivir.

As told with lifeless tongue but living word.
I'll tell it to the valleys near at hand
Where never shines the sun upon the land;
By venomous serpents shall my tale be heard
On the low-lying, marshy river plain.
And yet, the telling will not be in vain;
For the reverberations of my plight,
Thy matchless austerity and this my pain,
Through the wide world shall go, thee to indict.

    Disdain may kill; suspicion false or true
May slay all patience; deadliest of all
Is jealousy; while absence renders life
Worse than a void; Hope lends no roseate hue
Against forgetfulness or the dread call
Of death inevitable, the end of strife.
Yet—unheard miracle!—with sorrows rife,
My own existence somehow still goes on;
The flame of life with me doth rise and fall.
Jealous I am, disdained; I know the gall
Of those suspicions that will not be gone,
Which leave me not the shadow of a hope,
And, desperate, I will not even grope
But rather will endure until the end,
And with despair eternally I'll cope,
Knowing that things for me will never mend.

    Can one both hope and fear at the same season?
Would it be well to do so in any case,
Seeing that fear, by far, hath the better excuse?
Confronting jealousy, is there any reason
For me to close my eyes to its stern face,
Pretend to see it not? What is the use,
When its dread presence I can still deduce
From countless gaping wounds deep in my heart?
When suspicion—bitter change!—to truth gives place,
And truth itself, losing its virgin grace,
Becomes a lie, is it not wisdom's part
To open wide the door to frank mistrust?
When disdain's unveiled, to doubt is only just.
O ye fierce tyrants of Love's empery!
Shackle these hands with stout cord, if ye must.
My pain shall drown your triumph—woe is me!

    I die, in short, and since nor life nor death
Yields any hope, to my fancy will I cling.
That man is freest who is Love's bond slave:
I'll say this with my living-dying breath,
And the ancient tyrant's praises I will sing.
Love is the greatest blessing Heaven e'er gave.

What greater beauty could a lover crave
Than that which my fair enemy doth show
In soul and body and in everything?
E'en her forgetfulness of me doth spring
From my own lack of grace, that I well know.
In spite of all the wrongs that he has wrought,
Love rules his empire justly as he ought.
Throw all to the winds and speed life's wretched span
By feeding on his self-deluding thought.
No blessing holds the future that I scan.

  Thou whose unreasonableness reason doth give
For putting an end to this tired life of mine,
From the deep heart wounds which thou mayest plainly see,
Judge if the better course be to die or live.
Gladly did I surrender my will to thine,
Gladly I suffered all thou didst to me;
And now that I'm dying, should it seem to thee
My death is worth a tear from thy bright eyes,
Pray hold it back, fair one, do not repine,
For I would have from thee no faintest sign
Of penitence, e'en though my soul thy prize.
Rather, I'd have thee laugh, be very gay,
And let my funeral be a festive day—
But I am very simple! knowing full well
That thou art bound to go thy blithesome way,
And my untimely end thy fame shall swell.

  Come, thirsting Tantalus from out Hell's pit;
Come, Sisyphus with the terrifying weight
Of that stone thou rollest; Tityus, bring
Thy vulture and thine anguish infinite;
Ixion[5] with thy wheel, be thou not late;
Come, too, ye sisters ever laboring;[6]
Come all, your griefs into my bosom fling,
And then, with lowered voices, intone a dirge,
If dirge be fitting for one so desperate,
A body without a shroud, unhappy fate!
And Hell's three-headed gateman,[7] do thou emerge
With a myriad other phantoms, monstrous swarm,
Beings infernal of fantastic form,
Raising their voices for the uncomforted
In a counterpoint of grief, harmonious storm.
What better burial for a lover dead?

5. In Greek myth, all four are proverbial images of mortals punished by the Gods with different forms of torture: *Tantalus*, craving water and fruit which he always fails to reach; *Sisyphus*, forever vainly trying to roll a stone upward to the top of a hill; *Tityus*, having his liver devoured by a vulture; and *Ixion*, being bound to a revolving wheel.   6. In classical mythology the three Fates (Moerae to the Greeks, Parcae to the Romans), spinners of man's destiny.   7. Cerberus, a dog-like three-headed monster, the mythological guardian of Hell.

> Despairing song of mine, do not complain,
> Nor let our parting cause thee any pain,
> For my misfortune is not wholly bad,
> Seeing her fortune's bettered by my demise.
> Then, even in the grave, be thou not sad.

Those who had listened to Grisóstomo's poem liked it well enough, but the one who read it remarked that it did not appear to him to conform to what had been told him of Marcela's modesty and virtue, seeing that in it the author complains of jealousy, suspicion, and absence, all to the prejudice of her good name. To this Ambrosio, as one who had known his friend's most deeply hidden thoughts, replied as follows:

"By way of satisfying, sir, the doubt that you entertain, it is well for you to know that when the unfortunate man wrote that poem, he was by his own volition absent from Marcela, to see if this would work a cure; but when the enamored one is away from his love, there is nothing that does not inspire in him fear and torment, and such was the case with Grisóstomo, for whom jealous imaginings, fears, and suspicions became a seeming reality. And so, in this respect, Marcela's reputation for virtue remains unimpaired; beyond being cruel and somewhat arrogant, and exceedingly disdainful, she could not be accused by the most envious of any other fault."

"Yes, that is so," said Vivaldo.

He was about to read another of the papers he had saved from the fire when he was stopped by a marvelous vision—for such it appeared—that suddenly met his sight; for there atop the rock beside which the grave was being hollowed out stood the shepherdess Marcela herself, more beautiful even than she was reputed to be. Those who up to then had never seen her looked on in silent admiration, while those who were accustomed to beholding her were held in as great a suspense as the ones who were gazing upon her for the first time.

No sooner had Ambrosio glimpsed her than, with a show of indignation, he called out to her, "So, fierce basilisk[8] of these mountains, have you perchance come to see if in your presence blood will flow from the wounds of this poor wretch whom you by your cruelty have deprived of life?[9] Have you come to gloat over your inhuman exploits, or would you from that height look down like another pitiless Nero upon your Rome in flames and ashes?[1] Or perhaps you would arrogantly tread under foot this poor corpse, as an ungrateful daughter did that of her father Tarquinius?[2] Tell us quickly why you have come and what it is that you want most; for I know that Grisóstomo's thoughts never failed to obey you in life, and though he is

---

8. A mythical lizard-like creature whose look and breath were supposed to be lethal.   9. According to folklore, the corpse of a murdered person was supposed to bleed in the presence of the murderer.
1. The Roman emperor Nero is supposed, in tale and proverb, to have been singing while from a tower he observed the burning of Rome in A.D. 64.   2. The inaccurate allusion is to Tullia, actually the wife of the last of the legendary kings of early Rome, Tarquinius; she let the wheel of her carriage trample over the body of her father—the previous king Servius Tullius—whom her husband Tarquinius had liquidated.

dead now, I will see that all those who call themselves his friends obey you likewise."

"I do not come, O Ambrosio, for any of the reasons that you have mentioned," replied Marcela. "I come to defend myself and to demonstrate how unreasonable all those persons are who blame me for their sufferings and for Grisóstomo's death. I therefore ask all present to hear me attentively. It will not take long and I shall not have to spend many words in persuading those of you who are sensible that I speak the truth.

"Heaven made me beautiful, you say, so beautiful that you are compelled to love me whether you will or no; and in return for the love that you show me, you would have it that I am obliged to love you in return. I know, with that natural understanding that God has given me, that everything beautiful is lovable; but I cannot see that it follows that the object that is loved for its beauty must love the one who loves it. Let us suppose that the lover of the beautiful were ugly and, being ugly, deserved to be shunned; it would then be highly absurd for him to say, 'I love you because you are beautiful; you must love me because I am ugly.'

"But assuming that two individuals are equally beautiful, it does not mean that their desires are the same; for not all beauty inspires love, but may sometimes merely delight the eye and leave the will intact. If it were otherwise, no one would know what he wanted, but all would wander vaguely and aimlessly with nothing upon which to settle their affections; for the number of beautiful objects being infinite, desires similarly would be boundless. I have heard it said that true love knows no division and must be voluntary and not forced. This being so, as I believe it is, then why would you compel me to surrender my will for no other reason than that you say you love me? But tell me: supposing that Heaven which made me beautiful had made me ugly instead, should I have any right to complain because you did not love me? You must remember, moreover, that I did not choose this beauty that is mine; such as it is, Heaven gave it to me of its grace, without any choice or asking on my part. As the viper is not to be blamed for the deadly poison that it bears, since that is a gift of nature, so I do not deserve to be reprehended for my comeliness of form.

"Beauty in a modest woman is like a distant fire or a sharp-edged sword: the one does not burn, the other does not cut, those who do not come near it. Honor and virtue are the adornments of the soul, without which the body is not beautiful though it may appear to be. If modesty is one of the virtues that most adorn and beautify body and soul, why should she who is loved for her beauty part with that virtue merely to satisfy the whim of one who solely for his own pleasure strives with all his force and energy to cause her to lose it? I was born a free being, and in order to live freely I chose the solitude of the fields; these mountain trees are my company, the clear-running waters in these brooks are my mirror, and to the trees and waters I communicate my thoughts and lend them of my beauty.

"In short, I am that distant fire, that sharp-edged sword, that does not burn or cut. Those who have been enamored by the sight of me I have disillusioned with my words; and if desire is sustained by hope, I gave none to Grisóstomo or any other, and of none of them can it be said that I killed them with my cruelty, for it was rather their own obstinacy that was to blame. And if you reproach me with the fact that his intentions were honorable and that I ought for that reason to have complied with them, I will tell you that when, on this very spot where his grave is now being dug, he revealed them to me, I replied that it was my own intention to live in perpetual solitude and that only the earth should enjoy the fruit of my retirement and the spoils of my beauty; and if he with all this plain-speaking was still stubbornly bent upon hoping against hope and sailing against the wind, is it to be wondered at if he drowned in the gulf of his own folly?

"Had I led him on, it would have been falsely; had I gratified his passion, it would have been against my own best judgment and intentions; but, though I had disillusioned him, he persisted, and though I did not hate him, he was driven to despair. Ask yourselves, then, if it is reasonable to blame me for his woes! Let him who has been truly deceived complain; let him despair who has been cheated of his promised hopes; if I have enticed any, let him speak up; if I have accepted the attentions of any, let him boast of it; but let not him to whom I have promised nothing, whom I have neither enticed nor accepted, apply to me such terms as cruel and homicidal. It has not as yet been Heaven's will to destine me to love any man, and there is no use expecting me to love of my own free choice.

"Let what I am saying now apply to each and every one of those who would have me for their own, and let it be understood from now on that if any die on account of me, he is not to be regarded as an unfortunate victim of jealousy, since she that cares for none can give to none the occasion for being jealous; nor is my plain-speaking to be taken as disdain. He who calls me a wild beast and a basilisk, let him leave me alone as something that is evil and harmful; let him who calls me ungrateful cease to wait upon me; let him who finds me strange shun my acquaintance; if I am cruel, do not run after me; in which case this wild beast, this basilisk, this strange, cruel, ungrateful creature will not run after them, seek them out, wait upon them, nor endeavor to know them in any way.

"The thing that killed Grisóstomo was his impatience and the impetuosity of his desire; so why blame my modest conduct and retiring life? If I choose to preserve my purity here in the company of the trees, how can he complain of my unwillingness to lose it who would have me keep it with other men? I, as you know, have a worldly fortune of my own and do not covet that of others. My life is a free one, and I do not wish to be subject to another in any way. I neither love nor hate anyone; I do not repel this one and allure that one; I do not play fast and loose with any. The modest conversation of these village lasses and the care of my goats is sufficient to occupy me. Those mountains there represent the bounds of my desire, and should my wishes go beyond them, it is but to contemplate the beauty of the heavens, that pathway by which the soul travels to its first dwelling place."

Saying this and without waiting for any reply, she turned her back and entered the thickest part of a near-by wood, leaving all present lost in admiration of her wit as well as her beauty. A few—those who had felt the powerful dart of her glances and bore the wounds inflicted by her lovely eyes—were of a mind to follow her, taking no heed of the plainly worded warning they had just had from her lips; whereupon Don Quixote, seeing this and thinking to himself that here was an opportunity to display his chivalry by succoring a damsel in distress, laid his hand upon the hilt of his sword and cried out, loudly and distinctly, "Let no person of whatever state or condition he may be dare to follow the beauteous Marcela under pain of incurring my furious wrath. She has shown with clear and sufficient reasons that little or no blame for Grisóstomo's death is to be attached to her; she has likewise shown how far she is from acceding to the desires of any of her suitors, and it is accordingly only just that in place of being hounded and persecuted she should be honored and esteemed by all good people in this world as the only woman in it who lives with such modesty and good intentions."

Whether it was due to Don Quixote's threats or because Ambrosio now told them that they should finish doing the things which his good friend had desired should be done, no one stirred from the spot until the burial was over and Grisóstomo's papers had been burned. As the body was laid in the grave, many tears were shed by the bystanders. Then they placed a heavy stone upon it until the slab which Ambrosio was thinking of having made should be ready, with an epitaph that was to read:

> Here lies a shepherd by love betrayed,
> His body cold in death,
> Who with his last and faltering breath
> Spoke of a faithless maid.
> He died by the cruel, heartless hand
> Of a coy and lovely lass,
> Who by bringing men to so sorry a pass
> Love's tyranny doth expand.

They then scattered many flowers and boughs over the top of the grave, and, expressing their condolences to the dead man's friend, Ambrosio, they all took their leave, including Vivaldo and his companions. Don Quixote now said good-by to the travelers as well, although they urged him to come with them to Seville, assuring him that he would find in every street and at every corner of that city more adventures than are to be met with anywhere else. He thanked them for the invitation and the courtesy they had shown him in offering it, but added that for the present he had no desire to visit Seville, not until he should have rid these mountains of the robbers and bandits of which they were said to be full.

Seeing that his mind was made up, the travelers did not urge him further but, bidding him another farewell, left him and continued on their way; and the reader may be sure that in the course of their journey they did not fail to discuss the story of Marcela and Grisóstomo as well as Don Quixote's madness. As for the good knight himself, he was resolved to go seek the shepherdess and offer her any service that lay in his power; but things did not turn out the way he expected. . . .

(Fighting the Sheep)

CHAPTER 18

In which is set forth the conversation that Sancho Panza had with his master, Don Quixote, along with other adventures deserving of record.

. . . . Don Quixote caught sight down the road of a large cloud of dust that was drawing nearer.

"This, O Sancho," he said, turning to his squire, "is the day when you shall see the boon that fate has in store for me; this, I repeat, is the day when, as well as on any other, shall be displayed the valor of my good right arm. On this day I shall perform deeds that will be written down in the book of fame for all centuries to come. Do you see that dust cloud rising there, Sancho? That is the dust stirred up by a vast army marching in this direction and composed of many nations."

"At that rate," said Sancho, "there must be two of them, for there is another one just like it on the other side."

Don Quixote turned to look and saw that this was so. He was overjoyed by the thought that these were indeed two armies about to meet and clash in the middle of the broad plain; for at every hour and every moment his imagination was filled with battles, enchantments, nonsensical adventures, tales of love, amorous challenges, and the like, such as he had read of in the books of chivalry, and every word he uttered, every thought that crossed his mind, every act he performed, had to do with such things as these. The dust clouds he had sighted were raised by two large droves of sheep coming along the road in opposite directions, which by reason of the dust were not visible until they were close at hand, but Don Quixote insisted so earnestly that they were armies that Sancho came to believe it.

"Sir," he said, "what are we to do?"

"What are we to do?" echoed his master. "Favor and aid the weak and needy. I would inform you, Sancho, that the one coming toward us is led and commanded by the great emperor Alifanfarón, lord of the great isle of Trapobana. This other one at my back is that of his enemy, the king of the Garamantas, Pentapolín of the Rolled-up Sleeve, for he always goes into battle with his right arm bare."

"But why are they such enemies?" Sancho asked.

"Because," said Don Quixote, "this Alifanfarón is a terrible pagan and in love with Pentapolín's daughter, who is a very beautiful and gracious lady and a Christian, for which reason her father does not wish to give her to the pagan king unless the latter first abjures the law of the false prophet, Mohammed, and adopts the faith that is Pentapolín's own."

"Then, by my beard," said Sancho, "if Pentapolín isn't right, and I am going to aid him all I can."

"In that," said Don Quixote, "you will only be doing your duty; for to engage in battles of this sort you need not have been dubbed a knight."

"I can understand that," said Sancho, "but where are we going to put this ass so that we will be certain of finding him after the fray is over? As for going into battle on such a mount, I do not think that has been done up to now."

"That is true enough," said Don Quixote. "What you had best do with him is to turn him loose and run the risk of losing him; for after we emerge the victors we shall have so many horses that even Rocinante will be in danger of being exchanged for another. But listen closely to what I am about to tell you, for I wish to give you an account of the principal knights that are accompanying these two armies; and in order that you may be the better able to see and take note of them, let us retire to that hillock over there which will afford us a very good view."

They then stationed themselves upon a slight elevation from which they would have been able to see very well the two droves of sheep that Don Quixote took to be armies if it had not been for the blinding clouds of dust. In spite of this, however, the worthy gentleman contrived to behold in his imagination what he did not see and what did not exist in reality.

Raising his voice, he went on to explain, "That knight in the gilded armor that you see there, bearing upon his shield a crowned lion crouched at the feet of a damsel, is the valiant Laurcalco, lord of the Silver Bridge; the other with the golden flowers on his armor, and on his shield three crowns argent on an azure field, is the dread Micocolembo, grand duke of Quirocia. And that one on Micocolembo's right hand, with the limbs of a giant, is the ever undaunted Brandabarbarán de Boliche, lord of the three Arabias. He goes armored in a serpent's skin and has for shield a door which, so report has it, is one of those from the temple that Samson pulled down, that time when he avenged himself on his enemies with his own death.

"But turn your eyes in this direction, and you will behold at the head of the other army the ever victorious, never vanquished Timonel de Carcajona, prince of New Biscay, who comes with quartered arms—azure, vert, argent, and or—and who has upon his shield a cat or on a field tawny, with the inscription *Miau,* which is the beginning of his lady's name; for she, so it is said, is the peerless Miulina, daughter of Alfeñquén, duke of Algarve. And that one over there, who weights down and presses the loins of that powerful charger, in a suit of snow-white armor with a white shield that bears no device whatever—he is a novice knight of the French nation, called Pierres Papin, lord of the baronies of Utrique. As for him you see digging his iron spurs into the flanks of that fleet-footed zebra courser and whose arms are vairs azure, he is the mighty duke of Nervia, Espartafilardo of the Wood, who has for device upon his shield an asparagus plant with a motto in Castilian that says 'Rastrea mi suerte.' "[3]

In this manner he went on naming any number of imaginary knights on either side, describing on the spur of the moment their arms, colors,

---

3. Probably a pun on *rastrear:* the meaning of the motto may be either "On Fortune's track" or "My Fortune creeps."

devices, and mottoes; for he was completely carried away by his imagination and by this unheard-of madness that had laid hold of him.

Without pausing, he went on, "This squadron in front of us is composed of men of various nations. There are those who drink the sweet waters of the famous Xanthus; woodsmen who tread the Massilian plain; those that sift the fine gold nuggets of Arabia Felix; those that are so fortunate as to dwell on the banks of the clear-running Thermodon, famed for their coolness; those who in many and diverse ways drain the golden Pactolus; Numidians, whose word is never to be trusted; Persians, with their famous bows and arrows; Medes and Parthians, who fight as they flee; Scythians, as cruel as they are fair of skin; Ethiopians, with their pierced lips; and an infinite number of other nationalities whose visages I see and recognize although I cannot recall their names.

"In this other squadron come those that drink from the crystal currents of the olive-bearing Betis; those that smooth and polish their faces with the liquid of the ever rich and gilded Tagus; those that enjoy the beneficial waters of the divine Genil; those that roam the Tartessian plains with their abundant pasturage; those that disport themselves in the Elysian meadows of Jerez; the men of La Mancha, rich and crowned with golden ears of corn; others clad in iron garments, ancient relics of the Gothic race; those that bathe in the Pisuerga, noted for the mildness of its current; those that feed their herds in the wide-spreading pasture lands along the banks of the winding Guadiana, celebrated for its underground course;[4] those that shiver from the cold of the wooded Pyrenees or dwell amid the white peaks of the lofty Apennines—in short, all those whom Europe holds within its girth."

So help me God! How many provinces, how many nations did he not mention by name, giving to each one with marvelous readiness its proper attributes; for he was wholly absorbed and filled to the brim with what he had read in those lying books of his! Sancho Panza hung on his words, saying nothing, merely turning his head from time to time to have a look at those knights and giants that his master was pointing out to him; but he was unable to discover any of them.

"Sir," he said, "may I go to the devil if I see a single man, giant, or knight of all those that your Grace is talking about. Who knows? Maybe it is another spell, like last night."[5]

"How can you say that?" replied Don Quixote. "Can you not hear the neighing of the horses, the sound of trumpets, the roll of drums?"

"I hear nothing," said Sancho, "except the bleating of sheep."

And this, of course, was the truth; for the flocks were drawing near.

"The trouble is, Sancho," said Don Quixote, "you are so afraid that you cannot see or hear properly; for one of the effects of fear is to disturb the senses and cause things to appear other than what they are. If you are so craven as all that, go off to one side and leave me alone, and I without your help will assure the victory to that side to which I lend my aid."

4. The Guadiana does run underground part of the way through La Mancha.   5. The inn where they had spent the previous night had been pronounced by Don Quixote an enchanted castle.

Saying this, he put spurs to Rocinante and, with his lance at rest, darted down the hillside like a flash of lightning.

As he did so, Sancho called after him, "Come back, your Grace, Señor Don Quixote; I vow to God those are sheep that you are charging. Come back! O wretched father that bore me! What madness is this? Look you, there are no giants, nor knights, nor cats, nor shields either quartered or whole, nor vairs azure or bedeviled. What is this you are doing, O sinner that I am in God's sight?"

But all this did not cause Don Quixote to turn back. Instead, he rode on, crying out at the top of his voice, "Ho, knights, those of you who follow and fight under the banners of the valiant Pentapolín of the Rolled-up Sleeve; follow me, all of you, and you shall see how easily I give you revenge on your enemy, Alifanfarón of Trapobana."

With these words he charged into the middle of the flock of sheep and began spearing at them with as much courage and boldness as if they had been his mortal enemies. The shepherds and herdsmen who were with the animals called to him to stop; but seeing it was no use, they unloosed their slings and saluted his ears with stones as big as your fist.

Don Quixote paid no attention to the missiles and, dashing about here and there, kept crying, "Where are you, haughty Alifanfarón? Come out to me; for here is a solitary knight who desires in single combat to test your strength and deprive you of your life, as a punishment for that which you have done to the valorous Pentapolín Garamanta."

At that instant a pebble from the brook struck him in the side and buried a couple of ribs in his body. Believing himself dead or badly wounded, and remembering his potion, he took out his vial, placed it to his mouth, and began to swallow the balm; but before he had had what he thought was enough, there came another almond, which struck him in the hand, crushing the tin vial and carrying away with it a couple of grinders from his mouth, as well as badly mashing two of his fingers. As a result of these blows the poor knight tumbled from his horse. Believing that they had killed him, the shepherds hastily collected their flock and, picking up the dead beasts, of which there were more than seven, they went off down the road without more ado.

Sancho all this time was standing on the slope observing the insane things that his master was doing; and as he plucked savagely at his beard he cursed the hour and minute when luck had brought them together. But when he saw him lying there on the ground and perceived that the shepherds were gone, he went down the hill and came up to him, finding him in very bad shape though not unconscious.

"Didn't I tell you, Señor Don Quixote," he said, "that you should come back, that those were not armies you were charging but flocks of sheep?"

"This," said Don Quixote, "is the work of that thieving magician, my enemy, who thus counterfeits things and causes them to disappear. You must know, Sancho, that it is very easy for them to make us assume any appearance that they choose; and so it is that malign one who persecutes me, envious of the glory he saw me about to achieve in this battle, changed the squadrons of the foe into flocks of sheep. If you do not believe me, I beseech you on my life to do one thing for me, that you may be unde-ceived and discover for yourself that what I say is true. Mount your ass and follow them quietly, and when you have gone a short way from here, you will see them become their former selves once more; they will no longer be sheep but men exactly as I described them to you in the first place. But do not go now, for I need your kind assistance; come over here and have a look and tell me how many grinders are missing, for it feels as if I did not have a single one left."

("To Right Wrongs and Come to the Aid of the Wretched")

CHAPTER 22

Of how Don Quixote freed many unfortunate ones who, much against their will, were being taken where they did not wish to go.

Cid Hamete Benengeli, the Arabic and Manchegan[6] author, in the course of this most grave, high-sounding, minute, delightful, and imaginative history, informs us that, following the remarks that were exchanged between Don Quixote de la Mancha and Sancho Panza, his squire, . . . the knight looked up and saw coming toward them down the road which they were following a dozen or so men on foot, strung together by their necks like beads on an iron chain and all of them wearing handcuffs. They were accompanied by two men on horseback and two on foot, the former car-rying wheel-lock muskets while the other two were armed with swords and javelins.

"That," said Sancho as soon as he saw them, "is a chain of galley slaves, people on their way to the galleys where by order of the king they are forced to labor."

"What do you mean by 'forced'?" asked Don Quixote. "Is it possible that the king uses force on anyone?"

"I did not say that," replied Sancho. "What I did say was that these are folks who have been condemned for their crimes to forced labor in the galleys for his Majesty the King."

"The short of it is," said the knight, "whichever way you put it, these people are being taken there by force and not of their own free will."

"That is the way it is," said Sancho.

"Well, in that case," said his master, "now is the time for me to fulfill the duties of my calling, which is to right wrongs and come to the aid of the wretched."

"But take note, your Grace," said Sancho, "that justice, that is to say, the king himself, is not using any force upon, or doing any wrong to, people like these, but is merely punishing them for the crimes they have committed."

The chain of galley slaves had come up to them by this time, whereupon

6. Of La Mancha.

Don Quixote very courteously requested the guards to inform him of the reason or reasons why they were conducting these people in such a manner as this. One of the men on horseback then replied that the men were prisoners who had been condemned by his Majesty to serve in the galleys, whither they were bound, and that was all there was to be said about it and all that he, Don Quixote, need know.

"Nevertheless," said the latter, "I should like to inquire of each one of them, individually, the cause of his misfortune." And he went on speaking so very politely in an effort to persuade them to tell him what he wanted to know that the other mounted guard finally said, "Although we have here the record and certificate of sentence of each one of these wretches, we have not the time to get them out and read them to you; and so your Grace may come over and ask the prisoners themselves, and they will tell you if they choose, and you may be sure that they will, for these fellows take a delight in their knavish exploits and in boasting of them afterward."

With this permission, even though he would have done so if it had not been granted him, Don Quixote went up to the chain of prisoners and asked the first whom he encountered what sins had brought him to so sorry a plight. The man replied that it was for being a lover that he found himself in that line.

"For that and nothing more?" said Don Quixote. "And do they, then, send lovers to the galleys? If so, I should have been rowing there long ago."

"But it was not the kind of love that your Grace has in mind," the prisoner went on. "I loved a wash basket full of white linen so well and hugged it so tightly that, if they had not taken it away from me by force, I would never of my own choice have let go of it to this very minute. I was caught in the act, there was no need to torture me, the case was soon disposed of, and they supplied me with a hundred lashes across the shoulders and, in addition, a three-year stretch in the *gurapas,* and that's all there is to tell."

"What are *gurapas?*" asked Don Quixote.

"*Gurapas* are the galleys," replied the prisoner. He was a lad of around twenty-four and stated that he was a native of Piedrahita.

The knight then put the same question to a second man, who appeared to be very downcast and melancholy and did not have a word to say. The first man answered for him.

"This one, sir," he said, "is going as a canary—I mean, as a musician and singer."

"How is that?" Don Quixote wanted to know. "Do musicians and singers go to the galleys too?"

"Yes, sir; and there is nothing worse than singing when you're in trouble."

"On the contrary," said Don Quixote, "I have heard it said that he who sings frightens away his sorrows."

"It is just the opposite," said the prisoner; "for he who sings once weeps all his life long."

"I do not understand," said the knight.

One of the guards then explained. "Sir Knight, with this *non sancta*[7] tribe, to sing when you're in trouble means to confess under torture. This singer was put to the torture and confessed his crime, which was that of being a *cuatrero*, or cattle thief, and as a result of his confession he was condemned to six years in the galleys in addition to two hundred lashes which he took on his shoulders; and so it is he is always downcast and moody, for the other thieves, those back where he came from and the ones here, mistreat, snub, ridicule, and despise him for having confessed and for not having had the courage to deny his guilt. They are in the habit of saying that the word no has the same number of letters as the word *sí*, and that a culprit is in luck when his life or death depends on his own tongue and not that of witnesses or upon evidence; and, in my opinion, they are not very far wrong."

"And I," said Don Quixote, "feel the same way about it." He then went on to a third prisoner and repeated his question.

The fellow answered at once, quite unconcernedly. "I'm going to my ladies, the *gurapas*, for five years, for the lack of five ducats."

"I would gladly give twenty," said Don Quixote, "to get you out of this."

"That," said the prisoner, "reminds me of the man in the middle of the ocean who has money and is dying of hunger because there is no place to buy what he needs. I say this for the reason that if I had had, at the right time, those twenty ducats your Grace is now offering me, I'd have greased the notary's quill and freshened up the attorney's wit with them, and I'd now be living in the middle of Zocodover Square in Toledo instead of being here on this highway coupled like a greyhound. But God is great; patience, and that's enough of it."

Don Quixote went on to a fourth prisoner, a venerable-looking old fellow with a white beard that fell over his bosom. When asked how he came to be there, this one began weeping and made no reply, but a fifth comrade spoke up in his behalf.

"This worthy man," he said, "is on his way to the galleys after having made the usual rounds clad in a robe of state and on horseback."[8]

"That means, I take it," said Sancho, "that he has been put to shame in public."

"That is it," said the prisoner, "and the offense for which he is being punished is that of having been an ear broker, or, better, a body broker. By that I mean to say, in short, that the gentleman is a pimp, and besides, he has his points as a sorcerer."

"If that point had not been thrown in," said Don Quixote, "he would not deserve, for merely being a pimp, to have to row in the galleys, but rather should be the general and give orders there. For the office of pimp is not an indifferent one; it is a function to be performed by persons of discretion and is most necessary in a well-ordered state; it is a profession that should be followed only by the wellborn, and there should, moreover, be a supervisor or examiner as in the case of other offices, and the number

7. Unholy.   8. After having been flogged in public, with all the ceremony that accompanied that punishment.

of practitioners should be fixed by law as is done with brokers on the exchange. In that way many evils would be averted that arise when this office is filled and this calling practiced by stupid folk and those with little sense, such as silly women and pages or mountebanks with few years and less experience to their credit, who, on the most pressing occasions, when it is necessary to use one's wits, let the crumbs freeze between their hand and their mouth and do not know which is their right hand and which is the left.

"I would go on and give reasons why it is fitting to choose carefully those who are to fulfill so necessary a state function, but this is not the place for it. One of these days I will speak of the matter to someone who is able to do something about it. I will say here only that the pain I felt at seeing those white hairs and this venerable countenance in such a plight, and all for his having been a pimp, has been offset for me by the additional information you have given me, to the effect that he is a sorcerer as well; for I am convinced that there are no sorcerers in the world who can move and compel the will, as some simple-minded persons think, but that our will is free and no herb or charm can force it.[9] All that certain foolish women and cunning tricksters do is to compound a few mixtures and poisons with which they deprive men of their senses while pretending that they have the power to make them loved, although, as I have just said, one cannot affect another's will in that manner."

"That is so," said the worthy old man; "but the truth is, sir, I am not guilty on the sorcery charge. As for being a pimp, that is something I cannot deny. I never thought there was any harm in it, however, my only desire being that everyone should enjoy himself and live in peace and quiet, without any quarrels or troubles. But these good intentions on my part cannot prevent me from going where I do not want to go, to a place from which I do not expect to return; for my years are heavy upon me and an affection of the urine that I have will not give me a moment's rest."

With this, he began weeping once more, and Sancho was so touched by it that he took a four-real piece from his bosom and gave it to him as an act of charity.

Don Quixote then went on and asked another what his offense was. The fellow answered him, not with less, but with much more, briskness than the preceding one had shown.

"I am here," he said, "for the reason that I carried a joke too far with a couple of cousins-german of mine and a couple of others who were not mine, and I ended by jesting with all of them to such an extent that the devil himself would never be able to straighten out the relationship. They proved everything on me, there was no one to show me favor, I had no money, I came near swinging for it, they sentenced me to the galleys for six years, and I accepted the sentence as the punishment that was due me. I am young yet, and if I live long enough, everything will come out all right. If, Sir Knight, your Grace has anything with which to aid these poor

9. Here Don Quixote despises charms and love potions though often elsewhere, in his own vision of himself as a knight-errant, he accepts enchantments and spells as part of his world of fantasy.

creatures that you see before you, God will reward you in Heaven, and we here on earth will make it a point to ask God in our prayers to grant you long life and good health, as long and as good as your amiable presence deserves."

This man was dressed as a student, and one of the guards told Don Quixote that he was a great talker and a very fine Latinist.

Back of these came a man around thirty years of age and of very good appearance, except that when he looked at you his eyes were seen to be a little crossed. He was shackled in a different manner from the others, for he dragged behind a chain so huge that it was wrapped all around his body, with two rings at the throat, one of which was attached to the chain while the other was fastened to what is known as a keep-friend or friend's foot, from which two irons hung down to his waist, ending in handcuffs secured by a heavy padlock in such a manner that he could neither raise his hands to his mouth nor lower his head to reach his hands.

When Don Quixote asked why this man was so much more heavily chained than the others, the guard replied that it was because he had more crimes against him than all the others put together, and he was so bold and cunning that, even though they had him chained like this, they were by no means sure of him but feared that he might escape from them.

"What crimes could he have committed," asked the knight, "if he has merited a punishment no greater than that of being sent to the galleys?"

"He is being sent there for ten years," replied the guard, "and that is equivalent to civil death. I need tell you no more than that this good man is the famous Ginés de Pasamonte, otherwise known as Ginesillo de Parapilla."

"Señor Commissary," spoke up the prisoner at this point, "go easy there and let us not be so free with names and surnames. My just name is Ginés and not Ginesillo; and Pasamonte, not Parapilla as you make it out to be, is my family name. Let each one mind his own affairs and he will have his hands full."

"Speak a little more respectfully, you big thief, you," said the commissary, "unless you want me to make you be quiet in a way you won't like."

"Man goes as God pleases, that is plain to be seen," replied the galley slave, "but someday someone will know whether my name is Ginesillo de Parapilla or not."

"But, you liar, isn't that what they call you?"

"Yes," said Ginés, "they do call me that; but I'll put a stop to it, or else I'll skin their you-know-what. And you, sir, if you have anything to give us, give it and may God go with you, for I am tired of all this prying into other people's lives. If you want to know anything about my life, know that I am Ginés de Pasamonte whose life story has been written down by these fingers that you see here."

"He speaks the truth," said the commissary, "for he has himself written his story, as big as you please, and has left the book in the prison, having pawned it for two hundred reales."

"And I mean to redeem it," said Ginés, "even if it costs me two hundred ducats."

"Is it as good as that?" inquired Don Quixote.

"It is so good," replied Ginés, "that it will cast into the shade *Lazarillo de Tormes*[1] and all others of that sort that have been or will be written. What I would tell you is that it deals with facts, and facts so interesting and amusing that no lies could equal them."

"And what is the title of the book?" asked Don Quixote.

"*The Life of Ginés de Pasamonte.*"

"Is it finished?"

"How could it be finished," said Ginés, "when my life is not finished as yet? What I have written thus far is an account of what happened to me from the time I was born up to the last time that they sent me to the galleys."

"Then you have been there before?"

"In the service of God and the king I was there four years, and I know what the biscuit and the cowhide are like. I don't mind going very much, for there I will have a chance to finish my book. I still have many things to say, and in the Spanish galleys I shall have all the leisure that I need, though I don't need much, since I know by heart what it is I want to write."

"You seem to be a clever fellow," said Don Quixote.

"And an unfortunate one," said Ginés; "for misfortunes always pursue men of genius."

"They pursue rogues," said the commissary.

"I have told you to go easy, Señor Commissary," said Pasamonte, "for their Lordships did not give you that staff in order that you might mistreat us poor devils with it, but they intended that you should guide and conduct us in accordance with his Majesty's command. Otherwise, by the life of— But enough. It may be that someday the stains made in the inn will come out in the wash. Meanwhile, let everyone hold his tongue, behave well, and speak better, and let us be on our way. We've had enough of this foolishness."

At this point the commissary raised his staff as if to let Pasamonte have it in answer to his threats, but Don Quixote placed himself between them and begged the officer not to abuse the man; for it was not to be wondered at if one who had his hands so bound should be a trifle free with his tongue. With this, he turned and addressed them all.

"From all that you have told me, my dearest brothers," he said, "one thing stands out clearly for me, and that is the fact that, even though it is a punishment for offenses which you have committed, the penalty you are about to pay is not greatly to your liking and you are going to the galleys very much against your own will and desire. It may be that the lack of spirit which one of you displayed under torture, the lack of money on the part of another, the lack of influential friends, or, finally, warped judgment

1. A picaresque or rogue novel, published anonymously about the middle of the fifteenth century.

on the part of the magistrate, was the thing that led to your downfall; and, as a result, justice was not done you. All of which presents itself to my mind in such a fashion that I am at this moment engaged in trying to persuade and even force myself to show you what the purpose was for which Heaven sent me into this world, why it was it led me to adopt the calling of knighthood which I profess and take the knightly vow to favor the needy and aid those who are oppressed by the powerful.

"However, knowing as I do that it is not the part of prudence to do by foul means what can be accomplished by fair ones, I propose to ask these gentlemen, your guards, and the commissary to be so good as to unshackle you and permit you to go in peace. There will be no dearth of others to serve his Majesty under more propitious circumstances; and it does not appear to me to be just to make slaves of those whom God created as free men. What is more, gentlemen of the guard, these poor fellows have committed no offense against you. Up there, each of us will have to answer for his own sins; for God in Heaven will not fail to punish the evil and reward the good; and it is not good for self-respecting men to be executioners of their fellow-men in something that does not concern them. And so, I ask this of you, gently and quietly, in order that, if you comply with my request, I shall have reason to thank you; and if you do not do so of your own accord, then this lance and this sword and the valor of my arm shall compel you to do it by force."

"A fine lot of foolishness!" exclaimed the commissary. "So he comes out at last with this nonsense! He would have us let the prisoners of the king go free, as if we had any authority to do so or he any right to command it! Be on your way, sir, at once; straighten that basin that you have on your head, and do not go looking for three feet on a cat."[2]

"You," replied Don Quixote, "are the cat and the rat and the rascal!" And, saying this, he charged the commissary so quickly that the latter had no chance to defend himself but fell to the ground badly wounded by the lance blow. The other guards were astounded by this unexpected occurrence; but, recovering their self-possession, those on horseback drew their swords, those on foot leveled their javelins, and all bore down on Don Quixote, who stood waiting for them very calmly. Things undoubtedly would have gone badly for him if the galley slaves, seeing an opportunity to gain their freedom, had not succeeded in breaking the chain that linked them together. Such was the confusion that the guards, now running to fall upon the prisoners and now attacking Don Quixote, who in turn was attacking them, accomplished nothing that was of any use.

Sancho for his part aided Ginés de Pasamonte to free himself, and that individual was the first to drop his chains and leap out onto the field, where, attacking the fallen commissary, he took away that officer's sword and musket; and as he stood there, aiming first at one and then at another, though without firing, the plain was soon cleared of guards, for they had taken to their heels, fleeing at once Pasamonte's weapon and the stones

2. Looking for the impossible ("five feet" in the more usual form of the proverb).

which the galley slaves, freed now, were hurling at them. Sancho, mean-while, was very much disturbed over this unfortunate event, as he felt sure that the fugitives would report the matter to the Holy Brotherhood, which, to the ringing of the alarm bell, would come out to search for the guilty parties. He said as much to his master, telling him that they should leave at once and go into hiding in the near-by mountains.

"That is all very well," said Don Quixote, "but I know what had best be done now." He then summoned all the prisoners, who, running riot, had by this time despoiled the commissary of everything that he had, down to his skin, and as they gathered around to hear what he had to say, he addressed them as follows:

"It is fitting that those who are wellborn should give thanks for the ben-efits they have received, and one of the sins with which God is most offended is that of ingratitude. I say this, gentlemen, for the reason that you have seen and had manifest proof of what you owe to me; and now that you are free of the yoke which I have removed from about your necks, it is my will and desire that you should set out and proceed to the city of El Toboso and there present yourselves before the lady Dulcinea del Toboso and say to her that her champion, the Knight of the Mournful Countenance, has sent you; and then you will relate to her, point by point, the whole of this famous adventure which has won you your longed-for freedom. Having done that, you may go where you like, and may good luck go with you."

To this Ginés de Pasamonte replied in behalf of all of them, "It is abso-lutely impossible, your Grace, our liberator, for us to do what you have commanded. We cannot go down the highway all together but must sep-arate and go singly, each in his own direction, endeavoring to hide our-selves in the bowels of the earth in order not to be found by the Holy Brotherhood, which undoubtedly will come out to search for us. What your Grace can do, and it is right that you should do so, is to change this service and toll that you require of us in connection with the lady Dulcinea del Toboso into a certain number of Credos and Hail Marys which we will say for your Grace's intention, as this is something that can be accom-plished by day or night, fleeing or resting, in peace or in war. To imagine, on the other hand, that we are going to return to the fleshpots of Egypt, by which I mean, take up our chains again by setting out along the highway for El Toboso, is to believe that it is night now instead of ten o'clock in the morning and is to ask of us something that is the same as asking pears of the elm tree."

"Then by all that's holy!" exclaimed Don Quixote, whose wrath was now aroused, "you, Don Son of a Whore, Don Ginesillo de Parapilla, or whatever your name is, you shall go alone, your tail between your legs and the whole chain on your back."

Pasamonte, who was by no means a long-suffering individual, was by this time convinced that Don Quixote was not quite right in the head, seeing that he had been guilty of such a folly as that of desiring to free them; and so, when he heard himself insulted in this manner, he merely gave the wink to his companions and, going off to one side, began raining so many stones upon the knight that the latter was wholly unable to protect himself with his buckler, while poor Rocinante paid no more attention to the spur than if he had been made of brass. As for Sancho, he took refuge behind his donkey as a protection against the cloud and shower of rocks that was falling on both of them, but Don Quixote was not able to shield himself so well, and there is no telling how many struck his body, with such force as to unhorse and bring him to the ground.

No sooner had he fallen than the student was upon him. Seizing the basin from the knight's head, he struck him three or four blows with it across the shoulders and banged it against the ground an equal number of times until it was fairly shattered to bits. They then stripped Don Quixote of the doublet which he wore over his armor, and would have taken his hose as well, if his greaves had not prevented them from doing so, and made off with Sancho's greatcoat, leaving him naked; after which, dividing the rest of the battle spoils amongst themselves, each of them went his own way, being a good deal more concerned with eluding the dreaded Holy Brotherhood than they were with burdening themselves with a chain or going to present themselves before the lady Dulcinea del Toboso.

They were left alone now—the ass and Rocinante, Sancho and Don Quixote: the ass, crestfallen and pensive, wagging its ears now and then, being under the impression that the hurricane of stones that had raged about them was not yet over; Rocinante, stretched alongside his master, for the hack also had been felled by a stone; Sancho, naked and fearful of the Holy Brotherhood; and Don Quixote, making wry faces at seeing himself so mishandled by those to whom he had done so much good.

("Set Free at Once That Lovely Lady . . .")

CHAPTER 52[3]

Of the quarrel that Don Quixote had with the goatherd, together with the rare adventure of the penitents, which the knight by the sweat of his brow brought to a happy conclusion.

All those who had listened to it were greatly pleased with the goatherd's story, especially the canon,[4] who was more than usually interested in noting the manner in which it had been told. Far from being a mere rustic herdsman, the narrator seemed rather a cultured city dweller; and the canon accordingly remarked that the curate had been quite right in saying that the mountain groves bred men of learning. They all now offered their services to Eugenio, and Don Quixote was the most generous of any in this regard.

"Most assuredly, brother goatherd," he said, "if it were possible for me

---

3. Last chapter of Part I. Through various devices, including the use of Don Quixote's own belief in enchantments and spells, the curate and the barber have persuaded the knight to let himself be taken home in an ox cart.　　4. A canon from Toledo who has joined Don Quixote and his guardians on the way; conversing about chivalry with the knight, he has had cause to be "astonished at Don Quixote's well-reasoned nonsense." Eugenio, a very literate goatherd met on the way, has just told them the story of his unhappy love for Leandra: the girl, instead of choosing one of her local suitors, had eloped with a flashy and crooked soldier; robbed and abandoned by him, she had been put by her father in a convent.

to undertake any adventure just now, I would set out at once to aid you and would take Leandra out of that convent, where she is undoubtedly being held against her will, in spite of the abbess and all the others who might try to prevent me, after which I would place her in your hands to do with as you liked, with due respect, however, for the laws of chivalry, which command that no violence be offered to any damsel. But I trust in God, Our Lord, that the power of one malicious enchanter is not so great that another magician may not prove still more powerful, and then I promise you my favor and my aid, as my calling obliges me to do, since it is none other than that of succoring the weak and those who are in distress."

The goatherd stared at him, observing in some astonishment the knight's unprepossessing appearance.

"Sir," he said, turning to the barber who sat beside him, "who is this man who looks so strange and talks in this way?"

"Who should it be," the barber replied, "if not the famous Don Quixote de la Mancha, righter of wrongs, avenger of injustices, protector of damsels, terror of giants, and champion of battles?"

"That," said the goatherd, "sounds to me like the sort of thing you read of in books of chivalry, where they do all those things that your Grace has mentioned in connection with this man. But if you ask me, either your Grace is joking or this worthy gentleman must have a number of rooms to let inside his head."

"You are the greatest villain that ever was!" cried Don Quixote when he heard this. "It is you who are the empty one; I am fuller than the bitch that bore you ever was." Saying this, he snatched up a loaf of bread that was lying beside him and hurled it straight in the goatherd's face with such force as to flatten the man's nose. Upon finding himself thus mistreated in earnest, Eugenio, who did not understand this kind of joke, forgot all about the carpet, the tablecloth, and the other diners and leaped upon Don Quixote. Seizing him by the throat with both hands, he would no doubt have strangled him if Sancho Panza, who now came running up, had not grasped him by the shoulders and flung him backward over the table, smashing plates and cups and spilling and scattering all the food and drink that was there. Thus freed of his assailant, Don Quixote then threw himself upon the shepherd, who, with bleeding face and very much battered by Sancho's feet, was creeping about on his hands and knees in search of a table knife with which to exact a sanguinary vengeance, a purpose which the canon and the curate prevented him from carrying out. The barber, however, so contrived it that the goatherd came down on top of his opponent, upon whom he now showered so many blows that the poor knight's countenance was soon as bloody as his own.

As all this went on, the canon and the curate were laughing fit to burst, the troopers[5] were dancing with glee, and they all hissed on the pair as men do at a dog fight. Sancho Panza alone was in despair, being unable

---

5. Law officers from the Holy Brotherhood. They had wanted to arrest Don Quixote on account of his having attempted the liberation of the galley slaves but had been persuaded not to do so, considering the knight's state of insanity.

to free himself of one of the canon's servants who held him back from going to his master's aid. And then, just as they were all enjoying themselves hugely, with the exception of the two who were mauling each other, the note of a trumpet fell upon their ears, a sound so mournful that it caused them all to turn their heads in the direction from which it came. The one who was most excited by it was Don Quixote; who, very much against his will and more than a little bruised, was lying pinned beneath the goatherd.

"Brother Demon," he now said to the shepherd, "for you could not possibly be anything but a demon, seeing that you have shown a strength and valor greater than mine, I request you to call a truce for no more than an hour; for the doleful sound of that trumpet that we hear seems to me to be some new adventure that is calling me."

Tired of mauling and being mauled, the goatherd let him up at once. As he rose to his feet and turned his head in the direction of the sound, Don Quixote then saw, coming down the slope of a hill, a large number of persons clad in white after the fashion of penitents; for, as it happened, the clouds that year had denied their moisture to the earth, and in all the villages of that district processions for prayer and penance were being organized with the purpose of beseeching God to have mercy and send rain. With this object in view, the good folk from a near-by town were making a pilgrimage to a devout hermit who dwelt on these slopes. Upon beholding the strange costumes that the penitents wore, without pausing to think how many times he had seen them before, Don Quixote imagined that this must be some adventure or other, and that it was for him alone as a knight-errant to undertake it. He was strengthened in this belief by the sight of a covered image that they bore, as it seemed to him this must be some highborn lady whom these scoundrelly and discourteous brigands were forcibly carrying off; and no sooner did this idea occur to him than he made for Rocinante, who was grazing not far away.

Taking the bridle and his buckler from off the saddletree, he had the bridle adjusted in no time, and then, asking Sancho for his sword, he climbed into the saddle, braced his shield upon his arm, and cried out to those present, "And now, valorous company, you shall see how important it is to have in the world those who follow the profession of knight-errantry. You have but to watch how I shall set at liberty that worthy lady who there goes captive, and then you may tell me whether or not such knights are to be esteemed."

As he said this, he dug his legs into Rocinante's flanks, since he had no spurs, and at a fast trot (for nowhere in this veracious history are we ever told that the hack ran full speed) he bore down on the penitents in spite of all that the canon, the curate, and the barber could do to restrain him— their efforts were as vain as were the pleadings of his squire.

"Where are you bound for, Señor Don Quixote?" Sancho called after him. "What evil spirits in your bosom spur you on to go against our Catholic faith? Plague take me, can't you see that's a procession of penitents and that lady they're carrying on the litter is the most blessed image of the

Immaculate Virgin? Look well what you're doing, my master, for this time it may be said that you really do not know."

His exertions were in vain, however, for his master was so bent upon having it out with the sheeted figures and freeing the lady clad in mourning that he did not hear a word, nor would he have turned back if he had, though the king himself might have commanded it. Having reached the procession, he reined in Rocinante, who by this time was wanting a little rest, and in a hoarse, excited voice he shouted, "You who go there with your faces covered, out of shame, it may be, listen well to what I have to say to you."

The first to come to a halt were those who carried the image; and then one of the four clerics who were intoning the litanies, upon beholding Don Quixote's weird figure, his bony nag, and other amusing appurtenances, spoke up in reply.

"Brother, if you have something to say to us, say it quickly, for these brethren are engaged in macerating their flesh, and we cannot stop to hear anything, nor is it fitting that we should, unless it is capable of being said in a couple of words."

"I will say it to you in one word," Don Quixote answered, "and that word is the following: 'Set free at once that lovely lady whose tears and mournful countenance show plainly that you are carrying her away against her will and that you have done her some shameful wrong. I will not consent to your going one step farther until you shall have given her the freedom that should be hers.' "

Hearing these words, they all thought that Don Quixote must be some madman or other and began laughing heartily; but their laughter proved to be gunpowder to his wrath, and without saying another word he drew his sword and fell upon the litter. One of those who bore the image, leaving his share of the burden to his companions, then sallied forth to meet the knight, flourishing a forked stick that he used to support the Virgin while he was resting; and upon this stick he now received a mighty slash that Don Quixote dealt him, one that shattered it in two, but with the piece about a third long that remained in his hand he came down on the shoulder of his opponent's sword arm, left unprotected by the buckler, with so much force that the poor fellow sank to the ground sorely battered and bruised.

Sancho Panza, who was puffing along close behind his master, upon seeing him fall cried out to the attacker not to deal another blow, as this was an unfortunate knight who was under a magic spell but who had never in all the days of his life done any harm to anyone. But the thing that stopped the rustic was not Sancho's words; it was, rather, the sight of Don Quixote lying there without moving hand or foot. And so, thinking that he had killed him, he hastily girded up his tunic and took to his heels across the countryside like a deer.

By this time all of Don Quixote's companions had come running up to where he lay; and the penitents, when they observed this, and especially when they caught sight of the officers of the Brotherhood with their cross-

bows, at once rallied around the image, where they raised their hoods and
grasped their whips as the priests raised their tapers aloft in expectations of
an assault; for they were resolved to defend themselves and even, if possible, to take the offensive against their assailants, but, as luck would have
it, things turned out better than they had hoped. Sancho, meanwhile,
believing Don Quixote to be dead, had flung himself across his master's
body and was weeping and wailing in the most lugubrious and, at the same
time, the most laughable fashion that could be imagined; and the curate
had discovered among those who marched in the procession another curate whom he knew, their recognition of each other serving to allay the
fears of all parties concerned. The first curate then gave the second a very
brief account of who Don Quixote was, whereupon all the penitents came
up to see if the poor knight was dead. And as they did so, they heard
Sancho Panza speaking with tears in his eyes.

"O flower of chivalry,"[6] he was saying, "the course of whose well-spent
years has been brought to an end by a single blow of a club! O honor of
your line, honor and glory of all La Mancha and of all the world, which,
with you absent from it, will be full of evil-doers who will not fear being
punished for their deeds! O master more generous than all the Alexanders,
who after only eight months of service presented me with the best island
that the sea washes and surrounds! Humble with the proud, haughty with
the humble, brave in facing dangers, long-suffering under outrages, in love
without reason, imitator of the good, scourge of the wicked, enemy of the
mean—in a word, a knight-errant, which is all there is to say."

At the sound of Sancho's cries and moans, Don Quixote revived, and
the first thing he said was, "He who lives apart from thee, O fairest Dulcinea, is subject to greater woes than those I now endure. Friend Sancho,
help me onto that enchanted cart, as I am in no condition to sit in Rocinante's saddle with this shoulder of mine knocked to pieces the way it is."

"That I will gladly do, my master," replied Sancho, "and we will go
back to my village in the company of these gentlemen who are concerned
for your welfare, and there we will arrange for another sally and one, let
us hope, that will bring us more profit and fame than this one has."

"Well spoken, Sancho," said Don Quixote, "for it will be an act of great
prudence to wait until the present evil influence of the stars has passed."

The canon, the curate, and the barber all assured him that he would be
wise in doing this; and so, much amused by Sancho Panza's simplicity,
they placed Don Quixote upon the cart as before, while the procession of
penitents re-formed and continued on its way. The goatherd took leave of
all of them, and the curate paid the troopers what was coming to them,
since they did not wish to go any farther. The canon requested the priest
to inform him of the outcome of Don Quixote's madness, as to whether it
yielded to treatment or not; and with this he begged permission to resume
his journey. In short, the party broke up and separated, leaving only the
curate and the barber, Don Quixote and Panza, and the good Rocinante,

6. Note how Sancho has absorbed some of his master's speech mannerisms.

who looked upon everything that he had seen with the same resignation as his master. Yoking his oxen, the carter made the knight comfortable upon a bale of hay, and then at his customary slow pace proceeded to follow the road that the curate directed him to take. At the end of the six days they reached Don Quixote's village, making their entrance at noon of a Sunday, when the square was filled with a crowd of people through which the cart had to pass.

They all came running to see who it was, and when they recognized their townsman, they were vastly astonished. One lad sped to bring the news to the knight's housekeeper and his niece, telling them that their master had returned lean and jaundiced and lying stretched out upon a bale of hay on an ox-cart. It was pitiful to hear the good ladies' screams, to behold the way in which they beat their breasts, and to listen to the curses which they once more heaped upon those damnable books of chivalry, and this demonstration increased as they saw Don Quixote coming through the doorway.

At news of the knight's return, Sancho Panza's wife had hurried to the scene, for she had some while since learned that her husband had accompanied him as his squire; and now, as soon as she laid eyes upon her man, the first question she asked was if all was well with the ass, to which Sancho replied that the beast was better off than his master.

"Thank God," she exclaimed, "for all his blessings! But tell me now, my dear, what have you brought me from all your squirings? A new cloak to wear? Or shoes for the young ones?"

"I've brought you nothing of the sort, good wife," said Sancho, "but other things of greater value and importance."

"I'm glad to hear that," she replied. "Show me those things of greater value and importance, my dear. I'd like a sight of them just to cheer this heart of mine which has been so sad and unhappy all the centuries that you've been gone."

"I will show them to you at home, wife," said Sancho. "For the present be satisfied that if, God willing, we set out on another journey in search of adventures, you will see me in no time a count or the governor of an island, and not one of those around here, but the best that is to be had."

"I hope to Heaven it's true, my husband, for we certainly need it. But tell me, what is all this about islands? I don't understand."

"Honey," replied Sancho, "is not for the mouth of an ass. You will find out in good time, woman; and you're going to be surprised to hear yourself called 'my Ladyship' by all your vassals."

"What's this you are saying, Sancho, about ladyships, islands, and vassals?" Juana Panza insisted on knowing—for such was the name of Sancho's wife, although they were not blood relatives, it being the custom in La Mancha for wives to take their husbands' surnames.

"Do not be in such a hurry to know all this, Juana," he said. "It is enough that I am telling you the truth. Sew up your mouth, then; for all I will say, in passing, is that there is nothing in the world that is more pleasant than being a respected man, squire to a knight-errant who goes in search of adventures. It is true that most of the adventures you meet with do not come out the way you'd like them to, for ninety-nine out of a hundred will prove to be all twisted and crosswise. I know that from experience, for I've come out of some of them blanketed and out of others beaten to a pulp. But, all the same, it's a fine thing to go along waiting for what will happen next, crossing mountains, making your way through woods, climbing over cliffs, visiting castles, and putting up at inns free of charge, and the devil take the maravedi that is to pay."

Such was the conversation that took place between Sancho Panza and Juana Panza, his wife, as Don Quixote's housekeeper and niece were taking him in, stripping him, and stretching him out on his old-time bed. He gazed at them blankly, being unable to make out where he was. The curate charged the niece to take great care to see that her uncle was comfortable and to keep close watch over him so that he would not slip away from them another time. He then told them of what it had been necessary to do in order to get him home, at which they once more screamed to Heaven and began cursing the books of chivalry all over again, praying God to plunge the authors of such lying nonsense into the center of the bottomless pit. In short, they scarcely knew what to do, for they were very much afraid that their master and uncle would give them the slip once more, the moment he was a little better, and it turned out just the way they feared it might.

Part II

("Put Into a Book")

CHAPTER 3

Of the laughable conversation that took place between Don Quixote, Sancho Panza, and the bachelor Sansón Carrasco.

Don Quixote remained in a thoughtful mood as he waited for the bachelor Carrasco,[7] from whom he hoped to hear the news as to how he had been put into a book, as Sancho had said. He could not bring himself to believe that any such history existed, since the blood of the enemies he had slain was not yet dry on the blade of his sword; and here they were trying to tell him that his high deeds of chivalry were already circulating in printed form. But, for that matter, he imagined that some sage, either friend or enemy, must have seen to the printing of them through the art of magic. If the chronicler was a friend, he must have undertaken the task in order to magnify and exalt Don Quixote's exploits above the most notable ones achieved by knights-errant of old. If an enemy, his purpose would have been to make them out as nothing at all, by debasing them below the

---

7. The bachelor of arts Sansón Carrasco, an important new character who appears at the beginning of Part II and will play a considerable role in the story with his attempts at "curing" Don Quixote (the first one a failure, the second one a success; see our following selections). Just now he has been telling Sancho about a book relating the adventures of Don Quixote and his squire, by which the two have been made famous; the book is, of course, *Don Quixote*, Part I.

meanest acts ever recorded of any mean squire. The only thing was, the knight reflected, the exploits of squires never were set down in writing. If it was true that such a history existed, being about a knight-errant, then it must be eloquent and lofty in tone, a splendid and distinguished piece of work and veracious in its details.

This consoled him somewhat, although he was a bit put out at the thought that the author was a Moor, if the appellation "Cid" was to be taken as an indication,[8] and from the Moors you could never hope for any word of truth, seeing that they are all of them cheats, forgers, and schemers. He feared lest his love should not have been treated with becoming modesty but rather in a way that would reflect upon the virtue of his lady Dulcinea del Toboso. He hoped that his fidelity had been made clear, and the respect he had always shown her, and that something had been said as to how he had spurned queens, empresses, and damsels of every rank while keeping a rein upon those impulses that are natural to a man. He was still wrapped up in these and many other similar thoughts when Sancho returned with Carrasco.

Don Quixote received the bachelor very amiably. The latter, although his name was Sansón, or Samson, was not very big so far as bodily size went, but he was a great joker, with a sallow complexion and a ready wit. He was going on twenty-four and had a round face, a snub nose, and a large mouth, all of which showed him to be of a mischievous disposition and fond of jests and witticisms. This became apparent when, as soon as he saw Don Quixote, he fell upon his knees and addressed the knight as follows:

"O mighty Don Quixote de la Mancha, give me your hands; for by the habit of St. Peter that I wear[9]—though I have received but the first four orders—your Grace is one of the most famous knights-errant that ever have been or ever will be anywhere on this earth. Blessings upon Cid Hamete Benengeli who wrote down the history of your great achievements, and upon that curious-minded one who was at pains to have it translated from the Arabic into our Castilian vulgate for the universal entertainment of the people."

Don Quixote bade him rise. "Is it true, then," he asked, "that there is a book about me and that it was some Moorish sage who composed it?"

"By way of showing you how true it is," replied Sansón, "I may tell you that it is my belief that there are in existence today more than twelve thousand copies of that history. If you do not believe me, you have but to make inquiries in Portugal, Barcelona, and Valencia, where editions have been brought out, and there is even a report to the effect that one edition was printed at Antwerp. In short, I feel certain that there will soon not be a nation that does not know it or a language into which it has not been translated."

"One of the things," remarked Don Quixote, "that should give most satisfaction to a virtuous and eminent man is to see his good name spread

8. The allusion is to Cid Hamete Benengeli; the word *cid*, "chief," is of Arabic derivation.   9. The dress of one of the minor clerical orders.

abroad during his own lifetime, by means of the printing press, through translations into the languages of the various peoples. I have said 'good name,' for if he has any other kind, his fate is worse than death."

"If it is a matter of good name and good reputation," said the bachelor, "your Grace bears off the palm from all the knights-errant in the world; for the Moor in his tongue and the Christian in his have most vividly depicted your Grace's gallantry, your courage in facing dangers, your patience in adversity and suffering, whether the suffering be due to wounds or to misfortunes of another sort, and your virtue and continence in love, in connection with that platonic relationship that exists between your Grace and my lady Doña Dulcinea del Toboso."

At this point Sancho spoke up. "Never in my life," he said, "have I heard my lady Dulcinea called 'Doña,' but only 'la Señora Dulcinea del Toboso'; so on that point, already, the history is wrong."

"That is not important," said Carrasco.

"No, certainly not," Don Quixote agreed. "But tell me, Señor Bachelor, what adventures of mine as set down in this book have made the deepest impression?"

"As to that," the bachelor answered, "opinions differ, for it is a matter of individual taste. There are some who are very fond of the adventure of the windmills—those windmills which to your Grace appeared to be so many Briareuses and giants. Others like the episode at the fulling mill. One relishes the story of the two armies which took on the appearance of droves of sheep, while another fancies the tale of the dead man whom they were taking to Segovia for burial. One will assert that the freeing of the galley slaves is the best of all, and yet another will maintain that nothing can come up to the Benedictine giants and the encounter with the valiant Biscayan."

Again Sancho interrupted him. "Tell me, Señor Bachelor," he said, "does the book say anything about the adventure with the Yanguesans, that time our good Rocinante took it into his head to go looking for tidbits in the sea?"

"The sage," replied Sansón, "has left nothing in the inkwell. He has told everything and to the point, even to the capers which the worthy Sancho cut as they tossed him in the blanket."

"I cut no capers in the blanket," objected Sancho, "but I did in the air, and more than I liked."

"I imagine," said Don Quixote, "that there is no history in the world, dealing with humankind, that does not have its ups and downs, and this is particularly true of those that have to do with deeds of chivalry, for they can never be filled with happy incidents alone."

"Nevertheless," the bachelor went on, "there are some who have read the book who say that they would have been glad if the authors had forgotten a few of the innumerable cudgelings which Señor Don Quixote received in the course of his various encounters."

"But that is where the truth of the story comes in," Sancho protested.

"For all of that," observed Don Quixote, "they might well have said nothing about them; for there is no need of recording those events that do not alter the veracity of the chronicle, when they tend only to lessen the reader's respect for the hero. You may be sure that Aeneas was not as pious as Vergil would have us believe, nor was Ulysses as wise as Homer depicts him."

"That is true enough," replied Sansón, "but it is one thing to write as a poet and another as a historian. The former may narrate or sing of things not as they were but as they should have been; the latter must describe them not as they should have been but as they were, without adding to or detracting from the truth in any degree whatsoever."

"Well," said Sancho, "if this Moorish gentleman is bent upon telling the truth, I have no doubt that among my master's thrashings my own will be found; for they never took the measure of his Grace's shoulders without measuring my whole body. But I don't wonder at that; for as my master himself says, when there's an ache in the head the members have to share it."

"You are a sly fox, Sancho," said Don Quixote. "My word, but you can remember things well enough when you choose to do so!"

"Even if I wanted to forget the whacks they gave me," Sancho answered him, "the welts on my ribs wouldn't let me, for they are still fresh."

"Be quiet, Sancho," his master admonished him, "and do not interrupt the bachelor. I beg him to go on and tell me what is said of me in this book."

"And what it says about me, too," put in Sancho, "for I have heard that I am one of the main presonages in it—"

"*Personages*, not *presonages*, Sancho my friend," said Sansón.

"So we have another one who catches you up on everything you say," was Sancho's retort. "If we go on at this rate, we'll never be through in a lifetime."

"May God put a curse on *my* life," the bachelor told him, "if you are not the second most important person in the story; and there are some who would rather listen to you talk than to anyone else in the book. It is true, there are those who say that you are too gullible in believing it to be the truth that you could become the governor of that island that was offered you by Señor Don Quixote, here present."

"There is still sun on the top of the wall," said Don Quixote, "and when Sancho is a little older, with the experience that the years bring, he will be wiser and better fitted to be a governor than he is at the present time."

"By God, master," said Sancho, "the island that I couldn't govern right now I'd never be able to govern if I lived to be as old as Methuselah. The trouble is, I don't know where that island we are talking about is located; it is not due to any lack of noddle on my part."

"Leave it to God, Sancho," was Don Quixote's advice, "and everything will come out all right, perhaps even better than you think; for not a leaf on the tree stirs except by His will."

"Yes," said Sansón, "if it be God's will, Sancho will not lack a thousand islands to govern, not to speak of one island alone."

"I have seen governors around here," said Sancho, "that are not to be compared to the sole of my shoe, and yet they call them 'your Lordship' and serve them on silver plate."

"Those are not the same kind of governors," Sansón informed him. "Their task is a good deal easier. The ones that govern islands must at least know grammar."

"I could make out well enough with the *gram*," replied Sancho, "but with the *mar* I want nothing to do, for I don't understand it at all. But leaving this business of the governorship in God's hands—for He will send me wherever I can best serve Him—I will tell you, Señor Bachelor Sansón Carrasco, that I am very much pleased that the author of the history should have spoken of me in such a way as does not offend me; for, upon the word of a faithful squire, if he had said anything about me that was not becoming to an old Christian, the deaf would have heard of it."

"That would be to work miracles," said Sansón.

"Miracles or no miracles," was the answer, "let everyone take care as to what he says or writes about people and not be setting down the first thing that pops into his head."

"One of the faults that is found with the book," continued the bachelor, "is that the author has inserted in it a story entitled *The One Who Was Too Curious for His Own Good*. It is not that the story in itself is a bad one or badly written; it is simply that it is out of place there, having nothing to do with the story of his Grace, Señor Don Quixote."[1]

"I will bet you," said Sancho, "that the son of a dog has mixed the cabbages with the baskets."[2]

"And I will say right now," declared Don Quixote, "that the author of this book was not a sage but some ignorant prattler who at haphazard and without any method set about the writing of it, being content to let things turn out as they might. In the same manner, Orbaneja,[3] the painter of Ubeda, when asked what he was painting would reply, 'Whatever it turns out to be.' Sometimes it would be a cock, in which case he would have to write alongside it, in Gothic letters, 'This is a cock.' And so it must be with my story, which will need a commentary to make it understandable."

"No," replied Sansón, "that it will not; for it is so clearly written that none can fail to understand it. Little children leaf through it, young people read it, adults appreciate it, and the aged sing its praises. In short, it is so thumbed and read and so well known to persons of every walk in life that no sooner do folks see some skinny nag than they at once cry, 'There goes Rocinante!' Those that like it best of all are the pages; for there is no lord's antechamber where a *Don Quixote* is not to be found. If one lays it down, another will pick it up; one will pounce upon it, and another will beg for it. It affords the pleasantest and least harmful reading of any book that has

---

1. The story, a tragic tale about a jealousy-ridden husband, occupies several chapters of Part I. Here, as elsewhere in this chapter, Cervantes echoes criticism currently aimed at his book. 2. Has jumbled together things of different kinds. 3. This painter is known only through the present allusion in *Don Quixote*.

been published up to now. In the whole of it there is not to be found an indecent word or a thought that is other than Catholic."

"To write in any other manner," observed Don Quixote, "would be to write lies and not the truth. Those historians who make use of falsehoods ought to be burned like the makers of counterfeit money. I do not know what could have led the author to introduce stories and episodes that are foreign to the subject matter when he had so much to write about in describing my adventures. He must, undoubtedly, have been inspired by the old saying, 'With straw or with hay . . . .'[4] For, in truth, all he had to do was to record my thoughts, my sighs, my tears, my lofty purposes, and my undertakings, and he would have had a volume bigger or at least as big as that which the works of El Tostado[5] would make. To sum the matter up, Señor Bachelor, it is my opinion that, in composing histories or books of any sort, a great deal of judgment and ripe understanding is called for. To say and write witty and amusing things is the mark of great genius. The cleverest character in a comedy is the clown, since he who would make himself out to be a simpleton cannot be one. History is a near-sacred thing, for it must be true, and where the truth is, there is God. And yet there are those who compose books and toss them out into the world as if they were no more than fritters."

"There is no book so bad," opined the bachelor, "that there is not some good in it."

"Doubtless that is so," replied Don Quixote, "but it very often happens that those who have won in advance a great and well-deserved reputation for their writings, lose it in whole or in part when they give their works to the printer."

"The reason for it," said Sansón, "is that, printed works being read at leisure, their faults are the more readily apparent, and the greater the reputation of the author the more closely are they scrutinized. Men famous for their genius, great poets, illustrious historians, are almost always envied by those who take a special delight in criticizing the writings of others without having produced anything of their own."

"That is not to be wondered at," said Don Quixote, "for there are many theologians who are not good enough for the pulpit but who are very good indeed when it comes to detecting the faults or excesses of those who preach."

"All of this is very true, Señor Don Quixote," replied Carrasco, "but, all the same, I could wish that these self-appointed censors were a bit more forbearing and less hypercritical; I wish they would pay a little less attention to the spots on the bright sun of the work that occasions their fault-finding. For if *aliquando bonus dormitat Homerus*,[6] let them consider how much of his time he spent awake, shedding the light of his genius with a minimum of shade. It well may be that what to them seems a flaw is but one of those moles which sometimes add to the beauty of a face. In any event,

---

4. The proverb concludes either "the mattress is filled" or "I fill my belly."   5. Alonso de Madrigal, bishop of Avila, a prolific author of devotional works.   6. "Good Homer sometimes nods too." (Horace, *Art of Poetry*, l. 359.)

I insist that he who has a book printed runs a very great risk, inasmuch as it is an utter impossibility to write it in such a manner that it will please all who read it."

"This book about me must have pleased very few," remarked Don Quixote.

"Quite the contrary," said Sansón, "for just as *stultorum infinitus est numerus*,[7] so the number of those who have enjoyed this history is likewise infinite. Some, to be sure, have complained of the author's forgetfulness, seeing that he neglected to make it plain who the thief was who stole Sancho's gray;[8] for it is not stated there, but merely implied, that the ass was stolen; and, a little further on, we find the knight mounted on the same beast, although it has not made its reappearance in the story. They also say that the author forgot to tell us what Sancho did with those hundred crowns that he found in the valise on the Sierra Morena, as nothing more is said of them and there are many who would like to know how he disposed of the money or how he spent it. This is one of the serious omissions to be found in the work."

To this Sancho replied, "I, Señor Sansón, do not feel like giving any account or accounting just now; for I feel a little weak in my stomach, and if I don't do something about it by taking a few swigs of the old stuff, I'll be sitting on St. Lucy's thorn.[9] I have some of it at home, and my old woman is waiting for me. After I've had my dinner, I'll come back and answer any questions your Grace or anybody else wants to ask me, whether it's about the loss of the ass or the spending of the hundred crowns."

And without waiting for a reply or saying another word, he went on home. Don Quixote urged the bachelor to stay and take potluck with him, and Sansón accepted the invitation and remained. In addition to the knight's ordinary fare, they had a couple of pigeons, and at table their talk was of chivalry and feats of arms.

(A Victorious Duel)

CHAPTER 12

Of the strange adventure that befell the valiant Don Quixote with the fearless Knight of the Mirrors.[1]

The night following the encounter with Death was spent by Don Quixote and his squire beneath some tall and shady trees,[2] the knight having been persuaded to eat a little from the stock of provisions carried by the gray.

7. "Infinite is the number of fools." (Ecclesiasticus 1:15.)   8. In Part I, Chapter 23.   9. I shall be weak and exhausted.   1. He will duly earn this title only in Chapter 15. In between, the author will be referring to him as the Knight of the Wood.   2. Don Quixote and his squire are now in the woody region around El Toboso, Dulcinea's town. Sancho has been sent to look for his knight's lady and has saved the day by pretending to see the beautiful damsel in a "village wench, and not a pretty one at that, for she was round-faced and snub-nosed." But by his imaginative lie he has succeeded, as he had planned, in setting in motion Don Quixote's belief in spells and enchantments: enemy magicians, envious of him, have hidden his lady's splendor only from his sight. While the knight was still under the shock of this experience, farther along their way he and his squire have met a group of itinerant players dressed in their proper costumes for a religious play, *The Parliament of Death*.

"Sir," said Sancho, in the course of their repast, "how foolish I'd have been if I had chosen the spoils from your Grace's first adventure rather than the foals from the three mares.[3] Truly, truly, a sparrow in the hand is worth more than a vulture on the wing."

"And yet, Sancho," replied Don Quixote, "if you had but let me attack them as I wished to do, you would at least have had as spoils the Empress's gold crown and Cupid's painted wings;[4] for I should have taken them whether or no and placed them in your hands."

"The crowns and scepters of stage emperors," remarked Sancho, "were never known to be of pure gold; they are always of tinsel or tinplate."

"That is the truth," said Don Quixote, "for it is only right that the accessories of a drama should be fictitious and not real, like the play itself. Speaking of that, Sancho, I would have you look kindly upon the art of the theater and, as a consequence, upon those who write the pieces and perform in them, for they all render a service of great value to the State by holding up a mirror for us at each step that we take, wherein we may observe, vividly depicted, all the varied aspects of human life; and I may add that there is nothing that shows us more clearly, by similitude, what we are and what we ought to be than do plays and players.

"Tell me, have you not seen some comedy in which kings, emperors, pontiffs, knights, ladies, and numerous other characters are introduced? One plays the ruffian, another the cheat, this one a merchant and that one a soldier, while yet another is the fool who is not so foolish as he appears, and still another the one of whom love has made a fool. Yet when the play is over and they have taken off their players' garments, all the actors are once more equal."

"Yes," replied Sancho, "I have seen all that."

"Well," continued Don Quixote, "the same thing happens in the comedy that we call life, where some play the part of emperors, others that of pontiffs—in short, all the characters that a drama may have—but when it is all over, that is to say, when life is done, death takes from each the garb that differentiates him, and all at last are equal in the grave."

"It is a fine comparison," Sancho admitted, "though not so new but that I have heard it many times before. It reminds me of that other one, about the game of chess. So long as the game lasts, each piece has its special qualities, but when it is over they are all mixed and jumbled together and put into a bag, which is to the chess pieces what the grave is to life."

"Every day, Sancho," said Don Quixote, "you are becoming less stupid and more sensible."

"It must be that some of your Grace's good sense is sticking to me," was Sancho's answer. "I am like a piece of land that of itself is dry and barren, but if you scatter manure over it and cultivate it, it will bear good fruit. By this I mean to say that your Grace's conversation is the manure that has been cast upon the barren land of my dry wit; the time that I spend in your

---

3. Don Quixote has promised them to Sancho as a reward for bringing news of Dulcinea. The following sentence is a proverb roughly corresponding to "a bird in the hand is worth two in the bush."   4. The Empress and Cupid were among the characters in *The Parliament of Death*.

service, associating with you, does the cultivating; and as a result of it all, I hope to bring forth blessed fruits by not departing, slipping, or sliding, from those paths of good breeding which your Grace has marked out for me in my parched understanding."

Don Quixote had to laugh at this affected speech of Sancho's, but he could not help perceiving that what the squire had said about his improvement was true enough; for every now and then the servant would speak in a manner that astonished his master. It must be admitted, however, that most of the time when he tried to use fine language, he would tumble from the mountain of his simple-mindedness into the abyss of his ignorance. It was when he was quoting old saws and sayings, whether or not they had anything to do with the subject under discussion, that he was at his best, displaying upon such occasions a prodigious memory, as will already have been seen and noted in the course of this history.

With such talk as this they spent a good part of the night. Then Sancho felt a desire to draw down the curtains of his eyes, as he was in the habit of saying when he wished to sleep, and, unsaddling his mount, he turned him loose to graze at will on the abundant grass. If he did not remove Rocinante's saddle, this was due to his master's express command; for when they had taken the field and were not sleeping under a roof, the hack was under no circumstances to be stripped. This was in accordance with an old and established custom which knights-errant faithfully observed: the bridle and saddlebow might be removed, but beware of touching the saddle itself! Guided by this precept, Sancho now gave Rocinante the same freedom that the ass enjoyed.

The close friendship that existed between the two animals was a most unusual one, so remarkable indeed that it has become a tradition handed down from father to son, and the author of this veracious chronicle even wrote a number of special chapters on the subject, although, in order to preserve the decency and decorum that are fitting in so heroic an account, he chose to omit them in the final version. But he forgets himself once in a while and goes on to tell us how the two beasts when they were together would hasten to scratch each other, and how, when they were tired and their bellies were full, Rocinante would lay his long neck over that of the ass—it extended more than a half a yard on the other side—and the pair would then stand there gazing pensively at the ground for as much as three whole days at a time, or at least until someone came for them or hunger compelled them to seek nourishment.

I may tell you that I have heard it said that the author of this history, in one of his writings, has compared the friendship of Rocinante and the gray to that of Nisus and Euryalus and that of Pylades and Orestes;[5] and if this be true, it shows for the edification of all what great friends these two peace-loving animals were, and should be enough to make men ashamed, who are so inept at preserving friendship with one another. For this reason it has been said:

5. Famous examples of friendship in Virgil's *Aeneid* and in Greek tradition and drama.

> There is no friend for friend,
> Reeds to lances turn . . .[6]

And there was the other poet who sang:

> Between friend and friend the bug . . .[7]

Let no one think that the author has gone out of his way in comparing the friendship of animals with that of men; for human beings have received valuable lessons from the beasts and have learned many important things from them. From the stork they have learned the use of clysters; the dog has taught them the salutary effects of vomiting as well as a lesson in gratitude; the cranes have taught them vigilance, the ants foresight, the elephants modesty, and the horse loyalty.[8]

Sancho had at last fallen asleep at the foot of a cork tree, while Don Quixote was slumbering beneath a sturdy oak. Very little time had passed when the knight was awakened by a noise behind him, and, starting up, he began looking about him and listening to see if he could make out where it came from. Then he caught sight of two men on horseback, one of whom, slipping down from the saddle, said to the other, "Dismount, my friend, and unbridle the horses; for there seems to be plenty of grass around here for them and sufficient silence and solitude for my amorous thoughts."

Saying this, he stretched himself out on the ground, and as he flung himself down the armor that he wore made such a noise that Don Quixote knew at once, for a certainty, that he must be a knight-errant. Going over to Sancho, who was still sleeping, he shook him by the arm and with no little effort managed to get him awake.

"Brother Sancho," he said to him in a low voice, "we have an adventure on our hands."

"God give us a good one," said Sancho. "And where, my master, may her Ladyship, Mistress Adventure, be?"

"Where, Sancho?" replied Don Quixote. "Turn your eyes and look, and you will see stretched out over there a knight-errant who, so far as I can make out, is not any too happy; for I saw him fling himself from his horse to the ground with a certain show of despondency, and as he fell his armor rattled."

"Well," said Sancho, "and how does your Grace make this out to be an adventure?"

"I would not say," the knight answered him, "that this is an adventure in itself, but rather the beginning of one, for that is the way they start. But listen; he seems to be tuning a lute or guitar, and from the way he is spitting and clearing his throat he must be getting ready to sing something."

"Faith, so he is," said Sancho. "He must be some lovesick knight."

"There are no knights-errant that are not lovesick," Don Quixote informed

6. From a popular ballad.   7. The Spanish "a bug in the eye" implies keeping a watchful eye on somebody.   8. All folkloristic beliefs about the "virtues" of animals.

him. "Let us listen to him, and the thread of his song will lead us to the
yarn-ball of his thoughts; for out of the abundance of the heart the mouth
speaketh."

Sancho would have liked to reply to his master, but the voice of the
Knight of the Wood, which was neither very good nor very bad, kept him
from it; and as the two of them listened attentively, they heard the following:

Sonnet

Show me, O lady, the pattern of thy will,
That mine may take that very form and shape;
For my will in thine own I fain would drape,
Each slightest wish of thine I would fulfill.
If thou wouldst have me silence this dead ill
Of which I'm dying now, prepare the crape!
Or if I must another manner ape,
Then let Love's self display his rhyming skill.
Of opposites I am made, that's manifest:
In part soft wax, in part hard-diamond fire;
Yet to Love's laws my heart I do adjust,
And, hard or soft, I offer thee this breast:
Print or engrave there what thou may'st desire,
And I'll preserve it in eternal trust.[9]

With an Ay! that appeared to be wrung from the very depths of his heart,
the Knight of the Wood brought his song to a close, and then after a brief
pause began speaking in a grief-stricken voice that was piteous to hear.

"O most beautiful and most ungrateful woman in all the world!" he
cried, "how is it possible, O most serene Casildea de Vandalia,[1] for you to
permit this captive knight of yours to waste away and perish in constant
wanderings, amid rude toils and bitter hardships? Is it not enough that I
have compelled all the knights of Navarre, all those of León, all the Tartes-
sians and Castilians, and, finally, all those of La Mancha, to confess that
there is no beauty anywhere that can rival yours?"

"That is not so!" cried Don Quixote at this point. "I am of La Mancha,
and I have never confessed, I never could nor would confess a thing so
prejudicial to the beauty of my lady. The knight whom you see there,
Sancho, is raving; but let us listen and perhaps he will tell us more."

"That he will," replied Sancho, "for at the rate he is carrying on, he is
good for a month at a stretch."

This did not prove to be the case, however; for when the Knight of the
Wood heard voices near him, he cut short his lamentations and rose to his
feet.

"Who goes there?" he called in a loud but courteous tone. "What kind

---

9. The poem intentionally follows affected conventions of the time.   1. The Knight of the Wood's
counterpart to Don Quixote's Dulcinea del Toboso.

of people are you? Are you, perchance, numbered among the happy or among the afflicted?"

"Among the afflicted," was Don Quixote's response.

"Then come to me," said the one of the Wood, "and, in doing so, know that you come to sorrow's self and the very essence of affliction."

Upon receiving so gentle and courteous an answer, Don Quixote and Sancho as well went over to him, whereupon the sorrowing one took the Manchegan's arm.

"Sit down here, Sir Knight," he continued, "for in order to know that you are one of those who follow the profession of knight-errantry, it is enough for me to have found you in this place where solitude and serenity keep you company, such a spot being the natural bed and proper dwelling of wandering men of arms."

"A knight I am," replied Don Quixote, "and of the profession that you mention; and though sorrows, troubles, and misfortunes have made my heart their abode, this does not mean that compassion for the woes of others has been banished from it. From your song a while ago I gather that your misfortunes are due to love—the love you bear that ungrateful fair one whom you named in your lamentations."

As they conversed in this manner, they sat together upon the hard earth, very peaceably and companionably, as if at daybreak they were not going to break each other's heads.

"Sir Knight," inquired the one of the Wood, "are you by any chance in love?"

"By mischance I am," said Don Quixote, "although the ills that come from well-placed affection should be looked upon as favors rather than as misfortunes."

"That is the truth," the Knight of the Wood agreed, "if it were not that the loved one's scorn disturbs our reason and understanding; for when it is excessive scorn appears as vengeance."

"I was never scorned by my lady," said Don Quixote.

"No, certainly not," said Sancho, who was standing near by, "for my lady is gentle as a ewe lamb and soft as butter."

"Is he your squire?" asked the one of the Wood.

"He is," replied Don Quixote.

"I never saw a squire," said the one of the Wood, "who dared to speak while his master was talking. At least, there is mine over there; he is as big as your father, and it cannot be proved that he has ever opened his lips while I was conversing."

"Well, upon my word," said Sancho, "I have spoken, and I will speak in front of any other as good—but never mind; it only makes it worse to stir it."

The Knight of the Wood's squire now seized Sancho's arm. "Come along," he said, "let the two of us go where we can talk all we like, squire fashion, and leave these gentlemen our masters to come to lance blows as they tell each other the story of their loves; for you may rest assured, day-break will find them still at it."

"Let us, by all means," said Sancho, "and I will tell your Grace who I am, so that you may be able to see for yourself whether or not I am to be numbered among the dozen most talkative squires."

With this, the pair went off to one side, and there then took place between them a conversation that was as droll as the one between their masters was solemn.

<h2>CHAPTER 13</h2>

In which is continued the adventure of the Knight of the Wood, together with the shrewd, highly original, and amicable conversation that took place between the two squires.

The knights and the squires had now separated, the latter to tell their life stories, the former to talk of their loves; but the history first relates the conversation of the servants and then goes on to report that of the masters. We are told that, after they had gone some little distance from where the others were, the one who served the Knight of the Wood began speaking to Sancho as follows:

"It is a hard life that we lead and live, *Señor mio*, those of us who are squires to knights-errant. It is certainly true that we eat our bread in the sweat of our faces, which is one of the curses that God put upon our first parents."[2]

"It might also be said," added Sancho, "that we eat it in the chill of our bodies, for who endures more heat and cold than we wretched ones who wait upon these wandering men of arms? It would not be so bad if we did eat once in a while, for troubles are less where there is bread; but as it is, we sometimes go for a day or two without breaking our fast, unless we feed on the wind that blows."

"But all this," said the other, "may very well be put up with, by reason of the hope we have of being rewarded; for if a knight is not too unlucky, his squire after a little while will find himself the governor of some fine island or prosperous earldom."

"I," replied Sancho, "have told my master that I would be satisfied with the governorship of an island, and he is so noble and so generous that he has promised it to me on many different occasions."

"In return for my services," said the Squire of the Wood, "I'd be content with a canonry. My master has already appointed me to one—and what a canonry!"

"Then he must be a churchly knight," said Sancho, "and in a position to grant favors of that sort to his faithful squire; but mine is a layman, pure and simple, although, as I recall, certain shrewd and, as I see it, scheming persons did advise him to try to become an archbishop. However, he did not want to be anything but an emperor. And there I was, all the time trembling for fear he would take it into his head to enter the Church, since

2. Cf. Genesis 3:19.

I was not educated enough to hold any benefices. For I may as well tell your Grace that, though I look like a man, I am no more than a beast where holy orders are concerned."

"That is where you are making a mistake," the Squire of the Wood assured him. "Not all island governments are desirable. Some of them are misshapen bits of land, some are poor, others are gloomy, and, in short, the best of them lays a heavy burden of care and trouble upon the shoulders of the unfortunate one to whose lot it falls. It would be far better if we who follow this cursed trade were to go back to our homes and there engage in pleasanter occupations, such as hunting or fishing, for example; for where is there in this world a squire so poor that he does not have a hack, a couple of greyhounds, and a fishing rod to provide him with sport in his own village?"

"I don't lack any of those," replied Sancho. "It is true, I have no hack, but I do have an ass that is worth twice as much as my master's horse. God send me a bad Easter, and let it be the next one that comes, if I would make a trade, even though he gave me four fanegas[3] of barley to boot. Your Grace will laugh at the price I put on my gray—for that is the color of the beast. As to greyhounds, I shan't want for them, as there are plenty and to spare in my village. And, anyway, there is more pleasure in hunting when someone else pays for it."

"Really and truly, Sir Squire," said the one of the Wood, "I have made up my mind and resolved to have no more to do with the mad whims of these knights; I intend to retire to my village and bring up my little ones— I have three of them, and they are like oriental pearls."

"I have two of them," said Sancho, "that might be presented to the Pope in person, especially one of my girls that I am bringing up to be a countess, God willing, in spite of what her mother says."

"And how old is this young lady that is destined to be a countess?"

"Fifteen," replied Sancho, "or a couple of years more or less. But she is tall as a lance, fresh as an April morning, and strong as a porter."

"Those," remarked the one of the Wood, "are qualifications that fit her to be not merely a countess but a nymph of the verdant wildwood. O whore's daughter of a whore! What strength the she-rogue must have!"

Sancho was a bit put out by this. "She is not a whore," he said, "nor was her mother before her, nor will either of them ever be, please God, so long as I live. And you might speak more courteously. For one who has been brought up among knights-errant, who are the soul of courtesy, those words are not very becoming."

"Oh, how little your Grace knows about compliments, Sir Squire!" the one of the Wood exclaimed. "Are you not aware that when some knight gives a good lance thrust to the bull in the plaza, or when a person does anything remarkably well, it is the custom for the crowd to cry out, 'Well done, whoreson rascal!' and that what appears to be vituperation in such a

---

3. About 1.6 bushels.

case is in reality high praise? Sir, I would bid you disown those sons or daughters who do nothing to cause such praise to be bestowed upon their parents."

"I would indeed disown them if they didn't," replied Sancho, "and so your Grace may go ahead and call me, my children, and my wife all the whores in the world if you like, for everything that they say and do deserves the very highest praise. And in order that I may see them all again, I pray God to deliver me from mortal sin, or, what amounts to the same thing, from this dangerous calling of squire, seeing that I have fallen into it a second time, decoyed and deceived by a purse of a hundred ducats that I found one day in the heart of the Sierra Morena.[4] The devil is always holding up a bag full of doubloons in front of my eyes, here, there—no, not here, but there—everywhere, until it seems to me at every step I take that I am touching it with my hand, hugging it, carrying it off home with me, investing it, drawing an income from it, and living on it like a prince. And while I am thinking such thoughts, all the hardships I have to put up with serving this crackbrained master of mine, who is more of a madman than a knight, seem to me light and easy to bear."

"That," observed the Squire of the Wood, "is why it is they say that avarice bursts the bag. But, speaking of madmen, there is no greater one in all this world than my master; for he is one of those of whom it is said, 'The cares of others kill the ass.' Because another knight has lost his senses, he has to play mad too[5] and go hunting for that which, when he finds it, may fly up in his snout."

"Is he in love, maybe?"

"Yes, with a certain Casildea de Vandalia, the rawest[6] and best-roasted lady to be found anywhere on earth; but her rawness is not the foot he limps on, for he has other and greater schemes rumbling in his bowels, as you will hear tell before many hours have gone by."

"There is no road so smooth," said Sancho, "that it does not have some hole or rut to make you stumble. In other houses they cook horse beans, in mine they boil them by the kettleful.[7] Madness has more companions and attendants than good sense does. But if it is true what they say, that company in trouble brings relief, I may take comfort from your Grace, since you serve a master as foolish as my own."

"Foolish but brave," the one of the Wood corrected him, "and more of a rogue than anything else."

"That is not true of my master," replied Sancho. "I can assure you there is nothing of the rogue about him; he is as open and aboveboard as a wine pitcher and would not harm anyone but does good to all. There is no malice in his make-up, and a child could make him believe it was night at midday. For that very reason I love him with all my heart and cannot bring myself to leave him, no matter how many foolish things he does."

---

4. When Don Quixote retired there in Part I, Chapter 23.   5. In the Sierra Morena, Don Quixote had decided to imitate Amadis de Gaul and Ariosto's Roland "by playing the part of a desperate and raving madman" as a consequence of love (Part I, Chapter 25).   6. The original has a pun on *crudo*, meaning both "raw" and "cruel."   7. Meaning that his misfortunes always come in large quantities.

"But, nevertheless, good sir and brother," said the Squire of the Wood, "with the blind leading the blind, both are in danger of falling into the pit. It would be better for us to get out of all this as quickly as we can and return to our old haunts; for those that go seeking adventures do not always find good ones."

Sancho kept clearing his throat from time to time, and his saliva seemed rather viscous and dry; seeing which, the woodland squire said to him, "It looks to me as if we have been talking so much that our tongues are cleaving to our palates, but I have a loosener over there, hanging from the bow of my saddle, and a pretty good one it is." With this, he got up and went over to his horse and came back a moment later with a big flask of wine and a meat pie half a yard in diameter. This is no exaggeration, for the pasty in question was made of a hutch-rabbit of such a size that Sancho took it to be a goat, or at the very least a kid.

"And are you in the habit of carrying this with you, Señor?" he asked.

"What do you think?" replied the other. "Am I by any chance one of your wood-and-water[8] squires? I carry better rations on the flanks of my horse than a general does when he takes the field."

Sancho ate without any urging, gulping down mouthfuls that were like the knots on a tether, as they sat there in the dark.

"You are a squire of the right sort," he said, "loyal and true, and you live in grand style as shown by this feast, which I would almost say was produced by magic. You are not like me, poor wretch, who have in my saddlebags only a morsel of cheese so hard you could crack a giant's skull with it, three or four dozen carob beans, and a few nuts. For this I have my master to thank, who believes in observing the rule that knights-errant should nourish and sustain themselves on nothing but dried fruits and the herbs of the field."

"Upon my word, brother," said the other squire, "my stomach was not made for thistles, wild pears, and woodland herbs. Let our masters observe those knightly laws and traditions and eat what their rules prescribe; I carry a hamper of food and a flask on my saddlebow, whether they like it or not. And speaking of that flask, how I love it! There is scarcely a minute in the day that I'm not hugging and kissing it, over and over again."

As he said this, he placed the wine bag in Sancho's hands, who put it to his mouth, threw his head back, and sat there gazing up at the stars for a quarter of an hour. Then, when he had finished drinking, he let his head loll on one side and heaved a deep sigh.

"The whoreson rascal!" he exclaimed, "that's a fine vintage for you!"

"There!" cried the Squire of the Wood, as he heard the epithet Sancho had used, "do you see how you have praised this wine by calling it 'whoreson'?"

"I grant you," replied Sancho, "that it is no insult to call anyone a son of a whore so long as you really do mean to praise him. But tell me, sir, in the name of what you love most, is this the wine of Ciudad Real?"[9]

---

8. Of low quality.   9. The main town in La Mancha and the center of a wine region.

"What a winetaster you are! It comes from nowhere else, and it's a few years old, at that."

"Leave it to me," said Sancho, "and never fear, I'll show you how much I know about it. Would you believe me, Sir Squire, I have such a great natural instinct in this matter of wines that I have but to smell a vintage and I will tell you the country where it was grown, from what kind of grapes, what it tastes like, and how good it is, and everything that has to do with it. There is nothing so unusual about this, however, seeing that on my father's side were two of the best winetasters La Mancha has known in many a year, in proof of which, listen to the story of what happened to them.

"The two were given a sample of wine from a certain vat and asked to state its condition and quality and determine whether it was good or bad. One of them tasted it with the tip of his tongue while the other merely brought it up to his nose. The first man said that it tasted of iron, the second that it smelled of Cordovan leather. The owner insisted that the vat was clean and that there could be nothing in the wine to give it a flavor of leather or of iron, but, nevertheless, the two famous winetasters stood their ground. Time went by, and when they came to clean out the vat they found in it a small key attached to a leather strap. And so your Grace may see for yourself whether or not one who comes of that kind of stock has a right to give his opinion in such cases."

"And for that very reason," said the Squire of the Wood, "I maintain that we ought to stop going about in search of adventures. Seeing that we have loaves, let us not go looking for cakes, but return to our cottages, for God will find us there if He so wills."

"I mean to stay with my master," Sancho replied, "until he reaches Saragossa, but after that we will come to an understanding."

The short of the matter is, the two worthy squires talked so much and drank so much that sleep had to tie their tongues and moderate their thirst, since to quench the latter was impossible. Clinging to the wine flask, which was almost empty by now, and with half-chewed morsels of food in their mouths, they both slept peacefully; and we shall leave them there as we go on to relate what took place between the Knight of the Wood and the Knight of the Mournful Countenance.

CHAPTER 14

Wherein is continued the adventure of the Knight of the Wood.

In the course of the long conversation that took place between Don Quixote and the Knight of the Wood, the history informs us that the latter addressed the following remarks to the Manchegan:

"In short, Sir Knight, I would have you know that my destiny, or, more properly speaking, my own free choice, has led me to fall in love with the peerless Casildea de Vandalia. I call her peerless for the reason that she has no equal as regards either her bodily proportions or her very great beauty. This Casildea, then, of whom I am telling you, repaid my worthy affections and honorable intentions by forcing me, as Hercules was forced by his stepmother, to incur many and diverse perils;[1] and each time as I overcame one of them she would promise me that with the next one I should have that which I desired; but instead my labors have continued, forming a chain whose links I am no longer able to count, nor can I say which will be the last one, that shall mark the beginning of the realization of my hopes.

"One time she sent me forth to challenge that famous giantess of Seville, known as La Giralda,[2] who is as strong and brave as if made of brass, and who without moving from the spot where she stands is the most changeable and fickle woman in the world. I came, I saw, I conquered her, I made her stand still and point in one direction only, and for more than a week nothing but north winds blew. Then, there was that other time when Casildea sent me to lift those ancient stones, the mighty Bulls of Guisando,[3] an enterprise that had better have been entrusted to porters than to knights. On another occasion she commanded me to hurl myself down into the Cabra chasm[4]—an unheard-of and terribly dangerous undertaking—and bring her back a detailed account of what lay concealed in that deep and gloomy pit. I rendered La Giralda motionless, I lifted the Bulls of Guisando, and I threw myself into the abyss and brought to light what was hidden in its depths; yet my hopes are dead—how dead!—while her commands and her scorn are as lively as can be.

"Finally, she commanded me to ride through all the provinces of Spain and compel all the knights-errant whom I met with to confess that she is the most beautiful woman now living and that I am the most enamored man of arms that is to be found anywhere in the world. In fulfillment of this behest I have already traveled over the greater part of these realms and have vanquished many knights who have dared to contradict me. But the one whom I am proudest to have overcome in single combat is that famous gentleman, Don Quixote de la Mancha; for I made him confess that my Casildea is more beautiful than his Dulcinea, and by achieving such a conquest I reckon that I have conquered all the others on the face of the earth, seeing that this same Don Quixote had himself routed them. Accordingly, when I vanquished him, his fame, glory, and honor passed over and were transferred to my person.

> The brighter is the conquered one's lost crown,
> The greater is the conqueror's renown.[5]

Thus, the innumerable exploits of the said Don Quixote are now set down to my account and are indeed my own."

Don Quixote was astounded as he listened to the Knight of the Wood, and was about to tell him any number of times that he lied; the words were on the tip of his tongue, but he held them back as best he could, thinking

---

1. Son of Zeus and Alcmena, Hercules was persecuted by Zeus's wife Hera.   2. Actually a statue on the Moorish belfry of the cathedral at Seville.   3. Statues representing animals and supposedly marking a place where Caesar defeated Pompey. (Cf. the use of Caesar's famous words a few lines above.) 4. Possibly an ancient mine in the Sierra de Cabra near Cordova.   5. From the *Araucana*, a poem by Alonso de Ercilla y Zúñiga on the Spanish struggle against the Araucanian Indians of Chile.

that he would bring the other to confess with his own lips that what he had said was a lie. And so it was quite calmly that he now replied to him.

"Sir Knight," he began, "as to the assertion that your Grace has conquered most of the knights-errant in Spain and even in all the world, I have nothing to say, but that you have vanquished Don Quixote de la Mancha, I am inclined to doubt. It may be that it was someone else who resembled him, although there are very few that do."

"What do you mean?" replied the one of the Wood. "I swear by the heavens above that I did fight with Don Quixote and that I overcame him and forced him to yield. He is a tall man, with a dried-up face, long, lean legs, graying hair, an eagle-like nose somewhat hooked, and a big, black, drooping mustache. He takes the field under the name of the Knight of the Mournful Countenance, he has for squire a peasant named Sancho Panza, and he rides a famous steed called Rocinante. Lastly, the lady of his heart is a certain Dulcinea del Toboso, once upon a time known as Aldonza Lorenzo, just as my own lady, whose name is Casildea and who is an Andalusian by birth, is called by me Casildea de Vandalia. If all this is not sufficient to show that I speak the truth, here is my sword which shall make incredulity itself believe."

"Calm yourself, Sir Knight," replied Don Quixote, "and listen to what I have to say to you. You must know that this Don Quixote of whom you speak is the best friend that I have in the world, so great a friend that I may say that I feel toward him as I do toward my own self; and from all that you have told me, the very definite and accurate details that you have given me, I cannot doubt that he is the one whom you have conquered. On the other hand, the sight of my eyes and the touch of my hands assure me that he could not possibly be the one, unless some enchanter who is his enemy— for he has many, and one in particular who delights in persecuting him— may have assumed the knight's form and then permitted himself to be routed, by way of defrauding Don Quixote of the fame which his high deeds of chivalry have earned for him throughout the known world. To show you how true this may be, I will inform you that not more than a couple of days ago those same enemy magicians transformed the figure and person of the beauteous Dulcinea del Toboso into a low and mean village lass, and it is possible that they have done something of the same sort to the knight who is her lover. And if all this does not suffice to convince you of the truth of what I say, here is Don Quixote himself who will maintain it by force of arms, on foot or on horseback, or in any way you like."

Saying this, he rose and laid hold of his sword, and waited to see what the Knight of the Wood's decision would be. That worthy now replied in a voice as calm as the one Don Quixote had used.

"Pledges," he said, "do not distress one who is sure of his ability to pay. He who was able to overcome you when you were transformed, Señor Don Quixote, may hope to bring you to your knees when you are your own proper self. But inasmuch as it is not fitting that knights should perform their feats of arms in the darkness, like ruffians and highwaymen, let us wait until it is day in order that the sun may behold what we do. And the condition governing our encounter shall be that the one who is vanquished must submit to the will of his conqueror and perform all those things that are commanded of him, provided they are such as are in keeping with the state of knighthood."

"With that condition and understanding," said Don Quixote, "I shall be satisfied."

With this, they went off to where their squires were, only to find them snoring away as hard as when sleep had first overtaken them. Awakening the pair, they ordered them to look to the horses; for as soon as the sun was up the two knights meant to stage an arduous and bloody single-handed combat. At this news Sancho was astonished and terrified, since, as a result of what the other squire had told him of the Knight of the Wood's prowess, he was led to fear for his master's safety. Nevertheless, he and his friend now went to seek the mounts without saying a word, and they found the animals all together, for by this time the two horses and the ass had smelled one another out. On the way the Squire of the Wood turned to Sancho and addressed him as follows:

"I must inform you, brother, that it is the custom of the fighters of Andalusia, when they are godfathers in any combat, not to remain idly by, with folded hands, while their godsons fight it out. I tell you this by way of warning you that while our masters are settling matters, we, too, shall have to come to blows and hack each other to bits."

"The custom, Sir Squire," replied Sancho, "may be all very well among the fighters and ruffians that you mention, but with the squires of knights-errant it is not to be thought of. At least, I have never heard my master speak of any such custom, and he knows all the laws of chivalry by heart. But granting that it is true and that there is a law which states in so many words that squires must fight while their masters do, I have no intention of obeying it but rather will pay whatever penalty is laid on peaceable-minded ones like myself, for I am sure it cannot be more than a couple of pounds of wax,[6] and that would be less expensive than the lint which it would take to heal my head—I can already see it split in two. What's more, it's out of the question for me to fight since I have no sword nor did I ever in my life carry one."

"That," said the one of the Wood, "is something that is easily remedied. I have here two linen bags of the same size. You take one and I'll take the other and we will fight that way, on equal terms."

"So be it, by all means," said Sancho, "for that will simply knock the dust out of us without wounding us."

"But that's not the way it's to be," said the other squire. "Inside the bags, to keep the wind from blowing them away, we will put a half-dozen nice smooth pebbles of the same weight, and so we'll be able to give each other a good pounding without doing ourselves any real harm or damage."

"Body of my father!" cried Sancho, "just look, will you, at the marten

6. In some confraternities, penalties were paid in wax, presumably to make church candles.

and sable and wads of carded cotton that he's stuffing into those bags so that we won't get our heads cracked or our bones crushed to a pulp. But I am telling you, *Señor mio*, that even though you fill them with silken pellets, I don't mean to fight. Let our masters fight and make the best of it, but as for us, let us drink and live; for time will see to ending our lives without any help on our part by way of bringing them to a close before they have reached their proper season and fall from ripeness."

"Nevertheless," replied the Squire of the Wood, "fight we must, if only for half an hour."

"No," Sancho insisted, "that I will not do. I will not be so impolite or so ungrateful as to pick any quarrel however slight with one whose food and drink I've shared. And, moreover, who in the devil could bring himself to fight in cold blood, when he's not angry or vexed in any way?"

"I can take care of that, right enough," said the one of the Wood. "Before we begin, I will come up to your Grace as nicely as you please and give you three or four punches that will stretch you out at my feet; and that will surely be enough to awaken your anger, even though it's sleeping sounder than a dormouse."

"And I," said Sancho, "have another idea that's every bit as good as yours. I will take a big club, and before your Grace has had a chance to awaken my anger I will put yours to sleep with such mighty whacks that if it wakes at all it will be in the other world; for it is known there that I am not the man to let my face be mussed by anyone, and let each look out for the arrow.[7] But the best thing to do would be to leave one's anger to its slumbers, for no one knows the heart of any other, he who comes for wool may go back shorn, and God bless peace and curse all strife. If a hunted cat when surrounded and cornered turns into a lion, God knows what I who am a man might not become. And so from this time forth I am warning you, Sir Squire, that all the harm and damage that may result from our quarrel will be upon your head."

"Very well," the one of the Wood replied, "God will send the dawn and we shall make out somehow."

At that moment gay-colored birds of all sorts began warbling in the trees and with their merry and varied songs appeared to be greeting and welcoming the fresh-dawning day, which already at the gates and on the balconies of the east was revealing its beautiful face as it shook out from its hair an infinite number of liquid pearls. Bathed in this gentle moisture, the grass seemed to shed a pearly spray, the willows distilled a savory manna, the fountains laughed, the brooks murmured, the woods were glad, and the meadows put on their finest raiment. The first thing that Sancho Panza beheld, as soon as it was light enough to tell one object from another, was the Squire of the Wood's nose, which was so big as to cast into the shade all the rest of his body. In addition to being of enormous size, it is said to have been hooked in the middle and all covered with warts of a mulberry hue, like eggplant; it hung down for a couple of inches below his mouth,

7. A proverbial expression from archery: let each one take care of his own arrow. Other obviously proverbial expressions follow, as is typical of Sancho's speech.

and the size, color, warts, and shape of this organ gave his face so ugly an appearance that Sancho began trembling hand and foot like a child with convulsions and made up his mind then and there that he would take a couple of hundred punches before he would let his anger be awakened to a point where he would fight with this monster.

Don Quixote in the meanwhile was surveying his opponent, who had already adjusted and closed his helmet so that it was impossible to make out what he looked like. It was apparent, however, that he was not very tall and was stockily built. Over his armor he wore a coat of some kind or other made of what appeared to be the finest cloth of gold, all bespangled with glittering mirrors that resembled little moons and that gave him a most gallant and festive air, while above his helmet were a large number of waving plumes, green, white, and yellow in color. His lance, which was leaning against a tree, was very long and stout and had a steel point of more than a palm in length. Don Quixote took all this in, and from what he observed concluded that his opponent must be of tremendous strength, but he was not for this reason filled with fear as Sancho Panza was. Rather, he proceeded to address the Knight of the Mirrors,[8] quite boldly and in a highbred manner.

"Sir Knight," he said, "if in your eagerness to fight you have not lost your courtesy, I would beg you to be so good as to raise your visor a little in order that I may see if your face is as handsome as your trappings."

"Whether you come out of this emprise the victor or the vanquished, Sir Knight," he of the Mirrors replied, "there will be ample time and opportunity for you to have a sight of me. If I do not now gratify your desire, it is because it seems to me that I should be doing a very great wrong to the beauteous Casildea de Vandalia by wasting the time it would take me to raise my visor before having forced you to confess that I am right in my contention, with which you are well acquainted."

"Well, then," said Don Quixote, "while we are mounting our steeds you might at least inform me if I am that knight of La Mancha whom you say you conquered."

"To that our[9] answer," said he of the Mirrors, "is that you are as like the knight I overcame as one egg is like another; but since you assert that you are persecuted by enchanters, I should not venture to state positively that you are the one in question."

"All of which," said Don Quixote, "is sufficient to convince me that you are laboring under a misapprehension; but in order to relieve you of it once and for all, let them bring our steeds, and in less time than you would spend in lifting your visor, if God, my lady, and my arm give me strength, I will see your face and you shall see that I am not the vanquished knight you take me to be."

With this, they cut short their conversation and mounted, and, turning Rocinante around, Don Quixote began measuring off the proper length of field for a run against his opponent as he of the Mirrors did the same. But

8. See note 1, page 1908.   9. Note the dignified, "majestic" plural form.

the Knight of La Mancha had not gone twenty paces when he heard his adversary calling to him, whereupon each of them turned halfway and he of the Mirrors spoke.

"I must remind you, Sir Knight," he said, "of the condition under which we fight, which is that the vanquished, as I have said before, shall place himself wholly at the disposition of the victor."

"I am aware of that," replied Don Quixote, "not forgetting the provision that the behest laid upon the vanquished shall not exceed the bounds of chivalry."

"Agreed," said the Knight of the Mirrors.

At that moment Don Quixote caught sight of the other squire's weird nose and was as greatly astonished by it as Sancho had been. Indeed, he took the fellow for some monster, or some new kind of human being wholly unlike those that people this world. As he saw his master riding away down the field preparatory to the tilt, Sancho was alarmed; for he did not like to be left alone with the big-nosed individual, fearing that one powerful swipe of that protuberance against his own nose would end the battle so far as he was concerned and he would be lying stretched out on the ground, from fear if not from the force of the blow.

He accordingly ran after the knight, clinging to one of Rocinante's stirrup straps, and when he thought it was time for Don Quixote to whirl about and bear down upon his opponent, he called to him and said, "Señor mio, I beg your Grace, before you turn for the charge, to help me up into that cork tree yonder where I can watch the encounter which your Grace is going to have with this knight better than I can from the ground and in a way that is much more to my liking."

"I rather think, Sancho," said Don Quixote, "that what you wish to do is to mount a platform where you can see the bulls without any danger to yourself."

"The truth of the matter is," Sancho admitted, "the monstrous nose on that squire has given me such a fright that I don't dare stay near him."

"It is indeed of such a sort," his master assured him, "that if I were not the person I am, I myself should be frightened. And so, come, I will help you up."

While Don Quixote tarried to see Sancho ensconced in the cork tree, the Knight of the Mirrors measured as much ground as seemed to him necessary and then, assuming that his adversary had done the same, without waiting for sound of trumpet or any other signal, he wheeled his horse, which was no swifter nor any more impressive-looking than Rocinante, and bore down upon his enemy at a mild trot; but when he saw that the Manchegan was busy helping his squire, he reined in his mount and came to a stop midway in his course, for which his horse was extremely grateful, being no longer able to stir a single step. To Don Quixote, on the other hand, it seemed as if his enemy was flying, and digging his spurs with all his might into Rocinante's lean flanks he caused that animal to run a bit for the first and only time, according to the history, for on all other occasions a simple trot had represented his utmost speed. And so it was that, with an unheard-of-fury, the Knight of the Mournful Countenance came down upon the Knight of the Mirrors as the latter sat there sinking his spurs all the way up to the buttons without being able to persuade his horse to budge a single inch from the spot where he had come to a sudden standstill.

It was at this fortunate moment, while his adversary was in such a predicament, that Don Quixote fell upon him, quite unmindful of the fact that the other knight was having trouble with his mount and either was unable or did not have time to put his lance at rest. The upshot of it was, he encountered him with such force that, much against his will, the Knight of the Mirrors went rolling over his horse's flanks and tumbled to the ground, where as a result of his terrific fall he lay as if dead, without moving hand or foot.

No sooner did Sancho perceive what had happened than he slipped down from the cork tree and ran up as fast as he could to where his master was. Dismounting from Rocinante, Don Quixote now stood over the Knight of the Mirrors, and undoing the helmet straps to see if the man was dead, or to give him air in case he was alive, he beheld—who can say what he beheld without creating astonishment, wonder, and amazement in those who hear the tale? The history tells us that it was the very countenance, form, aspect, physiognomy, effigy, and image of the bachelor Sansón Carrasco!

"Come, Sancho," he cried in a loud voice, "and see what is to be seen but is not to be believed. Hasten, my son, and learn what magic can do and how great is the power of wizards and enchanters."

Sancho came, and the moment his eyes fell on the bachelor Carrasco's face he began crossing and blessing himself a countless number of times. Meanwhile, the overthrown knight gave no signs of life.

"If you ask me, master," said Sancho, "I would say that the best thing for your Grace to do is to run his sword down the mouth of this one who appears to be the bachelor Carrasco; maybe by so doing you would be killing one of your enemies, the enchanters."

"That is not a bad idea," replied Don Quixote, "for the fewer enemies the better." And, drawing his sword, he was about to act upon Sancho's advice and counsel when the Knight of the Mirrors' squire came up to them, now minus the nose which had made him so ugly.

"Look well what you are doing, Don Quixote!" he cried. "The one who lies there at your feet is your Grace's friend, the bachelor Sansón Carrasco, and I am his squire."

"And where is your nose?" inquired Sancho, who was surprised to see him without that deformity.

"Here in my pocket," was the reply. And, thrusting his hand into his coat, he drew out a nose of varnished pasteboard of the make that has been described. Studying him more and more closely, Sancho finally exclaimed, in a voice that was filled with amazement, "Holy Mary preserve me! And is this not my neighbor and crony, Tomé Cecial?"

"That is who I am!" replied the de-nosed squire, "your good friend

Tomé Cecial, Sancho Panza. I will tell you presently of the means and snares and falsehoods that brought me here. But, for the present, I beg and entreat your master not to lay hands on, mistreat, wound, or slay the Knight of the Mirrors whom he now has at his feet; for without any doubt it is the rash and ill-advised bachelor Sansón Carrasco, our fellow villager."

The Knight of the Mirrors now recovered consciousness, and, seeing this, Don Quixote at once placed the naked point of his sword above the face of the vanquished one.

"Dead you are, knight," he said, "unless you confess that the peerless Dulcinea del Toboso is more beautiful than your Casildea de Vandalia. And what is more, you will have to promise that, should you survive this encounter and the fall you have had, you will go to the city of El Toboso and present yourself to her in my behalf, that she may do with you as she may see fit. And in case she leaves you free to follow your own will, you are to return to seek me out—the trail of my exploits will serve as a guide to bring you wherever I may be—and tell me all that has taken place between you and her. These conditions are in conformity with those that we arranged before our combat and they do not go beyond the bounds of knight-errantry."

"I confess," said the fallen knight, "that the tattered and filthy shoe of the lady Dulcinea del Toboso is of greater worth than the badly combed if clean beard of Casildea, and I promise to go to her presence and return to yours and to give you a complete and detailed account concerning anything you may wish to know."

"Another thing," added Don Quixote, "that you will have to confess and believe is that the knight you conquered was not and could not have been Don Quixote de la Mancha, but was some other that resembled him, just as I am convinced that you, though you appear to be the bachelor Sansón Carrasco, are another person in his form and likeness who has been put here by my enemies to induce me to restrain and moderate the impetuosity of my wrath and make a gentle use of my glorious victory."

"I confess, think, and feel as you feel, think, and believe," replied the lamed knight. "Permit me to rise, I beg of you, if the jolt I received in my fall will let me do so, for I am in very bad shape."

Don Quixote and Tomé Cecial the squire now helped him to his feet. As for Sancho, he could not take his eyes off Tomé but kept asking him one question after another, and although the answers he received afforded clear enough proof that the man was really his fellow townsman, the fear that had been aroused in him by his master's words—about the enchanters' having transformed the Knight of the Mirrors into the bachelor Sansón Carrasco—prevented him from believing the truth that was apparent to his eyes. The short of it is, both master and servant were left with this delusion as the other ill-errant knight and his squire, in no pleasant state of mind, took their departure with the object of looking for some village where they might be able to apply poultices and splints to the bachelor's battered ribs.

Don Quixote and Sancho then resumed their journey along the road to Saragossa, and here for the time being the history leaves them in order to

give an account of who the Knight of the Mirrors and his long-nosed squire
really were.

CHAPTER 15

Wherein is told and revealed who the Knight of the Mirrors and his
squire were.

Don Quixote went off very happy, self-satisfied, and vainglorious at having achieved a victory over so valiant a knight as he imagined the one of
the Mirrors to be, from whose knightly word he hoped to learn whether or
not the spell which had been put upon his lady was still in effect; for,
unless he chose to forfeit his honor, the vanquished contender must of
necessity return and give an account of what had happened in the course
of his interview with her. But Don Quixote was of one mind, the Knight
of the Mirrors of another, for, as has been stated, the latter's only thought
at the moment was to find some village where plasters were available.

The history goes on to state that when the bachelor Sansón Carrasco
advised Don Quixote to resume his feats of chivalry, after having desisted
from them for a while, this action was taken as the result of a conference
which he had held with the curate and the barber as to the means to be
adopted in persuading the knight to remain quietly at home and cease
agitating himself over his unfortunate adventures. It had been Carrasco's
suggestion, to which they had unanimously agreed, that they let Don Quixote
sally forth, since it appeared to be impossible to prevent his doing so, and
that Sansón should then take to the road as a knight-errant and pick a
quarrel and do battle with him. There would be no difficulty about finding
a pretext, and then the bachelor knight would overcome him (which was
looked upon as easy of accomplishment), having first entered into a pact
to the effect that the vanquished should remain at the mercy and bidding
of his conqueror. The behest in this case was to be that the fallen one
should return to his village and home and not leave it for the space of two
years or until further orders were given him, it being a certainty that, once
having been overcome, Don Quixote would fulfill the agreement, in order
not to contravene or fail to obey the laws of chivalry. And it was possible
that in the course of his seclusion he would forget his fancies, or they
would at least have an opportunity to seek some suitable cure for his madness.

Sansón agreed to undertake this, and Tomé Cecial, Sancho's friend and
neighbor, a merry but featherbrained chap, offered to go along as squire.
Sansón then proceeded to arm himself in the manner that has been described,
while Tomé disguised his nose with the aforementioned mask so that his
crony would not recognize him when they met. Thus equipped, they followed the same route as Don Quixote and had almost caught up with him
by the time he had the adventure with the Cart of Death. They finally
overtook him in the wood, where those events occurred with which the
attentive reader is already familiar; and if it had not been for the knight's
extraordinary fancies, which led him to believe that the bachelor was not

the bachelor, the said bachelor might have been prevented from ever attaining his degree of licentiate, as a result of having found no nests where he thought to find birds.

Seeing how ill they had succeeded in their undertaking and what an end they had reached, Tomé Cecial now addressed his master.

"Surely, Señor Sansón Carrasco," he said, "we have had our deserts. It is easy enough to plan and embark upon an enterprise, but most of the time it's hard to get out of it. Don Quixote is a madman and we are sane, yet he goes away sound and laughing while your Grace is left here, battered and sorrowful. I wish you would tell me now who is the crazier: the one who is so because he cannot help it, or he who turns crazy of his own free will?"

"The difference between the two," replied Sansón, "lies in this: that the one who cannot help being crazy will be so always, whereas the one who is a madman by choice can leave off being one whenever he so desires."

"Well," said Tomé Cecial, "since that is the way it is, and since I chose to be crazy when I became your Grace's squire, by the same reasoning I now choose to stop being insane and to return to my home."

"That is your affair," said Sansón, "but to imagine that I am going back before I have given Don Quixote a good thrashing is senseless; and what will urge me on now is not any desire to see him recover his wits, but rather a thirst for vengeance; for with the terrible pain that I have in my ribs, you can't expect me to feel very charitable."

Conversing in this manner they kept on until they reached a village where it was their luck to find a bonesetter to take care of poor Sansón. Tomé Cecial then left him and returned home, while the bachelor meditated plans for revenge. The history has more to say of him in due time, but for the present it goes on to make merry with Don Quixote.

CHAPTER 16

Of what happened to Don Quixote upon his meeting with a prudent gentleman of La Mancha.

With that feeling of happiness and vainglorious self-satisfaction that has been mentioned, Don Quixote continued on his way, imagining himself to be, as a result of the victory he had just achieved, the most valiant knight-errant of the age. Whatever adventures might befall him from then on he regarded as already accomplished and brought to a fortunate conclusion. He thought little now of enchanters and enchantments and was unmindful of the innumerable beatings he had received in the course of his knightly wanderings, of the volley of pebbles that had knocked out half his teeth, of the ungratefulness of the galley slaves and the audacity of the Yanguesans whose poles had fallen upon his body like rain. In short, he told himself, if he could but find the means, manner, or way of freeing his lady Dulcinea of the spell that had been put upon her, he would not envy the greatest good fortune that the most fortunate of knights-errant in ages past had ever by any possibility attained.

He was still wholly wrapped up in these thoughts when Sancho spoke to him.

"Isn't it strange, sir, that I can still see in front of my eyes the huge and monstrous nose of my old crony, Tomé Cecial?"

"And do you by any chance believe, Sancho, that the Knight of the Mirrors was the bachelor Sansón Carrasco and that his squire was your friend Tomé?"

"I don't know what to say to that," replied Sancho. "All I know is that the things he told me about my home, my wife and young ones, could not have come from anybody else; and the face, too, once you took the nose away, was the same as Tomé Cecial's, which I have seen many times in our village, right next door to my own house, and the tone of voice was the same also."

"Let us reason the matter out, Sancho," said Don Quixote. "Look at it this way: how can it be thought that the bachelor Sansón Carrasco would come as a knight-errant, equipped with offensive and defensive armor, to contend with me? Am I, perchance, his enemy? Have I given him any occasion to cherish a grudge against me? Am I a rival of his? Or can it be jealousy of the fame I have acquired that has led him to take up the profession of arms?"

"Well, then, sir," Sancho answered him, "how are we to explain the fact that the knight was so like the bachelor and his squire like my friend? And if this was a magic spell, as your Grace has said, was there no other pair in the world whose likeness they might have taken?"

"It is all a scheme and a plot," replied Don Quixote, "on the part of those wicked magicians who are persecuting me and who, foreseeing that I would be the victor in the combat, saw to it that the conquered knight should display the face of my friend the bachelor, so that the affection which I bear him would come between my fallen enemy and the edge of my sword and might of my arm, to temper the righteous indignation of my heart. In that way, he who had sought by falsehood and deceits to take my life, would be left to go on living. As proof of all this, Sancho, experience, which neither lies nor deceives, has already taught you how easy it is for enchanters to change one countenance into another, making the beautiful ugly and the ugly beautiful. It was not two days ago that you beheld the peerless Dulcinea's beauty and elegance in its entirety and natural form, while I saw only the repulsive features of a low and ignorant peasant girl with cataracts over her eyes and a foul smell in her mouth. And if the perverse enchanter was bold enough to effect so vile a transformation as this, there is certainly no cause for wonderment at what he has done in the case of Sansón Carrasco and your friend, all by way of snatching my glorious victory out of my hands. But in spite of it all, I find consolation in the fact that, whatever the shape he may have chosen to assume, I have laid my enemy low."

"God knows what the truth of it all may be," was Sancho's comment. Knowing as he did that Dulcinea's transformation had been due to his own scheming and plotting, he was not taken in by his master's delusions. He was at a loss for a reply, however, lest he say something that would reveal his own trickery.

As they were carrying on this conversation, they were overtaken by a man who, following the same road, was coming along behind them. He was mounted on a handsome flea-bitten mare and wore a hooded greatcoat of fine green cloth trimmed in tawny velvet and a cap of the same material, while the trappings of his steed, which was accoutered for the field, were green and mulberry in hue, his saddle being of the *jineta* mode.[1] From his broad green and gold shoulder strap there dangled a Moorish cutlass, and his half-boots were of the same make as the baldric. His spurs were not gilded but were covered with highly polished green lacquer, so that harmonizing as they did with the rest of his apparel, they seemed more appropriate than if they had been of purest gold. As he came up, he greeted the pair courteously and, spurring his mare, was about to ride on past when Don Quixote called to him.

"Gallant sir," he said, "If your Grace is going our way and is not in a hurry, it would be a favor to us if we might travel together."

"The truth is," replied the stranger, "I should not have ridden past you if I had not been afraid that the company of my mare would excite your horse."

"In that case, sir," Sancho spoke up, "you may as well rein in, for this horse of ours is the most virtuous and well mannered of any that there is. Never on such an occasion has he done anything that was not right—the only time he did misbehave, my master and I suffered for it aplenty. And so, I say again, your Grace may slow up if you like; for even if you offered him your mare on a couple of platters, he'd never try to mount her."

With this, the other traveler drew rein, being greatly astonished at Don Quixote's face and figure. For the knight was now riding along without his helmet, which was carried by Sancho like a piece of luggage on the back of his gray, in front of the packsaddle. If the green-clad gentleman stared hard at his new-found companion, the latter returned his gaze with an even greater intensity. He impressed Don Quixote as being a man of good judgment, around fifty years of age, with hair that was slightly graying and an aquiline nose, while the expression of his countenance was half humorous, half serious. In short, both his person and his accouterments indicated that he was an individual of some worth.

As for the man in green's impression of Don Quixote de la Mancha, he was thinking that he had never before seen any human being that resembled this one. He could not but marvel at the knight's long neck, his tall frame, and the leanness and the sallowness of his face, as well as his armor and his grave bearing, the whole constituting a sight such as had not been seen for many a day in those parts. Don Quixote in turn was quite conscious of the attentiveness with which the traveler was studying him and could tell from the man's astonished look how curious he was; and so,

---

1. A saddle with a high pommel and short stirrups.

being very courteous and fond of pleasing everyone, he proceeded to anticipate any questions that might be asked him.

"I am aware," he said, "that my appearance must strike your Grace as
being very strange and out of the ordinary, and for that reason I am not
surprised at your wonderment. But your Grace will cease to wonder when
I tell you, as I am telling you now, that I am a knight, one of those

> Of whom it is folks say,
> They to adventures go.

I have left my native heath, mortgaged my estate, given up my comfortable
life, and cast myself into fortune's arms for her to do with me what she
will. It has been my desire to revive a knight-errantry that is now dead, and
for some time past, stumbling here and falling there, now throwing myself
down headlong and then rising up once more, I have been able in good
part to carry out my design by succoring widows, protecting damsels, and
aiding the fallen, the orphans, and the young, all of which is the proper
and natural duty of knights-errant. As a result, owing to my many valiant
and Christian exploits, I have been deemed worthy of visiting in printed
form nearly all the nations of the world. Thirty thousand copies of my
history have been published, and, unless Heaven forbid, they will print
thirty million of them.

"In short, to put it all into a few words, or even one, I will tell you that
I am Don Quixote de la Mancha, otherwise known as the Knight of the
Mournful Countenance. Granted that self-praise is degrading, there still
are times when I must praise myself, that is to say, when there is no one
else present to speak in my behalf. And so, good sir, neither this steed nor
this lance nor this buckler nor this squire of mine, nor all the armor that I
wear and arms I carry, nor the sallowness of my complexion, nor my
leanness and gauntness, should any longer astonish you, now that you
know who I am and what the profession is that I follow."

Having thus spoken, Don Quixote fell silent, and the man in green was
so slow in replying that it seemed as if he was at a loss for words. Finally,
however, after a considerable while, he brought himself to the point of
speaking.

"You were correct, Sir Knight," he said, "about my astonishment and
my curiosity, but you have not succeeded in removing the wonderment
that the sight of you has aroused in me. You say that, knowing who you
are, I should not wonder any more, but such is not the case, for I am now
more amazed than ever. How can it be that there are knights-errant in the
world today and that histories of them are actually printed? I find it hard
to convince myself that at the present time there is anyone on earth who
goes about aiding widows, protecting damsels, defending the honor of wives,
and succoring orphans, and I should never have believed it had I not
beheld your Grace with my own eyes. Thank Heaven for that book that
your Grace tells me has been published concerning your true and exalted
deeds of chivalry, as it should cast into oblivion all the innumerable stories

of fictitious knights-errant with which the world is filled, greatly to the detriment of good morals and the prejudice and discredit of legitimate histories."

"As to whether the stories of knights-errant are fictitious or not," observed Don Quixote, "there is much that remains to be said."

"Why," replied the gentleman in green, "is there anyone who can doubt that such tales are false?"

"I doubt it," was the knight's answer, "but let the matter rest there. If our journey lasts long enough, I trust with God's help to be able to show your Grace that you are wrong in going along with those who hold it to be a certainty that they are not true."

From this last remark the traveler was led to suspect that Don Quixote must be some kind of crackbrain, and he was waiting for him to confirm the impression by further observations of the same sort; but before they could get off on another subject, the knight, seeing that he had given an account of his own station in life, turned to the stranger and politely inquired who his companion might be.

"I, Sir Knight of the Mournful Countenance," replied the one in the green-colored greatcoat, "am a gentleman, and a native of the village where, please God, we are going to dine today. I am more than moderately rich, and my name is Don Diego de Miranda. I spend my life with my wife and children and with my friends. My occupations are hunting and fishing, though I keep neither falcon nor hounds but only a tame partridge[2] and a bold ferret or two. I am the owner of about six dozen books, some of them in Spanish, others in Latin, including both histories and devotional works. As for books of chivalry, they have not as yet crossed the threshold of my door. My own preference is for profane rather than devotional writings, such as afford an innocent amusement, charming us by their style and arousing and holding our interest by their inventiveness, although I must say there are very few of that sort to be found in Spain.

"Sometimes," the man in green continued, "I dine with my friends and neighbors, and I often invite them to my house. My meals are wholesome and well prepared and there is always plenty to eat. I do not care for gossip, nor will I permit it in my presence. I am not lynx-eyed and do not pry into the lives and doings of others. I hear mass every day and share my substance with the poor, but make no parade of my good works lest hypocrisy and vainglory, those enemies that so imperceptibly take possession of the most modest heart, should find their way into mine. I try to make peace between those who are at strife. I am the devoted servant of Our Lady, and my trust is in the infinite mercy of God Our Savior."

Sancho had listened most attentively to the gentleman's account of his mode of life, and inasmuch as it seemed to him that this was a good and holy way to live and that the one who followed such a pattern ought to be able to work miracles, he now jumped down from his gray's back and,

2. Used as a decoy.

running over to seize the stranger's right stirrup, began kissing the feet of the man in green with a show of devotion that bordered on tears.

"Why are you doing that, brother?" the gentleman asked him. "What is the meaning of these kisses?"

"Let me kiss your feet," Sancho insisted, "for if I am not mistaken, your Grace is the first saint riding *jineta* fashion that I have seen in all the days of my life."

"I am not a saint," the gentleman assured him, "but a great sinner. It is you, brother, who are the saint; for you must be a good man, judging by the simplicity of heart that you show."

Sancho then went back to his packsaddle, having evoked a laugh from the depths of his master's melancholy and given Don Diego fresh cause for astonishment.

Don Quixote thereupon inquired of the newcomer how many children he had, remarking as he did so that the ancient philosophers, who were without a true knowledge of God, believed that mankind's greatest good lay in the gifts of nature, in those of fortune, and in having many friends and many and worthy sons.

"I, Señor Don Quixote," replied the gentleman, "have a son without whom I should, perhaps, be happier than I am. It is not that he is bad, but rather that he is not as good as I should like him to be. He is eighteen years old, and for six of those years he has been at Salamanca studying the Greek and Latin languages. When I desired him to pass on to other branches of learning, I found him so immersed in the science of Poetry (if it can be called such) that it was not possible to interest him in the Law, which I wanted him to study, nor in Theology, the queen of them all. My wish was that he might be an honor to his family; for in this age in which we are living our monarchs are in the habit of highly rewarding those forms of learning that are good and virtuous, since learning without virtue is like pearls on a dunghill. But he spends the whole day trying to decide whether such and such a verse of Homer's *Iliad* is well conceived or not, whether or not Martial is immodest in a certain epigram, whether certain lines of Vergil are to be understood in this way or in that. In short, he spends all of his time with the books written by those poets whom I have mentioned and with those of Horace, Persius, Juvenal, and Tibullus. As for our own moderns, he sets little store by them, and yet, for all his disdain of Spanish poetry, he is at this moment racking his brains in an effort to compose a gloss on a quatrain that was sent him from Salamanca and which, I fancy, is for some literary tournament."

To all this Don Quixote made the following answer:

"Children, sir, are out of their parents' bowels and so are to be loved whether they be good or bad, just as we love those that gave us life. It is for parents to bring up their offspring, from the time they are infants, in the paths of virtue, good breeding, proper conduct, and Christian morality, in order that, when they are grown, they may be a staff to the old age of the ones that bore them and an honor to their own posterity. As to compelling them to study a particular branch of learning, I am not so sure as to that, though there may be no harm in trying to persuade them to do so. But where there is no need to study *pane lucrando*[3]—where Heaven has provided them with parents that can supply their daily bread—I should be in favor of permitting them to follow that course to which they are most inclined; and although poetry may be more pleasurable than useful, it is not one of those pursuits that bring dishonor upon those who engage in them.

"Poetry in my opinion, my dear sir," he went on, "is a young and tender maid of surpassing beauty, who has many other damsels (that is to say, the other disciplines) whose duty it is to bedeck, embellish, and adorn her. She may call upon all of them for service, and all of them in turn depend upon her nod. She is not one to be rudely handled, nor dragged through the streets, nor exposed at street corners, in the market place, or in the private nooks of palaces. She is fashioned through an alchemy of such power that he who knows how to make use of it will be able to convert her into the purest gold of inestimable price. Possessing her, he must keep her within bounds and not permit her to run wild in bawdy satires or soulless sonnets. She is not to be put up for sale in any manner, unless it be in the form of heroic poems, pity-inspiring tragedies, or pleasing and ingenious comedies. Let mountebanks keep hands off her, and the ignorant mob as well, which is incapable of recognizing or appreciating the treasures that are locked within her. And do not think, sir, that I apply that term 'mob' solely to plebeians and those of low estate; for anyone who is ignorant, whether he be lord or prince, may, and should, be included in the vulgar herd.

"But," Don Quixote continued, "he who possesses the gift of poetry and who makes the use of it that I have indicated, shall become famous and his name shall be honored among all the civilized nations of the world. You have stated, sir, that your son does not greatly care for poetry written in our Spanish tongue, and in that I am inclined to think he is somewhat mistaken. My reason for saying so is this: the great Homer did not write in Latin, for the reason that he was a Greek, and Vergil did not write in Greek since he was a Latin. In a word, all the poets of antiquity wrote in the language which they had imbibed with their mother's milk and did not go searching after foreign ones to express their loftiest conceptions. This being so, it would be well if the same custom were to be adopted by all nations, the German poet being no longer looked down upon because he writes in German, nor the Castilian or the Basque for employing his native speech.

"As for your son, I fancy, sir, that his quarrel is not so much with Spanish poetry as with those poets who have no other tongue or discipline at their command such as would help to awaken their natural gift; and yet, here, too, he may be wrong. There is an opinion, and a true one, to the effect that 'the poet is born,' that is to say, it is as a poet that he comes forth from his mother's womb, and with the propensity that has been

3. Earning one's bread.

bestowed upon him by Heaven, without study or artifice, he produces those compositions that attest the truth of the line: '*Est deus in nobis,*' etc.[4] I further maintain that the born poet who is aided by art will have a great advantage over the one who by art alone would become a poet, the reason being that art does not go beyond, but merely perfects, nature; and so it is that, by combining nature with art and art with nature, the finished poet is produced.

"In conclusion, then, my dear sir, my advice to you would be to let your son go where his star beckons him; for being a good student as he must be, and having already successfully mounted the first step on the stairway of learning, which is that of languages, he will be able to continue of his own accord to the very peak of humane letters, an accomplishment that is altogether becoming in a gentleman, one that adorns, honors, and distinguishes him as much as the miter does the bishop or his flowing robe the learned jurisconsult. Your Grace well may reprove your son, should he compose satires that reflect upon the honor of other persons; in that case, punish him and tear them up. But should he compose discourses in the manner of Horace, in which he reprehends vice in general as that poet so elegantly does, then praise him by all means; for it is permitted the poet to write verses in which he inveighs against envy and the other vices as well, and to lash out at the vicious without, however, designating any particular individual. On the other hand, there are poets who for the sake of uttering something malicious would run the risk of being banished to the shores of Pontus.[5]

"If the poet be chaste where his own manners are concerned, he would likewise be modest in his verses, for the pen is the tongue of the mind, and whatever thoughts are engendered there are bound to appear in his writings. When kings and princes behold the marvelous art of poetry as practiced by prudent, virtuous, and serious-minded subjects of their realm, they honor, esteem, and reward those persons and crown them with the leaves of the tree that is never struck by lightning[6]—as if to show that those who are crowned and adorned with such wreaths are not to be assailed by anyone."

The gentleman in the green-colored greatcoat was vastly astonished by this speech of Don Quixote's and was rapidly altering the opinion he had previously held, to the effect that his companion was but a crackbrain. In the middle of the long discourse, which was not greatly to his liking, Sancho had left the highway to go seek a little milk from some shepherds who were draining the udders of their ewes near by. Extremely well pleased with the knight's sound sense and excellent reasoning, the gentleman was about to resume the conversation when, raising his head, Don Quixote caught sight of a cart flying royal flags that was coming toward them down the road and, thinking it must be a fresh adventure, began calling to Sancho in a loud voice to bring him his helmet. Whereupon Sancho hastily left the shepherds and spurred his gray until he was once more alongside

4. "There is a god in us." (Ovid, *Fasti*, VI, 5.)   5. As Ovid was by Augustus in A.D. 8.   6. The laurel tree.

his master, who was now about to encounter a dreadful and bewildering ordeal.

("For I Well Know the Meaning of Valor")

CHAPTER 17

Wherein Don Quixote's unimaginable courage reaches its highest point, together with the adventure of the lions and its happy ending.

The history relates that, when Don Quixote called to Sancho to bring him his helmet, the squire was busy buying some curds from the shepherds and, flustered by his master's great haste, did not know what to do with them or how to carry them. Having already paid for the curds, he did not care to lose them, and so he decided to put them into the headpiece, and, acting upon this happy inspiration, he returned to see what was wanted of him.

"Give me that helmet," said the knight; "for either I know little about adventures or here is one where I am going to need my armor."

Upon hearing this, the gentleman in the green-colored greatcoat looked around in all directions but could see nothing except the cart that was approaching them, decked out with two or three flags which indicated that the vehicle in question must be conveying his Majesty's property. He remarked as much to Don Quixote, but the latter paid no attention, for he was always convinced that whatever happened to him meant adventures and more adventures.

"Forewarned is forearmed," he said. "I lose nothing by being prepared, knowing as I do that I have enemies both visible and invisible and cannot tell when or where or in what form they will attack me."

Turning to Sancho, he asked for his helmet again, and as there was no time to shake out the curds, the squire had to hand it to him as it was. Don Quixote took it and, without noticing what was in it, hastily clapped it on his head; and forthwith, as a result of the pressure on the curds, the whey began running down all over his face and beard, at which he was very much startled.

"What is this, Sancho?" he cried. "I think my head must be softening or my brains melting, or else I am sweating from head to foot. If sweat it be, I assure you it is not from fear, though I can well believe that the adventure which now awaits me is a terrible one indeed. Give me something with which to wipe my face, if you have anything, for this perspiration is so abundant that it blinds me."

Sancho said nothing but gave him a cloth and at the same time gave thanks to God that his master had not discovered what the trouble was. Don Quixote wiped his face and then took off his helmet to see what it was that made his head feel so cool. Catching sight of that watery white mass, he lifted it to his nose and smelled it.

"By the life of my lady Dulcinea del Toboso!" he exclaimed. "Those are curds that you have put there, you treacherous, brazen, ill-mannered squire!"

To this Sancho replied, very calmly and with a straight face, "If they are curds, give them to me, your Grace, so that I can eat them. But no, let the devil eat them, for he must be the one who did it. Do you think I would be so bold as to soil your Grace's helmet? Upon my word, master, by the understanding that God has given me, I, too, must have enchanters who are persecuting me as your Grace's creature and one of his members, and they are the ones who put that filthy mess there to make you lose your patience and your temper and cause you to whack my ribs as you are in the habit of doing. Well, this time, I must say, they have missed the mark; for I trust my master's good sense to tell him that I have neither curds nor milk nor anything of the kind, and if I did have, I'd put it in my stomach and not in that helmet."

"That may very well be," said Don Quixote.

Don Diego was observing all this and was more astonished than ever, especially when, after he had wiped his head, face, beard, and helmet, Don Quixote once more donned the piece of armor and, settling himself in the stirrups, proceeded to adjust his sword and fix his lance.

"Come what may, here I stand, ready to take on Satan himself in person!" shouted the knight.

The cart with the flags had come up to them by this time, accompanied only by a driver riding one of the mules and a man seated up in front.

"Where are you going, brothers?" Don Quixote called out as he placed himself in the path of the cart. "What conveyance is this, what do you carry in it, and what is the meaning of those flags?"

"The cart is mine," replied the driver, "and in it are two fierce lions in cages which the governor of Oran is sending to court as a present for his Majesty. The flags are those of our lord the King, as a sign that his property goes here."

"And are the lions large?" inquired Don Quixote.

It was the man sitting at the door of the cage who answered him. "The largest," he said, "that ever were sent from Africa to Spain. I am the lion-keeper and I have brought back others, but never any like these. They are male and female. The male is in this first cage, the female in the one behind. They are hungry right now, for they have had nothing to eat today; and so we'd be obliged if your Grace would get out of the way, for we must hasten on to the place where we are to feed them."

"Lion whelps against me?" said Don Quixote with a slight smile. "Lion whelps against me? And at such an hour? Then, by God, those gentlemen who sent them shall see whether I am the man to be frightened by lions. Get down, my good fellow, and since you are the lionkeeper, open the cages and turn those beasts out for me; and in the middle of this plain I will teach them who Don Quixote de la Mancha is, notwithstanding and in spite of the enchanters who are responsible for their being here."

"So," said the gentleman to himself as he heard this, "our worthy knight has revealed himself. It must indeed be true that the curds have softened his skull and mellowed his brains."

At this point Sancho approached him. "For God's sake, sir," he said, "do something to keep my master from fighting those lions. For if he does, they're going to tear us all to bits."

"Is your master, then, so insane," the gentleman asked, "that you fear and believe he means to tackle those fierce animals?"

"It is not that he is insane," replied Sancho, "but, rather, foolhardy."

"Very well," said the gentleman, "I will put a stop to it." And going up to Don Quixote, who was still urging the lionkeeper to open the cages, he said, "Sir Knight, knights-errant should undertake only those adventures that afford some hope of a successful outcome, not those that are utterly hopeless to begin with; for valor when it turns to temerity has in it more of madness than of bravery. Moreover, these lions have no thought of attacking your Grace but are a present to his Majesty, and it would not be well to detain them or interfere with their journey."

"My dear sir," answered Don Quixote, "you had best go mind your tame partridge and that bold ferret of yours and let each one attend to his own business. This is my affair, and I know whether these gentlemen, the lions, have come to attack me or not." He then turned to the lionkeeper. "I swear, Sir Rascal, if you do not open those cages at once, I'll pin you to the cart with this lance!"

Perceiving how determined the armed phantom was, the driver now spoke up. "Good sir," he said, "will your Grace please be so kind as to let me unhitch the mules and take them to a safe place before you turn those lions loose? For if they kill them for me, I am ruined for life, since the mules and cart are all the property I own."

"O man of little faith!" said Don Quixote. "Get down and unhitch your mules if you like, but you will soon see that it was quite unnecessary and that you might have spared yourself the trouble."

The driver did so, in great haste, as the lionkeeper began shouting, "I want you all to witness that I am being compelled against my will to open the cages and turn the lions out, and I further warn this gentleman that he will be responsible for all the harm and damage the beasts may do, plus my wages and my fees. You other gentlemen take cover before I open the doors; I am sure they will not do any harm to me."

Once more Don Diego sought to persuade his companion not to commit such an act of madness, as it was tempting God to undertake anything so foolish as that; but Don Quixote's only answer was that he knew what he was doing. And when the gentleman in green insisted that he was sure the knight was laboring under a delusion and ought to consider the matter well, the latter cut him short.

"Well, then, sir," he said, "if your Grace does not care to be a spectator at what you believe is going to turn out to be a tragedy, all you have to do is to spur your flea-bitten mare and seek safety."

Hearing this, Sancho with tears in his eyes again begged him to give up the undertaking, in comparison with which the adventure of the windmills and the dreadful one at the fulling mills—indeed, all the exploits his master had ever in the course of his life undertaken—were but bread and cakes.

"Look, sir," Sancho went on, "there is no enchantment here nor anything of the sort. Through the bars and chinks of that cage I have seen a real lion's claw, and judging by the size of it, the lion that it belongs to is bigger than a mountain."

"Fear, at any rate," said Don Quixote, "will make him look bigger to you than half the world. Retire, Sancho, and leave me, and if I die here, you know our ancient pact: you are to repair to Dulcinea—I say no more."

To this he added other remarks that took away any hope they had that he might not go through with his insane plan. The gentleman in the green-colored greatcoat was of a mind to resist him but saw that he was no match for the knight in the matter of arms. Then, too, it did not seem to him the part of wisdom to fight it out with a madman; for Don Quixote now impressed him as being quite mad in every way. Accordingly, while the knight was repeating his threats to the lionkeeper, Don Diego spurred his mare, Sancho his gray, and the driver his mules, all of them seeking to put as great a distance as possible between themselves and the cart before the lions broke loose.

Sancho already was bewailing his master's death, which he was convinced was bound to come from the lions' claws, and at the same time he cursed his fate and called it an unlucky hour in which he had taken it into his head to serve such a one. But despite his tears and lamentations, he did not leave off thrashing his gray in an effort to leave the cart behind them. When the lionkeeper saw that those who had fled were a good distance away, he once more entreated and warned Don Quixote as he had warned and entreated him before, but the answer he received was that he might save his breath as it would do him no good and he had best hurry and obey. In the space of time that it took the keeper to open the first cage, Don Quixote considered the question as to whether it would be well to give battle on foot or on horseback. He finally decided that he would do better on foot, as he feared that Rocinante would become frightened at sight of the lions; and so, leaping down from his horse, he fixed his lance, braced his buckler, and drew his sword, and then advanced with marvelous daring and great resoluteness until he stood directly in front of the cart, meanwhile commending himself to God with all his heart and then to his lady Dulcinea.

Upon reaching this point, the reader should know, the author of our veracious history indulges in the following exclamatory passage:

"O great-souled Don Quixote de la Mancha, thou whose courage is beyond all praise, mirror wherein all the valiant of the world may behold themselves, a new and second Don Manuel de León,[7] once the glory and the honor of Spanish knighthood! With what words shall I relate thy terrifying exploit, how render it credible to the ages that are to come? What eulogies do not belong to thee of right, even though they consist of hyperbole piled upon hyperbole? On foot and singlehanded, intrepid and with greathearted valor, armed but with a sword, and not one of the keen-edged Little Dog[8] make, and with a shield that was not of gleaming and polished

---

7. Don Manuel Ponce de León, a paragon of gallantry and courtesy, belonging to the time of Ferdinand and Isabella.   8. The trademark of a famous armorer of Toledo and Saragossa.

steel, thou didst stand and wait for the two fiercest lions that ever the African forests bred! Thy deeds shall be thy praise, O valorous Manchegan; I leave them to speak for thee, since words fail me with which to extol them."

Here the author leaves off his exclamations and resumes the thread of the story.

Seeing Don Quixote posed there before him and perceiving that, unless he wished to incur the bold knight's indignation there was nothing for him to do but release the male lion, the keeper now opened the first cage, and it could be seen at once how extraordinarily big and horribly ugly the beast was. The first thing the recumbent animal did was to turn round, put out a claw, and stretch himself all over. Then he opened his mouth and yawned very slowly, after which he put out a tongue that was nearly two palms in length and with it licked the dust out of his eyes and washed his face. Having done this, he stuck his head outside the cage and gazed about him in all directions. His eyes were now like live coals and his appearance and demeanor were such as to strike terror in temerity itself. But Don Quixote merely stared at him attentively, waiting for him to descend from the cart so that they could come to grips, for the knight was determined to hack the brute to pieces, such was the extent of his unheard-of madness.

The lion, however, proved to be courteous rather than arrogant and was in no mood for childish bravado. After having gazed first in one direction and then in another, as has been said, he turned his back and presented his hind parts to Don Quixote and then very calmly and peaceably lay down and stretched himself out once more in his cage. At this, Don Quixote ordered the keeper to stir him up with a stick in order to irritate him and drive him out.

"That I will not do," the keeper replied, "for if I stir him, I will be the first one he will tear to bits. Be satisfied with what you have already accomplished, Sir Knight, which leaves nothing more to be said on the score of valor, and do not go tempting your fortune a second time. The door was open and the lion could have gone out if he had chosen; since he has not done so up to now, that means he will stay where he is all day long. Your Grace's stoutheartedness has been well established; for no brave fighter, as I see it, is obliged to do more than challenge his enemy and wait for him in the field; his adversary, if he does not come, is the one who is disgraced and the one who awaits him gains the crown of victory."

"That is the truth," said Don Quixote. "Shut the door, my friend, and bear me witness as best you can with regard to what you have seen me do here. I would have you certify: that you opened the door for the lion, that I waited for him and he did not come out, that I continued to wait and still he stayed there, and finally went back and lay down. I am under no further obligation. Away with enchantments, and God uphold the right, the truth, and true chivalry! So close the door, as I have told you, while I signal to the fugitives in order that they who were not present may hear of this exploit from your lips."

The keeper did as he was commanded, and Don Quixote, taking the cloth with which he had dried his face after the rain of curds, fastened it to the point of his lance and began summoning the runaways, who, all in a body with the gentleman in green bringing up the rear, were still fleeing and turning around to look back at every step. Sancho was the first to see the white cloth.

"May they slay me," he said, "if my master hasn't conquered those fierce beasts, for he's calling to us."

They all stopped and made sure that the one who was doing the signaling was indeed Don Quixote, and then, losing some of their fear, they little by little made their way back to a point where they could distinctly hear what the knight was saying. At last they returned to the cart, and as they drew near Don Quixote spoke to the driver.

"You may come back, brother, hitch your mules, and continue your journey. And you, Sancho, may give each of them two gold crowns to recompense them for the delay they have suffered on my account."

"That I will, right enough," said Sancho. "But what has become of the lions? Are they dead or alive?"

The keeper thereupon, in leisurely fashion and in full detail, proceeded to tell them how the encounter had ended, taking pains to stress to the best of his ability the valor displayed by Don Quixote, at sight of whom the lion had been so cowed that he was unwilling to leave his cage, though the door had been left open quite a while. The fellow went on to state that the knight had wanted him to stir the lion up and force him out, but had finally been convinced that this would be tempting God and so, much to his displeasure and against his will, had permitted the door to be closed.

"What do you think of that, Sancho?" asked Don Quixote. "Are there any spells that can withstand true gallantry? The enchanters may take my luck away, but to deprive me of my strength and courage is an impossibility."

Sancho then bestowed the crowns, the driver hitched his mules, and the lionkeeper kissed Don Quixote's hands for the favor received, promising that, when he reached the court, he would relate this brave exploit to the king himself.

"In that case," replied Don Quixote, "if his Majesty by any chance should inquire who it was that performed it, you are to say that it was the Knight of the Lions; for that is the name by which I wish to be known from now on, thus changing, exchanging, altering, and converting the one I have previously borne, that of Knight of the Mournful Countenance; in which respect I am but following the old custom of knights-errant, who changed their names whenever they liked or found it convenient to do so."

With this, the cart continued on its way, and Don Quixote, Sancho, and the gentleman in the green-colored greatcoat likewise resumed their journey. During all this time Don Diego de Miranda had not uttered a word but was wholly taken up with observing what Don Quixote did and listening to what he had to say. The knight impressed him as being a crazy sane man and an insane one on the verge of sanity. The gentleman did not happen to be familiar with the first part of our history, but if he had read it he would have ceased to wonder at such talk and conduct, for he would then have known what kind of madness this was. Remaining as he did in ignorance of his companion's malady, he took him now for a sensible individual and now for a madman, since what Don Quixote said was coherent, elegantly phrased, and to the point, whereas his actions were nonsensical, foolhardy, and downright silly. What greater madness could there be, Don Diego asked himself, than to don a helmet filled with curds and then persuade oneself that enchanters were softening one's cranium? What could be more rashly absurd than to wish to fight lions by sheer strength alone? He was roused from these thoughts, this inward soliloquy, by the sound of Don Quixote's voice.

"Undoubtedly, Señor Don Diego de Miranda, your Grace must take me for a fool and a madman, am I not right? And it would be small wonder if such were the case, seeing that my deeds give evidence of nothing else. But, nevertheless, I would advise your Grace that I am neither so mad nor so lacking in wit as I must appear to you to be. A gaily caparisoned knight giving a fortunate lance thrust to a fierce bull in the middle of a great square makes a pleasing appearance in the eyes of his king. The same is true of a knight clad in shining armor as he paces the lists in front of the ladies in some joyous tournament. It is true of all those knights who, by means of military exercises or what appear to be such, divert and entertain and, if one may say so, honor the courts of princes. But the best showing of all is made by a knight-errant who, traversing deserts and solitudes, crossroads, forests, and mountains, goes seeking dangerous adventures with the intention of bringing them to a happy and successful conclusion, and solely for the purpose of winning a glorious and enduring renown.

"More impressive, I repeat, is the knight-errant succoring a widow in some unpopulated place than a courtly man of arms making love to a damsel in the city. All knights have their special callings: let the courtier wait upon the ladies and lend luster by his liveries to his sovereign's palace; let him nourish impoverished gentlemen with the splendid fare of his table; let him give tourneys and show himself truly great, generous, and magnificent and a good Christian above all, thus fulfilling his particular obligations. But the knight-errant's case is different.

"Let the latter seek out the nooks and corners of the world; let him enter into the most intricate of labyrinths; let him attempt the impossible at every step; let him endure on desolate highlands the burning rays of the midsummer sun and in winter the harsh inclemencies of wind and frost; let no lions inspire him with fear, no monsters frighten him, no dragons terrify him, for to seek them out, attack them, and conquer them all is his chief and legitimate occupation. Accordingly, I whose lot it is to be numbered among the knights-errant cannot fail to attempt anything that appears to me to fall within the scope of my duties, just as I attacked those lions a while ago even though I knew it to be an exceedingly rash thing to do, for that was a matter that directly concerned me.

"For I well know the meaning of valor: namely, a virtue that lies between the two extremes of cowardice on the one hand and temerity on the other.

It is, nonetheless, better for the brave man to carry his bravery to the point of rashness than for him to sink into cowardice. Even as it is easier for the prodigal to become a generous man than it is for the miser, so is it easier for the foolhardy to become truly brave than it is for the coward to attain valor. And in this matter of adventures, you may believe me, Señor Don Diego, it is better to lose by a card too many than a card too few, and 'Such and such a knight is temerarious and overbold' sounds better to the ear than 'That knight is timid and a coward.' "

"I must assure you, Señor Don Quixote," replied Don Diego, "that everything your Grace has said and done will stand the test of reason; and it is my opinion that if the laws and ordinances of knight-errantry were to be lost, they would be found again in your Grace's bosom, which is their depository and storehouse. But it is growing late; let us hasten to my village and my home, where your Grace shall rest from your recent exertions; for if the body is not tired the spirit may be, and that sometimes results in bodily fatigue."

"I accept your offer as a great favor and an honor, Señor Don Diego," was the knight's reply. And, by spurring their mounts more than they had up to then, they arrived at the village around two in the afternoon and came to the house that was occupied by Don Diego, whom Don Quixote had dubbed the Knight of the Green-colored Greatcoat.

(Last Duel)

CHAPTER 64

Which treats of the adventure that caused Don Quixote the most sorrow of all those that have thus far befallen him.

. . . One morning, as Don Quixote went for a ride along the beach,[9] clad in full armor—for, as he was fond of saying, that was his only ornament, his only rest the fight, and, accordingly, he was never without it for a moment—he saw approaching him a horseman similarly arrayed from head to foot and with a brightly shining moon blazoned upon his shield.

As soon as he had come within earshot the stranger cried out to Don Quixote in a loud voice. "O illustrious knight, the never to be sufficiently praised Don Quixote de la Mancha, I am the Knight of the White Moon whose incomparable exploits you will perhaps recall. I come to contend with you and try the might of my arm, with the purpose of having you acknowledge and confess that my lady, whoever she may be, is beyond comparison more beautiful than your own Dulcinea del Toboso. If you will admit the truth of this fully and freely, you will escape death and I shall be spared the trouble of inflicting it upon you. On the other hand, if you choose to fight and I should overcome you, I ask no other satisfaction

9. Don Quixote and Sancho, after numberless encounters and experiences (of which the most prominent have been Don Quixote's descent into the cave of Montesinos, and their residence at the castle of the playful ducal couple who give Sancho the "governorship of an island" for ten days), are now in Barcelona. Famous as they are, they meet the viceroy and the nobles; their host is Don Antonio Moreno, "a gentleman of wealth and discernment who was fond of amusing himself in an innocent and kindly way."

than that, laying down your arms and seeking no further adventures, you retire to your own village for the space of a year, during which time you are not to lay hand to sword but are to dwell peacefully and tranquilly, enjoying a beneficial rest that shall redound to the betterment of your worldly fortunes and the salvation of your soul. But if you are the victor, then my head shall be at your disposal, my arms and steed shall be the spoils, and the fame of my exploits shall go to increase your own renown. Consider well which is the better course and let me have your answer at once, for today is all the time I have for the dispatching of this business."

Don Quixote was amazed at the knight's arrogance as well as at the nature of the challenge, but it was with a calm and stern demeanor that he replied to him.

"Knight of the White Moon," he said, "of whose exploits up to now I have never heard, I will venture to take an oath that you have not once laid eyes upon the illustrious Dulcinea; for I am quite certain that if you had beheld her you would not be staking your all upon such an issue, since the sight of her would have convinced you that there never has been, and never can be, any beauty to compare with hers. I do not say that you lie, I simply say that you are mistaken; and so I accept your challenge with the conditions you have laid down, and at once, before this day you have fixed upon shall have ended. The only exception I make is with regard to the fame of your deeds being added to my renown, since I do not know what the character of your exploits has been and am quite content with my own, such as they are. Take, then, whichever side of the field you like, and I will take up my position, and may St. Peter bless what God may give."

Now, as it happened, the Knight of the White Moon was seen by some of the townspeople, who informed the viceroy that he was there, talking to Don Quixote de la Mancha. Believing this to be a new adventure arranged by Don Antonio Moreno or some other gentleman of the place, the viceroy at once hastened down to the beach, accompanied by a large retinue, including Don Antonio, and they arrived just as Don Quixote was wheeling Rocinante to measure off the necessary stretch of field. When the viceroy perceived that they were about to engage in combat, he at once interposed and inquired of them what it was that impelled them thus to do battle all of a sudden.

The Knight of the White Moon replied that it was a matter of beauty and precedence and briefly repeated what he had said to Don Quixote, explaining the terms to which both parties had agreed. The viceroy then went up to Don Antonio and asked him if he knew any such knight as this or if it was some joke that they were playing, but the answer that he received left him more puzzled than ever; for Don Antonio did not know who the knight was, nor could he say as to whether this was a real encounter or not. The viceroy, accordingly, was doubtful about letting them proceed, but inasmuch as he could not bring himself to believe that it was anything more than a jest, he withdrew to one side, saying, "Sir Knights, if there is nothing for it but to confess or die, and if Señor Don Quixote's mind is

made up and your Grace, the Knight of the White Moon, is even more
firmly resolved, then fall to it in the name of God and may He bestow the
victory."

The Knight of the White Moon thanked the viceroy most courteously
and in well-chosen words for the permission which had been granted them,
and Don Quixote did the same, whereupon the latter, commending himself with all his heart to Heaven and to his lady Dulcinea, as was his
custom at the beginning of a fray, fell back a little farther down the field
as he saw his adversary doing the same. And then, without blare of trumpet
or other warlike instrument to give them the signal for the attack, both at
the same instant wheeled their steeds about and returned for the charge.
Being mounted upon the swifter horse, the Knight of the White Moon
met Don Quixote two-thirds of the way and with such tremendous force
that, without touching his opponent with his lance (which, it seemed, he
deliberately held aloft) he brought both Rocinante and his rider to the
ground in an exceedingly perilous fall. At once the victor leaped down and
placed his lance at Don Quixote's visor.

"You are vanquished, O knight! Nay, more, you are dead unless you
make confession in accordance with the conditions governing our encounter."

Stunned and battered, Don Quixote did not so much as raise his visor
but in a faint, wan voice, as if speaking from the grave, he said, "Dulcinea
del Toboso is the most beautiful woman in the world and I the most unhappy
knight upon the face of this earth. It is not right that my weakness should
serve to defraud the truth. Drive home your lance, O knight, and take my
life since you already have deprived me of my honor."

"That I most certainly shall not do," said the one of the White Moon.
"Let the fame of my lady Dulcinea del Toboso's beauty live on undimin-
ished. As for me, I shall be content if the great Don Quixote will retire to
his village for a year or until such a time as I may specify, as was agreed
upon between us before joining battle."

The viceroy, Don Antonio, and all the many others who were present
heard this, and they also heard Don Quixote's response, which was to the
effect that, seeing nothing was asked of him that was prejudicial to Dulcinea, he would fulfill all the other conditions like a true and punctilious
knight. The one of the White Moon thereupon turned and with a bow to
the viceroy rode back to the city at a mild canter. The viceroy promptly
dispatched Don Antonio to follow him and make every effort to find out
who he was; and, in the meanwhile, they lifted Don Quixote up and
uncovered his face, which held no sign of color and was bathed in perspiration. Rocinante, however, was in so sorry a state that he was unable to
stir for the present.

Brokenhearted over the turn that events had taken, Sancho did not know
what to say or do. It seemed to him that all this was something that was
happening in a dream and that everything was the result of magic. He saw
his master surrender, heard him consent not to take up arms again for a
year to come as the light of his glorious exploits faded into darkness. At the

same time his own hopes, based upon the fresh promises that had been made him, were whirled away like smoke before the wind. He feared that Rocinante was maimed for life, his master's bones permanently dislocated—it would have been a bit of luck if his madness also had been jolted out of him.[1]

Finally, in a hand litter which the viceroy had them bring, they bore the knight back to town. The viceroy himself then returned, for he was very anxious to ascertain who the Knight of the White Moon was who had left Don Quixote in so lamentable a condition.

CHAPTER 65

Wherein is revealed who the Knight of the White Moon was.

The Knight of the White Moon was followed not only by Don Antonio Moreno, but by a throng of small boys as well, who kept after him until the doors of one of the city's hostelries had closed behind him. A squire came out to meet him and remove his armor, for which purpose the victor proceeded to shut himself up in a lower room, in the company of Don Antonio, who had also entered the inn and whose bread would not bake until he had learned the knight's identity. Perceiving that the gentleman had no intention of leaving him, he of the White Moon then spoke.

"Sir," he said, "I am well aware that you have come to find out who I am; and, seeing that there is no denying you the information that you seek, while my servant here is removing my armor I will tell you the exact truth of the matter. I would have you know, sir, that I am the bachelor Sansón Carrasco from the same village as Don Quixote de la Mancha, whose madness and absurdities inspire pity in all of us who know him and in none more than me. And so, being convinced that his salvation lay in his returning home for a period of rest in his own house, I formed a plan for bringing him back.

"It was three months ago that I took to the road as a knight-errant, calling myself the Knight of the Mirrors, with the object of fighting and overcoming him without doing him any harm, intending first to lay down the condition that the vanquished was to yield to the victor's will. What I meant to ask of him—for I looked upon him as conquered from the start—was that he should return to his village and not leave it for a whole year, in the course of which time he might be cured. Fate, however, ordained things otherwise; for he was the one who conquered me and overthrew me from my horse, and thus my plan came to naught. He continued on his wanderings, and I went home, defeated, humiliated, and bruised from my fall, which was quite a dangerous one. But I did not for this reason give up the idea of hunting him up once more and vanquishing him as you have seen me do today.

"Since he is the soul of honor when it comes to observing the ordinances of knight-errantry, there is not the slightest doubt that he will keep the

---

1. The original has an untranslatable pun on *deslocado*, which means "out of joint" ("dislocated") and also "cured of madness" (from *loco*, "mad").

promise he has given me and fulfill his obligations. And that, sir, is all that I need to tell you concerning what has happened. I beg you not to disclose my secret or reveal my identity to Don Quixote, in order that my well-intentioned scheme may be carried out and a man of excellent judgment be brought back to his senses—for a sensible man he would be, once rid of the follies of chivalry."

"My dear sir," exclaimed Don Antonio, "may God forgive you for the wrong you have done the world by seeking to deprive it of its most charming madman! Do you not see that the benefit accomplished by restoring Don Quixote to his senses can never equal the pleasure which others derive from his vagaries? But it is my opinion that all the trouble to which the Señor Bachelor has put himself will not suffice to cure a man who is so hopelessly insane; and if it were not uncharitable, I would say let Don Quixote never be cured, since with his return to health we lose not only his own drolleries but also those of his squire, Sancho Panza, for either of the two is capable of turning melancholy itself into joy and merriment. Nevertheless, I will keep silent and tell him nothing, that I may see whether or not I am right in my suspicion that Señor Carrasco's efforts will prove to have been of no avail."

The bachelor replied that, all in all, things looked very favorable and he hoped for a fortunate outcome. With this, he took his leave of Don Antonio, after offering to render him any service that he could; and, having had his armor tied up and placed upon a mule's back, he rode out of the city that same day on the same horse on which he had gone into battle, returning to his native province without anything happening to him that is worthy of being set down in this veracious chronicle.

(Homecoming and Death)

CHAPTER 73

Of the omens that Don Quixote encountered upon entering his village, with other incidents that embellish and lend credence to this great history.

As they entered the village, Cid Hamete informs us, Don Quixote caught sight of two lads on the communal threshing floor who were engaged in a dispute.

"Don't let it worry you, Periquillo," one of them was saying to the other; "you'll never lay eyes on it again as long as you live."

Hearing this, Don Quixote turned to Sancho. "Did you mark what that boy said, my friend?" he asked. " 'You'll never lay eyes on it[2] again . . .' "

"Well," replied Sancho, "what difference does it make what he said?"

"What difference?" said Don Quixote. "Don't you see that, applied to the one I love, it means I shall never again see Dulcinea."

Sancho was about to answer him when his attention was distracted by a

---

2. The same as "her" in the original, since the reference is to a cricket cage, denoted in Spanish by a feminine noun; hence the Don's inference concerning Dulcinea.

hare that came flying across the fields pursued by a large number of hunters with their greyhounds. The frightened animal took refuge by huddling down beneath the donkey, whereupon Sancho reached out his hand and caught it and presented it to his master.

"*Malum signum, malum signum,*"[3] the knight was muttering to himself. "A hare flees, the hounds pursue it, Dulcinea appears not."

"It is very strange to hear your Grace talk like that," said Sancho. "Let us suppose that this hare *is* Dulcinea del Toboso and the hounds pursuing it are those wicked enchanters that transformed her into a peasant lass; she flees, I catch her and turn her over to your Grace, you hold her in your arms and caress her. Is that a bad sign? What ill omen can you find in it?"

The two lads who had been quarreling now came up to have a look at the hare, and Sancho asked them what their dispute was about. To this the one who had uttered the words "You'll never lay eyes on it again as long as you live," replied that he had taken a cricket cage from the other boy and had no intention of returning it ever. Sancho then brought out from his pocket four cuartos and gave them to the lad in exchange for the cage, which he placed in Don Quixote's hands.

"There, master," he said, "these omens are broken and destroyed, and to my way of thinking, even though I may be a dunce, they have no more to do with what is going to happen to us than the clouds of yesteryear. If I am not mistaken, I have heard our curate say that sensible persons of the Christian faith should pay no heed to such foolish things, and you yourself in the past have given me to understand that all those Christians who are guided by omens are fools. But there is no need to waste a lot of words on the subject; come, let us go on and enter our village."

The hunters at this point came up and asked for the hare, and Don Quixote gave it to them. Continuing on their way, the returning pair encountered the curate and the bachelor Carrrasco, who were strolling in a small meadow on the outskirts of the town as they read their breviaries. And here it should be mentioned that Sancho Panza, by way of sumpter cloth, had thrown over his gray and the bundle of armor it bore the flame-covered buckram robe in which they had dressed the squire at the duke's castle, on the night that witnessed Altisidora's[4] resurrection; and he had also fitted the miter over the donkey's head, the result being the weirdest transformation and the most bizarrely appareled ass that ever were seen in this world. The curate and the bachelor recognized the pair at once and came forward to receive them with open arms. Don Quixote dismounted and gave them both a warm embrace; meanwhile, the small boys (boys are like lynxes in that nothing escapes them), having spied the ass's miter, ran up for a closer view.

"Come, lads," they cried, "and see Sancho Panza's ass trigged out finer than Mingo,[5] and Don Quixote's beast is skinnier than ever!"

Finally, surrounded by the urchins and accompanied by the curate and

3. A bad sign. "Meeting a hare is considered an ill omen."   4. Altisidora was a girl in the duke's castle where Quixote and Sancho were guests for a time; she dramatically pretended to be in love with Don Quixote.   5. The allusion is to the opening lines of a fifteenth-century satire, *Mingo Revulgo.*

the bachelor, they entered the village and made their way to Don Quixote's house, where they found the housekeeper and the niece standing in the doorway, for the news of their return had preceded them. Teresa Panza, Sancho's wife, had also heard of it, and, half naked and disheveled, dragging her daughter Sanchica by the hand, she hastened to greet her husband and was disappointed when she saw him, for he did not look to her as well fitted out as a governor ought to be.

"How does it come, my husband," she said, "that you return like this, tramping and footsore? You look more like a vagabond than you do like a governor."

"Be quiet, Teresa," Sancho admonished her, "for very often there are stakes where there is no bacon. Come on home with me and you will hear marvels. I am bringing money with me, which is the thing that matters, money earned by my own efforts and without harm to anyone."

"You just bring along the money, my good husband," said Teresa, "and whether you got it here or there, or by whatever means, you will not be introducing any new custom into the world."

Sanchica then embraced her father and asked him if he had brought her anything, for she had been looking forward to his coming as to the showers in May. And so, with his wife holding him by the hand while his daughter kept one arm about his waist and at the same time led the gray, Sancho went home, leaving Don Quixote under his own roof in the company of niece and housekeeper, the curate and the barber.

Without regard to time or season, the knight at once drew his guests to one side and in a few words informed them of how he had been overcome in battle and had given his promise not to leave his village for a year, a promise that he meant to observe most scrupulously, without violating it in the slightest degree, as every knight-errant was obliged to do by the laws of chivalry. He accordingly meant to spend that year as a shepherd,[6] he said, amid the solitude of the fields, where he might give free rein to his amorous fancies as he practiced the virtues of the pastoral life; and he further begged them, if they were not too greatly occupied and more urgent matters did not prevent their doing so, to consent to be his companions. He would purchase a flock sufficiently large to justify their calling themselves shepherds; and, moreover, he would have them know, the most important thing of all had been taken care of, for he had hit upon names that would suit them marvelously well. When the curate asked him what these names were, Don Quixote replied that he himself would be known as "the shepherd Quixotiz," the bachelor as "the shepherd Carrascón," the curate as "the shepherd Curiambro," and Sancho Panza as "the shepherd Pancino."

Both his listeners were dismayed at the new form which his madness had assumed. However, in order that he might not go faring forth from

6. Since the knight-errant's life has been forbidden him by his defeat, Don Quixote for a time plans to live according to another and no less "literary" code, that of the pastoral. In the following paragraphs the author, especially through the bachelor Carrasco, refers humorously to some of the conventions of pastoral literature.

the village on another of his expeditions (for they hoped that in the course of the year he would be cured), they decided to fall in with his new plan and approve it as being a wise one, and they even agreed to be his companions in the calling he proposed to adopt.

"What's more," remarked Sansón Carrasco, "I am a very famous poet, as everyone knows, and at every turn I will be composing pastoral or courtly verses or whatever may come to mind, by way of a diversion for us as we wander in those lonely places; but what is most necessary of all, my dear sirs, is that each one of us should choose the name of the shepherd lass to whom he means to dedicate his songs, so that we may not leave a tree, however hard its bark may be, where their names are not inscribed and engraved as is the custom with lovelorn shepherds."

"That is exactly what we should do," replied Don Quixote, "although, for my part, I am relieved of the necessity of looking for an imaginary shepherdess, seeing that I have the peerless Dulcinea del Toboso, glory of these brookside regions, adornment of these meadows, beauty's mainstay, cream of the Graces—in short, one to whom all praise is well becoming however hyperbolical it may be."

"That is right," said the curate, "but we will seek out some shepherd maids that are easily handled, who if they do not square with us will fit in the corners."

"And," added Sansón Carrasco, "if we run out of names we will give them those that we find printed in books the world over: such as Fílida, Amarilis, Diana, Flérida, Galatea, and Belisarda; for since these are for sale in the market place, we can buy them and make them our own. If my lady, or, rather, my shepherdess, should be chance be called Ana, I will celebrate her charms under the name of Anarda; if she is Francisca, she will become Francenia; if Lucía, Luscinda; for it all amounts to the same thing. And Sancho Panza, if he enters this confraternity, may compose verses to his wife, Teresa Panza, under the name of Teresaina."

Don Quixote had to laugh at this, and the curate then went on to heap extravagant praise upon him for his noble resolution which did him so much credit, and once again he offered to keep the knight company whenever he could spare the time from the duties of his office. With this, they took their leave of him, advising and beseeching him to take care of his health and to eat plentifully of the proper food.

As fate would have it, the niece and the housekeeper had overheard the conversation of the three men, and as soon as the visitors had left they both descended upon Don Quixote.

"What is the meaning of this, my uncle? Here we were thinking your Grace had come home to lead a quiet and respectable life, and do you mean to tell us you are going to get yourself involved in fresh complications—

Young shepherd, thou who comest here,
Young shepherd, thou who goest there . . .[7]

7. From a ballad.

For, to tell the truth, the barley is too hard now to make shepherds' pipes of it."[8]

"And how," said the housekeeper, "is your Grace going to stand the midday heat in summer, the winter cold, the howling of the wolves out there in the fields? You certainly cannot endure it. That is an occupation for robust men, cut out and bred for such a calling almost from their swaddling clothes. Setting one evil over against another, it is better to be a knight-errant than a shepherd. Look, sir, take my advice, for I am not stuffed with bread and wine when I give it to you but am fasting and am going on fifty years of age: stay at home, attend to your affairs, go often to confession, be charitable to the poor, and let it be upon my soul if any harm comes to you as a result of it."

"Be quiet, daughters," said Don Quixote. "I know very well what I must do. Take me up to bed, for I do not feel very well; and you may be sure of one thing: whether I am a knight-errant now or a shepherd to be, I never will fail to look after your needs as you will see when the time comes."

And good daughters that they unquestionably were, the housekeeper and the niece helped him up to bed, where they gave him something to eat and made him as comfortable as they could.

CHAPTER 74

Of how Don Quixote fell sick, of the will that he made, and of the manner of his death.

Inasmuch as nothing that is human is eternal but is ever declining from its beginning to its close, this being especially true of the lives of men, and since Don Quixote was not endowed by Heaven with the privilege of staying the downward course of things, his own end came when he was least expecting it. Whether it was owing to melancholy occasioned by the defeat he had suffered, or was, simply, the will of Heaven which had so ordained it, he was taken with a fever that kept him in bed for a week, during which time his friends, the curate, the bachelor, and the barber, visited him frequently, while Sancho Panza, his faithful squire, never left his bedside.

Believing that the knight's condition was due to sorrow over his downfall and disappointment at not having been able to accomplish the disenchantment and liberation of Dulcinea, Sancho and the others endeavored to cheer him up in every possible way. The bachelor urged him to take heart and get up from bed that he might begin his pastoral life, adding that he himself had already composed an eclogue that would cast in the shade all that Sannazaro[9] had ever written, and had purchased with his own money from a herdsman of Quintanar two fine dogs to guard the flock, one of them named Barcino and the other Butrón. All this, however, did not serve to relieve Don Quixote's sadness; whereupon his friends called in the doctor, who took his pulse and was not very well satisfied with it. In any

8. A proverb.   9. The Italian poet Jacopo Sannazaro (1456?–1530), whose *Arcadia* is one of the milestones in the pastoral tradition.

case, the physician told them, they should attend to the health of his soul as that of his body was in grave danger.

Don Quixote received this news calmly enough, but not so his house-keeper, niece, and squire, who began weeping bitterly, as if he were already lying dead in front of them. It was the doctor's opinion that melancholy and depression were putting an end to his patient's life. The knight then requested them to leave him alone as he wished to sleep a little, and they complied. He slept for more than six hours at a stretch, as the saying is, and so soundly that the housekeeper and niece thought he would never wake.

At last he did, however, and at once cried out in a loud voice, "Blessed be Almighty God who has given me so many blessings! Truly His mercy is boundless and is not limited or restrained by the sins of men."

The niece listened carefully to what her uncle said, and it seemed to her that he was speaking more rationally than was his wont, at least during his illness.

"Sir," she said to him, "what does your Grace mean? Has something occurred that we know nothing about? What is this talk of mercy and sins?"

"The mercy that I speak of," replied Don Quixote, "is that which God is showing me at this moment—in spite of my sins, as I have said. My mind now is clear, unencumbered by those misty shadows of ignorance that were cast over it by my bitter and continual reading of those hateful books of chivalry. I see through all the nonsense and fraud contained in them, and my only regret is that my disillusionment has come so late, leaving me no time to make any sort of amends by reading those that are the light of the soul. I find myself, niece, at the point of death, and I would die in such a way as not to leave the impression of a life so bad that I shall be remembered as a madman; for even though I have been one, I do not wish to confirm it on my deathbed. And so, my dear, call in my good friends: the curate, the bachelor Sansón Carrasco, and Master Nicholas the barber; for I want to confess my sins and make my last will and testament."

The niece, however, was relieved of this errand, for the three of them came in just then.

"I have good news for you, kind sirs," said Don Quixote the moment he saw them. "I am no longer Don Quixote de la Mancha but Alonso Quijano, whose mode of life won for him the name of 'Good.' I am the enemy of Amadis of Gaul and all his innumerable progeny; for those pro-fane stories dealing with knight-errantry are odious to me, and I realize how foolish I was and the danger I courted in reading them; but I am in my right senses now and I abominate them."

Hearing this, they all three were convinced that some new kind of mad-ness must have laid hold of him.

"Why, Señor Don Quixote!" exclaimed Sansón. "What makes you talk like that, just when we have received news that my lady Dulcinea is disen-chanted? And just when we are on the verge of becoming shepherds so that we may spend the rest of our lives in singing like a lot of princes, why does your Grace choose to turn hermit? Say no more, in Heaven's name, but be sensible and forget these idle tales."

"Tales of that kind," said Don Quixote, "have been the truth for me in the past, and to my detriment, but with Heaven's aid I trust to turn them to my profit now that I am dying. For I feel, gentlemen, that death is very near; so, leave all jesting aside and bring me a confessor for my sins and a notary to draw up my will. In such straits as these a man cannot trifle with his soul. Accordingly, while the Señor Curate is hearing my confession, let the notary be summoned."

Amazed at his words, they gazed at one another in some perplexity, yet they could not but believe him. One of the signs that led them to think he was dying was this quick return from madness to sanity and all the additional things he had to say, so well reasoned and well put and so becoming in a Christian that none of them could any longer doubt that he was in full possession of his faculties. Sending the others out of the room, the curate stayed behind to confess him, and before long the bachelor returned with the notary and Sancho Panza, who had been informed of his master's condition, and who, finding the housekeeper and the niece in tears, began weeping with them. When the confession was over, the curate came out.

"It is true enough," he said, "that Alonso Quijano the Good is dying, and it is also true that he is a sane man. It would be well for us to go in now while he makes his will."

At this news the housekeeper, niece, and the good squire Sancho Panza were so overcome with emotion that the tears burst forth from their eyes and their bosoms heaved with sobs; for, as has been stated more than once, whether Don Quixote was plain Alonso Quijano the Good or Don Quixote de la Mancha, he was always of a kindly and pleasant disposition and for this reason was beloved not only by the members of his household but by all who knew him.

The notary had entered along with the others, and as soon as the preamble had been attended to and the dying man had commended his soul to his Maker with all those Christian formalities that are called for in such a case, they came to the matter of bequests, with Don Quixote dictating as follows:

"ITEM. With regard to Sancho Panza, whom, in my madness, I appointed to be my squire, and who has in his possession a certain sum of money belonging to me: inasmuch as there has been a standing account between us, of debits and credits, it is my will that he shall not be asked to give any accounting whatsoever of this sum, but if any be left over after he has had payment for what I owe him, the balance, which will amount to very little, shall be his, and much good may it do him. If when I was mad I was responsible for his being given the governorship of an island, now that I am of sound mind I would present him with a kingdom if it were in my power, for his simplicity of mind and loyal conduct merit no less."

At this point he turned to Sancho. "Forgive me, my friend," he said, "for having caused you to appear as mad as I by leading you to fall into the same error, that of believing that there are still knights-errant in the world."

"Ah, master," cried Sancho through his tears, "don't die, your Grace, but take my advice and go on living for many years to come; for the greatest madness that a man can be guilty of in this life is to die without good reason, without anyone's killing him, slain only by the hands of melancholy. Look you, don't be lazy but get up from this bed and let us go out into the fields clad as shepherds as we agreed to do. Who knows but behind some bush we may come upon the lady Dulcinea, as disenchanted as you could wish. If it is because of worry over your defeat that you are dying, put the blame on me by saying that the reason for your being overthrown was that I had not properly fastened Rocinante's girth. For the matter of that, your Grace knows from reading your books of chivalry that it is a common thing for certain knights to overthrow others, and he who is vanquished today will be the victor tomorrow."

"That is right," said Sansón, "the worthy Sancho speaks the truth."

"Not so fast, gentlemen," said Don Quixote. "In last year's nests there are no birds this year. I was mad and now I am sane; I was Don Quixote de la Mancha, and now I am, as I have said, Alonso Quijano the Good. May my repentance and the truth I now speak restore to me the place I once held in your esteem. And now, let the notary proceed:

"ITEM. I bequeath my entire estate, without reservation, to my niece Antonia Quijana, here present, after the necessary deductions shall have been made from the most available portion of it to satisfy the bequests that I have stipulated. The first payment shall be to my housekeeper for the wages due her, with twenty ducats over to buy her a dress. And I hereby appoint the Señor Curate and the Señor Bachelor Sansón Carrasco to be my executors.

"ITEM. It is my will that if my niece Antonia Quijana should see fit to marry, it shall be to a man who does not know what books of chivalry are; and if it shall be established that he is acquainted with such books and my niece still insists on marrying him, then she shall lose all that I have bequeathed her and my executors shall apply her portion to works of charity as they may see fit.

"ITEM. I entreat the aforementioned gentlemen, my executors, if by good fortune they should come to know the author who is said to have composed a history now going the rounds under the title of *Second Part of the Exploits of Don Quixote de la Mancha*, to beg his forgiveness in my behalf, as earnestly as they can, since it was I who unthinkingly led him to set down so many and such great absurdities as are to be found in it; for I leave this life with a feeling of remorse at having provided him with the occasion for putting them into writing."

The will ended here, and Don Quixote, stretching himself at length in the bed, fainted away. They all were alarmed at this and hastened to aid him. The same thing happened very frequently in the course of the three days of life that remained to him after he had made his will. The household was in a state of excitement, but with it all the niece continued to eat her meals, the housekeeper had her drink, and Sancho Panza was in good spirits; for this business of inheriting property effaces or mitigates the sorrow which the heir ought to feel and causes him to forget.

Death came at last for Don Quixote, after he had received all the sacraments and once more, with many forceful arguments, had expressed his abomination of books of chivalry. The notary who was present remarked that in none of those books had he read of any knight-errant dying in his own bed so peacefully and in so Christian a manner. And thus, amid the tears and lamentations of those present, he gave up the ghost; that is to say, he died. Perceiving that their friend was no more, the curate asked the notary to be a witness to the fact that Alonso Quijano the Good, commonly known as Don Quixote, was truly dead, this being necessary in order that some author other than Cid Hamete Benengeli might not have the opportunity of falsely resurrecting him and writing endless histories of his exploits.

Such was the end of the Ingenious Gentleman of La Mancha, whose birthplace Cid Hamete was unwilling to designate exactly in order that all the towns and villages of La Mancha might contend among themselves for the right to adopt him and claim him as their own, just as the seven cities of Greece did in the case of Homer. The lamentations of Sancho and those of Don Quixote's niece and his housekeeper, as well as the original epitaphs that were composed for his tomb, will not be recorded here, but mention may be made of the verses by Sansón Carrasco:

> Here lies a gentleman bold
> Who was so very brave
> He went to lengths untold,
> And on the brink of the grave
> Death had on him no hold.
> By the world he set small store—
> He frightened it to the core—
> Yet somehow, by Fate's plan,
> Though he'd lived a crazy man,
> When he died he was sane once more.

CHRISTOPHER MARLOWE
1564–1593

The information we have on Christopher Marlowe's life is haunting and fragmentary; there seems to be no doubt that he entertained unorthodox religious views, that he had a violent temper, and that he engaged in some sort of spying activities for Queen Elizabeth. Born in Canterbury on February 6, 1564, the son of a shoemaker, Marlowe studied at the King's School in his native city and from 1581 on a scholarship at Corpus Christi College (then Benet College), Cambridge, where he received his B. A. in 1584 and his M.A. in 1587. There was some opposition to the granting of his degree but the Queen's Privy Council intervened in his favor, a fact that has been used to support the hypothesis that Marlowe was already affiliated with the Queen's secret service (a diplomatic and intelligence operation). After Cambridge he lived in London, where little is known about his life; we obviously do know of his connections with the theatrical world and of his four great dramatic successes between 1587 and 1593, *Tamburlaine the Great, The Jew of Malta, Edward II,* and *Dr. Faustus* (ca. 1592–93). Besides the plays Marlowe also wrote a mythological poem, "Hero and Leander," and translations of the Latin poets Ovid and Lucan.

Marlowe was accused of atheism and treason by a one-time friend and fellow-playwright, Thomas Kyd. He was involved in a bloody brawl with an innkeeper named William Bradley, and at 29, in an inn at Deptford, was stabbed to death by one Ingram Frizer in an argument over the bill; Frizer was pardoned on the grounds that he had acted in self-defense.

Of the plays that make him one of the most prominent Elizabethan dramatists, *Dr. Faustus* is still the most famous, probably because the legend of Faust has occupied an important place in literature since the Renaissance. Like Don Juan, Faust is one of the characters to whom authors have returned again and again as to convenient epitomes of certain traits and aspirations. The human story of Faust has been varied and adapted to suit the intellectual needs of various times, much as both ancient and modern poets have used the stories of Greek mythology for their own purposes.

Marlowe's *Dr. Faustus* powerfully exemplifies the intellectual aspirations of the Renaissance, but he is haunted by a sense of their vanity and sinfulness. Whereas the tension of opposites produces in other instances some sort of compromise, and often fruitful results, here the outcome of inner conflict is tragedy and ruin. In our gallery of Renaissance heroes Dr. Faustus represents an extreme case, almost the reverse of Rabelais's exuberant and satisfied sensualist-scholar; to him the fruit of knowledge is not the confirmation of our dignity and divine nature, but despair and destruction.

The popular tendency to identify Faust with magic and witchcraft, suffering a final punishment for having followed the unorthodox and sinful black arts, is of course justified. But such a simple scheme, while it may have been the whole "point" of earlier versions of the story, does not account for the obviously larger and deeper implications we discern in Marlowe's tragedy. With this in mind, it may be particularly illuminating to ask ourselves what Dr. Faustus's knowledge and aspirations are. We then realize that both in the hero's initial phase, where he expresses his satiety and dissatisfaction with humanity's accumulated knowledge, and in the later one, where he embraces magic and the devil's arts, he is actually concerned with the proudest intellectual values of the Renaissance. Such well-known attitudes as excitement in discovery and delight in intellectual and physical power are expressed with an unmatched imaginative and metric splendor: "Faustus, these books, thy wit, and our experience/Shall make all nations to canónize us." Yet they are also presented as temptations of the devil.

In this light, the progression by which Dr. Faustus, scientist and scholar, arrives at his decision to "sell his soul to the devil" is not clear-cut. We can, of course, trace the route he travels, the crucial episode of which is his decision to give himself to the arts of Mephistophilis. As the play opens, Dr. Faustus is presented in his study, feeling the vanity of his intellectual pursuits. These studies are, to him, vain and dusty; but in his enumeration of them we recognize the very culture on which many intellectuals of the time would have securely counted: Greek philosophy and physics, the laws of the Roman empire, the Vulgate version of the Scriptures. Yet, in the opening monologue of Marlowe's play Faustus reviews and discards these pillars of humanistic culture and turns to the "metaphysics of magicians." He has tried, as it were, to cure his thirst for knowledge and power by orthodox means, but the cure, as far as he is concerned, has failed. He then turns to less usual and less reputable means to satisfy himself, somewhat in the same way that a patient dissatisfied with physicians turns to a brilliant "quack." Magic, he hopes, will "resolve" him "of all ambiguities."

But if we ask ourselves what magic promises Dr. Faustus, we come to the realization that what it promises is a more colorful and adventurous side of that same Renaissance body of values to which his discarded studies and books also belong. In this second phase, Dr. Faustus can exercise his fertile imagination and his instinctive longing for beauty and power—the "magic" of the period. Instead of plodding through the traditional texts he can imagine thrilling voyages, the "Venetian argosies," and express his desire for vast earthly conquest: "I'll join the hills that bind the Afric shore/And make that country continent to Spain,/And both contributory to my crown. . . ." This imperial dream is more than once expressed with references to antiquity, as a new vision of ancient myth ("from America the golden fleece"; "Instead of Troy shall Wittenberg be sacked"). Similarly, he sees in the image of Helen the supreme figuration of beauty and aspires to it as to a culminating fulfillment of his desires.

Such aspirations and visions, doomed to a catastrophic end, give the figure of Dr. Faustus a heroic stature, as we can clearly see by comparing him to the Scholars. The Scholars hold the position that the Chorus in Greek tragedy often does—middle-of-the-road, conformist, prudent; in contrast, Dr. Faustus seems to possess the grandeur of some of Dante's damned. He lives for higher stakes and falls harder; there is greatness in the very extent of his final hopelessness. In the end it becomes clear, as we have suggested, that the sense of doom has presided over both phases, both means, fair and foul, of Faustus's search for knowledge. Not only his "magic" visions but his whole past come back to haunt him, and at this point we no longer have the lyric beauty of the Helen passage, but the panting, colloquial, extraordinarily effective monologue in which all Faustus's science, all his knowledge, are desperately rejected: "O would I had never seen Wittenberg, never read book. And what wonders I have done all Germany can witness, yea all the world, for which Faustus hath lost both Germany and the world, yea heaven itself. . . ."

Marlowe's *Dr. Faustus*, then, is considerably more interesting to the modern reader than the simple story of how a necromancer lost his soul by dabbling with magic. The nature of the hero's despair cuts deeper than that; as a Renaissance character he embodies a more deeply earned dissatisfaction. Here is more than ordinary "melancholy"; the drama seems to suggest that the seeds of damnation are implicit in some of the most cherished and proud pursuits and attitudes of the period; their depiction as devilish temptations is a concrete way of symbolizing their comprehensively damning nature. In this light, the play becomes one of the most contemporary statements we have of human terror at the daring of our own thoughts and the need for "limits" that Montaigne so eloquently expounds.

Frederick S. Boas, *Christopher Marlowe: A Biographical and Critical Study* (1940), is the standard account of Marlowe's life and literary career. A helpful anthology of criticism is *Twentieth Century Interpretations of Doctor Faustus* (1969), edited by Willard Farnham. A. Bartlett Giamatti's brilliant essay "Marlowe, the Arts of Illusion" is chapter 6 of his *Exile and Change in Renaissance Literature* (1984). Harry Levin, *The Overreacher: A Study of Christopher Marlowe* (1952), stresses the dramatist's modern spirit. Charles Norman, *The Muses' Darling: Christopher Mar-*

lowe (1950), contains illustrations, maps, and facsimilies. A. L. Rowse provides a very readable account of Marlowe's life in *Christopher Marlowe: A Biography* (1964).

The Tragical History
of the Life and Death of Doctor Faustus

Dramatis Personae

CHORUS

DR. JOHN FAUSTUS, *of the University of Wittenberg*

WAGNER, *his servant*

GOOD ANGEL *and* BAD ANGEL

VALDES *and* CORNELIUS, *magicians and friends of* FAUSTUS

THREE SCHOLARS, *students at the university*

LUCIFER, MEPHISTOPHILIS, *and* BELZEBUB, *devils*

ROBIN *and* DICK, *rustic clowns*

THE SEVEN DEADLY SINS

POPE ADRIAN

RAYMOND, *King of Hungary*

BRUNO, *a rival Pope, appointed by the* EMPEROR

CARDINALS OF FRANCE *and* PADUA

ARCHBISHOP OF RHEIMS

MARTINO, FREDERICK, *and* BENVOLIO, *gentlemen at the* EMPEROR'*s court*

CAROLUS (CHARLES) THE FIFTH, EMPEROR

DUKE OF SAXONY

DUKE *and* DUCHESS OF VANHOLT

HORSE-COURSER

CARTER

HOSTESS *of a tavern*

OLD MAN

SPIRITS *of* DARIUS, ALEXANDER *and his* PARAMOUR, *and* HELEN OF TROY

ATTENDANTS, MONKS *and* FRIARS, SOLDIERS, PIPER, *two* CUPIDS

Act I

[*Enter* CHORUS.[1]]

CHORUS: Not marching in the fields of Trasimene
Where Mars did mate[2] the warlike Carthagens,
Nor sporting in the dalliance of love
In courts of kings where state[3] is overturned,
Nor in the pomp of proud audacious deeds   5
Intends our Muse to vaunt his heavenly verse:
Only this, gentles, we must now perform,
The form of Faustus' fortunes good or bad.
And so to patient judgments we appeal
And speak for Faustus in his infancy.   10
Now is he born, his parents base of stock,

---

1. A single actor who recited a prologue to an act or a whole play, and occasionally delivered an epilogue.   2. Join with. The battle of Lake Trasimene (217 B.C.) was one of the Carthaginian leader Hannibal's great victories.   3. Political power.

In Germany within a town called Rhode;
At riper years to Wittenberg[4] he went
Whereas[5] his kinsmen chiefly brought him up;
So much he profits in divinity,   15
The fruitful plot of scholarism graced,[6]
That shortly he was graced with Doctor's name,
Excelling all whose sweet delight disputes[7]
In th' heavenly matters of theology,
Till, swollen with cunning,[8] of a self-conceit,   20
His waxen wings did mount above his reach
And melting, heavens conspired his overthrow.[9]
For, falling to a devilish exercise
And glutted more with learning's golden gifts,
He surfeits upon curséd necromancy;   25
Nothing so sweet as magic is to him,
Which he prefers before his chiefest bliss[1]—
And this the man that in his study sits.
    [*Draws the curtain*[2] *and exit.*]

SCENE 1

    [FAUSTUS *in his study.*]
FAUSTUS: Settle thy studies, Faustus, and begin
To sound the depth of that thou wilt profess.
Having commenced, be a divine in show,
Yet level[3] at the end of every art
And live and die in Aristotle's works: 5
Sweet Analytics,[4] 'tis thou hast ravished me!
    [*Reads.*]
Bene disserere est finis logicis—
Is to dispute well logic's chiefest end?
Affords this art no greater miracle?
Then read no more; thou hast attained that end.   10
A greater subject fitteth Faustus' wit:
Bid *ὄν χαὶ μὴ ὄν*[5] farewell, Galen come,
Seeing *ubi desinit philosophus, ibi incipit medicus;*[6]
Be a physician, Faustus, heap up gold
And be eternized for some wondrous cure.   15
    [*Reads.*]
Summum bonum medicinae sanitas—[7]

4. The famous university where Martin Luther studied, as did Shakespeare's Hamlet and Horatio. *Rhode:* Roda.   **5.** Where.   **6.** Grazed. In the next line it refers to the Cambridge word for permission to proceed to a degree.   **7.** The usual academic exercises were disputations, which took the place of examinations.   **8.** Learning.   **9.** In Greek myth Icarus flew too near the sun on wings of feathers and wax; the wax melted and he fell into the sea and was drowned.   **1.** The salvation of his soul.   **2.** The curtain to the inner stage which serves here as Faustus's study. *Draws:* Draws apart.   **3.** Aim. *Commenced:* Graduated, i.e., received the doctor's degree. *In show:* In external appearance.   **4.** A treatise on logic by Aristotle. The Latin: "To carry on a disputation well is the purpose of logic."   **5.** "Being and not being," i.e., philosophy. *Galen:* The ancient authority on medicine (2nd century A.D.).   **6.** "Where the philosopher leaves off the physician begins."   **7.** "Good health is the object of medicine" (or "physic").

The end of physic is our bodies' health:
Why, Faustus, hast thou not attained that end?
Is not thy common talk sound aphorisms?[8]
Are not thy bills hung up as monuments   20
Whereby whole cities have escaped the plague
And thousand desperate maladies been eased?
Yet art thou still but Faustus, and a man.
Couldst thou make men to live eternally
Or, being dead, raise them to life again,   25
Then this profession were to be esteemed.
Physic, farewell. Where is Justinian?[9]
        [Reads.]
Si una eademque res legatur duobus,
Alter rem, alter valorem rei, etc.[1]—
A pretty case of paltry legacies!   30
Exhaereditare filium non potest pater nisi[2]
Such is the subject of the Institute
And universal body of the law.
This study fits a mercenary drudge
Who aims at nothing but external trash,   35
Too servile and illiberal for me.
When all is done, divinity is best.
Jerome's Bible,[3] Faustus, view it well:
        [Reads.]
Stipendium peccati mors est—Ha! *Stipendium, etc.*
The reward of sin is death? That's hard.   40
Si pecasse negamus, fallimur, et nulla est in nobis veritas[4]—
If we say that we have no sin
We deceive ourselves, and there's no truth in us.
Why then belike
We must sin and so consequently die,   45
Aye, we must die an everlasting death.
What doctrine call you this, *Che sera, sera.*
What will be, shall be? Divinity, adieu!
These metaphysics of magicians
And necromantic books are heavenly: 50
Lines, circles, signs, letters, and characters—
Aye, these are those that Faustus most desires.
O what a world of profit and delight,
Of power, of honor, of omnipotence,
Is promised to the studious artisan!   55
All things that move between the quiet[5] poles

8. I.e., reliable medical pronouncements. *Bills:* Prescriptions.   9. Roman emperor and authority on
law (483–565), author of the *Institutes.*   1. "If something is bequeathed to two persons, one shall have
the thing itself, the other something of equal value."   2. "A father cannot disinherit his son unless."
3. The Latin translation, or "Vulgate," of St. Jerome (ca. 340–420). The Latin (Romans 6:23) is translated
in line 40.   4. I John 1:8, translated in the next two lines.   5. Unmoving. *Artisan:* A master of the
occult arts.

Shall be at my command. Emperors and kings
Are but obeyed in their several provinces,
Nor can they raise the wind or rend the clouds;
But his dominion that exceeds in this   60
Stretcheth as far as doth the mind of man.
A sound magician is a demigod:
Here tire my brains to gain a deity!
Wagner!
    [*Enter* WAGNER.]
Commend me to my dearest friends,   65
The German Valdes and Cornelius;
Request them earnestly to visit me.
WAGNER: I will, sir.
    [*Exit.*]
FAUSTUS: Their conference will be a greater help to me
Than all my labors, plod I ne'er so fast.   70
    [*Enter the* GOOD ANGEL *and the* BAD ANGEL.]
GOOD ANGEL: O Faustus, lay that damnèd book aside
And gaze not on it, lest it tempt thy soul
And heap God's heavy wrath upon thy head.
Read, read the Scriptures! That is blasphemy.
BAD ANGEL: Go forward, Faustus, in that famous art   75
Wherein all nature's treasury is contained:
Be thou on earth, as Jove[6] is in the sky,
Lord and commander of these elements.
    [*Exeunt* ANGELS.]
FAUSTUS: How am I glutted with conceit[7] of this!
Shall I make spirits fetch me what I please,   80
Resolve me of all ambiguities,
Perform what desperate enterprise I will?
I'll have them fly to India[8] for gold,
Ransack the ocean for orient pearl,
And search all corners of the new-found world   85
For pleasant fruits and princely delicates;
I'll have them read me strange philosophy
And tell the secrets of all foreign kings;
I'll have them wall all Germany with brass
And make swift Rhine circle fair Wittenberg;   90
I'll have them fill the public schools[9] with silk
Wherewith the students shall be bravely clad;
I'll levy soldiers with the coin they bring,
And chase the Prince of Parma[1] from our land
And reign sole king of all our provinces;   95
Yea, stranger engines for the brunt of war

6. God (a common substitution in Elizabethan drama).   7. Filled with the idea.   8. "India" could mean the West Indies, America, or Ophir (in the east).   9. The university lecture rooms.   1. The Duke of Parma was the Spanish governor general of the Low Countries from 1579 to 1592.

Than was the fiery keel[2] at Antwerp's bridge
I'll make my servile spirits to invent!
   [*Enter* VALDES *and* CORNELIUS.]
Come, German Valdes and Cornelius,
And make me blest with your sage conference.   100
Valdes, sweet Valdes and Cornelius,
Know that your words have won me at the last
To practice magic and concealèd arts;
Yet not your words only, but mine own fantasy
That will receive no object,[3] for my head   105
But ruminates on necromantic skill.
Philosophy is odious and obscure,
Both law and physic are for petty wits,
Divinity is basest of the three,
Unpleasant, harsh, contemptible, and vile;   110
'Tis magic, magic, that hath ravished me!
Then, gentle friends, aid me in this attempt,
And I, that have with concise syllogisms
Graveled[4] the pastors of the German church,
And made the flowering pride of Wittenberg   115
Swarm to my problems[5] as the infernal spirits
On sweet Musaeus when he came to hell,
Will be as cunning as Agrippa[6] was
Whose shadows made all Europe honor him.
VALDES: Faustus, these books, thy wit, and our experience   120
Shall make all nations to canonize us.
As Indian Moors[7] obey their Spanish lords
So shall the spirits of every element
Be always serviceable to us three:
Like lions shall they guard us when we please,   125
Like Almain rutters[8] with their horsemen's staves,
Or Lapland giants trotting by our sides;
Sometimes like women, or unwedded maids,
Shadowing more beauty in their airy brows
Then in the white breasts of the queen of love;   130
From Venice shall they drag huge argosies
And from America the golden fleece
That yearly stuffs old Philip's[9] treasury,
If learned Faustus will be resolute.
FAUSTUS: Valdes, as resolute am I in this   135
As thou to live; therefore object it not.

2. The burning ship sent by the Netherlanders in 1585 against the barrier on the river Scheldt which Parma had built as a part of the blockade of Antwerp.   3. That will pay no attention to physical reality.   4. Confounded.   5. Lectures in logic and mathematics.   6. Cornelius Agrippa, German author of *The Vanity and Uncertainty of Arts and Sciences*, popularly supposed to have the power of calling up shades ("shadows") of the dead. *Musaeus*: Mythical singer, son of Orpheus; it was, however, the latter who charmed the denizens of hell with his music.   7. I.e., dark-skinned American Indians.   8. German horsemen.   9. Philip II, king of Spain.

CORNELIUS: The miracles that magic will perform
   Will make thee vow to study nothing else.
   He that is grounded in astrology,
   Enriched with tongues, well seen[1] in minerals,   140
   Hath all the principles magic doth require.
   Then doubt not, Faustus, but to be renowned
   And more frequented for this mystery
   Than heretofore the Delphian oracle.[2]
   The spirits tell me they can dry the sea   145
   And fetch the treasure of all foreign wrecks—
   Aye, all the wealth that our forefathers hid
   Within the massy entrails of the earth.
   Then tell me, Faustus, what shall we three want?
FAUSTUS: Nothing, Cornelius. O this cheers my soul!   150
   Come, show me some demonstrations magical
   That I may conjure in some lusty[3] grove
   And have these joys in full possession.
VALDES: Then haste thee to some solitary grove
   And bear wise Bacon's and Abanus'[4] works,   155
   The Hebrew Psalter and New Testament;
   And whatsoever else is requisite
   We will inform thee ere our conference cease.
CORNELIUS: Valdes, first let him know the words of art,
   And then, all other ceremonies learned,   160
   Faustus may try his cunning by himself.
VALDES: First I'll instruct thee in the rudiments,
   And then wilt thou be perfecter than I.
FAUSTUS: Then come and dine with me, and after meat
   We'll canvass every quiddity[5] thereof;   165
   For ere I sleep I'll try what I can do:
   This night I'll conjure though I die therefore.
     [*Exeunt.*]

SCENE 2

   [*Enter two* SCHOLARS.]
1 SCHOLAR: I wonder what's become of Faustus, that was wont to make
   our schools ring with *sic probo*.[6]
2 SCHOLAR: That shall we presently know; here comes his boy.[7]
   [*Enter* WAGNER *carrying wine.*]
1 SCHOLAR: How now, sirrah; where's thy master?
WAGNER: God in heaven knows.   5
2 SCHOLAR: Why, dost not thou know then?

---

1. Expert.   2. The oracle of Apollo at Delphi, much frequented in antiquity. *Mystery:* Craft.
3. Flourishing, beautiful.   4. Pietro d'Albano, 13th-century alchemist. *Bacon:* Roger Bacon, the medieval friar and scientist, popularly throught a magician.   5. Essential feature.   6. "Thus I prove," a
phrase in scholastic disputation.   7. Poor student earning his keep.

WAGNER: Yes, I know; but that follows not.

1 SCHOLAR: Go to, sirrah; leave your jesting and tell us where he is.

WAGNER: That follows not by force of argument, which you, being
    licentiate,[8] should stand upon; therefore acknowledge your error   10
    and be attentive.

2 SCHOLAR: Then you will not tell us?

WAGNER: You are deceived, for I will tell you. Yet if you were not
    dunces you would never ask me such a question, for is he not *corpus*
    naturale, and is not that *mobile?*[9] Then wherefore should you ask   15
    me such a question? But that I am by nature phlegmatic, slow to wrath
    and prone to lechery (to love, I would say), it were not for you to
    come within forty foot of the place of execution,[1] although I do not
    doubt to see you both hanged the next sessions. Thus having
    triumphed over you, I will set my countenance like a precisian,[2]   20
    and begin to speak thus: Truly, my dear brethren, my master is
    within at dinner with Valdes and Cornelius, as this wine, if it could
    speak, would inform your worships; and so the Lord bless you, pre-
    serve you, and keep you, my dear brethren.
    [*Exit.*]

1 SCHOLAR: O Faustus, then I fear that which I have long suspected,   25
    That thou art fallen into that damnèd art
    For which they two are infamous through the world.

2 SCHOLAR: Were he a stranger, not allied to me,
    The danger of his soul would make me mourn.
    But come, let us go and inform the Rector,[3]   30
    It may be his grave counsel may reclaim him.

1 SCHOLAR: I fear me nothing will reclaim him now.

2 SCHOLAR: Yet let us see what we can do.
    [*Exeunt.*]

SCENE 3

[*Enter* FAUSTUS *to conjure.*]

FAUSTUS: Now that the gloomy shadow of the night,
    Longing to view Orion's drizzling look,[4]
    Leaps from the antarctic world unto the sky
    And dims the welkin with her pitchy breath,
    Faustus, begin thine incantations   5
    And try if devils will obey thy hest,
    Seeing thou hast prayed and sacrificed to them.
    Within this circle is Jehovah's name
    [*He draws the circle*[5] *on the ground.*]

8. I.e., graduate students.   9. *Corpus naturale et mobile* (natural, movable matter) was a scholastic
definition of the subject matter of physics. Wagner is here parodying the language of learning he hears
around the university.   1. I.e., the dining room.   2. A Puritan. The rest of his speech is in the style
of the Puritans.   3. Head of a German university.   4. Orion appears at the beginning of winter.
5. Within which the spirits rise.

Forward and backward anagrammatized,
The breviated names of holy saints,   10
Figures of every adjunct[6] to the heavens
And characters of signs[7] and erring stars,
By which the spirits are enforced to rise.
Then fear not, Faustus, but be resolute
And try the uttermost magic can perform.   15
     [*Thunder.*]
Sint mihi dei Acherontis propitii! Valeat numen triplex Iehovae! Ignei
aerii aquatici terreni spiritus, salvete! Orientis princeps Lucifer Bel-
zebub, inferni ardentis monarcha, et Demogorgon, propitiamus vos,
ut appareat et surgat Mephistophilis![8]
     [FAUSTUS *pauses. Thunder still.*]
Quid tu moraris?[9] *Per Iehovam, Gehennam et consecratam aquam*   20
quam nunc spargo, signumque crucis quod nunc facio, et per vota
nostra, ipse nunc surgat nobis dicatus Mephistophilis!
     [MEPHISTOPHILIS *in the shape of a dragon rises from the earth outside*
     the circle.]
I charge thee to return and change thy shape;
Thou art too ugly to attend on me.
Go, and return an old Franciscan friar;   25
That holy shape becomes a devil best.
     [*Exit* MEPHISTOPHILIS.]
I see there's virtue in my heavenly words:
Who would not be proficient in this art?
How pliant is this Mephistophilis,
Full of obedience and humility!   30
Such is the force of magic and my spells.
Now, Faustus, thou art conjurer laureate
That canst command great Mephistophilis:
Quin redis, Mephistophilis, fratris imagine![1]
     [*Re-enter* MEPHISTOPHILIS *like a Friar.*]
MEPHISTOPHILIS: Now, Faustus, what wouldst thou have me do?   35
FAUSTUS: I charge thee wait upon me whilst I live
     To do whatever Faustus shall command,
     Be it to make the moon drop from her sphere
     Or the ocean to overwhelm the world.
MEPHISTOPHILIS: I am a servant to great Lucifer   40
     And may not follow thee without his leave:
     No more than he commands must we perform.
FAUSTUS: Did not he charge thee to appear to me?

6. Heavenly body, thought to be joined to the solid firmament.   7. Signs of the zodiac and the planets.
Erring: Wandering.   8. "May the gods of the lower regions favor me! Goodbye to the Trinity! Hail,
spirits of fire, air, water, and earth! Prince of the East, Belzebub, monarch of burning hell, and Demogorgon, we pray to you that Mephistophilis may appear and rise."   9. Nothing has happened, so Faustus
asks, "What are you waiting for?" and continues to conjure: "By Jehovah, Gehenna, and the holy water
which I now sprinkle, and the sign of the cross which I now make, and by our vows, may Mephistophilis
himself now rise to serve us."   1. "Return, Mephistophilis, in the shape of a friar."

MEPHISTOPHILIS: No, I came now hither of my own accord.
FAUSTUS: Did not my conjuring speeches raise thee?   45
    Speak!
MEPHISTOPHILIS: That was the cause, but yet *per accidens,*[2]
    For when we hear one rack the name of God,
    Abjure the Scriptures and his Saviour Christ,
    We fly in hope to get his glorious soul;   50
    Nor will we come unless he use such means
    Whereby he is in danger to be damned;
    Therefore the shortest cut for conjuring
    Is stoutly to abjure the Trinity
    And pray devoutly to the prince of hell.   55
FAUSTUS: So I have done, and hold this principle,
    There is no chief but only Belzebub
    To whom Faustus doth dedicate himself.
    This word "damnation" terrifies not me
    For I confound hell in Elysium;   60
    My ghost be with the old philosophers![3]
    But leaving these vain trifles of men's souls—
    Tell me, what is that Lucifer thy lord?
MEPHISTOPHILIS: Arch-regent and commander of all spirits.
FAUSTUS: Was not that Lucifer an angel once?   65
MEPHISTOPHILIS: Yes, Faustus, and most dearly loved of God.
FAUSTUS: How comes it, then, that he is prince of devils?
MEPHISTOPHILIS: O, by aspiring pride and insolence,
    For which God threw him from the face of heaven.
FAUSTUS: And what are you that live with Lucifer?   70
MEPHISTOPHILIS: Unhappy spirits that fell with Lucifer,
    Conspired against our God with Lucifer,
    And are forever damned with Lucifer.
FAUSTUS: Where are you damned?
MEPHISTOPHILIS: In hell.   75
FAUSTUS: How comes it, then, that thou art out of hell?
MEPHISTOPHILIS: Why, this is hell, nor am I out of it:
    Thinkst thou that I who saw the face of God
    And tasted the eternal joys of heaven
    Am not tormented with ten thousand hells   80
    In being deprived of everlasting bliss?
    O Faustus, leave these frivolous demands
    Which strike a terror to my fainting soul!
FAUSTUS: What, is great Mephistophilis so passionate[4]
    For being deprivèd of the joys of heaven?   85
    Learn thou of Faustus' manly fortitude
    And scorn those joys thou never shalt possess.

2. By the immediate, not ultimate, cause. *Rack:* Torture (by anagrammatizing).   3. I.e., I regard heaven and hell indifferently; if the old (pre-Christian) philosophers are damned, let me be damned with them.   4. Overcome by emotion.

Go, bear these tidings to great Lucifer:
Seeing Faustus hath incurred eternal death
By desperate thoughts against Jove's deity,   90
Say he surrenders up to him his soul
So he will spare him four and twenty years,
Letting him live in all voluptuousness,
Having thee ever to attend on me:
To give me whatsoever I shall ask,   95
To tell me whatsoever I demand,
To slay mine enemies and aid my friends,
And always be obedient to my will.
Go, and return to mighty Lucifer,
And meet me in my study at midnight   100
And then resolve me of thy master's mind.[5]
MEPHISTOPHILIS: I will, Faustus.
     [*Exit.*]
FAUSTUS: Had I as many souls as there be stars
     I'd give them all for Mephistophilis!
     By him I'll be great emperor of the world,   105
     And make a bridge through the moving air
     To pass the ocean with a band of men;
     I'll join the hills that bind the Afric shore
     And make that country continent to Spain,
     And both contributory to my crown;   110
     The Emperor[6] shall not live but by my leave,
     Nor any potentate of Germany.
     Now that I have obtained what I desire
     I'll live in speculation[7] of this art
     Till Mephistophilis return again.   115
     [*Exit.*]

SCENE 4

[*Enter* WAGNER *and the* CLOWN (ROBIN).[8]]
WAGNER: Come hither, sirrah boy.
CLOWN: Boy! O disgrace to my person! Zounds, boy in your face! You
     have seen many boys with such pickadevaunts,[9] I am sure.
WAGNER: Sirrah, hast thou no comings in?[1]
CLOWN: Yes, and goings out too; you may see, sir.   5
WAGNER: Alas, poor slave. See how poverty jests in his nakedness: the
     villain's out of service, and so hungry that I know he would give his
     soul to the devil for a shoulder of mutton, though it were blood-
     raw.

5. Give me his decision.   6. The Holy Roman Emperor.   7. Contemplation.   8. Not a court jester
(as in some of Shakespeare's plays), but the older-fashioned stock character, a rustic buffoon. The name
"Robin" has been interpolated by later editors of the text.   9. Beards. *Zounds*: An oath ("God's
wounds").   1. Income, but the Clown then puns on the literal meaning by showing the rents in his
clothes.

CLOWN: Not so, neither; I had need to have it well-roasted, and good   10
  sauce to it, if I pay so dear, I can tell you.

WAGNER: Sirrah, wilt thou be my man and wait on me? And I will
  make thee go like *Qui mihi discipulus.*[2]

CLOWN: What, in verse?

WAGNER: No, slave, in beaten silk and staves-acre.[3]   15

CLOWN: Staves-acre! that's good to kill vermin. Then, belike, if I serve
  you I shall be lousy.

WAGNER: Why, so thou shalt be, whether thou dost it or no; for, sirrah,
  if thou dost not presently bind thyself to me for seven years, I'll turn
  all the lice about thee into familiars[4] and make them tear thee in   20
  pieces.

CLOWN: Nay, sir, you may save yourself a labor, for they are as familiar
  with me as if they paid for their meat and drink, I can tell you.

WAGNER: Well, sirrah, leave your jesting and take these guilders.[5]

CLOWN: Yes, marry, sir, and I thank you, too.   25

WAGNER: So, now thou art to be at an hour's warning[6] whenever and
  wheresoever the devil shall fetch thee.

CLOWN: Here, take your guilders again, I'll none of 'em.

WAGNER: Not I, thou art pressed;[7] prepare thyself, for I will presently
  raise up two devils to carry thee away. Banio! Belcher!   30

CLOWN: Belcher? And[8] Belcher come here I'll belch him. I am not
  afraid of a devil.

  [*Enter two* DEVILS, *and the* CLOWN *runs up and down crying.*]

WAGNER: How now, sir! Will you serve me now?

CLOWN: Aye, good Wagner, take away the devils then.

WAGNER: Spirits, away!

  [DEVILS *exeunt.*]

                        Now, sirrah, follow me.   35

CLOWN: I will, sir. But hark you, master, will you teach me this conjuring occupation?

WAGNER: Aye, sirrah, I'll teach thee to turn thyself to a dog, or a cat,
  or a mouse, or a rat, or anything.

CLOWN: A dog, or a cat, or a mouse, or a rat! O brave[9] Wagner!   40

WAGNER: Villain, call me Master Wagner; and see that you walk attentively, and let your right eye be always diametrally fixed upon my
  left heel, that thou mayst *quasi vestigiis nostris insistere.*[1]

CLOWN: Well, sir, I warrant you.

  [*Exeunt.*]

---

2. "One who is my pupil." I.e., dress you in a style befitting a scholar's pupil.   3. A powder made from delphinium seeds and used for killing vermin.   4. Devils.   5. Coins.   6. Ready for service.   7. Impressed, i.e., hired.   8. If.   9. Marvelous, wonderful.   1. A pedantic way of saying "follow my footsteps."

Act II

SCENE 1

[*Enter* FAUSTUS *in his study.*]

FAUSTUS: Now, Faustus, must thou needs be damned,
  And canst thou not be saved.
  What boots[2] it, then, to think of God or heaven?
  Away with such vain fancies, and despair—
  Despair in God and trust in Belzebub.   5
  Now go not backward, no, be resolute!
  Why waverest thou? O something soundeth in mine ears:
  "Abjure this magic, turn to God again!"
  Aye, and Faustus will turn to God again.
  To God? He loves thee not;   10
  The God thou servest is thine own appetite,
  Wherein is fixed the love of Belzebub.
  To him I'll build an altar and a church
  And offer lukewarm blood of newborn babes.

    [*Enter* GOOD ANGEL *and* BAD ANGEL.]

GOOD ANGEL: Sweet Faustus, leave that execrable art.   15
BAD ANGEL: Go forward, Faustus, in that famous art.
FAUSTUS: Contrition, prayer, repentance—what of them?
GOOD ANGEL: O they are means to bring thee unto heaven!
BAD ANGEL: Rather illusions, fruits of lunacy,
  That makes men foolish that do use them most.   20
GOOD ANGEL: Sweet Faustus, think of heaven and heavenly things.
BAD ANGEL: No, Faustus, think of honor and of wealth.

    [*Exeunt* ANGELS.]

FAUSTUS: Of wealth!
  Why, the signiory of Emden[3] shall be mine.
  When Mephistophilis shall stand by me   25
  What power can hurt me? Faustus, thou art safe;
  Cast no more doubts. Come, Mephistophilis,
  And bring glad tidings from great Lucifer.
  Is't not midnight? Come, Mephistophilis!
  Veni, veni, Mephistophile![4]   30

    [*Enter* MEPHISTOPHILIS.]

  Now tell me what saith Lucifer, thy lord?
MEPHISTOPHILIS: That I shall wait on Faustus whilst I live,
  So he will buy my service with his soul.
FAUSTUS: Already Faustus hath hazarded that for thee.
MEPHISTOPHILIS: But, Faustus, thou must bequeath it solemnly   35
  And write a deed of gift with thine own blood,
  For that security craves Lucifer.

2. Avails.   3. A wealthy German trade center.   4. "Come, come Mephistophilis!"

If thou deny it, I must back to hell.
FAUSTUS: Stay, Mephistophilis, and tell me what good
     Will my soul do thy lord?
MEPHISTOPHILIS.   Enlarge his kingdom.   40
FAUSTUS: Is that the reason why he tempts us thus?
MEPHISTOPHILIS: *Solamen miseris socios habuisse doloris.*[5]
FAUSTUS: Why, have you any pain that tortures others?
MEPHISTOPHILIS: As great as have the human souls of men.
     But tell me, Faustus, shall I have thy soul?   45
     And I will be thy slave, and wait on thee,
     And give thee more than thou hast wit to ask.
FAUSTUS: Aye, Mephistophilis, I'll give it him.
MEPHISTOPHILIS: Then, Faustus, stab thine arm courageously,
     And bind thy soul that at some certain day   50
     Great Lucifer may claim it as his own,
     And then be thou as great as Lucifer.
FAUSTUS: Lo, Mephistophilis, for love of thee
     [*Stabbing his arm.*]
     Faustus hath cut his arm, and with his proper[6] blood
     Assures his soul to be great Lucifer's.   55
     Chief lord and regent of perpetual night,
     View here the blood that trickles from mine arm
     And let it be propitious for my wish!
MEPHISTOPHILIS: But, Faustus,
     Write it in manner of a deed of gift.   60
FAUSTUS: Aye, so I do. [*Writes.*] But, Mephistophilis,
     My blood congeals and I can write no more.
MEPHISTOPHILIS: I'll fetch thee fire to dissolve it straight.
     [*Exit.*]
FAUSTUS: What might the staying of my blood portend?
     Is it unwilling I should write this bill?[7]   65
     Why streams it not, that I may write afresh?
     "Faustus gives to thee his soul"—ah, there it stayed.
     Why shouldst thou not? Is not thy soul thine own?
     Then write again: "Faustus gives to thee his soul."
     [*Enter* MEPHISTOPHILIS *with a chafer*[8] *of fire.*]
MEPHISTOPHILIS: See, Faustus, here is fire; set it on.   70
FAUSTUS: So: now the blood begins to clear again;
     Now will I make an end immediately.
     [*Writes.*]
MEPHISTOPHILIS: [*Aside.*] What will not I do to obtain his soul!
FAUSTUS: *Consummatum est*[9]—this bill is ended;
     And Faustus hath bequeathed his soul to Lucifer.   75
     But what is this inscription on mine arm?
     "*Homo, fuge!*"[1] Whither should I fly?

5. "Misery loves company."   6. Own.   7. Contract.   8. A portable grate.   9. "It is finished." A
blasphemy, as these are the words of Jesus on the Cross (see John 19:30).   1. "Man, fly!"

If unto God, he'll throw me down to hell.
My senses are deceived; here's nothing writ.
O yes, I see it plain: even here is writ   80
"*Homo, fuge!*" Yet shall not Faustus fly.
MEPHISTOPHILIS: I'll fetch him somewhat to delight his mind.
    [*Exit. Re-enter* MEPHISTOPHILIS *with* DEVILS, *giving crowns and rich*
    apparel to FAUSTUS, *and dance, and then depart.*]
FAUSTUS: What means this show?
  Speak, Mephistophilis.
MEPHISTOPHILIS: Nothing, Faustus, but to delight thy mind   85
  And let thee see what magic can perform.
FAUSTUS: But may I raise such spirits when I please?
MEPHISTOPHILIS: Aye, Faustus, and do greater things than these.
FAUSTUS: Then, Mephistophilis, receive this scroll,
  A deed of gift of body and of soul;   90
  But yet conditionally that thou perform
  All covenant-articles between us both.
MEPHISTOPHILIS: Faustus, I swear by hell and Lucifer
  To effect all promises between us made.
FAUSTUS: Then hear me read it, Mephistophilis.   95
    [*Reads.*]
  "On these conditions following:
  First, that Faustus may be a spirit in form and substance.
  Secondly, that Mephistophilis shall be his servant and at his command.
  Thirdly, that Mephistophilis shall do for him, and bring him what-   100
  soever.
  Fourthly, that he shall be in his chamber or house invisible.
  Lastly, that he shall appear to the said John Faustus at all times, in
  what form or shape soever he please.
  I, John Faustus of Wittenberg, Doctor, by these presents do give 105
  both body and soul to Lucifer, Prince of the East, and his minister
  Mephistophilis, and furthermore grant unto them, that four and
  twenty years being expired, the articles above written inviolate, full
  power to fetch or carry the said John Faustus, body and soul, flesh,
  blood, or goods, into their habitation wheresoever.   110
                        By me John Faustus."
MEPHISTOPHILIS: Speak, Faustus, do you deliver this as your deed?
FAUSTUS: Aye, take it, and the devil give thee good of it.
MEPHISTOPHILIS: Now, Faustus, ask what thou wilt.
FAUSTUS: First will I question with thee about hell.   115
  Tell me, where is the place that men call hell?
MEPHISTOPHILIS: Under the heavens.
FAUSTUS: Aye, but whereabout?
MEPHISTOPHILIS: Within the bowels of these elements,
  Where we are tortured and remain forever.
  Hell hath no limits, nor is circumscribed   120

In one self place, for where we are is hell,
And where hell is there must we ever be;
And, to be short, when all the world dissolves
And every creature shall be purified,
All places shall be hell that is not heaven.   125
FAUSTUS: I think hell's a fable.
MEPHISTOPHILIS: Aye, think so still, till experience change thy mind.
FAUSTUS: Why, thinkst thou that Faustus shall be damned?
MEPHISTOPHILIS: Aye, of necessity, for here's the scroll
In which thou hast given thy soul to Lucifer.   130
FAUSTUS: Aye, and body too; but what of that?
Thinkst thou that Faustus is so fond[2] to imagine
That after this life there is any pain?
Tush no, these are trifles and mere old wives' tales.
MEPHISTOPHILIS: But I am an instance to prove the contrary,   135
For I tell thee I am damned and now in hell.
FAUSTUS: Nay, and this be hell I'll willingly be damned.
What, sleeping, eating, walking, and disputing?
But leaving off this, let me have a wife,
The fairest maid in Germany,   140
For I am wanton and lascivious
And cannot live without a wife.
MEPHISTOPHILIS: I prithee, Faustus, talk not of a wife.[3]
FAUSTUS: Nay, sweet Mephistophilis, fetch me one, for I will have one.
MEPHISTOPHILIS: Well, thou shalt have a wife. Sit there till I come.   145
    [Exit. Re-enter MEPHISTOPHILIS with a DEVIL dressed like a woman,
    with fireworks.]
FAUSTUS: What sight is this?
MEPHISTOPHILIS: Now Faustus, how dost thou like thy wife?
FAUSTUS: Here's a hot whore indeed! No, I'll no wife.
MEPHISTOPHILIS: Marriage is but a ceremonial toy,
And if thou lovest me, think no more of it.   150
I'll cull thee out the fairest courtesans
And bring them every morning to thy bed;
She whom thine eye shall like thy heart shall have,
Were she as chaste as was Penelope,
As wise as Saba,[4] or as beautiful   155
As was bright Lucifer before his fall.
Hold, take this book: peruse it thoroughly.
The iterating of these lines brings gold,
The framing of this circle on the ground
Brings whirlwinds, tempests, thunder, and lightning;   160
Pronounce this thrice devoutly to thyself
And men in harness shall appear to thee,

---

2. Foolish.   3. Mephistophilis cannot produce a wife for Faustus because marriage is a sacrament.
4. Queen of Sheba. *Penelope:* Wife of Ulysses, famed for chastity and fidelity.

Ready to execute what thou desirest.
FAUSTUS: Thanks, Mephistophilis, yet fain would I have a book wherein
I might behold all spells and incantations, that I might raise up   165
spirits when I please.
MEPHISTOPHILIS: Here they are in this book.
   [*There turn to them.*]
FAUSTUS: Now would I have a book where I might see all characters
and planets of the heavens, that I might know their motions and
dispositions.   170
MEPHISTOPHILIS: Here they are too.
   [*Turn to them.*]
FAUSTUS: Nay, let me have one book more, and then I have done,
wherein I might see all plants, herbs, and trees that grow upon the
earth.
MEPHISTOPHILIS: Here they be.   175
FAUSTUS: O thou art deceived!
MEPHISTOPHILIS: Tut, I warrant thee.
   [*Turn to them. Exeunt.*][5]

SCENE 2

   [*Enter* FAUSTUS *in his study and* MEPHISTOPHILIS.]
FAUSTUS: When I behold the heavens then I repent
And curse thee, wicked Mephistophilis,
Because thou hast deprived me of those joys.
MEPHISTOPHILIS: 'Twas thine own seeking, Faustus, thank thyself.
But thinkest thou heaven is such a glorious thing?   5
I tell thee, Faustus, it is not half so fair
As thou or any man that breathes on earth.
FAUSTUS: How provest thou that?
MEPHISTOPHILIS: 'Twas made for man; then he's more excellent.
FAUSTUS: If heaven was made for man 'twas made for me.   10
I will renounce this magic and repent.
   [*Enter* GOOD ANGEL *and* BAD ANGEL.]
GOOD ANGEL: Faustus, repent; yet God will pity thee.
BAD ANGEL: Thou art a spirit; God cannot pity thee.
FAUSTUS: Who buzzeth in mine ears I am a spirit?[6]
Be I a devil, yet God may pity me.   15
Yea, God will pity me, if I repent.
BAD ANGEL: Aye, but Faustus never shall repent.
   [*Exeunt* ANGELS.]
FAUSTUS: My heart is hardened; I cannot repent.
Scarce can I name salvation, faith, or heaven,
But fearful echoes thunder in mine ears: 20

5. After this a comic scene has been lost from the text. In it, apparently the Clown stole one of Faustus' conjuring books and left Wagner's service. He then became an hostler at an inn. 6. I.e., a devil (having signed away his human soul).

"Faustus, thou are damned!" Then guns and knives,
Swords, poison, halters, and envenomed steel
Are laid before me to dispatch myself,
And long ere this I should have done the deed
Had not sweet pleasure conquered deep despair.   25
Have I not made blind Homer sing to me
Of Alexander's[7] love and Oenon's death,
And hath not he that built the walls of Thebes
With ravishing sound of his melodious harp[8]
Made music with my Mephistophilis?   30
Why should I die, then, or basely despair?
I am resolved Faustus shall not repent.
Come, Mephistophilis, let us dispute again
And reason of divine astrology.
Speak, are there many spheres above the moon?   35
Are all celestial bodies but one globe
As is the substance of this centric earth?
MEPHISTOPHILIS: As are the elements, such are the heavens,
    Even from the moon unto the empyreal orb,
    Mutually folded in each other's spheres,[9]   40
    And jointly move upon one axletree
    Whose termine[1] is termed the world's wide pole;
    Nor are the names of Saturn, Mars, or Jupiter
    Feigned, but are erring stars.
FAUSTUS: But tell me, have they all one motion, both *situ et tempore?*[2]   45
MEPHISTOPHILIS: All move from east to west in four and twenty hours
    upon the poles of the world, but differ in their motions upon the
    poles of the zodiac.
FAUSTUS: These slender questions Wagner can decide.
    Hath Mephistophilis no greater skill?   50
    Who knows not the double motion of the planets?
    That the first is finished in a natural day;
    The second thus, Saturn in thirty years, Jupiter in twelve, Mars in
    four, the Sun, Venus, and Mercury in a year, the moon in twenty-
    eight days. These are freshmen's suppositions. But tell me, hath 55
    every sphere a dominion or *intelligentia?*[3]
MEPHISTOPHILIS: Aye.
FAUSTUS: How many heavens or spheres are there?
MEPHISTOPHILIS: Nine; the seven planets, the firmament, and the
    empyreal heaven.   60
FAUSTUS: But is there not *coelum igneum, et crystallinum?*[4]

7. Another name for Paris, the lover of Oenone; later he deserted her and abducted Helen, causing the
Trojan War. Oenone refused to heal the wounds Paris received in battle, and when he died of them she
killed herself in remorse.   8. I.e., the legendary musician Amphion.   9. In Ptolemaic astronomy,
the sun, moon, and stars were believed set into spherical shells, transparent, concentric, and revolving
within one another.   1. End.   2. In direction and duration of revolutions.   3. Ruling spirit.
4. The "heaven of fire" and the "crystalline sphere," introduced by some of the old authorities to explain
the precession of the equinoxes.

MEPHISTOPHILIS: No, Faustus, they be but fables.

FAUSTUS: Resolve me then in this one question: why are not conjunctions, oppositions, aspects, eclipses, all at one time, but in some years we have more, in some less? 65

MEPHISTOPHILIS: *Per inequalem motum respectu totius.*[5]

FAUSTUS: Well, I am answered. Tell me, who made the world?

MEPHISTOPHILIS: I will not.

FAUSTUS: Sweet Mephistophilis, tell me.

MEPHISTOPHILIS: Move me not, Faustus. 70

FAUSTUS: Villain, have I not bound thee to tell me anything?

MEPHISTOPHILIS: Aye, that is not against our kingdom; this is. Thou art damned; think thou of hell.

FAUSTUS: Think, Faustus, upon God that made the world!

MEPHISTOPHILIS: Remember this! 75
    [*Exit.*]

FAUSTUS: Aye, go, accursèd spirit, to ugly hell;
    'Tis thou has damned distressèd Faustus' soul.
    Is 't not too late?
    [*Enter* GOOD ANGEL *and* BAD ANGEL.]

BAD ANGEL: Too late.

GOOD ANGEL: Never too late, if Faustus will repent. 80

BAD ANGEL: If thou repent, devils will tear thee in pieces.

GOOD ANGEL: Repent, and they shall never raze thy skin.
    [*Exeunt* ANGELS.]

FAUSTUS: O Christ, my Saviour! my Saviour!
    Help to save distressèd Faustus' soul.
    [*Enter* LUCIFER, BELZEBUB, *and* MEPHISTOPHILIS.]

LUCIFER: Christ cannot save thy soul, for he is just; 85
    There's none but I have interest in the same.

FAUSTUS: O what art thou that lookst so terrible?

LUCIFER: I am Lucifer,
    And this is my companion prince in hell.

FAUSTUS: O Faustus, they are come to fetch thy soul! 90

BELZEBUB: We are come to tell thee thou dost injure us.

LUCIFER: Thou call'st on Christ, contrary to thy promise.

BELZEBUB: Thou shouldst not think on God.

LUCIFER: Think on the devil.

BELZEBUB: And his dam too.[6] 95

FAUSTUS: Nor will I henceforth. Pardon me in this,
    And Faustus vows never to look to heaven,
    Never to name God or pray to him,
    To burn his Scriptures, slay his ministers,
    And make my spirits pull his churches down. 100

LUCIFER: So shalt thou show thyself an obedient servant, and we will highly gratify thee for it.

5. "Because of their unequal velocities within the system." 6. "The devil and his dam" was a common colloquial expression—the devil's dam, or mother, being sin.

BELZEBUB: Faustus, we are come from hell in person to show thee some pastime. Sit down, and thou shalt behold the Seven Deadly Sins appear to thee in their own proper shapes and likeness. 105

FAUSTUS: That sight will be as pleasant to me as Paradise was to Adam, the first day of his creation.

LUCIFER: Talk not of Paradise or Creation, but mark the show. Go, Mephistophilis, fetch them in.

[*Enter the* SEVEN DEADLY SINS, *led by a piper.*]

Now, Faustus, question them of their names and dispositions. 110

FAUSTUS: That shall I soon. What art thou, the first?

PRIDE: I am Pride. I disdain to have any parents. I am like to Ovid's flea:[7] I can creep into every corner of a wench; sometimes like a periwig I sit upon her brow; next like a necklace I hang about her neck; then like a fan of feathers I kiss her lips; and then turning 115 myself to a wrought smock[8] do what I list. But fie, what a smell is here! I'll not speak another word except the ground be perfumed and covered with cloth of arras.

FAUSTUS: Thou art a proud knave indeed. What art thou, the second?

COVETOUSNESS: I am Covetousness, begotten of an old churl in a leather 120 bag; and, might I now obtain my wish, this house, you and all, should turn to gold, that I might lock you safe into my chest. O my sweet gold!

FAUSTUS: And what art thou, the third?

ENVY: I am Envy, begotten of a chimney-sweeper and an oyster-wife. 125 I cannot read, and therefore wish all books were burned. I am lean with seeing others eat. O that there would come a famine over all the world, that all might die, and I live alone; then thou shouldst see how fat I'd be! But must thou sit and I stand? Come down, with a vengeance! 130

FAUSTUS: Out, envious wretch! But what art thou, the fourth?

WRATH: I am Wrath. I had neither father nor mother; I leapt out of a lion's mouth when I was scarce an hour old, and ever since have run up and down the world with these case[9] of rapiers, wounding myself when I could get none to fight withal. I was born in hell; 135 and look to it, for some of you shall be my father.

FAUSTUS: And what art thou, the fifth?

GLUTTONY: I am Gluttony. My parents are all dead, and the devil a penny they have left me but a small pension, and that buys me thirty meals a day and ten bevers—a small trifle to suffice nature. I 140 come of a royal pedigree: my father was a gammon[1] of bacon, and my mother was a hogshead of claret wine. My godfathers were these: Peter Pickle-herring and Martin Martlemas-beef. But my god-mother, O, she was a jolly gentlewoman, and well beloved in every good town and city: her name was mistress Margery March-beer. 145

---

7. A salacious medieval poem *Carmen de Pulice* ("The Flea") was attributed to Ovid.   8. A decorated or ornamented petticoat.   9. Pair.   1. The lower side of pork, including the leg. *Bevers:* Snacks.

Now, Faustus, thou hast heard all my progeny; wilt thou bid me to
supper?

FAUSTUS: Not I. Thou wilt eat up all my victuals.

GLUTTONY: Then the devil choke thee!

FAUSTUS: Choke thyself, glutton. What art thou, the sixth?   150

SLOTH: Heigh ho! I am Sloth. I was begotten on a sunny bank, where
I have lain ever since, and you have done me great injury to bring
me from thence; let me be carried thither again by Gluttony and
Lechery. Heigh ho! I'll not speak word more for a king's ransom.

FAUSTUS: And what are you, mistress minx, the seventh and last?   155

LECHERY: Who, I, sir? I am one that loves an inch of raw mutton[2]
better than an ell of fried stockfish, and the first letter of my name
begins with Lechery.

LUCIFER: Away, to hell, away! On, piper!

    [*Exeunt the* SINS.]

FAUSTUS: O how this sight doth delight my soul!   160

LUCIFER: Tut, Faustus, in hell is all manner of delight.

FAUSTUS: O might I see hell and return again safe, how happy were I
then!

LUCIFER: Faustus, thou shalt. At midnight I will send for thee. In
meantime peruse this book, and view it throughly, and thou shalt   165
turn thyself into what shape thou wilt.

FAUSTUS: Thanks, mighty Lucifer; this will I keep as chary[3] as my life.

LUCIFER: Now Faustus, farewell.

FAUSTUS: Farewell, great Lucifer. Come, Mephistophilis.

    [*Exeunt* OMNES.]

SCENE 3

[*Enter the* CLOWN (ROBIN).]

ROBIN: What, Dick, look to the horses there till I come again. I have
gotten one of Dr. Faustus' conjuring books, and now we'll have
such knavery as 't passes.

    [*Enter* DICK.]

DICK: What, Robin, you must come away and walk the horses.

ROBIN: I walk the horses! I scorn 't, faith: I have other matters in hand;   5
let the horses walk themselves and they will. "A *per se*[4] a; t, h, e,
the; o *per se* o; deny orgon, gorgon." Keep further from me, O thou
illiterate and unlearned hostler.

DICK: 'Snails,[5] what has thou got there? a book? Why, thou canst not
tell ne'er a word on 't.   10

ROBIN: That thou shalt see presently. Keep out of the circle, I say, lest
I send you into the ostry[6] with a vengeance.

---

2. Here, the penis. *Ell*: 45 inches; *stockfish*: dried cod.   3. Carefully.   4. "A by itself," a method of
reading the letters of the alphabet taught to children. Robin's semiliteracy is being satirized. *Deny orgon,
gorgon*: A parody of Faustus' invocation of Demogorgon in Act I, sc. 3.   5. I.e., God's nails (on the
Cross).   6. Stable.

DICK: That's like, faith! You had best leave your foolery, for an my
master come, he'll conjure you, faith.

ROBIN: My master conjure me! I'll tell thee what; an my master come   15
here, I'll clap as fair a pair of horns on 's head as e'er thou sawest
in thy life.[7]

DICK: Thou needst not do that, for my mistress hath done it.

ROBIN: Aye, there be of us here have waded as deep into matters as
other men, if they were disposed to talk.   20

DICK: A plague take you! I thought you did not sneak up and down
after her for nothing. But I prithee tell me in good sadness, Robin,
is that a conjuring book?

ROBIN: Do but speak what thou 't have me do, and I'll do 't. If thou 't
dance naked, put off thy clothes, and I'll conjure thee about pres-   25
ently. Or if thou 't but to the tavern with me, I'll give thee white
wine, red wine, claret wine, sack, muscadine, malmesey, and
whippincrust,[8] hold-belly-hold, and we'll not pay one penny for it.

DICK: O brave! Prithee let's to it presently, for I am as dry as a dog.

ROBIN: Come then, let's away.   30

    [*Exeunt.*]

Act III

[*Enter* CHORUS.]

CHORUS: Learned Faustus,
To find the secrets of astronomy
Graven in the book of Jove's high firmament,
Did mount himself to scale Olympus' top.
Where sitting in a chariot burning bright   5
Drawn by the strength of yokèd dragons' necks,
He views the clouds, the planets, and the stars,
The tropics, zones, and quarters of the sky
From the bright circle of the hornèd moon
Even to the height of *Primum Mobile;*[9]   10
And whirling round with this circumference
Within the concave compass of the pole,
From east to west his dragons swiftly glide
And in eight days did bring him home again.
Not long he stayed within his quiet house   15
To rest his bones after his weary toil
But new exploits do hale him out again;
And mounted then upon a dragon's back
That with his wings did part the subtle air,
He now is gone to prove cosmography[1]   20
That measures coasts and kingdoms of the earth:

7. A wife's infidelity was supposed to cause her husband to grow horns.   8. Robin's pronunciation of
"hippocras," a spiced wine.   9. The outermost sphere, the empyrean.   1. I.e., to test the accuracy of
maps.

And, as I guess, will first arrive at Rome
To see the Pope and manner of his court
And take some part of holy Peter's feast,
The which this day is highly solemnized.   25
    [*Exit.*]

SCENE 1

[*Enter* FAUSTUS *and* MEPHISTOPHILIS.]

FAUSTUS: Having now, my good Mephistophilis,
    Passed with delight the stately town of Trier[2]
    Environed round with airy mountain tops,
    With walls of flint and deep-entrenchèd lakes,[3]
    Not to be won by any conquering prince;   5
    From Paris next coasting the realm of France,
    We saw the river Main fall into Rhine,
    Whose banks are set with groves of fruitful vines;
    Then up to Naples, rich Campania,
    With buildings fair and gorgeous to the eye,   10
    Whose streets straight forth and paved with finest brick
    Quarter the town in four equivalents
    There saw we learned Maro's[4] golden tomb,
    The way he cut, an English mile in length,
    Through a rock of stone in one night's space.   15
    From thence to Venice, Padua, and the rest,
    In midst of which a sumptuous temple[5] stands
    That threats the stars with her aspiring top,
    Whose frame is paved with sundry colored stones
    And roofed aloft with curious work in gold.   20
    Thus hitherto hath Faustus spent his time.
    But tell me now, what resting place is this?
    Hast thou, as erst I did command,
    Conducted me within the walls of Rome?
MEPHISTOPHILIS: I have, my Faustus, and for proof thereof   25
    This is the goodly palace of the Pope,
    And 'cause we are no common guests
    I choose his privy chamber for our use.
FAUSTUS: I hope his Holiness will bid us welcome.
MEPHISTOPHILIS: All's one, for we'll be bold with his venison.   30
    But now, my Faustus, that thou mayst perceive
    What Rome contains for to delight thine eyes,
    Know that this city stands upon seven hills
    That underprop the groundwork of the same;
    Just through the midst runs flowing Tiber's stream,   35

2. Treves (in Prussia).   3. Moats.   4. Virgil's. In medieval legend the Roman poet Virgil was considered a magician, and a tunnel ("way") on the promontory of Posillipo at Naples, near his tomb, was accredited to his supposed magical powers.   5. St. Mark's in Venice.

With winding banks that cut it in two parts
Over the which four stately bridges lean
That make safe passage to each part of Rome.
Upon the bridge called Ponte Angelo
Erected is a castle passing strong,   40
Where thou shalt see such store of ordnance
As that the double cannons forged of brass
Do match the number of the days contained
Within the compass of one complete year;
Besides the gates and high pyramides⁶   45
That Julius Caesar brought from Africa.
FAUSTUS: Now by the kingdoms of infernal rule,
Of Styx, Acheron, and the fiery lake
Of ever-burning Phlegethon,⁷ I swear
That I do long to see the monuments   50
And situation of bright-splendent Rome.
Come, therefore, let's away.
MEPHISTOPHILIS: Nay, stay, my Faustus; I know you'd see the Pope
And take some part of holy Peter's feast,
The which in state and high solemnity   55
This day is held through Rome and Italy
In honor of the Pope's triumphant victory.
FAUSTUS: Sweet Mephistophilis, thou pleasest me;
Whilst I am here on earth let me be cloyed
With all things that delight the heart of man.   60
My four and twenty years of liberty
I'll spend in pleasure and in dalliance,
That Faustus' name, whilst this bright frame doth stand,
May be admirèd through the furthest land.
MEPHISTOPHILIS: 'Tis well said, Faustus; come then, stand by me   65
And thou shalt see them come immediately.
FAUSTUS: Nay, stay, my gentle Mephistophilis,
And grant me my request, and then I go.
Thou knowst, within the compass of eight days
We viewed the face of heaven, of earth, of hell;   70
So high our dragons soared into the air
That, looking down, the earth appeared to me
No bigger than my hand in quantity.
There did we view the kingdoms of the world,
And what might please mine eye I there beheld.   75
Then in this show let me an actor be,
That this proud Pope may Faustus' cunning see.
MEPHISTOPHILIS: Let it be so, my Faustus, but first stay
And view their triumphs⁸ as they pass this way,
And then devise what best contents thy mind,   80

6. *Py-rám-i-des*, a singular noun, meaning an obelisk. 7. Classical names for rivers of the underworld. 8. Parades.

By cunning of thine art to cross the Pope
Or dash the pride of this solemnity,
To make his monks and abbots stand like apes
And point like antics⁹ at his triple crown,
To beat the beads about the friars' pates   85
Or clap huge horns upon the cardinals' heads,
Or any villainy thou canst devise,
And I'll perform it, Faustus. Hark, they come!
This day shall make thee be admired in Rome.

> [*Enter the* CARDINALS *and* BISHOPS, *some bearing crosiers, some the
> pillars;*¹ MONKS *and* FRIARS *singing their procession; then the* POPE *and*
> RAYMOND, *King of Hungary, with* BRUNO² *led in chains.*]

POPE: Cast down our footstool.
RAYMOND: Saxon Bruno, stoop,   90
Whilst on thy back his Holiness ascends
St. Peter's chair and state pontifical.
BRUNO: Proud Lucifer, that state belongs to me;
But thus I fall, to Peter, not to thee.
POPE: To me and Peter shalt thou groveling lie   95
And crouch before the papal dignity.
Sound trumpets, then, for thus St. Peter's heir
From Bruno's back ascends St. Peter's chair.

> [*A flourish while he ascends.*]

Thus as the gods creep on with feet of wool
Long ere with iron hands they punish men,   100
So shall our sleeping vengeance now arise
And smite with death thy hated enterprise.
Lord Cardinals of France and Padua,
Go forthwith to our holy consistory
And read among the statutes decretal   105
What, by the holy council held at Trent,³
The sacred synod hath decreed for him
That doth assume the papal government
Without election and a true consent.
Away and bring us word with speed.   110
1 CARDINAL: We go, my lord.

> [*Exeunt* CARDINALS.]

POPE: Lord Raymond—
FAUSTUS: Go, haste thee, gentle Mephistophilis,
Follow the cardinals to the consistory,
And as they turn their superstitious books,   115
Strike them with sloth and drowsy idleness
And make them sleep so sound that in their shapes
Thyself and I may parley with this Pope,

---

9. Grotesque figures.   1. Columnlike objects carried as marks of office.   2. Like Raymond, fictitious; he is the German pretender to the papal throne over whom the Pope has just triumphed (l. 57).
3. 1545–1563.

This proud confronter of the Emperor,[4]
And in despite of all his holiness   120
Restore this Bruno to his liberty
And bear him to the states of Germany.
MEPHISTOPHILIS: Faustus, I go.
FAUSTUS: Dispatch it soon.
The Pope shall curse that Faustus came to Rome.
    [*Exeunt* FAUSTUS *and* MEPHISTOPHILIS.]
BRUNO: Pope Adrian, let me have some right of law;   125
I was elected by the Emperor.
POPE: We will depose the Emperor for that deed
And curse the people that submit to him;
Both he and thou shalt stand excommunicate
And interdict from church's privilege   130
And all society of holy men.
He grows too proud in his authority,
Lifting his lofty head above the clouds,
And like a steeple overpeers the church,
But we'll pull down his haughty insolence.   135
And as Pope Alexander,[5] our progenitor,
Trod on the neck of German Frederick,
Adding this golden sentence to our praise,
That Peter's heirs should tread on emperors
And walk upon the dreadful adder's back,   140
Treading the lion and the dragon down,
And fearless spurn the killing basilisk;
So will we quell that haughty schismatic,
And by authority apostolical
Depose him from his regal government.   145
BRUNO: Pope Julius swore to princely Sigismond,
For him and the succeeding popes of Rome,
To hold the emperors their lawful lords.
POPE: Pope Julius did abuse the church's rights,
And therefore none of his decrees can stand.   150
Is not all power on earth bestowed on us?
And therefore though we would we cannot err.
Behold this silver belt, whereto is fixed
Seven golden keys fast sealed with seven seals
In token of our sevenfold power from heaven,   155
To bind or loose, lock fast, condemn, or judge,
Resign or seal, or whatso pleaseth us.
Then he and thou and all the world shall stoop,
Or be assurèd of our dreadful curse
To light as heavy as the pains of hell.   160

4. Holy Roman Emperor. Faustus refers to the conflict between the Pope and the Emperor; the former
was victorious and captured the Emperor's choice for Pope, "Saxon Bruno."   5. Alexander III (1159–
1181) compelled the Emperor Frederick Barbarossa to submit to him.

[*Enter* FAUSTUS *and* MEPHISTOPHILIS *like cardinals.*]
MEPHISTOPHILIS: Now tell me, Faustus, are we not fitted well?
FAUSTUS: Yes, Mephistophilis, and two such cardinals
  Ne'er served a holy pope as we shall do.
  But whilst they sleep within the consistory
  Let us salute his reverend Fatherhood.   165
RAYMOND: Behold, my lord, the cardinals are returned.
POPE: Welcome, grave fathers, answer presently;[6]
  What have our holy council there decreed
  Concerning Bruno and the Emperor
  In quittance of their late conspiracy   170
  Against our state and papal dignity?
FAUSTUS: Most sacred patron of the church of Rome,
  By full consent of all the synod
  Of priests and prelates it is thus decreed:
  That Bruno and the German Emperor   175
  Be held as lollards[7] and bold schismatics
  And proud disturbers of the church's peace.
  And if that Bruno by his own assent,
  Without enforcement of the German peers,
  Did seek to wear the triple diadem   180
  And by your death to climb St. Peter's chair,
  The statutes decretal have thus decreed:
  He shall be straight condemned of heresy
  And on a pile of fagots burned to death.
POPE: It is enough. Here, take him to your charge   185
  And bear him straight to Ponte Angelo,
  And in the strongest tower enclose him fast.
  Tomorrow, sitting in our consistory
  With all our college of grave cardinals,
  We will determine of his life or death.   190
  Here, take his triple crown along with you
  And leave it in the church's treasury.
  Make haste again, my good lord cardinals,
  And take our blessing apostolical.
MEPHISTOPHILIS: So, so. Was never devil thus blessed before!   195
FAUSTUS: Away, sweet Mephistophilis, be gone;
  The cardinals will be plagued for this anon.
  [*Exeunt* FAUSTUS *and* MEPHISTOPHILIS *with* BRUNO.]
POPE: Go presently and bring a banquet forth,
  That we may solemnize St. Peter's feast
  And with Lord Raymond, King of Hungary,   200
  Drink to our late and happy victory.
  [*Exeunt.*]

6. Immediately.   7. Protestants, usually English followers of Wycliffe, fourteenth-century religious reformer.

SCENE 2

[*The banquet is brought in, and then enter* FAUSTUS *and* MEPHISTO-
PHILIS *in their own shapes.*]

MEPHISTOPHILIS: Now Faustus, come prepare thyself for mirth;
    The sleepy cardinals are hard at hand
    To censure Bruno, that is posted hence
    And on a proud-paced steed as swift as thought
    Flies o'er the Alps to fruitful Germany,   5
    There to salute the woeful Emperor.
FAUSTUS: The Pope will curse them for their sloth today
    That slept both Bruno and his crown away.
    But now, that Faustus may delight his mind
    And by their folly make some merriment,   10
    Sweet Mephistophilis, so charm me here
    That I may walk invisible to all
    And do whate'er I please unseen of any.
MEPHISTOPHILIS: Faustus, thou shalt; then kneel down presently,

                    Whilst on thy head I lay my hand   15
                    And charm thee with this magic wand.
                    First wear this girdle, then appear
                    Invisible to all are here.
                    The planets seven, the gloomy air,
                    Hell, and the Furies' forkèd hair,   20
                    Pluto's blue fire and Hecate's[8] tree
                    With magic spells so compass thee
                    That no eye may thy body see.

    So, Faustus, now, for all their holiness,
        Do what thou wilt thou shalt not be discerned.   25
FAUSTUS: Thanks, Mephistophilis. Now friars, take heed
    Lest Faustus make your shaven crowns to bleed.
MEPHISTOPHILIS: Faustus, no more; see where the cardinals come.
        [*Enter* POPE *and all the lords, with* KING RAYMOND *and the* ARCHBISHOP
        OF RHEIMS. *Enter the two* CARDINALS *with a book.*]
POPE: Welcome, lord cardinals; come, sit down.
    Lord Raymond, take your seat. Friars, attend,   30
    And see that all things be in readiness
    As best beseems this solemn festival.
1 CARDINAL: First may it please your sacred holiness
    To view the sentence of the reverend synod
    Concerning Bruno and the Emperor.   35
POPE: What needs this question? Did I not tell you
    Tomorrow we would sit i' th' consistory
    And there determine of his punishment?
    You brought us word, even now, it was decreed

8. Goddess of magic and witchcraft, whose name the Elizabethans pronounced *Héc-at. Tree* may be a
mistake for "three," since she was often represented as a triple goddess—of heaven, earth, and hell.

That Bruno and the cursèd Emperor   40
Were by the holy council both condemned
For loathèd lollards and base schismatics;
Then wherefore would you have me view that book?
1 CARDINAL: Your Grace mistakes; you gave us no such charge.
RAYMOND: Deny it not; we all are witnesses   45
That Bruno here was late delivered you,
With his rich triple crown to be reserved
And put into the church's treasury.
BOTH CARDINALS: By holy Paul we saw them not.
POPE: By Peter, you shall die   50
Unless you bring them forth immediately.
Hale them to prison! Lade their limbs with gyves![9]
False prelates, for this hateful treachery,
Cursed be your souls to hellish misery.
          [*Exeunt* CARDINALS.]
FAUSTUS: So they are safe. Now, Faustus, to the feast;   55
The Pope had never such a frolic guest.
POPE: Lord Archbishop of Rheims, sit down with us.
ARCHBISHOP: I thank your Holiness.
FAUSTUS: Fall to! The devil choke you an you spare!
POPE: Who's that spoke? Friars, look about.   60
Lord Raymond, pray fall to. I am beholden
To the Bishop of Milan for this so rare a present.
FAUSTUS: I thank you, sir.
          [FAUSTUS *snatches the meat from the* POPE.]
POPE: How now! Who snatched the meat from me? Villains, why
speak you not?   65
FRIAR: Here's nobody, if it like your Holiness.
POPE: My good Lord Archbishop, here's a most dainty dish.
Was sent me from a cardinal in France.
FAUSTUS: I'll have that, too.
          [FAUSTUS *snatches the dish from the* POPE.]
POPE: What lollards do attend our Holiness   70
That we receive such great indignity?
Fetch me some wine.
FAUSTUS: Aye, pray do, for Faustus is adry.
POPE: Lord Raymond, I drink unto your Grace.
FAUSTUS: I pledge your Grace.   75
          [FAUSTUS *snatches the cup from the* POPE.]
POPE: My wine gone, too? Ye lubbers, look about
And find the man that doth this villainy,
Or by my sanctitude you all shall die.
I pray, my lords, have patience at this troublesome banquet.
ARCHBISHOP: Please your Holiness, I think it be some ghost crept out of 80

9. I.e., load their limbs with prisoners' shackles.

purgatory and now is come unto your Holiness for his pardon.

POPE: It may be so;
Go then, command our priests to sing a dirge
To lay the fury of this same troublesome ghost.
Once again, my lord, fall to.   85
    [*The* POPE *crosses himself.*]

FAUSTUS: How now!
Must every bit be spiced with a cross?
Well, use that trick no more, I would advise you.
    [*The* POPE *crosses himself.*]
Well, there's the second time; aware the third;
I give you fair warning.   90
    [*The* POPE *crosses himself again.*]
Nay then, take that!
    [FAUSTUS *hits the* POPE *a box on the ear.*]

POPE: O, I am slain! Help me, my lords!
O come and help to bear my body hence!
Damned be his soul forever for this deed.
    [*Exeunt the* POPE *and his train.*]

MEPHISTOPHILIS: Now Faustus, what will you do now? For I can tell   95
you you'll be cursed with bell, book, and candle.[1]

FAUSTUS: Bell, book, and candle; candle, book, and bell
Forward and backward, to curse Faustus to hell!
    [*Enter all the* FRIARS *with bell, book, and candle to sing the dirge.*]

FRIAR: Come, brethren, let's about our business with good devotion.
    [ALL *sing this:*]
Cursèd be he that stole away his Holiness' meat from the table—   100
    maledicat dominus![2]
Cursèd be he that struck his Holiness a blow on the face—*maledicat
    dominus!*
Cursèd be he that took Friar Sandelo a blow on the face—*maledicat
    dominus!*   105
Cursèd be he that disturbeth our holy dirge—*maledicat dominus!*
Cursèd be he that took away his Holiness' wine—*maledicat domi-
    nus! Et omnes sancti!*[3] Amen.
    [FAUSTUS *and* MEPHISTOPHILIS *beat the* FRIARS, *and fling fireworks among
    them, and so exeunt.*]

SCENE 3

[*Enter* CLOWN (ROBIN) *and* DICK *with a cup.*]

DICK: Sirrah Robin, we were best look that your devil can answer the
stealing of this same cup, for the vintner's boy follows us at the hard
heels.

ROBIN: 'Tis no matter, let him come! An he follow us I'll so conjure

1. The traditional paraphernalia for cursing and excommunication.   2. "May the Lord curse him!"
3. And all the saints (also curse him).

him as he was never conjured in his life, I warrant him. Let me   5
see the cup.

[*Enter* VINTNER.]

DICK: Here 'tis. Yonder he comes. Now, Robin, now or never show
thy cunning.

VINTNER: O, are you here? I am glad I have found you. You are a
couple of fine companions! Pray, where's the cup you stole from   10
the tavern?

ROBIN: How, how? We steal a cup? Take heed what you say! We look
not like cup-stealers, I can tell you.

VINTNER: Never deny it, for I know you have it, and I'll search you.

ROBIN: Search me? Aye, and spare not. Hold the cup, Dick! Come,   15
come; search me, search me.

VINTNER: Come on, sirrah, let me search you now.

DICK: Aye, aye, do; do. Hold the cup, Robin. I fear not your searching. We scorn to steal your cups, I can tell you.

VINTNER: Never outface me for the matter, for sure the cup is between   20
you two.

ROBIN: Nay, there you lie. 'Tis beyond us both.

VINTNER: A plague take you! I thought 'twas your knavery to take it
away. Come, give it me again.

ROBIN: Aye, much! When, can you tell?[4] Dick, make me a circle, and   25
stand close at my back and stir not for thy life. Vintner, you shall
have your cup anon. Say nothing, Dick. O *per se* O; Demogorgon,
Belcher and Mephistophilis!

[*Enter* MEPHISTOPHILIS.]

MEPHISTOPHILIS: Monarch of hell, under whose black survey
Great potentates do kneel with awful fear,   30
Upon whose altars thousand souls do lie,
How am I vexèd with these villains' charms!
From Constantinople am I hither brought
Only for pleasure of these damnèd slaves.

[*Exit* VINTNER.]

ROBIN: By Lady, sir, you have had a shrewd journey of it; will it please   35
you to take a shoulder of mutton to supper and a tester[5] in your
purse, and go back again?

DICK: Aye, I pray you heartily, sir; for we called you but in jest, I
promise you.

MEPHISTOPHILIS: To purge the rashness of this cursèd deed,   40
First be thou turnèd to this ugly shape:
For apish deeds transformèd to an ape.

ROBIN: O brave! an ape! I pray, sir, let me have the carrying of him
about to show some tricks.

MEPHISTOPHILIS: And so thou shalt. Be thou transformed to a dog and   45
carry him upon thy back. Away! Be gone!

---

4. A common Elizabethan scornful retort.   5. Sixpence.

ROBIN: A dog! That's excellent! Let the maids look well to their por-
ridge pots, for I'll into the kitchen presently. Come, Dick, come.
   [*Exit* ROBIN *and* DICK.]
MEPHISTOPHILIS: Now with the flames of ever-burning fire
   I'll wing myself and forthwith fly amain   50
   Unto my Faustus, to the Great Turk's court.
   [*Exit.*]

Act IV

[*Enter* CHORUS.]
CHORUS: When Faustus had with pleasure ta'en the view
   Of rarest things and royal courts of kings,
   He stayed his course and so returnèd home,
   Where such as bear his absence but with grief,
   I mean his friends and nearest companións,   5
   Did gratulate his safety with kind words,
   And in their conference of what befell
   Touching his journey through the world and air,
   They put forth questions of astrology
   Which Faustus answered with such learned skill   10
   As they admired and wondered at his wit.
   Now is his fame spread forth in every land:
   Amongst the rest the Emperor is one,
   Carolus the Fifth,[6] at whose palace now
   Faustus is feasted 'mongst his noblemen.   15
   What there he did in trial of his art
   I leave untold, your eyes shall see performed.
   [*Exit.*]

SCENE 1

[*Enter* MARTINO *and* FREDERICK *at several doors.*[7]]
MARTINO: What ho! Officers, gentlemen!
   Hie to the presence[8] to attend the Emperor.
   Good Frederick, see the rooms be voided straight;
   His Majesty is coming to the hall.
   Go back, and see the state[9] in readiness.   5
FREDERICK: But where is Bruno, our elected Pope,
   That on a fury's back came post from Rome?
   Will not his Grace consort the Emperor?
MARTINO: O yes, and with him comes the German conjurer,
   The learned Faustus, fame of Wittenberg,   10
   The wonder of the world for magic art;
   And he intends to show great Carolus

6. Emperor Charles V (1519–1556).   7. At different entrances.   8. Chamber where royalty makes
ceremonial appearances.   9. Throne.

The race of all his stout progenitors
And bring in presence of his majesty
The royal shapes and warlike semblances   15
Of Alexander and his beauteous paramour.[1]
FREDERICK: Where is Benvolio?
MARTINO: Fast asleep, I warrant you;
  He took his rouse with stoups[2] of Rhenish wine
  So kindly yesternight to Bruno's health   20
  That all this day the sluggard keeps his bed.
FREDERICK: See, see; his window's ope; we'll call to him.
MARTINO: What ho, Benvolio!
    [*Enter* BENVOLIO *above at a window, in his nightcap, buttoning.*]
BENVOLIO: What a devil ail you two?
MARTINO: Speak softly, sir, lest the devil hear you;   25
  For Faustus at the court is late arrived
  And at his heels a thousand furies wait
  To accomplish whatsoever the Doctor please.
BENVOLIO: What of this?
MARTINO: Come, leave thy chamber first and thou shalt see   30
  This conjurer perform such rare exploits
  Before the Pope[3] and royal Emperor
  As never yet was seen in Germany.
BENVOLIO: Has not the Pope enough of conjuring yet?
  He was upon the devil's back late enough,   35
  And if he be so far in love with him
  I would he would post home to Rome with him again.
FREDERICK: Speak, wilt thou come and see this sport?
BENVOLIO: Not I.
MARTINO: Wilt thou stand in thy window and see it, then?   40
BENVOLIO: Aye, and I fall not asleep i' th' meantime.
MARTINO: The Emperor is at hand, who comes to see
  What wonders by black spells may compassed be.
BENVOLIO: Well, go you attend the Emperor. I am content for this
  once to thrust my head out a window, for they say if a man be drunk   45
  overnight the devil cannot hurt him in the morning. If that be true,
  I have a charm in my head shall control him as well as the conjurer,
  I warrant you.
    [*Exit* MARTINO *and* FREDERICK.]

SCENE 2

[*A sennet. Enter* CHARLES THE GERMAN EMPEROR, BRUNO, *the* DUKE
OF SAXONY, FAUSTUS, MEPHISTOPHILIS, FREDERICK, MARTINO, *and*
ATTENDANTS. BENVOLIO *remains at his window.*]
EMPEROR: Wonder of men, renowned magician,

1. Alexander the Great and his mistress Thais. 2. Drank many full glasses. 3. Bruno.

Thrice-learned Faustus, welcome to our court.
This deed of thine, in setting Bruno free
From his and our professèd enemy,
Shall add more excellence unto thine art   5
Than if by powerful necromantic spells
Thou couldst command the world's obedience.
Forever be beloved of Carolus;
And if this Bruno thou hast late redeemed
In peace possess the triple diadem   10
And sit in Peter's chair despite of chance,
Thou shalt be famous through all Italy
And honored of the German Emperor.
FAUSTUS: These gracious words, most royal Carolus,
Shall make poor Faustus to his utmost power   15
Both love and serve the German Emperor
And lay his life at holy Bruno's feet.
For proof whereof, if so your Grace be pleased,
The Doctor stands prepared by power of art
To cast his magic charms that shall pierce through   20
The ebon gates of ever-burning hell
And hale the stubborn furies from their caves
To compass whatsoe'er your Grace commands.
BENVOLIO: [Aside.] Blood! He speaks terribly, but for all that I do not
greatly believe him. He looks as like a conjurer as the Pope to a   25
costermonger.
EMPEROR: Then Faustus, as thou late didst promise us,
We would behold that famous conqueror,
Great Alexander and his paramour,
In their true shapes and state majestical,   30
That we may wonder at their excellence.
FAUSTUS: Your Majesty shall see them presently.
Mephistophilis, away!
And with a solemn noise of trumpets' sound
Present before this royal Emperor   35
Great Alexander and his beauteous paramour.
MEPHISTOPHILIS: Faustus, I will.
    [Exit.]
BENVOLIO: [Aside.] Well, master Doctor, an your devils come not away
quickly, you shall have me asleep presently. Zounds, I could eat
myself for anger to think I have been such an ass all this while to   40
stand gaping after the devil's governor, and can see nothing.
FAUSTUS: [Aside.] I'll make you feel something anon if my art fail me
not.—
My lord, I must forewarn your Majesty
That when my spirits present the royal shapes
Of Alexander and his paramour,   45
Your Grace demand no questions of the King,

But in dumb silence let them come and go.

EMPEROR: Be it as Faustus please; we are content.

BENVOLIO: [*Aside.*] Aye, Aye, and I am content, too. And thou bring   50
Alexander and his paramour before the Emperor, I'll be Actaeon[4]
and turn myself into a stag.

FAUSTUS: [*Aside.*] And I'll play Diana and send you the horns presently.

> [*Sennet. Enter at one door the emperor* ALEXANDER, *at the other* DAR-
> IUS. *They meet;* DARIUS *is thrown down;* ALEXANDER *kills him, takes
> off his crown and, offering to go out, his* PARAMOUR *meets him; he
> embraceth her and sets* DARIUS' *crown upon her head and, coming
> back, both salute the* EMPEROR, *who, leaving his state,[5] offers to embrace
> them, which* FAUSTUS *seeing, suddenly stays him. Then trumpets cease
> and music sounds.*]

FAUSTUS: My gracious lord, you do forget yourself;   55
These are but shadows, not substantial.

EMPEROR: O pardon me; my thoughts are ravished so
With sight of this renownèd Emperor
That in mine arms I would have compassed him.
But Faustus, since I may not speak to them   60
To satisfy my longing thoughts at full,
Let me this tell thee: I have heard it said
That this fair lady, whilst she lived on earth,
Had on her neck a little wart or mole.
How may I prove that saying to be true?   65

FAUSTUS: Your Majesty may boldly go and see.

EMPEROR: Faustus, I see it plain;
And in this sight thou better pleasest me
Than if I gained another monarchy.

FAUSTUS: Away, be gone!   70
[*Exit* SHOW.]
See, see, my gracious lord, what strange beast is yon, that thrusts
its head out at the window!

EMPEROR: O wondrous sight! See, Duke of Saxony, two spreading horns
most strangely fastened upon the head of young Benvolio.

SAXONY: What, is he asleep, or dead?   75

FAUSTUS: He sleeps, my lord, but dreams not of his horns.

EMPEROR: This sport is excellent. We'll call and wake him. What ho!
Benvolio!

BENVOLIO: A plague upon you! Let me sleep a while.

EMPEROR: I blame thee not to sleep, much, having such a head of   80
thine own.

SAXONY: Look up, Benvolio. 'Tis the Emperor calls.

BENVOLIO: The Emperor! Where? O zounds, my head!

---

4. The hunter of classical legend who happened to see the goddess Diana bathing. In punishment he was
changed into a stag and pursued by his own hounds.   5. Throne.

EMPEROR: Nay, and thy horns hold 'tis no matter for thy head, for
  that's armed sufficiently.   85
FAUSTUS: Why, how now, sir knight! What, hanged by the horns? This
  is most horrible. Fie, fie! Pull in your head, for shame! Let not all
  the world wonder at you.
BENVOLIO: Zounds, Doctor, is this your villainy?
FAUSTUS: O, say not so, sir. The Doctor has no skill,   90
  No art, no cunning to present these lords
  Or bring before this royal Emperor
  The mighty monarch, warlike Alexander?
  If Faustus do it, you are straight resolved
  In bold Actaeon's shape to turn a stag?   95
  And therefore, my lord, so please your Majesty,
  I'll raise a kennel of hounds shall hunt him so
  As all his footmanship shall scarce prevail
  To keep his carcass from their bloody fangs.
  Ho, Belimote, Argiron, Asterote!   100
BENVOLIO: Hold, hold! Zounds, he'll raise up a kennel of devils, I
  think, anon. Good my lord, entreat for me. 'Sblood, I am never
  able to endure these torments.
EMPEROR: Then good master Doctor,
  Let me entreat you to remove his horns;   105
  He has done penance now sufficiently.
FAUSTUS: My gracious lord, not so much for injury done to me, as to
  delight your Majesty with some mirth, hath Faustus justly requited
  this injurious knight; which, being all I desire, I am content to
  remove his horns.—Mephistophilis, transform him.—And here-   110
  after, sir, look you speak well of scholars.
BENVOLIO: [Aside.] Speak well of ye! 'Sblood, and scholars be such
  cuckoldmakers to clap horns of honest men's heads o' this order,
  I'll ne'er trust smooth faces and small ruffs[6] more. But an I be not
  revenged for this, would I might be turned to a gaping oyster and   115
  drink nothing but salt water!
EMPEROR: Come, Faustus. While the Emperor lives,
  In recompense of this thy high desert,
  Thou shalt command the state of Germany
  And live beloved of mighty Carolus.   120
  [Exeunt OMNES.]

SCENE 3

[Enter BENVOLIO, MARTINO, FREDERICK, and SOLDIERS.]
MARTINO: Nay, sweet Benvolio, let us sway thy thoughts
  From this attempt against the conjurer.
BENVOLIO: Away! You love me not to urge me thus.

6. Scholars were often smooth shaven and did not wear the large "ruffs" (collars) of courtiers. But Faustus
has a beard; see the next scene.

Shall I let slip so great an injury
When every servile groom jests at my wrongs   5
And in their rustic gambols proudly say,
"Benvolio's head was graced with horns today"?
O, may these eyelids never close again
Till with my sword I have that conjurer slain.
If you will aid me in this enterprise,   10
Then draw your weapons and be resolute;
If not, depart. Here will Benvolio die,
But Faustus' death shall quit[7] my infamy.

FREDERICK: Nay, we will stay with thee, betide what may,
And kill that Doctor if he come this way.   15

BENVOLIO: Then gentle Frederick, hie thee to the grove
And place our servants and our followers
Close in an ambush there behind the trees.
By this I know the conjurer is near;
I saw him kneel and kiss the Emperor's hand   20
And take his leave laden with rich rewards.
Then, soldiers, boldly fight. If Faustus die,
Take you the wealth, leave us the victory.

FREDERICK: Come, soldiers, follow me unto the grove;
Who kills him shall have gold and endless love.   25
    [*Exit* FREDERICK *with the* SOLDIERS.]

BENVOLIO: My head is lighter than it was by th' horns,
But yet my heart's more ponderous than my head
And pants until I see that conjurer dead.

MARTINO: Where shall we place ourselves, Benvolio?

BENVOLIO: Here will we stay to bide the first assault.   30
O, were that damnèd hell-hound but in place
Thou soon shouldst see me quit my foul disgrace.
    [*Enter* FREDERICK.]

FREDERICK: Close, close! The hated conjurer is at hand
And all alone comes walking in his gown;
Be ready then and strike the peasant down.   35

BENVOLIO: Mine be that honor then. Now, sword, strike home!
For horns he gave I'll have his head anon.
    [*Enter* FAUSTUS *wearing a false head.*]

MARTINO: See, see, he comes.

BENVOLIO: No words; this blow ends all;
Hell take his soul, his body thus must fall.

FAUSTUS: O!   40

FREDERICK: Groan you, master Doctor?

BENVOLIO: Break may his heart with groans. Dear Frederick, see
Thus will I end his griefs immediately.
    [*Cuts off the false head.*]

7. Avenge.

MARTINO: Strike with a willing hand! His head is off.

BENVOLIO: The devil's dead; the furies now may laugh. 45

FREDERICK: Was this that stern aspect, that awful frown,
Made the grim monarch of infernal spirits
Tremble and quake at his commanding charms?

MARTINO: Was this that damnèd head whose art conspired
Benvolio's shame before the Emperor? 50

BENVOLIO: Aye, that's the head, and here the body lies
Justly rewarded for his villainies.

FREDERICK: Come, let's devise how we may add more shame
To the black scandal of his hated name.

BENVOLIO: First, on his head, in quittance of my wrongs, 55
I'll nail huge forkèd horns and let them hang
Within the window where he yoked me first,
That all the world may see my just revenge.

MARTINO: What use shall we put his beard to?

BENVOLIO: We'll sell it to a chimney-sweeper; it will wear out ten birchen 60
brooms, I warrant you.

FREDERICK: What shall his eyes do?

BENVOLIO: We'll put out his eyes, and they shall serve for buttons to
his lips to keep his tongue from catching cold.

MARTINO: An excellent policy. And now, sirs, having divided him, 65
what shall the body do?

[FAUSTUS rises.]

BENVOLIO: Zounds, the devil's alive again!

FREDERICK: Give him his head, for God's sake!

FAUSTUS: Nay, keep it. Faustus will have heads and hands,
Aye, all your hearts, to recompense this deed. 70
Knew you not, traitors, I am limited
For four and twenty years to breathe on earth?
And had you cut my body with your swords
Or hewed this flesh and bones as small as sand,
Yet in a minute had my spirit returned 75
And I had breathed a man made free from harm.
But wherefore do I dally my revenge?
Asteroth, Belimoth, Mephistophilis!

[Enter MEPHISTOPHILIS and other DEVILS.]

Go, horse these traitors on your fiery backs
And mount aloft with them as high as heaven, 80
Then pitch them headlong to the lowest hell.
Yet stay, the world shall see their misery,
And hell shall after plague their treachery.
Go, Belimoth, and take this caitiff hence
And hurl him in some lake of mud and dirt; 85
Take thou this other, drag him through the woods
Amongst the pricking thorns and sharpest briars,
Whilst with my gentle Mephistophilis

This traitor flies unto some steepy rock
That rolling down may break the villain's bones   90
As he intended to dismember me.
Fly hence, dispatch my charge immediately.
FREDERICK: Pity us, gentle Faustus; save our lives!
FAUSTUS: Away!
FREDERICK: He must needs go that the devil drives.   95
          [*Exeunt* SPIRITS *with the* KNIGHTS. *Enter the ambushed* SOLDIERS.]
1 SOLDIER: Come, sirs, prepare yourselves in readiness;
          Make haste to help these noble gentlemen;
          I heard them parley with the conjurer.
2 SOLDIER: See where he comes; dispatch, and kill the slave!
FAUSTUS: What's here? An ambush to betray my life?   100
          Then, Faustus, try thy skill. Base peasants, stand!
          For lo, these trees remove at my command
          And stand as bulwarks 'twixt yourselves and me
          To shield me from your hated treachery;
          Yet to encounter this, your weak attempt,   105
          Behold an army comes incontinent. [8]
          [FAUSTUS *strikes the door, and enter a* DEVIL *playing on a drum; after
          him another bearing an ensign, and divers with weapons;* MEPHISTO-
          PHILIS *with fireworks. They set upon the* SOLDIERS *and drive them
          out. Exeunt.*]

                              SCENE 4

          [*Enter at several doors* BENVOLIO, FREDERICK, *and* MARTINO, *their heads
          and faces bloody and besmeared with mud and dirt, all having horns
          on their heads.*]
MARTINO: What ho, Benvolio!
BENVOLIO: Here! What, Frederick, ho!
FREDERICK: O help me, gentle friend. Where is Martino?
MARTINO: Dear Frederick, here—
          Half smothered in a lake of mud and dirt   5
          Through which the furies dragged me by the heels.
FREDERICK: Martino, see! Benvolio's horns again.
MARTINO: O misery! How now, Benvolio!
BENVOLIO: Defend me, heaven! Shall I be haunted still?
MARTINO: Nay, fear not, man; we have no power to kill.   10
BENVOLIO: My friends transformèd thus! O hellish spite!
          Your heads are all set with horns.
FREDERICK: You hit it right;
          It is your own you mean; feel on your head.
BENVOLIO: Zounds, horns again!   15
MARTINO: Nay, chafe not, man; we are all sped. [9]

8. Immediately.   9. "Don't fret, man, we are all done for."

BENVOLIO: What devil attends this damned magician
  That spite of spite our wrongs are doublèd?
FREDERICK: What may we do that we may hide our shames?
BENVOLIO: If we should follow him to work revenge,   20
  He'd join long asses' ears to those huge horns
  And make us laughingstocks to all the world.
MARTINO: What shall we then do, dear Benvolio?
BENVOLIO: I have a castle joining near these woods,
  And thither we'll repair and live obscure   25
  Till time shall alter this our brutish shapes.
  Sith black disgrace hath thus eclipsed our fame,
  We'll rather die with grief than live with shame.
    [*Exeunt* OMNES.]

SCENE 5

[*Enter* FAUSTUS *and the* HORSE-COURSER.[1]]
HORSE-COURSER: I beseech your Worship, accept of these forty dollars.[2]
FAUSTUS: Friend, thou canst not buy so good a horse for so small a
  price. I have no great need to sell him, but if thou likest him for
  ten dollars more, take him, because I see thou hast a good mind to
  him.   5
HORSE-COURSER: I beseech you, sir, accept of this; I am a very poor
  man and have lost very much of late by horseflesh, and this bargain
  will set me up again.
FAUSTUS: Well, I will not stand with thee; give me the money. Now,
  sirrah, I must tell you that you may ride him o'er hedge and ditch   10
  and spare him not; but—do you hear?—in any case ride him not
  into the water.
HORSE-COURSER: How, sir, not into the water? Why, will he not drink
  of all waters?
FAUSTUS: Yes, he will drink of all waters, but ride him not into the   15
  water; o'er hedge and ditch or where thou wilt, but not into the
  water. Go bid the hostler deliver him unto you, and remember
  what I say.
HORSE-COURSER: I warrant you, sir. O joyful day! Now am I a made
  man forever.   20
    [*Exit.*]
FAUSTUS: What art thou, Faustus, but a man condemned to die?
  Thy fatal time draws to a final end;
  Despair doth drive distrust into my thoughts.
  Confound these passions with a quiet sleep.
  Tush, Christ did call the thief upon the cross;[3]   25
  Then rest thee, Faustus, quiet in conceit.

---

1. Horse trader, traditionally a sharp bargainer or a cheat.   2. Common German coins; the word originally comes from the German *Joachimsthaler*.   3. In Luke 23:39–43 one of the two thieves crucified with Jesus is promised Paradise. *In conceit*: In mind.

[*He sits to sleep in his chair. Enter the* HORSE-COURSER *wet.*]

HORSE-COURSER: O, what a cozening Doctor was this! I riding my horse
    into the water, thinking some hidden mystery had been in the horse,
    I had nothing under me but a little straw, and had much ado to
    escape drowning. Well, I'll go rouse him and make him give me   30
    my forty dollars again. Ho! sirrah Doctor, you cozening scab! Mas-
    ter Doctor, awake and rise, and give me my money again, for your
    horse is turned to a bottle[4] of hay. Master Doctor—
    [*He pulls off his leg.*]
    Alas, I am undone! What shall I do? I have pulled off his leg.

FAUSTUS: O help! Help! The villain hath murdered me!   35

HORSE-COURSER: Murder or not murder, now he has but one leg I'll
    outrun him and cast this leg into some ditch or other.
    [*Exit.*]

FAUSTUS: Stop him, stop him, stop him! Ha ha ha! Faustus hath his
    leg again, and the horse-courser a bundle of hay for his forty dollars.
    [*Enter* WAGNER.]

FAUSTUS: How now, Wagner! What news with thee?   40

WAGNER: If it please you, the Duke of Vanholt doth earnestly entreat
    your company and hath sent some of his men to attend you with
    provision fit for your journey.

FAUSTUS: The Duke of Vanholt's an honorable gentleman, and one to
    whom I must be no niggard of my cunning. Come, away!   45

SCENE 6

[*Enter* ROBIN, DICK, HORSE-COURSER, *and a* CARTER.]

CARTER: Come, my masters, I'll bring you to the best beer in Europe—
    What ho, Hostess!—Where be these whores?[5]
    [*Enter* HOSTESS.]

HOSTESS: How now! What lack you? What, my old guests, welcome.

ROBIN: Sirrah Dick, dost thou know why I stand so mute?

DICK: No, Robin, why is 't?   5

ROBIN: I am eighteen pence on the score,[6] but say nothing; see if she
    have forgotten me.

HOSTESS: Who's this that stands so solemnly by himself? What, my
    old guest!

ROBIN: O, hostess, how do you do? I hope my score stands still.   10

HOSTESS: Aye, there's no doubt of that, for methinks you make no
    haste to wipe it out.

DICK: Why, hostess, I say, fetch us some beer.

HOSTESS: You shall presently; look up into th' hall. There, ho!
    [*Exit.*]

DICK: Come, sirs; what shall we do now till mine hostess comes?   15

---

4. Bundle.   5. I.e., the hostess and maids of the inn.   6. Charged, not paid for.

CARTER: Marry, sir, I'll tell you the bravest tale how a conjurer served me. You know Dr. Faustus?

HORSE-COURSER: Aye, a plague take him! Here's some on 's have cause to know him. Did he conjure thee too?

CARTER: I'll tell you how he served me. As I was going to Wittenberg   20
t' other day, he met me and asked me what he should give me for as much hay as he could eat. Now, sir, I, thinking that a little would serve his turn, bade him take as much as he would for three farthings. So he presently gave me my money and fell to eating; and, as I am a cursen man, he never left eating till he had eat up   25
all my load of hay.

ALL: O monstrous; eat a whole load of hay!

ROBIN: Yes, yes; that may be, for I have heard of one that has eat a load of logs.[7]

HORSE-COURSER: Now, sirs, you shall hear how villainously he served   30
me. I went to him yesterday to buy a horse of him, and he would by no means sell him under forty dollars. So, sir, because I knew him to be such a horse as would run over hedge and ditch and never tire, I gave him his money. So, when I had my horse, Dr. Faustus bade me ride him night and day and spare him no time; "But,"   35
quoth he, "in any case ride him not into the water." Now sir, I thinking the horse had had some quality that he would not have me know of, what did I but ride him into a great river, and when I came just in the midst my horse vanished away and I sat straddling upon a bottle of hay.   40

ALL: O brave Doctor!

HORSE-COURSER: But you shall hear how bravely I served him for it. I went me home to his house, and there I found him asleep; I kept a hallowing and whooping in his ears, but all could not wake him. I seeing that, took him by the leg and never rested pulling till I had   45
pulled me his leg quite off, and now 'tis at home in mine hostry.[8]

DICK: And has the Doctor but one leg then? That's excellent, for one of his devils turned me into the likeness of an ape's face.

CARTER: Some more drink, hostess!

ROBIN: Hark you, we'll into another room and drink awhile, and then   50
we'll go seek out the Doctor.

    [*Exeunt* OMNES.]

SCENE 7

[*Enter the* DUKE OF VANHOLT, *his* DUCHESS, FAUSTUS, *and* MEPHISTO-PHILIS.]

DUKE: Thanks, master Doctor, for these pleasant sights; nor know I how sufficiently to recompense your great deserts in erecting that

7. Comic expression for being drunk—to carry a jag (or load) of logs.   8. Inn.

enchanted castle in the air, the sight whereof so delighted me as
nothing in the world could please me more.

FAUSTUS: I do think myself, my good lord, highly recompensed that it   5
pleaseth your Grace to think but well of that which Faustus hath
performed. But gracious lady, it may be that you have taken no
pleasure in those sights; therefore I pray you tell me what is the
thing you most desire to have; be it in the world it shall be yours. I
have heard that great-bellied women do long for things that are rare   10
and dainty.

DUCHESS: True, master Doctor, and since I find you so kind, I will
make known unto you what my heart desires to have; and were it
now summer, as it is January, a dead time of winter, I would request
no better meat than a dish of ripe grapes.   15

FAUSTUS: This is but a small matter.—Go, Mephistophilis, away!—
    [*Exit* MEPHISTOPHILIS.]
Madam, I will do more than this for your content.
    [*Enter* MEPHISTOPHILIS *again with the grapes.*]
Here, now taste ye these; they should be good, for they come from
a far country, I can tell you.

DUKE: This makes me wonder more than all the rest, that at this time   20
of year, when every tree is barren of his fruit, from whence you had
these ripe grapes.

FAUSTUS: Please it your Grace, the year is divided into two circles over
the whole world, so that when it is winter with us, in the contrary
circle it is likewise summer with them, as in India, Saba, and such   25
countries that lie far east, where they have fruit twice a year. From
whence, by means of a swift spirit that I have, I had these grapes
brought as you see.

DUCHESS: And trust me they are the sweetest grapes that e'er I tasted.
    [*The* CLOWNS *bounce*[9] *at the gate within.*]

DUKE: What rude disturbers have we at the gate?   30
Go pacify their fury, set it ope,
And then demand of them what they would have.
    [*They knock again and call out to talk with* FAUSTUS.]

A SERVANT: Why, how now, masters, what a coil[1] is there!
What is the reason you disturb the Duke?

DICK: We have no reason for it, therefore a fig[2] for him!   35

SERVANT: Why, saucy varlets! Dare you be so bold?

HORSE-COURSER: I hope, sir, we have wit enough to be more bold than
welcome.

SERVANT: It appears so; Pray be bold elsewhere
And trouble not the Duke.   40

DUKE: What would they have?

SERVANT: They all cry out to speak with Dr. Faustus.

9. Bang.   1. Disturbance.   2. An obscene gesture, implying contempt.

CARTER: Aye, and we will speak with him.

DUKE: Will you, sir? Commit[3] the rascals!

DICK: Commit with us? He were as good commit with his father as   45
commit with us.

FAUSTUS: I do beseech your Grace, let them come in;
They are good subject for a merriment.

DUKE: Do as thou wilt, Faustus; I give thee leave.

FAUSTUS: I thank your Grace.

        [*Enter* ROBIN, DICK, CARTER, *and* HORSE-COURSER.]
                        Why, how now, my good friends?   50
'Faith you are too outrageous; but come near,
I have procured your pardons. Welcome all!

ROBIN: Nay, sir, we will be welcome for our money, and we will pay
for what we take. What ho! Give 's half a dozen of beer here, and
be hanged.   55

FAUSTUS: Nay, hark you, can you tell me where you are?

CARTER: Aye, marry, can I; we are under heaven.

SERVANT: Aye, but, sir saucebox, know you in what place?

HORSE-COURSER: Aye, aye, the house is good enough to drink in.
Zounds, fill us some beer, or we'll break all the barrels in the house   60
and dash out all your brains with your bottles.

FAUSTUS: Be not so furious; come, you shall have beer.
My lord, beseech you give me leave awhile;
I'll gage my credit 'twill content your Grace.

DUKE: With all my heart, kind Doctor, please thyself;   65
Our servants and our court's at thy command.

FAUSTUS: I humbly thank your Grace. Then fetch some beer.

HORSE-COURSER: Aye, marry, there spake a doctor indeed; and, faith,
I'll drink a health to thy wooden leg for that word.

FAUSTUS: My wooden leg! What dost thou mean by that?   70

CARTER: Ha ha ha, dost hear him, Dick? He has forgot his leg.

HORSE-COURSER: Aye, he does not stand much upon that.

FAUSTUS: No, faith, not much upon a wooden leg.

CARTER: Good lord, that flesh and blood should be so frail with your
worship! Do you not remember a horse-courser you sold a horse to?   75

FAUSTUS: Yes, I remember I sold one a horse.

CARTER: And do you remember you bid he should not ride him into
the water?

FAUSTUS: Yes, I do very well remember that.

CARTER: And do you remember nothing of your leg?   80

FAUSTUS: No, in good sooth.

CARTER: Then I pray remember your courtesy.

FAUSTUS: I thank you, sir.

CARTER: 'Tis not so much worth. I pray you tell me one thing.

---

3. Put in jail. Dick puns on its other meaning ("commit adultery"), from the Ten Commandments.

FAUSTUS: What's that?   85

CARTER: Be both of your legs bedfellows every night together?

FAUSTUS: Wouldst thou make a colossus[4] of me, that thou askest me
such questions?

CARTER: No, truly, sir, I would make nothing of you, but I would fain
know that.   90

[*Enter* HOSTESS *with drink.*]

FAUSTUS: Then I assure thee certainly they are.

CARTER: I thank you; I am fully satisfied.

FAUSTUS: But wherefore dost thou ask?

CARTER: For nothing, sir; but methinks you should have a wooden
bedfellow to one of 'em.   95

HORSE-COURSER: Why, do you hear, sir, did not I pull off one of your
legs when you were asleep?

FAUSTUS: But I have it again now I am awake; look you here, sir.

ALL: O horrible! Had the doctor three legs?

CARTER: Do you remember, sir, how you cozened me and eat up my   100
load of——

[FAUSTUS *charms him dumb.*]

DICK: Do you remember how you made me wear an ape's——

HORSE-COURSER: You whoreson conjuring scab, do you remember how
you cozened me of a ho——

ROBIN: Ha' you forgotten me? You think to carry it away with your   125
hey-pass and your re-pass;[5] do you remember the dog's fa——

[*Exeunt* CLOWNS.]

HOSTESS: Who pays for the ale? Hear you, master Doctor, now you
have sent away my guests, I pray who shall pay me for my a——

[*Exit* HOSTESS.]

DUCHESS: My lord,
We are much beholding to this learned man.   130

DUKE: So are we, madam, which we will recompense
With all the love and kindness that we may;
His artful sport drives all sad thoughts away.

[*Exeunt.*]

Act V

SCENE 1

[*Thunder and lightning. Enter* DEVILS *with covered dishes;* MEPHIS-
TOPHILIS *leads them into* FAUSTUS' *study. Then enter* WAGNER.]

WAGNER: I think my master means to die shortly;
He has made his will and given me his wealth,
His house, his goods, and store of golden plate,
Besides two thousand ducats ready coined.

---

4. The huge statue that stood at the entrance to the harbor at Rhodes; boats sailed between its legs, and
Dr. Faustus is suggesting that the clowns are making his legs as important.   **5.** Traditional exclamations
of a conjurer.

And yet I wonder, for if death were nigh   5
He would not banquet and carouse and swill
Amongst the students as even now he doth,
Who are at supper with such belly-cheer
As Wagner ne'er beheld in all his life.
See where they come; belike the feast is ended.   10
    [*Exit. Enter* FAUSTUS *and* MEPHISTOPHILIS *with two or three* SCHOL-
ARS.]

1 SCHOLAR: Master Doctor Faustus, since our conference about fair
ladies, which was the beautifullest in all the world, we have determined with ourselves that Helen of Greece was the admirablest lady
that ever lived. Therefore, master Doctor, if you will do us that
favor as to let us see that peerless dame of Greece whom all the   15
world admires for majesty, we should think ourselves much beholding unto you.

FAUSTUS: Gentlemen,
    For that I know your friendship is unfeigned,
    And Faustus' custom is not to deny   20
    The just requests of those that wish him well,
    You shall behold that peerless dame of Greece,
    No otherways for pomp and majesty
    Than when Sir Paris crossed the seas with her
    And brought the spoils to rich Dardania.[6]   25
    Be silent, then, for danger is in words.
    [*Music sounds, and* HELEN *passes over the stage.*]

2 SCHOLAR: Too simple is my wit to tell her praise
    Whom all the world admires for majesty.

3 SCHOLAR: No marvel though the angry Greeks pursued
    With ten years' war the rape of such a queen   30
    Whose heavenly beauty passeth all compare.

1 SCHOLAR: Since we have seen the pride of Nature's works
    And only paragon of excellence,
    Let us depart, and for this glorious deed
    Happy and blest be Faustus evermore.   35

FAUSTUS: Gentlemen, farewell; the same I wish to you.
    [*Exeunt* SCHOLARS.—*Enter an* OLD MAN.]

OLD MAN: O gentle Faustus, leave this damnèd art,
    This magic, that will charm thy soul to hell
    And quite bereave[7] thee of salvation.
    Though thou hast now offended like a man,   40
    Do not persèver in it like a devil.
    Yet, yet, thou hast an amiable soul
    If sin by custom grow not into nature;
    Then, Faustus, will repentance come too late;
    Then thou art banished from the sight of heaven.   45

6. Troy.   7. Deprive.

No mortal can express the pains of hell.
It may be this my exhortation
Seems harsh and all unpleasant; let it not;
For, gentle son, I speak it not in wrath
Or envy of thee, but in tender love   50
And pity of thy future misery,
And so have hope that this my kind rebuke,
Checking thy body, may amend thy soul.
FAUSTUS: Where are thou, Faustus? Wretch, what hast thou done?
  Damned art thou, Faustus, damned! Despair and die.   55
      [MEPHISTOPHILIS *gives him a dagger.*]
  Hell claims his right, and with a roaring voice
  Says, "Faustus, come; thine hour is almost come!"
  And Faustus now will come to do thee right.
OLD MAN: O stay, good Faustus, stay thy desperate steps!
  I see an angel hovers o'er thy head   60
  And with a vial full of precious grace
  Offers to pour the same into thy soul:
  Then call for mercy and avoid despair.
FAUSTUS: Ah my sweet friend, I feel thy words
  To comfort my distressèd soul.   65
  Leave me awhile to ponder on my sins.
OLD MAN: Faustus, I leave thee, but with grief of heart,
  Fearing the ruin of thy hapless soul.
      [*Exit.*]
FAUSTUS: Accursèd Faustus, where is mercy now?
  I do repent and yet I do despair: 70
  Hell strives with grace for conquest in my breast.
  What shall I do to shun the snares of death?
MEPHISTOPHILIS: Thou traitor, Faustus, I arrest thy soul
  For disobedience to my sovereign lord.
  Revolt, or I'll in piecemeal tear thy flesh.   75
FAUSTUS: I do repent I e'er offended him.
  Sweet Mephistophilis, entreat thy lord
  To pardon my unjust presumption,
  And with my blood again I will confirm
  The former vow I made to Lucifer.   80
MEPHISTOPHILIS: Do it then, Faustus, with unfeignèd heart
  Lest greater danger do attend thy drift.
FAUSTUS: Torment, sweet friend, that base and aged man
  That durst dissuade me from thy Lucifer,
  With greatest torments that our hell affords.   85
MEPHISTOPHILIS: His faith is great; I cannot touch his soul;
  But what I may afflict his body with
  I will attempt, which is but little worth.
FAUSTUS: One thing, good servant, let me crave of thee
  To glut the longing of my heart's desire: 90

That I might have unto my paramour
That heavenly Helen which I saw of late,
Whose sweet embracings may extinguish clear
These thoughts that do dissuade me from my vow,
And keep mine oath I made to Lucifer.   95
MEPHISTOPHILIS: This, or what else my Faustus shall desire
    Shall be performed in twinkling of an eye.
        [*Enter* HELEN *again, passing over between two* CUPIDS.]
FAUSTUS: Was this the face that launched a thousand ships
    And burnt the topless[8] towers of Ilium?
    Sweet Helen, make me immortal with a kiss.   100
    Her lips suck forth my soul—see where it flies!
    Come, Helen, come, give me my soul again.
    Here will I dwell, for heaven is in these lips
    And all is dross that is not Helena.
        [*Enter* OLD MAN *and stands watching* FAUSTUS.]
    I will be Paris, and for love of thee   105
    Instead of Troy shall Wittenberg be sacked,
    And I will combat with weak Menelaus
    And wear thy colors on my plumèd crest;
    Yea, I will wound Achilles in the heel
    And then return to Helen for a kiss.   110
    O thou art fairer than the evening air
    Clad in the beauty of a thousand stars!
    Brighter art thou than flaming Jupiter
    When he appeared to hapless Semele,[9]
    More lovely than the monarch of the sky   115
    In wanton Arethusa's[1] azured arms,
    And none but thou shalt be my paramour!
        [*Exeunt* ALL *except the* OLD MAN.]
OLD MAN: Accursèd Faustus, miserable man,
    That from thy soul exclud'st the grace of heaven
    And fliest the throne of his tribunal seat.   120
        [*Enter the* DEVILS *to torment him.*]
    Satan begins to sift me with his pride.[2]
    As in this furnace God shall try my faith,
    My faith, vile hell, shall triumph over thee!
    Ambitious fiends, see how the heavens smiles
    At your repulse, and laughs your state to scorn.   125
    Hence, hell! for hence I fly unto my God.
        [*Exeunt.*]

8. So high they seemed to have no tops.   9. A Theban girl, loved by Jupiter and destroyed by the fire
of his lightning when he appeared to her in his full splendor.   1. The nymph of a fountain, as well as
the fountain itself; no classical myth, however, records her love affair with Jupiter, the "monarch of the
sky."   2. To test me with his strength.

SCENE 2

[*Thunder. Enter* LUCIFER, BELZEBUB, *and* MEPHISTOPHILIS.]

LUCIFER: Thus from infernal Dis[3] do we ascend
    To view the subjects of our monarchy,
    Those souls which sin seals the black sons of hell.
    'Mong which as chief, Faustus, we come to thee,
    Bringing with us lasting damnation   5
    To wait upon thy soul; the time is come
    Which makes it forfeit.
MEPHISTOPHILIS: And this gloomy night
    Here in this room will wretched Faustus be.
BELZEBUB: And here we'll stay
    To mark him how he doth demean himself.   10
MEPHISTOPHILIS: How should he but with desperate lunacy?
    Fond worldling, now his heart-blood dries with grief,
    His conscience kills it, and his laboring brain
    Begets a world of idle fantasies
    To overreach the devil, but all in vain.   15
    His store of pleasure must be sauced with pain.
    He and his servant Wagner are at hand;
    Both come from drawing Faustus' latest will.
    See where they come!

    [*Enter* FAUSTUS *and* WAGNER.]

FAUSTUS: Say, Wagner, thou hast perused my will;   20
    How dost thou like it?
WAGNER: Sir, so wondrous well
    As in all humble duty I do yield
    My life and lasting service for your love.

    [*Enter the* SCHOLARS.]

FAUSTUS: Gramercies, Wagner.—Welcome, gentlemen.
1 SCHOLAR: Now, worthy Faustus, methinks your looks are changed.   25
FAUSTUS: Ah, gentlemen!
2 SCHOLAR: What ails Faustus?
FAUSTUS: Ah, my sweet chamber-fellow, had I lived with thee, then
    had I lived still, but now must die eternally. Look, sirs! Comes he
    not? Comes he not?   30
1 SCHOLAR: O my dear Faustus, what imports this fear?
2 SCHOLAR: Is all our pleasure turned to melancholy?
3 SCHOLAR: He is not well with being over-solitary.
2 SCHOLAR: If it be so, we'll have physicians, and Faustus shall be
    cured.   35
3 SCHOLAR: 'Tis but a surfeit,[4] sir; fear nothing.
FAUSTUS: A surfeit of deadly sin that hath damned both body and soul.

---

3. The underworld.   4. Indigestion; the effects of overindulgence.

2 SCHOLAR: Yet, Faustus, look up to heaven: remember God's mercies are infinite.

FAUSTUS: But Faustus' offense can ne'er be pardoned; the Serpent [40] that tempted Eve may be saved, but not Faustus. Ah, gentlemen, hear me with patience, and tremble not at my speeches. Though my heart pants and quivers to remember that I have been a student here these thirty years, O would I had never seen Wittenberg, never read book! And what wonders I have done [45] all Germany can witness, yea all the world, for which Faustus hath lost both Germany and the world, yea heaven itself— heaven the seat of God, the throne of the blessed, the kingdom of joy, and must remain in hell forever, hell, ah hell, forever! Sweet friends, what shall become of Faustus, being in hell [50] forever?

3 SCHOLAR: Yet, Faustus, call on God.

FAUSTUS: On God, whom Faustus hath abjured? on God, whom Faustus hath blasphemed? Ah, my God, I would weep, but the devil draws in my tears! Gush forth, blood, instead of tears, yea life and [55] soul! O he stays my tongue; I would lift up my hands but, see, they hold 'em, they hold 'em!

ALL: Who, Faustus?

FAUSTUS: Why, Lucifer and Mephistophilis.
Ah, gentlemen, I gave them my soul for my cunning. [60]

ALL: God forbid!

FAUSTUS: God forbade it indeed, but Faustus hath done it: for vain pleasure of four and twenty years hath Faustus lost eternal joy and felicity. I writ them a bill with mine own blood; the date is expired, this is the time, and he will fetch me. [65]

1 SCHOLAR: Why did not Faustus tell us of this before, that divines might have prayed for thee?

FAUSTUS: Oft have I thought to have done so, but the devil threatened to tear me in pieces if I named God, to fetch both body and soul if I once gave ear to divinity; and now 'tis too late. Gentlemen, away, [70] lest you perish with me!

2 SCHOLAR: O what may we do to save Faustus?

FAUSTUS: Talk not of me, but save yourselves and depart.

3 SCHOLAR: God will strengthen me: I will stay with Faustus.

1 SCHOLAR: Tempt not God, sweet friend, but let us into the next [75] room, and there pray for him.

FAUSTUS: Aye, pray for me, pray for me! And what noise soever ye hear, come not unto me, for nothing can rescue me.

2 SCHOLAR: Pray thou, and we will pray that God may have mercy upon thee. [80]

FAUSTUS: Gentlemen, farewell. If I live till morning I'll visit you; if not, Faustus is gone to hell.

ALL: Faustus, farewell.

[*Exeunt* SCHOLARS.]

MEPHISTOPHILIS: Aye, Faustus, now thou hast no hope of heaven;
   Therefore despair, think only upon hell,   85
   For that must be thy mansion, there to dwell.
FAUSTUS: O thou bewitching fiend, 'twas thy temptation
   Hath robbed me of eternal happiness.
MEPHISTOPHILIS: I do confess it, Faustus, and rejoice.
   'Twas I, that when thou wert i' the way to heaven   90
   Damned up thy passage; when thou tookest the book
   To view the scriptures, then I turned the leaves
   And led thine eye.
   What, weepst thou? 'tis too late. Despair, farewell!
   Fools that will laugh on earth must weep in hell.   95
      [*Exit. Enter the* GOOD ANGEL *and the* BAD ANGEL *at several doors.*]
GOOD ANGEL: Ah Faustus, if thou hadst given ear to me,
   Innumerable joys had followed thee,
   But thou didst love the world.
BAD ANGEL: Gave ear to me
   And now must taste hell's pains perpetually.
GOOD ANGEL: O what will all thy riches, pleasures, pomps   100
   Avail thee now?
BAD ANGEL: Nothing but vex thee more,
   To want in hell, that had on earth such store.
      [*Music while the throne descends.*[5]]
GOOD ANGEL: O, thou hast lost celestial happiness,
   Pleasures unspeakable, bliss without end.
   Hadst thou affected sweet divinity   105
   Hell or the devil had had no power on thee.
   Hadst thou kept on that way, Faustus, behold
   In what resplendent glory thou hadst sit
   In yonder throne, like those bright shining saints,
   And triumphed over hell; that hast thou lost.   110
   And now, poor soul, must thy good angel leave thee;
   The jaws of hell are open to receive thee.
      [*Exit. Hell is discovered.*]
BAD ANGEL: Now Faustus, let thine eyes with horror stare
   Into that vast perpetual torture-house.
   There are the furies, tossing damnèd souls   115
   On burning forks; their bodies boil in lead.
   There are live quarters[6] broiling on the coals
   That ne'er can die; this ever-burning chair
   Is for o'ertortured souls to rest them in;
   These that are fed with sops of flaming fire   120
   Were gluttons and loved only delicates
   And laughed to see the poor starve at their gates.

---

5. A throne suspended by ropes descended to the stage near the end of many Elizabethan plays and was an expected theatrical display. Here the throne clearly symbolizes heaven, as the next speech shows.
6. Bodies.

But yet all these are nothing; thou shalt see
Ten thousand tortures that more horrid be.
FAUSTUS: O, I have seen enough to torture me.   125
BAD ANGEL: Nay, thou must feel them, taste the smart of all;
He that loves pleasure must for pleasure fall.
And so I leave thee, Faustus, till anon;
Then wilt thou tumble in confusión.[7]
[*Exit. The clock strikes eleven.*]
FAUSTUS: Ah, Faustus,   130
Now hast thou but one bare hour to live
And then thou must be damned perpetually!
Stand still, you ever-moving spheres of heaven,
That time may cease and midnight never come;
Fair Nature's eye, rise, rise again, and make   135
Perpetual day; or let this hour be but
A year, a month, a week, a natural day,
That Faustus may repent and save his soul!
O *lente lente currite noctis equi.*[8]
The stars move still, time runs, the clock will strike,   140
The devil will come, and Faustus must be damned.
O, I'll leap up to my God! Who pulls me down?
See, see, where Christ's blood streams in the firmament!—
One drop would save my soul—half a drop! ah, my Christ!
Rend not my heart for naming of my Christ;   145
Yet will I call on him—O, spare me, Lucifer!
Where is it now? 'Tis gone; and see where God
Stretcheth out his arm and bends his ireful brows.
Mountains and hills, come, come and fall on me
And hide me from the heavy wrath of God,   150
No, no—
Then will I headlong run into the earth:
Earth, gape! O no, it will not harbor me.
You stars that reigned at my nativity,
Whose influence hath allotted death and hell,   155
Now draw up Faustus like a foggy mist
Into the entrails of yon laboring clouds
That when they vomit forth into the air,
My limbs you issue from your smoky mouths,
So that my soul may but ascend to heaven.   160
[*The watch strikes.*]
Ah, half the hour is past; 'twill all be past anon.
O God,
If thou wilt not have mercy on my soul,
Yet for Christ's sake whose blood hath ransomed me
Impose some end to my incessant pain: 165

7. Destruction, perdition.   8. "Slowly, slowly run, O horses of the night," adapted from a line in Ovid's *Amores.*

Let Faustus live in hell a thousand years,
A hundred thousand, and at last be saved!
O, no end is limited to damnèd souls!
Why wert thou not a creature wanting soul?
Or why is this immortal that thou hast?   170
Ah, Pythagoras' *métempsýchosis*[9]—were that true,
This soul should fly from me, and I be changed
Unto some brutish beast. All beasts are happy,
For when they die
Their souls are soon dissolved in elements,   175
But mine must live still[1] to be plagued in hell.
Cursed be the parents that engendered me!
No, Faustus, curse thyself, curse Lucifer
That hath deprived thee of the joys of heaven.
    [*The clock strikes twelve.*]
It strikes, it strikes! Now, body, turn to air   180
Or Lucifer will bear thee quick[2] to hell!
    [*Thunder and lightning.*]
O soul, be changed to little water drops
And fall into the ocean, ne'er be found.
My God, my God, look not so fierce on me!
    [*Enter* DEVILS.]
Adders and serpents, let me breathe awhile!   185
Ugly hell, gape not—come not, Lucifer—
I'll burn my books—ah, Mephistophilis!
    [*Exeunt* DEVILS *with* FAUSTUS.]

SCENE 3

[*Enter the* SCHOLARS.]
1 SCHOLAR: Come, gentlemen, let us go visit Faustus,
    For such a dreadful night was never seen
    Since first the world's creation did begin,
    Such fearful shrieks and cries were never heard.
    Pray heaven the Doctor have escaped the danger.   5
2 SCHOLAR: O, help us heaven! See, here are Faustus' limbs
    All torn asunder by the hand of death.
3 SCHOLAR: The devils whom Faustus served have torn him thus;
    For 'twixt the hours of twelve and one, methought
    I heard him shriek and call aloud for help.   10
    At which self[3] time the house seemed all on fire
    With dreadful horror of these damnèd fiends.
2 SCHOLAR: Well, gentlemen, though Faustus' end be such
    As every Christian heart laments to think on,
    Yet for he was a scholar once admired   15

9. Pythagoras's doctrine of the transmigration of souls.   1. Always.   2. Alive.   3. Same, exact.

For wondrous knowledge in our German schools,
We'll give his mangled limbs due burial;
And all the students, clothed in mourning black,
Shall wait upon his heavy[4] funeral.
    [*Exeunt. Enter* CHORUS.]
CHORUS: Cut is the branch that might have grown full straight,   20
    And burnèd is Apollo's laurel bough[5]
    That sometime grew within this learnèd man.
    Faustus is gone: regard his hellish fall,
    Whose fiendful fortune may exhort the wise
    Only to wonder at[6] unlawful things   25
    Whose deepness doth entice such forward wits
    To practice more than heavenly power permits.
    [*Exit.*]

WILLIAM SHAKESPEARE
1564–1616

When William Shakespeare was born in April 1564 at Stratford-on-Avon in War-
wickshire, Stratford was a rural community with a population of less than two
thousand—of which his father, John Shakespeare, was a prominent and prosperous
member. Little is known of Shakespeare's early life beyond conjecture or legend;
he probably received the education offered by the good local grammar school, with
emphasis on Latin; at eighteen he married a farmer's daughter, Anne Hathaway,
seven or eight years his senior; there are baptismal records of their children, Susanna
(1583) and the twins Hamnet and Judith (1585). After a gap of seven years, records
show Shakespeare in 1592 already a successful and many-talented playwright in
London; in 1594 he was a shareholder in a prominent players' company of which
the Lord Chamberlain was patron and the famous actors Burbage and Kempe were
members, while literary distinction of a type that was then more highly respected
came from successful poems ("Venus and Adonis," 1593; "The Rape of Lucrece,"
1594). By 1596, of his now best-known plays he had written *The Taming of the
Shrew, Richard III, Romeo and Juliet,* and *The Merchant of Venice;* in 1597–1598,
with the two parts of *Henry IV* he added Falstaff to his growing list of famous
characters.

The Chamberlain's men had been playing at the Theatre, north of the city of
London, and later at the Curtain; in 1598 the Theatre was demolished, and the
Globe, a large playhouse south of the Thames, was built, Shakespeare sharing in
the expenses. Increased prosperity had brought social advancement: in 1596 the
College of Heralds had sanctioned Shakespeare's claim to a gentleman's station by
recognizing the family's coat of arms; in the same period he had bought New Place,
a large house in his hometown. In 1599, *Henry V,* the last of the plays centering
on the Lancastrian kings, was followed by the first of the great Roman tragedies,
Julius Caesar. The Globe period saw most of Shakespeare's mature work; this is a

---

4. Tragic, sorrowful.   5. Symbol of wisdom and learning; Apollo was the god of divination.   6. To
be content with observing with awe. *Fiendful fortune:* Devilish fate.

usual dating of the most famous plays: *Hamlet*, 1601; *Othello*, 1603–1604; *King Lear*, 1605; *Macbeth*, 1606; *Antony and Cleopatra*, 1607; *The Tempest*, 1611. Queen Elizabeth had favored the players, and her successor, James I, directly patronized them; the Lord Chamberlain's company thus became the King's Men. In 1608, besides the Globe, they acquired an enclosed playhouse in Blackfriars, in the city of London, for winter entertainment. At about that time Shakespeare seems to have retired from the stage, and certainly from then on he wrote fewer plays. He lived most of the time at Stratford until his death there on April 23, 1616.

Shakespeare's plays constitute the most important body of dramatic work in the history of literature, and no character in literature is more familiar to world audiences than Hamlet. He belongs to the world also in the sense that some of the influential interpretations of his character have been developed outside the country and language of his origin, the most famous being the one offered by Goethe in *Wilhelm Meister*. The unparalleled reputation of the work may also have certain nonliterary causes. For instance, it is a play whose central role is singularly cherished by actors in all languages as the test of their skill; and, conversely, audiences sometimes content themselves with a rather vague notion of the work as a whole and concentrate on the attractively problematical and eloquent hero, and on the actor impersonating him, waiting for his famous soliloquies as a certain type of operagoer waits for the next aria of a favorite singer. But along with the impact of the protagonist, there are other and deeper reasons why the world should naturally have given *Hamlet* its leading place in our literary heritage. Though it is a drama that concerns personages of superior station, and the conflicts and problems associated with men and women of high degree, it reveals these problems in terms of a particular family, presenting an individual and domestic dimension along with a public one—the pattern of family conflict within the larger pattern of the *polis*—like the plays of antiquity that deal with the Theban myth, such as *Oedipus* and *Antigone*.

This public dimension of *Hamlet* helps us see it, for our present purposes, in relation to the literature of the Renaissance—for the framework within which the characters are presented and come into conflict is a court. In spite of the Danish locale and the relatively remote period of the action, it is plainly a Renaissance court exhibiting the structure of interests to which Machiavelli's *Prince* has potently drawn our attention. There is a ruler holding power, and much of the action is related to questions concerning the nature of that power—the way in which he had acquired it and the ways in which it can be preserved. Moreover, there is a courtly structure: the king has several courtiers around him, among whom Hamlet, the heir apparent, is only the most prominent.

We have seen some of the forms of the Renaissance court pattern in earlier selections—in Castiglione, Rabelais, Machiavelli. The court, the ruling nucleus of the community, was also an arena for conflicts of interest and of wit, a setting for the cultivation and codification of aristocratic virtues (valor, physical and intellectual brilliance, "courtesy"). The positive view of human achievement on earth, so prominent in the Renaissance, was given in courtly life its characteristic setting and testing ground. And as we have observed, the negative view (melancholy, sense of void and purposelessness) also emerged there.

Examining *Hamlet*, we soon realize that its temper belongs more to the negative than to the positive Renaissance outlook. Certain outstanding forms of human endeavor (the establishment of earthly power, the display of gallantry, the confident attempt of the mind to acquire knowledge and to inspire purposeful action), which elsewhere are presented as highly worthwhile, or are at least soberly discussed in terms of their value and limits, seem to be caught here in a condition of disorder and imbued with a sense of vanity and emptiness.

The way in which the state and the court of Denmark are presented in *Hamlet* is significant: they are shown in images of disease and rottenness. And here again, excessive stress on the protagonist himself must be avoided. His position as denouncer of the prevailing decadence, and the major basis for his denunciation—the murder of his father, which leads to his desire to obtain revenge and purify the court by destroying the present king—are central elements in the play; but they are not the *whole* play. The public situation is indicated, and Marcellus has pronounced his famous "Something is rotten . . ." before Hamlet has talked to the Ghost and learned the Ghost's version of events. Moreover, the sense of outside dangers and internal disruption everywhere transcends the personal story of Hamlet, of his revenge, of Claudius's crime; these are rather the signs of the breakdown, portents of a general situation. In this sense, we may tentatively say that the general theme of the play has to do with a kingdom, a society, a *polis*, going to pieces—or even more, with its realization that it has already gone to pieces. Concomitant with this is a sense of the vanity of those forms of human endeavor and power of which the kingdom and the court are symbols.

The tone Shakespeare wants to establish is evident from the opening scenes: the night air is full of dread premonitions; sentinels turn their eyes toward the threatening outside world; meanwhile, the Ghost has already made his appearance, a sinister omen. The kingdom, as we proceed, is presented in terms that are an almost point by point reversal of the ideal. Claudius, the *pater patriae* and *pater familias*, whether we believe the Ghost's indictment or not (Hamlet does not necessarily, and some of his famous indecision has been attributed to his seeking evidence of the Ghost's truthfulness before acting), has by marrying the queen committed an act that by Elizabethan standards is incestuous. There is an overwhelming sense of disintegration in the body of the state, evident in the first court assembly and in all subsequent ones. In their various ways the two courtiers, Hamlet and Laertes, are strangers, contemplating departure; they offer, around their king, a picture quite unlike that of the conventional paladins, supports of the throne, in a well-manned and well-mannered court. (In Rabelais's "kingdom," when Grangousier is ruler, the pattern is also a courtly and knightly one, but the young heir, Gargantua, who is like Hamlet a university student, readily abandons his studies to answer the fatherland's call; here the direction is reversed.)

On the other hand, as in all late and decadent phases of a social or artistic structure (the court in a sense is both), we have semblance instead of substance, ornate and empty façades, of which the more enlightened members of the group are mockingly aware. Thus Polonius, who after Hamlet is the major figure in the king's retinue, is presented satirically in his empty formalities of speech and conventional patterns of behavior. And there are numerous instances (Osric is one) of manners being replaced by mannerisms. Hence the way courtly life is depicted in the play suggests always the hollow, the fractured, the crooked. The traditional forms and institutions of gentle living, and all the pomp and solemnity, are marred by corruption and distortion. Courtship and love are reduced to Hamlet's mockery of a "civil conversation" in the play scene, his phrases presenting not Castiglione's Platonic loftiness and the repartee of "gentilesse," but punning undercurrents of bawdiness. The theater, a traditional institution of court life, is "politically" used by the hero as a device to expose the king's crime. There are elements of macabre caricature in Shakespeare's treatment of the solemn theme of death (see, for instance, the manner of Polonius's death, which is a sort of sarcastic version of a cloak-and-dagger scene; or the effect of the clownish gravediggers' talk). Finally, the arms tournament, the typical occasion for the display of courtiers' gallantry in front of their king, is here turned by the scheming of the king himself into the play's conclusive scene of carnage. And the person who, on the king's behalf, invites Hamlet to that feast is Osric, the "waterfly," the caricature of the hollow courtier.

This sense of corruption and decadence dominates the temper of the play and obviously qualifies the character of Hamlet, his indecision, his sense of vanity and disenchantment with the world in which he lives. In Hamlet the relation between thought and deed, intent and realization, is confused in the same way that the norms and institutions that would regulate the life of a well-ordered court have been deprived of their original purpose and beauty. He and the king are "mighty opposites," and it can be argued that against Hamlet's indecision and negativism the king presents a more positive scheme of action, at least in the purely Machiavellian sense, at the level of practical power politics. But even this conclusion will prove only partly true. There are indeed moments in which all that the king seems to wish for himself is to forget the past and rule honorably. He advises Hamlet not to mourn his father excessively, for melancholy is not in accord with "nature." On various occasions the king shows a high and competent conception of his office: a culminating instance is the courageous and cunning way in which he confronts and handles Laertes's wrath. The point can be made that since his life is obviously threatened by Hamlet (who was seeking to kill him when by mistake he killed Polonius instead), the king acts within a legitimate pattern of politics in wanting to have Hamlet liquidated. But this argument cannot be carried so far as to demonstrate that he represents a fully positive attitude toward life and the world, even in the strictly amoral terms of political technique. For in fact his action is corroded by an element alien to that technique—the vexations of his own conscience. In spite of his energy and his extrovert qualities he too becomes part of the negative picture of disruption and lacks concentration of purpose. The images of decay and putrescence that characterize his court extend to his own speech: his "offense," in his own words, "smells to heaven."

To conclude, *Hamlet* as a Renaissance tragedy presents a world particularly "out of joint," a world that, having long ago lost the sense of a grand extratemporal design that was so important to the medieval man (to Hamlet the thought of the afterlife is even more puzzling and dark than that of this life), looks with an even greater sense of disenchantment at the circle of temporal action symbolized by the kingdom and the court. These could have offered certain codes of conduct and objects of allegiance that would have given individual action a purposeful meaning. But now their order has been destroyed. Ideals that once had power and freshness have lost their vigor under the impact of satiety, doubt, and melancholy.

Since communal values are so degraded, it is natural to ask in the end whether some alternative attempt at a settlement could be imagined, with Hamlet—like other Renaissance heroes—adopting an individual code of conduct, however extravagant. On the whole, Hamlet seems too steeped in his own hopelessness, and in the courtly mechanism to which he inevitably belongs, to be able to find personal intellectual and moral compromise or his own version of total escape or total dream; for his "antic disposition" is a strategy, his "folly" is politically motivated. Still, the tone of his brooding and often moralizing speech, his melancholy and dissatisfaction, his very desire for revenge do seem to imply an aspiration toward some form of moral beauty, a nostalgia for a world—as the king his father's must have been—of clean allegiances and respected codes of honor. One thing worth examining in this connection is Hamlet's attitude toward Fortinbras. Fortinbras is a marginal character, but our attention is emphatically drawn to him both at the very opening and at the very close of the play. There is no doubt that while in the play certain positive virtues—such as friendship, loyalty, and truthfulness—are represented by the very prominent Horatio, who will live on to give a true report of Hamlet, in Fortinbras the ideals of gallant knighthood, which in the present court have been so corrupted and lost, seem to be presented at their purest. And he has, of course, Hamlet's "dying voice." Earlier, in act 4, scene 4, Hamlet has seen Fortinbras move with his army toward an enterprise characterized by the flimsiness of its material rewards. In a world where all matter seems corrupt, Hamlet's qualified sympathy for that gratuitous display of honor for honor's sake, of valor "even for an eggshell," of death braved "for a fantasy," calls to mind some of the serious aspects of the Quixotic code.

William Shakespeare's Hamlet, edited and with an introduction by Harold Bloom (1986), contains some unconventional critical approaches. A biography placing Shakespeare in his social context is M. C. Bradbrook, Shakespeare the Poet in His World (1978), while E. K. Chambers, William Shakespeare, A Study of Facts and Problems, 2 vols. (1930), is considered the most fully documented biography. The student will find several views in Shakespeare: Modern Essays in Criticism (1957), edited by Leonard F. Dean. More advanced interpretations and critical methods are presented in Paul Gottschalk, The Meanings of Hamlet. Modes of Literary Interpretation Since Bradley (1972). Another valuable work is Harry Levin, The Question of Hamlet (1959). Cedric Watts, Hamlet (1988), besides critical interpretation, offers stage history, critical history, and a selected bibliography.

Hamlet, Prince of Denmark

Characters

CLAUDIUS, *king of Denmark*	VOLTIMAND,
HAMLET, *son to the late, and*	CORNELIUS,
nephew to the present king	ROSENCRANTZ,
POLONIUS, *lord chamberlain*	GUILDENSTERN, *courtiers*
HORATIO, *friend to Hamlet*	OSRIC,
LAERTES, *son of Polonius*	GENTLEMAN,
PRIEST	ENGLISH AMBASSADORS
MARCELLUS, *officers*	GERTRUDE, *queen of Denmark,*
BERNARDO,	*and mother to Hamlet*
FRANCISCO, *a soldier*	OPHELIA, *daughter of Polonius*
REYNALDO, *servant to Polonius*	LORDS, LADIES, OFFICERS, SOL-
PLAYERS	DIERS, SAILORS, MESSENGERS,
TWO CLOWNS, *grave-diggers*	*and* OTHER ATTENDANTS
FORTINBRAS, *prince of Norway*	GHOST OF HAMLET'S FATHER
CAPTAIN	

SCENE—*Denmark.*

Act I

SCENE 1—*Elsinore. A platform before the castle.*

[FRANCISCO *at his post. Enter to him* BERNARDO.]

BERNARDO: Who's there?

FRANCISCO: Nay, answer me: stand, and unfold yourself.

BERNARDO: Long live the king!

FRANCISCO: Bernardo?

BERNARDO: He.   5

FRANCISCO: You come most carefully upon your hour.

BERNARDO: 'Tis now struck twelve; get thee to bed, Francisco.

FRANCISCO: For this relief much thanks: 'tis bitter cold,
    And I am sick at heart.

BERNARDO: Have you had quiet guard?

FRANCISCO: Not a mouse stirring.   10

BERNARDO: Well, good night.
    If you do meet Horatio and Marcellus,
    The rivals[1] of my watch, bid them make haste.

FRANCISCO: I think I hear them. Stand, ho! Who is there?

    [*Enter* HORATIO *and* MARCELLUS.]

HORATIO: Friends to this ground.

MARCELLUS: And liegemen to the Dane.[2]   15

FRANCISCO: Give you good night.

MARCELLUS: O, farewell, honest soldier:
    Who hath relieved you?

FRANCISCO: Bernardo hath my place.
    Give you good night.
    [*Exit.*]

MARCELLUS: Holla! Bernardo!

BERNARDO: Say,
    What, is Horatio there?

HORATIO: A piece of him.

BERNARDO: Welcome, Horatio; welcome, good Marcellus.   20

MARCELLUS: What, has this thing appeared again to-night?

BERNARDO: I have seen nothing.

MARCELLUS: Horatio says 'tis but our fantasy,
    And will not let belief take hold of him
    Touching this dreaded sight, twice seen of us: 25
    Therefore I have entreated him along
    With us to watch the minutes of this night,
    That if again this apparition come,
    He may approve our eyes[3] and speak to it.

HORATIO: Tush, tush, 'twill not appear.

BERNARDO: Sit down a while;   30
    And let us once again assail your ears,

---

1. Partners.   2. The king of Denmark.   3. Confirm what we saw.

That are so fortified against our story,
What we have two nights seen.

HORATIO: Well, sit we down,
And let us hear Bernardo speak of this.

BERNARDO: Last night of all,   35
When yond same star that's westward from the pole
Had made his course to illume that part of heaven
Where now it burns, Marcellus and myself,
The bell then beating one,—
    [*Enter* GHOST.]

MARCELLUS: Peace, break thee off; look, where it comes again!   40
BERNARDO: In the same figure, like the king that's dead.
MARCELLUS: Thou art a scholar; speak to it, Horatio.
BERNARDO: Looks it not like the king? mark it, Horatio.
HORATIO: Most like it: it harrows me with fear and wonder.
BERNARDO: It would be spoke to.
MARCELLUS: Question it, Horatio.   45
HORATIO: What art thou, that usurp'st this time of night,
    Together with that fair and warlike form
    In which the majesty of buried Denmark
    Did sometimes[4] march? by heaven I charge thee, speak!
MARCELLUS: It is offended.
BERNARDO: See, it stalks away!   50
HORATIO: Stay! speak, speak! I charge thee, speak!
    [*Exit* GHOST.]
MARCELLUS: 'Tis gone, and will not answer.
BERNARDO: How now, Horatio! you tremble and look pale:
    Is not this something more than fantasy?
    What think you on't?   55
HORATIO: Before my God, I might not this believe
    Without the sensible and true avouch
    Of mine own eyes.
MARCELLUS: Is it not like the king?
HORATIO: As thou art to thyself:
    Such was the very armor he had on   60
    When he the ambitious Norway[5] combated;
    So frown'd he once, when, in an angry parle,[6]
    He smote the sledded Polacks on the ice.
    'Tis strange.
MARCELLUS: Thus twice before, and jump[7] at this dead hour,   65
    With martial stalk hath he gone by our watch.
HORATIO: In what particular thought to work I know not;
    But, in the gross and scope of my opinion,[8]
    This bodes some strange eruption to our state.
MARCELLUS: Good now, sit down, and tell me, he that knows,   70

4. Formerly. *Denmark:* The king of Denmark.   5. The king of Norway (the elder Fortinbras).   6. Parley.
Sledded: Who travel in sledges.   7. Just.   8. Taking a general view.

Why this same strict and most observant watch
So nightly toils the subject[9] of the land,
And why such daily cast of brazen cannon,
And foreign mart for implements of war;
Why such impress of shipwrights,[1] whose sore task   75
Does not divide the Sunday from the week;
What might be toward,[2] that this sweaty haste
Doth make the night joint-laborer with the day:
Who is't that can inform me?
HORATIO: That can I;
At least the whisper goes so. Our last king,   80
Whose image even but now appear'd to us,
Was, as you know, by Fortinbras of Norway,
Thereto pricked on by a most emulate pride,
Dared to the combat; in which our valiant Hamlet—
For so this side of our known world esteem'd him—   85
Did slay this Fortinbras; who by a seal'd compact
Well ratified by law and heraldry,[3]
Did forfeit, with his life, all those his lands
Which he stood seized of, to the conqueror:
Against the which, a moiety competent[4]   90
Was gagèd by our king; which had returned
To the inheritance of Fortinbras,
Had he been vanquisher; as, by the same covenant
And carriage[5] of the article design'd,
His fell to Hamlet. Now, sir, young Fortinbras,   95
Of unimprovèd[6] metal hot and full,
Hath in the skirts of Norway here and there
Shark'd up a list of lawless resolutes,
For food and diet, to some enterprise
That hath a stomach in't:[7] which is no other—   100
As it doth well appear unto our state—
But to recover of us, by strong hand
And terms compulsatory, those foresaid lands
So by his father lost: and this, I take it,
Is the main motive of our preparations,   105
The source of this our watch and the chief head
Of this post-haste and romage[8] in the land.
BERNARDO: I think it be no other but e'en so:
Well may it sort,[9] that this portentous figure
Comes armèd through our watch, so like the king   110
That was and is the question of these wars.
HORATIO: A mote it is to trouble the mind's eye.

9. Makes the people (the subjects) toil.   1. Forcing of ship carpenters into service. *Mart*: Trading.
2. Impending.   3. Duly ratified and proclaimed through heralds.   4. Equal share. *Seized*: Possessed.
Gagèd: Pledged.   5. Purport.   6. Untested. *Skirts*: Outskirts, border regions.   7. Calls for courage.
8. Bustle. *Head*: Origin, cause.   9. Fit with the other signs of war.

In the most high and palmy state of Rome,
A little ere the mightiest Julius fell,
The graves stood tenantless, and the sheeted dead   115
Did squeak and gibber in the Roman streets:
As stars with trains of fire and dews of blood,
Disasters in the sun; and the moist star,[1]
Upon whose influence Neptune's empire stands,[2]
Was sick almost to doomsday with eclipse: 120
And even the like precurse[3] of fierce events,
As harbingers preceding still the fates
And prologue to the omen coming on,
Have heaven and earth together demonstrated
Unto our climatures[4] and countrymen.   125
    [Re-enter GHOST.]
But soft, behold! lo, where it comes again!
I'll cross it, though it blast me. Stay, illusion!
If thou hast any sound, or use of voice,
Speak to me:
If there be any good thing to be done,   130
That may to thee do ease and grace to me,
Speak to me:
If thou art privy to thy country's fate,
Which, happily, foreknowing may avoid,
O, speak!   135
Or if thou hast uphoarded in thy life
Extorted treasure in the womb of earth,
For which, they say, you spirits oft walk in death,
Speak of it: stay, and speak! [The cock crows.] Stop it, Marcellus.
MARCELLUS: Shall I strike at it with my partisan?   140
HORATIO: Do, if it will not stand.
BERNARDO: 'Tis here!
HORATIO: 'Tis here!
    [Exit GHOST.]
MARCELLUS: 'Tis gone!
We do it wrong, being so majestical,
To offer it the show of violence;
For it is, as the air, invulnerable,   145
And our vain blows malicious mockery.
BERNARDO: It was about to speak, when the cock crew.
HORATIO: And then it started like a guilty thing
Upon a fearful summons. I have heard
The cock, that is the trumpet to the morn,   150
Doth with his lofty and shrill-sounding throat
Awake the god of day, and at his warning,
Whether in sea or fire, in earth or air,

1. The moon. *Disasters:* Ill omens.   2. The moon regulates the sea tides.   3. Foreboding.
4. Regions.

The extravagant[5] and erring spirit hies
To his confine: and of the truth herein   155
This present object made probation.[6]
MARCELLUS: It faded on the crowing of the cock.
  Some say that ever 'gainst[7] that season comes
  Wherein our Saviour's birth is celebrated,
  The bird of dawning singeth all night long: 160
  And then, they say, no spirit dare stir abroad,
  The nights are wholesome, then no planets strike,
  No fairy takes[8] nor witch hath power to charm,
  So hallowed and so gracious[9] is the time.
HORATIO: So have I heard and do in part believe it.   165
  But look, the morn, in russet mantle clad,
  Walks o'er the dew of yon high eastward hill:
  Break we our watch up; and by my advice,
  Let us impart what we have seen to-night
  Unto young Hamlet; for, upon my life,   170
  This spirit, dumb to us, will speak to him:
  Do you consent we shall acquaint him with it,
  As needful in our loves, fitting our duty?
MARCELLUS: Let's do't, I pray; and I this morning know
  Where we shall find him most conveniently.   175
    [*Exeunt.*]

SCENE 2—*A room of state in the castle.*

  [*Flourish. Enter the* KING, QUEEN, HAMLET, POLONIUS, LAERTES, VOL-
  TIMAND, CORNELIUS, LORDS, *and* ATTENDANTS.]
KING: Though yet of Hamlet our dear brother's death
  The memory be green, and that it us befitted
  To bear our hearts in grief and our whole kingdom
  To be contracted in one brow of woe,
  Yet so far hath discretion[1] fought with nature   5
  That we with wisest sorrow think on him,
  Together with remembrance of ourselves.
  Therefore our sometime sister, now our queen,
  The imperial jointress to this warlike state,
  Have we, as 'twere with a defeated joy,—   10
  With an auspicious and a dropping eye,
  With mirth in funeral and with dirge in marriage,
  In equal scale weighing delight and dole,—
  Taken to wife: nor have we herein barr'd[2]
  Your better wisdoms, which have freely gone   15
  With this affair along. For all, our thanks.

5. Wandering out of its confines.   6. Gave proof.   7. Just before.   8. Bewitches. *Strike*: Exercise
evil influence (compare "moon struck").   9. Full of blessing.   1. Restraint (here, on grief).
2. Ignored. *Dole*: Grief.

Now follows, that[3] you know, young Fortinbras,
Holding a weak supposal of our worth,
Or thinking by our late dear brother's death
Our state to be disjoint and out of frame,   20
Colleaguèd with this dream[4] of his advantage,
He hath not failed to pester us with message,
Importing the surrender of those lands
Lost by his father, with all bonds of law,
To our most valiant brother. So much for him.   25
Now for ourself, and for this time of meeting:
Thus much the business is: we have here writ
To Norway, uncle of young Fortinbras,—
Who, impotent and bed-rid, scarcely hears
Of this his nephew's purpose,—to suppress   30
His further gait[5] herein; in that the levies,
The lists and full proportions,[6] are all made
Out of his subject:[7] and we here dispatch
You, good Cornelius, and you, Voltimand,
For bearers of this greeting to old Norway,   35
Giving to you no further personal power
To business with the king more than the scope
Of these delated[8] articles allow.
Farewell, and let your haste commend your duty.

CORNELIUS: ⎫
VOLTIMAND: ⎭   In that and all things will we show our duty.   40

KING: We doubt it nothing: heartily farewell.

     [*Exeunt* VOLTIMAND *and* CORNELIUS.]

And now, Laertes, what's the news with you?
You told us of some suit; what is't, Laertes?
You cannot speak of reason to the Dane,[9]
And lose your voice: what wouldst thou beg, Laertes,   45
That shall not be my offer, not thy asking?
The head is not more native to[1] the heart,
The hand more instrumental to the mouth,
Than is the throne of Denmark to thy father.
What wouldst thou have, Laertes?

LAERTES: My dread lord,   50
Your leave and favor to return to France,
From whence though willingly I came to Denmark,
To show my duty in your coronation,
Yet now, I must confess, that duty done,
My thoughts and wishes bend again toward France   55
And bow them to your gracious leave and pardon.

KING: Have you your father's leave? What says Polonius?

POLONIUS: He hath, my lord, wrung from me my slow leave

---

3. What.   4. Combined with this fantastic notion.   5. Proceeding.   6. Amounts of forces and
supplies.   7. Subjects, people.   8. Detailed.   9. King of Denmark.   1. Naturally bound to.

By laborsome petition, and at last
Upon his will I sealed my hard consent: 60
I do beseech you, give him leave to go.
KING: Take thy fair hour, Laertes; time be thine,
And thy best graces spend it at thy will!
But now, my cousin Hamlet, and my son,—
HAMLET: [*Aside.*] A little more than kin, and less than kind.   65
KING: How is it that the clouds still hang on you?
HAMLET: Not so, my lord; I am too much i' the sun.[2]
QUEEN: Good Hamlet, cast thy nighted color off,
And let thine eye look like a friend on Denmark.
Do not for ever with thy vailèd[3] lids   70
Seek for thy noble father in the dust:
Thou know'st 'tis common; all that lives must die,
Passing through nature to eternity.
HAMLET: Aye, madam, it is common.
QUEEN: If it be,
Why seems it so particular with thee?   75
HAMLET: Seems, madam! nay, it is; I know not 'seems.'
'Tis not alone my inky cloak, good mother,
Nor customary suits of solemn black,
Nor windy suspiration of forced breath,
No, nor the fruitful river in the eye,   80
Nor the dejected havior of the visage,
Together with all forms, moods, shapes of grief,
That can denote me truly: these indeed seem,
For they are actions that a man might play:
But I have that within which passeth show;   85
These but the trappings and the suits of woe.
KING: 'Tis sweet and cómmendàble in your nature, Hamlet,
To give these mourning duties to your father:
But, you must know, your father lost a father,
That father lost, lost his, and the survivor bound   90
In filial obligation for some term
To do obsequious[4] sorrow: but to persevere
In obstinate condolement is a course
Of impious stubborness; 'tis unmanly grief:
It shows a will most incorrect[5] to heaven,   95
A heart unfortified, a mind impatient,
An understanding simple and unschool'd:
For what we know must be and is as common
As any the most vulgar thing to sense,
Why should we in our peevish opposition   100
Take it to heart? Fie! 'tis a fault to heaven,

2. The cue to Hamlet's irony is given by the King's "my cousin . . . my son." Hamlet is punning on "son."   3. Downcast.   4. Dutiful, especially concerning funeral rites (obsequies).   5. Not subdued.

A fault against the dead, a fault to nature,
To reason most absurd, whose common theme
Is death of fathers, and who still hath cried,
From the first corse till he that died to-day,   105
'This must be so.' We pray you, throw to earth
This unprevailing[6] woe, and think of us
As of a father: for let the world take note,
You are the most immediate to our throne,
And with no less nobility of love   110
Than that which dearest father bears his son
Do I impart toward you. For your intent
In going back to school in Wittenberg,[7]
It is most retrograde[8] to our desire:
And we beseech you, bend you to remain   115
Here in the cheer and comfort of our eye,
Our chiefest courtier, cousin and our son.
QUEEN: Let not thy mother lose her prayers, Hamlet:
  I pray thee, stay with us; go not to Wittenberg.
HAMLET: I shall in all my best obey you, madam.   120
KING: Why, 'tis a loving and a fair reply:
  Be as ourself in Denmark. Madam, come;
  This gentle and unforced accord of Hamlet
  Sits smiling to my heart: in grace whereof,
  No jocund health that Denmark drinks to-day,   125
  But the great cannon to the clouds shall tell,
  And the king's rouse the heaven shall bruit[9] again,
  Re-speaking earthly thunder. Come away.
    [*Flourish. Exeunt all but* HAMLET.]
HAMLET: O, that this too too sullied flesh would melt,
  Thaw and resolve itself into a dew!   130
  Or that the Everlasting had not fixed
  His canon[1] 'gainst self-slaughter! O God! God!
  How weary, stale, flat and unprofitable
  Seem to me all the uses of this world!
  Fie on't! ah fie! 'tis an unweeded garden,   135
  That grows to seed; things rank and gross in nature
  Possess it merely. That it should come to this!
  But two months dead! nay, not so much, not two:
  So excellent a king; that was, to this,
  Hyperion[2] to a satyr: so loving to my mother,   140
  That he might not beteem[3] the winds of heaven
  Visit her face too roughly. Heaven and earth!
  Must I remember? why, she would hang on him,
  As if increase of appetite had grown

6. Useless.   7. The seat of a university; at the peak of fame in Shakespeare's time because of its connection with Martin Luther.   8. Opposed.   9. Proclaim, echo. *Rouse:* Carousal, revel.   1. Law.
2. The sun god.   3. Allow.

By what it fed on: and yet, within a month—   145
Let me not think on't—Frailty, thy name is woman!—
A little month, or ere those shoes were old
With which she followed my poor father's body,
Like Niobe,[4] all tears:—why she, even she,—
O God! a beast that wants discourse of reason[5]   150
Would have mourned longer,—married with my uncle,
My father's brother, but no more like my father
Than I to Hercules: within a month;
Ere yet the salt of most unrighteous tears
Had left the flushing in her gallèd[6] eyes,   155
She married. O, most wicked speed, to post
With such dexterity to incestuous sheets![7]
It is not, nor it cannot come to good:
But break, my heart, for I must hold my tongue!
　　[*Enter* HORATIO, MARCELLUS, *and* BERNARDO.]
HORATIO: Hail to your lordship!
HAMLET:　　　　　　　　　　I am glad to see you well: 160
　　Horatio,—or I do forget myself.
HORATIO: The same, my lord, and your poor servant ever.
HAMLET: Sir, my good friend; I'll change[8] that name with you:
　　And what make you from Wittenberg, Horatio?
　　Marcellus?   165
MARCELLUS: My good lord?
HAMLET: I am very glad to see you. [*To* BERNARDO.] Good even, sir.
　　But what, in faith, make you from Wittenberg?
HORATIO: A truant disposition, good my lord.
HAMLET: I would not hear your enemy say so,   170
　　Nor shall you do my ear that violence,
　　To make it truster of your own report
　　Against yourself: I know you are no truant.
　　But what is your affair in Elsinore?
　　We'll teach you to drink deep ere you depart.   175
HORATIO: My lord, I came to see your father's funeral.
HAMLET: I pray thee, do not mock me, fellow-student;
　　I think it was to see my mother's wedding.
HORATIO: Indeed, my lord, it followed hard upon.
HAMLET: Thrift, thrift, Horatio! the funeral baked-meats   180
　　Did coldly furnish forth the marriage tables.
　　Would I had met my dearest[9] foe in heaven
　　Or ever I had seen that day, Horatio!
　　My father!—methinks I see my father.
HORATIO: O where, my lord?

---

4. A proud mother who boasted of having more children than Leto; her seven sons and seven daughters were slain by Apollo and Artemis, children of Leto. The grieving Niobe was changed by Zeus into a continually weeping stone.　　5. Lacks the reasoning faculty.　　6. Inflamed.　　7. According to principles which Hamlet accepts, marrying one's brother's widow is incest.　　8. Exchange.　　9. Bitterest.

HAMLET: In my mind's eye, Horatio.   185
HORATIO: I saw him once; he was a goodly king.
HAMLET: He was a man, take him for all in all,
    I shall not look upon his like again.
HORATIO: My lord, I think I saw him yesternight.
HAMLET: Saw? who?   190
HORATIO: My lord, the king your father.
HAMLET: The king my father!
HORATIO: Season your admiration[1] for a while
    With an attent ear, till I may deliver,
    Upon the witness of these gentlemen,
    This marvel to you.
HAMLET: For God's love, let me hear.   195
HORATIO: Two nights together had these gentlemen,
    Marcellus and Bernardo, on their watch,
    In the dead vast and middle of the night,
    Been thus encountered. A figure like your father,
    Armed at point exactly, cap-a-pe,[2]   200
    Appears before them, and with solemn march
    Goes slow and stately by them: thrice he walked
    By their oppressed and fear-surprisèd eyes,
    Within his truncheon's length; whilst they, distilled
    Almost to jelly with the act of fear,   205
    Stand dumb, and speak not to him. This to me
    In dreadful secrecy impart they did;
    And I with them the third night kept the watch:
    Where, as they had delivered, both in time,
    Form of the thing, each word made true and good,   210
    The apparition comes: I knew your father;
    These hands were not more like.
HAMLET: But where was this?
MARCELLUS: My lord, upon the platform where we watched.
HAMLET: Did you not speak to it?
HORATIO: My lord, I did.
    But answer made it none: yet once methought   215
    It lifted up its head and did address
    Itself to motion, like as it would speak:
    But even then the morning cock crew loud,
    And at the sound it shrunk in haste away
    And vanished from our sight.
HAMLET: 'Tis very strange.   220
HORATIO: As I do live, my honored lord, 'tis true,
    And we did think it writ down in our duty
    To let you know of it.

1. Restrain your astonishment.   2. From head to foot. *At point:* Completely.

HAMLET: Indeed, indeed, sirs, but this troubles me.
  Hold you the watch to-night?

MARCELLUS: }
BERNARDO: }   We do, my lord.   225

HAMLET: Armed, say you?

MARCELLUS: }
BERNARDO: }   Armed, my lord.

HAMLET: From top to toe?

MARCELLUS: }
BERNARDO: }   My lord, from head to foot.

HAMLET: Then saw you not his face?

HORATIO: O, yes, my lord; he wore his beaver[3] up.   230

HAMLET: What, looked he frowningly?

HORATIO: A countenance more in sorrow than in anger.

HAMLET: Pale, or red?

HORATIO: Nay, very pale.

HAMLET: And fixed his eyes upon you?

HORATIO: Most constantly.

HAMLET: I would I had been there.   235

HORATIO: It would have much amazed you.

HAMLET: Very like, very like. Stayed it long?

HORATIO: While one with moderate haste might tell[4] a hundred.

MARCELLUS: }
BERNARDO: }   Longer, longer.

HORATIO: Not when I saw't.

HAMLET: His beard was grizzled?[5] no?   240

HORATIO: It was, as I have seen it in his life,
  A sable silvered.[6]

HAMLET: I will watch to-night;
  Perchance 'twill walk again.

HORATIO: I warrant it will.

HAMLET: If it assume my noble father's person,
  I'll speak to it, though hell itself should gape   245
  And bid me hold my peace. I pray you all,
  If you have hitherto concealed this sight,
  Let it be tenable in your silence still,[7]
  And whatsoever else shall hap to-night,
  Give it an understanding, but no tongue: 250
  I will requite your loves. So fare you well:
  Upon the platform, 'twixt eleven and twelve,
  I'll visit you.

ALL: Our duty to your honor.

HAMLET: Your loves, as mine to you: farewell.
  [*Exeunt all but* HAMLET.]

3. Visor.   4. Count.   5. Gray.   6. Black and white.   7. Consider it still a secret.

My father's spirit in arms! all is not well;   255
I doubt[8] some foul play: would the night were come!
Till then sit still, my soul: foul deeds will rise,
Though all the earth o'erwhelm them, to men's eyes.
    [*Exit.*]

SCENE 3—*A room in Polonius's house.*

[*Enter* LAERTES *and* OPHELIA.]
LAERTES: My necessaries are embarked: farewell:
    And, sister, as the winds give benefit
    And convoy[9] is assistant, do not sleep,
    But let me hear from you.
OPHELIA: Do you doubt that?
LAERTES: For Hamlet, and the trifling of his favor,   5
    Hold it a fashion,[1] and a toy in blood,
    A violet in the youth of primy[2] nature,
    Forward, not permanent, sweet, not lasting,
    The perfume and suppliance of a minute;
    No more.
OPHELIA: No more but so?
LAERTES: Think it no more: 10
    For nature crescent[3] does not grow alone
    In thews and bulk; but, as this temple[4] waxes,
    The inward service of the mind and soul
    Grows wide withal. Perhaps he loves you now;
    And now no soil nor cautel[5] doth besmirch   15
    The virtue of his will: but you must fear,
    His greatness weighed,[6] his will is not his own;
    For he himself is subject to his birth:
    He may not, as unvalued persons do,
    Carve for himself, for on his choice depends   20
    The safety and health of this whole state,
    And therefore must his choice be circumscribed
    Unto the voice and yielding[7] of that body
    Whereof he is the head. Then if he says he loves you,
    It fits your wisdom so far to believe it   25
    As he in his particular act and place
    May give his saying deed; which is no further
    Than the main voice of Denmark goes withal.[8]
    Then weigh what loss your honor may sustain,
    If with too credent ear you list his songs,   30
    Or lose your heart, or your chaste treasure open
    To his unmastered importunity.

8. Suspect.   9. Conveyance, means of transport.   1. A passing mood.   2. Early, young. *Forward:*
Early.   3. Growing.   4. The body.   5. No foul or deceitful thoughts. *Will:* Desire.   6. When
you consider his rank.   7. Assent.   8. Goes along with, agrees. *Main:* Powerful.

Fear it, Ophelia, fear it, my dear sister,
And keep you in the rear of your affection,
Out of the shot and danger of desire.   35
The chariest maid is prodigal enough
If she unmask her beauty to the moon:
Virtue itself 'scapes not calumnious strokes:
The canker galls the infants of the spring
Too oft before their buttons be disclosed,   40
And in the morn and liquid dew of youth
Contagious blastments[9] are most imminent.
Be wary then; best safety lies in fear:
Youth to itself[1] rebels, though none else near.

OPHELIA: I shall the effect of this good lesson keep,   45
As watchman to my heart. But, good my brother,
Do not, as some ungracious pastors do,
Show me the steep and thorny way to heaven,
Whilst, like a puffed and reckless libertine,
Himself the primrose path of dalliance treads   50
And recks not his own rede.[2]

LAERTES: O, fear me not.
I stay too long; but here my father comes.
    [*Enter* POLONIUS.]
A double blessing is a double grace;
Occasion smiles upon a second leave.

POLONIUS: Yet here, Laertes! Aboard, aboard, for shame!   55
The wind sits in the shoulder of your sail,
And you are stayed for. There; my blessing with thee!
And these few precepts in thy memory
See thou chárácter.[3] Give thy thoughts no tongue,
Nor any unproportioned thought his act.   60
Be thou familiar, but by no means vulgar.
Those friends thou hast, and their adoption tried,
Grapple them to thy soul with hoops of steel,
But do not dull thy palm[4] with entertainment
Of each new-hatched unfledged comrade. Beware   65
Of entrance to a quarrel; but being in,
Bear't, that the opposèd may beware of thee.
Give every man thy ear, but few thy voice:
Take each man's censure,[5] but reserve thy judgment.
Costly thy habit as thy purse can buy,   70
But not expressed in fancy; rich, not gaudy:
For the apparel oft proclaims the man;
And they in France of the best rank and station
Are of a most select and generous chief[6] in that.

9. Blights.   1. Against its better self.   2. Does not follow his own advice.   3. Engrave in your
memory. *Unproportioned*: Unsuitable.   4. Make the palm of your hand callous (by indiscriminate
handshaking).   5. Opinion.   6. Preeminence.

Neither a borrower nor a lender be: 75
For loan oft loses both itself and friend,
And borrowing dulls the edge of husbandry.[7]
This above all: to thine own self be true,
And it must follow, as the night the day,
Thou canst not then be false to any man.   80
Farewell: my blessing season[8] this in thee!
LAERTES: Most humbly do I take my leave, my lord.
POLONIUS: The time invites you; go, your servants tend.[9]
LAERTES: Farewell, Ophelia, and remember well
    What I have said to you.
OPHELIA: 'Tis in my memory locked,   85
    And you yourself shall keep the key of it.
LAERTES: Farewell.
    [*Exit.*]
POLONIUS: What is't, Ophelia, he hath said to you?
OPHELIA: So please you, something touching the Lord Hamlet.
POLONIUS: Marry, well bethought:
    'Tis told me, he hath very oft of late   90
    Given private time to you, and you yourself
    Have of your audience been most free and bounteous:
    If it be so—as so 'tis put on me,
    And that in way of caution—I must tell you,
    You do not understand yourself so clearly   95
    As it behoves my daughter and your honor.
    What is between you? give me up the truth.
OPHELIA: He hath, my lord, of late made many tenders
    Of his affection to me.
POLONIUS: Affection! pooh! you speak like a green girl,   100
    Unsifted[1] in such perilous circumstance.
    Do you believe his tenders, as you call them?
OPHELIA: I do not know, my lord, what I should think.
POLONIUS: Marry, I'll teach you: think yourself a baby,
    That you have ta'en these tenders for true pay,   105
    Which are not sterling. Tender yourself[2] more dearly;
    Or—not to crack the wind of the poor phrase,
    Running it thus—you'll tender me a fool.[3]
OPHELIA: My lord, he hath importuned me with love
    In honorable fashion.   110
POLONIUS: Aye, fashion you may call it; go to, go to.
OPHELIA: And hath given countenance[4] to his speech, my lord,
    With almost all the holy vows of heaven.
POLONIUS: Aye, springes to catch woodcocks. I do know,
    When the blood burns, how prodigal the soul   115

---

7. Thriftiness.   8. Ripen.   9. Wait.   1. Untested.   2. Regard yourself.   3. You'll furnish me with a fool (a foolish daughter).   4. Authority.

Lends the tongue vows: these blazes, daughter,
Giving more light than heat, extinct in both,
Even in their promise, as it is a-making,
You must not take for fire. From this time
Be something scanter of your maiden presence; 120
Set your entreatments[5] at a higher rate
Than a command to parley. For Lord Hamlet,
Believe so much in him, that he is young,
And with a larger tether may he walk
Than may be given you: in few, Ophelia, 125
Do not believe his vows; for they are brokers,
Not of that dye which their investments[6] show,
But mere implorators of unholy suits,
Breathing like sanctified and pious bawds,
The better to beguile. This is for all: 130
I would not, in plain terms, from this time forth,
Have you so slander any moment[7] leisure,
As to give words or talk with the Lord Hamlet.
Look to't, I charge you: come your ways.
OPHELIA: I shall obey, my lord. 135
    [*Exeunt.*]

SCENE 4—*The platform.*

[*Enter* HAMLET, HORATIO, *and* MARCELLUS.]
HAMLET: The air bites shrewdly; it is very cold.
HORATIO: It is a nipping and an eager[8] air.
HAMLET: What hour now?
HORATIO: I think it lacks of twelve.
MARCELLUS: No, it is struck.
HORATIO: Indeed? I heard it not: it then draws near the season 5
  Wherein the spirit held his wont to walk.
    [*A flourish of trumpets, and ordnance shot off within.*]
  What doth this mean, my lord?
HAMLET: The king doth wake to-night, and takes his rouse,
  Keeps wassail, and the swaggering up-spring[9] reels;
  And as he drains his draughts of Rhenish[1] down, 10
  The kettle-drum and trumpet thus bray out
  The triumph of his pledge.[2]
HORATIO: Is it a custom?
HAMLET: Aye, marry, is't:
  But to my mind, though I am native here
  And to the manner born, it is a custom 15
  More honored[3] in the breach than the observance.

---

5. Conversation, company. 6. Clothes. *Brokers:* Procurers, panders. 7. Use badly any momentary. 8. Sharp. 9. Wild dance. 1. Rhine wine. 2. In downing the cup in one draught. 3. Honorable.

2030   WILLIAM SHAKESPEARE

This heavy-headed revel east and west
Makes us traduced and taxed of other nations:
They clepe[4] us drunkards, and with swinish phrase
Soil our addition;[5] and indeed it takes   20
From our achievements, though performed at height,[6]
The pith and marrow of our attribute.
So, oft it chances in particular men,
That for some vicious mole of nature in them,
As, in their birth,—wherein they are not guilty,   25
Since nature cannot choose his origin,—
By the o'ergrowth of some complexion,[7]
Oft breaking down the pales and forts of reason,
Or by some habit that too much o'er-leavens[8]
The form of plausive manners, that these men,—   30
Carrying, I say, the stamp of one defect,
Being nature's livery, or fortune's star,—
Their virtues else[9]—be they as pure as grace,
As infinite as man may undergo—
Shall in the general censure take corruption   35
From that particular fault: the dram of evil
Doth all the noble substance often dout
To his own scandal.[1]

    [*Enter* GHOST.]
HORATIO: Look, my lord it comes!
HAMLET: Angels and ministers of grace defend us!
Be thou a spirit of health or goblin damned,   40
Bring with thee airs from heaven or blasts from hell,
Be thy intents wicked or charitable,
Thou comest in such a questionable shape
That I will speak to thee: I'll call thee Hamlet,
King, father, royal Dane: O, answer me!   45
Let me not burst in ignorance; but tell
Why thy canónized bones, hearsèd in death,
Have burst their cerements; why the sepulchre,
Wherein we saw thee quietly inurned,
Hath oped his ponderous and marble jaws,   50
To cast thee up again. What may this mean,
That thou, dead corse, again, in complete steel,
Revisit'st thus the glimpses of the moon,
Making night hideous; and we fools of nature
So horridly to shake our disposition   55
With thoughts beyond the reaches of our souls?
Say, why is this? Wherefore? what should we do?

---

4. Call. *Taxed:* Blamed.   5. Reputation.   6. Done in the best possible manner. *Attribute:* Reputation.   7. Excess in one side of their temperament.   8. Modifies, as yeast changes dough. *Plausive:* Agreeable.   9. The rest of their qualities.   1. To its own harm. *Dout:* Extinguish, nullify.

[GHOST *beckons* HAMLET.]

HORATIO: It beckons you to go away with it,
  As if it some impartment did desire
  To you alone.

MARCELLUS: Look, with what courteous action   60
  It waves you to a more removèd ground:
  But do not go with it.

HORATIO: No, by no means.

HAMLET: It will not speak; then I will follow it.

HORATIO: Do not, my lord.

HAMLET: Why, what should be the fear?
  I do not set my life at a pin's fee;   65
  And for my soul, what can it do to that,
  Being a thing immortal as itself?
  It waves me forth again: I'll follow it.

HORATIO: What if it tempt you toward the flood, my lord,
  Or to the dreadful summit of the cliff   70
  That beetles o'er[2] his base into the sea,
  And there assume some other horrible form,
  Which might deprive your sovereignty of reason
  And draw you into madness? think of it:
  The very place puts toys[3] of desperation,   75
  Without more motive, into every brain
  That looks so many fathoms to the sea
  And hears it roar beneath.

HAMLET: It waves me still.
  Go on; I'll follow thee.

MARCELLUS: You shall not go, my lord.

HAMLET: Hold off your hands.   80

HORATIO: Be ruled; you shall not go.

HAMLET: My fate cries out,
  And makes each petty artery in this body
  As hardy as the Nemean lion's nerve.[4]
  Still am I called, unhand me, gentlemen;
  By heaven, I'll make a ghost of him that lets[5] me: 85
  I say, away! Go on; I'll follow thee.
      [*Exeunt* GHOST *and* HAMLET.]

HORATIO: He waxes desperate with imagination.

MARCELLUS: Let's follow; 'tis not fit thus to obey him.

HORATIO: Have after. To what issue will this come?

MARCELLUS: Something is rotten in the state of Denmark.   90

HORATIO: Heaven will direct it.

MARCELLUS: Nay, let's follow him.
      [*Exeunt.*]

---

2. Juts over.   3. Fancies.   4. Sinew, muscle. *Nemean lion:* Slain by Hercules as one of his twelve
labors.   5. Hinders.

SCENE 5—*Another part of the platform.*

[*Enter* GHOST *and* HAMLET.]

HAMLET: Whither wilt thou lead me? speak; I'll go no further.

GHOST: Mark me.

HAMLET: I will.

GHOST: My hour is almost come,
When I to sulphurous and tormenting flames[6]
Must render up myself.

HAMLET: Alas, poor ghost!

GHOST: Pity me not, but lend thy serious hearing   5
To what I shall unfold.

HAMLET: Speak; I am bound to hear.

GHOST: So art thou to revenge, when thou shalt hear.

HAMLET: What?

GHOST: I am thy father's spirit;
Doomed for a certain term to walk the night,   10
And for the day confined to fast in fires,
Till the foul crimes done in my days of nature
Are burnt and purged away. But that I am forbid
To tell the secrets of my prison-house,
I could a tale unfold whose lightest word   15
Would harrow up thy soul, freeze thy young blood,
Make thy two eyes, like stars, start from their spheres,[7]
Thy knotted and combinèd locks to part
And each particular hair to stand on end,
Like quills upon the fretful porpentine:[8]   20
But this eternal blazon[9] must not be
To ears of flesh and blood. List, list, O, list!
If thou didst ever thy dear father love—

HAMLET: O God!

GHOST: Revenge his foul and most unnatural murder.   25

HAMLET: Murder!

GHOST: Murder most foul, as in the best it is,
But this most foul, strange, and unnatural.

HAMLET: Haste me to know't, that I, with wings as swift
As meditation or the thoughts of love,   30
May sweep to my revenge.

GHOST: I find thee apt;
And duller shouldst thou be than the fat weed
That roots itself in ease on Lethe[1] wharf,
Wouldst thou not stir in this. Now, Hamlet, hear:
'Tis given out that, sleeping in my orchard,   35
A serpent stung me; so the whole ear of Denmark

6. Of purgatory.   7. Transparent revolving shells in each of which, according to Ptolemaic astronomy, a planet or other heavenly body was placed.   8. Porcupine.   9. Publication of the secrets of the other world (i.e., of eternity).   1. The river of forgetfulness in Hades.

Is by a forgèd process of my death
Rankly abused: but know, thou noble youth,
The serpent that did sting thy father's life
Now wears his crown.

HAMLET: O my prophetic soul!   40
    My uncle!

GHOST: Aye, that incestuous, that adulterate beast,
    With witchcraft of his wit, with traitorous gifts,—
    O wicked wit and gifts, that have the power
    So to seduce!—won to his shameful lust   45
    The will of my most seeming-virtuous queen:
    O Hamlet, what a falling-off was there!
    From me, whose love was of that dignity
    That it went hand in hand even with the vow
    I made to her in marriage; and to decline   50
    Upon a wretch, whose natural gifts were poor
    To those of mine!
    But virtue, as it never will be moved,
    Though lewdness court it in a shape of heaven,[2]
    So lust, though to a radiant angel linked,   55
    Will sate itself in a celestial bed
    And prey on garbage.
    But, soft! methinks I scent the morning air;
    Brief let me be. Sleeping within my orchard,
    My custom always of the afternoon,   60
    Upon my secure hour thy uncle stole,
    With juice of cursed hebenon[3] in a vial,
    And in the porches of my ears did pour
    The leperous distilment; whose effect
    Holds such an enmity with blood of man   65
    That swift as quicksilver it courses through
    The natural gates and alleys of the body;
    And with a sudden vigor it doth posset[4]
    And curd, like eager droppings into milk,
    The thin and wholesome blood: so did it mine;   70
    And a most instant tetter barked about,[5]
    Most lazar-like, with vile and loathsome crust,
    All my smooth body.
    Thus was I, sleeping, by a brother's hand
    Of life, of crown, of queen, at once dispatched: 75
    Cut off even in the blossoms of my sin,
    Unhouseled, disappointed, unaneled;[6]
    No reckoning made, but sent to my account
    With all my imperfections on my head:

2. A heavenly, angelic form. 3. Henbane, a very poisonous herb. 4. Coagulate. *Eager:* Sour.
5. The skin immediately became thick like the bark of a tree. *Lazar-like:* Leper-like (from the beggar
Lazarus, "full of sores," in Luke 16:20). 6. Without sacrament, unprepared, without extreme unction.

O, horrible! O, horrible! most horrible!   80
If thou hast nature in thee, bear it not;
Let not the royal bed of Denmark be
A couch for luxury and damned incest.
But, howsoever thou pursuest this act,
Taint not thy mind, nor let thy soul contrive   85
Against thy mother aught: leave her to heaven,
And to those thorns that in her bosom lodge,
To prick and sting her. Fare thee well at once!
The glow-worm shows the matin to be near,
And 'gins to pale his uneffectual fire: 90
Adieu, adieu, adieu! remember me.
    [*Exit.*]
HAMLET: O all you host of heaven! O earth! what else?
And shall I couple hell? O, fie! Hold, hold, my heart;
And you, my sinews, grow not instant old,
But bear me stiffly up. Remember thee!   95
Aye, thou poor ghost, while memory holds a seat
In this distracted globe.[7] Remember thee!
Yea, from the table[8] of my memory
I'll wipe away all trivial fond records,
All saws of books, all forms, all pressures past,   100
That youth and observation copied there:
And thy commandment all alone shall live
Within the book and volume of my brain,
Unmixed with baser matter: yes, by heaven!
O most pernicious woman!   105
O villain, villain, smiling, damnèd villain!
My tables,—meet it is I set it down,
That one may smile, and smile, and be a villain;
At least I'm sure it may be so in Denmark.
    [*Writing.*]
So, uncle, there you are. Now to my word;   110
It is 'Adieu, adieu! remember me.'
I have sworn't.
HORATIO: } [*Within*] My lord, my lord!
MARCELLUS: }
    [*Enter* HORATIO *and* MARCELLUS.]
MARCELLUS: Lord Hamlet!
HORATIO: Heaven secure him!
HAMLET: So be it!
MARCELLUS: Illo,[9] ho, ho, my lord!   115
HAMLET: Hillo, ho, ho, boy! come, bird, come.
MARCELLUS: How is't, my noble lord?

---

7. Head.   8. Writing tablet. The word is used in the same sense in line 107.   9. A falconer's call.

HORATIO: What news, my lord?
HAMLET: O, wonderful!
HORATIO: Good my lord, tell it.
HAMLET: No; you will reveal it.
HORATIO: Not I, my lord, by heaven.
MARCELLUS: Nor I, my lord.   120
HAMLET: How say you, then; would heart of man once think it?
   But you'll be secret?
HORATIO: }
                           Aye, by heaven, my lord.
MARCELLUS: }
HAMLET: There's ne'er a villain dwelling in all Denmark
   But he's an arrant knave.
HORATIO: There needs no ghost, my lord, come from the grave   125
   To tell us this.
HAMLET: Why, right; you are i' the right;
   And so, without more circumstance[1] at all,
   I hold it fit that we shake hands and part:
   You, as your business and desire shall point you;
   For every man hath business and desire,   130
   Such as it is; and for my own poor part,
   Look you, I'll go pray.
HORATIO: These are but wild and whirling words, my lord.
HAMLET: I'm sorry they offend you, heartily;
   Yes, faith, heartily.
HORATIO: There's no offense, my lord.   135
HAMLET: Yes, by Saint Patrick, but there is, Horatio,
   And much offense too. Touching this vision here,
   It is an honest[2] ghost, that let me tell you:
   For your desire to know what is between us,
   O'ermaster't as you may. And now, good friends,   140
   As you are friends, scholars and soldiers,
   Give me one poor request.
HORATIO: What is't, my lord? we will.
HAMLET: Never make known what you have seen tonight.
MARCELLUS: }
                  My lord, we will not.
HORATIO: }
HAMLET: Nay, but swear't.
HORATIO: In faith,
   My lord, not I.
MARCELLUS: Nor I, my lord, in faith.   145
HAMLET: Upon my sword.
MARCELLUS: We have sworn, my lord, already.
HAMLET: Indeed, upon my sword, indeed.
GHOST: [*Beneath*]   Swear.

1. Ceremony.   2. Genuine.

HAMLET: Ah, ha, boy! say'st thou so? art thou there, true-penny?[3]
  Come on: you hear this fellow in the cellarage:
  Consent to swear.
HORATIO: Propose the oath, my lord.   150
HAMLET: Never to speak of this that you have seen,
  Swear by my sword.
GHOST: [*Beneath*] Swear.
HAMLET: Hic et ubique?[4] then we'll shift our ground.
  Come hither, gentlemen,   155
  And lay your hands again upon my sword:
  Never to speak of this that you have heard,
  Swear by my sword.
GHOST: [*Beneath*] Swear.
HAMLET: Well said, old mole! canst work i' the earth so fast?   160
  A worthy pioner![5] Once more remove, good friends.
HORATIO: O day and night, but this is wondrous strange!
HAMLET: And therefore as a stranger give it welcome.
  There are more things in heaven and earth, Horatio,
  Than are dreamt of in your philosophy.   165
  But come;
  Here, as before, never, so help you mercy,
  How strange or odd soe'er I bear myself,
  As I perchance hereafter shall think meet
  To put an antic[6] disposition on,   170
  That you, at such times seeing me, never shall,
  With arms encumbered[7] thus, or this head-shake,
  Or by pronouncing of some doubtful phrase,
  As 'Well, well, we know,' or 'We could, an if we would,'
  Or 'If we list to speak,' or 'There be, an if they might,'   175
  Or such ambiguous giving out, to note
  That you know aught of me: this not to do,
  So grace and mercy at your most need help you,
  Swear.
GHOST: [*Beneath*] Swear.   180
HAMLET: Rest, rest, perturbèd spirit!
  [*They swear.*]
  So, gentlemen,
  With all my love I do commend[8] me to you:
  And what so poor a man as Hamlet is
  May do, to express his love and friending to you,   185
  God willing, shall not lack. Let us go in together;
  And still your fingers on your lips, I pray.
  The time is out of joint: O cursèd spite,
  That ever I was born to set it right!

---

3. Honest fellow. 4. Here and everywhere. 5. Miner. 6. Odd, fantastic. 7. Folded.
8. Entrust.

Nay, come, let's go together.   190
    [*Exeunt.*]

Act II

SCENE 1—*A room in Polonius's house.*

[*Enter* POLONIUS *and* REYNALDO.]
POLONIUS: Give him this money and these notes, Reynaldo.
REYNALDO: I will, my lord.
POLONIUS: You shall do marvelous wisely, good Reynaldo,
    Before you visit him, to make inquire
    Of his behavior.
REYNALDO: My lord, I did intend it.   5
POLONIUS: Marry, well said, very well said. Look you, sir,
    Inquire me first what Danskers are in Paris,
    And how, and who, what means, and where they keep,[9]
    What company, at what expense, and finding
    By this encompassment[1] and drift of question   10
    That they do know my son, come you more nearer
    Than your particular demands will touch it:
    Take you, as 'twere, some distant knowledge of him,
    As thus, 'I know his father and his friends,
    And in part him': do you mark this, Reynaldo?   15
REYNALDO: Aye, very well, my lord.
POLONIUS: 'And in part him; but,' you may say, 'not well:
    But if 't be he I mean, he's very wild,
    Addicted so and so'; and there put on him
    What forgeries you please; marry, none so rank   20
    As may dishonor him; take heed of that;
    But, sir, such wanton, wild and usual slips
    As are companions noted and most known
    To youth and liberty.
REYNALDO: As gaming, my lord.
POLONIUS: Aye, or drinking, fencing, swearing, quarreling,   25
    Drabbing:[2] you may go so far.
REYNALDO: My lord, that would dishonor him.
POLONIUS: Faith, no; as you may season it in the charge.[3]
    You must not put another scandal on him,
    That he is open to incontinency;   30
    That's not my meaning: but breathe his faults so quaintly[4]
    That they may seem the taints of liberty,
    The flash and outbreak of a fiery mind,
    A savageness in unreclaimèd blood,
    Of general assault.[5]

9. Dwell. *Danskers:* Danes.   1. Roundabout way.   2. Whoring.   3. Qualify it in making the
accusation.   4. Delicately, skillfully. *Incontinency:* Extreme sensuality.   5. Assailing all men. *Unre-
claimèd:* Untamed.

REYNALDO: But, my good lord,—   35
POLONIUS: Wherefore should you do this?
REYNALDO: Aye, my lord,
  I would know that.
POLONIUS: Marry, sir, here's my drift,
  And I believe it is a fetch of warrant:[6]
  You laying these slight sullies on my son,
  As 'twere a thing a little soiled i' the working,   40
  Mark you,
  Your party in converse, him you would sound,
  Having ever seen in the prenominate[7] crimes
  The youth you breathe of guilty, be assured
  He closes with you in this consequence;[8]   45
  'Good sir,' or so, or 'friend,' or 'gentleman,'
  According to the phrase or the addition[9]
  Of man and country.
REYNALDO: Very good, my lord.
POLONIUS: And then, sir, does he this—he does—what was I about to
  say? By the mass, I was about to say something: where did I leave?   50
REYNALDO: At 'closes in the consequence,' at 'friend or so,' and
  'gentleman.'
POLONIUS: At 'closes in the consequence,' aye, marry;
  He closes with you thus: 'I know the gentleman;
  I saw him yesterday, or t' other day,
  Or then, or then, with such, or such, and, as you say,   55
  There was a' gaming, there o'ertook in 's rouse,[1]
  There falling out at tennis': or perchance,
  'I saw him enter such a house of sale,'
  Videlicet,[2] a brothel, or so forth.   60
  See you now;
  Your bait of falsehood takes this carp of truth:
  And thus do we of wisdom and of reach,[3]
  With windlasses and with assays of bias,[4]
  By indirections find directions out: 65
  So, by my former lecture and advice,
  Shall you my son. You have me, have you not?
REYNALDO: My lord, I have.
POLONIUS: God be wi' ye; fare ye well.
REYNALDO: Good my lord!
POLONIUS: Observe his inclination in yourself.[5]   70
REYNALDO: I shall, my lord.
POLONIUS: And let him ply his music.
REYNALDO: Well, my lord.

6. Allowable stratagem.   7. Aforementioned. *Having ever:* If he has ever.   8. You may be sure he
will agree in this conclusion.   9. Title.   1. Intoxicated in his reveling.   2. Namely.   3. Wise
and farsighted.   4. Sending the ball indirectly (in bowling), devious attacks. *Windlasses:* Winding ways,
roundabout courses.   5. Ways of procedure by yourself.

POLONIUS: Farewell!

   [*Exit* REYNALDO.—*Enter* OPHELIA.]

  How now, Ophelia! what's the matter?

OPHELIA: O, my lord, I have been so affrighted!   75

POLONIUS: With what, i' the name of God?

OPHELIA: My lord, as I was sewing in my closet,[6]
  Lord Hamlet, with his doublet all unbraced,
  No hat upon his head, his stockings fouled,
  Ungartered and down-gyvèd[7] to his ankle;   80
  Pale as his shirt, his knees knocking each other,
  And with a look so piteous in purport
  As if he had been loosèd out of hell
  To speak of horrors, he comes before me.

POLONIUS: Mad for thy love?

OPHELIA: My lord, I do not know,   85
  But truly I do fear it.

POLONIUS: What said he?

OPHELIA: He took me by the wrist and held me hard;
  Then goes he to the length of all his arm,
  And with his other hand thus o'er his brow,
  He falls to such perusal of my face   90
  As he would draw it. Long stayed he so;
  At last, a little shaking of mine arm,
  And thrice his head thus waving up and down,
  He raised a sigh so piteous and profound
  As it did seem to shatter all his bulk   95
  And end his being: that done, he lets me go:
  And with his head over his shoulder turned,
  He seemed to find his way without his eyes;
  For out o' doors he went without their help,
  And to the last bended their light on me.   100

POLONIUS: Come, go with me: I will go seek the king.
  This is the very ecstasy of love;
  Whose violent property fordoes itself[8]
  And leads the will to desperate undertakings
  As oft as any passion under heaven   105
  That does afflict our natures. I am sorry.
  What, have you given him any hard words of late?

OPHELIA: No, my good lord, but, as you did command,
  I did repel his letters and denied
  His access to me.

POLONIUS: That hath made him mad.   110
  I am sorry that with better heed and judgment
  I had not quoted[9] him: I fear'd he did but trifle
  And meant to wreck thee; but beshrew my jealousy![1]

---

6. Private room. *Doublet:* Jacket.   7. Pulled down like fetters on a prisoner's leg.   8. Which, when violent, destroys itself. *Ecstasy:* Madness.   9. Noted.   1. Curse my suspicion.

By heaven, it is as proper to our age
To cast beyond ourselves[2] in our opinions   115
As it is common for the younger sort
To lack discretion. Come, go we to the king:
This must be known; which, being kept close, might move
More grief to hide than hate to utter love.[3]
Come.   120
    [*Exeunt.*]

SCENE 2—*A room in the castle.*

[*Flourish. Enter* KING, QUEEN, ROSENCRANTZ, GUILDENSTERN, *and*
ATTENDANTS.]

KING: Welcome, dear Rosencrantz and Guildenstern!
  Moreover that we much did long to see you,
  The need we have to use you did provoke
  Our hasty sending. Something have you heard
  Of Hamlet's transformation; so call it,   5
  Sith[4] nor the exterior nor the inward man
  Resembles that it was. What it should be,
  More than his father's death, that thus hath put him
  So much from the understanding of himself,
  I cannot dream of: I entreat you both,   10
  That, being of so young days brought up with him
  And sith so neighbored to his youth and behavior,
  That you vouchsafe your rest[5] here in our court
  Some little time: so by your companies
  To draw him on to pleasures, and to gather   15
  So much as from occasion you may glean,
  Whether aught to us unknown afflicts him thus,
  That opened[6] lies within our remedy.
QUEEN: Good gentlemen, he hath much talked of you,
  And sure I am two men there are not living   20
  To whom he more adheres.[7] If it will please you
  To show us so much gentry[8] and good will
  As to expend your time with us awhile
  For the supply and profit of our hope,
  Your visitation shall receive such thanks   25
  As fits a king's remembrance.
ROSENCRANTZ: Both your majesties
  Might, by the sovereign power you have of us,
  Put your dread pleasures more into[9] command
  Than to entreaty.
GUILDENSTERN: But we both obey,

---

2. Overshoot, go too far.   3. If Hamlet's love is revealed. *To hide:* If kept hidden.   4. Since.
5. Consent to stay.   6. Once revealed.   7. Is more attached.   8. Courtesy.   9. Give your sovereign wishes the form of.

And here give up ourselves, in the full bent[1] 30
To lay our service freely at your feet,
To be commanded.
KING: Thanks, Rosencrantz and gentle Guildenstern.
QUEEN: Thanks, Guildenstern and gentle Rosencrantz:
And I beseech you instantly to visit 35
My too much changéd son. Go, some of you,
And bring these gentlemen where Hamlet is.
GUILDENSTERN: Heavens make our presence and our practices
Pleasant and helpful to him!
QUEEN: Aye, amen!
[*Exeunt* ROSENCRANTZ, GUILDENSTERN, *and some* ATTENDANTS.—*Enter*
POLONIUS.]
POLONIUS: The ambassadors from Norway, my good lord, 40
Are joyfully returned.
KING: Thou still[2] hast been the father of good news.
POLONIUS: Have I, my lord? I assure my good liege,
I hold my duty as I hold my soul,
Both to my God and to my gracious king: 45
And I do think, or else this brain of mine
Hunts not the trail of policy so sure
As it hath used to do, that I have found
The very cause of Hamlet's lunacy.
KING: O, speak of that; that do I long to hear. 50
POLONIUS: Give first admittance to the ambassadors;
My news shall be the fruit[3] to that great feast.
KING: Thyself do grace[4] to them, and bring them in.
[*Exit* POLONIUS.]
He tells me, my dear Gertrude, he hath found
The head and source of all your son's distemper. 55
QUEEN: I doubt it is no other but the main;
His father's death and our o'erhasty marriage.
KING: Well, we shall sift him.
[*Re-enter* POLONIUS, *with* VOLTIMAND *and* CORNELIUS.]
Welcome, my good friends!
Say, Voltimand, what from our brother Norway?
VOLTIMAND: Most fair return of greetings and desires. 60
Upon our first,[5] he sent out to suppress
His nephew's levies, which to him appeared
To be a preparation 'gainst the Polack,
But better looked into, he truly found
It was against your highness: whereat grieved, 65
That so his sickness, age and impotence
Was falsely borne in hand,[6] sends out arrests
On Fortinbras; which he, in brief, obeys,

1. Bent (as a bow) to the limit. 2. Always. 3. Dessert. 4. Honor. 5. As soon as we made the
request. 6. Deceived, deluded.

Receives rebuke from Norway, and in fine[7]
Makes vow before his uncle never more   70
To give the assay[8] of arms against your majesty.
Whereon old Norway, overcome with joy,
Gives him three thousand crowns in annual fee
And his commission to employ those soldiers,
So levied as before, against the Polack: 75
With an entreaty, herein further shown,
          [*Giving a paper.*]
That it might please you to give quiet pass
Through your dominions for this enterprise,
On such regards of safety and allowance
As therein are set down.
KING: It likes us well,   80
And at our more considered time we'll read,
Answer, and think upon this business.
Meantime we thank you for your well-took labor:
Go to your rest; at night we'll feast together:
Most welcome home!
          [*Exeunt* VOLTIMAND *and* CORNELIUS.]
POLONIUS: This business is well ended.   85
My liege, and madam, to expostulate
What majesty should be, what duty is,
Why day is day, night night, and time is time,
Were nothing but to waste night, day and time.
Therefore, since brevity is the soul of wit   90
And tediousness the limbs and outward flourishes,
I will be brief. Your noble son is mad:
Mad call I it; for, to define true madness,
What is 't but to be nothing else but mad?
But let that go.
QUEEN: More matter, with less art.   95
POLONIUS: Madam, I swear I use no art at all.
That he is mad, 'tis true: 'tis true 'tis pity,
And pity 'tis 'tis true: a foolish figure;[9]
But farewell it, for I will use no art.
Mad let us grant him then: and now remains   100
That we find out the cause of this effect,
Or rather say, the cause of this defect,
For this effect defective comes by cause:
Thus it remains and the remainder thus.
Perpend.[1]   105
I have a daughter,—have while she is mine,—
Who in her duty and obedience, mark,
Hath given me this: now gather and surmise.

7. Finally.   8. Test.   9. Of speech.   1. Consider.

[*Reads.*] 'To the celestial, and my soul's idol, the most beautified
Ophelia,'—That's an ill phrase, a vile phrase; 'beautified' is a vile   110
phrase; but you shall hear. Thus:
    [*Reads.*] 'In her excellent white bosom, these,' &c.
QUEEN: Came this from Hamlet to her?
POLONIUS: Good madam, stay awhile; I will be faithful.
    [*Reads.*]   'Doubt thou the stars are fire;   115
                Doubt that the sun doth move;
                Doubt truth to be a liar;
                But never doubt I love.
'O dear Ophelia, I am ill at these numbers;[2] I have not art to reckon
my groans: but that I love thee best, O most best, believe it. Adieu.   120
           'Thine evermore, most dear lady, whilst this
                    machine is to him,[3] HAMLET.'
This in obedience hath my daughter shown me;
And more above,[4] hath his solicitings,
As they fell out by time, by means and place,   125
All given to mine ear.
KING: But how hath she
Received his love?
POLONIUS: What do you think of me?
KING: As of a man faithful and honorable.
POLONIUS: I would fain prove so. But what might you think,
When I had seen this hot love on the wing,—   130
As I perceived it, I must tell you that,
Before my daughter told me,—what might you,
Or my dear majesty your queen here, think,
If I had played the desk or table-book,[5]
Or given my heart a winking, mute and dumb,   135
Or looked upon this love with idle sight;
What might you think? No, I went round[6] to work,
And my young mistress thus I did bespeak:
'Lord Hamlet is a prince, out of thy star;[7]
This must not be:' and then I prescripts gave her,   140
That she should lock herself from his resort,
Admit no messengers, receive no tokens.
Which done, she took the fruits of my advice;
And he repulsed, a short tale to make,
Fell into a sadness, then into a fast,   145
Thence to a watch, thence into a weakness,
Thence to a lightness,[8] and by this declension
Into the madness wherein now he raves
And all we mourn for.
KING: Do you think this?

2. Verses.   3. Body is attached.   4. Moreover.   5. If I had acted as a desk or notebook (in keeping
the matter secret). *Given my heart a winking:* Shut my heart's eye.   6. Straight.   7. Sphere.
8. Lightheadedness. *Watch:* Insomnia.

QUEEN: It may be, very like. 150

POLONIUS: Hath there been such a time, I'd fain know that,
That I have positively said ' 'tis so,'
When it proved otherwise?

KING: Not that I know.

POLONIUS: [*Pointing to his head and shoulder.*] Take this, from this,
if this be otherwise:
If circumstances lead me, I will find
Where truth is hid, though it were hid indeed
Within the center.[9]

KING: How may we try it further?

POLONIUS: You know, sometimes he walks for hours together
Here in the lobby.

QUEEN: So he does, indeed. 160

POLONIUS: At such a time I'll loose my daughter to him:
Be you and I behind an arras then;
Mark the encounter: if he love her not,
And be not from his reason fall'n thereon,[1]
Let me be no assistant for a state, 165
But keep a farm and carters.

KING: We will try it.

QUEEN: But look where sadly the poor wretch comes reading.

POLONIUS: Away, I do beseech you, both away:
I'll board him presently.[2]

[*Exeunt* KING, QUEEN, *and* ATTENDANTS. —*Enter* HAMLET, *reading.*]

O, give me leave: how does my good Lord Hamlet? 170

HAMLET: Well, God-a-mercy.

POLONIUS: Do you know me, my lord?

HAMLET: Excellent well; you are a fishmonger.[3]

POLONIUS: Not I, my lord.

HAMLET: Then I would you were so honest a man. 175

POLONIUS: Honest, my lord!

HAMLET: Aye, sir; to be honest, as this world goes, is to be one man
picked out of ten thousand.

POLONIUS: That's very true, my lord.

HAMLET: For if the sun breed maggots in a dead dog, being a good 180
kissing carrion[4]— Have you a daughter?

POLONIUS: I have, my lord.

HAMLET: Let her not walk i' the sun: conception is a blessing; but as
your daughter may conceive,—friend, look to 't.

POLONIUS: [*Aside*] How say you by that? Still harping on my daughter: 185
yet he knew me not at first; he said I was a fishmonger: he is far
gone: and truly in my youth I suffered much extremity for love; very
near this. I'll speak to him again.—What do you read, my lord?

HAMLET: Words, words, words.

9. Of the earth. 1. For that reason. 2. Approach him at once. 3. Seller of fish, but also slang
for procurer. 4. Good bit of flesh for kissing.

POLONIUS: What is the matter,[5] my lord?   190

HAMLET: Between who?

POLONIUS: I mean, the matter that you read, my lord.

HAMLET: Slanders, sir: for the satirical rogue says here that old men
have gray beards, that their faces are wrinkled, their eyes purging
thick amber and plum-tree gum, and that they have a plentiful lack   195
of wit, together with most weak hams: all which, sir, though I most
powerfully and potently believe, yet I hold it not honesty to have it
thus set down; for yourself, sir, shall grow old as I am, if like a crab
you could go backward.

POLONIUS: [Aside] Though this be madness, yet there is method in   200
't.—Will you walk out of the air, my lord?

HAMLET: Into my grave.

POLONIUS: Indeed, that's out of the air.

     [Aside]
How pregnant sometimes his replies are! a happiness[6] that often
madness hits on, which reason and sanity could not so prosperously   205
be delivered of. I will leave him, and suddenly contrive the means
of meeting between him and my daughter.—My honorable lord, I
will most humbly take my leave of you.

HAMLET: You cannot, sir, take from me any thing that I will more
willingly part withal: except my life, except my life, except my life.   210

POLONIUS: Fare you well, my lord.

HAMLET: These tedious old fools.

     [Re-enter ROSENCRANTZ and GUILDENSTERN.]

POLONIUS: You go to seek the Lord Hamlet; there he is.

ROSENCRANTZ: [To POLONIUS.] God save you, sir!

     [Exit POLONIUS.]

GUILDENSTERN: My honored lord!   215

ROSENCRANTZ: My most dear lord!

HAMLET: My excellent good friends! How dost thou, Guildenstern?
Ah, Rosencrantz! Good lads, how do you both?

ROSENCRANTZ: As the indifferent[7] children of the earth.

GUILDENSTERN: Happy, in that we are not over-happy;   220
On Fortune's cap we are not the very button.[8]

HAMLET: Nor the soles of her shoe?

ROSENCRANTZ: Neither, my lord.

HAMLET: Then you live about her waist, or in the middle of her favors?

GUILDENSTERN: Faith, her privates[9] we.   225

HAMLET: In the secret parts of Fortune? O, most true; she is a strumpet. What's the news?

ROSENCRANTZ: None, my lord, but that the world's grown honest.

HAMLET: Then is doomsday near: but your news is not true. Let me
question more in particular: what have you, my good friends, deserved   230

---

5. The subject matter of the book; Hamlet responds as if he referred to the subject of a quarrel.
6. Aptness of expression.   7. Average.   8. Top.   9. Ordinary men (with obvious play on the sexual term "private parts").

at the hands of Fortune, that she sends you to prison hither?

GUILDENSTERN: Prison, my lord!

HAMLET: Denmark's a prison.

ROSENCRANTZ: Then is the world one.

HAMLET: A goodly one; in which there are many confines, wards[1] and 235
dungeons, Denmark being one o' the worst.

ROSENCRANTZ: We think not so, my lord.

HAMLET: Why, then, 'tis none to you; for there is nothing either good
or bad, but thinking makes it so: to me it is a prison.

ROSENCRANTZ: Why, then your ambition makes it one; 'tis too narrow 240
for your mind.

HAMLET: O God, I could be bounded in a nut-shell and count myself
a king of infinite space, were it not that I have bad dreams.

GUILDENSTERN: Which dreams indeed are ambition; for the very substance of the ambitious is merely the shadow of a dream. 245

HAMLET: A dream itself is but a shadow.

ROSENCRANTZ: Truly, and I hold ambition of so airy and light a quality
that it is but a shadow's shadow.

HAMLET: Then are our beggars bodies, and our monarchs and outstretched heroes the beggars' shadows. Shall we to the court? for, 250
by my fay, I cannot reason.

ROSENCRANTZ: } We'll wait upon you.
GUILDENSTERN: }

HAMLET: No such matter: I will not sort you[2] with the rest of my servants; for, to speak to you like an honest man, I am most dreadfully
attended. But, in the beaten way of friendship, what make you at 255
Elsinore?

ROSENCRANTZ: To visit you, my lord; no other occasion.

HAMLET: Beggar that I am, I am even poor in thanks; but I thank you:
and sure, dear friends, my thanks are too dear a halfpenny.[3] Were
you not sent for? Is it your own inclining? Is it a free visitation? 260
Come, deal justly[4] with me: come, come; nay, speak.

GUILDENSTERN: What should we say, my lord?

HAMLET: Why, any thing, but to the purpose. You were sent for; and
there is a kind of confession in your looks, which your modesties
have not craft enough to color: I know the good king and queen 265
have sent for you.

ROSENCRANTZ: To what end, my lord?

HAMLET: That you must teach me. But let me conjure you, by the
rights of our fellowship, by the consonancy of our youth, by the
obligation of our ever-preserved love, and by what more dear a bet- 270
ter proposer[5] could charge you withal, be even and direct with me,
whether you were sent for, or no.

ROSENCRANTZ: [Aside to GUILDENSTERN] What say you?

1. Cells. *Confines:* Places of confinement.   2. Put you together.   3. If priced at a halfpenny.
4. Honestly.   5. Speaker.

HAMLET: [*Aside*] Nay then, I have an eye of[6] you.—If you love me, hold not off.   275

GUILDENSTERN: My lord, we were sent for.

HAMLET: I will tell you why; so shall my anticipation prevent your discovery,[7] and your secrecy to the king and queen moult no feather. I have of late—but wherefore I know not—lost all my mirth, forgone all custom of exercises; and indeed it goes so heavily with my   280 disposition that this goodly frame, the earth, seems to me a sterile promontory; this most excellent canopy, the air, look you, this brave o'erhanging firmament, this majestical roof fretted[8] with golden fire, why, it appears no other thing to me than a foul and pestilent congregation of vapors. What a piece of work is a man! how noble in   285 reason! how infinite in faculty! in form and moving how express[9] and admirable! in action how like an angel! in apprehension how like a god! the beauty of the world! the paragon of animals! And yet, to me, what is this quintessence of dust? man delights not me; no, nor woman neither, though by your smiling you seem to say   290 so.

ROSENCRANTZ: My lord, there was no such stuff in my thoughts.

HAMLET: Why did you laugh then, when I said 'man delights not me'?

ROSENCRANTZ: To think, my lord, if you delight not in man, what lenten entertainment the players shall receive from you: we coted[1]   295 them on the way; and hither are they coming, to offer you service.

HAMLET: He that plays the king shall be welcome; his majesty shall have tribute of me; the adventurous knight shall use his foil and target; the lover shall not sigh gratis; the humorous[2] man shall end his part in peace; the clown shall make those laugh whose lungs are   300 tickle o' the sere,[3] and the lady shall say her mind freely, or the blank verse shall halt for 't. What players are they?

ROSENCRANTZ: Even those you were wont to take such delight in, the tragedians of the city.

HAMLET: How chances it they travel? their residence, both in reputa-   305 tion and profit, was better both ways.

ROSENCRANTZ: I think their inhibition comes by means of the late innovation.[4]

HAMLET: Do they hold the same estimation they did when I was in the city? are they so followed?   310

ROSENCRANTZ: No, indeed, are they not.

HAMLET: How comes it? do they grow rusty?

ROSENCRANTZ: Nay, their endeavor keeps in the wonted pace: but there is, sir, an eyrie of children, little eyases,[5] that cry out on the top of question[6] and are most tyrannically clapped for 't: these are now the   315 fashion, and so berattle[7] the common stages—so they call them—

6. On.   7. Precede your disclosure.   8. Adorned.   9. Precise.   1. Overtook.   2. Eccentric, whimsical.   3. Ready to shoot off at a touch.   4. The introduction of "an eyrie of children," as Rosencrantz explains in his subsequent replies to Hamlet. *Inhibition*: Prohibition.   5. Nest of children, nestling hawks.   6. Above others on matter of dispute.   7. Berate.

that many wearing rapiers are afraid of goose-quills,[8] and dare scarce come thither.

HAMLET: What, are they children? who maintains 'em? how are they escoted? Will they pursue the quality[9] no longer than they can sing? will they not say afterwards, if they should grow themselves to common players—as it is most like, if their means are no better,—their writers do them wrong, to make them exclaim against their own succession?[1]   320

ROSENCRANTZ: Faith, there has been much to-do on both sides, and the nation holds it no sin to tarre[2] them to controversy: there was for a while no money bid for argument unless the poet and the player went to cuffs in the question.[3]   325

HAMLET: Is 't possible?

GUILDENSTERN: O, there has been much throwing about of brains.   330

HAMLET: Do the boys carry it away?[4]

ROSENCRANTZ: Aye, that they do, my lord; Hercules and his load too.[5]

HAMLET: It is not very strange; for my uncle is king of Denmark, and those that would make mows[6] at him while my father lived, give twenty, forty, fifty, a hundred ducats a-piece, for his picture in little. 'Sblood, there is something in this more than natural, if philosophy could find it out.   335

[Flourish of trumpets within.]

GUILDENSTERN: There are the players.

HAMLET: Gentlemen, you are welcome to Elsinore. Your hands, come then: the appurtenance of welcome is fashion and ceremony: let me comply with you in this garb, lest my extent[7] to the players, which, I tell you, must show fairly outwards, should more appear like entertainment[8] than yours. You are welcome: but my uncle-father and aunt-mother are deceived.   340

GUILDENSTERN: In what, my dear lord?   345

HAMLET: I am but mad north-north-west: when the wind is southerly I know a hawk from a handsaw.[9]

[Re-enter POLONIUS.]

POLONIUS: Well be with you, gentlemen!

HAMLET: Hark you, Guildenstern; and you too: at each ear a hearer: that great baby you see there is not yet out of his swaddling clouts.[1]   350

ROSENCRANTZ: Happily he's the second time come to them; for they say an old man is twice a child.

HAMLET: I will prophesy he comes to tell me of the players; mark it. You say right, sir: o' Monday morning; 'twas so, indeed.[2]

POLONIUS: My lord, I have news to tell you.   355

8. Gentlemen are afraid of pens (i.e., of poets satirizing the "common stages"). 9. Profession of acting. *Escoted:* Financially supported. 1. Recite satiric pieces against what they are themselves likely to become, common players. 2. Incite. 3. No offer to buy a plot for a play if it did not contain a quarrel between poet and player on that subject. 4. Win out. 5. The sign in front of the Globe theater showing Hercules bearing the world on his shoulders. 6. Faces, grimaces. 7. Welcoming behavior. *Garb:* Style. 8. Welcome. 9. A hawk from a heron, as well as a kind of ax from a handsaw. 1. Clothes. 2. Hamlet, for Polonius's sake, pretends he is deep in talk with Rosencrantz.

HAMLET: My lord, I have news to tell you. When Roscius[3] was an
    actor in Rome,—
POLONIUS: The actors are come hither, my lord.
HAMLET: Buz, buz![4]
POLONIUS: Upon my honor,—   360
HAMLET: Then came each actor on his ass,—
POLONIUS: The best actors in the world, either for tragedy, comedy,
    history, pastoral, pastoral-comical, historical-pastoral, tragical-his-
    torical, tragical-comical-historical-pastoral, scene individable, or
    poem unlimited:[5] Seneca cannot be too heavy, nor Plautus too light. 365
    For the law of writ and the liberty,[6] these are the only men.
HAMLET: O Jephthah,[7] judge of Israel, what a treasure hadst thou!
POLONIUS: What a treasure had he, my lord?
HAMLET: Why,
          'One fair daughter, and no more,   370
          The which he lovèd passing well.'[8]
POLONIUS: [Aside] Still on my daughter.
HAMLET: Am I not i' the right, old Jephthah?
POLONIUS: If you call me Jephthah, my lord, I have a daughter that I
    love passing well.   375
HAMLET: Nay, that follows not.
POLONIUS: What follows, then, my lord?
HAMLET: Why,
          'As by lot, God wot.'
    and then you know,
          'It came to pass, as most like it was,'—   380
    the first row of the pious chanson will show you more; for look,
    where my abridgment[9] comes.
    [Enter four or five PLAYERS.]
    You are welcome, masters; welcome, all. I am glad to see thee well.
    Welcome, good friends. O, my old friend! Why thy face is valanced[1]
    since I saw thee last; comest thou to beard me in Denmark? What, 385
    my young lady and mistress! By'r lady, your ladyship is nearer to
    heaven than when I saw you last, by the altitude of a chopine. Pray
    God, your voice, like a piece of uncurrent[2] gold, be not cracked
    within the ring.[3] Masters, you are all welcome. We'll e'en to 't like
    French falconers, fly at any thing we see: we'll have a speech straight: 390
    come, give us a taste of your quality; come, a passionate speech.
FIRST PLAYER: What speech, my good lord?
HAMLET: I heard thee speak me a speech once, but it was never acted;
    or, if it was, not above once; for the play, I remember, pleased not

3. A famous Roman comic actor.   4. An expression used to stop the teller of a stale story.   5. For
plays governed and those not governed by classical rules.   6. A possible meaning is, "For both written
and extemporized plays." *Seneca*: Roman writer of tragedies (ca. 4 B.C.–A.D. 65). *Plautus*: Roman writer
of comedies (ca. 254–184 B.C.).   7. Who was compelled to sacrifice a dearly beloved daughter (Judges
11).   8. From an old ballad about Jephthah.   9. I.e., the players interrupting him. *Row . . . chanson*: Stanza . . . song.   1. Draped (with a beard).   2. Unfit for currency. *Chopine*: A thick-soled
shoe.   3. A pun on the "ring" of the voice and the "ring" around the king's head on a coin.

the million; 'twas caviare to the general:[4] but it was—as I received 395
it, and others, whose judgments in such matters cried in the top of
mine[5]—an excellent play, well digested in the scenes, set down
with as much modesty as cunning. I remember, one said there were
no sallets[6] in the lines to make the matter savory, nor no matter in
the phrase that might indict the author of affection; but called it an 400
honest method, as wholesome as sweet, and by very much more
handsome than fine.[7] One speech in it I chiefly loved: 'twas Æneas'
tale to Dido;[8] and thereabout of it especially, where he speaks of
Priam's slaughter: if it live in your memory, begin at this line; let
me see, let me see; 405
'The rugged Pyrrhus, like th' Hyrcanian beast,'[9]—
It is not so: it begins with 'Pyrrhus.'
'The rugged Pyrrhus, he whose sable arms,
Black as his purpose, did the night resemble
When he lay couchèd in the ominous horse,[1] 410
Hath now this dread and black complexion smeared
With heraldry more dismal: head to foot
Now is he total gules; horridly tricked[2]
With the blood of fathers, mothers, daughters, sons,
Baked and impasted with the parching streets, 415
That lend a tyrannous[3] and a damnèd light
To their lord's murder: roasted in wrath and fire,
And thus o'er-sizèd[4] with coagulate gore,
With eyes like carbuncles, the hellish Pyrrhus
Old grandsire Priam seeks.' 420
So, proceed you.

POLONIUS: 'Fore God, my lord, well spoken, with good accent and
good discretion.

FIRST PLAYER: 'Anon he finds him
Striking too short at Greeks; his antique sword, 425
Rebellious to his arm, lies where it falls,
Repugnant to command: unequal matched,
Pyrrhus at Priam drives; in rage strikes wide;
But with the whiff and wind of his fell sword
The unnervèd father falls. Then senseless Ilium,[5] 430
Seeming to feel this blow, with flaming top
Stoops to his base, and with a hideous crash
Takes prisoner Pyrrhus' ear: for, lo! his sword,
Which was declining on the milky[6] head
Of reverend Priam seemed i' the air to stick: 435
So, as a painted tyrant, Pyrrhus stood,

---

4. A delicacy wasted on the general public. 5. Were louder (more authoritative than) mine. 6. Salads
(i.e., relish, spicy passages). *Affection:* Affectation. 7. More elegant than showy. 8. The story of the
fall of Troy, told by Aeneas to queen Dido. Priam was the king of Troy. 9. Tiger. *Pyrrhus:* Achilles'
son (also called Neoptolemus). 1. The wooden horse in which Greek warriors were smuggled into
Troy. 2. Adorned. *Gules:* Heraldic term for red. 3. Savage. 4. Glued over. 5. Troy's
citadel. 6. White-haired.

And like a neutral to his will and matter,
Did nothing.
But as we often see, against some storm,
A silence in the heavens, the rack[7] stand still,   440
The bold winds speechless and the orb below
As hush as death, anon the dreadful thunder
Doth rend the region, so after Pyrrhus' pause
Aroused vengeance sets him new a-work;
And never did the Cyclops'[8] hammers fall   445
On Mars's armor, forged for proof[9] eterne,
With less remorse than Pyrrhus' bleeding sword
Now falls on Priam.
Out, thou strumpet, Fortune! All you gods,
In general synod take away her power,   450
Break all the spokes and fellies from her wheel,
And bowl the round nave[1] down the hill of heaven
As low as to the fiends!
POLONIUS: This is too long.
HAMLET: It shall to the barber's, with your beard. Prithee, say on: he's   455
for a jig[2] or a tale of bawdry, or he sleeps: say on: come to Hecuba.
FIRST PLAYER: 'But who, O, who had seen the mobled[3] queen—'
HAMLET: 'The mobled queen'?
POLONIUS: That's good; 'mobled queen' is good.
FIRST PLAYER: 'Run barefoot up and down, threatening the flames   460
With bisson rheum; a clout[4] upon that head
Where late the diadem stood; and for a robe,
About her lank and all o'er-teemèd loins,[5]
A blanket, in the alarm of fear caught up:
Who this had seen, with tongue in venom steeped   465
'Gainst Fortune's state[6] would treason have pronounced:
But if the gods themselves did see her then,
When she saw Pyrrhus make malicious sport
In mincing with his sword her husband's limbs,
The instant burst of clamor that she made,   470
Unless things mortal move them[7] not at all,
Would have made milch the burning eyes of heaven[8]
And passion in the gods.'
POLONIUS: Look, whether he has not turned his color and has tears in
's eyes. Prithee, no more.   475
HAMLET: 'Tis well; I'll have thee speak out the rest of this soon. Good
my lord, will you see the players well bestowed?[9] Do you hear, let

7. Clouds. *Against:* Just before.   8. The gigantic workmen of Hephaestus (Vulcan), god of blacksmiths and fire.   9. Protection.   1. Hub. *Fellies:* Rims.   2. Ludicrous sung dialogue, short farce.
3. Muffled.   4. Cloth. *Bisson rheum:* Blinding moisture, tears.   5. Worn out by childbearing.
6. Government.   7. The gods.   8. The stars. *Milch:* Moist (milk-giving).   9. Taken care of, lodged.

them be well used, for they are the abstracts and brief chronicles of the time: after your death you were better have a bad epitaph than their ill report while you live. 480

POLONIUS: My lord, I will use them according to their desert.

HAMLET: God's bodykins,[1] man, much better: use every man after his desert, and who shall 'scape whipping? Use them after your own honor and dignity: the less they deserve, the more merit is in your bounty. Take them in. 485

POLONIUS: Come, sirs.

HAMLET: Follow him, friends: we'll hear a play to-morrow. [*Exit* POLONIUS *with all the* PLAYERS *but the first.*] Dost thou hear me, old friend; can you play the Murder of Gonzago?

FIRST PLAYER: Aye, my lord. 490

HAMLET: We'll ha 't to-morrow night. You could, for a need, study a speech of some dozen or sixteen lines, which I would set down and insert in 't, could you not?

FIRST PLAYER: Aye, my lord.

HAMLET: Very well. Follow that lord; and look you mock him not. 495 [*Exit* FIRST PLAYER.] My good friends, I'll leave you till night: you are welcome to Elsinore.

ROSENCRANTZ: Good my lord!

HAMLET: Aye, so, God be wi' ye! [*Exeunt* ROSENCRANTZ *and* GUILDEN-STERN.] Now I am alone. 500
O, what a rogue and peasant slave am I!
Is it not monstrous that this player here,
But in a fiction, in a dream of passion,
Could force his soul so to his own conceit
That from her[2] working all his visage wanned; 505
Tears in his eyes, distraction in 's aspect,
A broken voice, and his whole function[3] suiting
With forms to his conceit? and all for nothing!
For Hecuba![4]
What's Hecuba to him, or he to Hecuba, 510
That he should weep for her? What would he do,
Had he the motive and the cue for passion
That I have? He would drown the stage with tears
And cleave the general air with horrid speech,
Make mad the guilty and appal the free, 515
Confound the ignorant, and amaze indeed
The very faculties of eyes and ears.
Yet I,
A dull and muddy-mettled rascal, peak,[5]
Like John-a-dreams, unpregnant of my cause,[6] 520

---

1. By God's little body. 2. His soul's. 3. Bodily action. *Conceit:* Imagination, conception of the role played. 4. Queen of Troy, Priam's wife. 5. Mope. *Muddy-mettled:* Of poor metal (spirit, temper), dull-spirited. 6. Not really conscious of my cause, unquickened by it. *John-a-dreams:* A dreamy, absent-minded character.

And can say nothing; no, not for a king,
Upon whose property and most dear life
A damn'd defeat was made. Am I a coward?
Who calls me villain? breaks my pate across?
Plucks off my beard, and blows it in my face?   525
Tweaks me by the nose? gives me the lie i' the throat,
As deep as to the lungs? who does me this?
Ha!
'Swounds, I should take it: for it cannot be
But I am pigeon-livered and lack gall   530
To make oppression bitter, or ere this
I should have fatted all the region kites[7]
With this slave's offal: bloody, bawdy villain!
Remorseless, treacherous, lecherous, kindless[8] villain!
O, vengeance!   535
Why, what an ass am I! This is most brave,
That I, the son of a dear father murdered,
Prompted to my revenge by heaven and hell,
Must, like a whore, unpack my heart with words,
And fall a-cursing, like a very drab,   540
A scullion!
Fie upon 't! About,[9] my brain! Hum, I have heard
That guilty creatures, sitting at a play,
Have by the very cunning of the scene
Been struck so to the soul that presently   545
They have proclaimed their malefactions;
For murder, though it have no tongue, will speak
With most miraculous organ. I'll have these players
Play something like the murder of my father
Before mine uncle: I'll observe his looks;   550
I'll tent him to the quick: if he but blench,[1]
I know my course. The spirit that I have seen
May be the devil; and the devil hath power
To assume a pleasing shape; yea, and perhaps
Out of my weakness and my melancholy,   555
As he is very potent with such spirits,
Abuses me to damn me. I'll have grounds
More relative[2] than this. The play's the thing
Wherein I'll catch the conscience of the king.
  [*Exit.*]

---

7. Kites (hawks) of the air.   8. Unnatural.   9. To work!   1. Flinch. *Tent:* Probe.   2. Relevant.

Act III

SCENE 1—*A room in the castle.*

[*Enter* KING, QUEEN, POLONIUS, OPHELIA, ROSENCRANTZ, *and* GUIL-
DENSTERN.]

KING: And can you, by no drift of circumstance,[3]
 Get from him why he puts on this confusion,
 Grating so harshly all his days of quiet
 With turbulent and dangerous lunacy?
ROSENCRANTZ: He does confess he feels himself distracted,   5
 But from what cause he will by no means speak.
GUILDENSTERN: Nor do we find him forward to be sounded;
 But, with a crafty madness, keeps aloof,
 When we would bring him on to some confession
 Of his true state.
QUEEN: Did he receive you well?   10
ROSENCRANTZ: Most like a gentleman.
GUILDENSTERN: But with much forcing of his disposition.
ROSENCRANTZ: Niggard of question, but of our demands
 Most free in his reply.
QUEEN: Did you assay[4] him
 To any pastime?   15
ROSENCRANTZ: Madam, it so fell out that certain players
 We o'er-raught[5] on the way: of these we told him,
 And there did seem in him a kind of joy
 To hear of it: they are about the court,
 And, as I think, they have already order   20
 This night to play before him.
POLONIUS: 'Tis most true:
 And he beseeched me to entreat your majesties
 To hear and see the matter.
KING: With all my heart; and it doth much content me
 To hear him so inclined.   25
 Good gentlemen, give him a further edge,[6]
 And drive his purpose on to these delights.
ROSENCRANTZ: We shall, my lord.

[*Exeunt* ROSENCRANTZ *and* GUILDENSTERN.]

KING: Sweet Gertrude, leave us too;
 For we have closely[7] sent for Hamlet hither,
 That he, as 'twere by accident, may here   30
 Affront[8] Ophelia:
 Her father and myself, lawful espials,
 Will so bestow[9] ourselves that, seeing unseen,
 We may of their encounter frankly judge,
 And gather by him, as he is behaved,   35

3. Turn of talk, or roundabout way.   4. Try to attract him.   5. Overtook.   6. Incitement.
7. Privately.   8. Confront.   9. Place. *Espials:* Spies.

If 't be the affliction of his love or no
That thus he suffers for.

QUEEN: I shall obey you:
And for your part, Ophelia, I do wish
That your good beauties be the happy cause
Of Hamlet's wildness: so shall I hope your virtues   40
Will bring him to his wonted way again,
To both your honors.

OPHELIA: Madam, I wish it may.
     [*Exit* QUEEN.]

POLONIUS: Ophelia, walk you here. Gracious, so please you,
We will bestow ourselves. [*To* OPHELIA.] Read on this book;
That show of such an exercise may color[1]   45
Your loneliness. We are oft to blame in this,—
'Tis too much proved—that with devotion's visage
And pious action we do sugar o'er
The devil himself.

KING: [*Aside*]   O, 'tis too true!
How smart a lash that speech doth give my conscience!   50
The harlot's cheek, beautied with plastering art,
Is not more ugly to the thing that helps it
Than is my deed to my most painted word:
O heavy burthen!

POLONIUS: I hear him coming: let's withdraw, my lord.   55
     [*Exeunt* KING *and* POLONIUS. *—Enter Hamlet.*]

HAMLET: To be, or not to be: that is the question:
Whether 'tis nobler in the mind to suffer
The slings and arrows of outrageous fortune,
Or to take arms against a sea of troubles,
And by opposing end them. To die: to sleep;   60
No more; and by a sleep to say we end
The heart-ache, and the thousand natural shocks
That flesh is heir to, 'tis a consummation[2]
Devoutly to be wished. To die, to sleep;
To sleep: perchance to dream: aye, there's the rub;[3]   65
For in that sleep of death what dreams may come,
When we have shuffled off this mortal coil,[4]
Must give us pause: there's the respect
That makes calamity of so long life[5];
For who would bear the whips and scorns of time,   70
The oppressor's wrong, the proud man's contumely,
The pangs of despisèd love, the law's delay,
The insolence of office, and the spurns
That patient merit of the unworthy takes,
When he himself might his quietus make   75

1. Excuse.   2. Final settlement.   3. The impediment (a bowling term).   4. Have rid ourselves of
the turmoil of mortal life. *Respect:* Consideration.   5. So long-lived.

With a bare bodkin? who would fardels[6] bear,
To grunt and sweat under a weary life,
But that the dread of something after death,
The undiscovered country from whose bourn[7]
No traveler returns, puzzles the will,   80
And makes us rather bear those ills we have
Than fly to others that we know not of?
Thus conscience does make cowards of us all,
And thus the native hue of resolution
Is sicklied o'er with the pale cast of thought,   85
And enterprises of great pitch[8] and moment
With this regard their currents turn awry
And lose the name of action. Soft you now!
The fair Ophelia! Nymph, in thy orisons[9]
Be all my sins remembered.

OPHELIA: Good my lord,   90
How does your honor for this many a day?

HAMLET: I humbly thank you: well, well, well.

OPHELIA: My lord, I have remembrances of yours,
That I have longed to re-deliver;
I pray you, now receive them.

HAMLET: No, not I;   95
I never gave you aught.

OPHELIA: My honored lord, you know right well you did;
And with them words of so sweet breath composed
As made the things more rich: their perfume lost,
Take these again; for to the noble mind   100
Rich gifts wax poor when givers prove unkind.
There, my lord.

HAMLET: Ha, ha! are you honest?

OPHELIA: My lord?

HAMLET: Are you fair?   105

OPHELIA: What means your lordship?

HAMLET: That if you be honest and fair, your honesty should admit no
    discourse to your beauty.

OPHELIA: Could beauty, my lord, have better commerce[1] than with
    honesty?   110

HAMLET: Aye, truly; for the power of beauty will sooner transform hon-
    esty from what it is to a bawd than the force of honesty can translate
    beauty into his[2] likeness: this was sometime a paradox, but now the
    time gives it proof.[3] I did love you once.

OPHELIA: Indeed, my lord, you made me believe so.   115

HAMLET: You should not have believed me; for virtue cannot so
    inoculate[4] our old stock, but we shall relish[5] of it: I loved you not.

OPHELIA: I was the more deceived.

---

6. Burdens. *Bodkin*: Poniard, dagger.   7. Boundary.   8. Height.   9. Prayers.   1. Intercourse.
2. Its.   3. In his mother's adultery.   4. Graft itself onto.   5. Retain the flavor of.

HAMLET: Get thee to a nunnery: why wouldst thou be a breeder of
sinners? I am myself indifferent honest; but yet I could accuse me   120
of such things that it were better my mother had not borne me: I
am very proud, revengeful, ambitious; with more offenses at my
beck than I have thoughts to put them in, imagination to give them
shape, or time to act them in. What should such fellows as I do
crawling between heaven and earth! We are arrant knaves all; believe   125
none of us. Go thy ways to a nunnery. Where's your father?
OPHELIA: At home, my lord.
HAMLET: Let the doors be shut upon him, that he may play the fool
no where but in 's own house. Farewell.
OPHELIA: O, help him, you sweet heavens!   130
HAMLET: If thou dost marry, I'll give thee this plague for thy dowry: be
thou as chaste as ice, as pure as snow, thou shalt not escape calumny. Get thee to a nunnery, go: farewell. Or, if thou wilt needs
marry, marry a fool; for wise men know well enough what monsters[6]
you make of them. To a nunnery, go; and quickly too. Farewell.   135
OPHELIA: O heavenly powers, restore him!
HAMLET: I have heard of your paintings too, well enough; God hath
given you one face, and you make yourselves another: you jig, you
amble, and you lisp, and nick-name God's creatures, and make
your wantonness your ignorance.[7] Go to, I'll no more on 't; it hath   140
made me mad. I say, we will have no more marriages: those that
are married already, all but one, shall live; the rest shall keep as
they are. To a nunnery, go.
      [*Exit.*]
OPHELIA: O, what a noble mind is here o'erthrown!
    The courtier's, soldier's, scholar's, eye, tongue, sword: 145
    The expectancy and rose of the fair state,
    The glass of fashion and the mould of form.[8]
    The observed of all observers, quite, quite down!
    And I, of ladies most deject and wretched,
    That sucked the honey of his music vows,   150
    Now see that noble and most sovereign reason,
    Like sweet bells jangled, out of tune and harsh;
    That unmatched form and feature of blown[9] youth
    Blasted with ecstasy:[1] O, woe is me,
    To have seen what I have seen, see what I see!   155
      [*Re-enter* KING *and* POLONIUS.]
KING: Love! his affections do not that way tend;
    Nor what he spake, though it lacked form a little,
    Was not like madness. There's something in his soul
    O'er which his melancholy sits on brood,

6. Cuckolds bear imaginary horns and "a horned man's a monster" (*Othello*, Act IV, sc. I).   7. Misname
(out of affectation) the most natural things, and pretend that this is due to ignorance instead of
affectation.   8. The mirror of fashion and the model of behavior.   9. In full bloom.   1. Madness.

And I do doubt[2] the hatch and the disclose   160
Will be some danger: which for to prevent,
I have in quick determination
Thus set it down:—he shall with speed to England,
For the demand of our neglected tribute:
Haply the seas and countries different   165
With variable objects shall expel
This something-settled matter in his heart,
Whereon his brains still beating puts him thus
From fashion of himself.[3] What think you on 't?
POLONIUS: It shall do well: but yet do I believe   170
The origin and commencement of his grief
Sprung from neglected love. How now, Ophelia!
You need not tell us what Lord Hamlet said;
We heard it all. My lord, do as you please;
But, if you hold it fit, after the play,   175
Let his queen mother all alone entreat him
To show his grief: let her be round[4] with him;
And I'll be placed, so please you, in the ear
Of all their conference. If she find him not,
To England send him, or confine him where   180
Your wisdom best shall think.
KING: It shall be so:
Madness in great ones must not unwatched go.
    [*Exeunt.*]

SCENE 2—A *hall in the castle.*

[*Enter* HAMLET *and* PLAYERS.]

HAMLET: Speak the speech, I pray you, as I pronounced it to you,
    trippingly on the tongue: but if you mouth it, as many of your
    players do, I had as lief the town-crier spoke my lines. Nor do not
    saw the air too much with your hand, thus; but use all gently: for
    in the very torrent, tempest, and, as I may say, whirlwind of your   5
    passion, you must acquire and beget a temperance that may give it
    smoothness. O, it offends me to the soul to hear a robustious peri-
    wig-pated fellow tear a passion to tatters, to very rags, to split the
    ears of the groundlings,[5] who, for the most part, are capable of
    nothing but inexplicable dumb-shows and noise: I would have such   10
    a fellow whipped for o'er doing Termagant;[6] it out-herods Herod:
    pray you, avoid it.
FIRST PLAYER: I warrant your honor.
HAMLET: Be not too tame neither, but let your own discretion be your
    tutor: suit the action to the word, the word to the action; with this   15

2. Fear.   3. Makes him behave unusually.   4. Direct.   5. Spectators in the pit, where admission
was cheapest.   6. God of the Mohammedans in old romances and morality plays. He was portrayed as
being noisy and excitable.

special observance, that you o'erstep not the modesty[7] of nature: for
anything so overdone is from the purpose of playing, whose end,
both at the first and now, was and is, to hold, as 'twere, the mirror
up to nature; to show virtue her own feature,[8] scorn her own image,
and the very age and body of the time his form and pressure.[9] Now   20
this overdone or come tardy off, though it make the unskillful laugh,
cannot but make the judicious grieve; the censure of the which one
must in your allowance o'erweigh a whole theater of others. O,
there be players that I have seen play, and heard others praise, and
that highly, not to speak it profanely,[1] that neither having the accent   25
of Christians nor the gait of Christian, pagan, nor man, have so
strutted and bellowed, that I have thought some of nature's jour-
neymen had made men, and not made them well, they imitated
humanity so abominably.

FIRST PLAYER: I hope we have reformed that indifferently[2] with us, sir.   30

HAMLET: O, reform it altogether. And let those that play your clowns
speak no more than is set down for them: for there be of them that
will themselves laugh, to set on some quantity of barren[3] spectators
to laugh too, though in the mean time some necessary question of
the play be then to be considered: that's villainous, and shows a   35
most pitiful ambition in the fool that uses it. Go, make you ready.

[*Exeunt* PLAYERS. —*Enter* POLONIUS, ROSENCRANTZ, *and* GUILDEN-
STERN.]

How now, my lord! will the king hear this piece of work?

POLONIUS: And the queen too, and that presently.

HAMLET: Bid the players make haste.

[*Exit* POLONIUS.]

Will you two help to hasten them?   40

ROSENCRANTZ: ⎫
GUILDENSTERN: ⎭ We will, my lord.

[*Exeunt* ROSENCRANTZ *and* GUILDENSTERN.]

HAMLET: What ho! Horatio!

[*Enter* HORATIO.]

HORATIO: Here, sweet lord, at your service.

HAMLET: Horatio, thou art e'en as just a man
As e'er my conversation coped withal.[4]   45

HORATIO: O, my dear lord,—

HAMLET: Nay, do not think I flatter;
For what advancement may I hope from thee,
That no revenue hast but thy good spirits,
To feed and clothe thee? Why should the poor be flattered?
No, let the candied tongue lick absurd pomp,   50
And crook the pregnant hinges of the knee
Where thrift may follow fawning.[5] Dost thou hear?

7. Moderation.   8. Form.   9. Impress, shape. *His:* Its   1. Hamlet apologizes for the profane
implication that there could be men not of God's making.   2. Pretty well.   3. Silly.   4. As I ever
associated with.   5. Material profit may be derived from cringing. *Pregnant hinges:* Supple joints.

WILLIAM SHAKESPEARE

Since my dear soul was mistress of her choice,
And could of men distinguish, her election
Hath sealed thee for herself: for thou hast been   55
As one, in suffering all, that suffers nothing;
A man that fortune's buffets and rewards
Hast ta'en with equal thanks: and blest are those
Whose blood and judgment[6] are so well commingled
That they are not a pipe for fortune's finger   60
To sound what stop she please.[7] Give me that man
That is not passion's slave, and I will wear him
In my heart's core, ay, in my heart of heart,
As I do thee. Something too much of this.
There is a play to-night before the king;   65
One scene of it comes near the circumstance
Which I have told thee of my father's death:
I prithee, when thou sees that act a-foot,
Even with the very comment of thy soul[8]
Observe my uncle: if his occulted guilt   70
Do not itself unkennel in one speech
It is a damned ghost that we have seen,
And my imaginations are as foul
As Vulcan's stithy.[9] Give him heedful note;
For I mine eyes will rivet to his face,   75
And after we will both our judgments join
In censure of his seeming.[1]

HORATIO: Well, my lord:
If he steal aught the whilst this play is playing,
And 'scape detecting. I will pay the theft.

HAMLET: They are coming to the play: I must be idle:[2]   80
Get you a place.

[*Danish march. A flourish. Enter* KING, QUEEN, POLONIUS, OPHELIA,
ROSENCRANTZ, GUILDENSTERN, *and other* LORDS *attendant, with the*
GUARD *carrying torches.*]

KING: How fares our cousin Hamlet?

HAMLET: Excellent, i' faith; of the chameleon's dish: I eat the air,[3]
promise-crammed: you cannot feed capons so.

KING: I have nothing with this answer, Hamlet; these words are not   85
mine.[4]

HAMLET: No, nor mine now. [*To* POLONIUS.] My lord, you played
once i' the university, you say?

POLONIUS: That did I, my lord, and was accounted a good actor.

HAMLET: What did you enact?   90

POLONIUS: I did enact Julius Cæsar: I was killed i' the Capitol; Brutus
killed me.

---

6. Passion and reason.   7. For Fortune to put her finger on any windhole she may please of the pipe.
8. With all your powers of observation.   9. Smithy.   1. To judge his behavior.   2. Crazy.   3. The
chameleon was supposed to feed on air.   4. Have nothing to do with my question.

HAMLET: It was a brute part of him to kill so capital a calf there. Be the
     players ready?

ROSENCRANTZ: Aye, my lord; they stay upon your patience.   95

QUEEN: Come hither, my dear Hamlet, sit by me.

HAMLET: No, good mother, here's metal more attractive.

POLONIUS: [*To the* KING.] O, ho! do you mark that?

HAMLET: Lady, shall I lie in your lap? [*Lying down at* OPHELIA'S *feet.*]

OPHELIA: No, my lord.   100

HAMLET: I mean, my head upon your lap?

OPHELIA: Aye, my lord.

HAMLET: Do you think I meant country matters?

OPHELIA: I think nothing, my lord.

HAMLET: That's a fair thought to lie between maids' legs.   105

OPHELIA: What is, my lord?

HAMLET: Nothing.[5]

OPHELIA: You are merry, my lord.

HAMLET: Who, I?

OPHELIA: Aye, my lord.   110

HAMLET: O God, your only jig-maker.[6] What should a man do but be
     merry? for, look you, how cheerfully my mother looks, and my
     father died within 's two hours.

OPHELIA: Nay, 'tis twice two months, my lord.

HAMLET: So long? Nay then, let the devil wear black, for I'll have a   115
     suit of sables.[7] O heavens! die two months ago, and not forgotten
     yet? Then there's hope a great man's memory may outlive his life
     half a year: but, by 'r lady, he must build churches then; or else
     shall he suffer not thinking on, with the hobby-horse,[8] whose epi-
     taph is, 'For, O, for, O, the hobby-horse is forgot.'   120

     [*Hautboys play. The dumb-show enters. —Enter a King and a Queen
     very lovingly; the Queen embracing him and he her. She kneels, and
     makes show of protestation unto him. He takes her up, and declines
     his head upon her neck; lays him down upon a bank of flowers: she,
     seeing him asleep, leaves him. Anon comes in a fellow, takes off his
     crown, kisses it, and pours poison in the King's ears, and exits. The
     Queen returns; finds the King dead, and makes passionate action.
     The Poisoner, with some two or three Mutes comes in again, seeming
     to lament with her. The dead body is carried away. The Poisoner
     woos the Queen with gifts: she seems loath and unwilling awhile, but
     in the end accepts his love. —Exeunt.*]

OPHELIA: What means this, my lord?

HAMLET: Marry, this is miching mallecho;[9] it means mischief.

OPHELIA: Belike this show imports the argument of the play.

     [*Enter* PROLOGUE.]

---

5. A sexual pun: no thing.   6. Maker of comic songs.   7. Hamlet notes sarcastically the lack of mourning
for his father in the fancy dress of court and king.   8. A figure in the old May-day games and Morris
dances.   9. Sneaking misdeed.

HAMLET: We shall know by this fellow: the players cannot keep coun-
 sel;[1] they'll tell all.   125
OPHELIA: Will he tell us what this show meant?
HAMLET: Aye, or any show that you'll show him: be not you ashamed
 to show, he'll not shame to tell you what it means.
OPHELIA: You are naught,[2] you are naught: I'll mark the play.
PROLOGUE: For us, and for our tragedy,   130
          Here stooping to your clemency,
          We beg your hearing patiently.
HAMLET: Is this a prologue, or the posy[3] of a ring?
OPHELIA: 'Tis brief, my lord.
HAMLET: As woman's love.   135
          [Enter two PLAYERS, KING and QUEEN.]
PLAYER KING: Full thirty times hath Phœbus' cart[4] gone round
     Neptune's salt wash and Tellus' orbed ground,
     And thirty dozen moons with borrowed sheen
     About the world have times twelve thirties been,
     Since love our hearts and Hymen did our hands   140
     Unite commutual in most sacred bands.
PLAYER QUEEN: So many journeys may the sun and moon
     Make us again count o'er ere love be done!
     But, woe is me, you are so sick of late,
     So far from cheer and from your former state,   145
     That I distrust you.[5] Yet, though I distrust,
     Discomfort you, my lord, it nothing must:
     For women's fear and love holds quantity,[6]
     In neither aught, or in extremity.
     Now, what my love is, proof hath made you know,   150
     And as my love is sized, my fear is so:
     Where love is great, the littlest doubts are fear,
     Where little fears grow great, great love grows there.
PLAYER KING: Faith, I must leave thee, love, and shortly too;
     My operant powers their functions leave[7] to do: 155
     And thou shalt live in this fair world behind,
     Honored, beloved; and haply one as kind
     For husband shalt thou—
PLAYER QUEEN: O, confound the rest!
     Such love must needs be treason in my breast:
     In second husband let me be accurst!   160
     None wed the second but who killed the first.
HAMLET: [Aside] Wormwood, wormwood.
PLAYER QUEEN: The instances that second marriage move
     Are base respects of thrift,[8] but none of love:
     A second time I kill my husband dead,   165

1. A secret. 2. Naughty, improper. 3. Motto, inscription. 4. The chariot of the sun. 5. I
am worried about you. 6. Maintain mutual balance. 7. Cease. 8. Considerations of material
profit. *Instances*: Motives.

When second husband kisses me in bed.
PLAYER KING: I do believe you think what now you speak,
    But what we do determine oft we break.
    Purpose is but the slave to memory,
    Of violent birth but poor validity: 170
    Which now, like fruit unripe, sticks on the tree,
    But fall unshaken when they mellow be.
    Most necessary 'tis that we forget
    To pay ourselves what to ourselves is debt:
    What to ourselves in passion we propose,   175
    The passion ending, both the purpose lose.
    The violence of either grief or joy
    Their own enactures[9] with themselves destroy:
    Where joy most revels, grief doth most lament;
    Grief joys, joy grieves, on slender accident.   180
    This world is not for aye, nor 'tis not strange
    That even our loves should with our fortunes change,
    For 'tis a question left us yet to prove,
    Whether love lead fortune or else fortune love.
    The great man down, you mark his favorite flies;   185
    The poor advanced makes friends of enemies:
    And hitherto doth love on fortune tend;
    For who not needs shall never lack a friend,
    And who in want a hollow friend doth try
    Directly seasons[1] him his enemy.   190
    But, orderly to end where I begun,
    Our wills and fates do so contrary run,
    That our devices still are overthrown,
    Our thoughts are ours, their ends none of our own:
    So think thou wilt no second husband wed,   195
    But die thy thoughts when thy first lord is dead.
PLAYER QUEEN: Nor earth to me give food nor heaven light!
    Sport and repose lock from me day and night!
    To desperation turn my trust and hope!
    An anchor's cheer[2] in prison be my scope!   200
    Each opposite, that blanks[3] the face of joy,
    Meet what I would have well and it destroy!
    Both here and hence pursue me lasting strife,
    If, once a widow, ever I be wife!
HAMLET: If she should break it now!   205
PLAYER KING: 'Tis deeply sworn. Sweet, leave me here a while;
    My spirits grow dull, and fain I would beguile
    The tedious day with sleep.
        [Sleeps.]
PLAYER QUEEN: Sleep rock thy brain;

9. Their own fulfillment in action.   1. Matures.   2. Hermit's, or anchorite's, fare.   3. Makes pale.

And never come mischance between us twain!

[*Exit.*]

HAMLET: Madam, how like you this play? 210

QUEEN: The lady doth protest[4] too much, methinks.

HAMLET: O, but she'll keep her word.

KING: Have you heard the argument?[5] Is there no offense in 't?

HAMLET: No, no, they do but jest, poison in jest; no offense i' the
world. 215

KING: What do you call the play?

HAMLET: The Mouse-Trap. Marry, how? Tropically.[6] This play is the
image of a murder done in Vienna: Gonzago is the duke's name;
his wife, Baptista: you shall see anon; 'tis a knavish piece of work;
but what o' that? your majesty, and we that have free souls, it touches 220
us not: let the galled jade wince, our withers are unwrung.[7]

[*Enter* LUCIANUS.]

This is one Lucianus, nephew to the king.

OPHELIA: You are as good as a chorus, my lord.

HAMLET: I could interpret[8] between you and your love, if I could see
the puppets dallying. 225

OPHELIA: You are keen,[9] my lord, you are keen.

HAMLET: It would cost you a groaning to take off my edge.

OPHELIA: Still better and worse.

HAMLET: So you must take[1] your husbands. Begin, murderer; pox,
leave thy damnable faces, and begin. Come: the croaking raven 230
doth bellow for revenge.

LUCIANUS: Thoughts black, hands apt, drugs fit, and time agreeing;
Confederate[2] season, else no creature seeing;
Thou mixture rank, of midnight weeds collected,
With Hecate's ban[3] thrice blasted, thrice infected, 235
Thy natural magic and dire property,
On wholesome life usurp immediately.

[*Pours the poison into the sleeper's ear.*]

HAMLET: He poisons him i' the garden for his estate. His name's Gonzago: the story is extant, and written in very choice Italian: you shall
see anon how the murderer gets the love of Gonzago's wife. 240

OPHELIA: The king rises.

HAMLET: What, frighted with false fire![4]

QUEEN: How fares my lord?

POLONIUS: Give o'er the play.

KING: Give me some light. Away! 245

POLONIUS: Lights, lights, lights!

[*Exeunt all but* HAMLET *and* HORATIO.]

---

4. Promise.   5. Plot of the play in outline.   6. By a trope, figuratively.   7. Not wrenched. *Galled
jade:* Injured horse. *Withers:* The part between the shoulders of a horse.   8. Act as interpreter (regular
feature in puppet shows).   9. Bitter—but Hamlet chooses to take the word sexually.   1. I.e., for better
or for worse, as in the marriage service—but in fact you "mis-take," deceive them.   2. Favorable.
3. Goddess of witchcraft's curse.   4. Blank shot.

HAMLET: Why, let the stricken deer go weep,
    The hart ungallèd play;
      For some must watch, while some must sleep:
        Thus runs the world away.   250
Would not this, sir, and a forest of feathers—if the rest of my for-
tunes turn Turk with me[5]—with two Provincial roses on my razed
shoes,[6] get me a fellowship in a cry of players, sir?
HORATIO: Half a share.
HAMLET: A whole one, I.   255
    For thou dost know, O Damon dear,
      This realm dismantled was
        Of Jove himself; and now reigns here
          A very, very—pajock.
HORATIO: You might have rhymed.[7]   260
HAMLET: O good Horatio, I'll take the ghost's word for a thousand
pound. Didst perceive?
HORATIO: Very well, my lord.
HAMLET: Upon the talk of the poisoning?
HORATIO: I did very well note him.   265
HAMLET: Ah, ha! Come, some music! come, the recorders!
    For if the king like not the comedy,
      Why then, belike, he likes it not, perdy.[8]
Come, some music!
    [*Re-enter* ROSENCRANTZ *and* GUILDENSTERN.]
GUILDENSTERN: Good my lord, vouchsafe me a word with you.   270
HAMLET: Sir, a whole history.
GUILDENSTERN: The king, sir—
HAMLET: Aye, sir, what of him?
GUILDENSTERN: Is in his retirement marvelous distempered.
HAMLET: With drink, sir?   275
GUILDENSTERN: No, my lord, rather with choler.[9]
HAMLET: Your wisdom should show itself more richer to signify this to
    the doctor; for, for me to put him to his purgation would perhaps
    plunge him into far more choler.
GUILDENSTERN: Good my lord, put your discourse into some frame,   280
    and start not so wildly from my affair.
HAMLET: I am tame, sir: pronounce.
GUILDENSTERN: The queen, your mother, in most great affliction of
    spirit, hath sent me to you.
HAMLET: You are welcome.   285
GUILDENSTERN: Nay, good my lord, this courtesy is not of the right
    breed. If it shall please you to make me a wholesome[1] answer, I
    will do your mother's commandment: if not, your pardon and my
    return shall be the end of my business.

5. Betray me.   6. Occasionally, parts of an actor's apparel. *Cry*: Company (term generally used with a pack of hounds).   7. "Ass" would have rhymed. *Pajock*: Peacock.   8. By God *(per Dieu)*.   9. Bile, anger.   1. Sensible.

HAMLET: Sir, I cannot.   290
GUILDENSTERN: What, my lord?
HAMLET: Make you a wholesome answer; my wit's diseased: but, sir,
   such answer as I can make, you shall command; or rather, as you
   say, my mother: therefore no more, but to the matter: my mother,
   you say,—   295
ROSENCRANTZ: Then thus she says; your behavior hath struck her into
   amazement and admiration.[2]
HAMLET: O wonderful son, that can so astonish a mother! But is there
   no sequel at the heels of this mother's admiration? Impart.
ROSENCRANTZ: She desires to speak with you in her closet, ere you go   300
   to bed.
HAMLET: We shall obey, were she ten times our mother. Have you any
   further trade with us?
ROSENCRANTZ: My lord, you once did love me.
HAMLET: So I do still, by these pickers and stealers.[3]   305
ROSENCRANTZ: Good my lord, what is your cause of distemper? you do
   surely bar the door upon your own liberty, if you deny your griefs
   to your friend.
HAMLET: Sir, I lack advancement.[4]
ROSENCRANTZ: How can that be, when you have the voice of the king   310
   himself for your succession in Denmark?
HAMLET: Aye, sir, but 'while the grass grows,'[5]—the proverb is some-
   thing musty.
   [Re-enter PLAYERS with recorders.]
   O, the recorders! let me see one. To withdraw[6] with you:—why do
   you go about to recover the wind of me,[7] as if you would drive me   315
   into a toil?
GUILDENSTERN: O, my lord, if my duty be too bold, my love is too
   unmannerly.
HAMLET: I do not well understand that. Will you play upon this pipe?
GUILDENSTERN: My lord, I cannot.   320
HAMLET: I pray you.
GUILDENSTERN: Believe me, I cannot.
HAMLET: I do beseech you.
GUILDENSTERN: I know no touch of it, my lord.
HAMLET: It is as easy as lying: govern these ventages[8] with your fingers   325
   and thumb, give it breath with your mouth, and it will discourse
   most eloquent music. Look you, these are the stops.
GUILDENSTERN: But these cannot I command to any utterance of har-
   mony; I have not the skill.
HAMLET: Why, look you now, how unworthy a thing you make of me!   330
   You would play upon me; you would seem to know my stops; you
   would pluck out the heart of my mystery; you would sound me from

---

2. Confusion and surprise.   3. The hands.   4. Hamlet pretends that the cause of his "distemper" is
frustrated ambition.   5. The proverb ends, "oft starves the silly steed."   6. Retire (talk in private).
7. Get to windward of me. Toil: Snare.   8. Windholes.

my lowest note to the top of my compass: and there is much music,
excellent voice, in this little organ; yet cannot you make it speak.
'Sblood, do you think I am easier to be played on than a pipe? Call   335
me what instrument you will, though you can fret[9] me, yet you
cannot play upon me.
   [*Re-enter* POLONIUS.]
   God bless you, sir!
POLONIUS: My lord, the queen would speak with you, and presently.
HAMLET: Do you see yonder cloud that's almost in shape of a camel?   340
POLONIUS: By the mass, and 'tis like a camel, indeed.
HAMLET: Methinks it is like a weasel.
POLONIUS: It is backed like a weasel.
HAMLET: Or like a whale?
POLONIUS: Very like a whale.   345
HAMLET: Then I will come to my mother by and by. They fool me to
   the top of my bent.[1] I will come by and by.
POLONIUS: I will say so.
   [*Exit* POLONIUS.]
HAMLET: 'By and by' is easily said. Leave me, friends.
   [*Exeunt all but* HAMLET.]
   'Tis now the very witching time of night,   350
When churchyards yawn, and hell itself breathes out
Contagion to this world: now could I drink hot blood,
And do such bitter business as the day
Would quake to look on. Soft! now to my mother.
O heart, lose not thy nature; let not ever   355
The soul of Nero[2] enter this firm bosom:
Let me be cruel, not unnatural:
I will speak daggers to her, but use none;
My tongue and soul in this be hypocrites;
How in my words soever she be shent,   360
To give them seals[3] never, my soul, consent!
   [*Exit.*]

SCENE 3—*A room in the castle.*

   [*Enter* KING, ROSENCRANTZ, *and* GUILDENSTERN.]
KING: I like him not, nor stands it safe with us
To let his madness range. Therefore prepare you;
I your commission will forthwith dispatch,
And he to England shall along with you:
The terms of our estate[4] may not endure   5
Hazard so near us as doth hourly grow

9. Vex, with a pun on "frets," meaning the ridges placed across the finger board of a guitar to regulate the fingering.   1. Straining, tension (as of a bow).   2. This Roman emperor was the murderer of his mother.   3. Ratify them by action. *Shent:* Reproached.   4. My position as king.

Out of his lunacies.
GUILDENSTERN: We will ourselves provide:
  Most holy and religious fear it is
  To keep those many many bodies safe
  That live and feed upon your majesty.   10
ROSENCRANTZ: The single and peculiar[5] life is bound
  With all the strength and armor of the mind
  To keep itself from noyance; but much more
  That spirit upon whose weal depends and rests
  The lives of many. The cease[6] of majesty   15
  Dies not alone, but like a gulf doth draw
  What's near it with it; it is a massy wheel,
  Fixed on the summit of the highest mount,
  To whose huge spokes ten thousand lesser things
  Are mortised[7] and adjoined; which, when it falls,   20
  Each small annexment, petty consequence,
  Attends the boisterous ruin. Never alone
  Did the king sigh, but with a general groan.
KING: Arm you, I pray you, to this speedy voyage,
  For we will fetters put about this fear,   25
  Which now goes too free-footed.
ROSENCRANTZ: ⎫
            ⎬ We will haste us.
GUILDENSTERN: ⎭
    [*Exeunt* ROSENCRANTZ *and* GUILDENSTERN. —*Enter* POLONIUS.]
POLONIUS: My lord, he's going to his mother's closet:
  Behind the arras I'll convey myself,
  To hear the process: I'll warrant she'll tax him home:[8]   30
  And, as you said, and wisely was it said
  'Tis meet that some more audience than a mother,
  Since nature makes them partial, should o'erhear
  The speech, of vantage.[9] Fare you well, my liege:
  I'll call upon you ere you go to bed,   35
  And tell you what I know.
KING: Thanks, dear my lord.
    [*Exit* POLONIUS.]
  O, my offense is rank, it smells to heaven;
  It hath the primal eldest curse[1] upon 't,
  A brother's murder. Pray can I not,
  Though inclination be as sharp as will: 40
  My stronger guilt defeats my strong intent,
  And like a man to double business bound,
  I stand in pause where I shall first begin,
  And both neglect. What if this cursed hand
  Were thicker than itself with brother's blood,
  Is there not rain enough in the sweet heavens   45

---

5. Individual.   6. Decease, extinction.   7. Fastened.   8. Take him to task thoroughly.   9. From
a vantage point.   1. Cain's.

To wash it white as snow? Whereto serves mercy
But to confront the visage of offense?[2]
And what's in prayer but this twofold force,
To be forestalled ere we come to fall,   50
Or pardoned being down? Then I'll look up;
My fault is past. But O, what form of prayer
Can serve my turn? 'Forgive me my foul murder?'
That cannot be, since I am still possessed
Of those effects for which I did the murder,   55
My crown, mine own ambition and my queen.
May one be pardoned and retain the offense?[3]
In the corrupted currents of this world
Offense's gilded hand may shove by justice,
And oft 'tis seen the wicked prize itself   60
Buys out the law:[4] but 'tis not so above;
There is no shuffling, there the action lies
In his[5] true nature, and we ourselves compelled
Even to the teeth and forehead of our faults
To give in evidence. What then? what rests?[6]   65
Try what repentance can: what can it not?
Yet what can it when one can not repent?
O wretched state! O bosom black as death!
O limèd soul, that struggling to be free
Art more engaged! Help, angels! make assay![7]   70
Bow, stubborn knees, and, heart with strings of steel,
Be soft as sinews of the new-born babe!
All may be well.
        [*Retires and kneels. —Enter* HAMLET.]
HAMLET: Now might I do it pat,[8] now he is praying
And now I'll do 't: and so he goes to heaven: 75
And so am I revenged. That would be scanned;[9]
A villain kills my father; and for that,
I, his sole son, do this same villain send
To heaven.
O, this is hire and salary, not revenge.   80
He took my father grossly, full of bread,
With all his crimes broad blown, as flush as May;
And how his audit[1] stands who knows save heaven?
But in our circumstance and course of thought,
'Tis heavy with him: and am I then revenged,   85
To take him in the purging of his soul,
When he is fit and seasoned[2] for his passage?
No.

2. Guilt.   3. The things obtained through the offense.   4. The wealth unduly acquired is used for
bribery.   5. Its.   6. What remains?   7. Make the attempt! *Limèd:* Caught as with birdlime.
8. Conveniently.   9. Would have to be considered carefully.   1. Account. *Broad blown:* In full
bloom.   2. Ripe, ready.

Up, sword, and know thou a more horrid hent:[3]
When he is drunk asleep, or in his rage, 90
Or, in the incestuous pleasure of his bed;
At game, a-swearing, or about some act
That has no relish of salvation in 't;
Then trip him, that his heels may kick at heaven
And that his soul may be as damned and black 95
As hell, whereto it goes. My mother stays:
This physic but prolongs thy sickly days.
　　[*Exit.*]
KING: [*Rising*] My words fly up, my thoughts remain below:
Words without thoughts never to heaven go.
　　[*Exit.*]

SCENE 4—*The Queen's closet.*

[*Enter* QUEEN *and* POLONIUS.]
POLONIUS: He will come straight. Look you lay home to him:
Tell him his pranks have been too broad[4] to bear with,
And that your grace hath screen'd and stood between
Much heat and him. I'll sconce me even here.
Pray you, be round[5] with him.
HAMLET: [*Within*]　　　　　Mother, mother, mother! 5
QUEEN: I'll warrant you; fear me not. Withdraw,
I hear him coming.
　　[POLONIUS *hides behind the arras.* —*Enter* HAMLET.]
HAMLET: Now, mother, what's the matter?
QUEEN: Hamlet, thou hast thy father much offended.
HAMLET: Mother, you have my father much offended. 10
QUEEN: Come, come, you answer with an idle tongue.
HAMLET: Go, go, you question with a wicked tongue.
QUEEN: Why, how now, Hamlet!
HAMLET:　　　　　　What's the matter now?
QUEEN: Have you forgot me?
HAMLET:　　　　　No, by the rood,[6] not so:
You are the queen, your husband's brother's wife; 15
And—would it were not so!—you are my mother.
QUEEN: Nay, then, I'll set those to you that can speak.
HAMLET: Come, come, and sit you down; you shall not budge:
You go not till I set you up a glass[7]
Where you may see the inmost part of you. 20
QUEEN: What wilt thou do? thou wilt not murder me?
Help, help, ho!
POLONIUS: [*Behind*] What, ho! help, help, help!

3. Grip.　4. Unrestrained. *Lay home:* Give him a stern lesson.　5. Straightforward.　6. Cross.
7. Mirror.

HAMLET: [*Drawing*] How now! a rat? Dead, for a ducat, dead!
  [*Makes a pass through the arras.*]
POLONIUS: [*Behind*] O, I am slain!
  [*Falls and dies.*]
QUEEN: O me, what hast thou done?   25
HAMLET: Nay, I know not: is it the king?
QUEEN: O, what a rash and bloody deed is this!
HAMLET: A bloody deed! almost as bad, good mother,
  As kill a king, and marry with his brother.
QUEEN: As kill a king!
HAMLET: Aye, lady, 'twas my word.   30
  [*Lifts up the arras and discovers* POLONIUS.]
Thou wretched, rash, intruding fool, farewell!
I took thee for thy better: take thy fortune;
Thou find'st to be too busy[8] is some danger.
Leave wringing of your hands: peace! sit you down,
And let me wring your heart: for so I shall,   35
If it be made of penetrable stuff;
If damned custom have not brassed it so,
That it be proof and bulwark against sense.[9]
QUEEN: What have I done, that thou darest wag thy tongue
  In noise so rude against me?
HAMLET: Such an act   40
  That blurs the grace and blush of modesty,
  Calls virtue hypocrite, takes off the rose
  From the fair forehead of an innocent love,
  And sets a blister there; makes marriage vows
  As false as dicers' oaths: O, such a deed   45
  As from the body of contraction[1] plucks
  The very soul, and sweet religion makes
  A rhapsody of words: heaven's face doth glow;[2]
  Yea, this solidity and compound mass,
  With tristful visage, as against the doom,[3]   50
  Is thought-sick at the act.
QUEEN: Aye me, what act,
  That roars so loud and thunders in the index?[4]
HAMLET: Look here, upon this picture, and on this,
  The counterfeit presentment[5] of two brothers.   55
  See what a grace was seated on this brow;
  Hyperion's curls, the front of Jove himself,
  An eye like Mars, to threaten and command;
  A station[6] like the herald Mercury
  New-lighted on a heaven-kissing hill;   60
  A combination and a form indeed,

8. Too much of a busybody.   9. Feeling.   1. Duty to the marriage contract.   2. Blush with shame.   3. Doomsday. *Tristful:* Sad.   4. Prologue, table of contents.   5. Portrait.   6. Posture.

Where every god did seem to set his seal
To give the world assurance of a man:
This was your husband. Look you now, what follows:
Here is your husband; like a mildewed ear,[7]   65
Blasting his wholesome brother. Have you eyes?
Could you on this fair mountain leave to feed,
And batten[8] on this moor? Ha! have you eyes?
You cannot call it love, for at your age
The hey-day in the blood is tame, it's humble,   70
And waits upon[9] the judgment: and what judgment
Would step from this to this? Sense[1] sure you have,
Else could you not have motion: but sure that sense
Is apoplexed: for madness would not err,
Nor sense to ecstasy[2] was ne'er so thralled   75
But it reserved some quantity of choice,
To serve in such a difference. What devil was 't
That thus hath cozened you at hoodman-blind?[3]
Eyes without feeling, feeling without sight,
Ears without hands or eyes, smelling sans[4] all,   80
Or but a sickly part of one true sense
Could not so mope.[5]
O shame! where is thy blush? Rebellious hell,
If thou canst mutine in a matron's bones,
To flaming youth let virtue be as wax   85
And melt in her own fire: proclaim no shame
When the compulsive ardor gives the charge,[6]
Since frost itself as actively doth burn,
And reason panders[7] will.
QUEEN: O Hamlet, speak no more:
Thou turn'st mine eyes into my very soul,   90
And there I see such black and grained spots
As will not leave their tinct.[8]
HAMLET: Nay, but to live
In the rank sweat of an enseamèd[9] bed,
Stew'd in corruption, honeying and making love
Over the nasty sty,—
QUEEN: O, speak to me no more;   95
These words like daggers enter in my ears;
No more, sweet Hamlet!
HAMLET: A murderer and a villain;
A slave that is not twentieth part the tithe[1]
Of your precédent lord; a vice of kings;
A cutpurse[2] of the empire and the rule,   100

7. Ear of corn.   8. Gorge, fatten. *Leave:* Cease.   9. Is subordinated to.   1. Sensibility, feeling.
2. Madness.   3. Blindman's buff. *Cozened:* Tricked.   4. Without.   5. Be stupid.   6. Attacks.
7. Becomes subservient to.   8. Lose their color. *Grained:* Dyed in.   9. Greasy.   1. Tenth.
2. Pickpocket. *Vice:* Clown (from the custom in the old morality plays of having a buffoon take the part of Vice, or of a particular vice).

That from a shelf the precious diadem stole
And put it in his pocket!
QUEEN: No more!
HAMLET: A king of shreds and patches—
    [*Enter* GHOST.]
    Save me, and hover o'er me with your wings,
    You heavenly guards! What would your gracious figure?   105
QUEEN: Alas, he's mad!
HAMLET: Do you not come your tardy son to chide,
    That, lapsed in time and passion, lets go by
    The important acting of your dread command?
    O, say!
GHOST: Do not forget: this visitation   110
    Is but to whet thy almost blunted purpose.
    But look, amazement on thy mother sits:
    O, step between her and her fighting soul:
    Conceit[3] in weakest bodies strongest works:
    Speak to her, Hamlet.
HAMLET: How is it with you, lady?   115
QUEEN: Alas, how is 't with you,
    That you do bend your eye on vacancy
    And with the incorporal air do hold discourse?
    Forth at your eyes your spirits wildly peep;
    And, as the sleeping soldiers in the alarm,   120
    Your bedded hairs, like life in excrements,[4]
    Start up and stand on end. O gentle son,
    Upon the heat and flame of thy distemper
    Sprinkle cool patience. Whereon do you look?
HAMLET: On him, on him! Look you how pale he glares!   125
    His form and cause conjoined, preaching to stones,
    Would make them capable.[5] Do not look upon me,
    Lest with this piteous action you convert
    My stern effects:[6] then what I have to do
    Will want true color; tears perchance for[7] blood.   130
QUEEN: To whom do you speak this?
HAMLET: Do you see nothing there?
QUEEN: Nothing at all; yet all that is I see.
HAMLET: Nor did you nothing hear?
QUEEN: No, nothing but ourselves.
HAMLET: Why, look you there! look, how it steals away!
    My father, in his habit as he lived!   135
    Look, where he goes, even now, out at the portal!
        [*Exit* GHOST.]
QUEEN: This is the very coinage of your brain:
    This bodiless creation ecstasy[8]

---

3. Imagination.   **4.** Outgrowths. *Alarm:* Call to arms.   **5.** Capable of feeling.   **6.** You make me change my purpose.   **7.** Instead of.   **8.** Madness.

Is very cunning in.

HAMLET: Ecstasy!
My pulse, as yours, doth temperately keep time,   140
And makes as healthful music: it is not madness
That I have uttered: bring me to the test,
And I the matter will re-word, which madness
Would gambol from. Mother, for love of grace,
Lay not that flattering unction to your soul,   145
That not your trespass but my madness speaks:
It will but skin and film the ulcerous place,
Whiles rank corruption, mining all within,
Infects unseen. Confess yourself to heaven;
Repent what's past, avoid what is to come,   150
And do not spread the compost on the weeds,
To make them ranker. Forgive me this my virtue,
For in the fatness of these pursy⁹ times
Virtue itself of vice must pardon beg,
Yea, curb¹ and woo for leave to do him good.   155

QUEEN: O Hamlet, thou hast cleft my heart in twain.

HAMLET: O, throw away the worser part of it,
And live the purer with the other half.
Good night: but go not to my uncle's bed;
Assume a virtue, if you have it not.   160
That monster, custom, who all sense doth eat,
Of habits devil, is angel yet in this,
That to the use of actions fair and good
He likewise gives a frock or livery,
That aptly is put on.² Refrain to-night,   165
And that shall lend a kind of easiness
To the next abstinence; the next more easy;
For use almost can change the stamp³ of nature,
And either curb the devil, or throw him out
With wondrous potency. Once more, good night: 170
And when you are desirous to be blest,
I'll blessing beg of you. For this same lord,
    [*Pointing to* POLONIUS.]
I do repent: but heaven hath pleased it so,
To punish me with this, and this with me,
That I must be their scourge and minister.   175
I will bestow⁴ him, and will answer well
The death I gave him. So, again, good night.
I must be cruel, only to be kind:
Thus bad begins, and worse remains behind.

9. Swollen from pampering.   1. Bow.   2. I.e., habit, though like a devil in establishing evil ways in us, is like an angel in doing the same for virtues. *Aptly:* Easily.   3. Cast, form. *Use:* Habit.   4. Stow away. *Minister:* Agent of punishment.

One word more, good lady.

QUEEN: What shall I do?   180

HAMLET: Not this, by no means, that I bid you do:
  Let the bloat[5] king tempt you again to bed;
  Pinch wanton on your cheek, call you his mouse;
  And let him, for a pair of reechy[6] kisses,
  Or paddling in your neck with his damned fingers,   185
  Make you to ravel all this matter out,
  That I essentially am not in madness,
  But mad in craft.[7] 'Twere good you let him know;
  For who, that's but a queen, fair, sober, wise,
  Would from a paddock, from a bat, a gib,[8]   190
  Such dear concernings hide? who would do so?
  No, in despite of sense and secrecy,
  Unpeg the basket on the house's top,
  Let the birds fly, and like the famous ape,[9]
  To try conclusions, in the basket creep   195
  And break your own neck down.

QUEEN: Be thou assured, if words be made of breath
  And breath of life, I have no life to breathe
  What thou hast said to me.

HAMLET: I must to England; you know that?

QUEEN: Alack,   200
  I had forgot: 'tis so concluded on.

HAMLET: There's letters sealed: and my two schoolfellows,
  Whom I will trust as I will adders fanged,
  They bear the mandate; they must sweep my way,
  And marshal[1] me to knavery. Let it work;   205
  For 'tis the sport to have the enginer[2]
  Hoist with his own petar:[3] and 't shall go hard
  But I will delve one yard below their mines,
  And blow them at the moon: I, 'tis most sweet
  When in one line two crafts directly meet.   210
  This man shall set me packing:
  I'll lug the guts into the neighbor room.
  Mother, good night. Indeed this counselor
  Is now most still, most secret and most grave,[4]
  Who was in life a foolish prating knave.   215
  Come, sir, to draw toward an end with you.
  Good night, mother.

      [*Exeunt severally;* HAMLET *dragging in* POLONIUS.]

_____

5. Bloated with drink.   6. Fetid.   7. Simulation.   8. Tomcat. *Paddock:* Toad. *Concernings:* Matters with which one is closely concerned.   9. The ape in the unidentified animal fable to which Hamlet alludes; apparently the animal saw birds fly out of a basket and drew the conclusion that by placing himself in a basket he could fly too.   1. Lead.   2. Military engineer.   3. Petard, a variety of bomb. *Hoist:* Blow up.   4. Hamlet is punning on the word.

Act IV

SCENE 1—A *room in the castle.*

[*Enter* KING, QUEEN, ROSENCRANTZ, *and* GUILDENSTERN]

KING: There's matter in these sighs, these profound heaves:
  You must translate: 'tis fit we understand them.
  Where is your son?

QUEEN: Bestow this place on us[5] a little while.

    [*Exeunt* ROSENCRANTZ *and* GUILDENSTERN.]

  Ah, mine own lord, what have I seen to-night!   5

KING: What, Gertrude? How does Hamlet?

QUEEN: Mad as the sea and wind, when both contend
  Which is the mightier: in his lawless fit,
  Behind the arras hearing something stir,
  Whips out his rapier, cries 'A rat, a rat!'   10
  And in this brainish apprehension[6] kills
  The unseen good old man.

KING: O heavy deed!
  It had been so with us, had we been there:
  His liberty is full of threats to all,
  To you yourself, to us, to every one.   15
  Alas, how shall this bloody deed be answered?
  It will be laid to us, whose providence
  Should have kept short,[7] restrained and out of haunt,
  This mad young man: but so much was our love,
  We would not understand what was most fit,   20
  But, like the owner of a foul disease,
  To keep it from divulging, let it feed
  Even on the pith of life. Where is he gone?

QUEEN: To draw apart the body he hath killed:
  O'er whom his very madness, like some ore[8]   25
  Among a mineral[9] of metals base,
  Shows itself pure; he weeps for what is done.

KING: O Gertrude, come away!
  The sun no sooner shall the mountains touch,
  But we will ship him hence: and this vile deed   30
  We must, with all our majesty and skill,
  Both countenance[1] and excuse. Ho, Guildenstern!

    [*Re-enter* ROSENCRANTZ *and* GUILDENSTERN.]

  Friends both, go join you with some further aid:
  Hamlet in madness hath Polonius slain,
  And from his mother's closet hath he dragged him: 35
  Go seek him out; speak fair, and bring the body
  Into the chapel. I pray you, haste in this.

    [*Exeunt* ROSENCRANTZ *and* GUILDENSTERN.]

5. Leave us alone. 6. Imaginary notion. 7. Under close watch. 8. Gold. 9. Mine.
1. Recognize.

Come, Gertrude, we'll call up our wisest friends;
And let them know, both what we mean to do,
And what's untimely done. . . .[2]   40
Whose whisper o'er the world's diameter
As level as the cannon to his blank[3]
Transports his poisoned shot, may miss our name
And hit the woundless air. O, come away!
My soul is full of discord and dismay.

    [*Exeunt.*]

SCENE 2—*Another room in the castle.*

    [*Enter* HAMLET.]

HAMLET: Safely stowed.

ROSENCRANTZ: ⎫
GUILDENSTERN: ⎬ [*Within*] Hamlet! Lord Hamlet!

HAMLET: But soft, what noise? who calls on Hamlet?
    O, here they come.

    [*Enter* ROSENCRANTZ *and* GUILDENSTERN.]

ROSENCRANTZ: What have you done, my lord, with the dead body?   5

HAMLET: Compounded[4] it with dust, whereto 'tis kin.

ROSENCRANTZ: Tell us where 'tis, that we may take it thence
    And bear it to the chapel.

HAMLET: Do not believe it.

ROSENCRANTZ: Believe what?   10

HAMLET: That I can keep your counsel and not mine own. Besides, to
be demanded of a sponge! what replication[5] should be made by the
son of a king?

ROSENCRANTZ: Take you me for a sponge, my lord?

HAMLET: Aye, sir; that soaks up the king's countenance,[6] his rewards,   15
his authorities. But such officers do the king best service in the end:
he keeps them, like an ape, in the corner of his jaw; first mouthed,
to be last swallowed: when he needs what you have gleaned, it is
but squeezing you, and sponge, you shall be dry again.

ROSENCRANTZ: I understand you not, my lord.   20

HAMLET: I am glad of it: a knavish speech sleeps in a foolish ear.

ROSENCRANTZ: My lord, you must tell us where the body is, and go
with us to the king.

HAMLET: The body is with the king, but the king is not with the body.
    The king is a thing—   25

GUILDENSTERN: A thing, my lord?

HAMLET: Of nothing: bring me to him. Hide fox, and all after.[7]

    [*Exeunt.*]

---

2. This gap in the text has been guessingly filled in with "So envious slander . . ."   **3.** His target.
4. Mixed.   **5.** Formal reply. *Demanded:* Questioned by.   **6.** Favor.   **7.** The name of a children's
game.

SCENE 3—*Another room in the castle.*

[*Enter* KING, *attended.*]

KING: I have sent to seek him, and to find the body.
How dangerous is it that this man goes loose!
Yet must not we put the strong law on him:
He's loved of the distracted multitude,
Who like not in their judgment, but their eyes;   5
And where 'tis so, the offender's scourge[8] is weighed,
But never the offense. To bear[9] all smooth and even,
This sudden sending away must seem
Deliberate pause:[1] diseases desperate grown
By desperate appliance[2] are relieved,   10
Or not at all.

[*Enter* ROSENCRANTZ.]

How now! what hath befall'n?

ROSENCRANTZ: Where the dead body is bestowed, my lord,
We cannot get from him.

KING: But where is he?

ROSENCRANTZ: Without, my lord; guarded, to know your pleasure.

KING: Bring him before us.   15

ROSENCRANTZ: Ho, Guildenstern! bring in my lord.

[*Enter* HAMLET *and* GUILDENSTERN.]

KING: Now, Hamlet, where's Polonius?

HAMLET: At supper.

KING: At supper! where?

HAMLET: Not where he eats, but where he is eaten: a certain convo-   20
cation of public worms are e'en at him. Your worm is your only
emperor for diet:[3] we fat all creatures else to fat us, and we fat ourselves for maggots: your fat king and your lean beggar is but variable
service,[4] two dishes, but to one table: that's the end.

KING: Alas, alas!   25

HAMLET: A man may fish with the worm that hath eat of a king, and
eat of the fish that hath fed of that worm.

KING: What dost thou mean by this?

HAMLET: Nothing but to show you how a king may go a progress[5]
through the guts of a beggar.   30

KING: Where is Polonius?

HAMLET: In heaven; send thither to see: if your messenger find him
not there, seek him i' the other place yourself. But indeed, if you
find him not within this month, you shall nose[6] him as you go up
the stairs into the lobby.   35

KING: [*To some* ATTENDANTS.] Go seek him there.

HAMLET: He will stay till you come.

8. Punishment.   9. Conduct.   1. The result of careful arrangement.   2. Treatment.   3. Possibly
a punning reference to the Diet (assembly) of the Holy Roman Empire at Worms.   4. I.e., the service
varies, not the food.   5. Royal state journey.   6. Smell.

[*Exeunt* ATTENDANTS.]

KING: Hamlet, this deed, for thine especial safety,
  Which we do tender,[7] as we dearly grieve
  For that which thou hast done, must send thee hence   40
  With fiery quickness: therefore prepare thyself;
  The bark is ready and the wind at help,
  The associates tend, and every thing is bent
  For England.
HAMLET: For England?
KING: Aye, Hamlet.
HAMLET: Good.
KING: So is it, if thou knew'st our purposes.   45
HAMLET: I see a cherub that sees them. But, come; for England!
  Farewell, dear mother.
KING: Thy loving father, Hamlet.
HAMLET: My mother: father and mother is man and wife; man and
  wife is one flesh, and so, my mother. Come, for England!   50
  [*Exit.*]
KING: Follow him at foot;[8] tempt him with speed aboard;
  Delay it not; I'll have him hence to-night:
  Away! for every thing is sealed and done
  That else leans on[9] the affair: pray you, make haste.
  [*Exeunt* ROSENCRANTZ *and* GUILDENSTERN.]
  And, England,[1] if my love thou hold'st at aught—   55
  As my great power thereof may give thee sense,[2]
  Since yet thy cicatrice looks raw and red
  After the Danish sword, and thy free awe
  Pays homage to us—thou mayst not coldly set[3]
  Our sovereign process; which imports at full,   60
  By letters conjuring[4] to that effect,
  The present death of Hamlet. Do it, England;
  For like the hectic[5] in my blood he rages,
  And thou must cure me; till I know 'tis done,
  Howe'er my haps, my joys were ne'er begun.   65
  [*Exit.*]

SCENE 4—A *plain in Denmark.*

[*Enter* FORTINBRAS, *a* CAPTAIN *and* SOLDIERS, *marching.*]

FORTINBRAS: Go, captain, from me greet the Danish king;
  Tell him that by his license Fortinbras
  Craves the conveyance[6] of a promised march
  Over his kingdom. You know the rendezvous.
  If that his majesty would aught with us,
  We shall express our duty in his eye;[7]   5

7. Care for. 8. At his heels. 9. Pertains to. 1. The king of England. 2. Make you feel.
3. Regard with indifference. 4. Enjoining. 5. Fever. 6. Convoy. 7. Presence.

And let him know so.

CAPTAIN: I will do 't, my lord.

FORTINBRAS: Go softly on.

[*Exeunt* FORTINBRAS *and* SOLDIERS. —*Enter* HAMLET, ROSENCRANTZ, GUILDENSTERN, *and others.*]

HAMLET: Good sir, whose powers[8] are these?

CAPTAIN: They are of Norway, sir.   10

HAMLET: How purposed, sir, I pray you?

CAPTAIN: Against some part of Poland.

HAMLET: Who commands them, sir?

CAPTAIN: The nephew to Old Norway, Fortinbras.

HAMLET: Goes it against the main[9] of Poland, sir,   15
   Or for some frontier?

CAPTAIN: Truly to speak, and with no addition,
   We go to gain a little patch of ground
   That hath in it no profit but the name.
   To pay five ducats, five, I would not farm it;   20
   Nor will it yield to Norway or the Pole
   A ranker rate, should it be sold in fee.[1]

HAMLET: Why, then the Polack never will defend it.

CAPTAIN: Yes, it is already garrisoned.

HAMLET: Two thousand souls and twenty thousand ducats   25
   Will not debate the question of this straw!
   This is the imposthume[2] of much wealth and peace,
   That inward breaks, and shows no cause without
   Why the man dies. I humbly thank you, sir.

CAPTAIN: God be wi' you, sir.

   [*Exit.*]

ROSENCRANTZ: Will 't please you go, my lord?   30

HAMLET: I'll be with you straight. Go a little before.

   [*Exeunt all but* HAMLET.]

   How all occasions do inform against[3] me,
   And spur my dull revenge! What is a man,
   If his chief good and market[4] of his time
   Be but to sleep and feed? a beast, no more.   35
   Sure, he that made us with such large discourse,[5]
   Looking before and after, gave us not
   That capability and god-like reason
   To fust[6] in us unused. Now, whether it be
   Bestial oblivion, or some craven scruple   40
   Of thinking too precisely on the event,[7]—
   A thought which, quartered, hath but one part wisdom
   And ever three parts coward,—I do not know
   Why yet I live to say 'this thing's to do,'

---

8. Armed forces.   9. The whole of.   1. For absolute possession. *Ranker:* Higher.   2. Ulcer.
3. Denounce.   4. Payment for, reward.   5. Reasoning power.   6. Become moldy, taste of the
cask.   7. Outcome.

Sith[8] I have cause, and will, and strength, and means,   45
To do 't. Examples gross as earth exhort me:
Witness this army, of such mass and charge,[9]
Led by a delicate and tender prince,
Whose spirit with divine ambition puffed
Makes mouths[1] at the invisible event,   50
Exposing what is mortal and unsure
To all that fortune, death, and danger dare,
Even for an egg-shell. Rightly to be great
Is not to stir without great argument,
But greatly to find quarrel in a straw   55
When honor's at the stake. How stand I then,
That have a father killed, a mother stained,
Excitements of my reason and my blood,
And let all sleep, while to my shame I see
The imminent death of twenty thousand men,   60
That for a fantasy and trick[2] of fame
Go to their graves like beds, fight for a plot
Whereon the numbers cannot try the cause,[3]
Which is not tomb enough and continent
To hide the slain? O, from this time forth,   65
My thoughts be bloody, or be nothing worth!
    [*Exit.*]

SCENE 5—*Elsinore. A room in the castle.*

[*Enter* QUEEN, HORATIO, *and a* GENTLEMAN.]
QUEEN: I will not speak with her.
GENTLEMAN: She is importunate, indeed distract:
    Her mood will needs be pitied.
QUEEN: What would she have?
GENTLEMAN: She speaks much of her father, says she hears
    There's tricks i' the world, and hems and beats her heart,   5
    Spurns enviously at straws;[4] speaks things in doubt,
    That carry but half sense: her speech is nothing,
    Yet the unshapèd use of it doth move
    The hearers to collection; they aim[5] at it,
    And botch the words up fit to their own thoughts;   10
    Which, as her winks and nods and gestures yield them,
    Indeed would make one think there might be thought,
    Though nothing sure, yet much unhappily.
HORATIO: 'Twere good she were spoken with, for she may strew
    Dangerous conjectures in ill-breeding minds.[6]   15
QUEEN: Let her come in.

8. Since.   9. Cost.   1. Laughs at.   2. Trifle of.   3. So small that it cannot hold the men who fight for it. *Continent:* Container.   4. Gets angry at trifles.   5. Guess. *Collection:* Gathering up her words and trying to make sense of them. *Botch:* Patch.   6. Minds breeding evil thoughts.

[*Exit* GENTLEMAN.]

[*Aside*] To my sick soul, as sin's true nature is,
Each toy seems prologue to some great amiss:[7]
So full of artless jealousy is guilt,
It spills itself in fearing to be spilt.   20

[*Re-enter* GENTLEMAN, *with* OPHELIA.]

OPHELIA: Where is the beauteous majesty of Denmark?

QUEEN: How now, Ophelia!

OPHELIA: [*Sings*] How should I your true love know
                          From another one?
                          By his cockle hat and staff   25
                          And his sandal shoon.[8]

QUEEN: Alas, sweet lady, what imports this song?

OPHELIA: Say you? nay, pray you, mark.

[*Sings*] He is dead and gone, lady,
                 He is dead and gone;   30
            At his head a grass-green turf,
                 At his heels a stone.

Oh, oh!

QUEEN: Nay, but Ophelia,—

OPHELIA: Pray you, mark.

[*Sings*] White his shroud as the mountain snow,—

[*Enter* KING.]

QUEEN: Alas, look here, my lord.   35

OPHELIA: [*Sings*]   Larded[9] with sweet flowers;
                    Which bewept to the grave did—not—go
                    With true-love showers.

KING: How do you, pretty lady?

OPHELIA: Well, God 'ild you![1] They say the owl was a baker's daugh-   40
ter. Lord, we know what we are, but know not what we may be.[2]
God be at your table!

KING: Conceit upon her father.

OPHELIA: Pray you, let's have no words of this; but when they ask you
what it means, say you this: 45

[*Sings*] To-morrow is Saint Valentine's day
                 All in the morning betime,
            And I a maid at your window,
                 To be your Valentine.
            Then up he rose, and donned his clothes,   50
                 And dupped[3] the chamber-door;
            Let in the maid, that out a maid
                 Never departed more.

KING: Pretty Ophelia!

7. Misfortune. *Toy*: Trifle. *Jealousy*: Uncontrolled suspicion.   8. Typical signs of pilgrims traveling to
places of devotion. *Shoon*: Shoes.   9. Garnished.   1. God yield (i.e., repay) you.   2. An allusion
to a folk tale about a baker's daughter changed into an owl for having shown no charity to those in need.
3. Opened.

OPHELIA: Indeed, la, without an oath, I'll make an end on 't: 55
   [*Sings*] By Gis[4] and by Saint Charity,
            Alack, and fie for shame!
         Young men will do 't, if they come to 't;
            By Cock,[5] they are to blame.
         Quoth she, before you tumbled me,   60
            You promised me to wed.
He answers:
         So would I ha' done, by yonder sun,
            An thou hadst not come to my bed.
KING: How long hath she been thus?   65
OPHELIA: I hope all will be well. We must be patient: but I cannot
   choose but weep, to think they should lay him i' the cold ground.
   My brother shall know of it: and so I thank you for your good coun-
   sel. Come, my coach! Good night, ladies; good night, sweet ladies;
   good night, good night.   70
      [*Exit.*]
KING: Follow her close; give her good watch, I pray you.
      [*Exit* HORATIO.]
   O, this is the poison of deep grief; it springs
   All from her father's death. O Gertrude, Gertrude,
   When sorrows come, they come not single spies,
   But in battalions! First, her father slain: 75
   Next, your son gone; and he most violent author
   Of his own just remove: the people muddied,[6]
   Thick and unwholesome in their thoughts and whispers,
   For good Polonius' death; and we have done but greenly
   In hugger-mugger[7] to inter him: poor Ophelia   80
   Divided from herself and her fair judgment,
   Without the which we are pictures, or mere beasts:
   Last, and as much containing as all these,
   Her brother is in secret come from France,
   Feeds on his wonder,[8] keeps himself in clouds,   85
   And wants not buzzers[9] to infect his ear
   With pestilent speeches of his father's death;
   Wherein necessity, of matter beggared,[1]
   Will nothing stick our person to arraign[2]
   In ear and ear. O my dear Gertrude, this,   90
   Like to a murdering-piece,[3] in many places
   Gives me superfluous death.
      [*A noise within.*]
QUEEN: Alack, what noise is this?
KING: Where are my Switzers?[4] Let them guard the door.

4. By Jesus.   5. Corruption of "God," but with a sexual undermeaning.   6. Confused, their thoughts
made turbid (as water by mud).   7. Hasty secrecy. *Greenly*: Foolishly.   8. Broods, keeps wondering.
9. Lacks not tale-bearers.   1. The necessity to build up a story without the materials for doing so.
2. Will not hesitate to accuse me.   3. A variety of cannon which scattered its shot in many directions.
4. Swiss guards.

[*Enter another* GENTLEMAN.]
What is the matter?

GENTLEMAN: Save yourself, my lord:
The ocean, overpeering of his list,[5]   95
Eats not the flats with more impetuous haste
Than young Laertes, in a riotous head,[6]
O'erbears your officers. The rabble call him lord;
And, as the world were now but to begin,
Antiquity forgot, custom not known,   100
The ratifiers and props of every word,
They cry 'Choose we; Laertes shall be king!'
Caps, hands and tongues applaud it to the clouds,
'Laertes shall be king, Laertes king!'

QUEEN: How cheerfully on the false trail they cry!   105
O, this is counter,[7] you false Danish dogs!
[*Noise within.*]

KING: The doors are broke.
[*Enter* LAERTES, *armed;* DANES *following.*]

LAERTES: Where is this king? Sirs, stand you all without.

DANES: No, let's come in.

LAERTES: I pray you, give me leave.

DANES: We will, we will.   110
[*They retire without the door.*]

LAERTES: I thank you: keep the door. O thou vile king,
Give me my father!

QUEEN: Calmly, good Laertes.

LAERTES: That drop of blood that's calm proclaims me bastard;
Cries cuckold to my father; brands the harlot
Even here, between the chaste unsmirchèd brows   115
Of my true mother.

KING: What is the cause, Laertes,
That thy rebellion looks so giant-like?
Let him go, Gertrude; do not fear[8] our person:
There's such divinity doth hedge a king,
That treason can but peep to what it would,[9]   120
Acts little of his will. Tell me, Laertes,
Why thou art thus incensed: let him go, Gertrude:
Speak, man.

LAERTES: Where is my father?

KING: Dead.

QUEEN: But not by him.

KING: Let him demand his fill.   125

LAERTES: How came he dead? I'll not be juggled with:
To hell, allegiance! vows, to the blackest devil!

5. Overflowing above the high-water mark.   6. Group of rebels.   7. Following the scent in the wrong
direction.   8. Fear for.   9. Look from a distance at what it desires. *His:* Its.

    Conscience and grace, to the profoundest pit
    I dare damnation: to this point I stand,
    That both the worlds I give to negligence,[1]   130
    Let come what comes; only I'll be revenged
    Most thoroughly for my father.
KING: Who shall stay you?
LAERTES: My will, not all the world:
    And for my means, I'll husband them so well,
    They shall go far with little.
KING: Good Laertes,   135
    If you desire to know the certainty
    Of your dear father's death, is 't writ in your revenge
    That, swoopstake,[2] you will draw both friend and foe,
    Winner and loser?
LAERTES: None but his enemies.
KING: Will you know them then?   140
LAERTES: To his good friends thus wide I'll ope my arms;
    And, like the kind life-rendering pelican,[3]
    Repast them with my blood.
KING: Why, now you speak
    Like a good child and a true gentleman.
    That I am guiltless of your father's death,   145
    And am most sensibly in grief for it,
    It shall as level to your judgment pierce
    As day does to your eye.
DANES: [*Within.*]   Let her come in.
LAERTES: How now! what noise is that?
    [*Re-enter* OPHELIA.]
    O heat, dry up my brains! tears seven times salt,   150
    Burn out the sense and virtue[4] of mine eye!
    By heaven, thy madness shall be paid with weight,
    Till our scale turn the beam. O rose of May!
    Dear maid, kind sister, sweet Ophelia!
    O heavens! is 't possible a young maid's wits   155
    Should be as mortal as an old man's life?
    Nature is fine in love, and where 'tis fine[5]
    It sends some precious instance of itself
    After the thing it loves.
OPHELIA: [*Sings.*] They bore him barefaced on the bier: 160
             Hey non nonny, nonny, hey nonny:
             And in his grave rained many a tear,—
    Fare you well, my dove!
LAERTES: Hadst thou thy wits, and didst persuade revenge,
    It could not move thus.   165

---

1. I don't care what may happen to me in either this world or the next.   2. Without making any distinction, as the winner takes the whole stake in a card game.   3. In myth, the pelican is supposed to feed its young with its own blood.   4. Power, faculty.   5. Refined. *Instance:* Sample, token.

OPHELIA: [*Sings.*] You must sing down a-down,
         An you call him a-down-a.
O, how the wheel becomes it![6] It is the false steward, that stole his
master's daughter.

LAERTES: This nothing's more than matter.[7]   170

OPHELIA: There's rosemary, that's for remembrance: pray you, love,
remember: and there is pansies,[8] that's for thoughts.

LAERTES: A document[9] in madness; thoughts and remembrance fitted.

OPHELIA: There's fennel for you, and columbines: there's rue[1] for you:
and here's some for me: we may call it herbs of grace o' Sundays: 175
O, you must wear your rue with a difference. There's a daisy: I
would give you some violets,[2] but they withered all when my father
died: they say he made a good end,—
[*Sings.*] For bonnie sweet Robin is all my joy.

LAERTES: Thought and affliction, passion, hell itself,   180
She turns to favor[3] and to prettiness.

OPHELIA: [*Sings.*] And will he not come again?
         And will he not come again?
            No, no, he is dead,
            Go to thy death-bed,   185
         He never will come again.
         His beard was as white as snow,
         All flaxen was his poll:
            He is gone, he is gone,
            And we cast away moan: 190
         God ha' mercy on his soul!
And of all Christian souls, I pray God. God be wi' you.
    [*Exit.*]

LAERTES: Do you see this, O God?

KING: Laertes, I must commune with your grief,
Or you deny me right. Go but apart,   195
Make choice of whom your wisest friends you will.
And they shall hear and judge 'twixt you and me:
If by direct or by collateral hand
They find us touched,[4] we will our kingdom give,
Our crown, our life, and all that we call ours,   200
To you in satisfaction; but if not,
Be you content to lend your patience to us,
And we shall jointly labor with your soul
To give it due content.

LAERTES: Let this be so;
His means of death, his obscure funeral,   205
No trophy, sword, nor hatchment[5] o'er his bones,

---

6. I.e., how well the refrain fits. *The false steward*: An allusion (probably to a lost ballad) further expressing Ophelia's preoccupation with betrayal, lost love, and death.   7. This nonsense is more indicative than sane speech.   8. The symbol of thought.   9. Lesson.   1. Emblem of sorrow and repentance (compare the verb "rue"). *Fennel*: Emblem of flattery. *Columbines*: Emblem of cuckoldom.   2. For faithfulness.   3. Charm.   4. Involved (in the murder). *Collateral*: Indirect.   5. Coat of arms.

No noble rite nor formal ostentation,
Cry to be heard, as 'twere from heaven to earth,
That I must call 't in question.
KING: So you shall;
And where the offense is let the great axe fall.   210
I pray you, go with me.
    [*Exeunt.*]

SCENE 6—*Another room in the castle.*

    [*Enter* HORATIO *and a* SERVANT.]
HORATIO: What are they that would speak with me?
SERVANT: Sea-faring men, sir: they say they have letters for you.
HORATIO: Let them come in.
    [*Exit* SERVANT.]
    I do not know from what part of the world
    I should be greeted, if not from Lord Hamlet.   5
    [*Enter* SAILORS.]
FIRST SAILOR: God bless you, sir.
HORATIO: Let him bless thee too.
FIRST SAILOR: He shall, sir, an 't please him.
    There's a letter for you, sir; it comes from the ambassador that was
    bound for England; if your name be Horatio, as I am let to know it   10
    is.
HORATIO: [*Reads.*] 'Horatio, when thou shalt have overlooked[6] this,
    give these fellows some means to the king: they have letters for him.
    Ere we were two days old at sea, a pirate of very warlike appoint-
    ment gave us chase. Finding ourselves too slow of sail, we put on a   15
    compelled valor, and in the grapple I boarded them: on the instant
    they got clear of our ship; so I alone became their prisoner. They
    have dealt with me like thieves of mercy:[7] but they knew what they
    did; I am to do a good turn for them. Let the king have the letters I
    have sent; and repair thou to me with as much speed as thou wouldst   20
    fly death. I have words to speak in thine ear will make thee dumb;
    yet are they much too light for the bore[8] of the matter. These good
    fellows will bring thee where I am. Rosencrantz and Guildenstern
    hold their course for England: of them I have much to tell thee.
    Farewell.   25
        'He that thou knowest thine, HAMLET.'
    Come, I will make you way for these your letters;
    And do 't the speedier, that you may direct me
    To him from whom you brought them.
    [*Exeunt.*]

---

6. Read over.   7. Merciful.   8. Caliber, i.e., importance.

SCENE 7—*Another room in the castle.*

[*Enter* KING *and* LAERTES.]

KING: Now must your conscience my acquittance seal,
  And you must put me in your heart for friend,
  Sith you have heard, and with a knowing ear,
  That he which hath your noble father slain
  Pursued my life.
LAERTES: It well appears: but tell me   5
  Why you proceeded not against these feats,
  So crimeful and so capital in nature,
  As by your safety, wisdom, all things else,
  You mainly⁹ were stirred up.
KING: O, for two special reasons,
  Which may to you perhaps seem much unsinewed,¹   10
  But yet to me they're strong. The queen his mother
  Lives almost by his looks; and for myself—
  My virtue or my plague, be it either which—
  She's so conjunctive² to my life and soul,
  That, as the star moves not but in his sphere,   15
  I could not but by her. The other motive,
  Why to a public count I might not go,
  Is the great love the general gender³ bear him;
  Who, dipping all his faults in their affection,
  Would, like the spring that turneth wood to stone,   20
  Convert his gyves⁴ to graces; so that my arrows,
  Too slightly timber'd for so loud a wind,
  Would have reverted to my bow again
  And not where I had aim'd them.
LAERTES: And so have I a noble father lost;   25
  A sister driven into desperate terms,
  Whose worth, if praises may go back again,
  Stood challenger on mount of⁵ all the age
  For her perfections: but my revenge will come.
KING: Break not your sleeps for that: you must not think   30
  That we are made of stuff so flat and dull
  That we can let our beard be shook with danger
  And think it pastime. You shortly shall hear more:
  I loved your father, and we love ourself;
  And that, I hope, will teach you to imagine—   35
    [*Enter a* MESSENGER, *with letters.*]
  How now! what news?
MESSENGER: Letters, my lord, from Hamlet:
  This to your majesty; this to the queen.
KING: From Hamlet! who brought them?

---

9. Powerfully.   1. Weak.   2. Closely joined.   3. Common people. *Count:* Accounting, trial.
4. Leg irons (i.e., shames).   5. Above. *Go back:* I.e., to what she was before her madness.

MESSENGER: Sailors, my lord, they say; I saw them not:
   They were given me by Claudio; he received them   40
   Of him that brought them.
KING: Laertes, you shall hear them.
   Leave us.
     [*Exit* MESSENGER.]
   [*Reads*] 'High and mighty, you shall know I am set naked on your
   kingdom. To-morrow shall I beg leave to see your kingly eyes: when
   I shall, first asking your pardon thereunto, recount the occasion of   45
   my sudden and more strange return.   HAMLET.'
   What should this mean? Are all the rest come back?
   Or is it some abuse, and no such thing?[6]
LAERTES: Know you the hand?
KING: 'Tis Hamlet's character.[7] 'Naked'!   50
   And in a postscript here, he says 'alone.'
   Can you advise me?
LAERTES: I'm lost in it, my lord. But let him come;
   It warms the very sickness in my heart,
   That I shall live and tell him to his teeth,   55
   'Thus diddest thou.'
KING: If it be so, Laertes,—
   As how should it be so? how otherwise?—
   Will you be ruled by me?
LAERTES: Aye, my lord;
   So you will not o'errule me to a peace.
KING: To thine own peace. If he be now returned,   60
   As checking[8] at his voyage, and that he means
   No more to undertake it, I will work him
   To an exploit now ripe in my device,
   Under the which he shall not choose but fall:
   And for his death no wind of blame shall breathe;   65
   But even his mother shall uncharge the practice,[9]
   And call it accident.
LAERTES: My lord, I will be ruled;
   The rather, if you could devise it so
   That I might be the organ.[1]
KING: It falls right.
   You have been talked of since your travel much,   70
   And that in Hamlet's hearing, for a quality
   Wherein, they say, you shine; your sum of parts[2]
   Did not together pluck such envy from him,
   As did that one, and that in my regard
   Of the unworthiest siege.[3]
LAERTES: What part is that, my lord?   75
KING: A very riband in the cap of youth,

6. A delusion, not a reality.   7. Handwriting.   8. Changing the course of, refusing to continue.
9. Not recognize it as a plot.   1. Instrument.   2. The sum of your gifts.   3. Seat, i.e., rank.

Yet needful too; for youth no less becomes[4]
The light and careless livery that it wears
Than settled age his sables and his weeds,[5]
Importing health and graveness. Two months since   80
Here was a gentleman of Normandy:—
I've seen myself, and served against, the French,
And they can well on horseback: but this gallant
Had witchcraft in 't; he grew unto his seat,
And to such wondrous doing brought his horse   85
As had he been incorpsed and demi-natured[6]
With the brave beast: so far he topped my thought
That I, in forgery of shapes and tricks,[7]
Come short of what he did.

LAERTES: A Norman was 't?
KING: A Norman.   90
LAERTES: Upon my life, Lamord.
KING: The very same.
LAERTES: I know him well: he is the brooch[8] indeed
And gem of all the nation.
KING: He made confession of you,
And gave you such a masterly report,   95
For art and exercise in your defense,[9]
And for your rapier most especial,
That he cried out, 'twould be a sight indeed
If one could match you: the scrimers[1] of their nation,
He swore, had neither motion, guard, nor eye,   100
If you opposed them. Sir, this report of his
Did Hamlet so envenom with his envy
That he could nothing do but wish and beg
Your sudden coming o'er, to play with him.
Now, out of this—
LAERTES: What out of this, my lord?   105
KING: Laertes, was your father dear to you?
Or are you like the painting of a sorrow,
A face without a heart?
LAERTES: Why ask you this?
KING: Not that I think you did not love your father,
But that I know love is begun by time,   110
And that I see, in passages of proof,[2]
Time qualifies the spark and fire of it.
There lives within the very flame of love
A kind of wick or snuff[3] that will abate it;

---

4. Is the appropriate age for. *Riband*: Ribbon, ornament.   5. Furs (also meaning "blacks," dark colors)
and robes.   6. Incorporated and split his nature in two.   7. In imagining methods and skills of
horsemanship.   8. Ornament.   9. Report of your mastery in the theory and practice of fencing.
1. Fencers.   2. Instances that prove it. *Qualifies*: Weakens.   3. Charred part of the wick.

And nothing is at a like goodness still, 115
For goodness, growing to a plurisy, [4]
Dies in his own too much: that we would do
We should do when we would; for this 'would' changes
And hath abatements and delays as many
As there are tongues, are hands, are accidents, 120
And then this 'should' is like a spendthrift sigh,
That hurts by easing. [5] But, to the quick o' the ulcer:
Hamlet comes back: what would you undertake,
To show yourself your father's son in deed
More than in words?
LAERTES: To cut his throat i' the church. 125
KING: No place indeed should murder sanctuarize;
Revenge should have no bounds. But, good Laertes,
Will you do this, keep close within your chamber.
Hamlet returned shall know you are come home:
We'll put on[6] those shall praise your excellence 130
And set a double varnish on the fame
The Frenchman gave you; bring you in fine together
And wager on your heads: he, being remiss,[7]
Most generous and free from all contriving,
Will not peruse[8] the foils, so that with ease, 135
Or with a little shuffling, you may choose
A sword unbated, and in a pass of practice[9]
Requite him for your father.
LAERTES: I will do 't;
And for that purpose I'll anoint my sword.
I bought an unction of a mountebank,[1] 140
So mortal that but dip a knife in it,
Where it draws blood no cataplasm[2] so rare,
Collected from all simples[3] that have virtue
Under the moon, can save the thing from death
That is but scratched withal: I'll touch my point 145
With this contagion, that, if I gall[4] him slightly,
It may be death.
KING: Let's further think of this;
Weigh what convenience both of time and means
May fit us to our shape:[5] if this should fail,
And that our drift look through[6] our bad performance, 150
'Twere better not assayed: therefore this project
Should have a back or second, that might hold
If this did blast in proof.[7] Soft! let me see:

4. Excess. *Still:* Constantly.   5. A sigh that gives relief but is harmful (according to an old notion that it draws blood from the heart).   6. Instigate.   7. Careless. *In fine:* Finally.   8. Examine closely. 9. Treacherous thrust. *Unbated:* Not blunted (as a rapier for exercise ordinarily would be).   1. Ointment of a peddler of quack medicines.   2. Plaster.   3. Healing herbs.   4. Scratch.   5. Plan.   6. Our design should show through.   7. Burst (like a new firearm) once it is put to the test.

We'll make a solemn wager on your cunnings:
I ha 't: 155
When in your motion you are hot and dry—
As make your bouts more violent to that end—
And that he calls for drink, I'll have prepared him
A chalice for the nonce;[8] whereon but sipping,
If he by chance escape your venomed stuck,[9]   160
Our purpose may hold there. But stay, what noise?
   [*Enter* QUEEN.]
How now, sweet queen!
QUEEN: One woe doth tread upon another's heel,
  So fast they follow: your sister's drowned, Laertes.
LAERTES: Drowned! O, where?   165
QUEEN: There is a willow grows aslant[1] a brook,
  That shows his hoar leaves in the glassy stream;
  There with fantastic garlands did she come
  Of crow-flowers, nettles, daisies, and long purples,
  That liberal shepherds give a grosser name,   170
  But our cold maids do dead men's fingers call them:
  There, on the pendent boughs her coronet weeds
  Clambering to hang, an envious sliver[2] broke;
  When down her weedy trophies and herself
  Fell in the weeping brook. Her clothes spread wide,   175
  And mermaid-like a while they bore her up:
  Which time she chanted snatches of old tunes,
  As one incapable of[3] her own distress,
  Or like a creature native and indued[4]
  Unto that element: but long it could not be   180
  Till that her garments, heavy with their drink,
  Pulled the poor wretch from her melodious lay
  To muddy death.
LAERTES: Alas, then she is drowned!
QUEEN: Drowned, drowned.
LAERTES: Too much of water hast thou, poor Ophelia,   185
  And therefore I forbid my tears: but yet
  It is our trick;[5] nature her custom holds,
  Let shame say what it will: when these are gone,
  The woman[6] will be out. Adieu, my lord:
  I have a speech of fire that fain would blaze,   190
  But that this folly douts[7] it.
   [*Exit.*]
KING: Let's follow, Gertrude:
  How much I had to do to calm his rage!
  Now fear I this will give it start again;

---

8. For that particular occasion.   9. Thrust.   1. Across.   2. Malicious bough.   3. Insensitive
to.   4. Adapted, in harmony with.   5. Peculiar trait.   6. The softer qualities, the woman in me.
7. Extinguishes.

Therefore let's follow.
   [*Exeunt.*]

Act V

SCENE 1—A *churchyard*.

[*Enter two* CLOWNS, *with spades, &c.*]

FIRST CLOWN: Is she to be buried in Christian burial that willfully seeks
  her own salvation?

SECOND CLOWN: I tell thee she is; and therefore make her grave straight:[8]
  the crowner[8] hath sat on her, and finds it Christian burial.

FIRST CLOWN: How can that be, unless she drowned herself in her own   5
  defense?

SECOND CLOWN: Why, 'tis found so.

FIRST CLOWN: It must be 'se offendendo;'[9] it cannot be else. For here
  lies the point: if I drown myself wittingly, it argues an act: and an
  act hath three branches; it is, to act, to do, to perform: argal,[1] she   10
  drowned herself wittingly.

SECOND CLOWN: Nay, but hear you, goodman delver.

FIRST CLOWN: Give me leave. Here lies the water; good: here stands
  the man; good: if the man go to this water and drown himself, it is,
  will he, nill he,[2] he goes; mark you that; but if the water come to   15
  him and drown him, he drowns not himself: argal, he that is not
  guilty of his own death shortens not his own life.

SECOND CLOWN: But is this law?

FIRST CLOWN: Aye, marry, is 't; crowner's quest[3] law.

SECOND CLOWN: Will you ha' the truth on 't? If this had not been a   20
  gentlewoman, she should have been buried out o' Christian burial.

FIRST CLOWN: Why, there thou say'st: and the more pity that great folk
  should have countenance[4] in this world to drown or hang themselves, more than their even Christian.[5] Come, my spade. There is
  no ancient gentlemen but gardeners, ditchers and gravemakers: they   25
  hold up Adam's profession.

SECOND CLOWN: Was he a gentleman?

FIRST CLOWN: A' was the first that ever bore arms.

SECOND CLOWN: Why, he had none.

FIRST CLOWN: What, art a heathen? How dost thou understand the   30
  Scripture? The Scripture says Adam digged: could he dig without
  arms? I'll put another question to thee: if thou answerest me not to
  the purpose, confess thyself—

SECOND CLOWN: Go to.

FIRST CLOWN: What is he that builds stronger than either the mason,   35
  the shipwright, or the carpenter?

---

8. Coroner. *Straight*: Right away.   9. The Clown's blunder for *se defendendo*, "in self-defense."
1. Blunder for *ergo*, "therefore."   2. Willy-nilly.   3. Inquest.   4. Sanction.   5. Fellow Christian.

SECOND CLOWN: The gallows-maker; for that frame outlives a thousand tenants.

FIRST CLOWN: I like thy wit well, in good faith: the gallows does well; but how does it well? it does well to those that do ill: now, thou dost ill to say the gallows is built stronger than the church: argal, the gallows may do well to thee. To 't again, come.   40

SECOND CLOWN: 'Who builds stronger than a mason, a shipwright, or a carpenter?'

FIRST CLOWN: Aye, tell me that, and unyoke.[6]   45

SECOND CLOWN: Marry, now I can tell.

FIRST CLOWN: To 't.

SECOND CLOWN: Mass, I cannot tell.

    [*Enter* HAMLET *and* HORATIO, *afar off.*]

FIRST CLOWN: Cudgel thy brains no more about it, for your dull ass will not mend his pace with beating, and when you are asked this question next, say 'a grave-maker:' the houses that he makes last till doomsday. Go, get thee to Yaughan;[7] fetch me a stoup of liquor.   50

    [*Exit* SECOND CLOWN.—FIRST CLOWN *digs and sings.*]

In youth, when I did love, did love,
    Methought it was very sweet,
To contract, O, the time, for-a my behove,[8]   55
    O, methought, there-a was nothing-a meet.[9]

HAMLET: Has this fellow no feeling of his business that he sings at grave-making?

HORATIO: Custom hath made it in him a property of easiness.[1]

HAMLET: 'Tis e'en so: the hand of little employment hath the daintier[2] sense.   60

FIRST CLOWN: [*Sings.*] But age, with his stealing steps,
          Hath clowed me in his clutch,
          And hath shipped me intil[3] the land,
          As if I had never been such.   65

    [*Throws up a skull.*]

HAMLET: That skull had a tongue in it, and could sing once: how the knave jowls[4] it to the ground, as if it were Cain's jaw-bone, that did the first murder! It might be the pate of a politician,[5] which this ass now o'er-reaches;[6] one that would circumvent God, might it not?

HORATIO: It might, my lord.   70

HAMLET: Or of a courtier, which could say, 'Good morrow, sweet lord! How dost thou, sweet lord?' This might be my lord such-a-one, that praised my lord such-a-one's horse, when he meant to beg it; might it not?

HORATIO: Aye, my lord.   75

HAMLET: Why, e'en so: and now my Lady Worm's; chapless, and

---

6. Call it a day.   7. Mug. *Yaughan:* Apparently a tavern-keeper's name.   8. Profit. *Contract:* Shorten.   9. Fitting.   1. Has made it a matter of indifference to him.   2. Finer sensitivity. *Of little employment:* Which does little labor.   3. Into.   4. Knocks.   5. The word has a pejorative sense. *First murder:* Possible an allusion to the legend according to which Cain slew Abel with an ass's jawbone.   6. Outwits.

knocked about the mazzard[7] with a sexton's spade: here's fine revolution, an we had the trick[8] to see 't. Did these bones cost no more
the breeding, but to play at loggats[9] with 'em? mine ache to think
on 't.   80

FIRST CLOWN: [*Sings.*] A pick-axe, and a spade, a spade,
                              For a shrouding sheet:
                          O, a pit of clay for to be made
                          For such a guest is meet.
      [*Throws up another skull.*]

HAMLET: There's another: why may not that be the skull of a lawyer?   85
      Where be his quiddities now, his quillets, his cases, his tenures,[1]
      and his tricks? why does he suffer this rude knave now to knock him
      about the sconce with a dirty shovel, and will not tell him of his
      action of battery?[2] Hum! This fellow might be in 's time a great
      buyer of land, with his statutes, his recognizances,[3] his fines, his   90
      double vouchers, his recoveries: is this the fine[4] of his fines and the
      recovery of his recoveries, to have his fine pate full of fine dirt? will
      his vouchers vouch him no more of his purchases, and double ones
      too, than the length and breadth of a pair of indentures? The very
      conveyances[5] of his lands will hardly lie in this box; and must the   95
      inheritor himself have no more, ha?

HORATIO: Not a jot more, my lord.

HAMLET: Is not parchment made of sheep-skins?

HORATIO: Aye, my lord, and of calf-skins too.

HAMLET: They are sheep and calves which seek out assurance[6] in that.   100
      I will speak to this fellow. Whose grave's this, sirrah?

FIRST CLOWN: Mine, sir.
      [*Sings.*] O, a pit of clay for to be made
                          For such a guest is meet.

HAMLET: I think it be thine indeed, for thou liest in 't.   105

FIRST CLOWN: You lie out on 't, sir, and therefore 'tis not yours: for my
      part, I do not lie in 't, and yet it is mine.

HAMLET: Thou dost lie in 't, to be in 't and say it is thine: 'tis for the
      dead, not for the quick;[7] therefore thou liest.

FIRST CLOWN: 'Tis a quick lie, sir; 'twill away again, from me to you.   110

HAMLET: What man dost thou dig it for?

FIRST CLOWN: For no man, sir.

HAMLET: What woman then?

FIRST CLOWN: For none neither.

HAMLET: Who is to be buried in 't?   115

FIRST CLOWN: One that was a woman, sir; but, rest her soul, she's
      dead.

7. Pate. *Chapless:* The lower jawbone missing.   8. Faculty.   9. A game resembling bowls.   1. Real-
estate holdings. *Quiddities:* Subtle definitions. *Quillets:* Quibbles.   2. Assault. *Sconce:* Head.
3. Varieties of bonds. Following are legal terms relating to the transfer of estates.   4. End. Hamlet is
punning on the legal and nonlegal meanings of the word.   5. Deeds. *Indentures:* Contracts drawn in
duplicate on the same piece of parchment, the two copies separated by an "indented" line.   6. Security;
another pun, since the word is also a legal term.   7. Living.

HAMLET: How absolute the knave is! we must speak by the card,[8] or
equivocation will undo us. By the Lord. Horatio, these three years
I have taken note of it; the age is grown so picked[9] that the toe of
the peasant comes so near the heel of the courtier, he galls his kibe.[1]
How long hast thou been a grave-maker?

FIRST CLOWN: Of all the days i' the year, I came to 't that day that our
last King Hamlet o'ercame Fortinbras.

HAMLET: How long is that since?

FIRST CLOWN: Cannot you tell that? every fool can tell that: it was that
very day that young Hamlet was born: he that is mad, and sent into
England.

HAMLET: Aye, marry, why was he sent into England?

FIRST CLOWN: Why, because a' was mad; a' shall recover his wits there:
or, if a' do not, 'tis no great matter there.

HAMLET: Why?

FIRST CLOWN: 'Twill not be seen in him there; there the men are as
mad as he.

HAMLET: How came he mad?

FIRST CLOWN: Very strangely, they say.

HAMLET: How 'strangely'?

FIRST CLOWN: Faith, e'en with losing his wits.

HAMLET: Upon what ground?

FIRST CLOWN: Why, here in Denmark: I have been sexton here, man
and boy, thirty years.

HAMLET: How long will a man lie i' the earth ere he rot?

FIRST CLOWN: I' faith, if a' be not rotten before a' die—as we have
many pocky corses now-a-days, that will scarce hold the laying in[2]—
a' will last you some eight year or nine year: a tanner will last you
nine year.

HAMLET: Why he more than another?

FIRST CLOWN: Why, sir, his hide is so tanned with his trade that a' will
keep out water a great while; and your water is a sore decayer of
your whoreson dead body. Here's a skull now: this skull has lain in
the earth three and twenty years.

HAMLET: Whose was it?

FIRST CLOWN: A whoreson mad fellow's it was: whose do you think it
was?

HAMLET: Nay, I know not.

FIRST CLOWN: A pestilence on him for a mad rogue! a' poured a flagon
of Rhenish[3] on my head once. This same skull, sir, was Yorick's
skull, the king's jester.

HAMLET: This?

FIRST CLOWN: E'en that.

HAMLET: Let me see. [*Takes the skull.*] Alas, poor Yorick! I knew him,

Horatio: a fellow of infinite jest, of most excellent fancy: he hath
borne me on his back a thousand times; and now how abhorred in
my imagination it is! my gorge rises at it. Here hung those lips that
I have kissed I know not how oft. Where be your gibes now? your   165
gambols? your songs? your flashes of merriment, that were wont to
set the table on a roar? Not one now, to mock your own grinning?
quite chop-fallen?[4] Now get you to my lady's chamber, and tell her,
let her paint an inch thick, to this favor[5] she must come; make her
laugh at that. Prithee, Horatio, tell me one thing.   170
HORATIO: What's that, my lord?
HAMLET: Dost thou think Alexander looked o' this fashion i' the earth?
HORATIO: E'en so.
HAMLET: And smelt so? pah!
    [*Puts down the skull.*]
HORATIO: E'en so, my lord.   175
HAMLET: To what base uses we may return, Horatio! Why may not
    imagination trace the noble dust of Alexander, till he find it stop-
    ping a bung-hole?
HORATIO: 'Twere to consider too curiously, to consider so.
HAMLET: No, faith, not a jot; but to follow him thither with modesty   180
    enough[6] and likelihood to lead it: as thus: Alexander died, Alexan-
    der was buried, Alexander returneth into dust; the dust is earth; of
    earth we make loam; and why of that loam, whereto he was con-
    verted, might they not stop a beer-barrel?
        Imperious Caesar, dead and turned to clay,   185
        Might stop a hole to keep the wind away:
        O, that that earth, which kept the world in awe,
        Should patch a wall to expel the winter's flaw!
    But soft! but soft! aside: here comes the king.
        [*Enter* PRIESTS &c, *in procession; the Corpse of Ophelia,* LAERTES *and*
        MOURNERS *following;* KING, QUEEN, *their trains,* &c.]
    The queen, the courtiers: who is this they follow?   190
    And with such maimèd rites?[7] This doth betoken
    The corse they follow did with desperate hand
    Fordo its own life: 'twas of some estate.[8]
    Couch we awhile, and mark.
        [*Retiring with* HORATIO.]
LAERTES: What ceremony else?   195
HAMLET: That is Laertes, a very noble youth: mark.
LAERTES: What ceremony else?
FIRST PRIEST: Her obsequies have been as far enlarged
    As we have warranty: her death was doubtful;
    And, but that great command o'ersways the order[9]   200
    She should in ground unsanctified have lodged

4. The lower jaw fallen down, hence dejected.   5. Appearance.   6. Without exaggeration.
7. Incomplete, mutilated ritual.   8. Rank. *Fordo:* Destroy.   9. The king's command prevails against
ordinary rules. *Doubtful:* Of uncertain cause (i.e., accident or suicide).

Till the last trumpet; for[1] charitable prayers,
Shards, flints and pebbles should be thrown on her:
Yet here she is allowed her virgin crants,
Her maiden strewments and the bringing home[2]   205
Of bell and burial.

LAERTES: Must there no more be done?

FIRST PRIEST: No more be done:
We should profane the service of the dead
To sing a requiem and such rest to her
As to peace-parted souls.

LAERTES: Lay her i' the earth: 210
And from her fair and unpolluted flesh
May violets spring! I tell thee, churlish priest,
A ministering angel shall my sister be,
When thou liest howling.

HAMLET: What, the fair Ophelia!

QUEEN: [Scattering flowers.] Sweets to the sweet: farewell!   215
I hoped thou shouldst have been my Hamlet's wife;
I thought thy bride-bed to have decked, sweet maid,
And not have strewed thy grave.

LAERTES: O, treble woe
Fall ten times treble on that cursed head
Whose wicked deed thy most ingenious sense   220
Deprived thee of! Hold off the earth a while,
Till I have caught her once more in mine arms.
    [Leaps into the grave.]
Now pile your dust upon the quick and dead,
Till of this flat a mountain you have made
To o'ertop old Pelion[3] or the skyish head   225
Of blue Olympus.

HAMLET: [Advancing.] What is he whose grief
Bears such an emphasis? whose phrase of sorrow
Conjures the wandering stars and makes them stand
Like wonder-wounded hearers? This is I,   230
Hamlet the Dane.
    [Leaps into the grave.]

LAERTES: The devil take thy soul!
    [Grappling with him.]

HAMLET: Thou pray'st not well.
I prithee, take thy fingers from my throat;
For, though I am not splenitive[4] and rash,
Yet have I in me something dangerous,   235
Which let thy wisdom fear. Hold off thy hand.

1. Instead of. 2. Laying to rest. *Crants*: Garland. *Strewments*: Strewing of the grave with flowers.
3. The mountain upon which the Aloadae, two rebellious giants in Greek mythology, piled up Mount
Ossa in their attempt to reach Olympus. 4. Easily moved to anger.

KING: Pluck them asunder.
QUEEN: Hamlet, Hamlet!
ALL: Gentlemen,—
HORATIO: Good my lord, be quiet.
   [*The* ATTENDANTS *part them, and they come out of the grave.*]
HAMLET: Why, I will fight with him upon this theme
   Until my eyelids will no longer wag.   240
QUEEN: O my son, what theme?
HAMLET: I loved Ophelia: forty thousand brothers
   Could not, with all their quantity of love,
   Make up my sum. What wilt thou do for her?
KING: O, he is mad, Laertes.   245
QUEEN: For love of God, forbear him.
HAMLET: 'Swounds, show me what thou 'lt do:
   Woo't weep? woo't fight? woo't fast? woo't tear thyself?
   Woo't drink up eisel?[5] eat a crocodile?
   I'll do't. Dost thou come here to whine?   250
   To outface me with leaping in her grave?
   Be buried quick with her, and so will I:
   And, if thou prate of mountains, let them throw
   Millions of acres on us, till our ground,
   Singeing his pate against the burning zone,   255
   Make Ossa like a wart! Nay, an thou 'lt mouth,
   I'll rant as well as thou.
QUEEN: This is mere madness:
   And thus a while the fit will work on him;
   Anon, as patient as the female dove
   When that her golden couplets are disclosed,[6]   260
   His silence will sit drooping.
HAMLET: Hear you, sir;
   What is the reason that you use me thus?
   I loved you ever: but it is no matter;
   Let Hercules himself do what he may,
   The cat will mew, and dog will have his day.   265
   [*Exit.*]
KING: I pray thee, good Horatio, wait upon him.
   [*Exit* HORATIO.]
   [*To* LAERTES.] Strengthen your patience in our last night's speech;
   We'll put the matter to the present push.[7]
   Good Gertrude, set some watch over your son.
   This grave shall have a living monument: 270
   An hour of quiet shortly shall we see;
   Till then, in patience our proceeding be.
   [*Exeunt.*]

5. Vinegar (the bitter drink given to Christ). Woo't: Wilt thou.   6. Twins are hatched.   7. We will push the matter on immediately.

SCENE 2—*A hall in the castle.*

[*Enter* HAMLET *and* HORATIO.]

HAMLET: So much for this, sir: now shall you see the other;
    You do remember all the circumstance?
HORATIO: Remember it, my lord?
HAMLET: Sir, in my heart there was a kind of fighting,
    That would not let me sleep: methought I lay   5
    Worse than the mutines in the bilboes.[8] Rashly,
    And praised be rashness for it, let us know,
    Our indiscretion sometime serves us well
    When our deep plots do pall;[9] and that should learn us
    There's a divinity that shapes our ends,   10
    Rough-hew them how we will.
HORATIO: That is most certain.
HAMLET: Up from my cabin,
    My sea-gown scarfed about me, in the dark
    Groped I to find out them; had my desire,
    Fingered their packet, and in fine withdrew   15
    To mine own room again; making so bold,
    My fears forgetting manners, to unseal
    Their grand commission; where I found, Horatio,—
    O royal knavery!—an exact command,
    Larded with many several sorts of reasons,   20
    Importing[1] Denmark's health and England's too,
    With, ho! such bugs and goblins in my life,
    That, on the supervise, no leisure bated,[2]
    No, not to stay the grinding of the axe,
    My head should be struck off.
HORATIO: Is't possible?   25
HAMLET: Here's the commission: read it at more leisure.
    But wilt thou hear now how I did proceed?
HORATIO: I beseech you.
HAMLET: Being thus be-netted round with villainies,—
    Ere I could make a prologue to my brains,   30
    They had begun the play,—I sat me down;
    Devised a new commission; wrote it fair:
    I once did hold it, as our statists[3] do,
    A baseness to write fair, and labored much
    How to forget that learning; but, sir, now   35
    It did me yeoman's service:[4] wilt thou know
    The effect of what I wrote?
HORATIO: Aye, good my lord.
HAMLET: An earnest conjuration from the king,

---

8. Mutineers in iron fetters.   9. Become useless.   1. Concerning.   2. As soon as the message was read, with no time subtracted for leisure. *Bugs:* Imaginary horrors to be expected if I lived. 3. Statesmen.   4. Excellent service.

As England was his faithful tributary,
As love between them like the palm might flourish,   40
As peace should still her wheaten garland wear
And stand a comma[5] 'tween their amities,
And many such-like 'As'es[6] of great charge,
That, on the view and knowing of these contents,
Without debatement further, more or less,   45
He should the bearers put to sudden death,
Not shriving-time[7] allowed.
HORATIO: How was this sealed?
HAMLET: Why, even in that was heaven ordinant.[8]
I had my father's signet in my purse,
Which was the model of that Danish seal: 50
Folded the writ up in the form of the other;
Subscribed it; gave 't the impression;[9] placed it safely,
The changeling never known. Now, the next day
Was our sea-fight; and what to this was sequent
Thou know'st already.   55
HORATIO: So Guildenstern and Rosencrantz go to 't.
HAMLET: Why, man, they did make love to this employment;
They are not near my conscience; their defeat
Does by their own insinuation[1] grow:
'Tis dangerous when the baser nature comes   60
Between the pass and fell[2]-incensèd points
Of mighty opposites.
HORATIO: Why, what a king is this!
HAMLET: Does it not, think'st thee, stand me now upon[3]—
He that hath killed my king, and whored my mother;
Popped in between the election and my hopes;   65
Thrown out his angle for my proper life,[4]
And with such cozenage—is't not perfect conscience,
To quit[5] him with this arm? and is't not to be damned,
To let this canker of our nature come
In further evil?   70
HORATIO: It must be shortly known to him from England
What is the issue of the business there.
HAMLET: It will be short: the interim is mine;
And a man's life's no more than to say 'One.'
But I am very sorry, good Horatio,   75
That to Laertes I forgot myself;
For, by the image of my cause, I see
The portraiture of his: I'll court his favors:
But, sure, the bravery[6] of his grief did put me

---

5. Connecting element.   6. A pun on "as" and "ass," which extends to the following *of great charge*, signifying both "moral weight," and "ass's burden."   7. Time for confession and absolution.   8. Ordaining.   9. Of the seal.   1. Meddling. *Defeat:* Destruction.   2. Fiercely. *Pass:* Thrust. *Baser:* Lower in rank than the king and Prince Hamlet.   3. Is it not my duty now?   4. Angling line for my own life.   5. Pay back.   6. Ostentation, bravado.

Into a towering passion.

HORATIO: Peace! who comes here? 80

[*Enter* OSRIC.]

OSRIC: Your lordship is right welcome back to Denmark.

HAMLET: I humbly thank you, sir. Dost know this waterfly?

HORATIO: No, my good lord.

HAMLET: Thy state is the more gracious, for 'tis a vice to know him.
He hath much land, and fertile: let a beast be lord of beasts, and 85
his crib shall stand at the king's mess: 'tis a chough,[7] but, as I say,
spacious in the possession of dirt.

OSRIC: Sweet lord, if your lordship were at leisure, I should impart a
thing to you from his majesty.

HAMLET: I will receive it, sir, with all diligence of spirit. Put your 90
bonnet to his right use; 'tis for the head.

OSRIC: I thank your lordship, it is very hot.

HAMLET: No, believe me, 'tis very cold; the wind is northerly.

OSRIC: It is indifferent[8] cold, my lord, indeed.

HAMLET: But yet methinks it is very sultry and hot, or my complex- 95
ion—

OSRIC: Exceedingly, my lord; it is very sultry, as 'twere,—I cannot tell
how. But, my lord, his majesty bade me signify to you that he has
laid a great wager on your head: sir, this is the matter—

HAMLET: I beseech you, remember— 100

[HAMLET *moves him to put on his hat.*]

OSRIC: Nay, good my lord; for mine ease, in good faith. Sir, here is
newly come to court Laertes; believe me, an absolute gentleman,
full of most excellent differences, of very soft society and great
showing:[9] indeed, to speak feelingly of him, he is the card or calendar of gentry, for you shall find in him the continent[1] of what part 105
a gentleman would see.

HAMLET: Sir, his definement suffers no perdition[2] in you; though, I
know, to divide him inventorially would dizzy the arithmetic[3] of
memory, and yet but yaw neither,[4] in respect of his quick sail. But
in the verity of extolment,[5] I take him to be a soul of great article, 110
and his infusion of such dearth and rareness, as, to make true diction of him, his semblable is his mirror, and who else would trace
him, his umbrage,[6] nothing more.

OSRIC: Your lordship speaks most infallibly of him.

HAMLET: The concernancy, sir? why do we wrap the gentleman[7] in 115
our more rawer breath?

7. Jackdaw. *Mess:* Table.　8. Fairly.　9. Agreeable company, and handsome in appearance. *Differences:* Distinctions.　1. Container. *Card or calendar of gentry:* Chart and model of gentlemanly manners. *What part:* Whatever quality.　2. Loss. *Definement:* Definition.　3. Arithmetical power.
Inventorially: Make an inventory of his virtues.　4. And yet would only be able to steer unsteadily
(unable to catch up with the "sail" of Laertes's virtues).　5. To prize Laertes truthfully. *Article:* Importance. *Infusion:* The virtues fused into him.　6. Keep pace with him, his shadow.　7. Laertes. *Concernancy:* Meaning.

OSRIC: Sir?

HORATIO: Is 't not possible to understand in another tongue?[8] You will do 't, sir, really.

HAMLET: What imports the nomination of this gentleman? 120

OSRIC: Of Laertes?

HORATIO: His purse is empty already; all's golden words are spent.

HAMLET: Of him, sir.

OSRIC: I know you are not ignorant—

HAMLET: I would you did, sir; yet, in faith, if you did, it would not 125 much approve me.[9] Well, sir?

OSRIC: You are not ignorant of what excellence Laertes is—

HAMLET: I dare not confess that, lest I should compare with him in excellence; but, to know a man well, were to know himself.[1]

OSRIC: I mean, sir, for his weapon; but in the imputation laid on him 130 by them, in his meed he's unfellowed.[2]

HAMLET: What's his weapon?

OSRIC: Rapier and dagger.

HAMLET: That's two of his weapons: but, well.

OSRIC: The king, sir, hath wagered with him six Barbary horses: against 135 the which he has imponed, as I take it, six French rapiers and poniards, with their assigns,[3] as girdle, hanger, and so: three of the carriages, in faith, are very dear to fancy, very responsive[4] to the hilts, most delicate carriages, and of very liberal conceit.[5]

HAMLET: What call you the carriages? 140

HORATIO: I knew you must be edified by the margent[6] ere you had done.

OSRIC: The carriages, sir, are the hangers.

HAMLET: The phrase would be more germane to the matter if we could carry a cannon by our sides:[7] I would it might be hangers till then. 145 But, on: six Barbary horses against six French swords, their assigns, and three liberal-conceited carriages; that's the French bet against the Danish. Why is this 'imponed,' as you call it?

OSRIC: The king, sir, hath laid, sir, that in a dozen passes between yourself and him, he shall not exceed you three hits: he hath laid 150 on twelve for nine; and it would come to immediate trial, if your lordship would vouchsafe the answer.[8]

HAMLET: How if I answer 'no'?

OSRIC: I mean, my lord, the opposition of your person in trial.

HAMLET: Sir, I will walk here in the hall: if it please his majesty, it is 155 the breathing time[9] of day with me; let the foils be brought, the

8. In a less affected jargon; or, in the same jargon when spoken by another (i.e., Hamlet's) tongue. 9. Be to my credit. 1. To know others one has to know oneself. 2. In the reputation given him by his weapons, his merit is unparalleled. 3. Appendages. *Imponed:* Wagered. 4. Corresponding, closely matched. *Carriages:* Ornamented straps by which the rapiers hung from the belt. *Very dear to fancy:* Agreeable to the taste. 5. Elegant design. 6. Instructed by the marginal note. 7. Hamlet is playfully criticizing Osric's affected application of the term "carriage," more properly used to mean "gun carriage." 8. The terms of this wager have never been satisfactorily clarified. 9. Time for exercise.

gentleman willing, and the king hold his purpose, I will win for him an I can; if not, I will gain nothing but my shame and the odd hits.

OSRIC: Shall I redeliver you e'en so?[1]   160

HAMLET: To this effect, sir, after what flourish your nature will.

OSRIC: I commend my duty to your lordship.

HAMLET: Yours, yours. [*Exit* OSRIC.] He does well to commend it himself; there are no tongues else for's turn.

HORATIO: This lapwing[2] runs away with the shell on his head.   165

HAMLET: He did comply[3] with his dug before he sucked it. Thus has he—and many more of the same breed that I know the drossy[4] age dotes on—only got the tune of the time and outward habit of encounter; a kind of yesty collection, which carries them through and through the most fond and winnowed opinions;[5] and do but   170 blow them to their trial, the bubbles are out.

[*Enter a* LORD.]

LORD: My lord, his majesty commended him[6] to you by young Osric, who brings back to him, that you attend him in the hall: he sends to know if your pleasure hold to play with Laertes, or that you will take longer time.   175

HAMLET: I am constant to my purposes; they follow the king's pleasure: if his fitness speaks, mine is ready; now or whensoever, provided I be so able as now.

LORD: The king and queen and all are coming down.

HAMLET: In happy time.   180

LORD: The queen desires you to use some gentle entertainment[7] to Laertes before you fall to play.

HAMLET: She well instructs me.

[*Exit* LORD.]

HORATIO: You will lose this wager, my lord.

HAMLET: I do not think so; since he went into France, I have been in   185 continual practice; I shall win at the odds. But thou wouldst not think how ill all's here about my heart: but it is no matter.

HORATIO: Nay, good my lord,—

HAMLET: It is but foolery; but it is such a kind of gaingiving[8] as would perhaps trouble a woman.   190

HORATIO: If your mind dislike anything, obey it. I will forestall their repair[9] hither, and say you are not fit.

HAMLET: Not a whit; we defy augury: there is special providence in the fall of a sparrow. If it be now, 'tis not to come; if it be not to come, it will be now; if it be not now, yet it will come: the readiness is all;   195 since no man has aught of what he leaves, what is't to leave betimes?[1] Let be.

---

1. Is that the reply you want me to carry back?   2. A bird supposedly able to run as soon as it is out of its shell.   3. Use ceremony.   4. Degenerate. *Yesty:* Frothy.   5. Makes them pass the test of the most refined judgment.   6. Sent his regards.   7. Kind word of greeting.   8. Misgiving. 9. Coming.   1. What is wrong with dying early (leaving "betimes") since man knows nothing of life ("what he leaves")?

[*Enter* KING, QUEEN, LAERTES, *and* LORDS, OSRIC *and other* ATTEN-
DANTS *with foils and gauntlets; a table and flagons of wine on it.*]
KING: Come, Hamlet, come, and take this hand from me.
    [*The* KING *puts* LAERTES' *hand into* HAMLET'*s.*]
HAMLET: Give me your pardon, sir: I've done you wrong;
    But pardon't, as you are a gentleman.   200
    This presence[2] knows,
    And you must needs have heard, how I am punished
    With sore distraction. What I have done,
    That might your nature, honor and exception[3]
    Roughly awake, I here proclaim was madness.   205
    Was't Hamlet wronged Laertes? Never Hamlet:
    If Hamlet from himself be ta'en away,
    And when he's not himself does wrong Laertes,
    Then Hamlet does it not, Hamlet denies it.
    Who does it then? His madness: if't be so,   210
    Hamlet is of the faction that is wronged;
    His madness is poor Hamlet's enemy.
    Sir, in this audience,
    Let my disclaiming from a purposed evil
    Free me so far in your most generous thoughts,   215
    That I have shot mine arrow o'er the house,
    And hurt my brother.
LAERTES: I am satisfied in nature,
    Whose motive, in this case, should stir me most
    To my revenge: but in my terms of honor[4]
    I stand aloof, and will no reconcilement,   220
    Till by some elder masters of known honor
    I have a voice and precedent[5] of peace,
    To keep my name ungored.[6] But till that time
    I do receive your offered love like love
    And will not wrong it.
HAMLET: I embrace it freely,   225
    And will this brother's wager frankly play.
    Give us the foils. Come on.
LAERTES: Come, one for me.
HAMLET: I'll be your foil,[7] Laertes: in mine ignorance
    Your skill shall, like a star i' the darkest night,
    Stick fiery off[8] indeed.
LAERTES: You mock me, sir.   230
HAMLET: No, by this hand.
KING: Give them the foils, young Osric. Cousin Hamlet,
    You know the wager?

2. Audience.   3. Objection.   4. Laertes answers separately each of the two points brought up by
Hamlet in line 86; "nature" is Laertes's natural feeling toward his father, and "honor" the code of honor
with its conventional rules.   5. Competent opinion based on precedent.   6. Unwounded.   7. A
pun, since the word means both "rapier" and "a thing which sets off another to advantage" (as gold leaf
under a jewel).   8. Stand out brilliantly.

HAMLET: Very well, my lord;
  Your grace has laid the odds o' the weaker side.
KING: I do not fear it; I have seen you both: 235
  But since he is bettered, we have therefore odds.
LAERTES: This is too heavy; let me see another.
HAMLET: This likes me well. These foils have all a length?
  [*They prepare to play.*]
OSRIC: Aye, my good lord.
KING: Set me the stoups⁹ of wine upon that table.   240
  If Hamlet give the first or second hit,
  Or quit in answer of the third exchange,¹
  Let all the battlements their ordnance fire;
  The king shall drink to Hamlet's better breath;
  And in the cup an union² shall he throw,   245
  Richer than that which four successive kings
  In Denmark's crown have worn. Give me the cups;
  And let the kettle³ to the trumpet speak,
  The trumpet to the cannoneer without,
  The cannons to the heavens, the heaven to earth,   250
  'Now the king drinks to Hamlet.' Come, begin;
  And you, the judges, bear a wary eye.
HAMLET: Come on, sir.
LAERTES: Come, my lord.
  [*They play.*]
HAMLET: One.
LAERTES: No.
HAMLET: Judgment.
OSRIC: A hit, a very palpable hit.
LAERTES: Well; again.
KING: Stay; give me drink. Hamlet, this pearl is thine;   255
  Here's to thy health.
  [*Trumpets sound, and cannon shot off within.*]
                          Give him the cup.
HAMLET: I'll play this bout first; set it by awhile.
  Come. [*They play.*] Another hit; what say you?
LAERTES: A touch, a touch, I do confess.
KING: Our son shall win.
QUEEN: He's fat⁴ and scant of breath.   260
  Here, Hamlet, take my napkin,⁵ rub thy brows:
  The queen carouses to thy fortune, Hamlet.
HAMLET: Good madam!
KING: Gertrude, do not drink.
QUEEN: I will, my lord; I pray you, pardon me.
KING: [*Aside.*] It is the poisoned cup; it is too late.   265
QUEEN: Come, let me wipe thy face.

9. Cups.   1. Requite, or repay (by scoring a hit) on the third bout.   2. A large pearl.
3. Kettledrum.   4. Sweaty, or soft, because out of training.   5. Handkerchief.

LAERTES: My lord, I'll hit him now.

KING: I do not think't.

LAERTES: [*Aside.*] And yet it is almost against my conscience.

HAMLET: Come, for the third, Laertes: you but dally;
I pray you, pass with your best violence;   270
I am afeard you make a wanton[6] of me.

LAERTES: Say you so? come on.
[*They play.*]

OSRIC: Nothing, neither way.

LAERTES: Have at you now!
[LAERTES *wounds* HAMLET; *then, in scuffling, they change rapiers,
and* HAMLET *wounds* LAERTES.]

KING: Part them; they are incensed.

HAMLET: Nay, come, again.
[*The* QUEEN *falls.*]

OSRIC: Look to the queen there, ho!   275

HORATIO: They bleed on both sides. How is it, my lord?

OSRIC: How is't, Laertes?

LAERTES: Why, as a woodcock to mine own springe,[7] Osric;
I am justly killed with mine own treachery.

HAMLET: How does the queen?   280

KING: She swounds to see them bleed.

QUEEN: No, no, the drink, the drink,—O my dear Hamlet,—
The drink, the drink! I am poisoned.
[*Dies.*]

HAMLET: O villainy! Ho! let the door be locked:
Treachery! seek it out.   285
[LAERTES *falls.*]

LAERTES: It is here, Hamlet: Hamlet, thou art slain;
No medicine in the world can do thee good,
In thee there is not half an hour of life;
The treacherous instrument is in thy hand,
Unbated and envenomed: the foul practice[8]   290
Hath turned itself on me; lo, here I lie,
Never to rise again: thy mother's poisoned:
I can no more: the king, the king's to blame.

HAMLET: The point envenomed too!   295
Then, venom, to thy work.
[*Stabs the* KING.]

ALL: Treason! treason!

KING: O, yet defend me, friends; I am but hurt.

HAMLET: Here, thou incestuous, murderous, damnèd Dane,
Drink off this potion: is thy union here?
Follow my mother.
[KING *dies.*]

6. Weakling, spoiled child.   7. Snare.   8. Plot.

LAERTES: He is justly served;   300
  It is a poison tempered[9] by himself.
  Exchange forgiveness with me, noble Hamlet:
  Mine and my father's death come not upon thee,
  Nor thine on me!
  [*Dies.*]
HAMLET: Heaven make thee free of it! I follow thee.   305
  I am dead, Horatio. Wretched queen, adieu!
  You that look pale and tremble at this chance,
  That are but mutes or audience to this act,
  Had I but time—as this fell sergeant, death,
  Is strict in his arrest—O, I could tell you—   310
  But let it be. Horatio, I am dead;
  Thou livest; report me and my cause aright
  To the unsatisfied.
HORATIO: Never believe it:
  I am more an antique Roman than a Dane:
  Here's yet some liquor left.
HAMLET: As thou'rt a man,   315
  Give me the cup: let go; by heaven, I'll have 't.
  O good Horatio, what a wounded name,
  Things standing thus unknown, shall live behind me!
  If thou didst ever hold me in thy heart,
  Absent thee from felicity a while,   320
  And in this harsh world draw thy breath in pain,
  To tell my story.
  [*March afar off, and shot within.*]
                   What warlike noise is this?
OSRIC: Young Fortinbras, with conquest come from Poland,
  To the ambassadors of England gives
  This warlike volley.
HAMLET: O, I die, Horatio;   325
  The potent poison quite o'er-crows[1] my spirit:
  I cannot live to hear the news from England;
  But I do prophesy the election lights
  On Fortinbras: he has my dying voice;
  So tell him, with the occurrents, more and less,   330
  Which have solicited.[2] The rest is silence.
  [*Dies.*]
HORATIO: Now cracks a noble heart. Good night sweet prince,
  And flights of angels sing thee to thy rest;
  [*March within.*]
  Why does the drum come hither?   215
  [*Enter* FORTINBRAS, *and the* ENGLISH AMBASSADORS, *with drum, colors, and* ATTENDANTS.]

9. Compounded.   1. Overcomes.   2. Which have brought all this about. *Occurrents:* Occurrences.

FORTINBRAS: Where is this sight?

HORATIO: What is it you would see?   335
  If aught of woe or wonder, cease your search.

FORTINBRAS: This quarry cries on havoc.[3] O proud death,
  What feast is toward[4] in thine eternal cell,
  That thou so many princes at a shot
  So bloodily hast struck?

FIRST AMBASSADOR: The sight is dismal;   340
  And our affairs from England come too late:
  The ears are senseless that should give us hearing,
  To tell him his commandment is fulfilled,
  That Rosencrantz and Guildenstern are dead:
  Where should we have our thanks?

HORATIO: Not from his mouth   345
  Had it the ability of life to thank you:
  He never gave commandment for their death.
  But since, so jump upon[5] this bloody question,
  You from the Polack wars, and you from England
  Are here arrived, give order that these bodies   350
  High on a stage be placèd to the view;
  And let me speak to the yet unknowing world
  How these things came about; so shall you hear
  Of carnal, bloody and unnatural acts,
  Of accidental judgments, casual slaughters,   355
  Of deaths put on[6] by cunning and forced cause,
  And, in this upshot, purposes mistook
  Fall'n on the inventors' heads: all this can I
  Truly deliver.

FORTINBRAS: Let us haste to hear it,
  And call the noblest to the audience.   360
  For me, with sorrow I embrace my fortune:
  I have some rights of memory[7] in this kingdom,
  Which now to claim my vantage doth invite me.

HORATIO: Of that I shall have also cause to speak,
  And from his mouth whose voice will draw on more[8]:   365
  But let this same be presently performed,
  Even while men's minds are wild; lest more mischance
  On[9] plots and errors happen.

FORTINBRAS: Let four captains
  Bear Hamlet, like a soldier, to the stage;   370
  For he was likely, had he been put on,[1]
  To have proved most royal: and, for his passage,[2]
  The soldiers' music and the rites of war
  Speak loudly for him.

---

3. This heap of corpses proclaims a carnage.   4. Imminent.   5. So immediately upon.   6. Prompted.
Casual: Chance.   7. Still remembered. *Vantage:* Advantageous position, opportunity.   8. More
voices.   9. Following on.   1. Tried (as a king).   2. Death.

Take up the bodies: such a sight as this   375
Becomes the field, but here shows much amiss.
Go, bid the soldiers shoot.

[*A dead march. Exeunt, bearing off the bodies: after which a peal of ordnance is shot off.*]

JOHN DONNE
1572–1631

John Donne was born in London in 1572 in a Catholic family and attended Oxford, Cambridge, and Lincoln's Inn (law school) without obtaining degrees or becoming a lawyer. His intellectual energy, his voracious reading, his wide traveling (including expeditions to Cadiz and to the Azores with Raleigh and Essex) all helped to prepare him for a brilliant career at court. In 1598 he was appointed private secretary to the Lord Keeper, Sir Thomas Egerton; but a couple of years later he destroyed his prospects of advancement by secretly marrying Ann More, the sixteen-year-old niece of Lady Egerton. When, after long inner debate, Donne left the Catholic Church and joined the Church of England, his decision bore no trace of opportunism. In 1615 he took sacred orders and was appointed Dean of St. Paul's in 1621. He died in 1631 a few weeks after having preached what is known as his own death sermon. His collected *Songs and Sonnets* were first published two years after his death.

The revaluation of Donne's poetry has been one of the crucial experiences in the history of poetic taste in our century. And there seems to be no doubt that his place among the most effective and original poets in any language is now firmly assured. The main reasons for this can be summarized under two general headings: the poet's tone of voice, the feeling of lively, vibrantly "spoken" language; and the use of varied, startling situations and images, especially in the sense that elements supposedly belonging to diverse areas of knowledge and sensibility are combined, with the result of stirring imagination and reason, senses and mind.

In our present context, briefly trying to elaborate on those two aspects of Donne's genius, we can see that they fit quite well within some of the definitions of the Renaissance that we have been using. If we say that Donne gathers images and situations from many different areas of knowledge and human experience—which in Donne's case, as we have indicated, were of extraordinary breadth and variety—our emphasis is not on the scattered diversity of his objects and themes, but on his effectiveness in combining them; his startling associations are his way of encompassing large segments of that knowledge and experience, and of giving them poetic shape and impact. So Donne's poetic voice is that of an individual who has absorbed with intelligence and gusto the culture of a time of great historical and psychological upheaval and of equally great intellectual achievement.

His mode of expression, his poetic manner, is correspondingly varied and authoritative. In Donne at his best, we first of all find the famous, irresistible openings—"I wonder, by my troth, what thou and I/Did, till we loved"; "For God's sake hold your tongue, and let me love"; "Death, be not proud, though some have callèd thee/Mighty and dreadful"—and then the characteristic developments, unpredictable yet logical, studded with images that for all their seeming oddity will prove wholly functional. For instance, in the opening of his song, "Go and catch a falling star," he uses six different images, all of them appropriate and interesting, to express the idea of impossibility. But this is no mere display of bravura and wit; it is a cultivated, incisive, and attractive way of making a point.

Indeed, behind the speaking voice of Donne's best poems we can easily imagine a character in a drama, convincingly and imaginatively addressing his interlocutors. To do so he draws from such diverse sources as theology, myth, the sciences, folklore, geography, war, court litigation. Donne studied the law, traveled quite extensively, was a man of the world who experienced the beginnings of a courtier's career with its implications of intellectual brilliance and sensual pleasures; his daring secret marriage to an aristocratic woman, though socially and professionally ruinous to him, was based on deep, lasting, fully requited love; and of course he ended his life on the pulpit as one of the most powerful orators of all time. The situations, the language, the metaphors of his worldly and sacred poems are rooted in experience and are perfectly plausible in his human and cultural circumstances; he is eminently fit to use them as instruments of his rhetoric—the rhetoric of someone very much alive in an age of discovery and controversy, of ever widening physical and intellectual perspectives.

Donne's method of conciliating disparate objects and concepts to make important points about the human condition applies to his worldly as well as to his religious poems. In fact, a distinction between the two types seems irrelevant on that score. As our selections will indicate, the same poetic and intellectual vigor is found in the first category—where the major theme is love—as in the second— where the main themes are death and resurrection. The effectiveness of both depends on love and death never being handled as abstractions but as events contemplated and discussed anew against the background of concrete human reality, tested against the variety of experience. Random examples—the lovers in "The Canonization": "Soldiers find wars, and lawyers find out still/Litigious men, which quarrels move,/ Though she and I do love"; or the dead in Holy Sonnet 7: "All whom war, dearth, age, agues, tyrannies/Despair, law, chance hath slain . . ."

In poems such as "The Good-Morrow" or "The Canonization" the idea of lovers discovering in their intimacy and in their exchange of looks the universal and the eternal—a situation that in itself is potentially a cliché—is wholly renovated through the poet's vision and skill. Holy Sonnets 7 and 10—undoubtedly two of the most beautiful devotional poems in world literature—perform a similar operation on the orthodox idea of death as awakening to eternal life. In both cases the poet is a believer whose faith is poetically (i.e., intelligently) realized, expressed, and made perceptible.

R. C. Bald, *John Donne. A Life* (1970), gives the general reader a thorough biography; more advanced students will find a detailed stylistic study of Donne's poetry and prose in Astley Cooper Partridge, *John Donne. Language and Style* (1978). Helpful studies of Donne include Peter Amadeus Fiore, ed., *Just So Much Honor: Essays Commemorating the Four-Hundredth Anniversary of the Birth of John Donne* (1972), William Zunder, *The Poetry of John Donne: Literature and Culture in the Elizabethan and Jacobean Period* (1982), and Helen Gardner, ed., *John Donne: A Collection of Critical Essays* (1962). C.A. Patrides, ed., *The Complete English Poems of John Donne* (1985), contains good biographical material, criticism, and an annotated bibliography.

The Good-Morrow

I wonder, by my troth, what thou and I
Did, till we loved? Were we not weaned till then,
But sucked on country pleasures, childishly?
Or snorted we in the seven sleepers' den?[1]
'Twas so; but[2] this, all pleasures fancies be.   5
If ever any beauty I did see,
Which I desired, and got, 'twas but a dream of thee.

And now good morrow to our waking souls,
Which watch not one another out of fear;
For love all love of other sights controls,   10
And makes one little room an everywhere.
Let sea-discoverers to new worlds have gone,
Let maps to others,[3] worlds on worlds have shown
Let us possess one world; each hath one, and is one.

My face in thine eye, thine in mine appears,   15
And true plain hearts do in the faces rest;
Where can we find two better hemispheres
Without sharp North, without declining West?
Whatever dies was not mixed equally;[4]
If our two loves be one, or thou and I   20
Love so alike that none do slacken, none can die.

Song

Go and catch a falling star,
     Get with child a mandrake root,
Tell me where all past years are,
     Or who cleft the Devil's foot,
Teach me to hear mermaids singing,   5
Or to keep off envy's stinging,
         And find
         What wind
Serves to advance an honest mind.

If thou beest born to strange sights,   10
     Things invisible to see,
Ride ten thousand days and nights,
     Till age snow white hairs on thee,
Thou, when thou return'st, wilt tell me

---

1. Both Christian and Mohammedan authors recite the legend of seven youths of Ephesus, who hid in a cave from the persecutions of Decius, and slept there for 187 years.   2. Except.   3. I.e., let us concede that maps to other investigators have shown, etc. ("other" is an archaic plural form).   4. Scholastic philosophy taught that when the elements were imperfectly ("not equally") mixed, matter was mortal and mutable; but when they were perfectly mixed, it was undying and unchanging.

All strange wonders that befell thee,   15
　　　And swear
　　　No where
Lives a woman true, and fair.

If thou find'st one, let me know,
　　　Such a pilgrimage were sweet;   20
Yet do not, I would not go,
　　　Though at next door we might meet;
Though she were true when you met her,
And last till you write your letter,
　　　Yet she   25
　　　Will be
False, ere I come, to two, or three.

The Indifferent

I can love both fair and brown,[5]
Her whom abundance melts, and her whom want betrays,
Her who loves loneness best, and her who masks and plays,
Her whom the country formed, and whom the town,
Her who believes, and her who tries,   5
Her who still weeps with spongy eyes,
And her who is dry cork, and never cries;
I can love her, and her, and you, and you,
I can love any, so she be not true.

Will no other vice content you?   10
Will it not serve your turn to do as did your mothers?
Or have you all old vices spent, and now would find out others?
Or doth a fear that men are true torment you?
O we are not, be not you so;
Let me, and do you, twenty know.   15
Rob me, but bind me not, and let me go.
Must I, who came to travail thorough you[6]
Grow your fixed subject, because you are true?

Venus heard me sigh this song,
And by love's sweetest part, variety, she swore,   20
She heard not this till now; and that it should be so no more.
She went, examined, and returned ere long,
And said, Alas, some two or three
Poor heretics in love there be,
Which think to 'stablish dangerous constancy.   25
But I have told them, Since you will be true,
You shall be true to them who are false to you.

---

5. Both blonde and brunette.   6. Through.

The Canonization

For God's sake hold your tongue, and let me love,
    Or chide my palsy, or my gout,
My five gray hairs, or ruined fortune, flout,
    With wealth your state, your mind with arts improve,
        Take you a course,[7] get you a place,   5
        Observe[8] His Honor, or His Grace,
Or the King's real, or his stampèd face[9]
    Contemplate; what you will, approve,[1]
    So you will let me love.

Alas, alas, who's injured by my love?   10
    What merchant's ships have my sighs drowned?
Who says my tears have overflowed his ground?
    When did my colds a forward spring remove?
        When did the heats which my veins fill
        Add one man to the plaguy bill?[2]   15
Soldiers find wars, and lawyers find out still
    Litigious men, which quarrels move,
    Though she and I do love.

Call us what you will, we are made such by love;
    Call her one, me another fly,   20
We're tapers too, and at our own cost die,[3]
    And we in us find the eagle and the dove.[4]
        The phoenix riddle hath more wit
        By us: we two being one, are it.[5]
So, to one neutral thing both sexes fit.   25
    We die and rise the same, and prove
    Mysterious by this love.

We can die by it, if not live by love,
    And if unfit for tombs and hearse
Our legend be, it will be fit for verse;   30
    And if no piece of chronicle we prove,
        We'll build in sonnets pretty rooms;
        As well a well-wrought urn becomes
The greatest ashes, as half-acre tombs,
    And by these hymns, all shall approve   35
    Us canonized[6] for love:

And thus invoke us: You whom reverend love
    Made one another's hermitage;

7. A direction (for life). *Place*: An appointment, at court or elsewhere. 8. Pay court to. 9. On coins. 1. Try. 2. List of those dead from bubonic plague, always worst in summer. 3. Here and in lines 26 and 28 the sexual sense is relevant. 4. Representing meekness and purity, as the eagle represents strength and wisdom. 5. Like flies we burn up in the candle flame; like candles we are consumed as we burn; like the phoenix we are reborn from our ashes. (A fabulous Arabian bird, the phoenix was alleged to make its own pyre, die in song, and arise new.) 6. Made saints, whose aid other lovers will invoke.

You, to whom love was peace, that now is rage;
    Who did the whole world's soul contract, and drove   40
        Into the glasses of your eyes
        (So made such mirrors, and such spies,
That they did all to you epitomize)
    Countries, towns, courts: Beg from above
    A pattern of your love!   45

The Apparition

When by thy scorn, O murderess, I am dead,
    And that thou thinkst thee free
    From all solicitation from me,
Then shall my ghost come to thy bed,
And thee, feigned vestal, in worse arms shall see;   5
Then thy sick taper will begin to wink,
And he whose thou art then, being tired before,
Will, if thou stir, or pinch to wake him, think
    Thou call'st for more,
And in false sleep will from thee shrink,   10
And then, poor aspen[7] wretch, neglected thou
Bathed in a cold quicksilver sweat[8] wilt lie
    A verier ghost than I;
What I will say, I will not tell thee now,
Lest that preserve thee; and since my love is spent,   15
I had rather thou shouldst painfully repent,
Than by my threatenings rest still innocent.

The Funeral

Whoever comes to shroud me, do not harm
    Nor question much
That subtle wreath of hair which crowns my arm;
The mystery, the sign you must not touch,
    For 'tis my outward soul,   5
Viceroy to that, which then to heaven being gone,
    Will leave this to control,
And keep these limbs, her provinces, from dissolution.

For if the sinewy thread[9] my brain lets fall
    Through every part   10
Can tie those parts and make me one of all;
These hairs which upward grew, and strength and art
    Have from a better brain,

---

7. Aspen leaves flutter in the slightest breeze.   8. Sweating in terror; quicksilver (mercury) was a stock prescription for venereal disease.   9. Network of nerves.

Can better do it: except she meant that I
    By this should know my pain,   15
As prisoners then are manacled, when they're condemned to die.

Whate'er she meant by it, bury it with me,
    For since I am
Love's martyr, it might breed idolatry,
If into others' hands these relics came: 20
    As 'twas humility
To afford to it all that a soul can do,
    So 'tis some bravery,
That since you would save none of me, I bury some of you.

Holy Sonnets

7

At the round earth's imagined corners, blow
Your trumpets, angels;[1] and arise, arise
From death, you numberless infinities
Of souls, and to your scattered bodies go:
All whom the flood did, and fire shall, o'erthrow,   5
All whom war, dearth, age, agues, tyrannies,
Despair, law, chance hath slain, and you whose eyes
Shall behold God, and never taste death's woe.
But let them sleep, Lord, and me mourn a space;
For, if above all these, my sins abound,
'Tis late to ask abundance of Thy grace
When we are there. Here on this lowly ground,
Teach me how to repent; for that's as good
As if Thou hadst sealed my pardon with Thy blood.

10

Death, be not proud, though some have callèd thee
Mighty and dreadful, for thou art not so;
For those whom thou think'st thou dost overthrow
Die not, poor Death, nor yet canst thou kill me.
From rest and sleep, which but thy pictures be,   5
Much pleasure; then from thee much more must flow,
And soonest our best men with thee do go,
Rest of their bones, and soul's delivery.
Thou art slave to fate, chance, kings, and desperate men,
And dost with poison, war, and sickness dwell,   10
And poppy or charms can make us sleep as well
And better than thy stroke; why swell'st[2] thou then?

---

1. Donne may have been thinking of the angels on old maps, who blow their trumpets to the four points
of the compass. See also Revelation 7:1.   2. Puff up with pride.

One short sleep past, we wake eternally
And death shall be no more; Death, thou shalt die.

PEDRO CALDERÓN DE LA BARCA
1600–1681

By virture of his talents and of a longevity quite exceptional for his time, Pedro Calderón de la Barca had a remarkably varied career, primarily as a playwright and also as a courtier, soldier, and clergyman.

Born in Madrid on January 17, 1600, Calderón spent his early childhood at Valladolid, where the king and his court had then moved, his father being a secretary to the Council of the Treasury. It has been argued that the severity with which Calderón's father exercised his authority may be related to the themes of some of his son's plays, including his masterpiece, *Life Is a Dream*. Calderón studied from 1609 to 1614 at a Jesuit college, and later at the universities of Alcalá de Henares and Salamanca. His earliest known work was a result of his participation in 1620 in a poetic competition to celebrate the canonization of Saint Isidore; Lope de Vega, then the leading Spanish dramatist, was the principal judge. In the following year, Calderón and one of his brothers were accused of having killed a servant in the household of the Duke of Frias and both were fined. Calderón's first play, *Love, Honor, and Power*, was performed at the royal palace in 1623. Between 1623 and 1625 he may have served in the army in Italy or in Flanders; in 1626 he was again in Madrid. King Philip IV had assembled around the court a small number of playwrights, and Calderón soon became the most prominent among them. His plays were widely performed not only at court, but also in the public theaters. In 1635, when Lope de Vega died, Calderón became the leading dramatist in Spain. In 1636 King Philip knighted him. At the outbreak of the Catalonian rebellion in 1640, Calderón enrolled in one of the troops of knights supplied by the military orders and served at various battlefields and in different capacities until 1642. From 1644 to 1649 his theatrical production practically ceased, as the theaters were closed from the queen's death until the king's remarriage. In 1645 Calderón entered the service of the duke of Alba. In 1648 or 1649, Calderón's mistress (whose identity is unknown) died, possibly in bearing his son, whom he recognized and raised in his own house until his early death in 1657. Calderón's sorrow at his mistress's death may have contributed to his decision to enter the priesthood. He was appointed to a Toledo parish, but could not serve because his superior objected to his being a playwright. For several years he was chaplain to the Brotherhood of the Refugio at Toledo, an order dedicated to charity work among the sick. Throughout this period and to the end of his life, Calderón wrote *autos sacramentales* (theological one-act allegories) for the court. In 1663 he was appointed honorary chaplain to the king. Thereafter he lived a retired life of writing, study, and meditation in Madrid, gathering in his house a rare collection of religious works of art and devotional objects. He died on May 25, 1681.

Calderón's theatrical output was immense and varied. Among the secular plays, there are dramas of honor and jealousy like *The Physician of His Own Honor* and *Secret Offense*; of cloak-and-dagger intrigue like *A House with Two Doors Is Hard to Guard* and *The Phantom Lady*; on classical and mythological themes like *The Daughter of the Air*; and on historical and legendary themes like *The Mayor of*

Zalamea. Calderón's deep preoccupation with religious themes shows itself in such complex melodramas as *The Devotion of the Cross* and such strictly religious plays as the seventy *autos sacramentales*, the most famous of which is *The Great Theater of the World*. One of the *autos sacramentales* has the same title, though hardly the same content and meaning, as the selection here, *Life Is a Dream*.

Considered by many to be the most important play of the Spanish theater, *Life Is a Dream* was written as a comedy, yet it has tragic overtones and its leading characters meditate on such serious questions as moral behavior, destiny, and the nature and purpose of human life in general. The play presents, albeit in new and extreme versions, some of the motifs that we have encountered in previous selections. Here the notion that the world is a stage and life an apparition, a dream, is not simply a poetic image or metaphor; it is presented as a philosophy, a design for living. Even if one should occasionally suspect that life is real and substantial, one must still think of it as a dream so that one may live it properly and achieve moral salvation.

The place of the action is a kingdom that, without even the remotest trace of historical justification, is called Poland. Its king, Basil, is a sage, but his sagacity is peculiar and somewhat sinister: he regulates his life by astrology. He has confined his son and heir apparent, Segismund, to a remote tower dungeon because before and during his birth the stars and heavens showed awful portents:

> The whole earth overflowed with conflagrations
> So that it seemed the final paroxysm
> Of existence. The skies grew dark. Buildings shook.
> The clouds rained stones. The rivers ran with blood.

But King Basil is sufficiently reasonable and orthodox to pay at least lip service to the notion of free will. He knows that

> Violent inclination, the most impious
> Planet—all can but influence, not force,
> The free will which man holds direct from God.

Consequently he decides to "test" Segismund, allowing him to be brought to the palace in a trance and there to be given courtly homage and royal powers. His conduct will show whether he is of royal timber or, as the stars have predicted, a dangerous monster.

The experiment fails: Segismund behaves like an unruly tyrant; the beast prevails. For example, after a brief exchange with a servant of the household concerning what amounts to a point of courtly etiquette (the impropriety of wooing a lady as boldly as Segismund woos Stella), he throws the man out of a window into "the sea" to prove that it is he who decides what is "just." Basil does not consider that his confinement of the prince may have contributed something to the prince's misbehavior; he simply considers the experiment a failure and a confirmation of his dire forecast. Nevertheless, he plants in Segismund's mind the first seeds of his redemption by warning him that *all* royal splendor and power may be a dream. Clotaldo, the hero's guardian-mentor, draws the moral of the lesson more precisely: "even in dreams, I warn you / Nothing is lost by trying to do good." This prompts Segismund's most celebrated speech at the end of the second act, and anticipates his full enlightenment in the last act.

The subplot, which interlocks with the main plot from the very first scene, is filled with the typical coincidences and implausibilities of a comedy of intrigue. The main character of the subplot is Rosaura, who has come to "Poland" disguised as a man to search for her seducer, Astolfo. There she finds not only her faithless lover—he has already taken up with his cousin, Stella, a possible heir to Basil's throne—but her father as well, and *he* turns out to have been the seducer of her mother. The subplot proceeds with the help of crude devices and props (the sword and the portrait) and elaborate debates on points of honor, very typical of Spanish plays of the period. What, for example, is the honorable behavior for Clotaldo, when he is caught on the horns of the dilemma that Astolfo saved his life during Segismund's tyrannical phase, but that the same Astolfo is the seducer of Clotaldo's daughter?

The dénouement is, of course, happy; Astolfo will marry Rosaura and Segismund will marry Stella. The only casualty, oddly enough, is the talkative clown, Clarion. The central issue as the final knots are tied is Segismund's moral development; the happy ending of the subplot parallels, at the higher level, Segismund's successful passing of the second "test." This test of Segismund's royal fitness is brought about by the action of insurgents against King Basil. They liberate Segismund from his renewed confinement and recognize him as their leader. He discourses upon his predicament at some length (it is not altogether unlike Clotaldo's) and then decides to act, equipped as he now is with new wisdom. For Segismund now accepts not only the principle that life is a dream—and an incomprehensible one at that, as he has suggested in the closing speech of the second act—but also the idea, expressed earlier by Clotaldo and now paraphrased by the hero, that "good actions, / Even in a dream, are not entirely lost." Segismund promises to lead the rebels "bravely and skillfully," even though he knows that life is an illusion. The implication is that in spite of the purposelessness of life, or perhaps *because* of it, life should be lived with dignity, courage, and a sense of purpose.

It would be easy to superimpose a strictly orthodox interpretation of Calderón's theme: life is an illusion and a test and is followed by revelation and a just reward. But the language and impact of the play hardly warrant it. After all, Calderón wrote this as a comedy, not as an *auto sacramental* (the type of religious allegory of which he was to become a master later in life). This play is about human conduct and carries a twofold "message": life is a dream, yet it must not be lived irresponsibly. Each of us must discover his or her own idea of virtue and honor and practice it, as it were, gratuitously. This interpretation has a lingering flavor of Quixotism and at the same time a haunting suggestion of modernity.

Even so, the "meanings" of *Life Is a Dream* are difficult to summarize. Its tone, yet more difficult, mixes elements of fairy tale with a tragic awareness of reality. There are cloak-and-dagger routines and debates on points of honor that, for all their conventions, suddenly seem authentic and strangely relevant to real life. The plot is that of a routine comedy, full of disguises and surprise recognitions; yet it is carried on by characters whose main purpose seems to be to meditate on human destiny and to contemplate death, while their speech, at once formal and exuberant, full of rich imagery, expresses their vitality and earthly attachment. The general truth that no commentary can ever replace or even approach the effect of direct immersion in a literary text is particularly relevant to this play. *Life Is a Dream* is its own haunting "meaning," and thus confirms in a splendid manner the nature of literary art.

Gerald Brenan, *The Literature of the Spanish People* (1951), includes an excellent chapter on "Calderón and the Late Drama." A good general introduction is Everett W. Hesse, *Calderón de la Barca* (1967). Bruce W. Wardropper, ed., *Critical Essays on the Theater of Calderón* (1965), devotes the entire Part II to *La Vida Es Sueño*, with four essays, including A. E. Sloman, "The Structure of Calderón's

La Vida Es Sueño," and Everett W. Hesse, "Calderón's Concept of the Perfect
Prince in *La Vida Es Sueño."* Recent and valuable is Alexander Augustine Parker,
The Mind and Art of Calderón: Essays on the Comedias (1988), with bibliograph-
ical references.

Life Is a Dream[1]

Dramatis Personae

BASIL, *King of Poland*   ROSAURA, *a lady*
SEGISMUND, *Prince*   STELLA, *a princess*
ASTOLFO, *Duke of Muscovy*   *Soldiers, guards, musicians, ser-*
CLOTALDO, *old man*   *vants, retinues, women*
CLARION, *a comical servant*

*The scene is laid in the court of Poland, a nearby fortress, and the
open country.*

Act I

*On one side a craggy mountain: on the other side a rude tower
whose base serves as a prison for* SEGISMUND. *The door facing the
spectators is open. The action begins at nightfall.*

[ROSAURA, *dressed as a man, appears on the rocks climbing down to
the plain: behind her comes* CLARION.]

ROSAURA: You headlong hippogriff[2] who match the gale
In rushing to and fro, you lightning-flicker
Who give no light, you scaleless fish, you bird
Who have no coloured plumes, you animal
Who have no natural instinct, tell me whither   5
You lead me stumbling through this labyrinth
Of naked crags! Stay here upon this peak
And be a Phaëthon[3] to the brute-creation!
For I, pathless save only for the track
The laws of destiny dictate for me,   10
Shall, blind and desperate, descend this height
Whose furrowed brows are frowning at the sun.
How rudely, Poland, you receive a stranger
(Hardly arrived, but to be treated hardly)
And write her entry down in blood with thorns.   15
My plight attests this well, but after all,
Where did the wretchèd ever pity find?
CLARION: Say *two* so wretchèd. Don't you leave me out

---

1. English version by Roy Campbell.   2. A fantastic creature (a winged horse with an eagle's head and
a lion's forelegs) invented by Italian Renaissance poets. Its most famous use was for Astolfo's flight to the
moon in Ariosto's *Orlando Furioso*.   3. In Greek mythology, the driver of the chariot of his father, the
Sun; he came too close to earth and nearly burned it up.

When you complain! If we two sallied out
From our own country, questing high adventure,   20
And after so much madness and misfortune
Are still two here, and were two when we fell
Down those rough crags—shall I not be offended
To share the trouble[4] yet forego the credit?

ROSAURA: I did not give you shares in my complaint   25
So as not to rob you of the right to sorrow
Upon your own account. There's such relief
In venting grief that a philosopher
Once said that sorrows should not be bemoaned
But sought for pleasure.

CLARION: Philosopher?   30
I call him a long-bearded, drunken sot
And would they'd cudgelled him a thousand blows
To give him something worth his while lamenting!
But, madam, what should we do, by ourselves,
On foot and lost at this late hour of day,   35
Here on this desert mountain far away—
The sun departing after fresh horizons?

ROSAURA: Clarion, how can I answer, being both
The partner of your plight and your dilemma?

CLARION: Would anyone believe such strange events?   40

ROSAURA: If there my sight is not deceived by fancy,
In the last timid light that yet remains
I seem to see a building.

CLARION: Either my hopes
Are lying or I see the signs myself.

ROSAURA: Between the towering crags, there stands so small   45
A royal palace that the lynx-eyed sun
Could scare perceive it at midday, so rude
In architecture that it seems but one
Rock more down-toppled from the sun-kissed crags
That form the jaggèd crest.

CLARION: Let's go closer,   50
For we have stared enough: it would be better
To let the inmates make us welcome.

ROSAURA: See:
The door, or, rather, that funereal gap,
Is yawning wide—whence night itself seems born,
Flowing out from its black, rugged centre.   55

[A sound of chains is heard.]

CLARION: Heavens! What's that I hear?

ROSAURA: I have become
A block immovable of ice and fire.

---

4. Plays on words are not infrequent in Calderón, as, for that matter, in Shakespeare. Here, for example, the untranslatable pun is on the double meaning of *pesar* ("trouble" and "to weigh").

CLARION: Was that a little chain? Why, I'll be hanged
  If that is not the clanking ghost of some
  Past galley-slave—my terror proves it is!   60
SEGISMUND: Oh, miserable me! Unhappy me!
ROSAURA: How sad a cry that is! I fear new trials
  And torments.
CLARION: It's a fearful sound.
ROSAURA: Oh, come,
  My Clarion, let us fly from suffering!
CLARION: I'm in such sorry trim, I've not the spirit   65
  Even to run away.
ROSAURA: And if you had,
  You'd not have seen that door, not known of it.
  When one's in doubt, the common saying goes
  One walks between two lights.
CLARION: I'm the reverse.
  It's not that way with me.
ROSAURA: What then disturbs you?   70
CLARION: I walk in doubt between two darknesses.
ROSAURA: Is not that feeble exhalation there
  A light? That pallid star whose fainting tremors,
  Pulsing a doubtful warmth of glimmering rays,
  Make even darker with its spectral glow   75
  That gloomy habitation? Yes! because
  By its reflection (though so far away)
  I recognise a prison, grim and sombre,
  The sepulchre of some poor living carcase.
  And, more to wonder at, a man lies there   80
  Clothed in the hides of savage beasts, with limbs
  Loaded with fetters and a single lamp
  For company. So, since we cannot flee,
  Let us stay here and listen to his plaint
  And what his sorrows are.
SEGISMUND: Unhappy me!   85
  Oh, miserable me! You heavens above,
  I try to think what crime I've done against you
  By being born. Although to have been born,
  I know, is an offence, and with just cause
  I bear the rigours of your punishment: 90
  Since to be born is man's worst crime. But yet
  I long to know (to clarify my doubts)
  What greater crime, apart from being born,
  Can thus have earned my greater chastisement.
  Aren't others born like me? And yet they seem   95
  To boast a freedom that I've never known.
  The bird is born, and in the hues of beauty
  Clothed with its plumes, yet scarce has it become

A feathered posy—or a flower with wings—
When through ethereal halls it cuts its way,   100
Refusing the kind shelter of its nest.
And I, who have more soul than any bird,
Must have less liberty?
The beast is born, and with its hide bright-painted,
In lovely tints, has scarce become a spangled   105
And starry constellation (thanks to the skilful
Brush of the Painter) than its earthly needs
Teach it the cruelty to prowl and kill,
The monster[5] of its labyrinth of flowers.
Yet I, with better instincts than a beast,   110
Must have less liberty?
The fish is born, the birth of spawn and slime,
That does not even live by breathing air.
No sooner does it feel itself a skiff
Of silver scales upon the wave than swiftly   115
It roves about in all directions taking
The measure of immensity as far
As its cold blood's capacity allows.
Yet I, with greater freedom of the will,
Must have less liberty?   120
The brook is born, and like a snake unwinds
Among the flowers. No sooner, silver serpent,
Does it break through the blooms than it regales
And thanks them with its music for their kindness,
Which opens to its course the majesty   125
Of the wide plain. Yet I, with far more life,
Must have less liberty?
This fills me with such passion, I become
Like the volcano Etna,[6] and could tear
Pieces of my own heart out of my breast!   130
What law, justice, or reason can decree
That man alone should never know the joys
And be alone excepted from the rights
God grants a fish, a bird, a beast, a brook?
ROSAURA: His words have filled me full of fear and pity.   135
SEGISMUND: Who is it overheard my speech? Clotaldo?
CLARION: Say "yes!"
ROSAURA: It's only a poor wretch, alas,
Who in these cold ravines has overheard
Your sorrows.
SEGISMUND: Then I'll kill you
    [Seizes her.]

---

5. An allusion to the Minotaur, a monster with a bull's head and a man's body, kept by King Minos in the Cretan Labyrinth, until killed by the Greek hero Theseus.   6. The highest active volcano in Europe, on the island of Sicily.

So as to leave no witness of my frailty.   140
I'll tear you into bits with these strong arms!
CLARION: I'm deaf. I wasn't able to hear that.
ROSAURA: If you were human born, it is enough
    That I should kneel to you for you to spare me.   144
SEGISMUND: Your voice has softened me, your presence halted me,
    And now, confusingly, I feel respect
    For you. Who are you? Though here I have learned
    So little of the world, since this grim tower
    Has been my cradle and my sepulchre;
    And though since I was born (if you can say   150
    I really have been born) I've only seen
    This rustic desert where in misery
    I dwell alone, a living skeleton,
    An animated corpse; and though till now,
    I never spoke, save to one man who hears   155
    My griefs and through whose converse I have heard
    News of the earth and of the sky; and though,
    To astound you more, and make you call me
    A human monster, I dwell here, and am
    A man of the wild animals, a beast   160
    Among the race of men; and though in such
    Misfortune, I have studied human laws,
    Instructed by the birds, and learned to measure
    The circles of the gentle stars, you only
    Have curbed my furious rage, amazed my vision,   165
    And filled with wonderment my sense of hearing.
    Each time I look at you, I feel new wonder!
    The more I see of you, the more I long
    To go on seeing more of you. I think
    My eyes are dropsical, to go on drinking   170
    What it is death for them to drink, because
    They go on drinking that which I am dying
    To see and that which, seen, will deal me death.
    Yet let me gaze on you and die, since I
    Am so bewitched I can no longer think   175
    What not seeing you would do to me—the sight
    Itself being fatal! that would be more hard
    Than dying, madness, rage, and fiercest grief:
    It would be life—worst fate of all because
    The gift of life to such a wretchèd man   180
    Would be the gift of death to happiness![7]
ROSAURA: Astonished as I look, amazed to hear,
    I know not what to say nor what to ask.
    All I can say is that heaven guided me

---

7. The gift of life, to a wretched man like himself, is like giving death to a happy one.

Here to be comforted, if it is comfort   185
To see another sadder than oneself.
They say a sage philosopher of old,
Being so poor and miserable that he
Lived on the few plain herbs he could collect,
One day exclaimed: "Could any man be poorer   190
Or sadder than myself?"—when, turning round,
He saw the very answer to his words.
For there another sage philosopher
Was picking up the scraps he'd thrown away.
I lived cursing my fortune in this world   195
And asked within me: "Is there any other
Suffers so hard a fate?" Now out of pity
You've given me the answer. For within me
I find upon reflection that my griefs
Would be as joys to you and you'd receive them   200
To give you pleasure. So if they perchance
In any measure may afford relief.
Listen attentively to my misfortune
And take what is left over for yourself.
I am . . .
CLOTALDO: [*Within*] Guards of the tower! You sluggards   205
  Or cowards, you have let two people pass
  Into the prison bounds . . .
ROSAURA: Here's more confusion!
SEGISMUND: That is Clotaldo, keeper of my prison.
  Are my misfortunes still not at an end?
CLOTALDO: Come. Be alert, and either seize or slay them   210
  Before they can resist!
VOICES: [*Within*]   Treason! Betrayal!
CLARION: Guards of the tower, who let us pass unhindered,
  Since there's a choice, to seize us would be simpler.
  [*Enter* CLOTALDO *with soldiers. He holds a pistol and they all wear
  masks.*]
CLOTALDO: [*Aside to the soldiers*] Cover your faces, all! It's a precaution
  Imperative that nobody should know us   215
  While we are here.
CLARION: What's this? A masquerade?
CLOTALDO: O you, who ignorantly passed the bounds
  And limits of this region, banned to all—
  Against the king's decree which has forbidden
  That any should find out the prodigy   220
  Hidden in these ravines—yield up your weapons
  Or else this pistol, like a snake of metal,
  Will spit the piercing venom of two shots
  With scandalous assault upon the air.
SEGISMUND: Tyrannic master, ere you harm these people   225

Let my life be the spoil of these sad bonds
In which (I swear it by Almighty God)
I'll sooner rend myself with hands and teeth
Amid these rocks than see them harmed and mourn
Their suffering.

CLOTALDO: Since you know, Segismund,   230
That your misfortunes are so huge that, even
Before your birth, you died by heaven's decree,
And since you know these walls and binding chains
Are but the brakes and curbs to your proud frenzies,
What use is it to bluster?
[*To the guards*]   Shut the door   235
Of this close prison! Hide him in its depths!

SEGISMUND: Ah, heavens, how justly you denied me freedom!
For like a Titan[8] I would rise against you,
Pile jasper mountains high on stone foundations
And climb to burst the windows of the sun!   240

CLOTALDO: Perhaps you suffer so much pain today
Just to forestall that feat.

ROSAURA: Now that I see
How angry pride offends you, I'd be foolish
Not to plead humbly at your feet for life.
Be moved by me to pity. It would be   245
Notoriously harsh that neither pride
Nor humbleness found favour in your eyes!

CLARION: And if neither Humility nor Pride
Impress you (characters of note who act
And motivate a thousand mystery plays)   250
Let me, here, who am neither proud nor humble,
But merely something halfway in between,
Plead to you both for shelter and for aid.

CLOTALDO: Ho, there!

SOLDIER: Sir?

CLOTALDO: Take their weapons. Bind their eyes
So that they cannot see the way they're led.   255

ROSAURA: This is my sword. To nobody but you
I yield it, since you're, after all, the chief.
I cannot yield to one of meaner rank.

CLARION: My sword is such that I will freely give it
To the most mean and wretched.
[*To one soldier*]   Take it, you!   260

ROSAURA: And if I have to die, I'll leave it to you
In witness of your mercy. It's a pledge
Of great worth and may justly be esteemed
For someone's sake who wore it long ago.

---

8. The Titans were primeval gods of Greek myth, sons of Uranus (Heaven) and Gaea (Earth).

CLOTALDO: [*Apart*] Each moment seems to bring me new misfortune!   265
ROSAURA: Because of that, I ask you to preserve
    This sword with care. Since if inconstant Fate
    Consents to the remission of my sentence,
    It has to win me honour. Though I know not
    The secret that it carries, I do know   270
    It has got one—unless I trick myself—
    And prize it just as the sole legacy
    My father left me.
CLOTALDO: Who then was your father?
ROSAURA: I never knew.
CLOTALDO: And why have you come here?
ROSAURA: I came to Poland to avenge a wrong.   275
CLOTALDO: [*Apart*] Sacred heavens!
    [*On taking the sword he becomes very perturbed.*]
                  What's this? Still worse and worse.
    I am perplexed and troubled with more fears.
    [*Aloud*] Tell me: who gave that sword to you?
ROSAURA: A woman.
CLOTALDO: Her name?
ROSAURA: A secret I am forced to keep.
CLOTALDO: What makes you think this sword contains a secret?   280
ROSAURA: That she who gave it to me said: "Depart
    To Poland. There with subtlety and art
    Display it so that all the leading people
    And noblemen can see you wearing it,
    And I know well that there's a lord among them   285
    Who will both shelter you and grant you favour."
    But, lest he should be dead, she did not name him.
CLOTALDO: [*Aside*] Protect me, heavens! What is this I hear?
    I cannot say if real or imagined
    But here's the sword I gave fair Violante   290
    In token that, whoever in the future
    Should come from her to me wearing this sword,
    Would find in me a tender father's love.
    Alas, what can I do in such a pass,
    When he who brings the sword to win my favour   295
    Brings it to find his own red death instead
    Arriving at my feet condemned already?
    What strange perplexity! How hard a fate!
    What an inconstant fortune to be plagued with!
    This is my son[9] not only by all signs   300
    But also by the promptings of my heart,
    Since, seeing him, my heart seems to cry out
    To him, and beat its wings, and, though unable

---

9. Rosaura, of course, is disguised as a man.

To break the locks, behaves as one shut in,
Who, hearing noises in the street outside,   305
Cranes from the window-ledge. Just so, not knowing
What's really happening, but hearing sounds,
My heart runs to my eyes which are its windows
And out of them flows into bitter tears.
Protect me, heaven! What am I to do?   310
To take him to the king is certain death.
To hide him is to break my sacred oath
And the strong law of homage. From one side
Love of one's own, and from the other loyalty—
Call me to yield. Loyalty to my king   315
(Why do I doubt?) comes before life and honour.
Then live my loyalty, and let him die!
When I remember, furthermore, he came
To avenge an injury—a man insulted
And unavenged is in disgrace. My son   320
Therefore he is not, nor of noble blood.
But if some danger has mischanced, from which
No one escapes, since honour is so fragile
That any act can smash it, and it takes
A stain from any breath of air, what more   325
Could any nobleman have done than he,
Who, at the cost of so much risk and danger,
Comes to avenge his honour? Since he's so brave
He is my son, and my blood's in his veins.
And so betwixt the one doubt and the other,   330
The most important mean between extremes
Is to go to the king and tell the truth—
That he's my son, to kill, if so he wishes.
Perhaps my loyalty thus will move his mercy
And if I thus can merit a live son,   335
I'll help him to avenge his injury.
But if the king prove constant in his rigour
And deal him death, he'll die in ignorance
That I'm his father.
          [*Aloud to* ROSAURA *and* CLARION.]
                    Come then, strangers, come!
And do not fear that you have no companions   340
In your misfortunes, since, in equal doubt,
Tossed between life and death, I cannot guess
Which is the greater evil or the less.

A hall at the royal palace, in court

[*Enter* ASTOLFO *and soldiers at one side: from the other side* PRINCESS
STELLA *and ladies. Military music and salvos.*]

ASTOLFO: To greet your excellent bright beams

As brilliant as a comet's rays,   345
The drums and brasses mix their praise
With those of fountains, birds, and streams.
With sounds alike, in like amaze,
Your heavenly face each voice salutes,
Which puts them in such lively fettle,   350
The trumpets sound like birds of metal,
The songbirds play like feathered flutes.
And thus they greet you, fair señora—
The salvos, as their queen, the brasses,
As to Minerva[1] when she passes,   355
The songbirds to the bright Aurora,[2]
And all the flowers and leaves and grasses
As doing homage unto Flora,[3]
Because you come to cheat the day
Which now the night has covered o'er—   360
Aurora in your spruce array,
Flora in peace, Pallas in war,
But in my heart the queen of May.
STELLA: If human voice could match with acts
You would have been unwise to say   365
Hyperboles that a few facts
May well refute some other day
Confounding all this martial fuss
With which I struggle daringly,
Since flatteries you proffer thus   370
Do not accord with what I see.
Take heed that it's an evil thing
And worthy of a brute accursed,
Loud praises with your mouth to sing
When in your heart you wish the worst.   375
ASTOLFO: Stella, you have been badly misinformed
If you doubt my good faith. Here let me beg you
To listen to my plea and hear me out.
The third Eugtorgius died, the King of Poland.
Basil, his heir, had two fair sisters who   380
Bore you, my cousin, and myself. I would not
Tire you with all that happened here. You know
Clorilene was your mother who enjoys,
Under a better reign,[4] her starry throne.
She was the elder. Lovely Recisunda   385
(Whom may God cherish for a thousand years!)
The younger one, my mother and your aunt,
Was wed in Muscovy.[5] Now to return:

1. The Roman goddess of wisdom, corresponding to the Greeks' Athena.   2. The Roman goddess of
Dawn.   3. The Roman goddess of flowers and fruitfulness.   4. Heaven.   5. The grand duchy of
Moscow.

Basil has yielded to the feebleness
Of age, loves learnèd study more than women,   390
Has lost his wife, is childless, will not marry.
And so it comes that you and I both claim
The heirdom of the realm. You claim that you
Were daughter to the elder daughter. I
Say that my being born a man, although   395
Son of the younger daughter, gives me title
To be preferred. We've told the king, our uncle,
Of both of our intentions. And he answered
That he would judge between our rival claims,
For which the time and place appointed was   400
Today and here. For that same reason I
Have left my native Muscovy. With that
Intent I come—not seeking to wage war
But so that you might thus wage war on me!
May Love, wise god, make true what people say   405
(Your "people" is a wise astrologer)
By settling this through your being chosen queen—
Queen and my consort, sovereign of my will;
My uncle crowning you, for greater honour;
Your courage conquering, as it deserves;   410
My love applauding you, its emperor!
STELLA: To such chivalrous gallantry, my breast
    Cannot hold out. The imperial monarchy
    I wish were mine only to make it yours—
    Although my love is not quite satisfied   415
    That you are to be trusted since your speech
    Is somewhat contradicted by that portrait[6]
    You carry in the locket round your neck.
ASTOLFO: I'll give you satisfaction as to that.
    [Drums] But these loud instruments will not permit it   420
    That sound the arrival of the king and council.
    [Enter KING BASIL with his following.]
STELLA: Wise Thales[7] . . .
ASTOLFO: Learned Euclid . . .
STELLA: Among the signs . . .
ASTOLFO: Among the stars . . .
STELLA: Where you preside in power . . .
ASTOLFO: Where you reside . . .
STELLA: And plot their paths . . .
ASTOLFO: And trace their fiery trails . . .   425
STELLA: Describing . . .
ASTOLFO: . . . Measuring and judging them . . .
STELLA: Please read my stars that I, in humble bonds . . .

6. A picture of Rosaura.   7. An early Greek philosopher. *Euclid*: The great Alexandrian geometer. The
speech that follows is a long, flattering salutation to the king, shared by Stella and Astolfo.

ASTOLFO: Please read them, so that I in soft embraces . . .
STELLA: May twine as ivy to this tree!
ASTOLFO: May find
   Myself upon my knees before these feet!   430
BASIL: Come and embrace me, niece and nephew. Trust me,
   Since you're both loyal to my loving precepts,
   And come here so affectionately both—
   In nothing shall I leave you cause to cavil,
   And both of you as equals will be treated.   435
   The gravity of what I have to tell
   Oppresses me, and all I ask of you
   Is silence: the event itself will claim
   Your wonderment. So be attentive now,
   Belovèd niece and nephew, illustrious courtiers,   440
   Relatives, friends, and subjects! You all know
   That for my learning I have merited
   The surname of The Learnèd, since the brush
   Of great Timanthes,[8] and Lisippus' marbles—
   Stemming oblivion (consequence of time)—   445
   Proclaimed me to mankind Basil the Great.
   You know the science that I most affect
   And most esteem is subtle mathematics
   (By which I forestall time, cheat fame itself)
   Whose office is to show things gradually.   450
   For when I look my tables up and see,
   Present before me, all the news and actions
   Of centuries to come, I gain on Time—
   Since Time recounts whatever I have said
   After I say it. Those snowflaking haloes,   455
   Those canopies of crystal spread on high,
   Lit by the sun, cut by the circling moon,
   Those diamond orbs, those globes of radiant crystal
   Which the bright stars adorn, on which the signs
   Parade in blazing excellence, have been   460
   My chiefest study all through my long years.
   They are the volumes on whose adamantine
   Pages, bound up in sapphire, heaven writes,
   In lines of burnished gold and vivid letters,
   All that is due to happen, whether adverse   465
   Or else benign. I read them in a flash,
   So quickly that my spirit tracks their movements—
   Whatever road they take, whatever goal
   They aim at. Would to heaven that before
   My genius had been the commentary   470
   Writ in their margins, or the index to

8. Greek painter of the fourth century B.C. *Lisippus:* A Greek sculptor of the same period. The names are used symbolically to mean great artists in general.

Their pages, that my life had been the rubble,
The ruin, and destruction of their wrath,
And that my tragedy in them had ended,
Because, to the unlucky, even their merit   475
Is like a hostile knife, and he whom knowledge
Injures is but a murderer to himself.
And this I say myself, though my misfortunes
Say it far better, which, to marvel at,
I beg once more for silence from you all.   480
With my late wife, the queen, I had a son,
Unhappy son, to greet whose birth the heavens
Wore themselves out in prodigies and portents.
Ere the sun's light brought him live burial
Out of the womb (for birth resembles death)   485
His mother many times, in the delirium
And fancies of her sleep, saw a fierce monster
Bursting her entrails in a human form,
Born spattered with her lifeblood, dealing death,
The human viper[9] of this century!   490
The day came for his birth, and every presage
Was then fulfilled, for tardily or never
Do the more cruel ones prove false. At birth
His horoscope was such that the bright sun,
Stained in its blood, entered ferociously   495
Into duel with the moon above,
The whole earth seemed a rampart for the strife
Of heaven's two lights, who—though not hand-to-hand—
Fought light-to-light to gain the mastery!
The worst eclipse the sun has ever suffered   500
Since Christ's own death horrified earth and sky.
The whole earth overflowed with conflagrations
So that it seemed the final paroxysm
Of existence. The skies grew dark. Buildings shook.
The clouds rained stones. The rivers ran with blood.   505
In this delirious frenzy of the sun,
Thus, Segismund was born into the world,
Giving a foretaste of his character
By killing his own mother, seeming to speak thus
By his ferocity: "I am a man,   510
Because I have begun now to repay
All kindnesses with evil." To my studies
I went forthwith, and saw in all I studied
That Segismund would be the most outrageous
Of all men, the most cruel of all princes,   515
And impious of all monarchs, by whose acts

9. Reputedly the viper is killed and devoured by its offspring.

The kingdom would be torn up and divided
So as to be a school of treachery
And an academy of vices. He,
Risen in fury, amidst crimes and horrors,   520
Was born to trample me (with shame I say it)
And make of my grey hairs his very carpet.
Who is there but believes an evil Fate?
And more if he discovers it himself,
For self-love lends its credit to our studies.   525
So I, believing in the Fates, and in
The havoc that their prophecies predestined,
Determined to cage up this newborn tiger
To see if on the stars we sages have
Some power. I gave out that the prince had died   530
Stillborn, and well-forewarned, I built a tower
Amidst the cliffs and boulders of yon mountains
Over whose tops the light scarce finds its way,
So stubbornly their obelisks and crags
Defend the entry to them. The strict laws   535
And edicts that I published then (declaring
That nobody might enter the forbidden
Part of the range) were passed on that account.
There Segismund lives to this day, a captive,
Poor and in misery, where, save Clotaldo,   540
His guardian, none have seen or talked to him.
The latter has instructed him in all
Branches of knowledge and in the Catholic faith,
Alone the witness of his misery.
There are three things to be considered now: 545
Firstly Poland, that I love you greatly,
So much that I would free you from the oppression
And servitude of such a tyrant king.
He would not be a kindly ruler who
Would put his realm and homeland in such danger.   550
The second fact that I must bear in mind
Is this: that to deny my flesh and blood
The rights which law, both human and divine,
Concedes, would not accord with Christian charity,
For no law says that, to prevent another   555
Being a tyrant, I may be one myself,
And if my son's a tyrant, to prevent him
From doing outrage, I myself should do it.
Now here's the third and last point I would speak of,
Namely, how great an error it has been   560
To give too much belief to things predicted,
Because, even if his inclination should
Dictate some headlong, rash precipitancies,

PEDRO CALDERÓN DE LA BARCA

They may perhaps not conquer him entirely,
For the most accursèd destiny, the most   565
Violent inclination, the most impious
Planet—all can but influence, not force,
The free will which man holds direct from God.
And so, between one motive and another
Vacillating discursively, I hit   570
On a solution that will stun you all.
I shall tomorrow, but without his knowing
He is my son—your king—place Segismund
(For that's the name with which he was baptised)
Here on my throne, beneath my canopy,   575
Yes, in my very place, that he may govern you
And take command. And you must all be here
To swear him fealty as his loyal subjects.
Three things may follow from this test, and these
I'll set against the three which I proposed.   580
The first is that should the prince prove prudent,
Stable, and benign—thus giving the lie
To all that prophecy reports of him—
Then you'll enjoy in him your rightful ruler
Who was so long a courtier of the mountains   585
And neighbour to the beasts. Here is the second:
If he prove proud, rash, cruel, and outrageous,
And with a loosened rein gallop unheeding
Across the plains of vice, I shall have done
My duty, and fulfilled my obligation   590
Of mercy. If I then re-imprison him,
That's incontestably a kingly deed—
Not cruelty but merited chastisement.
The third thing's this: that if the prince should be
As I've described him, then—by the love I feel   595
For you, my vassals—I shall give you worthier
Rulers to wear the sceptre and the crown;
Because your king and queen will be my nephew
And niece, each with an equal right to rule,
Each gaining the inheritance he merits,   600
And joined in faith of holy matrimony.
This I command you as a king, I ask you
As a kind father, as a sage I pray you,
As an experienced old man I tell you,
And (if it's true, as Spanish Seneca[1]   605
Says, that the king is slave unto his nation)
This, as a humble slave, I beg of you.
ASTOLFO: If it behooves me to reply (being

1. The Roman dramatist and philosopher (4 B.C.?–A.D. 65) was born at Córdoba in Spain. The thought mentioned here is in his book *De clementia*, l. 19.

The person most involved in this affair)
Then in the name of all, let Segismund   610
Appear! It is enough that he's your son!
ALL: Give us our prince: we want him for our king!
BASIL: Subjects, I thank you for your kindly favour.
Accompany these, my two Atlases,[2]
Back to their rooms. Tomorrow you shall see him.   615
ALL: Long live the great King Basil! Long live Basil!

> [*Exeunt all, accompanying* STELLA *and* ASTOLFO: *The* KING *remains.*
> *Enter* CLOTALDO *with* ROSAURA *and* CLARION.]

CLOTALDO: May I have leave to speak, sire?
BASIL: Oh, Clotaldo!
You're very welcome.
CLOTALDO: Thus to kneel before you
Is always welcome, sire—yet not today
When sad and evil Fate destroys the joy   620
Your presence normally concedes.
BASIL: What's wrong?
CLOTALDO: A great misfortune, sire, has come upon me
Just when I should have met it with rejoicing.
BASIL: Continue.
CLOTALDO: Sire, this beautiful young man
Who inadvertently and daringly   625
Came to the tower, wherein he saw the prince,
Is my . . .
BASIL: Do not afflict yourself, Clotaldo.
Had it not been just now, I should have minded,
I must confess. But I've revealed the secret,
And now it does not matter if he knows it.   630
Attend me afterwards. I've many things
To tell you. You in turn have many things
To do for me. You'll be my minister,
I warn you, in the most momentous action
The world has ever seen. These prisoners, lest you   635
Should think I blame your oversight, I'll pardon.
   [*Exit.*]
CLOTALDO: Long may you live, great sire! A thousand years!
   [*Aside*] Heaven improves our fates. I shall not tell him
Now that he is my son, since it's not needed
Till he's avenged.   640
   [*Aloud.*] Strangers, you may go free.
ROSAURA: Humbly I kiss your feet.
CLARION: Whilst I'll just *miss* them—
Old friends will hardly quibble at one letter.
ROSAURA: You've granted me my life, sir. I remain

---

2. Astolfo and Stella, supporting him as the mythological Atlas supports the earth.

Your servant and eternally your debtor.   645
CLOTALDO: No! It was not your life I gave you. No!
Since any wellborn man who, unavenged,
Nurses an insult does not live at all.
And seeing you have told me that you came
For that sole reason, it was not life I spared—   650
Life in disgrace is not a life at all.
[*Aside*] I see this spurs him.
ROSAURA: Freely I confess it—
Although you spared my life, it was no life.
But I will wipe my honour's stain so spotless
That after I have vanquished all my dangers   655
Life well may seem a shining gift from you.
CLOTALDO: Take here your burnished steel: 'twill be enough,
Bathed in your enemies' red blood, to right you.
For steel that once was mine (I mean of course
Just for the time I've had it in my keeping)   660
Should know how to avenge you.
ROSAURA: Now, in your name I gird it on once more
And on it I will swear to take revenge
Although my foe were even mightier.
CLOTALDO: Is he so powerful?
ROSAURA: So much so that . . .   665
Although I have no doubt in your discretion . . .
I say no more because I'd not estrange
Your clemency.
CLOTALDO: You would have won me had you told me, since
That would prevent me helping him.   670
[*Aside*] If only I could discover who he is!
ROSAURA: So that you'll not think that I value lightly
Such confidence, know that my adversary
Is no less than Astolfo, Duke of Muscovy.
CLOTALDO: [*Aside*] (I hardly can withstand the grief it gives me   675
For it is worse than aught I could imagine!
Let us inquire of him some further facts.)
[*Aloud*] If you were born a Muscovite, your ruler
Could never have affronted you. Go back
Home to your country. Leave this headstrong valour.   680
It will destroy you.
ROSAURA: Though he's been my prince,
I know that he has done me an affront.
CLOTALDO: Even though he slapped your face, that's no affront.
[*Aside*] O heavens!
ROSAURA: My insult was far deeper.
CLOTALDO: Tell it:
Since nothing I imagine could be deeper.   685
ROSAURA: Yes. I will tell it, yet, I know not why,

With such respect I look upon your face,
I venerate you with such true affection,
With such high estimation do I weigh you,
That I scarce dare to tell you—these men's clothes   690
Are an enigma, not what they appear.
So now you know. Judge if it's no affront
That here Astolfo comes to wed with Stella
Although betrothed to me. I've said enough.
          [*Exeunt* ROSAURA *and* CLARION.]
CLOTALDO: Here! Listen! Wait! What mazed confusion!   695
It is a labyrinth wherein the reason
Can find no clue. My family's honour's injured.
The enemy's all powerful. I'm a vassal
And she's a woman. Heavens! Show a path
Although I don't believe there is a way!   700
There's nought but evil bodings in the sky.
The whole world is a prodigy, say I.

Act II

A Hall in the Royal Palace

          [*Enter* BASIL *and* CLOTALDO.]
CLOTALDO: All has been done according to your orders.
BASIL: Tell me, Clotaldo, how it went.
CLOTALDO: Why, thus:
I took to Segismund a calming drug
Wherein are mixed herbs of especial virtue,
Tyrannous in their overpowering strength,   5
Which seize and steal and alienate man's gift
Of reasoning, thus making a live corpse
Of him. His violence evaporated
With all his faculties and senses too.
There is no need to prove it's possible   10
Because experience teaches us that medicine
Is full of natural secrets, that there is no
Animal, plant, or stone that has not got
Appointed properties. If human malice
Explores a thousand poisons which deal death,   15
Who then can doubt, that being so, that other
Poisons less violent, cause only sleep?
But (leaving that doubt aside as proven false
By every evidence) hear then the sequel:
I went down into Segismund's close prison   20
Bearing the drink wherein, with opium,
Henbane and poppies had been mixed. With him
I talked a little while of the humanities,
In which dumb Nature has instructed him,

The mountains and the heavens and the stars,   25
In whose divine academies he learned
Rhetoric from the birds and the wild creatures.
To lift his spirit to the enterprise
Which you require of him I chose for subject
The swiftness of a stalwart eagle, who,   30
Deriding the base region of the wind,
Rises into the sphere reserved for fire,
A feathered lightning, an untethered comet.
Then I extolled such lofty flight and said:
"After all, he's the king of birds, and so   35
Takes precedence, by right, over the rest."
No more was needful for, in taking up
Majesty for his subject, he discoursed
With pride and high ambition, as his blood
Naturally moves, incites, and spurs him on   40
To grand and lofty things, and so he said
That in the restless kingdom of the birds
There should be those who swear obedience, too!
"In this, my miseries console me greatly,
Because if I'm a vassal here, it's only   45
By force, and not by choice. Of my own will
I would not yield in rank to any man."
Seeing that he grew furious—since this touched
The theme of his own griefs—I gave the potion
And scarcely had it passed from cup to breast   50
Before he yielded all his strength to slumber.
A chill sweat ran through all his limbs and veins.
Had I not known that this was mere feigned death
I would have thought him dead. Then came the men
To whom you've trusted this experiment,   55
Who placed him in a coach and brought him here
To your own rooms, where all things were prepared
In royalty and grandeur as befitting
His person. In your own bed they have laid him
Where, when the torpor wanes, they'll do him service   60
As if he were Your Majesty himself.
All has been done as you have ordered it,
And if I have obeyed you well, my lord,
I'd beg a favour (pardon me this freedom)—
To know what your intention is in thus   65
Transporting Segismund here to the palace.
BASIL: Your curiosity is just, Clotaldo,
And yours alone I'll satisfy. The star
Which governs Segismund, my son, in life,
Threatens a thousand tragedies and woes.   70
And now I wish to see whether the stars

(Which never lie—and having shown to us
So many cruel signs seem yet more certain)
May yet be brought to moderate their sentence,
Whether by prudence charmed or valour won,   75
For man does have the power to rule his stars.
I would examine this, bringing him here
Where he may know he is my son, and make
Trial of his talent. If magnanimously
He conquers and controls himself, he'll reign,   80
But if he proves a tyrant and is cruel,
Back to his chains he'll go. Now, you will ask,
Why did we bring him sleeping in this manner
For the experiment? I'll satisfy you,
Down to the smallest detail, with my answer.   85
If he knows that he is my son today,
And if tomorrow he should find himself
Once more reduced to prison, to misery,
He would despair entirely, knowing truly
Who, and whose son, he is. What consolation   90
Could he derive, then, from his lot? So I
Contrive to leave an exit for such grief,
By making him believe it was a dream.
By these means we may learn two things at once:
First, his character—for he will really be   95
Awake in all he thinks and all his actions;
Second, his consolation—which would be
(If he should wake in prison on the morrow,
Although he saw himself obeyed today)
That he might understand he had been dreaming,   100
And he will not be wrong, for in this world,
Clotaldo, all who live are only dreaming.
CLOTALDO: I've proofs enough to doubt of your success,
    But now it is too late to remedy it.
    From what I can make out, I think he's wakened   105
    And that he's coming this way, by the sound.
BASIL: I shall withdraw. You, as his tutor, go
    And guide him through his new bewilderments
    By answering his queries with the truth.
CLOTALDO: You give me leave to tell the truth of it?   110
BASIL: Yes, because knowing all things, he may find
    Known perils are the easiest to conquer.
        [*Exit* BASIL. *Enter* CLARION.]
CLARION: It cost me four whacks to get here so quickly.
    I caught them from a red-haired halberdier
    Sprouting a ginger beard over his livery,   115
    And I've come to see what's going on.
    No windows give a better view than those

A man brings with him in his head, not asking
For tickets of admission or paid seats,
Since at all functions, festivals, or feasts   120
He looks out with the same nice self-composure.
CLOTALDO: [Aside] Here's Clarion who's the servant of that person—
That trader in woes, importer from Poland
Of my disgrace.
[Aloud]   Come, Clarion what news?
CLARION: Item the first: encouraged by the fact   125
Your clemency's disposed to venge her insult,
Rosaura has resumed her proper clothing.
CLOTALDO: That's right: it's less indecorous and bold.
CLARION: Item: she's changed her name, and given out
That she's your niece. And now they've made so much   130
Of her that she's been raised to maid of honour
To the unique and only princess, Stella.
CLOTALDO: That's right: her honour stands to my account.
CLARION: Indeed she merely bides the time till you
Will settle all accounts about her honour.   135
CLOTALDO: Biding the time is wise, for in the end
It's Time that's going to settle all accounts!
CLARION: Item: that she's attended like a queen,
Because they take her for your niece. Item:
That I, who trudged along with her, am dying   140
Of hunger. Nobody remembers me,
Nor yet remembers that I'm like my name
And (should I sound my Clarion) could tell
All to the king and Stella and Astolfo.
For I am both a Clarion and a servant—   145
Two things which ill-accord with secrecy.
If silence should, by chance, let slip my hand,
Then there's a chorus which would fit me well:
"Dawn-breaking Clarion plays no better tune!"
CLOTALDO: You've reason for complaint. I'll satisfy it   150
If you'll but serve me . . .
CLARION: Hush, here's Segismund!
[Enter musicians, singing, and servants arraying SEGISMUND, who seems
amazed.]
SEGISMUND: Heavens above! What's this that I am seeing?
I wonder at it all, with naught of fear!
But with a mighty doubt, I disbelieve it!
I?—in a sumptuous palace? I—encircled   155
With rich brocades and silks? I—overwhelmed
With servants in such brilliant liveries?
I—to awake in such a gorgeous bed?
I—in the middle of so many footmen
Who clothe me in rich garments? I'm awake: 160

It would be false to take this for a dream.
Am I not Segismund? Heavens! disabuse me
If I'm mistaken. Say, what could have happened
In my imagination while I slept—
That I should find myself in such a place?   165
But why should I worry, whatever it was?
I'll let myself be served and entertained—
Befall what may.
FIRST SERVANT: [*Aside to* SECOND SERVANT *and* CLARION]
                He's very melancholy!
SECOND SERVANT: Who would not be, considering all that's happened
    To him?
CLARION: I would not be!
SECOND SERVANT: You, speak to him.   170
FIRST SERVANT: Shall they begin to sing again?
SEGISMUND: Why, no,
    I would not have them sing.
SECOND SERVANT: You're so distraught,
    I wish you entertained.
SEGISMUND: My griefs are such
    That no mere voices can amuse me now—
    Only the martial music pleased my mind.   175
CLOTALDO: Your Highness, mighty prince, give me your hand
    To kiss. I'm glad to be the first to offer
    Obedience at your feet.
SEGISMUND: [*Aside*]   This is Clotaldo.
    How is it he, that tyrannised my thralldom,
    Should now be treating me with such respect?   180
    [*Aloud*] Tell me what's happening all round me here.
CLOTALDO: With the perplexities of your new state,
    Your reason will encounter many doubts,
    But I shall try to free you from them all
    (If that may be) because you now much know   185
    You are hereditary Prince of Poland.
    If you have been withdrawn from public sight
    Under restraint, it was in strict obedience
    To Fate's inclemency, which will permit
    A thousand woes to fall upon this empire   190
    The moment that you wear the sovereign's crown.
    But trusting that you'll prudently defeat
    Your own malignant stars (since they can be
    Controlled by magnanimity) you've been
    Brought to this palace from the tower you knew   195
    Even while your soul was yielded up to sleep.
    My lord the king, your father, will be coming
    To see you, and from him you'll learn the rest.
SEGISMUND: Then, vile, infamous traitor, what have I

To know more than this fact of who I am,   200
To show my pride and power from this day onward?
How have you played your country such a treason
As to deny me, against law and right,
The rank which is my own?

CLOTALDO: Unhappy me!

SEGISMUND: You were a traitor to the law, a flattering liar   205
To your own king, and cruel to myself.
And so the king, the law, and I condemn you,
After such fierce misfortunes as I've borne,
To die here by my hands.

SECOND SERVANT: My lord!

SEGISMUND: Let none
Get in the way. It is in vain. By God!   210
If you intrude, I'll throw you through the window.

SECOND SERVANT: Clotaldo, fly!

CLOTALDO: Alas, poor Segismund!
That you should show such pride, all unaware
That you are dreaming this.
        [Exit.]

SECOND SERVANT: Take care! Take care!

SEGISMUND: Get out!

SECOND SERVANT: He was obeying the king's orders.   215

SEGISMUND: In an injustice, no one should obey
The king, and I'm his prince.

SECOND SERVANT: He had no right
To look into the rights and wrongs of it.

SEGISMUND: You must be mad to answer back at me.

CLARION: The prince is right. It's you who're in the wrong!   220

SECOND SERVANT: Who gave you right to speak?

CLARION: I simply took it.

SEGISMUND: And who are you?

CLARION: I am the go-between,
And in this art I think I am a master—
Since I'm the greatest jackanapes alive.

SEGISMUND: [To CLARION] In all this new world, you're the only one
Of the whole crowd who pleases me.

CLARION: Why, my lord,   226
I am the best pleaser of Segismunds[3]
That ever was: ask anybody here!
        [Enter ASTOLFO.]

ASTOLFO: Blessèd the day, a thousand times, my prince,
On which you landed here on Polish soil   230
To fill with so much splendour and delight
Our wide horizons, like the break of day!

3. There had been three kings of Poland by that name between the early sixteenth century and the time
of this play.

For you arise as does the rising sun
Out of the rugged mountains, far away.
Shine forth then! And although so tardily   235
You bind the glittering laurels on your brows,
The longer may they last you still unwithered.

SEGISMUND: God save you.

ASTOLFO: That you do not know me, sir,
Is some excuse for greeting me without
The honour due to me. I am Astolfo.   240
The Duke of Muscovy. You are my cousin.
We are of equal rank.

SEGISMUND: Then if I say,
"God save you," do I not display good feeling?
But since you take such note of who you are,
The next time that I see you, I shall say   245
"God save you *not*," if you would like that better.

SECOND SERVANT: [*To* ASTOLFO] Your Highness, make allowance for his
    breeding
Amongst the mountains. So he deals with all.
[*To* SEGISMUND] Astolfo does take precedence, Your Highness—

SEGISMUND: I have no patience with the way he came   250
To make his solemn speech, then put his hat on!

SECOND SERVANT: He's a grandee![4]

SEGISMUND: I'm grander than grandees!

SECOND SERVANT: For all that, there should be respect between you,
More than among the rest.

SEGISMUND: And who told you
To mix in my affairs?   255
    [*Enter* STELLA.]

STELLA: Many times welcome to Your Royal Highness,
Now come to grace the dais that receives him
With gratitude and love. Long may you live
August and eminent, despite all snares,
And count your life by centuries, not years!   260

SEGISMUND: [*Aside to* CLARION] Now tell me, who's this sovereign deity
At whose divinest feet Heaven lays down
The fleece of its aurora in the east?

CLARION: Sir, it's your cousin Stella.

SEGISMUND: She were better
Named "sun" than "star"![5]
[*To* STELLA]   Though your speech was fair,   265
Just to have seen you and been conquered by you
Suffices for a welcome in itself.
To find myself so blessed beyond my merit
What can I do but thank you, lovely Stella,

---

4. Etiquette allowed a grandee (in Spain, the highest rank of the nobility) to keep his hat on in the king's presence.   5. Stella is Latin for star.

For you could add more brilliance and delight   270
To the most blazing star? When you get up
What work is left the sun to do? O give me
Your hand to kiss, from out whose cup of snow
The solar horses drink the fires of day!

STELLA: Be a more gentle courtier.

ASTOLFO: I am lost.   275

SECOND SERVANT: I know Astolfo's hurt. I must divert him.
  [To SEGISMUND] Sir, you should know that thus to woo so boldly
  Is most improper. And, besides, Astolfo . . .

SEGISMUND: Did I not tell you not to meddle with me?

SECOND SERVANT: I only say what's just.

SEGISMUND: All this annoys me.   280
  Nothing seems just to me but what I want.

SECOND SERVANT: Why, sir, I heard you say that no obedience
  Or service should be lent to what's unjust.

SEGISMUND: You also heard me say that I would throw
  Anyone who annoys me from that balcony.   285

SECOND SERVANT: With men like me you cannot do such things.

SEGISMUND: No? Well, by God, I'll have to prove it then!
  [He takes him in his arms and rushes out, followed by many, to return
  soon after.]

ASTOLFO: What on earth have I seen? Can it be true?

STELLA: Go, all, and stop him!

SEGISMUND: [Returning]   From the balcony
  He's fallen in the sea. How strange it seems!   290

ASTOLFO: Measure your acts of violence, my lord:
  From crags to palaces, the distance is
  As great as that between man and the beasts.

SEGISMUND: Well, since you are for speaking out so boldly,
  Perhaps one day you'll find that on your shoulders   295
  You have no head to place your hat upon.
  [Exit ASTOLFO. Enter BASIL.]

BASIL: What's happened here?

SEGISMUND: Nothing at all. A man
  Wearied me, so I threw him in the sea.

CLARION: [To SEGISMUND] Be warned. That is the king.

BASIL: On the first day,   300
  So soon, your coming here has cost a life?

SEGISMUND: He said I couldn't: so I won the bet.

BASIL: It grieves me, Prince, that, when I hoped to see you
  Forewarned, and overriding Fate, in triumph
  Over your stars, the first thing I should see
  Should be such rigour—that your first deed here   305
  Should be a grievous homicide. Alas!
  With what love, now, can I offer my arms,
  Knowing your own have learned to kill already?

Who sees a dirk, red from a mortal wound,
But does not feat it? Who can see the place   310
Soaking in blood, where late a man was murdered,
But even the strongest must respond to nature?
So in your arms seeing the instrument
Of death, and looking on a blood-soaked place,
I must withdraw myself from your embrace,   315
And though I thought in loving bonds to bind
Your neck, yet fear withholds me from your arms.

SEGISMUND: Without your loving arms I can sustain
   Myself as usual. That such a loving father
   Could treat me with such cruelty, could thrust me   320
   From his side ungratefully, could rear me
   As a wild beast, could hold me for a monster,
   And pray that I were dead, that such a father
   Withholds his arms from winding round my neck,
   Seems unimportant, seeing that he deprives   325
   Me of my very being as a man.

BASIL: Would to heaven I had never granted it,
   For then I never would have heard your voice,
   Nor seen your outrages.

SEGISMUND: Had you denied
   Me being, then I would not have complained,   330
   But that you took it from me when you gave it—
   That is my quarrel with you. Though to give
   Is the most singular and noble action,
   It is the basest action if one gives
   Only to take away.

BASIL: How well you thank me   335
   For being raised from pauper to a prince!

SEGISMUND: In this what is there I should thank you for?
   You tyrant of my will! If you are old
   And feeble, and you die, what can you give me
   More than what is my own by right of birth?   340
   You are my father and my king, therefore
   This grandeur comes to me by natural law.
   Therefore, despite my present state, I'm not
   Indebted to you, rather can I claim
   Account of all those years in which you robbed me   345
   Of life and being, liberty, and honour.
   You ought to thank me that I press no claim
   Since you're my debtor, even to bankruptcy.

BASIL: Barbarous and outrageous brute! The heavens
   Have now fulfilled their prophecy: I call   350
   Them to bear witness to your pride. Although
   You know now, disillusioned, who you are,
   And see yourself where you take precedence,

Take heed of this I say: be kind and humble
Since it may be that you are only dreaming,   355
Although it seems to you you're wide-awake.
  [*Exit.*]
SEGISMUND: Can I perhaps be dreaming, though I seem
So wide-awake? No: I am not asleep.
Since I can touch, and realise what I
Have been before, and what I am today.   360
And if you even now relented, Father,
There'd be no cure since I know who I am
And you cannot, for all your sighs and groans,
Cheat me of my hereditary crown.
And if I was submissive in my chains   365
Before, then I was ignorant of what I am,
Which I now know (and likewise know that I
Am partly man but partly beast as well).
  [*Enter* ROSAURA *in woman's clothing.*]
ROSAURA: [*Aside*] I came in Stella's train. I am afraid
Of meeting with Astolfo, since Clotaldo   370
Says he must not know who I am, not see me,
Because (he says) it touches on my honour.
And well I trust Clotaldo since I owe him
The safety of my life and honour both.
CLARION: What pleases you, and what do you admire   375
Most, of the things you've seen here in the world?
SEGISMUND: Why, nothing that I could not have foreseen—
Except the loveliness of women! Once,
I read among the books I had out there
That who owes God most grateful contemplation   380
Is Man: who is himself a tiny world.
But I think who owes God more grateful study
Is Woman—since she is a tiny heaven,
Having as much more beauty than a man
As heaven than earth. And even more, I say,   385
If she's the one that I am looking at.
ROSAURA: [*Aside*] That is the prince. I'll go.
SEGISMUND: Stop! Woman! Wait!
Don't join the sunset with the breaking day
By fading out so fast. If east and west
Should clash like that, the day would surely suffer   390
A syncope. But what is this I see?
ROSAURA: What I am looking at I doubt, and yet
Believe.
SEGISMUND: [*Aside*] This beauty I have seen before.
ROSAURA: [*Aside*] This pomp and grandeur I have seen before
Cooped in a narrow dungeon.

SEGISMUND: [*Aside*] I have found 395
  My life at last.
  [*Aloud*] Woman (for that sole word
  Outsoars all wooing flattery of speech
  From one that is a man), woman, who are you?
  If even long before I ever saw you
  You owed me adoration as your prince, 400
  How much the more should you be conquered by me
  Now I recall I've seen you once before!
  Who are you, beauteous woman?
ROSAURA: [*Aside*] I'll pretend.
  [*Aloud*] In Stella's train, I am a luckless lady.
SEGISMUND: Say no such thing. You are the sun from which 405
  The minor star that's Stella draws its life,
  Since she receives the splendour of your rays.
  I've seen how in the kingdom of sweet odours,
  Commander of the squadrons of the flowers,
  The rose's diety presides, and is 410
  Their empress by divine right of her beauty.
  Among the precious stones which can be listed
  In the academy of mines, I've seen
  The diamond much preferred above the rest,
  And crowned their emperor, for shining brightest. 415
  In the revolving empire of the stars
  The morning star takes pride among the others.
  In their perfected spheres, when the sun calls
  The planets to his council, he presides
  And is the very oracle of day. 420
  Then if among stars, gems, planet, and flowers
  The fairest are exalted, why do you
  Wait on a lesser beauty than yourself
  Who are, in greater excellence and beauty,
  The sun, the morning star, the diamond, and the rose! 425
  [*Enter* CLOTALDO, *who remains by the stage-curtain.*]
CLOTALDO: [*Aside*] I wish to curb him, since I brought him up.
  But, what is this?
ROSAURA: I reverence your favour,
  And yet reply, rhetorical, with silence,
  For when one's mind is clumsy and untaught,
  He answers best who does not speak at all. 430
SEGISMUND: Stay! Do not go! How can you wish to go
  And leave me darkened by my doubts?
ROSAURA: Your Highness,
  I beg your leave to go.
SEGISMUND: To go so rudely
  Is not to beg my leave but just to take it.

ROSAURA: But if you will not grant it, I must take it.   435
SEGISMUND: That were to change my courtesy to rudeness.
 Resistance is like venom to my patience.
ROSAURA: But even if this deadly, raging venom
 Should overcome your patience, yet you dare not
 And could not treat me with dishonour, sir.   440
SEGISMUND: Why, just to see then if I can, and dare to—
 You'll make me lose the fear I bear your beauty,
 Since the impossible is always tempting
 To me. Why, only now I threw a man
 Over this balcony who said I couldn't: 445
 And so to find out if I can or not
 I'll throw your honour through the window too.
CLOTALDO: [Aside] He seems determined in this course. Oh, heavens!
 What's to be done that for a second time
 My honour's threatened by a mad desire?   450
ROSAURA: Then with good reason it was prophesied
 Your tyranny would wreak this kingdom
 Outrageous scandals, treasons, crimes, and deaths.
 But what can such a creature do as you
 Who are not even a man, save in the name—   455
 Inhuman, barbarous, cruel, and unbending
 As the wild beasts amongst whom you were nursed?
SEGISMUND: That you should not insult me in this way
 I spoke to you most courteously, and thought
 I'd thereby get my way; but if you curse me thus   460
 Even when I am speaking gently, why,
 By the living God, I'll really give you cause.
 Ho there! Clear out, the lot of you, at once!
 Leave her to me! Close all the doors upon us.
 Let no one enter!
  [Exeunt CLARION and other attendants.]
ROSAURA: I am lost . . . I warn you . . .   465
SEGISMUND: I am a tyrant and you plead in vain.
CLOTALDO: [Aside] Oh, what a monstrous thing! I must restrain him
 Even if I die for it.
 [Aloud]   Sir! Wait! Look here!
SEGISMUND: A second time you have provoked my anger,
 You feeble, mad old man! Do you prize lightly   470
 My wrath and rigour that you've gone so far?
CLOTALDO: Brought by the accents of her voice, I came
 To tell you you must be more peaceful
 If still you hope to reign, and warn you that
 You should not be so cruel, though you rule—   475
 Since this, perhaps, is nothing but a dream.
SEGISMUND: When you refer to disillusionment
 You rouse me near to madness. Now you'll see,

Here as I kill you, if it's truth or dreaming!
> [*As he tries to pull out his dagger,* CLOTALDO *restrains him and throws himself on his knees before him.*]

CLOTALDO: It's thus I'd save my life: and hope to do so—   480
SEGISMUND: Take your presumptuous hand from off this steel.
CLOTALDO: Till people come to hold your rage and fury
  I shall not let you go.
ROSAURA: O heavens!
SEGISMUND: Loose it,
> [*They struggle.*] I say, or else—you interfering fool—
  I'll crush you to your death in my strong arms!   485
ROSAURA: Come quickly! Here's Clotaldo being killed!
> [*Exit.* ASTOLFO *appears as* CLOTALDO *falls on the floor, and the former stands between* SEGISMUND *and* CLOTALDO.]

ASTOLFO: Why, what is this, most valiant prince? What? Staining
  Your doughty steel in such old, frozen blood?
  For shame! For shame! Sheathe your illustrious weapon!
SEGISMUND: When it is stained in his infamous blood!   490
ASTOLFO: At my feet here he has found sanctuary
  And there he's safe, for it will serve him well.
SEGISMUND: Then serve me well by dying, for like this
  I will avenge myself for your behaviour
  In trying to annoy me first of all.   495
ASTOLFO: To draw in self-defense offends no king,
  Though in his palace.
> [ASTOLFO *draws his sword and they fight.*]

CLOTALDO: [*To* ASTOLFO] Do not anger him!
> [*Enter* BASIL, STELLA, *and attendants.*]

BASIL: Hold! Hold! What's this? Fighting with naked swords?
STELLA: [*Aside*] It is Astolfo! How my heart misgives me!
BASIL: Why, what has happened here?
ASTOLFO: Nothing, my lord,   500
  Since you've arrived.
> [*Both sheathe their swords.*]

SEGISMUND: Much, though you *have* arrived.
  I tried to kill the old man.
BASIL: Had you no
  Respect for those white hairs?
CLOTALDO: Sire, since they're only
  Mine, as you well can see, it does not matter!
SEGISMUND: It is in vain you'd have me hold white hairs   505
  In such respect, since one day you may find
  Your own white locks prostrated at my feet
  For still I have not taken vengeance on you
  For the foul way in which you had me reared.
> [*Exit.*]

BASIL: Before that happens you will sleep once more   510

    Where you were reared, and where what's happened may
    Seem just a dream (being mere earthly glory).
      [*All save* ASTOLFO *and* STELLA *leave.*]
ASTOLFO: How seldom does prediction fail, when evil!
    How oft, foretelling good! Exact in harm,
    Doubtful in benefit! Oh, what a great   515
    Astrologer would be one who foretold
    Nothing but harms, since there's no doubt al all
    That they are always due! In Segismund
    And me the case is illustrated clearly.
    In him, crimes, cruelties, deaths, and disasters   520
    Were well predicted, since they all came true.
    But in my own case, to predict for me
    (As I foresaw beholding rays which cast
    The sun into the shade and outface heaven)
    Triumphs and trophies, happiness and praise,   525
    Was false—and yet was true: it's only just
    That when predictions start with promised favours
    They should end in disdain.
STELLA: I do not doubt
    Your protestations are most heartfelt; only
    They're not for me, but for another lady   530
    Whose portrait you were wearing round your neck
    Slung in a locket when you first arrived.
    Since it is so, she only can deserve
    These wooing flatteries. Let her repay you
    For in affairs of love, flatteries and vows   535
    Made for another are mere forged credentials.
      [ROSAURA *enters but waits by the curtain.*]
ROSAURA: [*Aside*] Thanks be to God, my troubles are near ended!
    To judge from what I see, I've naught to fear.
ASTOLFO: I will expel that portrait from my breast
    To make room for the image of your beauty   540
    And keep it there. For there where Stella is
    Can be no room for shade, and where the sun is
    No place for any star. I'll fetch the portrait.
    [*Aside*] Forgive me, beautiful Rosaura, that,
    When absent, men and women seldom keep   545
    More faith than this.
      [*Exit.* ROSAURA *comes forward.*]
ROSAURA: [*Aside*] I could not hear a word. I was afraid
    That they would see me.
STELLA: Oh, Astrea![6]
ROSAURA: My lady!
STELLA: I am delighted that you came. Because

---

6. The name assumed by Rosaura.

To you alone would I confide a secret.   550
ROSAURA: Thereby you greatly honour me, your servant.
STELLA: Astrea, in the brief time I have known you
  I've given you the latchkey of my will.
  For that, and being who you are, I'll tell you
  A secret which I've very often hidden   555
  Even from myself.
ROSAURA: I am your slave.
STELLA: Then, briefly:
  Astolfo, who's my cousin (the word cousin
  Suffices, since some things are plainly said
  Even by thinking them), is to wed me
  If Fortune thus can wipe so many cares   560
  Away with one great joy. But I am troubled
  In that, the day he first came here, he carried
  A portrait of a lady round his neck.
  I spoke to him about it courteously.
  He was most amiable, he loves me well,   565
  And now he's gone for it. I am embarrassed
  That he should give it me himself. Wait here,
  And tell him to deliver it to you.
  Do not say more. Since you're discreet and fair:
  You'll surely know just what love is.
    [Exit.]
ROSAURA: Great heavens!   570
  How I wish that I did not! For who could be
  So prudent or so skilful as would know
  What to advise herself in such a case?
  Lives there a person on this earth today
  Who's more beset by the inclement stars,   575
  Who has more cares besieging him, or fights
  So many dire calamities at once?
  What can I do in such bewilderment
  Wherein it seems impossible to find
  Relief or comfort? Since my first misfortune   580
  No other thing has chanced or happened to me
  But was a new misfortune. In succession
  Inheritors and heirs of their own selves
  (Just like the Phoenix,[7] his own son and father)
  Misfortunes reproduce themselves, are born,   585
  And live by dying. In their sepulchre
  The ashes they consume are not forever.
  A sage once said misfortunes must be cowards
  Because they never dare to walk alone
  But come in crowds. I say they are most valiant   590

7. The mythical bird that every 500 years is consumed by fire and then rises from its own ashes.

Because they always charge so bravely on
And never turn their backs. Who charges with them
May dare all things because there is no fear
That they'll ever desert him; and I say it
Because in all my life I never once   595
Knew them to leave me, nor will they grow tired
Of me till, wounded and shot through and through
By Fate, I fall into the arms of death.
Alas, what can I do in this dilemma?
If I reveal myself, then old Clotaldo,   600
To whom I owe my life, may take offence,
Because he told me to await the cure
And mending of my honour in concealment.
If I don't tell Astolfo who I am
And he detects me, how can I dissimulate?   605
Since even if I say I am not I,
The voice, the language, and the eyes will falter,
Because the soul will tell them that they lie.
What shall I do? It is in vain to study
What I should do, when I know very well   610
That, whatsoever way I choose to act,
When the time comes I'll do as sorrow bids,
For no one has control over his sorrows.
Then since my soul dares not decide its actions
Let sorrow fill my cup and let my grief   615
Reach its extremity and, out of doubts
And vain appearances, once and for all
Come out into the light—and Heaven shield me!
    [*Enter* ASTOLFO.]
ASTOLFO: Here, lady, is the portrait . . . but . . . great God!
ROSAURA: Why does Your Highness halt, and stare astonished?
ASTOLFO: Rosaura! Why, to see you here!
ROSAURA: Rosaura?   621
   Sir, you mistake me for some other lady.
   I am Astrea, and my humble station
   Deserves no perturbation such as yours.
ASTOLFO: Enough of this pretence, Rosaura, since   625
   The soul can never lie. Though as Astrea
   I see you now, I love you as Rosaura.
ROSAURA: Not having understood Your Highness' meaning
   I can make no reply except to say
   That Stella (who might be the star of Venus)   630
   Told me to wait here and to tell you from here
   To give to me the portrait you were fetching
   (Which seems a very logical request)
   And I myself will take it to my lady.
   Thus Stella bids: even the slightest things   635

Which do me harm are governed by some star.
ASTOLFO: Even if you could make a greater effort
  How poorly you dissimulate, Rosaura!
  Tell your poor eyes they do not harmonise
  With your own voice, because they needs must jangle   640
  When the whole instrument is out of tune.
  You cannot match the falshood of your words
  With the sincerity of what you're feeling.
ROSAURA: All I can say is—that I want the portrait.
ASTOLFO: As you require a fiction, with a fiction   645
  I shall reply. Go and tell Stella this:
  That I esteem her so, it seems unworthy
  Only to send the counterfeit to her
  And that I'm sending her the original.
  And you, take the original along with you,   650
  Taking yourself to her.
ROSAURA: When a man starts
  Forth on a definite task, resolved and valiant,
  Though he be offered a far greater prize
  Than what he seeks, yet he returns with failure
  If he returns without his task performed.   655
  I came to get that portrait. Though I bear
  The original with me, of greater value,
  I would return in failure and contempt
  Without the copy. Give it me, Your Highness,
  Since I cannot return without it.
ASTOLFO: But   660
  If I don't give it you, how can you do so?
ROSAURA: Like this, ungrateful man! I'll take it from you.
  [*She tries to wrest it from him.*]
ASTOLFO: It is in vain.
ROSAURA: By God, it shall not come
  Into another woman's hands!
ASTOLFO: You're terrifying!
ROSAURA: And you're perfidious!
ASTOLFO: Enough, my dear   665
  Rosaura!
ROSAURA: I, your dear? You lie, you villain!
  [*They are both clutching the portrait. Enter* STELLA.]
STELLA: Astrea and Astolfo, what does this mean?
ASTOLFO: [*Aside*] Here's Stella.
ROSAURA: [*Aside*]   Love, grant me the strength to win
  My portrait. [*To* STELLA] If you want to know, my lady,
  What this is all about, I will explain.   670
ASTOLFO: [*To* ROSAURA, *aside*] What do you mean?
ROSAURA: You told me to await
  Astolfo here and ask him for a portrait

On your behalf. I waited here alone
And as one thought suggests another thought,
Thinking of portraits, I recalled my own   675
Was here inside my sleeve. When one's alone,
One is diverted by a foolish trifle
And so I took it out to look at it.
It slipped and fell, just as Astolfo here,
Bringing the portrait of the other lady,   680
Came to deliver it to you as promised.
He picked my portrait up, and so unwilling
Is he to give away the one you asked for,
Instead of doing so, he seized upon
The other portrait which is mine alone   685
And will not give it back though I entreated
And begged him to return it. I was angry
And tried to snatch it back. That's it he's holding,
And you can see yourself if it's not mine.
STELLA: Let go the portrait.
        [*She snatches it from him.*]
ASTOLFO: Madam!
STELLA: The draughtsman   690
    Was not unkind to truth.
ROSAURA: Is it not mine?
STELLA: Why, who could doubt it?
ROSAURA: Ask him for the other.
STELLA: Here, take your own, Astrea. You may leave us.
ROSAURA: [*Aside*] Now I have got my portrait, come what will.
        [*Exit.*]
STELLA: Now give me up the portrait that I asked for   695
    Although I'll see and speak to you no more.
    I do not wish to leave it in your power
    Having been once so foolish as to beg it.
ASTOLFO: [*Aside*] Now how can I get out of this foul trap?
    [*To* STELLA] Beautiful Stella, though I would obey you,   700
    And serve you in all ways, I cannot give you
    The portrait, since . . .
STELLA: You are a crude, coarse villian
    And ruffian of a wooer. For the portrait—
    I do not want it now, since, if I had it,
    It would remind me I had asked you for it.
        [*Exit.*]
ASTOLFO: Listen! Look! Wait! Let me explain!
    [*Aside*]   Oh, damn
    Rosaura! How the devil did she get
    To Poland for my ruin and her own?

The prison of Segismund in the tower

[SEGISMUND *lying on the ground loaded with fetters and clothed in skins as before.* CLOTALDO, *two attendants, and* CLARION.]

CLOTALDO: Here you must leave him—since his reckless pride
  Ends here today where it began.
ATTENDANT: His chain   710
  I'll rivet as it used to be before.
CLARION: O Prince, you'd better not awake too soon
  To find how lost you are, how changed your fate,
  And that your fancied glory of an hour
  Was but a shade of life, a flame of death!   715
CLOTALDO: For one who knows so well to wield his tongue
  It's fit as worthy place should be provided
  With lots of room and lots of time to argue.
  This is the fellow that you have to seize   719
  [*To the attendants*] And that's the room in which you are to lock him.
  [*Points to the nearest cell.*]
CLARION: Why me?
CLOTALDO: Because a Clarion who knows
  Too many secrets must be kept in gaol—
  A place where even clarions are silent.
CLARION: Have I, by chance, wanted to kill my father
  Or thrown an Icarus[8] from a balcony?   725
  Am I asleep or dreaming? To what end
  Do you imprison me?
CLOTALDO: You're Clarion.
CLARION: Well, say I swear to be a cornet now,
  A silent one, a wretched instrument . . . ?
  [*They hustle him off.* CLOTALDO *remains. Enter* BASIL, *wearing a mask.*]
BASIL: Clotaldo.
CLOTALDO: Sire . . . and is it thus alone   730
  Your Majesty has come?
BASIL: Vain curiosity
  To see what happens here to Segismund.
CLOTALDO: See where he lies, reduced to misery!
BASIL: Unhappy prince! Born at a fatal moment!
  Come waken him, now he has lost his strength   735
  With all the opium he's drunk.
CLOTALDO: He's stirring
  And talking to himself.
BASIL: What is he dreaming?
  Let's listen now.
SEGISMUND: He who chastises tyrants
  Is a most pious prince . . . Now let Clotaldo
  Die by my hand . . . my father kiss my feet . . .   740
CLOTALDO: He threatens me with death!

8. Mythological figure who, in attempting to fly, came so close to the sun that his wax wings melted and
he fell into the sea.

BASIL:　　　　　　　　　　　　And me with insult
　　And cruelty.
CLOTALDO:　　He'd take my life away.
BASIL: And he'd humiliate me at his feet.
SEGISMUND: [*Still in a dream*]
　　Throughout the expanse of this world's theatre
　　I'll show my peerless valour, let my vengeance　　　　　745
　　Be wreaked, and the Prince Segismund be seen
　　To triumph—over his father . . . but, alas!
　　[*Awakening*] Where am I?
BASIL: [*To* CLOTALDO] Since he must not see me here,
　　I'll listen further off. You know your cue. [*Retires to one side.*]　750
SEGISMUND: Can this be I? Am I the same who, chained
　　And long imprisoned, rose to such a state?
　　Are you not still my sepulchre and grave,
　　You dismal tower? God! What things I have dreamed!
CLOTALDO: [*Aside*] Now I must go to him to disenchant him.　　755
　　[*Aloud*] Awake already?
SEGISMUND:　　　　　　　Yes: it was high time.
CLOTALDO: What? Do you have to spend all day asleep?
　　Since I was following the eagle's flight
　　With tardy discourse,[9] have you still lain here
　　Without awaking?
SEGISMUND:　　　　　No. Nor even now　　　　　760
　　Am I awake. It seems I've always slept,
　　Since, if I've dreamed what I've just seen and heard
　　Palpably and for certain, then I am dreaming
　　What I see now—nor is it strange I'm tired,
　　Since what I, sleeping, see, tells me that I　　　　　765
　　Was dreaming when I thought I was awake.
CLOTALDO: Tell me your dream.
SEGISMUND:　　　　　　　That's if it *was* a dream!
　　No, I'll not tell you what I dreamed; but what
　　I lived and saw, Clotaldo, I *will* tell you.
　　I woke up in a bed that might have been　　　　　770
　　The cradle of the flowers, woven by Spring.
　　A thousand nobles, bowing, called me Prince,
　　Attiring me in jewels, pomp, and splendour.
　　My equanimity you turned to rapture
　　Telling me that I was the Prince of Poland.　　　　　775
CLOTALDO: I must have got a fine reward!
SEGISMUND:　　　　　　　　　Not so:
　　For as a traitor, twice, with rage and fury,
　　I tried to kill you.
CLOTALDO:　　　Such cruelty to me?

9. See lines 28ff. at the opening of this act.

SEGISMUND: I was the lord of all, on all I took revenge,
  Except I loved one woman . . . I believe   780
  That *that* was true, though all the rest has faded.
    [*Exit* BASIL.]
CLOTALDO: [*Aside*] I see the king was moved, to hear him speak.
  [*Aloud*] Talking of eagles made you dream of empires,
  But even in your dreams it's good to honour
  Those who have cared for you and brought you up.   785
  For Segismund, even in dreams, I warn you
  Nothing is lost by trying to do good.
    [*Exit.*]
SEGISMUND: That's true, and therefore let us subjugate
  The bestial side, this fury and ambition,
  Against the time when we may dream once more,   790
  As certainly we shall, for this strange world
  Is such that but to live here is to dream.
  And now experience shows me that each man
  Dreams what he is until he is awakened.
  The king dreams he's a king and in this fiction   795
  Lives, rules, administers with royal pomp.
  Yet all the borrowed praises that he earns
  Are written in the wind, and he is changed
  (How sad a fate!) by death to dust and ashes.
  What man is there alive who'd seek to reign   800
  Since he must wake into the dream that's death.
  The rich man dreams his wealth which is his care
  And woe. The poor man dreams his sufferings.
  He dreams who thrives and prospers in this life.
  He dreams who toils and strives. He dreams who injures,   805
  Offends, and insults. So that in this world
  Everyone dreams the thing he is, though no one
  Can understand it. I dream I am here,
  Chained in these fetters. Yet I dreamed just now
  I was in a more flattering, lofty station.   810
  What is this life? A frenzy, an illusion,
  A shadow, a delirium, a fiction.
  The greatest good's but little, and this life
  Is but a dream, and dreams are only dreams.

Act III

The tower

[*Enter* CLARION.]
CLARION: I'm held in an enchanted tower, because
  Of all I know. What would they do to me
  For all I don't know, since—for all I know—

They're killing me by starving me to death.
O that a man so hungry as myself   5
Should live to die of hunger while alive!
I am so sorry for myself that others
May well say "I can well believe it," since
This silence ill accords with my name "Clarion,"
And I just can't shut up. My fellows here?   10
Spiders and rats—fine feathered songsters those!
My head's still ringing with a dream of fifes
And trumpets and a lot of noise humbug
And long processions as of penitents
With crosses, winding up and down, while some   15
Faint at the sight of blood besmirching others.
But now to tell the truth, I am in prison.
For knowing secrets, I am kept shut in,
Strictly observed as if I were a Sunday,
And feeling sadder than a Tuesday, where   20
I neither eat nor drink. They say a secret
Is sacred and should be as strictly kept
As any saint's day on the calendar.
Saint Secret's Day for me's a working day
Because I'm never idle then. The penance   25
I suffer here is merited, I say:
Because being a lackey, I was silent,
Which, in a servant, is a sacrilege.
            [A noise of drums and trumpets]
FIRST SOLDIER: [Within] Here is the tower in which he is imprisoned.
    Smash in the door and enter, everybody!   30
CLARION: Great God! They've come to seek me. That is certain
    Because they say I'm here. What can they want?
            [Enter several soldiers.]
FIRST SOLDIER: Go in.
SECOND SOLDIER: He's here!
CLARION: No, he's not here!
ALL THE SOLDIERS: Our lord!
CLARION: What, are they drunk?
FIRST SOLDIER: You are our rightful prince.
    We do not want and never shall allow   35
    A stranger to supplant our trueborn prince.
    Give us your feet to kiss!
ALL THE SOLDIERS: Long live the prince!
CLARION: Bless me, if it's not real! In this strange kingdom
    It seems the custom, every day, to take
    Some fellow and to make him prince and then   40
    Shut him back in this tower. That must be it!
    So I must play my role.
ALL THE SOLDIERS: Give us your feet.

CLARION: I can't. They're necessary. After all
   What sort of use would be a footless prince?
SECOND SOLDIER: All of us told your father, as one man,   45
   We want no prince of Muscovy but you!
CLARION: You weren't respectful to my father? Shame!
FIRST SOLDIER: It was our loyalty that made us tell him.
CLARION: If it was loyalty, you have my pardon.   49
SECOND SOLDIER: Restore your empire. Long live Segismund!
CLARION: [Aside] That is the name they seem to give to all
   These counterfeited princes.
      [Enter SEGISMUND.]
SEGISMUND: Who called Segismund?
CLARION: [Aside] I seem to be a hollow sort of prince.
FIRST SOLDIER: Which of you's Segismund?
SEGISMUND: I am.
SECOND SOLDIER: [To CLARION]   Then, why,
   Rash fool, did you impersonate the prince   55
   Segismund?
CLARION: What? I, Segismund? Yourselves
   Be-Segismunded me without request.
   All yours was both the rashness and the folly.
FIRST SOLDIER: Prince Segismund, whom we acclaim our lord,
   Your father, great King Basil, in his fear   60
   That heaven would fulfill a prophecy
   That one day he would kneel before your feet
   Wishes now to deprive you of the throne
   And give it to the Duke of Muscovy.
   For this he called a council, but the people   65
   Discovered his design and knowing, now,
   They have a native king, will have no stranger.
   So scorning the fierce threats of destiny,
   We've come to seek you in your very prison,
   That aided by the arms of the whole people,   70
   We may restore you to the crown and sceptre,
   Taking them from the tyrant's grasp. Come, then:
   Assembling here, in this wide desert region,
   Hosts of plebeians, bandits, and freebooters,
   Acclaim you king. Your liberty awaits you!   75
   Hark to its voice!
   [Shouts within]   Long life to Segismund!
SEGISMUND: Once more, you heavens will that I should dream
   Of grandeur, once again, 'twixt doubts and shades,
   Behold the majesty of pomp and power
   Vanish into the wind, once more you wish   80
   That I should taste the disillusion and
   The risk by which all human power is humbled,
   Of which all human power should live aware.

It must not be. I'll not be once again
Put through my paces by my fortune's stars.   85
And since I know this life is all a dream,
Depart, vain shades, who feign, to my dead senses,
That you have voice and body, having neither!
I want no more feigned majesty, fantastic
Display, nor void illusions, that one gust   90
Can scatter like the almond tree in flower,
Whose rosy buds, without advice or warning,
Dawn in the air too soon and then, as one,
Are all extinguished, fade, and fall, and wither
In the first gust of wind that comes along!   95
I know you well. I know you well by now.
I know that all that happens in yourselves
Happens as in a sleeping man. For me
There are no more delusions and deceptions
Since I well know this life is all a dream.   100
SECOND SOLDIER: If you think we are cheating, just sweep
    Your gaze along these towering peaks, and see
    The hosts that wait to welcome and obey you.
SEGISMUND: Already once before I've seen such crowds
    Distinctly, quite as vividly as these: 105
    And yet it was a dream.
SECOND SOLDIER: No great event
    Can come without forerunners to announce it
    And this is the real meaning of your dream.
SEGISMUND: Yes, you say well. It was the fore-announcement
    And just in case it was correct, my soul,   110
    (Since life's so short) let's dream the dream anew!
    But it must be attentively, aware
    That we'll awake from pleasure in the end.
    Forewarned of that, the shock's not so abrupt,
    The disillusion's less. Evils anticipated   115
    Lose half their sting. And armed with this precaution—
    That power, even when we're sure of it, is borrowed
    And must be given back to its true owner—
    We can risk anything and dare the worst.
    Subjects, I thank you for your loyalty.   120
    In me you have a leader who will free you,
    Bravely and skillfully, from foreign rule.
    Sound now to arms, you'll soon behold my valour.
    Against my father I must march and bring
    Truth from the stars.[1] Yes: he must kneel to me.   125
    [Aside] But yet, since I may wake before he kneels,
    Perhaps I'd better not proclaim what may not happen.

1. Proof that their predictions were truthful.

ALL: Long live Segismund!
   [*Enter* CLOTALDO.]
CLOTALDO: Gracious heavens! What is
  This riot here?
SEGISMUND: Clotaldo!
CLOTALDO: Sir!
  [*Aside*]   He'll prove
  His cruelty on me.
CLARION: I bet he throws him   130
  Over the mountain.
CLOTALDO: At your royal feet
  I kneel, knowing my penalty is death.
SEGISMUND: Rise, rise, my foster father, from the ground,
    For you must be the compass and the guide
    In which I trust. You brought me up, and I   135
  Know what I owe your loyalty. Embrace me!
CLOTALDO: What's that you say?
SEGISMUND: I know I'm in a dream,
  But I would like to act well, since good actions,
    Even in a dream, are not entirely lost.
CLOTALDO: Since doing good is now to be your glory,   140
  You will not be offended that I too
    Should do what's right. You march against your father!
    I cannot give you help against my king.
    Here at your feet, my lord, I plead for death.
SEGISMUND: [*Aloud*] Villain!
  [*Aside*]   But let us suffer this annoyance.
  Though my rage would slay him, yet he's loyal.   146
  A man does not deserve to die for that.
    How many angry passions does this leash
    Restrain in me, this curb of knowing well
    That I must wake and find myself alone!   150
SECOND SOLDIER: All this fine talk, Clotaldo, is a cruel
    Spurn of the public welfare. We are loyal
    Who wish our own prince to reign over us.
CLOTALDO: Such loyalty, after the king were dead,
    Would honour you. But while the king is living   155
  He is our absolute, unquestioned lord.
    There's no excuse for subjects who oppose
    His sovereignty in arms.
FIRST SOLDIER: We'll soon see well
  Enough, Clotaldo, what this loyalty
  Is worth.
CLOTALDO: You would be better if you had some.   160
  It is the greatest prize.
SEGISMUND: Peace, peace, I pray you.
CLOTALDO: My lord!

SEGISMUND: Clotaldo, if your feelings
   Are truly thus, go you, and serve the king;
      That's prudence, loyalty, and common sense.
      But do not argue here with anyone   165
   Whether it's right or wrong, for every man
      Has his own honour.
CLOTALDO: Humbly I take my leave.
   [*Exit.*]
SEGISMUND: Now sound the drums and march in rank and order
   Straight to the palace.
ALL: Long live Segismund!
SEGISMUND: Fortune, we go to reign! Do not awake me   170
   If I am dreaming! Do not let me fall
   Asleep if it is true! To act with virtue
   Is what matters, since if this proves true,
   That truth's sufficient reason in itself;
   If not, we win us friends against the time   175
   When we at last awake.

              A room in the royal palace

   [*Enter* BASIL *and* ASTOLFO.]
BASIL: Whose prudence can rein in a bolting horse?
   Who can restrain a river's pride, in spate?
   Whose valour can withstand a crag dislodged
   And hurtling downwards from a mountain peak?   180
   All these are easier by far than to hold back
   A crowd's proud fury, once it has been roused.
   It has two voices, both proclaiming war,
   And you can hear them echoing through the mountains,
   Some shouting "Segismund," others "Astolfo."   185
   The scene I set for swearing all allegiance
   Lends but an added horror to this strife:
   It has become the back cloth to a stage
   Where Fortune plays out tragedies in blood.
ASTOLFO: My lord, forget the happiness and wealth   190
   You promised me from your most blessèd hand.
   If Poland, which I hope to rule, refuses
   Obedience to my right, grudging me honour,
   It is because I've got to earn it first.
   Give me a horse, that I with angry pride   195
   May match the thunder in my voice and ride
   To strike, like lightning, terror far and wide.
   [*Exit.*]
BASIL: No remedy for what's infallible!
   What is foreseen is perilous indeed!
   If something has to be, there's no way out;   200
   In trying to evade it, you but court it.

This law is pitiless and horrible.
Thinking one can evade the risk, one meets it:
My own precautions have been my undoing,
And I myself have quite destroyed my kingdom.   205
    [*Enter* STELLA.]
STELLA: If you, my lord, in person do not try
    To curb the vast commotion that has started
    In all the streets between the rival factions,
    You'll see your kingdom, swamped in waves of crimson,
    Swimming in its own blood, with nothing left   210
    But havoc, dire calamity, and woe.
    So frightful is the damage to your empire
    That, seen, it strikes amazement; heard, despair.
    The sun's obscured, the very winds are hindered.
    Each stone is a memorial to the dead.   215
    Each flower springs from a grave while every building
    Appears a mausoleum, and each soldier
    A premature and walking skeleton.
        [*Enter* CLOTALDO.]
CLOTALDO: Praise be to God, I reach your feet alive!
BASIL: Clotaldo! What's the news of Segismund?   220
CLOTALDO: The crowd, a headstrong monster blind with rage,
    Entered his dungeon tower and set him free.
    He, now exalted for the second time,
    Conducts himself with valour, boasting how
    He will bring down the truth out of the stars.   225
BASIL: Give me a horse, that I myself, in person,
    May vanquish such a base, ungrateful son!
    For I, in the defence of my own crown,
    Shall do by steel what science failed to do.
        [*Exit.*]
STELLA: I'll be Bellona[2] to your Sun, and try   230
    To write my name next yours in history.
    I'll ride as though I flew on outstretched wings
    That I may vie with Pallas.
        [*Exit. Enter* ROSAURA, *holding back* CLOTALDO.]
ROSAURA: I know that all is war, Clotaldo, yet
    Although your valour calls you to the front,   235
    First hear me out. You know quite well that I
    Arrived in Poland poor and miserable,
    Where, shielded by your valour, I found mercy.
    You told me to conceal myself, and stay
    Here in the palace, hiding from Astolfo.   240
    He saw me in the end, and so insulted
    My honour that (although he saw me clearly)

2. The Roman war goddess.

He nightly speaks with Stella in the garden.
I have the key to it and I will show you
How you can enter there and end my cares.   245
Thus bold, resolved, and strong, you can recover
My honour, since you're ready to avenge me
By killing him.

CLOTALDO: It's true that I intended,
Since first I saw you (having heard your tale)
With my own life to rectify your wrongs.   250
The first step that I took was bid you dress
According to your sex, for fear Astolfo
Might see you as you were, and deem you wanton.
I was devising how we could recover
Your honour (so much did it weigh on me)   255
Even though we had to kill him. (A wild plan—
Though since he's not my king, I would not flinch
From killing him.) But then, when suddenly
Segismund tried to kill me, it was he
Who saved my life with his surpassing valour.   260
Consider: how can I requite Astolfo
With death for giving me my life so bravely,
And when my soul is full of gratitude?
So torn between the two of you I stand—
Rosaura, whose life I saved, and Astolfo,   265
Who saved my life. What's to be done? Which side
To take, and whom to help, I cannot judge.
What I owe you in that I gave you life
I owe to him in that he gave me life.
And so there is no course that I can take   270
To satisfy my love. I am a person
Who has to act, yet suffer either way.

ROSAURA: I should not have to tell so brave a man
That if it is nobility to give,
It's baseness to receive. That being so   275
You owe no gratitude to him, admitting
That it was he who gave you life, and you
Who gave me life, since he forced you to take
A meaner role, and through me you assumed
A generous role. So you should side with me: 280
My cause is so far worthier than his own
As giving is than taking.

CLOTALDO: Though nobility
Is with the giver, it is gratitude
That dwells with the receiver. As a giver
I have the name of being generous: 285
Then grant me that of being grateful too
And let me earn the title and be grateful,

As I am liberal, giving or receiving.
ROSAURA: You granted me my life, at the same time
  Telling me it was worthless, since dishonored,   290
  And therefore was no life. Therefore from you
  I have received no life at all. And since
  You should be liberal first and grateful after
  (Since so you said yourself) I now entreat you
  Give me the life, the life you never gave me!   295
  As giving magnifies the most, give first
  And then be grateful after, if you will!
CLOTALDO: Won by your argument, I will be liberal.
  Rosaura, I shall give you my estate
  And you shall seek a convent, there to live.   300
  This measure is a happy thought, for, see,
  Fleeing a crime, you find a sanctuary.
  For when the empire's threatened, with disasters
  And is divided thus, I, born a noble,
  Am not the man who would augment its woes.   305
  So with this remedy which I have chosen
  I remain loyal to the kingdom, generous
  To you, and also grateful to Astolfo.
  And thus I choose the course that suits you best.
  Were I your father, what could I do more?   310
ROSAURA: Were you my father, then I would accept
  The insult. Since you are not, I refuse.
CLOTALDO: What do you hope to do then?
ROSAURA: Kill the duke!
CLOTALDO: A girl who never even knew her father
  Armed with such courage?
ROSAURA: Yes.
CLOTALDO: What spurs you on?   315
ROSAURA: My good name.
CLOTALDO: In Astolfo you will find . . . .
ROSAURA: My honour rides on him and strikes him down!
CLOTALDO: Your king, too, Stella's husband!
ROSAURA: Never, never
  Shall that be, by almighty God, I swear!
CLOTALDO: Why, this is madness!
ROSAURA: Yes it is!
CLOTALDO: Restrain it.   320
ROSAURA : That I cannot.
CLOTALDO: Then you are lost forever!
ROSAURA: I know it!
CLOTALDO: Life and honour both together!
ROSAURA: I well believe it!
CLOTALDO: What do you intend?
ROSAURA: My death.

CLOTALDO: This is despair and desperation.
ROSAURA: It's honour.
CLOTALDO: It is nonsense.
ROSAURA: It is valour.   325
CLOTALDO: It's frenzy.
ROSAURA: Yes, it's anger! Yes, it's fury!
CLOTALDO: In short you cannot moderate your passion?
ROSAURA: No.
CLOTALDO: Who is there to help you?
ROSAURA: I, myself.
CLOTALDO: There is no cure?
ROSAURA: There is no cure!
CLOTALDO: Think well
   If there's not some way out . . . .
ROSAURA: Some other way   330
   To do away with me . . . .
      [*Exit.*]
CLOTALDO: If you are lost,
   My daughter, let us both be lost together!

In the country

[*Enter* SEGISMUND *clothed in skins. Soldiers marching.* CLARION. *Drums
   beating.*]

SEGISMUND: If Rome, today, could see me here, renewing
   Her olden triumphs, she might laugh to see
   A wild beast in command of mighty armies,   335
   A wild beast, to whose fiery aspirations
   The firmament were all too slight a conquest!
   But stoop your flight, my spirit. Do not thus
   Be puffed to pride by these uncertain plaudits
   Which, when I wake, will turn to bitterness   340
   In that I won them only to be lost.
   The less I value them, the less I'll miss them.
      [*A trumpet sounds.*]
CLARION:[3] Upon a rapid courser (pray excuse me,
   Since if it comes to mind I must describe it)
   In which it seems an atlas was designed   345
   Since if its body is earth, its soul is fire
   Within its breast, its foam appears the sea,
   The wind its breath, and chaos its condition,
   Since in its soul, its foam, its breath and flesh,
   It seems a monster of fire, earth, sea, and wind,   350
   Upon the horse, all of a patchwork colour,
   Dappled, and rushing forward at the will
   Of one who plies the spur, so that it flies

---

3. Clarion's speech is a parody of exaggerated style—including Calderón's. [Translator's note]

Rather than runs—see how a woman rides
Boldly into your presence.
SEGISMUND: Her light blinds me.   355
CLARION: Good God! Why, here's Rosaura!
SEGISMUND: It is heaven
That has restored her to my sight once more.
   [*Enter* ROSAURA *with sword and dagger in riding costume.*]
ROSAURA: Generous Segismund, whose majesty
Heroically rises in the lustre
Of his great deeds out of his night of shadows,   360
And as the greatest planet,[4] in the arms
Of his aurora, lustrously returns
To plants and roses, over hills and seas.
When, crowned with gold, he looks abroad, dispersing
Radiance, flashing his rays, bathing the summits,   365
And broidering the fringes of the foam.
So may you dawn upon the world, bright sun
Of Poland, that a poor unhappy woman
May fall before your feet and beg protection
Both as a woman and unfortunate—   370
Two things that must oblige you, sire, as one
Who prize yourself as valiant, each of them
More than suffices for your chivalry.
Three times you have beheld me now, three times
Been ignorant of who I am, because   375
Three times you saw me in a different clothing
The first time you mistook me for a man,
Within that rigorous prison, where your hardships
Made mine seem pleasure. Next time, as a woman,
You saw me, when your pomp and majesty   380
Were as a dream, a phantasm, a shade.
The third time is today when, as a monster
Of both the sexes, in a woman's costume
I bear a soldier's arms. But to dispose you
The better to compassion, hear my story.   385
My mother was a noble in the court
Of Moscow, who, since most unfortunate,
Must have been beautiful. Then came a traitor
And cast his eyes on her (I do not name him,
Not knowing who he is). Yet I deduce   390
That he was valiant too from my own valour,
Since he gave form to me—and I could wish
I had been born in pagan times, that I might
Persuade myself he was some god of those
Who rain in showers of gold, turn into swans   395

4. The sun.

Or bulls, for Danaës, Ledas, or Europas.[5]
That's strange: I thought I was just rambling on
By telling old perfidious myths, yet find
I've told you how my mother was cajoled.
Oh, she was beautiful as no one else   400
Has been, but was unfortunate like all.
He swore to wed her (that's an old excuse)
And this trick reached so nearly to her heart
That thought must weep, recalling it today.
The tyrant left her only with his sword   405
As Aeneas left Troy.[6] I sheathed its blade here
Upon my thigh, and I will bare it too
Before the ending of this history.
Out of this union, this poor link which neither
Could bind the marriage nor handcuff the crime,   410
Myself was born, her image and her portrait,
Not in her beauty, but in her misfortune,
For mine's the same. That's all I need to say.
The most that I can tell you of myself
Is that the man who robbed me of the spoils   415
And trophies of my honour is Astolfo.
Alas! to name him my heart rages so
(As hearts will do when men name enemies).
Astolfo was my faithless and ungrateful
Lord, who (quite forgetful of our happiness,   420
Since of a past love even the memory fades)
Came here to claim the throne and marry Stella
For she's the star who rises as I set.
It's hard to credit that a star should sunder
Lovers the stars had made conformable!   425
So hurt was I, so villainously cheated,
That I became mad, brokenhearted, sick,
Half wild with grief, and like to die, with all
Hell's own confusion ciphered on my mind
Like Babel's incoherence. Mutely I told   430
My griefs (since woes and griefs declare themselves
Better than can the mouth, by their effects),
When, with my mother (we were by ourselves),
She broke the prison of my pent-up sorrows
And from my breast they all rushed forth in troops.   435
I felt no shyness, for in knowing surely
That one to whom one's errors are recounted
Has also been an ally in her own,
One finds relief and rest, since bad example

5. To seduce them, Zeus assumed the shapes, respectively, of a gold shower, a swan, and a bull.
6. Probably Calderón was thinking of Carthage rather than Troy. Aeneas departed from Carthage in haste,
leaving behind the sword that queen Dido would use for her suicide.

Can sometimes serve for a good purpose too.   440
She heard my plaint with pity, and she tried
To palliate my sorrows with her own.
How easily do judges pardon error
When they've offended too! An example,
A warning, in herself, she did not trust   445
To idleness, or the slow cure of time,
Nor try to find a remedy for her honour
In my misfortunes, but, with better counsel,
She bade me follow him to Poland here
And with prodigious gallantry persuade him   450
To pay the debt to honour that he owes me.
So that it would be easier to travel,
She bade me don male clothing, and took down
This ancient sword which I am wearing now.
Now it is time that I unsheathe the blade   455
As I was bid, for, trusting in its sign,
She said: "Depart to Poland, show this sword
That all the nobles may behold it well,
And it may be that one of them will take
Pity on you, and counsel you, and shield you."   460
I came to Poland and, you will remember,
Entered your cave. You looked at me in wonder.
Clotaldo passionately took my part
To plead for mercy to the king, who spared me,
Then, when he heard my story, bade me change   465
Into my own clothes and attend on Stella,
There to disturb Astolfo's love and stop
Their marriage. Again you saw me in woman's dress
And were confused by the discrepancy.
But let's pass to what's new: Clotaldo, now   470
Persuaded that Astolfo must, with Stella,
Come to the throne, dissuades me from my purpose,
Against the interests of my name and honour.
But seeing you, O valiant Segismund,
Are claiming your revenge, now that the heavens   475
Have burst the prison of your rustic tower,
(Wherein you were the tiger of your sorrows,
The rock of sufferings and direful pains)
And sent you forth against your sire and country,
I come to aid you, mingling Dian's silks   480
With the hard steel of Pallas. Now, strong Captain,
It well behoves us both to stop this marriage—
Me, lest my promised husband should be wed.
You, lest, when their estates are joined, they weigh
More powerfully against your victory.   485
I come, as a mere woman, to persuade you

To right my shame; but, as a man, I come
To help you battle for your crown. As woman,
To melt your heart, here at your feet I fall;
But, as a man, I come to serve you bravely   490
Both with my person and my steel, and thus,
If you today should woo me as a woman,
Then I should have to kill you as a man would
In honourable service of my honour;
Since I must be three things today at once—   495
Passionate, to persuade you: womanly,
To ply you with my woes: manly, to gain
Honour in battle.

SEGISMUND: Heavens! If it is true I'm dreaming,
Suspend my memory, for in a dream
So many things could not occur. Great heavens!   500
If I could only come free of them all!
Or ever think of any! Who ever felt
Such grievous doubts? If I but dreamed that triumph
In which I found myself, how can this woman
Refer me to such sure and certain facts?   505
Then all of it was true and not a dream.
But if it be the truth, why does my past life
Call it a dream? This breeds the same confusion.
Are dreams and glories so alike, that fictions
Are held for truths, realities for lies?   510
Is there so little difference in them both
That one should question whether what one sees
And tastes is true or false? What? Is the copy
So near to the original that doubt
Exists between them? Then if that is so,   515
And grandeur, power, majesty, and pomp,
Must all evaporate like shades at morning,
Let's profit by it, this time, to enjoy
That which we only can enjoy in dreams.
Rosaura's in my power: my soul adores her beauty.   520
Let's take the chance. Let love break every law
On which she has relied in coming here
And kneeling, trustful, prostrate at my feet.
This is a dream. If so, dream pleasures now
Since they must turn to sorrows in the end!   525
But with my own opinions, I begin
Once again to convince myself. Let's think.
If it is but vainglory and a dream,
Who for mere human vainglory would lose
True glory? What past blessing is not merely   530
A dream? Who has known heroic glories,
That deep within himself, as he recalls them,

Has never doubted that they might be dreams?
But if this all should end in disenchantment,
Seeing that pleasure is a lovely flame   535
That's soon converted into dust and ashes
By any wind that blows, then let us seek
That which endures in thrifty, lasting fame
In which no pleasures sleep, nor grandeurs dream.
Rosaura's without honour. In a prince   540
It's worthier to restore it than to steal it.
I shall restore it, by the living God,
Before I win my throne! Let's shun the danger
And fly from the temptation which is strong!
Then sound to arms!   545
[*To a soldier*] Today I must give battle before darkness
Buries the rays of gold in green-black waves!

ROSAURA: My lord! Alas, you stand apart, and offer
   No word of pity for my plight. How is it
   You neither hear nor see me nor even yet   550
   Have turned your face on me?

SEGISMUND: Rosaura, for your honour's sake
   I must be cruel to you, to be kind.
   My voice must not reply to you because
   My honour must reply to you. I am silent
   Because my deeds must speak to you alone.   555
   I do not look at you since, in such straits,
   Having to see your honour is requited,
   I must not see your beauty.
     [*Exit with soldiers.*]

ROSAURA: What strange enigma's this? After such trouble
   Still to be treated with more doubtful riddles!   560
    [*Enter* CLARION.]

CLARION: Madam, may you be visited just now?
ROSAURA: Why, Clarion, where have you been all this time?
CLARION: Shut in the tower, consulting cards
   About my death: "to be or not to be."
   And it was a near thing.
ROSAURA: Why?
CLARION: Because I know   565
   The secret who you are: in fact, Clotaldo . . .
   [*Drums.*] But hush what noise is that?
ROSAURA: What can it be?
CLARION: From the beleaguered palace a whole squadron
   Is charging forth to harry and defeat
   That of fierce Segismund.
ROSAURA: Why, what a coward   570
   Am I, not to be at his side, the terror
   And scandal of the world, while such fierce strife

Presses all round in lawless anarchy.
    [*Exit.*]
VOICES OF SOME: Long live our king!
VOICES OF OTHERS: Long live our liberty!
CLARION: Long live both king and liberty. Yes, live!   575
    And welcome to them both! I do not worry
    In all this pother, I behave like Nero[7]
    Who never grieved at what was going on.
    If I had anything to grieve about
    It would be me, myself. Well hidden here,   580
    Now, I can watch the sport that's going on.
    This place is safe and hidden between crags,
    And since death cannot find me here, two figs for death!
        [*He hides. Drums and the clash of arms are heard. Enter* BASIL, CLO-
        TALDO, *and* ASTOLFO, *fleeing.*]
BASIL: Was ever king so hapless as myself
    Or, father more ill used?
CLOTALDO: Your beaten army   585
    Rush down, in all directions, in disorder.
ASTOLFO: The traitors win!
BASIL: In battles such as these
    Those on the winning side are ever "loyal,"
    And traitors the defeated. Come, Clotaldo,
    Let's flee from the inhuman cruelty   590
    Of my fierce son!
        [*Shots are fired within.* CLARION *falls wounded.*]
CLARION: Heavens, save me!
ASTOLFO: Who is this
    Unhappy soldier bleeding at our feet?
CLARION: I am a most unlucky man who, wishing
    To guard myself from death, have sought it out
    By fleeing from it. Shunning it, I found it,   595
    Because, to death, no hiding-place is secret.
    So you can argue that whoever shuns it
    Most carefully runs into it the quickest.
    Turn, then, once more into the thick of battle:
    There is more safety there amidst the fire   600
    And clash of arms than here on this secluded
    Mountain, because no hidden path is safe
    From the inclemency of Fate; and so,
    Although you flee from death, yet you may find it   604
    Quicker than you expect, if God so wills.
        [*He falls dead.*]
BASIL: "If God so wills" . . . With what strange eloquence
    This corpse persuades our ignorance and error

7. Roman emperor from A.D. 54 to A.D. 68 who was blamed by some for a destructive fire that burned
half of Rome in A.D. 64.

To better knowledge, speaking from the mouth
Of its fell wound, where the red liquid flowing
Seems like a bloody tongue which teaches us   610
That the activities of man are vain
When they are pitted against higher powers.
For I, who wished to liberate my country
From murder and sedition, gave it up
To the same ills from which I would have saved it.   615
CLOTALDO: Though Fate, my lord, knows every path, and finds
  Him whom it seeks even in the midst of crags
  And thickets, it is not a Christian judgment
  To say there is no refuge from its fury.
  A prudent man can conquer Fate itself.   620
  Though you are not exempted from misfortune,
  Take action to escape it while you can!
ASTOLFO: Clotaldo speaks as one mature in prudence,
  And I as one in valour's youthful prime.
  Among the thickets of this mount is hidden   625
  A horse, the very birth of the swift wind.
  Flee on him, and I'll guard you in the rear.
BASIL: If it is God's will I should die, or if
  Death waits here for my coming, I will seek
  Him out today, and meet him face to face.   630
    [*Enter* SEGISMUND, STELLA, ROSAURA, *soldiers, and their train.*]
A SOLDIER: Amongst the thickets of this mountain
  The king is hiding.
SEGISMUND: Seek him out at once!
  Leave no foot of the summit unexplored
  But search from stem to stem and branch to branch!
CLOTALDO: Fly, sir!
BASIL: What for?
ASTOLFO: What do you mean to do?   635
BASIL: Astolfo, stand aside!
CLOTALDO: What is your wish?
BASIL: To take a cure I've needed for sometime.
  [*To* SEGISMUND] If you have come to seek me, here I am.
  [*Kneeling*] Your father, prince, kneels humbly at your feet.
  The white snow of my hair is now your carpet.   640
  Tread on my neck and trample on my crown!
  Lay low and drag my dignity in dust!
  Take vengeance on my honour! Make a slave
  Of me and, after all I've done to thwart them,
  Let Fate fulfil its edict and claim homage   645
  And Heaven fulfil its oracles at last!
SEGISMUND: Illustrious court of Poland, who have been
  The witness of such unwonted wonders,
  Attend to me, and hear your prince speak out.

What Heaven decrees and God writes with this finger   650
(Whose prints and ciphers are the azure leaves
Adorned with golden lettering of the stars)
Never deceives nor lies. They only lie
Who seek to penetrate the mystery
And, having reached it, use it to ill purpose.   655
My father, who is here to evade the fury
Of my proud nature, made me a wild beast:
So, when I, by my birth of gallant stock,
My generous blood, and inbred grace and valour,
Might well have proved both gentle and forbearing,   660
The very mode of life to which he forced me,
The sort of bringing up I had to bear
Sufficed to make me savage in my passions.
What a strange method of restraining them!
If one were to tell any man: "One day   665
You will be killed by an inhuman monster,"
Would it be the best method he could choose
To wake that monster when it was asleep?
Or if they told him: "That sword which you're wearing
Will be your death," what sort of cure were it   670
To draw it forth and aim it at his breast?
Of if they told him: "Deep blue gulfs of water
Will one day be your sepulchre and grave
Beneath a silver monument of foam,"
He would be mad to hurl himself in headlong   675
When the sea highest heaved its showy mountains
And crystalline sierras plumed with spray.
The same has happened to the king as to him
Who wakes a beast which threatens death, to him
Who draws a naked sword because he fears it,   680
To him who dives into the stormy breakers.
Though my ferocious nature (hear me now)
Was like a sleeping beast, my inborn rage
A sheathèd sword, my wrath a quiet ripple,
Fate should not be coerced by man's injustice—   685
This rouses more resentment. So it is
That he who seeks to tame his fortune must
Resort to moderation and to measure.
He who foresees an evil cannot conquer it
Thus in advance, for though humility   690
Can overcome it, this it can do only
When the occasion's there, for there's no way
To dodge one's fate and thus evade the issue.
Let this strange spectacle serve as example—
This prodigy, this horror, and this wonder,   695
Because it is no less than one, to see,

After such measures and precautions taken
To thwart it, that a father thus should kneel
At his son's feet, a kingdom thus be shattered.
This was the sentence of the heavens above, 700
Which he could not evade, much though he tried.
Can I, younger in age, less brave, and less
In science than the king, conquer that fate?
[*To the* KING] Sire, rise, give me your hand, now that the heavens
Have shown you that you erred as to the method 705
To vanquish them. Humbly I kneel before you
And offer you my neck to tread upon.
BASIL: Son, such a great and noble act restores you
Straight to my heart. Oh, true and worthy prince!
You have won both the laurel and the palm. 710
Crown yourself with your deeds! For you *have* conquered!
ALL: Long live Segismund! Long live Segismund!
SEGISMUND: Since I have other victories to win,
The greatest of them all awaits me now:
To conquer my own self. Astolfo, give 715
Your hand here to Rosaura, for you know
It is a debt of honour and must be paid.
ASTOLFO: Although, it's true, I owe some obligations—
She does not know her name or who she is,
It would be base to wed a woman who . . . 720
CLOTALDO: Hold! Wait! Rosaura's of as noble stock
As yours, Astolfo. In the open field
I'll prove it with my sword. She is my daughter,
And that should be enough.
ASTOLFO: What do you say?
CLOTALDO: Until I saw her married, righted, honoured, 725
I did not wish for it to be discovered.
It's a long story but she is my daughter.
ASTOLFO: That being so, I'm glad to keep my word.
SEGISMUND: And now, so that the princess Stella here
Will not remain disconsolate to lose 730
A prince of so much valour, here I offer
My hand to her, no less in birth and rank.
Give me your hand.
STELLA: I gain by meriting
So great a happiness.
SEGISMUND: And now, Clotaldo,
So long so loyal to my father come 735
To my arms. Ask me anything you wish.
FIRST SOLDIER: If thus you treat a man who never served you,
What about me who led the revolution
And brought you from your dungeon in the tower?
What will you give me?

SEGISMUND: That same tower and dungeon   740
  From which you never shall emerge till death.
  No traitor is of use after his treason.
BASIL: All wonder at your wisdom!
ASTOLFO: What a change
  Of character!
ROSAURA: How wise and prudent!
SEGISMUND: Why
  Do you wonder? Why do you marvel, since   745
  It was a dream that taught me and I still
  Fear to wake up once more in my close dungeon?
  Though that may never happen, it's enough
  To dream it might, for thus I came to learn
  That all our human happiness must pass   750
  Away like any dream, and I would here
  Enjoy it fully ere it glide away,
  Asking (for noble hearts are prone to pardon)
  Pardon for faults in the actors or the play.[8]

JOHN MILTON
1608–1674

The quality of Milton's literary achievement places him, however late, still within the broad span of the Renaissance. His intellectual inclinations and the support of a learned and artistic father combined to make him, already in early life, a most accomplished exemplar of the Renaissance scholar and literary artist. Concomitant with this achievement, and inseparable from it, are Milton's views and activities as a reformed Christian humanist.

Milton was born in London on December 9, 1608. Encouraged by his father—a well-to-do notary, private banker, and distinguished musician—he was educated both at home by tutors and at excellent schools (St. Paul's in London and Christ's College, Cambridge). He took his B. A. in 1629 and his M. A. in 1632. Milton decided against taking holy orders and retired to his father's estate at Horton, near Windsor, where he rounded out his prodigiously vast education and reading. His view of education included science and the new discoveries, while his splendid knowledge of ancient languages, including Hebrew, permitted him to maintain a constant, deep familiarity with both Greek and Latin literature and the Scriptures, in their original texts. As a young student at Cambridge he exchanged letters in Latin verse with a friend. His early poetry culminated in the splendid elegy *Lycidas* (1637), commemorating a dead classmate. In 1638–39, now a highly educated man in his early thirties, he traveled on the continent, especially in Italy, where he conversed with prominent intellectuals, including scientists like Galileo, and wrote sonnets in Italian. Rumors of political trouble at home hastened his return to England.

8. This form of close, addressed to the audience and begging for its favor, is a well-established Renaissance convention.

The following twenty years were the period of Milton's involvement in doctrinal and governmental controversy. The major events of this period of his life are the writing of *Areopagitica* (1644), an eloquent defense of the right to print without a license, and his appointment as Latin Secretary to Cromwell's Council of State; Milton's writings in English and Latin defending the execution of King Charles I also belong to this period. The restoration of the monarchy brought him legal and financial difficulties, brief imprisonment, and loss of property. Milton's first wife, Mary Powell (who left him shortly after their marriage in 1642 and later returned to him), died in 1652. His second wife died in childbirth in 1658. In 1663 he married Elizabeth Minshull, who outlived him. Totally blind from 1651 on, the poet now attended to his major tasks: *Paradise Lost* was published in 1667; *Paradise Regained* and *Samson Agonistes* followed in 1671. In his late years Milton had passages of the Hebrew Bible read to him every morning. He died in 1674.

Quite understandably, then, the apex of Milton's career as a poet (his long commitment to public life does not directly concern us here) was ultimately represented by a monumental exercise in the grandest and most authoritative of the classic genres—the epic poem. His choice of subject matter is obviously significant as well. Milton, as a Protestant heroic poet reflecting a trend toward an individual humanistic relationship to the Scriptures, undertook an epic dramatization and a free poetic reappropriation of the story of "man's first disobedience."

Naturally, Milton believed in the superiority of his epic material to that of his ancient and medieval predecessors. Book IX of *Paradise Lost* and the latter part of Book X—which, with the opening and conclusion of the poem, constitute our selection from Milton—repeatedly illustrate this point. Mythological reference often provides support for action and characterization: Eve's divine touch and "goddess-like deport" not only recall but surpass those of the goddess Diana; and as she goes to work in the fields she is equated with the major Roman goddesses of agriculture. The fatal spot where she will be tempted is "more delicious" than the gardens of Adonis or of King Alcinous, both of which possess high mythological and epic credentials; to them, with full awareness of his higher theme, Milton adds a garden taken from Scriptural tradition. Even the serpent is lovelier than those sung by Ovid, and Eve's animals are "more duteous" than were Circe's pigs in the *Odyssey*. Indeed, in the proemium to Book IX and in the invocation to his muse (Urania, to be sure, not the Virgin Mary as in the poem of the Roman Catholic Counter-Reformation, Tasso's *Jerusalem Delivered*), Milton has declared his material to be "not less but more heroic" than the high points of the *Iliad* and the *Aeneid*, implying that his purpose is nobler than Homer's or Virgil's, not to mention that of the medieval chivalric poets with their "mastery to dissect/With long and tedious havoc fabled knights/In battles feigned. . . ."

Milton's battle, or drama, is not "feigned" for the preeminent reason that it is the basic inner drama of Christianity. Humanity is fallen, yet that fall is the precondition to human life as we know it, and it contains the promise of redemption; it is a happy fault, a *felix culpa*. So the subject of Milton's epic is not only the fall, of course, but also the transgressors' discovery and acceptance of their new mortal status, implying moral awareness and hope along with corruptibility and guilt.

Our major selection from *Paradise Lost* is the key moment in the action, the temptation and fall. Here Milton faced, among other problems, that of describing the fundamentally evil in ambiguously attractive terms. Without ever abandoning his grand manner or relenting in his highly literate sense of style, he handles blank verse with beautifully appropriate variety and mobility: passages such as lines 71 ff. or 1067–1080 speak for themselves. In some of his most felicitous moments Milton strikes a balance between sustained epic tone and quick, effective notation. Take, for example, some of the varying images of the Satanic serpent: "Stupidly good, of enmity disarmed," "his head / crested aloft, and carbuncle his eyes"; or observe the rapid effectiveness of the fatal act: "Forth reaching to the fruit, she plucked, she eat."

The two main stages in the dramatic sequence of events are the serpent successfully tempting Eve, and Eve convincing Adam to join her in the new knowledge. The dramatic situation demanded masterful handling, equal to its complexity and variety. For instance, Adam sins out of loyalty, out of chivalrous trust in his wife; and the poet does not shun such stagy lines as ". . . for with thee / Certain my resolution is to die," while Eve's rhetoric matches Adam's, in a lighter vein: "On my experience, Adam, freely taste, / And fear of death deliver to the winds." In all possible ways, the exchange of argumentation is given dramatic substance and vitality.

Milton was well acquainted with the arts of rhetoric and eloquence; and the story of the fall is largely told in terms of the use and misuse of those arts. From the serpent, Eve is not only taught evil action but also evil counseling, verbal cunning, sophistry. While before the tempter's success her speech was only externally twisted by an occasional pun or conceit, after the fall her rhetorical art becomes internally perverse, in perfect correspondence with the "distemper" in her now corrupt body.

On the other hand, new dimensions are added as the protagonists are now bound by "earthly" love and by mutual rancor and misery and also by the knowledge of a new delight, however dangerous; a line like "as with new wine intoxicated both" must work, so to speak, positively and negatively, strike a note at once joyful and ominous. Earthly attachments, though "corrupt," must be poetically perceptible, as in the pivotal consummation passage (lines 1034–1045). Hence the variety in Milton's use not only of his stylistic and prosodic instrument but also of his wide range of cultural reference, as when he adopts exotic imagery suggested by the new geographic discoveries in the comparison between the transgressors and "th'American, so girt / With feathered cincture, naked else and wild. . . ."

In brief, Milton is fully recognizable as a Renaissance literary artist: his service to his God is inseparable from his service to poetry, to the cultivated and esthetically beautiful handling of language fit to encompass and express a wide range of human experience. The work for which he had prepared himself through all of his life, a Biblical epic in the grand classic manner, is also a crowning product of ripe, autumnal Renaissance culture.

Particularly helpful to the new reader is Harry Blamires, *Milton's Creation: A Guide through Paradise Lost* (1971). Douglas Bush, *John Milton: A Sketch of His Life and Writings* (1964; 1967), provides a brief account of Milton's life. The standard modern biography is William Riley Parker, *Milton: A Biography*, 2 vols. (1981). A Bartlett Giamatti, *The Earthly Paradise and the Renaissance Epic* (1966), analyzes the "coalescence of classical and Christian material" in the poem. Michael Lieb, *Politics of the Holy: A Reading of Paradise Lost* (1981), deals with its basic religious context. Louis Lohr Martz, ed., *Milton: A Collection of Critical Essays* (1966), and Marjorie H. Nicolson, *John Milton: A Reader's Guide to His Poetry* (1975), will give the reader insight into his work.

Paradise Lost[1]

From BOOK I

("This Great Argument")

Of man's first disobedience, and the fruit[2]
Of that forbidden tree whose mortal taste[3]
Brought death into the world, and all our woe,
With loss of Eden, till one greater Man[4]
Restore us, and regain the blissful seat,   5
Sing, Heavenly Muse,[5] that, on the secret top
Of Oreb, or of Sinai,[6] didst inspire
That shepherd who first taught the chosen seed
In the beginning how the Heavens and Earth
Rose out of Chaos: or, if Sion hill   10
Delight thee more, and Siloa's brook that flowed
Fast by the oracle of God,[7] I thence
Invoke thy aid to my adventurous[8] song,
That with no middle flight intends to soar
Above th' Aonian mount,[9] while it pursues   15
Things unattempted yet in prose or rhyme.
And chiefly thou, O Spirit,[1] that dost prefer
Before all temples th' upright heart and pure,
Instruct me, for thou know'st; thou from the first
Wast present, and, with mighty wings outspread,   20
Dovelike sat'st brooding[2] on the vast abyss,
And mad'st it pregnant: what in me is dark
Illumine; what is low, raise and support;
That, to the height of this great argument,[3]
I may assert[4] Eternal Providence,   25
And justify the ways of God to men.[5]

---

1. Abridged.   2. The apple itself, and also the consequences of Adam and Eve's disobedience.
3. The tasting of which brought mortality into the world.   4. Christ.   5. The opening invocation to
the Muse who will inspire ("sing" to) the poet is a regular feature of epic poems. Milton's "Heavenly
Muse," elsewhere in the poem (the first line of Book VII), is given the name of the mythological Urania;
in another passage (see Book IX, line 21), she is given the adjective "celestial." Both words—of Greek and
Latin derivation, respectively—mean "heavenly." Clearly (see following lines), and typically, in Milton's
"Heavenly Muse" pagan elements and images are adopted and given new substance within the framework
of Judeo-Christian culture and beliefs.   6. The names Oreb and Sinai designate the mountain where
God spoke to Moses ("that shepherd"), who in Genesis taught the Hebrew people ("the chosen seed") the
story of the Creation.   7. The names of biblical localities suggested here as haunts for Milton's muse
are emblematic of his certainty about the higher nature of his theme in comparison with the epic subjects
of pagan antiquity. The fact that "Siloa's brook" is flowing by the Temple ("the oracle of God") suggests
the holy nature of Milton's subject. Typically also, the geographical symbolism is patterned on a similar
situation in Greek myth (see note 9 below).   8. Perilous, as the poet is daring something new (see line
16).   9. Helicon, the Greek mountain that was the seat of the nine Muses. A spring (Aganippe) giving
poetic power, and an altar of Zeus, were part of that landscape.   1. Described in Milton's Latin treatise
on Christian doctrine as "that impulse or voice of God by which the prophets were inspired," the "Spirit"
is a further source of inspiration over and above the "Heavenly Muse:" the poet asks not for song, but for
knowledge ("instruct me"), and identifies the "Spirit" with the Spirit of God that "moved upon the face of
the waters" in the opening lines of Genesis.   2. As a bird hatching eggs; the image is pursued in the
"pregnant" of the following line. *Dovelike*: The traditional figuration of the Holy Spirit (e.g., Luke 3:22:
". . . the Holy Ghost descended in a bodily shape like a dove . . ."").   3. Subject, theme.   4. Champion,
vindicate.   5. Demonstrate the justice of "the ways of God," i.e., of the course of God's providence.

BOOK IX

The Argument

Satan, having compassed the Earth, with meditated guile returns as a mist
by night into Paradise; enters into the serpent sleeping. Adam and Eve in
the morning go forth to their labors, which Eve proposes to divide in several places, each laboring apart: Adam consents not, alleging the danger
lest that enemy of whom they were forewarned should attempt her found
alone. Eve, loath to be thought not circumspect or firm enough, urges her
going apart, the rather desirous to make trial of her strength; Adam at last
yields. The serpent finds her alone: his subtle approach, first gazing, then
speaking, with much flattery extolling Eve above all other creatures. Eve,
wondering to hear the serpent speak, asks how he attained to human speech
and such understanding not till now; the serpent answers that by tasting of
a certain tree in the garden he attained both to speech and reason, till then
void of both. Eve requires him to bring her to that tree, and finds it to be
the Tree of Knowledge forbidden: the serpent, now grown bolder, with
many wiles and arguments induces her at length to eat. She, pleased with
the taste, deliberates a while whether to impart thereof to Adam or not; at
last brings him of the fruit; relates what persuaded her to eat thereof. Adam,
at first amazed, but perceiving her lost, resolves, through vehemence of
love, to perish with her, and, extenuating the trespass, eats also of the fruit.
The effects thereof in them both; they seek to cover their nakedness; then
fall to variance and accusation of one another.

(Temptation and Fall)

No more of talk where God or angel guest[6]
With man, as with his friend, familiar used
To sit indulgent, and with him partake
Rural repast, permitting him the while
Venial[7] discourse unblamed. I now must change   5
Those notes to tragic; foul distrust, and breach
Disloyal, on the part of man, revolt
And disobedience; on the part of Heaven,
Now alienated, distance and distaste,
Anger and just rebuke, and judgment given,   10
That brought into this world a world of woe,
Sin and her shadow Death, and Misery,
Death's harbinger. Sad task! yet argument
Not less but more heroic than the wrath
Of stern Achilles on his foe pursued   15
Thrice fugitive about Troy wall;[8] or rage

6. Raphael, the "affable archangel," who in preceding books (V–VIII) has sat with Adam sharing "rural
repast" and discoursing on such highly relevant matters as Lucifer's fall, the Creation, the structure of the
universe. To him, Adam has told of the warning he has received from God not to touch the Tree of
Knowledge.   7. Unblemished.   8. Achilles, whose "wrath" is the subject announced in the first line
of the *Iliad*, at the end of that epic will chase his enemy, the Trojan Hector, three times around the walls
of Troy before killing him.

Of Turnus for Lavinia disespoused;[9]
Or Neptune's ire, or Juno's, that so long
Perplexed the Greek, and Cytherea's son:[1]
If answerable style I can obtain   20
Of my celestial Patroness,[2] who deigns
Her nightly visitation unimplored,
And dictates to me slumbering, or inspires
Easy my unpremeditated verse,[3]
Since first this subject for heroic song   25
Pleased me,[4] long choosing and beginning late,
Not sedulous by nature to indite
War, hitherto the only argument
Heroic deemed, chief mastery to dissect[5]
With long and tedious havoc fabled knights   30
In battles feigned (the better fortitude
Of patience and heroic martyrdom
Unsung), or to describe races and games,[6]
Or tilting furniture, emblazoned shields,
Impresses[7] quaint, caparisons and steeds,   35
Bases and tinsel trappings, gorgeous knights
At joust and tournament; then marshaled feast
Served up in hall with sewers and seneschals:[8]
The skill of artifice or office mean;
Not that which justly gives heroic name   40
To person or to poem. Me,[9] of these
Nor skilled nor studious, higher argument
Remains, sufficient of itself to raise
That name, unless an age too late, or cold
Climate,[1] or years, damp my intended wing   45
Depressed; and much they may if all be mine,
Not hers who brings it nightly to my ear.
     The sun was sunk, and after him the star
Of Hesperus, whose office is to bring
Twilight upon the Earth, short arbiter   50
'Twixt day and night, and now from end to end
Night's hemisphere had veiled the horizon round,
When Satan, who late fled before the threats

9. In Virgil's *Aeneid*, Lavinia, fated to be Aeneas's wife, had earlier been promised to king Turnus.
1. In the *Odyssey*, Poseidon (Neptune) is the god hostile to Odysseus ("the Greek"). In the *Aeneid*, the hero is persecuted by the wrath of the goddess Juno who had quarreled with Aeneas's mother, Venus (Cytherea).   2. Urania, originally the Muse of Astronomy; to Milton, in a wider sense, the source of "celestial" inspiration. *Answerable*: Suitable.   3. In other passages of the poem, Milton refers to inspiration coming to him at night or at early dawn, with spontaneous ("unpremeditated") ease.   4. The choice of his present heroic theme had occurred early, as had the rejection of the kind of subject matter described in the subsequent lines.   5. To analyze, but also to cut up: a possible allusion to the abundance of bloody battle wounds described in classical epics.   6. There are long descriptions of games in the *Iliad* (Book XXIII) and in the *Aeneid* (Book V).   7. Fancy emblems on shields. *Tilting furniture*: The paraphernalia of arms tournaments. *Bases*: Skirtlike housings for warhorses.   8. Attendants at meals and stewards in noble households.   9. To me.   1. The notion that nordic climates "damp" (i.e., benumb) human wit was accepted by Milton and is as old as Aristotle. *That name*: That of epic poet. *An age too late*: A time no longer fit for epic poetry.

Of Gabriel out of Eden,[2] now improved
In meditated fraud and malice, bent   55
On man's destruction, mauger[3] what might hap
Of heavier on himself, fearless returned.
By night he fled, and at midnight returned
From compassing the Earth—cautious of day
Since Uriel, regent of the sun, descried   60
His entrance, and forewarned the Cherubim
That kept their watch.[4] Thence, full of anguish, driven,
The space of seven continued nights he rode
With darkness; thrice the equinoctial line
He circled, four times crossed the car of Night   65
From pole to pole, traversing each colure;[5]
On the eighth returned, and on the coast averse[6]
From entrance or cherubic watch by stealth
Found unsuspected way. There was a place
(Now not, though sin, not time, first wrought the change)   70
Where Tigris,[7] at the foot of Paradise,
Into a gulf shot under ground, till part
Rose up a fountain by the Tree of Life.
In with the river sunk, and with it rose,
Satan, involved in rising mist; then sought   75
Where to lie hid. Sea he had searched and land
From Eden over Pontus, and the pool
Maeotis, up beyond the river Ob;[8]
Downward as far antarctic; and, in length,
West from Orontes to the ocean barred   80
At Darien,[9] thence to the land where flows
Ganges and Indus.[1] Thus the orb he roamed
With narrow search, and with inspection deep
Considered every creature, which of all
Most opportune might serve his wiles, and found   85
The serpent subtlest beast of all the field.[2]
Him, after long debate, irresolute
Of thoughts revolved, his final sentence[3] chose
Fit vessel, fittest imp[4] of fraud, in whom
To enter, and his dark suggestions hide   90
From sharpest sight; for in the wily snake
Whatever sleights none would suspicious mark,

---

2. As described in the conclusion of Book IV.   3. In spite of.   4. The angel Uriel, possibly because
the name means "fire of God," according to a tradition used by Milton is the "Regent" of the sun and of
heat; in Book IV, he warns Gabriel and his troops (the Cherubim) against Satan entering Eden.   5. Satan
manages always to stay on the dark side of the earth by circling it three times along the equator ("the
equinoctial line") and twice on each of the two "colures," i.e., the two circles of longitude that intersect
at the poles.   6. The side opposite to the gate guarded by Gabriel.   7. Cf. the river that "went out of
Eden to water the garden" in Genesis 2:10.   8. Siberian river flowing into the Arctic Ocean. Pontus:
The Black Sea. Maeotis: The Sea of Azov.   9. The Isthmus of Panama. Orontes: A river in Syria.
1. Rivers in India.   2. Cf. Genesis 3:1.   3. Decision.   4. Offspring, with a devilish connotation.

As from his wit and native subtlety
Proceeding, which, in other beasts observed,
Doubt[5] might beget of diabolic power   95
Active within beyond the sense of brute.
Thus he resolved, but first from inward grief
His bursting passion into plaints thus poured:
    "O Earth, how like to Heaven, if not preferred
More justly, seat worthier of Gods, as built   100
With second thought, reforming what was old!
For what God, after better, worse would build?
Terrestrial Heaven, danced round by other Heavens,
That shine, yet bear their bright officious[6] lamps,
Light above light, for thee alone, as seems,   105
In thee concent'ring all their precious beams
Of sacred influence! As God in Heaven
Is center, yet extends to all, so thou
Cent'ring receiv'st from all those orbs; in thee,
Not in themselves, all their known virtue appears,   110
Productive in herb, plant, and nobler birth
Of creatures animate with gradual life
Of growth, sense, reason, all summed up in man.[7]
With what delight could I have walked thee round,
If I could joy in aught; sweet interchange   115
Of hill and valley, rivers, woods, and plains,
Now land, now sea, and shores with forest crowned,
Rocks, dens, and caves! But I in none of these
Find place or refuge; and the more I see
Pleasures about me, so much more I feel   120
Torment within me, as from the hateful siege[8]
Of contraries; all good to me becomes
Bane,[9] and in Heaven much worse would be my state.
But neither here seek I, no, nor in Heaven,
To dwell, unless by mastering Heaven's Supreme;   125
Nor hope to be myself less miserable
By what I seek, but others to make such
As I, though thereby worse to me redound.
For only in destroying I find ease
To my relentless thoughts, and him[1] destroyed,   130
Or won to what may work his utter loss,
For whom all this was made, all this[2] will soon
Follow, as to him linked in weal or woe:
In woe then, that destruction wide may range!
To me shall be the glory sole among   135
The infernal Powers, in one day to have marred

5. Suspicion.   6. Performing their function.   7. What Adam has called (in Book V. 509) "the scale
of Nature" ascends from the vegetable order (pure growth), to the animal (sensation), to the human (the
two, plus reason).   8. Seat, place.   9. Poison.   1. Man.   2. All of created nature.

What he, Almighty styled, six nights and days
Continued making, and who knows how long
Before had been contriving? though perhaps
Not longer than since I in one night freed   140
From servitude inglorious well-nigh half
Th' angelic name,[3] and thinner left the throng
Of his adorers. He, to be avenged,
And to repair his numbers thus impaired,
Whether such virtue,[4] spent of old, now failed   145
More angels to create (if they at least
Are his created),[5] or to spite us more,
Determined to advance into our room
A creature formed of earth, and him endow,
Exalted from so base original,   150
With heavenly spoils, our spoils. What he decreed
He effected; man he made, and for him built
Magnificent this World, and Earth his seat,
Him lord pronounced, and, O indignity!
Subjected to his service angel-wings   155
And flaming ministers, to watch and tend
Their earthy charge. Of these the vigilance
I dread, and to elude, thus wrapt in mist
Of midnight vapor, glide obscure, and pry
In every bush and brake, where hap may find   160
The serpent sleeping, in whose mazy folds
To hide me, and the dark intent I bring.
O foul descent! that I, who erst contended
With Gods to sit the highest, am now constrained
Into a beast, and, mixed with bestial slime,   165
This essence[6] to incarnate and imbrute,
That to the height of deity aspired!
But what will not ambition and revenge
Descend to? Who aspires must down as low
As high he soared, obnoxious,[7] first or last,   170
To basest things. Revenge, at first though sweet,
Bitter ere long back on itself recoils.
Let it; I reck not, so it light well aimed,
Since higher[8] I fall short, on him who next
Provokes my envy, this new favorite   175
Of Heaven, this man of clay, son of despite,
Whom, us the more to spite, his Maker raised
From dust: spite then with spite is best repaid."
    So saying, through each thicket, dank or dry,
Like a black mist low-creeping, he held on   180

3. Family, clan.   4. Power, force.   5. Inciting the angels to rebellion, Satan has pretended that they
are not God's creation, but "self-begot" (Book V. 860).   6. The supernatural substance of which he
considers himself to be made.   7. Exposed to.   8. Against God. *I reck not:* I don't mind.

His midnight search, where soonest he might find
The serpent. Him fast sleeping soon he found,
In labyrinth of many a round self-rolled,
His head the midst, well stored with subtle wiles:
Not yet in horrid shade or dismal den,   185
Nor nocent[9] yet, but on the grassy herb,
Fearless, unfeared, he slept. In at his mouth
The devil entered, and his brutal sense,
In heart or head, possessing soon inspired
With act intelligential;[1] but his sleep   190
Disturbed not, waiting close[2] th' approach of morn.
    Now, whenas sacred light began to dawn
In Eden on the humid flowers, that breathed
Their morning incense, when all things that breathe
From th' Earth's great altar send up silent praise   195
To the Creator, and his nostrils fill
With grateful smell, forth came the human pair,
And joined their vocal worship to the choir
Of creatures wanting[3] voice; that done, partake
The season, prime for sweetest scents and airs;   200
Then cómmune how that day they best may ply
Their growing work; for much their work outgrew
The hands' dispatch of two gardening so wide:
And Eve first to her husband thus began:
    "Adam, well may we labor still[4] to dress   205
This garden, still to tend plant, herb, and flower,
Our pleasant task enjoined; but, till more hands
Aid us, the work under our labor grows,
Luxurious by restraint: what we by day
Lop overgrown, or prune, or prop, or bind,   210
One night or two with wanton growth derides,
Tending to wild. Thou, therefore, now advise,
Or hear what to my mind first thoughts present.
Let us divide our labors; thou where choice
Leads thee, or where most needs, whether to wind   215
The woodbine round this arbor, or direct
The clasping ivy where to climb; while I
In yonder spring[5] of roses intermixed
With myrtle find what to redress till noon.
For, while so near each other thus all day   220
Our task we choose, what wonder if so near
Looks intervene and smiles, or objects new
Casual discourse draw on, which intermits
Our day's work, brought to little, though begun
Early, and th' hour of supper comes unearned!"   225

9. Harmful.   1. Intellectual activity.   2. Hidden.   3. Lacking.   4. Constantly.   5. Thicket, grove.

   To whom mild answer Adam thus returned:
"Sole Eve, associate sole, to me beyond
Compare above all living creatures dear!
Well hast thou motioned,[6] well thy thoughts employed
How we might best fulfil the work which here   230
God hath assigned us, nor of me shalt pass
Unpraised; for nothing lovelier can be found
In woman than to study household good,
And good works in her husband to promote.
Yet not so strictly hath our Lord imposed   235
Labor as to debar us when we need
Refreshment, whether food or talk between,
Food of the mind, or this sweet intercourse
Of looks and smiles; for smiles from reason flow,
To brute denied, and are of love the food,   240
Love, not the lowest end[7] of human life.
For not to irksome toil, but to delight,
He made us, and delight to reason joined.
These paths and bowers doubt not but our joint hands
Will keep from wilderness[8] with ease, as wide   245
As we need walk, till younger hands ere long
Assist us. But, if much converse perhaps
Thee satiate, to short absence I could yield;
For solitude sometimes is best society,
And short retirement urges sweet return.   250
But other doubt possesses me, lest harm
Befall thee, severed from me; for thou know'st
What hath been warned us, what malicious foe,
Envying our happiness, and of his own
Despairing, seeks to work us woe and shame   255
By sly assault, and somewhere nigh at hand
Watches, no doubt, with greedy hope to find
His wish and best adventage, us asunder,
Hopeless to circumvent us joined, where each
To other speedy aid might lend at need.   260
Whether his first design be to withdraw
Our fealty from God, or to disturb
Conjugal love, than which perhaps no bliss
Enjoyed by us excites his envy more;
Or this, or worse,[9] leave not the faithful side   265
That gave thee being, still shades thee and protects.
The wife, where danger or dishonor lurks,
Safest and seemliest by her husband stays,
Who guards her, or with her the worst endures."
   To whom the virgin[1] majesty of Eve,   270

6. Suggested.   7. Object.   8. Wildness.   9. Whether his design be this, or something even
worse.   1. Pure, sinless.

As one who loves, and some unkindness meets,
With sweet austere composure thus replied:
　　"Offspring of Heaven and Earth, and all Earth's lord!
That such an enemy we have, who seeks
Our ruin, both by thee informed I learn,   275
And from the parting angel[2] overheard,
As in a shady nook I stood behind,
Just then returned at shut of evening flowers.
But that thou shouldst my firmness therefore doubt
To God or thee, because we have a foe   280
May tempt it, I expected not to hear.
His violence thou fear'st not, being such
As we, not capable of death or pain,
Can either not receive, or can repel.
His fraud is, then, thy fear; which plain infers   285
Thy equal fear that my firm faith and love
Can by his fraud be shaken or seduced:
Thoughts, which how found they harbor in thy breast,
Adam, misthought of her to thee so dear?"[3]
　　To whom, with healing words, Adam replied: 290
"Daughter of God and man, immortal Eve,
For such thou art, from sin and blame entire;[4]
Not diffident of thee do I dissuade
Thy absence from my sight, but to avoid
Th' attempt itself, intended by our foe.   295
For he who tempts, though in vain, at least asperses[5]
The tempted with dishonor foul, supposed
Not incorruptible of faith,[6] not proof
Against temptation. Thou thyself with scorn
And anger wouldst resent the offered wrong,   300
Though ineffectual found; misdeem not, then,
If such affront I labor to avert
From thee alone, which on us both at once
The enemy, though bold, will hardly dare;
Or, daring, first on me th' assault shall light.   305
Nor thou his malice and false guile contemn—
Subtle he needs must be who could seduce
Angels—nor think superfluous others' aid.
I from the influence of thy looks receive
Access in every virtue;[7] in thy sight   310
More wise, more watchful, stronger, if need were
Of outward strength; while shame, thou looking on,
Shame to be overcome or overreached,[8]
Would utmost vigor raise, and raised unite.

2. Raphael. 3. A misjudgment ("misthought") of me ("of her to thee so dear"). 4. Intact.
5. Literally, "sprinkles." 6. Faithfulness, loyalty. 7. Increased strength. 8. Outdone.

Why shouldst not thou like sense[9] within thee feel 315
When I am present, and thy trial choose
With me, best witness of thy virtue tried?"
    So spake domestic Adam in his care
And matrimonial love; but Eve, who thought
Less[1] attributed to her faith sincere, 320
Thus her reply with accent sweet renewed:
    "If this be our condition, thus to dwell
In narrow circuit straitened[2] by a foe,
Subtle or violent, we not endued[3]
Single with like defence wherever met, 325
How are we happy, still in fear of harm?
But harm precedes not sin: only our foe
Tempting affronts us with his foul esteem
Of our integrity: his foul esteem
Sticks no dishonor on our front,[4] but turns 330
Foul on himself; then wherefore shunned or feared
By us, who rather double honor gain
From his surmise proved false, find peace within,
Favor from Heaven, our witness, from th' event?
And what is faith, love, virtue, unassayed 335
Alone, without exterior help sustained?[5]
Let us not then suspect our happy state
Left so imperfect by the Maker wise
As not secure to single or combined.
Frail is our happiness, if this be so; 340
And Eden were no Eden, thus exposed."
    To whom thus Adam fervently replied:
"O woman, best are all things as the will
Of God ordained them; his creating hand
Nothing imperfect or deficient left 345
Of all that he created, much less man,
Or aught that might his happy state secure,
Secure from outward force. Within himself
The danger lies, yet lies within his power;
Against his will he can receive no harm. 350
But God left free the will; for what obeys
Reason is free; and reason he made right,
But bid her well beware, and still erect,[6]
Lest, by some fair appearing good surprised,
She dictate false, and misinform the will 355
To do what God expressly hath forbid.
Not then mistrust, but tender love, enjoins
That I should mind[7] thee oft; and mind thou me.

9. Sensation. 1. Less than she deserves. 2. Confined. 3. Endowed. 4. Brow. 5. Without being put to test by outside forces. 6. On the alert against temptation, since God has "created Man free and able enough to have withstood his Tempter" (Book III, The Argument). 7. Remind.

Firm we subsist, yet possible to swerve,
Since reason not impossibly may meet   360
Some specious object by the foe suborned,[8]
And fall into deception unaware,
Not keeping strictest watch, as she was warned.
Seek not temptation, then, which to avoid
Were better, and most likely if from me   365
Thou sever not: trial will come unsought.
Wouldst thou approve[9] thy constancy, approve
First thy obedience; th' other who can know,
Not seeing thee attempted, who attest?
But if thou think trial unsought may find   370
Us both securer[1] than thus warned thou seem'st,
Go; for thy stay, not free, absents thee more.
Go in thy native innocence; rely
On what thou hast of virtue; summon all;
For God towards thee hath done his part: do thine."   375
     So spake the patriarch of mankind; but Eve
Persisted; yet submiss,[2] though last, replied:
     "With thy permission, then, and thus forewarned,
Chiefly by what thy own last reasoning words
Touched only, that our trial, when least sought,   380
May find us both perhaps far less prepared,
The willinger I go, nor much expect
A foe so proud will first the weaker seek;
So bent, the more shall shame him his repulse."
Thus saying, from her husband's hand her hand   385
Soft she withdrew, and like a wood nymph light,
Oread or dryad, or of Delia's train,[3]
Betook her to the groves, but Delia's self
In gait surpassed and goddesslike deport,
Though not as she with bow and quiver armed,   390
But with such gardening tools as art yet rude,
Guiltless of fire[4] had formed, or angels brought.
To Pales, or Pomona, thus adorned,
Likest she seemed, Pomona when she fled
Vertumnus, or to Ceres in her prime,   395
Yet virgin of Proserpina from Jove.[5]
Her long with ardent look his eye pursued
Delighted, but desiring more her stay.

8. Procured for treacherous purposes. 9. Give proof, test. 1. Less careful, less alert to danger.
2. Submissive. Eve's submissiveness, however, is qualified by Adam's reluctant tone as he agrees to let
her go; and by the fact that it is she who speaks the final words of their dialogue. 3. In Greek mythology,
the Oreads were nymphs of the mountains, the Dryads of the woods; Delia (i.e., born on the island of
Delos) is the goddess Diana (Artemis), the huntress with her train of nymphs. 4. The producing of fire
will become necessary only after the Fall. (Cf. Book X. 1070–1082.) 5. In practical-minded Roman
mythology, Pales and Pomona are deities who preside over flocks and fruit, respectively; Ceres is the
goddess of agriculture in general. Both Pomona and Ceres are presented here in virginal youth, Pomona
fleeing from her suitor Vertumnus (another agricultural deity), and Ceres before the time when Jupiter
made her the mother of Proserpina.

Oft he to her his charge of quick return
Repeated; she to him as oft engaged   400
To be returned by noon amid the bower,
And all things in best order to invite
Noontide repast, or afternoon's repose.
O much deceived, much failing, hapless Eve,
Of[6] thy presumed return! Event perverse!   405
Thou never from that hour in Paradise
Found'st either sweet repast, or sound repose;
Such ambush hid among sweet flowers and shades
Waited with hellish rancor imminent[7]
To intercept thy way, or send thee back   410
Despoiled of innocence, of faith, of bliss.
For now, and since first break of dawn, the fiend,
Mere serpent in appearance, forth was come,
And on his quest, where likeliest he might find
The only two of mankind, but in them   415
The whole included race, his purposed prey.
In bower and field he sought, where any tuft
Of grove or garden-plot more[8] pleasant lay,
Their tendance[9] or plantation for delight;
By fountain or by shady rivulet   420
He sought them both, but wished his hap might find
Eve separate; he wished, but not with hope
Of what so seldom chanced; when to his wish,
Beyond his hope, Eve separate he spies,
Veiled in a cloud of fragrance, where she stood,   425
Half spied, so thick the roses bushing round
About her glowed, oft stooping to support
Each flower of slender stalk, whose head though gay
Carnation, purple, azure, or specked with gold,
Hung drooping unsustained, them she upstays   430
Gently with myrtle band, mindless the while
Herself, though fairest unsupported flower,
From her best prop so far, and storm so nigh.
Nearer he drew, and many a walk traversed
Of stateliest covert, cedar, pine, or palm;   435
Then voluble[1] and bold, now hid, now seen
Among thick-woven arborets[2] and flowers
Embordered on each bank,[3] the hand of Eve:
Spot more delicious than those gardens feigned[4]
Or of revived Adonis, or renowned   440
Alcinous,[5] host of old Laertes' son,

6. About.   7. Ominously ready.   8. Particularly.   9. A spot that they tended.   1. Rolling.
2. Shrubbery.   3. Forming a border on each side of a walk. *Hand:* Handiwork.   4. Imagined by the
poets (cf. l. 31 above).   5. King of the Phaeacians and host to Odysseus, son of Laertes. His perpetually
flowering garden is described in Book VII of the *Odyssey. Of revived Adonis:* The mythical garden where
Aphrodite (Venus) nursed her lover Adonis, wounded by a boar. The most famous description of the
garden, certainly known to Milton, is in Book III of Spenser's *Faerie Queene.*

Or that, not mystic, where the sapient king[6]
Held dalliance with his fair Egyptian spouse.
Much he the place admired, the person more.
As one who long in populous city pent,   445
Where houses thick and sewers annoy[7] the air,
Forth issuing on a summer's morn to breathe
Among the pleasant villages and farms
Adjoined, from each thing met conceives delight,
The smell of grain, or tedded[8] grass, or kine,   450
Or dairy, each rural sight, each rural sound:
If chance[9] with nymphlike step fair virgin pass,
What pleasing seemed, for her[1] now pleases more,
She most, and in her look sums[2] all delight.
Such pleasure took the serpent to behold   455
This flowery plat,[3] the sweet recess of Eve
Thus early, thus alone; her heavenly form
Angelic, but more soft, and feminine,
Her graceful innocence, her every air
Of gesture or least action overawed   460
His malice, and with rapine[4] sweet bereaved
His fierceness of the fierce intent it brought:
That space the evil one abstracted[5] stood
From his own evil, and for the time remained
Stupidly good, of enmity disarmed,   465
Of guile, of hate, of envy, of revenge.
But the hot Hell that always in him burns,
Though in mid Heaven, soon ended his delight,
And tortures him now more, the more he sees
Of pleasure not for him ordained: then soon   470
Fierce hate he recollects, and all his thoughts
Of mischief, gratulating,[6] thus excites:
    "Thoughts, whither have ye led me? with what sweet
Compulsion thus transported to forget
What hither brought us? hate, not love, nor hope   475
Of Paradise for Hell, hope here to taste
Of pleasure, but all pleasure to destroy,
Save what[7] is in destroying; other joy
To me is lost. Then let me not let pass
Occasion which now smiles; behold alone   480
The woman, opportune to all attempts,[8]
Her husband, for I view far round, not nigh,
Whose higher intellectual more I shun,
And strength, of courage haughty, and of limb
Heroic built, though of terrestrial mold.[9]   485

6. Solomon. *Not mystic:* Not mythical like the previous "feigned" gardens of pagan antiquity. *Egyptian spouse:* Pharaoh's daughter (cf. I Kings, 3:1 and Song of Songs, 6:2).   7. Make noisome, pollute.
8. Spread out for drying.   9. If it should happen that.   1. Because of her.   2. Rounds out and brings to perfection.   3. Plot.   4. Theft.   5. Drawn off, separated.   6. Rejoicing.   7. Whatever pleasure.   8. In the appropriate situation for Satan's attempts on her.   9. Formed of earth.

Foe not informidable, exempt from wound,[1]
I not; so much hath Hell debased, and pain
Enfeebled me, to what I was in Heaven.
She fair, divinely fair, fit love for gods,
Not terrible, though terror be in love   490
And beauty, not approached by stronger hate,[2]
Hate stronger, under show of love well feigned,
The way which to her ruin now I tend."
    So spake the enemy of mankind, enclosed
In serpent, inmate bad, and toward Eve   495
Addressed his way, not with indented wave,[3]
Prone on the ground, as since, but on his rear,
Circular base of rising folds, that towered
Fold above fold a surging maze; his head
Crested aloft, and carbuncle[4] his eyes;   500
With burnished neck of verdant gold, erect
Amidst his circling spires,[5] that on the grass
Floated redundant. Pleasing was his shape,
And lovely; never since of serpent kind
Lovelier, not those that in Illyria changed   505
Hermione and Cadmus,[6] or the god
In Epidaurus; nor to which transformed
Ammonian Jove, or Capitoline was seen,
He with Olympias, this with her who bore
Scipio, the height of Rome.[7] With tract oblique   510
At first, as one who sought access, but feared
To interrupt, sidelong he works his way.
As when a ship by skillful steersman wrought
Nigh river's mouth or foreland, where the wind
Veers oft, as oft so steers, and shifts her sail: 515
So varied he, and of his tortuous train
Curled many a wanton wreath in sight of Eve,
To lure her eye: she busied heard the sound
Of rustling leaves, but minded not, as used
To such disport before her through the field,   520
From every beast, more duteous at her call,
Than at Circean call the herd disguised.[8]
He bolder now, uncalled before her stood:

1. Cf. line 283 above.   2. If not approached, and counteracted, by hate.   3. Zigzagging.   4. Fiery
red.   5. Coils, loops. *Redundant:* In great abundance.   6. Those that Hermione and Cadmus were
turned into. Cadmus, the founder of Thebes, and his wife Harmonia (Hermione), according to their story
as told by Ovid (*Metamorphoses* IV. 562–602), were transformed into snakes when they retired to Illyria
after much family tragedy. *Epidaurus:* The place in Greece where Aesculapius, the god of medicine, had
his major temple and appeared to worshipers in the form of an erect, flashy-eyed serpent (again as in Ovid,
Metamorphoses XV. 622–744).   7. According to hero-deifying legends, Jupiter (Jove), in his personification as Jupiter Ammon (a mingling of Greco-Roman and Egyptian cults), loved the Princess Olympias
and became the father of Alexander the Great. As the Capitoline Jupiter (worshiped in the major Roman
temple on the Capitol), he fathered Scipio, the supreme hero (the "height") of Rome's African wars. In
both cases, the father-god appeared in the form of a snake.   8. The enchantress Circe, in Book X of the
Odyssey, is surrounded by subjected beasts and transforms some of the hero's companions into swine.

But as in gaze admiring; oft he bowed
His turret⁹ crest, and sleek enameled neck,   525
Fawning, and licked the ground whereon she trod.
His gentle dumb expression turned at length
The eye of Eve to mark his play: he, glad
Of her attention gained, with serpent tongue
Organic, or impulse of vocal air,¹   530
His fraudulent temptation thus began.
  "Wonder not, sovereign mistress, if perhaps
Thou canst, who art sole wonder; much less arm
Thy looks, the heaven of mildness, with disdain,
Displeased that I approach thee thus, and gaze   535
Insatiate, I thus single, nor have feared
Thy awful brow, more awful thus retired.
Fairest resemblance of thy Maker fair,
Thee all things living gaze on, all things thine
By gift, and thy celestial beauty adore   540
With ravishment beheld, there best beheld
Where universally admired: but here
In this enclosure wild, these beasts among,
Beholders rude, and shallow² to discern
Half what in thee is fair, one man except,   545
Who sees thee? (and what is one?) who shouldst be seen
A goddess among gods, adored and served
By angels numberless, thy daily train."
  So glozed the tempter, and his proem³ tuned;
Into the heart of Eve his words made way,   550
Though at the voice much marveling: at length,
Not unamazed, she thus in answer spake.
"What may this mean? Language of man pronounced
By tongue of brute, and human sense expressed?
The first at least of these I thought denied   555
To beasts, whom God on their creation-day
Created mute to all articulate sound;
The latter I demur, for in their looks
Much reason, and in their actions oft appears.⁴
Thee, serpent, subtlest beast of all the field   560
I knew, but not with human voice endued:
Redouble then this miracle, and say,
How cam'st thou speakable of mute,⁵ and how
To me so friendly grown above the rest
Of brutal kind, that daily are in sight?   565
Say, for such wonder claims attention due."

9. Towering.   1. Producing a voice either by using his serpent's ("organic") tongue, or by some more
direct impulse on the air.   2. Mentally inadequate.   3. Preamble, introduction. *Glozed:* Flattered.
4. Eve, well acquainted with animals, which are "duteous at her call" (line 521 above), questions the
notion ("I demur") that they are wholly deprived of "human sense" and "reason."   5. How did you
acquire speech after being dumb.

To whom the guileful tempter thus replied:
"Empress of this fair world, resplendent Eve!
Easy to me it is to tell thee all
What thou command'st and right thou shouldst be obeyed: 570
I was at first as other beasts that graze
The trodden herb, of abject thoughts and low,
As was my food, nor aught but food discerned
Or sex, and apprehended nothing high:
Till on a day, roving the field, I chanced   575
A goodly tree far distant to behold
Loaden with fruit of fairest colors mixed,
Ruddy and gold; I nearer drew to gaze;
When from the boughs a savory odor blown,
Grateful to appetite, more pleased my sense   580
Than smell of sweetest fennel, or the teats
Of ewe or goat dropping with milk[6] at even,
Unsucked of lamb or kid, that tend their play.
To satisfy the sharp desire I had
Of tasting those fair apples, I resolved   585
Not to defer: hunger and thirst at once,
Powerful persuaders, quickened at the scent
Of that alluring fruit, urged me so keen.
About the mossy trunk I wound me soon,
For, high from ground, the branches would require   590
Thy utmost reach, or Adam's: round the tree
All other beasts that saw, with like desire
Longing and envying stood, but could not reach.
Amid the tree now got, where plenty hung
Tempting so nigh, to pluck and eat my fill   595
I spared not; for such pleasure till that hour
At feed or fountain never had I found.
Sated at length, ere long I might perceive
Strange alteration in me, to degree
Of reason[7] in my inward powers, and speech   600
Wanted not long,[8] though to this shape retained.
Thenceforth to speculations high or deep
I turned my thoughts, and with capacious mind
Considered all things visible in Heaven,
Or Earth, or middle,[9] all things fair and good: 605
But all that fair[1] and good in thy divine
Semblance, and in thy beauty's heavenly ray
United I beheld: no fair to thine
Equivalent or second, which compelled
Me thus, though importune perhaps, to come   610

6. According to old folklore, snakes were fond of fennel, which was supposed to sharpen their eyesight, and of goat's milk.   7. To the point of acquiring the faculty of reason.   8. The faculty of speech soon followed. *Retained:* Restrained, kept to his outward appearance.   9. The air.   1. Fairness, beauty.

And gaze, and worship thee of right declared
Sovereign of creatures, universal dame."[2]
  So talked the spirited[3] sly snake: and Eve
Yet more amazed, unwary thus replied:
  "Serpent, thy overpraising leaves in doubt   615
The virtue of that fruit, in thee first proved.
But say, where grows the tree, from hence how far?
For many are the trees of God that grow
In Paradise, and various, yet unknown
To us; in such abundance lies our choice,   620
As leaves a greater store of fruit untouched,
Still hanging incorruptible, till men
Grow up to their provision, and more hands
Help to disburden Nature of her bearth."[4]
  To whom the wily adder, blithe and glad: 625
"Empress, the way is ready, and not long,
Beyond a row of myrtles, on a flat,
Fast by a fountain, one small thicket past
Of blowing[5] myrrh and balm: if thou accept
My conduct, I can bring thee thither soon."   630
  "Lead then," said Eve. He leading swiftly rolled
In tangles, and made intricate seem straight,
To mischief swift. Hope elevates, and joy
Brightens his crest; as when a wandering fire
Compact of unctuous vapor,[6] which the night   635
Condenses, and the cold environs round,
Kindled through agitation to a flame
(Which oft, they say, some evil spirit attends),
Hovering and blazing with delusive light,
Misleads th' amazed night-wanderer from his way   640
To bogs and mires, and oft through pond or pool,
There swallowed up and lost, from succor far:
So glistered the dire snake, and into fraud
Led Eve our credulous mother, to the tree
Of prohibition,[7] root of all our woe: 645
Which when she saw, thus to her guide she spake:
  "Serpent, we might have spared our coming hither,
Fruitless to me, though fruit be here to excess,
The credit of whose virtue rest with thee;[8]
Wondrous indeed, if cause of such effects!   650
But of this tree we may not taste nor touch:
God so commanded, and left that command
Sole daughter of his voice;[9] the rest, we live

2. Mistress of this world.   3. Possessed by an evil spirit.   4. Products.   5. Blossoming.
6. Composed of greasy vapor. *Wandering fire*: Will-o'-the-wisp.   7. The forbidden Tree of
Knowledge.   8. Since the forbidden tree is as good as fruitless to Eve, the only proof of its power
("virtue") will remain with the Serpent.   9. God's command, elsewhere described (Book IV. 433) as
"one easy prohibition," in its present form is the translation of a Hebrew phrase. *The rest*: For the rest.

Law to ourselves; our reason is our law."
   To whom the tempter guilefully replied: 655
"Indeed? Hath God then said that of the fruit
Of all these garden trees ye shall not eat,
Yet lords declared of all in Earth or air?"
   To whom thus Eve, yet sinless: "Of the fruit
Of each tree in the garden we may eat,   660
But of the fruit of this fair tree amidst
The garden, God hath said, 'Ye shall not eat
Thereof, nor shall yet touch it, lest ye die.' "
   She scarce had said, though brief, when now more bold,
The tempter, but with show of zeal and love   665
To man, and indignation at his wrong,
New part[1] puts on, and as to passion moved,
Fluctuates[2] disturbed, yet comely, and in act
Raised,[3] as of some great matter to begin.
As when of old some orator renowned   670
In Athens or free Rome, where eloquence
Flourished, since mute, to some great cause addressed,
Stood in himself collected, while each part,[4]
Motion, each act, won audience ere the tongue,
Sometimes in height began, as no delay   675
Of preface brooking,[5] through his zeal of right.
So standing, moving, or to height upgrown
The tempter all impassioned thus began:
   "O sacred, wise, and wisdom-giving plant,
Mother of science![6] now I feel thy power   680
Within me clear, not only to discern
Things in their causes, but to trace the ways
Of highest agents, deemed however wise.
Queen of this universe! do not believe
Those rigid threats of death. Ye shall not die;   685
How should ye? By the fruit? it gives you life
To knowledge;[7] by the Threatener? look on me,
Me who have touched and tasted, yet both live,
And life more perfect have attained than Fate
Meant me, by venturing higher than my lot.   690
Shall that be shut to man, which to the beast
Is open? Or will God incense his ire
For such a petty trespass, and not praise
Rather your dauntless virtue, whom the pain
Of death denounced, whatever thing death be,   695
Deterred not from achieving what might lead
To happier life, knowledge of good and evil?

---

1. A new role, as of an actor in drama.   2. Undulates with his body.   3. Assuming the orator's posture.   4. Of the body.   5. Plunging into the middle of the subject (in medias res), without any preamble.   6. Knowledge.   7. Life as well as knowledge.

Of good, how just! Of evil, if what is evil
Be real, why not known, since easier shunned?
God therefore cannot hurt ye, and be just;   700
Not just, not God; not feared then, nor obeyed:
Your fear itself of death removes the fear.[8]
Why then was this forbid? Why but to awe,
Why but to keep ye low and ignorant,
His worshipers? He knows that in the day   705
Ye eat thereof, your eyes that seem so clear,
Yet are but dim, shall perfectly be then
Opened and cleared, and ye shall be as gods,
Knowing both good and evil, as they know.
That ye should be as gods, since I as man,   710
Internal man,[9] is but proportion meet,
I, of brute, human; ye, of human, gods.
So ye shall die perhaps, by putting off
Human, to put on gods:[1] death to be wished,
Though threatened, which no worse than this can bring.   715
And what are gods that man may not become
As they, participating godlike food?
The gods are first, and that advantage use
On our belief, that all from them proceeds.
I question it; for this fair Earth I see,   720
Warmed by the sun, producing every kind,
Them nothing: If they[2] all things, who enclosed
Knowledge of good and evil in this tree,
That whoso eats thereof forthwith attains
Wisdom without their leave? And wherein lies   725
Th' offense, that man should thus attain to know?
What can your knowledge hurt him, or this tree
Impart against his will if all be his?
Or is it envy, and can envy dwell
In heavenly breasts? These, these, and many more   730
Causes import[3] your need of this fair fruit.
Goddess humane, reach then, and freely taste!"
    He ended, and his words, replete with guile,
Into her heart too easy entrance won:
Fixed on the fruit she gazed, which to behold   735
Might tempt alone, and in her ears the sound
Yet rung of his persuasive words, impregned[4]
With reason, to her seeming, and with truth;
Meanwhile the hour of noon drew on, and waked
An eager appetite, raised by the smell   740

8. The Serpent's captious argument is that God is by definition just; but since a death-giving God would
not be just, he would not be God; consequently, he would not have to be feared and obeyed.   9. Cf.
"inward," line 600 above. The Serpent has acquired human faculties although his outer form has remained
unchanged.   1. *Human . . . gods:* Humanity . . . divinity.   2. If they produced.   3. Imply,
indicate.   4. Impregnated, filled.

So savory of that fruit, which with desire,
Inclinable[5] now grown to touch or taste,
Solicited her longing eye; yet first
Pausing a while, thus to herself she mused:
   "Great are thy virtues, doubtless, best of fruits,   745
Though kept from man, and worthy to be admired,
Whose taste, too long forborne, at first assay
Gave elocution to the mute, and taught
The tongue not made for speech to speak thy praise:
Thy praise he also who forbids thy use,   750
Conceals not from us, naming thee the Tree
Of Knowledge, knowledge both of good and evil;
Forbids us then to taste; but his forbidding
Commends thee more, while it infers[6] the good
By thee communicated, and our want: 755
For good unknown, sure is not had, or had
And yet unknown, is as not had at all.
In plain[7] then, what forbids he but to know?
Forbids us good, forbids us to be wise!
Such prohibitions bind not.[8] But if Death   760
Bind us with after-bands, what profits then
Our inward freedom?[9] In the day we eat
Of this fair fruit, our doom is, we shall die.
How dies the serpent? He hath eaten and lives,
And knows, and speaks, and reasons, and discerns,   765
Irrational till then. For us alone
Was death invented? Or to us denied
This intellectual food, for beasts reserved?
For beasts it seems: yet that one beast which first
Hath tasted, envies not, but brings with joy   770
The good befallen him, author unsuspect,[1]
Friendly to man, far from deceit or guile.
What fear I then, rather what know to fear
Under this ignorance of good and evil,[2]
Of God or death, of law or penalty?   775
Here grows the cure of all, this fruit divine,
Fair to the eye, inviting to the taste,
Of virtue[3] to make wise: what hinders then
To reach, and feed at once both body and mind?"
   So saying, her rash hand in evil hour,   780
Forth reaching to the fruit, she plucked, she eat.[4]

5. Favorably disposed.   6. Implies.   7. In plain words.   8. Eve, who has learned from the Serpent
the art of sophistical argument, claims that God himself, by naming the Tree, has indicated to us the
"good" in it; but a "good unknown" is as nothing; besides, forbidding the experience of the Tree of
Knowledge is forbidding man "to be wise"; hence the prohibition is not binding.   9. Death would
constitute a later bond ("after-bands"), after God has granted us free will ("inward freedom").   1. An
unsuspectable authority on the subject.   2. Having no knowledge of good and evil, Eve doesn't know
what is to be feared.   3. With the power.   4. Ate.

Earth felt the wound, and Nature from her seat
Sighing through all her works gave signs of woe,[5]
That all was lost. Back to the thicket slunk
The guilty serpent, and well might, for Eve   785
Intent now wholly on her taste, naught else
Regarded; such delight till then, as seemed,
In fruit she never tasted, whether true
Or fancied so, through expectation high
Of knowledge; nor was godhead from her thought.[6]   790
Greedily she engorged without restraint,
And knew not eating death:[7] satiate at length,
And heightened as with wine, jocund and boon,[8]
Thus to herself she pleasingly began:
    "O sovereign, virtuous, precious of all trees   795
In Paradise! of operation blest
To sapience,[9] hitherto obscured, infamed,
And thy fair fruit let hang, as to no end
Created; but henceforth my early care,
Not without song each morning, and due praise   800
Shall tend thee, and the fertile burden ease
Of thy full branches offered free to all;
Till dieted by thee I grow mature
In knowledge, as the gods who all things know;
Though others envy what they cannot give: 805
For had the gift been theirs, it had not here
Thus grown.[1] Experience, next to thee I owe,
Best guide; not following thee I had remained
In ignorance; thou open'st Wisdom's way,
And giv'st access, though secret she retire.   810
And I perhaps am secret; Heaven is high,
High and remote to see from thence distinct
Each thing on Earth; and other care perhaps
May have diverted from continual watch
Our great Forbidder, safe[2] with all his spies   815
About him. But to Adam in what sort[3]
Shall I appear? Shall I to him make known
As yet my change, and give him to partake
Full happiness with me, or rather not,
But keep the odds[4] of knowledge in my power   820
Without copartner? so to add what wants
In female sex, the more to draw his love,
And render me more equal, and perhaps,
A thing not undesirable, sometime

5. Natural "signs," omens, metaphorically given as—and punning with—the "sighs" of Nature; forebod-
ings of disaster.   6. She thought of acquiring divinity.   7. That she was eating death.
8. Cheerful.   9. Endowed with the power to give wisdom. *Infamed:* Made infamous.   1. For Satan's
argument (here adopted by Eve) about "the gods" not having created the forbidden tree, and their consequent envy, see lines 720–730 above.   2. Not dangerous.   3. Manner.   4. Advantage.

Superior: for, inferior, who is free?   825
This may be well: but what if God have seen
And death ensue? Then I shall be no more,
And Adam, wedded to another Eve,
Shall live with her enjoying, I extinct;
A death to think. Confirmed then I resolve,   830
Adam shall share with me in bliss or woe:
So dear I love him, that with him all deaths
I could endure, without him live no life."[5]
    So saying, from the tree her step she turned,
But first low reverence done, as to the power   835
That dwelt within, whose presence had infused
Into the plant sciential[6] sap, derived
From nectar, drink of gods. Adam the while
Waiting desirous her return, had wove
Of choicest flowers a garland to adorn   840
Her tresses, and her rural labors crown,
As reapers oft are wont their harvest queen.
Great joy he promised to his thoughts, and new
Solace in her return, so long delayed:
Yet oft his heart, divine of[7] something ill,   845
Misgave him; he the faltering measure[8] felt;
And forth to meet her went, the way she took
That morn when first they parted. By the Tree
Of Knowledge he must pass; there he her met,
Scarce from the tree returning; in her hand   850
A bough of fairest fruit that downy smiled,
New gathered, and ambrosial smell diffused.
To him she hastened, in her face excuse
Came prologue, and apology to prompt,[9]
Which with bland words at will she thus addressed: 855
    "Hast thou not wondered, Adam, at my stay?
Thee I have missed, and thought it long, deprived
Thy presence, agony of love till now
Not felt, nor shall be twice; for never more
Mean I to try, what rash untried I sought,   860
The pain of absence from thy sight. But strange
Hath been the cause, and wonderful to hear:
This tree is not as we are told, a tree

---

5. In the crucial lines 817–833, Eve's thoughts are shown moving through three stages: first, the idea of not sharing her knowledge with Adam, so as to enhance her own power, with the gratuitous notion that lesser power brings no freedom at all (ll. 817–820); then, jealously at the thought of her own possible death, and Adam "wedded to another Eve" (ll. 820–825); finally, with an opportune resurgence of "love," the resolve to be with Adam "in bliss or woe," i.e., to make him her partner in sin. Thus the passage is centrally representative of Milton's characterization of Eve in her relation to Adam, and possibly of some of the poet's own conceptions of femininity in general. Cf., in this same Book, such other characterizing passages as lines 377–384 above, 869–885 and 1155–1161 below.   6. Infusing knowledge.   7. Divining, foreseeing.   8. Irregularity of heartbeats.   9. A pleading expression on her face came as an introduction (the "prologue" to a play) to prepare for ("prompt" is also a theatrical term) the formal "apology."

Of danger tasted,[1] nor to evil unknown
Opening the way, but of divine effect   865
To open eyes, and make them gods who taste;
And hath been tasted such.[2] The serpent wise,
Or not restrained as we, or not obeying,
Hath eaten of the fruit, and is become,
Not dead, as we are threatened, but thenceforth   870
Endued with human voice and human sense,
Reasoning to admiration,[3] and with me
Persuasively hath so prevailed, that I
Have also tasted, and have also found
Th' effects to correspond, opener mine eyes,   875
Dim erst, dilated spirits, ampler heart,
And growing up to godhead; which for thee
Chiefly I sought, without thee can despise.
For bliss, as thou hast part, to me is bliss,
Tedious, unshared with thee, and odious soon.   880
Thou therefore also taste, that equal lot
May join us, equal joy, as equal love;
Lest, thou not tasting, different degree[4]
Disjoin us, and I then too late renounce
Deity for thee, when Fate will not permit."[5]   885
     Thus Eve with countenance blithe her story told;
But in her cheek distemper[6] flushing glowed.
On th' other side, Adam, soon as he heard
The fatal trespass done by Eve, amazed,
Astonied[7] stood and blank, while horror chill   890
Ran through his veins, and all his joints relaxed;[8]
From his slack hand the garland wreathed for Eve
Down dropped, and all the faded roses shed.
Speechless he stood and pale, till thus at length
First to himself he inward silence broke: 895
     "O fairest of creation, last and best
Of all God's works, creature in whom excelled
Whatever can to sight or thought be formed,
Holy, divine, good, amiable, or sweet!
How art thou lost, how on a sudden lost,   900
Defaced, deflowered, and now to death devote?[9]
Rather how hast thou yielded to transgress
The strict forbiddance, how to violate
The sacred fruit forbidden! Some cursèd fraud
Of enemy hath beguiled thee, yet unknown,[1]   905
And me with thee hath ruined, for with thee
Certain my resolution is to die.

---

1. When tasted.   2. Has been proved by tasting.   3. Admirably.   4. A difference in rank between
us.   5. Cf., and contrast, ll. 825–833 above.   6. Disharmony in the body's "humours"; disease.
7. Stunned.   8. Slackened.   9. Doomed.   1. Refers to "enemy."

How can I live without thee, how forgo
Thy sweet converse and love so dearly joined,
To live again in these wild woods forlorn?　　910
Should God create another Eve, and I
Another rib afford, yet loss of thee
Would never from my heart; no, no! I feel
The link of nature draw me: flesh of flesh,
Bone of my bone thou art, and from thy state　915
Mine never shall be parted, bliss or woe."
　　So having said, as one from sad dismay
Recomforted, and after thoughts disturbed
Submitting to what seemed remediless,
Thus in calm mood his words to Eve he turned:　920
　　"Bold deed thou hast presumed, adventurous Eve
And peril great provoked, who thus hath dared
Had it been only coveting to eye
That sacred fruit, sacred to abstinence,
Much more to taste it, under ban to touch.　925
But past who can recall, or done undo?
Not God omnipotent, nor Fate! Yet so
Perhaps thou shalt not die, perhaps the fact
Is not so heinous now, foretasted fruit,
Profaned first by the serpent, by him first　930
Made common and unhallowed ere our taste,
Nor yet on him found deadly; he yet lives,
Lives, as thou saidst, and gains to live as man
Higher degree of life: inducement strong
To us, as likely, tasting, to attain　935
Proportional[2] ascent, which cannot be
But to be gods, or angels, demigods.
Nor can I think that God, Creator wise,
Though threatening, will in earnest so destroy
Us his prime creatures, dignified so high,　940
Set over all his works, which in our fall,
For us created, needs with us must fail,
Dependent made; so God shall uncreate,
Be frustrate, do, undo, and labor lose;
Not well conceived of God,[3] who, though his power　945
Creation could repeat, yet would be loath
Us to abolish, lest the adversary
Triúmph and say: 'Fickle their state whom God
Most favors; who can please him long? Me first
He ruined, now mankind; whom will he next?'　950
Matter of scorn, not to be given the foe.
However, I with thee have fixed my lot.

2. Proportionate to our human status (cf. the Serpent's argument, ll. 710–12 above).　　3. That would be a wrong conception of God.

Certain[4] to undergo like doom: if death
Consort with thee, death is to me as life;
So forcible within my heart I feel   955
The bond of nature draw me to my own,
My own in thee, for what thou art is mine;
Our state cannot be severed; we are one,
One flesh; to lose thee were to lose myself."
  So Adam, and thus Eve to him replied: 960
"O glorious trial of exceeding love,
Illustrious evidence, example high!
Engaging me to emulate; but short
Of thy perfection, how shall I attain,
Adam? from whose dear side I boast me sprung,   965
And gladly of our union hear thee speak,
One heart, one soul in both; whereof good proof
This day affords, declaring thee resolved,
Rather than death or aught than death more dread
Shall separate us, linked in love so dear,   970
To undergo with me one guilt, one crime,
If any be, of tasting this fair fruit;
Whose virtue (for of good still good proceeds,
Direct, or by occasion)[5] hath presented
This happy trial of thy love, which else   975
So eminently never had been known.
Were it[6] I thought death menaced would ensue
This my attempt, I would sustain alone
The worst, and not persuade thee, rather die
Deserted, than oblige[7] thee with a fact   980
Pernicious to thy peace, chiefly assured
Remarkably so late of thy so true,
So faithful love unequaled; but I feel
Far otherwise th' event;[8] not death, but life
Augmented, opened eyes, new hopes, new joys,   985
Taste so divine, that what of sweet before
Hath touched my sense, flat seems to this, and harsh.
On my experience, Adam, freely taste,
And fear of death deliver to the winds."
  So saying, she embraced him, and for joy   990
Tenderly wept, much won that he his love
Had so ennobled, as of choice to incur
Divine displeasure for her sake, or death.
In recompense (for such compliance bad
Such recompense best merits), from the bough   995
She gave him of that fair enticing fruit
With liberal hand; he scrupled not to eat,

4. Resolved.   5. Indirectly.   6. If.   7. Involve (Adam in her guilty action).   8. The eventual
consequence of her transgression.

Against his better knowledge, not deceived,[9]
But fondly overcome with female charm.
Earth trembled from her entrails, as again 1000
In pangs, and Nature gave a second groan.
Sky lowered, and muttering thunder, some sad drops
Wept at completing of the mortal sin
Original; while Adam took no thought,
Eating his fill, nor Eve to iterate 1005
Her former trespass feared, the more to soothe
Him with her loved society; that now
As with new wine intoxicated both,
They swim in mirth, and fancy that they feel
Divinity within them breeding wings 1010
Wherewith to scorn the Earth. But that false fruit
Far other operation first displayed,
Carnal desire inflaming; he on Eve
Began to cast lascivious eyes, she him
As wantonly repaid; in lust they burn, 1015
Till Adam thus 'gan Eve to dalliance move:
    "Eve, now I see thou art exact of taste,[1]
And elegant, of sapience[2] no small part,
Since to each meaning savor we apply,
And palate call judicious. I the praise 1020
Yield thee, so well this day thou hast purveyed.
Much pleasure we have lost, while we abstained
From this delightful fruit, nor known till now
True relish, tasting; if such pleasure be
In things to us forbidden, it might be wished, 1025
For[3] this one tree had been forbidden ten.
But come; so well refreshed, now let us play,
As meet is, after such delicious fare;
For never did thy beauty, since the day
I saw thee first and wedded thee, adorned 1030
With all perfections, so enflame my sense
With ardor to enjoy thee, fairer now
Than ever, bounty of this virtuous[4] tree."
    So said he, and forbore not glance or toy[5]
Of[6] amorous intent, well understood 1035
Of Eve, whose eye darted contagious fire.
Her hand he seized, and to a shady bank,
Thick overhead with verdant roof embowered
He led her, nothing loath; flowers were the couch,
Pansies, and violets, and asphodel, 1040

9. Adam, unlike Eve, acts in full consciousness, not having been "deceived" by the Serpent.   1. Of exacting taste.   2. In both meanings of the word ("wisdom" and "taste") originating in the Latin *sapere*, as does "savour," similarly played on in the next line. *Elegant:* Choosy, refined.   3. Instead of.
4. Endowed with special power (the "virtue" of ll. 651 and 778 above).   5. Toying, playing.   6. With.

And hyacinth, Earth's freshest, softest lap.
There they their fill of love and love's disport
Took largely, of their mutual guilt the seal,
The solace of their sin, till dewy sleep
Oppressed them, wearied with their amorous play.   1045
    Soon as the force of that fallacious fruit,
That with exhilarating vapor bland
About their spirits had played, and inmost powers
Made err, was now exhaled, and grosser sleep
Bred of unkindly fumes,[7] with conscious dreams   1050
Encumbered, now had left them, up they rose
As from unrest, and each the other viewing,
Soon found their eyes how opened, and their minds
How darkened. Innocence, that as a veil
Had shadowed them from knowing ill, was gone;   1055
Just confidence, and native righteousness,
And honor from about them, naked left
To guilty Shame; he covered, but his robe
Uncovered more.[8] So rose the Danite strong,
Hercúlean Samson, from the harlot-lap   1060
Of Philístean Dáliláh, and waked
Shorn of his strength;[9] they destitute and bare
Of all their virtue. Silent, and in face
Confounded, long they sat, as strucken mute;
Till Adam, though not less than Eve abashed,   1065
At length gave utterance to these words constrained:
    "O Eve, in evil hour thou didst give ear
To that false worm,[1] of whomsoever taught
To counterfeit man's voice, true in our fall,
False in our promised rising; since our eyes   1070
Opened we find indeed, and find we know
Both good and evil, good lost, and evil got:
Bad fruit of knowledge, if this be to know,
Which leaves us naked thus, of honor void,
Of innocence, of faith, of purity,   1075
Our wonted ornaments now soiled and stained,
And in our faces evident the signs
Of foul concupiscence; whence evil store,[2]
Even shame, the last[3] of evils; of the first
Be sure then. How shall I behold the face   1080
Henceforth of God or angel, erst with joy
And rapture so oft beheld? Those heavenly shapes
Will dazzle now this earthly[4] with their blaze

---

7. Unnatural exhalations.   8. Shame (personified) covered them, but his cover ("robe") only made them aware of their nakedness ("uncovered more").   9. For the story of Samson betrayed by his wife Delilah see Judges 16:4–20. *Danite*: Of the tribe of Dan.   1. The Serpent, now disparaged.   2. An abundance of evils.   3. Extreme, ultimate.   4. Adam's now earthly nature and senses.

Insufferably bright. O might I here
In solitude live savage, in some glade   1085
Obscured, where highest woods, impenetrable
To star or sunlight, spread their umbrage broad,
And brown[5] as evening! Cover me, ye pines,
Ye cedars, with innumerable boughs
Hide me, where I may never see them[6] more!   1090
But let us now, as in[7] bad plight, devise
What best may for the present serve to hide
The parts of each from other, that seem most
To shame obnoxious,[8] and unseemliest seen;
Some tree whose broad smooth leaves together sewed,   1095
And girded on our loins, may cover round
Those middle parts, that this newcomer, Shame,
There sit not, and reproach us as unclean."
      So counseled he, and both together went
Into the thickest wood; there soon they chose   1100
The figtree,[9] not that kind for fruit renowned,
But such as at this day, to Indians known,
In Malabar or Deccan[1] spreads her arms
Branching so broad and long, that in the ground
The bended twigs take root, and daughters grow   1105
About the mother tree, a pillared shade
High overarched, and echoing walks between;
There oft the Indian herdsman, shunning heat,
Shelters in cool, and tends his pasturing herds
At loopholes cut through thickest shade. Those leaves   1110
They gathered, broad as Amazonian targe,[2]
And with what skill they had, together sewed,
To gird their waist; vain covering, if to hide
Their guilt and dreaded shame! O how unlike
To that first naked glory! Such of late   1115
Columbus found th' American, so girt
With feathered cincture,[3] naked else and wild
Among the trees on isles and woody shores.
Thus fenced, and, as they thought, their shame in part
Covered, but not at rest or ease of mind,   1120
They sat them down to weep; nor only tears
Rained at their eyes, but high winds worse within
Began to rise, high passions, anger, hate,
Mistrust, suspicion, discord, and shook sore
Their inward state of mind, calm region once   1125

5. Dark.   6. The "heavenly shapes" of line 1082.   7. As we are in.   8. Exposed to.   9. Identified
as the banyan or Indian fig tree, also classified in botany as *Ficus religiosa*.   1. Regions in southern
India.   2. Cf. "target": the shield of the Amazons, women warriors in Greco-Roman myth (and memorably in Virgil's *Aeneid*). Actually, the leaf of the "Indian fig tree" is small; Milton's inaccurate notion
comes from contemporary sources he knew, and goes back to antiquity.   3. Belt.

And full of peace, now tossed and turbulent:
For Understanding ruled not, and the Will
Heard not her lore, both in subjection now
To sensual Appetite, who, from beneath
Usurping over sovereign Reason, claimed   1130
Superior sway.[4] From thus distempered breast,
Adam, estranged in look and altered style,
Speech intermitted thus to Eve renewed:
   "Would thou hadst hearkened to my words, and stayed
With me, as I besought thee, when that strange   1135
Desire of wandering, this unhappy morn,
I know not whence possessed thee! we had then
Remained still happy, not as now, despoiled
Of all our good, shamed, naked, miserable.
Let none henceforth seek needless cause to approve   1140
The faith they owe;[5] when earnestly they seek
Such proof, conclude, they then begin to fail."
   To whom, soon moved with touch of blame, thus Eve:
"What words have passed thy lips, Adam severe?
Imput'st thou that to my default, or will   1145
Of wandering, as thou call'st it, which who knows
But might as ill have happened, thou being by,
Or to thyself perhaps? Hadst thou been there,
Or here th' attempt, thou couldst not have discerned
Fraud in the serpent, speaking as he spake;   1150
No ground of enmity between us known,
Why he should mean me ill, or seek to harm?
Was I to have never parted from thy side?
As good have grown there still a lifeless rib.
Being as I am, why didst not thou, the head,   1155
Command me absolutely not to go,
Going into such danger, as thou saidst?
Too facile then, thou didst not much gainsay,
Nay, didst permit, approve, and fair dismiss.
Hadst thou been firm and fixed in thy dissent,   1160
Neither had I transgressed, nor thou with me."[6]
   To whom, then first incensed, Adam replied:
"Is this the love, is this the recompense
Of mine to thee, ingrateful Eve, expressed[7]
Immutable when thou were lost, not I,   1165
Who might have lived and joyed immortal bliss,
Yet willingly chose rather death with thee?

4. The victory of "sensual Appetite" over "Reason," both here personified (cf. l. 113 above, and note 37), and over man's free will (cf. l. 351ff.), man's distinguishing traits, is of course, in brief abstract, the very history of the Fall.   5. Own. *Approve:* Prove by testing.   6. The notion of man's authority over woman—recognized by Milton's Eve (e.g., in Book IV. 442–443: "my guide / and head") and echoing St. Paul ("the head of the woman is the man," I Corinthians 10:13) is here used by her to make Adam her equal in guilt, accusing him of indulgence in letting her go ("too facile").   7. Demonstrated, proved.

And am I now upbraided as the cause
Of thy transgressing? not enough severe,
It seems, in thy restraint![8] What could I more?　　　　1170
I warned thee, I admonished thee, foretold
The danger, and the lurking enemy
That lay in wait; beyond this had been force,
And force upon free will hath here no place.
But confidence then bore thee on, secure　　　　1175
Either to meet no danger, or to find
Matter of glorious trial; and perhaps
I also erred in overmuch admiring
What seemed in thee so perfect, that I thought
No evil durst attempt thee! but I rue　　　　1180
That error now, which is become my crime,
And thou th' accuser. Thus it shall befall
Him who, to worth in women overtrusting,
Lets her will rule; restraint she will not brook,[9]
And, left to herself, if evil thence ensue,　　　　1185
She first his weak indulgence will accuse."
　　Thus they in mutual accusation spent
The fruitless hours, but neither self-condemning;
And of their vain contést appeared no end.

From BOOK X

The Argument

　　Man's transgression known, the guardian Angels forsake Paradise, and
return up to Heaven to approve their vigilance, and are approved; God
declaring that the entrance of Satan could not be by them prevented. He
sends his Son to judge the transgressors; who descends, and gives sentence
accordingly; then, in pity, clothes them both, and reascends. Sin and Death,
sitting till then at the gates of Hell, by wondrous sympathy feeling the
success of Satan in this new World, and the sin by Man there committed,
resolve to sit no longer confined in Hell, but to follow Satan, their sire, up
to the place of Man: to make the way easier from Hell to this World to and
fro, they pave a broad highway or bridge over Chaos, according to the track
that Satan first made; then, preparing for Earth, they meet him, proud of
his success, returning to Hell; their mutual gratulation. Satan arrives at
Pandemonium; in full assembly relates, with boasting, his success against
Man; instead of applause is entertained with a general hiss by all his audience, transformed, with himself also, suddenly into Serpents, according to
his doom given in Paradise; then, deluded with a show of the Forbidden
Tree springing up before them, they, greedily reaching to take of the fruit,
chew dust and bitter ashes. The proceedings of Sin and Death: God foretells the final victory of his Son over them, and the renewing of all things;

8. In restraining Eve.　　9. Put up with.

but, for the present, commands his Angels to make several alterations in the Heavens and Elements. Adam, more and more perceiving his fallen condition, heavily bewails,[1] rejects the condolement of Eve; she persists, and at length appeases him: then, to evade the curse likely to fall on their offspring, proposes to Adam violent ways; which he approves not, but, conceiving better hope, puts her in mind of the late promise made them, that her seed should be revenged on the Serpent, and exhorts her, with him, to seek peace of the offended Deity by repentance and supplication.

(Acceptance, Reconciliation, Hope)

Be it so, for I submit; his doom is fair,[2]
That dust I am and shall to dust return.   770
O welcome hour whenever! Why delays
His hand to execute what his decree
Fixed on this day? Why do I overlive?
Why am I mocked with death, and lengthened out
To deathless pain? How gladly would I meet   775
Mortality, my sentence, and be earth
Insensible! how glad would lay me down
As in my mother's lap![3] There I should rest
And sleep secure; his dreadful voice no more
Would thunder in my ears; no fear of worse   780
To me and to my offspring would torment me
With cruel expectation. Yet one doubt
Pursues me still, lest all I cannot die;
Lest that pure breath of life, the spirit of man
Which God inspired, cannot together perish   785
With this corporeal clod; then, in the grave,
Or in some other dismal place, who knows
But I shall die a living death? O thought
Horrid, if true![4] Yet why? It was but breath
Of life that sinned; what dies but what had life   790
And sin? the body properly hath neither.
All of me then shall die: let this appease
The doubt, since human reach no further knows.
For though the Lord of all be infinite,
Is his wrath also? Be it, man is not so,   795
But mortal doomed. How can he exercise
Wrath without end on man whom death must end?
Can he make deathless death? That were to make
Strange contradiction, which to God himself

1. Our selection starts toward the end of Adam's long lamentation.   2. In his inner debate, Adam has just been arguing to himself that God created us "of choice his own, / and of his own to serve him"; hence in the same way as reward "was of his [God's] grace," so punishment "justly is at his will," therefore acceptable.   3. The reference is to the earth (in Book XI. 536, Michael, addressing Adam, calls the earth "thy Mother's lap"), and is in part probably an echo of Job 3.   4. Adam fears that the soul, breathed (inspired) into the corporeal clod at creation, may be immortal and so suffer a "living death" in the grave.

Impossible is held, as argument   800
Of weakness, not of power.[5] Will he draw out,
For anger's sake, finite to infinite
In punished man, to satisfy his rigor
Satisfied never? That were to extend
His sentence beyond dust and Nature's law;   805
By which all causes else according still
To the reception of their matter act,
Not to th' extent of their own sphere.[6] But say
That death be not one stroke, as I supposed,
Bereaving sense,[7] but endless misery   810
From this day onward, which I feel begun
Both in me and without[8] me, and so last
To perpetuity—Ay me! that fear
Comes thundering back with dreadful revolution
On my defenseless head! Both death and I   815
Am[9] found eternal, and incorporate both:
Nor I on my part single; in me all
Posterity stands cursed. Fair patrimony
That I must leave ye, sons! O, were I able
To waste it all myself, and leave ye none!   820
So disinherited, how would ye bless
Me, now your curse! Ah, why should all mankind
For one man's fault thus guiltless be condemned,
If guiltless? But from me what can proceed,
But all corrupt, both mind and will depraved,   825
Not to do only, but to will the same
With me? How can they then acquitted stand
In sight of God?[1] Him, after all disputes,
Forced I absolve. All my evasions vain
And reasonings, though through mazes, lead me still   830
But to my own conviction: first and last
On me, me only, as the source and spring
Of all corruption, all the blame lights due;
So might the wrath! Fond[2] wish! Couldst thou support
That burden, heavier than the earth to bear;   835
Than all the world much heavier, though divided
With that bad woman? Thus, what thou desir'st,

---

5. Adam corrects himself, arguing (as Milton did in his theological writings) that since only the spirit ("breath of life") sinned, it shall die with the body (and, implicitly, await resurrection). Otherwise, according to the same theological line of thinking, there would be "strange contradiction," an inadmissable sign of weakness in God.   6. According to "Nature's law," the power of all agents, God excepted ("all causes else"), cannot be exercised to its utmost ("the extent of their own sphere"), but is limited by the capacity for "reception" that the object of that power possesses. I.e., once body *and* spirit die, further punishment is impossible.   7. Removing all sensory powers.   8. Outside.   9. The verb in the singular form stresses Adam's concentration on himself, and on the fact that he and Death are now united in one body ("incorporate").   1. Inheriting Adam's original sin, his descendants, like him ("with me"), are going to act sinfully by their own free will.   2. Foolish.

And what thou fear'st, alike destroys all hope[3]
Of refuge, and concludes thee[4] miserable
Beyond all past example[5] and future;   840
To Satan only like, both crime and doom.[6]
O Conscience! into what abyss of fears
And horrors hast thou driven me; out of which
I find no way, from deep to deeper plunged!"
    Thus Adam to himself lamented loud   845
Through the still night, not now, as ere man fell,
Wholesome and cool and mild, but with black air
Accompanied, with damps and dreadful gloom;
Which to his evil conscience represented
All things with double terror. On the ground   850
Outstretched he lay, on the cold ground, and oft
Cursed his creation; Death as oft accused
Of tardy execution, since denounced
The day of his offense. "Why comes not Death,"
Said he, "with one thrice-ácceptáble stroke   855
To end me? Shall Truth fail to keep her word,
Justice divine not hasten to be just?
But Death comes not at call; Justice divine
Mends not her slowest pace for prayers or cries.
O woods, O fountains, hillocks, dales, and bowers!   860
With other echo late I taught your shades
To answer, and resound far other song."
Whom thus afflicted when sad Eve beheld,
Desolate where she sat, approaching nigh,
Soft words to his fierce passion she essayed;   865
But her with stern regard he thus repelled:
    "Out of my sight, thou serpent! that name best
Befits thee, with him leagued, thyself as false
And hateful: nothing wants, but that thy shape,
Like his, and color serpentine, may show   870
Thy inward fraud, to warn all creatures from thee
Henceforth; lest that too heavenly form, pretended[7]
To hellish falsehood, snare them. But for thee
I had persisted happy, had not thy pride
And wandering vanity, when least was safe,   875
Rejected my forewarning, and disdained
Not to be trusted, longing to be seen
Though by the devil himself, him overweening
To overreach,[8] but, with the serpent meeting,

3. Actually, by his desperate self-accusation, and by wanting to assume, alone, the burden of guilt, Adam is shown to be already on the way to full repentance and to his own regeneration.   4. Demonstrates that you are.   5. That of the fallen angels.   6. The comparison is clearly invalid, Adam's remorse and repentant despair being opposite to Satan's choice, as seen for instance in Book IV, 109–110: "Farewell Remorse: all good to me is lost; / Evil be now my Good. . ."   7. Put up as a screen.   8. Overestimating your power to outwit him.

Fooled and beguiled; by him thou, I by thee,   880
To trust thee from my side, imagined wise,
Constant, mature, proof against all assaults;
And understood not all was but a show
Rather than solid virtue, all but a rib
Crooked by nature—bent, as now appears,   885
More to the part sinister—from me drawn;
Well if thrown out, as supernumerary
To my just number found!⁹ Oh, why did God,
Creator wise, that peopled highest Heaven
With spirits masculine, create at last   890
This novelty on earth, this fair defect
Of nature, and not fill the world at once
With men, as angels, without feminine;
Or find some other way to generate
Mankind?¹ This mischief had not then befallen,   895
And more that shall befall—innumerable
Disturbances on earth through female snares,
And strait conjunction with this sex. For either
He never shall find out fit mate, but such
As some misfortune brings him, or mistake;   900
Or whom he wishes most shall seldom gain,
Through her perverseness, but shall see her gained
By a far worse, or, if she love, withheld
By parents, or his happiest choice too late
Shall meet, already linked² and wedlock-bound   905
To a fell³ adversary, his hate or shame:
Which infinite calamity shall cause
To human life, and household peace confound."
      He added not, and from her turned; but Eve,
Not so repulsed, with tears that ceased not flowing,   910
And tresses all disordered, at his feet
Fell humble, and, embracing them, besought
His peace, and thus proceeded in her plaint:
      "Forsake me not thus, Adam! witness Heaven
What love sincere and reverence in my heart   915
I bear thee, and unweeting⁴ have offended,
Unhappily deceived! Thy suppliant⁵
I beg, and clasp thy knees; bereave me not,
Whereon I live, thy gentle looks, thy aid,
Thy counsel in this uttermost distress,   920
My only strength and stay: forlorn of thee,
Whither shall I betake me, where subsist?

9. Folklore has it that the rib from which Eve was created was an extra thirteenth rib on Adam's left (Latin
sinister) side. Note double meaning of "sinister."   1. Adam's frenzied speech belongs to a tradition of
misogynistic rhetoric that goes back to antiquity. Lines 888–895, in particular, seem to echo lines 617–
620 of the tragedy *Hippolytus* by Euripides, one of Milton's favorite poets.   2. When *he* is already
linked.   3. Fierce, bitter.   4. Unknowingly.   5. As thy suppliant.

While yet we live, scarce one short hour perhaps,
Between us two let there be peace; both joining,
As joined in injuries, one enmity   925
Against a foe by doom express assigned us,
That cruel serpent. On me exercise not
Thy hatred for this misery befallen;
On me already lost, me than thyself
More miserable. Both have sinned, but thou   930
Against God only; I against God and thee,
And to the place of judgment will return,
There with my cries importune Heaven, that all
The sentence, from thy head removed, may light
On me, sole cause to thee of all this woe,   935
Me, me only, just object of his ire."
    She ended weeping; and her lowly plight,
Immovable[6] till peace obtained from fault
Acknowledged and deplored, in Adam wrought
Commiseration. Soon his heart relented   940
Towards her, his life so late and sole delight,
Now at his feet submissive in distress,
Creature so fair his reconcilement seeking,
His counsel, whom she had displeased, his aid;
As one disarmed, his anger all he lost,   945
And thus with peaceful words upraised her soon:
    "Unwary, and too desirous, as before,
So now, of what thou know'st not,[7] who desir'st
The punishment all on thyself! Alas!
Bear thine own first, ill able to sustain   950
His full wrath, whose thou feel'st as yet least part,[8]
And my displeasure bear'st so ill. If prayers
Could alter high decrees, I to that place
Would speed before thee, and be louder heard,
That on my head all might be visited,   955
Thy frailty and infirmer sex forgiven,
To me committed, and by me exposed.[9]
But rise; let us no more contend, nor blame
Each other, blamed enough elsewhere,[1] but strive
In offices of love, how we may lighten   960
Each other's burden in our share of woe;
Since this day's death denounced, if aught I see,
Will prove no sudden, but a slow-paced evil,

6. Modifies both Eve in her lowly posture of repentance and Adam in his first reluctance to forgive.
7. Once more ("as before / so now") Eve is "too desirous" of the unknown; but her situation and her tone
are now totally different and so are Adam's, whose "counsel" and "aid" she has sought.   8. Eve would
not be able to bear the weight of God's full wrath, of which she has until now experienced only the smallest
part.   9. In the present atmosphere of reconciliation, Adam seems to accept Eve's earlier charge (cf.
Book IX. 1158–1161 and note 6): now he blames himself for having "exposed" her to temptation.
1. At the place of judgment (cf. ll. 932 and 953 above, 1098–1099 below).

A long day's dying to augment our pain,
And to our seed (O hapless seed!) derived."[2]   965
    To whom thus Eve, recovering heart, replied:—
"Adam, by sad experiment I know
How little weight my words with thee can find,
Found so erroneous, thence by just event
Found so unfortunate. Nevertheless,   970
Restored by thee, vile as I am, to place
Of new acceptance, hopeful to regain
Thy love, the sole contentment of my heart,
Living or dying from thee I will not hide
What thoughts in my unquiet breast are risen,   975
Tending to some relief of our extremes,
Or end, though sharp and sad, yet tolerable,
As in our evils,[3] and of easier choice.
If care of our descent[4] perplex us most,
Which must be born to certain woe, devoured   980
By Death at last (and miserable it is
To be to others cause of misery,
Our own begotten, and of our loins to bring
Into this cursed world a woeful race,
That, after wretched life, must be at last   985
Food for so foul a monster), in thy power
It lies, yet ere conception, to prevent
The race unblest, to being yet unbegot.[5]
Childless thou art; childless remain. So Death
Shall be deceived his glut,[6] and with us two   990
Be forced to satisfy his ravenous maw.
But, if thou judge it hard and difficult,
Conversing, looking, loving, to abstain
From love's due rites, nuptial embraces sweet,
And with desire to languish without hope   995
Before the present object[7] languishing
With like desire—which would be misery
And torment less than none of what we dread—
Then, both our selves and seed at once to free
From what we fear for both, let us make short;   1000
Let us seek Death, or, he not found, supply
With our own hands his office on ourselves.
Why stand we longer shivering under fears
That show no end but death, and have the power,
Of many ways to die the shortest choosing   1005
Destruction with destruction to destroy?"[8]

2. Transmitted.   3. We being in such evils.   4. Descendants, lineage.   5. To forestall, by abstinence, the birth of descendants.   6. Shall be cheated of its fill.   7. Eve herself, object of Adam's
love, and now in his presence.   8. Destroy "destruction" (i.e., Death's power to destroy future mankind)
by destroying ourselves now.

She ended here, or vehement despair
Broke off the rest; so much of death her thoughts
Had entertained as dyed her cheeks with pale.
But Adam, with such counsel nothing swayed,   1010
To better hopes his more attentive mind
Laboring had raised, and thus to Eve replied:—
"Eve, thy contempt of life and pleasure seems
To argue in thee something more sublime
And excellent than what thy mind contemns: 1015
But self-destruction therefore sought refutes
That excellence thought in thee, and implies
Not thy contempt, but anguish and regret
For loss of life and pleasure overloved.[9]
Or, if thou covet death, as utmost end   1020
Of misery, so thinking to evade
The penalty pronounced, doubt not but God
Hath wiselier armed his vengeful ire than so
To be forestalled. Much more I fear lest death
So snatched will not exempt us from the pain   1025
We are by doom to pay; rather such acts
Of contumacy will provoke the Highest
To make death in us live. Then let us seek
Some safer resolution—which methinks
I have in view, calling to mind with heed   1030
Part of our sentence,[1] that thy seed shall bruise
The Serpent's head. Piteous amends! unless
Be meant whom I conjecture,[2] our grand foe,
Satan, who in the Serpent hath contrived
Against us this deceit. To crush his head   1035
Would be revenge indeed—which will be lost
By death brought on ourselves, or childless days
Resolved as thou proposest; so our foe
Shall scape his punishment ordained, and we
Instead shall double ours upon our heads.   1040
No more be mentioned, then, of violence
Against ourselves, and wilful barrenness
That cuts us off from hope, and savors only
Rancor and pride, impatience and despite,
Reluctance[3] against God and his just yoke   1045
Laid on our necks. Remember with what mild

9. I.e., the suicide project excludes ("refutes") the idea that Eve be contemptuous of life and pleasure in view of "something more sublime;" it rather implies "anguish and regret" at the thought of losing those goods.   1. In lines 163–208 of this Book X (cf. The Argument), the Lord "gives sentence" on the Serpent and on the transgressors. The references in the following lines are to that passage (which in turn is quite literally based on Genesis 30), particularly to lines 179–181: "Between thee and the Woman I will put / Enmity, and between thine and her seed; / Her seed shall bruise thy head, thou bruise his heel."   2. The notion that Satan spoke through the Serpent was not at first given to Man (lines 170–171 of this Book: "Concerned not Man. . . . / Nor altered his offense"); Adam is late in coming to that conclusion ("I conjecture"); and on it he bases his following eloquent argument in favor of survival, hope, procreation, activity.   3. Resistance, opposition.

And gracious temper he both heard and judged,
Without wrath or reviling. We expected
Immediate dissolution, which we thought
Was meant by death that day; when, lo! to thee   1050
Pains only in child-bearing were foretold,
And bringing forth, soon recompensed with joy,
Fruit of thy womb. On me the curse aslope
Glanced on the ground.[4] With labor I must earn
My bread; what harm: Idleness had been worse;   1055
My labor will sustain me; and, lest cold
Or heat should injure us, his timely care
Hath, unbesought, provided, and his hands
Clothed us unworthy, pitying while he judged.
How much more, if we pray him, will his ear   1060
Be open, and his heart to pity incline,
And teach us further by what means to shun
The inclement seasons, rain, ice, hail, and snow!
Which now the sky, with various face, begins
To show us in this mountain,[5] while the winds   1065
Blow moist and keen, shattering the graceful locks
Of these fair spreading trees; which bids us seek
Some better shroud, some better warmth to cherish
Our limbs benumbed—ere this diurnal star[6]
Leave cold the night, how[7] we his gathered beams   1070
Reflected may with matter sere foment,[8]
Or by collision of two bodies grind
The air attrite to fire;[9] as late the clouds,
Justling, or pushed with winds, rude in their shock,
Tine[1] the slant lightning, whose thwart flame, driven down,   1075
Kindles the gummy bark of fir or pine,
And sends a comfortable heat from far,
Which might supply the Sun. Such fire to use,
And what may else be remedy or cure
To evils which our own misdeeds have wrought,   1080
He will instruct us praying,[2] and of grace
Beseeching him; so as we need not fear

4. I.e., the curse descending ("aslope") on Adam took an oblique course ("glanced") toward the ground.
Thus Adam is not only accepting the Lord's sentence (lines 201–202 and 205 of this Book: "Curs'd is the
ground for thy sake; thou in sorrow / Shalt eat thereof all the days of thy life; / . . . . In the sweat of thy
face thou shalt eat bread. . . ."), but turning it into a project for an active life after the Fall.   5. In his
description of "delicious Paradise" in Book IV, lines 132–158, Milton situates it on a high plateau at the
top of a "steep wilderness" which denies access to the "enclosure green" and its "insuperable height of
loftiest shade, / Cedar, and pine, and fir, and branching palm, / A sylvan scene, and, as the ranks ascend
/ Shade above shade, a woody theater / Of stateliest view . . . ," where "gentle gales / . . . dispense /
Native perfumes, and whisper whence they stole / Those balmy spoils." That stately and blissful order is
now disrupted, and after the radical alterations in the heavens and in the elements that God has commanded, Adam is preparing to cope with the hardships and the challenges of his mortal state in a time-
conditioned universe of season changes, dawns and sunsets, heat and ice, and shattering winds.   6. The
day-star, the sun.   7. "Seek" how.   8. Heat, warm.   9. The implied belief is that rubbing two
"bodies" (as two flints) against each other, the air thus "attrite" (i.e., "ground" down by the attrition) turns
into fire.   1. Kindle. That fire was produced by lightning is one of the ancient theories about its origin
on earth. *Thwart*: Passing across the sky.   2. If we pray to him.

To pass commodiously this life, sustained
By him with many comforts, till we end
In dust, our final rest and native home.   1085
What better can we do, than, to the place
Repairing where he judged us, prostrate fall
Before him reverent, and there confess
Humbly our faults, and pardon beg, with tears
Watering the ground, and with our sighs the air   1090
Frequenting,[3] sent from hearts contrite, in sign
Of sorrow unfeigned and humiliation meek?
Undoubtedly he will relent, and turn
From his displeasure, in whose look serene,
When angry most he seemed and most severe,   1095
What else but favor, grace, and mercy shone?"
    So spake our Father penitent; nor Eve
Felt less remorse. They, forthwith to the place
Repairing where he judged them, prostrate fell
Before him reverent, and both confessed   1100
Humbly their faults, and pardon begged, with tears
Watering the ground, and with their sighs the air
Frequenting, sent from hearts contrite, in sign
Of sorrow unfeigned and humiliation meek.

From BOOK XII

("The World Was All Before Them")

[After God's acceptance of the transgressors' prayers, and the decree that
"they must no longer abide in Paradise" (Book XI, The Argument), Michael
the Archangel, with a band of Cherubim, has been sent "to dispossess
them." After Eve's lamentation and his own pleading, Adam has submitted; Michael has led him up to a high hill where, in a mixture of prophecy
and instruction, he has set "before him in vision" the future of mankind,
from Cain and Abel through Noah (end of Book XI) and the Prophets,
thus coming "by degrees to explain who that Seed of Woman shall be
which was promised Adam and Eve in the Fall: his incarnation, death,
resurrection, and ascension; the state of the Church till his second coming" (Book XII, The Argument). Toward the close of his speech, Michael
has recommended the exercise of the basic Christian virtues, culminating
in love, "By name to come called Charity, the soul / Of all the rest: then
will thou not be loath / To leave this Paradise, but shalt possess / A Paradise
within thee, happier far" (lines 584–587). Michael has just ended his long
speech.]

. . . He ended, and they both descend the hill.
Descended, Adam to the bower where Eve

3. Filling.

Lay sleeping[4] ran before, but found her waked;
And thus with words not sad she him received:
    "Whence thou return'st and whither went'st, I know;   610
For God is also in sleep, and dreams[5] advise,
Which he hath sent propitious, some great good
Presaging, since, with sorrow and heart's distress
Wearied, I fell asleep. But now lead on;
In me is no delay; with thee to go   615
Is to stay here; without thee here to stay
Is to go hence unwilling; thou to me
Art all things under Heaven, all places thou,
Who for my willful crime art banished hence.
This further consolation yet secure   620
I carry hence: though all by me is lost,
Such favor I unworthy am vouchsafed,
By me the Promised Seed shall all restore."
    So spake our mother Eve; and Adam heard
Well pleased, but answered not; for now too nigh   625
Th' archangel stood, and from the other hill[6]
To their fixed station, all in bright array,
The cherubim descended; on the ground
Gliding meteorous, as evening mist
Risen from a river o'er the marish[7] glides,   630
And gathers ground fast at the laborer's heel
Homeward returning. High in front advanced,[8]
The brandished sword of God before them blazed,
Fierce as a comet; which with torrid heat,
And vapor as the Libyan air adust,[9]   635
Began to parch that temperate clime; whereat
In either hand the hastening angel caught
Our lingering parents, and to th' eastern gate[1]
Led them direct, and down the cliff as fast
To the subjected[2] plain; then disappeared.   640
They, looking back, all th' eastern side beheld
Of Paradise, so late their happy seat,[3]
Waved over by that flaming brand;[4] the gate
With dreadful faces thronged and fiery arms.
Some natural tears they dropped, but wiped them soon;   645

4. Michael has just said to Adam (ll. 594–597): ". . . Go, waken Eve; / Her also I with gentle dreams have calmed, / Portending good, and all her spirits composed / To meek submission. . ."   5. The fact that Adam was granted a "vision" and Eve a "dream" may symbolize a difference in the mode of perception between man and woman; at any rate, both are God's revelations.   6. The hill that Michael had indicated to Adam in lines 590–592: ". . . and, see! the guards, / By me encamped on yonder hill, expect / Their motion, at whose front a flaming sword, / In signal of remove, waves fiercely round."   7. Marsh.   8. Raised high, carried like a banner.   9. Burned up, as the air of the Sahara Desert in Libya.   1. Milton describes "the eastern gate" of Eden, guarded by Gabriel, in Book IV, lines 543ff.: "It was a rock / Of alabaster, piled up to the clouds, / Conspicuous far, winding with one ascent / Accessible from Earth, one entrance high; / The rest was craggy cliff. . ."   2. Lying below.   3. Abode.   4. The word "brand," here in its meaning of "sword," also conveys the image of "burning," "flaming."

The world was all before them, where to choose
Their place of rest,[5] and Providence their guide.
They, hand in hand, with wandering steps and slow,
Through Eden took their solitary way.

5. Not, of course, a place of repose, but their new, earthly abode.

A Note on Translation

Reading literature in translation is a pleasure on which it is fruitless to frown. The purist may insist that we ought always read in the original languages, and we know ideally that this is true. But it is a counsel of perfection, quite impractical even for the purist, since no one in a lifetime can master all the languages whose literatures it would be a joy to explore. Master languages as fast as we may, we shall always have to read to some extent in translation, and this means we must be alert to what we are about: if in reading a work of literature in translation we are not reading the "original," what precisely are we reading? This is a question of great complexity, to which justice cannot be done in a brief note, but the following sketch of some of the considerations may be helpful.

One of the memorable scenes of ancient literature is the meeting of Hector and Andromache in Book VI of Homer's *Iliad*. Hector, leader and mainstay of the armies defending Troy, is implored by his wife Andromache to withdraw within the city walls and carry on the defense from there, where his life will not be constantly at hazard. In Homer's text her opening words to him are these: δαιμόνιε, φθίσει σε τὸ σὸν μένος (daimonie, phthisei se to son menos). How should they be translated into English?

Here is how they have actually been translated into English by capable translators, at various periods, in verse and prose:

1. George Chapman, 1598

> O noblest in desire,
> Thy mind, inflamed with others' good, will set thy self on fire.

2. John Dryden, 1693

> Thy dauntless heart (which I foresee too late),
> Too daring man, will urge thee to thy fate.

3. Alexander Pope, 1715

> Too daring Prince! . . . .
> For sure such courage length of life denies,
> And thou must fall, thy virtue's sacrifice.

4. William Cowper, 1791

> Thy own great courage will cut short thy days,
> My noble Hector. . . .

5. Lang, Leaf, and Myers, 1883 (prose)

> Dear my lord, this thy hardihood will undo thee. . . .

6. A. T. Murray, 1924 (prose, Loeb Library)

> Ah, my husband, this prowess of thine will be thy doom. . . .

7. E. V. Rieu, 1950 (prose)

"Hector," she said, "you are possessed. This bravery of yours will be your end."

8. I. A. Richards, 1950 (prose)

"Strange man," she said, "your courage will be your destruction."

9. Richmond Lattimore, 1951

Dearest,
Your own great strength will be your death. . . .

10. Robert Fitzgerald, 1979

O my wild one, your bravery will be
Your own undoing!

11. Robert Fagles, 1990

reckless one,
Your own fiery courage will destroy you!

From these strikingly different renderings of the same six words, certain facts about the nature of translation begin to emerge. We notice, for one thing, that Homer's word μένος (menos) is diversified by the translators into "mind," "dauntless heart," "such courage," "great courage," "hardihood," "prowess," "bravery," "courage," "great strength," "bravery," and "fiery courage." The word has in fact all these possibilities. Used of things, it normally means "force"; of animals, "fierceness" or "brute strength" or (in the case of horses) "mettle"; of men and women, "passion" or "spirit" or even "purpose." Homer's application of it in the present case points our attention equally—whatever particular sense we may imagine Andromache to have uppermost—to Hector's force, strength, fierceness in battle, spirited heart and mind. But since English has no matching term of like inclusiveness, the passage as the translators give it to us reflects this lack and we find one attribute singled out to the exclusion of the rest.

Here then is the first and most crucial fact about any work of literature read in translation. It cannot escape the linguistic characteristics of the language into which it is turned: the grammatical, syntactical, lexical, and phonetic boundaries that constitute collectively the individuality or "genius" of that language. A Greek play or a Russian novel in English will be governed first of all by the resources of the English language, resources that are certain to be in every instance very different, as the efforts with μένος show, from those of the original.

Turning from μένος to δαιμόνιε (daimonie) in Homer's clause, we encounter a second crucial fact about translations. Nobody knows exactly what shade of meaning δαιμόνιε had for Homer. In later writers the word normally suggests divinity, something miraculous, wondrous; but in Homer it appears as a vocative of address for both chieftain and commoner, man and wife. The coloring one gives it must therefore be determined either by the way one thinks a Greek wife of Homer's era might actually address her husband (a subject on which we have no information whatever), or in the way one thinks it suitable for a hero's wife to address her husband in an epic poem, that is to say, a highly stylized and formal work. In general, the translators of our century will be seen to have abandoned formality in order to stress the intimacy, the wifeliness, and, especially in Lattimore's case, a certain chiding tenderness, in Andromache's appeal: (6) "Ah, my husband," (7)

"Hector" (with perhaps a hint, in "you are possessed," of the alarmed distaste with which wives have so often viewed their husbands' bellicose moods), (8) "Strange man," (9) "Dearest," (10) "O my wild one" (mixing an almost motherly admiration with reproach and concern), and (11) "reckless one." On the other hand, the older translators have obviously removed Andromache to an epic or heroic distance from her beloved, whence she sees and kindles to his selfless courage, acknowledging, even in the moment of pleading with him to be otherwise, his moral grandeur and the tragic destiny this too certainly implies: (1) "O noblest in desire, . . . inflamed by others' good"; (2) "Thy dauntless heart (which I foresee too late), / Too daring man"; (3) "Too daring Prince! . . . / And thou must fall, thy virtue's sacrifice"; (4) "My noble Hector." Even the less specific "Dear my lord" of Lang, Leaf, and Myers looks in the same direction because of its echo of the speech of countless Shakespearean men and women who have shared this powerful moral sense: "Dear my lord, make me acquainted with your cause of grief"; "Perseverance, dear my lord, keeps honor bright"; etc.

The fact about translation that emerges from all this is that just as the translated work reflects the individuality of the language it is turned into, so it reflects the individuality of the age in which it is made, and the age will permeate it everywhere like yeast in dough. We think of one kind of permeation when we think of the governing verse forms and attitudes toward verse at a given epoch. In Chapman's time, experiments seeking an "heroic" verse form for English were widespread, and accordingly he tries a "fourteener" couplet (two rhymed lines of seven stresses each) in his *Iliad* and a pentameter couplet in his *Odyssey*. When Dryden and Pope wrote, a closed pentameter couplet had become established as the heroic form *par excellence*. By Cowper's day, thanks largely to the prestige of *Paradise Lost*, the couplet had gone out of fashion for narrative poetry in favor of blank verse. Our age, inclining to prose and in verse to proselike informalities and relaxations, has, predictably, produced half a dozen excellent prose translations of the *Iliad*, but only three in verse (by Robert Fagles, Richmond Lattimore, and Robert Fitzgerald), all relying on rhythms that are much of the time closer to the verse of William Carlos Williams and some of the prose of novelists like Faulkner than to the swift firm tread of Homer's Greek. For if it is true that what we translate from a given work is what, wearing the spectacles of our time, we see in it, it is also true that we see in it what we have the power to translate.

Of course there are other effects of the translator's epoch on a translation besides those exercised by contemporary taste in verse and verse forms. Chapman writes in a great age of poetic metaphor and therefore almost instinctively translates his understanding of Homer's verb φθίσει (phthisei, "to cause to wane, consume, waste, pine") into metaphorical terms of flame, presenting his Hector to us as a man of burning generosity who will be consumed by his very ardor. This is a conception rooted in large part in the psychology of the Elizabethans, who had the habit of speaking of the soul as "fire," of one of the four temperaments as "fiery," of even the more material bodily processes, like digestion, as if they were carried on by the heat of fire ("concoction," "decoction"). It is rooted too in that characteristic Renaissance élan so unforgettably expressed in characters such as Tamburlaine and Dr. Faustus, the former of whom exclaims to the stars above:

> . . . I, the chiefest lamp of all the earth,
> First rising in the East with mild aspect,
> But fixèd now in the meridian line,
> Will send up fire to your turning spheres,
> And cause the sun to borrow light of you. . . .

Pope and Dryden, by contrast, write to audiences for whom strong metaphor has become suspect. They therefore reject the fire image (which we must recall is not present in the Greek) in favor of a form of speech more congenial to their age, the *sententia* or aphorism, and give it extra vitality by making it the scene of a miniature drama: in Dryden's case, the hero's dauntless heart "urges" him (in the double sense of physical as well as moral pressure) to his fate; in Pope's, the hero's courage, like a judge, "denies" continuance of life, with the consequence that he "falls"—and here Pope's second line suggests analogy to the sacrificial animal—the victim of his own essential nature, of what he is.

To pose even more graphically the pressures that a translator's period brings, consider the following lines from Hector's reply to Andromache's appeal that he withdraw, first in Chapman's Elizabethan version, then in Lattimore's twentieth-century one:

Chapman, 1598

> The spirit I did first breathe
> Did never teach me that—much less since the contempt of death
> Was settled in me, and my mind knew what a Worthy was,
> Whose office is to lead in fight and give no danger pass
> Without improvement. In this fire must Hector's trial shine.
> Here must his country, father, friends be in him made divine.

Lattimore, 1951

> and the spirit will not let me, since I have learned to be valiant
> and to fight always among the foremost ranks of the Trojans,
> winning for my own self great glory, and for my father.

If one may exaggerate to make a necessary point, the world of Henry V and Othello suddenly gives way here to our own, a world whose discomfort with any form of heroic self-assertion is remarkably mirrored in the burial of Homer's key terms (*spirit, valiant, fight, foremost, glory*)—five out of twenty-two words in the original, five out of thirty-six in the translation—in a cushioning huddle of harmless sounds.

Besides the two factors so far mentioned, language and period, as affecting the character of a translation, there is inevitably a third—the translator, with a particular degree of talent, a personal way of regarding the work to be translated, a special hierarchy of values, moral, esthetic, metaphysical (which may or may not be summed up in a "world view"), and a unique style or lack of it. But this influence all readers are likely to bear in mind, and it needs no laboring here. That, for example, two translators of Hamlet, one a Freudian, the other a Jungian, will produce impressively different translations is obvious from the fact that when Freudian and Jungian argue about the play in English they often seem to have different plays in mind.

We can now return to the question from which we started. After all allowances have been made for language, age, and individual translator, is anything of the original left? What, in short, does the reader of translations read? Let it be said at once that in utility prose—prose whose function is mainly referential—the reader who reads a translation reads everything that matters. "*Nicht Rauchen,*" "*Défense de Fumer,*" and "*No Smoking,*" posted in a railway car, make their point, and the differences between them in sound and form have no significance for us in that context. Since the prose of a treatise and of most fiction is preponderantly referential, we rightly feel, when we have paid close attention to Cervantes or Montaigne or Machiavelli or Tolstoy in a good English translation, that we have had roughly the same experience as a native Spaniard, Frenchman, Italian, or Russian. But "roughly" is the correct word; for good prose points iconically *to* itself as well as referentially beyond itself, and everything that it points to in itself in the original (rhythms, sounds, idioms, word play, etc.) must alter radically in being translated. The best analogy is to imagine a Van Gogh painting reproduced in the medium of tempera, etching, or engraving: the "picture" remains, but the intricate interanimation of volumes with colorings with brushstrokes has disappeared.

When we move on to poetry, even in its longer narrative and dramatic forms— plays like *Oedipus*, poems like the *Iliad* or the *Divine Comedy*—our situation as English readers worsens appreciably, as the many unlike versions of Andromache's appeal to Hector make very clear. But, again, only appreciably. True, this is the point at which the fact that a translation is *always* an interpretation explodes irresistibly on our attention; but if it is the best translation of its time, like John Ciardi's translation of the *Divine Comedy* for our time, the result will be not only a sensitive interpretation but also a work with intrinsic interest in its own right—at very best, a true work of art, a new poem. It is only when the shorter, primarily lyrical forms of poetry are presented that the reader of translations faces insuperable disadvantage. In these forms, the referential aspect of language has a tendency to disappear into, or, more often, draw its real meaning and accreditation from, the iconic aspect. Let us look for just a moment at a brief poem by Federico García Lorca and its English translation (by Stephen Spender and J. L. Gili):

> ¡Alto pinar!
> Cuatro palomas por el aire van.
>
> Cuatro palomas
> vuelan y tornan.
> Llevan heridas
> sus cuatro sombras.
>
> ¡Bajo pinar!
> Cuatro palomas en la tierra están.

> Above the pine trees:
> Four pigeons go through the air.
>
> Four pigeons
> fly and turn round.
> They carry wounded
> their four shadows.
>
> Below the pine trees:
> Four pigeons lie on the earth.

In this translation the referential sense of the English words follows with remarkable exactness the referential sense of the Spanish words they replace. But the life of Lorca's poem does not lie in that sense. It lies in such matters as the abruptness, like an intake of breath at a sudden revelation, of the two exclamatory lines (1 and 7), which then exhale musically in images of flight and death; or as the echoings of *palomas* in *heridas* and *sombras*, bringing together (as in fact the hunter's gun has done) these unrelated nouns and the unrelated experiences they stand for in a sequence that seems, momentarily, to have all the logic of a tragic action, in which *doves* become *wounds* become *shadows*; or as the external and internal rhyming among the five verbs, as though all motion must (as in fact it must) end with *están*.

Since none of this can be brought over into another tongue (least of all Lorca's rhythms), the translator must decide between leaving a reader to wonder why Lorca is a poet to be bothered about at all, and making a new but true poem, whose merit will almost certainly be in inverse ratio to its likeness to the original. Samuel Johnson made such a poem in translating Horace's famous *Diffugere nives*, and so did A. E. Housman. If we juxtapose the last two stanzas of each translation, and the corresponding Latin, we can see at a glance that each has the consistency and inner life of a genuine poem, and that neither of them (even if we consider only what is obvious to the eye, the line-lengths) is very close to Horace.

> *Cum semel occideris, et de te splendida Minos*
> *fecerit arbitria,*
> *non, Torquate, genus, non te facundia, non te*
> *restituet pietas.*
>
> *Infernis neque enim tenebris Diana pudicum*
> *liberat Hippolytum*
> *nec Lethaea valet Theseus abrumpere caro*
> *vincula Pirithoo.*

Johnson:

> Not you, Torquatus, boast of Rome,
> When Minos once has fixed your doom,
> Or eloquence, or splendid birth,
> Or virtue, shall restore to earth.
> Hippolytus, unjustly slain,
> Diana calls to life in vain;
> Nor can the might of Theseus rend
> The chains of hell that hold his friend.

Housman:

> When thou descendest once the shades among,
> The stern assize and equal judgment o'er,
> Not thy long lineage nor thy golden tongue,
> No, nor thy righteousness, shall friend thee more.
>
> Night holds Hippolytus the pure of stain,
> Diana steads him nothing, he must stay;
> And Theseus leaves Pirithous in the chain
> The love of comrades cannot take away.

The truth of the matter is that when the translator of short poems chooses to be literal, most or all of the poetry is lost; and when the translator succeeds in forging a new poetry, most or all of the original author is lost. Since there is no way out of this dilemma, we have always been sparing, in this anthology, in our use of short poems in translation.

We may assure ourselves, then, that the reading of literature in translation is not the disaster it has sometimes been represented. It is true that, however good the translation, we remain at a remove from the original, the remove becoming closest to impassable in the genre of the lyric poem. But with this exception, it is obvious that translation brings us closer by far to the work than we could be if we did not read it at all, or read it with a defective knowledge of the language. "To a thousand cavils," said Samuel Johnson, "one answer is sufficient; the purpose of a writer is to be read, and the criticism which would destroy the power of pleasing must be blown aside." Johnson was defending Pope's Homer for those marks of its own time and place that make it the great interpretation it is, but Johnson's exhilarating common sense applies equally to the problem we are considering here. Literature is to be read, and the criticism that would destroy the reader's power to make some form of contact with much of the world's great writing must indeed be blown aside.

MAYNARD MACK

Index

Abélard, Pierre, 1267
Aeneid, The (Virgil), 844
Aeschylus, 543, 548
Agamemnon (Aeschylus), 548
Alcuin, 1264
Antigone (Sophocles), 701
Apology for Raymond Sebond, from (Montaigne), 1808
Apology of Socrates, The (Plato), 807
Apparition, The (Donne), 2115
Aquinas, Thomas, 1272
Archpoet, The, 1267
Aristophanes, 772, 774
Aristotle, 831
"At the round earth's imagined corners, blow" (Donne), 2116
Aucassin and Nicolette, 1230, 1231
Augustine, St., 980, 982

Ballade (Villon), 1622
Beowulf, 1047, 1052
Blest Be the Day (Petrarch), 1677
"Blest be the day, and blest the month and year" (Petrarch), 1677
Boccaccio, Giovanni, 1467, 1470
Boethius, Anicius Manlius Severinus, 1260
Book of the Courtier, The (Castiglione), 1719
"Brother humans who live on after us" (Villon), 1622

"Caelius, my Lesbia, that one, that only Lesbia" (Catullus), 839
Calderón de la Barca, Pedro, 2117, 2120
Canonization (Donne), 2114
Canterbury Tales, The (Chaucer), 1558
Carmina Burana, 1270
Castiglione, Baldesar, 1718, 1719
Catullus, 835, 836
Cervantes, Miguel de, 1819, 1823
Chaucer, Geoffrey, 1551, 1558
"Come, Lesbia, let us live and love" (Catullus), 836
"Come, sweetheart, come," 1266
Confessions (St. Augustine), 982
Consolation of Philosophy, The (Boethius), 1260

Dante Alighieri, 1273, 1284
David's Lament for Jonathan (Abelard), 1267

"Death, be not proud, though some have callèd thee" (Donne), 2116
Decameron, The (Boccaccio), 1470
Dinner with Trimalchio (Satyricon) (Petronius), 963
Divine Comedy, The (Dante), 1284
Don Quixote (Cervantes): Part I, 1823; Part II, 1902
Donne, John, 2110, 2112

Eliduc (Marie de France), 1218
Epic of Gilgamesh, The, 11, 14
Erasmus, Desiderius, 1679, 1682
Essays (Montaigne), 1793
Eumenides, The (Aeschylus), 623
Euripides, 739, 740
Everyman, 1637, 1639

Father in Heaven (Petrarch), 1677
"Father in heaven, after each lost day" (Petrarch), 1677
First Day, The (Decameron) (Boccaccio), 1470
"For God's sake hold your tongue, and let me love" (Donne), 2114
Fortunatus, Saint Venantius, 1263
Funeral, The (Donne), 2115
"Furius, Aurelius, bound to Catullus" (Catullus), 839

Gargantua and Pantagruel (Rabelais): Book I, 1753; Book II, 1775
General Prologue (Canterbury Tales) (Chaucer), 1558
Genesis, 49
"Go and catch a falling star" (Donne), 2112
Go, Grieving Rimes of Mine (Petrarch), 1679
"Go, grieving rimes of mine, to that hard stone" (Petrarch), 1679
Good-Morrow, The (Donne), 2112
Great Is My Envy of You (Petrarch), 1678
"Great is my envy of you, earth, in your greed" (Petrarch), 1678

Hamlet, Prince of Denmark (Shakespeare), 2014
He Complains to Bishop Hartgar of Thirst (Scottus), 1265
Heptameron, The (Marguerite de Navarre), 1734

"He who has made his reckoning with life" (Boethius), 1260
His Confession (Archpoet), 1267
Holy Sonnets (Donne): no. 7, 2116; no. 10, 2116
Homer, 92, 98

"I can love both fair and brown" (Donne), 2113
"I hate and love" (Catullus), 838
"If man can find rich consolation, remembering his good deeds and all he has done" (Catullus), 840
Iliad, The (Homer), 98
Indifferent, The (Donne), 2113
Inferno (Dante), 1284
Isaiah, 89
It Was the Morning (Petrarch), 1676
"It was the morning of that blessèd day" (Petrarch), 1676
"I wonder, by my troth, what thou and I" (Donne), 2112

Job, 69
Jonah, 90

(Knight's Interruption of the Monk's Tale, The) (Canterbury Tales) (Chaucer), 1606
Koran, The, from, 1012, 1014

Lament for the Cuckoo (Alcuin), 1264
"Lesbia speaks evil of me with her husband near and he (damned idiot) loves to hear her" (Catullus), 837
"Let's away with study" (Carmina Burana), 1270
Letter to Dionisio da Borgo San Sepolcro (Petrarch), 1670
Letter to Francesco Vettori (Machiavelli), 1705
Libation Bearers, The (Aeschylus), 594
Life Is a Dream (Calderon), 2120
"Low in thy grave with thee" (Abelard), 1267
Luke, 948, 954
Lysistrata (Aristophanes), 774

Machiavelli, Niccolò, 1702, 1705
Marguerite de Navarre, 1730, 1734
Marie de France, 1216, 1218
Marlowe, Christopher, 1955, 1958
Matthew, 950, 956
Medea (Euripides), 740
Metamorphoses (Ovid), 918
Miller's Tale, The (Canterbury Tales) (Chaucer), 1578
Milton, John, 2176, 2179
Montaigne, Michel de, 1789, 1793
"My life, my love, you say our love will last forever" (Catullus), 837
"My woman says that she would rather wear the wedding veil for me" (Catullus), 838

New Testament, The, 947, 948
Ninth Tale of the Fifth Day, The (Decameron) (Boccaccio), 1488
"No woman, if she is honest, can say that she's" (Catullus), 837
Nun's Priest's Tale, The (Canterbury Tales) (Chaucer), 1607

"O happy hour" (Carmina Burana), 1271
Odyssey, The (Homer), 208
Oedipus the King (Sophocles), 658
Of Cannibals (Montaigne), 1793
Of Repentance (Montaigne), 1816
Of the Inconsistency of Our Actions (Montaigne), 1803
Old Testament, The, 45, 49
Oresteia, The (Aeschylus), 548
Ovid, 917, 918

Paradise Lost (Milton): Book I, 2179; Book IX, 2180; Book X, 2208; Book XII, 2217
Paradiso, from (Dante), 1447
Pardoner's Tale, The (Canterbury Tales) (Chaucer), 1595
Petrarch, Francis, 1668, 1670
Petronius, 961, 963
Phaedo, from (Plato), 827
Plato, 806, 807
Poetics, from (Aristotle), 831
"Poor damned Catullus, here's no time for nonsense" (Catullus), 839
Praise of Folly, The (Erasmus): Part I, 1682; Part II, 1683; Part IV, 1698
Prince, The (Machiavelli), 1706
Prologue to the Miller's Tale (Canterbury Tales) (Chaucer), 1577
Prologue to the Pardoner's Tale (Canterbury Tales) (Chaucer), 1592
Psalms, The: no. 8, 86; no. 19, 86; no. 23, 87; no. 104, 87; no. 137, 89
Purgatorio, from (Dante), 1423

Rabelais, François, 1750, 1753

Satyricon, The (Petronius), 963
Scottus, Sedulius, 1265
Second Tale of the Fourth Day, The (Decameron) (Boccaccio), 1482
"Seething over inwardly" (Archpoet), 1267
Shakespeare, William, 2010, 2014
She Used to Let Her Golden Hair Fly Free (Petrarch), 1677
Sir Gawain and the Green Knight, 1492, 1493

Song ("Go and catch a falling star")
  (Donne), 2112
Song of Roland, The, *from*, 1155, 1159
Song of the Seeress, The, 1136, 1137
Sophocles, 652, 658
Story of Deirdre, The, 1127, 1129

Testament, The, *from* (Villon), 1623
The Eyes That Drew from Me (Petrarch),
  1678
"The eyes that drew from me such fervent
  praise" (Petrarch), 1678
"There are many who think of Quintia in
  terms of beauty" (Catullus), 836
"There was a time, O Lesbia, when you
  said Catullus was the only man on
  earth who could understand you"
  (Catullus), 838
"The standards of the King go forth" (For-
  tunatus), 1263
"The standing corn is green, the wild in
  flower" (Scottus), 1265
"The Word went forth" (Aquinas), 1272

Thorstein the Staff-Struck, 1148, 1149
To the Lady Radegunde, with Violets (For-
  tunatus), 1264
Tragical History of the Life and Death of
  Doctor Faustus, The (Marlowe),
  1958

Villon, François, 1621, 1622
Virgil, 841, 844

Wanderer, The, 1123, 1124
"Were you born of a lioness in the Libyan
  Mountains" (Catullus), 838
"When at last after long despair, our hopes
  ring true again" (Catullus), 837
"When by thy scorn, O murderess, I am
  dead" (Donne), 2115
"Whoever comes to shroud me, do not
  harm" (Donne), 2115

"You are the cause of this destruction, Lesbia" (Catullus), 839